THE ALMANAC OF AMERICAN POLITICS 1996

The Senators, the Representatives and the Governors: Their Records and Election Results, Their States and Districts

Michael Barone and Grant Ujifusa with Richard E. Cohen

Washington, D.C.

NATIONAL JOURNAL INC.

President: John Fox Sullivan
Senior Vice President: Steve Hull
Vice President, Advertising: Linda Cheesman
Vice President, Finance: Brent Willman
Associate Publisher, Editorial Products: Eleanor Evans Kitfield
Marketing Director: Yvonne Miller
Circulation Director: Tish Billings

Publishers of:

National Journal: Richard S. Frank, Editor
Government Executive: Timothy Clark, Editor & Publisher
CongressDaily, CongressDaily/A.M.: Lou Peck, Editor
also
The Capital Source, The Federal Technology Source,
The Federal Internet Source, PoliticsUSA
also
National Journal Convention Daily, published every four years at the Democratic
and Republican National Conventions
and

The Almanac of American Politics

Printed in the United States of America by Arcata Graphics. Composition by
Applied Graphics Technologies. Distributed by Times Books, a division of Random
House Inc.

Photographs by John Eisele, Susan M. Muniak and Bruce Reedy. For information
regarding photographs, contact: National Journal, 1501 M Street, N.W., Washington, D.C. 20005. 202-739-8400. All rights reserved.

ISBN 0-89234-057-6 (Cloth)
ISBN 0-89234-058-4 (Paper)

National Journal Inc. is a wholly-owned subsidiary of the Times Mirror Co.
**A Times Mirror
Company**

THE ALMANAC OF AMERICAN POLITICS 1996

Authors: Michael Barone, Grant Ujifusa

Editor: Eleanor Evans Kitfield

Managing Editor: Cathryn M. Newson

Principal Contributing Editor: Richard E. Cohen

Senior Contributing Editors: Gary Cohen, Carol Matlack, Tracy McLoone

Contributing Editors: David Baumann, Graeme Browning, Jane Clark, Lou Peck, Troy Schneider, Kirk Victor

Research Associates: Mark Allen, John Buntin, Blair Campbell, Mike Donohue

Editorial Assistants: David Caliguiri, Charles Eaton, Chris Wise

Research Assistants: John Gallagher, Mary Lou Wendell

Photographers: John Eisele, Bruce Reedy

Page Layout: Shirley Yonce, Applied Graphics Technologies

Cover Design: Shirley Tibbetts

Election Results & State Maps: Election Data Services Inc.

Publisher: John Fox Sullivan

The Almanac especially would like to thank the entire staff of *National Journal* for their invaluable support and assistance during the production of this book.

CONTENTS

CONGRESS AT-A-GLANCE

GUIDE TO USAGE

The Almanac of American Politics is designed to be self-explanatory. The following guide provides a brief description of each section and a list of sources from which information was derived, both of which serve as a road map to understanding the meaning behind the figures.

The People

Population. All population figures, excluding unemployment rates and voter registration, are from the Bureau of the Census, U.S. Department of Commerce, Washington D.C. 20230, 301-763-4040.

Race and Ethnic Origin. For the 1990 Census, the Census Bureau asked people what their race or ethnic origin was. Race, as defined by the Bureau of the Census, reflects the individual respondents' perception of his or her racial identity and does not reflect any biological or anthropological definition. The basic racial categories are: American Indian or Alaska Native; Asian or Pacific Islander; Black; and White. Hispanic origin is defined as an ethnicity, and includes those who classified themselves in one of three specific Hispanic categories on the census form (Cuban, Mexican, Puerto Rican) or as of "other Spanish/Hispanic origin"; persons of Hispanic origin may be of any race. Origin can be viewed as ancestry, nationality group or country of birth. The "Other" category was intended to include those persons who do not consider themselves to be in the basic racial or ethnic categories.

Households and Housing Information. A Household is defined as including all persons occupying a housing unit; a Married Couple Family is a household of persons related by marriage. Owner occupied housing units include only single-family houses on less than ten acres with no business or medical office on the property. The value of a housing unit is the respondent's estimate of how much the unit would sell for if it were for sale, and determines Median House Value. Monthly rent is defined as the per-month contract rent agreed to for a unit, regardless of any goods or services that may be included (e.g. utilities), and determines Median Monthly Rent.

Age. The Bureau of the Census defines age as based on the number of years a person completed as of April 1, 1990. This definition was used to determine the voting age population, the percentage of population over 65 years of age, and the median age. Many people, however, provided their age as of the date they completed the census form rather than the definition provided by the Bureau of the Census.

Education. The level of higher education is measured by the Census from persons over 25 years of age who have pursued vocational, public, or private forms of college education not necessarily leading to graduation.

Unemployment. All unemployment figures are from the Bureau of Labor Statistics, U.S. Department of Labor, Washington, D.C. 20210, 202-606-7828. These figures represent the average rate of unemployment for each state for 1992.

Registered Voters. Registered voter numbers are from the individual states' election bureaus or political parties, and represent the number of voters officially registered as close as possible to the November, 1992 election. Some states have no voter registration.

Political Lineup. This block includes the names of top state officials as well as a breakdown by party of the state legislative bodies. The names of U.S. senators and a party breakdown of the state's congressional delegation are also provided.

Presidential Vote. The 1988 and 1992 presidential vote is included for each state and congressional district. Presidential vote on the state level was drawn from state election returns. Presidential vote by congressional district was derived from state, county and precinct results as compiled by the staff of the National Committee for an Effective Congress (NCEC), 507 Capitol Ct., N.E., Washington, D.C. 20002, 202-547-1151. Discrepancies exist between the state and district figures because of inconsistent reporting methods employed by the counties, the states and the FEC. Results of the presidential primaries were provided by the states and the FEC. Caucus results are not provided.

Biography. This section lists when each governor, senator and representative was elected or appointed, date and place of birth, home, college education and degrees obtained (if any), religion, marital status and, if applicable, spouse's name. Also listed is a brief outline of the politician's career, including military service in the Air Force, Army, Marine Corps, Navy, National Guard, or Reserves, and his or her office addresses and telephone numbers. Committee and subcommittee assignments are provided as well. (Note: On many committees, the chairman and ranking minority member are ex officio members of each subcommittee on which they do not hold a regular assignment.)

Ratings

Group Ratings. The congressional rating statistics of 11 lobby groups provide an idea of a legislator's general ideology and the degree to which the legislator represents different groups' interests. Not just a record of liberal/conservative voting behavior, these ratings come from a range of groups concerned with everything from single issues (environmental concerns) to the political interests of a particular sector (e.g., consumers). The order of the groups is such that the more "liberal" groups are on the left and the more "conservative" are on the right. Four groups, ACLU, NSI, NTLC and CHC release ratings only once every two years, the duration of one full congressional session. Following is a general description of each organization, its address and telephone number.

ADA   Americans for Democratic Action
1625 K St., N.W., #210, Washington, D.C. 20006, 202-785-5980.
    Liberal: Since its founding in 1947, ADA members have pushed for legislation designed to reduce inequality, curtail rising defense spending, prevent encroachments on civil liberties and promote international human rights. The ADA uses a broad spectrum of issues for its vote analysis.

ACLU   American Civil Liberties Union
122 Maryland Ave., N.E., Washington, D.C. 20002, 202-544-1681.
    Pro-individual liberties: ACLU seeks to protect individuals from legal, executive and congressional infringement on basic rights guaranteed by the Bill of Rights. The ACLU ratings are published for every Congress; the 1992 ratings include the years 1991 and 1992.

COPE   Committee on Political Education of the AFL-CIO
815 16th St., N.W., 6th Floor, Washington, D.C. 20006, 202-637-5122.
    Liberal-Labor: As the powerful and well-funded arm of the AFL-CIO, COPE is concerned with the economic interests of the American worker. While COPE covers a broad spectrum of issues, it monitors few votes on foreign policy and defense spending. These ratings are based on members' cumulative lifetime records.

CFA   Consumer Federation of America
1424 16th St., N.W., #604, Washington, D.C. 20036, 202-387-6121.
Pro-Consumer: CFA is a group spawned in the mid-sixties as a pro-consumer counterweight to various business-oriented lobbies. Their vote ratings concentrate on pocketbook consumer issues and health and safety concerns.

LCV   League of Conservation Voters
1707 L St., N.W., #550, Washington, D.C. 20036, 202-785-8683.
Environmental: Formed in 1970, LCV is the national, non-partisan arm of the environmental movement. LCV works to elect pro-environmental candidates to Congress. LCV ratings are based on key votes concerning energy, environment and natural resource issues, selected by leaders from major national environmental organizations.

CON   Concord Coalition
1025 Vermont Avenue, N.W., #810, Washington, D.C. 20005, 202-737-1077.
Pro-Balanced Budget: The Concord Coalition is a nonpartisan, grassroots organization dedicated to eliminating the federal budget deficit by the year 2000. The Coalition, with members and active chapters in all 50 states, is determined to educate the American public about the dangers of the federal deficit.

NSI   National Security Index of the American Security Council
1155 15th St., N.W., #1101, Washington, D.C. 20005, 202-484-1676.
Pro-strong defense: Founded in 1965, the Council feels that American security is best preserved by developing and maintaining large weapons systems to achieve strategic military superiority. The NSI rates members on their support of defense and foreign policy issues that affect the NSI strategy of peace through strength.

COC   Chamber of Commerce of the United States
1615 H Street, N.W., Washington, D.C. 20062, 202-659-6000.
Pro-business: Founded in 1912 as a voice for organized business, COC represents local, regional and state chambers of commerce in addition to trade and professional organizations.

ACU   American Conservative Union
38 Ivy St., S.E., Washington, D.C. 20003, 202-546-6555.
Conservative: Since 1971, ACU ratings have provided a means of gauging the conservatism of members of Congress. Foreign policy, social and budget issues are their primary concerns.

NTLC   National Tax-Limitation Committee
201 Massachusetts Ave., N.E., #C-7, Washington, D.C. 20002, 202-547-4196
Pro-tax limitation: NTLC was organized in 1975 to seek constitutional and other limits on taxes, spending and deficits at the state and federal levels. NTLC actively pursues a balanced budget/tax limitation amendment to the U.S. Constitution. These ratings are based on budget issue votes and bills which would have a major impact on long-term goverment taxing and spending programs.

CHC   Christian Coalition
227 Massachusetts Avenue, N.E., # 101, Washington, D.C. 20002, 202-547-3600.
Conservative: Pro-family citizen organization and national lobby founded in 1989 working for family-friendly public policy on a local, state and national level with 1.5 million members and activists.

National Journal Ratings. *National Journal*'s rating system establishes an objective method of analyzing congressional voting. A panel of *National Journal* editors and staff initially compiled a list of congressional roll call votes and classified them as either economic, social or foreign policy-related. Professor Garrison Nelson of the University of Vermont provided the computerized roll-call data. The interrelationship of these votes was shown by a statistical procedure called "principal components analysis," which revealed which "yea" votes and which "nay" votes fit a liberal or a conservative pattern. The votes in each of the three subject areas were computer-weighted to reflect the degree they fit the common pattern. All members of Congress who participated in at least half of the votes in each area received ratings; those who missed more that half the votes were not scored (shown as *). Absences and abstentions were not counted.

Members of Congress were then ranked according to relative liberalism and conservatism. Finally, they were assigned percentiles showing their rank relative to others in their chamber. Percentile scores range from a minimum of 0 to a maximum of 99. Because some members voted liberal or conservative on every roll call, however, there are ties at the liberal and conservative ends of each scale. For that reason, the maximum percentiles often turn out to be less than 99.

Election Results

Election Results. Listed for each member of the House are results of the 1994 general, runoff and primary elections, as well as the 1992 general elections (results of any special elections are also listed). Gubernatorial and senatorial results are presented in a like manner. Votes and percentages are included, indicating the margin of victory (due to the process of rounding up and rounding down, some totals may equal more or less than 100%). Candidates receiving less than 4% of the total vote are listed as "Other." Dollar amounts listed to the right of the vote totals are campaign expenditures as reported by the candidate to the Federal Election Commission. Election returns were provided by Election Data Services Inc., 1225 Eye Street, N.W., #200, Washington, D.C. 20005, 202-789-2004.

Campaign Finance

All data are derived from candidates' campaign finance reports and party reports, as well as other official and preliminary studies available from the Federal Election Commission (FEC), 999 E St., NW, Washington, D.C. 20463, 202-219-4140 (toll free, 1-800-424-9530). The dollar figure, in parentheses to the right of the election results, represent the candidates total expenditures for the period beginning January 1, 1993 and ending December 31, 1994 (1993–94 election cycle).

ABBREVIATIONS

A.A.	Administrative Assistant	CORE	Congress on Racial Equality
ABC	Americans for Better Childcare Act	D	Democrat
ACLU	American Civil Liberties Union	DCCC	Democratic Congressional Campaign Committee
ACP	A Connecticut Party	Dem.	Democratic
ACU	American Conservative Union	DFL	Democratic–Farmer–Labor Party (MN)
ADA	Americans for Democratic Action, Americans with Disabilities Act	DLC	Democratic Leadership Council
AI	Alaska Independent Party	DNC	Democratic National Committee
ANWR	Alaska National Wildlife Reserve	DOE	U.S. Department of Energy
AS	American Samoa	DOT	U.S. Department of Transportation
ASI	American Systems Independent Party (PA)	DSCC	Democratic Senatorial Campaign Committee
		DSOB	Dirksen Senate Office Building
BCCI	Bank of Credit and Commerce International		
Bd.	Board	EMILY	EMILY's List-Early Money is Like Yeast
BGH	Bovine Growth Hormone	EPA	U.S. Environmental Protection Agency
Btu	British thermal unit	ERISA	Employee Retirement Income Security Act
BVP	Brooklyn Voters Party (NY)	Expend.	Expenditure/s
C	Conservative Party (NY)		
CAB	Civil Aeronautics Board	FCP	Free Congress Political Action Committee
CAFE	Corporate Average Fuel Economy	FEC	Federal Election Commission
Cand.	Candidate	FY	Fiscal Year
CFA	Consumer Federation of America		
CCP	Change Congress Party	GREEN	Green Party
CHC	Christian Coalition		
CHOB	Cannon House Office Building	H	Capitol Building Room—House side
CIA	Central Intelligence Agency	HSOB	Hart Senate Office Building
COC	Chamber of Commerce of the United States		
COH	Cash-On-Hand	I, Ind., Indep.	Independent
COLA	Cost of Living Adjustment	IC	Independent Conservative
CON	Concord Coalition	IMF	International Monetary Fund
COPE	Committee on Political Education (AFL-CIO)	INF	Independent Fusion Party
		INN	Independent Neighbors Party

IR	Independent-Republican Party (MN)
IRA	Individual Retirement Account
ISTEA	Intermodal Surface Transportation Efficiency Act
IVP	Independent Voters Party
JBS	Jobs Party (NY)
JWP	Jim Wham Party (IL)
L	Liberal Party
LCV	League of Conservation Voters
LHOB	Longworth House Office Building
LIB	Libertarian Party
LIF	Long Island First Party (NY)
LWV	League of Women Voters
MFN	Most Favored Nation
MTV	Music Television
NAFTA	North American Free Trade Agreement
NAP	New Alliance Party (MA)
NARAL	National Abortion Rights Action League
NEA	National Endowment for the Arts
NRCC	National Republican Congressional Committee
NRSC	National Republican Senatorial Committee
NSI	National Security Index of the American Security Council
NTLC	National Tax-Limitation Committee
PAC	Political Action Committee
P & F	Peace & Freedom Party (CA)
PDP	Popular Democratic Party (PR)
POP	Populist Party
PR	Puerto Rico
R, Repub.	Republican
RC	Rainbow Coalition

Rep./s	Representative/s
RHOB	Rayburn House Office Building
RMM	Ranking Minority Member
RNC	Republican National Committee
RSOB	Russell Senate Office Building
RTL	Right-to-Life Party (NY)
S	Capitol Building Room, Senate side
S & L	Savings and Loan
SDI	Strategic Defense Initiative
Sen./s	Senator/s
SIS	Staten Island Secession Party (NY)
SOL	Solidarity Party (IL)
S.U.N.Y.	State University of New York
SWP	Socialist Workers Party (MN)
TXB	Tax Break Party (NY)
UAW	United Auto Workers
UDAG	Urban Development Action Grant
VA	Veterans' Administration
VRP	Voters Rights Party (NY)
WASP	White, Anglo-Saxon, Protestant
WIC	Women and Infant Children

Contract with America

The initial months of 1995 featured congressional votes on the Contract with America. That campaign document, which was presented by House Republicans in the fall of 1994, became an integral part of the biggest switch in party control since 1954. With that success behind them, the same Republicans sought to make good on their promise: a House vote—though not necessarily passage—on each piece of the Contract in the first 100 days of the new Congress. By the Easter recess, House Republicans delivered on the Contract; furthermore, they passed each part of the Contract with one exception—the constitutional amendment that limits the number of terms that Members of Congress may serve. Senate Republicans had not formally joined in presenting the Contract with America although many of them echoed its rhetoric during and following the campaign. In 1995, they moved more slowly than the House in voting on the Contract with America, both because they were less committed to its details and because the Senate's looser procedural rules permitted Democrats to slow progress on the agenda. By late spring, they had completed action on about half of the House-passed Contract items, passing some parts, defeating another (the balanced budget amendment to the Constitution) and watering down still others (especially, the line-item veto and product liability bills).

In this edition, each legislator's profile includes votes on the Contract with America in early 1995, which are described at the end of this section. As with the separate votes for 1993–94, the results were drawn from Legi-Slate; an asterisk means that the member was absent, voted present or abstained from voting on the issue. Although House Republicans during the 1994 campaign presented their Contract in 10 parts, they divided some of those pieces when they began to move the legislation through Congress. That explains why 15 votes—which cover virtually all parts of the agenda—are listed in this edition; for example, the balanced budget amendment and line-item veto had been listed together in the Contract but they were separate House votes. In addition, Senators' vote are listed for 6 issues, including the fiscal 1996 budget resolution. Each vote tally is for final passage of that measure.

An analysis of the votes shows a remarkable degree of legislative unity by Republicans. In the House, 148 of the 230 Republicans (nearly two-thirds) had a perfect voting record on Contract issues, excluding votes on which they were not present. Of the 54 Senate Republicans, 44 were united on the votes. (For purposes of this analysis, Nathan Deal of Georgia is counted as a Democrat because he switched to the Republican Party in April, after all the votes were cast; Ben Nighthorse Campbell, who switched in March during the middle of the Senate votes, is counted as a Republican.) Most of the Republican dissenters were sparing. In the House, only 10 Republicans voted "no" on passage of more than 2 of the 15 votes; Connie Morella of Maryland opposed 7 of the bills, 3 more than the next-highest total. Mark Hatfield of Oregon was the only Republican Senator who voted against more than one of the 6 Senate bills, including his celebrated vote against the balanced budget amendment, which resulted in its defeat in March; Majority Leader Robert Dole, the only other Republican who voted against the balanced budget proposal, did so only for procedural reasons to keep the issue open for a subsequent vote. Senate Republicans were unanimous on 3 of the 6 votes—Congressional Accountability, unfunded mandates and the fiscal 1996 budget resolution; their biggest source of division was the product liability bill, which 7 of them opposed. In the House, they were unanimous on Congressional Accountability and unfunded mandates; the most opposition came from the 40 Republicans opposing term limits and 23 against the bill compensating owners for the federal government's "takings" of private property.

As for the Democrats, the record was mixed. According to a vote analysis prepared by House Republican leaders, an average of 42% House Democrats voted for each Contract measure.

Because the Congressional Accountability Act passed unanimously (with 6 absentees) in the House and was opposed in the Senate by only Robert Byrd of West Virginia, very few Democrats had a perfect voting record in opposition—Byrd in the Senate and Corinne Brown of Florida and Pete Stark of California in the House. Another 8 Senators and 59 members of the House (including Bernie Sanders of Vermont, an Independent) voted for only one bill, the Congressional Accountability Act in virtually every case. In addition to the Accountability Act, the issues generating the most Democratic support in the Senate were unfunded mandates (35) and the line-item veto (19); in the House, Democrats gave the most support to unfunded mandates (130), the balanced budget amendment (72), the private property bill (72) and the line-item veto (71). Some Democrats were strong supporters of the Contract with America. In the Senate, Charles Robb of Virginia voted with Republicans on each of the 6 votes and Sam Nunn favored 5 issues. Following are the House Democrats, all but four of them from the South, with the strongest record of support on the 15 Contract votes.

Ralph Hall	TX-4	15
Billy Tauzin	LA-3	15
Nathan Deal	GA-9	14
Robert Cramer	AL-5	13
Pete Geren	TX-12	13
Jimmy Hayes	LA-7	13
Mike McNulty	NY-21	13
Sonny Montgomery	MS-3	13
Tom Bevill	AL-4	12
Bill Brewster	OK-3	12
Gary Condit	CA-18	12
Pat Danner	MO-6	12
Greg Laughlin	TX-14	12
Mike Parker	MS-4	12
James Traficant	OH-17	12

In addition to the strong Republican cohesion on its Contract, the start of the 104th Congress was marked by an unusually high number of hours in session and roll-call votes, especially in the House. The 487 hours and 279 votes were more than double the figures for the Democratic-controlled House in the comparable first three months of 1993.

Votes

Key Votes. The Key Votes section attempts to illustrate a legislator's stance on important votes where he or she must vote *for* or *against* a national issue. The process grossly oversimplifies the legislative system where months of debate, amendment, pressure, persuasion, and compromise go into a final floor vote. However, the voting record remains the best indication of a member's general ideologies and position on specific issues.

Following is a list of key votes used. A member who was absent, voted present, or who was not in office at the time of a particular vote receives an asterisk. The votes were drawn from Legi-Slate, a computer system tracking legislation, voting attendance, committee schedules, etc. For information on Legi-Slate or their vote recording process, please contact: Legi-Slate, 777 N. Capitol St., N.E., #900, Washington, D.C. 20002, 202-898-2300.

House Votes, 104th Congress:

1) **Congressional Compliance**   (H.R.1) House made certain laws applicable to the legislative branch of the Federal Government. January 4, 1995. House Vote No. 15: Passed 429-0; (D: 200-0; R: 228-0).

2) **Balanced Budget Amndmt.** (H.J.R.1) House passed H.J.R. 1, a balanced budget amendment to the Constitution of the United States. January 26, 1995. House Vote No. 51: Passed 300-132; (D: 72-129; R: 228-2).

3) **Bar Unfunded Mandates** (H.R.5) House curbed the practice of imposing unfunded Federal mandates on States and local governments, to ensure that the Federal Government pays the costs incurred by those governments in complying with certain Federal requirements. February 1, 1995. House Vote No. 83: Passed 360-74; (D: 130-73; R: 230-0).

4) **Pass Line Item Veto** (H.R.2) Line-Item Veto Act. House gave the President line-item authority over appropriation Acts and targeted tax benefits in revenue Acts. February 6, 1995. House Vote No. 95: Passed 294-134; (D: 71-129; R: 223-4).

5) **Relax Exclusionary Rule** (H.R.666) House reformed the crime exclusionary rule for illegally-obtained evidence. February 8, 1995. House Vote No. 103: Passed: 289-142; (D: 69-134; R: 220-7).

6) **Reform Crime Grant** (H.R.728) House approved a law to control crime by providing law enforcement block grants. February 14, 1995. House Vote No. 129: Passed 238-192; (D: 18-182; R: 220-9).

7) **National Security Act** (H.R.7) House changed various national security laws of the United States.
February 16, 1995. House Vote No. 145: Passed 241-181; (D: 18-176; R: 223-4)

8) **Moratorium on Regs.** (H.R.450) House established a moratorium on new Federal regulatory actions. February 24, 1995. House Vote No. 174: Passed 276-146; (D: 51-143; R: 225-2).

9) **Risk Assessment on Regs.** (H.R.1022) House passed regulatory reform including risk assessments of costs and benefits in major rules. February 28, 1995. House Vote No. 183: Passed 286-141; (D: 60-138; R: 226-2).

10) **Expnd. Priv. Prop. Rights** (H.R.925) House approved compensation of owners of private property for the effect of certain regulatory restrictions. March 3, 1995. House Vote No. 197: Passed 277-148; (D: 72-124; R: 205-23).

11) **Loser Pays Court Reform** (H.R.988) House reformed the Federal civil justice system. March 7, 1995. House Vote No. 207: Passed 232-193; (D: 16-181; R: 216-11).

12) **Product Liability Reform** (H.R.956) House established legal standards and procedures for product liability litigation. March 10, 1995. House Vote No. 229: Passed 265-161; (D: 45-154; R: 220-6).

13) **Welfare Reform** (H.R.4) House passed a bill to control welfare spending and reduce welfare dependence. March 24, 1995. House Vote No. 269: Passed 234-199; (D: 9-193; R: 225-5).

14) **Term Limits Amndmt.** (H.J.R.73) House failed to pass an amendment to the Constitution to limit the number of terms of office for Congress. March 29, 1995. House Vote No. 277: Failed two-thirds majority 227-204; (D: 38-163; R: 189-40).

15) **Tax Cuts** (H.R.1215) House passed tax changes to strengthen the American family and create jobs. April 5, 1995. House Vote No. 295: Passed 246-188; (D: 27-176; R: 219-11).

House Votes, 103d Congress:

1) **Clinton Deficit Plan** (H.R.2264) The House agreed to the conference report on H.R. 2264, to approve the Clinton Administration deficit reduction plan. August 5, 1993. House Vote No. 406: Passed 218-216; (D: 217-41; R: 0-175).

2) **NAFTA** (H.R.3450) North American Free Trade Agreement Implementation Act. November 17, 1993. House Vote No. 575: Passed 234-200; (D: 102-156; R: 132-43).

3) **Brady Handgun Purchase** (H.R.1025) House voted for a waiting period before the purchase of a handgun, and for a national instant criminal background check to be conducted by firearms dealers before the transfer of any firearm. November 10, 1993. House Vote No. 564: Passed 238-189; (D: 184-69; R: 54-119).

4) **Strike Race/Death Pnlty.**   (H.R.4092) House rejected the McCollum amendment that sought to strike provisions that bar execution of prisoners who demonstrate that their death sentence was imposed because of racial discrimination, and that permit the use of statistical evidence showing a significant racially discriminatory pattern in this determination. April 20, 1994. House Vote No. 131: Rejected 212-217; (D: 48-211; R: 164-5).

5) **Lmt. UN Cmnd. of Forces**   (H.R.2401) House rejected the Spence motion to restrict placing United States forces under operational control of a foreign national acting on behalf of the United Nations. September 29, 1993. House Vote No. 473: Rejected 192-238; (D: 20-236; R: 172-1).

6) **Cut Missile Funds**   (H.R.3116) House rejected the Penny amendment that sought to cut $1.2 billion from the Navy weapons procurement appropriation. September 30, 1993. House Vote No. 477: Rejected 178-248; (D: 144-111; R: 33-137).

Senate Votes, 104th Congress:

1) **Congressional Compliance** (S.2) Senate made certain laws applicable to the legislative branch. January 11, 1995. Senate Vote No. 14: Passed 98-1; (D: 45-1; R: 53-0).

2) **Bar Unfunded Mandates** (S.1) Senate curbed the practice of imposing unfunded Federal mandates on States and local governments and ensured that the Federal Government pays the costs incurred by those governments in complying with certain requirements. January 27, 1995. Senate Vote No. 61: Passed 086-10; (D: 35-10; R: 51-0).

3) **Balanced Budget Amendment** (H.J.R.1) Senate failed to pass a balanced budget amendment to the Constitution. March 2, 1995. Senate Vote No. 98: Failed two-thirds majority 65-35; (D: 14-33; R: 51-2).

4) **Pass Line Item Veto** (S.4) Senate gave the power to the President to reduce budget authority. March 23, 1995. Senate Vote No. 115: Passed 69-29; (D: 19-27; R: 50-2).

5) **Product Liability Reform** (H.R.956) Senate established legal standards and procedures for product liability litigation. May 10, 1995. Senate Vote No. 161: Passed 61-37; (D: 15-30; R: 46-7).

6) **FY96 Budget** (H.C.R.67) Senate passed HCR 67, approving the congressional budget designed to balance the budget in year 2002. May 25, 1995. Senate Vote No. 232: Passed 57-42; (D: 3-42; R: 54-0).

Senate Votes, 103d Congress:

1) **Clinton Deficit Plan** (H.R.2264) With the Vice President voting in favor, Senate agreed to the conference report on H.R. 2264, to approve the Clinton Administration deficit reduction plan. August 6, 1993. Senate Vote No. 247: Passed 50-50; (D: 50-6; R: 0-44).

2) **NAFTA** (H.R.3450) Implementation of the North American Free-Trade Agreement. November 20, 1993. Senate Vote No. 395: Passed 61-38; (D: 27-28; R: 34-10).

3) **Brady Handgun Purchase** (H.R.1025) Senate passed a law to provide for a waiting period before the purchase of a handgun, and for a national instant criminal background check to be conducted by firearms dealers before the transfer of any firearm. November 20, 1993. Senate Vote No. 394: Passed 63-36; (D: 47-8; R: 16-28).

4) **Strike Race/Death Pnlty.** (S.1935) Senate agreed to D'Amato Amendment to express the sense of the Senate that the conferees should reject the Racial Justice Act provisions for death penalty cases. May 11, 1994. Senate Vote No. 106: Passed 58-41; (D: 20-35; R: 38-6).

5) **Lmt. UN Cmnd. of Forces** (H.R.3116) Senate rejected the Nickles/Cochran Amendment to prohibit the use of funds to support U.S. military forces in certain international operations. October 19, 1993. Senate Vote No. 317: Rejected 33-65; (D: 1-54; R: 32-11).

6) **Cut Missile Funds** (H.R.4650) Senate rejected the Bumpers Amendment to reduce funds for the Trident II Missile program. August 10, 1994. Senate Vote No. 274: Rejected 40-60; (D: 34-22; R: 6-38).

INTRODUCTION

THE RESTORATION OF THE CONSTITUTIONAL ORDER AND THE RETURN TO TOCQUEVILLIAN AMERICA

The 1994 election, the first time Americans have selected national officeholders with terms extending into the 21st Century, has also marked a return to old traditions—in government a restoration of constitutional order, in society a return to a Tocquevillian America. Marked, it should be emphasized, not caused: for this single election did not entirely transform either the political opinion or civil society; it only provided an occasion and a setting in which opinions which had long been held could be expressed and a society that had been for some time reshaping itself could reveal its new form. Plus, it will seem implausible to many that a single election, and an offyear election at that, is the harbinger of a new era. Certainly it is possible that the new Republican majorities will fail miserably to keep their promises or, having kept them, have nothing more to offer that the voting public wants.

But the 1994 election does go a long way toward settling an argument that has been raging for at least a dozen years about where we stand in our history. The more familiar theory of our times is implicit in the narratives of the great New Deal historians and set forth as a cyclical theory by the best-known of them, Arthur Schlesinger Jr. According to this theory, American politics turns primarily on economic issues, and is a continuing struggle between the haves and have-nots. Every generation a new leader comes forward, supported by a generation of young idealists, proposing public action to solve national problems; that leader and his programs are embraced for a time by the people, who then sink back to support conservatives who try to maintain the status quo. In this view, history always moves to the left, lurching leftward when prodded by liberal leaders, then pausing, then lurching leftward again: Jefferson, Jackson, Lincoln, the two Roosevelts, Kennedy and, said Schlesinger hopefully after the 1992 election, Bill Clinton.

Another theory holds that politics divides Americans less often on economic than along cultural lines—according to race, religion, region, ethnic group and cultural values. It believes that Americans are looking to government not so much for economic redistribution—indeed, until the mid-20th century government did not seem capable of massive economic redistribution—but for the maintenance of basic order—not some authoritarian order, it must be added, but to an orderly framework in which people can make their livings, raise their families and work together in their communities. This theory holds that most Americans do not cast their votes just as a referendum on the performance of the macroeconomy, though some marginal number of votes, frequently enough to change the outcomes of otherwise close elections, often do so. Rather, their voting allegiance is determined by the accumulated effects of experiences over time that cut to the quick of their lives. Thus millions of Americans switched from the Republican to the Democratic Party in response to the economic disorder of the early 1930s, and millions of Americans switched from the Democratic to the Republican Party in response to the cultural disorder of the late 1960s. There is no inevitable cycle here, occurring at a certain place on the calendar. Rather, people respond to real events, and carry the experience of those events with them the rest of their lives, or until some other extended series of events cuts as deeply.

The presidential results of the last quarter century gave powerful support to the second theory. Republicans won five of the six presidential elections from 1968 to 1988 and lost the other, 1976, by only a 50%–48% margin. Republicans had an average margin of 53%–43%, a larger advantage than any party has won over any other six elections in American history. But Democrats won control of the Senate during most of this period and held the House for all of it: countervailing evidence. And in 1992, when Bill Clinton was elected, Schlesinger was only one of many who argued that his victory proved the cyclical theory was right: the new liberal leader had arrived, surrounded by a coterie of idealistic aides, and America was ready in this generation once again for a lurch to the left.

The 1994 election goes about as far as any election could toward settling the argument. Franklin Roosevelt, after his first victory in 1932, saw his party gain seats in the House and Senate in 1934—the only such offyear gain for the party in power in American history. John Kennedy, after his victory in 1960, saw his party gain four seats in the Senate and lose four in the House in 1962—a tradeoff any president would accept, and the second best showing of any party in history. In contrast, Bill Clinton, after his victory in 1992, saw his party lose control of both the Senate and the House in 1994, the most disastrous first term loss for a president since Herbert Hoover, in the Great Depression, in 1930. Since World War II, the average loss for the party in power during the first term after the election of a president has been zero seats in the Senate and 13 in the House. Bill Clinton's party lost eight seats in the Senate and 52 in the House. Moreover, these losses came at a time when the macroeconomy was growing and the United States was at peace. A clearer repudiation of the party in power cannot be imagined. Wherever history is headed, it is no longer headed left.

These results were no accident. They flowed logically from the election of 1992 and its aftermath, from the Democrats' past congressional victories and their performance as the majority in Congress and from voters' basic attitudes. Bill Clinton was elected in 1992 because he campaigned as a New Democrat, one who would use a combination of market and government mechanisms to reform public sector institutions that weren't working, and his party was repudiated in 1994 because he governed as an old Democrat, one who seeks an ever larger and more assertive public sector to solve problems. The most astonishing thing about Clinton's presidency is how this articulate, politically shrewd man utterly misread the lesson of his own election. It is said in his behalf that his campaign emphasized government "investments" and that his programs included some New Democratic initiatives. But the "investments" were only part of a market-government mix; when the Clinton general election campaign was in trouble, the ad that it put up on TV was the one that pledged to "end welfare as we know it." In office, it is true that Clinton adopted New Democrat initiative Vice President Al Gore's reinventing government and the national service plan. But the two issues which the President himself made number one were the budget and tax package of 1993, with its tax increases and faster-than-economic-growth increases in government spending, and Hillary Rodham Clinton's healthcare finance reform package of 1994, which political scientist Martha Derthick called the bossiest government program she had ever read.

The embrace of the Clinton front-row-center Old Democrat programs by the Democratic Congress enabled the Republicans to nationalize the congressional elections more than at any time since the Republicans lost control of the House in 1954. Democrats had denationalized House elections, starting around 1970, by building up institutional advantages—superior candidate skills, redistricting, artful employment of the perquisites of office and pork barrel projects and the camouflage of allowing members to cast showy moderate and conservative votes while a whip-cracking leadership insisted on loyalty on key procedural and rules votes. By the early 1990s the quality of all these institutional advantages was degrading. The Democrats' edge in superior candidate skills, greatest when self-starting young liberals energized by opposition to the Vietnam war and Richard Nixon were capturing and holding onto marginal and Republican districts, grew less as these baby boom liberals retired and no new generation of articulate young liberals appeared. Redistricting, controlled mostly by Democrats after the 1970 and 1980 Censuses, was controlled mostly by Republicans after the 1990 Census. And although their plans were seldom as egregiously partisan as those of the Democrats, they made up for that by allying themselves with blacks, especially in the South, and using the Voting Rights Amendments of 1982 as justification for maximizing the number of black-majority districts and removing from adjacent districts black voters whom white Democrats needed to win majorities. Perks and pork degraded, as voters' attention was focused on overdrafts at the House bank and post office and members' reserved parking places at Washington airports, and as voters came to be less interested in getting a new post office or national historic bike trail built than they were in reducing total federal spending. And congressional Democrats' camouflage was destroyed by the Clinton Administration. The fact that the Clinton budget and tax package was passed without a single Republican vote and by only one vote in both the Senate and the House made every Democrat who voted for it vulnerable to the charge of having cast the decisive vote. And too many Democrats, lulled by the widespread assumption in Washington that Hillary Rodham Clinton's healthcare package or something like it would inevitably pass, failed to separate themselves from this increasingly unpopular program until it was too late.

That moment came, ironically, when Democrats were poised to push through a piece of legislation they thought would make them widely popular, the 1994 crime package. But the House and Senate leadership, trying to please the liberals in their own caucuses who wanted social work and gun control measures more than the large majority of voters who wanted tough law enforcement and punishment, put together a package that House Republican Whip Newt Gingrich could portray as "social work" and "pork." All but 11 Republicans voted against the rule to consider the crime bill, while 58 Democrats, most of them opponents of the gun control measures insisted on by liberals, voted no also. The Clinton Administration and the Democratic leadership tactic of keeping liberals happy and using their whips to bludgeon enough moderate Democrats to produce 218 votes had definitively failed. It will not succeed again any time soon.

At this point, it soon became apparent that any Democratic healthcare plan could not pass. But it had been implausible for a long time that most members, remembering voters' fury when they passed a supposedly popular catastrophic healthcare plan in 1988, would vote for a thousand-plus-page piece of legislation which would inevitably have direct and intimate effects on their constituents' lives which could not be anticipated and some of which surely would be regarded as negative. Bringing the Democrats' policy aims out into the open was fatal for the Democrats' political ambitions.

So the forces nationalizing the election were already very busy at work when Newt Gingrich assembled 300-plus Republican incumbents and candidates on the steps of the Capitol September 27 to sign the House Republican Contract With America and when White House political strategists two weeks later decided to run against the Contract. Even before the Contract was signed, most Republican challenger and open seat candidates were running on platforms very much like it, emphasizing not the personal qualification and local issues Democrats had been campaigning on for years but their support for specific measures to discipline and cut the size of government—the balanced budget amendment, the line-item veto, term limits, applying to Congress the laws that it applies to everyone else. The Contract simply helped to standardize Republican campaigns even more, and to give the party a convenient label for a set of proposals that were widely popular. The Democrats' decision to run against the Contract is explicable only by observing they had nothing else to run on. Their institutional advantages, as already noted, were vanishing. The economic package, crime bill and healthcare plan they had counted on as assets turned out to be liabilities. The President whose support they expected might help them as Franklin Roosevelt's helped in 1934 and John Kennedy's in 1962 ended up traveling to the Middle East in October because he had so few invitations to the Middle West.

More evidence that the congressional results were no accident came in the elections for governor and other state offices. The eight largest states, with 49% of the nation's population, all had seriously contested elections for governor. Republicans won seven of these eight races, and the Democrat who won the other, Lawton Chiles of Florida, carried only voters age 65 and over and lost among voters under 65. Republicans won control of both houses of the legislature in Pennsylvania, Ohio, Michigan and Illinois; they won lower statewide offices in New York, Ohio, Michigan, Illinois, Florida, Texas and California. In all these contests there were personal and local factors and different personalities, but in all the basic contrast between the parties closely resembled the contrast between the parties nationally.

The Republican victory in 1994 arose from fundamental, not incidental causes. It was the result of voters' rational responses to the parties' differences on major issues, not to some accidental events or irrational paroxysm of anger. The long course of election results over the last quarter century proves, as much as these things can ever be proved, that 1992 was the exception and 1994 is the rule. We are moving away from, not toward, an ever-larger government; we are at the least uneasy about our renunciation of traditional cultural mores, and possibly ready to embrace them again; we cherish an inchoate, mostly unarticulated American nationalism that guides our unfocused, seeming contradictory impulses on foreign and defense and trade policy.

WHERE ARE WE HEADED?

In important respects, we seem to be returning to a Tocquevillian America, to something resembling the country that the French aristocrat Alexis de Tocqueville visited in 1831 and described in his *Democracy in America*. Tocqueville's America was egalitarian, individualistic, decentralized, religious, property-loving, lightly governed. Egalitarian, not in economic terms but in the sense that Americans are comfortable with the presumption of the moral equality of every citizen: we are not a servile people, in awe of any elite, though we are quick to recognize and honor talent. Individualistic, not rejecting common enterprise but insisting on the right to make personal decisions without interference from others. Decentralized, as the big units that dominated America in World War II and for decades afterward—big government, big business, big labor—have lost their hold on the economy and on people's imaginations. Religious, because the United States remains the one economically advanced country in which most people are religious. Property-loving, since ordinary people in the course of a lifetime expect to and do accumulate significant wealth, primarily in residential real estate but also in investments and pension. Lightly governed, because government leaves to voluntary associations of many kinds social functions which elsewhere and at other times have been performed by the state.

Centralization and hierarchy, which historian Robert Wiebe in *Self-Rule: A Cultural History of American Democracy* identifies as the dominant characteristics of American life for most of the 20th Century, seem to be yielding to decentralization and equality, as Wiebe shows they were, even more suddenly, in the early 19th Century. Then, when they were released from the threat of the Napoleonic wars, Americans liberated religion and medicine from central authorities, stopped working for big employers and surged west in great numbers to become independent farmers and merchants. That America developed a national two-party politics, but as Wiebe puts it, "Politics diffused government power and united a sprawling nation." In the 1990s, Americans once again have been released suddenly from the threat of world war. They are rejecting the authority of hierarchies in religion (compare the declining mainline denominations with the surging fundamentalist faiths or the New Age mentality) and medicine (look at the popularity of alternative healing and fads even in a time of great scientific progress).

Geographically, ordinary Americans have been spreading out to edge cities and beyond, in computer-equipped houses in low-priced subdivisions, living comfortably on credit extended in free if seemingly disorderly markets. Economically, they increasingly work for small businesses or hop from one job to another with dexterity and optimism and without generating political demands for economic redistribution or government guarantees. Americans are not a people yearning for security, although the G.I. generation who grew up in the Depression, served in

World War II and helped build prosperous postwar America do have a more than economic attachment to Social Security; when politicians have staked their all on claims to provide security, when Richard Nixon resisted Watergate investigations in the name of national security or when Bill Clinton offered voters what he claimed was health security, they have conspicuously failed to command voters' allegiance.

Intellectually, Americans take direction not from a cultural and educational elite that seeks to make the country obey abstract rules learned in prestigious universities—an elite that in many ways resembles the New England Federalists who were swept aside in the years following the Battle of New Orleans—but from self-help advisers, television evangelists and radio talk show hosts. The Ivy League elite that Christopher Lasch described in his posthumous *The Revolt of the Elites and the Betrayal of Democracy* no longer captures Americans' imaginations: compare the fascination with the Kennedys in the early 1960s with the vitriolic dislike for Bill and Hillary Rodham Clinton expressed by a very large minority of voters and the indifference of the rest.

This 21st Century Tocquevillian America is not necessarily Republican, any more than Tocqueville's 1830s America inevitably voted for the Jacksonian Democrats. The Whigs, when they escaped the thrall of their New England elites, won elections too, and in the 1990s Democrats can certainly win again, and not just because of Republican blunders. They can win if they develop a New Democratic politics that is an acceptable variant of the Republican faith, a set of policies with a more communitarian thrust but not one that attempts to impose centralized, hierarchical solutions on a country that resists centralization and hierarchy. Such a politics is what Bill Clinton seemed to be promising in 1992 but, in the opinion of most voters, failed to deliver in 1993 and 1994.

But in this new-old America the political rules are different from those most readers have grown up with and become accustomed to. Underlying much of today's political analysis and strategies is the assumption that the first things voters seek from government are economic—a smooth upward business cycle and a fairer distribution of income and wealth. But that is clearly wrong. The first thing voters seek of government is order—not some arbitrary, authoritarian order, but a rational, predictable order in which ordinary people can raise their families, make their livings, participate in their communities and go about their daily lives without fear of physical violence or economic disaster. Americans have had a happy history during most of which they took this basic order for granted. But they have reacted strongly when order is threatened. The economic disorder of the 1930s deprived the Republicans of their natural majority and gave Democrats the chance to become the majority party. The cultural disorder of the late 1960s deprived the Democrats of their natural majority and gave Republicans the chance to become the majority party.

The fallacy that the first things voters seek from government are economic is an idea that grew out of New Deal politics and Keynesian economics—specific responses to an episode of severe economic disorder. Yet even in the 1930s and the generation that followed that idea was never true except at the margins. In different elections 5% and sometimes even 10% of the voters would change their votes based on the performance of the macroeconomy or in response to policies of economic redistribution. And in an electorate closely divided between adherents of the two major parties, those 5% and 10% could easily make the difference in outcomes between one party or the other. But even at the height of what seemed to be class warfare politics—from 1935 to 1963, approximately—the very much larger blocs of the electorate adhered to party preferences that resulted from cultural issues. Southern whites were Democrats because Democrats opposed the issues of the Civil War. African-Americans, for three generations solidly Republican, became solidly Democratic, because Franklin Roosevelt seemed to back civil rights in the 1930s and 1940s as Abraham Lincoln and the radical Republicans had in the 1860s and 1870s. (Interestingly the New Dealers who were most favorable to civil rights were former Republicans—Eleanor Roosevelt, Harold Ickes, Henry Wallace.) Voters of New England Yankee stock were heavily Republican, as they had been since they founded the Republican Party in the 1850s; voters of immigrant stock were heavily Democratic, as they had been since they came to the great cities of the East and Midwest and found them run by unsympathetic Yankee Republicans. To these culturally defined blocs were added some defined by their stand on economic issues, most notably the militant members of the industrial CIO unions, the United Mine Workers, United Steelworkers and United Auto Workers, which transformed the industrial cities of the Great Lakes basin—Pittsburgh, Buffalo, Cleveland, Detroit—from Republican strongholds to Democratic bastions. But the politics of economic redistribution even at its height was a driving force to only a minority of voters.

Today it is a driving force for almost no one. For more than 20 years, since 1973, the income distribution has been growing less egalitarian—incidentally, not only in the United States but in other advanced countries as well. Yet there has grown up no political movement in this country to redistribute incomes or wealth. To the contrary, the redistributionist impulse has perceptibly withered. From 1935 to 1963 the CIO unions' heartland in the industrial cities of the Great Lakes basin were a dependable constituency for the economic redistribution advocated by great union leaders from John L. Lewis to Walter Reuther. But in 1994 every one of these great metropolitan areas—Buffalo, Pittsburgh, Cleveland, Detroit, Chicago—voted Republican for governor and, where there were contests, senator. And these were not liberal Republicans, of the sort who used to carry industrial areas in the heyday of the CIO, but Republicans calling for lower taxes and less government spending.

So we are moving from what has been the exception in American political life back to what has been the rule: a Tocquevillian politics in a Tocquevillian country. This is a country in which order exists because basic rules are accepted by the people, or insisted upon by them: government keeps the peace, lightly; government promotes a hard currency, indirectly; government enforces contracts, but not in the broad light of day. It is a country in which political forces and governmental mechanisms tend to ratchet the size of government down, not ratchet it up as did the political forces and governmental mechanisms operating from the New Deal years up through the 1980s. The political force ratcheting government down already existed by 1990: the people's widespread distrust of government as an instrumentality, measured in starkly different results to polling questions in the 1960s and 1990s. Voters in the 1990s have shown ingenuity and used unprecedented creativity to show they insist on compliance with George Bush's 1988 promise, "Read my lips—no new taxes!" In 1990, for the first time in a half century, they gave reduced percentages to House incumbents of both parties, after most members of both parties colluded with Bush in the budget summit tax increases. In 1992, they gave Bush a percentage 16% less than four years before, a loss almost as great as Herbert Hoover's during the Great Depression, after he broke his own promise. In 1994, they ousted Democrats from control of the House after 40 years, after they supported the Clinton tax increases of 1993. Just as Americans decided from long experience with the depression of the 1930s and the prosperity of the 1940s and after that markets don't work very well and government does, so Americans decided from long experience with the stagflation of the 1970s and the growth of the 1980s and after that government doesn't work very well and markets do.

Ronald Reagan, operating from the Executive Branch, was not able to put into place governmental mechanisms to ratchet government down, with one major exception, the large budget deficits which he tolerated and which placed downward pressure on spending. The Republicans of the 104th Congress came into office with a series of proposals which, if adopted, will exert much more downward pressure: the balanced budget amendment, the unfunded mandates law, the line-item veto, supermajorities for tax increases, abolition of the "current services" budget that gave every department an automatic increase and let it argue for more. In addition, there seems little support for the Keynesian policy of countercyclical government spending: note the utter failure of the Clinton stimulus package in the Democratic Congress in 1993. Not all the forces tending to ratchet down government will always succeed. But they are all working in the same direction.

The economic issues in the politics of a 21st Century Tocquevillian America will not concern the distribution of income or wealth or the care and tending of the macroeconomic business cycle. Both these tasks by the middle 1990s have come to be seen as largely beyond the competence of government. Rather, the goal of government in the economy will be seen as the maintenance of a reliable currency—a goal with deflationary tendencies, in contrast to the inflationary tendencies of the Keynesian goal of protection against recession—and an ordered environment in which consensual economic transactions can take place. There is room for argument here about just what these things mean: one side could argue that government should compensate citizens for any decision that affects their property, the other that government should require insurance against certain eventualities; such arguments are indeed the stuff of economic politics in the 1990s.

But it needs to be recognized that arguments which appear to be totally about economic issues are often arguments about cultural values. Consider the welfare issue. On the surface the debate seems to pit those who want to spend less of the government's (and ultimately their own) money on poor people and those who want to spend as much as or more than government is spending now. But the amounts of money involved, if not as trivial as some liberals suggest, are not as enormous as much popular rhetoric implies. The complaint of those who want to do away with or greatly alter the current welfare system is not so much that it costs too much as that it degrades the morals of the society by fostering the growth of a criminal underclass. Subsidizing single mothers puts an imprimatur of approval on unmarried parenthood by women and irresponsibility by men and creates whole neighborhoods where adolescent boys are unsupervised and are readily drawn into association with the criminals who are the real rulers.

Many voters suspect, with some accuracy, that the culture of caregiving professions has infected government and meant that programs originally intended to encourage middle class behavior instead tend to discourage the values that promote stability. Welfare programs are seen as run by social workers who do not believe in encouraging recipients to work; schools are seen as run by educators who do not believe in teaching basic skills and information; prisons are seen as maintained by penologists who do not believe in keeping people in jail. There is an element of exaggeration in these views but also, as those who are familiar with graduate schools of social work, education and penology know, large kernels of truth. Indeed, the body of graduate school-educated voters, among whom teachers and social workers with master's degrees are far more numerous than lawyers or doctors, has become the leftmost leaning segment of the electorate when it is stratified by education. In the 1994 exit poll, for example, voters with no high school diplomas voted 60% Democratic for Congress, in line with the historic tendency of least-educated voters to prefer Democrats; but this is a diminishing segment of the electorate, only 6% of the total in 1994, made up disproportionately of elderly blacks. The larger segment of voters with graduate school degrees, made up disproportionately of teachers, social workers and other highly credentialed public sector employees, voted 58% Democratic; and this group has been growing, and formed 17% of the electorate. In contrast, the voters in the educational middle, from high school graduates to college graduates, voted an average of 55% Republican.

When Americans were voting Republican in 1994, they were not voting against the economic elite, which was voting Republican also; they were voting against the educational elite, which was voting Democratic. That educational elite propagates ideas spread on a national basis, ideas which on their own could not win majority endorsement in the overwhelming majority of constituencies, ideas based on abstractions about human nature which have not held up in practice. We are indeed in the midst of a cultural war, as Pat Buchanan called it in 1992 (while seeming to relish it more than suited most voters), a struggle in which propagators of liberal cultural values have used government to impose them in every segment of American life—sometimes with success, as with the basic civil rights laws banning segregation of public accommodations, workplaces and the voting booth; often with controversy, as with abortion; sometimes with rejection, as in attempts to legalize marijuana and other euphoric drugs. In a country where politics has divided voters less often on economic lines than on cultural lines—along lines of race, region, religion, ethnic group and cultural values—this is the norm, and is the kind of politics we should expect in the future.

THE HOUSE OF REPRESENTATIVES

The 1994 election resulted in the restoration of the constitutional order: first—and for a limited period of time—in the most literal sense; second—and by no means with certainty—in the sense of imposing a political regime significantly closer to that envisaged by the Founding Fathers than the political regime which we have grown accustomed to in the sixty years following the New Deal of Franklin Roosevelt.

Article I of the Constitution is not about the President; it is about Congress, and the House of Representatives, not the Senate, comes first. Article I, describing how the Congress is constituted and specifying its powers, is also much longer than Article II or any other article; almost larger indeed than all the original articles put together. The Framers knew the presidency was an important office; they designed it after all for George Washington, than whom no man was more respected in America, and they hoped, and their hopes were fulfilled, that Washington in occupying the office first would define its powers and the limits thereon more powerfully than any abstract document could. The Framers' President had the veto, administrative powers, military authority; but he was not the center of things as he has been since 1933.

So let us begin with the institution which the Framers put first and expected would be the center: the House of Representatives. For years the House resisted change, as its majority Democrats used institutional advantages to hold their majorities regardless of public opinion on major national issues. But by 1994 those institutional advantages had degraded, and House elections served the function the Framers intended, registering public opinion on major national issues. This meant a change of political regimes, as the last months of 1994 and the first months of 1995 saw the collapse of the political regime created by, more than any one person, Phil Burton, and the establishment of a new regime created, again more than is usually true in our political history by one person, Newt Gingrich.

The collapse of the House Phil Burton built. Great turning points in history sometimes occur in events that in themselves are trivial: so it was on August 11, 1994, the House of Representatives voted down the rule on the crime bill—a procedural motion on a second-line piece of legislation—turned out to mark the end of the control of the House by liberal Democrats after precisely 20 years and two days. This was the collapse of the House Phil Burton built, the implosion of a political regime forged by a man who failed to achieve his own personal ambitions and had died 11 years before, but whose vision of who should control the House and to what ends had dominated the institution since the resignation of Richard Nixon on August 9, 1974.

Phil Burton started off on the left wing of the House; elected in February 1964, he not only had a perfect labor voting record and supported the Great Society but also voted against the House Un-American Activities Committee and the Vietnam war. But unlike other dreamy liberals of the time, he was a hard-nosed political operator who got his start campaigning among San Francisco's left-wing dock workers. Filling a vacuum left by aging Democratic leaders, he became a leader of the liberal Democratic Study Group and attracted new antiwar and environmental Democrats to his side; an expert on redistricting in California, he drew up its district lines for the 1970s to maximize Democratic representation and kibbitzed other states' redistricting as well. By 1974, everything was working Burton's way. The huge new crop of Democratic freshmen supported his reforms which established his political regime. The key was for the liberal majority of Democrats to control the Democratic caucus in order to produce 218 votes for rules and liberal legislation; that was secured in December 1974 when Burton got caucus secret ballot votes on all chairmen. Henceforward they would be disciplined by threat of liberal opposition. To maintain the overall Democratic majority in the House, Burton relied not on the popularity of his issues, about which he had no illusions, but on institutional advantages such as redistricting and teaching talented young candidates with superior skills to hold otherwise Republican-leaning seats; he encouraged Democrats to rely on the perquisites of office and pork barrel projects.

Burton failed in his own leadership ambitions, losing the majority leadership to Jim Wright by one vote in the December 1976 caucus; and he died of a heart attack, the victim of his unhealthy lifestyle, in March 1983. But his political regime continued, supported by Tip O'Neill, who never trusted him but agreed with him that Republicans should be ignored; Jim Wright, who had opposed him and learned from him; Thomas Foley, whom he had picked to head the DSG during a crucial period; and Richard Gephardt, who cast his first vote as a Democratic member for him in 1976. Democrats continued to win majorities in every election. They ignored Republicans, routinely used the rules to prevent direct votes on issues on which their stands were unpopular, maintained caucus solidarity and, under the leadership of Tony Coelho in the 1980s, bludgeoned business PACs into contributing to marginal Democrats and not contributing to Republican challengers. Democrats maintained their majorities through the Reagan years and, except for most of 1981 and occasional periods otherwise, maintained working control of the House until August 1994.

But over time their institutional advantages deteriorated. The Watergate era incumbents with their superior skills suffered attrition, as some ran for other office and others retired, with no similar cadre of talented Democrats appearing in districts. Redistricting, thanks to Republican control of federal judgeships, mostly went the Republicans' way for the 1990s. Perks and pork became less helpful in the anti-government early 1990s. Most of all, the Burton regime ultimately failed because it could not stand the light of day. Talk radio shows showed voters how overbearing and unfair the Democratic majorities were. Democratic scandals got great publicity. And voters became aware that, although most of them were voting for Republicans or for Democrats who professed to be moderates or conservatives, the House was continuing to produce liberal legislation year after year.

The Clinton Administration brought this out into the open. The spectacle of Democrats passing their budget and tax increases by one-vote margins in the House and Senate reduced to zero the credibility of Democratic incumbents who said they were moderates but who voted with the leadership. The prospect of Democrats passing on a party-line vote the unpopular healthcare plan was frightening. But even before that came up, Republicans argued plausibly that the Democrats' crime bill was a pork barrel measure—an impression strengthened by the fact that then-Judiciary Chairman Jack Brooks's alma mater announced it was getting a grant in the bill before members of the House were allowed to see it. The threat of liberal retaliation in the caucus could not overcome anti-gun control Democrats' fear of retribution from their constituents, while Republicans were united by the Democratic leadership's contemptuous treatment of them over many years—and by the skills of Newt Gingrich. The crime bill rule defeat, and the crash and burn of the Clinton healthcare plan, showed that the Burton political regime could no longer produce 218 votes.

The collapse of the House Phil Burton built left the House in ruins for only the few weeks from August to October 1994. Ready to rise in its place was a new political regime, just as soon as the Republicans won their almost universally unexpected majority in November 1994.

The construction of the House Newt Gingrich built. Newt Gingrich was elected to the House in 1978, after two unsuccessful races, as a reformist Republican—as unusual a position as Phil Burton's as a left-wing Democrat in 1964. He brought with him a broad and deep knowledge of history and a greater alertness to alternative contingencies than almost all of his Republican colleagues. They had been in the minority by then for 24 years, and with seemingly no prospects for reversing that status. In the early 1970s they might have hoped that Richard Nixon's big majorities could turn that around. But Democrats won a 2–1 advantage in the Watergate year of 1974, held it despite Jimmy Carter's narrow victory in 1976 and lost only a dozen seats in 1978. Democrats obviously had vast advantages in superior campaigning skills, and with a Democrat in the White House and liberals on the federal bench, Democrats seemed in control of the House forever. Republicans hunkered down in their committee seats, trying to mollify chairmen and get little advantages in policy or pork in return for bipartisan support.

Gingrich was confident that if Republicans could put the spotlight on the Democrats' methods and their ideas they could eventually prevail. But he had only a few allies among junior Republicans and almost none in the press. So he started appealing to a broader audience over C-SPAN and attacked House leaders head on. In 1984 his quotations of Democrats' absurd rhetoric against the invasion of Grenada spurred Speaker Tip O'Neill into violating the rules in attack. In 1987 Gingrich brought an ethics complaint against Speaker Jim Wright. In March 1989 he ran for Republican Whip over Minority Leader Robert Michel's choice, Edward Madigan, and won 87–85. Three months later Wright was forced to retire. In 1992 Gingrich was poised for big Republican gains, which did not occur because of the collapse of George Bush's candidacy. But he did succeed in getting Michel to agree to retire and in cinching the Republican leadership in November 1993. He worked hard to unite the Republican Conference, courting especially the relatively few moderate and liberal members, many of whom supported him for whip and almost all of whom stayed with him on the crucial crime bill rule vote. He attracted insurgent candidates around the country, sending out instructional audio tapes and teaching a course on American civilization designed for cable TV.

In September 1994 Gingrich got almost all Republican incumbents and challengers to sign his Contract With America. It raised few new issues; most Republicans were campaigning focusedly on Contract issues already. And it hazarded the risk of Democratic and media attacks, which soon arrived. But it also committed a Republican majority to holding votes on 10 issues in

HOUSE REPUBLICAN LEADERS

Position	Representative	Elected	Age*
Speaker of the House	Newt Gingrich (GA)	1978	52
House Majority Leader	Dick Armey (TX)	1984	55
House Majority Whip	Tom DeLay (TX)	1984	48
House Conference Chair	John Boehner (OH)	1990	45

COMMITTEE CHAIRMEN

Agriculture	Pat Roberts (KS)	1980	59
Appropriations	Bob Livingston (LA)	1977	52
Banking & Financial Services	Jim Leach (IA)	1976	52
Budget	John Kasich (OH)	1982	43
Commerce	Tom Bliley (VA)	1980	63
Economic & Educational Opportunities	Bill Goodling (PA)	1974	67
Government Reform & Oversight	Bill Clinger (PA)	1978	66
House Oversight	Bill Thomas (CA)	1978	53
Intelligence (Permanent Select)	Larry Combest (TX)	1984	50
International Relations	Ben Gilman (NY)	1972	72
Judiciary	Henry Hyde (IL)	1974	71
National Security	Floyd Spence (SC)	1970	67
Resources	Don Young (AK)	1973	62
Rules	Gerald Solomon (NY)	1978	65
Science	Bob Walker (PA)	1976	52
Small Business	Jan Meyers (KS)	1984	67
Standards of Official Conduct	Nancy Johnson (CT)	1982	60
Transportation & Infrastructure	Bud Shuster (PA)	1972	63
Veterans' Affairs	Bob Stump (AZ)	1976	68
Ways & Means	Bill Archer (TX)	1970	67

*as of July 1, 1995.

its first 100 days, a sort of public accountability unusual in American politics and directly contrary in spirit to the legislate-in-the-dark spirit of the Burton political regime. Throughout the fall Gingrich predicted Republicans would win a majority in the House—a prediction most in the media thought crazy. It turned out he was in close touch with American voters. The Newt Gingrich political regime was voted in on November 8, 1994.

How it will fare, and whether it will last anything like as long as the 20-year Phil Burton regime, is at this writing very far from clear. But it does seem to be a regime more in line with the constitutional order, in that it contemporaneously reflects public opinion on national issues as the Framers intended the House would, and with high-tech communications, for it has fared best on cable TV and worst in newspapers. It is beginning at least by advancing popular positions and at least initially has not relied on using the rules to prevent votes on issues where opinion favors the opposition. Like the Burton House, the Gingrich House is not a one-man show. Its success requires many hands. Gingrich took special care to choose the chairmen of the Budget and Appropriations Committee who would implement his party's plans to cut spending. He backed John Kasich over the more senior Alex McMillan for the ranking post on Budget in December 1992, recognizing Kasich's commitment, political skills and attractive television personality. And in December 1994 he stepped over four more senior members to announce that Bob Livingston would be chairman of Appropriations, valuing his conservative record and aggressiveness. On leadership positions, he went along with Dick Armey, though they are not entire allies, and did not strenuously oppose Tom DeLay, though he had opposed him back in 1989. The adjacent table shows the new House Republican leadership and committee chairmen, with age and year first elected.

THE SENATE

The Senate, first on the Sunday talk shows, is second in the constitutional order. As the 104th Congress assembled, the Senate's Majority Leader Bob Dole stood as the most respected political leader in America. But the Senate of which he was the formal leader was still very much second in setting the national agenda to Newt Gingrich's House, though ahead of Bill Clinton's Executive Branch. The Senate today is surely not "the greatest deliberative body in the world," as it likes to style itself; it is very seldom deliberative, and is often scarcely a body at all. This is a legislature where it is every member for him or herself, where the whole is equal to a fair lot less than the sum of its parts, where it is far easier to kill someone else's initiative than it is to get one going. But this is perhaps what the Framers intended. With only one-third of its members elected every two years, with a fair number of its members freed from political pressures because of their personal relationship with voters in small or one-party states, with its rules allowing even the politically weakest and personally least regarded of its members to stop the forward motion of legislation for some precious period of time, the Senate supplies some caution to the enthusiasms of the House.

What else it supplies is open to question. Partisan control of the Senate has been shifted as sharply, in percentage terms, as control of the House. As Bill Clinton was emerging ahead in the exit polls on election night 1992, his fellow Democrats seemed to have a 58–42 margin in the Senate, not quite filibuster-proof (that would have needed 60), but strong enough with a strong incumbent president. But the Democrats soon lost two more seats, significantly enough in the South. Democrat Wyche Fowler of Georgia, ahead 49%–48% in November 1992, lacked the absolute majority required by state law; in the runoff three weeks later he lost to Paul Coverdell, who though pro-choice had the support of the Christian right, 51%–49%. And after Lloyd Bentsen resigned to become Secretary of the Treasury, appointed Democrat Bob Krueger lost the seat to Republican Kay Bailey Hutchison 67%–33%. Then, in 1994, two incumbent Democratic senators were defeated, Jim Sasser of Tennessee, the Budget Committee chairman who had been running for Majority Leader, and Harris Wofford of Pennsylvania, whose election in November 1991 put the healthcare issue in the national spotlight. Republicans also won all six open seats, and the day after the election Richard Shelby of Alabama, a Democrat in the Clinton Administration's doghouse, switched parties, only to be followed in March by Colorado's Ben Nighthorse Campbell, ultimately giving the Republicans a 54–46 margin.   Over this Senate, Bob Dole looms as the colossus, not so much by virtue of his position as Majority Leader, but because the strength of his character. He is one of the few members of the World War II G.I. generation left in Congress, a connection to an older and in some ways more successful America, with his background in small town Kansas, his record as a war hero and his years of painful recovery. He first took his seat in Congress when Dwight Eisenhower was president and when Robert Taft was still an inspiration to Midwestern Republicans. Balancing budgets and holding down spending were their main goals in politics, reflecting the orderliness and thrift of the men who ran things in places like Russell, Kansas. Dole brought a conventional mindset and sharp partisanship to his first years in the House and Senate, but also showed—and continues to show—the ability to adapt to circumstances and learn from sometimes bitter experiences. He performed smoothly as Senate Finance chairman in the early 1980s and maneuvered smartly to win the Republican leadership in 1984 (which by late December 1995 he will have held longer than anyone else in history).

Dole has a bedrock of consistent beliefs: in the country and an assertive foreign policy, in the Republican party and something like fiscal probity, in small town America and some conservative cultural values. From these follow votes for defense spending, for domestic budget cuts, against abortion. But Dole has no ideological framework, no organizing vision, on which he can fall back. He is not good at strategy, brilliant at tactics. And he is a shrewd judge of the political winds. In mid-1993 it was widely assumed he would join with Democrats and fashion a bipartisan healthcare bill. But as the Clinton White House remained obdurate even as its plan became more unpopular, Dole pulled back and worked with Republicans who opposed it all the way. As Newt Gingrich stole the spotlight after the 1994 election, Dole proved quickly that he could speak the same language, and with some of his own accents.

Dole is pressed on all sides in the Senate. Most Senate Republicans are on the angry right, as was shown when Trent Lott ousted Al Simpson from the whip position by 27–26, despite Dole's support of Simpson; especially obstreperous is Phil Gramm, who sees Dole as a rival presidential candidate. But Dole has shown he can move their way without being intimidated. On the left, the Democrats who threaten Dole are not so much Minority Leader Tom Daschle, whose institutional powers are limited, but those who can out of conviction slow up the Senate, like Robert Byrd, or those who can out of originality command the spotlight, like Daniel Patrick Moynihan. But Dole has more to say on foreign policy than Foreign Affairs Chairman Jesse Helms or on defense than Armed Services Chairman Strom Thurmond; he overshadows other Republicans on domestic policy. He has the nation's, and therefore the Senate's, respectful attention because Americans have seen him over the years take blows and come back to fight stronger and smarter. Whatever the fate of his 1996 presidential ambitions, he remains a large figure on our political landscape.

Will the Republicans hold the Senate? There is nothing inevitable about Senate elections; there are not enough of them for the collection of outcomes to be statistically significant; contests depend often on personal factors that have little relation to national issues. Yet looking ahead from early 1995 Republicans appear to have the advantage in adding seats, unless opinion shifts quite sharply in the Democratic direction. True, the Democrats have fewer seats up in 1996 than Republicans, as the accompanying chart shows. But a dozen or so of the Republican seats seem very safe, as compared to a half dozen of the Democrats'. Moreover, Democratic senators unhappy that they are no longer in the majority are retiring in disproportionate numbers. Of the first three retirements announced, two were by Democrats in states that voted strongly Republican in 1994, Illinois and Louisiana, against one by a Republican where his colleague had switched parties: Colorado. The next three retirements came in Alabama, Arkansas and Nebraska—all states where Democrats will have uphill battles.

SENATE SEATS UP IN 1996

Democrats (15)

Max Baucus (MT)
Joseph R. Biden, Jr. (DE)
Bill Bradley (NJ)
J. James Exon (NE)
Tom Harkin (IA)
Howell Heflin (AL)
J. Bennett Johnston Jr. (LA)
John F. Kerry (MA)
Carl Levin (MI)
Sam Nunn (GA)
Claiborne Pell (RI)
David Pryor (AR)
John D. (Jay) Rockefeller (WV)
Paul Simon (IL)
Paul Wellstone (MN)

Republicans (18)

Hank Brown (CO)
Thad Cochran (MS)
William S. Cohen (ME)
Larry Craig (ID)
Pete Domenici (NM)
Phil Gramm (TX)
Mark O. Hatfield (OR)
Jesse A. Helms (NC)
James M. Inhofe (OK)
Nancy Landon Kassebaum (KS)
Mitch McConnell (KY)
Larry Pressler (SD)
Alan K. Simpson (WY)
Robert Smith (NH)
Ted Stevens (AK)
Fred D. Thompson (TN)
Strom Thurmond (SC)
John W. Warner (VA)

Italics indicates member retiring at end of term.

Then there is the South. Once upon a time, southern Democrats led the Senate, chaired its major committees, set its tone. Today, for the first time since Reconstruction, most senators from the South are Republicans. Only two southern states have two Democratic senators, Arkansas and Louisiana, and one in each state is retiring in 1996. Other southern Democratic senators include three old-timers (Ford; Heflin, retiring in 1996; Hollings, reelected with 51% in 1992), two with personal popularity far greater than their party (Nunn, Graham) and one who was reelected with a minority over a Republican with grave weaknesses (Robb). A solidly Republican South makes it hard for Democrats to win a majority in the Senate, as hard perhaps as it was for Republicans in the 40 years following 1932.

THE PRESIDENCY

The presidency was not expected to be an important office. Article I of the Constitution is about the Congress, and has 10 long Sections; Article II, establishing the presidency, has just four. The longest sets out how the president is elected—much of this had to be scrapped in 1804—and specifies the oath he must take. Section 2 says the President is Commander-in-Chief, that he can require the opinion in writing of officers of government, issue pardons and appoint ambassadors and Supreme Court judges and such other officers as Congress may provide for. Section 3 prescribes that he communicate annually to Congress, recommend laws to them, call Congress into session and "shall take care that the laws be faithfully executed." Section 4 is the impeachment clause. Interesting are the omissions. Article II doesn't say that the President can fire officers of government, or set public policy, much less that he "runs the country." Mostly, his powers are what Congress gives him. The Framers' scheme seems pretty simple. In peacetime the President presides, does what Congress requires and little more. In wartime he has greater powers, unspecified, indeed unlikely to be challenged in the midst of great exigencies.

This, one could argue, is how the Presidency has worked in practice. In wartime the President has terrible powers: Lincoln suspended habeas corpus and expanded federal powers vastly. But

PRESIDENT

President William Jefferson (Bill) Clinton (D)

Elected 1992, term expires Jan. 1997; born, August 19, 1946, Hope, AR; home, Little Rock, AR; Georgetown University, B.S. 1968; Rhodes Scholar, Oxford University, 1968–70; Yale University, J.D. 1973; Baptist; married (Hillary Rodham).

Career: Professor, University of Arkansas, 1974–76; Democratic Nominee for U.S. House of Representatives, 1974; Arkansas Attorney General, 1976–78; Practicing attorney, 1981–82; Governor of Arkansas, 1978–80, 1982–92.

Office: The White House, 1600 Pennsylvania Ave., NW, Washington, DC 20500, 202-456-1414.

VICE PRESIDENT

Vice President Albert (Al) Gore, Jr. (D)

Elected 1992, term expires, Jan. 1997; born, March 31, 1948, Washington, DC; home, Carthage, TN; Harvard University, B.A. 1969; Vanderbilt School of Religion, 1971–72; Vanderbilt Law School, 1974–76; Baptist; married (Tipper).

Career: Army, 1969–71 (Vietnam); Homebuilding business; Reporter, *Nashville Tennessean*, 1973–76; U.S. House of Representatives, 1976–84; U.S. Senate, 1984–92.

Office: The White House, 1600 Pennsylvania Ave., NW, Washington, DC 20500, 202-456-1414.

1992 Presidential Vote

Clinton (D) 44,908,233 (43%)
Bush (R) 39,102,282 (37%)
Perot (I)................. 19,741,048 (19%)

1988 Presidential Vote

Bush (R) 48,886,097 (53%)
Dukakis (D)............. 41,809,074 (46%)

The People: Est. Pop. 1994: 260,341,000; Pop. 1990: 248,709,873, up 4.7% 1990–1992. 24.8% rural. Median age: 32.9 years. 12.6% 65 years and over. 75.6% White, 12.1% Black, 9% Hispanic origin, 2.9% Asian, .8% American Indian. Households: 55.1% married couple families; 25.6% married couple fams. w. children; 45.3% college educ.; median household income: $30,056; per capita income: $14,420; 64.2% owner occupied housing; median house value: $79,100; median monthly rent: $374. 7.4% Unemployment. Voting age pop.: 185,105,441.

20 years later Woodrow Wilson, then a professor of political science, could argue that Congress runs the government and the President matters hardly at all. As a wartime President, Wilson himself exercised powers that would make us quail and, when peace came, saw his grandest policy frustrated when the Senate declined to ratify the peace treaties he had made. The power of the presidency subsided again in the 1920s, only to be revived by Franklin D. Roosevelt in the terrible economic disorder of the 1930s. Then came the extended experience of war—World War II, the Cold War, Korea, Vietnam—in which the Presidency became the center of American government—indeed, as the symbol of the whole country. We depended on presidents to preserve the nation, to prevent a world war; we were always aware that this one individual had the power to blow up the world. We spoke of "the Eisenhower era" or "the Johnson years"; a President's scandal could give its name to our times, "the Watergate era," or to a set of policies, "the Reagan revolution"; a record parodying the president and his family could soar to number one on the hit parade.

But after the American victories in the long Cold War in 1989 and the brief Gulf war in 1991, is the presidency so important any more? One never hears people talking of "the Bush years" or "the Clinton era." When Bill Clinton was elected president, he like almost all American adults had no living memory of a time when presidents were not utterly central in our politics and government, when the office was swelled up to its wartime dimension. But now it seems to have shrunk back to the size the Framers envisioned it would have in ordinary times. Bill Clinton has received low marks from the public for various substantive reasons—because he seemed to govern like an Old Democrat after campaigning as a New Democrat, because as Dan Quayle put it in the 1992 vice presidential debate he "has trouble telling the truth," because the public policies and cultural values he seems to represent are seen as immoral by a very large number of Americans. But not all his low standing is his own fault. In these times any president would be seen as a smaller figure than the presidents we have been used to. If the man is smaller than we expected, so is the office.

It could be added that this president is less suited to the smaller peacetime presidency than to the larger wartime presidency which he sought for most of his adult life. Bill Clinton's greatest gift is his way with words: he uses the language eloquently, sinuously, with down-home accents when he wants them and soaring elevation the next moment; when folks are angry at him, he can talk them back to his side, as he has done hundreds of times in rooms in Arkansas, a state small enough that he could speak to every important person and many not so important face to face. But a president today has a harder time getting and keeping our attention. And once he has forfeited it by failing to tell the truth or follow through on his commitments, we feel free to press the mute button every time we see his face on the screen. Americans have hung on the words of their presidents in crisis from Franklin Roosevelt during the banking crisis of 1933 to George Bush during the Gulf war of 1991. Now, it seems, they do not, and Bill Clinton, whose strongest weapon is words, is disarmed.

Another function of a wartime president is to hold people together in this always diverse and segmented nation. For this Clinton also seems eminently well prepared. He has genuine roots in many Americas: he is "the man from Hope," as he was touted at the 1992 Democratic National Convention, and the boy whose home town was the raffish gambling resort of Hot Springs; the charming son of the Bible-believing rural South and the alumnus of elite and skeptical Oxford and Yale Law School; the young man who when he took the oath seemed new to Washington and the grizzled political veteran who had been close to the center of power for more than 20 years, from 1966 when he was on Senator William Fulbright's Foreign Relations staff and 1972 when he was the McGovern coordinator in the not inconsiderable state of Texas. In 1963, at 17, he shook the hand of President Kennedy in the Rose Garden; in 1974, at 28, he was running for Congress, and almost won; in 1978, at 32, he was elected governor. His mixed background helped in Arkansas, a state with a taste for politicians of elite background: it elected the Oxford-educated Fulbright senator for 30 years, just after he had been fired by a politician as president of the University of Arkansas, and it elected Winthrop Rockefeller governor, to whom Bill

Clinton applied for help in avoiding the military draft. Clinton's elite credentials from Georgetown, Oxford and Yale and the well-connected friends he made there were assets, not liabilities, in his political career. He would not have been a plausible candidate for Congress at 28 or governor at 32—or for president at 46—if he had been locally educated and nationally unconnected.

Clinton has seemed less well suited to the diminished peacetime presidency, measured against the provisions of each section of Article II. His 1992 victory may have seemed to show he mastered the electoral process. But he owed that victory more than many of his admirers appreciated to contingencies which could scarcely have been predicted. One was the weakness of the Democratic field, a direct result of the opposition of most Democrats to the Gulf war—an opposition which was quickly revealed not only to be out of line with public opinion, but based on assumptions that were out of line with reality. If Clinton had an opponent of the stature of, say, Al Gore or Lloyd Bentsen, Gennifer Flowers's charges would surely have done him in by the New Hampshire primary. A totally unpredictable contingency was the candidacy of Ross Perot, who in spring 1992 "departisanized the critique of Bush" as no Democrat could have done, according to the late Paul Tully, a top Democratic strategist. Perot pushed Bush down in the polls at a time when Clinton was even lower, then left the race just at the moment that helped Clinton most. The third contingency was the weakness of Bush's campaign, which may reflect what the good grace with which he has taken to private life suggests: that he was ready to retire. All those things had to come together, and still Clinton won by only 43%–37%, a result that would have translated to approximately 51%–46% in a two-candidate race. Democrats who saw the Clinton victory as the natural result of the workings of a predictable political cycle naturally took it as a mandate for Democratic big government programs; analysts alert to these contingencies would certainly have been more cautious.

They would have been cautious also if they had known how poorly Clinton would measure up to the assignments the Constitution explicitly gives a president in peacetime. He is Commander-in-Chief, though in peacetime not one who can win credit for a successful war; Clinton's lies about his draft status and his obvious discomfort with things military obviously hurt him in 1993 and after. So did his dithering over his promise to allow gays in the military, the result of an improvident promise (this was not a high priority for gay rights lobbyists) and an ignorance of the mores of the career military. The Constitution also gives the president the power to appoint. But Clinton, more than any other recent president, has a hard time making up his mind, while his aides routinely and inexplicably leak evidence of his indecision to the press. And even when he does decide, appointments must be held up until they meet the standards of gender, race and ethnic balance set by First Lady Hillary Rodham Clinton. The Constitution requires the President to communicate to Congress. Clinton began his presidency with cordial relations with Democratic leaders—too cordial, it turned out; they persuaded him to support unpopular policies and oppose popular reforms. And the priorities the President set—the budget package with its tax increase in 1993, the healthcare plan in 1994—convinced voters he was an Old Democrat reneging on his 1992 promise to be a New Democrat.

Section 4 of Article II tells how the President can be impeached. This seems highly unlikely; even if Whitewater and other Arkansas scandals turn out to involve serious wrongdoing by the President, surely it will not rise to the level of high crimes and misdemeanors specified in the Constitution. But the scandals, even if nothing further turns up in 1995 and 1996, have already done Clinton much damage. The transparent lies and evasions of the White House on these issues have reduced Clinton's credibility to low levels. This affects substantive issues, because it means that the President cannot frame issues and define where he and his opponents stand. Thus in summer 1994, when the President of the United States said his crime bill was a crime bill and the number two leader of the minority party in the House said it was a pork bill, the voters split roughly equally on whether it was a crime bill or pork.

The weaknesses of Bill Clinton as a peacetime president were the proximate causes of the Democrats' debacle in fall 1994. Can he be reelected in 1996? The answer must surely be yes, if only because contingencies may arise that no one has foreseen. The Republican candidate could implode. A combination of third and fourth party candidates could enable Clinton to win with a plurality of electoral votes, as he did in 1992. He may win a military victory of the proportion of the Gulf war, a result so far above voters' expectations that their opinion of him will rise. There are other possibilities. But he begins with two major liabilities, and one handicap. The liabilities are that he is not trusted and that his party is on most national issues not the majority party. The handicap is that in this time of a diminished presidency voters will pay less attention to the President, so that those who have written him off are less likely to listen to him and give him a second chance.

If the presidency is a diminished office in a restored constitutional order, the means of selecting the president remain extraconstitutional. The Framers did not anticipate political parties—they thought and feared that there would be fluid, regionally based factions—and their own system of selection had to be scrapped after Thomas Jefferson's vice presidential nominee Aaron Burr intrigued to seize the presidency himself in 1800. In practice, our presidential selection system has been designed by able but not Rushmore-sized men: Martin Van Buren, who organized the first Democratic National Convention in 1831; Thurlow Weed, who engineered the first successful Republican nomination in 1860; Robert LaFollette, who enacted the first primary election in 1904 and the Wisconsin presidential primary in 1912; George McGovern and Donald Fraser, who led the redrafting of the Democratic Party's rules for the election of 1972. Ironically, it is the Republican Party which is sure to have a contested nomination in 1996, under rules mostly established by Democrats.

There is much to criticize in these rules. Two smallish states have disproportionate power to elevate little-known candidates to national fame in the two earliest contests. The Iowa caucuses are models of civic involvement; but they have also tilted Democrats toward candidates of extreme foreign policy dovishness and give an edge to Republicans who look favorably on farm subsidies. The New Hampshire primary attracts relatively large and well-informed electorates; but it gives an inordinate advantage to Democrats familiar in the Boston media market and Republicans implacably hostile to taxes.

The most important new fact for 1996 is this: several megastates, feeling left out of the process, have rescheduled their primaries to earlier dates for 1996. This means that the two parties' nominations are virtually certain to be decided in a 44-day period between the Iowa caucuses February 12 and the California primary March 26 during which over two-thirds of delegates will have been selected. This may have its advantages. The country will not bear the burden of lengthy primary campaigns, if that is a burden; the nominees will not be hectored by protracted opposition, as Jimmy Carter was in 1980, for example, since the contest will be hopeless and the goal of staying in to make a convention speech, as Edward Kennedy did, makes less sense as conventions' TV ratings go down every cycle; the Democrats will probably have renominated their president, or otherwise will have a new leader, while the Republicans will have a candidate who will have more time to gain the stature that leaders of the opposition often have in parliamentary systems.

Of course there is risk too. A nominee who comes to seem unsatisfactory cannot easily be removed; his campaign has, after all, selected most of the delegates. Electorates in big states will have little time to get to know candidates, having seen them up close only during the one- or two-week runups to their primaries. Little-known candidates will probably have to raise some $20 million before Iowa to get through the cycle, since there will be little time to raise money in the 44 days that follow. But that may be a good threshold test. In primaries following New Hampshire candidates will depend heavily on TV advertising and on their performance in local and national newscasts: not much civic involvement here. But there will be a great premium on focus and discipline; the candidate who fritters three days away "clarifying" an unfortunate statement or emphasizing an issue voters do not care about has probably ruined his chances. In both parties' primaries, and even more in the relatively few caucuses, the voters who form the largest core of enthusiasts in the two parties will have influence greater than their numbers: the religious right among Republicans, the feminist left among Democrats. It is all something of a crapshoot. Yet it would be hard to develop a system for parties to choose presidential nominees in a diverse country of 260 million people that is by some large quantum better, and it would be easy to design one that would be demonstrably worse.

What follows is a list of Republican presidential primaries and caucuses, according to the schedule as set in early 1995. It cannot be emphasized too strongly that this schedule is subject to change.

1996 REPUBLICAN PRIMARY AND CAUCUS SCHEDULE

Schedule is tentative and subject to change.
States holding primaries are in roman type, caucuses in italics.

February	6	Tuesday	*Louisiana*	**April**	2	Tuesday	Kansas
	12	Monday	*Iowa*				Minnesota
	20	Tuesday	New Hampshire		26	Friday	*Alaska*
	24	Saturday	Delaware	**May**	2	Thursday	*Nevada*
	27	Tuesday	Arizona		4	Saturday	*Wyoming*
			North Dakota		7	Tuesday	District of Columbia
			South Dakota				Indiana
March	2	Saturday	South Carolina		14	Tuesday	North Carolina
	5	Tuesday	Colorado				Nebraska
			Connecticut				West Virginia
			Georgia		21	Tuesday	Arkansas
			Maine				Oregon
			Maryland		28	Tuesday	Idaho
			Massachusetts				Kentucky
			Rhode Island	**June**	4	Tuesday	Alabama
			Vermont				Montana
	7	Thursday	New York				New Jersey
	12	Tuesday	Florida				New Mexico
			Louisiana				
			Mississippi				
			Oklahoma				
			Tennessee				
			Texas				
			Washington				
	17	Sunday	Puerto Rico				
	19	Tuesday	Illinois				
			Michigan				
			Ohio				
			Pennsylvania				
			Wisconsin				
	26	Tuesday	California				

"Why Great Men Are Not Chosen Presidents" is the title of a famous chapter of Lord Bryce's *The American Commonwealth,* first published in 1888 and revised in 1910—interestingly, just before the election of 1912, in which three of our most intellectually distinguished presidents, Theodore Roosevelt, William Howard Taft and Woodrow Wilson, ran against each other. Perhaps it is a characteristic of a decentralized, lightly governed Tocquevillian republic that the ablest people do not run; in happy times they may not be needed either. Still, there are stronger and weaker fields.

The Republican field for 1996 at this writing includes, in alphabetical order, Lamar Alexander, Pat Buchanan, Bob Dole, Robert Dornan, Phil Gramm, Alan Keyes, Richard Lugar,

Arlen Specter and Pete Wilson. Among the prominent Republicans who chose not to run are Dick Cheney, Jack Kemp and Dan Quayle. Bill Clinton, at this writing, has no declared Democratic challengers, but could. And, as Ross Perot showed in 1992, a third candidate could make a significant, possibly a winning, showing: Perot again or Colin Powell are the likeliest possibilities.

If the Republican field is not the strongest any party has ever had to choose from, it is by no means the weakest. Serious arguments can be made for the candidacies of most of the men in it, and most can write a plausible scenario of how he can win the nomination. Yet each also has a weakness which, the morning after he withdraws from the race, every pundit in the press will identify as his fatal flaw, the defect which meant that he never really had a chance to win. But if the presidential race is a zero-sum game so that all but one candidate must lose, it is also true that one of them must win and—if Republican optimism about the 1996 election turns out to be justified—become President in January 1997.

Lamar Alexander. Announcing on the steps of the Blount County Courthouse in Maryville, Tennessee, in his trademark red and black flannel shirt, Lamar Alexander stamped himself indelibly as the Beyond the Beltway candidate for president. He lives in Nashville and the only elective office he has held is governor of Tennessee; if he has served in Washington, in a minor post in the Nixon-Ford Administrations and as secretary of Education in George Bush's, he has always returned back home. In summer 1994 he drove around the country, staying with people involved in community work and talking late into the night about what is wrong with the country. One of Alexander's strengths is disciplined ambition. After Vanderbilt and New York University Law School, he clerked for Judge John Minor Wisdom in New Orleans and then came back to Tennessee where he quickly became a protege of Senator Howard Baker. In 1974, at 34, he ran for governor, and lost; in 1978, he ran again, walking across the state in his flannel shirt, picking up the trail at the same spot a few days after he was hit by a car. He had the advantage of running in the wake of Governor Ray Blanton's term in office, a crook who was selling pardons, and was sworn into office days early to stop the sales. His best-known achievement as governor was education reform—merit pay for teachers, opposed by teachers' unions, approved by voters. He also made Tennessee one of the leaders in attracting Japanese investment and new business generally.

What does Alexander believe? As Education Secretary he switched from a moderate stance to hard-line advocacy of school choice, and by 1994 he was sounding radical themes: cut Congress's pay and send it home half the year (something Howard Baker has urged for years), devolve responsibility for welfare and other programs from the federal government to the states. He calls for a reversal of the trend toward centralization and professional expertise called for by the progressive Herbert Croly in his 1909 *The Promise of American Life*; local communities and ordinary citizens with common sense can do a better job. If the force of his anti-Washington message is blunted by the Republican congressional victories of 1994, Alexander can also claim to have anticipated much of the Contract With America, and his ideas remain highly popular, especially among Republican voters. At the same time, his calm manner and his soothing music—he plays gospel songs and country music on the piano and other instruments—takes the Gingrichian hard edge off his proposals.

The first and obvious weakness of Alexander's candidacy is that voters may not want to take a chance again, after Bill Clinton and Michael Dukakis and Jimmy Carter, on a governor they know very little about. To which his answer is that Ronald Reagan turned out pretty well. The second defect is the sense that some in the press have that his candidacy is contrived; they started off imagining him to be a moderate and are startled to hear a message that is conservative. But every presidential candidacy is to some extent contrived—we do not want presidents sending out for pizzas at midnight while they decide what they think about welfare or whom they'll pick for vice president—and if Alexander is right in thinking that voters want someone from outside Washington he is the candidate who best fits that description.

Pat Buchanan. In 1992 Pat Buchanan left his post as *Crossfire* co-host and syndicated columnist to run against President George Bush; energized by the cheers he got on his way to a 37% showing in New Hampshire, he stayed in the race to the end and gave a fire-eating speech at the Republican National Convention that gave Democrats and media critics plenty of fodder and pushed former President Ronald Reagan's last major public address out of prime time. Now he is running again. Buchanan revived, after a 40-year absence from presidential politics, the conservative Republicanism of Senator Robert Taft. Like Taft and Republicans going back to the Civil War, he is protectionist, in favor of higher trade barriers to prop up American wages; like Republicans in the 1920s, he favors sharp restrictions on immigration, indeed a total ban on legal immigration for five years (would he have let Einstein in?); like Republicans between the two world wars and Taft when he voted against the NATO Treaty, he opposes the extension of American power abroad, as for example when he opposed the Gulf war resolution in 1991. Buchanan's views on these issues are shared by very few elected Republicans, but they may be— and the hopes of his candidacy are pinned on this—shared by very many Republican primary voters, and even by some erstwhile Democrats and Independents who may be persuaded to cross over and support him. Certainly he has a monopoly on them.

The obvious weakness of Buchanan's candidacy is that he has never run anything. As an editorial writer and speech writer and maker, he has a gift for vivid phrases and an impressive body of learning to draw from. But, as accounts of his service in the Nixon and Reagan White Houses suggest, he never made much of an effort to make his views prevail; there may be something of Machiavelli's lion to him, but nothing of Machiavelli's fox.

Robert Dole. In early 1995 the giant figure in American politics and government was Senate Majority Leader Bob Dole. He did not hold the government's major office like Bill Clinton nor was he the most vivid advocate of major policy changes like Newt Gingrich. But he stood above these two loquacious Baby Boomers with a gravitas and authority that comes from his membership in the G.I. Generation that led American government from 1960 to 1992 and from his own heroism and the grievous wound he suffered in the war in April 1945. He also stood above them in experience in government: if Dole was wounded in the first days of Harry Truman's Administration, he was sworn in as a member of Congress in the last days of Dwight Eisenhower's. Americans have seen Bob Dole perform under pressure for more than two decades now; they have seen him operate when his side is winning and they have seen him fall in defeat— and they have seen how every time he has risen back on his feet to fight again. There is a hard, bitter edge to Dole, apparent even in his quick and sometimes self-deprecating humor as well in his biting attacks on others; but it seems to have mellowed out somehow with age: it is hard to imagine Dole coming up today with jibes as angry as during his stint as Republican National chairman under Richard Nixon or in his debate as the vice presidential candidate of Gerald Ford.

Dole's greatest strength is an intellect honed by experience though unshaped by any general theory. He remains visibly uncomfortable articulating what George Bush picturesquely called "the vision thing." But he seems serenely comfortable executing political strategy on the national stage with an almost unerring sense of where the public is going and how his maneuvers in Washington can take him and his party there first. On health care during much of 1993, he sent out messages that he was prepared to compromise with the Clinton Administration and push a bipartisan bill through the Senate. But in January 1994, just as Bill Clinton's ratings started to founder, Dole started to say, in agreement with Republican strategist William Kristol, "There is no healthcare crisis," and began what turned out to be solid opposition to the key ingredients of the Clinton plan. In presidential campaigning Dole has moved smartly up the learning curve as well. In 1980 he ran without much of a campaign, and lost badly; in 1988 he ran without managing his campaign well, and lost to George Bush; in 1995 he started at least by assembling a fine campaign and running it well. On issues he adapted well to the Republican victory of 1994, taking up the cause of unfunded mandates in the Senate before Newt Gingrich did in the House, striving mightily for the balanced budget amendment. An old dog *can* learn new tricks. By mid-1995 he was leading other Republicans by wide margins and leading Bill Clinton by narrower margins in the polls. Inertia seemed to be leading Dole directly to the White House.

But there is one obvious weakness to the Dole candidacy: age. He turns 73 in 1996, the same age Ronald Reagan was when he was elected for his second term in 1984. Up through mid-1995 Dole showed himself to be vigorous, fully engaged, not at all diminished in his powers. But voters will be watching him as long as the campaign goes on for signs that he is no longer up to the job.

Robert Dornan. One of the surprise candidacies in 1995 was that of Robert Dornan, congressman from Orange County, California, who had already announced he would not run for the House again in 1996. In a time when the Republican message is transmitted most effectively by talk show hosts, his is perhaps an inevitable candidacy: for Dornan got his political start as a talk show host in Los Angeles in the 1970s, a fiery conservative who declared verbal war on liberals and cheered for things conservative. He likes to take the battle to the enemy: he was first elected to Congress in 1976, from a district on the showbiz liberal Westside of Los Angeles; defeated in a Senate primary (by Pete Wilson) in 1982, he captured his Orange County seat from a Democrat, with key support from Vietnamese-American voters who are, like Dornan, unhappy not that the United States went into Vietnam but that we got out. The military metaphor is apt: Dornan was an Air Force pilot, and his admiration for the military records of George Bush and Bob Dole is boundless. The strengths of Dornan's candidacy are his strong opposition to abortion, well-known to many pro-life activists, and his nationwide fame as a talk show host: he is the number one substitute host for Rush Limbaugh and has a direct mail list from which he has raised $2 million.

The obvious weakness of Dornan's candidacy is that almost no one (including, one suspects, the candidate himself) can see Bob Dornan as president. He argues that he uses his fieriness for effect in one-minutes on the floor of the House, and there is a goodhearted sincerity behind even his loudest attacks. He is obviously having a good time on the campaign trail, but adds "I know when to hold 'em and I know when to fold 'em."

Phil Gramm. The United States has had only one president with a Ph.D., Woodrow Wilson, of Johns Hopkins and Princeton; Phil Gramm, of the University of Georgia and Texas A&M, wants to be the second. Gramm combines steely ambition and measured discipline with a devotion to free market economics; his great political ability is to frame issues in a way which makes his answer seem not only attractive but inevitable. Gramm is very much a product of Texas A&M, as *Texas Monthly*'s Paul Burka has argued: he came there in 1967, when protests were raging on other campuses and riots flaring in big cities, and found a university that combined high intellectual standards with respect for military service and disdain for counter-cultural values. Like that other Ph.D. who has reached the highest levels of American politics, Newt Gingrich, Gramm started out in politics without any institutional support, without money, with influential personal connections, without much in the way of political organizing experiences. Instead he talked—to small town Texas audiences—about the virtues of free markets and the vices of government. He had the audacity to run in the Democratic primary against Senator Lloyd Bentsen in 1976, at 34, and got shellacked; he ran for Congress in 1978, and made the runoff by exactly 115 votes—a narrow margin by which to enter the history books. (But Lyndon Johnson won the 1948 Senate runoff by only 87 votes, and they were probably stolen.)

In Congress Gramm antagonized colleagues, nonplussed the press, operated without organizational backing—and made national policy nonetheless. In 1981 he was the Democratic co-sponsor of the Reagan budget cuts, distrusted ever after by his fellow Democrats. In 1983 he switched parties, resigned and won reelection triumphantly as a Republican. "I had to choose between Tip O'Neill and y'all," he said, "and I decided to stand with y'all." In 1984 he was elected to the Senate by a wide margin; in 1985 he proposed the Gramm-Rudman automatic budget-cutting mechanism, which dominated Washington policymaking and which in practice actually was followed by the cutting in half of the federal budget deficit until its enforcement mechanism was overturned by the courts. In time Gramm learned to pursue the institutional interests which back free market policies, and he was unembarrassed about representing Texas interests as well. He was easily reelected in 1990 and, from his campaign committee chairmanship, led Republicans in recapturing control of the Senate in 1994. Already he was planning his presidential race. It was Gramm who first made the argument that any serious candidate must raise $20 million in 1995 to compete in the brief seven-weeks primary period in 1996. Gramm argues as well that he is the strongest true conservative in the race and therefore is the logical nominee of the conservative Republican Party.

Two weaknesses are apparent in Gramm's candidacy. One is his reputation for meanness, earned among politicians for his readiness to disregard colleagues' political needs, earned among the press for the harshness of his rhetoric. But it may be that Bill Clinton has satiated the appetite of voters, particularly of Republican voters, for politicians who ingratiate themselves with voters and can "feel their pain." The other weakness is the sense that Gramm really cares only about economics, that his conservative voting record on cultural and foreign issues is not matched by the burning passion and impressive creativity he has brought to economic issues.

Alan Keyes. In early 1995, as presidential candidates spoke before Republican audiences, the one candidate who brought many conservatives to their feet cheering with his denunciations of cultural decay and insistence on stressing his opposition to abortion was Alan Keyes. That is the strength of his candidacy. The weakness is that he has never held elective office (he lost two races for senator in Maryland) and indeed has not held any office that comes remotely close to being considered a serious credential for the presidency.

Richard Lugar. The premise behind Richard Lugar's candidacy is that there are two important things a president needs to do in this post-Cold War, post-liberal era, and that Lugar is the candidate best qualified to do them. One is to maintain America's safety in the world, the other is to pare down the federal deficit. Lugar is probably the Republican candidate with the most experience in foreign policy. He chaired the Foreign Relations Committee in 1985 and 1986—Jesse Helms did not invoke seniority then to replace him, because of a campaign promise, but did later—and in that time took operative control of our policy toward the Philippines, easing President Ferdinand Marcos peacefully out office, preparing the way for the democratic election of Corazon Aquino. It was a masterful performance in all respects, a demonstration of Lugar's intellect, steadiness of character, capacity for hard work. He has taken a key role in foreign policy since, most notably in working with Sam Nunn on disarming the former Soviet nuclear arsenal: sensitive work in which both details and a grand strategy are important. On paring the budget, Lugar has been less centrally involved, though his votes on economic as on cultural and foreign issues have mostly been conservative. But in early 1995 he was preparing to use his post as chairman of the Senate Agriculture Committee not just to make deep cuts in the 1995 farm bill but to question the basic premises of farm subsidies: more radical reform than Newt Gingrich's House is likely to produce.

Lugar has no intention of raising $20 million in 1995 and admits that he lacks the personal charisma and the long acquaintance with conservative political activists which many argue are essential to winning the Republican nomination. These are his obvious weaknesses. But he has seen political tides, and his own political fortunes, come and go. In 1967, at 35, he was elected mayor of Indianapolis, and soon became a national figure as President Richard Nixon's favorite mayor; but in 1974 he lost a Senate race, before winning in 1976. As Foreign Relations chairman, he was a world leader for two years; then the Democratic victory in 1986 and Jesse Helms's decision pushed him aside. In 1988 he hoped to be George Bush's vice presidential candidate; instead the nomination went to Indiana's junior senator, Dan Quayle, whose likely national candidacies seemed to rule out a Lugar presidential candidacy forever. But in November 1994 Lugar started thinking about running and in February 1995 Quayle dropped out (it is revealing of their character that neither seems to have any animosity toward the other, despite their obvious rivalry); and now Lugar must be counted a serious candidate.

Arlen Specter. The one candidacy launched against the grain of the Republican Party is Arlen Specter's. He is one of the brainiest senators, and one of the most politically experienced—he was a key counsel to the Warren Commission in 1964 and was elected District Attorney in Philadelphia as a Republican, just after switching parties, in 1965. He has also lost some elections—for district attorney in 1973, for senator in 1976, for governor in 1978—before narrowly winning a Senate seat in 1980. He is running as a fiscal conservative and social moderate, though both labels are a stretch, overstating his conservatism on both counts. Specter's chief motivation seems to be to challenge the religious right, which by any measure is the leading source of enthusiasm and elan in the Republican Party (as the feminist left is in the Democratic Party). He also seems to be seeking absolution for his questioning in 1991 of Anita Hill in the hearings on the nomination of Justice Clarence Thomas. Specter's questions were fair and relevant, delivered in business-like tones, and his arguments well supported intellectually, but feminists have portrayed him as badgering the witness and in recent appearances he has refrained from defending his entirely defensible conduct and instead has confessed that the hearings taught him a lot about sexual harassment.

Specter's strategy seems aimed at corralling pro-choice and pro-feminist Republican voters and winning a plurality in early primaries. But it is hard to see how a candidate who challenges the central motivating beliefs of the largest number of activists for a party can hope to win its nomination without a total turnover in its ranks.

Pete Wilson. The governorship of the nation's largest state has long been a launching pad for the presidency: from 1813 until 1963 that state was New York, which produced dozens of candidates; since then it has been California, which has produced Richard Nixon, Ronald Reagan, Jerry Brown, Alan Cranston and now Pete Wilson. Wilson said he would not run for president as he was running for reelection as governor in 1994, then promptly reconsidered and got into the race in spring 1995; but then he ran for governor, at the urging of state party leaders, in 1990 just having been elected in 1988 to his second two-year term in the Senate. The strongest argument for Wilson's candidacy is that he brings a broad range of government experience, both in Washington and beyond the Beltway, and has issue positions widely acceptable in the nation's largest state and around the country. Republicans may be the anti-government party, but Wilson (like Bob Dole, Phil Gramm, Richard Lugar and Arlen Specter) has held elective office most of his adult life: he was elected to the California Assembly in 1966, the year Ronald Reagan was first elected governor; he was elected mayor of San Diego in 1971, and put environmental limits on its rapid growth; he was elected to the Senate in 1982 and 1988, beating Jerry Brown and Leo McCarthy, and was elected governor in 1990 and 1994, beating Dianne Feinstein and Kathleen Brown—all proven statewide winners. He is a master of detail who never loses sight of the larger message he is trying to deliver; he is a scrappy fighter, irritable but capable of keeping a clear vision through times of crisis. His great political talent earlier in his career was melding an appreciation of California's environment with a hardline stand on crime; his great talent more recently has been disciplining himself to stress very simple and basic themes which are the only messages a candidate can communicate over California's resolutely apolitical media.

Wilson has also shown flexibility in his views, accurately supplying what there is a demand for in the political marketplace, it can be argued. In 1990 he called for "preventive government," a mixture of market and government means to attack social problems, and in 1991 he sponsored a tax increase. In 1994 he was running hard against public spending for services for illegal immigrants—and, it should be added, emphasizing in every statement on the subject that he did not oppose legal immigrants, a distinction not at all lost on California voters. Always he has been strong for capital punishment—his grandfather was a police officer killed in the line of duty—and always he has backed a strong defense budget and interventionist foreign policy. A product of the Marine Corps as well as law school in Berkeley, he is a fighter, whether battling against Democrats in Washington or longtime Speaker Willie Brown in Sacramento, but is also willing to deal when the time comes.

The great weakness of Wilson's candidacy is that it is not clear if he has a constituency in Republican primaries. Even in California, in the 1994 primary he beat Ron Unz, an unknown conservative computer millionaire, by only 61%–34%: many California conservatives haven't forgiven him his tax bill, his resoundingly pro-choice position on abortion or his signing of a gay rights bill (less liberal than one he vetoed). Presumably he could win the March 26 California primary against anyone else who survived that far; but in mid-1995 California polls he was trailing Bob Dole. Outside California Wilson is largely unknown. He must share his beyond-the-Beltway credential with Lamar Alexander, whose claims to being outside government now ring truer, and his pro-choice and similar liberal cultural stands with Arlen Specter, who proclaims them more loudly. He may benefit from an expected endorsement by Massachusetts Governor William Weld, but Weld is disliked by some in New Hampshire for his much-publicized December 1994 approval of a legislative pay increase. Wilson's candidacy is premised on the collapse of Bob Dole's, which of course could happen, and the hope that Republican primary voters will calculate, as the Clinton White House was calculating in early 1995, that Wilson would be Clinton's toughest opponent because of his presumed ability to carry California, without which Clinton cannot be reelected. But it's not clear that voters, as opposed to politicians, make such calculations.

Gubernatorial Election Cycle

1995, 3 States

Kentucky (D)   Mississippi (R)
Louisiana (D)

1996, 11 States

Delaware (D)   North Dakota (R)
Indiana (D)   Utah (R)
Missouri (D)   Vermont (D)*
Montana (R)   Washington (D)
New Hampshire (R)*   **West Virginia (D)**
North Carolina (D)

1997, 2 States

New Jersey (R)   **Virginia (R)**

1998, 36 States

Alabama (R)   Minnesota (R)
Alaska (D)   **Nebraska (D)**
Arizona (R)   **Nevada (D)**
Arkansas (D)   New Hampshire*
California (R)   New Mexico (R)
Colorado (D)   New York (R)
Connecticut (R)   **Ohio (R)**
Florida (D)   Oklahoma (R)
Georgia (D)   Oregon (D)
Hawaii (D)   Pennsylvania (R)
Idaho (R)   Rhode Island (R)
Illinois (R)   South Carolina (R)
Iowa (R)   South Dakota (R)
Kansas (R)   Tennessee (R)
Maine (I)   Texas (R)
Maryland (D)   Vermont*
Massachusetts (R)   Wisconsin (R)
Michigan (R)   Wyoming (R)

30 Republicans, 19 Democrats, 1 Independent

*States with two year terms. All others are four-year.
Boldface indicates governors who may not suceed themselves in the election that year.

ALABAMA

On a hill overlooking downtown Montgomery stands Alabama's Greek Revival Capitol. This is the building where the Confederate Congress first met, and where Jefferson Davis in 1861 took the oath of office as President of the Confederate States of America; in 1993, when the Capitol reopened after seven years of renovation, controversy raged over whether to fly the Stars and Bars over its dome. (Governor Folsom had it removed shortly after taking office.) Down the hill is Martin Luther King, Jr.'s Dexter Avenue Baptist Church, where the young minister found himself leading the boycott that began when Rosa Parks refused to move to the back of the bus. Alabama poignantly honors both the Confederacy and the Civil Rights Revolution, those two uprisings that so moved America. Today, whatever flags may fly over the Capitol, it is the latter subject that gets the most attention: Maya Lin's circular Civil Rights Memorial in Montgomery, the Civil Rights Institute across the street from the 16th Street Baptist Church in Birmingham's Civil Rights District, the Pettus Bridge in Selma and the Dexter Avenue Baptist Church are among the many sites of civil rights and black history preserved and promoted by the state.

Yet the classic symmetry of the Capitol and the calm simplicity of the black churches are not the whole story. Thick-leaved trees and creeping vines clutter the view from the hill or the street below. In the interstices between old brick and new steel buildings, the countryside seems to be returning to a small urban space. Nature still seems untamed in Alabama, and the raw passions of the first settlers which gave life to these serene buildings always seem ready to break into violence.

A raucous tone has rung since the first Jacksonian farmers pushed the Indians west and plowed the steeply inclined red clay hills of northern Alabama and the first plantation owners shipped in hundreds of slaves to grow cotton in the dark Black Belt soil. It was the violent reactions of white Alabamans to desegregation in Tuscaloosa, Freedom Riders in Anniston, schoolchildren on the streets of Birmingham and marchers in Selma that finally turned national opinion in favor of the civil rights revolution. In Alabama's peaceful economic development are currents of raw innocence: the miners hacking away in the 1880s at the solid-iron rock of Red Mountain to feed newly cast steel mills glaring in the valley of Birmingham below; the motorists of the 1990s speeding past exposed red earth of gouged-out hillsides to interchanges where the small factories and Wal-Mart shopping centers have sprouted up.

A similar rawness can be seen in Alabama's politics. Half a century ago, Alabama produced some of the most populist American politicians, crusaders against Wall Street and against the local economic potentates they called the "Big Mules": Hugo Black, a senator until he became a Supreme Court justice in 1937; Lister Hill and John Sparkman—young congressmen who went on to the Senate and sponsored landmark health and housing legislation. And, young congressmen in the 1950s gave Alabama arguably the nation's most legislatively productive House delegation. On the state level, the foremost populist was Kissin' Jim Folsom, a huge, oratorically overpowering, personally flawed politician who was elected governor (back when consecutive terms were forbidden) in 1946 and 1954, and whose son was governor in 1993 and 1994. The elder Folsom was a serious candidate again in 1962 until he appeared drunk in a late campaign appearance on the new medium of television, and later watched his following taken over by his onetime protege, a young lawyer named George Wallace.

While Wallace was orating in the Capitol, Martin Luther King, at the Dexter Avenue Baptist Church, was leading what turned out to be a civil rights revolution. King initiated a seemingly hopeless bus boycott and soon became the leader of a national movement whose moral force he was one of the few to comprehend. In the southern standards of the time, what King demanded seemed impossible; it was unthinkable that blacks should ever vote. In short-run politics, it

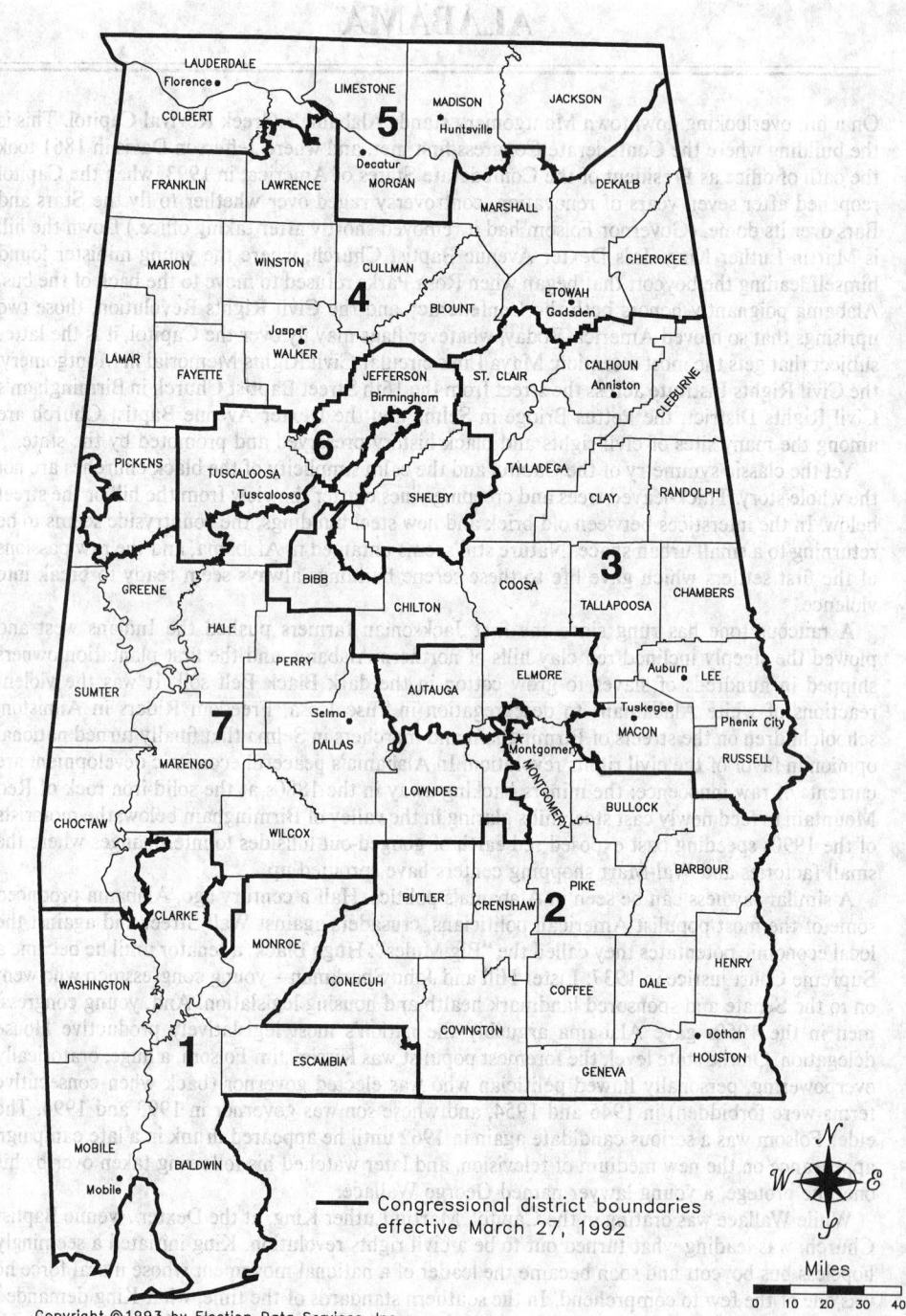

LAUDERDALE
Florence
COLBERT
LIMESTONE
5
MADISON
Huntsville
JACKSON

FRANKLIN
LAWRENCE
Decatur
MORGAN
MARSHALL
DEKALB

MARION
WINSTON
CULLMAN
BLOUNT
ETOWAH
Gadsden
CHEROKEE

4
Jasper
WALKER
JEFFERSON
Birmingham
ST. CLAIR
CALHOUN
Anniston

LAMAR
FAYETTE

PICKENS
TUSCALOOSA
Tuscaloosa
6
SHELBY
TALLADEGA
CLAY
RANDOLPH
CLEBURNE

GREENE
BIBB
CHILTON
COOSA
TALLAPOOSA
CHAMBERS

HALE
PERRY
AUTAUGA
ELMORE
Auburn
LEE

SUMTER
7
Selma
DALLAS
Tuskegee
MACON
Phenix City

MARENGO
Montgomery
MONTGOMERY
BULLOCK
RUSSELL

CHOCTAW
LOWNDES
WILCOX

CLARKE
BUTLER
CRENSHAW
2
PIKE
BARBOUR

MONROE
HENRY

WASHINGTON
CONECUH
COFFEE
DALE

COVINGTON
Dothan
HOUSTON

ESCAMBIA
GENEVA

1
MOBILE
BALDWIN
Mobile

Congressional district boundaries
effective March 27, 1992

N
W　E
S

Miles
0　10　20　30　40

helped the politicians who most strongly proclaimed their opposition to desegregation. But in the long run it changed public life in America—and in Alabama. But not before George Wallace made himself a national figure. He believed he had lost the 1958 governor's primary because he was "out-segged," and vowed that he never would be again. Elected governor in 1962, he pledged to stand in the schoolhouse door to prevent desegregation; this was a charade, but a dangerous one. And it encouraged the violent resistance of Alabama officials—Birmingham commissioner Bull Connor's police dogs and fire hoses in 1963, Sheriff Jim Clark's cordons in Selma in 1965—which, transmitted on evening newscasts, highlighted, as King expected it would, the evils of segregation. The North was no longer able to turn its eyes away from southern segregation, and most Americans decided they must support the Civil Rights Act of 1964 and the Voting Rights Act of 1965.

Despite his defeat, Wallace went national. With a shrewd sense of ordinary voters' resentment at elites' cultural liberalism, Wallace ran well in the 1964 and 1972 northern Democratic presidential primaries, and as a third-party candidate in the 1968 presidential race won 13.5% of the vote. Crippled by a gunshot wound while running again in May 1972, he lost all force as a national politician when he lost to Jimmy Carter in the March 1976 Florida primary. But he remained the key figure in Alabama, retiring as governor in 1978 but returning to office in 1982 until his final retirement in 1986. In time he became a sad figure, crippled and unable to hear much, often in dreadful pain, inspiring sympathy by seeking the support of the blacks he had once scorned. This longtime opportunist seemed now to be helping Alabama make peace with its past; "The South has changed," he said, "and for the better."

Unfortunately, in the Wallace years Alabama in some ways lost ground. While Atlanta was peacefully desegregating and beginning three decades of vibrant white-collar growth, Birmingham was violently resisting the civil rights movement, only to see the shrinkage of its once substantial blue-collar base—the steel industry—and an outflow of talented people of all races. The state's economy, regarded as progressive when manufacturing was the leading edge of growth, became positively backward during the Wallace era. The big steel mills of Birmingham turned cold as demand for steel fell; the shipyards of Mobile scrambled for work; the electric generators of TVA, once hailed as signs of progress, were condemned for burning dirty coal or allegedly hazardous nuclear fuel. Struggling to catch up, Alabama in 1993 managed to attract a new Mercedes plant to Tuscaloosa, but at a record cost of $300 million in concessions and incentives.

Politically, Wallace's ascendancy delayed a Republican emergence in Alabama during the late 1970s to 1980s, as his presidential candidacies delayed a Republican emergence in most of the South during that same time; and it may have helped atrophy the Democratic Party, as well. Alabama has always had a thin public sector, and the low income levels and growth rates of the Wallace years prevented any major strengthening. In the post-Wallace years, partisan struggles came to resemble the old intra-Democratic Party battles between populists and "Big Mules." The dominant forces in the Democratic Party—particularly as the party's gubernatorial primary electorate shrunk from 1 million in 1982 to 703,000 in 1994 and its black percentage rose nearer 50%—were the Alabama Education Association, trial lawyers and black organizations. They provided the main means of support for Senator Howell Heflin and gubernatorial candidacies of Bill Baxley, Paul Hubbert and Jim Folsom. On the other side is a Republican Party with a large reservoir of support in general elections, but little history as an organization and a small bench of officeholders. Alabama's current Republican Governor and Senator, Fob James and Richard Shelby, were both originally elected to office as Democrats, James as Governor in 1978 (the only non-Wallace elected in 20 years) and Shelby as Congressman beginning in 1978 and Senator in 1986 and 1992; James switched parties before running in 1994 and Shelby switched the day after the 1994 election. Alabama's previous two-term Republican Governor, Guy Hunt, a Primitive Baptist preacher and former Amway salesman from Holly Pond, was removed from office in April 1993 after he was convicted of converting $200,000 from an inaugural fund to personal use; he was immediately replaced by Jim Folsom Jr..

Partisan contests are decided along now familiar lines. Democrats carry black neighborhoods in the cities and the Black Belt counties in west central Alabama and just east of Montgomery; Greene County voted 88% for Jim Folsom in November 1994. Republicans win big margins among whites in the metropolitan areas, particularly in the new and relatively affluent subdivisions 10 miles or more beyond the old downtowns; Shelby County, outside Birmingham, voted 81% for Fob James in 1994. Democrats can still carry the virtually all-white hill counties north of Birmingham, but the Tennessee Valley, once solidly Democratic, now leans the other way as the area around Huntsville and Decatur vote heavily Republican. Demography favors the Republicans: the Black Belts have long been losing population, the suburban rings have been gaining fast. Even in 1992, George Bush carried Alabama, 48%–41%; in 1994, everything seemed to be working for Jim Folsom, but Fob James won instead. Republicans now hold three of Alabama's seven U.S. House seats, and made a serious challenge for a fourth in 1994; they gained seats in both houses of the legislature also, though are still far short of majorities. But the trend, which likely will be reinforced by the 1996 contest to succeed the retiring Heflin, is pretty clear.

Indeed, the Democrats have struggled to stay in power by staging what seem like banana republic coups—and have eventually lost anyway. In 1986, after Attorney General Charlie Graddick won a runoff by some 8,000 votes, the state Democratic Party stripped him of the gubernatorial nomination on the grounds that Republican primary voters had been allowed to vote in the runoff, and, therefore, gave it instead to liberal former Attorney General Bill Baxley; he lost in the fall to Guy Hunt. Then came the case brought in 1992 by Attorney General Jimmy Evans against Hunt for converting inaugural funds to personal use; Hunt did not dispute the facts but said his lawyers told him the transfer was legal, but a Montgomery jury evidently found he had criminal intent anyway. This verdict gave the Democrats the governorship they had not been able to win at the polls; but they lost it again in 1994. Jimmy Evans was then also defeated by Jeff Sessions, a lawyer rejected by the Senate Judiciary Committee for a federal judgeship in 1987, by a startling 57%–43% margin.

The pioneers' fighting spirit is still very much alive in Alabama politics. Democrats evidently feel so self-righteous in their opposition to a party that flies the Stars and Bars over the Capitol, that they feel entitled to steal one election after another. Republicans evidently feel so beleaguered by a political establishment that will steal elections, they feel no obligation to engage in any form of comity. Do not expect the fireworks to stop any time soon.

Governor. Fob James comes to the office of governor for the second time (in his second party) by a margin of 10,000, 50.4%–49.6%. He first gained fame as an All-American halfback at Auburn in 1954. He played pro ball for the Montreal Alouettes and at 28 started an athletic equipment business and made a fortune producing high-density plastic barbells. He ran for governor as a Democrat in 1978, though he had been active in Republican politics as late as 1976, and beat four experienced politicians in the primary and runoff. As governor, he claimed credit for raising student test scores and generating business investment, but he did not run for reelection in 1982, when George Wallace won his last term. He moved to the Gulf area and founded a new business and by 1994 was ready to run for governor again, as a Republican. Some 212,000 voters turned out for the Republican primary, nearly double the figure in 1990. James, better known and better financed than his opponents, won 40% in a six-candidate primary and then beat Mobile-based state Senator Ann Bedsole in the runoff 62%–38%.

The favorite still was Democratic incumbent, Jim Folsom, Jr. Folsom was born during his father's first term as governor; he ran for the Senate in 1980, at 31, and lost 50%–47% to Admiral Jeremiah Denton; he was reelected Lieutenant Governor in 1990 even as Guy Hunt was beating Democrat Paul Hubbert, former head of the Alabama Education Association. He became governor when Attorney General Jimmy Evans's prosecution produced a guilty verdict, eventually ousting Hunt from office in April 1993. Immediately Folsom ordered the Confederate flag to be taken down from atop the Capitol. He worked with the legislature on difficult issues of ethics, education financing and casino gambling. But in 1994 he was accused of giving a

Medicaid contract to a firm co-founded by his father-in-law and incorporated by 7th District Congressman Earl Hilliard. Folsom beat Hubbert 54%–41% in the primary and led in polls through the campaign, but was edged out in the end by James by 10,000 votes.

James evidently scored with his attack on Folsom's education reform as "Outcomes Based Education," which taught values rather than skills and cost $1 billion. He promised education reform that would teach basics and test students rigorously; he opposed casino gambling but said he would allow a referendum on it. And he promised to continue to encourage private economic development.

Senators. Alabama has two senators, both originally elected as Democrats. But one, Howell Heflin, has moved closer to the national Democratic party, providing its Senate leaders with critical votes while maintaining a conservative record on many issues, while the other, Richard Shelby, after voting conspicuously against the Clinton administration, switched to the Republican party immediately after the 1994 election. It is a measure of Alabama's current Republican trend that Heflin decided not to seek reelection in the face of what would have been a stern challenge in 1996, while polls show Shelby the strongest public figure in the state.

Howell Heflin looks more like a southern politician than any other member of Congress: he is a huge man, with a thick accent, an inveterate storyteller. He is the son of a Methodist minister and nephew of "Cotton Tom" Heflin, a fierce segregationist who served in the Senate from 1920 to 1931. Heflin was a successful trial lawyer in Tuscumbia, in the Tennessee Valley, before being elected in 1970 as the anti-George Wallace Chief Justice of the state Supreme Court. "I just try to be the country judge," he says, and certainly looks the part; but of course he has more political sophistication and wiliness than that. When Heflin ran for the Senate in 1978, he expected Wallace to be his opponent, but Wallace declined to run. Heflin beat Congressman Walter Flowers in the primary by running against "the Washington crowd." In 1984 he was reelected over a one-term congressman and in 1990 he beat a state Senator from Mountain Brook, an affluent suburb of Birmingham, whom he described as a "Gucci-clothed, Mercedes-driving, Jacuzzi-soaking, Perrier-drinking, Grey Poupon" Republican—even as Heflin, thanks to a crackerjack fundraising operation that mined liberal money in New York and Beverly Hills, was outspending him nearly 2–1. He won comfortably in each campaign.

From the cradle of TVA, Heflin is a believer in government programs. He supports rural electrification, for example, with rhetoric straight out of the New Deal. On the Agriculture Committee, he fights for the peanut program, federal crop insurance, the Boll Weevil Eradication Act, and flood relief. His Animal Enterprise Protection Act punishes violence by animal rights advocates against zoos, aquariums and livestock shows; he works to ease restrictions on pesticides. He outspokenly opposed NAFTA, which he saw as competition for Alabama's textile mills, and the Btu tax on energy, both favored projects of the Clinton Administration. Mindful of the space industry centered on Huntsville, he is a strong supporter of both the Space Shuttle and Space Station; he pledges to work to keep Anniston's Fort McClellan and Army Depot off the base-closings list (the former reprieved only at the last minute in 1991 and 1993). He tends to favor an assertive foreign policy—he cast a key vote for the Gulf war resolution—but is wary of free trade and wants a lower ceiling on immigration.

Heflin has gained his most national attention by serving on the Judiciary Committee, where he prides himself on being a careful lawyer who picks at the rules of law with the delicate touch of a watch repairman. He was the chief sponsor of the Bankruptcy Act revisions which were signed into law in 1994, the first major revision of this important but often invisible legislation in 16 years. He works hard on the mechanics of the federal court system. Mindful of Alabama's history, he is proud of his support for civil rights, but pushed the EEOC to withdraw its religious harassment guidelines, which he thought would inhibit free expression. He favors some abortion restrictions and supported the balanced budget amendment. He has participated in more than his share of high-profile nationally televised hearings. On Judiciary he asked Judge Robert Bork why he grew a beard and voted against him because of his "proclivity for extremism." He was an early opponent of Clarence Thomas in 1991, but his questions allowed Thomas to make his most effective responses. On these controversial judicial appointments, Heflin has seemed to work for the goals of the Washington civil rights lobby but he tried to find reasons for his votes that would appeal to rural Alabama voters. He may have had a partisan motive too when, as chairman of the Senate Ethics Committee in its investigation of the Keating Five, he kept the one Republican in the case, despite the weakness of the charges against him.

Heflin made a sensible decision to retire rather than seek reelection in 1996, at 75, in a state that has moved away from his party. He had an angioplasty in 1993 and he appears in good health but he said that he wants to return to Tuscumbia. Although Republicans were initially favored to win the seat, wide-open contests are likely in each party and the state's unpredictable politics could play a role. Among the Democrats being touted for the seat are Lieutenant Governor Don Siegelman (though he has said he wouldn't run), Congressman Glen Browder and Democrate state chair Bill Blount. On the Republican side, Congressman Terry Everett is considered a likely candidate, and 1994 gubernatorial candidate Winton Blount has also been mentioned.

Richard Shelby was one of the lesser known senators, popular back home but not famous nationally, until he switched parties the day after the 1994 election, and increased the Republicans' Senate margin from 52–48 to 53–47. The move was not out of line with his career. The son of a steelworker, Shelby stayed in Tuscaloosa after getting degrees from the University of Alabama; he went into law practice with Walter Flowers, later Congressman, and was politically well enough connected to be elected state Senator in 1970 and to succeed Flowers— who lost to Heflin in the Senate in the Democratic primary—in the House in 1978. The critical contest was the runoff against Chris McNair, a black legislator whose daughter had been killed in the 1963 Birmingham church bombing. The district had the highest percentage of black population of any Alabama district, but Shelby compiled a conservative voting record once he gained office, opposing the Voting Rights Act extension and the Martin Luther King Holiday. In the 1986 Senate race, he won the primary with 51% after getting a liberal to withdraw, then ran TV ads attacking incumbent Jeremiah Denton for voting to cut Social Security and owning two Mercedes; Shelby won by 7,000 votes.

In his first term, Shelby had probably the most conservative record of any Democratic senator. He voted for the confirmation of Clarence Thomas and for the Gulf war resolution. He voted against the campaign finance bill supported by almost all Democrats and he voted for the Strategic Defense Initiative. He supported oil drilling in the Arctic National Wildlife Refuge and opposed a 4,250-drum limit on nuclear waste stored underground. He was a major sponsor of a law to enforce court orders on fathers who default on child support payments. After a young Shelby aide was murdered a few blocks from the Capitol, Shelby pushed through a law requiring the District of Columbia to hold a referendum on capital punishment (it lost). In 1992 by beating political consultant Richard Sellers 65%–33%, Shelby broke the political jinx on this seat which, before his election in 1986, had four occupants in ten years.

Then, in February 1993, came the break with his party. Angered by Shelby's criticism of the president's just released economic plan—"the taxman cometh"—Clinton strategists ostentatiously decided to make an example of him and Shelby ostentatiously decided to make a display of his independence. At a meeting in which Vice President Al Gore tried to persuade Shelby to support the plan, Shelby turned to the 19 Alabama TV cameras there and, embarrassing Gore, further denounced the Clinton program as "high on taxes, low on spending cuts." As punishment, a multi-million dollar space facility was moved from Alabama to Texas. But, as the Clinton Administration's ratings slid downward, this only raised Shelby's popularity ratings to the highest level in the state, making a politician known more for his suppleness of maneuver appear an embattled defender of principle. In retrospect this was a harbinger of the 1994 elections: a state long hungry for federal largess was happy to give up pork in order to get less spending and a lower deficit. Relentlessly but without evident rancor, Shelby voted against the administration again and again and lined up with Republicans on almost every partisan issue. And he struck where it hurt. He was the first Democrat to call for the resignation of Deputy

Treasury Secretary Roger Altman. In August 1994 he went out of his way to criticize Majority Leader George Mitchell's healthcare plan as "ill-conceived, unworkable and unwanted by the American people" and worked with Texas Senator Phil Gramm to kill it.

So it was not much of a surprise when Shelby announced he was switching parties the day after the election. He was allowed to keep his seniority on committees, so he can remain active on national-security issues, perhaps his greatest policy interest. In his party-switching speech he pointed to the Democrats' support of "taxation, regulation and quotas" and the Clinton Administration's economic and healthcare packages. The first polls were highly favorable, and unlike Colorado colleague Ben Nighthorse Campbell who also made a switch to the Republicans, none of Shelby's staff resigned. Shelby does not come up for reelection until 1998, which gives him plenty of time to settle in, and much of his fundraising and activist base will probably be the same anyway. One thing is certain: next time he will carry the one jurisdiction he lost last time, the heavily Republican suburban overflow of Birmingham in Shelby County.

Presidential politics. Alabama is now one of the most Republican states in presidential politics. Although, with all its troubles, the Bush-Quayle campaign had to work it hard in 1992; for 1996 it is enough to quote one Democratic consultant, who quipped it was only a matter of time before the Secret Service wouldn't let Bill Clinton fly over the state. Alabama's presidential primary, held on Super Tuesday in the 1980s, was moved to June in 1992. Only some 400,000 Alabamans, perhaps half of them black, vote in the Democratic primary; some 200,000 have voted in the Republican primary when it was seriously contested.

Congressional districting. The Voting Rights Act, as revised in 1982, was the engine that drove Alabama's congressional redistricting in 1992. The plan adopted was proposed by Republicans and ordered into effect by a federal court. It resulted in the election of a black congressman in the new 68% black 7th District, which stretches from central Birmingham through the Black Belt counties to downtown Montgomery. It also resulted in victories by Republicans in two seats, the once-competitive 2d and the previously-Democratic 6th, from which tens of thousands of blacks had been removed to raise the black percentage in the 7th.

The People: Est. Pop. 1994: 4,219,000; Pop. 1990: 4,040,587, up 4.4% 1990–1994. 1.6% of U.S. total, 22d largest; 40% rural. Median age: 33.0 years. 12.9% 65 years and over. 73.6% White, 25.3% Black. Households: 57.0% married couple families; 27% married couple fams. w. children; 37% college educ.; median household income: $23,597; per capita income: $11,486; 70.5% owner occupied housing; median house value: $53,700; median monthly rent: $229. 7.3% Unemployment. 1994 Voting age pop.: 3,138,000. 1994 Turnout: 1,191,913; 38% of VAP. Registered voters (1994): 2,283,484; no party registration.

Political Lineup: Governor, Fob James (R); Lt. Gov., Don Siegelman (D); Secy. of State, Jim Bennett (D); Atty. Gen., Jeff Sessions (R); Treasurer, Lucy Baxler (D); Auditor, Pat Duncan (R); State Senate, 35 (23 D, 12 R); State House of Representatives, 105 (73 D, 32 R). Senators, Howell T. Heflin (D) and Richard C. Shelby (R). Representatives, 7 (4 D and 3 R).

1992 Presidential Vote

Bush (R)	804,283	(48%)
Clinton (D)	690,080	(41%)
Perot (I)	183,109	(11%)

1988 Presidential Vote

Bush (R)	815,576	(59%)
Dukakis (D)	549,506	(40%)

1992 Democratic Presidential Primary

Clinton	307,621	(68%)
Brown	30,626	(7%)
Other	21,789	(5%)
Uncommitted	90,863	(20%)

1992 Republican Presidential Primary

Bush	122,703	(74%)
Buchanan	12,588	(8%)
Uncommitted	29,830	(18%)

GOVERNOR

Gov. Fob James (R)

Elected 1994; term expires Jan. 1999. b. Sept. 15, 1934, Lanett; home, Magnolia Springs; Auburn U., B.S. 1955; Episcopalian; married (Bobbie).

Career: Army Corps. of Engineers, 1957–58; Pro football player, Montreal Allouettes, 1956–57; Construction superintendent, 1958–62; Founder & Chmn., Diversified Products Inc., 1962–78; AL Gov., 1979–82; Co-owner, Orange Beach Marina, 1982; CEO, Coastal Erosion Control Inc., 1988; CEO, Escambia Cnty. Environmental Corp., 1992.

Office: Alabama State Capitol, 11 S. Union St., Montgomery 36130, 334-242-7100; Fax: 334-242-4541.

Election Results

1994 gen.	Fob James (R)	604,926	(50%)
	James E. Folsom, Jr.(D)	594,169	(49%)
	Others	2,874	
1994 runoff	Fob James (R)	130,233	(62%)
	Ann Bedsole (R)	78,338	(38%)
1994 prim.	Fob James (R)	84,019	(40%)
	Ann Bedsole (R)	54,449	(26%)
	Winton Blount (R)	51,785	(24%)
	Mickey Kirkland (R)	18,538	(9%)
	Others	3,680	(2%)
1990 gen.	Harold Guy Hunt (R)	633,520	(52%)
	Paul R. Hubbert (D)	582,106	(48%)

SENATORS

Sen. Howell T. Heflin (D)

Elected 1978, seat up 1996; b. June 19, 1921, Poulan, GA; home, Tuscumbia; Birmingham-Southern Col., B.A. 1941, U. of AL, J.D. 1948; United Methodist; married (Elizabeth Ann).

Career: Marine Corps, 1942–46 (WWII); Practicing atty., 1948–71, 1977–79; Chief Justice, AL Supreme Court, 1971–77.

DC Office: 728 HSOB 20510, 202-224-4124; Fax: 202-224-3149.

State Offices: B-29 Fed. Crthse., 15 Lee St., Montgomery 36104, 334-832-7287; 104 W. 5th St., P.O. Box 228, Tuscumbia 35674, 205-381-7060; 341 Fed. Bldg., 1800 5th Ave., N., Birmingham 35203, 205-731-1500; and 437 Fed. Crthse., Mobile 36602, 334-690-3167.

Committees: *Agriculture, Nutrition & Forestry* (3rd of 8 D): Forestry, Conservation and Rural Revitalization (RMM); Marketing, Inspection and Product Promotion; Research, Nutrition and General Legislation. *Energy and Natural Resources* (8th of 9 D): Energy Research and Development; Parks, Historic Preservation and Recreation. *Judiciary* (4th of 8 D): Administrative Oversight and the Courts (RMM); Antitrust, Business Rights and Competition. *Small Business* (8th of 9 D).

Group Ratings

	ADA	ACLU	COPE	CFA	LCV	CON	NSI	COC	ACU	NTLC	CHC
1994	55	32	63	67	31	42	100	55	28	46	43
1993	35	—	90	80	31	4	—	45	48	—	—

National Journal Ratings

	1993 LIB — 1993 CONS		1994 LIB — 1994 CONS	
Economic	46% —	51%	47% —	52%
Social	35% —	64%	43% —	56%
Foreign	32% —	60%	42% —	57%

Key Votes of the 103d Congress

1. Clinton Deficit Plan	Y	3. Brady Handgun Purchase	N	5. Lmt. UN Cmnd. of Forces	N
2. NAFTA	N	4. Strike Race/Death Pnlty.	Y	6. Cut Missile Funds	N

Key Votes of the 104th Congress

1. Congressional Compliance	Y	3. Balanced Budget Amndt.	Y	5. Product Liability Reform	N
2. Bar Unfunded Mandates	Y	4. Pass Line Item Veto	Y	6. FY96 Budget	N

Election Results

1990 general	Howell T. Heflin (D)	717,814	(61%)	($3,437,073)
	Bill Cabaniss (R)	467,190	(39%)	($1,853,869)
1990 primary	Howell T. Heflin (D)	540,876	(81%)	
	Mrs. Frank Ross Stewart (D)	123,508	(19%)	
1984 general	Howell T. Heflin (D)	860,535	(63%)	($2,001,386)
	Albert Lee Smith, Jr. (R)	498,508	(36%)	($574,382)

Sen. Richard C. Shelby (R)

Elected 1986, seat up 1998; b. May 6, 1934, Birmingham; home, Tuscaloosa; U. of AL, B.A. 1957, LL.B. 1963; Presbyterian; married (Annette).

Career: Practicing atty., 1963–78; AL Senate, 1970–78; U.S. House of Reps., 1978–1986.

DC Office: 110 HSOB 20510, 202-224-5744; Fax: 202-224-3416.

State Offices: 113 St. Joseph St., 438 U.S. Crthse., Mobile 36602, 334-694-4164; 1000 Glenn Hearn Blvd., Huntsville 35824, 205-772-0460; 1800 5th Ave., N., 321 Fed. Blvdg., Birmingham 35203, 205-731-1384; 15 Lee St., 828 U.S. Crthse., Montgomery 36104, 334-223-7303; and 118 Greensboro Ave., #240, Tuscaloosa 35401, 205-759-5047.

Committees: *Appropriations* (12th of 15 R): Defense; Foreign Operations; Military Construction; Treasury, Postal Service and General Government (Chmn.); VA, HUD and Independent Agencies. *Banking, Housing & Urban Affairs* (3rd of 9 R): Financial Institutions and Regulatory Relief (Chmn.); Housing Opportunity and Community Development; Securities. *Intelligence (Select)* (3rd of 9 R). *Aging (Special)* (8th of 10 R).

Group Ratings

	ADA	ACLU	COPE	CFA	LCV	CON	NSI	COC	ACU	NTLC	CHC
1994	30	41	83	63	8	54	100	62	55	62	71
1993	35	—	73	30	19	12	—	82	64	—	—

National Journal Ratings

	1993 LIB — 1993 CONS			1994 LIB — 1994 CONS		
Economic	37%	—	62%	45%	—	54%
Social	40%	—	59%	29%	—	70%
Foreign	32%	—	60%	40%	—	59%

Key Votes of the 103d Congress

1. Clinton Deficit Plan	N	3. Brady Handgun Purchase	N	5. Lmt. UN Cmnd. of Forces	N
2. NAFTA	N	4. Strike Race/Death Pnlty.	*	6. Cut Missile Funds	N

Key Votes of the 104th Congress

1. Congressional Compliance	Y	3. Balanced Budget Amndt.	Y	5. Product Liability Reform	N
2. Bar Unfunded Mandates	Y	4. Pass Line Item Veto	Y	6. FY96 Budget	Y

Election Results

1992 general	Richard C. Shelby (D)	1,022,698	(65%)	($2,807,764)
	Richard Sellers (R)	522,015	(33%)	($149,578)
	Other	31,811	(2%)	
1992 primary	Richard C. Shelby (D)	304,957	(62%)	
	Chris McNair (D)	136,836	(28%)	
	Bob Miller (D)	28,432	(6%)	
	Mrs. Frank Ross Stewart (D)	25,956	(5%)	
1986 general	Richard C. Shelby (D)	609,360	(50%)	($2,258,547)
	Jeremiah Denton (R)	602,537	(50%)	($4,621,163)

FIRST DISTRICT

Mobile, where the Tombigbee and Alabama Rivers flow into the Gulf of Mexico, was once an American frontier. Held by the Spanish until after the Revolutionary War, it was wrested away by threats of war from Secretary of State John Quincy Adams. During the Civil War, Mobile was one of the blockaded ports of the Confederacy; it was while steaming into Mobile harbor in 1864 that Admiral David Farragut, lashed to his mast, cried, "Damn the torpedoes! Full speed ahead." Today, Mobile is full of graceful signs of its slightly exotic past: behind the docks and rail lines are downtown buildings and old houses with Spanish motifs, French accents, or tropical Art Deco lines. Further inland are neighborhoods with spacious houses, often with double porches, overhung by huge live oaks, graced sometimes with Spanish moss. Mobile is a Gulf Coast version of Charleston or a smaller, more comfortable New Orleans, with a taste for shellfish and spicy food. Its economy was based originally on docks and shipyards, factories and terminals, but with a determination to impose touches of beauty on its hot, flat landscape. Mobile is also, as befits a frontier city with a martial past, bristling with arms: one of the proudest possessions of the city is the battleship U.S.S. Alabama, moored at the head of Mobile Bay, with its guns aimed out toward the Gulf. For years this southern seaboard of the Confederacy and the Union has been one of the most hawkish parts of America, and today it is solidly Republican in national elections.

Mobile forms the heart of Alabama's 1st Congressional District, which extends north along the lazily flowing Tombigbee and Alabama rivers, near the old forts and mansions and miles of fields that once grew cotton (more likely now to be producing soybeans or scrub pine). Also here are surviving back-country settlements of blacks and Cajans (who may or may not be descended from Louisiana Cajuns). To the south, along the shores of the Gulf of Mexico, are fast-growing condominium communities; the glorious Gulf beaches are one of the South's best-kept secrets and this is one of the fastest-growing parts of Alabama—and the most Republican part of the Mobile area.

The congressman from the 1st District is Sonny Callahan, a Republican with a rags-to-riches biography and a Democrat-to-Republican political history. The oldest boy in a family of nine children whose father died young, Callahan went to work at the age of 12, during World War II; fortunately, the boss was his uncle who owned a warehouse company. After serving in the Navy during Korea, Callahan rose to become president of the company at 32 and expanded into real estate and insurance. Like so many go-getters, he ran for the state legislature and was elected at 38. A Democrat, he ran for lieutenant governor and lost the 1982 Democratic primary to liberal Bill Baxley. Then 1st District Republican Congressman Jack Edwards decided to retire in 1984 after 20 years and asked Callahan to run as a Republican; he did and won, though with smaller margins than expected, 61% in the Republican primary and 51% in the general. He has been reelected easily and has one of the most conservative voting records in the House.

Suddenly, after the 1994 elections, Callahan occupies a position of power in the House that will make his name known in governments around the world, as chairman of the Foreign Operations Appropriations Subcommittee, with power over the foreign aid budget. This comes despite the fact that he hip-hopped from one committee to another for a decade, with one term at Public Works, then three terms at Commerce, then an assignment to Appropriations in 1993. Just two years later, he unexpectedly gained a seat in the prestigious "college of Cardinals," when the three Republicans senior to him on the Foreign Operations Subcommittee each took a more powerful chairmanship elsewhere on the committee. He has been familiar with tending to district interests as a member of the minority, promoting the Dog River Bridge and pushing for more lenient recycling standards for paper manufacturers. Now he has a major say on international issues, on which he has often been hostile to major U.S. interests and largely unknown to the striped-pants set. One is aid to Russia. In June 1993 he tried to place strings on the aid, requiring Russian help in furthering democracy in Cuba and elsewhere; in May 1994 he moved to cut aid to Russia by $349 million—eliminating everything but humanitarian assistance. Both moves failed. Callahan probably does not have the votes to make such draconian cuts now, if the Clinton Administration insists they would badly damage U.S.-Russian relations; but, at the least, he has great leverage in ratcheting down aid to Russia.

Callahan was easily reelected in 1994, and there is no question how he interprets the 1994 elections results. The voters "said, and rather loudly, that we're tired of business as usual, we're sick of being asked to pay more, only to make the government bigger, not necessarily better, and we want to make certain that we really receive at least a dollar's worth of value for every dollar we spend." Unassuming and informal, Callahan is one of the few members of Congress who lives on a houseboat which, he explains, he can take back to the district when he retires.

The People: Pop. 1990: 577,375; 34% rural; 13% age 65+; 70% White; 29% Black; 1% Amer. Indian; 1% Asian; 1% Hispanic origin. Voting age pop.: 414,788; 26% Black; 1% Hispanic origin. Households: 57% married couple families; 27% married couple fams. w. children; 36% college educ.; median household income: $22,881; per capita income: $10,961; median gross rent: $322; median house value: $52,600.

1992 Presidential Vote

Bush (R)	118,420	(51%)
Clinton (D)	84,193	(36%)
Perot (I)	26,749	(12%)

1988 Presidential Vote

Bush (R)	119,249	(63%)
Dukakis (D)	69,315	(37%)

Rep. H. L. (Sonny) Callahan (R)

Elected 1984; b. Sept. 11, 1932, Mobile; home, Mobile; U. of AL; Catholic; married (Karen).

Career: Navy, 1952–54; Finch Cos. 1955–85, Pres., 1964–85; AL House of Reps., 1970–78; AL Senate, 1978–82.

DC Office: 2418 RHOB 20515, 202-225-4931; Fax: 202-225-0562.

District Offices: 2970 Cottage Hill Rd., #126, Mobile 36606, 334-690-2811.

Committees: *Appropriations* (16th of 32 R): Foreign Operations, Export Financing, and Related Programs (Chmn.); Military Construction; Transportation.

Group Ratings

	ADA	ACLU	COPE	CFA	LCV	CON	NSI	COC	ACU	NTLC	CHC
1994	5	9	13	0	0	83	100	92	100	92	100
1993	0	—	0	10	0	59	—	90	96	—	—

National Journal Ratings

	1993 LIB — 1993 CONS		1994 LIB — 1994 CONS	
Economic	23%	— 77%	26%	— 70%
Social	0%	— 89%	0%	— 89%
Foreign	15%	— 84%	14%	— 80%

Key Votes of the 103d Congress

1. Clinton Deficit Plan	N	3. Brady Handgun Purchase	N	5. Lmt. UN Cmnd. of Forces	Y
2. NAFTA	Y	4. Strike Race/Death Pnlty.	Y	6. Cut Missile Funds	N

Key Votes of the 104th Congress

1. Congressional Compliance	Y	6. Reform Crime Grant	Y	11. Loser Pays Court Reform	Y
2. Balanced Budget Amndmt.	Y	7. National Security Act	Y	12. Product Liability Reform	Y
3. Bar Unfunded Mandates	Y	8. Moratorium on Regs.	Y	13. Welfare Reform	Y
4. Pass Line Item Veto	Y	9. Risk Assessment on Regs.	Y	14. Term Limits Amndmt.	Y
5. Relax Exclusionary Rule	Y	10. Expnd. Priv. Prop. Rights	Y	15. Tax Cuts	Y

Election Results

1994 general	H. L. (Sonny) Callahan (R)	103,431	(67%)	($416,080)
	Don Womack (D)	50,227	(33%)	($55,721)
1994 primary	H. L. (Sonny) Callahan (R)	unopposed		
1992 general	H. L. (Sonny) Callahan (R)	128,874	(60%)	($383,760)
	William A. Brewer (D)	78,742	(37%)	($13,297)
	Other	6,548	(3%)	

SECOND DISTRICT

The countryside is everywhere apparent in southern Alabama. Even in Montgomery the stone and brick buildings that rise in the irregular downtown grid do not mask the contours of the hills or hide the lush foliage. You can look downhill from the recently renovated Greek Revival Capitol toward Dexter Avenue Baptist Church where Martin Luther King Jr. became pastor in 1954, or out toward the newer subdivisions and shopping complexes, and still sense that this was once cottonfields. The rural landscape is never far away either in the urban growth areas of southeast Alabama's wiregrass region, named for the stiff native grass: around the town of Dothan, whose major tourist attraction is the Farley Nuclear Visitors Center, past Daleville and the Army's Fort Rucker to Enterprise, site of the Boll Weevil Monument which commemorates the insect that destroyed two-thirds of the cotton crop here in 1915 and then spread throughout the South.

The 2d Congressional District of Alabama covers most of the southeast corner of the state. An 80% black segment of Montgomery County is part of the black-majority 7th District, and the 2d includes 78% white Elmore and Autauga Counties across the Alabama River. Naturally this tips the 2d District very much toward Republicans; for politics in southern Alabama remains racially polarized: blacks vote almost unanimously Democratic, whites vote very heavily (but not unanimously) Republican in national elections and, increasingly, in state and local contests as well. Blacks' party preference is rooted in 1960s era civil rights and in the Kennedy brothers' opposition to Governor George Wallace. The whites' preference has something to do with race but is also linked with foreign and military policy. They want from their leaders not a repudiation of the civil rights laws of the 1960s, but a validation of the proud nationalism and traditional moral values that are so strong here.

The congressman from the 2d District is Terry Everett, a businessman from the wiregrass region and a political neophyte first elected in 1992. He was doubly, really triply lucky; for he was running in an anti-incumbent year in a district in which longtime congressman, Republican Bill Dickinson, was in some political difficulty, and in which Everett's major opponents looked far more like a career politician than Everett did. After Dickinson decided to retire after 28 years of service, the favorite for the Republican primary was Montgomery state Representative Larry Dixon. But Everett, with 84% in the wiregrass region, beat Dixon 58%–42%. Then in the general he faced George Wallace, Jr., state treasurer and son of the former governor, who had black support and called his father's standing in the schoolhouse door in 1963 "a bad political stunt." Wallace had 49.7% in the primary and was forced into a runoff; during that campaign *People* came out with a story in which one of his three former wives claimed he was sometimes violently temperamental, and Wallace won with just 57%. In the general Wallace complained bitterly of "cruel lies" in an Everett ad claiming Wallace had been chauffeured around as a child; just 11 when his father was first elected governor, he was protected by security agents because of frequent death threats. Everett spent some $600,000 of his own money and, echoing an old George Wallace slogan, called on voters to "Send them a message, not a politician." Everett carried the Montgomery area 54%–43% and the Dothan-Enterprise corridor 57%–41%. Wallace carried the remaining third of the district 60%–37%, but that wasn't quite enough, as Everett won 49%–48%. Redistricting plainly made a difference: subtract Autauga and Elmore Counties and add back the part of Montgomery now in the 7th, and you have a 48%–46% Democratic victory.

Everett has an interesting background: he served in Air Force Intelligence in Germany in the 1950s, learned Russian, worked as a sports reporter and circulation manager for southern Alabama newspapers, then bought some newspapers himself and sold them for far more, and ended up heading a S&L and owning a large farm and real estate development firm. Though campaigning as an anti-incumbent, he has been as slavish a supporter of parochial interests as the most cynical insider: he went to Russia to promote the sale of Alabama peanuts, opposed the North American Free Trade Agreement because he felt it threatened local textile and agricultural jobs and got on the National Security Committee to protect Fort Rucker and Montgomery's Maxwell Air Force Base. He votes solidly conservative on cultural issues, and mostly conservative on economic and foreign issues. He works on local issues from bringing jobs to Maxwell to arguing that the Alabama sturgeon is not a separate species subject to the protection of the Endangered Species Act; he seeks federal subsidies for water service in rural communities up to 55,000 people; he opposed an Indian casino in Wetumpka; he proposed a new House Peanut Caucus. Everett favors term limits and his family remains in Alabama, but he has proved very popular in his district and was reelected by an overwhelming margin in 1994. His early interest in seeking Heflin's Senate seat suggests that he may not have to worry about violating his pledge to limit his terms in the House. His brief political history suggests that he would be a formidable candidate.

The People: Pop. 1990: 577,203; 42% rural; 13% age 65+; 75% White; 24% Black; 1% Asian; 1% Hispanic origin. Voting age pop.: 422,551; 21% Black; 1% Hispanic origin. Households: 59% married couple families; 28% married couple fams. w. children; 40% college educ.; median household income: $24,374; per capita income: $11,636; median gross rent: $329; median house value: $53,700.

1992 Presidential Vote			1988 Presidential Vote		
Bush (R)	123,856	(53%)	Bush (R)	133,819	(68%)
Clinton (D)	82,656	(35%)	Dukakis (D)	62,858	(32%)
Perot (I)	27,319	(12%)			

Rep. Terry Everett (R)

Elected 1992; b. Feb. 15, 1937, Dothan; home, Enterprise; Baptist; married (Barbara).

Career: Air Force, 1955–59; Newspaper reporter, 1959–61, 1966–68; Businessman, 1961–64; Editor and publisher, 1968–88; Real estate developer, 1988–92.

DC Office: 208 CHOB 20515, 202-225-2901; Fax: 202-225-8913; e-mail: everett@hr.house.gov.

District Offices: 3500 Eastern Blvd., #250, Montgomery 36116, 334-277-9113; 100 W. Troy St., #101, Dothan 36303, 334-794-9680; and City Hall Bldg., Opp 36487, 334-493-9253.

Committees: *Agriculture* (14th of 27 R): Risk Management and Specialty Crops. *National Security* (17th of 30 R): Military Procurement; Military Readiness. *Veterans' Affairs* (6th of 18 R): Compensation, Pension, Insurance and Memorial Affairs (Chmn.).

Group Ratings

	ADA	ACLU	COPE	CFA	LCV	CON	NSI	COC	ACU	NTLC	CHC
1994	0	13	33	20	0	55	100	75	100	93	100
1993	10	—	25	10	21	69	—	91	96	—	—

National Journal Ratings

	1993 LIB — 1993 CONS		1994 LIB — 1994 CONS	
Economic	34% —	65%	34% —	64%
Social	11% —	82%	0% —	89%
Foreign	31% —	67%	14% —	80%

Key Votes of the 103d Congress

1. Clinton Deficit Plan	N	3. Brady Handgun Purchase	N	5. Lmt. UN Cmnd. of Forces	Y
2. NAFTA	N	4. Strike Race/Death Pnlty.	Y	6. Cut Missile Funds	Y

Key Votes of the 104th Congress

1. Congressional Compliance	Y	6. Reform Crime Grant	Y	11. Loser Pays Court Reform	Y
2. Balanced Budget Amndmt.	Y	7. National Security Act	Y	12. Product Liability Reform	Y
3. Bar Unfunded Mandates	Y	8. Moratorium on Regs.	Y	13. Welfare Reform	Y
4. Pass Line Item Veto	Y	9. Risk Assessment on Regs.	Y	14. Term Limits Amndmt.	Y
5. Relax Exclusionary Rule	Y	10. Expnd. Priv. Prop. Rights	Y	15. Tax Cuts	Y

Election Results

1994 general	Terry Everett (R)	124,465	(74%)	($224,606)
	Brian Dowling (D)	44,694	(26%)	($22,742)
1994 primary	Terry Everett (R)	unopposed		
1992 general	Terry Everett (R)	112,906	(49%)	($1,042,083)
	George C. Wallace, Jr. (D)	109,335	(48%)	($637,773)
	Others	5,906	(3%)	

THIRD DISTRICT

Fanning out in all directions from Horseshoe Bend, where Andrew Jackson won a climactic battle against the Indians, is the 3d Congressional District of Alabama. It stretches across the central part of the state from the Black Belt in the south to the red clay hills in the north, through land that is densely populated but not much urbanized. In the south is Tuskegee, a black-majority town in a black-majority county, home of Booker T. Washington's Tuskegee Institute. Nearby is Auburn, home of Auburn University, with its nationally renowned athletic teams and veterinary school. In the northern part of the district is the small industrial city of Anniston and the Army's Fort McClellan. Only occasionally does central Alabama make national news: when a high school principal in Wedowee bans interracial dating and cancels the prom, or when Talladega, home of the Alabama Institute for the Deaf and Blind, turns out to be perhaps America's most user-friendly place for the disabled. This is rural Alabama, yet modern technologies from the Internet to the Interstates keep people here in touch with the outside world, and year after year the red hills sprout small subdivisions filled with young parents who may work far away but want to raise their children in a country environment.

Politically, this has been Democratic country, the home of those conservative white Democrats—patriotic supporters of the military, cautious supporters of some domestic programs—who have historically been the heart of the party's support in the South. But the towns where the interstates have brought in new businesses and new families—Auburn, Talladega, Pell City—have been trending Republican, and in the close 1994 governor's race the 3d District split almost evenly. In congressional politics, it has been represented by southern Democrats ever since Reconstruction. The current Congressman, Glen Browder, chosen in a special election in 1989, is part of that tradition; but, despite his efforts to make conservative Democrats more of a force, it is not clear how much power he will wield in a Republican House. Browder has certainly shown political skills. He holds a political science Ph.D. from Emory University and taught at Jacksonville State University near Anniston; in 1982 he was elected to the state House and in 1986 Secretary of State. He was obviously a strong candidate in the 1989 special—well connected in Montgomery, particularly with the teachers' union and the trial lawyers, the two main Democratic lobbies, but also conservative on issues like the death penalty, school prayer, abortion and gun control. He led the primary with 25%, won the runoff with 63% against Tuskegee Mayor Johnny Ford, and in the general beat state Senator John "Hand Grenade" Rice 65%–35%. In the House, Browder joined the National Security Committee and the Conservative Democratic Forum.

Browder has a voting record that was at the midpoint of the 103d Congress on economic, cultural and foreign issues; he has also shown considerable legislative creativity. One obvious priority is to prevent the closure of Fort McClellan, which was only narrowly averted in the 1991 and 1993 base closings; Browder's strategy has been to strengthen its chemical defense preparedness mission so it stay's off the list. On campaign finance reform, he pressed hard for a Democratic alternative with a 100% tax credit on contributions under $50 and a tax on candidates who spend over a certain amount; but no bill ever passed the Democratic House. He is one of the Democrats who has voted with his party less than 80% of the time, for example supporting inclusion of a Republican welfare plan in the 1994 budget resolution. Though he is part of the Democratic Leadership Council once headed by Bill Clinton, he has opposed the Clinton Administration on major issues, including the 1993 economic package and NAFTA. In the 104th Congress, Browder will not be a terribly important vote when Republicans maintain party discipline. But if they do not, he is one of the Democrats they will look to on many issues and, with his legislative creativity, he could be one of the key votes in the House. Along with the two other white House Democrats from Alabama, he was a charter member of The Coalition, a group of mostly southern Democrats who seek to stress their independence from their national party.

Browder has been reelected by solid margins in the 1990s. Following Heflin's retirement announcement, he made known his interest in running for the Senate seat and announced an exploratory committee in May. His record could make him the Democrat with the best chance of holding the seat for his party, but the prospects will be uphill for any Democrat.

The People: Pop. 1990: 577,116; 47% rural; 13% age 65+; 73% White; 26% Black; 1% Hispanic origin. Voting age pop.: 429,034; 24% Black. Households: 58% married couple families; 27% married couple fams. w. children; 32% college educ.; median household income: $21,594; per capita income: $10,204; median gross rent: $296; median house value: $46,600.

1992 Presidential Vote		
Bush (R)	104,928	(47%)
Clinton (D)	91,983	(41%)
Perot (I)	23,733	(11%)

1988 Presidential Vote		
Bush (R)	109,093	(61%)
Dukakis (D)	69,634	(39%)

Rep. Glen Browder (D)

Elected Apr., 1989; b. Jan. 15, 1943, Sumter, SC; home, Jacksonville; Presbyterian Col., B.A. 1965; Emory U., M.A., Ph.D. 1971; United Methodist; married (Becky).

Career: P.R., Presbyterian Col., 1965; Sportswriter, *Atlanta Journal,* 1966; Investigator, U.S. Civil Service Comm., 1966–68; Asst. Prof., Jacksonville St. U., 1971–1987; AL House of Reps., 1982–86; AL Secy. of State, 1987–89.

DC Office: 2344 RHOB 20515, 202-225-3261; Fax: 202-225-9020.

District Offices: 107 Fed. Bldg., Opelika 36801, 205-745-6221; P.O. Box 2042, Anniston 36202, 205-236-5655; and 115 E. Northside, #205, Tuskegee 36083, 205-727-6490.

Committees: *Budget* (12th of 18 D). *National Security* (11th of 25 D): Military Installations and Facilities; Military Readiness.

Group Ratings

	ADA	ACLU	COPE	CFA	LCV	CON	NSI	COC	ACU	NTLC	CHC
1994	25	13	78	50	39	57	100	75	62	54	79
1993	20	—	58	40	43	11	—	36	52	—	—

National Journal Ratings

	1993 LIB — 1993 CONS		1994 LIB — 1994 CONS	
Economic	48% —	51%	47% —	51%
Social	40% —	60%	40% —	59%
Foreign	51% —	42%	49% —	49%

Key Votes of the 103d Congress

1. Clinton Deficit Plan	N	3. Brady Handgun Purchase	N	5. Lmt. UN Cmnd. of Forces	N
2. NAFTA	N	4. Strike Race/Death Pnlty.	Y	6. Cut Missile Funds	N

Key Votes of the 104th Congress

1. Congressional Compliance Y	6. Reform Crime Grant N	11. Loser Pays Court Reform N
2. Balanced Budget Amndt. Y	7. National Security Act N	12. Product Liability Reform Y
3. Bar Unfunded Mandates Y	8. Moratorium on Regs. Y	13. Welfare Reform N
4. Pass Line Item Veto Y	9. Risk Assessment on Regs. Y	14. Term Limits Amndt. Y
5. Relax Exclusionary Rule Y	10. Expnd. Priv. Prop. Rights Y	15. Tax Cuts Y

Election Results

1994 general	Glen Browder (D)	93,924	(64%)	($171,912)
	Ben Hand (R)	53,757	(36%)	($41,265)
1994 primary	Glen Browder (D)	88,473	(85%)	
	Leamon (Lea) Fite Jr. (D)	15,167	(15%)	
1992 general	Glen Browder (D)	119,175	(60%)	($108,814)
	Don Sledge (R)	73,800	(37%)	($22,160)
	Other	4,570	(2%)	

FOURTH DISTRICT

The corduroy ridges of the Appalachian mountains dividing the Atlantic coast from the interior are the nation's coal-and-steel industrial spine, from the black coal country of western Pennsylvania to the red hill country of northern Alabama. Here rose America's two premier steel cities, Pittsburgh and Birmingham; around both, and for many miles in between them, is hill country settled by feisty Scotch-Irish farmers in the years between the Revolution and the Civil War. In valley land accessible to railroads are the great steel factories built in the 80 years after the Civil War and smaller factories that produce underwear and tires, socks and chickens. Politically, the two regions were separated by the Civil War: western Pennsylvania was overwhelmingly Republican until the 1930s, while northern Alabama, except for a few mountain communities that remained loyal to the Union (one called itself the Free State of Winston), was solidly Democratic through the 1950s. Then both changed. Western Pennsylvania became Democratic during the New Deal years and again as the steel industry collapsed in the 1980s. Northern Alabama left the national Democratic Party over civil rights in the 1960s, then returned to vote for Jimmy Carter in 1976; now it supports local Democrats but gave George Bush a narrow victory over Bill Clinton in 1992. Counties close to Birmingham and along the interstates became Republican in the 1980s, with young families seeking city affluence and country values; more remote hill counties are still voting heavily for populists running against the "Big Mules."

Alabama's 4th Congressional District covers both areas, from the gritty factory town of Gadsden in the east, across the counties just north of Birmingham, to the hill counties of the west represented by onetime (1937–40) Speaker William Bankhead. Currently it is represented by Tom Bevill, first elected in 1966, one of the most senior Democrats in the House. Bevill is one of the strongest—and for years has been one of the most effective—believers in old-fashioned pork barrel politics. From 1977 to 1995, he chaired the Appropriations Subcommittee on Energy and Water Development—a fancy name for public works. Growing up in northern Alabama during the Depression, Bevill naturally came to believe in government spending on dams and buildings and highways—often the only source of employment in those communities then, and their only hope for developing jobs in the future.

As a subcommittee chairman, Bevill was in a position to amass personal power by granting and withholding projects, as some chairmen of the authorizing committees have done. But he is a pleasant man, of humble temperament, who preferred to work in tandem with others in the Alabama delegation and with members of both parties on his subcommittee; in 1994 he boasted that he never brought a bill to the full committee or the floor without the support of then-ranking

Republican John Myers. He has encountered many challenges. In 1977 President Jimmy Carter tried to cancel several water projects; Bevill resisted and eventually won. In the 1980s environmentalists and fiscal conservatives combined to challenge various projects. Bevill had to struggle hard to finish the Tennessee-Tombigbee Waterway project which passes through western Alabama and whose economic justification is pathetically weak. Budgetary limits have hurt him as well. In 1994 he had to eliminate funding for 30 projects and cut funding for 300 more. And in June 1993 he was beaten on the floor on one of his largest projects, the Superconducting Supercollider, despite support from Bush and Clinton Administrations and the big Texas delegation. Now, after the 1994 election, he is ranking minority member rather than chairman, which should prove even more frustrating. But he is not likely to quit working for Alabama projects, from the port of Mobile to the Jasper Bypass in the hills (its destination: the Tom Bevill industrial park). He will work on funding Corridor X, a freeway to repair the inexplicable failure of the Interstate Highway system to include a road from Birmingham to Memphis. And he can take satisfaction in the University of Alabama at Huntsville's optics research lab and its Tom Bevill Center, the local headquarters of the Army Corps of Engineers.

Bevill returns often to the district, never takes on airs, but always gets credit for the federal money he has brought home: he has been reelected easily. But it's possible that minority status, or simply the toll of age (he will be 75 in 1996), may convince him to retire. If he does, Democrats will find it difficult to keep the seat.

The People: Pop. 1990: 577,058; 66% rural; 15% age 65+; 92% White; 7% Black; 1% Amer. Indian. Voting age pop.: 432,040; 6% Black. Households: 65% married couple families; 29% married couple fams. w. children; 26% college educ.; median household income: $20,877; per capita income: $10,170; median gross rent: $262; median house value: $42,800.

1992 Presidential Vote			**1988 Presidential Vote**		
Bush (R)	107,064	(44%)	Bush (R)	110,149	(57%)
Clinton (D)	104,526	(43%)	Dukakis (D)	83,950	(43%)
Perot (I)	28,558	(12%)			

Rep. Tom Bevill (D)

Elected 1966; b. Mar. 27, 1921, Townley; home, Jasper; U. of AL, B.S. 1943, LL.B. 1948; Baptist; married (Lou).

Career: Army, 1943–46 (WWII); Practicing atty., 1948–66; AL House of Reps., 1958–66.

DC Office: 2302 RHOB 20515, 202-225-4876; Fax: 202-225-1604.

District Offices: 107 Fed. Bldg., Gadsden 35901, 205-546-0201; 1710 Alabama Ave. #247, Fed. Bldg., Jasper 35501, 205-221-2310; and 102 Fed. Bldg., Cullman 35055, 205-734-6043.

Committees: *Appropriations* (4th of 24 D): Energy and Water Development (RMM); Interior.

Group Ratings

	ADA	ACLU	COPE	CFA	LCV	CON	NSI	COC	ACU	NTLC	CHC
1994	35	23	56	60	53	5	90	50	50	27	64
1993	45	—	92	70	50	4	—	18	38	—	—

National Journal Ratings

	1993 LIB	—	1993 CONS	1994 LIB	—	1994 CONS
Economic	61%	—	37%	67%	—	29%
Social	43%	—	56%	41%	—	59%
Foreign	44%	—	55%	57%	—	37%

Key Votes of the 103d Congress

1. Clinton Deficit Plan	Y	3. Brady Handgun Purchase	N	5. Lmt. UN Cmnd. of Forces	N
2. NAFTA	N	4. Strike Race/Death Pnlty.	Y	6. Cut Missile Funds	N

Key Votes of the 104th Congress

1. Congressional Compliance	Y	6. Reform Crime Grant	N	11. Loser Pays Court Reform	N
2. Balanced Budget Amndmt.	Y	7. National Security Act	Y	12. Product Liability Reform	Y
3. Bar Unfunded Mandates	Y	8. Moratorium on Regs.	Y	13. Welfare Reform	N
4. Pass Line Item Veto	Y	9. Risk Assessment on Regs.	Y	14. Term Limits Amndmt.	Y
5. Relax Exclusionary Rule	Y	10. Expnd. Priv. Prop. Rights	Y	15. Tax Cuts	Y

Election Results

1994 general	Tom Bevill (D)	unopposed		($274,164)
1994 primary	Tom Bevill (D)	unopposed		
1992 general	Tom Bevill (D)	157,907	(69%)	($519,416)
	Mickey Strickland (R)	66,934	(29%)	($20,117)
	Other.............................	5,646	(2%)	

FIFTH DISTRICT

Twice in this century, major projects of the federal government have transformed the northern Alabama counties along the Tennessee River. The first was the Tennessee Valley Authority, created in 1933. The government needed to do something with its World War I munitions plant at Muscle Shoals, on the then unnavigable, often-flooding Tennessee River. Nebraska Senator George Norris proposed a series of dams and power plants, and President Franklin Roosevelt embraced it and pushed it through Congress in 1933. This was then one of the poorest parts of the country: poor white farmers scratched a living out of hardscrabble land, were housed in shacks without electricity or running water, and lived off a diet that produced pellagra and rickets. TVA proceeded to dam the wild river, control flooding, produce cheap electric power and for years served as a proud example of what an active government could do. Northern Alabama voters became staunch New Deal Democrats, supporters of liberal (on everything but race) Congressman and Senator John Sparkman, who served for 42 years.

The second major federal project here was the space program. After the Soviets put up Sputnik in 1957, the Redstone Arsenal in Huntsville became our major missile development center. NASA built its Marshall Space Flight Center nearby in the 1960s, and Huntsville changed from a quaint courthouse town of 14,000 in 1950 to a metropolitan area of 250,000 by the 1990s. Huntsville also developed in the 1980s a scientific and technical community of sufficient competence and critical mass to make this the center for research and development on both the manned space station and the Strategic Defense Initiative. Historically, the biggest boosters of the space program were Democrats, but the professional and technical people in the space business tend toward Newt Gingrich's combination of high tech and traditional values, and increasingly vote Republican. This has moved Madison and Morgan Counties, around Huntsville and nearby Decatur, from the Democratic to the Republican column.

The 5th Congressional District of Alabama includes most of the state's TVA and space counties, including Huntsville and Decatur. Historically it has elected Democratic congressmen who vote with their party on economics and work to strengthen TVA and the space program. That has indeed been the formula of its congressman in the 1990s, Democrat Bud Cramer. But

Cramer's close shave in the 1994 election suggests that politics may be changing here. The problem was not any Cramer weakness, but the fact that his strength counted for little. He has a fine local base, having served as Madison County District Attorney from 1981 to 1990, and a splendid personal issue: as DA in 1985, he set up a Child Advocacy Center, a child-friendly environment for abused children; as congressman, he set up a $5 million federal program to encourage such centers across the country. "We are the Mayo Clinic there in Huntsville of child abuse," he boasted.

Cramer won his first congressional elections easily. When incumbent Ronnie Flippo ran for governor in 1990, Cramer won 44% in the Democratic primary and 60% in the runoff. Against state Agriculture Commissioner Al McDonald, who had switched to the Republican Party, Cramer won 67%–33%. In the House, he got on the Transportation and Infrastructure and Science Committees, the better to tend to his district's federal interests, and became a tireless lobbyist for the beleaguered Space Station, which was challenged in seven floor votes and which survived by only a 216–215 margin in June 1993. He got a 1995 review of a decision to close a National Weather Service radar station in Huntsville. He won funding to start an Atlanta-Memphis highway. At the same time, he warned people that "a community like this is too tied to federal spending."

For 1994, Cramer may have been tied too closely to the Democratic leadership, which in his first term he supported more than any other Alabama congressman. He supported the Clinton economic package with its five cent gas-tax increase and opposed the Penny-Kasich budget cuts. He supported the Clinton crime bill with its gun control provisions. Two serious Republicans ran to oppose him, with Wayne Parker, Huntsville native and son-in-law of Texas Congressman Bill Archer, winning the primary narrowly. Parker called for spending cuts, school choice, tougher sentences and put up billboards saying "Cramer, Clinton, Congress. We won't be fooled again! Vote Parker," while Clinton's job rating was 68% negative. Cramer criticized Parker for living off a trust fund and suggested that Parker, if elected, would move the space-station program to Houston, because of his ties with Archer. (Actually, another local NASA project was transferred to Texas by the Clinton Administration in retaliation for opposition from Alabama Senator Richard Shelby). With $288,000 from PACs, Cramer outspent Parker 2–1, and he had massive support from local media. But the issues worked against him, and he barely won, 50%–49%.

The closeness of the result suggests that the 5th District may be seriously contested again in 1996, and that Cramer's formula may no longer be a winning one. Republican control of the House means he can no longer rely on a huge advantage in PAC contributions, and the argument that he is needed to save the Space Station is undercut by the fact that on key votes it got more support from Republicans than Democrats. Wherever opinion goes nationally, the Clinton Administration is likely to be a millstone here. And the 1994 result shows that this district, so heavily impacted by major federal projects, seems now to be more interested in disciplining a federal government that is seen as overlarge and over-liberal than it is in channeling some of the money home.

The People: Pop. 1990: 577,235; 39% rural; 11% age 65+; 83% White; 15% Black; 1% Amer. Indian; 1% Asian; 1% Hispanic origin. Voting age pop.: 433,205; 14% Black; 1% Hispanic origin. Households: 62% married couple families; 29% married couple fams. w. children; 44% college educ.; median household income: $28,364; per capita income: $13,268; median gross rent: $361; median house value: $63,000.

1992 Presidential Vote			1988 Presidential Vote		
Bush (R)	110,268	(44%)	Bush (R)	108,499	(60%)
Clinton (D)	102,130	(41%)	Dukakis (D)	73,579	(40%)
Perot (I)	36,921	(15%)			

Rep. Robert E. (Bud) Cramer (D)

Elected 1990; b. Aug. 22, 1947, Huntsville; home, Huntsville; U. of AL, B.S. 1969, J.D. 1972; Methodist; widowed.

Career: Army, 1972; Army Reserves, 1976–78; Intructor, U. of AL Law Schl., Dir., Clinical Studies Program, 1972–73; Madison Cnty. Asst. Dist. Atty., 1973–75; Practicing atty., 1975–80; Madison Cnty. Dist. Atty., 1981–1990; Founder, Natl. Children's Advocacy Ctr., 1985.

DC Office: 236 CHOB 20515, 202-225-4801; Fax: 202-225-4392.

District Offices: 737 E. Avalon Ave., Muscle Shoals 35661, 205-381-3450; 403 Franklin St., Huntsville 35801, 205-551-0190; and Morgan Cnty. Crthse., P.O. Box 668, Decatur 35602, 205-355-9400.

Committees: *Science* (8th of 23 D): Energy and Environment; Space and Aeronautics. *Transportation & Infrastructure* (15th of 27 D): Railroads; Surface Transportation.

Group Ratings

	ADA	ACLU	COPE	CFA	LCV	CON	NSI	COC	ACU	NTLC	CHC
1994	40	26	78	60	39	21	90	58	38	24	57
1993	45	—	83	70	57	11	—	18	38	—	—

National Journal Ratings

	1993 LIB — 1993 CONS		1994 LIB — 1994 CONS	
Economic	57%	— 42%	67%	— 29%
Social	47%	— 53%	46%	— 53%
Foreign	46%	— 53%	57%	— 37%

Key Votes of the 103d Congress

1. Clinton Deficit Plan	Y	3. Brady Handgun Purchase	N	5. Lmt. UN Cmnd. of Forces	N
2. NAFTA	N	4. Strike Race/Death Pnlty.	Y	6. Cut Missile Funds	N

Key Votes of the 104th Congress

1. Congressional Compliance	Y	6. Reform Crime Grant	N	11. Loser Pays Court Reform	N
2. Balanced Budget Amndmt.	Y	7. National Security Act	Y	12. Product Liability Reform	Y
3. Bar Unfunded Mandates	Y	8. Moratorium on Regs.	Y	13. Welfare Reform	Y
4. Pass Line Item Veto	Y	9. Risk Assessment on Regs.	Y	14. Term Limits Amndmt.	Y
5. Relax Exclusionary Rule	Y	10. Expnd. Priv. Prop. Rights	Y	15. Tax Cuts	Y

Election Results

1994 general	Robert E. (Bud) Cramer (D)	88,693	(50%)	($565,457)
	Wayne Parker (R)	86,923	(49%)	($430,822)
1994 primary	Robert E. (Bud) Cramer (D)	unopposed		
1992 general	Robert E. (Bud) Cramer (D)	160,060	(66%)	($389,349)
	Terry Smith (R)	77,951	(32%)	($28,225)
	Other	6,006	(2%)	

SIXTH DISTRICT

Birmingham, Alabama, a city that for years liked to think of itself as new and modern, now has a great deal of history behind it—and prospects for the future far more hopeful than seemed possible even a decade ago. Birmingham's old reputation as a new city makes sense in the southern context. For there was no settlement here before the Civil War, just a few creeks running below Red Mountain. But Red Mountain is almost pure iron ore, and Birmingham soon became a steel center; by 1890 it had the South's largest steel mills. By the early 20th Century, as the statue of Vulcan, Roman god of fire and metalworking, looked out over the smokestack-rich city in the valley, Birmingham seemed the most up-to-date and progressive city in the South. But the worldwide overcapacity in steel and technological obsolescence at home sent the American steel industry into long-term decline starting in the 1950s. And in the years when commercial Atlanta was billing itself as "The City Too Busy to Hate" and building its giant airport, industrial Birmingham's political leaders were plotting to avoid desegregation. Birmingham's violent reaction to civil rights—police commissioner Bull Connor set dogs and firehoses against peaceful demonstrators, and Ku Klux Klansmen bombed the 16th Street Baptist Church killing four young girls in 1963—made a vivid impression over the new medium of television news, helping to pass the Civil Rights Act of 1964, and created a reputation from which Birmingham was still suffering a generation later.

Today's Birmingham has developed a new economic base to generate growth and has worked to improve amicable race relations. Health care is one major industry: Birmingham has one of the largest and most advanced medical care centers in the South. Banking is the other: while Atlanta's banks foundered and were acquired by outsiders, Birmingham became the largest southern banking center after Charlotte, North Carolina, with headquarters of SouthTrust, AmSouth Bancorp, First Alabama Bancshares and Central Bancshares of the South. There is still racial polarization: most blacks live in Birmingham itself and the series of factory towns north of Red Mountain; this area is about two-thirds black. A whole new Birmingham has grown up along the freeways south of Red Mountain, starting with the old high-income suburb of Mountain Brook and spreading south into fast-growing Shelby County; this is over 90% white.

The 6th Congressional District of Alabama, which once included all of Birmingham and most of its suburbs, is now, thanks to prevailing interpretations of the 1982 Voting Rights Act amendments, the white Birmingham-area district. It includes only a small part of the city, plus the high-income suburbs south of Red Mountain and in Shelby County and the middle-income white suburbs north of Birmingham. It runs south to the white areas of the university town of Tuscaloosa. This is one of the most Republican districts in the nation, 77% for George Bush in 1988, just 1% less than his home district in Houston, and 64% for Bush in 1992.

The congressman from the 6th District is Spencer Bachus, a Republican first elected in 1992. He owned a sawmill company and practiced law, and boasts that he was a good enough trial-lawyer to have produced four straight acquittals in murder trials. He was elected to the state legislature in 1982, at 35, and was an active legislator for a Republican in a heavily Democratic body. He ran for attorney general in 1990 and got 36% of the vote; he was Republican state chairman in 1991 and 1992. But Bachus had to fight to win the district. First he had to win a Republican runoff, with 59% over Marty Connors. Then he faced incumbent Democrat Ben Erdreich, first elected in 1982, popular beyond party lines for his economically moderate record and because he was, early on, among the few prominent Birmingham whites who supported civil rights at a time when that was not only politically courageous but physically dangerous. Erdreich outspent Bachus nearly 2–1 and led in polls, but Bachus won 52%–45%. This is one seat Democrats lost to racial gerrymandering: Erdreich lost the 6th District portion of Jefferson County by 17,000 votes, but the rest of the county went Democratic by 57,000 votes in the adjacent 7th District race.

In the House, Bachus has been a solid and enthusiastic conservative on economic, cultural and foreign issues. In his first term, he proposed saving 25% of government printing costs and co-sponsored $32 billion in spending cuts. He got a seat on the Banking Committee to tend Birmingham's banking interests, and there questioned Treasury Secretary Lloyd Bentsen during the Whitewater hearings about his knowledge of potential White House conflict of interest. He sponsored an amendment to ban National Endowment for the Arts grants for art that portrayed religious, sexual or excretory activities "in a patently offensive way." He was reelected easily, with almost 80% of the vote, and in his second term won a seat on the Transportation and

Infrastructure Committee where he is interested in building a third bridge over the Black Warrior River in Tuscaloosa. As General Oversight and Investigations Subcommittee chairman on Banking, he likely will be an enthusiastic and active member of Newt Gingrich's majority and an aggressive partisan.

The People: Pop. 1990: 577,170; 23% rural; 12% age 65+; 90% White; 9% Black; 1% Asian; 1% Hispanic origin. Voting age pop.: 441,588; 8% Black. Households: 61% married couple families; 28% married couple fams. w. children; 51% college educ.; median household income: $31,864; per capita income: $16,033; median gross rent: $405; median house value: $72,800.

1992 Presidential Vote			1988 Presidential Vote		
Bush (R)	183,127	(64%)	Bush (R)	170,697	(77%)
Clinton (D)	73,463	(26%)	Dukakis (D)	51,732	(23%)
Perot (I)	28,196	(10%)			

Rep. Spencer Bachus (R)

Elected 1992; b. Dec. 28, 1947, Birmingham; home, Birmingham; Auburn U., B.A. 1969, U. of AL, J.D. 1972; Baptist; divorced.

Career: Natl. Guard, 1969–71; Owner, Lumber Co.; Practicing atty., 1972–92; AL Senate, 1983–84; AL House of Reps., 1984–87; AL Repub. Party Chmn., 1991–92.

DC Office: 127 CHOB 20515, 202-225-4921; Fax: 202-225-2082.

District Offices: 1900 Intl. Park Dr., #107, Birmingham 35243, 205-969-2296; and 3500 McFarland Blvd., P.O. Drawer 569, Northport 35476, 205-333-9894.

Committees: *Banking & Financial Services* (8th of 27 R): Capital Markets, Securities and Government Sponsored Enterprises; General Oversight and Investigations (Chmn.). *Transportation & Infrastructure* (24th of 33 R): Aviation; Railroads. *Veterans' Affairs* (9th of 18 R): Hospitals and Health Care.

Group Ratings

	ADA	ACLU	COPE	CFA	LCV	CON	NSI	COC	ACU	NTLC	CHC
1994	15	17	22	10	0	85	100	82	95	100	100
1993	0	—	0	0	36	69	—	100	100	—	—

National Journal Ratings

	1993 LIB — 1993 CONS		1994 LIB — 1994 CONS	
Economic	0% —	88%	0% —	80%
Social	0% —	89%	11% —	85%
Foreign	24% —	72%	25% —	71%

Key Votes of the 103d Congress

1. Clinton Deficit Plan	N	3. Brady Handgun Purchase	N	5. Lmt. UN Cmnd. of Forces	Y
2. NAFTA	Y	4. Strike Race/Death Pnlty.	Y	6. Cut Missile Funds	N

Key Votes of the 104th Congress

1. Congressional Compliance	Y	6. Reform Crime Grant	Y	11. Loser Pays Court Reform	Y
2. Balanced Budget Amndmt.	Y	7. National Security Act	Y	12. Product Liability Reform	Y
3. Bar Unfunded Mandates	Y	8. Moratorium on Regs.	Y	13. Welfare Reform	Y
4. Pass Line Item Veto	Y	9. Risk Assessment on Regs.	Y	14. Term Limits Amndmt.	Y
5. Relax Exclusionary Rule	Y	10. Expnd. Priv. Prop. Rights	Y	15. Tax Cuts	Y

Election Results

1994 general	Spencer Bachus (R)	155,047	(79%)	($332,233)
	Larry Fortenberry (D).................	41,030	(21%)	
1994 primary	Spencer Bachus (R)	unopposed		
1992 general	Spencer Bachus (R)	146,599	(52%)	($502,793)
	Ben Erdreich (D)	126,062	(45%)	($1,015,731)
	Others	7,357	(3%)	

SEVENTH DISTRICT

More than any other state, Alabama has taken to celebrating its black heritage, building striking memorials to the civil rights movement in Montgomery and Birmingham, promoting tourism to these and other black history sites, commemorating with dignified restraint a history that was full of raucous hatred and moving sacrifice. Blacks first came here as slaves; the last slave ship to the United States, the *Clotilde*, docked in Mobile in 1859, where its cargo was then set free. Blacks were part of the great migration into the cottonlands after the Jacksonians swept the Indians out of the Southeast and sent them on their Trail of Tears to what is now Oklahoma. Today, Alabama's rural blacks are still clustered in the Black Belt of fertile dark soil across the center of the state: around Montgomery, where Rosa Parks refused to move to the back of a city bus in 1955 and a young minister named Martin Luther King, Jr., led a bus boycott; around Selma, founded by Alabama's one vice president, William Rufus King, and where Sheriff Jim Clark's troops beat up peaceful marchers on the Edmund Pettus Bridge in demonstrations that led to the march on Montgomery and the 1965 Voting Rights Act. All 10 of Alabama's majority-black counties are in the rich farm country of the Black Belt. But most Alabama blacks now live in urban areas, one-quarter in metropolitan Birmingham.

The 7th Congressional District of Alabama, with its convoluted boundaries, was created as a black-majority district. Some 45% of its people live in the narrow valley of Birmingham where the population is 75% black; another 13% are in an 80% black portion of Montgomery County. The rest of the district includes Black Belt counties where the Alabama and Tombigbee Rivers flow lazily past old plantations, plus part of Tuscaloosa, home of the University of Alabama, and nearby Vance, site of the much sought-after new Mercedes factory. It thus combines the remnants of Alabama's old cotton economy with neighborhoods built in the shadows of Birmingham's once booming steel mills.

The 7th District was obviously meant to elect a black congressman, Alabama's first since Republican Jeremiah Haralson retired in 1876. The white 7th District incumbent Claude Harris retired. The decisive 1992 Democratic primary was a "friends and neighbors" contest reminiscent of the old days of southern white politics. State Senator Earl Hilliard of Birmingham led the primary with 31%, winning 58% in Jefferson County but running far behind elsewhere. In second place with 24%, with solid wins in his home Black Belt, was State Senator Hank Sanders. Montgomery County Commissioner John Knight, got 72% in Montgomery County, but his 20% overall was good only for third place. In the runoff, Jefferson County cast only one-third of the votes, but Hilliard got 71% there, and carried two small rural counties as well. He held Sanders to a 53% edge in Montgomery County, enough for a 50.5%–49.5% victory. Sanders claimed vote fraud but decided not to contest the result.

Hilliard was first elected to the Alabama legislature in 1974 and rose to committee chairman in 1982. He pushed for horse racing in Birmingham and sponsored tax abatement bills. In the House Hilliard has a solidly liberal voting record, backed single-payer health insurance and is pro-choice. He is also interested in local projects, from encouraging catfish farms in the Black Belt to building a new international airport east of Birmingham. He also has become an outspoken member of the Congressional Black Caucus, frequently taking to the floor to defend the achievements of the civil-rights revolution. He fought for the racial justice death penalty provision and pressed the postal service to issue a stamp honoring Mary Eliza Mahoney, the first black professional nurse. He won easily in 1994.

The People: Pop. 1990: 577,430; 27% rural; 14% age 65+; 32% White; 67% Black. Voting age pop.: 407,380; 64% Black. Households: 44% married couple families; 20% married couple fams. w. children; 32% college educ.; median household income: $16,560; per capita income: $8,135; median gross rent: $276; median house value: $40,200.

1992 Presidential Vote			1988 Presidential Vote		
Clinton (D)	151,129	(69%)	Dukakis (D)	138,438	(68%)
Bush (R)	56,620	(26%)	Bush (R)	64,070	(32%)
Perot (I)	11,633	(5%)			

Rep. Earl F. Hilliard (D)

Elected 1992; b. Apr. 9, 1942, Birmingham; home, Birmingham; Morehouse Col., B.A. 1964; Howard U., J.D. 1967; Atlanta U., M.B.A. 1969; Baptist; married (Mary).

Career: Practicing atty., 1972–92; AL House of Reps., 1974–80; AL Senate, 1980–92.

DC Office: 1007 LHOB 20515, 202-225-2665; Fax: 202-226-0772.

District Offices: Vance Fed. Bldg., #305, 1800 5th Ave., Birmingham 35203, 205-328-2841; P.O. Box 2627, Tuscaloosa 35403, 205-752-3578; Fed. Bldg., #109, Selma 36701, 205-872-2684; and Fed. Bldg., 15 Lee St., #301, Montgomery 36104, 334-262-4724.

Committees: *Agriculture* (12th of 22 D): Department Operations, Nutrition and Foreign Agriculture; Livestock, Dairy and Poultry. *Small Business* (12th of 19 D): Procurement, Exports and Business Opportunities.

Group Ratings

	ADA	ACLU	COPE	CFA	LCV	CON	NSI	COC	ACU	NTLC	CHC
1994	80	87	100	50	73	1	20	25	29	11	7
1993	90	—	100	70	64	11	—	9	4	—	—

National Journal Ratings

	1993 LIB — 1993 CONS		1994 LIB — 1994 CONS	
Economic	88%	0%	83%	0%
Social	68%	29%	76%	23%
Foreign	84%	16%	54%	45%

Key Votes of the 103d Congress

1. Clinton Deficit Plan	Y	3. Brady Handgun Purchase	N	5. Lmt. UN Cmnd. of Forces	N
2. NAFTA	N	4. Strike Race/Death Pnlty.	N	6. Cut Missile Funds	Y

Key Votes of the 104th Congress

1. Congressional Compliance	Y	6. Reform Crime Grant	N	11. Loser Pays Court Reform	N
2. Balanced Budget Amndmt.	N	7. National Security Act	N	12. Product Liability Reform	*
3. Bar Unfunded Mandates	N	8. Moratorium on Regs.	N	13. Welfare Reform	N
4. Pass Line Item Veto	N	9. Risk Assessment on Regs.	N	14. Term Limits Amndmt.	N
5. Relax Exclusionary Rule	N	10. Expnd. Priv. Prop. Rights	Y	15. Tax Cuts	N

Election Results

1994 general	Earl F. Hilliard (D)	116,150	(77%)	($337,772)
	Alfred J. Middleton (R)	34,814	(23%)	
1994 primary	Earl F. Hilliard (D)	unopposed		
1992 general	Earl F. Hilliard (D)	144,320	(70%)	($352,237)
	Kervin Jones (R)	36,086	(17%)	($11,963)
	James Lewis (I)	12,461	(6%)	($58,470)
	James Chambliss (I)	11,466	(6%)	
	Others	3,300	(2%)	

ALASKA

"The purchase of Alaska," wrote historian Henry Clark of William Seward's 1867 agreement, "was not made in any spirit of farsighted policy, but by almost stumbling into a treaty." This immense land mass, so remote from the rest of the United States, has puzzled Americans ever since. It has never had a self-sustaining private sector economy, and its growth came almost entirely from government spending and mineral extraction. Alaska was opened up to settlement by the surprise discovery of gold in Canada's Klondike in 1897. Its interior around Fairbanks was connected to the port of Anchorage by the Alaska Railroad built by the government in the 1920s; it was connected to the rest of North America by the Alcan Highway, built (like most of Alaska's roads) by the Army in eight months during the grim war days of 1942. After a valiant campaign, Alaska was admitted to the Union in 1959 with a statehood act that promised state government a choice of public lands, and for many years afterwards it remained the least populated of American states.

Then, the day after Christmas 1967, at Prudhoe Bay on the Arctic coast, an undulating roar as loud as four jumbo jets directly overhead drew a crowd of 40 men, heavily clothed against the 30-below, 30-knot weather, to an oil rig. Suddenly a natural gas flare shot 30 feet straight up: this was oil, the great 11 billion barrel North Slope oil field. The greatest oil strike ever in the United States, it has made this country a major (though not self-sufficient) producer during the years after the oil shocks of the 1970s, and has made Alaska what it is—and is not—today. It was another accident: oil companies had drilled seven dry wells on Prudhoe Bay, and ARCO chief executive Robert Anderson wouldn't have ordered this one last try, except that he had a drilling rig nearby. Yet this spurting up of the lifeblood of western civilization in the cold darkness of Arctic winter was not the end of the story of this improbable American commonwealth.

Just half a million of 260 million Americans live in this gigantic land mass, larger than all the Northeastern and Great Lakes states put together; almost half are in the Anchorage area, the others scattered in a few small towns and Native settlements over an area so vast that, if superimposed on the Lower 48, it would stretch from Florida to southern California to Lake Superior. Alaska was the only part of the nation occupied by the enemy in World War II (Japan held the Aleutian islands of Attu and Kiska) and is the only part to border Russia, just across the Bering Strait. Alaskans are closer to these Siberian neighbors geographically and, for Natives, ethnically and culturally, than to Americans in the Lower 48. Physically, there is something slapdash about Alaska's civilization: much of the housing is flimsily built, garbage is left outside to freeze in the winter, moose nibble shrubbery in suburban Anchorage backyards, and caribou breed in record numbers near the Trans-Alaska oil pipeline. If a whole town, like Kivalina on the Chukchi Sea, runs out of room, it moves somewhere else. This is still a frontier state with few old people and more males than females. Every American has heard of Alaska and has some image of its wildness; but fewer than 10% of Americans have ever been there.

Finding oil in Prudhoe Bay was something like finding it on the moon: it was not clear in 1967 who owned the oil or how it could be taken out. Ownership was in question because the Statehood Act of 1959 provided for the state to choose its own public lands, but only after settling Native land claims. Congress, not Alaska, settled such claims in the 1971 Alaska Native Claims Act which set up 12 regional and 220 village Native corporations, gave them $962 million and time to select their own 44 million acres, and ended the Interior Department's freeze that enabled the state to stake claims to mineral-rich acreage. The only feasible way to get the oil out—the Beaufort Sea remains frozen much of the year—was a pipeline, but that was opposed by environmentalists for fear it would destroy the delicate permafrost and interfere with caribou migrations. Development-minded Alaskans got a pipeline bill through Congress in 1973 by just a one-vote margin in the Senate, but the pipeline had to be built on stilts and wasn't opened until 1977, and Congress banned oil exports to Japan and other obvious East Asian markets. Then in 1980, after brilliant lobbying by environmentalists, Congress passed over the objections of Alaska's two senators and in the face of tears from its single Congressman, Don Young, the Alaska Lands Act, which set aside 159 million acres as wilderness.

There were some happy accidents here: the pipeline came on line just as oil prices were approaching their peak, thus generating maximum revenues to the state, which gets 100% of the royalties; the environment was protected and the caribou thrived; the Natives got more autonomy than the non-Native majority of Alaskans would have given them. With oil providing 85% of its revenue, the state abolished its income tax in 1980 and voted lavish benefits, subsidized mortgage interest rates and 25-year residents' housing, granted low-interest college loans and forgave half the debt of students if they would return to Alaska for five years—all for a relatively affluent population, even as the cost-of-living differential from the Lower 48 was being vastly reduced. In the 1970s, Alaska established a Permanent Fund for most of the oil money, totalling $13.2 billion by 1993, and every one-year resident of Alaska gets an annual check—in 1994, $983.90.

Alaska now faces other tough decisions—which often enough depend on Washington, and therefore on national political trends. In 1993 and 1994, with the White House and Congress in Democratic hands, Alaskans eager to exploit their natural resources, like Governor Walter Hickel, were thwarted by Washington. The national Republican sweep of 1994 changed the calculus: now Alaska's Senators Ted Stevens and Frank Murkowski and Congressman Don Young all chair key committees and subcommittees where they will be in a position to deliver on issues vital to their home state. But in 1994 Alaska elected by a plurality of 536 votes a Democratic Governor, Tony Knowles, who is less development-minded than any governor in at least a dozen years. And the Clinton Administration, with no hope of ever winning Alaska's electoral votes, may use its powers to limit development, as it did in April 1994 when the Forest Service canceled the 50-year contract to harvest timber in the Tongass National Forest on Alaska's panhandle. Most Alaskans hope the Republican victory will resurrect plans for oil exploration on a narrow coastal strip of the Arctic National Wildlife Refuge (ANWR), a plot of land they claim is no bigger than the state of Delaware, which may have the potential to be another Prudhoe Bay. Congress seemed about to approve ANWR drilling when the Exxon *Valdez* went aground in Prince William Sound in March 1989. But the disaster—spilling 11 million gallons of crude oil and killing some 400,000 waterfowl and shore birds, at least 3,500 sea otters and 900 bald eagles—changed its mind. ANWR drilling was narrowly defeated in November 1991; it had no chance in the 103d Congress, and if passed by the 104th might be vetoed by President Clinton. The Exxon *Valdez* disaster surely increased the risks of oil production: Exxon spent $2.5 billion on cleanup and lost a $5 billion judgment in court in 1994, on top of a 1991 settlement in which it agreed to pay an additional $900 million over 11 years to restore Prince William Sound and $100 million in restitution—half to Alaska and half to the federal government. A happy side effect is that the state is spending much of its money buying up land.

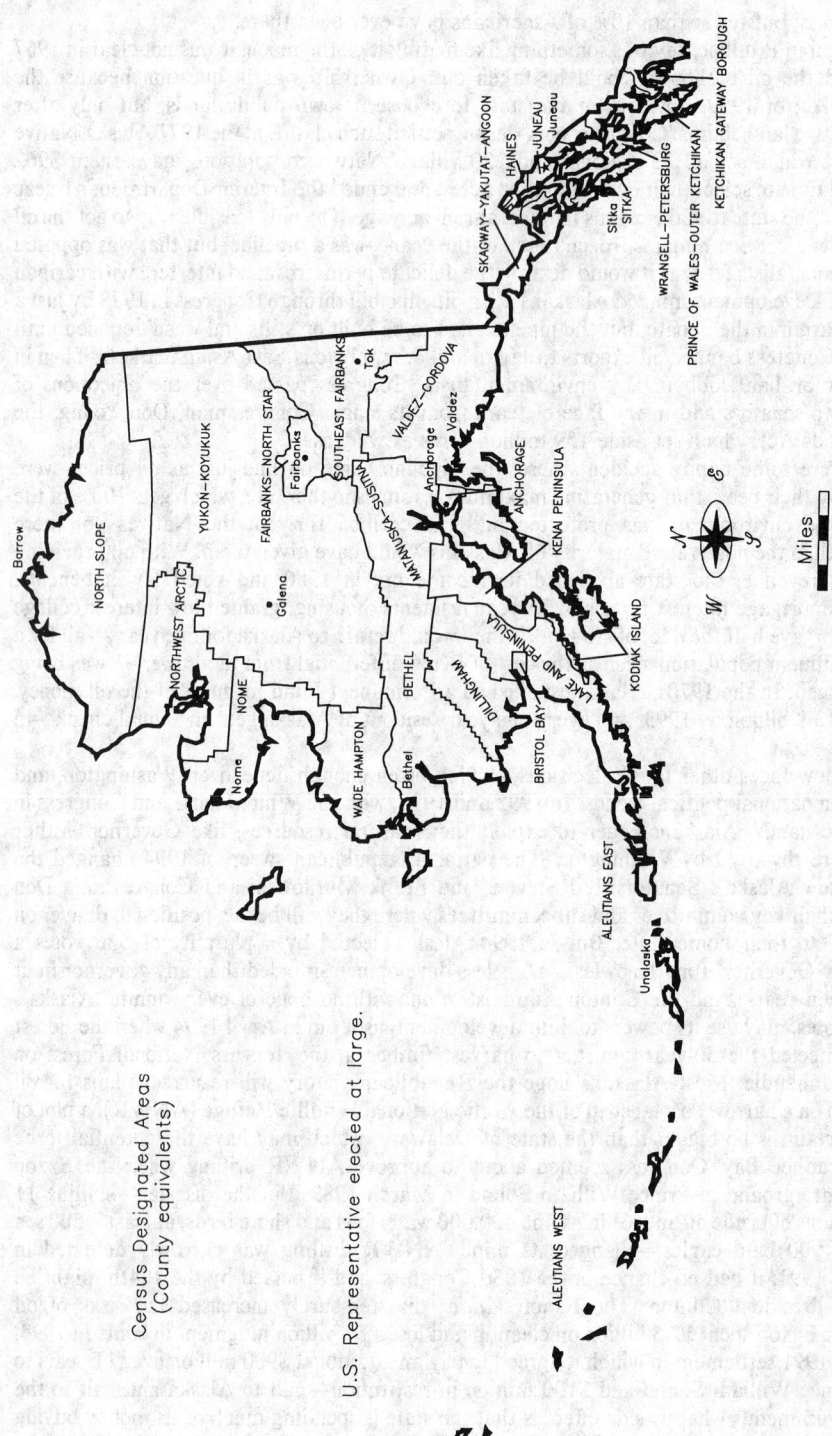

Census Designated Areas
(County equivalents)

U.S. Representative elected at large.

Meantime, the character of this state, with its disproportionate numbers of airplanes and convicts, its earthquakes and surging glaciers, seems slowly to be changing: life on the frontier is becoming more routinized and regulated, and the free spirit evidenced in large votes for the Libertarian Party a dozen or more years ago may be vanishing. This is apparent in the 1990 vote to revoke Alaska's 1975 decriminalization of marijuana, in the charging of fees for climbing Mount McKinley in Denali National Park, in the 1994 change from open 48-hour harvests of fish to set quotas, in restrictions against RVs camping out in shopping center parking lots. The Alaska bush in the 1970s attracted hippies and eccentrics looking for elbow room; "end-of-the-roaders" in the 1990s are more likely to be offbeat strangers drawn by escapist fantasies and prone to violence. It is not "Northern Exposure." Some of the Native corporations are thriving, but others have fallen on hard times and are selling timber and other resources their creators hoped they would preserve; poverty and alcoholism are high in the bush, and native languages like *Tlingit* are dying out. Other institutions remain weak. Unions, which were politically pivotal 20 years ago, aren't any more. The oil companies, while not so unpopular as Lower 48ers thought they would be after the oil spill, were not able to stop higher state oil taxes. Political party organizations have never been strong and voters don't follow party lines—as was shown spectacularly by the election of Walter Hickel as an Independent in 1990. As for the legislature—well, just about any kind of candidate can get elected, and has. In national politics, Alaska is solidly Republican, because national Democrats are seen as wanting to lock up Alaska's resources; no Democrat has been elected to Congress here since 1974, though some contests have been close.

Important regional differences persist. Anchorage, with 40% of the population, is much like a prosperous Rocky Mountains' metropolis with longer summer days and winter nights; it is affluent and booming, with 70% of women in the work force here, the highest in the country. Politically, it is solidly Republican. So are the smaller settlements in a 200-mile arc around Anchorage, which have been growing even more rapidly—the Matanuska Valley (one of the few places in Alaska where farming is possible), Seward, the Kenai peninsula, the little port of Valdez at the southern terminus of the pipeline, the town of Wasilla where a local legislator wanted to relocate the state capital, a move defeated in a 1994 referendum 55%–45%. This was strong Ross Perot territory in 1992; overall, Alaska cast the nation's second highest Perot percentage, 28%. Fairbanks, Alaska's second largest city, is a pipeline and mineral service center deep in the interior, unprotected from Arctic winds in winter and fierce crowds of mosquitoes in the brief but hot summer. Once solidly Republican, it now seems disgruntled.

The old Alaska, first settled by Russians, can be seen in the fishing towns of the Panhandle and in the capital of Juneau, located on an inlet of the Pacific up against a steep mountain; Alaskans voted to move the capital to a site near Anchorage in 1974 but defeated referenda to pay for it in 1978 and 1982, and Juneau survived once again in 1994. The Panhandle usually votes Democratic. Far away to the north and west is the Alaska bush, the villages where Natives—Indians, Aleuts, Eskimos—live, often in poverty. Natives make up 16% of Alaska's population and 70% in the vast lands north and west of Anchorage and Fairbanks, but they are only 51,000 people living in an area larger than the northeast United States.

Governor. Alaska has had a colorful array of governors in its nearly four decades of statehood, from its first governor, Democrat William Egan, through bush pilot Jay Hammond, elected in 1974 and 1978, and Walter Hickel, Anchorage developer, elected in 1966, appointed Richard Nixon's Interior secretary in 1969 (he resigned in 1970 in protest against the invasion of Cambodia) and elected again, as a member of the Alaska Independence Party, at 71 in 1990. None, incidentally, has won an absolute majority of the vote since Egan did in 1970; independent and third party candidates have abounded, and this national Republican state has elected Democratic governors in three of the last four contests. The current Governor is Tony Knowles, a Democrat who lost to Hickel in 1990 and then, after Hickel retired, was elected by substantially less than a landslide in 1994: the one governorship that year picked up by the Democrats.

As usual in Alaska, it was a rough and ready contest. Senator Frank Murkowski was urged to run, but decided not to. Hickel teased voters by switching back to the Republican Party, bowing out of the race while threatening to run as an independent, then finally retiring eight days before the all-party primary. The Republican nomination went unopposed to Jim Campbell, a loser in 1990; Democrats picked Tony Knowles, former Anchorage Mayor, over former Lieutenant Governor Steve McAlpine. Lieutenant Governor Jack Coghill, whose maneuverings got Hickel into the race in 1990, ran on the Alaska Independence ticket. Campbell started out with big leads and popular issue stands but squandered them with two astonishingly foolish tactics. The first was a telephone poll which stated that Knowles supported gay marriage and adoption—though he had never done so. The second was an ad in which Campbell said, "I was watching the news last night and I noticed something—President Bill Clinton is tall, has a shy smile, good hair. Some women tell me he's really good-looking. And then I noticed Tony Knowles—tall, shy smile, good hair—same thing with women. But it doesn't stop there. Bill Clinton wants more environmental restrictions in Alaska. Tony Knowles says he thinks we need more environmental restrictions in Alaska. Coincidence? Or is this always the way it is when a guy's handsome and has good hair. Jim Campbell doesn't have good hair, but he says Tony Knowles is wrong." The "good hair" line was witty self-deprecation: Campbell is bald and wore a toupee until he ran in 1990. But the "same thing with women" line was baseless innuendo, and shifted the focus from development, on which Campbell's stand was popular, to campaign tactics. Knowles surged to a big lead in polls but on election day won by only 41.1%–40.8%, with 13% for Coghill—a 536-vote margin after all the ballots were in. Knowles had huge leads in the bush and Juneau, but ran behind in urban areas.

Once in office, Knowles proclaimed that "Alaska is open for business" and called for "adding value to our resources in Alaska and enhancing—not detracting from—the beauty and cleanliness of our home." He pledged to emphasize education and made national news in his first weeks by stopping a wolf-shooting program (initiated by Hickel to increase caribou and attract hunters) after a wildlife biologist critical of the policy videotaped state officials inhumanely trapping and killing wolves.

Senators. Few senators occupy as central a place in their state's public and economic life as Ted Stevens. "They sent me here," Stevens said in one impassioned debate, "to stand up for the state of Alaska." Alaska's special dependence on the federal government makes Stevens more like an ambassador than a run-of-the-mill legislator. "We ask for special consideration," Stevens is not too shy to say, "because no one else is that far away, no one else has the problems that we have or the potential that we have, and no one else deals with the federal government day in and day out the way we do." Stevens spends plenty of time on national issues, but much of his time and energy over the last quarter century has been necessarily consumed dealing with parochial Alaska issues. With his often prickly personality, that persistence has not endeared him to many colleagues, but he has demanded the Senate's attention during the many battles over his state's interests in his quarter-century in the Senate.

He has had plenty of training. Stevens moved to Alaska in 1950, was U.S. Attorney and worked in the Interior Department in Washington, served in the legislature in Juneau and was appointed to the Senate by Governor Walter Hickel in December 1968, at 45. In the Senate, he has not been entirely successful. He could not stop the Alaska Lands Act in 1980 and could not push through ANWR oil drilling in 1991. But he did get the pipeline through by one vote in 1973, he managed the oil spill bill of 1989 in response to the *Valdez* accident, requiring double hulls and compensating Alaska and, with impressive mastery of detail, he has worked on Alaska issues of all description. He has worked on fishing legislation: to ban monofilament nets and to reduce waste and bycatch, to reauthorize the 200-mile limit, to ratify the International Salmon Treaty and the treaty to preserve pollock stocks in the area known as the "Doughnut Hole" in the central Bering Sea. He worked for more health and sanitation aid to bush villages and funding for health research on fetal alcohol syndrome and cancers common among Natives. He got funding for Alaska Native's cultural programs and for the American Russian Center and restoration of Russian Orthodox churches in Alaska. With Republican majorities, he will try to get approval for ANWR oil drilling and exports of Alaskan oil to East Asia, and to relax the wetlands law in Alaska.

Stevens is the second ranking Republican on Appropriations, and chairs the Defense Subcommittee. He works hard to fund the National Guard, to raise military salaries and to keep troops in readiness. After surgery for prostate cancer in 1991, he has pushed for more funding for breast, cervical and prostate cancer research. He voted against GATT, charging that it would jeopardize Alaska's unitary business tax on oil producers. Though his voting record is mostly conservative (he opposed the Brady bill and the assault weapon ban), he takes some un-Republican stands. He supports the Corporation for Public Broadcasting: Alaska's public TV stations have the nation's largest audience shares. And, with the large government work force in high-cost Alaska, he supports increased salaries and benefits for federal workers and argues volubly for higher salaries for senators and Senate staffers. In 1995, he became chairman of the Senate Rules Committee, in which capacity he will preside over the 1997 Inauguration. But that also has put him into the uncomfortable position of forcing cutbacks in the Senate's staff payroll and other office perquisites. The fact that he does not chair a more important Senate committee is odd, especially given that he is the third-most senior Republican; it also reflects his committee-switching in the 1970s on behalf of Alaska projects and some favors that he granted to other GOP Senators, which Stevens cited after the 1994 election in his unsuccessful bid to take the Commerce, Science and Transportation Committee chairmanship.

Stevens served as Republican whip from 1981 to 1984, and ran for majority leader in 1984; he lost 28–25 to Bob Dole. But he rebounded quickly from this disappointment and remains part of the Senate's old guard. Back home in 1990, he won reelection by a 66%–32% margin, down slightly from his previous showings. He is regarded as a solid favorite to win reelection in 1996.

Frank Murkowski, after two terms as junior senator, is now a major figure, chairman of the Energy and Natural Resources Committee and his party's point man on one of our stickiest foreign policy problems, North Korea, where hs is anxious to facilitate "meaningful dialogue" between North and South Korea. Murkowski grew up in Seattle and Ketchikan, served in the Coast Guard in Alaska, and became a banker in Fairbanks. A department head under Governor Walter Hickel in the 1960s, he ran for Congress and lost in 1970. He was elected to the Senate in 1980 by winning 54% against liberal Democrat Clark Gruening. He got a seat on Energy, which handles many Alaska issues, and has worked cooperatively with Stevens, with many successes and some failures. The former include a ban on driftnet fishing in international waters, the Native Languages Preservation Act, initiating contacts between Alaska and Siberia and a law allowing Native corporation shareholders to retain control of their lands. He led the so-far unsuccessful fight for ANWR oil drilling and backed the timber harvest in the Tongass forest suspended by the Clinton Administration. On the Foreign Relations Committee, he has worked on East Asia issues, from Taiwan to Vietnam to North Korea, which he visited; in late 1994 he criticized the Clinton Administration's accord with North Korea, but declined to try to overturn it. But he gave up that assignment to join the Finance Committee, part of Bob Dole's cabal to prevent Phil Gramm from gaining a seat on that high-profile panel.

Murkowski has been reelected twice in contests that attracted little attention outside Alaska. In 1986 he beat former Alaska Pacific University president Glenn Olds 54%–44%. In 1992, he attracted strong opposition from Native leader Willie Hensley, who filed late but got on the ballot, and former Commissioner of Economic Development Tony Smith, who attacked Murkowski as ineffective on ANWR and the Exxon clean-up money. Smith edged Hensley in the primary, 45%–40%, but Murkowski ran an ad showing a farmer with a wheelbarrow full of manure, a reference to Smith's allegedly liberal promises; there were some nasty charges and countercharges, and Murkowski greatly outspent Smith, winning 53%–38%. Murkowski has never received as much as 55% of the vote, but his chairmanship is highly valuable to Alaska and his views in line with those of most Alaska voters; he should be in a strong position in 1998.

Representative-At-Large. Alaska's Don Young, onetime tugboat captain on the Yukon and the only licensed mariner in Congress, is, in his words, "not one of these smooth, namby-pamby politicians." He is a hot-tempered, salty-tongued true believer, given to malapropisms ("Pribilof's dog" and "bladderdash") and blunders (he settled a libel lawsuit brought by his 1988 opponent whom Young accused of using "laundered funds" from environmental groups). He was elected to the legislature in 1966 and ran for Congress in 1972; his opponent, incumbent Nick Begich, was killed in a plane crash, and Young won the March 1973 special election to succeed him. For two decades, Young served in the minority on the Resources Committee, which handles many Alaska issues, and was ranking minority member from 1985 to 1995. This was frustrating service: one development-minded Alaskan facing off against 434 mostly environment-minded Lower 48ers; and Young served on a committee even more dominated by environmentalists, including Chairmen Morris Udall, who pushed through the Alaska Lands Act of 1980, and the hot-tempered George Miller. Young was continually frustrated that he could not make his fellow legislators see reason, while back home he was fiercely attacked as ineffective. While Alaska's two senators could often stop action in the Senate, House rules allowed the Democratic majority easily to roll over Young. He lost one battle after another: to open up ANWR to oil drilling, to continue full logging of the Tongass forest, to stop the Alaska Lands Act, to allow Alaska oil exports to East Asia. He could point to some successes, too: the driftnet law which would limit foreign fishing techniques and thereby help Alaska fishermen; laws to help the Alaska Natives; raising Payments In Lieu of Taxes (PILT) by 140%; blocking reforms to the 1872 Mining Law which, in Young's view, would make it harder to stake a mining claim here than in Russia. Young is not entirely a free market conservative, though: he supported the Family and Medical Leave Act and Hatch Act repeal.

Over the years Young's stormy personality and lack of strong successes on Alaska issues inspired stronger opposition than his party label and national issue stands would suggest. He had significant opposition in 1978, 1984, 1986 and 1990, winning only 52% that year against John Devens, the mayor of Valdez, known statewide because of the oil spill cleanup. In 1992, Devens ran again, and led in most polls. Young apologized for his volatile behavior and used the Clinton-Gore opposition to ANWR drilling against the Democrat. The *Anchorage Daily News*'s constant criticisms of Young depressed his vote in that usually Republican city, but his work for Native causes helped him carry the combined rural and bush vote, enough for a statewide victory of 47%–43%.

Over the next two years, things moved very much Young's way. His Democratic opponent was former Commerce Commissioner Tony Smith, fresh from a respectable 53%–38% loss to Senator Frank Murkowski. But the Clinton Administration was unpopular, and Young did not hobble himself with any inconvenient stands on national issues: because of his opposition to term limits and his concern over the cost of its other pieces, he was one of three Republican incumbents who didn't sign the Contract With America. Young won by a solid 57%–33% vote, not his best showing ever but a solid recovery from 1992. As the returns were coming in, he also had the pleasure of learning that he would no longer be in the minority, but would be holding the Resources chairmanship so long held by his scornful adversaries. "Suddenly, the former trapper from Fort Yukon is a celebrity, attracting a steady stream of visitors who come away with stories about his salty language and the animal trophies on his wall," *National Journal* reported in April 1995. Young argued unsuccessfully for the retention of the Merchant Marine and Fisheries Committee, on which he also served. But the Republicans' reorganization gave Resources control of all Alaska federal non-military lands as well as some of the maritime issues that are so important to his home state. Now Young will be tested as never before: can he get ANWR drilling and oil exports and other longtime Alaska causes through his much more sympathetic committee and the House? In his early months as chairman, he showed that he would not be shy in pushing his agenda. Environmentalists are going to have to compromise, he told *National Journal*. "If not, I'm just going to ram it down their throats." He installed pro-development allies to head new task forces on his committee in order to work around potentially reluctant subcommittee chairmen on wetlands issues and the Endangered Species Act, of which Young has been a harsh critic. It also will be interesting to watch how Young gets along with

Murkowski when the House and Senate seek to settle differences on bills from their two committees. Although Young is far more flamboyant, the two have said that they expect to cooperate and they obviously share many views.

Presidential politics. In presidential elections, Alaska votes Alaska issues, but this was not always so: in 1960 and 1968 its vote came eerily close to the national average. Since then, it has voted for development and against the national Democrats: in the year of the Alaska Lands Act, it gave only 26% of its votes to Jimmy Carter, who in some places ran behind Libertarian Ed Clark. In 1988 and 1992, Alaska joined the Pacific Rim shift away from the Republicans, but not necessarily toward the Democrats. In 1992, Bush carried the state with only 40% of the vote, Clinton had only 30% and Ross Perot had 28%, his second best showing after Maine.

Alaska has no presidential primary. Party true believers tend to dominate the caucuses.

The People: Est. Pop. 1994: 606,000; Pop. 1990: 550,043, up 10.2% 1990–1994. 0.2% of U.S. total, 48th largest; 33% rural. Median age: 29.4 years. 4.1% 65 years and over. 75.5% White, 15.6% American Indian, 4.1% Black, 3.6% Asian, 3.2% Hispanic origin, 1.2% Other. Households: 56.2% married couple families; 34% married couple fams. w. children; 58% college educ.; median household income: $41,408; per capita income: $17,610; 56.1% owner occupied housing; median house value: $94,400; median monthly rent: $503. 9.1% Unemployment. 1994 Voting age pop.: 429,000. 1994 Turnout: 182,982; 43% of VAP. Registered voters (1994): 340,415; 59,772 D (18%), 78,183 R (23%), 202,460 unaffiliated and minor parties (59%).

Political Lineup: Governor, Tony Knowles (D); Lt. Gov., Fran Ulmer (D); Atty. Gen., Bruce M. Botelho (R); Commissioner of Revenue, Wilson L. Condon (R). State Senate, 20 (12 R and 8 D). State House of Representatives, 40 (22 R, 17 D and 1 I). Senators, Ted Stevens (R) and Frank H. Murkowski (R). Representative, 1 R at large.

1992 Presidential Vote		
Bush (R)	102,000	(40%)
Clinton (D)	78,294	(30%)
Perot (I)	73,481	(28%)

1988 Presidential Vote		
Bush (R)	119,251	(60%)
Dukakis (D)	72,584	(36%)
Others	8,281	(4%)

GOVERNOR

Gov. Tony Knowles (D)

Elected 1994; term expires Jan. 1999. b. Jan. 1, 1943, Tulsa, OK; home, Anchorage; Yale U., B.A. 1968; Christian; married (Susan).

Career: Army, 1962–64 (Vietnam). Restaurant owner, 1968–present; Anchorage Assembly, 1975–79; Anchorage Mayor, 1982–87.

Office: P.O. Box 110001, Juneau 99811, 907-465-3500; Fax: 907-465-3532.

Election Results

1994 gen.	Tony Knowles (D)	87,693	(41%)
	James O. (Jim) Campbell (R)	87,157	(41%)
	John B. (Jack) Coghill (I)	27,838	(13%)
	Jim Sykes (Green)	8,727	(4%)
	Others	2,020	(1%)
1994 prim.	Tony Knowles (D)	24,727	(44%)
	Stephen McAlpine (D)	17,482	(31%)
	Sam Cotten (D)	13,899	(25%)
	Others	550	(1%)
1990 gen.	Walter J. Hickel (AI)	68,181	(39%)
	Tony Knowles (D)	53,998	(31%)
	Arliss Sturgulewski (R)	46,553	(27%)
	Other	6,832	(3%)

SENATORS

Sen. Ted Stevens (R)

Appointed Dec. 1968, seat up 1996; b. Nov. 18, 1923, Indianapolis, IN; home, Girdwood; U.C.L.A., A.B. 1947, Harvard, LL.B. 1950; Episcopalian; married (Catherine).

Career: Army Air Corps, 1943–46 (WWII); Practicing atty., 1950–53, 1961–68; U.S. Atty., 1953–56; U.S. Dept. of Interior, Legis. Cnsl., 1956–58, Asst. to Secy., 1958–60, Solicitor, 1960–61; AK House of Reps., 1964–68.

DC Office: 522 HSOB 20510, 202-224-3004; Fax: 202-224-2354.

State Offices: Fed. Bldg., Box 4, 101 12th Ave., Fairbanks 99701, 907-456-0261; 222 W. 7th Ave., Anchorage 99513, 907-271-5915; Fed. Bldg., Box 020149, Juneau 99802, 907-586-7400; 120 Trading Bay Rd., #260, Kenai 99611, 907-283-5808; and 109 Main St., Ketchikan 99901, 907-225-6880.

Committees: *Appropriations* (2nd of 15 R): Commerce, Justice, State and Judiciary; Defense (Chmn.); Interior; Military Construction; VA, HUD and Independent Agencies. *Commerce, Science & Transportation* (3rd of 10 R): Aviation; Communications; Oceans and Fisheries (Chmn.); Science, Technology and Space; Surface Transportation and Merchant Marine. *Governmental Affairs* (2nd of 8 R): Investigations; Post Office and Civil Service (Chmn.). *Rules & Administration* (Chmn. of 9 R).

Group Ratings

	ADA	ACLU	COPE	CFA	LCV	CON	NSI	COC	ACU	NTLC	CHC
1994	25	44	43	33	8	21	100	70	77	67	64
1993	25	—	55	17	6	46	—	91	86	—	—

National Journal Ratings

	1993 LIB — 1993 CONS			1994 LIB — 1994 CONS		
Economic	40%	—	58%	37%	—	61%
Social	34%	—	65%	33%	—	66%
Foreign	0%	—	92%	23%	—	74%

Key Votes of the 103d Congress

1. Clinton Deficit Plan	N	3. Brady Handgun Purchase	N	5. Lmt. UN Cmnd. of Forces	Y
2. NAFTA	N	4. Strike Race/Death Pnlty.	Y	6. Cut Missile Funds	N

Key Votes of the 104th Congress

1. Congressional Compliance	Y	3. Balanced Budget Amndt.	Y	5. Product Liability Reform	Y
2. Bar Unfunded Mandates	Y	4. Pass Line Item Veto	*	6. FY96 Budget	Y

Election Results

1990 general	Ted Stevens (R)	125,806	(66%)	($1,618,098)
	Michael Beasley (D)	61,115	(32%)	($445)
	Other	2,999	(2%)	
1990 primary	Ted Stevens (R)	81,968	(70%)	
	Bob Bird (R)	34,824	(30%)	
1984 general	Ted Stevens (R)	146,919	(71%)	($1,323,218)
	John E. Havelock (D)	58,804	(29%)	($90,685)

Sen. Frank H. Murkowski (R)

Elected 1980, seat up 1998; b. Mar. 28, 1933, Seattle, WA; home, Fairbanks; U. of Santa Clara, Seattle U., B.A. 1955; Catholic; married (Nancy).

Career: Coast Guard, 1955–56; Pacific Natl. Bank of Seattle, 1957–58; Natl. Bank of AK, 1959–67; Commissioner, AK Dept. of Econ. Devel., 1966–70; Pres., AK Natl. Bank, 1971–80.

DC Office: 706 HSOB 20510, 202-224-6665; Fax: 202-224-5301.

State Offices: 222 W. 7th Ave., Box 1, Anchorage 99513, 907-271-3735; 101 12th Ave., Fairbanks 99701, 907-456-0233; Box 21647 Fed. Bldg, Juneau 99802, 907-586-7400; 130 Trading Bay Rd., #350, Kenai 99611, 907-283-5808; and 109 Main St., Ketchikan 99901, 907-225-6880.

Committees: *Energy & Natural Resources* (Chmn. of 10 R). *Finance* (10th of 11 R): International Trade; Long-Term Growth, Debt and Deficit Reduction; Taxation and IRS Oversight. *Veterans' Affairs* (3rd of 7 R). *Indian Affairs* (2nd of 9 R).

Group Ratings

	ADA	ACLU	COPE	CFA	LCV	CON	NSI	COC	ACU	NTLC	CHC
1994	10	28	0	25	0	61	100	81	96	83	100
1993	20	—	20	30	6	63	—	100	80	—	—

National Journal Ratings

	1993 LIB	—	1993 CONS	1994 LIB	—	1994 CONS
Economic	25%	—	70%	12%	—	82%
Social	14%	—	85%	21%	—	75%
Foreign	15%	—	84%	6%	—	86%

Key Votes of the 103d Congress

1. Clinton Deficit Plan	N	3. Brady Handgun Purchase	N	5. Lmt. UN Cmnd. of Forces	Y
2. NAFTA	Y	4. Strike Race/Death Pnlty.	Y	6. Cut Missile Funds	N

Key Votes of the 104th Congress

1. Congressional Compliance	Y	3. Balanced Budget Amndt.	Y	5. Product Liability Reform	Y
2. Bar Unfunded Mandates	Y	4. Pass Line Item Veto	Y	6. FY96 Budget	Y

Election Results

1992 general	Frank H. Murkowski (R)	127,163	(53%)	($1,910,759)
	Tony Smith (D).......................	92,065	(38%)	($910,138)
	Mary Jordan (Green)	20,019	(8%)	($4,091)
1992 primary	Frank H. Murkowski (R)	37,486	(81%)	
	Jed Whittaker (R).....................	9,065	(19%)	
1986 general	Frank H. Murkowski (R)	97,674	(54%)	($1,514,628)
	Glenn Olds (D)	79,727	(44%)	($412,074)

REPRESENTATIVE

Rep. Don Young (R)

Elected Mar. 1973; b. June 9, 1933, Meridian, CA; home, Fort Yukon; Yuba Jr. Col., A.A. 1952, Chico St. Col., B.A. 1958; Episcopalian; married (Lula).

Career: Army, 1955–57; Fort Yukon City Cncl., 1960–64; Fort Yukon Mayor, 1964–68; AK House of Reps., 1966–70; AK Senate, 1970–73.

DC Office: 2331 RHOB 202-225-5765; Fax: 202-224-0425.

District Offices: 222 W. 7th Ave., #3, Anchorage 99513, 907-271-5978; 401 Fed. Bldg., Box 1247, Juneau 99802, 907-586-7400; Fed. Bldg., Box 10, 101 12th Ave., Fairbanks 99701, 907-456-0210; and 109 Main St., Ketchikan 99901, 907-225-6880.

Committees: *Resources* (Chmn. of 25 R): Fisheries, Wildlife and Oceans; Native American and Insular Affairs. *Transportation & Infrastructure* (2nd of 33 R): Coast Guard and Maritime Transportation; Water Resources and Environment.

Group Ratings

	ADA	ACLU	COPE	CFA	LCV	CON	NSI	COC	ACU	NTLC	CHC
1994	10	27	33	20	0	50	100	92	100	73	100
1993	15	—	64	30	8	59	—	73	85	—	—

National Journal Ratings

	1993 LIB	—	1993 CONS	1994 LIB	—	1994 CONS
Economic	42%	—	57%	34%	—	64%
Social	19%	—	77%	15%	—	84%
Foreign	17%	—	83%	13%	—	87%

Key Votes of the 103d Congress

1. Clinton Deficit Plan	N	3. Brady Handgun Purchase	N	5. Lmt. UN Cmnd. of Forces	Y
2. NAFTA	N	4. Strike Race/Death Pnlty.	*	6. Cut Missile Funds	N

Key Votes of the 104th Congress

1. Congressional Compliance	Y	6. Reform Crime Grant	Y	11. Loser Pays Court Reform	Y
2. Balanced Budget Amndmt.	Y	7. National Security Act	Y	12. Product Liability Reform	Y
3. Bar Unfunded Mandates	Y	8. Moratorium on Regs.	Y	13. Welfare Reform	Y
4. Pass Line Item Veto	Y	9. Risk Assessment on Regs.	Y	14. Term Limits Amndmt.	Y
5. Relax Exclusionary Rule	Y	10. Expnd. Priv. Prop. Rights	Y	15. Tax Cuts	N

Election Results

1994 general	Don Young (R)	118,537	(57%)	($930,513)
	Tony Smith (D)	68,172	(33%)	($343,879)
	Jonni Whitmore (Green)	21,277	(10%)	
1994 primary	Don Young (R)	unopposed		
1992 general	Don Young (R)	111,849	(47%)	($873,486)
	John Devens (D)	102,378	(43%)	($469,738)
	Michael States (AI)	15,049	(6%)	($6,835)
	Mike Milligan (Green)	9,529	(4%)	

ARIZONA

In the mid-1990s, the desert republic of Arizona is once again on the rise, as one of America's fastest-growing states, rich with innovative technology and creative entrepreneurs. It is the home of most members of America's largest Indian tribe, the Navajo, and of the ancient Hopi; yet Arizona is largely a product of the 20th Century, indeed of its second half. Only 700,000 people lived here at the end of World War II, compared to 3,900,000 by 1994: an almost entirely new society has been built from scratch on mile-square grids in the desert. It is a society whose fundaments owe much to a federal government that still owns most of Arizona's land. But it is also a society on which the public sector sits lightly and sometimes clumsily—the Arizona Patriots, of Timothy McVeigh fame, rail against the federal government on shortwave radio broadcasts. In the last decade, Arizona was the home base of the most spectacular of the savings and loan crooks, Charles Keating; it saw the impeachment and removal from office of a governor; it discovered its state legislature was laced with corruption. Arizona is a place where a relatively unregulated private sector has produced bounteous growth and the change and disorder which are its inevitable byproducts, in an environment with few established community institutions or traditions.

From the start, Arizona was long on opportunity and thin on establishment. Its first builders were copper barons and southern-accented politicians, men like Lewis Douglas, copper heir and congressman, briefly Franklin Roosevelt's budget director and for a longer time Harry Truman's ambassador to Britain; and Carl Hayden, Democratic congressman from statehood in 1912 and senator from 1927 until 1969, whose public works projects watered Arizona's cotton, citrus and cattle farms. The second wave of Arizona's builders were the businessmen, lawyers and developers who shaped the new metropolis of Phoenix and the smaller city of Tucson in the decades after World War II. Their major national figure was Barry Goldwater and the Arizona they built was not based on resources (today, only 1% of the work force is in mining). It was a polity based on something like the opposite of New Deal principles: with minimal government and precious little regulation of business, a welcoming of the new technological ideas and disinterest in the new cultural liberalism. With conservative politicians like Goldwater, these new Arizonans built a society that, like Disneyland, seemed a more gleaming and spotless embodiment of old values than America had ever been. They also made this a solidly Republican state, the only state to have voted Republican in every presidential election since 1948.

Economically, the mainstay of this Arizona is technology: Phoenix has been attracting high-tech industries since Motorola built a research center for military electronics there in 1948, and big employers now include Motorola's semiconductor operation, Garret aircraft, Honeywell flight systems, and Tucson's Hughes aircraft. Arizona's dry climate is good for precision manufacturing and the cultural environment attracts well-educated technicians, people who like certainty, order and discipline. That is true also of Arizona's retirees, who tend to be affluent—though they do not form an unusually large percentage of the state's population.

The result is a state untraditional as much as it is conservative. There is something vibrant and chaotic about Phoenix's explosive growth. This is a city with plenty of money but few standards; plenty of crooked land salesmen, fast-buck artists and drifters who would have been at home in Raymond Chandler's Los Angeles: Charles Keating was not the only one of his kind. And Arizona is still building—the I-10 Freeway, the direct route to Los Angeles, was completed only in 1990—and momentous decisions need to be made, notably on water. "Shadow governments," to use author Joel Garreau's term, have arisen to make many of these decisions. The Salt River Project, for example, has expanded beyond rationing water to provide a sort of regional government; the city of Phoenix gave different urban cores various powers; private developers, most visibly in the huge Sun City retirement community, make regulations more binding than most governments can. The biggest public policy question facing Arizona, now that the Central Arizona Project is virtually complete, is how to allocate water. The CAP, whose board members are elected, was originally intended to subsidize growers of cotton and other thirsty crops and replace underground water. But farmers say CAP water is too expensive, and Governor Fife Symington's commission on the subject proposed to reduce the price to farmers from $61 to $17 an acre-foot; otherwise, the CAP would not have enough revenue to pay off its debt. That would place higher costs, say opponents, who may include Interior Secretary and former Arizona Governor Bruce Babbitt, on urban users, Indian tribes and the federal government; others fear that in a purely economic market Californians would outbid Arizonans, and Arizona would lose the Colorado River water allocation its politicians have long fought for. But this may make sense: why should taxpayers subsidize water for farmers to produce subsidized cotton, a commodity easily available on world markets? Already, cottonfields are going back to desert; even as metro Phoenix grows outward, especially west along I-10, but also north where it is not hemmed in by Indian reservations, much of the desert may revert to something much like its natural condition when Arizona became a state in 1912.

Governor. Arizona's Governor Fife Symington is perhaps the nation's purest free marketeer in executive office, a man whose basic instincts are in line with his constituents. So is his background: like most Arizona voters, he is from somewhere else, the hunt country of Maryland; he is a distant relative of the late Senator Stuart Symington of Missouri and graduated from Harvard in 1968. But he is not a Democrat like the Senator nor a revolutionary like so many '68 Harvardites: rather to the contrary. Fife Symington made millions as a Phoenix developer and had a reputation for erecting tasteful buildings. He has also been the target of charges by the RTC that he misused his power as director of a savings and loan that ultimately has cost taxpayers $1 billion; additionally, charges were aired by Senator Howard Metzenbaum in the February 1991 run-off campaign that Symington had violated S&L conflict of interest rules by forming a partnership between the S&L and a development project in which he had financial interest. Symington and other directors were sued by the RTC for $197 million. In May 1994, Symington and the others settled for $12.1 million, none of which is to be payed by Symington personally, who admits no wrongdoing.

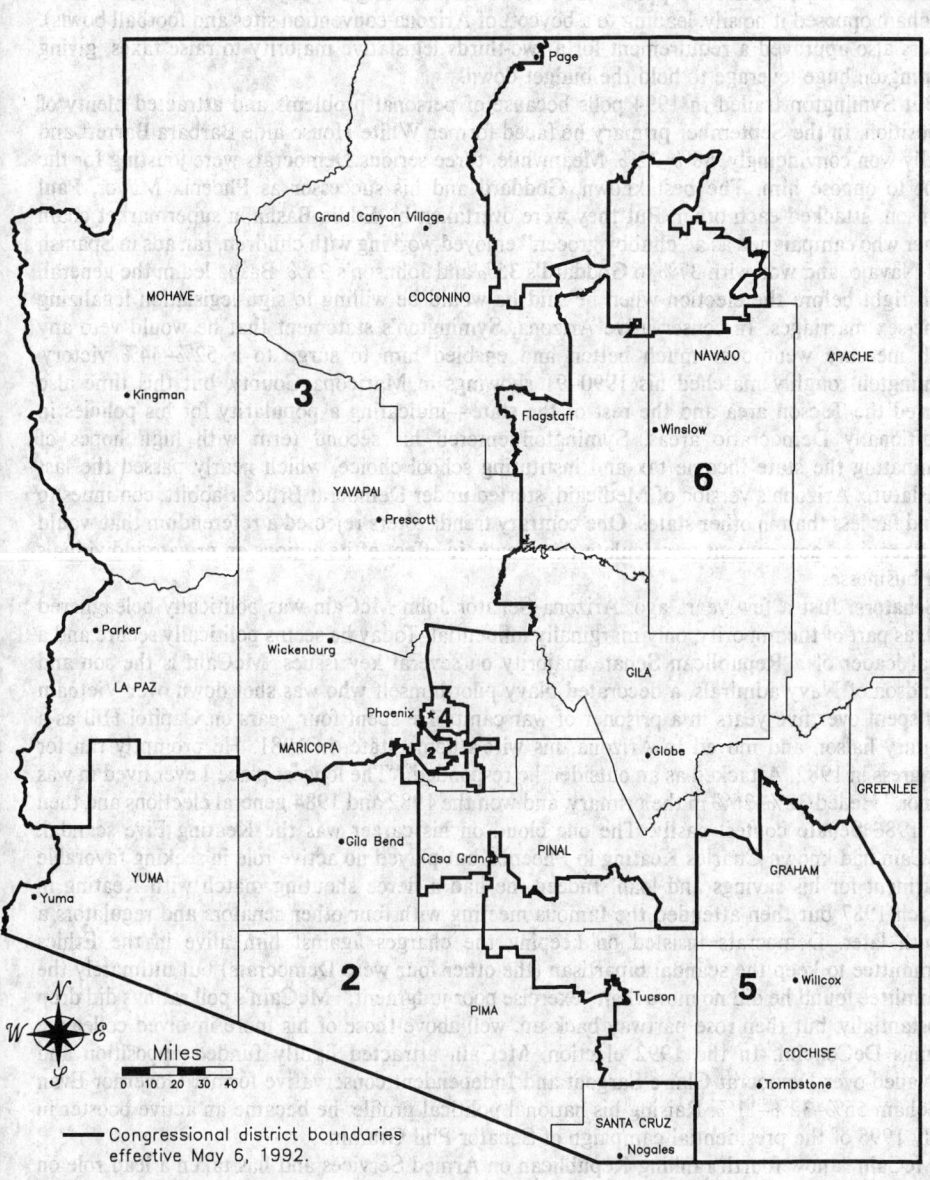

MOHAVE

COCONINO

NAVAJO

APACHE

• Kingman

3

Flagstaff

• Winslow

6

YAVAPAI

• Prescott

• Parker

Wickenburg

GILA

LA PAZ

Phoenix ★ **4**

MARICOPA

2 **1**

• Globe

GREENLEE

• Gila Bend

PINAL

GRAHAM

• Casa Grande

YUMA

• Yuma

2

Tucson

5

• Willcox

PIMA

COCHISE

• Tombstone

SANTA CRUZ

• Nogales

Page

Grand Canyon Village

N
W   E
S

Miles
0 10 20 30 40

—— Congressional district boundaries
    effective May 6, 1992.

These charges have hurt—the 1994 exit poll showed 45% said the S&L investigation made them doubt Symington's honesty while a bare majority of 51% remained supportive—but his issue positions have enabled him to win. In 1990 he edged former Phoenix Mayor Terry Goddard by less than 1% in November; but no one had a majority, and in February 1991 Symington won the runoff 52%–48%. It was a typical partisan pattern: the Republican carried Phoenix's Maricopa County, where most votes are cast, and lost the rest of the state. In office Symington cut taxes, held down spending, helped Republicans gain control of both houses of the legislature and got voters to approve the Martin Luther King holiday (former Governor Evan Mecham opposed it noisily, leading to a boycott of Arizona convention sites and football bowls). Voters also approved a requirement for a two-thirds legislative majority to raise taxes, giving Symington huge leverage to hold the budget down.

But Symington trailed in 1994 polls because of personal problems and attracted plenty of opposition. In the September primary he faced former White House aide Barbara Barrett and finally won convincingly, 68%–32%. Meanwhile, three serious Democrats were jousting for the right to oppose him. The best known, Goddard and his successor as Phoenix Mayor, Paul Johnson, attacked each other. But they were overtaken by Eddie Basha, a supermarket chain owner who campaigned as a "chubby grocer," enjoyed working with children, ran ads in Spanish and Navajo, and won with 37% to Goddard's 35% and Johnson's 28%. Basha led in the general, until right before the election when he said he would be willing to sign legislation legalizing same-sex marriages. In conservative Arizona, Symington's statement that he would veto any such measure went over much better, and enabled him to surge to a 52%–44% victory. Symington roughly matched his 1990–91 showings in Maricopa County, but this time also carried the Tucson area and the rest of the state—indicating a popularity for his policies in traditionally Democratic areas. Symington entered his second term with high hopes of eliminating the state income tax and instituting school choice, which nearly passed the last legislature. Arizona's version of Medicaid, started under Democrat Bruce Babbitt, continues to spend far less than in other states. One contrary trend: voters rejected a referendum that would have required government to calculate the economic effect of its actions on private individuals and businesses.

Senators. Just a few years ago, Arizona Senator John McCain was politically beleaguered and, as part of the minority, only marginally influential. Today he seems politically secure and a vocal leader of a Republican Senate majority on several key issues. McCain is the son and grandson of Navy admirals, a decorated Navy pilot himself who was shot down over Vietnam and spent over five years in a prisoner of war camp. He spent four years on Capitol Hill as a military liaison and moved to Arizona, his wife's home state, in 1981. He promptly ran for Congress in 1982. Attacked as an outsider, he responded, "The longest place I ever lived in was Hanoi." He led 32%–26% in the primary, and won the 1982 and 1984 general elections and then the 1986 Senate contest easily. The one cloud on his career was the Keating Five scandal. McCain had known Charles Keating in Phoenix, but played no active role in seeking favorable treatment for his savings and loan. Indeed, he had a fierce shouting match with Keating in March 1987 but then attended the famous meeting with four other senators and regulators a month later. Democrats insisted on keeping the charges against him alive in the Ethics Committee to keep the scandal bipartisan (the other four were Democrats) but ultimately the committee found he did no more than "exercise poor judgment." McCain's poll ratings did drop substantially, but then rose partway back up, well above those of his more involved colleague Dennis DeConcini. In the 1992 election, McCain attracted lightly funded opposition and prevailed over Democrat Claire Sargent and Independent conservative former Governor Evan Mecham 56%–32%–11%. Raising his national political profile, he became an active booster in early 1995 of the presidential campaign of Senator Phil Gramm.

McCain is now fourth ranking Republican on Armed Services and has taken a lead role on military issues. He has criticized the Clinton Administration for stinting on defense but has worked to hold down funding for some projects—the Sea Wolf submarine, B-2 bomber, the

Strategic Defense Initiative. He wants to maintain funds for readiness and stop military add-ons, especially for the home-state pork that has long been a part of congressional spending for the Pentagon. He has shown a professional military officer's caution about committing American troops without a clear end in sight, most notably in Bosnia. But he has supported lifting the embargo on arms sales to the Bosnian Muslims. His fear is "failure reinforcing failure": another Vietnam. In early 1994 he criticized Clinton for taking "every possible" stand on Bosnia and has consistently opposed sending American troops or fliers, invoking his own experience: "the use of air power alone has never determined the outcome of a military conflict." McCain has favored a more assertive policy in other areas, particularly when there is a danger of nuclear proliferation. In spring 1994, while Jimmy Carter was negotiating with North Korean President Kim Il Sung, he called administration policy on North Korea appeasement and sponsored a resolution calling for "all necessary and prudent actions" to deter a North Korean attack on South Korea; he has said that sanctions against North Korean nuclear proliferation should be backed by explicit threats of airstrikes. And he has criticized relaxation of restrictions on exports of nuclear-sensitive materials and on promoting proliferation for commercial gain. The same combination of caution, boldness and concern about proliferation came out in his comments on Iraq: he urged caution in committing American troops in August 1990, strongly backed the Gulf war resolution in January 1991 and all along threatened a crackdown on Iraq for its nuclear program. McCain does not talk about his experiences as a POW, but has worked on Vietnam issues: he favored releasing reports of POW sightings and, with fellow decorated Vietnam veteran John Kerry, sponsored the successful lifting of the embargo on Vietnam in 1994.

McCain's other major committee post is the chair of the Indian Affairs Committee. Here he has worked with Hawaii's Daniel Inouye to increase Native American self-governance. The major issues are Indian gaming—to what extent can states regulate the burgeoning number of Indian casinos?—and religious freedom. On the latter, McCain has been cautious about giving tribes great leeway in designating burial grounds and other sacred sites not already on Indian lands. He has also worked to clean up the 600-some hazardous waste dumps on reservations.

On environmental issues, McCain favored banning flights in the Grand Canyon and opposed construction of Cliff Dam; his 1992 campaign spots described him as "the Grand Canyon's best friend in Congress." His record on most domestic issues is conservative. He wants to require 60 votes in the Senate to raise federal taxes, favors the more sweeping version of a line-item veto (leading him to contest a more limited version backed by Senate Budget Committee Chairman Pete Domenici), opposes congressional earmarks for highways and other pork barrel projects and sponsored an amendment to eliminate D.C. airport parking places for Members of Congress, which failed. One change McCain favors would actually raise the deficit: repealing the Social Security earnings test, which hits hard in Sun City.

Arizona's junior senator, Republican Jon Kyl, was elected in 1994 to the seat from which Democrat Dennis DeConcini retired after three terms. DeConcini made a name in the Senate in several ways: he cast a critical vote for the Panama Canal Treaties in 1978; he cast a critical vote against Judge Robert Bork; he was the central figure in the Keating Five scandal when he interceded with federal regulators on behalf of S&L operator Charles Keating; and, as chairman of the Intelligence Committee in 1993–94, he was a caustic critic of CIA Director James Woolsey. Opposition for 1994 lined up even before DeConcini announced his retirement: Kyl was obviously poised to run and Secretary of State Dick Mahoney, a former academic and congressional staffer, said he'd run in the Democratic primary. Kyl, with a solid base on the affluent east side of Phoenix and an activist conservative record which ranged from support of the Strategic Defense Initiative to sponsoring a limit on federal spending of 19% of GDP, had no opposition in the Republican primary; Mahoney was opposed by Phoenix Congressman Sam Coppersmith and by state Senate Minority Leader Cindy Resnick in a race that turned out to be excruciatingly close. Resnick, carrying Tucson, got 30%; Coppersmith, carrying Phoenix, and Mahoney, carrying the rest of the state, got 32% each. It took two weeks before a recount showed Coppersmith the winner by 59 votes of 255,000 cast. Kyl, with far more money, ran ads with home movie texture showing him travelling through the desert countryside in a Chevy Suburban, dressed in jeans and working on ranches, while talking about how he and his wife first fell in love with the state. Coppersmith stressed his pro-choice stand on abortion and said he would welcome a campaign visit from President Clinton. Kyl prevailed solidly in the general, winning 54%–40%; Coppersmith ran only slightly ahead of the weak 1992 Clinton showing in each area of the state but did win in Tuscon's Pima County.

Kyl is the son of Iowa Congressman John Kyl (1959–65, 1967–73), who eventually lost his seat in redistricting; the son moved to a state that, in effect, was gaining the Republican seats Great Plains states like Iowa were losing. He practiced law, worked on Republican campaigns and headed the Phoenix Chamber of Commerce; he won an open House seat in 1986 by beating 60%–28% former (1973–77) Congressman John Conlan, who had support from the religious right. In the House, Kyl was a leader among Republicans on three issues. One was the Strategic Defense Initiative; SDI has little institutional backing in the Pentagon, but Kyl was its devoted supporter on the Armed Services Committee. Another was the balanced budget amendment, for which he has been a leading advocate; also, he would limit federal spending to 19% of GDP. From his seat on the Ethics Committee, he insisted in spring 1993 on disclosure of the names of House members with overdrafts on the House bank. He also supported the "three-strikes" crime legislation and—a hot issue in Arizona—school vouchers. In the Senate, Kyl is likely to be not only a solid conservative vote but an activist seizing upon new conservative causes and challenging old liberal certainties. He took early steps to join the growing corps of Republicans seeking to repeal federal controls on western lands, a role that should be enhanced by his committee assignments.

Presidential politics. For a few moments in fall 1992, when Bill Clinton was leading in polls here, it looked like Arizona might break the longest string of any state in American presidential politics: it had voted Republican in every presidential election since Harry Truman won here in 1948. But in the end George Bush won by the underwhelming margin of 38%–37%, as Ross Perot picked up 24%. Metro Phoenix, where Perot got 25%, was one of his best million-plus metro area, and he got over 30% in retirement-heavy Mojave and LaPaz Counties along the Colorado River—in line with the national pattern of Perot running strongest where voters have the weakest local roots.

Arizona's precinct caucuses late in the spring typically have attracted little attention: too late, too few delegates, too far away from anywhere else. That explains why Governor Symington led a move to put Arizona at the front of the 1996 primary calendar; after objections from New Hampshire, he agreed to schedule it a week after the traditionally first state. A Republican presidential straw poll garnered some attention here in early 1995, when Phil Gramm received more that 50% of the vote; this was the second such contest (the first was Louisiana) that he had won. The state is more noteworthy for having produced for its size so many presidential candidates—Barry Goldwater in 1964, Morris Udall in 1976, Bruce Babbitt in 1988. Of different politics and temperament, they are all intellectually honest, personally candid, genuinely engaged in ideas while retaining a lively sense of how the real world works; each has a good sense of humor and is refreshingly unfull of himself; each lost big.

Congressional districting. Arizona gained one congressional district from the 1990 Census, as it did in 1980, 1970 and 1960, increasing its delegation during that time from two House members to six. The divided state legislature couldn't agree on a plan for 1992, so a federal court drew the lines, with the 2d District—now represented by the delegation's only Democrat—continuing to be heavily Hispanic and the new 6th District drawn to maximize the Indian population (though the Hopis, who have had a furious land dispute with the much more numerous Navajo, were carefully placed in the 3d). Democrats, down 4–1 before redistricting, got a 3–3 tie in 1992, then fell to a 5–1 deficit after 1994.

The People: Est. Pop. 1994: 4,075,000; Pop. 1990: 3,665,228, up 11.2% 1990–1994. 1.6% of U.S. total, 23d largest; 12% rural. Median age: 32.2 years. 13.1% 65 years and over. 80.8% White, 18.8% Hispanic origin, 5.6% American Indian, 3.0% Black, 1.5% Asian, 9.1% Other. Households: 54.6% married couple families; 25% married couple fams. w. children; 53% college educ.; median household income: $27,540; per capita income: $13,461; 64.4% owner occupied housing; median house value: $80,100; median monthly rent: $370. 7.4% Unemployment. 1994 Voting age pop.: 2,923,000. 1994 Turnout: 715,619; 37% of VAP. Registered voters (1994): 1,963,492; 833,997 D (43%), 889,644 R (45%), 239,851 unaffiliated and minor parties (12%).

Political Lineup: Governor, Fife Symington (R); Secy. of State, Jane Dee Hull (R); Atty. Gen., Grant Woods (R); Treasurer, Tony West (R); Auditor General, Douglas Norton (I). State Senate, 30 (19 R and 11 D); State House of Representatives, 60 (38 R and 22 D). Senators, John McCain (R) and Jon Kyl (R). Representatives, 6 (5 R and 1 D).

1992 Presidential Vote		
Bush (R)	572,086	(38%)
Clinton (D)	543,050	(37%)
Perot (I)	353,741	(24%)

1988 Presidential Vote		
Bush (R)	702,541	(60%)
Dukakis (D)	454,029	(39%)

GOVERNOR

Gov. Fife Symington (R)

Elected Feb., 1991, term expires Jan. 1999; b. Aug. 12, 1945, New York, NY; home, Phoenix; Harvard, B.A. 1968; Episcopalian; married (Ann).

Career: Air Force, 1968–71 (Vietnam); Commercial and industrial real estate developer, 1972–91.

Office: Office of the Governor, 1700 W. Washington, 9th Fl., Phoenix 85007, 602-542-4331; Fax: 602-542-7601.

Election Results

1994 gen.	Fife Symington (R)	593,492	(53%)
	Eddie Basha (D)	500,702	(44%)
	Others	35,413	(3%)
1994 prim.	Fife Symington (R)	202,588	(68%)
	Barbara Barrett (R)	94,740	(32%)
1991 runoff	Fife Symington (R)	492,569	(52%)
	Terry Goddard (D)	448,168	(48%)
1990 gen.	Fife Symington (R)	523,964	(50%)
	Terry Goddard (D)	519,653	(50%)

SENATORS
Sen. John McCain (R)

Elected 1986, seat up 1998; b. Aug. 29, 1936, Panama Canal Zone; home, Phoenix; U.S. Naval Acad., 1958, Natl. War Col., 1973–74; Episcopalian; married (Cindy).

Career: Navy, 1958–80 (Vietnam); Dir., Navy Senate Liaison Ofc., 1977–81; U.S. House of Reps., 1982–1986.

DC Office: 241 RSOB 20510, 202-224-2235; Fax: 202-228-2862.

State Offices: 1839 S. Alma School Rd., #375, Mesa 85210, 602-491-4300; 450 W. Pasco Redondo, #200, Tucson 85701, 602-670-6334; and 2400 E. Arizona Biltmore Cir., #1150, Phoenix 85016, 602-952-2410.

Committees: *Armed Services* (4th of 11 R): Personnel; Readiness (Chmn.); Seapower. *Commerce, Science & Transportation* (4th of 10 R): Aviation (Chmn.); Communications; Consumer Affairs, Foreign Commerce and Tourism. *Governmental Affairs* (7th of 8 R): Oversight of Government Management and the District of Columbia; Investigations; Post Office and Civil Service. *Indian Affairs* (Chmn. of 9 R).

Group Ratings

	ADA	ACLU	COPE	CFA	LCV	CON	NSI	COC	ACU	NTLC	CHC
1994	10	16	0	17	15	96	100	83	96	92	93
1993	15	—	18	20	19	63	—	82	83	—	—

National Journal Ratings

	1993 LIB — 1993 CONS	1994 LIB — 1994 CONS
Economic	22% — 75%	0% — 88%
Social	19% — 78%	0% — 85%
Foreign	31% — 68%	18% — 80%

Key Votes of the 103d Congress

1. Clinton Deficit Plan	N	3. Brady Handgun Purchase N	5. Lmt. UN Cmnd. of Forces N
2. NAFTA	Y	4. Strike Race/Death Pnlty. Y	6. Cut Missile Funds N

Key Votes of the 104th Congress

1. Congressional Compliance Y	3. Balanced Budget Amndt. Y	5. Product Liability Reform Y
2. Bar Unfunded Mandates *	4. Pass Line Item Veto Y	6. FY96 Budget Y

Election Results

1992 general	John McCain (R)	771,395	(56%)	($3,766,588)
	Claire Sargent (D)	436,321	(32%)	($287,682)
	Evan Mecham (I)	145,361	(11%)	($86,433)
	Others	28,974	(2%)	
1992 primary	John McCain (R) .... unopposed			
1986 general	John McCain (R)	521,850	(60%)	($2,228,498)
	Richard Kimball (D).................	340,965	(40%)	($657,908)

Sen. Jon Kyl (R)

Elected 1994, seat up 2000; b. Apr. 25, 1942, Oakland, NE; home, Phoenix; U. of AZ, B.A. 1964, LL.B. 1966; Presbyterian; married (Caryll).

Career: Practicing atty., 1966–86; Chmn., Phoenix Chamber of Commerce, 1985–86, U.S. House of Reps., 1986–94.

DC Office: 702 HSOB 20510, 202-224-4521; Fax: 202-224-2207.

State Offices: 2200 E. Camelback, #120, Phoenix 85016, 602-840-1891; and 7315 N. Oracle, #220, Tucson 85704, 520-575-8633.

Committees: *Energy & Natural Resources* (7th of 10 R): Energy Research and Development; Forests and Public Land Management (Vice Chmn.). *Judiciary* (8th of 10 R): Constitution, Federalism and Property Rights; Immigration. *Intelligence (Select)* (5th of 9 R).

Group Ratings (as Member of U.S. House of Representatives)

	ADA	ACLU	COPE	CFA	LCV	CON	NSI	COC	ACU	NTLC	CHC
1994	5	10	0	83	6	79	100	83	90	96	93
1993	5	—	0	10	21	74	—	100	96	—	—

National Journal Ratings (as Member of U.S. House of Representatives)

	1993 LIB — 1993 CONS		1994 LIB — 1994 CONS	
Economic	0% —	88%	0% —	80%
Social	11% —	82%	34% —	66%
Foreign	0% —	91%	0% —	88%

Key Votes of the 103d Congress (as Member of U.S. House of Representatives)

1. Clinton Deficit Plan N	3. Brady Handgun Purchase N	5. Lmt. UN Cmnd. of Forces Y
2. NAFTA Y	4. Strike Race/Death Pnlty. Y	6. Cut Missile Funds N

Key Votes of the 104th Congress

1. Congressional Compliance Y	3. Balanced Budget Amndt. Y	5. Product Liability Reform Y
2. Bar Unfunded Mandates Y	4. Pass Line Item Veto Y	6. FY96 Budget Y

Election Results

1994 general	Jon Kyl (R)	600,999	(54%)	($4,138,203)
	Sam Coppersmith (D)	442,510	(40%)	($1,577,556)
	Scott Grainger (Lib)	75,493	(7%)	
1994 primary	Jon Kyl (R)	unopposed		
1988 general	Dennis DeConcini (D)	660,403	(57%)	($2,640,650)
	Keith DeGreen (R)	478,060	(41%)	($238,369)

FIRST DISTRICT

Barry Goldwater, Phoenix's great elder statesman, lives in the midst of one of America's great metropolitan areas. Yet he surely knew some of the men and women who could remember when it was founded in 1881 as a haymarket for cavalry horses at Fort McDowell 40 miles away; and he must remember well what it was like when he returned from World War II half a century ago, when that Phoenix was not much more than a railroad stop. But in 1948 Motorola built a research center here for military electronics—the first of many such companies that would make Phoenix one of the nation's important high-tech centers and one of America's large metropolitan areas. The 1950 Census counted just 106,000 residents in Phoenix and 331,000 in all of Maricopa County. But new businesses, symbolized by Motorola, changed Phoenix from the sleepy whistle-stop, where the small tufa stone turn-of-the-century Capitol was the most prominent building, to today's high-rise studded metropolis, with one million people in Phoenix and 2.3 million in Maricopa County.

This almost instant city was created not in response to geographical imperative but in spite of it. Neither the copper mines of southern Arizona nor the cotton farms irrigated by the Salt River needed a city the size of Phoenix, nor is there any thickly populated hinterland in the vast area between the Rio Grande and Los Angeles for which this is the natural commercial center. Nor is Phoenix a giant retirement village, though there are huge retirement developments northwest of town. Phoenix's economic base has been in research and development and high-tech manufacturing, and its population tends to be young and family-oriented, on the way up from whatever level of society they were born into.

Over the years, Phoenix's growth has oozed outward along its mile-square grid streets and its few freeways, blocked off here and there by mountains and Indian reservations. Much of that growth has been to the east, south of the Salt River and east of South Mountain, along today's Superstition Freeway, where metro Phoenix has merged into old towns. One is Tempe, founded in 1871 as Hayden's Ferry and renamed in 1879 for an ancient Greek vale, home of Arizona State University and the Fiesta Bowl; it had 7,000 people in 1950 and 142,000 in 1990. Farther east is Mesa, whose central focus is one of the nation's few Mormon temples, and whose Mormon founders used irrigation ditches dug by Indians in 700 A.D.; Mesa had 16,000 people in 1950 and 288,000 in 1990. North of the Salt River, directly east of Phoenix and in the shadows of Camelback Mountain, is Scottsdale, with its trendy shops carefully decked out in Old West style, for this is the site of the annual U.S.-Canada Wrangler Jeans Rodeo Showdown; Scottsdale had no recorded population in 1950, 130,000 in 1990.

The 1st Congressional District of Arizona consists of much of this eastern part of metropolitan Phoenix. Geographically, it is centered on Tempe, and includes Chandler, once a desert crossroads and now a 91,000-strong suburb. The 1st also includes about half of Mesa, plus the southern portion of Scottsdale and much of the east side of Phoenix—mostly affluent territory south of Camelback Road. These lines were carefully drawn for 1992 to leave heavily Hispanic and black neighborhoods in the 2d District, and to keep the Salt River and Gila River Indian Reservations in the 6th District. As a result, the 1st is 80% non-Hispanic white, mostly affluent, and heavily Republican.

Nevertheless, the 1st District has had a robust bipartisan politics since its current boundaries were set after the 1990 Census. In 1992, it was the site of protest politics, directed at incumbent Republican John Rhodes III, whose father had represented Maricopa County and was the House minority leader from 1973 to 1980. The younger Rhodes angered conservatives by coming out early for impeachment of Governor Evan Mecham in 1987, and he had 32 overdrafts on the House bank. In 1992, he barely won his Republican primary against two state legislators and lost the general to Sam Coppersmith, former top aide to Phoenix Mayor Terry Goddard and head of the Phoenix Planned Parenthood chapter. Coppersmith campaigned as a "new-generation Democrat," calling for deficit reduction and public investment, congressional reform and preserving the environment; he beat Rhodes 51%–45%. In the House, Coppersmith made a "new Democrat" record, opposing the Clinton budget and tax package and backing the "A-to-Z" spending-cut reform. Feeling that reelection to the House might be as problematic as a Senate bid, Coppersmith decided to go for the Senate seat but lost to Republican Jon Kyl.

The new congressman, who was one of five serious candidates for the seat, is Matt Salmon, former state senator and head of community affairs for U S West. He had serious primary competition: cable TV lobbyist Susan Bitter Smith had more money and endorsements; attorney Linda Rawles attacked Salmon misleadingly for favoring higher taxes; his anti-abortion stand was a potential liability. But he won 39% of the vote, compared to 19% to 22% for his major rivals. In the general, Salmon ran on the Contract with America even before the Contract was signed, boosting the $500 dependent tax credit, the medical savings account and a buydown of the national debt. "Moses wandered in the desert for 40 years," he said, in an opaque metaphor. "I think the Democratic leadership has been wandering in the desert." His opponent, Democrat Chuck Blanchard, also a state senator and a former clerk for Supreme Court Justice Sandra Day O'Connor, was proud of passing an anti-parole bill in Phoenix and took some moderate stands on national issues. But Blanchard was co-chair of the 1992 Clinton-Gore campaign in Arizona, was enthusiastically boosted by the national party and rose to defend the House Democrats' crime bill. He accused Salmon of being "partisan," but, in this Republican area in a partisan Republican year, Salmon won 56%–39%.

In the House Salmon should be a reliable member of Newt Gingrich's Republican Conference. But he did not get a seat on the Commerce Committee as his former employer must have wished.

The People: Pop. 1990: 610,817; 9% age 65+; 80% White; 3% Black; 2% Amer. Indian; 2% Asian; 6% Other; 13% Hispanic origin. Voting age pop.: 458,227; 3% Black; 11% Hispanic origin. Households: 49% married couple families; 24% married couple fams. w. children; 64% college educ.; median household income: $31,288; per capita income: $15,144; median gross rent: $478; median house value: $88,300.

1992 Presidential Vote			1988 Presidential Vote		
Bush (R)	105,784	(40%)	Bush (R)	131,093	(65%)
Clinton (D)	88,247	(33%)	Dukakis (D)	70,881	(35%)
Perot (I)	68,143	(26%)			

Rep. Matt Salmon (R)

Elected 1994; b. Jan. 21, 1958, Salt Lake City, UT; home, Mesa; AZ St. U., B.A. 1981, Brigham Young U., M.A. 1986; Mormon; married (Nancy).

Career: Public Affairs Mgr., U.S. West, 1981–94; AZ Senate, 1990–94; Asst. Majority Leader, 1993–94.

DC Office: 115 CHOB 20515, 202-225-2635; Fax: 202-225-3405.

District Offices: 401 W. Baseline Rd., #209, Tempe 85282, 602-831-2900.

Committees: *International Relations* (22nd of 23 R): Africa; International Operations and Human Rights. *Science* (17th of 27 R): Energy and Environment; Space and Aeronautics. *Small Business* (15th of 22 R): Procurement, Exports and Business Opportunities.

Group Ratings and 103d Congress Votes: Newly Elected

Key Votes of the 104th Congress

1. Congressional Compliance Y	6. Reform Crime Grant Y	11. Loser Pays Court Reform Y
2. Balanced Budget Amndmt. Y	7. National Security Act Y	12. Product Liability Reform Y
3. Bar Unfunded Mandates Y	8. Moratorium on Regs. Y	13. Welfare Reform Y
4. Pass Line Item Veto Y	9. Risk Assessment on Regs. Y	14. Term Limits Amndmt. N
5. Relax Exclusionary Rule Y	10. Expnd. Priv. Prop. Rights Y	15. Tax Cuts Y

Election Results

1994 general	Matt Salmon (R)	101,350	(56%)	($508,421)
	Chuck Blanchard (D)	70,627	(39%)	($440,372)
	Bob Howarth (Lib)	8,890	(5%)	
1994 primary	Matt Salmon (R)	19,862	(39%)	
	Susan Bitter Smith (R)	11,359	(22%)	
	Linda Rawles (R)	9,596	(19%)	
	Bev Hermon (R)	8,030	(16%)	
	Bert Tollefson (R)	2,119	(4%)	
1992 general	Sam Coppersmith (D).................	130,715	(51%)	($244,633)
	John J. Rhodes III (R)	113,613	(45%)	($336,768)
	Ted Goldstein (Natural Law)	10,461	(4%)	

SECOND DISTRICT

Southern Arizona, although technically a part of Mexico for hundreds of years, was not a site of Hispanic civilization like New Mexico; this hot desert land was inhabited mainly by Indians who kept their native ways and language until English-speaking whites came in on cavalry horses, miners' wagons and railroad cars in the late 19th Century. Today's Hispanic Arizonans are mostly descendants of immigrants from Mexico, people who came over the border in the sleepier days before World War II when it was scarcely patrolled, or who have come more recently to take part in the dazzling economic growth which has served as both an attraction and an example to so many *norteno* Mexicans. The 2d District of Arizona was designed to be the state's Hispanic district; its population is 50% Hispanic and includes nearly two-thirds of the state's Hispanic population. On a map, it looks like a regularly-shaped district, but in fact it is a collection of distant communities connected only by many miles of uninhabited desert.

The largest of these communities is central Phoenix, including the old downtown, the state Capitol to the west and the skyscraper districts on North Central Avenue and out toward Camelback Road. The stereotypical Hispanic neighborhood here is a collection of 1940s and 1950s bungalows, unpainted for years and spaced out by empty lots, not far from the railroad or Sky Harbor Airport or nestling within view of South Mountain. In fact, this is a diverse area, with affluent and comfortable neighborhoods, where Hispanics have been moving in scatterings as well as clumps. The west side of Tucson, the next-largest gathering of people in the 2d, is similar. The 2d also includes Yuma, on a Colorado River crossing, in an irrigated agricultural valley, often the hottest place in the country. (It's also the spring training site for the Yakult Swallows, a Japanese baseball team.) A desalination plant, proposed to protect Mexican farmlands, was opened here in 1992, 14 years behind schedule. Across the desert, past the Luke Air Force Base shooting range, the Organ Pipe Cactus National Monument, and the Papago Indian Reservation, is the Mexican border town of Nogales, 75% Hispanic and near many maquiladora plants.

The 2d is the one solidly Democratic district in Arizona and the one which, in previous boundaries, for three decades elected Morris Udall, presidential candidate in 1976 and major legislator on issues from campaign finance to nuclear waste, until his retirement due to illness in May 1991. In the September 1991 special election, Republican Pat Conner, a Yuma County Supervisor, seriously contested the seat, but came up short with 44%. The winner with 56% was Democrat and career politician Ed Pastor of Phoenix, since 1976 a Maricopa County supervisor and, before that, an aide to Governor Raul Castro. "The fact is I am Hispanic, the fact is there is a lot of pride in the Hispanic community," he said on winning. "And I join in that enthusiasm. But as an elected official for 16 years, you represent the entire community."

In the House Pastor has been a faithful follower of the Democratic leadership and now his delegation's only Democrat. He has passed some minor amendments—promoting education for the deaf, passing flood control projects for the district and sponsoring a Morris Udall Scholarship Act, setting up grants at the University of Arizona for the study of natural resources as well as for training of professionals for health care for Indians and Alaska Natives. But he saved his emphasis for family medical leave, Hatch Act reform and the motor voter act—and the national service act, the Clinton budget and tax package and the North American Free Trade Agreement. He lost his Appropriations seat when the new Republican majority downsized Democratic slots on committees in 1995. And Pastor was elected chairman of the Hispanic Caucus in November 1994—a position of potential influence—but just in time for the cutoff of House funding of the caucuses by the new leadership. However, Pastor is working to keep the Hispanic caucus alive in the form of a nonprofit.

The 2d District is safe for Pastor, but his tenure may be limited by Arizona's term limits law, which if upheld would keep him off the ballot in 1998. A loyal party man, he says he has worked to boost turnout in the district, though he scarcely needs more votes himself; however, because of low registration and high numbers of non-citizens, 1994 turnout here was 100,000 compared to 180,000 to 220,000 in Arizona's five other districts.

The People: Pop. 1990: 610,266; 10% rural; 10% age 65+; 38% White; 7% Black; 5% Amer. Indian; 1% Asian; 27% Other; 50% Hispanic origin. Voting age pop.: 414,274; 6% Black; 45% Hispanic origin. Households: 52% married couple families; 28% married couple fams. w. children; 33% college educ.; median household income: $20,258; per capita income: $8,424; median gross rent: $366; median house value: $54,500.

1992 Presidential Vote			1988 Presidential Vote		
Clinton (D)	74,588	(51%)	Dukakis (D)	70,995	(57%)
Bush (R)	41,757	(28%)	Bush (R)	52,572	(43%)
Perot (I)	28,767	(20%)			

Rep. Ed Pastor (D)

Elected Sept. 1991; b. June 28, 1943, Claypool; home, Phoenix; AZ St. U., B.A. 1966, J.D. 1974; Catholic; married (Verma).

Career: High schl. teacher, 1966–69; Asst., AZ Gov. Castro, 1975; Maricopa Cnty. Bd. of Supervisors, 1976–91.

DC Office: 223 CHOB 20515, 202-225-4065; Fax: 202-225-1655; e-mail: edpastor@hr.house.gov.

District Offices: 802 N. Third Ave., Phoenix 85003, 602-256-0551; 2432 E. Broadway, Tucson 85719, 602-624-9986; and 281 W. 24th St., Yuma 85364, 602-726-2234.

Committees: *Agriculture* (21st of 22 D): General Farm Commodities; Risk Management and Specialty Crops. *House Oversight* (5th of 5 D).

Group Ratings

	ADA	ACLU	COPE	CFA	LCV	CON	NSI	COC	ACU	NTLC	CHC
1994	80	78	78	100	67	4	20	42	14	11	7
1993	90	—	92	100	64	16	—	27	4	—	—

National Journal Ratings

	1993 LIB — 1993 CONS			1994 LIB — 1994 CONS		
Economic	60%	—	39%	83%	—	0%
Social	80%	—	13%	70%	—	28%
Foreign	74%	—	22%	64%	—	33%

Key Votes of the 103d Congress

1. Clinton Deficit Plan	Y	3. Brady Handgun Purchase	Y	5. Lmt. UN Cmnd. of Forces	N
2. NAFTA	Y	4. Strike Race/Death Pnlty.	N	6. Cut Missile Funds	N

Key Votes of the 104th Congress

1. Congressional Compliance	Y	6. Reform Crime Grant	N	11. Loser Pays Court Reform	N
2. Balanced Budget Amndmt.	N	7. National Security Act	N	12. Product Liability Reform	N
3. Bar Unfunded Mandates	N	8. Moratorium on Regs.	N	13. Welfare Reform	N
4. Pass Line Item Veto	N	9. Risk Assessment on Regs.	N	14. Term Limits Amndmt.	N
5. Relax Exclusionary Rule	N	10. Expnd. Priv. Prop. Rights	N	15. Tax Cuts	N

Election Results

1994 general	Ed Pastor (D)	62,589	(62%)	($349,627)
	Robert MacDonald (R)	32,797	(33%)	
	James Bertrand (Lib)	5,060	(5%)	
1994 primary	Ed Pastor (D)	26,426	(74%)	
	Robert Molina (D)	9,330	(26%)	
1992 general	Ed Pastor (D)	90,693	(66%)	($266,660)
	Don Shooter (R)	41,257	(30%)	($27,260)
	Dan Detaranto (L)	5,423	(4%)	

THIRD DISTRICT

The physical landscape of Arizona, for all the vibrant metropolitan growth of Phoenix and Tucson, remains much as it was when white men first settled here. Beneath mountains and along occasionally-running creeks, they built towns that have as Old West a look as anywhere in America, like Prescott, originally a gold mining camp, home since 1888 of America's oldest annual rodeo and now, to the distress of some, the home of many ex-Californians. The landscape retains a beauty that can overpower mere buildings and parking lots: think of the red rocks of Sedona, an esoteric resort between Prescott and Flagstaff. And some landscape is intentionally preserved, like the sere uplands of the Hopi Indian Reservation. There are some abrupt juxtapositions of settlement and nature: the real London Bridge transplanted to Lake Havasu City, a retirement community on the Colorado River; or Bullhead City, one-third of whose people work in "family gambler" casinos in Laughlin, Nevada, just across the bridge over the rock-lined, piping-hot river. Just west, and a bit north, of Bullhead City is the last known address of Timothy McVeigh, arrested in April 1995 for the Oklahoma City bombing.

All these areas are part of the 3d Congressional District of Arizona, which stretches from the west side of Phoenix to cover most of the northwest quadrant of the state. Most of its people are clustered in its southeast corner, in metro Phoenix. Here, west of the Black Canyon Freeway, is the mushrooming suburb of Glendale, not so long ago just a crossroads but now home to 148,000 people; just west are Peoria, as Middle American as its namesake in Illinois, and the huge retirement community of Sun City, with a dozen or so golf courses and many dozens of shuffleboard courts. The 3d District also includes the corridor along the westbound I-10 Papago Freeway, past Litchfield Park and its Wigwam resort to the now open spaces of Goodyear and Buckeye, the likely site of Phoenix's fastest growth in the next decade. This is heavily Republican territory: the retirees here remember—and the upwardly-striving, family-oriented young migrants who have populated these new towns in the desert still try to live—the culturally conservative, Ozzie-and-Harriet lifestyle of the 1950s. This more than affluence, which by national standards is not all that striking here, accounts for their political conservatism. Similarly Republican are the Colorado River new cities and Prescott, where Barry Goldwater used to end all his campaigns.

The 3d District's congressman is Bob Stump, a Republican who quietly and without much notice has become one of the more senior members of the House and is now chairman of the Veterans' Affairs Committee. He has a political history similar to many older Arizonans': he was a "pinto" (conservative) Democrat, a cotton and grain farmer in the rich irrigated lands west of Phoenix, and a member of the legislature, elected to Congress as a Democrat in 1976. In 1981, after voting for the Reagan budget and tax cuts, he switched parties, to reflect both his constituency and his convictions. It was one of the smoothest party switches of recent times: he won 64% as a Democrat in 1980 and 63% as a Republican in 1982. When Stump switched, Republicans gave him seats on the Armed Services and Veterans' Affairs Committees, whose conservatism was compatible with his own. Tight-lipped in public (he has no press secretary), he lets his conservative voting record and style speak for him, as they do eloquently.

Stump's accession to the chair long occupied by Mississippi Democrat Sonny Montgomery does not signal a change in policy. Both are World War II veterans, and they have long been friends and allies on veterans' issues. Sometimes their work has been innovative, as with the Montgomery G.I. veterans' benefits package of the 1980s. Sometimes it is more retrograde, when they try to resist modernization of the troubled veterans' hospitals—aging facilities for aging beneficiaries. Stump in 1994 angrily insisted that the Republicans' Contract with America wouldn't force sharp cuts in veterans' services despite opponents' arguments otherwise. Stump is also the second ranking Republican, behind South Carolina's Floyd Spence, on the renamed National Security Committee, where he has been cautious about steep defense spending cuts. On other issues, Stump has filed bills to bar states from taxing pension incomes of residents of other states and to repeal the Social Security earnings tax—popular causes in Sun City. He favors four-year terms for representatives, with term limits, and in January 1995 advocated dropping the anti-abortion plank from the GOP platform.

Stump eschews the common course of seeking pork-barrel projects for his district or backing publicity-worthy causes; but he returns to the district often, spending only one weekend a year in Washington. Except for 1990, when his percentage dipped to 57%, he has been reelected easily in this strongly Republican district.

The People: Pop. 1990: 610,424; 18% rural; 20% age 65+; 82% White; 2% Black; 3% Amer. Indian; 1% Asian; 6% Other; 12% Hispanic origin. Voting age pop.: 457,328; 2% Black; 9% Hispanic origin. Households: 63% married couple families; 24% married couple fams. w. children; 49% college educ.; median household income: $27,627; per capita income: $13,185; median gross rent: $457; median house value: $79,700.

1992 Presidential Vote

Bush (R)	109,840	(40%)
Clinton (D)	86,060	(31%)
Perot (I)	73,356	(27%)

1988 Presidential Vote

Bush (R)	132,289	(67%)
Dukakis (D)	66,106	(33%)

Rep. Bob Stump (R)

Elected 1976; b. Apr. 4, 1927, Phoenix; home, Tolleson; AZ St. U., B.S. 1951; Seventh Day Adventist; divorced.

Career: Navy, 1943–46 (WWII); Cotton and grain farmer; AZ House of Reps., 1958–66; AZ Senate, 1966–76, Senate Pres., 1975–76.

DC Office: 211 CHOB 20515, 202-225-4576; Fax: 202-225-6328.

District Offices: 230 N. First Ave., #2001, Phoenix 85025, 602-379-6923.

Committees: *National Security* (2nd of 30 R): Military Installations and Facilities; Military Procurement. *Veterans' Affairs* (Chmn. of 18 R): Hospitals and Health Care.

Group Ratings

	ADA	ACLU	COPE	CFA	LCV	CON	NSI	COC	ACU	NTLC	CHC
1994	0	13	11	0	6	67	100	75	100	93	100
1993	0	—	0	0	14	50	—	91	100	—	—

National Journal Ratings

	1993 LIB — 1993 CONS	1994 LIB — 1994 CONS
Economic	14% — 80%	0% — 80%
Social	0% — 89%	0% — 89%
Foreign	0% — 91%	0% — 88%

Key Votes of the 103d Congress

1. Clinton Deficit Plan	N	3. Brady Handgun Purchase N	5. Lmt. UN Cmnd. of Forces Y
2. NAFTA	Y	4. Strike Race/Death Pnlty. Y	6. Cut Missile Funds N

Key Votes of the 104th Congress

1. Congressional Compliance Y	6. Reform Crime Grant Y	11. Loser Pays Court Reform Y
2. Balanced Budget Amndt. Y	7. National Security Act Y	12. Product Liability Reform Y
3. Bar Unfunded Mandates Y	8. Moratorium on Regs. Y	13. Welfare Reform Y
4. Pass Line Item Veto Y	9. Risk Assessment on Regs. Y	14. Term Limits Amndt. Y
5. Relax Exclusionary Rule Y	10. Expnd. Priv. Prop. Rights Y	15. Tax Cuts Y

Election Results

1994 general	Bob Stump (R)	145,396	(70%)	($152,718)
	Howard Lee Sprague (D)	61,939	(30%)	($5,851)
1994 primary	Bob Stump (R)	unopposed		
1992 general	Bob Stump (R)	158,906	(62%)	($303,208)
	Roger Hartstone (D)...................	88,830	(34%)	($99,133)
	Pamela Volponi (Natural Law)..........	10,767	(4%)	

FOURTH DISTRICT

From Camelback Mountain, 1800 feet high above the Valley of the Sun, you can look north over one of America's fastest-growing and most affluent metropolises, spread out over what was clumps of sagebrush a few decades ago. That was what Frank Lloyd Wright saw from his Taliesin West home and studio when he looked out toward the Biltmore Hotel he designed in the 1930s. Now the same area—northern Scottsdale, the town of Paradise Valley, the northern section of Phoenix between Camelback and Lookout Mountains—includes many of the most upscale parts of fast-growing metropolitan Phoenix. There is still very much of a Western air to these neighborhoods: grass is discouraged, when not prohibited by subdivision covenant; planting anything but desert flora is frowned upon; the architecture of the houses tends toward unadorned stucco with picture windows facing away from the sun; the idea is to suggest that there is a horse corral over in the next lot and sometimes, especially in the northern edges of Phoenix, there is.

The 4th Congressional District of Arizona consists of this northern part of Phoenix, most of Scottsdale and Paradise Valley and part of Glendale, bounded approximately by Camelback Road on the south, Pima Road and the Salt River Indian Reservation on the east, Pinnacle Peak Road on the north and 47th and Grand Avenues on the west. For all its rustic and unplanned air, this is a highly affluent district, and a heavily Republican one; there is scarcely a Democratic precinct to be found.

The congressman from the 4th is John Shadegg, a freshman elected in 1994, but with a fine Arizona Republican pedigree. His father, Stephen Shadegg, managed Barry Goldwater's first campaign for the Senate in 1952, when he upset Senate Majority Leader Ernest McFarland; the senior Shadegg also wrote a guide to political campaigning for conservatives, first published in 1964, titled *How to Win an Election: The Art of Political Victory*. John Shadegg helped deliver campaign press releases in those pre-fax days. He is a lawyer and, well connected in Phoenix, was a special assistant in the state attorney general's office and a special counsel to the Arizona House Republican caucus. When 4th District congressman Jon Kyl decided to run for the Senate in 1994, Shadegg was one of three strong Republicans candidates for the seat. Another was former state Representative Trent Franks, a former aide to controversial conservative Governor Evan Mecham, who tried unsuccessfully in 1992 to ban abortion in Arizona; a third was Maricopa Supervisor Jim Bruner, who ran as a "tough law-and-order candidate." But the Maricopa Treasurer, Assessor and Recorder all endorsed Shadegg, saying that Bruner helped run up a $62 million deficit in Maricopa County. Shadegg won with 43%, to 30% for Franks and 21% for Bruner.

In the general, Shadegg was attacked by Democrat Carol Cure as an "extremist" in seeking to cut back government programs; she called herself a "different kind of Democrat," backed a balanced budget amendment and took tough stands on crime. Shadegg took the standard Republican position on health care and welfare, and opposed most forms of gun control and abortion. But he emphasized that the economic issues of the Contract with America should come first. The result was unambiguous: Shadegg won 60%–36% and will likely be a solid conservative vote in the House for as long as term limits let him serve. He showed early interest in budget issues, including his leadership of freshmen who wanted the balanced budget constitutional amendment to include a requirement that three-fifths of House and Senate members approve any tax increase. "The freshmen aren't interested in coming here to be reasonable and to settle for what they can get. They don't want to go along to get along," he said after that measure's failure. The issue, which was an early test of House Republican cohesion, showed the pressure from the political right on Speaker Newt Gingrich and Majority Leader Dick Armey.

The People: Pop. 1990: 610,708; 11% age 65+; 87% White; 2% Black; 1% Amer. Indian; 2% Asian; 3% Other; 8% Hispanic origin. Voting age pop.: 465,000; 2% Black; 6% Hispanic origin. Households: 54% married couple families; 24% married couple fams. w. children; 62% college educ.; median household income: $33,681; per capita income: $18,331; median gross rent: $473; median house value: $90,700.

1992 Presidential Vote

Bush (R) 118,927 (43%)
Clinton (D) 86,922 (31%)
Perot (I) 70,682 (25%)

1988 Presidential Vote

Bush (R) 154,375 (68%)
Dukakis (D) 72,943 (32%)

Rep. John Shadegg (R)

Elected 1994; b. Oct. 22, 1949, Phoenix; home, Phoenix; U. of AZ, B.A. 1972, J.D. 1975; Episcopalian; married (Shirley).

Career: Air Natl. Guard, 1969–75; Practicing atty., 1975–present; US Spec. Asst. Atty. Gen., 1983–90; Spec. Cnsl., AZ House Republican Caucus, 1991–92; Cnsl., AZ Wildlife Conservation, 1992.

DC Office: 503 CHOB 20515, 202-225-3361; Fax: 202-225-3462.

District Offices: 1158 E. Missouri Ave., #100, Phoenix 85014, 602-248-7779.

Committees: *Budget* (22nd of 24 R). *Government Reform & Oversight* (22nd of 27 R): National Economic Growth, Natural Resources and Regulatory Affairs; National Security, International Affairs and Criminal Justice. *Resources* (25th of 25 R): National Parks, Forests and Lands; Water and Power Resources.

Group Ratings and 103rd Congress Votes: Newly Elected

Key Votes of the 104th Congress

1. Congressional Compliance	Y	6. Reform Crime Grant	Y	11. Loser Pays Court Reform	Y
2. Balanced Budget Amndmt.	Y	7. National Security Act	Y	12. Product Liability Reform	Y
3. Bar Unfunded Mandates	Y	8. Moratorium on Regs.	Y	13. Welfare Reform	Y
4. Pass Line Item Veto	Y	9. Risk Assessment on Regs.	Y	14. Term Limits Amndmt.	Y
5. Relax Exclusionary Rule	Y	10. Expnd. Priv. Prop. Rights	Y	15. Tax Cuts	Y

Election Results

1994 general	John Shadegg (R)	116,714	(60%)	($590,725)
	Carol Cure (D)	69,760	(36%)	($281,562)
	Others	7,428	(4%)	
1994 primary	John Shadegg (R)	26,489	(43%)	
	Trent Franks (R)	18,574	(30%)	
	Jim Bruner (R)	12,718	(21%)	
	Joan Jugloff (R)	3,678	(6%)	
1992 general	Jon Kyl (R)	156,330	(59%)	($458,358)
	Walter R. Mybeck II (D)	70,572	(27%)	
	Debbie Collings (I)	25,553	(10%)	($14,744)
	Tim McDermott (L)	11,611	(4%)	

FIFTH DISTRICT

The first frontier in what now is Arizona was in the southeast corner of the state. Here, just south of today's Tucson, Franciscan friars built San Xavier del Bac mission in the 18th Century. Here in the late 19th Century the mining towns of Tombstone and Bisbee sprang up on desert mountainsides, where miners dug up gold and silver and, for many years, much of America's copper; Cochise County, including those two towns, was the most populous county when Arizona became the 48th state in 1912. Here the white man last subdued the Indians, when the Apache leader Geronimo faced the U.S. Army in 1900. Southern Arizona remains pioneer country today: this was the site of the Biosphere II project, the greenhouse-like structure in the desert in which eight men and women lived more or less self-sufficiently, sealed from outside contact, from September 1991 until September 1993. Biosphere has now joined Tombstone as a tourist attraction; both are within the orbit of Tucson, Arizona's second metropolis, much smaller, more rough-hewn and more liberal than Phoenix. Tucson is a high-tech city, and its economy has been hurt by defense cuts. It is also home to the University of Arizona. For nearly 40 years, it was the political base of the brothers Udall: Stewart, congressman in the 1950s, Interior Secretary in the 1960s, now an Arizona lawyer again; Morris, congressman for 30 years and Interior Committee chairman, forced to retire in 1991 by Parkinson's disease.

The 5th Congressional District of Arizona includes most, but not all of Tucson and Pima County—the heavily Democratic Hispanic precincts are in the 2d District. It also includes much southeastern Arizona desert real estate: all of Cochise County, including Tombstone and Bisbee and Sierra Vista near Fort Huachuca; and some small farming and mining towns in Pinal and Graham Counties. It is smaller than the pre-1990 census 5th District, and is ordinarily solidly Republican, despite Tucson's historic Democratic preference. The political beneficiary of this is Republican congressman Jim Kolbe. First elected in 1984, when this was one of the most fiercely contested seats in the country, he has been reelected without difficulty ever since.

Kolbe has a reputation as a moderate Republican, yet on most issues has been conservative, sometimes aggressively so. In the Arizona legislature, he helped craft the statewide Medicaid program that is now the least costly in the country and worked on groundwater legislation; he is pro-choice on abortion. On economic issues, he is an Arizona free marketeer, against tax increases, for the balanced-budget constitutional amendment and line-item veto and for elimination of baseline budgeting; he has been a strong ally of Budget Chairman John Kasich and called the Democratic-run Congressional Budget Office a "budgetary brothel." He strongly opposed the Clinton healthcare plan. His greatest economic cause was the North American Free Trade Agreement, on which he was a leader in the bipartisan coalition for approval. He was one of the three Republicans who pushed their party to provide most of the votes to pass NAFTA in the House in November 1993, and has remained an enthusiast for it since. He has long admired the maquiladora program, through which U.S.-made components shipped to Mexico for assembly can reenter the U.S. without paying full duty, and believes that more trade can boost the economies of both countries. He was also a strong supporter of the General Agreement on Tariffs and Trade in November 1994. Separately, he has put pressures on Japan to lower its tariffs on copper and Motorola cellular phones—Arizona products.

Kolbe has other causes. He worked to expand the Saguaro National Monument and make it a national park, and he passed a bill to establish the Cave Creek Canyon Wilderness Area in Cochise County. He favors a dollar coin. He has been willing to risk offending some constituents: he voted against a cost of living increase for the military, and he voted for the crime bill negotiated by moderate Republicans with the Clinton Administration in August 1994. He returns to Arizona almost every weekend and in 1994, despite the Republican leanings of the district, exerted some effort against Democratic opponent Gary Auerbach, who was once Morris Udall's chiropractor. Kolbe criticized him for flip-flopping on the Clinton healthcare plan and made a point of inviting the President to the district to campaign for his opponent "in case he has neglected to invite you to Arizona." Kolbe won 68%–29% and—given that he is close to chairing an Appropriations subcommittee—seems likely to be a prominent member of the Republican House.

The People: Pop. 1990: 611,128; 13% rural; 15% age 65+; 78% White; 3% Black; 1% Amer. Indian; 2% Asian; 6% Other; 16% Hispanic origin. Voting age pop.: 466,689; 3% Black; 14% Hispanic origin. Households: 55% married couple families; 23% married couple fams. w. children; 59% college educ.; median household income: $27,047; per capita income: $14,361; median gross rent: $404; median house value: $81,100.

1992 Presidential Vote		
Clinton (D)	116,226	(42%)
Bush (R)	104,509	(37%)
Perot (I)	56,516	(20%)

1988 Presidential Vote		
Bush (R)	127,572	(56%)
Dukakis (D)	100,900	(44%)

Rep. Jim Kolbe (R)

Elected 1984; b. June 28, 1942, Evanston, IL; home, Tucson; Northwestern U., B.A. 1965, Stanford U., M.B.A. 1967; United Methodist; divorced.

Career: Navy, 1967–69 (Vietnam), Naval Reserves, 1970–77; Asst., IL Bldg. Authority Architect, 1970–72; Asst., IL Gov. Ogilvie, 1972–73; Vice Pres., land planning firm; Real estate consultant; AZ Senate, 1976–82.

DC Office: 205 CHOB 20515, 202-225-2542; Fax: 202-225-0378.

District Offices: 1661 N. Swan Rd., #112, Tucson 85712, 602-881-3588; and 77 Calle Portal, #B-160, Sierra Vista 85635, 602-459-3115.

Committees: *Appropriations* (12th of 32 R): Commerce, Justice, State, and Judiciary; Interior. *Budget* (4th of 24 R).

Group Ratings

	ADA	ACLU	COPE	CFA	LCV	CON	NSI	COC	ACU	NTLC	CHC
1994	15	39	11	20	6	73	100	100	80	70	57
1993	5	—	8	10	25	82	—	100	88	—	—

National Journal Ratings

	1993 LIB — 1993 CONS	1994 LIB — 1994 CONS
Economic	0% — 88%	26% — 70%
Social	44% — 55%	44% — 55%
Foreign	24% — 72%	34% — 63%

Key Votes of the 103d Congress

1. Clinton Deficit Plan	N	3. Brady Handgun Purchase	N	5. Lmt. UN Cmnd. of Forces	Y
2. NAFTA	Y	4. Strike Race/Death Pnlty.	Y	6. Cut Missile Funds	N

Key Votes of the 104th Congress

1. Congressional Compliance	Y	6. Reform Crime Grant	Y	11. Loser Pays Court Reform	Y
2. Balanced Budget Amndmt.	Y	7. National Security Act	Y	12. Product Liability Reform	Y
3. Bar Unfunded Mandates	Y	8. Moratorium on Regs.	Y	13. Welfare Reform	Y
4. Pass Line Item Veto	Y	9. Risk Assessment on Regs.	Y	14. Term Limits Amndmt.	Y
5. Relax Exclusionary Rule	N	10. Expnd. Priv. Prop. Rights	Y	15. Tax Cuts	Y

Election Results

1994 general	Jim Kolbe (R)	149,514	(68%)	($478,730)
	Gary Auerbach (D)	63,436	(29%)	($113,889)
	Others	7,821	(4%)	
1994 primary	Jim Kolbe (R)	42,239	(80%)	
	Joseph Sweeney (R)	10,350	(20%)	
1992 general	Jim Kolbe (R)	172,867	(67%)	($469,053)
	Jim Toevs (D)	77,256	(30%)	($103,589)
	Perry Willis (L)	9,690	(4%)	

SIXTH DISTRICT

Each time Arizona has created a new congressional district, as it has in each of the last three decades, it has resulted in some new configuration of the area that stretches from Phoenix and Scottsdale to the Navajo Indian Reservation in the northeast corner of the state. So it is with the new 6th Congressional District of Arizona, whose boundaries are just a bit more irregular than those of its predecessors. The current district includes just the northern edges of Scottsdale and Phoenix, with the suburbs of Carefree and Cave Creek, rustic areas where the mile-square grids are far from filled in and the local stores are more likely to feature horse feed than designer clothes. The 6th also takes in the old mining towns of Globe and Clifton and the sparsely-populated, wind-swept desert up to, and including, the Navajo Reservation. The district includes seven Indian reservations total, but its erose boundaries exclude the Hopis, who have a longstanding, sometime violent and continuing boundary dispute with the Navajo which is currently in federal court. There is vast cultural and economic disparity here; average household income levels vary from $64,000 in the Scottsdale area to below $20,000 in the northern Indian country. Politically, the 6th's portions of Phoenix and Scottsdale are heavily Republican, but the mining towns and the Navajo Reservation are heavily Democratic, and so sometimes is the more recently added Flagstaff. The result is a district leaning Republican, but potentially competitive.

So it has proved to be in Arizona's roller coaster politics of the 1990s. In 1992, when the national tide was running toward Bill Clinton's Democrats, local Republicans seemed to assume the seat was automatically theirs and had a fractious primary. The winner was Doug Wead, an Assemblies of God minister and former Bush White House liaison to the religious right, who moved to Arizona in 1990 to run for Congress and relocated four times to stay in the new district. He appeared opportunistic next to the Democrat, Karan English, a state legislator from Flagstaff who created an Arizona Conservation Corps and worked on water issues. She ran as a moderate Democrat supporting the line-item veto and a balanced budget amendment, and beat the state Senate majority leader in the primary. In the general, Wead was attacked as a carpetbagger and his aggressive pro-life stance on abortion aroused the ire of Barry Goldwater, who doesn't like government getting into personal issues: he loudly endorsed English, and she won 53%–41%, carrying the district's Maricopa County portion as well as every other county in the district.

Then the atmosphere changed as the Clinton budget and tax package of 1993 and healthcare plan of 1994 convinced people the President was an old-style Democrat. English's vote for the Clinton budget inspired J. D. Hayworth, sportscaster for seven years on Phoenix's Channel 10, to run against her. Well known from his TV work and an articulate conservative speaker, he framed the race as "between a citizen who pays taxes and a career politician who raises them." Long before the Contract with America, Hayworth issued his Action Plan for Arizona, full of denunciations of federal programs and praise for state and private initiatives. In the primary, Hayworth won 45% of the primary vote, to 21% for former legislative leader David Schweikert and 14% for drug prosecutor Gary Husk. In the general, Hayworth enthusiastically signed the Contract with America and blasted English for supporting the Clinton Administration. Hayworth carried Maricopa County 65%–32%, enough to easily overcome deficits on the Indian reservations and around Flagstaff; overall it was a 55%–41% Republican victory.

Hayworth seems likely to be a solid vote and booming voice in Newt Gingrich's Republican Conference. And with that voice and his sportscaster enthusiasm, he became a spokesman for the freshman in his early months but—like many of the newcomers who lacked previous government experience—he seemed thin on the details.

The People: Pop. 1990: 611,885; 33% rural; 13% age 65+; 64% White; 1% Black; 22% Amer. Indian; 1% Asian; 6% Other; 13% Hispanic origin. Voting age pop.: 424,927; 1% Black; 11% Hispanic origin. Households: 62% married couple families; 28% married couple fams. w. children; 45% college educ.; median household income: $25,710; per capita income: $11,322; median gross rent: $426; median house value: $75,700.

58   ARIZONA

Rep. J. D. Hayworth (R)

Elected 1994; b. July 12, 1958, High Point, NC; home, Scottsdale; NC St. U., B.A. 1980; Baptist; married (Mary).

Career: Sports Reporter/Anchor: WPTF-TV Raleigh, NC, 1980–81; WTFF-TV Greenville, SC, 1981–86; WLWT-TV, Cincinnati, OH, 1986–87; WKTSP-TV Phoenix, AZ, 1987–94; Insurance Agent & PR Consultant, 1994.

DC Office: 1023 LHOB 20515, 202-225-2190; Fax: 202-225-3263.

District Offices: 1818 E. Southern Ave., #3-B, Mesa 85204, 602-926-4151; and 1300 S. Milton, #207, Flagstaff 85001, 602-556-8760.

Committees: *Banking & Financial Services* (14th of 27 R): Capital Markets, Securities and Government Sponsored Enterprises; Housing and Community Opportunity. *Resources* (13th of 25 R): Energy and Mineral Resources; National Parks, Forests and Lands. *Veterans' Affairs* (16th of 18 R): Compensation, Pension, Insurance and Memorial Affairs.

Group Ratings and 103d Congress Votes: Newly Elected

Key Votes of the 104th Congress

1. Congressional Compliance Y	6. Reform Crime Grant Y	11. Loser Pays Court Reform Y
2. Balanced Budget Amndmt. Y	7. National Security Act Y	12. Product Liability Reform Y
3. Bar Unfunded Mandates Y	8. Moratorium on Regs. Y	13. Welfare Reform Y
4. Pass Line Item Veto Y	9. Risk Assessment on Regs. Y	14. Term Limits Amndmt. Y
5. Relax Exclusionary Rule Y	10. Expnd. Priv. Prop. Rights Y	15. Tax Cuts Y

Election Results

1994 general	J.D. Hayworth (R)	107,060	(55%)	($538,650)
	Karan English (D)	81,321	(41%)	($785,765)
	Others	7,687	(4%)	
1994 primary	J. D. Hayworth (R)	21,109	(45%)	
	David Schweikert (R)	9,565	(21%)	
	Gary Husk (R)	6,500	(14%)	
	David Smith (R)	5,093	(11%)	
	Ramona Liston (R)	4,376	(9%)	
1992 general	Karan English (D)	124,251	(53%)	($391,015)
	Doug Wead (R)	97,074	(41%)	($667,690)
	Sarah Stannard (I)	13,047	(6%)	($5,785)

ARKANSAS

In the 1990s America has come to know Arkansas as never before. One view, from a Bush campaign ad, showed a buzzard looking out over a bleak landscape, with an unseen voice reciting statistics ranking Arkansas at the bottom of the nation in education, health and crime. The brighter view came from Bill Clinton's ceremonial appearances in front of the old State House, whose Greek Revival columns were festooned with flags for his announcement in October 1991, or at the red-brick Governor's Mansion where he and Al Gore baked in the heat as the running mate was introduced in July 1992, or from the same mansion which was bathed in thousands of lights set in place by his Hollywood friends for Clinton's 1992 election night victory celebration. And then there was the view as the various scandals and episodes labelled as Whitewater were uncovered, of a poor state in which a few rich people knew and took care of each other. Which Arkansas is real? This is like asking which Bill Clinton is authentic—the responsive New Democrat, the cynical insider, the caring campaigner, the articulate intellectual, the indulger in fast food and other vices. They are all real, depending on the time, place and circumstances.

Arkansas, like Clinton, began life without many advantages. In area, it's the smallest state between the Mississippi and the Pacific; in population, it's the smallest state in the South; it has not been blessed with any great natural resource or any growing major industry. Arkansas is the land left over when Louisiana and Missouri were carved out of the Louisiana Purchase and what is now Oklahoma was fenced off as Indian Territory. Settled by poor farmers with large families, few slaves and little cash, it has had no Atlanta or Dallas or even Memphis to be a focus of growth. As Arkansas political scientist Diane Blair notes, Arkansas never had a power elite of great plantation owners or economic robber barons. That has left it a heritage without honored traditions or tight standards, but has also made Arkansas a land of great opportunities, where talented people can move up fast—like Blair and her husband, the house counsel at Tyson Foods, who guided the young Hillary Rodham Clinton in the commodities trading that resulted in unbelievable profits. Or like Jim McDougal, the onetime political prodigy and proprietor of the now-defunct Madison Guaranty Savings & Loan.

This Arkansas produced old style politicians like John McClellan and William Fulbright, who represented Arkansas in the Senate for a total of 60 years from the 1940s to the 1970s, while chairing the Appropriations and Foreign Relations Committees, and Wilbur Mills, chairman of the House Ways and Means Committee from 1958 to 1974; Governor Orval Faubus, who shamed Little Rock and Arkansas around the world by resisting integration at Central High School in 1957; and Governor Winthrop Rockefeller, who steered the state toward integration a dozen years later. Its current politicos include Dale Bumpers and David Pryor, who each served four years as governor before being elected to the Senate in the 1970s; top Clinton aides Mack McLarty and Bruce Lindsey and politicians whose careers were sidetracked by Clinton's rise, like Governor Jim Guy Tucker. Arkansas has also produced men who have made huge fortunes by taking break-through ideas and making them work: Sam Walton believed that rural and small town America would support a chain of giant discount stores which, through tough bargaining with vendors and ultra-quick distribution, could undersell competitors, but through demanding management and employee profit-sharing could embody small town friendliness and service; he was the richest American when he died in April 1992. Jack Stephens and his late brother Witt started an investment banking house in Little Rock specializing in underwriting municipal bonds and investing in businesses that are a mix of private enterprise, government subsidies and public regulation; their success—and political connections in Arkansas and elsewhere—amassed a billion dollar fortune. Don Tyson took his father's chicken business and

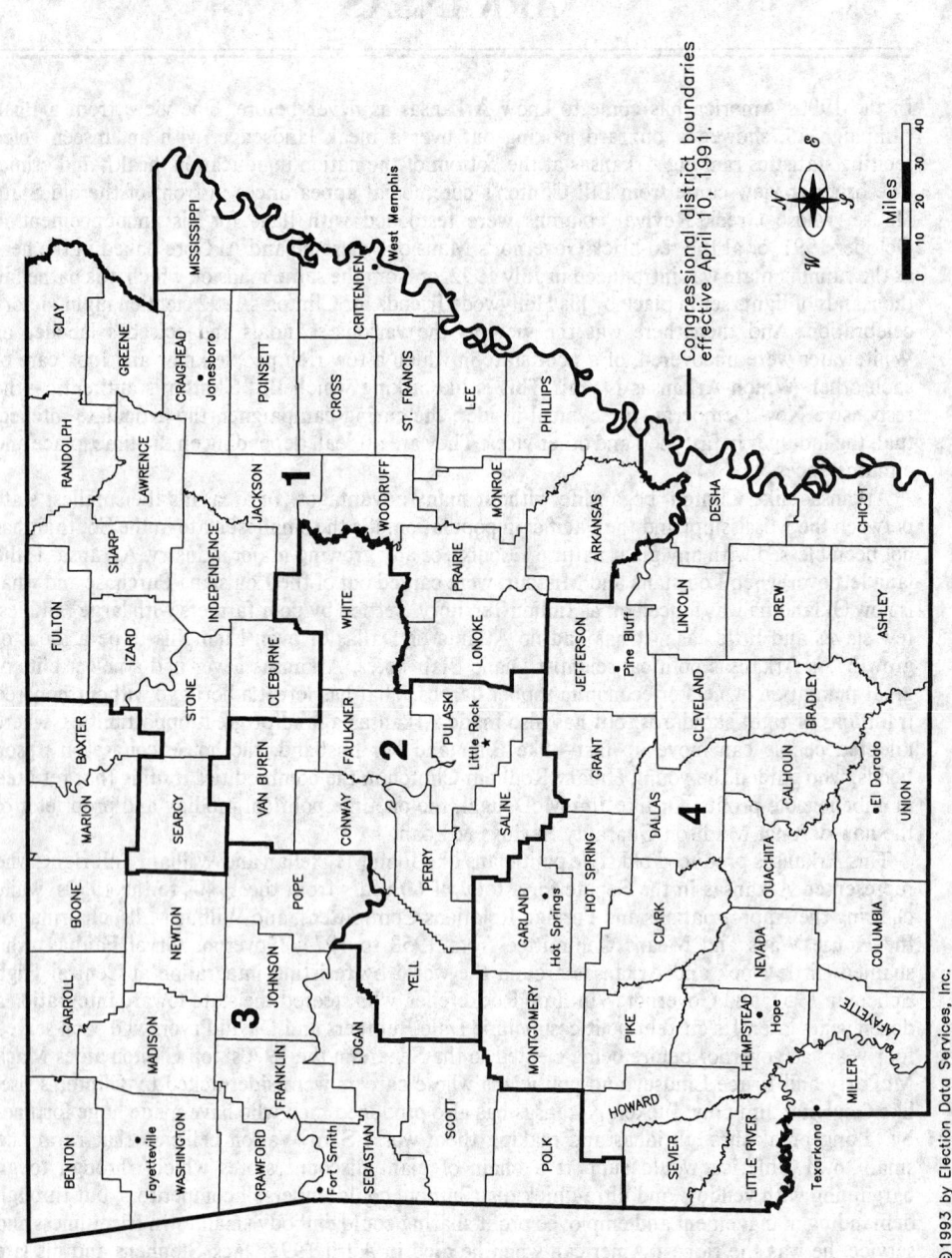

Congressional district boundaries effective April 10, 1991.

made it one of the biggest food producers in America. Other big Arkansas operations include TCBY (The Country's Best Yogurt) and J.B. Hunt's trucking empire. Yet these business giants, like most of Arkansas's successful politicians, have kept a down home, laid-back style. Sam Walton could be seen in Bentonville, driving his pickup truck with cages for his bird dogs in the back, stopping off to eat breakfast in a greasy spoon, just as president-elect Bill Clinton could be seen jogging around Little Rock, on his way to a giant cup of coffee and perhaps a sausage biscuit at McDonald's.

For all these Arkansans' successes, there is still an uncomfortable contrast here between billionaires and backwardness, presidents and poverty. Income levels remain stubbornly near the bottom of the nation; taxes and spending per capita remain low; achievement in schools and public health indicators rank low nationally. The government programs which Bill Clinton championed as governor—education reform, with teacher and pupil testing that began in 1983, workfare experiments, attracting new businesses and jobs—have produced some significant results, but have not totally transformed everyday life. Arkansas is the nation's number one producer of chickens and rice, but they have not generated many high-wage jobs; neither have lumbering and forest products. Yet life here is ever so much better than it was a couple of generations ago.

So it may not be surprising that Arkansas, for all its pride in its president, has had turbulent politics in the 1990s and that Bill Clinton has been at the center of much of the tussling. Indeed, for a time in 1990 it looked like his political career was over. He had been governor for 10 of 12 previous years, but with some rocky going. After being elected in 1978, at 32, he lost his first reelection campaign in 1980 after raising license plate fees and incurring anger by housing Cuban refugees in Fort Chaffee. He rebounded and won again in 1982 (his wife started calling herself Hillary Clinton during the campaign rather than Hillary Rodham), but his school reform program won him bitter opposition from the teachers' union in 1983, and his support of higher taxes earned him political opposition from Jack Stephens. His obvious national ambitions went unrealized in 1988, except for his overlong nominating speech for Michael Dukakis and his graceful recovery on the *Tonight* show. He had passed on the 1988 presidential race and admitted he lacked fire in his belly for 1990. He had opposition from the state's dominant newspaper, the *Arkansas Democrat-Gazette*, and its editor Paul Greenberg, who first called him "Slick Willie." And he had serious opponents in both the primary and general, whom he beat by only 55%–39% and 54%–46%. Through all this there were lurid charges against Clinton, of the sort that later became national news at Gennifer Flowers's press conference in January 1992.

There was similar turbulence underneath Clinton's success in carrying Arkansas in 1992. The national anti-incumbent trend was apparent in the defeat of two of Arkansas's four congressmen, veteran Democrats Bill Alexander and Beryl Anthony; another, Republican John Paul Hammerschmidt retired, leaving the Arkansas delegation with less seniority than probably any time since it was readmitted to the Union after the Civil War. In the general, Clinton carried Arkansas by a large margin, but his 53% of the vote was not spectacular, identical to what Michael Dukakis got in Massachusetts in 1988. Exit polling showed Clinton running far ahead of George Bush with voters 45 and over, 70%–26%, but Bush actually carried voters under 45, 43%–41%, not a sign of good long-term strength for the Democratic Party. Neither was the passage of term limits by a 60%–40% margin—the law which became the subject of the key Supreme Court test of term limits in 1995. Arkansas reelected Senator Dale Bumpers, but not overwhelmingly. Subsequent results were even more ominous for Democrats. Republican Mike Huckabee was elected lieutenant governor in a 1993 special, and in 1994 both Republican congressmen were reelected and one of the Democrats was given a serious challenge. Turnout rose especially in the heavily Republican northwest corner of the state. On balance there still seems to be a pro-Clinton majority in Arkansas. But it has not been a large majority at any point in the 1990s, and Arkansas voters, familiar with the President's strengths and his weaknesses, still seem discontented.

Governor. Jim Guy Tucker, another smart Arkansas politician of Bill Clinton's generation, has finally arrived at the governorship only to encounter serious problems. Tucker grew up in Little Rock, went to Harvard and served in the Marine Reserves. He was elected prosecutor in Little Rock in 1970, at 26, while Clinton was still at Oxford. In 1972 he was elected Attorney General, the office Clinton would win four years later when Tucker was elected to succeed Wilbur Mills in Congress. 1978 was the crucial year for both: Clinton ran for governor and won the nomination and election without serious competition; Tucker ran for senator, finishing second in the first primary, just ahead of then (and now) Congressman Ray Thornton, then lost the runoff 55%–45% to then-Governor David Pryor. How would history have been different if Clinton and Tucker had each run for the other office? Tucker did run against Clinton for governor in 1982, when the Republican who beat Clinton in 1980 was the incumbent; Clinton finished first with 42% and Tucker third with 23%. Clinton won that runoff against the second-place finisher 54%–46%.

Tucker was elected lieutenant governor in 1990 and cooperated with Clinton during the 1992 campaign. After the election, there was a moment of untidiness in the transition: Tucker's succession was challenged because of differing sections of the state Constitution. Only in early December 1992 was it established that Tucker would be governor. Tucker does not represent a major shift from Clinton's politics in substance or style. Like Clinton, he backs education reforms to which the teachers' union has been reconciled. He looks probably more for economic growth and new jobs than environmental purity. He stands for racial justice, but favors the death penalty. But like Clinton he has had his disappointments. In the July 1993 special election for lieutenant governor, Republican Mike Huckabee beat the impeccably pro-Clinton Democrat, Nate Coulter, an ex-aide to Senator Bumpers. Despite his eventual impressive victory, Tucker's reelection effort was more challenging than expected. In August Tucker was in intensive care at the Mayo Clinic for internal bleeding, a situation that threatened his shoo-in status. Tucker was also dogged by charges of scandal. In his years out of office his net worth increased from zero to $5.5 million. He was a business partner of Madison Guaranty Savings & Loan operator James McDougal; it was alleged that companies he controlled failed to pay back more than $1 million to failed McDougal entities. Tucker labored through the 1994 election year under this burden. He was nominated without opposition—the first time that happened since 1914—and got a crime package through the legislature (zero tolerance for teenagers with guns). Republican Sheffield Nelson, who had won 42% against Bill Clinton in 1990, accused Tucker of not repaying the McDougal loans and of raising money from nursing homes for whom he had done favors. But not all of Nelson's charges were substantiated and, ironically, Nelson himself had also profited from business dealings with McDougal. Tucker won 60%–40%, even while Lieutenant Governor Mike Huckabee was reelected 59%–41%.

After the election, there was press speculation that Tucker would be indicted. But by May 1995 he had not been. His biggest governmental problem was the state education aid formula which, it had been discovered in 1994, was being misapplied. After an Arkansas court rejected Tucker's solution, a temporary solution was eventually hammered out during the 1995 legislative session. For the next two years, the governor's efforts to rewrite the anachronistic 1874 state constitution, as well as revamping the financing systems for highway construction and school aid, are likely to dominate state politics.

Senators. Dale Bumpers and David Pryor, the two governors who preceded Bill Clinton, have much in common with him. All three grew up in small towns, in successive decades, without any particular political connections. All have always been moderate liberals, notably on race issues. All rose quite quickly in politics, though not without some disappointments. At least one soon will be heading home.

Dale Bumpers sprang directly from a small-town law practice to statewide office and for a time some thought he was headed to the White House. He was elected governor in 1970, beating Orval Faubus in the primary and Winthrop Rockefeller in the general, and was reelected in 1972; then in 1974, he ran for the Senate and beat 30-year incumbent William Fulbright in the primary. Bumpers has the eloquence and gift for the pungent phrase of a trial lawyer who knows how to sway a jury; he can speak the language of ordinary people, reducing complicated arguments to simple statements. But he is also the town iconoclast, with his idiosyncratic, often unpopular ideas, who is nonetheless respected and even loved. The Dale Bumpers who served on the committee that quietly integrated the schools in Charleston, Arkansas, is the same Dale Bumpers who loudly proclaimed integration as Arkansas's official state policy and as senator calls for "leveling the playing field" with affirmative action. Bumpers was raised a Roosevelt liberal Democrat; growing up in the 1930s, he saw FDR's federal government as the one institution working for the common man. But he has bucked organized labor, as when he voted against cloture on filibusters on labor law reform in 1978 and the striker-replacement ban in 1994.

In the Senate, Bumpers picks and chooses his issues, making him something like a cat: seemingly lazy while he naps but dangerous when he pounces. "Certain senators seem to have an opinion on everything," he says. "I don't like to get involved unless I have very strong feelings and am very prepared." In the 1990s, he has spent much time opposing major federal science and defense projects, leading battles to cut funds for the Strategic Defense Initiative, the Space Station, the Supercollider, with varying success: the Supercollider is dead, SDI limited, but the Space Station survived as Bumpers lost 64–36. He also argues for stretching out or canceling defense systems—the Trident submarine, the Milstar II satellite, the F-22, the C-17, the Advanced Neutron Source research reactor. He has led the so far unsuccessful crusade to reform the Mining Act of 1872, to require mining companies to pay much higher royalties to the government. He has also tried to reform concessions policy for national parks, again attacking well-entrenched interests. He backs a capital gains tax cut for small business investments held for five years. He wants mail order companies to collect sales taxes for all states. He sponsored the 1994 law, sought by Arkansas food producers, to delay nutrition labelling requirements.

After more than 20 years in Congress, Bumpers has not held a major chairmanship—although the announced retirement of Bennett Johnston will make Bumpers the top Democrat on Energy and Natural Resources. He is capable of swaying colleagues with his oratory, as in 1988 when he made a brilliant speech in favor of preserving the Manassas, Virginia, Civil War battlefield from a shopping center project. He can claim to have been early to spot key issues (warning about aerosol cans in 1975, pushing for childhood immunizations in the 1980s) but has been late in abandoning lost causes (battling long and hard against decontrol of energy prices in the early 1980s). He was one of the three senators (Bradley and Hollings were the others) who voted for the 1981 Reagan budget cuts and against the 1981 tax cuts—a set of positions which, if adopted, would have just about eliminated the budget deficits of the 1980s. Bumpers was urged to run for president in 1984 and 1988, but declined both times, partly because he didn't relish the grueling process and partly because he feared "a total disruption of the closeness my family has cherished."

Bumpers's phenomenal popularity as governor has cooled a bit in his years in Washington but has not burnt out altogether. He was reelected with 59% in 1980, 62% in 1986, 60% in 1992. His 1992 opponent was Mike Huckabee, a minister and former president of the Arkansas Baptist Convention, who operates and appears on a community television channel; in 1993 he was elected Lieutenant Governor. Huckabee grew up in Hope, the small town where Bill Clinton was born, but has little in common with him on issues. "We need to give the people of Arkansas a senator who does more than talk cornbread and catfish in Arkansas, but votes Kennedy and Cranston in Washington," Huckabee proclaimed, boosting the balanced budget amendment and term limits and twitting Bumpers for opposing the campaign finance reform measures Clinton backs. Huckabee may be an opponent in 1998, if he does not become a colleague before then.

Senator David Pryor by common consent is President Bill Clinton's best friend in Congress. He has followed Clinton's career since he saw him as a teenager handing out political buttons in 1966, and he gave him wholehearted and energetic support in the 1992 campaign. But he announced in April 1995 that, like many other Arkansas Democrats recently, he soon will be heading home, setting off a flurry of speculation about possible successors.

Pryor got his start in politics while Clinton was still in college. His father and grandfather were Sheriffs of Ouachita County, from which he was elected to the state legislature in 1960, at 26. He won a House seat in 1966, where he was one of the very few members from the Deep South to support civil rights. He ran for the Senate in 1972 and was only narrowly defeated in the runoff by 76-year-old conservative John McClellan. Pryor was elected governor in 1974 and 1976, where he became known as something of a cost-cutter.

In 1978, he won the Senate seat after a close three-way primary contest against House members Jim Guy Tucker and Ray Thornton. All three now hold high office: Pryor as senator, Tucker as governor and Thornton after a 12-year hiatus is back in the House. Pryor has seen many political cycles by now. He left a Washington in 1972 dominated by liberals bent on increasing public spending; he returned in 1979 when pressure was increasing to cut domestic spending and step up defense. He surely rejoiced at the 1992 Clinton victory and was dismayed by the Republicans' success in 1994.

Pryor has long been interested in issues concerning the elderly. As a young House member, he investigated nursing homes by going undercover as an orderly. When the House refused to hold hearings on the elderly, Pryor held his own hearings in a trailer near the Capitol and eventually won establishment of the Special Committee on Aging. For many years he has criticized pharmaceutical companies for what he considers unduly high drug prices, and with Oregon's Representative Ron Wyden, he pushed through a bill to force drug companies to give their most favorable prices to Medicare and Medicaid purchasers. In early 1993 he seemed about to advance these causes further. He beat back an attempt to abolish the Special Committee on Aging he had chaired since 1989. And he was pleased to see President Clinton in March 1993 attack the pharmaceutical industry as greedy and suggest caps on drug price increases. Pryor worked hard over the next 18 months at the Finance Committee to forge a compromise on the Clinton healthcare plan, but was unsuccessful. Similarly, his proposals to provide "incentives or inducements" to pharmaceuticals to hold down their prices did not produce legislation.

Pryor has had successes in other crusades. He has long criticized the IRS for overharsh enforcement methods and in 1988 steered to passage a taxpayer bill of rights. He has run dozens of hearings and demanded more than 40 GAO reports on government use of private consultants, which he sees as a "shadow government," and in 1992 he successfully limited consultant payments on the Strategic Defense Initiative. He has a bill to require groups that raise money through direct mail to disclose what they do with the money; this was aimed at conservative direct mail czar Richard Viguerie's groups of elderly, which are attacking the AARP and other organizations long allied with Pryor. He is attentive to Arkansas interests, holding up the 1986 savings and loan recapitalization bill because of what he regarded as "a deliberate system of harassment" against Arkansas S&Ls, which then had the nation's highest insolvency rate. He voted against cloture on striker replacement and in 1994 switched to support product liability reform, both measures backed by many Arkansas businesses. But he will work against local interests on occasion. As a vocal opponent of chemical weapons, Pryor has fought against production of both the Big-Eye nerve gas bomb and the 155 millimeter artillery shell which can be used to launch chemical weapons, and was successful in halting construction of the Big-Eye, which was slated for production in the Arkansas Pine Bluff weapons plant.

Overall Pryor has a moderate record on economic issues and, like his colleague Dale Bumpers, a very liberal record on foreign policy. Pryor was elected Conference Secretary, the number three position in the Democratic leadership, in 1988. But he bowed out of a race for Whip in 1990 and in 1994 relinquished the secretary job—after having opposed Tom Daschle's election as Democratic leader. Pryor's 1995 retirement announcement was not entirely unexpected, given the serious heart attack that he suffered in 1991. Although his popularity remained high and he probably would have had no trouble winning reelection, he said that he wanted to spend more time back home with his family.

Pryor's son, Mark Pryor, a state Representative from the Little Rock area, ran for Attorney General in 1994 and narrowly lost the Democratic runoff to incumbent Winston Bryant, who figured prominently in the early speculation for the Democratic nomination to succeed Pryor. On the Republican side, attention focused chiefly on Lieutenant Governor Mike Huckabee, who ran against Dale Bumpers in 1992. But Republicans have gained a strong enough bench that they will be competitive in 1996, regardless of who is their nominee. National Republican Senatorial Committee Chairman D'Amato has promised the maximum financial support allowed by federal law—$212,000—to help capture the seat.

Presidential politics. Arkansas was Bill Clinton's strongest state in 1994, one of the three places where his percentage most exceeded Michael Dukakis's (the other two: Al Gore's Tennessee and the District of Columbia). Arkansas has long been one of the southern states least negatively disposed to national Democratic tickets, and even a northern candidate might have hoped to carry it. For 1992, Arkansas moved its primary from Super Tuesday in March back to May, when state candidates run as well. Its early primary hadn't attracted much attention, since it's the smallest southern state, and neither did the primary in May 1992, since the results were not in doubt. There is no party registration in Arkansas and turnout in Republican primaries is usually very low.

Congressional districting. Arkansas made only minor changes in its district boundaries to meet the equal-population standard in the 1990s.

The People: Est. Pop. 1994: 2,453,000; Pop. 1990: 2,350,725, up 4.3% 1990–1994. 1.0% of U.S. total, 33d largest; 46% rural. Median age: 33.8 years. 14.9% 65 years and over. 82.7% White, 15.9% Black. Households: 59.2% married couple families; 27% married couple fams. w. children; 34% college educ.; median household income: $21,147; per capita income: $10,520; 69.6% owner occupied housing; median house value: $46,300; median monthly rent: $230. 7.2% Unemployment. 1994 Voting age pop.: 1,729,594; Registered voters (1994): 1,317,944; no party registration.

Political Lineup: Governor, Jim Guy Tucker (D); Lt. Gov., Mike Huckabee (R); Secy. of State, Sharon Priest (D); Atty. Gen., Winston Bryant (D); Treasurer, Jimmie Lou Fisher (D); Auditor, Guss Wingfield (D). State Senate, 35 (28 D and 7 R); State House of Representatives, 100 (88 D and 12 R). Senators, Dale Bumpers (D) and David Pryor (D). Representatives, 4 (2 R and 2 D).

1992 Presidential Vote

Clinton (D)	505,823	(53%)
Bush (R)	337,324	(35%)
Perot (I)	99,132	(10%)

1992 Democratic Presidential Primary

Clinton	342,017	(68%)
Brown	55,184	(11%)
Other	14,656	(3%)
Uncommitted	90,710	(18%)

1988 Presidential Vote

Bush (R)	466,578	(56%)
Dukakis (D)	349,237	(42%)

1992 Republican Presidential Primary

Bush	45,590	(83%)
Buchanan	6,551	(12%)
Uncommitted	2,735	(5%)

GOVERNOR

Gov. Jim Guy Tucker (D)

Assumed office, Dec. 1992, term expires Jan. 1999; b. June 13, 1943, Oklahoma City, OK; home, Little Rock; Harvard, A.B. 1964, U. of AR, J.D. 1968; Presbyterian; married (Betty).

Career: Marine Corps Reserves, 1962–64; News reporter, Vietnam, 1965, 1967; Teacher, American U. of Beirut, Lebanon, 1966; Practicing atty., 1968–71; Prosecuting Atty., 6th Judicial District of AR, 1971–73; AR Atty. Gen., 1973–77; U.S. House of Reps., 1976–78; Chmn., Cablevision Management Inc., 1982–present; AR Lt. Gov., 1990–92.

Office: State Capitol, #250, Little Rock 72201, 501-682-2345; Fax: 501-682-1382.

Election Results

1994 gen.	Jim Guy Tucker (D).	428,936	(60%)
	Sheffield Nelson (R)	287,904	(40%)
1994 prim.	Jim Guy Tucker (D) . unopposed		
1990 gen.	Bill Clinton (D)	400,326	(57%)
	Sheffield Nelson (R)	295,883	(42%)

SENATORS

Sen. Dale Bumpers (D)

Elected 1974, seat up 1998; b. Aug. 12, 1925, Charleston; home, Charleston; U. of AR, Northwestern U., LL.B. 1951; Methodist; married (Betty).

Career: Marine Corps, 1943–46 (WWII); Practicing atty., 1951–70; AR Gov., 1970–74.

DC Office: 229 DSOB 20510, 202-224-4843; Fax: 202-224-6435; e-mail: senator@bumpers.senate.gov.

State Offices: 2527 Fed. Bldg., 700 W. Capitol, Little Rock 72201, 501-324-6286.

Committees: *Appropriations* (6th of 13 D): Agriculture, Rural Development and Related Agencies (RMM); Commerce, Justice, State and Judiciary; Defense; Interior; Labor, Health and Human Services, Education. *Energy & Natural Resources* (2nd of 8 D): Forests and Public Land Management; Parks, Historic Preservation and Recreation (RMM). *Small Business* (RMM of 9 D).

Group Ratings

	ADA	ACLU	COPE	CFA	LCV	CON	NSI	COC	ACU	NTLC	CHC
1994	80	53	63	83	77	21	20	31	4	8	14
1993	80	—	73	80	69	46	—	18	8	—	—

National Journal Ratings

	1993 LIB — 1993 CONS		1994 LIB — 1994 CONS	
Economic	59% —	34%	50% —	48%
Social	67% —	32%	60% —	38%
Foreign	87% —	8%	94% —	0%

Key Votes of the 103d Congress

1. Clinton Deficit Plan	Y	3. Brady Handgun Purchase	Y	5. Lmt. UN Cmnd. of Forces	N
2. NAFTA	Y	4. Strike Race/Death Pnlty.	Y	6. Cut Missile Funds	Y

Key Votes of the 104th Congress

1. Congressional Compliance	Y	3. Balanced Budget Amndt.	N	5. Product Liability Reform	N
2. Bar Unfunded Mandates	N	4. Pass Line Item Veto	N	6. FY96 Budget	N

Election Results

1992 general	Dale Bumpers (D).....................	553,635	(60%)	($2,016,112)
	Mike Huckabee (R)	366,373	(40%)	($910,212)
1992 primary	Dale Bumpers (D).....................	322,458	(65%)	
	Julia Hughes Jones (D)...............	177,273	(35%)	
1986 general	Dale Bumpers (D).....................	433,092	(62%)	($1,797,370)
	Asa Hutchinson (R)	262,300	(38%)	($939,342)

Sen. David Pryor (D)

Elected 1978, seat up 1996; b. Aug. 29, 1934, Camden; home, Little Rock; U. of AR, B.A. 1957, LL.B. 1964; Presbyterian; married (Barbara).

Career: Editor and Publisher, *Ouachita Citizen*, 1957–61; AR House of Reps., 1960–66; Practicing atty., 1964–66, 1972–75; U.S. House of Reps., 1966–72; AR Gov., 1974–78.

DC Office: 267 RSOB 20510, 202-224-2353; Fax: 202-228-3973.

State Offices: 3030 Fed. Bldg., Little Rock 72201, 501-378-6336.

Committees: *Agriculture, Nutrition & Forestry* (2nd of 8 D): Marketing, Inspection & Product Promotion; Production & Price Competitiveness (RMM); Research, Nutrition & General Legislation. *Finance* (4th of 9 D): Long-Term Growth, Debt & Defict Reduction (RMM); Medicare, Long-Term Care & Health Insurance; Taxation & IRS Oversight. *Governmental Affairs* (4th of 7 D): Oversight of Government Management and the District of Columbia; Investigations; Post Office and Civil Service (RMM). *Aging (Special)* (RMM of 9 D).

Group Ratings

	ADA	ACLU	COPE	CFA	LCV	CON	NSI	COC	ACU	NTLC	CHC
1994	80	50	50	75	69	19	20	44	4	4	14
1993	70	—	70	90	63	29	—	10	9	—	—

National Journal Ratings

	1993 LIB — 1993 CONS		1994 LIB — 1994 CONS	
Economic	83%	0%	46%	53%
Social	65%	34%	62%	37%
Foreign	87%	8%	94%	0%

Key Votes of the 103d Congress

1. Clinton Deficit Plan	Y	3. Brady Handgun Purchase	Y	5. Lmt. UN Cmnd. of Forces	N
2. NAFTA	Y	4. Strike Race/Death Pnlty.	Y	6. Cut Missile Funds	Y

Key Votes of the 104th Congress

1. Congressional Compliance Y   3. Balanced Budget Amndt. N   5. Product Liability Reform Y
2. Bar Unfunded Mandates   Y   4. Pass Line Item Veto   N   6. FY96 Budget   N

Election Results

1990 general	David Pryor (D) .... unopposed			($622,479)
1990 primary	David Pryor (D) .... unopposed			
1984 general	David Pryor (D)	502,341	(57%)	($1,838,352)
	Ed Bethune (R).	373,615	(43%)	($1,072,879)

FIRST DISTRICT

The flat, mushy lowlands known as the Delta, on both sides of the lower Mississippi River, were some of the country's first industrial farmlands. This land was uncultivated in the 19th Century, when plows were still pulled by mules and muddy flatlands were impassable. Then, around 100 years ago, big landowners used machines to drain the marshlands and used capital to attract poor blacks to tend fields of cotton, rice and later soybeans. The results were bountiful agriculture and impoverished people. Around 1940, the Delta began to change slowly: national minimum wage legislation drew young people out of the Delta and mechanization forced many people off the farms. But this land—stretching flat as far as the eye can see, past rows of telephone poles and ribbons of asphalt that shimmer in the heat—remains poor by national standards and the people undereducated and underemployed.

The 1st Congressional District of Arkansas includes most of the state's Delta lands and stretches west to the cool green Ozarks. The Delta started off heavily Democratic, while some of the hill counties are ancestrally Republican. That changed as partisan preferences oscillated wildly just after the civil rights revolution, but the district returned to its historical norm by the late 1980s, and the Delta provided critical support for, perhaps saving the career of, Bill Clinton in 1990. In 1992, Delta counties voted 58% to 69% for Clinton, some of his best county showings anywhere in the United States.

The Congresswoman from the 1st District is Blanche Lambert Lincoln, who first won the seat in a 1992 contest that was a prime example of national anti-incumbent sentiment. Lincoln grew up in Helena, in the Delta, where her father and brothers are the sixth and seventh generations running a farm raising rice, wheat, soybeans and cotton, and where she stayed in public schools after they were integrated. "My parents raised independent-minded kids," she said. Immediately after college, in 1982, she got a staff job on Capitol Hill; she worked, among other jobs, as a receptionist for 1st District Congressman Bill Alexander and as a lobbyist in Washington for Billy Broadhurst, Gary Hart's host on his "Monkey Business" cruise. By 1992 Alexander, a member of the Democratic leadership from 1976 to 1986, was in political trouble. He won his 1986 and 1990 primaries with 52% and 54%; he was named in a 1991 lawsuit to recover a $308,000 debt; he had 487 overdrafts totalling $208,000 on the House bank. "I'll promise you one thing," the 31-year-old challenger said. "I can sure enough balance my checkbook." She won the primary 61%–39%, carrying 23 of 25 counties.

Lincoln is cheerful, active, endowed with good political sense; her recreations, she says, are duck hunting, fishing and yard sales. In the House she compiled a moderate record, rather liberal on foreign policy in the Arkansas Democrat mode. In her first term, she got seats on the Commerce and Democratic Steering and Policy Committees. She co-sponsored a major Superfund reform bill in May 1994, endorsed by the Chemical Manufacturers and National Federation of Independent Business; she ranked as the 8th lowest-spending Democrat according to the National Taxpayers Union Foundation. She must have been cheered when Japan opened its market to rice imports. State Representative Wayne Wagner, an Alexander ally thinking of challenging her in the Democratic primary, decided not to. In the general election she raised

$312,000 from PACs and outspent Republican Warren DuPwe $505,453 to $210,360. But that contest turned out closer than expected. She lost five mountain counties and also the fast-growing county around Jonesboro, which casts more than any other county in the district. Lincoln won 53%–47%, a result suggesting this seat may be seriously contested again.

Lincoln quickly showed some good political moves in the 104th Congress. After voicing initial concerns that a Republican moratorium on regulations might prevent the government from issuing guidelines for the duck hunting season, Lincoln eventually came out in support for the regulations moratorium and for other parts of the Contract. She denounced the SSI program paying disability checks to kids who act up in school—"crazy checks," they call them in the Delta. She enlisted in The Coalition, a group of 23 conservative Democrats. She certainly seems likely to be the strongest candidate the Democrats could run here.

The People: Pop. 1990: 588,588; 53% rural; 15% age 65+; 81% White; 18% Black; 1% Hispanic origin. Voting age pop.: 425,209; 15% Black. Households: 60% married couple families; 28% married couple fams. w. children; 26% college educ.; median household income: $18,180; per capita income: $9,148; median gross rent: $290; median house value: $39,800.

1992 Presidential Vote			1988 Presidential Vote		
Clinton (D)	131,585	(59%)	Bush (R)	101,784	(51%)
Bush (R)	71,160	(32%)	Dukakis (D)	93,331	(47%)
Perot (I)	20,116	(9%)			

Rep. Blanche Lambert Lincoln (D)

Elected 1992; b. Sept. 30, 1960, Helena; home, Helena; U. of AR, 1979–80, Randolph Macon Col., B.S. 1982; Episcopalian; married (Steve).

Career: Staff Asst., U.S. Rep. Bill Alexander, 1982–84; Lobbyist and govt. affairs rep., 1985–91.

DC Office: 1204 LHOB 20515, 202-225-4076; Fax: 202-225-4654.

District Offices: 615 S. Main, #211, Jonesboro 72401, 501-972-4600.

Committees: *Commerce* (14th of 21 D): Commerce, Trade and Hazardous Materials; Energy and Power; Health and Environment.

Group Ratings

	ADA	ACLU	COPE	CFA	LCV	CON	NSI	COC	ACU	NTLC	CHC
1994	60	52	33	70	50	93	40	83	10	43	36
1993	65	—	75	60	86	88	—	45	25	—	—

National Journal Ratings

	1993 LIB — 1993 CONS		1994 LIB — 1994 CONS	
Economic	52% —	48%	50% —	46%
Social	56% —	42%	55% —	44%
Foreign	79% —	16%	68% —	29%

Key Votes of the 103d Congress

1. Clinton Deficit Plan	Y	3. Brady Handgun Purchase	N	5. Lmt. UN Cmnd. of Forces	N
2. NAFTA	Y	4. Strike Race/Death Pnlty.	N	6. Cut Missile Funds	Y

Key Votes of the 104th Congress

1. Congressional Compliance Y	6. Reform Crime Grant Y	11. Loser Pays Court Reform N
2. Balanced Budget Amndmt. Y	7. National Security Act N	12. Product Liability Reform Y
3. Bar Unfunded Mandates Y	8. Moratorium on Regs. Y	13. Welfare Reform N
4. Pass Line Item Veto N	9. Risk Assessment on Regs. Y	14. Term Limits Amndmt. N
5. Relax Exclusionary Rule N	10. Expnd. Priv. Prop. Rights Y	15. Tax Cuts Y

Election Results

1994 general	Blanche Lambert Lincoln (D)	95,290	(53%)	($505,453)
	Warren DuPwe (R)	83,147	(47%)	($210,360)
1994 primary	Blanche Lambert Lincoln (D)	unopposed		
1992 general	Blanche Lambert Lincoln (D)	149,558	(70%)	($327,100)
	Terry Hayes (R)	64,618	(30%)	($30,571)

SECOND DISTRICT

Little Rock, the central focus of Arkansas for a century and a half, twice in the 20th Century became the central focus of the United States and the world. The first time was in September 1957, when Governor Orval Faubus, eager for a third term, sent in the National Guard to block a desegregation order at Central High School. President Eisenhower sent in U.S. troops and federalized the Guard to enforce the order, and Little Rock became a synonym for bigotry around the world—not quite fairly, since in many ways Little Rock has been more tolerant and fair than many other places. Little Rock's second moment in the international spotlight came in late 1992, when it was the headquarters of Democratic nominee and President-elect Bill Clinton. Television viewers became familiar with the Old State House and the Governor's Mansion the Rose Law Firm and McDonald's. Bill Clinton grew up in Hope and Hot Springs, went to college in Washington, D.C., Oxford and New Haven, then lived and ran for Congress in the university town of Fayetteville, in the northwest corner of the state; he has lived in Little Rock only as the official resident of the Governor's Mansion, and in 1981–82 after he was defeated for reelection. Yet Little Rock more than anywhere else seems his home.

Little Rock is in any case the center of Arkansas, geographically and, even more, politically. It sets the tone of the public life of its state as do only a few other state capitals—Boston, Providence, Atlanta, Denver, Honolulu. Little Rock is home to the *Arkansas Democrat*, the feistily conservative paper that forced the liberal *Arkansas Gazette* out of business in 1991. Its television stations reach to within a few counties of the state's boundaries. It is home to the state government and to Jack Stephens's investment banking firm and Worthen Bank, to Dillards department stores and the TCBY yogurt chain and to the Rose Law Firm at which Hillary Rodham Clinton was a partner. Little Rock may not be upscale by national standards, but it is in Arkansas. And the bad name it earned internationally when Governor Orval Faubus forcibly resisted the desegregation of Central High School in 1957 has surely been overshadowed by the good name it has won as Bill Clinton's home.

The 2d Congressional District of Arkansas includes Little Rock, with its large black and affluent white neighborhoods, and North Little Rock, a kind of industrial suburb across the Arkansas River known informally for years as Dog Town. (At the turn of the century, Little Rock officials, peeved that North Little Rock was allowed to incorporate separately, dumped all their stray dogs there.) It also includes surrounding counties which have grown rapidly as people move farther out the freeways. Politically, Little Rock has been a progressive force in a state with widely divergent political tendencies; it provided key support to Clinton when he was in political trouble in the 1990 primary and general, and again in 1992. The 2d also includes several hill counties to the north and, in the flat southeast, part of the cotton, rice and soybean-growing Mississippi plain. While the 2d has tended to favor moderate establishment politicians, it also has produced some odd-duck results. In 1958, after the Central High crisis, it elected a segregationist with write-in votes. For three elections starting in 1984 it elected Tommy Robinson, whose antics as sheriff earned him notoriety and popularity, who switched to the Republican Party in 1989 and ran unsuccessfully for governor in 1990, and later was found to have had 996 overdrafts on the House bank.

The congressman now from the 2d District is Ray Thornton, who has had a public career since he was president of the University of Arkansas student body. He is a nephew of Little Rock financier Jack Stephens; Thornton wrote a book about his grandfather A. J. Stephens, a farmer, woodsman, and state representative who could recite Tennyson and Scott and who instilled a sense of public service in Thornton. After working for Stephens interests, Thornton was elected Attorney General in 1970 and Congressman from the 4th District in 1972. There he served on the Judiciary Committee when it voted for the impeachment of Richard Nixon. He ran for the Senate in 1978 and lost the Democratic runoff to David Pryor. In 1980, he became president of Arkansas State University and in 1984 president of the University of Arkansas system. Elected in the 2d District without difficulty in 1990, he is the only recent Arkansas politician, surely, who has lived or worked in all of the state's four congressional districts.

Thornton has some big ideas: he calls for a "Marshall Plan for America," to invest 2% of GNP, about $110 billion, in rebuilding the nation's infrastructure and economy. He favors a capital budget, is against abortion funding and gun control, favored a "modest" health care reform. He is also for term limits, but only if they're uniform nationally; he is one of the defendants in the Supreme Court case challenging Arkansas's term limits that will almost certainly be a landmark case. He works on local projects—Little Rock Airport improvements, the National Center for Toxicological Research at Pine Bluff, Children's Hospital in Little Rock. Thornton's biggest moment in the national spotlight since the impeachment hearings came in August 1993, when he was one of the last three Democrats to vote on the Clinton budget and tax package. He voted no, after which Marjorie Margolies Mezvinsky voted yes—to her likely (and, as it turned out, actual) political peril. Given the home-state ties, Thornton was widely criticized for not voting for the President's proposal. But he had notified the White House some time before that he would not vote for a gas tax increase, and in fact his stand was in line with his moderate voting record (he was the only Arkansas Democrat to vote for the Gulf war resolution).

Thornton was probably in greater peril than anyone thought. True, in 1992 he had been reelected with 74%—the only Arkansas House incumbent to be reelected that year. But in 1994 he was opposed by former talk radio host Bill Powell, who accused him of delaying his vote until he was sure Clinton's package would pass and called him a liberal. Powell, with two sons who had drug problems, favored decriminalization of hard drugs; Thornton attacked that. Thornton outspent Powell by a wide (6–1) margin. He won by 57%–43%, a safe margin for many members, but far less than was expected. Thornton returned to his first Republican Congress at 67 and, despite rumors, insisted, "I'm not planning to retire."

The People: Pop. 1990: 587,412; 31% rural; 12% age 65+; 81% White; 18% Black; 1% Asian; 1% Hispanic origin. Voting age pop.: 434,412; 15% Black; 1% Hispanic origin. Households: 58% married couple families; 27% married couple fams. w. children; 43% college educ.; median household income: $25,142; per capita income: $12,334; median gross rent: $383; median house value: $56,300.

1992 Presidential Vote			1988 Presidential Vote		
Clinton (D)	130,435	(55%)	Bush (R)	117,477	(56%)
Bush (R)	84,922	(36%)	Dukakis (D)	89,526	(43%)
Perot (I)	19,348	(8%)			

Rep. Ray Thornton (D)

Elected 1990; b. July 16, 1928, Conway; home, Little Rock; Yale, B.A. 1950, U. of AR, J.D. 1956; Church of Christ; married (Betty Jo).

Career: Navy, 1951–54 (Korea); Dep. Prosecutor, Pulaski and Perry Cntys., 1956–57; Practicing atty., 1957–71; AR Atty. Gen., 1971–73; U.S. House of Reps., 1972–78; Pres., AR St. U., 1980–84; Pres., U. of AR, 1984–89.

DC Office: 1214 LHOB 20515, 202-225-2506; Fax: 202-225-9273.

District Offices: 1527 Fed. Bldg., 700 W. Capitol, Little Rock 72201, 501-324-5941.

Committees: *Appropriations* (24th of 24 D): Agriculture, Rural Development, FDA, and Related Agencies; Legislative Branch.

Group Ratings

	ADA	ACLU	COPE	CFA	LCV	CON	NSI	COC	ACU	NTLC	CHC
1994	75	43	78	70	63	5	70	50	19	24	36
1993	50	—	83	80	62	0	—	45	30	—	—

National Journal Ratings

	1993 LIB — 1993 CONS	1994 LIB — 1994 CONS
Economic	54% — 45%	73% — 17%
Social	53% — 46%	63% — 37%
Foreign	51% — 42%	64% — 33%

Key Votes of the 103d Congress

1. Clinton Deficit Plan	N	3. Brady Handgun Purchase	N	5. Lmt. UN Cmnd. of Forces	N
2. NAFTA	Y	4. Strike Race/Death Pnlty.	N	6. Cut Missile Funds	N

Key Votes of the 104th Congress

1. Congressional Compliance	Y	6. Reform Crime Grant	N	11. Loser Pays Court Reform	N
2. Balanced Budget Amndmt.	N	7. National Security Act	*	12. Product Liability Reform	N
3. Bar Unfunded Mandates	Y	8. Moratorium on Regs.	N	13. Welfare Reform	N
4. Pass Line Item Veto	N	9. Risk Assessment on Regs.	Y	14. Term Limits Amndmt.	Y
5. Relax Exclusionary Rule	N	10. Expnd. Priv. Prop. Rights	Y	15. Tax Cuts	N

Election Results

1994 general	Ray Thornton (D)	97,580	(57%)	($423,597)
	Bill Powell (R)	72,473	(43%)	($60,918)
1994 primary	Ray Thornton (D)	unopposed		
1992 general	Ray Thornton (D)	154,946	(74%)	($206,328)
	Dennis Scott (R)	53,978	(26%)	($6,212)

THIRD DISTRICT

The Ozarks of northwestern Arkansas, once one of the most isolated and backward parts of America, are now in important ways one of the country's leading edges. Much of the scenery remains the same: rounded green mountains spotted with farmhouses, little towns and small cities in valleys, man-made lakes glistening in the sunlight. People are still friendly and lifestyles tradition-minded and family-oriented—qualities that have made the Ozarks one of the nation's favorite retirement areas. Tourists throng to attractions like the Bible Museum and Cosmic Cavern near Eureka Springs. But the Ozarks have also become an engine of economic growth. Sam Walton put the headquarters of his Wal-Mart chain in Bentonville, which has the small town ambience that is so much a part of Wal-Mart's success even though profit-sharing and stock prices have made some Wal-Mart employees millionaires. And down the road near the University of Arkansas in Fayetteville, is Don Tyson's Tyson Foods in Springdale, now the leading chicken producer and processor in the nation: once again, an Arkansas entrepreneur has taken insights gained from his knowledge of Arkansas and enriched the nation as well as the state.

The 3d Congressional District of Arkansas occupies the northwest part of the state, including Bentonville, Fayetteville and the city of Fort Smith on the Oklahoma line, plus several mountain and upcountry counties to the east and south. This is the most Republican part of Arkansas, 2–1 for George Bush in 1988 and for Bill Clinton in 1992 by a bare 42.9%–42.2% margin. The mountain counties have historically been heavily Republican: they had few slaves and were opposed to secession and remained hostile to the Democratic flatlands. Fort Smith is also a Republican stronghold and, while Wal-Mart had Hillary Rodham Clinton on its board and Don Tyson's house counsel put her in the way of making unbelievable profits in commodities trades, the area around Bentonville and Springdale is very heavily Republican.

The Congressman from the 3d District is Tim Hutchinson, a Republican elected in 1992 to replace 24-year veteran (and victor over Bill Clinton in 1974) John Paul Hammerschmidt. Hutchinson grew up in northwest Arkansas, attended Bob Jones University and became a Baptist Minister; he also owned and managed a radio station and was founder and administrator of a christian school in Rogers. In 1984 he was elected to the Arkansas House, where Clinton called him "No-Tax Tim." His brother Asa Hutchinson was the Republican nominee against Senator Dale Bumpers in 1986 and is now Republican state chairman. In 1992 Tim Hutchinson ran for Congress and won the three-candidate Republican primary impressively, 53%–32% over a fellow legislator. The winner of the four-candidate Democratic primary, John VanWinkle, was the Fort Smith Democratic chairman and a Clinton-appointed judge; with plenty of Clinton connections, he raised more money than Hutchinson and called for healthcare reform. Hutchinson backed term limits, the line-item veto and the balanced budget amendment—all Contract items two years before the Contract; he called for Dick Armey's process for closing military bases to be applied to cutting waste in all parts of government. He said he would follow Hammerschmidt's voting record and claimed attacks on him as a religious extremist were "scare tactics" reflecting "a kind of intolerance." In the last week of the campaign, Hutchinson was endorsed by local Perot supporters who dismissed VanWinkle as a "waffler." Hutchinson won by just 50%–47%, carrying the counties around Bentonville, Fayetteville and Fort Smith.

In the House Hutchinson has had a very conservative voting record. He supported the Clinton position for NAFTA, after watching U.S. exports sell in a Mexico City Wal-Mart. At the same time he decried the "mean-spirited partisanship" he found in Congress. He served on Hammerschmidt's committees—Transportation and Infrastructure and Veterans' Affairs—and said his voting record was similar to his predecessor's. He was one of the originators of the Contract With America's promise of a $500 per child tax credit (and points out that 90% of the benefit goes to families with incomes under $60,000). After winning narrowly in 1992, Hutchinson did not attract strong opposition in 1994 and won with 68% of the vote. He is now Chairman of the Veterans' Subcommittee on Hospitals and Health Care—a proprietor of one of the nation's socialized medicine systems—and on Transportation he promises to work for an I-49 stretching from the Louisiana border near Texarkana to the Missouri border near Bentonville: "I don't have a higher priority." He lost a race for Republican Conference Secretary to Barbara Vucanovich of Nevada and is a deputy whip. He was one of eight House members to attend the White House conference on welfare in January 1995. Hutchinson has pledged to serve no more than 12 years in the House.

The People: Pop. 1990: 589,523; 49% rural; 16% age 65+; 96% White; 2% Black; 1% Amer. Indian; 1% Asian; 1% Hispanic origin. Voting age pop.: 440,426; 1% Black; 1% Hispanic origin. Households: 64% married couple families; 28% married couple fams. w. children; 36% college educ.; median household income: $21,903; per capita income: $10,876; median gross rent: $328; median house value: $48,900.

1992 Presidential Vote

Clinton (D) 109,111 (43%)
Bush (R) 107,351 (42%)
Perot (I)................... 35,991 (14%)

1988 Presidential Vote

Bush (R) 137,239 (66%)
Dukakis (D)................. 67,856 (33%)

Rep. Tim Hutchinson (R)

Elected 1992; b. Aug. 11, 1949, Gravette; home, Bentonville; Bob Jones U., B.A. 1979, U. of AR, M.A. 1990; Baptist; married (Donna Jean).

Career: Baptist Minister; Founder and Admin., Benton Cnty. Christian Schl., 1975–85; Co-owner and Mgr., KBCV Radio, 1982–89; Prof., John Brown U., 1989–92; AR House of Reps., 1984–92.

DC Office: 1005 LHOB 20515, 202-225-4301; Fax: 202-226-2263.

District Offices: 30 S. 6th St., #248, Ft. Smith 72901, 501-782-7787; 422 Fed. Bldg., 35 E. Mountain, #422, Fayetteville 72701, 501-442-5258; and 210 Fed. Bldg., 425 N. Walnut, Harrison 72601, 501-741-6900.

Committees: *Economic & Educational Opportunities* (16th of 24 R): Workforce Protections. *Transportation & Infrastructure* (14th of 33 R): Aviation; Surface Transportation. *Veterans' Affairs* (5th of 18 R): Education, Training, Employment and Housing; Hospitals and Health Care (Chmn.).

Group Ratings

	ADA	ACLU	COPE	CFA	LCV	CON	NSI	COC	ACU	NTLC	CHC
1994	5	17	22	20	11	81	100	75	95	100	100
1993	5	—	0	10	14	63	—	100	100	—	—

National Journal Ratings

	1993 LIB — 1993 CONS		1994 LIB — 1994 CONS	
Economic	14%	— 80%	0%	— 80%
Social	0%	— 89%	11%	— 85%
Foreign	17%	— 76%	14%	— 80%

Key Votes of the 103d Congress

1. Clinton Deficit Plan	N	3. Brady Handgun Purchase	N	5. Lmt. UN Cmnd. of Forces	Y
2. NAFTA	Y	4. Strike Race/Death Pnlty.	Y	6. Cut Missile Funds	N

Key Votes of the 104th Congress

1. Congressional Compliance	Y	6. Reform Crime Grant	Y	11. Loser Pays Court Reform	Y
2. Balanced Budget Amndmt.	Y	7. National Security Act	Y	12. Product Liability Reform	Y
3. Bar Unfunded Mandates	Y	8. Moratorium on Regs.	Y	13. Welfare Reform	Y
4. Pass Line Item Veto	Y	9. Risk Assessment on Regs.	Y	14. Term Limits Amndmt.	Y
5. Relax Exclusionary Rule	Y	10. Expnd. Priv. Prop. Rights	Y	15. Tax Cuts	Y

Election Results

1994 general	Tim Hutchinson (R)	129,800	(68%)	($288,412)
	Berta L. Seitz (D)	61,883	(32%)	($61,131)
1994 primary	Tim Hutchinson (R)	unopposed		
1992 general	Tim Hutchinson (R)	125,295	(50%)	($339,772)
	John VanWinkle (D)	117,775	(47%)	($489,833)
	Others	6,424	(3%)	

FOURTH DISTRICT

Southern Arkansas runs the gamut of the state, from the Delta flatlands along the Mississippi River, where the water-soaked fields produce America's largest rice crop, across small cities with antique pasts like Pine Bluff and El Dorado, west to the Ouachita Mountains and the border town of Texarkana, where the main street divides two states and Texan Ross Perot grew up five blocks west of Arkansas. This is the northwestern corner of the Deep South. There is still a large black population here, a reminder that parts of southern Arkansas were once plantation country; but oil is also in production here, a reminder that this is the beginning of the Southwest. The broiler chicken industry looms large in these parts, and the accent is clearly Arkansan: El Dorado, Nevada and Lafayette are all pronounced with long *A*s and penultimate syllable accents, and Ouachita is, with a bow to the original French, *waSHEEta*. The district also includes the little railroad-crossing, county seat town of Hope, where President Bill Clinton and his first White House chief of staff Mack McLarty were classmates at Miss Mary's Kindergarten, and Hot Springs, the spa resort and gambling haven where Bill Clinton's stepfather sold Buicks, his mother bet on the horses and he excelled in high school as he began his climb from southern Arkansas to world eminence.

The 4th Congressional District of Arkansas occupies almost all of the southern geographical half of the state, from the Mississippi River to the Ouachita Mountains, the Delta to Texarkana. It is historically a Democratic district, and one which for most of this century has elected a young man to the House and kept him there for years, to cut deals with the Democratic leadership and bring home the bacon. In 50 years the 4th District had four congressmen, all Democrats. But now it has a very different congressional politics: bipartisan, with rancorous debates on national issues followed by narrow election victories—and something in the nature of repudiation of the politics of this district's most famous native son.

The Congressman from the 4th District is Jay Dickey, a Republican twice elected by narrow margins. He replaced Beryl Anthony, Chairman of the Democratic Congressional Campaign Committee and member of Ways and Means, Washington insider and brother-in-law of the late White House counsel Vincent Foster; despite spending $1 million, Anthony the 1992 primary 51%–49%. Dickey is from Pine Bluff, where his uncle and grandfather were both state Senators; he caught polio in 1960, but recovered and became a top college tennis player and runs 5K races today. Practicing law in Pine Bluff, Dickey represented the Arkansas Fox and Coon Hunters Association challenging state restrictions on running dogs; he won the case in the Arkansas Supreme Court and there are no restrictions on the running of dogs in Arkansas today. In the 1970s and 1980s, Dickey ran Baskin Robbins and Taco Bell franchises and formed an advertising sign company and a travel agency. He won the ordinarily worthless Republican nomination in 1992, but in the general attacked Secretary of State Bill McCuen, who had beaten Anthony, for giving out a $324,000 no-bid contract on computers for his office. McCuen countered by charging that Dickey's pro-life views meant he condoned incest. Dickey won 52%–48%.

In the House Dickey made a mostly conservative voting record. He sits on Appropriations' Agriculture, Labor-HHS and Transportation Subcommittees. He sponsored a crime bill to allow flogging of prisoners and to remove color televisions and other "conveniences for criminals" from prisons. Like many new Republicans, he returns to his district almost every weekend. The 1994 Democratic primary made national headlines when Whitewater's Jim McDougal entered the race, but he won only 22% of the vote, far behind Pine Bluff state Senator Jay Bradford, who won with 54%. Locally popular, well connected in Washington (he took in large sums from PACs), Bradford raised about as much as Dickey. But his support of the Brady bill and the assault weapons ban triggered a $17,000 independent expenditure by the National Rifle Association. Bradford carried Pine Bluff and most of the smaller counties. But Dickey carried Hot Springs, Texarkana and El Dorado and won, again with 52%–48%.

Dickey looked forward to working on the 1995 farm bill and arranged a meeting of Tyson Food's lobbyist with Agriculture Chairman Pat Roberts, on the subject of the independent counsel investigating former Agriculture Secretary Mike Espy's connections with Tyson, whose Democratic ties are evidently no longer so helpful. Dickey—who briefly considered a bid for David Pryor's open Senate seat in 1996—can scarcely be regarded as a sure bet for reelection with his 52% majorities and in this historically Democratic area. But Bradford is probably as strong a candidate as Democrats could find, and now that they are in the minority they will likely find it harder to raise money. Bill Clinton's home district is likely to be seriously contested again as he himself seeks reelection.

The People: Pop. 1990: 585,202; 52% rural; 16% age 65+; 72% White; 27% Black; 1% Hispanic origin. Voting age pop.: 429,410; 24% Black; 1% Hispanic origin. Households: 59% married couple families; 26% married couple fams. w. children; 30% college educ.; median household income: $19,621; per capita income: $9,723; median gross rent: $299; median house value: $39,900.

1992 Presidential Vote

Clinton (D) 134,692 (57%)
Bush (R) 73,891 (31%)
Perot (I) 23,677 (10%)

1988 Presidential Vote

Bush (R) 110,078 (52%)
Dukakis (D). 98,524 (46%)

Rep. Jay Dickey (R)

Elected 1992; b. Dec. 14, 1939, Pine Bluff; home, Pine Bluff; U. of AR, B.A. 1961, J.D. 1963; Methodist; divorced.

Career: Practicing atty., 1963–92; Pine Bluff City Atty., 1968–70; Small business and franchise owner, 1982–present.

DC Office: 230 CHOB 20515, 202-225-3772; Fax: 202-225-1314; e-mail: jdickey@hr.house.gov.

District Offices: 100 E. 8th St., #2521, Pine Bluff 71601, 501-536-3376; 100 Reserve, #201, Hot Springs 71913, 501-623-5800; and 100 S. Jackson, #201, El Dorado 71730, 501-862-0236.

Committees: *Appropriations* (24th of 32 R): Agriculture, Rural Development, FDA, and Related Agencies; Labor, Health and Human Services, and Education; Transportation.

Group Ratings

	ADA	ACLU	COPE	CFA	LCV	CON	NSI	COC	ACU	NTLC	CHC
1994	0	23	22	20	18	59	100	75	95	96	100
1993	10	—	8	20	36	74	—	91	100	—	—

National Journal Ratings

	1993 LIB — 1993 CONS			1994 LIB — 1994 CONS		
Economic	0%	—	88%	26%	—	70%
Social	23%	—	77%	11%	—	85%
Foreign	33%	—	65%	25%	—	71%

Key Votes of the 103d Congress

1. Clinton Deficit Plan	N	3. Brady Handgun Purchase	N	5. Lmt. UN Cmnd. of Forces	Y
2. NAFTA	Y	4. Strike Race/Death Pnlty.	Y	6. Cut Missile Funds	N

Key Votes of the 104th Congress

1. Congressional Compliance	Y	6. Reform Crime Grant	Y	11. Loser Pays Court Reform	Y
2. Balanced Budget Amndmt.	Y	7. National Security Act	Y	12. Product Liability Reform	Y
3. Bar Unfunded Mandates	Y	8. Moratorium on Regs.	Y	13. Welfare Reform	Y
4. Pass Line Item Veto	Y	9. Risk Assessment on Regs.	Y	14. Term Limits Amndmt.	Y
5. Relax Exclusionary Rule	Y	10. Expnd. Priv. Prop. Rights	Y	15. Tax Cuts	Y

Election Results

1994 general	Jay Dickey (R)	87,469	(52%)	($832,117)
	Jay Bradford (D).....................	81,370	(48%)	($797,708)
1994 primary	Jay Dickey (R)	unopposed		
1992 general	Jay Dickey (R)	113,009	(52%)	($397,841)
	W. J. (Bill) McCuen (D)..............	102,918	(48%)	($357,911)

CALIFORNIA

California, where everything seemed to be going wrong in the early 1990s, now seems to be going right, in two senses: its economy is headed upward again and its politics is moving in a conservative direction. The first development is almost universally welcomed, the second of course controversial; both seem to be a return to the pattern of the 1980s. Yet there is still little here of the rosy optimism and cheery chipperness of the state's most influential politician, Ronald Reagan. California may be recovering, but it remains in a sour mood. The California economy, it turns out, has been stronger all along than its political and big business establishment proclaimed. But its culture seems less resilient, more tattered, far more segmented than the California culture that made this an advanced state in the first half of the 20th century and then produced the nation's most rapid and creative growth in the first 40 years of the second half.

Few states in recent times have had to weather the disasters, economic, natural and social, that hit California in the past few years. First came the Loma Prieta earthquake, shaking San Francisco's Candlestick Park as the 1989 World Series was about to start; then came the torrential Central Valley floods of 1991; in May 1992, South Central Los Angeles broke out in rioting after the policemen who assaulted Rodney King were acquitted in Simi Valley; in September 1992 came the terrible fires of Malibu, sweeping down from the mountains toward the ocean; in January 1994, the Northridge earthquake shook the San Fernando Valley and Santa Monica; in June 1994, O.J. Simpson's former wife was murdered in Brentwood. Overhanging all this was the California recession. Relatively untouched by the recessions of the 1970s, creating 300,000 new jobs a year in the 1980s, the state was suddenly hit hard by defense cutbacks as the Cold War ended, and lost 500,000 jobs. But by the 1990s, more people were moving to other states than coming from them to California, the reversal of a 60-year pattern; the state's unemployment rate climbed to well over the national average; real estate values, wondrously high in the 1980s, plummeted. Articulate opinion back East and in elite quarters in the state itself gave up on California, decided the Golden State was irretrievably tarnished, proclaimed the end of its affluence and success.

History should have taught them another lesson. For California, ever since it suddenly became American in 1848, has always been a place of economic vitality and personal creativity. Legend has it that California grew because of blind luck, and that it was built by big aggregations of wealth and power. It is true that in the Gold Rush of 1849 San Francisco grew from nothing to one of the largest American cities in one year. And it can also be said that California was given its shape by big units: the Southern Pacific and Union Pacific Railroads, the giant agri-business combines who controlled the vast Central Valley acreage, giant engineering projects like the Los Angeles Aqueduct and the California water plan of the 1960s, huge aircraft factories and shipyards and steel plants built to win World War II. But these large entities worked because they created a framework in which individuals could work, innovate and prosper, inventing their own styles and technologies, new economies and lifestyles. Compare today's California, the hugely prosperous and most creative place on the face of the earth, where the richest nation meets the world's fastest-growing region, the Pacific Rim, with the California of the 1940s, when there were just seven million Californians, when it was always convertible weather and no one had yet named smog. "California is an island," Carey McWilliams wrote then: America's lightly populated outpost on the Pacific, thousands of miles across plains, mountains and desert from thickly settled parts of the country, separated from hostile Japan only by the open waters of the ocean, a Yankee commonwealth with a Mission veneer.

Then came the explosive change of World War II, when California became one of the great defense industry states, making steel and aluminum for the first time, building ships and airplanes by the thousands. Millions of Americans came here and millions stayed. California's economy was expected to collapse when the big firms shut down after the war, a much greater defense cutback than in the 1990s. Instead, as urbanologist Jane Jacobs points out, one-eighth of all the new jobs in the nation in the late 1940s were created in metro Los Angeles. This small scale growth, multiplied thousands of times over, made California into the nation's most populous state by 1963. And so Los Angeles in the 20th Century became a great city, the nation's second biggest, with a metropolitan population of 14.8 million people—behind New York's 19.3 million but well ahead of Chicago's 8.3 million—not so much because of geography (LA has no natural harbor and had to build one) or natural resources (it once exported oil, but has imported it since the 1940s) or its historical eminence (Los Angeles had 102,000 people in 1900), but because people wanted it to be. Similarly, San Francisco and the Bay Area around it, now the nation's fourth largest metropolis with 6.4 million people, grew initially because it was California's great port and the processor of its agricultural produce; but it owes its standard of living, arguably the nation's highest, primarily to products of the mind.

In that context, what is remarkable is not that California rebounded from the defense cutbacks and recession, but that so many doubted it would. The defense cuts of the early 1990s were a much smaller share of the state's economy than in the late 1940s and were largely concentrated in Los Angeles County; the rest of the state's economy lost only 1.2% of jobs—far below the 7–10% of New York or New England. One thing slowing recovery was tax increases, all proposed by politicians California voted for: George Bush's budget summit in 1990, Pete Wilson's state tax hikes in 1991, Bill Clinton's budget and tax package of 1993. California's nominal incomes (and living costs) are higher than the rest of the country's, and many more people are self-employed or own small businesses, so these soak-the-rich measures were really soak-California. Plus, California was relentlessly talked down by national media back East and even by the Los Angeles Times; Pete Wilson, decrying high taxes and tort costs, lent his voice to this opera. Every earthquake, flood, fire was the end; the collapse of real estate prices in

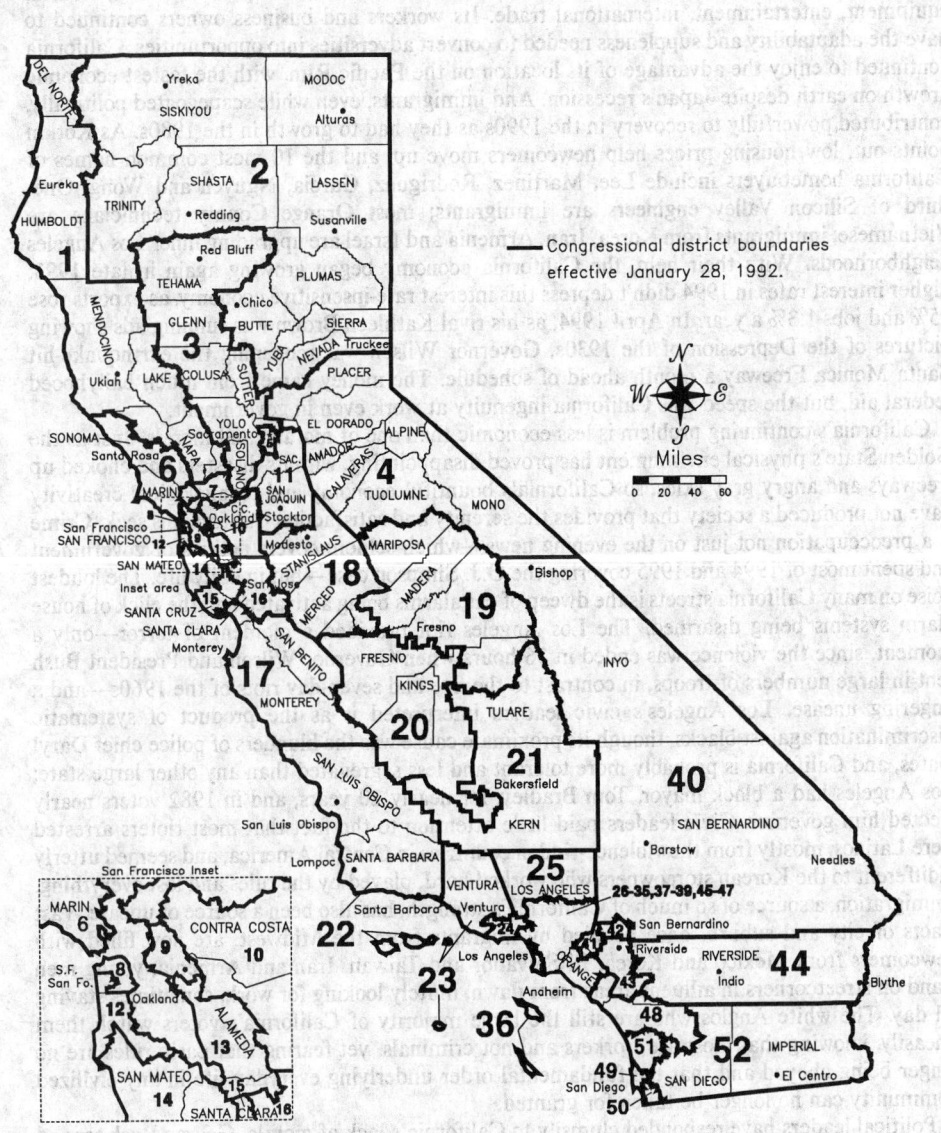

Congressional district boundaries
effective January 28, 1992.

DEL NORTE

SISKIYOU

Yreka

Alturas

MODOC

Eureka

HUMBOLDT

TRINITY

SHASTA

Redding

LASSEN

Susanville

1

Red Bluff

TEHAMA

2

Chico

PLUMAS

MENDOCINO

GLENN

BUTTE

SIERRA

NEVADA

Truckee

3

LAKE

COLUSA

SUTTER

YUBA

PLACER

Ukiah

YOLO

Sacramento

EL DORADO

ALPINE

SONOMA

NAPA

SOLANO

11

SAC.

AMADOR

Santa Rosa

6

MARIN

C.C.

Oakland

10

SAN JOAQUIN

Stockton

CALAVERAS

4

TUOLUMNE

MONO

San Francisco
SAN FRANCISCO

12

SAN MATEO

14

Inset area

13

Modesto

STANISLAUS

MARIPOSA

SANTA CRUZ

15

16

San Jose

18

MERCED

MADERA

19

Bishop

SANTA CLARA

Monterey

SAN BENITO

Fresno

17

MONTEREY

FRESNO

INYO

KINGS

20

TULARE

SAN LUIS OBISPO

21

Bakersfield

40

San Luis Obispo

KERN

SAN BERNARDINO

Barstow

Needles

Lompoc

25

SANTA BARBARA

VENTURA

Santa Barbara

LOS ANGELES

26-35,37-39,45-47

San Bernardino

22

Ventura

24

23

Los Angeles

ORANGE

Riverside

RIVERSIDE

44

Indio

Blythe

36

Anaheim

43

48

52

IMPERIAL

51

SAN DIEGO

El Centro

49

San Diego

50

San Francisco Inset

MARIN
6

CONTRA COSTA

S.F.
San Fo.

8

9

10

12

Oakland

ALAMEDA

13

SAN MATEO

14

SANTA CLARA

16

15

N
W   E
S

Miles

0   20   40   60

Westside Los Angeles meant the economy could never recover; the last white Californians were leaving for Utah; and so on.

Yet all the while, California's population kept growing faster than the nation's. Net job losses, estimated at over one million, turned out to have been 500,000; while the press headlined every layoff by a large defense contractor, neither the media nor government did a good job of tracking the self-employed or the cash economy. They failed to understand what analyst Joel Kotkin calls "the new economy's dynamism and lack of structure." California's knowledge-intensive industries were still thriving—telecommunications, biomedical research, computer software, medical equipment, entertainment, international trade. Its workers and business owners continued to have the adaptability and suppleness needed to convert adversities into opportunities. California continued to enjoy the advantage of its location on the Pacific Rim, with the fastest economic growth on earth despite Japan's recession. And immigrants, even while scapegoated politically, contributed powerfully to recovery in the 1990s as they had to growth in the 1980s. As Kotkin points out, low housing prices help newcomers move up, and the 10 most common names of California homebuyers include Lee, Martinez, Rodriguez, Garcia, Nguyen and Wong. One-third of Silicon Valley engineers are immigrants; most Orange County technicians are Vietnamese; immigrants from Korea, Iran, Armenia and Israel are upgrading inner Los Angeles neighborhoods. With their help, the California economy began growing again in late 1993; higher interest rates in 1994 didn't depress this interest rate-insensitive economy, as exports rose 15% and jobs 1.3% a year. In April 1994, as his rival Kathleen Brown was running ads showing pictures of the Depression of the 1930s, Governor Wilson was reopening the earthquake-hit Santa Monica Freeway a month ahead of schedule. The money came from much ballyhooed federal aid, but the speed was California ingenuity at work even in government.

California's continuing problem is less economic than one of morale, and morals. Just as the Golden State's physical environment has proved disappointing, with its disasters and choked-up freeways and angry gray skies, so California's bountiful economy and technological creativity have not produced a society that provides the serenity and satisfaction Californians seek. Crime is a preoccupation not just on the evening news—which seldom covers politics or government and spent most of 1994 and 1995 covering the O.J. Simpson case—but in daily life. The loudest noise on many California streets is the dweep of car alarms being activated and the click of house alarm systems being disarmed. The Los Angeles riot provided a moment of terror—only a moment, since the violence was ended in 36 hours when Governor Wilson and President Bush sent in large numbers of troops, in contrast to the five and seven-day riots of the 1960s—and a lingering unease. Los Angeles's civic leaders interpreted it as the product of systematic discrimination against blacks, though its proximate cause was the blunders of police chief Daryl Gates, and California is probably more tolerant and less segregated than any other large state; Los Angeles had a black mayor, Tom Bradley, for nearly 20 years, and in 1982 voters nearly elected him governor. Civic leaders paid little attention to the fact that most rioters arrested were Latinos, mostly from the violence-ridden countries in Central America, and seemed utterly indifferent to the Korean storeowners who worked hard, played by the rules and lost everything. Immigration, a source of so much of California's strength, has also been a source of unease. Vast tracts of city and suburb, once peopled by migrants from the Midwest, are now filled with newcomers from Mexico and Korea, El Salvador and Taiwan, Iran and Armenia; young men stand on streetcorners in affluent areas from dawn, mutely looking for work, sometimes staying all day. The white Anglos who are still the large majority of California's voters watch them uneasily, knowing that most are workers and not criminals, yet fearing that basic rules are no longer being obeyed and that the fundamental order underlying everyday life in any civilized community can no longer be taken for granted.

Political leaders have responded clumsily to California's lack of morale. George Bush tended to ignore California—in his autobiography, he said the few months he lived in the state as a young man were the unhappiest of his life—and was punished by the voters just as they had punished a president of the other party who seemed to have no feel for the state, Jimmy Carter.

Carter's share of California's votes dropped from 48% to 36% between 1976 and 1980; Bush's dropped from 51% to 32% between 1988 and 1992. Bill Clinton, knowing that he could not hope to win the presidency without California's 54 electoral votes, has given California plenty of attention and treated its problems as if they could be solved by a combination of government aid and personal therapy—"I feel your pain." He carried California by the wide margin of 46%–33% and had better poll numbers here than nationally for 18 months. But by summer 1994 California voters were cooling towards him, and in November his job approval was only 47%, just 2% better than nationally, and Republicans won more votes in congressional races than Democrats. Pete Wilson, running for governor in 1990, talked about "preventive government," putting social services into schools to help children. He attacked economic problems, in 1991 passing a major tax increase, in 1992 reducing burdens on business. His job rating plummeted amid recession and disasters, and most observers assumed the new governor would be Treasurer Kathleen Brown, with her soothing proposals to use government to spur economic growth, or possibly Insurance Commissioner John Garamendi, with his harsh attacks on big companies.

But in 1993 Wilson began to emphasize discipline over therapy. He emphasized his support for capital punishment, opposed by Brown and many Democratic legislators but favored by 80% of voters. He attacked the federal government for foisting on California the cost of caring for illegal immigrants in prisons, hospitals and schools. There were other signs of a shift in values. In the June 1993 election for mayor, Los Angeles chose Richard Riordan, a successful businessman who called for privatizing LAX airport and hiring more police, over Councilman Michael Woo, who preached leftish multiculturalism and big government. In June 1994 voters rejected four bond issues, including one for earthquake relief, a sign of lack of confidence in the government aid Clinton and Democratic Senator Dianne Feinstein boasted of providing. That same spring, they responded positively to a TV ad from Republican Senate candidate Michael Huffington promoting William Bennett's *The Book of Virtues*. This struck a chord in a state seeking, if not traditional values, some moral compass or sense of virtue. California is far more secular than most of America, "post-Christian" in Joel Kotkin's phrase, with fewer church members and fewer pillars of traditional morality, a state that has led America in preferring therapy to discipline, getting in touch with oneself to obeying the rules (the ultimate example may be the Menendez trial, where two rich boys escaped conviction for killing their parents by portraying themselves as victims). Huffington, though mostly scorned by media elites and with no record of civic involvement and slender credentials for the office he sought, nonetheless caught the wave of opinion as people searched for order in a California that suddenly seemed—with recession and disasters, crime and illegal immigration—dangerously disorderly. California has long been marvelously tolerant—pro-choice and pro-gay rights, ready to tolerate marijuana use and alternative lifestyles, racially tolerant and inclusive—but in the 1990s, it seemed to be yearning for strong principles, for reasonable rules to be obeyed.

This helps to explain voters' 59%–41% vote in November 1994 for Proposition 187, which would ban state spending on illegal immigrants; opponents made the point that in the short run this would just put students on the street and suggested that backers were acting out of dislike for people with different colored skin. But as Susan Estrich, Michael Dukakis's campaign manager in 1988 and now a law professor at the University of Southern California pointed out, few voters here are bigots and most Proposition 187 supporters just wanted the rules to be obeyed: why should the public pay for people who the law says aren't supposed to be here? "They just keep coming," said one Pete Wilson ad, showing Mexicans illegally crossing the border. Anti-187 Democratic Senators Feinstein and Barbara Boxer and gubernatorial candidate Brown called for tougher border enforcement, which turns out to be eminently feasible: In 1993, deployment of large numbers of Immigration and Naturalization Service patrolmen on the border stopped most illegal immigrants in El Paso, Texas. Curiously, the INS has resisted such tactics, insisting that it can stop more illegals by tracking them down once they are in the United States. Opponents of 187 shrewdly ran ads targeting the measure's details, but they were overshadowed when anti-187 demonstrators in a Los Angeles rally waved huge Mexican flags.

The important lesson here is that 187 was not a vote against immigration, but against illegal immigration—a distinction that Wilson has been careful to make and that ordinary Californians, so many of them immigrants, readily volunteer themselves.

California promises to have another important referendum in 1996, on affirmative action. Two professors are backing a proposition echoing the language of the Civil Rights Act of 1964 and banning use of race and gender in hiring, schooling, and the like. This would outlaw the quotas for blacks, Latinos, Asians and women that are used routinely by government units, universities and corporations. Wilson and other Republicans have come out for the measure, and Democrats like Assembly Speaker Emeritus Willie Brown have been forced to defend it in public policies which they are happier to promote surreptitiously. It may well drive a national debate between presidential candidates, too. If it passes, will it and 187 be taken as attempts to shut people out or as attempts to enforce fair rules?

California in the 1990s has gone through two political revolutions—and may be ready for another. From the election of Reagan as governor in 1966, up through 1990, California voting behavior was steady and, in retrospect at least, predictable. Voters chose Republicans, usually seemingly boring middle-aged men, for their top political offices, while picking Democrats, often baby boom liberals, for the state legislature and Congress. In effect, voters were ratifying the choices they made during the nation's last period of economic turmoil, when they passed property-tax-cutting Proposition 13 in 1978 and elected Reagan president with a solid 53%–36% margin in 1980 and George Deukmejian governor by 49%–48% in 1982. The Republican executives were inert, content to give lip service to traditional values and to watch government coffers fill from the state's economic growth. But the state's Democratic legislators were clandestinely activist, working to further the causes of their clients—like teachers' unions, trial lawyers and the criminal defense bar—in ways that undercut the values the executives were preaching.

In 1990, as the economy started to contract, voters revolted. Gubernatorial candidates Pete Wilson and Dianne Feinstein presented themselves as activist public sector reformers determined to make schools and social services better and ready to impose capital punishment. Wilson won 49%–46%, while voters approved term limits for the legislature—a stunning repudiation of Willie Brown and all his works. Then after two years of economic turmoil and natural disaster, California veered left. They voted for Clinton (and for Ross Perot in significant numbers) rather than Bush; they made this "the year of the woman," as they elected Feinstein overwhelmingly and Boxer narrowly to the U.S. Senate. These were the first top-of-the-ticket Democratic wins since 1978 except for Alan Cranston's easy victory in 1980 and his narrow 1986 reelection. But the 1992 numbers suggested that they were not so much an endorsement of the Democrats as a repudiation of the Republicans, a window of opportunity for the minority party rather than the inauguration of a new majority. Clinton's winning 46% was still less than Dukakis's losing 48%; Clinton ran about even with Dukakis in southern California, but in northern California outside the San Francisco Bay Area—the fastest-growing part of the state since 1980—he won only 39%–36%, while Perot got 21%. Clinton owed his victory as much to Bush's devastating collapse in southern California: Bush only barely carried Orange County, lost San Diego County and the fast-growing Inland Empire of San Bernardino-Riverside, and carried by 38%–35% an area he had carried 63%–36% four years earlier.

But this was not a vote for more government. Californians turned on Clinton as they looked more closely at his healthcare plan, and in November 1994 they voted 73%–27% against a single-payer healthcare initiative just as in November 1990 they rejected the highly regulatory "Big Green" environmental initiative 64%–36%. And as Wilson exalted discipline over therapy and Huffington praised traditional virtues rather than liberation theologies, Californians moved toward Republicans, not just at the top of the ticket, but in other races as well, for the first time since Ronald Reagan's heyday in the late 1960s. Wilson won 55%–41%, the second time he had beaten a member of the same family: he beat Kathleen's brother, Jerry Brown, for U.S. Senate in 1982, 52%–45%. Republicans won most of the statewide offices for the first time since 1966.

The Republican's major disappointment was the election of Lieutenant Governor Gray Davis, who a dozen years before was chief aide to Governor Jerry Brown. Republicans carried elections for U.S. House and California Assembly by identical 49%–48% margins, even though they left a couple of seats in both chambers uncontested. The results here and in most statewide races were eerily similar, statewide and in each region, to the 47%–45% Feinstein-Huffington race. That gave Republicans a three seat gain in the House delegation and a 41–39 majority in the Assembly, much to everyone's surprise—though those had been the intended results of Wilson's successful maneuverings on redistricting in 1991. But Speaker Brown got one renegade Republican assemblyman to vote with him on a ruling that another Republican, who had also been elected to the state Senate, must vacate his seat. Wilson retaliated successfully by recalling the renegade in May 1995 and Brown resigned from the speaker position. He was able to install in his place, however, another Republican renegade, Doris Allen. Brown is barred by term limits from running for the Assembly again in 1996.

Through all this tumult, the basic divides in California's electorate, as to a great extent in the nation as a whole, are cultural. This makes sense in a nation where personal beliefs tend to endure while economic conditions change. The cultural division in California today follows geographical lines, not the historic north-south contrast, but the division that has developed over two decades between coast and inland. Coastal California, the big population gainer in the 1970s, tends toward cultural liberalism. The Big Sur coast or the Redwood Empire, San Francisco and Marin County or Westside Los Angeles—this was the political base of Jerry and Kathleen Brown in the 1992 presidential and 1994 gubernatorial primaries and of Democrats in general elections. But go inland, even a few miles, and the cultural climate changes as rapidly as the weather. This California is sunnier in summer, colder in winter, more arid. And from the Central Valley and the Sierra foothills to the San Ramon Valley, or the "Inland Empire" at the east end of the Los Angeles basin around San Bernardino, Riverside and the desert beyond, this big growth area of the 1980s has attracted cultural conservatives. While coastal California protected itself from growth with environmental restrictions, new subdivisions and factories and cities proliferated inland. This cultural politics turns partisan history on its head. The affluent coastal counties were solidly Republican as late as the 1960s, while the dusty roads of the Central Valley and the inland industrial suburbs were the heartland of the Democratic Party that carried California for Lyndon Johnson in 1964, when Democrats like Governor Pat Brown—Kathleen's dad—stood for building highways and massive water systems and financing universities to uphold American values, not deconstruct them.

Culturally, if no state is more diverse than California, no county is more diverse than Los Angeles County, which is to the America of 1990 what New York City was to the America of 1910: the great entry point for immigrants and the venue of their rapid upward mobility. It is also inevitably, as was New York, messy and disorganized, crime-ridden and anxiety-prone. During the 1980s, Los Angeles County's population zoomed upward, not typical behavior for a central city jurisdiction any time after World War II, but exactly what was happening to New York before World War I. Los Angeles now, like New York then, is the starting point not only of the immigrant but of the small-time entrepreneur—often the same person—who starts a small business in a garage, hires people newly-arrived into town, sells products out of a van, and makes enough money to expand the business and buy a home. Low-lying stucco buildings all over the Los Angeles basin house these businesses, run and staffed by Mexicans, Koreans, Vietnamese, Soviet Jews, Armenians and Iranians. This Los Angeles, like the great surging cities of the past—Dickens's London, Balzac's Paris or Dreiser's New York and Chicago—is not a comfortable place. Traffic is choking; the air has a sour, burnt look. Housing is cramped, with most people living in stucco houses in tightly-packed subdivisions or garden apartments on tiny plots of land that a midwesterner would find claustrophobic. There is increasingly a New Yorkish surliness and lack of neighborliness in daily life.

Los Angeles County was hit hard by 1990s defense cutbacks, the 1992 riot and the 1994 earthquake; but like New York after the panic of 1907 and the Triangle fire of 1911, it surges ahead. Los Angeles's boom, as Joel Kotkin points out, was based less on big defense contractors than on small factories, less on highly visible tenants of downtown office towers than on the self-employed, who are more numerous than union members. Demographically, the areas where blacks and recent Central American migrants rioted are a small part of LA County, far smaller than heavily Mexican East Los Angeles or affluent black Baldwin Hills where there was no rioting. The entrepreneurial impulse among Koreans, Armenians, Iranians and many other newcomers remains vibrant; they have not looked to government for aid as Irish-Americans and African-Americans did historically. As a whole Los Angeles County votes Democratic, and the many Jewish and cultural liberal voters on the Westside plus the rather small number of blacks here remain solidly Democratic. But other groups have become more conservative. Asians moved Republican in 1992—presumably in reaction to civic leaders' sympathy for rioters and indifference toward Asian storeowners—and again in 1994; they would surely have voted for Riordan in 1993 if Woo had not been of Chinese ancestry. Latinos still vote in small numbers, because so many are children or non-citizens: In 1990, one central Los Angeles Assembly district cast only 25,000 votes, while a Westside district that had the same population—but many Anglos and singles—cast 154,000. Latinos are by no means a solid Democratic bloc; in 1994, 22% voted for Wilson in 1994, despite his support of 187; indeed, 22% also voted for 187. Latinos have high rates of family formation and work and low rates of divorce and (outside a few central neighborhoods) crime; they resemble the white Anglo young families who voted for Pat Brown in 1958 and Reagan in 1966.

While Los Angeles fills up with immigrants, the rest of southern California looks more like the Los Angeles of the 1940s: predominantly white, middle class, of midwestern origin, although with more Asians and Hispanics than East Coast experts usually imagine. Essentially, the old Los Angeles has grown out past the freeways into Orange County and the east end of the Los Angeles basin, and out into the desert, past the San Fernando Valley into Ventura County, down south of San Juan Capistrano and Camp Pendleton, where it merges with fast-growing San Diego. Of the four major regions, this is now the most populous, casting 28% of the state's votes, with 350,000 more votes than LA County in 1992. Until the early 1990s Southern California radiated the optimism, the somewhat innocent confidence and the know-how of its pioneers, contemporaries of its natural hero, Reagan, who came out here in hard times and created a new Middle America more tidy and square and cheerful than the original Middle America ever was. Then it soured—first on the Republicans for their indifference and next on the Democrats for their indiscipline. In 1992, Southern California outside LA voted only 38%–35%–24% for Bush over Clinton and Perot. In 1994 it voted 68% for Proposition 187 and 65%–31% for Wilson over Brown. This is the most Republican part of the state now, and one of the most Republican parts of America again.

A very different cultural atmosphere animates the San Francisco Bay area. Here is an affluent, high-tech civilization preoccupied with the physical environment and self-realization. The Bay Area is environmentalist, dovish and therapy-minded, but not much interested in income redistribution; this fifth largest American metropolitan area refutes Karl Marx's economic theories of politics, since it is arguably the richest of America's great metropolises and also one of the most Democratic. For years, not just San Francisco, but the East Bay and the Peninsula, attracted those who felt their personal lifestyles were not accepted elsewhere or who relished the atmosphere of counter-culture and revolt here that has roots in the turn-of-the-century artists and writers and the Beat Generation of the 1950s—gays and perpetual graduate students, radicals and perennial rebels. It has lots of voters with graduate degrees—the most Democratic educational group in California—and they voted 55%–27% for Clinton over Bush in 1992, similar to his 55%–24% Bay Area margin. California's Democratic base is made up less of blacks and factory workers than it is of teachers, lawyers, nurses, environmental enthusiasts and public sector administrators. The Bay Area majority must have hoped after 1992 that it was leading opinion in the state, as voters chose for the Senate Dianne Feinstein, longtime (1978–87) mayor of San Francisco, and Barbara Boxer, who got her political start on the Marin County

Board of Supervisors. But in 1994 Feinstein had to scramble to get reelected, and Boxer is widely regarded as a political endangered species.

The fastest-growing part of California in recent years has been northern California outside the Bay Area. There are some eight million people here, more than in North Carolina or Massachusetts; the media markets of Sacramento and Fresno in the Central Valley, if added together, would be the ninth largest in the country. This is the most culturally conservative part of the state; many new residents are young families fleeing from the smog and crime of the Los Angeles basin to the cleaner and safer Central Valley or Mother Lode country or Sacramento area. They have helped turn this historically Democratic area toward the Republicans; John Kennedy carried it in 1960, but Pete Wilson beat Kathleen Brown here 61%–35% in 1994.

Where is California headed? In partisan terms, toward Republicans, but not by any wide margin, and not irrevocably; Bill Clinton certainly has this state targeted for 1996, and he should run ahead of his national average here. Economically, California seems headed for growth again; with its creativity, suppleness, Pacific Rim location and brains, it cannot be kept permanently down. Culturally, Californians have moved some distance from therapy toward discipline; having looked into the abyss, in Gertrude Himmelfarb's phrase, they seek to enforce basic rules and strengthen the order without which decent lives are not possible. But there is a danger that California voters, in their desire to punish criminals, restore national borders and treat people as individuals rather than as members of victim groups, will forget the traditions of openness, friendliness and optimism which are so central to the success of their state.

Governor. Pete Wilson is completing the third decade of a political career that has been extraordinarily successful—and may be even more so—but that has attracted little notice outside California. In two successive elections in 1988 and 1990, he won more votes for senator than anyone else in history and was elected governor of the nation's largest state; in 1994 he was reelected 55%–41% after trailing by 23% in the polls. Like so many Californians, Wilson grew up back East; after attending Yale on scholarship, he came to Camp Pendleton as a Marine and to Boalt Hall in Berkeley as a law student—seeing two very different parts of California—and then settled in San Diego. He was elected to the Assembly in 1966 and became mayor of San Diego in 1971; he was known as a problem solver and moderate, supporting Gerald Ford over Ronald Reagan in 1976, opposing Proposition 13 in 1978. He ran for governor in 1978 and finished fourth in the primary with 9%, about the San Diego media market's share of the statewide vote. In 1982, he ran for senator, won a five-candidate primary with 38%, and beat outgoing Governor Jerry Brown in the general. Brown was under attack for refusing to use a harmless pesticide to subdue the citrus-destroying Mediterranean fruit fly, and Wilson's 52%–45% win was typical of Republican top-of-the-ticket margins in the 1980s. In the Senate Wilson opposed coastal oil drilling, but favored agribusiness positions inland. He enthusiastically backed the Reagan defense buildup and took up the role of defending California interests that Alan Cranston let slip while running for president in 1983. In 1988 he was reelected 53%–44%. When Governor George Deukmejian announced he was retiring in 1990, Republican leaders, fearful of giving Democrats full control of redistricting, urged Wilson to run. He agreed: being governor was his first choice all along.

He did not get a free ride. The Democratic nominee was Dianne Feinstein, former mayor of San Francisco, who beat the more liberal Attorney General John Van de Kamp 52%–41% by stressing her support of abortion rights and capital punishment. Her first TV spot recalled how she took charge when Mayor George Moscone and Supervisor Harvey Milk were murdered in 1978; after her primary win, she was hailed as a possible national candidate. Wilson and Feinstein sounded similar and in fact had worked together: both were pro-choice and pro-death penalty, pro-defense spending and against offshore oil drilling. Both spoke of actively using government to help children. Referenda made a difference, as they often do in California; Wilson supported term limits, which passed 52%–48%; Feinstein backed Tom Hayden's Big Green, which lost 64%–36%. Wilson won 49%–46%, with Feinstein carrying only the San Francisco Bay Area and other coastal areas.

In office, Wilson was confronted with recession and revenue shortfalls and backed a major tax increase in 1991, which alienated many conservative Republicans. Gays were angered when he vetoed a gay rights law in 1991; conservatives were angered when he signed another in 1992. In that year Wilson and the legislature wrangled for months over the budget, which in California must be approved by a two-thirds vote; they also passed some of his "preventive government" programs, but there were no vast new sums for California's tattered public school systems or its sometimes suffering infrastructure. Wilson bitterly attacked the Democratic legislature for its softness on crime, its obeisance to trial lawyers and the absurdly expensive workmen's comp system which paid benefits (and lawyers' fees) for psychological loss—the logical outgrowth of the goofiness that produced a legislative task force on self-esteem. Wilson was surely correct that high costs were sending a lot of businesses elsewhere, often to booming Rocky Mountain states like Nevada and Utah, but his criticisms may have accelerated the migration. Wilson was disappointed when his redistricting plans failed to produce anticipated Republican gains in 1992 (they would, however, in 1994) and when voters turned down a welfare measure he put on the ballot. But he may have noted that voters were also leery of higher taxes, repealing his snack tax 67%–33% and rejecting the Democrats' soak-the-rich initiative 59%–41%; in 1993 he worked with Willie Brown and other legislators to reduce taxes and regulations and reform workmen's comp.

It was widely assumed that Wilson was finished, and Kathleen Brown started her campaign with the assumption that 1994 would be like 1992, another "Year of the (Democratic) Woman," in which an electorate tired of a lackluster Republican executive indifferent to a troubled economy would embrace an energetic woman. But Brown was weak on details when she got off message. Her primary opponent, Insurance Commissioner John Garamendi, a onetime Berkeley quarterback and Peace Corps volunteer, attacked her sharply for opposing the death penalty—a sore issue in her family: her father as San Francisco district attorney and governor carried out the death penalty, but in his old age wrote a book regretting it; Jerry Brown as governor vetoed death penalties and appointed Rose Bird, a chief justice who voted to overturn every death penalty verdict before her. Kathleen Brown said she opposed the death penalty but would carry it out. This might have defeated her even among Democrats, except that Garamendi ran out of money and went off the air; Brown won 48%–33%. Meanwhile, Wilson was fending off a challenge from conservative Ron Unz, a 32-year old computer millionaire, who held him to a 61%–34% majority. But exit polls showed Unz voters would happily support Wilson over Brown, while half of Garamendi voters would also support Wilson over Brown. In other words, Wilson was ahead by June. He relentlessly pressed his advantage, stressing capital punishment over and over again and calling for the federal government to reimburse California for services to illegal immigrants. He came out for Proposition 187, designed to cut state spending on illegals, while Brown opposed it—and pointed out correctly that the immigration law provision sponsored in 1986 by Wilson (and then-Rep. Leon Panetta) to admit farm workers is how many illegals got to California in the first place. In November, Wilson easily won 55%–41%. He ran ahead of his 1990 showing and was especially strong in the Central Valley and the Mother Lode country in the foothills of the Sierra, beating Brown outside the big metropolitan areas.

Early in his second term Wilson went on the offensive against the federal government, suing it for unfunded mandates on services for illegal immigrants before Washington could sue him for refusing to spend state money enforcing the federal "motor-voter" act. (California's Democrats had already made voter registration much easier; one result is that the Mexican who murdered presidential candidate Luis Donaldo Colosio is a registered Democrat in Long Beach.) He was frustrated in translating Replicans' 41–39 edge in the Assembly into control, but by early 1995 he seemed likely to prevail. Indeed, he and his allies seems to be dismantling the Democratic system of control. Term limits are important here: Democrats kept control of the legislature for years by monopolizing information and campaign funds and by grooming staffers to step into their places when they retired. Term limits will force them out, as Brown will be forced out of the Assembly in 1996. Wilson—and the flagging economy—have also cut the growth in state government that proceeded through the 1980s under Republican executives. As Wilson points out, under the projections made when he took office, state spending in 1995 would have been $60 billion; instead it is $40 billion. For 1995 Wilson was proposing a 15% cut in taxes and was taking aim at laws favoring trial lawyers. A Democratic regime that continued, despite Ronald Reagan, for one-third of a century after Pat Brown's election in 1958 seemed to be coming to an end.

Up through the 1994 campaign, Wilson said he would not run for president; afterwards, he dropped the denials, even though Democrat Gray Davis had been elected lieutenant governor. In late March 1995, Wilson formed an exploratory committee, was backed by Governor William Weld in April, and made his official announcement in May. It was then revealed that Wilson and his ex-wife hired an undocumented Mexican domestic worker in the late 1970s. But, Wilson is undeniably able, disciplined and hard-working; he is a fighter, with gritty determination and few illusions, curiously unoptimistic and unsunny for a Californian, but not a hater or one fixated on his adversaries. He takes pro-choice and some pro-gay rights stands almost for granted, which may be natural for a Californian; he is exceedingly tough on crime and contemptuous of criminals, which may be natural for a man whose grandfather was a policeman killed in the line of duty. He seems serious, even plodding, on TV, but he and his wife sing duets, of songs they've written themselves. Without becoming well-known nationally and without an enthusiastic core constituency, he has become a major influence in national politics, one entitled to take some satisfaction in welcoming the 1996 Republican National Convention to his chosen home town of San Diego.

Senators. California has two Democratic senators, both women, both from the San Francisco Bay Area, both first elected in 1992, both with considerable talents. But neither is politically invincible. Dianne Feinstein, elected 54%–38% to Pete Wilson's unexpired term in 1992, nearly lost to the previously unknown Michael Huffington in 1994. Barbara Boxer, elected by 48%–43% in a good Democratic year, has made one of the most liberal records in Congress and must depend on some major turn in public opinion to be reelected in 1998.

Twenty years ago, Dianne Feinstein was a member of the San Francisco County Board of Supervisors, a moderate Democrat whose training was in criminology, appointed by Governor Pat Brown to the women's parole board in 1960; in 1992, she was elected to the United States Senate with more votes than any other senator in American history. In between, her government service was entirely in San Francisco, a sometimes daffily leftish city where she was a force for moderation, backing more police and the death penalty, vetoing a gay marriage ordinance and opposing commercial rent control. In taking over as mayor after the murders of Mayor Moscone and Supervisor Milk in 1978, she showed steadiness and a sense of command that calmed the city. In 1984, Walter Mondale seriously considered her for vice president, passing over her for Geraldine Ferraro because of qualms about the business dealings of her husband, Richard Blum. Feinstein presided gracefully that year over the Democratic National Convention in San Francisco—while Ferraro juggled questions about *her* family's business. In fact, Feinstein and Blum's investments have thrived; the Capitol Hill newspaper *Roll Call* estimated their net worth in 1995 at $50 million, the fourth highest in Congress. Ineligible for a third full term in 1987, Feinstein ran for governor in 1990, won the Democratic primary impressively, then lost 49%–46% to Pete Wilson. When Wilson appointed Orange County state Senator John Seymour—an unknown and colorless choice—to replace him, Feinstein quickly announced for the seat, even though the 1992 race was for only the last two years of Wilson's term, and she could have run for the seat being vacated by Alan Cranston the same year. Presumably, she wanted to forestall primary competition and guarantee herself an easy reelection two years later.

Feinstein won, but she had primary competition in 1992 and a tough race in 1994. Seymour turned out to be a disappointment to Republicans. He was pro-choice, but only because he just switched on the issue, just as he switched to oppose offshore oil drilling after the Exxon *Valdez* crash; his statewide electoral experience was losing the 1990 primary for lieutenant governor. He was mistrusted on the right and was challenged in the primary by a fellow Orange Countian, the conservative Congressman William Dannemeyer; but he won no backing on the left, either.

Feinstein was opposed by Controller (and now Lieutenant Governor) Gray Davis, who ran a spot focusing on her apparent violations of campaign finance laws in 1990 and comparing her to Leona Helmsley; that raised some hackles, and she won solidly 58%–33%. Nothing worked for Seymour—not Feinstein's arguably tricky financing of her 1990 gubernatorial campaign (which resulted in a $190,000 fine), nor fears of immigration, nor recoil against the 1992 Los Angeles riot, nor Seymour's tending to agricultural interests. California was determined to embrace the Democrats' core constituency, and Feinstein won 54%–38%. She won 59% in Los Angeles County, 68% in the Bay Area, and almost carried Southern California, losing 44%–47%.

California has a long tradition of having one senator who expresses ideological views and another who works hard to represent the state's economic interests. Feinstein chose the latter workhorse role, as did Pete Wilson, Alan Cranston and Thomas Kuchel before. She got a seat on the Appropriations Committee, where she could funnel money to California, and on the Judiciary Committee, where she was one of the women chosen by then-chairman Joseph Biden sought to spare him the flak he got for allowing cross-examination of Anita Hill. Feinstein has a generally but not uniformly liberal voting record; she also has a tough, prosecutorial demeanor, and on the podium she is one of the best speakers in American politics today. She has usually been an ally of the Clinton Administration, but not always an uncritical one. She wangled changes to help California in the 1993 Clinton budget and tax proposal before she supported it. She voted against the North American Free Trade Agreement. Despite being one of the 30 original co-sponsors of the Clinton healthcare plan, she quietly withdrew her support in May 1994. She supported the Clinton crime bill enthusiastically, in large part because she succeeded in attaching her assault weapon ban to it—one of two major legislative achievements in her two-year term. When Idaho's Larry Craig argued that her definition of assault weapons was not rigorous and challenged her knowledge of firearms, she responded by saying: "I know something about what firearms can do; I came to be Mayor of San Francisco as a product of assassination." The measure was good politics for her, but it helped split apart the Democratic party in the House in August 1994. Feinstein's other major achievement was a California desert protection act. Similar measures had been stymied by the state's Republican senators as too restrictive, but now that there was no Republican senator, Feinstein managed it through enactment. In October 1994, the retiring Republican Malcolm Wallop of Wyoming tried to kill the bill by end-of-session filibuster, but other senators, apparently sympathetic to Feinstein's case or her political plight, passed it.

Feinstein surely hoped that she would face weak competition in 1994 and that her early and hard work raising money would enable her to win essentially unopposed. But then came Michael Huffington, with the determination and the cash to be the biggest spending Senate candidate of all time. Huffington grew up in modest circumstances in Houston, graduated from Stanford and Harvard Business School and made his fortune in his father's oil and natural gas business. In 1988 his wife Arianna Stassinopolous, a biographer of Maria Callas and Pablo Picasso, moved to Santa Barbara, and he commuted there from Houston; in 1991 he moved, too, and immediately ran against 18-year Republican Congressman Robert Lagomarsino. Huffington spent over $3 million in the 1992 primary and attacked Lagomarsino for intervening on behalf of a firm selling torture instruments to the Chinese—the kind of constituent service that congressmen usually brag about. Huffington won the primary 49%–43% and the general 53%–35%. In the 103d Congress, he was quiet and uninfluential, like most Republican freshman, and had a fairly liberal voting record. Nothing made him a plausible Senate candidate but his money—and his message. Huffington started off with an ad in which he promoted William Bennett's *The Book of Virtues*, addressing Californians' sense of moral deficiency; he followed by attacking Feinstein for providing the deciding vote for the 1993 tax increase, which of course hit Californians quite heavily with their high nominal incomes. Feinstein ran an ad accusing Huffington of refusing to act as an advocate for Raytheon in Congress, a company located in his district; he responded with an ad showing that Feinstein had received contributions from the same company and that she immediately wrote letters to government agencies on behalf of the company. This was political jujitsu, using her strength of constituency service to prove his claim that she was a "career politician."

Feinstein was clearly flustered and angry that a politician who had put in so little time and effort had pulled even with her in the polls by September, and that she could not count on heavily outspending her opponent, even using her own money, as so many incumbent Democrats were used to doing. By her own standards and those of voters in 1992, she had done an excellent job; shouldn't that be enough? The press took an intense dislike to Huffington and his wife, calling her the "Sir Edmund Hillary of social climbing" and the front page of The *Los Angeles Times* took on the appearance of an anti-Huffington bulletin board, with stories about Arianna's involvement with the Movement for Spiritual Awareness (MSIA) and that the Huffingtons had a racially restrictive covenant on their property, though, as it turned out, so did Feinstein. (Many of these covenants have been on the books for ages, but now mostly go ignored.)

It was suggested that Huffington was some kind of programmed automaton, though his two campaigns with different consultants advanced similar ideas and used similar tactics, and he seems about as intelligent and articulate as Jay Rockefeller or Herb Kohl, who spent larger sums per capita of their own money to be elected senators from West Virginia or Wisconsin. But the result did not hinge on these things. In October, Huffington made a big point of endorsing Proposition 187; Feinstein was opposed to it. Then it was revealed that the Huffingtons had employed an illegal alien as a nanny. Huffington's poll numbers went down. On the Thursday before the election, it was revealed that Feinstein, despite her earlier denials, had employed a woman whose work permit had expired. But the news media ran stories saying that federal officials cast doubt on whether the woman was an illegal. This alibi turned out to be false, but it probably made the difference; it is a sign of Democratic weakness that Feinstein, for all her strength and achievements, was reelected with the help of the Clinton Administration. Feinstein won 47%–45%, carrying the Bay Area 63%–30% and Los Angeles County 52%–40%—a nasty drop from 1992. Huffington carried the south 56%–35% and the north outside the Bay Area 51%–40%.

Feinstein seems sure to remain an active and influential senator and must surely be relieved at not having to run a fourth statewide campaign in 1996—especially since she will not have to explain to the voters her early 1995 vote reversing her earlier support for the balanced-budget constitutional amendment. The Huffingtons remain active in Washington, and he also retained a presence in California, where he says he plans to run again, either against Feinstein in 2000 or against Boxer or for governor in 1998. Indeed, in 1995 Huffington had already begun running the first negative campaign ads of the 2000 election cycle.

California's junior senator is Barbara Boxer, by most measures one of the most liberal members of Congress. Boxer grew up in Brooklyn, where she was sexually harassed by a professor and was refused work as a stockbroker; she moved to California in 1965 and worked on civic and political campaigns and ultimately for Democratic Congressman John Burton. In 1972 she ran for the Marin County Board of Supervisors, in the ultra-trendy suburbs nestled between Mount Tamalpais and the Bay, north of the Golden Gate Bridge. She lost, but in 1976, when woman candidates were more accepted, she won a seat on the board. Boxer is energetic, good-humored, unafraid to challenge authority but able to work harmoniously with others. When Burton retired unexpectedly in 1982, she ran for the House and was easily elected. She made many splashes in the House, unearthing the Air Force's $7,622 coffee pot in 1984, denouncing the Persian Gulf war with more ardor than anyone, and leading a march of angry women on the Senate when Anita Hill was testifying against Clarence Thomas. She also compiled the highest-dollar voting record in the House on spending in 1992.

Boxer began the 1992 Senate campaign not as the best-known or best-financed candidate, but as the most distinctive in a year in which the enthusiasm of the feminist left energized the Democratic Party and sped it to victory. In the Democratic primary, she faced Lieutenant Governor Leo McCarthy, who had high name identification after four statewide races, and Congressman Mel Levine, who had strong financial backing from the so-called "Berman-

Waxman machine" on Los Angeles's Westside. Levine ran tough ads in favor of the Gulf war resolution and taking a tough stand against the Los Angeles riot, but only managed to alienate liberal voters—who went to Boxer—without winning over moderates who stuck with the better-known but more liberal McCarthy. Boxer, despite 143 overdrafts at the House bank, won with 44% of the vote, to 31% for McCarthy and 22% for Levine. Her general election opponent was Bruce Herschensohn, a Los Angeles TV and radio commentator, Nixon speechwriter and Reagan enthusiast, backer of a flat tax and offshore oil drilling and opponent of abortion. Herschensohn had edged Silicon Valley moderate Congressman Tom Campbell 38%–36% in the primary, with the help of then-Palm Springs Mayor Sonny Bono, who picked up 17% of the vote. The Boxer-Herschensohn race was a battle of opposites, the far left versus the far right of the American electoral spectrum. Herschensohn ran an effective ad attacking Boxer for charging the government $1,565 for limousine service to the airport, and his gentle, friendly persona contrasted with Boxer's avoidance of unguarded public appearances. But Boxer was helped by the collapse of the Bush candidacy in California, by hearty support from Feinstein and by the revelation by the state Democratic political director during the last week of the campaign that Herschensohn attended nude dancer night clubs. Herschensohn was the only statewide Republican who rallied a big margin in the south outside LA County, and he ran well enough there to carry southern California as a whole; he also carried the north outside the Bay Area. But he lost the Bay Area 61%–30%, and lost statewide 48%–43%.

As Senator, Boxer serves not on the Judiciary Committee she once stormed but on the Budget, Banking and Environment and Public Works Committees—where she had few notable accomplishments in her first two years. In contrast to Feinstein, she is more of a Capitol Hill insider. She had hoped to win a Finance Committee seat by playing an active role in the 1994 contest to select the new Senate Democratic leader but she failed after siding with the losing candidate, Chris Dodd, against Tom Daschle. Her voting record continues to be on the left, but she has also worked to save Edwards Air Force Base by linking it with others, and she got funds appropriated for National Guard troops to patrol the Mexican border, though by August 1994 no troops had been assigned there. She defended the Clintons against scandal charges in the 1994 Whitewater hearings; her warm feelings toward them may have been understandably strengthened by the fact that her daughter married Hillary Rodham Clinton's brother in a White House wedding. In 1995, she said that loan guarantees to Mexico should be conditioned on cooperation on stopping illegal immigration. It is widely assumed in California political circles that Boxer cannot be reelected in 1998, and many Republicans are lining up to run against her, hoping that a plurality primary win can catapult them into the Senate. But if opinion shifts again as sharply as it has already in California in the 1990s, Boxer could reemerge as a strong competitor.

Presidential politics. With 54 electoral votes, California is the gorilla of American politics: it may be geographically far away from all the other action, but you ignore it at your peril. In the 1970s and 1980s, it was the state that Republicans had to carry to win the White House; they did so handily when they nominated Californians—Richard Nixon in 1972 and Ronald Reagan in 1980 and 1984—but they lost the state in 1976 and won it by only a narrow margin in 1988 when they didn't. Now it is the Democrats who cannot afford to lose California. Bill Clinton, leading in California polls by wide margins, was able to prospect for votes in the Midwest and South in 1992; now, with southern electoral votes seemingly out of reach, he must carry California in 1996 or relinquish any hope of winning.

California reacts strongly against presidents who seem to neglect it: Jimmy Carter got 36% here in 1980, George Bush 33% in 1992. It also tends to cast lower than average percentages for national landslide winners (Johnson in 1964, Nixon in 1972, Reagan in 1984), as if it were in a hurry to get to the next national trend before everyone else. The great Democratic success of 1992, followed by the Republican recoil of 1994, looks like the same pattern. That must seem ominous for Clinton, who entered the White House determined not to make Bush's and Carter's mistake. He has visited California frequently, showered it with federal aid and kept in particularly close touch with the Hollywood figures whose company he obviously likes to keep. For 18 months it worked, and his popularity here was well above national levels. Then in 1994 it foundered.

Where is California going next? Start with the cultural issues always important here. California has been open to liberation movements, even when it has been market-oriented on economics, and it is the most secular and least churched of the megastates. Of the major sources of energy in the two parties in 1992—the feminist left and the religious right—California had no problem embracing the former and scorning the latter. But in 1994, California seemed to be yearning for virtues more than self-esteem, moving away from therapy and toward discipline: toward strictly enforcing rules against crime and illegal immigration and racial quotas. This clearly does not help Clinton, who can plausibly claim to be somewhere near the midpoint on the continuums between socialism and free markets and between tradition and liberation, but who appears to be all therapy and no discipline. On economics, California is not on the left: it has rejected big-government solutions on health and the environment and taxation, and its high nominal incomes and large number of small businesses and self-employed people lead it to value free markets even if its articulate elites do not. But the numbers do not permit any strong prediction. Even if the 1994 trend continues into 1996—and remember that Democrats suffered here because they assumed the 1992 trend would continue into 1994—Republicans have no overwhelming strength. In 1994, they carried statewide and district races by an average margin of only 48%–45%, no landslide. It is generally assumed that Republicans will carry the state if Pete Wilson is on the ticket, and certainly his hard-edged, unsentimental style embodies the discipline California seeks. But it should be remembered that he has no personally loyal core constituency (the unknown Ron Unz got 34% against him in the 1994 Republican primary) and is more respected than loved by most voters.

California's presidential primary was held for years in June, and it often attracted national attention, as when Robert Kennedy beat Eugene McCarthy in 1968 or when George McGovern edged Hubert Humphrey in 1972. But since 1976, the primary has not mattered much, and for 1996 the legislature rescheduled it to March 26. It is still the latest of the early primaries, and so possibly a clincher and possibly an irrelevancy.

Congressional districting. California grows so fast and is so populous that redistricting matters here more than anywhere else. The tradition of partisan redistricting goes way back: Republicans drew the lines to their advantage in the 1940s and 1950s, Democrats in the 1960s, 1970s and 1980s, as the California House delegation grew from 23 in the 1940s to 30, 38, 43, 45 and 52, the largest for any state in history. The great genius of redistricting here was Democratic Congressman Phillip Burton, who dominated the line-drawing for House seats and state Senate and Assembly as well; his 1982 plan, slightly revised for 1984–90, left Democrats in secure control of the delegation even though he died in 1983. Thus, in 1984 Democrats had a 27–18 edge in the House delegation, even though Republicans won the popular vote 49%–48%. In contrast, in 1994, when Republicans won the popular vote again 49%–48%, the district lines again produced 27 Democrats but now also 25 Republicans.

The man who made the difference more than anyone else was Governor Pete Wilson, elected in 1990; he was a hard-nosed bargainer with the Democratic legislature in 1991 and persuaded the state Supreme Court (Republican since voters threw out three Jerry Brown appointees in 1986) to adopt a plan drawn up by his appointed commission in 1992. This was a relatively evenhanded plan, with generally regular boundaries. There are no black-majority districts (California is only 7% black, and the Los Angeles area's former black ghettos are now heavily Hispanic) and seven Hispanic-majority districts (though in at least three of them, few Hispanics are registered to vote and the congressmen's names are Dooley, Berman, and Dornan). The state also includes five districts that are 20% or more Asian—but these are not the districts that elect the state's two Japanese American and one Korean-American congressmen.

92   CALIFORNIA

The People: Est. Pop. 1994: 31,431,000; Pop. 1990: 29,760,021, up 5,6% 1990–1994. 12.1% of U.S. total, 1st largest; 7% rural. Median age: 31.5 years. 10.5% 65 years and over. 69.0% White, 25.8% Hispanic origin, 9.6% Asian, 7.4% Black, 13.2% Other. Households: 52.7% married couple families; 26% married couple fams. w. children; 54% college educ.; median household income: $35,798; per capita income: $16,409; 55.6% owner occupied housing; median house value: $195,500; median monthly rent: $561. 9.1% Unemployment. 1994 Voting age pop.: 23,225,000. 1994 Turnout: 7,881,562; 34% of VAP. Registered voters (1994): 14,723,784; 7,219,635 D (49%); 5,472,391 R (37%); 1,566,144 unaffiliated and minor parties (11%).

Political Lineup: Governor, Pete Wilson (R); Lt. Gov., Gray Davis (D); Secy. of State, Bill Jones (R); Atty. Gen., Daniel E. Lungren (R); Treasurer, Matt Fong (D); Controller, Kathleen Connell (D). State Senate, 40 (21 D, 17 R, 2 I); State Assembly, 80 (40 R, 39 D and 1 vacancy). Senators, Dianne Feinstein (D) and Barbara Boxer (D). Representatives, 52 (25 R and 27 D).

1992 Presidential Vote

Clinton (D)	5,121,249	(46%)
Bush (R)	3,630,566	(33%)
Perot (I)	2,296,004	(21%)

1992 Democratic Presidential Primary

Clinton	1,359,112	(47%)
Brown	1,150,460	(40%)
Tsongas	212,522	(7%)
Other	141,515	(5%)

1988 Presidential Vote

Bush (R)	5,054,917	(51%)
Dukakis (D)	4,702,233	(48%)

1992 Republican Presidential Primary

Bush	1,587,369	(74%)
Buchanan	568,892	(26%)

GOVERNOR

Gov. Pete Wilson (R)

Elected 1990, term expires Jan. 1999; b. Aug. 23, 1933, Lake Forest, IL; home, San Diego; Yale, B.A. 1955, U. of CA at Berkeley, J.D. 1962; Presbyterian; married (Gayle).

Career: Marine Corps, 1955–58; Practicing atty., 1963–66; CA Assembly, 1966–71, Minority Whip, 1967–69; San Diego Mayor, 1970–83; U.S. Senate, 1982–90.

Office: State Capitol Bldg., Sacramento 95814, 916-445-2841; Fax: 916-445-4633.

Election Results

1994 gen.	Pete Wilson (R)	4,777,674	(55%)
	Kathleen Brown (D)	3,517,777	(41%)
	Others	363,430	(4%)
1994 prim.	Pete Wilson (R)	1,266,832	(61%)
	Ron Unz (R)	707,431	(34%)
	Others	87,528	(4%)
1990 gen.	Pete Wilson (R)	3,791,904	(49%)
	Dianne Feinstein (D)	3,525,197	(46%)
	Other	383,316	(5%)

SENATORS

Sen. Dianne Feinstein (D)

Elected 1992, seat up 2000; b. June 22, 1933, San Francisco; home, San Francisco; Stanford U., B.A. 1955; Jewish; married (Richard C. Blum).

Career: CA Women's Parole Bd., 1960–66; San Francisco Bd. of Supervisors, 1970–78, Pres., 1970–71, 1974–75, 1978; San Francisco Mayor, 1978–88.

DC Office: 331 HSOB 20510, 202-224-3841; Fax: 202-228-3954.

State Offices: 1700 Montgomery St., #305, San Francisco 94111, 415-249-4777; 750 B St., #1030, San Diego 92101, 619-231-9712; 11111 Santa Monica Blvd., #915, Los Angeles 90025, 310-914-7300; and 1130 O St., #4015, Fresno 93721, 209-485-7430.

Committees: *Foreign Relations* (8th of 8 D): African Affairs; East Asian and Pacific Affairs; Near Eastern and South Asian Affairs (RMM). *Judiciary* (7th of 8 D): Immigration; Terrorism, Technology and Government Information. *Rules & Administration* (7th of 7 D).

Group Ratings

	ADA	ACLU	COPE	CFA	LCV	CON	NSI	COC	ACU	NTLC	CHC
1994	70	63	63	67	77	28	40	24	8	20	8
1993	85	—	100	80	63	22	—	9	13	—	—

National Journal Ratings

	1993 LIB — 1993 CONS		1994 LIB — 1994 CONS	
Economic	55%	— 44%	72%	— 18%
Social	68%	— 29%	66%	— 32%
Foreign	64%	— 35%	51%	— 46%

Key Votes of the 103d Congress

1. Clinton Deficit Plan	Y	3. Brady Handgun Purchase	Y	5. Lmt. UN Cmnd. of Forces	N
2. NAFTA	N	4. Strike Race/Death Pnlty.	Y	6. Cut Missile Funds	N

Key Votes of the 104th Congress

1. Congressional Compliance	Y	3. Balanced Budget Amndt.	N	5. Product Liability Reform	Y
2. Bar Unfunded Mandates	Y	4. Pass Line Item Veto	Y	6. FY96 Budget	N

Election Results

1994 general	Dianne Feinstein (D)	3,977,063	(47%)	($14,407,179)
	Michael Huffington (R)	3,811,501	(45%)	($29,969,695)
	Others	714,500	(8%)	
1994 primary	Dianne Feinstein (D)	1,635,837	(74%)	
	Ted Andromidas (D)	297,128	(13%)	
	Daniel O'Dowd (D)	271,615	(12%)	
1992 general	Dianne Feinstein (D)	5,853,621	(54%)	($8,054,222)
	John Seymour (R)	4,093,488	(38%)	($6,849,805)
	Five Others	832,581	(8%)	
1992 primary	Dianne Feinstein (D)	1,775,730	(58%)	
	Gray Davis (D)	1,009,761	(33%)	
	David Kearns (D)	149,918	(5%)	
	Joseph M. Alioto (D)	139,410	(5%)	

Sen. Barbara Boxer (D)

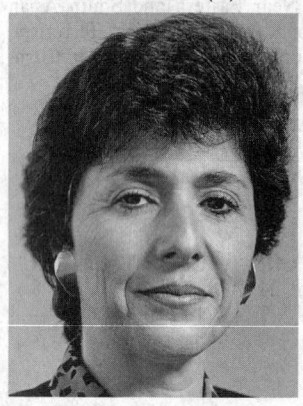

Elected 1992, seat up 1998; b. Nov. 11, 1940, Brooklyn, NY; home, Greenbrae; Brooklyn Col., B.A. 1962; Jewish; married (Stewart).

Career: Stockbroker, researcher, 1962–65; Journalist, *Pacific Sun*, 1972–74; Dist. aide, U.S. Rep. John Burton, 1974–76; Marin Cnty. Bd. of Supervisors, 1976–82; U.S. House of Reps., 1982–92.

DC Office: 112 HSOB 20510, 202-224-3553; Fax: 202-228-0026.

State Offices: 1700 Montgomery St., #240, San Francisco 94111, 415-403-0100; and 2250 E. Imperial Hwy., #545, El Segundo 90245, 310-414-5700.

Committees: *Banking, Housing & Urban Affairs* (5th of 7 D): Financial Institutions and Regulatory Relief; International Finance (RMM); Securities. *Budget* (9th of 10 D). *Environment & Public Works* (7th of 7 D): Clean Air, Wetlands, Private Property and Nuclear Safety; Drinking Water, Fisheries and Wildlife; Superfund, Waste Control and Risk Assessment.

Group Ratings

	ADA	ACLU	COPE	CFA	LCV	CON	NSI	COC	ACU	NTLC	CHC
1994	95	74	88	83	100	26	0	20	0	12	0
1993	90	—	91	90	88	16	—	9	12	—	—

National Journal Ratings

	1993 LIB — 1993 CONS		1994 LIB — 1994 CONS	
Economic	70% —	29%	84% —	0%
Social	79% —	19%	75% —	24%
Foreign	78% —	13%	78% —	15%

Key Votes of the 103d Congress

1. Clinton Deficit Plan	Y	3. Brady Handgun Purchase	Y	5. Lmt. UN Cmnd. of Forces	N
2. NAFTA	N	4. Strike Race/Death Pnlty.	N	6. Cut Missile Funds	Y

Key Votes of the 104th Congress

1. Congressional Compliance	Y	3. Balanced Budget Amndt.	N	5. Product Liability Reform	N
2. Bar Unfunded Mandates	N	4. Pass Line Item Veto	N	6. FY96 Budget	N

Election Results

1992 general	Barbara Boxer (D)	5,173,443	(48%)	($10,415,811)
	Bruce Herschensohn (R)...............	4,644,139	(43%)	($7,649,072)
	Six Others.........................	981,781	(9%)	
1992 primary	Barbara Boxer (D)	1,339,126	(44%)	
	Leo McCarthy (D)	935,209	(31%)	
	Mel Levine (D)......................	667,359	(22%)	
	Charles Greene (D)...................	122,954	(4%)	
1986 general	Alan Cranston (D)	3,646,672	(50%)	($11,037,707)
	Ed Zschau (R)	3,541,804	(47%)	($11,781,316)

FIRST DISTRICT

The North Coast of California is unlike any other place in America. It is the only part of the Lower 48 states first settled by Russians, who built Fort Ross in 1812; they sold it in 1841 to a Swiss named John Augustus Sutter, whose discovery of gold near Sacramento started the Gold Rush eight years later. It is the only part of the world with large numbers of redwood trees, shooting up in the moist and drizzly air hundreds of feet toward the sky. It is wet country, and for years it has been one of America's prime lumbering areas: Eureka and smaller lumber towns are filled with filigreed Victorian houses and old lumber mills, saloons and waterfront hotels. It has moved on to other crops: in sunny valleys sealed off the from Coast Range ridges grow some of the nation's premium wine grapes, and Mendocino County has been known from the late 1960s for its premier marijuana fields. Twenty years ago, there were only 20 wineries in Napa Valley; today there are about 200, with another 100 just west of the ridges in Sonoma County. These valleys were some of California's earliest literary haunts: Robert Louis Stevenson took his honeymoon near Calistoga (named for California plus Saratoga, for the spring water) in Napa, and Jack London owned a giant house in Sonoma which mysteriously burned down in 1913.

California's 1st Congressional District consists of most of the North Coast (though just missing Fort Ross), plus much of the wine-growing area inland and just a bit of the vast Central Valley interior. The North Coast lumbering area from Mendocino on north, once filled with rough-hewn working men, was historically Democratic country, but it backlashed toward the Republicans on cultural issues. As veterans of the counterculture settled in Mendocino County and along the coast, it has moved toward the cultural left. Inland, the wine-growing country around Healdsburg and in Napa County is politically more conservative, with neither the blue-collar tradition nor the counterculture past of the coast, though there is often partisan competition. The district's inland portion is around Fairfield, home of Travis Air Force Base. The mix of different economies and cultures, of generations with sharply different experiences and outlooks, makes this one of California's politically most unstable districts, and it has changed partisan hands three times in the last three elections.

The current Congressman from the 1st is Frank Riggs, a Republican first elected in 1990, defeated in 1992, then returned to office in 1994. His background is in law enforcement; he was an MP in the Army and worked for the Santa Barbara and Healdsburg police departments and the Sonoma County sheriff's office. In 1983 he went into real estate in fast-growing Sonoma County and served several years on school boards. In 1990 he ran for Congress, targeting Democrat Doug Bosco, who tended to favor the growth forces in the Redwood Empire more than the Sonoma County enviros. Riggs accused Bosco of selling an interest in a farm to a lobbyist who represented the purchaser of 15 Texas S&Ls. At the same time, Bosco was attacked from the left by a Peace & Freedom candidate who got 15% of the vote. Riggs won 43%–42%. He quickly won attention, first when he reneged on his pledge not to take the "obscene" congressional pay raise and voted against the Gulf war resolution, then as one of the freshman Republican Gang of Seven who insisted on disclosure of the names of House bank check-bouncers. But Riggs then discovered that he had three overdrafts himself.

In 1992 he was opposed by Dan Hamburg, a Democrat who spent the late 1960s at Stanford, then moved to Mendocino County and founded an "alternative school." He served a term on the Board of Supervisors favoring "managed growth," then moved to Quangdong province, China, to teach Chinese to Americans, Britons and New Zealanders. After returning to California, he worked for an antipoverty agency and as a computer typesetter while earning advanced degrees, at one point collecting $87 a week in unemployment. A clearer contrast of lifestyles and values is hard to imagine. As Hamburg put it, "He was a narc. I favor growing your own"—and indeed he favored legalization of marijuana, a major crop in Mendocino, for personal and medicinal use. With help from rock stars, Hamburg nearly outraised the incumbent and won 48%–45% in a district Bill Clinton was carrying 46%–29%. Riggs was the only Gang of Seven member to be defeated in 1992.

1994 was a rematch. Hamburg made a stir in the House with his rugged good looks (he was named "one of the 50 most beautiful people in the world" by *People* magazine) and bolo ties; he called for defense reconversion in Fairfield and for acquiring 44,000 acres of Headwaters timberland near Eureka for an environmental preserve, despite opposition from loggers. He maintained he had no interest in a lifetime career and cast the most liberal voting record in the House while representing this very divided district. Once again, he raised more money than Riggs, with a big edge among PACs. But Bosco ran against him in the primary and, although Hamburg won 62%–38%, Bosco carried the North Coast and most Bosco voters said they'd support Riggs. Riggs attacked Hamburg for supporting Bill Clinton and the "job killer" Headwaters forest: "I say jobs first and not earth first like Dan Hamburg and other environmentalists do." Hamburg abjured negative campaigning and Riggs called for more bipartisanship, but this was a hard-fought race between two candidates who represented very different cultural segments of our society. Riggs carried the northern North Coast by wide margins and held Hamburg even in Mendocino and Sonoma; he also carried Napa and the military-dependent area around Fairfield and Vacaville. This was good enough for a 53%–47% victory—the first absolute majority for anyone in this district since 1988.

Riggs returned to the House with a little extra seniority among the not very seniority-conscious Republican freshmen. His earlier contacts helped him to get a seat on Appropriations, where he can work for the diminishing pie of local economic development projects. His past record suggests that he could be an occasional maverick from conservative orthodoxy.

The People: Pop. 1990: 572,870; 33% rural; 13% age 65+; 79% White; 4% Black; 3% Amer. Indian; 4% Asian; 5% Other; 11% Hispanic origin. Voting age pop.: 423,536; 4% Black; 10% Hispanic origin. Households: 58% married couple families; 27% married couple fams. w. children; 52% college educ.; median household income: $30,943; per capita income: $14,298; median gross rent: $512; median house value: $136,200.

1992 Presidential Vote

Clinton (D)	119,491	(46%)
Bush (R)	74,597	(29%)
Perot (I)	61,160	(24%)

1988 Presidential Vote

Dukakis (D)	110,832	(52%)
Bush (R)	100,825	(48%)

Rep. Frank D. Riggs (R)

Elected 1994; b. Sept. 5, 1950, Louisville, KY; home, Windsor; Golden Gate U., B.A. 1980; Episcopalian; married (Cathy).

Career: Army, 1972–75; Police officer & Deputy Sheriff, Sonoma Cnty, 1976–83; Owner, Duncan Enterprises, 1985–present; Vice Pres. & Gen. Mr., Learning Tools Educ. Software Co., 1993–94.

DC Office: 1714 LHOB 20515, 202-225-3311; Fax: 202-225-3403.

District Offices: 1700 2nd St., #378, Napa 94559, 707-254-7308; and 710 E St., #100, Eureka 95501, 707-441-8701.

Committees: *Appropriations* (26th of 32 R): Agriculture, Rural Development, FDA, and Related Agencies; Energy and Water Development; Labor, Health and Human Services, and Education. *Economic & Educational Opportunities* (18th of 24 R): Early Childhood, Youth and Families; Postsecondary Education, Training and Life-Long Learning.

Group Ratings and 103d Congress Votes: Newly Elected

Key Votes of the 104th Congress

1. Congressional Compliance Y	6. Reform Crime Grant Y	11. Loser Pays Court Reform Y
2. Balanced Budget Amndmt. Y	7. National Security Act Y	12. Product Liability Reform Y
3. Bar Unfunded Mandates Y	8. Moratorium on Regs. Y	13. Welfare Reform Y
4. Pass Line Item Veto Y	9. Risk Assessment on Regs. Y	14. Term Limits Amndmt. Y
5. Relax Exclusionary Rule Y	10. Expnd. Priv. Prop. Rights Y	15. Tax Cuts Y

Election Results

1994 general	Frank D. Riggs (R)	106,870	(53%)	($605,185)
	Dan Hamburg (D)	93,717	(47%)	($834,611)
1994 primary	Frank D. Riggs (R)	31,572	(63%)	
	Morton S. Levine (R)	9,976	(20%)	
	Glen A. Deronde (R)	8,300	(17%)	
1992 general	Dan Hamburg (D)	119,676	(48%)	($647,532)
	Frank D. Riggs (R)	113,266	(45%)	($716,401)
	Phil Baldwin (P&F)	10,764	(4%)	($10,588)
	Other	7,500	(3%)	

SECOND DISTRICT

Rising 14,000 feet over low foothills and the Central Valley, visible for 100 miles, is the lone snow-capped volcanic cone of Mount Shasta, one of a string of (presumably) burnt-out volcanoes that march up and down the Pacific Coast states. This is the far northern end of California, where truck traffic on Interstate 5 is the only reminder of the choked metropolitan areas where most of the state's people live. It is lumber country mostly, where the mountains that rise on all sides—the Coast Range to the east, the Sierra Nevada to the west, the scattered mountains sealing off the Central Valley north of Redding—are carpeted with trees; rough flannel-shirt, two-lane-road country that was left behind economically when greater Los Angeles and San Francisco boomed after World War II.

In the last dozen years, however, the northern end of California has been attracting people, mostly young families who come here to raise their children in a small town atmosphere, but also retirees looking for a calm atmosphere and low cost of living. There are few minorities here; the population is 88% white Anglo, the highest in any California district. The political result is that an area which from 1943 to 1980 elected rough-and-ready Democrats who pulled strings in

Sacramento and Washington to build roads and dams, now elects abstemious and circumspect Republicans who have solidly conservative voting records and tend to local needs. That is certainly the case in the 2d Congressional District, which takes in the northern end of the state, except for the coastal counties in the 1st District. The district has two major population areas: one around Redding, just below Mount Shasta, and the other farther south, at the edge of the Sierra foothills, around the Butte County communities of Chico and Paradise.

The congressman from the 2d District is Wally Herger, a solidly conservative Republican, businessman and rancher first elected to the Assembly in 1980. In 1986 he came to Congress after winning solid margins over the mayor of Redding in the primary and a Shasta County supervisor in the general. He has served rather quietly on the Ways and Means Committee, though as part of the majority he will be much more a part of the action than before 1995. He is less of an ideologue than many of the state's other lawmakers and has shown signs of enjoying the legislative give-and-take on his committee. He was an early critic of the Endangered Species Act, which he wants amended to account for economic effects; the spotted owl controversy centers on Oregon, but there are plenty of people here dependent on lumbering whose livelihoods might be endangered by a designation of another species as endangered. Herger served on the conference committee on the Central Valley Project water bill, the final version of which he opposed, saying that it "legislates a permanent drought."

Herger seems in a strong position politically. Redistricting changed the shape of the district in 1992, but he has had no trouble winning before or after; in 1994 he was reelected 64%–26%.

The People: Pop. 1990: 573,226; 40% rural; 16% age 65+; 88% White; 1% Black; 3% Amer. Indian; 2% Asian; 2% Other; 6% Hispanic origin. Voting age pop.: 425,392; 1% Black; 5% Hispanic origin. Households: 58% married couple families; 24% married couple fams. w. children; 51% college educ.; median household income: $24,807; per capita income: $12,458; median gross rent: $429; median house value: $94,000.

1992 Presidential Vote		
Bush (R)	101,505	(38%)
Clinton (D)	93,823	(35%)
Perot (I)	67,298	(25%)

1988 Presidential Vote		
Bush (R)	125,793	(58%)
Dukakis (D)	91,390	(42%)

Rep. Wally Herger (R)

Elected 1986; b. May 20, 1945, Yuba City; home, Marysville; American River Comm. Col., A.A. 1967; CA St. U., 1968–69; Mormon; married (Pamela).

Career: Rancher; Owner, Herger Gas Inc. 1969–80; CA Assembly, 1980–86.

DC Office: 2433 RHOB 20515, 202-225-3076; Fax: 202-225-3245.

District Offices: 55 Independence Cir., #104, Chico 95926, 916-893-8363; and 410 Hemsted Dr., #115, Redding 96002, 916-223-5898.

Committees: *Budget* (6th of 24 R). *Ways & Means* (8th of 21 R); Oversight.

Group Ratings

	ADA	ACLU	COPE	CFA	LCV	CON	NSI	COC	ACU	NTLC	CHC
1994	5	14	0	20	6	79	100	91	100	93	100
1993	5	—	0	0	21	74	—	91	100	—	—

National Journal Ratings

	1993 LIB — 1993 CONS			1994 LIB — 1994 CONS		
Economic	20%	—	80%	0%	—	80%
Social	0%	—	89%	0%	—	89%
Foreign	16%	—	84%	0%	—	88%

Key Votes of the 103d Congress

1. Clinton Deficit Plan	N	3. Brady Handgun Purchase	N	5. Lmt. UN Cmnd. of Forces	Y
2. NAFTA	Y	4. Strike Race/Death Pnlty.	Y	6. Cut Missile Funds	*

Key Votes of the 104th Congress

1. Congressional Compliance	Y	6. Reform Crime Grant	Y	11. Loser Pays Court Reform	Y
2. Balanced Budget Amndmt.	Y	7. National Security Act	Y	12. Product Liability Reform	Y
3. Bar Unfunded Mandates	Y	8. Moratorium on Regs.	Y	13. Welfare Reform	Y
4. Pass Line Item Veto	Y	9. Risk Assessment on Regs.	Y	14. Term Limits Amndmt.	Y
5. Relax Exclusionary Rule	Y	10. Expnd. Priv. Prop. Rights	Y	15. Tax Cuts	Y

Election Results

1994 general	Wally Herger (R)	137,863	(64%)	($572,629)
	Mary Jacobs (D)	55,958	(26%)	($167,907)
	Devvy Kidd (AI)	15,569	(7%)	
	Others	5,417	(3%)	
1994 primary	Wally Herger (R)	unopposed		
1992 general	Wally Herger (R)	167,247	(65%)	($533,861)
	Elliot Roy Freedman (D)	71,780	(28%)	($4,947)
	Harry H. Pendery (Lib)	17,529	(7%)	($5,900)

THIRD DISTRICT

California's Sacramento Valley is one of nature's—and man's—miracles. Nature has sculpted a floor of almost perfectly flat land, surrounded on three sides by mountains, alternately purple and brown in the light. To this fertile lush black loam, man has added roads and fences—as straight as the lines in a geometry text—and, most important, water. Pacific clouds pour rain into the mountains, but the water used to run off quickly before it was penned in reservoirs and distributed through a system of canals and aqueducts, levees and pumping plants. The Sacramento and Central Valleys now produce a marvelous variety of crops—rice, plums, almonds, olives, asparagus, pears, hops, beans, celery, onions, potatoes. The Sacramento Valley has always guarded its water jealously and in the days before one-person-one-vote, it had enough seats in the California Senate to veto water decisions it didn't like; today it must fight to keep enough for its farms against the demands of the cities to the south.

The metropolis of this valley is Sacramento. Its historic foundation is apparent, coming into town on the West Sacramento Freeway, elevated above utterly flat rice lands painstakingly drained by a network of canals. As you hurtle over the Sacramento River on the M Street Bridge you see, framed perfectly in its arch, California's glorious golden-domed Capitol. On this landing Sacramento was born, and the state government, along with the agriculture symbolized by those rice fields, were for years its lifeblood. Now Sacramento spreads far to the south, east and north, with 1.5 million people—one of the fastest-growing major metropolitan areas in the last 15 years.

The 3d Congressional District includes part of metropolitan Sacramento and much of the Sacramento Valley to the north. It takes in many of the suburbs just north of Sacramento and the American River—all or part of Carmichael, Citrus Heights, North Highlands and Foothills Farms. Sacramento is historically Democratic, but these suburbs are increasingly Republican. The 3d also includes heavily Democratic Yolo County, with industrial West Sacramento just across the Sacramento River from the Capitol and, on the flat farmlands, the tree-shaded, bicycle-pathed town of Davis, with its University of California campus. In the Sacramento Valley it extends north along I-5 to Red Bluff.

This is a district that leans Republican in most elections but is represented by one of the leaders of the Democratic Party, Vic Fazio. Fazio's life work has been politics and legislation: he was a lobbyist in Sacramento, long California's most political locale, a staffer for Assembly Speaker Bob Moretti in the early 1970s and a founder of the *California Journal*. He was elected to the Assembly in 1974, the great breakthrough year for liberal Democrats. In 1978 he was elected to the House, replacing an incumbent who was discovered to have two wives and families, one in California and the other back East. After only two years, Fazio became chairman of the Legislative Appropriations Subcommittee, the panel that handles Congress's own budget—the mayor of Capitol Hill. Fazio is a consummate political insider, always personable and articulate, entirely presentable outside the back rooms and private hallways; knowledgeable without being cynical, a sharp operator who keeps score and remembers friends and enemies, a politician who is anything but an innocent but who retains a certain idealism and a willingness to take serious risks for what he believes. He sponsored congressional pay raises in 1982, 1987 and 1989, and took much heat back home; he served on the Ethics Committee, where in 1989 he found violations of rules by Speaker Jim Wright. After Wright and Tony Coehlo resigned in 1989, Fazio became vice chairman of the Democratic Caucus, technically the number five position in the Democratic leadership. And after the 1994 elections, he easily moved up to become the caucus chairman.

The 1990s have been much more perilous politically for Fazio than the 1970s or 1980s: he became more powerful and more imperiled, all at the same time. In the late 1980s he headed the Democrats' national redistricting operation and in 1991 he was California House Democrats' chief agent in redistricting negotiations in Sacramento. But he and Speaker Willie Brown were unable to outmaneuver Governor Pete Wilson, and Fazio ended up with a new 3d District that was markedly less Democratic than those he had run in before. After the 1990 elections, he became chairman of the Democratic Congressional Campaign Committee, a post he had sought in 1986; the collapse of George Bush's candidacy on the West Coast helped him avoid great losses, but House Democrats lost 10 seats nationally, even as Bill Clinton was winning the presidency. The institutional advantages that Democrats had enjoyed were deteriorating, despite Fazio's best efforts; the extent of the rot became starkly apparent in his second term as campaign committee chairman, when Democrats lost 52 seats and control of the House in 1994. Despite grumbling about his campaign criticism of the "religious right," few Democrats believed that Fazio could have done much to avoid the debacle.

This same trend was apparent back home. In 1986 Fazio was reelected with 70% of the vote; in 1988 he was unopposed. In 1990 he spent $1 million to his opponent's $40,000 and won 55%–39%. Then came redistricting and in 1992 a better-known opponent, Bill Richardson, a longtime (1966–86) state Senator from Southern California who settled in the Sacramento area. Richardson, a former member of the John Birch Society, started Gun Owners of America; he attacked Fazio for spending $945,000 on office expenses, more than any other member. Richardson backed term limits and attacked Fazio for the House bank scandal (though Fazio had no overdrafts) and the pay raise. Fazio responded that Richardson "doesn't want to govern and solve problems," and he stressed local issues such as the threatened loss of McClellan Air Force Base, levee protection and keeping the north's water in the Valley (he noted that Richardson, as a Southern California legislator, had supported measures to import water from the north). He argued emotionally for the proposed Auburn Dam to protect Sacramento from the possibility of floods and said he wanted the Endangered Species Act to take economic factors into account. Richardson spent $853,000, but Fazio far outpaced him, raising $786,000 from individuals and $1.1 million from PACs and parties, spending a total of $1.9 million and an extraordinary $587,000 in the last three weeks. All that netted him a handsome 51%–40% victory: he carried Yolo County 64%–30% and ran unspectacularly ahead in the Sacramento

County suburbs, 49%–41%. But despite his stress on agriculture and water, he lost, 45%–46%, in the Sacramento Valley.

In 1993 and 1994 Fazio became a more visible member of the Democratic leadership as it came increasingly under attack. But his prominence did not always produce success—the Auburn Dam was defeated by a coalition of environmentalists and Republicans—and the demands on his time from the campaign committee and his faraway district became fierce. Fazio got national notice in June when he attacked Republicans for accepting support from the "radical" and "intolerant" religious right, and in response was attacked for "religious bigotry." At home, his Republican opponent was Tim Lefever, an unheralded 33-year-old real estate broker who attacked him for supporting environmentalism and gun control; he spent only $251,000 while Fazio raised over $1 million from PACs, second only to Speaker Thomas Foley. Fazio again spent $1.9 million, the eighth highest among House candidates. With all that, he won by only 50%–46%, carrying Yolo County 61%–35%, but running only narrowly ahead in Sacramento County (50%–46%) and trailing 53%–43% in the Sacramento Valley.

None of this deterred Fazio from continuing on his course. After the election, he gave up the campaign committee post to run for Democratic Caucus Chairman, the number three leadership position, and beat Black Caucus Chairman Kweisi Mfume 149–57. With the Republican takeover, he no longer chairs the Legislative Subcommittee but was installed as ranking Democrat on the House Oversight Committee, replacing leadership critic Charlie Rose of North Carolina. If the anti-Democratic trend of 1994 continues, Fazio will surely have another tough race and could easily lose reelection. The PAC money is not likely to come in so easily now that he is in the minority, and it will be much harder for him to engage in the constructive incremental legislating which he has seen as his work in Congress. But he seems determined to fight and in the early days of the 104th Congress worked with Minority Leader Dick Gephardt to orchestrate criticism of Speaker Newt Gingrich.

The People: Pop. 1990: 571,545; 18% rural; 11% age 65+; 76% White; 3% Black; 1% Amer. Indian; 6% Asian; 8% Other; 14% Hispanic origin. Voting age pop.: 418,655; 3% Black; 12% Hispanic origin. Households: 56% married couple families; 27% married couple fams. w. children; 53% college educ.; median household income: $30,296; per capita income: $13,786; median gross rent: $498; median house value: $118,300.

1992 Presidential Vote			1988 Presidential Vote		
Clinton (D)	99,781	(41%)	Bush (R)	110,174	(55%)
Bush (R)	90,799	(37%)	Dukakis (D)	90,437	(45%)
Perot (I)	53,323	(22%)			

Rep. Vic Fazio (D)

Elected 1978; born Oct. 11, 1942, Winchester, MA; home, West Sacramento; Union Col., B.A. 1965, CA St. U., 1969–72; Episcopalian; married (Judy).

Career: Legis. Consult., 1966–75; Co-founder, *The California Journal*; Consult. & Asst., CA Assembly Speaker, 1971–74; CA Assembly, 1975–78.

DC Office: 2113 RHOB 20515, 202-225-5716; Fax: 202-225-3076.

District Offices: 722-B Main St., Woodland 95695, 916-666-5521; and 332 Pine St., #F, Red Bluff 96080, 916-529-5629.

Committees: *Democratic Caucus Chairman. Appropriations* (10th of 24 D): Energy and Water Development; Legislative (RMM). *House Oversight* (RMM of 5 D).

Group Ratings

	ADA	ACLU	COPE	CFA	LCV	CON	NSI	COC	ACU	NTLC	CHC
1994	75	87	78	90	61	11	50	42	14	11	7
1993	85	—	92	100	50	11	—	27	8	—	—

National Journal Ratings

	1993 LIB — 1993 CONS	1994 LIB — 1994 CONS
Economic	68% — 26%	73% — 17%
Social	80% — 13%	73% — 26%
Foreign	59% — 38%	57% — 37%

Key Votes of the 103d Congress

1. Clinton Deficit Plan	Y	3. Brady Handgun Purchase	Y	5. Lmt. UN Cmnd. of Forces	N
2. NAFTA	Y	4. Strike Race/Death Pnlty.	N	6. Cut Missile Funds	N

Key Votes of the 104th Congress

1. Congressional Compliance	Y	6. Reform Crime Grant	N	11. Loser Pays Court Reform	N
2. Balanced Budget Amndmt.	N	7. National Security Act	N	12. Product Liability Reform	N
3. Bar Unfunded Mandates	Y	8. Moratorium on Regs.	Y	13. Welfare Reform	N
4. Pass Line Item Veto	N	9. Risk Assessment on Regs.	N	14. Term Limits Amndmt.	N
5. Relax Exclusionary Rule	N	10. Expnd. Priv. Prop. Rights	Y	15. Tax Cuts	N

Election Results

1994 general	Vic Fazio (D)	97,093	(50%)	($1,972,033)
	Tim Lefever (R)	89,964	(46%)	($251,369)
	Ross Crain (Lib)	8,100	(4%)	
1994 primary	Vic Fazio (D)	42,896	(75%)	
	Rodger McAfee (D)	14,219	(25%)	
1992 general	Vic Fazio (D)	122,149	(51%)	($1,906,584)
	H. L. (Bill) Richardson (R)	96,092	(40%)	($853,730)
	Ross Crain (Lib)	20,444	(9%)	

FOURTH DISTRICT

California sprang suddenly into existence: the Gold Rush of 1849 was followed by statehood and the creation of the first 27 counties in 1850. The new state's first boom area was the Mother Lode country in the foothills of the Sierras above Sacramento. Mining camps the size of eastern cities grew up in vacant valleys locked amid steep hills, with thousands of would-be millionaires gathered to find gold—though most of those who actually got rich did so by catering to miners' needs. In Placerville, John Studebaker had a buggy shop, Phillip Armour ran a butcher shop and Mark Hopkins had a dry goods store. The biggest mine in California was sunk in Grass Valley in 1857 and worked for half a century. But long before that, most of the Mother Lode country emptied out, leaving ghost towns and villages with hundreds of deserted houses—an antique vacation country left behind in time.

In the last 20 years the Mother Lode country has become a boom area again. Thousands of Californians—many of them families from smog-filled, middle-class suburbs of the Los Angeles basin and the San Francisco Bay area—looking for a more pleasant, small-town, orderly environment, found it here along fast-flowing creeks where the '49ers camped. For the first time since the 1860 Census, county populations rose and old Victorian houses were renovated even as new subdivisions were built. Politically, this migration has changed the Mother Lode country from Democrat to Republican. The new migrants are tired of the cultures of therapy of the big metro areas and ready for more discipline. In 1976, the Mother Lode counties from Placer to Tuolumne cast 98,000 votes, 50% for Jimmy Carter and 47% for Gerald Ford—close to the

California average. By 1992, they cast 217,000 votes, 40% for George Bush, 34% for Bill Clinton and 25% for Ross Perot—results more like Idaho than coastal California.

The 4th Congressional District consists of most of the Mother Lode country plus the northeastern suburbs of Sacramento—Fair Oaks, Citrus Heights, Orangevale—and the old town of Folsom. The district runs northeast along I-80 into Auburn and Roseville in Placer County where the Mother Lode hills start, then up to the crest of the Sierra Nevada and over to the California shore of Lake Tahoe and the arid salt flats around Mono Lake. Politically, this is a solidly Republican area, though in 1992 Ross Perot cut deeply into the Republican vote.

The Congressman from the 4th District is John Doolittle, a Republican with one of the most conservative voting records in the House. Doolittle is from Rocklin, at the edge of the Sacramento metro area where the foothills begin, and for 10 years he represented a state Senate district that stretched up to the Oregon border. Doolittle's conservatism was annealed in the fires of adversity; he graduated from the University of California in Santa Cruz in 1972, when the campus was 97% for George McGovern. His first victory in 1980, when he was 30, was evidence of the area's Republican trend; he made a record against gun control and abortion, and for a crime victims' bill of rights and widespread AIDS testing. When the incumbent retired in 1990 in a district that then stretched from the Mother Lode country to Stockton, Doolittle ran for the seat. He had tougher competition than expected from Democrat Patricia Malberg, a former ski champion and onetime health care worker in Africa who was pro-choice on abortion, against nuclear power and for defense spending cuts; Doolittle won by just 50%–46%.

In the 102d Congress Doolittle was one of the less prominent members of the Gang of Seven freshman Republicans who demanded full disclosure of House bank overdrafts. But he was also the House's top user of franked mail, and in 1991 he joined Democrat Maxine Waters in calling for Sacramento-style perks: more staff, $92 daily expense allowances, and more cellular phones for members. He was California House Republicans' point man on redistricting, but he supported a plan that only protected Republican incumbents and gave them no shot at California's seven new seats; this was nixed by Governor Pete Wilson. In 1992 he had a second matchup with Malberg and won again by 50%–46%. In the 103d Congress he made fewer headlines and again had a very conservative record. Perhaps to curry favor with the 25% of the district who voted for Ross Perot in 1992, Doolittle joined his group "United We Stand America" His Democratic opponent in 1994 was Katie Hirning, a manager at New Generation Software. She campaigned to "give entrepreneurs the freedom they need and deserve to keep and create jobs" and called the federal government "bloated, inefficient and unresponsive." But the Republican tide was too much in this district, which cast more votes than any California district except the leftish Marin-Sonoma 6th, and Doolittle won 61%–35%. He is now part of the majority for the first time in his legislative career. Historically, the Water and Power Resources Subcommittee, which he chairs, has been a source of major legislative influence in the House. But the downsizing of federal spending and the Republicans' aversion to pork-barrel projects will make it tougher for Doolittle to establish the post as a power base.

The People: Pop. 1990: 571,027; 38% rural; 12% age 65+; 88% White; 2% Black; 1% Amer. Indian; 2% Asian; 2% Other; 7% Hispanic origin. Voting age pop.: 427,008; 2% Black; 7% Hispanic origin. Households: 63% married couple families; 28% married couple fams. w. children; 58% college educ.; median household income: $35,772; per capita income: $16,263; median gross rent: $569; median house value: $152,400.

1992 Presidential Vote

Bush (R)	117,155	(40%)
Clinton (D)	97,501	(34%)
Perot (I)	73,060	(25%)

1988 Presidential Vote

Bush (R)	136,618	(60%)
Dukakis (D)	89,522	(40%)

Rep. John T. Doolittle (R)

Elected 1990; b. Oct. 30, 1950, Glendale; home, Rocklin; U. of CA at Santa Cruz, B.A. 1972, U. of the Pacific, J.D. 1978; Mormon; married (Julia).

Career: CA Senate, 1980–90, Repub. Caucus Chmn., 1987–90.

DC Office: 1526 LHOB 20515, 202-225-2511; Fax: 202-225-5444.

District Offices: 2130 Professional Dr., Roseville 95661, 916-786-5560.

Committees: *Agriculture* (9th of 27 R): Resource Conservation, Research and Forestry; Risk Management and Specialty Crops. *Resources* (7th of 25 R): National Parks, Forests and Lands; Water and Power Resources (Chmn.).

Group Ratings

	ADA	ACLU	COPE	CFA	LCV	CON	NSI	COC	ACU	NTLC	CHC
1994	5	14	13	0	6	87	100	82	100	100	100
1993	10	—	8	0	21	82	—	91	100	—	—

National Journal Ratings

	1993 LIB — 1993 CONS	1994 LIB — 1994 CONS
Economic	20% — 77%	0% — 80%
Social	0% — 89%	0% — 89%
Foreign	9% — 85%	0% — 88%

Key Votes of the 103d Congress

1. Clinton Deficit Plan	N	3. Brady Handgun Purchase N	5. Lmt. UN Cmnd. of Forces Y
2. NAFTA	N	4. Strike Race/Death Pnlty. Y	6. Cut Missile Funds N

Key Votes of the 104th Congress

1. Congressional Compliance Y	6. Reform Crime Grant Y	11. Loser Pays Court Reform Y
2. Balanced Budget Amndmt. Y	7. National Security Act Y	12. Product Liability Reform Y
3. Bar Unfunded Mandates Y	8. Moratorium on Regs. Y	13. Welfare Reform Y
4. Pass Line Item Veto Y	9. Risk Assessment on Regs. Y	14. Term Limits Amndmt. Y
5. Relax Exclusionary Rule Y	10. Expnd. Priv. Prop. Rights Y	15. Tax Cuts Y

Election Results

1994 general	John T. Doolittle (R).................	144,936	(61%)	($664,109)
	Katie Hirning (D)....................	82,505	(35%)	($354,786)
	Others..............................	8,882	(4%)	
1994 primary	John T. Doolittle (R)...............	unopposed		
1992 general	John T. Doolittle (R).................	141,155	(50%)	($622,071)
	Patricia Malberg (D)	129,489	(46%)	($376,190)
	Patrick Lee McHargue (Lib)	12,705	(4%)	

FIFTH DISTRICT

Sacramento, capital of the nation's largest state, focus of California's third-largest media market, home of a national sports franchise (the NBA's Sacramento Kings) and an 18-mile light rail system, is no longer just a small city with a lot of civil servants and a vegetable-packing economy. It is a vibrant major American metropolis, with some of the nation's highest job growth. Sacramento started as a river port on the sluggish waters of the Sacramento and American Rivers. It was the destination of many overland migrants, the site of Sutter's Fort where John Augustus Sutter found the gold that set off the Gold Rush of 1849, and the western terminus of the Pony Express in 1860. This was the natural choice to be California's capital, halfway between the San Francisco Bay and the Mother Lode country in the foothills of the Sierras, and in the middle of California's vast valley. Agriculture continues to be important today in Sacra-tomato (as some call it)—it has the world's largest almond processing plant.

In the old days, government was not a big business. Just a few lobbyists hung out in saloons on K or J Streets, the governor's mansion was a musty antique, and the 100-plus degree summers emptied out what there was of the city. But air conditioning has replaced awnings, freeways and shopping malls have followed the city's growth east and north toward the Sierra foothills, and affluence has made this one of America's higher income metropolitan areas. In the 1980s metropolitan Sacramento grew 35%, more than any other large metro area except that other western capital, Phoenix, to more than 1.5 million. Even military base closedowns have not stopped the surge; the city extended benefits to get the computer maker Packard Bell, the number-three U.S. PC manufacturer to move to the Sacramento Army Depot after its headquarters was destroyed in the 1994 Northridge earthquake. Government expanded, too, even under conservative Republican governors Ronald Reagan and George Deukmejian, and Sacramento is now the home of platoons of lobbyists, lawyers and consultants.

As Sacramento has grown, it has also become more Republican: this once Democratic, pro-government, working-class bastion has become something very close to an upscale Sun Belt boom town. Sacramento voted against Ronald Reagan for governor in 1966 and 1970, but voted for him for president in 1980 and 1984; it spurned Richard Nixon and Gerald Ford in the 1970s but voted for George Bush in 1988 and gave Bill Clinton only a mediocre 44% plurality in 1992. Civil servants and the *Sacramento Bee* once made the city Democratic, but private sector growth, immigration and competition from the peppery, conservative *Sacramento Union* all have helped Republicans.

The 5th District consists of the center of metropolitan Sacramento; the metro area now includes parts of three other districts. The 5th contains affluent neighborhoods on older grid streets and scattered low-income black, Mexican-American and Hmong neighborhoods, as well as new condominiums north of the American River and middle-class subdivisions south of downtown. Politically, this includes most of Sacramento's remaining Democratic neighborhoods, and it is now one of the most Democratic district in the great valley from Bakersfield north to Oregon.

The Congressman from the 5th is Robert Matsui, a Democrat first elected in 1978, a member of the Ways and Means Committee and one of the most influential House Democrats on a number of important issues. Born in 1941, the infant Matsui and his family were among the West Coast Japanese Americans forced into internment camps in 1942, and although he has no memory of the experience himself, he does remember the silence his family and others maintained about it. It was Asian shame, when none of the victims had anything to be ashamed about. He was one of the lead sponsors of the 1988 Japanese American redress law which apologized for the internment policy and provided monetary compensation for every survivor of the camps and for so-called "voluntary evacuees."

Most of Matsui's work comes out of Ways and Means. He was a hard-working supporter of the 1986 rate-lowering, preference-cutting tax reform. He has favored targeted capital gains tax cuts, has tried to encourage mass transit use by limiting the deductibility of parking and advocates a tax credit for using energy from wind and crop incineration. In 1993 he passed a program to deal with child abuse and neglect and to encourage family preservation. In 1994 he advanced his own welfare reform plan providing for job training and education requirements, without the Clinton plan's two-year time limit.

Matsui is one of the House's leading free traders, although he has been willing to get tough with Japan on its import restrictions. He was a strong backer of free trade with Mexico for years, and in early 1993 took the lead among House Democrats in seeking approval of the North American Free Trade Agreement, even when the Clinton Administration was lukewarm, then-Majority Leader Dick Gephardt was opposed and then-Minority Whip Newt Gingrich was not engaged in the issue. Working with Republican Jim Kolbe of Arizona, he rallied support and let the White House know that NAFTA was foundering and would not pass without a major push. Communication was made easier because his wife Doris Matsui was the deputy director of public affairs in the Clinton White House—"the season's hot couple," *The New York Times* called them. But Matsui depends for his influence not on connections and favors but on intensity and discipline; and without him NAFTA might not have passed. Fittingly, he became acting chairman of the Trade Subcommittee when Sam Gibbons became Ways and Means chairman in June 1994. In the 104th Congress, in a sign of the internal tensions within the party, Charlie Rangel of New York asserted his right to the senior-Democratic position on the Trade Subcommittee.

Matsui has shown political astuteness over the years. He was the first non-Massachusetts House member to support Michael Dukakis in 1987. He has pondered statewide races— against then-Senator Pete Wilson in 1988, for attorney general in 1990, for the Senate seat Alan Cranston vacated in 1992—but decided each time not to run. In 1991 he became treasurer of the Democratic National Committee, giving him a good opportunity to mix with big contributors. He was critical of Speaker Thomas Foley in the early 1990s for not defending incumbents, and the Republican takeover of the House has diminished his long-time hope that he will be chairman of Ways and Means, on which he is now the sixth ranking Democrat. Back home, Matsui's voting record—liberal on cultural issues, more moderate on economic and foreign issues—has been popular, and at one point he accumulated $1.4 million in his campaign treasury. He won reelection easily, by 68%–29% in 1994, when he spent $909,000 to $64,000 for his opponent. Matsui can probably remain in the House as long as he wants, but as part of the minority party he must seek new roles.

The People: Pop. 1990: 573,659; 11% age 65+; 59% White; 13% Black; 1% Amer. Indian; 13% Asian; 7% Other; 14% Hispanic origin. Voting age pop.: 421,533; 11% Black; 12% Hispanic origin. Households: 45% married couple families; 21% married couple fams. w. children; 57% college educ.; median household income: $29,974; per capita income: $14,661; median gross rent: $505; median house value: $121,000.

1992 Presidential Vote

Clinton (D)	120,577	(50%)
Bush (R)	73,562	(31%)
Perot (I)	42,566	(18%)

1988 Presidential Vote

Dukakis (D)	118,468	(55%)
Bush (R)	97,313	(45%)

Rep. Robert T. Matsui (D)

Elected 1978; b. Sept. 17, 1941, Sacramento; home, Sacramento; U. of CA at Berkeley, A.B. 1963, J.D. 1966; United Methodist; married (Doris).

Career: Practicing atty., 1967–78; Sacramento City Cncl., 1971–78.

DC Office: 2311 RHOB 20515, 202-225-7163; Fax: 202-225-0566.

District Offices: 8058 Fed. Bldg., 650 Capitol Mall, Sacramento 95814, 916-498-5600.

Committees: *Ways & Means* (6th of 15 D): Oversight (RMM); Trade.

Group Ratings

	ADA	ACLU	COPE	CFA	LCV	CON	NSI	COC	ACU	NTLC	CHC
1994	75	78	67	90	78	4	50	42	11	11	0
1993	80	—	92	100	71	7	—	27	8	—	—

National Journal Ratings

	1993 LIB	—	1993 CONS	1994 LIB	—	1994 CONS
Economic	68%	—	26%	73%	—	17%
Social	87%	—	0%	86%	—	14%
Foreign	69%	—	30%	71%	—	29%

Key Votes of the 103d Congress

1. Clinton Deficit Plan	Y	3. Brady Handgun Purchase	Y	5. Lmt. UN Cmnd. of Forces	N
2. NAFTA	Y	4. Strike Race/Death Pnlty.	N	6. Cut Missile Funds	Y

Key Votes of the 104th Congress

1. Congressional Compliance	Y	6. Reform Crime Grant	*	11. Loser Pays Court Reform	N
2. Balanced Budget Amndmt.	N	7. National Security Act	N	12. Product Liability Reform	N
3. Bar Unfunded Mandates	N	8. Moratorium on Regs.	N	13. Welfare Reform	N
4. Pass Line Item Veto	N	9. Risk Assessment on Regs.	N	14. Term Limits Amndmt.	N
5. Relax Exclusionary Rule	Y	10. Expnd. Priv. Prop. Rights	N	15. Tax Cuts	N

Election Results

1994 general	Robert T. Matsui (D)	125,042	(68%)	($929,464)
	Robert S. Dinsmore (R)	52,905	(29%)	($74,212)
	Others	4,649	(3%)	
1994 primary	Robert T. Matsui (D)	unopposed		
1992 general	Robert T. Matsui (D)	158,250	(69%)	($1,421,123)
	Robert S. Dinsmore (R)	58,698	(25%)	($32,826)
	Others	13,612	(6%)	

SIXTH DISTRICT

When the Golden Gate bridge was opened in 1937, San Francisco was one of the nation's best-known cities, but few knew much about the land beyond the bridge's north pierhead. There were fewer than 50,000 people in Marin County then and another 65,000 just to the north in Sonoma County. For San Franciscans, Marin was known for the ferry terminus in Sausalito, a fishing village and art colony, and as the beginning of the Redwood Empire, with its giant trees in Muir Woods; near the Bay was the state prison at San Quentin, with its infamous gas chamber. Farther north, in a sunny valley protected from the fog by the Coast Range, was Santa Rosa, site of agronomist Luther Burbank's laboratory, a town that looked Middle American enough to be the set for dozens of movies. Politically, the area was then typical of the nation: traditionally Republican, but favoring Franklin Roosevelt in the 1930s.

Today this part of California is far more populous, with 230,000 people in Marin and 388,000 in Sonoma, solidly a part of the San Francisco Bay Area, affluent beyond the dreams of the Americans of 50 years ago and extreme in its cultural attitudes. Trendy Marin, with its hot tubs and its fashionable people getting in touch with themselves, became a national caricature in the late 1970s; the interesting question is how such an affluent area could move politically so far to the left. It is an illustration of the primacy of cultural over economic factors and of a cultural identity consuming an entire metropolitan area. For even as metro San Francisco's economy has generated increasing numbers of professional jobs, its reputation for cultural tolerance has attracted many people willing and able to pay its far-above-average real estate prices, and at the same time repelled many others, who are happier in the Central Valley or Sierras or Idaho, where they can live cheaply. The result is that affluent Bay Area residents are increasingly self-selected cultural liberals—averse to traditional religion, derisive of traditional sexual and marriage mores, viscerally anti-military. And over the years Marin, with its mountain-bound subdivisions of contemporary houses, and southern Sonoma County, with its rolling countryside and picturesque small towns, have attracted the most liberal of the affluent liberal. Consider the election returns: Marin and Sonoma, both Republican as recently as 1980, voted 59% for Michael Dukakis in 1988 and 56% for Bill Clinton in 1992—a dozen points above the national average and perhaps double the percentage in similar income areas nationally.

The 6th Congressional District includes all of Marin County and most of Sonoma. It is represented by Lynn Woolsey, a Democrat chosen in 1992 when 10-year incumbent Barbara Boxer, the personification of trendy liberalism since she was elected to the Marin County Board of Supervisors in 1976, was elected to the U.S. Senate. Woolsey came to Marin 30 years ago and was a housewife with three children under age 6 when her marriage ended in 1968. She went on welfare, got a low-paying job and left her children with 13 different babysitters in a year. Deliverance appeared in the form of a job with a high-tech startup firm where she rose to become a top executive. She remarried and moved to a house in Petaluma where her mother could live and look after the kids. As she wrote in her campaign literature, "Finally I could concentrate on work. The children had good care at last!" She put herself through business school at night, earned a degree in human resources and started her own personnel service. She won a seat on the Petaluma Council in 1984 and is proud of its record in limiting growth (Marin and Sonoma, with their low-growth policies, are becoming lesser political forces in California), setting up affirmative action programs and a Women of Color Task Force, requiring that 15% of new housing be reserved for low-income buyers and establishing a voucher system for low-income families' child care. "I know what it means to have an effective safety net to help people get back on their feet," she campaigned. "I know what a bottom line means. I have made the tough decisions to keep our City prosperous in the post-Proposition 13 era."

Woolsey was one of nine Democrats running for the seat in 1992; also running was Marin Assemblyman Bill Filante, a liberal Republican: serious competition all round. One Democrat was J. Bennett Johnston III, son of the Louisiana senator, whose Oil Patch friends raised

$400,000; also running were well-known members of the Marin and Sonoma Boards of Supervisors. But Woolsey won with 26% of the vote, well ahead of the second place finisher's 19%. In the general, she unexpectedly became unbeatable after Filante had surgery which removed only part of a cancerous brain tumor. He stopped campaigning and Woolsey won 65%–34%.

Woolsey won seats on the Budget and Economic and Educational Opportunities Committees. As the first welfare recipient known to be in Congress, she sponsored a bill to help welfare mothers achieve "financial independence" and another (co-sponsored by conservative Henry Hyde) to let the Internal Revenue Service collect child support payments. She lobbied against banning gays in the military, accompanied by her son who is gay; she moved to expand the Point Reyes National Seashore into Sonoma County; and she backed a single-payer health care program.

Overall, Woolsey has one of the most liberal voting records in the House. Her enthusiasm for liberal programs unabated by the problems of the Clinton Administration, she was reelected 58%–38% over a spunky moderate Republican who spent $204,000 of his own money. She seems sure to persevere in her opposition to Speaker Newt Gingrich and his Republicans.

The People: Pop. 1990: 571,360; 19% rural; 13% age 65+; 85% White; 2% Black; 1% Amer. Indian; 3% Asian; 3% Other; 9% Hispanic origin. Voting age pop.: 444,348; 2% Black; 8% Hispanic origin. Households: 53% married couple families; 23% married couple fams. w. children; 67% college educ.; median household income: $40,564; per capita income: $21,603; median gross rent: $709; median house value: $255,900.

1992 Presidential Vote		
Clinton (D)	169,301	(56%)
Bush (R)	71,564	(24%)
Perot (I)	60,920	(20%)

1988 Presidential Vote		
Dukakis (D)	152,467	(59%)
Bush (R)	107,374	(41%)

Rep. Lynn Woolsey (D)

Elected 1992; b. Nov. 3, 1937, Seattle, WA; home, Petaluma; U. of San Francisco, B.A. 1980; Presbyterian; divorced.

Career: Human Resources Mgr., Harris Digital Telephone, 1969–80; Owner, Woolsey Personnel Svc., 1980–92; Petaluma City Cncl., 1985–92, Vice Mayor, 1986, 1991.

DC Office: 439 CHOB 20515, 202-225-5161; Fax: 202-225-5161; e-mail: woolsey@hr.house.gov.

District Offices: 1101 College Ave., #200, Santa Rosa 95404, 707-542-7182; and 1050 Northgate Dr., #140, San Rafael 94903, 415-507-9554.

Committees: *Budget* (13th of 18 D). *Economic & Educational Opportunities* (17th of 19 D): Postsecondary Education, Training and Life-Long Learning; Workforce Protections.

Group Ratings

	ADA	ACLU	COPE	CFA	LCV	CON	NSI	COC	ACU	NTLC	CHC
1994	100	87	100	90	94	18	0	25	0	14	0
1993	100	—	100	100	100	39	—	9	4	—	—

National Journal Ratings

	1993 LIB — 1993 CONS			1994 LIB — 1994 CONS	
Economic	88%	—	0%	83%	—	0%
Social	87%	—	0%	90%	—	6%
Foreign	93%	—	0%	85%	—	0%

Key Votes of the 103d Congress

1. Clinton Deficit Plan	Y	3. Brady Handgun Purchase	Y	5. Lmt. UN Cmnd. of Forces	N
2. NAFTA	N	4. Strike Race/Death Pnlty.	N	6. Cut Missile Funds	Y

Key Votes of the 104th Congress

1. Congressional Compliance	Y	6. Reform Crime Grant	N	11. Loser Pays Court Reform	N
2. Balanced Budget Amndmt.	N	7. National Security Act	N	12. Product Liability Reform	N
3. Bar Unfunded Mandates	N	8. Moratorium on Regs.	N	13. Welfare Reform	N
4. Pass Line Item Veto	N	9. Risk Assessment on Regs.	N	14. Term Limits Amndmt.	N
5. Relax Exclusionary Rule	N	10. Expnd. Priv. Prop. Rights	N	15. Tax Cuts	N

Election Results

1994 general	Lynn C. Woolsey (D)	137,642	(58%)	($649,388)
	Michael J. Nugent (R)	88,940	(38%)	(456,901)
	Others	10,258	(4%)	
1994 primary	Lynn Woolsey (D)	unopposed		
1992 general	Lynn Woolsey (D)	190,322	(65%)	($584,913)
	Bill Filante (R)	98,171	(34%)	($436,752)
	Others	3,293	(1%)	

SEVENTH DISTRICT

The journey inward from the Pacific Ocean to the vast flatness of California's Central Valley passes through wondrous terrain. The traveler starts at the Golden Gate, with the lush green Presidio on one side and the bluff of the Marin mountains on the other; through the waters of San Francisco Bay, looked down upon by ridges above the East Bay on one side and the cone of Mount Tamalpais on the other; through the narrow Carquinez Strait to Suisun Bay, with its sloughs and marshes, fed by the sluggish waters of the Sacramento and San Joaquin Delta; and finally past the mountains and waters, to the flat, fertile expanse of California's great interior. This is not a journey most tourists make, but it was a familiar route to the first Californians and it passes by much of the industrial base of the Bay Area. On the east side of the bay is Richmond, developed almost instantaneously during World War II when Henry J. Kaiser built a shipyard in its deep water port and 91,000 people from all over the country were put to work building ships for the Pacific theater; it now has a large black population and is attracting high-tech spinoffs. Across Carquinez Strait is Vallejo, named for a Mexican general and member of the first California Senate, the site since 1853 of the giant Mare Island Naval Shipyard. Across the strait are tank farms and factories in Rodeo and Pittsburg and Martinez, the seat of Contra Costa County (literally, the coast opposite San Francisco).

Politically, this industrial area was blue-collar, labor-union Democratic back in the days when San Francisco, with its larger white-collar and professional population, often voted Republican. More recently, as San Francisco has moved to the left on cultural issues, this area has become a bit more conservative, but only by Bay Area standards. The current 7th Congressional District includes most of this area, from Richmond and El Cerrito along both sides of Carquinez Strait and Suisun Bay to Vallejo, Rodeo, Martinez and Pittsburg. It also proceeds inland through the intermountain interstices of Contra Costa County to include most of middle-income Concord, but excludes the heavily Republican and higher-income interior Contra Costa communities around Walnut Hill and the San Ramon Valley.

The Congressman from the 7th District is George Miller, one of the few remaining Democrats of the Watergate class of 1974, the first baby-boom liberal to chair a House committee. He is also heir to a tradition of Bay Area working-class politics. His father was chairman of the state Senate Finance Committee; when he died in 1969, Miller lost the race to succeed him, but became a staffer for Senate leader (and later San Francisco Mayor) George Moscone. In the House, Miller brings to his work an aggressiveness and zest for political combat, a self-righteousness and a set of convictions not worn down by Capitol Hill clubbiness. Miller is one of several proteges of the late San Francisco Congressman Phillip Burton, who did so much to establish liberal hegemony in the House roundabout 1974; he backed Miller in his first race and saw to it that he served on the same two committees, then called Interior and Education and Labor.

In 1991, Miller became chairman of Interior (in 1993, he changed its name to Natural Resources, and Republicans changed it to Resources in 1995) just before his side started losing political strength. Miller has long seen his job as protecting the government's natural resources from greedy private sector operators who would exploit them and scar the environment, and get off without paying for their economic value. He approaches his work with pugnacity—"People sent me to Congress to kick ass and take names, and I'm not going to roll over," he once said—and perseverance. One great success of his chairmanship built on his work, as Water Subcommittee chairman, crusading against the big subsidies received by farmers in California's Central Valley and elsewhere in the West. In 1992, taking advantage of concern over the California drought, he passed a major water bill, with projects for most western states and a revision of California's Central Valley Project that channels one-fifth of the state's usable water supply, requires farmers to pay prices closer to those of urban water users and enforces fish and wildlife protection measures. This was passed with the help of Senator Bill Bradley and over furious opposition from Valley politicians and Governor Pete Wilson. The victory was sealed when the Clinton Administration appointed a top Miller aide, Dan Beard, as head of the Bureau of Reclamation, the largest supplier of water to 17 states.

Miller was less successful on other fronts. He stood up for the Endangered Species Act in the controversy over the spotted owl and logging in the Pacific Northwest, and tried to stop logging in a wide swath of land while providing aid to laid-off loggers. But as endangered species proceedings have interfered with farmers and businessmen all across the country, Miller was increasingly on the defensive. He strongly backs higher mining, grazing and timber fees for companies operating on federal lands and was pleased when incoming Interior Secretary Bruce Babbitt endorsed this, but was dismayed in March 1993 when the Clinton Administration abandoned the proposal, under pressure from senators from the Rocky Mountain states: "This is absolutely spoonfeeding the special interests," Miller said. In July 1993, he said government would have to spend at least $150 billion cleaning up environmental contamination on federal lands caused by government agencies and private companies. In September 1993 he called for expanding the boundaries of the Yellowstone and Rocky Mountain National Park ecosystems. Neither seems likely any time soon. He did achieve an important success in the California desert bill, which passed the House in late 1993 and, after Dianne Feinstein beat a filibuster by Wyoming's Malcolm Wallop, the Senate in October 1994. But the month before, Miller had to admit that Senate inaction would prevent revision of the Mining Act of 1872; he believes that it allows mining companies to stake claims and extract resources from federal lands for minuscule fees. That cause is certainly dead now that Don Young of Alaska, who long chafed under Miller, is now chairman of Resources. For the 104th Congress, Miller seems to be shifting inevitably from assembling complex legislation to sponsoring bills to make a political point with the subtlety of a Bronx cheer—including legislation to recover $3 billion purportedly lost to the government through mining, timber, grazing and water subsidies, and a bill for hearings on withdrawal from NAFTA.

Miller has a liberal voting record on almost all issues, though in the 1980s, as chairman of a special committee on children, he opposed the ABC child care bill supported by Hillary

Rodham Clinton's ally Marian Wright Edelman, backing instead a measure with greater parent choice and less government supervisory power. At home, Miller has remained highly popular; after a cloud of sulfuric acid blanketed Richmond in 1993, he protested loudly at the practice of storing tank cars with toxic chemicals on tracks in Contra Costa County. Miller was one Democrat who was helped by Pete Wilson's redistricting plans: he lost high-income inland parts of Contra Costa County to the new 10th District represented by Republican Bill Baker, and he gained Vallejo and the north shore of the Carquinez Strait, all heavily Democratic, from Vic Fazio's old district. So he can count on being reelected by wide margins.

The People: Pop. 1990: 572,857; 10% age 65+; 56% White; 17% Black; 1% Amer. Indian; 14% Asian; 6% Other; 13% Hispanic origin. Voting age pop.: 421,835; 15% Black; 11% Hispanic origin. Households: 54% married couple families; 26% married couple fams. w. children; 57% college educ.; median household income: $38,608; per capita income: $16,006; median gross rent: $625; median house value: $167,000.

1992 Presidential Vote

Clinton (D)	140,159	(60%)
Bush (R)	51,356	(22%)
Perot (I)	39,038	(17%)

1988 Presidential Vote

Dukakis (D)	126,704	(62%)
Bush (R)	76,561	(38%)

Rep. George Miller (D)

Elected 1974; b. May 17, 1945, Richmond; home, Martinez; San Francisco St. U., B.A. 1968, U. of CA at Davis, J.D. 1972; Catholic; married (Cynthia).

Career: Legis. aide, CA Sen. Majority Ldr., 1969–74; Practicing atty., 1972–74.

DC Office: 2205 RHOB 20515, 202-225-2095; Fax: 202-225-5609; e-mail: gmiller@hr.house.gov

District Offices: 367 Civic Dr., #14, Pleasant Hill 94523, 510-602-1880; and 3220 Blume Dr., #281, Richmond 94806, 510-262-6500.

Committees: *Economic & Educational Opportunities* (2nd of 19 D): Early Childhood, Youth and Families; Workforce Protections. *Resources* (RMM of 20 D): Fisheries, Wildlife and Oceans; Water and Power Resources.

Group Ratings

	ADA	ACLU	COPE	CFA	LCV	CON	NSI	COC	ACU	NTLC	CHC
1994	90	86	100	90	89	42	0	25	0	12	7
1993	100	—	100	90	93	47	—	0	8	—	—

National Journal Ratings

	1993 LIB — 1993 CONS		1994 LIB — 1994 CONS	
Economic	88% —	0%	65% —	34%
Social	80% —	13%	94% —	0%
Foreign	84% —	13%	85% —	0%

Key Votes of the 103d Congress

1. Clinton Deficit Plan	Y	3. Brady Handgun Purchase	Y	5. Lmt. UN Cmnd. of Forces	N
2. NAFTA	N	4. Strike Race/Death Pnlty.	N	6. Cut Missile Funds	Y

Key Votes of the 104th Congress

1. Congressional Compliance Y	6. Reform Crime Grant N	11. Loser Pays Court Reform N
2. Balanced Budget Amndmt. N	7. National Security Act N	12. Product Liability Reform N
3. Bar Unfunded Mandates N	8. Moratorium on Regs. N	13. Welfare Reform N
4. Pass Line Item Veto N	9. Risk Assessment on Regs. N	14. Term Limits Amndmt. N
5. Relax Exclusionary Rule N	10. Expnd. Priv. Prop. Rights N	15. Tax Cuts N

Election Results

1994 general	George Miller (D)	116,105	(70%)	($442,581)
	Charles V. Hughes (R)	45,698	(27%)	($2,432)
	Others	4,798	(3%)	
1994 primary	George Miller (D)	unopposed		
1992 general	George Miller (D)	153,320	(70%)	($651,360)
	Dave Scholl (R)	54,822	(25%)	($62,047)
	David L. Franklin (P&F)	9,840	(5%)	

EIGHTH DISTRICT

On February 20, 1915, Governor Hiram Johnson and Mayor James Rolph led 150,000 people onto the grounds of the Panama-Pacific International Exposition to see the Spanish-Italian baroque style building built on reclaimed land in what became San Francisco's Marina district. The Exposition ostensibly celebrated the completion of the Panama Canal, but it was clearly intended to show off San Francisco's recovery from the 1906 earthquake. It also spotlighted San Francisco as the central focus of an America that was becoming, with its acquisition of Hawaii and the Philippines and its interest in an open door policy with China and trade with Japan, a power in what we now call the Pacific Rim.

The Exposition set the physical style of San Francisco: it encouraged the use of Mediterranean color, accent and detail that characterizes most post-Victorian houses and commercial structures in The City (as the *San Francisco Examiner* still calls it). It created the picturesque Marina district, whose old buildings were among the few damaged in the 1989 earthquake, and today's tourist waterfront around Fisherman's Wharf and Ghirardelli Square. This San Francisco has many facets: on a sunny day it looks almost tropical, with brown mountains baking in the sun and light shining off the pastel stucco buildings; when the clouds scud in from the Pacific, it can look sinister, full of dark corners where a private detective's partner might be ambushed by a pretty girl. The buildings can be majestic, like the monumental Beaux Arts City Hall, or tawdry, like the hotels of the Tenderloin; it is a city that looks exotic at first but, when you look closely, can only be American.

San Francisco has been a dynamic city, capable of great growth, carrying the American tradition of tolerance of diversity to new lengths; it grew from nothing to a major city in the single year of 1850; its American origins are obvious from the regular grids of streets named after politicians and local developers. The San Francisco of 1915 was proud of the writers who had flourished there—Jack London, Ambrose Bierce, Frank Norris—and of the home-town traditions of the arts and crafts movement, just as San Francisco later would have a Herb Caenish pride in the beats of the 1950s North Beach, the hippies who thronged Haight-Ashbury in 1967, and the gays of the Castro in the 1970s and 1980s. Over the years, the city's booming economy, based initially on food processing, but now on finance, high-tech and clothing (Levi Strauss, The Gap) has attracted talented newcomers, weighted increasingly toward those who find its liberation-minded cultural attitudes congenial.

Politically, San Francisco was a progressive Republican town, like the two men who led the way into the Exposition. The sour-tempered Hiram Johnson made his name as a reformer throwing out crooked city politicians; his administration gave California primary elections, referenda and recall, and strong civil service laws. "Sunny Jim" Rolph, mayor from 1911 to 1930 and then governor, built the civic center, parks, schools, streetcars and the Hetch Hetchy power lines—the antique infrastructure of San Francisco today. Sympathetic to the conservation movement, willing to deal with organized labor in a union town that had America's only general strike in 1934, tolerant of the diversity of California as the anti-Chinese working class movements of the 19th Century were not, these progressive Republicans were the recognizable ancestors of, though certainly not identical to, the San Franciscans who in the 1970s and 1980s became increasingly liberal and even radical.

But San Francisco's hipness can be overstated. For if its distinctive style attracted liberal singles and gays in increasing numbers, its economic dynamism on the Pacific Rim has attracted Asians—as indeed San Francisco did from 1850 until immigration was shut off by the Chinese Exclusion Act in 1882. The city has elected strong liberal politicians at least since the 1975 elections of Mayor George Moscone and openly gay Supervisor Harvey Milk, who were shot to death in 1978 by a political opponent who was acquitted of murder by a liberal jury on the bizarre theory that he had been crazed by junk food. Over the next ten years, the city's cultural liberalism was tempered by Mayor Dianne Feinstein, who vetoed a gay marriage ordinance and opposed commercial rent control. When her successor Art Agnos promised shelter to every homeless person in the city and allowed a homeless colony ("Camp Agnos") across from City Hall, he was ousted in 1991 by former police chief Frank Jordan, backed by Asian-Americans and white homeowners. Jordan's crackdown on the homeless was attacked by liberals on the Board of Supervisors, but Jordan entered the 1995 campaign season as the favorite, and faced probable liberal opposition from former assistant HUD secretary Roberta Achtenberg and Assembly Speaker Willie Brown.

The 8th Congressional District of California takes in four-fifths of San Francisco, all but the southwest corner. It has all of San Francisco's high-rise downtown, the increasingly crowded and bustling Chinatown, Telegraph, Nob and Russian Hills, North Beach (which was once really a beach), Pacific Heights (which is still on heights) and the Marina District (which does not have a very big marina). It extends to the ocean to include Sea Cliff overlooking the Golden Gate Bridge, and the Richmond area with its many Asian-Americans. In the valleys are the mostly black Fillmore and Western Addition areas, but only 13% of the district's residents are black, as compared to 15% Hispanic and 28% Asian—the highest Asian percentage of any district outside Hawaii. The 8th also has the gay Castro district and Noe Valley, Haight-Ashbury, once the bedraggled center of hippiedom and now another yup-and-coming San Francisco neighborhood, and Portrero Hill with its restored houses overlooking downtown. Farther south are the old residential areas between Candlestick Park, the Cow Palace and I-280, with pastel houses strewn out along grid streets which hug the steep hills.

The 8th District is represented by Nancy Pelosi, a Democrat with deep political roots and a capacity for keeping all parts of her party happy. She has the energy and shrewdness of one who has handled the most delicate political chores and the charm and unflappability of one who has been the parent of five children. Pelosi grew up in Maryland; her father, Thomas D'Alessandro, served in the House from 1939 to 1947 and was mayor of Baltimore for 12 years after that, and her brother, Thomas D'Alessandro Jr., was mayor from 1967 to 1971. Married to a successful San Francisco businessman, she was California Democratic Party chair in the early 1980s, chaired the national party's Compliance Review Commission on delegate rules for 1984, and served as the Democratic Senatorial Campaign Committee's finance chair in 1985. She never considered running for the House when San Francisco's congressional politics was dominated by Phillip Burton, congressman since 1964, an old-fashioned labor-liberal Democrat and opponent of the Vietnam war from the beginning. But Burton died in 1983 and his widow Sala, elected to succeed him, died in 1987. Pelosi ran and won 35%–31% in an April 1987 special primary against gay supervisor Harry Britt.

Pelosi's highest-profile work in the House has come not on left-liberal but on Asian issues. She took the lead, in her first full term, in opposing President Bush's treatment of Chinese students after Tiananmen Square, sponsoring an amendment to give them protective immigration status—which passed the House overwhelmingly but was vetoed by Bush. In 1991 she was the lead sponsor of the bill to condition China's Most Favored Nation status on human rights reforms; it passed both houses, and Bush's veto was overridden in the House 357–61 but upheld in the Senate 60–38. She has continued to sponsor bills to condition MFN status on human rights improvements and to protect Chinese students here from being forcibly returned to China, and she was disappointed in May 1994 when President Clinton renewed MFN status without her conditions, and called Clinton's 1995 round of trade talks with China "a failure." Pelosi's other great cause is AIDS funding; she uses her seat on Appropriations to get money for research, treatment and housing for people with AIDS. The former military base at San Francisco's Presidio has occupied much of her time, too. Years ago, Burton got a law turning over the Presidio to the Interior Department if it was abandoned by the military; it got on the 1993 base closing list, despite Pelosi's efforts, and was transferred to the National Park Service in 1995. There is no more stunning piece of urban property in America, but restoring its dilapidated buildings could absorb most of the Park Service budget when it is cutting elsewhere. Pelosi proposed a nonprofit trust to renovate and lease out buildings, and it passed the House in 1994 but was killed by Republicans in the Senate; she will be challenged to come up with a solution in the 104th Congress.

Pelosi has one of the most liberal voting records in the House; she supported the Clinton Administration on the North American Free Trade Agreement as well as the 1993 budget and tax package. She was reelected with 82% of the vote in 1992 and 1994.

The People: Pop. 1990: 573,192; 14% age 65+; 44% White; 13% Black; 28% Asian; 7% Other; 15% Hispanic origin. Voting age pop.: 481,195; 11% Black; 14% Hispanic origin. Households: 31% married couple families; 12% married couple fams. w. children; 58% college educ.; median household income: $31,659; per capita income: $19,377; median gross rent: $631; median house value: $270,100.

1992 Presidential Vote

Clinton (D)	187,201	(75%)
Bush (R)	39,396	(16%)
Perot (I)	21,180	(8%)

1988 Presidential Vote

Dukakis (D)	162,192	(76%)
Bush (R)	50,277	(24%)

Rep. Nancy Pelosi (D)

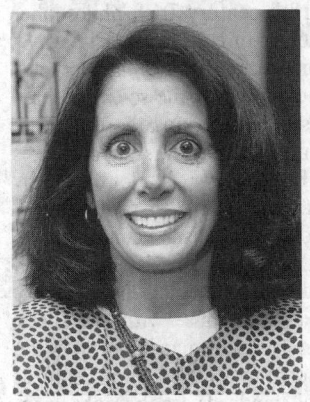

Elected June, 1987; b. Mar. 26, 1940, Baltimore, MD; home, San Francisco; Trinity College, B.A. 1962; Catholic; married (Paul).

Career: CA Dem. Party, Northern Chmn., 1977–81, St. Chmn., 1981–83; Finance Chmn., DSCC, 1985–87; PR exec., Ogilvy & Mather, 1986–87.

Office: 2457 RHOB 20515, 202-225-4965; Fax: 202-225-8259.

District Offices: 450 Golden Gate Ave., #45378, San Francisco 94102, 415-556-4862.

Committees: *Appropriations* (19th of 24 D): Foreign Operations, Export Financing, and Related Programs; Labor, Health and Human Services, and Education. *Standards of Official Conduct* (3rd of 5 D). *Intelligence (Permanent Select)* (6th of 7 D): Technical and Tactical Intelligence (RMM).

Group Ratings

	ADA	ACLU	COPE	CFA	LCV	CON	NSI	COC	ACU	NTLC	CHC
1994	90	87	89	100	94	32	0	25	0	4	0
1993	95	—	92	100	100	32	—	18	0	—	—

National Journal Ratings

	1993 LIB — 1993 CONS		1994 LIB — 1994 CONS	
Economic	78% —	12%	83% —	0%
Social	87% —	0%	87% —	11%
Foreign	79% —	21%	85% —	0%

Key Votes of the 103d Congress

1. Clinton Deficit Plan	Y	3. Brady Handgun Purchase	Y	5. Lmt. UN Cmnd. of Forces	N
2. NAFTA	Y	4. Strike Race/Death Pnlty.	N	6. Cut Missile Funds	Y

Key Votes of the 104th Congress

1. Congressional Compliance	Y	6. Reform Crime Grant	N	11. Loser Pays Court Reform	N
2. Balanced Budget Amndmt.	N	7. National Security Act	N	12. Product Liability Reform	N
3. Bar Unfunded Mandates	N	8. Moratorium on Regs.	N	13. Welfare Reform	N
4. Pass Line Item Veto	N	9. Risk Assessment on Regs.	N	14. Term Limits Amndmt.	N
5. Relax Exclusionary Rule	N	10. Expnd. Priv. Prop. Rights	N	15. Tax Cuts	N

Election Results

1994 general	Nancy Pelosi (D).....................	137,642	(82%)	($370,000)
	Elsa C. Cheung (R)	30,528	(18%)	($19,882)
1994 primary	Nancy Pelosi (D).....................	58,426	(91%)	
	Robert Ingraham (D)	5,476	(9%)	
1992 general	Nancy Pelosi (D).....................	191,906	(82%)	($443,238)
	Marc Wolin (R)......................	25,693	(11%)	($49,566)
	Others	15,092	(7%)	

NINTH DISTRICT

Oakland and Berkeley, the two best-known cities on the East Bay opposite San Francisco, stand today on one of the lushest sites in America, overlooking the Bay Bridge and the Golden Gate, basking in the sunshine that is more common here than across the Bay. Both cities are still the homes of great institutions, but in different ways they are also museum pieces, antiques from a moment in the 1960s when both, especially Berkeley, gained an identity that is hard to shake. Berkeley was founded as a university town, named after the 18th century Irish philosopher Bishop George Berkeley, for his proclamation, "Westward the course of empire takes its way." Famous for years as the home of first-rate scholarship at the University of California, Berkeley became famous politically in 1964 as the home of student rebellion when the so-called Free Speech Movement, protesting an administrator's refusal to let students set up a card table to sign up volunteers for Lyndon Johnson's 1964 campaign, led to months of riots, student strikes and classroom confrontation. In 1969, students led protests at "People's Park," a lot owned by the university, and Governor Ronald Reagan sent in the National Guard to protect state property from conversion to a playground: an episode in which both sides relished confrontation more than success. Berkeley in the 1960s gave birth to a street culture that still exists (in 1993, a student went about campus naked and was expelled only when administrators had the ingenuity to charge him with sexual harassment). Its denizens made common cause with the Black Panthers, a violent quasi-political gang from nearby Oakland and smoked marijuana with the Hell's Angels motorcycle gang, also once based in Oakland. Berkeley's city council features bizarre political wars in which Democrats very liberal by national standards are the right wing.

The Berkeley campus, with its view of the Bay, remains beautiful, and old buildings like the shingled Claremont Hotel are grand. Undergraduate students, about one-third Asian (a number sharply up after administrators adjusted racial quotas under pressure), are studying hard to get ahead in a high-tech economy. But Berkeley has had little commercial development, and its public facilities have a low-maintenance, almost Third World look, as if people want to live forever in 1969.

Oakland has a different history, centered around commerce and building its own civic institutions (Gertrude Stein was wrong: there is a there there). It became the western terminus of the transcontinental railroad in 1870 and was connected by ferry to San Francisco; it has always had heavy industry, and its port today is the busiest on the bay. The docks attracted young roustabouts like the writer Jack London, after whom a downtown square is named; civic affairs were run by the local elite, like the Knowland family who owned the *Oakland Tribune*. With the Bay Area's largest black community, Oakland spawned the Black Panthers in the 1960s; blacks took control of city government in the 1970s and, through the late editor-owner Bob Maynard, the *Tribune* in the 1980s. The city has a high crime rate and more than its share of tragedy, like the firestorm that broke out in the hills in October 1991, killing 25 people and destroying 2,500 homes. But Oakland, more than Berkeley, seems to be looking ahead, with Mayor Elihu Harris pledging better law enforcement and local civic leaders trying to spark new businesses.

The 9th Congressional District consists of Oakland and Berkeley, plus adjacent towns—notably Alameda, site of an old Navy base on the bay. It has the largest black percentage of any northern California district, but not a majority (32%); it is 16% Asian and 12% Hispanic. Politically, it is leftish Democratic: George Bush got only 12% of the vote here in 1992.

The congressman from the 9th is Ronald Dellums, a product of the radical politics of the late 1960s. Dellums grew up in Oakland, enlisted in the Marine Corps at 18, then became the first member of his family to attend college. He was a psychiatric social worker in San Francisco when friends got him to run for the Berkeley Council in 1967; in 1970 he challenged Congressman Jeffrey Cohelan, a six-term Democrat who had one of the most liberal voting records in Congress but wasn't sufficiently radical to suit the Berkeley left. Dellums has a faith in the domestic public sector which owes something to his career as a social worker and a ramrod-straight bearing and a faithfulness to duty which may owe something to his service as a Marine. He won a seat on the Armed Services Committee (now National Security) upon arrival in Washington in 1971 but found that he had no place to sit during meetings; the chairman had assigned the same chair to both Dellums and another newcomer. He persevered, though, and in 1993, became National Security chairman. Dellums has consistently favored lower defense spending than the House as a whole has supported; he opposed the MX missile, the Pershing II, the Midgetman, B-1 and B-2; he did not vote for a defense authorization bill until 1993. But as chairman first of the Acquisitions Subcommittee and then of the full committee, he never used his power to obstruct projects he opposed. And he worked hard to see that his bills reflected the views of his colleagues, even when they were different from his own. In 1993 he insisted on a vote on eliminating the ban on gays in the military, and lost 43–12 in committee; he lost another vote 29–27 on antimissile defense. His performance should stand for years as a prime example of how a chairman can preside fairly and with dignity while conscientiously disagreeing with the views of his colleagues. He also answered those who jibed that he and other Bay Area congressmen were happy to vote for defense cuts while protecting local defense installations. The 9th District had six facilities on the 1993 base closing list, including the Alameda Naval Air Station, with 11,000 employees. Dellums did not fight the list, but instead promoted defense reconversion legislation and pilot programs in Alameda as well as suggesting new research projects for the Lawrence Livermore Labs.

Dellums's views have mellowed a bit over the years, even as on one issue—South Africa—his views have helped to change the world. Dellums came to Congress convinced, as many were at the time, that the extension of U.S. military power was dangerous and evil—dangerous to us and evil to others. He once told a Berkeley symposium, "We should dismantle every intelligence agency in this country piece by piece, brick by brick, nail by nail." But by 1991, when he was serving on the Intelligence Committee, he said, "Intelligence acquisition enjoys a rightful place; but responsible agencies must be required to respect both the nation's laws and international laws that we have, by treaty, incorporated into the body of our own jurisprudence." He was among the harshest critics of the 1983 Grenada invasion, which he saw as hurting the Grenadans; one of his staffers, it turned out, had close ties with the pro-Communist New Jewel movement there. He vehemently opposed U.S. military action in the Persian Gulf in 1990 and 1991, leading the lawsuit against President Bush brought by 54 members of Congress to reaffirm that only Congress can declare war. But he did not argue that Saddam Hussein was progressive and, after the speedy success of U.S. forces, he no longer seems to argue that any U.S. military intervention will prove futile.

Dellums first proposed sanctions against South Africa in 1971, finally winning the fight for their passage in 1986; he had the satisfaction of seeing South Africa end apartheid and institute democracy, and of having President Nelson Mandela address Congress. Dellums's leadership on South Africa was singled out for praise by Newt Gingrich in his first speech as Speaker in 1995. And in other places Dellums sees the United States as a force for good. He urged the Clinton Administration to take action to restore President Aristide to power in Haiti; he was more cautious, however, than other Black Caucus members about recommending the dispatch of U.S. troops.

The Republican victory of 1994 deprived Dellums of his chairmanship and put him back in the role of protester. He will continue to work, probably with mixed success, on National Security projects like streamlining acquisition and relaxing export controls on technology. At home he has pushed an anti-crime project and dredging not to create ship channels but to re-create tidal wetlands. For years he has had one of the most liberal, often the most liberal, voting record in the House. This suits the 9th District just fine. Before 1992, his districts contained suburbs over the ridge from Berkeley and Oakland where Dellums regularly lost, and he never won with more than 61% of the vote. In 1992, after it was revealed he had 851 overdrafts on the House bank, he might have been in more trouble but for redistricting, which kept the district entirely in the East Bay. In 1992 and 1994 he was reelected with 72%.

The People: Pop. 1990: 573,669; 12% age 65+; 41% White; 32% Black; 1% Amer. Indian; 16% Asian; 6% Other; 11% Hispanic origin. Voting age pop.: 447,239; 29% Black; 10% Hispanic origin. Households: 37% married couple families; 17% married couple fams. w. children; 62% college educ.; median household income: $30,067; per capita income: $16,833; median gross rent: $538; median house value: $220,200.

1992 Presidential Vote			1988 Presidential Vote		
Clinton (D)	186,714	(78%)	Dukakis (D)	178,152	(80%)
Bush (R)	29,394	(12%)	Bush (R)	44,112	(20%)
Perot (I)	21,207	(9%)			

Rep. Ronald V. Dellums (D)

Elected 1970; b. Nov. 24, 1935, Oakland; home, Oakland; Oakland City Col., A.A. 1958, San Francisco St. Col., B.A. 1960, U. of CA, M.S.W. 1962; Protestant; married (Leola).

Career: Marine Corps, 1954–56; Psychiatric social worker, CA Dept. of Mental Hygiene, 1962–64; Prog. Dir., Bayview Community Ctr., 1964–65; Dir., Hunter's Pt. Bayview Youth Oppor. Ctr., 1965–66; Consultant, Bay Area Social Plng. Cncl., 1966–67; Dir., San Francisco Econ. Oppor. Cncl. Employment Prog., 1967–68; Berkeley City Cncl., 1967–71.

DC Office: 2108 RHOB 20515, 202-225-2661; Fax: 202-225-9817.

District Offices: 1301 Clay St., Oakland 94612, 510-763-0370.

Committees: *National Security* (RMM of 25 D): Military Procurement.

Group Ratings

	ADA	ACLU	COPE	CFA	LCV	CON	NSI	COC	ACU	NTLC	CHC
1994	100	91	100	100	100	16	0	17	5	11	0
1993	100	—	100	100	86	39	—	0	4	—	—

National Journal Ratings

	1993 LIB — 1993 CONS		1994 LIB — 1994 CONS	
Economic	88%	— 0%	83%	— 0%
Social	87%	— 0%	86%	— 14%
Foreign	93%	— 0%	85%	— 0%

Key Votes of the 103d Congress

1. Clinton Deficit Plan	Y	3. Brady Handgun Purchase	Y	5. Lmt. UN Cmnd. of Forces	N
2. NAFTA	N	4. Strike Race/Death Pnlty.	N	6. Cut Missile Funds	Y

Key Votes of the 104th Congress

1. Congressional Compliance	Y	6. Reform Crime Grant	N	11. Loser Pays Court Reform	N
2. Balanced Budget Amndmt.	N	7. National Security Act	N	12. Product Liability Reform	N
3. Bar Unfunded Mandates	N	8. Moratorium on Regs.	N	13. Welfare Reform	N
4. Pass Line Item Veto	N	9. Risk Assessment on Regs.	N	14. Term Limits Amndmt.	N
5. Relax Exclusionary Rule	N	10. Expnd. Priv. Prop. Rights	N	15. Tax Cuts	N

Election Results

1994 general	Ronald V. Dellums (D)	129,233	(72%)	($482,877)
	Deborah Wright (R)	40,448	(23%)	($18,453)
	Emma Wong Mar (P&F)	9,194	(5%)	
1994 primary	Ronald V. Dellums (D)	unopposed		
1992 general	Ronald V. Dellums (D)	164,265	(72%)	($921,771)
	G. William (Billy) Hunter (R)	53,707	(24%)	($73,659)
	Dave Linn (P&F)	10,472	(5%)	

TENTH DISTRICT

In the 1950s, when the streets of San Francisco and Oakland were already crowded, the rolling grasslands on the east of the mountain ridges, over the hill and through the tunnel from Oakland, were still mostly empty. In the years since, they have started to fill up. Freeways took the first commuters through the Caldecott Tunnel to the woodsy trail-like roads of Orinda and Lafayette; Interstate 580 brought people east from the southern East Bay towns to the Amador Valley and Livermore, site of one of the nation's nuclear laboratories; Interstate 680 running north-south provided a spine for businesses and shopping centers up and down the San Ramon Valley, from burgeoning Concord through Walnut Creek, Danville and Dublin; BART stations in Walnut Creek and Orinda took commuters to downtown San Francisco. Not all this area is filled in yet, and there is resistance to overdevelopment. But what has evolved in this sunny land, shielded by the mountains from the ocean fogs and rains, is an advanced civilization of highly skilled and educated people. Affluent and generally tolerant of—if a little put off by—what happens in San Francisco, they are respectful of economic markets and wary of government, but concerned about preserving a physical environment that can be one of America's most pleasant.

This is the land of the 10th Congressional District, a seat newly created by the court-ordered redistricting of 1992. It consists almost entirely of the interior portion of the Bay Area, with just a few salients beyond—the suburb of Castro Valley on the East Bay, the working class town of Antioch on the San Joaquin River Delta. This area had been voting Republican for years but was split up between four Democratic districts. It is easily now the most Republican Bay Area district.

The Congressman from the 10th is Bill Baker, a Republican who has made a career as an expert in government who wants to cut it back. He grew up in Oakland, served in the Coast Guard, worked as a budget analyst for the Department of Finance in Sacramento, and became Executive Vice President of the Contra Costa Taxpayers Association. He used to write a newspaper column called "The Angry Taxpayer," and in 12 years in the Assembly he became known as an expert budget-cutter. As one observer wrote, "Baker makes any list of the legislature's quickest minds, tartest tongues and most doctrinaire conservatives." He also helped the city of Oakland with its budget problems; he was criticized for saying in 1980 that he would tell welfare mothers if they had more children, "If you're going to be a breeder, we're not going to subsidize it." An opponent of abortion rights, Baker hailed a high school delegation in 1991 as "17 survivors of abortion"—a comment for which he later apologized. None of this was helpful in 1992, as Californians, even suburban fiscal conservatives, seemed disgusted with George Bush and the religious right in the Republican Party. Baker won his primary 64%–36%, but in the general, faced Democrat Wendell Williams, who had run against him twice for the Assembly, holding him to 55% in 1990. Williams attacked Baker for being antiabortion and for the "breeder" and "17 survivors" lines; he also accused Baker, apparently without evidence, of having ties to the religious right. Baker talked about budget-cutting and called for lower capital gains taxes, measures to spur home construction and "government that is user-friendly to investors." He won with only 52% of the vote—not a stunning showing for a clear favorite in this favorable district.

In the House, Baker became vice chair of the now-defunct, conservative-activist Republican Study Committee and served on the Science Committee, important for thousands of voters employed at the Livermore Lab and a branch of the Sandia Lab here, and on Transportation and Infrastructure, where he promoted San Ramon Valley roads. He worked to repeal the"must-carry" provision of the 1992 Cable Act and compiled an almost perfectly conservative voting record, risking wrath at his opposition to abortion and gun control, though he supported the Brady Bill. Baker continued to write witty columns attacking the Clinton healthcare plan and crime bills. His Democratic opponent in 1994, businesswoman Ellen Schwartz, hit Baker on his opposition to gun control and abortion, but was almost disqualified from running in the Democratic primary as she had registered in the Green Party a year earlier. Baker beat her 59%–39%. In the 104th Congress, Baker was successful in incorporating a proposal for a "stay at home" spousal IRA into the 1995 tax bill. He has also introduced a bill giving companies a $500 tax credit for each employee it allows to "telecommute."

The People: Pop. 1990: 571,979; 3% rural; 10% age 65+; 82% White; 2% Black; 1% Amer. Indian; 6% Asian; 3% Other; 9% Hispanic origin. Voting age pop.: 431,696; 2% Black; 8% Hispanic origin. Households: 63% married couple families; 29% married couple fams. w. children; 68% college educ.; median household income: $52,378; per capita income: $23,972; median gross rent: $746; median house value: $273,800.

1992 Presidential Vote			1988 Presidential Vote		
Clinton (D)	127,450	(42%)	Bush (R)	144,386	(58%)
Bush (R)	107,191	(35%)	Dukakis (D)	104,199	(42%)
Perot (I)	66,180	(22%)			

Rep. Bill Baker (R)

Elected 1992; b. June 14, 1940, Oakland; home, Danville; San Jose St. U., B.S. 1963; Catholic; married (Joanne).

Career: Coast Guard Reserves, 1957–65; Budget Analyst, CA Dept. of Finance 1968–72; Exec. V.P., Contra Costa Taxpayers Assn., 1972–78; CA Assembly, 1980–92.

DC Office: 1724 LHOB 20515, 202-225-1880; Fax: 202-225-1868.

District Offices: 1801 N. California Blvd., Walnut Creek 94596, 510-932-8899; and Dublin City Hall, 100 Civic Plz., Dublin 94568, 510-829-0813.

Committees: *Transportation & Infrastructure* (15th of 33 R): Coast Guard and Maritime Transportation; Surface Transportation. *Science* (11th of 27 R): Basic Research; Energy and Environment.

Group Ratings

	ADA	ACLU	COPE	CFA	LCV	CON	NSI	COC	ACU	NTLC	CHC
1994	0	13	11	20	13	67	100	83	100	96	100
1993	10	—	0	20	14	74	—	100	96	—	—

National Journal Ratings

	1993 LIB — 1993 CONS		1994 LIB — 1994 CONS	
Economic	14%	— 80%	0%	— 80%
Social	11%	— 82%	0%	— 89%
Foreign	0%	— 91%	0%	— 88%

Key Votes of the 103d Congress

1. Clinton Deficit Plan	N	3. Brady Handgun Purchase Y	5. Lmt. UN Cmnd. of Forces Y
2. NAFTA	Y	4. Strike Race/Death Pnlty. Y	6. Cut Missile Funds N

Key Votes of the 104th Congress

1. Congressional Compliance Y	6. Reform Crime Grant Y	11. Loser Pays Court Reform Y
2. Balanced Budget Amndmt. Y	7. National Security Act Y	12. Product Liability Reform Y
3. Bar Unfunded Mandates Y	8. Moratorium on Regs. Y	13. Welfare Reform Y
4. Pass Line Item Veto Y	9. Risk Assessment on Regs. Y	14. Term Limits Amndmt. Y
5. Relax Exclusionary Rule Y	10. Expnd. Priv. Prop. Rights Y	15. Tax Cuts Y

Election Results

1994 general	Bill Baker (R)	138,916	(59%)	($909,065)
	Ellen Schwartz (D)	90,523	(39%)	($440,805)
	Others	4,802	(2%)	
1994 primary	Bill Baker (R)	44,771	(77%)	
	Dave Williams (R)	13,587	(23%)	
1992 general	Bill Baker (R)	145,702	(52%)	($697,982)
	Wendell H. Williams (D)	134,635	(48%)	($238,906)

ELEVENTH DISTRICT

People from back East looking for clues about California might consider avoiding Beverly Hills and Nob Hill and taking a look at Stockton. For Stockton, just 50 miles south of Sacramento, is in the middle of the Central Valley, which saw much of California's most rapid growth in the 1980s and is now subject to some growing problems of it own. This is not a new part of the state: Stockton was named after Robert Stockton, the second U.S. military governor of California, who captured Santa Barbara and Los Angeles from Mexico and proclaimed California United States territory. Founded in 1847, Stockton was an important trading town during the Gold Rush. The Central Valley, criss-crossed with railroads and canals, became one of the world's greatest agriculture areas; the San Joaquin River channel was deepened to 37 feet and Stockton today is the Central Valley's ocean port. The rich farming attracted immigrants from all over: Mexicans coming up Route 99 joined North Dakotans flocking to the town of Lodi; Italian and Yugoslav immigrants bringing their Old World crops; Yankees and Okies bringing their distinct churches and systems of belief; and now Southeast Asian refugees crowd into the older streets of Stockton. The 1980s growth brought traffic congestion and air quality problems to the Central Valley, and some fear that development will gobble up the best farmland. It also brought many voters, tilting a longtime Democratic area noticeably to the right.

The 11th Congressional District includes Stockton and most of surrounding San Joaquin County, plus the southern part of Sacramento County, an area of farms and a few subdivisions, dredge tailings and marshy, rich-soiled islands in the delta of the Sacramento and San Joaquin Rivers. The district was widely thought to have been intended by Governor Pete Wilson for former Sacramento County Supervisor Sandy Smoley—like Wilson a moderate and pro-choice Republican—who had lost to Robert Matsui in a Sacramento-based district in 1978. But Smoley lost the Republican primary to Richard Pombo, a 31-year-old rancher and Tracy council member who was known for bringing a Safeway distribution center to town. With his trademark cowboy hat and mustache, he looked the part of the fourth-generation San Joaquin County rancher. Pombo called Smoley "the surefire choice of the hard-line feminists" and attacked her support of Wilson's gay rights bill; when liberal Massachusetts Congressman Barney Frank called Pombo a "low-rent Pat Buchanan," Pombo embraced the label. Pombo won 36%–27%, with 24% going to a former aide to a former Stockton congressman. In the general, Pombo faced Patti Garamendi, a onetime Peace Corps volunteer, mother of six and wife of Insurance Commissioner and and unsuccessful 1994 Democratic gubernatorial aspirant John Garamendi. She was well known but suffered from a reputation as a perpetual candidate: she ran unsuccessfully to succeed her husband in the state Senate in 1990 and then lost a 1991 special election for the Assembly. Pombo, far from being defensive about his conservative stands, emblazoned them: this was a Contract With America candidate two years before the Contract. He stressed his opposition to abortion, his support of property rights and opposition to the Endangered Species Act. He denounced the lyrics of rap singer Ice-T's song "Cop Killer," and attacked Garamendi when she accused him of racism for it. Though solidly outspent, Pombo won 48%–46%.

In the House Pombo compiled a perfectly conservative record, tilting with environmentalists on the Resources Committee and with subsidy advocates on Agriculture. Pombo is known to be tough on crime, supporting longer sentences for criminals, and in May 1994 voted against the bill banning the sale of military-style assault weapons. "I'm not going to fit in too well," he predicted, "because I'm anything but politically correct." He and like-minded Republicans helped prove that prediction wrong. Pombo attacked the Clinton Administration hard and was reelected 62%–35%. He fit in perfectly with the new Republican freshmen and became an enthusiastic supporter of the Contract. In early 1995 Resources Committee chairman Don Young appointed Pombo chairman of a special task force charged with reauthorization of the Endangered Species Act.

The People: Pop. 1990: 571,650; 15% rural; 11% age 65+; 62% White; 6% Black; 1% Amer. Indian; 12% Asian; 7% Other; 20% Hispanic origin. Voting age pop.: 404,873; 5% Black; 18% Hispanic origin. Households: 58% married couple families; 29% married couple fams. w. children; 46% college educ.; median household income: $31,605; per capita income: $13,299; median gross rent: $499; median house value: $123,000.

1992 Presidential Vote		
Clinton (D)	79,432	(40%)
Bush (R)	75,319	(38%)
Perot (I)	41,006	(21%)

1988 Presidential Vote		
Bush (R)	97,325	(56%)
Dukakis (D)	76,929	(44%)

Rep. Richard W. Pombo (R)

Elected 1992; b. Jan. 8, 1961, Tracy; home, Tracy; CA Polytechnic Inst., 1979–82; Catholic; married (Annette).

Career: Cattle rancher; Co-founder, Citizens Land Alliance, 1986; Tracy City Cncl., 1990–92.

DC Office: 1519 LHOB 20515, 202-225-1947; Fax: 202-225-0861.

District Offices: 2495 W. March La., #104, Stockton 95207, 209-951-3091.

Committees: *Agriculture* (11th of 27 R): Livestock, Dairy and Poultry; Resource Conservation, Research and Forestry; Risk Management and Specialty Crops. *Resources* (11th of 25 R): National Parks, Forests and Lands; Water and Power Resources.

Group Ratings

	ADA	ACLU	COPE	CFA	LCV	CON	NSI	COC	ACU	NTLC	CHC
1994	5	13	25	20	6	78	100	92	100	96	100
1993	10	—	8	10	14	74	—	91	100	—	—

National Journal Ratings

	1993 LIB — 1993 CONS		1994 LIB — 1994 CONS	
Economic	20% —	77%	0% —	80%
Social	0% —	89%	0% —	89%
Foreign	9% —	85%	0% —	88%

Key Votes of the 103d Congress

1. Clinton Deficit Plan	N	3. Brady Handgun Purchase	N	5. Lmt. UN Cmnd. of Forces	Y
2. NAFTA	N	4. Strike Race/Death Pnlty.	Y	6. Cut Missile Funds	N

Key Votes of the 104th Congress

1. Congressional Compliance	Y	6. Reform Crime Grant	Y	11. Loser Pays Court Reform	Y
2. Balanced Budget Amndmt.	Y	7. National Security Act	Y	12. Product Liability Reform	Y
3. Bar Unfunded Mandates	Y	8. Moratorium on Regs.	Y	13. Welfare Reform	Y
4. Pass Line Item Veto	Y	9. Risk Assessment on Regs.	Y	14. Term Limits Amndmt.	Y
5. Relax Exclusionary Rule	Y	10. Expnd. Priv. Prop. Rights	Y	15. Tax Cuts	Y

Election Results

1994 general	Richard W. Pombo (R)	99,302	(62%)	($657,627)
	Randy A. Perry (D)	55,794	(35%)	($146,682)
	Others	4,718	(3%)	
1994 primary	Richard W. Pombo (R)	unopposed		
1992 general	Richard W. Pombo (R)	94,453	(48%)	($528,989)
	Patricia Garamendi (D)	90,539	(46%)	($864,411)
	Christine Roberts (Lib)	13,498	(7%)	

TWELFTH DISTRICT

Running south from San Francisco is the Peninsula, which connects the city with the mainland of the United States. This is geologically interesting, and active, country: the San Andreas Fault runs just east of the Coast Range, underneath the reservoirs that store San Francisco's water supply. To the west are green mountains splashing down into the foggy ocean. To the east is a zone of flat land between mountain and bay, an unbroken chain of suburbs and urban settlement, with light industry and salt flats along the bay front, and residential neighborhoods and some commercial strips from the Bayshore Freeway up through the Junipero Serra Freeway atop the mountain ridge. Historically, the Peninsula has seemed separate from San Francisco; Dashiell Hammett, writing before the advent of freeways, gets his detective Sam Spade out of the city for most of a day when he follows a false tip down the Peninsula. But today, the Peninsula suburbs are demographically an extension of the city.

The 12th Congressional District consists of the northern Peninsula suburbs plus the southwest quadrant of San Francisco—the city's middle-income Sunset district, with older houses amid unburied telephone and electric wires, lying on curving hills that were once sand dunes. Just to the south, across the San Mateo County line at the southern extension of the BART lines, is Daly City with substantial numbers of Mexican-Americans and Asians; nearby, South San Francisco proclaims itself "the industrial city" in big letters on San Bruno Mountain near the Bayshore Freeway; the streets lined with boxy houses in San Bruno and Pacifica wind over sweeping hillsides facing cemeteries where many San Franciscans and veterans of Pacific wars are buried. That is the view from one side of the Junipero Serra Freeway; from the other, the vista is of San Francisco Bay, broader than one might expect, and the airport next door, connecting this metropolis with others on the Pacific Rim; to the south is the neat suburban city of San Mateo and, on twisting streets in the hills above the Burlingame Country Club, the rich suburb of Hillsborough, home to much of the city's WASP elite.

This is an ethnically diverse and economically prosperous constituency. Fully 26% of its residents are Asian—the second highest of any mainland district, after San Francisco's 8th just to the north—and another 14% are Hispanic. Income levels are, if not among the highest in the country, very far above average: one-third of Hispanic households in San Mateo County in 1990 made over $50,000 a year. The economic orientation here is more toward San Francisco to the north than south toward Silicon Valley; the political heritage here is Democratic, from ethnic heritage and historic labor union ties. San Mateo gave Bill Clinton a large margin in 1992 and was one of only seven counties to vote for Democrat Kathleen Brown for governor in 1994.

The congressman from the 12th District, Tom Lantos, has several distinctions, but none more important than the fact that he is one of the few members of Congress with personal experience living under tyranny. Lantos was born in Hungary and as a teenager fought in the underground against the Nazis; he was one of the Jews saved by Swedish diplomat Raoul Wallenberg. He has the confidence of an intellectual (he taught economics at San Francisco State) who has also shrewdly made some money, and who has moved up politically (he chose to run against a Republican incumbent in the Republican year of 1980 and won), and who has seen first hand in his own lifetime the rise and then the rollback of totalitarianism.

Lantos has spent much of his time in the House on foreign policy. Unlike other Bay Area Democrats, he did not bring to his work an instinctive mistrust of American policy or doubts of American good intentions. He founded the Congressional Human Rights Caucus, focusing on Communist regimes as well as the right-wing dictatorships other liberal Democrats denounced. He is among the most enthusiastic supporters of Israel and called for economic sanctions against Iraq back in 1988 for its gassing of the Kurds. He was an enthusiastic supporter of the Gulf war resolution and was criticized by some back in his district for holding hearings where an unidentified 15-year-old Kuwaiti girl told of Iraqi atrocities; it turned out that she was the daughter of the Kuwaiti ambassador, and Lantos was accused of whipping up war fever. Lantos stayed in close touch with Eastern Europe, especially Hungary, as Communism collapsed and new democracies rose up; in 1990 he was the first American official to visit Albania since 1946. He has strongly advocated a more active American role in Bosnia. As chairman of the Foreign Affairs International Operations Subcommittee in 1993 and 1994, he conducted 50 hearings on United Nations peacekeeping operations. He is concerned about any Republican plans that may slash foreign aid, in light of increasing terrorism and nuclear proliferation.

Lantos has displayed a flair for showmanship on his Government Operations subcommittee investigations. In 1989 and 1990 he conducted hearings on alleged misconduct under Reagan HUD Secretary Samuel Pierce, which attracted great attention; an independent counsel was appointed and 16 guilty pleas resulted, although no action was taken against Pierce. His high-publicity hearings on labor law violations by the Food Lion supermarket chain led to legal charges, and he attacked West Coast-based Jack in the Box for child labor law violations. He was a founder of the Congressional Friends of Animals Caucus.

Lantos raised and spent a total of $1.7 million on his 1980 and 1982 campaigns. He has by far the most moderate voting record of Bay Area Democrats and since 1984 has been reelected easily. Redistricting helped by moving the district north into even more Democratic territory. He had the satisfaction of seeing his son-in-law Dick Swett elected to the House from the 2d District of New Hampshire in 1990 and 1992 and the disappointment of seeing him lose in 1994. He also must have been disappointed to see Democrats lose control and to lose his subcommittee chairmanship; it will be interesting to see how this active, publicity-minded Democrat applies his energies in Newt Gingrich's House.

The People: Pop. 1990: 571,667; 14% age 65+; 56% White; 4% Black; 26% Asian; 5% Other; 14% Hispanic origin. Voting age pop.: 456,457; 4% Black; 13% Hispanic origin. Households: 53% married couple families; 23% married couple fams. w. children; 62% college educ.; median household income: $44,720; per capita income: $20,984; median gross rent: $780; median house value: $320,400.

1992 Presidential Vote

Clinton (D) 139,281 (57%)
Bush (R) 64,984 (27%)
Perot (I). 38,129 (16%)

1988 Presidential Vote

Dukakis (D). 127,565 (59%)
Bush (R) 88,994 (41%)

Rep. Tom Lantos (D)

Elected 1980; b. Feb. 1, 1928, Budapest, Hungary; home, San Mateo; U. of WA, B.A. 1949, M.A. 1950, U. of CA, Ph.D. 1953; Jewish; married (Annette).

Career: Economist, Bank of America, 1952–53; TV Commentator, San Francisco, 1955–63; Dir. of Intl. Programs, CA St. U., 1962–71; Advisor, U.S. Sen. Joseph R. Biden Jr., 1978–79; Mbr., Pres. Task Force on Defense & Foreign Policy, 1976; Prof., San Francisco St. U., 1950–80.

DC Office: 2217 RHOB 20515, 202-225-3531; Fax: 202-225-7900; e-mail: talk2tom@hr.gov.

District Offices: 400 El Camino Real, #800, San Mateo 94402, 415-342-0300.

Committees: *International Relations* (3rd of 19 D): International Operations and Human Rights (RMM); Western Hemisphere. *Government Reform & Oversight* (3rd of 22 D): Human Resources and Intergovernmental Affairs; National Security, International Affairs and Criminal Justice.

Group Ratings

	ADA	ACLU	COPE	CFA	LCV	CON	NSI	COC	ACU	NTLC	CHC
1994	70	70	88	90	94	29	40	50	24	17	0
1993	90	—	100	100	100	47	—	18	9	—	—

National Journal Ratings

	1993 LIB — 1993 CONS	1994 LIB — 1994 CONS
Economic	75% — 22%	66% — 34%
Social	87% — 0%	72% — 27%
Foreign	59% — 38%	57% — 37%

Key Votes of the 103d Congress

1. Clinton Deficit Plan	Y	3. Brady Handgun Purchase	Y	5. Lmt. UN Cmnd. of Forces	N
2. NAFTA	N	4. Strike Race/Death Pnlty.	N	6. Cut Missile Funds	N

Key Votes of the 104th Congress

1. Congressional Compliance	Y	6. Reform Crime Grant	N	11. Loser Pays Court Reform	N
2. Balanced Budget Amndmt.	N	7. National Security Act	N	12. Product Liability Reform	N
3. Bar Unfunded Mandates	Y	8. Moratorium on Regs.	N	13. Welfare Reform	N
4. Pass Line Item Veto	Y	9. Risk Assessment on Regs.	N	14. Term Limits Amndmt.	N
5. Relax Exclusionary Rule	N	10. Expnd. Priv. Prop. Rights	Y	15. Tax Cuts	N

Election Results

1994 general	Tom Lantos (D)	118,408	(67%)	($322,016)
	Deborah Wilder (R)	57,228	(33%)	($146,133)
1994 primary	Tom Lantos (D)	unopposed		
1992 general	Tom Lantos (D)	157,205	(69%)	($600,656)
	Jim Tomlin (R)	53,278	(23%)	($5,554)
	Mary Weldon (P&F)	10,142	(4%)	
	Other	7,782	(3%)	

THIRTEENTH DISTRICT

The East Bay is the workaday, unglamorous side of metropolitan San Francisco—the margin of land perhaps five miles wide between San Francisco Bay and the surprisingly high mountains that rise just to the east. The shoreline is not picturesque, with its closed-down Navy bases, docks, airports and salt evaporators; the skyscrapers of Oakland are unimpressive compared to those of San Francisco; the Bay Bridge, bisected by Yerba Buena Island, cuts an inspiring figure, but the San Mateo Bridge to the south is at best utilitarian. Fifty years ago, when the shipyards of Richmond and the Navy yard in Oakland were buzzing, the East Bay south of Oakland was still largely uninhabited farm fields. In the postwar years, it has filled up, south along Route 17: San Leandro, originally settled by Portuguese, Castro Valley with its Japanese Gardens, Hayward with its Cal State University campus, Union City with its rail yards, and Fremont, home of the famous NUMMI auto plant where Chevrolets and Toyotas are produced together, and of the California School for the Deaf.

The 13th Congressional District is made up of this string of East Bay towns, somewhat lower income than the Peninsula towns across the Bay. The district is racially and ethnically mixed in the California manner—19% Asian, 18% Hispanic, 7% black—and with a Democratic heritage not yet dampened by high crime (crime rates are much lower here than in Oakland) or revulsion toward cultural liberalism (these people are used to TV newscasts from San Francisco). This area looks like much of the Bay Area, with stucco houses and shopping centers, but house prices are below the ridiculously high Bay Area average and the stores are discount chains more than upscale. Still, income levels are well above the national average.

The Congressman from the 13th District is Pete Stark, a liberal Democrat and product of the peace movement of the 1960s who in the first half of the 1990s was one of four senior Democratic House committee and subcommittee chairmen elected from four East Bay districts. Now, in the second half of the 1990s, he is only a senior member of the minority party. Stark grew up in Wisconsin, served in the Air Force, got an engineering degree at M.I.T. and an M.B.A. at Berkeley and in 1961 started a bank in Walnut Creek. He first attracted attention all over the Bay Area when he put a giant peace symbol atop the bank headquarters and peace symbols on all checks. In 1972 he ran for Congress, spending his own money freely; he beat an 81-year-old incumbent in the primary 56%–22% and held on in the McGovern undertow to win the general with 53%. He sold his bank stock when he got on the Banking Committee, whose members often used their committee positions to enrich themselves, and by his third term he was on Ways and Means, chairing its Health Subcommittee from 1985 to 1995.

Stark brought to that post a desire to use government powers to make health care more available—and a habit of infelicitous quips that got him into trouble. He was not always successful on policy. His major achievement was the Catastrophic Health Care Act of 1988, which created a new benefit for Medicare recipients but was repealed by an overwhelming vote in 1989 after an outpouring of public protest: the problem was that its tax on the high-income elderly was very unpopular while benefits seemed puny, a reminder that in constructing a healthcare system, even a small mistake can be politically devastating. In 1991 he offered a bill for universal health care access, to be financed by higher payroll taxes and a 2% gross income tax; in 1993 he worked toward a "global" budget imposing limits on health costs. All this was overtaken by the Clinton healthcare plan, from whose formulation Stark and other members of Congress complained that they were shut out. In the spring of 1994, Stark worked his subcommittee hard, eventually producing a majority for a bill that modified the Clinton plan with some Stark features; after alterations, it narrowly passed Ways and Means. But, with moderate swing Democrats fearful of its big-government features, it never had majority support in the House and was not brought to the floor.

In the 103d Congress Stark also served as chairman of the District of Columbia Committee, now abolished; he seemed to defer its problems to others, as the District plunged into insolvency.

In the new Republican Congress Stark will likely remain vocal on healthcare issues, but not very influential; the brokering from the left which he did in 1994 was not able to produce a passable bill then, and is far less likely to do so now. He is likely to be the Democrats' point man against Republican efforts to reform and restructure Medicare.

Stark's sharp tongue has gotten him in trouble. In 1990 he called Health and Human Services Secretary Louis Sullivan "a disgrace to his race" for supporting Bush Administration health policies; in 1991, he attacked "Jewish colleagues" for voting for the Gulf war resolution to help Israel. In 1994, when Republican Nancy Johnson, who is married to a physician, attacked Stark's proposals, he said, "The gentlelady got her medical degree through pillow talk and the gentleman from Washington [Jim McDermott, a committee member trained as a psychiatrist] got his medical degree by going to school." Johnson said that was insulting, and 35 Republicans insisted Stark apologize; after an uncomfortable interval he did. Then in March 1995, Stark again insulted Johnson by calling her a "whore" for the insurance industry. This time women members from both sides of the aisle banded together to demand an apology.

Before 1992, Stark's district extended east over the mountains to the Republican-leaning Livermore Valley, and in 1990 he was reelected by only 58%–42%. The 1992 redistricting confined the 13th to the East Bay, and his margin rose to 65%–30% in 1994.

The People: Pop. 1990: 572,333; 9% age 65+; 55% White; 7% Black; 1% Amer. Indian; 19% Asian; 8% Other; 18% Hispanic origin. Voting age pop.: 426,247; 7% Black; 16% Hispanic origin. Households: 59% married couple families; 29% married couple fams. w. children; 55% college educ.; median household income: $43,877; per capita income: $17,335; median gross rent: $726; median house value: $222,700.

1992 Presidential Vote			1988 Presidential Vote		
Clinton (D)	116,829	(54%)	Dukakis (D)	106,561	(56%)
Bush (R)	55,100	(25%)	Bush (R)	83,883	(44%)
Perot (I)	43,026	(20%)			

Rep. Fortney H. (Pete) Stark (D)

Elected 1972; b. Nov. 11, 1931, Milwaukee, WI; home, Hayward; MIT, B.S. 1953, U. of CA at Berkeley, M.B.A. 1960; Unitarian; married (Deborah).

Career: Air Force, 1955–57; Founder, Beacon Savings & Loan Assn., 1961; Founder and Pres., Security Natl. Bank, Walnut Creek, 1963–72.

DC Office: 239 CHOB 20515, 202-225-5065; Fax: 202-225-5065; e-mail: petemail@hr.house.gov.

District Offices: 22320 Foothill Blvd., Hayward 94541, 510-247-1388.

Committees: *Ways & Means* (3rd of 15 D): Health (RMM); Human Resources. *Joint Economic Committee* (7th of 10 Reps.).

Group Ratings

	ADA	ACLU	COPE	CFA	LCV	CON	NSI	COC	ACU	NTLC	CHC
1994	95	86	100	100	94	41	0	27	0	7	0
1993	100	—	100	100	93	47	—	0	4	—	—

National Journal Ratings

	1993 LIB — 1993 CONS			1994 LIB — 1994 CONS		
Economic	88%	—	0%	83%	—	0%
Social	87%	—	0%	94%	—	0%
Foreign	84%	—	13%	85%	—	0%

Key Votes of the 103d Congress

1. Clinton Deficit Plan	Y	3. Brady Handgun Purchase	Y	5. Lmt. UN Cmnd. of Forces	N
2. NAFTA	N	4. Strike Race/Death Pnlty.	N	6. Cut Missile Funds	*

Key Votes of the 104th Congress

1. Congressional Compliance	*	6. Reform Crime Grant	N	11. Loser Pays Court Reform	N
2. Balanced Budget Amndmt.	N	7. National Security Act	N	12. Product Liability Reform	N
3. Bar Unfunded Mandates	N	8. Moratorium on Regs.	N	13. Welfare Reform	N
4. Pass Line Item Veto	N	9. Risk Assessment on Regs.	N	14. Term Limits Amndmt.	N
5. Relax Exclusionary Rule	N	10. Expnd. Priv. Prop. Rights	N	15. Tax Cuts	N

Election Results

1994 general	Fortney H. (Pete) Stark (D)	97,344	(65%)	($391,319)
	Larry Molton (R)	45,555	(30%)	($26,249)
	Robert (Bob) Gough (Lib)	7,743	(5%)	
1994 primary	Fortney H. (Pete) Stark (D)	34,103	(77%)	
	Jim Mills (D)	10,337	(23%)	
1992 general	Fortney H. (Pete) Stark (D)	123,795	(60%)	($589,500)
	Verne Teyler (R)	64,953	(32%)	($43,435)
	Roslyn A. Allen (P&F)	16,768	(8%)	

FOURTEENTH DISTRICT

Silicon Valley is a place and a state of mind, an area that had no distinctive identity two decades ago but is now recognized, admired and imitated all over the world. For Silicon Valley has been the center of America's computer and microprocessor industry, a place where creative minds have produced products that large corporations never thought would sell. Its beginnings can be traced back to 1939, when William Hewlett and David Packard started their electronics firm in a Palo Alto garage, or perhaps to 1891, when Stanford University was founded on the estate of a California governor and senator. But Silicon Valley did not achieve critical mass until the late 1970s and early 1980s, when Steve Jobs started Apple in a garage in Cupertino with the idea of making a computer ordinary people could use, and Gordon Moore, Robert Noyce and Andrew Grove started Intel in nearby Santa Clara to make the microchips that let computers process data much faster than almost anyone thought possible. The office parks of Silicon Valley are unremarkable-looking, in Cupertino and Sunnyvale and Mountain View and Palo Alto, the line of towns between the Junipero Serra and Bayshore Freeways running south from San Francisco to San Jose. Yet this is where computer hackers have turned tinkerer's dreams into multi-billion dollar companies and innovators have produced business after business that out-think public planners and out-compete subsidized foreign consortiums.

Of course there is much hand-wringing and worrying about Silicon Valley's future, since rapidly growing businesses are inherently unstable, but it has proved amazingly adaptable. And in good times there are complaints about clogged traffic and high housing prices. But Silicon Valley has great assets. One is Stanford, which has encouraged its faculty in high-tech experimentation. Another is venture capital, widely available from innovation-minded San Francisco WASPs. A third, perhaps the greatest, is that Silicon Valley is the kind of place where smart young innovators like to live. Counterculture veterans may cluster around the liberal university towns; elite law and medical school graduates head to the prestigious, high-salary jobs of central cities; but techies are free to live in this pleasant, healthy environment. Sheltered by hills from coastal fogs and rains, Silicon Valley boasts a sunny climate with perceptible but gentle seasons, perfect for year-round outdoor sports; there may well be more jogging trails and bicycle paths here than anywhere else in the country. There is a sort of pure Americana here: these communities were rustic but never poor, rural but never bigoted, country-like but still easily accessible to the luxuries of civilization. People here were ahead of the rest of the nation in fighting to preserve the environment, in favoring natural over processed foods, and in indulging in regular exercise. Innovation extends even to government. The city of Sunnyvale, with its results-oriented management, and flexible job definitions in the semi-conductor, aerospace and biotechnology firms, is the hero of David Osborne's *Reinventing Government*, and President Clinton and Vice President Gore visited here in September 1993 for instruction.

The 14th Congressional District coincides almost exactly with Silicon Valley. Though it reaches to the Pacific and homey Half Moon Bay with its pumpkin farms, the 14th's population lies mostly on the San Francisco Bay side of the mountains, in the strip of flat land from Belmont, not far south of San Francisco Airport, through Redwood City, Menlo Park, Palo Alto (home of Stanford), Mountain View, Sunnyvale and Cupertino. There are a few high-income enclaves: Atherton, with its stone-walled lots; Woodside, with its 1850s country store and mansions dotting the hills; Portola Valley and Los Altos Hills, with stark contemporary homes overlooking the Bay. The 14th's political heritage is Republican—a sort of environmentalist, dovish, healthy-lifestyle, but entrepreneurial Republicanism, typified by former Congressmen Pete McCloskey (1967–83), Ed Zschau (1983–87) and Tom Campbell (1989–93); each of the three ran unsuccessfully for statewide office, so the district has elected five congressmen in the last eight elections. But on national issues, the trend here is very Democratic: Silicon Valley is increasingly culturally liberal, has long been dovish on foreign policy and is so rich that it doesn't greatly mind higher taxes and government spending.

The Congresswoman from the 14th District is Anna Eshoo, elected in 1992's "year of the woman," but with a political pedigree that goes back before that. Born back East, she is the only member of Congress of Assyrian descent. She was a full time homemaker, then chaired the San Mateo County Democratic Party and was elected to the San Mateo Board of Supervisors in 1982. In 1988, she ran for the House, facing Republican Tom Campbell, who had upset one-term Republican Congressman Ernest Konnyu in the primary. Campbell, an economics Ph.D. and Stanford law professor, was supported by David Packard; Eshoo and Campbell spent a total of $2.5 million. In that campaign, Eshoo originated the technique of distributing videotapes—100,000 copies—complete with hip music, showing her in a postmodern office, telling voters that the Silicon Valley, unlike Orange County or Iowa, should be represented by someone special. But Campbell had strong appeal, too, and won 52%–46%. In 1992 he ran for the Senate and lost the Republican primary 38%–36% to Bruce Herschensohn, a share of the vote almost identical to the 37% Ed Zschau had when he beat Herschensohn in 1986 (and then lost to Alan Cranston 50%–47%). With the seat open, Eshoo ran for the House again, and in the primary beat Assemblyman Ted Lempert, redistricted out of his seat at age 30, by 40%–36%; the Republican nominee was Tom Huening, a former airline pilot and San Mateo Supervisor who had Packard's backing. In true 1992 style, Eshoo distributed a 58-page booklet of her issue positions, "First Things First" and boasted of her work on setting up a managed-competition health plan for county government (which she touted as a national model), her opposition to coastline development, and her gender in a year when two female Democrats carried this area solidly in Senate races. She also spent $909,000, much more than Huening, and profited from the collapse of George Bush's candidacy here (he won only 26% in the 14th, scarcely ahead of Ross Perot's 20%). Eshoo won 57%–39%, and seems to have a safe seat.

In the House Eshoo compiled a liberal record on cultural and foreign issues, but a somewhat more moderate one on economics. After serving in her first term on the Science Committee, which is potentially important to the Silicon Valley, she secured a once-prime Democratic seat on the Commerce Committee, where she could eventually become a partner to LA's Henry

Waxman. She seemed a bit nervous about supporting the Clinton budget and tax package, which hit this high-income area hard, and hesitated long before supporting the North American Free Trade Agreement. She promised to back managed-competition healthcare reform but was not a major player on the issue. Some of these stands seemed risky back home. But the 1994 campaign moved culturally liberal voters farther to the left, even as the larger electorate moved right, and that meant that the once-Republican Silicon Valley was one of the most Democratic parts of California. Eshoo was reelected 61%–39%. Her challenge now will be to find opportunities to apply her creativity effectively to the legislative process in a House whose majority has values and interests so different from hers.

The People: Pop. 1990: 571,058; 2% rural; 11% age 65+; 69% White; 5% Black; 12% Asian; 4% Other; 13% Hispanic origin. Voting age pop.: 457,209; 4% Black; 12% Hispanic origin. Households: 52% married couple families; 22% married couple fams. w. children; 73% college educ.; median household income: $50,078; per capita income: $26,047; median gross rent: $777; median house value: $401,600.

1992 Presidential Vote			1988 Presidential Vote		
Clinton (D)	143,765	(53%)	Dukakis (D)	137,090	(55%)
Bush (R)	71,754	(26%)	Bush (R)	112,059	(45%)
Perot (I)	53,047	(20%)			

Rep. Anna G. Eshoo (D)

Elected 1992; b. Dec. 13, 1942, New Britain, CT; home, Atherton; Canada Col., A.A. 1976; Catholic; divorced.

Career: Chmn., San Mateo Cnty Dem. Party, 1980; Chief of Staff, CA Assembly Speaker McCarthy, 1981; San Mateo Cnty. Bd. of Supervisors, 1982–92, Pres., 1986.

DC Office: 308 CHOB 20515, 202-225-8104; Fax: 202-225-8890; e-mail: annagram@hr.house.gov.

District Offices: 698 Emerson St., Palo Alto 94301, 415-323-2984.

Committees: *Commerce* (19th of 21 D): Oversight and Investigations; Telecommunications and Finance.

Group Ratings

	ADA	ACLU	COPE	CFA	LCV	CON	NSI	COC	ACU	NTLC	CHC
1994	95	87	89	100	94	21	20	33	0	14	0
1993	95	—	92	100	100	19	—	27	4	—	—

National Journal Ratings

	1993 LIB — 1993 CONS		1994 LIB — 1994 CONS	
Economic	68% —	26%	73% —	17%
Social	87% —	0%	82% —	15%
Foreign	74% —	22%	85% —	0%

Key Votes of the 103d Congress

1. Clinton Deficit Plan	Y	3. Brady Handgun Purchase	Y	5. Lmt. UN Cmnd. of Forces	N
2. NAFTA	Y	4. Strike Race/Death Pnlty.	N	6. Cut Missile Funds	Y

Key Votes of the 104th Congress

1. Congressional Compliance Y	6. Reform Crime Grant N	11. Loser Pays Court Reform N
2. Balanced Budget Amndmt. N	7. National Security Act N	12. Product Liability Reform N
3. Bar Unfunded Mandates Y	8. Moratorium on Regs. N	13. Welfare Reform N
4. Pass Line Item Veto Y	9. Risk Assessment on Regs. N	14. Term Limits Amndmt. Y
5. Relax Exclusionary Rule N	10. Expnd. Priv. Prop. Rights N	15. Tax Cuts N

Election Results

1994 general	Anna G. Eshoo (D)	120,713	(61%)	($487,660)
	Ben Brink (R)	78,475	(39%)	($223,118)
1994 primary	Anna G. Eshoo (D)	47,373	(87%)	
	Donald Tirey (D)	7,338	(13%)	
1992 general	Anna G. Eshoo (D)	146,873	(57%)	($909,604)
	Tom Huening (R)	101,202	(39%)	($670,277)
	Others	11,147	(4%)	

FIFTEENTH DISTRICT

The broad valley of Santa Clara County around San Jose a few decades ago was mostly orchards and vineyards. Sheltered by mountains from the chilly ocean fogs, with soil incredibly fertile once it was irrigated, this valley produced peaches, plums, prunes, apricots and grapes and made San Jose half a century ago the nation's biggest fruit-packing center. Today, almost all the orchards have been replaced by subdivisions and shopping centers and office buildings, for Santa Clara County has become a metropolitan area of 1.5 million people. San Jose, with a growing downtown, an arena rising for its own major league hockey team (the San Jose Sharks), and a population of 782,000, has become a major American city. Santa Clara County is also the center of Silicon Valley, site of many creative firms that have made the United States the world's computer and microchip industry center, a phenomenon predicted by few if any national policymakers or corporate leaders a quarter-century ago.

The 15th Congressional District is made up of the central slice of Santa Clara County plus, over the mountains to the south, a portion of Santa Cruz County. Downtown San Jose is in the 16th District to the east, and Silicon Valley towns like Cupertino and Mountain View are in the 14th District to the west; the 15th District lies in between. At its northern end, near the salt evaporators and wetlands around San Francisco Bay, is the Great America theme park, not far from where a huge Lockheed plant was once one of the nation's largest defense contractors. Just to the south is Santa Clara, with its old mission and Santa Clara University. The 15th includes much of the upscale and middle-income neighborhoods of western San Jose, with over 300,000 people. It also has high-income suburbs nestled in what used to be vineyards beneath the encroaching mountains: Saratoga, Los Gatos, Monte Sereno. After all this settlement, the mountains remain surprisingly wild, a haunt of Ken Kesey's Merry Pranksters in the 1960s, now inhabited with rustic cabins and high-income houses in narrow valleys. Prosperous and pleased with its environment, confident in free-market economics and uneasy about the performance of the public sector, people here have been somewhat more conservative than in other quadrants of the Bay Area. There are fewer singles and gays here than farther north, fewer Mexican-Americans than farther east; the 11% who are Asian-Americans are far likelier to be high-income producers than to be low-income supplicants. But the 1990s trend here, as elsewhere in the Bay Area and in contrast to most of the country, has been toward the Democrats. This is a place where any traces of cultural conservatism hurt the Republicans.

The Congressman from the 15th District is Norman Mineta, who parlayed a less-than-a-decade career in San Jose city politics into more than two decades in the House. Mineta grew up in San Jose; as a child in World War II, he was shipped off, wearing his Cub Scout uniform, to one of the internment camps in Wyoming where the government confined West Coast Japanese Americans; his family lost their home and his father's insurance business. While in Wyoming, Mineta met Alan Simpson, with whom he would later work on the Japanese American redress bill. After college, he went into the insurance business, joined the San Jose Council in 1967, when the city was rapidly expanding, and became mayor in 1971. He called for slowing down development—but not to zero, as in Marin County—and was widely popular. When a 22-year Republican incumbent retired in the Democratic year of 1974, Mineta ran and was easily elected. He was one of the leaders of the Watergate-era class of Democrats, promoting their House reforms and opposing Republican administrations on foreign and cultural policies.

Mineta has combined a fairly liberal voting record, more moderate than other Bay Area Democrats on foreign issues, with a practical-minded concentration on the Transportation and Infrastructure Committee which he joined in 1975 and of which he became chairman in 1993. The committee authorizes highway and other transportation projects, often in conflict with the Appropriations subcommittees; it also handled major environmental legislation, including the Clean Water Act and the Superfund. Mineta was named chairman of the Aviation Subcommittee in 1981 and became an expert on airports and air safety. In 1989 he became chairman of the Surface Transportation Subcommittee, which handles highways and railroads. His major achievement here was passage of the Surface Transportation Act of 1991, which reversed the longtime bias toward highways and let states spend trust fund dollars on subways, light rail and even magnetic levitation systems if they chose. Of course the specifics of allocation formulas and project definitions are always argued over, and senior members make sure federal money goes to local projects. Mineta, representing the prosperous Silicon Valley, has been less preoccupied with this than some, including the longtime ranking Republican and now chairman, Bud Shuster, who represents a low-income and geographically isolated district in Pennsylvania.

Mineta first sought the full committee chairmanship in 1990, after the Democratic Caucus ousted an aging chairman, but was beaten 121–107 by the more senior Robert Roe of New Jersey; when Roe retired in 1992, the way was open for Mineta. He must have been pleased that Transportation was the number one committee choice of incoming Democratic freshmen, many of whom, like him, had experience in local government. But he was frustrated in reshaping major laws. He efforts to reauthorize the Clean Water Act and get stronger pollution runoff provisions foundered, as pressure from farm interests and conservatives to restrict government "takings," require agency to make risk assessments and cost-benefit analyses and to ban unfunded mandates to state and local governments prevented agreement. Similar arguments stopped Superfund authorization. Transportation had often produced bipartisan bills, with local benefits for members of both parties; now, partisan politics and principled differences on policy were preventing Mineta from exerting control. That is likely to remain true under the chairmanship of Shuster, who took control of the bill referral process within the committee over Mineta's objection.

Mineta has other legislative causes and has served stints on the Budget and Intelligence Committees, but one of his great accomplishments was as lead House sponsor of the 1988 Japanese American redress bill, which officially apologized for the internment and provided a $20,000 payment to each survivor of the camps and to so-called voluntary evacuees. Since then, he has worked to make sure enough money was appropriated for the payments which have now all been completed.

Mineta has remained popular in the 15th District, and the national conservative trend of the 1990s has been less visible here as the area's cultural liberalism has worked for the Democrats. He took no chances in 1994, spending $971,000 on his campaign, and was reelected 60%–40%.

The People: Pop. 1990: 572,360; 4% rural; 9% age 65+; 76% White; 2% Black; 1% Amer. Indian; 11% Asian; 3% Other; 10% Hispanic origin. Voting age pop.: 444,624; 2% Black; 9% Hispanic origin. Households: 57% married couple families; 25% married couple fams. w. children; 68% college educ.; median household income: $50,823; per capita income: $22,833; median gross rent: $794; median house value: $290,200.

1992 Presidential Vote

Clinton (D) 127,060 (46%)
Bush (R) 83,301 (30%)
Perot (I) 64,192 (23%)

1988 Presidential Vote

Bush (R) 126,310 (51%)
Dukakis (D) 119,300 (49%)

Rep. Norman Y. Mineta (D)

Elected 1974; b. Nov. 12, 1931, San Jose; home, San Jose; U. of CA at Berkeley, B.S. 1953; United Methodist; married (Danealia).

Career: Army, 1953–56 (Korea); Owner, Mineta Insur. Agcy.; San Jose City Cncl., 1967–71; San Jose Vice Mayor, 1969–71; Mayor, 1971–74.

DC Office: 2221 RHOB 20515, 202-225-2631; Fax: 202-225-6788; e-mail: tellnorm@hr.house.gov.

District Offices: 1245 S. Winchester Blvd., #310, San Jose 95128, 408-984-6045.

Committees: *Transportation & Infrastructure* (RMM of 27 D).

Group Ratings

	ADA	ACLU	COPE	CFA	LCV	CON	NSI	COC	ACU	NTLC	CHC
1994	90	83	75	100	83	20	40	33	10	11	0
1993	80	—	92	100	71	1	—	27	8	—	—

National Journal Ratings

	1993 LIB — 1993 CONS	1994 LIB — 1994 CONS
Economic	78% — 12%	83% — 0%
Social	87% — 0%	94% — 0%
Foreign	66% — 31%	72% — 25%

Key Votes of the 103d Congress

1. Clinton Deficit Plan	Y	3. Brady Handgun Purchase	Y	5. Lmt. UN Cmnd. of Forces	N
2. NAFTA	Y	4. Strike Race/Death Pnlty.	N	6. Cut Missile Funds	N

Key Votes of the 104th Congress

1. Congressional Compliance	Y	6. Reform Crime Grant	N	11. Loser Pays Court Reform	N
2. Balanced Budget Amndmt.	N	7. National Security Act	N	12. Product Liability Reform	N
3. Bar Unfunded Mandates	N	8. Moratorium on Regs.	N	13. Welfare Reform	N
4. Pass Line Item Veto	N	9. Risk Assessment on Regs.	N	14. Term Limits Amndmt.	N
5. Relax Exclusionary Rule	N	10. Expnd. Priv. Prop. Rights	N	15. Tax Cuts	N

Election Results

1994 general	Norman Y. Mineta (D)	119,921	(60%)	($1,009,947)
	Robert Wick (R)	80,266	(40%)	($13,759)
1994 primary	Norman Y. Mineta (D)	unopposed		
1992 general	Norman Y. Mineta (D)	168,617	(64%)	($1,112,414)
	Robert Wick (R)	82,875	(31%)	($62,961)
	Duggan Dieterly (Lib)	13,293	(5%)	

SIXTEENTH DISTRICT

With more people than San Francisco, higher per capita incomes than San Diego, a tradition of high-tech innovation that rivals any on earth, and a major league sports team housed in California's biggest indoor arena, San Jose has great claims on national attention and respect. Yet San Jose—with the 11th largest population within city limits in the United States—does not yet bulk as large in the national consciousness as it should. At the southern end of the Bay, it remains in San Francisco's shadow. San Francisco is every tourist's idea of a city: geographically compact, with picturesque public transportation, old-time immigrant groups and new, an economy historically based on heavy industry and sea trade, a large city bureaucracy symbolized by a monumental city hall. San Jose is quite different. It got its start as a farm-market town, with canneries and fruit-packing operations for the produce from the fertile plains around. It sits not on the Bay, but on the Southern Pacific line above the marshes and salt evaporators; its major transportation arteries are the freeways—U.S. 101, Interstates 280 and 680, California 17— which encircle its revitalized downtown. The main minority group here is Mexican-Americans, who initially came as farm workers but now inhabit every occupational niche and, while concentrated on the east side, are also scattered throughout San Jose and adjacent towns; there are also increasing numbers of Asian-Americans. And scattered is the right word to describe San Jose's growth. It has a downtown, now spruced up, and a civic center graced by a cost-overrun indoor arena for the San Jose Sharks hockey team. But starting in the 1950s, San Jose has grown out in every direction, developers hip-hopping across the farmland, putting up subdivisions faster sometimes than the few city employees could update the street map. Economically, San Jose has been sustained by everything from its traditional agriculture to the high-tech businesses that are centered in Silicon Valley towns just to the west but are omnipresent here: an American city, 21st century style.

The 16th Congressional District consists of the larger part of San Jose, plus its urban fringe to the east and the still agricultural Santa Clara Valley to the south, including Gilroy, the garlic capital of the United States. It includes the old and new downtown and the heavily Mexican-American areas to the east. This is the most heavily Hispanic district in the Bay Area (37%) and is also heavily Asian (21%), with the largest concentration of Vietnamese in the U.S. Politically, it has become Democratic, although perhaps not overwhelmingly so, and its future leanings depend on the trends among Latinos, who are family-oriented and not nearly so favorable to big government as blacks, and Asians, who are more often the victims than the beneficiaries of liberals' quota schemes.

The Congresswoman from the 16th District is Zoe Lofgren, a Democrat and Santa Clara County Supervisor who was elected in 1994 when incumbent Don Edwards retired after 32 years. Edwards, perhaps the House's most faithful liberal, never chaired the Judiciary Committee, but as a longtime member played major parts in squelching constitutional amendments and criminal law provisions sought by conservatives and in extending civil rights laws into some now controversial areas. Edwards's retirement set up a major Democratic primary contest between Lofgren, a supervisor for 14 years, and Tom McEnery, mayor of San Jose from 1983 to 1990. McEnery was probably better known, for his efforts to build up San Jose's downtown with business towers, a shopping mall, the sports arena, and for starting a Police Corps and building Guadalupe River Park, the McEnery Convention Center and a 15-mile trolley to southern San Jose. But Lofgren had her own achievements; she spearheaded a 1984 ballot proposition to give local governments control of freeway building and moved the jails from the sheriff's office to the local corrections department. And Lofgren had two other advantages, which were related: she is a woman and she raised more money. Her campaign literature noted that she is the daughter of a truck driver and a secretary, and she tried unsuccessfully to be listed on the ballot as a "Mother/County Supervisor." She won the support of the National Women's Political Caucus, the National Organization for Women, EMILY's List, Senator Barbara Boxer and Congresswomen Anna Eshoo and Lynn Woolsey. With their help, she vastly outraised McEnery, and in the primary outspent him $400,000 to $210,000. He had been leading in polls, but the money enabled her to overtake him and win 45%–42%. The general election was anticlimactic, and Lofgren surely has a safe seat.

The 104th Congress will surely prove frustrating to an activist-feminist like Lofgren, but she must hope that more of her gender and her party will join her in the House.

The People: Pop. 1990: 571,460; 4% rural; 7% age 65+; 37% White; 5% Black; 1% Amer. Indian; 21% Asian; 18% Other; 36% Hispanic origin. Voting age pop.: 408,987; 5% Black; 33% Hispanic origin. Households: 57% married couple families; 32% married couple fams. w. children; 49% college educ.; median household income: $42,223; per capita income: $14,614; median gross rent: $718; median house value: $233,600.

1992 Presidential Vote			1988 Presidential Vote		
Clinton (D)	86,418	(52%)	Dukakis (D)	80,194	(57%)
Bush (R)	44,693	(27%)	Bush (R)	60,379	(43%)
Perot (I)	33,882	(20%)			

Rep. Zoe Lofgren (D)

Elected 1994; b. Dec. 21, 1947, San Mateo; home, San Jose; Stanford U., B.A. 1970, U. of Santa Clara Law Schl., J.D. 1975; Protestant; married (John Collins).

Career: Staff Asst., U.S. Rep. Don Edwards, 1970–78; Practicing atty., 1978–80; Prof., U. of Santa Clara Law Schl., 1981–94; Santa Clara Bd. of Supervisors, 1980–94.

DC Office: 118 CHOB 20515, 202-225-3072; Fax: 202-225-3336.

District Offices: 635 N. 1st St., #B, San Jose 95112, 408-271-8700.

Committees: *Judiciary* (14th of 15 D): Crime. *Science* (19th of 23 D): Basic Research; Technology.

Group Ratings and 103rd Congress Votes: Newly Elected

Key Votes of the 104th Congress

1. Congressional Compliance Y	6. Reform Crime Grant N	11. Loser Pays Court Reform N
2. Balanced Budget Amndmt. N	7. National Security Act N	12. Product Liability Reform N
3. Bar Unfunded Mandates Y	8. Moratorium on Regs. N	13. Welfare Reform N
4. Pass Line Item Veto N	9. Risk Assessment on Regs. N	14. Term Limits Amndmt. N
5. Relax Exclusionary Rule N	10. Expnd. Priv. Prop. Rights N	15. Tax Cuts N

Election Results

1994 general	Zoe Lofgren (D)	74,935	(65%)	($646,764)
	Lyle J. Smith (R)	40,409	(35%)	
1994 primary	Zoe Lofgren (D)	16,168	(45%)	
	Tom McEnery (D)	15,037	(42%)	
	Richard R. Lane (D)	1,537	(4%)	
	Others	2,915	(8%)	
1992 general	Don Edwards (D)	96,661	(62%)	($291,251)
	Ted Bundesen (R)	49,843	(32%)	($505)
	Amani S. Kuumba (P&F)	9,370	(6%)	

SEVENTEENTH DISTRICT

The California coast around Monterey Bay is for many a working definition of paradise. This kernel of California history, where Spanish and then Mexicans governed a virtually empty land and Californians set up their first state capital, still makes a fine living, as it has for nearly 150 years, off the land and sea. The fields around Salinas supply much of the nation's lettuce and cauliflower, the fields around Castroville supply almost all of its artichokes, and the vast greenhouses around Watsonville supply a goodly portion of its roses. The fishing fleet and 18 canneries of Monterey are not the major industry they were half a century ago, but they have generated a new industry: Cannery Row is refurbished with upscale shops and hotels, and the magnificent Monterey Bay Aquarium has become one of California's top tourist destinations. There are other attractions on the Monterey peninsula as well, like the Pebble Beach golf courses and the Del Monte Lodge, and Carmel, whose restrictive laws—no house numbers, no door-to-door mail delivery, no live entertainment, no stop lights, no cutting trees without city council permission—reflect an effort to maintain the atmosphere of 80 years ago, when it really was an artists' colony.

The 17th Congressional District includes all the coast of Monterey Bay and then follows the Big Sur coastline south almost to William Randolph Hearst's castle, San Simeon, past perhaps the most beautiful scenery in America. The district extends inland, into sunny valleys sheltered from ocean mists, and covers some of the nation's richest farmland. This area is a prime example of how, while interior California became more Republican, the coast trended Democratic. The older residents—landowners in Salinas and the townspeople who sympathize with them, retirees in Santa Cruz and the Monterey Peninsula—still vote Republican. But an influx of liberation-minded young people now in their prime years, attracted less by the economy (though that has been vibrant) than by the atmosphere, moved the coast to the left. Also, the branch of the University of California at Santa Cruz is so liberal (97% for McGovern in 1972) that it has changed the political balance of the whole county. As late as 1980, Monterey and Santa Cruz Counties were voting less Democratic than the nation. But in 1984 they were 7% more Democratic, in 1988 9% and in 1992 10%.

The Congressman from the 17th is Sam Farr, a Democrat elected in June 1993 to replace Leon Panetta, who resigned after 16 years in the House, including four as Budget Committee chairman, to become President Clinton's Office of Management and Budget director and later White House chief of staff. Panetta's whole career—he switched from Republican to Democrat in 1970 and beat an incumbent Republican Congressman in 1976—tracked the political movement in the district. Farr also has roots in this area. His father, Fred Farr, was a state senator from Monterey County for many years, and Sam Farr has spent his adult life in politics and public service. He served two years in the Peace Corps, then was a staffer in the California Assembly for a decade, became a Monterey County Supervisor in 1975 and was elected to the Assembly in 1980. Farr is very much interested in preserving the environment that is so important here, and from his Natural Resources Committee seat in the state legislature, he wrote one of the nation's strictest oil-spill liability laws.

But Farr had serious competition for the seat, and the results in the special and the 1994 general suggest that the Democratic trend on the coast may be a thing of the past. Farr entered the 1993 race as the overwhelming favorite, although he had serious competition from County Supervisor Barbara Shipnuck and Salinas lawyer Bill Manning. He raised vastly more money than his opponents and won the all-party primary in April with 26% of the vote; Democrats took 59% in that contest and Republicans just 28%. In the runoff, he faced Bill McCampbell, who had won the Republican nomination with only 12% of the vote and had been beaten 72%–24% by Panetta in November 1992. McCampbell had worked for years in Washington, and he boasted about (and Democrats attacked him for) his work as a lobbyist for the South African "homeland" Transkei. Although Farr had much more money, the reputation of the Clinton

Administration was plummeting, and he ended up winning by only 52%–43%.

Farr got seats on the Agriculture and Resources Committees and worked on local projects. He was proud of getting $15 million to start a California State University campus at the Army's closed Fort Ord and a 700-employee Defense Department finance center there. In 1994 he again faced McCampbell, but this time the Republican raised as much money and spent more. In something of a surprise, McCampbell carried Monterey County 50%–47%; Farr depended on his 60%–35% margin in Santa Cruz County for an overall 52%–45% victory. This was about the same level of support as for the state Democratic ticket, in between the vote for Dianne Feinstein and that of Kathleen Brown. In the opening week of the new Congress, he summed up the feelings of many Democrats when he described a conversation with a San Benito County administrative officer concerning California flooding: "He asked me whether, being in the minority, I was able to handle disasters. I said becoming the minority was a disaster. I am disaster equipped." Farr is still strongly positioned in this district, but could well face serious competition again and a less favorable fundraising picture in 1996.

The People: Pop. 1990: 571,077; 15% rural; 10% age 65+; 58% White; 4% Black; 1% Amer. Indian; 6% Asian; 19% Other; 31% Hispanic origin. Voting age pop.: 420,688; 4% Black; 26% Hispanic origin. Households: 57% married couple families; 29% married couple fams. w. children; 54% college educ.; median household income: $33,911; per capita income: $15,006; median gross rent: $643; median house value: $219,100.

1992 Presidential Vote			**1988 Presidential Vote**		
Clinton (D)	111,937	(52%)	Dukakis (D)	103,346	(56%)
Bush (R)	57,990	(27%)	Bush (R)	82,214	(44%)
Perot (I)	42,317	(20%)			

Rep. Sam Farr (D)

Elected June 1993; b. July 4, 1941, San Francisco; home, Carmel; Willamette U., B.S. 1963; Episcopalian; married (Shary).

Career: Peace Corps, Columbia, 1963–65; Staff, CA Assembly, 1965–75; Monterey Cnty. Bd. of Supervisors, 1975–80, Chmn., 1979; CA Assembly, 1980–93.

DC Office: 1117 LHOB 20515, 202-225-2861; Fax: 202-225-6791.

District Offices: 380 Alvarado St., Monterey 93940, 408-649-3555; 701 Ocean Ave., Santa Cruz 95060, 408-429-1976; and 100 W. Alisal St., Salinas 93901, 408-424-2229.

Committees: *Agriculture* (20th of 22 D): Department Operations, Nutrition and Foreign Agriculture; Risk Management and Specialty Crops. *Resources* (20th of 20 D): Fisheries, Wildlife and Oceans; Water and Power Resources.

Group Ratings

	ADA	ACLU	COPE	CFA	LCV	CON	NSI	COC	ACU	NTLC	CHC
1994	90	85	88	90	100	19	13	45	0	21	0
1993	93	—	83	100	85	*		29	7	—	—

National Journal Ratings

	1993 LIB — 1993 CONS		1994 LIB — 1994 CONS	
Economic	*	—	*	83% — 0%
Social	87%	—	0%	90% — 6%
Foreign	84%	—	16%	85% — 0%

Key Votes of the 103d Congress

1. Clinton Deficit Plan	Y	3. Brady Handgun Purchase	Y	5. Lmt. UN Cmnd. of Forces	N
2. NAFTA	Y	4. Strike Race/Death Pnlty.	N	6. Cut Missile Funds	Y

Key Votes of the 104th Congress

1. Congressional Compliance	Y	6. Reform Crime Grant	N	11. Loser Pays Court Reform	N
2. Balanced Budget Amndmt.	N	7. National Security Act	N	12. Product Liability Reform	N
3. Bar Unfunded Mandates	N	8. Moratorium on Regs.	N	13. Welfare Reform	N
4. Pass Line Item Veto	N	9. Risk Assessment on Regs.	N	14. Term Limits Amndmt.	N
5. Relax Exclusionary Rule	N	10. Expnd. Priv. Prop. Rights	N	15. Tax Cuts	N

Election Results

1994 general	Sam Farr (D)	87,222	(52%)	($387,872)
	Bill McCampbell (R)	74,380	(44%)	($451,490)
	Others	5,591	(3%)	
1994 primary	Sam Farr (D)	42,720	(81%)	
	Art Dunn (D)	10,298	(19%)	
1993 runoff	Sam Farr (D)	53,675	(52%)	($806,332)
	Bill McCampbell (R)	43,774	(43%)	($170,305)
	Six Others	5,283	(5%)	
1993 special	Sam Farr (D)	23,600	(26%)	
	Bill Manning (D)	17,050	(19%)	
	Barbara Shipnuck (D)	12,982	(14%)	
	Bill McCampbell (R)	10,911	(12%)	
	Bob Ernst (R)	5,126	(6%)	
	Twenty-one Others	12,568	(14%)	
1992 general	Leon E. Panetta (D)	151,565	(72%)	($513,958)
	Bill McCampbell (R)	49,947	(24%)	($77,509)
	Others	8,855	(4%)	

EIGHTEENTH DISTRICT

The Central Valley of California is a miraculous man-made landscape, a horizontal factory stretching as far as the eye can see. Nature created the vast flatlands, rimmed by mountains rising surreally in the distant haze. But man in the last century has disciplined the land with a remorseless mile-square grid of roads, and the sluggish-flowing California Aqueduct and dozens of arrow-straight canals; pipes fitted with valves and gauges to pump water and fertilizer and pesticides to the fields in measured quantities give an air of industrial precision. The crops grow in carefully spaced rows, filling the fields, for the rich soil and the irrigated water are too precious to waste on decoration or vegetable patches or flower gardens: the Valley is business. Farming here has always been an industrial enterprise; in the 19th century the land was not given to 160-acre homesteaders but sold to thousands-of-acres capitalist enterprises.

The Central Valley was one of California's surprise boom areas in the 1980s, growing not just crops but people. Middle-wage employees in the San Francisco Bay area drive east at night on I-580, past surreal windmills whirling on the bare hills of the Altamont pass, across the Westlands fields to modestly priced homes in Modesto, the town immortalized (when it was much smaller) in *American Graffiti*. Water was scarce in the drought years of the late 1980s, and heavily subsidized water was cut off from cultivators of cotton (which after all can be grown in many states where nature provides the water for free), but the towns and countryside of the Central Valley have been generating a well-rounded economy. On the down side, traffic has become a problem, air pollution on bad days has approached coastal metropolitan levels, and the pace of life is getting more hectic and frazzled.

The 18th Congressional District includes a large chunk of the Central Valley from Modesto and Stanislaus County south through Merced almost to Fresno. The political tradition here is Democratic: Democrats in Washington and Democratic Governor Pat Brown built the irrigation canals and authorized the water subsidies; Democrats own the *Bee* newspapers, the predominant Valley chain; Democrats staffed the Bank of America, long the dominant financial force here; on the walls of insider law firms are signed pictures of Franklin Roosevelt and Pat Brown, not Ronald Reagan and Pete Wilson. Today the voters of the 18th District remain fairly heavily Democratic. There are many Latinos here, and an increasing number of Asians, though neither group produces the overwhelming Democratic majorities blacks do; there are some voters of white southern ancestry, used to voting for local Democrats though happy to vote Republican for president. The Central Valley is the part of California with the highest proportion of families and children, and there is a natural cultural conservatism here, shared by successful local Democratic politicians.

The current incumbent is Gary Condit, elected in a September 1989 special election to replace Tony Coelho, the House majority whip whose sudden resignation in June 1989 stunned most of Washington. Condit was the Democrats' natural choice for the seat. A native of Oklahoma and son of a Baptist minister, he was elected to the Ceres Council in 1972 at 24, the Stanislaus County Board of Supervisors in 1976, and the California Assembly in 1982, where he made an attractive moderate to conservative record on crime and taxes. He was one of the "Gang of Five" Democrats who threatened to topple Speaker Willie Brown in 1988. That challenge collapsed after the 1988 election, and when Coelho resigned Condit seized the chance to run for Congress. Republicans in the meantime elbowed out pro-choice Modesto Mayor Carol Whiteside for older former state Senator Clare Berryhill, who proved to be a less vigorous candidate. Condit raised money efficiently and ran an absentee voter drive which essentially won the election before it was held. Some 35% of all votes were cast absentee, the large majority Democratic, and Condit won 57%–35%.

Condit is the most conservative Democrat in the California delegation, with a *National Journal* voting record almost identical to 1994 Republican Senate nominee Michael Huffington's. He is the only California Democrat to vote for the Hyde amendment banning most publicly-funded abortions. He voted against the Clinton budget and economic package. He has long supported the balanced budget amendment and was one of three California Democrats, (along with Calvin Dooley and Jane Harman) to do so in 1995. He was the prime Democratic co-sponsor of the unfunded mandates bill, which passed in 1995, and when Gephardt refused to seat him (twice) on the conference committee, Gingrich appointed him instead. He backed regulatory reform, including risk assessment and cost-benefit analysis, before as well as after the 1994 election, but pushed Republican David McIntosh away from keeping his moratorium on regulations in effect until a permanent bill is passed.

Condit's independence cost him when Democrats were in control and made him something of a pariah in his party; he didn't get a seat on Commerce and failed to save a provision benefiting California dairy farmers. But now that Republicans are in control, he is a key member, at least when they want bipartisan support. He has worked on local issues in the past, like designating the lower portion of the Merced as a Wild and Scenic River, but seems to rely for his appeal largely on national issues. It has worked: he was reelected with 66% in 1990 and 1994 and had no Republican opposition in 1992.

The People: Pop. 1990: 571,358; 19% rural; 10% age 65+; 65% White; 3% Black; 1% Amer. Indian; 6% Asian; 14% Other; 26% Hispanic origin. Voting age pop.: 391,319; 3% Black; 22% Hispanic origin. Households: 61% married couple families; 33% married couple fams. w. children; 41% college educ.; median household income: $28,324; per capita income: $12,013; median gross rent: $462; median house value: $113,600.

1992 Presidential Vote

Clinton (D)	74,357	(41%)
Bush (R)	67,898	(37%)
Perot (I)	39,645	(22%)

1988 Presidential Vote

Bush (R)	75,832	(53%)
Dukakis (D)	66,366	(47%)

Rep. Gary A. Condit (D)

Elected Sept., 1989; b. Apr. 21, 1948, Salina, OK; home, Ceres; Modesto Jr. Col., A.A. 1970, CA St. U., B.A. 1972; Protestant; married (Carolyn).

Career: Ceres City Cncl., 1972–76; Ceres Mayor, 1974–76; Stanislaus Cnty. Bd. of Supervisors, 1976–82; CA Assembly, 1982–89.

DC Office: 2444 RHOB 20515, 202-225-6131; Fax: 202-225-0819.

District Offices: 415 W. 18th St., Merced 95340, 209-383-4455; and 920 16th St., Modesto 95354, 209-527-1914.

Committees: *Agriculture* (7th of 22 D): Department Operations, Nutrition and Foreign Agriculture (RMM); Resource Conservation, Research and Forestry. *Government Reform & Oversight* (10th of 22 D): National Economic Growth, Natural Resources and Regulatory Affairs; National Security, International Affairs and Criminal Justice.

Group Ratings

	ADA	ACLU	COPE	CFA	LCV	CON	NSI	COC	ACU	NTLC	CHC
1994	40	43	67	40	29	93	50	92	38	62	57
1993	60	—	67	60	36	91	—	55	50	—	—

National Journal Ratings

	1993 LIB — 1993 CONS		1994 LIB — 1994 CONS	
Economic	40% —	58%	39% —	60%
Social	52% —	47%	46% —	53%
Foreign	66% —	31%	45% —	55%

Key Votes of the 103d Congress

1. Clinton Deficit Plan	N	3. Brady Handgun Purchase	Y	5. Lmt. UN Cmnd. of Forces	Y
2. NAFTA	N	4. Strike Race/Death Pnlty.	Y	6. Cut Missile Funds	Y

Key Votes of the 104th Congress

1. Congressional Compliance	Y	6. Reform Crime Grant	Y	11. Loser Pays Court Reform	*
2. Balanced Budget Amndmt.	Y	7. National Security Act	N	12. Product Liability Reform	Y
3. Bar Unfunded Mandates	Y	8. Moratorium on Regs.	Y	13. Welfare Reform	N
4. Pass Line Item Veto	Y	9. Risk Assessment on Regs.	Y	14. Term Limits Amndmt.	Y
5. Relax Exclusionary Rule	Y	10. Expnd. Priv. Prop. Rights	Y	15. Tax Cuts	Y

Election Results

1994 general	Gary A. Condit (D)	91,105	(66%)	($387,494)
	Tom Carter (R)	44,046	(32%)	
	Others	3,901	(3%)	
1994 primary	Gary A. Condit (D)	unopposed		
1992 general	Gary A. Condit (D)	139,704	(85%)	($311,000)
	Kim R. Almstrom (Lib)	25,307	(15%)	

NINETEENTH DISTRICT

Fresno, in California's Central Valley, between the flat Westlands and the Sierras on the east, is a city agricultural and industrial, middle American and ethnically diverse. It is a creation of the industrial age, founded by the Central Pacific Railroad; its city fathers bred the local wine grape, developed the raisin industry and introduced the Smyrna fig. But these are not all of Fresno County's crops, which include cotton, lima beans, tomatoes, cantaloupes, plums, peaches and alfalfa: Fresno produces more farm products in dollar value than any other county in the United States. Central Valley agriculture is industrial in its precision, its thoroughness and its ownership by large corporations: the vineyards outside Fresno radiate in mechanical precision, with vines just 10 feet apart and exposed to the relentless summer sun—nothing romantic or quaint here. The city of Fresno started off as a farm-marketing center—one high-income neighborhood is called Fig Garden, because that's what it used to be—and as a tourists' stop-off point on the way to Yosemite. But it has long since grown out north, east and west from its old downtown, and its economy has diversified.

Like all the Central Valley, Fresno has always been ethnically diverse, with a telephone book that reads like the United Nations. It has America's second largest Armenian community, after Los Angeles; Fresno's great chronicler was William Saroyan. Its already large Latino population doubled to more than 100,000 in the 1980s; Asians, including Chinese, Filipinos, Vietnamese and Hmong, may number as many as 50,000. Fresno has had its troubles in the 1990s, as immigration continued despite high unemployment, violent teenage gangs and air pollution that made the Sierra Nevada invisible on many days. In spring 1993, voters voted for term limits after turning over the entire council in two elections. They ousted the incumbent Democratic mayor, who had built a sleek new city hall, and installed Republican Jim Patterson, a religious broadcaster who immediately got more policemen out patrolling without increasing taxes and set about reducing burdens on business. Patterson argues that liberals are dividing voters by stressing ethnic differences and conservatives should unite them by stressing common values. It was an anticipation of the state and national trends of 1994, of voters seeking discipline rather than therapy, enforcement of old moral rules rather than erection of new government buildings. Fresno County, long heavily Democratic, voted 63%–33% for Pete Wilson over Kathleen Brown, and Californians elected Fresno Republican Bill Jones Secretary of State, from which post he might run for governor in 1998.

There was also a change in the 19th Congressional District, which includes most of Fresno, all but the old downtown and a Latino area reserved for the Hispanic-majority 20th District. The 19th spreads with an erose boundary over the farm country below the foothills of the Sierras from Visalia, south of Fresno, to mountainous Mariposa County. Most of its land mass is part of the Sierra Nevada, and it contains most of three major national parks, Yosemite, Kings Canyon and Sequoia. Strongly Democratic historically, it trended Republican through the 1980s, and after a pause in 1992 trended even harder that way in 1994. And in a race between two candidates for Congress with deep Valley roots, the 19th chose the Republican.

The Congressman from the 19th District now is George Radanovich, a vintner who defeated Richard Lehman, who comes from a Fresno County farming family and has been in politics since he was part of Jesse Unruh's Robert Kennedy delegation to the 1968 Chicago convention. In 1970, Lehman became a staffer to a Fresno state senator; he was elected to the Assembly in 1976, at 28, and to the House in 1982. After redistricting he was nearly beaten in 1992 by 28-year-old Tal Cloud, winning 47%–46% with a spending edge of $915,000 to $150,000. Lehman opposed the Clinton budget and tax package and raised and spent over $1 million—he was the number 17 recipient of PAC money in the country. But it was to no avail, and Radanovich won 57%–40%, the biggest defeat of a non-freshman incumbent in 1994.

Radanovich is the son of Croatian immigrants, with relatives all over the Valley. In 1986, after studying the local microclimates, he opened the first winery in Mariposa County and made it work; the Radanovich Winery now ships 4,000 cases of sauvignon blanc, chardonnay, merlot, zinfandel and cabernet sauvignon and Radanovich is the first winemaker to be elected to the House. He served on the county planning commission, won a seat on the Board of Supervisors in 1989 and in 1992 ran for Congress, losing to Cloud in the primary by 33%–30%. In his 1994 campaign, Radanovich attacked Lehman for supporting the Clinton Administration 73% of the time—in fact, he invited Clinton to campaign for Lehman—and heartily endorsed the Contract With America. He called for more water for California agriculture—Lehman was hurt because the Bay Area Democrat George Miller has worked hard to increase the cost of water here—and called for collapsing federal departments. Lehman in turn attacked him for raising taxes locally. But Radanovich's appeal was stronger. "I have experience in the real world, and I'm trying to go back to Washington and make a difference," he said of Lehman. "He's a bureaucrat trying to protect his own job."

Now the job is Radanovich's, and in this Republican-leaning district he seems likely to hold it for a while. He has seats on the Budget and Resources Committees; on the latter, he can look after the district's national parks and federal lands.

The People: Pop. 1990: 573,077; 20% rural; 11% age 65+; 65% White; 3% Black; 1% Amer. Indian; 7% Asian; 14% Other; 23% Hispanic origin. Voting age pop.: 404,734; 3% Black; 20% Hispanic origin. Households: 57% married couple families; 28% married couple fams. w. children; 52% college educ.; median household income: $29,153; per capita income: $13,516; median gross rent: $450; median house value: $90,200.

1992 Presidential Vote			1988 Presidential Vote		
Bush (R)	97,124	(43%)	Bush (R)	103,142	(55%)
Clinton (D)	85,049	(38%)	Dukakis (D)	83,845	(45%)
Perot (I)	41,052	(18%)			

Rep. George P. Radanovich (R)

Elected 1994; b. June 20, 1955, Mariposa; home, Mariposa; CA Polytechnic U., B.S. 1978; Roman Catholic; single.

Career: Farmer; Mariposa Cnty. Planning Comm., 1982–86, Chmn., 1985–86; Mariposa Cnty. Bd. of Supervisors, 1989–92; Founder & Owner, Radanovich Winery, 1986–present.

DC Office: 313 CHOB 20515, 202-225-4540; Fax: 202-225-3402.

District Offices: 2377 W. Shaw, #105, Fresno 93711, 209-248-0800.

Committees: *Budget* (23rd of 24 R). *Resources* (19th of 25 R): National Parks, Forests and Lands; Water and Power Resources.

Group Ratings and 103rd Congress Votes: Newly Elected

Key Votes of the 104th Congress

1. Congressional Compliance Y	6. Reform Crime Grant Y	11. Loser Pays Court Reform Y
2. Balanced Budget Amndmt. Y	7. National Security Act Y	12. Product Liability Reform Y
3. Bar Unfunded Mandates Y	8. Moratorium on Regs. Y	13. Welfare Reform Y
4. Pass Line Item Veto Y	9. Risk Assessment on Regs. Y	14. Term Limits Amndmt. Y
5. Relax Exclusionary Rule Y	10. Expnd. Priv. Prop. Rights Y	15. Tax Cuts Y

Election Results

1994 general	George P. Radanovich (R)	104,435	(57%)	($468,818)
	Richard H. Lehman (D)	72,912	(40%)	($1,079,999)
	Others	6,579	(4%)	
1994 primary	George P. Radanovich (R)	25,191	(51%)	
	Michael Der Manouel Jr. (R)	14,551	(29%)	
	Ron Gulke (R)	9,883	(20%)	
1992 general	Richard H. Lehman (D)	101,620	(47%)	($915,504)
	Tal L. Cloud (R)	100,590	(46%)	($153,784)
	Dorothy L. Wells (P&F)	13,334	(6%)	
	Other	1,098	(1%)	

TWENTIETH DISTRICT

California's Central Valley on the map seems a monotonous landscape: mile after mile of farmland with mile-square grid roads, cut across by diagonal railroads and canals, with an occasional cluster town. The land is hilly and gets more water near the Sierra Nevada, and this is where the larger cities cluster. On the other side is the Westlands, where the land is flatter and the water scarcer. Here are huge farming operations, like the giant J.G. Boswell holdings, augmented by purchase of the rival Salyer acreage near Corcoran. This land was always developed and sold in giant plots. And it produces plenty: alfalfa, cantaloupes, cotton, grapes, lima beans, olives, peaches, plums, raisins, sugar beets, tomatoes, walnuts, wheat. The owners are a hardy lot, but like most entrepreneurs they are happy to use government help: crop price supports, agricultural research, exceptions to the immigration laws, irrigation systems and (most important) subsidized water. They have fought hard against liberals' efforts at change, from Governor Jerry Brown's attempts to encourage Cesar Chavez's United Farm Workers in the 1970s to former House Natural Resources Committee chairman George Miller's 1990s bill to draw off more water to the Sacramento delta and charge higher prices for it in the Valley. But the greatest threats may come from conservatives: in a free market for water, Los Angeles users may outbid the farmers, and restrictions on illegal immigrants, like 1994's Proposition 187, may cut off the supply of farm workers.

The 20th Congressional District includes most of the Westlands of the Central Valley, from south of Bakersfield to north of Fresno. Its irregular boundaries were drawn to maximize the Hispanic population, so the 20th includes the old downtown neighborhoods of both Bakersfield and Fresno, but none of their newer suburbs; it includes heavily Latino towns like Delano, long Chavez's headquarters, but not more Anglo places like Tulare. The 20th's Hispanic percentage is 55%, compared to 20%–26% in other Central Valley districts, but many Latinos don't vote; still, it is the most Democratic seat between Sacramento and Los Angeles.

The Congressman from the 20th is Calvin Dooley, a Democrat who is a fourth-generation farmer in the Valley and who has been the beneficiary of good luck in three elections. A former staffer for Tulare state Senator Rose Ann Vuich, he ran in 1990 against incumbent Republican Chip Pashayan, who had received contributions from S&L crook Charles Keating and then interceded with regulators on his behalf, and who had switched off the Resources Committee, which handles so many Valley issues, onto Rules in 1989. Dooley won with a solid 55%. In 1992, after new district lines were announced, Fresno area 10-year incumbent Democrat Richard Lehman decided not to run against Dooley in a primary but instead ran in the much more Republican 19th District; Lehman barely won in 1992, then lost in 1994. In the 20th, Dooley won with 65% in 1992.

Dooley has a moderate voting record and was a key vote on many issues in the 103d Congress. He tottered before voting for the Clinton budget and tax package, and he supported the balanced budget amendment and the line-item veto. But he is more liberal on foreign policy—

the only Central Valley vote against the Gulf war resolution. He opposed the employer mandates and backup price controls in Democratic healthcare plans. He has a seat on the Resources and Agriculture Committees and has concentrated on farm issues; he was touted by some state officials as a nominee for secretary of agriculture in 1993, but as a white Anglo male didn't fill anyone's quota and was not a serious contender. In 1994, when so many Democrats were in trouble, Dooley had a Republican opponent who spent all of $6,000 and was reelected 57%–43%.

The People: Pop. 1990: 573,555; 27% rural; 9% age 65+; 33% White; 6% Black; 1% Amer. Indian; 6% Asian; 38% Other; 55% Hispanic origin. Voting age pop.: 373,437; 7% Black; 50% Hispanic origin. Households: 60% married couple families; 35% married couple fams. w. children; 26% college educ.; median household income: $21,140; per capita income: $8,097; median gross rent: $379; median house value: $63,400.

1992 Presidential Vote			1988 Presidential Vote		
Clinton (D)	55,942	(47%)	Dukakis (D)	55,851	(53%)
Bush (R)	44,674	(37%)	Bush (R)	49,815	(47%)
Perot (I)	18,568	(16%)			

Rep. Calvin Dooley (D)

Elected 1990; b. Jan. 11, 1954, Visalia; home, Visalia; U. of CA at Davis, B.S. 1977, Stanford U., M.A. 1987; Methodist; married (Linda).

Career: Farmer, 1978–91; A.A., CA Sen. Rose Ann Vuich, 1987–89.

DC Office: 1227 LHOB 20515, 202-225-3341; Fax: 202-225-9308.

District Offices: 224 W. Lacey Blvd., Hanford 93230, 209-585-8171.

Committees: *Agriculture* (9th of 22 D): General Farm Commodities; Livestock, Dairy and Poultry. *Resources* (15th of 20 D): Energy and Mineral Resources; Water and Power Resources.

Group Ratings

	ADA	ACLU	COPE	CFA	LCV	CON	NSI	COC	ACU	NTLC	CHC
1994	50	65	22	50	33	88	22	92	22	33	28
1993	75	—	67	70	57	69	—	64	25	—	—

National Journal Ratings

	1993 LIB — 1993 CONS			1994 LIB — 1994 CONS		
Economic	50%	—	49%	49%	—	50%
Social	73%	—	23%	53%	—	46%
Foreign	79%	—	16%	83%	—	17%

Key Votes of the 103d Congress

1. Clinton Deficit Plan	N	3. Brady Handgun Purchase	Y	5. Lmt. UN Cmnd. of Forces	N
2. NAFTA	Y	4. Strike Race/Death Pnlty.	Y	6. Cut Missile Funds	Y

Key Votes of the 104th Congress

1. Congressional Compliance Y	6. Reform Crime Grant N	11. Loser Pays Court Reform N
2. Balanced Budget Amndmt. Y	7. National Security Act N	12. Product Liability Reform Y
3. Bar Unfunded Mandates Y	8. Moratorium on Regs. Y	13. Welfare Reform N
4. Pass Line Item Veto Y	9. Risk Assessment on Regs. Y	14. Term Limits Amndmt. N
5. Relax Exclusionary Rule Y	10. Expnd. Priv. Prop. Rights Y	15. Tax Cuts N

Election Results

1994 general	Calvin Dooley (D).....................	57,394	(57%)	($275,544)
	Paul Young (R).......................	43,836	(43%)	($10,346)
1994 primary	Calvin Dooley (D)...................	unopposed		
1992 general	Calvin Dooley (D)....................	72,679	(65%)	($504,352)
	Ed Hunt (R)	39,388	(35%)	($173,744)

TWENTY-FIRST DISTRICT

Bakersfield, at the apex of the southern end of California's Central Valley, has been the focus of great migrations four times—in a gold rush in 1885, when oil was discovered here in 1899, during the 1930s when so-called Okies drove their jalopies from the Dust Bowl of Oklahoma and Kansas and Texas across the Southwest on U.S. 66, and again in the 1980s, when Bakersfield and Kern County grew more rapidly than California's biggest metro areas. Bakersfield's gold is gone, its oil rigs still pump, but the migration that made the deepest imprint was in the 1930s. The Okies drove over one thousand miles of brown landscape, then through the Tehachapi Pass found the vast green valley, with its irrigated fields and its eucalyptus-shaded towns, the richest farming country in the world bright under the sun. The story is told vividly in John Steinbeck's *The Grapes of Wrath*, though his vision of the Okies as workers eager to join together with their fellow proletarians and rise up against their bosses did not get the picture quite right. More accurate is Dan Morgan's *Rising in the West*, which shows the strong Pentecostal beliefs which drove many migrants and, unlike Steinbeck, explains how they prospered in California. The area around Bakersfield has become the one southern-accented part of California, the home of country singers Buck Owens and Merle Haggard and a thriving contemporary country music scene, culturally conservative with a strong drive toward discipline and little empathy for the therapy that is so common in Los Angeles, 110 miles south. "I hope you all agree with me that Bakersfield is boring," LA Mayor Richard Riordan said on radio in July 1994—and then came up for a tour in 106-degree heat and heard the Kern County DA tell him that motorists are not fired at on Bakersfield's freeways, its citizens don't riot when they don't like a jury verdict and its celebrities are not on trial for murder.

The 21st Congressional District, the southernmost district in the Central Valley, is centered on Bakersfield and takes in most of Kern and Tulare Counties; it also includes Edwards Air Force Base where Chuck Yeager flew the X-1 and where the space shuttle frequently lands. The district's boundaries are irregular to maximize the Hispanic percentage of the next-door 20th District. The 21st includes most of Bakersfield and its surroundings, oil fields and high-income subdivisions, and Kern County desert and mountain communities. Politically, this was Democratic territory in the early 1960s—when, for that matter, so was Oklahoma; by the late 1960s, both had become solidly Republican in national politics, and today seem Republican up and down the ticket. In 1994, Kern and Tulare Counties favored Governor Pete Wilson over Kathleen Brown 70%–27% and Michael Huffington over Dianne Feinstein 63%-28%.

The congressman from the 21st, Bill Thomas, is now one of the senior Republicans in the House after years of frustration in the minority. He chairs the House Oversight Committee and is a senior member of Ways and Means and chairman of its Health Subcommittee. Thomas grew up in Orange County, graduated from San Francisco State and taught political science in the community college in Bakersfield. He was elected to the Assembly in 1974, a conservative in a liberal–run legislature; when Congressman Bill Ketchum died after the 1978 primary, he ran as the relative moderate at the party convention and won the seat. With his position on the House Oversight Committee, Thomas defended partisan positions with no chance of prevailing, on campaign finance and the contest over the Indiana 8th District in 1985; he worked with Democrat Al Swift on uniform poll closings but could reach no agreement on a motor voter bill. On campaign finance reform, Thomas called for restricting PAC and out-of-district contributions; he passed a bill restricting franked mail. Some younger conservatives considered him too accommodating, and—with the encouragement of then-Minority Whip Newt Gingrich—Paul Gillmor of Ohio ran against him for the ranking-member post on the House Oversight Committee in December 1992, losing by only 12 votes.

Since then Thomas has been an adamant opponent of the Democrats. He criticized their health care plans and called for more choices and innovations for consumers. He fought George Miller's Central Valley Water Project Act and the Desert Protection Act, unsuccessfully. He backed "super IRAs" for college and major medical expenses and a $2,500 first-time homebuyer tax credit. He has generally been a free trader, with an eye out for California pistachios; he voted for the North American Free Trade Agreement.

After Republicans won their majority, Newt Gingrich appointed Thomas chairman of House Oversight, but many of that post's administrative functions have been taken over by a new House administrative officer, who reports to the Speaker; Gingrich also named his ally Jim Nussle to work on internal House matters and named all the members of the committee. On the Health Subcommittee, Thomas has promised to do much to reshape Medicaid and Medicare and to salvage the depleting resources of the Medicare trust fund, and on the full committee he can promote super IRAs. He took a lead in backing the restoration of the 25% health care deduction for the self-employed, which Republicans packaged with repeal of the broadcast license racial preference in February 1995.

Thomas has not had serious competition for reelection in many years.

The People: Pop. 1990: 571,143; 19% rural; 11% age 65+; 71% White; 4% Black; 1% Amer. Indian; 3% Asian; 13% Other; 20% Hispanic origin. Voting age pop.: 398,049; 4% Black; 17% Hispanic origin. Households: 59% married couple families; 30% married couple fams. w. children; 47% college educ.; median household income: $29,943; per capita income: $12,983; median gross rent: $454; median house value: $84,600.

1992 Presidential Vote			1988 Presidential Vote		
Bush (R)	94,727	(46%)	Bush (R)	107,624	(64%)
Clinton (D)	66,284	(32%)	Dukakis (D)	60,740	(36%)
Perot (I)	43,016	(21%)			

Rep. William M. Thomas (R)

Elected 1978; b. Dec. 6, 1941, Wallace, ID; home, Bakersfield; San Francisco St. U., B.A. 1963, M.A. 1965; Baptist; married (Sharon).

Career: Prof., Bakersfield Comm. Col., 1965–74; CA Assembly, 1974–78.

DC Office: 2208 RHOB 20515, 202-225-2915; Fax: 202-225-2908.

District Offices: 4100 Truxtun Ave., #220, Bakersfield 93309, 805-327-3611; and 319 W. Murray St., Visalia 93291, 209-627-6549.

Committees: *House Oversight* (Chmn. of 7 R). *Ways & Means* (3rd of 21 R): Health (Chmn.); Trade. *Joint Committee on Taxation* (3rd of 5 Reps.).

Group Ratings

	ADA	ACLU	COPE	CFA	LCV	CON	NSI	COC	ACU	NTLC	CHC
1994	10	32	29	10	6	82	90	100	84	89	64
1993	5	—	17	20	29	64	—	100	78	—	—

National Journal Ratings

	1993 LIB — 1993 CONS		1994 LIB — 1994 CONS	
Economic	0%	— 88%	24%	— 75%
Social	42%	— 57%	32%	— 67%
Foreign	9%	— 85%	25%	— 71%

Key Votes of the 103d Congress

1. Clinton Deficit Plan	N	3. Brady Handgun Purchase	Y	5. Lmt. UN Cmnd. of Forces	Y
2. NAFTA	Y	4. Strike Race/Death Pnlty.	Y	6. Cut Missile Funds	N

Key Votes of the 104th Congress

1. Congressional Compliance	Y	6. Reform Crime Grant	Y	11. Loser Pays Court Reform	Y
2. Balanced Budget Amndmt.	Y	7. National Security Act	Y	12. Product Liability Reform	Y
3. Bar Unfunded Mandates	Y	8. Moratorium on Regs.	Y	13. Welfare Reform	Y
4. Pass Line Item Veto	Y	9. Risk Assessment on Regs.	Y	14. Term Limits Amndmt.	Y
5. Relax Exclusionary Rule	Y	10. Expnd. Priv. Prop. Rights	Y	15. Tax Cuts	Y

Election Results

1994 general	William M. Thomas (R)	116,874	(68%)	($434,146)
	John L. Evans (D)	47,517	(28%)	($31,101)
	Mike Hodges (Lib)	6,899	(4%)	
1994 primary	William M. Thomas (R)	38,947	(70%)	
	Nora (Jenkins) Weber (R)	16,730	(30%)	
1992 general	William M. Thomas (R)	127,758	(65%)	($615,587)
	Deborah A. Vollmer (D)	68,058	(35%)	($28,487)

TWENTY-SECOND DISTRICT

Santa Barbara is one of California's most paradisical cities, a collection of red tile roofs and leafy live oaks, sheltered by towering mountains just above the sea. The impression is a bit misleading, for Santa Barbara has its problems, and its Spanish style is a creation not of 18th-century Mission culture, but of the 20th century. Most of its red-tile-roofed, white stucco buildings were put up after a 1925 earthquake leveled much of the town, with the most distinguished of the Spanish Revival buildings designed by an architect with the marvelously un-Latin name of George Washington Smith (though the documents at the Santa Barbara Mission are authentic). Santa Barbara, like Disneyland, does not reproduce the past but presents a bigger, more attractive, cleaner version of it, maintained not by a company but (as in Santa Fe and Nantucket) by an architectural review board. But Santa Barbara's affluence isn't ersatz. This has long been one of the nation's richest retirement communities, and one increasingly devoted to preserving its environment and serenity. Both came under threat spectacularly in 1969, when an underwater oil well ruptured, coating the beach with oil; pictures of the oil slick in the channel and of volunteers trying to wash oil off grounded birds, as Interior Secretary Walter Hickel circled in a helicopter above, helped to launch the environmental movement of the 1970s. Almost all the wells are closed now (though some old 19th century wells still send globs of oil to the beach at nearby Summerland, where the Clintons rested in November 1992) but the oil spill did leave a residue in Santa Barbara's politics. This is a Republican community, uninterested in redistribution of wealth, but very concerned about the environment (it has built the nation's largest desalination plant) and moderate to liberal on cultural issues like abortion.

The 22d Congressional District consists of all of Santa Barbara County except the town of Carpinteria at its southeast corner, plus San Luis Obispo County to the north. Not all of this area resembles Santa Barbara. The most notable feature in northern Santa Barbara County, across the Santa Ynez Mountains from Ronald Reagan's ranch, is Vandenberg Air Force Base, and the nearby town of Santa Maria is pro-military and conservative. San Luis Obispo County is pleasant and as untrendy a place as you could find on this coast, culturally more Middle American than Santa Barbara.

The Congresswoman from the 22d District is Andrea Seastrand, a Republican elected in 1994 in the third close contest this area has seen in the last four elections. The first was in 1988, when longtime Republican incumbent Robert Lagomarsino was challenged by state Senator Gary K. Hart (no relation to the former Colorado senator); both candidates raised about $1.5 million, and Lagomarsino won 50%–49%. The second was in 1992, when Lagomarsino was challenged in the primary by Michael Huffington, then an unknown oil and natural gas millionaire from Texas who bought a Montecito mansion in 1988 and moved there in 1991. Huffington spent $3 million of his own money on the primary and attacked Lagomarsino for using influence to help a local company selling surveillance cameras to the Chinese government to track down Tiananmen Square protesters—the same anti-"career politician" theme he would use against Senator Dianne Feinstein in 1994. Huffington ran saturation TV ads, sent out 15 mailings and numerous videos, and won the primary 49%–43%, losing Santa Barbara County 42%–55% but carrying San Luis Obispo 60%–28%. In the House, Huffington had a moderate record, pro-choice on abortion and pro-gay rights, but conspicuously refused to lobby the government for constituents and soon started running for the Senate. When he ran for the Senate, much was made by the hostile press of hostility toward him by leading voices in Santa Barbara, but in fact he carried the 22d District in both primary and general, thanks to big margins in San Luis Obispo County. Within weeks of his defeat, he began to talk up another statewide race—for Senate or governor in 1998 or for the Feinstein seat in 2000.

With Huffington out, there was naturally serious competition for the seat. On the Republican side, Seastrand's experience and local base in San Luis Obispo helped her beat Santa Barbara Supervisor Mike Stoker 59%–36%. Seastrand grew up in the Chicago area and moved to Salinas to teach school. Her husband Eric Seastrand, a strong conservative, ran for Congress against Leon Panetta in 1978 and lost 61%–39%; in 1982 he was elected to the California Assembly and served until his death in 1990, when Andrea Seastrand was elected to fill his vacancy. Her chief project there was promoting Vandenberg Air Force Base as a Commercial Spaceport. Her Democratic opponent in 1994 was Walter Capps, winner of a three-way primary with 40% of the vote, a professor of religious studies at the University of California at Santa Barbara and author of *The New Religious Right*, of which he does not take a favorable view. The general election presented as nice a contrast of cultural views as any in the country. Seastrand strongly opposed abortion and gays in the military; Capps favored them and opposed the death penalty. Capps attacked Seastrand for delivering a sermon calling the Northridge earthquake, Malibu fires and California floods signs of God's judgements on the state's morality. He was described by a local newspaper as invoking "an abstract view of God to encourage a return to community and human relationships." This was a good example of how politics can become an argument between therapy and discipline. Therapy-minded Santa Barbara County voted 51%–47% for Capps, but discipline-minded San Luis Obispo voted 53%–44% for Seastrand: both closely tracked the Huffington-Feinstein numbers. Seastrand won 49.3%–48.5%, one of the closest races in the country. And while Huffington spent a total of $5.4 million to win this seat in 1992, Seastrand spent only $600,000.

In the House, Seastrand worked hard to promote the commercial spaceport idea, and in March 1995 the Western Commercial Space Center signed a 25 year lease with Vandenberg. She took time to read into the record statements supporting Speaker Newt Gingrich and voted solidly for the Contract With America. Her strong religious views and close margin seem certain to bring her spirited Democratic competition, perhaps even a primary challenge, in 1996.

The People: Pop. 1990: 572,956; 11% rural; 13% age 65+; 72% White; 3% Black; 1% Amer. Indian; 4% Asian; 11% Other; 21% Hispanic origin. Voting age pop.: 443,156; 3% Black; 18% Hispanic origin. Households: 54% married couple families; 24% married couple fams. w. children; 59% college educ.; median household income: $33,680; per capita income: $16,458; median gross rent: $621; median house value: $229,000.

1992 Presidential Vote			1988 Presidential Vote		
Clinton (D)	106,815	(41%)	Bush (R)	121,486	(56%)
Bush (R)	92,045	(35%)	Dukakis (D)	96,838	(44%)
Perot (I)	61,030	(23%)			

Rep. Andrea Seastrand (R)

Elected 1994; b. Aug. 5, 1941, Chicago, IL; home, Shell Beach; DePaul U., B.A. 1963; Catholic; widow.

Career: Elem. schl. teacher; CA House of Reps., 1990–94.

DC Office: 1216 LHOB 20515, 202-225-3601; Fax: 202-225-3426.

District Offices: 1525 State St., #206, Santa Barbara 93101, 805-899-3578; and 778 Osos St., #A-2, San Luis Obispo 93401, 805-541-0170.

Committees: *Transportation & Infrastructure* (29th of 33 R): Aviation; Public Buildings and Economic Development (Vice Chmn.). *Science* (21st of 27 R): Space and Aeronautics; Technology.

Group Ratings and 103rd Congress Votes: Newly Elected

Key Votes of the 104th Congress

1. Congressional Compliance Y	6. Reform Crime Grant Y	11. Loser Pays Court Reform Y
2. Balanced Budget Amndmt. Y	7. National Security Act Y	12. Product Liability Reform Y
3. Bar Unfunded Mandates Y	8. Moratorium on Regs. Y	13. Welfare Reform Y
4. Pass Line Item Veto Y	9. Risk Assessment on Regs. Y	14. Term Limits Amndmt. Y
5. Relax Exclusionary Rule Y	10. Expnd. Priv. Prop. Rights Y	15. Tax Cuts Y

Election Results

1994 general	Andrea Seastrand (R)................	102,987	(49%)	($630,933)
	Walter Holden Capps (D)..............	101,424	(49%)	($497,585)
	Others	4,597	(2%)	
1994 primary	Andrea Seastrand (R).................	39,938	(59%)	
	Mike Stoker (R)......................	24,405	(36%)	
	Wayne Reddoch (R)...................	3,394	(5%)	
1992 general	Michael Huffington (R)	131,242	(53%)	($5,435,177)
	Gloria Ochoa (D)	87,328	(35%)	($663,027)
	Mindy Lorenz (Green)	23,699	(9%)	($18,707)
	Others	7,657	(3%)	

TWENTY-THIRD DISTRICT

On a golden mountainside, looking westward over a valley hemmed in by mountains north and south, five United States presidents gathered in November 1991 to dedicate the Ronald Reagan Library. This was the first time in 202 years that five presidents had stood together in one place—one which the Founding Fathers surely did not imagine would ever be American and yet today seems quintessentially so. Simi Valley would become famous five months later as the site of the criminal trial of the four Los Angeles Police Department officers accused of assaulting Rodney King after a high-speed freeway chase; the verdict was criticized as an expression of racism, though given the evidence and argument the jury was presented with, it was a rational response. Simi Valley is just one of several communities in the valleys and narrow coastal margins of Ventura County, west of Los Angeles, that have been filling up with people leaving the Los Angeles Basin and the San Fernando Valley and building new communities in what had been an agricultural county with a gritty port and Navy base.

In fact, these new communities in Ventura County—Simi Valley, Moorpark and Thousand Oaks and Camarillo, running out toward the industrial port of Oxnard and the county seat of Ventura—are diverse in most respects; Ventura County in 1990 was 30% Hispanic and 5% Asian; its white Anglo residents include many with names and backgrounds that would have been recognized as ethnic a few years ago. It also has some of the nation's lowest crime rates, a stark contrast with gang warfare in Los Angeles, and some of the highest percentages of intact families in California, a vivid contrast with the showbiz lifestyles of Westside LA. And this is car country: Simi Valley claims to have more cars per capita than anywhere in the United States. But what is wrong with this?

The 23d Congressional District includes almost all of Ventura County (except Thousand Oaks) and just a corner of Santa Barbara County, the town of Carpinteria. Politically, this home of the Reagan Library was strong Reagan country when he was elected governor and president, though it lost some of its cheerful, upbeat optimism in the more downbeat years of his successors, Jerry Brown in California and George Bush in Washington. But the balance toward the Republicans, the yearning for the cheerful order Reagan was able to impart, remains.

The Congressman from the 23d District is Elton Gallegly. He grew up in a working class suburb of Los Angeles, dropped out of college and became a real estate broker. He was elected at 35 to the Simi Valley city council, became mayor in 1980, then ran for Congress in 1986 when the incumbent ran for the Senate. Gallegly's local ties and money prevailed 50%–34% in the

1986 primary over Tony Hope, son of comedian Bob Hope, who had spent the previous decade in Washington. In the 1988 and 1990 primaries, Gallegly withstood by solid margins primary challenges by a Korean-born entrepreneur who spent over $300,000 each time to win 14% and 32%.

In 1992, after redistricting had moved much of fellow incumbent Robert Lagomarsino's district into the new Ventura County-based seat, Gallegly moved fast to push Lagomarsino into running in the 22d District to the north, where he lost the primary to Michael Huffington's $3 million campaign. Gallegly had minimal primary opposition but a spirited challenge from Democrat Anita Perez Ferguson, who raised large sums from the feminist left in "the year of the woman" and held Gallegly to a 54%–41% margin. In 1994 he was reelected easily, 66%–27%.

Gallegly has compiled almost a perfectly conservative voting record and has emphasized three major issues. One is illegal immigration. In the first weeks of the new Congress he has called for a tougher Border Patrol, a tamperproof identification card for legal aliens and an end to welfare for illegal immigrants. He criticizes the current Immigration and Naturalization Service IDs as easily forgeable, carrying one around himself as evidence. In 1995, Speaker Newt Gingrich named him head of House Republicans' Immigration Reform Task Force; his emphasis on improving ID cards and border patrolling differs from that of Immigration Subcommittee Chairman Lamar Smith of Texas, who is bent on reducing legal immigration totals, and it will be interesting to see what comes out of the likely intra-party tension in this arrangement. His second major cause has been to minimize the labeling requirements on vitamins and dietary supplements issued by the Food and Drug Administration in response to a 1990 law sponsored by Los Angeles's Henry Waxman. Gallegly would allow the dietary supplements to make health claims without the documentation required for prescription drugs or foods. Gallegly became chairman of the Native Americans and Insular Affairs Subcommittee in 1995. This gives him possible superintendency over Indian affairs, always a quandary given their grave problems, the incompetence of the Bureau of Indian Affairs and the sudden importance of Indian gambling. He also has control of laws affecting the 4 million Americans who live in Puerto Rico, the Virgin Islands, Guam and American Samoa; Gallegly's impulse, symbolized by the 1995 closure of the Office of Territorial and International Affairs, is to let them run their own affairs. Incidentally, he turned down the Africa Subcommittee chair for this post. Gallegly has also worked on local issues, calling for $2,400 tax credits for companies that hire laid-off defense workers and getting the Port Nogu and Port Hueneme Naval Bases near Oxnard designated as a U.S. port of entry.

The People: Pop. 1990: 571,562; 5% rural; 9% age 65+; 62% White; 3% Black; 1% Amer. Indian; 5% Asian; 14% Other; 30% Hispanic origin. Voting age pop.: 413,051; 2% Black; 26% Hispanic origin. Households: 63% married couple families; 33% married couple fams. w. children; 54% college educ.; median household income: $42,989; per capita income: $16,617; median gross rent: $733; median house value: $234,200.

1992 Presidential Vote

Clinton (D) 82,613 (38%)
Bush (R) 74,106 (34%)
Perot (I). 58,177 (27%)

1988 Presidential Vote

Bush (R) 115,744 (61%)
Dukakis (D). 75,566 (39%)

Rep. Elton Gallegly (R)

Elected 1986; b. Mar. 7, 1944, Huntington Park; home, Simi Valley; Los Angeles St. Col., 1962–63; Protestant; married (Janice).

Career: Owner, real estate firm; Simi Valley City Cncl., 1979–80; Simi Valley Mayor, 1980–86.

DC Office: 2441 RHOB 20515, 202-225-5811; Fax: 202-225-1100.

District Offices: 300 Esplanade Dr., #1800, Oxnard 93030, 805-485-2300.

Committees: *International Relations* (10th of 23 R): Western Hemisphere. *Resources* (4th of 25 R): Native American and Insular Affairs (Chmn.). *Judiciary* (9th of 20 R): Courts and Intellectual Property; Immigration and Claims.

Group Ratings

	ADA	ACLU	COPE	CFA	LCV	CON	NSI	COC	ACU	NTLC	CHC
1994	10	9	25	20	6	58	100	92	95	93	86
1993	10	—	8	30	29	74	—	73	96	—	—

National Journal Ratings

	1993 LIB — 1993 CONS	1994 LIB — 1994 CONS
Economic	20% — 77%	0% — 80%
Social	11% — 82%	20% — 80%
Foreign	0% — 91%	14% — 80%

Key Votes of the 103d Congress

1. Clinton Deficit Plan	N	3. Brady Handgun Purchase Y	5. Lmt. UN Cmnd. of Forces Y
2. NAFTA	N	4. Strike Race/Death Pnlty. Y	6. Cut Missile Funds N

Key Votes of the 104th Congress

1. Congressional Compliance Y	6. Reform Crime Grant Y	11. Loser Pays Court Reform Y
2. Balanced Budget Amndmt. Y	7. National Security Act Y	12. Product Liability Reform Y
3. Bar Unfunded Mandates Y	8. Moratorium on Regs. Y	13. Welfare Reform Y
4. Pass Line Item Veto Y	9. Risk Assessment on Regs. Y	14. Term Limits Amndmt. Y
5. Relax Exclusionary Rule Y	10. Expnd. Priv. Prop. Rights Y	15. Tax Cuts Y

Election Results

1994 general	Elton Gallegly (R)	114,043	(66%)	($300,846)
	Kevin Ready (D)	47,345	(27%)	($24,813)
	Others	10,952	(6%)	
1994 primary	Elton Gallegly (R)	unopposed		
1992 general	Elton Gallegly (R)	115,504	(54%)	($862,061)
	Anita Perez Ferguson (D)	88,225	(41%)	($543,116)
	Jay C. Wood (Lib)	9,091	(4%)	

TWENTY-FOURTH DISTRICT

The San Fernando Valley, in the early 20th Century when the movie business was young, was a vast expanse of empty land, annexed to Los Angeles in 1915; moviemakers looking for filming sites for a western drove past the vacant lots of Westwood, up narrow roads through the Santa Monica Mountains and over into the vast Valley, sheltered from ocean breezes and rain-bearing clouds by the mountains. Over the past 80 years this vast bowl of land has been transformed, first into 1950s suburbia, then into a postmodern city of its own, economically vital and yeastily ethnic. Even in its suburban years the San Fernando Valley was not entirely residential: big factories—the General Motors Van Nuys assembly plant, the Anheuser Busch brewery, Rockwell and Litton defense plants—provided jobs. But in the 1950s and 1960s this was fast-growing, family-friendly territory; politically, turf fought over hard by Republicans and Democrats. By the 1970s young white Anglo families were fleeing, as the Los Angeles Unified school district was hit by a busing order. There is plenty of upscale territory left in the uplands in the rims of the Valley, in heavily Jewish Sherman Oaks and Encino and to the west in Woodland Hills and Chatsworth; and the office blocks and mini-malls along Ventura and Woodland Hills Boulevard show unmistakable signs of affluence. In the inner lowlands of the Valley, new immigrants have moved in. Some old neighborhoods have become rough Latino enclaves, with youth gangs and boarded-up houses and apartments weakened by the Northridge earthquake; in other neighborhoods Iranians and Chinese, Mexicans and Koreans, Israelis and Filipinos are keeping neighborhoods solidly middle-class.

The 24th Congressional District includes most of the southern and western San Fernando Valley, from the hillside mansions of Encino to the gang territory around the Van Nuys plant. Two-thirds of the 24th's people live in the Valley; another one-fifth live directly west, in new communities nestled amid mountains along U.S. 101—ranch-like Agoura, jewel-like Westlake Village and sprawling Thousand Oaks, home of the biotechnology giant, Amgen Inc. The 24th also takes in Malibu, recovering now from the fires and mudslides, with $1 million beach houses five feet from each other. Politically, this is a mixed area. The Jewish precincts are solidly Democratic, and got even more so in the 1994 campaign; Thousand Oaks is heavily Republican; the immigrant areas fluctuate and could go any which way; Malibu is trendy showbiz liberal.

The Congressman from the 24th is Anthony Beilenson, a Democrat and who has spent almost all his adult life as a legislator. He grew up in Westchester County, New York, moved to Beverly Hills after Harvard Law, and within five years had been elected to the California Assembly in 1962, at 30, two years before Willie Brown. He was elected to the state Senate in 1966, after redistricting gave Los Angeles County more than one state Senate district, and in 1968 lost the primary for U.S. Senate to Alan Cranston. In 1976, when an incumbent retired, he was elected to the House from a district south of the Santa Monica Mountains. For a lifetime professional politician, he comes off oddly like a straight arrow, telling uncomfortable truths to his colleagues and constituents, and yet he is shrewd enough to get away with it. Since 1978 he has been on the Rules Committee, which up through 1994 was a willing and pliant instrument of the Democratic leadership; but he labored on budget and intelligence and electoral process issues and made impolitic proposals like cutting Social Security and imposing a 50 cent gas tax. He chaired the Intelligence Committee for two years and tried unsuccessfully to promote bipartisan coopera-tion. He passed an African elephant protection law prohibiting ivory imports and has promoted elephant conservation. Quietly, he kept in touch with constituents as his district lines shifted northward. Sherman Oaks and Encino were added in the 1980s; many of their residents used to live on the Westside. For 1992, he had the choice of running against the well-financed and better-known Henry Waxman in the 29th or running in the more Republican 24th, and chose the latter. He has had serious competition in the district in 1992 and 1994.

In 1992, nine Republicans ran for the nomination; the winner, with 34%, was Ventura County Assemblyman Tom McClintock, a conservative who would privatize street lights and prisons, and a fierce critic of Governor Pete Wilson for his 1991 tax increases and pro-choice stands. Beilenson has stressed family-planning (he wrote California's 1967 liberalized abortion law, signed by Governor Ronald Reagan, and chaired the congressional delegation to the 1994 international population conference in Cairo) and the environment—his opposition to offshore oil drilling and sponsorship of continuing expansions of the Santa Monica Mountains National Recreation Area. He called for a national health service, with government payment and price-setting, and stressed his refusal to accept PAC contributions. McClintock's hard-edged conservatism did not go over well as the Bush candidacy was sinking, and Beilenson won 56%–39%. In 1994, the Republican nominee, Rich Sybert, was better suited to the district. A lawyer and department head for Pete Wilson, he spent liberally of his own money to win a five-candidate primary with 47%; he called for tough measures on crime, stricter border patrols and an end to aid to illegal immigrants. This was one race where the Republican challenger outspent the incumbent and, with personal door-to-door campaigning, outhustled him too. But residual goodwill toward the earnest Beilenson and his help in delivering federal disaster aid following the 1994 earthquake, plus Jewish and showbiz voters' antipathy to the cultural conservatism of national Republicans, worked for the Democrat. Sybert carried the Thousand Oaks area 62%–35%, but Beilenson won the Los Angeles County portion of the district 54%–43%, enough for a 49%–48% victory overall.

Beilenson has been in the minority before, in the California Senate in 1969 and 1970. "We have to experience it for a while," he said in early 1995, "and discover how best to serve the nation and our beliefs." He has a particular problem, since Democrats are likely to be routinely outvoted on the Rules Committee, which almost always operates by party-line votes, and he will have little leverage there to advance legislative projects. But his friendship with Minority Leader Dick Gephardt and his position as the second-senior Rules Committee Democrat behind aging Joe Moakley could move Beilenson back into a position of power if Democrats regain House control. And, given the close margin in 1994, it is almost certain that the 24th District will be seriously contested again in 1996; given Beilenson's win in tough circumstances, it is by no means a foregone conclusion that he will lose.

The People: Pop. 1990: 572,287; 3% rural; 11% age 65+; 78% White; 2% Black; 6% Asian; 7% Other; 13% Hispanic origin. Voting age pop.: 450,914; 2% Black; 12% Hispanic origin. Households: 55% married couple families; 25% married couple fams. w. children; 66% college educ.; median household income: $48,433; per capita income: $25,767; median gross rent: $779; median house value: $304,300.

1992 Presidential Vote		
Clinton (D)	128,572	(48%)
Bush (R)	79,728	(30%)
Perot (I)	57,625	(22%)

1988 Presidential Vote		
Bush (R)	132,750	(54%)
Dukakis (D)	112,531	(46%)

Rep. Anthony C. Beilenson (D)

Elected 1976; b. Oct. 26, 1932, New Rochelle, NY; home, Los Angeles; Harvard, A.B. 1954, LL.B. 1957; Jewish; married (Dolores).

Career: Practicing atty., 1957–59; Cnsl., CA Assembly Cmte. on Finance & Insurance, 1960; Atty., CA Compensation & Insurance Fund, 1961–62; CA Assembly, 1963–66; CA Senate, 1967–76.

DC Office: 2465 RHOB 20515, 202-225-5911; Fax: 202-225-0092.

District Offices: 21031 Ventura Blvd., #1010, Woodland Hills 91364, 818-999-1990; and 200 N. Westlake Blvd., #211, Thousand Oaks 91362, 805-496-4333.

Committees: *Rules* (2nd of 4 D): Rules of the House (RMM).

Group Ratings

	ADA	ACLU	COPE	CFA	LCV	CON	NSI	COC	ACU	NTLC	CHC
1994	95	78	89	100	89	20	20	33	0	7	7
1993	85	—	75	90	93	32	—	27	8	—	—

National Journal Ratings

	1993 LIB — 1993 CONS		1994 LIB — 1994 CONS	
Economic	68%	— 26%	73%	— 17%
Social	67%	— 33%	82%	— 15%
Foreign	87%	— 7%	72%	— 25%

Key Votes of the 103d Congress

1. Clinton Deficit Plan	Y	3. Brady Handgun Purchase	Y	5. Lmt. UN Cmnd. of Forces	N
2. NAFTA	Y	4. Strike Race/Death Pnlty.	N	6. Cut Missile Funds	Y

Key Votes of the 104th Congress

1. Congressional Compliance	Y	6. Reform Crime Grant	N	11. Loser Pays Court Reform	N
2. Balanced Budget Amndmt.	N	7. National Security Act	N	12. Product Liability Reform	N
3. Bar Unfunded Mandates	N	8. Moratorium on Regs.	N	13. Welfare Reform	N
4. Pass Line Item Veto	N	9. Risk Assessment on Regs.	N	14. Term Limits Amndt.	N
5. Relax Exclusionary Rule	N	10. Expnd. Priv. Prop. Rights	N	15. Tax Cuts	N

Election Results

1994 general	Anthony C. Beilenson (D)	95,342	(49%)	($587,641)
	Rich Sybert (R)	91,806	(48%)	($1,687,166)
	Others	6,031	(3%)	
1994 primary	Anthony C. Beilenson (D)	42,283	(87%)	
	Scott Gaulke (D)	6,467	(13%)	
1992 general	Anthony C. Beilenson (D)	141,742	(56%)	($786,463)
	Tom McClintock (R)	99,835	(39%)	($469,714)
	John Paul Lindblad (P&F)	13,690	(5%)	

TWENTY-FIFTH DISTRICT

One of the poignant tragedies of the 1994 Northridge earthquake was at the intersection of the I-5 and Route 14 Freeways at the north edge of the San Fernando Valley, where an overpass collapsed and a motorcycle patrolman hurtled to his death. The destruction of the interchange had an economic and personal impact for months afterwards, for the settled area of Los Angeles County no longer ends at the mountains at the northern rim of the San Fernando Valley. It continues along Route 14 past the mountain-surrounded city of Santa Clarita, with 110,000 people in 1990, and 25 miles beyond, where the mountains stop at the San Andreas Fault and the desert stretches out low and flat, divided into mile-square grids—the Antelope Valley, with huge aerospace plants and military bases around the fast-growing towns of Palmdale and Lancaster, where nearly 200,000 people live. Because of the mountain terrain, all these areas are connected by just one freeway, over which thousands commute and travel each way; when the chokepoint intersection was crushed, commuters lined up for hours to get to work every day.

The 25th Congressional District covers all three of these areas. It includes the northwest quadrant of the San Fernando Valley, Granada Hills and Chatsworth, with 180,000 mostly affluent and Republican white Anglos inside the LA city limits; it takes in Santa Clarita, with its Old West air and its industrial park, spreading subdivisions and Six Flags Magic Mountain theme park, home of a boosterish Republicanism; it includes the aerospace country of the Antelope Valley, with somewhat lower-income. All three parts of the district are heavily Republican, especially the desert area; when the 25th was newly created for 1992 it was assumed the Republican primary would choose the new congressman, and it did.

The Congressman from the 25th is Howard "Buck" McKeon, who grew up in Southern California, graduated from Brigham Young University and is the owner of Howard and Phil's Western Wear, a family business he helped expand from one store to 52 outlets in California, Arizona, Nevada and Utah. McKeon was the first mayor of Santa Clarita, when it was incorporated by joining several smaller towns, and served five years on the council. In the 1992 primary his main competitor was Assemblyman Phil Wyman, who had held office for 14 years and had a solid, even eccentric, conservative record; he once had a bill to ban the allegedly satanic practice of recording certain words into songs backwards. McKeon won 40%–38% and went on win the general 52%–33%. (In 1994 Wyman, by then a state Senator, was the only Republican legislator defeated west of the Mississippi River.)

McKeon talked about reforming government and was one of the first-term Republicans—he was freshman class president—who in 1993 helped abolish four select committees. He voted for the North American Free Trade Agreement after saying he opposed it. With the help of his seat on the National Security Committee, he worked to save local defense jobs—this is the production base for the B-1 and B-2 bombers, and the F-117 and SR-71 fighter planes. He opposed the Desert Protection Act, which, he said, "does little more than create pork projects." He fought an Equal Employment Opportunity Commission religious harassment guideline which, he felt, would bar people from keeping a bible on their desk or wear religious symbols like the Star of David at work. After the January 1994 Northridge earthquake, he worked to get a $9.6 billion emergency supplemental, $22 million for rebuilding the California Institute for the Arts and a $9 million Small Business Administration loan for a Chatsworth manufacturer.

McKeon was reelected overwhelmingly in 1994 against attorney James Gilmartin and had the satisfaction of seeing very many more freshmen Republicans elected than in 1992. He seems in line with the spirit of the new freshmen, though perhaps more interested than many of them in securing federal benefits for his district.

The People: Pop. 1990: 573,189; 10% rural; 8% age 65+; 72% White; 5% Black; 1% Amer. Indian; 6% Asian; 8% Other; 16% Hispanic origin. Voting age pop.: 415,109; 4% Black; 15% Hispanic origin. Households: 63% married couple families; 34% married couple fams. w. children; 59% college educ.; median household income: $46,480; per capita income: $18,849; median gross rent: $690; median house value: $213,000.

1992 Presidential Vote

Bush (R)	89,987	(39%)
Clinton (D)	83,305	(36%)
Perot (I)	57,398	(25%)

1988 Presidential Vote

Bush (R)	131,044	(67%)
Dukakis (D)	64,743	(33%)

Rep. Howard P. (Buck) McKeon (R)

Elected 1992; b. Sept. 9, 1939, Los Angeles; home, Santa Clarita; Brigham Young U., B.S. 1985; Mormon; married (Patricia).

Career: Small businessman; Owner, Howard and Phil's Western Wear, 1973–present; William S. Hart School District Bd., 1979–87; Chmn., Valencia Natl. Bank, 1987–88; Santa Clarita Mayor, 1987–88; Santa Clarita City Cncl., 1988–92.

DC Office: 307 CHOB 20515, 202-225-1956; Fax: 202-225-0683.

District Offices: 23929 W. Valencia Blvd., #410, Santa Clarita 91355, 805-254-2111; and 1008 West Ave., #E, Palmdale 93551, 805-948-7833.

Committees: *National Security* (19th of 30 R): Military Procurement; Military Readiness. *Economic & Educational Opportunities* (10th of 24 R): Oversight and Investigations; Postsecondary Education, Training and Life-Long Learning (Chmn.).

Group Ratings

	ADA	ACLU	COPE	CFA	LCV	CON	NSI	COC	ACU	NTLC	CHC
1994	5	17	11	20	6	54	100	100	95	96	93
1993	5	—	8	10	21	74	—	100	100	—	—

National Journal Ratings

	1993 LIB — 1993 CONS		1994 LIB — 1994 CONS	
Economic	14% —	80%	26% —	70%
Social	0% —	89%	11% —	85%
Foreign	0% —	91%	0% —	88%

Key Votes of the 103d Congress

1. Clinton Deficit Plan	N	3. Brady Handgun Purchase	N	5. Lmt. UN Cmnd. of Forces	Y
2. NAFTA	Y	4. Strike Race/Death Pnlty.	Y	6. Cut Missile Funds	N

Key Votes of the 104th Congress

1. Congressional Compliance	Y	6. Reform Crime Grant	Y	11. Loser Pays Court Reform	Y
2. Balanced Budget Amndmt.	Y	7. National Security Act	Y	12. Product Liability Reform	Y
3. Bar Unfunded Mandates	Y	8. Moratorium on Regs.	Y	13. Welfare Reform	Y
4. Pass Line Item Veto	Y	9. Risk Assessment on Regs.	Y	14. Term Limits Amndmt.	Y
5. Relax Exclusionary Rule	Y	10. Expnd. Priv. Prop. Rights	Y	15. Tax Cuts	Y

Election Results

1994 general	Howard P. (Buck) McKeon (R) 110,301	(65%)	($474,945)
	James H. Gilmartin (D) 53,445	(31%)	($34,857)
	Others 6,225	(4%)	
1994 primary	Howard P. (Buck) McKeon (R) 35,776	(82%)	
	Sandra Tulley (R) 7,777	(18%)	
1992 general	Howard P. (Buck) McKeon (R) 113,611	(52%)	($452,792)
	James H. (Gil) Gilmartin (D) 72,233	(33%)	($168,319)
	Rick Pamplin (I) 13,930	(6%)	($20,178)
	Others 18,941	(9%)	

TWENTY-SIXTH DISTRICT

A hiker looking north from the crest of the Santa Monica Mountains in 1910 would have seen spread out, almost totally empty and barren, 20 miles wide and 12 miles deep, the San Fernando Valley. Separated by the Cahuenga Pass from rapidly growing Los Angeles and Hollywood, the Valley was bought up in massive tracts by civic leaders even as they were urging city engineer William Mulholland to build a huge 250-mile aqueduct from the Owens Valley to give Los Angeles water and persuading the city in 1915 to annex 200 square miles of the Valley. In the years after World War II, this was modern suburbia, filled with *Leave It to Beaver* families. Today the San Fernando Valley is postmodern urban, with a look you can see in exaggerated form in the Disney headquarters buildings in Burbank or Universal City's CityWalk shopping mall: the driver topping the crest today sees office towers looming out over slightly hazy air, shopping centers and occasional palm trees, lines of grid streets stretching out into the distance beyond stucco subdivisions and the squat factory and warehouse buildings that make Los Angeles the nation's number one manufacturer.

The people in the Valley have also changed. The white Anglo families with stay-at-home moms in the 1950s have been replaced by hard-working Latino families, with children waiting at the bus stops for schools and parents juggling two jobs. But there is continuity: as in the 1950s, these are places where people work hard and try to raise families who will have better chances and make better livings than they have. Pacoima, mostly black and Latino, at the northern end of the Valley, is where Rodney King was pulled over and beaten and arrested, and where George Holliday took the video, 81 seconds of which did so much to change Los Angeles. It should be added that Pacoima and the heavily Hispanic Golden State Freeway corridor in the eastern Valley were not sites of major rioting in April 1992. The lower income areas here are farther from the central city; the southern rim of the Valley, around Studio City and North Hollywood, is still heavily Jewish and is attracting new families who often send their kids to religious schools.

The 26th Congressional District consists of the Golden State and Hollywood Freeway corridors of the Valley—roughly its eastern half—proceeding as far west as Van Nuys and the San Diego Freeway. Overall, the district was 53% Hispanic in 1990, but as yet Latinos are not the major voting bloc here; many are not citizens, many are children or young people not yet in the voting stream; and the tradition among Latinos in the 1990s, as among Italians in the 1910s, is to trust family and hard work, not politics and government, to get ahead. The high Democratic percentages here are due as much to Jewish as to Latino voters; indeed, the latter, despite 1994's Proposition 187 that calls for ending benefits to illegal immigrants, have been trending more to the Republicans than the former.

The congressman from the 26th is Howard Berman, one of the most aggressive and creative members of the House—and one of the most clear-sighted operators in American politics. He grew up in Los Angeles in modest circumstances, got involved in politics, and was elected to the Assembly from a formerly Republican Hollywood Hills district in 1972. This was the beginning of the so-called Berman-Waxman political machine—not so much a precinct organization as a group of consultants who raised money, redrew district lines and endorsed candidates through direct mail; their core constituency was liberal Westside Jews. In 1980 Berman tried to unseat Assembly Speaker Leo McCarthy; ultimately both lost out to Willie Brown, who in early 1995 was still clinging to the job though Republicans had won 41 seats to Democrats' 39. Berman's consolation prize was a Valley-based congressional seat in 1982, which he has held ever since with minimal competition. The Berman-Waxman machine fell on hard times in the 1990s, as Republicans seized control of redistricting, the feminist left became the driving force in the Democratic Party and Berman-Waxman ally Mel Levine lost the 1992 Senate primary to Barbara Boxer.

Berman has been an active legislator even more than a political operator, and on all manner of issues. On foreign policy, he started off less as a Vietnam war dove than as a backer of Israel, and he is not one of those Democrats who think America has habitually been on the wrong side in the world. For a decade he floor-managed foreign aid bills, defending aid to many countries as well as Israel. With Henry Hyde he wrote the law authorizing embargoes on nations that condone terrorism; in April 1990 he called for sanctions on Iraq, a position opposed as late as August 1 by the Bush Administration—a stance that George Bush himself said later he "absolutely" regretted. Berman voted for the Gulf war resolution, but was understandably critical of the Administration—if it had followed his advice there might well have been no need for war. Since then, Berman has worked to stop weapons proliferation, even while other Democrats seek to facilitate arms exports. He passed a law banning the double issuing of U.S. passports to coddle Arab countries who refuse to honor passports with Israeli marks. He pushed through the International Broadcasting Act of 1994, consolidating and downsizing agencies but maintaining Radio Free Europe and establishing Radio Free Asia. He worked hard to save the National Endowment for Democracy. Despite his close ties to organized labor, he voted for the North American Free Trade Agreement. He favors U.S. payments for United Nations peacekeeping and led the successful fight to scuttle the Republicans' Contract With America's call for reducing U.S. participation in UN-led peacekeeping operations.

Berman is also a major force on immigration. In 1988 he sponsored the provision allowing 20,000 immigrant visas for migrants without close relatives here, to be selected randomly by computer—"Berman visa applications" they are called. He got into the 1990 law more family reunification slots, to expedite the immigration of Soviet Jews (a vivid presence in L.A. these days), and to pass amnesty provisions allowing more family members to remain in this country. More recently, he worked to get the federal government to acknowledge responsibility for state spending on illegal immigrants, especially those in prison, and sought 4,000 more border patrols over the next four years. From his seat on the Judiciary Committee he is likely to oppose efforts to lower legal immigration, even as he acts to reduce illegal immigration.

Some of Berman's issues are local; others defy classification. He worked hard on earthquake relief after the January 1994 Northridge earthquake, getting the House of Representatives to approve $8.6 billion in emergency aid, the largest relief package in U.S. history. He tried to eliminate the 10% threshold on disaster deductibility. In 1991 he helped establish CALSTART, to produce electric cars in the Valley; with continued funding it has produced a prototype bus. With Senator Charles Grassley, he sponsored the 1986 False Claims Act rewarding whistleblowers in the government, which collected a record $1.09 billion in civil settlements in 1994. Berman has less leverage to get things done in a Republican House, but he is resourceful and capable of working with the other party. The question is how much he will continue to relish service in Newt Gingrich's House.

The People: Pop. 1990: 571,538; 8% age 65+; 34% White; 6% Black; 1% Amer. Indian; 7% Asian; 32% Other; 52% Hispanic origin. Voting age pop.: 410,180; 6% Black; 46% Hispanic origin. Households: 50% married couple families; 28% married couple fams. w. children; 40% college educ.; median household income: $32,134; per capita income: $12,198; median gross rent: $624; median house value: $185,300.

1992 Presidential Vote

Clinton (D) 72,673 (56%)
Bush (R) 31,013 (24%)
Perot (I)................... 24,167 (19%)

1988 Presidential Vote

Dukakis (D)................. 72,596 (56%)
Bush (R) 56,360 (44%)

Rep. Howard L. Berman (D)

Elected 1982; b. Apr. 15, 1941, Los Angeles; home, Sherman Oaks; U.C.L.A., B.A. 1962, LL.B. 1965; Jewish; married (Janis).

Career: Practicing atty., 1967–72; CA Assembly, 1973–82, Majority Ldr., 1974–79.

DC Office: 2231 RHOB 20515, 202-225-4695; Fax: 202-225-5279.

District Offices: 10200 Sepulveda Blvd., #130, Mission Hills 91345, 818-891-0543.

Committees: *International Relations* (5th of 19 D): Asia and the Pacific (RMM); International Operations and Human Rights. *Judiciary* (5th of 15 D): Courts and Intellectual Property; Immigration and Claims.

Group Ratings

	ADA	ACLU	COPE	CFA	LCV	CON	NSI	COC	ACU	NTLC	CHC
1994	90	86	88	80	94	39	20	30	0	4	7
1993	95	—	92	100	86	19	—	20	5	—	—

National Journal Ratings

	1993 LIB — 1993 CONS		1994 LIB — 1994 CONS	
Economic	75%	25%	64%	35%
Social	80%	13%	87%	11%
Foreign	79%	16%	83%	15%

Key Votes of the 103d Congress

1. Clinton Deficit Plan	Y	3. Brady Handgun Purchase	Y	5. Lmt. UN Cmnd. of Forces	N
2. NAFTA	Y	4. Strike Race/Death Pnlty.	N	6. Cut Missile Funds	Y

Key Votes of the 104th Congress

1. Congressional Compliance	Y	6. Reform Crime Grant	N	11. Loser Pays Court Reform	N
2. Balanced Budget Amndmt.	N	7. National Security Act	N	12. Product Liability Reform	N
3. Bar Unfunded Mandates	Y	8. Moratorium on Regs.	N	13. Welfare Reform	N
4. Pass Line Item Veto	N	9. Risk Assessment on Regs.	N	14. Term Limits Amndmt.	N
5. Relax Exclusionary Rule	N	10. Expnd. Priv. Prop. Rights	N	15. Tax Cuts	N

Election Results

1994 general	Howard L. Berman (D)	55,145	(63%)	($432,535)
	Gary E. Forsch (R)	28,423	(32%)	($38,922)
	Erich D. Miller (Lib)	4,570	(5%)	
1994 primary	Howard L. Berman (D)	20,104	(76%)	
	Jose P. Galvin (D)	4,169	(16%)	
	G.C. (Brodie) Broderson (D)	2,209	(8%)	
1992 general	Howard L. Berman (D)	73,807	(61%)	($722,606)
	Gary Forsch (R)	36,453	(30%)	($76,667)
	Margery Hinds (P&F)	7,180	(6%)	
	Other	3,468	(3%)	

TWENTY-SEVENTH DISTRICT

In the early years of the 20th Century, when Los Angeles was growing to become one of America's major cities, its richest citizens settled not on the beach (too clammy and cold) or on the west side (too dusty and remote), but in communities they built at the base of the San Gabriel Mountains that rise 10,000 feet above the city, their snow-capped peaks visible most of the year. The premier such community was Pasadena, with its institutions of national stature— the Rose Bowl, Cal Tech—and the premier structures were Pasadena's baroque-domed City Hall and railroader Henry Huntington's house in next-door San Marino, now the Huntington Library, one of the world's great scholarly institutions. Pasadena and South Pasadena have proudly preserved their bungalow neighborhoods, and Pasadena preserved and rebuilt the 80-year old curving Colorado Street Bridge over Arroyo Seco. Less elite but still comfortable is Glendale, north of downtown Los Angeles, site of Forest Lawn Cemetery; just west, beneath the Verdugo Mountains, is Burbank (named not for botanist Luther Burbank but for a local dentist-developer), famous now for the NBC Studios and Disney headquarters.

The 27th Congressional District takes in all these affluent foothill communities plus— sandwiched between the Verdugo and San Gabriel Mountains—La Canada, La Crescenta, Sunland and Tujunga. All these areas are traditionally, indeed clichedly, Republican. But the movement has been the other way in recent years. The black communities in Pasadena and Altadena, the boyhood home of Jackie Robinson, are expanding. Affluent Asians are moving into San Marino and style-conscious young couples are moving into South Pasadena, making it more—but not heavily—Democratic than it was in the last decade. Glendale is now the center of Los Angeles's large Armenian community and has many Iranians as well, and there are more singles in conveniently located Burbank. The result is a district still Republican, but capable of being seriously contested; Bill Clinton won here 44%–36% in 1992.

The congressman from the 27th is Carlos Moorhead, dean of the California delegation, one of the House's senior Republicans, but passed over for a full committee chairmanship after the party won control in 1994. He practiced law for years in Glendale and was elected to the California Assembly in 1968 and to the House in 1972. He has long served on Commerce and on Judiciary, where in his first term he dissented from the vote to impeach Richard Nixon. His voting record has long been one of the most conservative in the House. Like many Republicans of Robert Michel's generation, Moorhead has brought to his work the friendliness and cooperative attitude of civic luncheon clubs, and has worked with majority Democrats for marginal gains while mostly losing on the big issues. Thus he worked with Don Edwards to set up a California research institute and with Howard Berman to promote the CALSTART electric vehicle project in Burbank. He amended the 1990 immigration act to add 1,000 border patrol officers. He worked to open up electric transmission grids to independent and renewable energy producers. He got the Santa Fe Railroad to sell 370 miles of track to the LA area transit agency. He backed Hollywood interests in opposing cable reregulation and has worked hard to protect intellectual property and copyrights, major American assets in foreign trade.

But many conservatives feel he is not aggressive enough in taking on Democratic barons to represent them on the floor. In 1992 Thomas Bliley challenged him for the ranking position on Commerce and lost. After the 1994 election, though Moorhead was number one in seniority on both Commerce and Judiciary, Newt Gingrich passed over him for Bliley on Commerce and Henry Hyde on Judiciary. He got the chairmanship of the Intellectual Property Subcommittee of Judiciary instead—a priority for Moorhead since copyright issues are of vital importance to the Disney and Warner Brothers Studios in his district, but not a terrific consolation prize.

Will Moorhead—as he moves into his mid-70s—continue in the House after having been passed over? In this historically Republican but Democrat-trending district, he had spirited competition in 1992 and 1994 from Doug Kahn, a computer typography business owner, who formerly lived in Seattle, Miami, and New York—the three other corners of the continental United States. Moorhead won 50%–39% in 1992 and 53%–42% in 1994. He can probably keep winning, but the 27th District could be seriously contested again in 1996.

The People: Pop. 1990: 572,629; 13% age 65+; 61% White; 8% Black; 1% Amer. Indian; 11% Asian; 10% Other; 20% Hispanic origin. Voting age pop.: 445,763; 8% Black; 18% Hispanic origin. Households: 49% married couple families; 23% married couple fams. w. children; 61% college educ.; median household income: $37,929; per capita income: $20,344; median gross rent: $671; median house value: $293,200.

1992 Presidential Vote			1988 Presidential Vote		
Clinton (D)	98,057	(44%)	Bush (R)	119,543	(57%)
Bush (R)	80,986	(36%)	Dukakis (D)	89,998	(43%)
Perot (I)	42,071	(19%)			

Rep. Carlos J. Moorhead (R)

Elected 1972; b. May 5, 1922, Long Beach; home, Glendale; U. of CA, B.A. 1943, U. of Southern CA, J.D. 1949; Presbyterian; married (Valery).

Career: Army, 1942–45 (WWII), Army Reserves, 1945–82; Practicing atty., 1949–72; CA Assembly, 1967–72.

DC Office: 2346 RHOB 20515, 202-225-4176; Fax: 202-225-1279.

District Offices: 420 N. Brand Blvd., #304, Glendale 91203, 818-247-8445.

Committees: *Commerce* (2nd of 26 R): Energy and Power; Telecommunications and Finance. *Judiciary* (2nd of 20 R): Courts and Intellectual Property (Chmn.); Immigration and Claims.

Group Ratings

	ADA	ACLU	COPE	CFA	LCV	CON	NSI	COC	ACU	NTLC	CHC
1994	0	17	11	20	0	85	100	83	100	100	100
1993	0	—	0	20	21	74	—	91	100	—	—

National Journal Ratings

	1993 LIB — 1993 CONS		1994 LIB — 1994 CONS	
Economic	0%	— 88%	0%	— 80%
Social	0%	— 89%	11%	— 85%
Foreign	0%	— 91%	0%	— 88%

Key Votes of the 103d Congress

1. Clinton Deficit Plan	N	3. Brady Handgun Purchase	N	5. Lmt. UN Cmnd. of Forces	Y
2. NAFTA	Y	4. Strike Race/Death Pnlty.	Y	6. Cut Missile Funds	N

Key Votes of the 104th Congress

1. Congressional Compliance	Y	6. Reform Crime Grant	Y	11. Loser Pays Court Reform	Y
2. Balanced Budget Amndmt.	Y	7. National Security Act	Y	12. Product Liability Reform	Y
3. Bar Unfunded Mandates	Y	8. Moratorium on Regs.	*	13. Welfare Reform	Y
4. Pass Line Item Veto	Y	9. Risk Assessment on Regs.	Y	14. Term Limits Amndmt.	Y
5. Relax Exclusionary Rule	Y	10. Expnd. Priv. Prop. Rights	Y	15. Tax Cuts	Y

Election Results

1994 general	Carlos J. Moorhead (R)	88,341	(53%)	($968,212)
	Doug Kahn (D).	70,267	(42%)	($581,225)
	Others	8,166	(5%)	
1994 primary	Carlos J. Moorhead (R)	34,724	(77%)	
	Elizabeth Michael (R)	10,435	(23%)	
1992 general	Carlos J. Moorhead (R)	105,521	(50%)	($705,814)
	Doug Kahn (D).	83,805	(39%)	($167,898)
	Jesse A. Moorman (Green).	11,003	(5%)	($10,097)
	Others	12,121	(6%)	

TWENTY-EIGHTH DISTRICT

It is the great route west to California: passengers on the Santa Fe railroad's Super Chief or motorists on U.S. 66, after hours and days in barren desert, descended through the El Cajon Pass into the Los Angeles Basin, moving in a stately procession beneath the 10,000-foot snow-capped San Gabriel Mountains, marveling at orange groves and exotic plants. The railroad and highway ran through a line of towns, built by Midwestern Protestants as independent communities and now mostly high-income suburbs with their own civic institutions—Claremont, home of the academically strong Claremont Colleges; La Verne and Glendora; Azusa, named by a Chicago manufacturer for his wife; Duarte, with the City of Hope Medical Center; Monrovia and Arcadia, site of the Santa Anita race track and the Los Angeles County Arboretum. Today, the traveler arriving in Los Angeles can see the same sights, if the air is clear, as the jet glides down the flightpath to LAX.

The 28th Congressional District covers much of this territory, with the exception of Azusa, which is part of the Hispanic-majority 31st District. Its eastern end reaches south from Claremont and Glendora to include Covina and West Covina, classic 1950s suburbs now with many Mexican-Americans, where city ordinances require that lawns be kept watered: 1950s homeowner values continue to govern here. The District's western end reaches south from Monrovia and Arcadia to include Temple City. It is far from mono-cultural: 24% Hispanic and 13% Asian in 1990. The 28th remains a solidly Republican district, indeed by most measures the most Republican district in Los Angeles County.

David Dreier, the congressman from the 28th, grew up in Kansas City, Missouri, then spent a decade mostly on the Claremont campus, as a student and administrator, before he was elected to Congress in 1980. He personifies the intellectually rigorous conservatism and free market economics that thrive in his district and maintains a cheerfulness and good humor characteristic of California—even though he served for 14 years in the minority, and several of those on the Rules Committee, where Republicans were outnumbered 9–4 and lost almost every floor vote. An exception was notable enough to be remembered: when Dreier got a rule allowing a favorable vote on HUD Secretary Jack Kemp's tenant ownership proposal. A strong backer of free trade, he was one of the leading Republicans rounding up votes for the North American Free Trade

Agreement in 1993, was a leader in permanently extending most favored nation status to China and was chief Republican negotiator with the Clinton Administration in getting approval for the General Agreement on Tariffs and Trade. In 1993 he was appointed vice chairman of the short-lived Joint Committee on the Organization of Congress; despite his boosterism, however, not many of its December 1993 proposals were adopted by the Democratic House.

But Dreier's work came in handy when the Republicans won their majority in November 1994. Newt Gingrich appointed him to realign the committee structure of the House—a task attended with the greatest political and policy sensitivities. Dreier's reform proposals, based on proposals rejected by the joint committee and refined in Republican negotiations and sometimes partisan debate, were introduced on the first day of the 104th Congress and speedily approved. Three committees were abolished, almost half the other panels were renamed and saw some shifting of jurisdictional lines, committee staff was cut by one-third, and term limits were established on chairmen. Dreier is now second ranking member of the majority on Rules, and—as a continuing Gingrich ally—often the spokesman for the committee. He also is on the Republican steering committee; in a sop to the nation's largest GOP delegation, which ended up with no significant committee chairmanship or party leadership post, Gingrich named him head of a Republican task force on California created to respond to the state's legislative priorities.

Dreier lost his first race for Congress in 1978, at 25, against Democrat Jim Lloyd; but he beat Lloyd in 1980 and then fellow Republican Wayne Grisham after they were redistricted together in 1982. At that point, Dreier evidently decided never to be pressed for funds again; he raised plenty of money and spent little, which takes more self-discipline than one might think. After the 1994 campaign he had $2.28 million cash on hand, the most in the House. He has passed by chances to run for the Senate and seems genuinely dedicated to the institution of the House; if terms limits are ruled applicable, however, he might be in the stampede likely to run against Barbara Boxer in 1998. He wins reelection in the 28th District easily.

The People: Pop. 1990: 572,189; 11% age 65+; 57% White; 6% Black; 13% Asian; 10% Other; 24% Hispanic origin. Voting age pop.: 423,291; 5% Black; 21% Hispanic origin. Households: 60% married couple families; 30% married couple fams. w. children; 59% college educ.; median household income: $43,508; per capita income: $18,064; median gross rent: $705; median house value: $231,900.

1992 Presidential Vote			1988 Presidential Vote		
Bush (R)	90,644	(41%)	Bush (R)	135,359	(63%)
Clinton (D)	82,958	(38%)	Dukakis (D)	79,100	(37%)
Perot (I)	45,623	(21%)			

Rep. David Dreier (R)

Elected 1980; b. July 5, 1952, Kansas City, MO; home, San Dimas; Claremont McKenna Col., B.A. 1975, Claremont Graduate School M.A. 1976; Christian Scientist; single.

Career: Corp. Relations Dir., Claremont McKenna Col., 1975–78; Mktg. Dir., Industrial Hydrocarbons, 1979–80; Vice Pres., Dreier Development Co., 1985–present.

DC Office: 411 CHOB 20515, 202-225-2305; Fax: 202-225-7018.

District Offices: 112 N. 2d Ave., Covina 91723, 818-339-9078.

Committees: *Rules* (3rd of 9 R): Rules of the House (Chmn).

Group Ratings

	ADA	ACLU	COPE	CFA	LCV	CON	NSI	COC	ACU	NTLC	CHC
1994	5	14	0	20	6	93	100	92	100	96	86
1993	0	—	0	10	14	74	—	100	96	—	—

National Journal Ratings

	1993 LIB — 1993 CONS		1994 LIB — 1994 CONS	
Economic	0%	— 88%	0%	— 80%
Social	18%	— 82%	16%	— 81%
Foreign	17%	— 76%	30%	— 67%

Key Votes of the 103d Congress

1. Clinton Deficit Plan N	3. Brady Handgun Purchase N	5. Lmt. UN Cmnd. of Forces Y
2. NAFTA Y	4. Strike Race/Death Pnlty. Y	6. Cut Missile Funds N

Key Votes of the 104th Congress

1. Congressional Compliance Y	6. Reform Crime Grant Y	11. Loser Pays Court Reform Y
2. Balanced Budget Amndmt. Y	7. National Security Act Y	12. Product Liability Reform Y
3. Bar Unfunded Mandates Y	8. Moratorium on Regs. Y	13. Welfare Reform Y
4. Pass Line Item Veto Y	9. Risk Assessment on Regs. Y	14. Term Limits Amndmt. N
5. Relax Exclusionary Rule Y	10. Expnd. Priv. Prop. Rights Y	15. Tax Cuts Y

Election Results

1994 general	David Dreier (R)	110,179	(67%)	($279,050)
	Tommy Randle (D)	50,022	(30%)	($28,905)
	Others	4,076	(2%)	
1994 primary	David Dreier (R)	unopposed		
1992 general	David Dreier (R)	122,353	(58%)	($290,128)
	Al Wachtel (D)	76,525	(37%)	($25,261)
	Others	10,504	(5%)	

TWENTY-NINTH DISTRICT

The Westside: the term was not much used 20 years ago, but is now shorthand for what might be the biggest and flashiest concentration of affluence in the world. It is the heartland of one of America's most productive and creative industries—the persistence of the word "industry" here is a charming bit of antiquarianism—and one of the nation's major exports, show business. The first moviemakers came here earlier in the century, looking for a place to shoot silent films where the sunlight was more dependable than Astoria, Queens, or Englewood, New Jersey. They found it in Hollywood, a suburb just annexed by burgeoning Los Angeles when the first movie studio was built in 1911. In 1923 came the Hollywood sign, overlooking the soon-famous intersection of Hollywood and Vine. By the 1930s, the big studio lots were scattered around town, over the mountains in Burbank or out toward the ocean in Westwood and Culver City. Miraculously, the studio bosses of that era—most of them Jewish immigrants with little ancestral experience of America—created a popular culture that was universally accessible and that embodied the American spirit in a way that still captures the imagination. This was the universal American culture of the 1940s movies that Ronald Reagan understood and transferred into politics. Today's showbiz moguls, by contrast, have been absorbed in the enterprise of putting their own personal idiosyncrasies on the screen or the tube or on records or tapes or CDs. It's oft-times very lucrative work, but at best the creation of a niche culture, speaking to people very much like themselves, and hoping by force of fashion to attract a segment of the market in the great masses beyond.

Showbiz still sets the tone for the Westside. It remains tremendously profitable, in large part because it's not run by big business units but by thousands of craftsmen and entrepreneurs who keep it anchored in Los Angeles because so many of them remain here. People on the Westside like to portray themselves as artists in a garret, willing to risk starving to make art and speak truth to bourgeois society. But their disdain for traditional moral values and their yen for fashionable new moral standards—promiscuous sex and drug use are OK, but smoking cigarettes and failing to exercise are wrong—make them disdainful of the ordinary people who are the market of any mass entertainment. The Westside loves to congratulate itself on its moral daring when it makes a movie or TV show revealing businessmen or priests as criminals. But it reacted furiously to Dan Quayle's 1992 remarks about *Murphy Brown,* in which he made the unexceptionable points that children are better off with two parents and that glamorizing single motherhood can mislead and harm those less well-off than a fictional newscaster or Hollywood star. And yet the marketplace may be teaching show biz some lessons. As Michael Medved, movie critic and author of *Hollywood vs. America,* has pointed out, Hollywood's most obscene, anti-business and anti-religious products don't sell nearly as well as its family fare; the best box office movies of 1994 were *Forrest Gump* and *The Lion King.* Showbiz rejoiced in the election of Bill Clinton in 1992 and in the way Clinton courted Hollywood in 1993. But as his administration went sour, the hold of the Hollywood Left on popular culture seemed to be weakening and the O.J. Simpson trial reminded everyone that underneath the veneer of showbiz glamour there is real life, right and wrong.

Not everyone on the Westside is in show business, of course. This is also the home of thousands of small entrepreneurs, manufacturers, and inventors and marketers of everything imaginable, who sparked the Los Angeles Basin growth of the 1980s, and there are even traces of pre-show business, old Los Angeles money which is also plentiful. There are large numbers of singles and gays here: apartment-renters provided majorities for Santa Monica's radical city government, which thrived when it imposed rent control but foundered when it invited in more homeless; West Hollywood, where the major voting blocs are gays and seniors, is proud of its openly gay mayor. The core of Hollywood itself has gone seedy and is the home now of many Central American immigrants, a high-crime and riot zone, but the Fairfax neighborhood remains solidly middle-class Jewish, and just to the east there are many Russian Jewish migrants. Hancock Park looks as aristocratic as it did when it was built, when Beverly Hills was vacant land. The Westside has been the home of a former president who does not at all exemplify its politics, Ronald Reagan; it is also the home, notably on the former Fox lot that is now Century City where Reagan keeps his office, of some of the largest office buildings in the Los Angeles area. It is the center of the second largest Jewish community in the United States, as well as the focus of the 1980s immigration of Iranians to the United States. It is also the home of some of America's most expensive residential real estate, where people buy houses for $1 million, knock down the structure and build something new for another million or two, and of one of the world's premier high-priced shopping areas—Rodeo Drive, a quite ordinary shopping street 20 years ago.

The 29th Congressional District contains almost all the major elements of Westside Los Angeles, from old, high-income Los Feliz and the gay neighborhood around Silver Lake through Hollywood and Hancock Park, west through Beverly Hills and Westwood, Bel Air and Brentwood, Santa Monica and Pacific Palisades. It is solidly Democratic, and not just in votes: it probably contributes more money to Democratic candidates and liberal causes than any other district with the possible exception of Manhattan's New York 14th. Its boundaries are carefully sculpted to put blacks in the 32nd District to the south and Hispanics and Asians in the 30th to the east; far from being racially diverse, it has the highest percentage of non-Hispanic whites (76%) of any Los Angeles Basin district except the 24th on the other side of Mulholland Drive.

The congressman from the 29th, Henry Waxman, is one of the ablest members of the House and for 16 years was one of the most powerful, a shrewd political operator who is a skilled and idealistic policy entrepreneur. There is no Westside glitz about him: he grew up over his family's store in Watts, his personal demeanor is quiet, he has never attended the Oscars ceremony. He first learned politics at UCLA with the likes of Howard Berman, Willie Brown, David Roberti and John Burton. At each stage of his career, he has seen political openings before others did and gone smartly through them. He ran against Assemblyman Lester McMillan in the mostly Jewish Fairfax area in 1968 and won 64% in the primary; incidentally, he served his first two years in the minority. In 1971–72 he chaired the redistricting committee, a good place to make friends, and he went to Congress in 1974 in a district designed, he likes to point out, not by his committee but by a court. Waxman's biggest break came after the 1978 election, when he was elected chairman of the Commerce Committee's Health and Environment Subcommittee. This was one of the first times House Democrats decided not to observe seniority in handing out subcommittee chairs, and Waxman's opponent, Richardson Preyer of North Carolina, was competent and widely respected. Nevertheless, Waxman argued his case on the issues and—in a move quite unprecedented at the time, though common in Sacramento and now also in Washington—made campaign contributions to other Democrats on the full committee, and won the post, 15–12.

The campaign contributions were no accident. Waxman and his friends Howard Berman and former area congressman Mel Levine built their own political machine in Los Angeles. Its power came not from patronage but from fundraising and savvy. Their specialty was targeted direct mail, with hundreds of customized letters and endorsement slates sent out to different lists of people. In the apolitical commonwealth of California, where television advertising is exceedingly expensive and people seem to avoid politics, this made them critical though not always successful players. But the 1990s have been tough for the machine. In 1992, "the year of the woman," when so much of the energy in the Democratic Party came from the feminist left, Levine lost the Senate primary to Barbara Boxer; that, plus term limits and Republican redistricting put the Berman-Waxman operation largely out of business in 1994.

Waxman became less involved in local politics as he became a major national policymaker. He played a critical role on the Clean Air Act, first in 1981–82 by preventing the Reagan Administration and then-Energy and Commerce Chairman John Dingell from relaxing the law's provisions, and then in 1989 and 1990, when he spearheaded the major revisions. He and Dingell—frequent shouting match partners who nevertheless maintained a working relationship—hammered out a compromise, delaying stricter California-type auto standards until 1994 and moving more aggressively on non-auto issues. Waxman and Dingell, in the House and in conference with the Senate, largely shaped the amendments signed by George Bush in 1990.

Another great project of Waxman's has been expanding Medicaid for the poor. His strategy was to expand coverage by threatening to hold up budget reconciliation bills unless they required states to expand Medicaid eligibility. Between 1984 and 1990, he got coverage for all poor children up to 18, all children under seven, and pregnant women in families under 133% of poverty income. He also got Medicare to pay deductibles for the poor and for mammograms, and he got a health care tax credit, similar to the earned income tax credit, for the working poor. This helped raise Medicaid from 9% to 14% of state spending in the 1980s, and helps to explain why Waxman is hated by many governors. Then-Arkansas Governor Clinton once attacked him for plotting to impose universal health care, "using Medicaid as the vehicle and the states' credit cards as the financing mechanism." Waxman's response to the governors: "These are legitimate expenses. States have objected to mandates to cover some of the most vulnerable population groups, yet they haven't given us any other solution as to how to deal with that overwhelming need. I'm unmoved by their plea." More than anything else, Waxman's Medicaid increases and the Republicans' desire to prevent his return to power sparked the demand for the unfunded mandates legislation passed by Congress in early 1995.

Waxman had less success on reforming national health care when the issue came out in the open. He wanted to move to something like a single-payer, government-paid program; but when that idea foundered in 1994, Waxman typically was careful not to criticize Clinton publicly and to insist that the battle would continue. He has secured more funding for AIDS research, a burning issue in the 29th District with its large gay population (West Hollywood and surrounding neighborhoods have a higher per-capita AIDS rate than New York or San Francisco), and he has criticized Republican administrations harshly for neglecting the disease.

He passed a law providing damages to children injured by required immunizations, sponsored measures to require testing of mammography devices, expanded the availability of generic drugs, extended patent protection for drugs during part of the regulatory process, and tried unsuccessfully to legalize the use of heroin to reduce the pain of terminal cancer patients. He has worked hard to allow fetal tissue research.

In early 1994, in widely publicized hearings, he lined up the chief executive officers of leading tobacco companies and accused them of adding nicotine and other substances to cigarettes and of lying in their testimony; he was hoping to impose restrictions on the production and consumption of the evil weed. After the Republican victory in November, he held one more hearing on smokeless tobacco before Thomas Bliley of Richmond, Virginia, home of Philip Morris's big cigarette factory, took over the Commerce Committee chair. Bliley told reporters the first week after the election: "I don't think we need any more legislation regulating tobacco," prompting Waxman to respond "He's acting like he's taking over the Tobacco Committee, not the Health Committee." He was obviously surprised and dismayed by the Republicans' win, and in the first months of the 104th Congress this man who had been able to channel billions of dollars into Medicaid was unable to prevail on just about any issue. "We have to recognize that we will be a permanent minority unless we put forward our agenda in a way the American people can understand it," he said, and proceeded to make his case eloquently against provisions of the Contract With America.

Waxman, unlike many of his Westside show business constituents, is not at all solipsistic or dilettantish. He has no personal taste for gaudy luxury. He cares about results in the real world and is unmoved by opposition. As one of the House's most senior and influential liberals, he carefully assesses his colleagues and their motives, gauging their weaknesses and appreciating their strengths, waiting for the right moment to outsmart them and staying unflappable. He did that after the 1992 redistricting, which he didn't control. Much of his old district went to make up the new majority-Hispanic 30th, and when colleague Anthony Beilenson said he might run in the new 29th, Waxman coolly said that it was a natural constituency for him and that he could win any primary; he offered to help Beilenson if he ran in the much less Democratic 24th, which Beilenson successfully did. Waxman always wins reelection with more than 60% of the vote, and he is one California congressman who could survive the state's term limits law, if it goes into effect in 1998. The law would only prohibit listing a candidate on the ballot, and Waxman has strong enough support that he could easily win as a write-in. In short, it's too early to count out this forceful and persistent lawmaker.

The People: Pop. 1990: 571,386; 16% age 65+; 76% White; 3% Black; 8% Asian; 5% Other; 13% Hispanic origin. Voting age pop.: 497,153; 3% Black; 11% Hispanic origin. Households: 34% married couple families; 12% married couple fams. w. children; 71% college educ.; median household income: $37,540; per capita income: $34,253; median gross rent: $678; median house value: $500,001.

1992 Presidential Vote

Clinton (D)	183,233	(66%)
Bush (R)	55,924	(20%)
Perot (I)	37,217	(13%)

1988 Presidential Vote

Dukakis (D)	162,917	(64%)
Bush (R)	91,595	(36%)

Rep. Henry A. Waxman (D)

Elected 1974; b. Sept. 12, 1939, Los Angeles; home, Los Angeles; U.C.L.A., B.A. 1961, J.D. 1964; Jewish; married (Janet).

Career: Practicing atty., 1965–68; CA Assembly, 1968–74.

DC Office: 2408 RHOB 20515, 202-225-3976; Fax: 202-225-4099.

District Offices: 8425 W. 3d St., #400, Los Angeles 90048, 213-651-1040.

Committees: *Commerce* (2nd of 21 D): Health and Environment (RMM); Oversight and Investigations. *Government Reform & Oversight* (2nd of 22 D): Human Resources and Intergovernmental Affairs; National Economic Growth, Natural Resources and Regulatory Affairs.

Group Ratings

	ADA	ACLU	COPE	CFA	LCV	CON	NSI	COC	ACU	NTLC	CHC
1994	90	86	100	100	100	34	10	25	0	7	7
1993	100	—	100	100	92	32	—	18	4	—	—

National Journal Ratings

	1993 LIB — 1993 CONS		1994 LIB — 1994 CONS	
Economic	88% —	0%	73% —	17%
Social	79% —	20%	87% —	11%
Foreign	87% —	7%	85% —	0%

Key Votes of the 103d Congress

1. Clinton Deficit Plan	Y	3. Brady Handgun Purchase	Y	5. Lmt. UN Cmnd. of Forces	N
2. NAFTA	N	4. Strike Race/Death Pnlty.	N	6. Cut Missile Funds	Y

Key Votes of the 104th Congress

1. Congressional Compliance	Y	6. Reform Crime Grant	N	11. Loser Pays Court Reform	N
2. Balanced Budget Amndmt.	N	7. National Security Act	N	12. Product Liability Reform	N
3. Bar Unfunded Mandates	N	8. Moratorium on Regs.	N	13. Welfare Reform	N
4. Pass Line Item Veto	N	9. Risk Assessment on Regs.	N	14. Term Limits Amndmt.	N
5. Relax Exclusionary Rule	N	10. Expnd. Priv. Prop. Rights	N	15. Tax Cuts	N

Election Results

1994 general	Henry A. Waxman (D)	129,413	(68%)	($186,127)
	Paul Stepanek (R)	53,801	(28%)	($70,777)
	Others	7,162	(4%)	
1994 primary	Henry A. Waxman (D)	54,694	(80%)	
	Jon Rappoport (D)	13,557	(20%)	
1992 general	Henry A. Waxman (D)	160,312	(61%)	($718,695)
	Mark A. Robbins (R)	67,141	(26%)	($148,274)
	David Davis (I)	15,445	(6%)	($23,849)
	Susan C. Davies (P&F)	13,888	(5%)	
	Others	4,700	(2%)	

THIRTIETH DISTRICT

Surrounding downtown Los Angeles are neighborhoods just now becoming antique, as the early 20th Century buildings stop looking familiar and start taking on the patina of the historic. Downtown LA, with its 1980s marble slabs and pink cylinders jutting up to 70 stories from what was once a low-rise business district, seems soulless and detached from the neighborhoods around, which change character with every few years' changes in immigration flow.

East of the Los Angeles River is Boyle Heights, once an entry neighborhood for Irish and Jewish immigrants and for the last 30 years predominantly Mexican-American, poor in income terms but with enough community cohesion not to riot in April 1992. To the north of downtown is Lincoln Heights, a heavily Hispanic area centering on the shopping street of North Broadway, plus the neighborhoods of Highland Park and Eagle Rock, white middle-class 30 years ago, now mostly Hispanic but with Asians as well. West of downtown are lower Sunset Boulevard, the Koreatown strip along Western Avenue, and much of Hollywood and some of South Central. Koreatown was the area worst hurt in the riots, and as elites empathized with the rioters more than the hard-working, law-abiding merchants whose property was destroyed, there is residual bitterness here of unknown proportions. Much of Hollywood has become an entry point for Central American migrants, as has the northern edge of South Central; coming from societies where violence is more common and endemic than in Mexico or the United States, they rioted in very substantial numbers. These are all neighborhoods populated more thickly than they were a quarter-century ago, with small houses and garden apartments full of large families and many children; new migrants stay with those who have been here a few years, with beds assigned to family members working different shifts so they're slept in 24 hours a day. To most American eyes, these look like poverty neighborhoods, but this is the snapshot view; in the video version they are the first frames on the way to prosperity, the first way-station on the Santa Ana and San Bernardino Freeways to middle-income American comfort.

All these areas, centering geographically on Dodger Stadium, are part of California's 30th Congressional District. The population here in 1990 was recorded as 60% Hispanic and 21% Asian. But many of these are recent immigrants; only 34% of registered voters were Latino and 7% Asian. Indeed, of 572,000 residents, only 32,700 voted in the crucial Democratic primary and 83,000 in the general election, compared to 85,000 in the Democratic primary and 261,000 in the general in the Westside 29th District just to the west. Newly created for the 1992 election, the 30th was expected to reelect 30-year Congressman Edward Roybal; his daughter, Assemblywoman Lucille Roybal-Allard, was running in (and won) the neighboring 33d District. But Roybal announced late in the game that he was retiring, and when his former aide Henry Lozano dropped out of the race, Roybal endorsed the Democrat who proved to be his successor, 34-year-old Assemblyman Xavier Becerra.

Becerra did not win without a struggle, conducted along Latino factional lines. His best-known opponent, Leticia Quezada, was a member of the Los Angeles school board, a powerful engine for publicity, and had the endorsement of Councilman Richard Alatorre and Assemblyman Richard Polanco. Becerra had held elective office as a member of the Assembly for only two years, and from the suburb of Monterey Park, outside the district. But Becerra had the endorsements of Roybal, 34th District Congressman Esteban Torres and County Supervisor Gloria Molina. And he had impressive credentials: he is a graduate of Stanford Law, worked for state Senator Art Torres and then served on Attorney General John Van de Kamp's staff. He had a liberal record on environment and making AIDS drugs available; he backed campaign finance reform and tougher penalties for gang activities near schools. His supposed carpetbagging evidently didn't matter much; after all, most LA area Latinos are less than a generation away from somewhere else. In this low-turnout primary, Becerra won 32% of the vote, well ahead of Quezada's 22%, Albert Lum's 16% and businessman Jeff Penichet's 13%. He won the general election 58%–24%.

The fast-moving Becerra initially was slowed down in the House. He did not get on the Commerce Committee, where he had hoped to work on healthcare reform, but he does serve on Judiciary. His voting record, as liberal as any, came in a House that was becoming more conservative. He spoke competently but had no major legislative successes. He won reelection easily, but Democrats lost their majority. By early 1995, Becerra was quick to complain about the Republicans' rules and was becoming a more forceful spokesman for liberal causes, but he was not in a position to do much about them.

The People: Pop. 1990: 572,604; 8% age 65+; 15% White; 3% Black; 21% Asian; 31% Other; 60% Hispanic origin. Voting age pop.: 415,907; 4% Black; 56% Hispanic origin. Households: 45% married couple families; 27% married couple fams. w. children; 35% college educ.; median household income: $23,435; per capita income: $9,637; median gross rent: $525; median house value: $187,400.

1992 Presidential Vote		
Clinton (D)	56,378	(62%)
Bush (R)	21,750	(24%)
Perot (I)	11,842	(13%)

1988 Presidential Vote		
Dukakis (D)	54,576	(64%)
Bush (R)	31,250	(36%)

Rep. Xavier Becerra (D)

Elected 1992; b. Jan. 26, 1958, Sacramento; home, Los Angeles; Stanford U., B.A. 1980, J.D. 1984; Catholic; married (Carolina Reyes).

Career: Staff Atty., Legal Assistance Corp. of Central MA; Dist. Dir., CA Sen. Art Torres, 1986; CA Dep. Atty. Gen., 1987–90; CA Assembly, 1990–92.

DC Office: 1119 LHOB 20515, 202-225-6235; Fax: 202-225-2202.

District Offices: 2435 Colorado Blvd., #200, Los Angeles 90041, 213-550-8962.

Committees: *Economic & Educational Opportunities* (14th of 19 D): Postsecondary Education, Training and Life-Long Learning. *Judiciary* (12th of 15 D): Courts and Intellectual Property; Immigration and Claims.

Group Ratings

	ADA	ACLU	COPE	CFA	LCV	CON	NSI	COC	ACU	NTLC	CHC
1994	100	86	78	90	94	20	0	36	0	8	0
1993	95	—	92	100	100	32	—	20	4	—	—

National Journal Ratings

	1993 LIB — 1993 CONS		1994 LIB — 1994 CONS	
Economic	74%	— 25%	83%	— 0%
Social	87%	— 0%	94%	— 0%
Foreign	79%	— 16%	85%	— 0%

Key Votes of the 103d Congress

1. Clinton Deficit Plan	Y	3. Brady Handgun Purchase	Y	5. Lmt. UN Cmnd. of Forces	N
2. NAFTA	Y	4. Strike Race/Death Pnlty.	N	6. Cut Missile Funds	Y

Key Votes of the 104th Congress

1. Congressional Compliance Y	6. Reform Crime Grant *	11. Loser Pays Court Reform N
2. Balanced Budget Amndmt. N	7. National Security Act *	12. Product Liability Reform N
3. Bar Unfunded Mandates *	8. Moratorium on Regs. *	13. Welfare Reform N
4. Pass Line Item Veto *	9. Risk Assessment on Regs. N	14. Term Limits Amndmt. N
5. Relax Exclusionary Rule N	10. Expnd. Priv. Prop. Rights N	15. Tax Cuts N

Election Results

1994 general	Xavier Becerra (D)	43,943	(66%)	($234,096)
	David A. Ramirez (R)	18,741	(28%)	
	R. William Weilberg (Lib)	3,741	(6%)	
1994 primary	Xavier Becerra (D)	18,790	(82%)	
	Oscar C. Valdes (D)	4,263	(18%)	
1992 general	Xavier Becerra (D)	48,800	(58%)	($373,551)
	Morry Waksberg (R)	20,034	(24%)	($57,063)
	Blase Bonpane (Green)	6,315	(8%)	($40,115)
	Elizabeth A. Nakano (P&F)	6,173	(7%)	
	Other	2,221	(3%)	

THIRTY-FIRST DISTRICT

Anyone interested in the future of America and today's immigrants should drive straight east from downtown Los Angeles on the San Bernardino Freeway, through the string of suburbs that grew up in the 1940s and 1950s. These were once white middle-class communities, with grids of stucco houses above the dry river beds; they were filled with Midwest and East Coast migrants who discovered California during World War II and decided to stay, or who learned of its golden reputation from the new medium of television in the days before smog became part of the language. The atmosphere then was Midwestern, cheerful, busy, with children always underfoot. Over the next generation or so, there has been almost a complete population turnover here, but some things remain the same. Mexican-Americans have spread out from their original East Los Angeles base to become majorities in blue-collar suburbs like El Monte, Baldwin Park and Azusa; all these towns have many more residents than in their Anglo days. But these are not mono-ethnic communities, and East Los Angeles has not become a slum. There are no empty storefronts, but busy shops with new signs; no housing riddled with vandalism and neglect, but newly painted homes with carefully tended gardens; these are neighborhoods still filled with children whose parents believe in traditional values. When blacks and Latinos were rioting in South Central and Hollywood, East Los Angeles was quiet and orderly.

Latinos are not the only migrants here; there are also Asians. Monterey Park and San Gabriel have sprouted Chinese and Korean shopping centers and storefronts, and have become the American center for Taiwanese. In next-door Alhambra, the Asians have made the local high school "an academic giant," reports *The Washington Post*'s Jay Mathews. "Its name is ... at the top of lists of the leading science and mathematics programs in American education." Sometime in the 21st Century, novels will be written describing the by-then vanished atmosphere of these immigrant suburbs, that will surely tell more about the human condition than the 1980s minimalist novels (like the eponymous *Less Than Zero*) did about the horrors of growing up rich in Beverly Hills.

In the 1950s, these were Democratic areas—New Dealers bringing their voting habits west— but the new Latinos and Asians seem up for grabs. They voted strongly for Ronald Reagan in 1984 and were only 5% to 8% more Democratic than average in the 1988 and 1990 elections; in 1992, Latinos moved toward the Democrats, but Asians, dismayed by responses to the riot, seemed to have trended Republican. In 1994, Governor Pete Wilson's support of Proposition 187 probably prevented much of a Republican trend, though it seems not to have created a

Democratic one. The promise of increased government benefits could help the Democrats. But working against them are these new Americans' hard work in building small businesses and their bad experiences with government here and where they came from.

The 31st Congressional District covers much of this territory, from the LA city limit east through East Los Angeles, Alhambra, San Gabriel, Rosemead, El Monte, Baldwin Park and Azusa; it brushes, but excludes, higher-income suburbs up against the San Gabriel Mountains. It was 59% Hispanic in 1990 and 23% Asian, with one of the lowest percentages of non-Hispanic whites (17%) in California. Its congressman, Marty Martinez, is a Democrat who has been in the right place with the right political patrons at the right time. The owner of an upholstery company, he was elected to the Monterey Park City Council in 1974 and became Mayor of Monterey Park in 1976. He was tapped in 1980 to run for the Assembly by Howard Berman, who was running for speaker, and the Berman-Waxman machine superintended Martinez's campaign to a win. Their ally, Phil Burton, in the 1982 redistricting plan forestalled a Republican-Hispanic alliance by creating two Hispanic districts in the eastern Los Angeles Basin. One of them was for Martinez, and after a desultory campaign he beat incumbent Republican and onetime John Birch Society organizer John Rousselot 54%–46%.

Seniority raised Martinez to a subcommittee chairmanship in the 103d Congress. Although his influence was rarely visible, he was technically the lead sponsor of the Clinton Administration's National Community Service Bill, which offers educational incentives for community service. Also, of the reauthorizations of the Older Americans Act and the Juvenile Justice Act and Delinquency Prevention Act, all signed into law. He also passed a Native American Languages Act to record these languages before they die out. His pet cause is a proposed Private Security Officer's Quality Assurance Act which requires states to set minimum training and screening standards for private security officers: will it attract Republican support? Martinez was called "one of Congress's lesser lights" by the December 1992 *California Journal*, and his hold on the seat seems a bit shaky: in four-candidate Democratic primaries he won with 43% in 1992 and 55% in 1994. His general election percentage fell from 63% in 1992 to 59% in 1994. It seems unlikely that Martinez could be beaten by a Republican, though the Republican base here is bigger than one might think; he might have a problem against a serious primary challenger, though.

The People: Pop. 1990: 572,758; 9% age 65+; 18% White; 2% Black; 23% Asian; 27% Other; 58% Hispanic origin. Voting age pop.: 403,292; 2% Black; 53% Hispanic origin. Households: 57% married couple families; 33% married couple fams. w. children; 36% college educ.; median household income: $30,667; per capita income: $10,264; median gross rent: $622; median house value: $178,400.

1992 Presidential Vote

Clinton (D)	59,616	(51%)
Bush (R)	37,250	(32%)
Perot (I)	18,449	(16%)

1988 Presidential Vote

Dukakis (D)	61,374	(54%)
Bush (R)	52,500	(46%)

Rep. Matthew G. (Marty) Martinez (D)

Elected 1982; b. Feb. 14, 1929, Walsenburg, CO; home, Monterey Park; Los Angeles Trade Tech. Col., 1950; Catholic; married (Elvira).

Career: Marine Corps, 1947–50; Businessman, 1950–70; Monterey Park Planning Cmte., 1971–74; Monterey Park City Cncl., 1974–80; Monterey Park Mayor, 1976, 1980; CA Assembly, 1980–82.

DC Office: 2239 RHOB 20515, 202-225-5464; Fax: 202-225-5467.

District Offices: 320 S. Garfield Ave., #214, Alhambra 91801, 818-458-4524.

Committees: *Economic & Educational Opportunities* (5th of 19 D): Employer-Employee Relations (RMM); Oversight and Investigations. *International Relations* (10th of 19 D): International Economic Policy and Trade; Western Hemisphere.

Group Ratings

	ADA	ACLU	COPE	CFA	LCV	CON	NSI	COC	ACU	NTLC	CHC
1994	70	68	67	80	56	39	44	58	15	11	7
1993	90	—	100	80	69	11	—	30	13	—	—

National Journal Ratings

	1993 LIB — 1993 CONS		1994 LIB — 1994 CONS	
Economic	61%	37%	67%	29%
Social	68%	29%	66%	33%
Foreign	66%	31%	71%	29%

Key Votes of the 103d Congress

1. Clinton Deficit Plan	Y	3. Brady Handgun Purchase	N	5. Lmt. UN Cmnd. of Forces	N
2. NAFTA	N	4. Strike Race/Death Pnlty.	N	6. Cut Missile Funds	N

Key Votes of the 104th Congress

1. Congressional Compliance	*	6. Reform Crime Grant	N	11. Loser Pays Court Reform	N
2. Balanced Budget Amndmt.	N	7. National Security Act	N	12. Product Liability Reform	N
3. Bar Unfunded Mandates	N	8. Moratorium on Regs.	N	13. Welfare Reform	N
4. Pass Line Item Veto	N	9. Risk Assessment on Regs.	*	14. Term Limits Amndmt.	N
5. Relax Exclusionary Rule	N	10. Expnd. Priv. Prop. Rights	Y	15. Tax Cuts	N

Election Results

1994 general	Matthew G. (Marty) Martinez (D)	50,541	(59%)	($123,767)
	John V. Flores (R)	34,926	(41%)	($81,517)
1994 primary	Matthew G. (Marty) Martinez (D)	15,422	(55%)	
	Bonifacio Bonny Garcia (D)	6,402	(23%)	
	Maria Escalante (D)	4,653	(17%)	
	David Romero (D)	1,447	(5%)	
1992 general	Matthew G. (Marty) Martinez (D)	68,324	(63%)	($149,441)
	Reuben D. Franco (R)	40,873	(37%)	($54,817)

THIRTY-SECOND DISTRICT

One of the myths of the Los Angeles riots of 1992 and 1965 is that black Angelenos live in conditions of isolation and poverty. Some do, of course. But in levels of income and in degree of residential integration with non-blacks, Los Angeles blacks rank among the top in the United States, and its black-owned businesses have the highest revenues of any city in the nation. Californians have historically shown less prejudice against blacks than most Americans, and job opportunities in Los Angeles—up to and including the office of mayor for 20 years—have been plenteous for blacks. This is apparent in the hills just west of Crenshaw, an Art Deco neighborhood built in the 1920s and 1930s in vacant flat land southwest of downtown LA. Here, in Baldwin Hills, where on clear days you can see the towers of downtown and the snow-capped San Gabriel Mountains beyond, is a high-income black neighborhood, one of the strongest in the country; to the north and west are other comfortable black-majority neighborhoods; on the flatlands south of Beverly Hills and the Fairfax district not far away, affluent blacks are buying houses as much as anyone else. There was little or no rioting here in April 1992.

This part of Los Angeles is the heart of the 32d Congressional District, which runs approximately from the Harbor Freeway west past Baldwin Hills to Culver City and almost to the ocean, and south from Olympic Boulevard past the Santa Monica Freeway down almost to Inglewood and the LAX airport. The 32d vies with the Maryland 4th and New York 6th for the largest numbers of affluent blacks. Politically there has been no serious trend toward Republicans. Indeed, affluent, well-educated blacks seem if anything to be culturally more liberal than low-income black voters who may have closer ties to church and tradition. Any affection that upper-income blacks may have for free market economics is tempered by the knowledge that many of them have profited on the way up from some form of government intervention—a student loan, a public sector job, an affirmative action program. And whites here seem immune to racial backlash.

The Congressman from the 32d District is Julian Dixon, a political veteran who has had an uncomfortable but honorable moment in the national spotlight. Dixon practiced law in Los Angeles and was elected in 1972 to the Assembly, where he was an ally of Henry Waxman, four years his senior; in 1978, when incumbent Yvonne Burke ran for attorney general, Dixon was elected to the House. Intelligent, politically savvy, a team player with high ethics, he got good positions and tough assignments. Early on he got a seat on the Appropriations Committee and rose quickly to become chairman of the District of Columbia Subcommittee—a thankless post, and one in which he was supposed to superintend Mayor Marion Barry and a city government that could never say how many employees it had or how much it was spending. By 1994 Dixon was saying, "The problem is just plain old overspending" and became a harsh critic of Barry, after he returned from prison and regained the Mayor's office. In 1984 he chaired the rules committee at the Democratic National Convention and dealt effectively with Jesse Jackson's challenges to the rules. In 1989, as chairman of the House Ethics Committee, he had to supervise the task of passing judgment on Speaker Jim Wright. This was as high-pressure an assignment as could be imagined: Republicans were baying that the Democrats were going to let their leader off; Wright and his loyalists were pooh-poohing the charges; the press was watching closely for signs of partiality or error. Dixon proceeded deliberately, and Wright was forced to resign once it became clear that his reservoir of support had dried up. No one can accuse Dixon of partisan tilt: while he was chairman, Wright's accuser (and ultimate successor) Newt Gingrich was found not to have violated the rules on a book contract and Barney Frank was reprimanded for bad judgment in fixing parking tickets.

As an Appropriations subcommittee chairman—a member of the "college of cardinals"—he was ready to step in with "dire emergency" supplementals for Los Angeles after the riots in 1992 and the Northridge earthquake in January 1994, and to put a lot of money into its Metro Rail subway, making sure the system reaches all parts of the city. His voting record, very liberal on most things, is more moderate on foreign issues, reflecting perhaps the area's heavy defense industries and his own recent service on the Defense Subcommittee. Along with Dianne Feinstein, Dixon introduced the Small Business Defense Loan Guarantee Act, which would provide loans to small businesses adversely affected by the closing of military bases or the termination of defense contracts. He supported a bill calling for federal assistance for research and development of new rail technology, boosted the bone marrow transplant program, supports defense reconversion programs and (a sign that he represents an affluent district) wants unemployed people permitted to withdraw money from their IRAs without penalty. In 1993, he got another challenging, but this time quiet, assignment: a seat on the Intelligence Committee.

Dixon is regularly reelected without significant opposition. He was criticized in 1990 because his wife was part of a joint venture that, on an investment of at most $15,000, won a minority set-aside contract for a Los Angeles Airport duty-free shop that yielded some $150,000 in two years; he resisted an Ethics Committee investigation and was not hurt electorally. He has passed up chances to run for major local office—the Board of Supervisors seat (representing America's most populous legislative district) for which Yvonne Burke edged state Senator Diane Watson in 1992, and the Los Angeles mayoralty in 1993.

The People: Pop. 1990: 572,630; 11% age 65+; 24% White; 40% Black; 8% Asian; 19% Other; 30% Hispanic origin. Voting age pop.: 435,528; 40% Black; 26% Hispanic origin. Households: 38% married couple families; 18% married couple fams. w. children; 50% college educ.; median household income: $28,332; per capita income: $14,520; median gross rent: $592; median house value: $231,400.

1992 Presidential Vote

Clinton (D)	147,623	(77%)
Bush (R)	23,956	(13%)
Perot (I)	17,561	(9%)

1988 Presidential Vote

Dukakis (D)	146,787	(79%)
Bush (R)	38,062	(21%)

Rep. Julian C. Dixon (D)

Elected 1978; b. Aug. 8, 1934, Washington, D.C.; home, Culver City; CA St. U., B.S. 1962, Southwestern U., LL.B. 1967; Episcopalian; married (Betty).

Career: Army, 1957–60; Practicing atty., 1960–73; CA Assembly, 1972–78.

DC Office: 2252 RHOB 20515, 202-225-7084; Fax: 202-225-4091.

District Offices: 5100 W. Goldleaf Cir., #208, Los Angeles 90056, 213-678-5424.

Committees: *Appropriations* (9th of 24 D): Commerce, Justice, State, and Judiciary; District of Columbia (RMM); Legislative. *Intelligence (Permanent Select)* (3rd of 7 D): Human Intelligence, Analysis, and Counterintelligence.

Group Ratings

	ADA	ACLU	COPE	CFA	LCV	CON	NSI	COC	ACU	NTLC	CHC
1994	75	83	88	100	72	7	40	33	10	5	0
1993	80	—	100	100	79	1	—	18	8	—	—

National Journal Ratings

	1993 LIB — 1993 CONS			1994 LIB — 1994 CONS		
Economic	88%	—	0%	83%	—	0%
Social	87%	—	0%	90%	—	6%
Foreign	51%	—	42%	71%	—	28%

Key Votes of the 103d Congress

1. Clinton Deficit Plan	Y	3. Brady Handgun Purchase	Y	5. Lmt. UN Cmnd. of Forces	N
2. NAFTA	N	4. Strike Race/Death Pnlty.	N	6. Cut Missile Funds	N

Key Votes of the 104th Congress

1. Congressional Compliance	Y	6. Reform Crime Grant	N	11. Loser Pays Court Reform	N
2. Balanced Budget Amndmt.	N	7. National Security Act	N	12. Product Liability Reform	N
3. Bar Unfunded Mandates	Y	8. Moratorium on Regs.	N	13. Welfare Reform	N
4. Pass Line Item Veto	N	9. Risk Assessment on Regs.	N	14. Term Limits Amndmt.	N
5. Relax Exclusionary Rule	*	10. Expnd. Priv. Prop. Rights	N	15. Tax Cuts	N

Election Results

1994 general	Julian C. Dixon (D)	98,017	(78%)	($141,941)
	Ernie A. Farhat (R)	22,190	(18%)	($43,910)
	John Honigsfeld (P&F)	6,099	(5%)	
1994 primary	Julian C. Dixon (D)	51,291	(90%)	
	Peter J. Duvall (D)	3,994	(7%)	
	Others	1,904	(3%)	
1992 general	Julian C. Dixon (D)	150,644	(87%)	($140,461)
	Bob Weber (Lib)	12,384	(7%)	
	William R. Williams (P&F)	9,782	(6%)	

THIRTY-THIRD DISTRICT

A block from Los Angeles's "modern architecture" City Hall, whose 452-foot white tower—long the symbol of the city but now dwarfed by 60- and 70-story postmodern marble slabs and pink cylinders a few blocks away—is Broadway, America's biggest volume retail shopping street west of Chicago. The sidewalks are thronged, the signs are mostly in Spanish, the merchandise is often strewn on tables: this could be Mexico City or Lima, Latin America transplanted a block from a gleaming symbol of Yankee propriety and gaudy emblems of North American prosperity. Broadway is neither the geographical nor spiritual center of Los Angeles's Latino communities and it is by no means their only major shopping area. But it is an emblem of the entry-level Latino neighborhoods of the nation's second largest city, the places where many immigrants, not so much from Mexico as from Central and South America, come to find a cheap place to live, doubled and tripled up with other families and single newcomers, close enough to drive in an old car to work in factories and warehouses that fill so much of the acreage south and east of downtown.

Broadway and many of these entry-level neighborhoods make up much of the 33d Congressional District. It includes downtown and MacArthur Park, once beautiful and now a drug dealers' hangout, and Pico Union, where many Central and South American immigrants make their first homes; it includes the giant factories south of downtown along the Southern Pacific Railroad and Santa Ana Freeway; it takes in part of East Los Angeles. To the south it includes what were in the 1940s working-class, southern-white suburbs—Huntington Park, South Gate, Bell and Bell Gardens, Commerce and Vernon, Maywood and Cudahy—which in the 1960s were nervously aware that they were separated by just Alameda Street from the black ghettos of Watts and Florence. Today newcomer Latinos have replaced blacks in Florence and Watts, while longer-settled Latinos inhabit the working-class bungalows east of Alameda. The 33d District in 1990 was 84% Hispanic, by far the highest figure of any California district, and the only district that can be truly claimed mono-cultural; it was only 4% black, 4% Asian and 8% non-Hispanic white. Politically, these neighborhoods are more Democratic than when they were white but less Democratic than when they were black. More important, this is mostly a non-voting constituency: newcomers may not be citizens, many residents are children, workers at two jobs may be too busy to register and Latinos tend to see private sector work, not public sector protections, as their way up in the world. As a result, in 1992 only 18,935 people voted in the 33d District's crucial Democratic primary and only 50,779 in the general election, compared to 261,000 in the Westside 29th District and 120,000, 83,000, 109,000 and 149,000 in the Hispanic-majority 26th, 30th, 31st and 34th Districts. The 33d District looks like a late 20th Century version of a rotten borough, Old-Sarum-on-the-Pacific-Rim; but it is a district where people work hard and play by the American rules and, vote or not, are as entitled to representation as anyone else who lives in the United States.

The 33d District's Congresswoman is Lucille Roybal-Allard, first elected in 1992, the daughter of 30-year Congressman Edward Roybal, whose roots were in New Mexico, not Mexico. Roybal-Allard was elected to the Assembly in 1986 and there sponsored bills on sexual assault, domestic violence and such causes as requiring more environmental impact reports for toxic waste incinerators (a move prompted by protests against a proposed incinerator in Vernon.) She entered the 1992 House race even before her father announced his retirement, and she won 75% in the Democratic primary and 63% in the general election. She says she is "dedicated to community empowerment at all levels," and compiled an almost perfectly liberal voting record. She worked to set the terms of minority- and woman-setaside programs and worked for an enterprise zone in her district. Roybal-Allard organized a meeting on healthcare reform among hispanics with Hillary Rodham Clinton. She worked for the Violence Against Women Act, the Family and Medical Leave Act and the Child Support Recovery Act, and investigated whether tobacco advertising targeted women. Roybal-Allard easily won reelection in 1994, only to face serving in a Republican House. "What I see us doing is mainly damage control," she said. "A lot of damage control."

The People: Pop. 1990: 570,893; 6% age 65+; 8% White; 4% Black; 1% Amer. Indian; 4% Asian; 55% Other; 83% Hispanic origin. Voting age pop.: 384,472; 5% Black; 79% Hispanic origin. Households: 49% married couple families; 34% married couple fams. w. children; 17% college educ.; median household income: $20,708; per capita income: $6,997; median gross rent: $484; median house value: $154,400.

1992 Presidential Vote			**1988 Presidential Vote**		
Clinton (D)	33,642	(63%)	Dukakis (D)	34,710	(64%)
Bush (R)	12,607	(23%)	Bush (R)	19,706	(36%)
Perot (I)	7,149	(13%)			

Rep. Lucille Roybal-Allard (D)

Elected 1992; b. June 12, 1941, Los Angeles; home, Los Angeles; CA St. U., B.A. 1965; Catholic; married (Edward Allard).

Career: CA Assembly, 1987–92.

DC Office: 324 CHOB 20515, 202-225-1766.

District Offices: Edward Roybal Fed. Bldg., 255 E. Temple St., #1860, Los Angeles 90012, 213-628-9230.

Committees: *Banking & Financial Services* (14th of 22 D): Domestic and International Monetary Policy; Housing and Community Opportunity. *Budget* (15th of 18 D).

Group Ratings

	ADA	ACLU	COPE	CFA	LCV	CON	NSI	COC	ACU	NTLC	CHC
1994	100	87	78	100	100	13	20	33	0	11	0
1993	95	—	92	100	100	16	—	20	4	—	—

National Journal Ratings

	1993 LIB — 1993 CONS			1994 LIB — 1994 CONS		
Economic	75%	—	22%	83%	—	0%
Social	87%	—	0%	94%	—	0%
Foreign	87%	—	7%	83%	—	15%

Key Votes of the 103d Congress

1. Clinton Deficit Plan	Y	3. Brady Handgun Purchase	Y	5. Lmt. UN Cmnd. of Forces	N
2. NAFTA	Y	4. Strike Race/Death Pnlty.	N	6. Cut Missile Funds	Y

Key Votes of the 104th Congress

1. Congressional Compliance	Y	6. Reform Crime Grant	N	11. Loser Pays Court Reform	N
2. Balanced Budget Amndmt.	N	7. National Security Act	N	12. Product Liability Reform	N
3. Bar Unfunded Mandates	N	8. Moratorium on Regs.	N	13. Welfare Reform	N
4. Pass Line Item Veto	N	9. Risk Assessment on Regs.	N	14. Term Limits Amndmt.	N
5. Relax Exclusionary Rule	N	10. Expnd. Priv. Prop. Rights	N	15. Tax Cuts	N

Election Results

1994 general	Lucille Roybal-Allard (D)	33,814	(81%)	($124,271)
	Kermit Booker (P&F)	7,694	(19%)	
1994 primary	Lucille Roybal-Allard (D)	10,842	(79%)	
	Charles E. Greene (D)	2,941	(21%)	
1992 general	Lucille Roybal-Allard (D)	32,010	(63%)	($264,755)
	Robert Guzman (R)	15,428	(30%)	($166,756)
	Tim Delia (P&F)	2,135	(4%)	
	Other	1,206	(2%)	

THIRTY-FOURTH DISTRICT

One of the great population surges in the United States is the upward social and outward geographic movement of the hundreds of thousands of immigrants to the Los Angeles Basin in recent decades, from crowded entry-level neighborhoods out freeways to the suburbs. It is visible east and southeast of Los Angeles, in suburbs that over a generation have changed from solidly white Anglo to largely Latino. Many have made their way up working in small smokeless factories along railroad tracks and near river beds, beneath roaring freeways and on grid streets near stucco garden apartment blocks—the factories that have made Los Angeles the nation's number one manufacturing metro area—and in small business offices and stores. These people came to the United States not to re-create their Third World environment but to rise above it, and they see this country not as a land of oppression but of opportunity. Their values resemble those of working-class Americans of the pre-Vietnam 1960s: pro-family and respectful of traditional personal morals (LA-area Latinos have lower than average divorce rates and are more likely to raise children in two-parent families), patriotic and pro-military (they are more likely than average to volunteer for military service).

Vast numbers of these new residents—whose rise through hard work has gone shamefully unnoticed in a mainline press which often seems convinced that only government can produce upward mobility—live in the 34th Congressional District of California. This is a swatch of suburban Los Angeles County anchored by three suburbs. On the northwest is Montebello, a working-class suburb since the 1940s just beyond East Los Angeles, now heavily Latino. To the east is La Puente, a center of the light-manufacturing economy that created hundreds of thousands of jobs in the Los Angeles Basin in the 1980s, and in which increasing numbers of small businesses are owned by Asians, Latinos and blacks. To the south is Whittier, a town founded by Midwestern Quakers, much of which is in the 34th District, where Richard Nixon grew up and went to Whittier College, and Norwalk, farther south astride the Santa Ana Freeway. The first 34th District was drawn in 1982, the result of redistricting politics; in the 1990s it has moved, like its people, outward from the central city; it was drawn not for partisan purposes but to maximize the Hispanic percentage, which was 62% in 1990, the second highest figure in California.

The new lines have worked out fine for Democrat Esteban Torres, the new 34th's one and only congressman. Torres rose from working on an auto assembly line through the ranks of the United Auto Workers, to head an antipoverty program in East Los Angeles. He worked in the Carter Administration, and in 1982, with support from the Waxman-Berman machine, scored a solid primary victory against former Congressman Jim Lloyd and won the general election by a 57%–43% margin. On economic issues, Torres is a liberal in the UAW tradition, favoring government action to help the poor move up into the middle class; on foreign issues, he is somewhat more moderate—the B-2 is built in a Northrop Grumman plant in Pico Rivera. On cultural issues he is mostly liberal, though not on abortion. He represents, after all, the number one family district in Los Angeles, a place where people are committed to family patterns and where high hopes for the future depend on the progress of their children in school and in the workplace. They are interested in having a secure government safety net but seem to believe that their children will get somewhere—as their parents or grandparents emerged from rural Mexico—largely through their own efforts. Torres has worked to clean up groundwater, especially in the San Gabriel Valley. He has bills to allow more spending to stop gang activity. He successfully knocked out of the 1990 immigration law a pilot program to create a forgery-proof driver's license—a civil rights issue and threat to privacy, Torres felt. Probably more than any member of the House, he was torn both ways on the North American Free Trade Agreement; his UAW roots were against it, his Latino roots in favor. At first he opposed it, then eventually voted for it after the Clinton Administration agreed to create a $225 million North American Development Bank to help workers adversely affected by NAFTA. In January 1993, Torres introduced a bill that would strip major league baseball of its exemption from anti-trust laws; professional baseball has been free of such laws since 1922.

Torres has been reelected with 60% or more since 1984; he had some interest in running for County Board of Supervisors in 1990, but had already filed for reelection when the vacancy came up. He won with 61% in 1992 and 62% in 1994. After the 1992 election, he won a seat on the Appropriations Committee, a good spot to pursue his groundwater issues and from which he says he will remain interested in fair credit legislation.

The People: Pop. 1990: 573,456; 9% age 65+; 27% White; 2% Black; 1% Amer. Indian; 9% Asian; 31% Other; 62% Hispanic origin. Voting age pop.: 402,525; 2% Black; 57% Hispanic origin. Households: 61% married couple families; 33% married couple fams. w. children; 37% college educ.; median household income: $36,224; per capita income: $12,012; median gross rent: $637; median house value: $172,900.

1992 Presidential Vote		
Clinton (D)	78,889	(51%)
Bush (R)	48,181	(31%)
Perot (I)	27,944	(18%)

1988 Presidential Vote		
Dukakis (D)	79,426	(52%)
Bush (R)	72,423	(48%)

Rep. Esteban E. Torres (D)

Elected 1982; b. Jan. 27, 1930, Miami, AZ; home, West Covina; E. Los Angeles Commun. Col., 1959, CA St. U., 1963, U. of MD, 1965, American U., 1966; No religious affiliation; married (Arcy).

Career: Army, 1949–53; Assembly-line worker, Chrysler Corp., 1953–63; Chief Steward, UAW Local 230, 1961–63; UAW Intl. Rep., Region 6, 1963–64, Inter-Amer. Rep., 1965–68; Dir., E. Los Angeles Commun. Union, 1968–74; UAW Intl. Affairs Dept., 1974–77; U.S. Permanent Rep., UNESCO, 1977–79, Special Asst., Pres. Jimmy Carter, 1979–81; Pres., Intl. Enterprise and Devel. Corp., 1981–82.

DC Office: 2368 RHOB 20515, 202-225-5256; Fax: 202-225-9711.

District Offices: 8819 Whittier Blvd., #101, Pico Rivera 90660, 310-695-0702.

Committees: *Appropriations* (22nd of 24 D): Foreign Operations, Export Financing, and Related Programs; Military Construction.

Group Ratings

	ADA	ACLU	COPE	CFA	LCV	CON	NSI	COC	ACU	NTLC	CHC
1994	75	82	75	100	72	9	20	42	10	8	7
1993	90	—	92	100	83	16	—	20	0	—	—

National Journal Ratings

	1993 LIB — 1993 CONS		1994 LIB — 1994 CONS	
Economic	74%	— 25%	83%	— 0%
Social	80%	— 13%	77%	— 21%
Foreign	74%	— 22%	67%	— 32%

Key Votes of the 103d Congress

1. Clinton Deficit Plan	Y	3. Brady Handgun Purchase Y	5. Lmt. UN Cmnd. of Forces N
2. NAFTA	Y	4. Strike Race/Death Pnlty. N	6. Cut Missile Funds N

Key Votes of the 104th Congress

1. Congressional Compliance Y	6. Reform Crime Grant N	11. Loser Pays Court Reform N
2. Balanced Budget Amndmt. N	7. National Security Act N	12. Product Liability Reform N
3. Bar Unfunded Mandates N	8. Moratorium on Regs. N	13. Welfare Reform N
4. Pass Line Item Veto N	9. Risk Assessment on Regs. N	14. Term Limits Amndmt. N
5. Relax Exclusionary Rule N	10. Expnd. Priv. Prop. Rights N	15. Tax Cuts N

Election Results

1994 general	Esteban E. Torres (D)	72,439	(62%)	($178,972)
	Albert J. Nunez (R)	40,068	(34%)	($5,115)
	Carl M. (Marty) Swinney (Lib)	4,921	(4%)	
1994 primary	Esteban E. Torres (D)	unopposed		
1992 general	Esteban E. Torres (D)	91,738	(61%)	($254,092)
	J. (Jay) Hernandez (R)	50,907	(34%)	($131,271)
	Carl M. (Marty) Swinney (Lib)	7,072	(5%)	

THIRTY-FIFTH DISTRICT

In April 1992, the corner of Florence and Normandie in South Central Los Angeles became for a moment the most famous intersection in America: the epicenter of the Los Angeles riot. This was not, as was commonly said, simply an outpouring of anger at the Rodney King verdict; if it were, there would have been rioting everywhere in the Los Angeles Basin, since few citizens agreed with the Simi Valley jury. It was rather, like the urban riots of the 1960s, a collection of criminal acts suddenly committed by people in the expectation that so many others would be doing the same thing that all would have impunity; and even so, the rioting this time clearly would have been stopped but for the dereliction of LAPD Chief Daryl Gates, who had prepared no contingency plan and spent hours on his way to and from a political fundraiser as the rioting broke out. The rioting did in fact stop once Governor Pete Wilson and President George Bush announced that some 25,000 troops were being ordered to Los Angeles, eliminating potential rioters' expectation of immunity.

The commitment of troops was much greater than in the big 1960s riots, and this riot ended far sooner. But in the meantime great damage was done. Most visible was the harm to individuals: black and Latino onlookers were killed and injured by rioters and law enforcement personnel; a white truck driver was viciously beaten at Florence and Normandie; Asian and Latino storeowners were singled out by black and Central American rioters and treated as oppressors, when in fact they were providing goods and services which no one else—for reasons now painfully apparent—was willing to provide. Even more harmful may be the damage to Los Angeles's civic culture. For in the aftermath of the riot it was widely repeated that blacks were helpless victims of racism and poverty, when in fact most LA area blacks have moved upward economically and out geographically from the old South Central and Watts ghettos in the 27 years since the 1965 riots, and African-Americans are well-represented in LA and California politics.

Among those commenting most vociferously on the riot was Congresswoman Maxine Waters, whose 35th Congressional District includes Florence and Normandie as well as much of the South Central and Watts corridors which formed California's first black-majority district 30 years ago. The 35th also includes the majority-black middle-income suburb of Inglewood, home of the Los Angeles Forum; Hawthorne, birthplace of the Beach Boys; and Gardena, with California's first licensed poker clubs at which some of the most cutthroat games in the country are played. Latinos have been moving for two decades into South Central and Watts, and the 35th District was 42% Hispanic in 1990. But 43% of its residents and a solid majority of its voters were black, and Waters seems to regard her constituency as essentially black, whatever the Census numbers. Waters came to California in 1961, worked in a garment factory and raised two children, got a sociology degree at California State University and became an assistant Head Start teacher after the Watts riot. A political activist, in 1976 she won a seat in the California Assembly. There she supported Willie Brown and passed minority, women's and tenants' rights laws, limits on police strip searches, and a provision mandating divestiture of state pension funds from South Africa. She was consulted on the 1982 redistricting by Phillip Burton, and when Congressman Augustus Hawkins retired in 1990 after 28 years in the House and 28 years in the California Assembly, capped by six years as chairman of the House Education and Labor Committee, Waters was the obvious choice for the seat and won it easily. She had already made a national name for herself as a vocal supporter of Jesse Jackson in 1984 and 1988 and was probably the most prominent freshman in the 102d Congress.

Waters brings to her work a wrath that is almost palpable, and an insistence that she will assert herself regardless of protocol, partly perhaps a result of anger but also a weapon she uses shrewdly and cynically to get both publicity and results. "I don't have time to be polite," she says, beginning her career by getting herself included in a post-riot White House meeting with George Bush after learning of the meeting on a morning TV show. She told Speaker Tom Foley she was going over there no matter what anyone else did. Sometimes she over-blusters: she missed the chance to demand a roll call for one of her amendments, which was beaten, because she was outside the House participating in a press conference. But she has pushed specific legislation, including the Community Reinvestment Act racial quotas, a "Youth Fair Chance Act" with job training and counseling for unemployed young men 17 to 30, and a Center for Women Veterans within the Department of Veterans Affairs. She was successful in getting legislation passed in 1992 which assures preference to low-income veterans in purchasing foreclosed properties from failed banks and S&Ls. She also succeeded in passing amendments, some of them even making laws more acceptable to conservatives, on Banking and Financial Services. Waters comes from a poor background and believes with fervor in federal aid for the poor and for racial preferences to help blacks overcome years of slavery, segregation and discrimination; she favors drastic reductions in defense spending and was one of six members who voted against supporting the Gulf war once it started, asking how urban gang members could be expected to stop fighting when America's own leaders were waging battles. She was an early but unillusioned supporter of Bill Clinton for the Democratic nomination, and traveled often with Clinton, who was happy to have the support of such an outspoken former Jesse Jackson backer. At the 1992 Democratic convention, insisting that "this is the last time I support an all-white anything," she said she would support the Democratic ticket in 2000 only if it has a black or a woman on it. Her husband, a former Mercedes Benz salesman, became President Clinton's Ambassador to the Bahamas. Even so, she voted against the crime bill rule in August 1994 when the administration desperately needed votes, because she said she "could not vote for a crime bill that sweepingly expands the death penalty to include sixty new crimes."

The Los Angeles riot was occasion for both Waters' best and worst moments. She flew home immediately and roused the Department of Water and Power to restore water to the riot area, and was effective in gaining provisions to the post-riot emergency act that eventually made it through Congress and was signed into law. But she also over-emotionally claimed, "Los Angeles is under siege . . . the violence could spill over to many other cities in this country." Which, of course, it didn't. And she made statements suggesting that the rioters were morally justified, that somehow street thugs were speaking for the black community instead of destroying it. She herself spoke in the accents of the street in the summer 1994 Banking Committee Whitewater hearings when Congressman Peter King was interrogating Maggie Williams, Mrs. Clinton's chief of staff, and Waters told King to "Shut up." Later, on the floor, she was gaveled down for talking beyond her alloted one minute by the Speaker Pro Tem, Congresswoman Carrie Meek.

Waters, though reelected easily in the past, cannot count on this for the future in a Republican House. And her power is likely to be diminished now that the majority is no longer in the hands of those who believe she speaks with some special moral authority.

The People: Pop. 1990: 570,697; 7% age 65+; 10% White; 43% Black; 6% Asian; 30% Other; 42% Hispanic origin. Voting age pop.: 389,120; 44% Black; 37% Hispanic origin. Households: 42% married couple families; 25% married couple fams. w. children; 35% college educ.; median household income: $25,481; per capita income: $9,761; median gross rent: $573; median house value: $148,700.

1992 Presidential Vote			1988 Presidential Vote		
Clinton (D)	100,432	(77%)	Dukakis (D)	101,310	(78%)
Bush (R)	16,685	(13%)	Bush (R)	28,119	(22%)
Perot (I)	11,950	(9%)			

Rep. Maxine Waters (D)

Elected 1990; b. Aug. 31, 1938, St. Louis, MO; home, Los Angeles; CA St. U., B.A. 1970; Christian; married (Sidney Williams).

Career: CA Assembly, 1976–90.

DC Office: 330 CHOB 20515, 202-225-2201; Fax: 202-225-7854.

District Offices: 10124 S. Broadway, #1, Los Angeles 90003, 213-757-8900.

Committees: *Banking & Financial Services* (10th of 22 D): Capital Markets, Securities and Government Sponsored Enterprises; Housing and Community Opportunity. *Veterans' Affairs* (5th of 15 D): Education, Training, Employment and Housing (RMM).

Group Ratings

	ADA	ACLU	COPE	CFA	LCV	CON	NSI	COC	ACU	NTLC	CHC
1994	100	91	89	90	89	13	10	25	10	14	0
1993	100	—	100	90	100	7	—	9	4	—	—

National Journal Ratings

	1993 LIB — 1993 CONS		1994 LIB — 1994 CONS	
Economic	88%	0%	83%	0%
Social	87%	0%	80%	20%
Foreign	79%	16%	83%	15%

Key Votes of the 103d Congress

1. Clinton Deficit Plan	Y	3. Brady Handgun Purchase	Y	5. Lmt. UN Cmnd. of Forces	N
2. NAFTA	N	4. Strike Race/Death Pnlty.	N	6. Cut Missile Funds	Y

Key Votes of the 104th Congress

1. Congressional Compliance	Y	6. Reform Crime Grant	N	11. Loser Pays Court Reform	N
2. Balanced Budget Amndmt.	N	7. National Security Act	N	12. Product Liability Reform	N
3. Bar Unfunded Mandates	N	8. Moratorium on Regs.	N	13. Welfare Reform	N
4. Pass Line Item Veto	N	9. Risk Assessment on Regs.	N	14. Term Limits Amndmt.	N
5. Relax Exclusionary Rule	N	10. Expnd. Priv. Prop. Rights	N	15. Tax Cuts	N

Election Results

1994 general	Maxine Waters (D)	65,688	(78%)	($177,791)
	Nate Truman (R)	18,390	(22%)	($9,580)
1994 primary	Maxine Waters (D)	unopposed		
1992 general	Maxine Waters (D)	102,941	(83%)	($207,954)
	Nate Truman (R)	17,417	(14%)	($7,143)
	Others	4,418	(4%)	

THIRTY-SIXTH DISTRICT

For many southern Californians, there is no better place to be than the beach. It is not a perfect environment: in the morning there may be mists, the winter air is damp and clammy, even in summer the weather can be chilly, the water is never very warm and is sometimes polluted. But for many this is echt-California, and in this democratic polity, there is a beach to suit the taste of just about everyone. The funkiest of all is surely Venice, with its beach houses jammed together and the canals dug by a developer in 1904, long stagnant and mudlined but slated to be reconstructed in 1994, with the boardwalk where skateboarding got its start and where the latest crazes are chainsaw juggling and outdoor massages. Right behind is Marina Del Rey, with sleek modern apartment complexes and expensive yacht moorings. Just south, across an inlet, is LAX, the only American airport commonly known by its three-letter code; the swooping arches of its theme building, intended in 1961 to symbolize the jet era, are now a historic landmark, like Disneyland's Tomorrowland or the *Jetsons*, an antique version of a surpassed future. To the south is El Segundo, named for Socal's second oil refinery, and the home of the huge Hughes radar and laser plant, one of many big defense plants just behind the beach. Next are Manhattan Beach, one of the favorites three decades ago of the original Beach Boys who grew up a couple of miles inland in Hawthorne, and tiny Hermosa Beach, with tightly packed frame houses originally the homes of elderly retirees; the current attitude here is suggested by Councilman Robert (Burgie) Benz, who sponsors a beer drinking and vomiting fest every Fourth of July. To the south are the flower-planted rises of Redondo Beach and Torrance, whose vast inland expanse is filled with the American headquarters of Japanese companies. The South Bay beaches end where the Palos Verdes Peninsula looms high over the ocean, seismically active and socioeconomically upscale. Just to the east is the harbor town of San Pedro, once working-class, but moving up as well, overlooking LA's eerily modern containerport.

All this beach territory, from Venice south to San Pedro (both of which technically are part of Los Angeles, though the area in between is not), makes up the 36th Congressional District. Historically Republican, this area is still leery of taxes, but culturally it is libertarian—against restrictions or even aspersions on its various lifestyles. From 1982 to 1992, when the South Bay district included black precincts inland, it elected Democrat Mel Levine by wide margins. But with Democrats no longer in charge of redistricting, the new 36th was only 3% black and had more registered Republicans than Democrats, usually a sure indication of being safe Republican. Yet even before George Bush's candidacy collapsed in California, it was apparent that the 36th would be competitive in 1992.

The Congresswoman from the 36th is Jane Harman, who has won two close victories since the district was created in its present form. Harman grew up in Los Angeles and remembers sitting as a teenager in the gallery at the 1960 Democratic National Convention in Los Angeles. After law school, she worked on Senator John Tunney's staff and made headlines when she quit a White House job to stay home with her children. Shortly afterwards, she divorced her first husband and in 1980 married Sidney Harman, who made a fortune manufacturing audio equipment; she has maintained a Washington residence ever since. But when she saw the new district lines, she returned to California and ran for the House—one of seven Democrats and 11 Republicans running. It turned out to be the year of the woman on the macho beach: women got 73% of Democratic and 68% of Republican primary votes in this district. Harman, spending her own money liberally, won with 45%; the second-place finisher, the daughter-in-law of the late Speaker and Treasurer Jesse Unruh, got 16%. In the Republican primary Los Angeles Councilwoman Joan Milke Flores beat Maureen Reagan, daughter of the former President, 34%–31%. In the general Harman campaigned as "pro-choice and pro-change"; Flores was pro-life and had the burden of George Bush's flagging candidacy. Harman also argued that she could do more to protect defense jobs in the area, and supported a targeted capital gains tax cut and the line-item veto. She spent $2.3 million, the fourth highest of any campaign in the country. The Republican registration advantage eroded from 5% to 2% during the campaign, an unusual shift in a short time, and Harman won 48%–42%.

Harman showed political acumen in the House, winning seats on the Science and National Security Committees, where she is an unabashed supporter of the defense industry within her district by supporting a ballistic missile defense system there. She was well connected on the Hill and in the Clinton Administration—she threw a birthday party for her husband in Speaker Foley's office, with Defense Secretary Les Aspin and then White House adviser, now Treasury Secretary, Robert Rubin, attending. She had a moderate voting record but was leftish on some key issues: she cast a decisive vote for the Clinton budget and tax package in August 1993 and voted against the North American Free Trade Agreement. She supported the balanced budget amendment, President Clinton's proposal to raise the cigarette tax to 99 cents a pack, and also the C-17 transport and missile defense. Her opponent in 1994 was Susan Brooks, a social worker and Rancho Palos Verdes councilwoman, a pro-choicer who won the Republican primary 51%–49%. She attacked Harman for supporting the Clinton tax increase, which hits hard in this high-income area, and for voting with Maxine Waters 95% of the time. Brooks campaigned door-to-door while Harman used her money to buy TV ads in the hugely expensive Los Angeles media market. This turned out to be one of the closest races in the nation. Out of 172,667 votes cast, Brooks was 93 votes ahead on election night, but the absentee ballots went heavily for Harman—either the result of organization or because upscale voters here are liberal. The state certified Harman as the winner by 812 votes; Brooks challenged the result, arguing that California's loose registration laws allow many illegal aliens to vote. The House Oversight Committee held a hearing on the case in May, and gave each candidate more time to produce more definitive statements.

In the Republican House, Harman voted for the balanced budget amendment and line-item veto, and she will surely continue to try to use her Clinton Administration connections to help South Bay defense industries. Her political skills and personal checkbook are formidable. But she has won only 48% of the vote twice in this district, and Brooks says she will run again in 1996: the beach district will have probably have its third serious contest in a row.

The People: Pop. 1990: 573,665; 10% age 65+; 69% White; 3% Black; 13% Asian; 6% Other; 15% Hispanic origin. Voting age pop.: 462,697; 3% Black; 13% Hispanic origin. Households: 49% married couple families; 20% married couple fams. w. children; 67% college educ.; median household income: $48,522; per capita income: $25,534; median gross rent: $812; median house value: $369,800.

1992 Presidential Vote

Clinton (D)	111,014	(41%)
Bush (R)	95,646	(35%)
Perot (I)	62,458	(23%)

1988 Presidential Vote

Bush (R)	150,984	(60%)
Dukakis (D)	102,061	(40%)

Rep. Jane Harman (D)

Elected 1992; b. June 28, 1945, New York, NY; home, Marina del Rey; Smith Col., B.A. 1966, Harvard, J.D. 1969; Jewish; married (Sidney).

Career: Legis. Dir., U.S. Sen. John Tunney, 1972–73; Chief Cnsl. & Staff Dir., Senate Judiciary Subcmtee., 1973–77; Dep. Cabinet Secy., White House, 1977; Defense Dept. Special Cnsl., 1979; Harman Intl. Industries, Corp. Secy., 1985–92, Dir., 1990–92; Practicing atty., 1987–92.

DC Office: 325 CHOB 20515, 202-225-8220; Fax: 202-225-0684; e-mail: jharman@hr.house.gov.

District Offices: 5200 W. Century Blvd., #960, Los Angeles 90045, 310-348-8220; 3031 Torrance Blvd., Torrance 90503, 310-787-0767.

Committees: *National Security* (18th of 25 D): Military Personnel; Military Research and Development. *Science* (11th of 23 D): Space and Aeronautics.

Group Ratings

	ADA	ACLU	COPE	CFA	LCV	CON	NSI	COC	ACU	NTLC	CHC
1994	60	82	67	60	56	37	60	83	19	31	14
1993	85	—	92	90	92	55	—	18	17	—	—

National Journal Ratings

	1993 LIB — 1993 CONS			1994 LIB — 1994 CONS		
Economic	59%	—	41%	55%	—	44%
Social	79%	—	20%	65%	—	35%
Foreign	59%	—	38%	51%	—	47%

Key Votes of the 103d Congress

1. Clinton Deficit Plan	Y	3. Brady Handgun Purchase	Y	5. Lmt. UN Cmnd. of Forces	N
2. NAFTA	N	4. Strike Race/Death Pnlty.	N	6. Cut Missile Funds	N

Key Votes of the 104th Congress

1. Congressional Compliance	Y	6. Reform Crime Grant	N	11. Loser Pays Court Reform	N
2. Balanced Budget Amndmt.	Y	7. National Security Act	N	12. Product Liability Reform	Y
3. Bar Unfunded Mandates	Y	8. Moratorium on Regs.	Y	13. Welfare Reform	N
4. Pass Line Item Veto	Y	9. Risk Assessment on Regs.	N	14. Term Limits Amndmt.	Y
5. Relax Exclusionary Rule	Y	10. Expnd. Priv. Prop. Rights	Y	15. Tax Cuts	N

Election Results

1994 general	Jane Harman (D)	93,939	(48%)	($1,300,855)
	Susan M. Brooks (R)	93,127	(48%)	($580,837)
	Others	8,742	(4%)	
1994 primary	Jane Harman (D)	unopposed		
1992 general	Jane Harman (D)	124,751	(48%)	($2,285,356)
	Joan Milke Flores (R)...............	109,684	(42%)	($811,592)
	Richard H. Greene (Green)	13,297	(5%)	
	Others	11,025	(4%)	

THIRTY-SEVENTH DISTRICT

Los Angeles is the creation not of nature but of man: there is little natural water supply here and no natural port, little in the way of natural resources except for oil which turned out not to be enough for California; it is a place for people who plan big. Nearly a century ago Los Angeles's city fathers decided to build a port where the usually-dry Los Angeles River debouches into the ocean; in 1906 they annexed an eight-mile-long, four-block-wide corridor of land (christened Harbor Gateway in 1984) and the harbor areas of Wilmington and San Pedro, and converted a shallow bay with a few marshy inlets into the biggest port on the West Coast, ahead of the splendid natural harbors of San Francisco and San Diego. Inland, along the rail lines that hug the river bed, grew up heavy and light industry—oil tank farms and big factories, small job shops and warehouses. Interspersed were subdivisions and to the north was Watts, the epicenter of the 1965 riot and also the site of one of the strangest made-by-man structures in this made-by-man city, the 107-foot-high Watts Tower, built from 1921 to 1954 by Simon Rodia out of all manner of salvaged material.

The 37th District takes in a swath of low-income industrial suburbs from Watts and the new Century Freeway, the most expensive road in history, south to Wilmington and the port. Here are Compton and Lynwood, which switched from all-white to all-black in the 1960s and in the 1980s became heavily Latino; here is Carson, with recent subdivisions amid freeway interchanges and tank farms; here is Wilmington, facing a spankingly modern port. Overall, the 37th District in 1990 was 34% black and 44% Hispanic, but blacks far outnumber Latinos as registered voters.

The Congressman from the 37th District is Democrat Walter Tucker, former Mayor of Compton, who won the seat in 1992 and has held it since, amid some turbulence. Tucker grew up in Compton and served as Los Angeles County deputy district attorney from 1984 to 1986, when he was dismissed after changing the date on photographic evidence in a drug case. In 1990, he was a criminal lawyer in Compton and associate pastor of the Bread of Life Christian Center in Carson. Then his father, the longtime mayor of Compton, suddenly died, and the younger Tucker was elected to take his place in April 1991. In 1992 longtime Congressman and onetime Lieutenant Governor (1974–78) Mervyn Dymally suddenly announced his retirement and endorsed his daughter Lynn Dymally, a member of the Compton School Board. Tucker jumped into what soon became a spirited primary. A group called Truth in Politics, advised by Mervyn Dymally, accused Tucker of being a convicted felon; in fact, in 1988 he pleaded no contest to the misdemeanor charge of altering an official document. Tucker said that the slogan "Dymally: a name we can depend on" should be supplemented with "to do nothing." Tucker won 39% of the votes to Dymally's 37%; he easily won the general election.

In the House Tucker compiled a solidly liberal voting record and claimed credit for getting $5.9 million in police funds for Southern California. But in August 1994 he made headlines when he was indicted for soliciting and taking $30,000 in bribes while Mayor of Compton. The indictment also said he sought $250,000 in return for approving the building of a refuse incinerator. Tucker "unequivocally and categorically" denied the charges and hired Johnnie Cochran to defend him; but Cochran had to drop the case in 1995 because of his prolonged committment to the O.J. Simpson trial, and Tucker's case now goes to court in September. Under the Hobbs Act, Tucker could be sentenced to 20 years in prison and fined $250,000 for each of the eight bribery counts. Tucker had already won the June 1994 Democratic primary with 84% of the vote and was reelected with 77% in November. But he must be considered to be serving in the 104th Congress under a cloud.

The People: Pop. 1990: 572,191; 7% age 65+; 12% White; 34% Black; 11% Asian; 29% Other; 44% Hispanic origin. Voting age pop.: 375,081; 34% Black; 40% Hispanic origin. Households: 51% married couple families; 30% married couple fams. w. children; 32% college educ.; median household income: $27,127; per capita income: $9,104; median gross rent: $548; median house value: $140,800.

1992 Presidential Vote			1988 Presidential Vote		
Clinton (D)	90,523	(73%)	Dukakis (D)	94,248	(76%)
Bush (R)	19,299	(16%)	Bush (R)	29,714	(24%)
Perot (I)	12,905	(10%)			

Rep. Walter R. Tucker, III (D)

Elected 1992; b. May 28, 1957, Compton; home, Compton; Princeton U., 1976–78, U. of Southern CA, B.A. 1978, Georgetown Law Schl., J.D. 1981; Baptist; married (Robin).

Career: LA Cnty. Dep. Dist. Atty, 1984–86; Practicing atty., 1986–92; Compton Mayor, 1991–92.

DC Office: 419 CHOB 20515, 202-225-7924; Fax: 202-225-7926; e-mail: tucker96@hr.house.gov.

District Offices: 145 E. Compton Blvd., Compton 90220, 310-884-9989.

Committees: *Transportation & Infrastructure* (25th of 27 D): Coast Guard and Maritime Transportation; Surface Transportation. *Small Business* (11th of 19 D): Tax and Finance.

Group Ratings

	ADA	ACLU	COPE	CFA	LCV	CON	NSI	COC	ACU	NTLC	CHC
1994	90	73	89	90	79	10	20	42	11	8	14
1993	90	—	100	100	83	25	—	18	4	—	—

National Journal Ratings

	1993 LIB	—	1993 CONS	1994 LIB	—	1994 CONS
Economic	68%	—	26%	83%	—	0%
Social	67%	—	33%	75%	—	25%
Foreign	74%	—	22%	77%	—	22%

Key Votes of the 103d Congress

1. Clinton Deficit Plan	Y	3. Brady Handgun Purchase Y	5. Lmt. UN Cmnd. of Forces N
2. NAFTA	N	4. Strike Race/Death Pnlty. N	6. Cut Missile Funds	N

Key Votes of the 104th Congress

1. Congressional Compliance Y	6. Reform Crime Grant	N	11. Loser Pays Court Reform N
2. Balanced Budget Amndmt. N	7. National Security Act	N	12. Product Liability Reform N
3. Bar Unfunded Mandates N	8. Moratorium on Regs.	N	13. Welfare Reform	N
4. Pass Line Item Veto	*	9. Risk Assessment on Regs. N	14. Term Limits Amndmt.	N
5. Relax Exclusionary Rule N	10. Expnd. Priv. Prop. Rights N	15. Tax Cuts	N

Election Results

1994 general	Walter R. Tucker III (D)	64,166	(77%)	($269,976)
	Guy Wilson (Lib)	18,502	(22%)	($34,640)
1994 primary	Walter R. Tucker III (D)	27,590	(84%)	
	Lew Prulitsky (D)	5,197	(16%)	
1992 general	Walter R. Tucker III (D)	97,159	(86%)	($277,586)
	B. Kwaku Duren (P&F)	16,178	(14%)	($4,129)

THIRTY-EIGHTH DISTRICT

Long Beach, founded in 1888, with 434,000 people in 1990, would be a major metropolis anywhere but in Los Angeles County where it seems just the largest of many suburbs. But it has an identity of its own. Started as a beach resort, it soon became a port when Los Angeles civic leaders decided that if their town were to be a world-class city it must have a world-class harbor; nature not having provided one, they built it where the Los Angeles River merges into the ocean at Long Beach. By 1909, Los Angeles had annexed the harbor towns of San Pedro and Wilmington next to Long Beach; over the next decades the two cities persuaded the government to dredge channels and build a breakwater and turning basins. Long Beach was developing other businesses as well: it sprouted oil derricks in the 1920s and briefly became one of the nation's big oil producers; it was the site of major aircraft plants in the 1940s and after. By the 1980s, the Los Angeles-Long Beach port was the nation's largest, the fastest-growing major cargo center in the world, with huge steel-gray container ships pulling quietly up to enormous automated loading facilities—a 21st Century contrast to the rotting docks of New York and San Francisco. Long Beach even acquired the *Queen Mary*, which became its biggest tourist attraction, and, until it was sawed apart and taken to a museum in Oregon, Howard Hughes's "Spruce Goose," the huge cargo seaplane that was piloted just once across this harbor in 1946. Long Beach's downtown, once full of rundown 1920s buildings and pawn shops, now has an array of glittering 1980s high-rises and the area has become a favorite for Japanese and Asian companies' American headquarters. Long Beach stands to be hurt by closure of its naval shipyard and cutbacks at the huge McDonnell Douglas plant, but it has shown it has the vitality to overcome setbacks and grow again.

The 38th Congressional District includes most of Long Beach, the beachfront and harbor and airport. It extends north and inland to include the post-World War II suburbs of Lakewood, Paramount, Bellflower and Downey. This is middle-class country, but not monochromatic; the 38th excludes some black areas of Long Beach but in 1990 was 26% Hispanic and 9% Asian.

Defense contracts and bases are important in Long Beach, and Downey has the Rockwell plant that builds the space shuttle. Politically, the 38th has a Republican tilt; it voted for Bill Clinton in 1992 but gave larger margins to Pete Wilson in 1990 and 1994.

The Congressman from the 38th is Steve Horn, a Republican first elected in 1992, at 61, and one with a background unusual in his party's conference. Horn was an aide to President Eisenhower's labor secretary in the 1950s and to California Senator Thomas Kuchel in the 1960s. He was in Everett Dirksen's office helping draft the language of the Voting Rights Act in those stirring days of 1965, and he served on the U.S. Commission on Civil Rights from 1969 to 1982. Horn is also a political scientist Ph.D., who has written books on parliamentary procedures, the Senate Appropriations Committee and campaign finance. He worked at the Brookings Institution, was a dean at American University in Washington, and then from 1970 to 1988 was president of Cal State at Long Beach, leaving the job when he first ran for Congress. That race was in a district that stretched from Long Beach far into Orange County, and he ran third, with 20%, behind the more conservative and flamboyant Dana Rohrabacher. In 1992 he ran in the newly drawn 38th. In the primary the pro-choice Horn beat pro-life former Assemblyman Dennis Brown by 105 votes out of 45,000 cast, 29.8%–29.5%. In the general he faced Long Beach Councilman Evan Anderson Braude, stepson of Congressman Glenn Anderson, who was retiring at 79 after 22 years in Congress and 44 years in elective office, including the chairmanship of the Public Works Committee from 1988 to 1991. Horn emphasized his pro-choice stand and took solid Republican stands on a spending freeze, workfare, tort reform and trade; he accepted no PAC money and ran his campaign out of his son's apartment, sending out 50,000 15-minute videos to voters. He won by a 49%–43% margin.

In the 103d Congress Horn was moderate on issues but critical of the heavyhandedness of the Democratic leadership. He was one of the Republican freshmen who got select committees abolished and discharge petitions open to the public. With Representative Jane Harman he worked to get funding for the C-17 transport plane and pushed unsuccessfully for campaign finance reform. He supported the North American Free Trade Agreement and the General Agreement on Tariffs and Trade. He worked to preserve Long Beach oil production and to build a new transportation technology center there. After winning in 1994 by a 58%–37% margin, he worked with Californians of both parties to curb illegal immigration by urging a tamperproof social security card, strengthening the border patrol and sending prisoners back to their home countries. In 1995 he was named chairman of the Subcommittee on Government Management on the Government Reform and Oversight Committee. Bipartisan when possible, but supporting the Republicans in partisan disputes, Horn with his scholarly background is an interesting and almost unique member in the 104th Congress.

The People: Pop. 1990: 572,676; 12% age 65+; 58% White; 8% Black; 1% Amer. Indian; 9% Asian; 13% Other; 25% Hispanic origin. Voting age pop.: 435,490; 7% Black; 22% Hispanic origin. Households: 46% married couple families; 21% married couple fams. w. children; 53% college educ.; median household income: $34,364; per capita income: $16,497; median gross rent: $636; median house value: $222,700.

1992 Presidential Vote

Clinton (D)	88,728	(44%)
Bush (R)	66,647	(33%)
Perot (I)	43,596	(22%)

1988 Presidential Vote

Bush (R)	108,815	(56%)
Dukakis (D)	85,262	(44%)

Rep. Stephen Horn (R)

Elected 1992; b. May 31, 1931, San Juan Bautista; home, Long Beach; Stanford U., A.B. 1953, Harvard U., M.P.A. 1955, Stanford U., Ph.D. 1958; Protestant; married (Nini).

Career: Army Reserves, Strategic Intelligence, 1954–62; A.A., U.S. Labor Secy. James Mitchell, 1959–60; Legis. Asst., U.S. Sen. Thomas Kuchel, 1960–66; Sr. Fellow, Brookings Inst., 1966–69; Dean, Grad. Studies, American U., 1969–70; Vice Chmn./Mbr., U.S. Commission on Civil Rights, 1969–82; Pres., CA St. U. at Long Beach, 1970–88; Chmn., Amer. Assn. of State Cols. and Universities, 1985–86; Prof., CA St. U. at Long Beach 1988–92.

DC Office: 129 CHOB 20515, 202-225-6676; Fax: 202-225-1012.

District Offices: 4010 Watson Plaza Dr., #160, Lakewood 90712, 310-425-1336.

Committees: *Government Reform & Oversight* (10th of 27 R): Government Management, Information and Technology (Chmn.). *Transportation & Infrastructure* (17th of 33 R): Surface Transportation; Water Resources and Environment.

Group Ratings

	ADA	ACLU	COPE	CFA	LCV	CON	NSI	COC	ACU	NTLC	CHC
1994	30	48	33	40	33	52	70	91	57	71	43
1993	40	—	58	60	57	16	—	91	63	—	—

National Journal Ratings

	1993 LIB — 1993 CONS	1994 LIB — 1994 CONS
Economic	39% — 61%	37% — 61%
Social	49% — 50%	42% — 58%
Foreign	17% — 76%	33% — 67%

Key Votes of the 103d Congress

1. Clinton Deficit Plan	N	3. Brady Handgun Purchase Y	5. Lmt. UN Cmnd. of Forces Y
2. NAFTA	Y	4. Strike Race/Death Pnlty. Y	6. Cut Missile Funds	N

Key Votes of the 104th Congress

1. Congressional Compliance Y	6. Reform Crime Grant Y	11. Loser Pays Court Reform Y
2. Balanced Budget Amndmt. Y	7. National Security Act Y	12. Product Liability Reform Y
3. Bar Unfunded Mandates Y	8. Moratorium on Regs. Y	13. Welfare Reform Y
4. Pass Line Item Veto Y	9. Risk Assessment on Regs. Y	14. Term Limits Amndmt. Y
5. Relax Exclusionary Rule Y	10. Expnd. Priv. Prop. Rights Y	15. Tax Cuts Y

Election Results

1994 general	Stephen Horn (R)	85,225	(58%)	($442,982)
	Peter Mathews (D)	53,681	(37%)	($433,706)
	Others	6,863	(5%)	
1994 primary	Stephen Horn (R)	28,323	(76%)	
	John B. Duke (R)	8,886	(24%)	
1992 general	Stephen Horn (R)	92,038	(49%)	($441,198)
	Evan Anderson Braude (D)	82,108	(43%)	($514,381)
	Paul Burton (P&F)	8,391	(4%)	
	Blake Ashley (Lib)	6,756	(4%)	

THIRTY-NINTH DISTRICT

When Walt Disney began planning Disneyland in the late 1940s, he did not have to drive far southeast of downtown Los Angeles before coming into agricultural land. Dairy farms and orange groves covered most of southeast Los Angeles County and Orange County, which had only 216,000 people in 1950, five years before Disneyland opened there in 1955. As Disneyland became a vast success, the area around it, a mass of flat land surrounded by mountains and sea, found itself directly in the path of settlement of the most explosively growing metropolitan area in the United States. Orange County's population rose to 703,000 in 1960, 1.4 million in 1970, 1.9 million in 1980 and 2.4 million in 1990.

Always Republican, Orange County became a symbol of conservatism first in California and then nationally; in the 1988 election, only three counties in the nation cast more votes, and Orange County produced the largest plurality, 317,000, for George Bush. Orange County's conservatism reflected a belief in technological progress and traditional values as unyielding as the mile-square grid the county's founders imposed on most of its land, a belief in the market economics that had produced such wonders as Disneyland and the area's advanced military technologies. But these faiths have been tried on occasion. In 1992, with Orange County deep in recession and defense industry layoffs commonplace, Bill Clinton actually led George Bush in some Orange County polls during the summer campaign; and in November Bush won only a 119,000-vote plurality, a disaster not only for him but for Republicans generally in California. As it turned out, that vote was a precursor to a shocking loss of faith in the county's tradition of market economics: In December 1994, the county was forced to declare bankruptcy because of sloppy investment and bookkeeping practices. Although the political impact was uncertain (the top financial official in charge was a Democrat, but Republicans controlled most offices), the financial impact initially appeared likely to weaken public confidence in government, across the state and perhaps beyond. Shortly afterwards, Walt Disney shelved plans for a two billion dollar resort development that would have doubled the size of Disneyland, a further blow to local officials and businesses.

The 39th Congressional District consists of an area that was mostly farmland when Disneyland was being laid out. In Los Angeles County, its largest community is Cerritos, once all dairy farms, now a suburb with a marvelous Angeleno mix: 45% Asian, 36% white Anglos, 12% Hispanic. La Mirada to the north is more upscale, as are the La Habra communities which span the LA-Orange County line. The biggest Orange County city here is Fullerton, with its own branch of Cal State University and its closed Hughes plant; to the southwest are Buena Park, home of the earliest theme park, Knott's Berry Farm, plus Cypress, Los Alamitos and Rossmoor. The 39th also pushes east of Fullerton to include, by just a few blocks, the Richard Nixon Library and birthplace in Yorba Linda.

The 39th District's Congressman, Ed Royce, was four years old and growing up in Anaheim when Disneyland opened; his life almost precisely covers the post-World War II growth of Orange County. Like Orange County, he has long been conservative: he was in the Young Americans for Freedom at Cal State Fullerton; he worked several years as a tax and capital projects manager for a cement company. In 1982, a bunch of conservative legislators known as "the Cave Men" took him to a Black Angus restaurant—no avocado and bean sprout sandwiches for them—and after a few beers persuaded him to run for the state Senate. He did and at age 31 won. The *California Political Almanac* called him "one of the quieter members of the Senate," but he did have an impact. He sponsored a law making stalking a crime, now copied in many other states. When the legislature refused to pass his legislation allowing crime victims to object to trial delays, giving grand juries more power and ending shopping for juries, he put it on the ballot as an initiative and it passed by a wide margin in 1990. He helps crime victims get jobs and encourages them to attend Republican fundraisers. Many Vietnamese have moved to Orange County, and Royce passed a law making it easier for University of Saigon graduates to practice medicine in California.

Royce was the natural choice to run for the 39th District seat when its incumbent, William Dannemeyer, a fierce opponent of gay rights and critic of gay activist groups, decided to make what turned out to be a quixotic race against his fellow Orange Countian, Senator John Seymour, in the 1992 U.S. Senate primary. With the blessing of Orange County Republican leaders and his own strength, Royce had no opposition in the decisive Republican primary. In a bad Republican year Royce won the general 57%–38%. In the House, he amassed an unspectacular but solidly conservative record, except on foreign policy issues where he appears leery of U.S. involvement abroad; he surprised many when he voted against the North American Free Trade Agreement. On the Science Committee, he was a champion of high technology such as digital compression technology, and he wants to pass the Federal Anti-Stalking bill and Repeat Offenders Accountability Act, provisions of which were incorporated in the Crime Bill adopted by the Senate in 1994. He also introduced a constitutional amendment to outlaw retroactive taxation. He joined the Banking Committee in 1995, in part to help Orange County deal with its major financial problems—another example of a politician casting aside anti-government rhetoric when his constituents are in need. He was reelected without difficulty in 1994.

The People: Pop. 1990: 573,941; 9% age 65+; 61% White; 3% Black; 1% Amer. Indian; 14% Asian; 10% Other; 22% Hispanic origin. Voting age pop.: 430,720; 2% Black; 20% Hispanic origin. Households: 62% married couple families; 29% married couple fams. w. children; 58% college educ.; median household income: $46,196; per capita income: $18,190; median gross rent: $736; median house value: $236,600.

1992 Presidential Vote			1988 Presidential Vote		
Bush (R)	100,669	(44%)	Bush (R)	149,866	(66%)
Clinton (D)	78,305	(34%)	Dukakis (D)	76,137	(34%)
Perot (I)	50,834	(22%)			

Rep. Edward R. Royce (R)

Elected 1992; b. Oct. 12, 1951, Los Angeles; home, Fullerton; CA St. U., B.S. 1977; Catholic; married (Marie).

Career: Tax Manager, 1978–81; CA Senate, 1982–92.

DC Office: 1133 LHOB 20515, 202-225-4111; Fax: 202-225-0335.

District Offices: 305 N. Harbor Blvd., #300, Fullerton 92632, 714-992-8081.

Committees: *Banking & Financial Services* (11th of 27 R): Domestic and International Monetary Policy; Financial Institutions and Consumer Credit. *International Relations* (15th of 23 R): Asia and the Pacific; International Operations and Human Rights.

Group Ratings

	ADA	ACLU	COPE	CFA	LCV	CON	NSI	COC	ACU	NTLC	CHC
1994	10	14	11	0	13	94	90	83	95	96	100
1993	20	—	8	0	29	91	—	91	96	—	—

National Journal Ratings

	1993 LIB — 1993 CONS	1994 LIB — 1994 CONS
Economic	12% — 87%	0% — 80%
Social	0% — 89%	0% — 89%
Foreign	33% — 65%	25% — 75%

Key Votes of the 103d Congress

1. Clinton Deficit Plan N	3. Brady Handgun Purchase N	5. Lmt. UN Cmnd. of Forces Y
2. NAFTA N	4. Strike Race/Death Pnlty. Y	6. Cut Missile Funds Y

Key Votes of the 104th Congress

1. Congressional Compliance Y	6. Reform Crime Grant Y	11. Loser Pays Court Reform Y
2. Balanced Budget Amndmt. Y	7. National Security Act Y	12. Product Liability Reform Y
3. Bar Unfunded Mandates Y	8. Moratorium on Regs. Y	13. Welfare Reform Y
4. Pass Line Item Veto Y	9. Risk Assessment on Regs. Y	14. Term Limits Amndmt. Y
5. Relax Exclusionary Rule Y	10. Expnd. Priv. Prop. Rights Y	15. Tax Cuts Y

Election Results

1994 general	Edward R. Royce (R)	113,037	(66%)	($403,335)
	Bob Davis (D)	49,459	(29%)	($3,755)
	Jack Dean (Lib)	7,862	(5%)	
1994 primary	Edward R. Royce (R)	unopposed		
1992 general	Edward R. Royce (R)	122,472	(57%)	($529,196)
	Molly McClanahan (D)	81,728	(38%)	($92,510)
	Jack Dean (Lib)	9,484	(4%)	

FORTIETH DISTRICT

Over the last two decades the great American movement west has turned back east, at least in California. As settlement reached the Pacific Coast, young families looking for affordable houses and neighborhoods and schools, where traditional values are respected, moved away from the liberation-minded and high-crime coast and toward the sunny, often hot, valleys inland. This impulse has resulted in rapid growth in the Central Valley, the repopulation of the Mother Lode country in the foothills of the Sierras and the startling growth in the eastern end of the Los Angeles Basin, around San Bernardino and Riverside, and east and north past the mountain rims into the desert. This "Inland Empire" of San Bernardino grew so robustly in the 1980s, from 1.6 million to 2.6 million, that it increased from three congressional districts to five.

One of these is the 40th Congressional District, which covers most of the land area of America's physically largest county, San Bernardino, though its population is concentrated in just a few places. About one-third of its people live on the eastern edge of San Bernardino itself, or around Loma Linda, Redlands and Yucaipa—small towns formed by pious Midwesterners at the base of 10,000-foot mountains, now part of the expanding Los Angeles suburban strip. North of the mountains, out beyond the wind-torn El Cajon Pass in the scorching desert, are Victorville and Apple Valley, once tiny gas station stops on the road to Las Vegas; Roy Rogers and Dale Evans lived for years on a ranch here, with their stuffed Trigger, Buttermilk and Bullet in a nearby museum. Now vast subdivisions and the new city of Hesperia have grown up here, housing more than 150,000 people. The rest of the people of the 40th are scattered across the desert, in ghost towns and weapons testing sites, in Twentynine Palms and its Marine base. The 40th has some of the nation's hottest temperatures and some of its lowest rainfall, the lower 48 states' highest point at Mount Whitney and lowest point in Death Valley.

The congressman from the 40th is Jerry Lewis, a House member since 1978, an assemblyman for 10 years before that and a House Republican leader from 1984 to 1992. Up to that point his career followed the usual path of House Republican leaders of earlier generations. He was an insurance agent in Redlands, a joiner in civic causes, when he was elected to the Assembly at 34. In the House, he got a seat on the Appropriations Committee, where bipartisan cooperation was the norm, enabling even minority members to confer favors on their districts. He eventually became ranking Republican on the Legislative Subcommittee, working amicably on Congress's budget with fellow Californian, chairman Vic Fazio. This was Robert Michel's route to the minority leadership, and Lewis seemed to be moving up the ladder: chairman of the Republican Research Committee in 1984, chairman of the Republican Policy Committee in 1986, Conference chairman (by three votes over Lynn Martin) in 1988.

But there he stalled. As House Republicans were becoming hungrier for confrontation with Democrats, Lewis was becoming more accommodation-minded. In March 1989, when Republican Whip Dick Cheney was appointed Secretary of Defense, Lewis was squeezed between Edward Madigan, who had Michel's support, and party rebel Newt Gingrich, and decided not to run. In 1990, Lewis loyally supported President Bush's budget summit agreement with tax increases, while Gingrich opposed them and backbencher Dick Armey forced a Conference vote against them. After the 1990 election, Gingrich supported the challenge by Carl Pursell of Michigan to Lewis for the House Republican Conference chair; Lewis won by a clear but unimpressive 98–64 vote. But he was removed by California Republicans as their representative on the party's committee on committees. In 1991 he continued to boast how well he got along with Democrats. So Armey challenged him for Conference chairman in December 1992 and won 88–84: that put Gingrich and Armey in line to become Speaker and Majority Leader when Republicans won their majority and Lewis to win the not inconsequential consolation prize of becoming an Appropriations subcommittee chairman.

Ironically, Lewis is a solid conservative on some, though not all, issues. He supported the balanced budget amendment with a supermajority to raise taxes. He fought hard against the George Miller-Dianne Feinstein version of the 1994 Desert Protection Act and claimed partial credit (giving some to Democrats) for amendments protecting hunting, private property rights, law enforcement access and "guzzlers," water sources critical to desert species, in protected lands, much of which falls in his district. On local issues, he worked hard to get a Defense Department finance center at closed Norton Air Force Base and to help the local development authority redevelop it and George Air Force Base. He worked for a medical facility at Loma Linda University and on behalf of a national bone marrow transplant registry. He backs tough clean air standards (smog backs up against the mountains in the Inland Empire) but in 1995 seeks to remove federal control of California's clean air plans. He wants to widen I-15 and I-40 in fast-growing desert areas.

In 1995 he not only became chairman of the VA-HUD-Independent Agencies Appropriations Subcommittee which regulates funding for NASA and the EPA, but also gained influence on the Intelligence Committee, chairing the Subcommittee on Intelligence and Counterintelligence—both serious assignments. As an appropriations "cardinal," he supervises housing funds that most Republicans, including himself, view as a prime target for spending cuts. And he has not lost a certain aggressiveness: one evening in May 1994 he saw a thief driving his 1984 Oldsmobile away from a parking place on Capitol Hill and chased the car down Pennsylvania Avenue until it crashed and police arrested the man two blocks away. In 1994, as in other years, Lewis won reelection by a wide margin.

The People: Pop. 1990: 573,939; 18% rural; 12% age 65+; 74% White; 5% Black; 2% Amer. Indian; 4% Asian; 7% Other; 16% Hispanic origin. Voting age pop.: 407,775; 5% Black; 13% Hispanic origin. Households: 60% married couple families; 30% married couple fams. w. children; 49% college educ.; median household income: $30,408; per capita income: $13,568; median gross rent: $507; median house value: $110,300.

1992 Presidential Vote

Bush (R)	86,453	(39%)
Clinton (D)	76,363	(35%)
Perot (I)	53,955	(25%)

1988 Presidential Vote

Bush (R)	108,755	(64%)
Dukakis (D)	60,975	(36%)

Rep. Jerry Lewis (R)

Elected 1978; b. Oct. 21, 1934, Seattle, WA; home, Redlands; U. of CA, B.A. 1956; Presbyterian; married (Arlene).

Career: Insurance exec., 1959–78; Field rep., U.S. Rep. Jerry Pettis, 1968; CA Assembly, 1968–78.

DC Office: 2112 RHOB 20515, 202-225-5861; Fax: 202-225-6498.

District Offices: 1150 Brookside Ave., Redlands 92374, 909-862-6030.

Committees: *Appropriations* (6th of 32 R): National Security; VA, HUD, and Independent Agencies (Chmn.). *Intelligence (Permanent Select)* (5th of 9 R): Human Intelligence, Analysis, and Counterintelligence (Chmn.); Technical and Tactical Intelligence.

Group Ratings

	ADA	ACLU	COPE	CFA	LCV	CON	NSI	COC	ACU	NTLC	CHC
1994	0	22	13	20	6	46	100	82	88	7	100
1993	0	—	8	0	29	64	—	100	88	—	—

National Journal Ratings

	1993 LIB — 1993 CONS			1994 LIB — 1994 CONS		
Economic	20%	—	77%	42%	—	58%
Social	28%	—	71%	23%	—	76%
Foreign	17%	—	76%	34%	—	63%

Key Votes of the 103d Congress

1. Clinton Deficit Plan	N	3. Brady Handgun Purchase	N	5. Lmt. UN Cmnd. of Forces	Y
2. NAFTA	Y	4. Strike Race/Death Pnlty.	Y	6. Cut Missile Funds	N

Key Votes of the 104th Congress

1. Congressional Compliance	Y	6. Reform Crime Grant	Y	11. Loser Pays Court Reform	Y
2. Balanced Budget Amndmt.	Y	7. National Security Act	Y	12. Product Liability Reform	Y
3. Bar Unfunded Mandates	Y	8. Moratorium on Regs.	Y	13. Welfare Reform	Y
4. Pass Line Item Veto	Y	9. Risk Assessment on Regs.	Y	14. Term Limits Amndmt.	N
5. Relax Exclusionary Rule	Y	10. Expnd. Priv. Prop. Rights	Y	15. Tax Cuts	Y

Election Results

1994 general	Jerry Lewis (R)	115,728	(71%)	($209,763)
	Donald M. Rusk (D)	48,003	(29%)	($39,544)
1994 primary	Jerry Lewis (R)	34,311	(69%)	
	George Craig (R)	9,217	(19%)	
	Richard E. Schmitter (R)	3,708	(8%)	
	John D. Henderson (R)	2,235	(5%)	
1992 general	Jerry Lewis (R)	129,563	(63%)	($546,541)
	Donald M. Rusk (D)	63,881	(31%)	($21,555)
	Margie Akin (P&F)	11,839	(6%)	

FORTY-FIRST DISTRICT

One of the areas of explosive growth in the 1980s boom years in California was in the eastern end of the Los Angeles Basin—the Inland Empire, as it is now called. Mostly orange groves a couple of decades ago, this territory now is the site of rapid economic growth, personal upward mobility and ethnic and cultural harmony. The secret of the economic growth is small entrepreneurial businesses, usually started by people with no particular connections or advantages—increasingly, of Asian or Latino immigrant background. California has never been a land of leisure, as stereotype would have it, but rather a place for hard work, where neither the amazing fertility of the soil nor the amazing productivity of the people has happened without a lot of effort and, one might add, a tolerant and welcoming attitude toward newcomers. California hasn't always welcomed people from strange places—a strain of anti-Asian feeling expressed itself in the Chinese Exclusion Act of 1882 and the Japanese American relocation camps of 1942–44—but certainly since World War II this has been one of the least prejudiced and most welcoming places on earth, a reason why it has been receiving more immigrants than any other American state.

The 41st Congressional District, in the Inland Empire, is one place where such trends are visible. The 41st is centered on the point where Los Angeles, San Bernardino and Orange Counties come together. In San Bernardino County it includes most of Ontario and its airport and industrial zone, plus the higher income towns of Montclair and Upland; it includes the old town of Pomona, now much expanded, site of the Los Angeles County Fair, and fast-growing Diamond Bar; it includes Chino, site of a low security prison, and subdivisions below the Chino Hills; over the hills in Orange County, it includes Yorba Linda, site (just beyond the district line) of the birthplace of Richard Nixon in 1913 (when Orange County had only 40,000 residents), and the site of the Richard Nixon Library now (when Orange County has 2.4 million and Yorba Linda 52,000). This was all rapidly growing country in the 1980s, filling up with two-worker households, parents scurrying to get their kids to school and drive dozens of miles on freeways to their jobs. Ethnically diverse, in the 1980s its residents were 32% Hispanic and 10% Asian, believers still in traditional values, working their way up through the private sector—and mostly strong Republicans.

The Congressman from the 41st, a new district created after the 1990 Census, is Jay Kim, one of the most distinctive members of the House. He was born in Korea, where his father managed a restaurant; their house was destroyed in the Korean war and they had to walk 90 miles to safety. He came to California in 1961, got an engineering degree from Southern California in 1967 and became city engineer for Ontario and Compton. In 1976, with a Small Business Administration loan, he started Jaykim Engineers, designing highways, water reclamation plants and other big projects—mostly government contracts, some minority set-asides. In 1984 he got an Army Corps of Engineers contract for the Los Angeles district and later an $8.7 million contract for Los Angeles's Metro Rail. In 1990 he built a $1 million dreamhouse in Diamond Bar and immediately ran for City Council, placing first in a nine-candidate race, and ultimately serving as mayor from 1991–92. This was perhaps characteristic: friends remember he was always interested in politics. In 1992, even while his firm was having problems, he ran for Congress. He campaigned for lower taxes and privatizing government services, against illegal immigration and for abortion rights. He loaned his campaign some $169,000 and raised about an equal amount, outspending two seasoned Republican primary opponents, Pomona Assemblyman Charles Bader and former Washington lawyer James Lacy. Kim won the primary with 30% to 28% for Bader and 27% for Lacy; in the general he prevailed 60%–34%.

That made Kim the first Korean-American member of Congress (but not the first Asian immigrant in Congress: that was Dalip Saund, from California's Imperial Valley, in 1956). Then a cloud appeared: in July 1993 the *Los Angeles Times* reported that his company had spent $400,000 on his campaign, a supposedly illegal corporate contribution. But $300,000 of that was his salary, which is not extraordinary: candidates can be paid salaries when they run and usually are, and he wholly owned the company anyway, though he sold it after he was elected. He did admit that he should have paid the company rent for office facilities and did so. In the end, no legal or ethics charges were brought. On issues Kim made a mostly conservative record, though one somewhat liberal on economics. But he also sought more money for transportation projects—the kind of work he had done while in the private sector—and had bills to help entrepreneurs in their relations with government, by redefining independent contractors under the tax law, allowing repair shops as well as car dealers to operate on-board diagnostic systems under the Clean Air Act and getting federal money to keep Orange County transit running after the county government's bankruptcy in December 1994. He opposed welfare for illegal immigrants but warned against backlash against legal immigrants. At the same time he spoke frequently in hard-line tones. "In a free enterprise system, hard work pays off. I've always believed that. If you don't work hard, too bad, you're going to fall behind." After refusing in his first term to join the International Relations Committee, noting that he had no special agenda for Koren-Americans, he finally became a member in 1995, with a seat on the Asia and the Pacific Subcommittee.

The controversy about Kim's campaign spending spurred primary opposition in 1994 and raised Republican fears that he would not survive. In the three-candidate Republican primary, which featured extremely negative campaigning focused on Kim's alleged improprieties, he won with only 41%—far below what incumbents usually get, though well ahead of the next finisher. He won the general election in this very Republican district with 62%. He has pledged to serve no more than three terms, but may have serious competition for a third in 1996.

The People: Pop. 1990: 572,529; 1% rural; 6% age 65+; 52% White; 7% Black; 1% Amer. Indian; 10% Asian; 14% Other; 31% Hispanic origin. Voting age pop.: 400,202; 7% Black; 28% Hispanic origin. Households: 65% married couple families; 38% married couple fams. w. children; 55% college educ.; median household income: $44,607; per capita income: $16,002; median gross rent: $656; median house value: $202,700.

1992 Presidential Vote			1988 Presidential Vote		
Bush (R)	78,902	(42%)	Bush (R)	110,058	(66%)
Clinton (D)	64,666	(35%)	Dukakis (D)	55,645	(34%)
Perot (I)	41,112	(22%)			

Rep. Jay Kim (R)

Elected 1992; b. Mar. 27, 1939, Seoul, Korea; home, Diamond Bar; U. of Southern CA, B.S. 1967, M.S., 1973, CA St. U., M.P.A. 1980; Methodist; married (June).

Career: Founder & Pres., Jaykim Engineers, 1977–93; Diamond Bar City Cncl., 1990–91, Diamond Bar Mayor, 1991–92.

DC Office: 435 CHOB 20515, 202-225-3201; Fax: 202-225-1485.

District Offices: 1131 W. 6th St., #160-A, Ontario 91762, 909-988-1055; and 18200 Yorba Linda Blvd., #203-A, Yorba Linda 92686, 714-572-8574.

Committees: *International Relations* (17th of 23 R): Asia and the Pacific. *Transportation & Infrastructure* (16th of 33 R): Aviation; Railroads; Surface Transportation.

Group Ratings

	ADA	ACLU	COPE	CFA	LCV	CON	NSI	COC	ACU	NTLC	CHC
1994	5	13	0	20	6	67	90	100	95	93	93
1993	10	—	0	10	36	91	—	100	92	—	—

National Journal Ratings

	1993 LIB — 1993 CONS		1994 LIB — 1994 CONS	
Economic	25%	— 72%	34%	— 64%
Social	11%	— 82%	16%	— 81%
Foreign	9%	— 85%	0%	— 88%

Key Votes of the 103d Congress

1. Clinton Deficit Plan	N	3. Brady Handgun Purchase	N	5. Lmt. UN Cmnd. of Forces	Y
2. NAFTA	Y	4. Strike Race/Death Pnlty.	Y	6. Cut Missile Funds	N

Key Votes of the 104th Congress

1. Congressional Compliance	Y	6. Reform Crime Grant	Y	11. Loser Pays Court Reform	Y
2. Balanced Budget Amndmt.	Y	7. National Security Act	Y	12. Product Liability Reform	Y
3. Bar Unfunded Mandates	Y	8. Moratorium on Regs.	Y	13. Welfare Reform	Y
4. Pass Line Item Veto	Y	9. Risk Assessment on Regs.	Y	14. Term Limits Amndmt.	Y
5. Relax Exclusionary Rule	Y	10. Expnd. Priv. Prop. Rights	Y	15. Tax Cuts	Y

Election Results

1994 general	Jay Kim (R)	81,854	(62%)	($810,211)
	Ed Tessier (D)	49,924	(38%)	($73,244)
1994 primary	Jay Kim (R)	14,028	(41%)	
	Valerie Romero (R)	7,077	(21%)	
	Bob Kerns (R)	6,528	(19%)	
	Todd R. Thakar (R)	5,422	(16%)	
	Ronald L. Curtis (R)	1,388	(4%)	
1992 general	Jay Kim (R)	101,753	(60%)	($764,895)
	Bob Baker (D)	58,777	(34%)	
	Mike Noonan (P&F)	10,136	(6%)	($35)

FORTY-SECOND DISTRICT

The gateway to the Los Angeles Basin for decades was San Bernardino, situated on flat land where the route through the twisting, windy El Cajon Pass took passengers on the Santa Fe Railroad and motorists on U.S. 66 from the hot and dusty desert to the greener, tree-lined basin. There were orange groves around the little railroad towns and vineyards to the west; this was an agricultural zone until World War II, when Henry J. Kaiser built the West Coast's first major steel mill between the Santa Fe and Southern Pacific lines in Fontana, just west of San Bernardino. Today, these lands have largely filled up. This Inland Empire, as it is called, may be where the smog piles up against the mountains, but it also has some of the lowest real estate prices in the Los Angeles Basin and in the 1980s a thriving small business economy.

The 42d Congressional District consists of most of San Bernardino and the towns running west—low-income Rialto, Fontana with many other businesses replacing the closed steel mill (the blast furnaces were dismantled and reassembled in China), fast-growing Rancho Cucamonga. It is 34% Hispanic, 11% black and only 4% Asian. Politically this area trended Republican in the 1980s, as the cultural liberalism of California Democrats repelled the family oriented here, but when the economy slowed and real estate prices plummeted in the early 1990s, it swung toward Bill Clinton and the Democrats.

The Congressman from the 42d District is George Brown, a Democrat who in 1995 was serving his 31st year in the House. An engineer with a Quaker upbringing who has long cared about arms control issues, Brown worked for 17 years for the city of Los Angeles. In 1958 he was Mayor of Monterey Park, far to the west; in that banner Democratic year, he was elected to the California Assembly and served on the redistricting committee. Lo and behold, he got one of California's eight new districts in 1962. He ran for the Senate in 1970 and almost beat John Tunney in the primary; if he had, he might well have won the general. Brown found a new district in 1972 in the Inland Empire, and Phillip Burton redrew the lines in 1982 to help him through another decade. But Brown has not won by landslides: against a religious fundamentalist, a small town businessman and a San Bernardino County supervisor, he won between 53% and 57% in the 1980s. His military dovishness over the years has moderated into support for local defense installations, and he has long been a supporter of space exploration. In 1990 he inherited the chairmanship of the House Science Committee. There he supported both manned and unmanned space exploration, backing a new space launch vehicle and the space shuttle. He worked to restructure the national weapons laboratories and maintain the Landsat remote-sensing system. He supported federal aid for emerging technologies and development of electric vehicles and solar energy. He looked forward to working with Vice President Albert Gore, a former Science Committee member, as "heaven on earth," and he had the pleasure of seeing Science become a sought-after assignment in 1993. The space shuttle did survive serious challenges, and Brown showed his feistiness by getting into a dispute with John Murtha of the Appropriations Committee over what Brown regarded as undue earmarking of projects.

Brown has continued to have serious challenges at home in the 1990s. The new district lines in 1992 were not as favorable as the old, and in 1992 he faced Dick Rutan, the developer and pilot (with partner Jeana Yeager) of the Voyager plane which in 1986 circled the earth without refueling. With gobs of PAC money, Brown outspent Rutan 2–1 and even netted Yeager's support. Brown won 51%–44%. In 1994 he was opposed by Rob Guzman, his first Latino opponent, who owned a workplace training business called Templo Calvario Legalization & Education. Two years before, Guzman had run against Lucille Roybal-Allard in the 33d District in Los Angeles, a hopeless race. In this race he supported tough crime measures, ending aid for illegal immigrants, more funding for schools and vocational education through the congressional review process rather than the earmarking of funds and IRAs for first-time homebuyers. Brown outspent him, and again his luck held: he won 51%–49%. He is no longer chairman of Science but ranks first among Democrats there and second on Agriculture. Despite his low margin and Republicans' continuing efforts to unseat him, he cannot be counted out in 1996. But some Democrats worry that he might retire and that the party will have a hard time holding his seat.

The People: Pop. 1990: 571,595; 7% age 65+; 51% White; 11% Black; 1% Amer. Indian; 4% Asian; 18% Other; 34% Hispanic origin. Voting age pop.: 380,921; 10% Black; 30% Hispanic origin. Households: 58% married couple families; 35% married couple fams. w. children; 46% college educ.; median household income: $33,737; per capita income: $12,308; median gross rent: $562; median house value: $125,600.

1992 Presidential Vote

Clinton (D) 76,964 (45%)
Bush (R) 54,978 (32%)
Perot (I) 35,828 (21%)

1988 Presidential Vote

Bush (R) 77,923 (54%)
Dukakis (D) 65,735 (46%)

Rep. George E. Brown, Jr. (D)

Elected 1972; b. Mar. 6, 1920, Holtville; home, San Bernardino; U.C.L.A., B.A. 1946; United Methodist; married (Marta).

Career: Army, 1942–46 (WWII); Monterey Park City Cncl., 1954–58, Monterey Park Mayor, 1955–56; Personnel, Engineering and Mgmt. Consult., City of Los Angeles, 1957–61; CA Assembly, 1958–62; U.S. House of Reps., 1962–70.

DC Office: 2300 RHOB 20515, 202-225-6161; Fax: 202-225-8671.

District Offices: 657 La Cadena Dr., Colton 92324, 909-825-2472.

Committees: *Agriculture* (2nd of 22 D): Department Operations, Nutrition and Foreign Agriculture; Resource Conservation, Research and Forestry. *Science* (RMM of 23 D).

Group Ratings

	ADA	ACLU	COPE	CFA	LCV	CON	NSI	COC	ACU	NTLC	CHC
1994	80	83	78	80	76	1	20	33	10	8	0
1993	90	—	92	80	92	16	—	27	0	—	—

National Journal Ratings

	1993 LIB — 1993 CONS		1994 LIB — 1994 CONS	
Economic	78% —	12%	83% —	0%
Social	87% —	0%	87% —	13%
Foreign	87% —	7%	63% —	36%

Key Votes of the 103d Congress

1. Clinton Deficit Plan	Y	3. Brady Handgun Purchase	Y	5. Lmt. UN Cmnd. of Forces	N
2. NAFTA	Y	4. Strike Race/Death Pnlty.	N	6. Cut Missile Funds	Y

Key Votes of the 104th Congress

1. Congressional Compliance	Y	6. Reform Crime Grant	N	11. Loser Pays Court Reform	N
2. Balanced Budget Amndmt.	N	7. National Security Act	N	12. Product Liability Reform	N
3. Bar Unfunded Mandates	N	8. Moratorium on Regs.	N	13. Welfare Reform	*
4. Pass Line Item Veto	Y	9. Risk Assessment on Regs.	N	14. Term Limits Amndmt.	N
5. Relax Exclusionary Rule	N	10. Expnd. Priv. Prop. Rights	*	15. Tax Cuts	N

Election Results

1994 general	George E. Brown, Jr. (D)	58,888	(51%)	($485,455)
	Rob Guzman (R)	56,259	(49%)	($308,574)
1994 primary	George E. Brown, Jr. (D)	unopposed		
1992 general	George E. Brown, Jr. (D)	79,780	(51%)	($907,227)
	Dick Rutan (R).......................	69,251	(44%)	($443,272)
	Fritz R. Ward (Lib)	8,424	(5%)	

FORTY-THIRD DISTRICT

Riverside was a sleepy town of 34,000, a couple hours' drive from Los Angeles, when Richard and Pat Nixon were married in 1940 in the gaudy Mission Inn, with its bell towers, altars, fountains, rotunda, stained-glass windows and wrought-iron grilles. It was not much larger, with 46,000 people, when Ronald and Nancy Reagan spent their honeymoon, also at the Mission Inn, in 1952. Riverside was known then, if at all, as a citrus center, a market town amid orange groves, where the local agricultural college developed among other things the navel orange. Today the Mission Inn is still doing business, but Riverside has changed completely. The city has expanded to 226,000 people, and Riverside County, which had 105,000 people in 1940, had 663,000 in 1980 and 1.17 million in 1990—a 76% increase in one decade. Riverside County stretches east to Arizona, so some of this increase was in the desert, but much was in the Inland Empire around Riverside, where the flat Los Angeles Basin plains are interrupted by odd-shaped hills and ridges and the vegetation has an other-worldly air. There are odd by-products from such rapid development, like the dozens of 300-pound pigs that live in the river bed just outside Riverside. This was one of the boom parts of California in the 1980s, where modest-income families found new houses in inexpensive developments and small businesses expanded mightily; it was hit hard by the recession of the early 1990s, when the growth suddenly stopped.

The 43d Congressional District is one of two that were formed from the old 37th District which included most of Riverside County and was the fastest-growing in the country in the 1980s. This was a seat without an incumbent and with great political volatility—not accidental in an area where few voters have deep roots, where neither ethnic ties nor economic security produces strong commitment to either party, and where the economy has changed so sharply. The 43d District includes all of Riverside and the towns immediately around; another population node just to the west, around Corona; and new subdivisions scattered around I-215 and I-15, which run south from Riverside and Corona until they join at Murietta Hot Springs, just north of the new town of Temecula.

The Congressman from the 43d is Ken Calvert, a Republican who won the district by a narrow margin in 1992 and retained it under embarrassing circumstances in 1994. Calvert grew up in Corona; after college, he ran a restaurant there and in 1980 started in the commercial real estate business. In 1982, at 29, he ran for Congress and in the old Riverside County district lost a nine-candidate primary to Al McCandless by a 25%–24% margin: 868 votes kept him out of Congress for 10 years. He continued to be active in civic affairs and chaired the local Republican Party. In 1992 he ran for Congress in the new 43d—one of seven Republicans and seven Democrats—and won the primary with 28%, followed by business professor Joseph Khoury (who ran ads featuring Milton Berle), with 21%, and Larry Arnn, president of Claremont Institute, with 18%. His opponent, who won 29% of the Democratic votes, was Mark Takano, a 33-year-old eighth grade teacher and Riverside Community College trustee with institutional support from teachers' unions and financial support from Japanese-Americans; he edged the one woman and Latino candidate, Raven Workman, who had 20%. The general was close fought and along national lines: George Bush beat Bill Clinton in the district by 797 votes and Calvert beat Takano by 519 votes.

In the House, Calvert compiled a fairly moderate voting record and voted contentedly with Democrats on the Science Committee; he also served on the Resources Committee. But he ran into trouble back home. In November 1993 he was stopped by the Corona police with a convicted prostitute in his car; not much was reported about the incident but the *Riverside Press-Enterprise* brought suit to recover police records, and in April 1994 it revealed the police reports, which showed that Calvert had been partly undressed. Calvert responded that he was upset because his wife had divorced him the month before and his father had recently committed suicide. "I realize now that this, or a similar incident, was probably inevitable," he said. "My conduct that evening was inappropriate. It was inappropriate, not because it was illegal or violated the office I hold, but because it violated the values of the person I strive to be." Also, it was reported that Calvert and his ex-wife owed $16,000 in back taxes on a nine-acre lot. He argued that the tax liability had been overlooked during his divorce, and his ex-wife defended him against charges of intentional tax avoidance. But it was, as he said, "an extremely embarrassing situation," which his opponents rushed to take advantage of. Joseph Khoury, running again, was already attacking him as insufficiently conservative and chimed in on the scandal. Calvert won the primary 51%–49%, with only an 884-vote margin. Mark Takano, running again in the general, ran an ad with the song *The Liar* and accused him of "flagrant womanizing." At a public meeting, Republican Assemblyman Ray Haynes called Takano a "nutzoid" liberal homosexual. And so a contest of relative moderates—Takano called himself a "business-friendly Democrat"—became one of acerbic personal attacks. Calvert was rated the most endangered incumbent by *Roll Call*. But the Republican tide of the year showed up in the election results, with Calvert winning by a thumping 55%–38%.

In 1995 Calvert found himself, after several political near-death experiences, chairman of the Resources Committee's Energy and Mineral Resources Subcommittee, with jurisdiction over the Mining Act and geothermal energy; he will be in a position to deliver on his promise to modify and ease the Endangered Species Act. "We'd like to come up with something more reasonable within this year," Calvert told reporters just after taking office. "Government has to recognize that people have rights as property owners." He also got a waiver of rules so he could take a seat on Agriculture. He seemed enthusiastic, despite his moderate voting record, about the Contract With America. Most of all, he should be relieved that he had survived.

The People: Pop. 1990: 571,090; 14% rural; 8% age 65+; 65% White; 6% Black; 1% Amer. Indian; 4% Asian; 13% Other; 25% Hispanic origin. Voting age pop.: 400,969; 6% Black; 21% Hispanic origin. Households: 63% married couple families; 35% married couple fams. w. children; 50% college educ.; median household income: $37,806; per capita income: $14,449; median gross rent: $595; median house value: $153,200.

1992 Presidential Vote

Bush (R)	76,837	(38%)
Clinton (D)	76,040	(38%)
Perot (I)	48,197	(24%)

1988 Presidential Vote

Bush (R)	97,970	(60%)
Dukakis (D)	64,860	(40%)

Rep. Ken Calvert (R)

Elected 1992; b. June 8, 1953, Corona; home, Corona; San Diego St. U., B.A. 1975; Protestant; divorced.

Career: Restaurant Owner, 1975–80; Real estate broker, 1980–92; Chmn, Riverside Cnty. Repub. Party, 1984–88.

DC Office: 1034 LHOB 20515, 202-225-1986; Fax: 202-225-2004.

District Offices: 3400 Central Ave., #200, Riverside 92506, 909-784-4300.

Committees: *Agriculture* (19th of 27 R): Department Operations, Nutrition and Foreign Agriculture. *Resources* (10th of 25 R): Energy and Mineral Resources (Chmn.). *Science* (10th of 27 R): Space and Aeronautics; Technology.

Group Ratings

	ADA	ACLU	COPE	CFA	LCV	CON	NSI	COC	ACU	NTLC	CHC
1994	5	13	13	20	6	48	100	100	90	88	100
1993	0	—	0	10	36	74	—	100	96	—	—

National Journal Ratings

	1993 LIB — 1993 CONS		1994 LIB — 1994 CONS	
Economic	25% —	72%	34% —	64%
Social	25% —	73%	16% —	84%
Foreign	9% —	85%	33% —	67%

Key Votes of the 103d Congress

1. Clinton Deficit Plan	N	3. Brady Handgun Purchase	N	5. Lmt. UN Cmnd. of Forces	Y
2. NAFTA	Y	4. Strike Race/Death Pnlty.	Y	6. Cut Missile Funds	N

Key Votes of the 104th Congress

1. Congressional Compliance	Y	6. Reform Crime Grant	Y	11. Loser Pays Court Reform	Y
2. Balanced Budget Amndmt.	Y	7. National Security Act	Y	12. Product Liability Reform	Y
3. Bar Unfunded Mandates	Y	8. Moratorium on Regs.	Y	13. Welfare Reform	Y
4. Pass Line Item Veto	Y	9. Risk Assessment on Regs.	Y	14. Term Limits Amndt.	Y
5. Relax Exclusionary Rule	Y	10. Expnd. Priv. Prop. Rights	Y	15. Tax Cuts	Y

Election Results

1994 general	Ken Calvert (R)	84,500	(55%)	($768,290)
	Mark A. Takano (D).................	59,342	(38%)	($562,401)
	Gene L. Berkman (Lib)	9,636	(6%)	
	Others	908	(1%)	
1994 primary	Ken Calvert (R)	22,149	(51%)	
	Joe Khoury (R)......................	21,265	(49%)	
1992 general	Ken Calvert (R)	88,987	(47%)	($422,717)
	Mark A. Takano (D).................	88,468	(46%)	($303,691)
	Others	13,184	(7%)	

FORTY-FOURTH DISTRICT

From the air two decades ago, a night flight east from Los Angeles showed the lights of 10 million people's streets and houses and then almost perfect darkness: a vast metropolis surrounded by almost uninhabited territory. Today the sprinkled pattern of white lights is more dense in the Inland Empire around Riverside and San Bernardino and is multiplying outward into the desert. The Inland Empire has filled up with instant towns like Moreno Valley, which did not exist in 1980 and had 118,000 people in 1990. The surreal landscape to the south and east, around the old towns of Perris and Hemet, is filling up with new places like Sun City and Valle Vista. Over the 10,000-foot San Jacinto Mountains, desert communities have boomed: Palm Springs, once the lone winter resort for the stars, is now one of a string of communities along Highway 111 and Frank Sinatra and Bob Hope Drives. Among rich retirees, the vogue for the coast lessened as beach cities filled up with enviro-activists and rent control crusaders; the clean, dry, roomy desert, where the days are almost always crystal clear and the sky usually blue and cloudless, became more attractive, and, with everything air-conditioned, a comfortable year-round home for more than 150,000 in 1990. That's 200,000 if you count Indio, the heavily Latino center of the Coachella Valley which has 98% of the country's date palms and which features camel races at its annual date festival. Two presidents have retired to the desert, Dwight Eisenhower in Palm Desert for the winters and Gerald Ford in nearby Rancho Mirage, which is also the home of Frank Sinatra and Spiro Agnew.

The 44th Congressional District is one of two that were created from the fastest-growing district (the old 37th) in the United States in the 1980s, which included all the desert and most of the rest of Riverside County. The 44th covers all the desert and proceeds west to Moreno Valley, including most of the region around Perris and Hemet. It is heavily Republican in most elections, though it voted for Bill Clinton in 1992. Republican Congressman Al McCandless, first elected from the larger district, was pressed while winning reelection in 1990 and 1992; in 1994 he decided to retire.

The new Congressman from the 44th District is onetime showbiz celebrity Sonny Bono, more recently mayor of Palm Springs and a U.S. Senate candidate in 1992. Bono, born in Detroit, moved with his family to southern California in World War II; after high school he became a songwriter and drove a meat delivery truck to make money. He wrote *Needles and Pins*, worked with Phil Spector and the Righteous Brothers and in 1964 borrowed $175 to record *Baby Don't Go* with his then-girlfriend Cherilyn Sarkisian: Sonny and Cher. They became stars. By 1965, Sonny had recorded five songs ranked in the Billboard Top 100, an achivement unmatched by anyone except the Beatles. As rock went drugward, they called for abstinence and named their daughter Chastity, made a couple of flop movies, then developed the mainline *Sonny and Cher* TV show. After they were divorced in 1974, Sonny dropped out of showbiz, started restaurants and settled in Palm Springs, where he got angry when city bureaucrats stalled his building plans; he ran for mayor and was elected in 1988. He claimed credit for erasing a $2.5 million deficit without new taxes and for starting a local film festival. He survived controversies over development and a recall attempt and ran for the Senate in 1992. He got 17% of the vote, placing him third in the primary for the full six-year term, behind conservative Bruce Herschensohn, who got 38%, and moderate Tom Campbell, with 36%. Afterwards, he became friends with the good-natured Herschensohn and started to run for lieutenant governor. Then, when McCandless announced his retirement, Bono ran for the House. In a six-candidate Republican primary, he won with 49% of the vote to 28% for Riverside County Supervisor Corky Larson. The Democratic nominee, Steve Clute, had served 10 years in the Assembly from 1982 to 1992; a former Navy pilot, he promised to work on the area's closed military bases. Despite initial Democratic optimism about winning the seat, the Republican tide and Bono's attractiveness gave him a 56%–38% win.

In his showbiz days, Bono always portrayed himself as a worse singer than Cher and the subject of her putdowns and that image has carried over into his political career. After the election, he said, "The last thing in the world I thought I would be is a U.S. Congressman, given all the bobcat vests and Eskimo boots I used to wear." But behind his seeming klutziness is a sense of humor that suggests a shrewdness as well. "That's a tricky one," he said in a 1992 Senate campaign debate when asked about trade—not such a bad answer in a state ambivalent on the subject. When asked about illegal immigration, he replied, "What's to talk about? It's illegal"—a response that nicely anticipated the success of Proposition 187. He opposed the Clinton health plan and called for less government regulation that "automatically says industry is the bad guy." He also vowed to fight the Endangered Species Act, saying, "If you can't build here in Palm Springs because there might be a fringe toad lizard on the property, and you lose jobs in Moreno Valley because the kangaroo rat is on the site for your proposed plant, something is dead wrong with the system." He continued the common-man approach after he was elected, complaining that the lawyers on the Judiciary Committee, where he now serves, play too many rhetorical games and hinder the law-enforcement process. In February 1995, Bono convulsed a Washington audience and C-SPAN viewers as an after-dinner speaker, talking about Bob Dornan and Phil Gramm and asking bewildered questions about their rhetorical excesses. For all his celebrity, Bono sounds very much like the small businessmen and lawyers outraged by heavyhanded bureaucracy who make up most of the freshman Republican class of 1994. He will likely win reelection easily, and he might eventually take another shot at a statewide race.

The People: Pop. 1990: 571,843; 14% rural; 18% age 65+; 64% White; 5% Black; 1% Amer. Indian; 3% Asian; 14% Other; 28% Hispanic origin. Voting age pop.: 417,142; 4% Black; 23% Hispanic origin. Households: 58% married couple families; 25% married couple fams. w. children; 45% college educ.; median household income: $29,049; per capita income: $14,417; median gross rent: $545; median house value: $121,800.

1992 Presidential Vote			1988 Presidential Vote		
Clinton (D)	87,180	(40%)	Bush (R)	97,391	(59%)
Bush (R)	76,772	(36%)	Dukakis (D)	66,685	(41%)
Perot (I)	50,867	(24%)			

Rep. Sonny Bono (R)

Elected 1994; b. Feb. 16, 1935, Detroit, MI; home, Palm Springs; Roman Catholic; married (Mary).

Career: Entertainer, Songwriter, Producer, 1959–88; Restaurateur, 1982–92; Palm Springs Mayor, 1988–92.

DC Office: 512 CHOB 20515, 202-225-5330; Fax: 202-225-2961.

District Offices: 1555 S. Palm Canyon Dr., #G-101, Palm Springs 92264, 619-320-1076; and 23119-A Cottonwood Ave., #208, Moreno Valley 92553, 909-653-4466.

Committees: *Banking & Financial Services* (16th of 27 R): Financial Institutions and Consumer Credit; Housing and Community Opportunity. *Judiciary* (15th of 20 R): Courts and Intellectual Property; Immigration and Claims.

Group Ratings and 103rd Congress Votes: Newly Elected

Key Votes of the 104th Congress

1. Congressional Compliance Y	6. Reform Crime Grant Y	11. Loser Pays Court Reform Y
2. Balanced Budget Amndmt. Y	7. National Security Act Y	12. Product Liability Reform Y
3. Bar Unfunded Mandates Y	8. Moratorium on Regs. Y	13. Welfare Reform Y
4. Pass Line Item Veto Y	9. Risk Assessment on Regs. Y	14. Term Limits Amndmt. Y
5. Relax Exclusionary Rule Y	10. Expnd. Priv. Prop. Rights Y	15. Tax Cuts Y

Election Results

1994 general	Sonny Bono (R)	95,521	(56%)	($731,238)
	Steve Clute (D)	65,370	(38%)	($340,587)
	Donald Cochran (AI)	10,885	(6%)	
1994 primary	Sonny Bono (R)	25,709	(49%)	
	Patricia (Corky) Larson (R)	14,897	(28%)	
	Kent DeLong (R)	5,746	(11%)	
	Phil Bretz (R)	2,883	(5%)	
	Bud Mathewson (R)	2,256	(4%)	
	Others	1,378	(3%)	
1992 general	Alfred A. (Al) McCandless (R)	110,333	(54%)	($278,880)
	Georgia Smith (D)	81,693	(40%)	($5,748)
	Phil Turner (Lib)	11,515	(6%)	

FORTY-FIFTH DISTRICT

In the 1950s, when the Beach Boys were at Hawthorne High School, surfers would drive far down the coast to the vast expanse of Huntington Beach in Orange County to catch huge waves. This was empty country then, vegetable fields and orange groves, with nary a freeway or shopping center in sight. Today the beach itself is eerily empty, with swampland across the highway where surfers' pickups are parked; but the rest of Orange County is pretty much filled in. Huntington Beach is a city of 181,000, a mixture of family subdivisions and garden apartments. To the north are Stanton and Westminster, the latter the center of the biggest Vietnamese-American community in the nation. South along the San Diego Freeway is Fountain Valley, the central focus now of many Asian-owned high-tech businesses, an engine of Southern California growth. Near the coast again is Costa Mesa, site of South Coast Plaza, with its luxury stores, America's first mall to offer valet parking and Newport Beach, with its large harbor and expensive mansions a block or two from the ocean.

The 45th Congressional District includes all this territory. Politically, it is heavily Republican, though Democrats have sometimes been competitive in Stanton and Westminster. The Vietnamese here are conservative, angry with America not for going into Vietnam but for leaving it. There is confidence here in free enterprise despite the early 1990s recession and despite the Orange County bankruptcy of December 1994 (the work of the county's one Democratic officeholder, Treasurer Robert Citron, but accepted by local government Republicans greedy for revenue). There is also a desire, despite the wildness of the beach and the seeming anarchy of the freeway, for discipline to supplant therapy and reassert the order that seemed so solid when Orange County was starting to grow in the 1950s.

The Congressman from the 45th is Dana Rohrabacher, who might be called a surfer Republican if there were such a thing. Rohrabacher, who actually is a surfer, is one Republican who confesses to a past of drug use and still takes libertarian stands on some cultural issues—a Reaganite with a *Saturday Night Live* attitude. He was purged from the Young Americans for Freedom for libertarian stands on the draft and drugs and once had a folk band called The Goldwaters. He worked on the 1976 and 1980 Reagan presidential campaigns, wrote editorials for *The Orange County Register* and served in the Reagan White House speechwriting shop. He returned to Southern California in 1988 when Long Beach-based Congressman Dan Lungren decided not to run again (Lungren went on to be elected attorney general in 1990). Rohrabacher, with fundraising help from Oliver North, won the primary with 35%, compared to 22% for an Orange County supervisor who had padded her resume and 20% for Steve Horn, now Congressman from the Long Beach-based 38th District. After easy reelection in 1990, redistricting posed a problem: Rohrabacher did not want to run to the north in the marginal 36th or in the 38th (neither of which had an incumbent), and he had to elbow aside Robert Dornan in the new, heavily Republican 45th in which neither lived but both wanted to run. (Dornan agreed to run in the 46th District.) Rohrabacher persuaded the mayor of Huntington Beach not to run and won the primary with 48% of the vote, to 28% for Costa Mesa Councilman Peter Buffa and 24% for Huntington Beach Councilman Peter Green. He won the general 55%–39%, not especially impressive; in 1994, he did much better, 69%–31%.

Rohrabacher has made waves—or is that an inapt surfer metaphor?—on several issues in the House. One is the subsidization of obscene and religiously offensive art by the National Endowment for the Arts. That may seem out of sync with his libertarian spirit, but why should the government pay for *Piss Christ*? Another great interest is space. The McDonnell Douglas plant in Huntington Beach builds the space shuttle, and Rohrabacher on the Science Committee and on the floor has worked for the single stage-to-orbit vehicle and the national aerospace plane. He admits that NASA is mismanaged but insists that low orbit space vehicles are scientifically important, because "once you're in low Earth orbit, you're halfway to anywhere else in the solar system." He is now the number two Republican on the Space Subcommittee, in a good position to push his views. His third major issue is illegal immigration. He was a vocal supporter of 1994's Proposition 187, arguing "we can no longer afford to provide a treasure chest of benefits to every person who manages to cross our border illegally." And he wants to move ahead on a tamperproof identification card. At the same time he insists on a sharp distinction between legals and illegals: he is not against government benefits for aliens legally resident in the United States, and he opposed the forcible return of refugees to Haiti when many liberals as well as conservatives were demanding it. When then-Minority Whip Newt Gingrich encouraged moderate Republicans in August 1994 to work out a deal with President Clinton on the crime bill, Rohrabacher went ballistic, though to little avail. Actively opposing Gingrich has not been a wise tactic within the Republican Conference.

The People: Pop. 1990: 570,991; 10% age 65+; 73% White; 1% Black; 1% Amer. Indian; 11% Asian; 5% Other; 15% Hispanic origin. Voting age pop.: 450,774; 1% Black; 13% Hispanic origin. Households: 52% married couple families; 23% married couple fams. w. children; 63% college educ.; median household income: $45,074; per capita income: $21,046; median gross rent: $815; median house value: $264,200.

1992 Presidential Vote

Bush (R) 105,893 (42%)
Clinton (D) 80,646 (32%)
Perot (I). 63,609 (25%)

1988 Presidential Vote

Bush (R) 148,999 (68%)
Dukakis (D). 71,027 (32%)

Rep. Dana Rohrabacher (R)

Elected 1988; b. June 21, 1947, Coronado; home, Huntington Beach; Long Beach St. Col. B.A. 1969, U. of Southern CA, M.A. 1971; Baptist; single.

Career: Radio and print journalist, 1970–80; Sr. Speechwriter, Special Asst. to Pres. Reagan, 1981–88.

DC Office: 2338 RHOB 20515, 202-225-2415; Fax: 202-225-0145.

District Offices: 16162 Beach Blvd., Huntington Beach 92647, 714-847-2433.

Committees: *International Relations* (13th of 23 R): Asia and the Pacific; International Economic Policy and Trade. *Science* 7th of 27 R): Energy and Environment (Chmn.); Space and Aeronautics.

Group Ratings

	ADA	ACLU	COPE	CFA	LCV	CON	NSI	COC	ACU	NTLC	CHC
1994	10	30	22	0	6	93	70	75	86	96	79
1993	20	—	0	0	29	91	—	100	92	—	—

National Journal Ratings

	1993 LIB — 1993 CONS		1994 LIB — 1994 CONS	
Economic	0%	— 88%	0%	— 80%
Social	19%	— 77%	36%	— 64%
Foreign	33%	— 65%	23%	— 76%

Key Votes of the 103d Congress

1. Clinton Deficit Plan	N	3. Brady Handgun Purchase	N	5. Lmt. UN Cmnd. of Forces	Y
2. NAFTA	Y	4. Strike Race/Death Pnlty.	Y	6. Cut Missile Funds	Y

Key Votes of the 104th Congress

1. Congressional Compliance	Y	6. Reform Crime Grant	Y	11. Loser Pays Court Reform	Y
2. Balanced Budget Amndmt.	Y	7. National Security Act	Y	12. Product Liability Reform	Y
3. Bar Unfunded Mandates	Y	8. Moratorium on Regs.	Y	13. Welfare Reform	Y
4. Pass Line Item Veto	Y	9. Risk Assessment on Regs.	Y	14. Term Limits Amndmt.	Y
5. Relax Exclusionary Rule	Y	10. Expnd. Priv. Prop. Rights	Y	15. Tax Cuts	Y

Election Results

1994 general	Dana Rohrabacher (R)	124,006	(69%)	($187,656)
	Brett Williamson (D)	55,489	(31%)	($85,803)
1994 primary	Dana Rohrabacher (R)	unopposed		
1992 general	Dana Rohrabacher (R)	123,731	(55%)	($321,912)
	Patricia McCabe (D)	88,508	(39%)	($32,473)
	Gary D. Copeland (Lib)	14,777	(7%)	

FORTY-SIXTH DISTRICT

Orange County is the fifth most populous county in the United States, having grown from 130,000 in 1940 to 216,000 in 1950, 703,000 in 1960, 1.4 million in 1970, 1.9 million in 1980 and 2.4 million in 1990. It is now a mature community with the patina of age—and in some ways an aging community, fraying around the edges. The county is no longer capable of its early growth, when Disneyland sprung up on empty land and mile-square grids of orange groves and bean fields were transformed into one suburban subdivision and shopping center and office tower after another. A distinctive civilization was implanted here: mostly white and middle-class, confident of its traditional values and its market capitalism, proud of American principles and American military might. Orange County has been troubled in years since, by the downfall of its native son Richard Nixon and the rejection of its core values by an articulate media elite, and it has been transformed by its own openness to economic and ethnic change. Its economy was constantly being reshaped by the inevitable upheavals of capitalism: there is no single industry here—not even defense—which is totally responsible for the prosperity of Orange County, and people here must be ready to adapt almost as deftly as the Taiwanese on the other side of the Pacific Rim. It was hit hard by the defense cutbacks and recession of the early 1990s but seems to be bouncing back, pitched forward by new startups and small entrepreneurial successes not anticipated by government or corporate planners. It also was shaken by the bankruptcy of the county government in December 1994, caused by the improvident investments of County Treasurer Robert Citron. Orange County's position on the Pacific Rim is apparent in its people: widely perceived as homogeneously white, Orange County has for years been home to large numbers of Latinos and Asians. Quietly, without political hubbub, they have moved out along the freeways, building ethnic cores like the Mexican-American precincts of Santa Ana and the Vietnamese corridor in Westminster and Garden Grove, working hard at jobs, commuting on freeways and living in stucco subdivisions like anyone else. By 1990 Orange County was about one-quarter Hispanic and one-tenth Asian—scarcely homogeneous. These changes have made for some political wobble—but not as much as one might think. Latinos tend to be Democrats, but many do not vote, and Vietnamese are staunchly Republican. Voters here flirted with the Democrats in 1992, ultimately giving George Bush only a small margin over Bill Clinton.

The 46th Congressional District is the geographic heart of Orange County. About half its people are in the county seat of Santa Ana, now heavily Latino, full of large families and many workers. It also includes most of Garden Grove, with many Latinos and some Vietnamese—though the main Vietnamese shopping area is across the line in Westminster—and most of Anaheim, including the site of Disneyland and territory just across the street from Orange County landmarks Anaheim Stadium, Knott's Berry Farm and John Wayne Airport. Overall, the district is 50% Hispanic and 12% Asian. For years this has been the least Republican part of Orange County, and from 1962 to 1982 redistricters carefully sculpted Democratic districts here. But the emergence of Vietnamese in the electorate moved the balance away from the Democrats: they are angry not that the United States got into Vietnam but that it got out.

The Congressman from the 46th is one of the leading firebrands among American politicians, loud and pugnacious and impossible to ignore, and a presidential candidate in 1996: Robert Dornan. He is now one of the senior Republicans in the House, first elected in 1976 in a Westside L.A. district and reelected twice there, an unsuccessful candidate for the Senate in 1982 (he finished fourth in the primary with 8% of the vote) and the 1984 upset winner over an incumbent Democrat in the 46th District's predecessor. Dornan is easier to understand if you remember that he was a fighter pilot. He volunteered for pilot training while in college, went on active duty in the Air Force in October 1952 and served as a fighter pilot until 1958. Then, with showbiz connections (his uncle Jack Haley was the Tin Man in *The Wizard of Oz*), he became a TV talk show host in Los Angeles and was a civilian combat photographer on five of his eight trips to wartime Vietnam. He has a taste for invective, perhaps because he often finds himself fighting in hostile arenas: the trendy and often mindless liberalism of the Westside was infuriating to this true believer in the B-1 bomber and a ban on abortion, and the political adeptness and verbal cleverness of House liberals enrage him as well. Dornan's temper sometimes enables him to accomplish things others dismiss as impossible; at other times it gets him and his causes in trouble. But it usually gets him on the air.

Dornan is if not the spiritual father—for he is more speaker than organizer—the spiritual uncle of the freshman Republicans elected in 1994. He has several passionate causes. One is the military. He has special respect for combat veterans, especially pilots: this was the first reason for his passionate support of George Bush in 1988 and 1992, and the basis of his respect for Bob Dole. He backs higher military pay and benefits; he has urged more investigations into POW/MIAs in Vietnam and continues to strongly oppose normalizing relations with Vietnam until such an accounting is given. His passion for things military also helps explain his vitriolic feelings toward Bill Clinton, who he believes is a liar and a draft-dodger. "The Chicken Little of Little Rock," he called him, "a nerdy little flower child." And in January 1995 he lost his floor privileges for a day after saying, "Clinton gave aid and comfort to the enemy." When Democrat Vic Fazio, a fellow Californian, demanded that he apologize, Dornan said, "I've had friends beaten to death in Hanoi, tortured and beaten—you have not. I will not withdraw my remarks. I will not apologize; I believe the President did give aid and comfort in London to the enemy in Hanoi." This may have helped Dornan with his Republican base. But his speeches in the fall of 1992 raising questions about Clinton's trips to the Soviet Union and Eastern Europe in 1969 made it seem that the Bush campaign was making unsubstantiated charges, all of which boomeranged against the Republicans.

Dornan now has much more opportunity to work substantively on these issues. In the 104th Congress he chairs two panels, the National Security Subcommittee on Military Personnel and the Intelligence Subcommittee on Technical and Tactical Intelligence. He likes to get first-hand experience flying military planes and visiting areas of engagement like Somalia. He has tried to prevent what he considers excessive defense spending cuts, especially in California. He has supported the Police Corps and a program to help former military personnel become teachers.

Another of Dornan's motivating forces is his fervent opposition to abortion and homosexuality. He once said every "lesbian spear-chucker" was against him, and he strongly opposed federal funding of fetal tissue research at N.I.H. and ending the ban on gays in the military. He called early for the resignation of Surgeon General Joycelyn Elders. On other issues, he added an amendment to the 1994 crime bill that imposes the death penalty for espionage that leads to the death of U.S. agents. He favors tort reform, and he opposed the Environmental Protection Agency's centralization of vehicle emission test centers in California.

Dornan has had many stormy campaigns and has been the target of some unfair charges by Democrats. Former House Democratic Whip Tony Coelho once suggested that he took pilot training to avoid combat, which could only have been true if he had advance knowledge of the Korean war armistice. His 1994 Democratic opponent dredged up old charges that he had beaten his wife; Sallie Dornan says that under the influence of painkillers and bad lawyers she made false accusations 30-some years ago, and the fact that their marriage has lasted 40 years is evidence supporting her denial. Dornan regularly spends about $1.5 million in his campaigns and often raises over $2 million, almost entirely from small contributors across the country who like his views and style. In the last two elections he has won 60%–40% and 57%–37%.

In 1993, Dornan said he would run for only one more House term (he says he hopes a Latino or Asian Republican will succeed him) and would look at the 1996 presidential race; in February 1995 he went up to New Hampshire and in April formally announced his decision to run. To many he seems a preposterous candidate, in fact, few potential candidates were lining up to succeed him in the district, believing that he may drop out of the presidential race in time to re-file for his House seat by March 12, 1996. But he is nationally known—the number one substitute host for Rush Limbaugh, he notes, including during the first week of the 104th Congress—and has a direct mail constituency from which he has consistently raised $2 million a cycle. He insists that he is reflective and not out of control, that the anger he seems to generate on the floor of the House is a product of the genre of one-minute speeches and his desire to get people's attention. He believes he has a base among the retired and career military, among people concerned about POW/MIAs, in the right-to-life movement. "Only God knows the outcome, but I'm ready for what may be the toughest mission of my life," he said, though he has also said, "I know when to hold 'em and know when to fold 'em. I'm going up there to have the time of my life."

The People: Pop. 1990: 570,963; 7% age 65+; 36% White; 2% Black; 1% Amer. Indian; 12% Asian; 18% Other; 49% Hispanic origin. Voting age pop.: 405,366; 2% Black; 45% Hispanic origin. Households: 58% married couple families; 33% married couple fams. w. children; 38% college educ.; median household income: $35,416; per capita income: $11,297; median gross rent: $719; median house value: $187,900.

1992 Presidential Vote

Bush (R) 47,689 (40%)
Clinton (D) 44,352 (37%)
Perot (I). 27,542 (23%)

1988 Presidential Vote

Bush (R) 74,822 (62%)
Dukakis (D). 45,162 (38%)

Rep. Robert K. (Bob) **Dornan** (R)

Elected 1984; b. Apr. 3, 1933, New York, N.Y.; home, Garden Grove; Loyola U.; Catholic; married (Sallie).

Career: Air Force, 1952–58, Air Natl. Guard, 1958–61, Air Force Reserves, 1962–75; Broadcast Journalist, 1965–69; Talk show host, 1969–73; U.S. House of Reps., 1976–82.

DC Office: 1201 LHOB 20515, 202-225-2965; Fax: 202-225-2762.

District Offices: 300 Plaza Alicante, #360, Garden Grove 92642, 714-971-9292.

Committees: *National Security* (8th of 30 R): Military Personnel (Chmn.); Military Research and Development. *Intelligence (Permanent Select)* (2nd of 9 R): Technical and Tactical Intelligence (Chmn.).

Group Ratings

	ADA	ACLU	COPE	CFA	LCV	CON	NSI	COC	ACU	NTLC	CHC
1994	0	13	33	10	6	86	100	75	100	93	100
1993	0	—	0	0	14	52	—	91	96	—	—

National Journal Ratings

	1993 LIB — 1993 CONS	1994 LIB — 1994 CONS
Economic	0% — 88%	0% — 80%
Social	0% — 89%	0% — 89%
Foreign	0% — 91%	0% — 88%

Key Votes of the 103d Congress

1. Clinton Deficit Plan	N	3. Brady Handgun Purchase	N	5. Lmt. UN Cmnd. of Forces	Y
2. NAFTA	Y	4. Strike Race/Death Pnlty.	Y	6. Cut Missile Funds	N

Key Votes of the 104th Congress

1. Congressional Compliance Y	6. Reform Crime Grant Y	11. Loser Pays Court Reform Y
2. Balanced Budget Amndmt. Y	7. National Security Act Y	12. Product Liability Reform Y
3. Bar Unfunded Mandates Y	8. Moratorium on Regs. Y	13. Welfare Reform Y
4. Pass Line Item Veto Y	9. Risk Assessment on Regs. Y	14. Term Limits Amndmt. Y
5. Relax Exclusionary Rule Y	10. Expnd. Priv. Prop. Rights *	15. Tax Cuts Y

Election Results

1994 general	Robert K. (Bob) Dornan (R)	50,126	(57%)	($2,261,696)
	Michael P. Farber (D)	32,577	(37%)	($302,747)
	Richard G. Newhouse (Lib)	5,018	(6%)	
1994 primary	Robert K. (Bob) Dornan (R)	unopposed		
1992 general	Robert K. (Bob) Dornan (R)	55,659	(50%)	($1,581,503)
	Robert John Banuelos (D)	45,435	(41%)	
	Richard G. Newhouse (Lib)	9,712	(9%)	

FORTY-SEVENTH DISTRICT

As one drives southeast in Orange County, there are still large patches of vacant land, places where one can see what this metropolis must have looked like before the vast growth starting in the 1950s. The Irvine Ranch, originally stretching 10 miles along the Pacific Coast and 22 miles inland to the mountains, was sold to developers by the Irvine family in the late 1970s but is still not entirely developed. Arrayed at the edges of the Irvine Ranch are Orange County landmarks. One is John Wayne Airport, named after the movie star who lived in Newport Beach and who symbolized patriotism though he never served in the military himself. Another is South Coast Plaza, the highest-volume upscale shopping center in southern California, standing in what not too long ago was a lima bean field. Another is the Irvine branch of the University of California, with 1,000 acres donated by the Irvine Ranch developers. On all sides are comfortable settlements—Orange, an orderly community, within sight of the hills, where even the street signs are orange; Newport Beach around its harbor; Irvine, with its planned communities, handsome clusters of office towers, landscaped shopping plazas and groups of houses and condominiums (but no cemeteries); artsy-craftsy Laguna Beach between mountains and the sea. Orange County is assailed by some as monotonous and sterile and boring, but for most of its residents it is a promised land, orderly without being authoritarian, crowded perhaps but with privacy, sunny without being too hot.

The 47th Congressional District is centered geographically on the Irvine Ranch lands. On the coast it includes about half of Newport Beach as well as most of Irvine and runs south to Laguna Beach. It includes the growing subdivisions of El Toro and Laguna Hills near the now closed El Toro Marine Corps Air Station. About half its residents live to the north, in and around Orange; the other half are split between the ocean communities and those inland. Politically, this is a conservative area, one of the most Republican districts in the United States, though one disillusioned with George Bush in 1992. Its people like the sense of order conveyed by its grid street patterns and the feeling of protection imparted by the subdivision walls. They have felt comfortable as well with the military nearby. Although there are some distinctively rich communities here, the people do not feel that they are some kind of elite; they tend to see themselves as ordinary Americans with classic values who have worked hard and are entitled to enjoy their comfort.

The Congressman from the 47th is Christopher Cox, a Republican who has become one of the intellectual leaders of his party in the House and now an elected leader, as well. Cox grew up in Minnesota; after Harvard Law, he practiced with a prestigious firm in Orange County, then was part of the counsel's staff in the Reagan White House. In 1988, when the local incumbent retired, he ran for the House—one of 14 candidates in the Republican primary. With the support of Oliver North, Robert Bork and members of the Irvine family, he won with 31%. He has won since without difficulty. Cox is not as pugnacious or as puckish as his Orange County colleagues Robert Dornan and Dana Rohrabacher, but is perhaps more rigorously conservative. His interests have ranged from the former Soviet Union (he and his father published an English translation of *Pravda* from 1984 to 1988) and Lithuanian independence (he supported it in 1990) to lobbying for more local control of highway funds and a proposed monorail system in Orange County. He has worked to eliminate the federal helium program (his co-sponsor was liberal Democrat Barney Frank of Massachusetts) and the Interstate Commerce Commission. He pushed to force a vote on military intervention in Haiti. He killed a proposal to require companies to deduct the inherently speculative value of stock options from their statements of current earnings. Cox did more than lament Orange County Treasurer Robert Citron's reckless investments, which bankrupted the county; he backed local Republican John Moorlach against the Democrat when Moorlach criticized Citron's practices. Afterwards, Cox proposed that public sector investors be required to make the same disclosures as private.

Well before the Contract With America, Cox was pushing for term limits and a balanced budget: he called for requiring the president and Congress to present a balanced budget, with a two-thirds vote required to exceed budget limits. He was a leader in attacking baseline budgeting, which in effect gave every federal department either an inflation increase or the previous year's increase, whichever was more, and then let them argue for even more: his radical idea was to state the budget in dollar terms, so that an increase would show up as an increase and a cut would mean an actual reduction in spending. He also took the lead in the Contract With America promise to cut down on "strike suits," stockholder derivative suits against corporations.

Cox considered running for the Senate in 1994 against Dianne Feinstein, but decided not to enter the primary against Michael Huffington, who was prepared to spend freely of his own money. He might run for Barbara Boxer's Senate seat in 1998, particularly if California's term limits law is upheld.

The People: Pop. 1990: 571,605; 11% age 65+; 75% White; 2% Black; 10% Asian; 5% Other; 13% Hispanic origin. Voting age pop.: 442,117; 2% Black; 12% Hispanic origin. Households: 58% married couple families; 27% married couple fams. w. children; 72% college educ.; median household income: $51,554; per capita income: $25,268; median gross rent: $845; median house value: $279,900.

1992 Presidential Vote

Bush (R)	127,700	(46%)
Clinton (D)	86,279	(31%)
Perot (I)	64,227	(23%)

1988 Presidential Vote

Bush (R)	162,104	(71%)
Dukakis (D)	67,579	(29%)

Rep. Christopher Cox (R)

Elected 1988; b. Oct. 16, 1952, St. Paul, MN; home, Newport Beach; U. of Southern CA, B.A. 1973, Harvard, M.B.A., J.D., 1977; Catholic; married (Rebecca).

Career: Clerk, U.S. Court of Appeals, Judge Hebert Choy, 1977; Practicing atty., 1978–86; Lecturer, Harvard Bus. Schl., 1982–83; Sr. Assoc. Cnsl., White House, 1986–88.

DC Office: 2402 RHOB 20515, 202-225-5611; Fax: 202-225-9177.

District Offices: 4000 MacArthur Blvd., #430, Newport Beach 92660, 714-756-2244.

Committees: *Republican Policy Committee Chairman. Commerce* (17th of 26 R): Oversight and Investigations; Telecommunications and Finance.

Group Ratings

	ADA	ACLU	COPE	CFA	LCV	CON	NSI	COC	ACU	NTLC	CHC
1994	0	14	11	10	11	84	100	82	100	100	79
1993	0	—	0	10	23	74	—	100	100	—	—

National Journal Ratings

	1993 LIB — 1993 CONS	1994 LIB — 1994 CONS
Economic	0% — 88%	0% — 80%
Social	19% — 81%	19% — 80%
Foreign	0% — 91%	0% — 88%

Key Votes of the 103d Congress

1. Clinton Deficit Plan	N	3. Brady Handgun Purchase N	5. Lmt. UN Cmnd. of Forces Y
2. NAFTA	Y	4. Strike Race/Death Pnlty. Y	6. Cut Missile Funds N

Key Votes of the 104th Congress

1. Congressional Compliance Y	6. Reform Crime Grant Y	11. Loser Pays Court Reform Y
2. Balanced Budget Amndmt. Y	7. National Security Act Y	12. Product Liability Reform Y
3. Bar Unfunded Mandates Y	8. Moratorium on Regs. Y	13. Welfare Reform Y
4. Pass Line Item Veto Y	9. Risk Assessment on Regs. Y	14. Term Limits Amndmt. Y
5. Relax Exclusionary Rule Y	10. Expnd. Priv. Prop. Rights Y	15. Tax Cuts Y

Election Results

1994 general	Christopher Cox (R)	152,413	(72%)	($246,400)
	Gary Kingsbury (D)	53,035	(25%)	($60,846)
	Others	7,175	(3%)	
1994 primary	Christopher Cox (R)	55,223	(86%)	
	Steven J. Frogue (R)	9,364	(15%)	
1992 general	Christopher Cox (R)	165,004	(65%)	($402,198)
	John F. Anwiler (D)	76,924	(30%)	
	Maxine B. Quirk (P&F)	12,297	(5%)	

FORTY-EIGHTH DISTRICT

The California coast between Los Angeles and San Diego has never entirely filled up with development and never will as long as the Marine Corps retains custody of Camp Pendleton, its giant training base just south of the Orange-San Diego County line. But on both sides of Pendleton up and down the coast and for miles inland on the pleasant hills and in sunny valleys, there has been tremendous growth over the past two decades. Little wonder: this area has perhaps the most agreeable climate in the continental United States, beautiful scenery, the physical infrastructure typical of California and much lower crime rates than Los Angeles or even San Diego. A quarter century ago, this was largely empty territory—never fertile enough to produce a large farm community, never endowed with much manufacturing, never actively promoted as a retirement community. In 1990 there were half a million people just north and south of Pendleton, and the Interior Department was struggling to come up with a district plan that would protect the ecosystem of the 4-inch gnat-catcher bird and other endangered species in the area without complete chaotic subdivision of the area.

The 48th Congressional District occupies the southernmost portion of Orange County, the North County part of San Diego County and a small slice of Riverside County, the instant town of Temecula. It includes the seaside communities of San Clemente, where Richard Nixon lived just after leaving the White House, and San Juan Capistrano, to which the swallows famously return every year. Inland, there are the newer condominium communities of Mission Viejo and Laguna Niguel; just south of Pendleton in San Diego County are Oceanside and Vista. Farther inland amid the hills are Fallbrook and, in Riverside County, Temecula, in the mid-1980s a corner-grocery town serving a vineyard district, now the center of an area with 100,000 people, mostly commuters to Orange County and Riverside attracted by low house prices and traditional values. People in all these areas tend to be Republicans; they are affluent enough to identify with the party of property, conventional enough in their personal lives to identify with what describes itself as the party of the family, undivided enough by ethnic differences to identify with the party that fancies it is made up of an unethnic majority.

The Congressman from the 48th, Ron Packard, is a Republican who first won when a new district was created for this area in 1982. Packard is a Mormon from Idaho, a dentist who served in the Navy Dental Corps in Camp Pendleton in the 1950s, then moved his growing family (now 7 children and 30 grandchildren) to Carlsbad. There he served on the school board, the Chamber of Commerce and city council, was a director of the North County Transit District and mayor: one of the people who keeps things working in these growing communities. He was mayor of Carlsbad in 1982 when he ran for Congress in the new district, losing an 18-candidate Republican primary by 92 votes to Johnnie Crean, who spent his own money on ads fraudulently claiming President Reagan's endorsement. Packard promptly ran as a write-in and won with 37% to 32% for the Democrat and 31% for Crean. He has been easily reelected since, winning 73%–22% in 1994.

Until 1994, Packard was a backbencher with a highly conservative voting record; now he is chairman of the Legislative Branch Appropriations Subcommittee, the panel that sets the budget for the House, which Speaker Gingrich has promised to cut substantially. His conservatism got him the California seat on the Republican Committee on Committees in 1990, when colleagues ousted the accommodationist Jerry Lewis. In 1993, he won a seat on Appropriations, where he attacked the convention of passing "emergency" spending measures. Packard has a bill to increase the border patrol by 10,000 in five years, so there would be no need for the highway checkpoints now in San Clemente and Temecula; he would deny all federal benefits except emergency medical care to illegal immigrants. He was an early supporter of the recently successful effort to cut down on unfunded mandates imposed by Washington on state and local governments. He also works on local matters, passing bills to set up a regional water reuse system in southern California and finance research on desalinization.

The People: Pop. 1990: 573,211; 11% rural; 10% age 65+; 74% White; 4% Black; 1% Amer. Indian; 5% Asian; 7% Other; 17% Hispanic origin. Voting age pop.: 426,696; 4% Black; 15% Hispanic origin. Households: 63% married couple families; 30% married couple fams. w. children; 65% college educ.; median household income: $42,389; per capita income: $19,435; median gross rent: $696; median house value: $237,300.

1992 Presidential Vote

Bush (R) 108,581 (44%)
Clinton (D) 71,621 (29%)
Perot (I). 65,980 (27%)

1988 Presidential Vote

Bush (R) 134,444 (70%)
Dukakis (D). 57,543 (30%)

Rep. Ron Packard (R)

Elected 1982; b. Jan. 19, 1931, Meridian, ID; home, Oceanside; Brigham Young U., Portland St. U., U. of OR, D.M.D. 1957; Mormon; married (Jean).

Career: Navy, 1957–59; Practicing dentist; Carlsbad Sch. Dist. Bd., 1962–74; Carlsbad City Cncl., 1976–78; Carlsbad Mayor, 1978–82.

DC Office: 2162 RHOB 20515, 202-225-3906; Fax: 202-225-0134; e-mail: rpackard@hr.house.gov.

District Offices: 221 E. Vista Way, #205, Vista 92084, 619-631-1364; and 629 Camino del los Mares, #204, San Clemente 92672, 714-496-2343.

Committees: *Appropriations* (15th of 32 R): Foreign Operations, Export Financing, and Related Programs; Legislative (Chmn.); Transportation.

Group Ratings

	ADA	ACLU	COPE	CFA	LCV	CON	NSI	COC	ACU	NTLC	CHC
1994	0	14	0	20	6	76	100	92	95	96	100
1993	0	—	0	0	8	55	—	100	96	—	—

National Journal Ratings

	1993 LIB — 1993 CONS	1994 LIB — 1994 CONS
Economic	0% — 88%	26% — 70%
Social	0% — 89%	16% — 81%
Foreign	0% — 91%	0% — 88%

Key Votes of the 103d Congress

1. Clinton Deficit Plan	N	3. Brady Handgun Purchase N	5. Lmt. UN Cmnd. of Forces Y
2. NAFTA	Y	4. Strike Race/Death Pnlty. Y	6. Cut Missile Funds N

Key Votes of the 104th Congress

1. Congressional Compliance Y
2. Balanced Budget Amndmt. Y
3. Bar Unfunded Mandates Y
4. Pass Line Item Veto Y
5. Relax Exclusionary Rule Y
6. Reform Crime Grant   Y
7. National Security Act   Y
8. Moratorium on Regs.   Y
9. Risk Assessment on Regs. Y
10. Expnd. Priv. Prop. Rights Y
11. Loser Pays Court Reform Y
12. Product Liability Reform Y
13. Welfare Reform   Y
14. Term Limits Amndmt.   Y
15. Tax Cuts   Y

Election Results

1994 general	Ron Packard (R)............................	143,275	(73%)	($210,125)
	Andrei Leschick (D).......................	43,446	(22%)	($3,726)
	Donna White (P&F).......................	8,520	(4%)	
1994 primary	Ron Packard (R)...........................	50,824	(81%)	
	Ed Mayerhofer (R)........................	12,129	(19%)	
1992 general	Ron Packard (R)..........................	140,935	(61%)	($363,341)
	Michael Farber (D).......................	67,415	(29%)	($65,944)
	Donna White (P&F)	13,396	(6%)	
	Ted Lowe (Lib)...........................	8,749	(4%)	

FORTY-NINTH DISTRICT

When the United States was dictating the terms of the Treaty of Guadalupe Hidalgo in 1848, after its successful war with Mexico, it made sure the southern boundary of its new California territory was just south of the port of San Diego. This is one of three splendid natural harbors on the Pacific Coast and the major West Coast U.S. Navy base for more than 50 years. The port and Navy base in the sheltered harbor are still the central focus of a metropolis which has grown tenfold over that time span and now stretches far inland and to the north. On one side is its downtown, blooming with post-modern buildings like the Horton Plaza amid a few well-preserved early 20th Century relics like the Spreckels Theatre. Across the harbor, on the sand spit that guards it against the ocean, is the white frame castle of the Hotel Del Coronado, with its surprisingly dark wooden interior, the world's largest wooden structure and a favored resort of past American presidents; the town of Coronado has long been a favorite retirement place for Navy admirals and captains.

But San Diego is not all harbor and Navy. To the north, the Pacific waves pound against the beach beneath erose cliffs of unique rock formations that stride up and down the coast on which stand some of San Diego's great cultural institutions: the Scripps Institute of Oceanography, the University of California San Diego campus, the Salk Institute and the Torrey Pines reserve, home of this unique, wide-spreading pine tree. They look out over the ocean through clear and gentle air south to La Jolla, the city's highest-income neighborhood, and north toward Del Mar and the race track that made San Diego a tourist mecca 50 years ago when it was owned by Bing Crosby and friends. The weather—sunny 70% of the time, arguably the most pleasant climate in the continental U.S.—has brought people to San Diego; the informal resort atmosphere of La Jolla and Mission Beach appeal to tourists. Among the visitors in August 1996 will be the delegates and guests of the Republican National Convention. But this is a working town as well, a sophisticated high-tech center with nearly 200,000 full- and part-time students at its colleges and universities and growing biotech, electronics and telecommunications industries; someone who looks like a professional surfer may turn out to be a high-tech engineer.

The 49th Congressional District, which includes about half the population of San Diego plus Coronado and Imperial Beach, takes in most of the harbor and Navy bases and much of its high-tech businesses and workers. It reaches as far south as the Mexican border and includes most of downtown San Diego and Balboa Park, with its justly famous zoo. It reaches inland where the city's freeway network, denser and more practical than San Francisco's or even Los Angeles's, efficiently shuttles commuters from scattered employment centers to their homes on hilltop subdivisions. San Diego under then-Mayor (1971–82) Pete Wilson wouldn't let developers build on the sides of the hills, so San Diego doesn't have the picturesque but precarious hillside streets of the Hollywood Hills or Pacific Heights—but rather the natural landscape that the Portuguese explorer Cabrillo saw in the 1500s and the American adventurer Richard Henry Dana saw three centuries later, though the hills are now topped unobtrusively by subdivisions. It includes Ocean Beach and Mission Bay and La Jolla and reaches as far north as Torrey Pines and as far inland as the outer boundary of Miramar Naval Air Station.

With its climate, scenery and friendliness, this should be paradise, but politically San Diego has been in a foul temper in the 1990s, kicking out incumbents of both parties all over town. Voters here tend to be Republican and free market on economics but liberal on cultural issues like abortion and the environment—much like Pete Wilson, who was elected U.S. Senator in 1982 and 1988 and governor in 1990 and 1994. But at the same time, this part of San Diego was rejecting incumbent Republicans, while the Democratic south side of town was throwing out a Democratic Congressman. The 49th District as drawn for the 1992 election contained the homes of three incumbents, but none ran here, and the 1992 winner was defeated after one term.

The current Congressman is Brian Bilbray, a Republican who was born in Coronado and grew up on naval bases and in Imperial Beach. He owns a tax service business and was elected to the Imperial Beach Council in 1976, at 25, then Mayor two years later, and to the San Diego County Board of Supervisors in 1984. He attracted some attention: when a city pier caught fire, he paddled out on his surfboard and fought the flames; though forbidden by a court, he commandeered a bulldozer and diverted sewage that was running from Mexico into the United States. In 1982 he lost a race for Assembly, but in 1994 he won the Republican primary for Congress. He faced strong opposition in first-term incumbent Democrat Lynn Schenk. In 1992, as two Republican incumbents moved out to run in safer seats and another retired after 300 overdrafts at the House bank, Schenk easily won the Democratic primary and faced nurse Judy Jarvis in the general. Schenk is a lawyer who co-founded a woman's bank and served in Governor Jerry Brown's cabinet; in 1989 she founded a San Diego Urban Corps and in 1990 became a San Diego port commissioner. "Schenk means business," she proclaimed; she raised large sums and defeated Jarvis 51%–42%. In the House, Schenk made a moderate record, especially on economic issues, worked on base closures with Republican Duncan Hunter and Mayor Susan Golding (from whom she once won a $150,000 libel judgment) and worked on John Dingell's Commerce Committee to encourage bioscience businesses.

But Schenk also voted for the 1993 Clinton budget and tax package and was associated with the president's overall record, while Bilbray supported the Contract With America. The 49th District swung toward the Republicans, and Bilbray won 49%–46%. (Curiously, he is a cousin of Nevada Democrat James Bilbray, who lost his seat the same day.) In the House, Bilbray joined the Commerce Committee, initially concentrated on Contract issues and worked with Democrat Bob Filner and other San Diego members to get an exclusion from Clean Water Act requirements because of the Mexican sewage being dumped via San Diego into the Pacific Ocean. With his election, Bilbray in effect moved Schenk's Commerce Committee seat to the other side of the aisle, and he probably will pursue some of her interests, though from a more conservative perspective.

The People: Pop. 1990: 573,437; 12% age 65+; 75% White; 5% Black; 1% Amer. Indian; 7% Asian; 5% Other; 12% Hispanic origin. Voting age pop.: 479,942; 5% Black; 11% Hispanic origin. Households: 41% married couple families; 16% married couple fams. w. children; 67% college educ.; median household income: $32,562; per capita income: $19,184; median gross rent: $607; median house value: $224,200.

1992 Presidential Vote

Clinton (D) 114,081 (43%)
Bush (R) 82,834 (31%)
Perot (I) 65,856 (25%)

1988 Presidential Vote

Bush (R) 147,529 (57%)
Dukakis (D) 113,380 (43%)

Rep. Brian P. Bilbray (R)

Elected 1994; b. Jan. 28, 1951, Coronado; home, San Diego; Southwestern Commun. Col., 1972; Catholic; married (Karen).

Career: Imperial Beach Mayor, 1978–85; San Diego Cnty. Supervisor, 1985–94; Tax consultant, 1972–present.

DC Office: 1004 LHOB 20515, 202-225-2040; Fax: 202-225-2948.

District Offices: 1011 Camino de Rio South, San Diego 92108, 619-291-1430.

Committees: *Commerce* (20th of 26 R): Commerce, Trade and Hazardous Materials; Health and Environment.

Group Ratings and 103d Congress Votes: Newly Elected

Key Votes of the 104th Congress

1. Congressional Compliance Y	6. Reform Crime Grant Y	11. Loser Pays Court Reform Y
2. Balanced Budget Amndmt. Y	7. National Security Act Y	12. Product Liability Reform Y
3. Bar Unfunded Mandates Y	8. Moratorium on Regs. Y	13. Welfare Reform Y
4. Pass Line Item Veto Y	9. Risk Assessment on Regs. Y	14. Term Limits Amndmt. Y
5. Relax Exclusionary Rule Y	10. Expnd. Priv. Prop. Rights Y	15. Tax Cuts Y

Election Results

1994 general	Brian P. Bilbray (R)	90,283	(49%)	($750,654)
	Lynn Schenk (D)	85,597	(46%)	($1,392,948)
	Others	10,238	(6%)	
1994 primary	Brian P. Bilbray (R)	26,756	(51%)	
	John Steel (R)	19,125	(37%)	
	Ted Y. Joseph (R)	3,229	(6%)	
	Scot A. Conway (R)	3,039	(6%)	
1992 general	Lynn Schenk (D)	127,280	(51%)	($1,131,021)
	Judy Jarvis (R)	106,170	(43%)	($433,649)
	John Wallner (Lib)	10,706	(4%)	($8,153)
	Others	4,742	(2%)	

FIFTIETH DISTRICT

San Diego, at one corner of the continental United States, not so long ago a small Navy town known for its good harbor and splendid weather, is now a major metropolis, a city of 1.1 million people and the center of a metro area of 2.5 million. It is also—to its increasing discomfort—one of the largest cities anywhere directly on an international border and between countries with strikingly different economic conditions, political systems and cultural traditions. Not many other Americans think about it, but Mexican presidential candidate Luis Donaldo Colosio was murdered in March 1994 just a few blocks from the border in Tijuana.

This is, in fact, the busiest border crossing in the world, but most of San Diego seems to look away, toward the ocean. Tijuana, inland, looks to the United States, to the lower-income part of San Diego—the industrial zone on brown hills in Otay Mesa and San Ysidro, the industrial suburbs of Chula Vista and National City toward the bay and the grid streets south of downtown and behind the harbor in San Diego itself. Latinos are scattered in various parts of the city, in the southern corridor and in Encanto and Chollas Park in the east. Oddly, there is little evidences of

Mexican style in San Diego–less even than in Los Angeles, as if the border city was insisting on its Yanqui origins, just as San Diego's civic leaders bridle at the idea of a bi-national airport on the border. Even San Diego's favorite symbol, the red Tijuana Trolley that takes tourists from downtown to the San Ysidro-Tijuana border station, is as resolutely American as Main Street in Disneyland.

The 50th Congressional District—the first 50th district in the history of the House—covers the southern and eastern ends of San Diego and includes National City and Chula Vista down toward the border. The district was 40% Hispanic in 1990, and in partisan terms it is easily the most Democratic district in the San Diego area. Even so, districts in this general territory ousted incumbent Democratic Congressmen in 1980 and again in 1990, both times electing Republicans who after the ensuing redistricting chose to run in more heavily Republican seats farther from the central city: Duncan Hunter, who now represents the 52d District, and Duke Cunningham, who represents the 51st. It was apparent when the district lines were announced that the new member would likely be chosen in the Democratic primary, and the 1992 race attracted the yeasty cross-section of political operators one might expect in a city where there are few established political organizations or traditions.

The winner and the Congressman now is Bob Filner, the only Democratic member of Congress south of Los Angeles. He grew up in New York and was a Freedom Rider in 1961, imprisoned for two months in Mississippi. He taught history at San Diego State and directed the Lipinsky Institute for Judaic Studies; he took time off to work on Senator Hubert Humphrey's staff in the 1970s and was elected to the San Diego school board in 1979 and to the city council in 1987. On the school board he worked for mandatory homework, tougher graduation requirements, stricter discipline and attendance regulations. He gave up the seat to run for council in 1983 and lost. But in 1987, when Councilman Uvaldo Martinez pleaded guilty to misusing credit cards, Filner ran again and won; in 1991 he won reelection 70%–26%, despite a heavy Latino majority. Running for Congress in 1992, he had strong backing from blacks and Latinos although he had two better-known rivals. One was Jim Bates, the four-term Congressman beaten by Cunningham in 1990 after he was disciplined by the House on charges of sexual harassment. Bates also had 89 overdrafts at the House bank; he won 20% of the vote. Another was Wadie Deddeh, an assemblyman and state senator since 1966. But Deddeh was 71 and had recently had open heart surgery; he was against abortion and had apparently failed to make timely payment of income taxes. He got 23%. Juan Carlos Vargas ran primarily as the lone Latino, which was good for 19%. Filner won with 26%. In the general, Filner was irritated when the Republican nominee, Tony Valencia, made pointed references to his religion before Latino audiences; Filner won 57%–29%.

Filner is an aggressive activist, not afraid to break old rules. He told the 1993 Democratic freshmen they should vote as a bloc for reform; they did not, and ended up losing in large numbers as Filner foresaw. He used his seats on Transportation and Infrastructure and Veterans' Affairs to work on San Diego issues. He opposed the North American Free Trade Agreement, but once it passed, he tried to get trade facilities working on the border. He worked to fund construction of an international treatment plant for raw sewage coming into San Diego from Mexico and at the same time to get San Diego exempted from the Clean Water Act standards. He opposed the proposed bi-national Otay Mesa Airport, also opposed by Mayor Susan Golding and other civic leaders. Filner had an active Republican opponent in 1994, Mary Alice Acevedo, but won 57%–35%. After the election, he started working with San Diego's new Republican Congressman, Brian Bilbray, as well as the old ones. "The shaking up of the system probably helped me more than hurt me," he said, citing the Clean Water exemption. This resourceful liberal shows how Democrats can have political success by working hard to make sure government actually works and strengthens community values rather than just pouring money into government programs.

The People: Pop. 1990: 573,244; 1% rural; 8% age 65+; 32% White; 14% Black; 1% Amer. Indian; 15% Asian; 23% Other; 40% Hispanic origin. Voting age pop.: 398,117; 14% Black; 35% Hispanic origin.

Households: 54% married couple families; 30% married couple fams. w. children; 44% college educ.; median household income: $27,655; per capita income: $10,577; median gross rent: $540; median house value: $136,200.

1992 Presidential Vote

Clinton (D)	69,546 (48%)
Bush (R)	42,830 (30%)
Perot (I)...................	30,267 (21%)

1988 Presidential Vote

Dukakis (D)................	62,935 (52%)
Bush (R)	57,855 (48%)

Rep. Bob Filner (D)

Elected 1992; b. Sept. 4, 1942, Pittsburgh, PA; home, San Diego; Cornell U., B.A. 1963, U. of DE, M.A. 1969, Cornell U., Ph.D. 1973; Jewish; married (Jane).

Career: Prof., San Diego St. U., 1970-92; Legis. Asst., U.S. Sen. Hubert Humphrey, 1974; Legis. Asst., U.S. Rep. Don Fraser, 1975; San Diego Schl. Bd., 1979–83, Pres., 1982–83; San Diego City Cncl., 1987–92, Dep. Mayor, 1990.

DC Office: 504 CHOB 20515, 202-225-8045; Fax: 202-225-9073.

District Offices: 333 F St., #A, Chula Vista 91910, 619-422-5963.

Committees: *Transportation & Infrastructure* (24th of 27 D): Surface Transportation; Water Resources and Environment. *Veterans' Affairs* (7th of 15 D): Compensation, Pension, Insurance and Memorial Affairs.

Group Ratings

	ADA	ACLU	COPE	CFA	LCV	CON	NSI	COC	ACU	NTLC	CHC
1994	100	87	78	100	94	11	10	50	0	14	7
1993	100	—	100	90	79	19	—	9	8	—	—

National Journal Ratings

	1993 LIB — 1993 CONS		1994 LIB — 1994 CONS	
Economic	88% —	0%	83% —	0%
Social	80% —	13%	90% —	6%
Foreign	66% —	31%	80% —	17%

Key Votes of the 103d Congress

1. Clinton Deficit Plan	Y	3. Brady Handgun Purchase	Y	5. Lmt. UN Cmnd. of Forces	N
2. NAFTA	N	4. Strike Race/Death Pnlty.	N	6. Cut Missile Funds	Y

Key Votes of the 104th Congress

1. Congressional Compliance	Y	6. Reform Crime Grant	N	11. Loser Pays Court Reform	N
2. Balanced Budget Amndmt.	N	7. National Security Act	N	12. Product Liability Reform	N
3. Bar Unfunded Mandates	N	8. Moratorium on Regs.	N	13. Welfare Reform	N
4. Pass Line Item Veto	N	9. Risk Assessment on Regs.	N	14. Term Limits Amndmt.	N
5. Relax Exclusionary Rule	N	10. Expnd. Priv. Prop. Rights	N	15. Tax Cuts	N

Election Results

1994 general	Bob Filner (D)...........................	59,214	(57%)	($818,051)
	Mary Alice Acevedo (R)	36,955	(35%)	($352,091)
	Others	8,282	(8%)	
1994 primary	Bob Filner (D)....................	unopposed		
1992 general	Bob Filner (D).......................	77,293	(57%)	($856,046)
	Tony Valencia (R).....................	39,531	(29%)	($69,936)
	Barbara Hutchinson (Lib).............	15,489	(11%)	($19,534)
	Others	4,313	(3%)	

FIFTY-FIRST DISTRICT

When FBI director J. Edgar Hoover came to the races at Del Mar for two weeks every summer in the 1940s and 1950s, the rest of north San Diego County, from the track north to the Marine Corps's Camp Pendleton, was mostly uninhabited: there were a few thousand people in the beach towns of Oceanside and Carlsbad and a few thousand more scattered over the dry, brownish hills that rolled inland. Today about 650,000 people live in north San Diego County, and who can blame them? For this is one of America's most beautiful and comfortable environments, with ocean and mountain scenery, sunny and warm weather, no rural poverty and few (so far) urban problems. Here, amid dry but not desert landscape, you can see miles of rolling hills, with occasional surrealistic trees and sagebrush-like bushes; mountains clump up not in ridges, but here and there, seemingly at random. This land has attracted thousands of new migrants, many, but by no means all, retirees. Outside the Los Angeles media market, not frequented by many entertainment celebrities, North County does not have a high media profile, which probably suits the quietly successful people who have moved here just fine.

For the second time in two decades, North County grew enough to earn a new congressional seat. The new 51st Congressional District includes some 200,000 people in San Diego itself—not in its urbanized core, but in land it annexed during Governor Pete Wilson's long tenure as mayor, including the Rancho Bernardo planned community and Miramar Naval Air Station, whose Navy fliers were made famous in *Top Gun* and infamous in the Tailhook scandal. The 51st also includes the beach communities from Del Mar north to Carlsbad and the nearby La Costa resort. Inland, with its red-tile roofs filling a sunny valley, is fast-growing Escondido, with 108,000 people in 1990. Politically, this is overwhelmingly Republican territory, though with a taste for Ross Perot in 1992; rather conservative on cultural issues, against bigger government, patriotic and nationalistic on foreign policy.

The Congressman from the 51st is Randy (Duke) Cunningham, one of the most distinctive members of Congress. Born the day after Pearl Harbor, he taught and coached swimming in Hinsdale, Illinois, and San Diego; in 1966, at 25, he joined the Navy and became one of the most decorated pilots in the Vietnam war. He then trained pilots at Miramar in the Top Gun program; after retiring from the Navy in 1987, he started a business in San Diego. In 1990 he ran in a Democratic district against Democratic Congressman Jim Bates, who was charged with sexual harassment; Cunningham beat a former Ambassador to Qatar in the Republican primary 46%–30%, and in the general beat Bates 46%–45%. In 1992, faced with a choice of districts to run in, he passed up the marginal and culturally more liberal 49th on the coast and ran in the 51st in North County. Incumbent Bill Lowery, a Republican who had 300 overdrafts at the House bank (Cunningham had only one), ran but withdrew from the race in April 1992. Lowery's name remained on the ballot for the June primary; he got 15% of the vote and Cunningham 52%. In the general, Cunningham won 56%–34% over Democrat Bea Herbert, who raised only $23,315 to his $972,606.

In the House, where his military experience has generated widespread respect, Cunningham supported the Gulf war resolution, worked with California colleague Duncan Hunter to make

Filipino Gulf war veterans eligible to apply for U.S. citizenship and on the National Security Committee has worked to prevent base closings in the San Diego area. He has called for stricter enforcement of immigration laws and wants a 50-foot easement on the border so property owners can't stop the government from repairing and monitoring its fences. He voted for the North American Free Trade Agreement. He was one of four Congressmen who in October 1992 met with President Bush and prompted him to ask questions about Bill Clinton's student trip to Moscow and Eastern Europe, an issue that hurt the Republican ticket. He worked to allow U.S. sport fishermen to fish off the islands of Mexico's Revillagigedo Archipelago, an area that had been declared a "biosphere preserve." He cautioned that U.S. air strikes in Bosnia were a dangerous business. He got a Navy F/A-18 maintenance site returned to San Diego's North Island Depot. In 1995, after being reelected easily, he became chairman of the Economic and Educational Opportunities Subcommittee on Early Childhood, Youth and Families and vice-chairman of the National Security Committee's special oversight panel on Merchant Marine. Cunningham also wants to push the "No Frills Prison Act of 1995" which would take away the perks for criminals, including celebrity inmates.

The People: Pop. 1990: 572,850; 3% rural; 11% age 65+; 76% White; 2% Black; 1% Amer. Indian; 8% Asian; 5% Other; 13% Hispanic origin. Voting age pop.: 432,607; 2% Black; 12% Hispanic origin. Households: 61% married couple families; 28% married couple fams. w. children; 68% college educ.; median household income: $45,186; per capita income: $20,586; median gross rent: $730; median house value: $230,200.

1992 Presidential Vote			1988 Presidential Vote		
Bush (R)	108,470	(40%)	Bush (R)	149,926	(67%)
Clinton (D)	86,870	(32%)	Dukakis (D)	72,889	(33%)
Perot (I)	73,580	(27%)			

Rep. Randy (Duke) Cunningham (R)

Elected 1990; b. Dec. 8, 1941, Los Angeles; home, San Diego; U. of MO, B.A. 1964, M.S. 1966, National U., M.B.A. 1979; Baptist; married (Nancy).

Career: Navy, 1966–87 (Vietnam); Businessman, 1987–90.

DC Office: 227 CHOB 20515, 202-225-5452; Fax: 202-225-2558.

District Offices: 613 W. Valley Pkwy., #320, Escondido 92025, 619-737-6960.

Committees: *Economic & Educational Opportunities* (8th of 24 R): Early Childhood, Youth and Families (Chmn.); Oversight and Investigations. *National Security* (11th of 30 R): Military Readiness; Military Research and Development.

Group Ratings

	ADA	ACLU	COPE	CFA	LCV	CON	NSI	COC	ACU	NTLC	CHC
1994	15	17	22	20	11	76	100	100	95	96	100
1993	0	—	0	10	36	69	—	91	100	—	—

National Journal Ratings

	1993 LIB — 1993 CONS			1994 LIB — 1994 CONS		
Economic	0%	—	88%	0%	—	80%
Social	0%	—	89%	16%	—	81%
Foreign	9%	—	85%	12%	—	87%

Key Votes of the 103d Congress

1. Clinton Deficit Plan	N	3. Brady Handgun Purchase	N	5. Lmt. UN Cmnd. of Forces	Y
2. NAFTA	Y	4. Strike Race/Death Pnlty.	Y	6. Cut Missile Funds	N

Key Votes of the 104th Congress

1. Congressional Compliance	Y	6. Reform Crime Grant	Y	11. Loser Pays Court Reform	Y
2. Balanced Budget Amndmt.	Y	7. National Security Act	Y	12. Product Liability Reform	Y
3. Bar Unfunded Mandates	Y	8. Moratorium on Regs.	Y	13. Welfare Reform	Y
4. Pass Line Item Veto	Y	9. Risk Assessment on Regs.	Y	14. Term Limits Amndmt.	Y
5. Relax Exclusionary Rule	*	10. Expnd. Priv. Prop. Rights	Y	15. Tax Cuts	Y

Election Results

1994 general	Randy (Duke) Cunningham (R)	138,547	(67%)	($395,144)
	Rita K. Tamerius (D)	57,374	(28%)	($65,035)
	Others	11,067	(5%)	
1994 primary	Randy (Duke) Cunningham (R)	60,160	(86%)	
	Donald J. Pando (R)	10,045	(14%)	
1992 general	Randy (Duke) Cunningham (R)	141,890	(56%)	($972,606)
	Bea Herbert (D)	85,148	(34%)	($23,315)
	Bill Holmes (Lib)	10,309	(4%)	
	Miriam E. Clark (P&F)	10,307	(4%)	
	Others	5,341	(2%)	

FIFTY-SECOND DISTRICT

San Diego began as a port, but today most metropolitan area residents live out of sight of the sea, in hilltop neighborhoods inland that look out over distant ridges and freeways in the valley or in warm, sunny valleys amid the mountains which become denser and higher as one travels east from the Pacific. There is a discernible difference in attitudes and values between those who have settled inland and those nearer the ocean, part of the coastal-inland split which became critical in California's political struggles and culture wars in the 1980s. In San Diego, both groups tend to identify as Republicans, and coastal people may be more affluent. But those who settle inland are more likely to be conventionally religious and to have traditional moral values; they tend to be more supportive of the military and of an assertive foreign policy; they are more dubious about the ability of government to shape poor citizens' lives. They are, in a word, more conservative on most of the cultural and foreign issues of recent times, and therefore more reliably Republican: when oceanfront voters in San Diego shifted sharply toward Democrats in 1992, those in inland suburbs shifted more to Ross Perot but stayed Republican in other races.

The 52d Congressional District—the highest-numbered House district in American history—takes in many of the inland San Diego suburbs and proceeds eastward across mountains and desert and the man-made Salton Sea to the drained-dry Colorado River on the Arizona border. More than half its people are clustered in suburbs directly east of San Diego, off I-8 and Routes 94 and 67: Lemon Grove, La Mesa, Spring Valley, El Cajon, Santee. The rest are scattered in pockets around rural San Diego County and in the Imperial Valley, irrigated desert land where low-paid farm workers harvest some of America's most bounteous crops.

The congressman from the 52d is Duncan Hunter, who came to the House in 1980 as an upset winner in the Reagan landslide and now is the leader of a strain of Republicanism which is not represented in large numbers in the House but which Hunter thinks has greater support among ordinary voters. Hunter served in the Army in Vietnam, in helicopter combat assaults, and was an antipoverty lawyer afterwards. In 1980, at 32, he beat an incumbent Democrat and came to the House brash and confident he had the right answers. On the National Security Committee, he was an ardent backer of the Strategic Defense Initiative and of a large Navy, and he fought hard for San Diego naval facilities during the recent base-closing rounds, with some success. Although San Diego—where an estimated 1.4% of the entire defense budget is spent—was hit hard in 1991 and 1993, it stands to pickup jobs in 1995, and to benefit in the future from the Navy's new emphasis on developing mega-ports. He also worked hard to block relaxation of controls on exports of high-technology products. He has called for greater willingness to receive Vietnamese refugees and worked for U.S. citizenship for the 4,000 Filipinos who served with U.S. forces in the Persian Gulf. But he is also a strong backer of measures to crack down on illegal immigration. He called for the 10-foot steel wall being built to replace the chain link fence between San Diego and Tijuana, and he worked to use military personnel to repair border fences and improve border roads; he calls for 10,750 border guards to keep people from crossing in the San Diego area. And he enacted a "return-to-sender" system to intercept sewage flows from across the border in Tijuana and return them to Mexico before sewage can enter the Tijuana River and pollute San Diego beaches.

In 1993, Hunter emerged as the Republicans' most ardent opponent of the North American Free Trade Agreement, taking a leading part in the debate and decrying Mexican abuses of human rights. He also vociferously opposed the General Agreement on Tariffs and Trade in 1994 and the Mexican bailout in 1995. In many ways he is the House member who comes closest in substantive views to Patrick Buchanan or to older conservative Republicans like former Senator Robert Taft. Once a strong follower of Newt Gingrich, he is no longer a member of the Republican leadership or of Newt's team. But Hunter has retreated to his work on the National Security Committee, where he been a strong backer of Republican proposals to keep U.S. troops out from under U.N. command; he also led the fight for greater missile defense spending than the Clinton Administration wanted but was beaten in February 1995—the first Contract With America item that failed to win a majority.

Hunter had some problems in the 1992 election. The new 52d District was heavily Republican, but he had 399 overdrafts at the House bank, totalling some $129,000. At first he denied any overdrafts, then said the problem was his charitable contributions; he was reduced to sitting behind a card table for three days in front of the El Cajon courthouse with copies of his checks, ready to explain each one to voters. In the fall of 1992, Hunter accompanied Bob Dornan and Duke Cunningham on their trip to the Oval Office to urge George Bush to follow their lead in criticizing Bill Clinton for not revealing the full facts of his trip to the Soviet Union as a student in 1969. Although Hunter did not charge Clinton with misconduct or disloyalty, the mere act of making of such charges in a campaign sounded like an accusation of something on that order. Meanwhile, Democrat Janet Gastil, an apple orchard owner and violist, was conducting a vigorous, if lightly financed campaign against Hunter, accusing him of voting for the congressional pay raise and against increasing the minimum wage and of attacking Clinton and being supported by the religious right. Hunter, who won only 60% against two primary opponents, beat Gastil by an unimpressive 53%–41%. Democrats later wished that they had given Gastil more attention. But in the more Republican environment of 1994, Hunter had no primary opposition and beat Gastil 64%–31%.

The People: Pop. 1990: 573,355; 11% rural; 11% age 65+; 71% White; 3% Black; 1% Amer. Indian; 3% Asian; 9% Other; 22% Hispanic origin. Voting age pop.: 415,404; 3% Black; 19% Hispanic origin. Households: 58% married couple families; 29% married couple fams. w. children; 52% college educ.; median household income: $33,046; per capita income: $14,075; median gross rent: $566; median house value: $155,100.

1992 Presidential Vote

Bush (R)	81,421	(37%)
Clinton (D)	74,913	(34%)
Perot (I)	63,176	(29%)

1988 Presidential Vote

Bush (R)	120,811	(65%)
Dukakis (D)	65,488	(35%)

Rep. Duncan Hunter (R)

Elected 1980; b. May 31, 1948, Riverside; home, Alpine; U. of MT, U. of CA, Western St. U., B.S.L & J.D. 1976; Baptist; married (Lynne).

Career: Army, 1969–71 (Vietnam); Practicing atty., 1976–80.

DC Office: 2265 RHOB 20515, 202-225-5672; Fax: 202-225-0235.

District Offices: 366 S. Pierce St., El Cajon 92020, 619-579-3001; and 1101 Airport Rd., #G, Imperial 92251, 619-353-5420.

Committees: *National Security* (3rd of 30 R): Military Installations and Facilities; Military Personnel; Military Procurement (Chmn.).

Group Ratings

	ADA	ACLU	COPE	CFA	LCV	CON	NSI	COC	ACU	NTLC	CHC
1994	0	13	33	0	6	70	100	73	100	92	100
1993	5	—	8	0	15	65	—	91	100	—	—

National Journal Ratings

	1993 LIB — 1993 CONS		1994 LIB — 1994 CONS	
Economic	14%	86%	0%	80%
Social	0%	89%	0%	89%
Foreign	16%	83%	12%	87%

Key Votes of the 103d Congress

1. Clinton Deficit Plan	N	3. Brady Handgun Purchase N	5. Lmt. UN Cmnd. of Forces Y
2. NAFTA	N	4. Strike Race/Death Pnlty. Y	6. Cut Missile Funds N

Key Votes of the 104th Congress

1. Congressional Compliance Y	6. Reform Crime Grant Y	11. Loser Pays Court Reform Y
2. Balanced Budget Amndmt. Y	7. National Security Act Y	12. Product Liability Reform Y
3. Bar Unfunded Mandates Y	8. Moratorium on Regs. Y	13. Welfare Reform Y
4. Pass Line Item Veto Y	9. Risk Assessment on Regs. *	14. Term Limits Amndmt. N
5. Relax Exclusionary Rule Y	10. Expnd. Priv. Prop. Rights Y	15. Tax Cuts Y

Election Results

1994 general	Duncan Hunter (R)............................ 109,201	(64%)	($559,926)
	Janet M. Gastil (D)..................... 53,024	(31%)	($181,855)
	Others 8,461	(5%)	
1994 primary	Duncan Hunter (R)................. unopposed		
1992 general	Duncan Hunter (R)................... 112,995	(53%)	($559,970)
	Janet M. Gastil (D)................... 88,076	(41%)	($164,480)
	Others 12,713	(6%)	

COLORADO

Colorado has many claims on being the typical American state, except that in so many other ways it is atypical. For starters, it's far away from almost every other population center, an island of 3 million people surrounded by the sea of the Great Plains and the ramparts of the Rocky Mountains. Colorado has been called stodgy and set in its ways (author John Gunther in the 1940s) and a national trendsetter (columnist Joseph Kraft in the 1970s). It is mostly Republican in its politics (though it voted for Bill Clinton in 1992) yet is the home base of nationally prominent Democrats (Patricia Schroeder, Timothy Wirth, Gary Hart). Functionally it is a city-state: despite its expanse of plains and hundreds of snow-clad peaks, over half its people live in metropolitan Denver and four-fifths in the urban strip paralleling the Front Range, where the Rockies rise suddenly from the mile-high plateau.

It was not always so: Colorado started off as a collection of raucous mining camps and has gone through cycles of boom and calm. Evidence of the mining boom is seen still in the opera houses and storefronts of Cripple Creek and Central City, Aspen and Telluride; the quiet growth of much of the 20th Century is evident in the orderly neighborhoods and lush trees of Denver. Then came the booms of the 1960s and the high-energy-prices 1970s, when the Denver skyline sprouted new buildings overlooking the Capitol's golden dome and winter sports entrepreneurs built ever more ski resorts and year-round mountain condominiums. Young people looking for a splendid environment in which to live settled where the Front Range of the Rockies rears dramatically up over the High Plains; for them Colorado "represented the geography of hope," as then-newcomer Dick Lamm said (he went on to be elected governor three times).

Taking prosperity for granted, these young liberals in the early 1970s persuaded Colorado voters to reject the 1976 Winter Olympics and vote out hawkish and pro-development politicians for Vietnam war opponents and environmentalists. They had personal political successes, electing Schroeder and Wirth to the House, Hart to the Senate and Lamm governor in 1972 and 1974. Republicans surged back to take the legislature in 1976 (they have held it ever since) and to retain an open Senate seat in 1978, as Colorado partook thirstily of the gushings of the energy boom of 1974–82. Then came the energy bust, leaving many new Denver skyscrapers empty and oil operators and lenders ruined, notably Silverado Savings and Loan, even as the Front Range's air quality declined and the government's plutonium plant at Rocky Flats just north of Denver was shut down in 1989 for safety violations.

As the anti-Olympics crusaders of the 1970s saw the Los Angeles Olympics of 1984 become a focus of national attention and pride and a local money-maker, Colorado's new generation of leaders, more business-oriented Democrats like Governor Roy Romer and then-Denver Mayor Federico Pena, planned a new convention center, baseball stadium and a giant new Denver International Airport 25 miles from downtown. By 1994 all these initiatives had gone sour: the convention center was half-empty, major league baseball set attendance records in its new locale but then went on strike, and DIA was unopened and on its way to becoming a case study in public sector bungling. The airport was probably misbegotten from the start (predictions that Stapleton Airport would be outgrown were based on projections for a couple of years that proved atypical) and its cost vastly underestimated (initially predicted to be $1.7 billion when voters approved it in 1990, by late 1994 it was $4.9 billion). Its opening, first scheduled for December 1993, was postponed four times, because of a $186 million high-tech baggage handling system that ended up mangling suitcases ("a momentary glitch," Pena said), and finally opened February 28, 1995. One major airline reduced flights and another stayed out entirely because of high costs; as delay costs reached $350 million, DIA bonds were dropped to junk bond status. The airport is now in the midst of slew of investigations for contract frauds, payroll padding and

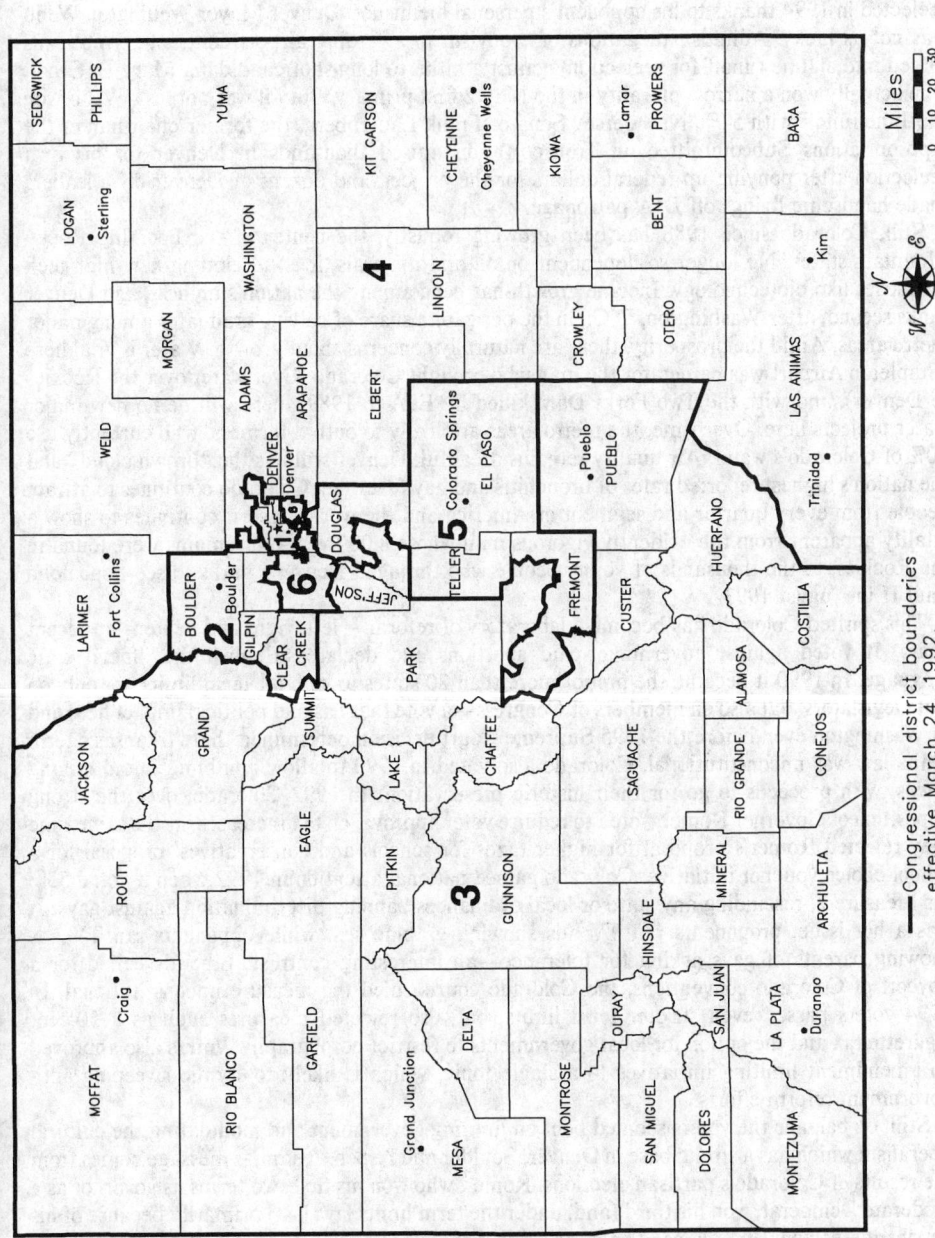

Congressional district boundaries
effective March 24, 1992.

Miles
0 10 20 30

Copyright © 1993 by Election Data Services, Inc.

other improprieties by the FAA, SEC, FBI and the Denver attorney general. The 34 white masts of its fiberglass roof loom up, a handsome counterpoint to the Rockies and a monument to ineptitude. But Pena went on to become Bill Clinton's Transportation Secretary and Romer was reelected in 1994 thanks to his opponent's personal blemishes. Denver Mayor Wellington Webb was not as lucky. Admidst allegations of cronyism in awarding airport contracts, Webb was forced into a June runoff for reelection against a hitherto long-shot candidate, Mary DeGroot, who actually won a narrow plurality in the May 2 first primary. But all was not lost. Webb won the June runoff with 54%, New Jersey Senator Frank Lautenberg, the former chairman of the Appropriations Subcommittee on Transportation, raised thousands in Denver for his own reelection after ponying up federal dollars for the project, and dozens of Denver civic leaders made handsome livings off DIA patronage.

Still, Colorado since 1988 has been growing robustly, the center of the booming Rocky Mountain states. No longer so dependent on oil and minerals, it is developing new high-tech industries like biotechnology. Income growth has been among the nation's highest, and Denver ranks second, after Washington, D.C., in the per capita share of college graduates among major metro areas. Amid the prosperity, there are naturally concerns about growth. Water is vital here (Stapleton Airport was named for the man who brought Colorado River water over the Rockies to Denver), and with the Two Forks Dam killed by EPA in 1989, there will be no new major water projects here. Over time, the metro areas are likely to outbid farmers, who currently use 90% of Colorado's water. Air quality remains dreadful: Denver still has the "brown cloud" and the nation's highest reported rates of bronchitis and hay fever. Yet Colorado continues to attract people from every quarter and segment of America and the world. And it continues to show a vitality apparent from the evidently vigorous man whose 8,000-year-old remains were found in the Rockies, to the thousands of young people who thronged Denver's parks to see Pope John Paul II in August 1993.

This spirited Colorado has become a laboratory of reform— left, right and center—in recent years. It voted against government-paid abortions and declared English the official state language. In 1990 it became the first of more than 20 states to vote for term limits not only on state legislators, but also on members of Congress—a vote that has had political impact here and in Washington even before the 1995 Supreme Court decision determined that Arkansas's term limits law was unconstitutional. Colorado also voted in 1990 to allow gambling in old mining towns, with proceeds to go for their historic preservation. In 1992 Colorado, over the strong opposition of Governor Romer, voted to require voter approval on tax increases; at the same time they rejected Romer's proposal for higher taxes for schools and conservatives' proposal for a school-choice voucher initiative. Colorado gained national attention in 1992 when it voted 53% for Measure 2, rescinding any state or local ordinances banning discrimination against gays. It was a hot issue: proponents ran TV ads showing graphic sex, while opponents ran TV ads showing parents of gays asking for tolerance—an interesting contrast. Liberals called for a boycott of Colorado conventions; the Colorado courts ruled the measure unconstitutional. In 1994 voters passed even stricter term limits, but also rejected measures such as a 50-cent cigarette tax and the option for local governments to restrict pornography. Voters also approved an amendment limiting initiatives to a single topic, which is likely to stymie sweeping anti-government reform efforts.

Still, on balance the voters seemed bent on limiting government and modulating the cultural liberalism which has a strong base in Denver, Boulder and Aspen. A similar message comes from the results of Colorado's partisan elections. Romer, who won his first two terms as governor as a moderate Democrat, won his third (and, under the term limits law, last) primarily because of his opponent's personal problems. The state's two Senate seats are held by freshmen, both with reputations as unconventional moderates. Republicans hold four of six U.S. House seats and majorities in the state legislature by solid margins.

Colorado was one of Ross Perot's best states: he was leading in polls when he left the race July 16 and won 23% of the vote in November, running over 30% in mountain and plains counties just beyond Denver. Similarly, in the primary season Colorado tilted to Jerry Brown and Paul Tsongas more than Bill Clinton while one-third of Republicans voted for Pat Buchanan over George Bush. Running through these results is a militant moderation, an angry rejection of much of the surface of public life together with an affection for the state and its ways of life. These are upscale voters (50% in 1994 were college graduates), tilted toward the baby boom generation (40% were age 30 to 44). Living in separate cultural enclaves, they yearn for a greater sense of community even as they argue about common values; they celebrate the beauty of their environment, even amid traffic jams under the "brown cloud." Even more than most Americans, Coloradans have much to be thankful for. But like most Americans, they have a nagging sense that they are missing out on what's important—and are arguing and trying to figure out what that can be.

Governor. Governor Roy Romer is the nation's second oldest governor (Idaho's Phil Batt is #1)—he turns 68 in 1996—but he remains refreshingly brusque, forceful, energetic, a man of impressive capacity and force of character. He grew up in a small town four miles from the Kansas border, built a chain of construction equipment stores and went into politics early on. He was elected to the legislature in 1958 and, as an opponent of the Vietnam war, ran and lost for a Senate seat against Republican Gordon Allott in 1966. In 1975 he became chief of staff to Governor Dick Lamm, who was younger and skeptical of growth. In 1976 he was elected state Treasurer and in 1986 won his first term as governor. Unlike some Democrats, Romer does not see economic growth solely as a menace to the environment. He has actually sought foreign investment and was a big booster of the troubled Denver International Airport and the Two Forks Dam, which was canceled by the Environmental Protection Agency.

Romer has played a national role on education as chairman until 1991 of the National Education Goals Panel, a bipartisan body set up between President Bush and the governors (led by Bill Clinton) as a result of a 1989 education summit. As National Governors' Association chairman he pushed for Goals 2000 education reform and urged President-elect Clinton to propose a national health insurance overhaul in his first 100 days. He took the response to that, as well as Colorado voters' decisions on two 1992 referenda—to reject his education tax and require a referendum on tax increases—as rebukes to his work. Prohibited from raising taxes, he squeezed down spending; he helped pass juvenile crime and "three strikes" laws; his fiscal policies were rated second best in the country by the libertarian Cato Institute. But Democrats were unpopular here, in part for national land and energy policies; in the 1994 exit polls only 24% said they helped and 24% said they hurt Colorado. In summer 1994 Romer was trailing Republican nominee Bruce Benson, a rich businessman, who attacked him for his support of the then-unopened Denver International Airport. But Benson had his own problems—a couple of drunk driving arrests more than a decade earlier and, it was revealed when his 1993 divorce records were opened, a threat that he was "going to kill" his wife. Also, in October Romer's car was mysteriously chased at over 100 mph on I-25 until a policeman finally shook the pursuer. Later, Ross Perot came in to endorse Romer. Benson plunged in the polls, and Romer won by 55–40% with exit polls showing the race close among men but Romer leading nearly 2–1 among women. Interestingly, Romer did much better with those with graduate degrees than with the less educated. In his third term Romer said he wanted to work on five "American dream" issues: jobs, education, crime, community stability for families and controlled growth, by maintaining open spaces around Colorado's fast-growing communities. He has thus far rejected urgings from national Democrats to run for Hank Brown's Senate seat in 1996.

Senators. Colorado was a pioneer in voting for term limits for Members of Congress, but it need hardly have bothered—or, perhaps, the voters' message has gotten through. In the 1990s, Republican Bill Armstrong retired after two terms, Democrat Tim Wirth in 1992 after one, Republican Hank Brown in 1994 announced he was retiring in 1996 after one, and Democrat-turned-Republican Ben Nighthorse Campbell, elected in 1992, supported the term limits initiative and pledged to retire after no more than two. None ever gained much seniority, but each has made a distinctive impact on national policy, Armstrong in indexing income tax rates and Wirth in overhauling the nation's communication policy and advocating policies to respond to global warming.

Hank Brown, who became Colorado's senior senator after just two years (while Ernest Hollings and Bob Packwood remain junior senators after 28 and 26 years respectively) has been in public life for many years. He was a star football player and student body president at the University of Colorado. He was a Navy aviator and served in Vietnam. After law school, he went to work for Monfort of Colorado, the world's largest cattle feed operation; Ken Monfort, its head, was an anti-war Democrat at the time. Brown served four years in the Colorado Senate, was out of office four years, and was then elected to the House in 1980. There he was activist who did not always fit the conservative mold. He was pro-choice on abortion and sponsored the first wild and scenic river designation for the Cache La Poudre River. He was a sharp critic, on the Ways and Means Committee, of the Democrats' welfare reform proposal in 1987–88 and got the House to endorse instead the workfare measure that became law instead. He argued strongly for allowing recipients to take low-paying jobs, and he fought hard against efforts to insulate even two-parent families from a work requirement. He was part of the House Ethics Committee that took on Speaker Jim Wright and was a leader in urging that Congress be covered by the civil rights and labor laws it imposes on others. He has tried to help Republicans out of their dilemma on term limits by offering a statutory alternative giving each state the option to pass its own law; that would require only a simple majority for approval, rather than the two-thirds for a constitutional amendment. When Senator Bill Armstrong announced his surprise retirement, Brown clinched the Republican nomination quickly. The upset winner of the Democratic nomination, former Boulder County Commissioner Josie Heath, turned out to be one of the few 1990 political casualties of the Gulf war; her loud advocacy of a 50% cut in the defense budget rang false when Saddam Hussein invaded Kuwait and hundreds of thousands of American troops were sent to the Gulf. Brown won by a solid 56%–42% margin.

Brown is pleasant and forthright, with a demeanor that seems in line with his moderate reputation; but he can also be a tough partisan and has a voting record which is in no danger of being confused for Democratic. He started off working with Democrats, agreeing on a Colorado wilderness bill and getting the Rocky Mountain Arsenal declared a national wildlife refuge. He was probably the least partisan Republican on Judiciary during the hearings on the Supreme Court nomination of Clarence Thomas; he got on amicably with Chairman John Kerry on the Foreign Relations subcommittee investigating the BCCI scandal.

Brown was a major party leader on important issues even before Republicans won their majority. On fiscal issues he sponsored "porkbuster" spending cuts and as early as March 1993 offered an alternative to the Clinton economic package; in November 1993 he sponsored with Nebraska's Bob Kerrey a $94 billion deficit-reduction package, including cuts in Medicare, the federal work force and federal retirees' COLAs. It was opposed by the Clinton Administration and defeated in February 1994. His March 1994 welfare bill, with more stringent work-based reforms and more flexibility for states than the Clinton plan, was endorsed by Bob Dole. On foreign policy, he has supported NATO entry for the Eastern European democracies, opposed U.S. intervention in Bosnia and been skeptical of U.S. involvement in Haiti, seeking an early withdrawal. He favors closer ties with Taiwan. He has taken some personal foreign-policy initiatives. One was a law to encourage Soviet nuclear scientists to emigrate to the United States, to stop nuclear proliferation. Another was his campaign against fellow Coloradan Sam Brown, who had been nominated by Clinton to head the U.S. delegation to the Conference on Security and Cooperation in Europe's arms control talks in Vienna; Sam Brown had been head of the antiwar Moratorium in 1969, and Hank Brown displayed posters of some of Sam's antiwar quotes and the nomination was killed. Hank Brown also got some attention in 1994 when he took Ralph Nader's dare and read the GATT treaty cover to cover; he took Nader's 10-question test, donated to charity the $10,000 he won from Nader and voted against GATT after he had said he was inclined to support it.

Practically every prominent Colorado politician has been mentioned as a candidate to succeed

Brown, who said soon after the 1994 election that he was retiring because he "never thought of this job as a lifetime career." Governor Roy Romer's announcement in December 1994 that he would not run, and Congressman David Skaggs' similar declaration in May 1995, leaves no clear Democratic frontrunner. Republican Attorney General Gale Norton has announced her candidacy and Congressman Wayne Allard seems certain to run as well. Congressmen Scott McInnis and Joel Hefley have both expressed an interest in the race, although McInnis appears more likely to wait for the 1998 contest for Ben Nighthorse Campbell's seat.

Colorado's junior senator is Ben Nighthorse Campbell from the Western Slope, who gave Bob Dole something of a consolation prize by announcing in March 1995, the day after the one-vote defeat of the balanced-budget constitutional amendment, that he was switching to the GOP. But that was not Campbell's first action that marked him as an eccentric, at least within the Senate. He is an Indian—only the eighth ever to serve in Congress—of the Northern Cheyenne tribe and attends tribal ceremonies every year in Montana. Campbell had a rough early life, being placed in an orphanage, dropping out of high school and joining the Air Force and serving in Vietnam. He studied judo for four years in Japan and was captain of the 1964 U.S. Olympic judo team. He bred hoses and built a successful jewelry-making business. He wears bolo ties and has his hair in a pony tail; he rides his motorcycle and resists mandatory helmet laws; on ceremonial occasions, notably at the 1993 Presidential Inaugural Parade, he rides his horse wearing full Indian headdress. He has taken up Indian causes, passing a law requiring that Indian-labelled arts and crafts must have been made by federally recognized American Indians and getting the Custer Battlefield Monument renamed as Little Bighorn; he wants to use government pressure to change the name of the Washington Redskins; he is irked that ethics specialists say he can't have an exemption from congressional income limits on his jewelry making, as writers in Congress can from book royalties. Campbell is not from one of the trendy "granola belt" ski resorts but from the small town of Ignacio on the plain below Durango, near the New Mexican border. He is a moderate on many issues, interested in economic growth perhaps even more than preserving the environment. He was elected to the Colorado legislature in 1982 and to the House in 1986, beating a Republican rancher with financial problems. He compiled a moderate Democratic voting record and, when Tim Wirth surprised just about everyone by announcing his retirement from the Senate in 1992, Campbell plunged into the race.

This was a furiously contested election. The Republican nominee was Terry Considine, entrepreneur and former state senator who had started the national term limits campaign. Democrats had three serious candidates: Campbell; 1990 nominee Josie Heath; and Dick Lamm, governor from 1974 to 1986, sponsor of one of the first laws legalizing abortion, proponent of zero population growth and immigration restrictions and a believer that the terminally ill have "a duty to die" rather than undergo elaborate medical treatment. Colorado holds party conventions and this one was close: Heath, with backing from feminists, had 25%; Lamm, with backing from environmentalists, had 37%; Campbell, with backing from the Western Slope and other non-upscale areas, had 38%. Then in the primary Campbell ended up losing Denver and its affluent suburbs and the "granola belt" ski counties to Lamm. But he carried 54 of 63 counties, and won with 46% to 36% for Lamm and 18% for Heath. In the general election, Campbell was put on the defensive by charges he'd accepted an oil company's plane ride to Alaska and stated falsely that he was trapped behind enemy lines for five weeks in Korea. In the weeks before his election, Campbell kept with him a ceremonial eagle feather tuft and Northern Cheyennes held a series of ritual ceremonies and prayer meetings on his behalf. Campbell benefited from Bill Clinton's victory in Colorado, from the endorsement of the active Colorado Perot organization and from the fact that he backed some of Considine's conservative reforms, notably term limits and the balanced budget amendment. All that was enough for a 52% Campbell victory. Once he switched parties, however, Democratic Senatorial Campaign Committee chairman Bob Kerrey took the unusual step of demanding that Campbell return the $255,000 that the committee spent to help get him elected in 1992. Campbell responded that the Democratic Party received sufficient benefit during the first two years of his term, but he did offer to return individual contributions to donors who disapproved of his switch.

As a Democrat, Campbell was one Senator who did not much mourn losing majority status. He has been a critic of Clinton environmental policies and is co-chairman of the Western States Senate Coalition; he has his own proposals for moderate grazing fee and mining law reforms. In Colorado he wants to open the Naval Oil Shale Reserves to drilling, to make the Black Canyon of the Gunnison into a national park and to add Old Spanish Trail to the national trails system. When he switched parties a few months after the election, his decision was due as much to local political jealousies as to grand national factors. Indeed, he warned that Republicans would grow uncomfortable with him. He is concerned that kids in trouble get a second chance, as he did, and was a key sponsor of the much-maligned midnight basketball provisions of the 1994 crime bill; he held a "gang summit" with gang leaders from around the nation to reduce violence and address the gang problem. He has worked for better housing for Indians and for a Fetal Alcohol Syndrome program to attack that disabling malady. He has worked on telecommunications issues, noting Colorado's prominence in the field (TCI's John Malone is based in Denver). Campbell has pledged to serve no more than two terms in the Senate but many in Colorado believe that his party switch was prompted, in part, by his hope to run for governor in 1998. If he does, he would become the third consecutive Colorado Senator to retire after one term—a sign of the times and an eccentric state.

Presidential politics. Colorado, for three decades heavily Republican in presidential races, was close to the national average in 1988 and 1992, which means that the Denver media market is as good a place as any in the country to see national candidates campaign and watch the ad wars in presidential races. Colorado's first ever presidential primaries, held in early March 1992, two weeks after New Hampshire and one week before Super Tuesday, were surprisingly uninfluential. The fact that Pat Buchanan got 30% despite never campaigning in the state attracted little attention. Jerry Brown's win here was deemed not to have precedential value; in fact, his candidacy proved more durable than expected, but he still seemed an inconceivable nominee. In 1996, with its early schedule, Colorado's March 5 primary may attract more attention.

Congressional districting. Colorado did not gain a new House seat out of the 1990 Census, for the first time in three decades; population growth had sagged in the mid-1980s and Arizona passed Colorado to become the most populous Mountain state. Under pressure from a nonpartisan court-appointed master plan, Democratic Governor Roy Romer and the Republican legislature agreed on a plan that didn't greatly change the character of the state's six districts, with three concentrated in metro Denver, another split between Denver suburbs and eastern Colorado, a fifth centered on Colorado Springs and the last covering the Western Slope and Pueblo.

The People: Est. Pop. 1994: 3,656,000; Pop. 1990: 3,294,394, up 11.0.1% 1990–1994. 1.4% of U.S. total, 26th largest; 18% rural. Median age: 32.5 years. 10.0% 65 years and over. 88.0% White, 12.9% Hispanic origin, 4.0% Black, 1.8% Asian, 5.1% Other. Households: 53.8% married couple families; 27% married couple fams. w. children; 58% college educ.; median household income: $30,140; per capita income: $14,821; 62.2% owner occupied housing; median house value: 82,700; median monthly rent: $362. 5.9% Unemployment. 1994 Voting age pop.: 2,713,000. 1994 Turnout: 1,111,486; 41% of VAP. Registered voters (1994): 2,034,393; 668,872 D (33%), 696,566 R (34%), 668,935 unaffiliated and minor parties (33%).

Political Lineup: Governor, Roy Romer (D); Lt. Gov., Gail Schoettler (D); Secy. of State, Vikki Buckley (R); Atty. Gen., Gale A. Norton (R); Treasurer, Bill Owens (R). State Senate, 35 (19 R and 16 D); State House of Representatives, 65 (41 R and 24 D). Senators, Hank Brown (R) and Ben Nighthorse Campbell (R). Representatives, 6 (4 R and 2 D).

1992 Presidential Vote

Clinton (D) 629,681 (40%)
Bush (R) 562,850 (36%)
Perot (I)................. 366,010 (23%)

1992 Democratic Presidential Primary

Brown 69,073 (29%)
Clinton................... 64,470 (27%)
Tsongas 61,360 (26%)
Kerrey 29,572 (12%)
Other...................... 9,812   (4%)

1988 Presidential Vote

Bush (R) 728,155 (53%)
Dukakis (D)............... 621,453 (45%)

1992 Republican Presidential Primary

Bush 132,100 (68%)
Buchanan.................. 58,753 (30%)

GOVERNOR

Gov. Roy Romer (D)

Elected 1986, term expires Jan. 1999; b. Oct. 31, 1928, Garden City, KS; home, Denver; CO St. U., B.S. 1950, U. of CO, LL.B. 1952, Yale, 1954; Presbyterian; married (Bea).

Career: Air Force, 1952–53; CO House of Reps., 1958–62; CO Senate, 1962–1966, Asst. Minority Ldr., 1964–66; Practicing atty., businessman, 1966–75; CO Ag. Commissioner, 1975; Chief of Staff, Gov. Richard D. Lamm, 1975–1977, 1982–1983; CO Treasurer, 1977–1986.

Office: 136 State Capitol, Denver 80203, 303-866-2471; Fax: 303-866-2003.

Election Results

1994 gen.	Roy Romer (D)	619,205	(55%)
	Bruce Benson (R)	432,042	(39%)
	Others	65,060	(6%)
1994 prim.	Roy Romer (D)..... unopposed		
1990 gen.	Roy Romer (D)	626,032	(64%)
	John Andrews (R)	358,403	(36%)

SENATORS

Sen. Hank Brown (R)

Elected 1990, seat up 1996; b. Feb. 12, 1940, Denver; home, Greeley; U. of CO, B.S. 1961, J.D. 1969; George Washington U., LL.M. 1986; C.P.A. accreditation, 1988; Congregationalist; married (Nan).

Career: Navy, 1962–66 (Vietnam); Accountant, 1968–69; Vice Pres., Monfort of CO, Inc., 1969–80; CO Senate, 1972–76, Asst. Majority Ldr., 1974–76; Greeley City Plng. Comm., 1979; U.S. House of Reps., 1980–90.

DC Office: 716 HSOB 20510, 202-224-5941; Fax: 202-224-6471; e-mail: senator_brown@brown.senate.gov.

State Offices: 1200 17th St., #2727, Denver 80202, 303-844-2600; 1100 10th St., #201, Greeley 80631, 303-352-4112; 228 N. Cascade, #106, Colorado Springs 80903, 719-634-6071; 411 Thatcher Bldg., Pueblo 81003, 719-545-9751; and 215 Fed. Bldg., 400 Rood Ave., Grand Junction 81501, 303-245-9553.

Committees: *Budget* (7th of 12 R). *Foreign Relations* (4th of 10 R): European Affairs; International Operations; Near Eastern and South Asian Affairs (Chmn). *Judiciary* (6th of 10 R): Administrative Oversight and the Courts; Constitution, Federalism and Property Rights (Chmn). *Veterans' Affairs* (6th of 7 R).

Group Ratings

	ADA	ACLU	COPE	CFA	LCV	CON	NSI	COC	ACU	NTLC	CHC
1994	30	21	13	33	8	99	90	88	92	88	86
1993	15	—	0	20	13	86	—	91	92	—	—

National Journal Ratings

	1993 LIB — 1993 CONS	1994 LIB — 1994 CONS
Economic	13% — 81%	0% — 88%
Social	26% — 73%	16% — 81%
Foreign	32% — 60%	23% — 74%

Key Votes of the 103d Congress

1. Clinton Deficit Plan	N	3. Brady Handgun Purchase	N	5. Lmt. UN Cmnd. of Forces	Y
2. NAFTA	Y	4. Strike Race/Death Pnlty.	Y	6. Cut Missile Funds	Y

Key Votes of the 104th Congress

1. Congressional Compliance	Y	3. Balanced Budget Amndt.	Y	5. Product Liability Reform	Y
2. Bar Unfunded Mandates	Y	4. Pass Line Item Veto	Y	6. FY96 Budget	Y

Election Results

1990 general	Hank Brown (R)	569,048	(56%)	($3,684,020)
	Josie Heath (D)	425,746	(42%)	($1,943,422)
	Others	27,233	(3%)	
1990 primary	Hank Brown (R)	unopposed		
1984 general	William L. Armstrong (R)	833,821	(64%)	($3,098,129)
	Nancy Dick (D)	449,327	(35%)	($840,595)

Sen. Ben Nighthorse Campbell (R)

Elected 1992, seat up 1998; b. Apr. 13, 1933, Auburn, CA; home, Ignacio; San Jose St. U., B.A. 1957, Meiji U., Japan, 1960–64; no religious affiliation; married (Linda).

Career: Air Force, 1951–53 (Korea); Rancher, horse trainer, jewelry designer; CO House of Reps., 1982–86; U.S. House of Reps, 1987–92.

DC Office: 380 RSOB 20510, 202-224-5852; Fax: 202-224-1933.

State Offices: 1129 Pennsylvania St., Denver 80203, 303-866-1900; 720 N. Main St., #210, Pueblo 81003, 719-542-6987; 105 E. Vermijo, #600, Colorado Springs 80903, 719-636-9092; 743 Horizon Ct., #366, Grand Junction 81506, 303-241-6631; 835 2nd Ave., #228, Durango 81301, 303-247-1609; and 19 Old Town Sq, #238, Ft. Collins 80524, 303-224-1909.

Committees: *Agriculture* (10th of 10 R): Forestry, Conservation and Rural Revitalization; Research, Nutrition and General Legislation. *Energy & Natural Resources* (6th of 11 R): Forests and Public Land Management; Parks, Historic Preservation and Recreation (Chmn.); Oversight and Investigations. *Veterans' Affairs* (6th of 7 R). *Indian Affairs* (7th of 9 R).

Group Ratings

	ADA	ACLU	COPE	CFA	LCV	CON	NSI	COC	ACU	NTLC	CHC
1994	55	79	88	67	62	39	56	47	25	16	23
1993	75	—	80	70	38	53	—	18	12	—	—

National Journal Ratings

	1993 LIB — 1993 CONS	1994 LIB — 1994 CONS
Economic	56% — 41%	68% — 29%
Social	62% — 37%	68% — 31%
Foreign	53% — 39%	41% — 58%

Key Votes of the 103d Congress

1. Clinton Deficit Plan	Y	3. Brady Handgun Purchase	N	5. Lmt. UN Cmnd. of Forces	N
2. NAFTA	N	4. Strike Race/Death Pnlty.	N	6. Cut Missile Funds	N

Key Votes of the 104th Congress

1. Congressional Compliance	Y	3. Balanced Budget Amndt.	Y	5. Product Liability Reform	Y
2. Bar Unfunded Mandates	Y	4. Pass Line Item Veto	Y	6. FY96 Budget	Y

Election Results

1992 general	Ben Nighthorse Campbell (D)	803,725	(52%)	($1,561,347)
	Terry Considine (R)	662,893	(43%)	($2,215,791)
	Others	85,671	(6%)	
1992 primary	Ben Nighthorse Campbell (D)	117,634	(46%)	
	Richard D. Lamm (D)	93,599	(36%)	
	Josie Heath (D)	47,418	(18%)	
1986 general	Timothy E. Wirth (D)	529,449	(50%)	($3,787,202)
	Ken Kramer (R)	512,994	(48%)	($3,785,577)

FIRST DISTRICT

One mile above sea level, (as the plaque on the 14th step of the gold-domed Capitol reads), a few miles from where the High Plains yield to the sharp peaks of the Front Range of the Rockies, on no historic trade route and with a fresh water supply adequate for a town one-tenth of its size, stands the great metropolitan center of Denver. With 1.6 million people, it has been the economic and cultural capital for 100 years of the whole Rocky Mountain region that author Joel Garreau called "the Empty Quarter." Denver has a Western air. It hosts the National Western Stock Show every year; not long ago the May D&F store led a 2,500-pound bull through its china department. But it is not roughneck. Its neat grid of streets, slanted on a 45-degree angle in downtown to align with the South Platte River and the railroad lines next to it, its array of parks, the trees which line so many of its streets and are a lush contrast with the dried landscape of the high plains and the Rockies—all these give Denver a burnished, sedate air, despite the unembellished skyscrapers of the 1970s energy boom. Three-quarters of the metro area's people now live in the suburbs, but the central city of Denver still seems to have the yeasty diversity inherent to a central city. The black neighborhoods of northeastern Denver are filled with well maintained 1950s bungalows; the Hispanic quarter northwest of downtown has vitality and sends residents on to upward mobility; gentrified areas south of the Capitol include the elegant elite neighborhood where the Tattered Cover, long the nation's largest independent book store, sits opposite posh Cherry Creek Shopping Center.

Denver increasingly is the liberal heart of Colorado, heavily Democratic in partisan elections, strongly liberation-minded on cultural issues, cautiously liberal on economic issues. Though it remains majority white Anglo, it has elected Hispanic and black mayors since 1983—Federico Pena, who became Bill Clinton's Transportation Secretary in 1993, and Wellington Webb who out of funds, campaigned for 41 days in 1991 without going home or getting into an automobile, walking the streets and staying at homes of supporters. Denver's liberalism in the early 1970s took the form of skepticism about growth and boosterism, at a time when growth seemed likely to go on forever. After the 1980s energy boom collapsed, Denver's leaders decided to use public monies to spur private growth—with disappointing results. The new convention center down-town has been half-empty, partly because of a boycott protesting Colorado's (but not Denver's) vote for an initiative banning gay-rights laws; the new baseball stadium was temporarily left without a major league team by the 1994 baseball strike. Then there is the Denver International Airport, Pena's pet project, which may be one of the greatest public sector fiascos of all time: its cost rose from $1.7 billion to at least $4.9 billion, its opening date was postponed 14 months after the scheduled December 1993, its costs so high that critics said that it was sure to have fewer flights than the supposedly obsolescent Stapleton. As Webb said, with perhaps unintentional understatement, "I think the age of the megaproject is probably over."

The 1st Congressional District of Colorado includes all of Denver and extends northeast toward DIA, taking in Commerce City and the northern part of Aurora, places with warehouses and trucking terminals on main streets and curved-street subdivisions behind. The 1st remains a heavily Democratic district, including most of metro Denver's blacks and Hispanics, singles and gays: the percentage of households with married couples and children is among the lowest in America. In an era when cultural attitudes are a better clue to voting behavior than economic status, this once politically marginal area has become a solidly Democratic constituency.

Representing the 1st District in the House for more than 20 years has been Patricia Schroeder, an important national figure symbolically and in substance. Schroeder sees herself less as a liberal than as a partaker in a vibrant Old West skepticism about tradition and authority figures; in Washington, however, and around the country where she has become one of the best-known House members, she is a symbol of feminism and liberalism—a kind of authority figure herself. She still has the breezy air of a midwesterner, the Harvard Law School graduate and daughter of an aviation insurance adjuster who got her pilot's license and worked her way through school with her own flying service. Her gift for the pithy phrase, unequalled in today's politics—it was she who called Ronald Reagan the "Teflon President"—and her often flip demeanor has put people off and have led some to underestimate her.

Several intellectual strains run clearly through Schroeder's career. One is dovishness. Her candidacy originated when a group of anti-Vietnam war activists caucused in a living room and came up with the then unusual idea of running a woman against an incumbent Republican who had beaten a dovish male two years before. Her first act in Washington, getting a seat on the National Security Committee over the objections of then-Chairman Edward Hebert, was a sensation (and a harbinger: two years later, Hebert was voted out of the chair). Predictably, she opposed extension of U.S. military power from Vietnam to the Gulf war. "Those certainly aren't my democracies," she said in August 1990. "They aren't big on human rights, for women anyway, or for anybody who doesn't agree with the monarchy." Another thread running through Schroeder's career is thriftiness. She has called for years for greater military burden-sharing by our allies and has pushed dual-basing—keeping more U.S. troops at domestic bases and ferrying them to South Korea, Japan or Europe if needed; in less elevated tones, she urged colleagues to scuttle foreign bases so they can be sure to save "Camp Swampy" at home. But her cost-consciousness extends to some domestic issues as well.

Schroeder has also been persistent in thrusting women's issues forward. She was an early supporter of legalized abortion, the sponsor of the law to make a federal crime of obstructing access to abortion clinics, a crusader for abortions at military hospitals, one of the leaders of the bloc who pledged to oppose any healthcare finance reform that didn't cover abortion. Not all of these have been successful: in 1994 no military doctor would perform abortions, and the push for abortion coverage in national health care was mooted when Democrats' health bills crashed and burned. She was more successful as the lead sponsor of the 1992 Family and Medical Leave Act George Bush vetoed and Bill Clinton signed. She has pushed for stronger child support enforcement.

Schroeder has used her seat on the National Security Committee to civilianize the military. To the Joint Chiefs of Staff she argued that the standards of civilian personnel law should be applied to the military. Early on, she interested herself in the situation of military families and in the wives of servicemen, passing her Military Family Act in 1985. In 1991 she got the National Security Committee to vote to allow women in the military to fly combat missions. She strongly criticized the handling of the alleged sexual harassment at the Tailhook convention and worked to reduce the rank of Admiral Frank Kelso and to deny promotion to Admiral J. M. Boorda. She has worked hard to elect more Democratic women to Congress; fewer now face the obstacle of being unwilling to run with young children, as Schroeder did in 1972 (when she thought she wouldn't win).

The 1994 elections vastly reduced Schroeder's power in the House, just as she was gaining the clout of seniority. She had hailed the 1992 results as an "American perestroika" that would "restructure government so that it is thoughtful, practical, cost-efficient and people-friendly." During the 1994 campaign, she looked forward to the committee posts her seniority would allow her to claim: the chairmanship of Post Office and Civil Service, a Judiciary subcommittee chairmanship, a senior seat on National Security behind her ally, Ron Dellums. But the Republican victory eliminated her hopes of any chairmanship and Post Office and Civil Service was one of three committees abolished by incoming Speaker Newt Gingrich. She considered running against John Conyers for the ranking post on Judiciary, which lost six of its eight top Democrats to retirement or defeat, but decided not to—a case where racial politics may have trumped gender politics. She expressed some relish at being part of the minority and became an early critic of Speaker Gingrich's ethics problems. "It liberates me because it's a whole lot more fun to throw grenades than to have people from my own party say, 'Now, now, now we must govern. We must be responsible.' " But she warned that her party "has to get its game together fast" or "you'll see an awful lot of members a year from now—some of the most senior ones—aren't going to run."

Could one of those be Schroeder? She has given no signs of eagerness for another job and has stayed in close touch with Colorado and Denver and even in 1994 had no trouble whatsoever winning reelection; Colorado's term limits initiatives, however, would bar her from running again in 2000. She continues to be a nationally prominent figure, capable of taking a part in presidential politics as she has in the past, when she chaired Gary Hart's campaign until it ended abruptly in May 1987 (ever the family person, she was furious with him for the personal scandal it involved) and then considered running herself. For three months she traveled the country, raised some $787,000 and watched herself rise in the polls to third in a field of unknowns. Then in September 1987, she appeared before supporters in Denver and, choking back a few tears, announced she wouldn't run. "Tears signify compassion, not weakness," she said later—no false male stoicism—but Schroeder did not run again in 1992, even when Democrats were casting about rather desperately for a candidate. For 1996 she could play a major role in shoring up support for Bill Clinton—or encouraging a primary competitor.

The People: Pop. 1990: 549,053; 13% age 65+; 62% White; 13% Black; 1% Amer. Indian; 2% Asian; 10% Other; 22% Hispanic origin. Voting age pop.: 424,850; 11% Black; 18% Hispanic origin. Households: 39% married couple families; 16% married couple fams. w. children; 54% college educ.; median household income: $24,870; per capita income: $14,942; median gross rent: $382; median house value: $74,900.

1992 Presidential Vote

Clinton (D) 135,016 (55%)
Bush (R) 63,283 (26%)
Perot (I) 43,245 (18%)

1988 Presidential Vote

Dukakis (D) 142,535 (61%)
Bush (R) 91,405 (39%)

Rep. Patricia Schroeder (D)

Elected 1972; b. July 30, 1940, Portland, OR; home, Denver; U. of MN, B.A. 1961, Harvard, J.D. 1964; United Church of Christ; married (James).

Career: Field Atty., Natl. Labor Relations Bd., 1964–66; Practicing atty.; Lecturer, Law prof., Commun. Col. of Denver, 1969–70, U. of Denver, Denver Ctr., 1969, Regis Col., 1970–72; Hearing officer, CO Dept. of Personnel, 1971–72; Legal Counsel, CO Planned Parenthood.

DC Office: 2307 RHOB 20515, 202-225-4431; Fax: 202-225-5842.

District Offices: 1600 Emerson St., Denver 80218, 303-866-1230.

Committees: *National Security* (3rd of 25 D): Military Research and Development. *Judiciary* (2nd of 15 D): Constitution; Courts and Intellectual Property (RMM).

Group Ratings

	ADA	ACLU	COPE	CFA	LCV	CON	NSI	COC	ACU	NTLC	CHC
1994	100	87	78	80	100	41	0	42	5	19	7
1993	95	—	92	90	100	50	—	27	13	—	—

National Journal Ratings

	1993 LIB — 1993 CONS		1994 LIB — 1994 CONS	
Economic	64%	— 34%	56%	— 43%
Social	73%	— 23%	77%	— 21%
Foreign	74%	— 26%	85%	— 0%

Key Votes of the 103d Congress

1. Clinton Deficit Plan	Y	3. Brady Handgun Purchase	Y	5. Lmt. UN Cmnd. of Forces	N
2. NAFTA	Y	4. Strike Race/Death Pnlty.	N	6. Cut Missile Funds	Y

Key Votes of the 104th Congress

1. Congressional Compliance	Y	6. Reform Crime Grant	N	11. Loser Pays Court Reform	N
2. Balanced Budget Amndmt.	N	7. National Security Act	N	12. Product Liability Reform	N
3. Bar Unfunded Mandates	N	8. Moratorium on Regs.	N	13. Welfare Reform	N
4. Pass Line Item Veto	N	9. Risk Assessment on Regs.	N	14. Term Limits Amndmt.	N
5. Relax Exclusionary Rule	N	10. Expnd. Priv. Prop. Rights	N	15. Tax Cuts	N

Election Results

1994 general	Patricia Schroeder (D)	93,123	(60%)	($502,466)
	William F. Eggert (R)	61,978	(40%)	($117,935)
1994 primary	Patricia Schroeder (D)	17,095	(85%)	
	Tom Simpson (D)	2,960	(15%)	
1992 general	Patricia Schroeder (D)	156,629	(69%)	($398,749)
	Raymond Diaz Aragon (R)	70,902	(31%)	

SECOND DISTRICT

Up against the Front Range of the Rockies nestle some of the most distinctive parts of the Denver metro area. One of these is Boulder, home of the University of Colorado, and says the *Rocky Mountain News*'s Clifford May, an "international mecca for people who thrive on physical challenge and risk," the nation's leading center for bungee jumping, mountain biking, snowshoe running, rock and ice climbing, downhill skiing, land surfing and hot-air ballooning. This is not surprising in a university town that literally looks up at erose rows of peaks rising to 14,000 feet from a mile-high plain laid out in mile-square grids much farther than the eye can see. Just to the south is another high-risk site, the government's now closed-down Rocky Flats nuclear weapons plant, whose astonishing mismanagement over the years is now being detailed in disturbing news stories.

The 2d Congressional District of Colorado is centered on this part of metro Denver. It includes all of Boulder County, Rocky Flats, some lightly-populated but picturesque Rocky Mountains acreage, including Central City with its new gambling casino, and lower-middle to middle-income suburbs north and northwest of Denver—Arvada, Wheat Ridge, Westminster, Thornton, Northglenn, Broomfield. Here families of comfortable affluence and struggling finances, of fundamentalist religion and environment-loving liberalism, live in subdivisions with views of the mountains, close to metro Denver's biggest shopping malls. This Metro North area is politically marginal, while Boulder is typically heavily Democratic; overall, despite occasional Republican speculation to the contrary, this is basically a Democratic district.

The Congressman from the 2d District is David Skaggs, a Democrat who came to Colorado after serving as a Marine in Vietnam. He was one of those baby boom liberals who came to the fore in the 1970s; like the California Gold Rush generation who held most major offices there from 1850 when they were in their 30s to the 1890s when they were in their 70s, this generation of politicians threatens to hold most of Colorado's top offices for decades. Skaggs was an aide to Congressman Tim Wirth in the 1970s; in the 1980s he was elected to the Colorado legislature. In 1986 when Wirth ran for the Senate, Skaggs won the seat, beating Democratic National Committee Vice-chair Polly Baca in the primary and hard-campaigning Republican Mike Norton in the general election.

Skaggs has worked aggressively on local issues while taking a role in the Democratic leadership in fighting for principles. He worked for worker retraining and education programs at the now defunct Rocky Flats nuclear weapons plant. He worked to pass the Colorado wilderness bill in 1993. With a seat on Appropriations, he worked to fund the Denver International Airport, acquisitions of Colorado wilderness lands, the National Renewable Energy Laboratory and National Institute of Standards and Technology in Boulder. He was also active in rounding up votes for the 1990 budget summit package and the Clinton budget and tax increase in 1993. He took the lead in attacking Dan Quayle's Competitiveness Council and has been the lead opponent of Radio Marti, which broadcasts to Cuba; in retaliation, Florida Republican Lincoln Diaz-Balart killed a $23 million appropriation for NIST.

Skaggs came through the 1994 election with a reduced but still solid 57% of the vote. He remained undaunted enough to run for the chairmanship of the Democratic Study Group; the vote was 93–93, after which Rosa DeLauro withdrew in Skaggs's favor. This is a seat and a congressman Democrats can ill afford to lose. But if the Republican tide is still running in 1996, Skaggs may have serious opposition even in this Democrat-leaning seat, especially if the Republicans nominate a candidate who is moderate on social issues. After some speculation, Skaggs announced in May that he would not run for Hank Brown's open Senate seat in 1996.

The People: Pop. 1990: 548,953; 8% rural; 8% age 65+; 87% White; 1% Black; 1% Amer. Indian; 2% Asian; 3% Other; 9% Hispanic origin. Voting age pop.: 407,961; 1% Black; 8% Hispanic origin. Households: 56% married couple families; 28% married couple fams. w. children; 61% college educ.; median household income: $35,117; per capita income: $15,823; median gross rent: $477; median house value: $89,700.

1992 Presidential Vote			1988 Presidential Vote		
Clinton (D)	123,144	(45%)	Dukakis (D)	115,446	(51%)
Bush (R)	83,209	(30%)	Bush (R)	110,047	(49%)
Perot (I)	66,678	(24%)			

Rep. David E. Skaggs (D)

Elected 1986; b. Feb. 22, 1943, Cincinnati, OH; home, Boulder; Wesleyan U., B.A. 1964, Yale, LL.B. 1967; Congregationalist; married (Laura).

Career: Marine Corps, 1968–71, Marine Corps Reserves, 1971–77; A.A., Rep. Timothy E. Wirth, 1975–77, Campaign Dir., 1976; Practicing atty., 1977–86; CO House of Reps., 1980–86, Minority Ldr., 1982–85.

DC Office: 1124 LHOB 20515, 202-225-2161; Fax: 202-225-9127; e-mail: skaggs@hr.house.gov.

District Offices: 9101 Harlan, #130, Westminster 80030, 303-650-7886.

Committees: *Appropriations* (18th of 24 D): Commerce, Justice, State, and Judiciary; Interior.

Group Ratings

	ADA	ACLU	COPE	CFA	LCV	CON	NSI	COC	ACU	NTLC	CHC
1994	80	83	67	90	89	13	40	50	10	14	7
1993	75	—	92	80	86	19	—	36	13	—	—

National Journal Ratings

	1993 LIB — 1993 CONS			1994 LIB — 1994 CONS		
Economic	59%	—	40%	73%	—	17%
Social	73%	—	23%	90%	—	6%
Foreign	79%	—	16%	57%	—	37%

Key Votes of the 103d Congress

1. Clinton Deficit Plan	Y	3. Brady Handgun Purchase	Y	5. Lmt. UN Cmnd. of Forces	N
2. NAFTA	Y	4. Strike Race/Death Pnlty.	N	6. Cut Missile Funds	Y

Key Votes of the 104th Congress

1. Congressional Compliance	Y	6. Reform Crime Grant	N	11. Loser Pays Court Reform	N
2. Balanced Budget Amndmt.	N	7. National Security Act	N	12. Product Liability Reform	N
3. Bar Unfunded Mandates	N	8. Moratorium on Regs.	N	13. Welfare Reform	N
4. Pass Line Item Veto	N	9. Risk Assessment on Regs.	N	14. Term Limits Amndmt.	N
5. Relax Exclusionary Rule	N	10. Expnd. Priv. Prop. Rights	N	15. Tax Cuts	N

Election Results

1994 general	David E. Skaggs (D).................	105,938	(57%)	($576,719)
	Patricia (Pat) Miller (R)...............	80,723	(43%)	($83,999)
1994 primary	David E. Skaggs (D)...............	unopposed		
1992 general	David E. Skaggs (D).................	164,790	(61%)	($673,887)
	Bryan Day (R)	88,470	(33%)	($93,577)
	Vern Tharp (Green)	18,101	(6%)	

THIRD DISTRICT

On a clear night from the air they look like tiny mottled veins with small clots here and there, thicker near Denver but never very bright: the lights of the civilization Americans have built on the Western Slope of the Rockies in Colorado. The lights follow the trails of valley roads and mountainside switchbacks; the nodes mark the dozens of little towns built during mining boom years—the gold rush of the 1870s, the uranium boom of the 1950s, the oil shale boomlet of the 1970s. The Western Slope—everything west of the Front Range, with dozens of peaks over 14,000 feet—has always blocked east-west movement; but for mining and now skiing, no one would have settled here. The miners who tracked gold and silver and lead ores also built Victorian towns with opera houses and gingerbread storefronts in valleys and defiles scarcely accessible to the outside world. Now many of these towns have been restored by ski resort operators and joined by dozens of new condominiums and shopping malls.

The political map of the Western Slope is as diverse as its history. Aspen and Telluride, with Victorian houses and counter-cultural substrata, are liberal and Democratic: the "granola belt." Vail and Crested Butte, with contemporary condominiums, are conservative and Republican. The rough-handed mining area around Grand Junction, where piles of tailings still crackle with radioactivity and people remember the oil shale boom with nostalgia, is hostile to environmentalists, while the small Hispanic and Indian communities in the south are heavily Democratic.

The 3d Congressional District of Colorado includes all the Western Slope plus the small industrial city of Pueblo. There, on the banks of the Arkansas River, the Rockefellers built large steel factories before World War I to make barbed wire and rails; now this blue-collar town has attracted new plants from McDonnell Douglas, Unisys and B.F. Goodrich. Pueblo is heavily Democratic and so are the Hispanic counties just to the south. Hispanic, not Mexican-American: Spanish-speaking people have been living here, as in northern New Mexico, for 350 years.

The 3d District is a political bellwether, for George Bush in 1988 and Bill Clinton in 1992. The current Congressman is a Republican, Scott McInnis, who grew up in Glenwood Springs, in a crevassed valley west of Aspen and Vail. He worked as a local policeman and went to law school, practiced law and was elected to the legislature in 1982, at 29. Colorado was one of the few states in the 1980s with a Republican legislature, and McInnis became House Majority Leader in 1991. In 1992, when 3d District Congressman Ben Nighthorse Campbell ran for the Senate, McInnis won the Republican nomination unopposed and outworked and outcampaigned Lieutenant Governor Mike Callihan to win 55%–44%. In his campaign, he called for cutting both entitlements and defense spending and was the beneficiary of a $127,000 independent expenditure by the American Medical Association PAC and by Campbell's refusal to endorse Callihan. He was also helped by the water issue: he had worked to pass a Basin of Origin bill to protect Colorado's water rights and prevent export of water to other states, and he promoted a study of deep groundwater aquifers in the Eastern Slope areas.

McInnis entered the House as part of the minority, but sponsored four laws, including a Colorado wilderness bill. He became a party spokesman on the problems in Korea and visited South Korea. He has tried to return to the district every weekend, and his hard work paid off when he overwhelmingly defeated New York transplant (and cowboy boot wearer) state Senator Linda Powers. As part of the majority and after being rewarded by Speaker Newt Gingrich with a seat on the Rules Committee, the House's traffic cop, McInnis now is well-positioned to influence many laws. He has been mentioned as a possible candidate for Hank Brown's Senate seat in 1996.

The People: Pop. 1990: 549,120; 46% rural; 13% age 65+; 80% White; 1% Black; 1% Amer. Indian; 6% Other; 17% Hispanic origin. Voting age pop.: 403,814; 1% Black; 15% Hispanic origin. Households: 57% married couple families; 27% married couple fams. w. children; 49% college educ.; median household income: $24,521; per capita income: $12,115; median gross rent: $361; median house value: $62,000.

1992 Presidential Vote		
Clinton (D)	107,227	(40%)
Bush (R)	92,292	(34%)
Perot (I)	67,210	(25%)

1988 Presidential Vote		
Bush (R)	120,715	(53%)
Dukakis (D)	106,381	(47%)

Rep. Scott McInnis (R)

Elected 1992; b. May 9, 1953, Glenwood Springs; home, Grand Junction; Ft. Lewis Col., B.A. 1975, St. Mary's U., J.D. 1980; Catholic; married (Lori).

Career: Glenwood Springs police officer, 1976; Practicing atty., 1980–92; CO House of Reps., 1982–92, Majority Ldr., 1990–92.

DC Office: 215 CHOB 20515, 202-225-4761; Fax: 202-225-0622.

District Offices: 327 N. 7th St., Grand Junction 81501, 303-245-7107; 134 W. B St., Pueblo 81003, 719-543-8200; 1060 Main Ave., #107, Durango 81301, 303-259-2754; and 526 Pine St., #112, Glenwood Springs 81601, 303-928-0637.

Committees: *Rules* (8th of 9 R): Rules of the House.

Group Ratings

	ADA	ACLU	COPE	CFA	LCV	CON	NSI	COC	ACU	NTLC	CHC
1994	15	23	11	20	18	88	100	83	81	93	79
1993	15	—	8	10	21	52	—	91	88	—	—

National Journal Ratings

	1993 LIB — 1993 CONS		1994 LIB — 1994 CONS	
Economic	23% —	75%	0% —	80%
Social	29% —	69%	31% —	69%
Foreign	37% —	60%	14% —	80%

Key Votes of the 103d Congress

1. Clinton Deficit Plan	N	3. Brady Handgun Purchase	N	5. Lmt. UN Cmnd. of Forces	Y
2. NAFTA	Y	4. Strike Race/Death Pnlty.	Y	6. Cut Missile Funds	Y

Key Votes of the 104th Congress

1. Congressional Compliance	Y	6. Reform Crime Grant	Y	11. Loser Pays Court Reform	Y
2. Balanced Budget Amndmt.	Y	7. National Security Act	Y	12. Product Liability Reform	Y
3. Bar Unfunded Mandates	Y	8. Moratorium on Regs.	Y	13. Welfare Reform	Y
4. Pass Line Item Veto	Y	9. Risk Assessment on Regs.	Y	14. Term Limits Amndmt.	Y
5. Relax Exclusionary Rule	Y	10. Expnd. Priv. Prop. Rights	Y	15. Tax Cuts	Y

Election Results

1994 general	Scott McInnis (R)...................	145,365	(70%)	($387,210)
	Linda Powers (D)	63,427	(30%)	($241,305)
1994 primary	Scott McInnis (R)................	unopposed		
1992 general	Scott McInnis (R)...................	143,293	(55%)	($434,449)
	Mike Callihan (D)..................	114,480	(44%)	($326,185)

FOURTH DISTRICT

The High Plains of eastern Colorado are dusty brown, gently rolling land that seems flat but is actually sloping imperceptibly downward toward the Mississippi River. The land is fertile but dry: rainfall is rare, the rivers are just a trickle most of the year, and in many places groundwater is equally scarce. It is fine wheat country when irrigated and one of the foremost beef cattle regions. But wheat prices and exports fell in the 1980s and beef consumption declined from the red-meat days of the middle 1970s. Water prices, thanks to continued growth on the Front Range, are rising beyond what farmers can pay, and landowners are selling their water rights to middlemen and urban users. The free market that once peopled the High Plains with farmers and ranchers and made it the scene of farm protests and revolts is now causing it to empty out and revert to untamed land, ready again for now increasingly numerous buffalo.

The 4th Congressional District of Colorado contains almost all of the High Plains plus the medium-sized towns of Greeley, Fort Collins and Loveland—the northern end of the densely populated Front Range. By heritage and usually by inclination, this is Republican territory. The only Democratic part of the 4th is its small segment of metro Denver, northern Adams County around Brighton, with large Mexican-American and blue-collar populations.

The congressman from the 4th is Wayne Allard, a Republican with one of the most conservative records in the House. He is a veterinarian—a thriving business in an area with huge feedlots—who was elected to the state Senate in 1982. In 1990, when 4th District Congressman Hank Brown was running for the Senate, Allard ran for the House. Against a former local university president and legislator, he barely carried the Front Range and won 61% on the High Plains, for a 54% victory. In 1992, Allard's opponent tried to capitalize on anti-incumbent feeling by running a TV spot showing pigs at the trough and an old farmer who said he would vote for Allard "when pigs fly." But Allard won with 58% and celebrated by showing off inflatable pigs with wings.

As a minority member of the Agriculture, Resources and Budget Committees, Allard made points if not laws in the 103d Congress. He wanted to abolish Interior Secretary Bruce Babbitt's National Biological Survey, in order to weaken the Endangered Species Act. He wanted to keep the Soil Conservation Service in the Farm Service Agency, for fear it would be used to take away western water. He got an amendment regarding the Colorado River Compact, to protect Colorado water, added to the California Desert Protection Act. His attempt to limit spending on San Francisco's Presidio military post and his move to put all health care legislation on-budget were both defeated, at least when Democrats were in the majority.

But many of these will be live issues in the Republican 104th Congress. Allard, who held 170 community meetings in four years and faced an opponent with little knowledge of local issues, won easily in 1994. He declined a seat on the Ways and Means Committee and instead chairs the Agriculture Subcommittee on Research and Forestry. There, he seems certain to play a role on the 1995 farm bill and will surely work to protect Colorado's water rights and reduce federal restrictions on the use of its natural resources. His national political stature is expected to increase with his plan to seek the Senate seat of Hank Brown; if he runs, he may find himself the conservative alternative in the primary.

The People: Pop. 1990: 549,216; 35% rural; 11% age 65+; 83% White; 1% Black; 1% Amer. Indian; 1% Asian; 6% Other; 15% Hispanic origin. Voting age pop.: 396,692; 1% Black; 12% Hispanic origin. Households: 60% married couple families; 30% married couple fams. w. children; 50% college educ.; median household income: $26,577; per capita income: $12,387; median gross rent: $379; median house value: $70,100.

1992 Presidential Vote			1988 Presidential Vote		
Bush (R)	96,638	(38%)	Bush (R)	124,253	(56%)
Clinton (D)	94,234	(37%)	Dukakis (D)	99,575	(44%)
Perot (I)	63,203	(25%)			

Rep. Wayne Allard (R)

Elected 1990; b. Dec. 2, 1943, Fort Collins; home, Loveland; CO St. U., D.V.M. 1968; Protestant; married (Joan).

Career: Veterinarian, 1968–69; Owner & veterinarian, Allard Animal Hosp., 1970–90; Loveland City Health Officer, 1970–78; CO Senate, 1982–90.

DC Office: 422 CHOB 20515, 202-225-4676; Fax: 202-225-8630.

District Offices: Greeley Natl. Plz., #350, 822 7th St., Greeley 80631, 303-351-7582; 315 W. Oak, #307, Ft. Collins 80521, 303-493-9132; 212 E. Kiowa, Ft. Morgan 80701, 303-867-8909; and 19 W. 4th Ave., La Junta 81050, 719-384-7370.

Committees: *Agriculture* (5th of 27 R): Department Operations, Nutrition and Foreign Agriculture; Resource Conservation, Research and Forestry (Chmn.). *Budget* (9th of 24 R). *Resources* (8th of 25 R): National Parks, Forests and Lands; Water and Power Resources.

Group Ratings

	ADA	ACLU	COPE	CFA	LCV	CON	NSI	COC	ACU	NTLC	CHC
1994	5	13	0	0	28	88	80	83	95	93	100
1993	15	—	0	0	23	95	—	91	96	—	—

National Journal Ratings

	1993 LIB — 1993 CONS		1994 LIB — 1994 CONS	
Economic	0% —	88%	0% —	80%
Social	0% —	89%	11% —	85%
Foreign	35% —	63%	0% —	88%

Key Votes of the 103d Congress

1. Clinton Deficit Plan	N	3. Brady Handgun Purchase	N	5. Lmt. UN Cmnd. of Forces	Y
2. NAFTA	Y	4. Strike Race/Death Pnlty.	Y	6. Cut Missile Funds	Y

Key Votes of the 104th Congress

1. Congressional Compliance Y	6. Reform Crime Grant Y	11. Loser Pays Court Reform Y
2. Balanced Budget Amndmt. Y	7. National Security Act Y	12. Product Liability Reform Y
3. Bar Unfunded Mandates Y	8. Moratorium on Regs. Y	13. Welfare Reform Y
4. Pass Line Item Veto Y	9. Risk Assessment on Regs. Y	14. Term Limits Amndmt. N
5. Relax Exclusionary Rule Y	10. Expnd. Priv. Prop. Rights Y	15. Tax Cuts Y

Election Results

1994 general	Wayne Allard (R)	136,251	(72%)	($267,997)
	Cathy Kipp (D)	52,202	(28%)	($19,344)
1994 primary	Wayne Allard (R)	unopposed		
1992 general	Wayne Allard (R)	139,884	(58%)	($551,110)
	Tom Redder (D)	101,957	(42%)	($378,655)

FIFTH DISTRICT

A century ago Pike's Peak, first espied by Zebulon Pike in 1806, and nearby Colorado Springs were major tourist attractions. In the years since, Colorado Springs has become one of the military fortresses of the United States, safe in the fastness of the continent where the Rockies meet the High Plains, bristling with weapons and highly trained personnel. Here is the Army's Fort Carson; just to the north is the Air Force Academy, its striking modern buildings silhouetted against the mountains. Not far away is Falcon Air Force Base, the central planning site for the Strategic Defense Initiative, and Cheyenne Mountain, where NORAD, from its underground headquarters, patrols the skies for invading planes or missiles. Some of these are obsolete; but around them Colorado Springs has built a high-tech, innovative economy and a community whose scenic grandeur and suburb-like quietude have attracted new residents young and old.

Politically, Colorado Springs is far and away the most conservative part of Colorado. None of Denver's liberalism here: this is the home base of the activists who put the 1992 propositions requiring voter approval of state tax increases and barring gay rights laws on the ballot. The 5th Congressional District, which includes all of Colorado Springs and reaches north through fast-growing Douglas County (from 8,000 to 60,000 in the 1980s), is by any measure Colorado's most Republican district, and one of the nation's.

The Congressman from the 5th District, Joel Hefley, came to Colorado Springs in 1965, became a professional civic leader, served 10 years in the state Senate and was elected to Congress in 1986. On the National Security Committee, where he chairs the Subcommittee on Military Installations and Facilities, Hefley has been a staunch supporter of SDI research and development and in the Clinton years pushed for a commitment to maintain 12 active Army divisions; he worked to find new missions for Fort Carson, lest it get on the base closings list.

More important, Hefley was one of the little-noticed pioneer advocates of many of the issues featured in the 1994 Republican Contract With America. For years he has tried to cut federal spending, issuing a Porker of the Week Award for colleagues. He proposed specific cuts, many of them overwhelmingly defeated, to zero out the National Endowment for Democracy, the Advisory Commission on Intergovernmental Regulations, the Economic Development Administration. He was one of the leaders of the move to zero out the Interstate Commerce Commission, which has lost all regulatory authority; but it was John Kasich's amendment to do so which finally passed the House in 1994. He authored a bill to end unfunded mandates, to lower capital gains tax rates and expand IRAs, to provide greater rights to taxpayers, to limit tort liability, to require a three-fifths vote on taxes. He wants to limit spending on national parks. Fringe stuff all this seemed, until November 1994; then it became mainstream. With his committee seniority, he will be well-positioned to act on many of these issues.

Hefley, chosen in a contested primary in 1986, has been reelected easily since, without opposition in 1994. But in 1996 he might opt to run for Hank Brown's Senate seat.

The People: Pop. 1990: 549,264; 11% rural; 7% age 65+; 85% White; 6% Black; 1% Amer. Indian; 2% Asian; 3% Other; 7% Hispanic origin. Voting age pop.: 394,528; 5% Black; 6% Hispanic origin. Households: 63% married couple families; 33% married couple fams. w. children; 65% college educ.; median household income: $33,348; per capita income: $15,370; median gross rent: $432; median house value: $90,200.

1992 Presidential Vote

Bush (R)	125,749	(49%)
Clinton (D)	71,185	(28%)
Perot (I)	57,488	(22%)

1988 Presidential Vote

Bush (R)	141,893	(70%)
Dukakis (D)	61,038	(30%)

Rep. Joel Hefley (R)

Elected 1986; b. Apr. 18, 1935, Ardmore, OK; home, Colorado Springs; OK Baptist U., B.A. 1957, OK St. U., M.S. 1962; Baptist; married (Lynn).

Career: CO House of Reps., 1976–78; CO Senate, 1978–86; Exec. Dir., Community Planning and Research Cncl., 1966–86.

DC Office: 2351 RHOB 20515, 202-225-4422; Fax: 202-225-1942.

District Offices: 104 S. Cascade Ave., #105, Colorado Springs 80903, 719-520-0055; and 9605 Maroon Cir., #280, Englewood 80112, 303-792-3923.

Committees: *National Security* (9th of 30 R): Military Installations and Facilities (Chmn.); Military Research and Development. *Resources* (6th of 25 R): Energy and Mineral Resources; National Parks, Forests and Lands. *Small Business* (2nd of 22 R): Government Programs.

Group Ratings

	ADA	ACLU	COPE	CFA	LCV	CON	NSI	COC	ACU	NTLC	CHC
1994	0	17	22	10	11	70	100	75	100	93	100
1993	5	—	0	0	29	55	—	91	100	—	—

National Journal Ratings

	1993 LIB — 1993 CONS		1994 LIB — 1994 CONS	
Economic	14% —	80%	0% —	80%
Social	0% —	89%	11% —	85%
Foreign	0% —	91%	0% —	88%

Key Votes of the 103d Congress

1. Clinton Deficit Plan	N	3. Brady Handgun Purchase	N	5. Lmt. UN Cmnd. of Forces	Y
2. NAFTA	Y	4. Strike Race/Death Pnlty.	Y	6. Cut Missile Funds	N

Key Votes of the 104th Congress

1. Congressional Compliance	Y	6. Reform Crime Grant	N	11. Loser Pays Court Reform	Y
2. Balanced Budget Amndmt.	Y	7. National Security Act	Y	12. Product Liability Reform	Y
3. Bar Unfunded Mandates	Y	8. Moratorium on Regs.	Y	13. Welfare Reform	Y
4. Pass Line Item Veto	Y	9. Risk Assessment on Regs.	Y	14. Term Limits Amndmt.	N
5. Relax Exclusionary Rule	Y	10. Expnd. Priv. Prop. Rights	Y	15. Tax Cuts	Y

Election Results

1994 general	Joel Hefley (R)	unopposed		($137,960)
1994 primary	Joel Hefley (R)	unopposed		
1992 general	Joel Hefley (R)	173,096	(71%)	($162,718)
	Charles Oriez (D)	62,550	(26%)	($14,613)
	Other	7,769	(3%)	

SIXTH DISTRICT

A generation ago, most people in metro Denver lived in the city itself; at the city limits the tree-shaded sidewalks gave way to the empty High Plains. Today, three-quarters of metro Denver residents live outside the city. Just south of Denver, in Arapahoe County, Englewood, Littleton and Cherry Hills, pioneered in the 1940s and 1950s, are the homes of much of the city's elite. Aurora, to the east, benefited at first from the growth around Stapleton Airport, now about to be replaced, but has grown big enough—from 50,000 in 1965 to 220,000 in 1990—to support its own regional mall. West, in Jefferson County, which in 1992 cast more votes than Denver, Lakewood and Wheat Ridge are creations of the 1960s and 1970s, affluent but not elite suburbs with winding streets and office complexes, notably Lakewood's gigantic Denver Federal Center. Up against the Front Range is Golden, the headquarters of Coors beer and the Coors family which funds so many conservative causes.

The 6th Congressional District of Colorado covers most of this suburban territory. This is almost entirely Republican domain. The dominant tone is technical and managerial, and people here still yearn for the certainty of traditional limits. They value their environment, but they also see the need for economic growth and scientific innovation—both of which they think liberals tend to underrate. George Bush ran badly here in 1992 compared to 1988, as was the case in many affluent areas, but the Republican allegiance remained, as the 1994 election showed.

The 6th District has had only one congressman since its creation in 1982; astronaut Jack Swigert, elected in 1982, died before taking office, and Dan Schaefer, public relations consultant and six-year state legislator, won the special election in March 1983. After nearly a decade in the minority, he has become an influential legislator and now chairs the Commerce Subcommittee on Energy and Power. But even in the 103d Congress, he had begun to play a key role. He worked with Chairman John Dingell on the Rocky Flats cleanup, trying to ferret out more information from the Justice and Energy Departments, and working with Colorado Attorney General Gale Norton as well. A 1992 law written by Schaefer gives states authority to deal with environmental violations caused by the federal government; a Schaefer provision of the 1994 Superfund bill reasserted this authority. Schaefer has also been active on cable TV legislation, not surprising since Denver is the headquarters of John Malone and TCI, the biggest cable operator. He opposed the 1992 cable re-regulation, which was the only bill passed over George Bush's veto, and he predicted it would raise rates for many, which it did. He now argues that the regional phone companies should be able to enter the cable business outside their own service areas. He also complains that cable companies after the 1992 law can't raise capital to create the information superhighway, and that the regional Bells don't have the same technological access to homes, so they should make a natural combination. He supported the Bell Atlantic-TCI merger and the telecommunications bill that passed the House in 1994, but it died in the Senate. This issue will be revisited and could easily be the most heavily lobbied issue in the 104th Congress.

Schaefer has also put forward spending-cut initiatives. With Democrat Tim Penny he proposed in 1994 to freeze all federal COLAs in three of the next five years and to bar welfare benefits for illegal immigrants, in a $482 billion cut package; it didn't pass, of course. He played an active role in the balanced budget amendment by successfully urging conservative advocates not to insist on a proposed three-fifths requirement for tax increases. He has suggested an approach like the base closing commission for cutting entitlements.

Schaefer has moved from cloutless backbencher to front-rank legislator in just a few years. His constituents seem to like him in both roles, and he has won reelection easily.

The People: Pop. 1990: 548,788; 5% rural; 8% age 65+; 87% White; 3% Black; 1% Amer. Indian; 2% Asian; 2% Other; 6% Hispanic origin. Voting age pop.: 406,563; 3% Black; 6% Hispanic origin. Households: 56% married couple families; 28% married couple fams. w. children; 68% college educ.; median household income: $37,333; per capita income: $18,289; median gross rent: $473; median house value: $92,200.

1992 Presidential Vote			1988 Presidential Vote		
Bush (R)	101,679	(38%)	Bush (R)	139,864	(59%)
Clinton (D)	98,875	(37%)	Dukakis (D)	96,478	(41%)
Perot (I)	68,186	(25%)			

Rep. Dan Schaefer (R)

Elected Mar. 1983; b. Jan. 25, 1936, Guttenberg, IA; home, Lakewood; Niagara U., B.A. 1961, Potsdam St. U., 1963; Catholic; married (Mary).

Career: Marine Corps, 1955–57; Educator, 1961–67; PR consultant, 1967–83; CO House of Reps., 1977–78; CO Senate, 1979–83.

DC Office: 2353 RHOB 20515, 202-225-7882; Fax: 202-225-7885.

District Offices: 3615 S. Huron, #101, Englewood 80110, 303-762-8890.

Committees: *Commerce* (6th of 26 R): Energy and Power (Chmn.); Telecommunications and Finance. *Veterans' Affairs* (18th of 18 R): Education, Training, Employment and Housing.

Group Ratings

	ADA	ACLU	COPE	CFA	LCV	CON	NSI	COC	ACU	NTLC	CHC
1994	10	13	22	10	6	98	100	83	90	82	93
1993	5	—	8	0	15	52	—	91	92	—	—

National Journal Ratings

	1993 LIB — 1993 CONS		1994 LIB — 1994 CONS	
Economic	14% —	80%	0% —	80%
Social	11% —	82%	0% —	89%
Foreign	35% —	63%	14% —	80%

Key Votes of the 103d Congress

1. Clinton Deficit Plan	N	3. Brady Handgun Purchase	N	5. Lmt. UN Cmnd. of Forces	Y
2. NAFTA	Y	4. Strike Race/Death Pnlty.	Y	6. Cut Missile Funds	Y

Key Votes of the 104th Congress

1. Congressional Compliance	Y	6. Reform Crime Grant	Y	11. Loser Pays Court Reform	Y
2. Balanced Budget Amndmt.	Y	7. National Security Act	Y	12. Product Liability Reform	Y
3. Bar Unfunded Mandates	Y	8. Moratorium on Regs.	Y	13. Welfare Reform	Y
4. Pass Line Item Veto	Y	9. Risk Assessment on Regs.	Y	14. Term Limits Amndmt.	Y
5. Relax Exclusionary Rule	Y	10. Expnd. Priv. Prop. Rights	Y	15. Tax Cuts	Y

Election Results

1994 general	Dan Schaefer (R)	124,079	(70%)	($495,506)
	John Hallen (D)	49,701	(28%)	($52,171)
	Others	3,929	(2%)	
1994 primary	Dan Schaefer (R)	unopposed		
1992 general	Dan Schaefer (R)	142,021	(61%)	($332,317)
	Thomas A. Kolbe (D)	91,073	(39%)	($9,794)

CONNECTICUT

Connecticut is an odd duck—small and isolated, insular throughout much of its history, without significant natural resources, the last state to renounce an established church and one of the last to impose an income tax; yet also it is America's most affluent state. Connecticut's success has come, now and in the past, not from any windfall but from its knack for tinkering. In 1831, Alexis de Tocqueville was struck by how this spot on the map gave America "the clock-peddler, the schoolmaster, and the senator. The first gives you time, the second tells you what to do with it, and the third makes your law and civilization." Connecticut made clocks of wood and metal and hats of felt and invented vulcanized rubber; it produced combs, cigars, clocks, silk thread, pins, matches, furniture; it invented and still manufactures Pez candy in Orange, Pepperidge Farm bread and Nivea cream in Norwalk, the Stanley Powerlock tape measure in New Britain and the Wiffle ball in Shelton.

Most importantly, Connecticut—one of the least violent parts of America—has always specialized in arms. The quintessential Connecticut Yankee, Eli Whitney, was the inventor not only of the cotton gin—which may have been the proximate cause of the Civil War—but also of the rifles with interchangeable parts with which so many were killed in that tragic and bloody conflict. For more than a century, ever since Samuel Colt won a War Department contract to manufacture guns for the Mexican-American War, Connecticut has had a close relationship with the military—and at no time more than during the Reagan defense buildup of the 1980s. United Technologies' various subsidiaries made Air Force jets and the Army's Sikorsky helicopters; General Dynamics's Electric Boat Shipyard in New London made the Navy's nuclear submarines; dozens of other companies made other weaponry.

These arms industries, like Connecticut's civilian manufacturers, depend heavily on precision work. For years, the state was the center of the brass industry, the nation's main producer of precision instruments, a center for machine tools, and the home of Perkin Elmer—a principle contractor for the Hubble Telescope. And if Connecticut workers today are more likely the descendants of Irish and Italian immigrants than of Yankee tinkerers, they have not lost the Yankee knack: Connecticut ranks second in new patents per capita. Connecticut also has the skill of cannily assessing risk: that is the foundation for its great insurance companies, Aetna, Connecticut Mutual and ITT Hartford. This business requires not just managing money but understanding people. The poet Wallace Stevens, a Hartford resident all his life, worked for The Hartford Company investigating whether claims were valid or bogus.

Then, with the end of the Cold War and the stock market crash of the late 1980s, Connecticut's boom economy went bust. The state lost nearly 150,000 manufacturing jobs, from a peak of 450,000. United Technologies laid off thousands of workers, and Electric Boat was in danger of being shut down. Real estate values, among the highest in the country, dropped as much as 30%–40%, and homeowners who had borrowed on inflated values suddenly found themselves without their life's savings. Connecticut had avoided an income tax by levying the nation's highest sales and corporate taxes; then in 1991 it got an income tax as well and reduced the others.

For much of the 20th Century, Connecticut politics was an ethnic struggle between the flinty Connecticut Yankees delineated by Hartford resident Mark Twain, and the ethnics who were already streaming into the state's small industrial cities while Twain was writing *Huckleberry Finn* in his big house on Farmington Avenue. Connecticut Yankees, economically innovative, were ornery and reactionary in politics: the last Federalists, loyal enough Republicans to carry the state for Herbert Hoover in 1932. In the years that followed, Connecticut became more Democratic as it grew more Catholic. The key Democratic politician was John Bailey, state party chairman from 1946 to 1975. A master legislative strategist and ticket-balancer, Bailey's power was augmented by Connecticut's strong party and straight ticket voting traditions; he was one of the earliest endorsers of John F. Kennedy, seeing electoral advantage in his Catholicism when most other old-line bosses saw peril. Connecticut also had a vital Republican Party which generated national party chairmen and swept occasional elections from 1950 to 1970. But Republicans, except for Lowell Weicker, faltered in the 1970s and 1980s, and he eventually started his own party, A Connecticut Party (ACP). Now Connecticut has a Republican governor again, but he won only by plurality; the legislature is split; the state seems tottering every which way, torn between about half the voters who like government and don't mind high taxes and about half who think big government is choking off growth and innovation.

Governor. John Rowland, elected Governor in 1994, at 37, was already a grizzled veteran of Connecticut's political wars, with some scar tissue and some muscular strength he didn't have when he started. Rowland grew up in Waterbury, the high-skill factory town that had America's highest percentage of Italian-Americans in the 1990 Census. His family has owned an insurance firm for four generations, a business which requires gregariousness. John Rowland was elected to the state House, from one of Connecticut's tiny districts, in 1980, at 23. He was part of the minority, voting against taxes and for welfare reform. He ran for Congress in 1984, a good Republican year, and upset a Democratic incumbent in a seat where redistricting added high-income Republican towns far from Waterbury. Rowland was the youngest member of the 99th Congress, in the minority again, with a conservative voting record.

In 1990, Rowland got it into his head to run for governor. Incumbent Democrat William O'Neill's reputation was in shambles—the economic slowdown hit hard at a state government used to increasing spending 10% a year; O'Neill pushed through a big tax package in 1989 and then announced he wasn't running in 1990. Rowland had competition from Democratic Congressman Bruce Morrison and from Lowell Weicker, still smarting from his defeat in the 1988 Senate race; bursting with energy and indignation as always, Weicker formed a third party and refused to rule out a state income tax which, under the circumstances, was as good as ruling one in. Weicker won with 40% of the vote, to 37% for Rowland and 21% for Morrison. Weicker carried the Hartford area and eastern Connecticut; Morrison carried New Haven; Rowland carried almost the whole western part of the state, the working-class areas around Waterbury and Bridgeport and the high-income suburbs and villages of Fairfield and Litchfield Counties. Weicker pushed a 4.5% income tax through the legislature by August 1991. Democrats held the legislature in 1992 as Bill Clinton carried the state; Weicker's ACP elected no candidates. In October 1993 Weicker, who had earlier predicted he'd be a one-term governor, withdrew from the 1994 race.

It became a multicandidate contest. Rowland ran again, downplaying an income tax repeal. But when former legislator Tom Scott ran on his own Independence Party line as an anti-income tax crusader, Rowland recanted and committed to repealing the state income tax within five years. Rowland easily beat primary opponent Secretary of State Pauline Kezer, while Democrats had a tougher battle. State Senator John Larson ran as a cheerleader for more government and got the Democratic convention endorsement. But state Comptroller Bill Curry managed to run as an "outsider" candidate, though he comes from a political family and ran for Congress

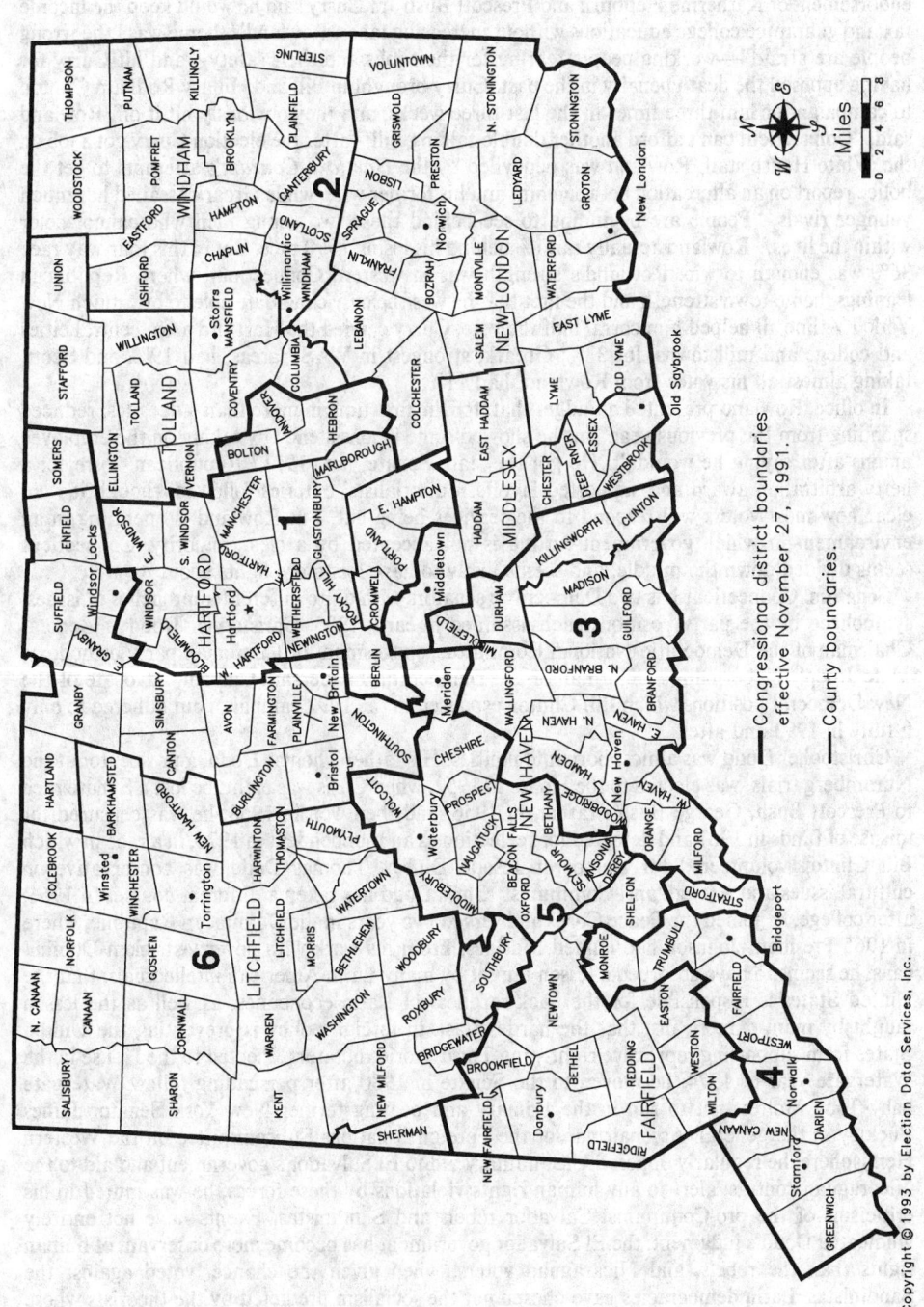

Congressional district boundaries
effective November 27, 1991.

County boundaries.

against Nancy Johnson in 1982, at 30. Curry's backing from labor unions and liberal citizens' groups, enabled him to upset Larson 55%–45%. Also running was Lieutenant Governor Eunice Groark, the candidate of Weicker's ACP, who claimed the reformer's mantle and had the endorsement of Katherine Hepburn and Prescott Bush Jr.. Curry said he would keep the income tax and guarantee college educations without increasing taxes. Rowland's theme was "the wrong people are afraid"—working people fearing for their jobs and their safety—and hit Curry for having opposed the death penalty in the past. Curry brought in Bill and Hillary Rodham Clinton to campaign for him three times in the last three weeks, and they obviously hit it off. Rowland said, "Connecticut can't afford another double-talking Bill;" after the election Curry got a job on the White House staff. Rowland was bedeviled by the *Hartford Courant*'s attempts to get the police report on an altercation between him and his former wife, while Groark assailed her much younger rivals, "People are beginning to see behind these two young men who cannot color within the lines." Rowland actually ran 1% behind his losing 1990 race. But in this four-way race 36% was enough to win. Rowland's strength was in western Connecticut, where Republican leanings, home-town strength and the fact that he was the only candidate able to buy much New York TV time all helped him corral half the vote. Curry carried the Hartford area, central cities and college and mill towns, for 33%; Groark, strongest in WASP areas, had 19%, and Scott, taking almost all his votes from Rowland, had 11%.

In office, Rowland presented a budget that, for the first time in more than 3 decades, reduced spending from the previous year. But he showed some inconsistency by taking on the employee unions after saying he wouldn't. He got the state Senate, now 19–17 Republican, to reject a hefty arbitration award and supported layoffs. Editorialists' outcries followed, though it's not clear how most voters will respond to the services being cut. But Rowland is operating in an environment in which government-cutting is not accepted by a clear majority. Connecticut seems divided down the middle, and seems likely to have lots more fights about it.

Senators. Connecticut has two Democratic senators with quite different approaches to issues, symbolized by the party positions each assumed in early 1995. Christopher Dodd is General Chairman of the Democratic National Committee, spokesman for Clintonian party orthodoxy, while Joseph Lieberman is Chairman of the Democratic Leadership Council, advocate of the New Democrat positions which Bill Clinton espoused in the 1992 campaign but adhered to only fitfully in 1993 and after.

Christopher Dodd was almost born into politics. His father Thomas Dodd, a prosecutor at the Nuremberg trials, was elected to the House in 1952, when Chris was eight; he lost a Senate race to Prescott Bush, George Bush's father, in 1956, and then won in 1958; he was censured for misuse of funds in 1967 and defeated for reelection as an Independent in 1970, in a race in which Bill Clinton volunteered for Democrat Joseph Duffey. Thomas Dodd was conservative on cultural issues and a tough anti-Communist; Chris Dodd has taken a different course. In 1966, after college, he joined the Peace Corps and served two years in the Dominican Republic, where in 1965 President Johnson had landed Marines. From his work with poverty-stricken Dominicans, he seems to have absorbed a lesson taught by many Latin American intellectuals, that the United States is responsible for the backwardness of Latin economies, as well as the lesson taught by many Americans, that the hardest task in foreign policy is preventing the United States from supporting repressive right-wing Third World dictators. Elected to the House in the Watergate year of 1974, he moved to the Senate in 1980 after persuading fellow Watergate baby Toby Moffett not to run in the primary and beating former New York Senator James Buckley in the general. As chairman of the Foreign Relations Subcommittee on the Western Hemisphere, he regularly opposed U.S. military aid to El Salvador's government and aid to the Nicaraguan contras; alert to any human rights violations by these forces, he was muted in his criticisms of the pro-Communist Salvador rebels and Sandinistas. Events have not entirely vindicated Dodd's judgment: the El Salvador government has become more observant of human rights than the rebels, and Nicaraguan voters, when given the chance, voted against the Sandinistas. Latin democracies have chosen not the socialism predicted by the theorists whose advice Dodd followed but free enterprise and the pro-U.S. policies championed by Ronald Reagan.

A major Dodd initiative on domestic policy was also unsuccessful: the ABC child care bill, supported by the AFL-CIO and the Children's Defense Fund, which sought to put preschooling into much the same institutional mold as elementary and secondary school, with federal aid aimed at national standards and promoting a corps of teachers trained in education schools and represented by teachers' unions. Dodd's bill passed the Senate but was rejected in the House in the late 1980s when liberal Democrats George Miller and Tom Downey opposed it and worked with the Bush Administration to pass their centrist alternative. Other Dodd legislation has been more successful. He sponsored the Family and Medical Leave Act vetoed by George Bush and signed by Bill Clinton. He worked on the Interstate Banking bill that became law in 1993. He put an Ounce of Prevention Council, which helps local groups cut through the red tape of government crime prevention programs, into the 1994 crime bill. He wrote a "safe schools" section of the Goals 2000 education law. On Capitol Hill, meanwhile, this one-time child of the Senate became part of what remains of the insider club.

When George Mitchell decided not to seek reelection in 1994, Dodd became an active supporter of Jim Sasser, who was backed by most of the senior Democrats in his campaign against Tom Daschle for what was then Majority Leader. As it became evident in October that Sasser was about to lose reelection in Tennessee, however, Dodd showed interest in taking on Daschle himself. The resulting month-long campaign for the less-important Minority Leader position was a nasty generational clash, which Dodd lost 24-23. Given continuing ferment among Senate Democrats, it is too early to rule out another Dodd bid. Meanwhile, he is a senior Democrat and a player on three Senate committees where he seeks a balance between occasional bipartisanship and advocacy of Clinton's interests.

Dodd's greatest strength, and what probably explains his selection as national chairman, is his easy, confident articulateness. In his third decade in Congress and his fifth decade of closeness to high office, he seems unfazed by opposition and approaches debate with a pleasant, affable air, deflating opponents' indignation and suggesting that they are all in this game together. Dodd is also capable of hard work, as he showed when he came up for reelection in 1992. The national anti-incumbent trend, the unpopularity of Lowell Weicker's income tax and the unsuccess of his two major policy initiatives seemed to make Dodd vulnerable, and his poll ratings were unspectacular. But in spring 1992, he fought to save Electric Boat's Seawolf submarine from extinction and in the fall ran one of 1992's best campaigns. His Republican opponent Brook Johnson was attacked for making money through 1980s leveraged buyouts, for investing in jobs overseas, for losing his cool with hecklers and reporters and for not voting in local elections. Dodd emphasized his work on child care and the family leave bill. Johnson, for all the talk of financing his own campaign, was heavily outspent. Dodd, incidentally, also had the ACP line on the ballot, which helped increase his winning margin; overall he won 59%–38%.

In his first term, Joseph Lieberman exerted influence far out of proportion to his seniority, committee position or political clout, an influence that came from respect for his independence of mind, civility of spirit and fidelity to causes in which he believes. Yet he is anything but a political innocent. He grew up in Stamford, the son of a liquor store owner, went to Yale, became president of the Yale Daily News, worked summers for Senator Abraham Ribicoff and the Democratic National Committee. In college he wrote a biography of that quintessential political boss John Bailey, which was both revealing and admiring. He helped found the Caucus of Connecticut Democrats, with liberal reformers and antiwar activists; in 1970 he ran for state Senate in New Haven against the Senate majority leader, and won with volunteer help from a Yale Law student named Bill Clinton. In 1980 he ran for an open House seat and lost 52%–46%; in 1982 he was elected Attorney General, where he took action against fake charities, crooked car dealers and gouging merchants.

In 1988, Lieberman decided to take on Senator Lowell Weicker, the Republican whose outspoken liberal views on some issues enabled him to win many Democrats' votes. Lieberman is an observant Orthodox Jew, who declined to appear at the convention that nominated him because it was held on Saturday, the Jewish sabbath. His religion is one force that makes him more respectful of cultural conservatism than many Democrats, and in 1988 on many issues he ran to Weicker's right, favoring the death penalty and a moment of silence in schools, and attacking Weicker's support of a 30-cent gas tax increase. He ran witty ads, one showing a bear sleeping through work—a nice take-off on the growling but erratic Weicker. The contest cut across party lines, with Lieberman running especially well in industrial towns and Weicker in Hartford, college towns and tony towns in Litchfield County.

In the Senate Lieberman was much less dovish than other Democrats on foreign issues, backing the use of force against Manuel Noriega in Panama and voting for some big defense programs. He was one of the leaders in the fight for the Gulf war resolution in January 1991, "a defining moment," he said—and without his earnest but vehement support it might not have passed. Presciently, he called for "final victory" over Saddam Hussein. He is a strong supporter of Israel but favored F-15 sales to Saudi Arabia in 1992 and interceded with the Clinton campaign to get a hearing for Arab-American Institute head James Zogby. He threatened to "strike and strike very hard" if the Serbs attack U.S. troops helping the U.N. troops withdraw. Lieberman favors capital gains tax cuts—"you can't be pro-jobs and anti-business"—and dissented when Majority Leader George Mitchell killed it in fall 1989. He is a leader for restricting product liability suits, which moved toward passage in 1995 despite fierce opposition from many Democrats. But he favored cable reregulation, wants to dismantle current airline reservation systems and supports many environmental laws. He worked hard for the Clean Air Act of 1990, against the 1991 energy law and against oil drilling in the Arctic National Wildlife Refuge. He was one of three Democrats to back a school choice demonstration project and one of three senators to switch and vote against Clarence Thomas after the testimony of Anita Hill.

Lieberman endorsed Bill Clinton for president in January 1992, and stuck with him through the Gennifer Flowers imbroglio. He supported the 1993 Clinton budget and tax package, although it contained a gas tax—which he had voted against in the 1990 budget summit. He also supported the 1994 crime bill, but he called the Clinton healthcare plan "a top-down, welfare-state kind of program." The Caucus of Connecticut Democrats declined to endorse him that year, but he had widespread support. Against retired physician and political neophyte Jerry Labriola, he was reelected 67%–31%—an extraordinary margin considering the national Republican trend; he carried almost every city and town in the state.

After the election, Lieberman called on Clinton to be more moderate on issues and to push welfare reform, with lots of work-oriented experimentation in the states; he said he would try to find common ground with a bipartisan caucus in the Senate. Lieberman kept to some partisan positions—he voted against the balanced budget amendment—but his good faith and lack of partisan rancor are widely acknowledged.

Presidential politics. Connecticut voted Democratic for president in the 1960s, Republican in the 1970s and 1980s, Democratic again in 1992—but not because the old Catholic-blue collar majority was reactivated but because Ross Perot cut deeply into the Republican vote. Clinton had only 42%, Bush a miserable 36%, Perot 22%, running strongest in suburbs and small towns at the far edges of Connecticut's metropolitan areas, where young voters with large families found themselves far behind in their yearly battle with credit card debt and their lifelong quest to build up equity.

The Connecticut presidential primary, once a vestige of party machine control, has become a vehicle for protest on the Democratic side. The 1992 primary was held March 24, a week after Illinois and Michigan had settled both parties' nominations. As usual, only about 100,000 voters showed up for the Republican primary. Democratic primary turnout was also low (173,000 voters), and resulted in an upset victory for Jerry Brown, who had 37% of the vote to 36% for Bill Clinton and 20% for a by-then withdrawn Paul Tsongas. This was less a show of strength for Brown than a sign of Clinton's weakness at that stage of the campaign. It also allowed the New York media, starved for national attention, to claim that their primary could determine the

Democratic nomination, which in fact Clinton had all but clinched.

Congressional districting. Connecticut's six districts' boundaries were drawn by a nine-member commission appointed by legislative leaders that made only minimal changes. Incidentally, three of Connecticut's six House members are women and one is black—a diversity that arose not from quotas but from candidates working their way up.

The People: Est. Pop. 1994: 3,275,000; Pop. 1990: 3,287,116, down 0.4% 1990–1994. 1.3% of U.S. total, 27th largest; 21% rural. Median age: 34.4 years. 13.6% 65 years and over. 8.3% Black, 6.5% Spanish origin, 1.5% Asian. Households: 55.6% married couple families; 25% married couple fams. w. children; 50% college educ.; median household income: $41,721; per capita income: $20,189; 65.6% owner occupied housing; median house value: $177,800; median median monthly rent: $510. 7.5% Unemployment. 1994 Voting age pop.: 2,486,000. 1994 Turnout: 1,139,575; 46% of VAP. Registered voters (1994): 1,795,895; 675,129 D (38%), 465,372 R (26%), 655,394 unaffiliated and minor parties (36%).

Political Lineup: Governor, John Rowland (R); Lt. Gov., M. Jodi Rell (R); Secy. of State, Miles S. Rapoport (D); Atty. Gen., Richard Blumenthal (D); Treasurer, Christoper Burnham (R); Comptroller, Nancy Wyman (D). State Senate, 36 (19 R and 17 D); State House of Representatives, 151 (90 D and 61 R). Senators, Christopher J. Dodd (D) and Joseph I. Lieberman (D). Representatives, 6 (3 R and 3 D).

1992 Presidential Vote			1988 Presidential Vote		
Clinton (D)	682,318	(42%)	Bush (R)	750,241	(52%)
Bush (R)	578,313	(36%)	Dukakis (D)	676,584	(47%)
Perot (I)	348,771	(22%)			

1992 Democratic Presidential Primary			1992 Republican Presidential Primary		
Brown	64,472	(37%)	Bush	66,356	(67%)
Clinton	61,698	(36%)	Buchanan	21,815	(22%)
Tsongas	33,811	(20%)	Uncommitted	9,008	(9%)
Other	7,708	(4%)			

GOVERNOR

Gov. John G. Rowland (R)

Elected 1994, term expires Jan. 1999; b. May 24, 1957, Waterbury; home, Waterbury; Villanova U., B.S. 1979; Roman Catholic; married (Patricia).

Career: Insurance Agent, 1979–84; CT House of Reps., 1980–84; U.S. House of Reps., 1984–90.

Office: Executive Chamber, State Capitol, Hartford 06106, 203-566-4840; Fax: 203-566-4677.

Election Results

1994 gen.	John G. Rowland (R)	415,201	(36%)
	Bill Curry (D)	375,133	(33%)
	Eunice Strong Groark (ACP)	216,585	(19%)
	Tom Scott (I)	130,128	(11%)
	Others	10,007	(1%)
1994 prim.	John G. Rowland (R)	78,051	(68%)
	Pauline R. Kezer (R)	37,010	(32%)
1990 gen.	Lowell P. Weicker, Jr. (ACP)	460,576	(40%)
	John G. Rowland (R)	427,840	(37%)
	Bruce Morrison (D)	236,641	(21%)
	Other	16,044	(1%)

SENATORS

Sen. Christopher J. Dodd (D)

Elected 1980, seat up 1998; b. May 27, 1944, Willimantic; home, East Haddam; Providence Col., B.A. 1966, U. of Louisville, J.D. 1972; Catholic; divorced.

Career: Peace Corps, Dominican Republic, 1966–68; Army Reserves, 1969–75; Practicing atty., 1972–74; U.S. House of Reps., 1974–80.

DC Office: 444 RSOB 20510, 202-224-2823; Fax: 202-224-1083; e-mail: sen_dodd@dodd.senate.gov.

State Offices: 100 Great Meadow Rd., Wethersfield 06109, 203-240-3470.

Committees: *Banking, Housing & Urban Affairs* (2nd of 7 D): Financial Institutions and Regulatory Relief; Housing Opportunity and Community Development; Securities (RMM). *Budget* (7th of 10 D). *Foreign Relations* (4th of 8 D): Western Hemisphere and Peace Corps Affairs (RMM). *Labor & Human Resources* (3rd of 7 D): Children & Families (RMM); Education, Arts & Humanities. *Rules & Administration* (6th of 7 D).

Group Ratings

	ADA	ACLU	COPE	CFA	LCV	CON	NSI	COC	ACU	NTLC	CHC
1994	80	68	75	67	69	4	10	26	0	8	0
1993	75	—	82	90	69	20	—	36	12	—	—

National Journal Ratings

	1993 LIB — 1993 CONS		1994 LIB — 1994 CONS	
Economic	71% —	17%	84% —	0%
Social	79% —	19%	85% —	7%
Foreign	61% —	38%	61% —	38%

Key Votes of the 103d Congress

1. Clinton Deficit Plan	Y	3. Brady Handgun Purchase	Y	5. Lmt. UN Cmnd. of Forces	N
2. NAFTA	Y	4. Strike Race/Death Pnlty.	N	6. Cut Missile Funds	N

Key Votes of the 104th Congress

1. Congressional Compliance	Y	3. Balanced Budget Amndt.	N	5. Product Liability Reform	Y
2. Bar Unfunded Mandates	Y	4. Pass Line Item Veto	N	6. FY96 Budget	N

Election Results

1992 general	Christopher J. Dodd (D-ACP)	882,569	(59%)	($4,553,792)
	Brook Johnson (R)	572,036	(38%)	($2,395,262)
	Others	46,104	(3%)	
1992 primary	Christopher J. Dodd (D-ACP), nom. by convention			
1986 general	Christopher J. Dodd (D)	632,695	(65%)	($2,276,764)
	Roger W. Eddy (R)	340,438	(35%)	($183,632)

Sen. Joseph I. Lieberman (D)

Elected 1988, seat up 2000; b. Feb. 24, 1942, Stamford; home, New Haven; Yale, B.A. 1964, LL.B. 1967; Jewish; married (Hadassah).

Career: CT Senate, 1970–80, Majority Ldr., 1974–80; CT Atty. Gen., 1983–88.

DC Office: 316 HSOB 20510, 202-224-4041; Fax: 202-224-9750; e-mail: senator_lieberman@lieberman-dc.senate.gov.

State Offices: One Commercial Plz., #2100, Hartford 06103, 203-240-3566.

Committees: *Armed Services* (9th of 10 D): Airland Forces; Seapower. *Environment & Public Works* (6th of 7 D): Clean Air, Wetlands, Private Property and Nuclear Safety; Drinking Water, Fisheries and Wildlife. *Governmental Affairs* (5th of 7 D): Oversight of Government Management and the District of Columbia; Investigations. *Small Business* (6th of 9 D).

Group Ratings

	ADA	ACLU	COPE	CFA	LCV	CON	NSI	COC	ACU	NTLC	CHC
1994	65	47	71	67	77	44	70	34	8	24	7
1993	65	—	82	80	100	22	—	45	20	—	—

National Journal Ratings

	1993 LIB — 1993 CONS		1994 LIB — 1994 CONS	
Economic	71%	— 17%	84%	— 0%
Social	61%	— 38%	53%	— 40%
Foreign	40%	— 57%	49%	— 50%

Key Votes of the 103d Congress

1. Clinton Deficit Plan	Y	3. Brady Handgun Purchase	Y	5. Lmt. UN Cmnd. of Forces	N
2. NAFTA	Y	4. Strike Race/Death Pnlty.	Y	6. Cut Missile Funds	N

Key Votes of the 104th Congress

1. Congressional Compliance	Y	3. Balanced Budget Amndt.	N	5. Product Liability Reform	*
2. Bar Unfunded Mandates	N	4. Pass Line Item Veto	Y	6. FY96 Budget	N

Election Results

1994 general	Joseph I. Lieberman (D)	723,842	(67%)	($4,017,520)
	Jerry Labriola (R)	334,833	(31%)	($166,064)
	Others	20,989	(2%)	
1994 primary	Joseph I. Lieberman (D). . nominated by convention			
1988 general	Joseph I. Lieberman (D)	688,499	(50%)	($2,570,779)
	Lowell P. Weicker, Jr. (R)	678,454	(49%)	($2,609,902)

FIRST DISTRICT

In 1871, Mark Twain moved to Hartford to become director of an insurance company, and ultimately became the Connecticut capital's most famous citizen. Hartford, already more than two centuries old, home of the nation's longest circulating newspaper (since 1764), the *Hartford Courant*, was becoming the nation's best-known insurance center. This was not a role envisioned by the harsh Puritans who established Hartford as a haven from backsliding Bostonians, but Connecticut's Yankees turned out to be shrewd businessmen. Thanks to the broad Connecticut River, Hartford became a seaport; its merchants, prevented from trading and writing marine insurance by Thomas Jefferson's Embargo Act of 1807, turned to writing fire insurance and using the capital they'd accumulated in the Napoleonic Wars to finance their ventures. They were also ready to finance tinkerers like Samuel Colt, whose gun factory just south of downtown Hartford became one of the nation's great arms plants—and whose company became a symbol of Connecticut's recession when it went into Chapter 11 in 1992.

Insurance and arms are still economic mainstays of Hartford, Connecticut's capital and the center of its largest metropolitan concentration. Though their economic clout and workforce have diminished, Hartford-headquartered Aetna, CIGNA and ITT Hartford are the biggest names among the state's insurers, with some $200 billion in assets. Just across the river is the Pratt and Whitney jet engine plant in East Hartford, cornerstone of Connecticut-based United Technologies, the huge defense contractor painfully downsizing in the 1990s.

The 1st Congressional District of Connecticut is centered on Hartford, though not dominated by it. As the central city's population has declined and become mostly black and Hispanic, it is far overshadowed by its suburbs: in 1994 West Hartford cast half again as many votes as Hartford, while Hartford public schools were taken over by a private firm. Politically, Hartford and its surrounding area have long been more Democratic than the rest of Connecticut, more favorably disposed to government and taxes; it voted for independent Lowell Weicker in 1990 and Democrat Bill Curry in 1994 for governor. Hartford in Connecticut is something like Boston in Massachusetts, a great commercial metropolis more statist than is its surroundings. But Hartford had a political leader more effective over a longer period than any in Boston—John Bailey, longtime state (1946–75) and national (1961–68) Democratic chairman, an old-fashioned political boss with a scandal-free career who promoted a raft of first-class candidates.

Representing the 1st District in the House today is Barbara Kennelly, John Bailey's daughter and wife of a former speaker of the Connecticut House. She grew up in Hartford, served on the Hartford Court of Common Council in the 1970s, was elected Secretary of State in 1978 and won her seat in the House in a January 1982 special election. In 1983 she got a seat on Ways and Means, whose jurisdiction over taxes is vital to the insurance industry. Balancing party loyalty and representing insurers is not easy: "You're never going to make everybody happy. That's how I've kept the respect of the committee. I won't be a flack without policy reasons." She fought successfully during tax reform against Chairman Dan Rostenkowski to save single-premium insurance policies from what the insurance companies consider overtaxation. She won approval of the proposal to eliminate taxes on accelerated death benefits, paid under insurance policies to terminally ill people who are expected to die within 12 months. She has worked to get annual mammograms for women over 65. The Clinton healthcare reform proposals hit Hartford hard, and Kennelly worked to maintain a role for private insurers and to allow them to sell policies to small companies based on experience rating rather than community rating. Although she preserved the interests of her local industry, she was keenly disappointed that Democrats failed to follow her urgings to pass a more incrementalist healthcare proposal.

Kennelly has other interests. She was the first woman to serve on the Intelligence Committee. She ran for Democratic Caucus chair in 1989, but lost to Steny Hoyer 165–82. She was appointed a chief deputy whip in 1991 and in November 1994 was elected Vice-Chairman of the Caucus over Louise Slaughter by a 93–90 vote. She was a lead sponsor of the successful Hate Crimes Statistics Act of 1990. She worked to save the historic preservation tax credit. She has worked for tougher child support enforcement, the Earned Income Tax Credit, a reform of the nanny tax and an extra standard deduction for the elderly.

Kennelly passed up the chance to run for governor in 1990, declining to challenge incumbent William O'Neill or to run when he bowed out. In the 1st District she has been reelected by impressive margins. Although she has become a national leader of her party, she is not a legislator who is accustomed or happy to serving in the minority.

The People: Pop. 1990: 547,979; 11% rural; 14% age 65+; 75% White; 14% Black; 2% Asian; 5% Other; 10% Hispanic origin. Voting age pop.: 423,623; 13% Black; 8% Hispanic origin. Households: 51% married couple families; 22% married couple fams. w. children; 49% college educ.; median household income: $39,961; per capita income: $18,644; median gross rent: $572; median house value: $170,700.

<table>
<tr><td colspan="2">1992 Presidential Vote</td><td colspan="2">1988 Presidential Vote</td></tr>
<tr><td>Clinton (D)</td><td>133,686 (50%)</td><td>Dukakis (D)</td><td>135,387 (55%)</td></tr>
<tr><td>Bush (R)</td><td>82,086 (31%)</td><td>Bush (R)</td><td>108,743 (45%)</td></tr>
<tr><td>Perot (I)</td><td>52,154 (19%)</td><td></td><td></td></tr>
</table>

Rep. Barbara B. Kennelly (D)

Elected 1982; b. Jul. 10, 1936, Hartford; home, Hartford; Trinity Col. (DC), B.A. 1958, Trinity Col. (Hartford), M.A. 1971; Catholic; married (James).

Career: Vice Chmn., Hartford Comm. on Aging, 1971–75; Hartford Court of Common Cncl., 1975–79; CT Secy. of State, 1979–82.

DC Office: 201 CHOB 20515, 202-225-2265; Fax: 202-225-1031.

District Offices: One Corporate Ctr., Hartford 06103, 203-278-8888.

Committees: *Democratic Caucus Vice Chairman. Ways & Means* (7th of 15 D): Human Resources; Social Security.

Group Ratings

	ADA	ACLU	COPE	CFA	LCV	CON	NSI	COC	ACU	NTLC	CHC
1994	85	78	67	80	94	13	30	50	10	14	7
1993	90	—	100	100	93	19	—	18	8	—	—

National Journal Ratings

	1993 LIB	—	1993 CONS		1994 LIB	—	1994 CONS
Economic	78%	—	12%		73%	—	17%
Social	80%	—	13%		75%	—	24%
Foreign	59%	—	38%		68%	—	29%

Key Votes of the 103d Congress

1. Clinton Deficit Plan	Y	3. Brady Handgun Purchase	Y	5. Lmt. UN Cmnd. of Forces	N
2. NAFTA	N	4. Strike Race/Death Pnlty.	N	6. Cut Missile Funds	Y

Key Votes of the 104th Congress

1. Congressional Compliance	Y	6. Reform Crime Grant	N	11. Loser Pays Court Reform	N
2. Balanced Budget Amndmt.	N	7. National Security Act	N	12. Product Liability Reform	Y
3. Bar Unfunded Mandates	Y	8. Moratorium on Regs.	N	13. Welfare Reform	N
4. Pass Line Item Veto	N	9. Risk Assessment on Regs.	N	14. Term Limits Amndmt.	N
5. Relax Exclusionary Rule	N	10. Expnd. Priv. Prop. Rights	N	15. Tax Cuts	N

Election Results

1994 general	Barbara B. Kennelly (D)	138,637	(73%)	($579,121)
	Douglas T. Putnam (R)	46,865	(25%)	($24,693)
	Others	3,405	(2%)	
1994 primary	Barbara B. Kennelly (D). . nominated by convention			
1992 general	Barbara B. Kennelly (D-ACP)	164,735	(67%)	($572,841)
	Philip L. Steele (R)	75,113	(31%)	($3,612)
	Others	5,582	(2%)	

SECOND DISTRICT

Eastern Connecticut, on its face a patchwork of small towns and rural land, now as it was 200 years ago, is actually one of the centers of innovation in America. This was always high-tech country: New London and Norwich were among the 13 colonies' leading workshops and ports, where in the 19th Century, factories sprang up in the little villages on the fast-flowing Quinebaug and Shetucket Rivers that provided waterpower. Sandbars kept ocean commerce out, and none of these cities grew large, but the technical Yankee knack of these towns and rocky hills remained, ever adapting itself to new technology and absorbing the talents of the children and grandchildren of mostly Catholic immigrants. (This was the boyhood home of Eugene O'Neill, and scene of some of his dramas.) There are four nuclear power plants here today, more than in any similarly-populated part of the United States, and here in Groton, across the Thames River from New London, is General Dynamics' Electric Boat Company, the major producer for four decades of nuclear submarines; employment is way down, but Clinton and the Democratic-controlled Congress pressed to keep the company going, lest we lose the capacity to produce these marvels of engineering and science that supporters claimed did so much to keep our nation's defense in a state of readiness. Not far away is another form of innovation, now thriving: the Foxwoods casino, with hotels and golf courses and a convention center, built by the 230-member Mashantucket Pequot tribe. The tribe has reaped enormous profits, donating $10 million to the National Museum of the American Indian and $500,000 to the Democratic Party before the 1994 elections; right afterwards, they ponied up some $250,000 to the Republicans.

The 2d Congressional District includes most of eastern Connecticut, centering on New London and Norwich, including mill towns and the college town of Storrs nestled in the rocky hills to the north, and stretching west to Middletown, once ethnic and now another college town, and picturesque towns like Old Lyme and Old Saybrook on Long Island Sound. For 40 years, from 1934 to 1974, the 2d District seat was passed back and forth between the parties. Since then, it has been held by baby boom liberal Democrats, who used the advantages of incumbency to build up personal popularity so that they could survive the bad years for their party as well as the good. The first was Christopher Dodd, son of a former Senator who was elected Senator himself in 1980; the other has been Sam Gejdenson, reelected by wide margins several times until he got into political trouble in the 1990s. Now the 2d is a closely contested seat again, as Gejdenson came close to losing in both 1992 and 1994. Indeed, Gejdenson holds his seat now largely because the Republicans are not as aggressively partisan in challenging elections as Gejdenson and other Democrats were in the 1980s.

Gejdenson was born in a German displaced persons camp, the son of concentration camp inmates, and grew up on a dairy farm in Bozrah, Connecticut; he likes to refer to himself wryly as "just a farm boy who spends his week in Washington." But he is also very much a Washington insider, a part of the Democratic leadership with one of the most liberal voting records in the House over the years. Gejdenson was elected to the state House in 1974, and carries the liberal beliefs of that era, the mistrust of American aims abroad as a senior member of the International Relations Committee and at home an appetite for government action and liberal cultural values. Naturally he supports Electric Boat and worked hard to continue building the Seawolf there; he is also a vocal supporter of the Coast Guard, whose academy is in New London. He was a strong supporter of Speaker Thomas Foley, chairman of his inside-the-House campaign for reelection as Speaker in 1992. Foley in return put Gejdenson in charge of campaign finance reform for his party—a classic example of the fox guarding the chicken coop. Despite House Democrats' success in passing modest reforms, there was no way that they or Gejdenson were going to dismantle a system which enabled them to gain such an advantage, and of course they didn't; but the blame for their failure surely can be shared with the intransigence of Senate Democrats. The irony, of course, is that Democrats fought for years to preserve an incumbency-favoring system, which now works against their party's interests. In 1992 Gejdenson won by just 51%–49% over

Republican Ed Munster, even though he outspent him by $1,014,000 to $140,000. In 1994, he faced Munster again, and this time—after the state Supreme Court's six-day hearing and final count—won by the less-than-landslide margin of 21 votes. In this contest Gejdenson spent $1,422,000 and Munster $426,000.

Munster, a biostatistician at Pfizer in Groton, was elected to the state Senate in 1990. He supported abortion rights and school vouchers and said that Gejdenson voted "against every weapons system except the bow and arrow" and that "Sam greased the wheels for Saddam" from his work on International Relations. Only Gejdenson's huge financial advantage and his margins in the college towns enabled him to win in 1992. In 1994 Munster returned, fortified by the Republican trend of the year. But the 2d was also one of Ross Perot's best districts in the country, and there was a third candidate, David Bingham, a Norwich area obstetrician and ice cream store owner, grandson of Connecticut Governor and Senator Hiram Bingham, environmentalist and pro-choicer, supporter of John Anderson in 1980, Lowell Weicker in 1990 and Perot in 1992. Gejdenson was clearly on the defensive; *The Day* of New London for the first time opposed him, saying Gejdenson had become "a career politician eager to protect the status quo." But the paper endorsed not Munster but Bingham, who on Weicker's A Connecticut Party line won 15% of the vote, running around the 20% level in the Norwich-New London area. Initial returns had Gejdenson ahead by 2 votes, out of more than 186,000 cast, with 43% to 43% for Munster and 15% for Bingham. Recounts raised his margin to 4 and finally, before the Supreme Court, 21. Partly because they were preoccupied with the larger task of passing the Contract With America, the new Republican majority agreed to seat Gejdenson at the start of the 104th Congress, pending further review.

In 1985 Gejdenson had been an enthusiastic member of the then-House Administration Committee majority that looked into a state-certified result and declared the Democrat, not the Republican, the winner in the Indiana 8th District. If the same standard had been applied to him, he would have been voted out of Congress. But Bill Thomas, new Chairman of the renamed House Oversight Committee, who had made the Republican case in 1985, said, "We're not the Democrats. We will not duplicate the Democrats' way of stealing seats." After Gejdenson was seated, a three-member task force headed by Jennifer Dunn was set up to look at the race. He evidently never considered applying his own former standards to himself and resigning. As the investigation dragged on and grew consumed by legalisms, Munster announced on April 28 that he was dropping the challenge, denying that he was influenced by local polls showing that district voters were tiring of the continued skirmishing and opposed a special election. But Gejdenson will surely be tested in the 1996 race. With Republicans in control, he is highly unlikely to enjoy the grotesque advantage in PAC money he and several dozen other Democrats in marginal districts have enjoyed under the campaign finance rules he defended against major reforms.

The People: Pop. 1990: 548,018; 45% rural; 12% age 65+; 93% White; 4% Black; 1% Asian; 1% Other; 3% Hispanic origin. Voting age pop.: 421,275; 3% Black; 2% Hispanic origin. Households: 59% married couple families; 27% married couple fams. w. children; 48% college educ.; median household income: $38,524; per capita income: $16,946; median gross rent: $564; median house value: $150,900.

1992 Presidential Vote

Clinton (D) 113,553 (43%)
Bush (R) 79,110 (30%)
Perot (I)................. 72,782 (27%)

1988 Presidential Vote

Bush (R) 115,314 (51%)
Dukakis (D)............... 111,939 (49%)

Rep. Samuel Gejdenson (D)

Elected 1980; b. May 20, 1948, Eschwege, Germany; home, Bozrah; Mitchell Col., A.S. 1966, U. of CT, B.A. 1970; Jewish; divorced.

Career: CT House of Reps., 1974–78; Legis. Liaison to Gov. Grasso, 1979–80.

DC Office: 2416 RHOB 20515, 202-225-2076; Fax: 202-225-4977; e-mail: bozrah@hr.house.gov

District Offices: 74 W. Main, Norwich 06360, 203-886-0139; and 94 Court St., Middletown 06457, 203-346-1123.

Committees: *International Relations* (2nd of 19 D): Asia and the Pacific; International Economic Policy and Trade (RMM). *House Oversight* (2nd of 5 D). *Resources* (6th of 20 D): Fisheries, Wildlife and Oceans; Water and Power Resources.

Group Ratings

	ADA	ACLU	COPE	CFA	LCV	CON	NSI	COC	ACU	NTLC	CHC
1994	80	87	89	90	94	4	30	36	10	11	0
1993	95	—	100	100	93	16	—	9	8	—	—

National Journal Ratings

	1993 LIB — 1993 CONS		1994 LIB — 1994 CONS	
Economic	78%	— 12%	72%	— 27%
Social	78%	— 22%	94%	— 0%
Foreign	70%	— 26%	72%	— 25%

Key Votes of the 103d Congress

1. Clinton Deficit Plan	Y	3. Brady Handgun Purchase	Y	5. Lmt. UN Cmnd. of Forces	N
2. NAFTA	N	4. Strike Race/Death Pnlty.	N	6. Cut Missile Funds	Y

Key Votes of the 104th Congress

1. Congressional Compliance	Y	6. Reform Crime Grant	N	11. Loser Pays Court Reform	N
2. Balanced Budget Amndmt.	N	7. National Security Act	N	12. Product Liability Reform	N
3. Bar Unfunded Mandates	N	8. Moratorium on Regs.	N	13. Welfare Reform	N
4. Pass Line Item Veto	N	9. Risk Assessment on Regs.	N	14. Term Limits Amndmt.	N
5. Relax Exclusionary Rule	N	10. Expnd. Priv. Prop. Rights	N	15. Tax Cuts	N

Election Results

1994 general	Samuel Gejdenson (D)	79,188	(43%)	($1,422,126)
	Edward W. Munster (R)	79,167	(43%)	($426,390)
	David Bingham (ACP)	27,716	(15%)	
1994 primary	Samuel Gejdenson (D) . . . nominated by convention			
1992 general	Samuel Gejdenson (D-ACP)	123,291	(51%)	($1,019,417)
	Edward W. Munster (R)	119,416	(49%)	($140,139)

THIRD DISTRICT

Nearly two centuries ago, in 1798, Eli Whitney, a young Yale graduate, won an order from the federal government to produce 10,000 muskets at $13.40 each: the beginning of Connecticut's defense industry. Six years before, Whitney had invented the cotton gin, which revolutionized the South but which for years only embroiled him in a patent suit. On the musket contract, he was determined to make a profit right off, so he set up a system of interchangeable parts and invented a milling machine and gauges: the beginning of standardized American manufacturing. It was also the beginning of New Haven, Connecticut, as a manufacturing center, for Whitney set up his factory along a small, rapidly flowing river just north of this town established more than 150 years before as a religious haven for Puritans. For the next 150 years or so, the town mass-produced rifles, clocks, locks, hardware and toys—anything its tinkerers and entrepreneurs could fashion. Manufacturing is less important than it used to be, and there is not a large white collar employment center as exists in Hartford. Yale, with its gothic spires, redbrick halls and modernist skating rink, has always been the visual focus of the city; now Yale is New Haven's largest employer and has put $50 million into civic projects over the last decade.

The 3d Congressional District of Connecticut covers the New Haven metropolitan area, which has long since spread beyond the narrow city limits over the hills of what were once Yankee villages and countryside; the population-losing city of New Haven cast only 13% of its votes in 1994. Politics in the New Haven area for years was a three-cornered battle, between Yankee Republicans, Irish Democrats and Italians who became its largest ethnic group and usually voted Republican: in effect each group joined the party not supported by the people who welcomed them at the docks. Though often regarded as a Democratic seat, the 3d has been marginal, changing partisan hands in the 1980s as well as the 1940s and 1950s.

The Congresswoman from the 3d is Rosa DeLauro, who is well connected in New Haven and Washington. She grew up in New Haven's Wooster Square, where her father Ted was Alderman; today her mother Luisa DeLauro is New Haven's longest-serving Alderman and her husband Stanley Greenberg is President Clinton's pollster. Rosa DeLauro has been in politics for years: she was a development administrator in New Haven in the 1970s, chief of staff to Senator Christopher Dodd from 1980 to 1987, then spent a year working to stop U.S. military aid to Nicaraguan contras before going on to become director of EMILY's List, the spectacularly successful liberal women's fundraising group. In 1990, when 3d District incumbent Bruce Morrison ran for governor, DeLauro ran for Congress, and won 52%–48% over anti-tax and anti-abortion legislator Tom Scott after spending an impressive $957,000.

In the House, DeLauro has been an active and enthusiastic supporter of feminist causes and the Democratic leadership. She was formally called down for demanding the Senate hold "a full and public hearing" on Anita Hill's charges (House rules forbid urging the Senate to do anything). She opposed a gas tax and the state income tax in 1991 but actively supported the 1993 Clinton budget package with its tax increases. She supported the Brady bill and assault weapons ban.

1992 was a marvelous year for DeLauro and Greenberg: his client Clinton won and she was reelected 66%–34%, again over Scott. In the House she became a strong Clinton supporter on most issues, though she voted against NAFTA. In 1994, she faced a Republican black woman raised in a New Haven project who attacked her as an insider; "I don't know what that means," said DeLauro, who certainly does. She won impressively, 63%–37%, and in December 1994 was appointed one of four chief deputy whips. From this position she had helped organize Democratic attacks on Gingrich by lining up colleagues for one-minute House floor speeches. She said her top goals are full employment—she chairs a Jobs Working Group—and a national healthcare plan. Although Democratic downsizing on committees forced her to lose her seat on Appropriations, she replaced that with a seat on National Security, important economically in Connecticut. Her prospects for continued reelection are very good.

The People: Pop. 1990: 547,904; 12% rural; 15% age 65+; 82% White; 12% Black; 1% Asian; 2% Other; 5% Hispanic origin. Voting age pop.: 426,862; 10% Black; 4% Hispanic origin. Households: 54% married couple families; 23% married couple fams. w. children; 48% college educ.; median household income: $39,815; per capita income: $18,243; median gross rent: $623; median house value: $173,300.

1992 Presidential Vote

Clinton (D)	121,163	(44%)
Bush (R)	96,085	(35%)
Perot (I)	54,147	(20%)

1988 Presidential Vote

Bush (R)	121,466	(50%)
Dukakis (D)	119,417	(50%)

Rep. Rosa L. DeLauro (D)

Elected 1990; b. Mar. 2, 1943, New Haven; home, New Haven; Marymount Col., B.A. 1964, London Sch. of Economics, 1962–63, Columbia U., M.A. 1966; Catholic; married (Stanley Greenberg).

Career: Exec. Asst., New Haven Mayor Frank Logue, 1976–77; Exec. Asst. and Development Admin., City of New Haven, 1977–79; Chief of Staff, U.S. Sen. Christopher Dodd, 1980–87; Exec. Dir., Countdown '87, 1987–88; Exec. Dir., EMILY's List, 1989.

DC Office: 436 CHOB 20515, 202-225-3661; Fax: 202-225-4890.

District Offices: 265 Church St., New Haven 06510, 203-562-3718.

Committees: *Chief Deputy Minority Whip. National Security* (23rd of 25 D): Military Personnel; Military Procurement.

Group Ratings

	ADA	ACLU	COPE	CFA	LCV	CON	NSI	COC	ACU	NTLC	CHC
1994	90	83	78	80	100	7	30	42	5	11	7
1993	95	—	100	90	93	19	—	9	4	—	—

National Journal Ratings

	1993 LIB	—	1993 CONS		1994 LIB	—	1994 CONS
Economic	78%	—	12%		73%	—	17%
Social	80%	—	13%		77%	—	21%
Foreign	66%	—	31%		75%	—	25%

Key Votes of the 103d Congress

1. Clinton Deficit Plan	Y	3. Brady Handgun Purchase	Y	5. Lmt. UN Cmnd. of Forces	N
2. NAFTA	N	4. Strike Race/Death Pnlty.	N	6. Cut Missile Funds	Y

Key Votes of the 104th Congress

1. Congressional Compliance	Y	6. Reform Crime Grant	N	11. Loser Pays Court Reform	N
2. Balanced Budget Amndmt.	N	7. National Security Act	N	12. Product Liability Reform	N
3. Bar Unfunded Mandates	Y	8. Moratorium on Regs.	N	13. Welfare Reform	N
4. Pass Line Item Veto	N	9. Risk Assessment on Regs.	N	14. Term Limits Amndmt.	N
5. Relax Exclusionary Rule	N	10. Expnd. Priv. Prop. Rights	N	15. Tax Cuts	N

Election Results

1994 general	Rosa L. DeLauro (D)	111,261	(63%)	($655,245)
	Susan E. Johnson (R)	64,094	(37%)	($8,297)
1994 primary	Rosa L. DeLauro (D) .... nominated by convention			
1992 general	Rosa L. DeLauro (D-ACP)	162,568	(66%)	($1,022,131)
	Thomas Scott (R)	84,952	(34%)	($219,786)

FOURTH DISTRICT

America's most affluent suburbs and some of America's biggest corporate headquarters now share what Americans in earlier centuries would have regarded as unlikely real estate: the hilly land rising from Long Island Sound in the southwest corner of Connecticut. This was lightly populated Yankee farm country in the 17th and 18th Centuries; in the 19th it became industrial as Bridgeport became a factory town, famous as the home of P. T. Barnum; by the early 20th, Greenwich and other Yankee villages clustered around commuter railroad stations became the home of some of New York's elite. Greenwich's beautifully manicured hills, its elaborately simple boat docks, its carefully casual roads, its good manners and dull haircuts, 16 private clubs and 10 private schools, give it a plainly American and understatedly affluent look. New York's corporate leaders, eager as always to minimize their own commutes, have moved their headquarters out to Greenwich and Stamford and Fairfield and points inland: General Electric, American Brands, Union Carbide, Champion International, Pitney Bowes, and Olin. Boom turned toward bust in the early 1990s, as big companies downsized; but by that time small businesses had grown up and were leading the recovery.

The 4th Congressional District of Connecticut covers all of Connecticut along Long Island Sound from industrial Bridgeport to Greenwich, plus several inland towns. It includes Stamford, chock full of office complexes; woodsy Darien and New Canaan; Norwalk, with its industrial zone and modest neighborhoods down by the tracks; artsy-craftsy Westport; Fairfield, home of GE; and Bridgeport, an odd duck, industrial and low-income. The basic political balance has been the same since the 1940s, when the heavily affluent suburbs attracted enough people to outvote Bridgeport and elect Clare Boothe Luce as congresswoman in 1942 and 1944. More than the rest of Connecticut, the 4th is oriented to New York rather than Hartford or Boston. People here watch New York TV stations: they are Yankee, not Red Sox, fans; their political attitudes are shaped by what is happening in the City as much as in Hartford. Hatred of the state income tax enabled Republican gubernatorial candidate John Rowland to carry this area heavily in 1990 against Greenwich native Lowell Weicker and again in 1994. But the specter of religious right domination of the Republican Party eroded the Episcopalian Republican vote and helped Bill Clinton make a dead heat of the race here against Greenwich native George Bush in 1992.

The 4th District's congressman, Christopher Shays, is a product of the upscale towns who sees the district as urban rather than suburban and who has one of the most liberal voting records of House Republicans. Shays volunteered for the Peace Corps with his wife and served in Fiji, and then served 12 years in the Connecticut House where he worked with Common Cause on rules reform. First elected to the legislature in 1974, he considers himself a Watergate baby. He won the House seat in a 1987 special election by beating a culturally conservative Democrat from Bridgeport after incumbent Stewart McKinney, a liberal Republican who left his name on an act to help the homeless, died of AIDS. Shays is a pleasant man with a stubborn streak and considerable legislative savvy. In 1985, he went to the length of going to jail for seven days to protest judicial system corruption. He tends toward the conservative on economic issues, is more liberal on cultural issues, mixed on foreign policy. Though not of a partisan bent—he says he always tries to find Democrats to work with—he was angry at the tactics of the Democratic leadership and cooperated with Newt Gingrich by threatening to withdraw his support in negotiating a tougher crime bill in August 1994.

In the new Congress, Shays's number one priority was his bill requiring Congress to obey the laws it imposes on others. He got this through the House, after much Democratic stalling, in 1994, only to see it die in the Senate. For the 104th Congress, Speaker Newt Gingrich made it the House's first order of business on opening day; the Republican House's first action was sponsored by a Republican the press hoped to see rebel against Gingrich's leadership. Shays did dissent from some Contract With America provisions, on crime and regulatory issues. Making clear that he would be a force attempting to keep Gingrich from the close embrace of the freshmen, he successfully held firm in March 1995 when anti-abortion Republicans sought to place a rider on an appropriations rescissions bill. But Shays can play an important role as a bridge between Republican leaders and the party's small moderate wing. On the Budget Committee, he was an active ally of John Kasich in drafting and selling the plan to downsize the federal government and reorganize major programs. Then, as a key member of the Government Reform and Oversight Committee, he planned to rewrite the organizing laws of large Cabinet departments. Over the years, he has worked on a bipartisan basis on other efforts, including Tom Lantos's extensive investigation of HUD, cable reregulation and the Clinton Administration's National Service legislation.

Shays has been reelected easily, with 74% in 1994—55% in usually Democratic Bridgeport and up to 87%, in New Canaan.

The People: Pop. 1990: 547,561; 4% rural; 14% age 65+; 74% White; 13% Black; 2% Asian; 4% Other; 11% Hispanic origin. Voting age pop.: 425,513; 12% Black; 9% Hispanic origin. Households: 55% married couple families; 23% married couple fams. w. children; 54% college educ.; median household income: $47,636; per capita income: $27,130; median gross rent: $706; median house value: $275,500.

1992 Presidential Vote

Bush (R)	110,072	(42%)
Clinton (D)	109,122	(42%)
Perot (I)	40,802	(16%)

1988 Presidential Vote

Bush (R)	138,369	(58%)
Dukakis (D)	101,232	(42%)

Rep. Christopher Shays (R)

Elected Aug. 1987; b. Oct. 18, 1945, Stamford; home, Stamford; Principia Col., B.A. 1968, NYU, M.B.A. 1974, M.P.A. 1978; Christian Scientist; married (Betsi).

Career: Peace Corps 1968–70; Aide, Trumbull Mayor, 1971–72; CT House of Reps., 1974–87.

DC Office: 1502 LHOB 20515, 202-225-5541; Fax: 202-225-9629; e-mail: cshays@hr.house.gov.

District Offices: 10 Middle St., Bridgeport 06604, 203-579-5870; 888 Washington Blvd., Stamford 06901, 203-357-8277.

Committees: *Budget* (5th of 24 R). *Government Reform & Oversight* (5th of 27 R): Human Resources and Intergovernmental Affairs (Chmn.); Postal Service.

Group Ratings

	ADA	ACLU	COPE	CFA	LCV	CON	NSI	COC	ACU	NTLC	CHC
1994	55	78	22	50	89	100	30	100	38	79	36
1993	60	—	42	80	93	100	—	64	58	—	—

National Journal Ratings

	1993 LIB — 1993 CONS		1994 LIB — 1994 CONS	
Economic	35%	— 63%	34%	— 64%
Social	58%	— 41%	60%	— 39%
Foreign	40%	— 57%	47%	— 52%

Key Votes of the 103d Congress

1. Clinton Deficit Plan	N	3. Brady Handgun Purchase	Y	5. Lmt. UN Cmnd. of Forces	Y
2. NAFTA	Y	4. Strike Race/Death Pnlty.	N	6. Cut Missile Funds	Y

Key Votes of the 104th Congress

1. Congressional Compliance Y	6. Reform Crime Grant N	11. Loser Pays Court Reform Y
2. Balanced Budget Amndmt. Y	7. National Security Act Y	12. Product Liability Reform Y
3. Bar Unfunded Mandates Y	8. Moratorium on Regs. Y	13. Welfare Reform Y
4. Pass Line Item Veto Y	9. Risk Assessment on Regs. N	14. Term Limits Amndmt. N
5. Relax Exclusionary Rule Y	10. Expnd. Priv. Prop. Rights N	15. Tax Cuts Y

Election Results

1994 general	Christopher Shays (R)	109,436	(74%)	($438,259)
	Jonathan D. Kantrowitz (D)	34,962	(24%)	
	Others	2,664	(2%)	
1994 primary	Christopher Shays (R) ... nominated by convention			
1992 general	Christopher Shays (R)	147,816	(67%)	($383,207)
	Dave Schropfer (D)	58,666	(27%)	($29,162)
	Al Smith (ACP)	11,679	(5%)	($24,518)
	Others	1,454	(1%)	

FIFTH DISTRICT

Central Connecticut could be called the Switzerland of America: its stony hills are physically isolated, the climate is forbidding, local manners are frosty, there is nothing to suggest lavishness. Yet in the last two hundred years, the mountains of Switzerland and the hills of Connecticut have been transformed from subsistence farmland to some of the most productive and affluent places on earth. Their secrets have been thrift, hard work, inventiveness and an intolerance for imprecision. Keeping time is a common motif: Switzerland was long the world's leading watchmaker, and Connecticut has long been America's leading clockmaker. The comparison at some point breaks down: Switzerland has prospered by closing others out, its political neutrality and financial probity reassuring investors and undergirding its banking industry. Connecticut, like the rest of America, is an open society, welcoming newcomers and imbuing immigrants with the Yankee knack for tinkering and precision work. It has also been quick to adapt to market changes. Danbury was once the nation's leading producer of hats; now it cuts almost no felt but is a major corporate headquarters city. Waterbury, once the nation's largest producer of brass, saw the last of its big three brass fabricators shut down in 1985, but has replaced that with health care and now two local hospitals are the city's biggest employers.

An irregularly shaped slice of central Connecticut, all inland from Long Island Sound, from Meriden west to Danbury and the high-income havens of Ridgefield and Wilton, makes up Connecticut's 5th Congressional District. This was the Federalist heartland in the early 19th Century. It voted Republican for nearly a century, then became Democratic as Catholics started outnumbering Protestants. Now, cultural conservatism and economic growth have made it mostly Republican again: it gave George Bush a 7% edge in 1992, voted 51% for Governor John Rowland in a four-way race in 1994 and has elected only Republican congressmen since 1984.

The current congressmen is one of the most distinctive members of the House, one of two black Republicans, Gary Franks. He is the son of a brass mill worker, all six of whose children went to college, he was captain of the Yale basketball team, he worked for three large companies, then invested in Waterbury real estate, making him a millionaire. He was elected to the Waterbury Board of Aldermen in 1985, and reelected twice; in 1986 he ran for state controller and, though he lost, carried the 5th District; in 1990, when 5th District incumbent John Rowland ran for governor, Franks ran on a mostly conservative (he's pro-choice) platform—for the flag amendment, capital gains cuts, for Bush's veto of the 1990 civil rights bill and against racial quotas. He was by no means the party's first pick, finishing last on the first round of balloting at the district convention and being selected as a compromise on the ninth ballot; he was able to win because the rule dropping the low man on each ballot was suspended. In the general, he faced Toby Moffett, one of the first successful baby boomer liberals, who won the 6th District House seat in the Watergate year of 1974, then lost statewide races in 1982 and 1986, and ended up a reporter on Hartford TV and later a Washington lobbyist. In a result in which race seemed to play little role—the district is only 4% black—Franks won 52%–47%, the first black Republican House victory since Oscar DePriest won his last term on the South Side of Chicago in 1932.

Franks had a tempestuous first term. His voting record was the most conservative in the Connecticut delegation. He had high staff turnover and routinely ignored many local politicians. At home, he was sued by an S&L for defaulting on loans totalling $471,000, but he settled on repayment terms. In 1992, he had serious opposition from Democrat Lynn Taborsak, a plumber, who ran as a liberal; as a state legislator she had supported the state income tax and (signs of later liberal dogma) proposed including discussion of masturbation in sex education curricula. Probate Judge James Lawlor, a more culturally conservative Democrat, had a strong base in Waterbury. Lawlor and Taborsak flailed at each other in the primary; after Lawlor narrowly won, Taborsak ran as the nominee of Lowell Weicker's A Connecticut Party. This was a break for Franks. His vote was down in the Waterbury area, where he is known best, and he lost to Lawlor, who carried the eastern half of the district. But Franks was able to carry the affluent towns around Danbury and Weston, which cast 35% of the votes; overall, Franks had 44% to 31% for Lawlor and 22% for Taborsak.

Franks's second term was stormy in different ways. In August 1993, Black Caucus members voted to exclude him after the first 30 minutes of meetings, because he opposed them on most issues. Franks said, "They think liberals have all the answers, and they don't," and threatened to resign from the Caucus, but didn't. He then enraged many black members by sponsoring a bill to stop requiring creation of black-majority districts and then testifying in a 1994 Georgia court case on the issue. He said his success and that of Douglas Wilder and Mike Espy showed blacks can win in white-majority districts; "my point is you can't win if you don't try." He also came forward with substantive proposals, to replace welfare checks with a debit card (a pilot program was scheduled for Waterbury in December 1995) and to order death penalties for carjackings that result in death. In 1994 Franks again was aided by Democrats who had a bitter primary. The winner, Danbury state Senator James Maloney, bragged of getting state funding for converting a Waterbury brass factory to a mall (Franks also got some federal money for it) and said he would take a moderate approach. His ads attacked Franks harshly on personal grounds; Franks's ads talked of his stands on issues. Franks ran behind Republican showings in high-income suburbs, but carried Waterbury with 53%, running better than Rowland, for a 52%–46% win.

In the 104th Congress, Franks was joined by another black Republican, J.C. Watts of Oklahoma, who refused to join the Black Caucus. Franks was a leading supporter for the Republicans' decision to eliminate House funding of the caucus. Given his past showings, he cannot be assumed to have an easy ride in 1996.

The People: Pop. 1990: 547,907; 21% rural; 13% age 65+; 88% White; 5% Black; 1% Asian; 2% Other; 6% Hispanic origin. Voting age pop.: 416,500; 4% Black; 5% Hispanic origin. Households: 61% married couple families; 28% married couple fams. w. children; 50% college educ.; median household income: $44,056; per capita income: $20,316; median gross rent: $574; median house value: $182,500.

1992 Presidential Vote

Bush (R)	111,327	(42%)
Clinton (D)	93,966	(35%)
Perot (I)	60,891	(23%)

1988 Presidential Vote

Bush (R)	137,962	(59%)
Dukakis (D)	95,236	(41%)

Rep. Gary A. Franks (R)

Elected 1990; b. Feb. 9, 1953, Waterbury; home, Waterbury; Yale, B.A. 1975; Baptist; married (Donna).

Career: Labor relations exec.: Continental Can Co., 1976–78; Cheesborough Ponds, 1978–82; Cadbury Schwepps, 1982–86; Real estate investor, 1981–90; Waterbury City Alderman, 1985–90.

DC Office: 133 CHOB 20515, 202-225-3822; Fax: 202-225-5085.

District Offices: 135 Grand St., #210, Waterbury 06701, 203-573-1418; 30 Main St., Danbury 06810, 203-790-1263; 1 First St., Seymour Town Hall, Seymour 06483, 800-556-5089; 142 E. Main St., #204, Meriden City Hall, Meriden 06450, 203-630-4130.

Committees: *Commerce* (14th of 26 R): Energy and Power (Vice Chmn.); Health and Environment; Oversight and Investigations.

Group Ratings

	ADA	ACLU	COPE	CFA	LCV	CON	NSI	COC	ACU	NTLC	CHC
1994	20	26	38	50	72	63	100	91	70	89	79
1993	10	—	8	20	64	74	—	82	92	—	—

National Journal Ratings

	1993 LIB — 1993 CONS	1994 LIB — 1994 CONS
Economic	14% — 80%	24% — 75%
Social	33% — 67%	29% — 70%
Foreign	0% — 91%	14% — 80%

Key Votes of the 103d Congress

1. Clinton Deficit Plan	N	3. Brady Handgun Purchase	N	5. Lmt. UN Cmnd. of Forces	Y
2. NAFTA	Y	4. Strike Race/Death Pnlty.	Y	6. Cut Missile Funds	N

Key Votes of the 104th Congress

1. Congressional Compliance	Y	6. Reform Crime Grant	Y	11. Loser Pays Court Reform	Y
2. Balanced Budget Amndmt.	Y	7. National Security Act	Y	12. Product Liability Reform	Y
3. Bar Unfunded Mandates	Y	8. Moratorium on Regs.	Y	13. Welfare Reform	Y
4. Pass Line Item Veto	Y	9. Risk Assessment on Regs.	Y	14. Term Limits Amndmt.	Y
5. Relax Exclusionary Rule	Y	10. Expnd. Priv. Prop. Rights	Y	15. Tax Cuts	Y

Election Results

1994 general	Gary A. Franks (R)	93,471	(52%)	($574,024)
	James H. Maloney (D)	81,523	(46%)	($896,785)
	Others	4,059	(2%)	
1994 primary	Gary A. Franks (R)...... nominated by convention			
1992 general	Gary A. Franks (R)	104,891	(44%)	($631,851)
	James J. Lawlor (D)	74,791	(31%)	($345,164)
	Lynn H. Taborsak (ACP)	54,022	(22%)	($493,563)
	Others	6,579	(3%)	

SIXTH DISTRICT

Ball bearings and sports broadcasts: these are some of the things that have made Connecticut, even in recession, the highest income state in the nation. Connecticut, from its Yankee past to its Ellis Islander present and ahead to its third wave of immigrants future, has been a land of tinkerers specializing in precision work; much of the American ball bearing industry is centered around the factory town of New Britain. Connecticut has also lived off ingenuity and adaptability, giving consumers what they want, even when they don't know what that is. As when Bill Rasmussen, a sports announcer in Bristol, down a two-lane country road from New Britain, had the idea in 1978 to put local sports and UConn games in Connecticut living rooms by transmitting satellite feeds on cable. RCA, eager to unload transponders, convinced him that for the same price he could beam sport broadcasts all over America. So ESPN was born; today its two channels beam sports 24 hours a day up from a high-tech satellite farm in Bristol.

New Britain and Bristol are the largest cities in the 6th Congressional District of Connecticut, which stretches from the urban corridor alongside the Connecticut River north of Hartford to the tiny Litchfield County towns north and west of industrial Waterbury and Danbury. Its Yankee towns, bearing witness to the prosperity of the Revolutionary era, have now become a country home mecca for ultra-rich New Yorkers. Nonetheless, this once entirely Yankee and Federalist land is now heavily ethnic and politically closely contested. Enfield and Windsor Locks, north of Hartford, are heavily Italian-American; New Britain is heavily Polish-American; the mill towns of Torrington and Winsted, in the clefts of river valleys, are a mixture.

Nancy Johnson, congresswoman from the 6th since 1982, has an interesting resume for a politician: a doctor's wife and a teacher, she raised three children and was active in charitable and community affairs before she was elected to the legislature in 1976 from heavily Democratic New Britain. When 6th District Congressman Toby Moffett ran against Senator Lowell Weicker in 1982, Johnson won the House seat, beating Bill Curry, then a 30-year-old nuclear freeze organizer and later the 1994 Democratic candidate for governor. It evidently helped that with her practical experience she was more woven into the fabric of everyday life than young campaign organizers who had done little else but politics.

Early on in her House career, Johnson proved herself an active and effective legislator; today, from her Oversight Subcommittee chairmanship on Ways and Means, she is, on several major issues, one of the most important members of the House. Her record is mostly market-oriented on economics, fairly liberal on foreign policy and cultural social issues, including abortion. She is pro-choice but has opposed what she considers statist legislation, from the Children's Defense Fund childcare bill in the 1980s to the Clinton healthcare package in 1994. She took the lead on eliminating the old child-care tax credit, which tended to help high-income parents, and replaced it with $300 million in vouchers to low-income working mothers. She also has worked on the unemployment benefits program, to get states to pay partial benefits for part-time workers and provide for temporary forgiveness of mortgage payments for persons who are "clearly going to regain their footing." Johnson weighed in early on welfare reform, backing a job requirement after two years on the rolls. She is a strong proponent of Superfund reform, eager to cut payments to lawyers and quicken the pace of cleanup at polluted sites. She supported NAFTA, voted for the Brady bill and the 1994 crime bill, and was one of the few Republican dissenters from the 1995 Contract With America crime package. She works on local projects, like the Farmington Wild and Scenic River designation and the Black Revolutionary War Patriots Memorial.

In 1995 Johnson became Chairman of the Ethics Committee—a hot seat, especially considering the charges, many of them insubstantial, Democrats have been hurling at Gingrich. Her own probity is not in doubt.

Johnson was a critical voice on health care in the 103d Congress. She had backed the Bush proposal for tax credits for low-income people to buy insurance, and she was eager for some legislation in the 103d; indeed her bill to continue low-cost health care for seniors was the only healthcare law passed by Congress in 1994. She met often with the Clinton healthcare task force and participated in markups in the Ways and Means Subcommittee, despite gratuitous and sexist insults from then-Chairman Pete Stark. In command of facts and arguments, she continued attacking as Stark and Ways and Means Chairman Sam Gibbons tried to paste a bill together, and her efforts contributed to its foundering later in the summer. Indeed, she had bowed out of the race for governor in 1993 so she could concentrate on health care—not the first time she decided against a statewide contest; in 1992, she had declined to run against Senator Christopher Dodd, despite favorable polls.

Johnson's moderation on many issues has the potential to put her at odds with Speaker Newt Gingrich and the conservative Republican freshmen, and on occasion she has opposed Gingrich sharply, as when he proposed to permanently deny AFDS funds to women who have additional children while still on welfare. But she and Gingrich have long been allies. He has consulted her often on issues; she gave him key support in his 1989 race for Republican whip, which he won by two votes. She shares with him a drive to express her market-oriented views, contentiously if necessary, and a conviction that the Democrats have not always played fair and must often be stoutly opposed. As a senior member of Ways and Means, Johnson now eagerly works to craft the new majority's program.

The People: Pop. 1990: 547,747; 32% rural; 14% age 65+; 93% White; 2% Black; 1% Asian; 2% Other; 3% Hispanic origin. Voting age pop.: 423,560; 2% Black; 3% Hispanic origin. Households: 60% married couple families; 26% married couple fams. w. children; 49% college educ.; median household income: $42,817; per capita income: $19,863; median gross rent: $571; median house value: $165,900.

1992 Presidential Vote			1988 Presidential Vote		
Clinton (D)	110,828	(40%)	Bush (R)	128,297	(53%)
Bush (R)	99,633	(36%)	Dukakis (D)	113,418	(47%)
Perot (I)	67,995	(24%)			

Rep. Nancy L. Johnson (R)

Elected 1982; b. Jan. 5, 1935, Chicago, IL; home, New Britain; U. of Chicago, 1951–53, Radcliffe Col., B.A. 1957, U. of London, 1957–58; Unitarian; married (Theodore).

Career: Pres., Sheldon Community Guidance Clinic; Adjunct Prof., Central CT St. Col., 1968–71; CT Senate, 1976–82.

DC Office: 343 CHOB 20515, 202-225-4476; Fax: 202-225-4488.

District Offices: 480 Myrtle St., #200, New Britain 06051, 203-223-8412.

Committees: *Standards of Official Conduct* (Chmn. of 5 R). *Ways & Means* (5th of 21 R): Health; Oversight (Chmn.).

Group Ratings

	ADA	ACLU	COPE	CFA	LCV	CON	NSI	COC	ACU	NTLC	CHC
1994	30	65	22	40	35	84	80	100	52	89	36
1993	40	—	45	60	71	96	—	91	65	—	—

National Journal Ratings

	1993 LIB —	1993 CONS		1994 LIB —	1994 CONS
Economic	38% —	61%		30% —	67%
Social	64% —	36%		53% —	47%
Foreign	37% —	60%		53% —	46%

Key Votes of the 103d Congress

1. Clinton Deficit Plan	N	3. Brady Handgun Purchase Y	5. Lmt. UN Cmnd. of Forces Y
2. NAFTA	Y	4. Strike Race/Death Pnlty. Y	6. Cut Missile Funds	Y

Key Votes of the 104th Congress

1. Congressional Compliance Y	6. Reform Crime Grant N	11. Loser Pays Court Reform *
2. Balanced Budget Amndmt. Y	7. National Security Act Y	12. Product Liability Reform Y
3. Bar Unfunded Mandates Y	8. Moratorium on Regs. Y	13. Welfare Reform Y
4. Pass Line Item Veto Y	9. Risk Assessment on Regs. Y	14. Term Limits Amndmt. N
5. Relax Exclusionary Rule Y	10. Expnd. Priv. Prop. Rights N	15. Tax Cuts Y

Election Results

1994 general	Nancy L. Johnson (R).................	123,101	(64%)	($597,703)
	Charlotte Koskoff (D).................	60,701	(32%)	($105,290)
	Patrick J. Danford (CC)...............	8,915	(5%)	($16,025)
1994 primary	Nancy L. Johnson (R).... nominated by convention			
1992 general	Nancy L. Johnson (R).................	166,967	(70%)	($570,046)
	Eugene F. Slason (D)	60,373	(25%)	($38,968)
	Daniel W. Plawecki (Concerned Citizens) ...	9,544	(4%)	
	Others	2,713	(1%)	

DELAWARE

Delaware, second smallest state in area, fifth smallest in population, has a fair claim to being typical of the country, despite a peculiar history. Delaware was explored by Henry Hudson, and the Dutch and Swedes built settlements there. But the three counties of Delaware owe their separate existence to the politics of the proprietors of William Penn's colony of Pennsylvania, and to Delawareans' own speed in ratifying the Constitution which made it literally the "First State." Delaware has not been typical in every way. Over much of its history, Delaware has been unusually affluent, with some of the nation's highest income levels during the early 20th Century; two-thirds of its people live in the mostly-wealthy, mostly-suburban county of New Castle. It houses, in beautiful cobblestone mansions in its chateau country, many members of the most numerous wealthy family in America, the du Ponts. Yet the United States today, after all, is mostly suburban and throughout its history has been by world standards affluent, and the du Ponts don't elevate the median income any more than a couple thousand more lawyers would. Delaware's ethnic and racial mixture is much like that along the rest of the East Coast and not that much different than the nation's, though with fewer than average Hispanics and Asians; there is a mixture here of suburbs, old immigrant neighborhoods, black slums and farmlands. If not all parts of the nation can follow Delaware's exact path to continued prosperity, perhaps they can get an idea of the direction to travel.

The central focus of Delaware's economy for two centuries has been the business started when Eleuthere Irenee du Pont, the practical business-minded son of a dreamy, idealistic French immigrant, built a gunpowder mill on the banks of Brandywine Creek in 1802. This was the first enterprise of the family du Pont, and it expanded to become one of America's great munitions and chemical companies. It grew especially rapidly during World War I, generating so much capital that the Du Pont Company bought control of General Motors in the 1920s and held GM for thirty years while it was America's largest corporation. That capital also financed what was arguably the world's finest research and development program. In the years during and after World War II, Du Pont prospered by bringing to the consumer and industrial market new synthetics and plastics like rayon, nylon, cellophane, polyethylene, lucite and teflon: "Better Living Through Chemistry." Delaware's other major business of note has been creating other businesses. In the late 19th Century, it pioneered liberal laws of incorporation, giving more flexibility and power to managers and owners. A large share of the nation's big companies are incorporated in Delaware—their legal births take place in a federal-style building near the Capitol in tiny Dover—which means that much of the nation's corporate law, especially on mergers and acquisitions and unfriendly takeovers, is made in Delaware courts.

In the last 20 years, Delaware's job growth, like that of the rest of the country, has been generated less by visible big business units than by the explosive growth of many small ones. Chemical manufacturing, always more capital- than labor-intensive, remains important, but now accounts for fewer than 10% of Delaware's jobs. More jobs were created in the 1980s after Governor Pete du Pont's successful fight for liberalizing Delaware's banking laws to encourage out-of-state banks to locate operations here. They did: Chase, Manufacturers Hanover, Morgan and other banks brought 14,000 jobs into Delaware, with the number of finance jobs more than doubling in just over a decade. Delaware has the best business climate of "high intensity" manufacturing states, according to a Grant Thornton study, which credits the rich climate of state-offered incentives for new businesses and the abundance of skilled workers. Delaware had its recession in the early 1990s, though unemployment did not rise or real estate values drop as sharply as elsewhere in the nation. But overall Delaware has made a mostly comfortable transition from the industrial state it was at the beginning of the 1970s to a 1990s services and professional economy.

Despite Delaware's mostly metropolitan character, there is still an intimacy to politics here. Most of Delaware is reached (though politically ignored) by Philadelphia TV, so personal campaigning is still important. The Thursday after the election is "Return Day," when winning and losing candidates—opponents ride in the same car—come back to the downstate town of Georgetown to receive the bipartisan cheers of the voters.

Governor. Tom Carper, the governor of Delaware, grew up in southside Virginia and went to college in Ohio. But out-of-state origins are not uncommon here: Delaware's two senators were born in Montana and Pennsylvania. Carper first came to Delaware as an ensign in the Navy, then returned after service in Southeast Asia to get his M.B.A. (He served in the Naval Reserves for nearly 20 years, retiring as a captain in 1991). In 1976, he was elected state treasurer; he ran for Congress in 1982 and beat a scandal-tarred incumbent. In the House, Carper had a moderate voting record and worked to let banks into the securities business and to prevent ocean sludge dumping, both causes supported by Delaware constituencies.

After 10 years in Congress, Carper was the favorite for governor when Republican Mike Castle had to step down in 1992 after two terms; with Castle elected to Congress, these two politicians of different parties changed places, seemingly postponing their inevitable showdown for a Senate seat. Carper won his primary with 89% and the general with 65% and pledged a partnership with Democratic Lieutenant Governor Ruth Ann Minner. After two years, he is proud that 20,000 more Delawareans have health insurance, and he also claims credit for placing 2,400 welfare recipients in full- or part-time employment and removing 1,300 people from the rolls altogether. He has taken an active approach to creating and preserving Delaware jobs, lobbying General Motors to keep its Boxwood plant, which employees 3,000 people, open until at least 1998, and quadrupling the state's economic development fund.

Senators. Senator William Roth, the sixth most senior Republican in the Senate, has now held

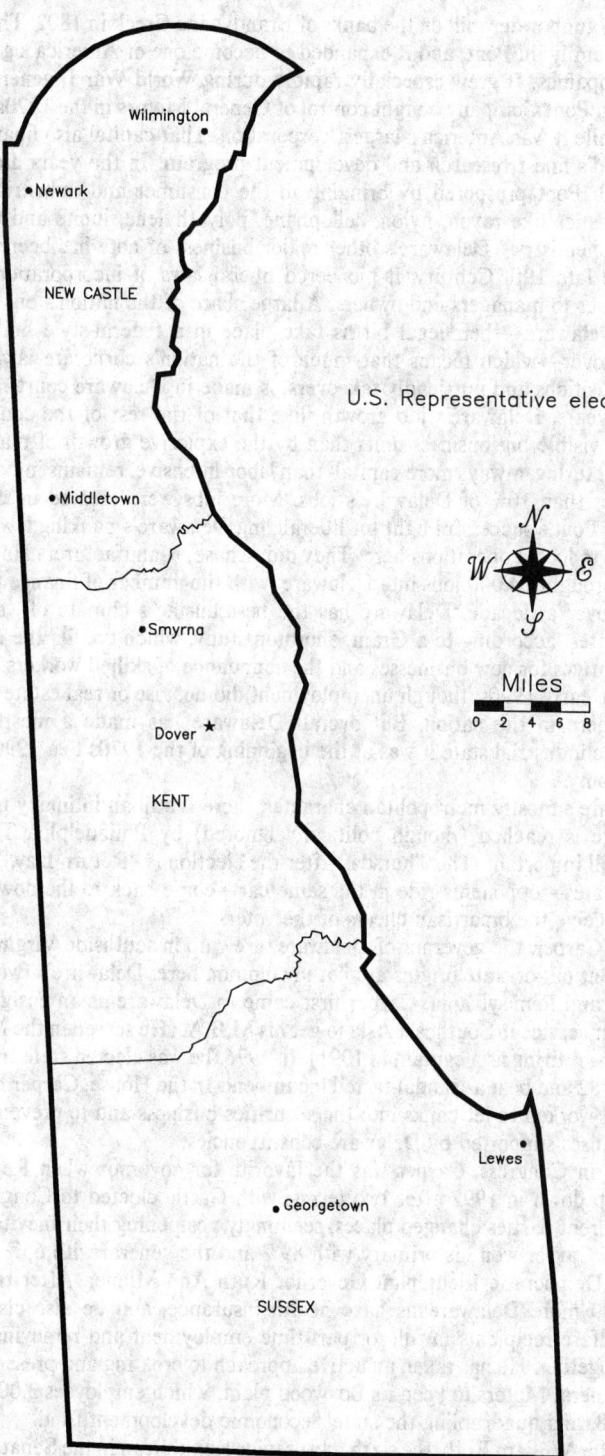

U.S. Representative elected at large.

high statewide office for longer than anyone else in Delaware's history. Reelected in 1994 at 73 over a serious opponent, he remains an elusive figure, at least in Washington. With his trademark toupee and a wife who is a federal judge back in Delaware, he does not cut a social figure nor is he dazzlingly articulate. Yet he has sponsored important legislation and advanced powerful political ideas. Practicing law in Wilmington, he became Republican state chairman in 1961 and ran for the state's at-large House seat in 1966, a marvelous Republican year and won. In 1970, when Senator John Williams retired after four terms, Roth was the obvious Republican choice. With his moderate voting record, friendly demeanor and frequent presence in Delaware with a St. Bernard by his side, he has been politically strong ever since.

Roth's major policy initiatives include the Kemp-Roth tax cut, of which he was the chief Senate sponsor, the 30% across-the-board cut in income tax rates first proposed and backed by almost every Republican in 1978 and then largely enacted in 1981 after Ronald Reagan won in 1980. In retrospect this was a rational response to bracket creep—the tendency of taxpayers to rise to higher tax brackets because of inflation although real income is stagnating. Another Roth cause is promoting IRAs. The 1986 tax reform cut back on such shelters, and Roth has been trying to extend them ever since. Again, his idea is to let middle-income earners in the high tax brackets hold onto more of their earnings. Roth has proposed creating a Mansfield-Roth Fellowship (with former Senate Majority Leader and later U.S. Ambassador to Japan Mike Mansfield) which would give recipients, after language training, one year of experience working for a Japanese government agency in Japan; Roth's son is also studying in Japan and writing a thesis in Japanese.

Roth's latest crusades have been on the Governmental Affairs Committee, where he regained in 1995 the chairmanship he held in the 1980s. For over a dozen years he pressed for government performance audits and in 1993 pushed to passage the Government Performance and Results Act, requiring federal agencies to specify strategic plans with measurable long-term goals and periodic evaluations; it was signed by President Clinton. He worked with the Clintonites on reinventing government, restructuring the Executive Branch and overhauling its personnel system; he pushed through a provision allowing the government to reduce personnel with buyouts of senior employees. On a few issues Roth tends to be liberal. He opposes ocean dumping and incineration of toxic waste, backs the Coastal Zone Management Act and wants to protect the striped bass; he is a leading Republican opponent of oil drilling in Alaska's Arctic National Wildlife Refuge and of logging in Alaska's Tongass National Forest; he pushed to allow women to serve as combat pilots. He voted for the 1994 crime bill, perhaps because it was sponsored by his Delaware colleague Joseph Biden. In 1995, conservative Republicans griped that he was too accommodating to Democrats on regulatory-reform provisions from the House-passed Contract With America; he responded that changes were needed to win Senate passage.

When Roth was first elected, he promised not to run after he turned 70, but he ran anyway in 1994. Democrats eyed this seat as one of their best targets. Their candidate, Attorney General Charles Oberly, was popular for his tough-on-crime record and well known. He spent over $1.5 million, competitive with Roth's $2.3 million. The attacks got a little tough, but Oberly never got much traction in a year in which Republicans won all statewide races, and Roth mostly stayed above the fray, winning 56%–42%. He is likely to concentrate on government reorganization and promises to consider deep cuts in government bureaucracy, like cutting 500,000 from the federal payroll or reducing agencies by up to half; he pledged to continue to work on a bipartisan basis, as he has been doing with Vice President Al Gore and others. Lurking in the back of his mind, no doubt, is the prospect that he would become Finance Committee chairman if Bob Packwood takes leave of the Senate and would improve prospects for placing his imprint on the tax code.

Delaware's junior senator, Joseph Biden, is in his third decade as a senator and even in the minority has influence on important policies. Nearly every working day he commutes from his home near Wilmington on the Amtrak Metroliner 80 minutes to and from Washington. His Delaware roots are deep, and more interesting than the way he distorted them in his brief presidential candidacy in 1987. He is not, as some suggested, a quintessential baby-boom liberal:

chronologically, he is just a tad too old and, more important, while they were attending elite colleges and marching in protests and organizing in precincts, Biden was winging it through law school and starting a family. Nor is he the son of an impoverished working class family held down for generations, as he suggested when he borrowed words from a speech by the British Labour Party leader Neil Kinnock. Biden grew up in 1950s white collar suburbia (his father was a car salesman and one grandfather was a state Senator in Pennsylvania), a Catholic when it was still assumed that only a Protestant could be president, and a teenager with a stutter who taught himself to deliver a speech to his whole school. Biden raised his children in Delaware after his first wife and daughter were killed in an auto accident in December 1972, a month after he was elected to the Senate; he remains a familiar figure in, and one familiar with, his constituency.

Biden's most visible gift is an articulateness that can verge on the mellifluous; he can inspire, but can also drone on at great length (being elected a senator at 29 does not curb a tendency to verbosity). He seems drawn again and again to try to reconcile the economic and cultural liberalism of the national Democratic Party, of which he is one of the leaders, with the economic and cultural conservatism of so many of those he grew up with: to explain one to the other, to reconcile them, to enable them to live happily together. This is not always easy work, and Biden has often been frustrated, as he showed vividly when the 1994 crime bill he had worked so hard to fashion—which had tough discipline to fight crime and tender therapy to prevent crime— seemed about to fail because of partisan opposition from Republican senators who had voted for it before. Biden responded with what one sage observer called the best speech of his career, or of any recent politician's. It was perhaps effective too: enough Republicans, including Delaware's William Roth, crossed lines to break the filibuster and pass Biden's bill.

More often Biden's position on the Judiciary Committee—Chairman from 1987 to 1995, ranking minority member from 1981 to 1987 and again today—has made his task of reconciliation harder. For the issues that arise here—abortion, flag-burning, capital punishment, the exclusionary rule—cut deeply, and on most the cultural liberals of Washington differ sharply from the moderate majority in America. Biden presided over the hearings of Supreme Court nominees in which such issues were pressed, with varying results. The outcomes were not always happy. The 1987 hearings on Robert Bork set a high intellectual standard for seriousness in much of the questioning, including Biden's, and Bork's responses were a high-level discourse on difficult constitutional issues. But many of Bork's opponents used his candor to vote against him for disgracefully dishonest reasons, from which Biden's attempts to construct an honestly based, anti-Bork rationale proved politically indistinguishable. At the same time, Biden used the power of the chair to undermine Bork and helped move critical votes on the committee away from him. Subsequent nominees have understandably refused to be as candid as Bork on judicial issues. Then the 1991 hearings on Clarence Thomas exploded when someone leaked charges of sexual harassment by Anita Hill against the nominee. Women members of the House marched over to the Senate in protest, and Biden was bitterly criticized for covering up this information. In fact, Biden had shared it with his Democratic committee colleagues and Republican Strom Thurmond, who agreed that Hill's initial unwillingness to testify publicly meant that any reference to it would be monstrously unfair to Thomas. Once the story was out though, Hill and then Thomas testified, changing few votes but mesmerizing the country; a majority of voters, and of women and blacks, believed Thomas over Hill, despite the strong pro-Hill bias of the press. Biden ran fair hearings, but became defensive against attacks from the feminist left, by then as strong a force in the Democratic Party as the religious right was in the Republican Party. Afterwards, he implored women senators to serve on Judiciary and pressed hard for a Violence Against Women Act, which became part of the 1994 crime bill. But he can be torn all ways. In February 1995, after divergent testimony on the number of abortions he performed, Biden angrily denounced Surgeon General nominee Henry Foster and Clinton's handling of the nomination; Biden quickly retracted his remark, though, and promised to withhold judgement until the vote. He also showed his independence from party dogma with his 1995 vote for the balanced budget amendment, whose approval he called essential for the nation's economy.

Biden worked effectively as Chairman to get more Democrats on the federal bench, delaying the filling of 115 judgeships in 1992, pressing the ever-tardy Clinton Administration to get its appointees approved by 1994, while expressing a certain dissatisfaction with some (he called Stephen Breyer's theories of economic regulation "presumptuous and elitist"). Should the Republicans recapture the White House, Biden will be on the lookout again for nominees who agree with conservative Richard Epstein that the Constitution protects property rights against government—an argument he pursued in the Bush years—although Republicans may try to legislate their theories instead.

Before 1994, Biden surely looked forward to chairing Foreign Relations after Claiborne Pell, who turns 78 in 1996 when his term is up. But now Biden must also wait until Democrats regain control. In the meantime, he is not shy about expressing views on policy. His four goals for the post-Cold War world are to promote democracy, contain nuclear weapons, rely on multilateral forces like the U.N. and protect the global environment. He is alert to human rights violations and often eager for the United States to act against them. He criticized the Bush Administration harshly for coddling "the butchers of Beijing," after Tiananmen Square. He has been one of the leading senators, with Bob Dole, to call for lifting the arms embargo against Bosnia while strongly criticizing Clinton's handling of the regional dispute. He has worked hard to preserve Radio Free Europe and Radio Liberty inside a new international broadcast organization and has been the real father of Radio Free Asia: he argues that these broadcast services can provide accurate information when little else is available and that foreign governments cannot in good faith oppose an information service which is forced on no one.

Biden is not likely to run for president again. He hoped to inspire a new generation in 1988. Instead, he left the race in the fall of 1987, in the midst of the Bork hearings, after an "attack video" circulated by a Dukakis staffer charged that he plagiarized the Kinnock speech. Then in 1988, Biden had a brush with death, suffering two sudden aneurysms. In Delaware his admirable personal qualities are well known and his issue positions not unpopular. Biden was first elected in 1972, against a popular incumbent who seemed ready to retire, while this young challenger had energy, an attractive extended family and an ability to connect with voters' emotions. He still has those assets, as he showed in 1990, when his opponent mailed out 40,000 copies of an 11-minute anti-Biden videotape, but Biden won with 63%—his best showing yet. He is one Democrat who seems a clear favorite to win reelection in 1996.

Representative-At-Large. In 1992, Mike Castle was elected to the House after eight years as Governor, where he was proud of starting a program to make healthcare services available to all children, developing an "Environmental Legacy" program to address issues in the coming decade, and increasing teacher salaries, as well as keeping taxes down. He won the primary by 56%–30% over state Treasurer Janet Rzewnicki in what many called the "year of the woman," and he won the general election 55%–43% over former Lieutenant Governor and Senate candidate S. B. Woo, beating the man who raised more in individual contributions (mostly from Chinese-Americans) than any other non-incumbent in 1992. In the House, it seemed hardly likely that Castle, as a moderate member of a conservative minority party, could be influential; yet he was. He was a leader of the bipartisan freshmen who offered their own budget cuts. But Castle's biggest moment came in August 1994 when, at Newt Gingrich's suggestion, he led a delegation of moderate Republicans to the White House to negotiate a deal to reduce spending on prevention in the Democrats' crime bill in exchange for their votes. His years as governor had made him one of the few Republicans with whom Bill Clinton was comfortable. Gingrich cleverly kept in close contact with Castle and his team, which was also led by John Kasich, signing off on each move without publicly endorsing them. Castle, who supported the assault-weapons ban, gained this position of leadership by sticking with the Republicans and voting against the August rule to bring the crime bill to the House floor without further revisions. In the end, Castle's high-stakes strategy for the Republicans succeeded on several terms—they pointed out the flaws in the original proposal, 46 Republicans voted for the revised bill, and the fight became an important issue to discredit Democrats on the eve of the historic election. Castle was reelected easily in 1994, and in early 1995 he was part of a group of moderates meeting again with White House Chief of Staff Leon Panetta, in Speaker Gingrich's office to discuss opportunities for bipartisan cooperation. Castle also has been a leader of efforts to cut congressional fat, including his 1995 bipartisan proposal to reduce funds for franking by more than half and prohibit mass mailings in an election year. His rapid rise in seniority also has made him a player to be reckoned with on the Banking Committee, where he deals with issues important to his bank-saturated home state. As a moderate willing to work with other Republicans on the Contract With America, Castle could end up one of the more influential members of the 104th Congress. Indeed, in April 1995 he led a bipartisan coalition of of moderates vowing to block passage of the Republican tax cut plan until the leadership agreed the cuts would not take effect until Congress completes work on a long-term budget to eliminate the deficit by 2002. And his work on welfare reform in the National Governors' Association leaves him well-positioned to influence welfare reform proposals in the 104th Congress.

Although Bill Roth's decision to seek reelection in 1994 temporarily squelched his desire to move to the Senate, it probably won't be many years before he has the opportunity.

Presidential politics. Delaware has had competitive state elections since the Federalists were battling the Jeffersonians, and in Presidential elections over the last 30 years it has come close to matching the national result. Wilmington and the downstate counties, blacks and southern-oriented whites, provide a divided base for the Democrats, counterbalanced by the Republican base in the affluent suburbs. Delaware voted for Kennedy in 1960, Nixon in 1968, Carter in 1976, Bush in 1988, Clinton in 1992, and by no more than a point or two off the national average—as good a barometer as any state. Yet Delaware with its three electoral votes gets little national attention, and other states did not rally to Delaware's two 1988 presidential candidates, Republican Pete du Pont and Democrat Joseph Biden.

In 1995 Delaware passed a law allowing political parties either to continue choosing their national convention delegates by caucus, or to switch to a presidential primary. Democrats are expected to stick with the caucus system, while Republicans have opted for a primary scheduled—to New Hampshire's chagrin—four days after the first-in-the-nation primary. (New Hampshire rules require that their primary be held seven ahead of the next state's.)

The People: Est. Pop. 1994: 705,000; Pop. 1990: 666,168, up 6.0% 1990–1994. 0.3% of U.S. total, 46th largest; 27% rural. Median age: 32.9. 12.1% 65 years and over. 80.3% White, 16.9% Black, 2.4% Hispanic origin, 1.4% Asian, 1.1% Other. Households: 55.8% married couple families; 26% married couple fams. w. children; 45% college educ.; median household income: $34,875; per capita income: $15,854; median house value: $100,100; median monthly rent: $425. 5.3% Unemployment. 1994 Voting age pop.: 534,000. 1994 Turnout 198,804; 37% of VAP. Registered voters (1994): 359,976; 154,603 D (43%), 130,715 R (36%); 74,658 unaffiliated and minor parties (21%).

Political Lineup: Governor, Thomas R. Carper (D); Lt. Gov., Ruth Ann Minner (D); Secy. of State, William T. Quillen (D); Atty. Gen., M. Jane Brady (R); Treasurer, Janet C. Rzewnicki (R); Controller General, Don Dryden (R); Auditor, R. Thomas Wagner, Jr. (R). State Senate, 21 (12 D and 9 R); State House of Representatives, 41 (27 R and 14 D). Senators, William V. Roth, Jr. (R) and Joseph R. Biden, Jr. (D). Representative, 1 R at large.

1992 Presidential Vote			1988 Presidential Vote		
Clinton (D)	126,054	(44%)	Bush (R)	139,689	(56%)
Bush (R)	102,313	(35%)	Dukakis (D)	108,532	(43%)
Perot (I)	59,213	(20%)			

GOVERNOR

Gov. Thomas R. Carper (D)

Elected 1992, term expires Jan. 1997; b. Jan. 23, 1947, Beckley, WV; home, Wilmington; OH St. U., B.A. 1968, U. of DE, M.B.A. 1975; Presbyterian; married (Martha).

Career: Navy, 1968–73 (Vietnam), Naval Reserves, 1973–91; Industrial Devel. Specialist, DE Div. of Econ. Devel., 1975–76; DE Treas., 1976–82; U.S. House of Reps., 1982–93.

Office: Legislative Hall, Dover 19901, 302-739-4101; and Carvel State Office Bldg., 12th Fl., 820 N. French St., Wilmington 19801, 302-577-3210. Fax: 302-577-3210.

Election Results

1992 gen.	Thomas R. Carper (D)	179,365	(65%)
	B. Gary Scott (R)	90,725	(33%)
	Others	6,944	(3%)
1992 prim.	Thomas R. Carper (D)	36,600	(89%)
	Daniel D. Rappa (D)	4,434	(11%)
1988 gen.	Michael N. Castle (R)	169,733	(71%)
	Jacob Kreshtool (D)	70,236	(29%)

SENATORS

Sen. William V. Roth, Jr. (R)

Elected 1970, seat up 2000; b. July 22, 1921, Great Falls, MT; home, Wilmington; U. of OR, B.A. 1944, Harvard U., M.B.A., LL.B. 1947; Episcopalian; married (Jane).

Career: Army, 1943–46 (WWII); Practicing atty., 1950–66; Chmn., DE Repub. State Cmte., 1961–64; U.S. House of Reps., 1967–70.

DC Office: 104 HSOB 20510, 202-224-2441; Fax: 202-224-0354.

State Offices: 3021 Fed. Bldg., 844 King St., Wilmington 19801, 302-573-6291; 2215 Fed. Bldg., 300 S. New St., Dover 19901, 302-674-3308; and 12 The Circle, Georgetown 19947, 302-856-7690.

Committees: *Finance* (3rd of 11 R): International Trade; Medicaid and Health Care for Low-Income Families; Taxation and IRS Oversight. *Governmental Affairs* (Chmn. of 8 R): Investigations (Chmn). *Joint Economic Committee* (2nd of 10 Sen.) *Joint Committee on Taxation* (2nd of 5 Sen.)

Group Ratings

	ADA	ACLU	COPE	CFA	LCV	CON	NSI	COC	ACU	NTLC	CHC
1994	35	21	38	50	69	88	90	79	68	92	79
1993	45	—	18	20	31	53	—	100	80	—	—

National Journal Ratings

	1993 LIB — 1993 CONS			1994 LIB — 1994 CONS		
Economic	25%	—	70%	26%	—	72%
Social	27%	—	71%	31%	—	67%
Foreign	24%	—	71%	32%	—	67%

Key Votes of the 103d Congress

1. Clinton Deficit Plan	N	3. Brady Handgun Purchase	Y	5. Lmt. UN Cmnd. of Forces	Y
2. NAFTA	Y	4. Strike Race/Death Pnlty.	Y	6. Cut Missile Funds	Y

Key Votes of the 104th Congress

1. Congressional Compliance	Y	3. Balanced Budget Amndt.	Y	5. Product Liability Reform	N
2. Bar Unfunded Mandates	Y	4. Pass Line Item Veto	Y	6. FY96 Budget	Y

Election Results

1994 general	William V. Roth, Jr. (R)	111,088	(56%)	($2,310,474)
	Charles M. Oberly III (D)	84,554	(42%)	($1,561,440)
	Others	3,387	(2%)	
1994 primary	William V. Roth, Jr. (R)	unopposed		
1988 general	William V. Roth, Jr. (R)	151,115	(62%)	($1,942,119)
	S.B. Woo (D).	92,378	(38%)	($2,235,318)

Sen. Joseph R. Biden, Jr. (D)

Elected 1972, seat up 1996; b. Nov. 20, 1942, Scranton, PA; home, Wilmington; U. of DE, B.A. 1965, Syracuse U., J.D. 1968; Catholic; married (Jill).

Career: Practicing atty., 1968–72; New Castle Cnty. Cncl., 1970–72.

DC Office: 221 RSOB 20510, 202-224-5042; Fax: 202-224-0139.

State Offices: Fed. Bldg., 844 King St., Wilmington 19801, 302-573-6345; 1101 Fed. Bldg, 300 S. New St., Dover 17901, 302-678-9483; and Box 109, The Circle, Georgetown 19947, 302-856-9275.

Committees: *Foreign Relations* (2nd of 8 D): East Asian and Pacific Affairs; European Affairs (RMM); International Economic Policy, Export and Trade Promotion; International Operations. *Judiciary* (RMM of 8 D): Youth Violence (RMM).

Group Ratings

	ADA	ACLU	COPE	CFA	LCV	CON	NSI	COC	ACU	NTLC	CHC
1994	80	61	86	92	85	14	10	28	0	18	14
1993	80	—	91	80	88	20	—	33	21	—	—

National Journal Ratings

	1993 LIB — 1993 CONS			1994 LIB — 1994 CONS		
Economic	71%	—	17%	65%	—	34%
Social	68%	—	29%	76%	—	19%
Foreign	53%	—	39%	87%	—	6%

Key Votes of the 103d Congress

1. Clinton Deficit Plan	Y	3. Brady Handgun Purchase	Y	5. Lmt. UN Cmnd. of Forces	N
2. NAFTA	Y	4. Strike Race/Death Pnlty.	N	6. Cut Missile Funds	Y

Key Votes of the 104th Congress

1. Congressional Compliance	Y	3. Balanced Budget Amndt.	Y	5. Product Liability Reform	N
2. Bar Unfunded Mandates	Y	4. Pass Line Item Veto	Y	6. FY96 Budget	N

Election Results

1990 general	Joseph R. Biden, Jr. (D)	112,918	(63%)	($2,550,061)
	M. Jane Brady (R)	64,554	(36%)	($240,669)
	Other	2,680	(1%)	
1990 primary	Joseph R. Biden, Jr. (D) . . nominated by convention			
1984 general	Joseph R. Biden, Jr. (D)	147,831	(60%)	($1,602,052)
	John M. Burris (R)	98,101	(40%)	($816,484)

REPRESENTATIVE

Rep. Michael N. Castle (R)

Elected 1992; b. July 2, 1939, Wilmington; home, Wilmington; Hamilton Col., B.A. 1961, Georgetown U., LL.B. 1964; Catholic; married (Jane).

Career: DE Dep. Atty. Gen., 1965–66; DE House of Reps., 1966–68; DE Senate, 1968–76, Minority Ldr., 1975–76; DE Lt. Gov., 1980–84; DE Gov., 1984–92.

DC Office: 1207 LHOB 20515, 202-225-4165; Fax: 202-225-2291.

District Offices: 3 Christina Ctr., 201 N. Walnut St., #1001, Wilmington 19801, 302-428-1902; and Freer Fed. Bldg., 300 S. New St., Dover 19901, 302-736-1666.

Committees: *Banking & Financial Services* (9th of 27 R): Domestic and International Monetary Policy (Chmn.); Housing and Community Opportunity. *Economic & Educational Opportunities* (11th of 24 R): Early Childhood, Youth and Families; Oversight and Investigations. *Intelligence (Permanent Select)* (9th of 9 R): Human Intelligence, Analysis, and Counterintelligence; Technical and Tactical Intelligence.

Group Ratings

	ADA	ACLU	COPE	CFA	LCV	CON	NSI	COC	ACU	NTLC	CHC
1994	20	30	33	30	22	74	100	100	67	89	79
1993	20	—	27	40	43	55	—	91	75	—	—

National Journal Ratings

	1993 LIB — 1993 CONS		1994 LIB — 1994 CONS	
Economic	23% —	75%	21% —	76%
Social	39% —	60%	36% —	62%
Foreign	31% —	67%	33% —	67%

Key Votes of the 103d Congress

1. Clinton Deficit Plan	N	3. Brady Handgun Purchase	Y	5. Lmt. UN Cmnd. of Forces	Y
2. NAFTA	Y	4. Strike Race/Death Pnlty.	Y	6. Cut Missile Funds	N

Key Votes of the 104th Congress

1. Congressional Compliance	Y	6. Reform Crime Grant	Y	11. Loser Pays Court Reform	Y
2. Balanced Budget Amndmt.	Y	7. National Security Act	Y	12. Product Liability Reform	Y
3. Bar Unfunded Mandates	Y	8. Moratorium on Regs.	Y	13. Welfare Reform	Y
4. Pass Line Item Veto	Y	9. Risk Assessment on Regs.	Y	14. Term Limits Amndmt.	Y
5. Relax Exclusionary Rule	Y	10. Expnd. Priv. Prop. Rights	N	15. Tax Cuts	Y

Election Results

1994 general	Michael N. Castle (R)	137,960	(71%)	($400,083)
	Carol Ann DeSantis (D)	51,803	(27%)	($45,863)
	Others	5,274	(3%)	
1994 primary	Michael N. Castle (R)	unopposed		
1992 general	Michael N. Castle (R)	153,037	(55%)	($690,740)
	S.B. Woo (D)	117,426	(43%)	($1,017,598)
	Other	5,661	(2%)	

DISTRICT OF COLUMBIA

Washington, D.C., the capital of the most successful democracy in the history of the world, has itself become a dysfunctional polity, a city with above-average incomes and a rapidly growing commercial property base but with a government so bloated with employees yet so indifferent to its duties that it is destroying one marginal neighborhood after another. The problem is not new—in the 1790s the framers of the Constitution, familiar with contemporary London and Paris mobs and remembering how crowds had threatened Congress in Philadelphia, purposely gave the new federal government control of the 10-mile-square enclave that came to be called the District of Columbia—but in the 1990s the irresponsibility of District officials, primarily of Mayor Marion Barry, led a reluctant Congress to turn control of the capital's city finances over to a federal financial control board.

Ironically, this has come more than 20 years after Congress relinquished the control of the District which it had exercised over most of its history, for its own advantage and out of distrust of the city's large black population. For blacks had consistently made up about one-quarter of metropolitan Washington's population since the 1790s, and the city was a center for free blacks before and after the Civil War and Emancipation. Radical Republicans gave the District self-government in the era of Reconstruction in 1871, but Governor Alexander "Boss" Shepherd built great public works and spent the District into bankruptcy, and local self-government ended in 1874. During the civil rights revolution of the 1960s, it began to seem absurd to deny the vote to Washington, which officially became majority-black in 1960. So in 1964, Washingtonians began to cast three electoral votes for president; in 1968 they were allowed to vote for their school board; in 1971, they finally got to elect a non-voting delegate to Congress; in 1974, they got home rule and could vote for a mayor and city council.

Since then city politics has mostly been dominated by Marion Barry, elected Mayor in 1978, 1982 and 1986, then disgraced in January 1990 when he was arrested and videotaped in a hotel using crack cocaine, a crime for which he was eventually convicted and imprisoned—and then, astonishingly, elected Mayor again in 1994. Barry is a man of great competence and charm, a Ph.D. candidate in chemistry from Tennessee who became a dashiki-clad protest leader in Washington, D.C. He inherited a government that was already overlarge and undermanaged, and increased the first tendency while eventually, as he came to spend most of his time drinking, womanizing and taking drugs, increasing the latter as well. There is no serious party competition here; Washington is overwhelmingly Democratic, more Democratic than any county in the United States; the District voted 85%–9% for Bill Clinton over George Bush in 1992, with 80% of whites voting for Clinton in exit polls. So Barry developed his own coalition of public employee unions and big real estate developers who ponied up votes and money and, until his arrest, seemed ready to make him Mayor-for-life.

Barry's downfall produced a surge for reform, of which the beneficiary in 1990 was Sharon

Pratt Dixon (Sharon Pratt Kelly, after her 1991 marriage), who challenged Barry when he was on top and called for sweeping cuts in District government. She won the September 1990 Democratic primary with 35% to 25% for Councilman John Ray and 21% for Councilwoman Charlene Drew Jarvis. By then the District government, as closely as anyone could figure, had 46,000 full-time employees for a city of 589,000, with outlays approaching $5 billion, about $8,000 per person; it had persistent, disguised budget deficits; it had a bureaucracy famously indifferent to the citizens it was supposed to serve, an attitude surely nourished by Barry's increasingly flagrant behavior as the 1980s went on. It had public schools so weak that the incoming Clintons did not even consider them for their daughter, but not because of lack of money. *The New York Times* noted without citation that District public schools were "notoriously underfinanced," but in fact per-pupil spending was higher than in 97% of over-20,000-pupil systems in the country. In her first year, Mayor Kelly seemed determined to cut government, but by 1993 she had flinched, built a palatial office for herself outside the flea-bitten District Building and even put a makeup artist on the city payroll. She started relying on the usual alibis: the federal payment the District receives in lieu of taxes on federal buildings wasn't large enough; Congress would not let the District tax suburbanites working in the city; Congress would not vote for statehood (the Democratic House voted against it 277–153 in November 1993). But the federal payment is actually generous and was increased for Kelly; the city has plenty of affluent white and black residents to soak with high taxes, and does; and Congress is not going to vote greater powers to a government plainly incompetent to handle those it has.

Under Barry the District developed—and Kelly did little to change—a public sector of Soviet magnitude and social problems of Third World dimensions—two facts that are surely related. The crime rate in the District is very high, and if it is not the nation's murder capital any more, there are many parts of the city which drug dealers rule, where murder is commonplace and women are routinely abused. The capital of the United States has a level of infant mortality twice the national average, and in poor neighborhoods the level is worse than in Sri Lanka, Panama or Jamaica. Drinking, drug use, simple neglect by unmarried mothers are the primary causes: the fatherless underclass seems in large parts of the District to have become self-sustaining and to have created a society which is literally hellish. Washington has a far lower percentage of people living in families than any state, or almost any central city, despite income levels well above the average (raised by affluent whites in Ward 3, west of Rock Creek Park, and affluent blacks in Ward 4, just east of the Park). The District government does deliver some services adequately, but most are carried out poorly, in vivid contrast to the high civic competence of suburban Maryland and Virginia jurisdictions (including majority-black Prince Georges County, Maryland). Most important, in the 1990s even more than in the 1980s, crime and poor schools have driven young, middle-income black families—exactly the people the city needs to have a decent civil society and become a workable polity—out to the suburbs. The rich stay, because the criminals seldom enter their neighborhoods and they can afford to supplement any services they need. And the welfare and criminal underclass stays and comes to dominate more and more territory.

Marion Barry, emerging from prison, immediately began running for office. In 1992 he was elected to the Council from Ward 8 east of the Anacostia River, the poorest part of the city, with many single mothers on welfare and very high rates of crime. Then in 1994 he ran again for mayor. Also running was Kelly, despite her failure to live up to her promises, and Councilman John Ray, who lost to her in 1990. Barry energetically built an organization in Anacostia and other poor areas, corralled support from public employees and built networks of families with imprisoned relatives. He won the September primary with 47% of the vote, to 37% for Ray and only 13% for Kelly; their combined vote would have beat him. A *Washington Post* headline said Barry's support "came from many classes, sections of the District," but the paper could not find space to print the ward by ward results (although it had space for county returns for Maryland's Republican primary). Actually support was highly uneven. Barry won 83% in Ward 8 and 66%

in Ward 7, also in Anacostia; Ray beat him in Ward 3, 83% to 3%. Councilman Bill Lightfoot, who said he would run as an Independent if Ray lost to Barry, changed his mind after the primary. In the general Barry faced Carol Schwartz, a former Councilwoman who also ran against him in 1986. Schwartz gamely campaigned in all parts of the city, talking issues and Barry's record, and ran better than almost anyone expected. Barry won 56%–42%, winning every ward but the 2nd and 3rd.

Barry's narrow but decisive victories may have come from the same impulse that is producing large numbers of nullification verdicts in D.C. criminal trials: older black jurors who, regardless of the evidence presented, are reluctant to send another black male to jail. Voters, especially in Anacostia where the large majority are older, often expressed a desire to forgive Barry and honor his "redemption." All societies need some balance between therapy and discipline, and so do all families; but voters in Washington's poorest areas, almost all from homes where men are conspicuously absent, seem possessed by motherly therapy and to be lacking fatherly discipline. The result is a dysfunctional polity: streets controlled by thugs let loose by nullifying jurors, the mayor's office in the hands of Marion Barry.

The task before Barry in early 1995 was to make deep cuts in the bureaucracy he had allowed to grow so large. He had cooperative-sounding meetings with Speaker Newt Gingrich and suburban Virginia Congressman Tom Davis, whom Gingrich designated to work with him; D.C.'s congressional Delegate Eleanor Holmes Norton was working closely and constructively with them as the ranking Democrat on the D.C. Subcommittee of Government Reform and Oversight (the old District of Columbia Committee was one of three eliminated by Gingrich when he became Speaker). But as the District's finances deteriorated to the point that it lost all capacity to borrow and its cash plunged toward zero, Barry left his first budget resolutely unbalanced. In effect, he invited the creation of a financial control board, preparing to blame white Republicans and anyone else he could for the District's problems and for the spending cutbacks and other tough medicine that would have to be administered. With little opposition (and without a roll-call vote in the House or Senate), Congress in April 1995 created the financial control board—modelled after bail-outs in other bankrupt cities during the past two decades—to oversee for the next several years the District's finances with an administrator responsible to the five members appointed by the President. The chief opposition appeared to come from D.C. Council members who resented their own loss of political influence. Meanwhile, the crisis of the District's finances and administration worsened, with growing numbers of local government bodies being placed in federal receivership. Looming on the horizon—with the encouragement of Gingrich—were more radical economic changes for the Nation's Capital, including discussion of tax-free zones and vouchers for children to attend private school.

The District's representative in the House of Representatives is Eleanor Holmes Norton, first elected in 1990. She was criticized during that campaign because her husband hadn't filed their income taxes for several years and in the primary beat Councilwoman Betty Anne Kane by only a 39%–33% margin. But she has won easily since and has proved herself to be hard-working, competent, intellectually honest, able to get along with opponents as well as fellow partisans, willing to take personal and political risks in the long-term interests of her community and constituency: a splendid representative. She established good relations with Republicans active on District matters long before they got their majority, and even though she led the drive, much resented by Republicans in 1993 and repealed by them in 1995, to give her and the four delegates to the House from territories—all of whom were then Democrats—votes on most legislation in the House. She also got on the good side of Bill Clinton, whose nomination she supported and whom she in turn helped persuade to back a little more money for the District government. During the District's 1995 fiscal crisis, she admitted that cuts were necessary, called on Barry to recommend them but said she would support a financial control board even if he did not. She proceeded with candor and skill, and at great political risk, for Barry could easily choose to blame her as well as the Republican Congress for any cuts in an effort to absolve himself of all responsibility.

The People: Est. Pop. 1994: 570,000; Pop. 1990: 606,900, down 6.1% 1990–1994. 0.2% of U.S. total, 50th largest. Median age: 33.5 years. 12.8% 65 years and over. 65.8% Black, 29.0% White, 5.4% Hispanic origin, 1.8% Asian, 2.4% Other. Households: 25.3% married couple families; 10% married couple fams. w. children; 52% college educ.; median household income: $30,727; per capita income: $18,881; 38.9% owner occupied housing; median house value: $123,900; median monthly rent: $441. 8.4% Unemployment. 1994 Voting age pop.: 452,000. 1994 Turnout: 179,023; 40% of VAP. Registered voters (1994): 365,472; 288,475 D (79%); 25,979 R (7%); 46,366 unaffiliated and minor parties (13%).

Political Lineup: Representative, 1 D at large.

1992 Presidential Vote

Clinton (D)	192,619	(85%)
Bush (R)	20,698	(9%)
Perot (I)	9,681	(4%)

1988 Presidential Vote

Dukakis (D)	159,407	(83%)
Bush (R)	27,590	(14%)

1992 Democratic Presidential Primary

Clinton	45,716	(74%)
Tsongas	6,452	(10%)
Brown	4,444	(7%)
Uncommitted	5,292	(9%)

1992 Republican Presidential Primary

Bush	4,265	(82%)
Buchanan	970	(19%)

DELEGATE

Del. Eleanor Holmes Norton (D)

Elected 1990; b. June 13, 1937, Washington, D.C.; home, Washington, D.C.; Antioch Col., B.A. 1960, Yale, M.A. 1963, LL.B. 1964; Episcopalian; divorced.

Career: Asst. Legal Dir., ACLU, 1965–70; New York City Comm. on Human Rights, 1970–77; Equal Empl. Oppor. Comm., 1977–81; Sr. Fellow, The Urban Inst., 1981–82; Prof., Georgetown U. Law Ctr., 1982–90.

DC Office: 1424 LHOB 20515, 202-225-8050; Fax: 202-225-3002.

District Offices: 815 15th St., NW, #100, Washington 20005, 202-783-5065; and 2041 MLK Ave., #300, Washington 20020, 202-678-8900.

Committees: *Government Reform & Oversight* (17th of 22 D): District of Columbia (RMM). *Transportation & Infrastructure* (17th of 27 D): Public Buildings and Economic Development; Water Resources and Environment.

Election Results

1994 general	Eleanor Holmes Norton (D)	154,988	(89%)	($72,830)
	Donald A. Saltz (R)	13,828	(8%)	
	Others	4,848	(3%)	
1994 primary	Eleanor Holmes Norton (D)	unopposed		
1992 general	Eleanor Holmes Norton (D)	166,808	(85%)	($143,853)
	Susan Emerson (R)	20,108	(10%)	($11,697)
	Susan Griffin (I)	7,253	(4%)	
	Other	2,585	(1%)	

FLORIDA

Florida, down in a far corner of the country, with a scorching tropical climate half the year and land that is mostly native swamp, is today one of the places where America is meeting its future. For many years, Florida has been what millions of retirees have looked forward to: the sunny year-round warmth after eternal gray skies over winter factories and rain pounding on office windows. And for millions of young families, from the South and various points north, Florida has been a booming economy, with jobs and opportunities in places that were recently just swampland. For refugees from Cuba and Haiti and immigrants from all over the Caribbean and Latin America, Florida has been a land of freedom and security from the armed thugs that control everyday life in police states; for immigrants from all over the Caribbean and Latin America, it has been a land of opportunity and upward mobility. For Americans and foreigners of all kinds—some 40 million of them in 1994, up from 23 million a dozen years before—Florida is the place to visit, with tourist attractions and year-round swimming and restaurants and rooms to suit every taste and pocketbook. Yet there can be trouble here as well: what seemed like paradise for some can be dystopia to others; a retirement haven can turn out to be a crime capital; a showplace of American creativity can turn out to be a place where naive foreigners are murdered by American criminals.

Florida is a creation not of America's elite—though a few millionaires like Henry Flagler and Marcus Plant pioneered tourism here—but a place for which ordinary people have voted with their feet. Half a century ago, it was the least populous state in the South, with 1.4 million people, swampy, isolated, disease-ridden, bigoted, with no mineral resources but phosphate mines, not much agriculture outside its citrus groves and hardly any manufacturing at all. Today it is America's fourth most populous state, with 14 million people (it passed Ohio in 1984, Illinois in 1986 and Pennsylvania in 1987). Florida is not a replica of the nation but an exaggeration: a state one-fifth of whose economy is based on tourism in a country where tourism is one of the great growth industries; a state with an economy based on services in a country increasingly service-oriented; the state with the largest proportion of elderly and retired citizens in a country where an increasing percentage will live many years in retirement; a state also with a growing number of school children in a country which, replenished by immigration, is growing faster and more robustly than any other advanced nation. Florida's architectural style once seemed exotic—Flagler's vast luxury hotels, the pink stucco motels of the 1940s and 1950s, the art deco hotels of Miami Beach—but now they have become leading edge: the Disney World Dolphin Hotel and Arquitectonica's Miami towers. And Florida is becoming a show business center, with actual movie production on the lots at the Universal and Disney World theme parks near Orlando: tourist attractions becoming workplaces, life imitating art imitating life.

Florida in the mid-1990s has had one of America's most buoyant economies, though its economic base may seem a mystery to outsiders—it can't all be tourism and retirees, can it? The answer is that it is also services and trade. Miami for two decades has been the economic and commercial capital of Latin America, as well as its mecca for political exiles. It is the one place from where you can fly nonstop to just about any place in Latin America, and the one place where you can be sure your money and your person are safe from government takeover. With its large Cuban community, Spanish is commonly spoken and understood. Miami is a truly international city, and getting more so. Quite appropriately, Miami was the site of the Summit of the Americas in December 1994. But international trade affects not just Miami, but all of south Florida, and the impact is likely to increase rather than decrease, particularly if the United States overcomes the Mexican currency crisis and makes progress on free trade agreements with other Latin American countries.

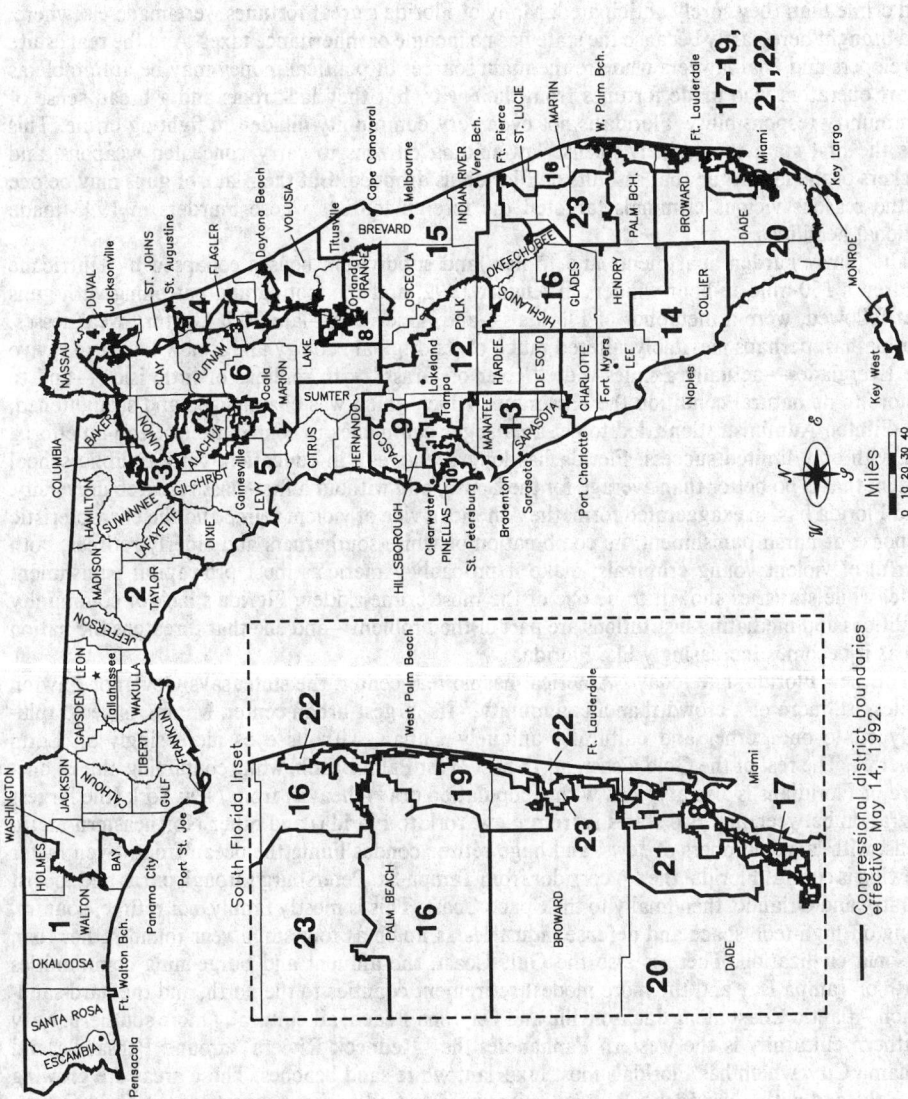

Congressional district boundaries effective May 14, 1992.

South Florida Inset

What may be more fragile in Florida than its economy is what the Eastern Europeans have accustomed us to call civil society. Most people here do not have deep roots in Florida, most communities sprang into existence within living memory and, if Florida gives people more freedom and options than they may ever have imagined, it has also given them more disorder and crime than they surely anticipated. Many of Florida's great fortunes were made elsewhere, and brought here partly because the state has no income or inheritance taxes. And the real estate developers and trial lawyers who are the main sources of political money may be admirable as smart operators who made fortunes from their wits, but they lack roots and a broad sense of community responsibility. Florida is not even very community-minded in fighting crime. This was the first state to routinely license law-abiding citizens to carry concealed weapons, and backers of the law argue that assaults on Floridians dropped. But their lack of guns may be one of the reasons vicious criminals targeted the foreign tourists whose murders in 1993 made national headlines.

The flimsy garden apartments and trailers and subdivision houses collapsed by Hurricane Andrew's 150-mile-an-hour winders in August 1992, and the looting and patrolling with guns that followed, were a metaphor of Florida's—and America's—late 20th Century weaknesses. Florida has, perhaps inevitably, altered much of its original ecology and is now trying to revive the Everglades—actually a miles-wide "River of Grass" with millions of little islets—and to restore to its natural condition the Kissimmee River which was channelized and straightened; the Clinton Administration tried to get area sugar companies to contribute to clean-up efforts, but with only limited success. Florida has long been weak in education, with a public school system that is no better than average for the South, and without a first-class research university. And Florida has, in exaggerated form, the American vice of violent crime and the characteristic response of harsh punishment: its combination of white southerners and elderly retirees, both fearful of violent young criminals, make it probably America's most pro-capital punishment state, while statistics show it to be one of the most crime-ridden. Florida's lack of community traditions and mediating institutions are part of the problem—and one that threatens the nation too as it becomes increasingly like Florida.

This new Florida, like today's America, has no real center; the state, says Governor Lawton Chiles, is "more of a crowd than a community." Its largest urban center, Miami, is geographically off to one corner and culturally uniquely Cuban, with its eyes increasingly on Latin America. The rest of the Gold Coast, north past West Palm Beach, while containing almost one-third of Floridians is also atypical, with a population drawn heavily from New York (the largest migration between any two states is from New York to Florida) and other Northeastern metro areas, with large numbers of Jews, and huge retiree condos lining the ocean front. Even faster growing is central Florida, the I-4 corridor from Tampa-St. Petersburg through citrus and tourist country and Orlando, then finally to the Space Coast. This is mostly family, not retiree, country, living off high-tech space and defense industries as much as tourism, a year-round rather than seasonal civilization. There is also the Gulf Coast, the affluent and burgeoning communities south of Tampa Bay and the more modest retirement counties to the north, and the hard-sand-beach Atlantic Coast along Jacksonville and Daytona Beach, all culturally more southern. Very southern culturally is the western Panhandle, the "Redneck Riviera" around Pensacola and Panama City, which has Florida's most luxuriant white sand beaches. These areas are growing robustly, and with a confidence and optimism hard to find in mature parts of the Gold Coast.

How does this diverse state add up politically? Differently every dozen years or so, it seems. Chiles, despite a growing economy and a moderate record, was nearly defeated by Republican Jeb Bush in 1994; the fact that it was so close reflected something like straight-ticket voting. This is on balance a Republican state now, in state as well as national politics: in eight 1994 statewide races Republicans led by an average of 52%–48%, while Democratic presidential candidates have averaged only 37% here in the last seven elections. Jimmy Carter got 52% in 1976, and Lyndon Johnson got 51% in 1964, but both were fellow Southerners. But the balance is in different places. The Panhandle and the Jacksonville area, once Dixiecrat, are now

Republican; Tallahassee and Gainesville, in between, with state government and universities, are Democratic. Retirees and refugees tend to bring their politics with them: Miami's Dade County moved from liberal Democratic to enthusiastically Republican as Cubans moved in and raised families and Jewish retirees kept moving further north along the Gold Coast; Fort Lauderdale's Broward County is now the most Democratic part of Florida and Palm Beach County is not far behind. The southern Gulf Coast counties, settled by affluent retirees, are strongly Republican; counties farther north, with many blue collar retirees, sometimes vote Democratic. From 1978 to 1992 total registration in Florida rose from 4.2 million to 6.5 million, with Republican registration up 1.5 million and Democratic registration up only 506,000. The Democrats' registration edge dropped from 64%–30% in 1980 to 51%–41% in 1992 to 50%–42% in 1994. They have counterbalanced this with strength at the top of the ticket and generally favorable media coverage, which may be especially important in a state with eight media markets and dozens of newspapers, and hundreds of thousands of new voters unacquainted with Florida government or politics and no established civic ladders for developing political talent. And Florida's political season is brief, tucked into hurricane season, with a primary in September, a runoff in October (and there often are runoffs), and then the November election. It's over in a flash: the wonder is that the results are as rational as they have been.

Governor. The governor of Florida technically has few powers. Many of his appointments and budget decisions must be approved by a cabinet made up of six separately elected officials. But he does set the agenda and tone of state government. For a quarter century, Florida has elected fairly liberal Democrats—Reubin Askew in 1970, Bob Graham 1978; Republican Bob Martinez won in 1986, then immediately sank in popularity when he pushed through a tax on services, which had to be repealed. That opened the way in 1990 for Lawton Chiles, who had retired in 1988 after 18 years in the Senate, to run for governor. Chiles grew up in Lakeland, in the citrus and phosphate country of central Florida. He was elected to the state House in 1958, at 28, to the state Senate in 1966. In 1970, he ran for governor by walking across the state, barely finishing second in the primary, beating a better-known Democrat in the runoff and then upsetting a Republican in the general. His demeanor and record were moderate, but well to the left of most Republicans. In 1990 he beat then-Congressman (and now Insurance Commissioner) Bill Nelson in the primary and whipped Martinez 57%–43%. Florida has never had an income tax—the state constitution bars it, and it would make little sense in the one state where outsiders pay one-third of sales tax revenues—but it had developed a large and sometimes overbearing state government, and the focus of Florida politics since Chiles was elected is to how rein it in.

Chiles, part of the Democratic Leadership Council, promised to reform government. He reduced spending increases, called for "right-sizing" the bureaucracy, settling a federal suit on the Everglades. Chiles was a late entry in 1990, brought in by his lieutenant governor, Buddy MacKay, a former congressman who nearly won the 1988 Senate race. He pushed through campaign finance reform with low contribution limits. He was proud of requiring "Healthy Start" to screen every pregnant woman and newborn for health risks and pushed a mandatory work program that he said cut state welfare rolls. MacKay worked on "reinventing government." But Chiles also called for $1.3 billion in new taxes in 1992, at which point his job rating plummeted. And in 1994 his healthcare reform plan was rejected by the legislature.

The Republicans had a spirited primary. Insurance Commissioner Tom Gallagher called for an increase in the sales tax to pay for new prison construction; it attracted some attention but bombed. Secretary of State Jim Smith, a former Democrat, campaigned on his well-known name. State Senator Ander Crenshaw tried to build on his Jacksonville base. But the best known candidate was presidential son Jeb Bush. Bush was a Miami real estate developer, Martinez's Commerce Commissioner, and head of the Dade County Republican Party; his wife Columba is a native of Mexico and he speaks fluent Spanish (and did so during one debate with Chiles). He campaigned indefatigably around the state, raised huge amounts of money and showed an impressive mastery of state and local government issues. He took some flak in the primary; Gallagher and Smith collaborated on an ad that insinuated that Bush walked away from an unpaid loan from a savings and loan. But on primary day he won an impressive 46% in a seven-candidate field and Smith, with only 18%, quickly announced he would not seek a runoff.

Bush zoomed to a lead in polls and presented a program of thoroughgoing conservative reform. "We need to change our entire relationship with government" until it plays "a useful but smaller role in our lives," he said. He called for fewer appeals for death row inmates and speedier executions, said Florida should withdraw from AFDC and replace it with limited temporary assistance, called for school choice and demanded voter approval of all state and local tax increases. A Constitutional amendment on this, supported by Bush, was on the Florida ballot until October 1994 when it was removed by the Florida Supreme Court on a technicality. Chiles responded that he had already started reforming welfare and education and had approved as many executions as Martinez. But his campaign only got revved up in October when he ran negative ads about Bush's ties with savings and loans and attacked a Bush ad which showed a mother whose daughter had been murdered accusing Chiles of not speeding executions. Chiles had other assets. In August 1994 he had called on the federal government to stop the flow of refugees from Cuba to Florida. Bill Clinton responded by reneging on his policy to provide refuge and he confined refugees at the Guantanamo Naval Base; Chiles got credit for keeping refugees out. And Chiles started emphasizing his "cracker" roots and calling himself "the he-coon (who) always walks before the light of day."

The result was a 51%–49% Chiles victory. The controversial crime ad may have hurt Bush, who otherwise ran no negative ads. But even more important may have been the mentions of savings and loans, as beloved by many older voters as Social Security. Chiles clearly cut into the elderly vote on the Gulf Coast and won big on the Gold Coast. Exit polls showed voters over 65 were 54% for Chiles and voters under 65 gave Bush a majority. Black turnout was high (the Democrats had a black running for Education Commissioner, who narrowly lost), with 94% going for Chiles; Jews were 79% for Chiles, Cubans 74% for Bush. Republicans won three of the six lower statewide offices, captured control of the state Senate and increased their seats in the House. "It's a question of time before we're in control," said Jeb Bush, who is considered likely to run again in 1998, following the election. In the meantime, Chiles continued to talk of cutting government. "Government can't work. People work," he said in his inaugural, and called for reducing government regulations by 50% in two years.

Senators. Florida has two senators not nationally well-known. But both are popular in Florida, though of different parties; and both are from families that have achieved fame in other fields. The senior senator, Bob Graham, is careful, methodical, thorough, hard-working, reliable—always wearing his Florida ties, recording every meeting he attends and meal he eats in notebooks, scheduling meetings with every member of the Florida House delegation and with lobbyists on both sides of environmental, banking and crime issues. He comes from a prominent Florida family. His father started out with a Miami area dairy farm and developed the planned mini-city of Miami Lakes; his half-brother Philip Graham was publisher of *The Washington Post*. He has been in politics almost all his adult life; he was elected to the state House in 1966, at 30, and to the state Senate in 1970. In 1978, after a come-from-behind win in the Democratic runoff and a solid 56% win in the general, he began the first of two terms as governor. The attention-getting device in that campaign (invented by Senator Tom Harkin for his 1974 House race) was work days: Graham worked one day a week at some local job, from bagging groceries to working construction. He keeps it up still, once a month, and by January 1995 had logged over 290 work days, all of course carefully recorded.

In the Senate, as in Tallahassee, Graham has proved to be middle of the road, efficient and popular. He has worked hard to restore the Kissimmee River to its natural state, to ban oil drilling off the southwest Florida coast and get the federal government to buy up existing leases, to expand the Everglades park and to make the Suwanee in north Florida a National Wild and Scenic River. He has been a hardliner on crime legislation, supporting capital punishment, opposing the measure that would try to impose quotas on jury verdicts, creating a juvenile delinquency program on federal lands. He pushed the Criminal Aliens Federal Responsibility

Act, requiring states to be reimbursed $350 million, and worked to cut foreign aid to countries that refuse to take back criminal aliens. He has worked on veterans issues in committee and on the floor. A staunch opponent of Fidel Castro, Graham has argued for continuing the embargo on Cuba, although he bucked his state's Cuban-American leaders in supporting Clinton's May 1995 deal to send additional refugees back to Cuba. He backed the Caribbean Basin Initiative. He wanted to stem the flow of Haitian refugees to Florida, and supported maintaining democracy in Haiti as a means to do this. He backed the dispatch of U.S. troops to Haiti. "The lesson of Haiti is going to be in terms of the resolve of the international community, specifically in the United States, for the protection of democracies."

On national issues, he is temperamentally a team player for Democrats, but with a decidedly moderate voting record and an independent streak on some matters. In March 1994, when the advice was not welcome, he urged Hillary Rodham Clinton to answer questions on Whitewater in "a calm rational forum"—advice she ultimately took. He dissents from the party line on some major issues: he voted for the Gulf war resolution and backs the balanced budget amendment. Naturally he has paid heed to issues like drug traffic, health care for elderly, and campaign finance reform (Florida has a tradition of "sunshine laws" requiring full disclosure). Graham has been mentioned as a national candidate—he was on one of Bill Clinton's short lists for the vice presidency in 1992—but he has not run, and seems unlikely to now.

Graham won the Senate seat in 1986 as he was leaving the governorship by beating Paula Hawkins, a sometimes eccentric but often popular Republican elected in 1980, 55%–45%. In 1992, he did not have a serious challenge; his opponent was a congressman who had switched to the Republican Party and then lost his Democratic-leaning House seat. Graham won 65%–35%. In the 1994 cycle, he chaired the Senate Democrats' campaign committee and raised a record amount of money. That was the good news. The bad news was that Democrats lost two incumbents, all six open seats and the majority—not Graham's fault, but a loss nevertheless. In 1995, for the first time in his political career, Graham was in the minority. But he finally got a seat on the Finance Committee, perhaps with an eye toward bipartisanship, and his standing in Florida seems to remain strong.

Connie Mack III, pleasant and unassuming, in a dozen years moved from being a banker in Cape Coral to second-term senator from the fourth largest state, Chairman of the Joint Economic Committee and on the leading edge of conservative economic issues. Mack is the grandson and namesake of the longtime owner and manager of the Philadelphia Athletics (his other grandfather was Morris Sheppard, senator from Texas from 1913 to 1941). He first ran for office in 1982, at 40, when he was president of the Florida National Bank of Lee County, and won a multi-candidate Republican primary for the House in a newly created Gulf Coast district. In the House, he became a supply-sider and one of the leaders of Newt Gingrich's Conservative Opportunity Society. He was lead sponsor in the House of the Gramm-Rudman deficit-cutting measure that originated in the Senate; pro-choice on abortion and for ERA, he switched on both issues when contemplating the 1988 Senate race. He entered that contest in October 1987, prior to the decisions of incumbent Lawton Chiles and former Governor Reubin Askew not to run. Against the Democratic nominee, Congressman (and now Lieutenant Governor) Buddy MacKay, Mack's campaign theme was, "Hey, Buddy, you're liberal." Mack called for "less taxing, less spending, less government, and more freedom" and attacked MacKay for opposing contra aid and the balanced budget amendment. Worries about social security clearly helped MacKay, who carried St. Petersburg and ran far ahead of most Democrats in Mack's own retiree-heavy House district. But Mack ran far ahead of other Republicans in the heavily military Jacksonville area and in the family-oriented I-4 corridor. Mack lost among those who went to the polls on election day, but with a big absentee margin won 50.4%–49.6%.

Mack has a very conservative voting record, with special attention to issues of importance in Florida. He has given special attention to early detection of cancer; both he and his wife are cancer survivors. He is a strong supporter of Israel and passed a law requiring the State Department to keep track of the PLO. He opposes offshore oil drilling and sponsored the Florida

Coastal Zone Protection Act; he favors restoration of the Everglades. He pushed successfully for tightening the economic embargo on Cuba and strongly favors TV Marti. He opposed the catastrophic healthcare bill in 1988, when almost everyone was for it, and reaped the political benefits in 1989, when almost everyone was against it. He was one of three Republicans who responded on national television to Bill Clinton's healthcare speech in September 1993. He was successful in helping Florida get two more baseball teams—the Florida Marlins in Miami and the Devil Rays in Tampa Bay—and called for revoking baseball's antitrust exemption. He and Bob Graham seem to have a kind of non-aggression pact; they work closely and amicably together on many Florida issues.

In 1994 Mack did not have tough opposition. Graham, though the Senate Democrats' campaign chairman, could not recruit a well-known candidate, and the Democratic nomination went in the runoff to Hugh Rodham, a Miami public defender better known as Hillary Rodham Clinton's brother. Rodham was subjected to ridicule for his inexperience and girth, and had in fact never voted until 1992; but he campaigned honorably and in good humor and with on-site campaigning from his sister and her husband. But Mack had affirmative popularity and far more money, and won with 70%, more than any other Republican senator in 1994.

In the Republican Senate, Mack could become a major force for the supply-side, market economics views he has long held. In 1990 he urged George Bush to stick to his "read my lips" pledge and he firmly opposed Bill Clinton's budget and tax package in 1993. As Joint Economic Committee Chairman, he can marshal statistics and arguments in favor of his positions. He has a bill to create an independent commission to develop an annual package of spending cuts, which Congress would have to accept or reject without amendments—much like Dick Armey's military base-closing law. Mack, who is Republican Conference Secretary, has sought to make Senate committee chairmen—including Mark Hatfield of Appropriations, on which Mack serves—more responsive to the party conference, a tougher task in the tradition-bound Senate than in the House. A man on the rise, he is chairman of two other subcommittees and a member of the Intelligence Committee.

Presidential politics. For reasons not readily apparent, Democratic presidential nominees seem to feel they have a chance to carry Florida, though their percentages in the last four elections have been 39%, 35%, 39%, 39%. Evidently its 25 electoral votes seem too much to pass up and the prospect of all those ex-New Yorkers on the Gold Coast (49% for Clinton in 1992, but only 28% of the state's votes) makes them ignore the rest of the state (35% for Clinton in 1992). But the disease resists cure: in March 1995, there was Bill Clinton on a campaign-like swing to Miami, Tallahassee and Tampa, on his way to Haiti. Any Republican who feels obliged to campaign in Florida, as George Bush did in 1992, is obviously in deep trouble nationally.

Florida's presidential primary is one of the early March Super Tuesday contests, and quite possibly the most important; Texas is larger, but could be preempted by Texas candidates, like Phil Gramm. In 1992 and 1988, Florida produced thumping victories for both parties' ultimate nominees. The Michael Dukakis victory in 1988 was evidence of how liberal and un-Dixiecrat Florida's Democratic electorate is. Its Republican electorate is hawkish, anti-tax, but with a soft spot for the environment.

Congressional districting. Florida gained four new House seats from the 1990 Census, going from 19 to 23 representatives, and redistricting was naturally fiercely contested. Democrats were so conflicted that they could not produce a plan even though they controlled both houses of the legislature and the governorship. So in May 1992, a federal court adopted a plan drawn by a Tulane University professor which created three black-majority (two of them new) and two Hispanic-majority districts (one new), some with very peculiar shapes; boundaries of the other 18 districts were not so driven by politics, but sometimes ended up grotesque because of next-door minority districts. As expected, Florida elected three black congressmen, the first here since Reconstruction, and two Cuban-Americans. That helped increase 1990's 10–9 Republican edge to 13–10 after 1992 and 15–8 after 1994—the most Republican megastate delegation. And, with several other seats that are competitive, Republicans might gain additional seats from the Democrats unless the once mighty majority party staunches its hemorrhaging in the South. In 1992, Florida voters overwhelmingly passed a term limits initiative barring members' names from appearing on the ballot after four terms in office.

The People: Est. Pop. 1994: 13,953,000; Pop. 1990: 12,937,926, up 7.8% 1990–1994. 5.4% of U.S. total, 4th largest; 15% rural. Median age: 36.4 years. 18.3% 65 years and over. 83.1% White, 13.6% Black, 12.2% Hispanic origin, 1.2% Asian, 1.8% Other. Households: 54.4% married couple families; 21% married couple fams. w. children; 44% college educ.; median household income: $27,483; per capita income: $14,698; 67.2% owner occupied housing; median house value: $77,100; median monthly rent: $402. 8.2% Unemployment. 1994 Voting age pop.: 10,856,000. 1994 Turnout: 4,177,391; 38% of VAP. Registered voters (1994): 6,560,429; 3,245,518 D (49%), 2,747,074 R (42%), 567,837 unaffiliated and minor parties (9%).

Political Lineup: Governor, Lawton Chiles (D); Lt. Gov., Buddy MacKay (D); Secy. of State, Sandy B. Mortham (R); Atty. Gen., Robert A. Butterworth (D); Treasurer and Insurance Commissioner, Bill Nelson (D); Comptroller, Bob Milligan (R); Auditor General, Charles L. Lester (D). State Senate, 40 (21 R and 19 D); State House of Representatives, 120 (63 D and 57 R). Senators, Bob Graham (D) and Connie Mack III (R). Representatives, 23 (15 R, 8 D).

1992 Presidential Vote

Bush (R)	2,171,781	(41%)
Clinton (D)	2,071,651	(39%)
Perot (I)	1,052,481	(20%)

1988 Presidential Vote

Bush (R)	2,618,885	(61%)
Dukakis (D)	1,656,701	(39%)

1992 Democratic Presidential Primary

Clinton	570,566	(51%)
Tsongas	388,124	(35%)
Brown	139,569	(12%)
Other	25,598	(2%)

1992 Republican Presidential Primary

Bush	608,077	(68%)
Buchanan	285,386	(32%)

GOVERNOR

Gov. Lawton Chiles (D)

Elected 1990, term expires Jan. 1999; b. Apr. 3, 1930, Lakeland; home, Tallahassee; U. of FL, B.S. 1952, LL.B. 1955; Presbyterian; married (Rhea).

Career: Army, 1953–54 (Korea); Practicing atty., 1955–71; Instructor, FL Southern Col., 1955–58; FL House of Reps., 1959–66; FL Senate, 1967–70; U.S. Senate, 1971–89; Dir., LeRoy Collins Ctr. for Pub. Policy, 1989–90.

Office: The Capitol, Tallahassee 32399, 904-488-7146; Fax: 904-487-0801.

Election Results

1994 gen.	Lawton Chiles (D)	2,135,008	(51%)
	Jeb Bush (R)	2,071,068	(49%)
1994 prim.	Lawton Chiles (D)	603,657	(72%)
	Jack Gargan (D)	232,757	(28%)
1990 gen.	Lawton Chiles (D)	1,988,341	(57%)
	Bob Martinez (R)	1,526,738	(43%)

SENATORS

Sen. Bob Graham (D)

Elected 1986, seat up 1998; b. Nov. 9, 1936, Coral Gables; home, Miami Lakes; U. of FL, B.A. 1959, Harvard, J.D. 1962; United Church of Christ; married (Adele).

Career: The Graham Cos., Sengra Development Corp., 1962–66; FL House of Reps., 1966–70; FL Senate, 1970–78; FL Gov., 1978–1986.

DC Office: 524 HSOB 20510, 202-224-3041; Fax: 202-224-2237.

State Offices: 44 W. Flagler St., #1715, Miami 33130, 305-536-7293; and 325 John Knox Rd., Bldg. 600, Tallahassee 32303, 904-422-6100; and 101 E. Kennedy Blvd., #3270, Tampa 33602, 813-228-2476.

Committees: *Environment & Public Works* (5th of 7 D): Clean Air, Wetlands, Private Property and Nuclear Safety (RMM); Transportation and Infrastructure. *Finance* (8th of 9 D): International Trade; Medicaid and Health Care for Low-Income Families (RMM); Medicare, Long-Term Care and Health Insurance. *Veterans' Affairs* (2nd of 5 D). *Intelligence (Select)* (4th of 8 D).

Group Ratings

	ADA	ACLU	COPE	CFA	LCV	CON	NSI	COC	ACU	NTLC	CHC
1994	75	47	75	75	92	55	90	31	8	8	28
1993	65	—	82	70	75	63	—	36	16	—	—

National Journal Ratings

	1993 LIB — 1993 CONS	1994 LIB — 1994 CONS
Economic	56% — 41%	55% — 40%
Social	58% — 41%	70% — 29%
Foreign	32% — 60%	63% — 35%

Key Votes of the 103d Congress

1. Clinton Deficit Plan	Y	3. Brady Handgun Purchase	Y	5. Lmt. UN Cmnd. of Forces	N
2. NAFTA	Y	4. Strike Race/Death Pnlty.	Y	6. Cut Missile Funds	N

Key Votes of the 104th Congress

1. Congressional Compliance	Y	3. Balanced Budget Amndt.	Y	5. Product Liability Reform	N
2. Bar Unfunded Mandates	Y	4. Pass Line Item Veto	Y	6. FY96 Budget	N

Election Results

1992 general	Bob Graham (D)	3,245,565	(65%)	($3,318,473)
	Bill Grant (R)	1,716,505	(35%)	($242,251)
1992 primary	Bob Graham (D)	968,618	(84%)	
	Jim Mahorner (D)	180,405	(16%)	
1986 general	Bob Graham (D)	1,877,231	(55%)	($6,173,663)
	Paula Hawkins (R)	1,551,888	(45%)	($6,723,729)

Sen. Connie Mack III (R)

Elected 1988, seat up 2000; b. Oct. 29, 1940, Philadelphia, PA; home, Cape Coral; U. of FL, B.A. 1966; Catholic; married (Priscilla).

Career: Banker, 1966–82; U.S. House of Reps., 1982–88.

DC Office: 517 HSOB 20510, 202-224-5274; Fax: 202-224-8022.

State Offices: 600 N. Westshore Blvd., #602, Tampa 33609, 813-225-7483.

Committees: *Republican Conference Secretary. Appropriations* (10th of 15 R): Defense; Foreign Operations; Interior; Labor, Health and Human Services, Education; Legislative Branch (Chmn). *Banking, Housing & Urban Affairs* (5th of 9 R): Financial Institutions and Regulatory Relief; Housing Opportunity and Community Development (Chmn.); International Finance. *Intelligence (Select)* (8th of 9 R). *Joint Economic Committee* (Chmn. of 10 Sens.)

Group Ratings

	ADA	ACLU	COPE	CFA	LCV	CON	NSI	COC	ACU	NTLC	CHC
1994	10	16	0	17	8	81	100	92	96	92	100
1993	10	—	0	10	6	77	—	100	92	—	—

National Journal Ratings

	1993 LIB — 1993 CONS		1994 LIB — 1994 CONS	
Economic	0%	— 87%	12%	— 82%
Social	8%	— 90%	26%	— 73%
Foreign	16%	— 77%	6%	— 86%

Key Votes of the 103d Congress

1. Clinton Deficit Plan	N	3. Brady Handgun Purchase	N	5. Lmt. UN Cmnd. of Forces	Y
2. NAFTA	Y	4. Strike Race/Death Pnlty.	Y	6. Cut Missile Funds	N

Key Votes of the 104th Congress

1. Congressional Compliance	Y	3. Balanced Budget Amndt.	Y	5. Product Liability Reform	Y
2. Bar Unfunded Mandates	Y	4. Pass Line Item Veto	Y	6. FY96 Budget	Y

Election Results

1994 general	Connie Mack III (R)	2,894,726	(71%)	($5,729,359)
	Hugh E. Rodham (D)	1,210,412	(29%)	($617,190)
1994 primary	Connie Mack III (R)	unopposed		
1988 general	Connie Mack III (R)	2,049,329	(50%)	($5,181,639)
	Buddy MacKay (D)	2,015,717	(50%)	($3,714,852)

FIRST DISTRICT

Widely known in the Southeast, scarcely heard of anywhere else, are the Gulf Coast beaches of Florida's Panhandle, from Pensacola east to Destin—the so-called "Redneck Riviera." This area has always been part of Dixie, an expanse of swamp and low farmland, and long heavily dependent on the military. Since John Quincy Adams persuaded Spain to sell Florida to the United States in 1819 to get the port of Pensacola, the United States Navy has had a base there (except during a spot of trouble in the 1860s). This was the site of the nation's first naval aviation training base, the birthplace of carrier aviation and a major base in World War II. Inland to the east is Eglin Air Force Base, which spreads over the lion's share of three counties. In the 1940s and 1950s, these facilities were the main engines of growth; since the 1960s, when the rural South started getting prosperous, this American Riviera has become a major vacation and retirement spot for southerners who enjoy its vast, fine-grained white sand beaches, perhaps the finest in the country, and its pleasant inlet-filled bays.

More than 1,000 miles from Miami, the Panhandle is economically, culturally and politically far from most of Florida. Culturally, it is very conservative, an area of large families and traditional churches. It also has violent anti-abortion fanatics, two of whom murdered doctors who performed abortions in March 1993 and July 1994. The Gulf Coast looks southward toward Castro's Cuba and unruly Caribbean and Latin republics, from a coast bristling with military installations, giant shipyards and huge air bases.

The 1st Congressional District of Florida includes the end of the Panhandle, so far west it's in the Central time zone. It stretches from Pensacola and the Alabama border east to include part of Panama City. Politically, this is Republican territory. George Bush may have been losing in the rest of the country, but even in 1992 he won a majority of the votes here, with only one in four for Bill Clinton. The Panhandle has become reliably Republican in statewide races now and elects only a few Democrats to the legislature.

The Congressman from the 1st is now a Republican, Joe Scarborough, elected in 1994 to replace retiring conservative Democrat Earl Hutto, who first won in 1978 and won with only 52% in 1990 and 1992. Scarborough, 31 in 1994, grew up in Pensacola and after college and law school, ran a beauty contest company and then practiced law and was active in community affairs. In October 1993 he helped collect 3,000 signatures to protest the city government's 65% property tax increase. He had not run for office, but had long been interested in politics. His family remembers him at five, in 1968, coloring in states red and blue depending on whether they went Democratic or Republican. When he entered the five-Republican, two-Democrat race for the 1st District, he was far from the best known candidate. The best-known Republican was Lois Benson, a one-term legislator and four-year Pensacola Council member, generally conservative but pro-choice on abortion. She won 31.4% in the first primary, but Scarborough, conservative, anti-abortion, built on petition contacts and bought 30-minute cable broadcasts and received 30.6%; in October he won the runoff 54%–46%.

The Democratic nominee, Vince Whibbs, Jr., was a fine example of the kind of candidate with whom his party had held southern seats for years. His father was mayor of Pensacola for 17 years, until 1991; he served in the Marines as a military lawyer with the rank of captain, then ran the family car dealership and practiced law. When the best-known local Democrats, Speaker Bo Johnson and state Representative Buzz Richie, declined to run, he did, and won the primary 55%–45%. He was against gun control, supported school prayer and the balanced budget amendment. "I'm one of those guys who's been registered Democrat all my life and I've never voted for a Democrat," he said, but added that he could do more for the district as part of the Democratic majority. Whibbs said government has "a responsibility" to show a "caring, concerned attitude."

Scarborough, in contrast, said, "The federal government should protect our shores and get out of citizens' way." He talked about "retaking America" and returning to the small government of Jefferson and Madison. "We need to send someone who will say 'no' when everyone else is saying 'yes.' " On health care: "You guys take care of the VA hospitals first." He advocated a five-year federal spending freeze, school vouchers and tax credits for home schoolers and a ban on offshore oil drilling. A friend of the family of Michael Griffin, the man convicted of the March 1993 shooting of Dr. David Gunn, who performed abortions, Scarborough was asked by the family to shield them from the prying media and to convince Griffin to get an attorney. Scarborough himself tried to sign on as Griffin's attorney, but a judge said he lacked the criminal law experience necessary for the case.

For 100 years districts like the 1st have elected congressmen like Whibbs. But in 1994, the 1st elected Scarborough, and it wasn't even close: he won 62%–38%. In the House he has been one of the most enthusiastic backers of the Contract With America. He has been a frequent speaker on the House floor, eager to defend the new Republican majority and its program, even at the risk of doing rhetorical battle with more experienced Democrats. Assuming he can avoid a primary, he should be able to hold this seat comfortably.

The People: Pop. 1990: 562,575; 26% rural; 11% age 65+; 84% White; 13% Black; 1% Amer. Indian; 2% Asian; 1% Other; 2% Hispanic origin. Voting age pop.: 419,727; 11% Black; 2% Hispanic origin. Households: 59% married couple families; 26% married couple fams. w. children; 49% college educ.; median household income: $25,866; per capita income: $12,505; median gross rent: $390; median house value: $61,800.

1992 Presidential Vote			1988 Presidential Vote		
Bush (R)	117,809	(51%)	Bush (R)	144,294	(73%)
Clinton (D)	59,316	(26%)	Dukakis (D)	52,230	(27%)
Perot (I)	53,250	(23%)			

Rep. Joe Scarborough (R)

Elected 1994; b. Apr. 9, 1963, Atlanta, GA; home, Pensacola; U. of AL, B.A. 1985; U. of FL, J.D. 1990; Baptist; married (Melanie).

Career: Practicing atty., 1990–94.

DC Office: 1523 LHOB 20515, 202-225-4136; Fax: 202-225-3414.

District Offices: 4300 Bayou Blvd., #37, Pensacola 32503, 904-479-1183; and 348 S.W. Miracle Strip Hwy., #21, Ft. Walton Beach 32548, 904-664-1266.

Committees: *Government Reform & Oversight* (21st of 27 R): Government Management, Information and Technology; Human Resources and Intergovernmental Affairs; National Economic Growth, Natural Resources and Regulatory Affairs. *National Security* (26th of 30 R): Military Readiness; Military Research and Development.

Group Ratings and 103rd Congress Votes: Newly Elected

Key Votes of the 104th Congress

1. Congressional Compliance	Y	6. Reform Crime Grant	N	11. Loser Pays Court Reform	Y
2. Balanced Budget Amndmt.	Y	7. National Security Act	Y	12. Product Liability Reform	Y
3. Bar Unfunded Mandates	Y	8. Moratorium on Regs.	Y	13. Welfare Reform	Y
4. Pass Line Item Veto	Y	9. Risk Assessment on Regs.	Y	14. Term Limits Amndmt.	Y
5. Relax Exclusionary Rule	Y	10. Expnd. Priv. Prop. Rights	Y	15. Tax Cuts	Y

Election Results

1994 general	Joe Scarborough (R)	112,901	(62%)	($345,687)
	Vince Whibbs Jr. (D)	70,389	(38%)	($271,953)
1994 runoff	Joe Scarborough (R)	18,713	(54%)	
	Lois Benson (R)	15,663	(46%)	
1994 primary	Lois Benson (R)	12,446	(31%)	
	Joe Scarborough (R)	12,114	(31%)	
	W.A. (Buck) Lee (R)	6,069	(15%)	
	Jim Paul (R)	4,682	(12%)	
	Basil Bethea (R)	4,284	(11%)	
1992 general	Earl Hutto (D)	118,941	(52%)	($308,621)
	Terry Ketchel (R)	100,349	(44%)	($166,762)
	Barbara Rodgers-Hendricks (Green)	9,342	(4%)	($4,797)

SECOND DISTRICT

Tallahassee, the small city that is capital of the nation's fourth largest state, was until recently a Spanish-mossed county seat with little to distinguish it but a handsome creole capitol, built in 1845 and preserved opposite its 1977 skyscraper replacement, and two state universities—sited here in the days when almost all Floridians lived along the state's northern edge and Tallahassee was near the population center. Ralph Waldo Emerson, visiting Tallahassee in the 19th Century, said it was a "grotesque place, rapidly settled by public officers, land speculators and desperadoes." The countryside around it is distinctly Dixie: cotton fields, soft pine stands, catfish farms, large families, small towns with big churches, both black and white. Madison County, 50% black, with Florida's lowest per capita income and losing population since 1930, is a noteworthy example. But Tallahassee itself and the subdivisions spreading beyond it are bringing to the state's north end some of the new urbanized Florida, with an additional pro-government tilt: 42% of Tallahassee area jobs are now in city and state government, compared to 15% statewide. Tallahassee has not attained the critical mass of the capitals of the three more populous states (Sacramento, Albany and Austin) but it is on its way.

The 2d Congressional District of Florida is centered on Tallahassee, but extends westward to Panama City and eastward almost to Jacksonville. Historically, this was Democratic country, Jeffersonian and segregationist. Today, it is still Democratic, though for different reasons; there is a large black percentage (23%, the largest in any non-black majority district in Florida) and a strong Democratic preference among state employees and those dependent on them. Tallahassee's Leon County voted 49%–33% for Bill Clinton over George Bush—the highest Clinton percentage in any big Florida county except for Broward, heavily Jewish, and Alachua, home of the University of Florida. This area supported liberals in Democratic primaries and Democrats in general elections with great consistency even in the Republican 1980s.

The congressman from the 2d District is a Democrat who won the seat in unusual circumstances. Pete Peterson entered the 1990 race as a classic political neophyte. He was an Air Force colonel who spent more than six years as a POW in Vietnam; after he retired he moved inland from Panama City to Marianna, his wife's home town. Peterson knew little about politics, but local Democrats were eager to teach him. The then-congressman, Bill Grant, had switched parties in February 1989, with hoopla from President Bush, Republican National Chairman Lee Atwater and Governor Bob Martinez; the switch was especially startling because, although Grant said he resented the national Democrats' liberalism, he had a rather moderate voting record himself. Some thought Grant was angling for statewide office, and he did become the Republican nominee against Senator Bob Graham in 1992. But the party switch was a loser in this still Democratic district. Democrats hammered at him and Peterson proved to be an appealing candidate, and was elected with 57% of the vote.

Peterson has had a moderate voting record, roughly at the midpoint of the Democratic House. But he backs term limits and the balanced budget amendment and voted against both NAFTA in November 1993 and the rule for the crime bill in August 1994 because he opposes gun control. Earnest and hard-working, he makes a good impression in town meetings. During his first term he made a trip to Vietnam to urge full access to information about possible Americans left behind. He was reelected with 73% in 1992 and, against an anti-pornography activist, with 61% in 1994.

Peterson got a seat on Appropriations in 1993. When Democrats lost their majority, he lost it in 1995, and got National Security instead. Although he opposed the Contract With America's defense provisions, he gave more support to the Republican program than did any other Florida Democrat. He also became head of the moderate Democratic Budget Group, a force for deficit reduction which lost much of its clout after the 1994 election.

The People: Pop. 1990: 562,410; 46% rural; 12% age 65+; 74% White; 23% Black; 1% Amer. Indian; 1% Asian; 1% Other; 2% Hispanic origin. Voting age pop.: 419,263; 21% Black; 2% Hispanic origin.

Households: 54% married couple families; 25% married couple fams. w. children; 42% college educ.; median household income: $23,388; per capita income: $11,491; median gross rent: $375; median house value: $57,500.

1992 Presidential Vote			1988 Presidential Vote		
Clinton (D)	100,723	(42%)	Bush (R)	115,959	(60%)
Bush (R)	92,805	(38%)	Dukakis (D)	76,695	(40%)
Perot (I)	46,958	(19%)			

Rep. Douglas (Pete) Peterson (D)

Elected 1990; b. June 26, 1935, Omaha, NE; home, Marianna; U. of Tampa, B.S. 1976, U. of Central MI, 1977; Catholic; married (Carlotta).

Career: Air Force, 1954–80 (Vietnam); Businessman; Co-owner, CRT Computers, 1984–90; Admin., FL St. U. Dozier Schl. for Boys, 1985–90.

DC Office: 306 CHOB 20515, 202-225-5235; Fax: 202-225-1586.

District Offices: 930 Thomasville Rd., #101, Tallahassee 32303, 904-561-3979; 30 W. Government St., #203, Panama City 32401, 904-785-0812.

Committees: *National Security* (21st of 25 D): Military Installations and Facilities; Military Procurement. *Small Business* (13th of 19 D): Regulation and Paperwork.

Group Ratings

	ADA	ACLU	COPE	CFA	LCV	CON	NSI	COC	ACU	NTLC	CHC
1994	50	43	67	50	50	21	70	67	38	21	36
1993	55	—	100	90	71	4	—	27	25	—	—

National Journal Ratings

	1993 LIB — 1993 CONS			1994 LIB — 1994 CONS		
Economic	78%	—	12%	59%	—	37%
Social	60%	—	38%	51%	—	49%
Foreign	46%	—	53%	57%	—	37%

Key Votes of the 103d Congress

1. Clinton Deficit Plan	Y	3. Brady Handgun Purchase	N	5. Lmt. UN Cmnd. of Forces	N
2. NAFTA	N	4. Strike Race/Death Pnlty.	Y	6. Cut Missile Funds	N

Key Votes of the 104th Congress

1. Congressional Compliance	Y	6. Reform Crime Grant	N	11. Loser Pays Court Reform	N
2. Balanced Budget Amndmt.	Y	7. National Security Act	N	12. Product Liability Reform	Y
3. Bar Unfunded Mandates	Y	8. Moratorium on Regs.	Y	13. Welfare Reform	N
4. Pass Line Item Veto	N	9. Risk Assessment on Regs.	Y	14. Term Limits Amndmt.	Y
5. Relax Exclusionary Rule	Y	10. Expnd. Priv. Prop. Rights	Y	15. Tax Cuts	N

Election Results

1994 general	Douglas (Pete) Peterson (D)	117,404	(61%)	($334,740)
	Carole Griffin (R)	74,011	(39%)	($102,221)
1994 primary	Douglas (Pete) Peterson (D)	unopposed		
1992 general	Douglas (Pete) Peterson (D)	167,215	(73%)	($376,786)
	Ray Wagner (R)	60,425	(27%)	($25,724)

THIRD DISTRICT

Florida was scarcely settled before the Civil War. The state had a few farms and plantations in the north and a few ports around the edges, but most of Florida was still an uncharted watery wilderness, festooned with exotic greenery, inhabited by unusual animals: a part of the United States so far out of the experience of most Americans as to seem foreign. As late as 1940, Florida had the smallest population of all the southern states and what population there was tended to be classic Dixie, in rural counties with courthouse towns, where civic affairs were run by the richest white men; blacks lived in poorly-constructed unpainted shotgun houses propped up on blocks, living with little money and without the vote. This was a land of swamps and lakes and orange groves, of Marjorie Kinnan Rawlings's Cross Creek, where she wrote the great children's classic *The Yearling*, and the Florida of the broad St. Johns River, one of the few rivers in North America that flow (if only sluggishly) north, through the orange grove country to the port of Jacksonville, for many years Florida's largest city.

The 3d Congressional District of Florida, drawn for 1992 to have a 55% percent black majority, occupies much of this old Florida terrain. The district collected the descendants of the slaves who worked on the plantations and farms of northern Florida over a century ago, plus blacks who have settled in the state since then. The district is a long thin chain of land tying together heavily black but widely separated neighborhoods of Jacksonville, Gainesville, Daytona Beach and Orlando. The Miami Herald called the 3rd the "ugliest district" in the state. Almost half the district's population lives in Jacksonville, almost one quarter in and near Orlando (including all-black Eatontown, home of author Zora Neale Hurston). Much of it follows Florida watercourses: it touches on Cross Creek, for example, and runs up along the St. Johns River as it makes its way past citrus trees toward Jacksonville. Necessarily, it includes some white areas, particularly around Palatka on the St. Johns.

The Congresswoman from the 3d is Corrine Brown, a Democrat who won the seat in 1992. She grew up in Jacksonville, taught at the community college and was a guidance counselor, and in 1982 was elected to the Florida House. With her Jacksonville base, she was the obvious favorite. In the 1992 primary she faced Andy Johnson, a white talk radio host who proclaimed himself "the blackest candidate in the race." Brown led Johnson 43%–31% in the primary, then polished him off 64%–36% in the runoff. In the general election she faced Republican nominee Don Weidner, executive director of the Florida Physicians Association, and won 59%–41%.

In her first term, Brown compiled a solid liberal record on most issues, though she tended to support defense spending. She stresses that the military can be a source of opportunity, a lesson many black Americans have learned from personal experience. She worked very hard, and used her seats on Transporation and Veterans' Affairs to bring economic development to her district, working to secure a $100 million federal courthouse for Jacksonville, to keep district facilities off the base closure list, and to create more healthcare facilities for veterans. Even so, in 1994 Brown faced a spirited primary challenge from Alvin Brown, who had worked for the Clinton Administration's Commerce Department and was endorsed by a Deputy Assistant Education Secretary. The administration quickly abstained, since Corrine Brown had mostly supported administration positions. She won 67%–33%. In the general, black Republican talk-show host Marc Little advocated a 2% cap on domestic spending increases and lower levels of immigration. Little carried some counties, Republican areas tied together with black neighborhoods, but was forced to change his registration back to the 4th District (he had registered for the 3d at his mother's house) and lost 58%–42%. Even so, that is a relatively close margin, and it will take all Brown's hard work on local projects to keep her in good shape, especially if federal court decisions force Florida to smooth out the district lines. Because she missed the vote on the first item on the Contract With America—the unanimously-approved bill to force Congress to comply with laws governing the private sector—she was one of only two Democrats, along with Pete Stark, not to vote for a single one of its pieces.

The People: Pop. 1990: 563,079; 16% rural; 12% age 65+; 42% White; 55% Black; 1% Asian; 1% Other; 3% Hispanic origin. Voting age pop.: 400,821; 50% Black; 3% Hispanic origin. Households: 43% married couple families; 19% married couple fams. w. children; 32% college educ.; median household income: $19,780; per capita income: $9,419; median gross rent: $372; median house value: $46,800.

1992 Presidential Vote

Clinton (D)	93,446	(57%)
Bush (R)	49,198	(30%)
Perot (I)	21,225	(13%)

1988 Presidential Vote

Dukakis (D)	76,611	(54%)
Bush (R)	64,586	(46%)

Rep. Corrine Brown (D)

Elected 1992; b. Nov. 11, 1946, Jacksonville; home, Jacksonville; FL A&M, B.A. 1969, M.S., 1974; Baptist; divorced.

Career: Prof., FL Commun. Col., 1977–82, Guidance Counselor, 1982–92; FL House of Reps., 1982–92.

DC Office: 1610 LHOB 20515, 202-225-0123; Fax: 202-225-2256.

District Offices: 815 S. Main St., Jacksonville 32207, 904-398-8567; 250 N. Beach St., #80-1, Daytona Beach 32114, 904-254-4622; 75 Ivanhoe Blvd., Orlando 32806, 407-872-0656; and 401 SE First Ave., #316, Gainesville 32601, 904-375-6003.

Committees: *Transportation & Infrastructure* (22nd of 27 D): Public Buildings and Economic Development; Surface Transportation. *Veterans' Affairs* (13th of 15 D): Hospitals and Health Care.

Group Ratings

	ADA	ACLU	COPE	CFA	LCV	CON	NSI	COC	ACU	NTLC	CHC
1994	85	65	78	100	83	1	60	50	24	15	7
1993	75	—	100	90	86	4	—	18	4	—	—

National Journal Ratings

	1993 LIB — 1993 CONS		1994 LIB — 1994 CONS	
Economic	88%	— 0%	83%	— 0%
Social	77%	— 23%	82%	— 15%
Foreign	69%	— 30%	54%	— 45%

Key Votes of the 103d Congress

1. Clinton Deficit Plan	Y	3. Brady Handgun Purchase	Y	5. Lmt. UN Cmnd. of Forces	N
2. NAFTA	N	4. Strike Race/Death Pnlty.	N	6. Cut Missile Funds	Y

Key Votes of the 104th Congress

1. Congressional Compliance	*	6. Reform Crime Grant	N	11. Loser Pays Court Reform	N
2. Balanced Budget Amndmt.	N	7. National Security Act	N	12. Product Liability Reform	N
3. Bar Unfunded Mandates	N	8. Moratorium on Regs.	N	13. Welfare Reform	N
4. Pass Line Item Veto	N	9. Risk Assessment on Regs.	N	14. Term Limits Amndmt.	N
5. Relax Exclusionary Rule	N	10. Expnd. Priv. Prop. Rights	N	15. Tax Cuts	N

Election Results

1994 general	Corrine Brown (D)	63,845	(58%)	($383,017)
	Marc Little (R)	46,895	(42%)	($212,235)
1994 primary	Corrine Brown (D)	29,843	(67%)	
	Alvin Brown (D)	14,659	(33%)	
1992 general	Corrine Brown (D)	91,918	(59%)	($275,705)
	Don Weidner (R)	63,115	(41%)	($258,394)

FOURTH DISTRICT

With nearly one million people in the surrounding area, Jacksonville is Florida's second major city, with a new National Football League (The Jaguars) franchise and bold new skyscrapers looming above a wide river and a shopping mall overshadowing grid streets of tiny shotgun houses. The wide freeways leading to huge beachfront properties are not far from primeval wetlands and citrus groves. Mayport, one of the Navy's biggest bases and other military installations are nearby. But Floridians tend to overlook Jacksonville. While its gleaming downtown is just one of a dozen in a state that had no commercial office development a generation ago, Jacksonville was known not long ago as a smelly, slow-growing insurance and paper mill town. Attracting big installations from AT&T, Brockway International, Prudential, Sears, UPS, American Express and the Mayo Clinic, Jacksonville grew in the 1980s, while still maintaining its big military bases and insurance headquarters. The city is solidly southern, with a large number of blue collar whites with southern accents, a large black population, lots of children and comparatively few retirees. The area has less tourism and high-tech industry than the rest of Florida and its work force is less well educated and its incomes lower. While it has a Democratic tradition, the area has been trending Republican in state and national elections.

The 4th Congressional District of Florida includes most of Jacksonville (minus the areas now in the majority-black 3d District) and beach areas to the north and south to St. Augustine, the oldest European-founded city in the United States, settled by the Spanish in the 16th Century. South of the area is Daytona Beach, made famous by racing cars and its hard-sand beach. The beaches were mostly vacant during the 1940s, when Jacksonville was the largest city in the state, but have now filled up with large subdivisions and giant developments.

The Congresswoman from the 4th District is Tillie Fowler, a Republican elected in 1992 after the retirement of 44-year Democratic incumbent Charles Bennett. Fowler grew up in Milledgeville, Georgia—where writer Carson McCullers lived—where her father was a druggist who served in the legislature. After law school she worked in Washington for Georgia Congressman Robert Stephens and the Nixon Administration. After marrying a Jacksonville businessman, she raised a family, did volunteer work and was elected to the City Council in 1985. In line with her support of Florida's successful term limit initiative, she believed that "eight is enough," and had planned to retire from the council by 1992. Then she ran for the House and left no doubt about her priorities: two retired admirals attended her announcement and she was armed with a promise from House Republican leaders that if elected she would get a seat on the National Security Committee. She pledged to make Mayport her top priority, while supporting abortion rights and the balanced budget amendment. Her Democratic opponent, Mattox Hair, hailed from rural Florida and had served as student body president at Florida State, served in the Army and in the legislature from 1972 to 1988, where he was a major committee chairman. He resigned a judgeship and campaigned as a conservative Democrat. But Fowler, bolstered by a strong showing in Jacksonville, won with 57%. She was unopposed in 1994.

In her first term, Fowler got that seat on National Security, long chaired by Carl Vinson who was also from Milledgeville. She was elected Co-Chair of the Freshman Republican Task Force on Reform and strongly backed term limits, pledging to serve no more than four terms. In 1995, she introduced an eight year term limits amendment, modeled after Florida's "eight is enough" initiative, and she sponsored a term limits statute that would allow states to impose their own limits. Although she was a strong supporter of the Republican term-limits goal, she was denied the opportunity to present her version to the House. She fought additional defense cuts, accusing the Administration of "ignoring the lessons of history," and also criticized Congress for including billions of dollars in non-defense projects in the defense appropriations bill. During the 104th Congress, she was selected to serve on the Republican Steering Committee, as a Deputy Whip and as a member of the Executive Committee of the National Republican Congressional Committee. As an active member of the new majority and with what seems a safe seat, she should continue to grow in influence as long as she remains in the House.

The People: Pop. 1990: 562,154; 13% rural; 14% age 65+; 89% White; 6% Black; 2% Asian; 1% Other; 3% Hispanic origin. Voting age pop.: 435,405; 5% Black; 3% Hispanic origin. Households: 58% married couple families; 25% married couple fams. w. children; 53% college educ.; median household income: $31,707; per capita income: $16,845; median gross rent: $483; median house value: $80,700.

1992 Presidential Vote			1988 Presidential Vote		
Bush (R)	132,023	(53%)	Bush (R)	132,762	(69%)
Clinton (D)	75,035	(30%)	Dukakis (D)	58,460	(31%)
Perot (I)	41,075	(17%)			

Rep. Tillie K. Fowler (R)

Elected 1992; b. Dec. 23, 1942, Milledgeville, GA; home, Jacksonville; Emory U., A.B. 1964, J.D. 1967; Episcopalian; married (Buck).

Career: Legis. Asst., U.S. Sen. Robert Stephens, 1967–70; White House Office of Consumer Affairs, 1970–71; Jacksonville City Cncl., 1985–92, Pres., 1989–90.

DC Office: 413 CHOB 20515, 202-225-2501; Fax: 202-225-9318.

District Offices: 4452 Hendricks Ave., Jacksonville 32207, 904-739-6600; and 533 N. Nova Rd., Ormond Beach 32174, 904-672-0754.

Committees: *National Security* (14th of 30 R): Military Installations and Facilities; Military Readiness. *Transportation & Infrastructure* (22nd of 33 R): Coast Guard and Maritime Transportation (Vice Chmn.); Surface Transportation.

Group Ratings

	ADA	ACLU	COPE	CFA	LCV	CON	NSI	COC	ACU	NTLC	CHC
1994	15	26	22	20	11	54	100	92	90	85	79
1993	15	—	0	40	36	50	—	82	83	—	—

National Journal Ratings

	1993 LIB — 1993 CONS			1994 LIB — 1994 CONS		
Economic	25%	—	72%	21%	—	76%
Social	38%	—	61%	24%	—	73%
Foreign	9%	—	85%	0%	—	88%

Key Votes of the 103d Congress

1. Clinton Deficit Plan	N	3. Brady Handgun Purchase	Y	5. Lmt. UN Cmnd. of Forces	Y
2. NAFTA	Y	4. Strike Race/Death Pnlty.	Y	6. Cut Missile Funds	N

Key Votes of the 104th Congress

1. Congressional Compliance Y	6. Reform Crime Grant Y	11. Loser Pays Court Reform Y
2. Balanced Budget Amndmt. Y	7. National Security Act Y	12. Product Liability Reform Y
3. Bar Unfunded Mandates Y	8. Moratorium on Regs. Y	13. Welfare Reform Y
4. Pass Line Item Veto Y	9. Risk Assessment on Regs. Y	14. Term Limits Amndmt. Y
5. Relax Exclusionary Rule Y	10. Expnd. Priv. Prop. Rights Y	15. Tax Cuts Y

Election Results

1994 general	Tillie K. Fowler (R)	.... unopposed		($103,233)
	Tillie K. Fowler (R)	.... unopposed		
1992 general	Tillie K. Fowler (R)	 135,883	(57%)	($512,267)
	Mattox Hair (D)	 103,531	(43%)	($427,480)

FIFTH DISTRICT

Florida's urban areas have grown in every unlikely direction during the past 25 years, occupying the high ground between the swamps and wetlands that still take up much of the state's peninsula. The pattern of development is clear in the Gulf Coast counties north of St. Petersburg and Tampa, where subdivisions and trailer parks and shopping centers with Eckerd drug stores and Winn Dixie markets sprang up in what were sleepy little towns with low brick buildings baking in the Florida sun. More than a half million people live in the towns starting with Clearwater and Tampa's northern suburbs that run up the spines of U.S. 19, just off the Gulf Coast, or U.S. 41 and Interstate 75 inland near the orange groves. Though there are plenty of working people here, this is retirement country. Though far from affluent, people are comfortable and if the existence of such communities is taken for granted by most Americans, their construction—the creation of an infrastructure of water and sewer lines, underground electricity, and phone and TV cables—is an example of the miracles of modern technology.

The 5th Congressional District of Florida, created after the 1990 census, occupies much of the fast growing area. In 1990 there were 562,000 people in land that held about 129,000 in 1960. The 5th travels northward to include most of Gainesville, home of the University of Florida, where students from the more wealthy urban corridors of central and south Florida study in a town occupied by flimsy houses from the impoverished South of 50 years ago; here they can become part of a Florida elite bonded by shared memories of the Gator Growl festivities. The district includes the still sparsely populated counties of Dixie, Gilchrist and Levy (the last named after Florida's first Senator, David Levy Yulee, who was Jewish). And it includes the New Port Richey area on the Pasco County coast and all of fast-growing Citrus, Hernando and Sumter Counties to the north. Three decades ago, this area was typically southern Democratic. Now the voting patterns reflect the presence of the newcomers. With many white- and blue-collar retirees, the Gulf Coast counties are mixed, while Gainesville is liberal and Democratic.

The Congresswoman from the 5th District is Karen Thurman, a Democrat who as chairman of the reapportionment committee drew the district lines and was careful to include her home town in Marion County. An Air Force brat, she grew up in Florida and elsewhere, worked as a middle school math teacher for eight years before being elected to the Dunnellon Council and then became mayor. Elected to the Florida Senate in 1982, she was reelected in 1986 with more votes than any other state senator. She sponsored an average of 60 bills a year on issues like education, the environment and agriculture. In 1992, she easily won the 5th District primary and in the general faced former prosecutor Tom Hogan who called her a "professional, big money politician." She outraised him 2–1 and won 49%–43%.

In the House Thurman has worked for funding for local water and sewer projects, pushing legislation to give the Tampa Bay area $29.9 million for water reuse projects. She was one of the chief Democratic advocates of requiring EPA on all proposed legislation to conduct risk-assessment studies before imposing new regulations. When proponents of a 1994 proposal to convert EPA into a cabinet agency refused to allow risk-assessment supporters to offer their amendment to the cabinet bill, Thurman and 59 other Democrats joined Republican colleagues to defeat a rule on the bill—scuttling the EPA department legislation for the 103rd Congress. Thurman had a moderate voting record and came close to chairing a subcommittee.

The 5th District race attracted nationwide attention in 1994, not because of Thurman, but because the Republican nominee was Don "Big Daddy" Garlits, a retired drag racing champion. In the GOP primary, Garlits, controversial because of his conservative views, was opposed by former Citrus County Judge Gary Graham, who had been stripped of his judgeship by the Florida Supreme Court because of official misconduct. The *Gainesville Sun* refused to endorse either one, saying the two "more closely fit the description of political buffoons than thoughtful public policy makers." Garlits won 58%–42%. Garlits called for "medieval-style prisons" and advocated public paddling of juveniles in town squares for truancy. He called homosexuality an "abomination," said Americans who do not believe the country is great should be charged with subversion—he later clarified that this suggestion referred only to the ACLU—and said blacks are more violent than whites. "A cross between David Koresh and David Duke," said the Democrats provocatively. Garlits got more publicity, but Thurman raised more money and won more votes. She carried every county but her home area, had a huge margin in Gainesville and won 57%–43%. In the 104th Congress, Thurman was immediately targeted by Republicans as a possible ally in their efforts toward "regulatory relief." She voted with the majority party on the Government Reform and Oversight Committee to freeze new federal regulations until Congress reviewed the underlying statutes—one of four Democrats to help achieve a 28-13 committee win on this issue. Thurman also was one of six Democrats in the Florida delegation to vote against term limits—a risky move in a state with a popular term-limits initiative and in a district that Republicans could make competitive with a more experienced opponent.

The People: Pop. 1990: 562,936; 42% rural; 26% age 65+; 90% White; 6% Black; 1% Asian; 1% Other; 3% Hispanic origin. Voting age pop.: 459,932; 5% Black; 3% Hispanic origin. Households: 58% married couple families; 17% married couple fams. w. children; 38% college educ.; median household income: $21,374; per capita income: $11,987; median gross rent: $403; median house value: $62,200.

1992 Presidential Vote			**1988 Presidential Vote**		
Clinton (D)	110,244	(41%)	Bush (R)	119,272	(57%)
Bush (R)	90,656	(34%)	Dukakis (D)	91,752	(43%)
Perot (I)	64,106	(24%)			

Rep. Karen L. Thurman (D)

Elected 1992; b. Jan. 12, 1951, Rapid City, SD; home, Dunnellon; U. of FL, B.A. 1973; Episcopalian; married (John).

Career: Middle schl. teacher, 1974–82; Dunnellon City Cncl., 1974–82; Dunnellon Mayor 1979–81; FL Senate 1982–92.

DC Office: 130 CHOB 20515, 202-225-1002; Fax: 202-226-0329.

District Offices: 2224 Hwy. 44 W., Inverness 34453, 904-344-3044; 5700 SW 34th St., #425, Gainesville 32608, 904-336-6614; and 5623 Rte. 19 S., #206, New Port Richey 34652, 813-849-4496.

Committees: *Agriculture* (17th of 22 D): Department Operations, Nutrition and Foreign Agriculture; Risk Management and Specialty Crops. *Government Reform & Oversight* (12th of 22 D): National Security, International Affairs and Criminal Justice (RMM).

Group Ratings

	ADA	ACLU	COPE	CFA	LCV	CON	NSI	COC	ACU	NTLC	CHC
1994	65	65	89	60	56	37	40	67	19	25	21
1993	80	—	100	90	86	39	—	18	17	—	—

National Journal Ratings

	1993 LIB — 1993 CONS		1994 LIB — 1994 CONS	
Economic	78%	— 12%	57%	— 42%
Social	54%	— 45%	53%	— 46%
Foreign	70%	— 26%	57%	— 37%

Key Votes of the 103d Congress

1. Clinton Deficit Plan	Y	3. Brady Handgun Purchase	N	5. Lmt. UN Cmnd. of Forces	N
2. NAFTA	N	4. Strike Race/Death Pnlty.	N	6. Cut Missile Funds	Y

Key Votes of the 104th Congress

1. Congressional Compliance	Y	6. Reform Crime Grant	N	11. Loser Pays Court Reform	N
2. Balanced Budget Amndmt.	N	7. National Security Act	N	12. Product Liability Reform	N
3. Bar Unfunded Mandates	Y	8. Moratorium on Regs.	Y	13. Welfare Reform	N
4. Pass Line Item Veto	Y	9. Risk Assessment on Regs.	Y	14. Term Limits Amndmt.	N
5. Relax Exclusionary Rule	Y	10. Expnd. Priv. Prop. Rights	Y	15. Tax Cuts	N

Election Results

1994 general	Karen L. Thurman (D)	125,780	(57%)	($564,265)
	Don Garlits (R)	94,093	(43%)	($308,963)
1994 primary	Karen L. Thurman (D)	unopposed		
1992 general	Karen L. Thurman (D)	129,698	(49%)	($352,607)
	Tom Hogan (R)	114,356	(43%)	($144,613)
	Cindy Munkittrick (I)	19,462	(7%)	($14,580)

SIXTH DISTRICT

The flat rolling grasslands of central Florida, once bypassed by southbound tourists heading for the coast, in the 1980s had become a prime growth area in the nation's prime growth state. In earlier decades, these areas depended economically on farming, on state institutions (the University of Florida in Gainesville, the big state prison in Raiford) and on passing tourists getting off the interstate to see attractions like Silver Springs, the world's largest formation of clear artesian springs. But as time went on, retirees began settling in places like the bluegrass country around Ocala (one of America's prime horse breeding grounds) and the plenteous lakes in Lake County to the south. These are not necessarily affluent developments: this part of central Florida has the highest percentage of mobile homes in the United States.

The 6th Congressional District of Florida takes up much of this territory. Its boundaries are a bit odd, since it is almost seven-eighths surrounded by the black-majority 3d District. About half of its people live around Ocala or in Lake County, marginal political territory. Another one-third live on the west side of Jacksonville or in suburban communities in Clay County just to the south, both heavily Republican.

The congressman from the 6th District is Cliff Stearns, a Republican first elected in 1988 when Democrat Buddy MacKay ran for the Senate (he lost but in 1990 was elected Lieutenant Governor). Stearns grew up and attended public schools in Washington, D.C., but he is a beyond-the-Beltway conservative, a self-made business success who ended up owning five motels, three restaurants and other real estate—"someone who works in the community, goes to church with his neighbors, and doesn't live in Tallahassee," as he put it in his 1988 campaign, when he beat the favorite, House Speaker Jon Mills, 54%–46%.

Stearns has a solid conservative voting record and has taken on interesting causes. He used to be hated on Capitol Hill for cutting congressional staff pay raises; now most of those fuming staffers are off the public payroll altogether. He sponsored a free market healthcare reform bill, pushed for funding cuts in the National Endowment for the Arts, chaired a Republican task force on gays in the military which surveyed generals and admirals and found 97% of them opposed to lifting the ban. In June 1994, he penned the letter signed by 87 Republicans calling for the resignation of then-Surgeon General Joycelyn Elders, declaring, "She should be using this office to fight sickness and disease and not using this office to fight parents and churches." He cut State Department funding to offset the cost of settling Iraqi prisoners of war in the United States. He worked out a consensus for a return to Florida state government of 77,000 acres set aside for the now-canceled Cross-Florida Barge Canal. He was able to convince HUD to issue rules protecting seniors-only housing developments from discrimination suits. But Stearns is also interested in funds which mean jobs for north Florida. He took credit for siting a new federal prison, to be the nation's largest, housing 3,000 inmates, in Sumter County, and putting a new veterans' psychiatric facility in Gainesville; both are now just slightly outside the 6th District lines. He was one of the leaders in urging recognition of Gulf war syndrome. He attempted to prevent the closure of the Cecil Field Naval Station, unsuccessfully, and earlier successful efforts to save the Jacksonville Naval Aviation Depot may now also prove fruitless. In February 1995, he introduced a resolution proposing an amendment to the Constitution in support of voluntary school prayer.

Stearns has worked the district hard and won easy reelection in the 1990s; he was unopposed in 1994. His major disappointment came in December 1994 when he lost the race for Vice Chair of the House Republican Conference to Susan Molinari of New York by a 124–100 margin. But with his growing seniority on the Commerce Committee, he has become an active player in the Republican crusade to cut back on federal regulatory controls.

The People: Pop. 1990: 561,464; 48% rural; 18% age 65+; 89% White; 7% Black; 1% Asian; 1% Other; 3% Hispanic origin. Voting age pop.: 427,270; 6% Black; 3% Hispanic origin. Households: 65% married couple families; 26% married couple fams. w. children; 37% college educ.; median household income: $26,025; per capita income: $12,274; median gross rent: $417; median house value: $66,400.

1992 Presidential Vote			1988 Presidential Vote		
Bush (R)	112,554	(47%)	Bush (R)	124,888	(70%)
Clinton (D)	74,328	(31%)	Dukakis (D)	52,714	(30%)
Perot (I)	50,914	(21%)			

Rep. Clifford B. Stearns (R)

Elected 1988; b. Apr. 16, 1941, Washington, DC; home, Ocala; George Washington U., B.S. 1963; Presbyterian; married (Joan).

Career: Air Force, 1963–67; Data Control Systems Inc., 1967–68; Negotiator, CBS, 1969–70; Pres., Stearns House Inc., 1972–present.

DC Office: 2352 RHOB 20515, 202-225-5744; Fax: 202-225-3973; e-mail: cstearns@hr.house.gov.

District Offices: 115 S.E. 25th Ave., Ocala 34471, 904-351-8777; 1726 Kingsley Ave., #8, Orange Park 32073, 904-269-3203; and 111 S. 6th St., Leesburg 34748, 904-326-8285.

Committees: *Commerce* (10th of 26 R): Energy and Power; Health and Environment; Telecommunications and Finance. *Veterans' Affairs* (10th of 18 R): Hospitals and Health Care.

Group Ratings

	ADA	ACLU	COPE	CFA	LCV	CON	NSI	COC	ACU	NTLC	CHC
1994	0	13	22	10	17	70	100	75	100	89	100
1993	15	—	17	30	36	39	—	73	96	—	—

National Journal Ratings

	1993 LIB — 1993 CONS	1994 LIB — 1994 CONS
Economic	23% — 77%	0% — 80%
Social	11% — 82%	0% — 89%
Foreign	9% — 85%	0% — 88%

Key Votes of the 103d Congress

1. Clinton Deficit Plan	N	3. Brady Handgun Purchase Y	5. Lmt. UN Cmnd. of Forces Y
2. NAFTA	N	4. Strike Race/Death Pnlty. Y	6. Cut Missile Funds N

Key Votes of the 104th Congress

1. Congressional Compliance Y	6. Reform Crime Grant Y	11. Loser Pays Court Reform Y
2. Balanced Budget Amndmt. Y	7. National Security Act Y	12. Product Liability Reform Y
3. Bar Unfunded Mandates Y	8. Moratorium on Regs. Y	13. Welfare Reform Y
4. Pass Line Item Veto Y	9. Risk Assessment on Regs. Y	14. Term Limits Amndmt. Y
5. Relax Exclusionary Rule Y	10. Expnd. Priv. Prop. Rights Y	15. Tax Cuts Y

Election Results

1994 general	Clifford B. Stearns (R) .... unopposed		($189,905)
1994 primary	Clifford B. Stearns (R) .... unopposed		
1992 general	Clifford B. Stearns (R) 144,195	(65%)	($309,532)
	Phil Denton (D) 76,419	(35%)	($2,333)

SEVENTH DISTRICT

In ever-changing Florida, new communities and towns continue to spring up on the landscape, replacing older town centers with which tourists have been familiar. Just down the road from Daytona Beach, where motorcyclists gather in February for Hog Week, is New Smyrna Beach, a new town established on the site of an old settlement. Fifteen miles inland, close to Sanford, where Amtrak's Auto-Train unloads its Florida-bound travelers, is Deltona, a vast five-mile square development that drained a part of Florida swamp and designed a grid of curving streets meandering around small lakes and golf courses, set aside land for shopping centers and office space, and then marketed the place nationwide. It created an instant city: in 1990, 51,000 people lived in Deltona—where there were 15,000 in 1980 and 4,800 in 1970.

The 7th Congressional District of Florida includes Deltona, New Smyrna Beach and part of Daytona Beach, as well as most of Sanford. Stretching from Daytona across the marshy St. Johns River basin to Seminole County, it includes large Orlando suburbs like Altamonte Springs and small old towns like Oviedo, and goes south to include part of Orlando itself. In most elections, this is a solidly Republican district, although the area around Daytona has a conservative Democratic heritage.

The Congressman from the 7th is John Mica, a spirited Republican and a political veteran who campaigns as an opponent of the status quo. He is from a bipartisan political family: his younger brother Dan Mica was a Democratic congressman from Palm Beach County from 1978 to 1988, when he lost a primary for U.S. Senate, and is now Bill Clinton's head of the Board for International Broadcasting; another brother worked for Democratic Governor Lawton Chiles. But John Mica has always been a conservative Republican. He served as state representative from the Orlando area from 1976 to 1980 and then as administrative assistant to Florida Senator

Paula Hawkins from 1981 to 1985. Mica made a small fortune by turning 360 feet of New Smyrna beachfront into a real estate business. He then became a lobbyist, representing American Specialty Chemical, Coopers & Lybrand and Harris computers; he was proud of his profession, commenting that "Some of the finest folks I've met are lobbyists." When attacked in the 1992 Republican primary as an insider representing special interests, Mica lobbied pro bono for the Daytona airport and got a runway extension, and won 53%–34%. Democrat Dan Webster attacked Mica as "the epitome of the professional politician," but Mica responded accurately that Webster was a liberal backed by trial lawyers and labor unions. Mica started his campaign with a $100,000 loan, raised plenty from former clients and outspent Webster, and won 56%–44%.

Mica is one of the Republican House members who led the reform charge to abolish House select committees and to make public the names of those signing petitions to discharge legislation. In 1993, Mica also pushed a plan to require the EPA to subject new regulations to a cost-benefit analysis. That stalled the bill to elevate EPA to cabinet status; a similar provision was passed as part of the Contract With America. He has sponsored a global environment cleanup act, to monitor other countries' environmental laws and encourage laggards to do better or risk losing U.S. aid. To the list of Republican policies he actively backs—capital gains cut, term limits, antiabortion—he adds support for Head Start. He wants to consolidate federal export programs into a single agency and to require broadcasters to spend 5% of commercial airtime combating drug abuse. He first advocated many of these ideas long before his party gained the House majority; now, they have moved to the political mainstream.

Mica portrays himself as willing to take political risks. "I've made a lot of money. I don't need the salary and I don't need the title." But in fact he has thrived politically. In 1994, against a Democrat who taught ballroom dancing on television—although he was primarily a stockbroker—Mica was reelected with 73%. In the 104th Congress, Mica became Chairman of the Government Reform and Oversight's Civil Service Subcommittee—a post he plans to use to develop legislation to shrink the size of the federal government. He attracted attention during the Contract With America welfare debate when he compared welfare recipients to alligators—"If left in their natural state, alligators can take care of themselves"—a metaphor that was denounced by many Democrats and caused many Republicans to wince.

The People: Pop. 1990: 563,552; 11% rural; 16% age 65+; 89% White; 4% Black; 1% Asian; 1% Other; 5% Hispanic origin. Voting age pop.: 436,780; 4% Black; 5% Hispanic origin. Households: 60% married couple families; 25% married couple fams. w. children; 51% college educ.; median household income: $30,921; per capita income: $15,132; median gross rent: $529; median house value: $80,400.

1992 Presidential Vote			1988 Presidential Vote		
Bush (R)	105,519	(45%)	Bush (R)	118,214	(67%)
Clinton (D)	81,180	(34%)	Dukakis (D)	58,846	(33%)
Perot (I)	49,588	(21%)			

Rep. John L. Mica (R)

Elected 1992; b. Jan. 27, 1943, Binghamton, NY; home, Winter Park; Miami-Dade Comm. Col., A.A. 1965, U. of FL, B.A. 1967; Episcopalian; married (Patricia).

Career: Exec. Dir., Palm Beach & Orange Cnty. Govt. Charter Study Commissions, 1970–74; Pres., MK Development, 1975–92; FL House of Reps., 1976–80; A.A., U.S. Sen. Paula Hawkins, 1981–85; Partner, Mica, Dudinsky & Assoc., 1985–92;

DC Office: 336 CHOB 20515, 202-225-4035; Fax: 202-226-0821.

District Offices: 1211 Semoran Blvd., Casselberry 32707, 407-657-8080; 840 Deltona Blvd., Deltona 32725, 407-866-1499; and 1396 Dunlawton Blvd., Port Orange 32127, 904-756-9798.

Committees: *Government Reform & Oversight* (11th of 27 R): Civil Service (Chmn.); National Security, International Affairs and Criminal Justice. *Transportation & Infrastructure* (20th of 33 R): Railroads; Surface Transportation.

Group Ratings

	ADA	ACLU	COPE	CFA	LCV	CON	NSI	COC	ACU	NTLC	CHC
1994	10	13	22	20	0	73	100	83	95	96	100
1993	5	—	8	0	29	69	—	82	96	—	—

National Journal Ratings

	1993 LIB — 1993 CONS	1994 LIB — 1994 CONS
Economic	12% — 87%	0% — 80%
Social	0% — 89%	16% — 81%
Foreign	17% — 76%	30% — 67%

Key Votes of the 103d Congress

1. Clinton Deficit Plan	N	3. Brady Handgun Purchase	N	5. Lmt. UN Cmnd. of Forces	Y
2. NAFTA	N	4. Strike Race/Death Pnlty.	Y	6. Cut Missile Funds	N

Key Votes of the 104th Congress

1. Congressional Compliance	Y	6. Reform Crime Grant	Y	11. Loser Pays Court Reform	Y
2. Balanced Budget Amndmt.	Y	7. National Security Act	Y	12. Product Liability Reform	Y
3. Bar Unfunded Mandates	Y	8. Moratorium on Regs.	Y	13. Welfare Reform	Y
4. Pass Line Item Veto	Y	9. Risk Assessment on Regs.	Y	14. Term Limits Amndmt.	Y
5. Relax Exclusionary Rule	Y	10. Expnd. Priv. Prop. Rights	Y	15. Tax Cuts	Y

Election Results

1994 general	John L. Mica (R)	131,711	(73%)	($300,058)
	Edward D. Goodard (D)	47,747	(27%)	($28,075)
1994 primary	John L. Mica (R)	unopposed		
1992 general	John L. Mica (R)	125,823	(56%)	($459,135)
	Dan Webster (D)	96,945	(44%)	($307,857)

EIGHTH DISTRICT

The center of one of America's, and the world's, great growth industries in the 1980s and surely into the 1990s, is a place few would have picked a generation ago as the center of anything except a bunch of orange groves. The industry is tourism, the place is Orlando and, at least a few people had an idea of its potential. The key decision was made by Walt Disney in the mid-1960s to put his vast theme park near the interchange of Florida's Turnpike and Interstate 4, the "crossroads of Florida," just a few miles west of Orlando. Today Orlando is the world's number one tourist destination, with more hotel rooms (over 80,000) than anywhere else in the country, attracting people not only to Disney World's Magic Kingdom, EPCOT Center and MGM Studios but also to Sea World, Universal Studios, Splendid China and dozens of other attractions. Orlando is the center of a one million-plus metropolitan area, with the biggest job gain, 74%, in the 1980s of any major metro area. But the economy has diversified beyond tourism: Martin Marietta built a big defense plant here way back in 1956, and greater Orlando has a high-tech economy and a population weighted toward young families with children rather than retirees.

The spirit of this place has been set by a man who never lived here but created something now taken for granted. Walt Disney invented the theme park in the flatlands of Orange County, California, but he perfected it in the 17,000 acres of swamp and lakes in Florida's Orange County. And while inventing the theme park, Disney also pioneered sophisticated communications, utility and waste disposal methods—all out of sight and underground. Yet Disney World does not work just by mechanics; it requires some 34,000 people with know-how and unfailing cheerfulness. Disney's vision of a future that was labor-intensive as well as high-tech, in which the critical ingredient is the provision of services, was a forecast of the service-driven economy that has grown so lustily for decades now.

The 8th Congressional District of Florida includes most of Orlando and surrounding Orange County. It excludes most heavily black neighborhoods and towns now placed in the grotesquely shaped 3d District. It includes central and eastern Orlando and all its suburbs directly to the east, plus most to the south and west. It also takes in most of the Kissimmee area in Osceola County just to the south and Disney World's Magic Kingdom. Politically, this Orange County, like the Orange County where the original Disneyland was built, is heavily Republican. Occasionally subject to spasms of Democratic sentiment, it remains heavily leavened to the party which seems friendlier to the wholesome spirit of this service industry and high-tech metropolis.

The congressman from the 8th District is Bill McCollum, one of the most active and articulate Republicans in the House, involved in one issue after another, and now chairman of Judiciary's Crime Subcommittee. McCollum is a native Floridian who after law school and Navy service practiced law in the Orlando area and was Seminole County Republican Chairman. In 1980, he ran for the House, in a district that went west to the Gulf of Mexico, and with his Orlando area base won the runoff and general. In the Democratic House he often lost on issues but was a force to be reckoned with. He led the fight against the Brady bill, winning in 1988, when he pushed an amendment to require a nationwide list of convicted felons, but lost in 1993. On immigration he was not happy with the higher quotas in the 1990 bill. His work on scaling back the RICO "racketeering" bill has not been rewarded with full success. He served on the Iran-contra committee, where he was a vocal critic of majority Democrats. He led the unsuccessful fight in 1992 to allow S&Ls to count goodwill as an asset. On all these controversies, McCollum's attention to detail and bulldog perseverance, even in unfashionable causes, has made him a strong contender.

In the mid-1990s McCollum's causes have had more success. When Democrats were still in the majority, he led the fight in the House against the so-called "racial justice" provision, which would impose something like racial quotas on executions by allowing capital defendants to use statistics to challenge a death sentence as biased based on race; he lost 217–212 in one vote but many House Democrats, embarrassed by the provision, switched and by a 264–149 vote took it out of the 1994 crime bill. In 1992 and 1993 he fought uphill battles for term limits; then in 1995 he was harshly criticized by some national term-limits backers for his plan, which would allow House members to serve 12 years. Three other alternatives were offered, but McCollum's amendment was the Contract With America version and won the most votes, including 82% of all Republicans. McCollum was less successful in his own leadership race. Since 1988 he had been Vice Chair of the Republican Conference. In 1994 he contributed over $1 million he raised to House Republican candidates, while making many local appearances on their behalf, and ran for Majority Whip. Perhaps because he was seen as a bit too earnest, he got only 28 votes, as Tom DeLay won with 119 and Bob Walker had 80.

In addition to his Judiciary subcommittee chairmanship, McCollum retains other important posts and likely will grow as one of the most influential Republican legislators. He is number two Republican on Banking, just behind Chairman Jim Leach, and he has a seat on the Intelligence Committee. McCollum had spirited competition from a "eight is enough" term limits backer in 1992, but won with 69%; he was unopposed in 1994.

The People: Pop. 1990: 562,244; 9% rural; 11% age 65+; 81% White; 5% Black; 2% Asian; 3% Other; 11% Hispanic origin. Voting age pop.: 436,385; 5% Black; 10% Hispanic origin. Households: 55% married couple families; 25% married couple fams. w. children; 52% college educ.; median household income: $31,251; per capita income: $15,464; median gross rent: $531; median house value: $84,600.

1992 Presidential Vote			1988 Presidential Vote		
Bush (R)	101,707	(48%)	Bush (R)	108,602	(71%)
Clinton (D)	68,840	(32%)	Dukakis (D)	43,910	(29%)
Perot (I)	42,901	(20%)			

Rep. Bill McCollum (R)

Elected 1980; b. July 12, 1944, Brooksville; home, Altamonte Springs; U. of FL, B.A. 1965, J.D. 1968; Episcopalian; married (Ingrid).

Career: Navy, 1969–72, Naval Reserves, 1972–92; Practicing atty., 1973–81; Chmn., Seminole Cnty. Repub. Cmte., 1976.

DC Office: 2266 RHOB 20515, 202-225-2176; Fax: 202-225-0999.

District Offices: 605 E. Robinson #650, Orlando 32801, 407-872-1962.

Committees: *Banking & Financial Services* (2nd of 27 R): Financial Institutions and Consumer Credit. *Judiciary* (4th of 20 R): Crime (Chmn.); Immigration and Claims. *Intelligence (Permanent Select)* (8th of 9 R): Human Intelligence, Analysis, and Counterintelligence; Technical and Tactical Intelligence.

Group Ratings

	ADA	ACLU	COPE	CFA	LCV	CON	NSI	COC	ACU	NTLC	CHC
1994	0	14	13	20	18	69	100	91	95	93	100
1993	0	—	0	10	31	65	—	100	96	—	—

National Journal Ratings

	1993 LIB — 1993 CONS		1994 LIB — 1994 CONS	
Economic	0% —	88%	0% —	80%
Social	0% —	89%	16% —	81%
Foreign	17% —	76%	21% —	78%

Key Votes of the 103d Congress

1. Clinton Deficit Plan	N	3. Brady Handgun Purchase	N	5. Lmt. UN Cmnd. of Forces	Y
2. NAFTA	Y	4. Strike Race/Death Pnlty.	Y	6. Cut Missile Funds	N

Key Votes of the 104th Congress

1. Congressional Compliance	Y	6. Reform Crime Grant	Y	11. Loser Pays Court Reform	Y
2. Balanced Budget Amndmt.	Y	7. National Security Act	Y	12. Product Liability Reform	Y
3. Bar Unfunded Mandates	Y	8. Moratorium on Regs.	Y	13. Welfare Reform	Y
4. Pass Line Item Veto	Y	9. Risk Assessment on Regs.	Y	14. Term Limits Amndmt.	Y
5. Relax Exclusionary Rule	Y	10. Expnd. Priv. Prop. Rights	Y	15. Tax Cuts	Y

Election Results

1994 general	Bill McCollum (R)	unopposed		($448,334)
1994 primary	Bill McCollum (R)	unopposed		
1992 general	Bill McCollum (R)	141,977	(69%)	($675,211)
	Chuck Kovaleski (D)	65,145	(32%)	($174,940)

NINTH DISTRICT

Half a century ago, the land north of St. Petersburg and Tampa was scarcely inhabited. The Gulf is lined with swamps and inland the land is spotted with lakes and covered with dense semitropical forests. Over the years, development has moved up the coast and up the major highways inland. Much of this originally was designed for retirees—condominiums, garden apartments, trailer parks. But this is working country as well. Businesses grew up around Clearwater in northern Pinellas County and inland in Pasco County off I-75. And people brought their ancestral political beliefs with them. In the 1950s and 1960s, only white-collar retirees could afford to buy new places in Florida, and they were heavily Republican. As blue-collar workers and union members became more affluent in the 1970s and 1980s, they came too, with their traditional Democratic Party identification and cultural conservatism.

The 9th Congressional District of Florida covers much of this area north of St. Petersburg and Tampa. About half its population is in northern Pinellas County around Clearwater and Tarpon Springs, an old resort first settled by Greek sponge divers early in the 20th Century. Another quarter is in northern Hillsborough County, on the suburban fringe of Tampa. The final quarter is the inland portion of Pasco County, north of Tampa, where former crossroads like Zephyrhills have become significant population centers.

The congressman from the 9th District is Michael Bilirakis, a Republican who grew up in Pittsburgh and worked his way through college toiling in a steel mill; he served in the Air Force, and then went to college. He believes strongly that Americans can work their way up, with occasional government assistance (like the G.I. Bill that helped him through school). Bilirakis switched to the Republican Party in 1980 and won this seat in 1982 though it had been designed for a Democrat. He had spirited competition from Democrat Cheryl Davis Knapp in 1990 and 1992, but won with 58% and 59%. He also easily survived a primary challenge after the 1992 redistricting.

Bilirakis has a somewhat moderate voting record, especially on economic issues. He favors generous Social Security benefits, government-funded research on Alzheimer's disease and cable reregulation—all issues with local resonance in this elderly district. He has made something of an environmental record, opposing western water subsidies and offshore oil drilling on the Gulf Coast. With a seat on the Commerce Committee, he has cast some key votes on regulatory and health issues, against the 1988 Catastrophic Health Care Act, for increased federal elderly home care money, for drug discounts for the VA and other federal purchasers. In 1994 he was the lead Republican sponsor of the Rowland-Bilirakis healthcare plan, which provided for portable health insurance and restricted preexisting condition exclusions and became the principal conservative alternative; it got wide bipartisan support, and some form of it probably could have passed if the Clinton Administration and House Democratic leadership had allowed it to come to a vote.

Bilirakis said some time ago that he would not run in 1994 unless he had major legislation pending. But he did, and was reelected without opposition. He returned as Chairman of Commerce's Health and Environment Subcommittee, one of the most important in Congress. With Republican leaders vowing to pass incremental legislation to deal with healthcare issues on a piece-meal basis, he may ironically find himself the author of more healthcare laws than was the likes of Henry Waxman. But with the new rules of the Republican Conference, he will not have the ability to wield single-handed influence as did Waxman and he probably will be forced to defer to committee chairman Tom Bliley on broad strategic decisions. If Bilirakis does choose to retire, this district could be seriously contested. Or he may decide that it's more fun to serve in the House majority.

The People: Pop. 1990: 562,814; 19% rural; 22% age 65+; 91% White; 3% Black; 1% Asian; 1% Other; 4% Hispanic origin. Voting age pop.: 448,534; 3% Black; 4% Hispanic origin. Households: 60% married couple families; 21% married couple fams. w. children; 48% college educ.; median household income: $29,293; per capita income: $15,797; median gross rent: $485; median house value: $84,800.

1992 Presidential Vote		
Bush (R)	113,853	(41%)
Clinton (D)	94,662	(34%)
Perot (I)	68,167	(25%)

1988 Presidential Vote		
Bush (R)	136,188	(63%)
Dukakis (D)	81,635	(37%)

Rep. Michael Bilirakis (R)

Elected 1982; b. July 16, 1930, Tarpon Springs; home, Palm Harbor; U. of Pittsburgh, B.S. 1959, U. of FL, J.D. 1963; Greek Orthodox; married (Evelyn).

Career: Air Force, 1951–55; Steelworker, 1955–59; Govt. contract negotiator, 1959–60; Petroleum engineer, 1960–63; Practicing atty., 1969–83.

DC Office: 2240 RHOB 20515, 202-225-5755; Fax: 202-225-4085.

District Offices: 1100 Cleveland St., #1600, Clearwater 34615, 813-441-3721; and 4111 Land O'Lakes Blvd., #306, Land O'Lakes 34639, 813-996-7441.

Committees: *Commerce* (5th of 26 R): Energy and Power; Health and Environment (Chmn.). *Veterans' Affairs* (3rd of 18 R): Hospitals and Health Care.

Group Ratings

	ADA	ACLU	COPE	CFA	LCV	CON	NSI	COC	ACU	NTLC	CHC
1994	20	26	56	20	6	85	90	75	86	93	93
1993	20	—	33	30	36	69	—	73	79	—	—

National Journal Ratings

	1993 LIB — 1993 CONS			1994 LIB — 1994 CONS		
Economic	29%	—	70%	37%	—	61%
Social	31%	—	68%	11%	—	85%
Foreign	17%	—	76%	0%	—	88%

Key Votes of the 103d Congress

1. Clinton Deficit Plan	N	3. Brady Handgun Purchase	Y	5. Lmt. UN Cmnd. of Forces	Y
2. NAFTA	N	4. Strike Race/Death Pnlty.	Y	6. Cut Missile Funds	N

Key Votes of the 104th Congress

1. Congressional Compliance	Y	6. Reform Crime Grant	Y	11. Loser Pays Court Reform	Y
2. Balanced Budget Amndmt.	Y	7. National Security Act	Y	12. Product Liability Reform	Y
3. Bar Unfunded Mandates	Y	8. Moratorium on Regs.	Y	13. Welfare Reform	Y
4. Pass Line Item Veto	Y	9. Risk Assessment on Regs.	Y	14. Term Limits Amndmt.	Y
5. Relax Exclusionary Rule	Y	10. Expnd. Priv. Prop. Rights	Y	15. Tax Cuts	Y

Election Results

1994 general	Michael Bilirakis (R)	unopposed		($191,717)
1994 primary	Michael Bilirakis (R)	unopposed		
1992 general	Michael Bilirakis (R)	158,028	(59%)	($779,818)
	Cheryl Davis Knapp (D).	110,135	(41%)	($269,617)

TENTH DISTRICT

Decisions made by pioneers of a community can shape it for decades afterwards. What shaped St. Petersburg, Florida, named after the city then the capital of Russia, was the decision in the early 1900s by *St. Petersburg Times* editor W. L. Straub to stop the industrialization of the waterfront, paving the way for St. Petersburg to become a tourist and, most importantly, a retirement mecca. By the 1950s, its name had become a national cliche, bringing to mind old folks on a park bench trying to drum up a game of chess or shuffleboard. Starting off on the grid streets facing Tampa Bay, spreading later toward the beaches on the Gulf Coast, St. Petersburg filled up to a greater extent than any other American city with retirees. They were at least modestly affluent and mostly from the North. They adapted easily to a city whose civic tone was set by the *St. Petersburg Times* and its longtime owners Nelson and Henrietta Poynter: sober, good-humored, supportive of clean government and civil rights, but not vociferously liberal.

Like any retirement center, St. Petersburg has had rapid population turnover, reflected in its political trends. White-collar Yankee retirees in the 1940s and 1950s made St. Petersburg the first Republican center in ancestrally Democratic Florida; it voted for Thomas E. Dewey in 1948 and elected a Republican congressman in 1954. Then, as more blue-collar workers could afford Florida retirement and the affluent moved farther down the Gulf Coast, St. Petersburg trended Democratic in the 1970s and 1980s. Pinellas County nearly voted for Jimmy Carter in 1976 and did vote for Bill Clinton in 1992 and for Governor Lawton Chiles in 1994. Also, businesses grew here, and St. Petersburg no longer has as high a percentage of the elderly as the Gulf Coast towns south of the Sunshine Skyway.

St. Petersburg and southern Pinellas County, including Largo and the string of barrier island beach towns from Mullet Key to Belleair Beach, make up the 10th Congressional District of Florida. The congressman here is Bill Young, tied for fifth in seniority among House Republicans; interestingly, neither he nor any of the four more senior is a full committee chairman. (Texan Bill Archer, elected in 1970, now chairs the Ways and Means Committee and classmate Floyd Spence now chairs National Security.) Young worked in the 1950s for St. Petersburg's first Republican congressman, William Cramer; was elected to the state Senate in 1960, at 29; then, when Cramer ran for the Senate in 1970 (and lost to Lawton Chiles), Young ran for the St. Petersburg House seat and won. In the early 1970s, Social Security was vastly increased and indexed to inflation and St. Petersburg basked in prosperity; Young delivered constituency services and had a moderate to conservative voting record, and was easily reelected.

Early on, Young got a seat on Appropriations, where he, like many Republicans, worked closely with the Democratic chairmen. Young's special project was the bone marrow donor program, originated by Dr. Robert Good of All Children's Hospital in St. Petersburg. Young was successful in a three-year effort to transfer authority for the program to the National Institutes of Health. He has backed child health research centers, juvenile diabetes centers and more money for pediatric AIDS. In 1980, he got on the National Security Appropriations Subcommittee, where he mostly supported the Reagan and Bush Administrations but had his own pet projects. Now he chairs the National Security Subcommittee, and thus has great leverage over military spending and policy.

The 1990s have not been entirely fulfilling politically for Young. In 1992 he was criticized in a series of articles in the *Tampa Tribune* for speech honoraria he received and trips he took, for buying a car with campaign funds, and for making inquiries at the Agency for International Development on a contract for a small firm whose owners later bought his North Carolina vacation house. Democrat Karen Moffitt, an expert on children with special health needs, ran as a New Democrat, calling for assessing government programs on their outputs, not inputs, and for cutting capital gains taxes. She lost, but held Young to 57%, his lowest percentage ever.

Young did not have opposition in 1994, but he did have disappointment. Speaker-designate Newt Gingrich, acting within a week of the November election, passed over four senior Appropriations Republicans—Joseph McDade because he was under indictment, John Myers because he opposed the Penny-Kasich tax cuts vigorously, and Young and Ralph Regula because they seemed too pro-spending and accommodationist—to pick the fire-breathing Bob Livingston as chairman. Gingrich had solid backing from most Republican members, especially the freshmen; there was nothing Young could do. The consolation prize of the National Security Subcommittee chairmanship is an important position, with the added plus that defense contractors are significant employers in the St. Petersburg area. But with the Republicans' plan to freeze defense spending at current levels, despite the protests of defense hawks, Young will find that he has a tough enough challenge to fund priority programs without having to also worry about local projects, both for his own district and for favored colleagues across the nation.

The People: Pop. 1990: 562,301; 26% age 65+; 87% White; 9% Black; 1% Asian; 2% Hispanic origin. Voting age pop.: 462,919; 8% Black; 2% Hispanic origin. Households: 49% married couple families; 15% married couple fams. w. children; 44% college educ.; median household income: $25,145; per capita income: $15,124; median gross rent: $448; median house value: $68,700.

1992 Presidential Vote			1988 Presidential Vote		
Clinton (D)	107,121	(40%)	Bush (R)	133,151	(56%)
Bush (R)	96,956	(36%)	Dukakis (D)	104,686	(44%)
Perot (I)	63,765	(24%)			

Rep. C. W. (Bill) Young (R)

Elected 1970; b. Dec. 16, 1930, Harmarville, PA; home, Indian Rocks Beach; United Methodist; married (Beverly).

Career: Aide, U.S. Rep. William Cramer, 1957–60; FL Senate, 1960–70, Minority Ldr., 1966–70.

DC Office: 2407 RHOB 20515, 202-225-5961; Fax: 202-225-9764.

District Offices: 627 Fed. Bldg., St. Petersburg 33701, 813-893-3191.

Committees: *Appropriations* (4th of 32 R): Labor, Health and Human Services, and Education; Legislative; National Security (Chmn). *Intelligence (Permanent Select)* (3rd of 9 R): Human Intelligence, Analysis, and Counterintelligence.

Group Ratings

	ADA	ACLU	COPE	CFA	LCV	CON	NSI	COC	ACU	NTLC	CHC
1994	25	18	33	30	14	65	100	83	81	86	93
1993	15	—	25	40	46	89	—	91	88	—	—

National Journal Ratings

	1993 LIB — 1993 CONS		1994 LIB — 1994 CONS	
Economic	28%	— 71%	37%	— 61%
Social	24%	— 76%	29%	— 71%
Foreign	24%	— 72%	0%	— 88%

Key Votes of the 103d Congress

1. Clinton Deficit Plan	N	3. Brady Handgun Purchase Y	5. Lmt. UN Cmnd. of Forces Y
2. NAFTA	Y	4. Strike Race/Death Pnlty. Y	6. Cut Missile Funds	N

Key Votes of the 104th Congress

1. Congressional Compliance Y	6. Reform Crime Grant Y	11. Loser Pays Court Reform Y
2. Balanced Budget Amndmt. Y	7. National Security Act Y	12. Product Liability Reform Y
3. Bar Unfunded Mandates Y	8. Moratorium on Regs. Y	13. Welfare Reform Y
4. Pass Line Item Veto Y	9. Risk Assessment on Regs. Y	14. Term Limits Amndmt. Y
5. Relax Exclusionary Rule Y	10. Expnd. Priv. Prop. Rights Y	15. Tax Cuts Y

Election Results

1994 general	C. W. (Bill) Young (R) .... unopposed		($146,246)
1994 primary	C. W. (Bill) Young (R) .... unopposed		
1992 general	C. W. (Bill) Young (R) 149,606	(57%)	($459,861)
	Karen Moffitt (D) 114,809	(43%)	($202,000)

ELEVENTH DISTRICT

Tampa, Florida, is one of America's contemporary boom towns. Its industrial past goes back to 1886, when Cuban cigar-makers left Key West for what became the Ybor City neighborhood of Tampa. Soon after, it was the major takeoff spot for U.S. troops in the Spanish-American War of 1898. It also became a major citrus distribution center. The old industrial city developed along the waterfront, where today you can find the world's longest sidewalk (6.5 miles along Bayshore Boulevard) and still see the 13 minarets of Tampa pioneer Henry B. Plant's 1890s

Arabian-style Tampa Bay Hotel (long since taken over by the University of Tampa). For a time, Tampa seemed drearily industrial. Now, with a diversified economy, a fast-growing service sector, tourist attractions led by Busch Gardens and a famously pleasant and convenient airport, it has moved ahead, with subdivisions and condominiums, office towers and low-rise commercial buildings spreading inland across swamps and lowlands.

Through all this, and in contrast to St. Petersburg with its many retirees, Tampa has remained a city of families and young people, a place with a blue-collar past which is quickly moving upscale as it expands. To be sure, it has had some setbacks: defense contractors here have been hurt by cutbacks. But the Tampa Bay area in 1995 finally won a new major league baseball franchise to fill the Thunderdome across Tampa Bay. And the local defense industry seems to have stabilized and may be expecting a boost from a GOP-controlled Congress. The smell of cigars still wafts over Ybor City (though pollution controllers want to get rid of it) and Tampa is still an important military command center: Central Command, which ran the Gulf war, is headquartered at the still-thriving MacDill Air Force Base, and General Norman Schwarzkopf remains a Tampa area resident.

The 11th Congressional District of Florida consists of Tampa and two-thirds of surrounding Hillsborough County. Tampa was historically Democratic as St. Petersburg was Republican, but in fact the two sides of Tampa Bay seem to have come together politically; if anything, they have both changed parties. In the close gubernatorial race in 1994, Pinellas County voted for Democratic Governor Lawton Chiles, while Hillsborough County voted for Republican Jeb Bush.

That trend has also affected congressional politics. The congressman from the 11th District is Sam Gibbons, a grizzled veteran Democrat who rose to become the Chairman of the Ways and Means Committee in June 1994 only to lose the post as a result of the Republican sweep five months later. Gibbons, who grew up in Tampa, parachuted into Normandy on D-Day as part of the 101st Airborne; after the war he practiced law and went into politics. He was elected to the state House in 1952 and the state Senate in 1958; in 1962, when Tampa got a separate House seat (it had been in with St. Petersburg), he was elected to represent it, and has held the seat ever since. Gibbons looks like an old-fashioned southern congressman, but in fact his voting record over the years has been quite liberal. He looks back fondly on his role as an Education and Labor Committee member in floor-managing Lyndon Johnson's anti-poverty package, including Head Start, through the House in 1965—fondly and ruefully, even angrily, as today's Republicans try to roll the Great Society back.

Gibbons is out of the southern tradition that produced Cordell Hull, who during decades in Congress and as secretary of state under Franklin Roosevelt toed the Democratic Party line and championed the cause of free trade. From studying the years before and after World War II, Gibbons carries the conviction that "a world bound together by the ties of trade is a world strongly inclined toward economic growth and peace." That too is a position under attack, as politicians, especially Democrats, have sought votes and campaign contributions with trade restrictions. Gibbons set himself, as Chairman of the Trade Subcommittee from 1981 to 1994, against that trend, not always with success. But Gibbons did have successes, from the Caribbean Basin Initiative to NAFTA and GATT. And on another issue, he sponsored the tax law that exempts homeowners over 55 from paying capital gains when selling their primary homes.

For almost 14 years, Gibbons ranked second on Ways and Means to forceful and domineering Chairman Dan Rostenkowski, a position of great frustration compounded by the fact that Gibbons is not a natural deal-maker or coalition-builder. Rostenkowski surely remembered that Gibbons considered a challenge to Tip O'Neill for majority leader in 1972, when Rostenkowski managed O'Neill's campaign. In early 1994, as Rostenkowski faced indictment, which would automatically deprive him of the chair, speculation abounded that Gibbons would not be up to replacing him, and might even be shoved aside. But Gibbons quickly took command of the committee and within a month reported out a healthcare bill—a task many thought impossible. Perhaps it was; Majority Leader Dick Gephardt altered some of Gibbons's bill, then declined even to bring it to the floor.

Gibbons, strong in Tampa for years, has had electoral problems in the 1990s. In 1992, he was opposed by Mark Sharpe, a former Navy intelligence officer born at MacDill Air Force Base where his father served in 1960, just two years before Gibbons was first elected. Until he resigned to run for Congress, Sharpe was one of four rotating briefers for the chief of Naval Operations. In 1992, Sharpe held Gibbons to a 53%–41% margin—not an outstanding result for the incumbent, particularly considering that Gibbons outspent Sharpe $960,000 to $51,000. Two years later, Sharpe ran again, this time spending more money ($472,000 in all) and attacked Gibbons for not supporting the balanced budget amendment and not protecting MacDill from cutbacks. In late September Gibbons sent out a letter ending, "I am asking you to provide an additional campaign contribution as soon as possible. Time is of the essence." In all, Gibbons raised $825,000 in PAC money, fifth highest in the House, and spent $1.1 million. For that, and despite the seeming prestige as Ways and Means chairman, he won 52%–48%.

The narrowness of his victory has not inhibited Gibbons from opposing most of the Contract With America with force. He rages like an old bull against the Republicans, stands long hours with only a few liberals like Barney Frank and Black Caucus members around; his handiwork, the things he most believes in, are being wrecked. In conscious contrast to Rostenkowski, Gibbons worked— with some success—to provide more democratic leadership to the now-Democratic minority. But in the absence of a change in the political mood, Gibbons's House seat is very much in jeopardy, for even as ranking minority member on Ways and Means, he will be hard put to raise the kind of PAC money that saved him in 1994.

The People: Pop. 1990: 562,293; 1% rural; 12% age 65+; 68% White; 17% Black; 1% Asian; 2% Other; 14% Hispanic origin. Voting age pop.: 430,969; 14% Black; 14% Hispanic origin. Households: 47% married couple families; 20% married couple fams. w. children; 46% college educ.; median household income: $26,166; per capita income: $13,578; median gross rent: $439; median house value: $66,000.

1992 Presidential Vote

Clinton (D)	81,849	(41%)
Bush (R)	77,942	(39%)
Perot (I)	39,148	(20%)

1988 Presidential Vote

Bush (R)	95,358	(56%)
Dukakis (D)	73,836	(44%)

Rep. Sam M. Gibbons (D)

Elected 1962; b. Jan. 20, 1920, Tampa; home, Tampa; U. of FL, J.D. 1947; Presbyterian; married (Martha).

Career: Army, 1941–45 (WWII); Practicing atty., 1947–62; FL House of Reps., 1952–58; FL Senate, 1958–62.

DC Office: 2204 RHOB 20515, 202-225-3376; Fax: 202-225-8016.

District Offices: 2002 N. Lois Ave., #260, Tampa 33607, 813-870-2101.

Committees: *Ways & Means* (RMM of 15 D): Trade. *Joint Committee on Taxation* (4th of 5 Reps.).

Group Ratings

	ADA	ACLU	COPE	CFA	LCV	CON	NSI	COC	ACU	NTLC	CHC
1994	70	65	63	80	76	7	40	42	16	15	21
1993	75	—	83	100	71	19	—	45	17	—	—

National Journal Ratings

	1993 LIB	—	1993 CONS	1994 LIB	—	1994 CONS
Economic	59%	—	41%	83%	—	0%
Social	72%	—	28%	69%	—	30%
Foreign	74%	—	22%	53%	—	47%

Key Votes of the 103d Congress

1. Clinton Deficit Plan	Y	3. Brady Handgun Purchase	Y	5. Lmt. UN Cmnd. of Forces	N
2. NAFTA	Y	4. Strike Race/Death Pnlty.	N	6. Cut Missile Funds	N

Key Votes of the 104th Congress

1. Congressional Compliance	Y	6. Reform Crime Grant	N	11. Loser Pays Court Reform	*
2. Balanced Budget Amndmt.	Y	7. National Security Act	N	12. Product Liability Reform	*
3. Bar Unfunded Mandates	N	8. Moratorium on Regs.	*	13. Welfare Reform	N
4. Pass Line Item Veto	Y	9. Risk Assessment on Regs.	N	14. Term Limits Amndmt.	N
5. Relax Exclusionary Rule	N	10. Expnd. Priv. Prop. Rights	N	15. Tax Cuts	N

Election Results

1994 general	Sam M. Gibbons (D)	76,814	(52%)	($1,155,373)
	Mark Sharpe (R)	72,119	(48%)	($472,871)
1994 primary	Sam M. Gibbons (D)	unopposed		
1992 general	Sam M. Gibbons (D)	100,984	(53%)	($960,511)
	Mark Sharpe (R)	77,640	(41%)	($51,393)
	Joe DeMinico (I).....................	12,730	(7%)	($35,534)

TWELFTH DISTRICT

With their skyscrapers rising over bays and rivers, the great gleaming cities of Florida are near the Atlantic or Gulf coasts. But parts of the state, including Polk County, the biggest inland county south of Orlando, that were most heavily settled half a century ago are inland. With its small cities of Lakeland, Bartow, Lake Wales and Winter Haven and small lakes scattered throughout the area, the citrus business is still a mainstay of the local economy and orange groves abound, although periodic freezes have convinced some growers to move south. Turpentine distilleries, dependent on the big stands of pine and phosphate mining businesses can be found and the area has proportionally more manufacturing jobs than almost anywhere else in the state. Retired *Ladies Home Journal* editor Edward Bok—father of former Harvard President Derek Bok—built the most prominent landmarks here, the gothic Bok Tower and the surrounding Mountain Lake Sanctuary and gardens. But little of Bok's wealth and prestige remains here and the area, unlike other parts of the state, is not filled with retirees, although the elderly population has grown in recent years.

In the past, Polk County was as solidly Democratic as the rest of the rural South, and the home of successive Democratic U.S. Senators Spessard Holland (1946–71) and Lawton Chiles (1971–89) (Holland was governor before he was senator, Chiles after). But like other areas, Republicans began to pick up strength in the area and by the end of the decade, appeared ready to take it over. It didn't happen in 1990, when Chiles's strength in his home county stopped Republicans from picking up two seats they needed for control of the Florida Senate. But in 1992, with Chiles's popularity low, George Bush handily carried Polk County over Bill Clinton, Democrats lost one of the Polk Senate seats, and Republicans held the local seat in the U.S. House.

The 12th District of Florida encompasses all but the northeast edge of Polk County, plus the western, rapidly suburbanizing edge of Tampa's Hillsborough County. It extends into old-fashioned Florida agricultural country north of Polk County, around Dade City in Pasco

County, and to the south, in Hardee, DeSoto and a slice of Highlands Counties. This was long a Democratic seat, until Congressman Andy Ireland switched parties in 1984. When Ireland retired in 1992, the seat went up for grabs, but even in a bad Republican year the Republicans held on.

The congressman from the 12th is Charles T. Canady. He grew up in Lakeland, went to school in the Northeast, and then practiced law in Lakeland; his father, Charles E. Canady, served for 18 years as Lawton Chiles's top staffer in Florida and Washington. The younger Canady was elected to the Florida House in 1984, at 30, and switched parties in 1989, saying he had little in common with liberal Democrats. In 1990 he ran for the state Senate and, as Chiles swept Polk County, lost. In 1992, Canady ran for Congress, unopposed in the Republican primary, and faced Tom Mims, a Democratic legislator supported by the teachers' union. Mims won the Democratic primary 2–1, and had an initial lead in polls. Canady attacked Mims sharply in mailings and in the end with TV spots calling him pro-tax and antibusiness, and won 52%–48%. Feelings between the two remained amicable enough for them to lunch together, as promised, the Friday after the election. In a similar spirit, Lakeland staged a straw poll in the old town square in October 1994, where Lawton Chiles and Jeb Bush harangued the crowd and Bush, foreshadowing the result in Polk County but not statewide, won in Chiles's hometown.

In the House, Canady has a solidly conservative voting record. On NAFTA he heeded citrus growers' concerns, and even after there was some accommodation voted no. He won reelection easily in 1994, with 65% of the vote. In the 104th Congress, he became Chairman of Judiciary's Constitution Subcommittee; after two years in the House he replaced a Democrat, Don Edwards, who had served 32 years. This is one of the hotter committee slots for Republicans. Canady reported out the balanced budget amendment and term limits during the Contract With America's 100 days; the former passed the House with 300 votes, but the latter had only 227, far short of the 290, or two-thirds, required. The soft-spoken Canady's subcommittee includes such caustic Democrats as Patricia Schroeder, Mel Watt and Barney Frank; but here, as in the 12th District, Canady has the votes.

The People: Pop. 1990: 562,381; 34% rural; 17% age 65+; 81% White; 13% Black; 1% Asian; 2% Other; 6% Hispanic origin. Voting age pop.: 419,888; 11% Black; 5% Hispanic origin. Households: 62% married couple families; 25% married couple fams. w. children; 35% college educ.; median household income: $25,315; per capita income: $12,277; median gross rent: $381; median house value: $61,800.

1992 Presidential Vote

Bush (R)	90,694	(45%)
Clinton (D)	68,487	(34%)
Perot (I)	39,770	(20%)

1988 Presidential Vote

Bush (R)	105,333	(67%)
Dukakis (D)	52,116	(33%)

Rep. Charles T. Canady (R)

Elected 1992; b. June 22, 1954, Lakeland; home, Lakeland; Haverford Col., B.A. 1976, Yale Law Schl., J.D. 1979; Presbyterian; single.

Career: Practicing atty., 1979–92; FL House of Reps., 1984–90.

DC Office: 1222 LHOB 20515, 202-225-1252; Fax: 202-225-2279; e-mail: canady@hr.house.gov

District Offices: Fed. Bldg., 124 S. Tennessee Ave., Lakeland 33801, 813-688-2651.

Committees: *Agriculture* (12th of 27 R): Department Operations, Nutrition and Foreign Agriculture. *Judiciary* (10th of 20 R): Constitution (Chmn.); Courts and Intellectual Property.

Group Ratings

	ADA	ACLU	COPE	CFA	LCV	CON	NSI	COC	ACU	NTLC	CHC
1994	5	9	0	20	11	58	100	92	90	96	100
1993	10	—	8	20	21	50	—	82	100	—	—

National Journal Ratings

	1993 LIB — 1993 CONS		1994 LIB — 1994 CONS	
Economic	25%	— 72%	0%	— 80%
Social	0%	— 89%	20%	— 77%
Foreign	9%	— 85%	0%	— 88%

Key Votes of the 103d Congress

1. Clinton Deficit Plan	N	3. Brady Handgun Purchase	N	5. Lmt. UN Cmnd. of Forces	Y
2. NAFTA	N	4. Strike Race/Death Pnlty.	Y	6. Cut Missile Funds	N

Key Votes of the 104th Congress

1. Congressional Compliance	Y	6. Reform Crime Grant	Y	11. Loser Pays Court Reform	Y
2. Balanced Budget Amndmt.	Y	7. National Security Act	Y	12. Product Liability Reform	Y
3. Bar Unfunded Mandates	Y	8. Moratorium on Regs.	Y	13. Welfare Reform	Y
4. Pass Line Item Veto	Y	9. Risk Assessment on Regs.	Y	14. Term Limits Amndmt.	Y
5. Relax Exclusionary Rule	Y	10. Expnd. Priv. Prop. Rights	Y	15. Tax Cuts	Y

Election Results

1994 general	Charles T. Canady (R)	106,123	(65%)	($333,623)
	Robert Connors (D)	57,203	(35%)	($192,849)
1994 primary	Charles T. Canady (R)	unopposed		
1992 general	Charles T. Canady (R)	100,484	(52%)	($156,984)
	Tom Mims (D)	92,346	(48%)	($349,895)

THIRTEENTH DISTRICT

Essentially, everyone else followed the circus to Sarasota. When the Ringling Brothers made a success of the circus they founded in the 1880s, they needed a place for performers and animals to rest during the winter months. They settled on the bayfront village behind a barrier island along the Gulf of Mexico. It was just far enough north to be reachable by railroad, just far enough south to be semitropical so the elephants would not get sick and die. Here, John Ringling established the Ringling Museum of Art, with its huge sculpture garden and built his own Venetian palace, the Ca'd'Zan. After World War II, when people began spending their retirement years in warmer climates, the Gulf Coast started attracting new settlers—affluent, WASPy Republicans from upper crust suburbs of northern cities. The population exploded, with Manatee and Sarasota Counties growing from 63,000 in 1950 to 489,000 in 1990.

The 13th Congressional District of Florida includes Sarasota County and Manatee County and slivers of Tampa's Hillsborough County on the north and Charlotte County on the south. It is mostly a collection of Gulf Coast towns, from Tampa Bay south past Venice (where the circus now has its winter quarters). It is retiree country: 31% of the people here are 65 or older. It is also very heavily Republican, with the second highest Republican registration of any Florida district (the highest is the 14th, just to the south).

The Congressman from the 13th District is Dan Miller, a Republican elected in 1992 when the seat had no incumbent; Andy Ireland, who had represented most of what is now the 13th and 12th, retired. Miller is a native of Michigan, with an M.B.A. and a Ph.D., who moved to Bradenton in the 1970s, where he started various businesses, including the Memorial Pier Restaurant, the Suncoast Manor Nursing Center, the Barnett Bank Building and Riverview Center. He served on local commissions, the hospital board of directors and the judicial nominating commission. He was not terribly specific on issues, calling mostly for less government and regulations and lower taxes: "The federal government does not need to solve all our problems." In 1992, he was one of five Republicans to run in the primary for Congress, while only two Democrats ran: a measure of how this is Republican country. In the first primary, Miller took second place, 143 votes behind former Bush Administration appointee Brad Baker; in the runoff, with Ireland's endorsement, Miller won 53%–47%. The Democratic nominee presented a nice contrast to Miller. Rand Snell is a native of Manatee County who had spent most of his adult life in politics. He became a staffer for Lawton Chiles right out of school; then for two years he directed a congressional study on "Biotechnology in a Global Economy." He was Chiles's director of cabinet affairs in Tallahassee in 1991 and 1992. While Snell sneered at Miller's lack of political experience and expertise, that probably worked in Miller's behalf, and he won 58%–42%. Two years later, he was reelected without opposition.

Miller came to Washington with friends in the Florida Republican delegation. Fellow freshman John Mica was his "big brother" at their University of Florida fraternity and another freshman, Tillie Fowler, was in his wife's class at Emory. Miller's voting record has been strongly conservative, with a few exceptions on cultural issues: he voted for the assault weapons ban and has been moderate on abortion. As a member of the Republican healthcare task force, Miller spearheaded opposition to the AARP's support for the Clinton health reform plan—a bit gutsy, given the large number of seniors in the 13th District. But he offered the AARP an olive branch in February 1995, by asking them to submit a list of spending cuts they would endorse to balance the budget. In the 104th Congress, Miller continues to serve on the Budget Committee, where he became an outspoken advocate and leader in the fight to balance the budget, including the politically risky cuts in Medicare. He also has been appointed to the Appropriations Committee and is an assistant majority whip. He has pushed for legislation establishing a bipartisan commission to reduce spending, patterned after Dick Armey's military base closure commission. He promised to lead the fight on the 1995 farm bill to eliminate subsidies for sugar, whose substantial harvests have posed a growing environmental hazard to the Everglades. Miller also sponsored legislation to cap congressional pensions after 12 years of service, to encourage House members to retire voluntarily rather than make lifetime careers of Congress.

The People: Pop. 1990: 562,501; 11% rural; 31% age 65+; 90% White; 5% Black; 1% Asian; 1% Other; 4% Hispanic origin. Voting age pop.: 464,980; 4% Black; 3% Hispanic origin. Households: 59% married couple families; 16% married couple fams. w. children; 45% college educ.; median household income: $27,616; per capita income: $16,254; median gross rent: $512; median house value: $81,300.

1992 Presidential Vote

Bush (R) 124,394 (43%)
Clinton (D) 100,831 (35%)
Perot (I).................. 65,283 (22%)

1988 Presidential Vote

Bush (R) 153,943 (66%)
Dukakis (D)................ 78,154 (34%)

Rep. Dan Miller (R)

Elected 1992; b. May 30, 1942, Highland Park, MI; home, Braden-ton; U. of FL, B.S.B.A. 1964, Emory U., M.B.A. 1965, Louisiana St. U., Ph.D. 1970; Episcopalian; married (Glenda).

Career: Businessman, Miller Enterprises, 1973–present; Asst. Prof., Georgia St. U., 1969–73; Adjunct Prof., U. of S. FL, 1975–83.

DC Office: 117 CHOB 20515, 202-225-5015; Fax: 202-226-0828.

District Offices: 2424 Manatee Ave., #104, Bradenton 34205, 813-747-9081; 1751 Mound St., #A-2, Sarasota 34236, 813-951-6643.

Committees: *Appropriations* (23rd of 32 R): Labor, Health and Human Services, and Education; Legislative. *Budget* (10th of 24 R).

Group Ratings

	ADA	ACLU	COPE	CFA	LCV	CON	NSI	COC	ACU	NTLC	CHC
1994	20	17	11	10	22	94	100	100	90	93	86
1993	10	—	17	20	50	82	—	91	88	—	—

National Journal Ratings

	1993 LIB — 1993 CONS	1994 LIB — 1994 CONS
Economic	0% — 88%	0% — 80%
Social	29% — 69%	24% — 73%
Foreign	31% — 67%	14% — 80%

Key Votes of the 103d Congress

1. Clinton Deficit Plan	N	3. Brady Handgun Purchase	N	5. Lmt. UN Cmnd. of Forces	Y
2. NAFTA	Y	4. Strike Race/Death Pnlty.	Y	6. Cut Missile Funds	Y

Key Votes of the 104th Congress

1. Congressional Compliance	Y	6. Reform Crime Grant	Y	11. Loser Pays Court Reform	Y
2. Balanced Budget Amndmt.	Y	7. National Security Act	Y	12. Product Liability Reform	Y
3. Bar Unfunded Mandates	Y	8. Moratorium on Regs.	Y	13. Welfare Reform	Y
4. Pass Line Item Veto	Y	9. Risk Assessment on Regs.	Y	14. Term Limits Amndmt.	Y
5. Relax Exclusionary Rule	Y	10. Expnd. Priv. Prop. Rights	N	15. Tax Cuts	Y

Election Results

1994 general	Dan Miller (R) .... unopposed		($278,042)
1994 primary	Dan Miller (R) 56,572	(81%)	
	Jeffrey R. Assmann (R) 13,086	(19%)	
1992 general	Dan Miller (R) 158,881	(58%)	($449,212)
	Rand Snell (D) 115,767	(42%)	($298,309)

FOURTEENTH DISTRICT

On the edge of the Tropics, in a physical environment teeming with diseases less than a century ago and inhospitable to advanced civilization only a generation ago, Florida's Gulf Coast has sprung up as a model of what America will be for many when they retire. The wide white sand beaches with gentle breakers, the inlets and broad estuaries that abound for boating, the wetlands filled with exotic birds, eventually made this prime resort country: Thomas Edison had his winter home in Fort Myers, Henry Ford used to visit here, Walter Reuther, after his gunshot wound, recuperated by building a modest house near the Caloosahatchee River. But the local economy could not support many permanent residents, and at the beginning of World War II, there were only 68,000 people living on the Gulf Coast from Sarasota south to Naples.

Now there are 1.1 million: the climate and environment attracted affluent suburbanites from the Midwest and Northeast, with the added lure of no state income or inheritance taxes. Developers like Barron Collier, who built the Tamiami Trail across the Everglades and designed Naples with the wealthy in mind (and gave his name to Collier County, the richest in Florida), were determined to avoid the high-rise canyons that line the Atlantic from Miami to Palm Beach. The alternative has been low-rise, city-sized developments like Cape Coral and Port Charlotte, with canals in most backyards, and thinly paved roads along the sand spits next to the sultry, lapping waves of the Gulf, or the luxurious town of Naples set amid preserved coastal islands and interior swamps. This is very much retirement country, with more than one in four residents over 65.

Florida's 14th Congressional District occupies the southern half of this Gulf Coast, from Charlotte County past Cape Coral and Fort Myers south to Naples. This district has the highest Republican registration of any in Florida, and continually casts among the highest Republican percentages.

The congressman from the 14th is Porter Goss, a Republican first elected in 1988, who worked 10 years in the CIA's Clandestine Services and then moved to Sanibel Island (whose famous shells are now scarce), where he founded a prize-winning newspaper, served on the city council and passed growth management laws and was appointed to the Lee County Commission by then-Governor Bob Graham. When incumbent Connie Mack III ran for the Senate in 1988, Goss ran for this seat and effectively won it in the Republican primary, leading 38%–29%–19% former Congressman Skip Bafalis and retired General Jim Dozier. In the runoff, Goss won with 72% and in the general beat Jack Conway, onetime top aide to UAW chief Reuther, 71%–29%, winning the largest number of votes of any House candidate in the country.

Goss has a largely conservative voting record in the House and has presented proposals suggesting an active and original mind. In 1993, he presented his own spending cuts package; in 1994, he worked for bipartisan healthcare reform. When other Republicans were attacking the Clinton budget in early 1993, Goss presented his own list of spending cuts totalling $200 billion over five years. In line with Gulf Coast opinion, he is something of an environmentalist, pushing to make permanent the moratorium on oil drilling in the Gulf; that position helps to explain his opposition to an important regulatory piece of the Contract With America. He is something of a reformer too; he proposed charging members $600 from their office accounts for each insertion of extraneous matter into the *Congressional Record*. He introduced legislation to repeal the Ramspeck Act, a measure passed in 1940 to make it easier for displaced Hill staffers to enter the civil service system, and which received notice and use when Congress changed hands in 1994. Since 1991, he has served on the Ethics Committee, staying on in 1995 pending resolution of charges against Newt Gingrich. He is not without guts, given his district's population: he served on Bob Kerrey's entitlements commission and called for "a comprehensive solution to fulfill the promises made to people currently in the system, while preparing future generations to plan ahead."

In 1993, Goss left the International Relations and the now-abolished Merchant Marine

Committees to become one of four Republicans on Rules. There, he led four of seven successful efforts on the House floor to defeat the Democrats' closed rules, most spectacularly on the crime bill conference report in August 1994. In 1995 he also was appointed to the Intelligence Committee and to a temporary panel on the future of intelligence.

He has been reelected easily. Redistricting was no problem: his original district grew so much it was in effect split in two, with the current 14th drawn as the southern and slightly more Republican half.

The People: Pop. 1990: 562,489; 18% rural; 26% age 65+; 87% White; 6% Black; 2% Other; 6% Hispanic origin. Voting age pop.: 455,734; 4% Black; 5% Hispanic origin. Households: 62% married couple families; 18% married couple fams. w. children; 44% college educ.; median household income: $29,620; per capita income: $17,165; median gross rent: $519; median house value: $90,500.

1992 Presidential Vote			1988 Presidential Vote		
Bush (R)	129,493	(46%)	Bush (R)	146,243	(70%)
Clinton (D)	87,978	(31%)	Dukakis (D)	63,885	(30%)
Perot (I)	63,175	(22%)			

Rep. Porter Johnston Goss (R)

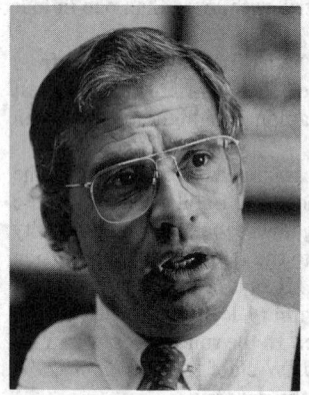

Elected 1988; b. Nov. 26, 1938, Waterbury, CT; home, Sanibel; Yale, B.A. 1960; Presbyterian; married (Mariel).

Career: Army Intelligence, 1960–62; CIA Clandestine Svcs. 1960–71; Businessman, Newspaper publ., 1973–78; Sanibel City Cncl., 1974–82; Sanibel Mayor, 1974–77, 1980; Lee Cnty. Commissioner 1983–88.

DC Office: 108 CHOB 20515, 202-225-2536; Fax: 202-225-6820.

District Offices: 2000 Main St., #303, Fort Myers 33901, 813-332-4677; and 3301 Tamiami Trail E., #212, Bldg. F, Naples 33962, 813-774-8060.

Committees: *Rules* (4th of 9 R): Legislative and Budget Process (Chmn.). *Standards of Official Conduct* (3rd of 5 R). *Intelligence (Permanent Select)* (6th of 9 R): Human Intelligence, Analysis, and Counterintelligence.

Group Ratings

	ADA	ACLU	COPE	CFA	LCV	CON	NSI	COC	ACU	NTLC	CHC
1994	10	13	22	10	39	87	100	92	86	93	93
1993	10	—	8	30	50	50	—	91	92	—	—

National Journal Ratings

	1993 LIB — 1993 CONS		1994 LIB — 1994 CONS	
Economic	14% —	80%	26% —	70%
Social	19% —	77%	24% —	73%
Foreign	0% —	91%	14% —	80%

Key Votes of the 103d Congress

1. Clinton Deficit Plan	N	3. Brady Handgun Purchase	Y	5. Lmt. UN Cmnd. of Forces	Y
2. NAFTA	Y	4. Strike Race/Death Pnlty.	Y	6. Cut Missile Funds	N

Key Votes of the 104th Congress

1. Congressional Compliance Y	6. Reform Crime Grant Y	11. Loser Pays Court Reform Y
2. Balanced Budget Amndmt. Y	7. National Security Act Y	12. Product Liability Reform Y
3. Bar Unfunded Mandates Y	8. Moratorium on Regs. Y	13. Welfare Reform Y
4. Pass Line Item Veto Y	9. Risk Assessment on Regs. Y	14. Term Limits Amndmt. Y
5. Relax Exclusionary Rule Y	10. Expnd. Priv. Prop. Rights N	15. Tax Cuts Y

Election Results

1994 general	Porter Johnston Goss (R) . . . . unopposed		($142,940)
1994 primary	Porter Johnston Goss (R) . . . . unopposed		
1992 general	Porter Johnston Goss (R) 220,351	(82%)	($414,185)
	James King (I) 48,160	(18%)	($18,310)

FIFTEENTH DISTRICT

When Cape Canaveral was chosen as the nation's rocket testing site in the 1940s, there were only 20,000 people in all of Brevard County, which stretches along 60 miles of the coast and includes the Cape. It was a backward place with no industry, picked because it was sunny and on the Atlantic coast: rockets here have to be launched eastward so spent parts fall into the ocean. Today, Brevard County north and south of the cape has 400,000 people. It is a prototype of America's future, with no city center but plenty of shopping centers along strip highways, with a white-collar and service economy, knit together by interest in the space program.

The 15th Congressional District of Florida includes all of the Space Coast and Brevard County and extends south into Indian River County and the fast-growing retirement areas around Vero Beach. It continues west past the vast new town of Palm Bay, now the district's largest city, to what is left of primeval Florida. But more may come: the Army Corps of Engineers, which straightened out the Kissimmee River in the early 1970s, is now seeking to restore it to its natural snake-like course, while nearby in the Three Lakes Wildlife Management Area, whooping cranes were released to propagate in the wild. The Space Coast is heavily Republican, distrustful of many national Democrats' disdain for the space program. But from 1978 until 1992, it elected Democratic congressmen: for 12 years, until he ran for governor in 1990, Bill Nelson, the first member of the House to go up in space; in 1990 and 1992, Jim Bacchus, onetime speechwriter to former Governor Reubin Askew, who capitalized on Republican splits and his own unique approach to community involvement to win narrow victories in 1990 and 1992.

The congressman now is a Republican, Dave Weldon, elected in 1994 after Bacchus retired. Weldon is a physician, educated in New York, who served six years in the Army in San Francisco and Fort Stewart, Georgia (two very different places!). In 1987, at 34, he went into private practice in Melbourne on the Space Coast. In 1989 he founded the Space Coast Family Forum, "to promote family-friendly issues and positions" and his strong Christian beliefs. When Weldon ran for the House in 1994, the conventional wisdom was that he would be a weak candidate, because the Republican nominee in the last three races, Bill Tolley, associated with the religious right, had lost. Weldon led the initial seven-candidate Republican primary, but with only 24% of the vote, not much ahead of Carole Jordan, pro-choice and more moderate. Publicity was also generated because Republican Sue Munsey, former head of the Space Coast Chamber of Commerce, switched parties and ran, with Bacchus's support, as a conservative Democrat on most issues and pro-choice on abortion. But it was not the year of the woman in the 15th District. In the Republican runoff, Jordan was unable to expand her appeal beyond her base in Indian River County, and Weldon won 54%–46%. In the general Munsey said Weldon was "radical right" and boasted that Speaker Thomas Foley promised her a seat on the Science Committee—both local candidates of course campaigned as great supporters of the space program—while on health care Weldon suggested phasing out welfare and was endorsed by the Florida Right to Life Committee. Weldon again won 54%–46%, this time with his biggest percentage in Indian River County, but carrying every part of the district.

Weldon not surprisingly got a seat on the Science Committee and was named vice chairman of the Space Subcommittee (seniority means relatively little in a party chock full of freshmen). He was a loyal supporter of the Contract With America and, despite his lack of political experience, seemed to move comfortably into his new profession. He was named the freshman representative on the Republican Policy Committee.

The People: Pop. 1990: 562,542; 18% rural; 19% age 65+; 88% White; 8% Black; 1% Asian; 1% Other; 3% Hispanic origin. Voting age pop.: 441,006; 6% Black; 3% Hispanic origin. Households: 61% married couple families; 22% married couple fams. w. children; 49% college educ.; median household income: $29,755; per capita income: $15,225; median gross rent: $485; median house value: $74,800.

1992 Presidential Vote			1988 Presidential Vote		
Bush (R)	117,206	(43%)	Bush (R)	144,236	(71%)
Clinton (D)	83,507	(31%)	Dukakis (D)	60,154	(29%)
Perot (I)	69,605	(26%)			

Rep. David J. Weldon (R)

Elected 1994; b. Aug. 31, 1953, Amityville, NY; home, Palm Bay; S.U.N.Y. Stonybrook, B.A. 1978, S.U.N.Y. Buffalo, M.D. 1981; Christian; married (Nancy).

Career: Army Medical Corps, 1981–87, Army Reserves, 1987–92; Practicing physician, 1987–94.

DC Office: 216 CHOB 20515, 202-225-3671; Fax: 202-225-3516.

District Offices: 2725 St. John St., P.O. Box 410007; Melbourne 32941; 407-632-1776.

Committees: *Economic & Educational Opportunities* (20th of 24 R): Early Childhood, Youth and Families; Employer-Employee Relations; Oversight and Investigations. *Science* (15th of 27 R): Basic Research; Space and Aeronautics.

Group Ratings and 103rd Congress Votes: Newly Elected

Key Votes of the 104th Congress

1. Congressional Compliance Y	6. Reform Crime Grant Y	11. Loser Pays Court Reform Y
2. Balanced Budget Amndmt. Y	7. National Security Act Y	12. Product Liability Reform Y
3. Bar Unfunded Mandates Y	8. Moratorium on Regs. Y	13. Welfare Reform Y
4. Pass Line Item Veto Y	9. Risk Assessment on Regs. Y	14. Term Limits Amndmt. Y
5. Relax Exclusionary Rule Y	10. Expnd. Priv. Prop. Rights Y	15. Tax Cuts Y

Election Results

1994 general	David J. Weldon (R)	117,027	(54%)	($478,303)
	Sue Munsey (D)	100,513	(46%)	($494,364)
1994 runoff	David J. Weldon (R)	18,739	(54%)	
	Carole Jean Jordan (R)	15,836	(46%)	
1994 primary	David J. Weldon (R)	13,969	(24%)	
	Carole Jean Jordan (R)	11,197	(19%)	
	Ed Stillie (R)	10,203	(17%)	
	Kevin McKeown (R)	7,633	(13%)	
	Gary Smith (R)	6,258	(11%)	
	Mike Shukdinas (R)	5,793	(10%)	
	Bill Wolfe (R)	3,654	(6%)	
1992 general	James L. Bacchus (D)	132,412	(51%)	($820,388)
	Bill Tolley (R)	128,873	(49%)	($215,538)

SIXTEENTH DISTRICT

Super-rich Palm Beach has spread outward from its original locus at the Breakers and into the always larger and once less fashionable city of West Palm Beach across Lake Worth: those are now just now neighborhoods in a vast metropolitan area. Old beach towns, such as Hobe Sound, located northward along the ocean, have become the hub of extremely affluent developments that stretch all the way to Stuart in Martin County. Farther north, near the old town of Fort Pierce are larger, but more modest developments like Port St. Lucie. Entire square miles west and northwest of West Palm Beach have been reclaimed from swampland and made into condo communities surrounded by golf courses or tracts of factories and warehouses. Once, metro Palm Beach was a narrow stretch along Lake Worth; now it runs inland halfway to Lake Okeechobee.

The 16th Congressional District of Florida does not include Palm Beach and only a portion of suburban West Palm, but it does include much of the metro area. Its boundaries include the beach towns from Jupiter north to Port St. Lucie, but they are convoluted to avoid the black-majority 23rd District. The district also takes in many recently and soon-to-be developed parcels in inland Palm Beach County. One-sixth of the district's residents live in citrus and vegetable growing areas around Lake Okeechobee, and as far away as Sebring, site of an auto racing track: here is the source of the Everglades, the 50-mile-wide and six-inch-deep "river of grass" that flows so slowly to the Gulf of Mexico. This is a Republican-leaning district, though much of Palm Beach County has been trending Democratic, and it can be competitive.

The congressman from the 16th District is Mark Foley, a Republican elected in 1994 to replace Tom Lewis. Lewis retired after 10 years as a conservative with a record as a problem-solver; for much of 1993 he led orchestrated citrus growers' opposition to NAFTA, then negotiated a modification of the agreement and orchestrated the switching of what turned out to be the key votes to approve it. Foley was born in Massachusetts, but moved to Florida at the age of three. He opened a restaurant in Lake Worth when he was 20, became the youngest member ever of the Lake Worth City Commission at 23, became a real estate broker in West Palm Beach, and then was elected to the state House in 1990 and the state Senate in 1992. In 1994 Lewis and the Palm Beach County Republican organization supported Foley, and he won the three-candidate primary with 61% of the vote. The Democrats had a closer race: financial manager John Comerford, the nominee against Lewis in 1992, led Ron Howard 36%–35%, then won the runoff 66%–34%. Comerford, also a Massachusetts native, had worked in the Carter White House and argued that Foley did not raise a family in the district, as had Lewis, and accused him of being beholden to special interests. Foley concentrated on immigration, arguing that the federal government should reimburse Florida for the tremendous costs associated with

Florida's immigrants and take steps to reduce illegal immigration. Foley far outraised and outpolled the Democrat, winning 58%–42%, though it was notably closer in Palm Beach County (52%–48%).

In the House, Majority Whip Tom DeLay appointed Foley an assistant whip and Speaker Newt Gingrich appointed him to the task force on immigration reform. Foley also joined House freshmen in organizing task forces to work for the abolition of the Commerce, Education and Energy Departments, plus HUD. He successfully sponsored an amendment to speed up the deportation of non-violent criminal aliens and promised to introduce legislation removing automatic citizenship for children of aliens born in the United States. Foley also attracted some attention when he proposed that members of Congress no longer receive free copies of the multi-volume U.S. Code; he argued that they and their staffs could use congressional libraries to do their research. But the freshman also demonstrated that he is willing to compromise, when he said House Republicans should abandon their position that the balanced budget amendment include a provision that income taxes could be increased only by a three-fifths supermajority.

The People: Pop. 1990: 561,856; 22% rural; 24% age 65+; 89% White; 4% Black; 1% Asian; 2% Other; 6% Hispanic origin. Voting age pop.: 446,860; 3% Black; 5% Hispanic origin. Households: 62% married couple families; 21% married couple fams. w. children; 45% college educ.; median household income: $30,582; per capita income: $16,952; median gross rent: $575; median house value: $87,900.

1992 Presidential Vote			1988 Presidential Vote		
Bush (R)	108,503	(39%)	Bush (R)	136,565	(65%)
Clinton (D)	98,154	(36%)	Dukakis (D)	74,865	(35%)
Perot (I)	68,543	(25%)			

Rep. Mark Foley (R)

Elected 1994; b. Sept. 8, 1954, Newton, MA; home, West Palm Beach; Palm Beach Comm. Col., 1974; Roman Catholic; single.

Career: Restauranteur, 1974–84; Real estate broker, 1984–90; Lake Worth City Comm., 1977–83; Vice Mayor, 1983–84; FL House of Reps., 1990–92; FL Senate, 1992–94.

DC Office: 506 CHOB 20515, 202-225-5792; Fax: 202-225-3132.

District Offices: 4440 PGA Blvd., #406, Palm Beach Gardens 33410, 407-627-6192; and 250 NW Country Club Dr., Port St. Lucie 34986, 407-878-3181.

Committees: *Agriculture* (25th of 27 R): Department Operations, Nutrition and Foreign Agriculture; Risk Management and Specialty Crops. *Science* (26th of 27 R): Energy and Environment; Space and Aeronautics.

Group Ratings and 103rd Congress Votes: Newly Elected

Key Votes of the 104th Congress

1. Congressional Compliance	Y	6. Reform Crime Grant	Y	11. Loser Pays Court Reform	Y
2. Balanced Budget Amndmt.	Y	7. National Security Act	Y	12. Product Liability Reform	Y
3. Bar Unfunded Mandates	Y	8. Moratorium on Regs.	Y	13. Welfare Reform	Y
4. Pass Line Item Veto	Y	9. Risk Assessment on Regs.	Y	14. Term Limits Amndmt.	Y
5. Relax Exclusionary Rule	Y	10. Expnd. Priv. Prop. Rights	Y	15. Tax Cuts	Y

Election Results

1994 general	Mark Foley (R)....................	122,734	(58%)	($629,406)
	John Comerford (D)...................	88,646	(42%)	($163,311)
1994 primary	Mark Foley (R)......................	29,891	(61%)	
	Audrey Vickers (R).....................	10,344	(21%)	
	John Anastasio (R).....................	8,848	(18%)	
1992 general	Tom Lewis (R)	157,422	(61%)	($363,795)
	John Comerford (D).................	101,237	(39%)	($97,871)

SEVENTEENTH DISTRICT

When 18 people died in a riot in 1980 after the acquittal of a police officer charged with killing a black insurance salesman, Miami's black neighborhood of Liberty City burst onto the national scene. The riot put the spotlight on the rising tension in Miami between a black community economically outdone and numerically outnumbered by Cuban-Americans and it was the first public crisis for Janet Reno, in her first term as Dade County Prosecutor. The tension still exists, though it may be ebbing. Another riot broke out in 1989, after a Colombian-born police officer shot a black motorcyclist; the police officer, originally convicted of manslaughter, won an appeal and was acquitted in May 1993. But there were no riots then, and it may be that the black-Cuban tension is being channeled away from the streets and into politics. For it remains true that blacks are the most Democratic voting group in Florida and Cuban-Americans, heavily concentrated in Miami, comprising 23% of the District, are the most Republican.

The 17th Congressional District of Florida, created to be a black-majority district, lies on the north side of Miami and its Dade County suburbs, running along the I-95 and 27th Avenue corridors from the Miami River north to the Dade County line. The mostly white high-rise condominiums on the shore of Biscayne Bay and heavily Cuban Hialeah were carefully excluded from the district. It extends south along a narrow corridor on either side of Dixie Highway, expanding here and there to bring in heavily black areas all the way south to Homestead, site of Hurricane Andrew's worst damage.

The congresswoman from the 17th is Carrie Meek, one of the most politically experienced of the freshman Democratic class of 1992. The granddaughter of a slave, Meek was born in 1926 in Tallahassee and grew up near the old Capitol in a neighborhood called the Bottom. She was a gifted athlete when she attended Florida A&M's lab school; she went to Florida A&M and the University of Michigan (Florida government paid the tuition because its graduate schools were segregated). When she came back to Miami, she taught physical education at a segregated community college. Here she became active in politics and, when pioneer black legislator Gwen Cherry died in an auto accident, Meek was elected to the Florida House in 1978. Particularly effective in the legislature, Meek passed legislation to criminalize stalking, a Minority Business Enterprise law, and promoted literacy and dropout prevention programs. In the State Senate for a decade, she helped to draw the district she would eventually serve. When the 17th was drawn with a black majority, she was clearly the best-known and best-liked politician in the Miami area and was nominated with 83% of the vote in the primary and elected with no Republican opposition.

In her first term, she demonstrated her own determination and savvy by being the only freshman Democrat to win a seat on the Appropriations Committee. She said her first priority was creating jobs through federal programs and private initiatives to help blacks develop their own businesses and banks as, she notes, Cuban-Americans have. Her voting record was liberal and she sponsored the law changing the rules for Social Security for household employees. The Republican capture of the House cost her her seat on Appropriations, though the Democratic leadership gave her a seat on the Budget Committee. In January 1995, she unexpectedly found herself as the central focus of Democrats' anger at how House Speaker Newt Gingrich's

Republicans were running the House. In a floor speech, Meek criticized Gingrich's book deal with Rupert Murdoch's HarperCollins publishing company. "News accounts tell us that while the speaker may have given up the $4.5 million advance, he stands to gain that amount and much more ... That is a whole lot of dust where I come from." She argued that Gingrich's earnings would depend directly on how hard the publishing house, owned by Rupert Murdoch, markets his book. Republicans demanded that her words be stricken from the Congressional Record as an impermissible criticism of another member. Although they may have had a point regarding House rules, they aroused a furor among Democrats, who started a two-hour shouting match on the floor. Meek was undaunted and will surely continue her attacks on Republican policy and politicians. But she will have a harder time achieving her positive goals, such as stimulating urban economic redevelopment through environmental cleanup.

The People: Pop. 1990: 563,284; 10% age 65+; 20% White; 59% Black; 1% Asian; 4% Other; 23% Hispanic origin. Voting age pop.: 391,574; 54% Black; 24% Hispanic origin. Households: 42% married couple families; 21% married couple fams. w. children; 32% college educ.; median household income: $21,899; per capita income: $9,157; median gross rent: $426; median house value: $63,900.

1992 Presidential Vote			1988 Presidential Vote		
Clinton (D)	99,422	(73%)	Dukakis (D)	87,289	(70%)
Bush (R)	25,873	(19%)	Bush (R)	37,800	(30%)
Perot (I)	9,913	(7%)			

Rep. Carrie P. Meek (D)

Elected 1992; b. April 29, 1926, Tallahassee; home, Miami; FL A&M U., B.A. 1946, U. of MI, M.S. 1948; Primitive Baptist; divorced.

Career: Admin., Miami-Dade Comm. Col., 1949–92; FL House of Reps, 1979–82; FL Senate 1982–92.

DC Office: 404 CHOB 20515, 202-225-4506; Fax: 202-226-0777.

District Offices: 25 W. Flagler St., #1015, Miami 33130, 305-381-9541.

Committees: *Budget* (16th of 18 D). *Government Reform & Oversight* (20th of 22 D): National Security, International Affairs and Criminal Justice; Postal Service.

Group Ratings

	ADA	ACLU	COPE	CFA	LCV	CON	NSI	COC	ACU	NTLC	CHC
1994	95	86	78	80	73	5	50	50	10	11	0
1993	75	—	92	90	79	1	—	18	9	—	—

National Journal Ratings

	1993 LIB — 1993 CONS		1994 LIB — 1994 CONS	
Economic	78% —	12%	83% —	0%
Social	87% —	0%	94% —	0%
Foreign	50% —	49%	75% —	23%

Key Votes of the 103d Congress

1. Clinton Deficit Plan	Y	3. Brady Handgun Purchase	Y	5. Lmt. UN Cmnd. of Forces	N
2. NAFTA	Y	4. Strike Race/Death Pnlty.	N	6. Cut Missile Funds	N

Key Votes of the 104th Congress

1. Congressional Compliance Y	6. Reform Crime Grant N	11. Loser Pays Court Reform *
2. Balanced Budget Amndmt. N	7. National Security Act N	12. Product Liability Reform N
3. Bar Unfunded Mandates N	8. Moratorium on Regs. *	13. Welfare Reform N
4. Pass Line Item Veto N	9. Risk Assessment on Regs. N	14. Term Limits Amndmt. N
5. Relax Exclusionary Rule N	10. Expnd. Priv. Prop. Rights N	15. Tax Cuts N

Election Results

1994 general	Carrie P. Meek (D)	unopposed	($166,452)
1994 primary	Carrie P. Meek (D)	unopposed	
1992 general	Carrie P. Meek (D)	unopposed	($461,115)

EIGHTEENTH DISTRICT

The *Miami Vice* image of Miami lingers on—the hum of orange and pink neon signs in hot night air, moonlight reflecting off Biscayne Bay onto surrealistic high rises, the pastel, random-shaped, sharp-angled style of clothes and furniture and the air of menace in streets where many are armed and vast quantities of drugs and cash regularly change hands. A resort city known for pseudo-Spanish mansions and art deco beach hotels two generations ago, on its way to becoming a fairly typical American metropolitan area one generation ago, Miami today cannot be mistaken for any other American—or Latin American—city. It lives on the cusp of two civilizations: Anglo and Latino, with different traditions, styles and sensibilities, converging here in Miami, despite some friction, toward an amalgam with many strengths of both. Miami has become commercially and economically the capital of Latin America, the one place from which it is easiest to fly directly to any other part of Latin America, where top business and banking services are available to a sophisticated Spanish-speaking (and usually also English-speaking) clientele. With NAFTA ratified, and other Latin nations eager for free trade with the United States, Miami stands to be at the center of the largest free-trade zone in the history of mankind, uniquely able to connect all sides.

In the meantime, there are inevitably frictions in a community divided between culturally defined groups with distinct histories and styles. Miami's Dade County in 1990 was 49% Hispanic (almost all Cuban), 32% white Anglo and 19% black. It is a city where you can rise to the top of your profession or business, patronize the best stores and restaurants, live in the best residential areas—all in Spanish, although most Cuban-Americans are fluent in English as well. There is friction on the streets between blacks and Cubans, and a resentment by some blacks of the success the hardworking, anything but fatalistic Cubans have achieved. And there is resentment by many Cuban-Americans of white liberals, reflected in Cuban activist Jorge Mas Canosa's charges that the *Miami Herald* "manipulates information just like *Granma*," the Castro paper in Havana. On its face, the charge is absurd, yet it should be added that many goodhearted liberals, for which the *Herald* is a proxy, have failed to appreciate the totalitarianism of Castro's regime, have overpraised its pathetically limited achievements and glossed over the brutality that has been its steady conduct.

Typical is the liberal Miami politician who calls the city's Cuban-Americans "emigres," the term leftists use to disparage supposedly rich and selfish opponents of supposedly progressive revolutions since the French Revolution 200 years ago. Anglo-Americans, after years of politics in which the shades of difference between candidates are often subtle and in which basic liberties and property are not threatened, have a hard time understanding the enthusiasm of Americans with backgrounds in Latin America, where the differences between political creeds can be enormous and where liberties have frequently been in danger. In U.S. politics, that has led to a friction between the Cuban-Americans, heavily Republican ever since John F. Kennedy refused to send air cover to the Bay of Pigs invasion, and Miami's blacks and Jews, overwhelmingly Democratic since they first came to the city.

The 18th Congressional District of Florida is one of two Hispanic-majority districts in Dade County, about two-thirds Cuban-American, and very heavily Republican. It includes the corridor along Southwest 8th Street—often called Calle Ocho—which was the original Cuban-American commercial strip when the first exiles from Castro's Communist regime came over in the early 1960s. Dade County's Latino population has increased from 50,000 in 1960 to 953,000 in 1990, and Calle Ocho remains a major Cuban-American thoroughfare, humming with commerce and activity. The 18th District spreads south and west toward Miami Airport and the suburb of Kendall. It stretches all the way down to Homestead, site of Hurricane Andrew's worst damage, and then extends back north, around the black-majority 17th, to include the neighborhoods of Coconut Grove and Miami Beach's South Beach, the hottest and hippest place in America at the moment, with old art deco hotels that used to house elderly retirees now a temporary home to the world's glitziest celebrities.

The representative from the 18th District is Ileana Ros-Lehtinen, the first Cuban-American elected to Congress. She was born in Cuba, became a teacher in Miami, then was the owner of a private school. Her husband, Dexter Lehtinen, was the controversial U.S. Attorney in Miami during the Bush Administration. She was elected to the Florida House in 1982, at 30, and to the state Senate in 1986. She ran for the House in the special election called after the death in May 1989 of Claude Pepper, one of the most enduring liberals in American politics, who served in the Senate from 1936 to 1950, was defeated in a bitter primary, then served in the House from 1962 and was a major political force, expanding Social Security and Medicare for the elderly, until his death (he was also a staunch opponent of Communism in Latin America). The contest made news when the Democratic nominee, Gerald Richman, proclaimed, "This isn't an Anglo seat, it isn't a Jewish seat, it isn't a Cuban-American seat. It's an American seat." This was taken as a challenge to Cuban-Americans. Voting ran almost entirely on ethnic lines: exit polls showed that 96% of blacks and 88% of non-Hispanic whites voted for Richman, while 90% of Hispanics voted for Ros-Lehtinen. Hispanic turnout was 58%, compared to 42% for non-Hispanic whites: this was the difference that enabled Ros-Lehtinen to win with 53%. She was reelected in 1990 by a 60%–40% margin. Redistricting has given her a much more solidly Cuban-American—and Republican—district, in which the only possible opposition could be in the Republican primary.

Ros-Lehtinen has a fairly moderate voting record, and often supports government spending. But one might add that free market economics has not had strong supporters in the Latin tradition until very recently. Despite the long-term local economic benefit, she opposed NAFTA (which extends only to Mexico), and spoke out against it. She harshly criticized the Clinton Administration for its decisions to route Cuban refugees to Guantanamo and then to force them back to Castro. "The message is very clear. Any time Castro has a problem in Cuba, he will do this again. We have once again rewarded him with the Carter Administration, the Clinton administration. But it did not happen under Reagan and Bush. They would have seen this as an act of aggression." Ros-Lehtinen was one of three incumbent Republicans running in 1994 who refused to sign the Contract With America. She opposed it because of its promise to deprive legal aliens of government benefits, and voted against the Contract's welfare reform for the same reason. Despite her independence, she is well-respected on the Republican side.

The People: Pop. 1990: 562,394; 17% age 65+; 29% White; 4% Black; 1% Asian; 6% Other; 67% Hispanic origin. Voting age pop.: 449,992; 3% Black; 67% Hispanic origin. Households: 50% married couple families; 20% married couple fams. w. children; 42% college educ.; median household income: $25,537; per capita income: $14,779; median gross rent: $460; median house value: $95,000.

1992 Presidential Vote

Bush (R)	93,870	(57%)
Clinton (D)	54,113	(33%)
Perot (I)	16,988	(10%)

1988 Presidential Vote

Bush (R)	106,697	(69%)
Dukakis (D)	47,975	(31%)

Rep. Ileana Ros-Lehtinen (R)

Elected Aug. 1989; b. July 12, 1952, Havana, Cuba; home, Miami; Miami-Dade Comm. Col., A.A. 1972, FL Intl. U., B.S. 1975, M.S. 1986; Catholic; married (Dexter).

Career: Teacher, Principal & Owner, Eastern Academy Elem. Schl., 1978–85; FL House of Reps., 1982–86; FL Senate, 1986–89.

DC Office: 2440 RHOB 20515, 202-225-3931; Fax: 202-225-5620.

District Offices: 5757 Blue Lagoon Dr., #240, Miami 33126, 305-262-1800.

Committees: *International Relations* (11th of 23 R): Africa (Chmn.); Western Hemisphere. *Government Reform & Oversight* (7th of 27 R): National Security, International Affairs and Criminal Justice.

Group Ratings

	ADA	ACLU	COPE	CFA	LCV	CON	NSI	COC	ACU	NTLC	CHC
1994	25	18	67	30	78	49	90	82	65	64	71
1993	30	—	75	70	79	19	—	82	79	—	—

National Journal Ratings

	1993 LIB — 1993 CONS		1994 LIB — 1994 CONS	
Economic	42%	— 58%	39%	— 61%
Social	35%	— 64%	38%	— 62%
Foreign	0%	— 91%	23%	— 76%

Key Votes of the 103d Congress

1. Clinton Deficit Plan	N	3. Brady Handgun Purchase	Y	5. Lmt. UN Cmnd. of Forces	Y
2. NAFTA	N	4. Strike Race/Death Pnlty.	Y	6. Cut Missile Funds	N

Key Votes of the 104th Congress

1. Congressional Compliance	Y	6. Reform Crime Grant	Y	11. Loser Pays Court Reform	N
2. Balanced Budget Amndmt.	Y	7. National Security Act	Y	12. Product Liability Reform	Y
3. Bar Unfunded Mandates	Y	8. Moratorium on Regs.	Y	13. Welfare Reform	N
4. Pass Line Item Veto	Y	9. Risk Assessment on Regs.	Y	14. Term Limits Amndmt.	Y
5. Relax Exclusionary Rule	Y	10. Expnd. Priv. Prop. Rights	Y	15. Tax Cuts	Y

Election Results

1994 general	Ileana Ros-Lehtinen (R)	unopposed		($148,341)
1994 primary	Ileana Ros-Lehtinen (R)	unopposed		
1992 general	Ileana Ros-Lehtinen (R)	104,755	(67%)	($669,350)
	Magda Montiel Davis (D)	52,142	(33%)	($335,408)

NINETEENTH DISTRICT

When the first millionaires came to Palm Beach in the 1920s to winter in their new Palm Beach Addison Mizner pseudo-Mediterranean mansions or when the first real estate speculators arrived in Miami, there was virtually nothing man-made between these two cites. In 1920, Dade, Broward and Palm Beach Counties had some 66,000 residents. Now, more than four million are wedged almost entirely in the 5- to 15-mile strip between the Atlantic Ocean and the protected Everglades. The contrast between the 1920s and today's vast state is especially glaring in Boca

Raton, where Mizner built what is now the Boca Raton Hotel and Club in 1926. Its azure-tiled fountains and red-tiled roofs, its pseudo-Moorish columns and pink stucco walls bespeak a vision of a holiday Florida, a bit mannered and antique to today's eye, but still exuberant. Today, Boca Raton has grown inland and is still solidly affluent, but also is more functional and workaday. Affluent retirees from New York and the rest of the northeast live in unadorned high-rise towers, enjoying the weather and the lack of a state income tax. But the headquarters of the troubled W.R. Grace conglomerate has relocated here from Manhattan and a joint venture between IBM and Intel also is here: high-tech and big money at work in what used to be just paradise.

The 19th Congressional District of Florida includes former swampland and citrus groves and it does not touch the ocean at all, kept from it by the majority-black 23d District which collects the black neighborhoods just inland from the Intracoastal Waterway. The district's population is evenly divided between Broward and Palm Beach Counties. It stretches from the edge of West Palm Beach, travels through the Lantana headquarters of the National Enquirer to Boynton Beach, Boca Raton, Deerfield Beach and Sunrise. With the growth in northern Broward and southern Palm Beach Counties during the 1970s and 1980s, the district's largest communities are no longer the beach towns, but new inland communities: Coral Springs, Margate, Tamarac. With one of the highest elderly percentages in the country, this is retiree country. But unlike the Gulf Coast, this is a Democratic area, with a large Jewish population from New York and the Northeast. (You'll also find "snowbirds" here, Jewish retirees from Canada whose primary language is French.) Liberal condominium associations are political powers.

The congressman from the 19th is Harry Johnston, a member of a prominent civic Palm Beach County family, who served 12 years in the legislature and became state Senate president. He ran for governor in 1986, but finished third in the primary and thus out of the runoff. In 1988, a Palm Beach County congressional district opened up when incumbent Dan Mica ran for the Senate. Johnston faced serious competition in the 1988 general from a Republican county commissioner, but won 55%–45%.

In the House, Johnston has had one of the most liberal records in the Florida delegation and has shown legislative skill. A man whose career connects the older, southern small town-oriented Florida with the gleaming, economically booming, environment-conscious metropolitan Florida of today, Johnston combines a reassuring demeanor with a voting record not far out of the House Democratic mainstream. He has worked hard on the Foreign Affairs Committee, especially on Latin America; he did not take as hard an anti-Communist line as most Florida legislators. He served as chairman of the Africa Subcommittee until the Republicans took over. Johnston also picked up a seat on Budget in 1993 and is an at-large member of the Democratic whip organization. He also serves as a co-chair of the Congressional Roundtable on Post-Cold War Relations, which focuses on the states of the former Soviet Union. That record has evidently suited his constituents fine. In 1994, against an inventor who spent more than $500,000 of his own money, Johnston won reelection with 66% of the vote.

In the 104th Congress, Johnston and two other Democrats filed an ethics complaint against Speaker Newt Gingrich, charging that he violated House rules by allowing his college course to be broadcast for free over a cable network whose owner had interests before Congress. The same theory could be used to argue that every member of Congress is violating the rules by appearing on C-SPAN. Johnston also introduced legislation which would change Medicare law to provide yearly mammograms for women over 65-years of age. Of the five white Democrats from Florida, he voted the least support for the Contract With America; it is a measure of his district's liberal bent that such a record will pose no political hazard.

The People: Pop. 1990: 562,978; 2% rural; 28% age 65+; 90% White; 3% Black; 1% Asian; 1% Other; 6% Hispanic origin. Voting age pop.: 462,963; 2% Black; 5% Hispanic origin. Households: 60% married couple families; 19% married couple fams. w. children; 50% college educ.; median household income: $34,396; per capita income: $20,029; median gross rent: $672; median house value: $107,100.

1992 Presidential Vote

Clinton (D)	159,284	(54%)
Bush (R)	89,698	(30%)
Perot (I)	46,946	(16%)

1988 Presidential Vote

Dukakis (D)	112,917	(51%)
Bush (R)	109,234	(49%)

Rep. Harry A. Johnston (D)

Elected 1988; b. Dec. 2, 1931, W. Palm Beach; home, W. Palm Beach; VA Military Inst., B.A. 1953; U. of FL, J.D. 1958; Presbyterian, married (Mary).

Career: Army, 1953–55; Practicing atty., 1958–88; FL Senate, 1974–86, Pres., 1985–86.

DC Office: 2458 RHOB 20515, 202-225-3001; Fax: 202-225-8791.

District Offices: 1501 Corporate Dr., Boynton Beach 33426, 407-732-4000.

Committees: *Budget* (8th of 18 D). *International Relations* (7th of 19 D): Africa; International Economic Policy and Trade.

Group Ratings

	ADA	ACLU	COPE	CFA	LCV	CON	NSI	COC	ACU	NTLC	CHC
1994	90	73	63	70	88	52	20	67	5	15	7
1993	90	—	92	100	86	32	—	18	8	—	—

National Journal Ratings

	1993 LIB	—	1993 CONS	1994 LIB	—	1994 CONS
Economic	68%	—	26%	58%	—	41%
Social	78%	—	21%	85%	—	14%
Foreign	87%	—	7%	85%	—	0%

Key Votes of the 103d Congress

1. Clinton Deficit Plan	Y	3. Brady Handgun Purchase	Y	5. Lmt. UN Cmnd. of Forces	N
2. NAFTA	Y	4. Strike Race/Death Pnlty.	N	6. Cut Missile Funds	Y

Key Votes of the 104th Congress

1. Congressional Compliance	Y	6. Reform Crime Grant	N	11. Loser Pays Court Reform	N
2. Balanced Budget Amndmt.	Y	7. National Security Act	*	12. Product Liability Reform	N
3. Bar Unfunded Mandates	N	8. Moratorium on Regs.	N	13. Welfare Reform	N
4. Pass Line Item Veto	N	9. Risk Assessment on Regs.	N	14. Term Limits Amndmt.	N
5. Relax Exclusionary Rule	N	10. Expnd. Priv. Prop. Rights	*	15. Tax Cuts	N

Election Results

1994 general	Harry A. Johnston (D)	147,591	(66%)	($288,073)
	Peter J. Tsakanikas (R)	75,779	(34%)	($615,927)
1994 primary	Harry Johnston (D)	unopposed		
1992 general	Harry A. Johnston (D)	177,423	(63%)	($235,412)
	Larry Metz (R)	103,867	(37%)	($63,200)

TWENTIETH DISTRICT

When Connie Francis and Paula Prentiss first made Fort Lauderdale famous in the 1960 spring break movie *Where the Boys Are*, it was just a small town with a strip of motels along the beach and some nice houses fronting canals. Now it is the center of a vast metropolitan area. Fort Lauderdale and Broward County had fewer than 100,000 people in 1950; by 1990 it was up to 1.3 million. The land from the strip of beach along the Atlantic Ocean west to the Sawgrass Expressway and the Everglades Wildlife Management Area filled up with subdivisions, shopping centers, office complexes, warehouses and trucking terminals. Broward County is no longer just vacation country; it is also a major port and business center with high-tech companies and startups that have become national giants, including Blockbuster Video. As it has grown, the ethnic composition of Broward County has changed. In the 1950s, it was understood that Jews couldn't buy houses or rent hotel rooms this far north of Miami. Today, after three decades of Cubans moving into the Miami area and many Jews moving out, Broward County is the most heavily Jewish part of Florida, indeed one of the most heavily Jewish parts of the United States. Nearer the coast, especially in the huge high-rises of Hollywood and Hallandale, most of Broward's Jews are retirees from New York and other northeastern metro areas. But inland, in towns like Pembroke Pines and Davie, and Plantation and Sunrise that didn't exist a few decades ago, there are many young Jewish parents raising families in communities that pride themselves on fine schools and high property values.

The 20th Congressional District of Florida includes most of southern Broward County, though not the precincts nearest the beach, which are in the 22d and 23d Districts. The district also includes much of the unpopulated Everglades west of the Sawgrass, connecting Broward County with southern Dade County, the outlying parts of the Miami area, and the Florida Keys. At the end of the Overseas Highway is Key West, now a bustling tropical outpost that little resembles its sleepy seafaring roots. This southern-most city in the continental United States was long accessible only by sea, and shipwrecks along the miles of coral reefs once gave its residents the highest per capita income in the nation. Key West has attracted famous residents—Ernest Hemingway, Tennessee Williams, Jimmy Buffett—and a large gay population, many living in restored "conch houses"—quaint clapboard bungalows. In 1982, some Key West citizens proclaimed the town as a separate Conch Republic. Politically, the Keys are Democratic; so is Broward County. The Miami area in between, with many Cuban-Americans, leans Republican.

The congressman from the 20th District is Peter Deutsch, a Democrat first elected in 1992. Deutsch grew up in New York, graduated from Yale Law School in June 1982, moved to Florida and by November was elected to the state legislature. Two years later, he was reelected with the largest vote in Florida and was unopposed in the next three elections. A *Miami Herald* reporter said Deutsch was "viewed by colleagues as bright but abrasive, and an expert at using procedural rules to advance or torpedo legislation." The newly drawn 20th District looked as if it were drawn for Deutsch. He became the first congressional candidate in Florida history to get on the ballot by petition, started off his campaign by loaning it $350,000 and allowed himself to be taped making fund-raising calls while in the presence of a reporter: "I raise money from special interests because they have a role to play in the process." He openly challenged incumbent and fellow Democrat and Foreign Affairs Committee chairman Dante Fascell, who, faced with the prospect of seeking reelection in a district dominated by unfamiliar Broward County, decided to retire after 38 years in the House. Deutsch won the primary nearly 2–1, and defeated Republican Beverly Kennedy in the general election, 55%–39%.

Deutsch is, unsurprisingly, pro-Israel, pro-choice and pro-universal health care. He is also a politician who does not waste time. On his first day in Congress, while most freshmen were attending swearing-in ceremonies, Deutsch held a press conference to announce he had introduced a bill to increase flood insurance benefits. He had a rather moderate voting record, but was more liberal on foreign and defense issues. Deutsch was easily reelected in 1994, although he was embarrassed by a contribution from former Broward County congressman and convicted felon Larry Smith. Deutsch's campaign is still one of the most debt-laden in the House, owing $312,000, but his personal loan has been repaid, and he appears to have a safe seat. In the Republican House, Deutsch got the Commerce Committee seat that eluded him as a freshman—a coveted post, but not quite the plum it would have been for him if John Dingell were still chairman. He sponsored the balanced budget amendment and a bill to regulate "cop-killer" ammunition, but this talented political entrepreneur is not likely to find as many opportunities in a Republican House as in a Democratic one.

The People: Pop. 1990: 562,673; 9% rural; 16% age 65+; 82% White; 4% Black; 2% Asian; 2% Other; 12% Hispanic origin. Voting age pop.: 440,902; 4% Black; 11% Hispanic origin. Households: 59% married couple families; 24% married couple fams. w. children; 51% college educ.; median household income: $35,378; per capita income: $18,285; median gross rent: $624; median house value: $102,300.

1992 Presidential Vote			1988 Presidential Vote		
Clinton (D)	116,568	(47%)	Bush (R)	106,798	(54%)
Bush (R)	83,485	(33%)	Dukakis (D)	92,804	(46%)
Perot (I)	48,687	(20%)			

Rep. Peter Deutsch (D)

Elected 1992; b. Apr. 1, 1957, New York, NY; home, Lauderhill; Swarthmore Col., B.A. 1979, Yale Law Schl., J.D. 1982; Jewish, married (Lori).

Career: FL House of Reps., 1982–92; Practicing atty., 1983–92.

DC Office: 204 CHOB 20515, 202-225-7931; Fax: 202-225-8456; e-mail: pdeutsch@hr.house.gov.

District Offices: 10100 Pines Blvd., Pembroke Pines 33025, 305-437-3936.

Committees: *Commerce* (17th of 21 D): Commerce, Trade and Hazardous Materials; Energy and Power; Health and Environment.

Group Ratings

	ADA	ACLU	COPE	CFA	LCV	CON	NSI	COC	ACU	NTLC	CHC
1994	60	68	67	70	100	63	40	75	19	32	7
1993	90	—	100	100	100	55	—	18	13	—	—

National Journal Ratings

	1993 LIB — 1993 CONS			1994 LIB — 1994 CONS		
Economic	61%	—	37%	59%	—	37%
Social	71%	—	28%	57%	—	43%
Foreign	51%	—	42%	80%	—	17%

Key Votes of the 103d Congress

1. Clinton Deficit Plan	Y	3. Brady Handgun Purchase	Y	5. Lmt. UN Cmnd. of Forces	N
2. NAFTA	N	4. Strike Race/Death Pnlty.	Y	6. Cut Missile Funds	N

Key Votes of the 104th Congress

1. Congressional Compliance Y	6. Reform Crime Grant N	11. Loser Pays Court Reform N
2. Balanced Budget Amndmt. Y	7. National Security Act N	12. Product Liability Reform N
3. Bar Unfunded Mandates Y	8. Moratorium on Regs. *	13. Welfare Reform N
4. Pass Line Item Veto Y	9. Risk Assessment on Regs. N	14. Term Limits Amndmt. Y
5. Relax Exclusionary Rule Y	10. Expnd. Priv. Prop. Rights N	15. Tax Cuts N

Election Results

1994 general	Peter Deutsch (D).................. 114,615	(61%)	($1,011,936)
	Beverly Kennedy (R) 72,516	(39%)	($111,869)
1994 primary	Peter Deutsch (D)................. unopposed		
1992 general	Peter Deutsch (D).................. 130,959	(55%)	($849,785)
	Beverly Kennedy (R) 91,589	(39%)	($88,811)
	James Blackburn (I)................. 15,341	(6%)	($14,664)

TWENTY-FIRST DISTRICT

As the Cuban-American and other Latino populations of Miami and Dade County increased from 50,000 in 1960 to 953,000 in 1990, Cuban-American neighborhoods centered along 8th Street—Calle Ocho—expanded to the southwest, west and northwest. Development moved out to the 1960s and 1970s, filling up the land all the way to the Palmetto Expressway; in the 1980s, development reached outward to the Homestead Extension of Florida's Turnpike. The Cuban-Americans moved out and beyond Hialeah, whose now-closed race track was constructed in the 1920s beyond the edge of urban development, and which now has the highest percentage of Cuban-Americans in the Miami area. To the south, Westwood and Kendall Lakes—southwest suburbs of Miami with large Cuban-American populations—have been growing outwards into what once was swampland. Here, planned communities and subdivisions often have just one, guarded entrance, with streets fanning out around lakes and golf courses.

The 21st Congressional District of Florida includes most of these new Cuban-American communities, taking in Hialeah and, just to the north, the planned community of Miami Lakes developed in 1962 by Senator Bob Graham and his father. To the south, it is centered on Kendall Lakes, and its boundaries go out to the Everglades Wildlife Management Area. The district is 70% Hispanic—almost all of it Cuban-American—and heavily Republican. Knowing first hand the evils of Communism, Cuban-Americans appreciate the blessings of free enterprise, cherish traditional moral values, and prefer Republicans to Democrats on all these counts. The 21st was a new district, created for the 1992 election; so far no Democrat has chosen to run here.

The congressman from the 21st District is Lincoln Diaz-Balart. Diaz-Balart was born in Cuba to a prominent family. His grandfather and father served in the Cuban Congress and the family left Cuba in 1959, shortly after Castro took over and their house was looted and burned. His aunt was the former wife of Fidel Castro and the mother of Castro's only recognized child. Lincoln Diaz-Balart started off as a poverty lawyer and a Democrat, but switched parties and has had great success as a Republican. He was elected to the state House as a Republican in 1986 with 78% of the vote and to the state Senate in 1989 with 82%, a year after his younger brother Mario was elected to the state House. In the legislature Lincoln Diaz-Balart sponsored laws toughening sentences for crimes against law enforcement officers, increasing penalties for drug money-laundering, providing low-interest home construction loans, creating a statewide substance abuse program, and requiring prospectuses of Florida firms issuing securities to disclose whether they do business with Cuba.

In 1989, Jorge Mas Canosa's Cuban American National Foundation convinced Diaz-Balart not to run against Ileana Ros-Lehtinen in the then-18th District special election to replace Claude Pepper. In 1992, the organization endorsed Diaz-Balart to run in the new 21st. But fellow Senator Javier Souto, also Cuban-born, opposed him in the primary, charging that Diaz-Balart was backed by wealthy contributors and was not a lifelong Republican. Diaz-Balart won 69%–31%.

Diaz-Balart has said he believes a hemispheric common market is inevitable, but he voted against the North American Free Trade Agreement because of his dissatisfaction with the Mexican government. He has pushed for stronger economic sanctions against Cuba and criticized the Democratic Party for selecting as its chairman Senator Christopher Dodd, because he felt that Dodd had been too cozy with Castro and other Latin leftists. When the Clinton Administration announced in May 1995 that it would no longer give automatic safe haven in the U.S. to Cuban refugees and instead would return them to Cuba—a reversal of previous U.S. policy—Diaz-Balart was one of two people arrested while protesting this policy switch. When Colorado Democrat David Skaggs tried to cut funding for Radio Marti and TV Marti broadcasts to Cuba, Diaz-Balart moved successfully to cut $23 million in funding for the National Institute of Standards and Technology in Skaggs's district. Diaz-Balart was one of three Republican incumbents running in 1994 who refused to sign the Contract With America; he opposed the section that called for denying government benefits to legal immigrants. For the same reason he voted against the Contract's welfare reform package. This apostasy was evidently understood by House Republican leaders, who welcome the cultural diversification of their ranks: Speaker Newt Gingrich named Diaz-Balart to the Rules Committee and has given him opportunities to gain attention in the House. With his ambition and skills, it may not be too early to contemplate Diaz-Balart as the first Hispanic-American member of the Senate.

The People: Pop. 1990: 562,402; 1% rural; 10% age 65+; 26% White; 4% Black; 1% Asian; 7% Other; 70% Hispanic origin. Voting age pop.: 424,125; 4% Black; 70% Hispanic origin. Households: 61% married couple families; 31% married couple fams. w. children; 45% college educ.; median household income: $32,043; per capita income: $13,173; median gross rent: $592; median house value: $91,100.

1992 Presidential Vote		
Bush (R)	85,292	(58%)
Clinton (D)	45,778	(31%)
Perot (I)	15,545	(11%)

1988 Presidential Vote		
Bush (R)	88,119	(72%)
Dukakis (D)	34,760	(28%)

Rep. Lincoln Diaz-Balart (R)

Elected 1992; b. Aug. 13, 1954, Havana, Cuba; home, Miami; U. of S. FL, B.S. 1977, Case Western Reserve U., J.D. 1979; Catholic; married (Cristina).

Career: Practicing atty., 1979–92; Asst. St. Atty., 1983–84; FL House of Reps., 1986–89; FL Senate 1990–92.

DC Office: 431 CHOB 20515, 202-225-4211; Fax: 202-225-8576.

District Offices: 8525 N.W. 53d Terr., #102, Miami 33166, 305-470-8555.

Committees: *House Oversight* (6th of 7 R). *Rules* (7th of 9 R): Rules of the House.

Group Ratings

	ADA	ACLU	COPE	CFA	LCV	CON	NSI	COC	ACU	NTLC	CHC
1994	25	17	78	50	39	49	90	83	71	72	71
1993	35	—	83	70	50	7	—	73	75	—	—

National Journal Ratings

	1993 LIB — 1993 CONS		1994 LIB — 1994 CONS	
Economic	45% —	55%	42% —	57%
Social	35% —	64%	38% —	61%
Foreign	0% —	91%	23% —	76%

Key Votes of the 103d Congress

1. Clinton Deficit Plan	N	3. Brady Handgun Purchase	Y	5. Lmt. UN Cmnd. of Forces	Y
2. NAFTA	N	4. Strike Race/Death Pnlty.	Y	6. Cut Missile Funds	N

Key Votes of the 104th Congress

1. Congressional Compliance	Y	6. Reform Crime Grant	Y	11. Loser Pays Court Reform	N
2. Balanced Budget Amndmt.	Y	7. National Security Act	Y	12. Product Liability Reform	N
3. Bar Unfunded Mandates	Y	8. Moratorium on Regs.	Y	13. Welfare Reform	N
4. Pass Line Item Veto	Y	9. Risk Assessment on Regs.	Y	14. Term Limits Amndmt.	Y
5. Relax Exclusionary Rule	Y	10. Expnd. Priv. Prop. Rights	Y	15. Tax Cuts	Y

Election Results

1994 general	Lincoln Diaz-Balart (R)	unopposed	($125,082)
1994 primary	Lincoln Diaz-Balart (R)	unopposed	
1992 general	Lincoln Diaz-Balart (R)	unopposed	($279,481)

TWENTY-SECOND DISTRICT

The barrier islands of Florida's Gold Coast have been developed in spasms of speculative frenzy, not just as vacation places and retirement homes but as embodiments of dreams and fantasies, bearing about the same relation to people's everyday lives as MTV videos. Consider Palm Beach, the great beach resort of the 1920s, where rich WASPs would leave their snow-covered Tudor or Georgian mansions and live in Addison Mizner's pseudo-Mediterranean confections. Or think of Miami Beach, the great resort of the 1950s, where Jews who had grown up amid prejudice and made their fortunes in ebullient postwar America vacationed in surrealistically curved and embellished skyscraper hotels—the Doral, Deauville, Eden Roc, Fontainebleau—giant variations on the themes set out in the much smaller Art Deco hotels at the beach's south end. Or think of the 1970s and 1980s, as the coastline of Dade, Broward and Palm Beach Counties were lined with one high-rise condo after another, a promised land for the retirees of New York and the northeast, free from winter frost and state and local income taxes.

Almost all of this beach area is now gathered together into Florida's 22d Congressional District, entirely different from any previous Florida district, and with the highest percentage of over 65 residents of any in the United States. Its shape was dictated by the governing interpretation of the Voting Rights Act, which required maximizing the black percentage in the 23d and 17th Districts just inland from the coast, sealing the beach towns off by themselves. Actually, the fit is not quite perfect. The 22d starts in the north in Juno Beach, north of Palm Beach, and reaches south to Miami Beach, but there exceeds the population limit and so excludes South Beach, at the moment arguably the trendiest place in North (or South: this is Miami) America. It is 91 miles long and never more than three miles wide.

The congressman from the 22d District is Clay Shaw, a Republican first elected in 1980, and now one of the senior Republicans handling one of the most important issues in the House. Shaw grew up in Fort Lauderdale, practiced law and served as a judge and councilman; in 1975 he became the city's Mayor. In 1980 he ran for the House, and had the good fortune of seeing the Democratic incumbent lose his primary to a Miami lawyer. He won the seat handily and has held it despite the Fort Lauderdale area's Democratic tilt. For eight years he served on the Judiciary Committee, working on drug and crime bills; he backed the death penalty for major drug dealers, a federal drug czar, and the use of the military to interdict drug smuggling, which became law in 1988. In July 1988 he switched to Ways and Means. There he found himself on the spot while debating the catastrophic healthcare program, and forced to cast decisive votes in committee; a supporter in 1988, he came out for repeal in 1989. With Democrat Charles Stenholm of Texas, he sponsored the tax credit alternative to the ABC child care bill on the theory that parents, rather than government bureaucrats, can best make decisions on child care; Stenholm-Shaw failed 195–225, but had a major effect on the bill that eventually passed the House in 1990. After the 1992 campaign, he came out sharply against allowing more Haitian refugees in south Florida. He co-sponsored the bill in March 1993 to make Social Security taxes for domestics "more reasonable" and easier to pay.

Most recently Shaw has been the House Republicans' point man on welfare reform. He came forward in early 1993 with a bill that would take most people off welfare rolls after two years and require them to work for continued benefits, as Bill Clinton promised to do in the 1992 campaign. This was not much noticed; Republicans were in the minority and Shaw not especially well-known. But in 1995, Republicans had a majority and Shaw's bill, modified over two years, was the basis of the Contract With America's welfare reform. Partly because of pressure from Republican governors and Speaker Gingrich, Shaw's bill would replace 45 social programs with five state block grants, thus allowing states to experiment without seeking federal approval. But it did impose some requirements: states could not give cash benefits to mothers under 18; they would have to require most welfare recipients to work within two years and require proof of paternity to receive benefits. Welfare reform passed in the House in March 1995, but its harsher edges seemed likely to be modified by the Senate and perhaps vetoed by Bill Clinton.

The coastal strand that makes up the 22d District has mixed political feelings. Its many Jewish residents tend to be ardent liberal Democrats; its affluent gentile residents tend to be equally ardent, economically conservative Republicans. Shaw has faced articulate opposition here twice. In 1992 his opponent was Gwen Margolis, president of the Florida Senate for four years, a Democrat from North Miami Beach who grew up in Philadelphia, an idealistic liberal who has also been a practical politician and a successful real estate investor. This was one of the most expensive races in the country, waged mostly over TV on both Miami and West Palm Beach stations. Shaw carried Palm Beach and Broward Counties, and won 52%–37%. In 1994, against a Democrat who spent $265,000 of her own money on the campaign, he won 63%–37%. Well-financed opponents may back off for a while: with his Ways and Means subcommittee chairmanship, Shaw will have no problems raising money.

The People: Pop. 1990: 560,959; 31% age 65+; 83% White; 3% Black; 1% Asian; 2% Other; 13% Hispanic origin. Voting age pop.: 489,631; 2% Black; 11% Hispanic origin. Households: 44% married couple families; 11% married couple fams. w. children; 51% college educ.; median household income: $29,595; per capita income: $24,663; median gross rent: $545; median house value: $117,300.

1992 Presidential Vote

Clinton (D)	115,912	(45%)
Bush (R)	96,986	(38%)
Perot (I)	44,845	(17%)

1988 Presidential Vote

Bush (R)	132,871	(58%)
Dukakis (D)	97,669	(42%)

Rep. E. Clay Shaw, Jr. (R)

Elected 1980; b. Apr. 19, 1939, Miami; home, Ft. Lauderdale; Stetson U., B.A. 1961, U. of AL, M.B.A. 1963, Stetson U., J.D. 1966; Catholic; married (Emilie).

Career: Practicing atty., 1966–68; Ft. Lauderdale Chf. City Prosecutor, 1968–69; Assoc. Municipal Judge, 1969–71; Ft. Lauderdale City Comm., 1971–73; Ft. Lauderdale Vice Mayor, 1973–75, Mayor, 1975–80.

DC Office: 2267 RHOB 20515, 202-225-3026; Fax: 202-225-8398.

District Offices: 1512 E. Broward Blvd., #101, Ft. Lauderdale 33301, 305-522-1800.

Committees: *Ways & Means* (4th of 21 R): Human Resources (Chmn.); Trade.

Group Ratings

	ADA	ACLU	COPE	CFA	LCV	CON	NSI	COC	ACU	NTLC	CHC
1994	15	4	13	30	22	76	100	92	74	85	86
1993	10	—	17	30	36	69	—	91	92	—	—

National Journal Ratings

	1993 LIB — 1993 CONS		1994 LIB — 1994 CONS	
Economic	0%	— 88%	25%	— 74%
Social	19%	— 77%	29%	— 70%
Foreign	28%	— 70%	20%	— 79%

Key Votes of the 103d Congress

1. Clinton Deficit Plan	N	3. Brady Handgun Purchase Y	5. Lmt. UN Cmnd. of Forces Y
2. NAFTA	Y	4. Strike Race/Death Pnlty. Y	6. Cut Missile Funds	N

Key Votes of the 104th Congress

1. Congressional Compliance Y	6. Reform Crime Grant Y	11. Loser Pays Court Reform Y
2. Balanced Budget Amndmt. Y	7. National Security Act Y	12. Product Liability Reform Y
3. Bar Unfunded Mandates Y	8. Moratorium on Regs. Y	13. Welfare Reform Y
4. Pass Line Item Veto Y	9. Risk Assessment on Regs. Y	14. Term Limits Amndmt. Y
5. Relax Exclusionary Rule Y	10. Expnd. Priv. Prop. Rights Y	15. Tax Cuts Y

Election Results

1994 general	E. Clay Shaw, Jr. (R)	119,690	(63%)	($808,984)
	Hermine L. Wiener (D)	69,215	(37%)	($522,269)
1994 primary	E. Clay Shaw, Jr. (R)	24,252	(78%)	
	John K. Stahl (R)	6,925	(22%)	
1992 general	E. Clay Shaw, Jr. (R)	128,400	(52%)	($1,138,425)
	Gwen Margolis (D)	91,625	(37%)	($936,960)
	Richard Stephens (I)	15,469	(6%)	($47,234)
	Others	11,594	(5%)	

TWENTY-THIRD DISTRICT

Behind the high-rise condominiums that line the Atlantic Ocean from Palm Beach to Miami Beach, behind the waterways that separate the barrier islands from the mainland, usually a few blocks off the coast and often off U.S. 1, the old highway that brought tourists here in the 1940s and 1950s, are the black neighborhoods of South Florida's Gold Coast. They are gatherings of older stucco homes and commercial storefronts, ranging from enclaves of upper-middle-class residents to rundown slums. Overlooked by the state's tourists, these neighborhoods generally do not loom large in the minds of most residents. The Gold Coast's blacks are vastly outnumbered by whites in Palm Beach and Broward Counties and by Cuban-Americans in Dade County.

The 23d Congressional District of Florida, created by the May 1992 court redistricting, gathers together many of these black neighborhoods in a constituency that is geographically grotesque but ethnically defined. A little more than half its residents live in Broward County, with a little more than one-third living in Palm Beach County and the rest scattered—some in north Dade County, more in a geographically expansive but lightly populated segment that includes migrant worker camps around Lake Okeechobee and the old black neighborhood of Fort Pierce, a small city 120 miles north of Miami.

The congressman from the 23d District is Alcee Hastings, a former federal judge and the only member of the House previously impeached and removed from office by Congress. He won the race in a turbulent Democratic primary in 1992. Hastings is articulate and charming, the son of a hotel maid, who rose to an appointment as a federal judge by President Carter. He was impeached by the House of Representatives by a vote of 426–3 in 1988 and convicted and removed from office by the Senate by a vote of 69–26. The impeachment arose from allegations that Hastings conspired with a friend to accept $150,000 for giving two convicted swindlers a break in sentencing. Hastings was acquitted in a criminal trial in 1983, but the friend, Washington attorney William Borders, was convicted. In the House the case for impeachment was made by John Conyers, senior member of the Congressional Black Caucus. Hastings was undefensive about all this. In 1990, he ran an abortive campaign for governor, then lost in the primary for Florida secretary of state, and when the 23d was created sprang into that race.

Despite his heavy name recognition, he almost lost. In the first Democratic primary, the leader with 35% was Lois Frankel, a white Palm Beach County state Representative with a liberal record. Hastings, with 28%, narrowly edged out Bill Clark, also black, with 27%. Hastings was helped in the runoff campaign by a ruling by federal Judge Stanley Sporkin that his removal from office was invalid since the charges were not heard by the full Senate; the Supreme Court ruled to the contrary in a case involving another federal judge in January 1993, but by that time, Hastings was in Congress. Frankel continually cited Hastings's legal difficulties in the runoff campaign, to which Hastings replied,"The bitch is a racist." He won the runoff 58%–42%, with voting closely following racial lines. His stated platform was "the elimination of racism, ageism, anti-Semitism and sexism." In the general election, Hastings won 59%–31%. He was unopposed in 1994.

After the election, a Florida law student brought suit charging that Hastings was barred from office by his conviction. The suit was dismissed on the grounds that the student did not live in Hasting's district and therefore did not have the standing to file. Hastings entered the House smiling, saying "I'm not a vengeful person. I get on with life. I didn't enter here with my arms and my elbows flying. I came here to work . . . I've met with nothing but pleasant exchanges." In his first term, Hastings compiled a liberal voting record, supporting many Clinton Administration initiatives, ranging from NAFTA to the Clinton health reform plan. He also became vice chairman of the Congressional Black Caucus. In the 104th Congress, Hastings ran for the chairmanship of the embattled caucus, whose public funding had been cut off by the new Republican majority, but lost 23–15 to the quieter Donald Payne of New Jersey. He has been a vociferous opponent on the House floor of the Contract With America, including its product-liability reform provisions, arguing that there is no "explosion in punitive damages," and citing a U.S. Supreme Court study that said only 355 punitive damage awards in product liability cases have been awarded over the last 25 years. Hastings is safe in this seat, designed for a Democrat, so long as he avoids intraparty problems.

The People: Pop. 1990: 563,645; 5% rural; 13% age 65+; 39% White; 52% Black; 1% Asian; 2% Other; 9% Hispanic origin. Voting age pop.: 407,766; 46% Black; 9% Hispanic origin. Households: 43% married couple families; 19% married couple fams. w. children; 32% college educ.; median household income: $23,039; per capita income: $10,511; median gross rent: $486; median house value: $67,200.

1992 Presidential Vote			1988 Presidential Vote		
Clinton (D)	94,873	(62%)	Dukakis (D)	82,738	(59%)
Bush (R)	35,265	(23%)	Bush (R)	57,772	(41%)
Perot (I)	22,084	(14%)			

Rep. Alcee L. Hastings (D)

Elected 1992; b. Sept. 5, 1936, Altamonte Springs; home, Miramar; Fisk U., B.A. 1958, Howard U., 1958–60, FL A&M, J.D. 1963; Methodist; divorced.

Career: Practicing atty., 1964–77; Broward Cnty. Circuit Court Judge, 1977–79; Federal Judge, U.S. District Court, 1979–89.

DC Office: 1039 LHOB 20515, 202-225-1313; Fax: 202-226-0690; e-mail: hastings@hr.house.gov.

District Offices: 2701 W. Oakland Park Blvd., Ft. Lauderdale 33311, 305-733-2800.

Committees: *International Relations* (16th of 19 D): Africa. *Science* (15th of 23 D): Basic Research; Space and Aeronautics.

Group Ratings

	ADA	ACLU	COPE	CFA	LCV	CON	NSI	COC	ACU	NTLC	CHC
1994	80	90	88	70	81	28	25	36	7	8	0
1993	90	—	92	100	89	11	—	18	4	—	—

National Journal Ratings

	1993 LIB — 1993 CONS		1994 LIB — 1994 CONS	
Economic	78% —	12%	83% —	0%
Social	87% —	0%	94% —	0%
Foreign	79% —	16%	83% —	17%

Key Votes of the 103d Congress

1. Clinton Deficit Plan	Y	3. Brady Handgun Purchase	Y	5. Lmt. UN Cmnd. of Forces	N
2. NAFTA	Y	4. Strike Race/Death Pnlty.	N	6. Cut Missile Funds	N

Key Votes of the 104th Congress

1. Congressional Compliance	Y	6. Reform Crime Grant	N	11. Loser Pays Court Reform	N
2. Balanced Budget Amndmt.	N	7. National Security Act	*	12. Product Liability Reform	N
3. Bar Unfunded Mandates	N	8. Moratorium on Regs.	N	13. Welfare Reform	N
4. Pass Line Item Veto	N	9. Risk Assessment on Regs.	N	14. Term Limits Amndmt.	N
5. Relax Exclusionary Rule	N	10. Expnd. Priv. Prop. Rights	N	15. Tax Cuts	N

Election Results

1994 general	Alcee L. Hastings (D)............. unopposed		($217,742)
1994 primary	Alcee L. Hastings (D)............. unopposed		
1992 general	Alcee L. Hastings (D)................. 84,249	(59%)	($427,931)
	Ed Fielding (R)..................... 44,807	(31%)	($15,622)
	Al Woods (I)....................... 14,879	(10%)	($7,097)

GEORGIA

In almost every important sense, Georgia is the heart of the South. It is only the fourth largest southern state, but Texas and Florida are at the edges of the region and North Carolina off to the side. It was not the South's historic leader: Virginia and South Carolina were the leading southern colonies, and Georgia was the last of the 13 states to be established. Nor was it the leader of the Confederacy: the first shots were fired in South Carolina and the Confederacy's capitals established in Montgomery and Richmond. But Georgia's position in the South was geographically central, and, after General William Tecumseh Sherman's "march to the sea" from Atlanta, it became a symbol—the worst of the ravaged South determined to rise again. Georgia was the center of Atlanta editor Henry Grady's "New South" in the 1870s and it was the subject of Atlanta writer Margaret Mitchell's *Gone with the Wind*. It was the center as well of the civil rights South: for if the first bus boycott was in Montgomery, Alabama, and the first lunch counter sit-in in Greensboro, North Carolina, the central command post of the civil rights movement, the headquarters in the time of Martin Luther King, Jr., and his lieutenants, of black colleges and universities and of most civil rights organizations that sprang up in the 1960s, was Atlanta.

But Atlanta is not just a regional headquarters and a state capital: it is a world-class city. It is the home base of Jimmy Carter, who first as governor and then as president ratified the reconciliation of black and white, and now has set himself up as a mediator of conflicts all over the world. Atlanta is the headquarters of Coca-Cola—that most southern of great worldwide corporations, of southern regional scholarship, of much of the southern timber and paper industries, of southern banking and legal services, and of course for Atlanta's Hartsfield Airport, the central transportation hub of the South. Ted Turner's Cable News Network has arguably made Atlanta the world's news capital, with Moscow, Baghdad, Washington and Peking all tuned in to watch broadcasts beamed from CNN's Atlanta headquarters. And Atlanta is the site of the 1996 Summer Olympics, and is aiming to make this a triumphal exhibition of the success of Atlanta and Georgia, the South and the United States.

The Atlanta and Georgia that were awarded the Olympics are places of optimism and economic growth. This was not always so. For many years after the Civil War, rural Georgia was a land of poverty, and metro Atlanta, for all its showy successes, had a standard of living lower than in big northern metropolises. The industrialized South that Grady proclaimed turned out to be filled with low-wage textile mills. The unionized South that 1940s liberal Governor Ellis Arnall envisioned never materialized. The desegregated South that Martin Luther King and so many others risked their lives for exists today at the ballot box, in public accommodations and at the workplace; but racial divisions and distrust persist. Even so, the overall picture in Georgia is one of great and mostly unpredicted growth. This has been one of the fastest-growing states in the 1980s and 1990s, generating jobs and businesses at record-high levels, attracting newcomers from all over the country and the world.

Georgia's progress is uneven. Atlanta is the center of a robust service economy, but the rest of

Georgia remains manufacturing country, with textile mills, apparel factories, carpet mills, paper plants and sawmills—still low-wage industries. And even while metro Atlanta's edge cities boom, much of the central city is plagued by high rates of crime and fatherlessness. And in the rest of Georgia there is a vivid contrast between the booming cities on the interstates and back country counties whose economies are still stagnant.

Historically, politics split Georgia on regional lines, between metropolitan Atlanta, where whites were willing to accept the civil rights revolution, and rural Georgia, where whites added the Confederate stars and bars on the state flag and voted for segregationists like Lester Maddox (elected governor in 1966) and George Wallace (who carried Georgia for president in 1968). This historical division ended abruptly in 1970, when Carter was elected governor—the first time a statewide candidate conspicuously supported by blacks still got enough white votes to win. Carter placed a portrait of Martin Luther King in the Capitol, and became one of the first white rural southern politicians to officially accept and honor the civil rights revolution. As Georgia followed him, other issues arose and new alignments emerged. The outlying parts of the Atlanta donut counties filled up with affluent young whites, conservative on economics and sometimes on cultural issues, heavily Republican in their politics.

Meanwhile whites in rural Georgia have soured on government spending: once seen as aid to farmers who work hard, it now looks like aid to city-dwellers who don't work at all. So rural Georgia has moved rapidly toward the Republican column in the 1990s. In partisan terms, the two Georgias have converged. Rural blacks and both blacks and whites in the urban core of Atlanta are the Democratic base in the state; young voters outside Atlanta's I-285 Perimeter road and affluent whites in smaller cities are the Republican base. The balance is clearly shifting toward the Republicans.

While it is true that Georgia voted for Bill Clinton in 1992 and reelected Democratic Governor Zell Miller in 1994, Clinton beat Bush by only a .2% margin, and almost no one expects him to carry Georgia in 1996 in a two-way race. And Miller, with a forceful personality and 24 years in statewide office, a booming state economy and an opponent who was attacked on ethics grounds, won by only 51%–49%—significantly less than his 53%–45% margin in 1990. As for Georgia's two senators, one is a Republican and one a very conservative Democrat. Sam Nunn was first elected in 1972, when he conspicuously shunned the McGovern-Shriver ticket; his record of supporting the military as Chairman of the Armed Services Committee gives him strength far beyond his party. Georgia's other Senate seat was won 51%–49% by liberal Democrat Wyche Fowler in 1986 and he led 49%–48% on Election Day 1992. But Georgia law requires a runoff when no one has an absolute majority, and in November 1992 Republican Paul Coverdell won 51%–49% It is almost as if Georgia has been shifting Republican by a certain amount each month.

And that trend is apparent in the Republicans' statewide percentage in U.S. House races, which rose from 39% in 1990 to 45% in 1992 and 55% in 1994. Georgia's House delegation in the 102d Congress had eight white Democrats, one black Democrat and one Republican, Newt Gingrich. In the 104th Congress it had zero white Democrats (after the last one switched parties), three black Democrats and eight Republicans, including the Speaker of the House, who was their unquestioned leader; not one of the voting Republicans voted against any piece of the Contract With America, a remarkable display of party discipline to match the remarkable shift of partisan balance. Georgia has become a two-party state; the question is whether it ever will be a one-party state again, this time Republican.

Governor. Zell Miller is a political veteran with a keen sense of public opinion. He grew up in the mountains of north Georgia, was elected to the Georgia Senate in 1960, at 28; he worked for Lester Maddox in his last two years as governor, ran the state Democratic Party when Jimmy Carter was governor, was elected lieutenant governor in 1974 and held the office 16 years. In 1990 he finally ran for governor. In the Democratic primary he faced former Atlanta Mayor, Congressman and Ambassador to the United Nations Andrew Young; in this first statewide contest with a major black candidate, Miller won 62%–38%. In the general he beat Republican

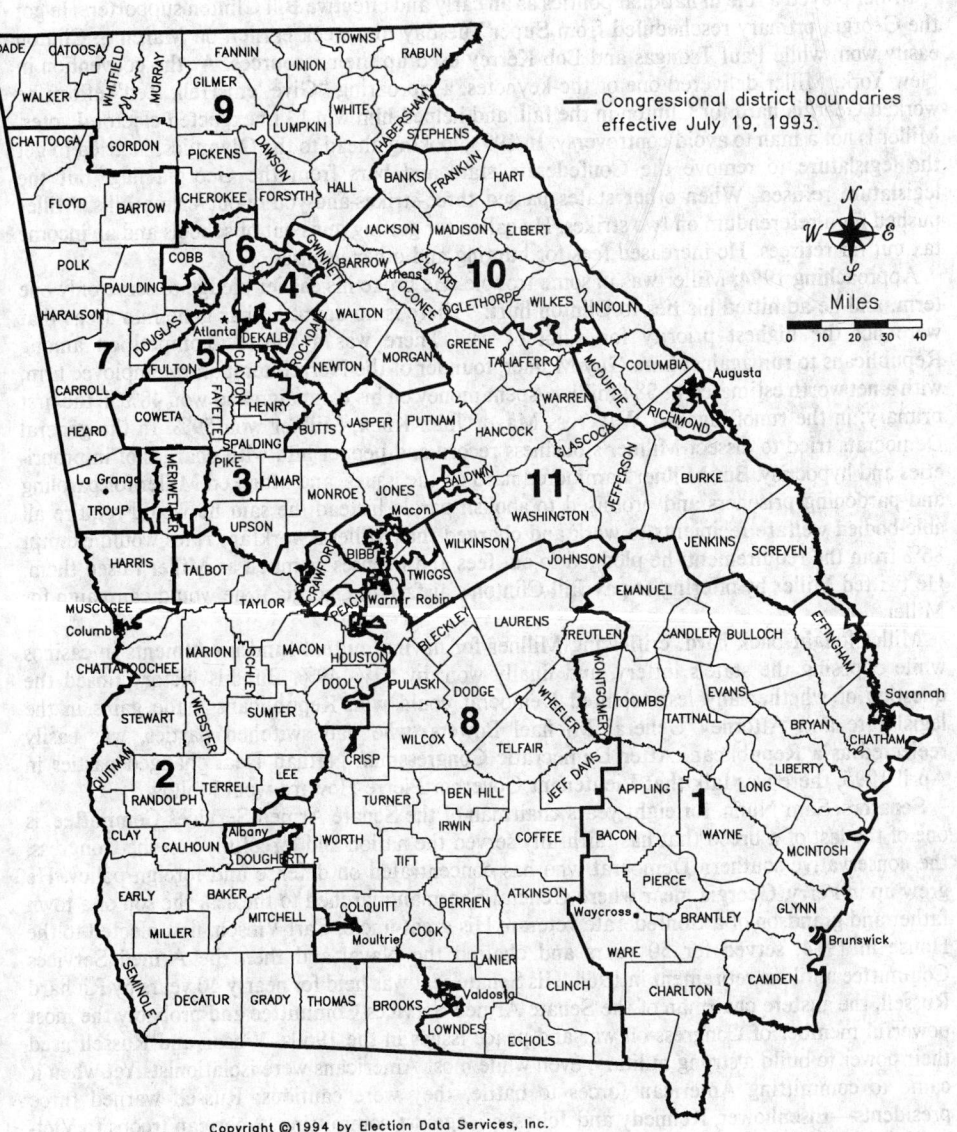

Congressional district boundaries effective July 19, 1993.

Miles
0 10 20 30 40

Johnny Isakson 53%–45%. He won by advocating a state lottery for increased education spending. He spoke in populist tones natural to him but, perhaps, was also inspired by—or helped inspire—consultant James Carville. In office Miller pushed through the lottery, appointed the first black woman to the state Supreme Court, strengthened drunk driving laws and started boot camps for first-time offenders.

Miller played a role in national politics as an early and effective Bill Clinton supporter. He got the Georgia primary rescheduled from Super Tuesday to a week earlier, on March 3; Clinton easily won, while Paul Tsongas and Bob Kerrey used up their resources. At the convention in New York, Miller delivered one of the keynotes, a riproaring "Give 'em Hell, Zell" effort; he worked Georgia hard for Clinton in the fall, and helped him win 13 unexpected electoral votes. Miller is not a man to avoid controversy. In 1993, looking ahead to the Olympics, he tried to get the legislature to remove the Confederate stars and bars from the Georgia flag; but the legislature refused. When other states passed three-strikes-and-you're-out crime bills, Miller pushed for a referendum on two strikes. He called for getting guns out of schools and an income tax cut for retirees. He increased fees for hunting and other licenses.

Approaching 1994, Miller was in some trouble. He broke his earlier pledge to serve only one term, and he admitted his ties to Clinton hurt: "There is no doubt he has gone into areas that were not the highest priority for a lot of us." There was a spirited competition among Republicans to run against him. Guy Millner, founder of the Norrell temporary employee firm, with a net worth estimated at $84 million, spent money on his campaign and won 48% in the first primary; in the runoff against Waycross Mayor John Knox, Millner won 59%. In the general Democrats tried to dissect Millner's business record and pepper him with charges of improprieties and hypocrisy. But Millner hammered hard on the issues, and attacked Miller for paroling and pardoning prisoners and promised to abolish parole instead; he said he would require all able-bodied welfare recipients to work and charged that Miller's workfare rules would exempt 86% from the requirement; he pledged to cut fees and licenses as much as Miller raised them. He twitted Miller by offering to pay Bill Clinton's airfare to Georgia if he would campaign for Miller.

Miller fought back hard, criticizing Millner for having mutual fund investments in casinos while opposing the state's lottery, and finally won, by 51%–49%. But his victory raised the question of whether any less talented Democrat could win. Republicans made gains in the legislature and Attorney General Michael Bowers, who had switched parties, was easily reelected as a Republican. After Democratic Congressman Nathan Deal changed parties in April 1995, there was talk that Lieutenant Governor Pierre Howard would follow.

Senators. Sam Nunn, for eight years chairman of the Senate Armed Services Committee, is one of the last of a breed that has faithfully served the nation and forcefully run the Congress, the conservative southern Democrat who has concentrated on defense and foreign policy. He grew up in Perry, Georgia, near where General Sherman marched to the sea, the son of a town father and grandson of a Confederate veteran. His great-uncle, Carl Vinson, first elected to the House in 1914, served for 50 years and chaired the Naval and then the Armed Services Committee until his retirement in 1964. His Senate seat was held for nearly 40 years by Richard Russell, the austere chairman of the Senate Armed Services Committee and probably the most powerful member of Congress on war and peace issues in the 1950s. Vinson and Russell used their power to build a strong military, even while most Americans were isolationist. Yet when it came to committing American forces to battle, they were cautious; Russell warned three presidents—Eisenhower, Kennedy and Johnson—against committing American troops to Vietnam. They also carefully hoarded their own power. Vinson was once mentioned as a candidate for secretary of defense; his apocryphal reply: "I'd rather run the Pentagon from up here." In many ways, he and Russell did; and to some extent Sam Nunn has as well, or has tried to.

Nunn's first move, after being elected senator in 1972 at 34 by beating a more liberal Democrat in the primary and a more conservative Republican in the general, was to get a seat on the Armed Services Committee. He studied military issues hard, worked quietly and made a solidly conservative voting record that protected him against criticism in rural Georgia. He chaired the Manpower Subcommittee in the 1970s, where he helped to reform the services and shape the reserve force structure and call-up procedures that proved themselves in the Gulf war in 1991. He supported the Carter defense buildup in 1979 and the bigger Reagan defense buildup beginning in 1981. He became ranking minority member on Armed Services in September 1983, when Henry Jackson died, and seemed content to work on defense issues as part of a bipartisan coalition. But around 1986 he became more partisan, campaigning against his Republican colleague Mack Mattingly, who lost to liberal Wyche Fowler, compiling a less conservative voting record. Ambition may have accounted for this: the only way Nunn could become Armed Services Chairman was if Democrats won a majority, as they did with his help in the 1986 election; the only way he could ever be president was as a Democrat, and indeed he did mull running in 1987 and preserved his options for a later national run by campaigning with Michael Dukakis in Hawkinsville, just down U.S. 341 from Perry.

What ideas animate Nunn? For much of the 1980s he was categorized as a hawk because he favored increased defense spending, fought for the B-2 stealth bomber and urged military readiness and modernization. But he has been cautious about actually using military power and he has been careful, as Carl Vinson may be noting with a smile, in preserving the prerogatives of Congress. He pushed for two-year DOD authorizations and supported Dick Armey's base-closing bill—both ways to rationalize defense spending. He fought hard against Ronald Reagan's interpretation of the ABM treaty, against George Bush's nomination of John Tower to be Defense Secretary and against Bill Clinton's promise to allow gays in the military—all assertions of Congress's, and Nunn's, power. Bush's mistrust and Nunn's partisanship form a backdrop to their actions and interactions in the Gulf war.

In July 1990 Nunn predicted that Saddam Hussein might do something that would require U.S. military action, and he supported the initial deployment of troops. But he was obviously angry about not being consulted on the dispatch of 250,000 more troops, two days after the November election, and he shared the caution many military leaders have had about armed conflict since Vietnam. In November Nunn orchestrated Armed Services hearings clearly stacked against military action and featuring testimony from advocates of caution like former Joint Chiefs Chairmen William Crowe and David Jones, leaving unstated the case for the other side. "The last thing we need," said this son of the land of Sherman's march, "is to have a war over there, a bloody war, and have American boys being sent and brought back in body bags and yet not have the American people behind them." But Nunn's initiative failed to persuade Bush to back off, and Nunn's own articulate opposition to military action made not only unanimity but a Senate majority difficult to attain. The Gulf war resolution did pass the Senate 52–47, however, and the rapid American military victory proved false Nunn's projections of military difficulties; he was proved far less prescient than House Armed Services Chairman Les Aspin. Nunn announced within days that he wasn't thinking about running for president in 1992 under any conceivable circumstances—something quite different from what he had said before January 1991 (when political reporters noted that he had switched his position on abortion and resigned from private clubs).

Nunn continued to stake out independent positions and to counter the executive branch during the Clinton years. Despite their common activity in the Democratic Leadership Council, Nunn did not support Clinton strenuously in the Georgia presidential primary as Governor Zell Miller did. In June 1992, after the Los Angeles riot, he called for using the military to assist civilians on "such needs as deteriorating infrastructure, the lack of role models for tens of thousands," and other domestic problems. In October 1992, he and Republican Pete Domenici presented a $2 trillion, 10-year plan to balance the budget, with a consumption tax to encourage savings and $376 billion in tax increases; it would have been shunned by Bush if he had been reelected and was ignored by Clinton and the Democratic Congress. Even before Clinton took office, Nunn forcefully opposed Clinton's campaign promise to end the ban on gays in the military, arguing with many military leaders that it would erode unit cohesion and the discipline necessary to weld together troops who must be ready to face combat and death. After Clinton backtracked on his promise, Nunn put forth a "Don't Ask, Don't Tell, Don't Investigate" compromise that was similar to Clinton's final order. Similarly, Nunn had concerns about Clinton's stimulus package and and voted against his budget and tax package. Nunn did cooperate with the administration in framing the law for national service, which he and Barbara Mikulski had been backing for some time. And Nunn staged investigations of the student loan program and health insurance industry, which generally helped Clinton proposals.

Working with Richard Lugar, Nunn supported aid to Russia and in December 1993 called for a cooperative rather than confrontational approach to Russia and opposed eastward expansion of NATO; he wanted to hold open the possibility of including Russia and Ukraine in an expanded NATO. He and Lugar also worked hard and effectively in getting the former Soviet republics, especially Ukraine, to relinquish their nuclear weapons. As on the Gulf war, he was hesitant about military involvement abroad. He called for rethinking our position in Somalia in summer 1993, but tried to calm demands for an immediate pullout after American Rangers were killed in October 1993. He was cautious about committing troops to Haiti, and agreed to accompany Jimmy Carter to negotiate with General Raoul Cedras, and suggested Colin Powell as the third member of the delegation. He opposed taking money from military operations to fund military retirees' benefits.

The Republican victory of course cost Nunn his chairmanship, but his conservative stands on many issues continued, usually against the preponderance of his own party. He voted for the balanced budget amendment after getting rhetorical assurance that the courts couldn't increase taxes or cut spending. He called for cuts in Medicare to balance the budget. Nunn has remained very popular in Georgia, and voters seem to distinguish his positions from those of national Democrats. But he must have been dismayed by the disappearance of conservative Democrats from the Georgia House delegation and by the loss of his chairmanship. In early 1995 there was speculation that he would not run again in 1996, when he turns 58, or promises that he would have serious Republican opposition for the first time since 1972. He will be the favorite if he runs; if not, Republicans will have a good chance to pick up the seat.

Georgia's junior Senator, Paul Coverdell, won his seat by the narrowest margin and in the last election of 1992, and quickly moved out onto the leading edge of political change. Like many newly elected Republicans, he is a small businessman, though he got a degree in journalism and served in the Army in Okinawa, Taiwan and Japan. In 1960, at 21, he started working in his parents' insurance marketing business in Atlanta. In 1970, when the Republican party seemed to be rising in the South, he was elected to the state Senate; in 1974, when the Republican rise seemed stalled, he became Minority Leader (of 5 Republicans versus 51 Democrats). He was Republican state chairman in the mid-1980s, supported George Bush in 1988 and served as Peace Corps Director from 1989 to 1991, leading the Peace Corps into Eastern Europe and Russia.

In 1992 he ran for the Senate, and battled through four elections before winning by 1%. In the July primary he ran first, with former U.S. Attorney and now 7th District Congressman Bob Barr just ahead of Waycross Mayor John Knox. In the August runoff, Coverdell beat Barr by 1,500 votes. In the general he faced incumbent Wyche Fowler, a politically savvy liberal who had represented the black-majority 5th District and then won statewide over Republican incumbent Mack Mattingly in 1986. Fowler had beaten Coverdell once before—in a 1977 House special election, in which Fowler had 40%, John Lewis 29% and Coverdell 22%—and, as a top lieutenant to Majority Leader George Mitchell, had much more money. But Coverdell attacked Fowler for opposing the Gulf war, supporting defense cuts, backing the congressional pay raise and defending the House bank ("Thankfully we have a bank that doesn't zap me when I bounce a check because we have our own bank," he told lawyers in his divorce case). Fowler's role as a key negotiator of the 1990 budget summit agreement was no asset. Coverdell's most memorable tactic was his "grandmother" ad, showing 73-year-old Margie Goode Lopp of Cuthbert, Georgia, sitting on a swing and singing a jingle she composed after being repelled by

Fowler's ads: "Let's put Paul Coverdell in the Senate and put Wyche Fowler out," it began. Fowler led in November, but only by 49%–48%, less than the absolute majority required by Georgia law; so there was a runoff November 24. Bill Clinton and Al Gore campaigned for Fowler; Coverdell got enthusiastic support from national and local Republicans, the Libertarian candidate who had deadlocked the first race, the Georgia Ross Perot organization, and from elite suburban Republicans who liked his pro-choice stand on abortion and the Christian Coalition pleased by his pledge to vote against the federal Freedom of Choice Act. Both national parties poured $1 million of soft money into the race, but Coverdell had the momentum. The runoff was the fourth straight time in which Georgia was almost evenly split on this Senate seat, as it was almost evenly split in the 1992 presidential race. But this time the Republican won, 51%–49%. Coverdell carried the suburban ring around Atlanta and also most of rural north Georgia and the rural counties in the southeast—economically booming areas like next-door South Carolina. He lost in the central and southwest parts of the state, economically ailing like Alabama. A lawsuit against the runoff law fizzled.

Despite his moderate credentials—Bush, the Peace Corps, pro-choice on abortion—Coverdell was a Contract With America Republican two years before the Contract. "The American people want a smaller and more efficient government, they want fewer economic pressures on their families and businesses from the government, and they want the federal government to be their partner and not their boss," he said. He quickly supported the balanced budget amendment and line-item veto; inspired by the Clinton budget and tax package, he sponsored a constitutional amendment to ban retroactive tax increases. He successfully stopped the Postal Service from "bullying" people with inspection audits and fines of businesses for using private express mail. He led the fight for release of secret Clinton healthcare task force documents. He called for repeal of the motor voter law because of its unfunded mandate, and called for relief from mandates in which the federal government forces local property taxes to be paid for complying with federal regulations. He was early in opposition to U.S. troops serving under United Nations command. He started a Repeal Initiative to encourage government officials and citizens out in the country to identify ways to cut government. Inside the Senate, he worked closely with Bob Dole to urge sympathetic interest groups to promote the Republican agenda and with Al D'Amato to boost party fundraising. Nevertheless, he announced his support early for Phil Gramm for president and is his National Vice Chair for the campaign.

It is too early to say how Coverdell will fare when his seat comes up in 1998, but this Atlanta businessman—in a state long suspicious of both businessmen and Atlanta—certainly seems to be in tune with where most Georgians were in November 1994.

Presidential politics. Georgia has voted Democratic the last three times Democrats ran a southerner with a moderate reputation—1976, 1980 and 1992—but the last time by a very close margin; in other circumstances, it seems to be heavily Republican.

Georgia's 1992 presidential primary was scheduled for one week before Super Tuesday at the insistence of Governor Zell Miller, who was intent on helping Bill Clinton. It worked: Clinton had a handsome victory to balance off his defeats the same day in Maryland and Colorado. At the same time, George Bush beat Pat Buchanan 64%–36%, not a great show of strength for Bush, but a clear indication that Buchanan would not be able to carry any southern states. Since there is no party registration, turnout gives some suggestion of each party's strength; the trend clearly favors Republicans. Their presidential primary turnout increased from 200,000 in 1980 to 400,000 in 1988 and 454,000 in 1992. Democratic primary turnout fell from 684,000 in 1984 to 612,000 in 1988 and 454,600 in 1992. The 1992 turnout turned out to be a good forecast of the close presidential and senatorial races in November. Will primary turnout in 1996 be a similarly good indicator?

Congressional districting. Georgia's robust growth in the 1980s meant that it gained a House seat for the 1990s, its first gain since the 1880s. This produced a robust redistricting fight. Georgia had just one black-majority district in the 1980s, in Atlanta, and the legislature drew another, in the southwest corner of the state; the Bush Justice Department pressured it to produce another, and the result was the elongated 11th, which goes from Atlanta to Savannah on something like the route of Sherman's March to the Sea in 1864. Speaker Tom Murphy also maneuvered to defeat Georgia's then only Republican congressman, Newt Gingrich, but to no avail, as Gingrich moved to a heavily Republican new seat in the north Atlanta suburbs.

The plan had two unintended consequences: huge Republican gains and a lawsuit that threatened the third black-majority seat. Republicans won four of the eight white-majority seats in 1992, two because black voters in adjacent areas were cordoned off into black-majority districts; they won three more of the white-majority seats in 1994, two of them seats made more Republican by the black-majority district lines; and they won the 9th district when Nathan Deal switched parties in April 1995. The lawsuit challenging the whole plan was argued before the Supreme Court in April 1995 and was expected to be decided by summer. If the plan is overturned, that will threaten the 11th's Cynthia McKinney, but given the 1994 results it is hard to see where a new white-majority Democratic district will be created; perhaps in DeKalb County east of Atlanta.

The People: Est. Pop. 1994: 7,055,000; Pop. 1990: 6,478,216, up 8.9% 1990–1994. 2.7% of U.S. total, 11th largest; 37% rural. Median age: 31.6 years. 10.1% 65 years and over. 71.0% White, 27.0% Black, 1.7% Hispanic origin, 1.2% Asian. Households: 55.2% married couple families; 27% married couple fams. w. children; 41% college educ.; median household income: $29,021; per capita income: $13,631; 64.9% owner occupied housing; median house value: $71,300; median monthly rent: $344. 6.9% Unemployment. 1994 Voting age pop.: 5,159,000. 1994 Turnout: 1,544,247; 30% of VAP. Registered voters (1994): 3,003,527; no party registration.

Political Lineup: Governor, Zell Miller (D); Lt. Gov., Pierre Howard (D); Secy. of State, Max Cleland (D); Atty. Gen., Michael J. Bowers (R); Auditor, Claude L. Vickers (D). State Senate, 56 (35 D and 21 R); State House of Representatives, 180 (114 D and 66 R). Senators, Sam Nunn (D) and Paul Coverdell (R). Representatives, 11 (8 R and 3 D).

1992 Presidential Vote

Clinton (D)	1,008,966	(43%)
Bush (R)	995,252	(43%)
Perot (I)	309,657	(13%)

1992 Democratic Presidential Primary

Clinton	259,907	(57%)
Tsongas	109,148	(24%)
Brown	36,808	(8%)
Kerrey	22,033	(5%)
Other	9,479	(2%)
Uncommitted	17,256	(4%)

1988 Presidential Vote

Bush (R)	1,081,331	(60%)
Dukakis (D)	714,792	(39%)

1992 Republican Presidential Primary

Bush	291,905	(64%)
Buchanan	162,085	(36%)

GOVERNOR

Gov. Zell Miller (D)

Elected 1990, term expires Jan. 1999; b. Feb. 24, 1932, Young Harris; home, Young Harris; U. of GA, A.B. 1957, M.A. 1958; Methodist; married (Shirley).

Career: Marine Corps, 1953–56; Young Harris Mayor, 1960–63; GA Senate, 1960–64; Dir., St. Board of Probation, Personnel Officer, GA Dept. of Corrections, 1965–66; Exec. Secy., Gov. Lester Maddox, 1969–71; Exec. Dir., GA Dem. Party, 1971–73; GA Lt. Gov., 1974–90.

Office: 203 State Capitol, Atlanta 30334, 404-656-1776; Fax: 404-656-2612.

Election Results

1994 gen.	Zell Miller (D)	788,926	(51%)
	Guy W. Millner (R)	756,371	(49%)
	Others	31	
1994 prim.	Zell Miller (D)	321,963	(70%)
	Jim Boyd (D)	78,444	(17%)
	Mark Tate (D)	30,749	(7%)
	Charles Poag (D)	28,623	(6%)
1990 gen.	Zell Miller (D)	766,662	(53%)
	Johnny Isakson (R)	645,625	(45%)
	Other	37,365	(3%)

SENATORS

Sen. Sam Nunn (D)

Elected 1972, seat up 1996; b. Sept. 8, 1938, Perry; home, Perry; Emory U., A.B. 1960, LL.B. 1962; United Methodist; married (Colleen).

Career: Coast Guard, 1959–60, Coast Guard Reserves, 1960–68; Farmer; Legal Cnsl., U.S. House Armed Svcs. Cmte., 1962–63; Practicing atty., 1963–72; GA House of Reps., 1968–72.

DC Office: 303 DSOB 20510, 202-224-3521; Fax: 202-224-0072.

State Offices: 75 Spring St. SW, #1700, Atlanta 30303, 404-331-4811; 915 Main St., Perry 31069, 912-987-1458; 130 Fed. Bldg., Gainesville 30501, 404-532-9976; 600 E. 1st St., Rome 30161, 404-291-5696; and 120 Barnard St., Savannah 31069, 912-944-4300.

Committees: *Armed Services* (RMM of 10 D): *Governmental Affairs* (2nd of 7 D): Investigations (RMM). *Small Business* (2nd of 9 D).

Group Ratings

	ADA	ACLU	COPE	CFA	LCV	CON	NSI	COC	ACU	NTLC	CHC
1994	50	21	25	33	46	44	100	61	33	40	43
1993	45	—	55	60	56	50	—	82	36	—	—

National Journal Ratings

	1993 LIB	—	1993 CONS	1994 LIB	—	1994 CONS
Economic	44%	—	55%	42%	—	57%
Social	45%	—	52%	41%	—	58%
Foreign	32%	—	60%	46%	—	51%

Key Votes of the 103d Congress

1. Clinton Deficit Plan	N	3. Brady Handgun Purchase	Y	5. Lmt. UN Cmnd. of Forces	N
2. NAFTA	Y	4. Strike Race/Death Pnlty.	Y	6. Cut Missile Funds	N

Key Votes of the 104th Congress

1. Congressional Compliance	Y	3. Balanced Budget Amndt.	Y	5. Product Liability Reform	Y
2. Bar Unfunded Mandates	Y	4. Pass Line Item Veto	N	6. FY96 Budget	Y

Election Results

1990 general	Sam Nunn (D)	.... unopposed		($1,214,695)
1990 primary	Sam Nunn (D)	.... unopposed		
1984 general	Sam Nunn (D)	 1,344,104	(80%)	($843,891)
	Mike Hicks (R)	 337,196	(20%)	

Sen. Paul Coverdell (R)

Elected 1992, seat up 1998; b. Jan. 20, 1939, Des Moines, IA; home, Atlanta; U. of MO, B.A., 1960; Methodist; married (Nancy).

Career: Army, 1962–64; Businessman, Coverdell & Co. Inc., Chmn., 1991–92; GA Senate, 1971–89, Minority Ldr., 1974–89; Chmn., GA Repub. Party, 1985–87; Dir., Peace Corps, 1989–91.

DC Office: 200 RSOB 20510, 202-224-3643; Fax: 202-228-3783; e-mail: senator_coverdell@coverdell.senate.gov.

State Offices: 100 Colony Sq., #300, 1175 Peachtree St., NE, Atlanta 30361, 404-347-2202.

Committees: *Agriculture, Nutrition & Forestry* (7th of 10 R): Forestry, Conservation and Rural Revitalization; Production and Price Competitiveness. *Foreign Relations* (5th of 10 R): East Asian and Pacific Affairs; International Operations; Western Hemisphere and Peace Corps Affairs (Chmn). *Indian Affairs* (8th of 9 R). *Small Business* (4th of 10 R).

Group Ratings

	ADA	ACLU	COPE	CFA	LCV	CON	NSI	COC	ACU	NTLC	CHC
1994	5	16	0	17	8	94	100	95	100	88	100
1993	10	—	0	20	13	86	—	100	92	—	—

National Journal Ratings

	1993 LIB	—	1993 CONS	1994 LIB	—	1994 CONS
Economic	0%	—	87%	0%	—	88%
Social	10%	—	88%	0%	—	85%
Foreign	24%	—	71%	16%	—	82%

Key Votes of the 103d Congress

1. Clinton Deficit Plan	N	3. Brady Handgun Purchase	N	5. Lmt. UN Cmnd. of Forces	Y
2. NAFTA	Y	4. Strike Race/Death Pnlty.	Y	6. Cut Missile Funds	N

Key Votes of the 104th Congress

1. Congressional Compliance Y   3. Balanced Budget Amndt. Y   5. Product Liability Reform Y
2. Bar Unfunded Mandates Y   4. Pass Line Item Veto   Y   6. FY96 Budget   Y

Election Results

1992 runoff	Paul Coverdell (R)	635,114	(51%)	($3,193,774)
	Wyche Fowler (D)	618,877	(49%)	($4,894,620)
1992 general	Wyche Fowler (D)	1,108,416	(49%)	
	Paul Coverdell (R)	1,073,282	(48%)	
	Others	69,889	(3%)	
1992 runoff	Paul Coverdell (R)	80,435	(50%)	
	Bob Barr (R)	78,887	(50%)	
1992 primary	Paul Coverdell (R)	100,016	(37%)	
	Bob Barr (R)	65,471	(24%)	
	John Knox (R)	64,514	(24%)	
	Charles Tanksley (R)	32,590	(12%)	
	Other	7,352	(1%)	
1986 general	Wyche Fowler (D)	623,705	(51%)	($2,779,297)
	Mack Mattingly (R)	601,235	(49%)	($5,119,249)

FIRST DISTRICT

Georgia's South Atlantic coast, long one of the poorest parts of the country, has been booming in recent years. The area was settled by James Oglethorpe as Britain's 13th coastal colony in the 1730s as a refuge and reformatory for convicts. It did not take long for the sea islands and lowlands along the wide rivers and inlets to become plantation country. Savannah, the state's first capital, was by the 1830s one of America's great cotton ports and, during the Civil War, the site of Confederate forts. After the Civil War, the area became impoverished, with many poor blacks still speaking Gullah dialects. Savannah languished, living off paper mills and chemical plants. Then, a few decades ago, preservationists started restoring houses and churches on the grid punctuated by 24 squares that Oglethorpe had laid out more than 200 years before. Today, Savannah, which calls itself the Hostess City of the South, is one of the most graciously preserved cities in the country. On the coast, some of the sea islands were preserved too, from the time they had been winter homes of the rich before they discovered Florida. Other islands filled up with expensive houses and condominiums. Today, prosperity has come rushing down I-95. The ports of Savannah and Brunswick doubled their tonnage, while the resorts of St. Simon's Island and Jekyll Island boomed. The tourism industry has exploded in Savannah following the publication of John Berendt's *Midnight in the Garden of Good and Evil* in 1994, a best-selling book that explores the eccentric characters in Savannah and has brought hordes of Yankees to the old port city—boosting tourism by 46%.

The 1st Congressional District of Georgia includes all the state's Atlantic coast and goes 50 or so miles inland, through cotton and tobacco fields and softwood forests. There are more exotic products here as well: Toombs County is the home of the fragrant Vidalia onion that folks say are so sweet that you can eat 'em like an apple, while Claxton in tiny Evans County has for nearly a century been home to two of the nation's prime fruitcake makers. Not all of Savannah is in the 1st District; black precincts are connected by a narrow corridor along the Savannah River to the black-majority 11th District, which extends all the way to Atlanta. The lawsuit challenging Georgia's district boundaries, if successful, would presumably return heavily black precincts of Savannah to the 1st. Though the counties in the 1st District are ancestrally Democratic, white voters here—more than 75% after redistricting—are conservative on cultural and military issues. That, plus coastal prosperity, has made this area Republican at the top of the ticket and even in statewide contests; the district voted for Republicans George Bush and Paul Coverdell in their statewide races in 1992.

The 1st District, represented by nothing but Democrats since Reconstruction, is now represented by a Republican, Jack Kingston, elected in 1992 when moderate Democrat Lindsay Thomas retired to work on the Atlanta Olympics. Kingston was an insurance agent in Savannah, elected to the Georgia House in 1984, where he was part of a vastly outnumbered Republican minority. There he sponsored an uninsured motorists' act and a bill allowing businesses to buy health insurance and workmen's compensation in a single policy. In 1992 he ran for Congress, winning the Republican nomination easily. His Democratic opponent was Barbara Christmas, a school principal in four counties over the years. Kingston won decisively—58%–42%, with a 2–1 margin in his home base of Savannah and Chatham County (though the results would have been about even if the 11th District portion of Savannah had remained). Kingston carried most of the rural counties as well, picking up the Christian, antiabortion vote.

On Capitol Hill Kingston joined in the Republicans' efforts to cut the budget and reform the welfare system and took the Gingrich route of speaking frequently during House special orders to help set the national partisan battle lines. He has also pushed to promote agricultural exports. He serves on the Appropriations Committee, where one of his three subcommittee assignments is Agriculture, Rural Development, Food and Drug Administration and Related Agencies—a good slot for this district. He has generally walked in lockstep with the Republican leadership, parting company with them only in opposing the North American Free Trade Agreement and the General Agreement on Tariffs and Trade. He criticized the high cost of implementing GATT and the loss of U.S. clout in joining a one-country, one-vote World Trade Organization, where it would have no more influence than the smallest country.

The affable, youthful-looking Kingston returned home virtually every weekend and held town meetings throughout the district. His strong victory in 1992 evidently discouraged any strong Democrat from running in 1994. Kingston won with 77% over a Democrat who called for abolition of the income tax and for tax deductions to companies with union contracts.

The People: Pop. 1990: 589,634; 45% rural; 11% age 65+; 76% White; 23% Black; 1% Asian; 1% Other; 2% Hispanic origin. Voting age pop.: 429,159; 20% Black; 1% Hispanic origin. Households: 60% married couple families; 30% married couple fams. w. children; 36% college educ.; median household income: $25,265; per capita income: $11,642; median gross rent: $373; median house value: $58,900.

1992 Presidential Vote			1988 Presidential Vote		
Bush (R)	88,703	(47%)	Bush (R)	97,277	(65%)
Clinton (D)	71,770	(38%)	Dukakis (D)	52,545	(35%)
Perot (I)	28,292	(15%)			

Rep. Jack Kingston (R)

Elected 1992; b. Apr. 24, 1955, Bryan, TX; home, Savannah; U. of GA, B.S. 1978; Episcopalian; married (Libby).

Career: Insurance agent, 1979–92; GA House of Reps., 1984–92.

DC Office: 1507 LHOB 20515, 202-225-5831; Fax: 202-226-2269.

District Offices: Enterprise Bldg., 6605 Abercorn St., #102, Savannah 31405, 912-352-0101; Statesboro Fed. Bldg., #220, Statesboro 30458, 912-489-8797; Thomas Henry Clarke Bldg., 208 Tebeau St., Waycross 31501, 912-287-1180; and Brunswick Fed. Bldg., 805 Gloucester St., #304, Brunswick 31520, 912-265-9010.

Committees: *Appropriations* (25th of 32 R): Agriculture, Rural Development, FDA, and Related Agencies; District of Columbia; Treasury, Postal Service, and General Government.

Group Ratings

	ADA	ACLU	COPE	CFA	LCV	CON	NSI	COC	ACU	NTLC	CHC
1994	5	13	11	20	17	65	80	83	100	93	100
1993	10	—	8	10	14	91	—	91	100	—	—

National Journal Ratings

	1993 LIB — 1993 CONS		1994 LIB — 1994 CONS	
Economic	12% —	87%	0% —	80%
Social	0% —	89%	0% —	89%
Foreign	24% —	72%	0% —	88%

Key Votes of the 103d Congress

1. Clinton Deficit Plan	N	3. Brady Handgun Purchase	N	5. Lmt. UN Cmnd. of Forces	Y
2. NAFTA	N	4. Strike Race/Death Pnlty.	Y	6. Cut Missile Funds	N

Key Votes of the 104th Congress

1. Congressional Compliance	Y	6. Reform Crime Grant	Y	11. Loser Pays Court Reform	Y
2. Balanced Budget Amndmt.	Y	7. National Security Act	Y	12. Product Liability Reform	Y
3. Bar Unfunded Mandates	Y	8. Moratorium on Regs.	Y	13. Welfare Reform	Y
4. Pass Line Item Veto	Y	9. Risk Assessment on Regs.	Y	14. Term Limits Amndmt.	Y
5. Relax Exclusionary Rule	Y	10. Expnd. Priv. Prop. Rights	Y	15. Tax Cuts	Y

Election Results

1994 general	Jack Kingston (R)	88,788	(77%)	($296,202)
	Raymond Beckworth (D)	27,197	(23%)	
1994 primary	Jack Kingston (R)	unopposed		
1992 general	Jack Kingston (R)	103,932	(58%)	($418,883)
	Barbara Christmas (D)	75,808	(42%)	($332,319)

SECOND DISTRICT

Southwest Georgia, pine lands and cotton fields and peanut acreage, is hallowed Democratic ground: Jimmy Carter was born here in October 1924, the same month that Franklin Roosevelt first visited the nearby bedraggled resort of Warm Springs, where he would build his little White House and where he would ultimately die in 1945. This is hardscrabble country: as recently as World War II, most people outside towns lived in clapboard cabins without power or running water, eking a living out of the over-tilled soil. Even in Albany, with its river-based shipping commerce, or Macon, named for 37-year Member of Congress Nathaniel Macon of North Carolina (who served in the Continental Congress and later became both Speaker of the House and president pro tem of the Senate) people lived a workaday life far removed from the gentility of Southern cities like Atlanta or Savannah. Even today Albany ranks among the lowest of the nation's metropolitan areas in years of education and among the highest in use of termite and pest control. And while slavery had long passed, as late as the early 1960s most people here thought racial segregation would never end.

In the years since Carter went off to Annapolis in 1942 and Roosevelt died at Warm Springs in 1945, economic growth and government works—rural electrification, the minimum wage, interstates, better schools, the military presence—have changed life vastly for the better here, and the Whites Only signs are a thing of the past. But sadly, the economy of southwest Georgia has not taken off. Farmers are hooked on the peanut subsidy—more of these dry-roasted legumes come from here than anywhere else in the world, and the jobs lost when the Americus Firestone plant closed have not come back. The 1994 summer floods sent the high-water mark to 100- and even 500-year levels all along the Flint river. Towns like tiny Montezuma, where Main Street stores were flooded nine feet deep, had not recovered months later. But Southwest

Georgia has its success stories too—its presidential heritage and famous sons like poet Sidney Lanier. And there are signs of economic movement. The soft pines that grow so rapidly here keep the paper and lumber mills busy; there are factories making things from aerospace equipment to zippers. Venerable Fort Benning, where General George Marshall held maneuvers to help him choose most of the Army's generals in World War II, seems likely to benefit from the latest round of base closings and realignments.

The 2d Congressional District of Georgia consists of most of southwest Georgia, including Warm Springs, Plains and Fort Benning. Its boundaries, however, are erose and convoluted, redrawn after the 1990 census to maximize the black percentage and make this Georgia's second black majority district. It includes heavily black parts of Columbus, Macon, Albany, Moultrie and Valdosta. Economically, this is the ninth-poorest district in the nation; politically, it is heavily Democratic, with almost every county going Democratic in Georgia's close statewide elections.

The Congressman from the 2d is Sanford Bishop, first elected in 1992 when the boundaries were changed to produce a black majority. Bishop grew up in Mobile, went to Morehouse College and was an award-winning student at Emory Law School. After a year in New York, he began practicing law in Columbus in 1972. He was elected to the state House in 1976, at 29, and the state Senate in 1990 and had prime committee positions in both, helping him to push through Georgia's tough ethics law. His style is not confrontational; he talks of cutting waste and foreign aid but also touts the millions he brought to southwest Georgia in the 103rd Congress. In 1992 he ran for the House, against incumbent Charles Hatcher, who gained his greatest public notice when it was revealed he had 819 overdrafts on the House bank. Bishop was urged into the race by Columbus business leaders, and in the primary he edged another Hatcher challenger by 21%–19% for a runoff slot. Hatcher had 40%, but could not get many more votes, and Bishop won the runoff 53%–47%. He won the general election easily.

Bishop's voting record in the House is moderate to liberal, far more moderate than most members of the Congressional Black Caucus; along with Mel Reynolds of Illinois, he voted for pieces of the Contract With America than did any other Democrat in the Caucus. He has sponsored public housing rent reform legislation with California's Maxine Waters. He showed his local political savvy by strongly supporting federal farm price-supports and by preserving—in the face of an amendment pushed in 1994 by Joe Kennedy—Fort Benning's School of the Americas, which Bishop says has promoted democracy in Latin America. To criticsms that it does nothing more than train future dictators, he says, "We might as well abolish the University of Pennsylvania because Michael Milken graduated from the Wharton School." He also worked to bring federal funds to Georgia for urban and rural economic development and education. In 1994 Bishop faced weak opposition, defeating a former Hatcher aide in the primary and the Republican in the general by wide margins. He has clearly been winning white as well as black votes. After Nathan Deal switched parties, there was local speculation that Bishop might be next. That seemed far-fetched given both his background and the district; Bishop responded that he was not considering the change but, "No one can speak about forever." His political savvy may be important if Georgia's 1992 redistricting is overturned by the Supreme Court. If the 2d's district lines are smoothed out and its black percentage reduced, Bishop will still be in a strong political position, even though he has to endure the frustration of being in the minority party for the first time in his almost 20-year legislative career.

The People: Pop. 1990: 592,011; 37% rural; 12% age 65+; 41% White; 57% Black; 1% Asian; 1% Other; 2% Hispanic origin. Voting age pop.: 415,776; 52% Black; 1% Hispanic origin. Households: 47% married couple families; 23% married couple fams. w. children; 27% college educ.; median household income: $17,942; per capita income: $8,532; median gross rent: $285; median house value: $42,200.

1992 Presidential Vote

Clinton (D) 96,684 (60%)
Bush (R) 47,692 (29%)
Perot (I). 17,248 (11%)

1988 Presidential Vote

Dukakis (D). 76,313 (56%)
Bush (R) 59,263 (44%)

Rep. Sanford D. Bishop, Jr. (D)

Elected 1992; b. Feb. 4, 1947, Mobile, AL; home, Columbus; Morehouse Col., B.A. 1968, Emory U., J.D. 1971; Baptist; divorced.

Career: Practicing atty., 1971–92; GA House of Reps., 1976–90; GA Senate, 1990–92.

DC Office: 1632 LHOB 20515, 202-225-3631; Fax: 202-225-2203.

District Offices: 225 Pine St., Albany 31701, 912-439-8067; 17 10th St., Columbus 31901, 706-323-6894; City Hall, Dawson 31742, 912-995-3991; 682 Cherry St., #1113, Macon 31201, 912-741-2221; and 401 N. Patterson St., #255, Valdosta 31601, 912-247-9705.

Committees: *Agriculture* (18th of 22 D): Department Operations, Nutrition and Foreign Agriculture; Risk Management and Specialty Crops. *Veterans' Affairs* (11th of 15 D): Hospitals and Health Care.

Group Ratings

	ADA	ACLU	COPE	CFA	LCV	CON	NSI	COC	ACU	NTLC	CHC
1994	75	62	56	70	56	35	56	64	25	19	14
1993	75	—	100	90	71	27	—	18	13	—	—

National Journal Ratings

	1993 LIB — 1993 CONS		1994 LIB — 1994 CONS	
Economic	88%	0%	57%	43%
Social	63%	36%	72%	28%
Foreign	59%	38%	57%	37%

Key Votes of the 103d Congress

1. Clinton Deficit Plan	Y	3. Brady Handgun Purchase	N	5. Lmt. UN Cmnd. of Forces	N
2. NAFTA	N	4. Strike Race/Death Pnlty.	N	6. Cut Missile Funds	N

Key Votes of the 104th Congress

1. Congressional Compliance	Y	6. Reform Crime Grant	N	11. Loser Pays Court Reform	N
2. Balanced Budget Amndmt.	*	7. National Security Act	N	12. Product Liability Reform	N
3. Bar Unfunded Mandates	Y	8. Moratorium on Regs.	N	13. Welfare Reform	N
4. Pass Line Item Veto	N	9. Risk Assessment on Regs.	Y	14. Term Limits Amndmt.	N
5. Relax Exclusionary Rule	N	10. Expnd. Priv. Prop. Rights	Y	15. Tax Cuts	N

Election Results

1994 general	Sanford D. Bishop, Jr. (D)	65,383	(66%)	($473,931)
	John Clayton (R)	33,429	(34%)	($9,736)
1994 primary	Sanford D. Bishop, Jr. (D)	33,862	(67%)	
	James C. Bush (D)	16,757	(33%)	
1992 general	Sanford D. Bishop, Jr. (D)	95,789	(64%)	($353,973)
	Jim Dudley (R).	54,593	(36%)	($222,806)

THIRD DISTRICT

Nearly a century ago, a boy named William Hartsfield, standing in Candler Racetrack eight miles south of Atlanta's Five Points, spotted his first flying machine. From this moment dates Atlanta's emergence as a world city. Hartsfield went on to become mayor of Atlanta for 24 years, from 1937 to 1961, the man who made "The City Too Busy to Hate" into the economic capital of the South. His two greatest achievements were Atlanta's acceptance of desegregation and the construction of what is now Hartsfield International Airport—if not the busiest in the nation, then certainly the biggest in the South, and the link between Atlanta's world corporations—Coca-Cola, CNN—its celebrations—the 1996 Olympics—and the rest of the world.

When Hartsfield saw his first plane, Candler Racetrack was far out in the country. Now it is at Atlanta's southern city limit and in the midst of one of the fastest growing metro areas in the country. For Atlanta's meteoric rise under Hartsfield's stewardship pales when compared to the torrid growth of the last decade: Clayton County has grown more than 20% since 1980—four times the state average. Running along the freeways stretching south are scores of new communities built in the last 20 years, transforming whole counties from rural outposts—the towns of Jonesboro and Fayetteville here both claim to be the spiritual home of *Gone with the Wind*. These new communities are affluent but not dominated by any establishment, liberation-minded in much of their lifestyles but often tradition-minded in their yearnings. Politically this is conservative country, full of young families moving up who prefer the relatively bucolic culture of the smaller counties. Mostly white, their ancestral politics may be Democratic but their current preferences lean Republican.

The 3d Congressional District of Georgia spans much of this territory from the Airport to rural south Georgia. More than 60% of its people are in five Atlanta metropolitan area counties, though back in Hartsfield's time few would have counted even one of them as metropolitan. To the south, the 3d sends two grotesquely shaped salients. One reaches down to the Alabama border and takes in most of the white precincts of Columbus. The other heads toward Macon, but stops just short of it, taking in a series of white-majority rural counties on either side of I-75. The 3d was redrawn for the 1992 elections with the assumption that Newt Gingrich would run there. It includes most of the 6th District Gingrich represented from 1982 to 1992, but Speaker Tom Murphy also tried to include enough Democrats, in the rural counties to the south and black neighborhoods around the airport, to give Gingrich a fight every two years. But Gingrich chose to run in the heavily Republican 6th District on the north side of Atlanta, and there were not enough Democratic voters left to reelect the incumbent who ran here, Richard Ray.

The Congressman from the 3d is Mac Collins, a switcher to the Republican party in the 1980s. Collins grew up in Jackson and started his trucking company at age 18, hauling logs for Georgia-Pacific; he is known, a local paper said, for "his lumbering stature and signature boots." He served as a Democrat on the Butts County Commission in the late 1970s, lost in 1980 then convinced the Republicans to elect him chairman. In 1988, he was elected to the state Senate, where he worked on welfare and ethics reforms and bills to fight drug dealing. In 1992, Collins capitalized on a fierce primary battle between the two Democrats Murphy had in mind for the seat, Richard Ray and David Worley, who came close to beating Gingrich in 1990. Ray won the Democratic primary 51%–32%. But Collins, like Worley, attacked Ray as an insider; he spent 10 years as an aide to Senator Sam Nunn before running for Congress himself. Ray, with a seat on Armed Services, spent $1.1 million. But Collins won in votes, 55%–45%.

In the House Collins combined a very conservative voting record with a constituent-based agenda. Hartsfield Airport was his chief early focus; he pushed for a repeal of the airline fuel tax slated for fall 1995, arguing the levy would cripple the industry. He voted to pare spending at almost every opportunity—defense projects and the 3d district being notable exceptions—and made a point of opting out of the congressional pension plan. Collins is not much of a free marketeer, however: he voted against NAFTA and made sour sounds about GATT and then voted no.

Collins was easily reelected in 1994, despite early predictions he would have serious competition. Indeed, his 66% of the vote—he carried every county—was 2% higher than Gingrich won in a much more Republican district. Collins' conservative credentials and staunch support for Gingrich were rewarded with a seat on Ways and Means in 1995. On the committee, he was an outspoken advocate for sweeping welfare reform and for broad-based tax cuts, just as Gingrich intended. With his down-home style and constituency-oriented record, he seems in strong shape to hold this seat.

The People: Pop. 1990: 592,002; 44% rural; 10% age 65+; 80% White; 18% Black; 1% Asian; 1% Hispanic origin. Voting age pop.: 429,264; 16% Black; 1% Hispanic origin. Households: 63% married couple families; 31% married couple fams. w. children; 38% college educ.; median household income: $32,380; per capita income: $13,849; median gross rent: $447; median house value: $70,300.

1992 Presidential Vote			1988 Presidential Vote		
Bush (R)	105,731	(48%)	Bush (R)	112,043	(68%)
Clinton (D)	80,628	(37%)	Dukakis (D)	51,982	(32%)
Perot (I)	32,285	(15%)			

Rep. Mac Collins (R)

Elected 1992; b. Oct. 15, 1944, Jackson; home, Hampton; Methodist; married (Julie).

Career: Army Natl. Guard, 1964–70; Founder & Pres., Collins Trucking Co., 1965–92; Chmn., Butts Cnty. Comm., 1977–80; Chmn., Butts Cnty. Repub. Party, 1981–82; GA Senate, 1988–92.

DC Office: 1130 LHOB 20515, 202-225-5901; Fax: 202-225-2515.

District Offices: 173 N. Main St., Jonesboro 30236, 404-603-3395; and 5704 Beallwood Connector, #200, Columbus 31904, 706-327-7728.

Committees: *Ways & Means* (17th of 21 R): Human Resources; Social Security.

Group Ratings

	ADA	ACLU	COPE	CFA	LCV	CON	NSI	COC	ACU	NTLC	CHC
1994	0	17	22	0	17	83	100	75	95	96	100
1993	10	—	25	10	29	94	—	82	100	—	—

National Journal Ratings

	1993 LIB — 1993 CONS			1994 LIB — 1994 CONS		
Economic	23%	—	75%	0%	—	80%
Social	11%	—	82%	20%	—	77%
Foreign	0%	—	91%	0%	—	88%

Key Votes of the 103d Congress

1. Clinton Deficit Plan	N	3. Brady Handgun Purchase	N	5. Lmt. UN Cmnd. of Forces	Y
2. NAFTA	N	4. Strike Race/Death Pnlty.	Y	6. Cut Missile Funds	N

Key Votes of the 104th Congress

1. Congressional Compliance Y	6. Reform Crime Grant Y	11. Loser Pays Court Reform Y
2. Balanced Budget Amndmt. Y	7. National Security Act Y	12. Product Liability Reform Y
3. Bar Unfunded Mandates Y	8. Moratorium on Regs. Y	13. Welfare Reform Y
4. Pass Line Item Veto Y	9. Risk Assessment on Regs. Y	14. Term Limits Amndmt. Y
5. Relax Exclusionary Rule Y	10. Expnd. Priv. Prop. Rights Y	15. Tax Cuts Y

Election Results

1994 general	Mac Collins (R)	94,717	(66%)	($503,867)
	Fred Overby (D)	49,828	(34%)	($1,284,414)
1994 primary	Mac Collins (R)	unopposed		
1992 general	Mac Collins (R)	114,107	(55%)	($246,007)
	Richard Ray (D)	94,271	(45%)	($1,127,731)

FOURTH DISTRICT

In 1920, when Gutzom Borglum began sculpting Jefferson Davis, Robert E. Lee and Stonewall Jackson into the side of Stone Mountain, the huge outcropping of granite was a day's drive into the country from central Atlanta. Even when the memorial (the largest single piece of sculpture in the world) was completed in 1972, suburban development barely reached this far. But today, after two decades of some of the most explosive metropolitan growth in the country, Stone Mountain is smack in the midst of metro Atlanta. Gwinnett County, just past Stone Mountain, cast 21,000 votes in 1972; it cast 150,000 in 1992, a level approaching that of Fulton County, which includes central Atlanta, or DeKalb just to the west of Gwinnett. In some ways, DeKalb and the area around Stone Mountain have become centers of the Atlanta metropolitan area. Emory University and the Centers for Disease Control, among the leading intellectual institutions in the South and nation, are in western DeKalb, just beyond the old mansions of Druid Hills, where *Driving Miss Daisy* was filmed. Not far away is Buckhead, the leading retail center of the South. All around are affluent subdivisions and condominiums, places where on the red clay soil of north Georgia styles of living descended from the finest in western tradition are established by the hard working people who have done much to make Atlanta a world-class city.

The 4th Congressional District of Georgia covers much of this territory. It includes the northern half of DeKalb County, mostly affluent, mostly white (the southern, mostly black half is in the black-majority 11th District), with a large Jewish and academic population. The district's Catholic contingent is small, although tens of thousands of believers have visited town of Conyers in recent years to hear spiritualist Nancy Fowler channel messages, allegedly from the Virgin Mary. It includes Stone Mountain and proceeds out I-85 to include most of Gwinnett County—parts of Lilburn, Snellville, Norcross and Lawrenceville. It moves east to Rockdale County, once clearly rural, now also suburban. The 4th District is very affluent, with a household median income exceeded in the South only by the next-door 6th District, three northern Virginia districts outside Washington, D.C., and five districts in Houston and Dallas-Fort Worth, Texas. Politically, the 4th is strongly Republican, but its university and Jewish populations provide a serious base for a liberal Democrat.

The Congressman from the 4th District is John Linder, a Republican elected by a narrow margin in 1992 and comfortably in 1994. Linder, like many in affluent Atlanta, is not from Georgia or the South at all. He grew up in Minnesota, got his degrees in dentistry there, then after military service moved to greater Atlanta and was in dental practice for 13 years. In 1977 he started Linder Financial, a lending institution for entrepreneurial ventures throughout the South. In 1976 he was elected to the Georgia House, where he served all but two years until 1990. Then he challenged Democratic Congressman Ben Jones, known to TV watchers as Cooter in the *Dukes of Hazzard*; Jones won 52%–48%. When redistricting removed black middle- and upper-income south DeKalb from the 4th, Jones decided to run in the new 10th, where he lost the Democratic primary; in 1994, Jones ran in the 6th against Newt Gingrich, and was whipped soundly. Linder stuck in 1992 with the 4th, where he finished first in a six-candidate primary with 38%, then won the runoff with 62%. In the general he faced Democratic state Senator Cathey Steinberg and, in a race that ran along national party lines, won by just 51%–49%.

Linder had a very conservative voting record but made no waves in the Democratic 103d Congress, except for sponsoring the Republicans' three-term limit on service as a committee's ranking minority member (more meaningful, now that Republicans are chairmen). In 1994, against an opponent who was encouraged by national Democrats and who attacked him as a tool of the National Rifle Association and as an opponent to abortion, Linder won 58%–42%. He narrowly lost DeKalb County, but won 69% in Gwinnett. In the Republican 104th Congress Linder was more in his element. He feels free to differ with Speaker (and 6th District neighbor) Newt Gingrich from both the right—he wanted a powerful line-item veto and a balanced budget amendment with a three-fifths vote to raise taxes—and the left—he called term limits "a bad idea whose time has come" but he voted for the proposal, which he played a role in drafting. Linder backs medical savings accounts and wants to move toward a tax code with a national sales tax. Linder is evidently trusted by Gingrich, who gave him a seat on the Rules Committee, where he can broaden his apparent leadership skills. But he seems to have his own compass. Gingrich has called on him to preside at sessions of the House on especially divisive issues such as welfare reform, and Linder in his serious, Minnesota-nice manner has insisted on the right of the minority to be respectfully heard. And when Gingrich was toying with the idea of running for president in 1996, Linder responded to his request to prepare a memo listing the pros and cons of whether he should run. Linder was mum on his recommendations and the memo was not released.

Linder is one Republican who stands to be hurt by any court decision that overthrows the Justice Department's insistence on maximizing the number of black-majority districts. Any remapping could put large parts of southern DeKalb County—heavily black middle class, heavily Democratic—into a new 4th District, which Linder would have great difficulty carrying.

The People: Pop. 1990: 589,293; 8% rural; 8% age 65+; 81% White; 12% Black; 4% Asian; 1% Other; 3% Hispanic origin. Voting age pop.: 448,249; 11% Black; 3% Hispanic origin. Households: 56% married couple families; 28% married couple fams. w. children; 64% college educ.; median household income: $40,303; per capita income: $18,607; median gross rent: $566; median house value: $96,600.

1992 Presidential Vote		1988 Presidential Vote	
Bush (R)	116,418 (46%)	Bush (R)	120,482 (64%)
Clinton (D)	101,990 (40%)	Dukakis (D)	66,557 (36%)
Perot (I)	33,226 (13%)		

Rep. John Linder (R)

Elected 1992; b. Sept. 9, 1942, Deer River, MN; home, Tucker; U. of MN, B.S. 1964, D.D.S., 1967; Presbyterian; married (Lynne).

Career: Air Force, 1967–69; Practicing dentist, 1969–82; Founder & Pres., Linder Financial, 1977–92; GA House of Reps., 1976–80, 1982–90.

DC Office: 1318 LHOB 20515, 202-225-4272; Fax: 202-225-4696; e-mail: jlinder@hr.house.gov.

District Offices: 3003 Chamblee-Tucker Rd., #140, Atlanta 30341, 404-936-9400.

Committees: *Rules* (5th of 9 R): Legislative and Budget Process.

Group Ratings

	ADA	ACLU	COPE	CFA	LCV	CON	NSI	COC	ACU	NTLC	CHC
1994	0	9	11	20	11	65	100	92	95	96	93
1993	5	—	0	0	29	74	—	100	100	—	—

National Journal Ratings

	1993 LIB — 1993 CONS	1994 LIB — 1994 CONS
Economic	0% — 88%	0% — 80%
Social	0% — 89%	0% — 89%
Foreign	17% — 76%	14% — 80%

Key Votes of the 103d Congress

1. Clinton Deficit Plan	N	3. Brady Handgun Purchase N	5. Lmt. UN Cmnd. of Forces Y
2. NAFTA	Y	4. Strike Race/Death Pnlty. Y	6. Cut Missile Funds	N

1. Clinton Deficit Plan   N   3. Brady Handgun Purchase N   5. Lmt. UN Cmnd. of Forces Y
2. NAFTA   Y   4. Strike Race/Death Pnlty. Y   6. Cut Missile Funds   N

Key Votes of the 104th Congress

1. Congressional Compliance Y   6. Reform Crime Grant   Y   11. Loser Pays Court Reform Y
2. Balanced Budget Amndmt. Y   7. National Security Act   Y   12. Product Liability Reform Y
3. Bar Unfunded Mandates   Y   8. Moratorium on Regs.   Y   13. Welfare Reform   Y
4. Pass Line Item Veto   Y   9. Risk Assessment on Regs. Y   14. Term Limits Amndmt.   Y
5. Relax Exclusionary Rule Y   10. Expnd. Priv. Prop. Rights Y 15. Tax Cuts   Y

Election Results

1994 general	John Linder (R)	90,063	(58%)	($671,801)
	Comer Yates (D)......................	65,566	(42%)	($521,432)
1994 primary	John Linder (R)	unopposed		
1992 general	John Linder (R)	126,495	(51%)	($542,137)
	Cathey Steinberg (D)	123,819	(49%)	($603,399)

FIFTH DISTRICT

Venture out of the quiet of the Ebenezer Baptist Church or the shade of Martin Luther King Jr.'s boyhood home two blocks away and into the steam-heat blast of the sun on Auburn Avenue—Sweet Auburn—and you can see, a mile away, downtown Atlanta's atrium-skyscrapers towering in their glory. They are evidence of the wealth and vibrant growth of "The City," as it boasted in the 1960s, "Too Busy To Hate," the commercial capital of the South, the metropolis that has grown up where there was little more than a railroad junction at the time of the War Between the States. But the awesome achievement that is downtown Atlanta is overshadowed by the revolution made in very large part by a man who grew up on Auburn Avenue, where people who never felt air conditioning moved slowly in the sweltering heat, and around Morehouse and Spelman Colleges, where proud professionals worked hard and raised their families and yet never saw more than a few dollars cash at a time. Atlanta's white establishment, led by Mayors William Hartsfield and Ivan Allen and Coca-Cola's Robert Woodruff, deserve credit for abandoning segregation, but it was King and other civil rights leaders who took the risks that led them to do so. Atlanta's city fathers acted out of good will, but also with an eye for the economic growth of their city, which they knew would be hurt by violent resistance. White Atlanta's decision to desegregate has helped Atlanta prosper, but King's vision and movement to change the way Americans behave have made it possible for a nation to live up to its ideals.

Yet, sadly, not all is entirely well in Atlanta—on Peachtree Street or on Sweet Auburn. Downtown Atlanta's primacy in office buildings is being eclipsed by north side Edge Cities in Buckhead and along I-285. Many of Atlanta's black neighborhoods today have been abandoned by the area's affluent families who have headed to subdivisions in DeKalb County, leaving to the mercies of a criminal underclass, the central city with its high rates of murder and infant mortality, abandoned housing and street crime. A caustic dispute arose in 1994 between the King family and the National Park Service: the Park Service promised to build in time for the Olympics an interpretive center across the street from the family's King Center; the family, led by the for-profit ventures of son Dexter opposed the Park Service plans and kicked them out of the Center; all parties were reconciled in April 1995 with the aide of Congressman John Lewis. But Atlanta has its glories. It is the headquarters of world-girdling Coca-Cola and CNN and Delta Airlines. And it is the host of the 1996 Summer Olympics.

The 5th Congressional District of Georgia includes most of Atlanta and a few suburbs, from posh white Sandy Springs in the north to middle-class and increasingly black East Point in the south, plus the rural precincts of southwest Fulton and a few precincts over the county line. It is a black-majority district, although when it first elected a black congressman, Andrew Young in 1972, most of its residents and voters were white.

The Congressman from the 5th District today is John Lewis, who made history a generation ago as a hero of the civil rights movement. A sharecropper's son from Troy, Alabama, he was the first in his family to finish high school; he wrote Ralph Abernathy for help in suing for the right to enter Troy State College; he met Martin Luther King when he was 18. In 1959, at age 19, he helped organize the first lunch-counter sit-in, which was received with open hostility hard to imagine today. In 1960, the day after John Kennedy was elected, Lewis sat in at the Krystal Diner in Nashville while a waitress poured cleansing powder down his back and water over his food; after eating, he went to talk to the manager, who turned a fumigating machine on him. In May 1961, he was on the first of the Freedom Rides, riding buses as they were attacked and burned; he was viciously beaten in Rock Hill, South Carolina, and Montgomery, Alabama. He spoke at the 1963 March on Washington. In 1964, he helped coordinate the Mississippi Freedom Project. In 1965, he led the Selma-to-Montgomery march to petition for voting rights and was attacked by policemen. Modestly, quietly, maintaining his poise and good judgment under harsh circumstances, Lewis was one of the people who risked their lives many times to make the civil rights revolution happen.

Lewis responded to these beatings with a stubborn determination to persevere with actions, not just words. His tenure as head of the Voter Education Project in Atlanta and his work at ACTION in the Carter Administration did not give him the publicity and fame, however, that made a national celebrity of Jesse Jackson, whose civil rights movement credentials are much thinner. Lewis's first foray into electoral politics was unsuccessful: he ran in 1977 to replace Andrew Young in the House and was soundly beaten by Wyche Fowler (but ran ahead of Republican Paul Coverdell, who beat Fowler in the 1992 Senate election). After winning a seat on the Atlanta Council in 1981, Lewis ran for Congress in 1986, and trailed Julian Bond 47%–35% in the first primary. But even though Bond won over 60% of the black vote, Lewis won the runoff because, thanks to his hard work on local issues like zoning and city ethics, he drew nearly 90% of the white vote. He has been reelected easily since.

Lewis approached House service saying, "I don't want to compromise my belief in interracial democracy," and working with members of many backgrounds. But he has also become a strong partisan: he is one of the Democrats' four chief deputy whips, and strongly supported Bill Clinton in spring 1992. In 1993 he got a seat on Ways and Means, where he backed Democrats' beleaguered healthcare plans. But as a strong opponent of capital punishment he opposed the Democrats' 1994 crime bill and cast a key vote against the rule for it in August 1994; under pressure, he switched on the rule later, saying, "I don't like voting against my president, against my party, against the leadership of the House." Just as he had good dealings with white Democratic leaders like Tom Foley and Dan Rostenkowski, Lewis had maintained pleasant relations for years with Newt Gingrich, whose district adjoins his. But he sharply attacked Gingrich in early 1995 for his book contract and called for an independent counsel on the issue. When Georgia Republicans John Linder and Mac Collins said his attitude made it harder to get bipartisan cooperation on the Olympics or Atlanta federal projects, Lewis insisted he would not be intimidated. He passionately opposed much of the Contract With America and insinuated comparison of the Republicans to Hitler's Nazis when citing a quote from a World War II German theologian. Similarly, he threatened "non-violent action" if Rules Chairman Gerald Solomon did not remove a portrait of former Chairman Howard Smith, a southern Democratic segregationist, from the committee's Capitol room; under pressure, Solomon took action to avert a showdown. Lewis has also devoted energy to commemorating the civil rights revolution in various ways. He got a federal building in Atlanta named for Martin Luther King and he sought to designate the route from Selma to Montgomery as a national trail.

The People: Pop. 1990: 586,526; 3% rural; 10% age 65+; 36% White; 62% Black; 1% Asian; 1% Other; 2% Hispanic origin. Voting age pop.: 440,803; 57% Black; 2% Hispanic origin. Households: 35% married couple families; 15% married couple fams. w. children; 49% college educ.; median household income: $25,892; per capita income: $15,831; median gross rent: $461; median house value: $74,800.

1992 Presidential Vote				1988 Presidential Vote			
Clinton (D)	140,175	(67%)		Dukakis (D)	117,881	(65%)	
Bush (R)	52,191	(25%)		Bush (R)	64,040	(35%)	
Perot (I)	15,241	(7%)					

Rep. John Lewis (D)

Elected 1986; b. Feb. 21, 1940, Troy, AL; home, Atlanta; Amer. Baptist Theological Seminary, B.A. 1961, Fisk U., B.A. 1963; Baptist; married (Lillian).

Career: Chmn., Student Nonviolent Coord. Cmte., 1963–66; Field Foundation, 1966–67; Community Organization Dir., Southern Regional Cncl., 1967–70; Exec. Dir., Voter Educ. Project, 1970–76; Assoc. Dir., ACTION, 1977–80; Community Affairs Dir., Natl. Coop. Bank, 1980–82; Atlanta City Cncl., 1981–86.

DC Office: 229 CHOB 20515, 202-225-3801; Fax: 202-225-0351.

District Offices: 100 Peachtree St., NW, #1920 Atlanta 30303, 404-659-0116.

Committees: *Chief Deputy Minority Whip. Ways & Means* (13th of 15 D): Health.

Group Ratings

	ADA	ACLU	COPE	CFA	LCV	CON	NSI	COC	ACU	NTLC	CHC
1994	100	91	100	70	100	19	0	25	5	14	0
1993	100	—	100	90	86	32	—	9	0	—	—

National Journal Ratings

	1993 LIB	—	1993 CONS	1994 LIB	—	1994 CONS
Economic	88%	—	0%	83%	—	0%
Social	87%	—	0%	80%	—	19%
Foreign	87%	—	7%	85%	—	0%

Key Votes of the 103d Congress

1. Clinton Deficit Plan	Y	3. Brady Handgun Purchase Y	5. Lmt. UN Cmnd. of Forces N
2. NAFTA	N	4. Strike Race/Death Pnlty. N	6. Cut Missile Funds	Y

Key Votes of the 104th Congress

1. Congressional Compliance Y	6. Reform Crime Grant N	11. Loser Pays Court Reform N
2. Balanced Budget Amndmt. N	7. National Security Act *	12. Product Liability Reform N
3. Bar Unfunded Mandates N	8. Moratorium on Regs. N	13. Welfare Reform N
4. Pass Line Item Veto N	9. Risk Assessment on Regs. N	14. Term Limits Amndmt. N
5. Relax Exclusionary Rule N	10. Expnd. Priv. Prop. Rights N	15. Tax Cuts N

Election Results

1994 general	John Lewis (D)	85,094	(69%)	($323,725)
	Dale Dixon (R)	37,999	(31%)	($47,726)
1994 primary	John Lewis (D)	unopposed		
1992 general	John Lewis (D)	147,445	(72%)	($246,913)
	Paul Stabler (R)	56,960	(28%)	($59,300)

SIXTH DISTRICT

In the red clay hills north of Atlanta, over the last three decades, an almost wholly new metropolitan quarter has grown up as affluent Atlanta has spread out from Ansley Park just north of downtown and the rolling hills of Buckhead within the city limit past the I-285 Perimeter into territory that was once just farms, small towns and little factory cities. Where there were perhaps 100,000 people in the 1950s, there are one million today. No longer is downtown Atlanta the only focus: the Edge Cities of Buckhead, Perimeter Center and the area near Cumberland Mall are now not just shopping but major office centers, rivaling downtown Atlanta in square footage. Cobb County around Marietta is the headquarters of Home Depot, and the Weather Channel; Dunwoody in northern DeKalb County, is the home of Holiday Inns. Yet physically this Golden Crescent north of the Perimeter and between I-75 in Cobb County and I-85 in Gwinnett County seems not to have changed greatly: the buildings are tree-shaded and lush foliage and large-lot requirements have given most of the communities a woodsy look; and for all their affluence they still have a folksy atmosphere and at least a hint of a southern accent.

The 6th Congressional District of Georgia occupies a large portion of this Golden Crescent north of Atlanta, including most of Cobb County, Fulton County north of the Perimeter, and to the east northern DeKalb County and a slice of Gwinnett. Its creation for the 1992 election was a recognition of the explosive growth of affluent suburban Atlanta. It would surely surprise Georgians a generation or two ago to learn that one of their congressional districts would rank among the nation's richest and most educated. The 6th ranks 11th of 435 districts in percentage of adults with a college degree, at 40%; it ranks 23d in median family income in 1990, behind districts all in larger metro areas. It is easily the most Republican district in Georgia, having voted 75% for George Bush in 1988; indeed, one of the most heavily Republican districts in the country.

The Congressman from the 6th District is Newt Gingrich, for years Georgia's lone Republican Congressman, now Speaker of the House of Representatives. In less than six years Gingrich moved from being a backbencher despised by Democratic House leaders and mistrusted by Republicans in the Executive Branch to the guiding if not commanding figure in American politics. This is all the more extraordinary because Gingrich in politics as in life is an autodidact, a scholar who has managed to bend the world to his own image. Gingrich grew up as the son of a Army officer, part of the career military world that in so many ways is more American than America itself. His political career, he says, dates from a visit to the ossuary at Verdun, France, where the sight of the bones of thousands of soldiers convinced him that politics matters. Gingrich went to college at Emory, got a Ph.D. in European history at Tulane, then in 1970 started teaching at West Georgia College in Carrollton. He had always been a Republican, supporting Nelson Rockefeller in 1968 because he always favored civil rights; he has always loved animals, and boosted zoos, and was something of an environmentalist; he has always been fascinated by space travel and science fiction, and is something of a futurist. In 1974 he ran for Congress in a still mostly rural district south and west of Georgia, challenging the conservative Democratic incumbent as unethical. He lost narrowly, ran again in 1976 and lost again as Jimmy Carter swept rural Georgia; he persevered and won in 1978, just as House Republicans were unanimously embracing the Kemp-Roth 30% tax cut.

Although Gingrich has changed positioning on a few issues like the environment, over a long career he has advocated steadily a coherent and consistent set of ideas. Gingrich is an American exceptionalist, a believer in the idea widely shared by American voters but widely rejected by American intellectuals that this is a uniquely good nation with a special mission in world history. While his liberal contemporaries disparaged traditional America in struggles over civil rights, he was living in the most integrated part of America, the career military, and during Vietnam he was married with children and saw no need to justify his lack of military service. Gingrich is also a believer in an energetic government that advances modern technology and promotes traditional values, a kind of American Gaullist. He is a cultural conservative who believes that liberal values are destroying the lives of the poor, a market capitalist who celebrates technological innovation.

Gingrich did not gain these beliefs either from the liberals who dominated campuses when he was a young man or Congress in his later years nor from the Republicans who came to celebrate him as their deliverer. Indeed, Gingrich infuriates congressional Democrats who insist that he believes in nothing but power (he has "an absolute ambition for power," says former Democratic leadership staffer George Stephanopoulos), though that is quite obviously wrong; he believes, whether you like them or not, in certain public policies. But the Democrats refuse to engage Gingrich's ideas: his attacks on things as they are pierce too deeply, wounding the Democrats' claims to intellectual and moral superiority, while his sloppiness in personal and political matters leaves him open to furious counterattack.

Nor was Gingrich brought forward by the older accommodationist Republicans who led the party when he came to the House. He argued for years that ranking Republicans should fight Democratic bills, not try to compromise with them for a few crumbs in return, and should frontally challenge Democratic ideas. In the early 1980s he formed the Conservative Opportunity Society—the opposite, he said, of the liberal welfare state—and recruited backbenchers like Robert Walker and organized them to give special orders speeches directed not at the House but at the C-SPAN audience. When he compiled a book of the angry comments of Democrats against the 1983 Grenada invasion and attacking the Democratic signers of the "Dear Commandante" letter to Nicaraguan leader Daniel Ortega, Speaker Tip O'Neill said Gingrich had "challenged the Americanism" of his colleagues and called it "the lowest thing that I've ever seen in my 32 years in Congress." O'Neill's words were ordered stricken from the record as violating House rules. Gingrich dared to challenge Speaker Jim Wright in December 1987 by bringing the ethics charges against him which, after bitter controversy, brought Wright's resignation in June 1989. In March 1989, after Dick Cheney was appointed secretary of defense, Gingrich ran for whip against Edward Madigan, an active legislator on the Health Subcommittee who was next in line in the leadership and had the support of fellow Illinoisan Minority Leader Robert Michel. But Gingrich rounded up support from conservatives, younger members, even some moderates, and won 87–85. The win was narrow but decisive, for the ranks of his opponents then started to thin, starting with Madigan who soon became secretary of agriculture; the numbers of Gingrich's kind increased in Republican ranks.

As a child Gingrich told people his goal was to become Speaker of the House, and for more than 20 years he worked steadily and shrewdly toward that goal, though for almost all that time no one else thought it was attainable. His courtship of Republican moderates, for example, was not just momentary but continual; he listened respectfully to their views and engaged in intellectually serious interchange. His use of ethics issues helped erode the Democrats' moral authority, but only because he was more careful than they have been to make charges that stick. Democrats attacked him for doing almost no work on legislation and dismissed his goal of achieving Republican control as ridiculous—an argument that is obsolete now. Colleagues mistrusted him because he seemed indifferent to the professional and sometimes personal ruin he has inflicted on politicians who got in his way. But Gingrich kept planning his way ahead. In 1992 he helped to engineer the election of Dick Armey and ouster of Jerry Lewis as Chairman of the Republican Conference and the selection of John Kasich over Alex McMillan as ranking Republican on the Budget Committee: both would become key leaders of his Republican majority. He used the GOPAC organization, which he inherited from Delaware Governor Pete duPont to raise money to help candidates when the Republicans' campaign committee was in financial trouble; Democrats attacked him for not disclosing donors, though the law did not require it. With logistical help from the Progress and Freedom Foundation, he taught his course "Renewing American Civilization," first at Kenesaw State College, then at Reinhardt College.

In October 1993, Robert Michel announced his retirement; Gingrich had refused to promise not to run against him for leader after the 1994 election. Gingrich announced he was running; Gerald Solomon announced against him, then two weeks later withdrew, admitting Gingrich had the commitments to win. Gingrich effectively became party leader. He worked closely with the Clinton White House and rounded up the promised number of votes for NAFTA, which passed with 132 Republicans and 102 Democrats. But he took a tough stand against the Clinton healthcare plan. He worked hard to recruit and raise money and campaign for 1994 candidates who shared his views. Although he received a lot of organizational help from other Republicans, chiefly Dick Armey, the Contract With America was Gingrich's initiative, more than anyone else's. Against conventional wisdom and the scorn of most reporters, he committed Republicans to voting on specific issues and bills; by staging a big Capitol rally September 27 and then stressing the Contract when Democrats criticized it, he helped nationalize the election and reduce the already declining political skills and institutional advantages of the Democrats. In May he thought Republicans might win House control; by August, with the Democrats' debacle on the crime and healthcare bills, he predicted they would; in November he seemed unsurprised by victory.

In the half-year after, Gingrich set the legislative course and political agenda as no other legislative leader—and few presidents—had in the 20th Century. The existence of the Contract avoided endless argument over an agenda and goaded Republicans toward radical reform when they might otherwise have quailed. Gingrich's strength among the 73 Republican freshmen, even greater than among incumbents, gave him the power to pass over the indicted Joseph McDade and three other senior Appropriations members to make Bob Livingston Chairman of Appropriations—a post from which, by pushing of bills with zero-appropriations for targeted programs, he can eliminate whole government agencies. Gingrich coolly ignored Bill Clinton's invitations to endless palavering sessions on welfare and other issues and proceeded to lead the House to take action. Nine of the ten Contract With America planks passed the House substantially intact; the one casualty was term limits, which was never close to the constitution-ally required two-thirds, although it was backed by 83% of House Republicans. "I think I am a transformational figure," he said. "I think I am trying to effect a change so large that the people who would be hurt by the change—the liberal, Democratic machine—have a natural reaction, which gets wearying sometimes." He parried Democratic attacks on his ethics and a largely hostile media, eventually agreeing to renounce his $4.5 million book advance from Rupert Murdoch, which even Republican allies conceded was insensitive to public appearances. The House Ethics Committee under Chairman Nancy Johnson deliberated at length on the four Democratic complaints that were filed against him. In the mid-1980s he had called Bob Dole "the tax collector of the welfare state," but in 1994 he deferred often to him and seemed to establish a good professional working relationship, as he had with Robert Michel. For the opening day of Congress he staged a kind of inaugural-cum-workday, delivering a 20-minute speech that fascinated those not familiar with his thinking, inviting talk show hosts into the Speaker's office, then gaveling the House to change its rules spreading power from committee chairmen to the Speaker and the whole Conference, and pass legislation applying to itself the laws that apply to the rest of the country.

Curiously, Gingrich has not had entirely clear political sailing back home; the same factors that made him unpopular in national polls in 1995—the professor's know-it-allness? the ethical lapses? the provocative statements?—have worked against him in Georgia. The 6th District which he represented in the 1980s covered south Atlanta suburbs near Hartsfield Airport and traditionally Democratic counties out in the country. In 1990 he nearly lost there, as Democrat David Worley attacked him for supporting the congressional pay raise and opposing government intervention in the Eastern Airlines strike; Gingrich won by only 974 votes after spending $1.5 million. In 1992, Speaker Tom Murphy tried to beat Gingrich by putting him in a new 3d District farther out from Atlanta with incumbent Democrat Richard Ray. Gingrich decided to run in the new, heavily Republican 6th District instead, but faced primary opposition from Herman Clark, who had resigned his seat in the legislature to run. Democrats joined in and urged Gingrich haters to cross party lines and vote for Clark, who attacked Gingrich for his 22 House bank overdrafts and for his "carpetbagging"; Gingrich won by only 980 votes, 51%–49%. In the general election Gingrich was also attacked on personal grounds. He won 58%–42%, comfortably but behind normal party lines. His opponent in the 1994 general was former Congressman Ben Jones, running in his third district in three elections. This time Gingrich won 64%–36%.

It is interesting to ponder how history would have been different if Gingrich had received 1,000 fewer votes in either of those two close contests. It is likely that without his vision, determination and hard work Republicans would not have won their majority. Yet now that they have achieved it and despite his sweeping power, his role is not quite so essential: the machine is in motion and others have shown they are capable of taking the controls. Gingrich has in fact given other Republicans lead roles on one issue after another and has nurtured talent and brought freshmen to the fore; he stepped down from his post at GOPAC in May 1995. But his role in getting them to the promised land is central. His success is proof of the permeability of American political institutions: here is a man who began without personal connections or wealth, without any institutional backing, who played and plays a major role in changing the direction of American politics and shaping America.

The People: Pop. 1990: 586,641; 11% rural; 5% age 65+; 90% White; 6% Black; 2% Asian; 1% Other; 2% Hispanic origin. Voting age pop.: 438,774; 6% Black; 2% Hispanic origin. Households: 62% married couple families; 32% married couple fams. w. children; 70% college educ.; median household income: $46,997; per capita income: $22,181; median gross rent: $600; median house value: $120,500.

1992 Presidential Vote

Bush (R) 155,739 (55%)
Clinton (D) 82,381 (29%)
Perot (I). 41,874 (15%)

1988 Presidential Vote

Bush (R) 150,405 (75%)
Dukakis (D). 50,297 (25%)

Rep. Newt Gingrich (R)

Elected 1978; b. June 17, 1943, Harrisburg, PA; home, Marietta; Emory U., B.A. 1965, Tulane U., M.A. 1968, Ph.D. 1971; Baptist; married (Marianne).

Career: Asst. Prof., W. GA Col., 1970–78.

DC Office: 2428 RHOB 20515, 202-225-4501; Fax: 202-225-4656; e-mail: georgia6@hr.house.gov.

District Offices: 3823 Roswell Rd., #200, Marietta 30062, 404-565-6398.

Committees: *Speaker of the House.*

Group Ratings

	ADA	ACLU	COPE	CFA	LCV	CON	NSI	COC	ACU	NTLC	CHC
1994	5	14	13	10	0	74	100	91	100	96	100
1993	0	—	0	20	25	69	—	91	96	—	—

National Journal Ratings

	1993 LIB — 1993 CONS		1994 LIB — 1994 CONS	
Economic	0% —	88%	0% —	80%
Social	11% —	82%	0% —	89%
Foreign	17% —	76%	25% —	71%

Key Votes of the 103d Congress

1. Clinton Deficit Plan	N	3. Brady Handgun Purchase N	5. Lmt. UN Cmnd. of Forces Y
2. NAFTA	Y	4. Strike Race/Death Pnlty. Y	6. Cut Missile Funds	N

Key Votes of the 104th Congress

1. Congressional Compliance *	6. Reform Crime Grant Y	11. Loser Pays Court Reform Y
2. Balanced Budget Amndmt. Y	7. National Security Act Y	12. Product Liability Reform *
3. Bar Unfunded Mandates Y	8. Moratorium on Regs. Y	13. Welfare Reform Y
4. Pass Line Item Veto Y	9. Risk Assessment on Regs. *	14. Term Limits Amndmt. Y
5. Relax Exclusionary Rule *	10. Expnd. Priv. Prop. Rights *	15. Tax Cuts Y

Election Results

1994 general	Newt Gingrich (R)	119,432	(64%)	($1,817,792)
	Ben Jones (D)	66,700	(36%)	($321,774)
1994 primary	Newt Gingrich (R)	43,254	(77%)	
	Bob Terrell (R)	12,683	(23%)	
1992 general	Newt Gingrich (R)	158,761	(58%)	($1,963,810)
	Tony Center (D)	116,196	(42%)	($411,794)

SEVENTH DISTRICT

The red clay hills of north Georgia, home of the Cherokee Nation before they were sent west in the 1830s on the Trail of Tears, have been manufacturing country for the last century. There are hundreds of textile mills and dozens of carpet mills located near the supply of natural cotton and along the railroad lines heading southwest at the base of the southern Appalachian chain. Factories were hailed as the vanguard of technological progress by the late 19th Century propagandists of the New South, and in fact they produced a higher standard of living than reliance on farming this stubborn land. But mill work put little premium on education or the cultivation of civic virtues and did little to bring in higher-skill white-collar work; all-white hiring practices maintained racial segregation in mostly white north Georgia. Today North Georgia is developing a different kind of economy, as the example of Atlanta shines to the south and spreads out interstate highways north into what used to be mill towns. Cobb County, once centered on the Lockheed aircraft factory in Marietta, has already been transformed into an upscale suburb and office center; places like the textile mill town of LaGrange or the carpet mill town of Rome have begun to be affected as well.

The 7th Congressional District of Georgia includes much of this part of north Georgia. It extends along the state's western boundary from LaGrange to Rome, and extends east to Cartersville, where U.S. 41 starts its four-lane roll toward Atlanta, and takes in part of western Cobb County, including the old center of Marietta. This was Democratic territory from the time General Sherman came through in the 1860s until the civil rights revolution of the 1960s; in the 1970s Carrollton, in the western part of the 7th, was the home of a West Georgia College professor who, in his third try, became a Republican Congressman: Newt Gingrich. Since Gingrich first won in 1978, north Georgia has become solidly Republican in national politics; now, after the 1994 election that made Gingrich Speaker of the House, it is Republican in congressional elections as well.

The Congressman from the 7th is Bob Barr, like Gingrich and several other Georgia Republicans, a transplanted Yankee. Barr was born in Iowa, graduated from USC, in 1970 went to work as an intelligence analyst for the CIA while in graduate school. In 1978 he left the agency and moved to Georgia, to practice law; in 1986 he became U.S. Attorney in Atlanta. That was a high-profile job and in 1992 Barr ran for the Senate, and with 24% in the primary just made it into a runoff with Paul Coverdell. He lost the runoff 50.5%–49.5%. Undaunted, in 1994 Barr ran for the 7th District House seat. Again he had primary opposition, from physician Brenda Fitzgerald; as the more conservative candidate, he won 57%–43%. In the general election, he faced Buddy Darden, an incumbent who won the seat after incumbent Larry McDonald was killed aboard the KAL 007 flight shot down by the Soviets. Darden is one of those Democrats who stayed in office in a Republican-leaning district with a mixed voting record, a congenial backslapping personality and close attention to district needs like Dobbins Air Force Base and the giant Lockheed plant near Marietta.

The thrust of Barr's campaign was apparent in the tee shirts it printed showing a photo of Darden jogging with Bill Clinton. Barr attacked Darden for voting for the Clinton budget and tax package, for the Brady bill, for the 1994 crime bill, for NAFTA, and said that his vote was always available to Democratic leaders when they needed it. Darden replied that he had voted against the assault weapons ban (though for the final crime bill), opposed Clinton on health care, federal funding for abortion, the balanced budget amendment and gays in the military. But, with his Appropriations Committee seat, he defended his votes on the budget and could not deny that he was the number one Clinton supporter among white Democrats in the Georgia delegation. Darden claimed that Barr's ex-wife "had to sue Barr for child support and medical bills"; she attacked Darden and defended Barr. Up through 1990 Darden won between 68% and 74% in north Georgia outside Cobb County; that was reduced to 56% in 1992 and 48% in 1994. Overall, Barr won 52%–48%.

Barr has been a prominent member of the 104th Congress. As a former federal prosecutor, he played a visible role on the Contract With America crime bill, and as head of Newt Gingrich's Task Force on Firearms persuaded Steve Stockman of Texas not to introduce repeal of the assault weapons ban into the Contract bill. Like almost all Republican freshmen, he opposed the Mexican bailout and the nomination of Henry Foster. As a former CIA agent, he believes the agency should continue to exist and should have more leeway to conduct covert operations. He seems politically strong in the 7th District; it is hard to imagine any future Democrat here running better than the personable, well-known, well-financed Darden.

The People: Pop. 1990: 587,917; 46% rural; 11% age 65+; 86% White; 13% Black; 1% Hispanic origin. Voting age pop.: 431,636; 12% Black; 1% Hispanic origin. Households: 62% married couple families; 30% married couple fams. w. children; 31% college educ.; median household income: $28,831; per capita income: $12,428; median gross rent: $403; median house value: $64,300.

1992 Presidential Vote			1988 Presidential Vote		
Bush (R)	93,175	(46%)	Bush (R)	101,310	(68%)
Clinton (D)	77,103	(38%)	Dukakis (D)	48,047	(32%)
Perot (I)	30,097	(15%)			

Rep. Bob Barr (R)

Elected 1994; b. Nov. 5, 1948, Iowa City, IA; home, Smyrna; U. of Southern CA, B.A. 1970, George Washington U., M.A. 1972, Georgetown U., J.D. 1977; Methodist; married (Jeri).

Career: CIA Analyst, 1971–78; Practicing atty., 1978–86, 1990–94; U.S. Atty., N. GA District, 1986–90; Dir., SE Legal Foundation, 1990–92.

DC Office: 1607 LHOB 20515, 202-225-2931; Fax: 202-225-2944.

District Offices: 1001 Whitlock Ave., #13, Marietta 30061, 404-429-1776; 200 Ridley Ave., LaGrange 30240, 706-812-1776; 600 E. 1st St., Rome 30161, 706-290-1776; and 423 College St., #503-B, Carrollton 30117, 404-836-1776.

Committees: *Banking & Financial Services* (19th of 27 R): Domestic and International Monetary Policy; General Oversight and Investigations. *Judiciary* (20th of 20 R): Commercial and Administrative Law; Crime. *Veterans' Affairs* (14th of 18 R): Compensation, Pension, Insurance and Memorial Affairs; Education, Training, Employment and Housing.

Group Ratings and 103rd Congress Votes: Newly Elected

Key Votes of the 104th Congress

1. Congressional Compliance	Y	6. Reform Crime Grant	Y	11. Loser Pays Court Reform	Y
2. Balanced Budget Amndmt.	Y	7. National Security Act	Y	12. Product Liability Reform	Y
3. Bar Unfunded Mandates	Y	8. Moratorium on Regs.	Y	13. Welfare Reform	Y
4. Pass Line Item Veto	Y	9. Risk Assessment on Regs.	Y	14. Term Limits Amndmt.	Y
5. Relax Exclusionary Rule	Y	10. Expnd. Priv. Prop. Rights	Y	15. Tax Cuts	Y

Election Results

1994 general	Bob Barr (R)	71,265	(52%)	($846,821)
	George (Buddy) Darden (D)	65,978	(48%)	($622,336)
1994 primary	Bob Barr (R)	16,165	(57%)	
	Brenda Fitzgerald (R)	12,217	(43%)	
1992 general	George (Buddy) Darden (D)	111,374	(57%)	($510,073)
	Al Beverly (R)	82,915	(43%)	($40,778)

EIGHTH DISTRICT

More than almost any part of America, south Georgia has been under attack and enemy occupation. Most famously, of course, when General William Tecumseh Sherman's troops set out from Atlanta, without supplies or lines of communication, to march through Georgia to the sea. The path they cut through south Georgia has been mostly poor country ever since, its antebellum mansions burned down, its leader captured (the Jefferson Davis Memorial in Ocilla marks the spot where Union troops took him in May 1865), its crops destroyed, and memories of slaves freed handed down as family lore for over a century. But the land bears, if only on its road signs, the memory of another invasion, when the poor white farmers, aided by Andrew Jackson's troops, drove the Cherokees and other Indians off this land west over the Trail of Tears to what is now Oklahoma. Only 50 years ago, archaeologists discovered near Macon a huge Indian earthlodge built nearly 1,000 years ago. And there was the oppression of blacks by whites under the old systems of slavery and legal segregation, the latter dead just one generation now—a past recalled by Macon's new Harriet Tubman Historical and Cultural Museum. More recently, many south Georgians, black and white, find themselves threatened by drug dealers heading north on I-75 from Florida, spreading addiction and AIDS to Macon and smaller towns that thought they were immune to these scourges.

The 8th Congressional District of Georgia runs down the southern center of the state along these lines of occupation, past immense stands of soft lumber pines, through counties where 60% of the world's kaolin (used for china and ceramics) is mined, all the way from Macon to the Okeefenokee Swamp and the Florida line. To place blacks in the next-door 2d District, the 8th's boundaries twist around Macon, home of music legends Otis Redding, Little Richard and the Allman brothers, a city proud of its restored houses and Japanese cherry trees (it has 20 times as many as Washington); the lines similarly wrap around the south Georgia county seats of Albany, Moultrie and Valdosta. There has been some growth in these towns and along the interstates, but in the more rural counties there is little sign of the Atlantic Coast prosperity apparent just a few miles east. This has been Democratic country since Sherman's troops came through, and many counties here remain Democratic in statewide contests; but the 8th District's erose boundaries put many black and therefore Democratic votes into the black-majority 2d District and make the 8th lean Republican.

The Congressman from the 8th District is Saxby Chambliss, a Republican elected in 1994 to replace the retiring Roy Rowland, one of the few physicians in Congress and co-sponsor of the Rowland-Bilirakis healthcare plan which could have passed in the 103d Congress if Bill Clinton and the Democratic leadership had allowed it to come up. Chambliss grew up in Shreveport, Louisiana, the son of an Episcopalian minister, went to college in Georgia, and practiced business and agriculture law in Moultrie since 1968. In 1992 he ran for the House and lost the Republican primary; in 1994 he was the sole Republican candidate, while Democrats, as in days of yore, had a multicandidate primary. In the lead with 26% was Craig Mathis, 32-year-old son of onetime (1971–81) Congressman Dawson Mathis; second, with 19% was attorney Tyron Spearman; trailing were, among others, former 8th District Congressman (1977–83) Billy Lee Evans. Mathis won the runoff on geographic lines, 54%–46%. But despite his congressional lineage he proved a weaker candidate than Chambliss. He had worked four years in Washington for Congressmen Ed Jenkins and Sonny Callahan (the latter a Republican). Chambliss had his home and career for 26 years in south Georgia, and for two decades coached boys' and girls' sports; one of his students is now the University of Georgia football coach. Chambliss also got good publicity because every Friday night he watched his son Bo play as a wide receiver for the Colquitt County Packers, who won the state AAAA Football championship in December 1994 over the Wildcats of Valdosta. On issues Chambliss called for targeting repeat offenders and reducing the deficit; he opposed Dick Armey's proposal to zero out peanut subsidies. He dismissed Mathis: "He's a nice young man. But as soon as he gets elected, he becomes an integral part of the Clinton team."

The interesting thing about the result is not that it was a Republican takeover but that it wasn't even close: Chambliss won 63%–37%. Except in three small counties, Chambliss won at least 47% everywhere and carried the Macon, Valdosta and Albany areas by 2–1. Like Georgia's other junior Republicans, he was well-positioned In the House with seats on the Agriculture and National Security Committees, where he will presumably continue to fight for peanut and cotton subsidies and Robins Air Force Base, which was added to the new base closing list in May 1995. He has been less visible than many other freshmen, which may be a sign that he is working to entrench himself back home.

The People: Pop. 1990: 590,835; 51% rural; 12% age 65+; 78% White; 21% Black; 1% Hispanic origin. Voting age pop.: 426,327; 18% Black; 1% Hispanic origin. Households: 60% married couple families; 29% married couple fams. w. children; 34% college educ.; median household income: $25,744; per capita income: $11,958; median gross rent: $341; median house value: $55,800.

1992 Presidential Vote			**1988 Presidential Vote**		
Bush (R)	93,643	(45%)	Bush (R)	107,034	(64%)
Clinton (D)	83,976	(40%)	Dukakis (D)	59,607	(36%)
Perot (I)	32,068	(15%)			

Rep. Saxby Chambliss (R)

Elected 1994; b. Nov. 10, 1943, Warrenton, NC; home, Moultrie; U. of GA, B.A. 1966; U. of TN, J.D. 1968; Episcopalian; married (Julianne).

Career: Practicing atty., 1968–94.

DC Office: 1708 LHOB 20515, 202-225-6531; Fax: 202-225-3013.

District Offices: 3312 Northside Dr., #232, Macon 31210, 912-475-0665; 1707 1st. Ave. SE, #B, Moultrie 31768, 912-891-3474.

Committees: *Agriculture* (26th of 27 R): General Farm Commodities; Risk Management and Specialty Crops. *National Security* (24th of 30 R): Military Personnel; Military Procurement.

Group Ratings and 103rd Congress Votes: Newly Elected

Key Votes of the 104th Congress

1. Congressional Compliance	Y	6. Reform Crime Grant	Y	11. Loser Pays Court Reform	Y
2. Balanced Budget Amndmt.	Y	7. National Security Act	Y	12. Product Liability Reform	*
3. Bar Unfunded Mandates	Y	8. Moratorium on Regs.	Y	13. Welfare Reform	Y
4. Pass Line Item Veto	Y	9. Risk Assessment on Regs.	Y	14. Term Limits Amndmt.	Y
5. Relax Exclusionary Rule	Y	10. Expnd. Priv. Prop. Rights	Y	15. Tax Cuts	Y

Election Results

1994 general	Saxby Chambliss (R)	89,591	(63%)	($680,075)
	Craig Mathis (D)	53,408	(37%)	($352,437)
1994 primary	Saxby Chambliss (R)	unopposed		
1992 general	J. Roy Rowland (D)	108,472	(56%)	($544,898)
	Bob Cunningham (R)	86,220	(44%)	($201,755)

NINTH DISTRICT

The mountains of north Georgia have become one of the boom areas of the state. But this is definitely a late 20th Century phenomenon. This part of Georgia had virtually no slaves before the Civil War; its people were mostly poor farmers, who sent their sons off to battle under the command of Confederate General Joe Johnston, and whose meager holdings were further devastated by U.S. General William T. Sherman's infamous March to the Sea (which included the burning of Atlanta) in 1864. After the Civil War this area lived in isolation, with some textile mill towns along the railroads, and hairpin curves leading up to remote hills where within living memory moonshine stills were more common than summer cabins. In 1912 Forsyth County, which forms the 9th District's southern boundary, drove out all of its black residents, and there are few blacks in the district even today.

As Atlanta became a boom town in the late 1960s, however, the city's economic good fortune began to spread north. Forsyth County is now a fast-growing part of the Atlanta metro area, as is Cherokee County, its neighbor to the west. A little to the north, poultry processing has become big business in Hall County around Gainesville, accessible to Atlanta on I-85 and with huge Lake Lanier close by. Dalton, in Whitfield County—the site of a key battle between U.S. and Confederate forces in May, 1864—has become a major carpet-making center, while the Georgia suburbs of Chattanooga, Tennessee, which gaze out from Lookout Mountain down to the Tennessee River below, form not only the 9th District's northern border but also its pillars of traditional conservatism. At the same time the north Georgia mountains, pleasantly cool in the summer when Atlanta swelters, with miles of shoreline on vast lakes formed by dams, have become vacation country, popularized by former President Jimmy Carter and connected to the Atlanta area by limited-access highways.

The 9th Congressional District sweeps across the northern border of the state from the Carolinas west to Alabama and dips south to include Forsyth and most of Cherokee Counties as well as Gainesville. From its Civil War heritage in the hills, from its cultural conservatism in the Chattanooga suburbs and the carpet country, from the economic conservatism of its affluent new migrants in Forsyth County and around Gainesville, the 9th is heavily Republican in national elections, by some measures second in the state to the very affluent 6th District. Still the 9th has not elected a Republican congressman in this century.

Yet the 9th is now represented by a Republican, Nathan Deal, who was elected as a Democrat in 1992 and 1994 but switched parties in April 1995. Deal is from Gainesville, and has been in public life since he was County Attorney in 1966, at 24; he was elected to the Georgia Senate in 1980 and was president pro tem when Congressman Ed Jenkins retired in 1992 and he ran for Congress. Deal won with 59% despite fierce campaigning by Republican Daniel Becker, an abortion foe. Deal quickly made a name for himself in his first term as a deficit hawk, founding the Fiscal Caucus, a group of 26 freshman Democrats who actively supported such fiscally conservative issues as the line-item veto and a balanced budget amendment. Deal opposed President Clinton's $496 billion anti-deficit package in August 1993, saying it didn't go far enough, and almost a year later co-sponsored a popular version of the "A to Z" spending cuts plan, which called for a special session of the House to consider lopping off additional parts of the federal budget.

Deal took such fiscally conservative positions, in fact, that his name topped lists of Southern Democrats likely to switch parties that began circulating on Capitol Hill prior to the 1994 election. But Deal won his second term by beating Republican Robert Castello 58%–42%, and said, "If I choose to switch during the term, I think the honest thing to do is resign and have a special election." Deal made no secret of his unhappiness with the House Democratic leadership, but soldiered on as a Democrat. He became Co-Chairman of The Coalition, a newly formed group of conservative House Democrats seeking bipartisan legislation, and he was the lead sponsor of one of the two Democratic alternatives to the Contract With America welfare plan, holding almost every Democrat and gaining a couple of Republicans as well, a feat which prompted considerable Democratic crowing, at least until he switched parties. He was also one of a handful of Democrats named to a House task force on immigration reform, and was a leading Democratic supporter of term limits. But he also was among the top Democratic supporters of the Contract With America.

Then in April 1995, the Monday after the House recessed for the Easter break, Deal announced he was switching parties. Angered by party leaders' opposition to efforts by many of its southerners to weaken the Clean Water Act, he said the national Democratic Party was unwilling to admit it was "out of touch with mainstream America" and "I think that it is important that at some point you get away from the schizophrenia I have had to deal with." Democrats were stunned and Newt Gingrich was clearly delighted; Deal was rewarded with a seat on the Commerce Committee. He also went from being the Georgia delegation's most conservative Democrat to its most liberal Republican. Some local Republicans, including former state House Minority Leader Steve Stancil were irritated, attacking Deal's pro-choice stand and threatening to oppose him in the 1996 primary.

The People: Pop. 1990: 586,310; 78% rural; 12% age 65+; 95% White; 4% Black; 1% Other; 1% Hispanic origin. Voting age pop.: 436,627; 3% Black; 1% Hispanic origin. Households: 66% married couple families; 31% married couple fams. w. children; 30% college educ.; median household income: $26,581; per capita income: $12,027; median gross rent: $365; median house value: $62,200.

1992 Presidential Vote

Bush (R) 98,205 (49%)
Clinton (D) 70,943 (35%)
Perot (I) 32,808 (16%)

1988 Presidential Vote

Bush (R) 109,872 (70%)
Dukakis (D). 46,007 (30%)

Rep. Nathan Deal (R)

Elected 1992; b. Aug. 25, 1942, Millen; home, Gainesville; Mercer U., B.A. 1964, J.D. 1966; Baptist; married (Sandra).

Career: Army, 1966–68; Hall Cnty. Atty., 1966–70; Asst. Dist. Atty., NE Judicial Circuit, 1970–71; Hall Cnty. Juvenile Court Judge, 1971–72; Practicing atty., 1971–92; GA Senate, 1980–92, Pres. Pro Tem, 1991–92.

DC Office: 1406 LHOB 20515, 202-225-5211; Fax: 202-225-8272.

District Offices: P.O. Box 1015, Gainesville 30503, 404-535-2592; 415 E. Walnut Ave., Dalton 30720, 706-226-5320; and 109 N. Main St., La Fayette 30728, 706-638-7042.

Committees: *Commerce* (18th of 26 R): Energy and Power; Telecommunications and Finance.

Group Ratings

	ADA	ACLU	COPE	CFA	LCV	CON	NSI	COC	ACU	NTLC	CHC
1994	15	22	33	40	47	96	80	92	67	71	86
1993	15	—	42	40	57	88	—	73	61	—	—

National Journal Ratings

	1993 LIB — 1993 CONS		1994 LIB — 1994 CONS	
Economic	38%	61%	43%	56%
Social	42%	58%	24%	73%
Foreign	40%	57%	41%	58%

Key Votes of the 103d Congress

1. Clinton Deficit Plan	N	3. Brady Handgun Purchase	*	5. Lmt. UN Cmnd. of Forces	N
2. NAFTA	Y	4. Strike Race/Death Pnlty.	Y	6. Cut Missile Funds	N

Key Votes of the 104th Congress

1. Congressional Compliance	Y	6. Reform Crime Grant	Y	11. Loser Pays Court Reform	Y
2. Balanced Budget Amndmt.	Y	7. National Security Act	Y	12. Product Liability Reform	Y
3. Bar Unfunded Mandates	Y	8. Moratorium on Regs.	Y	13. Welfare Reform	N
4. Pass Line Item Veto	Y	9. Risk Assessment on Regs.	Y	14. Term Limits Amndmt.	Y
5. Relax Exclusionary Rule	Y	10. Expnd. Priv. Prop. Rights	Y	15. Tax Cuts	Y

Election Results

1994 general	Nathan Deal (D).....................	79,145	(58%)	($368,648)
	Robert L. Castello (R).................	57,568	(42%)	($22,953)
1994 primary	Nathan Deal (D)....................	unopposed		
1992 general	Nathan Deal (D).....................	113,024	(59%)	($542,479)
	Daniel Becker (R).....................	77,919	(41%)	($161,060)

TENTH DISTRICT

Heading south from Atlanta, General Sherman and his Union troops avoided the towns of central Georgia—fortunately preserving a couple of America's loveliest small cities, Augusta and Athens. Founded in 1735 on the site of a fur-trading post, Augusta has grown into a regional manufacturing and medical center. It was the boyhood home of Woodrow Wilson, but is better known for the Augusta National golf course, site of the Masters' tournament every year. Augustans are proud as well of the antique Medical College of Georgia, dating to 1835, and the new Riverwalk where the old levee used to be. Once a cotton port on the Savannah River with its own Cotton Exchange, Augusta has built a paper industry, stoked by the pines that grow in profusion on the flat Piedmont land, and has grown out into adjoining counties. Athens, on a bluff over a river, is the home of the University of Georgia—the country's oldest chartered state university. Founded as a home for the university in the late 1700s, Athens is the site of one of America's finest collection of Greek Revival buildings—gleaming white columns, perfectly proportioned little Parthenons, flat-roofed square houses surrounded by fluted columns with Corinthian capitals, all dating from the 1830s to the 1850s. Athens too has been spreading outward, another little Atlanta.

The 10th Congressional District of Georgia takes in Athens and the surrounding area and the white precincts of Augusta and its suburbs. It stretches north toward the north Georgia mountains and east to take in the eastern end of fast-growing Gwinnett County, just outside Atlanta. This was once an almost entirely rural expanse, but now is increasingly metropolitan, with subdivisions and shopping centers springing up at interchanges. Politically, this was conservative Democratic country, the home base of longtime (1933–71) Senator Richard Russell. But its fastest-growing areas are affluent and Republican. Gwinnett County is one of the most Republican large counties in the country; the white suburbs of Augusta are heavily Republican; and while Athens, a pale replica of the liberalism of Northeastern university towns and home to the politically active rock band R.E.M., votes Democratic, the two fast-growing counties beyond go Republican. Yet it is a district that always elected Democratic congressmen—until 1994.

The Congressman from the 10th now is Charlie Norwood, a native of Valdosta who practiced dentistry in August for more than 20 years. A former president of the Georgia Dental Association, in 1993 he sold his practice when he decided to challenge incumbent Don Johnson. But first he faced a primary with Ralph Hudgens, a former propane business owner and US

Agriculture Department official who lost to Johnson 54%–46% in 1992. Hudgens led in the first primary, 47%–38%, but Norwood rallied and won the runoff 51%–49%. That turned out to be the hard part. Johnson, a former congressional staffer and state Senator, came under scathing criticism after he supported the Clinton budget and tax package in 1993 despite a 1992 promise to vote against any tax increase. *The Augusta Chronicle*, one of the surprisingly few small city newspapers with a conservative editorial policy, thundered unremittingly against him. In any case, as one Georgia Republican said, 1994 was "not a good year to be in the same party as Bill Clinton and Zell Miller." Norwood campaigned aggressively and hammered on the Clinton connection. Johnson tried unsuccessfully to associate himself with Senator Sam Nunn, and belatedly said that he only wanted Bill Clinton or Al Gore in the 10th District if "they are coming down to endorse my opponent." Norwood issued Clinton an invitation and offered to pay his plane fare. Norwood won 65%–35%, as Johnson took one of the worst lickings of a non-scandal-tarred incumbent in recent history. One small rural county and Athens's Clarke County voted narrowly for Johnson. Norwood carried all the rest, with 70% in Gwinnett County and 77% in the Augusta area.

In the House the folksy Norwood has worked to maintain his populist image, chastising the IRS for delaying tax refund checks and speaking vociferously for a three-fifths supermajority requirement for all federal tax increases. He also called for a more-prisons-less-pork revision of the 1994 crime bill. Norwood sits on the Economic and Educational Opportunities Committee, as well as the Commerce Committee's health panel—the first stop for any Republican healthcare reform bill and a good seat for a former dentist.

The People: Pop. 1990: 591,706; 53% rural; 10% age 65+; 80% White; 18% Black; 1% Asian; 1% Hispanic origin. Voting age pop.: 438,211; 16% Black; 1% Hispanic origin. Households: 60% married couple families; 29% married couple fams. w. children; 37% college educ.; median household income: $27,553; per capita income: $12,550; median gross rent: $390; median house value: $67,200.

1992 Presidential Vote			1988 Presidential Vote		
Bush (R)	99,336	(47%)	Bush (R)	104,251	(66%)
Clinton (D)	81,960	(38%)	Dukakis (D)	53,059	(34%)
Perot (I)	30,662	(14%)			

Rep. Charlie Norwood (R)

Elected 1994; b. July 27, 1941, Valdosta; home, Evans; GA Southern U., B.S. 1964; Georgetown U., D.D.S. 1967; Methodist; married (Gloria).

Career: Army, 1967–69 (Vietnam); Practicing dentist, 1969–93; Pres., GA Dental Assn., 1983.

DC Office: 1707 LHOB 20515, 202-225-4101; Fax: 202-225-3397.

District Offices: 1056 Clausson Rd., #226, Augusta 30807, 706-733-7066.

Committees: *Economic & Educational Opportunities* (24th of 24 R): Workforce Protections. *Commerce* (24th of 26 R): Energy and Power; Health and Environment.

Group Ratings and 103rd Congress Votes: Newly Elected

Key Votes of the 104th Congress

1. Congressional Compliance Y	6. Reform Crime Grant	Y	11. Loser Pays Court Reform Y
2. Balanced Budget Amndmt. Y	7. National Security Act	Y	12. Product Liability Reform Y
3. Bar Unfunded Mandates Y	8. Moratorium on Regs.	Y	13. Welfare Reform Y
4. Pass Line Item Veto Y	9. Risk Assessment on Regs. Y		14. Term Limits Amndmt. Y
5. Relax Exclusionary Rule Y	10. Expnd. Priv. Prop. Rights Y		15. Tax Cuts Y

Election Results

1994 general	Charlie Norwood (R)	96,099	(65%)	($787,441)
	Don Johnson (D)	51,192	(35%)	($773,927)
1994 runoff	Charlie Norwood (R)	16,048	(51%)	
	Ralph T. Hudgens (R)	15,506	(49%)	
1994 primary	Ralph T. Hudgens (R)	16,331	(47%)	
	Charlie Norwood (R)	13,238	(38%)	
	Bill Jackson (R)	5,307	(15%)	
1992 general	Don Johnson (D)	108,426	(54%)	($622,590)
	Ralph Hudgens (R)	93,059	(46%)	($182,637)

ELEVENTH DISTRICT

The 11th Congressional District, Georgia's third black-majority district, created after the 1990 Census, includes parts of the state recalling all the eras in local black history. Philanthropist James Oglethorpe didn't intend for the colony he founded in 1736 to permit slavery, but labor was hard to find in frontier settlements and by 1750 slaves were being shipped to farms along Georgia's seacoast. After Eli Whitney patented the cotton gin in 1794 and cotton became a hugely profitable crop, those farms grew into vast plantations. Slaves were common in southwest and central antebellum Georgia within a triangle formed by three succeeding state capitals: Augusta, the second capital, an old cotton town along the Savannah River that had been named after King George III's mother; Milledgeville, the third state capital; and Atlanta, the fourth. For many years after the Civil War, most freed blacks remained where they were; black immigration to the North remained only a trickle until the 1940s. By the 1950s, however, blacks as well as whites were migrating to Atlanta in droves. In large numbers they worked their way up in the city that was clearly the capital of the South and of the civil rights movement. Central Atlanta soon developed a black majority, and beginning in the 1970s affluent blacks flocked east of the city to comfortable new subdivisions in southern DeKalb County.

Black influence in Georgia's state legislature developed more slowly, but in the end as surely. One of the strongest voices for modern black interests in the state House has long been J.E. "Billy" McKinney, a civil rights activist who was elected to the legislature in 1973. Fifteen years later Billy McKinney's daughter, Cynthia, a political scientist who had taught at Clark Atlanta University and Agnes Scott College, a century-old woman's college in DeKalb County, won a seat in the state House as well. Together they became the only father-daughter legislative team in the country. Cynthia McKinney brought to her post the same commitment to defending minority interests her father had; she was just 10 when the Voting Rights Act was passed and she has recalled that, as a child, she often rode on her father's shoulders as he walked in civil rights marches. She got a seat on the Georgia legislature's redistricting committee and worked long and hard to craft the two new black-majority districts. In 1992 Cynthia McKinney ran as a Democrat for the right to represent one of the districts she had helped create. The real contest was for the Democratic nomination: she led the primary with 31%, then won the runoff over George DeLoach 56%–44%. She won in November with 73%.

As a freshman, McKinney called for balancing demands for budget-cutting with the needs of children and the working poor. She voted against the Superconducting Supercollider, but supported the Clinton crime bill provision for more police. One of her first acts upon taking office was to ask the U.S. Justice Department to investigate alleged price-fixing and fraud by large companies in her district that mine kaolin, the white clay used in white china, stationery and paint; in late September 1994 Justice launched an antitrust probe into the kaolin mining industry's activities.

At the same time, however, McKinney's district was running into danger. By any measure, the 11th District is a geographic monstrosity. It stretches across 260 miles and 22 counties from Atlanta to Savannah, linking by narrow corridors the black neighborhoods in Augusta, Savannah and southern DeKalb County. Demographically, it is 64% black and heavily Democratic. In a 1993 case called *Shaw v. Reno* the Supreme Court ruled that such districts may constitute "racial gerrymandering," and a federal court in September 1994 ordered that the 11th District must be redrawn. That case was appealed and argued before the Supreme Court in April 1995 with a decision expected by summer.

Meanwhile, McKinney was easily reelected, and in her second term emerged as a fiery opponent of her Georgia neighbor, Speaker Newt Gingrich. She was one of three members who brought the ethics complaint charging him with violating anti-gift rules by accepting free cable-TV time to broadcast his college course—on which theory every member of Congress is violating the rules in every appearance on C-SPAN. She attacked his book deal and told a satirical "children's tale" about "a little piglet who spent most of his days rolling around in a filthy ditch, throwing mud and insults at the giraffes walking around outside." When Georgia Republicans John Linder and Mac Collins said her attitude made it harder to get bipartisan cooperation on the Olympics or Atlanta federal projects, McKinney responded, "I have to speak with an even stronger voice now. And I will." In a similar spirit, she dismissed Nathan Deal when he switched parties as a "worried warrior" and said the Democratic Caucus would be more united without him. McKinney is undaunted. But the 1994 results showed that she won virtually no white votes, and her political future clearly depends on whether Georgia continues to have a third black-majority district.

The People: Pop. 1990: 585,341; 29% rural; 10% age 65+; 34% White; 64% Black; 1% Asian; 1% Hispanic origin. Voting age pop.: 412,740; 60% Black; 1% Hispanic origin. Households: 48% married couple families; 24% married couple fams. w. children; 35% college educ.; median household income: $24,763; per capita income: $10,381; median gross rent: $409; median house value: $58,200.

1992 Presidential Vote			1988 Presidential Vote		
Clinton (D)	121,356	(67%)	Dukakis (D)	92,497	(63%)
Bush (R)	44,419	(24%)	Bush (R)	55,354	(37%)
Perot (I)	15,676	(9%)			

Rep. Cynthia A. McKinney (D)

Elected 1992; b. Mar. 17, 1955, Atlanta; home, Lithonia; U. of Southern CA, B.A. 1978; Catholic; divorced.

Career: Diplomatic Fellow, Spelman Col., 1984; GA House of Reps., 1988–92; Atlanta Bd. of Health Svcs. Plng. Cncl., 1990–92; Adjunct Prof., Agnes Scott Women's Col., 1991–92.

DC Office: 124 CHOB 20515, 202-225-1605; Fax: 202-226-0691.

District Offices: 1 S. DeKalb Ctr., #9, 2853 Candler Rd., Decatur 30034, 404-244-9902; 120 Barnard St., #306-A, Savannah 31401, 912-652-4118; and 505 Courthouse La., #100, Augusta 30901, 706-722-7551.

Committees: *Agriculture* (15th of 22 D): Department Operations, Nutrition and Foreign Agriculture. *International Relations* (15th of 19 D): International Operations and Human Rights.

Group Ratings

	ADA	ACLU	COPE	CFA	LCV	CON	NSI	COC	ACU	NTLC	CHC
1994	100	87	100	100	100	23	0	33	0	4	0
1993	100	—	100	100	83	39	—	9	0	—	—

National Journal Ratings

	1993 LIB — 1993 CONS	1994 LIB — 1994 CONS
Economic	66% — 33%	83% — 0%
Social	87% — 0%	90% — 6%
Foreign	93% — 0%	85% — 0%

Key Votes of the 103d Congress

1. Clinton Deficit Plan	Y	3. Brady Handgun Purchase	Y	5. Lmt. UN Cmnd. of Forces	N
2. NAFTA	N	4. Strike Race/Death Pnlty.	N	6. Cut Missile Funds	Y

Key Votes of the 104th Congress

1. Congressional Compliance	Y	6. Reform Crime Grant	N	11. Loser Pays Court Reform	*
2. Balanced Budget Amndmt.	N	7. National Security Act	N	12. Product Liability Reform	N
3. Bar Unfunded Mandates	N	8. Moratorium on Regs.	N	13. Welfare Reform	N
4. Pass Line Item Veto	N	9. Risk Assessment on Regs.	N	14. Term Limits Amndmt.	N
5. Relax Exclusionary Rule	N	10. Expnd. Priv. Prop. Rights	*	15. Tax Cuts	N

Election Results

1994 general	Cynthia A. McKinney (D)	71,560	(66%)	($274,232)
	Woodrow Lovett (R)	37,533	(34%)	($12,091)
1994 primary	Cynthia A. McKinney (D)	unopposed		
1992 general	Cynthia A. McKinney (D)	120,168	(73%)	($306,978)
	Woodrow Lovett (R)	44,221	(27%)	($26,721)

HAWAII

The turning point in Hawaii's history came in 1819, closer to 200 than 100 years ago, when this volcanic island chain, first settled by Polynesians paddling across vast Pacific expanses in small outrigger canoes and united politically in 1779 by King Kamehameha I, came under American influence. For within a year of Kamehameha's death that year, his consort Kaahumanu outlawed the Hawaiian religious tabus and welcomed the American missionary Hiram Bingham. The New England missionaries and their trader cousins came—while British and Russian ships occasionally put into port—and established the predominate culture. They also brought in migrant laborers from Japan and Portugal and China and the Philippines. American planters and businessmen bridled at the caprices of the royal line and, in January 1893, with the help of U.S. Marines, ousted Queen Liliuokalani from the Iolani Palace and called on the United States to annex Hawaii. The new President, Grover Cleveland, demurred; so Hawaii became a republic July 1898.

This history is a source of regret for some; an Onipa'a ceremony remembering Liliuokalani's overthrow was staged by John Waihee, the first governor of native Hawaiian descent, in January 1993, with the American flag conspicuously absent. Yet Hawaii, with all its oddness and some of its recent discomforts, is a civilization both American and Pacific which has created a better life for its citizens than almost any island or native commonwealth of 100 years ago. Its ethnic mixing had already begun a century ago: Liliuokalani's Hawaii had a population of 3,000 Americans, 30,000 Hawaiians, 20,000 Chinese, 25,000 Japanese—a contrast with the pure Hawaiian population of 1819. It was well on it way to being "the gathering place of peoples," as Walter McDougall called it in his wonderful 1993 history of the North Pacific, *Let the Sea Make a Noise*, "filled up now with Japanese, Okinawans, Chinese, Filipinos, Portuguese and Mexican *paniolos*, African-Americans, Puerto Ricans, and just a smattering of more or less pure-blood Polynesians. And yet it's as American as the Beach Boys."

To that Americanness, each new group has made a positive contribution. The Asian migrant laborers brought traditions of hard work, family loyalty and group solidarity that found expression most vividly in the performance of the 442d "Go for Broke" Regimental Combat Team, made up mostly of sons of Japanese immigrants, which became the most decorated unit in U.S. military history. The Yankee spirit has been evident in Hawaii's commercial success, as a port and a tourist center, and in its attachment to the rule of Anglo-American law. And the Hawaiian spirit is alive in the vitality of the *aloha* ambience, the welcoming of others despite their differences and a willingness to absorb the teachings of others while maintaining a certain Polynesian attitude toward life. When Pearl Harbor was attacked by the Japanese in December 1941, no one in Hawaii or on the mainland doubted that this was part of America. Ironically, it was Hawaii's super-American tolerance that inspired segregationist southern Democrats to block its admission to the Union for years. Today, Hawaiians retain pride in their ethnic heritage—or heritages: 44% of non-military weddings are "out" marriages and 60% of babies born are of mixed racial background; in 1989, the state gave up trying to tabulate the ethnic origin of its legislators. The sensible future for Hawaii is not to create enclaves or racial preference for the 12% who call themselves Hawaiians or the 21% who have some Hawaiian ancestry—and few proposals for "native sovereignty" go so far—but to nurture the special strengths of all the peoples who have made Hawaii tolerant and affluent—just as Hawaii, to protect its 10,000 unique biologic and botanical species, needs not to put them under glass but to maintain the environment in which they have flourished.

Hawaii's economy was built first on agriculture; then on the Big Five trading companies who shipped out sugar and pineapple and shipped in almost anything else; then on the military, important for nearly 100 years in this strategic site in the middle of the world's largest ocean. But in recent years the real engine of Hawaii's economy has been tourism: like Nevada this is a million-person commonwealth that lives on serving tourists. It is booming now far beyond the dreams of the proprietors of the cruise ships and low stucco hotels of the Waikiki of the 1950s; yet it is also an unstable business, flourishing in the early 1990s, for example, and then stumbling as recession lingered in California and raged in Japan. Many tourism jobs are low-wage, and Hawaiians worry that educated young people will go to the mainland to find high-skill work. And there is a certain separatism: Waikiki with its world-class shopping seems sealed off from the rest of Hawaii.

Possibilities for diversification beyond tourism exist: ocean research, on these islands that are the tips of volcanic peaks; astronomy, in this land of clear air; securities markets, in one of the few inhabited places where it's daytime during the four hours when the New York Stock Exchange has closed and Tokyo has not yet opened. After all, Hawaii has American political stability and is sensitive to East Asian ways; it has first-rate transportation and communication facilities. It is a place where you can get Korean *kal bi* ribs on the same menu as hamburgers, where Filipino *lumpia*, Portuguese bread, and *poi* are staples; where Japanese holidays, religions, names and customs are all familiar.

As it seeks new growth, Hawaii needs to avoid being hurt by two special characteristics it shares with no other state. The first is its large landholdings, a product of its native and royal past. Eight public and private entities own 70% of Hawaii's land: the federal government 16%, the state 29%, six private landowners 25%. The Bishop Estate (Mrs. Bishop was the last surviving member of the Hawaiian royal family) owns 8% of the state's land; its five trustees, appointed by the state Supreme Court for life and paid roughly $650,000 a year, are supposed to

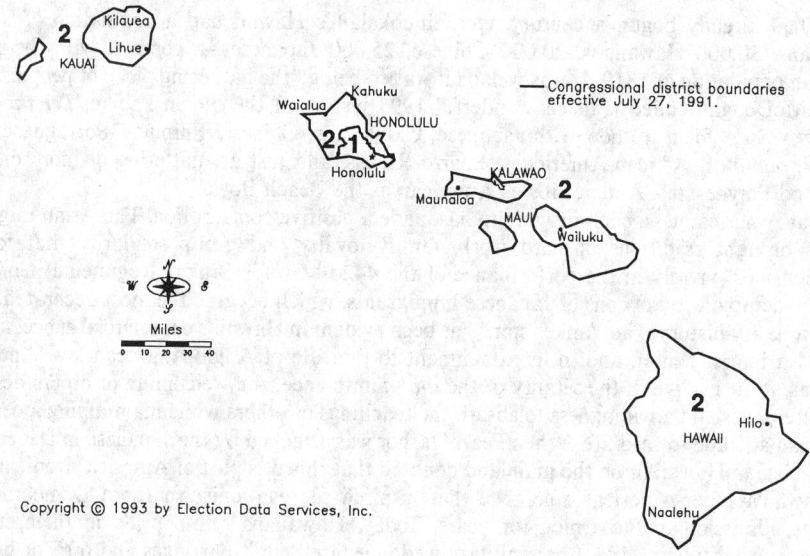

Congressional district boundaries effective July 27, 1991.

spend all the Estate's huge income on the Kamehameha School whose students are all native Hawaiians and whose teachers are supposed to be all Protestants. State government has been controlled by essentially the same Democratic machine since 1962, which clinched control of the Bishop Estate board in the 1980s. Most of this land is held on long-term leaseholds; since a state law forcing outright sales was upheld by the U.S. Supreme Court in 1984, the Bishop Estate has recently sought to diversify, buying a $250 million stake in the investment firm of Goldman Sachs and buying other businesses, but avoiding taxes by seeking favorable IRS rulings and using losses from some operations to offset profits from others.

The second peculiar characteristic of Hawaii is its *aloha* spirit. Hawaiians want to be Americans—if they didn't, the islands would have become independent, as the Philippines did, or might have sought a separate status, like Puerto Rico. But they have always had, in accentuated form, the tolerance of diversity that is a keynote of the American experience, and each group's traditions still remain distinctive. The Japanese, the largest single migrant group after whites (who are sometimes called *haoles*), are by most measures the most successful, doing well in professions and organizations such as unions, government and the Democratic Party. Whites still tend to have the highest incomes: many came to Hawaii after success on the mainland. Filipinos for years have tended to fill menial jobs, though the new governor is of Philippine descent; native Hawaiians have tended to have lower incomes and to have special medical and legal benefits. Politically, the whites have tended to be Republican, and Japanese and other groups Democratic.

Hawaii's dominant political institution is the Democratic Party which, under a single chain of leadership, has welded Hawaii's disparate groups together to win elections since territorial days. It had its beginning in the 1950s when returning World War II veterans like Daniel Inouye, Spark Matsunaga and George Ariyoshi joined forces with former mainlander John Burns, who as a policeman during the war helped prevent persecution of Japanese Americans. They allied themselves with the then powerful International Longshoremen's and Warehousemen's Union, and cemented the allegiance of Japanese American voters. In the 1950s, Hawaii, resenting mainland southern Democratic senators who delayed statehood, tended to vote Republican. But Inouye was elected to the House as a Democrat in 1959 and the Senate in 1962, and Republicans have won few elections since. Burns was elected governor in 1962 and retired because of illness in 1974; his chosen successor, George Ariyoshi, won in 1974, 1978 and 1982 and retired when he was ineligible for another term. In time, Inouye split with Ariyoshi, and the ILWU's power waned; the machine became centered on the governor's office and the patronage it controlled, from state judgeships to the trusteeship of the Bishop Estate. But the succession continued: John Waihee was Ariyoshi's man in 1986, and won after a rough campaign; Ben Cayetano, Waihee's lieutenant governor, won a three-way race in 1994. There are echoes here of a Pacific Rim political style—cool, competent, tough, unsentimental; Hawaii is one of the few states to prohibit write-in votes, a law the Supreme Court upheld in 1992.

Governor. Ben Cayetano's election as governor in 1994 was due less to the strength of his Democratic machine than to the weakness and division of his opponents. Former Congresswoman Pat Saiki, a strong though losing candidate against Senator Daniel Akaka in 1990, and of Japanese descent, seemed as potent a candidate as Republicans could field. But she split the anti-Democratic vote with Frank Fasi, longtime (1968–80, 1984–94) mayor of Honolulu. In 1994, Fasi formed his own The Best party, raised money from city employees and was endorsed by the carpenters' union; meanwhile, Lieutenant Governor Cayetano beat state healthcare program director Jack Lewin by only 55%–38% in the September primary. Cayetano said he was more concerned about education than prisons, and argued that Democrats' programs benefited ordinary people; Saiki talked tough on crime and promised a better business climate to "grow" the economy; Fasi combatively stressed his get-things-done record as mayor. Cayetano, relying on a half-hour ad telling his personal story, won with 37% of the vote; Saiki had 31% and Fasi 29%.

In office, Cayetano reluctantly cut spending increases sharply and declined to raise taxes: in tandem with mainland politics. But Hawaii does have its distinctive policies. Its healthcare plan, which since 1974 has had employer mandates and near-universal coverage, was cited in the 1994 healthcare debate. But its geographical discreteness, cultural group-mindedness and small size make it atypical: Blue Cross/Blue Shield and Kaiser Permanente cover 75% already, and costs have risen as on the mainland. Hawaii also has a native sovereignty commission, considering proposals from secession from the U.S. (not likely) to "nation within a nation" (something like an Indian reservation) to "state within a state." This may be brought to a vote in 1996; 1998 is the centennial of annexation.

Senators. The largest figure in Hawaii's public life remains Senator Daniel Inouye, who has held statewide elective office since Hawaii attained statehood in 1959—longer than many Hawaii voters can remember. Inouye was a severely wounded veteran of the 442d Regimental Combat Team, then became a lawyer, and was elected to the state legislature in 1954, the House in 1959 and the Senate in 1962. He was keynoter at the turbulent 1968 Democratic National Convention, a tenacious member of the Senate Watergate Committee in 1973–74 and the first chairman of the Senate Intelligence Committee, in 1976.

What does he believe in? The Senate, the Democratic Party, Hawaii, the armed services, American Indians—among other things. He is the fifth most senior member of the Senate, and a stickler for its prerogatives. He went out of his way to defend senators in his view unjustly attacked—Harrison Williams during the Abscam scandal, Dennis DeConcini of the Keating Five—but was also quick to call for the resignation of Bob Packwood after the Senate voted in 1993 to subpoena his diaries. As number two Democrat on Appropriations and number three in the Democratic leadership from 1979 to 1986, he has worked closely and loyally with Robert Byrd. But when Byrd relinquished the majority leadership in 1988, Inouye won only 14 votes for the post, tied with Bennett Johnston and well behind George Mitchell's 27.

On Appropriations, Inouye, hawkish in the Vietnam years and a critic of Reagan Administration policies in Nicaragua, Lebanon and Grenada in the 1980s, has been concerned in the 1990s that the Pentagon budget is "bare bones," stretched to the breaking point and that the Army is "eating its seed corn." He has always strongly favored aid to Israel. Inouye has long used his seat on Appropriations to fund projects he finds worthy, from his alma mater of George Washington University to the Pacific Island Technical Assistance Program to native Hawaiian education. He was successful in getting the island of Kahoolawe, a federal target range for many years, turned back to the state, with $445 million earmarked for cleanup. He pushed for $1.2 billion in aid after Hurricane Iniki struck Kauai in September 1991. And, after Hurricane Emilia, the strongest Pacific storm ever, narrowly missed Hawaii in August 1994, Inouye proposed a federal natural disaster reinsurance program to protect insurance companies whose reserves would be wiped out by such disasters. All of this is not inconsistent with his general support of federal spending. This is one senator who believes in the federal government and, according to the National Taxpayers Union Foundation, in the first session of the 103d Congress proposed more dollars of spending than any other senator: $561 billion.

On the Commerce Committee, Inouye has been deeply involved in communications issues and tends to favor government regulation over markets. He backed cable reregulation and opposed letting the Regional Bells enter the long-distance market before imposing a competition standard for local services; he wanted to set aside up to 20% of the information superhighway for libraries, schools, state and local governments and nonprofits. He chaired the Indian Affairs Committee, where he worked to authorize a new building on Washington's Mall to house part of the American Indian Museum collection. In 1990, he got $2 million for a drug-free schools program for American Indians and Hawaiian natives; in the 1990 crime bill, he also got Indian reservations exempted from the federal death penalty—although individuals there are still subject to tribal law. He backed Indian gaming in 1988 but is pushing to tighten federal control over it, with a tax of up to 2% of gross revenues. He wants to strengthen the 1978 American Indian Religious Freedom Act so that government must have a "compelling interest" before disturbing a sacred site. He sponsored a 1993 bill in which the United States apologized for helping to overthrow the Hawaiian monarchy, and is sympathetic to the claim of native Hawaiians for some form of sovereignty; in 1994, he moved to apply the religious practices bill to them.

Honolulu is a long two flights from Washington, and Inouye's local influence has varied. In 1986 and 1990, he supported John Waihee for governor and Daniel Akaka for senator; both won close races. But Inouye was subjected to attacks in his 1992 campaign as never before. He was opposed by brash Republican legislator Rick Reed, who started a newspaper in Maui in the 1970s and defended himself successfully in a libel suit by an alleged organized crime figure. Reed called Inouye a Washington insider and defender of the Keating Five and ran an ad with tapes of a woman barber, Lenore Kwock, who had cut Inouye's hair for 20 years, in which she accused Inouye of forcing himself on her sexually some 17 years ago. Kwock did not deny the charges but said she was taped without her consent and demanded the ad be pulled, and it was. But on election day Inouye won with a much reduced percentage, 57%, to 27% for Reed and 14% for the Green Party's Linda Martin. After the election, Democratic state Representative Annelle Amaral said she received calls from nine women alleging sexual harassment by Inouye. The issue was referred to the Senate Ethics Committee, but no witness would come forward; Amaral apologized to Inouye, and the Ethics Committee dropped the case in April 1993. It is not clear whether Inouye will run again in 1998, when he turns 74, especially if Democrats remain in the minority.

Daniel Akaka, native Hawaiian, congressman since 1976, loyal member of the Democratic machine, was appointed to the Senate by Governor Waihee after the death in April 1990 of Spark Matsunaga, 442d Regiment veteran and chief sponsor of the Japanese American Reparations Act. In the House, Akaka had been a quiet member of the Appropriations Committee; in the Senate, he has been a quiet member of Energy and Governmental Affairs. In fall 1990 he faced Republican Congresswoman Pat Saiki in a special election that hinged on local more than national issues. For instance, the target range on the island of Kahoolawe: Saiki got President Bush to order the bombing stopped; Akaka trumped her with a ban in an appropriations bill. Akaka also introduced two amendments to the crime bill for stiffer penalties for use and distribution of "ice," a drug even more addictive than cocaine that came to Hawaii from Korea and Taiwan. Saiki conceded that Akaka was congenial but suggested he was ineffective and not too bright; Akaka fought back hard, with a media campaign stressing his drug and bombing range amendments, with endorsements from environmental groups, and with a Democratic organizational effort as strong as any Hawaii has seen in years. Akaka won 54%–45%, carrying not just the Democratic Neighbor Islands and poorer areas of Honolulu, but most of Oahu as well.

Since 1990, Akaka has worked mostly on Hawaii issues. The island of Kahoolawe, the former government bombing range, was transferred to Hawaii, with $445 million for cleanup; a tropical forest recovery bill was passed; so was a law to stop the introduction of alien species to Hawaii, especially the brown tree snake which has devastated Guam. He orchestrated the authorization of direct V.A. home loans to native Americans and Hawaiians living on trust lands, and helped set up a Pacific Center for Post-Traumatic Stress Disorder for veterans. As chairman of the Mineral Resources Subcommittee, he supported the revision of the Mining Act of 1872 to impose mineral royalties; highly unpopular in the mountain West, the proposal died. Hawaii is one state where a high Clinton rating was not a liability in 1994: Akaka, at age 70, beat Molokai rancher Maria Hustace 72%–24% in a virtual non-contest. Under the new Republican regime, this reliable Democrat is not likely to be much of a player in the legislative mix.

Presidential politics. Hawaii's presidential voting over the years has been the product of two countervailing forces. One is the Islands' strong Democratic partisan preference, since voters tend to favor big government and value tolerance of diversity. This helps explain why Hawaii voted Democratic when most states didn't in 1980 and 1988. The other is an inclination to support incumbents in a state that takes patriotism very seriously, in part because the patriotism of so many of its citizens was once unjustly questioned and in part because, in these heavily fortified Pacific islands, foreign threats seem more menacing. This helps explain why Hawaii supported President Reagan solidly in 1984 and came close to voting for President Ford in 1976. But the pro-incumbent tilt here was not enough for George Bush in 1992: Ross Perot's military background, and the presence of Hawaiian Orson Swindle among his top leaders, gave him 14% and helped Bill Clinton carry Hawaii 48%–37%. Exit polling indicated that Bush's poor showing here, as on the West Coast, came from the collapse of his support among affluent whites: the white vote was 48%–32% for Clinton, while it was 42%–41% for Republican Rick Reed over Senator Daniel Inouye. But the Asian vote, which is mostly Japanese American, went only 50%–43% for Clinton, despite its usual strong Democratic preference, apparent in its 77%–17% vote for Inouye; Japanese American support for the commander-in-chief is still strong. Others, mainly Native Hawaiians and Filipinos, were solidly Democratic in both races: 61%–28% for Clinton, 73%–21% for Inouye. For 1996, Hawaii's Democratic and pro-incumbent tilt both point toward a Clinton victory here, whatever happens on the Mainland.

Hawaii chooses presidential delegates by caucus. In 1992, they quietly opted for Bill Clinton and George Bush—a contrast from 1988, when the Democrats' choice was Jesse Jackson and the Republican state party establishment, finding its membership ranks swelled by Pat Robertson supporters, canceled a scheduled straw poll for a week, but then let Robertson win.

Congressional districting. Hawaii has two congressional districts: the 1st includes urban Honolulu (city elections now cover all of Oahu) and extends westward to Pearl Harbor and the rural area beyond; the 2d includes the rest of Oahu and the Neighbor Islands. Redistricting by a bipartisan commission changed the lines only slightly. Both districts are represented by liberal Democrats who had served in the past, then lost elections, ran again and won in 1990 and have been reelected since.

The People: Est. Pop. 1994: 1,179,000; Pop. 1990: 1,108,229, up 6.3% 1990–1994. 0.5% of U.S. total, 40th largest; 11% rural. Median age: 32.6 years. 11.3% 65 years and over. 61.8% Asian, 33.4% White, 7.3% Hispanic origin, 2.5% Black, 1.9% Other. Households: 59.1% married couple families; 29% married couple fams. w. children; 51% college educ.; median household income: $38,829; per capita income: $15,770; 53.9% owner occupied housing; median house value: $245,300; median monthly rent: $599. 4.5% Unemployment. 1994 Voting age pop.: 900,000. 1994 Turnout: 369,013; 41% of VAP. Registered voters (1994): 488,889; no party registration.

Political Lineup: Governor, Benjamin J. Cayetano (D); Lt. Gov., Mazie Hirono (D); Atty. Gen., Robert Marks (D); Comptroller, Eugene Imia (D). State Senate, 25 (23 D and 2 R); State House of Representatives, 51 (46 D and 5 R). Senators, Daniel K. Inouye (D) and Daniel K. Akaka (D). Representatives, 2 (2 D).

1992 Presidential Vote			1988 Presidential Vote		
Clinton (D)	179,310	(48%)	Dukakis (D)	192,364	(54%)
Bush (R)	136,822	(37%)	Bush (R)	158,625	(45%)
Perot (I)	53,003	(14%)			

GOVERNOR

Gov. Benjamin J. Cayetano (D)

Elected 1994, term expires Jan. 1999. b. Nov. 14, 1939, Honolulu; home, Honolulu; U. of CA, B.A. 1968; Loyola Law Schl., J.D. 1971; Christian; married (Lorraine).

Career: Practicing atty., 1971–86; HI House of Reps., 1975–78; HI Senate 1979–86; HI Lt. Gov., 1986–90.

Office: State Capitol, Executive Chambers, Honolulu 96813, 808-586-0034; Fax: 808-586-0006.

Election Results

1994 gen.	Benjamin J. Cayetano (D)	134,978	(37%)
	Frank F. Fasi (Best)	113,158	(31%)
	Patricia F. Saiki (R)	107,908	(29%)
	Others	12,969	(4%)
1994 prim.	Benjamin J. Cayetano (D)	110,489	(55%)
	John (Jack) Lewin (D)	76,606	(38%)
	Others	14,305	(7%)
1990 gen.	John D. Waihee III (D)	203,491	(60%)
	Fred Hemmings (R)	131,310	(39%)
	Others	5,331	(2%)

SENATORS

Sen. Daniel K. Inouye (D)

Elected 1962, seat up 1998; b. Sept. 7, 1924, Honolulu; home, Honolulu; U. of HI, B.A. 1950, George Washington U., J.D. 1952; United Methodist; married (Margaret).

Career: Army, 1943–47 (WWII); Honolulu Dep. Public Prosecutor, 1953–54; HI House of Reps., 1954–58; HI Senate, 1958–59; U.S. House of Reps., 1959–62.

DC Office: 722 HSOB 20510, 202-224-3934; Fax: 202-224-6747.

State Offices: 7325 Prince Kuhio Fed. Bldg., 300 Ala Moana Blvd., Honolulu 96850, 808-541-2542.

Committees: *Appropriations* (2nd of 13 D): Commerce, Justice, State and Judiciary; Defense (RMM); Foreign Operations; Labor, Health and Human Services, Education; Military Construction. *Commerce, Science & Transportation* (2nd of 9 D): Aviation; Communications; Oceans and Fisheries; Surface Transportation and Merchant Marine (RMM). *Rules & Administration* (4th of 7 D). *Indian Affairs* (Vice Chmn. of 8 D).

Group Ratings

	ADA	ACLU	COPE	CFA	LCV	CON	NSI	COC	ACU	NTLC	CHC
1994	75	79	88	83	69	3	43	26	0	9	0
1993	85	—	100	80	56	2	—	20	13	—	—

National Journal Ratings

	1993 LIB — 1993 CONS		1994 LIB — 1994 CONS	
Economic	67%	32%	84%	0%
Social	92%	0%	76%	19%
Foreign	40%	57%	57%	42%

Key Votes of the 103d Congress

1. Clinton Deficit Plan	Y	3. Brady Handgun Purchase	Y	5. Lmt. UN Cmnd. of Forces	N
2. NAFTA	N	4. Strike Race/Death Pnlty.	N	6. Cut Missile Funds	N

Key Votes of the 104th Congress

1. Congressional Compliance	Y	3. Balanced Budget Amndt.	N	5. Product Liability Reform	N
2. Bar Unfunded Mandates	*	4. Pass Line Item Veto	N	6. FY96 Budget	N

Election Results

1992 general	Daniel K. Inouye (D)	208,266	(57%)	($3,515,722)
	Rick Reed (R)	97,928	(27%)	($438,851)
	Linda B. Martin (Green)	49,921	(14%)	($6,687)
	Other	7,547	(2%)	
1992 primary	Daniel K. Inouye (D)	94,827	(79%)	
	Wayne K. Nishiki (D)	25,782	(21%)	
1986 general	Daniel K. Inouye (D)	241,887	(74%)	($1,039,418)
	Frank Hutchinson (R)	86,910	(26%)	($31,843)

Sen. Daniel K. Akaka (D)

Appointed May, 1990, seat up 2000; b. Sept. 11, 1924, Honolulu; home, Honolulu; U. of HI, B.A. 1953, M.A. 1966; Congregationalist; married (Mary Mildred).

Career: Army Corps of Engineers, 1945–47 (WWII); Public schl. teacher, principal and admin., 1953–71; Dir., HI Office of Econ. Oppor., 1971–74; Asst., HI Gov. Ariyoshi, 1975–76; Dir., Progressive Neighborhoods Program, 1975–76; U.S. House of Reps., 1977–90.

DC Office: 720 HSOB 20510, 202-224-6361; Fax: 202-224-2126.

State Offices: 3104 Prince Kuhio Fed. Bldg., 300 Ala Moana Blvd., Honolulu 96850, 808-541-2534.

Committees: *Energy & Natural Resources* (6th of 8 D): Energy Production and Regulation; Oversight and Investigations (RMM). *Governmental Affairs* (6th of 7 D): Oversight of Government Management and the District of Columbia; Investigations; Post Office and Civil Service. *Veterans' Affairs* (3rd of 5 D). *Indian Affairs* (5th of 8 D).

Group Ratings

	ADA	ACLU	COPE	CFA	LCV	CON	NSI	COC	ACU	NTLC	CHC
1994	85	79	88	83	62	10	30	26	0	4	0
1993	90	—	91	90	81	16	—	18	4	—	—

National Journal Ratings

	1993 LIB — 1993 CONS			1994 LIB — 1994 CONS		
Economic	83%	—	0%	84%	—	0%
Social	87%	—	8%	76%	—	19%
Foreign	53%	—	39%	60%	—	39%

Key Votes of the 103d Congress

1. Clinton Deficit Plan	Y	3. Brady Handgun Purchase Y	5. Lmt. UN Cmnd. of Forces N
2. NAFTA	N	4. Strike Race/Death Pnlty. N	6. Cut Missile Funds N

Key Votes of the 104th Congress

1. Congressional Compliance	Y	3. Balanced Budget Amndt. N	5. Product Liability Reform N
2. Bar Unfunded Mandates	*	4. Pass Line Item Veto N	6. FY96 Budget N

Election Results

1994 general	Daniel K. Akaka (D)	256,189	(72%)	($1,017,872)
	Maria M. Hustace (R)	86,320	(24%)	($29,293)
	Richard O. Rowland (Lib)	14,393	(4%)	
1994 primary	Daniel K. Akaka (D)	unopposed		
1990 general	Daniel K. Akaka (D)	188,901	(54%)	($1,691,384)
	Patricia Saiki (R)	155,978	(45%)	($2,398,961)
	Other.......................	4,787	(1%)	
1990 primary	Daniel K. Akaka (D)	180,235	(91%)	
	Paul Snider (D).....................	18,427	(9%)	

FIRST DISTRICT

Tourists in Honolulu see the airport and adjacent Hickam Air Force Base, the Arizona monument in Pearl Harbor, perhaps the downtown with its wondrously Victorian Iolani Palace and early 20th Century buildings amid high-rises, and of course Waikiki, with its 40-story hotels rising within a few feet of one another, its restaurants and souvenir shops. But few of Hawaii's 1st District voters live in any of these places. The neighborhoods around Honolulu's downtown and the university campus are lower income and usually Democratic. To the west, around the harbor, are many military families in modest neighborhoods who may vote for Democrats but can be attracted to Republicans. To the east, past Waikiki, around Diamond Head and out to the Kahala and Koko Head beach areas, is higher-income territory, voting for Republicans when they seriously contest a race.

The 1st District is represented by Neil Abercrombie, a Democrat with a greying beard and pony tail; his home is decorated with leis and a Buddha statue; he debates with an aggressiveness and bombast tempered by enthusiasm and good humor. He is a sociology Ph.D. with a visceral skepticism about military spending; but he has also worked for more military housing in Hawaii. He is proud of passing a Humpback Whale Marine Sanctuary for Hawaii, a plutonium safety act, a renewal of the Native Hawaiian Health Care Act, and obtaining increased money for Child Advocacy Centers. He has a liberal voting record, tempered by a move to the middle on economics in 1993. He seems to relish controversial stands, from opposing the joint operating agreements Honolulu newspapers wanted, to protesting one of the many Clinton Haiti policies, to favoring new elevators to replace the slow-moving lifts in the Longworth Building.

Abercrombie first came to the House in 1986, when he won a special election, and served only three months; he lost a primary for the full term to a Democrat who attacked him unfairly and who then lost to Republican Pat Saiki. When she ran for the Senate, Abercrombie won a three-way primary for the House seat and won the 1990 and 1992 general elections easily. In 1994 he had serious competition from Orson Swindle, Marine Corps pilot and Vietnam POW, Reagan Administration appointee, national leader of Ross Perot's United We Stand America and co-founder of Jack Kemp's and William Bennett's Empower America. As head of the Economic Development Administration, Swindle blew the whistle on then-Speaker Jim Wright's seeking government financing for his benefactor George Mallick. Swindle campaigned hard against Abercrombie's pro-Clinton and dovish voting record, carried Republican areas and made serious inroads elsewhere. But Abercrombie raised over $200,000 from PACs, compared to $20,000 for Swindle, and with that financial advantage, and the Hawaiian proclivity to reelect the incumbent, won 54%–43%.

Given Abercrombie's readiness to vote his convictions without much regard for the political fallout, and unless national opinion shifts sharply to the Democrats, the 1st District could be seriously contested again in 1996.

The People: Pop. 1990: 554,174; 12% age 65+; 29% White; 2% Black; 67% Asian; 1% Other; 5% Hispanic origin. Voting age pop.: 431,736; 2% Black; 4% Hispanic origin. Households: 58% married couple families; 26% married couple fams. w. children; 54% college educ.; median household income: $40,257; per capita income: $17,508; median gross rent: $659; median house value: $307,800.

1992 Presidential Vote

Clinton (D)	87,664	(47%)
Bush (R)	72,182	(39%)
Perot (I)	23,442	(13%)

1988 Presidential Vote

Dukakis (D)	99,302	(54%)
Bush (R)	83,361	(46%)

Rep. Neil Abercrombie (D)

Elected 1990; b. June 26, 1938, Buffalo, NY; home, Honolulu; Union Col., B.A. 1959, U. of HI, M.A 1964, Ph.D. 1974; no religious affiliation; married (Nancie Caraway).

Career: Elem. and high schl. teacher, 1959–63; Probation Officer, Marin Cnty., CA, 1964–67; Sociologist, 1967–74; HI House of Reps., 1974–78; HI Senate, 1978–86; Asst. prof., HI Loa Col., 1979–80; Consultant, 1983–87, 1989–90; U.S. House of Reps., 1986–87; Asst., HI Superintendent of Educ., 1987–88; Honolulu City Cncl., 1988–90.

DC Office: 1233 LHOB 20515, 202-225-2726.

District Offices: 300 Ala Moana Blvd., #4104, Honolulu 96850, 808-541-2570.

Committees: *National Security* (13th of 25 D): Military Installations and Facilities; Military Procurement. *Resources* (11th of 20 D): Energy and Mineral Resources (RMM).

Group Ratings

	ADA	ACLU	COPE	CFA	LCV	CON	NSI	COC	ACU	NTLC	CHC
1994	100	83	89	100	89	15	0	25	0	4	0
1993	100	—	100	100	79	19	—	9	4	—	—

National Journal Ratings

	1993 LIB — 1993 CONS		1994 LIB — 1994 CONS	
Economic	66%	— 33%	83%	— 0%
Social	87%	— 0%	86%	— 13%
Foreign	87%	— 7%	85%	— 0%

Key Votes of the 103d Congress

1. Clinton Deficit Plan	Y	3. Brady Handgun Purchase	Y	5. Lmt. UN Cmnd. of Forces	N
2. NAFTA	N	4. Strike Race/Death Pnlty.	N	6. Cut Missile Funds	Y

Key Votes of the 104th Congress

1. Congressional Compliance	Y	6. Reform Crime Grant	N	11. Loser Pays Court Reform	N
2. Balanced Budget Amndmt.	N	7. National Security Act	N	12. Product Liability Reform	N
3. Bar Unfunded Mandates	N	8. Moratorium on Regs.	N	13. Welfare Reform	N
4. Pass Line Item Veto	N	9. Risk Assessment on Regs.	N	14. Term Limits Amndmt.	N
5. Relax Exclusionary Rule	N	10. Expnd. Priv. Prop. Rights	N	15. Tax Cuts	N

Election Results

1994 general	Neil Abercrombie (D)	94,754	(54%)	($391,451)
	Orson Swindle III (R)	76,623	(43%)	($276,355)
	Others	5,329	(3%)	
1994 primary	Neil Abercrombie (D)	65,145	(66%)	
	Dennis M. Nakasato (D)	32,851	(34%)	
1992 general	Neil Abercrombie (D).	129,332	(73%)	($359,681)
	Warner C. Sutton (R)	41,575	(23%)	($16,103)
	Rockne Hart Johnson (LIB)	6,569	(4%)	

SECOND DISTRICT

The 2d District of Hawaii includes not only the Neighbor Islands but most of Oahu's acreage except for Honolulu. It has Wheeler Air Force Base, still looking much as it did in December 1941, and the farmlands north of Pearl Harbor, between two jagged chains of mountains that lift the island out of the sea. Over the mountains to the west is the Leeward Coast—calm, sultry and lightly populated; over the mountains to the northeast is the Windward Coast—windy, as its name implies—with many prosperous and Republican subdivisions in and around Kaneohe and Kailua. The Neighbor Islands have distinct personalities. Hawaii, the Big Island, is large enough to boast huge cattle ranches, the active volcano of Kilauea, and Mauna Kea, the highest mountain in the world if you count from its base far under the ocean to the peak, rising in a slow slant from Hilo on the Kona Coast. On the north shore, with heavy rainfall and tropical foliage, is the old port of Hilo and Hawaii's macadamia nut industry; this is a blue-collar Democratic area. On the Kona Coast, where there is little rainfall and the landscape is dominated by lava flows, there are retirement condominiums and a higher-income, more Republican population. Maui in recent years has been the fastest-developing island, with dozens of luxury condominiums and vast upscale resorts. Kauai, much of which was devastated by Hurricane Iniki in 1991, is the least-developed and most agricultural of the main islands; parts of it have the nation's highest rainfall, while others seldom get wet. Its large farm work force makes it the most Democratic of the islands.

The 2d District is represented by Patsy Mink, still exuberant and enthusiastically liberal after a long congressional career: she was first elected in 1964, gave up the seat to run unsuccessfully for the Senate in 1976, then, after losing races for governor in 1986 and mayor of Honolulu in 1988, won the House seat again in 1990 after incumbent Daniel Akaka was appointed to the Senate. She helped feminism grow from a fringe cause to one of the main rallying cries for Democrats, and sponsored a gender equity act, which passed the House and then the Senate—though in a more diluted form—and women's healthcare measures. She wants the Pentagon to pay for "impact" education aid in locales, such as military bases, where there are a large number of families with children. She wants to expand Head Start to include full-day, full-year programs. The 1994 elections disappointed her. "I will not like having to just wait for the other side to make their move in order to get something done," she said, adding that she fears that the effect of medical care and Social Security cuts will not be felt until after the 1996 elections.

Mink won the seat in 1990 by narrowly edging former 1st District incumbent (1986–88) Mufi Hannemann in the primary; she has won easily ever since.

The People: Pop. 1990: 554,055; 22% rural; 10% age 65+; 35% White; 2% Black; 1% Amer. Indian; 57% Asian; 2% Other; 9% Hispanic origin. Voting age pop.: 396,268; 2% Black; 7% Hispanic origin. Households: 64% married couple families; 33% married couple fams. w. children; 48% college educ.; median household income: $37,247; per capita income: $14,032; median gross rent: $633; median house value: $189,700.

1992 Presidential Vote

Clinton (D)	91,646	(49%)
Bush (R)	64,640	(34%)
Perot (I)	29,561	(16%)

1988 Presidential Vote

Dukakis (D)	93,062	(55%)
Bush (R)	75,264	(45%)

Rep. Patsy T. Mink (D)

Elected Sept., 1990; b. Dec. 6, 1927, Paia, Maui; home, Honolulu; U. of HI, B.A. 1948, U. of Chicago, J.D. 1951; Protestant; married (John Francis).

Career: Practicing atty., 1953–64, 1987–90; HI House of Reps., 1956–58; HI Senate, 1959, 1963–64; U.S. House of Reps., 1964–76; U.S. Asst. Secy. of State for Oceans and Intl. Environment and Scientific Affairs, 1977–78; Pres., Americans for Democratic Action, 1978–81; Honolulu City Cncl., 1983–87.

DC Office: 2135 RHOB 20515, 202-225-4906; Fax: 202-225-4987.

District Offices: 5104 Prince Kuhio Fed. Bldg., P.O. Box 50124, Honolulu 96850, 808-541-1966.

Committees: *Budget* (9th of 18 D). *Economic & Educational Opportunities* (9th of 19 D): Early Childhood, Youth and Families; Workforce Protections.

Group Ratings

	ADA	ACLU	COPE	CFA	LCV	CON	NSI	COC	ACU	NTLC	CHC
1994	100	87	100	100	89	9	0	17	0	11	0
1993	100	—	100	100	86	25	—	0	4	—	—

National Journal Ratings

	1993 LIB — 1993 CONS	1994 LIB — 1994 CONS
Economic	88% — 0%	83% — 0%
Social	87% — 0%	94% — 0%
Foreign	93% — 0%	85% — 0%

Key Votes of the 103d Congress

1. Clinton Deficit Plan	Y	3. Brady Handgun Purchase	Y	5. Lmt. UN Cmnd. of Forces	N
2. NAFTA	N	4. Strike Race/Death Pnlty.	N	6. Cut Missile Funds	Y

Key Votes of the 104th Congress

1. Congressional Compliance	Y	6. Reform Crime Grant	N	11. Loser Pays Court Reform	N
2. Balanced Budget Amndmt.	N	7. National Security Act	N	12. Product Liability Reform	N
3. Bar Unfunded Mandates	N	8. Moratorium on Regs.	N	13. Welfare Reform	N
4. Pass Line Item Veto	N	9. Risk Assessment on Regs.	N	14. Term Limits Amndmt.	N
5. Relax Exclusionary Rule	N	10. Expnd. Priv. Prop. Rights	N	15. Tax Cuts	N

Election Results

1994 general	Patsy T. Mink (D)	124,431	(70%)	($157,523)
	Robert H. Garner (R)	42,891	(24%)	
	Larry R. Bartley (Lib)	10,074	(6%)	
1994 primary	Patsy T. Mink (D)	79,351	(85%)	
	David Louis Bourgoin (D)	14,221	(15%)	
1992 general	Patsy T. Mink (D)	131,454	(73%)	($287,017)
	Kamuela Price (R)	40,070	(22%)	($772)
	Lloyd (Jeff) Mallan (LIB)	9,431	(5%)	

IDAHO

Far off toward the northwest corner of the continental 48 states, little noticed on the national news and seldom thought of by most citizens, Idaho is nevertheless one of the success stories—maybe *the* success story—of America's 1990s. Its economy has been robust: employment was up 39% and personal income up 74% from 1987 to 1994. Idaho's biggest businesses—J. R. Simplot's potato empire, Micron Technology and Albertson's supermarkets—have grown and dozens of new high-tech and service businesses are springing up. Population is up 12.5% since 1990, as Idaho has attracted high-skill workers who like having wilderness so nearby and a family lifestyle where traditional values are respected and traditional rules enforced.

For the wilderness is never far away here, nor is the understanding of the life of the first settlers. Towering over the state Capitol in Boise is the vast peak of Shafer Butte, and a few miles away are impassable mountains; Idaho ranks third in National Wilderness lands behind California and Alaska. This was the last North American area European pioneers—fur traders—set eyes on. The first farmers in Idaho were New England Yankees led by ministers wending their way west on the Oregon Trail into the broad Snake River Valley. Idaho's northern panhandle, an extension of Washington's Columbia Valley, was first settled by miners seeking gold and silver; loggers followed. Mormons moved north from Utah and settled in eastern Idaho. But what brought the most settlers were federal water reclamation projects first authorized in 1894, which transformed the barren Snake River Valley into some of the nation's best volcanic soil-enriched farmland. Many Idahoans knew personally the people who pioneered this state, built the first towns and farms, established the first churches and schools and became its community leaders. Yet while Idaho remains close to its roots, it is also cosmopolitan. Its potato-based agriculture which uses more water per capita than any other state—a fact of political significance—makes this an exporting state, shipping foodstuffs as well as lumber to the other side of the Pacific Rim. Add Idaho's high-tech development, and you have a state very much connected to the world beyond.

Idaho politics for years was run by two bosses—Democrat Tom Boise from the panhandle and Republican Lloyd Adams from the Mormon east—who could patch together statewide alliances from the regional divisions still apparent today. Overall, Idaho is heavily Republican. Even in 1992, the Boise area and the Magic Valley east along the Snake and Pocatello Rivers voted for George Bush over Bill Clinton and Ross Perot by 44%–28%–26%. But the panhandle voted 37% for Clinton to 33% for Bush and 29% for Perot, a result similar to eastern Washington state. In contrast, the mostly Mormon counties in the east voted 48% for Bush, 28% for Perot and only 18% for Clinton, very much like Utah. Similar patterns, modified by the candidates' regional strengths, prevailed in 1990s statewide races.

Although its first settlers had a Republican heritage, silver-mining Idaho went for William Jennings Bryan and free silver in 1896, and then supported Woodrow Wilson and Franklin D. Roosevelt; as late as 1960, John F. Kennedy won 46% of the vote here. Idaho produced prominent national politicians of both parties—notably, Senate Foreign Relations Committee Chairmen William Borah, a Republican, and Frank Church, a Democrat. Then, ahead of the national trend, Idaho turned right. Idahoans began to think of themselves less as downtrodden employees of absentee corporations needing a protective federal government, and more as pioneering entrepreneurs who needed to get a bloated, bossy federal government off their backs. The federal government owns 65% of Idaho's land; when regulatory measures block exploitation of local resources to protect the environment—vetoing a logging operation or preventing sheep-ranchers from destroying coyotes—Washington can arouse fierce resentment here. In April 1995, soon after endangered grey wolves were let back into the wild in Idaho, one was found shot

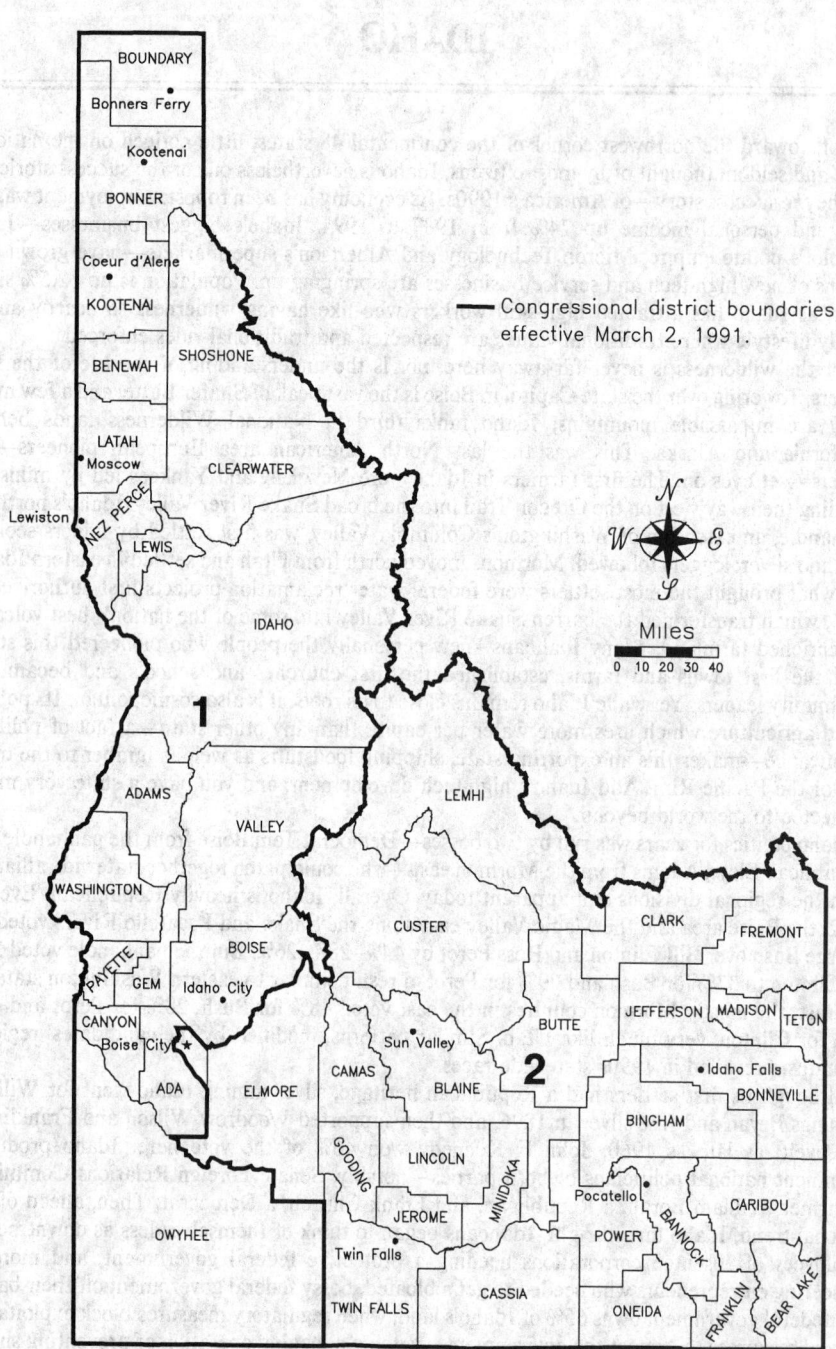

Congressional district boundaries
effective March 2, 1991.

BOUNDARY

Bonners Ferry

Kootenai

BONNER

Coeur d'Alene

KOOTENAI

BENEWAH

SHOSHONE

LATAH
Moscow

CLEARWATER

Lewiston

NEZ PERCE

LEWIS

IDAHO

1

ADAMS

VALLEY

LEMHI

WASHINGTON

CUSTER

CLARK

FREMONT

BOISE

JEFFERSON   MADISON   TETON

PAYETTE

GEM
Idaho City

BUTTE

CANYON
Boise City

Sun Valley

Idaho Falls

ADA

CAMAS

2

BONNEVILLE

ELMORE

BLAINE

BINGHAM

GOODING

LINCOLN

MINIDOKA

Pocatello

CARIBOU

JEROME

OWYHEE

Twin Falls

POWER

BANNOCK

CASSIA

ONEIDA

FRANKLIN   BEAR LAKE

TWIN FALLS

Miles
0 10 20 30 40

Copyright © 1993 by Election Data Services, Inc.

to death on a rancher's farm. When U.S. Fish and Wildlife officers (who routinely are armed) arrived to investigate and serve a search warrant on the rancher, 74-year old Gene Hussey, the local sheriff was called in to avoid a possible physical confrontation. Hundreds of people organized in central Idaho to protest the federal government's tactics, saying "We are not Waco, Texas," referring to federal raids at the Branch Davidian compound. Proposals to revise the Mining Act of 1872 and raise grazing fees on federal lands have in many Idahoans' minds become "Clinton's war on the West"; the 1994 network exit polls showed that voters felt the administration's environmental policies hurt rather than helped the state by a 54%–14% margin.

That strong anti-Washington and anti-Clinton feeling has had its effect on state politics. For nearly 40 years Democrats held either the governorship or one Senate seat in Idaho; the state elected nothing but Democratic governors from 1970 to 1990. But in 1994 Republican Phil Batt won the governorship over Democrat Larry EchoHawk, and Republicans now hold both of Idaho's Senate and House seats—the first time they have held all five of these posts since 1954.

Governor. Phil Batt is a potato grower from Canyon County, west of Boise; he was elected to the state House in 1964, at age 37, served 14 years in the state Senate, was elected lieutenant governor in 1978 and ran for governor and lost to John Evans in 1982 by a 51%–49% margin. (Evans's victory was part of a Democratic chain starting with Cecil Andrus's wins in 1970 and 1974; Evans then won two full terms in 1978 and 1982 after Andrus became Jimmy Carter's Secretary of the Interior, and Andrus came back for two more wins in 1986 and 1990.) In a state as sparsely populated as Idaho, genuinely talented politicians are fairly rare; Batt seems to have shown talent in the legislature and had great success as Republican state chairman in 1992. He believes "the private sector can do nearly anything better than the government," and opposes higher taxes and heavy regulation.

Batt's election in 1994 came only after a serious contest. He won his primary 48%–33% and then had to face Attorney General Larry EchoHawk. EchoHawk is a Pawnee Indian, and newspapers in and out of Idaho dwelled on the possibility that he would be the first Native American elected governor of any state. But other factors were more important. One was his profession of friendship for President Clinton—a distinct minus in the state, despite EchoHawk's opposition to gun control and some Clinton Interior policies. Another was the fact that EchoHawk is a Mormon, and he received many contributions from prominent Utah Republican Mormons. In November EchoHawk split the Idaho Mormon vote evenly and, as a result, ran even with Batt in usually Republican eastern Idaho. But Batt narrowly carried the often Democratic panhandle 48%–47%, for a 52%–44% final victory. During the campaign both candidates were able to agree on one issue: Idaho had a ballot proposition banning gay-rights laws; it was opposed by both Batt and EchoHawk and lost 50.4%–49.6.

Senators. Idaho is represented in the Senate by two Republican freshmen, who even before the 1994 election took the lead on major Republican initiatives—Larry Craig on the balanced budget amendment, Dirk Kempthorne on unfunded federal mandates.

Larry Craig, still in his first term, is one of the most conservative senators (he and Kempthorne tied for first place at the conservative end of the ideological spectrum in the 1994 *National Journal* ratings) and one of the most aggressive. Born on a farm owned by his family since 1899, he was elected to the state Senate at 29 and to the U.S. House at 35, in 1980. He is a crisp speaker, well-informed and tenacious in his advocacy. He started his battle for the balanced budget constitutional amendment in the House, working with Democrat Charles Stenholm of Texas. In the Senate, Craig's latest version of the amendment would require a three-fifths vote to raise the debt ceiling but, contrary to the views of tax-limitation advocates, it would not require a super-majority to raise taxes. Craig, who has worked closely in the Senate with Democrat Paul Simon, admits it is "not a cure-all" but argues it would "a fundamental change in the budget environment." In the 103rd Congress, he was supported by 41 of the then 44 Republicans. On March 2, 1995, the Senate on a cliff-hanger 65–35 vote fell barely short of gaining the two-thirds vote required to pass the amendment, with all of the 53 Republicans except for Mark Hatfield voting in favor. (Majority Leader Bob Dole subsequently switched and voted against the amendment, with the promise that he would exercise his procedural right to force another vote on the amendment in the 104th Congress.) Although Craig surely would have preferred victory, the outcome gave him further opportunity to play an active role in the high-profile battle over the proposal.

Craig will also play a critical role in battling what Republicans call "Clinton's war on the West." He wants to get federal agencies out of the law enforcement business—as in the grey wolf case—and have them just manage natural resources. He chairs two subcommittees with jurisdiction over forestry and mining, where he has been a staunch opponent of the Clinton Administration's proposed big increases in grazing fees and of revision of the 1872 Mining Act which would impose gross royalties on hard rock minerals, though he concedes that some modest change might be desirable. He seeks also to revise the Endangered Species Act, a moot cause in 1993–94 but a lively possibility in 1995–96. Craig also tends to local issues, such as expanding the Nez Perce Historical Park, site of the last official conflict between the U.S. government and Native Americans. Craig is also one of the most voluble opponents of gun control, not always to his advantage; when he challenged Dianne Feinstein's knowledge of specific guns, she responded by saying that she had had enough experience with guns when she discovered the body of her predecessor as mayor of San Francisco, who had been fatally shot. Craig also angered some when he argued to an Idaho crowd, "Easterners should stop interfering with environmental issues. It isn't a New York City problem. The only endangered species in New York City is probably a free white human being." He quickly and justifiably admitted making "a poor choice of words."

Craig was elected to the Senate in 1990 when James McClure retired after three terms. In the primary, Craig won 59% against Attorney General Jim Jones and in the general stumbled politically only once when he said that if his wife became pregnant by rape, it would be up to her to decide whether to have an abortion. Democrat Ron Twilegar claimed that was a contradiction to Craig's right-to-life votes, and was certainly an indication that abortion may look different as a personal dilemma than it does as a public policy matter for those on all sides of the issue. Craig still won with a solid 61% of the vote. He looks like an easy favorite for reelection in 1996.

The junior senator from Idaho is Dirk Kempthorne, the fourth most conservative senator in the 1993 *National Journal* ratings and tied for the top in 1994. Kempthorne has spent most of his adult life in the political arena, if not always in electoral politics: as Idaho public affairs director for FMC Corporation, an executive at the Idaho Home Builders Association, manager of Phil Batt's 1982 gubernatorial campaign and as mayor of Boise for seven boom years from 1986 to 1993. Kempthorne won the Senate seat in 1992 after two-term incumbent Republican Steve Symms announced his retirement in August 1991. After seven years as mayor of Boise, Kempthorne easily won the Republican primary, but had tough competition in the general from Democratic Congressman Richard Stallings, a former professor at Ricks College in Rexburg, whose conservative votes on abortion and gun control, and Mormon affiliation, helped him win the heavily Mormon 2d District seat four times. Already primed to run against Symms, Stallings easily won his primary. In the general, Kempthorne attacked Stallings for having eight overdrafts on the House bank, pledged never to vote to give away Idaho's water rights, called for a capital gains tax cut and for additional compensation to property owners for federal takings. With solid backing from Symms and McClure, Kempthorne was leading in polls by June 1992; Stallings's charges that Kempthorne raised taxes in Boise didn't turn it around. Kempthorne won with 57%, barely carrying the panhandle, but running far ahead in the Boise market and carrying the Mormon areas in the east.

Kempthorne's major cause in the Senate has been to stop unfunded mandates—when the federal government orders states or localities to do something but doesn't provide the money. In 1994 he worked on a compromise with Governmental Affairs Chairman John Glenn, which passed that committee and its House counterpart with bipartisan support late in the session but did not make it through either chamber. But that Kempthorne version was attacked by *The Wall Street Journal* editorial page as insufficient. In 1995, with the new Republican control,

Majority Leader Bob Dole committed to give the symbolically significant bill number, S. 1, to a strengthened unfunded mandates bill. After Democrat stalwart Robert Byrd, who challenged the proposal for infringing on congressional prerogatives, fought mightily against the proposal for three weeks, the Senate easily passed it with broad bipartisan support. As a junior Senator, Kempthorne impressed colleagues with his knowledgeable and calm demeanor and for holding his own against the experienced Byrd. Kempthorne pointed out that unless unfunded future mandates are banned, the balanced budget amendment might simply move Congress to thrust responsibilities but not resources on the states.

Presidential politics. Idaho remains one of the most Republican states in national politics. If George Bush won only 42% here in 1992, Bill Clinton barely edged Ross Perot out of second place, 28%–27%. Since 1988, Idaho's presidential primary has been held in late May but is not binding; the contest that counted was the caucus vote for delegates in early March. It seems unlikely that many candidates will be touching down at Idaho airports in 1996.

Congressional districting. Idaho has two congressional districts; redistricting for 1992 just shuffled nine Boise precincts between them.

The People: Est. Pop. 1994: 1,133,000; Pop. 1990: 1,006,749, up 12.5% 1990–1994. 0.4% of U.S. total, 42d largest; 43% rural. Median age: 31.5 years. 12.0% 65 years and over. 94.4% White, 5.3% Hispanic origin, 1.4% American Indian, 3.0% Other. Households: 62.2% married couple families; 32% married couple fams. w. children; 49% college educ.; median household income: $25,257; per capita income: $11,457; 70.1% owner occupied housing; median house value: $58,200; median monthly rent: $261. 6.5% Unemployment. 1994 Voting age pop.: 803,000. 1994 Turnout: 413,263; 51% of VAP. Registered voters (1994): 625,803; no party registration.

Political Lineup: Governor, Phil Batt (R); Lt. Gov., C. L. (Butch) Otter (R); Secy. of State, Pete T. Cenarrusa (R); Atty. Gen., Alan Lance (R); Treasurer, Lydia Justice Edwards (R); State Controller, J. D. Williams (D). State Senate, 35 (27 R and 8 D); State House of Representatives, 70 (57 R and 13 D). Senators, Larry Craig (R) and Dirk Kempthorne (R). Representatives, 2 (2 R).

1992 Presidential Vote

Bush (R)	202,645	(42%)
Clinton (D)	137,013	(28%)
Perot (I)	130,395	(27%)

1992 Democratic Presidential Primary

Clinton	27,004	(49%)
Brown	9,212	(17%)
Other	2,879	(5%)
Uncommitted	16,029	(29%)

1988 Presidential Vote

Bush (R)	253,881	(62%)
Dukakis (D)	147,272	(36%)

1992 Republican Presidential Primary

Bush	73,297	(63%)
Buchanan	15,167	(13%)
Uncommitted	27,038	(23%)

GOVERNOR

Gov. Phil Batt (R)

Elected 1994, term expires Jan. 1999; b. Mar. 4, 1927, Wilder; home, Boise; U. of ID, 1944–48; Baptist; married (Jacque).

Career: Army, 1945–46; Onion farmer; ID House of Reps., 1965–67; ID Senate, 1967–78; ID Lt. Gov., 1978–82.

Office: State House, Boise 83720, 208-334-2100; Fax: 208-334-2175.

Election Results

1994 gen.	Phil Batt (R).	216,123	(52%)
	Larry EchoHawk (D).	181,363	(44%)
	Ronald D. Rankin (I).	15,793	(4%)
1994 prim.	Phil Batt (R).	57,066	(48%)
	Larry Eastland (R).	38,664	(33%)
	Charles L. Winder (R).	16,063	(14%)
	Doug Dorn (R).	7,098	(6%)
1990 gen.	Cecil D. Andrus (D).	217,801	(68%)
	Roger Fairchild (R)	101,885	(32%)

SENATORS

Sen. Larry Craig (R)

Elected 1990, seat up 1996; b. July 20, 1945, Midvale; home, Payette; U. of ID, B.A. 1969; United Methodist; married (Suzanne).

Career: Army Natl. Guard, 1970–74; Rancher, farmer; ID Senate, 1974–80; U.S. House of Reps., 1980–90.

DC Office: 313 HSOB 20510, 202-224-2752; Fax: 202-224-2573; e-mail: larry_craig@craig.senate.gov.

State Offices: 304 N. 8th St., #149, Boise 83702, 208-342-7985; 103 N. 4th St., Coeur d'Alene 83814, 208-667-6130; 846 Main St., Lewiston 83501, 208-743-0792; 1292 Addison Ave. E., Twin Falls 83301, 202-734-6780; 250 S. 4th Ave., #216, Pocatello 83201, 208-236-6817; and 2539 Channing Way, Idaho Falls 83404, 208-523-5541.

Committees: *Agriculture, Nutrition & Forestry* (6th of 10 R): Forestry, Conservation and Rural Revitalization (Chmn.); Research, Nutrition and General Legislation. *Energy & Natural Resources* (5th of 10 R): Energy Research and Development; Forests and Public Land Management (Chmn); Oversight and Investigations. *Veterans' Affairs* (7th of 7 R). *Ethics* (3rd of 3 R). *Aging (Special)* (6th of 10 R). *Joint Economic Committee* (3rd of 10 Sen.)

Group Ratings

	ADA	ACLU	COPE	CFA	LCV	CON	NSI	COC	ACU	NTLC	CHC
1994	0	21	13	25	0	80	100	91	100	92	100
1993	5	—	18	20	13	63	—	91	100	—	—

National Journal Ratings

	1993 LIB — 1993 CONS			1994 LIB — 1994 CONS	
Economic	0%	—	87%	0% —	88%
Social	15%	—	84%	0% —	85%
Foreign	0%	—	92%	0% —	94%

Key Votes of the 103d Congress

1. Clinton Deficit Plan	N	3. Brady Handgun Purchase N	5. Lmt. UN Cmnd. of Forces Y
2. NAFTA	N	4. Strike Race/Death Pnlty. Y	6. Cut Missile Funds N

Key Votes of the 104th Congress

1. Congressional Compliance Y	3. Balanced Budget Amndt. Y	5. Product Liability Reform Y
2. Bar Unfunded Mandates Y	4. Pass Line Item Veto Y	6. FY96 Budget Y

Election Results

1990 general	Larry Craig (R).....................	193,641	(61%)	($1,620,304)
	Ron J. Twilegar (D)	122,295	(39%)	($544,419)
1990 primary	Larry Craig (R)......................	65,830	(59%)	
	Jim Jones (R)	45,733	(41%)	
1984 general	James A. McClure (R)...............	293,193	(72%)	($1,016,944)
	Peter Martin Busch (D)	105,591	(26%)	($31,001)

Sen. Dirk Kempthorne (R)

Elected 1992, seat up 1998; b. Oct. 29, 1951, San Diego, CA; home, Boise; U. of ID, B.A. 1975; Methodist; married (Patricia).

Career: Exec. Asst. to the Dir., ID Dept. of Public Lands, 1976–78; Exec. V.P., ID Home Builders Assn., 1978–81; Campaign Mgr., Phil Batt's gubernatorial campaign, 1982; ID Public Affairs Mgr., FMC Corp., 1983–86; Boise Mayor, 1986–93.

DC Office: 367 DSOB 20510, 202-224-6142; Fax: 202-224-5893; e-mail: dirk_kempthorne@kempthorne.senate.gov.

State Offices: 304 N. 8th St., #338, Boise 83701, 208-334-1776; 118 N. 2d St., Coeur d'Alene 83814, 208-664-5490; 633 Main St., #103, Lewiston 83501, 208-743-1492; 401 2d St. N., #106, Twin Falls 83301, 208-734-2515; 250 S. 4th, #207, Pocatello 83201, 208-236-6775; and 2539 Channing Way, #240, Idaho Falls 83404, 208-522-9779; 704 Blaine St., #1, Caldwell 83605, 208-955-0360; 220 E. 5th St., #105; Moscow 83843, 208-883-9783.

Committees: *Armed Services* (8th of 11 R): Acquisition and Technology; Airland Forces; Strategic Forces. *Environment & Public Works* (5th of 9 R): Drinking Water, Fisheries and Wildlife (Chmn.); Transportation and Infrastructure. *Small Business* (5th of 10 R).

Group Ratings

	ADA	ACLU	COPE	CFA	LCV	CON	NSI	COC	ACU	NTLC	CHC
1994	0	21	13	25	0	83	100	86	100	92	100
1993	5	—	9	20	6	93	—	91	100	—	—

National Journal Ratings

	1993 LIB — 1993 CONS			1994 LIB — 1994 CONS	
Economic	0%	—	87%	0% —	88%
Social	8%	—	90%	0% —	85%
Foreign	0%	—	92%	0% —	94%

Key Votes of the 103d Congress

1. Clinton Deficit Plan	N	3. Brady Handgun Purchase	N	5. Lmt. UN Cmnd. of Forces	Y
2. NAFTA	N	4. Strike Race/Death Pnlty.	Y	6. Cut Missile Funds	N

Key Votes of the 104th Congress

1. Congressional Compliance	Y	3. Balanced Budget Amndt.	Y	5. Product Liability Reform	Y
2. Bar Unfunded Mandates	Y	4. Pass Line Item Veto	Y	6. FY96 Budget	Y

Election Results

1992 general	Dirk Kempthorne (R)................	270,468	(57%)	($1,305,338)
	Richard Stallings (D)...............	208,036	(43%)	($1,222,222)
1992 primary	Dirk Kempthorne (R)................	67,001	(57%)	
	Rod Beck (R)......................	26,977	(23%)	
	Milton Erhart (R)...................	22,682	(19%)	
1986 general	Steven D. Symms (R)...............	196,958	(52%)	($3,229,939)
	John V. Evans (D)..................	185,066	(48%)	($2,135,537)

FIRST DISTRICT

The 1st District, which stretches from the Nevada border to Canada, includes most of usually Republican Boise and the panhandle where the dominant voice is Coeur d'Alene newspaper baron and resort developer Duane Hagadone. In statewide elections, it is the less Republican of the two districts because of the panhandle, though solidly Republican by national standards. But it was a key race in the 1994 cycle, as conservative Republican Helen Chenoweth defeated two-term Democratic incumbent Larry LaRocco in a campaign in which national themes and personal attacks both played a role.

LaRocco won the seat in 1990, when incumbent Larry Craig ran for the Senate; LaRocco worked for years for Senator Frank Church and held Craig to 54% in 1982. In 1990 he attacked his Republican opponent for opposing all abortions, education funding, living wills and day care standards, while himself opposing the budget summit tax increase. In office LaRocco compiled a middle-of-the-House voting record and worked on wilderness bills; he won reelection against state Senator Rachel Gilbert 58%–37% in 1992.

Helen Chenoweth has also labored long in the political vineyards, on the other side. Actually, apple orchards might be more appropriate; for she worked for apple rancher Steve Symms when he was a congressman in the 1970s. She was earlier a medical office manager and later a lobbyist for timber and mining industries. Chenoweth made her contempt for environmentalists apparent when she hosted an "endangered salmon bake" during her primary campaign. She started off as the underdog in the primary against former Lieutenant Governor David Leroy, whose nearly successful gubernatorial campaign she managed in 1986; but with support from the religious right she beat him 48%–28%, carrying all but one remote county.

A poll after the May primary showed Chenoweth leading incumbent LaRocco—a highly unusual result, and an early harbinger of the 1994 Republican tsunami. LaRocco attacked her as an extremist for opposing gay rights (a 1994 referendum issue in Idaho), and on school vouchers—an "out-of-state extremist agenda." She talked more about mining, timber and the "Clinton war on the West" stating, "Natural resources issues are a wedge into western family values." LaRocco rallied in several polls, but in late October the *Idaho Statesman* reported that LaRocco's former employer, the Boise brokerage firm of Piper Jaffrey, paid $40,000 to LaRocco's former assistant to settle a sexual discrimination complaint she brought after quitting the firm under pressure because of her relationship with LaRocco. Even more damaging was the fact that, when confronted with the story in a debate by his 1992 opponent Rachel Gilbert, he denied it and charged Gilbert with "sleaze." Chenoweth won with 55% of the vote, carrying 58%

in Boise's Ada County and losing the panhandle by only 51%–49%.

Chenoweth serves on the Agriculture and Resources Committees, plum assignments for this district, and in her early months she showed that she would be an outspoken advocate on Capitol Hill for cutting back the federal role in those areas. She intends to produce legislation that would require federal agents to get written authorization from local law enforcement officers before carrying out any federal actions. Her conservative views should be an asset in this basically Republican district in 1996, although Democrats will work to assure that she does not get a free ride.

The People: Pop. 1990: 503,141; 46% rural; 13% age 65+; 93% White; 1% Amer. Indian; 1% Asian; 2% Other; 5% Hispanic origin. Voting age pop.: 358,572; 4% Hispanic origin. Households: 63% married couple families; 30% married couple fams. w. children; 47% college educ.; median household income: $25,086; per capita income: $11,530; median gross rent: $332; median house value: $60,000.

1992 Presidential Vote			1988 Presidential Vote		
Bush (R)	101,787	(41%)	Bush (R)	120,011	(60%)
Clinton (D)	75,499	(30%)	Dukakis (D)	79,593	(40%)
Perot (I)	67,677	(27%)			

Rep. Helen Chenoweth (R)

Elected 1994; b. Jan. 27, 1938, Topeka, KS; home, Boise; Whitworth Col., B.A. 1962; Christian; divorced.

Career: Legal/Medical Mgmt. Consultant, 1964–75; Exec. Dir., ID Republican Party, 1975–77; Chief of Staff, U.S. Rep. Steve Symms, 1977–78; Founder & Pres., Consulting Associates Inc., 1978–94.

DC Office: 1719 LHOB 20515, 202-225-6611; Fax: 202-225-3029.

District Offices: 304 N. 8th St., #454, Boise 83702, 208-336-9831; 118 N. 2nd St., #2, Coeur d'Alene 83814, 208-667-0127; and 621 Main St., #G, Lewiston 83501, 208-746-4613.

Committees: *Agriculture* (20th of 27 R): Resource Conservation, Research and Forestry. *Resources* (17th of 25 R): Energy and Mineral Resources; National Parks, Forests and Lands; Water and Power Resources.

Group Ratings and 103rd Congress Votes: Newly Elected

Key Votes of the 104th Congress

1. Congressional Compliance	Y	6. Reform Crime Grant	Y	11. Loser Pays Court Reform	Y
2. Balanced Budget Amndmt.	Y	7. National Security Act	*	12. Product Liability Reform	Y
3. Bar Unfunded Mandates	Y	8. Moratorium on Regs.	Y	13. Welfare Reform	Y
4. Pass Line Item Veto	N	9. Risk Assessment on Regs.	Y	14. Term Limits Amndmt.	Y
5. Relax Exclusionary Rule	N	10. Expnd. Priv. Prop. Rights	Y	15. Tax Cuts	Y

Election Results

1994 general	Helen Chenoweth (R)	111,728	(55%)	($796,149)
	Larry LaRocco (D)	89,826	(45%)	($845,902)
1994 primary	Helen Chenoweth (R)	28,545	(48%)	
	David H. Leroy (R)	16,570	(28%)	
	Ron McMurray (R)	11,816	(20%)	
	Henry (Sonny) Kinsey (R)	2,606	(4%)	
1992 general	Larry LaRocco (D)	140,985	(58%)	($623,327)
	Rachel Gilbert (R)	90,983	(37%)	($222,604)
	Others	10,822	(5%)	

SECOND DISTRICT

The 2d District of Idaho, from central Boise east to the Utah border, is one of America's most Republican districts in presidential elections and, after several competitive years, in House elections as well. The congressman is Mike Crapo, first elected in 1992 when Democratic incumbent Richard Stallings ran for the Senate. Crapo had been a state Senator since 1984, the Senate leader since 1988, a bishop in the Mormon Church at age 31, "intelligent, approachable and even-tempered," said an Idaho Falls *Post Register* reporter. Crapo won his primary 68%–32%. "Cowboy Democrat" J. D. Williams, the state controller, ran on a "put America first" stand on industrial policy and trade; Crapo opposed all tax increases and favored spending cuts, a balanced budget amendment and the line-item veto, and won 61%–35%. Incidentally, Williams was the only statewide elected Democrat in Idaho to survive 1994; he was reelected with 50% of the vote.

Crapo came to Washington with "a passion for reform," he said, to change both the institution [Congress] and government. In 1993, freshmen Republicans voted him their class leader, he crusaded hard to make it easier for Members to sign the discharge petition in order to get bills out of recalcitrant committees, and he opposed the select committees, closed rules and closed committee meetings. On broader national issues, like many Republicans he favors simple, hard-and-fast rules—a balanced budget, term limits, across-the-board spending cuts (excluding social security)—to force tough decisions. He has seats on Commerce and Agriculture and has worked on local issues—for potato and other agricultural research programs, lifting water user fees, against the Delaney clause on pesticides and for the Idaho National Engineering Laboratory (INEL). A junior rebel just a short time ago, he works well with the Gingrich team and could become a power in the Republican House.

The People: Pop. 1990: 503,608; 39% rural; 11% age 65+; 92% White; 1% Amer. Indian; 1% Asian; 3% Other; 6% Hispanic origin. Voting age pop.: 340,340; 5% Hispanic origin. Households: 63% married couple families; 33% married couple fams. w. children; 51% college educ.; median household income: $25,446; per capita income: $11,384; median gross rent: $327; median house value: $55,900.

1992 Presidential Vote

Bush (R)	100,858	(43%)
Perot (I)	62,718	(27%)
Clinton (D)	61,514	(26%)
Other	8,925	(4%)

1988 Presidential Vote

Bush (R)	133,870	(66%)
Dukakis (D)	67,679	(34%)

Rep. Michael Crapo (R)

Elected 1992; b. May 20, 1951, Idaho Falls; home, Idaho Falls; Brigham Young U., B.A. 1973, Harvard, J.D. 1977; Mormon; married (Susan).

Career: Practicing atty., 1977–92; ID Senate, 1984–92.

DC Office: 437 CHOB 20515, 202-225-5531; Fax: 202-225-8216.

District Offices: 304 N. 8th St., #325, Boise 83702, 208-334-1953; 250 S. 4th St., #220, Pocatello 83201, 208-236-6734; 628 Blue Lakes Blvd., N., Twin Falls 83301, 208-734-7219; and 2539 Channing Way, #330, Idaho Falls 83404, 208-523-6701.

Committees: *Agriculture* (18th of 27 R): Department Operations, Nutrition and Foreign Agriculture; Resource Conservation, Research and Forestry. *Commerce* (16th of 26 R): Commerce, Trade and Hazardous Materials; Energy and Power; Oversight and Investigations.

Group Ratings

	ADA	ACLU	COPE	CFA	LCV	CON	NSI	COC	ACU	NTLC	CHC
1994	5	9	11	10	0	85	100	10	90	89	100
1993	5	—	8	0	21	65	—	91	96	—	—

National Journal Ratings

	1993 LIB — 1993 CONS			1994 LIB — 1994 CONS		
Economic	12%	—	87%	0%	—	80%
Social	0%	—	89%	16%	—	81%
Foreign	24%	—	72%	0%	—	88%

Key Votes of the 103d Congress

1. Clinton Deficit Plan	N	3. Brady Handgun Purchase	N	5. Lmt. UN Cmnd. of Forces	Y
2. NAFTA	N	4. Strike Race/Death Pnlty.	Y	6. Cut Missile Funds	N

Key Votes of the 104th Congress

1. Congressional Compliance	Y	6. Reform Crime Grant	*	11. Loser Pays Court Reform	Y
2. Balanced Budget Amndmt.	Y	7. National Security Act	Y	12. Product Liability Reform	Y
3. Bar Unfunded Mandates	Y	8. Moratorium on Regs.	Y	13. Welfare Reform	Y
4. Pass Line Item Veto	Y	9. Risk Assessment on Regs.	Y	14. Term Limits Amndmt.	Y
5. Relax Exclusionary Rule	N	10. Expnd. Priv. Prop. Rights	Y	15. Tax Cuts	Y

Election Results

1994 general	Michael Crapo (R)	143,593	(75%)	($352,461)
	Penny Fletcher (D)	47,936	(25%)	($26,862)
1994 primary	Michael Crapo (R)	unopposed		
1992 general	Michael Crapo (R)	139,783	(61%)	($572,532)
	J.D. Williams (D)	81,450	(35%)	($245,954)
	Others	8,724	(4%)	

ILLINOIS

One hundred years ago, American politics centered on Chicago; arguably, it still does today. Chicago was the site in 1896 of William Jennings Bryan's convention speech where he pleaded that mankind not be crucified on a cross of gold. Chicago was also where Marcus Hanna, the genius behind William McKinley's campaign, dispatched a 30-year-old lawyer named Charles Dawes to set up a headquarters for the Republican campaign the same year. It was a natural site: Chicago was already an economic center as the hub of the nation's railroad lines, and it was a political center sitting on the boundary between the Great Plains and the West, where Democrat Bryan was evangelizing the cause of free silver, and the industrial Great Lakes and Northeast, which Republican McKinley needed to carry to uphold the gold standard. In the 1860 election that split the Union, it was the home town of Stephen Douglas and the site of the convention that nominated Abraham Lincoln. Then Chicago was a city of 112,000, eighth in the nation, but Illinois was already the fourth largest state. By 1896, Chicago, with 1.4 million people, was one of the great metropolises of the world, the center, as William Cronon describes in his wonderful *Nature's Metropolis*, of the nation's trade in lumber, grain and meat.

A century later, Chicago may no longer be the nation's Second City (Los Angeles is), but O'Hare Airport is the nation's busiest: Chicago is an air as well as rail hub. And Chicago was chosen to host the 1996 Democratic National Convention. In commerce, Illinois remains a prime producer and processor of corn and soybeans, the home of the world's greatest commodities exchanges and futures markets, a great manufacturing center with the strongest white-collar and service economy between the coasts. Politically, Chicago and Illinois have not produced any presidents in the 20th Century, but they have produced pivotal politicians—and votes. Dawes himself was a major figure, as a World War I general, first Budget Bureau (now Office of Management and Budget) director, vice president under Calvin Coolidge; Chicago lawyer Harold Ickes was Franklin Roosevelt's great Interior secretary. Prominent Illinois Republicans have included Speaker Joseph Cannon, Senate Republican Leader Everett Dirksen, Senator Charles Percy and House Republican Leader Robert Michel; prominent Democrats include Governor Adlai Stevenson, Mayor Richard J. Daley and Ways and Means Chairman Dan Rostenkowski. As for votes, Illinois has 22 electoral votes and, with percentages near the national average of blacks and Hispanics, immigrants and pioneers, city-dwellers and suburbanites and farmers, the affluent and the impoverished, heavy industry and high-tech, they tend to reflect national divisions. Illinois is furiously contested in close presidential elections and, since Bryan orated and Dawes set up shop, it has voted for the losing presidential candidate only twice, in 1916 and 1976.

But politics has not always been central to life in Illinois, or America. This was a state of farmers, whose families, communities and churches absorbed more of their energies than politics or government. Chicago was established not by government but by markets; it has always been a free enterprise city, settled by pioneers from New England and Kentucky, by immigrant Irishmen who dug the first canal connecting Lake Michigan and the Illinois River, and by railroad promoters who saw its potential as the great connecting point between East and West and the Great Lakes and the Mississippi Valley. Its factories, built where iron ore from Great Lakes freighters and coal from inland hills came together, attracted migrants from near and far. To meet the demands of these masses and referee their cultural struggles, political machines sprang up, allied with the Republicans who predominated in northern Illinois and the Democrats who usually prevailed from Springfield south. Not until the Depression of the 1930s did Chicago become reliably Democratic, and that was in part because so many Republicans had moved to the Cook County suburbs and the Collar Counties surrounding Chicago—one of America's strongest Republican constituencies.

Over the last quarter-century, Illinois's politics have been the nation's writ large. For the two decades following 1968, when the Democrats held their disastrous national convention in Chicago, their party had trouble rallying the middle-class voters who were its historic base. Democrats failed to carry metro Chicago or Illinois for president or governor during most of those years. Chicagoland voters were split along racial lines following the election of black Mayor Harold Washington in 1983 and the "council wars" that followed; despite a farm recession Downstate, Illinois was mostly Republican in the Reagan years. Then racial animosities in Chicago eased after Washington's death and with the election of Richard M. Daley in 1989; Illinois gave two resounding victories to Democratic senators in the 1990s and voted 49%–34% for Bill Clinton in 1992. Chicago cast only 22% of the state's votes, but Clinton got 72% of it; he only barely lost the suburbs, which cast 40% of the votes, to George Bush, 39%–42%; he carried Downstate 45%–36%. This was not quite so smashing a victory as Senator Paul Simon's 65%–35% win over underfinanced Congresswoman Lynn Martin in 1990, but it roughly paralleled the 1992 victory of Carol Moseley-Braun, the first black woman elected to the Senate, who in a climate of racial reconciliation won 53%–43%.

In 1994, Illinois, like the nation, moved sharply to the right. Governor Jim Edgar, a moderate Republican with a earnest, low-key personality, succeeded the forceful, exuberant James Thompson in 1990 by only a 51%–48% margin, winning 61%–39% in the suburbs and only 51%–48% in his native Downstate (he is the first Downstater elected governor since the 1920s). In 1994, Edgar had articulate opposition from Comptroller Dawn Clark Netsch. But in a year when voters were skeptical of government, Netsch called for an income tax increase. The result

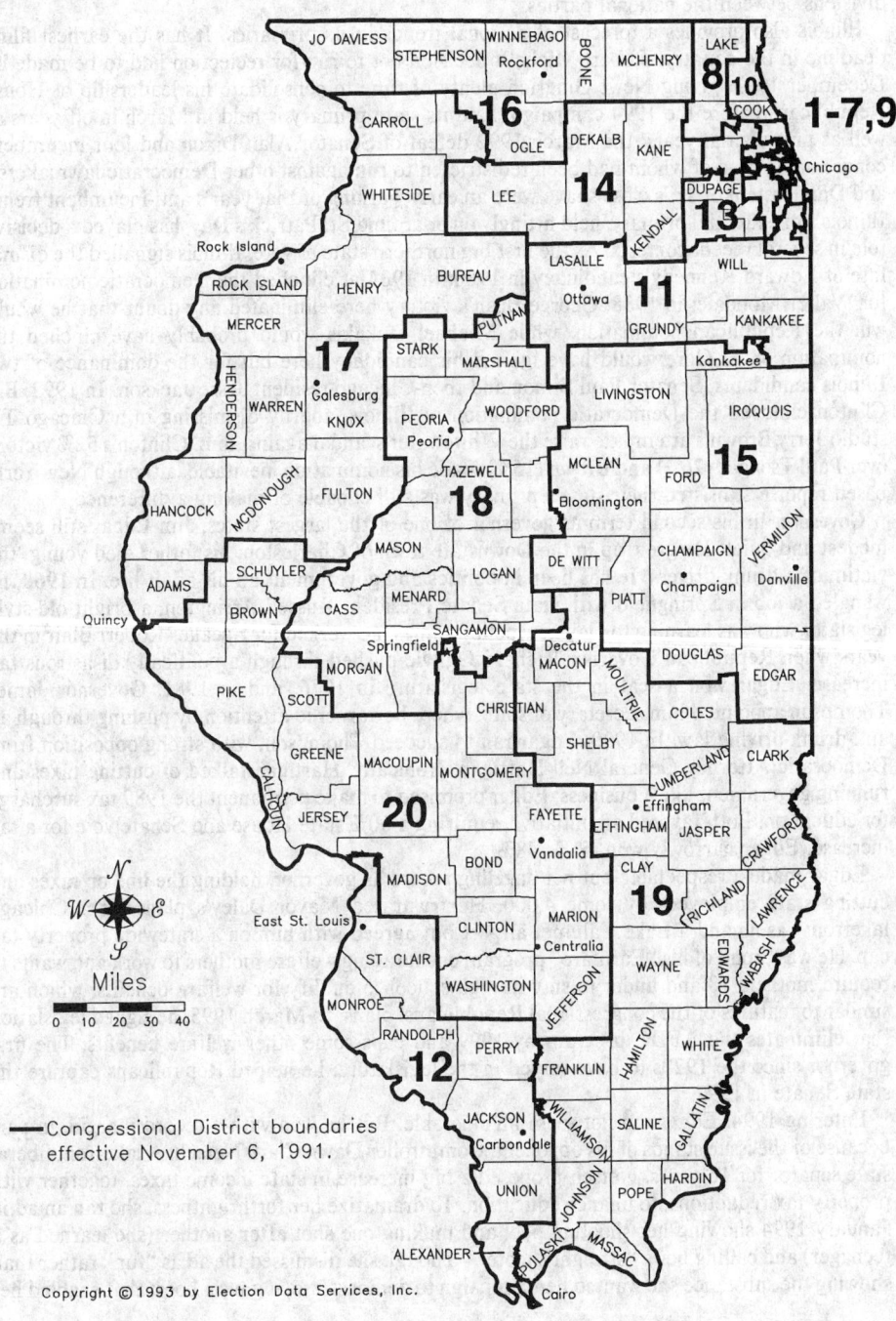

JO DAVIESS
STEPHENSON
WINNEBAGO
Rockford
BOONE
MCHENRY
LAKE
8
10
COOK
1-7,9
16
CARROLL
OGLE
DEKALB
KANE
Chicago
WHITESIDE
LEE
DUPAGE
13
ROCK ISLAND
HENRY
BUREAU
LASALLE
Ottawa
KENDALL
WILL
MERCER
PUTNAM
GRUNDY
KANKAKEE
HENDERSON
STARK
MARSHALL
Kankakee
17
Galesburg
KNOX
WOODFORD
LIVINGSTON
IROQUOIS
WARREN
PEORIA
Peoria
15
MCDONOUGH
FULTON
TAZEWELL
MCLEAN
Bloomington
FORD
HANCOCK
MASON
LOGAN
DE WITT
CHAMPAIGN
Champaign
VERMILION
Danville
18
ADAMS
SCHUYLER
MENARD
CASS
PIATT
Quincy
BROWN
SANGAMON
Springfield
MACON
Decatur
DOUGLAS
EDGAR
PIKE
SCOTT
MORGAN
CHRISTIAN
MOULTRIE
COLES
GREENE
MACOUPIN
SHELBY
CUMBERLAND
CLARK
20
MONTGOMERY
Effingham
FAYETTE
EFFINGHAM
JASPER
CRAWFORD
JERSEY
BOND
Vandalia
CLAY
RICHLAND
LAWRENCE
19
MADISON
CLINTON
MARION
Centralia
WAYNE
EDWARDS
WABASH
East St. Louis
ST. CLAIR
WASHINGTON
JEFFERSON
MONROE
PERRY
HAMILTON
WHITE
RANDOLPH
FRANKLIN
12
JACKSON
Carbondale
WILLIAMSON
SALINE
GALLATIN
UNION
JOHNSON
POPE
HARDIN
ALEXANDER
PULASKI
MASSAC
Cairo

N
W·E
S

Miles
0 10 20 30 40

—Congressional District boundaries
effective November 6, 1991.

was one of the two most one-sided governor's races in Illinois since 1848 (the other was Thompson's 1976 victory over a Chicago machine wheelhorse). Edgar won 64%–34%, with 70% Downstate and 71% in the suburbs; Netsch won Chicago 62%–36%. That's not necessarily a forecast for 1996, but the differences between Edgar and Netsch bear some resemblance to divisions between the national parties.

Illinois also provides a forecast of national trends in its primaries. It has the earliest filing deadline in the country: Robert Michel's decision not to run for reelection had to be made by December 1993, giving Newt Gingrich plenty of time to consolidate his leadership of House Republicans before the 1994 campaign. And its state primary is held in March in off years as well as presidential years: the March 1992 defeat of Senator Alan Dixon and four incumbent congressmen (two of whom had been redistricted to run against other Democratic lawmakers), and Dan Rostenkowski's close shave were an early warning of that year's anti-incumbent trend. Illinois's presidential primary, held fittingly on or around St. Patrick's Day, has played a decisive role in several recent contests. As the first big northern state to vote, Illinois signalled the dismal fate of Edward Kennedy's candidacy in 1980; in 1984, it clinched the Democratic nomination for Walter Mondale; in 1988, George Bush's victory here eliminated any doubt that he would win the Republican nomination, while Michael Dukakis would probably have cinched the nomination or Al Gore would have ignited his candidacy here but for the dominance of two Illinois candidates, Senator Paul Simon and then-Chicago resident Jesse Jackson. In 1992, Bill Clinton clinched the Democratic nomination in Illinois, angrily dismissing in a Chicago TV studio Jerry Brown's attempt to raise the Whitewater scandal against him. Clinton's 52% victory over Paul Tsongas (26%) and Brown (15%) made his nomination inevitable, although New York-based reporters insisted their state's primary was still capable of making a difference.

Governor. In his second term as governor of one of the largest states, Jim Edgar still seems modest and quiet. He grew up in the Downstate town of Charleston; his father died young, the victim of a drunk driver. He has been in politics and government all his adult life. In 1968, he wangled a job in Springfield with state Senate President Russell Arrington, a bright old-style legislator who was learning to play new policy games; he worked for Speaker Robert Blair in the years when Republican Governor Richard Ogilvie pushed through a politically disastrous tax increase. Edgar won a seat in the state legislature in 1976, and in 1981, Governor James Thompson appointed him secretary of state, where he garnered attention by pushing through an anti-drunk-driving law. In 1990, Edgar ran to succeed Thompson, with strong opposition from Democratic Attorney General Neil Hartigan. Ironically, Hartigan talked of cutting taxes and running government like a business; Edgar promised to make permanent the 1989 tax surcharge for education. Both favored an initiative requiring a 60% state House and Senate vote for a tax increase. Edgar narrowly won, 51%–48%.

Edgar made a respectable but not dazzling record as governor, holding the line on taxes and cutting state employees by some 4,000. He frustrated Mayor Daley's plans for a Chicago lakefront casino and a Lake Calumet airport but agreed with him on a statewide property tax cap. He was proud of his "Earnfare" program encouraging welfare mothers to work and wants to require mothers 18 and under to stay in high school to qualify for welfare benefits, which are similar to features of the congressional Republicans' plans. In March 1995, he signed legislation that eliminates the AFDC program by 1999 and caps some other welfare benefits. The first governor since the 1920s to have served in the legislature, he helped Republicans capture the state Senate in 1992.

Entering 1994, Edgar did not seem invulnerable. But he won with a record margin, in part because of the issue stands of his opponent, Comptroller Dawn Clark Netsch. A lakefront liberal state senator for 18 years, Netsch proposed a big increase in state income taxes, together with property tax reductions, to finance education. To dramatize her forthrightness, she ran an ad in January 1994 showing her shooting pool and making one shot after another (she learned as a teenager) and calling her a "straight shooter." Though she dismissed the ad as "fun" rather than showing the substance she wanted her campaign to demonstrate, it gave a boost that enabled her to beat Attorney General Roland Burris (who carried the black wards), 44%–36%; Cook County Board President Richard Phelan, who broke his own tax promise, was third, with 15%. But the tax plan hurt in the fall. So did Netsch's opposition to capital punishment (favored by 79% in the VNS exit poll) and the odd fact that she has never learned to drive—the latter became an issue when Netsch requested a security detail because she said she had received death threats. Edgar bragged of increased education funding and a lower-than-national unemployment rate. He survived a couple of potential setbacks. In July, he had emergency open heart surgery, just weeks after Lieutenant Governor Bob Kustra said he was leaving the ticket to become a radio talk show host. Kustra reconsidered as Edgar was recuperating. And in October it was revealed that a woman in an Edgar welfare-to-work program had been convicted of manslaughter in 1986. But Edgar won overwhelmingly anyway, carrying 101 of 102 counties (losing one southern Downstate county by 3 votes), and saw Republicans sweep all the statewide offices and capture control of the state House. He entered 1995 in a position of political strength not equalled in the last three generations, hoping to cut state government employment further, implement tort reform and try further reforms of the welfare system. He would be a strong candidate for the Senate, but quickly deferred to Kustra—at least for 1996.

Senators. Illinois has two Democratic senators, one in her first term and one in his last, with different backgrounds but similar voting records. Paul Simon, who a week after the 1994 election announced he would not run again in 1996, has been an important figure in Illinois politics for a quarter century, and was a presidential candidate in 1988. Carol Moseley-Braun was the Cook County Recorder of Deeds, unknown outside Chicago and Springfield inner political circles, until she won an upset victory in the 1992 Democratic primary and suddenly became a symbolic figure of national importance.

Paul Simon looks the part of the country editor he once was, with his horn-rimmed glasses and bow tie, his extra-flat midwestern accent and his habit of writing his own newsletters and books; his 15th book, published in January 1995, is about Elijah Lovejoy, the abolitionist editor killed at his press in 1837 in Alton, just 15 miles from where Simon got his start in public life when he bought the *Troy Tribune* in 1948, at age 19. There, he crusaded against local gangsters and machine politicians and was elected to the legislature in 1954; in 1968, he was elected lieutenant governor, and was prepared to take on politically ailing Republican Governor Richard Ogilvie when he lost the 1972 Democratic primary to anti-Daley, anti-spending Daniel Walker. In 1974, when Ken Gray retired from the state's southernmost Downstate congressional district, Simon ran and won. In 1984, he won a heavily contested Democratic primary for the Senate and, by running virtually even Downstate, beat Foreign Relations Committee Chairman Charles Percy 50%–48%.

Knitting together Simon's record on a miscellany of issues is a sort of perky reformism, which has made him a distinctive member of a party often tarred by corruption in a state where politics is usually a matter of hard-bitten self-interest. Simon was one of the first American politicians to disclose his personal finances, starting in the 1950s. He has been the Senate's lead sponsor of the balanced budget constitutional amendment, furiously opposed by Democratic leaders, especially Robert Byrd, but backed by 13 Democrats in the March 1995 showdown vote. But unlike so many Republicans who back it, he thinks it will require higher taxes—which seems to be OK by him. (He praised Dawn Clark Netsch's tax increase in her 1994 campaign for governor.) He was willing to consider government action against violent television programming, but held off any action in early 1994, after networks and cable operators promised to practice self-restraint. He worked on the 1994 education bill, sponsoring "school-to-work" programs for the non-college bound, fine tuning aid formulas, trying to compromise by making voluntary for states the "opportunity to learn" standards that would prescribe what schools should provide—not a popular concept with congressional conservatives seeking deregulation and loosening of federal standards. He was the Senate's lead sponsor of the direct student loan program, bypassing the banks and Sallie Mae, which President Clinton has cited as one of his major legislative achievements. Every Thursday morning he has a half-hour coffee and doughnut session in his office where any constituent can drop by.

Simon has sailed through varying political weather in the past. He ran for president in 1988 as an unabashed liberal, stressing issues like foreign-language education which struck some as peripheral. He finished second in the Iowa caucuses, third in New Hampshire, and out of the running in the South on Super Tuesday; but, at the importuning of Illinois politicos on his delegate slates, he stayed in the race and won the Illinois primary a week later, then retired from the field. In 1990, he was opposed by Congresswoman Lynn Martin, a sharp-tongued partisan in the House. But the news media did not celebrate Martin and other Republican women in 1990 as they did Democratic women running in 1992's "year of the woman." Martin ran out of money and was off the air most of October; Simon won 65%–35%, with 64% Downstate and 57% in the suburbs.

Simon's retirement leaves the seat wide open. After Governor Jim Edgar deferred, Lieutenant Governor Bob Kustra became the Republican frontrunner and seemed likely to raise the millions of dollars needed for a credible statewide race. Likely Democratic candidates Lane Evans and former Attorney General Neil Hartigan, a Chicago lawyer who became the favorite of many party regulars who viewed his prospective successful 1996 candidacy as a prelude to the more important recapture of the governor's office in 1998, decided not to run. Lesser-known Downstate Congressmen Richard Durbin now moves to the top of the list.

Carol Moseley-Braun is charming, politically experienced, well spoken, grounded in the reality of urban life. But it was inevitable she always would be described as the first black woman senator after she was elected in 1992. She grew up in a middle class neighborhood, the daughter of a policeman and a medical technician. She was elected to the legislature in 1978, at 31, and performed creditably even according to Republicans. She wanted to be slated for lieutenant governor in 1986 and, failing that, got elected Cook County Recorder of Deeds in 1989. Her great political intuition told her that Senator Alan Dixon, up for reelection in 1992 after 40 years in public office, would be vulnerable, and that an attractive candidate who built on the 25% of primary voters who are black could beat him. Dixon and Al Hofeld, a free-spending lawyer also in the race, traded charges; Moseley-Braun (she inserted the hyphen in 1993—in the campaign her last name was Braun) stayed, as consultant David Axelrod said, "really below the fray," and came on strong in the final week to win with 38% of the vote to 35% for Dixon and 27% for Hofeld. In the 1992 general, Chicago area voters were in a mood for racial reconciliation, and there was no easier way to signal that than to vote for the intelligent, always smiling Moseley-Braun. Meanwhile, her opponent, former Reagan aide Rich Williamson, was fending off attacks for switching his position on abortion just about the time he announced his candidacy. So strong was support for Moseley-Braun that she weathered the storm in September when it was revealed that in 1989 she split among herself and siblings a $28,750 timber royalty inheritance owed to her mother, a nursing home resident who was supposed to have reimbursed Medicaid with the money. Moseley-Braun's explanations were unconvincing at best, and a candidate of other race and gender might have lost the election right there. But she did well in debates and won 53%–43%.

Her record since has been mixed. After the election she was criticized for paying below-market rent for a posh lakefront apartment and for taking a month-long trip to Africa with her campaign manager and then-fiancé Kgosie Matthews (whom she did not end up marrying); when he was accused of sexual harassment by female campaign workers, Moseley-Braun called the charges "groundless." She was often late for appointments, had trouble managing her staff, and complained about negative press coverage. She got better notices in July 1993, when she confronted and defeated Jesse Helms when he sought to renew a patent for the insignia of the United Daughters of the Confederacy and when she helped to delete a commodities futures-exchange tax from the Clinton economic package. In her first term, Moseley-Braun took a seat on the Judiciary Committee only when pressed, despite feminists' interest in seeing a black woman on the panel that initially balked at hearing Anita Hill. But she left that panel two years later when she won a coveted seat on Finance, cleverly gaining the seat in exchange for her support of Tom Daschle, the one-vote winner for Minority Leader who gave her his own seat. On Finance, she planned to focus on local interests; she quickly took the initiative, winning committee approval and enactment of a plan to allow a team including composer Quincy Jones and publisher Rupert Murdoch to use a minority-ownership preference to purchase a group of television stations. She backed trying as adults teenagers as young as 13 for violent crimes, and in December 1994 she took the politically smart step of endorsing Mayor Richard Daley for reelection: she is willing to risk antagonizing the left and has made moves to appeal to the center. She gets some 500 requests a week to make speeches, but many Senate insiders question whether she has put in the hard work needed for long-term achievement. She is on the early list of incumbents who appear very vulnerable for reelection in 1998.

Mayor. Richard M. Daley, mayor of Chicago since 1989, who came to office with a reputation as an inarticulate heir, has proved to be an innovative, thoughtful and effective mayor—and, since the 1994 elections, one of the most successful Democratic public officials in the country. His father of course was Richard J. Daley, first elected in 1955 and mayor until his death in December 1976—and boss of the fabled Chicago machine. Richie Daley, as he is often called, was a state senator and Cook County state's attorney whose one major setback was his defeat in the 1983 mayoral primary by Harold Washington, an able mayor who was vociferously opposed by white politicians in "the council wars;" no able black successor appeared, and Daley was elected by winning the white "bungalow wards" plus Hispanic and lakefront wards his opponents took for granted. Daley's first achievement was racial reconciliation; he entered the 1995 campaign season with approval ratings over 50% among blacks and 70% overall. His second step was to downsize and privatize city government, eliminating 1600 jobs and privatizing 40 functions. The old Daley machine, in which city employees were expected to be Democratic precinct and ward committeemen, producing votes for the machine on election day, was rendered defunct by a 1970s court case that prohibited firing employees for political reasons, and it became obvious that the government bureaucracy was so inefficient that continuing to rely on it would mean ever-higher taxes and municipal ruin. Daley has hired 1,000 new police officers, but held the line on property taxes.

Daley's big projects have not all come to fruition. The new McCormick Place convention center has been built but he hasn't yet gotten permission for a gambling casino—although he hasn't quit trying. He is working on reforesting the city by planting half a million trees, but his plans for a new airport around Lake Calumet were abandoned when the legislature would not meet his terms, and he is now calling for modernization and expansion of O'Hare, to bring it into the next century, he explains. Chicago has suffered some job losses at big firms—Amoco, United Airlines, Inland Steel, the Sears catalogue division—but there is great vitality in the city as well. Small businesses are replacing large; old factories far from the lakefront are being rebuilt as luxury condominium complexes; immigrant communities are vibrant; South Side black neighborhoods, with help from Daley's SNAP (Strategic Neighborhood Assistance Program) zones, are well maintained and growing rather than being abandoned; the new United Center, replacing Chicago Stadium, is bringing signs of life to the bedraggled West Side, even as the old open-air Maxwell Street Market is moved and divided. And, once again, Chicago will be the site for the Democratic National Convention in 1996.

In early 1995, Daley was facing opposition from Water Reclamation District Commissioner Joseph Gardner in the February Democratic primary and from former Attorney General Roland Burris, who came close to winning the 1994 governor nomination and opposed Daley as an Independent, in the April general. He was handily reelected with 67% in the primary and 60% in the general. The greatest challenge ahead for Daley is improving Chicago's public schools, often called the nation's worst; even with local parent councils, test scores keep going downhill.

Although Daley has concentrated on local politics—like most Chicago politicians, notably his father, he seems to look down on Springfield, Washington and the rest of the world as "out of town"—his influence goes farther. Machine endorsements don't mean what they used to, but Daley made no secret of his backing of the embattled Dan Rostenkowski in the 1992 and 1994 primaries. Daley was obviously friendly to Bill Clinton's presidential candidacy: his own campaign manager, David Wilhelm, signed on to manage Clinton's campaign, and Daley had a well-publicized meeting with Clinton just before the crucial Illinois primary. But that support was not rewarded as it might have been. William Daley, the mayor's brother and a highly competent politician in his own right, lost out for Secretary of Transportation; he did, quietly but effectively, lead the administration's lobbying effort for NAFTA, but then promptly returned home. Wilhelm became Democratic National Committee chairman, but was undercut when Clinton brought Tony Coelho in for the 1994 campaign; Wilhelm resigned gracefully after the election and moved back to Chicago. The Daleys did get one prize: the 1996 Democratic National Convention will be held in Chicago, and they must hope that a harmonious gathering will erase the memories of 1968.

Presidential politics. Illinois is a presidential bellwether; it has voted for every presidential winner for 100 years except for southerners Jimmy Carter in 1976 and Woodrow Wilson in 1916. It could be especially important in 1996. If Democrats must write off the southern electoral votes Bill Clinton won in 1992, and depend on the two coasts for their base, then they must win votes in the Midwest. Illinois has the most electoral votes there—22—and has recently produced the biggest Democratic margins of any big Midwestern state in presidential elections. In other words, without Illinois, Bill Clinton can't win.

Illinois's March primary was arguably determinative for Republicans in 1976, 1980 and 1988 and for Democrats in 1980, 1984 and 1992. In 1996, it will be held on March 19, the same day as Ohio, Michigan and Wisconsin and most likely Pennsylvania also. Coming after New York and Super Tuesday, it could be too late to matter, or it could, once again, make all the difference. Illinois's Republican primary voters, by the way, are about evenly split between the suburbs, with their affluent free-marketeer dislike for taxes, and Downstate, with their old-fashioned, practical-minded Midwestern politics.

Congressional districting. A federal court redistricted Illinois's House seats in 1991, choosing a plan favoring Republicans; this was a counterbalance to the court decision 10 years before which favored Democrats. The 1991 plan caused a quick revolution in Illinois politics, for the filing deadline here is in December, the earliest in the nation. It forced two primaries between pairs of Democratic incumbents, one Downstate and one mostly in the Chicago suburbs; it would have forced another, in a mostly Chicago district, if Frank Annunzio had not retired. Four Democratic incumbents were defeated in the primary, two of them by other incumbents. A new Hispanic-majority seat was created with the effect of weakening next-door Dan Rostenkowski, who had tough primaries in March 1992 and 1994 and, scarred by indictment and loss of his Ways and Means chair, lost to a little-known Republican in November 1994. With the delegation's partisan balance now evenly split, Republicans are hoping that retirements Downstate will allow them to regain seats that they held before 1982.

The People: Est. Pop. 1994: 11,752,000; Pop. 1990: 11,430,602, up 2.8% 1990–1994. 4.5% of U.S. total, 6th largest; 15% rural. Median age: 32.8 years. 12.6% 65 years and over. 78.3% White, 14.8% Black, 7.9% Hispanic origin, 2.5% Asian, 4.2% Other. Households: 54.1% married couple families; 26% married couple fams. w. children; 46% college educ.; median household income: $32,252; per capita income: $15,201; 64.2% owner occupied housing; median house value: $80,900; median monthly rent: $369. 7.5% Unemployment. 1994 Voting age pop.: 8,712,000. 1994 Turnout: 3,076,292; 35% of VAP. Registered voters (1994): 6,119.001; no party registration.

Political Lineup: Governor, Jim Edgar (R); Lt. Gov., Bob Kustra (R); Secy. of State, George H. Ryan, Sr. (R); Atty. Gen., James E. Ryan (R); Treasurer, Judy Barr Topinka (R); Comptroller, Loleta Didrickson (R). State Senate, 59 (33 R and 26 D); State House of Representatives, 118 (65 R and 53 D). Senators, Paul Simon (D) and Carol Moseley-Braun (D). Representatives, 20 (10 R and 10 D).

1992 Presidential Vote

Clinton (D) 2,453,350 (49%)
Bush (R) 1,734,096 (34%)
Perot (I)................... 840,515 (17%)

1988 Presidential Vote

Bush (R) 2,310,939 (51%)
Dukakis (D).............. 2,215,940 (49%)

1992 Democratic Presidential Primary

Clinton.................... 776,829 (52%)
Tsongas 387,891 (26%)
Brown 220,346 (15%)
Uncommitted 67,612 (4%)

1992 Republican Presidential Primary

Bush 634,588 (76%)
Buchanan................. 186,915 (22%)

GOVERNOR

Gov. Jim Edgar (R)

Elected 1990, term expires Jan. 1999; b. July 22, 1946, Vinita, OK; home, Springfield; E. IL U., B.A. 1968; American Baptist; married (Brenda).

Career: Staff Aide, IL House of Reps. & IL Senate, 1968–76; IL House of Reps., 1976–79; Legis. Affairs Dir., IL Gov. Thompson, 1979–81; IL Secy. of St., 1981–90.

Office: 207 State House, Springfield 62706, 217-782-6830; Fax: 217-524-1676.

Election Results

1994 gen.	Jim Edgar (R)	1,984,318	(64%)
	Dawn Clark Netsch (D).......	1,069,850	(34%)
	Others....................	52,398	(2%)
1994 prim.	Jim Edgar (R)	521,590	(75%)
	Jack Roeser (R)	173,742	(25%)
1990 gen.	Jim Edgar (R)	1,653,126	(51%)
	Neil F. Hartigan (D)..........	1,569,217	(48%)
	Other	35,067	(1%)

SENATORS

Sen. Paul Simon (D)

Elected 1984, seat up 1996; b. Nov. 29, 1928, Eugene, OR; home, Makanda; U. of OR, 1945–46, Dana Col., 1946–48; Lutheran; married (Jeanne).

Career: Army, 1951–53; Editor-Publisher, *Troy Tribune*, 1948–66; Owner, weekly newspaper chain, 1948–66; IL House of Reps., 1954–62; IL Senate, 1962–68; IL Lt. Gov., 1968–72; Prof., Sangamon St. U., 1972–73; U.S. House of Reps., 1974–84; Author, 1964–present.

DC Office: 462 DSOB 20510, 202-224-2152; Fax: 202-224-0868; e-mail: senator@simon.senate.gov.

State Offices: Kluczynski Bldg., 230 S. Dearborn, #3800, Chicago 60604, 312-353-4952; 3 W. Old Capital Plz., #1, Springfield 62701, 217-492-4960; and 250 W. Cherry, #115B, Carbondale 62901, 618-457-3653.

Committees: *Budget* (5th of 10 D). *Judiciary* (5th of 8 D): Constitution, Federalism and Property Rights (RMM); Immigration. *Labor & Human Resources* (4th of 7 D): Aging; Disability Policy; Education, Arts and Humanities. *Indian Affairs* (4th of 8 D).

Group Ratings

	ADA	ACLU	COPE	CFA	LCV	CON	NSI	COC	ACU	NTLC	CHC
1994	95	84	75	92	77	49	10	26	4	16	7
1993	85	—	64	70	81	44	—	36	0	—	—

National Journal Ratings

	1993 LIB	—	1993 CONS		1994 LIB	—	1994 CONS
Economic	59%	—	34%		71%	—	28%
Social	87%	—	8%		93%	—	0%
Foreign	78%	—	13%		94%	—	0%

Key Votes of the 103d Congress

1. Clinton Deficit Plan	Y	3. Brady Handgun Purchase	Y	5. Lmt. UN Cmnd. of Forces	N
2. NAFTA	Y	4. Strike Race/Death Pnlty.	N	6. Cut Missile Funds	Y

Key Votes of the 104th Congress

1. Congressional Compliance	Y	3. Balanced Budget Amndt.	Y	5. Product Liability Reform	N
2. Bar Unfunded Mandates	Y	4. Pass Line Item Veto	N	6. FY96 Budget	N

Election Results

1990 general	Paul Simon (D).....................	2,115,377	(65%)	($8,665,789)
	Lynn Martin (R).....................	1,135,628	(35%)	($4,921,613)
1990 primary	Paul Simon (D).....................	unopposed		
1984 general	Paul Simon (D).....................	2,397,165	(50%)	($4,545,786)
	Charles H. Percy (R)	2,308,039	(48%)	($5,391,567)

Sen. Carol Moseley-Braun (D)

Elected 1992, seat up 1998; b. Aug. 16, 1947, Chicago; home, Chicago; U. of IL, B.A., 1969, U. of Chicago, J.D. 1972; Catholic; divorced.

Career: Asst. U.S. Atty., 1973–77; IL House of Reps., 1978–88, Asst. Majority Ldr., 1983; Cook Cnty. Recorder of Deeds, 1989–92.

DC Office: 320 HSOB 20515, 202-224-2854; Fax: 202-224-2626.

State Offices: Kluczynski Fed. Bldg., #3996, 230 S. Dearborn, Chicago 60604, 312-353-5420; 117 Fed. Bldg., 600 E. Monroe St., Springfield 62701, 217-492-4126; and Fed. Bldg., 105 S. 6th St., Mt Vernon 62864, 618-383-7920.

Committees: *Banking, Housing & Urban Affairs* (6th of 7 D): Financial Institutions and Regulatory Relief; HUD Oversight and Structure (RMM); International Finance. *Finance* (9th of 9 D): Medicaid and Health Care for Low-Income Families; Medicare, Long-Term Care and Health Insurance; Social Security and Family Policy. *Aging (Special)* (9th of 9 D).

Group Ratings

	ADA	ACLU	COPE	CFA	LCV	CON	NSI	COC	ACU	NTLC	CHC
1994	85	76	75	83	77	33	10	35	4	12	8
1993	85	—	73	90	69	8	—	36	0	—	—

National Journal Ratings

	1993 LIB	—	1993 CONS	1994 LIB	—	1994 CONS
Economic	71%	—	17%	66%	—	33%
Social	87%	—	8%	93%	—	0%
Foreign	78%	—	13%	72%	—	22%

Key Votes of the 103d Congress

1. Clinton Deficit Plan	Y	3. Brady Handgun Purchase Y	5. Lmt. UN Cmnd. of Forces N
2. NAFTA	Y	4. Strike Race/Death Pnlty. N	6. Cut Missile Funds Y

Key Votes of the 104th Congress

1. Congressional Compliance Y		3. Balanced Budget Amndt. Y	5. Product Liability Reform Y
2. Bar Unfunded Mandates Y		4. Pass Line Item Veto N	6. FY96 Budget N

Election Results

1992 general	Carol Moseley-Braun (D)	2,631,229	(53%)	($6,699,942)
	Richard S. Williamson (R)	2,126,833	(43%)	($2,300,924)
	Nine Others.	181,496	(4%)	
1992 primary	Carol Moseley-Braun (D)	557,694	(38%)	
	Alan J. Dixon (D)	504,077	(35%)	
	Albert F. Hofeld (D)	394,497	(27%)	
1986 general	Alan J. Dixon (D)	2,033,926	(65%)	($1,928,750)
	Judy Koehler (R)	1,053,793	(34%)	($851,305)

FIRST DISTRICT

The South Side of Chicago has been the nation's largest urban black community for nearly a century now. At first there were just a few blocks where black families from the South would settle; this ghetto grew rapidly with the first influx of blacks from the Mississippi Delta in the 1910s. By the 1920s, the South Side was well established, a center of blues music in America and of black-owned businesses. Politically, the South Side was a heavily Republican constituency throughout those years; the comfortable white Protestants who settled in solid brick houses here believed in the party of Yankee propriety, and the blacks had faith in the party of Lincoln. This was one of the heartlands of the Republican Party, represented in Congress by Republican Leader James Mann, and then Appropriations Chairman Martin Madden. After Madden died in the Appropriations Committee room in 1928, the 1st District elected Oscar DePriest, the first black elected to the House in the 20th Century. Blacks remained faithful to the party of Lincoln even during the Depression, voting for Herbert Hoover and DePriest in 1932.

The New Deal and the racial liberalism of New Dealers like Eleanor Roosevelt and Interior Secretary Harold Ickes (a former Chicago Republican himself) attracted blacks to the Democratic Party, and DePriest was beaten by a black Democrat in 1934. The South Side has been Democratic ever since. For 40 years, it was a cooperative part of Chicago's Democratic machine; then, after the death of longtime Congressman William Dawson, it rebelled against Mayor Richard J. Daley. Then the South Side seemed to take over the city when Congressman Harold Washington was elected mayor in 1983 and 1987. But control of political office does not mean what it once did. Patronage jobs became fewer as a result of court decisions. After Washington died in December 1987, other South Side black politicians flailed at each other, even though Chicago's electorate is only 40% black and a black candidate needs non-black voters to win. As these leaders fell, gang members came to fill the vacuum; the Gangster Disciples gang has a PAC called 21st Century VOTE (Voices of Total Empowerment) and one of its leaders even maneuvered himself into a group photograph with President Clinton. Yet the gangs do not rule everywhere. Many South Side neighborhoods are showing signs of vitality and growth. Citizens have banded together to fight crime using high-sodium streetlights and roadblocks. The South Shore Development Bank, much touted by Clinton in 1992, has provided loans to minority business owners.

The 1st Congressional District of Illinois includes about half of Chicago's South Side black community within its oddly shaped boundaries. It also extends out into the suburbs, and is no longer the nation's highest-percentage black district, but is by most measures Illinois's most Democratic. It includes the Gothic spires of the University of Chicago and the mansions of Kenwood, once the home of Chicago's Jewish aristocracy and more recently the headquarters of the Nation of Islam and home to its leader, Louis Farrakhan. Miles and miles of the district are made up of bungalow neighborhoods, with single-family houses lining arrow-straight streets. The 1st's odd shape follows historic patterns: the eastern half of the district roughly approximates the boundaries of 1st Districts going back to the 1960s; the western half, to which it is connected by a strip a mile wide, has some all-black neighborhoods, but also includes the high-income Irish-American neighborhoods of Morgan Park and Beverly, where the annual South Side Irish St. Patrick's Day Parade is held. It goes as far south as the industrial suburbs of Alsip and Blue Island.

The congressman from the 1st District is a man who has gone through several transformations. Bobby Rush grew up on the North Side, a Boy Scout whose mother was a Republican precinct captain. In the Army, he became involved in Student Non-Violent Coordinating Committee in the South, then founded the Illinois Black Panthers, where he recruited Fred Hampton, later killed in a raid by police in 1969. Rush served six months in prison for illegal possession of firearms, but also during his time with the Black Panthers he had run a medical clinic which developed the nation's first mass sickle cell anemia testing program. In 1983, he was elected 2d Ward alderman and became a strong Harold Washington supporter; after 1989, he worked amicably with Mayor Richard M. Daley as well. In 1992, with the district expanded, he decided to challenge the incumbent, Charles Hayes, an older generation politician with a more conventional background: a union official since the 1940s, elected in 1983 to replace Washington after he was elected mayor. Just before the March 1992 primary it was revealed that Hayes had 716 overdrafts on the House bank. Rush had acknowledged Hayes's past services but questioned his zeal and effectiveness; the checks may have made the difference. In a big primary turnout of 128,000, he beat Hayes 42%–39%, carrying eight of 12 black wards plus Morgan Park and Beverly, where many white police veterans live and where Rush was helped by then-House Speaker and 13th Ward Committeeman Michael Madigan.

Rush's rhetoric today is not what one might expect from his Panther days. "Most African-Americans just want a comfortable, middle-class lifestyle," he said in 1992. "Twenty-five years ago, I didn't know that." On crime, he said, "Blacks are killing blacks. Young blacks are killing other young blacks. We don't need to make excuses for our young people. We need to challenge them." He called for laws to reduce crime in high schools, increase youth employment and establish community-based organizations: articulating surely the yearnings of constituents struggling to keep safe neighborhoods where they can raise their families and work their way up.

In the House, Rush was elected freshman class whip in 1993, and worked to ban handguns generally and in housing projects and to pass a Community Development Banking Fund. He has argued for non-punitive welfare reform. In 1994, he was renominated without primary opposition and was mentioned as a candidate for mayor in 1995. But a week before the November 1994 election, his Republican opponent (who had been thrown out of a Chicago hotel for shouting questions at President Clinton about his promised tax cut in 1993), William Kelly, crashed a Rush press conference and accused Rush of owing $55,000 in back income taxes; the IRS had treated this as a civil matter, and Rush had paid off tax liens of $27,000 in October. Rush also settled $6,000 of back parking tickets with the city of Chicago for $2,500. He was easily reelected, but his 76% of the vote was below his 1992 percentage. Then in December, it was revealed that state computer records showed him owing $13,500 in "delinquent" child support payments. Rush said the income tax charges were persecution akin to newspaper stories about Fred Hampton before he was killed and that the child support records were incorrect, as the payments had long since been made—and the Illinois Department of Public Aid said it was conceivable that their records were inaccurate. Probably these charges won't hurt him too much in the 1st District; Harold Washington owed back income taxes, and won anyway. But Rush announced he would not run for mayor. Back in Washington, Rush secured a seat on the Commerce Committee, providing even more of an anchor for him at home.

The People: Pop. 1990: 571,908; 14% age 65+; 26% White; 70% Black; 1% Asian; 2% Other; 4% Hispanic origin. Voting age pop.: 418,848; 68% Black; 3% Hispanic origin. Households: 35% married couple families; 15% married couple fams. w. children; 45% college educ.; median household income: $24,140; per capita income: $11,709; median gross rent: $425; median house value: $72,400.

1992 Presidential Vote			1988 Presidential Vote		
Clinton (D)	214,104	(81%)	Dukakis (D)	202,182	(80%)
Bush (R)	32,803	(12%)	Bush (R)	50,575	(20%)
Perot (I)	17,355	(7%)			

Rep. Bobby Rush (D)

Elected 1992; b. Nov. 23, 1946, Albany, GA; home, Chicago; Roosevelt U., B.A. 1973, U. of IL, M.A. 1994; Protestant; married (Carolyn).

Career: Army, 1963–68; Student Non-Violent Coor. Cmtee., 1966–68; Co-founder, IL Black Panther Party, 1968; Chicago City Alderman, 1982–92.

DC Office: 131 CHOB 20515, 202-225-4372; Fax: 202-226-0333.

District Offices: 655 E. 79th St., Chicago 60619, 312-224-6500; and 9730 S. Western Ave., #237, Evergreen Park 60643, 708-422-4055.

Committees: *Commerce* (18th of 21 D): Energy and Power; Telecommunications and Finance.

Group Ratings

	ADA	ACLU	COPE	CFA	LCV	CON	NSI	COC	ACU	NTLC	CHC
1994	100	91	89	100	89	20	0	33	5	4	0
1993	95	—	100	100	92	39	—	9	0	—	—

National Journal Ratings

	1993 LIB — 1993 CONS			1994 LIB — 1994 CONS		
Economic	88%	—	0%	83%	—	0%
Social	87%	—	0%	94%	—	0%
Foreign	93%	—	0%	85%	—	0%

Key Votes of the 103d Congress

1. Clinton Deficit Plan	Y	3. Brady Handgun Purchase	Y	5. Lmt. UN Cmnd. of Forces	N
2. NAFTA	N	4. Strike Race/Death Pnlty.	N	6. Cut Missile Funds	Y

Key Votes of the 104th Congress

1. Congressional Compliance	Y	6. Reform Crime Grant	N	11. Loser Pays Court Reform	N
2. Balanced Budget Amndmt.	*	7. National Security Act	N	12. Product Liability Reform	N
3. Bar Unfunded Mandates	N	8. Moratorium on Regs.	*	13. Welfare Reform	N
4. Pass Line Item Veto	N	9. Risk Assessment on Regs.	*	14. Term Limits Amndmt.	N
5. Relax Exclusionary Rule	N	10. Expnd. Priv. Prop. Rights	N	15. Tax Cuts	N

Election Results

1994 general	Bobby Rush (D)	112,474	(76%)	($195,833)
	William J. Kelly (R)	36,038	(24%)	($37,066)
1994 primary	Bobby Rush (D)	unopposed		
1992 general	Bobby Rush (D)	209,258	(83%)	($260,389)
	Jay Walker (R)	43,453	(17%)	($13,740)

SECOND DISTRICT

Chicago is a great center of both commerce and industry, and if its white collar offices are heavily concentrated in the Loop, its blue collar heavy industries are most visible on the far south side. This heavy industry Chicago, diminished in importance economically now, is historically significant and, with the remnants of its great hulking factories around Lake Calumet and the nearby rail yards, has a certain undeniable majesty. Thomas Geoghegan, who writes more poetically than a lawyer ought to be able to, has told in his book, *Whose Side Are You On?*, of the fights to wrest severance benefits and pension rights for the workers whose steel mills shut down, of the decline in the labor movement in a place where it got much of its inspiration. For this is where the Pullman strike of 1894 was broken by federal troops and where policemen killed 10 union supporters in the Little Steel strike of 1937. Over the years, Chicago grew around the tight ethnic neighborhoods where workers went home at shift break each afternoon or midnight; today, they are mostly empty buildings that suburbanites speed by on the Calumet and Dan Ryan Expressways.

The 2d Congressional District of Illinois includes much of Chicago's old South Side industrial area plus many suburbs to the south. About two-thirds of its people live in Chicago, in widely separated neighborhoods. Some are in the old factory towns around Lake Calumet, some in the once heavily Jewish South Shore neighborhood, some in black wards west of Halsted Street. The Chicago portion of the 2d is overwhelmingly black; many blacks, especially young parents fleeing Chicago public schools, are moving into suburbs directly to the south—Harvey, Dolton, Posen (a reminder of its Polish origin), Markham. Farther south are Homewood and Flossmoor, with significant Jewish populations, high-income Olympia Fields, the planned town of Park Forest, and Chicago Heights, home town of America's premier political reporter for three decades now, David Broder. Two-thirds of the district's voters are black, and most are middle class. But there are signs everywhere of crime: a PAC called 21st Century VOTE (it stands for Voices of Total Empowerment) was run, according to ABC News and the *Los Angeles Times*, by the Gangster Disciples, a 30,000-member gang.

The 2d District is represented in Congress by Mel Reynolds, a Democrat whose primary victory in 1992 was hailed nationally as a deliverance. The reason: Reynolds defeated incumbent Gus Savage, whose 12-year career in the House was riddled with charges of absenteeism, blatantly incomplete campaign finance disclosure statements, nepotism, sexual harassment and bigotry against whites generally and Jews specifically. Reynolds, with a sparkling resume that included a Rhodes Scholarship, won by a resounding 63%–37%, carrying seven of the 11 wards in Chicago as well as the suburbs.

Reynolds started his first term well, but got into terrible trouble in his second year in the House and his problems steadily worsened. In 1993, he campaigned hard against fellow Chicago freshmen Bobby Rush and Luis Gutierrez for a seat on the Ways and Means Committee, and by carefully studying Chairman Dan Rostenkowski's 66-page list of committee issues and personally lobbying the 35 members of the Steering and Policy Committee, he won—the first and only freshman picked during Rostenkowski's tenure. But his victory was short lived: When the Republicans took hold of Congress after the 1994 elections, Reynolds, as the last-ranking Democrat on Ways and Means, lost his slot in committee downsizing. He currently holds a seat on the Economic and Educational Opportunities Committee, where Democrats were slow to take the legislative initiative.

In October 1993, Reynolds was highly critical of a "peace summit" with gang members praised by Jesse Jackson and then-NAACP head Benjamin Chavis. He had well-known opposition in the March 1994 primary, from state Senator Bill Shaw and Alderman Allan Streeter. President Clinton visited the 2d District the same day he came in to help Rostenkowski, and Reynolds won by a solid 56%–26%–18% margin. Then, in August 1994, Reynolds was indicted in Chicago on charges of rape and obstructing justice, for allegedly having had sex with a 16-year-old campaign worker. Reynolds denied that he had sex with the woman and said she had demanded money from him. Cook County State's Attorney Jack O'Malley, a Republican often mentioned as a candidate for higher office, accused Reynolds of giving false information to investigators and trying to influence witnesses before a grand jury. Reynolds responded with an affidavit from the complainant retracting the charges. "If I were a white congressman with the same background, would the same thing have happened?" Reynolds asked. "I think not." Later, after the trial on the initial charges was postponed until the summer of 1995, Reynolds was charged with additional counts of sex with a teenage girl and improper dealings with witnesses. Also, Reynolds's campaign finance reports failed to list many contributions; his former treasurer said he converted many contributions to cash. There doesn't seem to be much middle ground on Reynolds: depending on who you talk to, either he is a fraud who has committed serious offenses or he has been the victim of grave injustice by the prosecutor.

Reynolds's indictment had little effect in November 1994, since he had no Republican opponent. But unless he is vindicated in court, Reynolds seems sure to have serious opposition in 1996. Local Democratic officials have become more open in planning their candidacy for the 1996 primary or an earlier special election if he is convicted. They include state Senator Alice Palmer and state Represenative Monique Davis. Another rumored candidate is Jesse Jackson, Jr., son of Reverend Jesse Jackson.

The People: Pop. 1990: 572,188; 10% age 65+; 25% White; 68% Black; 1% Asian; 4% Other; 6% Hispanic origin. Voting age pop.: 402,161; 66% Black; 6% Hispanic origin. Households: 46% married couple families; 22% married couple fams. w. children; 42% college educ.; median household income: $30,217; per capita income: $11,468; median gross rent: $449; median house value: $64,200.

1992 Presidential Vote			1988 Presidential Vote		
Clinton (D)	194,639	(80%)	Dukakis (D)	167,574	(78%)
Bush (R)	31,634	(13%)	Bush (R)	48,467	(22%)
Perot (I)	16,950	(7%)			

Rep. Mel Reynolds (D)

Elected 1992; b. Jan. 8, 1952, Mound Bayou, MS; home, Chicago; Chicago City Cols., A.A. 1972; U. of IL, B.A. 1974; Rhodes Scholar, Oxford, Honor Schl. of Jurisprudence, J.D.S. 1976; Harvard JFK Schl. of Govt., 1984–86; Baptist; married (Marisol).

Career: Army Reserves, 1988–present; Founder & Pres., Amer. Scholars Against World Hunger, 1985–87; Asst. Prof., Roosevelt U., 1990–91; Exec. Dir., Community Econ. Devel. Foundation, 1990–91; Radio talk show host, 1990–91.

DC Office: 312 CHOB 20515, 202-225-0773.

District Offices: 525 E. 103rd St., Chicago 60628, 312-568-7900; and 17926 S. Halsted, #1-W, Homewood 60430, 708-957-9955.

Committees: *Economic & Educational Opportunities* (19th of 19 D): Employer-Employee Relations; Oversight and Investigations.

Group Ratings

	ADA	ACLU	COPE	CFA	LCV	CON	NSI	COC	ACU	NTLC	CHC
1994	85	83	63	80	85	*	11	50	0	13	7
1993	90	—	92	100	86	32	—	18	4	—	—

National Journal Ratings

	1993 LIB — 1993 CONS		1994 LIB — 1994 CONS	
Economic	78%	12%	*	*
Social	79%	20%	80%	20%
Foreign	87%	7%	85%	0%

Key Votes of the 103d Congress

1. Clinton Deficit Plan	Y	3. Brady Handgun Purchase	Y	5. Lmt. UN Cmnd. of Forces	N
2. NAFTA	Y	4. Strike Race/Death Pnlty.	N	6. Cut Missile Funds	Y

Key Votes of the 104th Congress

1. Congressional Compliance	Y	6. Reform Crime Grant	*	11. Loser Pays Court Reform	N
2. Balanced Budget Amndmt.	N	7. National Security Act	N	12. Product Liability Reform	N
3. Bar Unfunded Mandates	Y	8. Moratorium on Regs.	N	13. Welfare Reform	N
4. Pass Line Item Veto	N	9. Risk Assessment on Regs.	Y	14. Term Limits Amndmt.	N
5. Relax Exclusionary Rule	N	10. Expnd. Priv. Prop. Rights	Y	15. Tax Cuts	*

Election Results

1994 general	Mel Reynolds (D)	unopposed		($427,562)
1994 primary	Mel Reynolds (D)	50,179	(56%)	
	William (Bill) Shaw (D)	23,711	(26%)	
	Allan Streeter (D)	15,873	(18%)	
1992 general	Mel Reynolds (D)	182,614	(78%)	($542,911)
	Ron Blackstone (R)	31,957	(14%)	($35,848)
	Louanner Peters (LPP)	19,293	(8%)	($45,008)

THIRD DISTRICT

A century ago, Finley Peter Dunne's fictional Mr. Dooley pontificated on matters political in a saloon on Archery Avenue. This was, and is, Archer Avenue on the South Side of Chicago, one of Chicago's radial streets that cuts across what was once open prairie near the Loop and out the Chicago River and the Chicago and Sanitary Ship Canal. Archer Avenue was one of the paths of outward migration and upward mobility for the children and grandchildren of Chicago's different ethnic and cultural groups; and still is. Italians from the river wards along the Canal moved west; the South Side Irish moved west and south along Cicero Avenue toward Oak Lawn; the Bohemians (as they were called then; now Czechs) were heavily concentrated in the neat bungalows of the industrial suburbs of Berwyn and Cicero, famous as a haven for Al Capone's mobsters in the 1920s. Today, Hispanics of varying origin are driving these same avenues, up before dawn to arrive at large factories and small, or heading to the Loop on the CTA or to edge city jobs out the expressways or the Tollway, then home to old bungalows carefully refurbished and tended by kids home from school.

The 3d Congressional District of Illinois consists of much of this territory, criss-crossed by the Canal, the radial streets and the railroad lines and switching yards so common in this, the center of the nation's rail network. It includes the far west edge of Chicago and most of Cicero and Berwyn; Riverside, with its early 20th Century prairie-style houses; a few older affluent suburbs like Western Springs and the more recent and middle-income expanses of Oak Lawn and Palos Heights. Politically, this is marginal territory. Ancestral political preferences are mostly Democratic, but this is a culturally conservative area, with a sense of patriotism; Cicero, hostile to blacks in the 1960s, is now growing with an influx of Hispanic families. The conflict here now is between Democratic machine tradition and new Republican faith in traditional values.

The 3d District's congressman, William Lipinski, is an exemplar of the older Democratic allegiance. He started off as a patronage employee with the Parks District, was elected alderman, and evidently sees his primary job in Congress as lobbying for Chicago area transportation projects. Lipinski was elected (and remains) 23d Ward Democratic Committeeman in 1975—the key political post in a ward that includes Midway Airport and Chicago's westernmost stretch of Archer Avenue. In 1982, he ran for Congress and was slated against an aging incumbent, and won easily, 61%–36%—a classic example of old-time Chicago politics. Lipinski held the seat easily in the 1980s, using his post on Transportation and Infrastructure to get funding for the nearly completed Southwest Rapid Transit Line and $22 million for Midway and O'Hare Airports; in 1990, he passed a passenger facility charge to enable Midway and O'Hare to finance expansion or (as Mayor Daley then hoped) a third airport. Redistricting in 1992 put him in the same seat as another Democratic incumbent, Marty Russo, who since 1974 had used seats on the Commerce and Ways and Means committees to weigh in on national issues; he played a major role on the 1986 tax reform and was chief House sponsor of single-payer national health insurance. Russo vastly outspent Lipinski (over $1 million to $375,000), but Lipinski had the support of the committeemen from Chicago's 13th and 23d Wards (then-House Speaker Michael Madigan and himself) and portrayed himself as "a neighborhood guy" and Russo as a luxury-loving Washington insider who favored federal funding of obscene art and opposed federal funding of church-run day care. Mayor Richard Daley quietly and the *Chicago Tribune* openly endorsed Lipinski as "more important to the future of Illinois." Lipinski won 58%–37%.

But that does not necessarily mean Lipinski had the district sewed up for another decade. Issues like those he used against Russo were also turning this district, which Bill Clinton carried by only 41%–39%, toward the Republicans. Lipinski continued to work on transportation—building the Central Avenue Bypass, paying wages to employees of bankrupt trucking companies, opposing further deregulation of trucking, imposing additional fees on foreign ships docking at U.S. ports to help maritime unions whose cause he served on the now-defunct Merchant Marine and Fisheries Committee. In 1994, he had his first serious Republican opponent, Jim Nalepa, a retired Army officer and real estate developer. He put Lipinski's picture on a poster that said "WANTED for attempted robbery by trying to raise your property taxes" and attacked Lipinski's wife for working as a Washington lobbyist for the Chicago Transit Authority. Lipinski attacked Nalepa for paying low child support while spending much more on his campaign, and Lipinski profited from his own vociferous opposition to the Clinton budget in 1993 and to gays in the military. Lipinski, according to his office literature, is "not afraid to break from the Democratic Party when his views and the views of his neighbors diverge from the party's position."

Lipinski won 54%–46%, a showing 10 points lower than in 1992. He will surely continue to work hard on transportation issues, but Republican control hurts: the Merchant Marine Committee has been abolished and he is now in the minority on the Transportation and Infrastructure Committee. His votes on the Contract With America made him one of its biggest supporters among Democrats outside the South. But he resisted switching parties, saying, "I believe in an active government. There are things only the government can do—building highways, building bridges and maintaining transit." His electoral fate probably depends on whether he can continue, in the minority, to affect the way government does these things.

The People: Pop. 1990: 570,902; 16% age 65+; 89% White; 2% Black; 1% Asian; 3% Other; 7% Hispanic origin. Voting age pop.: 441,900; 2% Black; 6% Hispanic origin. Households: 58% married couple families; 25% married couple fams. w. children; 40% college educ.; median household income: $36,250; per capita income: $15,854; median gross rent: $489; median house value: $92,100.

1992 Presidential Vote

Clinton (D) 108,342 (41%)
Bush (R) 102,632 (39%)
Perot (I)................. 52,905 (20%)

1988 Presidential Vote

Bush (R) 157,477 (61%)
Dukakis (D)............... 100,124 (39%)

Rep. William O. Lipinski (D)

Elected 1982; b. Dec. 22, 1937, Chicago; home, Chicago; Loras Col., 1956–57; Catholic; married (Rose Marie).

Career: Army Reserves, 1961–67; Chicago Parks & Recreation Dept., 1958–75; Chicago 23d Ward Committeeman, 1975–present; Chicago City Alderman, 1975–83.

DC Office: 1501 LHOB 20515, 202-225-5701; Fax: 202-225-1012.

District Offices: 5832 S. Archer Ave., Chicago 60638, 312-886-0481; and 12717 W. Ridgeland Ave., Palos Heights 60463, 708-371-7460.

Committees: *Transportation & Infrastructure* (5th of 27 D): Aviation; Railroads (RMM).

Group Ratings

	ADA	ACLU	COPE	CFA	LCV	CON	NSI	COC	ACU	NTLC	CHC
1994	45	17	88	60	39	27	40	42	38	26	71
1993	45	—	83	70	71	1	—	27	33	—	—

National Journal Ratings

	1993 LIB — 1993 CONS		1994 LIB — 1994 CONS	
Economic	50%	— 49%	59%	— 37%
Social	31%	— 68%	46%	— 53%
Foreign	45%	— 55%	40%	— 60%

Key Votes of the 103d Congress

1. Clinton Deficit Plan	N	3. Brady Handgun Purchase	Y	5. Lmt. UN Cmnd. of Forces	Y
2. NAFTA	N	4. Strike Race/Death Pnlty.	Y	6. Cut Missile Funds	N

Key Votes of the 104th Congress

1. Congressional Compliance	Y	6. Reform Crime Grant	N	11. Loser Pays Court Reform	N
2. Balanced Budget Amndmt.	Y	7. National Security Act	Y	12. Product Liability Reform	N
3. Bar Unfunded Mandates	Y	8. Moratorium on Regs.	Y	13. Welfare Reform	Y
4. Pass Line Item Veto	N	9. Risk Assessment on Regs.	*	14. Term Limits Amndmt.	N
5. Relax Exclusionary Rule	Y	10. Expnd. Priv. Prop. Rights	N	15. Tax Cuts	Y

Election Results

1994 general	William O. Lipinski (D)	92,353	(54%)	($366,804)
	Jim Nalepa (R).....................	78,163	(46%)	($277,772)
1994 primary	William O. Lipinski (D)	unopposed		
1992 general	William O. Lipinski (D)	162,165	(64%)	($556,847)
	Harry C. Lepinske (R)	93,128	(36%)	($66,991)

FOURTH DISTRICT

Just west of the Loop, the Chicago River splits into North and South Branches, both penetrating the heart of old neighborhoods where immigrants fresh off the boat first got their start in Chicago. The South Branch is the guts of Chicago, the site of one of western civilization's astonishing engineering feats: here in 1900, the course of the river was reversed so that sewage flowed Downstate through a canal rather than out into Lake Michigan. Just blocks away was Maxwell Street, thronged with market stalls (just recently closed), long the arrival neighborhood for Chicago's Jews; not far away, in an Italian-American neighborhood on Halsted Street, was Jane Addams's Hull House, the original settlement house, where social workers told new immigrants not how to rebel against middle-class American mores, but how to live them. To the south were Bridgeport, home of the Irish and of the mayors of Chicago from 1933 to 1979 and again from 1989 until recently, when the Daleys moved to the South Loop, and Pilsen, arrival neighborhood for the Bohemians (Czechs). Off the North Branch of the River was Milwaukee Avenue, the main street of Polish-Americans and Ukrainian-Americans for a century now.

Today, many of these places are arrival neighborhoods again, mostly for Chicago's wide variety of Hispanic immigrants. On the South Side, in the old river wards, is Chicago's Mexican-American community, extending west into the once Bohemian suburb of Cicero; on the North Side are many Puerto Ricans and other Hispanics. Altogether, the 1990 Census counted 545,000 Hispanics in Chicago, by far the largest Latino concentration north of Texas and Florida and between the two coasts. They have been attracted, as immigrants were 100 years ago, by a vibrant economy that provides opportunity to those who work hard, and by a culture which can be portrayed as unwelcoming only because of its own high standards.

The 4th Congressional District of Illinois is the Hispanic-majority district which was deemed mandatory under the Voting Rights Act amendments of 1982. The problem was that the South Side Mexican-American and the North Side Puerto Rican communities were separated by the West Side black ghetto. The solution was today's 4th Congressional District, with arguably the most convoluted shape of any district in the country: essentially these two Latino communities, defined by erose boundaries to maximize the Hispanic percentage, are connected by a thin line of territory which stretches around the West Side black-majority 7th District to meet at the Cook-DuPage County line. Most of this salient consists of parkland, railroad yards and cemeteries; more than 95% of the votes are in Chicago or Cicero. The 4th's population is about two-thirds Hispanic, with Mexican-Americans outnumbering Puerto Ricans more than 2–1; but eligible voters are 58% white anglo and 39% Latino, with Mexican-Americans and Puerto Ricans about equally split. This is a solidly Democratic district, though by no means as Democratic as the black-majority 1st, 2d or 7th.

The congressman here, Luis Gutierrez, was effectively chosen in the 1992 Democratic primary. He is a politician who in his decade-long career has shown some skill at political maneuvering. Gutierrez grew up, the son of a cab driver and factory worker, in both Chicago, where he was a social worker, and Puerto Rico, where he taught school. He started off politically as a supporter of Harold Washington by defiantly running—and losing—against Dan Rostenkowski for 32d Ward Committeeman in 1983. Then Washington hired him as a staffer, and backed Gutierrez in a crucial 1986 special election for City Council in one of two new Hispanic seats. Gutierrez won and, with Juan Soliz on the South Side, gave control of the Council to Washington. Then Washington died in 1987 and, in the 1989 election to succeed him, Gutierrez backed (and Soliz opposed) Richard M. Daley. For that, Gutierrez was richly rewarded: he became chairman of the Housing Committee, pushed through his "New Homes for Chicago" plan authorizing the city to sell vacant lots to developers of affordable housing for $1; he was also author of a bill prohibiting discrimination against gays and the disabled. In both cases, he helped Daley cement his support with crucial groups in the middle 20% of the electorate, Latinos and gays.

Another "payback," as Gutierrez called it, came in the 1992 race for the new 4th Congressional District. Gutierrez and Soliz were again rivals. Gutierrez called crime the number one problem and bragged of his council record; Soliz talked about trade and health care and called Gutierrez a machine candidate. Certainly Gutierrez seemed a multi-ethnic candidate: "There is a Hispanic agenda . . . it's the same as the Polish, Irish and Lithuanian agenda. If you work hard, sweat and toil and play by the rules, you will be rewarded . . . with clean streets, safer and better schools, the opportunity to send your kids to college. Tell me who in America and in the 4th Congressional District doesn't want these things?" Gutierrez said, and won 60%–40%. The 1994 primary was a rematch and Gutierrez won again, 64%–36%. Gutierrez has a high profile in the district, running recycling drives, a Gutierrez Community Corps to paint out graffiti and citizenship enrollment meetings.

Gutierrez brought his in-your-face style to the House, with mixed results. His past independence kept him from a seat on the Ways and Means Committee, of which Dan Rostenkowski was still chairman; Gutierriez' call for a congressional pay freeze was not heeded. In February 1994, he was the subject of a *60 Minutes* profile, in which he called the House "the belly of the beast," charging that chairmen intimidated members and that the House Democratic leadership stifled reform, and that some freshmen Democrats "sold out" or "reneged on their reformist promises." These reasonably accurate observations were not appreciated by Democratic colleagues, to put it mildly. "I've gotten my rear end kicked around here," Gutierrez told *The Washington Post*. A leadership staffer said Gutierrez "will never get a choice committee assignment. . . . He will always end up on the Banking Committee." And at least for now, he has not been very successful legislatively. Gutierrez amendments to make abortions an available service in veterans' hospitals and to change the formula on anti-crime aid to local housing authorities both were rejected. So were Gutierrez causes like lobbying reform and single-payer health insurance. Gutierrez could perhaps take some satisfaction that voters in November 1994 seemed to endorse his critique of the Democratic House; but of course he is in the minority now, and disliked by many fellow Democrats. And he remains a member of the Banking Committee. But this spunky politician has picked himself up and dusted himself off after defeat before and, with a solid local base, seems likely to do so again.

The People: Pop. 1990: 571,162; 8% age 65+; 49% White; 6% Black; 3% Asian; 42% Other; 64% Hispanic origin. Voting age pop.: 383,285; 6% Black; 58% Hispanic origin. Households: 49% married couple families; 31% married couple fams. w. children; 24% college educ.; median household income: $23,083; per capita income: $8,352; median gross rent: $393; median house value: $64,300.

1992 Presidential Vote		
Clinton (D)	82,271	(65%)
Bush (R)	29,093	(23%)
Perot (I)	15,272	(12%)

1988 Presidential Vote		
Dukakis (D)	79,492	(63%)
Bush (R)	45,938	(37%)

Rep. Luis V. Gutierrez (D)

Elected 1992; b. Dec. 10, 1953, Chicago; home, Chicago; Northeastern IL U., B.A. 1975; Catholic; married (Soraida).

Career: Teacher, Puerto Rico, 1977–78; Social Wkr., Chicago Dept. of Children & Family Svcs., 1979–83; Advisor, Chicago Mayor Harold Washington, 1984–86; Chicago City Alderman, 1986–92, Pres. Pro Tem, 1989–92.

DC Office: 408 LHOB 20515, 202-225-8203; Fax: 202-225-7810.

District Offices: 3181 N. Elston Ave., Chicago 60618, 312-509-0999; 1751 W. 47th St., Chicago 60609, 312-247-9020; 3659 Halsted, Chicago 60609, 312-254-0797; and 2132 W. 21st St., Chicago 60608, 312-579-0886.

Committees: *Banking & Financial Services* (13th of 22 D): General Oversight and Investigations; Housing and Community Opportunity. *Veterans' Affairs* (9th of 15 D): Hospitals and Health Care.

Group Ratings

	ADA	ACLU	COPE	CFA	LCV	CON	NSI	COC	ACU	NTLC	CHC
1994	90	87	100	80	88	39	0	80	0	15	0
1993	100	—	100	90	93	39	—	9	4	—	—

National Journal Ratings

	1993 LIB — 1993 CONS			1994 LIB — 1994 CONS		
Economic	64%	—	34%	65%	—	34%
Social	87%	—	0%	89%	—	11%
Foreign	78%	—	21%	75%	—	25%

Key Votes of the 103d Congress

1. Clinton Deficit Plan	Y	3. Brady Handgun Purchase	Y	5. Lmt. UN Cmnd. of Forces	N
2. NAFTA	N	4. Strike Race/Death Pnlty.	N	6. Cut Missile Funds	Y

Key Votes of the 104th Congress

1. Congressional Compliance	Y	6. Reform Crime Grant	N	11. Loser Pays Court Reform	N
2. Balanced Budget Amndmt.	N	7. National Security Act	N	12. Product Liability Reform	N
3. Bar Unfunded Mandates	N	8. Moratorium on Regs.	N	13. Welfare Reform	N
4. Pass Line Item Veto	Y	9. Risk Assessment on Regs.	*	14. Term Limits Amndmt.	N
5. Relax Exclusionary Rule	N	10. Expnd. Priv. Prop. Rights	N	15. Tax Cuts	N

Election Results

1994 general	Luis V. Gutierrez (D)	46,695	(75%)	($367,811)
	Steven Valtierra (R)	15,384	(25%)	($12,603)
1994 primary	Luis V. Gutierrez (D)	31,100	(64%)	
	Juan M. Soliz (D)	17,696	(36%)	
1992 general	Luis V. Gutierrez (D)	90,452	(78%)	($420,227)
	Hildegarde Rodriguez-Schieman (R)	26,154	(22%)	($3,574)

FIFTH DISTRICT

No place in America today has more variety, ethnic and cultural, than the North Side of Chicago. From the air, the geometric grid streets lit by high-sodium lamps seem monotonous; on the ground, on a winter's day with snow swirling, its brick buildings look stolid and forbidding. This has been the homeland of one immigrant group after another and the chosen neighborhoods of all manner of successful middle-class people. Wooden workingman's cottages from the late 19th Century give way to sturdy huge brick houses of the early 1900s and then to the prairie bungalows of the 1920s and white-shuttered, orange-brick colonials of the 1950s. Chicago was America's number one immigrant destination for Poles, Lithuanians, Czechs, Slovaks, Ukrainians and Romanians; something about the heavy dull clouds of the long winters, the short hot summers, a climate suited to potatoes and cabbage and other earth vegetables, may have reminded them of central and eastern Europe. By the late 1980s, new upwardly mobile immigrants from Mexico and Guatemala, Korea and the Philippines, refugees and recent arrivals from Eastern Europe and the former Soviet Union moved into these melting pot precincts. Family ties, webs of acquaintance that reach back to ancestral villages, have made the North Side of Chicago a natural port of entry for Eastern bloc migrants coming to America.

The 5th Congressional District of Illinois covers an oddly-shaped slice of Chicago's North Side, running from the Lakefront all the way to the suburbs directly south of O'Hare Airport. Its boundaries were carefully drawn to put most Hispanics in the 4th District just to the south, but otherwise it reflects the full variety of the North Side. It includes Chicago's most glamorous lakefront apartments facing the Oak Street beach and the gentrified neighborhoods of Old Town, where old houses and factories are being converted into upscale condominiums. It takes in the Polish-American and Ukrainian-American neighborhoods around Milwaukee Avenue, and the old Italian neighborhoods running west on Grand Avenue. It includes, a couple of blocks from the Chicago River, the old church of St. Stanislaus Kostka, a traditional center of the Polish community since the 19th Century, and the residence across Pulaski Park of a man who until 1994 was one of America's most powerful politicians, Dan Rostenkowski.

Rostenkowski deserves at least a long footnote in history, something more than a mention of the May 1994 indictment for misusing his office stamp allowance, which as part of a 17-count indictment on charges of embezzlement, fraud and witness tampering, forced him from the Ways and Means chairmanship and led to his defeat by an unknown Republican in November 1994. For Rostenkowski was a product of the gritty Chicago machine who showed far greater skill and public spiritedness than his background could lead anyone to expect and who made important contributions to national public policy. Politics in Chicago was long a family matter; Joe Rostenkowski, 32d Ward Committeeman since 1935, was owed a favor by Mayor Richard J. Daley, and so in 1958 his 30-year-old son was elected to Congress. By 1980, Dan Rostenkowski had his choice of the chair of Ways and Means or the post of Whip, which would probably have made him speaker in 1989 instead of Tom Foley. He chose Ways and Means and, after losing on the Reagan tax cuts of 1981, came back to fashion the tax reform act of 1986, showing both a mastery of the technical details of the tax code and a broad view of the national interest: one of the best legislative performances of his generation. Sometimes frustrated on economic policy in the Bush years, he played a lead role in Bill Clinton's two major legislative successes, the 1993 deficit-reduction package and the North American Free Trade Agreement; the indictment forced him out of the chair just as the committee was about to consider the Clinton healthcare plan and when Democrats could have used his coalition-building skills.

Politically, the 1990s were more difficult for Rosty. The new 5th District was mostly new territory to him, and in 1992 he faced lakefront liberal Dick Simpson in the primary. Even with strong backing from Mayor Richard M. Daley, he won by only 57%–43%. Before his 1994 indictment, he had primary opposition from Simpson and state Senator John Cullerton, also a lakefront liberal but from a family that had produced many North Side politicians, notably longtime Assessor Parky Cullerton. (If you have to ask why that office was important, you are from out of town.) Cullerton edged up on Rostenkowski in polls until Daley stepped in; Rostenkowski started running hard in the last two weeks; President Clinton came in the last week for a "nonpolitical" appearance—ostensibly to discuss health care—with Rostenkowski, at which Republican Governor Jim Edgar was also present. The message was received: the chairman got 50% to 30% for Cullerton and 14% for Simpson.

Most observers, including Republican leaders, thought the primary was tantamount to election; 93,000 people voted in the Democratic primary, while 10,000 voted on the Republican side. Their nominee, Michael Flanagan, was a 31-year-old lawyer with a sense of humor and solid conservative views who had never held public office. In late October, local Republicans told national Republicans they had a poll showing Flanagan ahead of Rostenkowski—a volunteer poll that even Flanagan greeted with skepticism; the Republican National Committee hired a national pollster, who found the same thing and, not believing the result, polled again. The RNC then put in $55,000 for ads the last week; Democrats evidently didn't sense the trouble until too late. Flanagan won 54%–46%. It is widely assumed he is a one-term congressman. But the district is not that heavily Democratic: if it voted solidly for Bill Clinton in 1992, it went for George Bush in 1988, which the 1994 results suggest may be a better indicator. Flanagan has sought to concentrate on providing constituency service—the formula which enabled many Democrats to hold Republican-leaning seats in the 1970s and 1980s. Republican leaders, who obviously relish the symbolism of Flanagan's 1994 victory, will give him leeway in casting votes that buck the party line—he was the only Republican to vote against the budget resolution. And the Democratic contenders for the nomination are likely to have the leftish views obligatory on the lakefront but unpopular a mile or so inland. So this could be a seriously, and surprisingly, contested seat again in 1996.

The People: Pop. 1990: 571,053; 15% age 65+; 79% White; 1% Black; 6% Asian; 6% Other; 13% Hispanic origin. Voting age pop.: 467,192; 1% Black; 11% Hispanic origin. Households: 44% married couple families; 18% married couple fams. w. children; 47% college educ.; median household income: $33,262; per capita income: $19,242; median gross rent: $514; median house value: $109,200.

1992 Presidential Vote			1988 Presidential Vote		
Clinton (D)	124,273	(51%)	Bush (R)	123,159	(52%)
Bush (R)	80,036	(33%)	Dukakis (D)	115,011	(48%)
Perot (I)	39,113	(16%)			

Rep. Michael Patrick Flanagan (R)

Elected 1994; b. Nov. 9, 1962, Chicago; home, Chicago; Loyola U., B.A. 1984, J.D. 1991; Roman Catholic; single.

Career: Army, 1984–88, 1991–92; Practicing atty., 1991–94;

DC Office: 1407 LHOB 20515, 202-225-4061; Fax: 202-225-3128.

District Offices: 3538 W. Irving Park Rd., Chicago 60618, 312-588-2288.

Committees: *Government Reform & Oversight* (23rd of 27 R): District of Columbia; Government Management, Information and Technology. *Judiciary* (19th of 20 R): Commercial and Administrative Law; Constitution. *Veterans' Affairs* (13th of 18 R): Hospitals and Health Care.

Group Ratings and 103rd Congress Votes: Newly Elected

Key Votes of the 104th Congress

1. Congressional Compliance Y	6. Reform Crime Grant Y	11. Loser Pays Court Reform Y
2. Balanced Budget Amndmt. Y	7. National Security Act Y	12. Product Liability Reform Y
3. Bar Unfunded Mandates Y	8. Moratorium on Regs. Y	13. Welfare Reform Y
4. Pass Line Item Veto Y	9. Risk Assessment on Regs. Y	14. Term Limits Amndmt. Y
5. Relax Exclusionary Rule Y	10. Expnd. Priv. Prop. Rights Y	15. Tax Cuts Y

Election Results

1994 general	Michael Patrick Flanagan (R)	75,328	(54%)	($112,638)
	Dan Rostenkowski (D)	63,065	(46%)	($2,495,222)
1994 primary	Michael Patrick Flanagan (R)	3,890	(38%)	
	James S. Parker (R)	2,155	(21%)	
	Elias R. Non-Incumbent Zenkich (R)	2,152	(21%)	
	John Cleland (R).	1,323	(13%)	
	Michael A. Bendas (R).	588	(6%)	
1992 general	Dan Rostenkowski (D)	132,889	(57%)	($1,455,455)
	Elias R. Non-Incumbent Zenkich (R)	90,738	(39%)	($83,293)
	Blaise C. Grenke (Lib)	8,456	(4%)	

SIXTH DISTRICT

What is today the nation's busiest airport was half a century ago an airstrip in an apple orchard (hence its current three-letter code: ORD); to the east was the Forest Preserve along the Des Plaines River, to the west little suburban villages strung along rail lines, separated by cornfields. But in the 1950s, Mayor Richard J. Daley decided that Chicago needed a new airport, annexed the orchard, and named it after a World War II hero from a good Chicago Irish Catholic Democratic family. Today, O'Hare is surrounded on all sides by suburbs as densely settled as the bungalow wards of the city, with hotels and office buildings clustered near the interchanges in Rosemont, and characteristic Chicago yellow-orange brick houses in orderly rows in suburbs like Park Ridge, the childhood home of Hillary Rodham Clinton. Politically, these suburbs have long been solidly Republican, as were the Rodhams, convinced that civic virtues could best be realized by opposing the party of City Hall in Chicago and economic growth could best be assured by opposing the party that backed stifling government regulation. Indeed, Maine Township, which includes Park Ridge, has remained true to the principles which its most famous daughter has renounced, voting for Paul Tsongas over Bill Clinton in the 1992 Illinois primary and for Bush/Quayle over Clinton/Gore in the general election.

The 6th Congressional District of Illinois includes much of this suburban area. It includes Park Ridge and Des Plaines just north of O'Hare and to the west the newer suburb of Elk Grove Village, the headquarters of United Airlines. The larger part of the district is over the line in DuPage County, including the string of long-settled suburbs directly (though far) west of the Loop: Elmhurst, Villa Park, Lombard, Glen Ellyn, Wheaton. It also takes in the newer suburbs along I-290 and Lake Street: Bensenville, Addison, Wood Dale, Bloomingdale. Economically, this is high income territory; culturally, it is cautiously moderate; politically, it is one of the most Republican districts in Illinois and the nation.

The congressman from the 6th is Henry Hyde, one of the most senior Republicans in Congress, and now chairman of the House Judiciary Committee. He also is one of the most respected and intellectually honest members of the House. Hyde springs from Chicago earth, was raised a Catholic and a Democrat, but came to see a widening gulf between his core beliefs and his ancestral party. He was elected to the Illinois legislature in 1966 and in the Democratic year of 1974 was elected to the House. He first made his name in the House as an opponent of abortion, attaching to Appropriations subcommittee bills his Hyde Amendments prohibiting the use of federal funds to pay for abortions in various circumstances. These were regarded by many as regressive and by others as a diversion from real issues; for Hyde, who regards abortion as murder, the issue was saving children. Hyde is unhappy that efforts to overturn *Roe v. Wade* have failed. But the Hyde amendment banning federal funding of most Medicaid abortions has been law since 1978, and in 1993, over the opposition of the incoming Clinton Administration, it was passed again in the House and the Senate by solid margins of 255–178 and 59–40. The exceptions are limited, to save the woman's life and, starting again in 1993, for victims of rape and incest. Hyde also helped defeat the Freedom of Choice Act, an attempt to codify *Roe v. Wade*, by arguing for states' rights to impose some restrictions.

Hyde's regard for children and desire to strengthen families takes him beyond abortion issues. He was one of the few Republicans who supported the family leave bill, and even voted to override President Bush's veto of it in 1992; he felt it was logical to help mothers care for children. He wants to outlaw commercial surrogate motherhood contracts and he worked to facilitate adoption of Romanian children. Hyde also joined the bipartisan effort on the 1995 welfare bill to add tough measures against "deadbeat dads" who fail to support their family. He has proposed that the IRS collect child support through wage withholding, a step that Ways and Means Committee chairman Bill Archer found objectionable. "Denying a little kid food and clothes is like stealing; it's child abuse," Hyde said. "Capitalism with a human face isn't such a nutty idea." His stands seem to stem from deep religious beliefs combined with a trial lawyer's combative instincts, a respect for rules combined with a certain compassion.

For many years, Hyde was one of the leaders of House conservatives, and still sometimes is; yet by the middle 1990s he was out of sync with some of the policies of Newt Gingrich's Contract with America. In the 1980s, Hyde destroyed the nuclear freeze resolution, defended the Reagan Administration on Iran-contra, sponsored a ban on arms sales to terrorist nations like Iraq. He has spoken out eloquently in favor of an amendment to allow a ban on flag-burning and rules to limit convicted criminals' appeals. But Hyde has irritated fellow Republicans by voting for the Brady bill waiting period for gun purchases and the assault weapon ban (which he had voted against before), trying to constructively amend the independent counsel law and opposing term limits. "I think America is always going to need statesmen, and you don't get them out of the phone book," he said, winning plaudits for his eloquent challenge to the party dogma. He worked hard on the 1994 crime bill, but criticized the Democrats' version as pork-laden and voted against it and played little role in the Gingrich's effort to craft a bipartisan compromise.

When Republicans won the majority, Hyde had several choices. He could keep a position in the party leadership, possibly remaining as Republican Policy Committee chairman. (Earlier, he had been mentioned briefly as a candidate for higher posts when Robert Michel announced his retirement, but his support is not great, and he made no move to challenge Newt Gingrich or Dick Armey for the posts they now hold.) Some talked him up as International Relations Committee chairman. But in choosing to chair the Judiciary Committee, Hyde won the opportunity to make changes he has voted for unavailingly for as long as 20 years and benefited from the reputation for fairness and competence to withstand purely partisan attack. With his central-casting bearing for the chairmanship, he added some credibility and policy heft to the new Gingrich team. Despite his ambivalence on some parts, he played a major role in moving the Contract With America to the floor in the first 100 days: balanced budget amendment, several crime bills and the term-limits proposal, which he strongly opposed. Hyde won generally positive reviews, although he grumbled on more than one occasion that his influence was limited to that of "a subchairman," meaning that Gingrich was calling the shots on major elements of the policies and the schedule.

Hyde has had no trouble winning reelection in the Republican 6th District, so many of whose residents grew up in Democratic Chicago as he did, and have moved right as they moved out.

The People: Pop. 1990: 572,268; 12% age 65+; 88% White; 1% Black; 5% Asian; 2% Other; 5% Hispanic origin. Voting age pop.: 437,173; 1% Black; 4% Hispanic origin. Households: 62% married couple families; 29% married couple fams. w. children; 57% college educ.; median household income: $44,216; per capita income: $19,405; median gross rent: $605; median house value: $129,800.

1992 Presidential Vote

Bush (R) 121,868 (47%)
Clinton (D) 86,448 (33%)
Perot (I) 52,734 (20%)

1988 Presidential Vote

Bush (R) 158,513 (68%)
Dukakis (D) 75,931 (32%)

Rep. Henry J. Hyde (R)

Elected 1974; b. Apr. 18, 1924, Chicago; home, Wooddale; Georgetown U., B.S. 1947, Loyola U., J.D. 1949; Catholic; widowed.

Career: Navy, 1944–46 (WWII); Naval Reserves, 1946–68; Practicing atty., 1950–75; IL House of Reps., 1966–74, Majority Ldr., 1971–72.

DC Office: 2110 RHOB 20515, 202-225-4561; Fax: 202-225-1166.

District Offices: 50 E. Oak St., Addison 60101, 312-832-5950.

Committees: *International Relations* (5th of 23 R): International Operations and Human Rights. *Judiciary* (Chmn. of 20 R): Commercial and Administrative Law; Constitution.

Group Ratings

	ADA	ACLU	COPE	CFA	LCV	CON	NSI	COC	ACU	NTLC	CHC
1994	5	17	11	30	6	64	100	96	90	89	100
1993	10	—	17	40	21	85	—	82	87	—	—

National Journal Ratings

	1993 LIB — 1993 CONS	1994 LIB — 1994 CONS
Economic	30% — 68%	0% — 80%
Social	25% — 73%	20% — 77%
Foreign	16% — 83%	14% — 80%

Key Votes of the 103d Congress

1. Clinton Deficit Plan	N	3. Brady Handgun Purchase Y	5. Lmt. UN Cmnd. of Forces Y
2. NAFTA	Y	4. Strike Race/Death Pnlty. Y	6. Cut Missile Funds N

Key Votes of the 104th Congress

1. Congressional Compliance	Y	6. Reform Crime Grant	Y	11. Loser Pays Court Reform Y
2. Balanced Budget Amndmt.	Y	7. National Security Act	Y	12. Product Liability Reform Y
3. Bar Unfunded Mandates	Y	8. Moratorium on Regs.	Y	13. Welfare Reform Y
4. Pass Line Item Veto	Y	9. Risk Assessment on Regs.	Y	14. Term Limits Amndmt. N
5. Relax Exclusionary Rule	Y	10. Expnd. Priv. Prop. Rights	Y	15. Tax Cuts Y

Election Results

1994 general	Henry J. Hyde (R)	115,664	(73%)	($423,027)
	Tom Berry (D)	37,163	(24%)	($14,449)
	Others	4,551	(3%)	
1994 primary	Henry J. Hyde (R)	45,546	(82%)	
	David J. Czech (R)	9,760	(18%)	
1992 general	Henry J. Hyde (R)	165,009	(66%)	($408,987)
	Barry W. Watkins (D)	86,891	(34%)	($62,423)

SEVENTH DISTRICT

The cross-country flyer on a lucky day can get a clear view of the biggest man-made cityscape between the Atlantic and Pacific Oceans: Chicago's Loop. High-rise buildings were pioneered a century ago in the Loop—named in 1897 for the circle the "El" train forms around the city's center—by architects like Louis Sullivan and Daniel Burnham. International School modernists built their most impressive collection of buildings here and along the Lakeshore in the years after World War II; in the last dozen years, postmodernists have decorated the Chicago River and reinvented the skyscraper. The Loop now spreads beyond the El, up the wondrous shopping street of North Michigan Avenue with a peak at the John Hancock Tower, and west beyond the commodities exchanges to the Sears Tower on the Chicago River. This is the face Chicago likes to present to the world: giant structures rising where the prairies meet the inland sea, a vast concentration of brains and muscle, the nerve center of the markets of the nation and the world.

Behind the lakefront, where the air traveler sees the grid spread out below with occasional radials, is the muscle and sinew, gristle and fat of the city. And also the parts that do not work so well: houses and apartment buildings are abandoned; commercial space stands empty and vandalized; giant housing projects, like the Robert Taylor Homes off the Dan Ryan Expressway, rise starkly, their playgrounds empty because of the ever-present threat of gunfire. The West Side of Chicago, the vast acres directly west of the Loop, for years has been a dreadful slum. And the decay has spread west to the Austin neighborhood, just before the border of upper income—and for two decades racially integrated—Oak Park.

The 7th Congressional District of Illinois contains the Loop and most of the North Michigan corridor and the Near North Side, with the infamous Cabrini-Green housing project. It also goes south, past 19th Century Prairie Avenue mansions to the Taylor homes and takes in a few heavily black South Side neighborhoods. Its heart, demographically and spiritually, is the black ghetto of the West Side, far more depopulated and socially disorganized than the South Side. To the west are Oak Park and River Forest, and the much more modest Maywood, which is black-majority, and Broadview and Hillside. About two-thirds of the people here are black; there are few Hispanics since they were confined by painstaking boundary-drawing to the 4th District, which practically encircles the 7th on three sides.

Representing the 7th District is Cardiss Collins, a black Democrat first elected in 1973 to replace her husband after he was killed in a plane crash; he had been a routine machine backer and Cardiss Collins was expected to be the same. But Chicago politics has changed and Congresswoman Collins has been something more than a cipher. With a seat on the Commerce Committee, long a sought-after assignment for House Democrats, she was chairwoman of the Commerce, Consumer Protection and Competitiveness Subcommittee from 1991 to 1994. There she passed laws to clear the way for mass introduction of blank digital audio recording tapes into the U.S. On the Health Subcommittee, she worked to expand Medicare coverage for Pap smears and mammograms and to establish health clinics in high schools. She has been a supporter of the Chicago futures markets and got the Agriculture Department to agree to release crop reports at 7:30 a.m., before the Chicago exchanges open, rather than at 2:00 p.m., when they are closed and speculators did their trading in Tokyo instead. With Senator Carol Moseley-Braun, Collins conducted hearings on violent and demeaning images in "gangsta" rap and other popular music. She has called for more gender equity in college athletics and questioned whether higher NCAA academic standards would hurt blacks by making it more difficult to get their degree while also participating in sports, which opens other doors for many. She passed a bill aimed at combating insurance company "redlining"—when companies refuse to sell policies in certain areas. She has called for more gender equity in college athletics and questioned possible racial bias on the part of some researchers and the data they use in calling for tougher entrance requirements for college atheletes. And over some protests, she supported Chicago Housing Commissioner Vince Lane's proposal to redevelop the Cabrini-Green project as a public/private mixed project, with six buildings to be demolished.

With the Democrats' loss of the majority and the shuffling of ranking memberships at key committees and subcommittees, Collins gave up her membership on Commerce in 1995 so that she could focus on her new position as ranking Democrat on Government Reform and Oversight; John Conyers had been the committee's chairman but he switched to the top Democratic seat at Judiciary at the start of the 104th Congress. The Government Reform panel played an active role on such early initiatives as unfunded mandates, line-item veto and regulatory reform, putting Collins in the spotlight as she organized, with some success, the new minority party's response; her chief problems came in attempting to manage conservative Democrats such as Gary Condit and Collin Peterson, who were more interested in doing business with Republicans. Like senior Democrats at other committees, she learned that the skills required to preside over a committee were not easily transferred and that the loss of staff was especially painful. If Democrats regain control, Collins obviously would be a big winner and an important player.

Collins had serious competition in the mid-1980s, when she twice beat Alderman Danny Davis in primaries, 48%–39% and 60%–40%; she has had no problems since. In the 1990s redistricting fight, she resisted a new Hispanic-majority district for fear it would cut her district in two; thanks to its grotesque shape, it did not.

The People: Pop. 1990: 572,039; 10% age 65+; 27% White; 66% Black; 3% Asian; 2% Other; 4% Hispanic origin. Voting age pop.: 407,120; 60% Black; 4% Hispanic origin. Households: 33% married couple families; 15% married couple fams. w. children; 43% college educ.; median household income: $25,220; per capita income: $13,056; median gross rent: $449; median house value: $89,300.

1992 Presidential Vote

Clinton (D)	184,966	(78%)
Bush (R)	35,530	(15%)
Perot (I)	15,992	(7%)

1988 Presidential Vote

Dukakis (D)	166,350	(76%)
Bush (R)	51,139	(24%)

Rep. Cardiss Collins (D)

Elected 1973; b. Sept. 24, 1931, St. Louis, MO; home, Chicago; Northwestern U., B.A. 1967; Baptist; widowed.

Career: Stenographer, IL Dept. of Labor, 1950–58; Secy., accountant and auditor, IL Dept. of Revenue, 1958–72.

DC Office: 2308 RHOB 20515, 202-225-5006; Fax: 202-225-8396.

District Offices: 230 S. Dearborn St., #3880, Chicago 60604, 312-353-5754; and 328 Lake St., Oak Park 60302, 708-383-1400.

Committees: *Government Reform & Oversight* (RMM of 22 D).

Group Ratings

	ADA	ACLU	COPE	CFA	LCV	CON	NSI	COC	ACU	NTLC	CHC
1994	95	91	89	80	87	38	0	25	6	4	0
1993	100	—	100	100	86	32	—	9	0	—	—

National Journal Ratings

	1993 LIB — 1993 CONS			1994 LIB — 1994 CONS	
Economic	88%	—	0%	83%	—	0%
Social	87%	—	0%	94%	—	0%
Foreign	87%	—	7%	85%	—	0%

Key Votes of the 103d Congress

1. Clinton Deficit Plan	Y	3. Brady Handgun Purchase	Y	5. Lmt. UN Cmnd. of Forces	N
2. NAFTA	N	4. Strike Race/Death Pnlty.	N	6. Cut Missile Funds	Y

Key Votes of the 104th Congress

1. Congressional Compliance	Y	6. Reform Crime Grant	N	11. Loser Pays Court Reform	N
2. Balanced Budget Amndmt.	N	7. National Security Act	N	12. Product Liability Reform	N
3. Bar Unfunded Mandates	N	8. Moratorium on Regs.	N	13. Welfare Reform	N
4. Pass Line Item Veto	N	9. Risk Assessment on Regs.	N	14. Term Limits Amndmt.	N
5. Relax Exclusionary Rule	N	10. Expnd. Priv. Prop. Rights	*	15. Tax Cuts	N

Election Results

1994 general	Cardiss Collins (D)	93,457	(80%)	($200,544)
	Charles (Chuck) Mobley (R)	24,011	(20%)	
1994 primary	Cardiss Collins (D)	unopposed		
1992 general	Cardiss Collins (D)	182,811	(81%)	($390,942)
	Norman G. Boccio (R)	35,346	(16%)	($6,978)
	Others	7,124	(3%)	

EIGHTH DISTRICT

Schaumburg, Illinois, may not be nationally known, but it is one of America's major corporate headquarters cities, indeed one of several edge cities northwest of Chicago. Fifty years ago, this was farmland, half a dozen miles beyond the orchard which is now O'Hare Airport. Today Schaumburg, near the intersection of the Northwest Tollway and I-290, with lots of office space and miles of subdivisions, with moderately-priced apartments and with some black residents, is the site of the headquarters of Motorola, one of the most innovative large corporations, which has done much to wrest the technological edge from the Far East, and of Zurich American Life Insurance. In nearby Hoffman Estates is the headquarters to which the oft-troubled Sears moved from the Sears Tower in Chicago; in Lake Zurich, not too far away, is Kemper Insurance.

Schaumburg, the biggest city in the 8th Congressional District of Illinois, sits at the District's southern end on prairie and hilly lakelands northwest of Chicago. Around Schaumburg are Streamwood, Hoffman Estates, Arlington Heights, Rolling Meadows, Palatine: over 60% of the district's population is in the far northwest extremity of Cook County. The 8th also includes the filling-up western half of Lake County, with little lake communities being surrounded by new suburbs. The tone of life here is not elite, but it is highly affluent; culturally, this is part of the great rural Midwest as much as—perhaps more than—it is of yeasty, lusty Chicago. Economically, it is suspicious of government spending, which it associates with the corrupt big city of yore. By most measures, this is the most Republican district in Illinois, and one of the most Republican in the nation.

The congressman from the 8th District is Philip Crane, a conservative Republican first elected in a 1969 special election. Crane has supported the ideas which have been on the ascendant in the nation and the world since he first won the seat—free market economics, a strong national defense, traditional values. Yet for years, his influence was meager and he languished largely unnoticed on the back benches of the House. It is hard to remember now that in 1980, Crane ran for president, hoping, as the truer libertarian, to cut in on the elderly Ronald

Reagan's support and then take it over when the Reagan candidacy faded. By 1992, Crane was in political trouble back home. He was opposed in the Republican primary by businessman Gary Skoien, a former aide to then-Governor James Thompson, who hit hard at congressional perks and criticized Crane for opposing a highway bill with many Illinois projects and for his anti-abortion stance. Ever a purist, Crane declines PAC money and consistently votes against many large projects that would bring money into the district. He won by only 55%–45%.

In the 1992 general, an early October poll showed the race even between Crane and Democrat Sheila Smith, a onetime champion swimmer and owner of a lamp manufacturing company. Smith was endorsed by the *Chicago Tribune*, once (though no longer) the voice of conservative Republicanism, which wrote, "The real question is why Representative Philip Crane wants to remain in Congress. Once a fairly prominent voice in conservative circles, he has been disengaged from the political process and shown little interest in his district for several years." Crane campaigned desultorily, and won by the unimpressive margin of 56%–40%.

During the next two years, Crane seemed more vigorous in the House. Always a strong supporter of free trade, with high-ranking seats on the Ways and Means Committee and its Trade Subcommittee, he saw trade issues come to the fore, as the North American Free Trade Agreement in 1993 and the Uruguay Round of the General Agreement on Tariffs and Trade in 1994 were passed largely with Republican votes. But he played anything but a high-profile role, deferring to Bill Archer at Ways and Means and to Newt Gingrich, who has taken the role that Crane once filled of defining conservatism for House Republicans. And it is by no means certain that he would be the heir apparent as Ways and Means chairman in the event of Archer's departure. Crane has sponsored the Andean Trade Preference Act, reducing duties on various legal products of Colombia, Peru, Ecuador and Bolivia, to discourage the drug trade; he strongly supports including Chile in NAFTA and moving toward a western hemisphere free trade zone. On another issue, his crusades to defund the National Endowment for the Arts and the Corporation for Public Broadcasting didn't get anywhere in the first two Clinton years but they were taken up after the 1994 election by Speaker Newt Gingrich. Now, both agencies are on the chopping block, but mostly for financial reasons rather than the cultural standards that drove most of Crane's opposition.

Crane had serious primary opposition in 1994, from Skoien again and from state Senator Peter Fitzgerald, a young conservative whom Crane had supported earlier and whose father is the well-known head of Suburban Bank of Chicago. Fitzgerald spent plenty of his own money and did little to conceal statewide ambitions, but Crane won 40% of the vote to Fitzgerald's 33% and Skoien's 21%. Not a resounding victory, but enough to send Crane back to a Republican House, where he now chairs the Trade Subcommittee. In the 104th Congress, Crane has a chance to show that he is not a burnt-out case, as some have suggested since the collapse of his presidential campaign, and he can advance the cause of free trade and rally majorities against the NEA and CPB. But primary opposition remains a distinct possibility.

The People: Pop. 1990: 571,464; 6% rural; 7% age 65+; 89% White; 2% Black; 4% Asian; 2% Other; 5% Hispanic origin. Voting age pop.: 420,226; 1% Black; 5% Hispanic origin. Households: 65% married couple families; 33% married couple fams. w. children; 61% college educ.; median household income: $47,374; per capita income: $20,488; median gross rent: $667; median house value: $131,900.

1992 Presidential Vote

Bush (R)	118,714	(47%)
Clinton (D)	76,327	(31%)
Perot (I)	54,269	(22%)

1988 Presidential Vote

Bush (R)	143,724	(71%)
Dukakis (D)	59,507	(29%)

Rep. Philip M. Crane (R)

Elected Nov., 1969; b. Nov. 3, 1930, Chicago; home, Wauconda; DePauw U., Hillsdale Col., B.A. 1952, IN U., M.A. 1961, Ph.D. 1963; Protestant; married (Arlene).

Career: Army, 1954–56; Instructor, IN U., 1960–63; Asst. Prof., Bradley U., 1963–67; Dir., Westminster Academy, 1967–68.

DC Office: 233 CHOB 20515, 202-225-3711; Fax: 202-225-7830.

District Offices: 1450 S. New Wilke Rd., Arlington Heights 60005, 708-394-0790; and 300 N. Milwaukee Ave., #C, Lake Villa 60046, 708-265-9000.

Committees: *Ways & Means* (2nd of 21 R): Health; Trade (Chmn.). *Joint Committee on Taxation* (2nd of 5 Reps.).

Group Ratings

	ADA	ACLU	COPE	CFA	LCV	CON	NSI	COC	ACU	NTLC	CHC
1994	5	22	0	0	6	91	90	83	100	96	93
1993	15	—	0	0	14	94	—	91	96	—	—

National Journal Ratings

	1993 LIB — 1993 CONS		1994 LIB — 1994 CONS	
Economic	0%	88%	0%	80%
Social	0%	89%	15%	85%
Foreign	28%	70%	13%	86%

Key Votes of the 103d Congress

1. Clinton Deficit Plan	N	3. Brady Handgun Purchase N	5. Lmt. UN Cmnd. of Forces Y
2. NAFTA	Y	4. Strike Race/Death Pnlty. Y	6. Cut Missile Funds N

Key Votes of the 104th Congress

1. Congressional Compliance Y	6. Reform Crime Grant Y	11. Loser Pays Court Reform Y
2. Balanced Budget Amndmt. Y	7. National Security Act Y	12. Product Liability Reform Y
3. Bar Unfunded Mandates Y	8. Moratorium on Regs. Y	13. Welfare Reform Y
4. Pass Line Item Veto Y	9. Risk Assessment on Regs. Y	14. Term Limits Amndmt. Y
5. Relax Exclusionary Rule Y	10. Expnd. Priv. Prop. Rights Y	15. Tax Cuts Y

Election Results

1994 general	Philip M. Crane (R)	88,225	(65%)	($722,267)
	Robert C. Walberg (D)	47,654	(35%)	($66,960)
1994 primary	Philip M. Crane (R)	21,703	(40%)	
	Peter G. Fitzgerald (R)	17,937	(33%)	
	Gary J. Skoien (R)	11,080	(21%)	
	Judy McCracken Svenson (R)	3,282	(6%)	
1992 general	Philip M. Crane (R)	132,887	(56%)	($528,818)
	Sheila A. Smith (D)	96,419	(40%)	($138,921)
	Joe M. Diller (ICP)	9,327	(4%)	

NINTH DISTRICT

"Make no little plans," commanded architect Daniel Burnham, who made no little plans for the Chicago lakefront: the glorious parks he designed are still among America's urban jewels, and the row of high-rise apartment buildings—some austere works of masters of the international style, some in traditional styles evocative of some other place and time, some sleek Art Deco works of the 1920s and 1930s—are a splendid accompaniment. Behind the lakefront is all the diversity of Chicago. In sturdy brick houses, with scarcely a shoe horn's space between them, or in stubby apartment buildings, are ethnic and racial groups of all sorts, from Argentinians to Slavs, Plains Indians to Indian plainsmen. Two decades ago, the neighborhoods behind the lakefront seemed to be getting grimier and heading downhill. In the past dozen years, they have been busy gentrifying, as young marrieds and gays, professionals and entrepreneurs renovate old houses and open new businesses.

The lakefront has long been the most heavily Jewish part of Chicago. Chicago's Jewish community, prominent more than a century ago, has never been as much a force for increased government responsibility as in New York, nor is it connected as much to a glamorous industry as in Los Angeles. Yet among Jewish voters liberal impulses have been strong: the 19th Century impulse to resist state authority and imposition of cultural uniformity and the 20th Century impulse to increase state responsibility for individuals' lives. Chicago's North Side Jews, on the lakefront or in neighborhoods like Rogers Park and nearby suburbs like Skokie and Niles, have been a solidly Democratic voting bloc, involved with but skeptical of the old Democratic machine. In the racial city politics of the 1980s, as in state politics, Jewish voters and lakefront liberals of all backgrounds have been a key swing group.

The 9th Congressional District of Illinois covers most of Chicago's lakefront, from Diversey Harbor north to Evanston, the home of Northwestern University and a city which has moved gracefully from historic Yankee Republican-ness to trendy postgraduate Democratic-ness. The 9th presses inland from the Rogers Park neighborhood at the north end of Chicago west into Polish-American areas at the northwest edge of the city; from Evanston it reaches west through Skokie to Morton Grove and Niles.

The 9th District's congressman, Democrat Sidney Yates, is the only member of the House who can remember having served in a Republican House before. His father was a Jewish immigrant from Lithuania who drove a truck in Chicago; two of his brothers were vaudeville booking agents there. He went to the University of Chicago, practiced law mostly in public sector jobs, joined the Navy at 35 in 1944 and was elected to Congress from the Lakefront wards in 1948. Recalling the last time the Republicans took over the House, 42 years ago, he said in 1994: "Republicans fought what they called the socialistic measures of Democrats, and we tried just to stay alive in that Congress and come back. . . . In that session Republicans were much tougher on Democrats than the present Republicans say we were on them. There was no bipartisanship except on foreign policy." But Democrats did come back in 1954. Yates ran for the Senate in 1962, losing to Everett Dirksen 53%–47%; he returned to the House in 1964.

In Chicago and in Washington, Yates has combined liberal idealism and practical political sense. Back home he has been cordially supported by liberal reformers even while maintaining a cooperative relationship with Democratic machine politicians. When he had a tough primary challenge in 1990, both lakefront reformers and Mayor Richard M. Daley stood at his side. In the House, Yates has long been on the Appropriations Committee, where he has quietly furthered liberal causes while getting along with practical-minded colleagues. Had he not run for the Senate, he would have been in line to become chairman of Appropriations after Jamie Whitten was replaced in 1992, and perhaps sooner; instead, from 1975–94 he chaired the Interior Subcommittee. Here he exerted great influence over important public policies—and has channeled billions to Chicago and Illinois. Local projects range from $879,000 for the Cook County Forest Preserve to $2.5 billion for improving the Metropolitan Water District's Deep

Tunnel sewage system; he nurtured over many years projects like the Chicago Cultural Center and Navy Pier park restorations, and responded rapidly to the flooding of Chicago's old water tunnels in 1993. Nationally, Yates is known as an environmentalist with a detailed knowledge of government land use policy, who used his appropriating power to create new national parks, wildernesses, seashores, lakeshores, wild and scenic rivers—a kind of pork many members and voters regard as particularly kosher.

Yates for years was a kind of Maecenas, the House's chief defender of the National Endowments for the Arts and Humanities and the National Trust for Historic Preservation. The NEA has been attacked for years because of the fecklessness of administrators who fund artists whose work might be considered obscene by the taxpayers whose funds are being used. Yates has seen his duty as preserving the NEA budget, and has tried to sidestep both the dubious claims that a denial of grants would restrict artistic freedom (since artists may do whatever they like on their own dollar) and the graceless task of writing a code of conduct for the agency. His political maneuvering kept the NEA alive during the Bush years and thriving during the first two Clinton years. Whether he can save it in a Republican House is an even more severe test of his talents.

Those talents have also been tested recently at the polls. In the 1990 primary, Yates was challenged by 31-year-old Near North Side Alderman Edwin Eisendrath, a Daley supporter able to self-finance his campaign; Yates responded with top-level endorsements and won the primary 70%–27%. In 1992, he won 65% against two candidates and in 1994, 75% against one. Any number of local political figures have been eyeing the district, but Yates is unlikely to face serious competition so long as he retains, as he has, his health and vigor. Now in the minority, he obviously has less clout, and perhaps he will just "tread water" as he advised his Democratic colleagues just after the 1994 election. It seems likely he has a more active role in mind. He announced in May 1995 that, "barring any health problems," he would seek another term. In any case, the district seems certain to remain Democratic.

The People: Pop. 1990: 571,611; 16% age 65+; 68% White; 12% Black; 10% Asian; 4% Other; 9% Hispanic origin. Voting age pop.: 467,183; 11% Black; 8% Hispanic origin. Households: 42% married couple families; 17% married couple fams. w. children; 60% college educ.; median household income: $32,183; per capita income: $18,691; median gross rent: $508; median house value: $145,000.

1992 Presidential Vote			**1988 Presidential Vote**		
Clinton (D)	155,446	(61%)	Dukakis (D)	143,120	(58%)
Bush (R)	68,418	(27%)	Bush (R)	102,168	(42%)
Perot (I)	29,294	(12%)			

Rep. Sidney R. Yates (D)

Elected 1964; b. Aug. 27, 1909, Chicago; home, Chicago; U. of Chicago, Ph.D. 1931, J.D. 1933; Jewish; married (Adeline).

Career: Navy, 1944–46; Practicing atty.; Asst. Atty. for IL St. Bank Receiver, 1935–37; Asst. Atty. Gen. for IL Commerce Comm., 1937–40; U.S. House of Reps., 1948–62; U.N. Rep., Trusteeship Council, 1963–64.

DC Office: 2109 RHOB 20515, 202-225-2111; Fax: 202-225-3493.

District Offices: 230 S. Dearborn St., #3920, Chicago 60604, 312-353-4596; and 2100 Ridge Ave., #2700, Evanston, 60204, 708-328-2610.

Committees: *Appropriations* (2nd of 24 D): Foreign Operations, Export Financing, and Related Programs; Interior (RMM).

Group Ratings

	ADA	ACLU	COPE	CFA	LCV	CON	NSI	COC	ACU	NTLC	CHC
1994	100	87	89	100	89	16	0	25	0	7	7
1993	85	—	100	100	71	39	—	0	0	—	—

National Journal Ratings

	1993 LIB — 1993 CONS		1994 LIB — 1994 CONS	
Economic	88%	0%	83%	0%
Social	80%	13%	94%	0%
Foreign	93%	0%	85%	0%

Key Votes of the 103d Congress

1. Clinton Deficit Plan	Y	3. Brady Handgun Purchase	Y	5. Lmt. UN Cmnd. of Forces	N
2. NAFTA	N	4. Strike Race/Death Pnlty.	N	6. Cut Missile Funds	Y

Key Votes of the 104th Congress

1. Congressional Compliance	*	6. Reform Crime Grant	Y	11. Loser Pays Court Reform	N
2. Balanced Budget Amndmt.	N	7. National Security Act	N	12. Product Liability Reform	N
3. Bar Unfunded Mandates	N	8. Moratorium on Regs.	N	13. Welfare Reform	N
4. Pass Line Item Veto	N	9. Risk Assessment on Regs.	N	14. Term Limits Amndmt.	N
5. Relax Exclusionary Rule	N	10. Expnd. Priv. Prop. Rights	N	15. Tax Cuts	N

Election Results

1994 general	Sidney R. Yates (D)	94,404	(66%)	($217,952)
	George Edward Larney (R)	48,419	(34%)	($48,121)
1994 primary	Sidney R. Yates (D)	60,644	(75%)	
	Frank Edward Gardner (D)	20,629	(25%)	
1992 general	Sidney R. Yates (D)	162,942	(68%)	($228,812)
	Herbert Sohn (R)	64,760	(27%)	($12,599)
	Sheila A. Jones (ERP)	12,001	(5%)	

TENTH DISTRICT

Since 1855, when the first Chicago & Northwestern opened the railroad line from downtown Chicago north along the lakeshore, the North Shore suburbs along Lake Michigan have been the favorite residence for Chicago's elite. The North Shore starts in Evanston, founded by Methodists to promote temperance (a cause that has never prospered in Chicago), and goes on to Wilmette, Winnetka (the "home" in the *Home Alone* movies), Glencoe, Highland Park, Lake Forest—each with a slightly different personality and character, each long established, mightily prosperous and with a patina of age. Not far from the gritty, monosyllabic city, these are communities of pleasant, affluent, well-educated people living in an environment whose natural beauty—the long water vista and blue light off the Lake, the gentle hills and fine trees—is kept carefully disciplined.

The 10th Congressional District of Illinois is the North Shore district, starting at the Baha'i Temple on the Wilmette lakefront, just north of Evanston, reaching up past Fort Sheridan (which was closed in 1993) to the city of Waukegan (once famous as the home of comedian Jack Benny) and the Wisconsin border beyond. The district also goes inland to what for many years was just cornfields (some still are) to Northbrook and Deerfield, just west of Glencoe and Highland Park. Farther inland are suburbs like Arlington Heights, developed in the 1950s and 1960s on the Northwestern railroad line, and Wheeling, developed in the 1960s and 1970s near Interstate 294. To the north are Long Grove and Libertyville, near where the Adlai Stevensons, the late presidential candidate and his son the former senator, have what is now one of the last farms only a few miles from Lake Michigan and the Onwentsia Club.

The congressman from the 10th District is John Porter, a Republican who has long seemed to fit the district well. He is a North Shore native, the son of an Evanston judge, a graduate of Northwestern, a Republican who is against tax increases and looks with favor on free markets, but who takes liberal stands on some foreign and cultural issues. Elected in 1980, he was on some issues a minority of the minority. But now he is chairman of the Labor-HHS-Education Appropriations Subcommittee, with much say about vast flows of money. Some of it he may well cut off; he agrees with Appropriations Chairman Bob Livingston that some programs should simply be zeroed out. "We needn't deauthorize programs that don't work. You just don't fund them."

Porter has opposed some big defense programs, like the *Seawolf* submarine, and in June 1994, got a House majority to agree to shift national health monies to 125 new community health centers across the country—until the Democratic leadership reversed the vote with what soon became the limp plea that the vote threatened the enactment of broader healthcare legislation. He is a strong supporter of the National Institutes of Health and favors more money for biomedical research, comparing government's role here to Prince Henry the Navigator's encouragement of ocean exploration in 15th Century Portugal. He opposed the "gag rule" ban on abortion counseling in federally funded clinics, which President Clinton lifted. He voted against the crime bill rule in August 1994, but then was the only Illinois Republican to vote for the bill after changes were made; one reason is that he strongly supports gun control. The tighter budget will force him to make the first tough choices on funding priorities among health and education programs; that helps to explain why he opposed the Contract With America's tax cut, which he said would only further tighten the budget noose. He gets involved in foreign issues, supporting Radio Free Asia to beam U.S. broadcasts into China, and denouncing Turkey and Iran for their persecution of the Kurds and the Baha'i respectively. He tends to local matters as well, getting $2.5 million in additional federal aid for the North Chicago school district serving the Great Lakes Naval Training Center. He is a House reformer, sponsor of the limit on ranking Republican committee positions to six years which now limits their service as chairmen.

Porter's stands on some cultural issues have made him anathema to many on his party's right. He was challenged in 1992 and 1994 by Kathleen Sullivan, founder of Project Respect, a high school program counseling sexual abstinence, who attacked Porter for favoring abortion rights, gun control and for supporting the National Endowment for the Arts. Porter won 60%–40% in 1992, not an overwhelming margin for an incumbent. And, after a campaign visit from Jim and Sarah Brady in 1994, he won 66%–34%. Porter briefly considered a run for the Senate seat Paul Simon is vacating but ruled it out, leaving the door open for a 1998 challenge to Carol Moseley-Braun. His cultural issue stands might mean trouble in a primary, unless two or more opponents split the conservative vote. He would be an attractive candidate in the general, particularly to the media, though some of his stands leave him out of sync with conservative majorities in the Gingrich era. An interesting note: this seat was once held by White House Counsel Abner Mikva. He gave up the seat to accept a federal judgeship in Washington from Jimmy Carter.

The People: Pop. 1990: 571,501; 1% rural; 10% age 65+; 82% White; 6% Black; 4% Asian; 3% Other; 7% Hispanic origin. Voting age pop.: 425,723; 6% Black; 6% Hispanic origin. Households: 66% married couple families; 33% married couple fams. w. children; 66% college educ.; median household income: $50,355; per capita income: $26,405; median gross rent: $605; median house value: $180,200.

1992 Presidential Vote			1988 Presidential Vote		
Bush (R)	112,401	(43%)	Bush (R)	142,291	(61%)
Clinton (D)	108,149	(41%)	Dukakis (D)	89,696	(39%)
Perot (I)	40,719	(16%)			

Rep. John E. Porter (R)

Elected 1980; b. June 1, 1935, Evanston; home, Wilmette; M.I.T., 1953–54, Northwestern U., B.S.B.A. 1957, U. of MI, J.D. 1961; Presbyterian; married (Kathryn).

Career: Army Reserves, 1958–64; Atty., U.S. Dept. of Justice, 1961–63; Practicing atty., 1963–80; IL House of Reps., 1972–78.

DC Office: 2373 RHOB 20515, 202-225-4835; Fax: 202-225-0157.

District Offices: 102 Wilmot Rd., #200, Deerfield 60015, 708-940-0202; and 18 N. County St., #601-A County Bldg., Waukegan 60085, 708-662-0101.

Committees: *Appropriations* (7th of 32 R): Foreign Operations, Export Financing, and Related Programs; Labor, Health and Human Services, and Education (Chmn.); Military Construction.

Group Ratings

	ADA	ACLU	COPE	CFA	LCV	CON	NSI	COC	ACU	NTLC	CHC
1994	30	30	33	50	89	92	80	83	52	86	71
1993	25	—	0	40	57	99	—	91	71	—	—

National Journal Ratings

	1993 LIB — 1993 CONS	1994 LIB — 1994 CONS
Economic	25% — 72%	37% — 61%
Social	45% — 54%	44% — 55%
Foreign	40% — 60%	43% — 56%

Key Votes of the 103d Congress

1. Clinton Deficit Plan	N	3. Brady Handgun Purchase	Y	5. Lmt. UN Cmnd. of Forces	Y
2. NAFTA	Y	4. Strike Race/Death Pnlty.	Y	6. Cut Missile Funds	Y

Key Votes of the 104th Congress

1. Congressional Compliance	Y	6. Reform Crime Grant	Y	11. Loser Pays Court Reform	Y
2. Balanced Budget Amndmt.	Y	7. National Security Act	N	12. Product Liability Reform	Y
3. Bar Unfunded Mandates	Y	8. Moratorium on Regs.	Y	13. Welfare Reform	Y
4. Pass Line Item Veto	Y	9. Risk Assessment on Regs.	Y	14. Term Limits Amndmt.	N
5. Relax Exclusionary Rule	Y	10. Expnd. Priv. Prop. Rights	N	15. Tax Cuts	N

Election Results

1994 general	John E. Porter (R)	114,884	(75%)	($538,716)
	Andrew M. Krupp (D)	38,191	(25%)	($10,214)
1994 primary	John E. Porter (R)	28,467	(66%)	
	Kathleen M. Sullivan (R)	14,484	(34%)	
1992 general	John E. Porter (R)	155,230	(65%)	($485,778)
	Michael J. Kennedy (D)	85,400	(35%)	($34,948)

ELEVENTH DISTRICT

South of Chicago, sluggishly flowing rivers run circles around industrial sites. This low-lying land is a great divide, over which French explorers portaged, the easiest path from the inland oceans of the Great Lakes to the widened-out channels of communication through North America, the Mississippi River and all its tributaries. Today, there is still a kind of borderland here, as the factories and shopping centers and subdivisions stop around the Cook County line and Downstate Illinois prairies begin, cornfields bisected by highways and railroads radiating out from the Loop and the railyards of the nation's transportation hub. Politically, this is a borderland as well, between the traditionally Democratic Chicago metropolitan area, with its hard-bitten machine politics, and heavily Republican Downstate Illinois, with its tradition of governance by local civic leaders that stretches back to the days of Abraham Lincoln.

The 11th Congressional District of Illinois covers much of this borderland. It includes the old 10th Ward of Chicago plus the suburbs of South Holland, Calumet City and Lansing near the Indiana line. This is heavy industry country; many of the factories around Lake Calumet are empty now—if not torn down—but the rows of workers' houses on the grid streets remain. This is the home of the struggling white working class, ancestrally Democratic. To the west is Joliet. Once a canal boat town, and later the producer of one-third of America's wallpaper, Joliet now has two big prisons; it and surrounding Will County are politically marginal. To the south is Kankakee, a Downstate county seat amid rich prairie earth on the Illinois Central main line; this is heavily Republican territory. Farther west, on bluffs above the Illinois River heading down to the Mississippi, are the factory towns of Ottawa and LaSalle and, to the south, Streator; this is LaSalle County, the only sometimes Democratic part of heavily Republican northern Downstate Illinois.

The 11th Congressional District was the scene in 1994 of one of those open seat contests which returned control of the House to Republicans for the first time in 40 years. The seat was vacated by George Sangmeister, a six-year Democratic incumbent and longtime officeholder who quit because "I realize it is time to smell the proverbial roses, get reacquainted with your children and grandchildren, enjoy family activities and vacations and live a life that is impossible with a political career." Thirteen candidates ran. The Democratic race was a close contest with legislators Frank Giglio (21%) and Clem Balanoff (19%) running well in Cook County and Downstaters Dave Neal (19%), Jack Buchanan (15%) and Marty Gleason (12%) doing well there. Among Republicans, Sam Panayotovich, protege of Ward 10 boss Edward Vrdolyak, carried Cook County narrowly over 1992 nominee Robert Herbolsheimer, but got 16% overall to Herbolsheimer's 29%. But Grundy County legislator Jerry Weller came out ahead with 32%. Weller, running as a member of the party opposing insiders, had Washington experience as an aide to Agriculture Secretary John Block. At 37, Weller was a six-year veteran of the state legislature who boasted of reforming health care via market-based principles, holding criminals accountable and promoting markets for ethanol fuels and soybean inks. He was proud of replacing the "granny tax" on nursing home residents with a cigarette tax as a way to pay for health care. Democrat Frank Giglio, at 61, had been a state representative for 20 of the previous 22 years, a Democratic leader who backed family leave, comparable worth for women employees and worker retraining. Of Congress, he said, "Wouldn't this be a nice way to finish my career?" He attacked Weller for always voting 'no;' Weller called Giglio a Chicago-style politician.

In November, Giglio carried Cook County, but with only 51%; Weller ran way ahead everywhere else—64% in Will County, 70% in Kankakee, 74% in Grundy, 61% in LaSalle—for a 61% victory. He seems likely to temper his conservatism with concern for district needs, from the soybean industry to promoting the proposed third Chicago airport which Governor Jim Edgar wanted in the Will County hamlet of Peotone and Mayor Richard Daley wanted near Lake Calumet and which currently is not set to be built anywhere. A loyal, though low-profile, supporter of the Contract With America, he serves on the Veterans' Affairs, Transportation and Infrastructure and Banking Committees.

The People: Pop. 1990: 571,050; 20% rural; 13% age 65+; 84% White; 8% Black; 1% Asian; 3% Other; 6% Hispanic origin. Voting age pop.: 417,655; 7% Black; 5% Hispanic origin. Households: 62% married couple families; 30% married couple fams. w. children; 39% college educ.; median household income: $33,632; per capita income: $13,838; median gross rent: $414; median house value: $66,900.

1992 Presidential Vote

Clinton (D) 108,456 (43%)
Bush (R) 90,058 (36%)
Perot (I) 50,186 (20%)

1988 Presidential Vote

Bush (R) 125,874 (57%)
Dukakis (D) 96,131 (43%)

Rep. Jerry Weller (R)

Elected 1994; b. July 7, 1957, Streator; home, Morris; U. of IL, B.A. 1979; Christian; single.

Career: Farmer; Aide, U.S. Rep. Tom Corcoran, 1980–81; Aide, U.S. Agriculture Secy. John Block, 1981–85; IL House of Reps., 1988–94.

DC Office: 1710 LHOB 20515, 202-225-3635; Fax: 202-225-3521.

District Offices: 51 W. Jackson St., #100, Joliet 60432, 815-740-2028; 3331 Chicago Rd., #4-B, Steger 60475, 708-754-7552; and 628 Columbus St., #207, Ottawa 61350, 815-433-0085.

Committees: *Banking & Financial Services* (13th of 27 R): Financial Institutions and Consumer Credit; Housing and Community Opportunity. *Transportation & Infrastructure* (25th of 33 R): Aviation; Surface Transportation. *Veterans' Affairs* (15th of 18 R): Compensation, Pension, Insurance and Memorial Affairs.

Group Ratings and 103rd Congress Votes: Newly Elected

Key Votes of the 104th Congress

1. Congressional Compliance Y	6. Reform Crime Grant Y	11. Loser Pays Court Reform Y
2. Balanced Budget Amndmt. Y	7. National Security Act Y	12. Product Liability Reform Y
3. Bar Unfunded Mandates Y	8. Moratorium on Regs. Y	13. Welfare Reform Y
4. Pass Line Item Veto Y	9. Risk Assessment on Regs. Y	14. Term Limits Amndmt. Y
5. Relax Exclusionary Rule Y	10. Expnd. Priv. Prop. Rights Y	15. Tax Cuts Y

Election Results

1994 general	Jerry Weller (R)	97,241	(61%)	($877,429)
	Frank Giglio (D)	63,150	(39%)	($614,142)
1994 primary	Jerry Weller (R)	11,387	(32%)	
	Robert T. Herbolsheimer (R)	10,329	(29%)	
	Sam Panayotovich (R)	5,799	(16%)	
	Jeffrey J. (Jeff) Tomczak (R)	4,424	(12%)	
	James J. O'Connell (R)	3,025	(8%)	
	Others	960	(3%)	
1992 general	George E. Sangmeister (D)	135,387	(56%)	($344,786)
	Robert T. Herbolsheimer (R)	107,860	(44%)	($281,243)

TWELFTH DISTRICT

The nation's two mightiest streams, the Mississippi and Missouri Rivers, their waters roiling together join just a few miles above St. Louis and just a few miles below Alton, Illinois. Most views of this center of the Mississippi Valley focus on the Gateway Arch and the buildings of downtown St. Louis. But the Mississippi shoreline of Illinois is worthy of attention as well. Alton's 19th Century buildings recall its turbulent history, when it was the home of the antislavery agitator Elijah Lovejoy, murdered by a mob; today it is the home of conservative crusader and columnist Phyllis Schlafly. Just across from the Gateway Arch is East St. Louis, where dozens of rail lines and highways funnel into bridges over the river. Once a rail and stockyards center second only to Chicago, East St. Louis is now one of America's poorest and most troubled cities, a half-abandoned slum with one of the nation's highest crime rates and a rapidly declining tax base. South of East St. Louis and the industrial area around Belleville, the river counties are lightly inhabited, but they were not always unimportant: this was the site of the French Kaskaskia settlement that became Illinois's first capital in 1818. Farther south, the river abuts the coal country and the town of Carbondale, once a coal center but now notable as the home of Southern Illinois University. Here also is Egypt, the southern end of Illinois where the Ohio River meets the Mississippi: flat, fertile farmland, protected by giant man-made levees because it is susceptible to yearly floods. There is more than a touch of Dixie here: the unofficial capital of Egypt, Cairo (pronounced *KAYroh*), is a declining town closer to Mississippi than to Chicago with its own occasional racial violence.

The 12th Congressional District of Illinois covers all of this riverfront from Alton south to Cairo, with some inland territory as well. Most of its population is in St. Clair (East St. Louis and Belleville) and Madison (Alton) Counties, but as drawn for 1992 the district includes much of an old Egypt-based district, including Carbondale and Cairo. The congressman from the 12th District is Jerry Costello, a Democrat from an old St. Clair County political family who first won the seat in 1988, when it was vacated after 44 years by Democrat Mel Price. Costello came to politics naturally. His father was St. Clair County treasurer and sheriff and he has worked in the public sector just about all his adult life. In 1980, he became chairman of the St. Clair County Board of Supervisors. Experienced, well-connected, supported by organized labor, he was the obvious successor when Price finally retired. Costello won the three-way special primary 46%–27%–25%, then by 53%–47% won the general election.

Costello is as practical- and district-minded as any member of the House, with a liberal record on economics and a mixed record on cultural and foreign issues, a lawmaker who places loyalty to party leadership as a relatively low priority. He opposed George Bush's Clean Air Act and Bill Clinton's North American Free Trade Agreement. He trumpets his accomplishments without subtlety. A 1994 campaign ad lists "$300 million for light rail connection to St. Louis, $120 million for a new Clark Bridge, millions for Clean Coal Technology Center in Carterville, funds to rebuild the Len Small Levee, infrastructure dollars for the Super Max prison, cops on the beat in Carbondale, Cairo and elsewhere"—the last a reference to the 1994 crime bill. His biggest ongoing project is developing a Mid-America Airport at Scott Air Force Base near Belleville. It is not clear that the St. Louis area needs a second major airport or that it's feasible to clean up the mess left here by the military base. But if it can be done, Costello will surely do it.

How Costello will fare on these projects in a Republican Congress is not clear. His votes for the Contract With America will open the door for him to cut deals on some local matters; but most Republicans have both partisan and philosophic reasons to oppose his priorities. He makes a practice of returning home every weekend and was reelected handily in Republican 1994.

The People: Pop. 1990: 571,441; 22% rural; 14% age 65+; 82% White; 17% Black; 1% Asian; 1% Hispanic origin. Voting age pop.: 421,266; 15% Black; 1% Hispanic origin. Households: 54% married couple families; 25% married couple fams. w. children; 40% college educ.; median household income: $25,032; per capita income: $11,547; median gross rent: $360; median house value: $47,400.

1992 Presidential Vote			1988 Presidential Vote		
Clinton (D)	132,570	(54%)	Dukakis (D)	124,751	(56%)
Bush (R)	69,829	(28%)	Bush (R)	96,302	(44%)
Perot (I)	42,169	(17%)			

Rep. Jerry F. Costello (D)

Elected Aug. 1988; b. Sept. 25, 1949, East St. Louis; home, Belleville; Belleville Area Col. A.A. 1970, Maryville Col. B.A. 1972; Catholic; married (Georgia).

Career: Dir., IL Court Svcs. & Probation, 1973–80; Chmn., Region's Cncl. of Govts., 1980–84; Chmn., St. Clair Cnty. Bd. of Supervisors, 1980–88.

DC Office: 2454 RHOB 20515, 202-225-5661; Fax: 202-225-0285.

District Offices: 327 W. Main St., Belleville 62221, 618-233-8026.

Committees: *Budget* (7th of 18 D). *Transportation & Infrastructure* (11th of 27 D): Aviation; Water Resources and Environment.

Group Ratings

	ADA	ACLU	COPE	CFA	LCV	CON	NSI	COC	ACU	NTLC	CHC
1994	50	30	78	60	56	40	50	50	38	32	64
1993	65	—	100	70	79	47	—	9	29	—	—

National Journal Ratings

	1993 LIB — 1993 CONS		1994 LIB — 1994 CONS	
Economic	78%	12%	67%	29%
Social	33%	67%	48%	50%
Foreign	40%	57%	43%	56%

Key Votes of the 103d Congress

1. Clinton Deficit Plan	Y	3. Brady Handgun Purchase N	5. Lmt. UN Cmnd. of Forces N
2. NAFTA	N	4. Strike Race/Death Pnlty. N	6. Cut Missile Funds N

Key Votes of the 104th Congress

1. Congressional Compliance Y	6. Reform Crime Grant N	11. Loser Pays Court Reform N
2. Balanced Budget Amndmt. Y	7. National Security Act N	12. Product Liability Reform N
3. Bar Unfunded Mandates Y	8. Moratorium on Regs. *	13. Welfare Reform N
4. Pass Line Item Veto Y	9. Risk Assessment on Regs. Y	14. Term Limits Amndmt. N
5. Relax Exclusionary Rule Y	10. Expnd. Priv. Prop. Rights Y	15. Tax Cuts N

Election Results

1994 general	Jerry F. Costello (D)	101,391	(66%)	($499,844)
	Jan Morris (R)	52,419	(34%)	($43,779)
1994 primary	Jerry F. Costello (D)	unopposed		
1992 general	Jerry F. Costello (D)	168,762	(71%)	($606,383)
	Mike Starr (R)	68,115	(29%)	($21,024)

THIRTEENTH DISTRICT

Most residents of Chicagoland now live not in the city but in the suburbs, and increasingly in the Collar Counties around Cook County. DuPage County, straight west of Chicago, had 103,000 residents in 1940; in 1990, there were 781,000, with new subdivisions still springing up. Nor are these just bedroom communities. Here in Oak Brook are the headquarters of Ace Hardware, Federal Signal, Waste Management, the Spiegel catalogue and, most prominently, McDonald's and its Hamburger University, the company which virtually invented fast food and which has reached new heights of fame with Bill Clinton in the White House. One out of eight young Americans has worked at McDonald's, and millions have learned from this corporation the basics of arithmetic and literacy, good work habits and cheerful service, which are not always available in today's public schools (for examples, look a few miles east to Chicago). Nearby are gracefully older railroad commuter towns like Hinsdale and Downers Grove, but also Naperville, once a country village, now an edge city. And vast government laboratories have sprung up, sparking private research firms, the Argonne National Laboratory along the Sanitary and Ship Canal and the Des Plaines River and Fermilab National Accelerator Laboratory west of the late *Chicago Tribune* owner Colonel Robert McCormick's estate, Cantigny.

The 13th Congressional District of Illinois includes the southern slice of DuPage County, including Oak Brook, Downers Grove and Naperville, the southwest corner of Cook County around Palos Hills, and the northern slice of Will County north of Joliet. Politically, this is a heavily Republican area, always suspicious of the motives and operations of Chicago's Democrats, devoted to free enterprise and hostile to higher taxes. DuPage County has indeed become Illinois's Republican powerhouse, the home base of state Senate President Pate Philip and House Speaker Lee Daniels, a jurisdiction that cast 228,000 votes in 1994, 79% of them for Governor Jim Edgar.

The congressman from the 13th is Harris Fawell, a career politician (he served in the Illinois Senate from 1962 to 1976 and was first elected to the House in 1984) and fiscal conservative who spent a decade tilting at Democratic windmills. But now that he is in the majority, he has a chance to realize his goals and put his programs into action. In 1990, with Democrats Charles Stenholm and Tim Penny, he formed "Porkbusters," to attack what they considered pork barrel spending in Appropriations bills. This seemed quixotic: "It has been said that if one dies and goes to heaven and wants to come back to earth and have eternal life, come back as a federal program," Fawell said while fighting the federal honey subsidy. Altogether, Fawell claimed credit for $2.4 billion in rescissions from 1992–94, including the honey subsidy that eventually was voted out. More important, "pork" became a rallying cry with the public, to the point that Republicans were able to discredit a Democratic crime bill by calling it pork and removing several offending provisions before agreeing to send it to Clinton for his signature.

Ironically, now that Republicans are in the majority, Fawell may spend less time busting pork. He does not serve on Appropriations—although he didn't serve there in his Porkbuster days either—which can and probably will zero out existing programs. And he has a long agenda for the Economic and Educational Opportunities Committee on which he now chairs the Employer-Employee Relations Subcommittee. He will be working to repeal the Davis-Bacon Act, which increases federal construction costs by mandating that government contractors pay local prevailing wages to construction workers, to change OSHA to allow more flexibility for total quality management in the workplace and to apply fully the labor laws to Congress. He also wants to consolidate job training programs and to pass an "abandoned babies" law to encourage termination of parental rights for unfit parents, so babies can be put up for adoption earlier.

Fawell won this seat in the heavily contested 1984 Republican primary, 30%–23%–22%–12%. He has not had serious competition since nor has he given serious consideration to moving up to a statewide office.

The People: Pop. 1990: 571,344; 4% rural; 8% age 65+; 90% White; 3% Black; 4% Asian; 1% Other; 3% Hispanic origin. Voting age pop.: 412,913; 3% Black; 3% Hispanic origin. Households: 68% married couple families; 37% married couple fams. w. children; 65% college educ.; median household income: $50,087; per capita income: $20,912; median gross rent: $619; median house value: $139,800.

1992 Presidential Vote

Bush (R)	128,612	(47%)
Clinton (D)	88,314	(32%)
Perot (I)	58,123	(21%)

1988 Presidential Vote

Bush (R)	154,374	(69%)
Dukakis (D)	69,949	(31%)

Rep. Harris W. Fawell (R)

Elected 1984; b. Mar. 25, 1929, West Chicago; home, Naperville; North Central Col., B.A. 1949, Chicago-Kent Col. of Law, J.D. 1953; United Methodist; married (Ruth).

Career: Practicing atty., 1953–84; IL Senate, 1962–76.

DC Office: 2159 RHOB 20515, 202-225-3515; Fax: 202-225-9420; e-mail: hfawell@hr.house.gov.

District Offices: 115 W. 55th St., #100, Clarendon Hills 60514, 708-655-2052.

Committees: *Economic & Educational Opportunities* (5th of 24 R): Employer-Employee Relations (Chmn.); Oversight and Investigations; Workforce Protections. *Science* (4th of 27 R): Energy and Environment.

Group Ratings

	ADA	ACLU	COPE	CFA	LCV	CON	NSI	COC	ACU	NTLC	CHC
1994	25	26	11	50	44	94	100	92	81	100	86
1993	15	—	0	40	36	85	—	82	92	—	—

National Journal Ratings

	1993 LIB — 1993 CONS		1994 LIB — 1994 CONS	
Economic	14%	— 80%	21%	— 76%
Social	38%	— 61%	24%	— 73%
Foreign	28%	— 70%	30%	— 67%

Key Votes of the 103d Congress

1. Clinton Deficit Plan	N	3. Brady Handgun Purchase Y	5. Lmt. UN Cmnd. of Forces Y
2. NAFTA	Y	4. Strike Race/Death Pnlty. Y	6. Cut Missile Funds N

Key Votes of the 104th Congress

1. Congressional Compliance Y	6. Reform Crime Grant Y	11. Loser Pays Court Reform Y
2. Balanced Budget Amndmt. Y	7. National Security Act Y	12. Product Liability Reform Y
3. Bar Unfunded Mandates Y	8. Moratorium on Regs. Y	13. Welfare Reform Y
4. Pass Line Item Veto Y	9. Risk Assessment on Regs. Y	14. Term Limits Amndmt. N
5. Relax Exclusionary Rule Y	10. Expnd. Priv. Prop. Rights Y	15. Tax Cuts Y

Election Results

1994 general	Harris W. Fawell (R)	124,312	(73%)	($278,469)
	William A. Riley (D)	45,709	(27%)	
1994 primary	Harris W. Fawell (R)	unopposed		
1992 general	Harris W. Fawell (R)	179,257	(68%)	($657,908)
	Dennis Michael Temple (D)	82,985	(32%)	($4,327)

FOURTEENTH DISTRICT

A few dozen miles beyond Chicago's Loop there is an invisible line marking two different Chicagos. One is the Chicago dominated by blacks and descendants of the vast immigrations of 1840–1924 and 1970s–90s, a Chicago where certain loyalties are taken for granted: loyalty to ethnic group, to church (usually the Catholic Church, often with an ethnic prefix), and to party (almost always the Democratic Party, but occasionally the Republican). This Chicago is a gritty city, where personal cheerfulness and courtesy lighten up days otherwise as cold and impersonal as the gray Chicago winter sky. The other Chicago is the beginning of the Great Plains, originally a white Anglo-Saxon Protestant Chicago, a place whose residents are products of the first great wave of immigration to America. The tone of this Chicago is lighter, its streets and highways cleaner and neater, its daily life generally free from evidence of unpleasantness and deprivation. People in this Chicago think of themselves as typical Americans, and their geographical vision takes in the vast plains. Ronald Reagan grew up in Downstate Illinois within the orbit of this Chicago (though he did live in the city briefly), and its spirit helped to characterize his presidency. His migration to southern California, incidentally, is not atypical: you can see in the geometric grids and Republican voting patterns of Orange County or Phoenix almost exact replicas of the grids and patterns in Chicago's suburban "Collar Counties," transported to the once-empty Southwest on the Atchison, Topeka & Santa Fe or out U.S. 66 from their beginnings in Chicago's Loop.

The 14th Congressional District of Illinois straddles this line between metropolitan Chicago and Downstate Illinois. It gets as close as 30 miles to Chicago's Loop, in western DuPage County, with two great Chicagoland landmarks: Cantigny, the estate of Colonel Robert McCormick, longtime publisher of the *Chicago Tribune*, and Fermilab, the world's fastest energy particle accelerator and employer of some 2,000 people: icons of political conservatism and high technology within two miles of each other. The 14th also contains the Fox River Valley, and its industrial cities of Elgin and Aurora, and antique St. Charles in the heart of the Collar Counties. Farther west, amid what may be the world's richest cornfields, the 14th passes through DeKalb, long the world's leading manufacturer of barbed wire, and goes on to Kendall and Lee Counties, including Reagan's boyhood home in Dixon. This is one of the most heavily Republican belts of territory in the country. Northern Illinois was settled, when Chicago was just a frontier village, by Yankees from Ohio, Indiana, Upstate New York and New England: people who formed the heart of the Republican Party from its founding in 1854, and who would form the core of the Grand Army of the Republic a few years later. Their descendants, in this Anglo-Saxon extension of Chicagoland, remain solidly Republican today.

It is often the case that congressmen from high-income districts full of entrepreneurs and professionals are politicians with relatively modest backgrounds. One such is Dennis Hastert, Republican congressman from the 14th, who for 16 years taught government and history and coached wrestling at Yorkville High School in Kendall County. Starting in 1980, he served six years in the Illinois Assembly; he was chosen by the party to run for Congress after the March 1986 primary when the incumbent was fatally stricken with cancer. Hastert was attacked by some Republicans as insufficiently conservative and won with only 52% over Kane County Coroner Mary Lou Kearns, the Democrat. But he has won easily since and was strengthened in the 1992 redistricting.

Hastert emerged in the 1990s as one of the leaders of House Republicans. In 1994, as an active member of both his party's leadership and at the Commerce Committee, he helped produce the House Republican healthcare reform plan, which got more co-sponsors than any other healthcare bill. And he also worked on the bipartisan Rowland-Bilirakis insurance reform, which contains provisions to restrict malpractice lawsuits, reduce paperwork and fraud, and establish a system of community health centers for the uninsured, among other things. He crusaded to repeal the Social Security "earnings tax"—the deduction of benefits among senior citizens who earn over a certain figure. In 1992, the House did vote to raise the earnings limit $10,200 to $20,000 over five years; a total repeal was included in the Contract with America as the "Senior Equity Act." He is enough of a purist to have voted against the bill which included aid to Chicago after the underground flooding in 1992. After the 1994 election, he was appointed Chief Deputy Majority Whip, a position where he works closely with Majority Whip Tom DeLay—whose successful campaign for Whip was managed by Hastert—in counting the votes among Republicans and urging discipline, where appropriate. This personable law-maker—whose genial disposition should not be mistaken for a lack of commitment to issues—

seems likely to be an active and aggressive party leader, especially on health care, should Republicans decide to bring legislation forward. Newt Gingrich has asked him to chair the Speaker's Steering Committee on Health Care Reform.

At home, Hastert has been utterly secure. In 1992, he declined to try to get his Democratic opponent off the ballot for insufficient signatures—"We thought people ought to hear the issues"—and won with 67%. In 1994, he was opposed by Chicago Perot coordinator Steve Denari, and won with 76% of the vote.

The People: Pop. 1990: 571,540; 21% rural; 9% age 65+; 84% White; 4% Black; 2% Asian; 5% Other; 10% Hispanic origin. Voting age pop.: 407,410; 4% Black; 8% Hispanic origin. Households: 65% married couple families; 35% married couple fams. w. children; 50% college educ.; median household income: $39,815; per capita income: $15,769; median gross rent: $484; median house value: $100,100.

1992 Presidential Vote			1988 Presidential Vote		
Bush (R)	105,700	(44%)	Bush (R)	127,399	(65%)
Clinton (D)	83,109	(34%)	Dukakis (D)	67,476	(35%)
Perot (I)	52,914	(22%)			

Rep. Dennis Hastert (R)

Elected 1986; b. Jan. 2, 1942, Aurora, IL; home, Yorkville; Wheaton Col., B.A. 1964, N. IL U., M.S. 1967; Protestant; married (Jean).

Career: High schl. teacher and coach, 1964–80; IL House of Reps., 1980–86.

DC Office: 2453 RHOB 20515, 202-225-2976; Fax: 202-225-0697; e-mail: dhastert@hr.house.gov.

District Offices: 27 N. River St., Batavia 60510, 708-406-1114.

Committees: *Chief Deputy Majority Whip. Commerce* (8th of 26 R): Energy and Power; Health and Environment; Telecommunications and Finance.

Group Ratings

	ADA	ACLU	COPE	CFA	LCV	CON	NSI	COC	ACU	NTLC	CHC
1994	5	9	0	40	11	82	100	92	95	93	93
1993	5	—	8	20	7	74	—	91	100	—	—

National Journal Ratings

	1993 LIB — 1993 CONS		1994 LIB — 1994 CONS	
Economic	14% —	80%	0% —	80%
Social	11% —	82%	0% —	89%
Foreign	0% —	91%	0% —	88%

Key Votes of the 103d Congress

1. Clinton Deficit Plan	N	3. Brady Handgun Purchase	N	5. Lmt. UN Cmnd. of Forces	Y
2. NAFTA	Y	4. Strike Race/Death Pnlty.	Y	6. Cut Missile Funds	N

Key Votes of the 104th Congress

1. Congressional Compliance	Y	6. Reform Crime Grant	Y	11. Loser Pays Court Reform	Y
2. Balanced Budget Amndmt.	Y	7. National Security Act	Y	12. Product Liability Reform	Y
3. Bar Unfunded Mandates	Y	8. Moratorium on Regs.	Y	13. Welfare Reform	Y
4. Pass Line Item Veto	Y	9. Risk Assessment on Regs.	Y	14. Term Limits Amndmt.	Y
5. Relax Exclusionary Rule	Y	10. Expnd. Priv. Prop. Rights	Y	15. Tax Cuts	Y

Election Results

1994 general	Dennis Hastert (R)	110,204	(76%)	($696,217)
	Steve Denari (D)	33,891	(24%)	($54,330)
1994 primary	Dennis Hastert (R)	46,897	(80%)	
	Steven H. Perry (R)	11,730	(20%)	
1992 general	Dennis Hastert (R)	155,271	(67%)	($615,535)
	Jonathan Abram Reich (D)	75,294	(33%)	

FIFTEENTH DISTRICT

South from Chicago the Illinois Central Railroad heads to the city of New Orleans on a railbed elevated a few feet above the rich black soil of the Illinois prairie, topsoil reaching down not just inches but feet. This land dazzled its first settlers, who were used to the land further east that had to be cleared of trees and stumps before it could be plowed; this treeless prairie could be cultivated almost immediately, and with bounteous results. Today, this remains farming country, made up not of small family farms but of large commercial operations, typically of 1,000 acres or more. Cultivating this soil is a business, requiring informed decisions about crop selection (soybeans and corn are the current favorites), maximizing yields, proper pesticides, marketing decisions, taking advantage of government programs, watching farm export prospects. The landscape on the prairies of eastern Illinois is marked by only a few small towns; the largest of which, Champaign-Urbana and Bloomington-Normal, are the sites of universities (the University of Illinois and Illinois Normal). Politically, these prairie lands have been Republican, often very Republican; they incline much more to the politics of former Speaker Joseph Cannon, a Republican from the manufacturing city of Danville east of Urbana, than to that of Vice President Adlai Stevenson, a Democrat from Bloomington, who served under *laissez-faire* Democrat Grover Cleveland and was the grandfather of the Adlai Stevenson nominated by the Democrats for president in 1952 and 1956.

The 15th Congressional District of Illinois occupies much of this prairie, beginning 60 miles from Chicago, where the Illinois Central heads toward Kankakee, and moving over 150 miles of prairie to the courthouse town of Monticello. It includes Bloomington, Champaign-Urbana and Danville, and runs south almost to the National Road and U.S. 40, traditionally the line between northern Republican and southern Democratic Illinois. Today, the area is heavily Republican; indeed, this was by far George Bush's best Downstate district in 1988, and has been represented for years by Republicans who have been active in local businesses, civic affairs and state legislative politics.

The congressman from the 15th, Thomas Ewing, fits that description. He is a lawyer from Pontiac, between Kankakee and Bloomington, a director of the Chamber of Commerce and county prosecutor, who was elected to the Illinois House in 1974 and reelected eight times. Ewing owes his election to Congress indirectly to Newt Gingrich, for Gingrich beat Ewing's predecessor, Edward Madigan, 87–85 in the race for Minority Whip in March 1989, and in late 1990 Madigan was happy to accept George Bush's appointment as secretary of agriculture. (Madigan died in December 1994, as Gingrich was preparing to become Speaker.) Ewing, assistant and deputy Minority Leader in Springfield from 1982, quickly became the overwhelming favorite. He beat the Democrat 66%–31% in the July 1991 special election.

Ewing has a conservative record on all issues, according to *National Journal*. He got a seat on the Agriculture Committee, reserved by Illinois's Robert Michel. There, Ewing is a promoter of ethanol, produced from Illinois prairie grain and by Decatur-based Archer-Daniels-Midland, and a backer of higher premium subsidies for farmers who buy crop insurance above amounts provided by the government. As a subcommittee chairman on Agriculture, he has played an important role in the deal-making that will be required to win approval of the the 1995 farm bill. That task became all the more difficult because of the budget crunch on farm programs and the large number of new congressmen unfamiliar with—and many of them not disposed toward— the old-fashioned coalition-building that has accompanied such legislation for decades. His desire to maintain some semblance of government regulations and price-supports for farmers does not extend to other parts of the federal apparatus. He opposed the tax increases required by budget procedures to finance the 1994 GATT treaty, whose trade provisions were not universally praised in the ag community. His demeanor suggests the traditional Downstate Republican hands-on approach to legislation, more akin to Madigan and former Minority Leader Robert Michel than to Gingrich. But in late 1994 Ewing was named head of the Conservative Opportunity Society, a House Republican discussion group that was once Gingrich's vehicle for shaking up the House and the country and has become a group to line up support for the party's agenda.

In 1992, Ewing was reelected with 59% of the vote, not a stunning showing for a Republican in these parts. In 1994, he defeated by 68%–32% a Capitol Hill Democratic staffer and former aide to former Congressman George Sangmeister, who re-registered to vote in the district five days before filing for the congresssional race.

The People: Pop. 1990: 571,292; 34% rural; 13% age 65+; 89% White; 7% Black; 2% Asian; 1% Other; 1% Hispanic origin. Voting age pop.: 432,983; 7% Black; 1% Hispanic origin. Households: 55% married couple families; 26% married couple fams. w. children; 45% college educ.; median household income: $26,760; per capita income: $12,709; median gross rent: $372; median house value: $52,300.

1992 Presidential Vote			1988 Presidential Vote		
Clinton (D)	107,914	(42%)	Bush (R)	126,872	(57%)
Bush (R)	98,378	(39%)	Dukakis (D)	94,937	(43%)
Perot (I)	47,280	(19%)			

Rep. Thomas W. Ewing (R)

Elected July 1991; b. Sept. 19, 1935, Atlanta, GA; home, Pontiac; Milliken U., B.S. 1957, John Marshall Law Schl., J.D. 1968; Methodist; married (Connie).

Career: Army, 1957–59; Army Reserves, 1959–63; Exec. Dir., Pontiac and Harvey Chambers of Commerce, 1963–68; Asst. State Atty., Livingston Cnty., 1968–73; IL House of Reps., 1974–91.

DC Office: 1317 LHOB 20515, 202-225-2371; Fax: 202-225-8071.

District Offices: P.O. Box 20, Pontiac 61764, 815-844-7660; 2401 E. Washington St., #201, Bloomington 61704, 309-662-9371; 102 E. Madison, #307, Urbana 61801, 217-328-0165; and 120 N. Vermillion, #A, Danville 61832, 217-431-8230.

Committees: *Agriculture* (8th of 27 R): Department Operations, Nutrition and Foreign Agriculture; Risk Management and Specialty Crops (Chmn.). *Transportation & Infrastructure* (12th of 33 R): Aviation; Water Resources and Environment. *Joint Economic Committee* (2nd of 10 Reps.).

Group Ratings

	ADA	ACLU	COPE	CFA	LCV	CON	NSI	COC	ACU	NTLC	CHC
1994	10	13	0	20	6	74	100	92	90	100	100
1993	5	—	0	10	29	74	—	91	100	—	—

National Journal Ratings

	1993 LIB — 1993 CONS		1994 LIB — 1994 CONS	
Economic	0%	88%	21%	76%
Social	0%	89%	20%	77%
Foreign	17%	76%	12%	87%

Key Votes of the 103d Congress

1. Clinton Deficit Plan	N	3. Brady Handgun Purchase	N	5. Lmt. UN Cmnd. of Forces	Y
2. NAFTA	Y	4. Strike Race/Death Pnlty.	Y	6. Cut Missile Funds	N

Key Votes of the 104th Congress

1. Congressional Compliance	Y	6. Reform Crime Grant	Y	11. Loser Pays Court Reform	Y
2. Balanced Budget Amndmt.	Y	7. National Security Act	Y	12. Product Liability Reform	Y
3. Bar Unfunded Mandates	Y	8. Moratorium on Regs.	Y	13. Welfare Reform	Y
4. Pass Line Item Veto	Y	9. Risk Assessment on Regs.	Y	14. Term Limits Amndmt.	Y
5. Relax Exclusionary Rule	Y	10. Expnd. Priv. Prop. Rights	Y	15. Tax Cuts	Y

Election Results

1994 general	Thomas W. Ewing (R)	108,857	(68%)	($511,926)
	Paul Alexander (D)	50,874	(32%)	($144,040)
1994 primary	Thomas W. Ewing (R)	unopposed		
1992 general	Thomas W. Ewing (R)	142,167	(59%)	($309,131)
	Charles D. Mattis (D)	97,190	(41%)	($6,328)

SIXTEENTH DISTRICT

The far northwest corner of Illinois is one of the heartlands of the Republican Party. Here, in the town square of Freeport, some 15,000 people came to hear Abraham Lincoln and Stephen Douglas in one of their seven debates, and on terrain most partial to Lincoln. Settled by New England Yankees, northern Illinois was one of the strongest Republican constituencies in 1860 and for years after. Not far away, on a little river once navigable by Mississippi River steamboats, is Galena, one of the earliest settlements in northern Illinois, the home of Ulysses S. Grant before he became general and then president; not far away are Tampico and Dixon, birthplace and boyhood home of Ronald Reagan. Farther up on the Rock River is Rockford, the home town of John Anderson, a conservative Republican for most of the 20 years he served in Congress before he became known as the liberal reformist independent candidate for president in 1980. During all these years, northern Illinois, perhaps inspired by Democratic Chicago, remained steadfastly Republican; it backed Herbert Hoover in 1932, Barry Goldwater in 1964 and George Bush in 1992 when most of America and Illinois were going the other way.

The 16th Congressional District consists of much of northwest Illinois; the largest city here is Rockford, headquarters of the paleo-conservative Rockford Institute. The district extends west to the hilly, almost mountainous country around Galena and the Mississippi River, and east to McHenry County, full of new subdivisions surrounding old towns, where Motorola has been opening new cellular phone plants to supply Japan, which only recently opened its cellular phone market to U.S. manufacturers, and affluent young families make their way up through free enterprise and have conservative cultural values. Over the years, the Republican Party has adapted itself well to trends of opinion here, and has held this congressional seat every year since the party's founding except for 1912 and 1990. The past two elections, however, have produced results quite different from the likes of moderate Republicans such as Anderson who served from 1960 to 1980 and Lynn Martin, later Bush's secretary of labor, from 1980 to 1990.

This congressman here is Don Manzullo, an unsuccessful candidate in the 1990 primary who won the seat in 1992 and was reelected overwhelmingly in 1994. Manzullo grew up in Rockford, where his family owns Manzullo's Drive-In Restaurant and Italian Villa. While in college in Washington in the mid-1960s, he worked for Republican candidates, and he has practiced law in Illinois since 1970. He also lives on a cattle-breeding farm, writes poetry and books on constitutional law, and ran a radio talk show; he and his wife home-school their three young children. He lost the 1990 primary 54%–46% to a moderate, who after revelations of personal problems then lost the general to Democrat John Cox. Cox favored increased taxes, opposed capital punishment and was hurt when ultra-Republican McHenry County was added in redistricting. Democrats may have been heartened when the favorite in the 1992 primary, Jack Schaffer, was beaten 56%–44% by Manzullo, who attacked him for supporting gasoline, cigarette and computer software tax increases in the legislature. Cox campaigned for higher taxes; Manzullo for a 10% across-the-board income tax cut. Manzullo lost narrowly in Rockford and in Winnebago County but he won nearly 2–1 in McHenry County and won overall with 56%.

In the House, he criticized members for not reading lengthy bills before they voted and for piling onerous provisions into innocuously titled bills; he sharply criticized an amendment to the crime bill after reading it—a "Buy American" provision not crime-related. He weighed in on the home schooling provision of the 1994 education bill, although he voted against the final product. He strongly supported GATT and pointed to specific benefits for the district. He got improvements for the Rockford airport UPS hub. He got some publicity and results when he attacked the relocation to the U.S. of Iraqi POWs, while the needs of some Gulf war veterans were ignored. He seems to have found a happy medium between a solidly conservative voting record and helping people in the district, and he was reelected with 71% of the vote, the best showing for this seat since 1972.

The People: Pop. 1990: 571,488; 26% rural; 12% age 65+; 91% White; 5% Black; 1% Asian; 1% Other; 3% Hispanic origin. Voting age pop.: 415,364; 4% Black; 2% Hispanic origin. Households: 63% married couple families; 31% married couple fams. w. children; 43% college educ.; median household income: $34,668; per capita income: $15,107; median gross rent: $392; median house value: $73,300.

1992 Presidential Vote			1988 Presidential Vote		
Bush (R)	108,949	(42%)	Bush (R)	133,449	(61%)
Clinton (D)	95,103	(36%)	Dukakis (D)	84,349	(39%)
Perot (I)	56,169	(21%)			

Rep. Donald Manzullo (R)

Elected 1992; b. Mar. 24, 1944, Rockford; home, Egan; American U., B.S. 1967, Marquette U. Law Schl., J.D. 1970; Baptist; married (Freda).

Career: Practicing atty., 1970–92; author.

DC Office: 426 CHOB 20515, 202-225-5676; Fax: 202-225-5284.

District Offices: 415 S. Mulford Rd., Rockford 61108, 815-394-1231; and 191 Virginia Ave., Crystal Lake 60014, 815-356-9800.

Committees: *International Relations* (14th of 23 R): Asia and the Pacific; International Economic Policy and Trade. *Small Business* (5th of 22 R): Procurement, Exports and Business Opportunities (Chmn.). *Joint Economic Committee* (4th of 10 Reps.).

Group Ratings

	ADA	ACLU	COPE	CFA	LCV	CON	NSI	COC	ACU	NTLC	CHC
1994	5	13	0	10	6	88	90	92	95	100	100
1993	5	—	0	10	21	85	—	91	100	—	—

National Journal Ratings

	1993 LIB — 1993 CONS	1994 LIB — 1994 CONS
Economic	0% — 88%	21% — 76%
Social	0% — 89%	11% — 85%
Foreign	9% — 85%	0% — 88%

Key Votes of the 103d Congress

1. Clinton Deficit Plan	N	3. Brady Handgun Purchase N	5. Lmt. UN Cmnd. of Forces Y
2. NAFTA	Y	4. Strike Race/Death Pnlty. Y	6. Cut Missile Funds	N

Key Votes of the 104th Congress

1. Congressional Compliance Y	6. Reform Crime Grant	Y	11. Loser Pays Court Reform Y
2. Balanced Budget Amndmt. Y	7. National Security Act	Y	12. Product Liability Reform Y
3. Bar Unfunded Mandates	Y	8. Moratorium on Regs.	Y	13. Welfare Reform	Y
4. Pass Line Item Veto	Y	9. Risk Assessment on Regs. Y	14. Term Limits Amndmt.	Y
5. Relax Exclusionary Rule	Y	10. Expnd. Priv. Prop. Rights Y	15. Tax Cuts	Y

Election Results

1994 general	Donald Manzullo (R)	117,238	(71%)	($579,059)
	Pete Sullivan (D)	48,736	(29%)	($214,715)
1994 primary	Donald Manzullo (R)	unopposed		
1992 general	Donald Manzullo (R)	142,388	(56%)	($435,468)
	John W. Cox, Jr. (D)	113,555	(44%)	($491,002)

SEVENTEENTH DISTRICT

Illinois's western prairies are some of America's richest agricultural land. This land was first settled by Yankees coming overland from northern Indiana and Ohio and Upstate New York. After 1848, Germans, who left their homeland in search of better opportunities, settled this land that in so many ways resembles the flat, orderly plains of northern Germany. All these migrants farmed quarter-sections and built small towns, with banks and stores, community churches and libraries. In time, investors built farm machinery factories, and the Quad Cities of the Mississippi—Davenport, Iowa, and Rock Island, Moline and East Moline, Illinois—became one of the nation's biggest agricultural equipment manufacturing centers. These plants were unionized in the 1930s and 1940s, and in post-World War II America their wages went up as the demand for ever more sophisticated machines rose among the Midwest's government-subsidized farmers. But eventually the cost of subsidies rose too high and the market had its revenge. In the early 1980s, farm profits vanished, land values declined and orders for new machinery and equipment dried up. The result was a depression in western Illinois and neighboring Iowa, and a political swing toward the Democrats and away from the Republicans who had been the ancestral party in most of this area. Now Republicanism seems to be returning, but more slowly than in the rest of the country and Illinois.

The 17th Congressional District includes most of the state's Mississippi River border with Iowa plus half a dozen more prairie counties to the east. For years, its Democratic base in the Quad Cities was outvoted by Republican counties elsewhere. But in 1982, longtime Republican congressman Tom Railsback lost to a conservative in the primary; ready to take advantage of this opening was Democrat Lane Evans, a local legal services attorney angry at the Reagan recession who took a gamble in running and ended up winning with 53%. Evans has represented the district ever since. He brings to his work an earnestness that is almost squareness, a pleasant, boyish demeanor which will never be mistaken for East Coast slick. He served in the Marine Corps from 1969 to 1971, then went to college and law school and did most of his lawyering for the poor. He calls himself a "populist" rather than a liberal; by most standards, including the tallies on the Contract With America, his voting record is one of the most liberal in the House. He was a strong opponent of NAFTA and GATT. He strongly favored higher agricultural subsidies, but never got on the Agriculture Committee and saw farm subsidies cut back.

Increasingly, Evans has concentrated on veterans' issues. On the Veterans' Affairs Committee, he worked hard for years to get compensation for veterans who claimed they were harmed by their exposure to Agent Orange, and ultimately succeeded. In 1992, he passed measures to provide mental health services for women veterans who are sexually traumatized on active duty, to set up a study of health consequences of Gulf war service and to expand housing services to homeless veterans. In 1994, he worked for compensation for victims of the mysterious and yet-unidentified Gulf war syndrome. Evans bridled at Chairman Sonny Montgomery's lack of sympathy on Agent Orange and other issues and his closeness to traditional veterans' organizations, and decided to challenge him for the chair after the 1992 election; in the liberal Democratic Caucus, the conservative Montgomery won by only a narrow 127–123 margin. Throughout 1994, Evans was thinking about running for chairman again, but that option was mooted after Republicans won control of the House; and Evans decided not to challenge Montgomery for the ranking minority member position. (Perhaps this decision is related to his desire to run for the Senate seat.) Evans also serves on National Security where he has concentrated on finding alternatives to tritium production and banning the sale of anti-personnel land mines; he also questioned how much export controls should be relaxed on critical weapons materials and demanded tougher export controls.

In the years of agricultural unrest in western Illinois, Evans was reelected by impressive margins, especially given the area's Republican leanings. But they have been declining lately. In 1992, Evans won with 60%, a fine showing but a drop from 1988 and 1990. In 1994, he was opposed by Jim Anderson, who sold his interest in his Farmers Grain and Coal business and decided to run on a "spur of the moment deal." Anderson called for welfare reform, universal access to health care, and for free trade; he refused PAC money (and wasn't likely to get much anyway) and ran on a shoestring. Yet he carried five counties and held Evans to 55% of the vote, his lowest showing since he first won the seat.

Suddenly, Evans's political universe changed. The outlook for 1996 in the 17th District looked less favorable, while within a week after the election the possibility of running for the Senate appeared when Evans's fellow Downstate Democrat Paul Simon announced he would retire in 1996. Evans immediately announced he was interested. He would likely portray himself as one who will shake up the system, a man who challenged Ronald Reagan in the 1980s and Sonny Montgomery in the 1990s and who worked for veterans and farmers in need of help. Republicans portray Evans as one of the most liberal members of the House, a proponent of big government; if he is the Democratic nominee, they would hope that the earnestness and hard work which have endeared him to marginal voters in the 17th District would not be enough to win over many voters statewide, where he is not as well known. An Evans candidacy would be a gamble on a change in the political climate, for in the atmosphere of 1994 he would clearly lose, and with Republicans in control of Congress a Democrat like Evans will have a hard time raising funds. Certainly, Evans must have weighed all these factors before deciding in May 1995 to stay put. House Democratic campaign strategists were pleased that Evans decided not to run for the Senate; they feared that it would be difficult for another Democrat to hold an open seat.

The People: Pop. 1990: 571,585; 38% rural; 17% age 65+; 93% White; 3% Black; 1% Asian; 1% Other; 3% Hispanic origin. Voting age pop.: 428,001; 3% Black; 2% Hispanic origin. Households: 59% married couple families; 26% married couple fams. w. children; 38% college educ.; median household income: $25,195; per capita income: $12,052; median gross rent: $309; median house value: $41,200.

1992 Presidential Vote

Clinton (D) 124,175 (47%)
Bush (R) 95,554 (36%)
Perot (I). 45,566 (17%)

1988 Presidential Vote

Dukakis (D). 127,357 (51%)
Bush (R) 120,322 (49%)

Rep. Lane Evans (D)

Elected 1982; b. Aug. 4, 1951, Rock Island; home, Rock Island; Augustana Col., B.A. 1974, Georgetown U., J.D. 1978; Catholic; single.

Career: Marine Corps, 1969–71; Practicing atty., 1978–82.

DC Office: 2335 RHOB 20515, 202-225-5905; Fax: 202-225-5396.

District Offices: 1535 47th Ave., Moline 61265, 309-793-5760; and 1640 N. Henderson St., Galesburg 61401, 309-342-4411.

Committees: *National Security* (9th of 25 D): Military Procurement; Military Readiness. *Veterans' Affairs* (2nd of 15 D): Compensation, Pension, Insurance and Memorial Affairs (RMM); Education, Training, Employment and Housing.

Group Ratings

	ADA	ACLU	COPE	CFA	LCV	CON	NSI	COC	ACU	NTLC	CHC
1994	100	87	100	100	94	16	0	25	0	14	7
1993	100	—	100	90	93	52	—	0	4	—	—

National Journal Ratings

	1993 LIB — 1993 CONS	1994 LIB — 1994 CONS
Economic	88% — 0%	83% — 0%
Social	80% — 13%	90% — 6%
Foreign	74% — 22%	85% — 0%

Key Votes of the 103d Congress

1. Clinton Deficit Plan	Y	3. Brady Handgun Purchase	Y	5. Lmt. UN Cmnd. of Forces	N
2. NAFTA	N	4. Strike Race/Death Pnlty.	N	6. Cut Missile Funds	Y

Key Votes of the 104th Congress

1. Congressional Compliance	Y	6. Reform Crime Grant	N	11. Loser Pays Court Reform	N
2. Balanced Budget Amndmt.	N	7. National Security Act	N	12. Product Liability Reform	N
3. Bar Unfunded Mandates	N	8. Moratorium on Regs.	N	13. Welfare Reform	N
4. Pass Line Item Veto	N	9. Risk Assessment on Regs.	N	14. Term Limits Amndmt.	N
5. Relax Exclusionary Rule	N	10. Expnd. Priv. Prop. Rights	N	15. Tax Cuts	N

Election Results

1994 general	Lane Evans (D).	95,312	(55%)	($270,939)
	Jim Anderson (R)	79,471	(45%)	($15,583)
1994 primary	Lane Evans (D).	unopposed		
1992 general	Lane Evans (D).	156,233	(60%)	($374,415)
	Ken Schloemer (R)	103,719	(40%)	($117,624)

EIGHTEENTH DISTRICT

Old vaudeville bookers, presented with a new act, used to ask, "Will it play in Peoria?" The implication was that if an act went over in this small city on the bluffs above the Illinois River, 154 miles from Chicago and 171 miles from St. Louis, it would go over just about anywhere. In the first half of this century, Peoria did seem pretty typical of America. If its citizens were mostly of British or German descent, with a small percentage of blacks, that was the image of ordinary America that prevailed up through the 1960s, despite the great immigrations of 1880–1924 and the northward urban migrations of southern rural blacks of 1940–1965. And for years, Peoria was a good test market for commercial products. But Peoria's economy, arguably typical at mid-century, is less so today. For this is still a heavy manufacturing town, dominated by big plants that produce farm machinery and earth-moving equipment. Its biggest employer is Caterpillar, the world's standard producer of earth-moving and construction equipment, and one of America's major exporters. And there are more than just memories here of the sharp divide between blue collar and white collar, union and management, Democrat and Republican—the basis of the class warfare politics that was the norm in the heavy industrial metropolises of the Great Lakes region for three or four decades starting with the sitdown strikes of the late 1930s. But the blue collar workers now are not as numerous and the unions not as strong. The Peoria area went through terrible times in the 1980s, as big farm machinery plants laid off workers and even closed down; now employment seems permanently down. And Caterpillar, struck by the United Auto Workers in 1992, hired replacement workers and continued to operate—not without some friction and inefficiency, but profitably—something unheard of a dozen or more years before.

The 18th Congressional District of Illinois, variously configured, has been the Peoria district since the 1940s. It has been represented by two national Republican leaders: Everett McKinley Dirksen, who went on to be elected senator in 1950 and was Senate Republican Leader from 1959–69, and Robert Michel, who worked for Dirksen's successor in the House and then won the seat himself in 1956, and who served as House Republican Leader from 1981–95—retiring just as Republicans were about to win a majority for the first time in 40 years, a circumstance that some allies of Newt Gingrich said is more than a coincidence. Michel has been described as an accommodationist, a pleasant and decent man who tempered his partisanship during the day with a friendship after hours with Tip O'Neill, in contrast to the hard-edged partisanship of the man Michel did not want as his successor, Newt Gingrich.

But this is not quite the whole truth. For there was fierce partisanship on some issues when Michel came to Congress, as a staffer in 1949 and a member in 1957; and Michel himself was an effective and on occasion outraged partisan. But he also believed in working with Democrats to achieve immediate results—half a loaf, even a quarter—on the assumption that there was no way Republicans could ever win a majority themselves. As time went on, particularly after the budget summit agreement of 1990 was followed by Republican losses in the election, fewer Republicans agreed with those tactics or that assumption. A decisive moment came in March 1989, when Whip Dick Cheney was appointed Defense secretary. Michel backed his Illinois neighbor Edward Madigan to succeed him and opposed Newt Gingrich; but Gingrich won 87–85. After that, every election saw Madigan supporters retire and new Gingrich supporters lined up. Up through the 1992 election, Gingrich pledged he would not oppose Michel for leader. But in 1993, Gingrich said he would make no such pledge for the next Congress and in October 1993, Michel, pushed by Illinois's December filing deadline, announced he would retire. In the next 13 months, he had the satisfaction of pushing through two major bipartisan trade agreements, NAFTA and GATT, of seeing his party finally win a majority and of taking the gavel himself when Speaker Thomas Foley presented it to him on the final day of the 103d Congress.

Michel could also take satisfaction from the fact that the 18th District elected as his successor his own former chief of staff, Ray LaHood. It was not an uncontested race, however. In early

February, LaHood was sharply attacked in the primary by state Representative Judy Koehler for keeping his $108,000 job on Michel's staff while campaigning; he revealed just weeks before the March primary that he had gone on unpaid leave of absence February 1 and that he had taken vacation days while campaigning. LaHood won 50%–40%, carrying the Peoria area but running behind in the rest of the district, which now goes south to include much of the Springfield area. LaHood brought to the general a resume out of line with most Republicans' anti-insider rhetoric. He worked six years as a teacher, then with delinquent teens as head of the Rock Island County Youth Services Bureau. Then came a staff job with Congressman Tom Railsback; from 1983, he headed Michel's Peoria office and was named chief of staff in the Washington office in 1990. When LaHood became candidate, his Democratic opponent was Douglas Stephens, a labor lawyer and small businessmen, who held Michel to 52% and 55% in 1982 and 1988. Stephens favored school prayer, term limits and abortion limits, and called for House members to debate and vote from their districts via interactive television. As for LaHood's experience with Michel, "I'm not sure being Arnold Palmer's caddy makes you as good a golfer as he is," Stephens said. He put on an energetic campaign, but in this Republican year LaHood carried all but one county—Putnam—and won 60%–40%. LaHood did not sign the Contract with America, and the interesting question now is how comfortable he will be in Newt Gingrich's Republican Conference. Early signs were not favorable: LaHood lost his bid for a seat on the Appropriations Committee, which had been Michel's power base for years. His Capitol Hill experience was seen by many of his new colleagues as much less of an advantage than it was for Michel when he was elected. And LaHood continued to voice objections to the Gingrich agenda, including the tax cuts—an old-time Republican voice for fiscal responsibility but not one heard much these days in the party caucus. In at least one area, however, LaHood joined the freshmen chorus: he filed a bill to ban the mass mailing of newsletters, a subject with which his earlier career made him very familiar.

The People: Pop. 1990: 572,238; 37% rural; 14% age 65+; 94% White; 5% Black; 1% Asian; 1% Hispanic origin. Voting age pop.: 422,371; 4% Black; 1% Hispanic origin. Households: 61% married couple families; 28% married couple fams. w. children; 43% college educ.; median household income: $30,189; per capita income: $13,792; median gross rent: $352; median house value: $51,600.

1992 Presidential Vote

Clinton (D)	117,483	(42%)
Bush (R)	114,090	(41%)
Perot (I)	47,087	(17%)

1988 Presidential Vote

Bush (R)	141,485	(57%)
Dukakis (D)	108,191	(43%)

Rep. Ray LaHood (R)

Elected 1994; b. Dec. 6, 1945, Peoria; home, Peoria; Canton Jr. Col., 1963–65, Bradley U., B.S. 1971; Roman Catholic; married (Kathy).

Career: Jr. High Schl. Teacher, 1971–77; Dir., Rock Island Youth Svcs., 1972–74; Chief Planner, Bi-state Planning Comm., 1974–76; Dist. A.A., U.S. Rep. Tom Railsback, 1977–82; IL House of Reps., 1982; Dist. A.A., U.S. Rep. Bob Michel, 1983–90, Chief of Staff, 1990–94.

DC Office: 329 CHOB 20515, 202-225-6201; Fax: 202-225-9249.

District Offices: 100 N.E. Monroe, #100, Peoria 61602, 309-671-7027; 3050 Montvale Dr., #D, Springfield 62704, 217-793-0808; and 236 W. State St., Jacksonville 62650, 217-245-1431.

Committees: *Agriculture* (27th of 27 R): Department Operations, Nutrition and Foreign Agriculture; Resource Conservation, Research and Forestry. *Transportation & Infrastructure* (32nd of 33 R): Aviation; Surface Transportation.

Group Ratings and 103rd Congress Votes: Newly Elected

Key Votes of the 104th Congress

1. Congressional Compliance	Y	6. Reform Crime Grant	Y	11. Loser Pays Court Reform	Y
2. Balanced Budget Amndmt.	Y	7. National Security Act	Y	12. Product Liability Reform	Y
3. Bar Unfunded Mandates	Y	8. Moratorium on Regs.	Y	13. Welfare Reform	Y
4. Pass Line Item Veto	Y	9. Risk Assessment on Regs.	Y	14. Term Limits Amndmt.	Y
5. Relax Exclusionary Rule	Y	10. Expnd. Priv. Prop. Rights	Y	15. Tax Cuts	N

Election Results

1994 general	Ray LaHood (R)......................	119,838	(60%)	($697,727)
	G. Douglas Stephens (D)	78,332	(39%)	($345,701)
1994 primary	Ray LaHood (R)......................	33,956	(50%)	
	Judy Koehler (R)	26,809	(40%)	
	Dennis Lee Higgins (R)	6,959	(10%)	
1992 general	Robert H. Michel (R).................	156,533	(58%)	($636,430)
	Ronald C. Hawkins (D)	114,413	(42%)	

NINETEENTH DISTRICT

Southern Illinois is a land of prairies, of flat, treeless land sloping imperceptibly down to the Ohio and Mississippi Rivers. It was settled almost entirely from the south by farmers coming overland from Kentucky, such as Abraham Lincoln's family. Just beyond the Ohio River, they found hilly terrain, some of which turned out to have coal deposits. To the north they must have been astonished, after miles of thick forest, to see the great American prairie stretch before them, a vast sea of empty land extending past the horizon. For 200 years, settlers had to chop down trees and clear stumps—backbreaking work that slowed the frontier's march forward. The prairie lands proved wondrously rich, and were soon criss-crossed by rail lines taking their produce away and bringing in products of industrial civilization from Chicago and St. Louis and points east. About the same time, vast coal deposits were found in southern Illinois, producing one mining town after another: this was the home turf of John L. Lewis, the imperious leader of the United Mine Workers for half a century and, in the late 1930s and early 1940s, one of the most powerful and eloquent figures in American politics.

The 19th Congressional District of Illinois covers most of the eastern half of southern Illinois.

Mostly it is south of the old National Road, which became U.S. 40 and is paralleled by Interstate 70, the traditional boundary between the part of Downstate Illinois settled by southerners and the Downstate settled by Yankees—a boundary also between traditional Democrats and traditional Republicans. North of that line, the 19th includes Decatur, a small city that is home of the giant Archer-Daniels-Midland company, the major producer and promoter of government-subsidized ethanol. About a third of the 19th is prairie, straddling or south of the National Road line; the other third is far Downstate, the Egypt region as it is called, where people speak with what Yankees regard as southern accents and southern mores prevail, including an attachment to a conservatively inclined Democratic Party.

The congressman from the 19th District is Glenn Poshard, a Democrat whose politics is very much in line with the history of the district. Poshard's parents' first home was a corn crib, and at 16 he was a $1-an-hour farm laborer; he joined the Army at 17 and served in Korea in the early 1960s; he graduated from Southern Illinois University before the wave of lefty trendiness hit it; he taught history and government and coached high school sports in the coal country towns of Galatia and Thompsonville and got an education Ph.D. He was elected to the state Senate in 1984 and 1986, where he chaired a committee and worked to cut down on pollution from coal use. When longtime (1954–74, 1980–88) and colorful incumbent Ken Gray retired a second time, the earnest and hard-working Poshard was elected to the House in 1988.

In 1992, Poshard faced that politician's nightmare: he was redistricted in with another incumbent, and one of his own party, who had much more money in the bank and could easily raise more. Terry Bruce had been elected to the House in 1984, got a seat on the Commerce Committee and had $659,000 in his treasury by the December 1991 filing deadline. Poshard did not decide to run until just days before the deadline, then ran a campaign of lawn signs and personal campaigning while Bruce ran ads on TV. But Poshard's theme was stronger. He called Bruce a "classic Washington insider," and cited a memo Bruce had written regarding the House bank ("we need to protect our privacy and wrap up the investigation quickly"). Poshard ran well in the Decatur area with 40%, and cut deeply into Bruce's old district with 44% and won in his own old district areas 90%–10%, for a 62%–38% victory.

Poshard has reformer instincts: he refuses PAC contributions, won't take over $500 from anyone and pledged in 1994 to serve no more than two more terms if reelected, for a total of 12 years the House. He has 100% roll call attendance. He favors "the citizen-legislator, not the career legislator" type of government, he says. He combines this seeming naivete with a hard-working determination to look after local interests. He favors government subsidies of ethanol and federal government purchase of soybean-based ink. He opposed the Btu tax in the Clinton tax bill. He was for expanding the Shawnee National Forest. He has not participated actively in Democratic leadership strategy-setting, but he is sensitive to which way the political wind is blowing, as shown by his ample support for the Contract With America. Modest and hard-working, Poshard was a strong candidate even in Republican 1994. He won 60% in the counties around Decatur and 67% in the 11 counties in the south; he ran just even in the 12 prairie counties around U.S. 40. He is one Democrat who will be tough for Republicans to beat in 1996.

The People: Pop. 1990: 571,390; 51% rural; 17% age 65+; 96% White; 4% Black. Voting age pop.: 428,993; 3% Black. Households: 60% married couple families; 27% married couple fams. w. children; 34% college educ.; median household income: $22,979; per capita income: $11,333; median gross rent: $295; median house value: $38,500.

1992 Presidential Vote

Clinton (D)	131,396	(47%)
Bush (R)	95,759	(34%)
Perot (I)	50,706	(18%)

1988 Presidential Vote

Bush (R)	132,401	(52%)
Dukakis (D)	120,078	(48%)

Rep. Glenn Poshard (D)

Elected 1988; b. Oct. 30, 1945, Herald.; home, Marion; Southern IL U., B.A. 1970, M.S. 1974, Ph.D. 1984; Southern Baptist; married (Jo).

Career: Army, 1962–65; High schl. teacher, 1970–74, Dir., Regional Educ. Svc. Ctr. for Educators of the Gifted, 1974–84; IL Senate 1984–88.

DC Office: 2334 RHOB 20515, 202-225-5201; Fax: 202-225-1541.

District Offices: 201 E. Nolan St., W. Frankfort 62896, 618-937-6402; New Rte. #13-W., Marion 62959, 618-953-8532; 363 S. Main St., Decatur 62521, 217-362-9011; 800 Airport Rd., Mattoon 61938, 217-234-7032; 444 S. Willow St., Effingham 62401, 217-342-7220; and 606 N. 13th St., Lawrenceville 62439, 618-943-6036.

Committees: *Transportation & Infrastructure* (14th of 27 D): Surface Transportation; Water Resources and Environment. *Small Business* (6th of 19 D): Government Programs (RMM).

Group Ratings

	ADA	ACLU	COPE	CFA	LCV	CON	NSI	COC	ACU	NTLC	CHC
1994	55	30	56	40	39	84	50	83	38	43	79
1993	60	—	92	60	64	82	—	9	38	—	—

National Journal Ratings

	1993 LIB — 1993 CONS		1994 LIB — 1994 CONS	
Economic	64%	— 34%	44%	— 54%
Social	35%	— 64%	43%	— 56%
Foreign	46%	— 53%	47%	— 52%

Key Votes of the 103d Congress

1. Clinton Deficit Plan	Y	3. Brady Handgun Purchase	N	5. Lmt. UN Cmnd. of Forces	Y
2. NAFTA	N	4. Strike Race/Death Pnlty.	N	6. Cut Missile Funds	Y

Key Votes of the 104th Congress

1. Congressional Compliance	Y	6. Reform Crime Grant	N	11. Loser Pays Court Reform	N
2. Balanced Budget Amndmt.	Y	7. National Security Act	N	12. Product Liability Reform	Y
3. Bar Unfunded Mandates	Y	8. Moratorium on Regs.	Y	13. Welfare Reform	N
4. Pass Line Item Veto	Y	9. Risk Assessment on Regs.	Y	14. Term Limits Amndmt.	Y
5. Relax Exclusionary Rule	N	10. Expnd. Priv. Prop. Rights	Y	15. Tax Cuts	N

Election Results

1994 general	Glenn Poshard (D)	115,045	(58%)	($164,541)
	Brent Winters (R)	81,995	(42%)	($57,702)
1994 primary	Glenn Poshard (D)	unopposed		
1992 general	Glenn Poshard (D)	187,156	(69%)	($312,530)
	Douglas E. Lee (R)	83,526	(31%)	($25,303)

TWENTIETH DISTRICT

Springfield, Illinois, is one of our state capitals which has changed relatively little since its great moment in history—in Springfield's case, when it was the home of Abraham Lincoln, lawyer, unsuccessful candidate for Congress and 16th president of the United States. Today, beyond the suburban fringe, the prairie countryside outside Springfield is still mostly farmland with few towns. If farming technology has changed vastly, the patterns of cultivation, the contours of the land, even the shape of the ribbons of back country roads, cannot be entirely different from what Lincoln saw as a lawyer making his way from one county seat to another on the circuit. Nor has downtown Springfield changed as much since Lincoln's time as, say, downtown Columbus or Indianapolis or even Des Moines. If most of the officefronts and houses captured in the old photographs are gone, some remain; and the scale has not changed utterly. Lincoln's clapboard house is still in Springfield, and so is the courtroom where he argued cases before federal judges; the Greek revival downtown bloc where Lincoln & Herndon kept their law offices is open for inspection, as is the state Capitol building built here in 1839. Much of today's Springfield is tawdry, but unlike other state capitals it has not lost its 19th Century scale.

The 20th Congressional District of Illinois is one of only 19 districts which can claim to be the lineal descendant of a district whose representative was also a president of the United States. The 20th District includes the southern half of Springfield and much of the Downstate Illinois prairie, which in 1846 elected a 37-year-old railroad lawyer and Whig opponent of the Mexican War named Abraham Lincoln to his single term in the House. Lincoln's denunciation of the Mexican War was so strong that he gave up any chance of a second term, for the countryside south and west of Springfield, straddling the National Road and along the Illinois River, both avenues of migration from the South, were strongly supportive of that war. Similar sentiments—a certain hawkishness and predisposition to the Democratic Party—are apparent today.

The current congressman from the 20th is, unlike Lincoln, a Democrat and professional politician. Richard Durbin has spent his adult life working in politics: on Paul Simon's staff when he was lieutenant governor (1969–73) and as a state Senate staffer in the 1970s. He lost two races for office in the 1970s, but in 1982 won the nomination to oppose incumbent Paul Findley, who had characterized himself as Yasir Arafat's best friend in Congress; that helped Durbin raise large sums from Israel supporters and to attack Findley for concentrating on issues of no importance at home. Durbin won that race, got a seat on the Agriculture Committee, and then moved to Appropriations, where in January 1993 he became chairman of the Agriculture Appropriations Subcommittee, succeeding Jamie Whitten of Mississippi who had held the job since 1949 (except for 1953–55 when Republicans were in control). That made Durbin one of the "college of cardinals" (the Appropriations subcommittee chairmen), and along with Chicago's Sidney Yates, Durbin proceeded to work for Illinois projects—not just Downstate projects like the research center at the Lincoln home, but the $750 million Chicago Circulator trolley project as well. Durbin opened subcommittee hearings, which Whitten had held behind closed doors, and involved Republicans and other Democrats in decision-making.

But for all his political skill and success, Durbin found himself increasingly frustrated. His subcommittee kept running up against overall spending limitations that forced him to cut back or hold down spending on rural infrastructure, low-cost housing, wetland reserve, watershed improvement and flood control programs. He did work to promote ethanol use and soybean-based ink in government documents—big causes in southern Illinois where soybeans are the number one crop. But he made little progress in his longtime crusade against tobacco. Durbin's father died of lung cancer when he was 14, and Durbin was the prime mover in the 1988 ban on smoking in domestic airline flights. Ever since he has moved methodically to limit smoking and zero out tobacco subsidies. But his 1994 amendment to direct the Food and Drug Administration to regulate tobacco as a health hazard was ruled out of order; his attempt to eliminate the $4 million tobacco research program was killed as well. Durbin was an open supporter of David

Obey over the more senior Neal Smith for Appropriations chairman in April 1994. But the Republican victory in November deprived both Obey and Durbin of their chairmanships much sooner than they expected.

Durbin was affected back home by the Republican trend. In 1992, after redistricting gave him much more territory, he had a serious Republican opponent and won with 57%, a sharp drop from previous years. In 1994, his opponent was a construction worker and John Birch Society member who spent only $55,000 to Durbin's $692,000. But Durbin won with just 55% of the vote, carrying Springfield comfortably but winning the narrowest of margins along the U.S. 40 route where Bill Clinton's bus campaign electrified voters in 1992 but where they were reviling him by 1994. This is clear evidence that Durbin could face a serious challenge in the 20th District—and suggests that a better risk may be to run for the Senate seat now held by his old boss Paul Simon. Indeed, when Simon announced his retirement a week after the 1994 election, he mentioned Durbin as just the kind of successor he would like to see. But it will take more for Durbin to win. Unknown in the Chicago media market, likely to face serious competition in the primary, he would have to raise sums which, with Republicans controlling Congress, may be difficult. So this talented politician who rose under the old system faces difficult choices in a new political world.

The People: Pop. 1990: 571,138; 48% rural; 16% age 65+; 95% White; 4% Black; 1% Hispanic origin. Voting age pop.: 425,014; 4% Black; 1% Hispanic origin. Households: 60% married couple families; 27% married couple fams. w. children; 36% college educ.; median household income: $26,173; per capita income: $12,289; median gross rent: $337; median house value: $47,000.

1992 Presidential Vote		
Clinton (D)	129,865	(46%)
Bush (R)	94,038	(34%)
Perot (I)	55,712	(20%)

1988 Presidential Vote		
Bush (R)	129,010	(51%)
Dukakis (D)	123,734	(49%)

Rep. Richard J. Durbin (D)

Elected 1982; b. Nov. 21, 1944; East St. Louis; home, Springfield; Georgetown U., B.S. 1966, J.D. 1969; Catholic; married (Loretta).

Career: Staff, Lt. Gov. Paul Simon, 1969–72; Legal Cnsl., IL Sen. Judiciary Cmte., 1972–82; Prof., S. IL Schl. of Medicine, 1978–82.

DC Office: 2463 RHOB 20515, 202-225-5271; Fax: 202-225-0170.

District Offices: 525 S. 8th St., Springfield 62703, 217-492-4062; 221 E. Broadway, Centralia 62801, 618-532-4265; and 400 St. Louis St., #2, Edwardsville 62025, 618-492-1082.

Committees: *Appropriations* (13th of 24 D): Agriculture, Rural Development, FDA, and Related Agencies (RMM); District of Columbia; Transportation.

Group Ratings

	ADA	ACLU	COPE	CFA	LCV	CON	NSI	COC	ACU	NTLC	CHC
1994	95	70	78	90	78	13	10	25	0	14	14
1993	90	—	92	100	64	39	—	27	13	—	—

National Journal Ratings

	1993 LIB — 1993 CONS		1994 LIB — 1994 CONS	
Economic	68% —	26%	73% —	17%
Social	68% —	29%	75% —	25%
Foreign	87% —	7%	85% —	0%

Key Votes of the 103d Congress

1. Clinton Deficit Plan	Y	3. Brady Handgun Purchase	Y	5. Lmt. UN Cmnd. of Forces	N
2. NAFTA	Y	4. Strike Race/Death Pnlty.	N	6. Cut Missile Funds	Y

Key Votes of the 104th Congress

1. Congressional Compliance	Y	6. Reform Crime Grant	N	11. Loser Pays Court Reform	N
2. Balanced Budget Amndmt.	N	7. National Security Act	N	12. Product Liability Reform	N
3. Bar Unfunded Mandates	Y	8. Moratorium on Regs.	N	13. Welfare Reform	N
4. Pass Line Item Veto	N	9. Risk Assessment on Regs.	N	14. Term Limits Amndmt.	N
5. Relax Exclusionary Rule	N	10. Expnd. Priv. Prop. Rights	Y	15. Tax Cuts	N

Election Results

1994 general	Richard J. Durbin (D)	108,034	(55%)	($692,886)
	Bill Owens (R)	88,964	(45%)	($55,337)
1994 primary	Richard J. Durbin (D)	unopposed		
1992 general	Richard J. Durbin (D)	154,869	(57%)	($921,659)
	John M. Shimkus (R)	119,219	(43%)	($278,357)

INDIANA

On Memorial Day the nation's eyes turn to Indianapolis, to the center of a state with the nation's most distinctive nickname and some of its least distinctive borders, for a sports spectacle celebrating the knack for tinkering and the taste for powerful machines that made the Midwest the nation's manufacturing center: the Indianapolis 500. This auto race used to be run on a technologically ancient brick track, but it has slowly been paved over with asphalt from 1936–62, with only one original yard of brick still marking the start/finish line. Indiana is a city literally in the center of American manufacturing: almost precisely half the country's manufacturing jobs are east of Indiana and the other half west, almost half are north and half south. Indianapolis and Indiana are also the center of an economically, culturally and politically older America. Older economically, because Indiana's employment patterns in the early 1990s resemble those of the United States of the early 1970s: more manufacturing and fewer service and government jobs than average today. On the map, Indiana may look rural, with its large number of small counties and single major metropolitan area of Indianapolis, but it is still a factory state, from the steel mills of Gary and the ring of auto plants 50 or so miles around Indianapolis to the coal-fired power plants in the south. Which is not to say that Indiana is not prosperous: its incomes hover just below the national average, but so does its cost of living; it has a large class of affluent citizens and not much of an urban underclass. It has one of the nation's lowest tax levels and some of the most restrictive tort laws.

Indiana is also like an older America culturally, with low levels of social pathology—violent crime, unwed mothers, and divorce. It retains some of the old norms that in the 1920s and 1930s brought sociologists Robert and Helen Lynd in their search for the typical American place to "Middletown" (actually Muncie). The major metropolitan area, Indianapolis, now has 1.4

million people, but still doesn't have the big singles and gay neighborhoods of larger cities. Ethnically, Indiana seems older too: except for the steel area around Gary—really an extension of the Chicago metropolitan area—Indiana has relatively few descendants from the 1840–1924 wave of immigration, and few recent Hispanic or Asian migrants. Finally, Indiana is transfixed by American sports: Indianapolis's civic leaders have made sports the focus of their development plans, attracting the Colts professional football team to the Hoosier Dome, hosting the Pan-American games in 1987, several trials for the 1996 Olympics and the NCAA Final Four in 1991, the pro basketball Pacers, the Big Ten Women's Basketball Championship in 1995, and of course the Indianapolis 500 at the Speedway every Memorial Day.

Politically, Indiana is also typical of an older America, with partisan preferences anchored in the Civil War era and a small overlay of change from the union-organizing days of the 1930s. Indiana's cultural conservatism has kept it Republican in presidential elections for the last generation, but for many years before, it was a fulcrum point in partisan politics, a crucial state from the Civil War to the New Deal in the struggles between Republicans and Democrats. Party identification was handed down with religious affiliation—the Lynds noted that the Presbyterians had little to do with Methodists, but that was nothing next to divisions between Republicans and Democrats—in a state still peopled largely by descendants of its original settlers, Yankees from Ohio and New England and "Butternuts" (as they were called in the Civil War years) from Kentucky and the South. Most Yankees became Republicans and most Butternuts Democrats, and so the split has remained over generations.

In Indiana, as in the Sun Belt, the big city votes more Republican than the rest of the state, at least if you ignore the northwest industrial zone from Gary to South Bend. Greater Indianapolis favored the Bush-Quayle ticket by a solid 48%–32% margin in 1992, as it won statewide 43%–37%; in 1988, Indianapolis and suburbs favored the Republican gubernatorial candidate 55%–45%, while almost every other county voted for Governor Evan Bayh. Conversely, the heavily industrial and unionized belt from Gary to South Bend tends to vote Democratic, even against a big winner like Republican Senator Dan Coats. But auto factory towns like Kokomo, Anderson, Muncie and Fort Wayne have mostly stuck with Republicans at the top of the ticket. In the 1920s, the Lynds, liberal academics influenced by Marx's idea that political beliefs were determined by economic interests, were puzzled why the factory workers in "Middletown" didn't vote against the bosses; in the 1930s, they were cheered by signs that they did. But why don't they vote against the bosses now? The answer is that cultural identity and personal values tend to be permanent and so have usually been the critical determinants of political allegiance in an America where economic status can often be changeable.

Indiana's strong partisan allegiances may be breaking down—but only a little. In the late 1980s, the legislature banned the mandatory 2% contributions by state employees to finance whichever party was in power. The Republican machine, which had controlled the state government for 20 years, lost the governorship in 1988. But in 1992, Democrat Evan Bayh, despite great popularity, wasn't able to sweep in many Democrats; instead, Hoosiers split their ticket as never before, with at least 20% splitting between Senate and governor races. In 1994, Indiana was Republican with a vengeance: 67% for Senator Richard Lugar, 57% for Republican House candidates, an average of 59% for Republicans in downballot statewide offices. But Bayh's conservative achievements have shown how Democrats can be competitive here, and hint at how they could be nationally. Hoosiers' ancestral ties produce rotation in office—but never a revolution in policies or cultural values.

Governor. Evan Bayh, first elected governor of Indiana at 32, is now in his second term, one of the nation's senior governors, and with one of the best job ratings. He was reelected in 1992 by a wide margin, running 25% ahead of Bill Clinton. Being elected at a young age is a Hoosier tradition by now: the governor's father Birch Bayh was first elected senator in 1962 at 34, and was beaten in 1980 by Dan Quayle, who was then 33. Evan Bayh ran in 1988 as a determined opponent of higher taxes and a less venturesome government activist than his Republican opponent, Lieutenant Governor John Mutz.

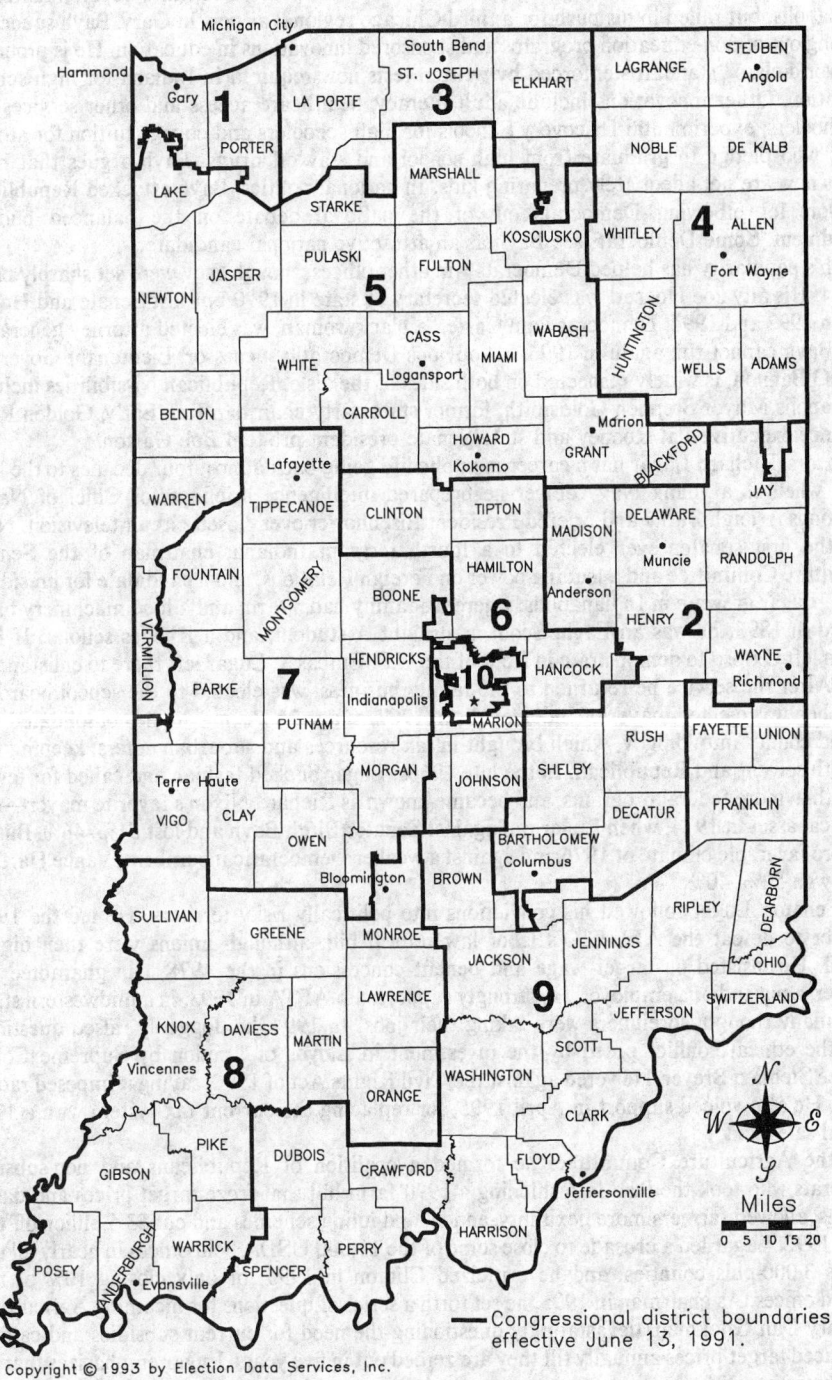

Congressional district boundaries
effective June 13, 1991.

Miles
0 5 10 15 20

In office, Bayh abolished the license plate fund and made Indiana one of only two states not to raise taxes since 1989. He helped attract a 7,500-worker United Airlines repair facility to Indianapolis, but failed in his push for a third Chicago regional airport in Gary. Bayh squeezed spending out of non-education programs and sponsored innovations in education. He is proud of the "world-class" standards enforced by written tests now required in Indiana for high school graduation. Other innovations include adult literacy, healthcare access and other services for pre-schoolers, experimental Discovery Schools for high schoolers and college tuition for at-risk youths who pledge to graduate from high school and stay off drugs. Bayh argues that high schools now are not adequately preparing kids. In national politics, Bayh attacked Republican governors for elbowing Democrats out of the national debate on the balanced budget amemdment. Some Democrats see Bayh as an attractive national candidate.

Bayh's popularity has helped Democrats win other offices, though they were set sharply back in 1994. His ally Joe Hogsett was elected secretary of state in 1990 but lost Senate and House races in 1992 and 1994; Democrat Pam Carter, a black woman, was elected attorney general in 1992. Bayh cannot run again in 1996; his obvious Democratic successor, Lieutenant Governor Frank O'Bannon, is widely respected on both sides of the aisle. Republican possibilities include Indianapolis Mayor Stephen Goldsmith, former state party chairman Rex Early, Golden Rule Insurance executive Pat Rooney and state Senate president pro-tem Bob Garton.

Senators. Richard Lugar has a career in public life going back almost four decades to the late 1950s, when as a young Navy officer he prepared intelligence briefings for Chief of Naval Operations Arleigh Burke and briefed President Eisenhower over closed-circuit television. Now he is the first senator ever elected to a fourth term in Indiana, chairman of the Senate Agriculture Committee and a leading power on Foreign Relations, and a candidate for president as well. Lugar grew up in Indianapolis, where his family had a farm and a food machinery firm, founded in 1893; he was an Eagle Scout, a straight A student, and a Rhodes scholar. If Bill Clinton left Oxford to demonstrate in front of the U.S. Embassy, Lugar left there to enlist in the Navy. After the service he returned to the family business, was elected to the school board in 1964, then was elected mayor of Indianapolis in 1967, at age 35. As mayor, he consolidated the city and county into Unigov, which brought in tax resources and suburban voters, keeping the city both solvent and Republican. In the late 1960s, Lugar bucked fashion and called for fewer rather than more federal programs, and became known as Richard Nixon's favorite mayor—not a political asset in 1974, when Lugar ran against Senator Birch Bayh and lost 51%–46%. But in the more favorable climate of 1976 and against a weaker Democratic incumbent, Vance Hartke, Lugar won 59%–40%.

As Senator, Lugar followed his convictions into politically risky territory. He led the 1978 filibuster to defeat the AFL-CIO's labor law reform bill, although unions were then big in Indiana. He insisted on larger wage and benefit concessions in the 1978 loan guarantee for Chrysler, a big Indiana employer. He strongly supported NAFTA in 1993, in a midwestern state where many thought foreigners were taking their jobs. In 1994, he doggedly raised questions about the ethical conflict posed by the investment in Lloyds of London by Supreme Court nominee Stephen Breyer. He voted against the Civil Rights Act of 1990, saying it imposed racial quotas. He also voiced support in April 1995, for replacing the current tax system with a 17% national sales tax.

On the Agriculture Committee, he formed a coalition of Republicans and non-subsidy Democrats who took the lead in fashioning a 1990 farm bill that froze target prices and dairy supports, allowed farmers more flexibility, ended land-idling schemes and cut $3.5 billion off the bill. In 1992, Lugar led a crusade to close some of the 11,000 USDA field offices in nearly all the nation's 3,000-plus counties, and he criticized Clinton in 1995 for only closing 10% of the targeted offices. As chairman in 1995, he set forth a series of questions for incoming Agriculture Secretary Dan Glickman, devastatingly questioning the need for current subsidies and calling for reduced target prices annually till they are zeroed out in five years. Lugar emphasizes that he is a farmer himself, raising corn, soybeans and wheat on a 600-acre spread outside Indianapolis.

But he sees no reason why taxpayers should subsidize a few crops when free markets work fine for others: "If we are serious about budget discipline, we cannot spare our friends."

Lugar's greatest interest has been foreign policy. In 1985 and 1986, he was chairman of the Foreign Relations Committee, where he quickly took command over a committee sharply divided between Jesse Helms of North Carolina, inclined to conduct his own foreign policy, and liberal Democrats. Lugar supported Reagan's foreign policy generally and was a vigorous advocate of aid to the Nicaraguan contras. But he favored sanctions on South Africa. And on the Philippines, Lugar was ahead of the administration. He quickly concluded that Ferdinand Marcos's 1986 "victory" over Corazon Aquino was fraudulent and, at a decisive point, called on Marcos to leave office; the administration followed. Lugar deserves credit for his foresight as well as his adroitness: he saw less reason to fear that protests against right-wing regimes would produce openings for Communism than reason to hope that the success of those protests would help spur the collapse of Communism that occurred in 1989 and 1990.

After the 1986 elections, Republicans lost control of the Senate, and Helms invoked his seniority to take the ranking minority position on Foreign Relations rather than on Agriculture. Lugar continued to play a role on major foreign issues. He worked with the Republican White House to manage the ratification of the INF Treaty in 1988 and of the START I Treaty for arms reduction in 1992. In 1991 he joined with Democrat Sam Nunn to encourage the dismantling and conversion of the Soviet nuclear stockpile; Nunn and Lugar sponsored a $7.8 billion commitment, funds for which helped secure the 1992 chemical weapons accord with Russia. In June 1992, Lugar called for the use of U.N. and, if necessary, U.S. military force in Bosnia. But by 1994 he was critical of those who would lift the arms embargo on the Bosnian Muslims, and in early 1995, said the United States should have intervened when Yugoslavia split into separate states in 1991. On Haiti, he said the Clinton Administration was "so wedded to the Aristide position" that it missed the chance for a peaceful transition much earlier. In 1995, Helms became Foreign Relations chairman, but immediately gave Lugar the job of managing the ratification of the START II Treaty.

Lugar has had disappointments too. In 1984, he ran to succeed his friend Howard Baker as Senate majority leader, and finished third behind Bob Dole and Ted Stevens. In 1986, Lugar was elbowed aside in Foreign Relations by Helms. And in August 1988, George Bush picked not Lugar, but his junior and less experienced Hoosier colleague, Dan Quayle, to be his vice president. But Lugar is a long-distance runner (literally) and does not quit. In Indiana he has remained vastly popular. He was reelected in 1988 with 68% of the vote, a record for Indiana, and in 1994 won with 67%. His opponent that time was former Congressman Jim Jontz, one of those energetic Democrats whose skill in winning Republican districts helped Democrats control the House for 40 years; but Jontz's energy and denunciations of NAFTA availed him little.

Right after that victory, Lugar started thinking about running for president again. His initial soundings among Indiana Republicans may have helped persuade Dan Quayle to decide suddenly not to run in February 1995. In any case, Lugar had strong home-state financial support; he denied it was necessary to raise $20 million to run—as Phil Gramm kept proclaiming—and he surely can raise $10 million. Lugar's message is simple. "Only the president can deal with the two challenges on which our future really depends—nuclear security and fiscal sanity." He argues that his foreign policy experience and his willingness to reduce farm spending show he fits that description better than anyone else.

The junior senator from Indiana is Dan Coats, a member of Congress for more than a dozen years who insists politics "is not really what I'd planned to do." He was a lawyer in Fort Wayne, then an aide to Dan Quayle when he served in the House in the 1970s. Coats was elected to succeed Quayle in that seat in 1980, was appointed to succeed him in the Senate in December 1988 and elected in his own right for the remainder of the term in 1990 and for a full term in 1992. Several themes emerge clearly from Coats's congressional career. One is a devotion to traditional values rooted in religious faith. Coats is strongly against abortion; he backed the ban on fetal tissue research and tried to block research on the abortifacient RU-486—lost causes now. He criticized Surgeon General Joycelyn Elders strongly and opposed Henry Foster as her successor. Coats backs school prayer and passed a law allowing parents to block dial-a-porn phone numbers. He wants to raise the dependent tax exemption to $4,000, supports the $500-per-child tax credit and he has led the fight for more money for shelters aiding victims of domestic violence. He has his own health plan, Medisave, which would encourage medical IRAs and, he says, give incentives for healthy lifestyles and preventive care.

Another thread in Coats's career is support for the military. He currently chairs the Armed Services Committee Personnel Subcommittee, and is supportive enough of defense needs to have acquiesced when Indiana's only two active bases were included on the 1991 base closure and realignment list. In 1993, he was the lead Republican seeking to block Clinton's plans to end the ban on gays in the military. Coats insisted he was not anti-gay and that the Clinton plan would, among other things, lead to harm for many gays.

Coats backed much of the Contract With America principles long before there was a Contract: term limits and the line-item veto were particular favorites; his work on those issues caused conflicts for him with more senior Senate Republicans. He has opposed many Clinton appointments in addition to Foster, including Justice Stephen Breyer. And Coats was firmly against the Clinton healthcare plan ("We may have to put one more stake through its heart," he said in August 1994 of the "mainstream alternative" measure sponsored by then-Majority Leader Mitchell and John Chafee) and the Clinton Haiti intervention ("Credibility lost by political bungling should not be redeemed by American blood"). One major cause in recent years is to let states and localities bar out-of-state waste, another issue on which he has sparred Chafee, who is the Environment and Public Works Committee chairman. "We want New Jersey students," he once said in debate. "We want New Jersey residents. We want New Jersey athletes. We want everything from New Jersey but your trash." But Coats is pleased with the version that cleared the Senate this year, and will continue to work to make it law.

In 1990 and 1992 Coats won two Senate races with increasing margins. In 1990, he was attacked by Democrat Baron Hill for mailing out 13 million franked letters; Hill campaigned by walking the length of the state, but didn't raise the abortion issue because he had just switched positions on it himself. Coats won 54%–46%, losing the northwest industrial corridor from Gary to South Bend, the old Butternut counties along the Ohio River, the Terre Haute area and Bloomington. Coats carried metro Indianapolis 57%–43% and ran even stronger in his old congressional district. In 1992, Democrat Joe Hogsett, who managed Governor Evan Bayh's first two campaigns and succeeded him as secretary of state by beating Indianapolis Mayor William Hudnut in 1990, ran, attacking Coats for accepting honoraria from speaking engagements, calling for an end to congressional pay raises and perks and criticizing NAFTA. But Coats challenged Hogsett for breaking his promise to serve a full term as secretary of state. Coats won 57%–41%, only barely losing the northwest industrial corridor and carrying greater Indianapolis 65%–34%.

Presidential politics. In recent presidential elections, Indiana has voted more Republican than any state that is larger, and is larger than any state that has voted more Republican. In 1988 and 1992 this owed something to the local popularity of Dan Quayle, but was more due to the statewide unpopularity of the cultural liberalism which to varying extents has characterized the national Democratic ticket since the late 1960s. Since 1968, Republicans have averaged 56% of Indiana's votes and the Democrats 38%. In 1992, George Bush got fewer votes than any Republican since Barry Goldwater, but even with higher turnout Bill Clinton did not win significantly more votes or a greater share of the vote than Michael Dukakis, Walter Mondale or Jimmy Carter. Indiana's May presidential primary has not been influential since 1968.

Congressional districting. Indiana's 1991 districting plan is a mild revision of a 1981 plan enacted by Republicans and upheld in a Supreme Court decision important to redistricting law. The 1980s districts surprised and disappointed Republicans by electing at one point eight Democrats and only two Republicans. When it came time for redistricting in 1991, legislative control was split between the parties and the lines were changed only marginally. The plan may be having its intended effect now that six out of ten seats are Republican—their party gained three seats in 1994, defeating two incumbents—with two others held by Democrats by only narrow margins.

The People: Est. Pop. 1994: 5,752,000; Pop. 1990: 5,544,159, up 3.8% 1990–1994. 2.2% of U.S. total, 14th largest; 35% rural. Median age: 32.8 years. 12.6% 65 years and over. 90.6% White, 7.8% Black, 1.8% Hispanic origin. Households: 58.2% married couple families; 28% married couple fams. w. children; 37% college educ.; median household income: $28,797; per capita income: $13,149; 70.2% owner occupied housing; median house value: $53,900; median monthly rent: $291. 6.5% Unemployment. 1994 Voting age pop.: 4,298,000. 1994 Turnout: 1,530,171; 36% of VAP. Registered voters (1994): 2,997,324; no party registration.

Political Lineup: Governor, Evan Bayh (D); Lt. Gov., Frank L. O'Bannon (D); Secy. of State, Sue Ann Gilroy (R); Atty. Gen., Pamela Fanning Carter (D); Treasurer, Joyce Brinkman (R); Auditor, Morris Wooden (R). State Senate, 50 (30 R and 20 D); State House of Representatives, 100 (56 R and 44 D). Senators, Richard G. Lugar (R) and Daniel R. Coats (R). Representatives, 10 (6 R and 4 D).

1992 Presidential Vote

Bush (R) 939,375 (43%)
Clinton (D) 848,420 (37%)
Perot (I). 455,934 (20%)

1992 Democratic Presidential Primary
Clinton. 301,905 (63%)
Brown 102,379 (21%)
Tsongas 58,215 (12%)

1988 Presidential Vote

Bush (R) 1,297,763 (60%)
Dukakis (D). 860,643 (39%)

1992 Republican Presidential Primary
Bush 374,666 (80%)
Buchanan. 92,949 (20%)

GOVERNOR

Gov. Evan Bayh (D)

Elected 1988, term expires Jan. 1996; b. Dec. 26, 1955, Terre Haute; home, Indianapolis; IN U., B.A. 1978, U. of VA, J.D. 1981; Episcopalian; married (Susan).

Career: Practicing atty., 1981–86; IN Secy. of State, 1986–89; Chmn., Democratic Governor's Assn., 1994.

Office: 206 State House, Indianapolis 46204, 317-232-4567; Fax: 317-232-3443.

Election Results

1992 gen.	Evan Bayh (D)	1,382,151	(62%)
	Linley E. Pearson (R).	822,853	(37%)
1992 prim.	Evan Bayh (D) . . . . . unopposed		
1988 gen.	Evan Bayh (D)	1,138,574	(53%)
	John Mutz (R)	1,002,207	(47%)

SENATORS

Sen. Richard G. Lugar (R)

Elected 1976, seat up 2000; b. Apr. 4, 1932, Indianapolis; home, Indianapolis; Denison U., B.A. 1954; Rhodes Scholar, Oxford U., M.A. 1956; Methodist; married (Charlene).

Career: Navy, 1957–60; Mgr., family farm; V.P. and Treas., Thomas L. Green & Co., 1960–67; Indianapolis Bd. of Schl. Commissioners, 1964–67; Indianapolis Mayor, 1968–75; Prof., U. of Indianapolis, 1976.

DC Office: 306 HSOB 20510, 202-224-4814.

State Offices: 1180 Market Tower, 10 W. Market St., Indianapolis 46204, 317-226-5555; Fed. Bldg., 1300 S. Harrison St., #3158, Fort Wayne 46802, 219-422-1505; 122 Fed. Bldg., 101 NW M.L.K. Blvd., Evansville 47708, 812-465-6313; 103 Fed. Ctr., 1201 E. 10th St., Jeffersonville 47132, 812-288-3377; and 8585 Broadway, #490, Merrillville 46410, 219-937-5380.

Committees: *Agriculture, Nutrition & Forestry* (Chmn. of 10 R). *Foreign Relations* (2nd of 10 R): East Asian and Pacific Affairs; European Affairs (Chmn.); Western Hemisphere and Peace Corps Affairs. *Intelligence (Select)* (2nd of 9 R).

Group Ratings

	ADA	ACLU	COPE	CFA	LCV	CON	NSI	COC	ACU	NTLC	CHC
1994	10	26	0	25	31	47	100	87	76	80	64
1993	10	—	0	40	6	83	—	100	72	—	—

National Journal Ratings

	1993 LIB	—	1993 CONS		1994 LIB	—	1994 CONS
Economic	0%	—	87%		18%	—	77%
Social	29%	—	69%		30%	—	69%
Foreign	24%	—	71%		34%	—	62%

Key Votes of the 103d Congress

1. Clinton Deficit Plan	N	3. Brady Handgun Purchase	Y	5. Lmt. UN Cmnd. of Forces	Y
2. NAFTA	Y	4. Strike Race/Death Pnlty.	Y	6. Cut Missile Funds	N

Key Votes of the 104th Congress

1. Congressional Compliance	Y	3. Balanced Budget Amndt.	Y	5. Product Liability Reform	Y
2. Bar Unfunded Mandates	Y	4. Pass Line Item Veto	Y	6. FY96 Budget	Y

Election Results

1994 general	Richard G. Lugar (R)...............	1,039,625	(67%)	($4,688,326)
	James Jontz (D)	470,799	(31%)	($472,788)
	Others	33,144	(2%)	
1994 primary	Richard G. Lugar (R)..............	unopposed		
1988 general	Richard G. Lugar (R)..............	1,430,525	(68%)	($3,244,601)
	Jack Wickes (D)	668,778	(32%)	($314,233)

Sen. Daniel R. Coats (R)

Appointed Jan. 1989, seat up 1998; b. May 16, 1943, Jackson, MI; home, Fort Wayne; Wheaton Col., B.A. 1965, IN U., J.D. 1971; Presbyterian; married (Marcia).

Career: Army Corps of Engineers, 1966–68; Asst. V.P. & Cnsl., Mutual Security Life Insurance Co., 1972–76; Dist. Rep., U.S. Rep. J. Danforth Quayle, 1976–80; U.S. House of Reps., 1980–88.

DC Office: 404 RSOB 20515, 202-224-5623; Fax: 202-228-4137.

State Offices: 1180 Market Tower, 10 W. Market St., Indianapolis 46204, 317-226-5555; Fed. Bldg., 1300 S. Harrison St., #3158, Fort Wayne 46802, 219-422-1505; 103 Fed. Ctr., 1201 E. 10th St., Jeffersonville 47132, 812-288-3377; 122 Fed. Bldg., 101 NW M.L.K. Blvd., Evansville 47708, 812-465-6313; and 5530 Sohl Ave., #103, Hammond 46320, 219-937-5380.

Committees: *Armed Services* (6th of 11 R): Airland Forces; Personnel (Chmn.); Readiness. *Labor & Human Resources* (3rd of 9 R): Aging; Children and Families (Chmn.); Education, Arts and Humanities.

Group Ratings

	ADA	ACLU	COPE	CFA	LCV	CON	NSI	COC	ACU	NTLC	CHC
1994	5	21	0	25	8	72	100	87	92	92	100
1993	20	—	18	30	6	93	—	100	88	—	—

National Journal Ratings

	1993 LIB — 1993 CONS		1994 LIB — 1994 CONS	
Economic	25%	— 70%	0%	— 88%
Social	29%	— 69%	21%	— 75%
Foreign	16%	— 77%	20%	— 78%

Key Votes of the 103d Congress

1. Clinton Deficit Plan	N	3. Brady Handgun Purchase	Y	5. Lmt. UN Cmnd. of Forces	Y
2. NAFTA	Y	4. Strike Race/Death Pnlty.	Y	6. Cut Missile Funds	N

Key Votes of the 104th Congress

1. Congressional Compliance	Y	3. Balanced Budget Amndt.	Y	5. Product Liability Reform	Y
2. Bar Unfunded Mandates	Y	4. Pass Line Item Veto	Y	6. FY96 Budget	Y

Election Results

1992 general	Daniel R. Coats (R)	1,267,972	(57%)	($3,802,077)
	Joseph H. Hogsett (D)	900,148	(41%)	($1,584,173)
	Others	43,306	(2%)	
1992 primary	Daniel R. Coats (R)	unopposed		
1990 general	Daniel R. Coats (R)	806,048	(54%)	($3,662,672)
	Baron P. Hill (D).....................	696,639	(46%)	($1,077,074)

FIRST DISTRICT

At the southernmost shore of Lake Michigan is a part of America made by steel. Here, in the northwest corner of Indiana, where the water highway of the Great Lakes comes closest to the steel highway of the transcontinental railroads, America's leading capitalists recognized nearly a century ago the best possible site for manufacturing steel. On empty sand dunes, United States Steel, then the nation's largest corporation, created only a few years before by financier J. P.

Morgan, established the city of Gary in 1906 and named it for the company's chairman, Chicago Judge Elbert Gary. For nearly 70 years, the steel mills attracted a diverse work force, like Chicago and quite unlike the rest of Indiana—Irish, Poles, Czechs, Ukrainians and blacks from the American South. Politics here has always been turbulent, from the Communist-led long and unsuccessful steel strike of 1919 to the racially polarized politics of the 1960s and 1970s. The tone of public life—the clash between union stewards and management foremen, between blacks and eastern European ethnics, between the stalwarts of different factions vying for control of Gary's massive City Hall—was always abrasive, like the clash of steel on steel.

Over all this time, only one thing brought people here: steel. In the 1920s, the merchants of Gary built massive storefronts along Broadway, looking north to the Gary Works; civic institutions were created and nurtured. Nearby Chicago was as culturally and economically diversified as any metropolis in the country. But Gary and Lake County always remained a bit remote, and always lived—and lived well for a time—on and for steel. Over time, steel management and union leaders tried to insulate the industry from the outside world, passing along high wage costs to users, building trade barriers to keep out competition. In the short run, this strategy worked: steel still employed 70,000 in Gary and northwest Indiana in 1979. But then economic disaster struck. Obsolete mills were closed and steel jobs fell to 35,000. In time, the steelmakers rebounded: U.S. Steel (renamed USX), Inland, Bethlehem and LTV spent nearly $3 billion modernizing their northwest Indiana plants; the number of man-hours needed to produce a ton of steel was cut by two-thirds; just-in-time methods were introduced; management and high-skill workers cooperated to build higher-quality, less expensive steel to meet customers' needs. By 1989, Indiana was the number one steel producing state in the nation, but with only a little more than 30,000 steel workers in this area. Nor has politics been Gary's salvation. Gary elected a black mayor, Richard Hatcher, as long ago as 1967, but racially polarized politics resulted in economic stagnation and flight to the suburbs; Gary's population fell 23% in the 1980s. Blocks of Broadway are now boarded up; there are no hotels or department stores in the city; the publicly financed convention center and airport do little business. The city's only hope right now is to try and lure casino gambling, which so far has been a less than successful venture.

The Gary area is the one overwhelmingly Democratic part of Indiana, though not out of any Civil War heritage, for this was heavily Republican territory until the United Steelworkers' late 1930s organizing drives. Racial friction in the 1960s and 1970s reduced the appeal of national Democrats, but the decline of the steel industry drove them up again.

Indiana's 1st Congressional District, stretching from Gary along the Lake Michigan shore east almost to Michigan City, has long been considered safely Democratic, with major battles only in Democratic primaries. Its current congressman, Pete Visclosky, has a career distinguished by earnestness and hard work. From a working class background, he worked for six years on the staff of Congressman Adam Benjamin, who died suddenly in 1982. Visclosky returned to Indiana and in 1984 ran against Katie Hall, a black state senator who had been given the 1982 nomination—and thus the election, in this area—by Richard Hatcher, then district party chairman. But Hall was able to win only 33% of the 1984 primary vote; Visclosky had 34% and another white candidate 31%. Visclosky beat Hall 57%–35% in 1986 and 51%–30% in 1990. He had only weak primary opposition in 1992 and 1994.

Visclosky is one of those congressmen whose constituents expect him to concentrate on strengthening the local economy. In the 1980s he worked for the misnamed Voluntary Restraint Agreements that barred many steel imports and helped delay modernization and to protect benefits for employees and retirees of bankrupt LTV. He pushed for a Little Calumet River flood control project, more acreage for the Indiana Dunes National Lakeshore, and transformation of the little-used Gary airport into the Chicago area's third major airport. The airport was stymied when Indiana Governor Evan Bayh supported Chicago Mayor Richard Daley's Lake Calumet site instead, which in turn was defeated by Illinois Senate President Pate Philip. Visclosky won a seat on the Appropriations Committee in 1991—an obvious place to work on local projects. He worked within the existing system of Democratic control; in the early 1990s he said, "In the end, the only people who are going to be able to make the thing work are the chairmen, in conjunction with the leadership."

Visclosky's record on cultural and foreign issues has been somewhat moderate, and even on economics he reflects concerns about deficits and spending more than old-time Democrats from similar districts. And indeed those concerns have become more important in the 1st District. The 1991 redistricting removed industrial Michigan City and added conservative inland suburbs south of Gary, which have become angrily Republican. In 1992 Visclosky was reelected easily, but in 1994 he faced for the first time a Republican who spent more than $100,000. John Larson campaigned for tough crime measures and against welfare, and actually carried Porter County, east of Gary, and held Visclosky to a 56%–44% victory.

Visclosky now must adapt to the new Republican House, where it will be much harder for him to work on district projects and where he must decide whether to vote for popular-sounding Republican measures. Perhaps a signal is that he voted for the balanced budget amendment and was one of six Democrats to vote for the Republican $17 billion recission bill in March 1995. But he seemed to show a greater commitment to Democratic core principles, with by far the lowest support of any Indiana Congressman for the Contract With America. It seems unlikely that he could lose this seat, but this district could be even more seriously contested than last time.

The People: Pop. 1990: 554,514; 9% rural; 12% age 65+; 70% White; 21% Black; 1% Asian; 4% Other; 8% Hispanic origin. Voting age pop.: 400,694; 19% Black; 7% Hispanic origin. Households: 57% married couple families; 27% married couple fams. w. children; 37% college educ.; median household income: $31,300; per capita income: $13,161; median gross rent: $399; median house value: $56,400.

1992 Presidential Vote

Clinton (D)	117,115	(52%)
Bush (R)	68,392	(31%)
Perot (I)	37,129	(17%)

1988 Presidential Vote

Dukakis (D)	118,554	(55%)
Bush (R)	98,656	(45%)

Rep. Peter J. Visclosky (D)

Elected 1984; b. Aug. 13, 1949, Gary; home, Merrillville; IN U. Northwest, B.S. 1970, U. of Notre Dame, J.D. 1973, Georgetown U., LL.M. 1982; Catholic; married (Anne Marie).

Career: Practicing atty., 1973–76, 1983–84; Aide, U.S. Rep. Adam Benjamin, 1976–82.

DC Office: 2464 RHOB 20515, 202-225-2461; Fax: 202-225-2493.

District Offices: 215 W. 35th Ave., Gary 46408, 219-884-1177; City Hall, 6070 Central Ave., Portage 46368, 219-763-2904; and City Hall, 166 Lincolnway, Valparaiso 46383, 219-464-0315.

Committees: *Appropriations* (20th of 24 D): Military Construction; Treasury, Postal Service, and General Government.

Group Ratings

	ADA	ACLU	COPE	CFA	LCV	CON	NSI	COC	ACU	NTLC	CHC
1994	75	70	78	80	78	31	60	50	19	14	14
1993	75	—	92	80	71	19	—	0	17	—	—

National Journal Ratings

	1993 LIB	—	1993 CONS		1994 LIB	—	1994 CONS
Economic	78%	—	12%		73%	—	17%
Social	66%	—	33%		76%	—	23%
Foreign	51%	—	42%		57%	—	37%

Key Votes of the 103d Congress

1. Clinton Deficit Plan	Y	3. Brady Handgun Purchase	Y	5. Lmt. UN Cmnd. of Forces N
2. NAFTA	N	4. Strike Race/Death Pnlty.	N	6. Cut Missile Funds N

Key Votes of the 104th Congress

1. Congressional Compliance Y	6. Reform Crime Grant	N	11. Loser Pays Court Reform N
2. Balanced Budget Amndmt. Y	7. National Security Act	N	12. Product Liability Reform N
3. Bar Unfunded Mandates N	8. Moratorium on Regs.	N	13. Welfare Reform N
4. Pass Line Item Veto N	9. Risk Assessment on Regs. N	14. Term Limits Amndmt. N
5. Relax Exclusionary Rule N	10. Expnd. Priv. Prop. Rights N	15. Tax Cuts N

Election Results

1994 general	Peter J. Visclosky (D).................	68,612	(56%)	($290,049)
	John Larson (R)	52,920	(44%)	($172,531)
1994 primary	Peter J. Visclosky (D).................	56,306	(77%)	
	Sandra Kay Smith (D)	11,726	(16%)	
	Cy Huerter (D)......................	4,723	(6%)	
1992 general	Peter J. Visclosky (D)................	147,054	(69%)	($268,786)
	David J. Vucich (R)	64,770	(31%)	

SECOND DISTRICT

Muncie, Indiana, became famous as the "Middletown" that sociologists Robert and Helen Lynd lived in and reported on in 1924–25 and again in 1935, and where a team of sociologists investigated again in 1976–78 (academic research, like so many other things, seems to require more people and take more time than it used to). The Lynds were attracted to Muncie by its typicalness—"every small city from Maine to California," *Life* said—but it wasn't exactly: it was a factory town in a country still almost half rural, it was almost entirely Protestant and northern in a country one-quarter Catholic and one-third southern. It was more typical in being culturally homogeneous but economically riven. In the 1920s, Muncie celebrated its common values and was loath to admit its economic disparities; in the 1930s, the latter came out into the open when Muncie, like most of the industrial Midwest, was unionized in what were sometimes violent uprisings. The business elite—local bankers, merchants, executives at General Motors and the Ball family's glass company—was fiercely opposed by workers who were joining CIO unions and voting Democratic. Partisan politics took on the sharp, bitter tone of a struggle for wealth between two rival classes whose claims seemed irreconcilable.

Now Muncie has changed again. As incomes tripled in real terms over 40 years, class antagonisms cooled; it turned out there was plenty for everyone. At the same time, increasing affluence and waning tradition allowed for more variety in personal life. As cultural issues came to the fore, the traditional values shared by the majority of Middletowners of various income levels tended to bring them together. The old factory economy was becoming less important: 35% of Muncie workers were in manufacturing in 1970, 21% in 1994. In partisan politics, Muncie was overwhelmingly Republican in the 1920s, voting its Civil War preference as so much of Indiana still does; it shifted toward the Democrats in the 1930s, on economic issues. As economic class conflict became less important, Muncie's cultural traditionalism moved it toward Republicans by the late 1960s. Yet voters were increasingly willing to split tickets, opening opportunities for Democrats—notably Philip Sharp, Democratic congressman for

Muncie and surrounding area from 1975–94.

The 2d Congressional District of Indiana is centered on Muncie and some similar small cities. Anderson, just to the west, has long had big General Motors factories, though some have closed down; Richmond was founded by a major branch of American Quakers, and is the home of their Earlham College; Columbus is the home of Cummins Engine, whose longtime head J. Irwin Miller paid major national architects to design most of the town's important buildings, public and private. Anderson sometimes leans Democratic; Richmond is ancestrally heavily Republican; Muncie and Columbus in between. Overall this is basically a Republican district, but Sharp's pleasant personality, hard work on energy and other issues and his fund-raising capability from his Commerce subcommittee chairmanship enabled him to win the seat from a Republican who voted against the impeachment of Richard Nixon—and hold it against serious challengers for 20 years in all. In February 1994, weary of the constant struggle to win reelection, Sharp announced he was retiring at age 52 and became director of the JFK School of Government's Institute of Politics at Harvard in May 1995.

The new Congressman is David McIntosh, a Republican who won the seat narrowly and within months became one of Newt Gingrich's key political operatives. McIntosh was born in California, moved to Indiana when his mother returned home after his father's death; he went to Yale and the University of Chicago Law School, where he was one of the founders of the conservative Federalist Society. He became interested in politics in 1976, at 18, when he saw the then 29-year-old Dan Quayle in his first campaign for Congress. McIntosh worked in the Reagan Justice Department and White House, then became director of the White House Council on Competitiveness headed by Vice President Quayle. After 1992, McIntosh worked for the Hudson Institute in Indianapolis and lived in Muncie, with a view of running against Sharp. He was not the only Republican interested in the race: State Auditor Ann DeVore was running. But astonishingly, her candidacy failed in February 1994 when she missed a noon deadline for filing nominating papers, though the office was down the hall from her own. Bill Frazier, Sharp's opponent in 1976, 1978 and 1980, also ran. While McIntosh showcased big-name endorsers like Robert Bork and Boyden Gray, Frazier spent $616,000 of his own money and attacked McIntosh as a Washington insider who only returned to Indiana to run. McIntosh won 43%–42%, with his biggest margin in Richmond.

Secretary of State Joe Hogsett won the Democratic nomination, getting two rivals with significant backing to leave the race after he won the convention. Hogsett was Governor Evan Bayh's campaign manager in 1988 and ran against Senator Dan Coats in 1992; he raised and spent nearly as much money as McIntosh. But McIntosh tied him to Bill Clinton—he called the 1994 crime bill "the Clinton/Hogsett hug-a-thug bill"—and the Democratic House leadership: "Joe says he's against taxes and for prayer in schools. But that first vote [that is cast at the start of each Congress] elects a speaker and chairs who are on the other side of those issues." Hogsett carried his home county, Rush County, but otherwise the vote went pretty much down straight ticket lines, and McIntosh won 54%–46%, a seat held by Democrats for 20 years.

McIntosh's expertise on regulatory matters and his fervor on the issue made him one of Speaker Newt Gingrich's key players in fulfilling the Contract With America. Regulations cost $600 billion a year, McIntosh said—"a hidden tax on family income." And "President Clinton is regulator-in-chief, leading an army of unelected bureaucrats whose sole job is to churn out red tape that destroys jobs and turns hard-working Americans into common criminals." Gingrich and Government Reform and Oversight Committee Chairman Bill Clinger created a new subcommittee called National Economic Growth, Natural Resources and Regulatory Affairs and, in a break with precedent, made the freshman McIntosh chairman. Noting that the administration had issued 4,300 regulations since the November election, McIntosh promptly proposed a moratorium on new regulations to retroactively take effect November 20. He also wrote bills requiring government agencies to make cost-benefit analyses, perform risk assessments, allow more court challenges—essentially to tie the government agencies in the same kind of red tape they have delighted in imposing on the private sector. This was complex, high-stakes stuff, lobbied heavily on all sides and attendant with political risks. But McIntosh, with help from Clinger and others, floor-managed the pieces of his regulatory bill to passage in the House in February 1995. It was an achievement in his first full month in office greater than what many members achieve in a political lifetime. Unlike four other Indiana Republicans, he was in complete support of the Contract With America.

McIntosh has probably got a pretty solid political base in the 2d District, where he will not always have to ask voters to cross party lines as Sharp did. But he seems less interested in a long career than in having a major impact on policy immediately, and seems to be doing so.

The People: Pop. 1990: 554,321; 43% rural; 14% age 65+; 95% White; 4% Black; 1% Hispanic origin. Voting age pop.: 416,245; 4% Black; 1% Hispanic origin. Households: 60% married couple families; 27% married couple fams. w. children; 32% college educ.; median household income: $26,185; per capita income: $12,311; median gross rent: $331; median house value: $43,000.

1992 Presidential Vote			1988 Presidential Vote		
Bush (R)	101,370	(43%)	Bush (R)	136,021	(61%)
Clinton (D)	82,008	(35%)	Dukakis (D)	88,521	(39%)
Perot (I)	50,458	(22%)			

Rep. David M. McIntosh (R)

Elected 1994; b. June 8, 1958, Oakton, CA; home, Muncie; Yale U., B.A. 1980; U. of Chicago Schl. of Law, J.D. 1983; Episcopalian; married (Ruthie).

Career: Spec. Asst. to U.S. Atty Gen., 1986–87; White House Spec. Asst. for Domestic Affairs, 1987–88; Spec. Asst., Vice Pres. Dan Quayle, 1989–91; Exec. Dir., Cncl of Competitiveness, 1989–92; Sr. Fellow, Hudson Inst., 1993–94.

DC Office: 1208 LHOB 20515, 202-225-3021. Fax: 202-225-3382.

District Offices: 2900 W. Jackson St., Muncie 47304, 317-747-5566.

Committees: *Economic & Educational Opportunities* (23rd of 24 R): Early Childhood, Youth and Families; Postsecondary Education, Training and Life-Long Learning. *Government Reform & Oversight* (14th of 27 R): National Economic Growth, Natural Resources and Regulatory Affairs (Chmn.); Postal Service.

Group Ratings and 103rd Congress Votes: Newly Elected

Key Votes of the 104th Congress

1. Congressional Compliance	Y	6. Reform Crime Grant	Y
2. Balanced Budget Amndmt.	Y	7. National Security Act	Y
3. Bar Unfunded Mandates	Y	8. Moratorium on Regs.	Y
4. Pass Line Item Veto	Y	9. Risk Assessment on Regs.	Y
5. Relax Exclusionary Rule	Y	10. Expnd. Priv. Prop. Rights	Y

11. Loser Pays Court Reform	Y
12. Product Liability Reform	*
13. Welfare Reform	Y
14. Term Limits Amndmt.	Y
15. Tax Cuts	Y

Election Results

1994 general	David M. McIntosh (R)	93,592	(54%)	($973,209)
	Joseph H. Hogsett (D)	78,241	(46%)	($794,684)
1994 primary	David M. McIntosh (R)	21,889	(43%)	
	Bill Frazier (R)	21,417	(42%)	
	Robert Marsh (R)	3,819	(8%)	
	Eddie K. Traylor (R)	3,617	(7%)	
1992 general	Philip R. Sharp (D)	130,881	(57%)	($623,400)
	William G. Frazier (R)	90,593	(40%)	($176,034)
	Other	7,821	(3%)	

THIRD DISTRICT

When Notre Dame University was founded in 1842, Catholics were still a rarity in most of America, and certainly rare on the limestone-bottomed plains of northern Indiana. This was still farm country then and South Bend no more than a crossroads on the St. Joseph River. By the 1920s, both had grown. Notre Dame, thanks to its football team, "the Fighting Irish," was the most famous Catholic university in the land, and South Bend was a significant industrial city, headquarters of Studebaker and Bendix and dozens of other factories. In the last 50 years, Notre Dame has grown in size and reputation, without giving up football; but South Bend has not done so well. Studebaker went out of business in the 1960s; other major factories closed; high-wage unionized jobs disappeared, replaced by lower-wage jobs with less protection. Elkhart, in the next county to the east, is still the nation's largest maker of "manufactured housing," i.e., trailers, and band instruments, but other plants have closed. The industrial swath from Michigan City on the Lake through South Bend to Elkhart is one of the few parts of the industrial Midwest that has suffered early 1980s-style job losses in the early 1990s.

The 3d Congressional District of Indiana has centered for decades on South Bend. This is an industrial and ethnic city—with the nation's largest percentage of Hungarian-Americans—which has long been Democratic; so is LaPorte County around Michigan City. Elkhart County, with more management people, is decidedly Republican.

The Congressman from the 3d District is Tim Roemer, a Democrat elected in 1990 over Republican John Hiler, a Reagan loyalist first elected 10 years earlier over then Democratic Whip John Brademas. Roemer grew up in South Bend and went to college in San Diego, then received a masters and Ph.D. from Notre Dame; he worked for Brademas and Arizona Senator Dennis DeConcini and is married to the daughter of Louisiana Senator Bennett Johnston, former Senate Energy Committee chairman. Roemer returned to South Bend in 1990, raised more PAC money than Hiler and sounded outsider themes with insider skill. Roemer has a moderate voting record, though more liberal on foreign affairs issues; he stresses his support of the balanced budget amendment, votes against pork barrel projects and support for much of the Contract With America. Counting the costs of the bills he has sponsored, the National Taxpayers Union Foundation rated him among the thriftiest 10% in Congress. With Republican Dick Zimmer, he has led opposition to funding of the Space Station, "not the Cinderella of NASA, but the ugly stepsister, cramming its enormous foot into the smaller NASA budget." He calls for nearly full funding of WIC, Head Start and child immunization programs.

Roemer also does a good job keeping in touch with voters. Recent job losses, which have not particularly helped other Democrats, probably help Roemer here. In 1992 and 1994, Roemer ran well ahead of his party, winning with 57% in 1992 while Bill Clinton was losing the district to George Bush. In 1994, while Republicans were carrying the area for all statewide offices, Roemer won 55%–45%, the second-best showing of any Indiana Democrat that year, and in a seat long considered marginal. Roemer's only problem is that there are no longer enough other talented political entrepreneurs in Democratic ranks to give them a majority.

The People: Pop. 1990: 554,482; 29% rural; 13% age 65+; 90% White; 7% Black; 1% Asian; 1% Other; 2% Hispanic origin. Voting age pop.: 407,598; 7% Black; 2% Hispanic origin. Households: 59% married couple families; 28% married couple fams. w. children; 37% college educ.; median household income: $29,470; per capita income: $13,385; median gross rent: $395; median house value: $55,000.

1992 Presidential Vote			1988 Presidential Vote		
Bush (R)	91,708	(42%)	Bush (R)	115,955	(58%)
Clinton (D)	82,483	(38%)	Dukakis (D)	83,789	(42%)
Perot (I)	41,358	(19%)			

Rep. Tim Roemer (D)

Elected 1990; b. Oct. 30, 1956, South Bend; home, South Bend; U. of CA at San Diego, B.A. 1979, U. of Notre Dame, M.A., 1981, Ph.D. 1985; Catholic; married (Sally).

Career: Staff Asst., U.S. Rep. John Brademas, 1980; Legis. Advisor, U.S. Sen. Dennis DeConcini, 1985–89; Instructor, American U., 1988.

DC Office: 407 CHOB 20515, 202-225-3915; Fax: 202-225-6798.

District Offices: 217 N. Main St., South Bend 46601, 219-288-3301.

Committees: *Economic & Educational Opportunities* (12th of 19 D): Oversight and Investigations; Postsecondary Education, Training and Life-Long Learning. *Science* (7th of 23 D): Energy and Environment; Space and Aeronautics.

Group Ratings

	ADA	ACLU	COPE	CFA	LCV	CON	NSI	COC	ACU	NTLC	CHC
1994	65	43	56	60	67	45	40	92	14	43	57
1993	45	—	73	80	79	59	—	55	38	—	—

National Journal Ratings

	1993 LIB — 1993 CONS		1994 LIB — 1994 CONS	
Economic	50%	— 49%	50%	— 46%
Social	46%	— 53%	52%	— 47%
Foreign	70%	— 26%	75%	— 23%

Key Votes of the 103d Congress

1. Clinton Deficit Plan	N	3. Brady Handgun Purchase	Y	5. Lmt. UN Cmnd. of Forces	N
2. NAFTA	N	4. Strike Race/Death Pnlty.	N	6. Cut Missile Funds	Y

Key Votes of the 104th Congress

1. Congressional Compliance	Y	6. Reform Crime Grant	N	11. Loser Pays Court Reform	N
2. Balanced Budget Amndmt.	Y	7. National Security Act	N	12. Product Liability Reform	Y
3. Bar Unfunded Mandates	Y	8. Moratorium on Regs.	Y	13. Welfare Reform	N
4. Pass Line Item Veto	Y	9. Risk Assessment on Regs.	Y	14. Term Limits Amndmt.	N
5. Relax Exclusionary Rule	Y	10. Expnd. Priv. Prop. Rights	Y	15. Tax Cuts	N

Election Results

1994 general	Tim Roemer (D)	72,497	(55%)	($350,594)
	Richard Burkett (R)	58,878	(45%)	($64,373)
1994 primary	Tim Roemer (D)	32,941	(86%)	
	Anthony V. Sims (D)	5,253	(14%)	
1992 general	Tim Roemer (D)	121,269	(57%)	($416,196)
	Carl H. Baxmeyer (R)	89,834	(43%)	($245,500)

FOURTH DISTRICT

The northeast corner of Indiana, in the center of flat agricultural area, can claim to be the center of Middle America. Its first settlers were of New England Yankee stock, establishing orderly communities with public schools and even colleges; they were joined by German immigrants, who built tidy farms and their own civic institutions. In the northern part of the state there are hills and lakes, and the strange swamp that is the central focus of Gene Stratton Porter's children's classic, *Girl of the Limberlost*. The one large city here, Fort Wayne, was built on flatter terrain, along the Maumee River that flows to Toledo, Ohio; it grew as a factory town, surging ahead and then falling back as large factories, often tied to the auto industry, opened and closed over the years. Now, Fort Wayne has more white collar jobs.

Politically, this area is ancestrally Republican from the Civil War years. Since the New Deal, it has sometimes veered to the Democrats in times of economic distress, and the mayoralty of Fort Wayne, the most visible local post, has alternated between the parties. This part of Indiana is also a cradle of vice presidents. Thomas Marshall, Woodrow Wilson's vice president, was born in North Manchester and practiced law in Columbia City; Dan Quayle spent his high school years and later practiced law in Huntington. Both VPs moved to the Hoosier metropolis of Indianapolis after their terms were over.

The 4th Congressional District of Indiana consists of nine counties in northeast Indiana, plus a bit of one other. It includes Fort Wayne, Huntington and Columbia City but not North Manchester. This is the district that Dan Quayle won from a Democratic incumbent in 1976 and represented for two terms; he was among the few who saw early on the potential of the anti-government, lower-taxes trend that dominated the 1980s, but was almost nowhere predicted in the 1970s. In 1980, when Quayle ran for the Senate, the 4th was won by Quayle aide Dan Coats, who in December 1988 succeeded him in the Senate. That set up a March 1989 special election which produced, as special elections early in a president's term often do, a political turnabout. The Republican candidate was Dan Heath, public safety director of Fort Wayne, whose mayor, Paul Helmke, had raised taxes. The Democrat, Jill Long, zeroed in on the tax issue, pledging not to vote to raise them. Long had lost twice, winning 39% in the 1986 Senate race against Quayle and 38% in the 1988 House race against Coats, but she ran dignified campaigns and her serious demeanor and farm background helped her win 51%.

Now the congressman is Mark Souder, a Republican who upset Long in 1994. He grew up in Grabill, 10 miles from Fort Wayne, where his Amish great-great-grandfather's family settled and started Souder's of Grabill in 1907, originally a harness shop and now a furniture store and manufacturer of store fixtures. Souder worked in the furniture business, returned to Grabill, went to work in 1984 for then-Congressman Dan Coats, as minority staff director of the Select Committee on Children, Youth and Families. In 1993 he returned to Fort Wayne and started running against Long. She was not an easy target. She voted against the Clinton budget and tax package and against NAFTA, and she won over 60% of the vote in 1990 and 1992. But Souder, who easily won the six-candidate Republican primary with 40% of the vote, raised more money and the state Republican ticket was running far ahead of the Democrats in the 4th District. The result was a 55%–44% Souder victory, sending Long to teach at the Kennedy School and keeping her name in the mix for various federal and state positions.

In the House, Souder was elected vice president of the freshman class and became one of its more outspoken advocates of change. He bluntly warned top Republicans that the leaders would be in jeopardy if they did not respond to the freshmen demand for change. He was one of only two Republicans—the other was another Hoosier freshman, John Hostettler—who voted against the balanced budget amendment, stating that "without a tax limitation provision . . . I'm skeptical of the spending cuts and certain of the tax hikes." Although Souder cast that vote as a matter of principle, it left him as something of a renegade on what became an issue demanding party loyalty. He also favors, and plans to introduce, Senator Arlen Specter's 20% flat tax with room for mortgage and charitable deductions. It is interesting to note the contrast of Souder with David McIntosh, a freshman from the district just to the south and another true-believer former top Washington aide, who moved more quickly to cast himself as a loyal insider and has been duly rewarded by Republican leaders. How will the difference play back home in Indiana?

The People: Pop. 1990: 554,577; 40% rural; 12% age 65+; 93% White; 5% Black; 1% Asian; 1% Other; 2% Hispanic origin. Voting age pop.: 396,425; 5% Black; 1% Hispanic origin. Households: 62% married couple families; 31% married couple fams. w. children; 40% college educ.; median household income: $30,859; per capita income: $13,436; median gross rent: $373; median house value: $56,200.

1992 Presidential Vote			1988 Presidential Vote		
Bush (R)	102,779	(46%)	Bush (R)	138,954	(67%)
Clinton (D)	69,292	(31%)	Dukakis (D)	68,371	(33%)
Perot (I)	49,565	(22%)			

Rep. Mark Edward Souder (R)

Elected 1994; b. July 18, 1950, Fort Wayne; home, Grabill; IN U., B.S. 1972; Notre Dame U., M.B.A. 1974; Protestant; married (Dianne).

Career: Furniture salesman, 1976–83; Staff Dir., U.S. House Select Cmte. on Children, Youth & Families, 1984–89; Legis. Dir., U.S. Sen. Dan Coats, 1989–91, Dep. Chief of Staff, 1991–93.

DC Office: 508 CHOB 20515, 202-225-4436; Fax: 202-225-3479.

District Offices: 1300 S. Harrison St., #3105, Ft. Wayne 46802, 219-424-3041.

Committees: *Economic & Educational Opportunities* (22nd of 24 R): Early Childhood, Youth and Families; Postsecondary Education, Training and Life-Long Learning. *Government Reform & Oversight* (19th of 27 R): Human Resources and Intergovernmental Affairs; National Security, International Affairs and Criminal Justice. *Small Business* (17th of 22 R): Regulation and Paperwork; Tax and Finance.

Group Ratings and 103rd Congress Votes: Newly Elected

Key Votes of the 104th Congress

1. Congressional Compliance	Y	6. Reform Crime Grant	Y	11. Loser Pays Court Reform	Y
2. Balanced Budget Amndmt.	N	7. National Security Act	Y	12. Product Liability Reform	Y
3. Bar Unfunded Mandates	Y	8. Moratorium on Regs.	Y	13. Welfare Reform	Y
4. Pass Line Item Veto	Y	9. Risk Assessment on Regs.	Y	14. Term Limits Amndmt.	Y
5. Relax Exclusionary Rule	Y	10. Expnd. Priv. Prop. Rights	Y	15. Tax Cuts	Y

Election Results

1994 general	Mark Edward Souder (R).	88,584	(55%)	($422,161)
	Jill L. Long (D).	71,235	(45%)	($410,299)
1994 primary	Mark Edward Souder (R).	17,948	(40%)	
	Mike Loomis (R)	8,359	(18%)	
	Bob Sedlmeyer (R).	7,344	(16%)	
	Denny Wright (R).	6,921	(15%)	
	Donna Kay Hagen (R)	2,543	(6%)	
	Michael A. Ripley (R)	2,111	(5%)	
1992 general	Jill Long (D)	134,907	(62%)	($346,011)
	Charles W. (Chuck) Pierson (R).	82,468	(38%)	($6,489)

FIFTH DISTRICT

Across the plains of northern Indiana runs the Hoosier Heartland Corridor—the HHC, a publicist's name for U.S. 24 as it runs west from Fort Wayne along the Wabash River through Wabash, Peru and Logansport, and then overland toward the Illinois prairie. Scattered on the major east-west railroad and highway lines that connect the East Coast and Chicago, the Hoosier Heartland's small cities and large towns display a geometric order that bespeaks virtues considered peculiarly American. And if they suffer from layoffs and unemployment, people here remain confident that most Americans are competent, decent, sensible people who will do the right thing in time of crisis. This is a part of America with little immigrant heritage from the early waves of immigration, relatively few blacks, and only a handful of the more recent Latin and Asian immigrants. Basic values have not been shaken so much here as in other parts of the nation: this area has one of the nation's highest percentages of households with families, married couples and children. It is also a place that has given America such icons as James Dean, who grew up in Fairmount (and would be in his 60s today if he had not smashed up his Porsche near the Pacific), and Cole Porter, who grew up in Peru.

The 5th Congressional District of Indiana occupies most of the land on either side of the HHC. There are no big cities within the district: it just skirts Indianapolis, Fort Wayne, South Bend and Gary. And, though farming is important here, factories employ many more people. There are big auto company factories in Marion and Kokomo (also the birthplace of stainless steel). Since the Civil War, this has mostly been Republican country, and the western part of the district was the home base of House Minority Leader (1959–65) Charles Halleck. But in much of the 1970s and 1980s Democrats were competitive.

The 5th District's congressman today is Steve Buyer (pronounced BOOyer), a Republican elected in 1992, defeating one of those natural-born Democratic politicos who for many years were responsible for their party's continuing majorities in the House. That was Jim Jontz, elected in 1974, at 22, to the legislature and in 1986 to the House; his resounding defeat in the 1994 Senate race suggests his perky, energetic Democratic politics has lost its appeal. Buyer grew up in White County, graduated from The Citadel and served in the Army, worked in Indianapolis and started a family law practice in Monticello, where he joined all the civic organizations. A major in the military reserves, he was called to active duty in fall 1990, serving as legal adviser at a prisoner-of-war camp in the Persian Gulf. Buyer was enraged that two-thirds of House Democrats, including Jontz, voted against the war. After he returned to Indiana, where he was White County Republican chairman, he began appearing in uniform around the Hoosier Heartland, attacking Jontz on his Gulf war stand. In October 1991, Buyer met with all of Jontz's former opponents, and then launched his campaign. By early 1992, as economic recovery stalled and interest in the Gulf war slackened, Buyer switched attacks to the "corruption" of the House bank and post office, calling for term limits and application of laws passed by Congress to Congress itself. He attacked Jontz for spending too much time protecting the spotted owl to the detriment of the timber industry—and American jobs—and for switching from the Veterans' Affairs Committee to Resources to do so. (According to a study by the Center for Public Integrity, Buyer was the top House recipient of timber industry PAC funds from 1991 to 1994, which is a signal of how much that industry wanted to replace Jontz.) Buyer won 51%–49%, carrying the Hoosier Heartland but losing counties at the edge of the district.

This result turned out to be a kind of preview of the 1994 elections. Buyer smoothed some of his rough rhetorical edges and compiled one of the most conservative voting records in the House. He got seats on the National Security and Veterans' Affairs Committees; he worked to protect Grissom Air Force Base near Peru from closure and argued in support of the existence of Gulf war syndrome. In 1994, Buyer was opposed by Kokomo Sheriff J. D. Beatty, who was invited to the White House for the signing of the 1994 crime bill which Buyer had voted against. Despite early Democratic optimism, Buyer won 70%–28%.

In the 104th Congress, Buyer is now chairman of the Veterans' Affairs Subcommittee on Education, Training, Employment and Housing where he is working closely with California Representative Maxine Waters to help veterans find work in the private sector. Noting that his district will receive between 1 and 1.5 million tons of out-of-state trash, Buyer introduced interstate waste legislation with Senator Dan Coats. In what may be a reflection of his background as a lawyer, Buyer supported all but the court-reform piece of the Contract With America.

The People: Pop. 1990: 554,240; 58% rural; 13% age 65+; 97% White; 2% Black; 1% Hispanic origin. Voting age pop.: 402,996; 2% Black; 1% Hispanic origin. Households: 64% married couple families; 30% married couple fams. w. children; 31% college educ.; median household income: $27,893; per capita income: $12,252; median gross rent: $335; median house value: $46,400.

1992 Presidential Vote		
Bush (R)	103,124	(45%)
Clinton (D)	70,891	(31%)
Perot (I)	52,354	(23%)

1988 Presidential Vote		
Bush (R)	138,464	(64%)
Dukakis (D)	77,198	(36%)

Rep. Steve Buyer (R)

Elected 1992; b. Nov. 26, 1958, Rensselaer; home, Monticello; The Citadel, B.S. 1980; Valparaiso U. Law Schl., J.D. 1984; Methodist; married (Joni).

Career: Army, 1984–87, 1990–91 (Persian Gulf); Army Reserves, 1980–84, 1988–present; IN Dep. Atty. Gen., 1987–88; Vice Chmn., White Cnty. Repub. Party, 1988–90; Practicing atty., 1988–92.

DC Office: 326 CHOB 20515, 202-225-5037.

District Offices: 120 E. Mulberry St., #106, Kokomo 46901, 317-454-7551; 204-A N. Main St., Monticello 47960, 219-583-9819.

Committees: *National Security* (12th of 30 R): Military Personnel; Military Procurement. *Judiciary* (13th of 20 R): Crime. *Veterans' Affairs* (7th of 18 R): Education, Training, Employment and Housing (Chmn.).

Group Ratings

	ADA	ACLU	COPE	CFA	LCV	CON	NSI	COC	ACU	NTLC	CHC
1994	0	14	22	20	0	65	100	100	100	96	93
1993	0	—	17	10	14	69	—	100	100	—	—

National Journal Ratings

	1993 LIB — 1993 CONS		1994 LIB — 1994 CONS	
Economic	0% —	88%	0% —	80%
Social	11% —	82%	0% —	89%
Foreign	9% —	85%	0% —	88%

Key Votes of the 103d Congress

1. Clinton Deficit Plan	N	3. Brady Handgun Purchase	N	5. Lmt. UN Cmnd. of Forces	Y
2. NAFTA	Y	4. Strike Race/Death Pnlty.	Y	6. Cut Missile Funds	N

Key Votes of the 104th Congress

1. Congressional Compliance	Y	6. Reform Crime Grant	Y	11. Loser Pays Court Reform	N
2. Balanced Budget Amndmt.	Y	7. National Security Act	Y	12. Product Liability Reform	Y
3. Bar Unfunded Mandates	Y	8. Moratorium on Regs.	Y	13. Welfare Reform	Y
4. Pass Line Item Veto	Y	9. Risk Assessment on Regs.	Y	14. Term Limits Amndmt.	Y
5. Relax Exclusionary Rule	Y	10. Expnd. Priv. Prop. Rights	Y	15. Tax Cuts	Y

Election Results

1994 general	Steve Buyer (R)	111,031	(70%)	($501,287)
	J.D. Beatty (D)	45,224	(28%)	($181,780)
	Others	3,403	(2%)	
1994 primary	Steve Buyer (R)	unopposed		
1992 general	Steve Buyer (R)	111,116	(51%)	($392,922)
	James Jontz (D)	105,209	(49%)	($583,029)

SIXTH DISTRICT

Indianapolis is one of America's most symmetric cities, sited in almost the exact center of Indiana, centered on Monument Circle with eight avenues radiating like wheel spokes, with the city occupying most of almost perfectly square Marion County. In the seven surrounding suburban counties, the irregularities of the physical landscape and the asymmetries of the original settlers' boundaries intrude; but a respected order has been established here. The more affluent areas are typically farther out, starting on the north side somewhere north of the home of Benjamin Harrison, Indiana's one president, and the 1920s-era Governor's Mansion built on North Meridian Street by the same man who more or less invented the gas station. Here are comfortable in-town neighborhoods built in the 1940s and 1950s, the cul-de-sac subdivisions and condominiums of the 1970s and 1980s, and new developments set out on hills in the once rural counties beyond.

The 6th Congressional District of Indiana includes most of the suburban territory around the core of Indianapolis, which forms the 10th District. The exception is to the west of the city, where most of Hancock and Boone Counties are in the 7th District. But the 6th includes the north side of Indianapolis and the affluent Hamilton County suburbs of Carmel, where Dan and Marilyn Quayle now reside, and Fishers; it includes Hancock County to the east and takes in the less affluent but still conservative suburban territory to the south. This is a very heavily Republican area, by far the most Republican in Indiana and indeed one of the most Republican districts in the country.

The congressman from the 6th District is Dan Burton, an active and enthusiastic Republican who has been running for office since he was in his 20s. He had a rough childhood and spent some time in the county guardian's home; he enlisted in the Army at 18 and never finished college. A hearty, bluff backslapper, he made his way up selling insurance. He was elected to the Indiana House in 1966, 1976 and 1978 and to the Indiana Senate in 1968 and 1980; he lost races for Congress in 1970 and 1972 and was first elected to the House in 1982 when the legislature created this heavily Republican suburban seat.

Burton is an enthusiastic conservative, confrontation-minded long before most of today's feisty young House Republicans appeared on the scene (or started shaving). He has served on the International Relations Committee and had the satisfaction of seeing his hard-line opposition to the Soviet Union crowned with success, and his critical approach to most sub-Saharan African regimes vindicated. He opposed sanctions on South Africa, and when Nelson Mandela came to the United States, Burton questioned why Mandela supported Yasir Arafat, Fidel Castro and Muammar Qaddafi. Burton, previously the ranking Republican on the Africa Subcommittee, was for years a strong backer of UNITA in Angola and Renamo in Mozambique; he seems to have as much faith in them as the leftish Democrats who have chaired the subcommittee have had in their opponents. While he now chairs the Western Hemisphere Subcommittee, had the new Republican majority not eliminated the old Post Office and Civil Service Committee, Burton probably would have been its chairman.

If Burton has been a precursor of today's Contract With America Republicans, he has not always been a steady leader, and his enthusiasm can become excitability. He has been a thorn in the side generally of the Clinton Administration, and the Whitewater investigation in particular, railing in a speech on the House floor in 1994 about the circumstances surrounding White House Deputy Counsel Vince Foster's death. In 1993, he became chairman of the Republican Study Committee, with 130 of the then-176 Republicans as members. But Newt Gingrich, then Minority Whip, was really providing the guidance for the party on issues, strategies and tactics. Burton's judgment on issues has been erratic. If he has been vindicated in many of his foreign policy stands and on the Catastrophic Healthcare Act, his proposal for universal mandatory AIDS testing is now seen as simply nonsense. If he showed political foresight in lambasting George Bush for breaking his no-new-taxes pledge, he brought forward many spending cut provisions which lost by wide margins. He has not been part of the inner circles of the Republican leadership.

Burton has been reelected easily in the 6th District, in 1994 with 77% of the vote. There were rumors in 1994 that Brose McVey, a former aide to Senator Dan Coats would run against Burton in the primary. But he did not, and Burton ended the 1994 race with $741,000 cash on hand, one of the highest figures in Congress; any opponent must start out that far behind. There was talk he would run for governor in 1996, but he seems happy serving in the Republican House.

The People: Pop. 1990: 553,865; 24% rural; 11% age 65+; 98% White; 1% Black; 1% Asian; 1% Hispanic origin. Voting age pop.: 407,482; 1% Black; 1% Hispanic origin. Households: 65% married couple families; 32% married couple fams. w. children; 52% college educ.; median household income: $38,644; per capita income: $17,971; median gross rent: $452; median house value: $81,200.

1992 Presidential Vote		
Bush (R)	153,269	(57%)
Clinton (D)	61,030	(23%)
Perot (I)	54,909	(20%)

1988 Presidential Vote		
Bush (R)	183,820	(75%)
Dukakis (D)	62,023	(25%)

Rep. Dan Burton (R)

Elected 1982; b. June 21, 1938, Indianapolis; home, Indianapolis; IN U., 1958–59, Cincinnati Bible Seminary, 1959–60; Protestant; married (Barbara).

Career: Army, 1956–57, Army Reserves, 1958–63; Founder, Dan Burton Insurance Agency, 1968; IN House of Reps., 1966–68, 1976–80; IN Senate, 1968–70, 1980–82.

DC Office: 2411 RHOB 20515, 202-225-2276; Fax: 202-225-0016.

District Offices: 8900 Keystone-at-the-Crossing, #1050, Indianapolis 46240, 317-848-0201; and 435 E. Main St., #J, Greenwood 46142, 317-882-3640.

Committees: *International Relations* (8th of 23 R): Asia and the Pacific; Western Hemisphere (Chmn.). *Government Reform & Oversight* (3rd of 27 R): Civil Service.

Group Ratings

	ADA	ACLU	COPE	CFA	LCV	CON	NSI	COC	ACU	NTLC	CHC
1994	0	13	22	0	6	74	100	73	100	96	100
1993	10	—	17	10	14	32	—	91	100	—	—

National Journal Ratings

	1993 LIB	—	1993 CONS	1994 LIB	—	1994 CONS
Economic	20%	—	77%	0%	—	80%
Social	11%	—	82%	0%	—	89%
Foreign	9%	—	85%	0%	—	88%

Key Votes of the 103d Congress

1. Clinton Deficit Plan	N	3. Brady Handgun Purchase	N	5. Lmt. UN Cmnd. of Forces	Y
2. NAFTA	N	4. Strike Race/Death Pnlty.	Y	6. Cut Missile Funds	N

Key Votes of the 104th Congress

1. Congressional Compliance	Y	6. Reform Crime Grant	Y	11. Loser Pays Court Reform	Y
2. Balanced Budget Amndmt.	Y	7. National Security Act	Y	12. Product Liability Reform	Y
3. Bar Unfunded Mandates	Y	8. Moratorium on Regs.	Y	13. Welfare Reform	Y
4. Pass Line Item Veto	Y	9. Risk Assessment on Regs.	Y	14. Term Limits Amndmt.	Y
5. Relax Exclusionary Rule	Y	10. Expnd. Priv. Prop. Rights	Y	15. Tax Cuts	Y

Election Results

1994 general	Dan Burton (R)......................	136,876	(77%)	($455,095)
	Natalie M. Bruner (D)	40,815	(23%)	
1994 primary	Dan Burton (R).......................	61,147	(87%)	
	George B. Tintera (R).................	9,004	(13%)	
1992 general	Dan Burton (R)......................	186,499	(72%)	($407,055)
	Natalie M. Bruner (D)	71,952	(28%)	($32,153)

SEVENTH DISTRICT

Of the railroad passenger trains that used to run on the lines criss-crossing the township grids of the Midwest, none had a more romantic name than the Wabash Cannonball that rumbled along the Wabash River, across the rolling farmland of northern Indiana on its way from Detroit to St. Louis, following the curve of the river and then crossing the old National Road, now U.S. 40, which runs in a nearly straight line from Indianapolis to St. Louis. The landscape here is some of the most prosaic in the United States, mostly flat, with neat farms and frame-bungalowed towns, looking unchanged from years ago. Today the Cannonball no longer runs; people bounce around the Midwest on commuter airlines or fly from one hub city to another; and the National Road and U.S. 40 have been replaced for through traffic by Interstate 70.

The 7th Congressional District of Indiana covers much of the routes of the Wabash Cannonball and the National Road in western Indiana, starting from the Indianapolis city limits. Its two largest towns are quite different in character. Terre Haute is an old manufacturing town, the boyhood home of Socialist Eugene Debs, and now has a Sony compact disc plant. It has not gained population in years and tends to vote Democratic—a lonely stand in central Indiana. The other major town is Lafayette, where the main business is Purdue University, Indiana's land-grant college and the alma mater of C-SPAN founder Brian Lamb. Growing and prosperous, Lafayette tends to vote Republican.

The congressman from the 7th District is John Myers, third in seniority among House Republicans (after Jimmy Quillen and Joseph McDade), who has survived many electoral perils, but despite his seniority was passed over for the chairmanship of the Appropriations Committee by Speaker Newt Gingrich. Like most Republican congressmen over the last century, Myers comes from a small town (Covington, on the Wabash 30 miles north of Terre Haute) where he was a bank officer entwined in local economic and civic affairs. He first won the seat in 1966, though it had been redistricted to elect a Democrat; he has held it through several redistrictings and in all types of political years. His voting record on cultural and foreign issues is entirely conservative; on economics, he is not always market oriented, and sometimes supports increased government spending. He is proud of having co-sponsored the Mammography Quality Standards Act of 1992, introducing Dan Coats's bill to let states stop out-of-state trash and a bill to lower taxes on capital gains for senior citizens.

Like so many old-time Republicans, especially those on Appropriations, Myers tends to be accommodationist, cooperating over the years with Democrats in return for some concessions, assuming that he was in a perpetual minority, settling disputes by giving both sides money. For years he was ranking minority member—and is now chairman—of the Energy and Water Development Subcommittee, a key dispenser of public works and dams and other local projects avidly sought by many members, working closely with Chairman Tom Bevill to maintain support for subcommittee bills and priorities. Their enemies include economizers, environmentalists and, often, the authorizing Transportation and Infrastructure Committee, the Appropriations subcommittee's rival as proprietor of the pork barrel. He was one of the few Republicans who opposed the Penny-Kasich budget cuts, and sent a letter to colleagues warning of local projects that might get axed if Penny-Kasich passed. That helps to explain why Gingrich looked elsewhere for a chairman of the full committee.

Myers can be tough and aggressive. In the late 1980s, he was the ranking Republican on the House Ethics Committee when it investigated Speaker Jim Wright. Myers was instrumental in hiring as chief counsel Richard Phelan, a Chicago lawyer and a Democrat (and now Cook County board president) who was fiercely critical of Wright; Myers was of the same mind, and showed steely determination to condemn Wright for what he felt were violations of House rules.

In the 1992 primary, retired farmer Charles Metzger had a rather high 39%, but Myers won, and beat a pro-choice Democratic woman in the general, with 59%. Those showings may have stimulated the talk that he might retire and the opposition Myers faced in 1994. With four Republican primary opponents, Myers won with 54%, to 22% for the next. In the general, he faced Greencastle Mayor Mike Harmless, whom Myers had appointed to West Point in 1967, and who made all the appropriate anti-incumbent sounds for the 1994 campaign. Harmless called for a part-time Congress, boasted of balancing city budgets and attracting business, and always carried General Colin Powell's "13 Rules" for effectiveness on a 3x5 card in his pocket. But central Indiana voters simply did not want to elect a Democrat or to repudiate a longtime representative. Myers won 65%–35%, carrying even Harmless's home county by that margin.

But Myers's more aggressive showing was not enough after Republicans won their majority in

November 1994. He knew that McDade, under indictment, would not be Appropriations chairman, and surely wanted the job himself. But Gingrich believed Myers would continue accommodating committee Democrats and would be unwilling to make the sharp cuts and zero-outs of Gingrich's ultimate choice, Bob Livingston of Louisiana. So in November, Gingrich simply announced that Livingston would be chairman, confident he had the votes in the Republican Conference to back him up. Myers, evidently also confident Gingrich had the votes, made clear that he was unhappy but he did not fight the decision. Myers did become chairman of the Energy and Water Development Subcommittee, but even there, Gingrich made it plain he wanted all subcommittees to meet their quota of spending cuts. (A loyal appropriator, Myers voted against the line-item veto, which targeted spending excesses.) Under these circumstances, it isn't clear whether Myers will run again in 1996, when he will have served 30 years and turns 69.

The People: Pop. 1990: 554,500; 48% rural; 12% age 65+; 96% White; 2% Black; 1% Asian; 1% Hispanic origin. Voting age pop.: 418,275; 2% Black; 1% Hispanic origin. Households: 62% married couple families; 29% married couple fams. w. children; 39% college educ.; median household income: $28,080; per capita income: $12,536; median gross rent: $358; median house value: $54,300.

1992 Presidential Vote			1988 Presidential Vote		
Bush (R)	103,801	(46%)	Bush (R)	134,308	(64%)
Clinton (D)	71,273	(32%)	Dukakis (D)	74,254	(36%)
Perot (I)	48,916	(22%)			

Rep. John T. Myers (R)

Elected 1966; b. Feb. 8, 1927, Covington; home, Covington; IN St. U., B.S. 1951; Episcopalian; married (Carol).

Career: Army, 1945–46 (WWII); Cashier & Trust Officer, Foundation Trust Co., 1954–66.

DC Office: 2372 RHOB 20515, 202-225-5805; Fax: 202-225-1649.

District Offices: 107 Fed. Bldg., Terre Haute 47808, 812-238-1619; and 107 Halleck Fed. Bldg., Lafayette 47901, 317-423-1661.

Committees: *Appropriations* (3rd of 32 R): Agriculture, Rural Development, FDA, and Related Agencies; Energy and Water Development (Chmn.); Military Construction.

Group Ratings

	ADA	ACLU	COPE	CFA	LCV	CON	NSI	COC	ACU	NTLC	CHC
1994	5	18	33	20	6	61	90	83	100	88	93
1993	10	—	36	20	14	50	—	80	91	—	—

National Journal Ratings

	1993 LIB — 1993 CONS		1994 LIB — 1994 CONS	
Economic	37%	— 62%	26%	— 70%
Social	19%	— 77%	0%	— 89%
Foreign	17%	— 76%	0%	— 88%

Key Votes of the 103d Congress

1. Clinton Deficit Plan	N	3. Brady Handgun Purchase N	5. Lmt. UN Cmnd. of Forces Y
2. NAFTA	N	4. Strike Race/Death Pnlty. Y	6. Cut Missile Funds N

Key Votes of the 104th Congress

1. Congressional Compliance Y	6. Reform Crime Grant Y	11. Loser Pays Court Reform Y
2. Balanced Budget Amndmt. Y	7. National Security Act Y	12. Product Liability Reform Y
3. Bar Unfunded Mandates Y	8. Moratorium on Regs. Y	13. Welfare Reform Y
4. Pass Line Item Veto N	9. Risk Assessment on Regs. Y	14. Term Limits Amndmt. N
5. Relax Exclusionary Rule Y	10. Expnd. Priv. Prop. Rights Y	15. Tax Cuts Y

Election Results

1994 general	John T. Myers (R)...................	104,359	(65%)	($543,967)
	Michael M. Harmless (D)	55,941	(35%)	($480,693)
1994 primary	John T. Meyers (R)...................	33,661	(54%)	
	Richard (Dick) Thompson (R)	14,015	(22%)	
	Dan L. Pool (R)	11,282	(18%)	
	Others	3,748	(6%)	
1992 general	John T. Myers (R)...................	129,189	(59%)	($369,882)
	Ellen E. Wedum (D).................	88,005	(41%)	($51,245)

EIGHTH DISTRICT

"Evansville," wrote John Bartlow Martin in 1947, "called the Pocket City (though not by loyal natives), is the capital of a tri-state area comprising the neglected tag ends of Indiana, Kentucky and Illinois." It was a factory town then, building car parts and refrigerators, drawing workers from Kentucky, Tennessee and the picturesque but not very fertile hills of southern Indiana. It was a town of hard-bitten politics, with plenty of partisan conflict. This was the boyhood home of Senator William Jenner, a McCarthy ally who once said General George Marshall would sell out his grandmother to the Communists, and the political base of Senator Vance Hartke, who inspired the not-quite-fair joke that Indiana had two senators, "Bayh and Bought."

Evansville is one of two major focuses of the 8th Congressional District of Indiana which, within irregular borders, covers most of the southwest portion of the state. The other is Bloomington, quite a different place, the home of Indiana University and a limestone quarrying center. This southwest corner of Indiana was the first part of the state settled by whites. Vincennes, now a small town on the banks of the Wabash River, was once the metropolis of Indiana, and the Scottish philanthropist and visionary, Robert Owen, established the town of New Harmony downstream. Owen's son was the first congressman from the area, elected in 1842 and 1844. Since then, it has been represented by both parties, at one point in the 1970s electing four different congressmen in four successive elections, the only congressional district to do so in that decade. The overall partisan tradition here has been Democratic since the Civil War, but the Democrats' cultural liberalism has cost them votes.

The Congressman from the 8th District is John Hostettler, elected in 1994, one of the young Contract With America Republicans who has worked to change the House almost beyond recognition. He beat Frank McCloskey, a Democrat who held the seat insecurely for 12 years. Once a dovish Bloomington mayor who ended up a leading advocate of bombing the Serbs, McCloskey was declared the loser by Indiana state officials in the 1984 election, but was seated in a partisan vote by the House in 1985. Hostettler is from the Evansville area; in 1994 he was a Southern Indiana Gas & Electric Company engineer, who at 33 had never run for office before. He was one of six Republican candidates in the 8th and had support from anti-abortion and Christian fundamentalist groups; he also had obvious regional strength in the western edge of the district, along the Wabash. He won the primary with 35%, to 23% for his next competitor.

In the general, Hostettler refused to take PAC money; McCloskey collected $368,000 of it, and outspent the Republican $565,000 to $309,000. In contrast, Hostettler's biggest fund raiser was a $100-per-family fried chicken dinner with Marilyn Quayle. Hostettler attacked McCloskey on taxes, gay rights, gun control, environment, school prayer and for having 65 overdrafts at the House bank, and constantly referred to him as Frank McClinton. McCloskey accused Hostettler of wanting to outlaw all abortions and called him John McGingrich. McCloskey's strategy was puzzling. At first he featured his opposition to Clinton Administration Bosnia policy; then he invited House Democratic leaders Dick Gephardt and David Bonior to campaign for him. Democratic National Chairman David Wilhelm listed Hostettler as one of 10 Republican challengers on "the extreme right;" eight of the 10 won. Hostettler was one of them. McCloskey carried Evansville and Bloomington by microscopic margins. But Hostettler carried most of the rural counties and won 52%–48%.

In the House, Hostettler serves on the National Security and Agriculture Committees, and he floor-managed an amendment to move toward zeroing out farm subsidies. Speaker Newt Gingrich, however, already had agreed with Agriculture Committee Chairman Pat Roberts of Kansas to preserve them, and so Hostettler led only a small band of purists. A true constitutional conservative, Hostettler opposed the balanced budget amendment, as he opposes changing the Constitution except where there is no alternative—the only Republican taking such a principled, if politically dubious, position. For the same reason, he opposed term limits, and opinion in line with the Supreme Court.

The People: Pop. 1990: 554,347; 42% rural; 14% age 65+; 96% White; 3% Black; 1% Asian; 1% Hispanic origin. Voting age pop.: 421,666; 3% Black. Households: 58% married couple families; 27% married couple fams. w. children; 37% college educ.; median household income: $25,242; per capita income: $12,153; median gross rent: $341; median house value: $48,800.

1992 Presidential Vote			1988 Presidential Vote		
Clinton (D)	103,844	(42%)	Bush (R)	129,324	(57%)
Bush (R)	97,062	(40%)	Dukakis (D)	98,539	(43%)
Perot (I)	43,177	(18%)			

Rep. John N. Hostettler (R)

Elected 1994; b. July 19, 1961, Evansville; home, Wadesville; Rose-Hulman Inst. of Tech., B.S. 1983; Baptist; married (Elizabeth).

Career: Mechanical Engineer, S. Indiana Gas & Electric Co., 1983–94.

DC Office: 1404 LHOB 20515, 202-225-4636; Fax: 202-225-3284.

District Offices: 101 M.L.K. Blvd., #124, Evansville 47708, 812-465-6484; and 120 W. 7th St., #208, Bloomington 47404, 812-334-1111.

Committees: *Agriculture* (21st of 27 R): Department Operations, Nutrition and Foreign Agriculture; Resource Conservation, Research and Forestry. *National Security* (23rd of 30 R): Military Installations and Facilities; Military Research and Development.

Group Ratings and 103rd Congress Votes: Newly Elected

Key Votes of the 104th Congress

1. Congressional Compliance	Y	6. Reform Crime Grant	Y
2. Balanced Budget Amndmt.	N	7. National Security Act	Y
3. Bar Unfunded Mandates	Y	8. Moratorium on Regs.	Y
4. Pass Line Item Veto	Y	9. Risk Assessment on Regs.	Y
5. Relax Exclusionary Rule	Y	10. Expnd. Priv. Prop. Rights	Y

11. Loser Pays Court Reform	Y
12. Product Liability Reform	Y
13. Welfare Reform	Y
14. Term Limits Amndmt.	N
15. Tax Cuts	Y

Election Results

1994 general	John N. Hostettler (R)	93,529	(52%)	($309,484)
	Frank McCloskey (D)	84,857	(48%)	($565,810)
1994 primary	John N. Hostettler (R)	12,557	(35%)	
	Howard Hubler (R)	8,213	(23%)	
	Leslie C. Shively (R)	6,466	(18%)	
	Phyllis N. Heuring (R)	4,036	(11%)	
	Jeff Devine (R)	3,563	(10%)	
	Others	1,156	(3%)	
1992 general	Frank McCloskey (D)	125,244	(53%)	($512,852)
	Richard Mourdock (R)	108,054	(45%)	($248,152)
	Others	5,099	(2%)	

NINTH DISTRICT

The southeastern corner of Indiana, something of a backwater now, was a busy place when white settlers rafted down the Ohio River in the early 19th Century. They were mostly southerners, "Butternuts," from across the river in Kentucky or over the mountains in Virginia, and they built the first large Indiana settlements. Today, you can see their work in the marvelous old buildings of Madison, now quiet but once one of the busiest ports on the Ohio River. Farther down the river is Corydon, from 1816 to 1825 the state capital. The early 19th Century buildings here have been well preserved because these towns were bypassed first by the railroads, then by U.S. routes and interstate highways, and they certainly are remote from major airports. The river is still an artery of commerce, but utilitarian barges have replaced steamers.

Butternut Indiana retained its affection for things southern into the Civil War and beyond. Local politician Jesse Bright was expelled from the U.S. Senate in 1862 for "supporting the rebellion." To this day, the hills along the Ohio River typically vote Democratic, as do the Indiana suburbs of Louisville. But to the east Indiana is now filling up with migrants from Cincinnati—a Yankee and German abolitionist bastion in Jesse Bright's time, an overwhelmingly Republican stronghold in ours—who are moving the southeast corner of Indiana away from its ancestral party.

The 9th Congressional District of Indiana is made up of most of the state's Ohio River counties and an oddly shaped collection of lightly populated counties to the north. Ancestrally Democratic, culturally conservative, recently Republican, idiosyncratically creative—like Columbus, where leading citizen J. Irwin Miller commissioned nationally recognized modern architects to design most of its public and many of its private buildings—this is a mixed political constituency.

For three decades, this district and its predecessors—the boundaries have shifted, often for political reasons—has been represented by Lee Hamilton, a Democrat elected in the 1964 anti-Barry Goldwater landslide and for two years chairman of the House International Relations Committee. Hamilton grew up in Evansville, studied in DePauw, postwar Germany and Indiana University, worked for a while for a big Chicago law firm but decided that he liked small town life and moved to Columbus; after eight years of law practice, he ran for the House in 1964, and was elected. Hamilton seems folksy and without urban savvy, has a strong intellect and capacity for hard work plus a sense of moral imperative. For a decade until the 1994 election, he was one of the leaders of the House—chairman of the Intelligence Committee in 1985–87; House chairman of the Iran-contra committee in 1987–88, in which capacity he sternly denounced Oliver North and the Reagan Administration; chairman of the Joint Economic Committee in 1989–90; chairman of International Relations in 1993–95. With Senator David Boren, he was appointed in 1992 to be co-chairman of the Joint Committee on the Organization of Congress, which he had suggested creating. Its recommendations went nowhere under the Democratic majority, a source of considerable frustration to Hamilton, but they became a useful starting point for the new Republican leaders. On economics, Hamilton urged higher taxes to reduce the deficit well before the 1990 budget summit and 1993 Clinton budget and tax package. Hamilton co-sponsored a bill to put the Treasury Secretary on the Federal Reserve Board, publish the Fed's budget, and subject it to tough GAO audits—attempts to make the Fed politically more responsive, with possible inflationary effects, and a classic small town cause. After the Iran-contra hearings made him well known nationally, Hamilton was seriously considered by both Michael Dukakis and Bill Clinton for the vice presidential nomination and was mentioned as a possible Clinton secretary of state.

The House, in foreign affairs, which Hamilton came to was something like Columbus, Indiana, in commerce: graced with fine architecture, but off the beaten track. It had its share of strong intellects, but it was largely ignored in favor of the more glamorous (treaty-ratifying and appointment-confirming) Senate. Hamilton has worked hard to change that. And with his moderate voting record—almost perfectly at the midpoint of the House in the 103d Congress on economic, cultural and foreign issues according to *National Journal*—he has usually provided a moderate rationale for the liberal foreign policy impulses of many House Democrats.

In the 1980s, Hamilton was opposed to contra aid and other help for anti-Communists in Latin America. He was strongly anti-administration on Iran-contra and his grant of immunity to leading witnesses ended up preventing their criminal prosecution. So too in the 1990s: he strongly opposed the Gulf war resolution and his dire predictions of the consequences of the Gulf war—massive American casualties, a fracturing of the allied coalition, rising anti-American-ism—almost entirely failed to come true. He conducted an investigation of the absurd "October surprise" theory in 1992 and exonerated President Bush of all involvement in July, though only after the election did he confirm that the conspiracy theory had no basis whatsoever.

In the post-Cold War world, Hamilton has tended to see weapons proliferation as a major problem, and the promotion of democracy, free markets and human rights as secondary. This is consistent with his long-term views: in the Middle East, for example, he was long considered evenhanded, certainly not tilting toward Israel, despite some Arab countries' dismal records on human rights. He sees protection of the environment as a major foreign policy goal, and also "the fight against hunger, disease and rapid population growth." In the Clinton years, Hamilton cautiously favored U.S. involvement in the former Yugoslavia and in February 1993, he called American participation in a multinational peacekeeping force "a prudent commitment of American power." He supported the Clinton (and Bush) stand on continuing trade ties to China and in 1994 called for delinking most favored nation status and human rights. He was not enthusiastic about intervention in Haiti. He opposed the trade embargo on Cuba. In October 1994, Hamilton showed himself the loyalist by listing Clinton foreign policy successes—Russia, the Middle East, Haiti, Asia, trade.

For years Hamilton had no serious opposition in the 9th District. In 1992 Republican Michael Bailey attracted attention by running television ads showing dead fetuses. This did not win him many votes—Hamilton won 70%–30%—but it was significant as the first time a Hamilton opponent ran TV ads. Then came 1994. State Senator Jean Leising beat Bailey 57%–35% in the Republican primary and began running a serious, aggressive campaign against Hamilton. She was anti-abortion, anti-gun control, pro-welfare reform. She mocked Hamilton's failure to achieve the House reforms he championed. "I'm so tired of hearing about Lee Hamilton and congressional reform. The great reformer fails with all his clout and experience." Hamilton conceded the Democratic House hadn't acted. He outspent Leising 2–1, but won by only 52%–48%, his lowest margin in all his 30 years. Leising carried the eastern counties, where new residents from the Cincinnati area increased turnout by up to 37% and voted Republican by as much as 63%. With Leising saying that she plans to run again, this is a district that could easily be seriously contested in 1996. Though he faces pressure from party leaders to seek another term, there is some question whether Hamilton, who has never been in the minority before and turns 65 that year, will run for reelection.

The People: Pop. 1990: 554,516; 59% rural; 13% age 65+; 98% White; 2% Black. Voting age pop.: 404,376; 2% Black. Households: 64% married couple families; 31% married couple fams. w. children; 29% college educ.; median household income: $26,900; per capita income: $11,727; median gross rent: $325; median house value: $49,200.

1992 Presidential Vote

Clinton (D)	97,970	(41%)
Bush (R)	97,412	(40%)
Perot (I)	44,839	(19%)

1988 Presidential Vote

Bush (R)	125,439	(58%)
Dukakis (D)	90,284	(42%)

Rep. Lee H. Hamilton (D)

Elected 1964; b. Apr. 20, 1931, Daytona Beach, FL; home, Nashville; DePauw U., B.A. 1952, Indiana U., J.D. 1956, Goethe U., Frankfurt, Germany, 1952–53; United Methodist; married (Nancy).

Career: Practicing atty., 1956–64; Instructor, American Banking Inst. 1960–61.

DC Office: 2314 RHOB 20515, 202-225-5315; Fax: 202-225-1101.

District Offices: 107 Fed. Ctr., 1201 E. 10th St., Jeffersonville 47130, 812-288-3999.

Committees: *International Relations* (RMM of 19 D). *Joint Economic Committee* (9th of 10 Reps.).

Group Ratings

	ADA	ACLU	COPE	CFA	LCV	CON	NSI	COC	ACU	NTLC	CHC
1994	60	43	44	60	61	36	70	67	38	43	50
1993	45	—	75	80	79	57	—	36	29	—	—

National Journal Ratings

	1993 LIB — 1993 CONS			1994 LIB — 1994 CONS		
Economic	57%	—	42%	54%	—	45%
Social	52%	—	47%	54%	—	45%
Foreign	51%	—	42%	51%	—	47%

Key Votes of the 103d Congress

1. Clinton Deficit Plan	Y	3. Brady Handgun Purchase	Y	5. Lmt. UN Cmnd. of Forces	N
2. NAFTA	Y	4. Strike Race/Death Pnlty.	N	6. Cut Missile Funds	N

Key Votes of the 104th Congress

1. Congressional Compliance	Y	6. Reform Crime Grant	N	11. Loser Pays Court Reform	N
2. Balanced Budget Amndmt.	Y	7. National Security Act	N	12. Product Liability Reform	Y
3. Bar Unfunded Mandates	Y	8. Moratorium on Regs.	Y	13. Welfare Reform	N
4. Pass Line Item Veto	N	9. Risk Assessment on Regs.	Y	14. Term Limits Amndmt.	N
5. Relax Exclusionary Rule	N	10. Expnd. Priv. Prop. Rights	Y	15. Tax Cuts	N

Election Results

1994 general	Lee H. Hamilton (D)	91,459	(52%)	($578,468)
	Jean Leising (R)	84,315	(48%)	($241,854)
1994 primary	Lee H. Hamilton (D)	67,007	(82%)	
	D. Keith Coats (D)	14,399	(18%)	
1992 general	Lee H. Hamilton (D)	160,980	(70%)	($477,591)
	Michael E. Bailey (R).	70,057	(30%)	($175,013)

TENTH DISTRICT

Indianapolis, radiating outward from the Soldiers and Sailors statue in Monument Circle, is precisely at the center of Indiana, dominating it as few other cities do a state. It is the political and governmental capital, industrial and financial center, and the intellectual center of Indiana as well. It is symmetrically laid out: just to the west of the circle is the state Capitol, to the north is the American Legion headquarters, to the east is the City-County building, to the south is the redeveloped Union Station, and the Hoosier Dome. The local papers are owned by former Vice President Dan Quayle's family, the Pulliams. Farther out is the huge and growing Indiana University Medical Center, and the state park along the creek-sized White River which is attracting new museums. Indianapolis has the world's biggest children's museum and has become one of the nation's top centers for religious conventions. In recent years, it has attracted a $1 billion United Airlines repair center and a $67 million Postal Service overnight mail hub—and the Hudson Institute, a leading conservative think tank.

Indianapolis has tried to make itself the amateur sports capital of the United States, and may have succeeded. In 1980, it started the Indiana Sports Corporation, a concept now copied by other U.S. cities. It showed off its amateur athletic facilities, probably the best in the nation, in the 1987 Pan American Games: a state-of-the-art natatorium, a track and field stadium, a velodrome for cycling, a soccer center, a horse park, plus the Hoosier Dome (renamed the RCA Dome) and Market Square Arena. And of course Indianapolis has its U.S. Track and Field Hall of Fame and the Speedway where the Indianapolis 500 is held every Memorial Day weekend. The cheerful, enthusiastic, healthful atmosphere of sports seems very much in tune with the civic tone of a state whose governor turns 40 in his second term and whose best known citizen is a former vice president known for, among other things, his athletic skill.

Politically, Indianapolis has long had robust competition, with Republicans very much ahead in national races but real battles for the offices below—a situation personified today by the eminence of Democratic Governor Evan Bayh and former Republican Vice President Dan Quayle. There is a Democratic core here, made up mostly of blacks in central city neighborhoods; Indianapolis lacks the yeasty ethnic mix of most midwestern cities, and has never had really big CIO unions nor large singles or gay communities. Almost all of this core is in the 10th Congressional District, bounded by an irregular line which runs about five miles out from Monument Circle in all directions.

The district is represented by one of the nation's quirkier and more distinctive politicians, Democrat Andy Jacobs. He is now something of an oldtimer: only five Democrats—John Dingell, Henry Gonzalez, Sam Gibbons, Sidney Yates and George Brown—served in the House before Jacobs was first elected in 1964. His service was interrupted when he lost reelection to William Hudnut in 1972; but he came back to beat Hudnut in 1974, paving the way for Hudnut's long service as mayor of Indianapolis. Jacobs is legendarily frugal: in 1974 he refused to board a plane because only first class seats were available; it crashed, killing all aboard. He translates that skinflintness into policy as well: he has supported a balanced budget constitutional amendment since 1976. He introduces a bill every term to withdraw the perquisites of former presidents. He wrote a law revoking Social Security benefits for prison inmates. He sympathizes with citizens who don't want to part with their money: he wrote a law barring the

IRS from garnishing 100% of a taxpayer's salary for delinquent taxes, and one giving volunteer fire departments the right to issue tax-free bonds to buy their equipment. Jacobs worked as a police officer in the Sheriff's Department while in law school and suggested a change in railroad grade crossings which virtually eliminated crossing accidents in Marion County. In Congress, he has introduced legislation to end PACs and publicly financed campaigns.

Overall, Jacobs's voting record is among the most moderate of northern Democrats. But not always predictably. He favors affirmative action as well as medical savings accounts, is for preventive anti-crime measures and against the death penalty, likes cognitive preschool programs and dislikes foreign aid. In May 1994, he switched his vote at the last minute and supported the ban on assault weapons. On foreign policy, he opposes U.S. military involvements abroad, including the Persian Gulf in 1990 and 1991, and wants a cost/benefit analysis included on any declaration of war. As a Marine veteran who sustained a back wound while in combat in Korea (but doesn't accept disability benefits), he coined the term "war wimps" to describe hawks who managed to avoid combat.

Jacobs is the fourth-ranking Democrat on Ways and Means. From 1987 to 1995 he chaired the Social Security Subcommittee. He sponsored laws making Social Security an independent agency, allowing employers to garnish the wages of federal employees, raising the salary level at which taxes must be withheld for household employees. But he says the agency is not working as competently as it used to. In December 1990, David Obey sponsored a rules change requiring Ways and Means subcommittee chairmen to be elected by the whole Democratic Caucus; many said this was aimed at Jacobs because he had opposed the congressional pay raise.

Jacobs's quirky ways have long made him popular. Embattled politically in the 1960s and early 1970s, he won easily through the 1980s and early 1990s, even though (or is it because?) he raises and spends little money, accepts no PAC contributions, sends out no mailings, runs no TV ads. It worked even in 1986, when the American Medical Association PAC made a $300,000 independent expenditure against him. In 1994 he was opposed by Marvin Scott, higher education director for the Eli Lilly pharmaceutical firm, a onetime Jimmy Carter and Michael Dukakis supporter who was converted to a conservative philosophy by his former colleague William Bennett. Scott spent $69,000—not much, but more than Jacobs's $27,000—and came out against gun control and GATT. In a Republican year (Senator Richard Lugar was carrying metro Indianapolis 74%–24%), Jacobs won by only 53%–47%. But he seems unlikely to change his ways. The prospect of defeat holds no terror for him: his father, elected here in 1948, lost in 1950; his former wife, Kansas Congresswoman Martha Keys, was defeated in 1978; he lost himself in 1972; he has two small children by his current marriage, and he has shown he does things his way.

The People: Pop. 1990: 554,797; 11% age 65+; 69% White; 30% Black; 1% Asian; 1% Hispanic origin. Voting age pop.: 410,877; 27% Black; 1% Hispanic origin. Households: 43% married couple families; 20% married couple fams. w. children; 40% college educ.; median household income: $25,304; per capita income: $12,562; median gross rent: $394; median house value: $45,700.

1992 Presidential Vote		
Clinton (D)	92,514	(47%)
Bush (R)	70,458	(36%)
Perot (I)	33,229	(17%)

1988 Presidential Vote		
Dukakis (D)	99,110	(51%)
Bush (R)	96,822	(49%)

Rep. Andy Jacobs, Jr. (D)

Elected 1974; b. Feb. 24, 1932, Indianapolis; home, Indianapolis; Catholic U., 1949, IN U., B.S. 1955, LL.B. 1958; Catholic; married (Kim).

Career: Marine Corps, 1950–52 (Korea); Police Officer, 1954–58; Practicing atty., 1958–65, 1973–74; IN House of Reps., 1959–60; U.S. House of Reps., 1964–72.

DC Office: 2313 RHOB 20515, 202-225-4011; Fax: 202-226-4093.

District Offices: 441-A Fed. Bldg., 46 E. Ohio St., Indianapolis 46204, 317-226-7331.

Committees: *Ways & Means* (4th of 15 D): Social Security (RMM).

Group Ratings

	ADA	ACLU	COPE	CFA	LCV	CON	NSI	COC	ACU	NTLC	CHC
1994	85	68	56	70	78	60	11	83	30	36	28
1993	90	—	100	90	64	11	—	18	25	—	—

National Journal Ratings

	1993 LIB — 1993 CONS	1994 LIB — 1994 CONS
Economic	47% — 52%	46% — 54%
Social	56% — 44%	67% — 32%
Foreign	40% — 57%	68% — 29%

Key Votes of the 103d Congress

1. Clinton Deficit Plan	Y	3. Brady Handgun Purchase Y	5. Lmt. UN Cmnd. of Forces Y
2. NAFTA	N	4. Strike Race/Death Pnlty. N	6. Cut Missile Funds Y

1. Clinton Deficit Plan Y 3. Brady Handgun Purchase Y 5. Lmt. UN Cmnd. of Forces Y
2. NAFTA N 4. Strike Race/Death Pnlty. N 6. Cut Missile Funds Y

Key Votes of the 104th Congress

1. Congressional Compliance Y 6. Reform Crime Grant N 11. Loser Pays Court Reform N
2. Balanced Budget Amndmt. Y 7. National Security Act Y 12. Product Liability Reform N
3. Bar Unfunded Mandates Y 8. Moratorium on Regs. Y 13. Welfare Reform N
4. Pass Line Item Veto N 9. Risk Assessment on Regs. N 14. Term Limits Amndmt. Y
5. Relax Exclusionary Rule Y 10. Expnd. Priv. Prop. Rights Y 15. Tax Cuts N

Election Results

1994 general	Andy Jacobs, Jr. (D)	58,573	(53%)	($27,544)
	Marvin Bailey Scott (R)	50,998	(47%)	($69,852)
1994 primary	Andy Jacobs, Jr. (D)	13,848	(61%)	
	Dwayne Marc Brown (D)	4,347	(19%)	
	Kenneth C. Bourke (D)	2,880	(13%)	
	Joe L. Turner (D)	1,140	(5%)	
	Others	644	(3%)	
1992 general	Andy Jacobs, Jr. (D)	117,604	(64%)	($14,373)
	Janos Horvath (R)	64,378	(35%)	($66,727)
	Other	1,849	(1%)	

IOWA

Corn-producing and corny, computer-literate yet still highly agricultural, traditional-looking and the first state to vote in the presidential race, Iowa was America's most downcast state in the upbeat 1980s and now seems to have turned frisky in the uncertain 1990s. In spirit, in temperament, in its preoccupation with issues and its partisan preferences, Iowa seems so often to be going just the other way from the rest of the nation—determinedly, with confidence in its own chipper rectitude, unembarrassed at being out of step. Back when onetime Des Moines radio announcer Ronald Reagan was president, Iowa gave him some of his lowest job ratings in the nation. The reason was the stalled economy: in the first seven years of the 1980s, Iowa saw 7% of its residents leave and its population fall more than any other state but West Virginia. It lost both incomes and wealth, as farmland prices dropped and farm implement factories shut down. These were exaggerations of the long-range trend, throughout this century, of outmigration.

Despite its proximity to major markets, despite its high levels of education—Iowa is dotted with colleges and boasts the nation's highest literacy rates—Iowa had trouble generating the new jobs it needed to employ its own young people, much less attract others. Iowa's very articulateness may have been working against it. For years Iowans seemed aggrieved that their economy, based on the wholesome business of farming, wasn't growing rapidly, even though history shows that one constant of economic growth is a long-term decline in commodity prices. For half a century, Iowa looked to the federal government to maintain agricultural profits, and demanded this with a fervor that began with Jeffersonian sentimentalism about the moral superiority of farming and ended up as a sense of entitlement and almost greed.

Iowa voters were coddled in these sentiments during ever-lengthier campaigns in this state's first-in-the-nation precinct caucuses. Starting in 1976, when Jimmy Carter's strategist Hamilton Jordan determined that intensive personal campaigning could produce national publicity for a little-known candidate, the Iowa caucuses were a major league event: Ronald Reagan avoided a debate here in 1980, only to be beaten by George Bush, while Carter was overwhelming Edward Kennedy; Walter Mondale won half the votes in an eight-candidate field in 1984, only to see the spotlight fall on the splinter vote for second-place finisher Gary Hart; attention fell for a moment on winners Bob Dole and Dick Gephardt in 1988, as George Bush was humiliated by coming in third behind Bob Dole and Pat Robertson in a rush of anti-Reagan feeling, and Michael Dukakis's spin team managed to convince the press that his third-place finish behind Gephardt and Paul Simon did not rule Dukakis out. In the 1970s, the Iowa caucuses were scheduled early by Democratic doves who wanted leverage for a dovish constituency (and there was hardly an electorate then more averse to the use of American military power than Iowa Democratic caucus-goers); but this tended to block hawkish Democrats nationally while reinforcing Iowa's preoccupation with the farm economy.

Now that has changed. It became apparent, as long ago as the 1985 farm bill, that wheat and corn subsidies couldn't be sustained, so they were cut way back. Iowa realized it needed to look elsewhere than Washington for growth. At which point, growth happened: in 1987 the economy turned upward. In the 1990–91 recession, Iowa's unemployment stayed low and farmland prices were stable; by 1994 Iowa had actually started generating jobs, farmland values and housing construction were sharply up and unemployment was around 3%. Not that the old Iowa was restored: most counties' population was well below 1980 levels, with growth robust only around Des Moines. The disastrous 1993 floods could have made Iowans victims of circumstance again, but with some federal aid they kept things going with pluck, ingenuity and community spirit. Plus, Iowa in the 1990s hasn't received the usual two years of sick calls from sympathetic-

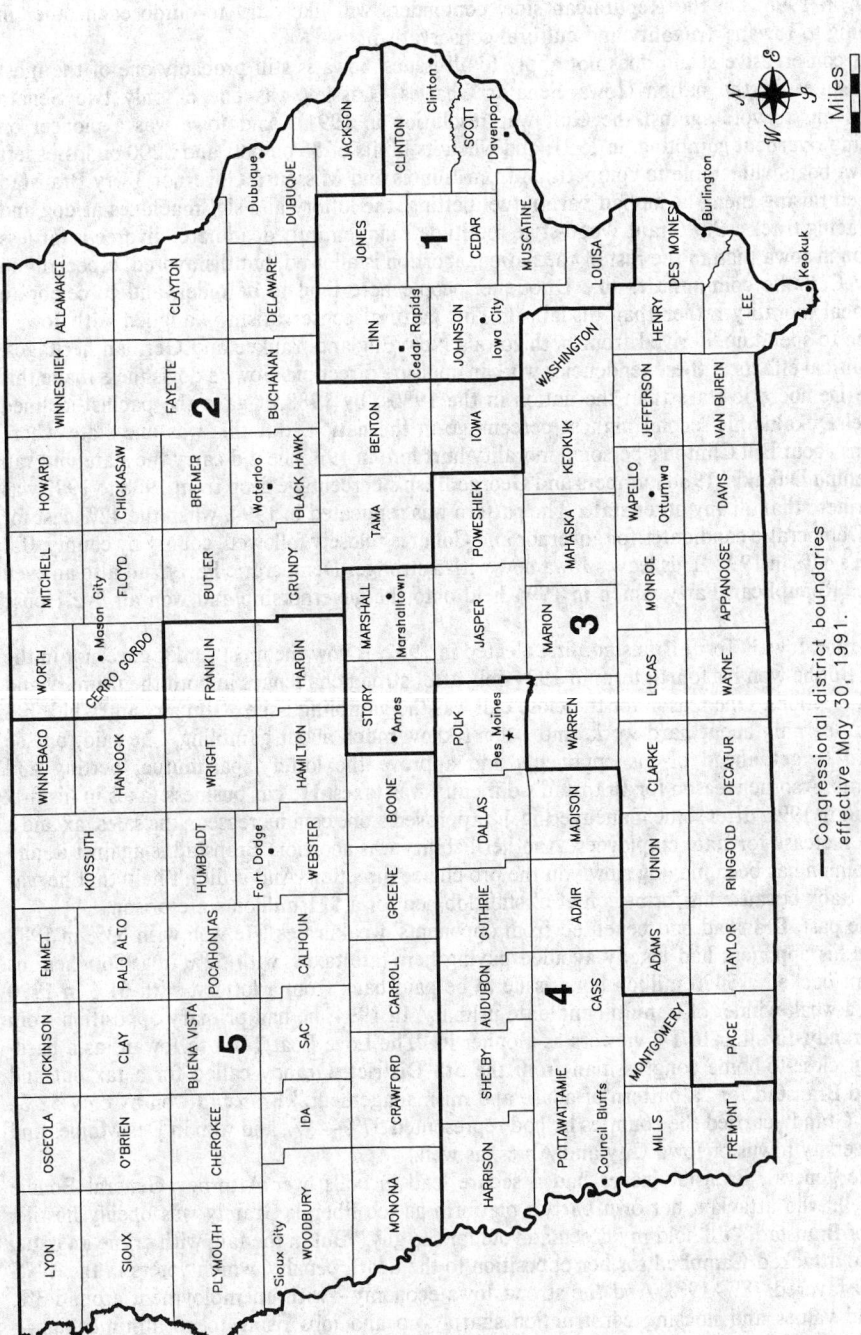

— Congressional district boundaries effective May 30, 1991.

Copyright © 1993 by Election Data Services, Inc.

physician presidential candidates. Iowa Senator Tom Harkin's 1992 candidacy kept other candidates out of the state for that cycle, and it's not clear that Iowa will see a challenger to Bill Clinton in 1996. On the Republican side, contenders will likely try to outdo each other in appealing to Iowans' frugality and cultural conservatism.

That conservative strain does not apply to all issues. Iowa is still probably one of the most dovish states in the nation (Iowa Senator Charles Grassley was one of only two Senate Republicans to vote against the Gulf war resolution in 1991). And Iowa was a pioneer on legalizing riverboat gambling, in 1991; and when its limits of $5 on bets and $200 on losses left the Iowa boats vulnerable to competition from Illinois and Missouri, Governor Terry Branstad approved raising them, as he had parimutuel betting, the lottery and slot machines at dog and horse racing tracks. But Grant Wood-style rectitude is not entirely dead here: divorce is far less common in Iowa than in the rest of the nation; abortion is allowed, but disfavored, especially in heavily Catholic communities like Dubuque; people here tend to be older, and to celebrate traditional morality rather than disdain it. This cultural conservatism is aligned with Iowa's aversion to spending, derived from both Iowa's New England Yankee and German heritages. The political effects of these tendencies work in opposite directions. Iowa's dovishness made this a more Democratic state than the nation in the 1980s; by 1988, it gave the pacifist-inclined Michael Dukakis his second highest percentage in the nation. But this was one state where concerns about Bill Clinton's personal morality hurt him in 1992: he did carry the state, but ran 12% behind Dukakis' 1988 numbers and George Bush's percentage drop from 1988 to 1992 was smaller here than in any other state. The pattern was replicated in 1994, when the 42% cast for losing Democratic candidates for governor and Congress closely followed, county by county, Bill Clinton's 43% in 1992. This leaves Iowa now with a stronger Democratic Party, but also an even stronger Republican Party which in 1994 held onto the governorship and won all five House seats.

Governor. Iowa's Terry Branstad, first elected in 1982, is now the most senior governor in the nation. But he won his fourth term in 1994 only after strong challenges in both the primary and general elections. One reason for the close call was the gambling issue. "I'm a country kid that grew up learning about hard work, and I don't know much about gambling," he said, but he skittered to get ahead of his opponents and approve the lottery, parimutuel betting and riverboats. Another reason for Branstad's difficulty was taxes. He cut business taxes in his first term, but in 1992, after some maneuvering, he approved a one cent increase in the sales tax and a big pay increase for state employees. Another liability was abortion: Branstad is against it, and Iowa opinion has been moving slowly in the pro-choice direction. And it didn't help that he was under attack because his former chief of staff lobbied for a $21 million state prison.

In the past, Branstad had benefited from opponents' weaknesses. He won with 53% in 1982 because his opponent had legally avoided paying her state taxes, with 52% in 1986 when his opponent backed a $400 million bond issue to be paid back from a lottery, with 61% in 1990 against a weak winner of a multi-candidate primary. In 1994, he had primary opposition from Fred Grandy, familiar to TV viewers as Gopher in "The Love Boat," but to Iowans as a hard-working, close-to-home congressman from the 5th District. Grandy called for a tax cut and attacked Branstad for "a pattern of abuse and mismanagement." Branstad won by only 52%–48%, as Grandy carried the counties he had represented 57%–43%, and won in Des Moines and the university towns of Iowa City and Ames, as well.

In the general, Branstad never had a secure lead in polls over Attorney General Bonnie Campbell, who attacked her own party's platform as too liberal; Grandy was openly hostile, saying of Branstad, "I'll hold my nose and vote for the guy." But in the fall, with crime an issue, Branstad attacked Campbell for her opposition to the death penalty, which voters in the VNS exit poll favored 78%–19%. And the strong Iowa economy—with unemployment around 3%, farmland values and housing construction sharply up and jobs rising to an all-time high—evidently worked for the incumbent. Branstad won 58%–42%, carrying all but four counties (Iowa City, Ames and the factory towns of Ottumwa and Fort Madison). In effect he carried both the Bush and Perot 1992 vote while Campbell carried Clinton's. Des Moines, the most vibrantly growing part of the state, which voted against Branstad in 1982 and 1986, voted for him this time. Branstad, who had the strength to win when Iowa seemed mostly Democratic, now has the opportunity to lead, for at least one more term, when it is trending Republican. Incidentally, Branstad has endorsed Bob Dole for president in 1996—the first time he has publicly endorsed a presidential candidate.

Senators. Iowa's senior senator, Charles Grassley, is a farmer who worked as a machinist, unquestionably honest, preternaturally thrifty. "The Eastern snobs of the Republican Party don't want someone like Chuck Grassley with a Midwestern twang speaking on national television," he told the 1992 Republican National Convention, with a straight face: he does not mind playing the part of the hayseed. But he is also a shrewd and successful Republican politician who has held public office for going on 40 years, winning a seat in the Iowa legislature in the Democratic year of 1958, a House seat in the Democratic year of 1974, and a Senate seat by beating a strong incumbent, John Culver, in 1980. Grassley's record in Congress has been guided by three issues: thrift, agriculture and dovishness on defense. He will abandon party lines to vote for higher farm spending and lower defense (the 1990 budget bill), or against extension of U.S. military power (the 1991 Gulf war resolution), or to force a vote on an energy bill with a coal tax (the 1992 energy bill). Working with Nebraska Democrat James Exon, he pushed in 1994 for lower caps on future federal spending; they won in the Senate Budget Committee and on the floor but were beaten on the House floor 216–202, when Democratic leaders put the heat on. Grassley also is alert to what he considers abuses of government power. He supports tough laws to protect whistleblower and in 1994 crusaded to deny promotion to Air Force Lieutenant General Buster Glosson for tampering with a promotion board to settle a grudge against a fellow officer, and not being honest about it; Grassley lost 59–30.

Grassley has been the leading senator to argue that Congress should be covered by the laws it imposes on others, and in 1991 achieved some success in getting the Senate covered by civil rights and sexual harassment laws. He finally won enactment in 1995 of a law applying other federal workplace laws to all of Congress. On the Judiciary Committee, where he is one of five non-lawyers, he skewered with good reason the American Bar Association as blatantly political in assessing Supreme Court nominees. He generally wants to discourage litigiousness, moving to deny attorney's fees to copyright infringement plaintiffs, but he was a major backer of the bill to let victims of rape and families of murder victims sue hard-core pornographers if a connection to the crime can be proved. He succeeded in getting a 25% tax deduction for health insurance for the self-employed and favors 100%. As always, Grassley advances his position soberly, in his own natural style; he is plainly sincere, yet more aware of the political repercussions of his actions than his manner suggests.

Since 1980, Grassley has been the most popular political figure in Iowa, with an appeal that goes far beyond party lines. In 1986, he became the first Iowa senator to win reelection in 20 years; no serious candidate filed to run against him, and he received 66% of the vote—more than any other Iowa senator in history. In 1988, his support helped Bob Dole win the Iowa presidential caucuses, and Grassley endorsed Dole again for the 1996 campaign. Grassley's 1992 opponent, Jean Lloyd-Jones, had started a peace institute, but she also had been an officer in the Iowa Senate which had declined to probe Senate President Joe Walsh's involvement in a banking scandal. Grassley carried even Lloyd-Jones' home base, the university town of Iowa City, and all the state's 99 counties, for a 70%–27% victory, a new record, and 33 points ahead of George Bush.

Tom Harkin, Iowa's junior senator, has also proved a durable political figure and, if he stands alone today as Iowa's single Democrat in major office, he has labored against great political odds before—and with some success. He is one of the Democrats' Watergate babies, first elected in 1974, but there is no smooth Ivy League smugness to him. He has a craggy and almost worn look; he grew up poor in a rural town, where his father was a coal miner and his mother, a Slovenian immigrant, died when he was 10. His desire to use government to help those who are struggling comes not from academic theory but from tough personal experience. He worked his way through college and law school, spent five years in the Navy during the 1960s, ferrying planes from Vietnam for repair. After a narrow loss in 1972, Harkin ran for Congress again in 1974 and invented "work days," a campaign technique widely imitated since: he spent a day working at each of a dozen or so local jobs. He won solidly and held the seat with good percentages. Well before the 1984 election, he cornered the Democratic nomination to run against Senator Roger Jepsen, who was gravely weakened by, among other things, insisting he was entitled to commute to work alone in the highway lane reserved for multiple passenger cars. In a tough year for Democrats elsewhere, Harkin was elected to the Senate with 55%.

In the Senate, Harkin has had disappointing defeats and unexpected successes. One disappointment was on farm policy. He came to the Senate as a self-styled populist, eager to expand government farm programs. But these programs became so expensive in the early 1980s that the 1985 and 1990 farm bills turned the trajectory downward. His biggest initiative was the 1987 Harkin-Gephardt supply management farm bill, which would have raised overall food costs in order to benefit small farmers with assets of half a million dollars or more; that died even before the demise of Gephardt's 1988 presidential campaign. At just about that point, Iowa's farm economy improved. Harkin has tried to help it along, supporting direct food aid to the old Soviet Union, on whatever terms, and more recently, despite his usual suspicion of free trade agreements, supporting the North American Free Trade Agreement (Mexicans eat vast amounts of corn and pork, Iowa's primary farm products).

Harkin's biggest success came from his work on the Americans with Disabilities Act (ADA). Influenced by the plight of his brother who became deaf at age nine, he has long been a champion of the disabled, using his chairmanship of the Labor-HHS Appropriations Subcommittee for that purpose; he has implemented grants for "assistive technology" for the handicapped and a new NIH Institute on Deafness and Other Communications Disorders. The ADA was a great achievement, one that required overcoming resistance based on cost and qualms about the real-world effect of regulations. At Gallaudet University in Washington, D.C., a noted school for the hearing impaired, Harkin gave part of his speech in sign language when he withdrew from the presidential race. Harkin's Appropriations seat has made him a major force on medical research, with specific interests. He created an Office of Alternative Medicines at NIH, after he got relief from allergies by eating morsels of bee pollen; then in 1994 essentially got its head to leave because he was dissatisfied with his performance. The office was dismantled a year later.

On foreign policy, Harkin is very much a product of the Vietnam experience, an opponent of U.S. military intervention and aid on behalf of right-wing governments, but in favor of aid to the left-wing government of Haiti. He opposed contra aid and verged on being an apologist for the Nicaraguan Sandinista government in the 1980s and fervently opposed the Gulf war in 1991, bringing a lawsuit against President Bush to try to prevent him from using force without congressional approval. But Harkin was just as fervent a sponsor of an embargo on Haiti in 1994 when the military was in power and of threatening to use force to install then exiled President Aristide.

In 1990, Harkin won reelection with 54% against a tough Republican opponent, Congressman Tom Tauke, a knowledgeable critic of government programs and a smart political operator. Harkin's pro-choice position on abortion was on balance an asset, and his fighting spirit impressed voters unhappy with Washington. Then, in 1991, Harkin surprised many by running for president. He did so more out of conviction than calculation: he sensed correctly there was no one in the race who would challenge George Bush as Harkin thought he should be. In angry phrases, with a Trumanesque zest, Harkin preached that George Bush and the Republicans helped only the rich and that government must get involved to help the poor and middle class. But Harkin was not always accurate and didn't play up to the modern media; his style and message came from a time when liberal politicians knew most of the media were against them and were confident that the people would support them if they could only shout their message loud enough. Harkin, however, failed to get solid support even from the AFL-CIO, which withheld an early endorsement of him despite his 90%-plus AFL-CIO voting record—a great tactical victory for Bill Clinton, governor of a right-to-work state. Harkin's sweep of the Iowa caucuses February 10, actually an impressive testimonial to his home state popularity, was mostly discounted by the media. But Harkin's greatest problem was that he just didn't strike a chord with many voters. He had a good New Hampshire organization, enough money to run a respectable campaign, and no scandal problems like Bill Clinton or health problems like Paul Tsongas. But New Hampshire, with its mania for low taxes, was not a good Harkin venue: he got only 10% of the vote in the February 18 contest. He won the Minnesota and Idaho caucuses March 3, but got only 7% in South Carolina March 7 after campaigning there with Jesse Jackson. In debt and ineligible for matching funds, Harkin decided to quit rather than contest Michigan and Illinois on March 17, despite pleas from some union leaders there.

But Harkin didn't entirely vanish from the scene. On March 26, he endorsed Bill Clinton, and campaigned gamely for him in primaries and with union audiences, despite the differences between their programs. This brought out the best side of Harkin. He showed none of the defensiveness he does when he's running himself; instead, he was a genuinely happy warrior. Clinton ultimately returned the favor by appointing his wife Ruth Harkin, a Washington lawyer who combines good humor, competence and strong beliefs, to head the Overseas Private Investment Corporation. In the Senate, Harkin has provided support for the Clinton Administration often. He tried in September 1994 to save the healthcare initiative by pushing a bill to provide coverage for children from families who earn up to 400% of the poverty level. But it was too late and went nowhere. Similarly, Harkin was frustrated in his desire to fully fund Head Start. His bill to prohibit import of products made with child labor went nowhere. His amendment to transfer Strategic Defense Initiative funds to state and local drug enforcement was defeated 59–40. And, he is likely to be more frustrated in the Republican Senate—and more feisty. His seat comes up in 1996, and he must expect it will be seriously contested, which helps to explain his 1995 vote for the balanced budget constitutional amendment. He is the first Iowa Democrat to win two consecutive six-year Senate terms; none has won a third.

Presidential politics. In November of an election year no presidential campaign cares very much about Iowa, with its seven electoral votes. But in the preceding January and February, eyes are very much on this state from which there is no direct flight from Washington, D.C.. One can argue that it is irrational to give two small and atypical states—Iowa and New Hampshire— such pivotal roles in the presidential selection process. In fact, they are guaranteed their first-in-the-nation status only by Democratic Party rules. The Republican Party, the only one sure to have a serious contest in 1996, could let any other states choose earlier; Arizona, in particular, had sought to move to the head of the calendar. But by early 1995 it seemed clear that Iowa would start the 38-day marathon in which most Republican delegates will be chosen.

Actually, what will happen in Iowa is that voters will gather in 2142 precinct caucus sites and choose delegates to county conventions, which will choose delegates to state conventions; state party officials and the press will scramble to discern the candidate preferences of those as measured in state-delegate-equivalents. The early favorite for 1996 is fellow farm stater Bob Dole, who had a solid victory here in 1988; he also came in first in a June 1994 Republican straw poll. Coming in second was former Tennessee Governor Lamar Alexander, followed by Phil Gramm, both of whom were already organizing the state. There are many Christian right voters here—Pat Robertson finished second to Dole in 1988: Iowa could end up being a race for second, with that finisher getting an edge in publicity that could help in New Hampshire and the big states voting soon after.

Congressional districting. In May 1991, Iowa's Democratic legislature and Governor Branstad approved congressional district lines drawn by the non-partisan Legislative Services Bureau. They ended up hurting the Democrats. Iowa lost one seat in the 1990 Census, and in the new 2d District Republican Jim Nussle beat Democrat Dave Nagle; Republican Jim Ross Lightfoot held on in the Democrat-leaning 3d District in 1992, while veteran Democrat Neal

Smith, given much new territory, lost in 1994. But all these results may be reversed before a new plan is adopted for 2002.

The People: Est. Pop. 1994: 2,829,000; Pop. 1990: 2,776,755, up 1.9% 1990–1994. 1.1% of U.S. total, 30th largest; 39% rural. Median age: 34.0 years. 15.3% 65 years and over. 96.9% White, 1.7% Black, 1.2% Hispanic origin. Households: 59.2% married couple families; 28% married couple fams. w. children; 42% college educ.; median household income: $26,229; per capita income: $12,422; 70.0% owner occupied housing; median house value: $45,900; median monthly rent: $261. 4.6% Unemployment. 1994 Voting age pop.: 2,112,000. 1994 Turnout: 986,371; 47% of VAP. Registered voters (1994): 1,588,772; 562,083 D (35%), 574,423 R (36%), 452,266 unaffiliated and minor parties (28%).

Political Lineup: Governor, Terry E. Branstad (R); Lt. Gov., Joy Corning (R); Secy. of State, Paul Danny Pate (R); Atty. Gen., Tom Miller (D); Treasurer, Michael L. Fitzgerald (D); Auditor, Richard D. Johnson (R). State Senate, 50 (27 D and 23 R); State House of Representatives, 100 (64 R and 36 D). Senators, Charles E. Grassley (R) and Tom Harkin (D). Representatives, 5 (5 R).

1992 Presidential Vote			1988 Presidential Vote		
Clinton (D)	586,353	(43%)	Dukakis (D)	670,557	(55%)
Bush (R)	504,891	(37%)	Bush (R)	545,355	(44%)
Perot (I)	253,468	(19%)			

GOVERNOR

Gov. Terry E. Branstad (R)

Elected 1982, term expires Jan. 1999; b. Nov. 17, 1946, Leland; home, Des Moines; U. of IA, B.A. 1969, Drake U., J.D. 1974; Catholic; married (Christine).

Career: Army, 1969–71; IA House of Reps., 1972–78; Practicing atty., Farmer, 1974–1982; IA Lt. Gov., 1978–82.

Office: State Capitol, Des Moines 50319, 515-281-5211; Fax: 515-281-6611.

Election Results

1994 gen.	Terry E. Branstad (R)	566,395	(57%)
	Bonnie J. Campbell (D)	414,453	(42%)
	Others	16,400	(2%)
1994 prim.	Terry E. Branstad (R)	161,228	(52%)
	Fred Grandy (R)	149,809	(48%)
1990 gen.	Terry E. Branstad (R)	591,852	(61%)
	Donald D. Avenson (D)	379,372	(39%)

SENATORS

Sen. Charles E. Grassley (R)

Elected 1980, seat up 1998; b. Sep. 17, 1933, New Hartford; home, New Hartford; U. of N. IA, B.A. 1955, M.A. 1956, U. of IA, 1957–58; Baptist; married (Barbara).

Career: Farmer; IA House of Reps., 1958–74; U.S. House of Reps., 1974–80.

DC Office: 135 HSOB 20510, 202-224-3744; Fax: 202-224-6020.

State Offices: 721 Fed. Bldg., 210 Walnut St., Des Moines 50309, 515-284-4890; 210 Waterloo Bldg., 531 Commercial St., Waterloo 50701, 319-232-6657; 116 Fed. Bldg., 131 E. 4th St., Davenport 52801, 319-322-4331; 103 Fed. Bldg., 320 6th St., Sioux City 51101, 712-233-3331; 307 Fed. Bldg., 8 S. 6th St., Council Bluffs 51501, 712-322-7103; and 206 Fed. Bldg., 101 1st St., SE, Cedar Rapids 52401, 319-399-2555.

Committees: *Budget* (2nd of 12 R). *Finance* (5th of 11 R): International Trade (Chmn.); Medicare, Long-Term Care and Health Insurance; Taxation and IRS Oversight. *Governmental Affairs* (6th of 8 R): Oversight of Government Management and the District of Columbia; Investigations. *Judiciary* (4th of 10 R): Administrative Oversight and the Courts (Chmn.); Immigration. *Aging (Special)* (3rd of 10 R).

Group Ratings

	ADA	ACLU	COPE	CFA	LCV	CON	NSI	COC	ACU	NTLC	CHC
1994	15	21	0	25	23	96	80	78	92	88	100
1993	20	—	0	30	6	68	—	91	88	—	—

National Journal Ratings

	1993 LIB — 1993 CONS	1994 LIB — 1994 CONS
Economic	13% — 81%	12% — 82%
Social	12% — 86%	0% — 85%
Foreign	53% — 39%	23% — 74%

Key Votes of the 103d Congress

1. Clinton Deficit Plan	N	3. Brady Handgun Purchase	N	5. Lmt. UN Cmnd. of Forces	Y
2. NAFTA	Y	4. Strike Race/Death Pnlty.	Y	6. Cut Missile Funds	Y

Key Votes of the 104th Congress

1. Congressional Compliance	Y	3. Balanced Budget Amndt.	Y	5. Product Liability Reform	Y
2. Bar Unfunded Mandates	Y	4. Pass Line Item Veto	Y	6. FY96 Budget	Y

Election Results

1992 general	Charles E. Grassley (R)	899,761	(70%)	($2,486,030)
	Jean Lloyd-Jones (D)	351,561	(27%)	($410,894)
	Others	40,879	(3%)	
1992 primary	Charles E. Grassley (R)	unopposed		
1986 general	Charles E. Grassley (R)	588,880	(66%)	($2,513,319)
	John P. Roehrick (D)	299,406	(34%)	($255,673)

Sen. Tom Harkin (D)

Elected 1984, seat up 1996; b. Nov. 19, 1939, Cumming; home, Cumming; IA St. U., B.S. 1962, Catholic U., J.D. 1972; Catholic; married (Ruth).

Career: Navy, 1962–67; Naval Reserves, 1969–72; Practicing atty., 1972–74; Staff Aide, House Select Cmte. on U.S. Involvement in SE Asia, 1973–74; U.S. House of Reps., 1974–84.

DC Office: 531 HSOB 20510, 202-224-3254; Fax: 202-224-9369; e-mail: tom_harkin@harkin.senate.gov.

State Offices: 733 Fed. Bldg., 210 Walnut St., Des Moines 50309, 515-284-4574; Fed. Bldg., Council Bluffs 51501, 712-325-0036; 150 1st Ave., NE, #370, Cedar Rapids 52401, 319-365-4504; 131 E. 4th St., 314B Fed. Bldg., Davenport, 52801, 319-322-1338; 350 W. 6th St., Dubuque 52001, 319-588-2130; and 110 Federal Bldg., 320 6th St., Sioux City 51101, 712-252-1550.

Committees: *Agriculture, Nutrition & Forestry* (4th of 8 D): Forestry, Conservation and Rural Revitalization; Research, Nutrition and General Legislation (RMM). *Appropriations* (8th of 13 D): Agriculture, Rural Development and Related Agencies; Defense; Foreign Operations; Labor, Health and Human Services, Education (RMM); Transportation. *Labor & Human Resources* (5th of 7 D): Children and Families; Disability Policy (RMM); Education, Arts and Humanities. *Small Business* (4th of 9 D).

Group Ratings

	ADA	ACLU	COPE	CFA	LCV	CON	NSI	COC	ACU	NTLC	CHC
1994	100	79	88	92	92	32	0	30	0	8	7
1993	90	—	73	80	88	2	—	27	0	—	—

National Journal Ratings

	1993 LIB — 1993 CONS		1994 LIB — 1994 CONS	
Economic	71%	— 17%	84%	— 0%
Social	86%	— 13%	93%	— 0%
Foreign	92%	— 0%	94%	— 0%

Key Votes of the 103d Congress

1. Clinton Deficit Plan	Y	3. Brady Handgun Purchase	Y	5. Lmt. UN Cmnd. of Forces	N
2. NAFTA	Y	4. Strike Race/Death Pnlty.	N	6. Cut Missile Funds	Y

Key Votes of the 104th Congress

1. Congressional Compliance	Y	3. Balanced Budget Amndt.	Y	5. Product Liability Reform	N
2. Bar Unfunded Mandates	Y	4. Pass Line Item Veto	Y	6. FY96 Budget	N

Election Results

1990 general	Tom Harkin (D)	529,571	(54%)	($5,628,242)
	Thomas J. Tauke (R)	453,273	(46%)	($5,060,104)
1990 primary	Tom Harkin (D)	unopposed		
1984 general	Tom Harkin (D)	716,883	(55%)	($2,838,277)
	Roger W. Jepsen (R)	564,381	(44%)	($3,420,153)

FIRST DISTRICT

A century and a half ago settlers surged west of the Mississippi River into the fertile hilly lands that became Iowa. There New England Yankees built on the strange, open terrain their characteristic farmhouses, barns, town halls, church spires and small colleges; Germans, after crossing the ocean, stopped at the river bluffs reminiscent of their native land and also built neat farmhouses and substantial towns; railroad builders, headquartered in Chicago, extended their networks of steel rails over the plains and rivers. Today some of the distinctiveness of these settlers remains in eastern Iowa, though the old ethnic distinctiveness is muted, the old river craft have been replaced by giant barges and riverboat casinos and the old rail lines have been modernized and employ fewer men. Davenport, on the hills over the Mississippi River (which, with Rock Island, Moline and East Moline, Illinois, is part of the Quad Cities) still has the look of the city where Ronald Reagan got his first radio announcing job more than 60 years ago. Cedar Rapids, a couple of counties west of the river, looks more up-to-date, with big high-tech employers (Rockwell has large avionics and electronics operations here); in 1992, PMX Industries, a metalworking company, opened a plant here, the largest single South Korean investment in the country. Iowa City, to the south, is a university town complete with trendy bookstores and vegetarian eateries.

Eight counties in eastern Iowa, with Davenport in one corner and Cedar Rapids in another, make up Iowa's 1st Congressional District. Historically, it has been Republican; in the 1970s and 1980s, it became Democratic, though not as much as the rest of the Quad Cities across the River in Illinois; now it can be labeled marginal. It is solidly Republican in House elections, however, thanks to Congressman Jim Leach, who was first elected in 1976 and has not had serious opposition since.

Leach is now one of the most senior and, on several issues, potentially most powerful Republicans in the House, and Chairman of the House Banking Committee. A few years ago, that might have perturbed some of his fellow Republicans, who regarded him as dangerously liberal. But his background and views were always more interesting than that. He was a foreign service officer assigned to the United Nations in 1972 when George Bush was U.S. ambassador there; they became friends and Leach supported him ever after. In 1973, Leach resigned out of dismay after President Nixon fired Watergate special prosecutor Archibald Cox, and went back to Iowa to run the family propane business. A believer in free enterprise with hands-on experience in a regulated business, he remains market-oriented on most economic issues. On cultural issues, almost in the tradition of mainline Protestant denominations, he looks with some favor on liberal-minded changes, supporting international family planning and sanctions on South Africa. He accused the 1992 Houston convention of supporting "an accelerating socialism of morality." On foreign policy, like many Iowa Republicans, he has been cautious about asserting U.S. military power. But he strenuously supported the Gulf war resolution.

But on two major issues that arose on the Banking Committee Leach, with his Iowa sense of rectitude, was in the vanguard of the Republican Party, and indeed the whole House: the savings and loan scandal and Whitewater. On S&Ls, he was closer to being correct than anyone else in Congress or the executive branch. He understood early that allowing the states to liberate S&Ls from their investment limits without increasing capital requirements would leave the federal government open to huge losses on federal deposit insurance. He tried unsuccessfully to raise capital requirements in 1987 and protested loudly while Speaker Jim Wright delayed the recapitalization bill for two years. In 1989, he voted against the S&L bailout measure when the House wouldn't accept his higher capital requirements, but managed to delete a list of provisions that helped specific special interests by 412–7. By then he had gained a considerable moral authority as it became apparent he had been solitarily right when so many others were expensively wrong.

Leach inherited the ranking Republican chair on Banking in 1993, in time for the Whitewater scandal. From early 1994 he said he feared that there was serious misconduct, perhaps by the Clintons, and that the committee should investigate; he said that he did not think any issue of impeachment would arise, but that voters ought to have the facts about the President's involvement in 1996, as they did not in 1992. Chairman Henry Gonzalez refused and accused Leach of conducting a political witch hunt. When Gonzalez wouldn't support a Leach subpoena of records, Leach sued in March 1994; he lost in court in August, but that was mooted by the November election. He charged that Resolution Trust Company regulators looking at Madison Guaranty S&L were being "gagged" by superiors. Gonzalez finally agreed to public hearings in July, but he and other Democrats blocked discussion of most issues, imposed tight limits on Republicans and did everything they could to make a mockery of the hearings. But in 1995 Leach no longer needed Gonzalez's permission to hold hearings. He was willing to defer for some time to Whitewater independent counsel Kenneth Starr, but seemed also determined to get at the facts. After the 1994 election, Democrats expressed fears about the aggressive, partisan new Senate Banking Chairman, Alfonse D'Amato. But Leach, with his reputation for probity and fairness, could prove more devastating.

On other financial issues, Leach could also prove important. He has tended to favor overhaul of Glass-Steagall, which keeps banks out of the investment business; some form of that is likely to pass the 104th Congress. He opposed the Clinton Administration's proposal to consolidate bank regulators in an agency responsible to the White House; he would prefer to leave more power to the independent Federal Reserve. On derivatives, he tends to favor some exercise of caution by banks in such high-risk investments, but does not want to ban them altogether. And he has kept an eye on the capital standards of Fannie Mae, Freddie Mae and other government-sponsored agencies .

Leach is also the third-ranking Republican on International Relations. There he has been willing to support some executive branch policies unpopular with the public—the Bush Administration's policy on China, for example. But most of his energies will probably go into Banking issues and hearings. And, abetted by his cordial relationship with Speaker Gingrich, little is likely to be heard of the criticisms Leach made of more conservative Republicans a decade ago, when he formed a "mainstream" group whose name, a reference to a Nelson Rockefeller battle cry of 1964, enraged many conservatives.

Before Leach first won this seat in 1976, the 1st District was one of the nation's prime marginal seats for a decade. Now, although he doesn't accept campaign contributions over $500 and takes no money from PACs or non-Iowans, he tends to win easily.

The People: Pop. 1990: 555,229; 24% rural; 12% age 65+; 95% White; 3% Black; 1% Asian; 1% Other; 2% Hispanic origin. Voting age pop.: 413,406; 2% Black; 1% Hispanic origin. Households: 58% married couple families; 27% married couple fams. w. children; 49% college educ.; median household income: $29,544; per capita income: $13,660; median gross rent: $365; median house value: $55,500.

1992 Presidential Vote		
Clinton (D)	128,655	(46%)
Bush (R)	95,660	(34%)
Perot (I)	52,983	(19%)

1988 Presidential Vote		
Dukakis (D)	136,716	(56%)
Bush (R)	105,683	(43%)

Rep. James A. Leach (R)

Elected 1976; b. Oct. 15, 1942, Davenport; home, Davenport; Princeton U., B.A. 1964, Johns Hopkins U., M.A. 1966, London Schl. of Econ., 1966–68; Episcopalian; married (Elisabeth).

Career: Staff Asst., U.S. Rep. Donald Rumsfeld, 1965–66; U.S. Foreign Svc., 1968–69, 1971–72; A.A. to Dir. of U.S. Office of Equal Opp., 1969–70; Pres., Flamegas Co., 1973–75; Dir., Fed. Home Loan Bank Bd., Midwest Reg., 1975–76.

DC Office: 2186 RHOB 20515, 202-225-6576; Fax: 202-226-1278.

District Offices: 209 W. 4th St., Davenport 52801, 319-326-1841; 102 S. Clinton, #505, Iowa City 52240, 319-351-0789; and 309 10th St., SE, Cedar Rapids 52403, 319-363-4773.

Committees: *Banking & Financial Services* (Chmn. of 27 R). *International Relations* (3rd of 23 R): Asia and the Pacific.

Group Ratings

	ADA	ACLU	COPE	CFA	LCV	CON	NSI	COC	ACU	NTLC	CHC
1994	40	61	22	40	39	90	40	100	33	73	43
1993	55	—	42	70	50	59	—	82	55	—	—

National Journal Ratings

	1993 LIB — 1993 CONS		1994 LIB — 1994 CONS	
Economic	30%	— 70%	30%	— 67%
Social	62%	— 38%	50%	— 49%
Foreign	69%	— 31%	51%	— 47%

Key Votes of the 103d Congress

1. Clinton Deficit Plan	N	3. Brady Handgun Purchase	Y	5. Lmt. UN Cmnd. of Forces	N
2. NAFTA	Y	4. Strike Race/Death Pnlty.	Y	6. Cut Missile Funds	Y

Key Votes of the 104th Congress

1. Congressional Compliance	Y	6. Reform Crime Grant	Y	11. Loser Pays Court Reform Y
2. Balanced Budget Amndmt.	Y	7. National Security Act	N	12. Product Liability Reform Y
3. Bar Unfunded Mandates	Y	8. Moratorium on Regs.	Y	13. Welfare Reform	Y
4. Pass Line Item Veto	Y	9. Risk Assessment on Regs.	Y	14. Term Limits Amndmt.	Y
5. Relax Exclusionary Rule	Y	10. Expnd. Priv. Prop. Rights	Y	15. Tax Cuts	Y

Election Results

1994 general	James A. Leach (R)	110,448	(60%)	($268,937)
	Glen Winekauf (D)	69,461	(38%)	($82,447)
	Others	3,552	(2%)	
1994 primary	James A. Leach (R)	unopposed		
1992 general	James A. Leach (R)	178,042	(68%)	($259,804)
	Jan J. Zonneveld (D)	81,600	(31%)	
	Others	1,667	(1%)	

SECOND DISTRICT

Northeast Iowa, along the Mississippi River and westward, has some of the loveliest landscape in America. Here bluffs rise above the Mississippi, which broadens out in great quiet pools and then flows fast in constricted narrows. Inland from the Mississippi are the rolling hills portrayed with surprisingly little exaggeration in the paintings of Iowa's Grant Wood. These were lands settled by immigrants in the late 19th Century. German Catholics settled Dubuque, whose giant Victorian courthouse looks down on the Mississippi and up at the Fenelon Place Elevator that rides up the bluff. North are the tiny towns of Allamakee County, settled by Swiss Germans, where former Senator John Culver restored his ancestral family home in McGregor. Just west of Dubuque is Dyersville, where *Field of Dreams* was filmed and to which baseball buffs now repair: "If you build it, they will come." Farther west is Waterloo, which grew rapidly after 1900 as the John Deere tractor factory expanded and the eight-floor Rath factory became the largest meatpacking plant in the world; Rath closed in 1984 and Deere had thousands of layoffs, but Waterloo has rebounded somewhat with new businesses from a dog track to telemarketing to a high-tech Iowa Beef Processing (IBP) factory. To the south are the Amana colonies, settled in the 1850s by the Community of True Inspiration, German pietists, who have retained many of their old customs even as they have built businesses like Amana appliances.

There is considerable political variation here. Dubuque, heavily German Catholic, was for years Iowa's most Democratic city, and still often is unless abortion is the issue. But the rural counties along the river and farther west—more German Protestant, Scandinavian and Yankee—were traditionally Republican. Waterloo, originally Republican, trended sharply Democratic as the Rath plant shut down and Deere had big layoffs.

The 2d Congressional District of Iowa covers most of northeast Iowa, including Dubuque and Waterloo, Allamakee County and Dyersville and the Amana colonies. This is an amalgam of the old 2d, centered on Dubuque, and the 3d, centered on Waterloo, and its creation in 1991 pitted two incumbents, both sharp partisans, against each other in 1992. The winner that year and in their rematch in 1994 was Republican Jim Nussle, the youngest member of Congress when he was first elected in 1990, at age 30, and four years later one of the leaders of the new Republican majority. Nussle grew up in Chicago, attended a Lutheran college (he is Danish-American and speaks Danish) and law school and then moved back to his native Iowa. In the small town way, he soon became Delaware County attorney, known for prosecuting a local day care employee for child abuse. He coupled his anti-abortion stance with support for helping expectant mothers with the expenses of parenthood. When Congressman Tom Tauke ran for the Senate in 1990, Nussle ran for his seat, narrowly winning the Republican primary and then facing a better-financed Democrat. Nussle emphasized his experience in law enforcement, called for more parental involvement in the drug war as well as choosing day care, and argued that "People make better decisions about things that affect their lives than does the government." This was enough for him to win 50%–49%, one of the closest margins in the country that year.

In the House, Nussle combined a friendly and personable demeanor with disgust at the Democrats' way of doing business. He became one of the Gang of Seven, a group of freshman Republican reformers who attacked the leadership. In October 1991, he made national political news by speaking on the House floor with a paper bag over his head to protest Democratic leaders' refusal to make full disclosure of House bank overdrafts. He voted against agricultural appropriations, to the dismay of senior Iowa Democrat Neal Smith, and moved to cut congressional salaries 5% every year the federal budget is not balanced. In May 1991, when new district lines were drawn, Nussle was thrown into the same district as Democratic incumbent Dave Nagle, a canny, sharp-tongued natural politician from Waterloo, Democratic state chairman during the 1984 Iowa presidential caucuses and Congressman since 1986. Nagle was a stalwart supporter of the Democratic leadership and when Speaker Jim Wright was under investigation in 1989 on charges brought by then-backbench Republican Newt Gingrich, Nagle convened secret strategy meetings for pro-Wright Democrats. In 1992, he denounced the subpoena of House bank records by special investigator Malcolm Wilkey as a violation of separation of powers, "public opinion be damned," as he put it. The clincher for the race was probably House reform, and the winner was Nussle, again by 50%–49%. Nagle had a turf advantage, having represented 56% of the new 2d to Nussle's 35%. But Nussle carried his old district with 54%, while Nagle carried his old district by just 51%–48%.

Nussle continued to be a scourge of the House Democratic leadership. Except on foreign issues, he made a strongly conservative record. Even after the 1993 Iowa floods, he held up a flood relief measure to demand offsetting spending cuts. Back in Iowa, Nagle, who had been thinking of running for governor, decided to run against Nussle again instead, and polls showed the race close. Nagle attacked Nussle on flood relief; Nussle attacked Nagle for not withholding taxes for his campaign employees. One big difference from 1992: both men raised and spent over $800,000 then; in 1994 Nussle spent about that again, but Nagle as a non-incumbent could raise and spend only about half that amount. Nussle won this time 56%–44%, carrying his old district with 61% and winning 54% in counties that were in Nagle's old district as well.

After the election, Newt Gingrich appointed Nussle as the director of the transition to Republican rule: from paper bag to power in just three years. Nussle immediately fired off letters to House officers demanding a freeze on hiring and detailed accounting of funding and activities. Then, he supervised a top-to-bottom administrative overhaul of the House. Personable and partisan, and with a seat on Ways and Means, Nussle is likely to play an important role in Newt Gingrich's inner circle and in the House of Representatives.

The People: Pop. 1990: 555,494; 49% rural; 16% age 65+; 97% White; 2% Black; 1% Hispanic origin. Voting age pop.: 408,421; 1% Black. Households: 62% married couple families; 28% married couple fams. w. children; 36% college educ.; median household income: $25,010; per capita income: $11,611; median gross rent: $300; median house value: $42,400.

1992 Presidential Vote			1988 Presidential Vote		
Clinton (D)	120,228	(44%)	Dukakis (D)	137,842	(55%)
Bush (R)	95,005	(35%)	Bush (R)	108,563	(44%)
Perot (I)	55,279	(20%)			

Rep. Jim Nussle (R)

Elected 1990; b. June 27, 1960, Des Moines; home, Manchester; Luther Col., B.A. 1983, Drake U., J.D. 1985; Lutheran; married (Leslie).

Career: Delaware Cnty. Atty., 1986–90.

DC Office: 303 CHOB 20515, 202-225-2911; Fax: 202-225-9129.

District Offices: 2300 JFK Rd., Dubuque 52002, 319-557-7740; 3356 Kimball Ave., Waterloo 50702, 310-235-1109; 1825 4th St., SW, Mason City 50401, 515-423-0303; and 223 W. Main St., Manchester 52057, 319-927-5141.

Committees: *Budget* (17th of 24 R). *Ways & Means* (14th of 21 R): Human Resources.

Group Ratings

	ADA	ACLU	COPE	CFA	LCV	CON	NSI	COC	ACU	NTLC	CHC
1994	25	22	22	100	22	98	40	100	70	89	93
1993	20	—	8	10	29	98	—	91	83	—	—

National Journal Ratings

	1993 LIB — 1993 CONS			1994 LIB — 1994 CONS		
Economic	0%	—	88%	0%	—	80%
Social	11%	—	82%	20%	—	77%
Foreign	40%	—	57%	34%	—	63%

Key Votes of the 103d Congress

1. Clinton Deficit Plan	N	3. Brady Handgun Purchase	N	5. Lmt. UN Cmnd. of Forces	Y
2. NAFTA	Y	4. Strike Race/Death Pnlty.	Y	6. Cut Missile Funds	Y

Key Votes of the 104th Congress

1. Congressional Compliance	Y	6. Reform Crime Grant	Y	11. Loser Pays Court Reform	Y
2. Balanced Budget Amndmt.	Y	7. National Security Act	Y	12. Product Liability Reform	Y
3. Bar Unfunded Mandates	Y	8. Moratorium on Regs.	Y	13. Welfare Reform	Y
4. Pass Line Item Veto	Y	9. Risk Assessment on Regs.	Y	14. Term Limits Amndmt.	Y
5. Relax Exclusionary Rule	Y	10. Expnd. Priv. Prop. Rights	Y	15. Tax Cuts	Y

Election Results

1994 general	Jim Nussle (R)	111,076	(56%)	($876,142)
	Dave Nagle (D)	86,087	(43%)	($491,552)
	Others	1,324	(1%)	
1994 primary	Jim Nussle (R)	unopposed		
1992 general	Jim Nussle (R)	134,536	(50%)	($865,838)
	David Nagle (D)	131,570	(49%)	($853,637)
	Others	1,786	(1%)	

THIRD DISTRICT

The rolling farmland of southern Iowa heads west, as settlers did more than a century ago, from the railroad towns perched below the bluffs on the Mississippi River to the dusty plains above the Missouri River looking over to Nebraska and the West. The southern two tiers of Iowa's counties have none of the state's large cities; the accent here sounds like rural Missouri, with a touch of the South. Population here has been declining for many years, as the numerous children of large farm families seek opportunity elsewhere, since mechanization and technology require fewer people on the land. The 3d Congressional District of Iowa covers much of the southern part of the state, including almost all of the southern tier, from the Mississippi River border with Illinois almost to the Missouri River border with Nebraska. The 3d also juts north to include a variety of noteworthy small towns: Pella, home of the Pella window firm; Newton, home of Maytag appliances; Grinnell, with Grinnell College; Marshalltown, memorialized in *The Music Man* and known more recently as the town first involved in the Iowa Trust scandal; and Ames, home of Iowa State University. The historical preference here is Republican. In the 1980s, when Iowans felt hard pressed economically, there was a trend toward the Democrats, even to Michael Dukakis in 1988. In the 1990s, the trend has been Republican, with Governor Terry Branstad carrying all but three scattered counties in 1994.

The congressman from the 3d District is conservative Republican Jim Ross Lightfoot, now a comparative veteran after a decade in office, with a career that resembles the "Perils of Pauline." Lightfoot has had an unusual career path: he was a Tulsa policeman at 21, farm editor (as Jim Ross) of KMA radio in his home town of Shenandoah in the 1960s, manager of a farm equipment company in the 1970s, then back again to KMA in 1976. He ran for Congress in 1984, when Democrat Tom Harkin gave up his seat to run for the Senate, and narrowly beat a prominent state legislator. He quickly became Iowa's most conservative member of Congress— he was one of only 28 House members to vote against Harkin's Americans With Disabilities Act—and won reelection easily until redistricting in 1992.

Then the nonpartisan plan took away most of the Republican southwest Iowa counties Lightfoot had represented and added the Democratic-leaning southern tier counties east to the Mississippi. Plus, he had 105 overdrafts on the House bank and serious opposition from Secretary of State Elaine Baxter. In the June primary, he got only 58% of the vote against a political unknown who said of his own showing, "There's only one explanation: God did it." *Roll Call* named him "America's most vulnerable incumbent." But Lightfoot counterattacked by running ads criticizing Baxter for her junkets to Hawaii, redecorating her office (paying $67 for an in-box), and supporting the increase in the sales and gas taxes. A 10-second ad showed a man's hand holding a wallet ("This is your wallet") and then a woman's hands taking the money out ("This is your wallet under Elaine Baxter"). Lightfoot ran a bus caravan across the district and won 49%–47%. Baxter ran again, with high hopes, in 1994, but this time she could raise only half as much money as Lightfoot—a forecast of how many Democratic candidates may fare in 1996—and Lightfoot won with 59%, carrying everything, even Ames, except for Baxter's home county. So Lightfoot will bring his conservative record, opposition to congressional pay raises and support of China's most favored nation status to the 104th Congress.

One of the unpredicted results of 1994 was that Lightfoot joined what used to be called the College of Cardinals: that is, he took over the chair of an Appropriations subcommittee— Treasury, Postal Service and General Government. So this farm radio broadcaster now oversees the White House budget, a delicious or sickening thought depending on where you stand. But power is ephemeral in Newt Gingrich's Washington. Despite his original pledge to serve only six terms, Lightfoot announced his intention to seek a seventh term, apparently enjoying his position as an Appropriations subcommittee chairman; he has ruled out challenging Tom Harkin for the Senate in 1996.

The People: Pop. 1990: 555,299; 46% rural; 16% age 65+; 98% White; 1% Black; 1% Asian; 1% Hispanic origin. Voting age pop.: 417,744; 1% Black; 1% Hispanic origin. Households: 61% married couple families; 27% married couple fams. w. children; 39% college educ.; median household income: $24,767; per capita income: $11,567; median gross rent: $315; median house value: $41,200.

1992 Presidential Vote			1988 Presidential Vote		
Clinton (D)	120,495	(45%)	Dukakis (D)	138,616	(56%)
Bush (R)	96,515	(36%)	Bush (R)	106,573	(43%)
Perot (I)	47,028	(18%)			

Rep. Jim Ross Lightfoot (R)

Elected 1984; b. Sept. 27, 1938, Sioux City; home, Shenandoah; Catholic; married (Nancy).

Career: Army, 1956, Army Reserves, 1957–64; Tulsa Police officer, 1959–61; Farm editor, KMA Radio, 1961–70, 1976–84; Mgr., farm equipment manufacturing co., 1970–76; Corsicana City Comm., 1974–76.

DC Office: 2161 RHOB 20515, 202-225-3806; Fax: 202-225-6973.

District Offices: 501 W. Lowell, Shenandoah 51601, 712-246-1984; 413 Kellogg, Ames 50010, 515-232-1288; 220 W. Salem, Indianola 50125, 515-961-0591; 347 E. 2d St., Ottumwa 52501, 515-683-3551; and 311 N. 3d St., Burlington 52601, 319-753-6415.

Committees: *Appropriations* (14th of 32 R): Foreign Operations, Export Financing, and Related Programs; Transportation; Treasury, Postal Service, and General Government (Chmn.).

Group Ratings

	ADA	ACLU	COPE	CFA	LCV	CON	NSI	COC	ACU	NTLC	CHC
1994	5	13	0	20	6	60	80	92	95	74	93
1993	10	—	8	20	15	16	—	91	91	—	—

National Journal Ratings

	1993 LIB	—	1993 CONS	1994 LIB	—	1994 CONS
Economic	30%	—	68%	36%	—	64%
Social	11%	—	82%	11%	—	85%
Foreign	17%	—	76%	25%	—	71%

Key Votes of the 103d Congress

1. Clinton Deficit Plan	N	3. Brady Handgun Purchase	N	5. Lmt. UN Cmnd. of Forces	Y
2. NAFTA	Y	4. Strike Race/Death Pnlty.	Y	6. Cut Missile Funds	N

Key Votes of the 104th Congress

1. Congressional Compliance	Y	6. Reform Crime Grant	Y	11. Loser Pays Court Reform	Y
2. Balanced Budget Amndmt.	Y	7. National Security Act	Y	12. Product Liability Reform	Y
3. Bar Unfunded Mandates	Y	8. Moratorium on Regs.	Y	13. Welfare Reform	Y
4. Pass Line Item Veto	Y	9. Risk Assessment on Regs.	Y	14. Term Limits Amndmt.	Y
5. Relax Exclusionary Rule	Y	10. Expnd. Priv. Prop. Rights	Y	15. Tax Cuts	Y

Election Results

1994 general	Jim Ross Lightfoot (R)	111,862	(58%)	($709,487)
	Elaine Baxter (D)	79,310	(41%)	($374,500)
	Others	2,359	(1%)	
1994 primary	Jim Ross Lightfoot (R)	unopposed		
1992 general	Jim Ross Lightfoot (R)	125,931	(49%)	($755,552)
	Elaine Baxter (D)	121,063	(47%)	($645,342)
	Larry Chroman (Natural Law)	10,181	(4%)	($129,096)

FOURTH DISTRICT

Iowa, which today seems very much in the middle of the country, was once part of the West. Iowa was home to sober farmers and pious burghers, but it was also the eastern terminus of the first Transcontinental Railroad, a waystop for people in a hurry to get to Nebraska and the Rockies and the Pacific or the Dakotas and the fastness of Montana. Those who stayed behind were determined to use the wealth accumulated by methodical husbandry of their fertile farmlands to implant firmly the glories of western civilization. You can feel that impulse today in Des Moines when you look across the river from downtown at the Victorian Capitol, its gold dome above a Corinthian pediment, or Terrace Hill, the beautifully restored governor's mansion, atop a hill overlooking the Raccoon River. The nearby Living History Farms, which recreate Indian villages, frontier towns and turn-of-the-century farms, show the effort the new settlers made to put their imprint on the environment. The same civilizing impulse can be seen farther west, in the city of Council Bluffs, in the mansion of General Grenville Dodge. Here in 1859, General Dodge lobbied Illinois lawyer Abraham Lincoln on the need for a transcontinental railroad; Lincoln got it through Congress in 1863, Dodge became its chief engineer, and Council Bluffs became its eastern terminus when it was completed in 1869.

Des Moines and Council Bluffs were among the few areas of Iowa which showed growth in the bedraggled 1980s. While small town bankers were foreclosing on farm mortgages, main street storefronts were going vacant one by one, and the meatpacking and tractor factories in Iowa's smaller cities were going dark and empty, these and a few other cities were growing. Their tidy shopping centers were gaining businesses that used to go to small towns, as Iowans got into the habit of driving 100 miles for a day's shopping; their office centers were filling up with new service jobs, as manufacturing jobs in other cities were disappearing; their insurance and printing companies were expanding as businesses elsewhere in Iowa were closing down. Now, in the 1990s, as all of Iowa is doing better, these cities continue to grow—though not as robustly and confidently as they did when they were the gateway to the West.

The 4th Congressional District of Iowa, greatly redesigned in the 1991 redistricting, includes Des Moines and Council Bluffs and their surrounding counties (Polk and Pottawattamie), plus 11 mostly rural counties in between, including the eponymous site of Robert James Waller's *The Bridges of Madison County*. There are varied political leanings here. Des Moines is in the center of corn and hog country, for years hankering for generous farm subsidies; its Iowa-ish cultural liberalism is strengthened by the liberal *Des Moines Register & Tribune*. Council Bluffs is surrounded by beef grazing country, where the federal government is seen as an officious intermeddler; it looks west to Omaha, taking on the culturally more conservative tone of Nebraska and the conservative politics of the *Omaha World-Herald*. Des Moines has more votes—Polk and next-door Dallas County cast 69% of the 4th District's votes—but in 1994 the balance of opinion was tilted more to the Council Bluffs side.

The 4th District was the scene of one of the biggest upsets of 1994, the defeat of 36-year incumbent Democrat Neal Smith by political newcomer Greg Ganske. To be sure, during all of that time until the 1991 redistricting, Smith had not represented Council Bluffs or most of the rural counties; but his margins in the Des Moines area were so high that he seemed unbeatable. Smith himself, with his persnickitiness about doing things by the rules and his liberal views on most issues, seemed quintessentially Iowan. He was the third ranking Democrat on Appropriations, chairing its Commerce-Justice-State-Judiciary Subcommittee. But in February 1994, when Appropriations Chairman William Natcher died, Smith lost out in the race for the post to the more junior David Obey of Wisconsin 152–106 (ironically, Smith sponsored the rule that chairmen be picked by caucus vote rather than seniority).

Meanwhile, back home, Ganske was campaigning hard. A small town boy from Manchester (the home now of 2d District Congressman Jim Nussle), Ganske was a reconstructive surgeon in Des Moines, performing both cosmetic surgery and also—what he liked to emphasize—reconstructive surgery for birth defects, and victims of accidents, burns and crimes. He decided to put some of his own money, ultimately $618,427, into his campaign and, at Newt Gingrich's suggestion, bought a rusty beige 1958 DeSoto, made in the year Smith first won, and drove it around the district. " '58 Nealmobile—WHY is it still running," a sign on its roof read. Ganske opposed the Clinton healthcare plan and demanded lawmakers read it before voting. He attacked Smith for "logrolling" (you support my bill, I'll support yours) and said, "What do 36-year career politicians like Neal Smith always do? They blame each other, spend more money and then raise your taxes." Smith seemed reluctant to speak in the idiom of 1994. "I am able to work on things that are important to Iowa," he said, in a year when pork barrel projects were not popular and his own clout seemed diminished, after his fellow Democrats turned him down for the Appropriations chairmanship. He was proud of restoring prairie lands Ganske derided as a "buffalo preserve."

By June Ganske had a poll showing Smith behind; Smith spent far more money than ever before, but won only 51% in the Des Moines area. Districtwide, Ganske won 53%–47%, with 65% in the Council Bluffs area and 62% in the rural counties. (Interestingly, Smith's two other lowest percentages, 53% in 1960 and 54% in 1980, came when he was opposed by physicians.) Although he showed some independence by leading Republican renegades seeking to scale back the proposed tax cut from the Contract With America, in order to keep the focus on reducing the federal deficit, Ganske is likely to be an enthusiastic follower of Newt Gingrich on most issues. His Commerce Committee seat gives him an opportunity to take advantage of his expertise on healthcare issues.

The People: Pop. 1990: 555,276; 26% rural; 14% age 65+; 95% White; 3% Black; 1% Asian; 1% Other; 2% Hispanic origin. Voting age pop.: 412,155; 2% Black; 1% Hispanic origin. Households: 58% married couple families; 27% married couple fams. w. children; 46% college educ.; median household income: $28,591; per capita income: $13,813; median gross rent: $405; median house value: $52,500.

1992 Presidential Vote			1988 Presidential Vote		
Clinton (D)	117,863	(43%)	Dukakis (D)	131,550	(55%)
Bush (R)	107,745	(39%)	Bush (R)	106,044	(44%)
Perot (I)	47,835	(17%)			

Rep. Greg Ganske (R)

Elected 1994; b. Mar. 31, 1949, New Hampton; home, Des Moines; U. of IA, B.S. 1972; M.D. 1976; Catholic; married (Corrine).

Career: Army Reserves, 1986–present; Farmer; Practicing surgeon, 1976–94;

DC Office: 1108 LHOB 20515, 202-225-4426; Fax: 202-225-3193.

District Offices: Fed. Bldg., 210 Walnut St., #717, Des Moines 50309, 515-284-4634; and 40 Pearl St., Council Bluffs 51503, 712-323-5976.

Committees: *Commerce* (22nd of 26 R): Commerce, Trade and Hazardous Materials; Health and Environment.

Group Ratings and 103rd Congress Votes: Newly Elected

Key Votes of the 104th Congress

1. Congressional Compliance	Y	6. Reform Crime Grant	Y	11. Loser Pays Court Reform	Y
2. Balanced Budget Amndmt.	Y	7. National Security Act	Y	12. Product Liability Reform	Y
3. Bar Unfunded Mandates	Y	8. Moratorium on Regs.	Y	13. Welfare Reform	Y
4. Pass Line Item Veto	Y	9. Risk Assessment on Regs.	Y	14. Term Limits Amndmt.	Y
5. Relax Exclusionary Rule	Y	10. Expnd. Priv. Prop. Rights	Y	15. Tax Cuts	Y

Election Results

1994 general	Greg Ganske (R)	111,935	(53%)	($1,195,525)
	Neal Smith (D)	98,824	(46%)	($1,005,498)
	Others	2,447	(1%)	
1994 primary	Greg Ganske (R)	45,915	(78%)	
	Paul Lunde (R)	12,968	(22%)	
1992 general	Neal Smith (D)	158,610	(62%)	($197,159)
	Paul Lunde (R)	94,045	(37%)	($11,178)
	Others	4,938	(2%)	

FIFTH DISTRICT

Nestled below and running up the loess bluffs above the Missouri River is one of the oldest market towns on the Great Plains, Sioux City. Although still the largest city on the Plains west of Des Moines and north of Omaha, Sioux City has not grown much in the last five decades. Its original economic base has become obsolete, and so has some of the city itself: the waterfront, once raucous with boatmen and stockyard workers, is now quiet; stockyards have been replaced by IBP's modern (and low-wage) beef factory across the river in Dakota City, Nebraska; downtown stores have been replaced by shopping malls at the edge of town where people will still drive for 100 miles to spend a day doing a season's shopping. In different form, Sioux City is still the main commercial center of the fertile plains of northwestern Iowa, and the leading city of Iowa's 5th Congressional District. The 5th District covers most of northern and northwest Iowa, politically an area that, on balance, is a few points more Republican than the rest of the state. Its biggest population centers are Sioux City in the west and Fort Dodge, just northwest of Des Moines, to the east. The counties on the gently rolling landscape in between are an ethnic melange: Irish Catholics in Palo Alto, Dutch in Sioux (the most heavily Republican county in Iowa), and the descendants of the English lords who built huge cattle ranches around Le Mars in Plymouth County.

The 5th District was the scene in 1994 of one of those open seat contests that produced a conservative freshman Republican. It was open because Republican Fred Grandy, known by C-SPAN viewers as an articulate House Republican but by cable rerun viewers as Gopher on *The Love Boat*, left the House to make a nearly successful primary run against Governor Terry Branstad. After losing, he voiced some sour notes about Branstad and at Newt Gingrich. One might have expected the two parties' nominations for the 5th District to be won by the two state legislators running; but in 1994, they were won instead by two candidates with interesting backgrounds typical of their parties' 1994 appeal.

The Republican was Tom Latham, a farmer who ran a seed company—a very Iowa business!—established by his family in rural Franklin County in 1947. Latham had been active in Republican politics, contributing, attending the national convention, and serving as a farm adviser to Grandy, but he had never run for office before. He opposed any government takeover of health care but favored continuation of farm support programs; he supported the Contract with America principles before the Contract existed. He easily beat Sioux City state Senator Brad Banks 62%–38% in the primary. The Democrat, Sheila McGuire, a health consultant in Boone, was trained as a dentist and has a doctorate in epidemiology; she has been an operative in many Democratic campaigns and was one of 47 medical care professionals selected to sit on a White House advisory panel to review the Clinton healthcare program. In early 1994 her campaign was going well: she billed herself as an expert who had helped draw up the Clinton healthcare plan and, with support from EMILY's List and other women's groups, she outraised other candidates of both parties. In the June primary, she beat state legislator Mike Peterson 53%–43% and seemed to be a strong contender.

But the growing unpopularity of the Clinton healthcare plan worked heavily against McGuire, while the rising popularity of the Republican platform, plus the 5th District's ancestral Republican leanings, worked strongly for Latham. Latham contrasted his farm and business background to McGuire's, noting that she had never been in a private practice of dentistry or medicine. "Professor McGuire helped write the Clinton healthcare plan that would put a bureaucrat between you and your doctor, raise your taxes and close many rural hospitals," a Latham ad said. "Everyone agrees the Clinton-McGuire plan was a bad idea." In reply McGuire said, "The economy is the main issue." The result was a resounding 61%–39% win for Latham in 1994, the best showing for any Iowa Republican, and in his first race. McGuire carried her home county with 52% and lost every other county; Latham won 87% in rural Sioux County and carried the Sioux City and Fort Dodge areas.

In the House Latham should be a strong Newt Gingrich Republican. He seems to have a safe seat for as long as his term limits conviction permits.

The People: Pop. 1990: 555,457; 52% rural; 18% age 65+; 98% White; 1% Black; 1% Asian; 1% Hispanic origin. Voting age pop.: 405,685; 1% Hispanic origin. Households: 62% married couple families; 28% married couple fams. w. children; 38% college educ.; median household income: $24,150; per capita income: $11,461; median gross rent: $285; median house value: $37,000.

1992 Presidential Vote

Bush (R) 109,966 (42%)
Clinton (D) 99,112 (38%)
Perot (I) 50,343 (19%)

1988 Presidential Vote

Dukakis (D) 125,833 (51%)
Bush (R) 118,492 (48%)

Rep. Tom Latham (R)

Elected 1994; b. July 14, 1948, Hampton; home, Alexander; Wartburg Col., 1966–67; IA St. U., 1967–70; Lutheran; married (Kathy).

Career: Farmer; Bank Teller/Bookkeeper, 1970–72; Independent Insurance Agent, 1972–74; Hartford Insurance Mktg. Rep., 1974–76; Co-Owner, Latham Seed Co., 1976–present.

DC Office: 516 CHOB 20515, 202-225-5476; Fax: 202-225-3301.

District Offices: 123 Albany Ave., SE. #1, Orange City 51041, 712-737-8708; 526 Pierce St., Sioux City 51101, 712-277-2114; 1411 1st Ave., S, Fort Dodge 50501, 515-573-2738; and 217 Grand Ave., Spencer 51301, 712-262-6480.

Committees: *Agriculture* (23rd of 27 R): Department Operations, Nutrition and Foreign Agriculture; General Farm Commodities. *Transportation & Infrastructure* (27th of 33 R): Surface Transportation; Water Resources and Environment.

Group Ratings and 103rd Congress Votes: Newly Elected

Key Votes of the 104th Congress

1. Congressional Compliance Y	6. Reform Crime Grant Y	11. Loser Pays Court Reform Y
2. Balanced Budget Amndmt. Y	7. National Security Act Y	12. Product Liability Reform Y
3. Bar Unfunded Mandates Y	8. Moratorium on Regs. Y	13. Welfare Reform Y
4. Pass Line Item Veto Y	9. Risk Assessment on Regs. Y	14. Term Limits Amndmt. Y
5. Relax Exclusionary Rule Y	10. Expnd. Priv. Prop. Rights Y	15. Tax Cuts Y

Election Results

1994 general	Tom Latham (R)	114,796	(61%)	($742,308)
	Sheila McGuire (D)	73,627	(39%)	($719,811)
1994 primary	Tom Latham (R)	47,454	(62%)	
	Brad Banks (R)	28,531	(38%)	
1992 general	Fred Grandy (R)	196,942	(99%)	($292,752)
	Others	1,424	(1%)	

KANSAS

"Like everyone else," James Dickenson writes of his grandmother Mary Phipps, who lived her 91 years in Kansas, "she was taught that the earth and the other planets circled the sun, but deep down she had the feeling that the sun and the rest of the cosmos really revolved around western Kansas. If anyone had suggested this in so many words, she'd have laughingly denied it, but it was implicit in her worldview. She took as the First Principle that bread, the staff of life, was one of the bases of existence itself, along with air and water. From this flowed the inescapable conclusion that wheat farmers were truly engaged in the Lord's work." These words open the book *Home on the Range*, in which Dickenson, for three decades a top national political reporter, starts with his own family and boyhood in Rawlins County to explain how Kansas came to be what it was, and how it is ceasing to be that and becoming something else. But Kansas has always been quintessentially American, which is not to say entirely placid or entirely unflavorful. Recall that in 1989 when Russian leader Yevgeny Primakov wanted to see "real Americans," he flew out with Bob Dole to Dodge City, to visit Boot Hill Museum and the Long Branch Saloon—and was questioned about, among other things, why his country continued to occupy the Baltic States. Kansas, like so much of Russia, may look quiet, full of solid farmers who work hard and have deep roots in the soil, the place around which the cosmos revolves. But Kansas's history, like Russia's, has also been punctuated by uprisings, intellectual and violent, by moments of anger and rage sweeping through the tall sheaves like a tornado wind. The difference, of course, is that Russian traditions of law and liberty, culture and civility are weak, while in Kansas as in all America they are remarkably strong.

Kansas literally began in a moment of violence, the Bleeding Kansas of the 1850s, that led proximately to the terrible war that split the whole nation: violence which broke out after the Kansas-Nebraska Act of 1854 left to local settlers the question of whether this new Kansas Territory would be a free or slave state. Pro-slavery "bushwhackers" rode over the line from Missouri, stealing elections and writing a pro-slavery constitution. But much larger numbers of free-soil "jayhawkers" from New England and the New England-Yankee-settled Great Lakes states put down roots and, despite the massacres of the mad John Brown, prevailed and established their own law and order. The effect on national politics was tumultuous: the Democratic Party was split, the Republican Party was created, the nation was plunged into Civil War. The effect on Kansas was calming: the anti-slavery majority bent the soil to the plow and built small towns thick with schools, churches and colleges, to the point that in the 1939 color movie, *Wizard of Oz*, Kansas was shot in dreary black and white as the image of dull, prim, old-fashioned Middle America. But the rebellious impulse did not totally die out. Kansas lived almost entirely on farming, and its livelihood was always at risk; hailstorms, grasshopper invasions, dry seasons or a drop in world farm prices could mean disaster for thousands of Kansans. The high-rainfall 1880s attracted hundreds of thousands of new settlers to Kansas; the low-rainfall 1890s produced a bust and a populist rebellion. "What you farmers should do," said orator Mary Ellen Lease, "is to raise less corn and more hell." For a few years in the 1890s, and then in farm rebellions of the 1930s, 1950s and 1970s, Kansans did, but afterwards always returned to jayhawker Republicanism.

At least a whiff of rebellion is apparent in the air of the 1990s. George Bush ended up carrying Kansas in 1992, but for much of the campaign he was running behind in polls, and Ross Perot won 27% of the vote here, his fifth best showing in the nation. Perot did not run that well in any of the five major urban counties, whose recent growth has made Kansas an increasingly urban state despite its wheat-farm heritage. But most of his strongest showings were not in the wheat country of central Kansas or the grazing lands of the southwest (where seven counties voted 84%

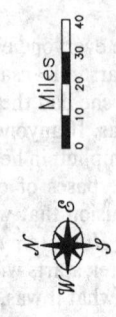

Miles
0 10 20 30 40

— Congressional district boundaries
effective June 3, 1992.

to secede from the state in April 1992), either; farm prices and profits have been relatively high and unemployment here very low. Instead, Perot ran best in counties just at the edge of metropolitan expansion and in the sparsely populated Flint Hills, where young families may live, but make their living commuting to two jobs in Wichita or Topeka or greater Kansas City and drive 50 or 100 miles to the nearest mall to shop. Historically, these counties are places where people have deep roots, but many of them have been moving out, and the new residents are oriented to the Interstates rather than the courthouse squares. It seems likely that the Perot vote comes in Kansas, as in other states, from the less deeply rooted, from newcomers with a tradition of civic involvement but with none of it in their lives until the Texas billionaire came along.

Governor. The governorship of Kansas is not very important to the rest of the nation, though once a Kansas governor—Alf Landon in 1936—was nominated for president; he lived to see his daughter Nancy Kassebaum serve in the United States Senate and died at age 100 in Topeka in 1987. In 1994 Kansas elected a governor as conservative on state issues as Landon was reputed (not quite accurately) to be on national issues when he ran against Franklin Roosevelt.

The new governor is Bill Graves, a Republican elected Secretary of State in 1986. Graves grew up in Salina, where his family had a trucking firm, Graves Truck Lines; he worked in the business from loading dock to management, even though he moved to a suburb of Kansas City (his wife practiced law in Missouri). Graves was not the favorite going into the race. That was probably Democratic Congressman Jim Slattery, one of those instinctively political Democrats who captures a Republican seat (as he did in 1982) and holds onto it indefinitely, with a voting record that promotes local interests and wobbles between moderate and liberal on national issues. Slattery was in fact a major national force in spring 1994 when he refused to support a healthcare plan with an employer mandate and forced Chairman John Dingell to admit that he could not report a bill out of his Energy and Commerce Committee. Slattery was able to win a five-candidate Democratic gubernatorial primary with an impressive 53%. But in the general he had little to say, slipping from one issue to another, then focusing on charges that Graves had received contributions from executives of an Alabama company owned by his father-in-law which was accused of misleading seniors about their insurance coverage. He sounded like Bill Clinton: he wanted to do government, but it wasn't clear what he wanted to do with it.

Graves, who won his six-candidate primary with 41%, had a more solid theme. "Load 'em high and tight," he repeated over and over again, as his family had loaded the trailers of 18-wheelers with cartons of goods. Graves pledged to keep spending down, to rein in government; he called Slattery a "double-dealing Washington congressman"—pretty tough stuff in 1994. The race blew open in the last weeks, and Graves won 64%–36%—the widest margin in over 20 years, and an astonishing showing against a man who had after all won election to Congress five times in a major portion of the state; Slattery carried three of 105 counties. The verdict was unambiguous. On taking office Graves pledged that "within a framework of limited government and careful allocation of resources we must give each Kansan an opportunity to experience a better quality of life." The state House was expected to concentrate on budget cutting, limiting abortion, school vouchers and Quality Performance Accreditation in the schools; the state Senate was working to repeal a 2.5% tax on labor used in new construction and utilities used in manufacturing. Liberals said Kansas had opted for a caretaker rather than a reformer; certainly it opted for less government.

Senators. Senator Bob Dole is one of the large political figures of our time, in the middle 1990s towering over everyone else in the political landscape, even the president. He became Senate Majority Leader in 1985 and again in 1995; in between, from 1987 to 1995, he was Senate Minority Leader. Overall, by December 1995, he will have been Senate Republican Leader longer than anyone else in history. In the early 1990s he was overshadowed by a Republican president and administration and the Democratic congressional leadership. But after the 1992 election he suddenly became the nation's most prominent Republican, immediately reminding the nation and Bill Clinton that 57% of Americans had voted against Clinton and that he, as leader of 44 Republicans in a Senate whose rules leave them far from powerless, would try to represent all of them. And after the 1994 election, after all eyes turned toward Newt Gingrich and the 73 freshman House Republicans, it became clear that Dole as Majority Leader in the Senate would have tremendous influence over how much of the new agenda passed and how much didn't. He was suddenly the front-running Republican presidential candidate, led Clinton in some national polls, and was the proven hero of the G.I. generation dwarfing loquacious baby boomers Newt and Bill.

For Dole is not only one of the most successful politicians of the second half of the 20th Century but also one of the most enduring. Grievously injured in World War II combat in the first days of Harry Truman's Administration, he took his seat in Congress in the last days of Dwight Eisenhower's. In the middle of his fifth Senate term in 1995, he had served 35 years in Congress, longer than all but four other Senators (Thurmond, Byrd, Pell, Inouye), longer as a Republican in Congress than anyone else. Dole has had his disappointments in national politics. He was the vice presidential candidate on Gerald Ford's losing ticket in 1976, and not an especially popular one. He got little support when he ran for president in 1980. When he did run a serious race in 1988, and seemed on the verge of winning, he lost the New Hampshire primary to George Bush, after which his campaign fell apart. Yet by 1995 he had emerged as the front-running candidate for president, even though in 1996 he turns 73, an age at which only Ronald Reagan has been elected, and will have to overcome the disadvantages that have prevented Senate leaders as talented as Robert Taft, Lyndon Johnson, and Dole himself from winning presidential nomination. But no one should count him out. How to account for Dole's endurance? He is a hard worker with an acerbic sense of humor, given to conciliatory language but with clear threats of political hardball; he has consistently held to certain basic principles, though he is not at all a political theorist; he has earned the respect that a politician can win only by persevering through hard times as well as good, by being bloodied by defeat and coming back to fight against the odds and win a victory.

The son of a cream-and-egg station operator in Russell, Kansas, Dole didn't seem headed for college when he went into the Army during World War II. In Italy in April 1945, just three weeks before V-E Day, he was seriously injured; this strong-bodied high school athlete lost nearly half his weight, almost died, and spent four years in hospital wards. Regarded by some as a hopeless case, he went through largely successful rehabilitation programs, although he does not have use of his right hand and still suffers considerable pain. This may help to explain his support for the handicapped. But the determination behind his recovery also explains how he moved forward from county attorney to congressman in a tough 1960 primary, from obscure congressman to a U.S. Senator in 1968, from a little-known freshman to Richard Nixon's Republican National Committee chairman in 1971, his first moment of national renown.

One consistent theme of Dole's career has been tough Republican partisanship. He came by it naturally—in Russell, Kansas, not just the banker and the country club member, but the mechanic at the garage and the clerk at the feed store are Republicans—and with no sense that the party excludes compassion for the helpless. It was this partisanship that propelled him to volunteer to defend the Nixon Administration when he first came to a very anti-Nixon Senate in 1969, that prompted Nixon to name him Republican National Committee chairman in 1971, and that led Gerald Ford's advisers to believe that Dole's nomination as vice president would propitiate Reagan conservatives in 1976. He was shoved out of the RNC when Richard Nixon needed a place for George Bush in 1973, he had his toughest Senate race and was nearly defeated by lawyer-doctor Bill Roy in 1974, and his vice presidential campaign brought him brickbats from the press without convincing Reagan Republicans that he was one of them.

In some important ways, he wasn't. He has the old Midwestern Republican's horror of budget deficits, and in the 1980s he was willing to raise taxes to prevent them. As Finance chairman, he loyally floor-managed the Reagan tax cuts of 1981. But, largely on his own hook, he came back in 1982 with the tax-raising TEFRA bill which he passed almost entirely with Republican votes. His disdain for supply-siders is legendary, and Newt Gingrich said in 1984, Bob Dole is "the tax collector for the welfare state." A decade later, Gingrich had become Dole's more cooperative partner but the underlying tension and contrasting political framework remained between them. On other issues, it should be added, Dole has been a consistent and hard-fighting conservative. He has always been antiabortion, as indeed every politician was when Dole was first elected to Congress, and he used the abortion issue sharply against Roy in 1974. He has always been a backer of big defense budgets and of an assertive foreign policy, and has thrown scorn on Democrats who in his view would not support U.S. troops in conflicts from Vietnam to Bosnia. He was the sharpest critic of Bill Clinton's statements about his draft record in the 1992 campaign and led the fight to codify the ban on gays in the military in early 1993. This combination of issue stands, and the knowledge that they are sincerely held, has positioned him well to lead Senate Republicans. He won the party leadership by a narrow margin in 1984, over Ted Stevens, Richard Lugar and James McClure, but his hold on it quickly became secure. His command of Senate procedure is ample, his word is reliable, his relations with different sorts of Republicans and with Democratic leaders amicable enough to keep the flow of business going, even with the many frustrations and difficulties of doing business in the Senate. He is an old-fashioned politician who does his own work and doesn't delegate much; this hurt his ill-fated 1988 presidential candidacy, but helps his floor leadership.

From his defeat in the 1988 presidential race, he rebounded as he has before. His bitterness at George Bush after the New Hampshire primary ("stop lying about my record," he said live on NBC) was genuine, but once Bush was in the White House he worked loyally for him. It surely helped that Bush appointed Elizabeth Dole as Secretary of Labor (she resigned to become head of the American Red Cross in late 1990). He got Republican senators to uphold all but one of Bush's vetoes, even on China, and provided key votes for Bush's version of the Clean Air Act. A civil rights supporter for years, and the man who fashioned the compromise that got the Voting Rights Act renewed in 1982, Dole followed the administration's lead in opposing several civil rights bills as quota measures and then backing a compromise in the fall of 1991. He supported Bush's policies in the Gulf war, despite some personal lobbying against them by Ross Perot. Dole did undercut Bush—or help him abandon his own promise—on taxes when during the 1990 budget summit talks, he helped ditch Bush's capital gains cut and thus increased pressure for income tax rises; Bush ended up repudiating the budget summit agreement in the 1992 campaign, but Dole didn't. Nevertheless, by the end of Bush's term, Dole was a strong Bush partisan, loudly criticizing independent counsel Lawrence Walsh's blatantly political Friday-before-election indictment of Caspar Weinberger and presiding over a tearful after-election dinner for the defeated President.

Dole realized instantly on election night 1992 that he held the key to his party's one source of power: if 41 of the 43 Republicans could stick together to sustain a filibuster, they could derail any Democratic initiative. (Republican numbers grew to 44 and 45 as Paul Coverdell won the Georgia runoff in November 1992 and Kay Bailey Hutchison won the Texas special in June 1993). In April 1993, Dole successfully held together Senate Republicans to filibuster Clinton's economic stimulus plan which the president eventually had to withdraw. He led Senate Republicans to unanimously oppose the Clinton budget and tax package—which put every Democrat contributing to its one-vote margin on the line as the decisive vote. He opposed military deployment in Haiti and tried to prevent it without a congressional vote. He showed an active interest in healthcare issues, and hinted during 1993 and early 1994 that he might be willing to negotiate a compromise with the Clinton healthcare plan, perhaps along the lines suggested by Rhode Island's John Chafee. But in January 1994 he called for Republican unity on a plan similar to what Lloyd Bentsen had proposed as a senator, for modest insurance reform; Hillary Rodham Clinton had missed her moment. Dole went on to effectively oppose Democrats' changing plans, causing rue among those who had banked on him for a compromise. He hit the Democrats hard on Whitewater issues—he remembers what Watergate did to his party—and he consistently urged lifting the arms embargo in Bosnia and seemed ready to intervene on the side of the Bosnian Muslims. In May 1994 he delivered the most moving and heartfelt eulogy of Richard Nixon: these two Republicans, only 10 years apart, had both once heard trains in the night, had both dreamed of making a great figure in the nation's capital, had both endured scorn from sophisticates to come back unyielding and prevail.

Dole campaigned hard for Republican candidates (and didn't stint Iowa or New Hampshire) and had the satisfaction of seeing Republicans fulfill his July 1993 prediction and pick up seven seats on November 8, 1994, for a majority of 52. (Republican numbers grew to 53 and 54 as Richard Shelby switched the day after the election and Ben Nighthorse Campbell joined the day after the balanced budget amendment vote). While reporters speculated that Dole would be overshadowed by and hostile to the new Speaker, Newt Gingrich, Dole came out aggressively for conservative reforms, promising to make unfunded mandates Senate Bill 1, encouraging welfare reform and devolution to the states (and the Republican governors), appearing amicably with Gingrich, who wisely deferred to him and noted that the chambers' differences in rules and custom meant that the Senate could not be expected to act as quickly or reliably on the Contract With America or other issues as the House. Dole did not always prevail: Trent Lott ousted Alan Simpson as Republican Whip by one vote, despite Dole's urgings; Phil Gramm, running hard for president, was clearly putting on the pressure; Dole could not deliver Mark Hatfield for the balanced budget amendment, and so lost by one vote.

But overall, Dole showed great adaptability and skill, emphasizing areas of agreement with the conservative freshmen, underplaying zones of dissent, campaigning for president hard across the country while keeping the reins tight on the Senate. Dole also raised vast sums and assembled a fine organization for his presidential campaign. His suppleness at tactics was greater than ever, and there was evidence that he was engaged in, rather than as in the past bored with, the larger strategy, framing the issues, setting the pace, building a set of governing ideas. The presidency itself has diminished since he started running, because after the Cold War the president no longer holds the fate of the world in his hands; and in that time Bob Dole is the one candidate who to many seems plainly larger than the office he seeks.

Dole has been reelected the last three times in Kansas without difficulty, and should he not be elected president could easily be reelected in 1998 at age 75 if he wants. Although he hopes that the nation's voters will act in 1996 so that he will not have to choose in 1998, he has hinted that this will be his last Senate term.

Nancy Kassebaum, first elected in 1978, is now one of the leading Republican senators, Chairman of the Labor and Human Resources Committee, originator of radical proposals to reshape domestic government. She came to the Senate with minimal experience in public office but a fine political legacy as the daughter of 1936 Republican presidential nominee Alf Landon, who died in 1987 at age 100; and she has shown shrewd political and policy instincts in office. Kassebaum's voting record tends to be moderate, though she is quite conservative on economics. She has made an important impact on foreign affairs. She was a key backer of sanctions against South Africa, and in determining when to scale them back. She and Democratic Congressman Dan Glickman came forward in June 1990 to urge a cutoff of $700 million in credit guarantees for Iraq for food purchases—money Saddam Hussein was using to buy arms. This was opposed heartily by the Bush Administration, a monumental blunder in retrospect. After a June 1992 trip, Kassebaum called for United Nations peacekeepers in famine-torn orderless Somalia; George Bush disagreed, but in November 1992 sent in U.S. troops. She supports international family planning abroad and is pro-choice at home. She is leery of the religious right in politics, as she showed in chairing confirmation hearings for Henry Foster as Surgeon General.

But it is a mistake to see her, as some have, as a liberal Republican close to Democrats on domestic issues. In 1994 she advanced a radical swap proposal, arguing that the federal government should give up welfare programs to the states, and take full responsibility from the states for Medicaid. Fiscally, the federal government might be more heavily burdened, should Medicaid costs keep rising rapidly; but that was less important than the fact that Kassebaum should be calling for such a radical change as devolution of power to the state. Similarly, in 1995 she called for giving states the authority to consolidate or eliminate job training programs, hitherto closely monitored by the feds. She also has sharp words for some constituencies on the left. In 1993 she opposed the Clinton Administration's national service plan, and proposed her own version. In 1994 she objected strongly to the Enola Gay exhibit on the atom bomb dropped over Hiroshima; the National Air and Space Museum had sponsored the project, which was withdrawn under considerable political protest in 1995. And in 1995 she spoke out angrily when the Clinton Administration without legal authority announced it would ban government contracts with firms that hire striker replacements, an action that she vowed to reverse.

Kassebaum has been very popular in Kansas. After winning a relatively close race against Bill Roy in 1978, she was easily reelected in 1984 and 1990, the latter time despite an earlier promise to serve only two terms; Bob Dole persuaded her to run. She can be easily reelected in 1996 should she run.

Presidential politics. Kansas is traditionally heavily Republican in presidential politics, and it is a measure more of George Bush's problems than of Kansas's partisanship that it was not in 1992. Ross Perot ran well in spring polls here, and won 27% in November; Bill Clinton led George Bush in some fall polls. The relatively low percentages for Bush in 1992 and 1988 may also reflect an adverse reaction to the man who dispatched Bob Dole's presidential hopes. You can see a similar disappointment factor in Edmund Muskie's Maine in 1972, George Romney's Michigan in 1968, Edward Kennedy's Massachusetts in 1980 and Gary Hart's Colorado in 1984, where the winning nominee did worse than expected in the nomination loser's state.

Congressional districting. Kansas lost one of its five seats in the 1990 Census. The losing congressman then was a freshman Republican, which left the delegation deadlocked at 2–2. But in 1994 Jim Slattery ran for governor and Dan Glickman was upset, and so in 1995 Kansas (like Iowa and Nebraska) has an all-Republican delegation, its first since Bob Dole's first two years in the Senate, 1969 and 1970.

The People: Est. Pop. 1994: 2,554,000; Pop. 1990: 2,477,574, up 3.1% 1990–1994. 1.0% of U.S. total, 32d largest; 31% rural. Median age: 32.9 years. 13.8% 65 years and over. 90.1% White, 5.8% Black, 3.8% Hispanic origin, 1.3% Asian. Households: 58.5% married couple families; 28% married couple fams. w. children; 48% college educ.; median household income: $27,291; per capita income: $13,300; 67.9% owner occupied housing; median house value: $52,200; median monthly rent: $285. 4.2% Unemployment. 1994 Voting age pop.: 1,889,000. 1994 Turnout: 819,140; 43% of VAP. Registered voters (1994): 1,314,213; 404,528 D (31%), 582,673 R (44%); 327,012 unaffiliated and minor parties (25%).

Political Lineup: Governor, Bill Graves (R); Lt. Gov., Sheila Frahm (R); Secy. of State, Ron Thornburgh (R); Atty. Gen., Carla Stovall (R); Treasurer, Sally Thompson (D); Commissioner of Insurance, Kathleen Sebellius (D). State Senate, 40 (27 R and 13 D); State House of Representatives, 125 (81 R and 44 D). Senators, Robert Dole (R) and Nancy Landon Kassebaum (R). Representatives, 4 (4 R).

1992 Presidential Vote		
Bush (R)	449,469	(39%)
Clinton (D)	389,704	(34%)
Perot (I)	311,316	(27%)

1988 Presidential Vote		
Bush (R)	549,049	(56%)
Dukakis (D)	422,636	(43%)

1992 Democratic Presidential Primary		
Clinton	82,145	(51%)
Tsongas	24,413	(15%)
Brown	20,811	(13%)
Other	10,723	(7%)
None of the Names Shown	22,159	(14%)

1992 Republican Presidential Primary		
Bush	132,131	(62%)
Buchanan	31,494	(15%)
Other	14,121	(7%)
None of the Names Shown	35,450	(17%)

GOVERNOR

Gov. Bill Graves (R)

Elected 1994, term expires Jan. 1999; b. Jan. 9, 1953, Salina; home, Lenexa; KS Wesleyan U., B.A. 1975, U. of KS, 1976–79; Methodist, married (Linda).

Career: Graves Truck Line; KS Deputy Secy. of State, 1980–84; KS Asst. Secy of State, 1984–85; KS Secy. of State, 1986–94.

Office: State Capitol, 2d Fl., Topeka 66617, 913-296-3232; Fax: 913-296-6231.

Election Results

1994 gen.	Bill Graves (R)	526,113	(64%)
	Jim Slattery (D)	294,733	(36%)
1994 prim.	Bill Graves (R)	115,608	(41%)
	Gene Bicknell (R)	79,816	(28%)
	Fred Kerr (R)	63,495	(22%)
	Others	23,706	(8%)
1990 gen.	Joan Finney (D)	380,609	(49%)
	Mike Hayden (R)	333,589	(43%)
	Christina Campbell-Cline (I)	69,127	(9%)

SENATORS

Sen. Robert Dole (R)

Elected 1968, seat up 1998; b. July 22, 1923, Russell; home, Russell; U. of KS, A.B., Washburn U., LL.B. 1952; United Methodist; married (Elizabeth).

Career: Army, 1943–48 (WWII); KS House of Reps., 1951–53; Russell Cnty. Atty., 1953–61; U.S. House of Reps., 1960–68; RNC Chmn., 1971–73; U.S. Senate Majority Ldr., 1984–86; Minority Ldr., 1986–1994.

DC Office: 141 HSOB 20510, 202-224-6521; Fax: 202-228-4569.

State Offices: 500 State Ave., #176, Kansas City 66101, 913-371-6108; 444 S.E. Quincy, #392, Topeka 66683, 913-295-2745; 100 N. Broadway, Wichita 67202, 316-263-4956.

Committees: *Majority Leader. Agriculture, Nutrition & Forestry* (2nd of 10 R): Marketing, Inspection and Product Promotion; Production and Price Competitiveness; Research, Nutrition and General Legislation. *Finance* (2nd of 11 R): Medicare, Long-Term Care and Health Insurance (Chmn.); Social Security and Family Policy; Taxation and IRS Oversight. *Rules & Administration* (5th of 9 R).

Group Ratings

	ADA	ACLU	COPE	CFA	LCV	CON	NSI	COC	ACU	NTLC	CHC
1994	0	26	0	25	0	82	100	84	100	88	100
1993	10	—	0	10	6	68	—	100	88	—	—

National Journal Ratings

	1993 LIB — 1993 CONS		1994 LIB — 1994 CONS	
Economic	0% —	87%	0% —	88%
Social	23% —	76%	0% —	85%
Foreign	8% —	86%	6% —	86%

Key Votes of the 103d Congress

1. Clinton Deficit Plan	N	3. Brady Handgun Purchase N	5. Lmt. UN Cmnd. of Forces Y
2. NAFTA	Y	4. Strike Race/Death Pnlty. Y	6. Cut Missile Funds N

Key Votes of the 104th Congress

1. Congressional Compliance Y	3. Balanced Budget Amndt. N	5. Product Liability Reform Y
2. Bar Unfunded Mandates Y	4. Pass Line Item Veto Y	6. FY96 Budget Y

Election Results

1992 general	Robert Dole (R)	706,246	(63%)	($3,542,989)
	Gloria O'Dell (D)	349,525	(31%)	($249,359)
	Christina Campbell-Cline (I)	45,423	(4%)	
	Other	25,253	(2%)	
1992 primary	Robert Dole (R)	244,480	(80%)	
	Richard Warren Rodewald (R)	59,589	(20%)	
1986 general	Robert Dole (R)	576,902	(70%)	($1,517,585)
	Guy MacDonald (D)	246,664	(30%)	

Sen. Nancy Landon Kassebaum (R)

Elected 1978, seat up 1996; b. July 29, 1932, Topeka; home, Burdick; U. of KS, B.A. 1954, U. of MI, M.A. 1956; Episcopalian; divorced.

Career: Maize Sch. Bd. Mbr., 1972–75; Staff, U.S. Sen. James Pearson, 1975.

DC Office: 302 RSOB 20510, 202-224-4774; Fax: 202-224-3514.

State Offices: 444 S.E. Quincy, Box 51, Topeka 66683, 913-295-2888; 911 N. Main, Garden City 67846, 316-276-3423; 4200 Somerset, #152, Prairie Village 66208, 913-648-3103; and 111 N. Market, #120, Wichita 67202, 316-269-6251.

Committees: *Foreign Relations* (3rd of 10 R): African Affairs (Chmn.); East Asian and Pacific Affairs; European Affairs. *Indian Affairs* (5th of 9 R). *Labor & Human Resources* (Chmn. of 9 R): Aging; Education, Arts and Humanities.

Group Ratings

	ADA	ACLU	COPE	CFA	LCV	CON	NSI	COC	ACU	NTLC	CHC
1994	45	32	13	33	46	72	90	70	48	80	57
1993	35	—	18	20	25	68	—	91	64	—	—

National Journal Ratings

	1993 LIB — 1993 CONS		1994 LIB — 1994 CONS	
Economic	13% —	81%	29% —	68%
Social	37% —	60%	42% —	57%
Foreign	49% —	49%	43% —	56%

Key Votes of the 103d Congress

1. Clinton Deficit Plan	N	3. Brady Handgun Purchase	Y	5. Lmt. UN Cmnd. of Forces	N
2. NAFTA	Y	4. Strike Race/Death Pnlty.	Y	6. Cut Missile Funds	Y

Key Votes of the 104th Congress

1. Congressional Compliance	Y	3. Balanced Budget Amndt.	Y	5. Product Liability Reform	Y
2. Bar Unfunded Mandates	Y	4. Pass Line Item Veto	Y	6. FY96 Budget	Y

Election Results

1990 general	Nancy Landon Kassebaum (R)	578,605	(74%)	($521,140)
	Dick Williams (D)	207,491	(26%)	($16,627)
1990 primary	Nancy Landon Kassebaum (R)	267,946	(87%)	
	R. Gregory Walstrom (R)	39,379	(13%)	
1984 general	Nancy Landon Kassebaum (R)	757,402	(76%)	($355,077)
	James R. Maher (D)	211,664	(21%)	($30,444)

FIRST DISTRICT

"A prairie is not any old piece of flatland in the Midwest," writes Kansas-born reporter Dennis Farney. "No, a prairie is wine-colored grass, dancing in the wind. A prairie is a sun-splashed hillside, bright with wild flowers. A prairie is a fleeting cloud shadow, the song of the meadowlark. It is the wild land that has never felt the slash of the plow." This prairie once covered almost all of Kansas. Now only a little virgin prairie can still be found, in the Flint Hills region west and south of Topeka, where the waist-deep sea of grass still waves in the wind as it did when the pioneers on the Santa Fe Trail went west through here some 150 years ago; there are proposals to make it a national park. Most of the Kansas prairie has long since been transformed by agriculture. Much of it was grazing land, first for buffalo, then for the cattle driven to Kansas railheads like Abilene and Dodge City in the 1870s and 1880s, a brief moment in history recaptured with varying accuracy in movies over a much longer span, and commemorated in Dodge City's Boot Hill Museum. Then, after the harsh winter of 1886–87 wiped out the cattle herds, came the plow and barbed wire (commemorated in LaCrosse's Barbed Wire Museum), which enabled farmers to keep livestock out of their wheatfields. The farmers also brought to this vacant landscape Yankee civilization, with its schools and churches and colleges, and some foreign traditions as well, like the Cathedral of the Plains built by German Catholics. Now this civilization is threatened. "My great-grandparents and grandparents were part of the stream of settlers who migrated to western Kansas after the Civil War to become wheat farmers," writes James Dickenson in his elegiac *Home on the Range.* "They broke the virgin sod, erected houses, barns, schools, churches and towns, and made the area one of the most agriculturally productive in the world. A little more than a century later, the population has ebbed away from this area and many of the farms, schools, churches and towns lie vacant, dilapidated and boarded up like old boomtowns."

The 1st Congressional District of Kansas consists of most of this expanse of the state, almost everything from the Flint Hills and Abilene west. Its 66 counties (only the Nebraska 3d and South Dakota at-large have more) increased from 76,000 people in 1870 to 570,000 in 1890; then growth slowed to 666,000 in 1940 and dropped to 619,000 in 1990. Population has dropped since 1980 almost everywhere except the natural gas exploration areas around Dodge City, its largest town, Salina, and German-Catholic Ellis County, with the high birth rates most Catholic communities had 30 years ago. Life isn't dismal in the "Big First," but community institutions are threatened by slow growth, and talented young people move elsewhere to get ahead in life.

The Congressman from the 1st is Pat Roberts, a Republican first elected in 1980 who has always specialized in farm issues, and is now chairman of the House Agriculture Committee.

Roberts comes from a fine Kansas Republican background: his great-grandfather founded Kansas's second oldest newspaper and his father, Wes Roberts, was briefly Republican National Committee chairman in the Eisenhower years. Pat Roberts has spent most of his adult life preparing for the place he is in now. After four years in the Marine Corps and five years running an Arizona newspaper, he worked for two years as an aide to Senator Frank Carlson and 12 years as chief aide to 1st District Congressman Keith Sebelius. When Sebelius retired in 1980, Roberts won the seat with 56% in a three-candidate Republican primary; ever since, he has traveled around the district in a van in which it takes two weeks to visit every county seat.

Roberts has always seen himself as the protector of Great Plains farm communities from ignorant outsiders who would upset the basis of their lives. That means of course that he is a protector of farm programs, and especially of wheat subsidy programs, on the Agriculture Committee. But that can get rather complicated, and no more so than in 1995. The huge and unanticipated costs of farm programs in the early 1980s were unsustainable, and subsidies have been cut back in the 1985 and 1990 farm bills: Roberts is painting an accurate picture when he says, "Only farm programs have declined an average of 9% since 1986 and are going to go on declining." He does not want to be recorded as the author of a 1995 bill that phases out wheat subsidies forever, and attacks somewhat bitterly Senate Agriculture Chairman Richard Lugar's incisive questioning of the theories behind farm programs: "When Senator Lugar puts agriculture through his personal inquisition, and has them in the confession box, we'll probably be holding hearings out in the field to see what farmers and ranchers want." But he has worked to let economic incentives play a greater role and government restrictions less. He has pushed for a more aggressive U.S. farm exports policy, and has attacked the Democrats' cargo preference provisions which increase export prices to help the maritime unions. He has worked on rural healthcare programs. He has challenged environmental regulations that infringe on property rights—like the Endangered Species Act and the wetlands act—in pungent terms. "It's time we protect the wetlands of true importance to the environment, not some low spot in your field where no self-respecting duck would ever land."

Roberts also keeps his eye on the bottom line. Noting that only 16% of agricultural spending goes to commodities programs and 63% to food stamps and other nutrition programs, he fought hard and successfully in early 1995 to keep food stamps from being included with other welfare measures in cash grants to the states. He won in part because he had his own package of reforms to reduce food stamp fraud and abuse: "I'm not trying to purge the food stamp program. I don't think it's a good thing to give it all back to the states." Roberts also had *bona fides* among less senior Republicans bent on changing the House's old ways because he led the fight to investigate the House Post Office and to publicize the $300,000 owed by members to the House restaurant. He also led the fight to defund the caucus organizations, which succeeded in late 1994. He also showed some deficit-consciousness and rural populism when he led an insurrection—unsuccessful, at least in the short term—to restrict the child tax credit in the Contract With America only to those families earning less than $95,000 annually. But the move, which some Republicans said had at least the implicit blessing of Speaker Newt Gingrich, did garner 106 signatures on a letter circulated by Roberts and freshman Greg Ganske. Despite the abortive effort, Roberts voted for each item in the Contract With America except for term limits.

Kansas lost a seat in the 1990 Census, and in 1992 Roberts was technically redistricted in with another Republican incumbent. But freshman Dick Nichols lived at the eastern edge of the district and chose to run in the 4th, where he lost. Hard-working, good-humored, knowledgeable about the district's number one concern and well-placed to do something about it, Roberts is reelected overwhelmingly.

The People: Pop. 1990: 619,371; 51% rural; 17% age 65+; 92% White; 1% Black; 1% Asian; 3% Other; 5% Hispanic origin. Voting age pop.: 452,347; 1% Black; 4% Hispanic origin. Households: 62% married couple families; 28% married couple fams. w. children; 43% college educ.; median household income: $23,433; per capita income: $11,328; median gross rent: $297; median house value: $38,000.

1992 Presidential Vote

Bush (R) 122,621 (42%)
Perot (I) 85,004 (29%)
Clinton (D) 81,423 (28%)

1988 Presidential Vote

Bush (R) 157,070 (61%)
Dukakis (D) 101,697 (39%)

Rep. Pat Roberts (R)

Elected 1980; b. Apr. 20, 1936, Topeka; home, Dodge City; KS St. U., B.A. 1958; United Methodist; married (Franki).

Career: Marine Corps, 1958–62; Co-owner, editor, *The Westsider* (AZ newspaper) 1962–67; A.A., U.S. Sen. Frank Carlson, 1967–68; A.A., U.S. Rep. Keith Sebelius, 1968–80.

DC Office: 1126 LHOB 20515, 202-225-2715; Fax: 202-225-5375; e-mail: emailpat@hr.house.gov

District Offices: P.O. Box 550, Dodge City 67801, 316-227-2244; P.O. Box 128, Norton 67654, 913-877-2454; P.O. Box 1128, Hutchinson 67502, 316-665-6138; and P.O. Box 1334, Salina 67402, 913-825-5409.

Committees: *Agriculture* (Chmn. of 27 R): *House Oversight* (3rd of 7 R).

Group Ratings

	ADA	ACLU	COPE	CFA	LCV	CON	NSI	COC	ACU	NTLC	CHC
1994	0	17	0	20	6	67	100	92	100	96	100
1993	0	—	0	10	21	59	—	100	100	—	—

National Journal Ratings

	1993 LIB — 1993 CONS	1994 LIB — 1994 CONS
Economic	0% — 88%	0% — 80%
Social	0% — 89%	11% — 85%
Foreign	28% — 70%	20% — 79%

Key Votes of the 103d Congress

1. Clinton Deficit Plan	N	3. Brady Handgun Purchase	N	5. Lmt. UN Cmnd. of Forces	Y
2. NAFTA	Y	4. Strike Race/Death Pnlty.	Y	6. Cut Missile Funds	N

Key Votes of the 104th Congress

1. Congressional Compliance	Y	6. Reform Crime Grant	Y	11. Loser Pays Court Reform	Y
2. Balanced Budget Amndmt.	Y	7. National Security Act	Y	12. Product Liability Reform	Y
3. Bar Unfunded Mandates	Y	8. Moratorium on Regs.	Y	13. Welfare Reform	Y
4. Pass Line Item Veto	Y	9. Risk Assessment on Regs.	Y	14. Term Limits Amndmt.	N
5. Relax Exclusionary Rule	Y	10. Expnd. Priv. Prop. Rights	Y	15. Tax Cuts	Y

Election Results

1994 general	Pat Roberts (R)	169,531	(77%)	($309,950)
	Terry L. Nichols (D)	49,477	(23%)	
1994 primary	Pat Roberts (R) .... unopposed			
1992 general	Pat Roberts (R)	94,165	(70%)	($601,655)
	Duane West (D)	37,826	(28%)	($64,850)
	Other	3,286	(2%)	

SECOND DISTRICT

The green plains of eastern Kansas have seen more than their share of American history. Here, on bluffs above the Missouri River, Fort Leavenworth was built in 1827, famous for years for its war college and military prison and now the oldest U.S. fort west of the Mississippi. In the 1850s, newly founded towns along the Kansas River and along the Missouri line were the centers of "Bleeding Kansas," where the pro-slavery bushwhackers set up a state capital in tiny Lecompton and anti-slavery New Englanders set up their stronghold down the river at Lawrence. Farther up the river is Fort Riley, once an outpost against the Indians, now a major Army base threatening, even after the end of the Cold War, to expand into adjacent farm fields, and Manhattan, home of Kansas State University. Topeka, the state capital, sits here on a low bluff above the river: it was the city whose system of legal segregation was overturned in the 1954 landmark case, *Brown v. Board of Education.* Farther south, on the Missouri border, are the hills called "the Balkans." Here coal miners, often of Eastern European origin, lived in and near towns like Pittsburg and Girard, once a center of American socialism, where Clarence Darrow and Upton Sinclair made pilgrimages, and its paper, *Appeal to Reason,* had a nationwide 750,000 circulation.

Most of these disparate areas, Topeka and Manhattan, Fort Riley and Fort Leavenworth, wheat-growing counties and the Balkans—most of eastern Kansas except the Kansas City metropolitan area—make up the 2d Congressional District of Kansas. The heritage here has been Republican ever since jayhawk Republicans defeated bushwhack Democrats once the votes were counted honestly in the 1850s. Yet for 20 of 24 years until 1994, the 2d District elected Democrats to the House—talented political entrepreneurs who often voted moderate but kept the liberal-dominated Democratic Caucus in control. Until 1994, that is, when incumbent Jim Slattery ran for governor and lost resoundingly, and the 2d elected a very different congressman, as typical of his new majority as his Democratic predecessors were of theirs.

The current Congressman is Sam Brownback, a leader of the 1994 freshman Republican class, and like many others with a more sophisticated background than his campaign rhetoric suggests. He grew up on a farm in Anderson County, some 50 miles from Kansas City, was student body president at Kansas State and briefly a farm broadcaster. After Kansas Law, he practiced law for four years in Manhattan in the 1980s; he was appointed secretary of the state Board of Agriculture in 1986 and served until it was abolished in 1993. He claims credit for encouraging the use of wheat to make plastics and cattle hides to make wound dressings. He was a White House Fellow, working 1990–91 for U.S. Trade Representative Carla Hills. In March 1994 he announced for Congress, condemning "a welfare system that discourages the work ethic and encourages the disintegration of families and a government that can't say no to spending or yes to reform." He won a three-way primary 48%–35%–16%. His opponent in the general was John Carlin, governor from 1978 to 1986. Carlin cited his experience and said he would "do what is right for the country" not what would get him reelected. But in anti-incumbent 1994 that appeal was weak. Brownback won 66%–34%, carrying every county. Carlin won from Clinton the promise of nomination to the long-vacant position of U.S. Archivist, with a vow of support from Dole.

After the election, Brownback took the lead in trying to sell off a House annex building, though it proved even more difficult than expected, and House leaders debated options on whether to sell, lease or just tear down the building. On opening day he sponsored a law to require an independent audit of the House. He heads a group of Republican freshman called the "New Federalists," whose mission is to eradicate the Departments of Commerce, Education, Energy and Housing and Urban Development.

The People: Pop. 1990: 619,385; 41% rural; 14% age 65+; 88% White; 6% Black; 1% Amer. Indian; 1% Asian; 1% Other; 3% Hispanic origin. Voting age pop.: 457,819; 6% Black; 2% Hispanic origin. Households: 60% married couple families; 29% married couple fams. w. children; 44% college educ.; median household income: $24,903; per capita income: $11,662; median gross rent: $344; median house value: $44,000.

1992 Presidential Vote

Bush (R) 98,884 (36%)
Clinton (D) 98,457 (36%)
Perot (I). 75,549 (28%)

1988 Presidential Vote

Bush (R) 126,878 (54%)
Dukakis (D). 107,003 (46%)

Rep. Sam Brownback (R)

Elected 1994; b. Sept. 12, 1956, Garnett; home, Topeka; KS St. U., B.S. 1978; U. of KS, J.D. 1982; Methodist; married (Mary).

Career: Radio broadcaster, KKSU, 1978–79; Practicing atty., 1982–86, 1993; Prof., KS St. U. Law Schl., 1982–86; Ogden & Leonardville City Atty., 1983–86; KS Secy. of Agriculture, 1986–93; White House Fellow, Office of USTR, 1990–91.

DC Office: 1313 LHOB 20515, 202-225-6601; Fax: 202-225-2983.

District Offices: 612 S. Kansas St., Topeka 66603, 913-233-2503; 1001 N. Broadway, Pittsburg 66762, 316-231-6040.

Committees: *Budget* (21st of 24 R). *International Relations* (18th of 23 R): Africa; International Economic Policy and Trade. *Small Business* (18th of 22 R): Procurement, Exports and Business Opportunities; Tax and Finance.

Group Ratings and 103rd Congress Votes: Newly Elected

Key Votes of the 104th Congress

1. Congressional Compliance Y	6. Reform Crime Grant Y	11. Loser Pays Court Reform Y
2. Balanced Budget Amndmt. Y	7. National Security Act Y	12. Product Liability Reform Y
3. Bar Unfunded Mandates Y	8. Moratorium on Regs. Y	13. Welfare Reform Y
4. Pass Line Item Veto Y	9. Risk Assessment on Regs. Y	14. Term Limits Amndmt. Y
5. Relax Exclusionary Rule Y	10. Expnd. Priv. Prop. Rights Y	15. Tax Cuts Y

Election Results

1994 general	Sam Brownback (R)	135,725	(66%)	($749,330)
	John Carlin (D).	71,025	(34%)	($526,315)
1994 primary	Sam Brownback (R)	35,415	(48%)	
	Bob Bennie (R)	26,008	(35%)	
	Joe Hume (R)	11,872	(16%)	
1992 general	Jim Slattery (D)	151,019	(56%)	($742,215)
	Jim Van Slyke (R)	109,801	(41%)	($36,704)
	Other.	7,986	(3%)	

THIRD DISTRICT

Kansas City is one of those metro areas that sits astride a state line. More than one-third of its residents live west of the line in Kansas, where the low-lying land near the Missouri River used to house one of the nation's largest stockyards. Kansas City, Kansas, is still a working-class town with a few dilapidated looking streets and lots of modest frame houses, the largest black neighborhood and old Catholic ethnic neighborhoods in Kansas, and an old Democratic machine politics. But Kansas City is losing population, while Johnson County, just to the south, is gaining rapidly, and now has nearly three times as many people. Its older neighborhoods are separated from the affluent Kansas City, Missouri, area around the old Country Club Plaza shopping center by just a single small street; the newer neighborhoods are arrayed along the interstates, and have grown to the point that Overland Park, Olathe, Shawnee and Lenexa—unfamiliar names to most Kansans—are among the largest municipalities in the state. Politically, Johnson

County is heavily Republican; on issues that pit metropolitan values against rural—liquor by the drink, the oil severance tax, property tax reassessment—Johnson County votes metropolitan, for bars, for taxing oilmen and against reassessors.

The 3d Congressional District consists of Johnson County, Kansas City and surrounding Wyandotte County, the town of Lawrence which is the home of Kansas University and one rural county to the south. A few decades ago Kansas City would have made this the most Democratic-leaning district in Kansas. But the balance has changed. Over the last 50 years, working-class Kansas City has hardly grown at all (and cast fewer votes in 1992 than in 1940), while Johnson County has grown explosively. In 1940, Kansas City's Wyandotte County cast 66,000 votes to Johnson's 16,000; in 1960, Wyandotte cast 76,000 to Johnson's 65,000; in 1988, Wyandotte's 61,000 was overwhelmed by Johnson's 195,000. In presidential-offyear 1994, Johnson County cast 116,000 votes, Wyandotte County 32,000. This makes the 3d a safe Republican district.

The Congresswoman from the 3d District is Jan Meyers, for some years a little-noticed member, now Chairman of the Small Business Committee and sponsor of a major welfare reform proposal. Like many women in Congress, Meyers started off working on local charitable and civic affairs. In 1967, at 29, she was on the Overland Park Council; in 1972 she was elected to the Kansas Senate, meeting part-time in Topeka, 60 miles away. In 1978, she ran for the U.S. Senate and finished fourth in a primary field of 10 with 10% of the vote. In 1984, she ran for the House and won a five-candidate primary with 35%; in the general, Johnson County's demographic strength enabled her to beat the mayor of Kansas City 63%–32%.

Meyers's record in the House has been moderate on cultural issues, pro-choice on abortion, conservative on economics and foreign policy. She worked quietly on local projects and foreign affairs. In the 1992 campaign she was attacked for using a special House Post Office box to collect campaign money in the 1980s; she beat her main primary opponent 56%–33% and won the general election with 58%. In 1993 Meyers introduced a welfare reform bill that would replace the AFDC entitlement with block grants to the states—the heart of the devolution approach that would become Republican policy in 1995. Her bill would have no federal work requirements but would leave that issue to the states.

Meyers was reelected with 57% of the vote in 1994: she lost Wyandotte County and ran only even in Douglas County, but won 64% in Johnson County. After the election she suddenly became something of a celebrity. Many Republicans had talked of abolishing the Small Business Committee, which has jurisdiction over only a few small government programs and is used by members as evidence of their concern for small business. But when it became apparent that Meyers was the only woman in line for a committee chairmanship, Small Business was retained—and Meyers became the first woman to chair a House standing committee since Leonor Sullivan retired in 1976.

The People: Pop. 1990: 619,445; 7% rural; 10% age 65+; 87% White; 9% Black; 1% Amer. Indian; 2% Asian; 1% Other; 3% Hispanic origin. Voting age pop.: 456,132; 8% Black; 3% Hispanic origin. Households: 57% married couple families; 28% married couple fams. w. children; 60% college educ.; median household income: $34,275; per capita income: $16,585; median gross rent: $454; median house value: $75,300.

1992 Presidential Vote		
Clinton (D)	116,396	(38%)
Bush (R)	113,963	(37%)
Perot (I)	75,413	(25%)

1988 Presidential Vote		
Bush (R)	134,809	(54%)
Dukakis (D)	113,511	(46%)

Rep. Jan Meyers (R)

Elected 1984; b. July 20, 1928, Lincoln, NE; home, Overland Park; Williams Wood Col., A.A. 1948, U. of NE, B.A. 1951; United Methodist; married (Louis).

Career: Overland Park City Cncl., 1967–72; KS Senate, 1972–84.

DC Office: 2303 RHOB 20515, 202-225-2865; Fax: 202-225-0554.

District Offices: 182 Fed. Bldg., Kansas City 66101, 913-621-0832; 7133 W. 95th St., #217, Overland Park 66212, 913-383-2013; and 708 W. 9th St., Lawrence 66044, 913-842-9313.

Committees: *Economic & Educational Opportunities* (12th of 24 R): Employer-Employee Relations. *International Relations* (9th of 23 R): International Economic Policy and Trade. *Small Business* (Chmn. of 22 R).

Group Ratings

	ADA	ACLU	COPE	CFA	LCV	CON	NSI	COC	ACU	NTLC	CHC
1994	30	35	22	50	65	61	100	100	57	93	64
1993	25	—	25	40	71	91	—	91	71	—	—

National Journal Ratings

	1993 LIB — 1993 CONS	1994 LIB — 1994 CONS
Economic	14% — 80%	37% — 61%
Social	50% — 49%	43% — 56%
Foreign	31% — 67%	38% — 61%

Key Votes of the 103d Congress

1. Clinton Deficit Plan	N	3. Brady Handgun Purchase	Y	5. Lmt. UN Cmnd. of Forces	Y
2. NAFTA	Y	4. Strike Race/Death Pnlty.	Y	6. Cut Missile Funds	N

Key Votes of the 104th Congress

1. Congressional Compliance	Y	6. Reform Crime Grant	Y	11. Loser Pays Court Reform Y
2. Balanced Budget Amndmt.	Y	7. National Security Act	Y	12. Product Liability Reform Y
3. Bar Unfunded Mandates	Y	8. Moratorium on Regs.	Y	13. Welfare Reform Y
4. Pass Line Item Veto	Y	9. Risk Assessment on Regs.	Y	14. Term Limits Amndmt. Y
5. Relax Exclusionary Rule	Y	10. Expnd. Priv. Prop. Rights	Y	15. Tax Cuts Y

Election Results

1994 general	Jan Meyers (R)	102,218	(57%)	($376,484)
	Judy Hancock (D)	78,401	(43%)	($340,859)
1994 primary	Jan Meyers (R)	31,852	(59%)	
	Tom Love (R)	16,486	(31%)	
	Kevin M. Johnson (R)	5,234	(10%)	
1992 general	Jan Meyers (R)	169,929	(58%)	($430,833)
	Tom Love (D)	110,076	(38%)	
	Frank Kaul (Lib)	12,791	(4%)	

FOURTH DISTRICT

Wichita is the largest Kansas-only metropolitan area, smaller than million-plus metro Kansas City, but a Great Plains metropolis of the magnitude of Omaha or Tulsa. It began as a farm market town and grew with local oil and gas discoveries in the 1920s. But its real impetus came during World War II and the years just after, when aircraft factories sprouted up here on the Kansas plains and Wichita suddenly became the nation's major producer of small planes. Today the big three—Cessna, Beechcraft and Learjet—are all located here; so is the bulk of Boeing's military business. This is the general aviation center of America. Wichita has also become a regional health center in the common Great Plains pattern, as rural counties are unable to attract new doctors or maintain hospitals, and people from miles around come to the metropolis for treatment. Wichita has also become a big center for franchising (Pizza Hut and Rent-A-Center are the two largest) and telemarketing. This economic mix has left Wichita vulnerable to the business cycle. General aviation is exquisitely sensitive to fluctuations in business profits: businessmen love buying company planes, but they're easily done without when times get tight or gas prices rise. Low oil prices hurt the Wichita area, with its dozens of stripper wells, and farm prices are notoriously volatile; the early 1990s were economically tough here. It didn't help that general aviation manufacturers were getting hit with liability suits for planes they had produced many years before.

Kansas's 4th Congressional District is centered around Wichita, covering wheat-growing areas to the east and west, but with most of its people in Wichita and Sedgwick County. Politically, it has voted Republican most years; even in 1992 it gave a plurality to George Bush. For 18 years, however, this district was represented by Democrat Dan Glickman, one of many politically talented young Democrats whose victories in such districts, taken together, explain why the Democrats were able to hold the House for so many years. Glickman's defeat in 1994, one of the biggest and most unexpected upsets of the year, also helps explain why the Republicans finally won control.

The Congressman from the 4th now is Todd Tiahrt who grew up on a farm in South Dakota and went to the same high school as South Dakota Congressman Tim Johnson. Tiahrt moved to the Wichita area to be closer to his wife's family and worked at Boeing as a proposal manager on the Space Station, Air Force One, KC-135, B-52, B-1, B-2, A-67, YF-22 and Comanche helicopter programs. Tiahrt lost a Kansas House seat in 1990 by only eight votes; in 1992 he was elected to the Kansas Senate, where his great cause was a concealed weapons law allowing citizens on application to carry firearms. In 1994 he got it into his head to run against Glickman, a task all the more daunting because Glickman seemed to be having a good ninth term: he became chairman of the House Intelligence Committee in 1993 and, with Senator Nancy Kassebaum, he passed legislation reducing the product liability of general aviation manufacturers in 1994. Tiahrt attacked Glickman for supporting the Clinton Administration, ran ads showing his face morphing into Clinton's, and targeted his vote for the 1994 crime bill with its gun control provisions. "I am a working man who cares about the financial bottom line," Tiahrt said. "I'm sick and tired of all the hype and all the waste. I don't have the Clinton Administration breaking their necks to get me into office."

In 1991 Wichita was the scene of antiabortion demonstrations by Operation Rescue, and religious conservatives won majorities in the local Republican Party in 1992. Tiahrt assembled a corps of 1,800 volunteers, including many from conservative churches; "I moved below radar and stayed low-key, so my opponent wouldn't start raising lots of money," he said. In fact, he was vastly outspent; Glickman spent $694,000, Tiahrt $200,000. On election day Glickman ran relatively well, as he had for years, in high-income Republican precincts; but he suffered serious losses in middle-income areas in Wichita and Sedgwick County and beyond. Tiahrt won a solid 53%–47% victory, and on election night his volunteers sang "What a Mighty God We Serve." Glickman did not make any alibis. With considerable class, he said, "Any candidate, no matter how perceptively strong, must stand for specific principles and articulate them to the public. I did not do that. I ran on my history, not on my future. Would that have made a difference in this race, I don't know. But ideas matter in politics."

Tiahrt won seats on the National Security and Science Committees. While he is a force for thoroughgoing reform in the House, he supports Kansas's Bob Dole for president. Glickman became Secretary of Agriculture in March 1995, with strong support from his suddenly powerful Kansas Republican friends.

The People: Pop. 1990: 619,373; 24% rural; 14% age 65+; 87% White; 7% Black; 1% Amer. Indian; 2% Asian; 2% Other; 3% Hispanic origin. Voting age pop.: 449,274; 6% Black; 3% Hispanic origin. Households: 59% married couple families; 28% married couple fams. w. children; 48% college educ.; median household income: $28,308; per capita income: $13,623; median gross rent: $376; median house value: $52,000.

1992 Presidential Vote			1988 Presidential Vote		
Bush (R)	114,001	(40%)	Bush (R)	135,292	(57%)
Clinton (D)	93,428	(33%)	Dukakis (D)	100,425	(43%)
Perot (I)	75,350	(27%)			

Rep. Todd Tiahrt (R)

Elected 1994; b. June 15, 1951, Vermillion, SD; home, Goddard; Evangel Col., B.A. 1975; SW MO St. U., M.B.A. 1989; Assembly of God; married (Vicki).

Career: Proposal Mgr., Boeing Co., 1985–94; KS Senate 1992–94.

DC Office: 1319 LHOB 20515, 202-225-6216; Fax: 202-225-3489.

District Offices: 155 N. Market, #400, Wichita 67202, 316-262-8992; and 325 N. Penn, #9, Independence 67301, 316-331-8056.

Committees: *National Security* (29th of 30 R): Military Personnel; Military Research and Development. *Science* (22nd of 27 R): Space and Aeronautics; Technology.

Group Ratings and 103rd Congress Votes: Newly Elected

Key Votes of the 104th Congress

1. Congressional Compliance	Y	6. Reform Crime Grant	Y	11. Loser Pays Court Reform	Y
2. Balanced Budget Amndmt.	Y	7. National Security Act	Y	12. Product Liability Reform	Y
3. Bar Unfunded Mandates	Y	8. Moratorium on Regs.	Y	13. Welfare Reform	Y
4. Pass Line Item Veto	Y	9. Risk Assessment on Regs.	Y	14. Term Limits Amndmt.	Y
5. Relax Exclusionary Rule	Y	10. Expnd. Priv. Prop. Rights	Y	15. Tax Cuts	Y

Election Results

1994 general	Todd Tiahrt (R)	111,653	(53%)	($199,973)
	Dan Glickman (D)	99,366	(47%)	($693,534)
1994 primary	Todd Tiahrt (R)	29,663	(54%)	
	David J. Roll (R)	12,939	(24%)	
	Bill Rauh (R)	12,360	(22%)	
1992 general	Dan Glickman (D)	143,671	(52%)	($1,046,769)
	Eric R. Yost (R)	117,070	(42%)	($396,254)
	Seth L. Warren (L)	17,275	(6%)	

KENTUCKY

Few states have stayed as close to their roots for as many years as Kentucky. This land was part of Virginia when it was first settled, in the years when Thomas Jefferson was writing his *Notes on Virginia*. It was admitted to the Union in 1792, when Jefferson was Secretary of State. Its one large county is named after Jefferson and its one large city after the monarch to whom he was credentialed as Ambassador to France, Louis XVI. Kentucky today is still recognizable as a Jeffersonian commonwealth. It still has a constitution informed by a jealousy of power, with a one-term limit on governors that will be raised to two starting in 1995 and strict limits on when the legislature can meet. It has long favored the Democratic Party, which can trace its ancestry at least tenuously back to Jefferson, though in 1994 Kentucky shifted sharply to Republicans who claim to be more faithful to Jeffersonian principles than their rivals. The agrarian Jefferson would approve of Kentucky's demography, which is still largely rural, with well under half its population in the big metropolitan areas of Louisville, Lexington and the Kentucky towns across the Ohio River from Cincinnati. And the tobacco planter who presided over what one historian called "the alcoholic republic" might not entirely disapprove of a Kentucky economy that remains heavily dependent on century-old industries such as coal, cigarettes, whiskey, heavy manufacturing and auto assembly. Many of the buildings here are old: the rickety cabins in the coal mining Appalachians, the unpainted houses in the soggy lowlands beneath the levees by the Mississippi River, the white-fenced bluegrass horse country farmhouses, the small-town 19th Century courthouses.

Satellite dishes and four-lane highways have brought modern civilization into hollows and lowland farms which lacked indoor plumbing and electricity within living memory, but people in this state still have a strong attachment to roots, to place and family. The continuity is real. Kentucky's population has grown just over 30% in the past 50 years; few outsiders have moved in, so today's Kentuckians are mostly descendants of settlers who poured over the mountains in the 40 years after Daniel Boone made his way through the Cumberland Gap in 1775. Kentucky's population rose from 73,000 in the Census of 1790 to 564,000 in 1820.

There has been great continuity politically as well. There has long been hearty, though lopsided, party competition, with most of the 120 counties voting today as they did in the Civil War era. The eastern mountains were pro-Union and remain Republican, except for counties where coal miners were organized by the United Mine Workers in the 1930s; the Bluegrass region and the western end of the state were slaveholding territory and have long been Democratic. Louisville, with many German immigrants, was an anti-slavery town, and supported a strong Republican organization. These patterns, which have prevailed now for more than 100 years, were plainly apparent in the returns for senator in 1990, governor in 1991 and president in 1992.

For years, that meant control by the Democratic Party, with the real battle in the Democratic primary. There was almost a party system within the dominant party, with factions that go back to the 1938 primary when Senate Majority Leader (and later Vice President) Alben Barkley was challenged by Governor (and later Senator and Baseball Commissioner) Happy Chandler. Barkley's faction was later led by Governor (1959–63) Bert Combs and Chandler's by Governor (1971–74) and Senator Wendell Ford, who were arrayed prominently on opposite sides in the 1987 primary. But Chandler and Combs both died in 1991, when the current governor, Brereton Jones, was elected, and intraparty struggles now are along new lines.

And, if 1994 is a good indicator, there are new party lines in other statewide elections as well. Kentucky Republicans, after holding the governorship and both Senate seats from 1967 to 1971, sagged badly; Bill Clinton carried Kentucky 45%–41% in 1992. But Clinton's popularity slid as

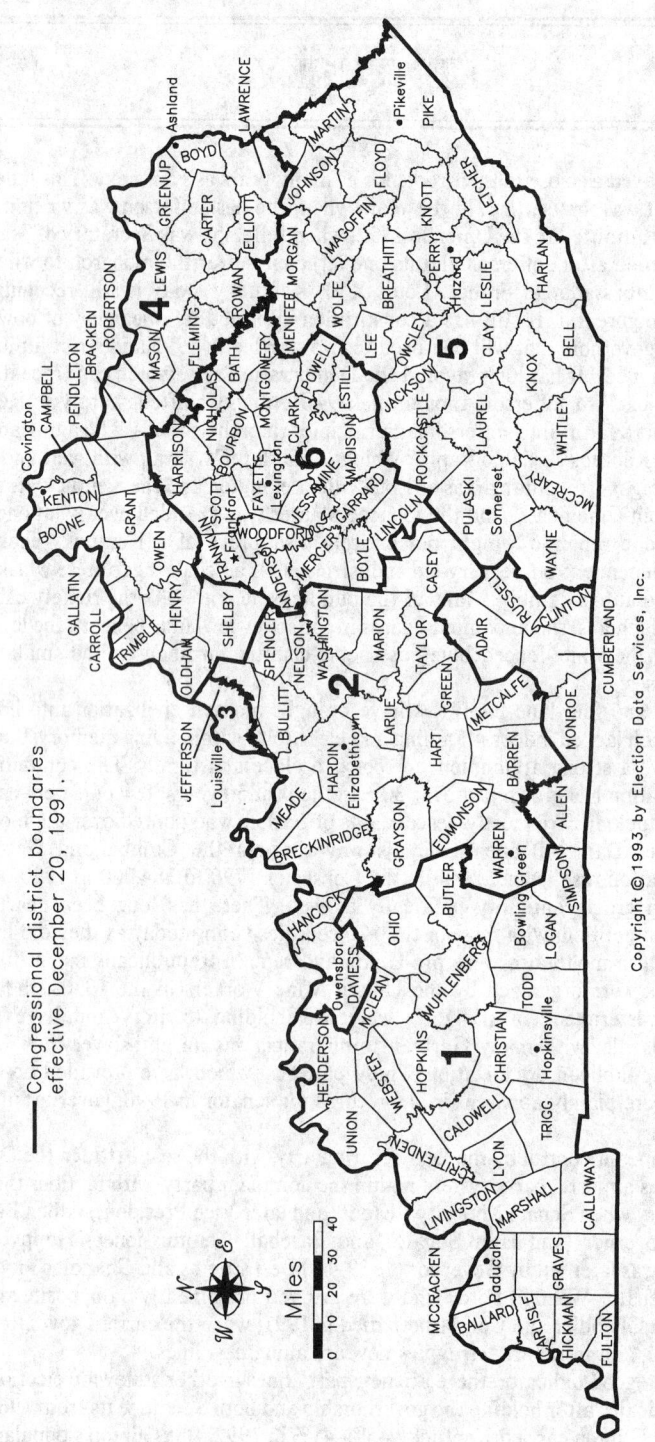

Congressional district boundaries
effective December 20, 1991.

Copyright © 1993 by Election Data Services, Inc.

it did in other border states and for the additional reason that his healthcare financing plan relied heavily on taxing one of Kentucky's most visible products, tobacco. Then, in May 1994, Republican Ron Lewis, a religious book store owner, won the 2d District seat left vacant by the death of House Appropriations Chairman William Natcher—a victory with national reverberations. In the fall, with active leadership from Senator Mitch McConnell, Republicans held the 2d District and won the 1st as well, giving them a 4–2 edge in the House delegation. And, by actively contesting legislative special elections, they reduced Democrats' edge to only 21–17 in the state Senate. Republicans won big margins in many historically Democratic counties, especially in the west, and in the big metro areas as well. "Western Kentucky is no longer the Gibraltar of the Democratic Party," one Republican Party leader said. Whether this Republican trend will prove evanescent or lasting will become clearer with the outcome of the 1995 election for governor.

Governor. There is no question who stands at the apex of Kentucky politics: the governor. The governor's appointment powers are wide; the legislature meets only 60 days every two years and the governor can then shift around line items in the state budget. The governor has almost always been the undisputed leader of his party. The one-term limit, applied to all statewide officials after Treasurer "Honest Dick" Tate absconded in 1888 with $250,000, has limited a governor's time, but not his powers. But now this is changing: in 1992 voters approved a second term for statewide officials, starting with those elected in 1995.

Democratic Governor Brereton Jones, elected in 1991, has acted in the tradition of his predecessors. He increased the generous tax incentives pioneered by Martha Layne Collins, elected in 1983, which brought the Toyota plant to the antique county seat of Georgetown, just north of Lexington. Jones and Lieutenant Governor Paul Patton's policy: "Locate your white-collar jobs in Kentucky, and the state will pay half your rent for 10 years and up to half your startup costs. Locate your manufacturing plant in Kentucky, and the state will reimburse your entire investment." Next-door Ohio quickly screamed foul, then passed its own incentives in self-defense. Jones has also continued the school reform program enacted under Wallace Wilkinson, elected in 1987, which, in response to a state Supreme Court decision, raised the dropout age to 18, added family resource centers in needy areas and computer-ready phone lines in each classroom, and increased aid to poorer districts with bonuses to those whose schools improve and penalties on those whose schools don't.

Jones's great initiative was healthcare reform. With Howard Dean of Vermont, he was the governor most supportive of the Clinton healthcare plan, and he wanted to expand Medicaid to provide universal coverage in Kentucky, with a health commission to set rates if costs exceed state-set limits. But no plan passed in the 1993 special legislative session, and in 1994, after Jones extended Medicaid coverage, he got through a bill to make insurance more portable from job to job and to make CommonHealth insurance available to the public on the same terms as state employees. He had greater success with ethics reform, demand for which was sharpened by a scandal that brought down former House Speaker Don Blandford. Jones and the legislature gave Kentucky a runoff primary which, with the increase in Republican strength, vastly reduced the chance of a little-known candidate winning with a flurry of advertising as Wilkinson did in 1987. Also, Kentucky will have a public financing system.

Jones came to office with an unusual background: he was a Republican legislator in West Virginia in the 1960s, moved to Kentucky in 1972 to take over his wife's family's horse farm and was elected lieutenant governor as a Democrat in 1987. His most publicized opponent, the wife of then-incumbent Wilkinson, withdrew just before the primary; Jones got 38%, enough to beat Scotty Baesler (30%), then Lexington mayor and now congressman, and Dr. Floyd Poore (27%). Republicans were handicapped by a primary between party choice Congressman Larry Hopkins and Larry Forgy, who had angered many by quitting the primary in 1987. This time Forgy, with 49%, nearly won and Hopkins had terrible liabilities—an inaccurate claim to have served in the Marines in Korea, and 321 overdrafts on the House bank.

Forgy ran again in 1995, winning the May gubernatorial primary handily 82%–14% over former state Republican Party Chairman Robert Gable. In the general he will face Lieutenant Governor Paul Patton, who beat four other Democrats with 45%, just enough to avoid a runoff; Secretary of State Bob Babbage came in second with 24%, just ahead of state Senate President John "Eck" Rose's 21%. Though party registration here is still 2–1 Democratic, Forgy's desire to be Kentucky's first Republican governor in 28 years must be bolstered by the 1994 Republican gains in the Congressional delegation which won statewide with 59%.

Senators. Wendell Ford is a canny veteran of Kentucky and Washington political wars who has usually been on the winning side, but now finds himself, for the second time in his Senate career, in the minority. Ford was chief aide to Governor Bert Combs from 1959 to 1963, was elected lieutenant governor in 1967, ran for governor in 1971 and beat Combs in the primary and the hand-picked successor of Governor Louie Nunn in the general. In 1974 he pondered long before giving up one year of the governorship to run for the Senate, but did and beat incumbent Republican Marlow Cook in 1974. Ford has a moderate but partisan voting record and has fought fiercely for what he regards as Kentucky's interests. He chaired the Democratic Senatorial Campaign Committee from 1976–82, chaired the Rules Committee for eight years after 1986, in which capacity he presided at the inaugurations of George Bush and Bill Clinton, ran unsuccessfully for whip against Alan Cranston in 1988, then seized the post unopposed when Cranston was hobbled by illness and the Keating Five case in 1990. But Majority Leader George Mitchell tended to use South Dakota Senator Tom Daschle, not Ford, as his deputy, and, when Mitchell retired in 1994, Ford, about to turn 70, announced he wasn't running for leader and kept his old post—now minority whip—unopposed.

Ford has worked hard on tobacco issues, from his first term when he got cigarettes excluded from the Consumer Product Safety Act to the Clinton years when he fought hard against the tobacco tax proposed to finance the Clinton healthcare plan. He fought Jay Rockefeller's coal tax for miners' health care because of the cost for Kentucky non-union coal operators; when Rockefeller complained about poor airline service in West Virginia, he asked, "Has the senator from West Virginia given any consideration to just buying your own airline?" He works for Kentucky projects from locks on the Kentucky River to an Atomic Vapor Laser Isotope Separation facility in Paducah and threatened "blood on the floor of the Senate" to backers of a coal slurry pipeline which would compete with Kentucky coal. He went to bat for UPS, whose hub is Louisville, against FedEx, whose hub is Memphis.

He was the chief sponsor of the Democrats' motor voter bill, which was finally enacted in 1993; he backed unions and opposed Clinton by voting against NAFTA. He surprised some by voting for Dianne Feinstein's ban on assault weapons. He spurned requests to set up a House bank-type operation in the Senate (although initially he did approve money to set up equipment for it) and used the issue in a 1992 campaign spot: "About five years ago a bunch of senators came to me and wanted to have a bank similar to the one they had in the House. And I said no way, we're not going to have a bank on our side. If it ain't good for Kentucky, it ain't good for Wendell Ford."

That was about all he needed that year—his third straight easy race. His opponent attacked him for opposing the Gulf war resolution and "waffling" on the balanced budget amendment (a criticism that later seemed prescient, given Ford's support of the amendment when it failed by several votes in the Senate in 1994, and his vote against a slightly different version in the 1995 razor-thin defeat); in the environment of 1992 that had little impact. But his percentage was lower than in 1986 or 1980, when he became the first opposed candidate to carry all 120 of Kentucky's counties. Will he run in 1998, when he turns 74? His decision not to seek the party leader position suggests that he will not. If not, and perhaps if so, this will be a seriously contested seat. The Republican National Committee took an early shot at Ford during the February 1995 balanced-budget debate by running TV ads that urged him to end the "taxing and spending."

Mitch McConnell, the only Republican to win a statewide race in Kentucky since 1968, is one of the most partisan Republicans in the Senate and recently one of the most effective, a hard-working defender of Republican causes and an assiduous attacker of Democrats. He also tends to Kentucky interests—backing tobacco causes and keeping horse shows operating despite criticism by animal rights activists. On campaign finance reform, he took the lead role for Senate Republicans, killing during the Bush and Clinton years any chance for Oklahoma Senator David Boren's bills to limit PAC contributions and introduce partial public financing. He may try to advance his own campaign finance reforms—no public financing, curbs on union activity, and curtailing out-of-state financing—and dare President Clinton to veto it—but the issue has low priority with Republicans. His arguments against his colleague Wendell Ford's motor voter bill—he called it "auto fraudo"—were less effective. He opposed the Democrats' gift ban rule in 1994 and has his own proposal. McConnell strongly backs product and malpractice liability reform, and wants to cap trial lawyers' contingent fees, but the Senate did not move as quickly as the House on those issues in early 1995. He sponsored a Pornography Victims Act, to let victims of sex crimes sue producers of hard-core pornography that motivated the offenders.

McConnell has been a serious player on foreign policy as well. In 1991, he and Democrat Paul Sarbanes piloted a foreign aid authorization through the Senate, the first since 1985, but it lost in the House. After leaving the Foreign Relations Committee, McConnell now chairs the Appropriations Subcommittee on Foreign Operations, where he strongly supports aid to Israel and has been skeptical about aid to Russia—and, not incidentally, has made clear that he, not Sen. Helms, plans to be Mr. Foreign Policy in the Senate. ("With all due respect to my good friend, Jesse," he told the *Los Angeles Times* in January 1995, "the Appropriations Committee would be where the action is.") He led Senate Republicans in February of 1994, assembling 31 votes against the confirmation of Strobe Talbott, presidential friend who has favored shoring up Russian leaders going back to the Cold War; that was a signal that Talbott could never be confirmed as secretary of State and that his Russophile policies were in trouble in the Senate. By late 1994, Talbott had moved some distance in McConnell's direction and, now that McConnell is chairman, may have to move more. McConnell has an even higher visibility assignment, as chairman of the Ethics Committee; he worked closely with former Chairman Richard Bryan on the long-running investigation of sexual harassment charges against Bob Packwood and in seizing Packwood's diaries.

McConnell, with a self-discipline that may derive from overcoming polio as a child, has devoted his adult life to politics. He served as a legislative aide to Senator Marlow Cook in the late 1960s, then moved back to Louisville and in 1977 won the office that had been Cook's political stepping stone, Jefferson County judge executive. McConnell ran for the Senate in 1984, highlighting the weakness in incumbent Democrat Dee Huddleston's low profile with ads that showed bloodhounds sniffing for Huddleston in vacation locales where he had collected fees for speeches while the Senate was in session. For the 1990 election, McConnell worked hard, built up chits with the Bush White House and pounced on the weaknesses of Democrat Harvey Sloane, onetime mayor of Louisville (1973–77, 1981–85) and Jefferson County judge executive (1986–89) and twice unsuccessful candidate for governor (1979, 1983). Sloane was hurt when the *Courier-Journal* (for years a Democratic and pro-Sloane paper) revealed that he had prescribed sleeping pills for himself after his DEA permit expired; McConnell interspersed his positive TV ads about show horses and the like with a spot showing a bottle of pills spilling onto a table as an announcer reminded viewers about Sloane's trouble. In the end, McConnell's long-accumulated money and political adeptness enabled him to eke out a 52%–48% victory.

Frustrated in applying his political skills to the National Republican Senatorial Committee—he lost the chairmanship to Phil Gramm of Texas by 26–17 in 1990 and 20–19 in 1992—he took them instead to Kentucky, overseeing Ron Lewis's capture of the 2d District House seat in a May 1994 special election, plus another House seat and several Republican legislative pickups in historically Democratic counties in western Kentucky in November. If Kentucky's Republican trend continues—and absent an obvious, well-financed alternative—he should be a solid favorite for reelection in 1996.

Presidential politics. After the 1988 election, Kentucky withdrew from the early March southern Super Tuesday primary and went back to its May primary, which was predictably ignored. In the general election, Kentucky is competitive when Democrats run a southerner or two, as it was in such widely separated years as 1952, 1980 and 1992. But the Republican resurgence in 1994 makes it plain that some major change in opinion (or a third party candidacy) is needed if the Clinton-Gore ticket is to be competitive here in 1996.

Congressional districting. Kentucky lost one district in the 1990 Census. Redistricting moved the 4th District out of the Jefferson County suburbs and east into the mountains and merged most of the old 5th and 7th mountain Districts, one very Republican and the other very Democratic, into a new 5th. Scandal, death, retirement and political upheaval have produced great turnover in what had been one of the House's most stable delegations: Kentucky's six districts have been represented by 11 congressmen already in the 1990s. All but two of the current group have taken office since 1992.

The People: Est. Pop. 1994: 3,627,000; Pop. 1990: 3,685,296, up 3.8% 1990–1994. 1.5% of U.S. total, 24th largest; 48% rural. Median age: 33.0 years. 12.7% 65 years and over. 92.0% White, 7.1% Black. Households: 59.2% married couple families; 29% married couple fams. w. children; 33% college educ.; median household income: $22,534; per capita income: $11,153; 69.6% owner occupied housing; median house value: $50,500; median monthly rent: $250. 6.9% Unemployment. 1994 Voting age pop.: 2,857,000. 1994 Turnout: 783,342; 27% of VAP. Registered voters (1994): 2,132,152; 1,398,854 D (65%), 644,709 R (30%), 88,589 unaffiliated and minor parties (4%).

Political Lineup: Governor, Brereton C. Jones (D); Lt. Gov., Paul E. Patton (D); Secy. of State, Bob Babbage (D); Atty. Gen., Chris Gorman (D); Treasurer, Francis Jones Mills (D); Auditor, Ben Chandler (D). State Senate, 38 (21 D and 17 R); State House of Representatives, 100 (63 D and 37 R). Senators, Wendell H. Ford (D) and Mitch McConnell (R). Representatives, 6 (4 R and 2 D).

1992 Presidential Vote

Clinton (D)	665,104	(45%)
Bush (R)	617,178	(41%)
Perot (I)	203,944	(14%)

1992 Democratic Presidential Primary

Clinton	207,804	(56%)
Brown	30,709	(8%)
Tsongas	18,097	(5%)
Uncommitted	103,590	(28%)

1988 Presidential Vote

Bush (R)	734,281	(56%)
Dukakis (D)	580,368	(44%)

1992 Republican Presidential Primary

Bush	75,371	(75%)
Uncommitted	25,748	(25%)

GOVERNOR

Gov. Brereton C. Jones (D)

Elected 1991, term expires, Dec. 1995; b. June 27, 1939, Pt. Pleasant, WV; home, Midway; U. of VA, B.S. 1961; Presbyterian; married (Libby).

Career: Real estate developer; Horse breeder; Founder, KY HealthCare Access Foundation; KY Lt. Gov., 1987–91.

Office: Office of the Governor, State Capitol, Frankfort 40601, 502-564-2611; Fax: 502-564-2735.

Election Results

1991 gen.	Brereton C. Jones (D).........	540,648	(65%)
	Larry J. Hopkins (R)	294,452	(35%)
1991 prim.	Brereton C. Jones (D).........	184,703	(38%)
	Scotty Baesler (D)	149,352	(30%)
	Dr. Floyd Poore (D)	132,060	(27%)
	Gatewood Galbraith (D)	25,834	(5%)
1987 gen.	Wallace G. Wilkinson (D)	504,674	(65%)
	John Harper (R).............	273,141	(35%)

SENATORS

Sen. Wendell H. Ford (D)

Elected 1974, seat up 1998; b. Sep. 8, 1924, Thruston; home, Owensboro; U. of KY, MD Schl. of Insurance; Baptist; married (Jean).

Career: Army, 1944–46 (WWII); Army Natl. Guard 1949–62; Family insur. business; Chief A.A., Gov. Bert Combs, 1959–63; KY Senate, 1965–67; KY Lt. Gov., 1967–71; KY Gov., 1971–74.

DC Office: 173-A RSOB 20510, 202-224-4343; Fax: 202-224-0046.

State Offices: 1072 New Fed. Bldg., Louisville 40202, 502-582-6251; 305 Fed. Bldg., Owensboro 42301, 502-685-5158; 343 Waller Ave., #204, Lexington 40504, 606-233-2484; and 19 U.S. P.O. and Crthse., Covington 41011, 606-491-7929.

Committees: *Minority Whip. Commerce, Science & Transportation* (3rd of 9 D): Aviation (RMM); Communications; Consumer Affairs, Foreign Commerce and Tourism. *Energy & Natural Resources* (3rd of 8 D): Energy Production and Regulation; Energy Research and Development (RMM). *Rules & Administration* (RMM of 7 D):

Group Ratings

	ADA	ACLU	COPE	CFA	LCV	CON	NSI	COC	ACU	NTLC	CHC
1994	60	32	75	67	46	17	60	37	24	12	50
1993	60	—	91	80	44	16	—	27	24	—	—

National Journal Ratings

	1993 LIB — 1993 CONS			1994 LIB — 1994 CONS		
Economic	83%	—	0%	72%	—	18%
Social	44%	—	55%	37%	—	62%
Foreign	53%	—	39%	46%	—	51%

Key Votes of the 103d Congress

1. Clinton Deficit Plan	Y	3. Brady Handgun Purchase	Y	5. Lmt. UN Cmnd. of Forces	N
2. NAFTA	N	4. Strike Race/Death Pnlty.	Y	6. Cut Missile Funds	N

Key Votes of the 104th Congress

1. Congressional Compliance	Y	3. Balanced Budget Amndt.	N	5. Product Liability Reform	N
2. Bar Unfunded Mandates	Y	4. Pass Line Item Veto	Y	6. FY96 Budget	N

Election Results

1992 general	Wendell H. Ford (D).................	836,888	(63%)	($2,321,131)
	David L. Williams (R)	476,604	(36%)	($335,304)
	Other.............................	17,366	(1%)	
1992 primary	Wendell H. Ford (D)...............	unopposed		
1986 general	Wendell H. Ford (D).................	503,755	(75%)	($1,201,624)
	Jackson M. Andrews (R)	173,330	(25%)	($58,572)

Sen. Mitch McConnell (R)

Elected 1984, seat up 1996; b. Feb. 20, 1942, Sheffield, AL; home, Louisville; U. of Louisville, B.A. 1964, U. of KY, J.D. 1967; Baptist; married (Elaine Chao).

Career: Chief Legis. Asst., U.S. Sen. Marlow Cook, 1967–70; Dep. Asst. Atty. Gen., 1974–75; Jefferson Cnty. Judge Exec., 1977–1984.

DC Office: 120 RSOB 20510, 202-224-2541; Fax: 202-224-2499.

State Offices: 601 W. Broadway, #630, Louisville 40202, 502-582-6304; 1185 Dixie Hwy., #345, Fort Wright 41011, 606-578-0188; Irvin Cobb Bldg., 602 Broadway, Paducah 42001, 502-442-4554; 1501-N S. Main St., London 40741, 606-864-2026; Fed. Bldg., 241 E. Main St., #102, Bowling Green 42101; and 155 E. Main St., #210, Lexington 40508, 606-252-1781.

Committees: *Agriculture, Nutrition & Forestry* (5th of 10 R): Marketing, Inspection and Product Promotion; Research, Nutrition and General Legislation (Chmn). *Appropriations* (9th of 15 R): Agriculture, Rural Development and Related Agencies; Commerce, Justice, State and Judiciary; Defense; Energy and Water Development; Foreign Operations (Chmn). *Environment & Public Works* (8th of 9 R): Clean Air, Wetlands, Private Property and Nuclear Safety; Superfund, Waste Control and Risk Assessment. *Rules & Administration* (6th of 9 R). *Ethics* (Chmn. of 3 R)

Group Ratings

	ADA	ACLU	COPE	CFA	LCV	CON	NSI	COC	ACU	NTLC	CHC
1994	5	32	0	25	0	72	90	89	92	83	93
1993	15	—	0	20	6	50	—	100	79	—	—

National Journal Ratings

	1993 LIB — 1993 CONS			1994 LIB — 1994 CONS		
Economic	0%	—	87%	18%	—	77%
Social	16%	—	81%	16%	—	81%
Foreign	32%	—	60%	26%	—	71%

Key Votes of the 103d Congress

1. Clinton Deficit Plan	N	3. Brady Handgun Purchase	N	5. Lmt. UN Cmnd. of Forces	N
2. NAFTA	Y	4. Strike Race/Death Pnlty.	Y	6. Cut Missile Funds	N

Key Votes of the 104th Congress

1. Congressional Compliance	Y	3. Balanced Budget Amndt.	Y	5. Product Liability Reform	Y
2. Bar Unfunded Mandates	Y	4. Pass Line Item Veto	Y	6. FY96 Budget	Y

Election Results

1990 general	Mitch McConnell (R)................	478,034	(52%)	($5,229,296)
	G. Harvey I. Sloane (D).............	437,976	(48%)	($2,929,641)
1990 primary	Mitch McConnell (R)................	64,063	(89%)	
	Tommy Klein (R)	8,310	(11%)	
1984 general	Mitch McConnell (R)................	644,990	(50%)	($1,767,114)
	Walter D. (Dee) Huddleston (D)	639,721	(49%)	($2,444,091)

FIRST DISTRICT

Where the Ohio River flows into the Mississippi—the intersection Huckleberry Finn and Jim missed in the fog—must have struck early settlers as a site for a great city. But no Pittsburgh or St. Louis grew up on this fertile black soil. Instead, the Kentucky land west of the dammed-up Tennessee and Cumberland Rivers, bought from the Chickasaw Indians by General Andrew Jackson and Governor Isaac Shelby in 1818—the Jackson Purchase, it is still called—was settled by farmers. Most people here today are the descendants of these farmers, with memories of earlier generations retained in family lore. Just to the east of the Tennessee and the Cumberland Rivers is the Pennyrile (after pennyroyal, a common variety of local wild mint), a land of low hills and small farms, where you find the west Kentucky coal fields, the site of much strip mining in recent years.

The 1st Congressional District of Kentucky is made up of the Jackson Purchase and much of the Pennyrile; following the 1992 redistricting, it stretches some 200 miles east of the Mississippi along the Tennessee border. There is a distinctive southern atmosphere here—in the crops that are grown, in the accents of the people, in the large number of blacks, in historically low wage levels and in the fact that the big city people look to is more often Nashville than Louisville. The Jackson Purchase and the Pennyrile have long been Democratic; Paducah, the 1st's largest city, produced one of the most enduring Democratic politicians of this century, Alben Barkley, whose career from 1912–56 included 14 years in the House, 24 in the Senate and four as vice president; he was Senate majority and minority leader and he keynoted four Democratic National Conventions. But far from the Mississippi is Kentucky mountain Republican country and this, combined with the Republican trend which reached north from Dixie to Paducah in 1994, has made the 1st District seriously contested political territory, a district that has so far had three congressmen in the 1990s.

One was almost a caricature of the venal career politician. Carroll Hubbard, a Democrat first elected in 1974, used his post on the Banking Committee to raise money and pocket speaking fees while doing lobbyists' bidding, as a series in the *Louisville Courier-Journal* pointed out just days before the 1992 primary. Hubbard had 152 overdrafts on the House bank; he also got the banking interests to contribute to his wife Carol, who was running for the 5th District seat in eastern Kentucky. Both Hubbards lost and their lives collapsed. In 1994, after bungling undercover work for the FBI (agents code-named him Elmer Fudd), he was sentenced to three years in jail. Hubbard was upset in the 1992 Democratic primary 48%–45% by Tom Barlow, one of the unlikelier winners of 1992. Raised and educated in the East, Barlow returned to his ancestral home, the town of Barlow, just west of Paducah, in the 1980s and sold phone equipment; he ran against Hubbard in 1986 and won 20% of the vote; then he ran again in a year when voters were looking for an honest outsider and were not ready for the anti-Congress campaign waged by Republican Steve Hamrick and won 61%–39%. Barlow's support of Clinton programs made him vulnerable, and though he beat a state senator in the primary 60%–33% he lost to Republican Ed Whitfield in the general 51%–49%.

In anti-insider 1994, Whitfield in fact had more political pedigree than the incumbent. He was elected to the legislature in 1973 as a Democrat and is close to former Governor Edward Breathitt, elected in 1963; he served as lobbyist for the CSX railroad and returned to Hopkinsville to run for Congress. He beat Hamrick in a light-turnout primary (8,000 voters while 57,000 voted on the Democratic side) and then, with the help of Senator Mitch McConnell, raised more money than the incumbent and evidently out-organized him as well. He won 70% in the mountain counties added after redistricting, but also carried traditionally Democratic areas around Hopkinsville in the Pennyrile, and Murray in the Jackson Purchase. Despite his Democratic past—or perhaps in line with so many of his constituents with Democratic pasts—he became a strong supporter of the Republican Contract with America. And he showed his political savvy by winning a seat on the influential Commerce Committee, where he surely will seek to protect the tobacco industry's interests. His political fate will be a good test of Republican strength, for the 1st District has many Democratic office holders who may be contemplating a challenge for this narrowly-won seat in 1996.

The People: Pop. 1990: 614,212; 61% rural; 15% age 65+; 91% White; 8% Black; 1% Hispanic origin. Voting age pop.: 460,440; 7% Black; 1% Hispanic origin. Households: 62% married couple families; 29% married couple fams. w. children; 28% college educ.; median household income: $20,331; per capita income: $10,238; median gross rent: $278; median house value: $40,200.

1992 Presidential Vote			1988 Presidential Vote		
Clinton (D)	116,637	(48%)	Bush (R)	120,522	(54%)
Bush (R)	96,602	(39%)	Dukakis (D)	101,957	(46%)
Perot (I)	30,869	(13%)			

Rep. Edward Whitfield (R)

Elected 1994; b. May 25, 1943, Hopkinsville; home, Hopkinsville; U of KY, B.S. 1965, J.D. 1969; Methodist; married (Connie).

Career: Army Reserves, 1967–73; Practicing atty., 1969–79; KY House of Reps. 1973–75; Owner, Rhodes Oil Co., 1975–79; Cnsl., Seaboard System Railroad, 1979–83; Vice Pres., CSX, 1983–91; Cnsl., Interstate Commerce Comm., 1991–93.

DC Office: 1541 LHOB 20515, 202-225-3115; Fax: 202-225-3547.

District Offices: 317 W. 9th St., Hopkinsville 42204, 502-885-0879; P.O. Box 717, Monroe Cnty. Courthouse, Tompkinsville 42617, 502-487-9509; 222 First St., #307, Henderson 42420, 502-826-4180; and 100 Fountain Ave., Paducah 42001, 502-442-6901.

Committees: *Commerce* (21st of 26 R): Commerce, Trade and Hazardous Materials; Health and Environment.

Group Ratings and 103rd Congress Votes: Newly Elected

Key Votes of the 104th Congress

1. Congressional Compliance Y	6. Reform Crime Grant Y	11. Loser Pays Court Reform Y
2. Balanced Budget Amndmt. Y	7. National Security Act Y	12. Product Liability Reform Y
3. Bar Unfunded Mandates Y	8. Moratorium on Regs. Y	13. Welfare Reform Y
4. Pass Line Item Veto Y	9. Risk Assessment on Regs. Y	14. Term Limits Amndmt. Y
5. Relax Exclusionary Rule Y	10. Expnd. Priv. Prop. Rights Y	15. Tax Cuts Y

Election Results

1994 general	Edward Whitfield (R)	64,849	(51%)	($349,472)
	Tom Barlow (D)	62,387	(49%)	($621,279)
1994 primary	Edward Whitfield (R)	4,212	(53%)	
	Steve Hamrick (R)	3,807	(47%)	
1992 general	Tom Barlow (D)	128,524	(61%)	($209,090)
	Steve Hamrick (R)	83,088	(39%)	($66,705)

SECOND DISTRICT

Americans began settling the limestone-soiled country of central Kentucky more than two centuries ago. In the 1770s and 1780s, they were staking out towns like Bardstown and Harrodsburg and starting academies and colleges; they were well-settled when Stephen Collins Foster wrote "My Old Kentucky Home" just before the Civil War. That conflict tore deeply here: this part of Kentucky gave birth to both Abraham Lincoln and Jefferson Davis, and in the Civil War it lost thousands of soldiers, Union and Confederate, and would suffer disproportionate casualties in the wars of the 20th Century as well. This area is also the home of several Kentucky landmarks—Fort Knox, the nation's gold depository; several of the nation's largest bourbon distilleries; and Mammoth Cave, the world's largest accessible cavern, in the south near Bowling Green.

The 2d Congressional District of Kentucky consists of much of the territory south and southwest of Louisville, starting with the southern Jefferson County suburbs and proceeding south to Bowling Green and west along the Ohio River to Owensboro. This is rural and small town country, where most people have family roots that go back generations and a connection with the past not often found in big metropolitan areas. Civil War loyalties are reflected in the election returns here; Kentucky was deeply split on secession, and a color-coded map of the current 2d District would show various splotches of counties pro-South and splotches pro-Union. But the bits of color would only hint at the deep and often bitter feelings caused by the splits over the War and the losses people suffered—feelings of which current partisan preferences are a dim but persistent reflection. Indeed, dimmer in the mid-1990s than ever, since in 1994 the balance here which had long favored Democrats turned Republican.

The occasion was the May 1994 special election to replace the legendary William Natcher, chairman of the House Appropriations Committee and one of the House's most hard-working and conscientious members; he missed not a single roll call vote after he won the seat in a special election in 1953 until he was mortally ill in March 1994. Meticulous and attentive to detail, scrupulously fair and totally honest, he campaigned by driving around the district and talking to voters, hiring only a small staff and accepting no campaign contributions. It was old-fashioned politics and it worked: he carried his appropriations bills through the House and was reelected by handsome margins.

It was generally assumed that Natcher would be succeeded by a Democrat with good political connections. The nomination went to former state Senate President Joe Prather, who had managed Governor Brereton Jones's campaign; before the election, Prather flew to Washington to go apartment hunting. The Republican nominee, Ron Lewis, a Baptist minister and Christian bookstore owner, had never won an election before. But the National Republican Congressional

Committee put in $200,000 and made the May 24 race a referendum on the Clinton Administration. Lewis ran ads showing Prather's face morphing into Bill Clinton's and saying that Prather had increased taxes and fees 40 times in the Kentucky legislature. Prather only belatedly raised campaign money and asserted that he was quite a different sort of Democrat than Clinton. Lewis won a solid 55%–45% victory, carrying Bowling Green heavily and running ahead in Owensboro and outside Louisville: the first Democratic loss of this seat in 129 years. Stunned House Democratic leaders retorted that Prather had run a weak campaign and had made a mistake by running away from the President and refusing party contributions, which were available.

In the House Lewis voted a predictably conservative line, though he objected to cuts in tobacco subsidies. He made news in August when he attended a smokers' rights rally where Hillary Rodham Clinton was burned in effigy—"inappropriate," he said, but "kind of a desperate act to get some attention to their cause." His November 1994 Democratic opponent, Owensboro Mayor David Adkisson, called it "an act of hate." Many Democrats had argued that Adkisson, a protege of Senator Wendell Ford, would have won in May and felt that Lewis, with his slow delivery, would now lose in the general. But Lewis projected sincerity, and his strong religious views and opposition to the Clinton tax increase and healthcare plan were pluses. "Simply put, I'm very much for reducing the size and intrusiveness of the federal government," he said. Lewis won by a resounding 60%–40% margin, carrying Owensboro's Daviess County and running ahead nearly 2–1 in exurban Bullitt and Hardin Counties south of Louisville. Lewis has pledged to serve no more than four full terms.

The People: Pop. 1990: 615,184; 56% rural; 11% age 65+; 93% White; 5% Black; 1% Asian; 1% Hispanic origin. Voting age pop.: 448,454; 5% Black; 1% Hispanic origin. Households: 65% married couple families; 33% married couple fams. w. children; 30% college educ.; median household income: $23,212; per capita income: $10,609; median gross rent: $310; median house value: $47,900.

1992 Presidential Vote

Bush (R) 107,318 (45%)
Clinton (D) 99,054 (41%)
Perot (I). 33,187 (14%)

1988 Presidential Vote

Bush (R) 122,880 (60%)
Dukakis (D). 83,022 (40%)

Rep. Ron Lewis (R)

Elected May 1994; b. Sept. 14, 1946, McKell; home, Stephensburg; U. of KY, B.A. 1969, Morehead State U., M.A. 1981; Baptist; married (Kayi).

Career: Navy OCS, 1972; Heavy Equip. Sales Rep., 1975–80; Baptist Minister, 1980-present; Prof., Watterson Col., 1980–85; Owner, Alpha Christian Bookstore, 1985–94.

DC Office: 412 CHOB 20515, 202-225-3501; Fax: 202-226-2019.

District Offices: 312 N. Mulberry St., Elizabethtown 42701, 502-765-4360; B-18 Fed. Bldg., 241 W. Main St., Bowling Green 42101, 502-842-9896; and B-17 Fed. Bldg., 423 Frederica St., Owensboro 42303, 502-688-8858.

Committees: *Agriculture* (16th of 27 R): Resource Conservation, Research and Forestry; Risk Management and Specialty Crops. *National Security* (20th of 30 R): Military Personnel; Military Procurement.

Group Ratings and 103rd Congress Votes: Served Only Partial Term

Key Votes of the 104th Congress

1. Congressional Compliance Y	6. Reform Crime Grant Y	11. Loser Pays Court Reform Y
2. Balanced Budget Amndmt. Y	7. National Security Act Y	12. Product Liability Reform Y
3. Bar Unfunded Mandates Y	8. Moratorium on Regs. Y	13. Welfare Reform Y
4. Pass Line Item Veto Y	9. Risk Assessment on Regs. Y	14. Term Limits Amndmt. Y
5. Relax Exclusionary Rule Y	10. Expnd. Priv. Prop. Rights Y	15. Tax Cuts Y

Election Results

1994 general	Ron Lewis (R)............................	90,535	(60%)	($393,266)
	David Adkisson (D)	60,867	(40%)	($493,564)
1994 primary	Ron Lewis (R).....................	unopposed		
1994 special	Ron Lewis (R).........................	40,126	(55%)	($215,037)
	Joseph W. (Joe) Prather (D).............	32,625	(45%)	($254,244)
1992 general	William H. Natcher (D)...............	126,894	(61%)	($6,624)
	Bruce R. Bartley (R)....................	79,684	(39%)	($1,125)

THIRD DISTRICT

At the falls of the Ohio River, Americans more than 200 years ago founded one of their first inland metropolises, the river port and industrial city of Louisville (pronounced *LOOuhv'l*). It is one of two major American cities today named for a man who was executed, King Louis XVI of France (the other is St. Paul). Far enough north for a temperate climate, Louisville has always retained an air of the South; when Kentucky decided not to secede in 1861, the decision was not unanimous, and the culture of tidewater Virginia is still visible in the Louisville lawn party. Steamboats are still tied up in front of Louisville's downtown, primed to follow the channel around the falls of the Ohio which prompted George Rogers Clark to found the town in 1778. Mint juleps are served on the verandas of mansions, especially (but not only) during Derby week in May; horse racing is a preoccupation not just then, but throughout the year. Although the Ohio River is crossed with many bridges and the accent across the river in Indiana may sound the same to outsiders, Louisville partakes of the cavalier culture that second sons of big landowners from the west of England brought to Virginia in the 17th Century and their heirs brought over the Appalachians to the valleys of Kentucky in the 18th Century.

Though Louisville's economy is not particularly southern, tobacco and cigarettes are a major business here, and so is distilling whiskey. Louisville still specializes in assembling large, clunky things like appliances and automobiles (Ford added jobs here in 1992), and Louisville airport is the hub for UPS. But its biggest business now is health: Columbia-HCA Healthcare Corp., the nation's largest operator of for-profit hospitals, has its headquarters here a few blocks from the riverfront in a Michael Graves building which is one of the monuments of post-modern architecture, and the Humana Festival is a creative mecca for playwrights. Politically, Louisville has always had some un-southern aspects and has often voted against the rest of Kentucky; if its elite were Virginia cavaliers, many of its burghers were Germans and Pennsylvanians who made this river town a Republican and anti-slavery island in a secessionist and pro-slavery sea. Locally, Louisville and Jefferson County have long had a robust two-party politics, with successive Jefferson County judge executives, Republican Mitch McConnell and Democrat Harvey Sloane, running against each other for the U.S. Senate in 1990.

The 3d Congressional District of Kentucky includes all of Louisville and almost all of the Jefferson County suburbs—the strip highway zone running south toward Fort Knox, then blue-collar factory zones south of Churchill Downs and the affluent suburbs in the hills to the east heading out toward Bluegrass country. Historically Louisville has had a strong Republican tradition, among its German and black voters; it also has a tradition of activist Democratic politics, personified in Mayors Wilson Wyatt, who served in the 1940s, Harvey Sloane, elected in 1973 and 1981, and Jerry Abramson, the highly popular current incumbent. The congressman from the 3d for almost a quarter century, from his election in 1970 by 211 votes to his retirement in 1994, was Romano Mazzoli, father of the immigration reform law of 1986 (though others disputed the parentage) who spent more time taking principled positions on national issues than tending to local projects or collecting special interest money and, as a result, had a series of close elections.

His successor, chosen in the most expensive congressional campaign in Kentucky history, by almost as narrow a margin as Mazzoli's first, is Democrat Mike Ward. Ward, a state representative from an affluent neighborhood southeast of downtown Louisville, had serious competition in the Democratic primary from cable TV investor Charles Owen, who spent over $800,000 of his own money, and from former Jefferson County human services director Dolores Delahanty. Ward, who stressed his legislative record, finished barely ahead, 27%–24%–24%. On the Republican side, Susan Stokes, former state representative and mayor of Rolling Fields, who held Mazzoli to a 53%–47% win in 1992, was attacked by pro-life opponent Tim Hardy as a "pro-abortion liberal feminist" and compared her to—slander in a Republican primary!—Hillary Rodham Clinton. She won by only 50%–44%. The general was even closer. Ward raised more money from unions and trial lawyers than Stokes did from businesses and doctors; a third, anti-abortion candidate Richard Lewis drained votes from Stokes. Ward opposed term limits and called himself an "old Democrat," and attacked the Clinton welfare proposal as too punitive, while Stokes signed the Contract with America. Ward came out ahead by 425 votes according to the official count, a victory, but not an impressive one, in a district that voted 50%–37% for Bill Clinton over George Bush. There was post-election speculation that the result could be overturned because a dip in electrical power knocked out the computers on some scanning machines, but it turned out to have affected only 74 ballots. Stokes carried the eastern suburbs heavily, but lost votes to third candidate Lewis in the west.

Will Ward, like Mazzoli, hold on for 24 years after winning a narrow victory? He enters a House where his party is at least temporarily in the minority, but has a constituency which has tended to lean his way, at least until 1994. He sits on the National Security Committee where he fought to keep the Naval Ordinance Station in Louisville off the base closure list. If he has a tough opponent in 1996, it will be someone other than Stokes, who has said she will not run again after two bruising races.

The People: Pop. 1990: 613,266; 2% rural; 14% age 65+; 81% White; 18% Black; 1% Asian; 1% Hispanic origin. Voting age pop.: 464,994; 16% Black. Households: 50% married couple families; 22% married couple fams. w. children; 44% college educ.; median household income: $26,614; per capita income: $14,072; median gross rent: $344; median house value: $56,300.

1992 Presidential Vote

Clinton (D)	143,824	(50%)
Bush (R)	105,520	(37%)
Perot (I)	35,902	(13%)

1988 Presidential Vote

Bush (R)	128,880	(51%)
Dukakis (D)	121,917	(49%)

Rep. Mike Ward (D)

Elected 1994; b. Jan. 7, 1951, White Plains, NY; home, Louisville; U. of Louisville, B.S. 1974; Episcopalian; married (Christina).

Career: Peace Corps, Gambia, 1978; Sales Rep., Matthew Bender, 1979–85; Spec. Asst. to Jefferson Cnty. Judge Exec., 1985–89; KY House of Reps., 1989–93; Gen. Mgr., P&C Media, 1990–94; Owner, Street Level Advertising, 1993–94.

DC Office: 1032 LHOB 20515, 202-225-5401; Fax: 202-225-3511; e-mail: mward2@hr.house.gov.

District Offices: 216 Fed. Bldg., 600 M.L.K. Jr. Pl., Louisville 40202, 502-582-5129.

Committees: *National Security* (24th of 25 D): Military Installations and Facilities; Military Personnel. *Science* (18th of 23 D): Energy and Environment; Space and Aeronautics.

Group Ratings and 103rd Congress Votes: Newly Elected

Key Votes of the 104th Congress

1. Congressional Compliance	Y	6. Reform Crime Grant	N	11. Loser Pays Court Reform	N
2. Balanced Budget Amndmt.	N	7. National Security Act	N	12. Product Liability Reform	N
3. Bar Unfunded Mandates	Y	8. Moratorium on Regs.	N	13. Welfare Reform	N
4. Pass Line Item Veto	Y	9. Risk Assessment on Regs.	*	14. Term Limits Amndmt.	N
5. Relax Exclusionary Rule	N	10. Expnd. Priv. Prop. Rights	N	15. Tax Cuts	N

Election Results

1994 general	Mike Ward (D)	67,663	(44%)	($565,022)
	Susan B. Stokes (R)	67,238	(44%)	($580,409)
	Richard A. Lewis (TXP)	17,591	(12%)	($25,472)
1994 primary	Mike Ward (D)	13,370	(27%)	
	Charles L. Owen (D)	11,970	(24%)	
	Dolores S. Delahanty (D)	11,951	(24%)	
	Bill Wilson (D)	3,699	(8%)	
	Shelby Lanier (D)	2,664	(5%)	
	Six Others	5,435	(11%)	
1992 general	Romano L. Mazzoli (D)	148,066	(53%)	($216,638)
	Susan B. Stokes (R)	132,689	(47%)	($364,659)

FOURTH DISTRICT

More than once the commonwealth of Kentucky has gone to court to stake its claim to all of the Ohio River up to its northern bank: this is the northernmost extension of the South. The Ohio sees many different parts of Kentucky. Ashland, near the West Virginia border, is industrial, the home of Ashland Oil, one of Kentucky's largest corporations; the river here is bound in by tight hills which hold smoke and soot close in the air. Farther down the river, the country is more bucolic: on frozen ice flotes in this part of the river, Harriet Beecher Stowe wrote, Eliza fled across the ice in *Uncle Tom's Cabin*. Farther west, between Louisville and Cincinnati, are counties which still look like they're in the 19th Century. But metropolitan growth obtrudes. Oldham County, just upriver from Louisville, has some of Kentucky's oldest homes, but the horse country is also sprouting affluent subdivisions. And the northern Kentucky "golden triangle," the three counties across the river from Cincinnati, saw rapid population growth and a sharp rise in incomes in the 1990s. Not far away is Cold Spring, where the predicted midnight appearance of the Virgin Mary brought many Catholics and others in September 1992 (some said they saw her; others did not).

The 4th Congressional District of Kentucky spans all these variations of Ohio River country, from Ashland west to Oldham County; it also includes the typically less populated counties just inland. Economically, it runs the gamut from coal mining towns to rich suburbs. Politically, it runs the gamut from some of the most Democratic counties in America, like Elliott County (this was the only county current Congressman Jim Bunning lost in 1994) in the mountains south of Ashland, or the three old counties along the river between Cincinnati and Louisville, to some of the most Republican territory in Kentucky, like Oldham County and the Cincinnati suburbs—not just the spanking-new towns but the old riverfront cities of Newport, long known for its gambling, and Covington, connected to Cincinnati by a suspension bridge built by John Roebling 16 years before the Brooklyn Bridge. This district was substantially changed by redistricting and lost the Jefferson County suburbs of Louisville. But it remains Republican, though more marginally so.

The congressman from the 4th District is Jim Bunning, who may go down in history first as a great baseball pitcher, but now has become a congressman of some power. Bunning's career in baseball was distinguished. He threw a no-hitter for the Detroit Tigers in 1958 and pitched a perfect game for the Philadelphia Phillies in 1964; he also played for the Pittsburgh Pirates and the Los Angeles Dodgers and retired in 1971 with a 224–184 record, a 3.24 ERA, 2,855 strikeouts and one of the highest totals in baseball history for hitting batters. Bunning brought that skill, energy and aggressiveness to politics in his native northern Kentucky (no, he never played for the Cincinnati Reds). He was elected to the state Senate in 1979 and won a respectable 44% against Martha Layne Collins in the 1983 race for governor (the best showing for a Republican gubernatorial candidate in the last 20 years). When incumbent 4th District Congressman Gene Snyder retired in 1986, Bunning won the general with 55%.

On Capitol Hill, Bunning has shown much of the aggressiveness that he had on the pitching mound and organizing the baseball players' union. Like that other union organizer, Ronald Reagan, Bunning is a solid conservative and once headed Newt Gingrich's Conservative Opportunity Society. He was a firm backer of the Gulf war; his son was an airman there, and several of his son's colleagues were killed. In 1990, he got a seat on Ways and Means, where he opposed higher taxes on earnings by Social Security beneficiaries—a hot issue in affluent older suburbs. In late 1991, he urged President Bush to focus on the economy before it was too late—not bad advice. In 1992 Bunning had his toughest challenge, from Dr. Floyd Poore, an appointee of two Democratic governors and a respectable third place finisher in the 1991 gubernatorial primary; Poore is a physician who changed his name legally so that the "Dr." would have to appear on the ballot. There was sharp clash on issues like healthcare reform, as well as nasty personal charges; Bunning won with 62%, establishing this as a safe district.

Bunning was not a fan of House Democratic leaders or President Clinton. He was outraged by his colleagues' overdrafts on the House bank, and on the Ethics Committee in March 1992 he led the successful charge against committee Chairman Matthew McHugh's proposal to identify only the 24 worst offenders. In September 1993, at a Republican rally in northern Kentucky, Bunning called Clinton "the most corrupt, the most amoral, the most despicable person I've ever seen in the presidency," and he didn't back down after criticism from Governor Brereton Jones, Senator Wendell Ford and Congressman William Natcher. In 1994 on the Ways and Means Committee, he fought the Clinton healthcare plan and the tobacco tax proposed to help finance it. He also fought against the plan's coverage of abortions. He did work with Democrats on making the nanny tax less oppressive—and Congress finally raised the limit to trigger coverage, which had not been changed since the 1930s. He also worked to pass the bill setting up the Social Security Administration as a separate agency, apart from HHS; President Clinton signed it in 1994.

Now, after an easy reelection victory, Bunning chairs the Ways and Means Social Security Subcommittee. Like other Republicans, he is pledged to oppose any reduction in Social Security benefits; he favors the Contract with America pledges to repeal 1993 Social Security tax increases and to raise the earnings limit on Social Security beneficiaries. Bunning seems exhilarated by serving in a Republican House and, with his considerable seniority, has vehemently denied that he is interested in running for governor.

The People: Pop. 1990: 614,410; 46% rural; 12% age 65+; 97% White; 2% Black. Voting age pop.: 449,656; 2% Black. Households: 62% married couple families; 31% married couple fams. w. children; 34% college educ.; median household income: $26,362; per capita income: $11,863; median gross rent: $336; median house value: $56,700.

1992 Presidential Vote			1988 Presidential Vote		
Bush (R)	106,685	(44%)	Bush (R)	125,832	(60%)
Clinton (D)	94,323	(39%)	Dukakis (D)	85,588	(40%)
Perot (I)	40,437	(17%)			

Rep. Jim Bunning (R)

Elected 1986; b. Oct. 23, 1931, Campbell County; home, Southgate; Xavier U., B.S. 1953; Catholic; married (Mary).

Career: Pro baseball player, 1950–71; Investment broker and agent, 1960–86; Ft. Thomas City Cncl., 1977–79; KY Senate, 1979–83.

DC Office: 2437 RHOB 20515, 202-225-3465; Fax: 202-225-0003.

District Offices: 1717 Dixie Hwy., #160, Ft. Wright 41011, 606-341-2602; 1408 Greenup Ave., #236, Ashland 41101, 606-325-9898; and 704 W. Jefferson St., #219, La Grange 40031, 502-222-2188.

Committees: *Budget* (7th of 24 R). *Standards of Official Conduct* (2nd of 5 R). *Ways & Means* (6th of 21 R): Social Security (Chmn.).

Group Ratings

	ADA	ACLU	COPE	CFA	LCV	CON	NSI	COC	ACU	NTLC	CHC
1994	5	14	11	20	11	72	100	83	95	96	100
1993	10	—	8	10	21	85	—	91	100	—	—

National Journal Ratings

	1993 LIB — 1993 CONS		1994 LIB — 1994 CONS	
Economic	20% —	77%	0% —	80%
Social	0% —	89%	0% —	89%
Foreign	0% —	91%	14% —	80%

Key Votes of the 103d Congress

1. Clinton Deficit Plan	N	3. Brady Handgun Purchase	N	5. Lmt. UN Cmnd. of Forces	Y
2. NAFTA	N	4. Strike Race/Death Pnlty.	Y	6. Cut Missile Funds	N

Key Votes of the 104th Congress

1. Congressional Compliance	Y	6. Reform Crime Grant	Y	11. Loser Pays Court Reform	Y
2. Balanced Budget Amndmt.	Y	7. National Security Act	Y	12. Product Liability Reform	Y
3. Bar Unfunded Mandates	Y	8. Moratorium on Regs.	Y	13. Welfare Reform	Y
4. Pass Line Item Veto	Y	9. Risk Assessment on Regs.	Y	14. Term Limits Amndmt.	Y
5. Relax Exclusionary Rule	Y	10. Expnd. Priv. Prop. Rights	Y	15. Tax Cuts	Y

Election Results

1994 general	Jim Bunning (R)	96,695	(74%)	($560,590)
	Sally Harris Skaggs (D)	33,717	(26%)	($20,141)
1994 primary	Jim Bunning (R)	unopposed		
1992 general	Jim Bunning (R)	139,634	(62%)	($984,180)
	Dr. Floyd Poore (D)	86,890	(38%)	($311,121)

FIFTH DISTRICT

The mountains of eastern Kentucky have been a special place since Daniel Boone came through the Cumberland Gap in 1775. As Virginians poured through and created their version of a Tidewater civilization in the Bluegrass country, the people who settled the counties of the mountains and the Cumberland Plateau, most of them of Irish Protestant or Border Scots descent, brought different values—an assertive egalitarianism, loyalty to family and community and passionate willingness to settle differences by feuds or violence. Most of the people in the mountains today are descendants of families who settled there in the two or three generations after Boone. Handed down are living memories of the old ways of doing things and personal values, from the time not so far distant when there was little contact here with the outside world and the ties to the rest of American civilization were secured mainly by school primers and the King James Bible.

Only when people's lives have been changed and uprooted by outside events and institutions have their basic political attitudes been changed—and in each case, changed with a lasting imprint. The first agent of such change was the Civil War; the second was the great United Mine Workers organizing drives in the coal mines around the 1930s. The Civil War made the mountains and the Cumberland Plateau a stronghold of the Republican Party. For this was never slave territory—hardly any blacks have ever lived here—and yet communities and families were riven by the rebellion of the South. People have not forgotten: the counties around Somerset and Corbin in south central Kentucky cast some of the highest Republican percentages in the nation in election after election.

Then came coal. Early in this century, vast seams of coal were discovered under the Kentucky mountains; representatives of eastern capitalists began prowling through these hills, hiring courthouse town lawyers to buy up mineral rights from unsuspecting farmers, building tiny industrial slum towns in hollows and creek beds beneath glowering, heavily forested mountainsides. The mines kept mountaineers home, but coal mining is harsh and deadly work: mine accidents, black lung disease and simple exhaustion killed tens of thousands of miners, while low wages and company stores kept them poor. Then John L. Lewis's United Mine Workers came in and something like open warfare followed, with neither mine operators nor union organizers loath to use violence and threats. The union mostly won in eastern Kentucky and in the short run raised wages and built hospitals for miners and their families; in the longer run, the UMW phased out many jobs in the mines, in return for job security and health benefits, as coal was replaced by oil as the nation's major fuel. Politically, the UMW counties in the eastern part of the state became heavily Democratic and have remained so even as underground mine jobs were phased out during the strip mining boom of the 1970s, and as UMW members have died out in the 1980s and 1990s.

The 5th Congressional District of Kentucky includes much of the Cumberland Plateau and most of the eastern mountains, a mixture of heavily Republican and heavily Democratic territory. It voted for George Bush in 1988 and Bill Clinton in 1992, but with huge internal differences: in the close 1990 Senate race Jackson County voted 79% Republican and Knott County a few mountain ridges away voted 72% Democratic. The current boundaries were a melding in the 1991 redistricting of two old districts: the old 5th, one of the most heavily Republican in the country, and the old 7th, reliably Democratic and represented for 35 years by

Carl Perkins, chairman of the Education and Labor Committee from 1967 to 1984.

The congressman now is Harold Rogers, a Republican first elected in the 5th District in 1980, with deep roots in the Cumberlands. He had won that district in a multicandidate primary and was spending much time on the Appropriations Committee helping district projects when the 1991 redistricting challenge brought on a serious Democratic opponent in 1992. At first it seemed that he would face 7th District Democrat Chris Perkins, son of the late chairman. But the younger Perkins had a lavish lifestyle that produced 514 overdrafts on the House bank; he retired before that was revealed, in January 1992, at 37; in December 1994 he pled guilty to federal charges of check-kiting. The winner of the six-candidate Democratic primary was state Senator John Doug Hays of Pike County, whose grandfather Doug "Sawloggin' " Hays was state senator before him. Hays attacked Rogers for supporting trickle-down economics and argued that as a Democrat he could get more money for the district in Bill Clinton's Washington. Rogers countered by pointing to his ongoing efforts to build the $250 million Cumberland Gap twin tunnels and Harlan County flood projects. Rogers won with 55%. He had 71% in his old 5th District, which cast 52% of the new district's votes; he lost 64%–36% in the old 7th District. The returns show the strength of partisan feelings in eastern Kentucky: Owsley County was 78% for Rogers; next-door Breathitt County was 68% for Hays.

Rogers continued to labor with business-as-usual on Appropriations and was one of three Republicans to vote for the ill-fated Clinton economic stimulus package in March 1993: no doctrinaire free marketeer he. He opposed any tobacco tax, called for the resignation of Surgeon General Joycelyn Elders, beat back an attempt to close the Appalachian Regional Commission, saved the Jackson weather station, worked for flood control projects in the Cumberland and Big Sandy River basins. In 1994, against another state senator, a dentist who became well-known while conducting Upward Bound programs for the underprivileged, Rogers won, even after canceling his last week of campaigning because of family illness, with an impressive 79% of the vote, carrying every county.

Now he is chairman of the Appropriations Subcommittee which handles budgets for the Commerce, Justice and State Departments, giving him the potential for great say over foreign policy. He advocates cuts in American support of the United Nations and a ban on U.S. troops serving under UN command; he seems cautious about U.S. interventions abroad. He voted against the GATT treaty. But one suspects much of his energy will be devoted to the pork-dispensing Energy and Water Subcommittee, on which he ranks second. In addition, he wants to fund a Kentucky portion of Interstate 66 through his district and other roads; he will pay close attention to tobacco laws and regulations. He supported the Contract with America but is a bit cautious about welfare reform; representing one of the lowest-income districts in the country, he said, "No simple solutions to getting people off welfare and into work—people of our region understand that." And he seems to understand them.

The People: Pop. 1990: 613,979; 87% rural; 12% age 65+; 99% White; 1% Black. Voting age pop.: 441,342; 1% Black. Households: 65% married couple families; 34% married couple fams. w. children; 20% college educ.; median household income: $15,052; per capita income: $7,717; median gross rent: $243; median house value: $35,400.

1992 Presidential Vote

Clinton (D)	109,607	(48%)
Bush (R)	95,843	(42%)
Perot (I)	23,890	(10%)

1988 Presidential Vote

Bush (R)	111,998	(53%)
Dukakis (D)	98,058	(47%)

Rep. Harold D. Rogers (R)

Elected 1980; b. Dec. 31, 1937, Barrier; home, Somerset; U. of KY, B.A. 1962, J.D. 1964; Baptist; married (Shirley).

Career: Army Natl. Guard, 1957–64; Practicing atty., 1964–69; Pulaski-Rockcastle Commonwealth atty., 1969–80.

DC Office: 2468 RHOB 20515, 202-225-4601; Fax: 202-225-0940.

District Offices: 203 E. Mount Vernon St., Somerset 42501, 606-679-8346; 601 Main St., Hazard 41701, 606-439-0794; and 806 Hambley Blvd., Pikeville 41501, 606-432-4388.

Committees: *Appropriations* (8th of 32 R): Commerce, Justice, State, and Judiciary (Chmn.); Energy and Water Development; Transportation.

Group Ratings

	ADA	ACLU	COPE	CFA	LCV	CON	NSI	COC	ACU	NTLC	CHC
1994	15	14	56	20	6	55	90	75	89	71	86
1993	20	—	42	30	23	11	—	82	83	—	—

National Journal Ratings

	1993 LIB — 1993 CONS		1994 LIB — 1994 CONS	
Economic	42%	— 57%	34%	— 64%
Social	19%	— 77%	19%	— 81%
Foreign	0%	— 91%	0%	— 88%

Key Votes of the 103d Congress

1. Clinton Deficit Plan	N	3. Brady Handgun Purchase	N	5. Lmt. UN Cmnd. of Forces	Y
2. NAFTA	N	4. Strike Race/Death Pnlty.	Y	6. Cut Missile Funds	N

Key Votes of the 104th Congress

1. Congressional Compliance	Y	6. Reform Crime Grant	Y	11. Loser Pays Court Reform	Y
2. Balanced Budget Amndmt.	Y	7. National Security Act	Y	12. Product Liability Reform	Y
3. Bar Unfunded Mandates	Y	8. Moratorium on Regs.	Y	13. Welfare Reform	Y
4. Pass Line Item Veto	Y	9. Risk Assessment on Regs.	Y	14. Term Limits Amndmt.	N
5. Relax Exclusionary Rule	Y	10. Expnd. Priv. Prop. Rights	Y	15. Tax Cuts	N

Election Results

1994 general	Harold D. Rogers (R)..................	82,291	(79%)	($348,243)
	Walter (Doc) Blevins (D)	21,318	(21%)	($52,377)
1994 primary	Harold D. Rogers (R)..............	unopposed		
1992 general	Harold D. Rogers (R)................	115,255	(55%)	($885,966)
	John Doug Hays (D)...................	95,760	(45%)	($274,753)

SIXTH DISTRICT

With its white picket-fenced horse farms and Georgian brick house-filled small towns, the Bluegrass country almost plumb in the middle of Kentucky is the most well-settled part of interior America: Lexington was founded in 1775; the town of Hopewell was renamed Paris in 1789 out of gratitude for French help during our Revolution and in a salute to theirs (though the county name remained Bourbon even after Louis XVI was executed). Tobacco farming started here in the 1770s, horse racing in 1787, and the first whiskey distillery, in Bourbon County, was built in 1790. Tobacco, whiskey and race horses remained the staples of the Bluegrass economy for six generations until 1956, when IBM built its typewriter plant and headquarters in Lexington. IBM's arrival "really was the beginning of Lexington's industrial revolution," as University of Kentucky historian Carl Cone put it. You imagine a Kentucky colonel sitting on the porch, dressed in a white suit and string tie and sipping a mint julep, as IBM engineers in their dark suits and white shirts file into their offices.

In the 1980s, another ingredient was added to the Bluegrass economic mix when Toyota located its $2 billion plant in Georgetown, a town with early 19th Century houses and lush countryside, just one county north of Lexington and west of Paris. Now in the seemingly timeless Bluegrass, economic change seems constant. IBM, finding the Selectric outclassed by the PC, put the business on the block in 1990, threatening all those jobs, while the horse racing industry suffered a slump symbolized by the bankruptcy of the late Leslie Combs's Spendthrift Farm. But just then, Toyota announced a doubling of its plant, so that its projected 4,100 (non-union) workers can keep using innovative methods to build the popular Camry and, when Calumet Farm went up for sale, it was snapped up by a Polish-born investor. From IBM to Toyota to even the Bluegrass horse farms, Lexington seems to be a focus of innovation and certainly of economic growth.

Lexington was the home base of the Whig party's great leader Henry Clay, but in the century and a half since his death the Bluegrass country has been Democratic, even into the 1990s. Jimmy Carter and Bill Clinton carried the Bluegrass counties, especially the small state capital of Frankfort, whose voters backed Democratic congressmen for years. But Lexington, as its metro area has grown to cover all of Fayette County and to spread out into others, has trended Republican and so has the 6th Congressional District, which includes Lexington and many of the Bluegrass counties, running south to the Cumberland Plateau and north halfway to Cincinnati. In 1978 the 6th, after a Democratic fumble, elected a Republican congressman, Larry Hopkins, who held on until he ran for governor in 1991 and it became known he had exaggerated his military service and had 32 overdrafts on the House bank; he retired in 1992. The new 6th District lines were intended by a Democratic legislature to elect a Democratic congressman, and it did. But it also narrowly voted for George Bush over Bill Clinton.

The congressman is Scotty Baesler, a celebrity in Lexington and the Bluegrass country for many years. He was captain of the University of Kentucky basketball team, class of 1963—the days of the legendary Coach Adolph Rupp. He went on to law school, then became administrator of Fayette County Legal Aid. He was elected Lexington mayor in 1982, where he created a statewide scholarship program called Sweet 16 Academic Showcase, brought the DARE program into schools to teach kids about drugs, sponsored downtown redevelopment, developed a Family Care Center for poor families, chaired a state commission to develop tourism and the arts and hosted major sports tourneys. In 1991 Baesler ran for governor and finished second in the Democratic primary, trailing Brereton Jones 38%–30%; if there had been a runoff, as there is now, he might have won. He was the obvious candidate in the 6th District. He won 82% in a five-candidate primary and then beat a little-known Republican 61%–39%.

In the House Baesler worked to put small-town amendments in the 1994 crime bill and serves on the Specialty Crops Subcommittee of Agriculture (by avocation he is a tobacco farmer; not a bad thing for a Kentucky politician). He has questioned the chemical weapons incineration proposal for Bluegrass Army Depot, established a 150-store "Country Store" rural communications network. He told voters he hoped the Clinton healthcare plan's tobacco tax could be scaled down, but said the biggest threat to tobacco was imports, not taxes. He criticized Surgeon General Joycelyn Elders for proposing to legalize marijuana but to outlaw tobacco.

Baesler did not have an altogether comfortable election year. He was embarrassed in April 1994 when it was revealed that on his last day as mayor he used two city employees to load furniture from his home onto a rental truck bound for Washington. After Republicans won the 2d District special election in May 1994, he decided to accept PAC money, even though his

Republican opponent was a political unknown. He refused support from the Democratic Congressional Campaign Committee after its chairman, Vic Fazio, criticized the religious right. Baesler won, but with 59% of the vote, 2% less than he garnered against a better-known opponent in 1992. That may have changed his mind on running for governor. In April 1994 Baesler said he would "probably" run for governor, "unless something untoward happens." But in December 1994, after the election and faced with the prospect of voting on the Republicans' Contract with America in the first 100 days of the new Congress, he opted out of the May gubernatorial primary.

The People: Pop. 1990: 614,245; 37% rural; 11% age 65+; 90% White; 8% Black; 1% Asian; 1% Hispanic origin. Voting age pop.: 464,792; 8% Black; 1% Hispanic origin. Households: 58% married couple families; 27% married couple fams. w. children; 41% college educ.; median household income: $25,377; per capita income: $12,419; median gross rent: $352; median house value: $61,200.

1992 Presidential Vote

Bush (R) 105,210 (42%)
Clinton (D) 101,659 (41%)
Perot (I). 39,659 (16%)

1988 Presidential Vote

Bush (R) 124,169 (58%)
Dukakis (D). 89,826 (42%)

Rep. Scotty Baesler (D)

Elected 1992; b. July 9, 1941, Athens; home, Lexington; U. of KY, B.S. 1963, J.D. 1966; Christian; married (Alice).

Career: Army Reserves, 1966–72; Tobacco farmer; Practicing atty., 1966–67; Fayette Cnty. Legal Aid Admin., 1967–73; Lexington Vice Mayor, 1974–78; Fayette Cnty. District Judge, 1978–82; Lexington Mayor, 1982–92.

DC Office: 113 CHOB 20515, 202-225-4706; Fax: 202-225-2122.

District Offices: 401 W. Main St., #318, Lexington 40507, 606-253-1124.

Committees: *Agriculture* (16th of 22 D): Department Operations, Nutrition and Foreign Agriculture; Risk Management and Specialty Crops. *Veterans' Affairs* (10th of 15 D): Hospitals and Health Care.

Group Ratings

	ADA	ACLU	COPE	CFA	LCV	CON	NSI	COC	ACU	NTLC	CHC
1994	45	43	56	40	39	44	70	92	33	36	57
1993	40	—	75	70	86	59	—	55	39	—	—

National Journal Ratings

	1993 LIB — 1993 CONS		1994 LIB — 1994 CONS	
Economic	46%	53%	59%	37%
Social	56%	44%	52%	47%
Foreign	63%	34%	42%	57%

Key Votes of the 103d Congress

1. Clinton Deficit Plan	N	3. Brady Handgun Purchase	Y	5. Lmt. UN Cmnd. of Forces	N
2. NAFTA	Y	4. Strike Race/Death Pnlty.	Y	6. Cut Missile Funds	N

Key Votes of the 104th Congress

1. Congressional Compliance Y	6. Reform Crime Grant N	11. Loser Pays Court Reform N
2. Balanced Budget Amndmt. Y	7. National Security Act N	12. Product Liability Reform Y
3. Bar Unfunded Mandates Y	8. Moratorium on Regs. Y	13. Welfare Reform N
4. Pass Line Item Veto Y	9. Risk Assessment on Regs. Y	14. Term Limits Amndmt. N
5. Relax Exclusionary Rule Y	10. Expnd. Priv. Prop. Rights Y	15. Tax Cuts N

Election Results

1994 general	Scotty Baesler (D)...................	70,085	(59%)	($223,327)
	Matthew Eric Wills (R)	49,032	(41%)	($23,190)
1994 primary	Scotty Baesler (D).................	unopposed		
1992 general	Scotty Baesler (D).................	135,613	(61%)	($273,727)
	Charles W. Ellinger (R)	87,816	(39%)	($65,643)

LOUISIANA

Louisiana often seems to be America's banana republic, with its charm and inefficiency, its communities interlaced by family ties and a public sector laced with corruption, with its own indigenous culture and its tradition of fine distinctions of class and caste. It is a state with an economy uncomfortably like that of an underdeveloped country, based on pumping minerals out of soggy ground, shipping grain produced in the vast hinterland drained by its great river, and increasingly dependent in recent years on the business typical of picturesque Third World countries—tourism. Its politics too has a third world quality, with its own peculiar election laws and a heritage of no-holds-barred conflict and demagoguery no other state can match: what other state has produced a Huey Long, or an Edwin Edwards? With a hereditary rich class and a large low-wage working class, conservative cultural attitudes (Louisiana, together with Utah, have the most conservative abortion laws in the U.S.) and a lazy tolerance of rule-breaking, Louisiana feels more like the Caribbean or the Mediterranean than the North Atlantic or the Pacific Rim. This is not an entirely original observation. Three decades ago, A. J. Liebling described Louisiana as an outpost of the Levant along the Gulf of Mexico. Most of the United States faces east toward the vast Atlantic Ocean or west toward the vast Pacific; Louisiana faces south, to the Gulf of Mexico and the steamy heat and volatile societies of Latin America.

New Orleans preserves the look and feel it had as a French and Spanish outpost in the New World. Traditions of centralized control and easygoing corruption—classic traits of colonialism—are part of this heritage. The *dirigiste* tradition comes from the fact that Louisiana is the only state that operates on the Napoleonic Code of France (which until 1990 required parents to leave a large percentage of their estate to their children), not the common law of England; the concept of civil liberties has shallower roots in Louisiana than in the other 49 states. Here abstract ideals have been overshadowed by the practical need for centralized action. This delta land—much of it below sea level, soggy, swampy, laced with tributaries and offshoots of the Mississippi and other major rivers like the Atchafalaya—requires vast capital expenditures for levees and drainage and causeways. Even today, houses in New Orleans don't have basements, people are buried in above-ground cemeteries in grandiose crypts, and swamp lands begin abruptly at the edges of subdivisions where people find alligators in their back yards.

The economy that grew up in these rich Delta lands has always been based on raw materials. Antebellum Louisiana produced and exported sugar, rice and cotton in enough abundance to generate the wealth which built grand plantation houses behind alleys of oaks running in from the Mississippi, and to make New Orleans the nation's fifth largest city by the time of the Civil War. Then came oil, found in the great Spindletop strike just over the Texas line in 1901 and in salt domes in Louisiana not long after; Jersey Standard (now Exxon) built the huge Baton Rouge refinery that became the training ground for generations of its top executives. When energy prices boomed after the oil shocks of 1973 and 1981, Louisiana, like an oil-rich Third World country, boomed too, reaching up toward national income levels, generating 500,000 new jobs between 1972 and 1981, only to lose 150,000 in the next six years as oil prices crashed and the rig count dropped from a peak of 455 in 1981 to 132 in 1994. Energy produced 41% of state government revenues in 1982, but only 13% in 1992. That economic turmoil has now abated: Louisiana's unemployment, the highest in the nation in the mid-1980s, was slightly above the national average in the early 1990s. But the instability produced violent tremors in Louisiana politics, with shocks heard around the country.

The shocks were the greater because Louisiana has greater income disparities than almost anywhere else in the United States, an economy more typical of a Caribbean sugar colony than an American state. New Orleans's rich are notoriously unventuresome and tight-knit, determined to hold on to their wealth against the grasp of the impecunious and unlearned masses. They have not hesitated to use the dirigiste tradition in their own interests, though others have not hesitated to use it against them. The most enduringly famous, and by far the most talented, was Huey P. Long, who in less than a single term each as governor (1928–32) and senator (1932–35), left an imprint on the state's public life and imposed an organization to its politics that have only in the last decade faded into history. Long's genius was not that he promised to tax the rich to help the poor—hundreds of idealists and demagogues in America have done that—but that, to an amazing extent, he actually delivered. He dominated the legislature so thoroughly that, as governor, he roamed the floors of both chambers at will, bringing to the podium bills he insisted be passed without changing a comma—and they were. He was ready to use bribery, intimidation and physical violence, to the point that his machine reminded many Americans of contemporary dictatorships in Europe. He built a new skyscraper Capitol, a new Louisiana State University, and more miles of roads than any state but rich New York and huge Texas. He also built a national following, and by 1935, he was planning to run for president on the platform of "Share the wealth, every man a king," when he was assassinated at age 42 in the hallway of the Capitol, where the bullet holes can still be seen in the marble.

For America, the Long threat may have moved Franklin Roosevelt to embrace the liberal programs—the Wagner Labor Act, social security, steeply graduated taxes—of the second New Deal. For Louisiana, Long delivered a political structure that revolved around him long after he was dead—and a class of political leaders who, lacking his talents, treated the state as Long's incompetent doctors had treated his fatal wound, leaving Louisiana without either a fully developed economy or a fully competent public sector. For 50 years, until Huey's son Senator Russell Long retired in 1986, Longs and Long proteges held high political office in Louisiana; for 20 years elections were run mostly on pro- and anti-Long lines. The Long experience has strengthened Louisiana's already strong predispositions—tolerance of corruption, disinterest in abstract reform, and taste for colorful extremists regardless of their short-term means or long-term ends—in a way that helps explain the rise and fall of former Ku Klux Klan leader David Duke in the early 1990s—and why Duke was never likely to run as well anywhere else in the country.

Louisiana has natural political divides. One divide is Cajuns and north Louisiana Baptists; the Cajun parishes cast about 30% of the state's vote, the New Orleans area around 25% or so, with about 45% in Protestant parishes from the Baton Rouge area and north. White Protestants these days want nothing to do with national Democrats, while Cajuns mull it over; about half of them voted for Bill Clinton and Michael Dukakis. Another divide is by race: blacks are overwhelmingly Democratic, whites split in state elections. A third divide is by income: with wide economic disparities, Louisiana's low- and high-income whites vote very differently, and are much less influenced than voters in most other states by candidates' cultural values, marital status,

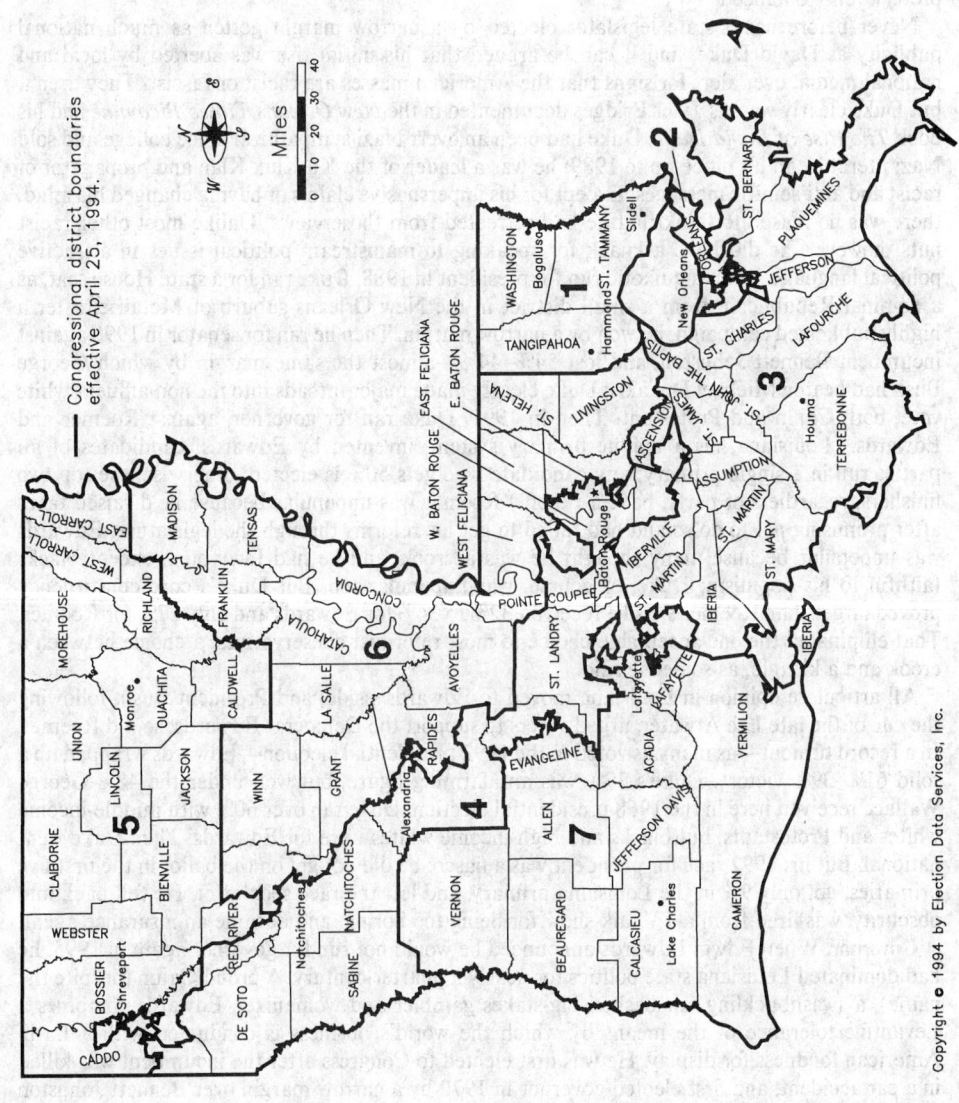

Congressional district boundaries effective April 25, 1994.

Miles
0 10 20 30 40

lifestyles and the like. As a result, Louisiana politics since Huey Long's time has often been a struggle between reformist and conservative forces on one side and roguish populists on the other, a struggle waged in lavishly financed campaigns and with grandiloquent rhetoric. In the last quarter-century, Governor Edwin Edwards has played the role of roguish populist, while his Republican counterparts like David Treen and Buddy Roemer (though he wasn't a Republican until he switched parties in March 1991) were cast as reformist conservatives; the sides were pretty evenly balanced.

Never before has a state legislator elected by a narrow margin gotten as much national publicity as David Duke, and it can be argued that his initial rise was abetted by local and national media, ever alert for signs that the American masses are racist or fascist. They aren't, but Duke clearly was: as Tyler Bridges documented in the *New Orleans Times-Picayune* and his book *The Rise of David Duke*, Duke had been an overt Nazi sympathizer since college and sold Nazi literature in his office up to 1989; he was a leader of the Ku Klux Klan and propagator of racist and anti-semitic messages. Except for his unpersuasive claims of having changed his mind, there was no reason to think that he had retreated from those views. Unlike most other racist nuts, however, he did have a knack for speaking to mainstream political issues in attractive political language. After a quixotic run for president in 1988, Duke ran for a state House seat, as a nominal Republican, from a small district in the New Orleans suburb of Metairie; after a highly publicized campaign, he won by a narrow margin. Then he ran for senator in 1990 against incumbent Bennett Johnston, and lost 54%–44%—almost the same margin by which George Bush had beaten Michael Dukakis; Duke clearly made major inroads into the non-affluent white vote, both Cajun and Protestant. Then in 1991, Duke ran for governor, against Roemer and Edwards. (Louisiana has a unique primary system, invented by Edwards: candidates of all parties run in a single primary; any candidate who gets 50% is elected; otherwise, the top two finishers, regardless of party, have a runoff.) Roemer was unpopular because he'd raised taxes after promising not to do so and had failed to get his reforms through the legislature; Edwards was unpopular because many thought he was a crook, and he had few voters except blacks faithful to his populism; Duke, of course, was unpopular too. But Duke's core constituency proved larger than Roemer's, as he received 32% to 34% for Edwards and only 27% for Roemer. That eliminated the one acceptable choice to most reformist conservatives; a choice between a crook and a kleagle, as someone said.

All articulate opinion in Louisiana moved to Edwards's side, and President Bush, following the cue of the late Lee Atwater, urged voters to support the Democrat Edwards; so did Roemer. In a record turnout—as many as voted in the 1992 presidential election—Edwards wrapped up a solid 61%–39% victory. Duke's 39% was an alarming figure, but well under the 48% George Wallace received here in the 1968 presidential election. Duke ran over 60% with middle-income whites and Protestants, but blacks and high-income whites were for Edwards. Then Duke went national. But his 1992 race for president was a fiasco: he did not get on the ballot in the first five primaries, got only 9% in the Louisiana primary, and left the race soon after. He fell back into obscurity, was fired from a TV talk show for being too boring, and became an insurance agent.

Governor. When Edwin Edwards announced he would not run for governor again in 1995, he had dominated Louisiana state politics for nearly a quarter-century. A proud Cajun (despite the name), a swashbuckling, unabashed big-stakes gambler and womanizer, Edwards combines a Levantine tolerance of the means by which the world's business is conducted with a Latin American fondness for display. He was first elected to Congress after the incumbent was killed in a car accident, and first elected governor in 1972 by a narrow margin over Bennett Johnston (whose consolation prize was a Senate seat) and David Treen (who was elected governor when Edwards was ineligible to run in 1979). The career of every other major figure in Louisiana politics is intertwined with his: Johnston was promptly elected to the Senate after he lost to Edwards; Treen succeeded Edwards in 1979; Senator John Breaux served as Edwards's top aide in the House; Governor Buddy Roemer's father was Edwards's top aide in Baton Rouge. Edwards came back and beat Treen in 1983, then spent much of 1986 and 1987 under trial for bribery charges. He was acquitted, but suffered significant political damage. In 1987 he was able to win only 28% against Buddy Roemer, and withdrew and left Roemer to win without a runoff. In 1991, he improved only slightly, winning 34% in the primary; both times his platform was vintage Edwards—a state lottery, casino gambling in New Orleans, one-man state budgeting. But the political misfortunes of Roemer and the rally against David Duke returned Edwards to the governorship.

In his last term Edwards got the legislature to approve casino gambling in New Orleans, after it already allowed riverboat gambling and video poker. He switched from a flat rate to a percentage tax on oil and gas, started two new Mississippi River bridges, and attracted new business that helped the state grow economically in the early 1990s. He got a larger share of state spending dedicated to education. In June 1994 he announced he was not running in 1995, leaving as wide open a field as Louisiana has had since 1979. Buddy Roemer, talking tough on crime, will run; so will Dave Treen, talking about $100 million for youth programs; other Republicans include legislator Quentin Dastugue, who has the nod from the state party, and anti-abortion activist Cary Kimbrell. Democrats include Lieutenant Governor Melinda Schwegmann, whose family owns New Orleans's biggest supermarket chain, Treasurer Mary Landrieu, whose father was mayor of New Orleans. Congressman Cleo Fields, who is black, announced in November 1994; Congressman Bill Jefferson, also black, was said to be mulling a run. There was speculation about another race by David Duke, and about a Fields- or Jefferson-versus-Duke runoff. Just about anything can happen in Louisiana.

Senators. Louisiana is, with Arkansas, the last state in Dixie with two Democratic senators, both moderates whose votes have been critical on many issues, both charming men and skilled political operators, both members who started their congressional careers in 1972, with help from Edwin Edwards.

Bennett Johnston announced in January 1995 that he would retire in 1996 after a career that, despite some disappointments, made him one of the most influential Senators. Within weeks he dropped hints of a possible race for the governorship, but in May 1995, decided not to run. Johnston leaves a Senate legacy that has taken on many different issues. One, quite naturally for a senator from Louisiana, is energy. After he was first elected in 1972, he got a seat on the Energy Committee, where he was the chief advocate of oil and gas price deregulation—a difficult cause at the time, but one which triumphed in theory and ultimately in practice. He was one of the backers of the Strategic Petroleum Reserve, whose salt dome storage areas are in Louisiana; that policy was nicely vindicated in the Gulf war. In the process of committee work, he has become a knowledgeable leader on issues from the Tongass National Forest in Alaska to the statehood status issue in Puerto Rico. He favored oil drilling in the Arctic National Wildlife Refuge, but dropped that from the 1992 energy bill after threat of filibuster; similarly, he bowed to opponents of raising the CAFE gas mileage standards on autos. In return he got abolition of the detritus of 1970s energy controls—taxes and controls on natural gas, the dormant windfall profits tax on oil—with new incentives for independent oil and gas drillers, moves toward building a nuclear waste dump in Nevada, and a requirement for the government to purchase cars that use alternate fuels. This was classic Johnston; as *National Journal*'s Margaret Kriz says, "an undisputed master of the give and take . . . happy to give his adversaries something to take away from the table. But they've learned to read the fine print as carefully as he's composed it."

Under the Clinton Administration, his projects have been both parochial—royalty relief for deepwater drillers, reform to remove restrictions on supposed wetlands—and far-ranging. He was a firm opponent of the Clinton Btu tax on energy, and one of several oil state Democrats who killed it in spring 1993. On several environmental bills, he has pushed amendments to require cost-benefit analysis and comparative risk assessment of government regulations, even before Newt Gingrich included the proposals in his Contract With America. Johnston also managed the bill to reform the Mining Act of 1872; he got the Senate to pass a mild measure, but as 1994 went on conservative opposition to the liberal House version mounted, and the bill was killed. A version favored by western state conservatives may pass the 104th Congress.

Johnston's voting record over the years has been among the most conservative of Democratic senators. But in the mid-1980s he moved toward the center as he also sought to become a Democratic leader. He came close to challenging Senator Robert Byrd for the majority leadership in 1986, and in 1987 was the first southern conservative to oppose the nomination of Judge Robert Bork—a key to his rejection. He also led the opposition to funding the Strategic Defense Initiative and called for unilateral troop reductions in South Korea. When Byrd relinquished the leadership in 1988, Johnston ran and got 14 votes to George Mitchell's 27 and another 14 for Daniel Inouye. In 1994, when Mitchell announced his retirement, he did not run but backed his colleague John Breaux, who withdrew a month later.

Johnston serves on Appropriations and has funded significant projects, national and local. He has sponsored five major national research centers for Louisiana universities, the National Wetlands Research Center and a new marine center in Lafayette. Having lost one Air Force base in Louisiana, Johnston has worked to keep enough B-52s and KC-10s at Barksdale Air Force Base to prevent it from being closed. After a Louisiana plant got a big subcontract, he supported the ill-fated Supercollider. He backed the Clinton Administration on striker replacement and family and medical leave but opposed the 1993 budget and tax package. He was criticized for trying to promote trade with China when his two sons were seeking business there. (One of them ran for the House in California in 1992, and lost; his son-in-law Tim Roemer won in Indiana in 1990 and still holds the 3d District seat.)

Johnston's Senate career started unpredictably. In 1971 he ran for governor and lost the Democratic nomination by only 4,488 votes to Edwin Edwards. Johnston then entered the August 1972 Democratic Senate primary for a long-shot bid against Allen Ellender, then Appropriations Committee Chairman. Ellender died after the filing date but three months before the primary, which Johnston won easily. Reelected easily in 1978 and 1984, Johnston was jerked into the limelight in 1990 as the incumbent targeted by David Duke. In a state with a great weakness for demagogues, at a time when white middle-class voters seemed especially hard pressed and were looking for a vehicle of protest, Duke struck a chord. Johnston fought back gamely and won 54%–44%. His retirement opens up the seat to all comers, but the lineup will surely not be complete until after the 1995 race for governor. Republicans looking at the seat before Johnston's announcement included conservative legislator Woody Jenkins, who lost to Johnston 59%–41% in 1978, and New Orleans Councilwoman-at-Large Peggy Wilson, who pushed through term limits there. Republican Congressmen Jim McCrery and Richard Baker might be interested in running; so might former Governors Buddy Roemer and David Treen. Democratic Congressman Billy Tauzin is strongly considering a run, but he's just as likely to run as a Republican than as a Democrat. Tauzin will evaluate his party affiliation and the Senate race at the end of the year.

John Breaux is a natural politician who in a short time became one of the pivotal members of the Senate. He is possessed of great political skills and a long political resume: he was first elected to the House at 28, in 1972, to replace Edwin Edwards. Breaux, like Edwards, is from the county seat of Crowley in Cajun country; he served four years on Edwards's staff, and won the Cajun country House seat when Edwards was elected governor in 1972. Quietly in the House, more publicly in the Senate, he has become a natural dealmaker, with contacts developed everywhere from the tennis court (he is one of Congress's best players) to the Democratic Leadership Council (where he followed Bill Clinton as chairman in 1992). His views on issues have a Louisiana Cajun accent: market-oriented with populist twists on economics, rather conservative on cultural issues. But he is not heavily encumbered with narrow principles. As he told the *Los Angeles Times*, "I see myself not as a philosopher, but somebody who is interested in making government work. More and more people in Congress . . . have an all-or-nothing attitude. All-or-nothing attitudes generally wind up getting nothing."

In the House, Breaux used seats on Public Works and Merchant Marines to get money to battle coastal wetlands erosion and defeat the Law of the Sea Treaty; to get sugar and natural gas concessions for Louisiana in the 1981 tax bill he uttered his famed statement that his vote was not for sale "but it is available for rent." He ran for the Senate in 1986, initially trailing his Republican House colleague Henson Moore, who was denouncing the then highly unpopular Edwards. But Breaux nurtured his Cajun base and won 61% in the Cajun parishes, mobilized blacks by attacking a hamhanded national Republican "ballot security" program targeted at black precincts, and won enough low-income whites to carry metro New Orleans and run not far behind in Baton Rouge and Baptist north Louisiana. Breaux held Moore under 50% in the September primary and then overtook him by November.

In the narrowly Democratic Senate, he was a key vote and knew it. He has tended to local interests with his seat on Commerce, and has focused on national issues at Finance. In 1989–90 he headed the Democratic Senatorial Campaign Committee, picking up one seat. He bucked Majority Leader George Mitchell by voting for the Gulf war resolution and the Clarence Thomas nomination and against the 1992 Democratic campaign finance bill. He actively supported Bill Clinton in the 1992 primaries, and succeeded him at the DLC, saying, presciently, "I worry that people in the interest groups will try to pull him away from the mainstream positions that got him elected." With good entree to Clinton and a seat on the Finance Committee, he played key roles on Clinton initiatives in 1993. He advised Clinton to put spending cuts before his stimulus package in March 1993; he warned him against the Btu tax. But Clinton went ahead, losing Breaux's vote, and the Senate, on both. Having got the Btu tax replaced with a gas tax, Breaux voted against the 1993 budget and tax package anyway. In 1994 he worked to pass some kind—almost any kind—of healthcare bill. Opposed to an employer mandate, he was the lead Senate sponsor of Representative Jim Cooper's managed care bill, while clearly deferring to Cooper's expertise. When Congressional Budget Office rulings in May 1994 weakened it greatly, he sponsored three other healthcare measures, but was not able to get negotiations going, and refused to support the Clinton or Mitchell plans. Similarly, on the Commerce Committee, he co-sponsored a bill to allow the regional Bells to offer long distance and cable within a year, an extreme position he hoped would spark negotiation, and didn't. That measure died in 1994, only to be revived for yet another showdown after Republicans won Senate control.

A key player on the two most heavily lobbied issues, an intimate of the President while opposing and negotiating with him, Breaux was highly visible in 1993 and 1994. Now, with Republicans in the majority, and with fewer members in the political center, he is less likely to be a pivotal figure, though on some issues, like communications, his policy instincts may be more likely to prevail. His 1995 support for the balanced budget amendment showed his continuing instinct to be at the center of legislative action. Breaux declined to run for Democratic leader in April 1994, and supported the liberal Tom Daschle, a fellow member of the class of 1986. He seems highly popular in Louisiana and he did not draw serious opposition in 1992; it is too soon to say how he will fare in 1998.

Presidential politics. Louisiana, perhaps because of its economic distress was more Democratic than the southern average; it came closer than any other southern state to backing Michael Dukakis in 1988 and cast the highest percentage for Bill Clinton and Al Gore of any southern state except their own Arkansas and Tennessee. But it is generally considered tough territory for Clinton in 1996.

The Louisiana presidential primary, held on southern Super Tuesday in 1992, produced a huge victory for Bill Clinton and a big margin for George Bush.

Congressional districting. Thanks to the 1982 amendments to the Voting Rights Act, the story of Louisiana's redistricting for the 1990s is as tangled as any state's. It was assumed that the law required the legislature to create two black-supermajority districts, and so it did, albeit under pressure from the Justice Department and a federal court: one was placed in New Orleans, which was easy; the other, the 4th, was a Z-shaped monstrosity, trekking through bayous and the Atchafalaya swamp from black precincts of Lafayette to Baton Rouge, along the Mississippi and the northern edge of the state, dipping down to black neighborhoods in Monroe and

Shreveport. That plan was ruled unconstitutional in federal court in December 1993; under Edwards's guidance the legislature in April 1994 drew a new plan with a new 4th, with a lower black majority, extending from the Mississippi River parishes south of Baton Rouge northwest to Shreveport. In August 1994 that new plan was disallowed by a federal court, but the Supreme Court kept it in effect for the 1994 elections. This is not likely to be the last court ruling, or perhaps the last plan; the 4th District's Cleo Fields, reelected in 1994 but facing an uphill fight if redistricting gives him a white majority, announced he plans to run for governor.

The People: Est. Pop. 1994: 4,315,000; Pop. 1990: 4,219,973, up 2.2% 1990–1994. 1.7% of U.S. total, 21st largest; 32% rural. Median age: 31.0 years. 11.1% 65 years and over. 67.3% White, 30.8% Black, 2.2% Hispanic origin, 1.0% Asian. Households: 53.6% married couple families; 28% married couple fams. w. children; 37% college educ.; median household income: $21,949; per capita income: $10,635; 65.9% owner occupied housing; median house value: $58,500; median monthly rent: $260. 8.1% Unemployment. 1994 Voting age pop.: 3,100,000. 1994 Turnout: 826,837; 27% of VAP. Registered voters (1994): 2,213,752; 1,563,989 D (71%); 428,597 R (19%); 221,168 unaffiliated and minor parties (10%).

Political Lineup: Governor, Edwin W. Edwards (D); Lt. Gov., Melinda Schwegmann (D); Secy. of State, W. Fox McKeithen (R); Atty. Gen., Richard P. Ieyoub (D); Treasurer, Mary L. Landrieu (D). State Senate, 39 (32 D and 7 R); State House of Representatives, 105 (87 D, 17 R, and 1 I). Senators, J. Bennett Johnston (D) and John B. Breaux (D). Representatives, 7 (3 R and 4 D).

1992 Presidential Vote			1988 Presidential Vote		
Clinton (D)	815,971	(46%)	Bush (R)	883,702	(54%)
Bush (R)	733,386	(41%)	Dukakis (D)	717,460	(44%)
Perot (I)	211,478	(12%)			

1992 Democratic Presidential Primary			1992 Republican Presidential Primary		
Clinton	267,002	(69%)	Bush	83,744	(62%)
Tsongas	42,508	(11%)	Buchanan	36,525	(27%)
Brown	25,480	(7%)	Duke	11,955	(9%)
McCarthy	15,129	(4%)			
Other	34,298	(9%)			

GOVERNOR
Gov. Edwin W. Edwards (D)

Elected 1991, term expires January 1996; b. Aug. 7, 1927, Marksville; home, Baton Rouge; LA St. U., 1943–45, LL.B. 1949; Catholic; married (Candace).

Career: Navy, 1945–46; Practicing atty., 1949–64; Crowley City Cncl., 1954–62; LA Senate, 1964–65; U.S. House of Reps., 1965–72; LA Gov., 1972–80, 1984–88; LA Supreme Court, 1980.

Office: State Capitol, P.O. Box 94004, Baton Rouge 70804, 504-342-7015; Fax: 504-342-7099.

Election Results

1991 gen.	Edwin W. Edwards (D)	1,057,031	(61%)
	David Duke (R)	671,009	(39%)
1991 prim.	Edwin W. Edwards (D)	523,195	(34%)
	David Duke (R)	491,342	(32%)
	Buddy Roemer (R)	410,690	(27%)
	Clyde C. Holloway (R)	82,683	(5%)
	Eight Others	41,444	(2%)
1987 gen.	Buddy Roemer (D) .. unopposed		

SENATORS

Sen. J. Bennett Johnston (D)

Elected 1972, seat up 1996; b. Jun. 10, 1932, Shreveport; home, Shreveport; Washington and Lee U., 1950–51, 1952–53, U.S. Military Acad. at West Point, 1951–52, LA St. U., LL.B. 1956; Baptist; married (Mary).

Career: Army, 1956–59; Practicing atty., 1959–72; LA House of Reps., 1964–68; LA Senate, 1968–72.

DC Office: 136 HSOB 20510, 202-224-5824; Fax: 202-224-2952.

State Offices: 1010 Hale Boggs Fed. Bldg., 501 Magazine St., New Orleans 70130, 504-589-2427; 300 Fannin St., #2240, Shreveport 71101, 318-676-3085; and 1 American Pl., #1510, Baton Rouge 70825, 504-389-0395.

Committees: *Appropriations* (4th of 13 D): Agriculture, Rural Development and Related Agencies; Defense; Energy and Water Development (RMM); Interior; VA, HUD and Independent Agencies. *Budget* (3rd of 10 D). *Energy & Natural Resources* (RMM of 8 D): *Intelligence (Select)* (7th of 8 D). *Aging (Special)* (4th of 9 D).

Group Ratings

	ADA	ACLU	COPE	CFA	LCV	CON	NSI	COC	ACU	NTLC	CHC
1994	55	12	75	83	23	2	50	53	22	16	43
1993	45	—	73	70	50	0	—	45	28	—	—

National Journal Ratings

	1993 LIB — 1993 CONS		1994 LIB — 1994 CONS	
Economic	49% —	47%	67% —	32%
Social	36% —	63%	38% —	61%
Foreign	53% —	39%	51% —	46%

Key Votes of the 103d Congress

1. Clinton Deficit Plan	N	3. Brady Handgun Purchase	N	5. Lmt. UN Cmnd. of Forces	N
2. NAFTA	Y	4. Strike Race/Death Pnlty.	Y	6. Cut Missile Funds	N

Key Votes of the 104th Congress

1. Congressional Compliance	Y	3. Balanced Budget Amndt.	N	5. Product Liability Reform	Y
2. Bar Unfunded Mandates	Y	4. Pass Line Item Veto	N	6. FY96 Budget	N

Election Results

1990 primary	J. Bennett Johnston (D)	752,902	(54%)	($5,389,624)
	David Duke (R)	607,391	(44%)	($2,615,267)
	Others	35,820	(3%)	
1984 primary	J. Bennett Johnston (D)	838,181	(86%)	($1,046,293)
	Robert M. Ross (R)	86,546	(9%)	
	Larry Napoleon Cooper (R)	52,746	(5%)	

Sen. John B. Breaux (D)

Elected 1986, seat up 1998; b. Mar. 1, 1944, Crowley; home, Lafayette; U. of S.W. LA, B.A. 1964, LA St. U., J.D. 1967; Catholic; married (Lois).

Career: Practicing atty., 1967–68; Legis. Asst. & Dist. Mgr., U.S. Rep. Edwin W. Edwards, 1968–72; U.S. House of Reps., 1972–87.

DC Office: 516 HSOB 20510, 202-224-4623; Fax: 202-224-4268.

State Offices: 705 Jefferson, #13, Lafayette 70501, 318-264-6871; Hale Boggs Fed. Bldg., #1005, 501 Magazine St., New Orleans 70130, 504-589-2531; and 211 N. 3d St., Monroe 71201, 318-325-3320.

Committees: *Chief Deputy Whip. Commerce, Science & Transportation* (7th of 9 D): Aviation; Communications; Oceans and Fisheries; Surface Transportation and Merchant Marine. *Finance* (6th of 9 D): Intl. Trade; Social Security and Family Policy (RMM); Taxation and IRS Oversight. *Aging (Special)* (5th of 9 D).

Group Ratings

	ADA	ACLU	COPE	CFA	LCV	CON	NSI	COC	ACU	NTLC	CHC
1994	55	24	63	58	31	34	50	60	17	12	50
1993	40	—	82	80	50	4	—	27	24	—	—

National Journal Ratings

	1993 LIB — 1993 CONS		1994 LIB — 1994 CONS	
Economic	71%	— 17%	60%	— 39%
Social	37%	— 60%	40%	— 59%
Foreign	51%	— 47%	66%	— 29%

Key Votes of the 103d Congress

1. Clinton Deficit Plan	Y	3. Brady Handgun Purchase	N	5. Lmt. UN Cmnd. of Forces	N
2. NAFTA	Y	4. Strike Race/Death Pnlty.	N	6. Cut Missile Funds	N

Key Votes of the 104th Congress

1. Congressional Compliance	Y	3. Balanced Budget Amndt.	Y	5. Product Liability Reform	N
2. Bar Unfunded Mandates	Y	4. Pass Line Item Veto	Y	6. FY96 Budget	N

Election Results

1992 primary	John B. Breaux (D)	616,021	(73%)	($2,007,675)
	Jon Khachaturian (I)	74,785	(9%)	($94,919)
	Lyle Stockstill (R)	69,986	(8%)	($34,711)
	Nick Accardo (D)	45,839	(6%)	
	Fred Clegg Strong (R)	36,406	(4%)	
1986 general	John B. Breaux (D)	723,586	(53%)	($2,958,313)
	W. Henson Moore (R)	646,311	(47%)	($5,986,460)
1986 primary	W. Henson Moore (R)	529,433	(44%)	
	John B. Breaux (D)	447,328	(37%)	
	Samuel B. Nunez (D)	73,505	(6%)	
	J.E. Jumonville (D)	53,394	(5%)	
	Sherman A. Bernard (D)	52,479	(5%)	

FIRST DISTRICT

New Orleans, founded in 1718, the nation's fifth largest city during the Civil War, is ancient for an American metropolis; yet it is still closely girded by the peculiar wilderness of the mushy delta lands of the sluggish Mississippi River. Climb the levee overlooking the Mississippi and you will see an expanse of water with untidy clumps of trees and disorganized-looking, seemingly abandoned docks—what Mark Twain had in his mind's eye while writing *Life on the Mississippi* in the 1870s. Or drive just past the last block of a suburban subdivision, and you are in unreclaimed swamp, vegetation and wetness, thick with herons and alligators, extending flatly as far as the eye can see. For years the river funneled the products of half a continent down to a single port with an international heritage and flair; the New Orleans metropolitan area is still living off that geography and history, with an inward-looking elite preoccupied with who is in which Mardi Gras krewe and interested more in old families' genealogy than in Oil Patch geology. The old buildings of New Orleans are finely proportioned and its old neighborhoods charming, like those in France; and its early 20th Century improvements, like Olmstead's City Park, are grand. But its middle and late 20th Century streetscapes and subdivisions, like those of France, are without ornament or charm, utilitarian works of man made to master the below-sea-level environment.

The 1st Congressional District of Louisiana includes most of the newer part of the New Orleans metropolitan area, spread over the soggy lands of the lower Mississippi and Lake Pontchartrain. It includes some affluent white neighborhoods and the vast suburb of Metairie in Jefferson Parish, divided by slanting grids and elevated only where bridges jut out over the many canals. The 1st extends across the 26-mile Lake Pontchartrain Causeway to include fast-growing St. Tammany Parish, with old towns lush with trees and clusters of new growth around giant intersections. It extends north and west, to parts of the Florida Parishes—so called because, even after the United States purchased Louisiana, they were part of the West Florida colony retained by Spain until it was annexed in 1810. The boundaries of the 1st District are liable to be only marginally changed by court decree; the 1st will have about half its voters on either side of Lake Pontchartrain and will be the most upscale, affluent, highly educated district in Louisiana. In Louisiana politics, this means it will be supportive of reform and against redistribution, and unabashedly Republican.

This is the district represented by Bob Livingston, who wields great power as chairman of the House Appropriations Committee. Livingston bears the name of the New York aristocrat who as chancellor administered the oath of office to George Washington 200 years ago and who as Ambassador to France helped negotiate the Louisiana Purchase, and some of whose relatives became Louisiana planters and politicians. But this Livingston grew up in modest circumstances, enlisting in the Navy after high school, working his way through school at the Avondale Shipyard. He spent most of his pre-congressional career as a prosecutor and approaches politics with a prosecutorial—aggressive, conservative—frame of mind. He won the seat in a 1977 special election, after a Democrat was forced to resign (and eventually jailed) due to fraud, and he went on to be a tough judge of his colleagues while on the House Ethics Committee during the Abscam investigation.

Livingston's rise to the chairmanship of Appropriations was rapid and unexpected. He started the 103d Congress as the fifth ranking Republican on the committee, and ranking minority member on the Foreign Operations Subcommittee. He had played little role in setting overall appropriations, though he did help get money for Louisiana defense projects, like the Navy sealift vessels, Navy/Marine amphibious ships and Coast Guard icebreakers built in Jefferson Parish's Avondale shipyard. And he worked to fund Louisiana projects such as the Harvey Canal flood control levee on the west bank of the Mississippi, and the 12-plane fleet stationed at Keesler Air Force Base for hurricane reconnaissance flights. Then Republicans won control of the House, and Speaker-to-be Newt Gingrich wanted a sympathetic chairman, willing to eliminate federal programs by giving them a zero appropriation and sticking to it in conference. The highest ranking Republican, Joseph McDade, was under indictment, and had been happy to work with Democrats to increase spending of most kinds; the next three Republicans had similar accommodationist attitudes. Livingston was then running for Republican conference chairman, the post being vacated by Dick Armey; Gingrich persuaded him to withdraw, and to become Appropriations chairman instead. Livingston also told the men he passed over that if they could not go along with the zero appropriations strategy they should leave the committee. Not surprisingly, all stayed.

So Livingston now has a key post after nearly 20 years in the House and a disappointing run for governor in 1987. His strongly conservative voting record on almost every issue and tough demeanor suggest he will perform as Gingrich imagined and intended. "I have become The Grinch that stole Christmas," he told *The New York Times*. "But it has its compensation; I have also gone from 18 years in the wilderness to suddenly a center of attraction, for good or bad." Local interests shouldn't be too much of a problem; "we'll still be in a good position for Avondale," a top Livingston aide said, "because we've always been so pro-defense." But Livingston has shown a bit of caution, during his career, hesitating in 1994 on whether to join most Republicans in supporting the A-to-Z spending cut plan (which would have bypassed Appropriations) and calling for a "lean but not mean budget." He is likely to have problems with some of his subcommittee chairmen, who will want to retain pet spending projects; with colleagues seeking to protect local projects; with the leadership and with Budget Chairman John Kasich who may invade what Livingston regards as Appropriations' turf. From 1964 to 1993 this chairmanship was held by just two men, George Mahon and Jamie Whitten; in the 103d Congress it was held by William Natcher and David Obey. Now Livingston has the potential to turn government in a very different direction, symbolized by the alligator skinning knife, a "Cajun scalpel," he brought to his first meeting; it remains to be seen whether he has the skill, the nerve and the conviction to do so.

Livingston is a beneficiary of the Voting Rights Act interpretation he has attacked; his district is so heavily white and Republican that he has no problem whatsoever winning reelection.

The People: Pop. 1990: 602,848; 28% rural; 12% age 65+; 85% White; 10% Black; 1% Asian; 1% Other; 4% Hispanic origin. Voting age pop.: 444,877; 9% Black; 4% Hispanic origin. Households: 58% married couple families; 28% married couple fams. w. children; 46% college educ.; median household income: $27,877; per capita income: $13,860; median gross rent: $420; median house value: $74,500.

1992 Presidential Vote		
Bush (R)	154,584	(56%)
Clinton (D)	87,429	(31%)
Perot (I)	34,402	(12%)

1988 Presidential Vote		
Bush (R)	169,539	(70%)
Dukakis (D)	72,424	(30%)

Rep. Robert L. (Bob) **Livingston (R)**

Elected Aug., 1977; b. Apr. 30, 1943, Colorado Springs, CO; home, Metairie; Tulane U., B.A. 1967, J.D. 1968; Episcopalian; married (Bonnie).

Career: Navy, 1961–63; Practicing atty., 1968–70, 1976–77; Asst. U.S. Atty., 1970–73; Chief Special Prosecutor, Orleans Parish Dist. Atty.'s Ofc., 1974–75; Chief Prosecutor, LA Atty. Gen.'s Ofc. Organized Crime Unit, 1975–76.

DC Office: 2406 RHOB 20515, 202-225-3015; Fax: 202-225-0739.

District Offices: 111 Veterans Blvd., #700, Metairie 70005, 504-589-2753.

Committees: *Appropriations* (Chmn.): Foreign Operations, Export Financing, and Related Programs; National Security.

Group Ratings

	ADA	ACLU	COPE	CFA	LCV	CON	NSI	COC	ACU	NTLC	CHC
1994	0	17	25	10	0	55	100	83	95	89	93
1993	0	—	8	0	21	65	—	100	96	—	—

National Journal Ratings

	1993 LIB — 1993 CONS		1994 LIB — 1994 CONS	
Economic	0%	— 88%	26%	— 70%
Social	19%	— 77%	15%	— 84%
Foreign	9%	— 85%	29%	— 70%

Key Votes of the 103d Congress

1. Clinton Deficit Plan	N	3. Brady Handgun Purchase	N	5. Lmt. UN Cmnd. of Forces	Y
2. NAFTA	Y	4. Strike Race/Death Pnlty.	Y	6. Cut Missile Funds	N

Key Votes of the 104th Congress

1. Congressional Compliance	Y	6. Reform Crime Grant	Y	11. Loser Pays Court Reform	Y
2. Balanced Budget Amndmt.	Y	7. National Security Act	Y	12. Product Liability Reform	Y
3. Bar Unfunded Mandates	Y	8. Moratorium on Regs.	Y	13. Welfare Reform	Y
4. Pass Line Item Veto	Y	9. Risk Assessment on Regs.	Y	14. Term Limits Amndmt.	N
5. Relax Exclusionary Rule	Y	10. Expnd. Priv. Prop. Rights	Y	15. Tax Cuts	Y

Election Results

1994 primary	Robert L. (Bob) Livingston (R)	83,928	(81%)	($348,081)
	Forest McNeir (D)	12,336	(12%)	
	Clark Simmons (I)	7,139	(7%)	
1992 primary	Robert L. (Bob) Livingston (R)	83,685	(73%)	($321,487)
	Anne Thompson (R)	11,620	(10%)	
	Vincent J. Bruno (R)	7,874	(7%)	($7,294)
	Richie Martin (R)	4,789	(4%)	($16,671)
	Jules W. Hillery (I)	4,442	(4%)	
	Other	2,641	(2%)	

SECOND DISTRICT

New Orleans, founded by the French in 1718, ruled by the Spanish from 1763 to just days before the French took over to sell it in 1803, was a Creole city—part French, a bit Spanish, more than a touch Caribbean—when the American flag was raised over what is now Jackson Square. The statue of Andrew Jackson still seems an alien intrusion in a square set off by a French Market, the Cabildo, the Presbytere, the Pontalba apartments and Cathedral St. Louis. New Orleans was the fifth largest American city from 1840 until the Civil War and the only sizable city in the South; yet even as it was sending southern cotton out to the mills of Lancashire, it was an alien cultural force in both the nation and region. Urbanized, yet poor and in many ways primitive, New Orleans had yellow fever epidemics late in the 19th Century, even as it was installing electric lights; it had a riot in which Italian immigrants were massacred, even as it was laying streetcar tracks and telephone lines. This was one of the most corrupt American cities during Reconstruction and the Gilded Age, when its votes were regularly bid for and bought; like other southern cities, it became rigidly segregated after 1890. Today, New Orleans remains a major port, but is eclipsed in the oil business by Houston and in Latin American trade by Miami and is pinning its hopes for economic growth on Governor Edwin Edwards's huge gambling casino.

The 2d Congressional District of Louisiana today includes almost all of the city of New Orleans, everything except a few affluent white neighborhoods, plus the west bank towns of Jefferson Parish—Gretna, Harvey, Westwego, Waggaman—industrial enclosures between levee and swamp. Here is the New Orleans everyone wants to visit, centered on the French Quarter, its 19th Century homes still intact because the Americans who moved here after 1803 wanted to stay away from the snobbish Creoles and built a new downtown above Canal Street. North of the Quarter is the site of Storyville, where prostitution was legal until 1918 and where jazz was probably first played; the old frame houses have long since been torn down and replaced by housing projects. But many similar neighborhoods remain, where blacks and some working-class whites live in rickety frame houses which are not always strong enough to keep the rain out and never tight enough to keep out the summer humidity or the damp winter chill, along the vividly named streets—Elysian Fields, Spain, Desire, Arts—that go north from the river wharves. In the other direction is the downtown flecked with skyscrapers and the ominous Superdome, past the old slum known as the Irish Channel—a reminder that New Orleans had more foreign immigrants than any other part of the South—to the Garden District. This was the home of the rich, early American settlers, and its antebellum homes are still covered with vines and Spanish moss. Quaintly named trolley cars still roll out St. Charles Avenue to Tulane University and Audubon Park.

New Orleans, for many years a speckled black-and-white city, now has a solid black majority, making the 2d District heavily Democratic. The congressman here is Bill Jefferson, first elected in 1990 after the retirement of Lindy Boggs, a charming Louisiana lady with perfect manners and perfect political pitch, who won majorities from blacks and whites alike. Jefferson was then a state senator, a skillful political operator with high professional credentials: he graduated from Harvard Law, clerked for a well-respected federal judge, worked for Senator Bennett Johnston and set up what became the largest black law firm in the South. Jefferson was elected to the state Senate in 1979; he twice ran for mayor and lost. In 1990 Jefferson was endorsed by then-Mayor Sidney Barthelemy, and in the primary won 25% of the vote to 22% for Marc Morial, whose father was New Orleans's first black Mayor and who was elected Mayor himself in March 1994. In the November runoff, charges flew: Jefferson was dogged by reports of defaults on outstanding loans and mortgages, while Morial admitted he was the father of an eight-year-old girl living in the Ivory Coast. Jefferson won with 52% and became the first Louisiana black elected to Congress since Reconstruction.

In the House Jefferson has shown impressive political skills. He was active in the Democratic Leadership Council and got to know its chairman, a young southern governor named Bill

Clinton. In November 1991, Jefferson and Mississippi Congressman Mike Espy endorsed Clinton, and both began campaigning hard for him across the country, including a southern bus tour in August—for which rewards would in time be coming. In December 1992, Jefferson won a seat on the Ways and Means Committee where he chalked up some successes. He got Ways and Means to halve Clinton's one dollar increase on inland waterway tolls. In August 1993, in a conversation with Clinton on Air Force One, Jefferson got him to save a tax break for venture capital companies dealing solely with minority-owned small businesses, generating, Jefferson claims, $1.2 billion in investment. In June 1994, on health care, he sponsored a compromise eliminating employer mandates for four million small businesses; this passed, and helped Ways and Means stitch together a Democratic healthcare bill. Jefferson also claimed credit for a law giving state and local governments priority in acquiring surplus Defense Department property.

Jefferson will have trouble equalling this record in a Republican House, not least because the downsizing of the Democratic ranks at Ways and Means left him and three other junior Democrats without a seat. But he has no trouble winning reelection in the 2d District. Originally thought to be interested in running for mayor, he announced in the spring of 1995 that he was running for governor.

The People: Pop. 1990: 602,774; 11% age 65+; 35% White; 61% Black; 2% Asian; 1% Other; 3% Hispanic origin. Voting age pop.: 425,475; 56% Black; 4% Hispanic origin. Households: 38% married couple families; 19% married couple fams. w. children; 40% college educ.; median household income: $18,367; per capita income: $9,790; median gross rent: $372; median house value: $61,800.

1992 Presidential Vote

Clinton (D)	153,134	(68%)
Bush (R)	55,362	(25%)
Perot (I)	13,895	(6%)

1988 Presidential Vote

Dukakis (D)	134,320	(66%)
Bush (R)	68,166	(34%)

Rep. William J. Jefferson (D)

Elected 1990; b. Mar. 14, 1947, Lake Providence; home, New Orleans; Southern U., B.A. 1969, Harvard, J.D. 1972; Baptist; married (Andrea).

Career: Army Reserves, 1969–78, Army Judge Advocate Corps, 1975; Law clerk, U.S. Dist. Judge Alvin Rubin, 1972–73; Legis. aide, U.S. Sen. Bennett Johnston, 1973–75; Practicing atty., 1975–90; LA Senate, 1979–90.

DC Office: 240 CHOB 20515, 202-225-6636; Fax: 202-225-1988.

District Offices: 501 Magazine St., #1012, New Orleans 70130, 504-589-2274.

Committees: *House Oversight* (4th of 5 D). *National Security* (22nd of 25 D): Military Personnel; Military Procurement.

Group Ratings

	ADA	ACLU	COPE	CFA	LCV	CON	NSI	COC	ACU	NTLC	CHC
1994	90	73	78	90	94	1	33	33	15	11	0
1993	95	—	92	90	79	11	—	18	4	—	—

National Journal Ratings

	1993 LIB — 1993 CONS		1994 LIB — 1994 CONS	
Economic	64% —	34%	83% —	0%
Social	87% —	0%	87% —	11%
Foreign	93% —	0%	68% —	32%

Key Votes of the 103d Congress

1. Clinton Deficit Plan	Y	3. Brady Handgun Purchase	Y	5. Lmt. UN Cmnd. of Forces	N
2. NAFTA	Y	4. Strike Race/Death Pnlty.	N	6. Cut Missile Funds	Y

Key Votes of the 104th Congress

1. Congressional Compliance	Y	6. Reform Crime Grant	N	11. Loser Pays Court Reform	*
2. Balanced Budget Amndmt.	N	7. National Security Act	N	12. Product Liability Reform	*
3. Bar Unfunded Mandates	N	8. Moratorium on Regs.	N	13. Welfare Reform	N
4. Pass Line Item Veto	*	9. Risk Assessment on Regs.	N	14. Term Limits Amndmt.	N
5. Relax Exclusionary Rule	N	10. Expnd. Priv. Prop. Rights	N	15. Tax Cuts	N

Election Results

1994 primary	William J. Jefferson (D)	60,906	(75%)	($608,567)
	Robert (Bob) Namer (R)	15,113	(19%)	($3,789)
	Others	5,549	(7%)	
1992 primary	William J. Jefferson (D)	67,030	(73%)	($352,058)
	Wilma Knox Irvin (D)	14,121	(15%)	($23,640)
	Roger C. Johnson (I)	10,090	(11%)	

THIRD DISTRICT

Below sea level, veined with bayous and creeks and wide streams of water, crossed by only an occasional road or railroad, the wetlands of southern Louisiana are one of America's unique landscapes. Technically, most of this waterlogged land rests on islands in a broad river mouth, through which the waters of the Mississippi and its tributaries drain into the Gulf of Mexico. It is rich with animal life, herons and egrets, shrimp and crawfish, muskrats and alligators, and supports more people than the casual observer would think. There are cabins along the bayous and crossroad towns where Cajun French remains the first language, and roadside diners feature crawfish etouffe. But the steep-roofed Cajun houses are not the only structures: here and there, jutting out of the swampy land, are huge elaborate metal sculptures—refineries and petrochemical plants, processing the oil and natural gas trapped under these wetlands and the shallow continental shelf of the Gulf, and released through 20th Century oil rig technology. In the 1960s and 1970s, the oil industry, by providing good jobs for young people here, helped preserve Cajun culture and built a Cajun pride that was seldom articulated a generation ago. That pride and the curiosity of tourists have helped maintain the way of life in the Cajun parishes in the 1980s and 1990s, as oil payrolls have gone way down and the wetlands seem threatened by coastal erosion—and by Hurricane Andrew, which did $1 billion worth of damage here in August 1992.

The 3d Congressional District of Louisiana includes about half the Cajun country, plus St. Bernard and Plaquemines Parishes downriver from New Orleans. St. Bernard is now working class suburbia and cast among the state's highest percentages in 1990 and 1991 for David Duke's statewide races. The 3d District then spreads west over the swamplands, covering Houma, where seven bayous converge; St. Charles, St. John the Baptist, St. James and Ascension Parishes on both sides of the Mississippi, once the greatest sugar producers in America, are now studded with refineries and petrochemical plants; roughneck Morgan City services many offshore oil rigs; Iberia Parish is home to McIlhenny's Tabasco sauce. This is one part of Louisiana where quite a few whites vote Democratic; it voted for Bill Clinton in 1992 and gave a good percentage to Michael Dukakis in 1988.

The 3d District is represented by Billy Tauzin, who brings Cajun caginess and charm to his work. Despite occasional clashes with his friend John Dingell, he is one of the most senior and influential Democrats on the Commerce Committee and, after the 1994 elections, was one of the Democrats tottering most conspicuously on the brink of switching parties. He was first elected to the legislature in 1971, at 28; he won the 3d District seat in a May 1980 special election. Tauzin ran for governor in 1987, but was doomed when Edwin Edwards entered the race, squeezing him out in Cajun country; he finished fourth, with 10%. In 1989 he inherited a Merchant Marine subcommittee chairmanship, just in time to handle legislation inspired by the Exxon *Valdez* oil spill in Alaska; Tauzin got an oil spill bill through in August 1990. He also drew up plans to allow a drawdown of the Strategic Petroleum Reserve (which is mostly in southern Louisiana) to help pay for Persian Gulf troop deployments, and was able to get Congress to build the Reserve back up to one billion barrels. On Commerce he has been active on cable reregulation (anti-cable operators) and telecommunications (pro-regional Bells). His biggest legislative project has been to revise environmental laws, especially the wetlands law which he believes unduly limits property rights in southern Louisiana and the Endangered Species Act; he voted for the unfunded mandates bill, and would require risk assessment by government agencies and do more to protect property rights. Fishermen, shrimpers and rice farmers in the 3d District surely agree with him.

Tauzin's views have even more currency in the 104th. In November 1994 he publicly mulled switching parties; after milking the decision for every ounce of publicity, in December 1994 he decided for now not to change parties, citing concessions by Democratic leaders and because as a Democrat he could work on a bipartisan basis with Republicans to fulfill their Contract With America. In fact, he was one of only two House Democrats to vote with Republicans on 15 key pieces of the Contract (the other was Ralph Hall of Texas). He may also have been miffed that Republicans abolished Merchant Marine out from under him; and he said he felt "honor bound" to serve out the term he was elected to as a Democrat. In February 1995, Tauzin and 22 other conservative Democrats banded together to form The Coalition, to serve as an outlet of opinion not in step with either side of the aisle. The Coalition insisted this wasn't a prelude to party switching, but Tauzin still has his options open: the 3d is one district that he could probably win as a member of either party in 1996, and he would be even stronger if his private property rights legislation goes through. Though he seems uninterested in running for governor, it seems likely he will make a run for retiring Senator Bennett Johnston's seat—possibly as a Republican. In short, this tough Cajun is working hard to prosper politically at a time when many Democrats were barely surviving.

The People: Pop. 1990: 603,258; 34% rural; 9% age 65+; 74% White; 22% Black; 1% Amer. Indian; 1% Asian; 2% Hispanic origin. Voting age pop.: 415,060; 19% Black; 2% Hispanic origin. Households: 63% married couple families; 34% married couple fams. w. children; 27% college educ.; median household income: $23,813; per capita income: $9,911; median gross rent: $338; median house value: $57,900.

1992 Presidential Vote

Clinton (D) 115,063 (44%)
Bush (R) 105,982 (40%)
Perot (I). 36,193 (14%)

1988 Presidential Vote

Bush (R) 128,518 (54%)
Dukakis (D). 108,353 (46%)

Rep. W. J. (Billy) Tauzin (D)

Elected May 1980; b. June 14, 1943, Chackbay; home, Thibodaux; Nicholls St. U., B.A. 1964, LA St. U., J.D. 1967; Catholic; married (Cecile).

Career: Practicing atty., 1968–80; LA House of Reps., 1971–79.

DC Office: 2183 RHOB 20515, 202-225-4031; Fax: 202-225-0563.

District Offices: 1041 Hale Boggs Bldg., 501 Magazine St., New Orleans 70130, 504-589-6366; 107 Fed. Bldg., Houma 700360, 504-876-3033; 210 E. Main St., New Iberia 70560, 318-367-8231; and 828 S. Irma Blvd., #212-A, Gonzales 70737, 504-621-8490.

Committees: *Commerce* (4th of 21 D): Commerce, Trade and Hazardous Materials (RMM); Energy and Power. *Resources* (13th of 20 D): Energy and Mineral Resources; Fisheries, Wildlife and Oceans.

Group Ratings

	ADA	ACLU	COPE	CFA	LCV	CON	NSI	COC	ACU	NTLC	CHC
1994	15	23	33	50	25	76	90	100	76	93	93
1993	35	—	42	30	29	96	—	73	78	—	—

National Journal Ratings

	1993 LIB — 1993 CONS		1994 LIB — 1994 CONS	
Economic	40%	— 58%	41%	— 58%
Social	27%	— 72%	11%	— 85%
Foreign	33%	— 67%	30%	— 67%

Key Votes of the 103d Congress

1. Clinton Deficit Plan	N	3. Brady Handgun Purchase	N	5. Lmt. UN Cmnd. of Forces	Y
2. NAFTA	N	4. Strike Race/Death Pnlty.	Y	6. Cut Missile Funds	N

Key Votes of the 104th Congress

1. Congressional Compliance	Y	6. Reform Crime Grant	Y	11. Loser Pays Court Reform	Y
2. Balanced Budget Amndmt.	Y	7. National Security Act	Y	12. Product Liability Reform	Y
3. Bar Unfunded Mandates	Y	8. Moratorium on Regs.	Y	13. Welfare Reform	Y
4. Pass Line Item Veto	Y	9. Risk Assessment on Regs.	Y	14. Term Limits Amndmt.	Y
5. Relax Exclusionary Rule	Y	10. Expnd. Priv. Prop. Rights	Y	15. Tax Cuts	Y

Election Results

1994 primary	W. J. (Billy) Tauzin (D)	90,536	(76%)	($680,211)
	Nick Accardo (I).	28,250	(24%)	
1992 primary	W. J. (Billy) Tauzin (D)	82,047	(82%)	($311,112)
	Paul I. Boynton (R).	18,402	(18%)	

FOURTH DISTRICT

Louisiana, founded by the French, ruled for a generation by the Spanish, run for half a century after statehood by a planter and cotton trader elite that included Creoles, Yankees and Jews, was a slave commonwealth. The money to build iron-balconied New Orleans townhouses and the grand riverfront plantation mansions came from rice and cotton and sugar grown in this soggy soil, none of which would have been possible without the labor of African-American slaves. There was slavery in other southern states, but in Louisiana it evolved with a French rigor and pitilessness; remember that the other French slave commonwealth in the New World became the Republic of Haiti. Louisiana's blacks, enfranchised after the Civil War, for a moment took political power in what was then a black-majority state. But they were soon driven from power—there is a monument in New Orleans to the laws that accomplished this—and left without the vote or any claim on the political system. Louisiana economically was one of the most backward states, with few paved roads and not much electricity until Huey Long became governor in 1928. Yet Louisiana blacks produced some of the nation's greatest popular culture: jazz music may have had its commercial start in the parlors of the legal houses of prostitution in the New Orleans neighborhood of Storyville, but it had deeper roots in the centuries-long experience of black people working hard in the wet soil, under the hot sun of Louisiana.

Today 31% of Louisianians are black and, since the Voting Rights Act of 1965, they have been part of the political culture of the state. And by no means an ignored part: black voters were key in electing Edwin Edwards governor four times and black state legislators have become power brokers in Baton Rouge. But Louisiana did not have a black congressman until 1990, because the black-majority New Orleans district in the 1980s elected the redoubtable Lindy Boggs. Then, when she retired in 1990, Bill Jefferson was elected in the 2d District, and in 1992 the prevailing interpretation of the Voting Rights Act caused the creation of a second black-majority district in the rest of the state. But the boundaries of this 4th Congressional District of Louisiana have been under judicial attack, and were modified twice for two elections. For 1992 the 4th was a Z-shaped district—actually a capital Z in cursive writing—taking in most of Louisiana's prominent cities outside New Orleans. The Z's tail was in Lafayette, it crossed the trackless Atchafalaya Swamp to "petroleum alley" along the Mississippi and Baton Rouge, then squiggled north along the Mississippi and proceeded west just south of Arkansas to take in parts of Monroe and Shreveport. But after a 1993 Supreme Court decision questioning a similarly grotesque black-majority district in North Carolina, a lower court ruled the Z-shaped district overly "race-conscious," and the legislature drew more benign boundaries, creating a 4th District that ran northwest from Baton Rouge through Natchitoches to Shreveport. To some surprise, in July 1994 a federal court ruled that district "bizarre and irregular" and race-motivated; the Supreme Court stayed that decision pending appeal, ordering an election within boundaries which may change again for 1996.

Meanwhile, the Congressman from the 4th is Cleo Fields, a political prodigy who as state Senator from Baton Rouge chaired the redistricting committee that drew the Z-shaped 4th. Fields, born exactly one year before the assassination of John F. Kennedy, went straight into politics while still in law school, became the youngest state legislator in Louisiana history and then the youngest member of the 103d Congress. At home he worked for drug-free zones near schools and inner city economic development programs. He ran for the House unsuccessfully in 1990, winning 30% in a white-majority district; in 1992, he won 48% in an eight-candidate field in the October primary, with absolute majorities in such far-flung places as Lafayette, Alexandria and Baton Rouge. Against state Senator Charles D. Jones, Fields won 74% in the runoff, with 84% in Shreveport and 87% in Lafayette, at opposite ends of the district. Fields, slight and youthful looking, often presided over the House and introduced some amendments in the Banking Committee; he had a mostly liberal record and voted against NAFTA and the 1994 crime bill. At home he created a Congressional Classroom to get students debating issues.

The reduction of the 4th's voting-age population from 63% black in the Z-shaped district to 55% in the 1994 version did not hurt Fields; he beat a Republican in October with 70%. But with his liberal voting record and concern with issues popular with blacks, he did not seem eager to run in a white-majority district, as the 4th might become in 1996. Yet, somewhat ironically, he is interested in running in a statewide, white-majority constituency. In November 1994, as he turned 32, he announced he was running for governor, in a reception with a display of pictures of 32-year-old governors (Bill Clinton was one). He promised a major voter registration drive and denied that the prospect of a David Duke candidacy influenced his decision. Though black Congressman Bill Jefferson's entry into the race poses a problem, Fields would have a good chance of finishing in the top two in the primary, but it will be a challenge for him to win a runoff. He has shown the ability, however, to win white votes in the 4th.

The People: Pop. 1990: 603,072; 30% rural; 11% age 65+; 33% White; 67% Black; 1% Hispanic origin. Voting age pop.: 413,858; 63% Black; 1% Hispanic origin. Households: 44% married couple families; 22% married couple fams. w. children; 28% college educ.; median household income: $14,515; per capita income: $7,270; median gross rent: $287; median house value: $40,200.

1992 Presidential Vote			1988 Presidential Vote		
Clinton (D)	150,800	(66%)	Dukakis (D)	139,950	(65%)
Bush (R)	57,286	(25%)	Bush (R)	75,676	(35%)
Perot (I)	17,298	(8%)			

Rep. Cleo Fields (D)

Elected 1992; b. Nov. 22, 1962, Baton Rouge; home, Baton Rouge; Southern U., B.A. 1984; Southern U. Law Schl., J.D. 1987; Baptist; married (Debra).

Career: LA Senate, 1986–92.

DC Office: 218 CHOB 20515, 202-225-8490; Fax: 202-225-8959.

District Offices: 700 N. 10th St., Baton Rouge 70802, 504-343-9773; 301 N. Main St., Opelousas 70570, 318-942-9691; and 610 Texas St., #201, Shreveport 71101, 318-221-9924; 515 Murrey St., #317, Alexandria 71301, 318-445-0632.

Committees: *Banking & Financial Services* (18th of 22 D): Domestic and International Monetary Policy; Housing and Community Opportunity. *Small Business* (10th of 19 D): Government Programs.

Group Ratings

	ADA	ACLU	COPE	CFA	LCV	CON	NSI	COC	ACU	NTLC	CHC
1994	90	91	100	90	83	17	10	30	5	15	0
1993	95	—	100	100	79	11	—	9	4	—	—

National Journal Ratings

	1993 LIB — 1993 CONS			1994 LIB — 1994 CONS		
Economic	68%	—	26%	83%	—	0%
Social	87%	—	0%	77%	—	21%
Foreign	79%	—	16%	80%	—	17%

Key Votes of the 103d Congress

1. Clinton Deficit Plan	Y	3. Brady Handgun Purchase	Y	5. Lmt. UN Cmnd. of Forces	N
2. NAFTA	N	4. Strike Race/Death Pnlty.	N	6. Cut Missile Funds	Y

Key Votes of the 104th Congress

1. Congressional Compliance	Y	6. Reform Crime Grant	N	11. Loser Pays Court Reform	N
2. Balanced Budget Amndmt.	*	7. National Security Act	N	12. Product Liability Reform	N
3. Bar Unfunded Mandates	Y	8. Moratorium on Regs.	N	13. Welfare Reform	N
4. Pass Line Item Veto	N	9. Risk Assessment on Regs.	N	14. Term Limits Amndmt.	N
5. Relax Exclusionary Rule	N	10. Expnd. Priv. Prop. Rights	N	15. Tax Cuts	N

Election Results

1994 primary	Cleo Fields (D)	88,288	(70%)	($271,463)
	Patricia Slocum (R)	37,935	(30%)	($25,978)
1992 general	Cleo Fields (D)	143,980	(74%)	($305,336)
	Charles Jones (D)	50,851	(26%)	($129,003)

FIFTH DISTRICT

Northern Louisiana, from the low-lying delta lands along the Mississippi River west to the Red River and Texas, is part of the Deep South. Unlike southern Louisiana, most people here are Protestant, not Catholic; they live in strait-laced small towns or small cities like Shreveport or Monroe, not the wide-open metropolis of New Orleans. Traditional and fundamentalist religion is still strong here; most people still live in traditional two-parent family units; pride in country is still strong. The countryside is agricultural, though there are few vestiges of either large riverfront plantations or backward farm country. Oil provided the basis for much of the economic growth of the 20th Century; defense facilities also helped; more recently there has been some high-tech and local entrepreneurialism. Politically, northern Louisiana voters for more than 100 years have been voting against cosmopolitan New Orleans and the Catholic Cajun south, sometimes for riproaring populists, and more often, as the economy grows more sophisticated, for market-oriented Republicans.

The 5th Congressional District of Louisiana includes most of the northern parishes, except for the black-majority areas cordoned off in the 4th District, whose boundaries were different for the 1992 and 1994 election and, depending on court rulings, may be different again in 1996. The current 5th has a large white majority, and since Louisiana's national voting patterns are racially polarized—the 1992 VRS exit poll showed blacks voting for Bill Clinton over George Bush 87%–7% and white Protestants voting for Bush over Clinton 61%–25%—this means it is heavily Republican, with especially high Republican margins in Caddo and Bossier (pronounced *bohzh-yer*) Parishes in Shreveport. But in 1992 there was a serious two-party contest here, since two incumbents were thrown into the same seat by redistricting.

The winner was Jim McCrery, the Republican, who hails from Shreveport and who in the early 1980s worked for 4th District Congressman Buddy Roemer when they were both Democrats. After Roemer was elected governor in 1987, McCrery ran for the seat as a Republican and won the April 1988 special election with 51%. In the October 1988 primary for the full term, he beat Roemer's mother, by a 55%–45% margin. In 1992 McCrery faced 16-year incumbent Jerry Huckaby, a conservative Democrat who worked on the Agriculture Committee to preserve cotton subsidies and sugar quotas. But Huckaby had 88 overdrafts on the House bank, totalling $41,000, while McCrery in the Louisiana conservative-reformist tradition bounced no checks, refused to take honoraria and backed term limits. In late August a gay publication charged that McCrery was a homosexual; he denied it and was supported by local newspapers. McCrery led the October primary 44%–29%, with 22% for an anti-incumbent third candidate; McCrery had a solid 57% in his old district. In the runoff McCrery won overwhelmingly, 63%–37%, with Huckaby running only 1% ahead of Bill Clinton. In 1994, though the district had an increased black percentage, McCrery was elected with 80% in the October primary.

McCrery has compiled a solid conservative record in the House and, with a seat on the Ways and Means Committee, worked on important issues. In 1994, on the Health Subcommittee, and armed with the intuitions that made him one of only 72 House members to vote against the disastrous 1988 catastrophic healthcare bill, he advanced much of the Republican alternative to the Democrats' version of the Clinton healthcare bill: capping deductibility of health insurance, opposing the Democrats' cost control measures, limiting medical malpractice and instituting medical savings accounts. Prompted by complaints from constituents, he pushed to replace the

SSI cash benefit with a voucher for children with emotional problems who came from poor families; he was told parents were coaching kids to act out, to be eligible for the checks. He also worked with Jim Talent of Missouri to write the welfare reform plank of the Contract With America. With a safe seat, and with as much experience on difficult legislative problems as many Republicans have, as he demonstrated by taking an active role on the welfare reform bill, McCrery has the potential to be an influential member of the 104th Congress. Or he may shift his focus to be a candidate for Bennett Johnston's Senate seat in 1996.

The People: Pop. 1990: 603,213; 44% rural; 13% age 65+; 77% White; 22% Black; 1% Hispanic origin. Voting age pop.: 436,413; 19% Black; 1% Hispanic origin. Households: 58% married couple families; 28% married couple fams. w. children; 41% college educ.; median household income: $22,903; per capita income: $11,349; median gross rent: $344; median house value: $54,900.

1992 Presidential Vote		
Bush (R)	125,965	(48%)
Clinton (D)	94,936	(36%)
Perot (I)	36,121	(14%)

1988 Presidential Vote		
Bush (R)	162,630	(69%)
Dukakis (D)	72,384	(31%)

Rep. Jim McCrery (R)

Elected Apr. 1988; b. Sept. 18, 1949, Shreveport; home, Shreveport; LA Tech. U., B.A. 1971, LA St. U., J.D. 1975; Methodist; married (Johnette).

Career: Practicing atty. 1975–78; Asst. Shreveport City Atty., 1979–80; Legis. Dir., U.S. Rep. Buddy Roemer, 1981–84; Regional Mgr., Georgia-Pacific Corp., 1984–88.

DC Office: 225 CHOB 20515, 202-225-2777; Fax: 202-225-8039.

District Offices: 6425 Youree Dr., #350, Shreveport 71105, 318-798-2254; and 1900 N. 18th St., #3, Monroe 71201, 318-388-6105.

Committees: *Ways & Means* (9th of 21 R): Health; Human Resources.

Group Ratings

	ADA	ACLU	COPE	CFA	LCV	CON	NSI	COC	ACU	NTLC	CHC
1994	5	18	13	20	22	65	100	100	90	93	93
1993	0	—	0	10	15	87	—	100	92	—	—

National Journal Ratings

	1993 LIB	—	1993 CONS	1994 LIB	—	1994 CONS
Economic	0%	—	88%	0%	—	80%
Social	11%	—	82%	24%	—	73%
Foreign	17%	—	76%	25%	—	71%

Key Votes of the 103d Congress

1. Clinton Deficit Plan	N	3. Brady Handgun Purchase	N	5. Lmt. UN Cmnd. of Forces	Y
2. NAFTA	Y	4. Strike Race/Death Pnlty.	Y	6. Cut Missile Funds	N

Key Votes of the 104th Congress

1. Congressional Compliance Y	6. Reform Crime Grant Y	11. Loser Pays Court Reform Y
2. Balanced Budget Amndmt. Y	7. National Security Act Y	12. Product Liability Reform Y
3. Bar Unfunded Mandates Y	8. Moratorium on Regs. Y	13. Welfare Reform Y
4. Pass Line Item Veto Y	9. Risk Assessment on Regs. Y	14. Term Limits Amndmt. Y
5. Relax Exclusionary Rule Y	10. Expnd. Priv. Prop. Rights Y	15. Tax Cuts Y

Election Results

1994 primary	Jim McCrery (R)	106,204	(80%)	($459,098)
	Paul Henry Kidd (D)	21,467	(16%)	
	E. Austin Simmons (I)	5,365	(4%)	
1992 general	Jim McCrery (R)	153,501	(63%)	($743,254)
	Jerry Huckaby (D)	90,079	(37%)	($792,318)

SIXTH DISTRICT

Across the geographic midriff of Louisiana runs an invisible line between Cajun and Catholic southern Louisiana and Anglo-Saxon and Protestant northern Louisiana, a line that separates accents, attitudes and tastes in music and cuisine. It was approximately along that line that the one Louisiana politician who straddled it got his start and met his end: Huey Long, born and raised in Winn Parish north of Alexandria, became governor at age 36 in the old (and still-standing) Gothic Capitol in Baton Rouge when the city had 30,000 people. He was shot and killed, allegedly by a young doctor but quite possibly by his own bodyguards, in the 34-story Art Deco Capitol he built, from which you can look south along the Mississippi River to Louisiana State University, which Long also mostly built, and north to the Exxon (once Jersey Standard) refinery, which he taxed to finance his public works. Baton Rouge is now the center of a metro area of half a million, almost all on the east bank of the Mississippi, and reaching far inland to Livingston Parish. Baton Rouge tries to maintain all of Louisiana's traditions; according to political consultant James Carville, who comes from nearby Carville in Iberville Parish, it has "the best restaurants per capita of any city in the United States."

The 6th Congressional District of Louisiana is centered on Baton Rouge, running south to the "petroleum alley" parishes along the Mississippi River, north to the river parishes opposite Mississippi and northwest to Alexandria and Winn Parish, with black neighborhoods shorn off and attached to the black-majority 4th District. More than half the people here live in Baton Rouge and its suburban fringe, which by now spreads east out I-12 to Livingston Parish. Historically Democratic, redistricting has helped to make this a solidly Republican area, particularly in and around Baton Rouge.

The Congressman from the 6th District is Richard Baker, one of those instinctive politicians who has spent most of his adult life in public office. He was elected as a Democrat to the Louisiana House from a blue-collar district in Baton Rouge in 1972, at 24, and rose to become chairman of the roads committee. He became a Republican in 1985, and in 1986, when Baton Rouge Republican Congressman Henson Moore ran for the Senate, Baker ran for the House and beat a Democratic state senator 51%–46%. Unopposed in 1988 and 1990, he found himself redistricted in the same district with Republican Congressman Clyde Holloway in 1992 and opposed as well by the Democratic mayor of Alexandria. The new district lines put Baker at a disadvantage. Holloway, who had been elected against black opponents three times (including the 4th District's Cleo Fields), got some publicity when he ran for governor in 1991, though he finished fourth; he was chief sponsor of the Republicans' child care tax credit targeted at low-income working families, and was endorsed by New Orleans suburban Congressman Bob Livingston. But Baker played off Holloway's tradition of urging squirrel hunters to vote for him absentee, because their season starts on primary day, with an ad showing squirrel hunters ticking off reasons to vote against Holloway. And he attacked Holloway for getting a disaster loan for his business while on the Agriculture Committee, for not paying withholding taxes to the government and for not donating his salary increase to a recognized charity as promised. Holloway hit Baker for living outside the district (his house is 200 yards from the line). Baker stressed economic issues—job creation, freeing up credit for businesses, reducing regulation. Holloway stressed cultural issues—abortion, gays, school prayer. In the October primary, both had majorities in their old districts; Holloway won 37% to Baker's 33%, and the third candidate, Democrat Ned Randolph, was eliminated with 30%. In the November runoff, Baker carried only East Baton Rouge and Livingston Parishes, but got 71% there, for a 51%–49% victory. 1994 was easier: Baker was reelected in October with 81% of the vote.

Baker is now chairman of the Banking subcommittee on Capital Markets, Securities and Government Sponsored Enterprises. He has been described by *The American Banker* as a "flagbearer for deregulation," and now will have a major say on legislation addressing bank sales of securities, mutual funds and insurance. Banks have been kept out of such businesses by the Glass-Steagall Act of 1933, but there has been a strong movement for repeal and in early 1995 Baker introduced legislation to reform Glass-Steagall, which critics say has been overtaken by time and business efficiencies but its defenders say is needed to protect against bankers' abuses. He also has superintendency over Fannie Mae and Freddie Mac. He favors raising the FHA home mortgage loan limit and opposes the requirement that public housing units be replaced one-for-one. On practically all issues Baker has a strongly conservative voting record; in *National Journal*'s 1993 ratings he was, with seven others, the most conservative member of the House. He has worked on local projects like expansion of the Port Hudson National Cemetery and recognition of the Jena Band of Choctaw Indians. He has been mentioned as a candidate for governor in 1995 or senator in 1996, although he has said he would defer to Jim McCrery in the Senate contest.

The People: Pop. 1990: 602,129; 45% rural; 11% age 65+; 82% White; 14% Black; 1% Amer. Indian; 1% Asian; 2% Hispanic origin. Voting age pop.: 434,108; 13% Black; 2% Hispanic origin. Households: 62% married couple families; 32% married couple fams. w. children; 42% college educ.; median household income: $25,251; per capita income: $12,042; median gross rent: $374; median house value: $63,100.

1992 Presidential Vote			1988 Presidential Vote		
Bush (R)	134,222	(50%)	Bush (R)	157,341	(68%)
Clinton (D)	91,273	(34%)	Dukakis (D).	74,534	(32%)
Perot (I).	35,325	(13%)			

Rep. Richard H. Baker (R)

Elected 1986; b. May 22, 1948, New Orleans; home, Baton Rouge; LA St. U., B.A. 1971; United Methodist; married (Kay).

Career: Real estate developer, 1972–86; LA House of Reps., 1972–86.

DC Office: 434 CHOB 20515, 202-225-3901; Fax: 202-225-7313.

District Offices: 5555 Hilton Ave., #100, Baton Rouge 70808, 504-929-7711; 3406 Rosalino St., Alexandria 71301, 318-445-5504.

Committees: *Agriculture* (17th of 27 R): General Farm Commodities. *Banking & Financial Services* (6th of 27 R): Capital Markets, Securities and Government Sponsored Enterprises (Chmn.); Housing and Community Opportunity.

Group Ratings

	ADA	ACLU	COPE	CFA	LCV	CON	NSI	COC	ACU	NTLC	CHC
1994	0	13	13	20	6	86	100	100	100	100	100
1993	0	—	0	20	21	69	—	91	100	—	—

National Journal Ratings

	1993 LIB — 1993 CONS	1994 LIB — 1994 CONS
Economic	0% — 88%	0% — 80%
Social	0% — 89%	0% — 89%
Foreign	0% — 91%	14% — 80%

Key Votes of the 103d Congress

1. Clinton Deficit Plan	N	3. Brady Handgun Purchase	N	5. Lmt. UN Cmnd. of Forces	Y
2. NAFTA	Y	4. Strike Race/Death Pnlty.	Y	6. Cut Missile Funds	N

Key Votes of the 104th Congress

1. Congressional Compliance	Y	6. Reform Crime Grant	Y	11. Loser Pays Court Reform	Y
2. Balanced Budget Amndmt.	Y	7. National Security Act	Y	12. Product Liability Reform	Y
3. Bar Unfunded Mandates	Y	8. Moratorium on Regs.	Y	13. Welfare Reform	Y
4. Pass Line Item Veto	Y	9. Risk Assessment on Regs.	Y	14. Term Limits Amndmt.	N
5. Relax Exclusionary Rule	Y	10. Expnd. Priv. Prop. Rights	Y	15. Tax Cuts	Y

Election Results

1994 primary	Richard H. Baker (R)................	103,174	(81%)	($518,945)
	Darryl Paul Ward (D).................	24,033	(19%)	
1992 general	Richard H. Baker (R)................	123,953	(51%)	($770,203)
	Clyde C. Holloway (R)...............	121,225	(49%)	($424,870)

SEVENTH DISTRICT

More than 200 years ago, French-speaking settlers were forced to leave their land of Acadie, which the British had taken over and renamed Nova Scotia, and make their way to the wetlands of southern Louisiana. Here, without much notice, they built steep-roofed houses to slough off nonexistent snow and adapted French cuisine to the crawfish and muskrat they found in abundance in the pelican-tended swamps. The heart of the Cajun country is around Lafayette, just west of the Atchafalaya Basin, where Mississippi waters pour through bayous and canals, with only occasional bits of solid land visible on the 30-mile section of Interstate 10 built on elevated stilts. For half a century the Cajun country thrived, thanks to the oil and gas plentiful here and just off shore in the Gulf of Mexico; oil rigs are common, and every once in a while the swampy foliage parts to reveal a giant refinery or petrochemical plant. In the past two decades, Cajun pride has grown; Cajun French is being kept alive and Cajun cooking has become a tourist attraction here and, in watered-down form, familiar all over the United States. Both Cajun culture and the oil business are particularly evident in Lafayette, with its Acadian Village and plethora of oil exploration firms.

The oil price crash of the middle 1980s hit the Cajun country hard. Rising expectations, and the giddy sense that the oil industry promised lasting prosperity, suddenly collapsed, leaving borrowers overextended and ordinary homeowners unable to maintain the standard of living they expected. Politically, the Cajun country seemed to move then toward national Democrats, whom it had shunned because their cultural liberalism seemed alien to the Cajun tradition of respecting the authority of Church and state while tolerating a certain amount of *laissez les bons temps rouler* spirit. The Cajun country voted more than the national average for Michael Dukakis in 1988 and was carried by Bill Clinton in 1992; it gave key support to Edwin Edwards, the most famous Cajun politician, in his 1991 race against David Duke.

The 7th Congressional District of Louisiana covers much of the Cajun country, from Lafayette and the Atchafalaya west along I-10 to Lake Charles and the Texas border. Its boundaries have changed due to litigation and varying interpretations of the Voting Rights Act amendments of 1982; for 1992 it included most of St. Martin Parish, east of Lafayette; for 1994, it included Vernon Parish, home of the Army's Fort Polk. It is the descendant of the district represented from 1965 to 1972 by Edwin Edwards and from 1972 to 1986 by John Breaux, both from Acadia Parish, who became governor and senator, respectively.

The current Congressman from the 7th is Jimmy Hayes of Lafayette, a successful real estate developer, prosecutor and Edwards ally, and a member of that increasingly rare species, the moderate-to-conservative southern Democrat. Hayes got his political start as a prosecutor in Lafayette and then as Edwards's head of the state banking department in 1983, where he rewrote the Louisiana Bank Code and Louisiana Securities law. In 1986, when John Breaux ran for the Senate, Hayes ran for the House. He won 30% in the primary, eliminating a more liberal Democrat, then beat a pro-business, anti-union state senator in the runoff. The AMA and Realtor PACs made independent expenditures against Hayes, but he was able to outspend them and his opponent out of his own pocket. In 1990, Hayes nearly lost Lafayette Parish but won 58%–38% in the October primary. In 1992, Hayes's brother Fredric, a onetime state legislator, ran as a Republican and attacked his brother as "part of the tax-and-spend Democratic elite which has bankrupted this nation"; but his real grievance seemed to be a family matter, a dispute over their father's will. Fredric Hayes got 27% in Lafayette Parish; Jimmy Hayes won district-wide with 73%.

Up through 1993, Hayes was going with the political flow in his district. His chairmanship of a Science Subcommittee on Energy and Environment enabled him to spotlight his telemedicine project, allowing doctors to talk over interactive video in order to increase efficiency and reduce costs. His seat on Transportation and Infrastructure enabled him to champion the property rights of local wetland owners and rice farmers from what they consider overregulation under wetlands laws and to get disaster relief after the area was hit by Hurricane Andrew in August 1992. He was an ethical straight arrow, having no overdrafts on the House bank and declining the congressional pay raise and pension. But the advent of the Clinton Administration put him in uncomfortable positions. He opposed the Btu tax and the Clinton budget and tax package and, when criticized by other House Democrats, said angrily, "I don't owe them a damn thing to be a Democrat. Most of them don't come from places like I do where being a Democrat is a liability." He voted for NAFTA and said he didn't seek any local road projects for doing so; he opposed the Clinton healthcare plan and came up with his own 18-page insurance reform bill; he opposed the Democrats' crime bill as well.

In October 1994 Hayes faced former Congressman Clyde Holloway, a Republican elected three times from a district where nearly half of the population was black. Holloway carried several parishes near his home area, but Hayes won solidly in Democratic Lake Charles and Lafayette, whose Republican tendencies are increasing because its black neighborhoods are now in the black-majority 4th District. Overall Hayes won 53%–40%, decisive but not entirely comfortable. Hayes is now no longer a chairman, but the issue to which he seems most dedicated, the property rights movement, has fared better in the Republican 104th than the Democratic 103d. Hayes has been mentioned as a candidate for governor in 1995 or senator in 1996, but with two black Democratic candidates running—the 4th's Cleo Fields and the 2nd's William Jefferson—he would have a hard time making the runoff.

The People: Pop. 1990: 602,679; 42% rural; 11% age 65+; 79% White; 19% Black; 1% Asian; 1% Hispanic origin. Voting age pop.: 420,905; 18% Black; 1% Hispanic origin. Households: 60% married couple families; 31% married couple fams. w. children; 33% college educ.; median household income: $21,442; per capita income: $10,226; median gross rent: $305; median house value: $49,700.

1992 Presidential Vote

Clinton (D) 123,336 (46%)
Bush (R) 99,985 (38%)
Perot (I)................... 38,244 (14%)

1988 Presidential Vote

Bush (R) 121,832 (51%)
Dukakis (D)............... 115,495 (49%)

Rep. James A. (Jimmy) Hayes (D)

Elected 1986; b. Dec. 21, 1946, Lafayette; home, Lafayette; U. of S.W. LA, B.A. 1967, Tulane U., J.D. 1970; Methodist; married (Leslie).

Career: Air Natl. Guard, 1968–74; Asst. Lafayette City Atty., 1971–72; Asst. Dist. Atty., Lafayette Parish, 1974–83; Real estate developer, 1978–86; LA Commissioner of Financial Inst., 1983–85.

DC Office: 2432 RHOB 202-225-2031; Fax: 202-225-1175.

District Offices: 100 E. Vermilion, Lafayette 70501, 318-233-4773; and 901 Lake Shore Dr., #402, Lake Charles 70601, 318-433-1613.

Committees: *Transportation & Infrastructure* (9th of 27 D): Aviation; Water Resources and Environment. *Science* (4th of 23 D): Energy and Environment (RMM).

Group Ratings

	ADA	ACLU	COPE	CFA	LCV	CON	NSI	COC	ACU	NTLC	CHC
1994	20	23	38	30	21	51	90	91	83	76	86
1993	20	—	50	40	29	57	—	90	70	—	—

National Journal Ratings

	1993 LIB — 1993 CONS	1994 LIB — 1994 CONS
Economic	42% — 58%	37% — 63%
Social	33% — 67%	15% — 84%
Foreign	51% — 49%	30% — 67%

Key Votes of the 103d Congress

1. Clinton Deficit Plan	N	3. Brady Handgun Purchase	N	5. Lmt. UN Cmnd. of Forces	N
2. NAFTA	Y	4. Strike Race/Death Pnlty.	Y	6. Cut Missile Funds	N

Key Votes of the 104th Congress

1. Congressional Compliance	Y	6. Reform Crime Grant	N	11. Loser Pays Court Reform	N
2. Balanced Budget Amndmt.	Y	7. National Security Act	Y	12. Product Liability Reform	Y
3. Bar Unfunded Mandates	Y	8. Moratorium on Regs.	Y	13. Welfare Reform	Y
4. Pass Line Item Veto	Y	9. Risk Assessment on Regs.	Y	14. Term Limits Amndmt.	Y
5. Relax Exclusionary Rule	Y	10. Expnd. Priv. Prop. Rights	Y	15. Tax Cuts	Y

Election Results

1994 primary	James A. (Jimmy) Hayes (D)............	72,424	(53%)	($436,254)
	Clyde C. Holloway (R)................	54,253	(40%)	
	Ron Ceasar (I)	9,937	(7%)	
1992 primary	James A. (Jimmy) Hayes (D)............	84,149	(73%)	($436,331)
	Fredric Hayes (R).....................	23,870	(21%)	($18,675)
	Robert J. (Bob) Nain (R)	7,184	(6%)	

MAINE

There is something ornery, contrary-minded, almost bullheaded about Maine. The state closest geographically to Europe was not settled heavily until the mid-19th Century, and then by people coming from the south and west—the opposite of America's usual westward thrust. In an urbanizing and rapidly changing country, Maine was famous for its pointed firs and steady habits, and if it developed a few dozen small factory and mill towns, it has nothing like a major metropolis. Maine grew in a rush and then mostly stopped: there were 600,000 people here in 1860 and its population did not top one million until the 1970s. Then, in the 1980s, the New England high-tech boom reached up Interstate 95 and the simple, back-to-nature Yankee style came into vogue, and Maine boomed. The antique dockside buildings on Portland's waterfront were restored and fern-filled; the Maine Mall expanded and saw office parks spring up nearby, a miniature Edge City; real estate prices rose by hundreds of percents, not just in vacation coves, but in Portland and small towns that had never considered themselves picturesque. The L.L. Bean headquarters in Freeport, open 24 hours a day, 365 days a year, symbolized the boom: the Anglo-Saxon monosyllable and two chaste initials suggesting the dry understatement of archetypical Down East Yankees; the 24-hour-a-day schedule recalling the hard work needed to eke out a living in this cold soil, between the lobster-laden North Atlantic and the pine-covered north woods; the commercial success of the enterprise a prime example of Maine's unexpected 1980s boom.

That boom had its costs, of course. Maine's manufacturing sector withered as service jobs increased; its main roads were suddenly jammed with cars waiting for the green arrow so they could turn into the mall. Not all of Maine has disappeared into high-tech glitter: farmers, though fewer every year, still try to scratch the small Maine boiling potatoes out of the far northern fields of Aroostook County, and many of Maine's paper and textile mill towns have the air of neglect and abandonment that comes to places that have been losing jobs and young people for a generation. Not far from neat town squares and picturesque seascapes you can find tarpaper- and plastic-clad homes of poor, uneducated, ill-clothed swamp Yankees. In the early 1990s Maine lost 40,000 jobs and saw real estate values crash. It saw the state budget cut three times and humiliating stoppages of state services. Increasingly, people wondered if they had let their forest and coast environments and their town Main Streets deteriorate because of development whose benefits seemed ephemeral. And after the Halloween 1991 storm damaged much waterfront property, including George Bush's house in Kennebunkport, nothing seemed safe.

Politically, Maine responded with anger and by flailing out in all directions. For decades this state has been an odd duck politically, often running contrary to national cycles. It held state elections in September, a date originally chosen because it followed the state's early harvest, up through 1958; in the days before polls, the results here were taken as a gauge of national partisan movement—hence the saying, "As Maine goes, so goes the nation." However in September 1936, Maine voted 56% for Republican Governor Lewis Barrows and in November only Maine and Vermont voted for Alf Landon over Franklin Roosevelt, prompting Roosevelt's campaign manager to observe, "As Maine goes, so goes Vermont"; its adherence to flinty Yankee Republicanism and Prohibition was echoed almost nowhere else in the nation. Since then, Maine has voted for the loser in the close presidential elections of 1948, 1960, 1968 and 1976, and nearly did so again in 1980—a record equalled by no other state. In 1992, it had the nation's highest voter turnout and highest percentage for Ross Perot, 30%, nearly within range of Bill Clinton's 39% and narrowly ahead of lifelong Maine vacationer George Bush. In 1994 Maine elected an independent candidate as governor—not the first time. It did in 1974 too—and saw both congressional districts switch parties; the Maine 2d was one of only four districts in the

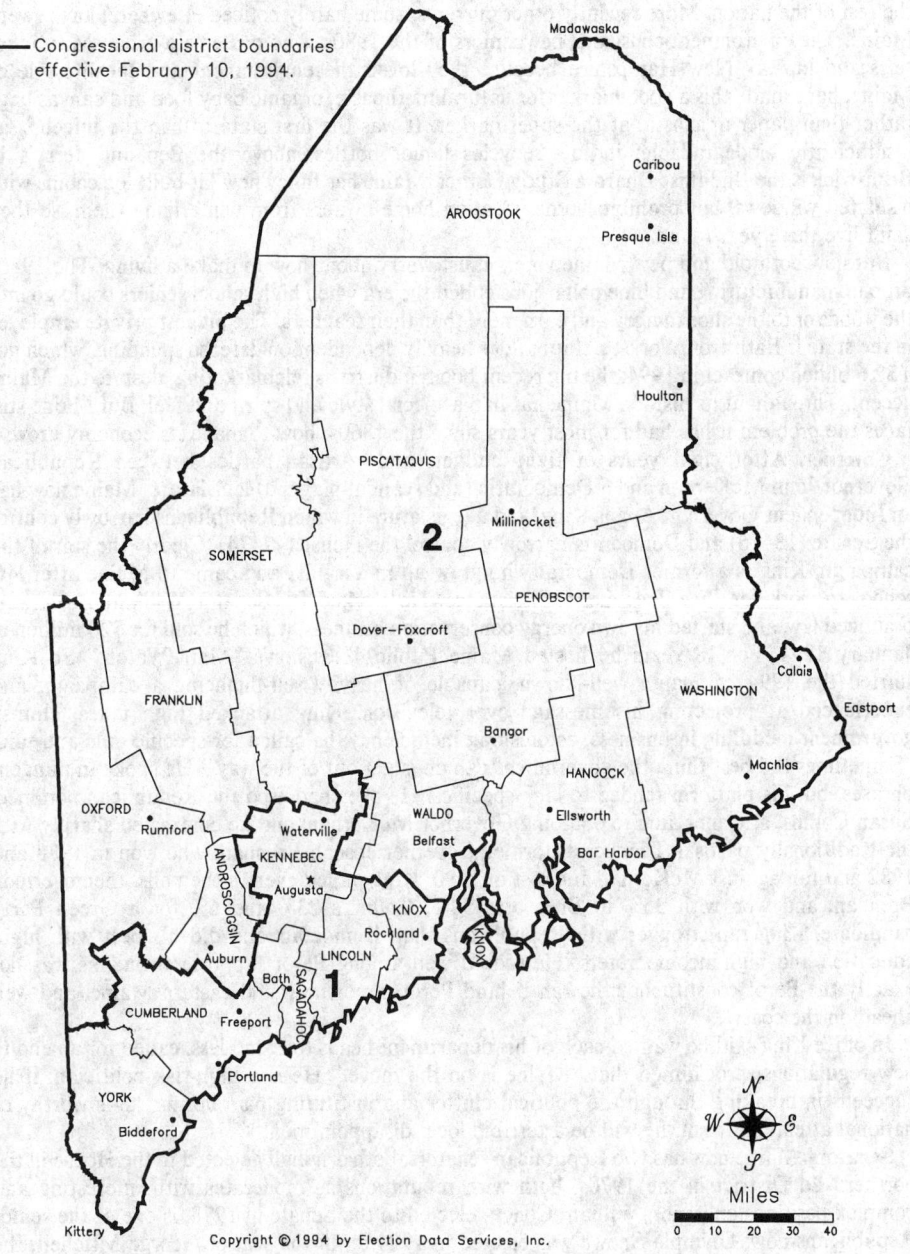

Congressional district boundaries effective February 10, 1994.

MADAWASKA

AROOSTOOK

CARIBOU

PRESQUE ISLE

HOULTON

PISCATAQUIS

SOMERSET

MILLINOCKET

2

PENOBSCOT

DOVER—FOXCROFT

FRANKLIN

BANGOR

WASHINGTON

CALAIS

EASTPORT

HANCOCK

MACHIAS

OXFORD

RUMFORD

WALDO

ELLSWORTH

WATERVILLE

BELFAST

ANDROSCOGGIN

KENNEBEC

BAR HARBOR

AUGUSTA

KNOX

AUBURN

ROCKLAND

KNOX

LINCOLN

BATH

1

SAGADAHOC

CUMBERLAND

FREEPORT

PORTLAND

YORK

BIDDEFORD

KITTERY

N W E S

Miles

0 10 20 30 40

country that voted for a Republican in 1992 and a Democrat in 1994.

If Maine's tradition-minded Yankees kept the state Republican long after the nation embraced the New Deal, the sons and daughters of its ethnics—Irish, French Canadian, Greek and Arab immigrants have come to equal the numbers of pure WASPs, though these new Mainers in many ways share traditional Yankee traits and values—made the Democrats competitive, perhaps even dominant, here in the 1970s and 1980s as they were losing ground in the rest of the nation. More recently other currents, some barely noticed elsewhere, have swept Maine. The environment-conscious newcomers of the 1980s, who passed up urban Massachusetts and low-tax New Hampshire because they loved the environment and the lifestyle of Maine, have made this a good market for natural toothpaste, organic baby food and canvas bags rather than paper or plastic at the supermarket. It was the first state to ban the juicebox as insufficiently biodegradable; it now recycles liquor bottles; above the Ben and Jerry's in Brunswick is the Buddhist Dharma Study Center. Maine has fancy new kit-built log cabins with insulated windows, but prohibits some vacation home owners from winterizing them, so they can't live there year-round.

But now both old and new Maine voters must worry about how to make a living. The 1980s drop in manufacturing and blue-collar jobs ended the era when high school seniors could go into the woods or to the shoe factory and earn more than their teachers. The biggest private employer in the state is Bath Iron Works, a shipbuilder heavily dependent on defense spending, which got a $2.6 billion contract in 1994; the big recent boom industry is telemarketing, despite the Maine accent. Throughout its history, Maine has had a special style and spirit and feel. But Maine still faces the problem it has had for most years since the 1860s: how to make its economy grow.

Governor. After eight years of tight budgets and partisan battles between Republican Governor John McKernan and a Democratic (and scandal-plagued) legislature, Maine now has an Independent Governor, Angus King, and a legislature in which Republicans narrowly control the Senate (18–16) and Democrats narrowly control the House (77–74). Clearly the star of the campaign, King is a former Democrat who grew up in Virginia and came to Maine after law school to work for Pine Tree Legal Assistance. He worked for Senator William Hathaway, practiced law, and started his own energy conservation business, which he sold for $20 million in January 1994. For 18 years he hosted Maine Public Television's "MaineWatch." So King started the 1994 campaign well-known, capable of heavily self-financing a campaign, and experienced at projecting his message over television. King attacked high taxes, clumsy government meddling in business, astonishing inefficiency; he called for specific cuts and said, "Sometimes the best thing the government can do is get out of the way." He spoke in pungent phrases, but his platform tended to lack specifics. He overshadowed the Republican nominee, Susan Collins, a former aide to outgoing Governor McKernan; and he contrasted sharply with the traditionally partisan Democrat, former Governor Joseph Brennan, who won in 1978 and 1982 and ran against McKernan and lost in 1990. King pulled even in the polls, then overtook Brennan, and won with 35% to Brennan's 34%, Collins's 23% and 6% for a Green Party candidate. King ran stronger with Republicans than Democrats and did his best with high-education and high-income voters. He scored well among Perot supporters, but his was not exactly the Perot constituency; he ran behind Perot in northern and eastern Maine, and well ahead on the coast.

In office King said he wanted each of his department heads to spend less, called for an end to new regulations, proclaimed that "Maine is on the move." He is a high-risk politician: if he succeeds in breaking through the political clutter and instituting his reforms, he is worthy of national attention; if not, he will be a terrible local disappointment.

Senators. Maine now has two Republican senators, both originally elected to the House in the northern 2d District in the 1970s, both with reputations as moderates with interesting and complex positions on issues. William Cohen, elected to the Senate in 1978, is one of the senior Republicans now; Olympia Snowe was elected in 1994 to fill the seat of George Mitchell, the outgoing Senate Majority Leader. Mitchell's partisan fervor and skill helped undermine George

Bush's Administration by killing his capital gains cut and forcing him into the 1990 budget summit tax increase, but he could not pass Bill Clinton's healthcare plan or rescue the Democratic Party from electoral disaster in 1994.

William Cohen grew up in Bangor, where his father owned a bakery; after law school he returned home, practiced law, and became a member of the city council in his 20s, in 1969. In 1972 he ran for Congress and won. That put him on the Judiciary Committee, where he was one of the Republicans who voted to bring impeachment charges against Richard Nixon. He was twice reelected easily and in 1978 ran for the Senate and beat incumbent Democrat William Hathaway. Throughout his career, Cohen has had something of a literary bent: he published books of poetry in 1978 and 1986, a journal of his first Senate year in 1981, spy novels (the first co-written with Senator Gary Hart) in 1985 and 1993 and an account of the Iran-contra investigation, co-written by Senator George Mitchell, in 1988.

Cohen's career has been characterized by pretty steady adherence to a set of principles. One such principle is purity of the political process. This came out in his impeachment vote in 1974 and in his stern condemnation of many in the Reagan Administration during the Iran-contra affair in 1987; to him and Mitchell, Oliver North and his colleagues were "men of zeal" who undermined the Constitution and the legal process. With Michigan's Carl Levin, he sponsored the independent counsel law in 1993—reauthorizing the special prosecutors who proponents think are necessary to ferret out Executive Branch crime and opponents think are irresponsible and oppressive inquisitors. He and Levin also sponsored the lobby disclosure and gift ban bill that died in the final days of the 1994 session after the House had agreed to final passage; the bill was revived in 1995, but with a low priority on Bob Dole's legislative agenda.

Cohen's stands are more conservative on military issues. When he challenged Hathaway in 1978, Cohen's platform was military preparedness. He has served on Armed Services, where he supported the Reagan defense buildup, opposed the nuclear freeze, backed the MX missile and a large Navy, and expressed alarm at Russian military operations in the former Soviet Republics. He looks after the big Navy shipbuilding operations at Bath Iron Works, which got a $2.6 billion destroyer contract in 1994, and has recently worked for money for defense reconversion. He argues strongly that the U.S. must not abandon a forward military strategy even after the Cold War, and backs bigger sealift capacity, more mobile forces and missile defense. He urged economic sanctions against Iraq even before Saddam Hussein invaded Kuwait and strongly backed the Gulf war resolution. Cohen doesn't back every big project; he opposes building further B-2s and has opposed the space station as "a financial black hole."

On economic issues, Cohen is not always market-oriented. From a state that uses lots of gasoline and home heating oil, he has backed oil price controls and a windfall profits tax. From his position as chairman of the Aging Committee, he wants to outlaw telemarketing scams against the elderly, protect Medicare against physician overcharges and penalize drug companies whose prices increase more than inflation. He worked with the bipartisan "Mainstream" coalition of senators to come up with a healthcare plan in 1994 while opposing the "bureaucratic overload and massive restructuring" of the Clinton plan. He also co-sponsored the bill to deny Social Security disability benefits to alcoholics and drug abusers, whose use of them was documented by his Aging Committee staff. He won passage of a law setting higher standards for medical equipment for Medicare beneficiaries. He also gets into messy details of government: how the Defense Department spends more processing travel vouchers than on travel; how the government makes generous deals with concessionaires. He opposed the U.S.-Canada Free Trade Agreement after attacking Canada for exporting "short" (i.e., underweight) lobsters. But he voted for GATT and has promoted Maine exports, such as blueberries going to Taiwan. On some cultural issues, he sides with liberals. He is pro-choice on abortion and voted to override Bush vetoes of the 1990 civil right bill and the 1992 Family and Medical Leave Act.

Cohen, like many veteran politicians, saw his percentage of the vote decline in the early 1990s. In 1990, his opponent, businessman Neil Rolde, spent more than $1 million of his own money, most of it on TV ads in which he argued effectively for national health insurance: this was one of the few Senate races in which the challenger outspent the incumbent. Cohen spent less, and his percentage fell from 73% in 1984 to a still impressive 61%. He appears to be in strong shape for reelection in 1996.

Olympia Snowe, Maine's junior Senator, has a long career now in politics, but got into it unexpectedly. Snowe grew up in Auburn, worked as a legislative staffer after college; in 1973, after her husband state Representative Peter Snowe died in an auto accident, she was elected to the legislature. In 1978, when Cohen ran for the Senate, she ran for the House in the northern 2d District, and won. She made a moderate record on issues and won by large margins in the 1980s but more narrowly in the 1990s; in 1989 she married Governor John McKernan, her former House colleague.

When George Mitchell announced his retirement in March 1994, Snowe quickly jumped into the race and began attacks on her Democratic opponent, 1st District Congressman Tom Andrews, even before he got into the race. Andrews was personally attractive and had been a strong vote-getter; he lost a leg to cancer as a teenager and headed a Maine handicapped organization. He raised money to help Central American farmers and demonstrated against the Seabrook nuclear plant in New Hampshire. He campaigned hard and won the House seat in 1990, and had an ultraliberal record—for progressive tax increases, a 50% defense spending cut and mass transit subsidies.

Snowe attacked him for voting for the base-closing bill that closed Loring Air Force Base in northern Maine and for opposing the balanced budget amendment. To judge from their performance in House races, Andrews should have won easily: in 1992, Snowe won by 22,000 votes, Andrews by 107,000. Indeed, in 1990 she won by just 51%–49% while Andrews was winning his first term with 61%. But when the spotlight shifted from Andrews's personal character and activism to his stand on national issues, the balance changed. Andrews attacked her for anti-education votes, but made no impact. Snowe won 60%–36%, carrying every county, losing only Portland, Lewiston and a few mill towns. In the Senate, she supported Republican positions on most economic issues, but also has backed abortion rights and family leave. Although she is the least conservative of the 11 freshmen Republicans elected in 1994, she is comfortable with their smaller-government rhetoric, at least in general terms; "The people of Maine have sent clear and unequivocal signals that we must have the courage and the will to balance the federal budget," she said in January. The problem that she has faced, more than most others, has been the perceived need to respond to her state's dependence on federal support, whether it is the home-heating assistance for low-income groups or the Portsmouth Naval Shipyard, which the base-closing commission in May 1995 added to its list for review. But she told *The New York Times* she saw no inconsistency: "We all fight for the things we think are important." She also has shown her moderate credentials by raising opposition to the ban on cash benefits to unwed teenage mothers, which House Republicans approved. Given her experience and her centrist proclivities, if she can maintain her skill as a party loyalist and work on the inside to smooth some of the rough edges of her party's program, she could become one of the Senate's most influential members.

Presidential politics. One of the most stunning rebukes of the 1992 presidential election was the fact that George Bush ran third in Maine, the site of his family summer home in Kennebunkport, where he has spent every summer of his life (except during World War II) and made many of the memorable appearances of his presidency. In York County around Kennebunkport, the home town appeal Bush demonstrated in the 1988 caucuses and in November 1988 evaporated after Maine's economy collapsed. The Kennebunk paper endorsed Bill Clinton, who carried York County. Ross Perot ran ahead of Bush statewide and carried three of Maine's 16 counties.

Maine's caucuses, coming just after the New Hampshire primary, made something of a ruckus in 1992. The state's economic trauma made it receptive to the message of Jerry Brown, who barnstormed little towns and inspired volunteers and ended up winning the caucuses. On the Republican side, Bush dominated a caucus process run largely by his supporters—a result that gave little indication of the rebellion which, as November's results showed, was more intense and angry in Maine than just about anywhere else in the United States.

Congressional districting. Maine did not bother redistricting for 1992, waiting for 1994 instead. It hardly matters: Maine's district lines have not changed much since the state lost its 3d District in the 1960 Census. The idea then was to split areas of Democratic strength, but now Maine is politically homogeneous enough that party makes less difference than the personal strengths of the candidates. 1994 lines put the 1st District half of Waldo County into the 2d District which also picked up a bit of Kennebec County. Maine is one of two states (Nebraska is the other) where the electoral vote can be divided if one congressional district votes for a candidate who loses statewide.

The People: Est. Pop. 1994: 1,240,000; Pop. 1990: 1,227,928, up 1.0% 1990–1994. 0.5% of U.S. total, 39th largest; 55% rural. Median age: 33.9 years. 13.3% 65 years and over. 98.4% White. Households: 58.1% married couple families; 28% married couple fams. w. children; 42% college educ.; median household income: $27,854; per capita income: $12,957; 70.5% owner occupied housing median house value: $87,400; median monthly rent: $358. 7.1% Unemployment. 1994 Voting age pop.: 931,000. 1994 Turnout: 506,864; 54% of VAP. Registered voters (1994): 940,569; 311,476 D (33%), 274,245 R (29%), 354,848 unaffiliated and minor parties (38%).

Political Lineup: Governor, Angus S. King, Jr. (I); Lt. Governor, Jeffrey H. Butland (R); Secy. of State, G. William Diamond (D); Atty. Gen., Michael E. Carpenter (D); Treasurer, Samuel Shapiro (D); Controller, David Bourne (D); Auditor, Rodney L. Scribner (D). State Senate, 35 (18 R, 16 D and 1 I); State House of Representatives, 151 (77 D and 74 R). Senators, William S. Cohen (R) and Olympia J. Snowe (R). Representatives, 2 (1 R and 1 D).

1992 Presidential Vote			1988 Presidential Vote		
Clinton (D)	263,420	(39%)	Bush (R)	307,131	(55%)
Perot (I)	206,820	(30%)	Dukakis (D)	243,569	(44%)
Bush (R)	206,504	(30%)			

GOVERNOR

Gov. Angus S. King, Jr. (I)

Elected 1994, term expires Jan. 1999; b. Mar. 31, 1944, Alexandria, VA; home, Brunswick; Dartmouth Col., A.B. 1966; U. of VA Law Schl., J.D. 1969; Episcopalian; married (Mary).

Career: Staff Atty., Pine Tree Legal Assistance, 1969–72; Chief Cnsl., U.S. Sen. William Hathaway, 1972–75; Practicing atty., 1975–83; Vice Pres. & Gen. Cnsl., Swift River/Hafslund Co., 1983–89; TV talk show host, 1975–93; Founder & Pres., Northeast Energy Management Inc., 1989–94.

Office: State House, Sta. 1, Augusta 04333, 207-287-3531; Fax: 207-287-1034.

Election Results

1994 gen.	Angus S. King, Jr. (I)	180,829	(35%)
	Joseph E. Brennan (D)	172,951	(34%)
	Susan M. Collins (R)	117,990	(23%)
	Jonathan K. Carter (IMG)	32,695	(6%)
	Others	6,843	(1%)
1990 gen.	John R. McKernan, Jr. (R)	243,766	(47%)
	Joseph E. Brennan (D)	230,038	(44%)
	Andrew Adam (I)	48,377	(9%)

SENATORS

Sen. William S. Cohen (R)

Elected 1978, seat up 1996; b. Aug. 28, 1940, Bangor; home, Bangor; Bowdoin Col., A.B. 1962, Boston U., LL.B. 1965; Unitarian; divorced.

Career: Practicing atty., 1966–72; Asst. Penobscot Cnty. Atty., 1968; Instructor, Husson Col., 1968, U. of ME, 1968–72; Bangor City Cncl., 1969–72, Bangor Mayor, 1971–72; U.S. House of Reps., 1972–78; Author.

DC Office: 322 HSOB 20510, 202-224-2523; Fax: 202-224-2693.

State Offices: 150 Capitol St., P.O. Box 347, Augusta 04332, 207-622-8414; Fed. Bldg., #204, 202 Harlow St., Bangor 04402, 207-945-0417; 109 Alfred St., Biddeford 04005, 207-283-1101; 11 Lisbon St., Lewiston 04240, 207-784-6969; 10 Moulton St., P.O. Box 1938, Portland 04104, 207-780-3575; and 169 Academy St., Presque Isle 04769, 207-764-3266.

Committees: *Armed Services* (3rd of 11 R): Airland Forces; Readiness; Seapower (Chmn.); Strategic Forces. *Governmental Affairs* (3rd of 8 R): Oversight of Government Management and the District of Columbia (Chmn.); Investigations. *Intelligence (Select)* (9th of 9 R). *Aging (Special)* (Chmn. of 10 R).

Group Ratings

	ADA	ACLU	COPE	CFA	LCV	CON	NSI	COC	ACU	NTLC	CHC
1994	40	53	29	58	85	77	100	57	45	84	43
1993	40	—	36	40	56	96	—	82	76	—	—

National Journal Ratings

	1993 LIB — 1993 CONS		1994 LIB — 1994 CONS	
Economic	30%	— 67%	36%	— 63%
Social	41%	— 56%	65%	— 34%
Foreign	16%	— 77%	15%	— 84%

Key Votes of the 103d Congress

1. Clinton Deficit Plan	N	3. Brady Handgun Purchase	Y	5. Lmt. UN Cmnd. of Forces	Y
2. NAFTA	N	4. Strike Race/Death Pnlty.	N	6. Cut Missile Funds	N

Key Votes of the 104th Congress

1. Congressional Compliance	Y	3. Balanced Budget Amndt.	Y	5. Product Liability Reform	N
2. Bar Unfunded Mandates	Y	4. Pass Line Item Veto	Y	6. FY96 Budget	Y

Election Results

1990 general	William S. Cohen (R)	319,167	(61%)	($1,628,292)
	Neil Rolde (D)	201,053	(39%)	($1,630,894)
1990 primary	William S. Cohen (R)	unopposed		
1984 general	William S. Cohen (R)	404,414	(73%)	($1,063,188)
	Elizabeth H. Mitchell (D)	142,626	(26%)	($410,611)

Sen. Olympia J. Snowe (R)

Elected 1994, seat up 2000; b. Feb. 21, 1947, Augusta; home, Auburn; U. of ME, B.A. 1969; Greek Orthodox; married (John R. McKernan).

Career: Dir., Superior Concrete Co.; Auburn Bd. of Voter Registration, 1971–73; ME House of Reps., 1972–76; ME Senate, 1976–78; U.S. House of Reps., 1978–94.

DC Office: 495 RSOB 20510, 202-224-5344; Fax: 202-224-1946.

State Offices: 2 Great Falls Plz., #78, Auburn 04210, 207-786-2451; 68 Sewall St., #101-C, Augusta 04330, 207-622-8292; 1 Cumberland Pl., #306, Bangor 04401, 207-945-0432; 231 Main St., #2, Biddeford 04005, 207-282-4144; 3 Canal Plz., #601, Portland 04112, 207-874-0833; and 169 Academy St., #3, Presque Isle 04769, 207-764-5124.

Committees: *Budget* (10th of 12 R). *Commerce, Science & Transportation* (9th of 10 R): Consumer Affairs, Foreign Commerce and Tourism; Oceans and Fisheries; Surface Transportation and Merchant Marine. *Foreign Relations* (6th of 10 R): African Affairs; European Affairs; International Operations (Chmn.); Near Eastern and South Asian Affairs. *Small Business* (10th of 10 R).

Group Ratings (as Member of U.S. House of Representatives)

	ADA	ACLU	COPE	CFA	LCV	CON	NSI	COC	ACU	NTLC	CHC
1994	30	39	56	50	65	52	80	67	57	75	57
1993	40	—	42	40	71	99	—	64	67	—	—

National Journal Ratings (as Member of U.S. House of Representatives)

	1993 LIB — 1993 CONS		1994 LIB — 1994 CONS	
Economic	35%	— 63%	40%	— 59%
Social	43%	— 56%	42%	— 58%
Foreign	35%	— 63%	25%	— 71%

Key Votes of the 103rd Congress (as Member of U.S. House of Representatives)

1. Clinton Deficit Plan	N	3. Brady Handgun Purchase	N	5. Lmt. UN Cmnd. of Forces	Y
2. NAFTA	N	4. Strike Race/Death Pnlty.	Y	6. Cut Missile Funds	Y

Key Votes of the 104th Congress

1. Congressional Compliance	Y	3. Balanced Budget Amndt.	Y	5. Product Liability Reform	Y
2. Bar Unfunded Mandates	Y	4. Pass Line Item Veto	Y	6. FY96 Budget	Y

Election Results

1994 general	Olympia J. Snowe (R)	308,244	(60%)	($2,041,834)
	Thomas H. Andrews (D)	186,042	(36%)	($1,482,060)
	Others	17,447	(3%)	
1994 primary	Olympia J. Snowe (R)	unopposed		
1988 general	George J. Mitchell (D)	452,590	(81%)	($1,471,426)
	Jasper S. Wyman (R)	104,758	(19%)	($147,760)

FIRST DISTRICT

The 1st District of Maine stretches from southernmost Kittery and nearby Kennebunkport to the craggy-shored ancestrally Republican counties to the east. The historic center is Portland, revived and renovated during its 1980s boom, with yuppies, bankers and courthouse lawyers. The commercial center now, for shoppers and office employees and drivers, is Maine Mall, spanning the Portland and Scarborough lines, just off the Maine Turnpike and I-295 and near the airport—the state's heaviest concentration of retail and office space. Most voters in the 1st District, except those far Down East, live within a couple hours drive of this area. Politically, the 1st votes very much like the state as a whole: it cast a large Perot vote in 1992 and was carried by Independent Governor Angus King in 1994. From 1968 to 1994 it elected three Democrats and three Republicans, with each side serving 14 years.

The new congressman from the 1st District is James Longley, Jr., a Republican whose father was the Independent elected Governor in 1974. This Longley graduated from college that year, went on to law school at the University of Maine and then joined the Marine Corps, serving three years on active duty; he later practiced law in Lewiston in the 2d District and moved to Falmouth in the 1st in early 1994. Raised a Democrat, he switched to the Republicans after deciding Democrats were out of control on taxes. As a Marine reservist, he was called to active duty in Operation Desert Storm, serving in Camp Lejeune and in Iraq. When Tom Andrews announced he was running for the Senate, Longley became one of four Republicans running for the open House seat. He called for changes in the payroll tax and, as a newcomer to elective politics, attacked the state legislature; his primary opponents included state party chairman Kevin Keogh, state Senator Charles D. Summers and former Portland City Council member Ted Rand, but Longley won the race with 43%. The Democratic nominee was state Senate President Dennis Dutremble, member of a prominent York County political family, but he had only 33% in his four-candidate primary and his political experience was a dubious asset in an anti-Democratic-incumbent year. Dutremble raised vastly more money and attacked Longley rather condescendingly; Longley backed the Contract With America and attacked Dutremble for trying to balance the state budget with gimmicks. Longley was supported by the local Perot organization and by right-to-lifers who accused Dutremble of flip-flopping.

Longley won 52%–48%, carrying most towns and cities; Dutremble carried Portland and a few blue collar towns. In the House Longley got seats on National Security—important for Bath Iron Works and other local defense industries—and Resources, where he can help revitalize local fisheries. With his independence and candid style, he quickly impressed House Republican leaders. But he will have to work hard to entrench himself with voters in this volatile district.

The People: Pop. 1990: 636,528; 51% rural; 13% age 65+; 98% White; 1% Asian; 1% Hispanic origin. Voting age pop.: 478,473; 1% Hispanic origin. Households: 59% married couple families; 28% married couple fams. w. children; 47% college educ.; median household income: $30,952; per capita income: $14,362; median gross rent: $474; median house value: $106,400.

1992 Presidential Vote

Clinton (D)	145,191	(40%)
Bush (R)	115,697	(32%)
Perot (I)	102,828	(28%)

1988 Presidential Vote

Bush (R)	169,292	(56%)
Dukakis (D)	131,078	(44%)

Rep. James B. Longley, Jr. (R)

Elected 1994; b. July 7, 1951, Lewiston; home, Yarmouth; Holy Cross Col., A.B. 1974, U. of ME, J.D. 1980; Catholic; separated.

Career: Marine Corps, 1976–79; Marine Corps Reserves, 1980–present (Persian Gulf); Practicing atty., 1980–94.

DC Office: 226 CHOB 20515, 202-225-6116; Fax: 202-225-3353.

District Offices: 4 Moulton St., Portland 04101, 207-774-5019; and 168 Capitol St., Augusta 04330, 207-626-3608.

Committees: *National Security* (28th of 30 R): Military Procurement. *Resources* (24th of 25 R): Fisheries, Wildlife and Oceans; Native American and Insular Affairs. *Small Business* (13th of 22 R): Regulation and Paperwork.

Group Ratings and 103rd Congress Votes: Newly Elected

Key Votes of the 104th Congress

1. Congressional Compliance Y	6. Reform Crime Grant Y	11. Loser Pays Court Reform N
2. Balanced Budget Amndmt. Y	7. National Security Act Y	12. Product Liability Reform Y
3. Bar Unfunded Mandates Y	8. Moratorium on Regs. Y	13. Welfare Reform Y
4. Pass Line Item Veto Y	9. Risk Assessment on Regs. Y	14. Term Limits Amndmt. N
5. Relax Exclusionary Rule Y	10. Expnd. Priv. Prop. Rights Y	15. Tax Cuts Y

Election Results

1994 general	James B. Longley, Jr. (R)	136,316	(52%)	($196,048)
	Dennis L. Dutremble (D)	126,373	(48%)	($514,071)
1994 primary	James B. Longley, Jr. (R)	19,705	(43%)	
	Charles E. Summers (R)	11,533	(25%)	
	Kevin Keogh (R)	8,327	(18%)	
	Theodore T. Rand (R)	6,490	(14%)	
1992 general	Thomas H. Andrews (D)	232,696	(65%)	($850,122)
	Linda Bean (R)	125,236	(35%)	($1,464,720)

SECOND DISTRICT

The 2d District covers the northern three-quarters of the state. In the more thickly populated part of southern Maine, however, the boundary line with the 1st is actually rather jagged, and the 2d takes in the traditionally Democratic mill town of Lewiston as well as the traditionally Republican coastal area down east. Its largest city is Lewiston, the blue-collar industrial town which Olympia Snowe did not carry in her Senate race. In contrast to the coastal south, which boomed in the 1980s, much of the north lagged or lost population, especially potato-growing Aroostook County, whose Loring Air Force Base was closed down in 1994. Things can get a little wacky here: one famous restaurant is the Roadkill Cafe, on Moosehead Lake, with backtalking waitresses and cooks. Anger was strong here in 1992; Ross Perot finished a solid second in the district, with one-third of the votes—his best congressional district in the United States.

The congressman from the 2d District is John Baldacci, a Democrat elected to replace Senator Olympia Snowe in 1994—one of only four Democrats elected that year in districts Republicans won in 1992. He grew up in Bangor, where his family ran Momma Baldacci's, a restaurant started by his grandparents in 1933; he is also of Italian and Lebanese descent, and distantly related to former Senator George Mitchell. He followed his father on the Bangor

County Council in 1978, at 23; in 1982, he was elected to the state Senate, where he often dissented from Democrats, had an anti-environmental record and eventually chaired the tax committee. He ran for the House in 1994, he said, because of concern about high local unemployment; he campaigned by holding spaghetti dinners at $2 a head (children under 12 free) around the district. In a seven-candidate primary, with lots of support around Bangor, Baldacci won with 27% to 23% for former Democratic state chairman James Mitchell, George Mitchell's nephew. The Republican nominee was Richard Bennett, a former director of the Maine Republican Party who worked for a local economic development group in western Maine. He won 30% in the four-candidate primary, calling for a balanced federal budget (pledging to take no pay raise until that happened) and economic development in northern Maine. Baldacci opposed the Clinton healthcare employer mandate; Bennett was iffy about the Contract With America's defense spending increase; both were pressed by Green and Independent Party candidates, who ended up winning 5% and 9% respectively. Baldacci ran ads showing him running the restaurant and calling for more jobs ("I'm not going to skimp on the sauce or jobs for Maine"); he was proud of running no negative ads. Baldacci won with 46% to Bennett's 41%. Bennett carried the western area and much of the coast, but Baldacci won solidly in Aroostook and carried the Bangor area as well.

In the House, Baldacci voted against the balanced budget amendment and pushed the gift ban—both positions supported by the Democratic leadership. But his independence in voting for key parts of the Contract With America could serve him well in this district.

The People: Pop. 1990: 591,400; 60% rural; 13% age 65+; 98% White; 1% Amer. Indian; 1% Hispanic origin. Voting age pop.: 440,155. Households: 60% married couple families; 28% married couple fams. w. children; 36% college educ.; median household income: $24,672; per capita income: $11,446; median gross rent: $365; median house value: $66,500.

1992 Presidential Vote			**1988 Presidential Vote**		
Clinton (D)	118,229	(38%)	Bush (R)	137,839	(55%)
Perot (I)	103,992	(33%)	Dukakis (D)	112,491	(45%)
Bush (R)	90,807	(29%)			

Rep. John Elias Baldacci (D)

Elected 1994; b. Jan. 30, 1955, Bangor; home, Bangor; U. of ME, B.A. 1986; Roman Catholic; married (Karen).

Career: Restauranteur; Bangor City Cncl., 1978–81; ME Senate, 1982–94.

DC Office: 1740 LHOB 20515, 202-225-6306; Fax: 202-225-2943.

District Offices: 202 Harlow St., P.O. Box 858, Bangor 04402, 207-942-6935; 157 Main St., Lewiston 04240, 207-782-3704; and 445 Main St., Presque Isle 04769, 207-764-1036.

Committees: *Agriculture* (22nd of 22 D): Department Operations, Nutrition and Foreign Agriculture; Resource Conservation, Research and Forestry.

Group Ratings and 103rd Congress Votes: Newly Elected

Key Votes of the 104th Congress

1. Congressional Compliance Y	6. Reform Crime Grant N	11. Loser Pays Court Reform N
2. Balanced Budget Amndmt. N	7. National Security Act N	12. Product Liability Reform N
3. Bar Unfunded Mandates Y	8. Moratorium on Regs. N	13. Welfare Reform N
4. Pass Line Item Veto Y	9. Risk Assessment on Regs. N	14. Term Limits Amndmt. Y
5. Relax Exclusionary Rule N	10. Expnd. Priv. Prop. Rights Y	15. Tax Cuts N

Election Results

1994 general	John Elias Baldacci (D)	109,615	(46%)	($442,226)
	Richard A. Bennett (R)	97,754	(41%)	($258,813)
	John M. Michael (I)	21,117	(9%)	($33,486)
	Charles FitzGerald (IMG)	11,353	(5%)	($647)
1994 primary	John Elias Baldacci (D)	12,191	(27%)	
	James F. Mitchell (D)	10,042	(23%)	
	Janet T. Mills (D)	7,896	(18%)	
	James P. Howaniec (D)	6,311	(14%)	
	Mary B. Cathcart (D)	5,606	(13%)	
	Jean Hay (D)	2,046	(5%)	
	Others	423	(1%)	
1992 general	Olympia J. Snowe (R)	153,022	(49%)	($746,611)
	Patrick K. McGowan (D)	130,824	(42%)	($382,410)
	Jonathan K. Carter (Green)	27,526	(9%)	($16,793)

MARYLAND

Maryland, at the midpoint of the 13 Colonies, just south of the Mason-Dixon Line and north of the lines between Union and Confederacy, lays claim to being the typical American state, yet stands out for its particularities. This was the only one of the 13 colonies founded by Roman Catholics—the Calvert family—and its embrace of religious tolerance came less from abstract principle than from the Calverts' desire to protect their property from Protestant monarchs. It was one of the two big Chesapeake colonies, overshadowed by Virginia, but with the same economy—one that traded directly with Britain and was based on tobacco cultivated by slave labor. In time, Virginia and Maryland went their separate ways, Virginia to become the capital of the Confederacy, Maryland to remain part of the Union, though grudgingly ("Maryland, My Maryland" condemns Abraham Lincoln's suppression of pro-Confederate rioters), and to become identified with the North.

The puritan impulse never was lively here: Prohibition was enforced only laxly in Baltimore, to the delight of its great journalist-cum-lexicographer, H.L. Mencken; slot machines were legal in the rural counties of the Western Shore. The state's law guaranteeing blacks equal access to public accommodations specifically excluded the Eastern Shore. By not pursuing any one course rigorously, Maryland could be many things at once: northern as well as southern, moralistic as well as libertine, industrial as well as rural, leaving people to their own devices yet with a heavy government presence. Perhaps as a result, much of Maryland's political history reads like a chronicle of rogues, from Luther Martin, the drunken haranguer at the Constitutional Convention, to Spiro Agnew, who took cash bribes as governor and vice president and resigned in 1973.

Maryland's genial tolerance may have given it a history a little too savory, but this state, perhaps because it is in so many ways typical, cherishes its sense of uniqueness. The Chesapeake Bay, for example, is the nation's largest estuary, with water saltier than a river but fresher than the ocean, with its unique watermen and shellfish. The terrapin and Chesapeake oyster may be so endangered as to be rare today, but Maryland blue crabs are still common, and the rockfish, once dwindling, can now be fished. Maryland likes its state bird (the Baltimore oriole), state flower (the black-eyed Susan), state dog (the Chesapeake Bay retriever), even if today's political correctness has made it convenient to forget the words to "Maryland, My Maryland."

Maryland also has some reason to be proud of the economy, or economies, it has built over the years. Half a century ago, half the state's population lived in the city of Baltimore and only one-fifth in suburbs. Now the proportions are the other way around, and then some: 15% Baltimore, 65% suburbs. And in 1992, the Census Bureau defined Washington and Baltimore as a single metropolitan area, the fourth largest in the country, with more than six million people. But this is a case of statistical definition at odds with practical reality. Baltimore and Washington are not fraternal, if sometimes quarrelsome, twins like Dallas and Fort Worth or Minneapolis and St. Paul; they are two quite separate cities, with different economic bases, and different attitudes toward public life. Baltimore started off as a port and an industrial city, and has managed to stay diversified and successful as it has spread out into the countryside from its new central core at the Inner Harbor and the solidly built edifices of its downtown grid streets. It makes spices and writes insurance; it headquarters one of the nation's giant power tool makers, Black & Decker, and one of its great investment banks, Alex Brown & Sons; it has big government operations, the headquarters of the Social Security Administration and, quietly down the road, the National Security Agency; it is home to the Orioles in their new, intentionally old-fashioned Oriole Park at Camden Yards and to Johns Hopkins University in Georgian buildings along the affluent corridor that runs directly north from downtown all the way to the developing edge city of Hunt Valley. "Bawlmer" retains its local accent and a fierce local pride, and is celebrated by artists as vivid in their own ways as Mencken was in his: the novelist Anne Tyler, and moviemaker Barry Levinson, who brings to life a Baltimore of the 1950s and 1960s that is at once both unique and universal—the Calverts' achievement all over again.

Baltimore remains the focus of Maryland's public life, for 50% of Marylanders still live in its metropolitan area, and its influence is far greater than Washington's on the Eastern Shore or in the western counties. Almost all of Maryland's successful statewide politicians—Governor Parris Glendening is an exception—come from the city of Baltimore or its very near suburbs. Many residents of suburban Washington counties—Montgomery and Prince George's—in contrast, have their focus elsewhere: Montgomery has a very large percentage of people from all over the nation, who moved here to be near the nation's capital and for whom residence in Maryland is a convenience, not a commitment; Prince George's has more black middle- and upper-income residents than any other county in America, most of them with roots in Washington or somewhere farther south. The Eastern Shore and the Western Shore counties south of Annapolis, in contrast, remain as fixated on things Maryland-ish as they are addicted to steamed crabs with characteristic Chesapeake spices: the Chesapeake origins of Maryland are never very far away. The uplands of the western counties, in contrast, are getting harder to distinguish from adjacent parts of Pennsylvania, Virginia and West Virginia.

Maryland is by most measures one of the nation's most Democratic states. Democratic presidential candidates ran relatively well here in the 1980s, with 47%, 47% and 48% of the vote; Maryland was one of Bill Clinton's very best states, as he won 50%–36% over George Bush. In statewide elections Democrats have not lost an election for senator or governor since liberal Republican Charles Mathias was reelected to the Senate in 1980. One reason for this is that 27% of Marylanders are black, according to 1995 Census Bureau projections, the highest percentage of any state outside the Deep South; even the prosperous blacks of Prince George's County still vote overwhelmingly Democratic. Another, overlapping reason is that this state and neighboring Virginia have by far the two highest percentages of federal and public employees, natural backers of the party of government. They help to keep the Washington suburbs solidly Democratic. The Eastern Shore and the western counties may go Republican; whites in the Baltimore metropolitan area may favor the Republicans, and often do; but the Democratic

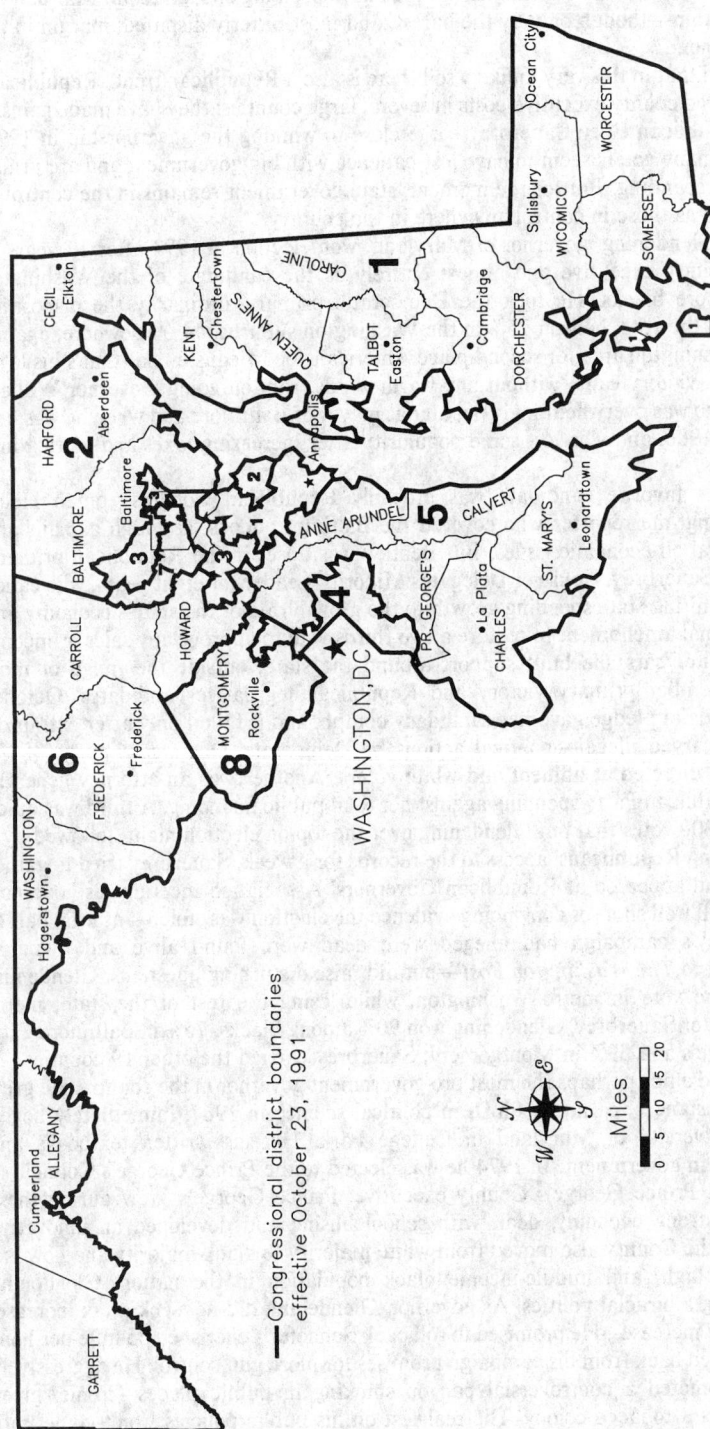

— Congressional district boundaries
effective October 23, 1991.

Copyright © 1993 by Election Data Services, Inc.

margins among blacks and in the Washington suburbs have been big enough to put Maryland in the Democratic column—though only by the barest, and most bitterly disputed, margin in the 1994 race for governor.

For it must be said that in this very unlikely soil there is also a Republican trend. Republicans have recently captured county executive posts in several large counties; they have made gains in the legislature; Republican Ellen Sauerbrey came close to winning the governorship in 1994. Even in Maryland, many voters seem to have lost patience with big government and are urging lower taxes and less spending. But for the moment, state government remains in the control of Democrats as liberal as those in control anywhere in the country.

Governor. Parris Glendening, governor of Maryland, won election in 1994 after 12 years as Prince George's County executive and almost entirely as the candidate of the Washington suburbs and Baltimore blacks. He took the Democratic primary, ordinarily the dispositive contest, with 54% of the vote; he won 75% in the Washington suburbs, 44% elsewhere, against 24% outside the Washington area for second-place American Joe Miedusiewski (that's his legal name). Glendening's victory came without any warm words from outgoing Governor William Donald Schaefer, who was overwhelmingly popular as mayor of Baltimore and when he was first elected governor in 1986, and who lost some popularity after increasing taxes and getting into various squabbles.

Indeed, Schaefer's favorite candidate was probably Republican Congresswoman Helen Delich Bentley, a longtime reporter who covered the Baltimore docks, as tough as nails and something of a liberal on economic issues. But Bentley was upset in the Republican primary, 52%–38%, by Ellen Sauerbrey, House of Delegates Minority Leader for eight years, who called for a 24% tax cut, limiting state spending growth to the growth rate of the state's economy and passing a constitutional amendment to require a two-thirds vote to approve any sales or income tax increase. For four years she built support around the state, outside the range of most reporters. Her September primary victory and Republican legislative candidates' October Contract With Maryland pledge gave her candidacy oomph, and it failed only after extraordinary—some have charged illegal—political actions by Democrats. One was a purge of the Baltimore City polls directed at affluent and white voters. Another was an attorney general's ruling counting Republican Party spending against her total public financing. A third was quick reporting of some 9,000 votes that put Glendening over the top on election night, followed by a court decision blocking Republicans' access to the records for a week. Sauerbrey tried to gather evidence of fraud and appeared at Republican Governors' Association meetings as governor-elect. Her findings fell well short of convincing evidence the election was stolen—at least half of the voters Sauerbrey's campaign had alleged were dead were found alive and living in Baltimore, according to *The Washington Post*—but did raise disturbing questions. Glendening won with 63% of the vote in metro Washington, while losing the rest of the state; metro Baltimore went 52% for Sauerbrey. Glendening won 90% among blacks, 75% in Baltimore City, 68% in Prince George's and 59% in Montgomery; Sauerbrey carried the other 19 counties.

Glendening entered office perhaps the most pro-government governor in the country. He grew up in modest circumstances, earned a Ph.D. in political science in 1967, immediately began teaching at the University of Maryland in College Park. He has written textbooks and participated actively in government. In 1974 he was elected to the Prince George's Council; in 1982 he was elected Prince George's County executive. Prince George's grew during these years, developed a strong economy, dealt with school busing and developed an innovative magnet school plan; the County also moved from white-majority to black-majority and now has perhaps the largest high- and middle-income black population in the nation. Glendening succeeded in building a biracial politics. As governor, Glendening did not seek a tax increase, but did seek spending increases. He promised to roll back Schaefer's cherished 55 mile-per-hour speed limit and stepped back from his campaign promises for more gun control. He aggressively and successfully promoted a controversial ban on smoking in public places—ironic, given Maryland's history as a tobacco colony. The real test on his public policies won't come until

1998: Maryland elects its legislators as well as its governor to four-year terms.

Senators. Paul Sarbanes was first elected to the Maryland House of Delegates in 1966, to the House in 1970, to the Senate in 1976: three decades as a legislator. His liberalism is rooted in his experience growing up in Salisbury on the Eastern Shore, the son of a Greek immigrant who owned the Mayflower Grill and taught himself enough on the side to discuss philosophy with his son's Princeton professors. As a big-firm lawyer in Baltimore, Paul Sarbanes got started in local politics campaigning in small groups, talking to voters and leaders, listening gravely to what they had to say. Tabbed early as a reformer, in the state legislature he voted against Marvin Mandel to replace Spiro Agnew as governor in 1969—not the most politic move. He beat a long-time incumbent congressman in the 1970 primary and in 1976 defeated former Senator Joseph Tydings in the primary and incumbent Senator Glenn Beall in the general by 59%–41%.

Sarbanes has been one of the most durable champions of the liberal politics of the early years of his career. He has pushed liberal economic policies on the Joint Economic Committee and the Budget Committee. In 1991 and 1992, he proposed a short-term economic stimulus package and extended unemployment benefits; he had long argued that the growth in the 1980s was illusory or confined to the rich. He also has sought more power by elected politicians over the Federal Reserve, but his bill to take the 12 regional bank presidents off the Federal Open Market Committee and make them advisers there never made it out of committee in the 103d Congress, and such a proposal has faint prospect in the 104th. However, Sarbanes clearly wants more stimulative monetary policies over time. "I have a sense of excitement," Sarbanes said just before the 1992 election, anticipating the result. "We've been through 12 years of sheer torture . . . Now, I think that we can show the country that we can govern." He must have been disappointed with the results. The Clinton economic stimulus package failed in the Senate, and while interest rates stayed low in 1993, they were increased in 1994 by a Fed whose independence Clinton expressly recognized. The 1994 Republican takeover brought more disappointment, denying him the Banking Committee chairmanship that was within his grasp. Sarbanes could take satisfaction, however, in the passage of the Family and Medical Leave Act and extended unemployment compensation. On foreign policy, Sarbanes has been mostly faithful to the liberalism of the 1970s, skeptical of foreign military involvement, eager for nuclear disarmament. He is a senior member of the Foreign Relations Committee, where one of his big projects has been reforming the foreign aid program, which has been carried over year to year without reauthorization until 1991. Given foreign aid's current unpopularity, and the particular interests of various countries, this is a tough job.

Sarbanes is an unusually quiet senator. He lives in Baltimore but actively disdains publicity: he sponsors relatively few bills and seldom seeks the limelight. Yet he was reelected in 1982 and 1988 with 63% and 62%, carrying Baltimore area whites and blacks and running mostly on party lines elsewhere—stronger around his boyhood home of Salisbury. In 1994, as his hopes for the success of the Clinton Administration turned sour, several Republicans ran against Sarbanes. The best known was Bill Brock, elected congressman from Tennessee in 1962 and senator in 1970, defeated in 1976. He then did a stint as Republican National Committee chairman and as a Special U.S. Trade Representative; he moved to the Annapolis area in 1988, became a lobbyist, and started paying Maryland taxes in 1990. Naturally he was attacked as a carpetbagger, first by primary opponent Ruthann Aron, a Montgomery County developer, and then by Sarbanes. Brock won over Aron unimpressively, 38%–26%. Sarbanes campaigned very little and refused to debate until the last two weeks. He vowed to fight for economic growth and lower interest rates and said Brock was "not really into this state." Brock, seeking to become the first popularly elected senator from two different states, spent $1.6 million of his own money, ran ads on crime and argued that our "value-free education" was not inculcating a sense of right and wrong or teaching the value of institutions. But while Ellen Sauerbrey's anti-tax gubernatorial campaign captured voters' attention, Brock's, for whatever reasons, did not. Sarbanes won 59%– 41%, slightly less than in the 1980s, but still convincingly. His 1994 margin was greatest in metro Washington, and he carried metro Baltimore as well. But once again he found himself in the

Senate minority.

Barbara Mikulski came to the Senate with deep roots in immigrant urban America, and more than most there she seems fascinated by the new technology and jobs growing on the outer edges of the urban areas, many of which are held by people with backgrounds like her own. Her roots are in east Baltimore, where her Polish immigrant parents ran a bakery. She got her start in politics as a social worker, organizing in Highlandtown to stop a highway from going through. She won, and in the process was elected to the Baltimore City Council in 1971, in time to serve (and spar) with the then new mayor, Donald Schaefer. As a local official with genuine ethnic roots and a woman with genuine liberal impulses, she was chosen head of the Democratic National Committee's Commission on Delegate Selection in 1972. She ran for the Senate in 1974, and got a respectable 43% against Charles Mathias; when Paul Sarbanes ran for the other Senate seat in 1976, Mikulski ran for his 3d District seat and won. Ten years later, she gave up that seat for what seemed like a chancy Senate race, and won handily, with 50% in the primary to 31% for Montgomery County Congressman Michael Barnes and 14% for Governor Harry Hughes. In the general, she beat former White House aide Linda Chavez, 61%–39%.

Mikulski is loud and brash, humorous and warm, brusque and aggressive when she feels it is necessary, curious and thoughtful when encountering another new part of the world. She knows Baltimore warp and woof—its neighborhoods and government agencies, charitable institutions and ethnic politicians—and she still lives there, in the Fells Point neighborhood being restored on the waterfront. Fells Point and Don Schaefer's Harborplace, she points out, stand where the highway she opposed was supposed to pass. But she also became, thanks to the Appropriations subcommittee chairmanship she held for six years and lots of hard work, the Senate's chief superintendent of the space program and an enthusiast for space exploration. An ardent backer of the manned Space Station *Freedom* often attacked by other liberals, she has battled to keep it alive, despite her sympathy for veterans' and housing programs also funded by her subcommittee which, under current budget procedures, tend to be competitors for the same fixed pool of funds. She also wants to change the culture of science agencies while defending them against attacks by budget-cutters. On foreign policy, she usually votes with the doves and opposed the Gulf war resolution, but was attentive even in the Cold War years to human rights violations in left-wing as well as right-wing countries.

On domestic policy, Mikulski is a liberal who insists that "where there are rights there are responsibilities." With Sam Nunn, she was a major Senate backer of Ted Kennedy's national service bill that produced AmeriCorps in 1993; two years later, when the program came under Republican attack, she made a lengthy floor speech in its defense. Overall, her voting record is somewhat less liberal than Sarbanes's. She supported workfare before Bill Clinton took office, and in 1995 said welfare reform "should replace welfare with work, reward those who practice self-help, eliminate the disincentives that undercut people getting off and staying off welfare." She added, "I believe the role of men is key to reforming welfare." More generally, she has criticized her fellow Democrats for being "angst-addicted" and wrote, "Being politically effective means helping those who are not middle class get there through hard work and practicing self-help. Democrats must figure out what works." On housing, an area where she has expertise, she said, "A series of complicated rules and boutique programs have rewarded the wrong kind of behavior and made housing projects Zip Codes of pathology."

Mikulski has been a strong proponent of policies to stop sexual harassment: she vocally defended Anita Hill during the Clarence Thomas hearings; with other woman senators of both parties, she opposed the retirement of Admiral Frank Kelso with four-star rank because of the Tailhook scandal; she chastised the allegedly discriminatory employment practices of Architect of the Capitol George White, making it politically impossible for him to win reappointment. She also co-sponsored Texas Republican Kay Bailey Hutchison's bill to make it easier for homemakers to set up IRAs. Mikulski has not been shy about using her Appropriations seat to help Maryland projects, from the National Institutes of Health in Bethesda to the Baltimore Veterans Affairs program to the Goddard Space Flight Center in Prince George's County to a new $130 million marine biotechnology center in Baltimore.

In 1992, Mikulski was opposed by Alan Keyes, a former Reagan appointee who ran against Sarbanes in 1988 and in 1995 announced for president. Articulate and angry, Keyes did not get much attention, while Mikulski remained affirmatively popular and won with 71%. Now she is in the minority for the first time in her congressional career. But she is also part of the leadership, having supported Tom Daschle for Minority Leader and then winning the position of Secretary of the Democratic Conference in December 1994.

Presidential politics. Maryland is one of the most Democratic states in presidential elections. It voted for Jimmy Carter in 1980, came close to voting for Walter Mondale and Michael Dukakis in 1984 and 1988 and, with New York, gave Bill Clinton his highest percentage in the country after the District of Columbia and Arkansas. Black voters and liberal Washington suburbanites have provided the key votes for this trend. Yet the Democratic percentages—47%, 47%, 48%, 50%—suggest that there may be a ceiling for national Democrats, or at least one they can't exceed until they win over more Baltimore-area whites.

In 1992, Maryland held its primary a week before Super Tuesday, on March 3, to avoid being ignored as it mostly was on Super Tuesday 1988. Paul Tsongas led Bill Clinton 41%–33%, with all his margin and more coming from suburban Baltimore and Montgomery County.

Congressional districting. Population movements to the suburbs and the Voting Rights Act mandate to maximize the number of black-majority districts made 1992 redistricting a politically wrenching process for Maryland. The legislature worked hard to create a new black-majority Prince George's County seat and still leave a Democratic district for House power Steny Hoyer; so far it has succeeded. The loser was Democrat Tom McMillen, who was put in with Republican Wayne Gilchrest and lost. That and the defeat of Beverly Byron in the primary removed the last conservative Democrats from the Maryland delegation and created a House delegation evenly balanced between the two parties.

The People: Est. Pop. 1994: 5,006,000; Pop. 1990: 4,781,468, up 4.7% 1990–1994. 2.0% of U.S. total, 19th largest; 19% rural. Median age: 33.0 years. 10.8% 65 years and over. 71.0% White, 24.9% Black, 2.9% Asian, 2.6% Hispanic origin. Households: 54.2% married couple families; 26% married couple fams. w. children; 50% college educ.; median household income: $39,386; per capita income: $17,730; 65.0% owner occupied housing; median house value: $116,500; median monthly rent: $473. 6.6% Unemployment. 1994 Voting age pop.: 3,750,000. 1994 Turnout: 1,361,803; 36% of VAP. Registered voters (1994): 2,367,166; 1,442,927 D (61%); 694,982 R (29%); 229,257 unaffiliated and minor parties (10%).

Political Lineup: Governor, Parris N. Glendening (D); Lt. Gov., Kathleen Kennedy Townsend (D); Secy. of State, Tyras Athey (D); Atty. Gen., J. Joseph Curran, Jr. (D); Treasurer, Lucille Maurer (D); Comptroller, Louis L. Goldstein (D). State Senate, 47 (32 D and 15 R); State House of Delegates, 141 (100 D and 41 R). Senators, Paul S. Sarbanes (D) and Barbara A. Mikulski (D). Representatives, 8 (4 R and 4 D).

1992 Presidential Vote

Clinton (D)	988,571	(50%)
Bush (R)	707,094	(36%)
Perot (I)	281,414	(14%)

1992 Democratic Presidential Primary

Tsongas	230,490	(41%)
Clinton	189,906	(33%)
Brown	46,480	(8%)
Harkin	32,899	(6%)
Kerrey	27,035	(5%)
Uncommitted	36,155	(6%)

1988 Presidential Vote

Bush (R)	876,167	(51%)
Dukakis (D)	826,304	(48%)

1992 Republican Presidential Primary

Bush	168,364	(70%)
Buchanan	71,647	(30%)

GOVERNOR

Gov. Parris N. Glendening (D)

Elected 1994, term expires Jan. 1999; b. June 11, 1942, Bronx, NY; home, University Park; FL St. U., B.A. 1964, M.A. 1965, Ph.D. 1967; Roman Catholic; married (Frances).

Career: Prof., U. of MD, 1967–94; Hyattsville City Cncl., 1973–74; Prince George's Cnty. Council, 1974–82; Prince George's Cnty. Exec., 1982–94.

Office: State House, Annapolis 21401, 410-974-3901; Fax: 410-974-2542.

Election Results

1994 gen.	Parris N. Glendening (D)......	708,094	(50%)
	Ellen R. Sauerbrey (R).......	702,101	(50%)
1994 prim.	Parris N. Glendening (D)......	293,314	(54%)
	American Joe Miedusiewski (D)	100,326	(18%)
	Melvin Steinberg (D)..........	82,308	(15%)
	Mary Boergers (D)............	46,888	(9%)
	Others.....................	24,567	(4%)
1990 gen.	William Donald Schaefer (D) ..	664,015	(60%)
	William S. Shepard (R).......	446,980	(40%)

SENATORS

Sen. Paul S. Sarbanes (D)

Elected 1976, seat up 2000; b. Feb. 3, 1933, Salisbury; home, Baltimore; Princeton, A.B. 1954, Rhodes Scholar, Oxford U., B.A. 1957, Harvard, LL.B. 1960; Greek Orthodox; married (Christine).

Career: Law Clerk, Judge Morris A. Soper, U.S. 4th Circuit Crt. of Appeals, 1960–61; Practicing atty., 1961–62, 1965–70; A.A., Pres. Kennedy's Cncl. of Econ. Advisers, 1962–63; Exec. Dir., Baltimore Charter Revision Comm., 1963–64; MD House of Delegates, 1966–70; U.S. House of Reps., 1971–77.

DC Office: 309 HSOB 20510, 202-224-4524; Fax: 202-224-1651.

State Offices: 100 S. Charles St., #1010, Baltimore 21201, 410-962-4436; 1110 Bonifant St., #450, Silver Spring 20910, 301-589-0797; 111 Baptist St., #115, Salisbury 21801, 410-860-2131; 47 S.E. Crain Hwy., Box 331, Cobb Island 20625, 301-259-2404; and 141 Baltimore St., #206, Cumberland 21502, 301-724-4660.

Committees: *Banking, Housing & Urban Affairs* (RMM of 7 D): Budget (8th of 10 D). *Foreign Relations* (3rd of 8 D): European Affairs; International Economic Policy, Export and Trade Promotion (RMM); Near Eastern and South Asian Affairs. *Joint Economic Committee* (8th of 10 Sen.)

Group Ratings

	ADA	ACLU	COPE	CFA	LCV	CON	NSI	COC	ACU	NTLC	CHC
1994	95	79	88	83	92	8	0	19	0	4	0
1993	95	—	91	90	88	12	—	18	0	—	—

National Journal Ratings

	1993 LIB — 1993 CONS	1994 LIB — 1994 CONS
Economic	71% — 17%	84% — 0%
Social	82% — 15%	76% — 19%
Foreign	87% — 8%	87% — 6%

Key Votes of the 103d Congress

1. Clinton Deficit Plan	Y	3. Brady Handgun Purchase	Y	5. Lmt. UN Cmnd. of Forces	N
2. NAFTA	N	4. Strike Race/Death Pnlty.	N	6. Cut Missile Funds	Y

Key Votes of the 104th Congress

1. Congressional Compliance	Y	3. Balanced Budget Amndt.	N	5. Product Liability Reform	N
2. Bar Unfunded Mandates	N	4. Pass Line Item Veto	N	6. FY96 Budget	N

Election Results

1994 general	Paul S. Sarbanes (D)	809,125	(59%)	($2,767,187)
	William Brock (R)	559,908	(41%)	($3,201,650)
1994 primary	Paul S. Sarbanes (D)	382,115	(79%)	
	John B. Liston (D)	52,031	(11%)	
	Dennard A. Gayle (D)	30,665	(6%)	
	Leonard E. Trout (D)	19,393	(4%)	
1988 general	Paul S. Sarbanes (D)	999,166	(62%)	($1,466,477)
	Alan L. Keyes (R)	617,537	(38%)	($662,651)

Sen. Barbara A. Mikulski (D)

Elected 1986, seat up 1998; b. July 20, 1936, Baltimore; home, Baltimore; Mt. St. Agnes Col., B.A. 1958, U. of MD, M.S.W. 1965; Catholic; single.

Career: Social worker, admin., Baltimore Dept. of Social Svcs., 1965–70; Baltimore City Cncl., 1971–76; Adjunct prof., Loyola Col., 1972–76; Chmn., DNC Delegate Selection Comm., 1972; U.S. House of Reps., 1976–86.

DC Office: 709 HSOB 20510, 202-224-4654; Fax: 202-224-8858.

State Offices: 253 World Trade Ctr., 401 E. Pratt St., Baltimore 21202, 410-962-4510; 60 West St., #202, Annapolis 21401, 410-263-1805; 9658 Baltimore Ave., #208, College Park 20740, 301-345-5517; 1201 Pemberton, Salisbury 21801, 410-546-7711; and 82 W. Washington St., #301, Hagerstown 21740, 301-797-2826.

Committees: *Democratic Conference Secretary. Appropriations* (9th of 13 D): Foreign Operations; Legislative Branch; Transportation; Treasury, Postal Service and General Government; VA, HUD and Independent Agencies (RMM). *Labor & Human Resources* (6th of 7 D): Aging (RMM); Education, Arts and Humanities. *Ethics* (2nd of 3 D).

Group Ratings

	ADA	ACLU	COPE	CFA	LCV	CON	NSI	COC	ACU	NTLC	CHC
1994	85	74	75	75	85	1	10	25	0	8	0
1993	85	—	100	80	75	1	—	27	4	—	—

National Journal Ratings

	1993 LIB	—	1993 CONS	1994 LIB	—	1994 CONS
Economic	71%	—	17%	68%	—	29%
Social	73%	—	25%	71%	—	26%
Foreign	71%	—	24%	65%	—	34%

Key Votes of the 103d Congress

1. Clinton Deficit Plan	Y	3. Brady Handgun Purchase Y	5. Lmt. UN Cmnd. of Forces N
2. NAFTA	N	4. Strike Race/Death Pnlty. N	6. Cut Missile Funds N

Key Votes of the 104th Congress

1. Congressional Compliance Y	3. Balanced Budget Amndt. N	5. Product Liability Reform Y
2. Bar Unfunded Mandates Y	4. Pass Line Item Veto N	6. FY96 Budget *

Election Results

1992 general	Barbara A. Mikulski (D)	1,307,610	(71%)	($3,623,974)
	Alan L. Keyes (R)	533,688	(29%)	($1,175,682)
1992 primary	Barbara A. Mikulski (D)	376,444	(77%)	
	Thomas M. Wheatley (D)	31,214	(6%)	
	Walter Boyd (D)	26,467	(5%)	
	Don Allensworth (D)	19,731	(4%)	
	Others	36,621	(8%)	
1986 general	Barbara A. Mikulski (D)	675,225	(61%)	($2,097,216)
	Linda Chavez (R)	437,411	(39%)	($1,699,175)

FIRST DISTRICT

The largest estuary in North America, the Chesapeake Bay, was the central focus of the most thickly settled of the 13 colonies, and today it remains a central focus for much of booming Maryland—and a backwater where remnants of an older civilization live on. The first British here were amazed at the Chesapeake's oysters and terrapin turtles and crabs and rockfish; despite pollution, watermen still make hardy livings bringing them to shore. This was an estuary civilization in colonial days, every little hamlet tied to mother England by the highways of bays and creeks and inlets off the Chesapeake. Old settlements like Chestertown, Oxford, St. Michaels and Cambridge don't look much different from when George Washington slept there. On the Western Shore, Annapolis was laid out as a capital in 1694, with one circle planned for the State House and one for the Church; the marble-halled State House, built in 1772, where the Continental Congress ratified the Treaty of Paris, is the oldest state capitol in continuous use. Annapolis is the home of the United States Naval Academy and its waterfront, though gentrified, is a waterman's as well as a yachter's port.

In post-colonial times, when most Americans were caught up in the romance of westward movement, these estuaries and peninsulas were forgotten, off the main lines of railroads and highways. Some of the Chesapeake has been changed beyond recognition—Baltimore, for instance, or the condominiums and strip malls spread out along Kent Island at the eastern foot of the Bay Bridge. But much has evolved slowly and with a certain continuity. The Eastern Shore counties of Maryland in the 160 years between 1790 and 1950 only doubled in population, perhaps the slowest growth rate on the Eastern Seaboard; and if its towns are industrial today, with little factories and mechanized farms, they still seem antique and the landscape is not vastly different from a century or two ago. There is some change now, as northeastern metropolitan expansion reaches south from the northern end of the Bay or east across the Bridge, and the Eastern Shore becomes increasingly second-home and vacation country, and businesses like Frank Perdue's chicken empire around Salisbury grow. But this is still an old-fashioned

America, a country left behind which many would like to find again.

The 1st Congressional District of Maryland includes all of the Eastern Shore and a segment of Maryland west of the Bay, including Annapolis and a strip of four-lane highway suburbs up to the southern rowhouse tip of Baltimore. In national elections, this is a solidly Republican area—George Bush carried it handily in 1992—and it tends toward the conservative on issues like gun control and abortion.

The congressman from the 1st District is Wayne Gilchrest, a Republican with an unusual political history and some unusual political views. Gilchrest served in the Marine Corps in Vietnam, taught high school for 17 years and painted houses in the summer. In 1988, Gilchrest ran for Congress and lost to incumbent Democrat Roy Dyson 50.4%–49.6%; Dyson spent vastly more money but was embarrassed by a *Washington Post* story on his personnel practices. In 1990, Gilchrest ran again, again was vastly outspent, but won 57%–43%. Then redistricting placed him in the same district with Democratic incumbent Tom McMillen, former Rhodes Scholar and star basketball player for the University of Maryland and the NBA's Capital Bullets. McMillen spent over $1.5 million to Gilchrest's $395,000 and had a moderate record and celebrity status. Gilchrest won his primary against two serious opponents with an unimpressive 47%. But Gilchrest represented 53% of the new district, and the Eastern Shore has a certain clannishness, which increased when insulted by Governor William Donald Schaefer. Probably decisive was a Gilchrest radio ad accusing McMillen of taking many congressional junkets; one ad had McMillen on a plane to Japan, with a flight attendant asking, "More sushi, Mr. McMillen?" The ad went on to assert that Gilchrest took only one trip, driving his pickup to Ocean City, to address fellow members of the Order of the Purple Heart: "Box of saltwater taffy, Mr. Gilchrest?" Gilchrest won 52%–48%, carrying 60% on the Eastern Shore.

In the House, Gilchrest has a moderate record for a Republican. He was the first Maryland congressman to endorse NAFTA, he was the only Maryland member to vote for D.C. statehood, and he voted for the assault weapons ban—in a district assumed to be vehemently opposed to gun control. But in 1994 this seemed to suit 1st District voters just fine, and he was reelected with 68% of the vote. Gilchrest serves on the Transportation and Infrastructure Committee, where he chairs the Public Buildings and Economic Development Subcommittee. He also sits on the Resources Committee, from which he threatened to resign in March 1995 when committee Chairman Richard Pombo of California refused to let Gilchrest invite scientists to testify in support of the Endangered Species Act at field hearings held in his district. Although he supported most of the Contract With America, he subsequently revealed his unhappiness with the new majority's handling of the Clean Water Act revision when he wrote in *The Baltimore Sun* that the bill "moved too quickly for members to know what they were voting on." He despaired that "the environmental movement has to start all over again," adding of his opponents, "I have never seen so many people afraid of information in my life [or] so extravagantly funded by interest groups that stand to make a lot of money from misinformation." Although national conservatives criticize him as out of step with his district's opposition to excessive federal regulation of wetlands, his political performance suggests otherwise.

The People: Pop. 1990: 597,821; 46% rural; 12% age 65+; 83% White; 15% Black; 1% Asian; 1% Hispanic origin. Voting age pop.: 455,221; 14% Black; 1% Hispanic origin. Households: 59% married couple families; 26% married couple fams. w. children; 42% college educ.; median household income: $35,115; per capita income: $16,104; median gross rent: $487; median house value: $100,500.

1992 Presidential Vote		
Bush (R)	109,039	(44%)
Clinton (D)	93,165	(37%)
Perot (I)	47,188	(19%)

1988 Presidential Vote		
Bush (R)	132,532	(63%)
Dukakis (D)	77,331	(37%)

Rep. Wayne T. Gilchrest (R)

Elected 1990; b. Apr. 15, 1946, Rahway, NJ; home, Kennedyville; Wesley Col., A.A. 1971, DE St. Col., B.A. 1973, Loyola Col., 1984; Methodist; married (Barbara).

Career: Marine Corps, 1964–67 (Vietnam); High schl. teacher, 1973–90.

DC Office: 332 CHOB 20515, 202-225-5311; Fax: 202-225-0254.

District Offices: 1 Plaza E., Salisbury 21801, 410-749-3184; 521 Washington Ave., Chestertown 21620, 410-778-9407; and 101 Crain Hwy., NW, #509, Glen Burnie 21061, 410-760-3372.

Committees: *Resources* (9th of 25 R): Fisheries, Wildlife and Oceans; Native American and Insular Affairs. *Transportation & Infrastructure* (13th of 33 R): Public Buildings and Economic Development (Chmn.); Water Resources and Environment.

Group Ratings

	ADA	ACLU	COPE	CFA	LCV	CON	NSI	COC	ACU	NTLC	CHC
1994	30	35	22	40	88	90	80	100	62	85	71
1993	30	—	33	50	93	96	—	90	63	—	—

National Journal Ratings

	1993 LIB — 1993 CONS	1994 LIB — 1994 CONS
Economic	32% — 66%	30% — 67%
Social	52% — 48%	43% — 56%
Foreign	37% — 60%	47% — 52%

Key Votes of the 103d Congress

1. Clinton Deficit Plan	N	3. Brady Handgun Purchase Y	5. Lmt. UN Cmnd. of Forces Y
2. NAFTA	Y	4. Strike Race/Death Pnlty. Y	6. Cut Missile Funds Y

Key Votes of the 104th Congress

1. Congressional Compliance Y	6. Reform Crime Grant Y	11. Loser Pays Court Reform Y
2. Balanced Budget Amndmt. Y	7. National Security Act Y	12. Product Liability Reform Y
3. Bar Unfunded Mandates Y	8. Moratorium on Regs. Y	13. Welfare Reform Y
4. Pass Line Item Veto Y	9. Risk Assessment on Regs. Y	14. Term Limits Amndmt. Y
5. Relax Exclusionary Rule Y	10. Expnd. Priv. Prop. Rights N	15. Tax Cuts Y

Election Results

1994 general	Wayne T. Gilchrest (R)	120,975	(68%)	($153,133)
	Ralph T. Gies (D)	57,712	(32%)	($30,612)
1994 primary	Wayne T. Gilchrest (R)	24,358	(65%)	
	Scott L. Meredith (R)	6,152	(16%)	
	Bradlyn McClanahan (R)	4,419	(12%)	
	George Williams (R)	2,504	(7%)	
1992 general	Wayne T. Gilchrest (R)	120,084	(52%)	($395,104)
	Thomas McMillen (D)	112,771	(48%)	($1,553,849)

SECOND DISTRICT

The spokes of Baltimore's streets spread out in all directions from the downtown centered on the Inner Harbor, connecting the central city with the suburbs where most residents of metropolitan Baltimore now live. The streets reach east to Dundalk and Essex, industrial suburbs where the tone of life was set for years by the giant Sparrows Point steel mill, long the biggest in the country. Northeast they extend to modest working class suburbs and the small towns of the Baltimore and Harford County countryside which are now speckled with suburban developments—Bel Air, Joppatowne, Aberdeen, Edgewood, the last two near the Aberdeen Proving Grounds and Edgewood Arsenal military installations. Straight north from downtown are the higher-income suburbs, the county seat of Towson, and farther north are Lutherville, Timonium, Cockeysville, Hunt Valley, all flanked by the Baltimore County hunt country. The McCormick food company is headquartered in Hunt Valley; Black and Decker is in Towson.

The 2d Congressional District of Maryland takes up most of this territory. The Sparrows Point area political tradition is union and Democratic, but that has been tempered lately. The northeast suburbs are ancestrally Democratic, but culturally rather conservative; the suburbs to the north are solidly Republican. Legislative and local offices are mostly held by Democrats, but a Republican won the Baltimore County executive post in 1990, which the party had not held since Spiro Agnew became governor in 1966; and a Republican has represented the 2d in the House since 1984.

The current congressman from the 2d is Bob Ehrlich, a Republican first elected in 1994, to succeed the tough-as-nails Helen Bentley, aggressive promoter of the port of Baltimore, who ran for governor and was upset in the Republican primary by tax-cut advocate Ellen Sauerbrey. Ehrlich has an appealing personal story and good political skills. He grew up in a rowhouse in the modest suburb of Arbutus, the son of a car salesman. A six footer at 13, he got a football scholarship to the elite Gilman School in Baltimore and then to Princeton; he went to law school at Wake Forest and practiced law in Baltimore. He volunteered in Republican campaigns in 1982 and 1984 and then ran for House of Delegates in 1986 and was elected. There he worked on tough sentencing and child pornography laws, but also opposed some bills as unneeded or unconstitutional. In a heavily Democratic House, "I was successful because I built coalitions between Democrats and Republicans." Running against an anti-abortion candidate in the primary, Ehrlich said he was pro-business, a military hawk, libertarian and wanted to continue in Bentley's path; he won 57%–38%. Meanwhile, there was a close Democratic primary between Delegates Gerry Brewster and Connie Galiazzo DeJuliis. Brewster, the son of former Congressman and Senator Daniel Brewster, was more moderate; Galiazzo, from Dundalk, portrayed herself as a fighter, and held Brewster to a 38%–35% victory.

There were eerie similarities between Ehrlich and Brewster: they were classmates at the private Gilman School and Princeton, served together in the House of Delegates and on the Judiciary Committee, spent almost identical amounts in the campaign (except that Brewster spent $92,000 of his own money). Ehrlich campaigned against the House Democratic leadership and signed the Contract With America, though he opposed term limits. He was enthusiastic about tax cuts, which fit in with Ellen Sauerbrey's surprisingly successful gubernatorial campaign. He ran ads showing the rowhouse where he grew up and saying the most important lessons he learned were around the dining room table. The race was expected to be close, but Maryland's Democratic tradition and the Brewster family background led insiders to overestimate Brewster's chances. This was a Republican-leaning district with a strong Republican candidate in a very Republican year, and Ehrlich won 63%–37%.

In the 104th Congress, Ehrlich serves on the Banking and Government Reform and Oversight Committees. True to his word, he was one of six freshmen to break with the GOP leadership and oppose term limits.

The People: Pop. 1990: 597,450; 18% rural; 12% age 65+; 92% White; 6% Black; 2% Asian; 1% Hispanic origin. Voting age pop.: 456,798; 5% Black; 1% Hispanic origin. Households: 62% married couple families; 28% married couple fams. w. children; 47% college educ.; median household income: $40,120; per capita income: $17,931; median gross rent: $507; median house value: $110,500.

1992 Presidential Vote			1988 Presidential Vote		
Bush (R)	121,087	(44%)	Bush (R)	146,902	(64%)
Clinton (D)	98,267	(36%)	Dukakis (D)	83,490	(36%)
Perot (I)	52,668	(19%)			

Rep. Robert L. Ehrlich, Jr. (R)

Elected 1994; b. Nov. 25, 1957, Arbutus; home, Timonium; Princeton U., B.A. 1979, Wake Forest U., J.D. 1982; Methodist; married (Kendel).

Career: Practicing atty., 1982–94; MD House of Delegates, 1986–94.

DC Office: 315 CHOB 20515, 202-225-3061; Fax: 202-225-3094.

District Offices: 1407 York Rd., Lutherville 21093, 410-337-7222; and 45 N. Main St., Bel Air 21014, 410-838-2517.

Committees: *Banking & Financial Services* (18th of 27 R): Financial Institutions and Consumer Credit; Housing and Community Opportunity. *Government Reform & Oversight* (27th of 27 R): National Economic Growth, Natural Resources and Regulatory Affairs; National Security, International Affairs and Criminal Justice; Postal Service.

Group Ratings and 103rd Congress Votes: Newly Elected

Key Votes of the 104th Congress

1. Congressional Compliance	Y	6. Reform Crime Grant	Y	11. Loser Pays Court Reform	N
2. Balanced Budget Amndmt.	Y	7. National Security Act	Y	12. Product Liability Reform	Y
3. Bar Unfunded Mandates	Y	8. Moratorium on Regs.	Y	13. Welfare Reform	Y
4. Pass Line Item Veto	Y	9. Risk Assessment on Regs.	Y	14. Term Limits Amndmt.	N
5. Relax Exclusionary Rule	Y	10. Expnd. Priv. Prop. Rights	Y	15. Tax Cuts	Y

Election Results

1994 general	Robert L. Ehrlich, Jr. (R)	125,162	(63%)	($562,892)
	Gerry L. Brewster (D)	74,275	(37%)	($550,471)
1994 primary	Robert L. Ehrlich, Jr. (R)	21,397	(57%)	
	William J. Frank (R)	14,218	(38%)	
	John Michael Fleig (R)	1,817	(5%)	
1992 general	Helen Delich Bentley (R)	165,443	(65%)	($956,821)
	Michael C. Hickey (D)	88,658	(35%)	($48,841)

THIRD DISTRICT

Baltimore is no longer a well-kept secret. Its Inner Harbor and new Camden Yards baseball stadium are now national tourist attractions. Its charms have been emblazoned on the national consciousness by Anne Tyler's novels and Barry Levinson's and John Waters's movies. Even its cuisine—steamed crabs with Baltimore spices, crab cakes—has become known beyond the watershed of the Chesapeake Bay. The central city of Baltimore certainly has its problems—high crime, poor schools, fiscal problems—but the greater Baltimore that slops over both sides of the Baltimore City and County lines retains a distinctive character. There is a patina of age, as on its Washington Monument, built in 1829 and recently refurbished, and the townhouses of Mount Vernon Square and an atmosphere of tolerance and diversity nurtured by Maryland's founding Catholics in search of liberty; the nation's first Catholic diocese and cathedral were built here when America was overwhelmingly and militantly Protestant. And this is a city built solidly on commerce which has always known how to reap its pleasures.

The 3d Congressional District of Maryland is centered on Baltimore and consists of three portions that extend outward like spokes of a wheel from the focus of metropolitan Baltimore at the Inner Harbor. The three spokes are connected by narrow bridges of land, with boundaries designed to build a black-majority 7th District next door. From the harbor, the 3d extends northeast out into the Polish Highlandtown neighborhood and the mostly white Catholic northeast precincts and close-in suburbs of Overlea and Parkville. It extends northwest to the heavily Jewish suburbs of Pikesville and Owings Mills, past the array of temples and synagogues on Park Heights Avenue to the open subdivisions where the newest Jewish neighborhoods are being built. And it extends southwest, past old rowhouse neighborhoods overlooking Fort McHenry, where Francis Scott Key saw by the dawn's early light the star-spangled banner, out past Arbutus and Lansdowne into Linthicum and Fort Meade in Anne Arundel County and Elkridge and Columbia in Howard County. Here lies the cusp of the Baltimore-Washington boundary; for Columbia, now a 30-something "new town" draws from both metro areas. Ancestrally Democratic, this district is now contested territory. Pikesville and Columbia are solidly liberal on most issues; the northeast and close-in southeast areas are culturally more conservative.

The congressman from the 3d is Benjamin Cardin, former speaker of the Maryland House of Delegates and one of the many bright politicos produced by the Jewish neighborhoods of northwest Baltimore, where he grew up. He was elected to the House of Delegates in 1966, at 23, the first time he was eligible to run; after serving there for 20 years, he was easily elected to Congress in 1986 when Barbara Mikulski ran for the Senate. In the House, Cardin has been an inside player. He got a seat on Ways and Means in October 1989, with the support of Chairman Dan Rostenkowski; he worked to revise 401(k) savings plans and to simplify pension rules, as well as developing his own Flexible Medical Access Act healthcare plan. In January 1995, he advanced a bill to restore the tax deduction for health insurance for the self-employed, which the new Republican-controlled Ways and Means Committee quickly drafted and President Clinton signed. He also worked with committee Republicans to pass a cap on medical malpractice damages, and to increase the tax on tobacco. He sponsored the Chesapeake Bay Restoration Act. Cardin serves on the Ethics Committee and worked to clean up the House bank scandal, but as an insider is leery of some proposed reforms: getting rid of perks, he says, is "nowhere near as important as taking a look at the way Congress does its business." His record is generally liberal, though more moderate on economic issues. Despite longstanding ties with organized labor, however, Cardin sided with President Clinton in the 103d Congress and supported NAFTA.

Cardin is able and businesslike. He chaired the Democratic Transition Team after the Republicans won control of the House in 1994, pushing for a uniform severance package for out-of-work Democratic committee staff members. He is an Assistant Democratic Whip and has worked to rebuild party enthusiasm. He has had no trouble at all winning his own reelection and has been mentioned, most recently in 1994, as a candidate for governor, but has not run. After 26 years as a hard-working and sometimes powerful member of the majority, crafting legislation and guiding procedure, he surely must find it frustrating to be in the minority.

The People: Pop. 1990: 597,712; 2% rural; 13% age 65+; 80% White; 17% Black; 2% Asian; 2% Hispanic origin. Voting age pop.: 459,046; 16% Black; 2% Hispanic origin. Households: 52% married couple families; 23% married couple fams. w. children; 49% college educ.; median household income: $35,970; per capita income: $17,779; median gross rent: $506; median house value: $90,000.

1992 Presidential Vote

Clinton (D)	136,829	(54%)
Bush (R)	82,494	(32%)
Perot (I)	34,973	(14%)

1988 Presidential Vote

Dukakis (D)	116,906	(51%)
Bush (R)	110,861	(49%)

Rep. Benjamin L. Cardin (D)

Elected 1986; b. Oct. 5, 1943, Baltimore; home, Baltimore; U. of Pittsburgh, B.A. 1964, U. of MD, LL.B., J.D. 1967; Jewish; married (Myrna).

Career: MD House of Delegates, 1966–86, Speaker, 1979–86; Practicing atty., 1967–86.

DC Office: 104 CHOB 20515, 202-225-4016; Fax: 202-225-9219; e-mail: cardin@hr.house.gov.

District Offices: 540 E. Belvedere Ave., #201, Baltimore 21212, 410-433-8886.

Committees: *Standards of Official Conduct* (2nd of 5 D). *Ways & Means* (10th of 15 D): Health; Oversight.

Group Ratings

	ADA	ACLU	COPE	CFA	LCV	CON	NSI	COC	ACU	NTLC	CHC
1994	75	73	89	80	89	35	30	50	10	18	7
1993	90	—	92	100	100	47	—	18	4	—	—

National Journal Ratings

	1993 LIB — 1993 CONS		1994 LIB — 1994 CONS	
Economic	68% —	26%	58% —	41%
Social	80% —	13%	74% —	26%
Foreign	70% —	26%	80% —	17%

Key Votes of the 103d Congress

1. Clinton Deficit Plan	Y	3. Brady Handgun Purchase	Y	5. Lmt. UN Cmnd. of Forces	N
2. NAFTA	Y	4. Strike Race/Death Pnlty.	N	6. Cut Missile Funds	Y

Key Votes of the 104th Congress

1. Congressional Compliance	Y	6. Reform Crime Grant	N	11. Loser Pays Court Reform	N
2. Balanced Budget Amndmt.	N	7. National Security Act	N	12. Product Liability Reform	N
3. Bar Unfunded Mandates	Y	8. Moratorium on Regs.	N	13. Welfare Reform	N
4. Pass Line Item Veto	Y	9. Risk Assessment on Regs.	N	14. Term Limits Amndmt.	N
5. Relax Exclusionary Rule	N	10. Expnd. Priv. Prop. Rights	N	15. Tax Cuts	N

Election Results

1994 general	Benjamin L. Cardin (D)	117,269	(71%)	($550,172)
	Robert Ryan Tousey (R)	47,966	(29%)	($10,439)
1994 primary	Benjamin L. Cardin (D)	64,742	(87%)	
	Dan Hiegel (D)	9,987	(13%)	
1992 general	Benjamin L. Cardin (D)	163,354	(74%)	($646,863)
	William T. S. Bricker (R)	58,869	(26%)	($8,832)

FOURTH DISTRICT

Prince George's County, Maryland, once tobacco land below the fall line, just north and east of Washington, D.C., is now metropolitan, with tentacles of settlement reaching out from Washington, growing larger and coming together. Today, Prince George's is home to some 729,000 people, a place that gives a hopeful glimpse of the future. This is not official Washington's conventional view, where Prince George's is seen as a working-class haven, overshadowed by faster-growing and higher-income Montgomery County to the west and Fairfax County in Virginia. But Prince George's is affluent by national standards, with one of the highest percentages of women in the work force in the nation (over 70%). All this is especially interesting because Prince George's is the nation's largest black suburban community. The black percentage here increased from 14% in 1970 to 37% in 1980; by the early 1990s it reached 50%, as blacks moved outward from the District of Columbia not only to nearby, modest-income suburbs, but out Routes 450, 214 and 5 to newly minted, more affluent subdivisions. More than any other place in America, Prince George's County is the home of the black middle class.

The 4th Congressional District of Maryland includes most of Prince George's County and a portion of Montgomery County to the west; it is mostly, but not entirely, inside the Capital Beltway. The biggest industry here is still government: in 1990, 21.5% of its workers were employed by the federal government, the highest percentage of any congressional district in the nation. The district is 58% black and also 6% Hispanic; it is overwhelmingly Democratic, and its current congressman was effectively chosen in the 1992 Democratic primary.

The race attracted 13 Democrats and seven Republicans; the two major contenders were state Senator Albert Wynn and Prince George's County prosecutor Alex Williams. Williams was probably the best known, from his county-wide state attorney victory; Wynn was the best funded. Wynn ran on a "put America first" platform, emphasizing domestic issues, with ads attacking President Bush; Williams called himself "a strong, independent voice for Congress" in his ads. Wynn spent much effort in Montgomery County, while Williams seemed to be targeting primarily Prince George's blacks. Prince George's County Councilwoman Hilda Pemberton highlighted her pro-choice stand, and Montgomery state Delegate Dana Dembrow, one of four white Democrats in the race, attacked the concept of a mandatory black-majority district. Wynn was endorsed by the *Prince George's Journal* and *The Washington Post* and won with 28% of the vote; Williams had 26%, Dembrow 15%, almost all from Montgomery, and Pemberton 13%. The general election was anticlimactic, with Wynn taking 75% of the vote against black businesswoman Michele Dyson.

Like many of the blacks elected from new black-majority districts, Wynn seems not to be making a monoracial appeal. He eschews expressions of militancy for pronouncements on national issues. He was key in bringing about hearings in 1993 to investigate allegations of racial bias at the National Institutes of Health, at the close of which Congress and an NIH task force pledged to monitor the agency. In May 1994 the NAACP, along with NIH's chapter of Blacks in Government, called for the resignation of NIH Director Harold Varmus, citing lack of progress in racial equity since the hearings. Although Wynn did not advocate Varmus' removal, he did express frustration at the slow pace of change at NIH. Wynn's voting record remains solidly liberal, and he serves on the Banking and International Relations Committees. He emerged victorious from his 1994 rematch with Dyson, again garnering 75% of the vote.

The People: Pop. 1990: 597,791; 1% rural; 7% age 65+; 31% White; 58% Black; 5% Asian; 3% Other; 6% Hispanic origin. Voting age pop.: 447,136; 56% Black; 6% Hispanic origin. Households: 47% married couple families; 24% married couple fams. w. children; 56% college educ.; median household income: $41,081; per capita income: $17,251; median gross rent: $643; median house value: $122,600.

1992 Presidential Vote

Clinton (D)	149,262	(74%)
Bush (R)	37,716	(19%)
Perot (I)	14,160	(7%)

1988 Presidential Vote

Dukakis (D)	121,421	(68%)
Bush (R)	56,346	(32%)

Rep. Albert R. Wynn (D)

Elected 1992; b. Sept. 10, 1951, Philadelphia, PA; home, Largo; U. of Pittsburgh, B.S. 1973, Howard U., 1973–74; Georgetown U. Law Schl., J.D. 1977; Baptist; married (Jessie).

Career: Exec. Dir., PG Cnty. Consumer Protection Comm., 1977–81; Chmn., Metro Washington Cncl. of Consumer Agencies, 1980–81; Practicing atty., 1981–92; MD House of Delegates, 1982–87; MD Senate 1987–92.

DC Office: 418 CHOB 20515, 202-225-8699; Fax: 202-225-8714.

District Offices: 9200 Basil Ct., #316, Landover 20785, 301-773-4094; 6009 Oxon Hill Rd., #208, Oxon Hill 20745, 301-839-5570; and 8061 Georgia Ave., #201, Silver Spring 20910, 301-558-7328.

Committees: *Banking & Financial Services* (17th of 22 D): Financial Institutions and Consumer Credit; General Oversight and Investigations. *International Relations* (17th of 19 D): Western Hemisphere.

Group Ratings

	ADA	ACLU	COPE	CFA	LCV	CON	NSI	COC	ACU	NTLC	CHC
1994	95	74	89	100	100	21	0	42	0	11	14
1993	100	—	100	100	93	39	—	9	4	—	—

National Journal Ratings

	1993 LIB	—	1993 CONS	1994 LIB	—	1994 CONS
Economic	88%	—	0%	83%	—	0%
Social	80%	—	13%	73%	—	26%
Foreign	93%	—	0%	85%	—	0%

Key Votes of the 103d Congress

1. Clinton Deficit Plan	Y	3. Brady Handgun Purchase	Y	5. Lmt. UN Cmnd. of Forces	N
2. NAFTA	N	4. Strike Race/Death Pnlty.	N	6. Cut Missile Funds	Y

Key Votes of the 104th Congress

1. Congressional Compliance	Y	6. Reform Crime Grant	N	11. Loser Pays Court Reform	N
2. Balanced Budget Amndmt.	N	7. National Security Act	N	12. Product Liability Reform	N
3. Bar Unfunded Mandates	Y	8. Moratorium on Regs.	N	13. Welfare Reform	N
4. Pass Line Item Veto	Y	9. Risk Assessment on Regs.	N	14. Term Limits Amndmt.	N
5. Relax Exclusionary Rule	N	10. Expnd. Priv. Prop. Rights	N	15. Tax Cuts	N

Election Results

1994 general	Albert R. Wynn (D)	93,148	(75%)	($358,607)
	Michele Dyson (R)	30,999	(25%)	($119,749)
1994 primary	Albert R. Wynn (D)	52,708	(84%)	
	Robert Bates (D)	9,919	(16%)	
1992 general	Albert R. Wynn (D)	136,902	(75%)	($386,186)
	Michele Dyson (R)	45,166	(25%)	($135,945)

FIFTH DISTRICT

Southern Maryland is a part of the United States with a distinctive history and not much of a national image. It was first settled by Catholics, the Calvert family of the Lords Baltimore, who founded their capital of St. Marys in 1634, not long after Jamestown and Plymouth Rock. Maryland became one of the two great tobacco colonies, and plantation houses grew up on every inlet off the broad Potomac and Patuxent Rivers, with docks where ships tied up straight from London. For years, none of these towns grew much, and even today many people here are directly descended from the old families. The biggest growth came from government installations like the Point Lookout prisoner-of-war camp in the Civil War or Patuxent Naval Air Test Center where many astronauts got their first training. This was never puritanical country: liquor flowed even during Prohibition and slot machines were specifically allowed by Maryland law until the 1940s.

The 5th Congressional District of Maryland, with lines redrawn completely in 1991, includes the three counties of southern Maryland, now attracting people who grew up in metro Washington and Baltimore, plus large slices of suburban Prince George's and Anne Arundel Counties between Washington and Annapolis. Its lines are drawn to make the adjacent 4th District in Prince George's majority-black, though with blacks moving outward in Prince George's and southern Maryland's historic black population, the 5th now is 19% black. Many of its people live north of Washington, in College Park, home of the University of Maryland, and Hyattsville, Greenbelt, Beltsville and Laurel. The 5th also includes southern Prince George's, from Clinton (heavily Democratic, unlike most Clinton Counties) south, and the suburbs of Bowie, Crofton and Davidsonville just west of Annapolis. Historically, this is a Democratic area. But southern Maryland has been conservative on many issues and voted for George Bush over Bill Clinton, and many Prince George's and Anne Arundel whites are Republicans as well.

The congressman from the 5th District is Steny Hoyer, a veteran Democrat who in the 1980s won in a seat with a large black percentage based in Prince George's and then relocated following redistricting to this south Maryland seat. Hoyer was elected to the Maryland Senate in 1966, at 27, just after graduating from law school. He was Senate President from 1975 to 1978; he made a misstep running for lieutenant governor on a losing ticket in 1978. But when the 5th District was declared vacant in 1981, after Representative Gladys Spellman went into an irreversible coma, Hoyer edged out Spellman's husband and several other Democrats in the primary and beat a well-financed, competent Republican candidate in the general.

In the House, Hoyer became an accomplished constituency service politician in the metropolitan Washington tradition and also a leader of the Democratic Party in the House. He won a seat on the Appropriations Committee, where he became a key man not only for Prince George's County but for Maryland and the overall D.C. metropolitan area, pushing for completion of the Metro subway system, money for the Baltimore-Washington Parkway reconstruction and for the National Archives research center at the University of Maryland. Hoyer also was the chief House sponsor of the Americans with Disabilities Act, skillfully shepherding it through substantive and procedural obstacles in 1989 and 1990. When Speaker Jim Wright and Whip Tony Coelho resigned from Congress in June 1989 because of ethics problems, Hoyer moved up and won a leadership position as chairman of the Democratic Caucus. In June 1991, when Democratic Whip William Gray retired, Hoyer tried to move up again. But this time he was opposed by Chief Deputy Whip David Bonior and, while Hoyer had the support of many younger members and the Conservative Democratic Forum, Bonior got the backing of most committee chairmen supportive of the seniority system and won the post, 160–109. Hoyer remains an integral part of the minority party leadership, as Democratic Steering Committee chairman, rallying to its support when necessary, as when he came out at a critical time for NAFTA.

In his old district, which nearly had a black majority, Hoyer had a very liberal voting record and courted black constituents ably; opposed by a candidate supported by Louis Farrakhan in the 1990 primary, he won 79% of the vote and carried every precinct. With the current district lines, his *National Journal* voting record has been more conservative, roughly at the midpoint of the 103d Congress. When Democrats had control, Hoyer chaired the Treasury, Postal Service and General Government Appropriations Subcommittee, which oversees several major components of the federal work force—17% of 5th District workers are federal employees—and the White House budget. He used the panel to prohibit changes in federal workers' health plans and to get $6 million for flexiplace telecommuting centers to allow long-commuting feds to work closer to home. He used his influence to get $100 million in federal money in south Maryland Navy installations and $150,000 in state money for St Mary's College.

Since redistricting, Hoyer has twice had serious opposition and has twice been reelected—after spending the astonishing sums of $1.6 million in 1992 and $1.3 million in 1994. In 1992, the Republican was Lawrence Hogan, Jr., whose father was a Prince George's congressman from 1968 to 1974 and Prince George's County executive, and who himself had chaired the local Reagan campaign. Hogan tried to tie Hoyer to the House bank and post office scandals and the federal deficit. Hogan won 50%–45% in the half of the district outside Prince George's. But Hoyer had a 60%–38% margin in Prince George's, for a 53%–44% win. In 1994, the Republican was Donald Devine, director of the Office of Personnel Management in the first Reagan term, heartily hated by civil service unions and cheered by many conservatives. Devine ran an ad quoting Hoyer on the House floor calling himself a "tax-tax, spend-spend Democrat" and defying opponents to "make of it what you will." Hoyer responded with a radio ad claiming Devine asked an aide to "lie under oath to Congress." Devine spent $581,000, but Hoyer outgunned him with $1,295,000—and had $172,000 cash on hand after the election. After two years of working the district, Hoyer led outside Prince George's County 53%–47% and in Prince George's 65%–35%, for a 59%–41% overall win. He was one of the few Democrats to noticeably increase his percentage between the two elections. It is unclear whether he will have serious opposition again, or whether he will be able to raise as much money now that he's in the minority.

Interestingly, Hoyer is of Danish descent, like former Treasury Secretary Lloyd Bentsen, Attorney General Janet Reno and the original eponym of Prince George's County, Prince George of Denmark, the husband of Queen Anne.

The People: Pop. 1990: 597,573; 30% rural; 8% age 65+; 77% White; 19% Black; 3% Asian; 1% Other; 2% Hispanic origin. Voting age pop.: 449,879; 18% Black; 2% Hispanic origin. Households: 62% married couple families; 31% married couple fams. w. children; 53% college educ.; median household income: $46,936; per capita income: $18,178; median gross rent: $674; median house value: $131,300.

1992 Presidential Vote		
Clinton (D)	107,618	(45%)
Bush (R)	95,356	(39%)
Perot (I)	37,441	(15%)

1988 Presidential Vote		
Bush (R)	115,062	(58%)
Dukakis (D)	84,162	(42%)

Rep. Steny H. Hoyer (D)

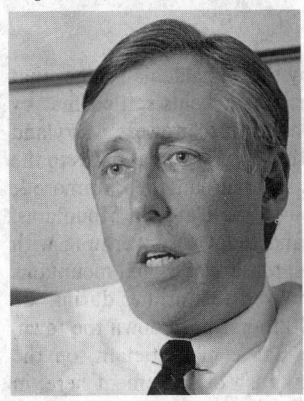

Elected May 1981; b. June 14, 1939, New York, NY; home, Mitchellville; U. of MD, B.S. 1963, Georgetown U., J.D. 1966; Baptist; married (Judith).

Career: Practicing atty., 1966–80; MD Senate, 1966–78, Pres., 1975–78; MD Bd. of Higher Educ., 1978–81.

DC Office: 1705 LHOB 20515, 202-225-4131; Fax: 202-225-4300.

District Offices: 6500 Cherrywood Ln., #310, Greenbelt 20770, 301-474-0119; and 21-A Industrial Park Dr., #101, Waldorf 20602, 301-843-1577.

Committees: *Democratic Steering Committee Chairman. Appropriations* (12th of 24 D): Labor, Health and Human Services, and Education; Treasury, Postal Service, and General Government (RMM). *House Oversight* (3rd of 5 D).

Group Ratings

	ADA	ACLU	COPE	CFA	LCV	CON	NSI	COC	ACU	NTLC	CHC
1994	70	64	78	70	65	32	70	42	24	15	7
1993	70	—	92	100	69	4	—	27	17	—	—

National Journal Ratings

	1993 LIB — 1993 CONS		1994 LIB — 1994 CONS	
Economic	68%	26%	67%	29%
Social	73%	23%	72%	28%
Foreign	51%	42%	57%	37%

Key Votes of the 103d Congress

1. Clinton Deficit Plan	Y	3. Brady Handgun Purchase	Y	5. Lmt. UN Cmnd. of Forces	N
2. NAFTA	Y	4. Strike Race/Death Pnlty.	N	6. Cut Missile Funds	N

Key Votes of the 104th Congress

1. Congressional Compliance	Y	6. Reform Crime Grant	N	11. Loser Pays Court Reform	N
2. Balanced Budget Amndmt.	Y	7. National Security Act	N	12. Product Liability Reform	N
3. Bar Unfunded Mandates	Y	8. Moratorium on Regs.	N	13. Welfare Reform	N
4. Pass Line Item Veto	N	9. Risk Assessment on Regs.	N	14. Term Limits Amndmt.	N
5. Relax Exclusionary Rule	N	10. Expnd. Priv. Prop. Rights	N	15. Tax Cuts	N

Election Results

1994 general	Steny H. Hoyer (D)	98,821	(59%)	($1,295,542)
	Donald Devine (R)	69,211	(41%)	($581,198)
1994 primary	Steny H. Hoyer (D)	47,644	(82%)	
	Harold Glynn Dial (D)	6,459	(11%)	
	Ricardo V. Johnson (D)	2,609	(4%)	
	Others	1,715	(3%)	
1992 general	Steny H. Hoyer (D)	118,312	(53%)	($1,584,271)
	Lawrence J. Hogan (R)	97,982	(44%)	($265,065)
	Other	6,990	(3%)	

SIXTH DISTRICT

The long green sloping fields of western Maryland, cut through by the Appalachian ridges that diagonally cross the state, were America's first western frontier: wheat fields settled first by Pennsylvania Dutch and Scots-Irish hill people, not Chesapeake Bay tobacco growers. Maryland is where the fall line comes closest to an ocean port, where the 19th Century's great paths to the interior were staked out: first the National Road, then the nation's first railroad, the Baltimore & Ohio, crossed the wide valleys of bounteous farms and climbed over the Catoctin Mountains. Towns grew up on single narrow streets lined with rowhouses and today are overhung with telephone and streetcar wires, overlooking long vistas of cornfields, pasturelands and mountains of ancient stone rising above the plains. Across this placid land moved vast armies during the Civil War. In Frederick, city officials paid Confederates $200,000 to not burn down the town, and near Sharpsburg, blue- and gray-clad soldiers fought the Battle of Antietam, on the bloodiest day in American military history. Today, there is a new rush of settlement here, in Carroll and Howard Counties, long parts of metro Baltimore, and Frederick County, which grew 31% in the 1980s and is now classified as part of metro Washington; growth remains slow, however, west of the Catoctins.

The 6th Congressional District of Maryland includes all of western Maryland, to mountainous Cumberland and Garrett County, and runs east to Carroll County northwest of Baltimore and the old town of Ellicott City in Howard County. The political tradition in most of this area, unlike the rest of Maryland, is Republican: this was Union country in the Civil War and has been mostly Republican ever since. The new rush of settlement seems to come from those seeking respite from metropolitan crime and values, strengthening the area's already conservative leanings. In 1994, the 6th voted Republican for gubernatorial candidate Ellen Sauerbrey and legislative candidates by wide margins.

The congressman from the 6th District is a Republican who matches its current mood, Roscoe Bartlett. He is an interesting character, a descendant of a signer of the Declaration of Independence and a Seventh Day Adventist with 10 children. He invented life support equipment for pilots and astronauts, ran his own business and taught at Frederick Community College—old values and high tech. In early 1992, when he first ran for Congress, he was a 65-year-old retired University of Maryland physiology professor. At first he seemed to have no chance of winning. Democrat Beverly Byron had represented the district for 14 years, had a conservative voting record, and chaired a subcommittee on National Security. But Byron was upset in the primary by Delegate Thomas Hattery, 56%–44%, who called for a middle class tax cut and national health insurance and was pro-choice on abortion. Meanwhile, Bartlett won his primary by only 42%–41%. But Bartlett had a big advantage on issues. He is solidly conservative and strongly anti-abortion; he campaigned with help from Oliver North and Tom Clancy and attacked Hattery for his perks as a legislator and accused him of expense account fraud. Hattery unveiled a healthcare plan, called for a federal "job czar," sounded many Clintonesque notes and hit Bartlett for accepting $4,000 in farm subsidies. But in a district that gave George Bush a solid margin over Bill Clinton, Bartlett won 54%–46%, carrying every county but Howard.

To many in the press, Bartlett seemed an odd duck and likely political loser. Washington reporters made a big deal when Bartlett told an audience that not more than a third of scholarship winners have "normal American" names. He apologized later, explaining that he should have said "European" and added that he meant to compliment Americans of Asian background. They said he was squandering votes when he refused to back disaster relief after a 1993 blizzard. But his style evidently suited his constituents quite well, and he was helped by Clinton Administration missteps, such as in May 1994 when a local newspaper photographed Clinton aide David Watkins boarding a helicopter at a Frederick County golf course: "The photo of two Marine guards saluting a golf bag as it was carried up the helicopter stairs is truly a picture that is worth a thousand words," said Bartlett, who represents the district where the golf course is located. In November 1994, Bartlett won 84% in the Republican primary and 66% in the general election—landslide victories. He is one older Republican who anticipated and seems to relish the Contract With America—the only Marylander to vote for all its provisions.

The People: Pop. 1990: 597,660; 47% rural; 11% age 65+; 94% White; 4% Black; 1% Asian; 1% Hispanic origin. Voting age pop.: 447,554; 4% Black; 1% Hispanic origin. Households: 65% married couple families; 31% married couple fams. w. children; 44% college educ.; median household income: $36,883; per capita income: $15,979; median gross rent: $448; median house value: $113,100.

1992 Presidential Vote			1988 Presidential Vote		
Bush (R)	125,494	(48%)	Bush (R)	140,008	(66%)
Clinton (D)	88,196	(34%)	Dukakis (D)	72,572	(34%)
Perot (I)	46,376	(18%)			

Rep. Roscoe G. Bartlett (R)

Elected 1992; b. June 3, 1926, Moreland, KY; home, Frederick; Columbia Union Col., B.A. 1947; U. of MD, M.S. 1949, Ph.D. 1952; Seventh Day Adventist; married (Ellen).

Career: Farmer; Prof., U. of MD, 1948–52; Asst. Prof., Loma Linda Schl. of Medicine, 1952–54; Asst. Prof., Howard U. Medical Schl., 1954–56; Research scientist, N.I.H., 1956–58; Research scientist, U.S. Naval Aerospace Medical Inst., 1958–62; Research scientist, Johns Hopkins U., 1962–67; Research Mgr., IBM, 1967–74; Pres., Roscoe Bartlett & Assoc., 1974–86.

DC Office: 322 CHOB 20515, 202-225-2721; Fax: 202-225-2193.

District Offices: 5831 Buckeystown Pk., Frederick 21701, 301-694-3030; 15 E. Main St., #110, Westminster 21157, 410-857-1115; 100 W. Franklin St., Hagerstown 21740, 301-797-6043; and 50 Broadway, Frostburg 21532, 301-689-0034.

Committees: *National Security* (18th of 30 R): Military Procurement; Military Readiness. *Science* (12th of 27 R): Basic Research; Energy and Environment. *Small Business* (7th of 22 R): Procurement, Exports and Business Opportunities; Tax and Finance.

Group Ratings

	ADA	ACLU	COPE	CFA	LCV	CON	NSI	COC	ACU	NTLC	CHC
1994	0	13	0	10	11	65	100	92	100	100	100
1993	5	—	18	10	29	74	—	91	100	—	—

National Journal Ratings

	1993 LIB — 1993 CONS		1994 LIB — 1994 CONS	
Economic	12% —	87%	0% —	80%
Social	11% —	82%	0% —	89%
Foreign	9% —	85%	14% —	80%

Key Votes of the 103d Congress

1. Clinton Deficit Plan	N	3. Brady Handgun Purchase	N	5. Lmt. UN Cmnd. of Forces	Y
2. NAFTA	N	4. Strike Race/Death Pnlty.	Y	6. Cut Missile Funds	N

Key Votes of the 104th Congress

1. Congressional Compliance	Y	6. Reform Crime Grant	Y	11. Loser Pays Court Reform	Y
2. Balanced Budget Amndmt.	Y	7. National Security Act	Y	12. Product Liability Reform	Y
3. Bar Unfunded Mandates	Y	8. Moratorium on Regs.	Y	13. Welfare Reform	Y
4. Pass Line Item Veto	Y	9. Risk Assessment on Regs.	Y	14. Term Limits Amndmt.	Y
5. Relax Exclusionary Rule	Y	10. Expnd. Priv. Prop. Rights	Y	15. Tax Cuts	Y

Election Results

1994 general	Roscoe G. Bartlett (R)	122,809	(66%)	($369,904)
	Paul Muldowney (D)	63,411	(34%)	($257,690)
1994 primary	Roscoe G. Bartlett (R)	41,438	(84%)	
	Fredric M. Parker (R)	5,345	(11%)	
	David R. Yurus (R)	2,320	(5%)	
1992 general	Roscoe G. Bartlett (R)	125,564	(54%)	($307,885)
	Thomas H. Hattery (D)	106,224	(46%)	($596,051)

SEVENTH DISTRICT

Baltimore, at the junction of North and South, terminus of America's first railroad and still the East Coast port closest to the great West, is one of the few American cities to have had large numbers of both blacks and European immigrants throughout its history. Its black community has a notable history: the *Afro-American* newspaper has been published here for more than 100 years; there was once a black symphony orchestra; and the city's black neighborhood west of downtown had a vital shopping district before World War II. Eubie Blake, the famous black musician and one of the founders of ragtime music, grew up here and now has a museum to honor him on Charles Street. Near downtown on the west side is the childhood home of Babe Ruth and the home of H.L. Mencken—two famous white Americans. Baltimore was the home of Clarence Mitchell, for many years the NAACP's lobbyist in Washington, and white Republicans like Mayor and Governor Theodore McKeldin competed zestfully with Democrats for black votes.

Baltimore has been a black-majority city since the late 1970s, and most of its west side neighborhoods are heavily black. Black Republicanism has long since died out, and William Donald Schaefer, who carried west Baltimore for mayor as late as 1983, went on to become governor. Black Democrats are the key politicians here, notably Mayor Kurt Schmoke, first elected in 1987. Schmoke's abilities—he is a Rhodes Scholar—and good intentions sparked hopes he could help Baltimore lessen the pathologies of violent crime, single parenthood and labor force non-participation that plague cities elsewhere. Schmoke has launched controversial initiatives: in 1988, he called for a full debate on drug decriminalization, and in 1992, the city made available Norplant implants as a contraceptive to public school teenagers. One hopeful initiative was developer James Rouse's five-year project to rebuild a 72-block area called Sandtown. But in the meantime, middle- and upper-income blacks have left behind the marble-stepped rowhouses of the city and moved to the suburbs.

Maryland's 7th Congressional District includes almost all of Baltimore City's black neighborhoods and extends into the heavily black suburbs running west from the city, Catonsville along the old Baltimore National Pike and Randallstown out Liberty Heights Avenue; 79% of the people and 70% of the votes are in the city. The congressman here is Kweisi Mfume, former councilman and radio talk show host, whose name ("Conquering Son of Kings") has echoes of the Black Power 1960s and whose personal history was touched by the social pathology that is at the root of the problems of the black underclass—and whose life shows how it can be overcome. Mfume's original name was Frizzell Gray; he was 16 when his mother died, at which point he dropped out of school, held low-paying jobs and fathered five sons out of wedlock. Then he had a conversion-like experience on a Baltimore street corner, took control of his life and moved it in another direction. He adopted his current African name, studied radio broadcasting, eventually graduating from Morgan State, and was elected to the Baltimore City Council in 1979, at 30; he also helped raise his sons, three of whom have gone on to college. On the council, he was a political critic of Mayor Schaefer, but he was also a stern critic of drug use and destructive behavior. In 1986, when 7th District Congressman Parren Mitchell retired, Mfume won 44% in the crucial Democratic primary, to 23% for Clarence Mitchell III, the retiring incumbent's nephew and a veteran state Senator with many legal problems, and 17% for minister and legislator Wendell Phillips.

Mfume seems to be a classic example of a black politician who has moved from demanding black power to emphasizing the need for individual self-discipline. He has sponsored laws requiring the government to use "underutilized" minority-owned banks and hire more lower-income people, to count only actual income toward determining public housing rents; he wants to restrict beeper use by people under 21. In late 1992, he was elected chairman of the Congressional Black Caucus, 27–9, which he used as a springboard for national influence and publicity. In that capacity, he got Democratic leaders to relax a subcommittee limitation rule to keep a separate Africa Subcommittee on International Relations. He also maneuvered the Black Caucus into blocking Charles Stenholm's rescission measure, the modified line-item veto, in April 1993, saying it gave up too much congressional authority. Mfume and the Black Caucus became important forces in the 103d Congress, though the Caucus was split on issues like Somalia and the crime bill. But its power was vastly reduced by the Republican capture of the House. Mfume's term as chairman was up, but he was infuriated when Republicans voted to end House financing of the caucuses. He ran for Democratic Caucus Chairman against Vic Fazio in November 1994, but lost 149–57. Mfume's forcefulness means he's unlikely to remain on the sidelines. In March 1995, he was appointed head of the Black Caucus task force to preserve affirmative action. Mfume is reelected every two years without difficulty.

The People: Pop. 1990: 597,701; 1% rural; 12% age 65+; 27% White; 71% Black; 1% Asian; 1% Hispanic origin. Voting age pop.: 447,777; 68% Black; 1% Hispanic origin. Households: 34% married couple families; 14% married couple fams. w. children; 37% college educ.; median household income: $25,684; per capita income: $11,718; median gross rent: $432; median house value: $59,400.

1992 Presidential Vote

Clinton (D)	159,191	(77%)
Bush (R)	32,431	(16%)
Perot (I)	13,009	(6%)

1988 Presidential Vote

Dukakis (D)	142,381	(77%)
Bush (R)	43,625	(23%)

Rep. Kweisi Mfume (D)

Elected 1986; b. Oct. 24, 1948, Baltimore; home, Baltimore; Morgan St. U., B.S. 1976, Johns Hopkins U., M.A. 1984; Baptist; divorced.

Career: Baltimore City Cncl., 1978–86. Adjunct Prof., Morgan St. U., 1984–85.

DC Office: 2419 RHOB 20515, 202-225-4741; Fax: 202-225-3178.

District Offices: 3000 Druid Park Dr., Baltimore 21215, 410-367-1900; and 1825 Woodlawn Dr., Baltimore 21207, 410-298-5997.

Committees: *Banking & Financial Services* (9th of 22 D): Financial Institutions and Consumer Credit; General Oversight and Investigations (RMM). *Small Business* (4th of 19 D): Government Programs. *Joint Economic Committee* (10th of 10 Reps.).

Group Ratings

	ADA	ACLU	COPE	CFA	LCV	CON	NSI	COC	ACU	NTLC	CHC
1994	95	83	100	90	83	34	0	33	0	14	0
1993	100	—	100	100	92	50	—	0	4	—	—

National Journal Ratings

	1993 LIB — 1993 CONS			1994 LIB — 1994 CONS		
Economic	66%	—	33%	66%	—	34%
Social	87%	—	0%	90%	—	6%
Foreign	79%	—	21%	79%	—	21%

Key Votes of the 103d Congress

1. Clinton Deficit Plan	Y	3. Brady Handgun Purchase	Y	5. Lmt. UN Cmnd. of Forces	N
2. NAFTA	N	4. Strike Race/Death Pnlty.	N	6. Cut Missile Funds	Y

Key Votes of the 104th Congress

1. Congressional Compliance	Y	6. Reform Crime Grant	N	11. Loser Pays Court Reform	N
2. Balanced Budget Amndmt.	N	7. National Security Act	N	12. Product Liability Reform	N
3. Bar Unfunded Mandates	N	8. Moratorium on Regs.	N	13. Welfare Reform	N
4. Pass Line Item Veto	N	9. Risk Assessment on Regs.	N	14. Term Limits Amndmt.	N
5. Relax Exclusionary Rule	N	10. Expnd. Priv. Prop. Rights	N	15. Tax Cuts	N

Election Results

1994 general	Kweisi Mfume (D)	97,016	(82%)	($161,285)
	Kenneth Kondner (R).................	22,007	(18%)	
1994 primary	Kweisi Mfume (D)	unopposed		
1992 general	Kweisi Mfume (D)	152,689	(85%)	($216,518)
	Kenneth Kondner (R).................	26,304	(15%)	

EIGHTH DISTRICT

One of America's most affluent and best-educated communities has grown up along an old road down which colonial farmers rolled barrels of tobacco to the port of Georgetown 200 years ago. The old road, now called Wisconsin Avenue and Rockville Pike, is the commercial spine of Montgomery County, Maryland. And this suburban jurisdiction just northwest of Washington, D.C. has for several decades ranked near the top of the list of counties in income and education. Today's Montgomery County is in large part a creation of the federal government, which has put huge facilities out here—Bethesda Naval Hospital, the National Institutes of Health, the Food and Drug Administration, the National Institute of Standards and Technology—to make it the center of America's fast-growing health industry. But the percentage of workers employed by government has been declining rapidly here, to about one in six in 1994—a figure only a percentage point or two above the national average. In the late 1970s or early 1980s, Montgomery seemed to have reached a critical mass, and started generating thousands of private sector health, high-tech, defense and service-industry jobs.

Wisconsin Avenue and Rockville Pike have become strip highways, with 1950s commercial development and 1960s shopping centers like so many in the country. But the stores are upscale, sometimes *very* upscale, and the new skyscrapers of downtown Bethesda and the office parks-cum-fitness centers of farther-out Gaithersburg are genuinely impressive. Not all of Montgomery County is exclusively high-income: there are some modest, mostly black and Jewish neighborhoods in Silver Spring and Wheaton. The 1980s saw a significant increase in foreign migration here—the Asian population alone increased 172% from 1980–90.

Historically, the typical Montgomery County voter was a high-ranking civil servant, but as private employment outpaces government work, the picture is changing. The fastest-growing parts of the county, out past Rockville in Gaithersburg and Germantown, are filling up with Republicans and conservatives. For nearly two decades, from 1960 to 1978, Montgomery County, most of which makes up Maryland's 8th Congressional District, had a run of liberal Republican congressmen. Then, in 1978, it elected liberal Democrat Michael Barnes, who became a leader of his party as chairman of the subcommittee handling Latin American policy. But when Barnes ran for the Senate in 1986, the increasing Republicanness of the newcomers may have tipped the balance back and helped elect current Congresswoman Connie Morella.

Morella is one of the three or four most liberal Republicans in the House by almost any gauge. Her votes against seven items of the Contract With America were three more than any other Republican. In the Montgomery County tradition, she takes liberal positions on social issues from abortion rights to gun control to contra aid. She was one of three Republicans to vote against the Gulf war resolution. She is more conservative on economic issues: the 8th has the second highest median household income of any district in the country (number one is the New Jersey 11th). But she favors more federal funding for early childhood intervention and after-school activities for at-risk kids. She now chairs the Science Subcommittee on Technology and favors protecting software produced by federal scientists with limited copyrights. Nevertheless, House Republican leaders have no desire to disown her, pointing to her as an example of their party's diversity. Despite some grumbling about her record by local Republicans—including Ruthann Aron, who ran unimpressively for the Senate nomination in 1994 and has threatened a primary challenge to Morella in 1996—most of the party's establishment knows that a conservative Republican couldn't win in Montgomery County (which gave Bill Clinton a 53%–35% margin over George Bush), and they appreciate her support on some partisan issues. She also has a genuine personal appeal: an ethnic background that not many old-line Republicans, but an increasing number of Montgomery voters, share; a personal history of raising nine children, six of them her late sister's; eight years' experience in the legislature. She is hard-working and cooperative with House colleagues and presses the flesh in friendly style throughout the district. Her experience raising a large family suggests she has the energy to tend to half a million local constituents who are only a local phone call away, and to make a mark on national issues—a regimen exhausting enough that three of the last four congressmen here relinquished their seats to retire or run for the more restful Senate.

Morella first won the seat in 1986, when she got 53% against liberal legislator Stewart Bainum, who spent a total of $1.5 million—much of it his own money. Redistricting made the 8th District marginally more Republican, adding high-income Potomac and putting most of Silver Spring and Takoma Park in the black-majority 4th District. Barring a destructive primary, the district appears to belong to Morella as long as she runs. She was reelected with 70% in 1994.

The People: Pop. 1990: 597,760; 6% rural; 10% age 65+; 78% White; 8% Black; 8% Asian; 2% Other; 6% Hispanic origin. Voting age pop.: 455,835; 8% Black; 6% Hispanic origin. Households: 61% married couple families; 30% married couple fams. w. children; 75% college educ.; median household income: $56,789; per capita income: $26,900; median gross rent: $777; median house value: $205,500.

1992 Presidential Vote

Clinton (D)	156,043	(53%)
Bush (R)	103,477	(35%)
Perot (I)	35,599	(12%)

1988 Presidential Vote

Bush (R)	130831	(51%)
Dukakis (D)	128041	(49%)

Rep. Constance A. Morella (R)

Elected 1986; b. Feb. 12, 1931, Somerville, MA; home, Bethesda; Boston U., A.B. 1954; American U., M.A. 1967; Catholic; married (Anthony).

Career: Teacher, Montgomery Cnty. Pub. Schls., 1956–60; Instructor, American U., 1968–70; Prof., Montgomery Col., 1970–86; MD House of Delegates, 1979–86.

DC Office: 106 CHOB 20515, 202-225-5341; Fax: 202-225-1389.

District Offices: 51 Monroe St., #507, Rockville 20850, 301-424-3501.

Committees: *Government Reform & Oversight* (4th of 27 R): Civil Service; Human Resources and Intergovernmental Affairs. *Science* (5th of 27 R): Basic Research; Technology (Chmn.).

Group Ratings

	ADA	ACLU	COPE	CFA	LCV	CON	NSI	COC	ACU	NTLC	CHC
1994	70	65	56	70	83	67	40	83	29	48	21
1993	60	—	67	90	93	19	—	73	39	—	—

National Journal Ratings

	1993 LIB — 1993 CONS		1994 LIB — 1994 CONS	
Economic	40%	— 58%	44%	— 54%
Social	73%	— 23%	56%	— 44%
Foreign	44%	— 55%	51%	— 47%

Key Votes of the 103d Congress

1. Clinton Deficit Plan	N	3. Brady Handgun Purchase	Y	5. Lmt. UN Cmnd. of Forces	Y
2. NAFTA	Y	4. Strike Race/Death Pnlty.	N	6. Cut Missile Funds	Y

Key Votes of the 104th Congress

1. Congressional Compliance	Y	6. Reform Crime Grant	N	11. Loser Pays Court Reform	Y
2. Balanced Budget Amndmt.	Y	7. National Security Act	N	12. Product Liability Reform	Y
3. Bar Unfunded Mandates	Y	8. Moratorium on Regs.	N	13. Welfare Reform	N
4. Pass Line Item Veto	Y	9. Risk Assessment on Regs.	Y	14. Term Limits Amndmt.	N
5. Relax Exclusionary Rule	Y	10. Expnd. Priv. Prop. Rights	N	15. Tax Cuts	N

Election Results

1994 general	Constance A. Morella (R)	143,449	(70%)	($306,968)
	Steven Van Grack (D)	60,660	(30%)	($10,802)
1994 primary	Constance A. Morella (R)	23,299	(70%)	
	Arnold Anderjaska (R)	9,918	(30%)	
1992 general	Constance A. Morella (R)	203,377	(73%)	($328,516)
	Edward J. Heffernan (D)	77,042	(27%)	($74,454)

MASSACHUSETTS

It would be a city on a hill, John Winthrop wrote of the Massachusetts Bay colony his Puritans were building, an example to the entire world. And Massachusetts in the more than three centuries since has always assumed it has a lot to teach others. The New World Puritans' austere creed, stemming from English Puritan Oliver Cromwell, taught that only the select would be saved and that they must extirpate the forces of Satan—Indians, Papists, tolerationists. For 150 years, New England was partial to learning, but also insular, hostile to outsiders and economically stagnant. Then, after the American Revolution, the international war between royal Britain and revolutionary and Napoleonic France allowed New England shipowners to cross enemy lines to become the world's leading merchants. They made vast profits in just a few brief years, and plowed the money made into textile mills, then railroads, then coal mining and steel-making: this was the capital that made industrial America.

Massachusetts made a new America in other ways. Intellectually, New England flowered: just a few writers from Boston and Concord—Ralph Waldo Emerson, Henry Wadsworth Longfellow, Henry David Thoreau, John Greenleaf Whittier, Nathaniel Hawthorne—created an American literary genre and popularized an American philosophy, more than 200 years after Plymouth Rock. Demographically, New England Yankees surged through Upstate New York, the Midwest, and across the continent. Long blocked from Upstate New York, they only reached Syracuse in the 1820s; by the 1850s they were in Iowa and Kansas and Oregon's Willamette Valley; by the 1880s they had settled Los Angeles. They built new cities and new colleges in the wilderness. They helped to start the Republican Party and did much to start—and win—the Civil War. They planted their economic system and their values, articulated in the "McGuffey Readers," across the continent: a nation looking to Massachusetts for instruction.

But in the meantime, Massachusetts itself and Boston, the Hub of the Universe, were being remade. The potato famine of the 1840s and an economy that continued imploding for decades sent Irishmen across the Atlantic, and many came to Boston, looking for work in the mills, docks and factories. Yankee Protestants had seen Catholics as their great cultural enemy for 200 years and felt their commonwealth was under siege. As the Irish became a majority, first in Boston and then statewide, Protestants feared the Irish would use their political clout to ladle out government jobs and benefits to their kind. And the Irish had a much better flair for politics than instinct for commerce; they yearned for the security of a government job. But they encountered such bigotry and rejection by the Yankees that even as successful an Irish Catholic as Joseph Kennedy felt obliged to move from Boston to New York in 1927. Politics in Massachusetts for years was a kind of cultural war between Yankee Republicans and Irish Democrats, an argument not so much over the distribution of income or the provision of services as over whose vision of Massachusetts should be honored, and whose version of history should be taught—not unlike battles being fought between liberals and conservatives today.

Sometimes, the stakes were concrete—control of patronage jobs, command of the Boston Police Department—but more often they were symbolic. Yankee Republicans tended to back activist government programs: public works and protective tariffs to help business, Civil War and Reconstruction to help suitably distant oppressed people like southern blacks, uplifting (and productivity-enhancing) social movements like temperance. The Irish found 19th Century Democrats—a party promoting laissez-faire—more congenial. The Irish had come from a place where the government was the enemy, and didn't want government spending money to help the rich or to stimulate commerce. They didn't want government to restrict immigration, to advance the blacks who might compete with them in the labor market, or to prohibit the consumption of liquor.

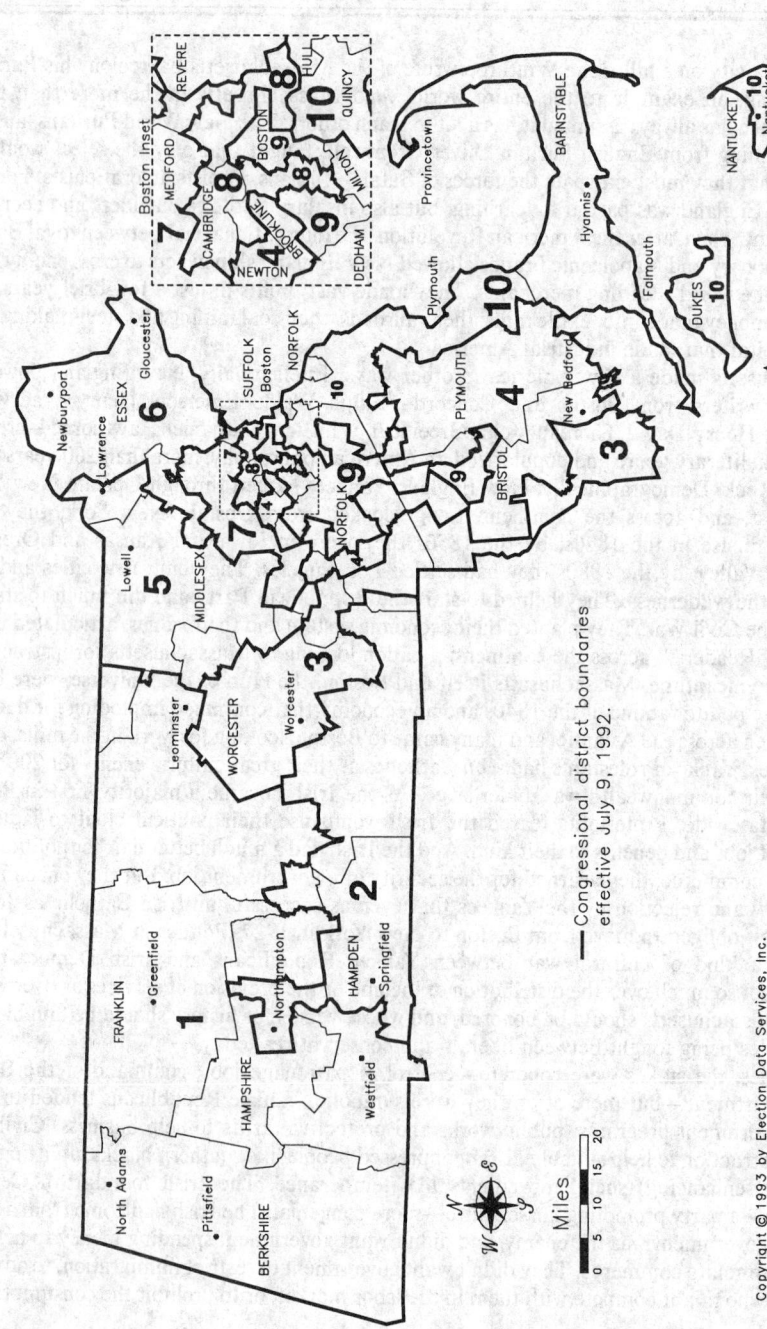

Congressional district boundaries effective July 9, 1992.

Copyright © 1993 by Election Data Services, Inc.

Over the years, the percentage of Irish and Catholics slowly rose. Yankees had smaller families, moved west, intermarried with people of immigrant stock and lost their Yankee identity. The Irish mostly stayed put, raising large families and eventually Massachusetts moved from being one of the most Republican states to one of the most Democratic. Economically, Massachusetts did not make much progress. The descendants of the Yankees who had been so venturesome in the early 19th Century became the most cautious investors in the early 20th, while the predominance of the textile mills in their home state meant that for a century beginning in the 1820s, Massachusetts imported low-skill labor and exported highly skilled people. As textile mills fled south in the 1920s, Massachusetts started exporting low-skill people as well; and from the waning of Yankee authority until the national rise of the Kennedys, Massachusetts seemed to run out of things to teach the rest of the nation. The state's Yankee Republicans were backward-looking, out of power in Washington, on the defensive at home, without a cause to champion. The Irish Democrats were hostile to Franklin Roosevelt's pro-British internationalism and receptive to the anti-Communism of the very Irish Joe McCarthy.

Then came the Kennedys. Their only residence in Massachusetts after 1927 was their summer home in Hyannis Port. Rose Kennedy was born in 1890 (and died in 1995 after a remarkable life that spanned nearly half this country's history), the daughter of John "Honey Fitz" Fitzgerald, elected to Congress at 31, mayor of Boston in 1906–07 and 1910–14; her husband Joseph Kennedy, first chairman of the Securities and Exchange Commission in the 1930s and ambassador to the Court of St. James from 1937–40, was perhaps the richest Catholic in the world and a shrewd and ruthless political operator. Joseph Kennedy moved his oldest surviving son, John, to Massachusetts, and engineered his election to the House in 1946, the Senate in 1952 and the Presidency in 1960. The Kennedys, with their elegant manners and great achievements, seemed like royalty to the Irish Catholics of Massachusetts and John Kennedy's election in 1960 certified to U.S. Catholics, 78% of whom voted for him, that they too were Americans. Joseph and John Kennedy were, on many issues, conservative or skeptical. But Kennedy's Administration was increasingly, even before his untimely death, identified as liberal, and his example and that of his brother, Edward, elected to the U.S. Senate at 30 in 1962, moved Massachusetts Catholics to the left. At the same time, Massachusetts Protestants were influenced by the leftward direction on the state's great campuses in the 1960s. The universities were also providing the basis for a surging high-tech economy, to the point that Massachusetts started importing high-skill people even as it continued to export those with low skills.

In the 1970s and 1980s Massachusetts, with one interval, had the most liberal governance and national politics of any state in the country. The expanding high-skill population, attracted initially by Massachusetts's many universities and colleges, not obliged to deal with the problems of a vast urban underclass, provided a political base of activists and money; Irish and other Catholics, won over by the Kennedys, provided most of the votes. Massachusetts was the only state to vote for George McGovern in 1972 and although it voted twice for Ronald Reagan, the son of an Irish Catholic, its Democratic percentage in presidential contests from 1968 to 1988 was 53%, just 0.4% behind Rhode Island and well ahead of every other state. The state's senators included Edward Kennedy, liberal Republican Edward Brooke, and liberal Democrats Paul Tsongas and John Kerry. Its governors, liberal Republican Francis Sargent and liberal Democrat Michael Dukakis, vastly increased spending and endorsed the inexplicable policies that sunk Dukakis's 1988 presidential campaign: prisoners sentenced to life without parole being given weekend furloughs—a policy that liberals in the press said it was racist to oppose— prisoners allowed to vote and be registered by state employees sent into prisons for that purpose, government spending that rose 9% a year in the 1980s. Rebellion against this resulted in Dukakis's defeat in 1978 and the election of conservative Democrat Edward King. As historian David Hackett Fischer points out in *Albion's Seed*, the mindset of the original settlers remains strong even when the ethnic origin of current residents is far different, and the spirit of the Puritans, the faith that they had much to teach the rest of the world, is strong in Massachusetts liberals: in the quietly smug liberalism of Michael Dukakis or the hearty and combative liberalism of Edward Kennedy.

Today, Massachusetts has largely rejected this politics, with a suddenness matched in its history by its merchants' sudden emergence as world traders in the 1790s and the appearance of Irish immigrants on Boston docks in the 1840s. It happened even as the country seemed to be going Massachusetts's way, as Michael Dukakis was winning the Democratic nomination for president and leading Massachusetts-born George Bush in the polls, and as "the Massachusetts miracle" was being celebrated by the *Boston Globe*, then as objective from the left as the old *Chicago Tribune* was on the right, although the *Globe* under its new editor, like the *Tribune* under its current leadership, comes closer to objectivity than most major dailies. But the state's financial problems were silently worsening as Dukakis campaigned across the country; he won only 53% of the vote in Massachusetts, running strong in the Berkshires and the Pioneer Valley in the west, but only running even in the Boston media market (which includes New Hampshire, a low-tax haven from high-tax Massachusetts since colonial times). Then in 1989, things fell apart. The state economy sagged badly: the slump in minicomputers hurt Massachusetts-based Wang and Digital; Cambridge's Lotus software was outflanked by Seattle's Microsoft; defense spending cutbacks, long sought by Massachusetts politicians, naturally produced job losses. More spectacular was the bursting of the Northeast real estate bubble and the resultant collapse of major New England banks: New Englanders relearned the old lesson that housing prices don't go up 25% a year indefinitely. The state government essentially went bankrupt, and Dukakis retired from office. It seemed that the rest of the country had something to teach Massachusetts.

In the 1990s the learning process has gone both ways. The 1990 general election for governor did not have a certifiable liberal candidate, as free marketeer and tough-on-crime Republican William Weld faced tough-talking back-to-basics Boston University President John Silber, who had beaten amiable liberal Frank Bellotti for the Democratic nomination. Republicans elected Joe Malone state treasurer and gained seats in the legislature and that colonial relic, the governor's council. Yet in 1992 Massachusetts, after backing native son Paul Tsongas in the Democratic primary, delivered a 48%–29% margin for Bill Clinton in November, and Democrats won veto-proof majorities in the legislature; even as Republicans picked up two congressional seats and seriously contested three others in 1992, Democrats won the total vote cast for Congress by 57%–35%, the largest margin in any big state. In 1994, Weld won reelection by a stunning 71%–28% margin, and Edward Kennedy was thrown sharply on the defensive before prevailing 58%–41% over Republican businessman Mitt Romney. But Democrats held all statewide offices except treasurer, led by 72%–28% in popular vote in House races, and held the largest Democratic percentage of seats in the legislature except in Rhode Island, Hawaii, Louisiana and Arkansas.

But what are Massachusetts's lessons? Talk radio hosts like WRKO's Jerry Williams and Howie Carr of the feisty *Boston Herald* helped delegitimize liberals' claims to moral superiority as Dukakisism collapsed. But, constantly complaining, they have not presented a countervailing order. William Weld presents a vision appealing to many of a government that taxes and spends lightly, that is friendly to feminism and gay rights, that exerts some effort to protect the environment. But he has not activated a core constituency or mustered an army of political followers—witness the pathetic Republican showing in legislative races even in 1994. Nor do the Democrats show the way. Liberal campuses still seem to be generating talented young Democratic politicos in Massachusetts, if not in the rest of the country. Even if their liberal rhetoric sounds hollow and unconvincing, their energy and political savvy, plus memories of the Kennedy family in the 1960s and the Irish potato famine of the 1840s, can still rally enough voters to win in most constituencies. Yet neither of their two guiding principles—tax and spend, liberation from restraint—seems capable of governance, which leaves only the Ivy League snob's condescension for the yahoos who for unfathomable reasons choose to live west of the Berkshires. Massachusetts undoubtedly will have more to teach the country, but for the moment it seems still to have some learning to do.

Governor. William Weld is the first Yankee Massachusetts Republican governor determined to hold down taxes and government spending since Christian Herter left the State House on Beacon Hill in 1956; he hangs a picture of James Michael Curley, the scampish mayor of Boston, congressman and one-term governor, in his office. Weld is not technically a Boston Brahmin: he grew up in New York and came to Massachusetts for prep school and college. He still lives in Cambridge (with his wife, a great-granddaughter of Theodore Roosevelt), just off fashionable Brattle Street. As U.S. attorney in Massachusetts, Weld prosecuted many local pols; as an assistant attorney general, he resigned in protest of the controversies surrounding Attorney General Edwin Meese. In the 1990 primary, Weld spent $1.1 million of his own money to overtake party-endorsed anti-abortion legislator Steven Pierce, 61%–39%. In the fall, he attacked Democratic opponent John Silber for his high salary at Boston University, his close ties to Senate President Billy Bulger and former Boston Mayor Kevin White and his refusal to support a tax-cutting ballot proposition. Silber hurt himself with his bluntness ("We have a generation of abused children by women who have thought a third-rate day care center was just as good as a first-rate home") and Weld won 50%–47%, with strong votes from women and baby boomers.

In 1991, Weld amazed Massachusetts by cutting state spending—not reducing increases from some projected level, but actually cutting spending. He privatized services, slashed public payrolls and set the way for nine tax cuts in four years—all things the Democrats did not think possible. At the same time, his outspoken pro-choice stand on abortion and his vehement support of gay rights—keep the government out of your pocketbook and your bedroom, he told the Republican National Convention in Houston—quieted Massachusetts's articulate cultural liberals. But he also combines a taste for rock and roll and poker parties with a streak of cultural conservatism enlivened perhaps by years of living in Cambridge: "Parents count! I cannot understand why people who expend so much energy telling the rest of us what not to eat, what not to drink, or where not to smoke become astoundingly silent when a couple who are utterly unprepared to raise a child become parents." Teachers, Weld said, should endorse "self-discipline, intellectual curiosity, courage, honesty, perseverance, compassion and justice."

Weld provided policy leadership, but he didn't attract many political followers. Republicans lost ground in the legislature in 1992 and don't have enough votes to uphold a Weld veto; he has been forced to cooperate with Bulger and, to some extent, Speaker Charles Flaherty. Weld has an aggressive program of charter schools, but has not achieved the full school choice he backs. His welfare program, unveiled in January 1994, was radical: replacing cash grants with day care, health care and child support, with beneficiaries given 90 days to find a job and then having to perform community service or forfeit benefits. But the Clinton Administration did not issues waivers and in January 1995, Weld was making concessions to Democratic legislators. Weld signed into law a revised plan in February 1995.

An avid hunter, Weld has supported environmental measures and boasts of protecting 44,000 acres of open land. Weld angered some conservatives when he changed his anti-gun control stand to back an assault weapons ban and waiting period for handgun purchases; he angered very many voters, in New Hampshire as well as Massachusetts, when he approved a 55% pay increase for legislators in December 1994.

That was just one month after Weld won an easy reelection victory in November, 1994. Congressman Joe Kennedy, Boston Mayor Ray Flynn, Attorney General Scott Harshbarger and John Silber all declined to run against him; the Democratic nominee was legislator Mark Roosevelt, a cousin of Weld's wife. Roosevelt emitted traditional liberal rhetoric of the sort that once swept all before it, calling Weld "indifferent, apathetic, feckless, aloof, passive and lazy. Did I say uncaring? He's uncaring." But it availed him nothing, and Weld won 71%–28%. Weld was immediately hailed as a presidential possibility, and may have rolled the idea around. But in February 1995, he announced he would not run, and in April announced he would serve as national finance chairman for the presidential campaign of California Governor Pete Wilson. As for the governorship, in 1993 Weld said: "Two terms is enough. After that, I just want to go back to the private practice of law." Probably he will and even if, as seems likely, a Democrat like

Harshbarger takes his place, Weld will have made Massachusetts a different place.

Senators. Edward Kennedy is now in his fourth decade as a national celebrity and a politician. He has had the highs and lows of his personal life followed by millions and criticized vitriolically by many; he has been a presidential candidate and, while still in his 30s, was widely assumed to be the next president. He is fourth in seniority in the Senate, behind Strom Thurmond, Robert Byrd and Claiborne Pell. His reputation as an idealistic champion of the poor has been burnished by the praise of first-rate celebrators that no American political family has attracted before. To millions of others, he is a symbol of personal immorality and unpunished criminal behavior, a man who has gotten away with things that would have ended anyone else's public career. There is some basis for both views, but neither is an entirely fair picture of this politician who was reelected by a smart margin in 1994 in a race whose outcome seemed by no means certain; Kennedy has been paid more attention in the 1990s as a scandal-beset celebrity than as a consistent and often effective advocate of a view of public policy.

For the luster of the Kennedys has worn off, in America and even in Massachusetts, and the percentage of Americans who look to the Kennedys for political leadership has grown small; most voters can't remember, or never knew, what made the Kennedys so exciting. He was first elected in 1962, at age 30, after a career of no discernible distinction: "He can do more for Massachusetts" was the winning political slogan of the president's brother. For three and a half years, from 1965 to 1968, Edward Kennedy was the Senate colleague of his brother Robert; after his brothers' assassinations, he was seen by many as their natural heir, and could conceivably have been nominated for president in 1968, at 36, or in 1972 had he chosen to run. Instead, in the latter year, he gave the first of several stirring convention speeches promoting his trademark liberalism. In 1980, he ran for president, and began the race against incumbent Jimmy Carter far ahead in the polls. But he was unable to articulate his reasons for running, and his candidacy was greeted with adverse reaction to him personally as well as to his policies. It ended in a crushing defeat, relieved only by another stirring convention speech, after which he pointedly refused to raise Carter's hand on the podium. In retrospect, it is plain that Edward Kennedy's presidential chances were ended in July 1969, with the accident at Chappaquiddick, even though the Kennedy family retainers managed to cast a cloud over the specifics in a way that would be considered outrageous if tried by anyone else. And after the Good Friday 1991 bar-hopping in Palm Beach and his nephew William Kennedy Smith's trial and acquittal for rape, Kennedy had to fight hard, with some low punches as well as fair hard lefts, to win reelection to represent in the Senate the Kennedy homeland of Massachusetts.

Kennedy has been a hardworking and practical politician who, after his brothers' deaths, took up the liberal causes and attention to the poor which had been the focus of Robert Kennedy in the last years of his life. He has worked hard for a quarter century on their behalf—and, until the election of Bill Clinton, without the friendship of a Democratic administration. On the Labor and Human Resources Committee during the Republican years, Kennedy supported private sector and teachers' unions; on the Judiciary Committee he supported pro-choice and feminist groups with energy and enthusiasm. He immediately pounced on Judge Robert Bork's nomination in 1987, but was precluded from a similarly loud role in the Clarence Thomas hearings in October 1991 because his personal shortcomings precluded him from pious disapproval of sexual harassment.

In October 1991, Kennedy gave a speech passionately defending liberalism at Harvard University's Kennedy School of Government. And in July 1992, he married Victoria Reggie. He supported Bill Clinton happily in 1992, and basked as President Clinton gave repeated homage to the Kennedy family. He sponsored the Family and Medical Leave Act vetoed by Bush in 1992 and signed by Clinton in February 1993, and he sponsored another bill signed by Clinton to criminalize blocking access to abortion clinics. But he was frustrated in achieving other goals—banning the death penalty when it is imposed disproportionately on members of different races, preventing states from regulating abortions. His record remained staunchly liberal, except for some moderate votes on foreign issues—a contrast with his harsh pre-1992 rhetoric against the

Gulf war resolution and for deep defense cuts.

His greatest frustration came on health care. Twenty years earlier, Kennedy had backed a Canadian-style single-payer system, and in May 1994 he got a healthcare bill resembling Clinton's, but without the bureaucratic alliances and with a less stringent employer mandate, through the Labor and Human Resources Committee he chaired. But the committee was much more liberal than the Senate and with characteristic political shrewdness Kennedy admitted "There's a bipartisan opportunity out there, but we haven't exactly been able to catch it." Alas, for Kennedy and the liberals, that was the high water mark of healthcare debate in the Senate.

In April 1994, a Massachusetts poll found 60% of voters favorable to Kennedy, but 62% saying it was time for a change: an opening for a Republican. Plus, Kennedy himself was visibly older, far heavier than ever, "all bloat and tremor," wrote *The New Yorker*'s Peter Boyer. Into the opening came Mitt Romney, son of former (1963–68) Michigan Governor George Romney, and a successful businessman in his own right. Romney is pro-choice on abortion, in favor of the death penalty, for Clinton's don't-ask-don't-tell policy on gays in the military, but market-oriented on economics. "The 1960s liberal agenda hasn't worked. It is time to reform the reforms." To which Kennedy said, "I stand for the idea that public service can make a difference in the lives of people." Romney loaned his campaign $3 million, won the Republican nomination easily, and in a September poll led Kennedy 43%–42%. That began the second most expensive Senate race in the country—Kennedy spent $10.4 million, Romney $7.6 million—and one of the most sharply contested. Kennedy showed signs of panic: he loaned his campaign $1.25 million, he brought in President Clinton to his house for a fund-raiser and took in $750,000, and he quietly pushed aside the family members who were nominally running the campaign in favor of professionals. Astonishingly for a man whose brother won the presidency while appealing against religious bigotry, Kennedy echoed questions, first raised by Joseph Kennedy, about Romney's Mormon faith, asking whether he had challenged that church's racially discriminatory beliefs before they were changed in 1978. The *Boston Globe* responded, "That line of attack makes no more sense than asking Kennedy how many times he has written to Rome demanding that the church change its stand on abortion."

More damaging were Kennedy ads attacking Romney's business practices. Romney claimed his work at Bain Capital produced 10,000 jobs. But Kennedy investigators found an Indiana factory where 350 workers had gone out on strike after their pay and benefits were cut after it was bought by Bain Capital. Romney claimed he severed his ties with Bain before the purchase was complete, but the damage was palpable. Also, in the campaign's first debate, Kennedy performed above expectations while pinning down Romney for being unable to say how much his healthcare plan would cost. By late October, a *Herald* poll had Kennedy ahead 50%–32%; he won 58%–41%. That is his lowest score ever, but roughly comparable to the 61%–38% by which he beat Ray Shamie in 1982. The campaign showed that his support is no longer automatic, but is rather more contingent on how he frames the issues and on the strengths and weaknesses of his opponent. It also reaffirmed that Kennedy will not be a serious candidate for president again.

Kennedy returned to a Senate in which he was in the minority, the ranking Democrat on the Labor Committee and the Judiciary Subcommittee on Immigration. He is certainly not going to be able to promote big government measures, but he is not without influence either. On immigration, for example, he could play a key role. The Immigration Act of 1965, the first piece of legislation he managed, eliminated the quotas of the 1920s laws and opened the way for vast increases in immigration in the 1970s and 1980s; by the mid-1980s he, like his labor union backers, was wary of more immigration. But in the 1990 act, prompted by increasing Irish immigration to Massachusetts, he provided key support for raising legal immigration levels. Kennedy and his sister, Ambassador to Ireland Jean Kennedy Smith, were also instrumental in getting Bill Clinton first to admit to the United States and then to receive in the White House Gerry Adams, the longtime leader of Sinn Fein, the political arm of the Irish Republican Army.

In January 1995, Kennedy made a major speech urging Democrats to stand for traditional liberalism. "If we become pale carbon copies of the opposition and try to act like Republicans, we will lose and we will deserve to lose." He defended Bill Clinton and said criticism of him came "with ill grace from those who abandoned him on critical votes in the last Congress, then ran from him in the last campaign and then lost, often by wide margins"—not so subtle references to House Democrats like Jim Cooper and Dave McCurdy who stymied health care but then failed in Senate bids. In Kennedy's view as in Clinton's, politics is entirely a matter of economics: the middle class is angry at the rich getting richer and the poor getting welfare, while their incomes stagnate; no attention at all is paid to the complaints they may voice about the liberal stands on cultural issues which Kennedy has so strongly taken. If there is an element of idealism here, a genuine desire to make the lot of the least of us better, there is also a certain condescension, that voters can be mollified with money to accept policies they think are morally questionable. But it still can be a winning formula in Massachusetts, if not the nation.

John Kerry, junior Senator from Massachusetts, first won fame as one of the organizers of Vietnam Veterans Against the War in 1971. His leadership attracted attention because of his background, unusual for a Vietnam veteran (he went to Yale and his mother is from the Brahmin Forbes family), and because of his record of genuine heroism in combat. "How do you ask a man to be the last to die for a mistake?" he asked in congressional testimony—a good question, and one which also suggested his future political ambitions. Yet his political career did not proceed straight ahead. He ran for Congress in 1972, after some widely observed district-shopping, and lost in a district carried by George McGovern. Chastened, Kerry went to law school, worked for a prosecutor, was elected lieutenant governor on the Dukakis ticket in 1982, and ran for senator in 1984; in both races, he upset a favored rival for the Democratic nomination. In 1982, Kerry won the general as part of a tied ticket with Dukakis; in the 1984 general, he beat Raymond Shamie, businessman and state Republican chairman, 55%–45%.

Kerry came to the Senate with a reputation as a strong liberal, and the similarity of his name to Kennedy's (his initials are J.F.K.) fed an assumption that the two Massachusetts senators would vote alike. They mostly have; but there are notable differences; Kerry has been more respectful of economic free markets and moved earlier than Kennedy toward supporting an expansive U.S. foreign and military policy. One of Kerry's first votes was for the Gramm-Rudman deficit-cutting measure. He has worked closely and cordially with William Weld to encourage new businesses in Massachusetts.

As a member of the majority in the Senate, Kerry made a name as an investigator, spending some time up blind alleys with klieg lights but also producing some important information regardless of political fallout. He used his Foreign Relations Terrorism, Narcotics and International Operations Subcommittee chairmanship to investigate the Bank of Credit & Commerce International—the now infamous BCCI scandal; his October 1992 report accused the Justice Department, British banking regulators and especially the CIA of "institutional failure" in recognizing the fraudulent nature of BCCI's operations. During that time, he did more than any American official except Manhattan District Attorney Robert Morgenthau to uncover what BCCI was up to. But the subcommittee also spent much time trying to pin drug-running charges on Central American rightists—convenient for American politicians supportive of Central American left-wingers. Kerry was on more solid ground, as later events made clear, in charging Manuel Noriega of Panama with drug-dealing, but failed to deliver on hinted-at revelations that George Bush somehow knew about Noriega's operations; he did support Bush's military action in Panama in December 1989.

Kerry's other great investigation was as chairman of the Select Committee on POW/MIA Affairs, on whether Americans were left behind in Vietnamese hands in 1973. Kerry and ranking Republican Bob Smith of New Hampshire tended to believe some were; they went to Vietnam and attempted to dig up new evidence. Kerry grilled former Secretary of State Henry Kissinger, bringing to light evidence and testimony showing that he and President Nixon understood that there could possibly be Americans left behind, but giving less credit than due to the defense that it was doves like Kerry himself who, by making American military retaliation impossible, forced Kissinger to negotiate with a very weak hand. But overall this was a serious effort, with an appropriately hedged conclusion: there is evidence "that indicates the possibility of survival, at least for a small number," after 1973, but also said, "there is at this time no compelling evidence that any American remains alive in captivity in southeast Asia." By May 1995, Kerry and fellow Vietnam veteran Senator John McCain's efforts in this area had convinced them that Hanoi was fully cooperating and they called on President Clinton to normalize relations.

Kerry has also spoken out interestingly on other issues. In 1992, just before the Los Angeles riot, he spoke at Yale on affirmative action, arguing that quota programs must be supplemented with initiatives that stress law and order, personal responsibility and the work ethic; in 1994, he backed substantial increases in funding for the crime bill. Similarly, Kerry opposed the Gulf war resolution, but for him it was a close call, and his speech against it was cautious and nuanced. Later, he worked to prohibit aid to Azerbaijan until it stopped its fight against Armenia. He is opposed to dolphin-killing drift net fishing, has called for a moratorium on mining in Antarctica. He has been a campaign finance reformer, refusing PAC money and championing voluntary public financing of congressional races. He successfully worked with Richard Bryan of Nevada to eliminate the wool and mohair subsidy in 1993 and he won a fight to eliminate the Advanced Liquid Metal Reactor nuclear disposal in 1994.

Kerry was reelected by a comfortable margin in 1990, but after a not entirely comfortable campaign. Republican Jim Rappaport spent $4.2 million of his own money in a year when voters were furious with Michael Dukakis; Rappaport ran an ad showing Kerry's face morphing into Dukakis's, probably the first morph ads in American political history. In mid-September, Rappaport trailed by only 45%–41% in a public poll. Kerry spoke plaintively in debate of his long record in public life; his campaign ads featured mostly 20-year-old TV footage showing his opposition to the Vietnam War, then switched to sharp and effective ridicule of Rappaport. Kerry finally won 57%–43%.

In December 1994, Kerry irritated some Democrats by saying that "screwups" by Clinton and other Democrats led to the Republican victory and that he was "delighted by the shakeup" of Congress, though adding, "I'm clearly not delighted the Republicans are running the show but I've been deeply concerned for a long time that there be changes in Congress and public policy." But Tom Daschle still made Kerry chairman of the newly-formed Senate Democratic Steering Committee. He also improved his political position when he announced he was going to marry Teresa Heinz, widow of the late Republican Senator John Heinz of Pennsylvania. H.J. Heinz Inc. stock has risen vastly in the last 20 years, and Teresa Heinz's net worth is estimated at $650 million; Kerry announced he expected to spend $8 million on his 1996 race. Late 1994 polls showed Kerry running even against Weld and leading Mitt Romney and Joe Malone with percentages hovering around 50%. But Malone has said he won't run, Weld has all but closed the door on speculation that he will challenge Kerry.

Presidential politics. Massachusetts is the most Democratic state in presidential elections with the arguable exception of Rhode Island. In 1992, it gave Bill Clinton one of his highest percentages in the nation, and his largest percentage margin of any state. It was also George Bush's worst state, though he was born and attended prep school here.

Massachusetts's presidential primary has long been in early March and is the leading northern Super Tuesday contest. Native sons have won the last four primaries here: Democrats Michael Dukakis and Paul Tsongas and Republican George Bush.

Congressional districting. Massachusetts's convoluted congressional district lines deserve their own biographer, someone with a sure political instinct and a touch of whimsy. The state lost one seat in each of the last two reapportionments. In 1982, Barney Frank beat Republican Margaret Heckler in their combined district; in 1992, carnage was avoided when Democrat Brian Donnelly retired and Governor William Weld reached agreement with the Democratic legislature on a set of grotesque district lines. Republicans now hold two seats, both of which they initially gained amid scandal and have held with difficulty.

The People: Est. Pop. 1994: 6,041,000; Pop. 1990: 6,016,425, up 0.4% 1990–1994. 2.3% of U.S. total, 13th largest; 16% rural. Median age: 33.6 years. 13.6% 65 years and over. 89.8% White, 5.0% Black, 4.8% Hispanic origin, 2.4% Asian, 2.6% Other. Households: 52.1% married couple families; 24% married couple fams. w. children; 50% college educ.; median household income: $36,952; per capita income: $17,224; 59.3% owner occupied housing; median house value: $162,800; median monthly rent: $506. 8.5% Unemployment. 1994 Voting age pop.: 4,564,000. 1994 Turnout: 2,165,647; 47% of VAP. Registered voters (1994): 3,153,178; 1,266,358 D (40%); 419,120 R (13%); 1,466,555 unaffiliated and minor parties (47%).

Political Lineup: Governor, William F. Weld (R); Lt. Gov., Argeo Paul Cellucci (R); Secy. of the Commonwealth, William Galvin (D); Atty. Gen., L. Scott Harshbarger (D); Treasurer, Joseph Malone (R); Comptroller, William Kilmartin (D); Auditor, A. Joseph DeNucci (D). State Senate, 40 (30 D and 10 R); State House of Representatives, 160 (124 D, 35 R and 1 I). Senators, Edward M. Kennedy (D) and John F. Kerry (D). Representatives, 10 (2 R and 8 D).

1992 Presidential Vote

Clinton (D)	1,318,639	(48%)
Bush (R)	805,039	(29%)
Perot (I)	630,731	(22%)

1992 Democratic Presidential Primary

Tsongas	526,297	(66%)
Brown	115,746	(15%)
Clinton	86,817	(11%)
Nader	32,881	(4%)

1988 Presidential Vote

Dukakis (D)	1,401,415	(53%)
Bush (R)	1,195,635	(45%)

1992 Republican Presidential Primary

Bush	176,868	(66%)
Buchanan	74,797	(28%)
No Preference	10,132	(4%)

GOVERNOR

Gov. William F. Weld (R)

Elected 1990, term expires Jan. 1999; b. July 31, 1945, Smithtown, NY; home, Cambridge; Harvard, B.A. 1966, J.D. 1970, Oxford U., 1967; Episcopalian; married (Susan).

Career: Practicing atty., 1970–80, 1988–90; U.S. Atty. for MA, 1981–86; U.S. Asst. Atty. Gen., Criminal Div., 1986–88.

Office: State House, Boston 02133, 617-727-3600; Fax: 617-727-9416.

Election Results

1994 gen.	William F. Weld (R)	1,533,380	(71%)
	Mark Roosevelt (D)	611,641	(28%)
	Others	19,238	(1%)
1994 prim.	William F. Weld (R) . unopposed		
1990 gen.	William F. Weld (R)	1,175,817	(50%)
	John Silber (D)	1,099,878	(47%)
	Other	67,167	(3%)

SENATORS

Sen. Edward M. Kennedy (D)

Elected 1962, seat up 2000; b. Feb. 22, 1932, Boston; home, Hyannis Port; Harvard, B.A. 1956, The Hague Intl. Law Schl., 1958, U. of VA, LL.B. 1959; Catholic; married (Vicki).

Career: Army, 1951–53; Western states coordinator, John F. Kennedy Pres. campaign, 1960; Asst. Dist. Atty., Suffolk Cnty., 1961–62.

DC Office: 315 RSOB 20510, 202-224-4543; Fax: 202-224-2417; e-mail: senator@kennedy.senate.gov.

State Offices: 2400 JFK Fed. Bldg., Boston 02203, 617-565-3170.

Committees: *Armed Services* (4th of 10 D): Acquisition and Technology; Personnel; Seapower (RMM). *Judiciary* (2nd of 8 D): Constitution, Federalism and Property Rights; Immigration (RMM). *Labor & Human Resources* (RMM of 7 D): Disability Policy; Education, Arts and Humanities. *Joint Economic Committee* (9th of 10 Sen.)

Group Ratings

	ADA	ACLU	COPE	CFA	LCV	CON	NSI	COC	ACU	NTLC	CHC
1994	90	79	88	75	92	10	10	18	0	4	0
1993	90	—	82	80	88	22	—	36	4	—	—

National Journal Ratings

	1993 LIB — 1993 CONS		1994 LIB — 1994 CONS	
Economic	83%	0%	84%	0%
Social	92%	0%	84%	15%
Foreign	62%	36%	66%	29%

Key Votes of the 103d Congress

1. Clinton Deficit Plan	Y	3. Brady Handgun Purchase	Y	5. Lmt. UN Cmnd. of Forces	N
2. NAFTA	Y	4. Strike Race/Death Pnlty.	N	6. Cut Missile Funds	N

Key Votes of the 104th Congress

1. Congressional Compliance	Y	3. Balanced Budget Amndt.	N	5. Product Liability Reform	N
2. Bar Unfunded Mandates	Y	4. Pass Line Item Veto	Y	6. FY96 Budget	N

Election Results

1994 general	Edward M. Kennedy (D)	1,265,997	(58%)	($11,493,735)
	W. Mitt Romney (R)	894,000	(41%)	($7,624,491)
	Others	19,948	(1%)	
1994 primary	Edward M. Kennedy (D)	391,637	(99%)	
	Others	4,498	(1%)	
1988 general	Edward M. Kennedy (D)	1,693,344	(65%)	($2,702,865)
	Joseph D. Malone (R)	884,267	(34%)	($587,323)

Sen. John F. Kerry (D)

Elected 1984, seat up 1996; b. Dec. 11, 1943, Denver, CO; home, Boston; Yale, A.B. 1966, Boston Col., LL.B. 1976; Catholic; married (Teresa Heinz).

Career: Navy, 1966–70 (Vietnam), Naval Reserves, 1972–78; Organizer, Vietnam Veterans Against the War; Asst. Dist. Atty., Middlesex Cnty., 1976–81; Practicing atty., 1981–82; MA Lt. Gov., 1982–84.

DC Office: 421 RSOB 20510, 202-224-2742; Fax: 202-224-8525.

State Offices: One Bowdoin Sq., #1000, Boston 02114, 617-565-8519; 222 Milliken Pl., #311, Fall River 02722, 508-677-0522; and 145 State St., #504, Springfield 01103, 413-785-4619.

Committees: *Banking, Housing & Urban Affairs* (3rd of 7 D): Financial Institutions and Regulatory Relief; Housing Opportunity and Community Development (RMM); International Finance. *Commerce, Science & Transportation* (6th of 9 D): Communications; Oceans and Fisheries (RMM); Science, Technology and Space. *Foreign Relations* (5th of 8 D): East Asian and Pacific Affairs; International Operations (RMM); Near Eastern and South Asian Affairs. *Intelligence (Select)* (5th of 8 D). *Small Business* (5th of 9 D).

Group Ratings

	ADA	ACLU	COPE	CFA	LCV	CON	NSI	COC	ACU	NTLC	CHC
1994	95	79	88	83	92	29	10	31	0	20	7
1993	90	—	82	70	100	29	—	45	12	—	—

National Journal Ratings

	1993 LIB — 1993 CONS		1994 LIB — 1994 CONS	
Economic	83% —	0%	72% —	18%
Social	87% —	8%	85% —	7%
Foreign	67% —	30%	72% —	22%

Key Votes of the 103d Congress

1. Clinton Deficit Plan	Y	3. Brady Handgun Purchase	Y	5. Lmt. UN Cmnd. of Forces	N
2. NAFTA	Y	4. Strike Race/Death Pnlty.	N	6. Cut Missile Funds	Y

Key Votes of the 104th Congress

1. Congressional Compliance	Y	3. Balanced Budget Amndt.	N	5. Product Liability Reform	N
2. Bar Unfunded Mandates	Y	4. Pass Line Item Veto	Y	6. FY96 Budget	N

Election Results

1990 general	John F. Kerry (D)	1,321,712	(57%)	($8,040,970)
	Jim Rappaport (R)	992,917	(43%)	($5,177,801)
1990 primary	John F. Kerry (D)	unopposed		
1984 general	John F. Kerry (D)	1,393,150	(55%)	($2,070,004)
	Raymond Shamie (R)	1,139,913	(45%)	($4,180,961)

FIRST DISTRICT

The stony hills and green-clad mountains of western Massachusetts, with more trees today than when Henry David Thoreau was writing in the 1840s, where stone wall fencing now passing through thick forest once bounded one working farm from another, probably looks today much like it did 300 years ago. This was the frontier in the 17th Century, where Puritan preachers formed new towns in the wilderness, farming the stony soil and preaching against declension. It was dangerous here as well, the site of the Indian uprising known as King Philip's War in 1676 and the Indian raid, supported by the French from Quebec, at Deerfield in 1704. This was Yankee New England's western frontier for nearly 200 years. In the 19th Century, western New England was the home of writers and artists, Emily Dickinson living quietly in Amherst, Edith Wharton grandly on her estate in Lenox, "The Mount," and the sculptor Augustus Saint Gaudens not far from where the Boston Symphony played in the Tanglewood Festival each summer. There were mill towns here as well, jammed in mountain crevasses or along the wide Connecticut River; but as the 20th Century went on, and trees grew up on stony land once farmed, western Massachusetts came to look less settled.

Western Massachusetts has also changed politically. For many years it was one of the heartlands of the Republican Party—flinty, thrifty and chilly just like the area's most famous politician, Calvin Coolidge, who worked his way up from mayor of Northampton to governor and president by lowering taxes and saying no to pleas for government action. But by the 1980s, western Massachusetts was one of the most left-wing parts of America. A town like Stockbridge could attract liberal artist Norman Rockwell (a solid New Dealer and peacenik) and baby boom radical Arlo Guthrie, whose Alice's Restaurant is there. The concentration of colleges and universities in the Pioneer Valley, around Amherst, Northampton and South Hadley, brought together a critical mass of leftish scholars and an even more leftish graduate student proletariat, people defying their Marxist philosophy of economic determinism by remaining in places where they could make little money in order to be surrounded by culturally congenial people and places. The results show up in the election returns: Hampshire County, dominated by Pioneer Valley college towns, voted 61%–37% for Michael Dukakis in 1988 and 54%–22% for Bill Clinton over George Bush in 1992.

The 1st Congressional District of Massachusetts, like all the state's districts, has convoluted boundaries which defy easy description. It includes almost all of the state west of the Connecticut River and the northern half of the state from the Connecticut River east to I-495. But its lines separate close neighbors. The 1st includes Amherst, but not Northampton or South Hadley; it includes West Springfield and Holyoke, but not Springfield just across the Connecticut River; it includes North Brookfield but not Brookfield, and so on. The result is a district that is Democratic, but not overwhelmingly so, and whose Democratic base is split among the Amherst radicals, low-income factory workers of Holyoke and the descendants of ethnic mill and blue-collar workers in factory towns from Pittsfield in the Berkshires to Fitchburg and Leominster in the eastern end of the district. For 32 years, until his death in February 1991, the 1st with somewhat different boundaries was represented by Silvio Conte, a liberal but still partisan Republican who was ranking member of the Appropriations Committee.

The congressman from the 1st is John Olver, a liberal Democrat and chemistry professor at the University of Massachusetts at Amherst. Olver was educated at Tufts and M.I.T. and came to UMass in 1961, at 25; his wife Rose is a professor of psychology and Women's and Gender Studies at Amherst College. John Olver was elected to the Massachusetts House in 1968 and to the Senate in 1972; altogether he served 23 years in Boston's State House. After Conte's death, Olver ran for the seat, and his Pioneer Valley base helped him win 31% in the fragmented Democratic primary. In the June 1991 general Olver faced Steven Pierce, former state House Republican leader, Governor William Weld's conservative opponent in the 1990 primary and a Weld cabinet appointee. With Massachusetts liberalism in grave disrepute, the race was close;

the election was scheduled for after students' summer vacation began. But Olver was able to eke out a 50%–48% win.

Olver has had one of the most liberal voting records in the House, modified only by some more conservative votes on foreign and defense issue in the 103d Congress. He boasts of working "to make federal government more responsive to people's needs by extending unemployment benefits, helping to ease the credit crunch on businesses and fighting to control the cost of health care." In his first term he passed a bill creating a network of Manufacturing Outreach Centers to help businesses tap into university resources—a bit of local pork?—and securing two-year funding for the Low-Income Home Energy Assistance Program. He was against NAFTA and for Canadian-style single-payer health insurance. Olver had a serious challenge in 1992, after Weld insisted on a redistricting plan that took Northampton and South Hadley out of the 1st District and put Fitchburg and Leominster in. The Republican candidate was Patrick Larkin, an aide to Conte supported by his widow; Olver was forced to apologize when he accused Larkin of holding two simultaneous Hill jobs (turns out there was another Patrick Larkin). Olver got help from big name Democrats and ended up winning 52%–43%, carrying Pittsfield and other Berkshire towns narrowly, winning big in the Pioneer Valley and carrying a plurality around Fitchburg.

In the Democratic 103d Congress Olver supported the Clinton Administration on most issues except NAFTA and, with help from Rules Chairman Joe Moakley of Boston, got a seat on Appropriations. The 1994 election worked out well for him—he was unopposed—but dreadfully for his party, and in 1995, he lost the Appropriations seat; instead, he gained a seat on the Budget Committee, where he helps to define the campaign against Newt Gingrich's fiscal plans. His remains a Democratic seat, and Gingrich's ascendancy in Washington may have hardened liberalism in the Pioneer Valley. But it will be harder for Olver to get programs and projects to aid the district.

The People: Pop. 1990: 601,721; 36% rural; 14% age 65+; 92% White; 2% Black; 1% Asian; 3% Other; 5% Hispanic origin. Voting age pop.: 458,088; 1% Black; 4% Hispanic origin. Households: 55% married couple families; 25% married couple fams. w. children; 45% college educ.; median household income: $31,903; per capita income: $14,200; median gross rent: $479; median house value: $123,200.

1992 Presidential Vote			1988 Presidential Vote		
Clinton (D)	130,308	(48%)	Dukakis (D)	138,999	(56%)
Bush (R)	72,238	(26%)	Bush (R)	111,242	(44%)
Perot (I)	68,545	(25%)			

Rep. John Olver (D)

Elected June 1991; b. Sept. 3, 1936, Homesdale, PA; home, Amherst; Rensselaer Polytechnic Inst., B.S. 1955, Tufts U., M.S. 1956, M.I.T., Ph.D. 1961; No religious affiliation; married (Rose).

Career: Prof., U. of MA, Amherst, 1961–69; MA House of Reps., 1968–72; MA Senate, 1972–91.

DC Office: 1027 LHOB 20515, 202-225-5335; Fax: 202-226-1224.

District Offices: 78 Center St. Arterial, Pittsfield 02101, 413-442-0946; 881 Main St., Philbin Fed. Bldg., Fitchburg 01420, 508-342-8722; and 187 High St., Holyoke 01040, 413-584-8108.

Committees: *Budget* (14th of 18 D). *Science* (14th of 23 D): Basic Research; Energy and Environment.

Group Ratings

	ADA	ACLU	COPE	CFA	LCV	CON	NSI	COC	ACU	NTLC	CHC
1994	100	87	89	100	100	33	0	33	0	11	0
1993	95	—	100	100	93	32	—	9	9	—	—

National Journal Ratings

	1993 LIB — 1993 CONS		1994 LIB — 1994 CONS	
Economic	88%	— 0%	83%	— 0%
Social	87%	— 0%	94%	— 0%
Foreign	63%	— 34%	85%	— 0%

Key Votes of the 103d Congress

1. Clinton Deficit Plan	Y	3. Brady Handgun Purchase	Y	5. Lmt. UN Cmnd. of Forces	N
2. NAFTA	N	4. Strike Race/Death Pnlty.	N	6. Cut Missile Funds	N

Key Votes of the 104th Congress

1. Congressional Compliance	Y	6. Reform Crime Grant	N	11. Loser Pays Court Reform	N
2. Balanced Budget Amndmt.	N	7. National Security Act	N	12. Product Liability Reform	N
3. Bar Unfunded Mandates	Y	8. Moratorium on Regs.	N	13. Welfare Reform	N
4. Pass Line Item Veto	N	9. Risk Assessment on Regs.	N	14. Term Limits Amndmt.	N
5. Relax Exclusionary Rule	N	10. Expnd. Priv. Prop. Rights	N	15. Tax Cuts	N

Election Results

1994 general	John W. Olver (D).................	unopposed		($317,317)
1994 primary	John W. Olver (D).................	unopposed		
1992 general	John Olver (D)	135,049	(52%)	($704,238)
	Patrick Larkin (R)	113,828	(43%)	($384,625)
	Others...........................	13,243	(5%)	

SECOND DISTRICT

As American as apple pie, the place where basketball was invented, the city where the Webster's unabridged dictionaries (2d and 3d editions) were edited and published, the site of the Armory where M-1 rifles were manufactured in World War II, the city with the highest percentage of Puerto Ricans: this is Springfield, Massachusetts. Springfield is the third largest city in the Bay State, but far from Boston; the second largest city in the Connecticut River Valley, but overshadowed by Hartford; a medium-sized American city built by New England Yankees, where immigrants from a dozen different countries worked their way up.

Springfield is the largest city in the 2d Congressional District of Massachusetts, whose irregular boundaries stretch north to South Hadley and Northampton, college towns of the Pioneer Valley, and east across stony hills and the antique center of Brimfield to the factory towns of the Blackstone Valley just north of Woonsocket, Rhode Island. Historically, this was a Yankee Republican district for much of the 20th Century, then a solidly Catholic Democratic district; now it is more marginal, but still leans Democratic.

The congressman from the 2d District is Richard Neal, mayor of Springfield from 1984–89. Neal grew up in Springfield, went to work for the mayor in 1973, was elected to the Council in 1978, meanwhile teaching high school and college history. As mayor himself, he boasted of both downtown rehabilitation and neighborhood revitalization. Neal was essentially bequeathed the seat by his predecessor, 36-year incumbent Edward Boland, longtime friend of Tip O'Neill. Boland announced his retirement just before the filing deadline, and after Neal had been making the rounds of the district for a year. Unopposed in the Democratic primary, Neal won 80% in the general.

Quiet, with a generally liberal record except on some cultural issues (abortion, the flag amendment), he seemed to do nothing politically risky. He sponsored the 1990 National Service Act based on his Service Learning Program in Springfield schools. In 1993, Joe Moakley of Boston helped Neal win a seat on the Ways and Means Committee, putting him in position to be a key vote on healthcare reform. But even from a district that previously had produced a stalwart leadership Democrat, Neal hesitated at supporting the Clinton plan. He worked with Ways and Means members Ben Cardin of Maryland and Bob Matsui of California to find some middle ground; he declared himself undecided on the Clinton plan in April 1994, noting that 2d District voters were telling him they were happy with what they had. With thousands of employees working in insurance companies in or nearby his district, he offered a successful amendment in committee in June 1994 to allow firms with more than 100 workers to self-insure. The bottom line is that, absent automatic support from Democrats like Neal, the Clinton plan failed in a Democratic House.

Neal has had some problems in elections, though not in 1994, mostly relating to charges arising out of his days as mayor. In 1990, he was opposed in the primary by the previous mayor, Theodore DiMauro, who attacked him for overspending as mayor, but Neal won 64%–36%. In 1992, after the district was considerably changed by redistricting, Neal had opposition again, and had to defend his 87 overdrafts on the House bank. He was challenged in the primary by Springfield Councilwoman Kateri Walsh and by systems design manager Charles Platten; Walsh won 34% of the vote and Platten 18%; Neal's 48% was good enough for a win, but below the 50% he would need to beat a single opponent. In the general election, 27-year-old Springfield Councilman Anthony Ravosa again harped on Neal's financial management as mayor. Ravosa won only 31%, but Thomas Sheehan of the For the People Party got 16% and Neal only 53%. In 1993, there were reports a federal prosecutor was looking into connections between contributions to Neal's 1988 campaign and a no-bid insurance contract he awarded as mayor; a Neal aide was indicted. But Neal was not, and now that he has been out of the mayor's office for seven years these issues seem moot. In 1994, he had no primary opposition and easily won the general; in 1995 he clung to his Ways and Means seat, as others below him lost theirs, leaving him the most junior Democrat.

The People: Pop. 1990: 601,490; 21% rural; 14% age 65+; 88% White; 6% Black; 1% Asian; 4% Other; 6% Hispanic origin. Voting age pop.: 453,960; 5% Black; 4% Hispanic origin. Households: 56% married couple families; 25% married couple fams. w. children; 42% college educ.; median household income: $33,401; per capita income: $14,652; median gross rent: $497; median house value: $128,800.

1992 Presidential Vote		
Clinton (D)	121,759	(46%)
Bush (R)	76,277	(29%)
Perot (I)	65,935	(25%)

1988 Presidential Vote		
Dukakis (D)	132,154	(55%)
Bush (R)	108,527	(45%)

Rep. Richard E. Neal (D)

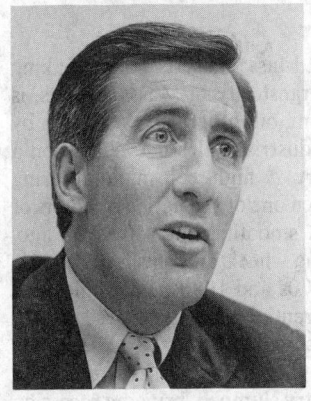

Elected 1988; b. Feb. 14, 1949, Springfield; home, Springfield; Amer. Intl. Col., B.A. 1972, U. of Hartford, M.A. 1976; Catholic; married (Maureen).

Career: Staff Asst., Springfield Mayor, 1973–78; Springfield City Cncl., 1978–83; Springfield Mayor, 1984–88.

DC Office: 2431 RHOB 20515, 202-225-5601; Fax: 202-225-8112.

District Offices: Fed. Office Bldg., #309, 1550 Main St., Springfield 01103, 413-785-0325; and 4 Congress St., Milford 01757, 508-634-8198.

Committees: *Ways & Means* (15th of 15 D): Social Security; Trade.

Group Ratings

	ADA	ACLU	COPE	CFA	LCV	CON	NSI	COC	ACU	NTLC	CHC
1994	95	78	89	70	94	27	20	42	0	11	14
1993	95	—	100	100	86	19	—	9	9	—	—

National Journal Ratings

	1993 LIB — 1993 CONS	1994 LIB — 1994 CONS
Economic	75% — 22%	64% — 35%
Social	73% — 23%	82% — 15%
Foreign	84% — 13%	85% — 0%

Key Votes of the 103d Congress

1. Clinton Deficit Plan	Y	3. Brady Handgun Purchase	Y	5. Lmt. UN Cmnd. of Forces	N
2. NAFTA	N	4. Strike Race/Death Pnlty.	N	6. Cut Missile Funds	Y

Key Votes of the 104th Congress

1. Congressional Compliance	Y	6. Reform Crime Grant	N	11. Loser Pays Court Reform	N
2. Balanced Budget Amndmt.	N	7. National Security Act	N	12. Product Liability Reform	N
3. Bar Unfunded Mandates	Y	8. Moratorium on Regs.	N	13. Welfare Reform	N
4. Pass Line Item Veto	N	9. Risk Assessment on Regs.	N	14. Term Limits Amndmt.	N
5. Relax Exclusionary Rule	N	10. Expnd. Priv. Prop. Rights	N	15. Tax Cuts	N

Election Results

1994 general	Richard E. Neal (D)	117,178	(59%)	($318,582)
	John M. Briare (R)	72,732	(36%)	($60,685)
	Kate Ross (NL)	10,167	(5%)	
1994 primary	Richard E. Neal (D)	unopposed		
1992 general	Richard E. Neal (D)	131,215	(53%)	($355,367)
	Anthony W. Ravosa, Jr. (R)	76,795	(31%)	($102,179)
	Thomas R. Sheehan (FTP)	38,963	(16%)	

THIRD DISTRICT

Worcester (its name still pronounced with a particularly pungent Massachusetts accent making it sound as if it had no *R*s), although technically the second-largest city in Massachusetts, is often overlooked. People may drive in for concerts at the Centrum, but otherwise they zoom by on I-495 or the Turnpike. Worcester is one of the few major industrial cities not located on a river, lake or sea coast, and it is far from a commercial airport. A high-tech manufacturing haven before the term was invented, for 200 years the city has been one of the nation's centers of tinkering, contriving and inventing. But it hasn't always been smooth going; 50 years ago, Worcester's biggest industries were wire-making, textiles, grinding wheels and envelopes: not on the cutting edge even then and certainly not now. But in the 1970s and 1980s, electronics and computer firms sprouted up along Interstate 495—the circumferential highway located just 20 miles east of Worcester, as they had earlier around Route 128, closer to Boston. The high-tech boom brought prosperity, labor shortages, new residents and higher housing prices to central Massachusetts. Then, in the early 1990s, the minicomputer industry slumped, bringing recession and a collapse of real estate values. But Worcester's ingenious entrepreneurs and skilled labor force have hustled and in the middle 1990s the local economy again is perking up.

The 3d Congressional District of Massachusetts, grotesquely shaped, has Worcester as its largest city if not its geographic center. The 3d includes towns north of Worcester up to Rutland and Princeton and east along the I-495 high-tech corridor, and it is connected by narrow land bridges running far to the southeast with Fall River, an old textile mill town on an inlet of Narragansett Bay, and to the towns of Westport and Dartmouth fronting on Buzzards Bay. It has been called the district that now makes inland Worcester a seaport town. While Worcester and the Fall River area are heavily Democratic, the area in between is Republican, and the I-495 corridor, once solidly Democratic, trended Republican: techies in Massachusetts tend to be Republican, lawyers and academics Democrats.

The congressman from the 3d District is Peter Blute, a Republican first elected in 1992 over scandal-plagued incumbent Joe Early, and reelected in 1994 over a different kind of Democrat. Blute is from the Worcester area, graduated from Boston College, did PR for the Boston Red Sox and owned a sports promotion firm; in 1986 he was elected to be part of the hardy minority of Republicans in Massachusetts's Great and General Court—their House of Representatives. In 1992, alerted by incumbent Early's weakness, Blute decided to run for Congress. Conservative on spending and anti-abortion, he defeated pro-choice colleague David Lionett in the Republican primary 49%–37%. Meanwhile, Early won a five-candidate primary with only 37%, as he carried the additional burden of 140 overdrafts on the House bank; in a speech on the floor of the House he said of the Ethics Committee members who released the list of violators, "They ran like rats!" In the general, Blute ran ads ridiculing Early for overdrafts, overseas junkets ("Tahiti Joe") and ducking debates; he had a Bart Simpson-like character speaking for Early ("Hey, dude. No big deal"). Blute won, 50%–44%.

In his first term, Blute compiled a moderate record, breaking with Republican leaders by supporting the Brady bill, the assault weapons ban, family leave legislation and the Clinton national service initiative. He voted against NAFTA and GATT. Still, he was naturally a Democratic target in 1994. Democrats had a serious primary between state Representative Kevin O'Sullivan of Worcester, fellow Massachusetts member Joe Moakley's press secretary, James McGovern of Worcester, as well as several others. O'Sullivan ran as a New Democrat, one not pledged to all party programs; he edged McGovern 38%–30% in the primary, largely on his margin in Worcester. In the general, O'Sullivan said Blute was too conservative for the district on abortion and other issues; Blute countered by reminding voters that O'Sullivan had switched on abortion and the death penalty for the campaign. O'Sullivan argued that Blute was "weak" on education and the environment and called the Contract With America "a big lie." But Blute touted his accomplishments and record and won 55%–44%, a solid victory in a district that had not elected a Republican between 1944 and 1992.

Blute was a leader on both the line-item veto and term limits in the 104th Congress; but he dissented from parts of the Contract With America, opposing the tax cut and the crime bill rewrite. He pushed successfully for a welfare amendment to cut benefits for fugitive felons and give law enforcement officials greater access to social service agencies to track down fugitives. He also has introduced legislation to stop the practice of putting former drug addicts in with senior citizens in formerly seniors-only public housing projects. Like most Republicans in Massachusetts, he can never rest easily, but he seems to have solidified his position in the 3rd District and should be a strong candidate for reelection.

The People: Pop. 1990: 601,852; 18% rural; 14% age 65+; 93% White; 2% Black; 2% Asian; 2% Other; 4% Hispanic origin. Voting age pop.: 459,291; 2% Black; 3% Hispanic origin. Households: 58% married couple families; 27% married couple fams. w. children; 48% college educ.; median household income: $36,873; per capita income: $15,917; median gross rent: $515; median house value: $150,500.

1992 Presidential Vote			1988 Presidential Vote		
Clinton (D)	123,724	(45%)	Dukakis (D)	127,607	(51%)
Bush (R)	85,047	(31%)	Bush (R)	123,250	(49%)
Perot (I)	62,667	(23%)			

Rep. Peter I. Blute (R)

Elected 1992; b. Jan. 28, 1956, Boston; home, Shrewsbury; Boston Col., B.A. 1978; Catholic; married (Robi).

Career: P.R., Boston Red Sox, 1979–80; Partner, Sports promotion firm; MA House of Reps., 1987–92.

DC Office: 1029 LHOB 20515, 202-225-6101; Fax: 202-225-2217.

District Offices: 100 Front St., #1079, Worcester 01608, 508-752-6789; 1039 S. Main St., Fall River 02724, 508-675-3400; and 7 N. Main St., Attleboro 02703, 508-223-3100.

Committees: *Government Reform & Oversight* (12th of 27 R): Government Management, Information and Technology; National Security, International Affairs and Criminal Justice. *Transportation & Infrastructure* (19th of 33 R): Public Buildings and Economic Development; Surface Transportation.

Group Ratings

	ADA	ACLU	COPE	CFA	LCV	CON	NSI	COC	ACU	NTLC	CHC
1994	20	26	56	30	39	76	80	92	67	79	71
1993	30	—	50	50	57	89	—	64	75	—	—

National Journal Ratings

	1993 LIB — 1993 CONS		1994 LIB — 1994 CONS	
Economic	35% —	65%	30% —	67%
Social	28% —	71%	46% —	54%
Foreign	28% —	70%	30% —	67%

Key Votes of the 103d Congress

1. Clinton Deficit Plan	N	3. Brady Handgun Purchase	Y	5. Lmt. UN Cmnd. of Forces	Y
2. NAFTA	N	4. Strike Race/Death Pnlty.	Y	6. Cut Missile Funds	N

Key Votes of the 104th Congress

1. Congressional Compliance Y	6. Reform Crime Grant N	11. Loser Pays Court Reform Y
2. Balanced Budget Amndmt. Y	7. National Security Act Y	12. Product Liability Reform Y
3. Bar Unfunded Mandates Y	8. Moratorium on Regs. Y	13. Welfare Reform Y
4. Pass Line Item Veto Y	9. Risk Assessment on Regs. Y	14. Term Limits Amndmt. Y
5. Relax Exclusionary Rule Y	10. Expnd. Priv. Prop. Rights N	15. Tax Cuts N

Election Results

1994 general	Peter I. Blute (R)	115,810	(55%)	($977,107)
	Kevin O'Sullivan (D)	93,689	(44%)	($495,645)
	Others	2,536	(1%)	
1994 primary	Peter I. Blute (R)	unopposed		
1992 general	Peter I. Blute (R)	131,473	(50%)	($435,911)
	Joseph D. Early (D)	115,587	(44%)	($924,384)
	Leonard J. Umina (I)	9,691	(4%)	
	Others	4,181	(2%)	

FOURTH DISTRICT

The political transformation of Massachusetts is nowhere better illustrated than in the Boston suburbs of Brookline and Newton. These were Yankee enclaves a century ago, with avenues built by developers to resemble the sweep of Haussmann's Grand Boulevards in Paris, and villages of giant clapboard houses clustering within a few blocks of a commuter railroad station. Brookline was where The Country Club (the very first one) was established in 1882, and where Joseph Kennedy, as an Irish Catholic 20-something banker seeking respectability, moved his family in 1914. Brookline and Newton then were solidly Republican in politics, the political base of leading politicians like Christian Herter, governor of Massachusetts and U.S. secretary of state in the 1950s; as late as 1960, Brookline and Newton and adjacent wards of Boston were electing a Republican congressman. Then came the transformation, personified by the election in 1962 of Michael Dukakis at 29 to the Great and General Court (the legislature). As Massachusetts's university-educated classes became more liberal, and as Brookline's and Newton's Jewish population grew, and as young liberal-minded families refurbished the graceful old houses, these became liberal Democratic bastions. By the 1970s, the Brookline Town Meeting was opening each year with debates over whether they should recite the Pledge of Allegiance; against that background, it is easier to understand how Dukakis could fail so utterly to understand the cultural attitudes of most Americans. And Brookline and Newton stayed loyal: 69%–29% for Dukakis in 1988, 68%–20% for Bill Clinton in 1992.

The 4th Congressional District of Massachusetts includes Brookline and Newton which form the political home base for its congressman, Barney Frank. But they cast only 25% of the district's votes, and this grotesquely shaped district is not all of one piece: indeed, one setting out to canvass entirely the district's bounds might have to get off the road and step over fences and trudge through marshes. The shape results from successive redistrictings: in 1982, Frank's district was extended south to the old textile mill city of Fall River; in 1992, it was adjusted to accommodate adjacent districts, so the 4th lost the western half of Fall River and gained New Bedford, a great 19th Century whaling port and still home to one of the largest fishing fleets in the United States and with the largest percentage of Portuguese-Americans in the nation. The 4th also curves north to the interior of Plymouth County, around old towns like Bridgewater. This is a Democratic district in national politics, but not nearly so Democratic nor as uniformly culturally liberal as Brookline and Newton; without those two, the district would have voted only about 40% for Dukakis and Clinton. There is a bit of most kinds of America here: high-income WASPy Wellesley, French Canadian mill worker Fall River, Foxboro with its football stadium,

Sharon with a middle-income Jewish population, countrified Dover.

Frank is one of the intellectual and political leaders of the Democratic Party in the House, political theorist and pit bull all at the same time. Frank grew up in Bayonne, New Jersey, went to Harvard, where he got to know local politicians as well as political scientists. In 1967, he went to work for newly elected Boston Mayor Kevin White; in 1971, Frank went to Washington to work for Congressman Michael Harrington. In 1972, Frank was elected to the Massachusetts House from the Back Bay of Boston, then just starting to be a liberal singles neighborhood. In 1980, when Congressman Robert Drinan retired after Pope John Paul II commanded Jesuits to leave elective office, Frank moved to Brookline and ran in the 4th Congressional District. With a strong base in Brookline and Newton he won and, keeping them together as redistricting moved the seat down to Fall River, beat Republican Margaret Heckler 60%–40% in 1982. He has been reelected by wide margins since.

In the House, Frank soon gained a reputation as one of the smartest talkers and best debaters in the chamber. At a time when so many members seem to rely on canned speeches produced by staffers and letterhead interest groups, Frank listens to others' arguments and engages them in his inimitable rapid-fire delivery. He has made some telling criticisms of conservatism over the years. But he also has been less rigidly partisan than many members and more willing to consider arguments on their intellectual merits. In his 1992 book, *Speaking Frankly*, he criticizes his fellow liberals for their "tyranny of the notsuppostas"—their unwillingness to criticize people who commit crimes or say that Communism is a terrible system—and chided them as "scolds" for opposing the 65-mile-an-hour speed limit or pursuing an impossible goal like federal gun control. He insists that "Democratic positions are fully consistent with the values of patriotism, free enterprise, working hard for one's self and one's family, and holding people to a standard of behavior fully respectful of the person and property of others."

But this was not how Frank made national headlines. In May 1987, in a seemingly casual answer to a reporter's question, Frank said he is gay. But in August 1989, the conservative *Washington Times* revealed that Frank had employed as a personal aide a male prostitute and convicted drug possessor, Steve Gobie, and let him live in his apartment where the man was allegedly carrying on his former trade. Frank admitted to paying Gobie, but was careful never to use official or campaign funds; he denied that he tolerated prostitution in his apartment and had thrown the man out when he suspected it was going on. The *Boston Globe* called on Frank to resign; his picture appeared on the cover of *Newsweek*; he called on the Ethics Committee to investigate. It did, and dismissed all but two minor charges. The committee recommended a reprimand but not censure; Frank agreed in a contrite appearance before the House in July 1990; the House voted 287–141 against censure (moved by Newt Gingrich); the vote for reprimand was 408–18. "I think members will agree that I have always had a reputation for honesty, not always tact or tolerance," Frank said to the House. That reputation was one reason he survived in the House; his brains, liberal stands, hard work and constituency service helped him survive in the 4th District.

Frank has been involved in many issues over the years. He took over the subcommittee handling the bill to provide redress to Japanese Americans interned in World War II and got it through the House and signed into law. In 1990, he worked to expand immigration limits and fought against the provision barring HIV-positive people from entering the country. On housing issues, he pushed successfully for amendments to the fair housing bill for AIDS victims and those with the HIV virus. He is proud of creating the HOME program providing housing block grants to states. He successfully stymied conservative attempts to undermine the Legal Services Corporation in the 1980s, only to find the program again under attack from the Gingrich Republicans.

In the early 1990s, Frank tended to work behind the scenes. He was active on the issue, raised by Bill Clinton and not by Frank or by gay rights groups in the 1992 campaign, of gays in the military. To the disappointment of many in the gay community, Frank admitted that allowing open homosexuals to serve in the military would not be accepted by most in Congress and the

Pentagon. Taking Senator Sam Nunn's "Don't Ask, Don't Tell" compromise a step further, Frank suggested that gays be allowed to conduct an openly gay lifestyle when off-base without fear of reprisal; but Clinton eventually declined to go so far. On the Budget Committee in 1993, Frank worked to make the budget both liberal and passable; enough, it turned out, to pass by one vote. He tried unsuccessfully to break down the firewalls and cut defense spending to increase domestic; he made a start toward requiring European allies to share more of the burden of stationing U.S. troops abroad. He pressed to use trade agreements and the World Bank to force higher labor standards and environmental rules on Mexico and other less developed countries. He is proud of the RTC program of selling low-end housing units acquired by bankrupt S&Ls to low and moderate income people, which he claims has enabled more poor people to become homeowners than any other federal program. Stung by Republicans' charges of institutional corruption and rot, Frank in 1993 tried to direct reformers' attention to the Senate's filibuster rule—a campaign that House Democrats soon would quietly drop—and in 1994 called for denial of frequent flier miles to members and staff.

After the Republican victory in November 1994, new Minority Whip David Bonior asked Frank to be the Democrats' point man in floor debates; Frank asked whether Bonior wanted him to be such a visible symbol of the party, and Bonior said yes. So during the Contract With America debate, Frank prowled the floor, ready to take up a microphone and deliver stinging attacks on Republicans' hypocrisy or cross-examine a freshman with all the mercy of a Harvard Law professor questioning a not quite prepared first-year student. His strong and orderly mind, his ability to argue abstract principles in rapid-fire but comprehensible words, were on display— and made him the most feared adversary on the Republican side. It was a dazzling performance and a bit out of character: Frank, long known for candor, was taking a purely partisan tack. Like many House Democrats, he professes to believe that the Republicans cannot succeed in fulfilling their campaign promises, that government spending simply cannot be cut without depriving voters of services and benefits they want, and that they will retaliate by installing Democratic majorities again. But the fury of his attacks on the other side suggest that he may in some corner of his brain fear that their strategy might work politically, and that he is laboring hard to prevent the demolition of the liberal government he has spent his lifetime supporting. If Frank is correct and Democrats regain the majority, his committee seniority will leave him well-positioned to influence many domestic issues.

The People: Pop. 1990: 601,392; 27% rural; 14% age 65+; 92% White; 2% Black; 2% Asian; 2% Other; 2% Hispanic origin. Voting age pop.: 461,137; 2% Black; 2% Hispanic origin. Households: 57% married couple families; 27% married couple fams. w. children; 51% college educ.; median household income: $39,005; per capita income: $18,963; median gross rent: $512; median house value: $170,200.

1992 Presidential Vote			1988 Presidential Vote		
Clinton (D)	143,595	(51%)	Dukakis (D)	147,309	(56%)
Bush (R)	74,769	(26%)	Bush (R)	114,414	(44%)
Perot (I)	62,746	(22%)			

Rep. Barney Frank (D)

Elected 1980; b. Mar. 31, 1940, Bayonne, NJ; home, Newton; Harvard, B.A. 1962, J.D. 1977; Jewish; companion, Herb Moses.

Career: Exec. Asst., Boston Mayor Kevin White, 1967–71; A.A., U.S. Rep. Michael Harrington, 1971–72; MA House of Reps., 1973–80; Lecturer, Harvard JFK Schl. of Govt., 1978–80.

DC Office: 2210 RHOB 20515, 202-225-5931; Fax: 202-225-0182.

District Offices: 29 Crafts St., Newton 02158, 617-332-3920; 558 Pleasant St., #309, New Bedford 02740, 508-999-6462; 222 Milliken Pl., #300, Fall River 02721, 508-674-3551; and 89 Main St., Bridgewater 02324, 508-697-9403.

Committees: *Banking & Financial Services* (5th of 22 D): Domestic and International Monetary Policy; Housing and Community Opportunity. *Judiciary* (3rd of 15 D): Constitution (RMM); Immigration and Claims.

Group Ratings

	ADA	ACLU	COPE	CFA	LCV	CON	NSI	COC	ACU	NTLC	CHC
1994	100	87	100	90	100	40	0	25	0	8	0
1993	100	—	100	100	93	39	—	9	4	—	—

National Journal Ratings

	1993 LIB — 1993 CONS		1994 LIB — 1994 CONS	
Economic	88%	— 0%	67%	— 29%
Social	87%	— 0%	94%	— 0%
Foreign	93%	— 0%	85%	— 0%

Key Votes of the 103d Congress

1. Clinton Deficit Plan	Y	3. Brady Handgun Purchase	Y	5. Lmt. UN Cmnd. of Forces	N
2. NAFTA	N	4. Strike Race/Death Pnlty.	N	6. Cut Missile Funds	Y

Key Votes of the 104th Congress

1. Congressional Compliance	Y	6. Reform Crime Grant	N	11. Loser Pays Court Reform	N
2. Balanced Budget Amndmt.	N	7. National Security Act	N	12. Product Liability Reform	N
3. Bar Unfunded Mandates	Y	8. Moratorium on Regs.	N	13. Welfare Reform	N
4. Pass Line Item Veto	N	9. Risk Assessment on Regs.	N	14. Term Limits Amndmt.	N
5. Relax Exclusionary Rule	Y	10. Expnd. Priv. Prop. Rights	N	15. Tax Cuts	N

Election Results

1994 general	Barney Frank (D) .... unopposed			($208,936)
1994 primary	Barney Frank (D) 43,865	(86%)		
	Denise B. Ham (D) 7,278	(14%)		
1992 general	Barney Frank (D) 182,633	(68%)	($376,829)	
	Edward J. McCormick, III (R) 70,665	(26%)	($51,350)	
	Luke Lumina (I) 13,670	(5%)		
	Others 2,844	(1%)		

FIFTH DISTRICT

The Merrimack River Valley at the northern edge of Massachusetts has had an erratic history: high-tech boom, bust, boom, bust. When Massachusetts was a kind of maritime republic in the 19th Century, with a few farmers struggling to scratch out a living from the stony soil, a few clever Yankees used their profits from the sea trade to try to tame the rapidly flowing Merrimack and build cotton spinning mills. Creating the cities of Lowell and Lawrence, they built model dormitories and recreation programs for their women. Because of the textile industry, which lasted here for nearly a century, Massachusetts continued to grow even after the maritime industry faded. But in the 1920s, the price of labor rose here and newly built mills in the Carolinas—much closer to the cotton supply—decimated the industry that Lawrence and Lowell built. Many residents—by then rather elderly—waited forlornly for an upturn in the local economy.

It eventually improved, largely due to an unexpected source. High-tech industry drove the growth, beginning in the 1960s in the area surrounding MIT, then moving out to the old Route 128 circular highway, and more recently along I-495, which passes through Lowell and Lawrence. Wang, headquartered in Lowell, grew steadily and former Congressman and Senator Paul Tsongas spearheaded a national historical restoration of the old mill area. When the rest of the nation was in a recession in the early 1980s, Massachusetts had one of the nation's lowest unemployment rates and in the middle of the decade, the state surged. But late that same decade, Wang's word processors and minicomputers slumped as businesses purchased personal computers and hooked them together in networks. The company's payroll fell from 31,500 in 1988 to a restructured 6,300 after declaring bankruptcy in 1992. Many of Lowell's restored buildings sprouted "now leasing" signs. Yet the overall prospects are surely better than they were in the 1920s. Lowell's new immigrants—mostly from Cambodia and Puerto Rico—provide vitality, and its recent growth shows the power of innovation and adaptability, much weaker ideas in the 1920s or 1950s.

The 5th Congressional District of Massachusetts includes Lawrence and Lowell, which with their suburbs accounts for about half the district's population. The remainder of the district includes the troubled high-tech corridor further south on I-495, running from the stony hills of Lawrence and Lowell to Maynard (headquarters of Digital) and Marlborough. The district also includes fancy suburbs like Concord, aging mill towns like Ayer, Fort Devens, which the Army is closing and the mountains along the New Hampshire state line. With the exception of Lowell and Lawrence, the area is ancestrally Yankee Republican. It is culturally liberal and trended toward the Democrats in the early 1970s. But in the 1980s and 1990s, with the area booming with high-tech growth, it went Republican in national and even statewide elections. Increasingly uneasy about George Bush's evident lack of interest in the domestic economy, it gave a plurality to Bill Clinton in 1992 but his lowest percentage in the state, and the real movement was to that high-tech pioneer Ross Perot. The 5th is the state's most Republican district, a kind of Baja New Hampshire; actually, a better way to put it would be to say it is the least Democratic.

The congressman from the 5th District is Martin Meehan, a Democrat first elected in 1992 when he polished off incumbent Chester Atkins in the primary and then handily beat long-ago incumbent Paul Cronin in the general. Meehan is more or less a lifelong politico; he was an aide to Congressman James Shannon while working on his masters degree, worked in the Massachusetts secretary of state's office after law school, was an assistant DA in Middlesex County from 1991 until he ran for Congress in 1992. His immediate target was Atkins, who had won in 1990 only after attacking his opponent's mother's religion, who had 127 overdrafts on the House bank and who voted for the 1990 pay raise. Atkins attacked an old ally, state Senate President Billy Bulger, and watched as Bulger and Governor William Weld kept Lawrence and Lowell, where Atkins was highly unpopular, in the district. Meehan beat Atkins by the astonishing margin of 65%–35%, winning the Lowell-Lawrence area 75%–25%. In the general, Meehan depicted

MASSACHUSETTS 651

Cronin as a perpetual loser (he lost the seat to Paul Tsongas in 1974 and had run for various offices since and mostly lost). Meehan had his own venturesome program—a 50% defense cut, targeted capital gains tax cuts and income tax increases—and backed the balanced budget amendment and term limits. He won 52%–38%, a solid margin but only a bit over the 50% mark.

As he showed again on the Contract With America, Meehan has compiled the most moderate voting record of Massachusetts Democrats—except on economic issues, where he seems to reflect the free market leanings of the district. He voted for NAFTA, helped establish a Manufacturing Task Force and early on supported the balanced budget amendment and the line-item veto. He committed himself to serving no more than four terms (which would put him off the public payroll practically for the first time at 44). Meehan raised an impressive $819,000 in 1994, and was number 10 in raising individual contributions; he was reelected with 70% over a nuisance candidate.

In December 1994, he asked Attorney General Janet Reno for a criminal investigation of the tobacco companies, charging they have engaged in a 40-year conspiracy to deceive the government and public. And he specifically blasted incoming Commerce Committee Chairman Thomas Bliley of Virginia, saying, "There is no member of Congress who has taken more money from the tobacco companies and that is inexcusable, indefensible and unethical." Meehan also promised to develop his own balanced budget plan, reducing Social Security benefits for the wealthy and slowing the growth of Medicare and Medicaid spending. But he didn't receive much encouragement from the Democratic Caucus.

The People: Pop. 1990: 601,527; 16% rural; 10% age 65+; 87% White; 2% Black; 4% Asian; 5% Other; 8% Hispanic origin. Voting age pop.: 446,128; 2% Black; 6% Hispanic origin. Households: 60% married couple families; 30% married couple fams. w. children; 52% college educ.; median household income: $42,701; per capita income: $18,293; median gross rent: $603; median house value: $174,100.

1992 Presidential Vote

Clinton (D)	113,073	(42%)
Bush (R)	85,366	(32%)
Perot (I)	70,474	(26%)

1988 Presidential Vote

Bush (R)	131,405	(53%)
Dukakis (D)	117,137	(47%)

Rep. Martin T. (Marty) Meehan (D)

Elected 1992; b. Dec. 30, 1956, Lowell; home, Lowell; U. of MA, B.S. 1978, Suffolk U., M.A. 1981, J.D. 1986; Catholic; divorced.

Career: Staff Asst., U.S. Rep. James Shannon, 1979–81; MA Dep. Secy. of State for Securities & Corps., 1986–90; Middlesex Cnty. 1st Asst. Dist. Atty., 1990–92.

DC Office: 318 CHOB 20515, 202-225-3411; Fax: 202-226-0771.

District Offices: 11 Kearney Sq., Lowell 01852, 508-459-0101; Bay State Bldg., 11 Lawrence St., #806, Lawrence 01840, 508-681-6200; and Walker Bldg., 255 Main St., #102, Marlborough 01752, 508-460-9292.

Committees: National Security (16th of 25 D): Military Readiness; Military Research and Development. Small Business (8th of 19 D): Tax and Finance (RMM).

Group Ratings

	ADA	ACLU	COPE	CFA	LCV	CON	NSI	COC	ACU	NTLC	CHC
1994	85	86	67	80	100	99	20	83	16	40	14
1993	90	—	83	90	93	89	—	27	17	—	—

National Journal Ratings

	1993 LIB — 1993 CONS			1994 LIB — 1994 CONS		
Economic	61%	—	39%	49%	—	51%
Social	73%	—	23%	77%	—	23%
Foreign	74%	—	22%	85%	—	0%

Key Votes of the 103d Congress

1. Clinton Deficit Plan	Y	3. Brady Handgun Purchase	Y	5. Lmt. UN Cmnd. of Forces	N
2. NAFTA	Y	4. Strike Race/Death Pnlty.	N	6. Cut Missile Funds	Y

Key Votes of the 104th Congress

1. Congressional Compliance	Y	6. Reform Crime Grant	N	11. Loser Pays Court Reform	N
2. Balanced Budget Amndmt.	Y	7. National Security Act	N	12. Product Liability Reform	N
3. Bar Unfunded Mandates	Y	8. Moratorium on Regs.	N	13. Welfare Reform	N
4. Pass Line Item Veto	Y	9. Risk Assessment on Regs.	N	14. Term Limits Amndmt.	Y
5. Relax Exclusionary Rule	N	10. Expnd. Priv. Prop. Rights	N	15. Tax Cuts	N

Election Results

1994 general	Martin T. (Marty) Meehan (D)	140,725	(70%)	($803,523)
	David E. Coleman (R)	60,734	(30%)	
1994 primary	Martin T. (Marty) Meehan (D)	35,739	(76%)	
	Thomas J. Quinn (D)	10,978	(23%)	
1992 general	Martin T. (Marty) Meehan (D)	133,844	(52%)	($831,544)
	Paul W. Cronin (R).....................	96,206	(38%)	($551,896)
	Mary J. Farinelli (I)	19,077	(7%)	($224)
	Others	7,437	(3%)	

SIXTH DISTRICT

The North Shore of Massachusetts Bay has a number of times been at the leading edge of the nation's economy. In 1640, the Saugus Iron Works was built here—the beginning of American heavy industry. When Europe's great powers were convulsed in international war from 1792 to 1815, American ship owners suddenly became the richest in the world and traders from Boston accumulated the capital needed to build textile mills and railroads and to finance much of the American industrial revolution. From the small port of Salem, ships left for the China trade, bringing back porcelain and artifacts, which helped change American styles forever. Salem, first settled in 1626, had the nation's first millionaire, Elias Hasket Derby and in 1900, it was the richest per capita city in the nation. But the North Shore is a quiet place, from Boston harbor north to the mouth of the Merrimack River, a collection of ethnic factory towns from Lynn on up through next-door Peabody to Newburyport, alternating with the high-income enclaves of Marblehead with its yachts and Beverly with its estates, artsy Rockport and the fishing port of Gloucester. Lynn is the largest town and its General Electric jet engine plant the largest employer, though its 6,300 workers in 1993 were less than half the work force during the 1980s defense buildup.

The 6th Congressional District of Massachusetts includes the North Shore from Lynn onward, plus towns and cities several miles inland. It is a varied area demographically and politically: its high-income Yankees towns are liberal Republicans, while Lynn, Salem, Peabody and the Merrimack mill towns are still Irish working-class Democratic. The 6th has been a Democratic district on balance since the 1960s; but in the 1980s and perhaps again, only marginally so. While this district is the site of the original gerrymander—named after Elbridge Gerry—the current 6th District boundaries are less grotesque and politically determined than those of any other Massachusetts district.

The congressman from the 6th District is Peter Torkildsen, a Republican who beat a scandal-tarred incumbent in 1992 and held on for a second term in 1994. Torkildsen is a young political veteran. In 1984, at 26, he beat the state House majority leader for the seat; in the legislature he was instrumental in the fight to repeal Michael Dukakis's services tax. He was the lieutenant governor candidate on Steven Pierce's unsuccessful 1990 ticket and Governor William Weld appointed Torkildsen commissioner of labor and industries. In 1992, he decided to take on 14-year Congressman Nicholas Mavroules. First he had a primary: former state party executive director Alexander Tennant attacked Torkildsen for switching to pro-choice on abortion the previous April; Torkildsen said he was prompted by the case of a 14-year-old rape victim in Ireland. With big margins in North Shore towns, Torkildsen won 56%–44%. Meanwhile, Mavroules was indicted for tax evasion, influence peddling and bribery two weeks before the primary, in which he nonetheless beat state Representative Barbara Hildt. Torkildsen criticized Mavroules for accepting PAC money and refused to take any himself. Torkildsen won 55%–45%. In April 1993, Mavroules plead guilty to 15 of the 17 charges against him.

In the Democratic House, Torkildsen had a middle-of-the-road record. He was attacked by conservatives for his support for ending the ban on gays in the military and by liberals for his opposition to gun control (although he voted for the Brady bill in 1993). He had a seat on the now-abolished Merchant Marine and Fisheries Committee and took a hand in fishing issues. In August 1994, he generated controversy when he charged that White House aide Susan Brophy told him she could get him a favorable column from Thomas Oliphant in the *Boston Globe* if he voted for the crime bill; Oliphant and Brophy denied the story. Oliphant, in fact, did write a column praising Massachusetts Republican Peter Blute's as a "stand-up guy" in voting for the bill and opposing the gun lobby, and attacking Torkildsen as a "smarmy . . . shadow-seeker" because he "succumbed to the pressure." Torkildsen did finally vote for the bill after the White House made some concessions. In 1994, Torkildsen was one of the Democrats' few major targets. Democrat John Tierney attacked him for voting against the crime bill and the ban on assault weapons; he backed single-payer healthcare reform and the banning of all handgun sales. Torkildsen boasted of his work on the Freshman Republican Task Force on Reform, his refusal of PAC money and his support of term limits, while attacking Tierney as "way too liberal for this district." Torkildsen won 51%–47%.

In the 104th Congress, Torkildsen opposed some Contract With America items, including the space-launched missile defense plank which lost and welfare reform which passed. He is currently the only Massachusetts member to chair a subcommittee, the Small Business Subcommittee on Government Programs. Nonetheless, he obviously has one of the shakiest Republican districts, in a commonwealth where the tenor of political talk has not moved very much in the Republicans' way.

The People: Pop. 1990: 601,811; 10% rural; 14% age 65+; 95% White; 2% Black; 1% Asian; 1% Other; 3% Hispanic origin. Voting age pop.: 466,764; 2% Black; 2% Hispanic origin. Households: 57% married couple families; 26% married couple fams. w. children; 54% college educ.; median household income: $40,836; per capita income: $18,549; median gross rent: $617; median house value: $181,400.

1992 Presidential Vote		
Clinton (D)	134,424	(43%)
Bush (R)	96,857	(31%)
Perot (I)	75,893	(25%)

1988 Presidential Vote		
Dukakis (D)	144,982	(51%)
Bush (R)	140,353	(49%)

Rep. Peter G. Torkildsen (R)

Elected 1992; b. Jan. 28, 1958, Milwaukee, WI; home, Danvers; U. of MA, B.A. 1982, Harvard JFK Schl. of Govt., M.A. 1990; Catholic; single.

Career: Svc. Coor., Visiting Nurses Assn., 1982–84; MA House of Reps., 1984–90; Commissioner, MA Dept. of Labor and Industry, 1991–92.

DC Office: 120 CHOB 20515, 202-225-8020; Fax: 202-225-8037.

District Offices: 70 Washington St., Salem 01970, 508-741-1600; 156 Broad St., #106, Lynn 01901, 617-599-2424; 160 Main St., Haverhill 01830, 508-521-0111; and 61 Center St., Burlington 01803, 617-273-4900.

Committees: *National Security* (13th of 30 R): Military Procurement; Military Readiness. *Resources* (12th of 25 R): Fisheries, Wildlife and Oceans; National Parks, Forests and Lands. *Small Business* (6th of 22 R): Government Programs (Chmn.).

Group Ratings

	ADA	ACLU	COPE	CFA	LCV	CON	NSI	COC	ACU	NTLC	CHC
1994	15	52	33	20	50	55	90	100	67	86	50
1993	30	—	42	40	71	59	—	73	75	—	—

National Journal Ratings

	1993 LIB — 1993 CONS		1994 LIB — 1994 CONS	
Economic	32%	66%	37%	61%
Social	49%	50%	44%	55%
Foreign	31%	67%	38%	61%

Key Votes of the 103d Congress

1. Clinton Deficit Plan	N	3. Brady Handgun Purchase Y	5. Lmt. UN Cmnd. of Forces Y
2. NAFTA	Y	4. Strike Race/Death Pnlty. Y	6. Cut Missile Funds N

Key Votes of the 104th Congress

1. Congressional Compliance Y	6. Reform Crime Grant N	11. Loser Pays Court Reform Y
2. Balanced Budget Amndmt. Y	7. National Security Act Y	12. Product Liability Reform Y
3. Bar Unfunded Mandates Y	8. Moratorium on Regs. Y	13. Welfare Reform N
4. Pass Line Item Veto Y	9. Risk Assessment on Regs. Y	14. Term Limits Amndmt. Y
5. Relax Exclusionary Rule Y	10. Expnd. Priv. Prop. Rights N	15. Tax Cuts Y

Election Results

1994 general	Peter G. Torkildsen (R)	120,952	(51%)	($768,072)
	John F. Tierney (D)	113,481	(47%)	($497,570)
	Others	5,011	(2%)	
1994 primary	Peter G. Torkildsen (R)	unopposed		
1992 general	Peter G. Torkildsen (R)	159,165	(55%)	($460,934)
	Nicholas Mavroules (D)	130,248	(45%)	($671,110)

SEVENTH DISTRICT

The Yankee Protestants and Irish Catholics who settled Massachusetts arrived by boat, the Yankees to a cold stony land with a few Indians, the Irish to a crowded city with Yankees who seemed even less welcoming. The Yankees whose ancestors once farmed the soil had, by the early 20th Century, founded suburbs filled with solid brick and white frame houses, furnished in Early American furniture, with a view out the paned windows. As the years went on, their local public schools were emptied as young people with children had moved out, and attendance at Protestant churches went down. The Irish, for decades heavily concentrated in the crowded wards of Boston, started moving out into the Yankee suburbs 50 years ago. There were other ethnic groups here and there (Jews, Italians, French Canadians) but the major conflict—fought out in neighborhood playgrounds, in school committee meetings and not least in political campaigns—was between Protestant Yankee Republicans and Catholic Irish Democrats.

The 7th Congressional District of Massachusetts is made up of northern and western suburbs of Boston where vestiges of this conflict can still be seen. Geographically, it forms an arc around Boston, starting with the clapboard beach towns of Winthrop and Revere just beyond Logan Airport, going north as far as Wakefield, west past working class Woburn and Medford, home of Tufts University, to the patriot town of Lexington that spans Route 128 and Waltham, home of Brandeis University, through high-income Lincoln and Weston to modest-income Natick and Framingham. Most of these towns were Yankee Republican up through the 1950s, but by the late 1960s they were pretty solidly Democratic; the high-tech suburbs trended Republican again in the 1980s but swung against George Bush in 1992. The highest income areas seem to run across the grain of their ethnic experience: Weston, with many Catholics, is pretty solidly Republican; Lincoln, with Yankees like Thomas Boylston Adams and George Bush's sister Nancy Ellis, is liberal and perversely countercyclical, voting for George McGovern and Gerald Ford in the 1970s, Walter Mondale and Michael Dukakis in the 1980s, finally striking a national chord with Bill Clinton in 1992.

The congressman in the 7th District is Edward Markey, first elected in 1976 at age 30, never having been to Washington before. From a modest economic background, very Irish, Markey is a graduate of Malden Catholic High, Boston College and the Massachusetts legislature. The Capitol he first laid eyes on was full of Democrats for whom Vietnam and Watergate were the paradigmatic events of all world history, a view Markey seemed to share. In his early House years, he was one of the fiercest opponents of nuclear power and a leading political organizer in 1983 for the nuclear freeze, which would have given away America's technological edge just as our defense buildup was overwhelming the Soviets. Markey's enthusiastic certainty and his thirst for publicity infuriated many colleagues, who saw him as a self-righteous grandstander.

But seniority and events have put Markey in position to be a productive and creative legislator. He is one of those lucky House members for whom the seniority system has clicked, opening up perhaps the choicest Commerce subcommittee chair, Telecommunications and Finance, after just 10 years. He got on Commerce because his predecessor had been there, with help from Tip O'Neill; he got on what was then called the Communications Subcommittee early because the high-tech boom on Route 128 convinced him that telecommunications issues would be critical. He met the high standards of then-Commerce Chairman John Dingell, who likes aggressive colleagues who are both productive and loyal. The voters of the 7th District also exerted some discipline, and when Markey started to run for the seat of retiring Senator Paul Tsongas in 1984, he jumped back into the House race when he failed to raise enough money and had to scramble to win his primary.

So from 1987–95, Markey chaired the Telecommunications and Finance Subcommittee; now he is ranking minority member. Either is a juicy position, with fabulous possibilities for campaign fund-raising (Markey doesn't take PAC money, but of course securities and communications executives can and do contribute, and for 1994 he got $956,000 in individual contributions) and with subject matter that is intellectually more demanding (and in lobbying terms more fiercely contested) than almost anything else in Congress. Markey's 1990 law responding to the 1987 market crash increased the power of the SEC to shut down markets or limit computer program trading in emergencies. Similarly, on derivatives, Markey sought not to shut the markets down but to provide more disclosure. In communications, Markey passed bills reducing commercial time on children's programs and requiring broadcasters to argue they are serving children's needs, requiring TVs to include decoder circuitry for close-captioned signals for the deaf, limiting dial-a-porn services and in 1994 making standard the V-chip, an electronic device allowing parents to block out violent programs. In 1992, he combined his penchant for regulation with political shrewdness to produce the cable TV reregulation bill which passed both houses, was vetoed by President Bush and then in October 1992 was passed over Bush's veto—the only bill passed over his veto in his four-year term. When it turned out that rates increased for one-third of subscribers, he sought more regulation. Another Markey achievement in 1993 was the law reallocating from public to private sector 200 megahertz of the radio frequency spectrum, four times as much as created the entire cellular phone industry, allocated by the most lucrative auction in human history.

Markey's biggest project is the Telecommunications bill, on which he has intermittently cooperated with Jack Fields, formerly ranking Republican and now subcommittee chairman. The basic idea is to allow long-distance companies to provide local phone services and to allow the regional Bells to provide long distance; the hope is that will result in digital service, through existing copper wires or ultimately fiber-optics, to every household: the information superhighway. The Markey-Fields bill passed the House 423–4 in June 1994, but was killed by Robert Dole in the Senate. By May 1995 another sweeping telecommunications bill passed out of committee, but Markey was one of 5 Democrats to oppose it. A key reason was the lifting of virtually all cable rate regulation, a reversal of his 1992 cable law. He hopes to create incentives for companies to develop hardware and software for video, data and voice to be transmitted over phone wires. This is likely to be fiercely opposed by newspapers, and financing is still uncertain unless utilities regulators allow the rewiring costs to be depreciated over much longer periods. Markey vowed to try to amend the bill to make it more "pro-consumer"; he objects to deregulating the cable industry without regard to the state of competition in the industry. He also worries that sweeping repeal of regulations will result in homoginized programming controlled by a few powerful interests.

Markey continues to compile one of the most liberal voting records in the House, and his earlier publicity-hunting days still pay dividends: his 1986 report on experiments with biological radiation without consent was given national publicity when it was picked up by the *Albuquerque Journal* and Energy Secretary Hazel O'Leary. He also tends to local issues, and has been easily reelected, by 64%–36% in 1994. His wife Susan Blumenthal is a Deputy Assistant Secretary for Health and Human Services. For the long term, Markey is another Democrat who would be well-positioned as a committee baron if Democrats regain their House majority sometime in the next decade.

The People: Pop. 1990: 601,476; 1% rural; 15% age 65+; 92% White; 2% Black; 3% Asian; 1% Other; 3% Hispanic origin. Voting age pop.: 485,578; 2% Black; 2% Hispanic origin. Households: 53% married couple families; 22% married couple fams. w. children; 53% college educ.; median household income: $41,318; per capita income: $19,825; median gross rent: $685; median house value: $192,700.

1992 Presidential Vote			1988 Presidential Vote		
Clinton (D)	150,073	(50%)	Dukakis (D)	161,506	(55%)
Bush (R)	87,418	(29%)	Bush (R)	129,649	(45%)
Perot (I)	61,963	(21%)			

Rep. Edward J. Markey (D)

Elected 1976; b. July 11, 1946, Malden; home, Malden; Boston Col., B.A. 1968, J.D. 1972; Catholic; married (Susan Blumenthal).

Career: Army Reserves, 1968–73; MA House of Reps., 1973–76.

DC Office: 2133 RHOB 20515, 202-225-2836; Fax: 202-225-1716.

District Offices: 5 High St., #101, Medford 02155, 617-396-2900.

Committees: *Commerce* (3rd of 21 D): Commerce, Trade and Hazardous Materials; Energy and Power; Telecommunications and Finance (RMM).

Group Ratings

	ADA	ACLU	COPE	CFA	LCV	CON	NSI	COC	ACU	NTLC	CHC
1994	85	87	88	80	100	11	0	33	0	4	0
1993	95	—	92	100	100	32	—	27	4	—	—

National Journal Ratings

	1993 LIB — 1993 CONS	1994 LIB — 1994 CONS
Economic	78% — 12%	83% — 0%
Social	87% — 0%	90% — 6%
Foreign	93% — 0%	85% — 0%

Key Votes of the 103d Congress

1. Clinton Deficit Plan	Y	3. Brady Handgun Purchase	Y	5. Lmt. UN Cmnd. of Forces	N
2. NAFTA	Y	4. Strike Race/Death Pnlty.	N	6. Cut Missile Funds	*

Key Votes of the 104th Congress

1. Congressional Compliance	Y	6. Reform Crime Grant	N	11. Loser Pays Court Reform	N
2. Balanced Budget Amndmt.	N	7. National Security Act	N	12. Product Liability Reform	N
3. Bar Unfunded Mandates	Y	8. Moratorium on Regs.	N	13. Welfare Reform	N
4. Pass Line Item Veto	N	9. Risk Assessment on Regs.	N	14. Term Limits Amndmt.	N
5. Relax Exclusionary Rule	N	10. Expnd. Priv. Prop. Rights	N	15. Tax Cuts	N

Election Results

1994 general	Edward J. Markey (D)	146,246	(64%)	($757,993)
	Brad Bailey (R)	80,674	(36%)	($360,370)
1994 primary	Edward J. Markey (D)	unopposed		
1992 general	Edward J. Markey (D)	174,837	(62%)	($928,883)
	Stephen A. Sohn (R)	78,262	(28%)	($290,304)
	Robert B. Antonelli (I)	28,421	(10%)	

EIGHTH DISTRICT

A long generation ago, Cambridge, Massachusetts was a plainly aging city, with a grayness in the air matching its gray winter skies. Its two great universities, Harvard and MIT, were closely hemmed in by a not very friendly town of Irish Catholics, Italians and a few Portuguese, living generation after generation in three-decker houses with cracked walls letting in the cold or letting out the heat. Boston was the nation's slowest-growing metropolitan area, economically stagnant, still caught in a 17th Century Puritan-Papist rivalry. Students from suburbs across the country exploring Boston from their dormitories and campuses felt they were pawing through the living remnants of 1920s America, a quaint place where people called traffic circles rotaries and milk shakes frappes. Massachusetts has since changed, and nowhere more than in Cambridge. As universities and high tech have become driving forces of economic growth, Cambridge has gone glitzy, with trendy restaurants and high-priced hotels, boutiques and upscale condominiums. Greater Boston may well have the heaviest concentration of graduate students and post-graduate hangers-on of any major city, and their world is centered on Cambridge, with outposts in low-income Somerville, tenured-faculty haven Belmont, Boston's Back Bay and Allston and Brighton near the Harvard Business School.

Cambridge is the center, and the rest of these communities are part, of Massachusetts's 8th Congressional District, a district with great historic sites from the gold dome of the State House on Beacon Hill to the frigate *Constitution* in the Charlestown docks; the district, with MIT and the software concentration in Cambridge's once downscale Lechmere Square, is one of the high-tech capitals of America. Redistricting has added the impoverished suburb of Chelsea, whose public schools were taken over by Boston University in 1984 and whose city government went into receivership in 1991, and much of the Roxbury black ghetto in Boston; this is by far the most Democratic district in Massachusetts. It has the further distinction of having elected as its two previous congressmen President John F. Kennedy and Speaker Thomas P. O'Neill.

The current congressman is Joseph P. Kennedy II, elected when O'Neill retired in 1986. He is the oldest son of the late Robert Kennedy, and won largely because of affection and veneration for his family. Before 1986, he was living on the South Shore and running the Citizens Energy Corporation he set up which bought oil in bulk and distributed it to low-income citizens. But when O'Neill announced his retirement, and half a dozen leftish candidates with various local bases filed, Kennedy ran, leading some of the other candidates to withdraw. Cambridge state senator George Bachrach made the mistake of charging Kennedy with having ties with Qaddafi's Libya, while O'Neill endorsed Kennedy; before that Kennedy had been running only even in the polls, but he beat Bachrach 52%–30%.

Like his uncle, Senator Edward Kennedy, Joe Kennedy seems to see himself as a tribune of the poor, and the three-decker house working-class as well; he tempers his liberalism with stands like supporting capital punishment and backing the balanced budget amendment (unlike the other two Kennedys in Congress, he voted for the amendment in January 1995). He oscillates between the boyish impulsiveness of a man who has never had to pay for his mistakes, and a determination to work hard and make a serious record as a mature politician; his admirers insist that he is now very little of the first and much of the second. On the Banking Committee, from which he has twice tried to be shifted, he chaired the Consumer Credit and Insurance Subcommittee in the 103d Congress. His major cause was strengthening the Community Reinvestment Act, requiring banks to disclose the race of those to whom they grant mortgages; the Clinton Administration in turn has used this information to pressure banks to agree to open new branches in minority neighborhoods and to grant more loans to blacks and other minorities. This attacks racial discrimination, proponents argue; opponents fear it could mean sinking depositors' money into high-risk loans and property. On the Veterans' Affairs Committee, Kennedy has worked to build a landmark shelter for homeless veterans in Boston and to increase nurses' pay in veterans' hospitals. He also has sponsored health warnings on alcohol bottles, indoor air quality standards and federal funding of bicycle paths and pedestrian walkways.

Kennedy has taken some controversial stands on foreign policy. He has long been critical of Britain's policy in Northern Ireland, and boycotted Queen Elizabeth's speech to Congress in 1991. He has joined his uncle Edward Kennedy in support of the mediation efforts of his aunt, Ambassador to Ireland Jean Kennedy Smith, and welcomed President Clinton's reception at the White House for Sinn Fein leader Gerry Adams, known to have terrorist ties but a member of parliament for several years. Kennedy worked to get humanitarian aid to Armenia (there's a big Armenian community in Watertown, west of Cambridge) and was a strong supporter of the

Aristide government in Haiti. On occasion he can be overwrought. In the Gulf war debate he asked, "Are we to be the international police force, the bully boys of the world?" Seeing America as the villain is congenial in some Cambridge precincts, but it was not a very mature way to see the world just at the moment when the United States's long twilight struggle had resulted in victory the breakup of the Soviet Union.

Kennedy has long been mentioned as a candidate for statewide office—for governor in 1990 and 1994, when he declined to run, and now for governor in 1998 or senator in 2000 should his uncle retire. He wins reelection easily, but spent $839,000 while having no opposition in 1994 and ended the campaign with $821,000 cash-on-hand, the fourth highest in the House. He played an unfortunate role in the 1994 Senate campaign, as the self-described "pit bull" for Edward Kennedy's campaign, attacking Republican nominee Mitt Romney's Mormon religion and charging him with backing that church's ban on blacks in their priesthood. It was a shameful contrast with the plea for religious toleration made by his uncle John Kennedy in the 1960 presidential campaign, and low-grade because the Mormon Church changed that tenet back in 1978. Joe Kennedy compounded the offense by writing an apology letter in which he attacked Romney for advice he had given to a single woman to give up a child for adoption. It is puzzling why a man with such a potential for public service before him would besmirch his record this way.

The People: Pop. 1990: 602,396; 11% age 65+; 61% White; 23% Black; 6% Asian; 5% Other; 10% Hispanic origin. Voting age pop.: 495,171; 20% Black; 9% Hispanic origin. Households: 32% married couple families; 13% married couple fams. w. children; 53% college educ.; median household income: $30,417; per capita income: $16,327; median gross rent: $636; median house value: $188,200.

1992 Presidential Vote		
Clinton (D)	136,438	(67%)
Bush (R)	39,368	(19%)
Perot (I)	25,423	(13%)

1988 Presidential Vote		
Dukakis (D)	145,843	(72%)
Bush (R)	57,591	(28%)

Rep. Joseph P. Kennedy, II (D)

Elected 1986; b. Sept. 24, 1952, Brighton; home, Brighton; U. of MA, B.A. 1976; Catholic; married (Beth).

Career: Community Svcs. Admin., 1977–79; Founder and Pres., Citizens Energy Corp., 1979–86, Citizens Conservation Corp., 1981.

DC Office: 2242 RHOB 20515, 202-225-5111; Fax: 202-225-9322.

District Offices: Schrafft Ctr., 529 Main St., Charlestown 02129, 617-242-0200.

Committees: *Banking & Financial Services* (7th of 22 D): Housing and Community Opportunity (RMM). *Veterans' Affairs* (3rd of 15 D): Compensation, Pension, Insurance and Memorial Affairs; Hospitals and Health Care.

Group Ratings

	ADA	ACLU	COPE	CFA	LCV	CON	NSI	COC	ACU	NTLC	CHC
1994	90	70	75	80	100	53	0	58	5	15	21
1993	95	—	92	100	100	39	—	20	4	—	—

National Journal Ratings

	1993 LIB	—	1993 CONS	1994 LIB	—	1994 CONS
Economic	75%	—	22%	63%	—	37%
Social	80%	—	13%	75%	—	25%
Foreign	93%	—	0%	85%	—	0%

Key Votes of the 103d Congress

1. Clinton Deficit Plan	Y	3. Brady Handgun Purchase	Y	5. Lmt. UN Cmnd. of Forces	N
2. NAFTA	Y	4. Strike Race/Death Pnlty.	N	6. Cut Missile Funds	Y

Key Votes of the 104th Congress

1. Congressional Compliance	Y	6. Reform Crime Grant	N	11. Loser Pays Court Reform	N
2. Balanced Budget Amndmt.	Y	7. National Security Act	N	12. Product Liability Reform	N
3. Bar Unfunded Mandates	Y	8. Moratorium on Regs.	N	13. Welfare Reform	N
4. Pass Line Item Veto	N	9. Risk Assessment on Regs.	N	14. Term Limits Amndmt.	N
5. Relax Exclusionary Rule	N	10. Expnd. Priv. Prop. Rights	N	15. Tax Cuts	N

Election Results

1994 general	Joseph P. Kennedy, II (D)............	unopposed		(839,725)
1994 primary	Joseph P. Kennedy, II (D)............	unopposed		
1992 general	Joseph P. Kennedy, II (D)..............	149,903	(83%)	($767,161)
	Alice Harriett Nakash (I)..............	30,402	(17%)	

NINTH DISTRICT

The "Hub of the Universe," the elder Oliver Wendell Holmes called it in the 19th Century, and so it seems again sometimes: when you reflect that Fidelity mutual funds and so many other big financial outfits are headquartered in modern towers built on streets laid out as 17th Century cowpaths; when you remember the 1988 campaign when Michael Dukakis, daily commuter on Boston's T, was leading George Bush and seemed likely to be the next president; when you walk on Beacon Street past the Bull and Finch Pub which is the original for TV's *Cheers* (and whose name is a play on the architect of the State House, Thomas Bulfinch). Today's Boston is a different city from the Boston of John Kennedy's time. Boston then was a gray city with no new buildings and dust on every windowsill; the sky was dark with pollution and the air was thick with ancient Yankee and Irish animosity. The old office buildings were full of Yankees seeking safe investments for their antique family fortunes; the State House and City Hall were full of Irishmen, scampering after good patronage jobs and regaling each other with political battle stories. Today, that Boston is mostly gone. The new skyscrapers are full of venture capitalists and lawyers of every ethnic description, looking for a turn-up in the high-tech economy; the advertising slogans crackle with a sauciness and *double entendre* you can find only here and maybe in New York and London.

Most of Boston's neighborhoods have changed. There are still vestiges of the old Irish neighborhoods, as in South Boston, but the central city is increasingly populated by blacks and young singles; its population is down from 801,000 in 1950 to 574,000 in 1990; over 80% of the metropolitan area is in the suburbs. The 9th Congressional District, historically anchored in Boston, has followed the move, and today only one-third of its residents are in Boston, mostly in still-Irish areas of South Boston, Hyde Park and West Roxbury. From there, the 9th heads southwest to Easton and the Patriots Stadium, southeast to Braintree, ancestral home of the presidential Adamses, Brockton, the old shoe manufacturing town, and the old textile mill town of Taunton. Politically, it is Democratic, but not overwhelmingly so for the descendant of a district which for 45 years was represented by Speaker of the House John McCormack.

The current congressman from the 9th is Joe Moakley, chairman from June 1989 to January

1995 of the House Rules Committee, a loyal son of South Boston, with an Irish face and a thick Boston accent. Joe Moakley volunteered for the Navy in 1943, at age 15. He came back home, practiced law, was elected to the Massachusetts House in 1952, at 25, then to the state Senate in 1964, to the Boston Council, with the highest vote, in 1971. In 1972, after losing the 1970 primary for this seat, he ran in the general as an Independent against anti-busing advocate Louise Day Hicks, and narrowly won. In his second term he got Tip O'Neill's former seat on the Rules Committee; he is not especially close to the Kennedys (he backed Edward McCormack, the speaker's nephew, against Edward Kennedy in the 1962 Senate primary). On the back benches in the 1970s, he moved up quickly in seniority and became chairman when Claude Pepper died in June 1989. As chairman of the Rules Committee, Moakley worked closely with Speaker Thomas Foley and Majority Leader Dick Gephardt; he helped Whip David Bonior, also a Catholic deeply opposed to U.S. Central American policy, win his leadership post. Under their lead, Rules increasingly passed closed rules, limiting amendments and debate, to the fury of the Republicans.

His one great cause has been El Salvador, on which he took the approach of Catholic liberation theologians. Acquainted with some of the nuns and priests who were murdered there, he worked to cut off military aid to the Salvadoran government and to grant refugee protection to Salvadorans in the United States. He headed a commission which in 1992 reported that some high-ranking Salvadoran military officials were involved in murder.

Moakley sees himself as a "bread and butter" politician and quotes Tip O'Neill's "All politics is local." He is proud that federal money is going into the rebuilding of Boston's Central Artery rebuilding (one of the largest highway projects ever in the United States), Boston Harbor cleanup and a third tunnel under the Harbor, and says he has created "countless jobs throughout the Commonwealth." Usually a humorous and gentle man, he abhors Newt Gingrich and the new Republican majority, especially on his Rules panel; "happy days aren't here again," he told the *Boston Herald* on opening day January 1995. There he found himself in the ironic position of criticizing Republicans for crafting restrictions on House debate—though usually not as tight as the ones that he had backed—with some of the same arguments that the other party had once used against him. He has been reelected easily, never running a TV ad; but he did spend $981,000 in 1994, on mailings and newspaper and radio ads. He could easily win again but he has had some health problems. If he chooses to retire, he might be replaced by Billy Bulger, the cultured, conservative and Yankee-twitting president of the state Senate, who followed Moakley in both houses of the legislature and is his longtime South Boston neighbor.

The People: Pop. 1990: 601,250; 2% rural; 15% age 65+; 86% White; 7% Black; 3% Asian; 3% Other; 5% Hispanic origin. Voting age pop.: 472,589; 6% Black; 4% Hispanic origin. Households: 51% married couple families; 22% married couple fams. w. children; 50% college educ.; median household income: $38,646; per capita income: $17,980; median gross rent: $616; median house value: $172,000.

1992 Presidential Vote

Clinton (D)	131,644	(48%)
Bush (R)	85,901	(31%)
Perot (I)	56,431	(21%)

1988 Presidential Vote

Dukakis (D)	140,852	(52%)
Bush (R)	127,638	(48%)

Rep. John Joseph (Joe) **Moakley (D)**

Elected 1972; b. Apr. 27, 1927, Boston; home, Boston; U. of Miami, Suffolk U., LL.B. 1956; Catholic; married (Evelyn).

Career: Navy, 1943–46 (WWII); MA House of Reps., 1953–65, Majority Whip, 1957; Practicing atty., 1957–72; MA Senate, 1965–69; Boston City Cncl., 1971.

DC Office: 235 CHOB 20515, 202-225-8273; Fax: 202-225-3984.

District Offices: 4 Court St., Taunton 02780, 617-824-6676; and World Trade Ctr., #220, Boston 02210, 617-565-2920.

Committees: *Rules* (RMM of 4 D): Legislative and Budget Process.

Group Ratings

	ADA	ACLU	COPE	CFA	LCV	CON	NSI	COC	ACU	NTLC	CHC
1994	95	81	100	90	88	31	0	25	0	4	7
1993	80	—	100	100	77	57	—	9	0	—	—

National Journal Ratings

	1993 LIB — 1993 CONS			1994 LIB — 1994 CONS		
Economic	88%	—	0%	73%	—	17%
Social	78%	—	22%	82%	—	15%
Foreign	74%	—	26%	85%	—	0%

Key Votes of the 103d Congress

1. Clinton Deficit Plan	Y	3. Brady Handgun Purchase	*	5. Lmt. UN Cmnd. of Forces	N
2. NAFTA	N	4. Strike Race/Death Pnlty.	N	6. Cut Missile Funds	N

Key Votes of the 104th Congress

1. Congressional Compliance	Y	6. Reform Crime Grant	N	11. Loser Pays Court Reform	N
2. Balanced Budget Amndmt.	N	7. National Security Act	N	12. Product Liability Reform	N
3. Bar Unfunded Mandates	Y	8. Moratorium on Regs.	N	13. Welfare Reform	N
4. Pass Line Item Veto	N	9. Risk Assessment on Regs.	N	14. Term Limits Amndmt.	N
5. Relax Exclusionary Rule	N	10. Expnd. Priv. Prop. Rights	*	15. Tax Cuts	N

Election Results

1994 general	John Joseph (Joe) Moakley (D)	146,287	(70%)	($981,247)
	Michael M. Murphy (R)	63,369	(30%)	($178,071)
1994 primary	John Joseph (Joe) Moakley (D)	57,471	(86%)	
	Dennis J. Ingalls (D)	9,204	(14%)	
1992 general	John Joseph (Joe) Moakley (D)	175,550	(69%)	($1,056,446)
	Martin B. Conboy (R)	54,291	(21%)	($12,616)
	Lawrence C. Mackin (I)	15,637	(6%)	
	Others	8,156	(3%)	

TENTH DISTRICT

The South Shore of Massachusetts Bay, from Boston southward to Plymouth and then down Cape Cod (there is a lot of dispute about which way is up and down on the Cape), is Massachusetts's oldest-settled territory and the site of its fastest-growing new communities. The Pilgrims landed here at Plymouth Rock in 1620; this stony land was farmed by John Adams's father, who was anything but the aristocrat some later members of the Adams family would have you believe. Daniel Webster lived in the South Shore town of Marshfield, today a high-income suburb of Boston far out the usually clogged Southeast Expressway; Joseph P. Kennedy used to summer with his young family on Nantasket Beach in Hull, and then moved out of Massachusetts when the Yankees wouldn't let them into their beach club in Cohasset in the 1920s; the Kennedy family continued to summer at their Hyannis Port compound. The Plymouth area and Cape Cod were originally farming country, with some industry; a railroad, now long-gone, steamed along the middle of the Cape. Provincetown (at the tip of the Cape) is still a fishing port, and also now one of the major gay vacation areas in the country; the islands of Martha's Vineyard and Nantucket, rich whaling ports in the early 19th Century, are now favored summer resorts for the trendy liberal rich of New York and Washington. Cape Cod is the site of the bogs which still produce half of America's cranberries, but it is also filled increasingly with retirees enjoying the relatively equable year-round climates and, to some longtime residents' dismay, is the fastest-growing part of Massachusetts.

The 10th Congressional District of Massachusetts, with grotesque boundaries like most other Bay State districts, follows the South Shore from Quincy to the Cape, jutting inland near Brockton, and including Martha's Vineyard and Nantucket. The South Shore and the Cape were once exclusively Protestant and Yankee, but in the Massachusetts way they have changed over the years, with Irish and Italian surnames as common as Yankee and the descendants of the Portuguese Azorean fishermen fanning out into the countryside. And trendy left politics, well established on the Vineyard and Nantucket, has spread inland as well.

The congressman from the 10th District is Gerry Studds, a Democrat first elected from the South Shore and Cape in 1972. His first name is pronounced Gary, a reminder that he is descended from Elbridge Gerry, fifth vice president of the United States and creator of the original gerrymander. Gerry Studds was a Foreign Service officer who landed a post in the Kennedy White House, then was a New Hampshire prep school teacher and a top volunteer for Eugene McCarthy in 1968. He returned home and ran for the House in 1970 and nearly won; in 1972, to woo the large Portuguese fisherman population in New Bedford, then in the district, he learned Portuguese, and won an ancestrally Republican seat in a nationally Republican year. Studds later got a seat on the International Relations Committee, but he started off first on the now-abolished Merchant Marine and Fisheries Committee, a body shunned by most members but of obvious importance to a coastal and fishing district. In his first term, Studds successfully sponsored legislation to extend U.S. territorial waters out to 200 miles, a great achievement; over the next 20 years he took this seemingly humdrum assignment and made important public policy and immense political capital out of it. The political capital came in handy in 1983, when Studds was censured for having had sex with a 17-year-old male page 10 years earlier. Under House rules, Studds lost his Merchant Marine subcommittee chairmanship, and many thought he could not be reelected. With characteristic stubbornness, Studds maintained he had done nothing wrong, and won reelection by beating two serious opponents in the 1984 primary and general. Over the years, he has compiled one of the most liberal voting records in the House, though in the 1990s he has been more moderate on economic issues.

Studds became Merchant Marine chairman in 1993; his succession after the death of Walter Jones, Sr., was uncontroversial, presumably because of his hard work and competence. He helped shape the oil spill bill passed after the 1989 Exxon *Valdez* disaster in Alaska and he pushed for a moratorium on oil drilling in the Georges Bank along the New England Coast until after 2000. He has passed through the House useful and bipartisan legislation penalizing prank distress calls to the Coast Guard and, working with Alaska Republican Don Young and the maritime industry, for stronger federal inspection of seafood. He pushed through a law to ban from U.S. ports for five years boats that use large-scale drift nets, which kill thousands of dolphins and sea tortoises. He is tough enough to push a bill halting federal flood insurance of most offshore barrier islands (let them build at their own risk, he says), and idealistic enough to spend time on a bill to preserve the environment in Antarctica.

Studds has mostly been reelected easily. Republican airline pilot Jon Bryan held him to 53% in 1990, but in 1992 Bryan ran as a third candidate and split the conservative vote, while Studds won with 61%; redistricting had made the seat a few points more Democratic, though it cost him New Bedford which he had long courted. In 1994 he won 69%–31%. But the 1994 election was surely a disaster for him. Merchant Marine, on which he lavished so much care, was abolished. He was given a middle-seniority seat on Resources, of which his Merchant Marine sometime partner Don Young is chairman, and he is ranking member of the Fisheries, Wildlife and Oceans Subcommittee. But the committee is now tilted very much against Studds's environmentalism; he is likely to see the Endangered Species Act rolled back, for example. Studds seems to be working more outside the congressional framework, trying to attract private investors to revitalize the Quincy Shipyard, which has been closed since 1986, and trying to create an environmental technology center with a "business incubator to test commercial applications of new technologies" on a Superfund site on Cape Cod. He was fortunate enough to get a sought-after seat on the Commerce Committee and the Telecommunications and Finance Subcommittee, a plum assignment with telecommunications issues so prevalent, and where he will undoubtedly work with fellow Massachusetts Democrat Ed Markey. He surely can be reelected in this district, but it is not clear whether he will want to continue serving in a Republican Congress. In early 1995 there was speculation that he may retire and, if so, Robert F. Kennedy's son Michael Kennedy, who now runs the Citizen's Energy Corporation started by his brother Joe, might seek to replace him.

The People: Pop. 1990: 601,510; 27% rural; 16% age 65+; 95% White; 2% Black; 1% Asian; 1% Other; 1% Hispanic origin. Voting age pop.: 466,334; 2% Black; 1% Hispanic origin. Households: 56% married couple families; 24% married couple fams. w. children; 54% college educ.; median household income: $37,489; per capita income: $17,535; median gross rent: $651; median house value: $163,200.

1992 Presidential Vote			1988 Presidential Vote		
Clinton (D)	133,601	(42%)	Bush (R)	150,566	(51%)
Bush (R)	101,798	(32%)	Dukakis (D)	145,026	(49%)
Perot (I)	80,654	(25%)			

Rep. Gerry E. Studds (D)

Elected 1972; b. May 12, 1937, Mineola, NY; home, Cohasset; Yale, B.A. 1959, M.A. 1961; Episcopalian; companion, Dean Hara.

Career: U.S. Foreign Svc., 1961–63; Exec. Asst., Domestic Peace Corps, 1963; Legis. Asst., U.S. Sen. Harrison Williams, 1964; High schl. teacher, 1965–69.

DC Office: 237 CHOB 20515, 202-225-3111; Fax: 202-225-2212.

District Offices: 1212 Hancock St., Quincy 02169, 617-770-3700; 146 Main St., Hyannis 02601, 508-771-0666; 166 Main St., Fed. Bldg., Brockton 02401, 508-584-6666; and 225 Water St., Plymouth 02360, 508-747-5500.

Committees: *Resources* (12th of 20 D): Fisheries, Wildlife and Oceans (RMM); National Parks, Forests and Lands. *Commerce* (11th of 21 D): Health and Environment; Telecommunications and Finance.

Group Ratings

	ADA	ACLU	COPE	CFA	LCV	CON	NSI	COC	ACU	NTLC	CHC
1994	95	87	89	80	100	16	10	33	0	8	0
1993	90	—	91	100	93	39	—	18	5	—	—

National Journal Ratings

	1993 LIB — 1993 CONS		1994 LIB — 1994 CONS	
Economic	68%	— 26%	73%	— 17%
Social	87%	— 0%	90%	— 6%
Foreign	93%	— 0%	85%	— 0%

Key Votes of the 103d Congress

1. Clinton Deficit Plan	Y	3. Brady Handgun Purchase Y	5. Lmt. UN Cmnd. of Forces N
2. NAFTA	Y	4. Strike Race/Death Pnlty. N	6. Cut Missile Funds Y

Key Votes of the 104th Congress

1. Congressional Compliance	Y	6. Reform Crime Grant	N	11. Loser Pays Court Reform	N
2. Balanced Budget Amndmt.	N	7. National Security Act	N	12. Product Liability Reform	N
3. Bar Unfunded Mandates	Y	8. Moratorium on Regs.	N	13. Welfare Reform	N
4. Pass Line Item Veto	N	9. Risk Assessment on Regs.	N	14. Term Limits Amndmt.	N
5. Relax Exclusionary Rule	N	10. Expnd. Priv. Prop. Rights	N	15. Tax Cuts	N

Election Results

1994 general	Gerry E. Studds (D).................	172,753	(69%)	($639,313)
	Keith Jason Hemeon (R)...............	78,487	(31%)	($10,990)
1994 primary	Gerry E. Studds (D)..................	37,393	(76%)	
	Roger P. Ham (D).....................	11,450	(23%)	
1992 general	Gerry E. Studds (D).................	189,342	(61%)	($1,440,376)
	Daniel W. Daly (R)...................	75,887	(24%)	($238,739)
	Jon L. Bryan (I)	39,265	(13%)	($230,617)
	Others............................	7,156	(2%)	

MICHIGAN

Michigan is one of America's laboratories of reform and innovation, busy now with overhauling government programs and cutting taxes just as it was once busy inventing the mass-production factory economy and then developing the giant industrial labor union and its version of the American welfare state. And to judge from the latest election returns, Michigan's most recent experiment is at least for the moment a success—a success all the more significant nationally because this state, once solidly Republican and then strongly Democratic, has become a political bellwether: It has voted within 1% of the national average for all major candidates in the last three presidential elections. Michigan's experiment is not only political. The state is also a laboratory of economic transformation, helping to show America how to move from an industrial to a post-industrial economy, from domination by big units—big business, big labor, big government—to growth increasingly derived from small units—small businesses, individual workers, flexible government.

Michigan is arguably going back to its roots in the Tocquevillian decade of the 1830s. These two peninsulas, explored and named by French explorers (which explains why Mackinac is pronounced with a silent final c), were settled in a rush by Yankee migrants from Upstate New York, who cut down trees and built farms and neat New Englandish towns complete with schools and colleges. Politically, Michigan was full of reformers who hated slavery, manned the Underground Railroad and promoted temperance—civilizing influences that in the 1850s made Michigan the first state to ban capital punishment. It was one of the birthplaces of the Republican Party, which was founded in Jackson in 1854 (Ripon, Wisconsin, also stakes a claim as the Republican Party birthplace) and swept the state in the elections later that year. Up through the 1920s, Michigan was one of the most Republican states in the nation.

Michigan also grew an industrial economy. Its Lower Peninsula was mostly covered with trees, and lumber was the first boom industry on which Michigan over-relied; forests were clear-cut or swept by blazes like the 1881 fire that burned out half the Thumb (look at the map). In the late 1800s huge copper deposits were discovered on the Keweenaw Peninsula, which juts from the Upper Peninsula into icy Lake Superior; immigrants from Italy and Finland, Cornwall and Croatia came to work in the mines. Then came the auto industry. A combination of accident and shrewdness, of bankers willing to finance auto startups and the prickly genius of Henry Ford, ensured that America's fastest-growing industry of the first 30 years of the 20th Century was centered in Michigan. Detroit became a boom town—the nation's fastest-growing metropolitan area after Los Angeles, zooming from 426,000 in 1900 to 2.2 million in 1930. The auto industry drew labor from the Outstate Michigan areas beyond Detroit, from southern Ontario and from the farms of Ohio and Indiana. It brought whites from the Kentucky and Tennessee mountains and (mostly after 1940) blacks from Alabama and Mississippi. It attracted Poles and Italians, Hungarians and Belgians, Greeks and Jews. This influx of a polyglot proletariat eventually changed Michigan's politics. The catalyst was the Great Depression of the 1930s and the company managers' desire to use machines efficiently, subsequently treating employees as extensions of the machines and with great distrust. The result was the 1937 sit-down strikes organized by the new United Auto Workers; management and labor fought, sometimes literally, for shares of what both sides feared was a shrinking pie. The UAW won and organized most of the companies after Democratic Governor Frank Murphy refused to send in troops to break the illegal strikes. In the years that followed, auto workers became a heavily Democratic voting bloc.

Michigan politics, during its big-unit years, was a species of class warfare, conducted with a bitterness that split families and neighbors. The union mostly won, because demographics benefited the Democrats: Auto workers and post-1900 immigrants produced more children than did Outstate Yankees or management. After Walter Reuther's election as UAW president in 1947, voters elected young, liberal G. Mennen Williams governor in 1948; by 1954 the Democrats, closely tied to the UAW, seemed to have become the natural majority in the state. And as growth continued economic issues became less bitter; by the early 1960s, the class-warfare atmosphere had dissipated. Republican and former auto executive George Romney was narrowly elected governor in 1962, and Henry Ford II joined Walter Reuther in backing Lyndon Johnson in 1964. Romney and his successor, William Milliken, accepted the welfare-state policies endorsed by the UAW leadership and the Democrats. The state government was one of the nation's most generous, and not just to the poor and the unemployed; it supported one of the nation's most distinguished and extensive higher education systems, built state parks and recreation areas, and pioneered efforts to end racial discrimination.

This system came crashing down with the collapse of the domestic auto industry after the oil shock of 1979. Union-management relations had been static since 1941, and there had been no major technological changes in American autos since the automatic transmission in 1940. Michigan incomes had grown as Americans grew more affluent; the one-car household became the two-car household, and consumers enjoyed the tailfins and chrome of new car styling. Michigan was the fastest-growing state in the Midwest from 1940 to 1965; except for Illinois, with its big white-collar job base in Chicago, Michigan had the highest incomes in the Midwest. Then, in 1979, this big-unit economy went bust. It became startlingly clear that the Big Three

Congressional district boundaries
effective April 6, 1992.

Miles
0 10 20 30 40

and the UAW did not have a captive market, that Americans did not *have* to buy a new full-sized, American-made car every two or three years, that foreign competitors were producing better and cheaper cars more responsive to changes in consumer preference. The big business and labor units, so well adapted for growth in the quarter century after World War II started, proved poorly adapted for the quarter century that followed. Auto employment in Michigan fell from 437,000 in October 1978 to 289,000 in October 1982. Chrysler nearly went bankrupt, Ford was in financial distress, General Motors had its first losses in years. As the recession passed, auto employment settled at 280,000, and wages and fringe benefits declined.

The collapse of the big-unit economy after 1979 forced the state to experiment. The first to try was Governor James Blanchard, a Democrat elected in 1982 with a record of supporting big units. His major achievement in eight years in Congress was managing the Chrysler bailout in the House. Blanchard worked to build a small-unit economy; he was proud of his efforts to stimulate high-skill, capital-intensive, flexible manufacturing, and he used $750 million of state pension funds as venture capital for manufacturers of items from tape drives for microcomputers to fiberglass coffins. Dodging his traditional labor allies, Blanchard made it clear that Michigan must learn how to nurture growth and that workers, instead of seeking more vacations and earlier retirements, would have to hustle and work harder than ever before. The second, and for the moment more successful, experiments came from John Engler, the Republican who beat Blanchard in 1990 and was resoundingly reelected in 1994. Engler believes in less government activism and industrial policy; he has cut or held the line on every state program but education. He zeroed out general assistance to nonworkers without children, cut off funding for the museums and arts, and closed a state mental clinic—all actions that sparked fierce protest and hostile media coverage. In 1993, while Republicans temporarily controlled the legislature, he reduced the powers of his great adversaries, the teachers' unions; in 1994 he pushed through a tax reform cutting property taxes by raising sales taxes and prodding school districts to reform. Under attack for months, Engler persevered. At first, progress was slow—in 1992 he helped defeat Democratic House Speaker Lew Dodak and deadlock the once overwhelmingly Democratic House 55–55. Then it was rapid—in 1994 he won reelection by 61%–38%, with Republicans narrowly carrying both houses of the legislature and Republican Spencer Abraham beating Democrat Bob Carr 52%–43% for a Senate seat held by Democrats for 36 years.

Historically, politics divided Michigan between labor and management and between the Detroit metro area and Outstate. Thus, in 1960 John Kennedy carried metro Detroit 62%–38% and Richard Nixon carried Outstate 60%–39%. Now that difference has diminished: George Bush in 1988 and Bill Clinton in 1992 carried both regions. New divisions have been created. In the Detroit area, the economically growing regions are voting Republican—almost all of Oakland County, much of western Wayne County and about half of Macomb County, which is no longer as blue-collar as its reputation. Though it voted 63%–37% for Kennedy, Macomb County was carried by Bush in both 1988 and 1992, and in 1994 it voted 70%–30% for Engler and 56%–36% for Abraham. Only central city Detroit, 70% black and rapidly losing population because of horrifying crime rates, and a few close-in working class suburbs are solidly Democratic. Outstate, Democrats still run well in the old auto factory corridor from Flint through Saginaw and Bay City, in the university town of Ann Arbor, in the capital-university town of Lansing, and in the Upper Peninsula, but nowhere else. Rapidly growing western Michigan around Grand Rapids is heavily Republican.

The results of Michigan's experiments are not final. Engler's critics say he has benefited from an upswing in domestic auto demand and will fare poorly when the inevitable downswing comes. The state's economy still depends heavily on the Big Three, despite the growth of a rich array of small specialist manufacturing companies. But in the long run, it seems that Michigan, having survived the downsizing of the auto industry, will survive the downsizing of government—and perhaps thrive as well.

Governor. John Engler grew up on a farm near Mount Pleasant, drove 50 miles south to go to Michigan State in East Lansing, then was elected to the state legislature in 1970, at 22, and remained there 20 years till he was elected governor. Most of that time he was in the minority. Even as Senate majority leader after 1983, when Republicans, reacting to Blanchard's tax increase, used recalls to seize control of the state Senate, Engler operated in a climate where liberals controlled most institutions. In that time he became a skillful political player, capable of keeping on civil terms with opponents and in marshaling his forces over the long run. In 1990 he ran for governor and lagged behind Blanchard in polls all though November. But his call for increasing education spending and cutting property taxes 20% was popular, and when Blanchard came forward with his own property tax cut, Engler effectively ridiculed it as saving a nickel a week per taxpayer. He won 50%–49%.

In office Engler relentlessly kept his campaign promises, cutting general assistance (welfare for able-bodied non-parents) and aid to the arts; he privatized services and started seeking federal waivers for welfare reform. Democrats and the *Detroit Free Press* habitually called him "mean-spirited." His efforts to change school financing failed in 1992; in 1993, when Democratic state Senator Debbie Stabenow pushed through a bill to abolish the current education funding system by the end of the year, Engler unexpectedly accepted the dare. Engler's proposal was a major cut in property taxes plus a sales tax increase; the legislature agreed to put it before the voters, with an alternative: increasing the income taxes. Democrats and the teachers' unions backed a higher income tax, but Engler's stand was endorsed by Detroit's incoming Mayor Dennis Archer and approved by voters 70%–30%. "Promises made, promises kept," was Engler's theme in 1994. He pointed out that Michigan's unemployment rate was below the national average and that the state was leading industrial states in creating new jobs and reducing unemployment. Small-unit economic growth, never heralded in the news media, was making itself felt in people's lives.

Meanwhile, Democrats had a four-candidate primary for governor, with no clear favorite: Howard Wolpe, an Outstate congressman for seven terms who retired in 1992 after redistricting sliced up his seat and now had the AFL-CIO's backing; Stabenow; Larry Owen, who was backed by the teachers' union; and Lynn Jondahl, who finished 4th. Wolpe won an upset 35% primary victory, to 30% for Stabenow, 26% for Owen, and promptly used large parts of the public financing that Michigan provides governor candidates on ads attacking Engler for approving a nuclear power plant and closing a mental health clinic. But 55% of voters thought the state was going in the right direction (while 62% thought the country was on the wrong track), and Engler's attacks on Wolpe's liberal House voting record were not diminished by Wolpe's attacks on Engler for an August 1994 prison break at Detroit's Ryan Correctional Facility, in which 10 prisoners escaped. Engler won 61%–38%, carrying all but two counties.

Engler, though mentioned sometimes for national office, is hardly likely to run; his wife gave birth to triplets days after the election. For 1995 he was pursuing a $1.5 billion tax cut, greater freedom for charter schools, more welfare reform. He won only a bare 56–54 margin in the state House but seems to have solid majorities on most issues. He stands clearly in command of state politics, and the success of his experiments in Michigan's laboratory of reform have made him a national political and governmental figure as well, one who has become a close adviser and role model to Speaker Gingrich and the new Republican majority.

Senators. Michigan's senior Senator, Carl Levin, is a durable and likable liberal Democrat, member of one of Michigan's most respected political families and a serious figure in Michigan politics for a quarter century. He is rumpled, unfashionable, speaks articulately but without apparent political artifice and takes unpopular stands on issues he cares about, without much regard for the political consequences. For these virtues, Michigan voters have been willing to forgive him a few sins. He grew up in Detroit, worked for the state civil rights commissioner and the appellate public defender's office, and was elected to Detroit's city council in 1969 and 1973, practically the only member with substantial support from both blacks and whites. In 1978 he ran for the Senate and was helped when incumbent Robert Griffin got out of the race and then back in; he won 52%–48%. In 1984 he won by a similar margin against a challenger who had given a public testimonial for his Japanese car, and he won a third term in 1990 despite an ad showing him aboard a battleship he had voted not to commission.

Levin has spent much of his time on process issues. He was chief sponsor of the lobbying regulation bill that passed the Senate early in 1993, stipulating that lobbyists disclose the identities of their clients and their income from them and requiring stringent detailing of government officials who are contacted and issues discussed. The bill also broadened the definition of lobbyist to cover those lobbying the Executive Branch as well as Congress. But it got tied up in Republican opposition at the end of the 1994 session and then was not included in House Republicans' reform package; on both counts Levin bitterly attacked House Speaker Newt Gingrich. Levin was also Congress's prime mover of the reenactment of the special counsel law, frustrated during the Bush years and signed by President Clinton. But he seemed genuinely surprised when the Whitewater special-counsel panel of federal judges chose Kenneth Starr, solicitor general of the Bush Administration. Levin vainly attempted to get him disqualified for partisan bias, though he was no more partisan and indeed had held the same position as Archibald Cox, the special prosecutor appointed to investigate Watergate in 1973. Cox had been the Kennedy Administration's solicitor general.

On issues Levin generally has one of the most liberal records in the Senate. He opposed NAFTA and favors a strong Super 301 provision to show that Japan has engaged in unfair trade practices. In September 1994 he scrambled to put together a healthcare plan with universal coverage for children to avoid the impending crash-and-burn of the Clinton health care plan. One issue on which he is passionate is capital punishment: Levin began his public career as head of Detroit's public defender office, and he has not only opposed capital punishment, but many times he has also led the fight against it in the Senate. This position is in line with Michigan tradition—the state constitution has outlawed the death penalty since 1855—but it has become a minority stand as Detroit's murder rate has skyrocketed. No Republican, certainly not 1990 Senate nominee Bill Schuette, has been able to take many votes away from Levin on this issue. Levin was one of the first Vietnam doves to join the Armed Services Committee. He characterizes his approach as supportive of basic, reliable weapons systems and conventional forces and skeptical of strategic weapons systems. He wants to cancel further B-2 construction and use the savings for the cleanup and reconditioning of closed military bases, and he is proud of a 1992 law cutting $3 billion in spending on clearly wasteful Defense Department inventory and purchasing practices. After the Republican takeover in 1994, he became a leading opponent of their agenda, including the unfunded-mandates bill that Clinton signed in March 1995.

Levin won reelection in 1990 by 57%–41% over then-Congressman Bill Schuette, who made several avoidable mistakes. His ads showed him looking much younger than his 37 years, and he tried to tie Levin to Donald Riegle's involvement in the Keating Five S&L scandal. This overstretch cost Schuette credibility later, when Levin gave him an opening by running an ad of himself in the Persian Gulf on the battleship *Wisconsin*. Schuette accurately pointed out that Levin had voted against the ship's recommissioning in 1985, and he noted that Levin had voted against the Maverick anti-tank missile, which was also being used successfully in the Gulf. Levin responded by citing his support of many technologically more simple weapons, notably the M-1 tank produced in Chrysler's plant in Warren, just north of Detroit; he also ran an ad showing a retired Reagan Administration Pentagon official saluting Levin for critically assaying defense spending requests. In February 1995 Levin announced that he was running for reelection in 1996. Initial polls showed him behind Governor John Engler, who surely will not run against him, and ahead of other Republicans, but not overwhelmingly so: this is likely to be one of the country's most seriously contested and perhaps most expensive races (California, Florida and New York have no contests). The best-known Republican possibility is Ronna Romney, former daughter-in-law of former Governor George Romney, who narrowly lost the 1994 Senate primary to Spencer Abraham; other possibilities include Congressmen Dave Camp and Fred Upton, and Republican National Committeewoman Betsy DeVos.

Michigan's junior Senator is Spencer Abraham, son of a Lansing "mom and pop" store owner and auto worker, who has never before held elective office. Abraham was elected in 1994 at 42 to the seat held for 18 years by Donald Riegle—once a young Republican himself, then a bombastic liberal Democrat who was reprimanded by the Senate for his involvement in the Keating Five scandal but who in his last year held dignified Whitewater hearings when other Democrats tried to make them a farce. Abraham grew up in Lansing, of Lebanese ancestry, and was always a conservative Republican. While at Michigan State in the 1970s he ran Clifford Taylor's nearly successful campaign against Democratic Congressman Bob Carr, and he became allies with a twenty-something legislator named John Engler. At Harvard Law School he founded the Federalist Society and a conservative law review; in 1982, at 30, he became state Republican chairman. The party was then out of power throughout the state. He helped it regain the state Senate in 1983 and helped Engler win in 1990. His efforts to make Michigan an early presidential-caucus state in 1988 backfired when Pat Robertson's forces won a plurality of delegates, and Abraham had to hide out from Robertson's process-servers while his allies were cementing a George Bush-Jack Kemp alliance, which prevailed at the February 1988 state convention. In 1990 he joined Vice President Dan Quayle's staff; he also was co-chair of the National Republican Congressional Committee. In 1993 he returned to Michigan and started running for the Senate, where he had anything but a clear field and trailed in initial polls for both the primary and general. In the primary he faced Ronna Romney, also a Republican party official; Abraham accused her of being less than strongly opposed to abortion and boasted of his endorsement by George Romney (made before Ronna entered the race). She lost 52%–48%, carrying metro Detroit but running far behind in western Michigan.

The multi-candidate Democratic primary was also almost a dead heat. Lansing Congressman Bob Carr, with a moderate record and a history of winning nine races and losing one in marginal districts, began slightly better known and with more money. He won 24%, to 23% for state Senator Lana Pollack, an Ann Arbor liberal; 20% for black businessman Joel Ferguson, who managed Jesse Jackson's 1988 primary win here; 14% to former Congressman Bill Brodhead; 11% for state Senator John Kelly; and 8% for Macomb County Prosecutor Carl Marlinga. In the fall an Abraham ad showed footage of President Clinton saying that he couldn't have gotten his budget and tax package through without Bob Carr; Carr sheepishly sat deep in the audience, not on the platform, at a Clinton appearance in Dearborn in October. In November, he appeared with Clinton, but both by then were flagging in popularity. Abraham ran a straightforward conservative candidacy, refusing even to rule out cuts in entitlements, opposing abortion, and favoring NAFTA and GATT, and he won by a solid 52%–43% margin. Incidentally, Michigan's Big Three auto executives—vestiges of the state's big-unit economy—mostly backed Carr and then scampered to make contributions to Abraham after the election: this is a small-business, not big-business, Republican.

In the Senate Abraham has a seat on the Judiciary Committee, where he should be a strong force for conservative views on criminal and regulatory law and in opposition to trial lawyers. He became an early advocate within the Republican Conference of a more activist party and was willing to challenge the moderate old bull Republicans when they clung too closely to the Democrats.

Presidential politics. Michigan, a bellwether state now for three presidential elections in a row and the eighth largest state, with 18 electoral votes, is an obvious target for candidates of both parties. In 1992, strategists hoped Michigan issues would turn the balance. Republicans claimed that Al Gore's positions in *Earth in the Balance* would cost thousands of auto jobs (though George Bush had signed the Clean Air Act); Democrats argued that George Bush's NAFTA would hurt Michigan (though Bill Clinton came out for it in September 1992). In the end, Michigan voted just like the nation as a whole. It should be added that Macomb County, supposedly the blue-collar bellwether of a blue-collar state, is not actually all that blue-collar any more (neither is Michigan), nor is it a bellwether; George Bush carried Macomb in 1992 but lost Michigan. For 1996, if 1994 is any indication, Bill Clinton will start off on the defensive here, primarily because his uncertain leadership and mixed results are in contrast to John Engler's sharp positions and clear achievements.

Having stumbled, tripped and fallen trying different ways of choosing its presidential delegates, Michigan finally opted in 1992 to have both parties run straight primaries and scheduled them for March 17, the same day as Illinois and a week after Super Tuesday. This was, in fact, the day both parties' nominations were decided and, if Illinois was more crucial, Michigan was still part of the mix. That outcome was a lot better than in 1988, when Michigan's selection process was an irrelevant farce: the Republican state convention was controlled by precinct delegates elected in 1986, and the main question was whether Bush strategists could wheedle enough Kemp delegates away from their alliance with Pat Robertson (they could). Democrats held an old-time "firehouse primary," in just few dozen polling places, in which blacks cast some 45% of the votes, many arriving by the dozen in church buses; Jesse Jackson won a victory with a handful of voters, which was misinterpreted by the press as an alliance of white blue-collar workers and blacks.

The Michigan 1992 primary contest was seized upon by underdogs of both parties who found Illinois too daunting. Jerry Brown came to Willow Run, where General Motors had announced the closure of an assembly plant after losing a much publicized contest for survival with another in Arlington, Texas, and donned a UAW jacket, which he wore every time he appeared in Michigan afterwards. Brown hoped to gain some of the union organizers who had earlier backed Tom Harkin. Paul Tsongas came in briefly, aiming to carry the affluent suburbs here. But Bill Clinton was far stronger and won 51% of the vote to Brown's 26% and Tsongas's 17%. The latter two did best in the Ann Arbor area, home of the University of Michigan, where Brown finished first and Tsongas tied for second.

On the Republican side, Pat Buchanan got it into his head that Michigan's rebellious auto workers were ready to come over to his side. The Sunday before the primary, he motorcaded from Bay City to Saginaw to Flint, a hopelessly Democratic area, and then made the mistake of appearing outside UAW Local 599 in Flint, where he was roundly jeered. Memories of the sitdown strikes of 1937 are still fresh in these precincts, and there are few places in America more partisanly anti-Republican. Buchanan lost to George Bush 67%–25%.

Congressional districting. Michigan, which lost one House seat after the 1980 Census and two after the 1990 Census, is now down to 16 House members, the same as after the 1930 Census. The current districting plan was drawn by a nonpartisan court and has rather regular lines. For the moment it seems to favor Democrats; they lost the popular vote for the House in 1994 51%– 47% but won nine seats to the Republicans' seven. Four of those Democrats' seats and only one of the Republicans' were seriously contested, however. As late as 1992, when Democrats were in control, Michigan had three committee chairmen and the House Majority Whip—one of the most powerful delegations in the House. Now its power mostly comes from the fact that some of its low-seniority Republicans are close to Newt Gingrich.

The People: Est. Pop. 1994: 9,496,000; Pop. 1990: 9,295,297, up 2.2% 1990–1994. 3.6% of U.S. total, 8th largest; 29% rural. Median age: 32.6 years. 11.9% 65 years and over. 83.4% White, 13.9% Black, 1.1% Asian, 2.2% Other. Households: 55.1% married couple families; 26% married couple fams. w. children; 44% college educ.; median household income: $31,020; per capita income: $14,154; 71.0% owner occupied housing; median house value: $60,600; median monthly rent: $343. 8.8% Unemployment. 1994 Voting age pop.: 6,983,000. 1994 Turnout: 3,080,079; 44% of VAP. Registered voters (1994): 6,207,662; no party registration.

Political Lineup: Governor, John M. Engler (R); Lt. Gov., Connie Binsfeld (R); Secy. of State, Candice Miller (R); Atty. Gen., Frank J. Kelley (D); Treasurer, Douglas B. Roberts (R). State Senate, 38 (22 R and 16 D); State House of Representatives, 110 (56 R and 54 D). Senators, Carl Levin (D) and Spencer Abraham (R). Representatives, 16 (7 R and 9 D).

1992 Presidential Vote

Clinton (D) 1,871,182 (44%)
Bush (R) 1,554,940 (36%)
Perot (I)................. 824,813 (19%)

1992 Democratic Presidential Primary

Clinton.................... 297,280 (51%)
Brown 151,400 (26%)
Tsongas 97,017 (17%)
Uncommitted 27,836 (5%)

1988 Presidential Vote

Bush (R) 1,965,485 (54%)
Dukakis (D).............. 1,675,783 (46%)

1992 Republican Presidential Primary

Bush 301,948 (67%)
Buchanan.................. 112,122 (25%)
Uncommitted 23,809 (5%)

GOVERNOR

Gov. John M. Engler (R)

Elected 1990, term expires Jan. 1999; b. Oct. 12, 1948, Mount Pleasant; home, Mount Pleasant; MI St. U., B.A. 1971, Cooley Law Schl., J.D. 1981; Catholic; married (Michelle).

Career: MI House of Reps., 1970–76; MI Senate, 1978–1990.

Office: Olds Plaza, 111 S. Capitol, Lansing 48933, 517-373-3400; Fax: 517-335-6863.

Election Results

1994 gen.	John M. Engler (R)	1,899,101	(61%)
	Howard Wolpe (D)...........	1,188,438	(38%)
1994 prim.	John M. Engler (R).. unopposed		
1990 gen.	John M. Engler (R)	1,276,134	(50%)
	James J. (Jim) Blanchard (D) ..	1,258,539	(49%)
	Other	29,890	(1%)

SENATORS

Sen. Carl Levin (D)

Elected 1978, seat up 1996; b. June 28, 1934, Detroit; home, Detroit; Swarthmore Col., B.A. 1956, Harvard, LL.B. 1959; Jewish; married (Barbara).

Career: Practicing atty., 1959–64, 1971–73, 1978–79; MI Asst. Atty. Gen. and Gen. Cnsl., MI Civil Rights Comm., 1964–67; Detroit Chief Appellate Defender, 1967–69; Detroit City Cncl., 1969–77, Pres., 1973–77.

DC Office: 459 RSOB 20510, 202-224-6221; Fax: 202-224-1388.

State Offices: 1860 McNamara Bldg., 477 Michigan Ave., Detroit 48226, 313-226-6020; Fed. Bldg., 145 Water St., #102, Alpena 49707, 517-354-5520; 623 Ludington St., #200, Escanaba 49829, 517-789-0052; Gerald R. Ford Fed. Bldg., 110 Michigan Ave. N.W., #134, Grand Rapids 49503, 616-456-2531; 1810 Michigan Natl. Tower, 124 Allegan St., Lansing 48933, 517-377-1508; P.O. Box 817, Saginaw 48606, 517-754-2494; 15100 Northline Rd., #107-A, Southgate 48195, 313-285-8596; 24580 Cunningham, #110, Warren 48091, 313-759-0477; and 207 Grandview Pkwy., #104, Traverse City 49685, 616-947-9569.

Committees: *Armed Services* (3rd of 10 D): Acquisition and Technology; Airland Forces (RMM); Strategic Forces. *Governmental Affairs* (3rd of 7 D): Oversight of Government Management and the District of Columbia (RMM); Investigations. *Small Business* (3rd of 9 D).

Group Ratings

	ADA	ACLU	COPE	CFA	LCV	CON	NSI	COC	ACU	NTLC	CHC
1994	95	74	88	83	85	15	0	23	0	12	7
1993	95	—	91	90	75	37	—	18	8	—	—

National Journal Ratings

	1993 LIB — 1993 CONS		1994 LIB — 1994 CONS	
Economic	83% —	0%	84% —	0%
Social	92% —	0%	85% —	7%
Foreign	71% —	24%	72% —	22%

Key Votes of the 103d Congress

1. Clinton Deficit Plan	Y	3. Brady Handgun Purchase	Y	5. Lmt. UN Cmnd. of Forces	N
2. NAFTA	N	4. Strike Race/Death Pnlty.	N	6. Cut Missile Funds	Y

Key Votes of the 104th Congress

1. Congressional Compliance	Y	3. Balanced Budget Amndt.	N	5. Product Liability Reform	N
2. Bar Unfunded Mandates	N	4. Pass Line Item Veto	N	6. FY96 Budget	N

Election Results

1990 general	Carl Levin (D)	1,471,753	(57%)	($7,066,832)
	Bill Schuette (R)...................	1,055,695	(41%)	($2,417,705)
	Other...........................	33,046	(1%)	
1990 primary	Carl Levin (D)	unopposed		
1984 general	Carl Levin (D)	1,915,831	(52%)	($3,569,330)
	Jack Lousma (R).................	1,745,302	(47%)	($1,765,786)

Sen. Spencer Abraham (R)

Elected 1994, seat up 2000; b. June 12, 1952, East Lansing; home, Auburn Hills; MI St. U., B.A. 1974, Harvard U., J.D. 1979; Eastern Orthodox; married (Jane).

Career: Asst. Prof., Thomas Cooley Law Schl., 1981–83; MI Repub. Party Chmn., 1982–90; Dep. Chief of Staff, V.P. Dan Quayle, 1990–91; Co-Chair, Natl. Repub. Cong. Cmte., 1991–92.

DC Office: 245 DSOB 20510, 202-224-4822; Fax: 202-224-8834.

State Offices: 30800 Van Dyke Ave., #307, Warren 48093, 810-573-9017; and 720 Fed. Bldg., 110 Michigan Ave., NW, Grand Rapids 49503, 616-456-2592.

Committees: *Budget* (11th of 12 R). *Judiciary* (10th of 10 R): Constitution, Federalism and Property Rights; Terrorism, Technology and Government Information. *Labor & Human Resources* (8th of 9 R): Children and Families; Education, Arts and Humanities.

Group Ratings and 103rd Congress Votes: Newly Elected

Key Votes of the 104th Congress

1. Congressional Compliance	Y	3. Balanced Budget Amndt.	Y	5. Product Liability Reform	Y
2. Bar Unfunded Mandates	Y	4. Pass Line Item Veto	Y	6. FY96 Budget	Y

Election Results

1994 general	Spencer Abraham (R).............	1,578,770	(52%)	($4,437,038)
	Bob Carr (D).....................	1,300,960	(43%)	($3,040,416)
	Jon Coon (Lib)	128,393	(4%)	($303,369)
	Others	35,262	(1%)	
1994 primary	Spencer Abraham (R)...............	292,399	(52%)	
	Ronna Romney (R).................	270,304	(48%)	
1988 general	Donald W. Riegle, Jr. (D)...........	2,116,865	(60%)	($3,383,849)
	Jim Dunn (R)	1,348,216	(39%)	($442,693)

FIRST DISTRICT

Michigan's Upper Peninsula, commonly known as the UP, is a land apart. Surrounded on three sides by frigid Lake Superior and Lake Michigan, it has its own flora, including the world's largest living object, a giant fungus that lives under 37 acres of a forest floor and is 1,500 years old. Although the UP is no farther north than Montreal or Seattle, it has one of the coldest climates in settled parts of North America."In October, usually, the first snow falls steady on the northland," writes Dixie Lee Franklin in *A Most Superior Land*, "whispering teasing promises of more to come"—for six months or more. Far away from any major city, with ground too frozen and a growing season too short for most crops, the Upper Peninsula was explored by French voyagers more than 300 years ago but was never thickly settled until prospectors found rich veins of ore here. Through 1987 the mineral veins of the Keweenaw Peninsula produced 13.3 billion pounds of copper; the Marquette, Menominee and Gogebic iron ranges have more than one billion tons of iron ore. Starting in the 1880s, immigrants flocked here to work the mines—Irish, Italians, Swedes, Norwegians, miners' sons from Wales and Cornwall, and most prominently Finns, who must have found this cold land with its lakes and hills much like their home. By 1900, the UP was a northern industrial belt, with a few bosses and some absentee overlords and a work force disposed to radical ideas and union movements.

A major strike in 1913–14 and falling ore prices after World War I—events that would be long forgotten elsewhere—are remembered in the UP as the beginning of its decline: The UP's population peaked at 332,000 in 1920. The copper veins were mostly depleted by then, mining iron ore became less labor-intensive, and lumber and farming provided only a few thousand jobs. In the last half century, there has been great migration to Detroit, Chicago and the West Coast; the UP's population has hovered around 300,000, rising to 318,000 in 1980 and dropping back to 313,000 in 1990. But "Yoopers" remain devoted to their land, which some say has its own dialect, "Yoopanese."

The 1st Congressional District of Michigan includes the Upper Peninsula and most of the three northern-tier counties in the Lower Peninsula. Just about half the people live in the UP; the other half live south of the breathtaking Mackinac Bridge. This is a vast area, geographically the second largest district east of the Mississippi and smaller than only 26 farther west; it is a 450-mile drive from Ironwood at the western end of the UP to the Sleeping Bear Dunes towering over Lake Michigan. The Lower Peninsula counties have two different personalities. On Lake Huron—the sunrise side—they are mostly industrial and slow growing. On Lake Michigan they comprise the affluent resort areas around Petoskey and Charlevoix, long summer places for people from Chicago (this is Ernest Hemingway's "up in Michigan"), and the boom area around Traverse City, with its burgeoning condominiums and resorts. Politically, the UP has long been Democratic, some parts more than others; the Lake Michigan shore of the Lower Peninsula is heavily Republican, the sunrise side marginally.

The congressman from the 1st District is Bart Stupak, a Democrat and a "Yooper" from Menominee on the Wisconsin border. He was a police officer in Escanaba, then became a Michigan state police trooper in 1974 and also earned a law degree; in 1984 he was injured in the line of duty and retired from the force. In 1988 he was elected to the Michigan House; in 1990 he lost a race for the state Senate. Stupak got into the 1992 race when incumbent Republican Bob Davis, with 878 overdrafts on the House bank, decided to drop out in May 1992. Stupak won the three-way primary with 58% in the UP, which cast 70% of Democratic primary votes; overall he beat restaurateur Mike McElroy 49%–43%. The Republican nominee was Philip Ruppe, member of a prominent UP family, who had represented the district from 1966–78; more recently his wife, Laurie, was Ronald Reagan's Peace Corps director and George Bush's ambassador to Norway. Ruppe won his primary handily but in the general was on the defensive as the Bush vote here plummeted to 35%. Stupak won 54%–44%.

In the House Stupak has been something of a maverick. Angered by the closing of K.I. Sawyer Air Force Base, the biggest employer in Marquette County in the UP, he threatened to vote against the Clinton budget and tax package; after some muscling, he voted for it. But he opposed NAFTA and the 1994 crime bill. He also sponsored the 1993 law limiting the sale of ephedrine, a legal drug that, when mixed with paint thinner, produces methcathinone (CAT), a highly addictive illegal drug that has become increasingly popular in the Midwest. He formed the Law Enforcement Caucus and tried to retain funding for Byrne Grant multijurisdiction drug task forces, zeroed out by Clinton. He boasted of obtaining $14 million in local disaster aid after the harsh winter of 1993–94. As an ally of John Dingell in the shrinking Democratic delegation, he gained a Commerce Committee seat, which could be especially useful if Democrats regain the majority. In 1994 Stupak had active opposition from Gil Ziegler, who made his fortune manufacturing "cold-formed" auto components like steel coils and transmission parts. He criticized Stupak for supporting the Clinton budget and tax package; he was pro-choice and Stupak anti-abortion, a reversal of the usual party positions these days. Ziegler spent $529,000 of his own money, but Stupak matched him and more by raising $519,000 from PACs. Stupak carried the UP by wide margins and the sunrise side as well; Ziegler carried his home area on the Lake Michigan shore, but Stupak won a solid 57%–42% victory. It is still possible, however, that this district will be seriously contested in 1996.

The People: Pop. 1990: 581,006; 69% rural; 16% age 65+; 96% White; 1% Black; 2% Amer. Indian; 1% Hispanic origin. Voting age pop.: 431,275; 1% Black. Households: 60% married couple families; 27% married couple fams. w. children; 39% college educ.; median household income: $22,788; per capita income: $10,846; median gross rent: $328; median house value: $44,700.

1992 Presidential Vote		1988 Presidential Vote	
Clinton (D)	118,983 (41%)	Bush (R)	133,946 (54%)
Bush (R)	101,110 (35%)	Dukakis (D)	115,350 (46%)
Perot (I)	65,402 (23%)		

Rep. Bart Stupak (D)

Elected 1992; b. Feb. 29, 1952, Milwaukee, WI; home, Menominee; NW MI Comm. Col., A.A. 1972, Saginaw Valley St. Col., B.S. 1977, Thomas Cooley Law Schl., J.D. 1981; Catholic; married (Laurie).

Career: Escanaba Police Officer, 1972–73; MI St. Trooper, 1974–84; Practicing atty., 1981–1992; MI House of Reps., 1989–90.

DC Office: 317 CHOB 20515, 202-225-4735; Fax: 202-225-4744.

District Offices: 1120 E. Front St., #D, Traverse City 49686, 616-929-4711; 111 E. Chisholm St., Alpena 49707, 517-356-0690; 1229 W. Washington St., Marquette 49855, 906-228-3700; 2501 14th Ave., Escanaba 49829, 906-786-4504; and 616 Sheldon Ave., #213, Houghton 49931, 906-482-1371.

Committees: *Commerce* (21st of 21 D): Commerce, Trade and Hazardous Materials; Health and Environment.

Group Ratings

	ADA	ACLU	COPE	CFA	LCV	CON	NSI	COC	ACU	NTLC	CHC
1994	70	43	100	70	69	23	40	42	24	29	36
1993	70	—	100	90	86	39	—	9	17	—	—

National Journal Ratings

	1993 LIB — 1993 CONS		1994 LIB — 1994 CONS	
Economic	78%	— 12%	73%	— 17%
Social	44%	— 55%	48%	— 50%
Foreign	70%	— 26%	68%	— 29%

Key Votes of the 103d Congress

1. Clinton Deficit Plan	Y	3. Brady Handgun Purchase	N	5. Lmt. UN Cmnd. of Forces	N
2. NAFTA	N	4. Strike Race/Death Pnlty.	N	6. Cut Missile Funds	Y

Key Votes of the 104th Congress

1. Congressional Compliance	Y	6. Reform Crime Grant	N	11. Loser Pays Court Reform	N
2. Balanced Budget Amndmt.	N	7. National Security Act	N	12. Product Liability Reform	N
3. Bar Unfunded Mandates	Y	8. Moratorium on Regs.	N	13. Welfare Reform	N
4. Pass Line Item Veto	Y	9. Risk Assessment on Regs.	Y	14. Term Limits Amndmt.	N
5. Relax Exclusionary Rule	Y	10. Expnd. Priv. Prop. Rights	Y	15. Tax Cuts	N

Election Results

1994 general	Bart Stupak (D)	121,433	(57%)	($678,925)
	Gil Ziegler (R)	89,660	(42%)	($665,398)
	Others	2,456	(1%)	
1994 primary	Bart Stupak (D)	unopposed		
1992 general	Bart Stupak (D)	144,857	(54%)	($225,572)
	Philip Ruppe (R)	117,056	(44%)	($449,464)
	Others	6,706	(2%)	

SECOND DISTRICT

The eastern shoreline of Lake Michigan, lined with giant sand dunes, where the lake winds temper the otherwise frigid Michigan climate, is one of the nation's lesser-known scenic areas. In the late 19th Century, this was America's greatest lumber country; the ports on the small rivers were choked with logs and full of lumbermen from Norway and Sweden, Ireland and Scotland, Quebec and New England. During the lumber boom, the shoreline just to the south was the locus of America's largest migration from the Netherlands and today still has the nation's largest concentration of Dutch-Americans. Wooden shoes are now seen only in the Tulip Festival in Holland, but here conscientious Dutch work habits have produced some of the most highly skilled workers in America, and major companies have grown up, like Gerber Foods in Fremont and Herman Miller furniture in Zeeland.

The 2d Congressional District of Michigan occupies the Lake Michigan shoreline counties, plus a tier of counties inland, from the lumber country around Manistee south to Holland and the resort town of Saugatuck. Some 25% of people here say they are of Dutch ancestry. Politically, the district is arguably Michigan's most Republican, roughly equal to the 3d and 11th. Its first Yankee settlers were part of the original Republican party, and Dutch-Americans with their innate conservatism seem to be the most heavily Republican ethnic group, with the possible exception of Cuban-Americans.

The congressman from the 2d is Peter Hoekstra (pronounced HOOKstra), who immigrated from the Netherlands at the age of three, graduated from Hope College in Grand Rapids (with a semester in Washington during Watergate) and got an MBA at the University of Michigan. Hoekstra went to work at Herman Miller, where he helped develop the "Equa Chair" seat in the early 1980s and became a vice president. In 1992, he decided to run what seemed like an improbable campaign for Congress against Guy Vander Jagt, 26-year incumbent, chairman of the National Republican Congressional Committee since 1975 and orator at political dinners around the country but who hadn't been a major presence in the district for years. Hoekstra saved up vacation time and in 1992 took off on a county-by-county bicycle tour of the district. With an earnestness that rang true, Hoekstra called for citizen, not career, politicians, refused PAC money and supported abolition of PACs, advocated 12-year term limits, and promised to uphold family values and to oppose abortion. He also advocated balancing the budget, protecting the environment and upholding the Second Amendment. Hoekstra spent only $55,600 to Vander Jagt's $725,000. But on primary day, Hoekstra carried the heavily Dutch Ottawa and Allegan Counties, which were newly added to the district, 53%–31%, while Vander Jagt won just 53%–36% in the rest of the district; since Ottawa and Allegan cast 59% of the primary vote, Hoekstra won 46%–40%. He won easily in 1992 and 1994.

Hoekstra brought to the House the new participatory-management ideas he had developed at Herman Miller which, according to a *National Journal* profile, "caught the eye of Newt Gingrich and propelled him into the new Speaker's coterie of advisers." He peppered the Democrats' healthcare bills with amendments, such as one to place a 1% tax on employers with healthcare plans negotiated by unions; he is strongly opposed to striker replacement and unsuccessfully pushed an amendment eliminating the requirement that employers who electronically monitor employees tell them so at initial job interviews. He supported NAFTA and opposed the Space Station. He worked closely with Gingrich on formulating the Contract With America and on planning how a Republican House would be managed, and was an early ally of Budget Committee Chairman John Kasich in seeking large cuts in federal spending. In 1995 he became chairman of the Oversight and Investigations Subcommittee on Economic and Educational Opportunities, where he surely will oppose laws sought by labor unions, whose rigidity and adversaryism, he thinks, work against efficiency and productivity. Gingrich also named him to lead a House task force to work with C-SPAN and television-industry officials who want more control of House cameras. But Hoekstra remains willing to dissent even from

Republican orthodoxy: he is one of the 24 Republicans whose votes killed the missile defense provision of the Contract With America.

The People: Pop. 1990: 581,017; 52% rural; 12% age 65+; 91% White; 4% Black; 1% Amer. Indian; 1% Asian; 1% Other; 3% Hispanic origin. Voting age pop.: 414,771; 4% Black; 2% Hispanic origin. Households: 64% married couple families; 31% married couple fams. w. children; 39% college educ.; median household income: $28,905; per capita income: $12,305; median gross rent: $383; median house value: $58,100.

1992 Presidential Vote			1988 Presidential Vote		
Bush (R)	126,969	(45%)	Bush (R)	154,305	(65%)
Clinton (D)	95,351	(34%)	Dukakis (D)	83,237	(35%)
Perot (I)	58,238	(21%)			

Rep. Peter Hoekstra (R)

Elected 1992; b. Oct. 30, 1953, Groningen, Netherlands; home, Holland; Hope Col., B.A. 1975, U. of MI, M.B.A. 1977; Christian Reformed; married (Diane).

Career: Furniture Exec., Herman Miller Co., 1977–92.

DC Office: 1122 LHOB 20515, 202-225-4401; Fax: 202-226-0779.

District Offices: 42 W. 10th St., Holland 49423, 616-395-0030; 900 Third St., #203, Muskegon 49440, 616-722-8386; and 120 W. Harris St., Cadillac 49601, 616-775-0050.

Committees: *Budget* (18th of 24 R). *Economic & Educational Opportunities* (9th of 24 R): Oversight and Investigations (Chmn.); Workforce Protections.

Group Ratings

	ADA	ACLU	COPE	CFA	LCV	CON	NSI	COC	ACU	NTLC	CHC
1994	20	22	0	20	17	96	100	100	86	86	100
1993	20	—	8	30	36	91	—	91	88	—	—

National Journal Ratings

	1993 LIB	—	1993 CONS	1994 LIB	—	1994 CONS
Economic	32%	—	66%	0%	—	80%
Social	24%	—	75%	33%	—	66%
Foreign	35%	—	63%	34%	—	63%

Key Votes of the 103d Congress

1. Clinton Deficit Plan	N	3. Brady Handgun Purchase	Y	5. Lmt. UN Cmnd. of Forces	Y
2. NAFTA	Y	4. Strike Race/Death Pnlty.	Y	6. Cut Missile Funds	Y

Key Votes of the 104th Congress

1. Congressional Compliance	Y	6. Reform Crime Grant	Y	11. Loser Pays Court Reform	Y
2. Balanced Budget Amndmt.	Y	7. National Security Act	Y	12. Product Liability Reform	Y
3. Bar Unfunded Mandates	Y	8. Moratorium on Regs.	Y	13. Welfare Reform	Y
4. Pass Line Item Veto	Y	9. Risk Assessment on Regs.	Y	14. Term Limits Amndmt.	Y
5. Relax Exclusionary Rule	Y	10. Expnd. Priv. Prop. Rights	Y	15. Tax Cuts	Y

Election Results

1994 general	Peter Hoekstra (R)	146,164	(75%)	($134,979)
	Marcus Peter Hoover (D)	46,097	(24%)	($9,792)
	Others	1,926	(1%)	
1994 primary	Peter Hoekstra (R)	unopposed		
1992 general	Peter Hoekstra (R)	155,577	(63%)	($100,278)
	John Miltner (D)	86,265	(35%)	($20,518)
	Others	4,919	(2%)	

THIRD DISTRICT

Grand Rapids today is the center of Michigan's most prosperous and confident metropolitan area. Known since the 19th Century as a major furniture producer, Grand Rapids was left behind in the 20th Century rush to develop Michigan's auto industry; once a demographic competitor of Detroit, it grew much more slowly. But with the decline of the auto industry in the last third of the century, Grand Rapids's slow-but-steady economy has gained speed without losing steadiness. The furniture business, started when Michigan was the nation's number-one lumber producer, still booms, with Grand Rapids now specializing in office and luxury residential furniture. Lumber is still important: Peter Secchia, ambassador to Italy during the Bush years and a possible Senate candidate in 1996, made his fortune in that business. Grand Rapids has sprouted other businesses, too, the flashiest of them being Amway, the door-to-door cosmetics and cleaning agent empire located in nearby Ada.

Grand Rapids was founded by New England Yankees, but much of its character was set by the Dutch immigrants who began arriving in western Michigan in the 1870s and are still coming today; 23% of people here claim Dutch ancestry. Politically, the Yankees were the original Republicans, but Dutch-Americans have become the nation's most heavily Republican identifiable ethnic group, except perhaps for Cuban-Americans; they believe strongly in free market economics and the rigorous cultural conservatism exemplified by the Christian Reform churches. Republican Grand Rapids has produced nationally important politicians, including Arthur Vandenberg, a newspaper editor who was U.S. senator from 1928 to 1951; though a one-time isolationist, he provided key support for the bipartisan internationalist foreign policies of Franklin Roosevelt and Harry Truman. It also yielded Gerald Ford, who was backed by Vandenberg in the 1948 primary, rose to become House Republican leader in 1965, vice president in 1973, and then President after Richard Nixon resigned in disgrace in 1974. Nixon got a bit of a nudge from the Grand Rapids district when, in an early 1974 special election, it voted to replace Vice President Ford with a Democrat, a clear sign that the Republican heartland was turning on the president.

The 3d Congressional District of Michigan includes all of Grand Rapids and surrounding Kent County, plus one and a half smaller counties east and southeast. It is probably tied with the 2d and 11th as Michigan's most Republican districts. The congressman from the 3d District is Vern Ehlers, a Republican elected in December 1993 following the death of Paul Henry, a thoughtful conservative with a fine Grand Rapids heritage. Henry had brain surgery in October 1992, was reelected 61%–36%, was sworn in in a wheelchair and died in July 1993. Ehlers is a physicist—unusual profession for a politician—with a Ph.D. from Berkeley who taught for 17 years at Calvin College in Grand Rapids. In 1974 he was elected to the county commission, in 1982 to the state House, and in 1986 to the state Senate, in each case following Henry. He is an environmentalist and co-author of two books on his Christian beliefs. Several prominent Republicans ran in the special primary in November 1993; Ehlers, with 33%, led state Representative Ken Sikkema, with 25%; state commerce official Marge Byington, with 19%; and furniture manufacturer Glenn Steil, with 16%. A month later Ehlers whipped the Democrat 67%–23%. Ehlers came from a district and a state Senate where Republicans were in the majority, and, once in Congress, he urged House Republicans to drop their minority mindset and seek a majority—very much Newt Gingrich's tune. He became part of Gingrich's circles; as he put it, "His circles are not concentric, but are overlapping and, to use a mathematical term, Newt is at the union of the sets ... In other words, he's part of every circle and some of us are part of more than one."

Not surprisingly, Ehlers became more prominent after Republicans captured the House. Gingrich named him to the Republican transition team and assigned him to lead efforts to revamp the House computer systems and to put every congressional office on the Internet. Gingrich's goal was to give ordinary citizens as much access as the best lobbyist, and Ehlers responded with a system making available to anyone vote tallies, public hearing transcripts and texts of amendments and bills. At the same time, he has had a mostly moderate voting record and was one of 24 Republicans who voted against and defeated the missile defense provisions of the Contract With America in 1995.

With his age and non-political demeanor, Ehlers does not seem to be seeking a lifetime career, despite his safe seat. But in 1995, his second full year, he was already an important member of the House.

The People: Pop. 1990: 580,874; 24% rural; 11% age 65+; 88% White; 7% Black; 1% Amer. Indian; 1% Asian; 1% Other; 3% Hispanic origin. Voting age pop.: 416,246; 7% Black; 2% Hispanic origin. Households: 59% married couple families; 30% married couple fams. w. children; 47% college educ.; median household income: $31,917; per capita income: $13,924; median gross rent: $425; median house value: $65,600.

1992 Presidential Vote		
Bush (R)	128,670	(46%)
Clinton (D)	94,715	(34%)
Perot (I)	52,773	(19%)

1988 Presidential Vote		
Bush (R)	149,772	(64%)
Dukakis (D)	85,467	(36%)

Rep. Vernon J. Ehlers (R)

Elected Dec. 1993; b. Feb. 6, 1934, Pipestone, MN; home, Grand Rapids; U. of CA Berkeley, A.B. 1956, Ph.D. 1960; U. of Heidelberg, Germany, 1961–62; Christian Reformed; married (Johanna).

Career: Prof., Calvin Col., 1966–82; Kent Cnty. Comm. 1975–82, Chmn., 1978–81; MI House of Reps 1983–85; MI Senate, 1985–93; Pres. Pro-Tem, 1990–93.

DC Office: 1717 LHOB 20515, 202-225-3831; Fax: 202-225-5144; e-mail: congehlr@hr.house.gov.

District Offices: 166 Fed. Bldg., 110 Michigan St. NW, Grand Rapids 49503, 616-451-8383.

Committees: *House Oversight* (2nd of 7 R). *Transportation & Infrastructure* (23rd of 33 R): Aviation; Coast Guard and Maritime Transportation. *Science* (13th of 27 R): Basic Research; Energy and Environment.

Group Ratings

	ADA	ACLU	COPE	CFA	LCV	CON	NSI	COC	ACU	NTLC	CHC
1994	25	30	0	40	61	81	100	100	81	86	100
1993	*	—	*	*	*	*	—	*	*	—	—

National Journal Ratings

	1993 LIB — 1993 CONS			1994 LIB — 1994 CONS	
Economic	*	—	*	26%	—	70%
Social	*	—	*	40%	—	59%
Foreign	*	—	*	38%	—	61%

Key Votes of the 103d Congress

1. Clinton Deficit Plan *	3. Brady Handgun Purchase *	5. Lmt. UN Cmnd. of Forces *
2. NAFTA *	4. Strike Race/Death Pnlty. Y	6. Cut Missile Funds *

Key Votes of the 104th Congress

1. Congressional Compliance Y	6. Reform Crime Grant Y	11. Loser Pays Court Reform Y
2. Balanced Budget Amndmt. Y	7. National Security Act Y	12. Product Liability Reform Y
3. Bar Unfunded Mandates Y	8. Moratorium on Regs. *	13. Welfare Reform Y
4. Pass Line Item Veto Y	9. Risk Assessment on Regs. Y	14. Term Limits Amndmt. Y
5. Relax Exclusionary Rule Y	10. Expnd. Priv. Prop. Rights N	15. Tax Cuts Y

Election Results

1994 general	Vernon J. Ehlers (R)	136,711	(74%)	($203,428)
	Betsy J. Flory (D)	43,580	(24%)	($20,402)
	Others	4,786	(3%)	
1994 primary	Vernon J. Ehlers (R)	unopposed		
1993 spec. gen.	Vernon J. Ehlers (R)	57,484	(67%)	($328,134)
	Dale R. Sprik (D)	19,993	(23%)	
	Dawn Ida Krupp (I)	8,759	(10%)	($22,281)
1993 spec. prim.	Vernon J. Ehlers (R)	28,260	(33%)	
	Ken Sikkema (R)	21,437	(25%)	
	Marge Byington (R)	16,343	(19%)	
	Glenn Steil (R)	13,853	(16%)	
	Michael G. Maxfield (R)	4,019	(5%)	
	Others	2,337	(3%)	
1992 general	Paul B. Henry (R)	162,451	(61%)	($282,472)
	Carol Kooistra (D)	95,927	(36%)	($44,866)
	Others	6,570	(3%)	

FOURTH DISTRICT

The central reaches of Michigan's Lower Peninsula are farm country, flat and treeless for endless miles, exposed to winter winds and snow drifts much of the year. Like the steppes of Eastern Europe, these are farmlands that produce hearty crops—potatoes, navy beans and sugar beets. The little cities here are often small factory towns, with neat tree-lined streets on a grid layout that suddenly end and turn to bare fields. Each city has some distinction. Midland in 1891 was a declining lumber town when Herbert Dow perfected an electrolytic process to extract chemicals like bromine from northern Michigan's extensive brine wells; that was the start of Dow Chemical, still headquartered in this now upscale town. Owosso in 1902 was the birthplace of Thomas E. Dewey, later New York governor and Republican candidate for president in 1944 and 1948. It was also the home of novelist James Oliver Curwood and his Curwood Castle writing studio, and today it hosts the Curwood Festival, lovingly chronicled by Thomas Mallon in his book, *Rockets and Rodeos*. Mount Pleasant, to the north, is the site of Central Michigan University, where parka-clad students stomp through snow to class; it is the home base of Governor John Engler.

The 4th Congressional District of Michigan includes much of this territory north of Lansing and Grand Rapids and west of Flint and Saginaw. It stretches north up the freeways, where thousands drive in fall to hunt and in winter to ski, into the rolling country around Houghton Lake, once lumbering country and now a retirement and resort area, with trailers and condominiums between knotty-pine cottages clustered around icy green lakes. Politically, it is mostly Republican territory, though retirees from the Detroit area and commuters to Flint and Saginaw have brought some Democratic tendencies with them.

The congressman from the 4th District is Dave Camp, a Republican first elected in 1990 when his former boss and predecessor Bill Schuette (now state senator) ran unsuccessfully against Senator Carl Levin. Camp grew up with Schuette in Midland and managed his first successful campaign in 1984. Camp's key victory was in the Republican primary, where he won 33% (62% in Midland County) to 30% for Al Cropsey, a former legislator and Pat Robertson supporter, and 19% and 18% for two other candidates. He has won since without difficulty.

Camp has compiled a conservative voting record, although he has sought aid for farmers whose crops are damaged by harsh weather, and has been a loyal and low-profile member of the Republican Conference. He served on the Agriculture Committee for two years, after the 1992 election won a seat on Ways and Means, and is now the number-two Republican on Human Resources, the subcommittee handling welfare reform. "Our current system is broken and desperately needs fixing. Our proposal will encourage independence, not dependence." He has been seriously considering a Senate bid in 1996, whereupon Bill Scheutte might seek his old congressional seat.

The People: Pop. 1990: 580,890; 72% rural; 12% age 65+; 97% White; 1% Black; 1% Amer. Indian; 1% Other; 2% Hispanic origin. Voting age pop.: 425,582; 1% Black; 1% Hispanic origin. Households: 64% married couple families; 30% married couple fams. w. children; 38% college educ.; median household income: $25,898; per capita income: $11,549; median gross rent: $360; median house value: $49,100.

1992 Presidential Vote

Clinton (D)	104,228	(38%)
Bush (R)	102,284	(37%)
Perot (I)	67,263	(24%)

1988 Presidential Vote

Bush (R)	135,597	(58%)
Dukakis (D)	98,197	(42%)

Rep. Dave Camp (R)

Elected 1990; b. July 9, 1953, Midland; home, Midland; Albion Col., B.A. 1975, U. of San Diego Law Schl., J.D. 1978; Catholic; married (Nancy).

Career: Practicing atty., 1978–90; MI Special Asst. Atty. Gen., 1980–84; A.A., U.S. Rep. Bill Schuette, 1984–87; MI House of Reps., 1988–90.

DC Office: 137 CHOB 20515, 202-225-3561; Fax: 202-225-9679; e-mail: davecamp@hr.house.gov.

District Offices: 135 Ashman St., Midland 48640, 517-631-2552; 308 W. Main St., Owosso 48867, 517-723-6759; and 3508 W. Houghton Lake Dr., Houghton Lake 48629, 517-366-4922.

Committees: *Ways & Means* (11th of 21 R): Human Resources; Trade.

Group Ratings

	ADA	ACLU	COPE	CFA	LCV	CON	NSI	COC	ACU	NTLC	CHC
1994	20	17	11	20	11	82	90	100	95	57	93
1993	5	—	0	10	21	91	—	91	92	—	—

National Journal Ratings

	1993 LIB — 1993 CONS		1994 LIB — 1994 CONS	
Economic	14% —	80%	21% —	76%
Social	18% —	82%	20% —	77%
Foreign	28% —	70%	23% —	76%

Key Votes of the 103d Congress

1. Clinton Deficit Plan N	3. Brady Handgun Purchase N	5. Lmt. UN Cmnd. of Forces Y
2. NAFTA Y	4. Strike Race/Death Pnlty. Y	6. Cut Missile Funds N

Key Votes of the 104th Congress

1. Congressional Compliance Y	6. Reform Crime Grant Y	11. Loser Pays Court Reform Y
2. Balanced Budget Amndmt. Y	7. National Security Act Y	12. Product Liability Reform Y
3. Bar Unfunded Mandates Y	8. Moratorium on Regs. Y	13. Welfare Reform Y
4. Pass Line Item Veto Y	9. Risk Assessment on Regs. Y	14. Term Limits Amndmt. Y
5. Relax Exclusionary Rule Y	10. Expnd. Priv. Prop. Rights Y	15. Tax Cuts Y

Election Results

1994 general	Dave Camp (R)..................... 145,176	(73%)	($444,419)
	Damion Frasier (D)................... 50,544	(25%)	($68,801)
	Others.............................. 2,814	(1%)	
1994 primary	Dave Camp (R)................... unopposed		
1992 general	Dave Camp (R)..................... 157,337	(63%)	($518,118)
	Lisa Donaldson (D)................. 87,573	(35%)	($15,650)
	Others.............................. 6,620	(3%)	

FIFTH DISTRICT

Saginaw Bay, the inlet of Lake Huron that separates Michigan's Thumb (people really call it that) from the mitten of its Lower Peninsula, was for a moment in the 1870s the site of the greatest flow of lumber in the United States. There were 36 sawmills in Bay City then, and logs were piled high along both banks of the Saginaw River for miles. Bay City and Saginaw, 15 miles upstream, handled logs from the wide area on both sides of Saginaw Bay drained by the Saginaw River and its tributaries. Neither city has since enjoyed such rapid growth. The automobile industry has also long been an important employer here; a General Motors plant in Saginaw is the world's largest manufacturer of power-steering mechanisms. And the flat broad fields around Saginaw Bay that once held so many trees are now the nation's leading producer of navy beans, the raw material of Senate bean soup. But boom growth has gone elsewhere.

The 5th Congressional District of Michigan includes Saginaw and Bay City and lands on both sides of Saginaw Bay. To the north it goes up past Oscoda on Lake Huron, where the 1993 closing of Wurtsmith Air Force Base resulted in a local economic boom rather than bust as new employers were attracted and property sold readily. To the east it includes most of the Thumb. To the south it reaches to the city limits of Flint, including both black and white working-class townships just north of the city. Bay City, with its large Polish population, has long been Democratic and, since the auto industry woes of the 1980s, so are Saginaw and the Flint suburbs. The Thumb historically is among the most Republican parts of Michigan, and the Oscoda area is Republican, but on balance this is a Democratic district.

The congressman from the 5th District is Jim Barcia, a Democrat elected in 1992 when incumbent Bob Traxler retired. Democrat Traxler first made national news when he won Gerald Ford's open Republican seat in April 1974; locally he was better known for bringing in pork from his post as head of the VA-HUD-Independent Agencies Appropriations Subcommittee. Barcia has always lived in the Saginaw Bay area; he worked in political staff jobs until he was elected to the state House in 1976, at 24, and the state Senate in 1982. Barcia was known in the legislature for his whistleblower protection law, and he was not an automatic vote for unions or management; he bucked organized labor by backing a measure to cut the cost of workers' compensation and bucked feminists by voting against abortion rights. In 1992 he had opposition from state Senator John Cherry of Saginaw, who had strong backing from organized labor, and from Don Hare, Traxler's district chief of staff. Barcia, with 72% in Bay County, won with 46% to 29% for Cherry and 25% for Hare. In the general election, Barcia beat Republican real estate developer Keith Muxlow 60%–38%, running ahead of party lines and carrying two Thumb counties.

In his first House term, Barcia had a moderate voting record, voting for one Republican budget alternative, opposing NAFTA and opposing the Clinton healthcare plan because of its employer mandate. He labored mightily to protect the CIESIN space project that Traxler managed to locate in Saginaw and worked for disaster relief for local farmers and for federal funding for highways M-53 and M-25. Opposed by an underfunded conservative in 1994, he won easily, 65%–32%. He is on the Transportation and Infrastructure and Science Committees and is one Democrat who may vote with Republicans on some issues, though his chief interest seems to be district matters.

The People: Pop. 1990: 580,981; 51% rural; 13% age 65+; 87% White; 8% Black; 1% Amer. Indian; 2% Other; 3% Hispanic origin. Voting age pop.: 418,692; 7% Black; 3% Hispanic origin. Households: 60% married couple families; 28% married couple fams. w. children; 36% college educ.; median household income: $26,312; per capita income: $11,891; median gross rent: $366; median house value: $47,100.

1992 Presidential Vote			**1988 Presidential Vote**		
Clinton (D)	119,086	(45%)	Dukakis (D)	120,804	(51%)
Bush (R)	85,603	(32%)	Bush (R)	118,247	(49%)
Perot (I)	61,544	(23%)			

Rep. James A. Barcia (D)

Elected 1992; b. Feb. 25, 1952, Bay City; home, Bay City; Saginaw Valley St. U., B.A. 1974; Catholic; married (Vicki).

Career: Staff Asst., U.S. Sen. Philip Hart, 1971; Commun. Svc. Coord., MI Commun. Blood Ctr., 1974–75; A.A., MI Rep. Donald Albosta, 1975–76; MI House of Reps., 1976–82, Majority Whip, 1979–82; MI Senate, 1982–92.

DC Office: 1410 LHOB 20515, 202-225-8171; Fax: 202-225-2168.

District Offices: 503 N. Euclid, #11., Bay City 48706, 517-667-0003; 5409 Pierson Rd., Flushing 48433, 313-732-7501; and 301 E. Genessee St., #502, Saginaw 48607, 517-754-6075.

Committees: *Science* (9th of 23 D): Energy and Environment; Space and Aeronautics. *Transportation & Infrastructure* (23th of 27 D): Surface Transportation; Water Resources and Environment.

Group Ratings

	ADA	ACLU	COPE	CFA	LCV	CON	NSI	COC	ACU	NTLC	CHC
1994	50	30	78	60	33	60	50	67	43	71	57
1993	65	—	100	70	54	47	—	36	42	—	—

National Journal Ratings

	1993 LIB	—	1993 CONS	1994 LIB	—	1994 CONS
Economic	78%	—	12%	56%	—	43%
Social	36%	—	62%	39%	—	61%
Foreign	47%	—	50%	43%	—	56%

Key Votes of the 103d Congress

1. Clinton Deficit Plan	Y	3. Brady Handgun Purchase	N	5. Lmt. UN Cmnd. of Forces Y
2. NAFTA	N	4. Strike Race/Death Pnlty.	N	6. Cut Missile Funds	Y

Key Votes of the 104th Congress

1. Congressional Compliance	Y	6. Reform Crime Grant	N	11. Loser Pays Court Reform Y
2. Balanced Budget Amndmt.	Y	7. National Security Act	N	12. Product Liability Reform Y
3. Bar Unfunded Mandates	Y	8. Moratorium on Regs.	Y	13. Welfare Reform	N
4. Pass Line Item Veto	Y	9. Risk Assessment on Regs.	Y	14. Term Limits Amndmt.	Y
5. Relax Exclusionary Rule	Y	10. Expnd. Priv. Prop. Rights	Y	15. Tax Cuts	N

Election Results

1994 general	James A. Barcia (D)	126,456	(65%)	($205,769)
	William Anderson (R)	61,342	(32%)	($5,856)
	Others	5,392	(3%)	
1994 primary	James A. Barcia (D)	unopposed		
1992 general	James A. Barcia (D)	147,618	(60%)	($288,755)
	Keith Muxlow (R)	93,098	(38%)	($93,557)
	Others	4,276	(2%)	

SIXTH DISTRICT

Michigan's southwest corner stands at the western end of the overland trail from Detroit, where the state's two southern tiers of counties were settled by New England Yankees and Upstate New Yorkers in the 1830s and 1840s. They built small towns with schools and churches and colleges, supported temperance and opposed capital punishment, and were original backers of the Republican Party. There are towns in southwest Michigan that still recall proudly their past as termini of the Underground Railroad, and black families with ancestors who made their way north out of slavery to freedom. Later, big industries transformed some of the small towns into large cities: Kalamazoo, started by Dutch-Americans who introduced celery to this country, became the home of Upjohn pharmaceuticals; Benton Harbor and St. Joseph, twin towns on Lake Michigan that were originally known for cherry and peach orchards, became the home of Whirlpool appliances. But this southwest corner is also where the influence of Michigan recedes: people here watch Chicago television and root for the Cubs or White Sox rather than the Tigers.

The 6th Congressional District of Michigan occupies this southwest corner of the state, with Kalamazoo and Benton Harbor-St. Joseph its two major urban areas, and three smaller counties besides. It was for many years arch-Republican territory, represented by a succession of congressmen who deplored federal spending and welfare state measures: New Deal opponent Clare Hoffman (1935–63), Nixon defender Edward Hutchinson (1963–77), and pork barrel critic and later Reagan Office of Management and Budget Director David Stockman (1977–81). More recently, Kalamazoo has trended toward the Democrats, and the 6th actually cast a small plurality for Bill Clinton in 1992.

The current congressman from the 6th District is Fred Upton. Grandson of one of the founders of Whirlpool, he grew up in St. Joseph, attended the University of Michigan and worked for David Stockman, first on his House staff, then from 1981–85 at OMB. He returned home and challenged Congressman Mark Siljander, a conservative and evangelical Christian, in the 1986 Republican primary and won 55%–45%. Upton is less like the congressional David

Stockman, who was a scourge of federal spending, and more like the OMB Stockman, who decided he must accommodate to Washington. He has a moderate voting record, perhaps the least conservative of Michigan Republicans, and has used his seat on the Commerce Committee to seek bipartisan compromises on regulatory issues. To the dismay of national and state Republicans, he voted for the Brady bill. Upton was one of the Republican congressmen who negotiated with the White House and then helped pass the crime bill rule on the second try in August 1994. Upton was later booed by delegates at the 1994 Michigan Republican Convention.

In the Clinton years, Upton moved toward cooperating with Democrats. In January 1993, apparently uncomfortable with the cultural conservatism of most House Republican leaders, he quit his deputy whip post under Newt Gingrich. He worked on the National Service bill: "We cannot be simple naysayers to proposals and plans simply because a Democrat is in the White House." He worked with Democrat Rick Boucher to prohibit interstate shipments of municipal solid waste without the authorization of the receiving jurisdiction, and with Boucher and Blanche Lambert to rewrite the Superfund law to use private allocators to lessen litigation on that cumbersome law. He was part of an informal bipartisan group on the Commerce Committee working unsuccessfully in 1994 to patch together a healthcare plan.

Upton's moderate record netted him primary opposition from anti-abortion state Senator Ed Fredricks in 1990; Upton won 63%–37%. In the general elections he has been reelected easily. Although his moderate tendencies are not likely to make him a team player in Newt Gingrich's Republican Conference, his knowledge of how Washington works and his search for bipartisan solutions could give him an important role.

The People: Pop. 1990: 580,973; 50% rural; 12% age 65+; 88% White; 10% Black; 1% Amer. Indian; 1% Asian; 1% Other; 2% Hispanic origin. Voting age pop.: 427,134; 8% Black; 1% Hispanic origin. Households: 57% married couple families; 26% married couple fams. w. children; 45% college educ.; median household income: $28,453; per capita income: $13,043; median gross rent: $385; median house value: $54,300.

1992 Presidential Vote			1988 Presidential Vote		
Clinton (D)	100,677	(39%)	Bush (R)	129,093	(59%)
Bush (R)	97,234	(38%)	Dukakis (D)	88,978	(41%)
Perot (I)	55,682	(22%)			

Rep. Fred Upton (R)

Elected 1986; b. Apr. 23, 1953, St. Joseph; home, St. Joseph; U. of MI, B.A. 1975; Protestant; married (Amey).

Career: Project coord., U.S. Rep. David Stockman, 1975–80; Legis. Affairs, O.M.B., 1981–83, Dir., 1984–85.

DC Office: 2333 RHOB 20515, 202-225-3761; Fax: 202-225-4986.

District Offices: 421 Main St., St. Joseph 49085, 616-982-1986; and 535 S. Burdick St., #225, Kalamazoo 49007, 616-385-0039.

Committees: *Commerce* (9th of 26 R): Commerce, Trade and Hazardous Materials; Energy and Power; Health and Environment.

Group Ratings

	ADA	ACLU	COPE	CFA	LCV	CON	NSI	COC	ACU	NTLC	CHC
1994	35	26	33	30	44	97	60	92	67	89	86
1993	35	—	33	50	64	96	—	82	67	—	—

National Journal Ratings

	1993 LIB	—	1993 CONS		1994 LIB	—	1994 CONS
Economic	32%	—	66%		30%	—	67%
Social	54%	—	45%		31%	—	68%
Foreign	37%	—	60%		43%	—	56%

Key Votes of the 103d Congress

1. Clinton Deficit Plan	N	3. Brady Handgun Purchase	Y	5. Lmt. UN Cmnd. of Forces	Y
2. NAFTA	Y	4. Strike Race/Death Pnlty.	Y	6. Cut Missile Funds	Y

Key Votes of the 104th Congress

1. Congressional Compliance	Y	6. Reform Crime Grant	Y	11. Loser Pays Court Reform	Y
2. Balanced Budget Amndmt.	Y	7. National Security Act	Y	12. Product Liability Reform	Y
3. Bar Unfunded Mandates	Y	8. Moratorium on Regs.	Y	13. Welfare Reform	Y
4. Pass Line Item Veto	Y	9. Risk Assessment on Regs.	Y	14. Term Limits Amndmt.	Y
5. Relax Exclusionary Rule	Y	10. Expnd. Priv. Prop. Rights	Y	15. Tax Cuts	Y

Election Results

1994 general	Fred Upton (R)........................	121,923	(73%)	($575,406)
	David Taylor (D).....................	42,348	(26%)	($71,609)
	Others...............................	1,695	(1%)	
1994 primary	Fred Upton (R).....................	unopposed		
1992 general	Fred Upton (R).....................	144,083	(62%)	($367,596)
	Andy Davis (D).....................	89,020	(38%)	($42,769)

SEVENTH DISTRICT

The small cities and towns spotting the southern-tier farmland counties of Michigan have been incubators of innovation since they were settled by Yankees from New England 150 years ago. The state's public school system was established by two politicians from Marshall, whose dashed hopes to have Marshall become the state capital resulted in the preservation of many of its 19th Century structures whose counterparts in Lansing, which won the contest, have long since been demolished. A few miles away, in Battle Creek, sanitarium operator W.K. Kellogg invented corn flakes as a health food; he and his one-time patient, C.W. Post, both established factories in the late 19th Century and created the American breakfast cereal industry. To the south is Hillsdale, where Hillsdale College has been proudly admitting blacks and women since the 1850s and refusing all federal aid. Politically, it has ordinarily been Republican territory since 1854, when the party was founded in nearby Jackson as a kind of reformist institution out of the same activist impulse that produced local support for women's rights, Prohibition and opposition to the death penalty. Southern Michigan mostly rejected New Deal tinkering and was hostile to the United Auto Workers, but the people here were receptive to moral claims made by later 20th Century reformers challenging racial segregation, the Vietnam war and the Watergate coverup. This is one part of the country where such cultural issues helped the Democrats.

The 7th Congressional District of Michigan covers all of six counties and parts of two others in Michigan's southern tier. It was a substantially new district for 1992, taking much territory represented by suburban Detroit Republican Carl Pursell and Lansing Democrat Howard Wolpe, but not including either incumbent's residence. Both decided to retire, though Wolpe ran, unsuccessfully, for governor in 1994. In fact, no Democrat at all filed in the 7th in 1992;

some Democrats there must be kicking themselves, since Bill Clinton edged George Bush in the district 38%–37%, and a Democrat might have had a chance.

The congressman from the 7th District is Nick Smith, the Republican who won his party's roughly fought primary in 1992. Smith is a farmer in Hillsdale County who was elected to the Somerset Township Board in 1962 and was involved in agriculture organizations; he was elected to the state House in 1978 and state Senate in 1982. In 1992 Smith's chief rival was fellow state Senator John Schwarz of Battle Creek, a physician accused by a third candidate of backing his car into a hospital security officer who had written him a ticket. Smith boasted of his 1992 property tax freeze and pro-life record and attacked Schwarz for raising money in Washington and from PACs while he took no PAC money. Smith won 43%–36%.

In the House Smith cast one of the most conservative voting records of any Michigan Republican. But he also fought successfully to save the Battle Creek Federal Center from the base-closing commission. He continues to refuse PAC money and would limit PAC contributions to $1,000. With seats on the Budget and Agriculture Committees, he has boasted of passing a law to provide farmers with remote sensing data that the government already processes and an amendment to reduce fraud in welfare assistance for housing. He wants to index depreciation schedules and capital gains. Smith dispatched a primary opponent 68%–32% in 1994 and won the general election 65%–32%. He seems likely to be a happy member of the Republican 104th Congress, though he is considering challenging Carl Levin for his Senate seat in 1996.

The People: Pop. 1990: 581,005; 52% rural; 12% age 65+; 92% White; 6% Black; 1% Amer. Indian; 1% Asian; 1% Other; 2% Hispanic origin. Voting age pop.: 423,899; 5% Black; 2% Hispanic origin. Households: 60% married couple families; 28% married couple fams. w. children; 43% college educ.; median household income: $29,976; per capita income: $12,900; median gross rent: $382; median house value: $50,500.

1992 Presidential Vote			1988 Presidential Vote		
Clinton (D)	96,872	(38%)	Bush (R)	130,165	(60%)
Bush (R)	96,253	(37%)	Dukakis (D)	87,289	(40%)
Perot (I)	62,657	(24%)			

Rep. Nick Smith (R)

Elected 1992; b. Nov. 5, 1934, Addison; home, Addison; MI St. U., B.A. 1957, U. of DE, M.S. 1959; Congregationalist; married (Bonnalyn).

Career: Air Force Intelligence, 1959–61; Businessman, farmer; Somerset Township Trustee, 1962–66, Supervisor, 1966–68; Hillsdale Cnty Bd. of Supervisors, 1966–68; Hillsdale Cnty. Repub. Chmn., 1966–68; MI Chmn., Agricultural Stabilization and Conservation Svc., 1969–72; Natl. Energy Dir., U.S. Dept. of Agriculture, 1972–74; MI Occup. Safety Standards Comm., 1975; MI House of Reps., 1978–82; MI Senate, 1982–92, Pres. Pro-Tem, 1983–90.

DC Office: 1530 LHOB 20515, 202-225-6276; Fax: 202-225-6281.

District Offices: 209 E. Washington St., #200-D, Jackson 49201, 517-783-4486; 121 S. Cochran Ave., Charlotte 48813, 517-543-0055; and 118 W. Church St., Adrian 49221, 517-263-5012; 81 S. 20th St., Battle Creek 29015, 616-965-9061.

Committees: *Agriculture* (13th of 27 R): General Farm Commodities; Livestock, Dairy and Poultry; Resource Conservation, Research and Forestry. *Budget* (13th of 24 R).

Group Ratings

	ADA	ACLU	COPE	CFA	LCV	CON	NSI	COC	ACU	NTLC	CHC
1994	5	13	13	10	18	88	100	100	95	93	93
1993	10	—	9	10	33	82	—	82	88	—	—

National Journal Ratings

	1993 LIB — 1993 CONS		1994 LIB — 1994 CONS	
Economic	0% —	88%	0% —	80%
Social	19% —	77%	24% —	73%
Foreign	30% —	69%	14% —	80%

Key Votes of the 103d Congress

1. Clinton Deficit Plan	N	3. Brady Handgun Purchase	Y	5. Lmt. UN Cmnd. of Forces	Y
2. NAFTA	Y	4. Strike Race/Death Pnlty.	Y	6. Cut Missile Funds	*

Key Votes of the 104th Congress

1. Congressional Compliance	Y	6. Reform Crime Grant	Y	11. Loser Pays Court Reform	Y
2. Balanced Budget Amndmt.	Y	7. National Security Act	Y	12. Product Liability Reform	Y
3. Bar Unfunded Mandates	Y	8. Moratorium on Regs.	Y	13. Welfare Reform	Y
4. Pass Line Item Veto	Y	9. Risk Assessment on Regs.	Y	14. Term Limits Amndmt.	Y
5. Relax Exclusionary Rule	Y	10. Expnd. Priv. Prop. Rights	Y	15. Tax Cuts	Y

Election Results

1994 general	Nick Smith (R)	115,621	(65%)	($289,573)
	Kim McCaughtry (D)	57,326	(32%)	($34,153)
	Others	4,553	(3%)	
1994 primary	Nick Smith (R)	23,146	(68%)	
	Mark Behnke (R)	11,128	(32%)	
1992 general	Nick Smith (R)	133,972	(88%)	($231,043)
	Kenneth Proctor (Lib)	18,751	(12%)	

EIGHTH DISTRICT

Lansing is the state capital, chosen in 1847 because of its geographic position halfway between Lake Huron and Lake Michigan and in ignorance of the fact that it has fewer days with sunshine than any place else in the state. It is nonetheless a tidy and pleasant city with more than its share of amenities. It has a beautifully restored capitol and a fine state history museum and is neighbor to Michigan State University in East Lansing, started in 1855 as America's first land-grant college. Its Oldsmobile plant brought in people and stimulated growth in the first half of this century, and state government did the same in the second half. Politically, Lansing has tended to go with the party controlling state government. When the legislature was apportioned to stay Republican, as it was until 1964, the Lansing area was usually Republican; when Democrats held control of the state House from 1968 to 1992, Lansing voted mostly Democratic.

The 8th Congressional District of Michigan includes Lansing and Ingham County but not the Lansing suburbs just across the line in Clinton and Eaton Counties, which are in the 4th and 7th Districts. It has two other very different population centers. One is the suburban fringe southwest of Flint, an area long Democratic and in deep trouble over the last dozen years with the shutdown of General Motors operations there. The other is Livingston County, where I-96 crosses U.S. 23. Strewn with lakes and hills, this has been one of the fastest-growing counties in Michigan, whose many new residents have left the Detroit area because they dislike its crime, high taxes and liberal politics. Livingston is very conservative and Republican; in 1992, only the heavily Dutch Ottawa County gave Bill Clinton a lower percentage of the state's vote. Such politically unlike areas leave the 8th District closely, even precariously, balanced, and in the last two elections it has elected congressmen of both parties.

The congressman from the 8th District now is Republican Dick Chrysler—no relation to the Big Three auto company, but the founder of a car customizing company that became Livingston County's largest employer, customizing 95,000 cars and grossing $158 million a year. His parents moved to Brighton in Livingston County when he was six; after high school he went to work on the assembly line at Willow Run. Then he got a job sweeping floors for the Hurst gearshift company and in 1968 started the line of Hurst Olds performance cars. In 1976 he started his Cars and Concepts, installing sun roofs and convertible tops; he invented the T-roof removable panels. He sold his firm to his employees in 1986 and started another company in 1991, building police cars and batteries for electric cars. In 1986 he also started his political career, "because when I was doing my plans, every time I turned around I bumped into government in some way, shape or form." He ran for governor and lost the Republican primary 45%–34% after newspaper stories criticized his employment practices.

In 1992 he ran for Congress against incumbent Democrat Bob Carr in the newly drawn 8th District. "Let's replace an old Carr with a new Chrysler," he proclaimed, though he is actually a year older than Carr. But first he had to win a primary, which he pulled out by a narrow 36%–30%–30% margin over two moderates. Chrysler loaned his campaign $1.6 million, took no PAC money and spent $1,763,000, saving $537,000 for the campaign's closing weeks. But Carr retaliated in kind, raising $568,000 from PACs (the 15th highest amount in the House that year) and spending $1,355,000 altogether and $476,000 after October 15. The result was practically a dead heat. Chrysler complained that Carr was a big-government spender and an insider politician; Carr, a member of the Appropriations Committee, claimed credit for creating 10,000 jobs in the district with $200 million in federal road projects. Carr won 48%–46%, carrying Ingham County 50%–42% and Flint's Genesee County 52%–43%; Chrysler carried Livingston 56%–39%. Carr returned to the House as chairman of the Transportation Appropriations Subcommittee. But after losing a key jurisdictional tussle to the authorizing committee and noting how narrow his 1992 margin was, he decided to run for the Senate in 1994, winning the Democratic nomination but losing the election.

This time Chrysler was unopposed for the Republican nomination. He decided not to spend any more of his own money and spent only $356,000 overall. But that was more than was spent by Democrat Bob Mitchell, one-time aide to Alaska Senator Mike Gravel and a high-level appointee of Governor James Blanchard as well as founder of a Michigan political leadership program at Michigan State. Mitchell stressed his independence from the Clinton Administration and refused to pledge to vote for a Democrat for Speaker; he attacked Chrysler for having been delinquent on taxes. Chrysler ran an ad saying "Just Do It" that showed him wearing a Nike-like T-shirt. Chrysler cruised to a 52%–45% victory. Mitchell won the Lansing area and ran even in the Flint area. But Chrysler carried Livingston County 64%–32%, where he got his entire district margin.

Chrysler briefly ran for president of the freshman Republican class and entered the House full of enthusiasm for reducing regulations on business and cutting capital gains taxes—for the Contract With America in general. This district is certainly favorable to him, but it does have a significant Democratic base. He could have serious competition in 1996, perhaps from Lansing state Senator Dianne Byrum, who won a four-year term in 1994.

The People: Pop. 1990: 581,072; 40% rural; 9% age 65+; 90% White; 6% Black; 1% Amer. Indian; 2% Asian; 1% Other; 3% Hispanic origin. Voting age pop.: 431,579; 5% Black; 2% Hispanic origin. Households: 58% married couple families; 29% married couple fams. w. children; 56% college educ.; median household income: $35,911; per capita income: $15,455; median gross rent: $435; median house value: $71,800.

1992 Presidential Vote

Clinton (D) 118,391 (40%)
Bush (R) 104,437 (36%)
Perot (I).................. 68,340 (23%)

1988 Presidential Vote

Bush (R) 132,642 (56%)
Dukakis (D)................ 105,153 (44%)

Rep. Dick Chrysler (R)

Elected 1994; b. Apr. 29, 1942, St. Paul, MN; home, Brighton; Presbyterian; married (Katie).

Career: Founder & Pres., Cars & Concepts, 1976–86; Founder & Pres., RCI, 1993–present.

DC Office: 327 CHOB 20515, 202-225-4872; Fax: 202-225-3034.

District Offices: 721 N. Capitol, #3, Lansing 48906, 514-484-1770; 10049 E. Grand River Ave. #900, Brighton 48116, 810-220-1002.

Committees: *Banking & Financial Services* (20th of 27 R): Domestic and International Monetary Policy; General Oversight and Investigations. *Government Reform & Oversight* (17th of 27 R): Human Resources and Intergovernmental Affairs. *Small Business* (12th of 22 R): Government Programs; Procurement, Exports and Business Opportunities.

Group Ratings and 103rd Congress Votes: Newly Elected

Key Votes of the 104th Congress

1. Congressional Compliance Y	6. Reform Crime Grant Y	11. Loser Pays Court Reform Y
2. Balanced Budget Amndmt. Y	7. National Security Act Y	12. Product Liability Reform Y
3. Bar Unfunded Mandates Y	8. Moratorium on Regs. Y	13. Welfare Reform Y
4. Pass Line Item Veto Y	9. Risk Assessment on Regs. Y	14. Term Limits Amndmt. Y
5. Relax Exclusionary Rule Y	10. Expnd. Priv. Prop. Rights Y	15. Tax Cuts Y

Election Results

1994 general	Dick Chrysler (R)....................	109,663	(52%)	($356,924)
	Bob Mitchell (D).....................	95,383	(45%)	($474,437)
	Others	7,435	(4%)	
1994 primary	Dick Chrysler (R).................	unopposed		
1992 general	Bob Carr (D)........................	135,517	(48%)	($1,355,199)
	Dick Chrysler (R)....................	131,906	(46%)	($1,762,766)
	Frank McAlpine (I)	12,155	(4%)	($21,529)
	Others	5,129	(2%)	

NINTH DISTRICT

General Motors was formed in 1918 as a merger of several smaller car companies; headquartered in Detroit, it had plants in several small cities in Michigan and Ohio. Foremost among them were Flint and Pontiac, two industrial county seats on the old Woodward Avenue route that led northwest from Detroit. Pontiac, named for the 18th Century Indian chief who sparked a rebellion that spread all the way to what is now Pittsburgh, produced Pontiacs and GMC Trucks; Flint, named for the flint from which Indians made arrowheads, produced Buicks and Chevrolets. For five decades after 1918, Flint and Pontiac grew lustily, attracting new workers from the mountains of Kentucky and Tennessee and the Black Belt of Alabama; country and black music and various southern accents became common in towns first settled by Yankees. There was turmoil, too. Flint was the scene in January 1937 of the great sitdown strike that, when Governor Frank Murphy refused to send National Guardsmen to enforce a court order, forced GM to recognize the United Auto Workers as the bargaining agent for all its workers. Yet in many ways these GM company towns built good lives for their citizens. The UAW-GM contracts produced the world's highest wages for industrial workers and lavish fringe benefits, including a healthcare plan as generous as any in the country. The Mott Foundation, started by GM's largest shareholder, Charles Stewart Mott, funded schools, historical exhibitions, even a university branch in Flint—an exemplary plowing-back of money into a one-industry town. Workers who were laid off got 65 weeks of benefits amounting to 90% of regular wages—a real safety net.

Then, starting in the late 1970s, came disaster. Auto sales plummeted with the oil shock of 1979, and imports, especially from Japan, that were higher in quality and cheaper in price than American cars were taking an increasing share of the market. The UAW leaders and GM managers assumed that increased labor costs could be passed along to consumers, that buyers were indifferent to quality and eager for new models. Those assumptions proved disastrously wrong: not even the cleverest advertising could persuade Americans to buy a new American car every two years. In 1979 GM employed more than 70,000 workers in its plants in Flint, a huge share of the labor force in a metro area of 430,000 people; by the early 1990s GM employment was down significantly. Thousands left Flint. Those who stayed found their real estate values—the store of wealth for most Americans—stagnant, and government attempts to develop an upscale shopping mall, a Hyatt hotel and the AutoWorld theme park all went bankrupt. Pontiac was also hurt in the late 1980s and early 1990s when GM closed plants there. But Pontiac has some advantages. The Detroit metro area has expanded, and surrounding Oakland County gained over 140,000 jobs, mainly in services and retail, in the 1980s. The city may sell the Silverdome, where the Detroit Lions play; nearby, in Auburn Hills, Chrysler has established a new technical center and plans to move its headquarters there from crime-plagued Highland Park in late 1995.

The 9th Congressional District of Michigan runs from Flint to Pontiac and has some diverse political territory. It includes the city of Flint and some of its suburbs to the southeast; this Genesee County portion amounts to 37% of the district population and is heavily Democratic. Pontiac, about half black, is heavily Democratic too. But it is only 12% of the district. Lake-strewn Waterford to the west was where many Pontiac whites moved when a school busing plan was ordered in the 1970s, and it tends to be Republican. Auburn Hills and Rochester Hills east of Pontiac are high-income and heavily Republican. Clarkston and other burgeoning communities to the north, where hills and lakes and large lots give new residents the advantages of Up North living with an easy commute on I-75, are heavily Republican also. Similarly, Lapeer County, north of Pontiac and east of Flint, has been growing and has long been Republican. That means that half the district is solidly Democratic, with a long union heritage; the other half is Republican, in some places very Republican.

The congressman from the 9th District is Dale Kildee, a Democrat first elected in 1976, whose district until 1992 clustered closely around Flint. He studied for the priesthood, and he brings to politics an intensity of conviction derived from the liberal tradition lively in the American Catholic church—a tradition with little regard for market economics and a strong obligation to care for the needy. He is solidly liberal on economics and always pro-union; he is against abortion and is something of a stickler on ethics. His door-to-door campaigning got him elected to a newly created state legislative seat in 1964 and enabled him to beat a 26-year veteran of the state Senate 10 years later. He won the House seat in 1976, when it was solidly Democratic, without a primary opponent and held the seat easily for his first 16 years.

In the House, he is a strong ally of organized labor and of teachers' unions in particular, a backer of increased federal aid for education and an opponent of school choice. He labored hard on the 1990 reauthorization of Head Start and on the 1990 child care bill, though the final version was considerably different from his. He worked on the 1994 elementary and secondary education reauthorization, downplaying President Clinton's proposal for national testing standards and promoting the "Opportunity to Learn" standards designed to ensure adequate learning resources for all, though he stops at calling for equal funding for all schools. On trade issues, he was the first House member to argue that imported minivans should be subject not to the 2.5% tariff for cars but to the 25% tariff for trucks, and was a strong opponent of NAFTA. His fastidiousness about ethics raised some hackles in March 1993 when, as a newly appointed member of the House Administration Committee, he attacked Chairman Charlie Rose in public hearings for being too heavyhanded in controlling House perks and for his proposal to hire former Florida Congressman Larry Smith as a consultant on the House restaurants while he was facing a federal prison sentence.

Kildee fit his old Flint-area district like a glove, but the new 9th District boundaries have presented him with a difficult political challenge. Except for Pontiac, most of the new area is strongly Republican. In both 1992 and 1994 Kildee attracted serious Republican challengers, and in both cases his opponent has been Megan O'Neill, a former Bush/Quayle advance staffer and administrator in her father's medical practice in Clarkston. In 1992 she won a multicandidate primary with 35%; in 1994 she upset Democratic former state Senator Kerry Kammer 53%–47%. Both general election campaigns took similar courses. O'Neill called Kildee a "career politician" and "Deficit Dale," who was "beholden to special interest groups" and who had (in 1992) 100 overdrafts on the House bank. Kildee's ads emphasized his parsimoniousness (he has voted against all pay increases, never took foreign junkets) and his conservative positions on some issues (he refused to co-sponsor the Clinton healthcare plan). "Washington might not be working, but Dale Kildee is," was the tag line on his ads. The biggest difference was money. In 1994 Kildee raised $631,000 from PACs and spent $963,000 altogether; O'Neill spent a total of $302,000. Both times Kildee carried Genesee County with over 70% but lost Lapeer narrowly; O'Neill carried Oakland 57%–42% in 1992 and 60%–38% in 1994. The overall results were Kildee wins, 54%–45% in 1992, 51%–47% in 1994. These are not likely to be the last serious contests in this district. Kildee has shown he can win even in a heavily Republican year, but the Republican areas in the district are growing while the Democratic areas are losing population, and it is doubtful that Democratic incumbents will continue to enjoy huge advantages in PAC money now that Republicans control the House.

The People: Pop. 1990: 580,908; 20% rural; 9% age 65+; 78% White; 18% Black; 1% Amer. Indian; 1% Asian; 1% Other; 3% Hispanic origin. Voting age pop.: 420,631; 16% Black; 2% Hispanic origin. Households: 54% married couple families; 26% married couple fams. w. children; 47% college educ.; median household income: $34,737; per capita income: $15,132; median gross rent: $448; median house value: $64,400.

1992 Presidential Vote		
Clinton (D)	117,872	(44%)
Bush (R)	92,262	(35%)
Perot (I)	55,077	(21%)

1988 Presidential Vote		
Bush (R)	113,351	(51%)
Dukakis (D)	107,485	(49%)

Rep. Dale E. Kildee (D)

Elected 1976; b. Sept. 16, 1929, Flint; home, Flint; Sacred Heart Seminary, B.A. 1952, U. of MI, M.A. 1961, Rotary Fellow, U. of Peshawar, Pakistan; Roman Catholic; married (Gayle).

Career: High schl. teacher, 1954–64; MI House of Reps., 1964–74; MI Senate, 1974–75.

DC Office: 2187 RHOB 20515, 202-225-3611; Fax: 202-225-6393.

District Offices: 316 W. Water St., Flint 48503, 313-239-1437; and 1829 N. Perry St., Pontiac 48340, 313-373-9337.

Committees: *Economic & Educational Opportunities* (3rd of 19 D): Early Childhood, Youth and Families (RMM); Employer-Employee Relations. *Resources* (4th of 20 D): National Parks, Forests and Lands.

Group Ratings

	ADA	ACLU	COPE	CFA	LCV	CON	NSI	COC	ACU	NTLC	CHC
1994	90	57	100	100	89	33	20	42	5	18	28
1993	90	—	100	90	79	39	—	18	13	—	—

National Journal Ratings

	1993 LIB — 1993 CONS	1994 LIB — 1994 CONS
Economic	78% — 12%	73% — 17%
Social	49% — 50%	80% — 19%
Foreign	63% — 34%	64% — 33%

Key Votes of the 103d Congress

1. Clinton Deficit Plan	Y	3. Brady Handgun Purchase Y	5. Lmt. UN Cmnd. of Forces Y
2. NAFTA	N	4. Strike Race/Death Pnlty. N	6. Cut Missile Funds Y

Key Votes of the 104th Congress

1. Congressional Compliance Y	6. Reform Crime Grant N	11. Loser Pays Court Reform N
2. Balanced Budget Amndmt. N	7. National Security Act N	12. Product Liability Reform N
3. Bar Unfunded Mandates Y	8. Moratorium on Regs. N	13. Welfare Reform N
4. Pass Line Item Veto N	9. Risk Assessment on Regs. N	14. Term Limits Amndmt. N
5. Relax Exclusionary Rule N	10. Expnd. Priv. Prop. Rights N	15. Tax Cuts N

Election Results

1994 general	Dale E. Kildee (D)	97,096	(51%)	($963,249)
	Megan O'Neill (R)	89,148	(47%)	($302,174)
	Others	3,319	(2%)	
1994 primary	Dale E. Kildee (D)	unopposed		
1992 general	Dale E. Kildee (D)	133,956	(54%)	($795,484)
	Megan O'Neill (R)	111,798	(45%)	($129,840)
	Others	3,776	(2%)	

TENTH DISTRICT

Macomb County, Michigan, on the billiard-table-flat shore of Lake St. Clair, northeast of Detroit, has become in the last several election cycles one of the most closely watched suburban areas in the nation—a political battleground where the electoral fate of Michigan and even the entire country may be determined. Macomb is considered the essence of blue-collar ethnic suburbia, and that is certainly its heritage, though today its people have higher incomes and are less likely to be foreign-born than the national average. Macomb is the product of the post-World War II boom: with just over 107,000 people in 1940, many of them in the old sulphur-water spa town of Mount Clemens, Macomb passed the 400,000 mark in 1960 and by 1990 had reached 717,000. Most people came here from Detroit: Polish-Americans marching out Van Dyke highway from Detroit and Hamtramck to Warren; Italian-Americans heading out Gratiot from Detroit's east side to Roseville and Clinton Township; Belgian-Americans from the Mack Avenue corridor moving out farther to St. Clair Shores. These new suburbanites were heavily Catholic, often blue collar, at least modestly affluent and ancestrally Democratic. They accepted the New Deal as part of their natural heritage but resented the efforts of Detroit politicians to tax them to pay for welfare, and they were fearful of the high crime rates in Detroit's black neighborhoods. Indeed, the suburb of East Detroit voted to change its name to Eastpointe to avoid any implication it is part of the central city.

In 1960, Macomb County was the most Democratic major suburban county in the United States, voting 63% for America's first Catholic president, John F. Kennedy. Since then, Macomb has been moving away from the national Democrats—in 1962, because they would let Detroit tax suburbanites, in 1972, because they didn't vehemently oppose a metropolitan school busing plan. The allegiance finally snapped; Macomb hasn't voted for a Democratic presidential candidate since Hubert Humphrey, and none has gotten more than 40% of its votes since Jimmy Carter in 1976. George Bush carried Macomb solidly in 1988, 60%–39%; his share of the vote dropped drastically in four years, but he still beat Bill Clinton there in 1992, 42%–37%, after appearances by both candidates. In 1994 Macomb voted 70%–30% for Republican Governor John Engler and 56%–36% for Republican Senator Spencer Abraham, while Macomb County Treasurer Candice Miller became the first Republican since 1956 to win lower statewide office, when she was elected Secretary of State. Democrats still hold most county offices and legislative seats in Macomb County, but not all, and Republicans ran ahead of Democrats in votes for state legislators in 1994.

The 10th Congressional District of Michigan includes most of Macomb County, everything but Warren, Sterling Heights and tiny Center Line and Utica, and it also takes in the much smaller St. Clair County to the northeast. Presidentially, it is a Republican district; in most state elections it is Republican as well. But it sends to Congress one of the Democratic Party's leaders in the House, David Bonior.

Bonior grew up in East Detroit (as it then was called), the grandson of Polish immigrants; he had an athletic scholarship to the University of Iowa, worked as a probation officer and social worker in Mount Clemens and served in the Air Force stateside in the Vietnam era (he came to oppose the war). He is a former seminarian sympathetic to liberal strains of Catholic thought and liberation theology; he is against abortion, though he has voted with most Democrats against the anti-abortion "gag rule" and fetal tissue research. In 1972 he was elected to the Michigan House, and in 1976, when Congressman James O'Hara ran for the Senate, he ran for the U.S. House. He had a knack for symbolism: that winter an ice storm killed many Macomb County trees, and in response he gave out thousands of pine seedlings as a campaign gimmick. This struck a chord with gun-toting sportsmen and baby-boomer environmentalists here, and by now he has handed out more than 400,000 seedlings and featured them in his TV ads. He does conspicuous work as well on local environmental problems—securing funds to study a replacement of the environmentally unsound Clinton River dam, taking credit for provisions in the Oil

Spill Liability Act that subjects foreign tanker pilots to the same operating standards as U.S. pilots.

Bonior brings to his work a great intensity and passion. Like many Catholic admirers of liberation theology, he opposed aid to the Nicaraguan contras and El Salvador government. It was Bonior's deep convictions and determination that probably commended him to Speaker Jim Wright, who appointed him chief deputy whip in 1986—an appointment underscoring to House Democrats who shared Bonior's views, Wright's sincerity in opposing the administration's Central America policy. That appointment put Bonior on the leadership ladder. He did not move up immediately: William Gray beat him for whip in June 1989, 134–97, after Wright and Whip Tony Coelho resigned; but when Gray retired in June 1991, Bonior beat Maryland's Steny Hoyer 160–109.

If Bonior sees himself representing Latin American peasants oppressed by U.S.-supported rightist military leaders abroad, he also sees himself representing a forgotten and scorned blue-collar working class at home. He organized an all-night vigil on the House floor in 1991, holding up aid to the former Soviet republics until Bush agreed to approve extended domestic unemployment benefits. With Marcy Kaptur of Ohio, he was one of the most passionate opponents of NAFTA, arguing that it was "basically the sellout of [American] workers" and that "we can't let jobs be our number one export." Others may argue that the Sandinista defeat in the Nicaraguan elections and the well-above-national income figures in Macomb County prove that Bonior's visions of the world are unrealistic. But he obviously feels a moral imperative to represent those who he believes need compassion and help from government. In these causes he does not stint in partisanship. After Republicans gained control of the House, the new Minority Leader, Dick Gephardt, took care to speak in conciliatory tones; not Bonior. He came out with blistering attacks on Republican policies as heartless and on the new Speaker Newt Gingrich as unethical. His work evidently pleases his Democratic colleagues. Challenged for the minority whip position in 1995 by conservative Charles Stenholm, he won 145–60.

Bonior's majorities are not necessarily so large at home. His principled politics puts him at risk in what is on balance a Republican constituency. As it happens, he has had serious challenges in each of the last three presidential years and has had easy races in off years, as in 1994, when his Republican opponent was a man who had been arrested repeatedly for disrupting antiwar demonstrations. His strongest opponent has been state Senator Doug Carl, a conservative Christian with ties to the evangelical movement, who ran against him in 1988 and 1992. Carl held him to nearly identical wins, 54%–45% in 1988 and 53%–44% in 1992. But in order to produce these numbers, Bonior had to raise much more money. In 1988, before he was elected whip, he spent $434,000. In 1992, he raised $934,000 from PACs and spent $1,345,000, to Carl's $258,000. Those figures meant that Bonior could buy lots of TV and the Republican none. In 1994, against nuisance opposition, Bonior still raised $768,000 from PACs and spent $1,123,000.

National Republicans, watching him harass Gingrich every day, would love to defeat him, and Republican state chairman Susy Heintz targeted him and John Dingell, calling Bonior a "whiny, wacky, wimpy, wasteful, worn-out, washed-up, windbag whip." Carl is one obvious candidate; he was reelected to the state Senate in 1994 with 70% of the vote. Bonior will find it more difficult to raise money from business PACs now that his party is not in the majority, but he should have very strong support from organized labor and liberals from around the country. Macomb County may not be as crucial in statewide Michigan races as pundits think, but it could be the scene of one of America's hardest-fought House races in 1996.

The People: Pop. 1990: 580,974; 17% rural; 12% age 65+; 97% White; 2% Black; 1% Asian; 1% Hispanic origin. Voting age pop.: 433,652; 2% Black; 1% Hispanic origin. Households: 62% married couple families; 29% married couple fams. w. children; 42% college educ.; median household income: $36,536; per capita income: $15,603; median gross rent: $471; median house value: $70,900.

1992 Presidential Vote

Bush (R) 115,849 (41%)
Clinton (D) 100,587 (36%)
Perot (I) 60,927 (22%)

1988 Presidential Vote

Bush (R) 136,944 (62%)
Dukakis (D) 85,674 (38%)

Rep. David E. Bonior (D)

Elected 1976; b. June 6, 1945, Detroit; home, Mt. Clemens; U. of IA, B.A. 1967, Chapman Col., M.A. 1972; Catholic; married (Judy).

Career: Air Force, 1968–72; Probation officer, adoption caseworker, 1967–68; MI House of Reps., 1973–76.

DC Office: 2207 RHOB 20515, 202-225-2106; Fax: 202-226-1169.

District Offices: 59 N. Walnut, #305, Mt. Clemens 48043, 313-469-3232; and 526 Water St., Port Huron 48060, 313-987-8889.

Committees: *Minority Whip.*

Group Ratings

	ADA	ACLU	COPE	CFA	LCV	CON	NSI	COC	ACU	NTLC	CHC
1994	95	78	100	100	83	20	20	25	5	4	7
1993	90	—	100	100	62	11	—	9	9	—	—

National Journal Ratings

	1993 LIB — 1993 CONS		1994 LIB — 1994 CONS	
Economic	88%	— 0%	83%	— 0%
Social	68%	— 29%	90%	— 6%
Foreign	78%	— 22%	80%	— 17%

Key Votes of the 103d Congress

1. Clinton Deficit Plan	Y	3. Brady Handgun Purchase Y	5. Lmt. UN Cmnd. of Forces N
2. NAFTA	N	4. Strike Race/Death Pnlty. N	6. Cut Missile Funds Y

Key Votes of the 104th Congress

1. Congressional Compliance Y	6. Reform Crime Grant N	11. Loser Pays Court Reform N
2. Balanced Budget Amndmt. N	7. National Security Act N	12. Product Liability Reform N
3. Bar Unfunded Mandates N	8. Moratorium on Regs. N	13. Welfare Reform N
4. Pass Line Item Veto N	9. Risk Assessment on Regs. N	14. Term Limits Amndmt. N
5. Relax Exclusionary Rule N	10. Expnd. Priv. Prop. Rights N	15. Tax Cuts N

Election Results

1994 general	David E. Bonior (D)	121,876	(62%)	($1,123,472)
	Donald J. Lobsinger (R)	73,862	(38%)	($18,084)
1994 primary	David E. Bonior (D) .... unopposed			
1992 general	David E. Bonior (D)	138,193	(53%)	($1,345,011)
	Douglas Carl (R)	114,918	(44%)	($258,057)
	Others	7,102	(3%)	

ELEVENTH DISTRICT

Only minutes on the Lodge Freeway from the empty, abandoned blocks of inner-city Detroit is one of the most affluent parts of the nation, with giant office buildings and multiplying small businesses, expensive houses on large lots and one shopping mall after another. This is southern Oakland County, north of the Eight Mile Road border with Detroit, where most people work in offices or stores and few in factories, and where crime is low and education levels are high. Even physically there is a distinction between the two areas: Detroit is on almost perfectly flat land, whereas many of the Oakland County suburbs run along a line of hills and lakes that marks the southernmost advance of an Ice Age glacier. Southfield, in southern Oakland County, is Michigan's largest office space center, far ahead of Detroit; Birmingham and Troy have major concentrations of luxury shopping, with additional big malls in Southfield and Novi; Bloomfield Hills has Michigan's highest incomes as well as the Cranbrook institutions with their distinctive architecture. Forty years ago, Detroit had 1.9 million people and Oakland County 396,000. In 1990 Oakland had over one million, and Detroit topped that mark only after Mayor Coleman Young pressured Census officials and presented names of people purportedly not counted.

The 11th Congressional District of Michigan includes almost half of Oakland County plus the comfortable suburbs of Redford Township and Livonia west of Detroit. This is mostly high-income Republican territory, where people generally believe in free market economics and fiercely oppose higher taxes. It is also home to most of the Detroit area's Jews, who have moved out the Lodge first to Southfield and then to West Bloomfield and are now scattered around most of these suburbs; they tend to remain Democratic and, together with affluent blacks who have moved to Southfield and other suburbs, form the district's chief Democratic bloc.

The congressman from the 11th District is Joe Knollenberg, a Republican first elected in 1992 when incumbent William Broomfield, ranking member of the International Relations Committee, retired after 36 years in office—and in the minority. The real contest for the seat came in the Republican primary. The most colorful candidates were state Senator David Honigman and former Judge Alice Gilbert, once called "Hanging Alice." Honigman, who had announced even before Broomfield retired, spent $1.3 million of his own money on the race, much of it attacking Gilbert. He ran one ad, a woman dressed in judge's robes doing the wave at a baseball game, mocking Gilbert's opening day attendance at a Detroit Tigers game, which she had attended on a day off during a highly publicized murder trial. Gilbert in turn plastered Honigman for taking a squishy, inconsistent position on abortion rights; she was pro-choice. Knollenberg, who grew up the fifth child in a family of 13 on a farm in Downstate Illinois, moved to Oakland County in 1967 as an insurance agent and became involved in civic affairs and Republican politics. He was anti-abortion, an advantage in Michigan Republican primaries, and ran ads denouncing free-spending millionaire candidates and career politicians and touting Broomfield's endorsement. Knollenberg won with 43% to 30% for Honigman and 27% for Gilbert. He won the general election easily.

Past 60, Knollenberg jogs several miles a week, and his wife, Sandie, hosts a TV aerobics show. Not dazzlingly articulate, he says of his constituents, "I am one of them . . . I raised a family . . . I built a business . . . I know something about the real world." In the Republican-controlled House he won a new seat on the Appropriations Committee, which will strengthen his influence as a Capitol Hill insider.

The People: Pop. 1990: 580,934; 5% rural; 12% age 65+; 93% White; 4% Black; 2% Asian; 1% Hispanic origin. Voting age pop.: 444,047; 4% Black; 1% Hispanic origin. Households: 63% married couple families; 28% married couple fams. w. children; 63% college educ.; median household income: $49,021; per capita income: $24,466; median gross rent: $638; median house value: $110,300.

1992 Presidential Vote

Bush (R) 147,786 (47%)
Clinton (D) 116,266 (37%)
Perot (I). 50,385 (16%)

1988 Presidential Vote

Bush (R) 173,339 (66%)
Dukakis (D). 91,266 (34%)

Rep. Joe Knollenberg (R)

Elected 1992; b. Nov. 28, 1933, Mattoon, IL; home, Bloomfield Township; E. IL U., B.S. 1955; Catholic; married (Sandie).

Career: Army, 1955–57; Insurance agent, 1958–92.

DC Office: 1221 LHOB 20515, 202-225-5802; Fax: 202-226-2356.

District Offices: 30833 Northwestern Hwy., #214, Farmington Hills 48334, 313-851-1366; and 15439 Middlebelt St., Livonia 48514, 313-425-7557.

Committees: *Appropriations* (22nd of 32 R): Energy and Water Development; Foreign Operations, Export Financing, and Related Programs; VA, HUD, and Independent Agencies. *Economic & Educational Opportunities* (17th of 24 R): Employer-Employee Relations.

Group Ratings

	ADA	ACLU	COPE	CFA	LCV	CON	NSI	COC	ACU	NTLC	CHC
1994	0	17	0	20	12	87	100	92	100	93	100
1993	5	—	0	10	29	85	—	91	96	—	—

National Journal Ratings

	1993 LIB — 1993 CONS		1994 LIB — 1994 CONS	
Economic	0%	— 88%	0%	— 80%
Social	0%	— 89%	11%	— 85%
Foreign	17%	— 76%	25%	— 71%

Key Votes of the 103d Congress

1. Clinton Deficit Plan	N	3. Brady Handgun Purchase	N	5. Lmt. UN Cmnd. of Forces	Y
2. NAFTA	Y	4. Strike Race/Death Pnlty.	Y	6. Cut Missile Funds	N

Key Votes of the 104th Congress

1. Congressional Compliance	Y	6. Reform Crime Grant	Y	11. Loser Pays Court Reform	Y
2. Balanced Budget Amndmt.	Y	7. National Security Act	Y	12. Product Liability Reform	Y
3. Bar Unfunded Mandates	Y	8. Moratorium on Regs.	Y	13. Welfare Reform	Y
4. Pass Line Item Veto	Y	9. Risk Assessment on Regs.	Y	14. Term Limits Amndmt.	Y
5. Relax Exclusionary Rule	Y	10. Expnd. Priv. Prop. Rights	Y	15. Tax Cuts	Y

Election Results

1994 general	Joe Knollenberg (R)	154,696	(68%)	($507,622)
	Mike Breshgold (D)	69,168	(30%)	($29,576)
	Others	3,020	(1%)	
1994 primary	Joe Knollenberg (R)	unopposed		
1992 general	Joe Knollenberg (R)	168,940	(58%)	($490,926)
	Walter Briggs, IV (D).	117,725	(40%)	($272,422)
	Others	6,433	(2%)	

TWELFTH DISTRICT

The flat expanse of land just north of Eight Mile Road, Detroit's northern city limit was mostly vacant in the years just after World War II. A string of suburbs in Oakland County ran along Woodward Avenue, Detroit's main street, already eight lanes wide, which led to the Shrine of the Little Flower church in Royal Oak. There, in the 1930s, Father Charles Coughlin made his radio broadcasts backing and then opposing Franklin Roosevelt and denouncing bankers and Jews. In Macomb County to the east was some industrial development along Van Dyke, but this was mostly empty land, too; Detroit's population was heading toward two million. Today, these areas are well-settled suburbs, entirely built up, some neighborhoods edging toward seediness, many others continually renovated and restored. Detroit, ripped apart by crime, saw its population fall below one million in 1992.

The 12th Congressional District of Michigan is in this suburban territory, with about half its population in two suburban counties. On the Oakland County side are Royal Oak and other Woodward Avenue suburbs, now attracting singles and gays as well as families; Oak Park, heavily Jewish in the 1950s and now perhaps the only small city in America with sizable numbers of Jews, Arabs and blacks; Hazel Park and Madison Heights, mostly peopled with descendants of the Appalachian migrants of a few decades ago; and Troy, once blank fields and now a major office center, with the Kmart world headquarters across Big Beaver Road from upscale Somerset Mall. On the Macomb County side are Warren and Sterling Heights, the destination often of Polish-Americans moving out from Hamtramck and the East Side of Detroit, and site of the General Motors Technical Center, a big Chrysler plant and the M-1 tank plant where Michael Dukakis took his famous ride in the 1988 campaign. Historically, Macomb County is Democratic, Oakland Republican, but Oak Park and Hazel Park have long been very Democratic, and Macomb has been trending Republican for years; their percentages have been virtually identical in the last three presidential elections.

The congressman from the 12th District is Sander Levin, member of one of Michigan's most respected political families, an elected politician for more than 30 years. Levin grew up in Detroit, settled in the Woodward Avenue suburb of Berkley after school and was elected state senator in 1964; in 1970 and 1974 he ran for governor and lost narrowly each time to Republican William Milliken. In the Carter Administration he was a top appointee at the Agency for International Development. In 1982 a House seat suddenly opened up, even though Michigan lost a seat in redistricting, when incumbent James Blanchard ran for governor and incumbent William Brodhead retired at 40. Levin won a spirited Democratic primary and held the seat without difficulty through 1990. The 1992 redistricting moved him east, into Macomb County, and placed him in the same district with Democrat Dennis Hertel, but Hertel, with 547 overdrafts on the House bank, retired, and Levin easily won the Democratic nomination.

Levin is a hard worker, a detail man, willing to spend endless hours with others working out a solution. He seems always to be seeking the mean between two extremes; he likes negotiations and dislikes issues that divide opponents by lines of principle. So it is not just for partisan reasons that he found the Democratic House more congenial than Newt Gingrich's regime. Levin has been one of the leading trade hawks on the Ways and Means Committee, but he insists he is not a protectionist; to expand U.S. trade overseas, he founded the Congressional Auto Parts Task Force with Marcy Kaptur and chairs the Competitiveness Caucus's Task Force on Japan with Republican Frank Wolf. In 1990, he published in the *Congressional Record* the controversial anti-American article, *The Japan That Can Say No*, by Akio Morita and Shintaro Ishihara, when the Japanese authors refused to allow it to appear in translation. Levin followed up by inviting Ishihara to a town meeting in his district to hear U.S. workers defend their products, after which he went to Japan to visit Ishihara's constituency. Even as U.S. automakers were competing more vigorously against Japanese companies, he pushed unsuccessfully for stringent measures—limits on Japanese car and truck sales, including those manufactured in U.S. plants, and a 25% rather than 2.5% tariff on Japanese minivans. He was a strong opponent of NAFTA in 1993, arguing that Mexican environmental and labor standards were so far below ours that the agreement did not make sense. But after it passed, he was in early 1995 one of the few House Democrats to back the original Mexican peso bailout proposed by the Clinton Administration and the bipartisan leadership.

On health care, Levin was a critical member of the Ways and Means Health Subcommittee, which hammered out a healthcare bill in spring 1994. Levin withheld his vote for the bill until Democratic panel members agreed to remove a payroll tax increase proposed by then-Health Subcommittee Chairman Fortney Stark. Needing Levin's vote to approve the measure, Democrats abandoned all general tax proposals and inserted a mix of smaller, health-related revenue raising measures. In addition, Levin fought to ease the bill's burden on businesses, and got an agreement to lengthen the phase in period under which employers would have begun contributing to the cost of employees' health insurance.

Levin's 12th District has fewer blacks and Jews than his seat in the 1980s. He was fortunate in 1992 to avoid a primary, but in both 1992 and 1994 he was hard pressed in the general election. His opponent was Oakland County Republican Party chairman John Pappageorge, a retired Army colonel and M-1 tank executive who had served in top-level diplomatic negotiations with Greece and Turkey in the late 1970s and early 1980s and after retiring was elected to the Oakland County Commission. Pappageorge argued that Democrats' policies on health care, crime, welfare and education have resulted in people losing control of their daily lives. In 1992 Levin campaigned in tandem with Bill Clinton, who narrowly carried the district; in 1994, he made little mention of him, instead stressing the local crime-fighting aid he had obtained in the 1994 crime bill, drug education projects and his work on trade. "We can't turn over the House of Representatives to 100-plus Newt Gingriches," he said, running ads that said Pappageorge was "just too extreme." To Levin, the Contract With America was crude and impractical, its proponents refusing to engage in the fine-tooled compromising he specializes in. "I'm in the mainstream. He's toying with the margins," he said of Pappageorge. Ideas mattered here, but so did money: both candidates had impressive volunteer support and on-the-ground campaigns, but both times Levin had enough money to run television advertising and Pappageorge did not. In 1994 Levin raised $731,000 from individuals and $684,000 from PACs and spent a total of $1,536,000 to $470,000 for Pappageorge.

The results were almost identical: Levin won 53%–46% in 1992 and 52%–47% in 1994. Levin won 54% in Oakland County both times, 51% in Macomb in 1992 and 50% in 1994. Given the numbers, this is likely to be a seriously contested seat again. Levin must hope that he will do better because he will be better known than he was in much of the district in 1992 and that Bill Clinton will not be so unpopular as he was in 1994. Republicans must hope that their 1994 issues advantage will stick and that Levin's ability to get funds to local projects and to raise money from PACs will be severely reduced now that Republicans control the House. Meanwhile, at least as long as Republican unity lasts, Levin will have less opportunity for the legislative compromising and craftsmanship he has specialized in.

The People: Pop. 1990: 580,987; 13% age 65+; 93% White; 4% Black; 2% Asian; 1% Hispanic origin. Voting age pop.: 442,555; 3% Black; 1% Hispanic origin. Households: 58% married couple families; 27% married couple fams. w. children; 48% college educ.; median household income: $38,760; per capita income: $16,796; median gross rent: $512; median house value: $75,300.

1992 Presidential Vote			1988 Presidential Vote		
Clinton (D)	119,055	(42%)	Bush (R)	143,088	(58%)
Bush (R)	115,065	(40%)	Dukakis (D)	104,832	(42%)
Perot (I)	49,519	(17%)			

Rep. Sander M. Levin (D)

Elected 1982; b. Sept. 6, 1931, Detroit; home, Royal Oak; U. of Chicago, B.A. 1952, Columbia U., M.A. 1954, Harvard, LL.B. 1957; Jewish; married (Victoria).

Career: Practicing atty., 1957–64, 1970–76; Oakland Bd. of Supervisors, 1961–64; MI Senate, 1965–70; Fellow, Harvard JFK Schl. of Govt., 1975; A.A., Agency for Intl. Devel., 1977–81.

DC Office: 2230 RHOB 20515, 202-225-4961; Fax: 202-226-1033.

District Offices: 2107 E. 14 Mile Rd., #130, Sterling Heights 48310, 810-268-4444.

Committees: *Ways & Means* (9th of 15 D): Human Resources; Oversight.

Group Ratings

	ADA	ACLU	COPE	CFA	LCV	CON	NSI	COC	ACU	NTLC	CHC
1994	85	78	89	80	89	16	40	50	5	18	7
1993	95	—	100	100	86	19	—	18	4	—	—

National Journal Ratings

	1993 LIB — 1993 CONS		1994 LIB — 1994 CONS	
Economic	78%	— 12%	73%	— 17%
Social	80%	— 13%	90%	— 6%
Foreign	87%	— 7%	68%	— 29%

Key Votes of the 103d Congress

1. Clinton Deficit Plan	Y	3. Brady Handgun Purchase	Y	5. Lmt. UN Cmnd. of Forces	N
2. NAFTA	N	4. Strike Race/Death Pnlty.	N	6. Cut Missile Funds	Y

Key Votes of the 104th Congress

1. Congressional Compliance	Y	6. Reform Crime Grant	N	11. Loser Pays Court Reform	N
2. Balanced Budget Amndmt.	N	7. National Security Act	N	12. Product Liability Reform	N
3. Bar Unfunded Mandates	N	8. Moratorium on Regs.	N	13. Welfare Reform	N
4. Pass Line Item Veto	N	9. Risk Assessment on Regs.	N	14. Term Limits Amndmt.	N
5. Relax Exclusionary Rule	N	10. Expnd. Priv. Prop. Rights	N	15. Tax Cuts	N

Election Results

1994 general	Sander M. Levin (D)	103,508	(52%)	($1,536,445)
	John Pappageorge (R)	92,762	(47%)	($470,616)
	Others	2,748	(1%)	
1994 primary	Sander M. Levin (D)	37,159	(80%)	
	Karen Roberts (D)	6,027	(13%)	
	Nat Pernick (D)	3,120	(7%)	
1992 general	Sander M. Levin (D)	137,514	(53%)	($1,185,400)
	John Pappageorge (R)	119,357	(46%)	($190,203)
	Others	4,478	(2%)	

THIRTEENTH DISTRICT

From Detroit's Metro Airport west to Ann Arbor runs what was once a key component in the "arsenal of democracy." Now the I-94 expressway, it was built in 1942 so workers from Detroit could drive to the huge Willow Run bomber plant 30 miles west; later it was known by travelers for its pothole-pocked pavement and the giant Goodyear tire over the billboard with the digital counter showing the year's (American) car production. Today, it is still a key link between factories and suppliers, workers and workplaces, between the blue-collar neighborhoods of southwest Wayne County and Ann Arbor, home of the University of Michigan. But the expressway symbolizes a shift that has been going on here for at least a dozen years, from many low-skill jobs assembling high-style but low-tech cars, to fewer higher-skill jobs in higher-tech manufacturing, often with smaller firms seeking out market niches. People here like to call I-94 "Automation Alley," and some people have done very well by the changes. Others have been left behind, such as the 2,460 workers at the General Motors plant in Ypsilanti, where UAW local leaders were so confident that they refused to make employment concessions when pitted against a plant in Arlington, Texas. The Texas UAW workers did make concessions, and GM closed the Ypsilanti plant in 1994.

The 13th Congressional District of Michigan covers much of this unpicturesque landscape from the airport to Ann Arbor. A few of its suburbs are distinctly downscale, like Romulus, where poorer residents have worked a little at a time to build their own houses, on land so flat it oozes water after a rain. Others are proudly middle-income, like Westland, which was named after a shopping center, and Canton Township, which grew robustly in the 1980s; Plymouth and Northville just to the north are high-income and fast-growing. Southwest Wayne County has been Democratic since the UAW forced an unwilling Henry Ford to sign a collective bargaining contract in 1941, but as working-class wages went up and working-class consciousness declined it has become less so. In Washtenaw County the district's largest city, Ann Arbor, has a Republican history going back to its beginnings as a haven for German veterans of the failed revolutions of 1848, but undergraduates in the 1970s and graduate students in the 1980s have swung it sharply to the left, making it one of the most dependably Democratic parts of Michigan. Ypsilanti, working class and home to Eastern Michigan University, is also Democratic. On balance the 13th leans Democratic but not overwhelmingly.

The congresswoman from the 13th District is Lynn Rivers, a Democrat who is one of the most atypical of 1994 freshmen. She was elected to replace William Ford, a 30-year, pro-labor incumbent, last chairman of the since-renamed Education and Labor Committee, and father of the plant-closing and family leave laws and the Hatch Act repeal. One reason he may have quit is that 1992 was the first year in which he had a district with a significant Republican base and faced a serious Republican opponent; in 1994 both parties had serious primary contests. On the Republican side was John Schall, who was already running when Ford bowed out in January 1994. Schall, former chief of staff to Labor Secretary Lynn Martin, narrowly won, 44%–42%, over Cynthia Hudgens Wilbanks, one-time aide to Plymouth Congressman Carl Pursell, who retired in 1992. The Democratic winner, over Ford aide Dave Geiss, was Lynn Rivers. Her story is an unusual one for an American politician. She was married and became a mother at 18; her husband is an auto worker and UAW member; she worked her way through school as her kids grew and got a bachelor's degree at University of Michigan in 1987 and a law degree in 1992. She entered politics as "a mom who got mad at the system" and was elected to the Ann Arbor school board in 1984. In 1992 she was elected to the state House.

Ann Arbor is a leftish constituency, and Rivers had one of the most liberal records in the House. That probably helped her in the primary: she beat Geiss 74%–15% in Ann Arbor's Washtenaw County while losing the Wayne County portion of the district, for a 56%–33% victory overall. In the general Schall portrayed himself as a "mainstream Republican" and called her an "ultra-liberal big-government Democrat," a fair if freighted description; she favored, among other things, a Canadian-style single-payer health plan and had voted against a bill to keep guns out of schools and for weakening a ban on child pornography. But Rivers, for all the genuine modesty of her personal background, raised far more money, including $240,000 from PACs, and spent $610,000 to Schall's $348,000. The result was not far different from Ford's 52%–43% win in 1992. If most of America was moving to the right in 1994, the hard core of the cultural left—places like Ann Arbor—were moving left as if in response. Rivers won Washtenaw County 62%–36%, while Schall carried the Wayne County portion 51%–46%. Overall, Rivers won 52%–45%.

In the House, Rivers has seats on the Budget and Science Committees; she did not get Ford's place on the renamed Economic and Educational Opportunities Committee, where she wanted to push for more school-to-work and vocational education programs. Being one of 13 Democratic freshmen was quite different from being one of 73 Republicans: "It's like when there's a war and you get in a foxhole with a lot of people. Then a grenade gets thrown in the foxhole and you become the only survivor. While you're elated to be alive, there's a tremendous sense of guilt and grief. There's not the usual jubilation." Given the strength of Rivers's support in Ann Arbor, she seems in good shape to hold this seat and to continue to present her distinctive perspective to the House.

The People: Pop. 1990: 580,882; 7% rural; 9% age 65+; 85% White; 11% Black; 3% Asian; 2% Hispanic origin. Voting age pop.: 442,363; 10% Black; 1% Hispanic origin. Households: 53% married couple families; 26% married couple fams. w. children; 55% college educ.; median household income: $36,596; per capita income: $16,267; median gross rent: $519; median house value: $76,600.

1992 Presidential Vote			1988 Presidential Vote		
Clinton (D)	129,113	(49%)	Bush (R)	112,085	(51%)
Bush (R)	89,040	(34%)	Dukakis (D)	108,488	(49%)
Perot (I)	43,946	(17%)			

Rep. Lynn N. Rivers (D)

Elected 1994; b. Dec. 19, 1956, Au Gres; home, Ann Arbor; U. of MI, B.A. 1987; Wayne St. U., J.D. 1992; Protestant; married (Joseph).

Career: Ann Arbor Schl. Bd., 1984–92; MI House of Reps., 1993–94.

DC Office: 1116 LHOB 20515, 202-225-6261; Fax: 202-225-3404.

District Offices: 106 E. Washington, Ann Arbor 48104, 313-741-4210; 3716 Newberry, Wayne 48184, 313-722-1411.

Committees: *Budget* (17th of 18 D). *Science* (16th of 23 D): Basic Research; Energy and Environment.

Group Ratings and 103rd Congress Votes: Newly Elected

Key Votes of the 104th Congress

1. Congressional Compliance	Y	6. Reform Crime Grant	N	11. Loser Pays Court Reform	N
2. Balanced Budget Amndmt.	N	7. National Security Act	N	12. Product Liability Reform	N
3. Bar Unfunded Mandates	Y	8. Moratorium on Regs.	N	13. Welfare Reform	N
4. Pass Line Item Veto	Y	9. Risk Assessment on Regs.	N	14. Term Limits Amndmt.	N
5. Relax Exclusionary Rule	N	10. Expnd. Priv. Prop. Rights	N	15. Tax Cuts	N

Election Results

1994 general	Lynn N. Rivers (D)	89,573	(52%)	($610,394)
	John A. Schall (R)	77,908	(45%)	($348,322)
	Others	5,197	(3%)	
1994 primary	Lynn N. Rivers (D)	24,426	(56%)	
	David Geiss (D)	14,386	(33%)	
	Fulton Eaglin (D)	4,423	(10%)	
1992 general	William D. Ford (D)	127,642	(52%)	($872,349)
	Robert Geake (R)	105,169	(43%)	($188,138)
	Randall Roe (I)	8,626	(4%)	
	Others	4,451	(2%)	

FOURTEENTH DISTRICT

The early auto factories of Detroit—Packard, Hudson, Ford Highland Park, Dodge Main, Briggs, Ford Rouge, Cadillac, Kelsey-Hayes, Chrysler, Plymouth, DeSoto—were built between 1905 and 1925 in an arc about five miles from the city's center, in green fields at what was then the edge of urban development. As they were going up, the flat farmlands all around were platted in grid streets and developed with houses. Some were wooden bungalows, but many neighborhoods were made up of massive brick one- and two-family houses, often with a driveway at the side and a single elm in front. Commercial developments lined the mile-square and radial main streets, stretching straight as far as the eye could see. Detroit was the nation's second fastest growing big city in those years, after Los Angeles, and with Los Angeles it was one of the first to be built to automobile scale. Its neighborhoods filled up with factory workers and civil servants, professionals and maintenance men, corner store owners and management personnel, Catholics and Protestants and Jews: a middle-class melting pot. With one exception: Detroit in those days had few blacks, who did not begin their big migrations here from the South, mainly Alabama, until around 1940, when defense plants began hiring in large numbers.

The history of black Detroit is one of conflict and uplift, inspiration and tragedy. The wartime mixture of Appalachian mountain whites and Deep South blacks proved volatile: There was a violent race riot in June 1943. Blacks were pent up in a few severely overcrowded neighborhoods during the war years, like the Black Bottom, which is now the Chrysler Freeway. After 1945, when blacks started moving outward, real estate agents played on racial fears to make sales, and in the 1950s whole square miles of Detroit changed racial composition in just a few years. In the 1960s there was hope that the civil rights movement, encouraged by Walter Reuther's United Auto Workers, and antipoverty programs would improve blacks' lot, and in fact many black Detroiters found good jobs and made good incomes, bought their own houses and built community institutions. Then came the riot of July 1967, followed by vast white flight, a huge proliferation of guns and terrible increases in crime. Detroit's first black mayor, Coleman Young, elected in 1973, responded with policies that may have seemed appropriate in the 1960s but had disastrous results in the 1970s and 1980s: He pressured major employers like the Big Three auto companies to build facilities in Detroit, raised taxes to support a vast army of city employees, and attributed city problems to white racism. Violent crime became a part of everyday life and arson became common, especially on "devil's night" before Halloween, with never a criticism from the mayor—for, in his view, to criticize blacks who commit crimes would have been blaming the victims and playing into the hands of white racists.

Detroit took on a garrison atmosphere. Crime reduced the value of residential real estate to near zero, and the city's population dropped from 1.7 million in 1960 to one million (perhaps) in 1990. Thousands of houses were abandoned to arsonists and drug dealers; in early 1993, the city's ombudsman proposed that large stretches of property be purchased by the city, fenced off and abandoned. In political dialogue, most black politicians called for, and most black voters seemed to support, an ever-increasing public sector. Yet the existing public sector, which takes a larger share of residents' income than almost anywhere else in the country, serves citizens very poorly. Detroit's new mayor, Dennis Archer, elected in 1993, seems determined both to fight crime and encourage private-sector growth. But he has inherited terrible problems.

The 14th Congressional District of Michigan consists of the northern half of Detroit, including most neighborhoods just beyond the auto plants. It also includes adjacent suburbs from high-income Grosse Pointe Woods and defiantly all-white Dearborn Heights to Highland Park, an enclave within the city, which had 52,000 people and fine city services in 1930 and 20,000 people and an essentially defunct government in 1990. There are some solid neighborhoods here, including high-income Palmer Woods and Sherwood Forest, and Rosedale Park, where many city employees live. On many blocks homeowners bravely install the big front-lawn lights Detroit Edison sells and patrol their streets, trying to protect them from the thugs that have dominion over most blocks nearby. Too often those nearby blocks are pockmarked by burnt-out hulks and empty lots where houses used to be. Politically, this is one of the most Democratic areas in the nation, with many precincts turning in percentages between 90% and 98%.

The congressman from the 14th District is John Conyers, senior member (and one of the founders) of the Congressional Black Caucus, chairman of the Government Operations Committee for six years when Democrats controlled the House and now ranking Democrat on Judiciary. The son of a left-wing operative in the UAW, he was first elected to Congress in 1964—one of six blacks in the House at the time, and the only one to take a militant approach to politics, distancing himself from the Johnson Administration, criticizing the Vietnam war from the beginning, charging that liberals were not doing enough for the poor. His response to the 1967 riot was to introduce the first bill for a guaranteed annual income. He supported reparations for the descendants of slaves. He stood by in disgust as his white Michigan Democratic colleagues opposed metropolitan school busing, and he has opposed most of the controversial parts of the crime bills of the 1970s, 1980s and 1990s, including the death penalty and abolishing the insanity defense after President Reagan was shot. In 1993 he helped kill the Youth Violence Initiative, a five-year study to determine which children are most likely to commit violent acts, and provide treatment to help. He charged that research on violent youths leads down "a dark path with potentially racially biased research"—as if it were not already apparent that young black males, for whatever reason, commit far more violent crimes proportionally than any other category of Americans. Over many years he has had one of the most liberal voting records in the House. He has often supported big-government solutions to problems, like a single-payer health care plan and massive public works projects.

Conyers has also had growing committee responsibilities. He chaired the hearings on the impeachment of Florida federal Judge Alcee Hastings and ruled against him; Hastings was removed from the bench but, ironically, elected to the House in 1992. As Government Operations chairman, Conyers installed chief financial officers in every government department, opposed oversight by OMB and the Competitiveness Council on government regulations, ferreted out waste in various agencies, and opposed many defense projects. He criticized Attorney General Janet Reno for her decision to storm the Branch Davidian compound in Waco.

Conyers's political standing at home has grown weaker. He abruptly ran for mayor against his longtime ally Coleman Young in 1989. His campaign was glitch-ridden and light on specifics, and he finished a dismal third in the primary. Inexplicably, he ran for mayor again in 1993, when Young retired, but did not conduct a serious campaign; he won a humiliating 3% of the vote. Not surprisingly, he attracted credible opposition in the 1994 primary from attorney Melvin Hollowell, a supporter of Mayor Dennis Archer, and city ombudsman Marie Farrell-Donaldson. They attacked Conyers for being out of touch with Detroit and for being absent from duty—his 71% voting record in 1993 was lower than any other member's except for one who was on trial. Conyers claimed credit for local projects—a downtown Drug Enforcement Administration building, a veterans' hospital in the Medical Center, funding for the Focus:HOPE jobs program.

"Here I am, working in the most exciting part of my career—with a new administration—on the local front and in the nation, and somebody is saying, let's start out all over again. It doesn't make sense," he said. He won 51% in the primary, to 28% for Hollowell and 21% for Farrell-Donaldson. It would be no surprise if local Democrats see him vulnerable in 1996.

The Republican takeover of the House cost Conyers his committee chairmanship, and a challenge from Patricia Schroeder threatened the ranking minority position on Judiciary to which seniority entitled him after the defeat of Jack Brooks and the retirement of Don Edwards. But Schroeder, evidently shy of the votes, withdrew her challenge, and Conyers stands to become Judiciary chairman if Democrats regain control of the House. In the meantime, he has been a vocal opponent of the Republicans' Contract With America measures.

The People: Pop. 1990: 580,977; 11% age 65+; 29% White; 69% Black; 1% Asian; 1% Hispanic origin. Voting age pop.: 409,188; 65% Black; 1% Hispanic origin. Households: 38% married couple families; 18% married couple fams. w. children; 40% college educ.; median household income: $25,079; per capita income: $11,462; median gross rent: $421; median house value: $29,400.

1992 Presidential Vote		
Clinton (D)	165,363	(79%)
Bush (R)	31,360	(15%)
Perot (I)	11,992	(6%)

1988 Presidential Vote		
Dukakis (D)	144,917	(76%)
Bush (R)	45,116	(24%)

Rep. John Conyers, Jr. (D)

Elected 1964; b. May 16, 1929, Detroit; home, Detroit; Wayne St. U., B.A. 1957, LL.B. 1958; Baptist; married (Monica).

Career: Army, 1950–54 (Korea); Legis. Asst., U.S. Rep. John Dingell, 1958–61; Practicing atty., 1959–61; Referee, MI Workmen's Compensation Dept., 1961–63.

DC Office: 2426 RHOB 20515, 202-225-5126; Fax: 202-225-0072; e-mail: jconyers@hr.house.gov.

District Offices: 669 Fed. Bldg., 231 W. Lafayette St., Detroit 48226, 313-961-5670.

Committees: *Judiciary* (RMM of 15 D): Constitution; Courts and Intellectual Property.

Group Ratings

	ADA	ACLU	COPE	CFA	LCV	CON	NSI	COC	ACU	NTLC	CHC
1994	100	86	100	60	85	29	0	25	5	10	7
1993	80	—	100	90	100	47	—	0	0	—	—

National Journal Ratings

	1993 LIB — 1993 CONS			1994 LIB — 1994 CONS		
Economic	88%	—	0%	83%	—	0%
Social	87%	—	0%	77%	—	21%
Foreign	*	—	*	85%	—	0%

Key Votes of the 103d Congress

1. Clinton Deficit Plan	Y	3. Brady Handgun Purchase	Y	5. Lmt. UN Cmnd. of Forces	N
2. NAFTA	N	4. Strike Race/Death Pnlty.	N	6. Cut Missile Funds	Y

Key Votes of the 104th Congress

1. Congressional Compliance Y	6. Reform Crime Grant N	11. Loser Pays Court Reform N
2. Balanced Budget Amndmt. N	7. National Security Act N	12. Product Liability Reform N
3. Bar Unfunded Mandates N	8. Moratorium on Regs. N	13. Welfare Reform N
4. Pass Line Item Veto N	9. Risk Assessment on Regs. N	14. Term Limits Amndmt. N
5. Relax Exclusionary Rule N	10. Expnd. Priv. Prop. Rights N	15. Tax Cuts N

Election Results

1994 general	John Conyers Jr. (D).................	128,463	(82%)	($575,696)
	Richard Charles Fournier (R)............	26,215	(17%)	
	Others...............................	2,953	(2%)	
1994 primary	John Conyers Jr. (D)...................	41,555	(51%)	
	Melvin Hollowell (D)	23,398	(28%)	
	Marie-Farrell Donaldson (D)	17,325	(21%)	
1992 general	John Conyers, Jr. (D)	165,496	(82%)	($332,818)
	John Gordon (R)......................	32,036	(16%)	
	Others...............................	3,347	(2%)	

FIFTEENTH DISTRICT

Few central cities in America have as vibrant a 20th Century history, and as sad a recent past, as Detroit. This was America's first automobile city, not just because it manufactured so many of the nation's cars but also because it was built to automobile scale. Detroit started the century as a second-rank city, no bigger than Milwaukee, with less than half a million people and extending no farther than four or five miles out from the site where the French built Fort Pontchartrain on the Detroit River in 1701. As the Motor City boomed it grew outward along wide avenues and freeways; the auto companies put their factories and headquarters near the edge of urban settlement. As early as 1954, the nation's first big suburban shopping center, with parking for 10,000 cars, started drawing retail trade from downtown. Metro Detroit expanded to four million people, each generation moving out the roadways rapidly in many directions, leaving behind the previous generation's neighborhoods and civic institutions.

Today, that rapid movement has left large parts of Detroit literally empty. The central city, which had nearly 1.9 million people in 1950, barely exceeded one million in 1990, and then only with the help of a city bureaucracy detailed to round up uncounted residents. It had the biggest rate of population loss of any 100,000-plus city in the 1980s except Gary and Newark and was in the congressional district with the biggest population decline of the 1980s—23%. The reason is obvious: crime. Detroit in 1990 had a murder rate *14 times* that in the suburbs, and over the years, whites and blacks who could afford to leave the city have done so. With more guns than people, personal altercations quickly become homicidal; innocent bystanders are killed by random gunfire. Downtown, the giant Hudson's department store is closed and several skyscrapers are all but empty, while the 70-story Renaissance Center is inaccessible from the sidewalk (you can only get there by car). Vacant fields where there were once five-story apartments or brick houses are populated by pheasants.

Detroit's fate is all the more tragic because it comes in a city where liberal reformers hoped to create model anti-poverty and anti-discrimination programs. Instead, they seem to have undermined the sense of individual responsibility and confidence in the legitimacy of institutions. Metro area jobs rose from 1.5 million at the trough of the 1980s to 2.0 million: the problem is not so much lack of jobs, but the fact that too many people don't seek them and live by crime instead. Detroit's mayor for 20 years, Coleman Young, spent his energy on courting the Big Three, bulldozing the viable Poletown neighborhood for a new Cadillac plant. Meanwhile, high taxes and high crime—never denounced by Young—meant that thousands of small-business jobs vanished. Dennis Archer, elected in 1993, takes a more intelligent and judicious approach, but it is uncertain whether he can stop Detroit's downward spiral and turn the city around.

The 15th Congressional District of Michigan includes the southern half of Detroit, plus a few adjacent suburbs, from Grosse Pointe Farms on Lake St. Clair to industrial Ecorse in the Downriver area, where the whole city government was privatized after it went bankrupt. The district also includes Hamtramck, the Polish-American enclave around the now demolished Dodge Main plant, which was America's fastest-growing city between 1910–20. The district is surely among the nation's top three or four in crime rates; median household income, at $15,264, is lower than in all but three other districts. Detroit's ombudsman in 1992 recommended that large parts of the city simply be abandoned and fenced off and its residents consolidated into better areas: This could be, as *Detroit News* editorial page editor Thomas Bray says, "America's first real ex-city." Politically, the district is overwhelmingly Democratic, but turnout is low— 142,000 in 1994, compared with 226,000 in the high-income 11th District.

The congresswoman from the 15th District is Barbara-Rose Collins, a Democrat first elected in 1990. She raised her children as a single mother after her husband died in 1972; a member of the Shrine of the Black Madonna, a pan-African Orthodox Christian Church, she was elected to the state House in 1974 and to the Detroit Council in 1981, where she supported Coleman Young. In 1988, she ran against Congressman George Crockett, a 78-year-old former judge and veteran of the labor movement who was general counsel of the UAW as part of its Communist-allied wing in the 1940s; she lost by only 46%–38%. Crockett bowed out of the 1990 race early. In the Democratic primary, Collins won the eight-candidate primary with a solid 34%.

She won the general election easily and weathered some problems with campaign finance (her campaign took out a $75,000 loan with three co-signers, who thus exceeded the contribution limit). She also had family trouble. In 1989 her 19-year-old son was jailed for using a sawed-off shotgun to rob a Bloomfield Township tennis shop of jogging suits and jewelry; he served time in jail and was released in 1992. This experience prompted Collins to declare that "we are in danger of becoming extinct as a black family." The breakup of the black family, she told the *Detroit Free Press*, "is something that you very seldom hear ministers preach about from the pulpit. This is something you very seldom hear social workers or teachers discuss. It's something that's almost whispered. I feel that as leaders of the African-American community, we have a responsibility to put it on the table and begin dealing with it, before it becomes too late." Of her own family, she said, "I could teach a girl how to be a woman, but I could not teach a boy how to be a man." Collins promised to introduce bills to promote community mentoring programs and programs to train foster parents and social workers in dealing with today's children, but she acknowledged that legislation would have a limited effect and that moral leadership from the black community was needed. Collins continues to have one of the most liberal voting record in Congress. But her expression of concern about the black family is a fascinating departure from the traditional political rhetoric of Detroit and an indication of how an elected representative's experiences can prompt a change in thinking.

The People: Pop. 1990: 580,933; 14% age 65+; 26% White; 70% Black; 1% Asian; 2% Other; 4% Hispanic origin. Voting age pop.: 417,646; 68% Black; 3% Hispanic origin. Households: 27% married couple families; 11% married couple fams. w. children; 33% college educ.; median household income: $15,264; per capita income: $9,650; median gross rent: $337; median house value: $22,900.

1992 Presidential Vote		1988 Presidential Vote	
Clinton (D)	159,284 (82%)	Dukakis (D)	143,942 (81%)
Bush (R)	24,552 (13%)	Bush (R)	32,722 (19%)
Perot (I)	8,998 (5%)		

Rep. Barbara-Rose Collins (D)

Elected 1990; b. Apr. 13, 1939, Detroit; home, Detroit; Wayne St. U., 1957; Pan-African Orthodox Christian; widowed.

Career: Detroit Schl. Bd., 1971–73; MI House of Reps., 1975–81; Detroit City Cncl., 1982–90.

DC Office: 401 CHOB 20515, 202-225-2261; Fax: 202-225-6645.

District Offices: 1155 Brewery Park Blvd., #353, Detroit 48207, 313-567-2233.

Committees: *Government Reform & Oversight* (16th of 22 D): District of Columbia; Postal Service (RMM). *Transportation & Infrastructure* (16th of 27 D): Aviation; Surface Transportation.

Group Ratings

	ADA	ACLU	COPE	CFA	LCV	CON	NSI	COC	ACU	NTLC	CHC
1994	100	87	100	100	86	15	0	25	0	4	0
1993	100	—	100	100	86	30	—	18	0	—	—

National Journal Ratings

	1993 LIB — 1993 CONS		1994 LIB — 1994 CONS	
Economic	88%	— 0%	83%	— 0%
Social	87%	— 0%	94%	— 0%
Foreign	87%	— 13%	85%	— 0%

Key Votes of the 103d Congress

1. Clinton Deficit Plan	Y	3. Brady Handgun Purchase Y	5. Lmt. UN Cmnd. of Forces N
2. NAFTA	N	4. Strike Race/Death Pnlty. N	6. Cut Missile Funds	Y

Key Votes of the 104th Congress

1. Congressional Compliance	Y	6. Reform Crime Grant	N	11. Loser Pays Court Reform	N
2. Balanced Budget Amndmt.	N	7. National Security Act	N	12. Product Liability Reform	N
3. Bar Unfunded Mandates	N	8. Moratorium on Regs.	N	13. Welfare Reform	N
4. Pass Line Item Veto	N	9. Risk Assessment on Regs.	N	14. Term Limits Amndmt.	N
5. Relax Exclusionary Rule	N	10. Expnd. Priv. Prop. Rights	N	15. Tax Cuts	N

Election Results

1994 general	Barbara-Rose Collins (D)	119,442	(84%)	($177,120)
	John W. Savage II (R)	20,074	(14%)	
	Others	2,498	(2%)	
1994 primary	Barbara-Rose Collins (D)	unopposed		
1992 general	Barbara-Rose Collins (D)	148,908	(81%)	($284,049)
	Charles Vincent (R)	31,849	(17%)	($94,260)
	Others	4,207	(2%)	

SIXTEENTH DISTRICT

One of America's great heavy-industry corridors is along the Detroit River, the choke point of the Great Lakes, in the Downriver communities below Detroit. Steel and chemical plants line the water, their dark and rusted hulks glaring across at Canada. A little ways up the sluggish Rouge River stands the giant Rouge complex, built by Henry Ford for $1 billion in the 1910s to take loads of iron ore, coal, limestone and sand from Great Lake freighters and railroad cars and convert them into automobiles in 48 hours. This swampy, low-lying land, along the nation's most heavily trafficked waterway and within easy reach of the great east-west rail lines, was a natural place for industry in the early 20th Century. Around the older factories and well within range of their sulfurous odors, the residential neighborhoods with their neat, tightly packed houses were homes of the migrants who came to work there—Polish, Hungarian, black, Italian, and more recently Mexican and Arab (the area has America's largest concentration of Arab-Americans). This industrial area has seen better times: many of the factories are dormant, and neighborhoods have been abandoned as the original migrants' children have moved outward. But there are also new factories, like Mazda's in Flat Rock, and smaller manufacturers are picking up the slack resulting from layoffs by corporate giants.

The 16th Congressional District of Michigan covers Dearborn and the Downriver communities, plus Monroe County directly to the south. The political tradition has been Democratic since the New Deal days, and while there is some cultural conservatism seen in top-of-the-ticket races, the basic preference remains much more Democratic here than in increasingly upscale Macomb County.

The congressman is John Dingell, the senior member of the House of Representatives. His father, John Dingell Sr., was elected to the House in 1932, from a new district created as a result of the Detroit area's auto boom. The first Congressman Dingell was one of the most productive urban liberals then, one of the sponsors of Social Security and, starting in 1943, of national health insurance. John Dingell, Jr., has been around Capitol Hill almost as long: he was a House page from 1938 to 1943, and after his father died, he was elected to succeed him in December 1955, at 29, from a district with large Polish, black and Jewish populations. He had one serious fight, because of redistricting, in 1964, against fellow Democrat John Lesinski, who opposed the Civil Rights Act. But although most of the district was new to Dingell, he won; he has been reelected easily since. He has had an interesting personal life, raising his children after his divorce (his son Christopher was elected to the Michigan Senate in 1986) and marrying in 1981 a granddaughter of one of General Motors's Fisher brothers (his wife, Debbie Dingell, is active and popular both in Washington and Michigan Democratic circles). In 1995 he was serving his 40th year in Congress—and his first in the minority party.

Whatever else he does, Dingell will go down in history as one of the most powerful and effective committee chairmen ever. From 1981 until 1995 he chaired the Energy and Commerce Committee (renamed Commerce) and its much-feared Investigations and Oversight Subcommittee. Dingell's committee, wrote *National Journal*'s Richard E. Cohen and Burt Solomon, "claims jurisdiction over anything that moves, burns or is sold"—clean air and securities markets, telecommunications and energy, railroads and toys, consumer protection and defense contracting. It handled up to 40% of all House bills, it had the largest budget and staff of any House committee and, for a decade, it was the House's most sought-after committee assignment. This institution took on the character of its leader, as institutions will: bright, pit-bull aggressive, domineering, determined. Commerce helped to create many of the big stories in the 1980s: the indictment of Reagan White House aide Michael Deaver, the ousting of EPA Administrator Anne Burford, and the clamor over the Pentagon's $640 toilet seat and General Dynamics' bill to the government for dog kennel fees. His investigations disgraced Nobel Prize-winning scientist David Baltimore and forced out Stanford President Donald Kennedy. Dingell and his committee superintended the breakup of AT&T and the sale of Conrail by public offering; studied insider trading, leveraged buyouts and hostile takeovers; and stimulated the growth of the generic drug industry and then swooped down to expose its misdeeds. After a decade of sparring with Health Subcommittee Chairman Henry Waxman over the Clean Air Act, Dingell and Waxman worked together to produce the Clean Air Act of 1990. Commerce's cable regulation law of 1992 was the only bill on which Congress overrode George Bush's presidential veto. Dingell also worked to reduce trial lawyer leverage on product liability and to increase the Securities and Exchange Commission's oversight of bond sales. These were complex, heavily lobbied matters on which Dingell often had jurisdictional fights with Jack Brooks of Judiciary and Henry Gonzalez of Banking.

On other issues, Dingell backed organized labor's agenda against NAFTA and other trade agreements. A well-known sportsman, he long opposed gun control but voted for the 1994 crime bill and resigned from the National Rifle Association board. In many ways, he is an old-fashioned Franklin Roosevelt Democrat, supporting big government and strenuous regulation, taking a conservative line on some cultural issues and backing an assertive foreign policy: he was the only Michigan Democrat to vote for the Gulf war resolution.

With a Democratic administration in office, Dingell should have been at the peak of his power in the 103rd Congress, but the political forces that produced the Republican sweep of 1994 also frustrated him on legislation. For years he had introduced his father's national health care bill at the beginning of each session, and he looked forward to passing some version of the Clinton health care plan. "Health care is the principal reason I came to Congress," he once said. But for all his efforts he could not put together a 23-vote majority on the committee for a bill with an employer mandate, and in June 1994 he confessed that Commerce was hopelessly deadlocked on health care. The fact that Dingell couldn't do it is pretty good proof that nobody could have. Similarly, he was stymied in October 1994 when Superfund reform was killed under time pressure ("a terrible set of circumstances") and as House-passed telecommunications reform went down in the Senate.

Dingell himself was reelected, after spending $1,075,000 to his opponent's $8,000, but by a less-than-usual margin of 59%–40%; the 16th District voted for Republican Governor John Engler. Worse for Dingell was the new Republican majority. Republicans vowed to give Dingell staff ratios as unfavorable as he had given them when he was chairman—though they were a bit more generous than his 10–1 share—and Republicans stripped Commerce of some of the jurisdiction Dingell had painstakingly amassed. The Glass-Steagall bill separating commercial and investment banking, which Dingell always protected against repeal, went to Banking, where the New Deal measure is likely to die. There was talk that a disconsolate Dingell would resign on the first day of Congress, presumably in the hope of turning the seat over to his son Chris, who represents Downriver in the Michigan Senate. But Dingell said that the seat is not his to hand down and insisted he had no intention of quitting. "Every goddamn time I go hunting or fishing, some son of a bitch starts a rumor like this." As the senior House member, he swore in the new Speaker Newt Gingrich with good grace. He took to his new place in the minority a remarkable good humor and sportsmanship and went after Republicans with unfeigned zest. He proved that he is a large man not only when he is in a position of power but also when things are not going his way. Michigan state Republican chairman Susy Heintz in early 1995 called on her party to go after Dingell in 1996. But he seems likely to be a pretty tough target.

The People: Pop. 1990: 580,884; 13% rural; 13% age 65+; 95% White; 1% Black; 1% Amer. Indian; 1% Asian; 1% Other; 2% Hispanic origin. Voting age pop.: 434,314; 1% Black; 2% Hispanic origin. Households: 60% married couple families; 28% married couple fams. w. children; 39% college educ.; median household income: $35,315; per capita income: $15,175; median gross rent: $456; median house value: $61,700.

714 MICHIGAN

1992 Presidential Vote

Clinton (D) 115,339 (43%)
Bush (R) 96,466 (36%)
Perot (I).................. 52,070 (20%)

1988 Presidential Vote

Bush (R) 125,074 (54%)
Dukakis (D)............... 104,704 (46%)

Rep. John D. Dingell (D)

Elected Dec. 1955; b. July 8, 1926, Colorado Springs, CO; home, Trenton; Georgetown U., B.S. 1949, J.D. 1952; Catholic; married (Deborah).

Career: Army, 1945–46 (WWII); Practicing atty., 1952–55; Wayne Cnty. Asst. Prosecuting Atty., 1953–55.

DC Office: 2328 RHOB 20515, 202-225-4071.

District Offices: 5465 Schaefer Rd., Dearborn 48126, 313-846-1276; and 23 E. Front St., #103, Monroe 48161, 313-243-1849.

Committees: *Commerce* (RMM of 21 D).

Group Ratings

	ADA	ACLU	COPE	CFA	LCV	CON	NSI	COC	ACU	NTLC	CHC
1994	70	48	75	70	63	4	56	33	15	4	14
1993	70	—	100	80	69	11	—	18	10	—	—

National Journal Ratings

	1993 LIB — 1993 CONS	1994 LIB — 1994 CONS
Economic	88% — 0%	73% — 17%
Social	59% — 40%	67% — 32%
Foreign	84% — 13%	53% — 46%

Key Votes of the 103d Congress

1. Clinton Deficit Plan	Y	3. Brady Handgun Purchase	N	5. Lmt. UN Cmnd. of Forces	N
2. NAFTA	N	4. Strike Race/Death Pnlty.	N	6. Cut Missile Funds	Y

Key Votes of the 104th Congress

1. Congressional Compliance	Y	6. Reform Crime Grant	N	11. Loser Pays Court Reform	N
2. Balanced Budget Amndmt.	N	7. National Security Act	N	12. Product Liability Reform	N
3. Bar Unfunded Mandates	N	8. Moratorium on Regs.	N	13. Welfare Reform	N
4. Pass Line Item Veto	N	9. Risk Assessment on Regs.	N	14. Term Limits Amndmt.	N
5. Relax Exclusionary Rule	N	10. Expnd. Priv. Prop. Rights	N	15. Tax Cuts	N

Election Results

1994 general	John D. Dingell (D) 105,849	(59%)	($1,075,063)
	Ken Larkin (R)....................... 71,159	(40%)	($8,074)
	Others 1,972	(1%)	
1994 primary	John D. Dingell (D) .... unopposed		
1992 general	John D. Dingell (D) 156,964	(65%)	($1,086,152)
	Frank Beaumont (R)................. 75,694	(31%)	($5,401)
	Others 8,278	(4%)	

MINNESOTA

Minnesota has long been an exemplary state, a distinctive commonwealth in America's frozen North which in commerce, culture and politics has set one example after another for the rest of the nation. It is the node of transcontinental railroads that linked the winter wheat fields of the northern prairies to the greatest grain milling center in the world, the birthplace of Scotch Tape and Betty Crocker and the Mall of America, the home base of chroniclers of small town America from Sinclair Lewis to Garrison Keillor. Politically, Minnesota over the last half century provided the nation with some of its most articulate and honorable leaders—Harold Stassen, Hubert Humphrey, Eugene McCarthy, Walter Mondale—and with traditions of probity, civic-mindedness and innovation which are second to none. Yet while commercially and culturally Minnesota has never been stronger, politically it has seen some hard times. Its recent electoral history has been one antic episode after another. Its two political parties, with their distinctive names—Democratic-Farmer-Labor, Independent Republican—have been dominated by activists extravagantly out of touch with ordinary voters. Its two senators, its spokesmen before the rest of the country, are a former professor and a former TV anchorman, neither from the top of his profession. Its primacy as a national policy-setter seems stuck in the past. But maybe these are signs of success, an indication that Minnesota and the nation are so secure that they no longer need the intense, impassioned, intellectually serious tutelage that Minnesota used to provide.

Minnesota's distinctive traditions come from a distinctive history. The far northern states were ignored by most Yankee immigrants, who headed straight west into Iowa, Nebraska and Kansas. But others saw opportunity in Minnesota's icy lakes and ferocious winters. James J. Hill, the builder of the Great Northern Railroad ("You can't interest me in any proposition in any place where it doesn't snow"), and others operating out of Minneapolis and St. Paul—already twin cities by 1860—worked to attract Norwegian, Swedish and German migrants who would find the terrain and climate congenial. By 1890, the Twin Cities—rivals that year in a Census competition—were the nerve center of a sprawling and rich agricultural empire stretching west from Minnesota through the Dakotas and eventually into Montana and beyond. Minneapolis and St. Paul became the termini of its rail lines and the site of its grain-milling companies.

The twin cities also became the center of a three-party politics and an economic radicalism reminiscent of the politics of Scandinavia. For our American regions seem a mirror image of the geography of Europe, with the East Coast resembling the British Isles and France, the industrial Midwest reminiscent of Germany and Poland, the relatively poor and always hawkish South a Baptist Mediterranean, and the Upper Midwest of Minnesota, Wisconsin and North Dakota as North American versions of Scandinavia. Like Scandinavia, these Upper Midwestern commonwealths pioneered their continent's welfare states, with an effect on public policy far out of proportion to their numbers. Alarmed by the unprecedented concentration of economic power and wealth into the hands of just a few identifiable millionaires who lived on St. Paul's Summit Avenue or the hill above Minneapolis's Hennepin Avenue, the immigrants drew on their native traditions of cooperative activity and bureaucratic socialism.

As in Wisconsin and North Dakota, a strong third party developed here in the years after the Populist era. This Farmer-Labor Party elected senators in the 1920s and dominated state politics in the 1930s. Hurt by their ties to Communists, the Farmer-Laborites were beaten by Harold Stassen's Republicans in 1938. But this was still a New Deal state and by 1944 the bedraggled local Democrats were merged with the anti-Communist faction of Farmer-Laborites to form the Democratic-Farmer-Labor party. A key role was played by Hubert Humphrey—mayor of Minneapolis in 1945, and the dazzling advocate of the civil rights plank at the 1948 Democratic

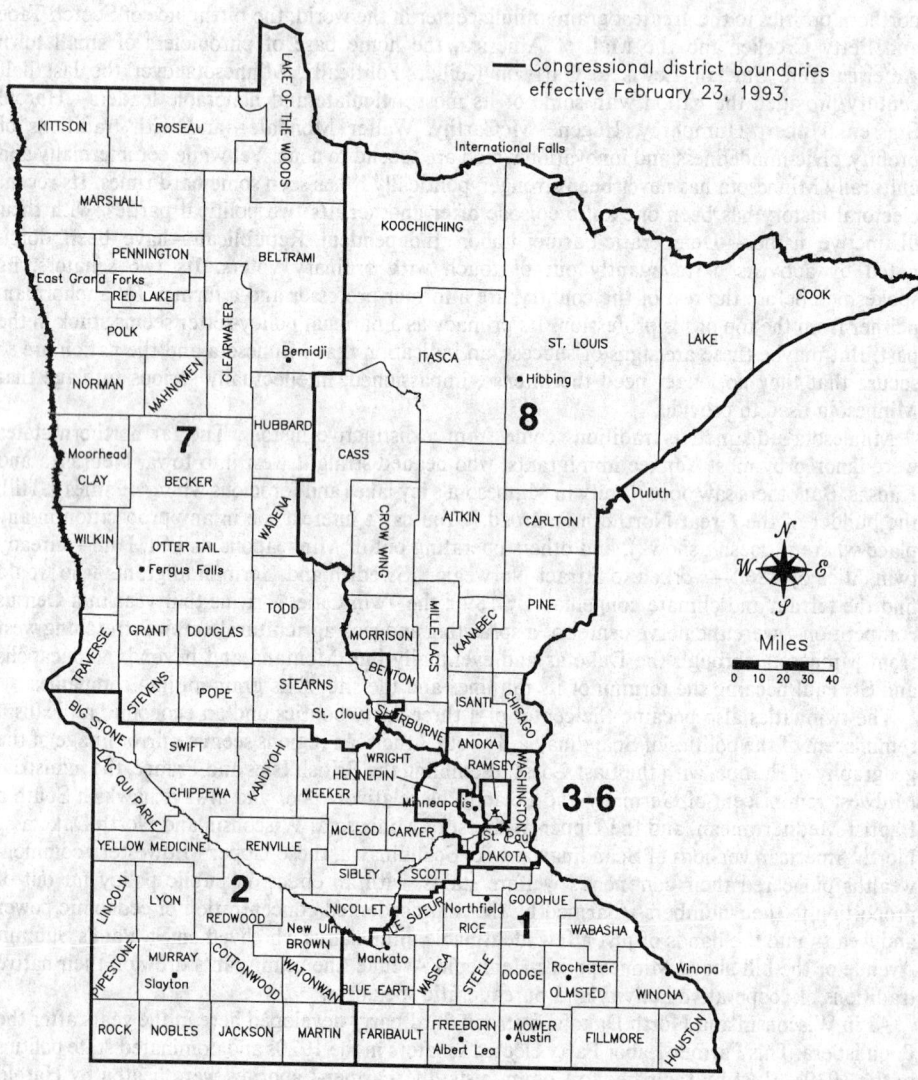

Congressional district boundaries
effective February 23, 1993.

KITTSON
ROSEAU
LAKE OF THE WOODS
International Falls
MARSHALL
KOOCHICHING
PENNINGTON
BELTRAMI
East Grand Forks
RED LAKE
COOK
POLK
CLEARWATER
LAKE
ST. LOUIS
Bemidji
ITASCA
Hibbing
NORMAN
MAHNOMEN
HUBBARD
7
BECKER
CASS
8
Moorhead
CLAY
WADENA
CROW WING
AITKIN
CARLTON
WILKIN
OTTER TAIL
Duluth
Fergus Falls
TODD
MILLE LACS
KANABEC
PINE
TRAVERSE
GRANT
DOUGLAS
MORRISON
BENTON
STEVENS
POPE
STEARNS
ISANTI
CHISAGO
BIG STONE
St. Cloud
SHERBURNE
SWIFT
WRIGHT
ANOKA
WASHINGTON
LAC QUI PARLE
KANDIYOHI
HENNEPIN
RAMSEY
3-6
CHIPPEWA
MEEKER
Minneapolis
St. Paul
YELLOW MEDICINE
RENVILLE
MCLEOD
CARVER
DAKOTA
LINCOLN
LYON
REDWOOD
SIBLEY
SCOTT
GOODHUE
2
NICOLLET
LE SUEUR
Northfield
RICE
WABASHA
PIPESTONE
MURRAY
New Ulm
BROWN
1
Slayton
COTTONWOOD
WATONWAN
Mankato
BLUE EARTH
WASECA
STEELE
DODGE
Rochester
OLMSTED
Winona
WINONA
ROCK
NOBLES
JACKSON
MARTIN
FARIBAULT
FREEBORN
MOWER
FILLMORE
HOUSTON
Albert Lea
Austin

N
W E
S

Miles
0 10 20 30 40

National Convention. Humphrey's DFL—clean, idealistic, closely tied to labor, backed by many farmers—attracted dozens of talented politicians, including Eugene McCarthy, Orville Freeman and Walter Mondale. In 1948, Humphrey's speech helped put the Democrats on record for civil rights, and he was elected to the Senate at age 37.

In the years following, the DFL dominated Minnesota politics, while a series of progressive companies led the development of a strong, diversified economy. The DFL stood for a generous, compassionate federal government, for strong labor unions and high wages, for an expansionist fiscal policy to encourage consumer-led economic growth, for civil rights, and for an anti-Communist but not bombastic foreign policy. Its base was among blue-collar workers in the Twin Cities, in Duluth and the Iron Range, and among farmers of Scandinavian origin. Minnesota's business leaders were conservative politically and innovation-minded in their work: 3M has been generating new products—more than 60,000 by 1995—since the abrasive material it was founded to sell proved a loser in 1903. (30% of 3M's sales is generated by products introduced after 1990.) Control Data was an early high-tech pioneer; IDS was one of the first mass-marketers of mutual funds; the Dayton family retail empire helped invent the indoor shopping mall and the national bookstore chain. Both the political and the business innovators built on a high-skill work force and a squeaky-clean ethic of honesty and integrity, low levels of crime and aberrant behavior—violent crime, children bearing children, substance abuse—with high wage and salary levels and a high percentage of women working outside the home. Over several decades, Minnesota has grown robustly in prosperous years and has not fallen much behind during recessions.

This has provided a basis for Minnesota's innovations in public policy in the 1980s and early 1990s. It produced the nation's first anti-smoking bill, one of the first public campaign financing schemes and the nation's first statewide educational choice plan. It was one of the first states to establish HMOs and in 1992 it passed a HealthRight plan to insure the uninsured, encouraging insurance pooling for small employers and setting targets for reducing spending, paid for by a cigarette tax and a 2% health services tax. Its generous state social services are supplemented by the commitment of 78 big Minnesota companies to donate 5% of their earnings to charity. The state government also has its version of industrial policy, pledging $840 million in credit and loan guarantees to Northwest Airlines in 1991, in return for a promise to keep its Twin Cities hub and build repair facilities in Duluth and the Iron Range. So just as Scandinavia is adapting its welfare state by lowering taxes and using market mechanisms, so Minnesota is building on the patchwork American welfare state by adding state protections and regulations. Both are continuing their search for a "third way" between unbridled market capitalism and regimented bureaucratic socialism.

Politically, that way has been led by mostly Democratic legislators and by governors who are not liberal Democrats—Democrat Rudy Perpich, elected in 1982 and 1986, and Republican Arne Carlson, elected in 1990 and 1994. In national politics, during the Democrats' quarter-century presidential dry spell, Minnesota was on average the most Democratic state, voting for Democrats in five of six elections and nearly backing George McGovern in 1972. Yet Minnesota now has a Republican governor and senator, and for 1994 increased its overall Republican percentage for congressional races by five points from 1992. Partly this represents the declining appeal of economic redistributionist politics in a robust post-industrial economy: workers and even (the much less numerous) farmers no longer feel at the mercy of a few big milling firms and railroads, young people starting out have many more career choices, and consumers have a much wider range of brand and product choices than they did 50 years ago. The need for New Deal-style intervention and regulation is less.

But it is also the result of the dominance of both parties' politics by enthusiastic party activists. Minnesota is proud of its tradition of party nominating conventions, whose choices can be challenged in primaries but for many years were honored. In the 1990s, however, the conventions have been dominated not by laborite Humphrey followers or the wives of management Republicans, but by left-wingers and counterculturites and right-wing abortion opponents and religious hardliners. Much national attention in 1994 was focused on the supposedly fatal capture of the IRs by the religious right. Actually, the capture had taken place some time ago and in 1994 was not fatal. Gubernatorial nominee Allen Quist was beaten in the primary by incumbent Arne Carlson—the strongest statewide vote-getter of recent years, which is not unconnected with the fact that he has never won at his party convention. The fatal capture of political parties by extremists—termed "endorsement horrors," by political scientist Steven Schier—can be seen in the DFL in 1994, when party liberals nominated two idealistic but impractical liberals from liberal Twin Cities neighborhoods. John Marty lost the gubernatorial race to Carlson 62%–33%. Ann Wynia, in a state where exit polls showed Bill Clinton's job rating higher than anywhere else but Massachusetts and Arkansas, lost the Senate race to the very conservative Rod Grams 49%–44%. The vote in the Senate race split along cultural lines, very much according to attitudes on abortion. Minnesota has one of the nation's most politically active anti-abortion movements, and support of abortion rights is not essential to winning here, as it is on the East and West Coasts.

Governor. Arne Carlson, elected governor twice without the support of a nominating convention and with the help of bizarre opposition, the son of Swedish immigrants, oddly enough, grew up in New York. Some 30 years ago he was on the Minneapolis City Council; he spent eight years in the state legislature and 12 as elected state auditor until he ran for governor in 1990. He bypassed the convention, already solidly conservative and anti-abortion, and lost to its designee Jon Grunseth in the primary 49%–32%. But in mid-October the *Minneapolis Star-Tribune* charged Grunseth with sexual improprieties; Grunseth hesitated, then withdrew. An IR delegation named Carlson as the party's nominee, and for two weeks he ran against embattled DFL incumbent Rudy Perpich, who first became governor in 1976 when incumbent Wendell Anderson named himself senator, then was elected in 1982 and 1986, and barely survived the 1990 primary. Carlson won the general 51%–47%, carrying the Twin Cities metro area, losing the rest of the state. In office, he made a liberal record, signing HealthRight, wetlands preservation and gay rights legislation. He succeeded in keeping the Minnesota Timberwolves basketball team in Minnesota by buying the Target Center arena for $55 million. He boasted of spending more for education and cutting taxes. It seemed a popular record, yet Carlson was also shy and aloof, especially from Republican activists. And his personal life was often the subject of his former wife Barbara Carlson, a radio talk show host, who occasionally broadcast her program while in a hot tub.

In 1994, Carlson was opposed by farmer and former legislator Allen Quist, a strong abortion opponent. Quist was endorsed by the IR party convention 69%–29%, but he was twitted by the media when he made controversial statements—he said men were "genetically predisposed" to head households—while Carlson was scarcely criticized when he likened Quist's intraparty victory to the rise of Hitler. Carlson won the primary 66%–34%. The DFL convention endorsed John Marty, an ultra-liberal state senator, over Hennepin County Attorney Mike Freeman. Marty displayed less than overwhelming strength in the primary, winning 38% to 36% for former Commerce Commissioner Mike Hatch and 25% for former Minneapolis Police Chief Tony Bouza. Marty limited his contributions to $100, refused to attend a big fundraiser with President Clinton, and eschewed negative TV spots. But he also went through four campaign managers and proposed to raise taxes on high income individuals and start new spending programs. Carlson won 62%–33%. On his agenda for a second term were welfare reform, scaling back workmen's compensation, term limits and more education spending.

Senators. Minnesota's two senators come from the extreme wings of their two parties, former Carleton College political science professor Paul Wellstone on the Democratic-Farmer-Labor left and former KMSP-TV news anchor Rod Grams on the Independent Republican right.

Paul Wellstone is a happy warrior of the campus left, good-humoredly bringing to the Senate the spirit of student protest that blazed in the late 1960s and, on some campuses at least, lives on in embers: the spirit of Woodstock 1969 come back to earth. Wellstone was a "rock-the-boat professor" at Carleton, where he taught the politics of protest and appeared at faculty meetings only to lead groups of students protesting something or other. He made a name for himself in local politics by leading protesters in sympathy with the Hormel meatpacker strikers in Austin and getting arrested while picketing a bank that had foreclosed on local farmers; he co-chaired Jesse Jackson's 1988 presidential campaign in Minnesota. He attracted little attention when he announced he was running in 1990 for the Senate seat held by Republican Rudy Boschwitz. But Walter Mondale did not run, as some thought he might, and Wellstone beat Agriculture Commissioner Jim Nichols, populist on economics but anti-abortion on abortion, 60%–34% in the DFL primary.

In the general, Wellstone's shrewd and humorous TV ads proclaimed that viewers wouldn't be seeing him as often as they saw Boschwitz (because he didn't accept PAC money), but his cute touches ("I'm better looking") guaranteed him more attention. His most-screened ad was a takeoff on the film *Roger and Me*, and like Michael Moore's movie on Flint, Michigan, the Wellstone ad was based on a dishonest premise: it purported to show Wellstone in pursuit of a confrontation-shy Boschwitz, even though Boschwitz had already agreed to a debate. But the ad's cleverness and the candidate's charm created an almost cuddly impression—the kind of feel-good, image-heavy politics of which Ronald Reagan was often accused. Boschwitz responded hamhandedly, needlessly involving himself in the controversy over gubernatorial nominee Jon Grunseth's personal problems, switching his stand on the veto override of the 1990 civil rights bill, sending out a letter to a Jewish mailing list suggesting that in this first Senate race between two Jewish candidates Boschwitz was the better Jew because Wellstone took no part in Jewish affairs and had not raised his children as Jews. Wellstone, the only candidate to beat an incumbent Senator in 1990, won 50%–48%, carrying metro Twin Cities 54%–45% while losing outstate Minnesota 51%–47%.

Like most politicians on either party's extreme wing, Wellstone was often frustrated in the Senate. He was dismayed that the first issue on which he voted was the Gulf war, and that the tide of opinion went against his views and the course of events against his prognostications. (He gave then-Vice President Dan Quayle a videotape of a Minnesota town meeting stacked with war opponents.) On several issues, Wellstone has gotten in front of other Democrats, in the hopes that they'll follow—with mixed results. He successfully led opposition to the 1991 energy bill that would have opened the Arctic National Wildlife Refuge to oil drilling. On campaign finance reform, this liberal who in 1990 spurned contributions over $100 (but who in a bow to realism and perhaps inflation has been accepting them for 1996) sponsored a purist bill, then let other Democrats lead. On health care, Wellstone has consistently favored a Canadian-style single-payer plan, successfully attached amendments to the bill in Edward Kennedy's committee markup, worked with the American Medical Association to oppose insurance companies' control and told Hillary Rodham Clinton not to take for granted the support of single-payer advocates like himself. But all these efforts were academic as healthcare legislation crashed and burned. Wellstone was more successful on the issue of lobbying reform and banning gifts, and co-sponsored with Frank Lautenberg of New Jersey a bill to prohibit lobbyists and their clients from providing gifts, meals and vacation trips to members of Congress and their staff. He advanced the idea in 1990 and, after the 1994 election, it emerged as one area on which Democrats were more pro-reform than Republicans. Along with other liberal senators, he favored a complete commercial embargo on Haiti except for humanitarian aid, he advocated waiting to see if sanctions would work before sending in troops, and he criticized Clinton for acting without the consent of Congress. He pressured for a study of Army chemical spraying over Minneapolis in the 1950s. And he pressed for a Violence Reduction Training Act to help healthcare professionals handle abused children.

Wellstone backers saw him as a harbinger of a new left politics, and the 1992 victories of Bill Clinton and Wisconsin Senator Russ Feingold, who ran similarly cute TV spots, must have given them hope. But the 1994 Republican sweep suggests their politics may be extinct. As Rod Grams's supporters shouted on election night, "Wellstone's next!" Rudy Boschwitz made it clear in 1994 that he was holding back in order to seek a rematch against the vulnerable Wellstone in

1996. But Minnesota is still one of the most Democratic states, and Wellstone can evoke some still lively Minnesota traditions—the 1960s protesters now grown older but still posing as angry rebels; the Farmer-Laborites of the 1930s, incremental socialists and foreign policy isolationists. Wellstone is highly motivated, determined to oppose the new Republicans, and has an enthusiastic core of support; this should be a hotly contested seat in 1996. And early 1995 polling suggested that Boschwitz, despite the resumption of his successful retail home-improvements business in Minnesota, retains significant negative baggage from the 1990 campaign. A March 1995 poll for the *St. Paul Pioneer Press* tested Weber, Ramstad, Boschwitz and Arne Carlson against Wellstone. Only Carlson bested him—by 1%; but Carlson says he won't run.

On the other side of the chamber, ideologically as well as on the seating chart, is Rod Grams, the conservative Republican who in 1994 won the seat of moderate Republican David Durenberger. Durenberger had an uneven Senate career: building on Minnesota's experience with HMOs, he developed impressive expertise on health care well before the Clintons came to Washington. But he was denounced by the Senate for ethics violations and faced an indictment on an improper Senate reimbursement claim for his Minneapolis condominium, which was dismissed in December 1993 but was later refiled by federal prosecutors. Durengerger tried to challenge the constitutionality of the indictment against him, but in February 1995, a federal appeals court panel denied his challenge and ordered him to stand trial. He had announced in September 1993 he would retire at the end of his term in 1994, ending an electoral career in which he won the seat vacated by the death of Hubert Humphrey in 1978, then beat millionaire Mark Dayton in a big-spending contest in 1982 and Hubert Humphrey III in 1988. The race to succeed Durenberger attracted many candidates, few of them well known. DFL leaders and activists were committed to running a woman, and their convention endorsed Ann Wynia, a serious-minded St. Paul liberal and former legislator. She was challenged in the DFL primary by Ramsey County Attorney Tom Foley, Minnesota leader of the moderate Democratic Leadership Council. But Wynia carried the Twin Cities area, more affluent and more liberal than the rest of the state, by more than 2–1 and won 62%–33%. The IRs had a robust, multi-ballot fight at their convention for the party endorsement. The winner was one-term Congressman and former Channel 9 anchor Rod Grams. He was challenged in the primary by pro-choice Lieutenant Governor Joanelle Dyrstad, who compared him to Ted Baxter, the mindless anchor on *The Mary Tyler Moore Show*, but the same electorate that chose Governor Arne Carlson 2–1 over anti-abortion Allen Quist gave anti-abortion Grams a 58%–35% victory.

The contrast between the two general election candidates was stark. Grams grew up on a dairy farm, married early and never graduated from college, worked while in school and held multiple jobs, and spent years as a radio and TV reporter, the last eight as a Twin Cities anchor. He also developed a home building and land development business in the Twin Cities suburbs. Unlike most reporters, he was solidly conservative, a fervent opponent of abortion, an angry critic of government regulation, staunchly against higher taxes. "Families are under attack from all angles—the media, in schools and from all levels of government," he said. In 1991, Grams left his broadcast job and ran for Congress in the 6th District, opposing incumbent Congressman Gerry Sikorski, who had 697 overdrafts on the House bank and had just switched from an anti-abortion to a pro-choice stance, and an Independent lawyer from an upscale suburb who called for a national sales tax. Sikorski got only 33% of the vote and the Independent 16%; Grams won with 44%. In the House Grams was elected a freshman Republican whip and pushed for the $500-per-child tax credit that was included in the Republican Contract With America; he backed term limits and proposed sunset amendments to dozens of laws.

Ann Wynia, in contrast, had an academic background; a native of Texas, she taught at a suburban community college and served in the Minnesota state House from 1976–90, where she made a solidly liberal record and became Majority Leader. "Every institution needs renewal," she said. "We need to be less focused on our egos and more focused on the problems Americans worry about every day, like job security, health care and safety." Grams was folksy, Wynia serious. Grams attacked her for voting 300 times for tax increases; she attacked him for opposing the Brady bill, family leave and single-payer healthcare reform. She also ran ads hitting Grams for not paying property taxes and not paying debts from his homebuilding business. He replied that he had not sought bankruptcy and had worked years to pay off $300,000 in debts; and it turned out that she also was late paying property taxes, which became the focus of Grams ads at the close of the campaign. Wynia was embarrassed at a press conference with retiring Congressman Tim Penny, when she admitted she would not have backed the Penny-Kasich budget cuts; Grams brandished a note from Penny thanking him for his vote and saying, "We did Minnesota proud!"

This was the Republicans' seat which national Democrats had the best chance to pick up. In the last three weeks leading up to the election, Bill Clinton came to Minnesota three times for Wynia. (Of course, in many other states Democrats didn't want him.) But Wynia won only a microscopic margin in metro Twin Cities and ran poorly outstate, carrying only seven counties there and losing dozens carried by DFL candidates for other offices. Grams won 49%–44%; his combination of fiscal and cultural conservatism sold better than Wynia's cultural and fiscal liberalism. He fit comfortably with the aggressive corps of freshman Republicans intent on changing the Senate's antiquated ways. By any measure, Grams is the most conservative senator elected in Minnesota for decades, a solid member of the new conservative Republican bloc, not dazzlingly articulate but determined to vote his convictions. He cannot count on a lifetime seat in liberal Minnesota; but he seems determined to vote his convictions for as long as he is there.

Presidential politics. Minnesota, still heavily Democratic, gave a wide margin to Bill Clinton in 1992. But with an above-average 24% of the voters choosing Ross Perot, Clinton had just 44%, Minnesota's lowest Democratic presidential percentage in 60 years. Perot ran strongest in the ring of fast-growing counties just beyond the Twin Cities and in some southwest farm counties— areas where the liberal DFL nominees ran dreadfully in 1994. But Minnesota is so Democratic that neither party is likely to contest it hard in 1996.

Minnesota has a tradition of making party decisions in caucuses, but in presidential as in state races there have been primaries as well, as in 1992. Tom Harkin won the early March DFL caucuses, largely because of the proximity of his native Iowa. The DFL also held a non-binding "beauty contest" primary in April; Bill Clinton won with 31.1% and Jerry Brown was right behind him with 30.9%. In the IR primary, Pat Buchanan got nearly one quarter of the vote—a harbinger of George Bush's lackluster performance in November.

Congressional districting. Minnesota has had three sets of congressional district lines in the 1990s. A federal court redistricted the eight seats in February 1992; that plan was left in place pending appeal for 1992. In February 1993, the Supreme Court ruled that the federal court should have let the state courts decide the issue. So the state court's plan was put into effect for 1994. Only minor changes were made, except for the suburban 3d and 6th Districts; the 3d became more upscale and Republican, the 6th less upscale and more Democratic. That surely made the difference, as the DFL's Bill Luther captured the 6th which was represented by IR Senate candidate Rod Grams.

The People: Est. Pop. 1994: 4,496,000; Pop. 1990: 4,375,099, up 2.2% 1990–1994. 1.8% of U.S. total, 20th largest; 30% rural. Median age: 32.5 years. 12.5% 65 years and over. 94.4% White, 2.2% Black, 1.8% Asian, 1.2% Hispanic origin, 1.1% American Indian. Households: 57.2% married couple families; 29% married couple fams. w. children; 49% college educ.; median household income: $30,909; per capita income: $14,389; 71.8% owner occupied housing; median house value: $74,000; median monthly rent: $384. 5.1% Unemployment. 1994 Voting age pop.: 3,362,000. 1994 Turnout: 1,769,835; 53% of VAP. Registered voters (1994): 2,678,103; no party registration.

Political Lineup: Governor, Arne H. Carlson (IR); Lt. Gov., Joanne Benson (IR); Secy. of State, Joan Anderson Growe (DFL); Atty. Gen., Hubert H. Humphrey, III (DFL); Treasurer, Michael McGrath (DFL); Auditor, Judith Dutcher (IR). State Senate, 67 (43 DFL and 24 IR); State House of Representatives, 134 (71 DFL and 63 IR). Senators, Paul D. Wellstone (DFL) and Rod Grams (IR). Representatives, 8 (2 IR and 6 DFL).

1992 Presidential Vote

Clinton (D)	1,020,997	(44%)
Bush (R)	747,841	(32%)
Perot (I)	562,506	(24%)

1992 Democratic Presidential Primary

Clinton	63,584	(31%)
Brown	62,706	(31%)
Tsongas	43,588	(21%)
Other	22,926	(11%)
Uncommitted	11,366	(6%)

1988 Presidential Vote

Dukakis (D)	1,109,471	(53%)
Bush (R)	962,337	(46%)

1992 Republican Presidential Primary

Bush	84,841	(64%)
Buchanan	32,094	(24%)
Other	11,723	(9%)

GOVERNOR

Gov. Arne H. Carlson (IR)

Elected 1990, term expires Jan. 1999; b. Sept. 24, 1934, New York, NY; home, St. Paul; Williams Col., B.A. 1957, U. of MN; Protestant; married (Susan).

Career: Control Data Corp., 1962–64; Minneapolis City Cncl., Majority Ldr., 1965–67; MN House of Reps., 1970–78; MN St. Auditor, 1978–90.

Office: 130 State Capitol Bldg., Aurora Ave., St. Paul 55155, 612-296-3391; Fax: 612-296-2089.

Election Results

1994 gen.	Arne H. Carlson (IR)	1,094,165	(62%)
	John Marty (DFL)	589,344	(33%)
	Others	82,081	(5%)
1994 prim.	Arne H. Carlson (IR)	321,084	(67%)
	Allen Quist (IR)	161,670	(33%)
1990 gen.	Arne H. Carlson (IR)	895,988	(51%)
	Rudy Perpich (DFL)	836,218	(47%)
	Others	45,016	(2%)

SENATORS

Sen. Paul D. Wellstone (DFL)

Elected 1990, seat up 1996; b. July 21, 1944, Washington, D.C.; home, St. Paul; U. of NC, B.A. 1965, Ph.D. 1969; Jewish; married (Sheila).

Career: Prof., Carleton Col., 1969–90.

DC Office: 717 HSOB 20510, 202-224-5641; Fax: 202-224-8438; e-mail: senator@wellstone.senate.gov.

State Offices: 2550 University Ave., #100, St. Paul 55114, 612-645-0323; 105 2nd Ave., S., Virginia 55792, 218-741-1074; and 417 Litchfield Ave., SW, Wilmar 56201, 612-231-0001.

Committees: *Energy & Natural Resources* (7th of 8 D): Energy Research and Development; Parks, Historic Preservation and Recreation. *Labor & Human Resources* (7th of 7 D): Aging; Children and Families; Education, Arts and Humanities. *Indian Affairs* (6th of 8 D). *Small Business* (7th of 9 D). *Veterans' Affairs* (5th of 5 D).

Group Ratings

	ADA	ACLU	COPE	CFA	LCV	CON	NSI	COC	ACU	NTLC	CHC
1994	100	79	100	100	100	29	0	13	4	4	0
1993	100	—	82	80	94	12	—	10	4	—	—

National Journal Ratings

	1993 LIB — 1993 CONS		1994 LIB — 1994 CONS	
Economic	83%	0%	82%	16%
Social	92%	0%	93%	0%
Foreign	92%	0%	87%	6%

Key Votes of the 103d Congress

1. Clinton Deficit Plan	Y	3. Brady Handgun Purchase	Y	5. Lmt. UN Cmnd. of Forces	N
2. NAFTA	N	4. Strike Race/Death Pnlty.	N	6. Cut Missile Funds	Y

Key Votes of the 104th Congress

1. Congressional Compliance	Y	3. Balanced Budget Amndt.	N	5. Product Liability Reform	N
2. Bar Unfunded Mandates	Y	4. Pass Line Item Veto	Y	6. FY96 Budget	N

Election Results

1990 general	Paul D. Wellstone (DFL)	911,999	(50%)	($1,338,708)
	Rudy Boschwitz (IR)	864,375	(48%)	($6,221,133)
	Other.............................	29,820	(2%)	
1990 primary	Paul D. Wellstone (DFL)	226,306	(60%)	
	James W. Nichols (DFL)	129,302	(34%)	
	Gene Schenk (DFL)..................	19,379	(5%)	
1984 general	Rudy Boschwitz (IR)	1,119,926	(56%)	($6,657,484)
	Joan Anderson Growe (DFL)...........	852,844	(43%)	($1,592,885)

Sen. Rod Grams (IR)

Elected 1994, seat up 2000; b. Feb. 4, 1948, Princeton; home, Ramsey; Brown Inst., 1966–68, Anoka-Ramsey Jr. Col., 1970–72, Carroll Col., 1974–75; Lutheran; married (Laurel).

Career: Engineering consultant, 1966–68, 1970–73; News Anchor: KFBB-TV, Great Falls, MT, 1976–78; WSAU-TV, Wausau, WI, 1978–81; WIFR-TV, Rockford, IL, 1981–83; Sr. News Anchor, KMSP-TV, Minneapolis, 1982–91; Pres. & CEO, Sun Ridge Builders, 1985–present; U.S. House of Reps., 1992–94.

DC Office: 261 DSOB 20510, 202-224-3244; Fax: 202-228-0956.

State Offices: 2013 2nd Ave., N., Anoka 55303, 612-427-5921.

Committees: *Banking, Housing & Urban Affairs* (8th of 9 R): Financial Institutions and Regulatory Relief; HUD Oversight and Structure; Securities. *Energy & Natural Resources* (8th of 10 R): Energy Research and Development; Parks, Historic Preservation and Recreation (Vice Chmn.) *Foreign Relations* (9th of 10 R): East Asian and Pacific Affairs; International Economic Policy, Export and Trade Promotion; Near Eastern and South Asian Affairs. *Joint Economic Committee* (6th of 10 Sen.)

Group Ratings (as Member of U.S. House of Representatives)

	ADA	ACLU	COPE	CFA	LCV	CON	NSI	COC	ACU	NTLC	CHC
1994	0	13	0	20	6	69	100	91	100	96	100
1993	0	—	0	10	14	82	—	91	100	—	—

National Journal Ratings (as Member of U.S. House of Representatives)

	1993 LIB — 1993 CONS	1994 LIB — 1994 CONS
Economic	0% — 88%	0% — 80%
Social	0% — 89%	0% — 89%
Foreign	9% — 85%	0% — 88%

Key Votes of the 103rd Congress (as Member of U.S. House of Representatives)

1. Clinton Deficit Plan	N	3. Brady Handgun Purchase	N	5. Lmt. UN Cmnd. of Forces	Y
2. NAFTA	Y	4. Strike Race/Death Pnlty.	Y	6. Cut Missile Funds	N

Key Votes of the 104th Congress

1. Congressional Compliance	Y	3. Balanced Budget Amndt.	Y	5. Product Liability Reform	Y
2. Bar Unfunded Mandates	Y	4. Pass Line Item Veto	Y	6. FY96 Budget	Y

Election Results

1994 general	Rod Grams (IR)	869,653	(49%)	($2,439,798)
	Ann Wynia (DFL)	781,860	(44%)	($2,659,423))
	Dean M. Barkley (I)	95,400	(5%)	($24,266)
	Others	26,016	(1%)	
1994 primary	Rod Grams (IR)	269,931	(58%)	
	Joanell M. Dyrstad (IR)	163,205	(35%)	
	Harold Edward Stassen (IR)	22,430	(5%)	
	Others	8,467	(2%)	
1988 general	Dave Durenberger (IR)	1,176,210	(56%)	($5,410,783)
	Hubert H. Humphrey, III (DFL)	856,694	(41%)	($2,477,068)

FIRST DISTRICT

The Mississippi River runs majestically southeast from Minneapolis and St. Paul, cutting a path through rolling hills and where it widens, forming calm lakes lapping at the bottomlands: one of the finest river landscapes of North America. This far north, the westward tide of Yankee migrants thinned out. After the Civil War, most settlers following the railroads on the floodplains west of the river were Germans and Scandinavians, bringing their families to this terrain so like the Rhine, and to the rolling uplands beyond which resemble the northern European plain. Southeastern Minnesota is a borderland between Yankee and German settlements—politically, between Civil War Republicans and Farmer-Laborites favoring interventionist economic and isolationist foreign policies.

The 1st Congressional District of Minnesota occupies the state's southeastern corner. Within its compact bounds is considerable diversity. Rochester has been home of the Mayo Clinic since it was founded in 1863 when English-born physician William Mayo set up a practice to examine inductees into the Union Army—early government involvement in medicine. Today, Rochester, with its large professional population, is prosperous and growing. Austin, a county away, is headquarters of the Hormel meatpacking firm that beat a bitter strike in 1986; this is one place where class warfare politics seems alive. Politically, Rochester is an IR stronghold, while Austin is solidly DFL. The 1st District extends north to new subdivisions spreading out from the Twin Cities and to Northfield, home of Carleton College and former professor Senator Paul Wellstone. The 1st also includes the river towns of Red Wing, Wabasha and Winona, with their 19th Century stone storefronts and mountain-like rock outcroppings that overlook the river.

There are farms here, but not the big—and troubled—commercial farms you find farther west.

This is on balance a Republican district, though for a dozen years it was represented by Tim Penny, an earnest moderate who was elected to the state Senate in 1976 at 24 and to the House, in a seat into which two Republican incumbents had been redistricted, in 1982 at 30; he was continually reelected by huge margins. Penny reached the national spotlight in 1993 when, in return for supporting the Clinton budget and tax package, he was allowed to bring to the floor the $103 billion in five-year spending cuts known as Penny-Kasich I. But House Democratic leaders and the Clinton White House pulled out all the stops to defeat it, and won 219–213; Penny-Kasich II was beaten in April 1994. Penny, bitter at Congress and his fellow Democrats, had announced in August 1993 he would not run again in 1994. The difference between the fate of Republicans and Democrats can be gauged by the fact that his co-sponsor, Ohio's John Kasich, now chairs the Budget Committee and Penny has returned home to small-town Minnesota to raise his family and teach at the University of Minnesota.

The new congressman is Gil Gutknecht, a Republican who won what seemed at times a competition to be the logical heir to Tim Penny. The name, he likes to explain, means "good hired hand," though "good indentured servant" might be closer to the mark. He grew up in Iowa, son of a union member, worked nine years as a school supply salesman, then became an auctioneer. He eventually handled large real estate auctions. He also was elected to the legislature in 1982 from Rochester and became floor leader for the IR Caucus. Partisan, engaging, he once told Iron Range DFLers that the state motto "L'etoile du Nord" did not mean "send the money north." His legislation includes a whistleblowing law, ethics issues and the 21-year-old drinking age. In 1993, he was aiming to run for the Senate in 1994; then, when Penny announced his retirement, he decided to run for the 1st District seat instead.

There was competition. In the IR primary, Arlen Erdahl, elected congressman in 1978 and defeated in 1982 after redistricting, was seeking a comeback after serving in the Reagan and Bush administrations. Gutknecht argued that the moderate Erdahl did not represent the increasing conservatism of the area or the party. Erdahl, 63, who was in office during a more bipartisan time, said he related more to Garrison Keillor than to Rush Limbaugh. Gutknecht won the primary 57%–36%. Meanwhile, the DFL nominated Mankato state Senator John Hottinger, who was endorsed by Penny: he favored a single-payer healthcare system. Gutknecht attacked him for voting 98% with the Democratic leadership and portrayed himself as "the Minnesota equivalent of Newt Gingrich." Hottinger, who believes "government is a tool of the people," had a 106-point budget-cutting plan; Gutknecht backed the balanced budget amendment. The verdict was split. Hottinger carried Austin and ran even in Mankato. But Gutknecht won big in Rochester and in the river counties, for a 55%–45% victory.

In the House, Gutknecht won seats on the Government Reform and Oversight and Science Committees. As his early record shows, he seems sure to be an ebullient, enthusiastic supporter of Speaker Newt Gingrich. But Democrats surely will seek a new edition of Penny who can win back the seat.

The People: Pop. 1990: 546,909; 48% rural; 14% age 65+; 97% White; 1% Asian; 1% Hispanic origin. Voting age pop.: 398,958; 1% Hispanic origin. Households: 62% married couple families; 30% married couple fams. w. children; 44% college educ.; median household income: $28,371; per capita income: $12,661; median gross rent: $342; median house value: $58,600.

1992 Presidential Vote			1988 Presidential Vote		
Clinton (D)	109,829	(38%)	Bush (R)	128,191	(51%)
Bush (R)	98,384	(34%)	Dukakis (D)	120,933	(49%)
Perot (I)	75,227	(26%)			

Rep. Gil Gutknecht (IR)

Elected 1994; b. Mar. 20, 1951, Cedar Falls, IA; home, Rochester; U. of N. IA, B.A. 1973; Catholic; married (Mary).

Career: Sales Rep., Latta School Supply Co., 1973–82; Real Estate Auctioneer, 1979–present; MN House of Reps. 1982–94.

DC Office: 425 CHOB 20515, 202-225-2472; Fax: 202-225-0051; e-mail: gil@hr.house.gov.

District Offices: 1530 Greenview Dr., #108, Rochester 55902, 507-252-9841.

Committees: *Government Reform & Oversight* (18th of 27 R): District of Columbia; National Economic Growth, Natural Resources and Regulatory Affairs. *Science* (20th of 27 R): Basic Research; Technology.

Group Ratings and 103rd Congress Votes: Newly Elected

Key Votes of the 104th Congress

1. Congressional Compliance Y	6. Reform Crime Grant Y	11. Loser Pays Court Reform Y
2. Balanced Budget Amndmt. Y	7. National Security Act Y	12. Product Liability Reform Y
3. Bar Unfunded Mandates Y	8. Moratorium on Regs. Y	13. Welfare Reform Y
4. Pass Line Item Veto Y	9. Risk Assessment on Regs. Y	14. Term Limits Amndmt. Y
5. Relax Exclusionary Rule Y	10. Expnd. Priv. Prop. Rights Y	15. Tax Cuts Y

Election Results

1994 general	Gil Gutknecht (IR)	117,613	(55%)	($581,099)
	John C. Hottinger (DFL)	95,328	(45%)	($347,084)
1994 primary	Gil Gutknecht (IR)	33,871	(57%)	
	Arlen I. Erdahl (IR)	21,541	(36%)	
	Doug Anderson (IR)	4,134	(7%)	
1992 general	Timothy J. Penny (DFL)	206,369	(74%)	($292,920)
	Timothy Droogsma (IR)	72,367	(26%)	($93,620)

SECOND DISTRICT

West of the Mississippi and Minnesota Rivers, where the plains rise above the gorges that the rivers have cut through them, is the great farming country of southwestern Minnesota. This is where Laura Ingalls Wilder's family came on the way west from their little house in the big woods in Wisconsin to the "Little House on the Prairie" in South Dakota, and stopped by the shores of Plum Creek, near Walnut Grove, Minnesota, not long after the Indians were forced out by U.S. troops following the Dakota rebellion of 1862. The creeks and rivers cut crevasses into these plains, spotted with occasional hills and towns settled 100 years ago by Yankee, German and Scandinavian farmers. This is a hard place to make a living; Laura's family, after all their struggles, left the farm for town as soon as they could. Even in the 1990s, farmers still struggle against the elements to make a profitable living, and even their successes hurt. With far higher farm productivity, far fewer people live on the land, and even in town, people here have had a hard time developing an economy that can provide jobs for all their children, much less attract newcomers.

The 2d Congressional District of Minnesota takes in roughly the southwestern quadrant of the state. The farm counties over the decades slowly have become depopulated, as young people move off farms into small towns and, more often, to the Twin Cities or other big metro areas. But now there is movement in the other direction. The 2d District's boundaries were shifted eastward after the 1990 Census and now take in outlying counties and townships of the Twin Cities metro area. Some, around Chanhassen and Shakopee southwest of Minneapolis, are relatively high income areas. Others, farther out, like Waverly where Hubert Humphrey had his lakeside home, are more humble—places where modest-income young families are moving into what was once open countryside punctuated by small villages. It is almost as if the southwestern Minnesota farmers who saw their children go off to the big city are now seeing their grandchildren move back out toward the farmlands, or at least into the same political constituency.

The 2d District on balance leans Republican, but—this is Minnesota—not very far, in national terms. The Congressman here is a Democrat, Dave Minge, with deep roots in the district, who won a narrow victory in 1992 when one of the House's leading Republicans, Vin Weber, retired; he won reelection by a solid though not overwhelming margin in 1994. Minge (pronounced with a hard *G*) is close to a personification of "Minnesota nice," the quiet cheerfulness and pleasantness which permeates much of life in Minnesota, though of late not much of its politics. Minge's father was a small town doctor who left Minnesota to be a medical missionary for five years. Minge practiced law in Minneapolis, taught law for seven years in Wyoming and worked briefly on Capitol Hill. He returned to Minnesota to practice law in Montevideo, the town where Walter Mondale grew up, where he worked with community organizations to clean up the Minnesota river and resettle Vietnamese refugees and served on the school board. In 1992, he decided to run against Weber. When Weber retired he found himself facing Cal Ludeman, conservative and antiabortion state legislator, Independent Republican nominee for governor in 1986. Ludeman began the race with more money, but showed less energy, while Minge rode 500 miles on his bicycle, stopping in 47 towns in nine days. He attacked Ludeman for voting against minimum wages, drug abuse programs, and federal disaster relief, and called for higher taxes on "anyone . . . who makes a good income." He called for handling the deficit with a commission like the one Congress used for military base closings and for a "unified" national healthcare plan. This was one of many districts where the party margin in the race for the House was close to the party margin in the race for president: Bill Clinton carried the district 37%–35%, and Minge won 47.9%–47.7%. Ludeman was proclaimed the winner on election night but Minge, with Norwegian stoicism, went to sleep and woke up to find out he had won by 569 votes.

In the House, Minge became very much a maverick in the mold of neighboring Tim Penny. He supported the Clinton stimulus package but opposed the budget and tax package and later NAFTA, saying it would hurt agricultural interests. He voted for the Brady bill and was attacked fiercely by the National Rifle Association. He backed the balanced budget amendment, line-item veto and A-to-Z spending cut plan. He worked for relief from the terrible floods of 1993 and for changes in the federal crop insurance program. He was one of several Democrats who initially pushed for budget reforms, but were muscled back by the leadership and in many cases defeated by the voters in 1994.

Minge ran better. Endorsed by most local newspapers—the stereotype of the crotchety conservative small town editor is outdated; most American editorial writers today are liberal— and far better financed than his IR opponent, Gary Revier, Minge ran well ahead of the much more liberal DFL state ticket and won reelection 52%–45%. A pivotal vote in the Democratic 103d Congress, he could be one again if the Republican majority fragments in the 104th. Republicans vow that they will produce a stronger candidate in 1996 to win back this district that they consider their own. Minge showed that he was aware of this threat with his many 1995 votes for the Contract With America. A supporter of term limits, he has promised to serve only 12 years.

The People: Pop. 1990: 546,874; 58% rural; 16% age 65+; 99% White; 1% Hispanic origin. Voting age pop.: 390,233; 1% Hispanic origin. Households: 65% married couple families; 32% married couple fams. w. children; 37% college educ.; median household income: $27,024; per capita income: $12,159; median gross rent: $309; median house value: $55,000.

1992 Presidential Vote

Clinton (D)	103,246	(37%)
Bush (R)	97,867	(35%)
Perot (I)	79,442	(28%)

1988 Presidential Vote

Bush (R)	131,863	(52%)
Dukakis (D)	121,837	(48%)

Rep. David Minge (DFL)

Elected 1992; b. Mar. 19, 1942, Clarkfield; home, Montevideo; St. Olaf College, B.A. 1964, U. of Chicago, J.D. 1967; Lutheran; married (Karen).

Career: Practicing atty., 1967–70, 1977–90; Professor, U. of WY Law Schl., 1970–77; Montevideo School Bd., 1990–92.

DC Office: 1415 LHOB 20515, 202-225-2331; Fax: 202-226-0836; e-mail: dminge@hr.house.gov.

District Offices: 542 1st St., Montevideo 56265, 612-269-9311; 405 E. 2nd St., Chaska 55318, 612-448-6567; and 938 4th Ave., Windom 56101, 507-831-0115.

Committees: *Agriculture* (11th of 22 D): General Farm Commodities; Resource Conservation, Research and Forestry. *Science* (13th of 23 D): Energy and Environment.

Group Ratings

	ADA	ACLU	COPE	CFA	LCV	CON	NSI	COC	ACU	NTLC	CHC
1994	60	71	33	50	61	100	30	92	14	50	28
1993	75	—	75	80	64	82	—	55	26	—	—

National Journal Ratings

	1993 LIB — 1993 CONS		1994 LIB — 1994 CONS	
Economic	44% —	56%	43% —	56%
Social	68% —	32%	63% —	36%
Foreign	87% —	7%	85% —	0%

Key Votes of the 103d Congress

1. Clinton Deficit Plan	N	3. Brady Handgun Purchase	Y	5. Lmt. UN Cmnd. of Forces	N
2. NAFTA	N	4. Strike Race/Death Pnlty.	N	6. Cut Missile Funds	Y

Key Votes of the 104th Congress

1. Congressional Compliance	Y	6. Reform Crime Grant	N	11. Loser Pays Court Reform	Y
2. Balanced Budget Amndmt.	Y	7. National Security Act	N	12. Product Liability Reform	Y
3. Bar Unfunded Mandates	Y	8. Moratorium on Regs.	Y	13. Welfare Reform	N
4. Pass Line Item Veto	Y	9. Risk Assessment on Regs.	Y	14. Term Limits Amndmt.	Y
5. Relax Exclusionary Rule	N	10. Expnd. Priv. Prop. Rights	N	15. Tax Cuts	N

Election Results

1994 general	David Minge (DFL)	114,289	(52%)	($622,920)
	Gary B. Revier (IR)	98,881	(45%)	($325,853)
	Others	6,615	(3%)	
1994 primary	David Minge (DFL)	unopposed		
1992 general	David Minge (DFL)	132,156	(48%)	($355,400)
	Cal Ludeman (IR)	131,587	(48%)	($429,100)
	Stan Bentz (I)	12,146	(4%)	

THIRD DISTRICT

Over the past half century, Minnesota's great twin metropolis has spread out from the neat streets inside the city limits of Minneapolis and St. Paul into the countryside all around. People have sorted themselves out geographically. In the lower lands along the Mississippi and Minnesota Rivers, where rail lines fan out from the Twin Cities heading toward the great farmlands of America, are the blue collar suburbs, with neat modest houses on grid streets and warehouses and factories near the tracks. Inland, around the lakes Minnesota is so proud of, in subdivisions with curved streets hugging the hills, are the Twin Cities' more affluent neighborhoods, quiet and unflashy in the Minnesota way, but comfortable whether blanketed with snow or when the lake is glinting in the summer sun. In between are the freeway interchanges where some of the Twin Cities' great innovations can be seen—Southdale Shopping Center in Edina, the first enclosed mall, and the site of the first B. Dalton store, the beginning of national book chains; and now the giant Mall of America, with its 4.2 million square feet, 400 stores, 45 restaurants, 14 theaters and 12,000 employees.

The 3d Congressional District of Minnesota takes in Hennepin County suburbs north, south and west of Minneapolis. On the north are working class Brooklyn Center and Brooklyn Park, still DFL strongholds; on the south is middle income Bloomington, home of the Mall of America; to the west are Edina, Plymouth, Wayzata and other towns around Lake Minnetonka. This is the largest lake and these are the most affluent communities in the Twin Cities area. The area also is home to headquarters of such diverse companies as Cargill and Radisson Hotels. The 3d also takes in fast-growing Burnsville across the Minnesota River from the airport and still vacant land northwest of Minneapolis. The boundaries of the 3d were changed substantially for 1994, leaving out marginal political territory in Dakota County south of St. Paul and adding northern Hennepin County. Overall, this is a heavily Republican district, the most so in Minnesota.

The congressman from the 3d District is Jim Ramstad, a Republican first elected in 1990, and now something of a power in the House. He has been in politics since childhood: raised in North Dakota, he used to go with his grandfather to visit Republican Senator Milton Young. He saw President Eisenhower in 1956 and met President Kennedy in 1963 at the same Rose Garden ceremony where a young Bill Clinton was photographed shaking Kennedy's hand (Ramstad is in the background of the now famous photo). He worked as an intern to Young and a staffer to Congressman Tom Kleppe while in his 20s. In 1980, at 34, he beat a Democratic state senator (spending a then record-breaking sum of $77,932) and worked on issues like chemical dependency in young people, "crack" babies and the handicapped, while favoring mandatory minimum sentences for drug dealers and boot camps for drug offenders. He used to spend time with police on all-night rounds.

In 1990, the 3d opened up when Bill Frenzel retired after 20 years. The crucial contest was the 1990 IR convention. Ramstad was pro-choice on abortion while most delegates were anti-abortion, but he had good endorsements, from then-Senator Rudy Boschwitz and Congressman Vin Weber, both anti-abortion, and won on the eighth ballot. In the House, Ramstad's record has been conservative on economics, moderate on some other issues. He gets Sierra Club support and led the fight against the Advanced Liquid Metal Reactor, for fiscal as well as environmental reasons. He sponsored provisions of the 1994 crime bill, including a national tracking system for convicted child abusers after they are released from prison. A recovering alcoholic, he backs drug tests for released federal prisoners. But he is also an aggressive reformer at home in the Republican Conference. He founded a medical technology caucus and rails against the Food and Drug Administration for stifling innovation. He favors tort reform. He demanded the firing of Joycelyn Elders long before it occurred and voted against the assault weapons ban. In 1995, as the senior Republican in the Minnesota delegation, he got a seat on the Ways and Means Committee, where he is likely to oppose any tax increase.

Ramstad has been easily reelected, and in 1994 had the third highest number of votes of any House candidate in the country. He has been mentioned as a possible candidate against Senator Paul Wellstone in 1996, though he says he won't run.

The People: Pop. 1990: 546,976; 2% rural; 8% age 65+; 96% White; 1% Black; 2% Asian; 1% Hispanic origin. Voting age pop.: 398,749; 1% Black; 1% Hispanic origin. Households: 63% married couple families; 32% married couple fams. w. children; 66% college educ.; median household income: $43,963; per capita income: $20,067; median gross rent: $577; median house value: $100,500.

1992 Presidential Vote				1988 Presidential Vote		
Clinton (D)	129,171	(39%)		Bush (R)	146,262	(54%)
Bush (R)	117,975	(36%)		Dukakis (D)	125,389	(46%)
Perot (I)	79,877	(24%)				

Rep. Jim Ramstad (IR)

Elected 1990; b. May 6, 1946, Jamestown, ND; home, Minnetonka; U. of MN, B.A. 1968, George Washington U., J.D. 1973; Protestant; single.

Career: Army Reserves, 1968–75; Special Asst., U.S. Rep. Tom Kleppe, 1970; Practicing atty., 1973–80; Adjunct Prof., American U., 1975–78; MN Senate, 1981–90.

DC Office: 103 CHOB 20515, 202-225-2871; Fax: 202-225-6351; e-mail: mn03@hr.house.gov.

District Offices: 8120 Penn Ave. S., #152, Bloomington 55431, 612-881-4600.

Committees: *Ways & Means* (12th of 21 R): Oversight; Trade.

Group Ratings

	ADA	ACLU	COPE	CFA	LCV	CON	NSI	COC	ACU	NTLC	CHC
1994	30	35	11	30	50	98	80	100	62	79	79
1993	35	—	33	50	50	98	—	82	67	—	—

National Journal Ratings

	1993 LIB	—	1993 CONS		1994 LIB	—	1994 CONS
Economic	14%	—	80%		21%	—	76%
Social	49%	—	50%		34%	—	65%
Foreign	37%	—	60%		30%	—	67%

Key Votes of the 103d Congress

1. Clinton Deficit Plan	N	3. Brady Handgun Purchase	Y	5. Lmt. UN Cmnd. of Forces	Y
2. NAFTA	Y	4. Strike Race/Death Pnlty.	Y	6. Cut Missile Funds	Y

Key Votes of the 104th Congress

1. Congressional Compliance Y	6. Reform Crime Grant Y	11. Loser Pays Court Reform Y
2. Balanced Budget Amndmt. Y	7. National Security Act Y	12. Product Liability Reform Y
3. Bar Unfunded Mandates Y	8. Moratorium on Regs. Y	13. Welfare Reform Y
4. Pass Line Item Veto Y	9. Risk Assessment on Regs. Y	14. Term Limits Amndmt. Y
5. Relax Exclusionary Rule Y	10. Expnd. Priv. Prop. Rights N	15. Tax Cuts Y

Election Results

1994 general	Jim Ramstad (IR)	173,223	(73%)	($498,146)
	Bob Olson (DFL)	62,211	(26%)	($35,839)
1994 primary	Jim Ramstad (IR)	unopposed		
1992 general	Jim Ramstad (IR)	200,240	(64%)	($695,521)
	Paul Mandell (DFL)	104,606	(33%)	($18,164)
	Other	9,164	(3%)	

FOURTH DISTRICT

Above the Mississippi River bluffs, forested when the first settlers arrived in the 1850s and one of America's great urban vistas today, stand the two great landmarks of St. Paul: the Minnesota Capitol and Archbishop Ireland's Cathedral. This is the older and smaller of the Twin Cities, settled mainly by Catholic Irish and German immigrants, while Minneapolis was attracting Protestant Swedes and Yankees. St. Paul became a major transportation hub, a railroad center and river port, while Minneapolis, farther up river at the Falls of St. Anthony, became the nation's largest grain milling center. St. Paul has a vibrant core. Beneath the Capitol and the cathedral, its skywalk-linked downtown is home to the Ordway Music Theater, the headquarters of Minnesota Public Radio and an active pop music industry. Beyond the cathedral is Summit Avenue, on which capitalists like the Great Northern Railway's James J. Hill built grandiose Romanesque houses, and which, with Monument Avenue in Richmond and Meridian Street in Indianapolis, remains one of America's grand residential boulevards.

Politically, St. Paul was one of the most Democratic parts of Minnesota even before the Democratic-Farmer-Labor Party was formed in 1944; St. Paul and Ramsey County are still solid DFL territory. The neighborhoods of St. Paul, soberly lined up on grid streets with solidly built houses, and the close-in suburbs, with their more irregular street patterns and shopping nodes, stayed Democratic in the 1980s, voting firmly in 1984 for Walter Mondale—who announced his candidacy in the State Capitol and lived during the campaign in the woodsy suburb of North Oaks just north of St. Paul—and voting Democratic for president in 1988 and 1992 as well.

Minnesota's 4th Congressional District is made up of St. Paul, the Ramsey County suburbs to the north, West St. Paul and South St. Paul (which are right next to each other) to the south, and Lake Elmo and Woodbury to the east. The 4th District has been held by the DFL since 1948, when Eugene McCarthy won it. The current congressman, Bruce Vento, was first elected in 1976. He came from a blue-collar, union background and a career as a science teacher, was elected to the state House in 1970 and then to a leadership post. He won the party endorsement at the 1976 district DFL convention with union support, and then won the primary easily.

Vento was one of the more senior and active members of the Democratic 103d Congress; he has fewer responsibilities in the Republican 104th. He used to chair the Resources subcommittee on National Parks, Forests and Lands, sorting through proposals for wilderness areas and national parks, national seashores, lakeshores and historic sites, wild and scenic rivers—attractive political plums for many members. Vento is a solid environmentalist. He favors severe restrictions on logging to protect the spotted owl in the Pacific Northwest, higher grazing fees on public lands and more money for urban parks. Now the subcommittee is under very different leadership, and Vento moved to a ranking position on the Banking Subcommittee on Financial Institutions and Consumer Credit, where he hopes that Republicans will welcome bipartisanship on the major financial-regulatory issues. His frosty relations with Henry Gonzalez—whom he challenged for the chairmanship, losing 89–163, in 1990—matter less now that Gonzalez is no longer Banking Chairman.

Vento has been reelected routinely, but by only 57%–37% in 1992 and 55%–42% in 1994, though he heavily outspent both opponents. While this seat does not look like a Republican target, one must wonder whether Vento, now denied the chance to wield power on issues which he knows well and cares about, will choose to remain in the House if Republican control seems more than temporary.

The People: Pop. 1990: 546,812; 12% age 65+; 89% White; 4% Black; 1% Amer. Indian; 5% Asian; 1% Other; 3% Hispanic origin. Voting age pop.: 410,506; 3% Black; 2% Hispanic origin. Households: 51% married couple families; 24% married couple fams. w. children; 55% college educ.; median household income: $32,670; per capita income: $15,863; median gross rent: $455; median house value: $83,700. 405,870.

1992 Presidential Vote

Clinton (D)	147,266	(51%)
Bush (R)	79,137	(28%)
Perot (I)	58,850	(21%)

1988 Presidential Vote

Dukakis (D)	162,016	(61%)
Bush (R)	102,725	(39%)

Rep. Bruce F. Vento (DFL)

Elected 1976; b. Oct. 7, 1940, St. Paul; home, St. Paul; U. of MN, A.A. 1961; WI St. U., B.S. 1965; Catholic; divorced.

Career: Teacher, 1965–76; MN House of Reps., 1970–76, Asst. Majority Ldr., 1974–76.

DC Office: 2304 RHOB 20515, 202-225-6631; Fax: 202-225-1968; e-mail: vento@hr.house.gov.

District Offices: 175 5th St. E., #727, Box 100, St. Paul 55101, 612-224-4503.

Committees: *Banking & Financial Services* (3rd of 22 D): Financial Institutions and Consumer Credit (RMM); Housing and Community Opportunity. *Resources* (3rd of 20 D): National Parks, Forests and Lands; Water and Power Resources.

Group Ratings

	ADA	ACLU	COPE	CFA	LCV	CON	NSI	COC	ACU	NTLC	CHC
1994	100	83	89	100	94	37	0	27	0	15	0
1993	100	—	100	100	100	39	—	9	4	—	—

National Journal Ratings

	1993 LIB — 1993 CONS			1994 LIB — 1994 CONS		
Economic	88%	—	0%	83%	—	0%
Social	87%	—	0%	94%	—	0%
Foreign	93%	—	0%	85%	—	0%

Key Votes of the 103d Congress

1. Clinton Deficit Plan	Y	3. Brady Handgun Purchase	Y	5. Lmt. UN Cmnd. of Forces	N
2. NAFTA	N	4. Strike Race/Death Pnlty.	N	6. Cut Missile Funds	Y

Key Votes of the 104th Congress

1. Congressional Compliance Y	6. Reform Crime Grant N	11. Loser Pays Court Reform N
2. Balanced Budget Amndmt. N	7. National Security Act N	12. Product Liability Reform N
3. Bar Unfunded Mandates N	8. Moratorium on Regs. N	13. Welfare Reform N
4. Pass Line Item Veto N	9. Risk Assessment on Regs. N	14. Term Limits Amndmt. N
5. Relax Exclusionary Rule N	10. Expnd. Priv. Prop. Rights N	15. Tax Cuts N

Election Results

1994 general	Bruce F. Vento (DFL)................	115,638	(55%)	($339,703)
	Dennis Newinski (IR)..................	88,344	(42%)	($93,457)
	Others................................	6,648	(3%)	
1994 primary	Bruce F. Vento (DFL).............	unopposed		
1992 general	Bruce F. Vento (DFL)................	159,796	(57%)	($348,920)
	Ian Maitland (IR)....................	101,744	(37%)	($82,563)
	Others............................	15,988	(6%)	

FIFTH DISTRICT

From almost nowhere in Minneapolis today can you see the geographic feature that put the city here—the Falls of St. Anthony, the head of navigation on the Mississippi River, where waters rush in rapids beneath low downtown bridges. In olden days every riverboat had to stop here, and the waterpower generated by the falls was the energy source first for pioneers' grist mills and then for the giant grain mills that processed the wheat of the northern Great Plains into food for the United States and the world. By 1890, Minneapolis and St. Paul made up one of America's largest urban areas, living mainly off grain. Today, Minneapolis is a center of high-tech industry and of banking and finance. It is a regional railroad center, and the headquarters of one the nation's largest airlines, Northwest; it is also the nerve center of an economic area that extends almost 1,000 miles west to the Rocky Mountains in Montana.

All of the city of Minneapolis, plus a few of its older suburbs directly west and south, make up the 5th District of Minnesota. In the southwest corner, in part of the suburb of Edina and the gracefully aged Minneapolis neighborhoods around Lake Calhoun and Lake Harriet—is the home of television's fictional heroine of the *Mary Tyler Moore Show*. These are affluent areas, long built-up and proudly maintained, not far from Minneapolis's skywalk-laced downtown skyscrapers and museum quarter up on the hill above Hennepin Avenue. But most of the 5th District is lower on the income scale. There are few blocks here as abandoned and ruined by crime as are square miles of Chicago or Detroit. But many of the working-class neighborhoods of small frame houses on grid streets are now kept up by elderly homeowners, while new immigrants have built small communities of their own. North of the Mississippi is the University of Minnesota; to the northeast, behind the railroad and warehouse district along the Mississippi, is the home of many Hmongs from Laos. Minneapolis's political liberalism is drawn from the Yankee tradition of clean government, the Scandinavian tradition of cooperative enterprise and the industrial labor tradition of economic redistribution. To this has been added in recent years, by feminists and the graduate student proletariat, an antic cultural liberalism notable for its ignorance not only of any conservative heritage but of many of the liberal traditions here as well. The 5th District is a solidly Democratic district, and one where the challenge to incumbent DFL politicians is as likely to come from the left as from the IRs.

The congressman from the 5th District is Martin Olav Sabo, son of Norwegian immigrants, a DFL leader who has spent all his adult life in politics: he was elected to the Minnesota legislature in 1960 at age 22, the minority leader at 30 and speaker at 34. In 1978, he was elected to the House and in his first year got a seat on the Appropriations Committee. It began as a quiet career: Sabo can be articulate, even humorous, and certainly is knowledgeable and averse to the cheap shot. But he pursued his career with a certain Scandinavian reticence and aversion to national publicity. Throughout the 1980s he delivered locally—new buses, bridges, job training programs, a Transportation Department study on promoting bicycles as an alternative mode of transportation, requiring the Pentagon to purchase only U.S. supercomputers. On the Budget Committee, he wrote the 1990 budget summit agreement's "firewalls" between defense and domestic spending, intended by liberals as an attempt to save domestic programs and by conservatives as a way of protecting the Pentagon. On national issues, he has backed environmental measures, a much higher minimum wage and healthcare reform similar to that pushed by former Congressman Jim Cooper of Tennessee.

In the 1990s, Sabo has been more visible. Back home, he was challenged at the 1992 DFL convention by Lisa Niebauer-Stall, a leftish liberal who kept him from getting the party endorsement until the eighth ballot; he won the primary 67%–28% and the general 63%–28%. After Leon Panetta was appointed OMB Director in January 1993, Sabo ran for Budget Chairman. He won by the solid but not overwhelming margin of 149–112 over John Spratt of South Carolina, who ran as a moderate. In that position it fell to him to defend the Clinton Administration budget, often from opposition in unexpected quarters. Thus in March 1993, Sabo was already cutting spending (from the increases mandated by "baseline" procedures) under pressure from Democrats; he had to fight hard to pass the budget resolution and the final spending and tax package passed by only 218–216 in August 1993. Sabo had to fight hard again against the spending cut packages proposed by his Minnesota colleague Tim Penny and Budget ranking Republican John Kasich in late 1993 and early 1994. The noncontroversial passage of the 1994 budget did not alter the fact that the 1993 votes were controversial and, as 1994 election results showed, unpopular.

Now Sabo is in the minority, as he was for a time in the Minnesota legislature. As ranking Democrat on Budget, he will still have some say on national budget issues—but less sway than new Chairman John Kasich had in 1993 and 1994. He also has become a senior member of the Appropriations Committee, where he is an ally of top Democrat David Obey. Sabo can certainly remain in Congress, unless he gives way to his local left, and since his life's work has been in legislatures it's not clear that he wants to leave. On the other hand, after years of productive work and two years of the spotlight in the majority, it must be frustrating for such an able and energetic legislator to be in the minority.

The People: Pop. 1990: 546,876; 14% age 65+; 84% White; 10% Black; 2% Amer. Indian; 4% Asian; 1% Other; 2% Hispanic origin. Voting age pop.: 434,447; 7% Black; 1% Hispanic origin. Households: 39% married couple families; 16% married couple fams. w. children; 57% college educ.; median household income: $28,634; per capita income: $15,794; median gross rent: $449; median house value: $77,900.

1992 Presidential Vote			1988 Presidential Vote		
Clinton (D)	167,941	(58%)	Dukakis (D)	181,948	(65%)
Bush (R)	68,072	(23%)	Bush (R)	98,200	(35%)
Perot (I)	52,374	(18%)			

Rep. Martin Olav Sabo (DFL)

Elected 1978; b. Feb. 28, 1938, Crosby, ND; home, Minneapolis; Augsburg Col., B.A. 1959; Lutheran; married (Sylvia).

Career: MN House of Reps., 1961–78, Minority Ldr., 1969–73, Speaker, 1973–78.

DC Office: 2336 RHOB 20515, 202-225-4755.

District Offices: 462 Fed. Courts Bldg., 110 S. 4th St., Minneapolis 55401, 612-348-1649.

Committees: *Appropriations* (8th of 24 D): National Security. *Budget* (RMM of 18 D).

Group Ratings

	ADA	ACLU	COPE	CFA	LCV	CON	NSI	COC	ACU	NTLC	CHC
1994	95	91	89	100	88	23	30	25	10	8	0
1993	100	—	100	100	79	19	—	9	0	—	—

National Journal Ratings

	1993 LIB — 1993 CONS		1994 LIB — 1994 CONS	
Economic	78%	— 12%	83%	— 0%
Social	87%	— 0%	82%	— 15%
Foreign	79%	— 16%	75%	— 23%

Key Votes of the 103d Congress

1. Clinton Deficit Plan	Y	3. Brady Handgun Purchase Y	5. Lmt. UN Cmnd. of Forces N
2. NAFTA	N	4. Strike Race/Death Pnlty. N	6. Cut Missile Funds Y

Key Votes of the 104th Congress

1. Congressional Compliance Y	6. Reform Crime Grant N	11. Loser Pays Court Reform N
2. Balanced Budget Amndmt. N	7. National Security Act N	12. Product Liability Reform N
3. Bar Unfunded Mandates N	8. Moratorium on Regs. N	13. Welfare Reform N
4. Pass Line Item Veto N	9. Risk Assessment on Regs. N	14. Term Limits Amndmt. N
5. Relax Exclusionary Rule N	10. Expnd. Priv. Prop. Rights N	15. Tax Cuts N

Election Results

1994 general	Martin Olav Sabo (DFL)	121,515	(62%)	($333,075)
	Dorothy L. LeGrand (IR)..............	73,258	(37%)	($148,799)
	Others.................................	1,399	(1%)	
1994 primary	Martin Olav Sabo (DFL)	unopposed		
1992 general	Martin Olav Sabo (DFL)	174,139	(63%)	($585,831)
	Stephen A. Moriarty (IR)..............	77,093	(28%)	($16,781)
	Others.................................	25,083	(9%)	

SIXTH DISTRICT

The earliest settlers to the Twin Cities of Minneapolis and St. Paul came up the Mississippi River, or up the rail lines which were soon enough built on the bottomlands beside. They lived in their first generation within walking distance of the mills and factories and railyards; as first streetcars and then automobiles allowed them to live farther from work, they spread out in St. Paul and Minneapolis and then over the lake-strewn countryside all around. The flat lands are bleak here when the winter sun struggles to shine through grey clouds. The lakes are often surrounded by, sometimes indistinguishable from, swamps. The old lumber mill towns which pioneers built, like Stillwater on the St. Croix, were for years economic backwaters, their antique structures ill-tended. But the creativity and productivity of Minnesotans have turned this not especially attractive environment into some of the most pleasant suburbs in the world. They have taken maximum advantage of their lakes and have refurbished old towns and farmhouses and have built comfortable homes in new subdivisions. Here live today's typical American families. Busy at home and at the workplace, communicating with each other by Post-it notes (invented at St. Paul's 3M), exhausted at the end of each day, winning through their efforts a material standard of living that would have dazzled their grandparents but at a price that might well have appalled them.

The 6th Congressional District of Minnesota includes much of the Twin Cities metropolitan area, suburbs and townships north, east and south of St. Paul and Minneapolis. To the northwest, the Anoka County suburbs along the Mississippi River, have attracted blue collar families. Incomes are below the high metro average, and politically this is a DFL area. Stillwater, facing Wisconsin on hills above the St. Croix River, with Victorian buildings from its days as a lumber port when it nearly became Minnesota's capital, and surrounding Washington County have attracted a mix of people and are politically marginal. South of St. Paul, the Dakota County towns along the Mississippi are blue collar and DFL; the newer, fast-growing Eagan and Apple Valley to the southwest are quite affluent and tend to vote Independent Republican. Altogether, this is perhaps Minnesota's most volatile district. Redistricting has arguably made the difference twice already in the 1990s. The 1992 plan, in which the 6th included some affluent suburbs west of Minneapolis, resulted in the election of Republican Rod Grams, who went on to be elected U.S. Senator in 1994. The altered 1994 plan shifted the district the other way, resulting in a narrow victory for the DFL's Bill Luther. This was one of only four districts which switched from Republican to Democrat in 1994, and would not have done so without redistricting.

The new congressman from the 6th District is Bill Luther, the winner of one of two turbulent races in Minnesota in 1994. He is another of Minnesota's talented career politicians. He grew up on a dairy farm, was elected to the state House in 1974 at 29 and to the state Senate in 1976. He ran for the 6th District seat in 1982, and lost the DFL endorsement to fellow legislator Gerry Sikorski. It was Sikorski's downfall—he had 697 overdrafts on the House bank and switched from anti-abortion to pro-choice in April 1992—that opened up the seat in the 1990s. Luther's life seems to be politics; his wife Darlene was elected to the state House in 1992 and 1994. He was Assistant Majority Leader in the state Senate, wrote the state's campaign finance laws, promoted a D.A.R.E. anti-crime initiative for children. He worked hard, kept quiet publicly, developed shrewd strategies, and was strongly partisan. He had been eyeing the 6th District ever since Sikorski lost to Grams, and when redistricting removed his home base of Brooklyn Center, he bought a second house north of St. Paul. Oddly, his IR opponent also had a residence outside the new 6th, and was a former DFLer as well. As Hennepin County Commissioner, and an opponent of abortion, Tad Jude had run and lost the DFL endorsement in 1980, then ran against Sikorski in the 1992 primary, losing by only a 49%–46% margin. Jude was also a career politician, elected to the state House in 1972 at 20 and to the state Senate in 1982. Though his father was a Humphrey DFLer and state Senator, he switched parties after the 1992 primary.

The campaign was fiercely contested. Both candidates won their 1994 primaries fairly easily,

Luther by 57%–30% and Jude 57%–36%. Luther painted Jude as an extremist on abortion and compared him to losing IR gubernatorial endorsee Allen Quist. Jude attacked Luther for voting against longer sentences for violent rapists and criminals attacking seniors. A late Jude ad attacked Luther for opposing a bill that would have prevented a convict from being paroled who had abducted and raped three women. Luther and local reporters said it was inaccurate, because the law would not have been retroactive, though of course it would have covered such offenders in the future. The final result was close: Luther won by 550 votes, carrying Washington and Anoka Counties and losing Dakota.

Luther is part of the small Democratic freshman class in the 103d Congress, well positioned if he can hold this seat to accumulate seniority ahead of Democrats who may make up the party's next House majority. But this seat could be seriously contested again.

The People: Pop. 1990: 547,055; 10% rural; 6% age 65+; 97% White; 1% Black; 1% Amer. Indian; 1% Asian; 1% Hispanic origin. Voting age pop.: 382,153; 1% Black; 1% Hispanic origin. Households: 67% married couple families; 38% married couple fams. w. children; 56% college educ.; median household income: $42,346; per capita income: $16,970; median gross rent: $513; median house value: $90,900.

1992 Presidential Vote			**1988 Presidential Vote**		
Clinton (D)	120,759	(39%)	Dukakis (D)	122,032	(50%)
Bush (R)	102,265	(33%)	Bush (R)	120,889	(50%)
Perot (I)	82,587	(27%)			

Rep. Bill Luther (DFL)

Elected 1994; b. June 27, 1945, Fergus Falls; home, Stillwater; U. of MN, B.S. 1967, J.D. 1970; Catholic; married (Darlene).

Career: Clerk, 8th Circuit U.S. Court of Appeals, 1970–71; Practicing atty., 1971–92; MN House of Reps., 1975–76; MN Senate, 1977–94.

DC Office: 1419 LHOB 20515, 202-225-2271; Fax: 202-225-3368.

District Offices: 1811 Weir Dr., #150, Woodbury 55125, 612-730-4940.

Committees: *Science* (23rd of 23 D): Basic Research; Space and Aeronautics. *Small Business* (18th of 19 D): Procurement, Exports and Business Opportunities; Regulation and Paperwork.

Group Ratings and 103rd Congress Votes: Newly Elected

Key Votes of the 104th Congress

1. Congressional Compliance	Y	6. Reform Crime Grant	N	11. Loser Pays Court Reform	N
2. Balanced Budget Amndmt.	Y	7. National Security Act	N	12. Product Liability Reform	N
3. Bar Unfunded Mandates	Y	8. Moratorium on Regs.	N	13. Welfare Reform	N
4. Pass Line Item Veto	Y	9. Risk Assessment on Regs.	N	14. Term Limits Amndmt.	Y
5. Relax Exclusionary Rule	Y	10. Expnd. Priv. Prop. Rights	N	15. Tax Cuts	N

Election Results

1994 general	Bill Luther (DFL).....................	113,740	(50%)	($1,133,977)
	Tad Jude (IR).......................	113,190	(50%)	($699,413)
1994 primary	Bill Luther (DFL).....................	20,170	(57%)	
	Daniel P. McCarthy (DFL).............	10,438	(30%)	
	Jennings B. Campbell (DFL)...........	4,641	(13%)	
1992 general	Rod Grams (IR).....................	133,564	(44%)	($439,718)
	Gerry Sikorski (DFL).................	100,016	(33%)	($1,217,832)
	Dean Barkley (I)....................	48,329	(16%)	($64,170)
	James H. Peterson (IFP)...............	16,411	(6%)	
	Other..............................	2,400	(1%)	

SEVENTH DISTRICT

The lake-strewn country along the upper stretches of the Mississippi River, settled by Norwegian and German immigrants, is the source of some prime American literary and political traditions. Here a century ago in the town of Sauk Centre grew up Sinclair Lewis, whose *Main Street* and *Babbitt* were greeted as the definitive satires of small town life, though on rereading they show surprising affection for their subjects. Not far north of Sauk Centre is Little Falls, the boyhood home of Charles Lindbergh, whose father was a progressive and isolationist congressman who opposed declaring war on Germany in 1917. In those years this seemingly placid country was seething with rage, as WASPy nationalists banned German from schools, renamed sauerkraut liberty cabbage, and boycotted German-American businesses. The rage simmered and became the source of the bitter isolationism of the 1930s and 1940s, of which Lindbergh was a national leader, and of the bitter anti-Communism of the 1950s. This part of Minnesota is also the home—though the actual location has somehow disappeared from the map—of Garrison Keillor's Lake Wobegon, whose history has an authentic ring: founded by New England Yankees as New Albion in 1852, renamed when Norwegians got a majority on the council in 1880, where the Norwegian flag still flies on holidays but no one has seen a German flag since 1917.

The 7th Congressional District of Minnesota, covering the northwest corner of the state, includes just about all this territory. It takes in the wheat-farming plains up near North Dakota and the German Catholic country, strewn with farm villages named for saints, around Sauk Centre and St. Cloud. This is a mixed area politically: some wheat counties are heavily DFL; heavily Norwegian Otter Tail County leans Republican; St. Cloud and Stearns County are volatile, dovish and anti-abortion. The 7th's political history reads like something out of *Lake Wobegon Days*. Back in 1958, Congresswoman Coya Knutson lost reelection when her husband Andy issued a plaintive statement urging her to come home and make his breakfast again; she was the only incumbent Democrat to lose in heavily Democratic 1958. Other Scandinavian names followed: Odin Langen, Bob Bergland (later Jimmy Carter's Secretary of Agriculture), Arlan Stangeland. None except Bergland won by any great margin. For most of the last 40 years this has been one of America's prime marginal districts.

The congressman from the 7th District today is Collin Peterson, onetime (1976–86) state Senator, who has run for this seat seven times and won three. He lost a DFL caucus in 1982; he lost to Stangeland in 1984 and 1986 (by only 121 votes the second time; he declared victory and went to Washington to set up an office); he lost the DFL primary again in 1988. But in 1990, when the *St. Cloud Times* reported that Stangeland made 341 credit card calls to a woman not his wife, Peterson won with a robust 54%. In office, he continued to do things his way, acting as his own press secretary, campaign consultant, and pilot on flights within the district. He said he modeled himself after veteran Kentucky Congressman William Natcher, who until his death in 1994 shunned publicity, had a small staff and had a locker next to Peterson's in the house gym.

Peterson got on the Agriculture Committee, where he pushed bills for rural economic development and wetland preservation. He is one of the last Farm Belt members favoring supply management and hoping for higher agriculture subsidies and price supports. He fiercely opposed the North America Free Trade Agreement and founded in 1993 the congressional anti-NAFTA caucus, both generally and on behalf of local sugar beet growers. Moderate to conservative on cultural issues, he favors parental consent abortion laws and opposes gun control measures, voting against the 1994 crime bill. His early 1995 votes made him one of the biggest supporters among northern Democrats of the Contract With America.

Since 1990, Peterson has been opposed twice by Bernie Omann, elected in 1990 at 25 to the legislature from Stearns County, and twice Peterson has won 51%–49%. Rhetorically these have been arguments as to who is more conservative. Omann has carried the southeast part of the 7th around St. Cloud by impressive margins. Peterson has had big margins in the north country, and cut into Republican votes there enough to carry Otter Tail County in 1992. This remains one of the most marginal seats in the nation, quite possibly the site of another serious contest in 1996.

The People: Pop. 1990: 547,021; 62% rural; 15% age 65+; 96% White; 2% Amer. Indian; 1% Hispanic origin. Voting age pop.: 394,259; 1% Hispanic origin. Households: 61% married couple families; 30% married couple fams. w. children; 40% college educ.; median household income: $22,893; per capita income: $10,294; median gross rent: $316; median house value: $50,200.

1992 Presidential Vote			1988 Presidential Vote		
Clinton (D)	104,359	(38%)	Bush (R)	129,301	(52%)
Bush (R)	103,624	(38%)	Dukakis (D)	119,049	(48%)
Perot (I)	63,610	(23%)			

Rep. Collin C. Peterson (DFL)

Elected 1990; b. June 29, 1944, Fargo, ND; home, Detroit Lakes; Moorhead St. U., B.A. 1966; Lutheran; divorced.

Career: Army Natl. Guard, 1963–69; Accountant, 1966–90; MN Senate, 1976–86.

DC Office: 1314 LHOB 20515, 202-225-2165; Fax: 202-225-1593.

District Offices: 714 Lake Ave., #107, Detroit Lakes 56501, 218-847-5056; 110 2nd St., #S-112, Waite Park 56387, 612-259-0559; and 2603 Wheat Dr., Red Lake Falls 56750, 218-253-4356.

Committees: *Agriculture* (8th of 22 D): Livestock, Dairy and Poultry; Resource Conservation, Research and Forestry. *Government Reform & Oversight* (11th of 22 D): National Economic Growth, Natural Resources and Regulatory Affairs (RMM).

Group Ratings

	ADA	ACLU	COPE	CFA	LCV	CON	NSI	COC	ACU	NTLC	CHC
1994	45	27	44	50	35	83	40	83	52	57	86
1993	60	—	83	60	57	39	—	27	38	—	—

National Journal Ratings

	1993 LIB — 1993 CONS			1994 LIB — 1994 CONS		
Economic	52%	—	47%	41%	—	58%
Social	35%	—	64%	33%	—	66%
Foreign	63%	—	34%	45%	—	54%

Key Votes of the 103d Congress

1. Clinton Deficit Plan	N	3. Brady Handgun Purchase	N	5. Lmt. UN Cmnd. of Forces	N
2. NAFTA	N	4. Strike Race/Death Pnlty.	Y	6. Cut Missile Funds	Y

Key Votes of the 104th Congress

1. Congressional Compliance	Y	6. Reform Crime Grant	N	11. Loser Pays Court Reform	Y
2. Balanced Budget Amndmt.	Y	7. National Security Act	N	12. Product Liability Reform	Y
3. Bar Unfunded Mandates	Y	8. Moratorium on Regs.	Y	13. Welfare Reform	N
4. Pass Line Item Veto	Y	9. Risk Assessment on Regs.	Y	14. Term Limits Amndmt.	Y
5. Relax Exclusionary Rule	Y	10. Expnd. Priv. Prop. Rights	Y	15. Tax Cuts	N

Election Results

1994 general	Collin C. Peterson (DFL)	108,023	(51%)	($584,092)
	Bernie Omann (IR)	102,623	(49%)	($507,325)
1994 primary	Collin C. Peterson (DFL)	unopposed		
1992 general	Collin C. Peterson (DFL)	133,886	(51%)	($495,882)
	Bernie Omann (IR)	130,396	(49%)	($218,951)

EIGHTH DISTRICT

In the 1860s, prospectors in the Arrowhead region of the new state of Minnesota, northwest of Lake Superior in the low hills of the Mesabi Range, happened upon the nation's largest veins of iron ore; they moved on, looking for gold. But in the 1880s, Duluth banker George Stone and Philadelphia financier Charlemagne Tower started mining the Iron Range and created the northern end of the lifeline of American heavy industry. The range runs south alongside rail lines to the port of Duluth nestled on dramatic bluffs over the always cold and, every winter, frozen waters of Lake Superior—one of the most beautiful settings for a city in North America. Duluth was a grain-shipping rival of Chicago and the premier iron-ore port. Its city plan was drawn up by Daniel Burnham and its splendid turn-of-the-century buildings still celebrate the triumph of technology and civilization over wilderness and the elements. Millions of tons of ore have been dug out of the Range, loaded into rail cars for the ride down to Duluth, and into Great Lakes freighters for shipment to Cleveland, Gary, Detroit, Chicago, Pittsburgh and Buffalo.

For most of this century, in this land where the Arctic winds blow down over the Canadian Shield's thousands of inland lakes, about 100,000 people have lived on the Iron Range and another 100,000 in Duluth, most of them the products of America's 1880–1924 wave of immigration—Italians, Poles, Serbs and Croats, Jews, Swedes and Finns. In this punishing environment, they worked to the point of exhaustion, built solid houses with staunch central heating, and wore layers of warm clothing to survive the winter. Life was rough: the work was hard, the hours long, and the pay low. The churches, a separate one for each ethnic group, were the main community institutions. Living conditions improved vastly in the decades of great economic growth after World War II, but life remains rough-hewn today, and there is still economic distress. As the iron and steel industry got more efficient, fewer workers were needed. When the American steel industry collapsed after 1979, it needed even fewer, or none at all. Unemployment topped 20% in the early 1980s; young people have been moving out for years.

The 8th Congressional District of Minnesota includes Duluth and the Iron Range, plus much of the north woods and lake country to the west and south. Under the 1990s redistricting, it moves all the way south to the boundaries of the Twin Cities metro area, to Isanti and Chisago Counties where young families are building new homes near pleasant old lakeside towns. The 8th District has been the bulwark of Minnesota's Democratic-Farmer-Labor Party since it was created in 1944, with turbulent primary and convention politics and solid DFL margins every November. The current congressman, James Oberstar, is from Chisholm in the Iron Range, where his father was a miner and union official. His views are in the liberal Catholic tradition: he believes government has an obligation to help the poor and disadvantaged and to stimulate economic growth, and has little faith in economic markets. He was long dubious about American military involvement abroad, especially in Central America, but favors involvement in Haiti; meanwhile, he is culturally traditional and an opponent of abortion. After serving in the Navy, he landed a job with Congressman John Blatnik in Washington and became his chief staffer in 1963: he has been working for the 8th District for 30 years. When Blatnik retired in 1974, Oberstar won the seat, beating Tony Perpich, brother of former Governor Rudy Perpich. He won tough primaries in 1980 and 1984, the latter after briefly running for the Senate.

Oberstar is the number-two Democrat on the Transportation and Infrastructure Committee, and until 1994 was successfully following the tradition of Blatnik, who chaired the panel when it was called Public Works. He concentrated on bringing projects into Duluth and the Iron Range and nurturing programs like EDA and UDAG, which did so. He claims credit for $80 million in highways, airports, high-tech research centers and the Voyageurs National Park visitor center. As chairman of the Aviation Subcommittee, he moved to overcome obstacles to KLM's investment in Minnesota-based Northwest Airlines, and pushed hard for the big repair facilities Northwest promised to build in Duluth and the Iron Range in return for $840 million of state investment. He proposed making the FAA a separate agency outside the Transportation Department. He fought hard against the Clinton Administration proposals to privatize air traffic control. An expert on Haiti—he lived there for over three years—he called for U.S. military intervention long before President Clinton ordered troops in.

This is a very Democratic district, and it was something of a surprise when Oberstar was held to a 59%–30% victory in 1992. He campaigned relatively little since his wife had just died and his daughter was finishing high school in the D.C. area. By 1994, he had remarried and was campaigning harder. IR candidate Phil Herwig again stressed term limits: a curious plank for a district which has chosen to be represented by only two men for a period of 50 years. Oberstar won in 1994 by 66%–34%. He will surely continue to work on aviation issues—he says he wants tougher safety standards for small commuter airline planes—and to bring projects home to Duluth and the Iron Range. But he will surely not be as pivotal in a Republican Congress. And he is one of several active senior Democrats—three in Minnesota alone—who if they conclude their party will not rebound soon may be questioning whether they want to keep serving in the minority, as Republicans had done for many years.

The People: Pop. 1990: 546,576; 60% rural; 15% age 65+; 97% White; 2% Amer. Indian; 1% Hispanic origin. Voting age pop.: 397,885. Households: 61% married couple families; 29% married couple fams. w. children; 40% college educ.; median household income: $24,667; per capita income: $11,302; median gross rent: $308; median house value: $49,000.

1992 Presidential Vote

Clinton (D)	138,426	(48%)
Bush (R)	80,517	(28%)
Perot (I)	70,539	(24%)

1988 Presidential Vote

Dukakis (D)	156,267	(60%)
Bush (R)	104,906	(40%)

Rep. James L. Oberstar (DFL)

Elected 1974; b. Sept. 10, 1934, Chisholm; home, Chisholm; St. Thomas Col., B.A. 1956, Col. of Europe, Bruges, Belgium, M.A. 1957; Catholic; married (Jean).

Career: Navy civilian language teacher, Haiti, 1959–63; A.A., U.S. Rep. John Blatnik, 1963–74; A.A., U.S. House Public Works Cmte., 1971–74.

DC Office: 2366 RHOB 20515, 202-225-6211; Fax: 202-225-0699.

District Offices: 231 Fed. Bldg., Duluth 55802, 218-727-7474; Chisolm City Hall, 316 Lake St., Chisholm 55719, 218-254-5761; City Hall, 13065 Orono Pkwy., Elk River 55330, 612-241-0188; and Brainerd City Hall, 501 Laurel St., Brainerd 56401, 218-828-4400.

Committees: *Transportation & Infrastructure* (2nd of 27 D): Aviation (RMM); Coast Guard and Maritime Transportation; Water Resources and Environment.

Group Ratings

	ADA	ACLU	COPE	CFA	LCV	CON	NSI	COC	ACU	NTLC	CHC
1994	80	70	89	80	83	33	0	25	15	11	28
1993	90	—	100	90	79	30	—	18	22	—	—

National Journal Ratings

	1993 LIB — 1993 CONS	1994 LIB — 1994 CONS
Economic	88% — 0%	73% — 17%
Social	45% — 54%	70% — 30%
Foreign	87% — 7%	85% — 0%

Key Votes of the 103d Congress

1. Clinton Deficit Plan	Y	3. Brady Handgun Purchase	N	5. Lmt. UN Cmnd. of Forces	N
2. NAFTA	N	4. Strike Race/Death Pnlty.	N	6. Cut Missile Funds	Y

Key Votes of the 104th Congress

1. Congressional Compliance	Y	6. Reform Crime Grant	N	11. Loser Pays Court Reform	N
2. Balanced Budget Amndmt.	N	7. National Security Act	N	12. Product Liability Reform	N
3. Bar Unfunded Mandates	N	8. Moratorium on Regs.	N	13. Welfare Reform	N
4. Pass Line Item Veto	N	9. Risk Assessment on Regs.	N	14. Term Limits Amndmt.	N
5. Relax Exclusionary Rule	N	10. Expnd. Priv. Prop. Rights	N	15. Tax Cuts	N

Election Results

1994 general	James L. Oberstar (DFL).............	153,161	(66%)	($488,411)
	Phil Herwig (IR).....................	79,818	(34%)	($31,673)
1994 primary	James L. Oberstar (DFL)...........	unopposed		
1992 general	James L. Oberstar (DFL)...........	167,104	(59%)	($386,646)
	Philip Herwig (IR)..................	83,823	(30%)	($32,416)
	Harry Robb Welty (PCP)..............	22,619	(8%)	
	Other.............................	8,602	(3%)	

MISSISSIPPI

"Only positive Mississippi spoken here." So say the signs Governor Kirk Fordice has ordered put up on highways at the state line, and the message reflects both the boisterous optimism of so many people in this state and a defensiveness against the reputation that Mississippi has suffered for so long. Is Mississippi moving toward a better future, or must it still be preoccupied with its fabled and fading past? For years no other state had such a painful contrast between image and reality, between an ideal sincerely strived for and the tawdry facts of everyday life. Magnolia trees on the lawns of antebellum mansions, golden-haired young women in white dresses on the veranda, faithful black servants and retainers: this was once the ideal. And behind it stood loose-jointed frame houses and unpainted back-country stores, cabins without indoor plumbing and poor white crossroads clustered with askew advertising signs. Mississippi for years ranked 50th among states in income, literacy, health and education levels, despite the best efforts of civic, political and business leaders. As Mississippi's greatest writer, William Faulkner, said of his state, "You don't love because: you love despite."

Today Mississippi still ranks 50th on many scales. But the gulf between Mississippi and the rest of America has narrowed enormously in the last half-century. In 1940 Mississippi had an economy based on low-wage, subsistence or sharecropper agriculture and a system of racial segregation enforced sometimes by violence. If history is, as Frederic Maitland wrote, the story of the progress from status to contract, then old Mississippi was still at the beginning, for status—race—meant just about everything. In the years since, Mississippi has moved, not always willingly, from status to contract, in its economy and in its race relations. Per capita income in Mississippi was 36% of the national average in 1940; in 1990, it was 67%, well below the norm, yet given the lower cost of living here they were producing a standard of living recognizably American. Daily life, thanks to cheap gas and air conditioning, national brands and the mechanization of farming, has changed drastically: most Mississippians of 50 years ago would be astonished by the physical comforts and mechanical marvels their grandchildren take for granted today. They would be astonished as well by relations between blacks and whites. As *The Washington Post's* William Raspberry wrote in the early 1990s, Mississippi "is one of the few places I know where racial relations are actually improving and where continuing the improvement has come to define the way residents think about their state . . . There is an easiness to relationships, a mutual respect and a willingness to move beyond race that, quite frankly, didn't exist during my years in the state. Mississippi," wrote this Mississippi native, "is finally a good place to be."

But how to make it better? There is still room for debate, sometimes acrimonious partisan debate, on public policy. One view, often summarized in the single word "education," is that government should spend more to improve basic skills. Its great proponents were Governor William Winter, elected in 1979, who finally made kindergarten mandatory and raised the dropout age to 14, and Governor Ray Mabus, elected in 1987, who proposed a major school reform package. But the uncomfortable fact is that most high taxpayers are white and most public school children are black, because many white children attend private academies. With about two-thirds of the state budget going to education and most of the rest to welfare, state government spending is genuine economic redistribution, desired by some but much resented by others.

The other view of public policy is taken by Republican Governor Kirk Fordice, who upset Mabus in 1991 and entered 1995 as a solid favorite for reelection. In this view, the public sector is an unreliable vehicle for progress. It is better to encourage private sector investment, by cutting taxes and regulation, and disciplining the public sector, with accountability and budget-

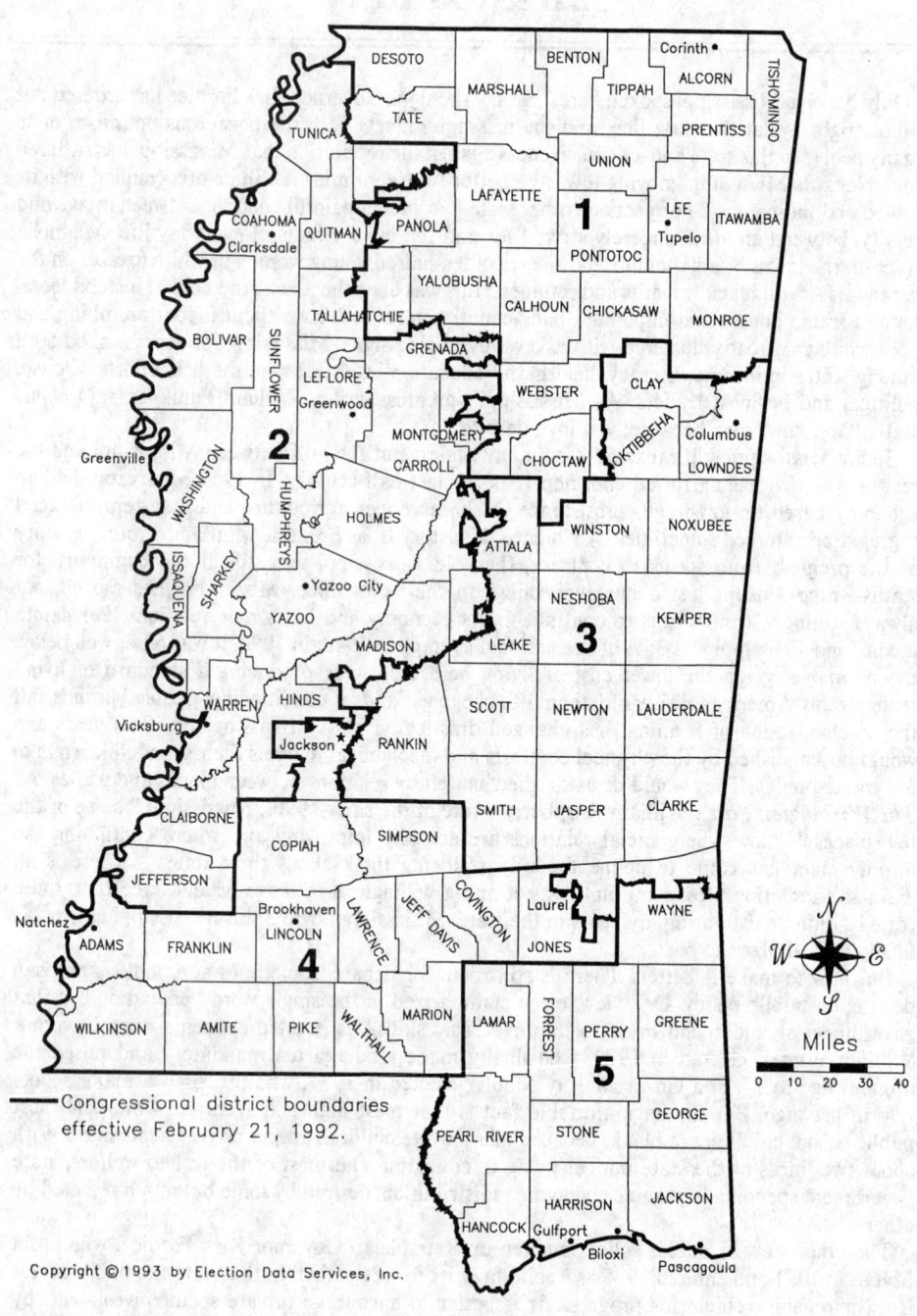

Congressional district boundaries
effective February 21, 1992.

tightening. Also important is encouraging traditional values, widely shared by blacks as well as whites. Fordice applauded when black Jackson high school principal Bishop Knox instituted school prayer; when Knox was fired by administrators, Fordice supported the legislature in authorizing student-initiated prayer in schools. Fordice also cheered when Jackson TV station owner Frank Melton, also black, went on the air and put up billboards calling on police to arrest certain named drug dealers; arrests were made and convictions followed. The argument here is that economic progress is possible only in a framework of traditional values and basic order, not where moral relativism prevails or the criminal underclass rules.

Such views appear to be widely shared in Mississippi. In national politics this is arguably the most Republican state: it gave George Bush his highest percentage in 1992; it is the home of Republican National Committee Chairman Haley Barbour; it elects by wide margins two Republican senators; and if it has a 4–1 Democratic House delegation, three of the four have voting records more conservative than many Republicans. To be sure, few blacks vote Republican and not very many whites in seriously contested races vote Democratic. But this political polarization does not mean blacks are excluded from political influence. Whites have voted for blacks like former Congressman and Agriculture Secretary Mike Espy and state Supreme Court Justice Fred Banks; blacks now hold 32 of 122 seats in the Mississippi House and 10 of 52 in the Senate; even with a Republican governor, blacks are part of the give-and-take of politics in a state where the legislature has long had great power. Mississippi has come a long way from the place where in 1964, civil rights workers were murdered for encouraging blacks to register and vote. By the 1980s, a state tourism brochure recalled the "oppression of the black population of the state," and said, "a change from the old racial status quo was necessary and morally correct." If some issues continue to split Mississippians along racial lines—education funding, the historically black colleges, capital punishment—they are being resolved with civility and there are signs of a convergence on basic values. "Positive Mississippi" is spoken here, and may have something to teach the rest of America as well.

Governor. Mississippi Governor Kirk Fordice, a businessman not entirely new to politics, is the first Republican governor elected here since 1874. He has the bluntness of an engineer and the self-assurance of a self-made man; he started his own construction company in Vicksburg at age 28 and in 1990 became head of the Associated General Contractors of America. He is capable of brusque and provocative language, such as his 1992 statement that the United States "is a Christian nation, which does not mean in any way to infer any kind of religious intolerance or any kind of particular dogma that is being forced on anyone"; he later apologized and said he only meant "the overwhelming majority of Americans say they are Christians and that Christian values and beliefs should not be denigrated." But he showed political skill in 1991, beating Auditor Pete Johnson, the grandson and nephew of governors, in the Republican primary, then zeroing in on Democratic incumbent Ray Mabus, one of several prominent young moderates, who had been elected governor just 11 years after finishing Harvard Law. Mabus's tax plan had been rejected by the legislature and a 24-hour waiting period on abortion passed over his veto; he beat former Congressman Wayne Dowdy by only 50%–41% in the Democratic primary. In the general, Fordice campaigned against welfare abusers and racial quotas—veiled racism, Mabus supporters said. He trailed in polls but won 51%–48%, losing the larger urban areas but carrying the white countryside solidly.

Fordice has not been entirely successful; a 1% increase in the sales tax was passed over his veto. But he did get a capital gains tax cut, tort reform and more prison cells. He wants to make Mississippi "the capital of capital punishment," and he eliminated air conditioning and television from prisons and required prisoners to wear stripes. He claims to have attracted thousands of jobs by "CEO-to-CEO recruitment" of corporate executives, and to have cut state spending while Mississippi's riverboat casinos were generating much new revenue. He installed an "empowerment" interactive telephone line with information on state issues and legislators' positions. Looking ahead to 1995, he proposed an income tax cut for married persons and families and announced an alliance with Lieutenant Governor Eddie Briggs (there was rumor of disharmony between the two), who backs a referendum to reduce the size of the legislature. In early 1995, Democratic Secretary of State Dick Molpus, another young moderate, was preparing to run against Fordice; he favors cutting the sales tax on groceries. Mississippi governors have been allowed to seek a second consecutive term since 1986, but scandal-tarred Bill Allain didn't run in 1987 and Mabus lost in 1991; Fordice hopes to break the jinx.

Senators. Mississippi has two Republican senators, both politically skilled, with similar, and very conservative, voting records; both were first elected to the House in 1972, when Mississippi was (as in 1992) the most Republican state in presidential politics. But they also have different temperaments and bases of support; and the more senior, Thad Cochran, who holds the number three Republican leadership post may resent the fact that his junior colleague, Trent Lott, leapfrogged him by winning the number two post in December 1994.

Thad Cochran has managed to amass a solidly conservative record with little controversy or acrimony. He won the House race in 1972 against a white Democrat and a black Independent; he was elected to the Senate in 1978 in a similar three-way contest. In both cases, he won with less than an absolute majority, but was reelected easily. His pleasant personal demeanor, his refusal to engage in racial politics, his conservative stands on almost all issues, and his Republican Party label in a state where most whites have been voting Republican for president for three decades, have made him broadly acceptable to voters.

Cochran is nonetheless a tougher partisan than he appears. In 1990, he challenged John Chafee of Rhode Island for the chairmanship of the Senate Republican Conference, the number three leadership position. "We need an aggressiveness in defining the differences between the two parties," he said, and won 22–21. He strongly supports the balanced budget amendment, limits on unfunded mandates, congressional staff reductions and tough anti-crime laws. In November 1994 Bob Dole named him leader of the Senate Republicans' transition team that struggled to assemble its response to the new hyperactive Republican majority.

Even as part of the leadership, Cochran gets little national publicity, and works hard on the Appropriations Committee—especially if it helps Mississippi. He is particularly active on farm issues, even at some cost to conservative principles. He worked on soybean provisions in the 1990 farm bill, helped kill an attempt to cut $75 million to promote sale of U.S. farm products abroad, pushed through $12 million in disaster relief for Mississippi pecan growers hurt by an ice storm, sought a delay in pesticide safety requirements, got more spending on flood control and added $200,000 for "entomology acoustics detection," i.e., finding noisy insects in Mississippi. He has worked for grants for historically black colleges and for vocational training for the disabled; he sponsored a bill to bring the latest computer technologies to the nation's schools. While capable of sharp partisanship—he called Ross Perot "a demagogue"—he is also practical-minded. "I always voted against subsidies for the maritime industry," he explained in 1993. "It was the conservative position to take. Then I was campaigning for reelection at the gates of the Ingalls shipyard in Pascagoula. I was handing out my leaflets and the union guys showed up with their leaflets, saying 'A vote for Cochran is a vote against your job.' Ever since then, I've voted for maritime subsidies."

Cochran has not had an electoral challenge since 1984, when former Governor William Winter started to run against him, then announced he would be chancellor of Ole Miss, then declined the post to run; Winter's dithering hurt, and Cochran won 61%–39%, winning white votes by a large margin and making inroads among blacks. In 1990, his only opponent, an unknown, withdrew before the filing deadline. For 1996 he is heavily favored.

Trent Lott, Mississippi's junior senator, has been one of the most effective and durable partisan Republicans on Capitol Hill, and the only one to have held his party's number two leadership position in both the House and the Senate. Lott started off from a modest background, with an eye for opportunity but also a strength of conviction that led him to take political risks which have turned out, in this increasingly Republican state, to have been political masterstrokes. Lott worked his way through law school by running the Ole Miss alumni affairs office, accumulating a bunch of good contacts along the way. He got a job on the staff of

Democratic Gulf Coast Congressman and Rules Committee chairman William Colmer, and when Colmer retired in 1972, Lott ran for the seat with Colmer's encouragement and endorsement—as a Republican. He was elected with 55% in what was the strongest Nixon district in the country that year. In 1974, Lott was the youngest member of the Judiciary Committee, loyally defending Richard Nixon in the impeachment hearings. In 1980, he was elected Republican whip, and he ran the Republican National Convention's platform committees in 1980 and 1984. He supported Jack Kemp for president in 1988, even as he was running for the Senate himself. Incidentally, Lott's decision to run for the Senate opened the way for Newt Gingrich's rise: Lott was succeeded as whip by Dick Cheney; when Cheney became Defense secretary in March 1989, Gingrich was elected whip 87–85.

Lott denies that he would have been speaker if he'd stayed in the House, modestly saying that the Republicans wouldn't have won a majority in 1994 because he wouldn't have highlighted broad philosophic issues as Gingrich did. Nevertheless, there is a discernible hard core of beliefs in Lott's career. His visceral dislike of taxes and big government made him a solid supporter of supply-side economics and deregulation; he abandoned his usual party loyalty to oppose the 1990 budget summit agreement. He believes in traditional moral values and he wants people to believe that America is good to the core, not riddled with rottenness. He argues for an assertive foreign policy and plenty of defense spending. He can be sharp in debate, aggressively partisan and combative. Gregarious and personable, he is on good terms with otherwise feuding conservatives, and has long cultivated his contemporaries among southern Democrats, looking for a vote here and a party switch there.

Lott certainly moved quickly to the leadership once he got into the Senate. He was asked by Republican Leader Bob Dole in 1993 to be the party's point man on Clinton Administration appointments, most of whom he ended up treating gently; he failed to ask tough questions of Ron Brown, and he decided not to raise what he considered unsubstantiated charges against Janet Reno. In budget hearings he came up with his own five-year plan for $216 billion in spending cuts and caps, though he declined to show it to OMB Director Leon Panetta; then he and Phil Gramm came out publicly with a list of $178 billion in spending cuts in March 1993. On the Senate Ethics Committee, he challenged Democrats when he felt they were keeping the charges against John McCain alive to keep the Keating Five scandal bipartisan. After the 1992 election, he declined to become top Republican on Ethics, and instead ran for conference secretary, the number four leadership post, and won, with 20 votes to 14 for Christopher Bond and five for Frank Murkowski.

After the 1994 election he sought to move up again, and challenged Whip Alan Simpson. Both are conservatives, but Simpson dissents on some issues (he is pro-choice on abortion). Simpson said of Lott, "It would be very difficult for Bob Dole to be free to do what he needs to do if he is looking over his shoulder and being second-guessed." Mary McGrory wrote, "Lott has a strain of border collie in his nature. He loves rounding up people." Bob Dole, comfortable that Simpson would back him up while he goes campaigning for president (as he did in 1988), and also that Simpson would not run for majority leader himself ("I don't have the patience for the job," he said), supported Simpson strongly, as did most Republican moderates. Lott had strong support from Dole's presidential and Senate rival Phil Gramm and from those who pointed to Lott's close relationship with Newt Gingrich in the House (although Lott was once Gingrich's senior and now gets much less national publicity). Lott won the post 27–26, and promised to be both an active vote-puller, with six regional whips and a whip of the day, but also to be loyal to Dole. Surely he will be careful not to cause umbrage, but he will also bring a hard partisan edge to the job, and some hurt feelings—from Simpson, from Dole and from Cochran, who let it be known he voted for Simpson. Although he has emphasized his loyalty to Dole, it didn't take long for Lott to cause intra-party friction when he criticized Appropriations Committee Mark Hatfield as "arrogant" in his early 1995 vote against the balanced-budget constitutional amendment, forcing a round of internal bloodletting. Still, Lott insists that he wants to respect the Senate's clubbish rules.

Lott gave up a safe seat and a chance at being speaker to run for the Senate in 1988, and he had something of a fight for it. Congressman Wayne Dowdy, who beat Secretary of State Dick Molpus in the primary 54%–42%, voiced populist themes and criticized Lott for having a chauffeur. Lott responded with an ad showing the employee in question, a black law enforcement professional named George Awkward, who explained he was guarding Lott because he was a member of the leadership: "I'm nobody's chauffeur, Mr. Dowdy." Lott outraised Dowdy and won a 61%–39% margin in the Jackson area, the Gulf Coast and other counties where turnout had increased 10% since 1980; in the rest of the state, Dowdy won only 51%–49%, giving Lott a 54%–46% win overall. In 1994, Lott faced former state Senator Ken Harper, who had support from labor unions and trial lawyers. Despite Senate Democrats' early hopes for a close race, Lott had far more money, a very high job rating and very many more votes.

Presidential politics. Mississippi was George Bush's number one state in 1992, though he won fractionally less than 50% of the vote, and Ross Perot's worst; just across the river from Bill Clinton's Arkansas, it gave Bush a larger percentage of the vote than did the other five southern states he carried. On balance, it must be regarded as a presidentially Republican state, and not because of race; it is other issues—defense, crime, cultural attitudes, taxes—on which majorities here shunned Walter Mondale, Michael Dukakis and Bill Clinton by decisive margins.

Other evidence of Mississippi's Republican strength is that it is the home of Republican National Committee Chairman Haley Barbour. Barbour got his start in Yazoo County and ran Mississippi for Richard Nixon in 1968. He became a leading Republican operative in the 1970s, ran unsuccessfully against Senator John Stennis in 1982 and was Reagan White House political director in 1985 and 1986. In 1993 he built on his ties to local politicians across the country to be elected chairman. In 1994, his gift for pungent sound bites made him an effective spokesman in public, while in private he worked with elected leaders to present a united front and with fundraisers to raise and distribute crucial funds. The Republican success in winning control of both Senate and House in 1994 owes much to him.

Congressional districting. In 1984, Mississippi was the first state to get a redistricting plan dictated by the dominant interpretation of the 1982 Voting Rights Amendments. The result was the black-majority 2d District, which duly elected Mike Espy in 1986; he went on to become Bill Clinton's Agriculture Secretary from 1993–94. Ironically, Espy wanted to hold down the black percentage in the 2d in the 1991 plan, because he was winning white votes and he wanted more black influence in other districts. But civil rights organization apparatchiks said no. The result is that the other four districts vote heavily Republican in national politics, and though three of them continue to elect conservative Democratic congressmen, all would probably elect Republicans if those incumbents were not on the ballot; indeed, that happened in the 1st District in 1994 when Jamie Whitten retired after the longest House career in history.

The People: Est. Pop. 1994: 2,689,000; Pop. 1990: 2,573,216, up 3.6% 1990–1994. 1.0% of U.S. total, 31st largest; 53% rural. Median age: 31.2 years. 12.5% 65 years and over. 63.5% White, 35.6% Black. Households: 54.7% married couple families; 27% married couple fams. w. children; 37% college educ.; median household income: $20,136; per capita income: $9,648; 71.5% owner occupied housing; median house value: $45,600; median monthly rent: $215. 8.1% Unemployment. 1994 Voting age pop.: 1,905,000. 1994 Turnout: 607,217; 32% of VAP. Registered voters (1994): 1,625,630; no party registration.

Political Lineup: Governor, Kirk Fordice (R); Lt. Gov., Eddie Briggs (R); Secy. of State, Dick Molpus (D); Atty. Gen., Mike Moore (D); Treasurer, Marshall Bennett (D); Auditor, Steven A. Patterson (D). State Senate, 52 (37 D and 15 R); State House of Representatives, 122 (89 D, 31 R, and 2 I). Senators, Thad Cochran (R) and Trent Lott (R). Representatives, 5 (1 R and 4 D)

1992 Presidential Vote

Bush (R) 487,793 (50%)
Clinton (D) 400,268 (41%)
Perot (I) 105,045 (9%)

1988 Presidential Vote

Bush (R) 557,921 (60%)
Dukakis (D) 363,921 (39%)

1992 Democratic Presidential Primary

Clinton 139,893 (73%)
Brown 18,396 (10%)
Tsongas 15,538 (8%)
Uncommitted 11,796 (6%)

1992 Republican Presidential Primary

Bush 111,794 (72%)
Buchanan 25,891 (17%)
Duke 16,426 (11%)

GOVERNOR

Gov. Kirk Fordice (R)

Elected 1991, term expires Jan. 1996; b. Feb. 10, 1934, Memphis, TN; home, Vicksburg; Purdue U., B.S. 1956, M.S. 1957; Methodist; married (Pat).

Career: Army, 1957–59, Army Reserves, 1959–77; Engineer, Exxon Corp., 1956, 1959–62; Exec., Fordice Construction Co., 1962–92; Pres., Assoc. General Contractors of Amer., 1989–91.

Office: State Capitol, P.O. Box 139, Jackson 39205, 601-359-3100; Fax: 601-359-3022.

Election Results

1991 gen.	Kirk Fordice (R)	361,500	(51%)
	Ray Mabus (D)	338,459	(48%)
	Other	11,253	(2%)
1991 runoff	Kirk Fordice (R)	31,753	(61%)
	Pete Johnson (R)	20,622	(39%)
1991 prim.	Kirk Fordice (R)	28,411	(45%)
	Pete Johnson (R)	27,561	(43%)
	Bobby Clanton (R)	7,589	(12%)
1987 gen.	Ray Mabus (D)	385,689	(61%)
	Jack Reed (R)	336,006	(39%)

SENATORS

Sen. Thad Cochran (R)

Elected 1978, seat up 1996; b. Dec. 7, 1937, Pontotoc; home, Jackson; U. of MS, B.A. 1959, J.D. 1965, Rotary Fellow, Trinity Col., Ireland, 1963–64; Baptist; married (Rose).

Career: Navy, 1959–61; Practicing atty., 1965–72; U.S. House of Reps., 1972–78.

DC Office: 326 RSOB 20510, 202-224-5054.

State Offices: 188 E. Capitol St., #164, Jackson 39201, 601-965-4459; and 911 Jackson St., #200, Oxford 38655, 601-236-1018.

Committees: *Republican Conference Chairman. Agriculture, Nutrition & Forestry* (4th of 10 R): Marketing, Inspection and Product Promotion; Production and Price Competitiveness (Chmn). *Appropriations* (3rd of 15 R): Agriculture, Rural Development and Related Agencies (Chmn.); Defense; Energy and Water Development; Interior; Labor, Health and Human Services, Education. *Governmental Affairs* (5th of 8 R): Oversight of Government Management and the District of Columbia; Investigations; Post Office and Civil Service. *Rules & Administration* (7th of 9 R).

Group Ratings

	ADA	ACLU	COPE	CFA	LCV	CON	NSI	COC	ACU	NTLC	CHC
1994	10	16	13	25	0	49	100	90	92	76	93
1993	0	—	9	30	6	57	—	91	84	—	—

National Journal Ratings

	1993 LIB — 1993 CONS		1994 LIB — 1994 CONS	
Economic	30% —	67%	33% —	65%
Social	12% —	86%	21% —	75%
Foreign	24% —	71%	14% —	85%

Key Votes of the 103d Congress

1. Clinton Deficit Plan	N	3. Brady Handgun Purchase	N	5. Lmt. UN Cmnd. of Forces	Y
2. NAFTA	Y	4. Strike Race/Death Pnlty.	Y	6. Cut Missile Funds	N

Key Votes of the 104th Congress

1. Congressional Compliance	Y	3. Balanced Budget Amndt.	Y	5. Product Liability Reform	Y
2. Bar Unfunded Mandates	Y	4. Pass Line Item Veto	Y	6. FY 96 Budget	Y

Election Results

1990 general	Thad Cochran (R)................. unopposed		($691,865)
1990 primary	Thad Cochran (R)................. unopposed		
1984 general	Thad Cochran (R)...................	580,314	(61%)	($2,870,894)
	William Winter (D)	371,926	(39%)	($738,739)

Sen. Trent Lott (R)

Elected 1988, seat up 2000; b. Oct. 9, 1941, Grenada; home, Pascagoula; U. of MS, B.A. 1963, J.D. 1967; Baptist; married (Tricia).

Career: Practicing atty., 1967–68; A.A., U.S. Rep. William Colmer, 1968–72; U.S. House of Reps., 1972–1988.

DC Office: 487 RSOB 20510, 202-224-6253; Fax: 202-224-2262.

State Offices: 1 Gov. Plaza, #428, Gulfport 39501, 601-863-1988; 245 E. Capitol St., #226, Jackson 39201, 601-965-4644; 3100 S. Pascagoula St., Pascagoula 39567, 601-762-5400; P.O. Box 1474, Oxford 38655, 601-234-3774; and 200 E. Washington St., #45, Greenwood 38930, 601-453-5681.

Committees: *Majority Whip. Armed Services* (5th of 11 R): Personnel; Seapower; Strategic Forces (Chmn). *Budget* (6th of 12 R). *Commerce, Science & Transportation* (7th of 10 R): Aviation; Communications; Science, Technology and Space; Surface Transportation and Merchant Marine (Chmn).

Group Ratings

	ADA	ACLU	COPE	CFA	LCV	CON	NSI	COC	ACU	NTLC	CHC
1994	5	16	0	25	0	79	100	90	100	83	100
1993	5	—	9	0	6	57	—	100	92	—	—

National Journal Ratings

	1993 LIB — 1993 CONS			1994 LIB — 1994 CONS	
Economic	13%	—	81%	23%	—	76%
Social	10%	—	88%	0%	—	85%
Foreign	0%	—	92%	6%	—	86%

Key Votes of the 103d Congress

1. Clinton Deficit Plan	N	3. Brady Handgun Purchase	N	5. Lmt. UN Cmnd. of Forces	Y
2. NAFTA	Y	4. Strike Race/Death Pnlty.	Y	6. Cut Missile Funds	N

Key Votes of the 104th Congress

1. Congressional Compliance	Y	3. Balanced Budget Amndt.	Y	5. Product Liability Reform	Y
2. Bar Unfunded Mandates	Y	4. Pass Line Item Veto	Y	6. FY 96 Budget	Y

Election Results

1994 general	Trent Lott (R).........................	418,333	(69%)	($2,516,189)
	Ken Harper (D)	189,752	(31%)	($345,379)
1994 primary	Trent Lott (R).........................	72,543	(95%)	
	Others	3,476	(5%)	
1988 general	Trent Lott (R).........................	510,380	(54%)	($3,405,242)
	Wayne Dowdy (D)	436,339	(46%)	($2,355,957)

FIRST DISTRICT

The university town of Oxford, the center of William Faulkner's fictional universe, sits on a divide between the hill country of Mississippi and the flat farmlands of the Mississippi Delta. The mostly white hill counties run up to where the Tennessee River nicks the northeast corner of Tishomingo County. The Tennessee Valley Authority brought electricity here, the Tennessee-Tombigbee Waterway provided construction jobs for years and a new shipping canal when it was completed in 1985. A big Yellow Creek plant producing advanced solid rocket motors for the Space Shuttle seemed likely to guarantee local prosperity until it was canceled in 1994. The focus, though, is different in the hill-country metropolis, Tupelo, which is a stronghold of private enterprise and traditional values. It excels at corporate recruitment, attracting new jobs without giving away the store—"probably the best small city in the South" at it, says one corporate recruiter—and is a major furniture manufacturer. Also, it is the home of the Reverend Donald Wildmon, who organizes boycotts of products advertised on television shows that he thinks have excessive sex or violence. West of Oxford is Mississippi's Delta, the swampy land pioneered by large planters around the turn of the century, with large black work forces little removed—in the conditions of their daily lives or long-term economic chances—from slavery. Oxford, home of Ole Miss, is also the home today of the Center for the Study of Southern Culture, and until recently, the home of mega-hit author John Grisham.

The 1st Congressional District of Mississippi includes most of the hill country and a little bit of the Delta plus the Memphis suburban fringe that has run over the Mississippi line. This was the district that elected the longest-ever serving member of the House, Jamie Whitten, first elected in November 1941, his last term ending in January 1995: 53 years and two months, the longest House service in history. Whitten served as chairman of the Agriculture Appropriations Subcommittee from 1949 to 1953 and then from 1955 until 1993, 42 years in which he knew the USDA better and had far more influence than most Agriculture secretaries. Whitten started off as a segregationist and for years voted conservative. Then when the Democratic Caucus started voting for committee chairmen, he voted more liberal, especially on economic issues. So he held the Appropriations chair which would have been his by seniority by winning elections, starting with 157–88 in 1978 to 218–34 in 1990. In February 1992, a month after he set the record for longest service in the House, Whitten suffered a stroke and was never able to floor-manage a bill again in his folksy, marbles-in-the-mouth manner. He was reelected in November 1992, but with just 59% of the vote; Kentucky's William Natcher was voted Appropriations chairman a month later (Natcher died in March 1994, so Whitten outlived him) and lost his Agriculture Subcommittee chair as well without a formal vote. Whitten announced his retirement in April 1994.

Even before that, Democratic House Speaker Tim Ford of Tupelo announced he was running. In decades past, a prominent conservative Democrat would be the obvious favorite, but there were several serious candidates in both parties; indeed, six Republicans to three Democrats. In the first primary, Ford trailed with 34% to 40% for state Representative Bill Wheeler, who walked across the district and had support from blacks, labor and teachers. In the runoff, Wheeler attacked Ford for raising money for a "slush fund" for the Speaker's office, and with better organization carried everything but the Tupelo area and won with 56%. Five Republicans were serious competitors in the primary, carrying their local bases; state Senator Roger Wicker led with 27% to 19% for Grant Fox, former aide to Senator Thad Cochran. In the runoff, Wicker campaigned as a conservative, but Fox, just 27, hit him hard for voting to override Governor Kirk Fordice's sales tax increase veto. Wicker won by just 53%–47%. Interestingly, Democratic turnout was not much higher than Republican in the primary (33,766 versus 26,607) or the runoff (29,871 versus 22,268).

In the general, Wicker said, "If you want more Bill Clinton, maybe you should vote for my opponent," while Wheeler campaigned as the candidate of working people against a "country club Republican" and insisted he too was against abortion and gun control. The result wasn't even close: a district held for 53 years by a Democratic leader voted 63% for the Republican. "A graying 43-year-old who wears Nikes and pressed khakis and drives a Chevrolet mini-van," *CongressDaily* wrote, "Wicker seems the model of New South conservatism." He has House experience, as a page in 1967 and an aide to Senator Trent Lott on the House Rules Committee for two years. He was student body president at Ole Miss and his father was a state senator and judge. Wicker practiced law in Tupelo and was elected to the legislature in 1987, as one of its few Republicans; there he sponsored a law requiring parental consent and a 24-hour waiting period for abortions. In the House he seems likely to be a strong supporter of Speaker Newt Gingrich and the Contract With America; and he showed his Capitol Hill savvy by gaining Whitten's old seat on the Appropriations Committee, though on the other side of the party aisle. He also displayed his political prowess by winning the chairmanship of the 73-member Republican freshman class—a position with no formal responsibilities but that gives Wicker an opportunity to step out from the crowd both within the House and in the national spotlight.

The People: Pop. 1990: 515,196; 67% rural; 13% age 65+; 77% White; 23% Black. Voting age pop.: 373,976; 20% Black. Households: 61% married couple families; 30% married couple fams. w. children; 30% college educ.; median household income: $20,867; per capita income: $9,639; median gross rent: $277; median house value: $43,700.

1992 Presidential Vote

Bush (R)	101,252	(50%)
Clinton (D)	84,765	(42%)
Perot (I)	17,984	(9%)

1988 Presidential Vote

Bush (R)	108,068	(60%)
Dukakis (D)	71,167	(40%)

Rep. Roger F. Wicker (R)

Elected 1994; b. July 5, 1951, Pontotoc; home, Tupelo; U. of MS, B.A. 1973, J.D. 1975; Baptist; married (Gayle).

Career: Air Force, 1976–80; Air Force Reserves, 1980–present; Staff, U.S. House Rules Cmte., 1980–82; Practicing atty., 1982–94; Lee Cnty. Public Defender, 1984–87; Tupelo City Judge Pro-Tem, 1986–87; MS Senate, 1988–94.

DC Office: 206 CHOB 20515, 202-225-4306; Fax: 202-225-3549.

District Offices: 500 W. Main St., #210, Tupelo 38802, 601-844-5437; and 8625 Hwy. 51-N, Southaven 38671, 601-342-3942.

Committees: *Appropriations* (28th of 32 R): Labor, Health and Human Services, and Education; Legislative; Military Construction.

Group Ratings and 103rd Congress Votes: Newly Elected

Key Votes of the 104th Congress

1. Congressional Compliance Y	6. Reform Crime Grant Y	11. Loser Pays Court Reform Y
2. Balanced Budget Amndmt. Y	7. National Security Act Y	12. Product Liability Reform Y
3. Bar Unfunded Mandates Y	8. Moratorium on Regs. Y	13. Welfare Reform Y
4. Pass Line Item Veto Y	9. Risk Assessment on Regs. Y	14. Term Limits Amndmt. N
5. Relax Exclusionary Rule Y	10. Expnd. Priv. Prop. Rights Y	15. Tax Cuts Y

Election Results

1994 general	Roger F. Wicker (R)	80,553	(63%)	($729,704)
	William R. Wheeler Jr. (D)	47,192	(37%)	($789,523)
1994 runoff	Roger F. Wicker (R)	11,905	(53%)	
	Grant Fox (R)	10,527	(47%)	
1994 primary	Roger F. Wicker (R)	7,156	(27%)	
	Grant Fox (R)	5,208	(19%)	
	Bob Whitwell (R)	4,606	(17%)	
	Clyde E. Whitaker (R)	4,602	(17%)	
	Larry Cobb (R)	4,162	(15%)	
	Bill Bowlin (R)	1,147	(4%)	
1992 general	Jamie L. Whitten (D)	121,664	(59%)	($267,223)
	Clyde E. Whitaker (R)	82,952	(41%)	($229,004)

SECOND DISTRICT

"The Mississippi Delta," wrote Delta native David Cohn, "begins in the lobby of the Peabody Hotel in Memphis and ends on Catfish Row in Vicksburg." For centuries, the flooding Mississippi and Yazoo Rivers left their sediments here, and "by slow accretion, without foundation of rock or shale, it laid down this land—pure soil endlessly dark, deep and sweet." Ironically, what may well be America's richest agricultural land has been home for more than a century of many of its poorest people. The Delta, criss-crossed by rivers and famously disease-ridden, wasn't much settled until after the Civil War; the tradition here is not of paternal masters and gracious mansions, but of sharp, profit-seeking operators who used 19th Century technology to drain the land, line the river with levees and build railroads on elevated tracks. Black sharecroppers and field hands worked here in conditions almost of bondage. From this episode of industrial farming came both great misery and great art: Clarksdale in Coahoma County was the home of W.C. Handy and Muddy Waters, the real birthplace of blues music; Greenville on the Mississippi has produced writers of the caliber of Walker Percy and Shelby Foote. Now Vicksburg's antebellum mansions, battlefield monuments and riverboat gambling bring in 1.5 million tourists annually from around the country.

Then 20th Century technology changed life in the Delta once again. The mechanical cotton-picking machine, invented in 1944, came along just as northern defense plants were seeking low-wage workers; the great exodus to Chicago and Memphis began, and the Delta's population has been declining ever since. Income levels remain very low, poverty is over 50% in some areas and infant mortality is at Third World levels; the crime and drugs of urban Chicago have been brought back by Delta migrants returning home. There are signs of hope: soybeans are now the big dollar crop here, although there is more acreage still in cotton, and catfish farms have become a major enterprise—the Delta produces 75% of the nation's catfish. Riverboat gambling was approved in 1992 in Tunica County, by some measures the nation's poorest county; in 1993 1.7 million people came in and spent $140 million in the casinos, which now have more square footage than Atlantic City's. There is still a gulf between the races, culturally and economically, but also positive signs: by 1990 a former state NAACP head was elected by a margin of 2–1 the mayor of Vicksburg, which is about half black; when Ku Klux Klansmen demonstrated in Greenwood and Clarksdale in 1994, they were promptly arrested and attracted no support. Still, the Delta has been unable to develop the self-propelling market economy that has brought growth to most of the nation.

The 2d Congressional District of Mississippi occupies the entire Mississippi Delta region, indeed the whole riverfront from Tunica almost to Natchez, plus black neighborhoods of Jackson. It is Mississippi's one black-majority district, first created as such in 1984, with modest changes in boundaries for 1992. Thirty years ago, when blacks were not allowed to vote in Mississippi, politics here was the politics of the big plantation owners, symbolized by James Eastland, U.S. senator from 1941 to 1979, Judiciary chairman from 1955 to 1979, an unyielding segregationist and conservative. Even after blacks got the vote, black registration was low and habits of deference in some places prevailed; voting was very racially polarized. In 1986, the district elected its first black congressman since Reconstruction, Mike Espy, whose grandfather and father built a chain of funeral homes and were among the biggest landowners in the state. Espy won narrowly then, with 50.1% in the Democratic primary and 52% in the general. He worked on farm issues, opposed gun control and appeared in National Rifle Association ads, and won reelection in succeeding years with 65%, 84% and 76%. He endorsed Bill Clinton early in the 1992 cycle and lobbied hard to become secretary of Agriculture.

That appointment changed both Espy's career and the politics of the 2d District. The new congressman is Bennie Thompson, a Jackson area politician who served 13 years on the Hinds County Board of Supervisors. In the special election to succeed Espy, Thompson won 28% in the March 1993 all-party first primary, to 20% for Henry Espy, the Agriculture secretary's older brother and mayor of Clarksdale in the northern Delta. The frontrunner with 34% was Republican Hayes Dent, a 31-year-old aide to Governor Kirk Fordice. In the April runoff, voting was mostly along racial lines, and Thompson won 55%–45%. Most of his margin came from Jackson and Hinds County; elsewhere he led only 51%–49%. Thompson, unlike Espy, made no particular attempt to win white votes and had a solidly liberal voting record, making as few concessions across the racial divide as had Eastland and his ilk in their day.

In 1994 there was another spirited race here—and some lament, for in October Espy announced he was resigning from the Cabinet amidst controversy over acceptance of Super Bowl tickets and transportation from Tyson Foods. Thompson, as a freshman member of the Agriculture Committee, played no role on major legislation, but did get the Jackson and Ruleville Post Offices named for civil rights pioneers Medgar Evers and Fannie Lou Hamer, and got an exemption from EPA for pesticide to kill the beet armyworm threatening cotton crops. He had spirited reelection competition from Bill Jordan, a black lawyer for Ingalls Shipbuilding for 17 years; Jordan said he agreed with Espy, who did not want to maximize the black percentage in the 2d. Thompson had 54% of the vote, down from 1993, but a Taxpayers' Party candidate got

7% and Jordan had only 39%. Whether Thompson will have such active competition again is unclear.

The People: Pop. 1990: 514,469; 55% rural; 13% age 65+; 36% White; 63% Black. Voting age pop.: 345,151; 58% Black. Households: 47% married couple families; 23% married couple fams. w. children; 33% college educ.; median household income: $15,530; per capita income: $7,771; median gross rent: $267; median house value: $39,700.

1992 Presidential Vote			1988 Presidential Vote		
Clinton (D)	105,185	(58%)	Dukakis (D)	101,337	(55%)
Bush (R)	66,905	(37%)	Bush (R)	81,598	(45%)
Perot (I)	9,879	(5%)			

Rep. Bennie G. Thompson (D)

Elected Apr., 1993; b. Jan. 28, 1948, Bolton; home, Bolton; Tougaloo Col., B.A. 1968, Jackson St. U., M.S. 1972; Methodist; married (London).

Career: Bolton Bd. of Aldermen, 1969–73; Bolton Mayor, 1973–79; Hinds Cnty. Supervisor, 1980–93.

DC Office: 1408 LHOB 20515, 202-225-5876; Fax: 202-225-5898.

District Offices: 137 Madison St., Bolton 39041, 601-859-5555.

Committees: *Agriculture* (19th of 22 D): Department Operations, Nutrition and Foreign Agriculture; General Farm Commodities. *Small Business* (14th of 19 D): Government Programs.

Group Ratings

	ADA	ACLU	COPE	CFA	LCV	CON	NSI	COC	ACU	NTLC	CHC
1994	80	84	88	80	88	1	22	36	20	5	0
1993	94	—	100	86	64	*	—	20	6	—	—

National Journal Ratings

	1993 LIB — 1993 CONS		1994 LIB — 1994 CONS	
Economic	88% —	0%	83% —	0%
Social	87% —	0%	89% —	11%
Foreign	87% —	7%	57% —	37%

Key Votes of the 103d Congress

1. Clinton Deficit Plan	Y	3. Brady Handgun Purchase	Y	5. Lmt. UN Cmnd. of Forces	N
2. NAFTA	N	4. Strike Race/Death Pnlty.	N	6. Cut Missile Funds	Y

Key Votes of the 104th Congress

1. Congressional Compliance	Y	6. Reform Crime Grant	N	11. Loser Pays Court Reform	N
2. Balanced Budget Amndmt.	N	7. National Security Act	N	12. Product Liability Reform	N
3. Bar Unfunded Mandates	N	8. Moratorium on Regs.	N	13. Welfare Reform	N
4. Pass Line Item Veto	N	9. Risk Assessment on Regs.	N	14. Term Limits Amndmt.	N
5. Relax Exclusionary Rule	N	10. Expnd. Priv. Prop. Rights	N	15. Tax Cuts	N

Election Results

1994 general	Bennie G. Thompson (D)	68,014	(54%)	($396,502)
	Bill Jordan (R)	49,270	(39%)	($279,234)
	Vince Thornton (TXP)	9,408	(7%)	
1994 primary	Bennie G. Thompson (D)	unopposed		
1993 runoff	Bennie G. Thompson (D)	72,561	(55%)	($498,397)
	Hayes Dent (R).	58,995	(45%)	($465,485)
1993 special	Hayes Dent (R).	34,766	(34%)	
	Bennie G. Thompson (D)	29,041	(28%)	
	Henry Espy (D).	20,800	(20%)	
	Unita Blackwell (D)	7,412	(7%)	
	David M. Halbrook (D)	6,027	(6%)	
	Others	3,915	(4%)	
1992 general	Mike Espy (D)	133,361	(76%)	($270,710)
	Dorothy (Dot) Benford (R).	41,248	(24%)	

THIRD DISTRICT

Mississippi, old and new: the old Mississippi is the Neshoba County fair, held every August since 1892 in the town of Philadelphia. This is traditionally the place where Mississippi politicians announce their candidacies, with the crowds watching to take their measure. When Ronald Reagan came here in 1980 and Michael Dukakis in 1988, neither mentioned what Philadelphia and Neshoba County are best known for in history, nor is there any memorial except engraved stones at two black churches: it was here in the "Freedom Summer" of 1964 that three civil rights workers, two white and one black, were murdered for the crime of urging black American citizens to register and vote. The new Mississippi is some 80 miles away, in Rankin County just east of Jackson, where subdivisions and shopping centers are sprouting up on lands which only a few years ago seemed out in the country.

The 3d Congressional District of Mississippi includes Rankin County and the Madison County suburbs of Jackson and Neshoba County. It stretches north to Starkville, home of Mississippi State University, and south to Laurel, an hour's drive from the Gulf Coast. In the middle is Meridian, a small city that may go down in history as the site of firings of White House Chiefs of Staff: on the last two presidential trips here, President Nixon informed Bob Haldeman that he was out as Chief of Staff in April 1973 and in December 1991 John Sununu penned his letter of resignation to President Bush. The political tradition here is southern Democratic, but the area's recent preference has been Republican: Mississippi, old and new.

A shining example of the conservative Democratic heritage is 3d District Congressman Sonny Montgomery, first elected in 1966, a veteran of the Army in World War II and a retired National Guard general who concentrates heavily on veterans' and military issues. Montgomery believes strongly in an assertive foreign policy, the all-volunteer military, a large reserve military force and generous veterans' benefits. From his different committee perches, he has made these policies work far better than many thought possible. Chairman of the Veterans' Affairs Committee from 1981 to 1995, he sponsored the 1985 Montgomery G.I. education bill, allowing servicemen to put aside $100 a month of their first 12 months pay and receive $300 a month in education aid for 36 months after leaving the service. As intended, this helped military recruitment and improved the skills and earnings of veterans. Its effect was seen in the high quality and performance of the military in the Gulf war—a vast improvement from a dozen years before. And it is likely to upgrade the civilian work force well into the 21st Century.

Montgomery's ability to shape legislation has been deep, because traditionally amendments are not allowed in votes on veterans' bills, and he has never lost a bill on the floor. But he has been challenged elsewhere. For years he resisted compensation for Vietnam veterans exposed to Agent Orange pesticide, arguing that scientific evidence of ill effects was lacking. But younger members persisted and he gave in. More recently, he strongly supported compensating Gulf war veterans for "Gulf war syndrome," though scientific evidence for it was even more vague; he prevailed over the Senate on this in October 1994. Montgomery passed a benefits package for Gulf war veterans, extended education benefits, broadened eligibility for VA home loans, expanded service to homeless veterans and improved healthcare programs for women veterans. Veterans' hospitals, poorly equipped and under-used, remain a troubling topic: Montgomery got the House to vote against a Clinton Administration move to cut their work force by 25,000. In between he was also challenged for the chairmanship by liberal, Vietnam-era veteran Lane Evans, who promised more activism; in December 1992 Montgomery won the Democratic Caucus vote by only 127–123.

On National Security, Montgomery has concentrated on strengthening the Reserves and National Guard. In the Vietnam era, the Reserves got much of their power from members of Congress in their ranks, and were never called up for service in the war; military leaders believed they were not anywhere near ready to serve. Not so today: Montgomery was determined that the U.S. have a truly ready reserve, and has made sure that units have necessary training and resources. He urged they be called for service in the Gulf, and they were; he worked hard to make sure they would not lose or be penalized in their jobs, and that their families would not lose medical insurance and other benefits. There are a couple of ironies here: this generally economically conservative Democrat has jurisdiction over the nation's major example of socialized medicine, the VA hospitals; and this representative from a district where history is stained with the murder of civil rights workers has played a major role in creating the most racially integrated institution in American society, the military.

Montgomery was not challenged for the chairmanship again in 1995, because Democrats lost their majority; Evans said he was considering running for the Senate and did not try to wrest away the ranking minority post. Nor has Montgomery ever challenged Ron Dellums, who jumped ahead of him on National Security; clearly a caucus vote would go against him. Montgomery has long been considered one of the Democrats most likely to switch parties; his voting record has been quite conservative and he has not hid his rapport with Republican presidents from Richard Nixon to George Bush. But he did not switch after the 1994 election and would not want to do so without getting the Veterans chairmanship, which presumably was not on offer. Now he may find it more congenial to work with the new Chairman Bob Stump, who is of the same generation and general views, than to have a Democratic majority with Lane Evans nipping at his heels.

Montgomery first won this seat in 1966 and has been reelected easily ever since; he won 68% of the vote in 1994. But this was his lowest percentage since he first won, and this district would almost surely go Republican were he not the Democratic candidate, a possibility in the not-so-distant future.

The People: Pop. 1990: 515,225; 61% rural; 12% age 65+; 67% White; 31% Black; 1% Amer. Indian. Voting age pop.: 370,288; 28% Black. Households: 57% married couple families; 28% married couple fams. w. children; 39% college educ.; median household income: $21,625; per capita income: $10,303; median gross rent: $324; median house value: $46,800.

1992 Presidential Vote			1988 Presidential Vote		
Bush (R)	116,973	(58%)	Bush (R)	122,510	(67%)
Clinton (D)	67,411	(34%)	Dukakis (D)	60,939	(33%)
Perot (I)	16,049	(8%)			

Rep. G. V. (Sonny) Montgomery (D)

Elected 1966; b. Aug. 5, 1920, Meridian; home, Meridian; MS St. U., B.S. 1943; Episcopalian; single.

Career: Army, 1943–46 (WWII), 1951–52, Army Natl. Guard, 1946–50, 1953–81; Owner, Montgomery Insurance Agency; MS Senate, 1956–66.

DC Office: 2184 RHOB 20515, 202-225-5031; Fax: 202-225-3375.

District Offices: Fed. Bldg., Meridian 39301, 601-693-6681; 110-D Airport Rd., Pearl 39208, 601-932-2410; and Golden Triangle Airport, Columbus 39701, 601-327-2766.

Committees: *National Security* (2nd of 25 D): Military Installations and Facilities; Military Personnel. *Veterans' Affairs* (RMM of 15 D): Compensation, Pension, Insurance and Memorial Affairs.

Group Ratings

	ADA	ACLU	COPE	CFA	LCV	CON	NSI	COC	ACU	NTLC	CHC
1994	35	17	50	50	38	48	100	58	57	36	71
1993	30	—	42	70	90	0	—	55	50	—	—

National Journal Ratings

	1993 LIB — 1993 CONS		1994 LIB — 1994 CONS	
Economic	45% —	55%	50% —	46%
Social	40% —	60%	36% —	62%
Foreign	47% —	50%	57% —	37%

Key Votes of the 103d Congress

1. Clinton Deficit Plan	N	3. Brady Handgun Purchase	N	5. Lmt. UN Cmnd. of Forces	N
2. NAFTA	Y	4. Strike Race/Death Pnlty.	Y	6. Cut Missile Funds	N

Key Votes of the 104th Congress

1. Congressional Compliance	Y	6. Reform Crime Grant	Y	11. Loser Pays Court Reform	Y
2. Balanced Budget Amndmt.	Y	7. National Security Act	N	12. Product Liability Reform	Y
3. Bar Unfunded Mandates	Y	8. Moratorium on Regs.	Y	13. Welfare Reform	Y
4. Pass Line Item Veto	Y	9. Risk Assessment on Regs.	Y	14. Term Limits Amndmt.	N
5. Relax Exclusionary Rule	Y	10. Expnd. Priv. Prop. Rights	Y	15. Tax Cuts	Y

Election Results

1994 general	G. V. (Sonny) Montgomery (D)	83,163	(68%)	($571,635)
	Dutch Dabbs (R)	39,826	(32%)	($106,706)
1994 primary	G. V. (Sonny) Montgomery (D)	unopposed		
1992 general	G. V. (Sonny) Montgomery (D)	162,864	(81%)	($174,165)
	Michael E. Williams (R)	37,710	(19%)	

FOURTH DISTRICT

A few decades ago, Jackson was a small town centered on a grand Beaux Arts 1901 state Capitol. Today, Jackson is clearly the metropolis of Mississippi, the pivot point between the Delta and the hills, the rivers flowing sluggishly to New Orleans and the Gulf of Mexico and the highways running north to Memphis and Chicago. Like Mississippi generally, it is racially divided, with a black, not-so-affluent south side and a white affluent north side; in its new subdivisions of pleasant, large colonial houses under huge, overhanging trees, you can get a sense of what growth has meant to Jackson—especially when you consider that at least some of the people in these neighborhoods came from humble rural Mississippi beginnings. This newer Mississippi contrasts with Natchez, where the finest collection of antebellum mansions sit on the bluffs overlooking the Mississippi River. Natchez had white millionaires and half the state's free blacks before the Civil War; it was content enough to oppose secession, and was spared major damage in the war because it was of no military importance. Both Jackson and Natchez went through an ugly decade during the civil rights revolution: Mississippi blacks were murdered for registering to vote or for seeking higher-paying jobs; today, the cities are more open, with more social contact between the races than in most northern metropolitan areas, but there is still yearning for economic growth and high-skill jobs.

The 4th Congressional District includes most of Jackson (excluding some black areas, which are in the black-majority 2d) and all of Natchez; it extends east to Laurel and south to the Louisiana line. This is an area that has trended Republican in national and state-wide elections, as newly affluent white Mississippians vote for a party they associate with economic growth and assertive foreign policy, while blacks remain pretty solidly Democratic. But in local contests, Democrats still win many races.

One example is 4th District Congressman Mike Parker, a conservative Democrat from Brookhaven, where he owned a funeral home, a business that often provides a base for a political career, since everyone in town goes through your doors sooner or later. Parker entered the wide open race here when incumbent Wayne Dowdy ran for the Senate in 1988; Parker ran second in the Democratic primary with 19%, then more than doubled his votes and won the runoff 61%–39%. In the general Parker refused to endorse presidential nominee Michael Dukakis and criticized Dukakis's mandatory health insurance proposal; he vastly outspent his opponent and won 55%–45%.

Parker has had one of the most conservative voting records among House Democrats, sometimes more so than Sonny Montgomery. He says his focus has been "on economic development efforts within my district along with an unequalled devotion to constituent casework rather than legislative initiatives." In 1994, Parker had competition in the primary from state Treasurer Marshall Bennett, who had support from labor unions and teachers' groups, and who attacked him for supporting NAFTA and opposing family leave and Head Start funding. Apparently Bennett hoped for a large black turnout. But Parker was well-funded and ran ads that showed his mother at a clothesline saying to him, "I'd rather see you lose a clean race than win a dirty one." He won 58%–35%. He won the general even more easily, 68%–32%. Parker has supported parts of the Contract With America and has often been mentioned as a possible party-switcher, but he didn't switch in 1994 and his victories suggest he has no political need to do so to assure reelection.

The People: Pop. 1990: 513,715; 47% rural; 13% age 65+; 59% White; 41% Black. Voting age pop.: 367,750; 36% Black. Households: 54% married couple families; 26% married couple fams. w. children; 42% college educ.; median household income: $20,234; per capita income: $10,411; median gross rent: $344; median house value: $47,500.

1992 Presidential Vote

Bush (R) 102,666   (50%)
Clinton (D) 84,089   (41%)
Perot (I) 16,758   (8%)

1988 Presidential Vote

Bush (R) 124,343   (61%)
Dukakis (D) 79,404   (39%)

Rep. Mike Parker (D)

Elected 1988; b. Oct. 31, 1949, Laurel; home, Brookhaven; William Carey Col., B.A. 1970; Presbyterian; married (Rosemary).

Career: Funeral home owner, 1971–88.

DC Office: 2445 RHOB 20515, 202-225-5865; Fax: 202-225-5886.

District Offices: 245 E. Capitol, #222, Jackson 39201, 601-352-1355; 230 S. Whitworth St., Brookhaven 39601, 601-835-0706; 118 N. Pearl St., #111, Natchez 39120, 601-446-7250; Chancery Ct. Annex, Columbia 39429, 601-731-1622; 728½ Sawmill Rd., Laurel 39440, 601-425-4999; and 176 W. Court St., Mendenhall 39114, 601-847-0873.

Committees: *Budget* (4th of 18 D). *Transportation & Infrastructure* (12th of 27 D): Surface Transportation; Water Resources and Environment.

Group Ratings

	ADA	ACLU	COPE	CFA	LCV	CON	NSI	COC	ACU	NTLC	CHC
1994	20	26	50	30	29	71	90	83	67	64	79
1993	20	—	33	70	50	32	—	73	67	—	—

National Journal Ratings

	1993 LIB — 1993 CONS	1994 LIB — 1994 CONS
Economic	42% — 58%	47% — 51%
Social	31% — 68%	27% — 73%
Foreign	44% — 55%	51% — 47%

Key Votes of the 103d Congress

1. Clinton Deficit Plan	N	3. Brady Handgun Purchase N	5. Lmt. UN Cmnd. of Forces Y
2. NAFTA	Y	4. Strike Race/Death Pnlty. N	6. Cut Missile Funds N

Key Votes of the 104th Congress

1. Congressional Compliance Y	6. Reform Crime Grant Y	11. Loser Pays Court Reform Y
2. Balanced Budget Amndmt. Y	7. National Security Act N	12. Product Liability Reform Y
3. Bar Unfunded Mandates Y	8. Moratorium on Regs. Y	13. Welfare Reform N
4. Pass Line Item Veto Y	9. Risk Assessment on Regs. Y	14. Term Limits Amndmt. N
5. Relax Exclusionary Rule Y	10. Expnd. Priv. Prop. Rights Y	15. Tax Cuts Y

Election Results

1994 general	Mike Parker (D)	82,939	(68%)	($672,593)
	Mike Wood (R)	38,200	(32%)	($13,239)
1994 primary	Mike Parker (D)	31,173	(58%)	
	Marshall Bennett (D)	18,561	(35%)	
	Bobby Smith (D)	3,702	(7%)	
1992 general	Mike Parker (D)	130,927	(67%)	($156,969)
	Jack L. McMillan (R)	43,705	(23%)	
	Liz Gilchrist (I)	10,523	(5%)	
	James H. Meredith (I)	9,389	(5%)	

FIFTH DISTRICT

The strand where Mississippi faces the Gulf of Mexico has gone through several transformations. French explorers here founded Biloxi in 1699, before New Orleans or St. Louis, and made it the capital of an empire extending to Yellowstone Park. It was on this strand 150 years later that Jefferson Davis built his "Beauvoir," a raised cottage house with sweeping front stairs, set on a broad lawn and shaded by ancient live oaks. In later decades, rich people from New Orleans came to this Gulf coast in summer to get away from yellow fever and to rest on Victorian verandas; six American presidents have vacationed here. More recently the Gulf Coast has been booming economically more than any other part of Mississippi. Biloxi and Gulfport, site of more than half a dozen casinos, are one of the boom areas of the country. And Biloxi's Keesler Air Force Base is one of the four largest bases in the country. Pascagoula, once a small town, is now home of Litton's 16,000-worker Ingalls Shipyard, whose gray hangar-like buildings and skeletons of ships under construction loom over the flat landscape. On nearby Singing River Island is a new naval station. To the west is the Stennis Space Center named for longtime (1947–88) Senator John Stennis, who died in 1995. Shopping centers and subdivisions are spreading back from the strand into the once lightly-inhabited piney woods.

This is the heart of the 5th Congressional District of Mississippi, some 60% of whose people live on the Gulf Coast; the rest are inland, in farm counties or around Hattiesburg. This was mostly scrub land, not much good for plantations, and thus has never had many black residents. With its low black percentage and mostly booming economy, the 5th District has become prime Republican territory. It gave Richard Nixon his highest percentage in all 435 districts in 1972, it voted twice against fellow southerner Jimmy Carter, and it was represented for 16 years in the House by Trent Lott until he was elected to the Senate in 1988.

The current congressman is Gene Taylor, a Democrat with a definite Gulf Coast twang. He started off as a boat salesman, served on the Bay St. Louis Council and was elected to the state Senate at age 30, in 1983. He ran for Congress in 1988, beating Attorney General Mike Moore in the primary, but lost to Republican Larkin Smith 55%–45%. Smith subsequently died in an August 1989 plane crash, and Trent Lott brushed aside Smith's widow and backed his own longtime aide Tom Anderson, who had spent little time in the district and proved to be an abrasive candidate. Taylor, combining a barely reined-in aggressiveness with a down-home manner, won 65%–35%.

In the House, Taylor has been the Democrat most often voting against his party's leadership, a peppery populist ("what Mississippians think is usually the right answer") with a reasonably consistent view on issues. He is pro-life, pro-defense and anti-gun control enough to have opposed the 1994 crime bill. Feisty to the point of being belligerent, he is a kind of isolationist, opposed to any U.S. military commitment that stops short of total victory: he opposed the Gulf war resolution, lifting the arms embargo on Bosnia, sending troops to Haiti. He is a protectionist, loudly opposing NAFTA and GATT. He voted against the Clinton economic package. He gives away his pay raise in local scholarships and cheers on lobbying reform. If there is anything that holds his record together, it is boats. He used to sell boats, he promotes Ingalls and other shipyards, he succeeded in widening and deepening the Gulfport shipping channel, he champions the seafood industry, he wants to prohibit foreign-flag ships from conducting passenger "voyages to nowhere" from U.S. ports. He served in the Coast Guard Reserves and his Washington residence is a 34-foot boat on the Anacostia River.

Why does he stay a Democrat, when it would probably be easier to win as a Republican? Before 1994 he said he liked being part of the majority party, with the clout it brings; that argument is now moot. More likely, this aggressive Mississippian sees that House Republicans are more cohesive and disciplined than Democrats, and he finds it easier to captain his own ship in the more choppy waters of the Democratic Party. Anyway, his constituents seem reasonably pleased; he won in 1992 and 1994 with 63% and 60% of the vote.

The People: Pop. 1990: 514,611; 35% rural; 11% age 65+; 78% White; 20% Black; 1% Asian; 1% Hispanic origin. Voting age pop.: 368,680; 18% Black; 1% Hispanic origin. Households: 59% married couple families; 29% married couple fams. w. children; 41% college educ.; median household income: $21,702; per capita income: $10,116; median gross rent: $329; median house value: $49,200.

1992 Presidential Vote			1988 Presidential Vote		
Bush (R)	99,997	(54%)	Bush (R)	121,371	(70%)
Clinton (D)	58,808	(32%)	Dukakis (D)	51,074	(30%)
Perot (I)	24,956	(14%)			

Rep. Gene Taylor (D)

Elected Oct., 1989; b. Sep. 17, 1953, New Orleans, LA; home, Bay St. Louis; Tulane U., B.A. 1974; Catholic; married (Margaret).

Career: Coast Guard Reserves, 1971–84; Sales rep., Stone Container Corp., 1977–89; Bay St. Louis City Cncl., 1981–83; MS Senate, 1983–89.

DC Office: 2447 RHOB 20515, 202-225-5772; Fax: 202-225-7074.

District Offices: 2424 14th St., Gulfport 39501, 601-864-7670; 701 Main St., Hattiesburg 39401, 601-582-3246; and 706 Watts Ave., Pascagoula 39567, 601-762-1770.

Committees: *Government Reform & Oversight* (15th of 22 D): National Security, International Affairs and Criminal Justice. *National Security* (12th of 25 D): Military Procurement; Military Research and Development.

Group Ratings

	ADA	ACLU	COPE	CFA	LCV	CON	NSI	COC	ACU	NTLC	CHC
1994	15	26	56	40	11	50	100	50	67	86	93
1993	25	—	42	50	36	63	—	73	79	—	—

National Journal Ratings

	1993 LIB — 1993 CONS		1994 LIB — 1994 CONS	
Economic	29% —	70%	44% —	54%
Social	31% —	68%	11% —	85%
Foreign	35% —	63%	37% —	62%

Key Votes of the 103d Congress

1. Clinton Deficit Plan	N	3. Brady Handgun Purchase	N	5. Lmt. UN Cmnd. of Forces	Y
2. NAFTA	N	4. Strike Race/Death Pnlty.	Y	6. Cut Missile Funds	N

Key Votes of the 104th Congress

1. Congressional Compliance	Y	6. Reform Crime Grant	Y	11. Loser Pays Court Reform	Y
2. Balanced Budget Amndmt.	Y	7. National Security Act	Y	12. Product Liability Reform	Y
3. Bar Unfunded Mandates	Y	8. Moratorium on Regs.	Y	13. Welfare Reform	Y
4. Pass Line Item Veto	N	9. Risk Assessment on Regs.	Y	14. Term Limits Amndmt.	N
5. Relax Exclusionary Rule	Y	10. Expnd. Priv. Prop. Rights	Y	15. Tax Cuts	N

Election Results

1994 general	Gene Taylor (D)	73,179	(60%)	($182,381)
	George Barlos (R)	48,575	(40%)	($71,860)
1994 primary	Gene Taylor (D)	unopposed		
1992 general	Gene Taylor (D)	120,766	(63%)	($340,311)
	Paul Harvey (R)	67,619	(35%)	($236,140)

MISSOURI

Missouri, the center of America in so many ways, has strong claims to being the typical American state. It is the geographic center of the nation's population—in central Washington County near the Mark Twain National Forest in 1990. Missouri is at once southern and northern, eastern and western. It is at the confluence of the continent's two greatest rivers, just beyond the boundary of the Louisiana Purchase, the starting point of the Santa Fe Trail, the Transcontinental Railroad and the Pony Express: in the mid-19th Century, it was the exciting frontier. Missouri's most important historical role was as a gateway to the West, an avenue for the great Yankee migrations west from Ohio, Indiana and Illinois and southerners' migration west from Kentucky (Missouri is where Daniel Boone finally stopped looking for elbow room). The northernmost slave state at the time of the civil war, Missouri in the 1850s sent pro-slavery raiders over the border into the Kansas Territory to fight abolitionist settlers; in the 1860s, it had its own mini-civil war in the hilly counties along the Missouri River. During the 19th Century, Americans turned away from their oceans and headed inward to settle the great interior of the continent, and there was Missouri, at its heart, with farmland and mines, rivers and railroads, a major manufacturing state—and in the days before tractors, the nation's leading breeder and trader of mules.

At the turn of the 20th Century, Missouri was the fifth largest state. St. Louis was the fourth largest city, site of the 1904 World's Fair, and one of the few cities with two major league baseball teams, the Cardinals and the Browns; Missouri, after the 1900 Census, had 16 congressional districts. But as the 20th Century went on, Americans—like the Browns who moved to Baltimore in the '50s and the football Cardinals who moved to Phoenix in the '80s—increasingly headed to the coasts, to the big cities of the East and to California, and eventually to Florida and Texas. Missouri has had below-average population growth since 1900, and today it is the 16th largest state, with just nine congressional districts. Yet Missouri has again captured Americans' imaginations: if Americans in 1904 flocked to St. Louis on the banks of the Mississippi, in the 1990s their vans and buses were jamming the two-lane road through the Ozarks to Branson, population 3,700, now America's number two tourist destination, with country music stars, soft rock veterans and violinist Shoji Tabuchi, more theater seats than Broadway and more seats for regularly scheduled music than anywhere else in America.

Politically, Missouri has remained one of our best bellwether states, having voted for every presidential winner but one (Eisenhower in 1956) in the 20th Century. From the 1960s to the 1980s it mirrored national trends by moving in its state and congressional politics from pretty solidly Democratic to pretty solidly Republican. In 1992, it moved sharply away from Republican chief executives and voted for a Democratic president and governor; in 1994, it shifted back toward the Republicans again. At the same time, turnout perked up: presidential year voting, stuck between 1.9 and 2.1 million from 1952–88, rose to 2.4 million in 1992; offyear turnout, stuck between 1.2 and 1.5 million, spiked to 1.8 million in 1994.

Missouri's ancient Civil War political divisions still hold in some rural areas: Little Dixie in the northeast, first settled by Virginians, is still Democratic; the Ozarks in the southwest, which was pro-Union, is Republican. Metro St. Louis, trending Republican in the 1980s, moved toward Democrats in 1992 and back to Republicans in 1994; the Kansas City area, more volatile in the 1980s, cast 25% of its votes in 1992 for Ross Perot and only 29% for George Bush, and tilted toward Democrats in 1994.

Missouri remains culturally more conservative than the rest of the country, indicated by its restrictions on abortion upheld in the 1989 *Webster* case, but still not always predictable; Webster himself lost the 1992 governor's race, though on ethics issues and not abortion. The political shift was greatest in the last two gubernatorial races: Republican Governor John Ashcroft won 64%–35% in 1988, while Democrat Mel Carnahan won 59%–41% in 1992. Meanwhile, Republican Senator Christopher Bond was elected with only 52% of the vote against a Democrat who had what is usually the disadvantage of being associated with St. Louis. The balance in the 1994 Senate race was like those of the 1980s: Ashcroft, after two years in private life, beat Kansas City Congressman Alan Wheat 60%–36%.

Governor. Missouri is one of the largest states with a Democratic governor. Mel Carnahan grew up in politics, the son of Congressman (1945–47, 1949–61) A.S.J. Carnahan, ambassador to newly independent Sierra Leone in the early 1960s. The younger Carnahan was elected municipal judge in 1960, at age 26; he was elected to the legislature in 1962, then became majority leader in 1965, and returned to full-time law practice two years later. In 1980, he was elected state treasurer and served four years; in 1988, he was elected lieutenant governor. His election as governor in 1992 came after one of the wildest and woolliest races in the nation. Carnahan won the Democratic primary over then-Mayor Vince Schoemehl of St. Louis, 55%–34%. Republican nominee William Webster was accused of awarding large fees to clients of campaign contributors in administering the workmen's compensation Second Injury Fund. Carnahan focused on education, calling for a tax increase to fund education reforms, reductions in class size, expansion of merit pay, and reorganization of higher education. Also, Carnahan wanted to regulate church day care centers, promised to stop defending the St. Louis and Kansas City school desegregation cases and called for active government direction of economic redevelopment. Carnahan won 59%–41%, with 63% in the metro areas and 53% outside.

There is a certain similarity between Carnahan's record as an executive and Bill Clinton's as president. In 1993, Carnahan got his education reform and tax increase through the Democratic legislature; in 1994 the legislature rejected his attempt to require health insurers to disregard preexisting conditions and make policies portable between jobs. He did claim credit for laws on welfare, campaign finance and crime. He spent much effort on avoiding federal control, to counter what some considered draconian federal sanctions imposed on the St. Louis area under the Clean Air Act. But his attempt to negotiate with the EPA proved unsuccessful, and the state attorney general has now taken the case to court. Carnahan also worked to reduce the expenditures required for years on the Kansas City schools by a federal judge in a desegregation case.

Carnahan opposed a tax limit initiative in November 1994 requiring public approval of tax increases, but by December was proposing a similar measure of his own. The tax limitation provision passed overwhelmingly in the 1995 legislative session; as a constitutional amendment, it must now be approved by statewide referendum. As governor, Carnahan can set the date for the referendum for any time before November 1996, and it would not be surprising to see it happen close to the election date. His job rating in early 1995 was much higher than Clinton's and one well-known challenger, former Secretary of State Roy Blunt, decided not to run. Possible 1996 opponents include former legislator David Steelman, Auditor Margaret Kelly, and state Senate Republican Leader Franc Flotron.

Senators. Missouri has two Republican senators, both former governors: Christopher Bond and John Ashcroft. Both are from outside the two major Missouri metro areas, Kansas City and St. Louis, although Ashcroft grew up in Springfield. Each brings different attitudes and

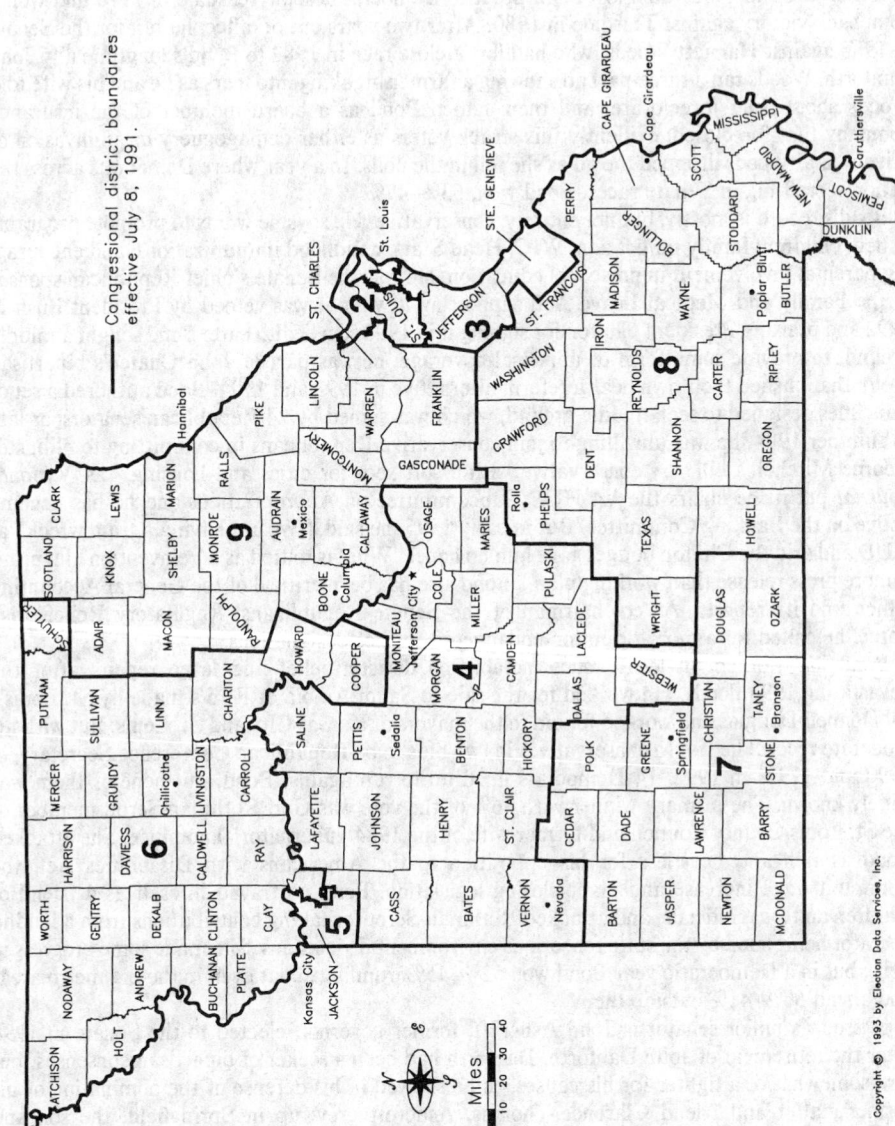

Congressional district boundaries effective July 8, 1991.

Copyright © 1993 by Election Data Services, Inc.

interests to his work.

Senator Christopher Bond has spent most of his adult life in politics. Bond grew up in the town of Mexico, Missouri, went to Princeton and the University of Virginia Law School, then ran for Congress in 1968, at age 29, and narrowly lost. He was elected state auditor in 1970, was elected governor at 33 in 1972, then lost in an upset to Democrat Joseph Teasdale in 1976 and won a comeback victory against Teasdale in 1980. After two years out of office, he ran for the Senate in 1986 against Harriett Woods, who had lost a close race in 1982 to Bond's longtime ally John Danforth. Woods ran a three-part ad showing a farmer breaking into tears as he and his wife told Woods about their foreclosure, and then named Bond as a board member of the insurance company that foreclosed; evidently this struck voters as either demagoguery or an invasion of privacy, and Woods dropped the ad as she fell in the polls. In a year where Democrats across the nation scored big in Senate races, Bond won, 53%–47%.

Bond's record is mostly, but not entirely, conservative. He says he wants to promote programs to help children: family unification, WIC, Head Start, childhood immunizations, and encouraging parental involvement in preschool education. He was the Senate's chief Republican sponsor of the Family and Medical Leave Act, supporting it when it was vetoed by President Bush in 1992 and praising President Clinton for signing it in 1993. On health care, Bond sought a middle ground, to provide some form of universal coverage; he was part of John Chafee's bipartisan group that pushed their own health reform alternative in 1993 and 1994. Bond authored a set of principles designed to seek middle ground, which was signed by 24 Republican senators; as late as summer 1994, he was unwilling to join conservative Republicans in committing to filibuster George Mitchell's bill. "A conservative with a soft spot for cities and housing," as *National Journal* put it, he chairs the VA-HUD Subcommittee on Appropriations and he has become active on the Banking Committee. But in early 1995, he said, "We are having a train wreck" at HUD and said the Clinton budget gave him no hope: "What is touted as a 'reinvention blueprint' is more press release than working plan." Bond also has been critical of the General Accounting Office and its reports. As co-chairman of the Senate Republicans' Regulatory Relief Task Force, he called for a moratorium on endangered species designations.

Bond has worked on local issues, notably on disaster relief and levee repairs after the devastating 1993 floods. He worked for the sale to Saudi Arabia of F-15's made by St. Louis's McDonnell-Douglas and worked for aid to the mayors of Kansas City and St. Louis. But with his moderate record, he lost to conservatives in two bids to be Republican Conference Secretary, in 1990 and 1992. In 1992, 14 Democrats lined up to run against Bond, but none of them was widely known. The primary winner with 36% of the vote was Geri Rothman-Serot, member of the St. Louis County Council and former wife of the 1984 gubernatorial nominee. She attacked Bond as rich and heartless for his opposition to the Americans with Disabilities Act, the minimum wage increase and plant closing legislation. Bond portrayed himself as a friend of children and local officials, and attacked Rothman-Serot for taking contributions from a landfill operator being sued by the state for serious environmental violations. She made some progress in polls, but in a Democratic year Bond won 52%–45%, running about even in the big metro areas and ahead 56%–41% outside them.

Missouri's junior senator is John Ashcroft, former governor, elected to the Senate in 1994 after the retirement of John Danforth. Danforth had been a seeker of bipartisan consensus, but also somewhat of a fighter for his causes, as he showed in his defense of the nomination of his former staffer and friend Clarence Thomas. Ashcroft grew up in Springfield, the son and grandson of ministers, graduated from Yale, met his wife when they were students at the University of Chicago Law School; they practiced law and wrote books together, raised a family and were active members of the Assemblies of God. He is serious, hard-working, abstemious; he sings gospel hymns and plays the piano. Ashcroft ran for Congress in 1972, at age 30, and lost the Republican primary 50%–45%; he was appointed state auditor in 1973, succeeding Christopher Bond when he became governor. Ashcroft went on to be elected attorney general in 1976 and 1980, governor in 1984 and 1988. As governor he held tax rates down and concentrated on creating a favorable job environment, establishing 50 enterprise zones, building new prison cells and starting a Learnfare program and education reform.

After two terms in the Statehouse, Ashcroft left for a St. Louis law practice, but Danforth soon announced his retirement and Ashcroft was the obvious and best known candidate to succeed him. Congressman Bill Emerson made a feint at running but decided not to, leaving Ashcroft with no serious opposition in the Republican primary. He raised vast sums and his conservative stands seemed increasingly in line with voters' views as the year went on. Democrats had a close primary between Kansas City Congressman Alan Wheat and Jackson County Executive Marsha Murphy, which Wheat eventually won 41%–38%, despite her attack on him for taking congressional perks. Wheat is black, and some speculated that his race hurt him against Ashcroft; a bigger problem was his solidly liberal voting record. Ashcroft ran ads against Wheat's votes on crime and welfare and about the House bank; Wheat had to pull one ad because it contained inaccuracies about Ashcroft. Wheat eventually raised a substantial amount of money—$3.4 million to Ashcroft's $4.1 million—but much of it came too late and Ashcroft won easily, 60%–36%, losing St. Louis City and Kansas City, but carrying all 115 counties.

In the Senate, Ashcroft soon established himself as a conservative activist in the mold of the 11-member freshman class. His first bill, introduced with Tennessee Senator Fred Thompson, was for term limits of 12 years for senators and six for representatives; he told the National Endowment for the Arts that Americans shouldn't "subsidize an assault on their values, religion or politics."

Presidential politics. Missouri's peculiar balance of northern and southern, urban and rural, has helped to make it a presidential bellwether and explains its one deviation in the 20th Century: it voted for Adlai Stevenson in 1956, who capitalized on farmer discontent and whose patent lukewarmness about civil rights helped him carry traditional southern Democrats. In recent presidential years, the economically hard-pressed northern part of the state has trended to the Democrats; George Bush carried Missouri in 1988 by only 52%–48%, and Bill Clinton won fairly easily in 1992, 44%–34%, with big margins in metro St. Louis and Kansas City and a 41%–38% edge in the rest of the state.

Missouri, which joined the Super Tuesday primary for 1988, went back to caucuses for 1992. Bill Clinton was the easy winner in the Democrats' contests, still held on Super Tuesday, with 45% to 39% uncommitted. George Bush, whose grandfather came from St. Louis and who has a brother and cousins living there now, won even more easily on the Republican side.

Congressional districting. Missouri did not lose any seats in the 1990 Census, but with continuing population loss in St. Louis and the northern rural counties (the state's best Democratic areas) the lines had to be redrawn. This cost the Democrats the 2d District, which lost black precincts to the black-majority 1st and expanded farther out into fast-growing Republican suburbs. In contrast to other states in the Midwest, its Democrats have survived—at least for now.

The People: Est. Pop. 1994: 5,278,000; Pop. 1990: 5,117,073, up 3.1% 1990–1994. 2.0% of U.S. total, 16th largest; 31% rural. Median age: 33.5 years. 14.0% 65 years and over. 87.7% White, 10.7% Black, 1.2% Hispanic origin. Households: 56.3% married couple families; 26% married couple fams. w. children; 41% college educ.; median household income: $26,362; per capita income: $12,989; 68.8% owner occupied housing; median house value: $59,800; median monthly rent: $282. 5.7% Unemployment. 1994 Voting age pop.: 3,902,000. 1994 Turnout: 1,773,633; 45% of VAP. Registered voters (1994): 2,952,642; no party registration.

Political Lineup: Governor, Mel Carnahan (D); Lt. Gov., Roger B. Wilson (D); Secy. of State, Judith K. Moriarty (D); Atty. Gen., Jay Nixon (D); Treasurer, Bob Holden (D); Auditor, Margaret Kelly (R). State Senate, 34 (19 D and 15 R); State House of Representatives, 163 (87 D and 76 R). Senators, Christopher S. (Kit) Bond (R) and John Ashcroft (R). Representatives, 9 (3 R and 6 D).

1992 Presidential Vote

Clinton (D) 1,053,873 (44%)
Bush (R) 811,159 (34%)
Perot (I). 518,741 (22%)

1988 Presidential Vote

Bush (R) 1,084,953 (52%)
Dukakis (D). 1,001,619 (48%)

GOVERNOR

Gov. Mel Carnahan (D)

Elected 1992, term expires Jan. 1997; b. Feb. 11, 1934, Birchtree; home, Rolla; George Washington U., B.A. 1954, U. of MO, J.D. 1959; Baptist; married (Jean).

Career: Air Force, 1954–56; Practicing atty., 1959–61, 1962–80, 1984–88; Rolla Municipal Judge, 1961–62; MO House of Reps., 1962–66; MO Treasurer, 1980–84; MO Lt. Gov., 1988–92.

Office: State Capitol Bldg., Jefferson City 65101, 314-751-3222; Fax: 314-751-1495.

Election Results

1992 gen.	Mel Carnahan (D)	1,375,425	(59%)
	William B. Webster (R)	968,574	(41%)
1992 prim.	Mel Carnahan (D)	388,098	(55%)
	Vince Schoemehl (D)	235,652	(34%)
	Sharon Rogers (D)	35,104	(5%)
	Others	42,134	(4%)
1988 gen.	John Ashcroft (R)	1,339,531	(64%)
	Betty Hearnes (D)	724,919	(35%)

SENATORS

Sen. Christopher S. (Kit) Bond (R)

Elected 1986, seat up 1998; b. Mar. 6, 1939, St. Louis; home, Mexico; Princeton, B.A. 1960, U. of VA, LL.B. 1963; Presbyterian; separated.

Career: Practicing atty., 1964–69, 1977–80; MO Asst. Atty. Gen., 1969–70; MO Auditor, 1970–72; MO Gov., 1972–76, 1980–84.

DC Office: 293 RSOB 20510, 202-224-5721; Fax: 202-224-8149.

State Offices: 1736 Sunshine, #705, Springfield 65804, 417-881-7068; 339 Broadway, #214, Cape Girardeau 63701, 314-334-7044; 600 Broadway, #420, Kansas City 64105, 816-471-7141; 312 Monroe St., Jefferson City 65101, 314-634-2488; and 8000 Maryland Ave., #1050, St. Louis 63105, 314-727-7773.

Committees: *Appropriations* (7th of 15 R): Agriculture, Rural Development and Related Agencies; Defense; Labor, Health and Human Services, Education; Transportation; VA, HUD and Independent Agencies (Chmn). *Banking, Housing & Urban Affairs* (4th of 9 R): Financial Institutions and Regulatory Relief; Housing Opportunity and Community Development; International Finance (Chmn). *Budget* (5th of 12 R). *Environment & Public Works* (9th of 9 R): Drinking Water, Fisheries and Wildlife; Transportation and Infrastructure. *Small Business* (Chmn. of 10 R).

Group Ratings

	ADA	ACLU	COPE	CFA	LCV	CON	NSI	COC	ACU	NTLC	CHC
1994	20	37	13	25	15	65	100	87	83	88	71
1993	25	—	10	40	6	53	—	100	80	—	—

National Journal Ratings

	1993 LIB — 1993 CONS		1994 LIB — 1994 CONS	
Economic	33% —	65%	32% —	67%
Social	19% —	78%	27% —	71%
Foreign	16% —	77%	16% —	82%

Key Votes of the 103d Congress

1. Clinton Deficit Plan	N	3. Brady Handgun Purchase	Y	5. Lmt. UN Cmnd. of Forces	Y
2. NAFTA	Y	4. Strike Race/Death Pnlty.	Y	6. Cut Missile Funds	N

Key Votes of the 104th Congress

1. Congressional Compliance	Y	3. Balanced Budget Amndt.	Y	5. Product Liability Reform	Y
2. Bar Unfunded Mandates	Y	4. Pass Line Item Veto	Y	6. FY96 Budget	Y

Election Results

1992 general	Christopher S. (Kit) Bond (R)	1,221,901	(52%)	($5,048,333)
	Geri Rothman-Serot (D)	1,057,967	(45%)	($1,112,187)
	Other	75,048	(3%)	
1992 primary	Christopher S. (Kit) Bond (R)	337,795	(83%)	
	Wes Hummel (R)	70,626	(17%)	
1986 general	Christopher S. (Kit) Bond (R)	777,612	(53%)	($5,376,255)
	Harriet Woods (D)	699,624	(47%)	($4,397,780)

Sen. John Ashcroft (R)

Elected 1994, seat up 2000; b. May 9, 1942, Chicago, IL; home, St. Louis; Yale U., B.A. 1964, U. of Chicago, J.D. 1967; Assembly of God; married (Janet).

Career: Practicing atty; Professor, 1968–73; MO Auditor, 1973–75; Asst. Atty. Gen. of MO. 1975–76; Atty Gen. of MO, 1976–84; MO Gov., 1984–92.

DC Office: 170 RSOB 20515, 202-224-6154; Fax: 202-228-5126.

State Offices: 1736 Sunshine, #705, Springfield 65804, 417-881-7068; 339 Broadway, #214, Cape Girardeau 63701, 314-334-7044; 600 Broadway, #420, Kansas City 64105, 816-471-7141; 312 Monroe St., Jefferson City 65101, 314-634-2488; and 8000 Maryland Ave., #1050, St. Louis 63105, 314-727-7773.

Committees: *Commerce, Science & Transportation* (10th of 10 R): Aviation; Communications; Consumer Affairs, Foreign Commerce and Tourism. *Foreign Relations* (10th of 10 R): African Affairs; International Economic Policy, Export and Trade Promotion; International Operations. *Labor & Human Resources* (7th of 9 R): Aging; Children and Families; Education, Arts and Humanities.

Group Ratings and 103rd Congress Votes: Newly Elected

Key Votes of the 104th Congress

1. Congressional Compliance	Y	3. Balanced Budget Amndt.	Y	5. Product Liability Reform	Y
2. Bar Unfunded Mandates	Y	4. Pass Line Item Veto	Y	6. FY96 Budget	Y

Election Results

1994 general	John Ashcroft (R)	1,060,149	(60%)	($4,063,927)
	Alan Wheat (D)	633,697	(36%)	($3,505,701)
	Bill Johnson (Lib)	81,264	(5%)	
1994 primary	John Ashcroft (R)	260,065	(83%)	
	Joyce Lea (R)	15,228	(5%)	
	Joseph A. Schwan (R)	14,713	(5%)	
	Others	22,642	(7%)	
1988 general	John C. Danforth (R)	1,407,416	(68%)	($4,060,441)
	Jeremiah W. Nixon (D)	660,045	(32%)	($880,160)

FIRST DISTRICT

For a century or more St. Louis seemed the center of America: the starting point for the Lewis and Clark expedition in 1804; the locus half a century later of the Dred Scott case, which produced a Supreme Court ruling that helped split the nation; the site of the 1904 World's Fair that introduced the hot dog and the ice cream cone and got 19 million people to "Meet Me in St. Louis." Its 630-foot-high Gateway Arch is just below the point where the waters of the Missouri surge into the Mississippi, about halfway between New Orleans and Lake Superior, the Atlantic and the Pacific. This first major American city west of the Mississippi River was the final resting place of Daniel Boone and for many years was Chicago's rival as the transportation hub of America. In 1904, St. Louis already had the Wainwright Building, one of Louis Sullivan's first skyscrapers, and Union Station, the world's largest train station when it opened in 1894; some 600,000 people lived in densely-packed brick houses on old street grids radiating outward from downtown. This was a heavily German city, with a teutonic solidity and orderliness which distinguished it from the surrounding southern-accented rural terrain; and from Mitteleuropa came the founders of St. Louis's great businesses—the Anheuser-Busch brewery, May Company department stores, Joseph Pulitzer's *St. Louis Post-Dispatch*—and its first great politician, Senator and Interior Secretary Carl Schurz. And there is almost a European aura to Forest Park, the site of the 1904 fair, and the dozen mansion-lined private streets nearby, like Portland Place.

St. Louis is still one of the 20 largest metro areas in the U.S., but today does not occupy as central a place in the national consciousness, and the central city itself has largely emptied out. The German order that made so many people comfortable living in such close quarters and commuting by streetcar seems to have yielded to an American desire for Daniel Boone's wide open (suburban) spaces and the less restrictive automobile. St. Louis's population peaked at 856,000 in 1950; in 1990, it was 396,000, dwarfed by the one million in suburban St. Louis County. Downtown St. Louis has been spruced up admirably: the Gateway Arch was finished in 1965; Union Station has been redeveloped; Laclede's Landing is stocked with shops. But most of St. Louis's old factories have closed and its once tight neighborhoods have emptied out.

Missouri's congressional districts have followed the people out of St. Louis. The 1st District, historically based on the north side of the city, now has 71% of its votes cast in suburban St. Louis County. It includes most of central and north St. Louis, the affluent and racially integrated suburbs of University City and Clayton just west of Forest Park, and the mostly black and mixed-race suburbs from the city limits north to Bellefontaine Neighbors, Florissant and the airport. In 1990, this district was 52% black, a figure likely to increase over the decade. This is easily Missouri's most Democratic district.

The congressman from the 1st District is the dean of the Missouri delegation, Bill Clay, a union staffer and firebrand civil rights activist in the 1960s known as "Wild Bill" (he served 105 days in jail in 1963 for participating in a civil rights demonstration), a House leader when Democrats were in control, now one of the angriest opponents of Newt Gingrich's Republicans and the Contract With America. Clay was first elected to the House in 1968, when the black members of the House could be counted on two hands. He weathered some serious ethical charges in the 1970s, when he billed the government for numerous auto trips home though he was apparently traveling on cheaper airline tickets. In 1992, it was revealed that he had 328 overdrafts on the House bank. But he has always won reelection, though on occasion he has shown political weakness in the suburbs.

Clay was also a major legislative force, as chairman of the now-abolished Post Office and Civil Service Committee and heir apparent to the Economic and Educational Opportunities Committee. He is one of the most faithful supporters of organized labor and public employee unions. One major Clay achievement was the Family and Medical Leave Act, vetoed by President Bush but signed by President Clinton in February 1993 as his first law. Hatch Act reform—allowing federal employees to be involved in politics—took only a bit longer; it passed the House in March 1993 and was signed by Clinton in October 1993. Less controversial was a Clay measure authorizing buyouts of senior federal employees, which passed the House 391–17 in February 1994 and became law the next month. But Clay was not as successful in pushing striker replacement, which would revise the 1935 Wagner Act and give more leverage to unions; although the bill passed the House in 1994, George Mitchell was unable to find the 60 votes required to break the Republicans' promised filibuster and it died without a Senate vote.

Clay's ferocity is apparent on several issues. He is a scathing critic of Postmaster General Marvin Runyon, and in 1994, called the agency "rudderless," saying the postal board of governors are "hoodwinked" about mail problems, and called unsuccessfully for a larger board staff to oversee Runyon. He criticized the postal inspection service for botching stings in drug cases and said the inspection service was biased against blacks. He also called for cancellation of the stamp honoring Richard Nixon. Clay requested the ouster of Republican Gary Franks from the Congressional Black Caucus, saying his voting record was "inimical to the permanent interests of black folk." Clay went on to tell Franks, "With your dismal record on the issues most critical to the welfare of black people, in my opinion, it would probably be better for all concerned if you did resign forthwith, admitting you should never have joined the ranks of black legislators who fight to protect the rights of black people."

Clay showed some weakness in the 1994 election, but emerged as aggressive as ever. He won only 53% in the Democratic primary, against scattered opposition from executive Patrick Cacchione (20%) and political operatives Eric Vickers (17%) and Dwight Billingsley (10%). In the general, he won solidly 63%–33%, but was pressed more closely than in 1992 in St. Louis County, winning there 54%–42%.

The big shock for Clay in 1994 was loss of Democratic control: instead of chairman of Education and Labor he became ranking minority member of Economic and Educational Opportunities. He denounced the Republican welfare plan, saying it will "potentially starve hundreds of thousands of children and impair the health of their mothers. This bill is not about welfare reform. This is a giant money laundering scheme. It's about writing blank checks to governors while imposing no standards or accountability." If denying cash assistance to unmarried teenagers, doesn't work, he asked, "What's next? Castration? Sterilization?"

The People: Pop. 1990: 568,472; 1% rural; 14% age 65+; 46% White; 52% Black; 1% Asian; 1% Hispanic origin. Voting age pop.: 418,960; 48% Black; 1% Hispanic origin. Households: 40% married couple families; 17% married couple fams. w. children; 44% college educ.; median household income: $24,963; per capita income: $12,632; median gross rent: $391; median house value: $55,200.

1992 Presidential Vote			1988 Presidential Vote		
Clinton (D)	161,447	(68%)	Dukakis (D)	162,714	(70%)
Bush (R)	45,231	(19%)	Bush (R)	69,059	(30%)
Perot (I)	29,682	(13%)			

Rep. William (Bill) Clay (D)

Elected 1968; b. Apr. 30, 1931, St. Louis; home, St. Louis; St. Louis U., B.S. 1953; Catholic; married (Carol).

Career: Real estate broker; Life insurance business, 1959–61; St. Louis City Alderman, 1959–64.

DC Office: 2306 RHOB 20515, 202-225-2406; Fax: 202-225-1725.

District Offices: 5261 Delmar Blvd., St. Louis 63108, 314-367-1970; and 49 Central City Shopping Ctr. N., St. Louis 63136, 314-388-0321.

Committees: *Economic & Educational Opportunities* (RMM of 19 D).

Group Ratings

	ADA	ACLU	COPE	CFA	LCV	CON	NSI	COC	ACU	NTLC	CHC
1994	85	91	100	80	85	4	20	18	14	11	0
1993	100	—	100	90	79	19	—	0	0	—	—

National Journal Ratings

	1993 LIB — 1993 CONS		1994 LIB — 1994 CONS	
Economic	88%	— 0%	83%	— 0%
Social	87%	— 0%	79%	— 21%
Foreign	87%	— 7%	78%	— 21%

Key Votes of the 103d Congress

1. Clinton Deficit Plan	Y	3. Brady Handgun Purchase	Y	5. Lmt. UN Cmnd. of Forces	N
2. NAFTA	N	4. Strike Race/Death Pnlty.	N	6. Cut Missile Funds	Y

Key Votes of the 104th Congress

1. Congressional Compliance	Y	6. Reform Crime Grant	N	11. Loser Pays Court Reform	N
2. Balanced Budget Amndmt.	N	7. National Security Act	*	12. Product Liability Reform	N
3. Bar Unfunded Mandates	N	8. Moratorium on Regs.	N	13. Welfare Reform	N
4. Pass Line Item Veto	N	9. Risk Assessment on Regs.	N	14. Term Limits Amndmt.	N
5. Relax Exclusionary Rule	N	10. Expnd. Priv. Prop. Rights	N	15. Tax Cuts	N

Election Results

1994 general	William (Bill) Clay (D)	97,061	(63%)	($349,528)
	Donald R. Counts (R)	50,303	(33%)	($7,408)
	Others	5,654	(4%)	
1994 primary	William (Bill) Clay (D)	34,656	(53%)	
	Patrick Cacchione (D)	13,062	(20%)	
	Eric E. Vickers (D)	11,224	(17%)	
	Z. Dwight Billingsly (D)	6,224	(10%)	
1992 general	William (Bill) Clay (D)	158,693	(68%)	($297,635)
	Arthur S. Montgomery (R)	74,482	(32%)	($21,862)

SECOND DISTRICT

Just as the U.S. population's geographic center has slowly crept westward into Missouri (the 1990 Census placed the axis just outside tiny Steelville), the greater St. Louis area continues to shift away from its Gateway Arch along the Mississippi River. The fulcrum now rests in St. Louis County, established in 1876 when the city, tired of paying for dusty back roads, separated itself from the sticks. There were then about 350,000 people in the city and 31,000 in the county. In 1990, the city, which once had 856,000 people, was down to 396,000, while the county was about 1 million. By the 1960s, the center of office employment had moved from downtown across the county line to Clayton; now even many Clayton office buildings seem half-empty, and the focus is fast moving out the Daniel Boone Expressway (U.S. 40) to Chesterfield, west of the I-270 ring road. Urban problems have headed in this direction too: McDonnell Douglas's big plant outside the St. Louis airport has been hit hard by defense cutbacks and has laid off thousands, while the area's once-booming auto assembly plants are now largely in mothballs. Compared to the troubles of downtown St. Louis, however, western St. Louis County and neighboring St. Charles County are an affluent suburban dream.

The 2d Congressional District of Missouri is made up of central and western St. Louis County, plus some St. Charles County suburbs northwest across the Missouri River. This is the Missouri district most changed by redistricting for 1992; in effect, it has followed its constituents farther out from the city, picking up a greater share of Republicans than previously. It covers a sociologically diverse terrain. In north St. Louis County, not far from McDonnell-Douglas and the airport, are blue-collar suburbs, full of whites who grew up on the north side of St. Louis and, in some areas, blacks as well: solidly Democratic. To the south are comfortable white-collar suburbs like Kirkwood, pleasant but not rich places filled mostly with older whites: solidly Republican. In the center of the county, along the Daniel Boone Expressway, are the old high-income suburbs of Ladue—still home to most of St. Louis's elite—and Creve Coeur and the newer Town and Country, Manchester and Chesterfield: Republican, and even more so in the newer family-oriented subdivisions than in the leafy precincts of the old rich.

The congressman from the 2d District is Jim Talent, a Republican who first won the seat against better-known opponents in both the primary and general in 1992. In 1994 the district beat its habit of changing parties in one election after another (1986, 1990, 1992). Talent grew up in Des Peres and lives in Chesterfield; he was a law clerk to Judge Richard Posner, one of the great free market legal minds, and was a management lawyer in St. Louis; in 1984, at age 28, he was elected to the state legislature, where he opposed taxes (even Republican Governor John Ashcroft's road tax) and backed reform of House rules. In 1992, Talent ran for the U.S. House, and in the primary beat George Bush's cousin, George Herbert Walker, by the unambiguous margin of 58%–32%. In the general, Talent faced incumbent Democrat Joan Kelly Horn, who in 1990 defeated Republican Jack Buechner by a grand total of 54 votes. Horn campaigned gamely and against the odds given redistricting changes, but Talent won 50%–48%.

In his first term, Talent compiled a solidly conservative voting record and focused on military readiness and welfare reform. In the 1994 election, he had no politically serious opposition and won 67%–31%—one of several Republicans elected narrowly in 1992 who were reelected overwhelmingly after two years of Bill Clinton. In the majority, Talent hammered hard on welfare reform; the Contract With America's welfare provisions were an echo of Talent's 1994 bill and, even though he did not sit on Ways and Means, he contributed actively to its provisions. He also has a seat on National Security and is chairman of the Small Business Committee's Regulation and Paperwork Subcommittee; he brings his legislative activism to Economic and Educational Opportunities as well.

The People:　Pop. 1990: 568,449; 3% rural; 10% age 65+; 94% White; 4% Black; 2% Asian; 1% Hispanic origin. Voting age pop.: 421,265; 3% Black; 1% Hispanic origin. Households: 65% married couple families; 31% married couple fams. w. children; 61% college educ.; median household income: $43,957; per capita income: $20,654; median gross rent: $519; median house value: $94,900.

1992 Presidential Vote

Bush (R)	126,621	(40%)
Clinton (D)	114,612	(36%)
Perot (I)	72,885	(23%)

1988 Presidential Vote

Bush (R)	167,072	(63%)
Dukakis (D)	99,268	(37%)

Rep. Jim Talent (R)

Elected 1992; b. Oct. 18, 1956, Des Peres; home, Chesterfield; Washington U., B.S. 1978, U. of Chicago Law Schl., J.D. 1981; Presbyterian; married (Brenda).

Career:　Practicing atty., 1981–92; Law Clerk, 7th Circuit Court of Appeals Judge Richard Posner, 1982–83; MO House of Reps., 1984–92, Minority Ldr., 1989–92.

DC Office: 1022 LHOB 20515, 202-225-2561; Fax: 202-225-2563.

District Offices:　555 N. New Balas, #315, St. Louis 63141, 314-872-9561; and 820 S. Main St., #206, St. Charles 63301, 314-949-6826.

Committees:　*Economic & Educational Opportunities* (13th of 24 R): Employer-Employee Relations. *National Security* (16th of 30 R): Military Procurement; Military Readiness. *Small Business* (4th of 22 R): Regulation and Paperwork (Chmn.).

Group Ratings

	ADA	ACLU	COPE	CFA	LCV	CON	NSI	COC	ACU	NTLC	CHC
1994	5	14	0	20	22	79	100	100	95	96	100
1993	10	—	8	0	29	85	—	82	96	—	—

National Journal Ratings

	1993 LIB	—	1993 CONS	1994 LIB	—	1994 CONS
Economic	20%	—	77%	0%	—	80%
Social	0%	—	89%	28%	—	71%
Foreign	17%	—	76%	14%	—	80%

Key Votes of the 103d Congress

1. Clinton Deficit Plan	N	3. Brady Handgun Purchase	N	5. Lmt. UN Cmnd. of Forces	Y
2. NAFTA	N	4. Strike Race/Death Pnlty.	Y	6. Cut Missile Funds	N

Key Votes of the 104th Congress

1. Congressional Compliance	Y	6. Reform Crime Grant	Y	11. Loser Pays Court Reform	Y
2. Balanced Budget Amndmt.	Y	7. National Security Act	Y	12. Product Liability Reform	Y
3. Bar Unfunded Mandates	Y	8. Moratorium on Regs.	Y	13. Welfare Reform	Y
4. Pass Line Item Veto	Y	9. Risk Assessment on Regs.	Y	14. Term Limits Amndmt.	Y
5. Relax Exclusionary Rule	Y	10. Expnd. Priv. Prop. Rights	Y	15. Tax Cuts	Y

Election Results

1994 general	Jim Talent (R)	154,882	(67%)	($773,953)
	Pat Kelly (D)	70,480	(31%)	($135,867)
	Others	4,925	(2%)	
1994 primary	Jim Talent (R)	unopposed		
1992 general	Jim Talent (R)	157,594	(50%)	($910,893)
	Joan Kelly Horn (D)	148,729	(48%)	($832,813)
	Other	6,119	(2%)	

THIRD DISTRICT

Middle America, in several senses of the word, lies in the 3d Congressional District of Missouri. The geographical center of the country's population was here in 1980, just south of St. Louis in once rural and now half-suburban Jefferson County; and while that point has moved a few miles southwest, St. Louis is still the metro area nearest the midpoint of a country most of whose people live in million-plus metro areas. Geographically, this is a node where some of the nation's main arteries come together. The Missouri River flows into the Mississippi a few miles north of St. Louis's Gateway Arch, the northern boundary of the 3d; the National Road and its successors, U.S. 40 and Interstate 70, cross the Mississippi just below the Arch. And the great tides of southerners migrating west up the Mississippi and Germans migrating overland met here to create one of the nation's largest and most bustling cities out of a town originally founded by the French in the years before the Revolutionary War. The south side of St. Louis is famous for its tight-knit, neat neighborhoods and pleasant parks; its most famous symbol is the Anheuser-Busch brewery just south of downtown and Grant's Farm, where Ulysses S. Grant lived in the 1850s and where Anheuser-Busch now keeps the Budweiser Clydesdales.

The 3d Congressional District was centered on the south side of St. Louis when its current congressman, Richard Gephardt, was growing up there 40 years ago. Now St. Louis City casts only 25% of its votes, and it stretches far south, through modest neighborhoods in the St. Louis County suburbs near the Mississippi River. In Jefferson County, old towns sitting near the banks of the fast-flowing Mississippi are now receiving an infusion of shopping centers, new subdivisions and apartment complexes. Since 1992, the 3d also includes lightly populated Ste. Genevieve County, whose name bespeaks its French origins; it is the site of Missouri's oldest permanent settlement, founded near a salt mine in 1730.

Gephardt, presidential candidate in 1988 and perhaps again someday, majority leader of the House from June 1989 to January 1995, still leads his party, but now as minority leader. Gephardt comes from the south side of St. Louis, from origins moderately humble. A bit too old to be part of the generation of Vietnam-era student rebels, Gephardt returned home from law school in 1965 to work in a large downtown law firm, but was clearly intent on a traditional political career; he moved to the south side and ran for alderman in 1971. In 1976, when 3d District Congresswoman Leonor Sullivan announced her retirement, Gephardt jumped into the race as an anti-establishment candidate. He beat a labor union official in the primary and a former board of aldermen president in the general. Gephardt started off in the House as one of the newer breed of Democrats who did not automatically favor big government and higher taxes. With the help of Missouri's Richard Bolling, Gephardt got a seat on the Ways and Means Committee—rare for a freshman. He voted for the 1981 Reagan tax cut and was the House co-sponsor of Bill Bradley's bill that was the basis of the 1986 tax reform. Gephardt was one of the founders of the moderate Democratic Leadership Council and opposed many popular Democratic causes such as abortion, busing and raising the minimum wage.

But around the mid-1980s he began to shift, perhaps reflecting the increasingly liberal tenor of the Democratic Caucus, of which he was elected chairman over David Obey in 1984. Gephardt has always been a superb caucus politician and a good listener, working with small universes—caucuses—of colleagues and constituents. He is a hard-working detail man, eager to absorb information and has a gift for molding compromises, for coming up with positions that hold together his caucus while dividing others.

When Gephardt started running for president in 1986, he had the enthusiastic support of dozens of House colleagues as he spent 144 days in Iowa between 1986 and the February 1988 caucuses. Iowa was the biggest population-losing state in the 1980s, bitterly anti-Reagan; to Iowans, and to many House Democrats in Washington, there was a sense the Reagan era was over. Gephardt adjusted to this new arena, sometimes to the dismay of his former allies. He played little role in the 1986 tax reform, which he had originally co-sponsored; he changed his stand on abortion to pro-choice. In Iowa, he supported mandatory agricultural production controls, a wackily impractical program that would have raised food prices to consumers in order to protect landowners' million-dollar equity. Even more prominently, he went on the offensive on the trade issue. The United Auto Workers are a major factor in Iowa caucuses, and Gephardt, who had opposed the UAW's domestic content bill, came up with his amendment requiring retaliation against countries (read: Japan) running large trade surpluses with the United States. It passed the House in late 1987 by a 218–214 margin—a gift to Gephardt's presidential campaign, for the bill clearly was going nowhere in the Senate.

Gephardt won the Iowa caucuses with 31% of the vote, to 27% for Paul Simon and 22% for Michael Dukakis. In New Hampshire found himself under attack for switching positions in a prosperous state that hates taxes and government regulation; he finished second with 20% to Dukakis's 36%. On Super Tuesday, Gephardt ran out of money and won only Missouri and he was out of the race.

In the House Gephardt rebounded when another leadership position came his way. In June 1989 Speaker Jim Wright and Majority Whip Tony Coelho resigned, and as Thomas Foley was elected speaker, Gephardt ran for majority leader and defeated Georgian Ed Jenkins 181–76. There, Gephardt went to work creating a sense of camaraderie in a dispirited Caucus. In the caucus-like setting of the 1990 budget summit talks, Gephardt used OMB Director Richard Darman's desire for agreement to frame the issue as a choice between the Democrats' plan to tax the rich more and Bush's refusal to do so—a contrast that at least momentarily hurt Republican candidates in October 1990 and prevented them from making gains in the November elections. In September 1990, Gephardt supported Bush's dispatch of troops to the Persian Gulf, but in December and into 1991, Gephardt led the opposition to the Gulf war resolution and uncharacteristically stumbled by threatening to cut off funds for American troops there.

In the first Clinton years, Gephardt combined ardent support for the administration on most issues with carefully calibrated dissent on others. He fought for the Clinton economic stimulus and for the budget and tax package which passed with exactly 218 votes in August 1993. His major dissent was on trade. He held off opposing NAFTA for several months as he sought more concessions from administration officials and he eventually came out against, though critics said his efforts were too late. He resisted demagoguery but called for side agreements on labor law, wage levels and the environment; but he did not get in the way as Clinton, his special aide William Daley and Republican Whip Newt Gingrich rounded up enough votes for passage in November 1993. In December 1993, Gephardt endorsed GATT; in February 1994, he came up with his own plan to force Japan to meet numerical goals in opening its markets, or face retaliation.

Gephardt vigorously supported the Clinton healthcare plan in 1994, and in the summer took the lead in putting together his own bill, which combined main features of the Clinton and Ways and Means health reform plans. His strategy, as always, was to assemble a 218-vote majority from the Democratic Caucus, starting with meeting members' substantive concerns, then squeezing out the last few votes by calling on party loyalty and implicitly threatening to use the caucus majority to deny dissenters committee posts, pork barrel projects and PAC money. But this had not worked when Gephardt was charged with producing a healthcare plan in 1991 and 1992, and it did not work in 1994. Indeed, even before the Gephardt health bill could come to the floor, on August 11 the Democratic leadership lost the vote on the crime bill rule. The crime bill, which they had hoped would be a political asset, became a liability; to propitiate liberals, gun control amendments were included, but these antagonized too many southern and western Democrats, and Newt Gingrich, shrewdly seizing on Democrats' high-handedness, got all but 11 Republicans to vote no. That delayed the crime bill for two weeks, and by late August it was apparent that the health bill would not pass; Gephardt had to admit a stinging defeat, not even bringing the bill to a House vote.

He had to admit an even more painful defeat when Democrats lost 52 seats in November and Republicans became the House majority. The long years of success in the House of the Gephardt strategy—grind out 218 votes in a cloud of dust—had blinded him and others to the unpopularity of the measures the Democrats in their camaraderie and/or obedience were passing. So when Democrats lost their institutional advantages—as candidate quality, redistricting, perquisites of office and pork barrel projects ceased working strongly in their favor—their majority disappeared, and the country gravitated toward Republicans in House races in 1994 as it had in presidential races in the 1980s.

Ironically, Gephardt's skills as a caucus leader, which delayed his party's defeat, made it all the more devastating when it came. And Gephardt himself had a serious challenge in the 3d District. Republican Gary Gill, an investment firm executive, put up lawn signs reading, "Fed up with Congress? Gephardt IS Congress. Vote Gary Gill." Gephardt, evidently reading trouble in the polls, spent over $2.6 million, the second most of any candidate in the country, raising $1,010,000 in PAC money (third, behind only Speaker Foley and Democratic Congressional Campaign Committee Chairman Vic Fazio). Gephardt campaigned door-to-door with the same perseverance that he had filled sandbags in the 1993 flood; he also ran blistering negative ads against Gill, linking him to Illinois gambling interests and an unpopular local landfill, and charging Gill would cut Social Security. Gill spent only $196,000, raising $15,000 from PACs. For all that, Gephardt won with just 58%, running behind in St. Louis City and Ste. Genevieve and carrying St. Louis County, with nearly half the votes, by only 53%–45%. It was not the first time Gephardt spent huge sums: in 1990, he spent $1.4 million and won with 57%; in more Democratic 1992, he spent $3.3 million and won with 64%.

Gephardt was challenged for minority leader by Charlie Rose, who charged Gephardt would be unable to reconcile the conservative and liberal wings of the Democratic Party in order to fight the GOP. But Gephardt won by 150–58 in the Democratic Caucus. He is not without influence in the Clinton White House—George Stephanopoulos once served on his staff, disastrously advising him that he could govern with 218 votes in the Democratic Caucus, and Leon Panetta, Tony Coelho and Abner Mikva all served with Gephardt in the House. But the new minority leader quickly set himself apart from the Clinton Administration. In January 1995, after the election, he said, "House Democrats are an independent organization, and we will present what we think is best for America's workers." In December 1994, two days before a scheduled Clinton speech, Gephardt called for a middle class tax credit on families with incomes under $75,000; in January 1995, he said he was developing a flat tax proposal. He also supported Clinton measures, like a higher minimum wage and college IRAs. But during the 1995 budget debate, he scrapped his middle class tax cut as most Democrats placed a greater emphasis on deficit reduction. Gephardt was not highly visible in the Democrats' fights against the Republicans' Contract With America, not nearly as vocal as Minority Whip David Bonior. But he remains one Democrat—along with his erstwhile ally, Bill Bradley—with the potential of challenging Bill Clinton in 1996, with some natural base of support, from organized labor perhaps and congressional liberals, and with some choice of ground. At the same time, he is not immune from challenge at home. The 3d District is not overwhelmingly Democratic and National Republican Congressional Committee Chairman Bill Paxon announced in early 1995 that Gephardt would be a target in 1996. That may be a bluff. But it's not clear that Gephardt will have his accustomed huge advantage in PAC money in 1996, and it's not clear how much of his 58% came from a financial advantage.

The People: Pop. 1990: 568,105; 16% rural; 15% age 65+; 96% White; 2% Black; 1% Asian; 1% Hispanic origin. Voting age pop.: 428,707; 2% Black; 1% Hispanic origin. Households: 56% married couple families; 26% married couple fams. w. children; 41% college educ.; median household income: $30,863; per capita income: $14,272; median gross rent: $390; median house value: $71,500.

1992 Presidential Vote

Clinton (D)	121,213	(44%)
Bush (R)	87,155	(32%)
Perot (I)	64,415	(24%)

1988 Presidential Vote

Bush (R)	128,331	(53%)
Dukakis (D)	113,349	(47%)

Rep. Richard A. Gephardt (D)

Elected 1976; b. Jan. 31, 1941, St. Louis; home, St. Louis; Northwestern U., B.S. 1962, U. of MI, J.D. 1965; Baptist; married (Jane).

Career: Air Natl. Guard, 1965–71; Practicing atty., 1965–71; St. Louis City Alderman, 1971–76. Dem. Candidate for Pres., 1988.

DC Office: 1226 LHOB 20515, 202-225-2671; Fax: 202-225-7452.

District Offices: 11140 S. Towne Sq., #201, St. Louis 63123, 314-894-3400.

Committees: *Minority Leader.*

Group Ratings

	ADA	ACLU	COPE	CFA	LCV	CON	NSI	COC	ACU	NTLC	CHC
1994	80	70	89	90	76	15	40	33	5	14	14
1993	90	—	100	100	62	25	—	9	8	—	—

National Journal Ratings

	1993 LIB — 1993 CONS		1994 LIB — 1994 CONS	
Economic	78% —	12%	83% —	0%
Social	73% —	23%	82% —	18%
Foreign	79% —	16%	78% —	22%

Key Votes of the 103d Congress

1. Clinton Deficit Plan	Y	3. Brady Handgun Purchase	Y	5. Lmt. UN Cmnd. of Forces	N
2. NAFTA	N	4. Strike Race/Death Pnlty.	N	6. Cut Missile Funds	Y

Key Votes of the 104th Congress

1. Congressional Compliance	Y	6. Reform Crime Grant	N	11. Loser Pays Court Reform	N
2. Balanced Budget Amndmt.	N	7. National Security Act	N	12. Product Liability Reform	N
3. Bar Unfunded Mandates	Y	8. Moratorium on Regs.	N	13. Welfare Reform	N
4. Pass Line Item Veto	N	9. Risk Assessment on Regs.	N	14. Term Limits Amndmt.	N
5. Relax Exclusionary Rule	N	10. Expnd. Priv. Prop. Rights	N	15. Tax Cuts	N

Election Results

1994 general	Richard A. Gephardt (D)	117,601	(58%)	($2,621,479)
	Gary Gill (R)	80,977	(40%)	($196,461)
	Others	5,362	(3%)	
1994 primary	Richard A. Gephardt (D)	54,582	(77%)	
	Leif Johnson (D)	11,619	(16%)	
	Lee Lehmuth (D)	4,718	(7%)	
1992 general	Richard A. Gephardt (D)	174,000	(64%)	($3,316,784)
	Mack Holekamp (R)	90,006	(33%)	($425,966)
	Other	7,828	(3%)	

FOURTH DISTRICT

Missouri was the first state settled west of the Mississippi, and the folk that settled it were a picture of pioneer diversity. Virginians and other southerners made their way to counties north of the Missouri River, while Germans settled around the still small capital city of Jefferson City. A taste of that variety can be found in the Capitol, with its mural by Thomas Hart Benton, great-grandnephew of Missouri's first senator, who championed hard money and westward expansion for 30 years and was thrown out of the Senate for opposing the expansion of slavery. The painting shows dance hall girls, black coal miners, a mother diapering an infant—all reminders that pioneer life was less homogeneous than one might imagine.

The 4th Congressional District of Missouri occupies much of this early-settled part of central and western Missouri. It penetrates into Kansas City's Jackson County and its metro overflow in Cass County, but the overall atmosphere here is rural and small town, with political traditions dating back to the community's early days. The rural counties around Kansas City were full of pro-slavery-expansion Bushwhackers who rode across the Kansas line to thwart the Yankee Jayhawks, and these areas today vote Democratic. The German area around Jefferson City was anti-slavery and remains among the most Republican parts of Missouri, and the new resort areas around Lake of the Ozarks tend also to be Republican. Indeed, Party Cove, at the lake's western end, is an archetypical example of deregulation—no curfew, speed or size limits for boats on the water—although the drunken flotilla parties and nude sunbathing might not be what Republican regulatory reformers have in mind. But this entire region is also Truman country: Harry Truman was born just south of the district and lived just northwest of it, spanning the gaps between country and city, South and North; Truman's mother could remember her house being attacked by Yankee soldiers, and she remained pro-Confederate even when her son was in the White House.

The congressman from the 4th District is Ike Skelton, who in many ways can be called a true Truman Democrat. A prosecutor and state senator first elected to Congress in 1976, Skelton looks—and votes—the part of an old-fashioned rural Missouri Democrat: his record on economics is in line with his party, but he is more tradition-minded on cultural issues. He supports the same expansive, assertive foreign and defense policies that the preponderance of Democrats supported in the days of Truman. Skelton serves on the National Security Committee where he has made great contributions to policy. He has long called for better strategic training in the services, particularly in the war colleges, and for improving the higher-level military educational programs; in 1994 he secured increased joint training programs for the four military branches—to be held at nearby Fort Leonard Wood. And though his work over the years has helped transform the American military into the high-performance force evident in the Gulf war, Skelton is not blindly pro-military; he warned President Clinton of a possible quagmire in the Balkans, and publicly opposed the invasion of Haiti.

Skelton also works on local issues, protecting farmers' use of pesticides and blocking reductions in rural mail service. He was instrumental in bringing B-2 bombers to Whiteman Air

Force Base—now one of the few military installations with booming growth—and expanding the Truman National Historical Site.

Now in his ninth term, Skelton's work for Missourians is reflected in his success at the polls. Redistricted with a Republican incumbent in 1982, he won with 55%; in anti-incumbent 1992, he was reelected with 70%. And in 1994, Skelton was barely buffeted by the Republican tidal wave. Facing token opposition in both the primary and general elections, he took all 23 counties both times. His centrism also is shown in his striking sympathy for the Contract With America, placing him at odds with fellow Missourian Dick Gephardt. Skelton has been replaced as Military Personnel Subcommittee chairman by Robert Dornan, but he remains an influential member and popular politician—and perhaps the last of a breed.

The People: Pop. 1990: 569,295; 61% rural; 15% age 65+; 95% White; 3% Black; 1% Amer. Indian; 1% Asian; 1% Hispanic origin. Voting age pop.: 420,487; 3% Black; 1% Hispanic origin. Households: 64% married couple families; 30% married couple fams. w. children; 34% college educ.; median household income: $23,064; per capita income: $10,984; median gross rent: $319; median house value: $49,400.

1992 Presidential Vote			1988 Presidential Vote		
Bush (R)	96,770	(38%)	Bush (R)	130,485	(59%)
Clinton (D)	94,948	(37%)	Dukakis (D)	88,890	(41%)
Perot (I)	65,233	(25%)			

Rep. Ike Skelton (D)

Elected 1976; b. Dec. 20, 1931, Lexington; home, Lexington; Wentworth Military Academy Jr. Col., 1949–51, U. of MO, A.B. 1953, LL.B. 1956; Disciples of Christ; married (Susan).

Career: Lafayette Cnty. Prosecuting atty., 1957–60; MO Special Asst. Atty. Gen., 1961–63; Practicing atty., 1963–76; MO Senate, 1971–76.

DC Office: 2227 RHOB 20515, 202-225-2876.

District Offices: 1616 Industrial Dr., Jefferson City 65109, 314-635-3499; 514-B N.W. 7 Hwy., Blue Springs 64014, 816-228-4242; 319 S. Lamine, Sedalia 65301, 816-826-2675; and 219 N. Adams St., Lebanon 65536, 417-532-7964.

Committees: *National Security* (4th of 25 D): Military Personnel; Military Procurement (RMM).

Group Ratings

	ADA	ACLU	COPE	CFA	LCV	CON	NSI	COC	ACU	NTLC	CHC
1994	35	18	56	20	25	26	80	67	62	44	64
1993	35	—	80	70	57	8	—	45	43	—	—

National Journal Ratings

	1993 LIB — 1993 CONS			1994 LIB — 1994 CONS		
Economic	52%	—	48%	59%	—	37%
Social	33%	—	66%	24%	—	73%
Foreign	47%	—	50%	45%	—	55%

Key Votes of the 103d Congress

1. Clinton Deficit Plan	Y	3. Brady Handgun Purchase	N	5. Lmt. UN Cmnd. of Forces	N
2. NAFTA	Y	4. Strike Race/Death Pnlty.	Y	6. Cut Missile Funds	N

Key Votes of the 104th Congress

1. Congressional Compliance Y	6. Reform Crime Grant Y	11. Loser Pays Court Reform N
2. Balanced Budget Amndmt. Y	7. National Security Act N	12. Product Liability Reform N
3. Bar Unfunded Mandates Y	8. Moratorium on Regs. Y	13. Welfare Reform *
4. Pass Line Item Veto Y	9. Risk Assessment on Regs. Y	14. Term Limits Amndmt. N
5. Relax Exclusionary Rule Y	10. Expnd. Priv. Prop. Rights Y	15. Tax Cuts Y

Election Results

1994 general	Ike Skelton (D).....................	137,876	(68%)	($427,184)
	James A. Noland Jr. (R)...............	65,616	(32%)	($15,666)
1994 primary	Ike Skelton (D)......................	45,715	(82%)	
	Alan E. (Gene) Allis (D)	5,473	(10%)	
	Ed Podhorn (D).......................	4,466	(8%)	
1992 general	Ike Skelton (D)......................	176,977	(70%)	($426,867)
	John Carney (R)......................	74,475	(30%)	($4,628)

FIFTH DISTRICT

Kansas City, Missouri, named after a state it isn't in and a river that doesn't touch it, is the center of one of America's large metro areas, the biggest on the central Great Plains. The first pioneers here started little towns on the bluffs above the Missouri River—Independence, Kansas City, Westport—which coalesced a few decades later. Here the Santa Fe Trail set out to cross the Sand Hills of Kansas and reach Mexican territory; here Jayhawks and Bushwhackers set out to fight for control of Bleeding Kansas. It was a rail center and had one of the largest stockyards in the country, a major commercial center that built Art Deco skyscrapers and the Country Club Plaza, the first shopping center in America, in the 1920s. It is famous for Harry Truman, whose family lived on a farm now in the suburb of Grandview and who himself lived in Independence, the old county seat just to the east. It is famous also for its black community, and jazz musicians like Scott Joplin, Charlie Parker and Count Basie, and for its much-praised barbecue.

The 5th Congressional District of Missouri includes most of Kansas City in Jackson County, plus Grandview and the bulk of Independence; most of the city's landmarks, including the Truman home, are here. It includes all of Kansas City's black neighborhoods and is 24% black. Solidly but not overwhelmingly Democratic, for 34 years it was represented by Richard Bolling—a Truman ally first elected in the Truman wave of 1948, junior partner of Sam Rayburn in the 1950s, one of the real scholars of the House and ultimately chairman of the Rules Committee. Then, starting in 1983, for 12 years it was represented by Alan Wheat, a Democrat elected at age 31, one of the few black congressmen to represent a white-majority district; he gave up the seat to run for the Senate in what turned out to be the un-Democratic year of 1994.

The congresswoman from the 5th now is Karen McCarthy, the winner of an 11-candidate Democratic primary in August 1994 and victor over a black Republican in November. McCarthy used to be a teacher and a government affairs consultant; in 1976 she was elected to the Missouri House, and stayed there until 1994, from 1983 chairing the Ways and Means Committee, in 1994 president of the National Conference of State Legislators. She managed the not inconsiderable feat of winning 41% in the primary, against 10 other candidates. The top three finishers all were women, one of the few places where the 1992 Year of the Woman survived two years later: pro-life Carole Roper Park won 17%, Jackie McGee, who is black, 13%. McCarthy was supported by unions, environmentalists, black organizations, Kansas City Mayor Emanuel Cleaver; she raised more than $350,000 for the primary.

By September, McCarthy had already arranged a place to live in Washington, but the general election turned out to be a little closer than expected. Republican Ron Freeman, in the 1980s a professional football player in the short-lived United States Football League, now works with the Fellowship of Christian Athletes. He backed term limits and attacked "a government which has refused to be accountable to the citizenship;" after the election, Republican leader Dick Armey called Freeman the best candidate that he had seen across the nation. McCarthy stressed her conciliatory skills: "I can put people with different views together in a room and help them come up with solutions." In Jefferson City she passed a clean air measure and a healthcare bill, which died in the Senate, and helped create the Office of Public Counsel to argue utility rate cases. She was supported by business leaders and her $250,000 edge in PAC money gave her an advantage in campaign spending. McCarthy won 57%–43%, carrying Kansas City 2–1 but losing the suburban half of the district.

In Washington McCarthy responded enthusiastically to Bill Clinton's State of the Union speech, but worked for passage of the balanced budget amendment and called for a more bipartisan approach to legislation. Unlike her two predecessors from the 5th district, who were skillful in assembling pieces of the Democratic coalition to pass major legislation, McCarthy faces the more demanding task of helping to rebuild a party and expand its appeal. As Dick Bolling helped Dick Gephardt get started in the 1970s, McCarthy could benefit from the help of Gephardt in the '90s. Her background should serve her well, but the challenge is great and the Republican takeover makes her committee assignments less appealing and her task more difficult.

The People: Pop. 1990: 569,289; 1% rural; 14% age 65+; 72% White; 24% Black; 1% Amer. Indian; 1% Asian; 2% Other; 3% Hispanic origin. Voting age pop.: 428,620; 21% Black; 3% Hispanic origin. Households: 47% married couple families; 20% married couple fams. w. children; 46% college educ.; median household income: $26,968; per capita income: $13,650; median gross rent: $398; median house value: $56,300.

1992 Presidential Vote			1988 Presidential Vote		
Clinton (D)	134,862	(52%)	Dukakis (D)	137,016	(60%)
Bush (R)	67,511	(26%)	Bush (R)	92,974	(40%)
Perot (I)	55,799	(22%)			

Rep. Karen McCarthy (D)

Elected 1994; b. Mar. 18, 1947, Haverhill, MA; home, Kansas City; U. of KS, B.A. 1969, M.B.A. 1986, U. of MO, M.A. 1976; Roman Catholic; divorced.

Career: High Schl. teacher, 1969–76; MO House of Reps., 1977–94; Financial analyst, 1984–86; Govt. affairs consultant, Marion Merrill Dow, 1986–94; Pres., Natl. Conf. of State Legislatures, 1994.

DC Office: 1232 LHOB 20515, 202-225-4535; Fax: 202-225-4403.

District Offices: 811 Grand Ave., #935, Kansas City 64106, 816-842-4545; and 301 W. Lexington, #217, Independence 64050, 816-833-4545.

Committees: *Science* (17th of 23 D): Energy and Environment; Technology. *Small Business* (17th of 19 D): Regulation and Paperwork; Tax and Finance.

Group Ratings and 103rd Congress Votes: Newly Elected

Key Votes of the 104th Congress

1. Congressional Compliance Y	6. Reform Crime Grant N	11. Loser Pays Court Reform N
2. Balanced Budget Amndmt. Y	7. National Security Act N	12. Product Liability Reform N
3. Bar Unfunded Mandates Y	8. Moratorium on Regs. *	13. Welfare Reform N
4. Pass Line Item Veto Y	9. Risk Assessment on Regs. N	14. Term Limits Amndmt. Y
5. Relax Exclusionary Rule N	10. Expnd. Priv. Prop. Rights N	15. Tax Cuts N

Election Results

1994 general	Karen McCarthy (D)	100,391	(57%)	($866,808)
	Ron Freeman (R)	77,120	(43%)	($458,373)
1994 primary	Karen McCarthy (D)	26,663	(41%)	
	Carole Roper Park (D)	11,097	(17%)	
	Jacqueline T. McGee (D)	8,143	(13%)	
	Edward (Gomer) Moody (D)	7,653	(12%)	
	Frank J. Smist Jr. (D)	4,134	(6%)	
	Others	6,642	(10%)	
1992 general	Alan Wheat (D)	151,014	(59%)	($673,086)
	Edward (Gomer) Moody (R)	93,562	(37%)	($57,400)
	Others	10,736	(4%)	

SIXTH DISTRICT

The rolling, surging fields along the Missouri River in the northwest Missouri were settled in a rush in the late 19th Century, and have been losing people ever since. Fewer hands are needed on farms than half a century ago, far fewer than at the turn of the century; and even the biggest town in northwest Missouri, St. Joseph, has lost population. In 1940, this area had the fifth largest meat-packing operation in the world, but the meat-packing business has generated no more new jobs than farming, and St. Joseph has fewer people than in 1900. The counties of northwest Missouri, aside from those in the Kansas City metro area, had 508,000 people in 1900, 452,000 in 1940 and under 300,000 in 1990.

All these counties, plus Clay and Platte Counties which include the parts of Kansas City north of the Missouri River, make up Missouri's 6th Congressional District: the two metro counties have gained people almost precisely to the extent that the rural counties have lost them. The Kansas City area has almost half the district's population, but newly developed, decentralized and without strong political organizations, it casts only 36% of its votes. The historic political tradition here is mostly Democratic, tempered by dislike for national Democrats' cultural liberalism, but strengthened in the 1980s by anger at what people regard as neglect of this salt-of-the-earth farming area—an attitude similar to that found across the border in more left-leaning Iowa. This area gave Bill Clinton a plurality in 1992, but Ross Perot got 27% here, and in 1994 it voted for Republican Senator John Ashcroft.

The congresswoman from the 6th District since 1992 has been Pat Danner, a state Senate veteran and former aide to Jerry Litton, congressman for four years here and the winner of the 1976 primary who was killed on a plane crash on primary night. Danner ran to succeed Litton that year, but placed second in the Democratic primary to Morgan Maxfield, who lost to Tom Coleman when it was discovered Maxfield had falsified his life story. Following her defeat, Danner became co-chair of the Ozark Regional Planning Commission under President Carter; in 1982 she was elected to the state Senate. In 1990, her son Stephen was elected in an adjoining district, and they became the only mother-son team in a state Senate in America; he ran for state auditor in 1994, and lost 58%–39%. Things went better for Pat Danner in 1992, when she won an eight-candidate Democratic primary with 52% of the vote, and defeated 16-year incumbent Republican Tom Coleman, 55%–45%, in a spirited campaign.

In her first term, Danner compiled a moderate-to-liberal voting record. She worked on Fiscal

Caucus efforts to cut outdated federal programs and worked for federal aid to repair the damage of the terrible 1993 floods. She opposed nationalized health care, and she balked at the House version of the Freedom of Choice Act, which gave states less leeway than the Senate version, having voted for the Missouri abortion law upheld in the 1989 *Webster* case. She voted against the Clinton budget and tax package in August 1993 and against NAFTA in October 1993. She contributed her pay raise to 6th District scholarships and returned much of her congressional office allowance to the treasury.

Danner was rewarded with this centrist record in 1994. Her Republican opponent, Tina Tucker, spent little money and Tucker's argument that NAFTA would benefit Missouri agriculture (after all, Mexican cuisine is based on corn) went mostly unheard. Danner won with 66% in a Republican year. In her second term she joined conservative House Democrats' "The Coalition," seeking grounds for bipartisanship and more appealing positions for their party. She favored a deficit-cutting "lock box" for receipts from new taxes. Because of Democrats' loss of seats and committee downsizing, the Agriculture Committee position she sought still eluded her—a bit surprising given the home-state connection to Minority Leader Gephardt. She raised the standard of one reform Speaker Newt Gingrich balked at: the wife of a retired airline pilot, she argued for restricting members' personal use of frequent flier miles. But as one of the strongest Democratic supporters of the Contract With America, she took a political profile very different from that of most other women first elected in 1992.

The People: Pop. 1990: 568,823; 37% rural; 14% age 65+; 96% White; 2% Black; 1% Asian; 1% Other; 2% Hispanic origin. Voting age pop.: 420,360; 2% Black; 1% Hispanic origin. Households: 62% married couple families; 29% married couple fams. w. children; 40% college educ.; median household income: $27,165; per capita income: $12,641; median gross rent: $362; median house value: $54,900.

1992 Presidential Vote

Clinton (D)	110,137	(40%)
Bush (R)	88,980	(32%)
Perot (I)	75,150	(27%)

1988 Presidential Vote

Bush (R)	119,494	(51%)
Dukakis (D)	116,582	(49%)

Rep. Pat Danner (D)

Elected 1992; b. Jan. 13, 1934, Louisville, KY; home, Smithville; NE MO St. U., B.A. 1973; Catholic; married (Markt Meyer).

Career: Dist. Asst., U.S. Rep. Jerry Litton, 1973–76; Co-Chmn., Ozarks Regional Plng. Comm., 1977–81; MO Senate, 1982–92.

DC Office: 1323 LHOB 20515, 202-225-7041; Fax: 202-225-8221.

District Offices: 5754 N. Broadway, Bldg. 3, Kansas City 64118, 816-455-2256; and 201 S. 8th St., #330, St. Joseph 64501, 816-233-9818.

Committees: *Transportation & Infrastructure* (19th of 27 D): Aviation; Surface Transportation.

Group Ratings

	ADA	ACLU	COPE	CFA	LCV	CON	NSI	COC	ACU	NTLC	CHC
1994	70	52	78	40	38	43	30	58	29	33	57
1993	60	—	92	80	57	10	—	27	25	—	—

National Journal Ratings

	1993 LIB — 1993 CONS			1994 LIB — 1994 CONS		
Economic	55%	—	43%	67%	—	29%
Social	54%	—	45%	48%	—	50%
Foreign	59%	—	38%	51%	—	47%

Key Votes of the 103d Congress

1. Clinton Deficit Plan	N	3. Brady Handgun Purchase	N	5. Lmt. UN Cmnd. of Forces	N
2. NAFTA	N	4. Strike Race/Death Pnlty.	N	6. Cut Missile Funds	Y

Key Votes of the 104th Congress

1. Congressional Compliance	Y	6. Reform Crime Grant	Y	11. Loser Pays Court Reform	N
2. Balanced Budget Amndmt.	Y	7. National Security Act	N	12. Product Liability Reform	Y
3. Bar Unfunded Mandates	Y	8. Moratorium on Regs.	Y	13. Welfare Reform	N
4. Pass Line Item Veto	Y	9. Risk Assessment on Regs.	Y	14. Term Limits Amndmt.	Y
5. Relax Exclusionary Rule	Y	10. Expnd. Priv. Prop. Rights	Y	15. Tax Cuts	Y

Election Results

1994 general	Pat Danner (D).....................	140,108	(66%)	($474,038)
	Tina Tucker (R)	71,709	(34%)	($42,378)
1994 primary	Pat Danner (D).....................	53,460	(77%)	
	Harold W. Ulmer (D)	15,819	(23%)	
1992 general	Pat Danner (D).....................	148,887	(55%)	($482,984)
	Tom Coleman (R)...................	119,637	(45%)	($533,305)

SEVENTH DISTRICT

The fastest-growing region of Missouri in the 1980s was neither of its big metropolitan areas, but the Ozarks region around Springfield. Filled with green hills sometimes labelled mountains and dam-made lakes sporting boats of all kinds, with small towns and the small city of Springfield, home of the fast-growing Assemblies of God, and Branson, the country and soft rock music center which has become America's number two tourist destination, the Ozarks region is the kind of place in which many Americans would like to live—and more do every day. New subdivisions pop up around Springfield, as do retirement developments and condominiums in the mountains to the south; the two-lane roads into Branson are choked with vans and tourist buses, full of people eager to see Mel Tillis and Louise Mandrell and Andy Williams and Shoji Tabuchi. Incomes are below average, but so is the cost of living and the crime rate. The climate here is relatively temperate and the cultural tone distinctly traditional. Historically, southwestern Missouri is Republican—against secession in 1861: pro-Union Springfield changed hands several times during Missouri own civil war. Its conservative response to the big-spending government of the 1960s and cultural liberalism of the 1970s reinforced its Republicanism.

The 7th Congressional District of Missouri covers most of the southwest corner of the state, centered on Springfield. It is a solidly Republican district and is held, sometimes less than solidly, by a very solid conservative, Mel Hancock. Hancock grew up in Carthage and Springfield, quit a job with International Harvester rather than be transferred out of southwest Missouri and started his own security equipment leasing business. In 1977 he found an anti-government speech his father had written in 1951, and was inspired to start a drive for an initiative mandating lower taxes: his Hancock Amendment was passed by the voters in 1980. He lost races for senator in 1982 and lieutenant governor in 1984; when the 7th District incumbent retired in 1988, he won the primary 39%–36% and the general 53%–46%. He has one of the most conservative voting records in the House, and has mostly abstained from introducing legislation. One exception: he proposed to cut off federal funds to schools that teach homosexuality is "a positive lifestyle alternative." As a Ways and Means Committee member, he is not a premier legislative craftsman but he has given solid rhetorical support to the Contract With America; with his business background, he has been quick to challenge the Democratic fiscal orthodoxies that had so long prevailed in the House. But much of his attention is directed to Missouri. When Democratic Governor Mel Carnahan got a tax increase for education in 1993 and did not submit it to referendum as Hancock believed the Hancock Amendment required, he put Hancock II on the ballot. Carnahan campaigned strongly against it, and retiring Republican Senator John Danforth opposed it as well; it was beaten badly. But in December 1994, Carnahan proposed his own tax limitation measure.

Hancock was reelected narrowly in 1990 and easily in 1992 and 1994. He favors term limits and in his first campaign promised to retire after four terms; in early 1995 he said he would keep his promise and retire in 1996. He added that he had no plans to run for governor then, either. Republicans should have no trouble holding his House seat. The first candidate into the race was conservative Gary Nodler, a regional official of the Small Business Administration during the Bush Administration who narrowly lost to Hancock in the 1988 primary and had been a long-time aide to Hancock predecessor Gene Taylor.

The People: Pop. 1990: 568,017; 48% rural; 16% age 65+; 97% White; 1% Black; 1% Amer. Indian; 1% Hispanic origin. Voting age pop.: 428,507; 1% Black; 1% Hispanic origin. Households: 61% married couple families; 27% married couple fams. w. children; 38% college educ.; median household income: $21,712; per capita income: $11,029; median gross rent: $315; median house value: $48,200.

1992 Presidential Vote			1988 Presidential Vote		
Bush (R)	118,817	(45%)	Bush (R)	139,627	(62%)
Clinton (D)	96,621	(36%)	Dukakis (D)	86,049	(38%)
Perot (I)	48,824	(18%)			

Rep. Mel Hancock (R)

Elected 1988; b. Sept. 19, 1929, Cape Fair; home, Springfield; SW MO St. Col., B.S. 1951; Church of Christ; married ("Sug").

Career: Air Force, 1951–53, Air Force Reserves, 1953–65; Intl. Harvester Co., 1947–51, 1953–59; Hardware Mutual Insurance, 1960–67; Owner & Pres., Federal Protection Inc., 1969–89.

DC Office: 438 CHOB 20515, 202-225-6536; Fax: 202-225-7700.

District Offices: 2840 E. Chestnut Expwy., Springfield 65802, 417-862-4317; and 302 Fed. Bldg., Joplin 64801, 417-781-1041.

Committees: *Ways & Means* (10th of 21 R): Oversight; Social Security; Trade.

Group Ratings

	ADA	ACLU	COPE	CFA	LCV	CON	NSI	COC	ACU	NTLC	CHC
1994	10	13	11	0	11	94	100	75	95	96	100
1993	5	—	0	0	14	52	—	91	100	—	—

National Journal Ratings

	1993 LIB — 1993 CONS		1994 LIB — 1994 CONS	
Economic	14%	80%	0%	80%
Social	0%	89%	0%	89%
Foreign	9%	85%	14%	80%

Key Votes of the 103d Congress

1. Clinton Deficit Plan	N	3. Brady Handgun Purchase	N	5. Lmt. UN Cmnd. of Forces	Y
2. NAFTA	Y	4. Strike Race/Death Pnlty.	Y	6. Cut Missile Funds	N

Key Votes of the 104th Congress

1. Congressional Compliance	Y	6. Reform Crime Grant	Y	11. Loser Pays Court Reform	Y
2. Balanced Budget Amndmt.	Y	7. National Security Act	Y	12. Product Liability Reform	Y
3. Bar Unfunded Mandates	Y	8. Moratorium on Regs.	Y	13. Welfare Reform	Y
4. Pass Line Item Veto	Y	9. Risk Assessment on Regs.	Y	14. Term Limits Amndmt.	Y
5. Relax Exclusionary Rule	Y	10. Expnd. Priv. Prop. Rights	Y	15. Tax Cuts	Y

Election Results

1994 general	Mel Hancock (R)	112,228	(57%)	($218,098)
	James R. Fossard (D)	77,836	(40%)	($239,681)
	Others	5,852	(3%)	
1994 primary	Mel Hancock (R)	unopposed		
1992 general	Mel Hancock (R)	160,303	(62%)	($426,525)
	Thomas Patrick Deaton (D)	99,762	(38%)	($310,658)

EIGHTH DISTRICT

Mark Twain might not recognize life on the Mississippi below St. Louis today, where the land flattens out and the river is hidden behind levees, which ordinarily—except during the terrible flood of 1993—screen small towns and river roads from the sight of rows of barges tethered together, full of coal or soybeans. The Mississippi today is an industrial waterway; but it was never really all that romantic, for Twain's steamboats, as he is at pains to point out, were dangerous, noisy contraptions, forever blowing up or getting embedded in roots and branches in the swirling river currents. This is one of the older-settled parts of the United States: French settlers founded Missouri towns like Cape Girardeau in the late 1700s. But the big influx started just a few years after the 1811 earthquake centered on New Madrid; the spongy Mississippi valley land is also seismically very active, and in this was the site of one of the most devastating earthquakes in U.S. history.

Outwardly, the southeast quadrant of Missouri—the river valley and the hills to the west, with coal and lead mines with their miles of tunnels, plus the Bootheel that hangs down in the far southeast—hasn't changed much in 50 years. The only big growth here in that time has been around Cape Girardeau and along the route of Interstate 44; there has been a big population outflow from the Bootheel, as machines replace low-wage farm workers, and from some mining communities, as ores give out or become uneconomical to extract. Politically, the heritage here is mostly Democratic, although with a strong southern accent. But Cape Girardeau, where Rush Limbaugh grew up, is Republican, and most counties have trended that way over time, reflected in presidential contests and in elections in the 8th Congressional District of Missouri, which covers most of the southeast quadrant of the state, and which since 1980 has elected Republican Bill Emerson.

Emerson's congressional career goes back arguably farther in his life than any other House Republican's. He was a congressional page in 1954, on the floor of the House when it was fired upon by Puerto Rican terrorists; in the 1960s, he was a staffer for Congressman Robert Ellsworth and Senator Charles Mathias. In the 1970s, Emerson was a Washington lobbyist, who upon spotting the personal vulnerability of the Democratic incumbent, in 1980 went back home to southeast Missouri to run, and won with 55%.

Emerson's voting record has been quite conservative, but he is not a purist. Emerson got a seat on the Agriculture Committee where he is now second-ranking Republican. This puts him on the spot, as the 1995 farm bill will affect rice and cotton farmers in the Bootheel and the Republican budget has promised sizable cuts in farm programs. In early 1995 he and Chairman Pat Roberts persuaded Newt Gingrich to drop the Contract With America proposal to put food stamps—a major part of Agriculture spending—into block grants to the states, with the committee promising some reforms of its own. But Emerson expressed "dismay" in a letter to Senate Republican leaders when they said that the House proposal did not go far enough in giving the states ample flexibility. Emerson worked against proposed EPA pesticide protection rules in 1994 and helped get them delayed until 1995. He has charged that the proposed National Biological Survey ultimately "will lead to the establishment of a militant eco Gestapo force." Emerson also serves on the Transportation and Infrastructure Committee. He has spent much time on highway and water projects for the district; he pushed for funding for the Mississippi Delta commission and for the Ozarks National Scenic Riverways visitors' center. He balked at the Clinton Administration's initial Mexico bailout proposal, and believes that affirmative action programs now amount to quotas.

Emerson won reelection in the late 1980s with less than 60%. But he appears to have secured the former "swing" district, with 63% in 1992 and 70% in 1994. He was mentioned as a candidate for the Senate in 1994, but declined to oppose former Governor John Ashcroft in the primary; he has also been mentioned as a possible candidate for governor in 1996, against incumbent Democrat Mel Carnahan, whose son he defeated in 1990.

The People: Pop. 1990: 568,385; 63% rural; 16% age 65+; 94% White; 4% Black; 1% Hispanic origin. Voting age pop.: 417,903; 4% Black. Households: 61% married couple families; 28% married couple fams. w. children; 25% college educ.; median household income: $18,207; per capita income: $9,300; median gross rent: $268; median house value: $37,500.

1992 Presidential Vote			1988 Presidential Vote		
Clinton (D)	109,858	(46%)	Bush (R)	116,668	(56%)
Bush (R)	89,238	(37%)	Dukakis (D)	92,880	(44%)
Perot (I)	41,558	(17%)			

Rep. Bill Emerson (R)

Elected 1980; b. Jan. 1, 1938, Hillsboro; home, Cape Girardeau; Westminster Col., B.A. 1959, U. of Baltimore, LL.B. 1964; Presbyterian; married (Jo Ann).

Career: Air Force Reserves, 1963–92; A.A., U.S. Rep. Bob Ellsworth, 1961–65; A.A., U.S. Sen. Charles Mathias, 1965–70; Govt. Affairs Dir., Fairchild Ind., 1970–73; Pub. Affairs Dir., Interstate Natural Gas Assn., 1974–75; Exec. Asst., FEC Chmn., 1975; Fed. Relations Dir., TRW Inc., 1975–79; Consultant, 1979–80.

DC Office: 2268 RHOB 20515, 202-225-4404; Fax: 202-225-9621.

District Offices: 339 Broadway, Cape Girardeau 63701, 314-335-0101; and 612 Pine, Rolla 65401, 314-364-2455.

Committees: *Agriculture* (2nd of 27 R): Department Operations, Nutrition and Foreign Agriculture (Chmn.); General Farm Commodities. *Transportation & Infrastructure* (7th of 33 R): Surface Transportation; Water Resources and Environment.

Group Ratings

	ADA	ACLU	COPE	CFA	LCV	CON	NSI	COC	ACU	NTLC	CHC
1994	0	17	0	20	0	56	100	100	100	86	100
1993	0	—	17	10	14	57	—	91	100	—	—

National Journal Ratings

	1993 LIB — 1993 CONS			1994 LIB — 1994 CONS		
Economic	25%	—	72%	0%	—	80%
Social	11%	—	82%	11%	—	85%
Foreign	9%	—	85%	33%	—	66%

Key Votes of the 103d Congress

1. Clinton Deficit Plan	N	3. Brady Handgun Purchase	N	5. Lmt. UN Cmnd. of Forces	Y
2. NAFTA	Y	4. Strike Race/Death Pnlty.	Y	6. Cut Missile Funds	N

Key Votes of the 104th Congress

1. Congressional Compliance	Y	6. Reform Crime Grant	Y	11. Loser Pays Court Reform	Y
2. Balanced Budget Amndmt.	Y	7. National Security Act	Y	12. Product Liability Reform	Y
3. Bar Unfunded Mandates	Y	8. Moratorium on Regs.	Y	13. Welfare Reform	Y
4. Pass Line Item Veto	Y	9. Risk Assessment on Regs.	Y	14. Term Limits Amndmt.	Y
5. Relax Exclusionary Rule	Y	10. Expnd. Priv. Prop. Rights	Y	15. Tax Cuts	Y

Election Results

1994 general	Bill Emerson (R)	129,320	(70%)	($396,967)
	James L. (Jay) Thompson (D)	48,987	(27%)	($3,752)
	Others	6,279	(3%)	
1994 primary	Bill Emerson (R)	unopposed		
1992 general	Bill Emerson (R)	147,398	(63%)	($488,949)
	Thad Bullock (D)	86,730	(37%)	($11,974)

NINTH DISTRICT

Little Dixie, the swath of northeast Missouri along the Mississippi River, was settled by southerners from Kentucky and Virginia. Its most famous native son is Mark Twain, born Sam Clemens in Hannibal, then as now a little town on bluffs overlooking the river. Hannibal also was the thinly disguised St. Petersburg of Tom Sawyer and Huckleberry Finn, loving created years later complete with Pike County and other dialect by Twain, then living in New England. Little Dixie has always been Democratic politically and was pro-Confederate during the Civil War; Callaway County declared its independence from the Union. Twain's view of politics was different, both darker and more optimistic: he created a vision of America that transcended region and a view of antebellum society that identified slavery as an evil without ever saying so; Twain himself was a Republican and close friend of Union General and President Ulysses S. Grant. But whatever the author's feelings for his birthplace, Hannibal loves Twain; some quarter-million tourists pour in to visit his boyhood home each year.

Faithfully Democratic Little Dixie has reared some notable politicians as well. One was Champ Clark, speaker of the House from 1911–19 and presidential candidate in 1912; another was Clarence Cannon, author of the definitive text on the House's parliamentary procedure and chairman of the House Appropriations Committee until his death in 1963. Since then the area has been represented in the House by only two other men, both Democrats.

The 9th Congressional District of Missouri includes Little Dixie and goes as far south as Franklin and outer St. Charles Counties in metro St. Louis. It has Columbia, home of the University of Missouri, and Fulton, home of Westminster College, where in 1946 Winston Churchill, accompanied by President Harry Truman, told the world that "from Stettin on the Baltic to Trieste on the Adriatic, an iron curtain has descended across the continent." It also includes the old German town of Hermann, laid out by members of the German settlement, Society of Philadelphia, who hoped to preserve the customs of their homeland in the isolation of the wilderness. Hermann and, to a lesser extent, the St. Louis suburbs tend to vote Republican, while conservative Little Dixie has mostly stayed faithful to the Democratic Party.

The congressman from the 9th District is Harold Volkmer, a contrary-minded Democrat who emerged from long obscurity to be one of the star attractions of the 104th Congress. Volkmer is from Hannibal, where he started practicing law in the 1950s; he was a prosecutor in the 1960s and a Missouri legislator for 10 years beginning in 1966. Those were years when Missouri's rural Democrats were on the defensive against young Republican reformers John Danforth and Christopher Bond; and Volkmer seems to thrive in opposition. He was elected to the House in 1976, when the incumbent retired; Democrats had a 2–1 edge, but his somewhat conservative record and irritable temperament set him apart. His biggest legislative achievement was passage in 1986 of the McClure-Volkmer amendments weakening federal gun control laws. On the Agriculture Committee, where he rose to chair (and is now the ranking minority member on) the Livestock panel, Volkmer worked to protect dairy farmers' federal aid and shield them from foreign competition.

The same conservative temperament and issue positions which made him unpopular in the Democratic caucus in the 1980s caused him problems in the university town of Columbia, even while his Democratic label hurt in some St. Louis suburbs. In 1992 he was opposed by Republican Rick Hardy, a political science professor at the University of Missouri, who caught Volkmer off guard. Although Bill Clinton was carrying the district, Volkmer won by only 48%–46%. In 1994 Hardy ran again, but after the primary filing deadline, he withdrew from the race because of depression and exhaustion. In August party leaders nominated state special prosecutor Kenny Hulsof as a replacement, but the late start gave him too little time with both voters and donors. Hulshof carried Columbia and Boone County, where the Libertarian candidate won 10% of the vote, but he lost almost everywhere else; Volkmer's huge advantage in PAC money helped him in the St. Louis area, and he carried all but two Little Dixie counties (Boone and Audrain), though some only narrowly, for a 50%–45% victory.

Volkmer's activist role in the 104th Congress arose out of happenstance: he was walking into the chamber when Republicans took down the words (a parliamentary challenge) of Florida Democrat Carrie Meek as she was attacking Newt Gingrich's book contract. Volkmer, contrary as always, was outraged by what he thought was unfairness; and ever after, he prowled the floor, pouncing to puncture the Republicans' arguments or pointing up their inconsistencies. His knowledge of parliamentary procedure, and his natural nitpickiness, made him a hero to leftish Democrats who used to shun him because they couldn't stand the smell of his cigarette smoke. For his part, Volkmer showed both humor and panache in the opposition, maintaining his record as an opponent of gun control by moving to exempt the Bureau of Alcohol, Tobacco and Firearms from Republicans' loosened search and seizure guidelines. More quietly, he voted for several other pieces of the Contract With America.

How will this play back home? Volkmer may well have a serious challenge and retirement is a possibility. But he is one rural Democrat who may be helped by obdurate opposition to Republicans. And his continued opposition to gun control may help him in Little Dixie. He may find it harder to raise money and buy St. Louis TV. But the traditional mascot of rural Missouri is the mule, and Volkmer in his stubbornness and prickliness may strike a mulish note that his constituents find appealing.

The People: Pop. 1990: 568,238; 51% rural; 13% age 65+; 95% White; 4% Black; 1% Asian; 1% Hispanic origin. Voting age pop.: 416,794; 3% Black; 1% Hispanic origin. Households: 62% married couple families; 30% married couple fams. w. children; 38% college educ.; median household income: $26,055; per capita income: $11,741; median gross rent: $338; median house value: $55,200.

1992 Presidential Vote

Clinton (D)	110,175	(41%)
Bush (R)	90,836	(34%)
Perot (I)	65,195	(24%)

1988 Presidential Vote

Bush (R)	121,243	(54%)
Dukakis (D)	104,871	(46%)

Rep. Harold L. Volkmer (D)

Elected 1976; b. Apr. 4, 1931, Jefferson City; home, Hannibal; Jefferson City Jr. Col., St. Louis U., U. of MO, LL.B. 1955; Catholic; married (Shirley).

Career: Army, 1955–57; Practicing atty., 1957–60; Marion Cnty. Prosecuting Atty., 1960–66; MO House of Reps., 1967–76.

DC Office: 2409 RHOB 20515, 202-225-2956; Fax: 202-225-7834.

District Offices: 370 Fed. Bldg., Hannibal 63401, 314-221-1200.

Committees: *Agriculture* (5th of 22 D): General Farm Commodities; Livestock, Dairy and Poultry (RMM).

Group Ratings

	ADA	ACLU	COPE	CFA	LCV	CON	NSI	COC	ACU	NTLC	CHC
1994	50	26	78	40	53	33	60	58	48	26	64
1993	60	—	100	90	50	19	—	18	29	—	—

National Journal Ratings

	1993 LIB — 1993 CONS	1994 LIB — 1994 CONS
Economic	61% — 37%	67% — 29%
Social	36% — 62%	45% — 54%
Foreign	66% — 31%	46% — 53%

Key Votes of the 103d Congress

1. Clinton Deficit Plan	Y	3. Brady Handgun Purchase	N	5. Lmt. UN Cmnd. of Forces	N
2. NAFTA	N	4. Strike Race/Death Pnlty.	N	6. Cut Missile Funds	Y

Key Votes of the 104th Congress

1. Congressional Compliance	Y	6. Reform Crime Grant	N	11. Loser Pays Court Reform	N
2. Balanced Budget Amndmt.	Y	7. National Security Act	N	12. Product Liability Reform	N
3. Bar Unfunded Mandates	Y	8. Moratorium on Regs.	N	13. Welfare Reform	N
4. Pass Line Item Veto	N	9. Risk Assessment on Regs.	Y	14. Term Limits Amndmt.	N
5. Relax Exclusionary Rule	Y	10. Expnd. Priv. Prop. Rights	Y	15. Tax Cuts	N

Election Results

1994 general	Harold L. Volkmer (D)	103,443	(50%)	($473,716)
	Kenny Hulshof (R)	92,301	(45%)	($185,418)
	Mitchell J. Moore (Lib)	9,198	(4%)	
1994 primary	Harold L. Volkmer (D)	45,125	(67%)	
	Anthony DeFranco (D)	21,741	(33%)	
1992 general	Harold L. Volkmer (D)	124,694	(48%)	($511,550)
	Rick Hardy (R)	118,811	(46%)	($139,860)
	Jeff Barrow (Green)	10,565	(4%)	($8,395)
	Other	7,265	(3%)	

MONTANA

Montana is America's Big Sky Country, a land of great empty vistas, with mountains in the west and hundreds of miles of plateaus and plains in the east—the 4th largest state in area and 44th in population. Montana seems mostly empty yet is growing lustily once again, a place that embodies the Old West of 19th Century cowboys but whose recent growth owes much to 21st Century electronic communications. Montana sits atop America, spanning the Rockies so that on Interstate 15 you can cross the Continental Divide three times. Here are the headwaters of the Missouri, from its source in Beaverhead County to its mouth in the Gulf of Mexico the longest river in North America, and of the Clark Fork which flows into the Columbia and eventually the Pacific. Not far away, at Egg Mountain near Choteau on the Deep Teton River, is the world's most plenteous source of dinosaur remains. But Montana's recorded history is recent: at its 1989 centennial, the son of one of its original cattleman-settlers watched 105 cowboys drive 4,000 cattle with 300 covered wagons trailing behind.

Statehood came less than a century after the first white Americans came here as agents of the government—the Lewis and Clark expedition in 1805. Next came the mountain men, seeking fur, and then came the miners seeking gold, silver and copper—sudden riches that would make them kings not of this barren land but of the metropolises back East. Raucous mining towns sprang up, complete with outlaws and vigilantes. The mining economy gave Montana a radical, class warfare politics. On one side was the Anaconda Mining Company, which from about 1900 to the 1940s bought up almost all of Montana's newspapers, many of its utilities, many of its politicians, and had strong allies in the Stockmen's Association and the Farm Bureau. On the other side were progressives like Senators Thomas Walsh, who exposed the Teapot Dome scandal, and Burton Wheeler, who backed the New Deal but broke with Franklin Roosevelt over court packing and isolationism, the labor unions (Montana has no right-to-work law and is the most pro-union state in the Rockies), and pork barrel beneficiaries (for a while in the 1930s, Montana received more federal money per capita than almost any other state). The locus of all this was Butte, with its gold and copper mines on "The Richest Hill on Earth," with its gamblers and bootleggers, company goons and union thugs, IWW organizers and Socialist mayor and millionaires who bought seats in the U.S. Senate. Today the mines are closed, the population depleted, and the stone temples of commerce and grim looming mineheads are being restored to a cleanliness they never enjoyed in the boom days.

Slowly Montana has changed. Butte's population peaked in 1920, mines slowly closed all over the state, and agriculture—wheat-growing and cattle grazing—became the mainstays of the economy and class warfare politics became a glimmer of what it was in the past. Other towns grew, though none is over 100,000 yet: Billings with its agricultural marketing in the east, the university town of Missoula, Great Falls just east of the Rockies, Kalispell near Lake Flathead, the university and resort town of Bozeman and the state capital of Helena. The muscular tone of a land settled by ranch hands, miners and railroad workers, of cowboy hats, boots and blue jeans, of men who do hard physical work and relax hard afterwards, remains a link with Montanans going back to the mountain men, miners and cowboys who drove herds of cattle across the open range. And there is still the sense of space. Hunting and fishing, as in *A River Runs Through It*, are never far away; development in the small cities and resort areas has not been enough to drive the game away. In the late 1970s, Montana started attracting affluent second home buyers, and by the mid-1990s they came in a rush, movie stars and Wall Street magnates but also just ordinary people buying large or small spreads near the Big Sky or McLeod, near Bozeman, or around Flathead Lake or Big Timber or the Big Mountain ski resort in Whitefish, where grizzlies come down to forage and the bars hold mouse races. Computers, modems and fax

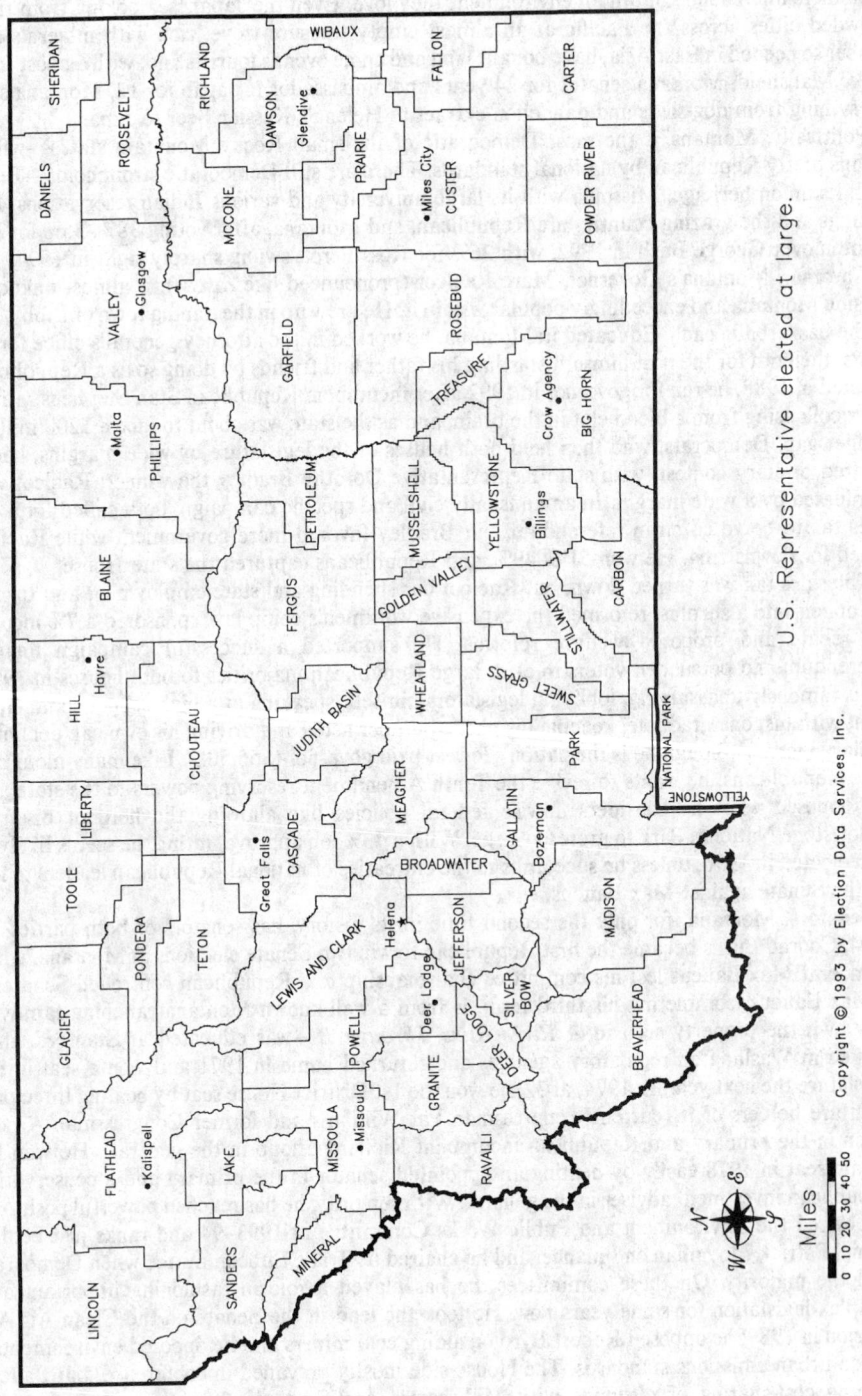

U.S. Representative elected at large.

Copyright © 1993 by Election Data Services, Inc.

machines make it possible for small businessmen and entrepreneurs to work here, far from their customers and clients, but in an environment they love. Even the Japanese, looking from their crowded cities across the Pacific at an almost empty treasure trove, rich with minerals and timber so needed in East Asia, have bought land and come over as tourists and, with a boost from Mike Mansfield, Montana senator for 24 years and ambassador to Japan for 12, Montana sells everything from dog sleds and dandelion extract to Helena's Kessler Beer to Japan.

Politically, Montana is the most Democratic of the small Rocky Mountain states—which means pretty Republican by national standards. There are still Democratic strongholds—Butte with its union heritage, Missoula with its large university and various Indian reservations. But Billings and the grazing counties are Republican, and Montana, after voting 38%–35% for Bill Clinton over George Bush in 1992, with 26% for Ross Perot, swung sharply right in 1994.

Governor. Montana's Governor, Marc Racicot (pronounced like *roscoe*), is almost unknown outside Montana and exceedingly popular within it. He grew up in the mining town of Libby, son of the basketball coach. Educated in Montana, he worked in the attorney general's office for 12 years, then ran for the post himself, startling his father and friends by doing so as a Republican. Elected in 1988, he ran for governor in 1992 after incumbent Republican Stan Stephens retired after collapsing from a blood clot in the brain, and as the state was about to face a $200 million budget gap. Democrats, who then held both houses of the legislature by wide margins, had a spirited primary contest, with state Representative Dorothy Bradley the winner; Racicot was nominated by a wide margin. In an unusually civil and specific campaign, both called for a 4% sales tax to be voted on in referendum, but Bradley favored more government while Racicot called for downsizing. He won 51%–49%, and Republicans captured the state House.

The sales tax was turned down, but Racicot cut spending and state employment and turned the deficit into a surplus, reformed the expensive workmen's comp law, sponsored a 7% income tax rebate and proposed welfare reforms. He supported a successful campaign finance referendum and persuaded voters to elect large Republican majorities to both houses in 1994. He is famously unassuming, lobbying legislators himself, speaking at a high school commencement with just one graduate, keeping his phone number listed and driving his own car, declining a salary increase though he is the nation's lowest paid governor ($55,502). Like many mountain state Republicans, he wants to revive the Tenth Amendment reserving powers to the state and has opposed what he considers unwise federal policies like allowing the herd of bison in Yellowstone National Park to grow too large. With a 73% job approval rating, he seems likely to be reelected in 1996, unless he succumbs to the entreaties of national Republican leaders to run for the Senate against Max Baucus.

Senators. Montana, for only the second time in its history, has senators of both parties. In 1994, Conrad Burns became the first Republican to win two Senate elections in Montana, while Democrat Max Baucus lost his committee chairmanship to a Republican controlled Senate.

Max Baucus, completing his third term, is from a well-known Montana ranching family— they own the property seen in *A River Runs Through It*—was educated at Stanford, then worked in Washington regulatory agencies and returned home in 1971 and won a seat in the legislature the next year. In 1974, at 32, he won the 1st District House seat by beating three past or future holders of it (current Congressman Pat Williams and former Congressman Arnold Olsen in the primary and Republican incumbent Richard Shoup in the general). He won his Senate seat in 1978 easily by beating an appointed senator in the primary and a conservative Republican investment adviser in the general. With seniority, he has reached powerful positions: he chaired the Environment and Public Works Committee in 1993–94 and ranks just behind Daniel Patrick Moynihan on Finance, and he chaired its Trade Subcommittee when Democrats held the majority. On these committees, he has played a role in fashioning important and complex legislation for some years now. He took the lead in the Senate on the Clean Air Act revision in 1989: he opposed Robert Byrd on aiding coal miners and he opposed environmentalists on urban emissions standards. The House side mostly prevailed in conference, but Baucus won no cost-sharing of cleanups with Midwestern coal-fired plants and no new scrubbers required on utility plants in cleaner western air. He has also worked on RCRA, the solid waste bill, in 1992 and 1994 and got the committee to give state governments veto power over solid waste imports from other states. On becoming chairman in 1993, he concentrated on the Safe Drinking Water reauthorization, proposing more flexibility for states and small water systems. He got a bill reported out of committee unanimously in March 1994, but was not able to get agreement with the House on a final bill in October 1994. One problem was Louisiana Senator Bennett Johnston's amendment requiring government risk assessment and cost-benefit analysis, resisted by House Democrats and incorporated in House Republicans' Contract With America. Two other Baucus causes: stopping the building of expensive federal courthouses, like the new one Justice Stephen Breyer supervised in Boston, and discouraging building on floodplains.

As chairman of the Trade Subcommittee, Baucus always kept his eye on Montana issues, seeking retaliation against Canada for its alleged subsidies of wheat, beef and lamb and for keeping U.S. products out of the Canadian market. He took the lead in backing Most Favored Nation status for China, an obvious market for Montana products. He supported NAFTA and GATT, but tried without success to get the retaliatory Super 301 provision reenacted after it was effectively repealed by GATT. On balance Baucus seems more free trader than protectionist. He was also alert to Montanans' qualms about the Clinton healthcare plan. Considered a likely Clinton vote on Finance, he became part of the bipartisan group seeking a compromise, then withdrew from that in June 1994, saying he opposed new taxes to pay for reform. Making what seemed like a local political calculation, he became in 1995 a supporter of the balanced budget constitutional amendment. "There has been a lot of rhetoric about the deficit, but not much action," he told *National Journal*.

On other matters, Baucus's initiatives have had varied success. He voted against the 1990 farm bill after his efforts to increase target prices and milk and wheat subsidies were soundly defeated. He crusades for more frequent airline service to Montana, restrictions on access to fossils from federal lands (Montana has the nation's greatest dinosaur remains) and for minting commemorative coins out of palladium (of which Nye, Montana is the only U.S. producer). Perhaps his greatest success for his home state came in March 1993, when he led the effort against the Clinton Administration's proposals to increase grazing fees and impose a 12.5% royalty on mining in public lands. Clinton, needing Baucus's vote in the Finance Committee for his budget and tax package, immediately buckled. This undercut Interior Secretary Bruce Babbitt's chances for major reforms, sending the message around Washington that this was a president who could be rolled. Even after that, Baucus was one of the senators who insisted on a much smaller tax increase than in the original Clinton package.

Hard-working, attentive to local issues, respected for his ability and deep Montana roots, Baucus was reelected with a solid majority in 1984 and overwhelmingly in 1990, despite what seemed like credible opposition. In 1996, with strong feeling against what many Montanans regard as the Clinton Administration's "war on the West" and the local Republican trend, Baucus may have a tougher race. He can argue that his seniority on the Finance Committee makes his seat an asset a small state like Montana should not squander. But a May 1995 poll showed him trailing by 26 points popular Governor Marc Racicot, who has seemed unlikely to run. Against two other Republicans, Lieutenant Governor Dennis Rehberg and 1994 House candidate Cy Jamison, Baucus had wide margins, but less than 55% of the total. Former Congressman Ron Marlenee is seriously considering the race as well. A little money, by national campaigning standards, buys a lot of TV time in Montana, and Baucus has kept up the personal campaigning Montanans expect. But this could be a serious contest and national Republicans began an early drumbeat that Baucus's views have been closer to those of Ted Kennedy than to Montanans.

Conrad Burns, Montana's junior senator, is almost a stereotypical Westerner, picking his teeth with a pocketknife, chewing tobacco, telling deadpan jokes. A native of Missouri, he started off as a livestock fieldman and auctioneer who became field representative of the *Polled Hereford World*; when he was reassigned back east (to Des Moines), he quit so he could stay in

Billings where he set up a farm news radio network. Piqued at a local politician, Burns ran for Yellowstone County Commissioner in 1986 and won; two years later, he ran against Democratic Senator John Melcher. Melcher had been in Congress for 19 years and Burns attacked him as "a liberal who is soft on drugs, soft on defense and very high on social programs." Melcher was hurt by a Reagan veto of a Melcher wilderness bill and by public opposition to the "let-it-burn" policy that resulted in the Yellowstone fires of summer 1988. Burns, who ended every speech with a Western "You bet!" won 52% of the vote.

In the Senate, Burns has made a mostly conservative voting record without taking a lead role on major legislation. His main issue is telecommunications—not so un-Montanan a cause when you think about it—and he has favored letting the regional Bells into cable and broadcast programming; that was beaten in 1994 but could pass in 1995. His ultimate goal is to encourage by 2015 a two-way interactive telecommunications "information superhighway" to every home, school and business. In November 1991, Burns finally reached agreement with Baucus on a Montana wilderness bill, with neutral language on water rights, but the bill was liberalized and then stalled in the House in 1992. He remains ready with quips: "Bureaucrats can make a lot of bad decisions, but they still get a check," and "We all do dumb things 15 minutes a day. The key is not to go over your quota!"

Burns was perhaps the Democrats' top target among Senate incumbents in 1994. They felt he had not returned to the state enough, had too conservative a voting record and was not strong enough to become the first Republican Senator to be reelected in Montana history. Democrats were nervous when former Senator Melcher entered the race after spending the previous five years in Washington, and when Becky Shaw (housemate of a Melcher adviser) ran as well; they were relieved when former University of Montana law dean Jack Mudd beat Melcher and Shaw, 47%–32%–21%. But Mudd ran an underfunded and puzzling campaign, saying he would have voted for the Clinton budget and tax package in 1993 and the assault weapon ban and crime bill in 1994. Burns attacked Mudd as an advocate of higher taxes and was only briefly thrown on the defensive when he repeated to a reporter a conversation he had with a constituent that included a racial slur about living in the District of Columbia. He apologized the next day and said he was only repeating the rancher's comments. On election day Bill Clinton's job approval in Montana was only 36%, and Burns won by an impressive 62%–38%.

Representative-At-Large. Montana's only congressman is Pat Williams, an old-fashioned liberal Democrat with ties to the state's past. He is from Butte and Helena, with roots in the labor movement, a former teacher, state legislator and Capitol Hill staffer; he is close to organized labor and teachers' unions. While Montana Republicans rail against federal bureaucrats, Williams believes that Montanans' real enemies are eastern corporations eager to exploit their resources, and he sees rational federal planning as a way to preserve the way of life that makes Montana special. This, he says, is the last state "in the lower 48 to have an opportunity to set our destiny in major and meaningful ways." Williams was first elected from the western half of the state (Montana had two districts until the 1992 redistricting) with its history of purists and radicals: half a century ago, it elected such diverse figures as Communist party-liner Jerry O'Connell, vicious anti-Semite Jacob Thorkelson, Jeanette Rankin, who voted against the declaration of war in 1941 as she had in 1917, and Mike Mansfield. Williams was elected to the state legislature in 1966, worked for John Melcher when he first came to Washington as a Congressman in 1969, ran for Congress himself and lost in the primary to Max Baucus in 1974 and was then elected to the House in 1978 when Baucus ran for the Senate.

In the House Williams has had a variedly liberal voting record, and has been a leader on several issues. On the Economic and Educational Opportunities Committee, he has been the staunchest opponent of aid to church schools, raising that issue with regards to child care when others wanted to slough over it, since so many existing day care centers and preschools are run by churches. As a subcommittee chairman, he defended the National Endowment of the Arts despite its grant for art as offensive as a crucifix submerged in the urine of the artist, fashioning a compromise allowing the NEA not to order the return of federal grant money, if courts decided the art was obscene. In 1995 he proposed a onetime $12 billion federal endowment in light of the congressional tide against the NEA.

Williams was reelected by good margins in the 1980s. But the 1990 Census, under the formula used by Congress and challenged in court by then-Attorney General Marc Racicot, eliminated Montana's second congressional district, and Williams was forced to run against Republican Ron Marlenee, with whom he shared incumbency but very little else. Marlenee loudly opposed federal intervention in Montana and for years blocked Montana wilderness bills sought by Williams and Baucus because they would limit mineral exploration and grazing. This was a battle between two philosophies, one using the federal government to limit and regulate land use and the other favoring private sector economic development. Both candidates had home-district strength, and the polls seemed to fluctuate with national trends. In the end, Williams won 50%–47%, the same 3% spread by which Bill Clinton beat George Bush.

Williams continued to work hard on programs he believes in, sponsoring the Family and Medical Leave Act, defending the NEA, advancing a wilderness bill killed by Senator Conrad Burns and sponsoring local measures like the Gallatin Range consolidation. In 1994 he had spirited opposition from former Bureau of Land Management head Cy Jamison, whom he accused of "a trail of mismanagement." Jamison attacked Williams for his support of liberal policies and the Clinton Administration. Williams outspent Jamison nearly 2–1, largely because he raised much more PAC money, and won 49%–42%, his lowest showing yet. This could be a seriously contested seat again in 1996. Interestingly, the Voter News Service exit poll showed that Williams got his biggest percentage margins not from the low income voters at the heart of his historic Democratic constituency (he won them 52%–35%) but from the highly educated, those with graduate degrees (he carried them 60%–33%). In the minority, he probably will not find as many opportunities to cut legislative deals.

If Montana keeps gaining population as it has in the 1990s, it will probably get its second House seat back after the 2000 Census.

Presidential politics. Montana, with only three electoral votes now, can't expect to see much of presidential candidates, particularly because its presidential primary is in early June, the same day as New Jersey's. Only Alaska, Idaho, Utah and North Dakota are farther out of the national political jetlanes. Yet this was the closest Rocky Mountain state in 1988, and one of the closest in 1992, and actually got visits from Bill Clinton and Dan Quayle, plus a Clinton TV buy. Clinton carried the state with 38% to George Bush's 35%, with a sizable 26% for Ross Perot, who ran second in 20 counties and got 36% in Phillips County on the Canadian border. But unless Clinton and his party rally impressively from their 1994 standing here, Montana is likely to go solidly Republican in the 1996 presidential race.

The People: Est. Pop. 1994: 850,000; Pop. 1990: 799,065, up 7.1% 1990–1994. 0.3% of U.S. total, 44th largest; 47% rural. Median age 33.8 years. 13.3% 65 years and over. 92.7% White, 6.0% American Indian, 1.5% Hispanic origin. Households: 57.7% married couple families; 28% married couple fams. w. children; 48% college educ.; median household income: $22,988; per capita income: $11,213; 67.3% owner occupied housing; median house value: $56,600; median monthly rent: $251. 6.7% Unemployment. 1994 Voting age pop.: 623,000. 1994 Turnout: 348,385; 56% of VAP. Registered voters (1994): 514,051; no party registration.

Political Lineup: Governor, Marc Racicot (R); Lt. Gov., Dennis Rehberg (R); Secy. of State, Mike Cooney (D); Atty. Gen., Joseph Mazurek (D); Auditor, Mark O'Keefe (D). State Senate, 50 (31 R and 19 D); State House of Representatives, 100 (67 R and 33 D). Senators, Max Baucus (D) and Conrad Burns (R). Representative, 1 D at large.

1992 Presidential Vote

Clinton (D)	154,507	(38%)
Bush (R)	144,207	(35%)
Perot (I)	107,225	(26%)

1988 Presidential Vote

Bush (R)	190,412	(52%)
Dukakis (D)	168,956	(46%)

1992 Democratic Presidential Primary

Clinton	54,989	(47%)
Brown	21,704	(18%)
Tsongas	12,614	(11%)
No Preference	28,164	(24%)

1992 Republican Presidential Primary

Bush	65,176	(72%)
Buchanan	10,701	(12%)
No Preference	15,098	(17%)

GOVERNOR

Gov. Marc Racicot (R)

Elected 1992, term expires Jan. 1997; b. July 24, 1948, Thompson Falls; home, Helena; Carroll Col., B.A. 1970, U. of MT Law Schl., J.D. 1973; Catholic; married (Theresa).

Career: Army Judge Advocate Corps, 1973–76; Dep. Missoula Cnty. Atty., 1976–77; MT Asst. Atty. Gen., 1977–88; MT Atty. Gen., 1988–92.

Office: Office of the Governor, State Capitol, Helena 59620, 406-444-3111; Fax: 406-444-4151.

Election Results

1992 gen.	Marc Racicot (R)	209,401	(51%)
	Dorothy Bradley (D)	198,421	(49%)
1992 prim.	Marc Racicot (R)	68,103	(69%)
	Andrea (Andy) Bennett (R)	31,038	(31%)
1988 gen.	Stan Stephens (R)	190,604	(53%)
	Tom Judge (D)	169,313	(47%)

SENATORS

Sen. Max Baucus (D)

Elected 1978, seat up 1996; b. Dec. 11, 1941, Helena; home, Helena; Stanford U., B.A. 1964, LL.B. 1967; Protestant; married (Wanda).

Career: Staff atty., Civil Aeronautics Bd., 1967–69; Legal Asst., Securities and Exchange Comm., 1969–71; Practicing atty., 1971–74; MT House of Reps., 1973–74; U.S. House of Reps., 1975–78.

DC Office: 511 HSOB 20510, 202-224-2651; e-mail: max@baucus.senate.gov.

State Offices: Granite Bldg., 23 S. Last Chance Gulch, Helena 59601, 406-449-5480; 202 Fratt Bldg., 2817 2d Ave. N., Billings 59101, 406-657-6970; Fed. Bldg., 32 E. Babcock, #114, P.O. Box 1689, Bozeman 59715, 406-586-6104; Silver Bow Ctr., 125 W. Granite, Butte 59701, 406-782-8700; 107 5th St. N., Great Falls 59401, 406-761-1574; 715 Main St., Kalispell 59901; and 211 N. Higgins, #102, Missoula 59802, 406-329-3123.

Committees: *Agriculture, Nutrition & Forestry* (7th of 8 D): Marketing, Inspection and Product Promotion; Production and Price Competitiveness. *Environment & Public Works* (RMM of 7 D): Transportation and Infrastructure (RMM). *Finance* (2nd of 9 D): International Trade; Medicare, Long-Term Care and Health Insurance; Social Security and Family Policy. *Intelligence (Select)* (6th of 8 D). *Joint Committee on Taxation* (5th of 5 Sen.)

Group Ratings

	ADA	ACLU	COPE	CFA	LCV	CON	NSI	COC	ACU	NTLC	CHC
1994	85	47	100	83	92	24	30	32	0	8	7
1993	85	—	73	70	63	37	—	20	16	—	—

National Journal Ratings

	1993 LIB — 1993 CONS		1994 LIB — 1994 CONS	
Economic	83%	— 0%	72%	— 18%
Social	55%	— 42%	53%	— 40%
Foreign	44%	— 52%	78%	— 15%

Key Votes of the 103d Congress

1. Clinton Deficit Plan	Y	3. Brady Handgun Purchase	Y	5. Lmt. UN Cmnd. of Forces	N
2. NAFTA	Y	4. Strike Race/Death Pnlty.	Y	6. Cut Missile Funds	Y

Key Votes of the 104th Congress

1. Congressional Compliance	Y	3. Balanced Budget Amndt.	Y	5. Product Liability Reform	N
2. Bar Unfunded Mandates	Y	4. Pass Line Item Veto	N	6. FY96 Budget	N

Election Results

1990 general	Max Baucus (D)	217,563	(68%)	($2,568,899)
	Allen C. Kolstad (R)	93,836	(29%)	($747,661)
	Other	7,937	(2%)	
1990 primary	Max Baucus (D)	81,687	(83%)	
	John Driscoll (D)	12,622	(13%)	
	Emmett (Curly) Thornton (D)	4,367	(4%)	
1984 general	Max Baucus (D)	215,704	(57%)	($1,386,561)
	Chuck Cozzens (R)	154,308	(41%)	($492,391)

Sen. Conrad Burns (R)

Elected 1988, seat up 2000; b. Jan. 25, 1935, Gallatin, MO; home, Billings; U. of MO, 1952–54; Lutheran; married (Phyllis).

Career: Marine Corps, 1955–57; TWA and Ozark Airlines, 1958–61; Field rep., *Polled Hereford World*, 1962; Mgr., Billings Livestock Show, 1968; Radio & TV broadcaster, 1968–86; Yellowstone Cnty. Commissioner, 1986–88.

DC Office: 183 DSOB 20510, 202-224-2644; Fax: 202-224-8594.

State Offices: 2708 First Ave. N., Billings 59101, 406-252-0550; 208 N. Montana Ave., #202-A, Helena 59601, 406-449-5401; 415 N. Higgins, Missoula 59802, 406-329-3528; 321 1st Ave. N, Great Falls 59401, 406-252-9585; 324 W. Towne, Glendive 59330, 406-365-2391; 10 E. Babcock, Fed. Bldg. #106, Bozeman 59715, 406-586-4450; 125 W. Granite, #211, Butte 59701, 406-723-3277; and 575 Sunset Blvd., #101, Kalispell 59901, 406-257-3360.

Committees: *Appropriations* (11th of 15 R): Agriculture, Rural Development and Related Agencies; Energy and Water Development; Interior; Military Construction (Chmn.); VA, HUD and Independent Agencies. *Commerce, Science & Transportation* (5th of 10 R): Aviation; Communications; Science, Technology and Space (Chmn.); Surface Transportation and Merchant Marine. *Energy & Natural Resources* (10th of 10 R): Energy Production and Regulation; Oversight and Investigations. *Small Business* (3rd of 10 R). *Aging (Special)* (7th of 10 R).

Group Ratings

	ADA	ACLU	COPE	CFA	LCV	CON	NSI	COC	ACU	NTLC	CHC
1994	0	26	13	25	0	58	100	87	92	84	100
1993	20	—	18	20	6	68	—	91	96	—	—

National Journal Ratings

	1993 LIB — 1993 CONS		1994 LIB — 1994 CONS	
Economic	25% —	70%	28% —	71%
Social	0% —	92%	16% —	81%
Foreign	8% —	86%	30% —	68%

Key Votes of the 103d Congress

1. Clinton Deficit Plan	N	3. Brady Handgun Purchase	N	5. Lmt. UN Cmnd. of Forces	Y
2. NAFTA	N	4. Strike Race/Death Pnlty.	Y	6. Cut Missile Funds	N

Key Votes of the 104th Congress

1. Congressional Compliance	Y	3. Balanced Budget Amndt.	Y	5. Product Liability Reform	Y
2. Bar Unfunded Mandates	Y	4. Pass Line Item Veto	Y	6. FY96 Budget	Y

Election Results

1994 general	Conrad Burns (R)	218,542	(62%)	($3,518,574)
	Jack Mudd (D)	131,845	(38%)	($1,107,591)
1994 primary	Conrad Burns (R)	unopposed		
1988 general	Conrad Burns (R)	189,445	(52%)	($1,076,010)
	John Melcher (D)	175,809	(48%)	($1,338,622)

REPRESENTATIVE

Rep. Pat Williams (D)

Elected 1978; b. Oct. 30, 1937, Helena; home, Helena; U. of MT, 1956–57, U. of Denver, B.A. 1961; Catholic; married (Carol).

Career: Army, 1960–61, Army Natl. Guard, 1962–69; Public schl. teacher; MT House of Reps., 1967, 1969; Reg. Dir., Humphrey Pres. campaign, 1968; Exec. Asst., U.S. Rep. John Melcher, 1969–71; MT Coord., Family Educ. Prog., 1971–78.

DC Office: 2329 RHOB 20515, 202-225-3211; Fax: 202-226-0244.

District Offices: 316 N. Park Ave., P.O. Box 1681, Helena 59624, 406-443-7878; 305 W. Mercury, #306, Butte 59701, 406-723-4404; 302 W. Broadway, Missoula 59802, 406-549-5550; 2806 3rd Ave. N., Billings 59101, 406-256-1019; and 325 2nd Ave. N., Great Falls 59401, 406-771-1242.

Committees: *Economic & Educational Opportunities* (4th of 19 D): Early Childhood, Youth and Families; Postsecondary Education, Training and Life-Long Learning (RMM). *Resources* (5th of 20 D): National Parks, Forests and Lands; Native American and Insular Affairs.

Group Ratings

	ADA	ACLU	COPE	CFA	LCV	CON	NSI	COC	ACU	NTLC	CHC
1994	75	73	78	60	50	38	20	64	19	20	14
1993	80	—	100	80	65	47	—	27	13	—	—

National Journal Ratings

	1993 LIB — 1993 CONS	1994 LIB — 1994 CONS
Economic	88% — 0%	72% — 27%
Social	58% — 42%	65% — 34%
Foreign	69% — 31%	51% — 47%

Key Votes of the 103d Congress

1. Clinton Deficit Plan	Y	3. Brady Handgun Purchase	N	5. Lmt. UN Cmnd. of Forces	N
2. NAFTA	N	4. Strike Race/Death Pnlty.	N	6. Cut Missile Funds	Y

Key Votes of the 104th Congress

1. Congressional Compliance	Y	6. Reform Crime Grant	N	11. Loser Pays Court Reform	N
2. Balanced Budget Amndmt.	N	7. National Security Act	N	12. Product Liability Reform	N
3. Bar Unfunded Mandates	N	8. Moratorium on Regs.	N	13. Welfare Reform	N
4. Pass Line Item Veto	N	9. Risk Assessment on Regs.	N	14. Term Limits Amndmt.	N
5. Relax Exclusionary Rule	N	10. Expnd. Priv. Prop. Rights	N	15. Tax Cuts	N

Election Results

1994 general	Pat Williams (D)	171,372	(49%)	($734,121)
	Cy Jamison (R)	148,715	(42%)	($436,943)
	Steve Kelly (I)	32,046	(9%)	($17,440)
1994 primary	Pat Williams (D)	unopposed		
1992 general	Pat Williams (D)	203,711	(50%)	($1,336,673)
	Ron Marlenee (R)	189,570	(47%)	($1,292,583)
	Other	10,454	(3%)	

NEBRASKA

"The sea of Nebraska" is what the first settlers coming west called the Platte River. It's actually not a single river but a braid of streams that weave a silver chain around sandbars and islands, flooding the level floor of the great plain—a mile wide, as the saying goes, and six inches deep. Nebraska was formed in one rush of settlement in the 1880s, when its population increased from 452,000 to 1,062,000, more than it has increased in the century since (it was 1,623,000 in 1994). That same decade Omaha became a major railroad center and Lincoln the state capital. Today, Nebraska remains heavily dependent on farming and related industries, and Omaha and Lincoln are still its only significant cities. This is a state that sprang suddenly into existence and has changed strikingly little since.

That is not what its founders intended: they hoped Nebraska would develop a diversified farming, industrial and commercial economy like Ohio, Illinois, Missouri or Minnesota. But while the 1880s were a time of plentiful rain here, the 1890s were a decade of drought, and Nebraska stopped growing. Many rural counties, and even Omaha, lost population and have been exporting people ever since. The creative energies in the economy seem to have skipped over the Great Plains and moved far to the West. Nebraska's settlers, like most migrants, were young people, optimistic and motivated, in search of opportunity, with families full of children. Some 48% of Nebraskans in 1890 were children; in 1990, only 27% were—which means there are actually 60,000 fewer children in this state today than there were 100 years ago.

The sudden boom of the 1880s and the bust of the 1890s produced the most colorful—and atypical—politics of Nebraska's history: the populist movement and William Jennings Bryan, the "silver tongued orator of the Platte." Bryan was only 36 when he delivered the famous Cross of Gold speech at the 1896 Democratic National Convention and was swept to the Democratic nomination. He was thought so radical that Democratic President Grover Cleveland wouldn't support him, but he still won 47% of the vote in the first of three attempts. Nebraskans supported Bryan, whose program may have been forward-looking, but whose purpose was retrograde: to restore Nebraska to the prosperity it had enjoyed a few years before. Since Bryan's time, Nebraska's most notable politician has been George Norris, who led the House rebellion against Speaker Joseph Cannon in 1911, and in the 1930s pushed through the Norris-LaGuardia Anti-Injunction Act, the first national pro-union legislation, and the Tennessee Valley Authority. But most Nebraskans were repelled by the New Deal, which seemed to threaten their stable society; despite its continuing proclivity to elect Democrats to statewide office, Nebraska for half a century has been among the most Republican of states in national elections.

And Nebraska has not been stagnant. Economically, it has shown some dynamism. Omaha is the home base of the fast-growing ConAgra food combine and of mega-investor Warren Buffett, whose down-home humor complements his knack for picking stocks that go up hundreds of percents. And after the nearby Strategic Air Command base brought the world's most advanced phone system to the Omaha area 40-odd years ago, hotel chains, credit card companies and telemarketers set up operations, making this the world's leading place to make a living by talking on the phone. Personal computers and the Internet have brought tiny Nebraska towns close to everywhere in the world or, as one mayor said, "With this thing [fiber optics] we're just another suburb of Chicago." Politically, Nebraska has shown some pizzazz too. It has produced one presidential contender and one of the nation's most popular governors—Bob Kerrey and Ben Nelson, both Democrats in this Republican state, and its unicameral nonpartisan legislature provides a steppingstone for politicians of both parties to challenge those in office.

Governor. Governor Ben Nelson, elected in 1990, was the third Democrat in a row to beat an incumbent Republican associated with tax increases; the first two went on to become senators. He was elected to office by a narrow margin and was retained in a landslide. Nelson is an insurance executive and lawyer from McCook, home town of George Norris and novelist Willa Cather. In the 1990 primary he defeated Bill Hoppner—who was supported by his former boss Bob Kerrey—by a 42-vote margin after a 48-day recount; in the general he beat Governor Kay Orr 50%–49% because she raised taxes and her political consultants failed to place many of her paid-for scheduled TV spots in October. In a pattern also seen in Senate contests, Nelson ran strongest in the eastern part of the state (though he lost Omaha's Douglas County—the only governor in the history of Nebraska to do so) and in the southern tier, while Orr ran strongest in the Platte Valley, the sparsely populated central and western counties, and around heavily Republican Madison. Nelson pledged to serve "one Nebraska," spreading economic growth outward from Omaha and Lincoln. His first budget increased spending less than 1%, and he reformed welfare, started a lottery (for creative education projects) and built more juvenile prisons. In Republican 1994, he was reelected by an unambiguous 73%–26% margin, and promised during the campaign to serve out his entire term. But Nelson subsequently came under strong pressure (notably, and with some irony, from DSCC Chairman Bob Kerrey) to run for the Senate seat Jim Exon is relinquishing in 1996. He is the Democrats best chance to retain the seat, but both Nelson and Lieutenant Governor Kim Robak seem reluctant to enter the race.

Senators. Jim Exon came to Nebraska after World War II and started an office equipment company, was active in politics and in 1970 was elected governor, where he cut deficits and became highly popular. After eight years in office he was elected to the Senate in 1978 and reelected twice. Coming to the Senate with a reputation as an economizer, he has mostly been a team-playing Democrat—not a down-the-line liberal vote by any means, but usually sticking with his party on tough issues and when his vote is needed. His voting record was just about at the midpoint of the Democratic Senate on all issues. He has had some significant achievements: the Exon-Florio bill that lets the president stop foreign takeovers that threaten national security,

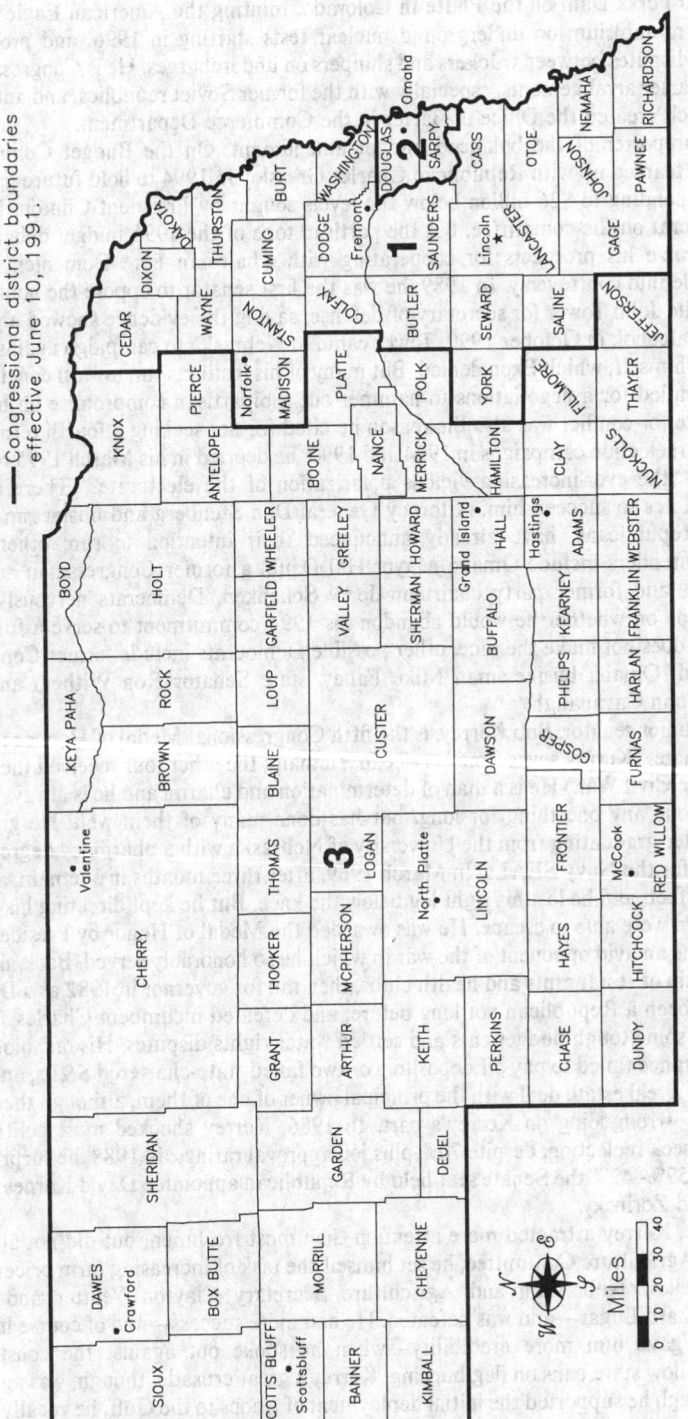

Copyright © 1993 by Election Data Services, Inc.

— Congressional district boundaries
effective June 10, 1991.

Miles

0 10 20 30 40

killing the Two Forks Dam on the Platte in Colorado, minting the American Eagle gold coin, authoring the moratorium on underground nuclear tests starting in 1996, and providing for settlements of disputes between truckers and shippers on undercharges. He is Congress's leading proponent of barter arrangements, especially with the former Soviet republics, and authored the legislation which created the Office of Barter in the Commerce Department.

Exon is a supporter of the balanced budget amendment. On the Budget Committee, he unsuccessfully teamed up with Republican Charles Grassley in 1994 to hold future increases in discretionary spending to $26 billion below the levels sought by President Clinton. Now he is ranking Democrat on the committee, but the partisan tone of the 1995 budget debate seemed likely to minimize his prospects for cooperating with Chairman Pete Domenici. Exon can sometimes wade into controversy. In 1989, he was the first senator to oppose the nomination of former colleague John Tower for secretary of defense, saying the evidence showed a pattern of problems with alcohol; in October 1990, Tower came to Nebraska to campaign against Exon as "a big boozer" himself, which Exon denied. But many of his instincts run toward conciliation. In July 1994 he called for a negotiations to hammer out a bipartisan compromise on healthcare reform. Distaste for conflict was also the reason he cited for not seeking a fourth term in 1996; after his rough reelection campaigns in 1984 and 1990, he decried in his March 1995 retirement announcement "the ever-increasing vicious polarization of the electorate." There are many possible candidates to succeed him. Attorney General Don Stenberg and businessman Chuck Hagel, both Republicans, have already announced their intention to run; other possible Republican contenders include Omaha Mayor Hal Daub, a former Congressman and Exon's 1990 opponent, and former party chairman Jerry Schenken. Democrats nervously awaited Nelson's decision on whether he would abandon his 1994 commitment to serve a full term as governor. If he does not make the race, other possible Democrats include former Congressman Peter Hoagland, Omaha businessman Mike Fahey, state Senator Ron Withem and former Congressman John Cavanaugh.

Nebraska's junior senator, Bob Kerrey, is the fifth Congressional Medal of Honor recipient to serve in the Senate. (Kerrey's was from service in Vietnam; the other four received their medals for service in the Civil War.) He is a man of determination and charm, and he is always evolving: he has never done any one thing for long, but has done many of them well. He grew up in Lincoln, and after graduating from the University of Nebraska with a pharmacy degree in 1966 he volunteered for the Navy SEALs. In March 1969, after three months in Vietnam, a grenade exploded at his feet, and he lost his right leg below the knee. But he kept directing his platoon's fire until his men were able to escape. He was awarded the Medal of Honor by President Nixon and later became an avid opponent of the war in which he so honorably served. Back in Lincoln, he started a chain of restaurants and health clubs, then ran for governor in 1982 as a Democrat, though he had been a Republican not long before, and defeated incumbent Charles Thone. In office, he made some tough budget cuts and settled water rights disputes. His one blotch came when state insurance failed to pay off depositors of two failed state-chartered S&Ls, and Kerrey was a partner in a real estate deal with the principal owner of one of them, although there was no evidence of any wrongdoing on Kerrey's part. In 1986, Kerrey shocked most politicians by deciding not to seek reelection, despite 70%-plus job approval ratings; in 1988, he surprised very few by winning 57%–42% the Senate seat held by Republican appointee David Karnes after the death of Edward Zorinsky.

In the Senate, Kerrey attracted more attention than most freshmen, but did not always get results. On the Agriculture Committee, he set himself the task of increasing farm price supports and took on fellow Nebraskan and Agriculture Secretary Clayton Yeutter and Indiana Republican Richard Lugar—and was defeated. He had more success—and of course his record as a war hero gave him more credibility—when he spoke out against the constitutional amendment to allow state bans on flag burning. Kerrey's great crusade, though, was against the Gulf war. Although he supported the initial deployment of troops to the Gulf, he vocally opposed military action, taking to the floor often with Terry Sanford of North Carolina to predict that there would be many casualties and that Bush's threats to Saddam Hussein was more the language of "a little league football coach than a commander in chief"—not prognostications of great foresight.

In September 1991 Kerrey abruptly decided to run for president, announcing on a brilliant day outside the skyscraper Capitol in Lincoln that he wanted to "lead America's fearless, restless voyage of generational progress." His great issue was his advocacy of national health insurance reform. In July 1991, with little publicity, he had introduced his national healthcare bill, a publicly financed system with total spending and minimum benefits determined by the federal government. States would set physician fees and spending targets and negotiate hospital budgets; funds would come from a 5% payroll tax, cigarette and alcohol taxes and a new top-bracket income tax. He presented his case articulately and in detail, but did not inspire audiences in New Hampshire. He finished third there, with only 11%, barely ahead of Tom Harkin and Jerry Brown. Then, despite his 40%–25% win over Harkin in South Dakota and his harsh attacks in Georgia on Bill Clinton's lack of candor on his experiences with the draft—he said of Clinton that Bush would "open him up like a soft peanut"—he finished fourth or fifth in five states a week later, and said "I just woke up Wednesday and said it was over." Unlike Tom Harkin, Kerrey did not endorse Clinton early or campaign for him, and Clinton never really seriously considered him for vice president, even though many Democrats relished the picture of a Medal of Honor winner debating former National Guardsman Dan Quayle.

In 1993 Kerrey continued to tussle with Clinton. He abandoned his government healthcare plan just as Hillary Rodham Clinton was designing hers. He called for a government restructuring bill to "do more with less," setting up a bipartisan commission to streamline the federal government, as Al Gore began his reinventing government efforts. And he balked at supporting the Clinton budget and tax package. In August 1993 he turned out to be the deciding vote in the Senate—the man who could make the administration fail, some said—and he had an angry shouting session with Clinton recounted in Bob Woodward's *The Agenda*. Finally Elizabeth Moynihan, wife of Daniel Patrick Moynihan, who had supported Kerrey's presidential candidacy, persuaded him to vote yes. His quid pro quo was creation of a bipartisan commission, headed by Kerrey and retiring Republican Senator John Danforth, on cutting federal spending for entitlements. In the meantime, Kerrey worked with Colorado Republican Hank Brown to get $109 billion more in budget cuts, unsuccessfully. In 1994 Kerrey and Danforth tried to persuade their fellow commissioners to recommend cuts in Social Security and Medicare. But their January 1995 report, which was short on specifics, was attacked by organized labor and leftist Democrats, and its calls for Social Security cuts were spurned by both Clinton and incoming Speaker Newt Gingrich. The effort must be counted a failure, though it might have succeeded if the Democrats, as almost everyone expected, had retained control of Congress. And Kerrey may be right in insisting that Social Security has to be cut sooner or later, and that cuts will be much deeper if they come later. Kerrey, along with Senators Chuck Robb and Sam Nunn, were the only Democrats to support the Senate Republican budget resolution in May 1995. An early supporter of Tom Daschle in the contest for Democratic Leader, Kerrey became his party's ranking member on the Intelligence Committee.

Kerrey faced a serious challenge back home in 1994. Republican Jan Stoney, who rose from telephone company clerk to executive vice president of U.S. West, attacked him for supporting the Clinton budget and tax package and for switching to favor the assault weapons ban. One summer poll showed her trailing by only 48%–40%. Kerrey cited his attempts to cut Clinton budgets, and ran an ad showing himself at a target range picking up an AK-47 and saying, "Twenty-five years ago, in the war in Vietnam, people hunted me. They needed a good weapon, like this AK-47. But you don't need one of these to hunt birds." Most importantly, he outspent Stoney by more than 2–1. He won 55%–45%, lower than his 1988 win; he carried eastern Nebraska and the southern tier of the state, ran the strongest around Lincoln, but won only 56% in greater Omaha. Stoney won large margins north and west of Columbus and Grand Island.

Kerrey remains changeable: he has moved from Republican to Democrat, from supporting national health insurance to opposing it, from anti-gun control to pro, from anti-abortion to pro-choice, from businessman to governor to senator. He has also clearly learned much at each stage, and his command of domestic and foreign policy seems greater than when he ran for president. The Clinton White House clearly sees him as a possible primary challenger to the President and urged other senators to prevail on him to take the chairmanship of the Democratic Senatorial Campaign Committee: a way to keep him usefully occupied and partisanly loyal. He reluctantly agreed. But by April 1995 the retirement of five Senate Democratic incumbents convinced Washington insiders that Democrats had no chance of regaining control, and it was unclear how deeply Kerrey would be engaged. His moderate voting record, personal history and increasing command of issues make him a plausible, quite possibly attractive national candidate.

Presidential politics. Over the last 50 years, Nebraska has voted more Republican in presidential elections than any other state—61% to Kansas's second place 57%. It was George Bush's best state outside the South in 1992, and Bill Clinton's third worst, after Utah and Idaho. There is an urban-rural split, with greater Lincoln and Omaha more Democratic; elsewhere in the state, Ross Perot outpolled Bill Clinton in 1992.

Nebraska has a presidential primary in May which once attracted attention; the whole national press followed Robert Kennedy and Eugene McCarthy out here in 1968 and took note when Frank Church won in 1976. No more: nominations are now sewn up long before May, and Nebraska has gone unnoticed. In 1992, its native son, Kerrey, was out of the running by then.

Congressional districting. Nebraska has had three congressional districts since the 1960s. Redistricting made only marginal changes for the 1990s.

The People: Est. Pop. 1994: 1,623,000; Pop. 1990: 1,578,385, up 2.8% 1990–1994. 0.6% of U.S. total, 37th largest; 34% rural. Median age: 33.0 years. 14.1% 65 years and over. 93.8% White 3.6% Black, 2.3% Hispanic origin. Households: 58.2% married couple families; 28% married couple fams. w. children; 47% college educ.; median household income: $26,016; per capita income: $12,452; 66.5% owner occupied housing; median house value: $50,400; median monthly rent: $282. 3.0% Unemployment. 1994 Voting age pop.: 1,192,000. 1994 Turnout: 572,859; 48% of VAP. Registered voters (1994): 919,321; 365,872 D (40%), 456,399 R (50%), 97,050 unaffiliated and minor parties (11%).

Political Lineup: Governor, E. Benjamin Nelson (D); Lt. Gov., Kim M. Robak (D); Secy. of State, Scott Moore (R); Atty. Gen., Donald Stenberg (R); Treasurer, David Heineman (R); Auditor, John Breslow (D). Unicameral Legislature, 49 (no party affiliation). Senators, J. James Exon (D) and Robert Kerrey (D). Representatives, 3 (3 R).

1992 Presidential Vote

Bush (R)	343,678	(47%)
Clinton (D)	216,864	(29%)
Perot (I)	174,104	(24%)

1992 Democratic Presidential Primary

Clinton	68,562	(46%)
Brown	31,673	(21%)
Tsongas	10,707	(7%)
Other	14,931	(10%)
Uncommitted	24,714	(16%)

1988 Presidential Vote

Bush (R)	397,956	(60%)
Dukakis (D)	259,235	(39%)

1992 Republican Presidential Primary

Bush	156,346	(81%)
Buchanan	25,847	(13%)
Other	9,905	(5%)

GOVERNOR

Gov. E. Benjamin Nelson (D)

Elected 1990, term expires Jan. 1999; b. May 17, 1941, McCook; home, Lincoln; U. of NE, B.A. 1963, M.A. 1965, LL.B. 1970; Methodist; married (Diane).

Career: Gen. Cnsl., Central Natl. Group Insurance, 1972–74, Pres. & CEO, 1977–81; NE Dir. of Insurance, 1975–76; Exec. V.P., Natl. Assn. of Insurance Commissioners, 1982–85; Practicing atty., 1985–90.

Office: State Capitol, P.O. Box 94848, Lincoln 68509, 402-471-2244; Fax: 401-471-6031.

Election Results

1994 gen.	E. Benjamin Nelson (D)	423,270	(73%)
	Gene Spence (R)	148,230	(26%)
	Others	8,061	(1%)
1994 prim.	E. Benjamin Nelson (D)	101,422	(88%)
	Robert Franklin Winingar (D)	6,993	(6%)
	Robb Nimic	6,373	(6%)
1990 gen.	E. Benjamin Nelson (D)	292,771	(50%)
	Kay A. Orr (R)	288,741	(49%)
	Other	5,030	(1%)

SENATORS

Sen. J. James Exon (D)

Elected 1978, seat up 1996; b. Aug. 9, 1921, Geddes, SD; home, Lincoln; U. of Omaha, 1939–41; Episcopalian; married (Patricia).

Career: Army, 1941–45 (WWII); Branch mgr., Universal Finance Corp., 1946–54; Pres., Exon's Inc. office equip., 1954–70; NE Gov., 1970–78.

DC Office: 528 HSOB 20510, 202-224-4224; Fax: 202-224-5213.

State Offices: 1623 Farnam St., #700, Omaha 68102, 402-341-1776; 287 Fed. Bldg., 100 Centennial Mall N., Lincoln 68508, 402-437-5591; 2106 1st St., Scottsbluff 69361, 308-632-3595; and 275 Fed. Bldg., North Platte 69101, 308-534-2006.

Committees: *Armed Services* (2nd of 10 D): Airland Forces; Seapower; Strategic Forces (RMM). *Budget* (RMM of 10 D): *Commerce, Science & Transportation* (4th of 9 D): Aviation; Communications; Consumer Affairs, Foreign Commerce and Tourism (RMM); Surface Transportation and Merchant Marine.

Group Ratings

	ADA	ACLU	COPE	CFA	LCV	CON	NSI	COC	ACU	NTLC	CHC
1994	65	16	63	67	69	35	80	46	25	20	71
1993	50	—	73	70	69	100	—	27	38	—	—

National Journal Ratings

	1993 LIB	—	1993 CONS		1994 LIB	—	1994 CONS
Economic	49%	—	47%		53%	—	46%
Social	37%	—	60%		44%	—	55%
Foreign	40%	—	57%		44%	—	55%

Key Votes of the 103d Congress

1. Clinton Deficit Plan	Y	3. Brady Handgun Purchase	Y	5. Lmt. UN Cmnd. of Forces	N
2. NAFTA	N	4. Strike Race/Death Pnlty.	Y	6. Cut Missile Funds	N

Key Votes of the 104th Congress

1. Congressional Compliance	Y	3. Balanced Budget Amndt.	Y	5. Product Liability Reform	Y
2. Bar Unfunded Mandates	Y	4. Pass Line Item Veto	Y	6. FY96 Budget	N

Election Results

1990 general	J. James Exon (D)...................	349,779	(59%)	($2,410,097)
	Hal Daub (R).......................	243,013	(41%)	($1,452,681)
1990 primary	J. James Exon (D)...................	157,959	(99%)	
	Other.............................	2,006	(1%)	
1984 general	J. James Exon (D)...................	332,217	(52%)	($886,760)
	Nancy Hoch (R)....................	307,147	(48%)	($583,632)

Sen. Robert Kerrey (D)

Elected 1988, seat up 2000; b. Aug. 27, 1943, Lincoln; home, Omaha; U of NE, M.S. 1966; Congregationalist; divorced.

Career: Navy, 1966–69 (Vietnam); Businessman, Restaurant owner, 1972–81; NE Gov., 1983–87.

DC Office: 303 HSOB 20510, 202-224-6551; Fax: 202-224-7645; e-mail: bob@kerrey.senate.gov.

State Offices: 7602 Pacific St. Omaha 68114, 402-391-3411; and 100 Centennial Mall N., #294, Fed. Bldg, Lincoln 68508, 402-437-5246.

Committees: *Democratic Senatorial Campaign Committee Chairman. Agriculture, Nutrition & Forestry* (8th of 8 D): Forestry, Conservation and Rural Revitalization; Production and Price Competitiveness. *Appropriations* (11th of 13 D): Agriculture, Rural Development and Related Agencies; Commerce, Justice, State and Judiciary; Energy and Water Development; Treasury, Postal Service and General Government (RMM); VA, HUD and Independent Agencies. *Intelligence (Select)* (RMM of 8 D).

Group Ratings

	ADA	ACLU	COPE	CFA	LCV	CON	NSI	COC	ACU	NTLC	CHC
1994	80	53	88	75	69	29	30	36	24	12	7
1993	75	—	64	70	75	89	—	45	8	—	—

National Journal Ratings

	1993 LIB	—	1993 CONS		1994 LIB	—	1994 CONS
Economic	56%	—	41%		55%	—	40%
Social	68%	—	29%		53%	—	40%
Foreign	62%	—	36%		54%	—	43%

Key Votes of the 103d Congress

1. Clinton Deficit Plan	Y	3. Brady Handgun Purchase	Y	5. Lmt. UN Cmnd. of Forces	N
2. NAFTA	Y	4. Strike Race/Death Pnlty.	N	6. Cut Missile Funds	Y

Key Votes of the 104th Congress

1. Congressional Compliance	Y	3. Balanced Budget Amndt.	N	5. Product Liability Reform	N
2. Bar Unfunded Mandates	Y	4. Pass Line Item Veto	N	6. FY96 Budget	Y

Election Results

1994 general	Robert Kerrey (D)	317,297	(55%)	($5,009,792)
	Jan Stoney (R)	260,668	(45%)	($1,821,778)
1994 primary	Robert Kerrey (D)	unopposed		
1988 general	Robert Kerrey (D)	378,717	(57%)	($3,461,148)
	David Karnes (R)	278,250	(42%)	($3,411,361)

FIRST DISTRICT

The eastern half of Nebraska, between the Missouri River and the 98th parallel, was laid out in remorseless Midwestern mile-square grids and became some of America's prime farmland in the single decade of the 1880s. The land here has contours just regular enough and weather just favorable enough to make farming economically viable. The plains here have completed most of their gentle decline from the Rockies to sea level; above the river bottoms the land is open to the winds. This land was settled by Yankee-descended Midwestern farmers and German immigrants. Politically it has long been Republican in national elections, but votes Democratic in seriously contested state races.

The 1st Congressional District of Nebraska includes 25 counties in eastern Nebraska. It does not include Omaha or its suburbs, which form the 2d District, but does take in Lincoln, the state capital and home of the University of Nebraska Cornhuskers. Lincoln, with the state government, the university and telemarketing, has been growing rapidly; big meatpacking operations have kept the population steady in smaller counties. Politically, Lincoln is fond of moderate-toned Republicans, and is more hospitable to Democrats than other part of the state; it split evenly between Bill Clinton and George Bush in 1992, when most of the rest of Nebraska gave Bush many more votes and split second-place between Clinton and Ross Perot.

The congressman from the 1st District is Douglas Bereuter (pronounced *BEEwriter*), a Republican first elected in 1978. He grew up in York, graduated from the University of Nebraska, then got degrees in planning and public policy from Harvard and worked as a planning consultant and part-time professor in Lincoln in the 1970s. He was elected to the Nebraska legislature in 1974 and to the U.S. House in 1978. He is of the same vintage as Newt Gingrich, but not as confrontational: "I work as effectively with people across party lines as any Republican. I think I'm far less partisan than almost any member of any party." He is part of the Society of Statesman, a two-dozen-member group of nonconfrontational Republicans; he has been active in the North Atlantic Assembly and in exchanges with the European Parliament. However, his voting record tilts pretty heavily to the conservative side.

As a senior member of two committees, Bereuter in 1995 was heavily involved in legislating. He chairs the Asia and Pacific Subcommittee of International Relations; he will surely continue his work encouraging farm exports and pressuring Europe to reduce agriculture subsidies. On the Banking Committee he was the sponsor of the 1995 regulatory relief bill, to cut bank reporting requirements. He sponsored the Section 502 home-loan guarantees for low- and moderate-income homebuyers in small towns and rural areas and has worked on Indian housing issues in several housing bills. He worked with Nebraska Democrats and against 3d District Republican Bill Barrett on the Niobrara Wild and Scenic River bill. He helped write the flood control bill in a way to reduce incentives for building in inherently unsafe coastal and shoreline areas, as well as floodplains.

Bereuter has been reelected with at least 60% since he first won the seat. After coming close to running for the Senate in other years, he seemed leaning towards a run for the seat Jim Exon is vacating in 1996, but decided to stay put in the House.

The People: Pop. 1990: 526,291; 39% rural; 15% age 65+; 96% White; 1% Black; 1% Amer. Indian; 1% Asian; 1% Other; 1% Hispanic origin. Voting age pop.: 389,907; 1% Black; 1% Hispanic origin. Households: 59% married couple families; 28% married couple fams. w. children; 46% college educ.; median household income: $25,763; per capita income: $12,088; median gross rent: $338; median house value: $49,700.

1992 Presidential Vote			1988 Presidential Vote		
Bush (R)	107,081	(43%)	Bush (R)	122,890	(56%)
Clinton (D)	80,696	(32%)	Dukakis (D)	96,015	(44%)
Perot (I)	59,974	(24%)			

Rep. Doug Bereuter (R)

Elected 1978; b. Oct. 6, 1939, York; home, Lincoln; U of NE, B.A. 1961, Harvard, M.C.P. 1966, M.P.A. 1973; Lutheran; married (Louise).

Career: Army, 1963–65; Urban planner, U.S. Dept. of HUD, 1965–66; Div. Dir., NE Econ. Devel. Dept., 1967–68; Dir., NE Office of Planning, 1968–70; NE Senate, 1974–78.

DC Office: 2348 RHOB 20515, 202-225-4806; Fax: 202-226-1148.

District Offices: 1045 K St., Lincoln 68508, 402-438-1598; and 502 N. Broad St., Fremont 68025, 402-727-0888.

Committees: *Banking & Financial Services* (4th of 27 R): Financial Institutions and Consumer Credit; Housing and Community Opportunity. *International Relations* (6th of 23 R): Asia and the Pacific (Chmn.); International Economic Policy and Trade.

Group Ratings

	ADA	ACLU	COPE	CFA	LCV	CON	NSI	COC	ACU	NTLC	CHC
1994	15	26	11	30	17	56	90	100	71	82	71
1993	10	—	8	40	36	59	—	91	88	—	—

National Journal Ratings

	1993 LIB — 1993 CONS			1994 LIB — 1994 CONS		
Economic	25%	—	72%	21%	—	76%
Social	36%	—	62%	36%	—	62%
Foreign	24%	—	72%	25%	—	71%

Key Votes of the 103d Congress

1. Clinton Deficit Plan	N	3. Brady Handgun Purchase	N	5. Lmt. UN Cmnd. of Forces	Y
2. NAFTA	Y	4. Strike Race/Death Pnlty.	Y	6. Cut Missile Funds	N

Key Votes of the 104th Congress

1. Congressional Compliance	Y	6. Reform Crime Grant	Y	11. Loser Pays Court Reform	Y
2. Balanced Budget Amndmt.	Y	7. National Security Act	Y	12. Product Liability Reform	Y
3. Bar Unfunded Mandates	Y	8. Moratorium on Regs.	Y	13. Welfare Reform	Y
4. Pass Line Item Veto	Y	9. Risk Assessment on Regs.	Y	14. Term Limits Amndmt.	Y
5. Relax Exclusionary Rule	Y	10. Expnd. Priv. Prop. Rights	Y	15. Tax Cuts	Y

Election Results

1994 general	Doug Bereuter (R)	117,967	(63%)	($334,598)
	Patrick Combs (D)	70,369	(37%)	($178,046)
1994 primary	Doug Bereuter (R)	unopposed		
1992 general	Doug Bereuter (R)	142,713	(60%)	($365,386)
	Gerry Finnegan (D)	96,309	(40%)	($84,533)

SECOND DISTRICT

Omaha, the commercial metropolis of Nebraska, the largest city on the Great Plains north of Kansas City and west of Minneapolis, the city that still produces one out of five American steaks, got its start from government: Abraham Lincoln picked it as the eastern terminus of the Union Pacific railroad, from which emerged the stockyards and livestock exchange that made it a top livestock town. Over the years, Omaha filled up with cattle hands from the West and European immigrants, especially Germans and Czechs; it developed fine civic institutions from the Joslyn Art Museum and the Ak-Sar-Ben (spell it backwards) Exhibition to the Boys Town of orphanage fame, founded by Father Flanagan in 1917, and its refurbished old theaters. Though a major city by the 1880s, Omaha has remained small enough (and famous on Wall Street as the place where Warren Buffett lives and works) to be readily comprehensible; you don't feel distant, physically or psychologically, from the other side of town, and you usually know people from a broader range of backgrounds than you would in a large homogeneous neighborhood within a big metropolitan area. The older, less affluent part of Omaha is near the river and Iowa; to the west, the city has been quietly booming, with affluent neighborhoods and new shopping areas. All over, Omaha's economy has been changing. It still has many processors of food products, like the hard-charging ConAgra company, and the giant Peter Kiewit construction firm; but it is also the nation's telecommunications center, handling 100 million '800' and '900' calls annually and employing 10,000 people in 24 telemarketing centers.

The 2d Congressional District of Nebraska is metropolitan Omaha: Douglas County with Omaha and its western suburbs; Sarpy County with suburbs to the south and the old Strategic Air Command headquarters at Offutt Air Force Base; and a sliver of Cass County just to the south. Politically, Omaha has long had competitive politics, with Democrats strong on the south side around the stockyards and the northeast and Republicans strong in the area west of 72d Street; the 2d District has been competitive more often than not over the last two decades.

The current Congressman from the 2d District is Jon Christensen, a Republican elected in a bitter contest in 1994 over three-term incumbent Democrat Peter Hoagland. Christensen grew up in rural Nebraska, attended Midland Lutheran College on a basketball scholarship, went to law school in Texas, returned to Nebraska to work as an insurance agent and marketing director, and owned a company marketing organic fertilizer. In 1994, Christensen waged an active door-to-door campaign, backing school prayer, the option to teach creationism and a ban on abortion, and he won the May Republican primary with 53% to 25% for state Senator Brad Ashford, pro-choice and moderate, and 23% for Ron Staskiewicz, the Republican nominee who lost 51%–49% to Hoagland in 1992. Right after the primary Christensen led Hoagland in both newspaper and Republican polls, though it is highly unusual for a non-scandal-tarred incumbent to trail so early in the campaign. Christensen showed up at Hoagland meetings in Omaha and committee hearings in Washington—"stalking," Democrats said. In June, Christensen sat in the front row at a Ways and Means hearing when Hoagland cast the decisive vote for employer mandates in health care; it passed 20–18, and Christensen was immediately on the phone to an Omaha radio station. This was all the more newsworthy, because Hoagland had opposed much of the Clinton plan, favoring managed competition instead, and had worked closely on the issue with officials of Mutual of Omaha, the city's largest employer. Christensen favored medical savings accounts.

More controversy came in August when a Hoagland TV ad showed a couple who said

Christensen, while campaigning door-to-door, told them Omaha public school textbooks taught immoral values. Christensen said he was never in that neighborhood, and took a lie detector test; Hoagland said he didn't ask anyone to lie, and also took a lie detector test; both passed. The ad was yanked when the couple claimed they received death threats, as did the daughter of a former Omaha mayor who in a Hoagland spot attacked Christensen's anti-abortion stand. More attacks followed. Christensen attacked Hoagland as a Clinton clone; Hoagland called him a right-wing extremist. Christensen attacked Hoagland for supporting "Rottenkowski" by voting against a House Post Office probe; Hoagland said Christensen supporters were cutting down his lawn signs with chain saws. Hoagland called Christensen a religious "extremist" and said his tax breaks for home schooling would be subsidies for Branch Davidians. Christensen pounded again and again on the moderate Hoagland's vote for the Clinton budget and tax package in August 1993 and on his record of 81% support of Clinton.

It became conventional wisdom among political reporters that this was one of the dirtiest campaigns in the country, and there were excesses. Yet the intensity of feeling reflected genuine and legitimate differences on important issues. Hoagland, who spent a total of $2.5 million in three previous campaigns, spent $1.1 million in this one, raising $780,000 from PACs (the seventh highest in the country). Christensen raised $779,000, with only $123,000 from PACs; he ended the campaign with $150,000 cash-on-hand, evidence perhaps of overconfidence. Fall polls showed him with narrow leads, and the final result was close. Hoagland carried Omaha's Douglas County but lost suburban Sarpy County by a wider margin, giving Christensen a 50%–49% victory.

Christensen is among the purists of Contract With America Republicans; he voted against term limits because the final version did not limit them enough and superseded state limits. He campaigned hard and was fortunate to get a seat on the powerful Ways and Means Committee, a rare plum for a freshman. Elected at 31, he is one of the youngest House members, and one with a limited and perhaps spotty past; he admitted past marital problems and flunking the bar exam. He may face spirited competition in the future, but not from Hoagland, who has said he may run for the Senate but not again for the House.

The People: Pop. 1990: 526,573; 6% rural; 10% age 65+; 86% White; 10% Black; 1% Amer. Indian; 1% Asian; 1% Other; 3% Hispanic origin. Voting age pop.: 379,295; 8% Black; 2% Hispanic origin. Households: 55% married couple families; 28% married couple fams. w. children; 56% college educ.; median household income: $30,889; per capita income: $14,322; median gross rent: $405; median house value: $60,700.

1992 Presidential Vote			1988 Presidential Vote		
Bush (R)	115,255	(47%)	Bush (R)	121,437	(58%)
Clinton (D)	78,701	(32%)	Dukakis (D)	88,547	(42%)
Perot (I)	48,657	(20%)			

Rep. Jon Christensen (R)

Elected 1994; b. Feb. 2, 1963, St. Paul, NE; home, Omaha; Midland Lutheran U., B.S. 1985; S. TX Col. of Law, J.D. 1989; Christian; married (Meredith).

Career: Vice Pres., COMReP Inc., 1989–91; Mktg. Dir., CT Mutual Insurance Co., 1991–94.

DC Office: 1020 LHOB 20515, 202-225-4155; Fax: 202-225-3032.

District Offices: 8712 Dodge St., #350, Omaha 68114, 402-397-9944.

Committees: *Ways & Means* (21st of 21 R): Health; Social Security.

Group Ratings and 103rd Congress Votes: Newly Elected

Key Votes of the 104th Congress

1. Congressional Compliance Y	6. Reform Crime Grant Y	11. Loser Pays Court Reform Y
2. Balanced Budget Amndmt. Y	7. National Security Act Y	12. Product Liability Reform Y
3. Bar Unfunded Mandates Y	8. Moratorium on Regs. Y	13. Welfare Reform Y
4. Pass Line Item Veto Y	9. Risk Assessment on Regs. Y	14. Term Limits Amndmt. N
5. Relax Exclusionary Rule Y	10. Expnd. Priv. Prop. Rights Y	15. Tax Cuts Y

Election Results

1994 general	Jon Christensen (R)	92,516	(50%)	($953,163)
	Peter Hoagland (D)	90,750	(49%)	($1,105,892)
	Others	2,044	(1%)	
1994 primary	Jon Christensen (R)	26,494	(53%)	
	Brad Ashford (R)	12,340	(25%)	
	Ron Staskiewicz (R)	11,436	(23%)	
1992 general	Peter Hoagland (D)	119,512	(51%)	($699,387)
	Ronald L. Staskiewicz (R)	113,828	(49%)	($378,721)

THIRD DISTRICT

West of Grand Island, Nebraska is wheat and livestock country. For miles on end you can see nothing but rolling brown fields, sectioned off here and there by barbed wire fences, and in the distance a grain elevator towering over a tiny town and its miniature railroad depot. The winds and rain and tornadoes that come suddenly out of the sky remind you that the original settlers likened this part of the country to an ocean and thought themselves in their wooden wagons almost as helpless as passengers at sea in a rowboat. Settlers passed through here on the Oregon Trail in the 1840s, then set down roots in the 1880s, but the rain they hoped for fell too unreliably, and wheatlands gave way to pasture and open range. It is a beautiful but hard land, exacting much from its people, as the novels of western Nebraska's Willa Cather make poignantly clear.

The 3d Congressional District of Nebraska has 33% of the state's people spread out over 82% of its acreage. And the land is emptying out: except along the interstate, the 3d has been losing population for decades; these 66 counties had 608,000 people in 1940, 525,000 in 1990. Geographically and politically, the 3d District is where the Midwest becomes the West. It has a Farm Belt demand for subsidies and the West's angry opposition to federal interference. It is heavily Republican: in 1994, when Senator Bob Kerrey carried the 1st District with 60% and the 2d District with 56%, Republican Jan Stoney carried the "Big Third" with 54%. In congressional elections, it has long been Republican, but is seriously contested when an incumbent retires, as in 1974 and 1990.

The current Congressman is Bill Barrett, who has lived all his life in Lexington, where he owned an insurance and real estate firm. In 1978 he was elected to Nebraska's unicameral legislature, where in 1987 he became Speaker. In 1990 he ran for the House and won a five-candidate Republican primary with 30%, running well in his home area and in the eastern end of the district, in the Lincoln media market. In the general he was hammered by Democratic state legislator Sandra Scofield for supporting Governor Kay Orr's 1987 tax package and for his antiabortion stand. Barrett charged that Scofield had missed a tax vote and, with vigorous campaigning from former Congresswoman Virginia Smith, won what proved to be a friends-and-neighbors contest, losing most of the western counties and carrying his home area in the southern tier of counties, with 51% of the vote.

In the House Barrett has compiled a solidly conservative voting record. He serves on the Agriculture Committee and is now chairman of the General Farm Commodities Subcommittee, a strategic position for his district. He has worked to promote planting flexibility and rural health care; he worked against a gas tax and for lower estate taxes on farms. He was president of the Republican freshman class in 1991—nothing as large as 1995's—and was on the six-member panel investigating the House Post Office scandal. Now he is on the spot. With Republicans slashing domestic spending, will he vote to reduce subsidies to local farmers on the 1995 farm bill, as he votes with other Republicans to reduce federal funding for other programs?

Barrett has been reelected easily with 72% and 79% of the vote. In March 1995, when Senator Jim Exon announced his retirement, Barrett said, "I have no intention of breaking my contract with the 'Big Third' and running for the U.S. Senate."

The People: Pop. 1990: 525,521; 56% rural; 18% age 65+; 96% White; 1% Amer. Indian; 1% Other; 3% Hispanic origin. Voting age pop.: 379,996; 2% Hispanic origin. Households: 62% married couple families; 29% married couple fams. w. children; 40% college educ.; median household income: $22,344; per capita income: $10,942; median gross rent: $284; median house value: $38,000.

1992 Presidential Vote			1988 Presidential Vote		
Bush (R)	121,342	(49%)	Bush (R)	153,629	(67%)
Perot (I)	65,473	(27%)	Dukakis (D)	74,673	(33%)
Clinton (D)	57,467	(23%)			

Rep. William (Bill) Barrett (R)

Elected 1990; b. Feb. 9, 1929, Lexington; home, Lexington; Hastings Col., B.A. 1951; Presbyterian; married (Elsie).

Career: Navy, 1951–52; Businessman, real estate and insurance, 1956–90; NE Legislature, 1978–90, Speaker, 1986–90.

DC Office: 1213 LHOB 20515, 202-225-6435; Fax: 202-225-0207.

District Offices: 312 W. 3d St., Grand Island 68801, 308-381-5555; and 1502 2d Ave., #2, Scottsbluff 69361, 307-632-3333.

Committees: *Agriculture* (6th of 27 R): General Farm Commodities (Chmn.); Resource Conservation, Research and Forestry. *Economic & Educational Opportunities* (7th of 24 R): Oversight and Investigations; Workforce Protections.

Group Ratings

	ADA	ACLU	COPE	CFA	LCV	CON	NSI	COC	ACU	NTLC	CHC
1994	5	17	11	20	6	79	100	92	95	85	86
1993	5	—	0	20	21	74	—	91	92	—	—

National Journal Ratings

	1993 LIB — 1993 CONS	1994 LIB — 1994 CONS
Economic	20% — 77%	0% — 80%
Social	11% — 82%	20% — 77%
Foreign	17% — 76%	14% — 80%

Key Votes of the 103d Congress

1. Clinton Deficit Plan	N	3. Brady Handgun Purchase	N	5. Lmt. UN Cmnd. of Forces	Y
2. NAFTA	Y	4. Strike Race/Death Pnlty.	Y	6. Cut Missile Funds	N

Key Votes of the 104th Congress

1. Congressional Compliance	Y	6. Reform Crime Grant	Y	11. Loser Pays Court Reform	Y
2. Balanced Budget Amndmt.	Y	7. National Security Act	Y	12. Product Liability Reform	Y
3. Bar Unfunded Mandates	Y	8. Moratorium on Regs.	Y	13. Welfare Reform	Y
4. Pass Line Item Veto	Y	9. Risk Assessment on Regs.	Y	14. Term Limits Amndmt.	Y
5. Relax Exclusionary Rule	Y	10. Expnd. Priv. Prop. Rights	Y	15. Tax Cuts	Y

Election Results

1994 general	William (Bill) Barrett (R)	154,919	(79%)	($232,013)
	Gil Chapin (D)	41,943	(21%)	($54,519)
1994 primary	William (Bill) Barrett (R)	unopposed		
1992 general	William (Bill) Barrett (R)	170,857	(72%)	($487,992)
	Lowell Fisher (D)	67,457	(28%)	($91,170)

NEVADA

Giant plinths, glass-covered towers, a pyramid and obelisk, all rising in a bowl-shaped desert valley rimmed by barren peaks: this surrealist landscape is today's Nevada. Nature left little here to encourage human settlement—lodes of gold and silver which attracted sudden agglomerations of miners and hangers-on for brief years, but almost no water, no arable land. So Nevada as a society is wholly the creation of man. Its existence as a state is happenstance: the discovery of the Comstock Lode silver mine in 1859—$500 million worth was taken out in 20 years—brought settlers, and Abraham Lincoln's Republicans made it a state in 1864 even though Nevada did not meet the population requirement for statehood when they thought they needed its 3 electoral votes. But Nevada's population dropped by the early 20th Century; in the early 1930s, there were only 91,000 Nevadans and the state government was about to go bankrupt. So Nevada decided to roll the dice. The state reduced its residency requirement for divorce to six weeks and legalized gambling. Catering to what most Americans considered sin— casinos, pawnshops, divorce mills, quick wedding chapels, even legal brothels—turned out to be good business. Nevada has been America's fastest growing state since 1960; in the 1980s its population rose 50%, from 800,000 to 1.2 million, adding 6,000 new residents every week; from 1990 to 1993, it added another 187,000, growing more than 15% over just three years.

Las Vegas, a mere spot on the map when gambling was legalized, is now a metro area of

971,000 and Reno, in the 1940s the divorce capital of America, has 269,000. Gaming—the industry word for gambling—generates most of this growth: Las Vegas's 28 million tourists spend $19 billion a year, Reno's nearly five million spend almost $4 billion; almost half Nevada's jobs are in services some way related to gambling or tourism. The 6.4% gambling receipts tax generates enough revenue so that Nevada has no income, corporate or inheritance tax, and the cost of living is low; half the houses in Las Vegas are valued at under $100,000 and many migrants from California cannot find a house that costs as much as the one they sold.

From mining to gaming, Nevada has been a second chance state, a place for outcasts and misfits to rebound. Some 11% of its adults are divorced, the highest rate in the nation. The four owners of the Comstock Lode—MacKay, Fair, Flood, O'Brien—were Irishmen; the first big hotel on the Las Vegas strip, the Flamingo, was built in 1946 by Jewish gangster Bugsy Siegel, later gunned down in his Beverly Hills home; most of the big casinos were owned by mobsters until Howard Hughes—a different kind of outcast—bought them up in the late 1960s. For years, the casinos catered to older tastes in entertainment, from Frank Sinatra to girlie shows, and depended on gamblers for all their trade. But in the early 1990s, Las Vegas became a family-friendly destination resort. Its huge and exuberantly tasteful hotels have glittering attractions: the 3,000-room Mirage with its tropical rainforest lobby has Siegfried and Roy's tiger-taming extravaganza; the MGM Grand, the largest hotel in the world, with its lion entry-hall, hosted Barbra Streisand's first live performance in decades in 1994; Caesars Palace has an upscale shopping center with Roman-style storefronts; the pyramid-shaped Luxor that looms over this desert has an amusement park and huge obelisk inside; out in front of the Treasure Island, a pirate ship battle occurs every 90 minutes. Slot machines no longer line every hallway, because that would mean keeping children out; Las Vegas has become decorous enough to attract the American Booksellers and Southern Baptist conventions. Will either political party ever dare to hold its national convention here?

There are other things going on in Nevada besides gambling and other places besides Las Vegas (though its Clark County contains nearly 62% of Nevadans). The state's low taxes have made it a regional distribution and credit card operations center and it has attracted warehouses and factories from California. There is still some mining, a little gold and silver, plus less glamorous diatomaceous earth, used for swimming pool filters and kitty litter. And the Wild West atmosphere remains, especially in the "Cow Counties" beyond Las Vegas and Reno. Near Elko, a Canadian company's subsidiary paid the federal government $9,765 for title to 1,949 acres of public lands with 30 million ounces of gold—all legal under the Mining Act of 1872. In Tonopah the federal government sued Nye County for claiming to own public lands and prosecuting federal officers enforcing federal land management laws.

For the past two decades, Nevada has had a volatile politics. Historically, it was Democratic, sending politically shrewd Democrats to Washington to protect the interests of a state always heavily dependent on the federal government. The most powerful were Key Pittman, chairman of the Senate Foreign Relations Committee, who backed FDR's foreign policy only after Roosevelt agreed to buy absurdly large amounts of silver, and penny-pinching Pat McCarran, author of the repressive McCarran Act, who shamelessly pushed aid for Reno and Las Vegas (the airport there is named for him) and became suddenly solicitous of civil liberties when mobsters and casino owners were called to testify before the Kefauver committee investigating crime and racketeering. In the 1980s Nevada trended sharply Republican, primarily because of newcomers. This came not out of devotion to family values, for Nevada is the least family-oriented state, with the nation's largest percentage of non-family households, but from people who think they are sharper than others, have a special angle, are a step ahead of the market, can and will beat the odds. In the 1990s the picture has been mixed. To the surprise of managers for both candidates, Bill Clinton carried Nevada in 1992, 37%–35%, and Democratic Senators Harry Reid and Richard Bryan have both been reelected. But in 1994, Nevada elected two Republicans to the U.S. House. The parties split the top statewide offices; Republicans hold the state Senate 13–8, but the state Assembly is evenly split, 21–21. Nevada may be vastly more

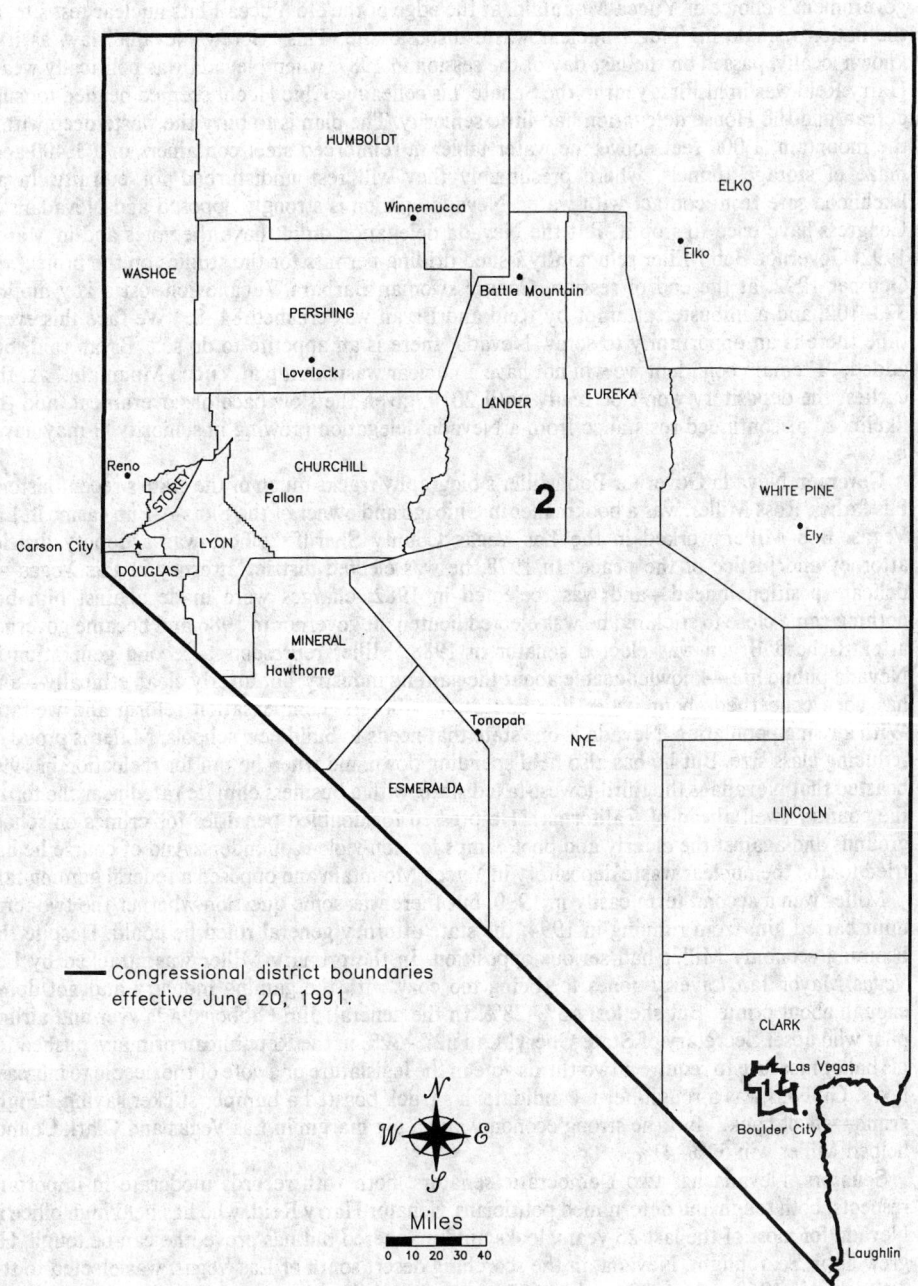

—Congressional district boundaries
effective June 20, 1991.

HUMBOLDT

Winnemucca

ELKO

WASHOE

Elko

PERSHING

Battle Mountain

LANDER

EUREKA

Reno

STOREY

CHURCHILL

WHITE PINE

Carson City

LYON

Fallon

Ely

DOUGLAS

MINERAL

Hawthorne

2

Tonopah

NYE

ESMERALDA

LINCOLN

CLARK

Las Vegas

Boulder City

1

Laughlin

N
W   E
S

Miles

0 10 20 30 40

populous than it used to be, but a few votes can still make a difference.

Politics can also make a difference, Nevadans have discovered, as they worry over the federal government's choice of Yucca Mountain, at the edge of the old Yucca Flats nuclear test site, as the nation's single high-level nuclear waste disposal site. This "Screw Nevada" law, as it is known locally, passed on the last day of the session in 1987, when Nevada was politically weak: Harry Reid was in his first year in the Senate, his colleague Chic Hecht seemed headed for sure defeat, and the House delegation had little seniority. The plan is to bury the waste deep within the mountain, 1,000 feet above the water table, in reinforced steel containers in a 1,400-acre maze of storage tunnels, where presumably they will rest undisturbed for eternity, in all likelihood safe from contact with water. Nevada opinion is strongly opposed and Nevadans in Congress have tried to stop it. But the Nevada delegation didn't have the votes and in March 1992, Governor Bob Miller reluctantly issued drilling permits for the studies on the project. In October 1992, at the end of session, Congresswoman Barbara Vucanovich lost a key motion 323–102, and a filibuster attempt by Reid and Bryan was crushed 84–8. "We face this every time there is an opportunity to screw Nevada, there is an appetite to do so," Bryan said, but added, "I remain confident we will not have a nuclear waste dump at Yucca Mountain." At the earliest the depository won't be ready until 2010; given the slow pace of government, and the likelihood of continued resistance from a Nevada delegation growing in seniority, it may never be.

Governor. Nevada Governor Bob Miller's biography tracks much of the state's recent history. His father, Ross Miller, was a bookmaker in Chicago and owner of the Slots-A-Fun casino in Las Vegas. Bob Miller worked in the Las Vegas County Sheriff's office, was a deputy district attorney and justice of the peace. In 1978, he was elected district attorney in Las Vegas—a delicate position indeed—and was reelected in 1982; charges were made against him but nothing came close to sticking; he was elected lieutenant governor in 1986 and became governor after Richard Bryan was elected senator in 1988. Miller represents a second generation in Nevada public life—knowledgeable about the gaming industry, but utterly clean ethically—and has been concerned about issues like education, workers' compensation reform and welfare. With a rising population, Nevada is one state that needs to build new schools; Miller is proud of reducing class size. But he has also held spending down and when he ran for reelection in 1994 boasted that Nevada is the third-lowest-taxed state, with a business climate rated near the top of the country (well ahead of California). He pressed for doubled penalties for crimes on school grounds and against the elderly and boot camps for non-violent offenders. And of course he has tried to stop the nuclear waste depository in Yucca Mountain and opposed a federal gaming tax.

Miller won a second term easily in 1990, but there was some question whether the two-term limit barred him from running in 1994; the state attorney general ruled he could. Despite the booming economy Miller had serious opposition. In the primary Miller was attacked by Las Vegas Mayor Jan Laverty Jones for being too cozy with the gaming industry and not doing enough about crime. But she lost 63%–28%. In the general, Jim Gibbons, a lawyer and airline pilot who upset Secretary of State Cheryl Lau 52%–32% in the Republican primary, pushed for his ballot measure to require a two-thirds vote in the legislature or a vote of the people to increase taxes. Gibbons was a rough-hewn candidate: his truck boasted a bumper sticker saying, "Fight crime—shoot back." But the strong economy and a big margin in Las Vegas and Clark County helped Miller win 53%–41%.

Senators. Nevada has two Democratic senators, both with records moderate in important respects, both tough and determined politicians. Senator Harry Reid, who has held high office in Nevada for most of the last 25 years, looks mild-mannered but has proved he can be tough. He grew up in Searchlight, Nevada, in the scorching desert south of Las Vegas, was elected to the Assembly in 1968, at age 28, and in 1970 was elected lieutenant governor. In 1974, he came within 624 votes of beating Paul Laxalt in the race for senator, lost for mayor of Las Vegas in 1976, and then became head of the Gaming Commission from 1977 to 1981—as sensitive a post as any in Nevada. In 1982, when Nevada got two House seats for the first time and

Congressman Jim Santini ran for the Senate, Reid ran for the Las Vegas 1st District seat and won. Laxalt retired in 1986, and Reid ran for the Senate again; his opponent turned out to be Santini, who had opportunistically switched parties at the last minute and was running as a Republican. Reid's ads depicted him as David to Santini's Goliath, and he won 50%–45%.

Reid combines a moderate-to-liberal voting record with a strong partisan commitment, tempered by a willingness to seek bipartisan solutions on occasion. He is antiabortion and was the first Democratic senator to support President Bush on the Gulf war resolution. He was prepared to vote for the Clarence Thomas nomination but changed his mind after the testimony of Anita Hill. He is not afraid to tackle tough local issues. Through two years of negotiation he produced an agreement on allocating water from Lake Tahoe and the Truckee River between Nevada and California; Reid got the Pyramid Lake Paiute Indians to agree to return their fisheries to the state for $25 million, plus $40 million in economic aid. He pushed through a Nevada Wilderness Protection Act in 1990, over the objections of Republican Congresswoman Barbara Vucanovich. He was successful in passing an amendment in the 1992 tax bill prohibiting states from taxing pension income of non-residents. In 1992 Reid had both primary and general opposition. In the September primary, Charles Woods, a businessman severely scarred in World War II, who had run for governor of Alabama and other offices there in the 1960s and 70s, ran TV ads that helped him win 39% to only 53% for Reid, who lost most of the Cow Counties (counties outside Las Vegas and Reno). In the general, against rancher Demar Dahl, Reid won by a similar margin, 51%–40%.

In his second term Reid has been feistier than ever. He took on David Pryor, Bill Clinton's best friend in the Senate, by moving to phase out his Special Committee on Aging; Pryor won that one. He took on Ross Perot, when he appeared before the Joint Committee on the Organization of Congress: "I think you should start checking your facts a little more and stop listening to the applause as much." He is one senator who relishes listening to unfriendly constituents. He took on the grazing fee issue, braving Cow County ranchers by negotiating with Interior Secretary Bruce Babbitt, who wanted to raise the animal unit month fee from $1.86 to $4.28, and Congressmen George Miller and Mike Synar for a compromise $3.45. This was stymied in November 1993 by a filibuster led by Pete Domenici of New Mexico. Reid allied himself with Hillary Rodham Clinton on healthcare reform, which turned out to be a risky position; he supported the Democrats' crime bill, despite its assault weapon ban. He called the possibility of mob control of poorly regulated Indian casinos "a national scandal in the making." Reid considered running for the Democratic leadership, but in April 1994 took himself out of the race and endorsed eventual winner Tom Daschle.

After the 1994 election, Reid said, "We have to all swallow a little bit of our pride and go toward the middle." He called for piecemeal healthcare reform and tightening legal immigration. In December 1994, Reid succeeded Daschle as co-chairman of the Senate Democratic Policy Committee, the lone westerner in the Democratic leadership. That same month he told Bill Clinton: "Our public lands policy is not working. You can't have a Secretary of Interior who can't campaign for senators in the West." (In March 1995, however, Reid did say that in 1996, Clinton could carry any number of Western states, although "it would be very tough in Nevada.") He rallied Democrats in February 1995 with Dianne Feinstein on the balanced budget amendment with his proviso that Social Security not be affected; it was defeated 57–41, but the argument gave cover to enough Democrats changing their votes to defeat it in March. The budget can't be balanced without Social Security funds, said Reid, "any more than I thought Evel Knievel could jump those fountains at Caesars Palace." But Reid also sought bipartisan solutions. With Frank Murkowski, he sponsored a mining bill requiring mining companies to pay market value for patented federal land and a 3% royalty on ore. With Don Nickles, he sponsored a plan to allow Congress to review federal regulations within a 45-day period. It is too soon to forecast how he will fare in 1998.

Senator Richard Bryan has been governor or senator for over 14 years. He grew up in Las Vegas, was a deputy district attorney in Clark County in 1964, at 27, then became the county's first public defender. In 1968 he was elected to the Assembly (the same year as Harry Reid), in 1972 to the state Senate. In 1978, he was elected attorney general; in 1982, he defeated incumbent Governor Robert List; and in 1988, he defeated incumbent Senator Chic Hecht. Bryan attacked Hecht for not fighting hard enough against the nuclear waste disposal site designation, and Hecht had indeed been rolled in the Senate. Bryan won 50%–46%.

Bryan's record was middle-of-the-road in the Democratic Senate. He voted for the Gulf war resolution and against the Clarence Thomas nomination, for the balanced budget amendment in 1995 and against the Clinton budget and tax package in 1993 (because of retroactive taxes and taxes on restaurants and tourism). Probably his number one cause in the Senate has been stopping the Yucca Mountain nuclear waste disposal site. His most recent proposals include a bill requiring a presidential commission to conduct an independent review of Yucca Mountain and another to allow nuclear power plants to store waste on-site—which may be the eventual solution. He has also opposed major changes in the Mining Act of 1872. But Bryan has other goals. He tried to raise the CAFE (Corporate Average Fuel Economy) standards on automakers to 40 miles per gallon by 2001. But the bill lost on the floor in 1990 and was not included in the 1992 energy act. He was more successful in sponsoring a law against telemarketing fraud with John McCain and another on airbags with Slade Gorton. He was successful in eliminating the mohair subsidy and the Search for Extraterrestrial Intelligence program. He has sponsored fair credit reporting legislation, a law to authorize more border patrol agents and wants to eliminate the tax break for products manufactured by corporations—generally the pharmaceutical industry—in Puerto Rico. In the 103d Congress, Bryan was most visible nationally as chairman of the Senate Ethics Committee, in which capacity he chaired the investigation of Bob Packwood and led the successful fight for access to his diaries. He is now vice chairman, the ranking minority slot, and is leading the effort in the Senate to reform congressional pensions.

Bryan won reelection in Republican 1994. Republicans had a primary. One candidate was Charles Woods, a free-spending businessman and severely scarred World War II veteran who ran for office many times as a Democrat in Alabama and in the Democratic primary against Senator Harry Reid in 1992; he led in polls for months. But in the end longtime Nevada Republican Hal Furman won 50%–26%. Furman served as a staffer to Senator Paul Laxalt in the 1970s and was an appointee in the Reagan Interior Department; in the private sector since 1985, he attacked Bryan for spending a lifetime in government. Bryan responded by calling Furman a lobbyist and asking what work the firm he was part of, public relations giant Hill and Knowlton, had done for the rogue international bank BCCI. In light of Bill Clinton's unpopularity, Bryan campaigned as an independent, strong voice, and he certainly was the louder one: he outspent Furman $3 million to $846,000. That was enough for a 51%–41% victory. Bryan lost the Cow Counties narrowly, 46%–44%, but won by a solid 53%–40% in Las Vegas's Clark County, which cast 57% of the state's votes.

Presidential politics. In the 1940s, Nevada was a Democratic state; in the 1960s, it was divided much as the nation was, voting narrowly for John Kennedy in 1960 and Richard Nixon in 1968. In the 1980s, it was heavily Republican, over 60% for Ronald Reagan and 59%–38% for George Bush in 1988. In 1992, it surprised just about everyone, including strategists for both candidates, by voting for Bill Clinton. But he won only a 37%–35% margin, with a thumping 26% for Ross Perot. Nevada at one time had a presidential primary, predictably ignored by the candidates, but now has caucuses.

Congressional districting. With a population increase of 50%, Nevada was the fastest growing state in the nation during the 1980s. It did not gain another seat, however, and the district lines were redrawn in the Las Vegas area.

The People: Est. Pop. 1994: 1,457,000; Pop. 1990: 1,201,833, up 21.2% 1990–1994. 0.6% of U.S. total, 38th largest; 12% rural. Median age: 33.3 years. 10.6% 65 years and over. 84.3% White, 10.4% Hispanic origin, 6.6% Black, 3.2% Asian, 1.6% American Indian, 4.4% Other. Households: 51.4% married couple families; 23% married couple fams. w. children; 47% college educ.; median household income: $31,011; per capita income: $15,214; 54.8% owner occupied housing; median house value: $95,700; median monthly rent: $445. 6.6% Unemployment. 1994 Voting age pop.: 1,088,000. 1994 Turnout: 379,584; 35% of VAP. Registered voters (1994): 630,615; 270,917 D (43%), 263,074 R (42%), 96,624 unaffiliated and minor parties (15%).

Political Lineup: Governor, Bob Miller (D); Lt. Gov., Lonnie Hammargren (R); Secy. of State, Dean Heller (R); Atty. Gen., Frankie Sue Del Papa (D); Treasurer, Robert L. Seale (R); Controller, Darrell Daines (R). State Senate, 21 (13 R and 8 D); State Assembly, 42 (21 D and 21 R). Senators, Harry Reid (D) and Richard H. Bryan (D). Representatives, 2 (2 R).

1992 Presidential Vote			1988 Presidential Vote		
Clinton (D)	189,148	(37%)	Bush (R)	206,040	(59%)
Bush (R)	175,828	(35%)	Dukakis (D)	132,738	(38%)
Perot (I)	132,580	(26%)			

GOVERNOR

Gov. Bob Miller (D)

Assumed office Jan. 1989, term expires Jan. 1999; b. Mar. 30, 1945, Chicago, IL; home, Carson City; U. of Santa Clara, B.A. 1967, Loyola U. Law Schl., J.D. 1971; Catholic; married (Sandy).

Career: Clark Cnty. Dep. Dist. Atty., 1971–73; Legal advisor, Las Vegas Metro. Police Dept., 1973–75; Justice of the Peace, Las Vegas Township, 1975–78; Clark Cnty. Dist. Atty., 1979–86; NV Lt. Gov., 1987–88; Chmn., Western Govs. Assn., 1992–94.

Office: Executive Chambers, Capitol Bldg., Carson City 89710, 702-687-5670; 702-687-4486.

Election Results

1994 gen.	Bob Miller (D)	200,026	(53%)
	Jim Gibbons (R)	156,875	(41%)
	Others	22,775	(6%)
1994 prim.	Bob Miller (D)	75,311	(63%)
	Jan Laverty Jones (D)	33,566	(28%)
	Others	11,309	(9%)
1990 gen.	Bob Miller (D)	207,878	(66%)
	Jim Gallaway (R)	95,789	(31%)
	Other	8,984	(3%)

SENATORS

Sen. Harry Reid (D)

Elected 1986, seat up 1998; b. Dec. 2, 1939, Searchlight; home, Searchlight; Southern UT St. Col., A.S. 1959; UT St. U., B.S. 1961, George Washington U., J.D. 1964; U. of NV, 1969–70; Mormon; married (Landra).

Career: Practicing atty., 1969–82; Henderson City Atty., 1964–66; NV Assembly, 1969–70; NV Lt. Gov., 1970–74; Chmn., NV Gaming Comm., 1977–81; U.S. House of Reps., 1982–86.

DC Office: 324 HSOB 20510, 202-224-3542; Fax: 202-224-7327; e-mail: senator_reid@reid.senate.gov.

State Offices: 245 E. Liberty St., #102, Reno 89501, 702-784-5568; 500 E. Charleston Blvd., Las Vegas 89104, 702-474-0041; and 600 E. Williams St., #302, Carson City 89701, 702-882-7343.

Committees: *Democratic Policy Committee Co-Chairman. Appropriations* (10th of 13 D): Energy and Water Development; Interior; Labor, Health and Human Services, Education; Military Construction (RMM); Transportation. *Environment & Public Works* (4th of 7 D): Drinking Water, Fisheries and Wildlife (RMM); Transportation and Infrastructure. *Indian Affairs* (3rd of 8 D). *Aging (Special)* (6th of 9 D).

Group Ratings

	ADA	ACLU	COPE	CFA	LCV	CON	NSI	COC	ACU	NTLC	CHC
1994	85	32	100	83	85	7	30	27	4	12	21
1993	60	—	82	90	69	44	—	18	24	—	—

National Journal Ratings

	1993 LIB — 1993 CONS	1994 LIB — 1994 CONS
Economic	59% — 34%	72% — 18%
Social	50% — 49%	53% — 40%
Foreign	71% — 24%	62% — 37%

Key Votes of the 103d Congress

1. Clinton Deficit Plan	Y	3. Brady Handgun Purchase Y	5. Lmt. UN Cmnd. of Forces N
2. NAFTA	N	4. Strike Race/Death Pnlty. Y	6. Cut Missile Funds	Y

Key Votes of the 104th Congress

1. Congressional Compliance Y	3. Balanced Budget Amndt. N	5. Product Liability Reform N
2. Bar Unfunded Mandates Y	4. Pass Line Item Veto N	6. FY96 Budget	N

Election Results

1992 general	Harry Reid (D)	253,150	(51%)	($3,259,802)
	Demar Dahl (R)	199,413	(40%)	($471,371)
	Others	43,333	(9%)	
1992 primary	Harry Reid (D)	64,828	(53%)	
	Charles Woods (D)	48,364	(39%)	
	Others	9,551	(8%)	
1986 general	Harry Reid (D)	130,955	(50%)	($2,055,756)
	Jim Santini (R)	116,606	(45%)	($2,656,747)
	Others	14,271	(5%)	

Sen. Richard H. Bryan (D)

Elected 1988, seat up 2000; b. July 16, 1937, Washington, D.C.; home, Carson City; U. of NV, B.A. 1959, U. of CA, Hastings Col. of Law., LL.B. 1963; Episcopalian; married (Bonnie).

Career: Army, 1959–60; Clark Cnty. Dep. Dist. Atty., 1964–66; Clark Cnty. Public Defender, 1966–68; Cnsl., Clark Cnty. Juvenile Court, 1968–69; NV Assembly, 1968–72; NV Senate, 1972–78; NV Atty. Gen., 1978–82; NV Gov., 1982–1988.

DC Office: 364 RSOB 20510, 202-224-6244; Fax: 202-224-1867.

State Offices: 300 Las Vegas Blvd. S., #1110, Las Vegas 89101, 702-388-6605; 300 Booth St., #2014, Reno 89509, 702-784-5007; and 600 E. William St., #304, Carson City 89701, 702-885-9111.

Committees: *Armed Services* (10th of 10 D): Airland Forces; Readiness; Strategic Forces. *Banking, Housing & Urban Affairs* (4th of 7 D): Financial Institutions and Regulatory Relief (RMM); Housing Opportunity and Community Development; Securities. *Commerce, Science & Transportation* (8th of 9 D): Aviation; Consumer Affairs, Foreign Commerce and Tourism; Science, Technology and Space; Surface Transportation and Merchant Marine. *Ethics* (Vice Chmn. of 3 D). *Intelligence (Select)* (3rd of 8 D).

Group Ratings

	ADA	ACLU	COPE	CFA	LCV	CON	NSI	COC	ACU	NTLC	CHC
1994	75	42	88	75	77	27	70	25	12	28	36
1993	60	—	73	90	63	22	—	36	29	—	—

National Journal Ratings

	1993 LIB — 1993 CONS	1994 LIB — 1994 CONS
Economic	46% — 51%	61% — 35%
Social	41% — 56%	52% — 47%
Foreign	53% — 39%	54% — 43%

Key Votes of the 103d Congress

1. Clinton Deficit Plan	N	3. Brady Handgun Purchase N	5. Lmt. UN Cmnd. of Forces N
2. NAFTA	N	4. Strike Race/Death Pnlty. Y	6. Cut Missile Funds Y

Key Votes of the 104th Congress

1. Congressional Compliance Y	3. Balanced Budget Amndt. Y	5. Product Liability Reform N
2. Bar Unfunded Mandates Y	4. Pass Line Item Veto N	6. FY96 Budget N

Election Results

1994 general	Richard H. Bryan (D)	193,804	(51%)	($3,021,834)
	Hal Furman (R)	156,020	(41%)	($845,340)
	Others	30,706	(8%)	
1994 primary	Richard H. Bryan (D)	unopposed		
1988 general	Richard H. Bryan (D)	175,548	(50%)	($2,957,789)
	Jacob (Chic) Hecht (R)	161,336	(46%)	($3,007,864)
	Others	12,765	(4%)	

FIRST DISTRICT

Nevada's congressional districts vastly differ in physical size; the 1st consists of the greater part of Las Vegas and its close-in suburbs; the 2d is the whole rest of the state. The 1st, something like a nervously drawn circle in the center of Clark County, takes in all of Las Vegas, most of Henderson, part of heavily black North Las Vegas and just a bit of the Las Vegas Colony Indian Reservation—added up, its just 0.2% of the state's land mass. It also is the more Democratic part of the state—though that was not very Democratic in 1994.

The congressman from the 1st District is John Ensign, a Republican elected in an upset in 1994. Ensign grew up in northern Nevada and moved to Las Vegas at 16; his family owns the Gold Strike Hotel, which he managed for some years, and he opened an around-the-clock veterinary hospital in 1987. In 1994, he decided to run against Congressman James Bilbray, a moderate Democrat on many issues. Ensign attacked Bilbray for voting for the Clinton budget and tax package in 1993 and for supporting the Clinton healthcare and crime bills in 1994. And Ensign also hit Bilbray for upgrading to first class on official flights home. Bilbray touted his opposition to Clinton on NAFTA and the Brady bill. Ensign called for medical savings accounts and truth in sentencing and opposed paying for day care for welfare mothers. Ensign started off little-known, but walked many precincts and spent $126,000 of his own money; this partially offset Bilbray's PAC money advantage, though he spent $914,000 to the Ensign's $687,000. Then in October, the *Las Vegas Review-Journal* reported that Bilbray political adviser Don Williams stood to gain $7 million on a land investment if Bilbray's bill to expand the Red Rock Canyon National Conservation Area passed. The House had already passed the bill; Senators Harry Reid and Richard Bryan held it for a while, but allowed it to pass, and it was signed into law six days before the election. This may have tipped the scale: Ensign won 48.5%–47.5%.

Ensign was one Republican freshman with almost no political or government experience. But he won a seat on the Ways and Means Committee, where he said he disliked other members' posturing questions, adding, "At the first hearing, you're just trying not to embarrass yourself." He also formed a House Gaming Caucus, with Nevada's Barbara Vucanovich and Atlantic City, New Jersey's Frank LoBiondo. Given the strong Democratic base here in North Las Vegas and north of the Strip, this will probably be a seriously contested seat in 1996.

The People: Pop. 1990: 601,042; 11% age 65+; 73% White; 10% Black; 1% Amer. Indian; 4% Asian; 5% Other; 12% Hispanic origin. Voting age pop.: 457,378; 9% Black; 11% Hispanic origin. Households: 49% married couple families; 21% married couple fams. w. children; 44% college educ.; median household income: $29,611; per capita income: $14,837; median gross rent: $505; median house value: $88,900.

1992 Presidential Vote

Clinton (D)	98,700	(43%)
Bush (R)	70,440	(31%)
Perot (I)	55,964	(24%)

1988 Presidential Vote

Bush (R)	86,736	(56%)
Dukakis (D)	67,413	(44%)

Rep. John Ensign (R)

Elected 1994; b. Mar. 25, 1958, Roseville, CA; home, Las Vegas; OR St. U., B.S. 1981; CO St. U., D.V.M. 1985; Christian; married (Darlene).

Career: Practicing veternarian, 1987–93; Gen. Mgr., Gold Strike Hotel, 1991–93.

DC Office: 414 CHOB 20515, 202-225-5965; Fax: 202-225-3119.

District Offices: 1000 E. Sahara Ave., #D, Las Vegas 89104, 702-731-1801.

Committees: *Ways & Means* (20th of 21 R): Health; Human Resources.

Group Ratings and 103rd Congress Votes: Newly Elected

Key Votes of the 104th Congress

1. Congressional Compliance Y	6. Reform Crime Grant Y	11. Loser Pays Court Reform Y
2. Balanced Budget Amndmt. Y	7. National Security Act Y	12. Product Liability Reform Y
3. Bar Unfunded Mandates Y	8. Moratorium on Regs. Y	13. Welfare Reform Y
4. Pass Line Item Veto Y	9. Risk Assessment on Regs. Y	14. Term Limits Amndmt. Y
5. Relax Exclusionary Rule Y	10. Expnd. Priv. Prop. Rights Y	15. Tax Cuts Y

Election Results

1994 general	John Ensign (R)	73,769	(48%)	($687,194)
	James H. Bilbray (D)	72,333	(48%)	($913,708)
	Others	6,065	(4%)	
1994 primary	John Ensign (R)	29,730	(83%)	
	Rex R. Weeks (R)	2,518	(7%)	
	William J. Schantz (R)	1,950	(5%)	
	Kish M. Marler (R)	1,566	(4%)	
1992 general	James H. Bilbray (D)	128,278	(58%)	($667,018)
	J. Coy Pettyjohn (R)	84,217	(38%)	($113,776)
	Scott A. Kjar (Lib)	8,993	(4%)	

SECOND DISTRICT

The 2d District is the more Republican of Nevada's two districts, and includes 99.8% of the state's land area. Reno, smaller than Las Vegas, surrounded by wooded mountains, is the 2d's largest city, but one-quarter of the district's votes are cast in Las Vegas suburbs. These are mostly Republican, as is Reno ordinarily. And dislike of Interior Secretary Bruce Babbitt's proposed grazing fees and Mining Act reform have made the Cow Counties heavily Republican.

The congresswoman from the 2d District is Barbara Vucanovich, a Republican first elected in 1982 when Nevada got its second district. She grew up back east, the daughter of a Catholic Democrat who was New York state's chief engineer under Al Smith and FDR. Widowed in her forties, Vucanovich owned a speed-reading school and a travel agency while raising five children. She worked on Paul Laxalt's staff after he was elected to the Senate in 1974 until she left to run for the House. Vucanovich has a conservative record, though not always pro-market on economic issues.

Vucanovich has made a name on several issues. One is breast cancer research and prevention. A breast cancer survivor herself, she has worked to expand Medicare and Medicaid coverage for breast cancer with annual mammograms and for prostate cancer. Representing perhaps the number one mining district in the country, she has waged a war against "extreme reform of the 1872 mining law, which would devastate Western mining and destroy Nevada jobs." She sharply opposed Bill Clinton's proposed 12.5% gross royalty on mining and invited him to Elko to see mining operations; cornering him at a meeting she asked if 12.5% was his final decision ("Well, I don't know yet," was his response). She also opposed the Clinton tax on gaming, and with freshmen John Ensign from Las Vegas and Frank LoBiondo from Atlantic City, New Jersey, she formed a House Gaming Caucus. In March 1995, she formed the Western Water Caucus with Senator Hank Brown of Colorado and California Democratic Congressman Calvin Dooley to make certain, she said, that Washington, D.C. hears westerners' concerns about federal water policy. She has fought hard against the Yucca Mountain nuclear waste depository. In April 1995, Vucanovich opposed House Resources Chairman Don Young's plan to give Nevada parcels of land to offset land taken for nuclear storage—"cash for trash"— reminding the Alaskan of his "Young Rule," which gives a state's delegation primary say on legislation directed at the state.

She was not always effective in the Democratic House—the 1990 Nevada Wilderness Act was passed over her opposition—but she seems likely to prevail now that the House is Republican. Speaker Newt Gingrich appointed Vucanovich to chair his "Corrections Day" steering group, to deal with setting aside specific days to repeal "dumb" laws and regulations. With pro-choice Republican Susan Molinari of New York, Vucanovich, who is anti-abortion, vowed not to let abortion   divide Republicans, stating, "We cannot allow a single issue to separate our party."

Vucanovich has had some serious challengers, but not in 1994. Two years before Reno Mayor Pete Sferrazza held her to a 48%–43% victory, with most of her margin in the Cow Counties. But this time Sferrazza ran, unsuccessfully, for state Controller, and Sparks Mayor Jim Spoo, Vucanovich's 1988 opponent, declined to run when he failed to raise much money. In this climate Vucanovich won 64%–29%. After the election, she was elected Secretary of the Republican Conference, making her part of Newt Gingrich's Republican leadership.

The People: Pop. 1990: 600,791; 23% rural; 10% age 65+; 84% White; 3% Black; 3% Amer. Indian; 3% Asian; 3% Other; 8% Hispanic origin. Voting age pop.: 449,696; 2% Black; 7% Hispanic origin. Households: 56% married couple families; 26% married couple fams. w. children; 51% college educ.; median household income: $32,413; per capita income: $15,592; median gross rent: $515; median house value: $103,900.

1992 Presidential Vote

Bush (R)	105,388	(38%)
Clinton (D)	90,448	(33%)
Perot (I)	76,616	(28%)

1988 Presidential Vote

Bush (R)	119,304	(65%)
Dukakis (D)	65,325	(35%)

Rep. Barbara F. Vucanovich (R)

Elected 1982; b. June 22, 1921, Camp Dix, NJ; home, Reno; Manhattanville Col., 1938–39; Catholic; married (George).

Career: NV franchise owner, Evelyn Wood Speed Reading Co., 1964–68; Owner, travel agcy., 1968–74; Dist. Rep., U.S. Sen. Paul Laxalt, 1974–81.

DC Office: 2202 RHOB 20515, 202-225-6155; Fax: 202-225-2319.

District Offices: 300 Booth St., Reno 89509, 702-784-5003; 700 Idaho St., Elko 89801, 702-738-4064; and 6900 Westcliff St., #509, Las Vegas 89128, 702-255-6470.

Committees: *Republican Conference Secretary. Appropriations* (13th of 32 R): Interior; Military Construction (Chmn.); VA, HUD, and Independent Agencies.

Group Ratings

	ADA	ACLU	COPE	CFA	LCV	CON	NSI	COC	ACU	NTLC	CHC
1994	0	14	22	10	11	56	100	100	100	81	100
1993	10	—	17	10	21	47	—	91	100	—	—

National Journal Ratings

	1993 LIB — 1993 CONS		1994 LIB — 1994 CONS	
Economic	35%	— 63%	39%	— 60%
Social	11%	— 82%	0%	— 89%
Foreign	0%	— 91%	21%	— 78%

Key Votes of the 103d Congress

1. Clinton Deficit Plan	N	3. Brady Handgun Purchase N	5. Lmt. UN Cmnd. of Forces Y
2. NAFTA	N	4. Strike Race/Death Pnlty. Y	6. Cut Missile Funds N

Key Votes of the 104th Congress

1. Congressional Compliance Y	6. Reform Crime Grant Y	11. Loser Pays Court Reform Y
2. Balanced Budget Amndmt. Y	7. National Security Act Y	12. Product Liability Reform Y
3. Bar Unfunded Mandates Y	8. Moratorium on Regs. Y	13. Welfare Reform Y
4. Pass Line Item Veto Y	9. Risk Assessment on Regs. Y	14. Term Limits Amndmt. Y
5. Relax Exclusionary Rule Y	10. Expnd. Priv. Prop. Rights Y	15. Tax Cuts Y

Election Results

1994 general	Barbara F. Vucanovich (R)	142,202	(64%)	($692,936)
	Janet Greeson (D)	65,390	(29%)	($58,191)
	Thomas F. Jefferson (IA)	9,615	(4%)	
	Others	6,725	(3%)	
1994 primary	Barbara F. Vucanovich (R)	58,378	(78%)	
	Joe Emmett Fay (R)	16,408	(22%)	
1992 general	Barbara F. Vucanovich (R)	129,575	(48%)	($688,379)
	Pete Sferrazza (D)	117,198	(43%)	($202,888)
	Daniel M. Hansen (IA)	13,285	(5%)	($17,015)
	Others	10,522	(4%)	

NEW HAMPSHIRE

New Hampshire, with four-tenths of 1% of the nation's population, in an odd corner of the country and with some most unusual public policies, has nonetheless done much to set the nation's political course over the last two decades. The mechanism of this influence is New Hampshire's first-in-the-nation presidential primary, a device specifically sanctioned by the Democratic rules reformers of the 1970s, which did much to defeat the Democratic presidential candidates of the 1980s. For good reason, George Bush ended his victory speech in November 1988 by saying, "Thank you, New Hampshire." But New Hampshire did not say, "You're welcome" when the recession of 1990–91 sent real estate values plunging and unemployment rising here: Bush's rather narrow 1992 primary victory over Pat Buchanan was an early warning signal, and his drop from 63% of New Hampshire's vote in 1988 to 38% in 1992 was greater than in any other state in the nation. Then in 1994, even as Republican presidential candidates were heading into New Hampshire, the state shifted back to the Republicans in record numbers, as the nation did likewise. What will New Hampshire do for, or to, America in 1996?

In a country that prides itself on its feistiness and freedom from outside direction, New Hampshire has always been even feistier and less fettered by authority. Before the Revolution, New Hampshire was almost an outlaw colony, its great fortunes made by poachers in the king's forests and smugglers avoiding taxes. It was the first colony with an independent government and was fighting the British before the Minutemen stood at Lexington and Concord. In this free environment, 19th Century entrepreneurs built textile mills along fast-flowing rivers; the Amoskeag Mills in Manchester, lining the Merrimack River for a mile, were once the largest cotton mills on the globe, employing 17,000 people and producing enough cloth every two months to put a band around the world. Around the mills grew a city of red brick dormitories and three-family frame houses filled with immigrants from Quebec, Ireland, Poland and Greece, set down amid dirt-roaded villages of flinty Yankee farmers and mechanics. New Hampshire held to its traditions of local government and little external control, and for years its refusal to join most other states and enact an income or sales tax or provide statewide guidance of schools and social services seemed to doom it to continued backwardness.

But low taxes proved to be New Hampshire's fortune. Starting in the 1960s, New Hampshire for 35 years had the fastest growth on the East Coast, attracting businesses from Massachusetts and other high-tax states. It became a location of choice for entrepreneurs and high-tech innovators, attracting an increasing number of people skeptical of government programs—like John Sununu, who grew up in New York and worked in Massachusetts but lived and made his political career in New Hampshire. From 1965 to 1990, Massachusetts grew from 5.5 million to 6.0 million, up 9%; New Hampshire grew from 676,000 to 1,137,000, up 64%. The bedraggled New Hampshire of 50 years ago, of poor Yankee farmers and French Canadian mill hands, has largely disappeared, and in its place one of the nation's most prosperous economic communities has arisen. This "Nouvelle Hampshire," to use *Washington Post* writer Henry Allen's term, has none of the architectural purity of Amoskeag: its shopping centers and new subdivisions have a slap-dash, half-built look, as if there were no time for details in the hurry to build. The boom was feverish in the late 1980s, producing more jobs per capita than any other state and fabulous increases in real estate value. Descendants of Amoskeag mill hands and stone-poor farmers found themselves with high-income jobs and perhaps even substantial wealth, property and interests in business worth hundreds of thousands of dollars.

The low taxes that spurred this growth, making New Hampshire a tax haven in Governor John Sununu's 1980s as it was in Governor Benning Wentworth's 1760s, would probably have been raised in the late 1960s or early 1970s, as they were in so many states at the time, but for the far

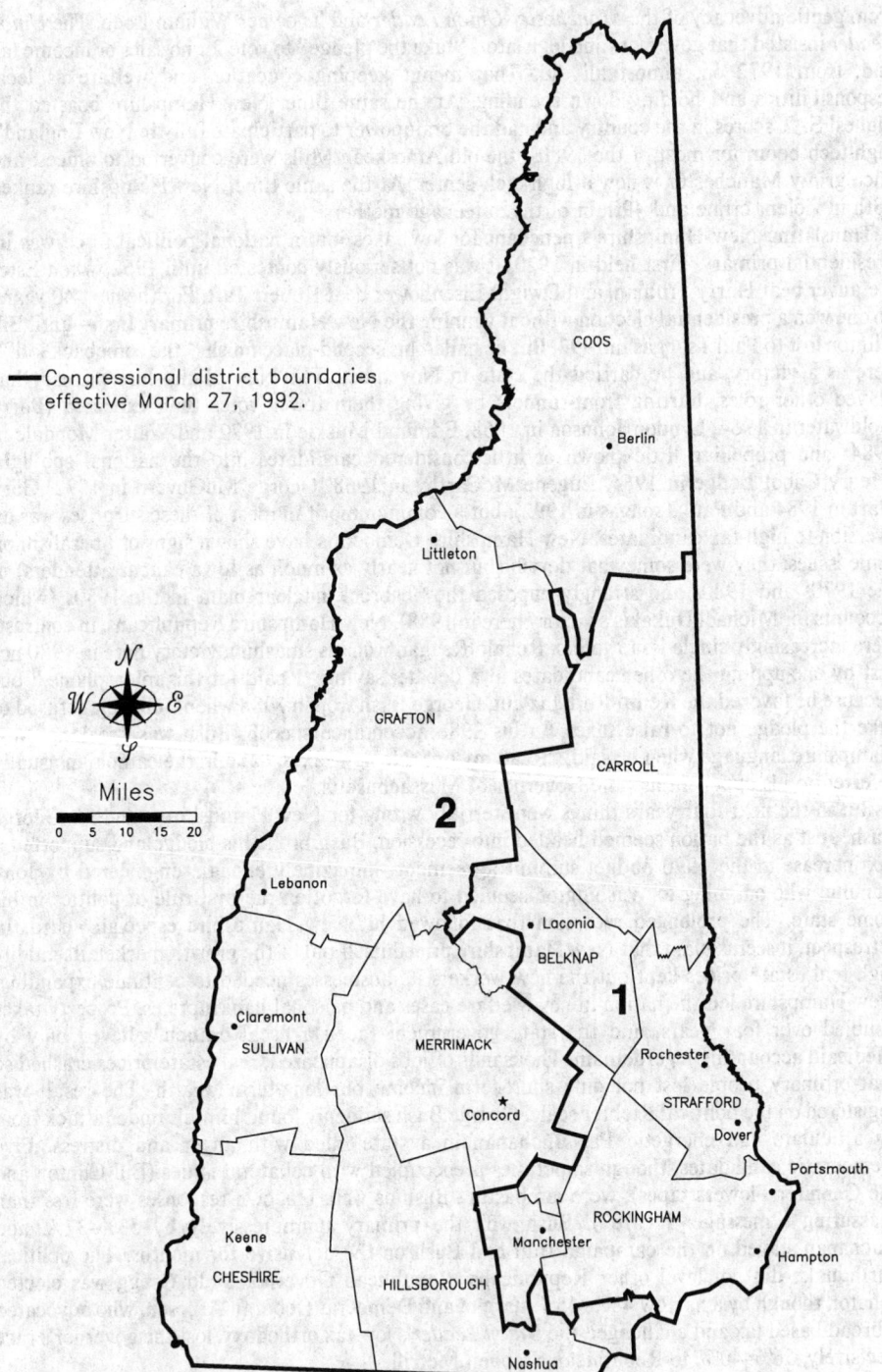

—Congressional district boundaries
effective March 27, 1992.

COOS

Berlin

Littleton

N
W E
S

Miles
0 5 10 15 20

GRAFTON

CARROLL

2

Lebanon

Laconia

BELKNAP

1

Claremont

SULLIVAN

MERRIMACK

Rochester

STRAFFORD

Concord

Dover

Portsmouth

ROCKINGHAM

Keene

Manchester

Hampton

CHESHIRE

HILLSBOROUGH

Nashua

from gentle advocacy of the *Manchester Union Leader* and its owner William Loeb. The *Union Leader* insisted that governors and legislators "take the pledge" to vote for no sales or income tax and, from 1972 on, almost all did. That meant keeping education and welfare as local responsibilities and holding down spending. At the same time, New Hampshire boasted the highest SAT scores in the country and had the brainpower to participate fully in New England's high-tech boom for most of the 1980s: the old Amoskeag Mills were converted to offices, and once grimy Manchester is now a high-tech center. At the same time, New Hampshire ranked 48th in violent crime and 49th in births to teenage mothers.

Translating New Hampshire's penchant for low taxes into a national political force was its presidential primary. First held in 1920, it was not seriously contested until 1952, when Estes Kefauver beat Harry Truman, and Dwight Eisenhower beat Robert Taft. For the next 40 years, no one won a presidential election without winning the New Hampshire primary first—until Bill Clinton lost to Paul Tsongas in 1992. But he hailed his second-place finish ("the comeback kid!") here as a victory, and he carried the state in November. The New Hampshire primary has played other roles, hurting front-runners by giving them fewer votes than expected (Barry Goldwater in 1964, Lyndon Johnson in 1968, Edmund Muskie in 1972 and Walter Mondale in 1984) and propelling little-known or little-considered candidates into the national spotlight (Henry Cabot Lodge in 1964, Eugene McCarthy in 1968, George McGovern in 1972, Gary Hart in 1984 and Paul Tsongas in 1992): but a common motif in most of these surprises was an aversion to high-tax candidates. New Hampshire Democrats have shown signs of liberalism on some issues: they were somewhat dovish (but not nearly as much as Iowa caucus attenders) in the 1970s and 1980s and strongly opposed the Seabrook nuclear plant in the 1980s (which accounts for Michael Dukakis's victory here in 1988). New Hampshire Republicans, in contrast, were increasingly single-issue voters. Ronald Reagan won his smashing victory here in 1980 not just by one-upping the other candidates at a debate, saying "I paid for this microphone," but because he favored the Kemp-Roth tax cut; George Bush won in 1988 when Bob Dole refused to take the pledge not to raise taxes. In his 1988 acceptance speech, Bush was speaking New Hampshire language when he said, "Read my lips. No new taxes," and in the campaign usually referred to his opponent as "the Governor of Massachusetts."

But in the next four years things went terribly wrong for New Hampshire—and for George Bush. Just as the nation seemed headed into recession, Bush broke his pledge and supported a tax increase in the 1990 budget summit agreement—amazingly enough, engineered by John Sununu, who on going to Washington seemed to have forgotten the first rule of politics in his home state. The prolonged recession that followed hit New Hampshire especially hard. In retrospect, it seems plain that New Hampshire priced itself out of the growth market: its giddily high real estate prices kept out the new workers its businesses needed to continue expanding. New Hampshire led the nation in new welfare cases and personal bankruptcies. Property taxes doubled over four years, and the state government faced a fiscal crunch relieved only by Medicaid accounting legerdemain. Thousands of jobs disappeared; real estate prices crashed so that ordinary people lost not only short-term income but long-term wealth. The result was registered on the political Richter scale. George Bush suddenly found himself under attack from an articulate and energetic Pat Buchanan in a state filled with anger and distress. Five Democratic candidates, though sometimes preoccupied with collateral issues (Bill Clinton and the Gennifer Flowers tapes), were lambasting Bush as well. His own responses were less than reassuring ("message: I care"). Bush won the primary unimpressively by 53%–37%, and Buchanan stayed on the campaign trail and Bush on the defensive for months. The political earthquake did not level other Republicans: Republican Governor Judd Gregg was elected senator, though by a narrow 48%–45% margin, and Democrat Deborah Arnesen, who advocated a broad-based tax and challenged the *Union Leader*'s low-tax orthodoxy, lost the governor's race decisively, 56%–40%, to Republican Stephen Merrill.

In two years New Hampshire shifted back to normal. With taxes still very much lower than other East Coast states, business boomed and unemployment fell from 8.1% to 3.5%. Confidence in the New Hampshire way returned, as national Democrats' confidence in the brilliance of Bill Clinton declined. The clearest evidence was Merrill's reelection in 1994 with 70% of the vote—the highest percentage since Samuel Bell won with 96% in 1822 in the Era of Good Feeling. Republicans recaptured the 2d District House seat they had lost to Democrat Dick Swett in 1990. Republican margins in the legislature increased to 18–6 in the state Senate and 286–112 in the state House—with 400 members, the largest state legislature in the country. And Republican presidential candidates poured into New Hampshire, eagerly taking the pledge (including Bob Dole, who attributed his change of mind from 1988 to the now Republican-controlled Congress) and describing how they will cut government. In April 1995, New Hampshire became the first state to enact term limits legislatively—a boon to supporters regrouping after the recent congressional defeat. New Hampshire seems to be moving America its way again.

Governor. Every four years in late February, within 24 hours after the primary returns are in, the national politicians and the press switch off Channel 9, stuff the *Union Leader* into the wastebasket and clear out of the Sheraton Wayfarer parking lot, not to be seen again for three or so years. New Hampshire then has its politics to itself. Its key issue is, was and probably always will be taxes; and its key politician, for the moment anyway, is Governor Stephen Merrill. For Merrill preached the New Hampshire gospel when it seemed suddenly imperilled and now seems a prophet whose divinations have come true. Merrill is from Hampton, on the Atlantic coast (the home of Timberland boots); after law school, he served four years in the Air Force, then practiced law and worked for two years as Governor John Sununu's counsel. In 1985 Sununu appointed him Attorney General, and he served in that post until 1989. If Sununu can be dismissive of others and angry, Merrill seems sunny and open; but his convictions are strong and he does not bend under pressure. He had four opponents in the September 1992 primary and won with 53%. He faced an articulate and attractive advocate of a broad-based statewide tax, State Representative Deborah "Arnie" Arnesen. She campaigned cheerfully as the "Tax Lady," called the *Union Leader*'s pledge a "pledge to fail" and argued that it robs the state of revenues necessary for education and economic development, and called for a 6% state income tax. She won her primary easily, but only 33% of New Hampshire voters are registered Democrats, and her message did not sell as well with the others. Merrill called for further government spending cuts and for the sale of some of the state's recently closed military bases. New Hampshire's basic convictions held, and Merrill won 56%–40%.

In office Merrill lowered the business profits, telecommunications and real estate transfer taxes and eliminated the savings bank and corporate franchise taxes altogether: the libertarian Cato Institute named him the nation's most fiscally responsible governor. He pushed through workmen's compensation reform, which lowered those rates 20%. He proposed banking, health care and education reforms based more on free market principles than on government precepts. By July 1994 his job approval was 76%, and he won the primary with 88%, the highest winning percentage at least since 1932. In November he beat state Senator Wayne King 70%–26%. In his second term (New Hampshire and Vermont are the last states with two-year gubernatorial terms) he called for eliminating welfare and replacing it with job placement and community work programs; he also proposed a budget that reduced spending. He has worked hard to maintain New Hampshire's national prominence: "My goal is to ensure that New Hampshire remains the first-in-the-nation primary state," repelling efforts by Phil Gramm allies in Arizona to hold their primary the same day. He arranged for the Republican Governors Association convention to meet in New Hampshire in November 1995, an obvious campaign event. His endorsement was much sought after, but up through spring he was keeping his options open. "Everyone in New Hampshire seems to think I will [endorse somebody]. I'm the only one who thinks I may not."

Senators. New Hampshire has two Republican senators, both freshmen, both solidly conservative. A dozen years ago, Bob Smith was a real estate agent in Tuftonboro; now his conservative principles have made him the senior senator from one of the nation's political trend-setting states: "Mr. Smith goes to Washington," as his campaign slogan put it. Smith grew up in New Jersey, served in the Navy in Vietnam, taught high school and managed Yankee Pedlar Real Estate in Wolfeboro, New Hampshire. Smith ran for the House and lost the primary in 1980, lost the general in 1982 and finally won the seat in 1984. In 1990, when Senator Gordon Humphrey honored a promise to retire after 12 years, Smith won the Republican nomination over a pro-choicer, 65%–29%, and in the general faced feisty former (1975–80) Senator John Durkin. Durkin attacked Smith for opposing abortion and (this worked better in the 1970s) supporting big oil companies, and called for $10 billion in new spending programs. Smith won overwhelmingly and went on to compile one of the most conservative voting records in the Senate.

Smith has carved out distinctive issues as well. He is seriously concerned that the United States left POWs and MIAs in Vietnam and in 1991 became vice chairman of the Select Committee on POW/MIA Affairs, which was chaired by fellow Vietnam veteran Massachusetts Democrat John Kerry. In June 1992, Smith concluded that the Pentagon was aware of scores left behind and later attacked the Defense Intelligence Agency's debunking of evidence to that effect. Despite support from other Republicans, he opposed reestablishing relations with Vietnam pending a full accounting. In January 1993, the committee's final report concluded there was "no compelling evidence" that POWs or MIAs are now in Southeast Asia, but the investigation brought to light disturbing evidence that some may have been left behind and could not rule out the possibility that some are still there against their will. In 1994, he opposed the Clinton Administration's lifting of the economic embargo against Vietnam.

Smith is co-sponsor with Congressman Bill Zeliff of a conservative Superfund reform bill, which would limit a company's liability for environmental damage. Now that he chairs the Senate subcommittee with jurisdiction over the issue, he is in a better position to get action on the long-stalled problem. He is the Senate sponsor of Pennsylvania Congressman Bob Walker's bill, supported by George Bush at the 1992 Republican Convention in Houston, to let taxpayers designate 10% of their taxes for deficit reduction. He was also a strong supporter of the successful Congressional Accountability Act which binds Congress to the rules and regulations it imposes on others.

In January 1993, while driving to work from suburban Virginia, Smith witnessed the murders outside CIA headquarters: "Coolly and methodically, with no emotion, no expression and no words, [the assailant] simply walked up to the automobiles and fired at point-blank range into the windows at these people. It was a pretty horrifying experience to witness." In the aftermath, Smith was criticized for opposing bans on the type of assault weapon used in that crime; his response was that the man, not the gun, did the killing.

Smith has endorsed Phil Gramm for president and appeared with him at his announcement in Texas. He is widely considered a shoo-in for reelection in 1996, although former 2d District Representative Dick Swett has said he is strongly considering the race.

New Hampshire's junior Senator is Judd Gregg. Politics is a family matter for him: his father Hugh Gregg was elected governor in 1952 and has since maintained an organization capable of turning out votes for presidential candidates, most recently George Bush. Judd Gregg was a student at Columbia during the student riots of 1968, but stayed true to New Hampshire Republicanism; after law school, he returned to Nashua and practiced law and politics. In 1978 he was elected to the Executive Council, which dates to the colonial era and approves state appointments and expenditures. In 1980 he was elected to the House, where he was an eager participant in the Reagan revolution. In 1988, Gregg ran for governor and won handily; he was easily reelected in 1990.

But then the New Hampshire economy turned sour, and the taciturn Gregg refused to exude the I-feel-your-pain empathy of a Bill Clinton. The state's banking industry "is going down the drain," he conceded, but "there is no magic wand" to cure the state's economy. He was "sure," he would win the 1992 Senate election for the seat vacated by Republican Warren Rudman. He did, but it was uncomfortably close. In the September primary he beat a construction company owner by only 50%–38%. In the general, Democrat John Rauh, who made money in Cincinnati with a plastic film business and then moved to New Hampshire, called for a line-item veto and balanced budget amendment, said he would produce "a prosperous economy, not legislative tinkering" and attacked Gregg for opposing abortion. Gregg was also attacked for having been deferred from the draft in 1969 for bad knees, sleepwalking and severe acne, and his father said the family doctor may have "exaggerated" his physical problems. (Gregg later said his father had been misquoted.) Gregg actually ran behind in some polls, and he won by an unimpressive 48%–45% margin.

In the Senate Gregg made a solidly conservative record, with just a few votes on the other side; however, as a junior member of the minority, his voice was not often heard. Then, in early 1995, he became head of the Senate Republicans' Working Group on Entitlement Reform and produced a seven-year plan to increase spending on Medicare and Medicaid by $495 billion less than projected. His method includes more co-insurance charges, lower reimbursements to doctors, an affluence test and encouraging seniors to enroll in managed care plans. "If we continue on our present course, around about the year 2010, your children and grandchildren are going to be faced with a country that goes bankrupt, just like Mexico," he said. Another way that he is making his voice heard is with his appointment as the Republican chief deputy whip, a position that shows his close connections to both Majority Leader Bob Dole and Majority Whip Trent Lott. Not a bad position for a young first-termer.

Presidential politics. That New Hampshire has had the first-in-the-nation presidential primary for almost half a century now will surely strike future Americans as bizarre; indeed, it strikes many foreigners that way today. To be sure, there are arguments for having early contests in small states which provide a venue for "retail politics," in which candidates meet voters in person, listening and talking to them, exchanging ideas and allowing them to gauge their character. In-person contact was one of the things that saved Bill Clinton in 1992, after the Gennifer Flowers charges; exit polls showed he did much better than average with voters who had personally met one or more of the candidates. But some might say that such retail campaigning places a premium on amiability rather than character. Then there is the more partisan argument, made even by many Republicans, that New Hampshire's aversion to taxes tilts the presidential contest toward the economic right. That is a complaint whose appeal depends on how much you share that taste. In any case, New Hampshire depends not on argument but on threats. When Democrats were changing their party rules in the 1970s and 1980s, New Hampshire insisted it would hold its primary outside "the window" in order to go first; it was confident candidates and voters would pay attention to the results, even if the miniscule New Hampshire delegation was denied its seats at the national convention. The Democrats caved. In 1994 and 1995 Arizona, led by Republicans friendly to Phil Gramm, threatened to hold its primary the same day as New Hampshire. Governor Stephen Merrill quickly put pressure on Gramm, who persuaded Arizona to pull back. But Gramm got into more hot water in May 1995 by speaking at Delaware's Republican Convention, but not publicly objecting to its primary plans—Delaware scheduled its 1996 primary four days after New Hampshire's, violating the seven-day buffer. Merrill said he had developed "a serious problem" with Phil Gramm, and speculation increased that his crucial endorsement may go to Bob Dole. Colonial-era Governor Benning Wentworth would have understood: New Hampshire does what it wants to, whatever the rules say, and dares the world to try to stop it.

A word should be said about New Hampshire media. The *Manchester Union Leader* has one of the nation's sharpest conservative tongues. Its owner Nackey Loeb (the widow of William) and its editorials scold Republicans who stray from the political right and excoriate almost all enemies. Its insistence that politicians take the pledge has set the course for New Hampshire state politics and government. But the *Union Leader* cannot automatically deliver votes on primary day, and its news coverage is more objective than that of many liberal-leaning national media outlets. New Hampshire's other great medium is Manchester's WMUR-TV, Channel 9, which also provides tons of information to a winter-bound audience. Channel 9's rule is to cover every candidate every day he is in New Hampshire, allowing each to present views and make arguments without the overlay of smirky, opinionated commentary that national network reporters use to promote the superiority of their intellects and moral character.

New Hampshire is ordinarily heavily Republican in general elections; when it is not, the Democratic nominee already has enough electoral votes to win, as in 1992. Indeed, this is one of the few states which has more registered Republicans (38%) than Democrats (32%). The Republican heart of the state is the Merrimack Valley, with the two biggest cities of Manchester and Nashua. Old Yankee towns farther north are also heavily Republican, and so are the suburbs just north of the Massachusetts line. More Democratic is the western edge of the state along the Connecticut River, which partakes a bit of the Ben & Jerry's Vermont liberalism, and Portsmouth and smaller old mill towns along the Maine border. The highest Democratic percentages in New Hampshire often come from Hanover, home of Dartmouth College; the highest Republican percentages from Dixville Notch in the far north, whose 30 voters, led in 1992 by 93-year-old Town Moderator Neil Tillotson, troop in at one minute after midnight and cast the nation's first recorded votes every presidential year.

Congressional districting. With only slight changes, New Hampshire's two congressional districts basically have had the same boundaries since 1881, neatly separating the Merrimack River mill towns of Manchester and Nashua, the state's largest cities. That was done originally to split the Catholic Democratic vote, but now both cities are high-tech Republican towns. So the split has the same political effect, giving Democrats a chance for upset victories in either seat.

The People: Est. Pop. 1994: 1,137,000; Pop. 1990: 1,109,252, up 2.5% 1990–1994. 0.4% of U.S. total, 41th largest; 49% rural. Median age: 32.8 years. 11.3% 65 years and over. 98.0% White, 1.0% Hispanic origin. Households: 59.7% married couple families; 30% married couple fams. w. children; 50% college educ.; median household income: $36,329; per capita income: $15,959; 68.2% owner occupied housing; median house value: $129,400; median monthly rent: $479. 7.5% Unemployment. 1994 Voting age pop.: 843,000. 1994 Turnout: 310,057; 37% of VAP. Registered voters (1994): 665,021; 210,865 D (32%), 252,199 R (40%), 201,927 unaffiliated and minor parties (30%).

Political Lineup: Governor, Steve Merrill (R); Lt. Gov., Joseph L. Delahunty (R); Secy. of State, William M. Gardner (D); Atty. Gen., Jeffrey R. Howard (R); Treasurer, Georgie A. Thomas (R); State Senate, 24 (18 R and 6 D); State House of Representatives, 400 (284 R, 112 D, and 1 L). Senators, Bob Smith (R) and Judd Gregg (R). Representatives 2 (2 R).

1992 Presidential Vote

Clinton (D)	209,040	(39%)
Bush (R)	202,484	(38%)
Perot (I)	121,337	(23%)

1992 Democratic Presidential Primary

Tsongas	55,638	(33%)
Clinton	41,522	(25%)
Kerrey	18,575	(11%)
Harkin	17,057	(10%)
Brown	13,654	(8%)
Cuomo	6,577	(4%)
Other	14,460	(9%)

1988 Presidential Vote

Bush (R)	281,537	(63%)
Dukakis (D)	163,696	(36%)

1992 Republican Presidential Primary

Bush	92,233	(53%)
Buchanan	65,087	(37%)
Other	16,845	(10%)

GOVERNOR

Gov. Steve Merrill (R)

Elected 1992, term expires Jan. 1997; b. June 21, 1946, Hampton; home, Manchester; U. of NH, B.A. 1969, Georgetown U., J.D. 1972; Episcopalian; married (Heather).

Career: Air Force, 1973–76; Practicing atty., 1976–82, 1989–92; Cnsl. & Chief of Staff, NH Gov. John Sununu, 1982–85; NH Atty. Gen., 1985–89.

Office: State House, Concord 03301, 603-271-2121; Fax: 603-271-2130.

Election Results

1994 gen.	Steve Merrill (R)	218,134	(70%)
	Wayne D. King (D)	79,686	(26%)
	Steve Winter (Lib)...........	13,709	(4%)
1994 prim.	Steve Merrill (R)	69,340	(89%)
	Fred Bramante (R)...........	6,623	(8%)
	Others.....................	2,267	(3%)
1992 gen.	Steve Merrill (R)	289,170	(56%)
	Deborah Arnesen (D).........	206,232	(40%)
	Miriam Luce (Lib)...........	20,663	(4%)

SENATORS

Sen. Bob Smith (R)

Elected 1990, seat up 1996; b. Mar. 30, 1941, Trenton, NJ; home, Tuftonboro; Trenton Jr. Col., A.A. 1963, Lafayette Col., B.A. 1965, Long Beach St. Col., 1968–69; Catholic; married (Mary Jo).

Career: Navy, 1965–67 (Vietnam), Naval Reserves, 1962–65, 1967–69; High schl. teacher, 1975–84; Real Estate agent, 1975–84; Chmn., Gov. Wentworth Schl. Bd., 1978–83; U.S. House of Reps., 1984–90.

DC Office: 332 DSOB 20510, 202-224-2841; Fax: 202-224-1353.

State Offices: 50 Phillippe Cote St., #200, Manchester 03101, 603-634-5000; 46 S. Main St., Concord 03301, 603-228-0453; and 1 Harbour Pl., Portsmouth 03801, 603-433-1667.

Committees: *Armed Services* (7th of 11 R): Acquisition and Technology (Chmn.); Seapower; Strategic Forces. *Environment & Public Works* (3rd of 9 R): Superfund, Waste Control and Risk Assessment (Chmn.); Transportation and Infrastructure. *Ethics* (2nd of 3 R). *Governmental Affairs* (8th of 8 R): Investigations; Post Office and Civil Service.

Group Ratings

	ADA	ACLU	COPE	CFA	LCV	CON	NSI	COC	ACU	NTLC	CHC
1994	5	16	14	25	8	88	100	90	100	96	100
1993	15	—	9	0	13	89	—	91	100	—	—

National Journal Ratings

	1993 LIB — 1993 CONS			1994 LIB — 1994 CONS		
Economic	0%	—	87%	0%	—	88%
Social	0%	—	92%	0%	—	85%
Foreign	0%	—	92%	0%	—	94%

Key Votes of the 103d Congress

1. Clinton Deficit Plan	N	3. Brady Handgun Purchase	N	5. Lmt. UN Cmnd. of Forces	Y
2. NAFTA	N	4. Strike Race/Death Pnlty.	Y	6. Cut Missile Funds	N

Key Votes of the 104th Congress

1. Congressional Compliance	Y	3. Balanced Budget Amndt.	Y	5. Product Liability Reform	Y
2. Bar Unfunded Mandates	Y	4. Pass Line Item Veto	Y	6. FY96 Budget	Y

Election Results

1990 general	Bob Smith (R)......................	189,792	(65%)	($1,419,127)
	John A. Durkin (D)..................	91,299	(32%)	($319,879)
	Other..............................	10,302	(3%)	
1990 primary	Bob Smith (R).......................	56,215	(65%)	
	Tom Christo (R)	25,286	(29%)	
	Others	4,777	(6%)	
1984 general	Gordon J. Humphrey (R).............	225,828	(59%)	($1,806,653)
	Norman E. D'Amours (D)	157,447	(41%)	($1,066,485)

Sen. Judd Gregg (R)

Elected 1992, seat up 1998; b. Feb. 14, 1947, Nashua; home, Greenfield; Columbia U., A.B. 1969, Boston U., J.D. 1972, LL.M. 1975; Protestant; married (Kathleen).

Career: Practicing atty., 1976–80; NH Exec. Cncl., 1978–80; U.S. House of Reps., 1980–88; NH Gov., 1988–92.

DC Office: 393 RSOB 20510, 202-224-3324; Fax: 202-224-4952.

State Offices: 125 N. Main St., Concord 03301, 603-225-7115; 28 Webster St., Manchester 03104, 603-622-7979; 136 Pleasant St., Berlin 03570, 603-752-2604; and 99 Pease Blvd., Portsmouth 03801, 603-431-2171.

Committees: *Chief Deputy Whip. Appropriations* (14th of 15 R): Commerce, Justice, State and Judiciary; Foreign Operations; Labor, Health and Human Services, Education; Military Construction; Treasury, Postal Service and General Government. *Budget* (9th of 12 R). *Labor & Human Resources* (4th of 9 R): Aging (Chmn.); Education, Arts and Humanities.

Group Ratings

	ADA	ACLU	COPE	CFA	LCV	CON	NSI	COC	ACU	NTLC	CHC
1994	15	28	0	25	38	100	100	87	79	96	85
1993	10	—	0	10	31	93	—	91	92	—	—

National Journal Ratings

	1993 LIB — 1993 CONS			1994 LIB — 1994 CONS		
Economic	25%	—	70%	0%	—	88%
Social	24%	—	75%	31%	—	67%
Foreign	16%	—	77%	30%	—	68%

Key Votes of the 103d Congress

1. Clinton Deficit Plan	N	3. Brady Handgun Purchase	N	5. Lmt. UN Cmnd. of Forces	Y
2. NAFTA	Y	4. Strike Race/Death Pnlty.	Y	6. Cut Missile Funds	N

Key Votes of the 104th Congress

1. Congressional Compliance	Y	3. Balanced Budget Amndt.	Y	5. Product Liability Reform	Y
2. Bar Unfunded Mandates	Y	4. Pass Line Item Veto	Y	6. FY96 Budget	Y

Election Results

1992 general	Judd Gregg (R)...............	249,591	(48%)	($875,675)
	John Rauh (D)	234,982	(45%)	($1,109,467)
	Katherine Alexander (LIB)	18,214	(4%)	
	Others	15,629	(3%)	
1992 primary	Judd Gregg (R)...............	57,141	(50%)	
	Harold Eckman (R)	43,264	(38%)	
	Jean T. White (R).............	10,642	(9%)	
	Others	3,690	(3%)	
1986 general	Warren Rudman (R)............	154,090	(63%)	($831,098)
	Endicott Peabody (D)	79,222	(32%)	($307,760)

FIRST DISTRICT

The 1st Congressional District of New Hampshire includes Manchester, its suburbs and the seacoast. Manchester was once a heavily French Canadian textile mill town, which also had the nation's largest percentage of Greek-Americans; in the 1980s it became a fast-growing high-tech city. There are new shopping malls here and in towns on the Massachusetts border. Portsmouth has restored its downtown to some of its historic splendor; Wal-Mart, drawn by the combination of new affluence and down-home tastes, built its first New England stores in this area. There is a Democratic heritage here, especially in Manchester, but in general elections this is usually Republican territory.

The congressman is Bill Zeliff, a Republican first elected in 1990 when incumbent Bob Smith was elected to the Senate. Zeliff has been something of a stormy petrel, buffeted by the hard and unpredictable winds of New Hampshire politics. An innkeeper from the north country, he won the 1990 primary by 314 votes in an eight-candidate race. Zeliff had the endorsement of John Sununu; second-place finisher and Reagan appointee Larry Brady had the endorsement of the *Manchester Union Leader*. But the perceived favorite was state legislator Douglas Scamman. Zeliff carried the north country, Scamman the coastal regions, and Brady the Manchester area—the three basic voting blocs here. Zeliff won with an unimpressive 55% in the general.

In the House, Zeliff's record was generally conservative, but he is pro-choice on abortion (though he opposes taxpayer-funded abortions), and for that reason was sharply opposed by the *Union Leader* in 1992, when he won the primary by only 50%–35% and the general by 53%–43%. But in the 103d Congress, an issue came his way which worked wonders in New Hampshire: the A-to-Z spending cuts proposal, which would have set aside 56 hours for House debate and roll call votes on spending cuts. This was to bypass committees which protect spending programs. Zeliff looked for a member whose name started with A to co-sponsor the measure and quickly came up with reform-minded New Jersey Democrat Rob Andrews. Intense pressure from Speaker Thomas Foley ("the most poorly thought out proposal for the consideration of public policy that I've seen in many years") prevented Zeliff and Andrews from getting enough signatures to discharge A-to-Z from committee in 1994. They promised to try again in 1995, after the Contract With America, but the pressure placed on Republicans to find major spending cuts in order to achieve their balanced-budget goal shifted the focus away from A-to-Z. Zeliff was also co-sponsor with New Hampshire Senator Bob Smith of a conservative Superfund reform bill.

A-to-Z and the change in New Hampshire's political climate clearly helped Zeliff in 1994. He was reelected by a 66%–29% margin, carrying every city and town except Durham, home of the University of New Hampshire.

The People: Pop. 1990: 554,303; 45% rural; 11% age 65+; 97% White; 1% Black; 1% Asian; 1% Hispanic origin. Voting age pop.: 415,779; 1% Black; 1% Hispanic origin. Households: 60% married couple families; 29% married couple fams. w. children; 51% college educ.; median household income: $36,511; per capita income: $16,044; median gross rent: $555; median house value: $132,600.

1992 Presidential Vote			1988 Presidential Vote		
Bush (R)	104,653	(39%)	Bush (R)	141,952	(64%)
Clinton (D)	101,415	(38%)	Dukakis (D)	78,235	(36%)
Perot (I)	61,571	(23%)			

Rep. William H. Zeliff, Jr. (R)

Elected 1990; b. June 12, 1936, East Orange, NJ; home, Jackson; U. of CT, B.S. 1958; Protestant; married (Sydna).

Career: Army Natl. Guard, 1958–64; Sales/Mktg. mgr., DuPont Co., 1961–76; Innkeeper, small business owner.

DC Office: 1210 LHOB 20515, 202-225-5456; Fax: 202-225-4370; e-mail: zeliff@hr.house.gov.

District Offices: 340 Commercial St., Manchester 03101, 603-669-6330; and 601 Spaulding Tnpk., #28, Portsmouth 03801, 603-433-1601.

Committees: *Government Reform & Oversight* (8th of 27 R): National Security, International Affairs and Criminal Justice (Chmn.). *Transportation & Infrastructure* (11th of 33 R): Aviation; Surface Transportation; Water Resources and Environment. *Small Business* (3rd of 22 R).

Group Ratings

	ADA	ACLU	COPE	CFA	LCV	CON	NSI	COC	ACU	NTLC	CHC
1994	5	22	0	20	7	66	100	100	86	92	86
1993	10	—	9	0	36	65	—	100	92	—	—

National Journal Ratings

	1993 LIB — 1993 CONS		1994 LIB — 1994 CONS	
Economic	0% —	88%	0% —	80%
Social	36% —	62%	24% —	73%
Foreign	0% —	91%	14% —	80%

Key Votes of the 103d Congress

1. Clinton Deficit Plan	N	3. Brady Handgun Purchase	N	5. Lmt. UN Cmnd. of Forces	Y
2. NAFTA	Y	4. Strike Race/Death Pnlty.	Y	6. Cut Missile Funds	N

Key Votes of the 104th Congress

1. Congressional Compliance Y	6. Reform Crime Grant	Y	11. Loser Pays Court Reform Y
2. Balanced Budget Amndmt. Y	7. National Security Act	Y	12. Product Liability Reform Y
3. Bar Unfunded Mandates Y	8. Moratorium on Regs.	Y	13. Welfare Reform	Y
4. Pass Line Item Veto Y	9. Risk Assessment on Regs. Y	14. Term Limits Amndmt.	Y
5. Relax Exclusionary Rule Y	10. Expnd. Priv. Prop. Rights Y	15. Tax Cuts	Y

Election Results

1994 general	William H. Zeliff, Jr. (R)	97,017	(66%)	($868,042)
	Bill Verge (D)	42,481	(29%)	($139,023)
	Others	8,324	(6%)	
1994 primary	William H. Zeliff, Jr. (R)	unopposed		
1992 general	William H. Zeliff, Jr. (R)	135,396	(53%)	($778,358)
	Bob Preston (D)	108,578	(43%)	($174,565)
	Others	11,339	(4%)	

SECOND DISTRICT

The 2d Congressional District includes Nashua, the state's second largest city, and Salem, both right on the Massachusetts line and solidly conservative: people came here to get away from "Taxachusetts." It also includes, farther from Boston and readier for taxes and government services, the state capital of Concord and towns in the Connecticut River Valley, from Keene near Mount Monadnock north to Hanover, home of Dartmouth College, an area of artist retreats: from that of sculptor August Saint Gaudens a century ago to writer J. D. Salinger's today. The 2d runs to the farthest north country: Dixville Notch and the paper mill town of Berlin, the Mount Washington Hotel and cog railway and the resort of Bretton Woods where the world monetary system, and the basis for post-World War II prosperity, was established in a conference in 1944.

The Congressman from the 2d District is Charles Bass, who has a long political pedigree: his grandfather Robert Bass was elected Governor in 1910 and his father Perkins Bass served in the House from 1955 to 1963. Charles Bass, after graduating from Dartmouth, worked for Maine Congressmen William Cohen and David Emery, then returned to New Hampshire to run for Congress in 1980: he finished third in the primary, with 22%, to 34% for now-Senator Judd Gregg and 25% for liberal Susan McLane. With his two brothers, he ran a factory making architectural products and served in the part-time state legislature—in the state House from 1982 and state Senate from 1988—where he wrote the state's voluntary campaign spending law which called on House candidates to observe $250,000 limits in primary and general elections. But he angered many when he bolted the party in 1990 to help elect a Democrat as Senate leader, and Bass was beaten by a conservative in the 1992 state Senate primary.

In 1994 Bass ran in the Republican primary for the right to oppose Democratic Congressman Dick Swett, elected in 1990 when party leaders and Nancy Sununu attacked the personal conduct of incumbent Chuck Douglas, and reelected as Bill Clinton carried the state in 1992. Bass ran as a moderate—pro-choice on abortion, but also a fiscal conservative, a supporter of welfare cuts and tougher sentencing. Bass ran only a few points better in the primary than he had in 1980, but his 29% this time was enough to beat former NRA consultant Mike Hammond (backed by the *Union Leader*) with 24%. Swett had a moderate voting record, but Bass attacked him for voting with Clinton 90% of the time and for supporting Democrats when his vote really mattered; Bass ran a TV spot of Swett and Clinton embracing. Swett was also attacked for switching from opposition to gun control to support for the assault weapons ban in 1994; Swett tried to make this a positive by cutting an ad in Newbury where several people were shot. Bass also attacked Swett for raising most of his money out of state—specifically charging that Swett received $67,000 from his father-in-law, California Congressman Tom Lantos, laundered through Democratic candidates and party treasuries. Swett denied the charges, but at the very least Lantos helped him raise money. Indeed, Swett spent over $1 million, while Bass adhered to the voluntary spending limits and spent $434,000. Bass won 51%–46%. Swett carried Concord, Hanover and other towns on the Connecticut River, the Keene area and the mill town of Berlin, but Bass carried practically everything else.

Bass is one Republican freshman who is interested in campaign finance reform and has promised to try to limit campaign spending and PAC contributions. He defected from Republicans on missile defense, but was mostly a loyal supporter of the Contract With America. With seats on Budget and Government Reform and Oversight, Bass should be able to solidify his position. And Dick Swett seems more interested in a possible 1996 Senate race against Bob Smith than in a rematch for this seat.

The People: Pop. 1990: 554,949; 53% rural; 11% age 65+; 97% White; 1% Black; 1% Asian; 1% Hispanic origin. Voting age pop.: 414,350; 1% Black; 1% Hispanic origin. Households: 61% married couple families; 30% married couple fams. w. children; 50% college educ.; median household income: $36,145; per capita income: $15,874; median gross rent: $541; median house value: $125,500.

1992 Presidential Vote			1988 Presidential Vote		
Clinton (D)	107,625	(40%)	Bush (R)	139,585	(62%)
Bush (R)	97,831	(37%)	Dukakis (D)	85,461	(38%)
Perot (I)	59,766	(22%)			

Rep. Charles F. Bass (R)

Elected 1994; b. Jan. 8, 1952, Boston, MA; home, Peterborough; Dartmouth, A.B. 1974; Episcopalian; married (Lisa).

Career: Field worker, U.S. Rep. William Cohen, 1974; Legis. Asst., U.S. Rep. David Emery, 1975–76, Chief of Staff, 1976–79; Vice Pres., High Standard Inc., 1980–93; Chmn., Columbia Architectural Products, 1980–93; NH House of Reps., 1982–88; NH Senate, 1988–92.

DC Office: 1728 LHOB 20515, 202-225-5206; Fax: 202-225-2946.

District Offices: 142 N. Main St., Concord 03301, 603-226-0249.

Committees: *Budget* (24th of 24 R). *Government Reform & Oversight* (24th of 27 R): Civil Service; Government Management, Information and Technology.

Group Ratings and 103rd Congress Votes: Newly Elected

Key Votes of the 104th Congress

1. Congressional Compliance	Y	6. Reform Crime Grant	Y	11. Loser Pays Court Reform	Y
2. Balanced Budget Amndmt.	Y	7. National Security Act	Y	12. Product Liability Reform	Y
3. Bar Unfunded Mandates	Y	8. Moratorium on Regs.	Y	13. Welfare Reform	Y
4. Pass Line Item Veto	Y	9. Risk Assessment on Regs.	Y	14. Term Limits Amndmt.	Y
5. Relax Exclusionary Rule	Y	10. Expnd. Priv. Prop. Rights	Y	15. Tax Cuts	Y

Election Results

1994 general	Charles F. Bass (R)	83,121	(51%)	($448,431)
	Dick Swett (D)	74,243	(46%)	($1,029,471)
	Others	4,209	(3%)	
1994 primary	Charles F. Bass (R)	12,526	(29%)	
	Mike Hammond (R)	10,340	(24%)	
	Ward Scott (R)	8,887	(21%)	
	Jim Bassett (R)	5,925	(14%)	
	Ted De Winter (R)	2,386	(6%)	
	Others	2,833	(7%)	
1992 general	Dick Swett (D)	157,328	(62%)	($785,452)
	Bill Hatch (R)	91,126	(36%)	($232,617)
	Others	6,731	(2%)	

NEW JERSEY

Named by King James II, then Duke of York, for the Channel Island on which he was sheltered during the English Civil War, plagued in its early years by rival claims from its neighbors and arguing even today with New York over who owns the Statue of Liberty and Ellis Island, New Jersey has spent much of its history betwixt and between. Its major cities lie on the swampy sides of America's two greatest harbor rivers, overshadowed for years by the metropolises of New York and Philadelphia—"a valley of humility between two mountains of conceit," its neighbor Benjamin Franklin called it. But New Jersey has much to say for itself. It is "a sort of laboratory in which the best blood is prepared for other communities to thrive on," Woodrow Wilson said when he was governor of New Jersey, just a tad defensively, it is "the fighting center of the most important social questions of our time." Today, New Jersey is the nation's ninth most populous state, one which fully enjoyed the 1980s boom, suffered sharply from the 1990s wealth recession and is now rebounding quietly. It is among the top half-dozen states in high-tech businesses and immigration, in pharmaceuticals and in tourism. Within its close boundaries is great diversity, geographically from beaches to mountains, demographically from old Quaker stock to new Hispanics, economically from inner city slums to hunt country mansions. New York writers are inclined to look on New Jersey as something quaint, but New Jersey comes far closer to resembling America than does Manhattan, even if its traffic signals are arrayed horizontally rather than vertically and its accents can be incomprehensible to outsiders. The row houses seen on emerging from the Holland Tunnel, many renovated by Wall Street commuters and Latin immigrants, give way within a few miles to the skyscrapers of Newark and middle-income suburbs. Nearby are the horse country around Far Hills, the university town of Princeton, old industrial towns like Paterson, and dozens of suburban towns and small factory cities where people work hard and raise their families over generations.

In the last 20 years, a new New Jersey has sprouted: the oil tank farms and swamplands of the Jersey Meadows have become sports palaces and office complexes; the intersection of I-78 and I-287 has become a major shopping and office center, one of the edge cities which grow up on the far sides of urban settlement; U.S. 1 north of Princeton has become one of the nation's high-tech centers; the flat vegetable fields once dotted with gas station junctions now have tourist attractions like Great Adventure park. For the first census year since 1840, New Jersey in 1990 had more people (7.7 million) than New York City (7.3 million); it had far more than metropolitan Philadelphia (5.9 million), and it was generating more new jobs than either New York or Pennsylvania. Growth is strongest in the interior away from New York City and Philadelphia, and New Jersey increasingly has an identity of its own. It is the home of Bruce Springsteen and of big league football, basketball and hockey franchises, of America's biggest gambling casinos outside Nevada, and of the world's longest expanse of boardwalks, on the Jersey Shore from Cape May to Sandy Hook.

Not that New Jersey hasn't had its problems. Waste disposal is one: this most densely populated of states is struggling to find ways to dispose sanitarily of its wastes, including pollutants left behind by its chemical industries. Another was the early 1990s recession. The reversals of the financial services industry hurt New Jersey, cutting job growth to zero and below, depressing commercial and residential real estate markets, playing havoc with the state government budget. State government played an important role in building state pride. Governor Brendan Byrne in the 1970s started the Meadowlands complex and got casino gambling legalized in Atlantic City. In the 1980s, Governor Tom Kean started education reforms and promoted the state shamelessly. But voters reacted angrily to Governor Jim Florio's tax increase of 1990 and in 1993 replaced him with Christine Todd Whitman, who promised to

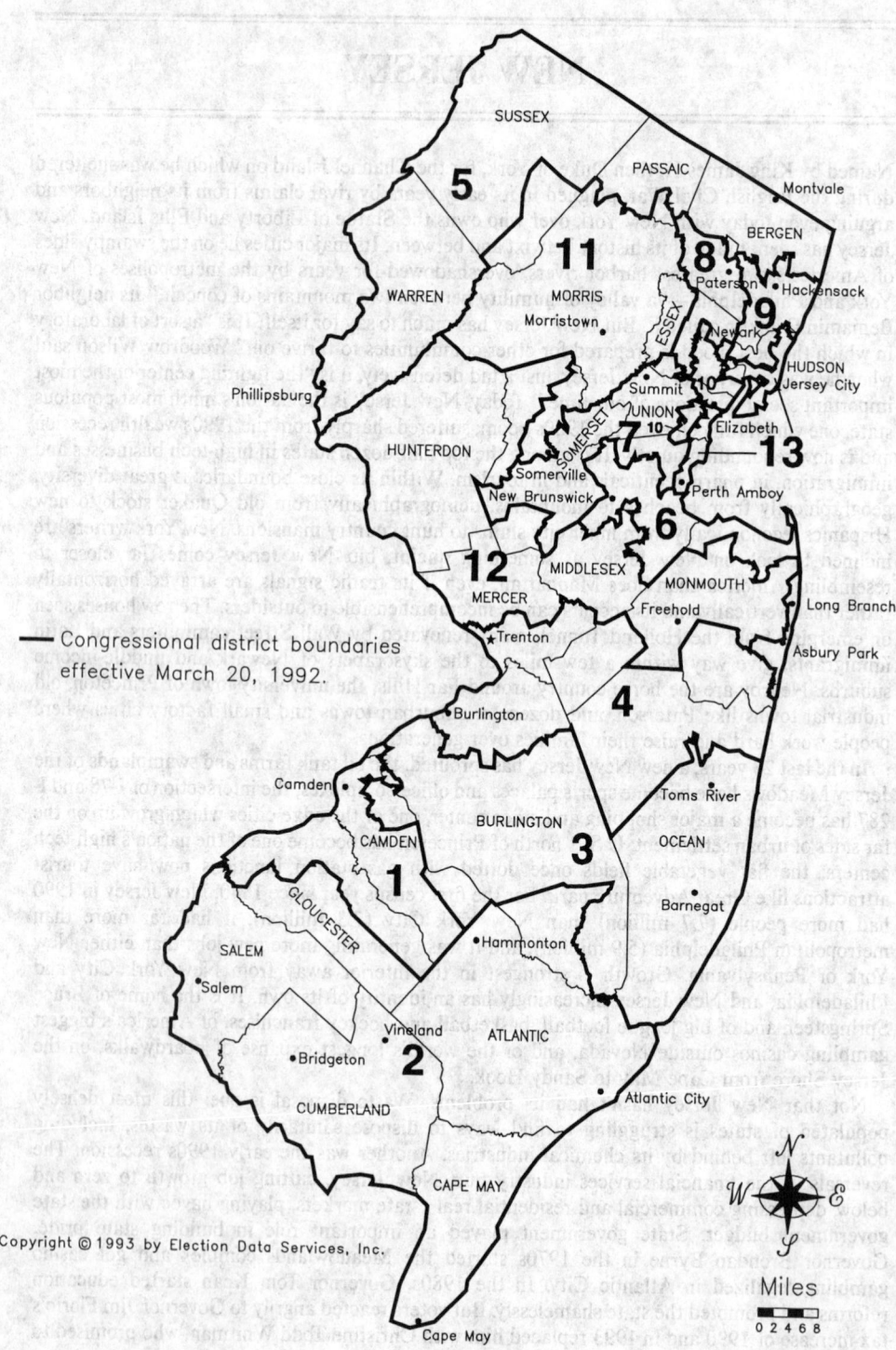

Congressional district boundaries
effective March 20, 1992.

Miles
0 2 4 6 8

cut tax rates: the laboratory rejected one experiment and embraced another.

The angry tone of public rhetoric may suggest that New Jersey's political system is flawed. Actually, in many ways it is exemplary. Its public financing of gubernatorial campaigns has, at last, made New Jersey politicians personally known statewide through TV ads and has produced a series of strong and distinctive governors—Byrne, Kean, Florio, Whitman—who are not beholden, as so many of their predecessors were, to county political bosses, a few of whom were shrewd political leaders but many of whom were hacks and even crooks. New Jersey, once corrupt, is now pretty well cleaned up. It also gives its governors more real power than any other state. They are the only statewide elected officials, unremovable by recall, with power to appoint all county prosecutors and judges and great clout in the budgetary process. This does insulate governors from pressure, which Florio's critics bemoaned in the early 1990s. But it also makes them accountable, as Florio's backers found in November 1993.

Governor. Christine Todd Whitman grew up in a political family, on an estate in the New Jersey horse country she now lives in. Her father, Webster Todd, was the New Jersey Republican chairman in 1964 and again in 1977; her mother was vice chairman of the Republican National Committee. Christie attended her first Republican National Convention in San Francisco in 1956, at age nine. She served five years on the Somerset County Board of Freeholders in the 1980s and was appointed to the Board of Public Utilities by Governor Tom Kean in 1988. In 1990 she took on the task of running against Senator Bill Bradley; it was just after Governor Jim Florio's big tax increases, and she attacked Bradley for taking no position on them. The result was a near-upset: Bradley won by only 50%–47%. Anti-Florio rage gave Republicans more than two-thirds legislative majorities in the 1991 elections. In 1993 Whitman ran for governor, winning the June primary with 40% of the vote to 33% for former Attorney General Cary Edwards and 24% for former state Senator James Wallwork.

The race between Florio and Whitman had national implications, not fully understood until 1994. Florio's 1990 tax package was very much like the 1993 Clinton tax increase, presented as an attempt to soak the rich and as the only way to pay for necessary government services. Clinton political advisers James Carville and Paul Begala ran Florio's campaign and Democratic National Chairman David Wilhelm said the race "will be a referendum on the type of leadership" both Florio and Clinton have provided. It was widely thought at the time that voters were resentful of the rich, and the two candidates' backgrounds presented a vivid contrast that the Florio campaign underlined. Florio grew up in working class Brooklyn, joined the Navy and became a boxer, practiced law and worked his way up in Camden County politics to the legislature in 1970 and Congress in 1974. Florio ads showed pictures of Whitman's house and attacked her for taking a farming deduction on her property taxes; she was ridiculed for saying "as funny as it seems, $500 is a lot of money" to many people. But Whitman trumped him by promising a 30% across-the-board income tax cut over three years.

Florio's tax increase on "the rich" had hit couples with $70,000 incomes and individuals with $35,000—people who shop at K-Mart, not Saks Fifth Avenue. Whitman did not apologize for her wealth, pointing out in debate that she and her husband paid more than $1 million in taxes; she said instead that high taxes were destroying businesses and depriving New Jerseyans of jobs, and that Florio was the worst New Jersey governor in history except for William Franklin, Ben's son, who supported the British in the Revolutionary War. Florio attacked her for not fully backing his assault weapon ban and for opposing a welfare bill that denies additional aid to mothers who do not identify the father of their child; newspapers attacked her tax cut promises as unrealistic. Under New Jersey's public finance law, each candidate has the same amount of money to spend in this second most expensive of media states (because you must buy New York and Philadelphia TV time). Whitman husbanded hers, withstanding pressure even as Florio built up a lead in polls, and then outspent him heavily the last two weeks. Carville and New Jersey reporters were ready to hail a Florio triumph as evidence that voters could be sold on higher taxes; instead they floundered to explain Whitman's 49%–48% victory. Days later she was embarrassed when her consultant Ed Rollins claimed money was spent to "depress" voter turnout in black areas; Whitman steadfastly denied it, and an embarrassed Rollins later repudiated his statement.

In office, Whitman delivered on her promises and became a national Republican star. Her tax cuts were proposed and passed ahead of schedule; some localities increased taxes in response, but not nearly as many or as much as critics had predicted. Whitman's crispness and steadiness were on view as she delivered from the State House in Trenton the Republican response to President Clinton's long State of the Union address in January 1995. On national issues, Whitman is very much for lower taxes and very pro-choice on abortion—positions that inspired speculation about a vice presidential nomination in 1996. She has downplayed the idea, and in fact it is hard to see how her stands on social issues—not just her positions, but her vehement tone—could fail to inspire a rebellion among many cultural conservatives at a Republican convention. She may or may not be a national candidate, but as governor of one of the largest states, popular politically and evidently successful in policy, she is a major national political force.

Senators. Bill Bradley, senior Senator from New Jersey, is in his second decade in politics and his fourth decade in public life. He is a politician and public policy maker of national stature, undeniably able, a student of and original thinker on major issues of economics and foreign policy—but in the last few years seemingly adrift and uncertain in his approach. Bradley was a celebrity before he was old enough to vote, when he was a star basketball player at Princeton. He always had steely self-discipline. He gave up two years of pro basketball for a Rhodes Scholarship and refused millions he could have made in commercial endorsements; instead he wrote a thoughtful memoir, *Life on the Run*. He listens closely to others, even opponents, engaging their ideas, and in response developing and sometimes even changing his own. When he first ran for the Senate in 1978, his Republican opponent, Jeffrey Bell, was championing the 30% Kemp-Roth federal income tax cut; Bradley, unlike most Democrats at the time, did not airily dismiss it but struggled to come up with an original response. He won with 55% of the vote, less than expected given his celebrity as a Princeton and New York Knicks basketball player. In the Senate, with Dale Bumpers and Ernest Hollings, he was one of three Democrats who voted for the Reagan budget and against the 1981 tax cuts—an approach that, had it prevailed, would have eliminated most of the 1980s deficit. Not satisfied with traditional Democratic economics, Bradley by 1982 came up with a proposal to cut tax rates sharply and eliminate most preferences and tax shelters. That led directly to the 1986 tax reform, which would surely never have happened without Bradley—a stunning achievement for a politician with little seniority on the minority side of the aisle at the time, and freighted with the kind of celebrity status other politicians usually resent. At each stage of the tax reform debate Bradley was there, quietly encouraging others, avoiding the spotlight but offering advice and lobbying key members.

Bradley has taken a similar approach—intensive study, original proposals supported by facts and strong argument, a willingness to fight for his goals—to other issues. He has traveled extensively in the former Soviet Union, was skeptical about aid during the Gorbachev years and called for more aid and student exchanges after Yeltsin came to power. He sponsored the student right-to-know act requiring publication of graduation rates. He used the chairmanship of the Water and Power Subcommittee in 1992 to insist that California farmers pay something closer to market cost for their heavily subsidized water. He called for major aid to cities in 1992, proposed an urban community building initiative in 1993, and warned against cutting welfare or affirmative action in 1994. His community policing, community schools (kept open after 3 p.m.) and community banking amendments passed in 1994. He did not weigh in noisily in the 1994 healthcare debate but participated in a centrist group on the Finance Committee. In 1994 he called for a "rules-based" approach to trade with Japan. He questioned ethanol subsidies and worked for direct universal student loans.

Bradley's political career was nearly ended and certainly transformed by his near-defeat for reelection in 1990. He won by only 50%–47% over Christine Todd Whitman, now governor but then almost totally unknown. Bradley ran only even in north Jersey, served by New York TV, while in South Jersey, served by Philadelphia TV, he won 54%–43%. His major problem was that he refused to express an opinion on the unpopular tax increase passed by Governor Jim Florio, by far the hottest issue that year; he was evidently torn between distaste for the Florio program and loyalty to a fellow Democrat. "He is a tax expert," Whitman said crisply in one ad. "This is the biggest tax increase in New Jersey history. I'd like to know what he thinks, how he differs from the governor, if at all." Bradley says that his electoral close call made him less cautious and more determined to speak from the heart; it also reduced the demand for him to run for president in 1992, and he made no moves to enter the race. He was one of three Democratic keynoters at the 1992 National Convention in the same Madison Square Garden where he played so many basketball games; he was mentioned briefly for Clinton's secretary of state, but evidently was not seriously considered. He has a mostly liberal voting record but is not a Clinton cheerleader; after the 1994 elections, he said: "I think the Democratic Party has got problems; the vote was a clear rejection of Bill Clinton, let's be honest about it." But he added that "two years is a lifetime in politics." He proposed radical public financing of campaigns, with no PACs, and called for a Neighborhood Reconstruction Corps, entrepreneurship training and individual development accounts to help inner cities. In an extraordinary speech in February 1995, Bradley argued that neither the Republicans' market nor the Democrats' governmental approaches can work without strong communal ties. He called for a stronger civil society and denounced the craving for a leader on a white horse to solve all of society's problems. This was taken by some as an indication that he was considering challenging Clinton in 1996; but its skepticism about the efficacy of government suggests that Bradley may be tiring of the political career he has pursued for 20 years. Some close to him believe he will not run for reelection; few think he will be the overwhelmingly strong candidate he seemed to be before 1990. Republican Congressman Dick Zimmer, a strong market conservative on economics but pro-choice on abortion, is planning to make the race, and Republican Congresswoman Marge Roukema has also been mentioned. If Bradley doesn't run, Democratic Congressmen Bob Torricelli, passed over by the Clinton White House for Democratic National Chairman, and Rob Andrews, a strong tax opponent himself, might run.

Frank Lautenberg is one of a species common for the last century and still today—the millionaire who becomes a Senator. In 1980 he was a Democratic moneygiver and member of the board of the New York and New Jersey Port Authority; in 1994 he was reelected to a third term in the Senate at 70. He has shown he knows how to play the game—and that it helps to come in with a large pile of chips. Lautenberg grew up poor, the son of an immigrant silk worker in Paterson who died young. He is a World War II veteran who would never have gone to college without the G.I. Bill of Rights. In 1952, he started a company called Automatic Data Processing, which by 1993 employed 21,000 people and processed the payroll for one of every 14 non-government workers in the United States. With an open Senate seat in New Jersey in 1982, the nation's second most expensive state to campaign in (because you have to buy New York and Philadelphia TV), Lautenberg decided to run, spending $5 million of his own money and spotlighting his high-tech experience. He beat several professional politicians in the primary and upset Republican Congresswoman Millicent Fenwick, 51%–48%, in the general. In 1988, he again showed good campaign skills, beating retired general and Wall Street executive Pete Dawkins with dollops of ridicule; he won 54%–46%.

Lautenberg believes that government helped him and many others work their way up, and he has a solid liberal voting record. But he is also willing to buck party lines when it is to his political advantage. Taking note of New Jersey's furious reaction to Governor Jim Florio's 1990 tax increase, he obdurately refused to vote for the Clinton budget and tax package in 1993. In 1994, he campaigned as a sponsor of the gift ban on lobbyists and denounced a charity ski event in Utah, though he had attended it three times in the past. In the meantime, a leaked memo showed that his fundraiser targeted people he had helped as Senator. As chairman of the Transportation Appropriations Subcommittee, he sponsored the laws that banned smoking first on two-hour, then on all domestic flights. He is a big booster of money for Amtrak and high-speed trains, mass transit and a footbridge from New Jersey to Ellis Island. He passed a radon bill that developed control standards and has backed the Superfund toxic waste cleanup program. In 1994, Lautenberg was an obvious Republican target; his opponent, after former Governor Tom Kean and Congressman Dick Zimmer decided not to run, was Assembly Speaker Chuck Haytaian. Haytaian had sponsored the rollback of Florio's sales tax and then helped pass Governor Christie Whitman's tax cuts. He came out for a flat tax, and raised plenty of money from his fellow Armenian-Americans. But he had opposed Florio's assault weapons ban, a symbolic but important issue. Lautenberg campaigned on ocean dumping, the Brady handgun-control bill, college loans for middle-class students and his opposition to Clinton's taxes; he got mileage from denouncing Haytaian for appearing on the program of WABC talk show host Bob Grant after Grant allegedly made racist remarks. Ross Perot, Lautenberg's fellow computer entrepreneur, endorsed him as "one of the few members of the Senate who know how the real world works," but Haytaian carried Perot voters. Money finally made the difference. Lautenberg spent $8 million altogether to $5 million for Haytaian; Lautenberg was left with a $4 million debt, mostly to himself, but he can raise much of that easily if he wants. Lautenberg won 50%–47%, exactly Bradley's margin in 1990. Lautenberg is no longer a subcommittee chairman and will have a harder time advancing his causes, and he does not have many warm allies, but he is for the next six years where he evidently wants to be.

Presidential politics. New Jersey has become a pivotal state in presidential politics, one that both Democrats and Republicans consider essential for victory. It is the one state that keeps presidential and vice presidential candidates in the northeast metropolitan corridor, hoping for New York and Philadelphia TV coverage no matter how safe for one party New York or Pennsylvania seems. New Jersey voted for Kennedy in 1960, Nixon in 1968, Reagan in 1980, Bush in 1988, and Clinton in 1992; in close elections over the last 50 years, it has voted for the loser only in 1948 and 1976. Mostly suburban, New Jersey has never had the urban Democratic base of New York, nor does it have the mass of unattached singles who move New York and California to the left. In 1988, it rejected the liberalism of Michael Dukakis and voted solidly for George Bush. In 1992, after three years of recession that lowered incomes and falling house prices, New Jersey deserted Bush, toyed with the idea of Ross Perot and finally gave Bill Clinton a 43%–41% victory. It is a must-win state for Republicans in 1996.

For years, New Jersey's June presidential primary was overshadowed by California's on the same day. Now California is voting in March, and New Jersey is likely to be voting long after the nominee is known.

Congressional districting. New Jersey grew 5% in the 1980s, well below the national average, and lost a congressional district in the 1990 census. The Democrats had full control of the process, with the governor and legislature, in calendar year 1991, but could not reach agreement. In November 1991 the Republicans, much to everyone's surprise, won veto-proof control of both houses; the Democrats, knowing Republicans could do what they liked, established a bipartisan commission like the one that draws legislative district lines. Republicans, confident that their population-gaining districts would fare better than the Democrats' population-losing ones, acquiesced. The commission plan joined the Jersey Shore and Middlesex County districts represented by Democrats into a new 6th District and created a new 38% Hispanic district linking parts of Jersey City, Newark and other cities facing New York City.

The People: Est. Pop. 1994: 7,904,000; Pop. 1990: 7,730,188, up 2.2% 1990–1994. 3.0% of U.S. total, 9th largest; 11% rural. Median age: 34.5 years. 13.4% 65 years and over. 79.3% White, 13.4% Black, 9.6% Hispanic origin, 3.5% Asian, 3.5% Other. Households: 56.5% married couple families; 26% married couple fams. w. children; 46% college educ.; median household income: $40,927; per capita income: $18,714; 64.9% owner occupied housing; median house value: $162,300; median monthly rent: $521. 8.4% Unemployment. 1994 Voting age pop.: 5,974,000. 1994 Turnout: 2,022,614; 34% of VAP. Registered voters (1994): 3,852,573; 1,109,565 D (29%), 851,798 R (22%), 1,891,210 unaffiliated and minor parties (49%).

Political Lineup: Governor, Christine Todd Whitman (R); Lt. Gov., Donald T. DiFrancesco (R); Secy. of State, Lonna R. Hooks (R); Atty. Gen., Deborah T. Poritz (R); Treasurer, Brian W. Clymer (R); Auditor, Richard L. Fair (D). State Senate, 40 (24 R and 16 D); General Assembly, 80 (52 R and 28 D). Senators, Bill Bradley (D) and Frank R. Lautenberg (D). Representatives, 13 (8 R and 5 D).

1992 Presidential Vote

Clinton (D)	1,436,206	(43%)
Bush (R)	1,356,865	(41%)
Perot (I)	521,829	(16%)

1992 Democratic Presidential Primary

Clinton	256,337	(63%)
Brown	79,877	(20%)
Tsongas	45,191	(11%)
Other	23,817	(6%)

1988 Presidential Vote

Bush (R)	1,743,192	(56%)
Dukakis (D)	1,320,352	(42%)

1992 Republican Presidential Primary

Bush	240,535	(78%)
Buchanan	46,432	(15%)
Write-In (Perot)	23,303	(8%)

GOVERNOR

Gov. Christine Todd Whitman (R)

Elected 1993, term expires Jan. 1997; b. Sept. 26, 1946, New York City, NY; home, Oldwick; Wheaton Col., B.A. 1968; Presbyterian; married (John).

Career: Staff Asst., Repub. Natl. Cmte., 1969–71; Pres., Public Utilities Bd., 1988–1990; Somerset Cnty. Bd. of Chosen Freeholders, 1983–88; U.S. Senate candidate, 1990.

Office: State House, 125 W. State St., #CN-001, Trenton 08625, 609-292-6000; Fax: 609-292-3454.

Election Results

1993 gen.	Christine Todd Whitman (R)	1,236,124	(49%)
	Jim Florio (D)	1,210,031	(48%)
	Others	59,809	(2%)
1993 prim.	Christine Todd Whitman (R)	159,765	(40%)
	Cary Edwards (R)	131,578	(33%)
	Jim Wallwork	96,034	(24%)
	Others	12,448	(3%)
1989 gen.	Jim Florio (D)	1,379,937	(61%)
	Jim Courter (R)	838,553	(37%)
	Others	34,563	(2%)

SENATORS

Sen. Bill Bradley (D)

Elected 1978, seat up 1996; b. July 28, 1943, Crystal City, MO; home, Montclair; Princeton, B.A. 1965, Rhodes Scholar, Oxford U., M.A. 1968; Presbyterian; married (Ernestine).

Career: Air Force Reserves, 1967–78; U.S. Olympic Team, 1964; Pro basketball player, New York Knicks, 1967–77.

DC Office: 731 HSOB 202-224-3224; Fax: 202-224-8567.

State Offices: 1 Newark Ctr., #1600, Newark 07102, 201-639-2860; and 1 Greentree Ctr., #303, Rte. #73, Marlton 08053, 609-983-4143.

Committee: *Energy & Natural Resources* (4th of 8 D): Forests and Public Land Management (RMM); Parks, Historic Preservation and Recreation. *Finance* (3rd of 9 D): International Trade; Long-Term Growth, Debt and Defict Reduction; Taxation and IRS Oversight (RMM). *Aging (Special)* (3rd of 9 D).

Group Ratings

	ADA	ACLU	COPE	CFA	LCV	CON	NSI	COC	ACU	NTLC	CHC
1994	85	72	88	100	92	49	0	27	4	12	0
1993	90	—	82	70	94	80	—	36	13	—	—

National Journal Ratings

	1993 LIB — 1993 CONS		1994 LIB — 1994 CONS	
Economic	83%	— 0%	55%	— 40%
Social	76%	— 23%	81%	— 16%
Foreign	87%	— 8%	78%	— 15%

Key Votes of the 103d Congress

1. Clinton Deficit Plan	Y	3. Brady Handgun Purchase	Y	5. Lmt. UN Cmnd. of Forces	N
2. NAFTA	Y	4. Strike Race/Death Pnlty.	N	6. Cut Missile Funds	Y

Key Votes of the 104th Congress

1. Congressional Compliance	Y	3. Balanced Budget Amndt.	N	5. Product Liability Reform	N
2. Bar Unfunded Mandates	N	4. Pass Line Item Veto	Y	6. FY96 Budget	N

Election Results

1990 general	Bill Bradley (D)	977,810	(50%)	($12,444,283)
	Christine Todd Whitman (R)	918,874	(47%)	($801,660)
	Others	41,770	(2%)	
1990 primary	Bill Bradley (D)	197,454	(92%)	
	Daniel Z. Seyler (D)	16,287	(8%)	
1984 general	Bill Bradley (D)	1,986,644	(64%)	($5,142,316)
	Mary V. Mochary (R)	1,080,100	(35%)	($956,398)

Sen. Frank R. Lautenberg (D)

Elected 1982, seat up 2000; b. Jan. 23, 1924, Paterson; home, Montclair; Columbia U., B.S. 1949; Jewish; separated.

Career: Army Signal Corps, 1942–46 (WWII); Co-founder, Automatic Data Processing, 1952–82; NY & NJ Port Authority Comm., 1978–82.

DC Office: 506 HSOB 20510, 202-224-4744; Fax: 202-224-9707.

State Offices: Barrington Commons, 208 Whitehorse Pk., #1819, Barrington 08007, 609-757-5353; and 1 Gateway Ctr., Newark 07102, 201-645-3030.

Committees: *Appropriations* (7th of 13 D): Commerce, Justice, State and Judiciary; Defense; Foreign Operations; Transportation (RMM); VA, HUD and Independent Agencies. *Budget* (4th of 10 D). *Environment & Public Works* (3rd of 7 D): Drinking Water, Fisheries and Wildlife; Superfund, Waste Control and Risk Assessment (RMM). *Small Business* (9th of 9 D).

Group Ratings

	ADA	ACLU	COPE	CFA	LCV	CON	NSI	COC	ACU	NTLC	CHC
1994	95	79	88	92	92	60	10	27	4	28	7
1993	95	—	82	70	100	4	—	45	24	—	—

National Journal Ratings

	1993 LIB — 1993 CONS		1994 LIB — 1994 CONS	
Economic	53%	— 45%	84%	— 0%
Social	82%	— 15%	81%	— 16%
Foreign	76%	— 23%	72%	— 22%

Key Votes of the 103d Congress

1. Clinton Deficit Plan	N	3. Brady Handgun Purchase	Y	5. Lmt. UN Cmnd. of Forces	N
2. NAFTA	N	4. Strike Race/Death Pnlty.	N	6. Cut Missile Funds	Y

Key Votes of the 104th Congress

1. Congressional Compliance	Y	3. Balanced Budget Amndt.	N	5. Product Liability Reform	N
2. Bar Unfunded Mandates	N	4. Pass Line Item Veto	N	6. FY96 Budget	N

Election Results

1994 general	Frank R. Lautenberg (D)	1,033,487	(50%)	($8,217,716)
	Garabed (Chuck) Haytaian (R)	966,244	(47%)	($5,110,378)
	Others	55,156	(3%)	
1994 primary	Frank R. Lautenberg (D)	151,416	(81%)	
	Bill Campbell (D)	26,066	(14%)	
	Lynne A. Speed (D)	9,563	(5%)	
1988 general	Frank R. Lautenberg (D)	1,599,905	(54%)	($7,298,663)
	Peter M. Dawkins (R).	1,349,937	(46%)	($7,616,249)

FIRST DISTRICT

There are few urban spaces that have been more ravaged, yet now have more signs of hope, than Camden, New Jersey. Across the Delaware River from Philadelphia's skyline, its closely built streets were jammed with immigrants in the 19th Century, when poet Walt Whitman lived here. In 1894, a Camden machinist named Eldridge Johnson produced the Victor Talking Machine—the birth of the company that became RCA Victor in 1929. In 1897, Camden was the site of the invention of condensed soup, and the Campbell Soup Company was founded soon afterwards. Thus Camden became a major industrial locus on the Jersey side of the Delaware River, not the broadest and certainly not the most picturesque of our Atlantic estuaries, but probably the East Coast's premier industrial waterway, with a concentration of steel factories, chemical plants and oil tank farms equal to any in the country. The flat lands of South Jersey all around, ignored in the 19th Century, had easy access to cheap water transport and plenty of skilled labor from the Philadelphia area, making them one of the country's fastest-growing industrial areas for a quarter-century starting in the 1940s. Camden tended to empty out, many of its factories closed, its neighborhoods were beset by crime. But local government has developed a riverfront park, with the New Jersey Aquarium and the Sony Music/Pace amphitheater, that takes advantage of Camden's site and attracts multiracial crowds. An aerospace complex and a Campbell Soup office tower have gone up; some factories are being revived. Camden may be coming back.

The 1st Congressional District is, more or less, greater Camden, the Delaware riverfront from Riverton south to a point across from the Delaware state line, and suburbs running southeast to the flat vegetable fields of South Jersey. Its boroughs and townships retain their separate identities; right next to Camden is Collingswood, with its middle-class porches still freshly painted and its shops prosperous. The district includes some underclass poor, but most people here are at some level of upward mobility from the grinding working-class life of 50 years ago, living in comfortable communities, worried that the petrochemical plants which have helped many of them move up may also be poisoning their land, water and air. Politically, this is an area with a Democratic heritage, the home base of Governor Jim Florio (though it was not happy with his 1990 tax increases), the most Democratic district in South Jersey.

The 1st District is represented by Rob Andrews, one of the most interesting young Democratic Congressmen. Andrews grew up in Bellmawr, the son of a shipyard worker, made a splendid record in college and law school, returned home and with Florio's support was elected to the Camden County Board of Chosen Freeholders (wonderful name!) before he was 30. There he reduced taxes to their lowest level since 1970, passed a recycling program that exceeded state requirements and established a Camden Alliance to replace welfare with jobs; his allies still control the Board and boast of producing better services while lowering taxes. When Florio resigned from Congress, he put off the special election to replace him until November 1990; he supported Andrews, though Andrews was silent on his tax increase. Andrews had other help. He spent $541,000 on his campaign, and he had a Republican opponent who switched positions on abortion and claimed to have attended a college he hadn't. Even so, in the anti-Florio climate, Andrews won by only 54%–43%.

Andrews entered the House as its youngest Democrat and has proved to be one of its most aggressive and independent-minded reformers. One big initiative was direct student loans. Andrews felt banks were making college loans inefficiently and that direct government loans would "save money for students, families, schools and the federal treasury." Against strong lobbying opposition, he got the House to approve direct loan demonstration projects, got candidate Bill Clinton to endorse the idea and then got it passed into law in 1993. He argues that it is a major success and it is one of the major achievements of the Clinton Administration. Locally, Andrews fought hard to save jobs at the Philadelphia Navy Yard, just across the Walt Whitman Bridge, and he made quite a flurry by accusing the Navy of illegally diverting repair work to foreign shipyards. He had a rather conservative record on economics and foreign policy and was more liberal on cultural issues. He voted against tax increases, including the Clinton budget and tax package of 1993 and announced early he would oppose the Clinton healthcare program. To some of Andrews's Democratic critics in the New Jersey delegation and elsewhere, he is a grandstander who would cut needed government programs. But his record in Camden and on direct student loans shows that he supports government that is vigorous and serves real needs—but that he insists on pruning government that isn't working and on not forcing voters to pay more in taxes for the same low level of services they've been getting.

Andrews's other major project in 1994 was the A-to-Z spending cut. This was the idea of New Hampshire Republican Bill Zeliff, and in looking for a Democrat whose name started with A as a co-sponsor he naturally came on Andrews. A-to-Z would set aside 56 hours of congressional debate during which any member could propose reducing or zeroing out spending on any program, with a guaranteed roll call vote. "It will put the onus on members of Congress to explain why programs should continue," Andrews said. Andrews and Zeliff got A-to-Z endorsed by 234 members and co-sponsored by 228. But Speaker Thomas Foley opposed it vehemently, as "probably the most poorly thought out proposal for the consideration of public policy that I've seen in many years—maybe the worst ever." A-to-Z needed the signatures of a majority of members on a discharge petition to come to a vote; thanks to a September 1993 reform forced over Foley's opposition, those signatures were public, but Foley still managed to get some co-sponsors to refuse to sign or withdraw their signatures, and A-to-Z failed in the summer of 1994 when Andrews and Zeliff could get only 204 signatures. They vowed to try again in 1995, but such a procedure may not seem necessary in a Republican House.

Andrews's political acumen has been apparent at election time. He has vastly outspent his opponents and, against the Gloucester County sheriff in a Republican year, he won with 72% of the vote in 1994. He has continued to show his political independence, as one of the strongest supporters of the Contract With America among northeastern Democrats. He has been mentioned frequently as a candidate against Governor Christie Whitman in 1997; he could conceivably run for the Senate in 1996 if Bill Bradley retires.

The People: Pop. 1990: 594,494; 4% rural; 12% age 65+; 77% White; 16% Black; 2% Asian; 4% Other; 6% Hispanic origin. Voting age pop.: 435,926; 14% Black; 5% Hispanic origin. Households: 55% married couple families; 27% married couple fams. w. children; 38% college educ.; median household income: $35,250; per capita income: $14,502; median gross rent: $514; median house value: $93,700.

1992 Presidential Vote			1988 Presidential Vote		
Clinton (D)	118,060	(48%)	Bush (R)	115,528	(53%)
Bush (R)	78,095	(32%)	Dukakis (D)	102,356	(47%)
Perot (I)	48,252	(20%)			

Rep. Robert E. Andrews (D)

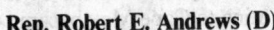

Elected 1990; b. Aug. 4, 1957, Camden; home, Haddon Heights; Bucknell U., B.A. 1979, Cornell U., J.D. 1982; Episcopalian; married (Camille).

Career: Practicing atty., 1982–87; Adjunct Prof., Rutgers Col. of Law, 1985–86, 1989–90; Dir., Camden Cnty. Bd. of Chosen Freeholders, 1987–90.

DC Office: 2439 RHOB 20515, 202-225-6501; Fax: 202-225-6583.

District Offices: 16 Somerdale Sq., Somerdale 08063, 609-627-9000; and 63 N. Broad St., Woodbury 08096, 609-848-3900.

Committees: *Economic & Educational Opportunities* (10th of 19 D): Postsecondary Education, Training and Life-Long Learning; Workforce Protections. *International Relations* (12th of 19 D): Asia and the Pacific.

Group Ratings

	ADA	ACLU	COPE	CFA	LCV	CON	NSI	COC	ACU	NTLC	CHC
1994	45	68	67	60	94	78	80	83	26	50	36
1993	60	—	83	70	86	1	—	27	25	—	—

National Journal Ratings

	1993 LIB —	1993 CONS	1994 LIB —	1994 CONS
Economic	48%	51%	42%	57%
Social	72%	27%	56%	43%
Foreign	35%	63%	39%	60%

Key Votes of the 103d Congress

1. Clinton Deficit Plan	N	3. Brady Handgun Purchase	Y	5. Lmt. UN Cmnd. of Forces	Y
2. NAFTA	N	4. Strike Race/Death Pnlty.	N	6. Cut Missile Funds	N

Key Votes of the 104th Congress

1. Congressional Compliance	Y	6. Reform Crime Grant	N	11. Loser Pays Court Reform	N
2. Balanced Budget Amndmt.	Y	7. National Security Act	Y	12. Product Liability Reform	N
3. Bar Unfunded Mandates	Y	8. Moratorium on Regs.	*	13. Welfare Reform	Y
4. Pass Line Item Veto	Y	9. Risk Assessment on Regs.	N	14. Term Limits Amndmt.	N
5. Relax Exclusionary Rule	Y	10. Expnd. Priv. Prop. Rights	N	15. Tax Cuts	Y

Election Results

1994 general	Robert E. Andrews (D)................	108,155	(72%)	($674,366)
	James N. Hogan (R)..................	41,505	(28%)	($78,028)
1994 primary	Robert E. Andrews (D).............	unopposed		
1992 general	Robert E. Andrews (D)................	153,525	(67%)	($762,588)
	Lee A. Solomon (R)	65,123	(29%)	($176,586)
	Others	9,424	(4%)	

SECOND DISTRICT

The builders of the Camden & Atlantic Railroad in 1852 may not have known it, but when they extended their line to the little inlet town of Absecon, they were starting America's biggest beach resort, Atlantic City. Like all resorts, it was a product of developments elsewhere: of industrialization and spreading affluence, of railroad technology and the conquest of diseases which used to make summer a time of terror for parents and doctors. In the years after the Civil War, first Atlantic City and then the whole Jersey Shore from Brigantine to Cape May became America's first seaside resort, and Atlantic City developed its characteristic features: the Boardwalk in 1870, the amusement pier in 1882, the rolling chair in 1884, salt water taffy in the 1890s, Miss America in 1921. By 1940, when 16 million Americans visited every summer, Atlantic City was a common man's resort of old traditions; it declined in the years after World War II as people could afford nicer vacations. By the early 1970s, Atlantic City was grim, with a bedraggled convention hall (site of the 1964 Democratic National Convention), empty hotels and bleak streets of rowhouses built in the ugliest Philadelphia style. Then in 1977, New Jersey voters legalized casino gambling in Atlantic City and gleaming new hotels sprang up, big name entertainers came in and Atlantic City became more glamorous than it had been in 90 years. But not for many of its residents: casino and hotel jobs tend to be low-wage, and the slums begin just feet from the massive parking lots of the casinos. The mayor tried to entice policemen to live in the city by offering no-interest home loans; no one bought. New York, Pennsylvania and Florida have not moved to legalize casino gambling, and Atlantic City seems to be holding on. But as Donald Trump's $1 billion Taj Mahal went up in 1990, some wondered whether the new Atlantic City would become as grimy as the old.

The Jersey Shore south of Atlantic City is a string of different resorts. There is the old Methodist town of Ocean City, where Gay Talese grew up the son of Italian immigrants, as he tells movingly in *Unto the Sons*. There is Wildwood, with its gritty boardwalk, and Cape May, with its beautifully preserved Victorian houses. Behind the Shore are swamp and flatland, the Pine Barrens and vegetable fields that gave New Jersey the name "Garden State." Growth has been slow in these small towns and gas station intersections, communities in whose eerie calmness in the summer you can hear mosquitoes whining. In the flatness, you can also find towns clustered around low-wage apparel factories or petrochemical plants on the Delaware estuary: the Northeast high-tech service economy has not reached this far south in Jersey yet.

This part of South Jersey makes up the 2d Congressional District. Politically, it was long marginal country, with strong Democratic presences in the chemical industry towns across from Wilmington, Delaware and in Atlantic City, and a strong Republican presence in Cape May. In the 1990s, Democrats have been dominant, as south Jersey voted for Senators Bill Bradley and Frank Lautenberg and President Bill Clinton. In House elections, the 2d District for 20 years reelected William Hughes, a moderate Democrat who was an Ocean County prosecutor and who in the 1980s and 1990s superintended crime bills and worked on copyright and ocean dumping issues as well. In 1994, after a 1992 challenge from Vineland Assemblyman Frank LoBiondo held him to a 56%–42% victory, his lowest margin ever, Hughes decided to retire.

Now Frank LoBiondo is the congressman. He grew up in South Jersey and worked for his family trucking company. In 1985 he got on the Cumberland County Board of Freeholders; in 1987 he was elected to the Assembly, where he stoutly opposed new taxes. LoBiondo also opposes gun control, and was backed by the National Rifle Association. In 1994, he had primary opposition from Atlantic County state Senator William Gormley, a party moderate who had run for governor in 1989; LoBiondo attacked him as a taxer and NRA ads called him "a liberal in Republican clothing"; to the surprise of many, LoBiondo won 54%–35%. The general election was not much of a contest: this 20-year Democratic district went Republican 65%–35%. LoBiondo seems very much in tune with the 1995 conservative Republican freshmen.

The People: Pop. 1990: 594,723; 30% rural; 15% age 65+; 78% White; 14% Black; 1% Asian; 4% Other; 6% Hispanic origin. Voting age pop.: 450,845; 13% Black; 5% Hispanic origin. Households: 54% married couple families; 24% married couple fams. w. children; 36% college educ.; median household income: $32,410; per capita income: $14,732; median gross rent: $525; median house value: $93,400.

1992 Presidential Vote		1988 Presidential Vote	
Clinton (D)	101,718 (40%)	Bush (R)	130,627 (59%)
Bush (R)	97,696 (39%)	Dukakis (D)	91,402 (41%)
Perot (I)	50,773 (20%)		

Rep. Frank A. LoBiondo (R)

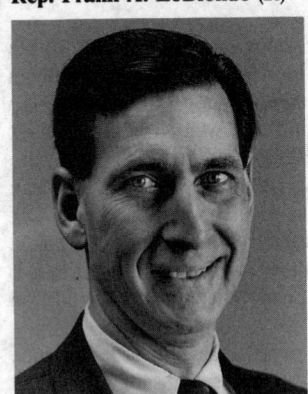

Elected 1994; b. May 12, 1946, Bridgeton; home, Vineland; St. Joseph's U., B.A. 1968; Roman Catholic; married (Jan).

Career: Operations Mgr., LoBiondo Bros. Motor Express Inc., 1968–94; Cumberland Cnty. Bd. of Chosen Freeholders, 1985–88; NJ Assembly, 1988–94.

DC Office: 513 CHOB 20515, 202-225-6572; Fax: 202-225-3318.

District Offices: 222 New Rd., #5, Linwood 08221, 609-927-4442.

Committees: *Banking & Financial Services* (25th of 27 R): Capital Markets, Securities and Government Sponsored Enterprises; Domestic and International Monetary Policy. *Small Business* (9th of 22 R): Regulation and Paperwork; Tax and Finance.

Group Ratings and 103rd Congress Votes: Newly Elected

Key Votes of the 104th Congress

1. Congressional Compliance Y	6. Reform Crime Grant　Y	11. Loser Pays Court Reform Y
2. Balanced Budget Amndmt. Y	7. National Security Act　Y	12. Product Liability Reform Y
3. Bar Unfunded Mandates　Y	8. Moratorium on Regs.　Y	13. Welfare Reform　　　Y
4. Pass Line Item Veto　Y	9. Risk Assessment on Regs. Y	14. Term Limits Amndmt.　Y
5. Relax Exclusionary Rule　Y	10. Expnd. Priv. Prop. Rights Y	15. Tax Cuts　　　　　Y

Election Results

1994 general	Frank A. LoBiondo (R)	102,566	(65%)	($757,681)
	Louis N. Magazzu (D)	56,151	(35%)	($168,428)
1994 primary	Frank A. LoBiondo (R)	23,152	(54%)	
	Bill Gormley (R)	14,989	(35%)	
	Robert D. Green (R)	4,364	(10%)	
1992 general	William J. Hughes (D)	132,465	(56%)	($608,150)
	Frank A. LoBiondo (R)	98,315	(42%)	($284,773)
	Others	6,247	(3%)	

THIRD DISTRICT

The Pine Barrens of New Jersey are one of the last vacant spots on the eastern seaboard; not quite *terra incognita*, but still not thickly populated. Encroached by the Philadelphia suburbs of South Jersey on the west and the burgeoning retirement developments of the Jersey Shore on the east, they are crossed even today mostly by narrow two-lane roads and is the site of McGuire Air Force Base. For years, the Barrens were seen as a barrier to civilization; only recently have environmentally-minded Jerseyites come to see them as a natural treasure.

The 3d Congressional District spans the Pine Barrens. Most of its residents live in the South Jersey suburbs of Philadelphia, in the spread-out suburb of Cherry Hill with its 1960s and 1970s shopping centers, or in the older towns along the Delaware River and newer ones inland toward McGuire. This is comfortable, but not hugely affluent, suburban country. East of the Pine Barrens is Ocean County, including the barrier islands from Normandy Beach south to Little Egg Harbor, with older beachfront communities and larger clusters of new subdivisions and condominium complexes inland. Ocean County grew rapidly in the 1980s, a kind of frost belt Florida, with many retirees from New York and north Jersey eager to leave behind the big cities with their high crime and high taxes, but still jealous of their Social Security benefits and concerned about the local environment. Politically, both the west and east ends of this district are solidly Republican.

The congressman from the 3d District is James Saxton, a former teacher and real estate broker who served nine years in the legislature, the kind of locally connected Republican politician who is conservative on most national issues and tends carefully to local concerns. Up through 1994 his profile was highest on local issues. With a seat on the now-abolished Merchant Marine Committee, he co-sponsored the ocean dumping law of 1988, when medical wastes were washing up against the Shore; in 1992 he sponsored a bill requiring uniform testing of ocean waters. On the National Security Committee he worked to save local bases; when Fort Dix ended up on the 1991 base closing list, he turned much of it into a federal prison and state police training center. When McGuire was on the 1993 list, Saxton convinced the commission that it needed not to be closed but to be expanded, as the East Coast air mobility hub for the armed forces.

On economic issues, Saxton has been a staunch conservative, a popular position at home since Governor Jim Florio's 1990 tax increases. "The old ways of carefree taxing and spending are no longer acceptable," he said after the 1994 elections. "Thank goodness!" He is now vice chairman of the Joint Economic Committee, an emerging advocate of the economic case for tax and spending cuts. He chairs the Resources subcommittee on Fisheries, Wildlife and Oceans, which has most of the jurisdiction of the old Merchant Marine Committee. But, in that position in 1995, he has sometimes found himself opposed to Republican dogma because he says he wants to make environmental decisions based on science, not emotions or political arm-twisting. Saxton has clashed occasionally with Committee Chairman Don Young, proposing a more moderate Clean Water Act reauthorization in April 1995.

Back home Saxton has been reelected by large margins.

The People: Pop. 1990: 594,667; 18% rural; 15% age 65+; 87% White; 8% Black; 2% Asian; 1% Other; 3% Hispanic origin. Voting age pop.: 451,844; 7% Black; 2% Hispanic origin. Households: 66% married couple families; 29% married couple fams. w. children; 47% college educ.; median household income: $41,257; per capita income: $18,138; median gross rent: $651; median house value: $128,300.

1992 Presidential Vote			1988 Presidential Vote		
Clinton (D)	114,503	(40%)	Bush (R)	154,804	(62%)
Bush (R)	113,583	(40%)	Dukakis (D)	94,963	(38%)
Perot (I)	54,996	(19%)			

Rep. H. James Saxton (R)

Elected 1984; b. Jan. 22, 1943, Scranton, PA; home, Vincentown; E. Stroudsburg St. Col., B.A. 1965, Temple U., 1967–68; United Methodist; separated.

Career: Jr. High Schl. teacher, 1965–68; Real estate broker, 1968–84; NJ Assembly, 1975–82; NJ Senate, 1982–84.

DC Office: 339 CHOB 20515, 202-225-4765; Fax: 202-225-0778.

District Offices: 100 High St., Mt. Holly 08060, 609-261-5800; 1 Maine Ave., Cherry Hill 08002, 609-428-0520; and 7 Hadley Ave., Toms River 08753, 908-914-2020.

Committees: *National Security* (10th of 30 R): Military Installations and Facilities; Military Procurement. *Resources* (3rd of 25 R): Fisheries, Wildlife and Oceans (Chmn.). *Joint Economic Committee* (Vice Chmn. of 10 Reps.).

Group Ratings

	ADA	ACLU	COPE	CFA	LCV	CON	NSI	COC	ACU	NTLC	CHC
1994	15	22	22	30	50	54	90	100	67	86	93
1993	20	—	42	40	64	69	—	82	79	—	—

National Journal Ratings

	1993 LIB — 1993 CONS		1994 LIB — 1994 CONS	
Economic	32% —	66%	30% —	67%
Social	28% —	71%	31% —	68%
Foreign	0% —	91%	25% —	71%

Key Votes of the 103d Congress

1. Clinton Deficit Plan	N	3. Brady Handgun Purchase	Y	5. Lmt. UN Cmnd. of Forces	Y
2. NAFTA	N	4. Strike Race/Death Pnlty.	Y	6. Cut Missile Funds	N

Key Votes of the 104th Congress

1. Congressional Compliance Y	6. Reform Crime Grant Y	11. Loser Pays Court Reform Y
2. Balanced Budget Amndmt. Y	7. National Security Act Y	12. Product Liability Reform Y
3. Bar Unfunded Mandates Y	8. Moratorium on Regs. Y	13. Welfare Reform Y
4. Pass Line Item Veto Y	9. Risk Assessment on Regs. Y	14. Term Limits Amndmt. Y
5. Relax Exclusionary Rule Y	10. Expnd. Priv. Prop. Rights Y	15. Tax Cuts Y

Election Results

1994 general	H. James Saxton (R)	115,750	(66%)	($356,108)
	James B. Smith (D)	54,441	(31%)	
	Others	4,137	(2%)	
1994 primary	H. James Saxton (R)	unopposed		
1992 general	H. James Saxton (R)	151,368	(59%)	($416,807)
	Timothy E. Ryan (D)	94,012	(37%)	($30,015)
	Eight Others	10,418	(4%)	

FOURTH DISTRICT

New Jersey, a state long thought to be split between a North Jersey that is an appanage of New York City and a South Jersey that has the distinctive accent of Philadelphia, is becoming a state with its own identity. In the 1980s, it bubbled over with pride at its growth and new civic institutions; in 1990, it raged with anger at Governor Jim Florio's tax increases. This shows a new unity: for the great medium of protest was the first New Jersey-oriented talk radio station, started in Trenton in 1989, and the symbolic event was the Hands Across New Jersey demonstration on a route approximating I-195, from the Jersey Shore west to the State House in Trenton overlooking the Delaware River. Trenton, an old manufacturing city ("Trenton Makes, The World Takes," the sign proclaims over the rooftops) where John Roebling of Brooklyn Bridge fame started making wire in 1848, and Walter Scott Lenox started making dishes in 1889, is now the anomalously gritty capital—the only state capital with no large downtown hotel—of a mostly white-collar state.

The 4th Congressional District covers approximately the same span as Hands Across New Jersey, from Trenton to the Jersey Shore, roughly following I-195 to the Shore communities of Manasquan and Point Pleasant and Mantoloking. It includes the old colonial town of Burlington on the Delaware River and the Great Adventure Safari and Entertainment Park in the Pine Barrens. This is one part of America where the population movement has been eastward, from the old neighborhoods of Trenton and its close-in suburbs to the new subdivisions of Ocean County and Wall Township. Trenton has long been a solidly Democratic town, but its suburbs are much less so, with the Jersey Shore parts of the district solidly Republican.

The congressman from the 4th District is Christopher Smith, a youthful-looking Republican with great seniority who has applied strong moral principles to practical politics with impressive results. Smith grew up in the Trenton area, worked in his family's sporting goods business, and was executive director of the New Jersey Right to Life Committee in the 1970s. In 1980 he ran for the House in a more Trenton-centered 4th District and beat 26-year incumbent Frank Thompson, a convicted Abscam defendant. A fluke, it seemed: but Smith proceeded to beat serious Democrats in the next five elections, with more than 60% each time. His motivation comes from religion: "Christ said it in Matthew 25: 'Whatsoever you do to the least of my brethren, you do likewise to me.' That was my motivating scripture through all of my years in Right to Life, and it continues to be," he said in 1992. He is concerned about children as well as victims of human rights violations. If his anti-abortion stance comes from his Catholicism, his concern for victims also is part of a lively Catholic tradition which does not count everything by its marketplace value.

Smith started with the abortion issue and has moved to help children born and unborn in other ways. He staunchly opposes federal funding of abortion and has worked to prevent abortions in military hospitals. He pushed for money for pregnant women and neonatal care in the developing world. He has strongly criticized China's human rights record, including forced sterilizations and abortions under its one-child-per-couple policy, as well as its slave labor and persecution of religious minorities. His $5,000 tax credit for adoption was passed by the House as part of the Contract With America.

Smith now chairs the International Operations and Human Rights Subcommittee, where he pursues his criticism of China as he called for trade sanctions against Romania in 1985 and criticized suppression of religious freedom in the Soviet bloc in the 1980s. He called Clinton's 1995 closing of the U.S. to Cuban refugees a "nightmare" scenario. He has been skeptical of funding United Nations operations, calling for cutbacks and criticizing what he considers immoral policies. In May 1995, he passed an amendment to the foreign aid bill barring funds to international organizations that support abortion. He also serves on Veterans' Affairs, where he favored recognition of Persian Gulf syndrome, wanted to protect VA hospitals in any national healthcare plan and has worked to build a VA outpatient clinic in Ocean County. He has also worked on other local projects—a wildlife refuge in Manasquan Cove, senior citizens' housing projects, the "weed and seed" anti-crime experiment in Trenton. Redistricting has made the 4th more Republican, and Smith has been reelected by handsome margins in the 1990s.

The People: Pop. 1990: 594,673; 16% rural; 17% age 65+; 81% White; 12% Black; 1% Asian; 2% Other; 5% Hispanic origin. Voting age pop.: 452,119; 11% Black; 4% Hispanic origin. Households: 58% married couple families; 26% married couple fams. w. children; 41% college educ.; median household income: $36,888; per capita income: $16,107; median gross rent: $583; median house value: $129,800.

1992 Presidential Vote

Bush (R)	109,907	(41%)
Clinton (D)	105,335	(39%)
Perot (I)	50,721	(19%)

1988 Presidential Vote

Bush (R)	140,170	(59%)
Dukakis (D)	97,182	(41%)

Rep. Christopher H. Smith (R)

Elected 1980; b. Mar. 4, 1953, Rahway; home, Washington Township; Trenton St. Col., B.S. 1975; Catholic; married (Marie).

Career: Sales exec., family-owned sporting goods business, 1975–80; Exec. Dir., NJ Right to Life, 1976–78.

DC Office: 2370 RHOB 20515, 202-225-3765; Fax: 202-225-7768.

District Offices: 1720 Greenwood, Trenton 08609, 609-890-2800; 427 High St., #1, Burlington City 08016, 609-386-5534; and 100 Lacey Rd., #38-A, Whiting 08759, 908-350-2300.

Committees: *International Relations* (7th of 23 R): International Operations and Human Rights (Chmn.); Western Hemisphere. *Veterans' Affairs* (2nd of 18 R): Hospitals and Health Care.

Group Ratings

	ADA	ACLU	COPE	CFA	LCV	CON	NSI	COC	ACU	NTLC	CHC
1994	30	24	56	40	53	59	100	83	70	82	100
1993	30	—	67	50	64	65	—	64	71	—	—

National Journal Ratings

	1993 LIB — 1993 CONS			1994 LIB — 1994 CONS		
Economic	38%	—	62%	21%	—	76%
Social	29%	—	69%	36%	—	64%
Foreign	24%	—	72%	38%	—	61%

Key Votes of the 103d Congress

1. Clinton Deficit Plan	N	3. Brady Handgun Purchase	Y	5. Lmt. UN Cmnd. of Forces	Y
2. NAFTA	N	4. Strike Race/Death Pnlty.	Y	6. Cut Missile Funds	N

Key Votes of the 104th Congress

1. Congressional Compliance	Y	6. Reform Crime Grant	Y	11. Loser Pays Court Reform	Y
2. Balanced Budget Amndmt.	Y	7. National Security Act	Y	12. Product Liability Reform	Y
3. Bar Unfunded Mandates	Y	8. Moratorium on Regs.	Y	13. Welfare Reform	Y
4. Pass Line Item Veto	Y	9. Risk Assessment on Regs.	Y	14. Term Limits Amndmt.	N
5. Relax Exclusionary Rule	Y	10. Expnd. Priv. Prop. Rights	Y	15. Tax Cuts	Y

Election Results

1994 general	Christopher H. Smith (R)	109,818	(68%)	($271,108)
	Ralph Walsh (D)	49,537	(31%)	($16,217)
	Others	2,412	(1%)	
1994 primary	Christopher H. Smith (R)	unopposed		
1992 general	Christopher H. Smith (R)	149,095	(62%)	($413,493)
	Brian M. Hughes (D)	84,514	(35%)	($164,038)
	Others	7,616	(3%)	

FIFTH DISTRICT

The northern edge of New Jersey was first settled three centuries ago by the Dutch, for whom this plateau of land behind the Hudson River Palisades seemed a natural part of Nieuw Amsterdam. The Dutch influence is still apparent in old steep-roofed farmhouses and in many of the place names—Bergen County, Cresskill, Closter. But overall, northernmost New Jersey has the well-settled look of so many northeastern suburbs, with touches both of affluence and small town hominess, criss-crossed at its edges with limited access highways lined with shopping centers—with five million square feet in Paramus, the home of Toys "R" Us. Not far away are Saddle River, with million-dollar houses on multi-acre lots, and Park Ridge, with office buildings and condominiums, the last two retirement homes of the late President Richard Nixon. This area may look like WASP suburbia on the surface, but in fact it is home to successful people of all ethnic groups, many descended from those who first saw the Statue of Liberty from the steerage deck and passed through the inspection queues at Ellis Island.

The 5th Congressional District consists of most of northern Bergen County, plus a swath of North Jersey stretching west to the hill-enclosed upper reaches of the Delaware, crossing one ridge of mountains after another, running south along I-78. Three-fifths of its population is clustered in Bergen; to the west, little subdivisions set amid the lakes of western Passaic County are filling up with young families; farther west are once rural, now fast-growing Sussex and Warren Counties. Politically, this area is solidly Republican, more so in the rapidly growing areas to the west than in the older areas near the George Washington Bridge.

Since 1980, the Congresswoman from this district has been Marge Roukema, a Republican whose Dutch name and Italian descent tell much of the district's ethnic history. She was a teacher who gave up her job to raise her children and was involved in community activities—founding a senior citizens' housing corporation and serving on a local school board—before becoming a political candidate. Like some other Republican congresswomen, she brings to politics maturity and experience in the actual workings of civic institutions. She tends to be market-oriented on economics but rather dovish on foreign policy: one of the key Republican moderates in this Congress.

Before Republicans won their majority, Roukema was most conspicuously active on student loan programs and family and medical leave. She was the lead Republican sponsor of the Family and Medical Leave Act which was vetoed by President Bush in 1990 and 1992 and then was passed and signed by President Clinton in February 1993. It requires employers of 50 or more people to give permanent workers 12 weeks unpaid leave per year for medical emergencies or the birth of a child. On student loans, Roukema in 1990 worked to make lenders and borrowers more accountable, and to crack down on for-profit trade schools that were generating many defaulted loans and in effect living off government guarantees. Here she was less successful. She got a change so that home equity is not counted in determining loan eligibility, which helps in North Jersey, but her crackdown on trade schools was rejected by Democrats, and her reform superseded by the direct student loan program boosted by New Jersey Democrat Rob Andrews and signed by President Clinton.

In the early Clinton years she was one of the Republicans who supported the assault weapon ban and the 1994 crime bill; there were so many good things in it, in her view, that she could not vote against it. In 1995, she joined Democrats in voting against restarting the Star Wars missile defense program—one of 24 Republicans who inflicted the first defeat of a Contract With America provision—and she worked to strip the anti-abortion language out of the $17 billion recission bill in March. Her biggest crusade recently has been tougher child support enforcement and she finally achieved success with House passage of the welfare-reform bill; she insists it must be part of any welfare reform and should require the identification of fathers, taking away driver's licenses and imposing interstate wage garnishment. As a senior majority-party member of two committees with broad swaths of domestic policy—Banking and Economic and Educational Opportunities—she is well-positioned to soften the harsher edges of the Republican plans to overhaul and downsize federal social and regulatory programs.

Roukema has been routinely reelected by wide margins and has swept primary opposition aside. The election of a veto-proof Republican legislative majority in 1991 guaranteed her a safe seat for the 1990s. She has been mentioned as a possible Senate candidate and, looking ahead to 1996 when Bill Bradley's Senate seat comes up, has said, "I'm keeping all my options open. It's no secret I would be interested in the Senate."

The People: Pop. 1990: 594,581; 19% rural; 13% age 65+; 91% White; 1% Black; 4% Asian; 3% Hispanic origin. Voting age pop.: 452,561; 1% Black; 3% Hispanic origin. Households: 69% married couple families; 33% married couple fams. w. children; 55% college educ.; median household income: $53,433; per capita income: $23,942; median gross rent: $717; median house value: $213,100.

1992 Presidential Vote		
Bush (R)	146,004	(49%)
Clinton (D)	99,733	(34%)
Perot (I)	48,661	(16%)

1988 Presidential Vote		
Bush (R)	178,419	(66%)
Dukakis (D)	91,227	(34%)

Rep. Marge Roukema (R)

Elected 1980; b. Sept. 19, 1929, W. Orange; home, Ridgewood; Montclair St. Col., B.A. 1951, Rutgers U.; Protestant; married (Richard).

Career: High schl. teacher, 1951–55; Ridgewood Board of Educ., 1970–73; Co-founder, Ridgewood Sr. Citizens Housing Corp., 1973.

DC Office: 2469 RHOB 20515, 202-225-4465; Fax: 202-225-9048.

District Offices: 1200 E. Ridgewood Ave., Ridgewood 07450, 201-447-3900; and 1500 Rte. 517, #105, Hackettstown 07840, 908-850-4747.

Committees: *Banking & Financial Services* (3rd of 27 R): Capital Markets, Securities and Government Sponsored Enterprises; Financial Institutions and Consumer Credit (Chmn.). *Economic & Educational Opportunities* (3rd of 24 R): Employer-Employee Relations; Postsecondary Education, Training and Life-Long Learning.

Group Ratings

	ADA	ACLU	COPE	CFA	LCV	CON	NSI	COC	ACU	NTLC	CHC
1994	35	41	17	50	67	92	40	100	50	63	71
1993	35	—	27	40	62	97	—	70	54	—	—

National Journal Ratings

	1993 LIB — 1993 CONS	1994 LIB — 1994 CONS
Economic	40% — 58%	24% — 75%
Social	42% — 58%	45% — 55%
Foreign	35% — 63%	47% — 52%

Key Votes of the 103d Congress

1. Clinton Deficit Plan	N	3. Brady Handgun Purchase	Y	5. Lmt. UN Cmnd. of Forces	Y
2. NAFTA	Y	4. Strike Race/Death Pnlty.	Y	6. Cut Missile Funds	Y

Key Votes of the 104th Congress

1. Congressional Compliance	Y	6. Reform Crime Grant	Y	11. Loser Pays Court Reform	Y
2. Balanced Budget Amndmt.	Y	7. National Security Act	Y	12. Product Liability Reform	Y
3. Bar Unfunded Mandates	Y	8. Moratorium on Regs.	Y	13. Welfare Reform	Y
4. Pass Line Item Veto	N	9. Risk Assessment on Regs.	Y	14. Term Limits Amndmt.	N
5. Relax Exclusionary Rule	Y	10. Expnd. Priv. Prop. Rights	N	15. Tax Cuts	Y

Election Results

1994 general	Marge Roukema (R)	139,964	(74%)	($497,345)
	Bill Auer (D)	41,275	(22%)	($160)
	Others	7,266	(4%)	
1994 primary	Marge Roukema (R)	20,394	(77%)	
	Lorraine Laneve (R)	6,138	(23%)	
1992 general	Marge Roukema (R)	196,198	(72%)	($504,596)
	Frank R. Lucas (D)	67,579	(25%)	($2,117)
	Others	10,594	(4%)	

SIXTH DISTRICT

For several generations, great transportation arteries have brought people out of the huge central cities of New York and Philadelphia and into the long-empty flatlands and hills of New Jersey— to vacation, to raise families and to work toward affluence and build communities. The railroads of the late 19th Century created the towns of the Jersey Shore, from 1874, when the first train from New York City reached Long Branch, which quickly became the summer home of presidents from Grant to Wilson (Garfield, convalescing after he was shot, died there in 1881) and of New York race horse owners and socialites. The great freight rail lines in the New York-Philadelphia corridor sparked big electrical and chemical industries here, building on the inventions of Thomas Edison, many produced in his Menlo Park laboratory, just off the rail lines. The same corridor was also the site of America's first cloverleaf intersection, at the junction of U.S. 1 and U.S. 9, and the intersection of two of America's great post-World War II highways, the New Jersey Turnpike and the Garden State Parkway. The Turnpike, now 12 lanes wide, roars past oil tank farms and petrochemical plants, major rail lines and Newark Airport and the oily waters of Raritan Bay; the Parkway links leafy affluent suburbs a dozen miles west of the Hudson with the Jersey Shore.

The 6th Congressional District of New Jersey ties together these great transportation nodes and the upward mobility and economic progress that have taken place around them. It includes the central core of Middlesex County—New Brunswick and Edison Township and the surrounding communities—a heavy industry area that also, since the time of Thomas Edison, has housed some of America's great research and development facilities. Here, immigrant factory workers in modest frame houses have raised their families in small towns that seem as far removed from Manhattan as any place in the Midwest. The 6th District includes a strip of territory overlooking Lower New York Bay, with spacious estates on highlands above little port towns. It takes in a strip of beach towns from Sandy Hook south to Sea Girt: Long Branch, with its seedy boardwalk amusements; Deal's grand mansions, windows always closed to save the air conditioning, now being bought up by Syrian Jews; Allenhurst, with its renovated clapboard Victorians; Asbury Park, once the vital center of this beachfront; Irish-American Spring Lake, with streets of neat houses; and Ocean Grove, founded in 1869 as a Methodist resort "free from the dissipation and follies of fashionable watering places," still for teetotalers who throng to its 10,000-seat 1894 Great Hall. The Shore is still a summer vacation area that attracts millions, but also has year-round communities, with their own upward-striving families, whose teenage energies have been expressed by the Shore's biggest celebrity, singer Bruce Springsteen.

The congressman from the 6th District is Frank Pallone, a Democrat who has had to meet severe political challenges to hold the seat. Pallone is the son of a disabled Long Branch policeman, an environmentalist since 1969, when as a college freshman in Vermont he worked for that state's first-in-the-nation bottle deposit law, and a professional politician who has run for office since law school. He was elected to the New Jersey Senate in 1983, where he did not always follow party lines and concentrated on environmental issues. When Congressman Jim Howard, chairman of the Transportation and Infrastructure Committee, died in March 1988, Pallone ran for the House. The district leaned Republican, but it was also angry about the untreated sludge, plastic containers and medical waste washing up on the beach in 1987 and 1988. This was ruining the Jersey Shore economy, and Pallone's bumper sticker, without mentioning his party affiliation, said "Stop Ocean Dumping." That, combined with his conservative stands on taxes and crime, helped him win 52% of the vote. In the House, Pallone got seats on the Transportation and Infrastructure and (now abolished) Merchant Marine Committees and continued to be a maverick, speaking out against the congressional pay raise and distancing himself from Governor Jim Florio's 1990 tax increase. Still, in 1990 he beat Asbury Park Councilman Paul Kapalko by only 49%–46%.

Redistricting nearly ended Pallone's career; he was the target of Republican redistricters, and

Democrats did not do much to help him. For 1992, the new 6th combined much of Pallone's Shore district in Monmouth County with much of the Middlesex County seat held by 71-year-old Democrat Bernard Dwyer. Dwyer announced his retirement the day the district lines were made public, but Pallone still won the primary with only 55% against a Middlesex opponent. In the general, against Republican legislator Joseph Kyrillos, Pallone depended on a huge money advantage and Bill Clinton's edge in the district to win 52%–45%.

After that marginal victory, Pallone took care to continue his moderate voting record. He supported the Clinton Administration on many budget votes but voted against the budget and tax package in August 1993; he was one of nine non-southern Democrats to vote for the Contract with America's tax cut provision in 1995. Pallone had supported single-payer health insurance in the 1992 campaign, but steered clear of the Clinton healthcare plan in 1994, helping to stymie its progress through John Dingell's Commerce Committee. In 1994 Pallone faced the youngest Republican congressional candidate, former Pentagon official Mike Herson, who refused PAC money and pledged to serve only three terms. But Pallone vastly outspent him, $672,000 to $252,000, by virtue of the $468,000 he raised from PACs. Pallone won 60%–38%, by far his best showing. Without the subcommittee showcases or the huge PAC money advantages he had when Democrats were in the majority, this could be a seriously contested district again.

The People: Pop. 1990: 594,650; 12% age 65+; 78% White; 11% Black; 5% Asian; 2% Other; 6% Hispanic origin. Voting age pop.: 465,588; 10% Black; 5% Hispanic origin. Households: 57% married couple families; 26% married couple fams. w. children; 47% college educ.; median household income: $42,309; per capita income: $18,135; median gross rent: $645; median house value: $159,500.

1992 Presidential Vote			1988 Presidential Vote		
Clinton (D)	110,821	(44%)	Bush (R)	132,480	(56%)
Bush (R)	98,397	(39%)	Dukakis (D)	105,023	(44%)
Perot (I)	41,867	(17%)			

Rep. Frank Pallone, Jr. (D)

Elected 1988; b. Oct. 30, 1951, Long Branch; home, Long Branch; Middlebury Col., B.A. 1973, Fletcher Schl. of Law and Diplomacy, M.A. 1974, Rutgers U., J.D. 1978; Catholic; married (Sarah).

Career: Asst. prof., Rutgers U., 1979–80; Practicing atty., 1981–83; Long Branch City Cncl., 1982–88; NJ Senate, 1983–88; Instructor, Monmouth Col., 1984–86.

DC Office: 420 CHOB 20515, 202-225-4671; Fax: 202-225-9665.

District Offices: IEI Airport Plz., #18, Hazlet 07703, 908-264-9104; 67/69 Church St., New Brunswick 08901, 908-249-8892; and 540 Broadway Ave., #119, Long Branch 07740, 201-571-1140.

Committees: *Commerce* (12th of 21 D): Energy and Power (RMM); Health and Environment.

Group Ratings

	ADA	ACLU	COPE	CFA	LCV	CON	NSI	COC	ACU	NTLC	CHC
1994	70	78	78	70	100	49	40	67	14	32	21
1993	90	—	92	80	93	8	—	36	13	—	—

National Journal Ratings

	1993 LIB	—	1993 CONS		1994 LIB	—	1994 CONS
Economic	52%	—	47%		50%	—	46%
Social	73%	—	23%		67%	—	32%
Foreign	74%	—	22%		57%	—	37%

Key Votes of the 103d Congress

1. Clinton Deficit Plan	N	3. Brady Handgun Purchase Y	5. Lmt. UN Cmnd. of Forces N
2. NAFTA	N	4. Strike Race/Death Pnlty. N	6. Cut Missile Funds Y

Key Votes of the 104th Congress

1. Congressional Compliance Y	6. Reform Crime Grant	N	11. Loser Pays Court Reform N
2. Balanced Budget Amndmt. Y	7. National Security Act	N	12. Product Liability Reform N
3. Bar Unfunded Mandates Y	8. Moratorium on Regs.	N	13. Welfare Reform N
4. Pass Line Item Veto Y	9. Risk Assessment on Regs. N		14. Term Limits Amndt. N
5. Relax Exclusionary Rule Y	10. Expnd. Priv. Prop. Rights N		15. Tax Cuts Y

Election Results

1994 general	Frank Pallone, Jr. (D).................	88,922	(60%)	($672,626)
	Mike Herson (R).....................	55,287	(38%)	($252,307)
	Others............................	3,122	(2%)	
1994 primary	Frank Pallone, Jr. (D).............	unopposed		
1992 general	Frank Pallone, Jr. (D)...............	118,266	(52%)	($929,541)
	Joseph M. Kyrillos (R)	100,949	(45%)	($403,153)
	Seven Others........................	6,878	(3%)	

SEVENTH DISTRICT

The transportation arteries beneath the curve of the First Watchung Mountain are one of New Jersey's historic lines of development. The rail lines of the late 19th Century opened up commuter suburbs; in the 1940s the four lanes of U.S. 22 created an automobile civilization; and finally Interstate 78, completed in the mid-1980s, put Newark only an hour's distance from the Pennsylvania line. This newest road stimulated the development of an Edge City called Bridgewater Commons, where a huge shopping mall and office developments that included the new headquarters of AT&T rose up amid the horse country around Far Hills and Bernardsville where the likes of Malcolm Forbes and Charles Engelhard owned huge estates.

The 7th Congressional District of New Jersey covers these several generations of suburban development. After the 1992 redistricting, the 7th no longer includes any of industrial Elizabeth, but begins just to the west, taking in affluent railroad commuter towns like Short Hills and Summit. It also includes more modest suburbs along U.S. 22 like Union and Westfield and the old city of Plainfield, with its large black community, plus the working class suburbs of Woodbridge and South Plainfield in Middlesex County. It then follows I-78 and the Watchung Mountains far into the countryside to the fields of Somerset County. Once this was all solidly Republican; now the closer-in suburbs are more mixed, with Democratic inner cities; the farther-out Edge City areas are, if anything, increasingly Republican. In the House, this area has been represented by Republicans for many years.

The congressman from the 7th is Bob Franks, who has been in politics most of his adult life. In 1979, three years after law school, he was elected to the New Jersey Assembly from a district including parts of all four counties now included in the 7th. He was state Republican chairman from 1988 to 1990 and one of the leaders of the revolt against Governor Jim Florio's 1990 tax increase. And he was a political ally of Matthew Rinaldo, the 7th District congressman for 20 years, who had a liberal voting record and a high-ranking spot on the Commerce Committee. When Rinaldo abruptly gave up his reelection effort in September 1992, after having been renominated three months before, to go into business, the local Republican organization chose Franks to take his place. But Franks had surprisingly serious competition from Democrat Leonard Sendelsky, a well-known local builder active in civic organizations. The two ran even in Middlesex, while Franks won 55% in the rest of the district, for a 53%–43% win.

In the House Franks has had a very conservative record on economics and has been more moderate on cultural and foreign issues. He serves on the Budget Committee as well as Transportation and Infrastructure, where he worked on Superfund and pipeline issues (there was a big pipeline explosion in Edison in March 1994). He served on Speaker Newt Gingrich's transition team after the 1994 election; it was then that he discovered and sought to dispose of a warehouse, leased by the House, full of old Agriculture Department yearbooks—evidence, he said, that the Democratic-run Congress was long overdue for a housecleaning. But Franks is not quite always party-loyal; he was one of the 24 Republicans who helped defeat the missile defense sections of the Contract With America in February 1995.

The People: Pop. 1990: 594,844; 4% rural; 14% age 65+; 80% White; 10% Black; 5% Asian; 1% Other; 5% Hispanic origin. Voting age pop.: 467,739; 9% Black; 4% Hispanic origin. Households: 64% married couple families; 27% married couple fams. w. children; 53% college educ.; median household income: $50,996; per capita income: $23,253; median gross rent: $699; median house value: $186,200.

1992 Presidential Vote			1988 Presidential Vote		
Bush (R)	125,592	(44%)	Bush (R)	160,286	(60%)
Clinton (D)	115,846	(41%)	Dukakis (D)	106,975	(40%)
Perot (I)	40,690	(14%)			

Rep. Bob Franks (R)

Elected 1992; b. Sept. 21, 1951, Hackensack; home, New Providence; DePauw U., B.A. 1973, S. Methodist U., J.D. 1976; Methodist; single.

Career: Political consultant, 1976–79; Med Data Inc., 1979–81; NJ Assembly, 1979–92; Co-owner, *County News*, 1982–84; NJ Repub. St. Chmn., 1988–89, 1990–92.

DC Office: 429 CHOB 20515, 202-225-5361; Fax: 202-225-9460; e-mail: franksnj@hr.house.gov.

District Offices: 2333 Morris Ave., #B-8, Union 07083, 908-686-5576; and 73 Main St., #4, Woodbridge 07095, 908-602-0075.

Committees: *Budget* (12th of 24 R). *Transportation & Infrastructure* (18th of 33 R): Railroads; Surface Transportation; Water Resources and Environment.

Group Ratings

	ADA	ACLU	COPE	CFA	LCV	CON	NSI	COC	ACU	NTLC	CHC
1994	25	35	0	40	59	86	80	91	62	92	79
1993	35	—	50	50	43	96	—	82	67	—	—

National Journal Ratings

	1993 LIB — 1993 CONS		1994 LIB — 1994 CONS	
Economic	30% —	68%	0% —	80%
Social	44% —	55%	38% —	61%
Foreign	33% —	65%	40% —	60%

Key Votes of the 103d Congress

1. Clinton Deficit Plan	N	3. Brady Handgun Purchase	Y	5. Lmt. UN Cmnd. of Forces	Y
2. NAFTA	Y	4. Strike Race/Death Pnlty.	Y	6. Cut Missile Funds	N

Key Votes of the 104th Congress

1. Congressional Compliance	Y	6. Reform Crime Grant	Y	11. Loser Pays Court Reform	Y
2. Balanced Budget Amndmt.	Y	7. National Security Act	Y	12. Product Liability Reform	Y
3. Bar Unfunded Mandates	Y	8. Moratorium on Regs.	Y	13. Welfare Reform	Y
4. Pass Line Item Veto	Y	9. Risk Assessment on Regs.	Y	14. Term Limits Amndmt.	Y
5. Relax Exclusionary Rule	Y	10. Expnd. Priv. Prop. Rights	N	15. Tax Cuts	Y

Election Results

1994 general	Bob Franks (R).....................	98,814	(60%)	($542,563)
	Karen Carroll (D)...................	64,231	(39%)	($15,667)
	Others.............................	2,812	(2%)	
1994 primary	Bob Franks (R)...................	unopposed		
1992 general	Bob Franks (R).....................	132,174	(53%)	($453,991)
	Leonard Sendelsky (D)..............	105,761	(43%)	($223,704)
	Others.............................	6,104	(3%)	

EIGHTH DISTRICT

Paterson, New Jersey, is one of few American cities that has turned out almost exactly as planned. The planner was Alexander Hamilton, who in the 1790s journeyed 20 miles from Manhattan into the interior of New Jersey to the Great Falls of the Passaic River. Watching the water surge down 72 feet—the highest falls along the East Coast—he predicted that an industrial city would rise on this site. He he formed the Society for Establishing Useful Manufactures, which opened a calico factory in 1794 and got Pierre L'Enfant, the designer of Washington, D.C., to design Paterson (named after then-Governor William Paterson). In 1836, Samuel Colt began manufacturing revolvers here; the first locomotive, the Sandusky, was built here in 1837, and a walkout of Paterson cottonworkers in 1828 was America's first factory strike. Paterson ultimately became America's "Silk City," employing 25,000 silk mill workers before the great strike of 1913 led by the radical Industrial Workers of the World, at a time when the city fathers were erecting imposing public buildings and the narrow streets were buzzing with rumors of anarchist plots. Paterson kept producing locomotives and, after the silk mills started closing down following another unsuccessful strike in 1924, became a cloth-dying center. Throughout, it attracted immigrants from England, Ireland and, after 1890, Italy and Poland. But now Paterson is a kind of misfit in time and place: still a manufacturing center at a time when manufacturing is no longer considered the nation's prime work, still an old fashioned central city, though it is surrounded by suburbs of New York and Newark and is an easy freeway ride from the George Washington Bridge.

The 8th Congressional District includes Paterson as its largest city, plus much suburban territory west and south of Paterson and north and west of Newark. It includes the mixed factory and middle-class towns south of Paterson on the Passaic River—Clifton, Passaic, Nutley, Belleville. On higher ground are Bloomfield and, up on a ridge with views of New York City, part of Montclair. An affluent part of the Oranges is also included, as well as Wayne Township west of Paterson. The political heritage of the 8th District is Democratic, partly from its radical past, but more from the allegiances of its immigrant groups. Recently, though, the central cities have been outvoted by increasingly Republican suburbs, and the district has been moving in a Republican direction.

The congressman from the 8th is Bill Martini, a Republican freshman elected in the party sweep of 1994. He has politics in the blood: his uncle Nicholas Martini was mayor of Passaic for many years. He became an assistant U.S. attorney at 27, and he was elected to the Clifton Council in 1990 and the Passaic County Board of Freeholders in 1992. He is also president of the Nicholas Martini Foundation, which awards grants to area charitable organizations. In 1994 he was well enough connected that when he decided to run against an obviously vulnerable incumbent, Democrat Herb Klein, he had no primary opposition. Klein, a well-off lawyer, had won the seat when Robert Roe, chairman of the Transportation and Infrastructure Committee, retired in 1992. Klein spent $580,000 of his own money and $1.2 million overall, beating Republican Joseph Bubba 47%–41%. Klein, an idealistic liberal and an Adlai Stevenson volunteer in the 1950s, had been an assemblyman for two terms, losing his seat in 1975 for supporting Governor Brendan Byrne's income tax. Martini attacked him for having supported the Clinton budget and tax proposals, and alleged that Klein was "allowed" to vote against it by party leaders only after it was clear that it had enough votes to pass. Klein campaigned against the Contract With America and said Martini had voted to raise local taxes. Klein spent over $1 million—this time, only $22,000 of it his own money; $392,000 was from PACs. Martini got only $80,000 from PACs, but spent $852,000 altogether. The result was a 50%–49% Martini victory.

Martini campaigned as a Republican with liberal positions on some cultural issues and some reservations about the Contract With America. He was dubious about defense spending increases and loser-pays in civil lawsuits, and he voted against the Contract's missile defense section when it was defeated. He has a seat on the Transportation and Infrastructure Committee—the new name for Roe's Public Works—but he switched from support to opposition to a $2.3 billion flood relief tunnel proposed for the Passaic River. This is a district that could easily be seriously contested again.

The People: Pop. 1990: 594,912; 15% age 65+; 67% White; 13% Black; 4% Asian; 8% Other; 17% Hispanic origin. Voting age pop.: 461,626; 12% Black; 15% Hispanic origin. Households: 55% married couple families; 24% married couple fams. w. children; 42% college educ.; median household income: $39,944; per capita income: $18,527; median gross rent: $595; median house value: $192,900.

1992 Presidential Vote

Clinton (D)	107,304	(45%)
Bush (R)	99,974	(42%)
Perot (I)	27,703	(12%)

1988 Presidential Vote

Bush (R)	123,358	(55%)
Dukakis (D)	101,357	(45%)

Rep. Bill Martini (R)

Elected 1994; b. Feb. 10, 1947, Passaic; home, Clifton; Villanova U., B.A. 1967, Rutgers U., J.D. 1971; Roman Catholic; married (Gloria).

Career: Practicing atty., 1971–present; Law Clerk, NJ Superior Ct., 1972–73; Hudson Cnty. Asst. Prosecutor, 1973–74; Asst. U.S. Atty. for NJ, 1974–77; Clifton City Cncl., 1990–94; Passaic Cnty. Freeholder, 1992–94.

DC Office: 1513 LHOB 20515, 202-225-5751; Fax: 202-225-3372.

District Offices: 200 Fed. Plz., #500, Paterson 07505, 201-523-5152.

Committees: *Government Reform & Oversight* (20th of 27 R): Human Resources and Intergovernmental Affairs. *Transportation & Infrastructure* (33rd of 33 R): Aviation; Surface Transportation; Water Resources and Environment.

Group Ratings and 103rd Congress Votes: Newly Elected

Key Votes of the 104th Congress

1. Congressional Compliance Y	6. Reform Crime Grant Y	11. Loser Pays Court Reform N
2. Balanced Budget Amndmt. Y	7. National Security Act Y	12. Product Liability Reform N
3. Bar Unfunded Mandates Y	8. Moratorium on Regs. Y	13. Welfare Reform Y
4. Pass Line Item Veto Y	9. Risk Assessment on Regs. Y	14. Term Limits Amndmt. Y
5. Relax Exclusionary Rule Y	10. Expnd. Priv. Prop. Rights N	15. Tax Cuts Y

Election Results

1994 general	Bill Martini (R)............................	70,494	(50%)	($851,781)
	Herb Klein (D)........................	68,661	(49%)	($1,116,614)
	Others..................................	2,213	(2%)	
1994 primary	Bill Martini (R)....................	unopposed		
1992 general	Herb Klein (D)......................	96,742	(47%)	($1,249,023)
	Joseph L. Bubba (R).................	84,674	(41%)	($432,784)
	Gloria J. Kolodziej (IFC)...............	16,170	(8%)	($3,850)
	Seven Others.........................	8,242	(4%)	

NINTH DISTRICT

The George Washington Bridge, one of several wondrous suspension bridges completed in America in the 1930s, strides across the Hudson, its west tower almost up against the green cliff of New Jersey's Palisades. It is one of the glories of modern engineering, enabling people and goods to be transported through the irregular terrain of metropolitan New York—tidal rivers and cliffs and broad expanses of swamp. The dramatic beauty of the Palisades contrasts with the ugly sprawl of the Hackensack River Valley and the Jersey Meadowlands. For a century or more, this giant swamp on both sides of the Hackensack River was the image of New Jersey for many New Yorkers, a landscape of giant gas station signs, oil tank farms, truck terminals and 12 lanes of New Jersey Turnpike—a smelly, ugly place that meant you were still not where you wanted to go, full of garbage and pig farms, briefly famous when Secaucus tavern owner Henry Krajewski ran for president in 1956 and commemorated in today's New Jersey Garbage Museum. But the Meadowlands were also the largest hunk of empty real estate near such a huge city center, and eventually they were developed. In the 1970s, the state built the Meadowlands Sports Complex—Giants Stadium (Giants and Jets now), the Meadowlands Racetrack, the Brendan Byrne Arena (Nets and Devils). Private development followed—hotels, warehouses, light industry, whole small cities.

The 9th Congressional District of New Jersey includes much of the Palisades and the Meadowlands. It runs from the high-rise towers of Fort Lee and Cliffside Park, where apartment houses brag about how close they are to New York City, to the west and north the leafy suburbs of Englewood and Teaneck, and southwest to the high land overlooking the Meadowlands and the Passaic River in old small towns like Rutherford, with Polish, German and Italian-Americans. Hackensack, an old industrial town that is the Bergen County seat, and much of Fair Lawn, a planned town with a large Jewish population, are also in the 9th. This area was growing in the 1950s and 1960s, as New Yorkers moved out of the City; it lost population in the 1970s and 1980s, as young people moved farther out and left empty nesters behind. Now there are new immigrants here: Englewood's schoolchildren are mostly black, Fort Lee's mostly Asian, many of Hackensack's Hispanic, though most of New Jersey's Cuban-American community is just to the south, around Union City in Hudson County.

This was Republican country in the New Deal years, an area of white-collar enclaves where people struggled to get by on their paychecks and resented the idea of their taxes going to the political machines of Hudson County and New York City. The towns near the bridge have become more Democratic as if they were extensions of the Upper West Side; old ethnic towns have trended Republican.

Bob Torricelli, congressman from the 9th, is an articulate and ambitious Democrat who started his political career while in his 20s. At 24 he was an aide to Governor Brendan Byrne; three years later he was working for Walter Mondale. He helped manage the Carter-Mondale victory over Edward Kennedy in Illinois and argued party rules with Kennedy's Harold Ickes (now Clinton's deputy chief of staff) in 1980. In 1982, at 31, he returned home to New Jersey, raised lots of money and beat an incumbent Republican congressman. In the House, he took politically beneficial committee assignments: International Relations (many of his ethnic constituents had particular interest in Israel, Greece, Korea, the Philippines and Cuba) and Science (North Jersey is one of the biggest high-tech areas in the country).

Torricelli combines high partisan intensity with a rather moderate voting record. He was one of the most outspoken defenders of Speaker Jim Wright in 1989 and one of the most vocal supporters of the Gulf war resolution in 1991. He became publicly critical of Speaker Tom Foley, as he had of other former mentors and allies, like Walter Mondale in 1984 and Governor Jim Florio in 1990. Perhaps because of his tendency to turn on former friends—and possibly because he's also seen as something of a grandstander—Torricelli is not especially well-liked by colleagues and has twice been denied major Democratic Party posts. In 1990, he lost out to Vic Fazio for the Democratic Congressional Campaign Committee chairmanship, and in early 1995, he was passed over for Senator Christopher Dodd for Democratic National Committee chairman—although he was willing to give up his House seat to take the job. In the latter case, there also was speculation that Vice President Al Gore thought Torricelli was too close to potential rival Dick Gephardt.

From 1991–95, Torricelli chaired the Western Hemisphere Subcommittee, and probably his most important national legislation is the 1992 Cuban Democracy Act that tightened trade restrictions on Cuba; it was opposed by many Democrats but publicly embraced by a campaigning Bill Clinton. If Torricelli's allies on that issue were mostly on the right, they were mostly on the left on Haiti, in which he favored sanctions and intervention. On other foreign policy issues, Torricelli seeks better treatment of Taiwan, to reward its moves toward democracy and to put pressure on China; he challenged the labeling of the Iranian Mujahedin as terrorist; he strongly opposed Clinton's 1995 agreement with Fidel Castro to restrict admission of Cuban refugees. He works on local issues as well, including removing thorium waste in Maywood, funding an environmental program in the Meadowlands and removing driftwood from New York Harbor. His amendment to the 1994 education bill authorized grants for longer school days and school years.

Torricelli was named to the Intelligence Committee in 1993. In the spring of 1995, he made national headlines when he announced that a Guatemalan military officer on the CIA payroll had been linked to the killings of an American innkeeper and a guerrilla leader in Guatemala. Colleagues in both parties were furious, saying that Torricelli had violated his oath not to disclose classified material; Speaker Newt Gingrich said he should be thrown off the Intelligence Committee. But Torricelli said he had gotten the information from outside sources—and in any case, he said, "no oath imposed by the leadership can ask a member of Congress to conceal criminal activity." But New Jersey Democrats see it as a no-lose issue for Torricelli—"if he ruffled the feathers of the Beltway crowd, all the better," one Democratic consultant said. The matter was referred to the Ethics Committee, which showed no hurry to resolve it. Torricelli's interest in the issue stemmed in part from his relationship with Bianca Jagger, a human rights activist and Nicaraguan native who's best known as the ex-wife of the *Rolling Stones*' Mick Jagger; she started dating Torricelli in 1993.

Torricelli, who has been reelected easily for years, has long been interested in statewide office. If Bill Bradley does not seek reelection in 1996, he's likely to run for the seat; or he might very well run against Governor Christie Whitman in 1997. He is keeping up with recent issues—he proposed his own welfare reform bill in March 1995, with time limits, a ban on aid to teens outside their homes and tougher child support enforcement—and he ranks number three among House members in campaign cash on hand, with $1.29 million.

The People: Pop. 1990: 594,790; 16% age 65+; 76% White; 6% Black; 7% Asian; 3% Other; 11% Hispanic origin. Voting age pop.: 481,031; 6% Black; 10% Hispanic origin. Households: 54% married couple families; 22% married couple fams. w. children; 44% college educ.; median household income: $40,816; per capita income: $20,012; median gross rent: $640; median house value: $194,500.

1992 Presidential Vote			1988 Presidential Vote		
Clinton (D)	122,676	(47%)	Bush (R)	134,923	(53%)
Bush (R)	102,578	(40%)	Dukakis (D)	117,314	(47%)
Perot (I)	31,534	(12%)			

Rep. Robert G. Torricelli (D)

Elected 1982; b. Aug. 26, 1951, Paterson; home, Englewood; Rutgers U., B.A. 1974, J.D. 1977, Harvard JFK Schl. of Govt., M.P.A. 1980; United Methodist; married (Susan).

Career: Asst., NJ Gov. Brendan Byrne, 1975–77; Cnsl., Vice Pres. Walter Mondale, 1978–81; Practicing atty., 1981–82.

DC Office: 1026 RHOB 20515, 202-225-5061; Fax: 202-225-0843.

District Offices: 25 Main St., Court Plz., Hackensack 07601, 201-646-1111.

Committees: *International Relations* (4th of 19 D): International Economic Policy and Trade; Western Hemisphere (RMM). *Intelligence (Permanent Select)* (4th of 7 D): Technical and Tactical Intelligence.

Group Ratings

	ADA	ACLU	COPE	CFA	LCV	CON	NSI	COC	ACU	NTLC	CHC
1994	65	82	78	80	81	51	33	58	6	16	7
1993	85	—	100	90	77	11	—	20	9	—	—

National Journal Ratings

	1993 LIB — 1993 CONS			1994 LIB — 1994 CONS		
Economic	75%	—	22%	58%	—	41%
Social	67%	—	33%	64%	—	35%
Foreign	47%	—	53%	56%	—	43%

Key Votes of the 103d Congress

1. Clinton Deficit Plan	Y	3. Brady Handgun Purchase	Y	5. Lmt. UN Cmnd. of Forces	*
2. NAFTA	N	4. Strike Race/Death Pnlty.	N	6. Cut Missile Funds	N

Key Votes of the 104th Congress

1. Congressional Compliance	Y	6. Reform Crime Grant	*	11. Loser Pays Court Reform	N
2. Balanced Budget Amndmt.	Y	7. National Security Act	N	12. Product Liability Reform	N
3. Bar Unfunded Mandates	Y	8. Moratorium on Regs.	N	13. Welfare Reform	N
4. Pass Line Item Veto	N	9. Risk Assessment on Regs.	N	14. Term Limits Amndmt.	N
5. Relax Exclusionary Rule	N	10. Expnd. Priv. Prop. Rights	N	15. Tax Cuts	Y

Election Results

1994 general	Robert G. Torricelli (D)	99,984	(63%)	($744,648)
	Peter J. Russo (R)	57,651	(36%)	($21,811)
	Others	2,253	(1%)	
1994 primary	Robert G. Torricelli (D)	15,564	(91%)	
	Matt Guice (D)	1,516	(9%)	
1992 general	Robert G. Torricelli (D)	139,188	(58%)	($1,001,343)
	Patrick J. Roma (R)	88,179	(37%)	($172,946)
	Six Others	11,337	(5%)	

TENTH DISTRICT

Newark is the hollow core of New Jersey, the city to which main transportation arteries once led and whose corporate headquarters buildings were the tallest in the state. In 1930, 442,000 people lived here, one of every nine in the state; in 1990, 275,000 did, one of every 28. Downtown Newark still has the Prudential and Public Service headquarters, there are still factories in the Ironbound district, the area around Newark airport has some industrial development, and the New Jersey Performing Arts Center is going up. But big corporation leaders and small businessmen alike have not put new jobs here since the 1967 riot. The reason is obvious: high crime. Some neighborhoods of Newark have retained their vitality, but very large parts are dominated by criminals and deserted by most law-abiding residents who can get out. In 1994 the state took over the public schools, abysmally run while spending more per pupil than almost any other district in the country.

Most of Newark—the Central, South and West Wards—plus Irvington, most of the Oranges and part of Montclair to the west, and much of Elizabeth, Rahway and Linden to the south, make up the 10th Congressional District. As drawn in 1992, the 10th is 60% black, and overwhelmingly Democratic; its boundary lines wiggle around to include blacks in Jersey City, Montclair and Elizabeth and leave Hispanics in the next-door 13th District.

The congressman from the 10th is Donald Payne. He was a teacher, worked for Prudential, served on the Board of Freeholders in the 1970s and was vice president of Urban Data Systems for 13 years. In 1980 and 1986, he ran against Congressman Peter Rodino, chairman of the House Judiciary Committee when it voted to impeach President Richard Nixon; he lost, even though the district had black majorities. But when Rodino retired in 1988, Payne got 73% in the Democratic primary and easily won the general, and has been returned routinely ever since.

Payne, the first black member of Congress from New Jersey, is a member of two major committees—International Relations and Economic and Educational Opportunities. He has had one of the most liberal voting records in the House. In 1993 he played a role in passing family and medical leave legislation and the motor voter bill; he was a strong supporter of "opportunity to learn" standards in the 1994 education bill—actually, requirements for state spending on equipment, teachers' salaries and other inputs. He has also expressed concern about heightened youth violence and supported tougher sentences for convicted drug pushers. He was elected Congressional Black Caucus chairman in December 1994, just as Republicans were defunding the legislative caucuses and just as the CBC's senior Democrats were having to relinquish their chairmanships to members of the new Republican majority. He was chosen by 23–15 over the more fiery Alcee Hastings of Florida, who had been impeached by the House for soliciting a bribe while a federal judge. Payne characterized himself as "a strong negotiator, a person that can compromise," and he had an early meeting with Speaker Gingrich to seek common ground. But within weeks he was vehemently opposing the Republicans' bill to cap increases in spending on food programs and convert them to block grants. He also opposed moves to end affirmative action because there are still "a great deal of barriers for minority people to move up the ladder to the top." The Black Caucus, he said, "will change as it has to so that it will not become obsolete."

The People: Pop. 1990: 593,876; 12% age 65+; 26% White; 60% Black; 2% Asian; 5% Other; 12% Hispanic origin. Voting age pop.: 444,082; 57% Black; 11% Hispanic origin. Households: 39% married couple families; 18% married couple fams. w. children; 34% college educ.; median household income: $28,849; per capita income: $12,833; median gross rent: $520; median house value: $136,100.

1992 Presidential Vote			1988 Presidential Vote		
Clinton (D)	126,415	(70%)	Dukakis (D)	128297	(72%)
Bush (R)	36,299	(20%)	Bush (R)	49043	(28%)
Perot (I)	14,887	(8%)			

Rep. Donald M. Payne (D)

Elected 1988; b. July 16, 1934, Newark; home, Newark; Seton Hall, B.A. 1957; Baptist; widowed.

Career: Elem. & High Schl. teacher, 1957–64; Exec., Prudential Insurance Co., 1964–72; Pres., YMCAs of the U.S., 1970; Essex Cnty. Board of Freeholders, 1972–78, Dir. 1977–78; Vice Pres., Urban Data Systems Inc., 1975–88; Newark Municipal Cncl., 1982–89.

DC Office: 417 CHOB 20515, 202-225-3436; Fax: 202-225-4160.

District Offices: 50 Walnut St., #1016, Newark 07102, 201-645-3213; and 333 N. Broad St., Elizabeth 07208, 908-629-0222.

Committees: *Economic & Educational Opportunities* (8th of 19 D): Early Childhood, Youth and Families; Employer-Employee Relations. *International Relations* (11th of 19 D): Africa; International Operations and Human Rights.

Group Ratings

	ADA	ACLU	COPE	CFA	LCV	CON	NSI	COC	ACU	NTLC	CHC
1994	95	91	100	90	100	20	0	18	10	11	0
1993	100	—	100	90	93	32	—	10	0	—	—

National Journal Ratings

	1993 LIB — 1993 CONS		1994 LIB — 1994 CONS	
Economic	88% —	0%	83% —	0%
Social	87% —	0%	86% —	13%
Foreign	93% —	0%	85% —	0%

Key Votes of the 103d Congress

1. Clinton Deficit Plan	Y	3. Brady Handgun Purchase	Y	5. Lmt. UN Cmnd. of Forces	N
2. NAFTA	N	4. Strike Race/Death Pnlty.	N	6. Cut Missile Funds	Y

Key Votes of the 104th Congress

1. Congressional Compliance	Y	6. Reform Crime Grant	N	11. Loser Pays Court Reform	N
2. Balanced Budget Amndmt.	N	7. National Security Act	N	12. Product Liability Reform	N
3. Bar Unfunded Mandates	N	8. Moratorium on Regs.	N	13. Welfare Reform	N
4. Pass Line Item Veto	N	9. Risk Assessment on Regs.	N	14. Term Limits Amndmt.	N
5. Relax Exclusionary Rule	N	10. Expnd. Priv. Prop. Rights	N	15. Tax Cuts	N

Election Results

1994 general	Donald M. Payne (D)	74,622	(76%)	($309,623)
	Jim Ford (R)	21,524	(22%)	($18,180)
	Others	2,222	(2%)	
1994 primary	Donald M. Payne (D)	unopposed		
1992 general	Donald M. Payne (D)	117,287	(78%)	($285,455)
	Alfred D. Palermo (R)	30,160	(20%)	($26,276)
	Others	2,185	(2%)	

ELEVENTH DISTRICT

New Jersey's Morris County, west of the Watchung Mountain ridges, was one of the first settled parts of the interior United States west of the Hudson. It has long been a place of comparative affluence, the home of skilled craftsmen in the Revolutionary War, with plenty of water mills and iron forges by the 19th Century. But only in the late 20th Century has it come into its own, as one of the most affluent quarters of the United States. And it is not just a collection of country estates with huddled small towns for the servants to live in, but a well-rounded community with all the appurtenances of urbanity except the high crime and poverty rates that city-lovers in places like Manhattan congratulate themselves for tolerating. The very rich have lived here for some time, connected to Manhattan by commuter rail lines, but in the 1970s and 1980s more rushed out the newly completed I-80 and I-280 or the ring road I-287. Today, more than 20 *Fortune* 500 companies are headquartered in Morris County, and the area has generated thousands of small businesses, filling new office parks and starting up in home offices, with business often conducted over car phones.

The 11th Congressional District includes all of Morris County plus similar adjacent areas. It is one of the wealthiest districts in the country: number one in median household income in 1990, at $57,219, with the highest median housing value in New Jersey, $214,600—exceeded only by four districts in the New York area, 25 in California and one in Hawaii. It is family territory, with relatively few singles; not a strongly culturally conservative area, but much more so than Manhattan. Politically, it is heavily Republican, the most Republican district in New Jersey, and one of the most in the Northeast.

The congressman from the 11th District is Rodney Frelinghuysen, a Republican and member of one of New Jersey's most durable political families: four Frelinghuysens served as Senator from New Jersey, starting in 1793 and as recently as 1923; Frederick Frelinghuysen was Chester Arthur's Secretary of State; Peter Frelinghuysen, the congressman's father, was elected to the House in 1952 and served until his retirement in 1974. After college, Rodney Frelinghuysen served in the Army in Vietnam and in 1972 was appointed an aide by then-Morris County Freeholder (and later Congressman) Dean Gallo; he served as a freeholder himself and was elected to the Assembly in 1983. There he supported one tax increase by Republican Governor Thomas Kean, but opposed Democratic Governor Jim Florio's 1990 tax increase and, as chairman of the Appropriations Committee, worked to control spending and roll back taxes after Republicans won legislative majorities in 1991 and Governor Christie Whitman was elected in 1993.

Frelinghuysen ran for Congress in the 12th District in 1990, when its boundaries were different, and lost the primary to Dick Zimmer. Then in August 1994, after the primary, Gallo—who had been elected to the House in 1984 and worked hard on many local issues—announced that he was retiring for health reasons; he died two days before the election. Frelinghuysen was chosen the Republican nominee at a September party convention and was elected with 71% of the vote. He showed his insider skills by winning a seat on the Appropriations Committee, where Gallo had also served. He generally favors lower spending and taxes, but he has been interested in veterans' programs, the disabled and preserving open space.

The People: Pop. 1990: 594,526; 13% rural; 11% age 65+; 89% White; 3% Black; 4% Asian; 1% Other; 4% Hispanic origin. Voting age pop.: 458,318; 3% Black; 4% Hispanic origin. Households: 67% married couple families; 31% married couple fams. w. children; 60% college educ.; median household income: $57,219; per capita income: $25,454; median gross rent: $730; median house value: $214,600.

1992 Presidential Vote			1988 Presidential Vote		
Bush (R)	153,731	(51%)	Bush (R)	182,282	(68%)
Clinton (D)	97,697	(33%)	Dukakis (D)	85,514	(32%)
Perot (I)	46,407	(16%)			

Rep. Rodney P. Frelinghuysen (R)

Elected 1994; b. Apr. 29, 1946, New York City; home, Morristown; Hobart Col., B.A. 1969; Episcopalian; married (Virginia).

Career: Army, 1970–71 (Vietnam); Morris Cnty. Bd. of Chosen Freeholders, 1974–83; NJ Assembly, 1983–94.

DC Office: 514 CHOB 20515, 202-225-5034; Fax: 202-225-3186.

District Offices: 1 Morris St., Morristown 07960, 201-984-0711; 18 W. Blackwell St., Dover 07801, 201-328-7413; and 3 Fairfield Ave., W. Caldwell 07006, 201-228-9262.

Committees: *Appropriations* (27th of 32 R): District of Columbia; Energy and Water Development; VA, HUD, and Independent Agencies.

Group Ratings and 103rd Congress Votes: Newly Elected

Key Votes of the 104th Congress

1. Congressional Compliance	Y	6. Reform Crime Grant	Y	11. Loser Pays Court Reform	Y
2. Balanced Budget Amndmt.	Y	7. National Security Act	Y	12. Product Liability Reform	Y
3. Bar Unfunded Mandates	Y	8. Moratorium on Regs.	Y	13. Welfare Reform	Y
4. Pass Line Item Veto	Y	9. Risk Assessment on Regs.	Y	14. Term Limits Amndmt.	Y
5. Relax Exclusionary Rule	Y	10. Expnd. Priv. Prop. Rights	N	15. Tax Cuts	Y

Election Results

1994 general	Rodney P. Frelinghuysen (R)	127,868	(71%)	($243,923)
	Frank Herbert (D)	50,211	(28%)	($43,614)
	Others	1,501	(1%)	
1994 special	Rodney P. Frelinghuysen (R)	nom. by convention		
1994 primary	Dean A. Gallo (R)	26,492	(65%)	
	Joe Pennacchio (R)	10,917	(27%)	
	Barry Fitzpatrick (R)	2,107	(5%)	
	Others	1,067	(3%)	
1992 general	Dean A. Gallo (R)	188,165	(70%)	($618,448)
	Ona Spiridellis (D)	68,871	(26%)	($132,520)
	Others	11,400	(4%)	

TWELFTH DISTRICT

It was once the main East Coast arterial highway, carrying the nation's highest volume of truck traffic. Today it is crowded with cars taking high-salaried workers and clerical help to one of the East Coast's thickest concentrations of office buildings in one of the bigger Edge Cities spawned in the 1980s. This is U.S. 1, which once just connected the industrial cities of Trenton and New Brunswick on its way from Philadelphia to New York; now it is better thought of as connecting the university towns around Princeton and Rutgers, and is a locus of telecommunications and pharmaceutical research. This had been empty bucolic country, looked out on by Scott Fitzgerald's undergraduates from their gothic Princeton towers; now it is filled with postmodern office campuses and hotels and restaurants clamoring for attention.

The 12th Congressional District of New Jersey extends several dozen miles on either side of this stretch of U.S. 1. To the west, it takes in the rolling country of Hunterdon County, around the old county seat town of Flemington, once the site of the Lindbergh kidnapping trial, now an outlet store center with many young families, affluent if not elite, modern but seeking traditional values. On the other side of U.S. 1, the 12th takes in modest-income suburbs like East Brunswick in Middlesex County and much of Monmouth County, almost to the beach resorts of the Jersey Shore. Some of these communities are long-settled, others are spanking new. What most of the district has in common politically is a Republican preference. Princeton, like so many university towns, is now politically liberal, and southern Middlesex County has vestiges of working-class Democratic sentiment. But Hunterdon and Monmouth in the east are solidly Republican.

The congressman from the 12th District is Dick Zimmer, a Republican raised in a garden apartment—"the New Jersey equivalent of a log cabin," he said—who worked his way through Yale. He was head of New Jersey Common Cause in the 1970s and was elected to the legislature in 1981; there he was a stickler for ethics, an environmentalist (with a law to preserve farmland from development) and a fierce opponent of higher government spending, opposing not only Governor Jim Florio's tax program in 1990 but the last budget of Republican Governor Thomas Kean in the 1989. In 1990, an off-year in state politics, the 12th District seat opened when incumbent Jim Courter retired after losing the 1989 governor's race. The two Republicans who vied with Zimmer had more celebrity: Rodney Frelinghuysen, scion of a New Jersey family that has been in politics since colonial times, and whose father represented much of the area for 22 years in the House; and former New York Giants football player Phil McConkey, who ran an anti-tax, anti-abortion campaign. But Zimmer's fiscal austerity (Frelinghuysen voted for Kean's budget), his pro-choice stand on abortion and environmental record evidently helped him to a 38% win, to 29% for Frelinghuysen and 31% for McConkey. The general election was the most expensive 1990 House race in the nation, with $2.9 million in spending because Democrat Marguerite Chandler spent liberally of her own money. But Zimmer's abortion rights stand deprived her of one major talking point, and she carried only Princeton.

Zimmer's record in the House has been fiercely market-oriented on economics and considerably more moderate on cultural and foreign issues. He has not only opposed Democratic projects, but also leads House opposition to the space station ("in its current scaled-down configuration, Space Station Freedom could better be called Space Station Lite—one-third of the mission for nearly four times the price") and new nuclear submarines. In 1994 he and Dick Armey persuaded the House to phase out the $190 million wool and mohair subsidy over three years. He got a committee to approve risk assessment guidelines for the Environmental Protection Agency in 1994—the germ of the Contract With America provision that passed the House in 1995. With his Common Cause roots, he objects to administration log-rolling to pass major programs, sponsoring a NAFTA Pork Repeal Act in 1993 and organizing a Health Care Pork Watch in 1994. In 1994 he got House proceedings put on the Internet and pushed for more debate to be open to the public and laws to be limited to a single subject. He sponsored the "Megan's law" provision in the 1994 crime bill, requiring community notification of the presence of sexually violent predators, plus a ban on a federal program providing bail to prisoners in Newark's Essex County. He has sponsored a No Frills Prisons Act, prohibiting weightlifting, coffee brewing and TV in prison cells. Zimmer has also worked on local environmental laws, trying to protect 19th-Century canals and ban oil and gas drilling off the Jersey Shore.

Zimmer was a critical vote on the 1994 crime bill—a forecast of his role in the Republican Congress. The fact that a moderate on cultural issues would stick with Newt Gingrich's Republican Conference on the crime bill rule showed the power of party cohesion, and how Democratic excess—opposing Megan's law because of concerns for the civil liberties of convicted sex predators—could promote it as well. He is the only Republican invited regularly to both moderates' and conservatives' lunch groups, and his vote is obviously critical to many measures. A new member of Ways and Means, he is in the center of even more issues and was a loyalist in the early legislative fights.

The Democrats in charge of redistricting in 1991 planned to eliminate his district, but Republicans won two-thirds veto-proof control of the legislature that fall and drew up a new 12th District that Zimmer could win easily. He gave some thought to running for the Senate in 1994 and has raised large sums: for his 1994 House campaign he raised over $1 million, an impressive $868,000 from individuals, and spent only $612,000 and so had $489,000 cash on hand at year's end. With his attractive combination of economic conservatism and cultural moderation, he moved in early 1995 to run for Bill Bradley's Senate seat in 1996, whether or not the incumbent seeks another term. Zimmer will be well-funded and should appeal to a broad cross-section of Republicans; in contrast to Chuck Haytaian against Frank Lautenberg in 1994, Zimmer's good-government, pro-choice on abortion also should allow him to reach across the political spectrum. In short, he should be a serious candidate.

The People: Pop. 1990: 594,577; 34% rural; 11% age 65+; 88% White; 5% Black; 4% Asian; 1% Other; 3% Hispanic origin. Voting age pop.: 455,866; 5% Black; 2% Hispanic origin. Households: 67% married couple families; 32% married couple fams. w. children; 62% college educ.; median household income: $54,630; per capita income: $24,615; median gross rent: $696; median house value: $205,200.

1992 Presidential Vote

Bush (R)	130,651	(43%)
Clinton (D)	121,447	(40%)
Perot (I)	50,357	(17%)

1988 Presidential Vote

Bush (R)	157,907	(61%)
Dukakis (D)	102,805	(39%)

Rep. Dick Zimmer (R)

Elected 1990; b. Aug. 16, 1944, Newark; home, Delaware Township; Yale, B.A. 1966, LL.B. 1969; Jewish; married (Marfy).

Career: Practicing atty., 1969–90; Chmn., NJ Common Cause, 1974–77; NJ Assembly, 1981–87; NJ Senate 1987–91; Chmn., NJ Repub. Platform Cmtee., 1989.

DC Office: 228 CHOB 202-225-5801; Fax: 202-225-9181; e-mail: dzimmer@hr.house.gov.

District Offices: 133 Franklin Corner Rd., Lawrenceville 08648, 609-895-1559; and 36 W. Main St., #201, Freehold 07728, 908-303-9020.

Committees: *Ways & Means* (13th of 21 R): Oversight; Trade.

Group Ratings

	ADA	ACLU	COPE	CFA	LCV	CON	NSI	COC	ACU	NTLC	CHC
1994	25	41	0	20	78	97	60	92	57	82	86
1993	40	—	33	50	86	98	—	73	71	—	—

National Journal Ratings

	1993 LIB — 1993 CONS		1994 LIB — 1994 CONS	
Economic	23% —	75%	0% —	80%
Social	41% —	58%	29% —	70%
Foreign	35% —	65%	30% —	67%

Key Votes of the 103d Congress

1. Clinton Deficit Plan	N	3. Brady Handgun Purchase	Y	5. Lmt. UN Cmnd. of Forces	Y
2. NAFTA	Y	4. Strike Race/Death Pnlty.	Y	6. Cut Missile Funds	Y

Key Votes of the 104th Congress

1. Congressional Compliance	Y	6. Reform Crime Grant	Y	11. Loser Pays Court Reform	Y
2. Balanced Budget Amndmt.	Y	7. National Security Act	Y	12. Product Liability Reform	Y
3. Bar Unfunded Mandates	Y	8. Moratorium on Regs.	Y	13. Welfare Reform	Y
4. Pass Line Item Veto	Y	9. Risk Assessment on Regs.	Y	14. Term Limits Amndmt.	Y
5. Relax Exclusionary Rule	Y	10. Expnd. Priv. Prop. Rights	N	15. Tax Cuts	Y

Election Results

1994 general	Dick Zimmer (R)	125,939	(68%)	($612,178)
	Joseph D. Youssouf (D)	55,977	(30%)	($49,395)
	Others	2,364	(1%)	
1994 primary	Dick Zimmer (R)	unopposed		
1992 general	Dick Zimmer (R)	174,216	(64%)	($911,638)
	Frank Abate (D)	83,035	(30%)	($62,937)
	Carl J. Mayer (I)	11,051	(4%)	($105,182)
	Others	4,455	(2%)	

THIRTEENTH DISTRICT

The Statue of Liberty, standing in New York Harbor since 1886, has been the great symbol of America welcoming immigrants to its shores. Actually, the statue is on the New Jersey side of the Harbor, and the shore on which many immigrants first settle—in the old days when they got off the boat and today when they are more likely to disembark at Kennedy or Newark Airports—is in New Jersey. The towns sitting on the granite and gneiss ridge of Hudson County, New Jersey, overlooking the Harbor, have in particular been immigrant territory. Today, as a century ago, they are the most densely populated part of urban America except for Manhattan, and with one of the largest percentages of immigrants. This was not always so during the years in between. After immigration was shut off by the laws of 1921 and 1924, many children and grandchildren of the Irish and Italian immigrants stayed in Hudson County, living in the same neighborhoods, working on the same docks or the same big factories—Maxwell House and Palmolive were here—and voting the dictates of the same political machine.

Hudson County was the setting of one of America's classic political machines, undisciplined by any metropolitan elite. From 1917 to 1949, the boss of Hudson County was Frank ("I am the law") Hague; his machine chose governors and U.S. Senators, prosecutors and judges, and had influence in the White House of Franklin D. Roosevelt. He collected high taxes from the industries clustered here—who then passed them on to consumers everywhere—and in return gave them an orderly city, free of most crime and vice, and a work force insulated against racketeers and militant unions. Hague's successor, John V. Kenny, was boss from 1949 to

1971—continuous power for 54 years, a record beaten only in Albany.

But Hudson County began changing again, in ways little noticed by either the local machine or Manhattan sophisticates. New immigrants were coming in—refugees from Castro's Cuba, other Latinos and Asians after the 1965 immigration law changed the rules. Union City became predominantly Cuban, Jersey City neighborhoods became heavily Latino. Upscale young singles looking for lower rents moved into Hoboken's five-story Victorian apartments that sparkle with light off the Hudson, and within a quick commute through the PATH tubes to Wall Street or Greenwich Village. The Jersey City waterfront is the scene of huge new condominium developments—Port Liberte, opposite the Statue of Liberty; Newport, with thousands of housing units and hundreds of thousands of square feet of office space; Liberty Place on the site of the old Colgate-Palmolive factory. This vibrant private sector contrasted with a somnolent public sector so incompetent and expensive that it gave an opening to Jersey City's Republican mayor, Bret Schundler, a former Wall Streeter who first won in 1992 after the incumbent went to jail and who was reelected in 1993 with 68%. Schundler cut taxes and vastly improved services, privatizing ingeniously; his major proposal is a school voucher program to shake up the public school system, one of the nation's most expensive yet so dreadful it was taken over by the state in 1989.

The 13th Congressional District of New Jersey includes most of Hudson County plus most of the immigrant entry ports along the water, from the Hackensack River and Newark Bay to Arthur Kill and Raritan Bay. It was designed to be an "Hispanic influence" district; 38% of its residents in 1990 were Hispanic and 14% black. With most of Jersey City and all of Union City and West New York and Weehawken, it includes 105,000 people in the old Ironbound area and North Ward of Newark, half of them Hispanic, and takes in the industrial city waterfront areas of Elizabeth, Linden, Carteret and Perth Amboy. It is still a Democratic district in congressional elections, despite the Cubans and despite Schundler.

The congressman from the 13th is Democrat Robert Menendez, a Cuban-American who grew up in Union City, America's most densely populated city (58,000 people in 1.3 square miles), and got into politics early: he was elected to the school board in 1974, at 20. He worked for Union City Mayor William Musto in the 1970s, but quit and testified against him in a corruption trial, and ran against him and lost in 1982. Then he was elected mayor in 1986 and to the legislature in 1987, serving in both places until he was elected to Congress. As mayor of Union City, he developed a drug education program bringing police into the schools, a child care program, and a recycling effort; in Trenton, he authored the anti-hate crime Ethnic Intimidation Act of 1990 and the Green Acres Bond Act of 1991. When the new district lines were created and incumbent Congressman Frank Guarini retired, Menendez won his primary 68%–32% and the general 64%–31%.

In the House, Menendez serves on International Relations. He opposes President Clinton's doing business with Fidel Castro, supports Bob Torricelli's tough Cuban embargo policies and has called for a policy of U.S. humanitarian aid to a post-Castro Cuba and help in downsizing its military. He sharply opposed NAFTA and the Mexico bailout. He has hailed the recognition of the I.R.A.'s controversial Gerry Adams by the U.S. government and was sent as a committee observer to the Sinn Fein Ard Fheis annual conference in Dublin. Overall, his voting record is liberal, but not totally so. He has been mentioned as a possible candidate against Governor Christie Whitman in 1997.

The People: Pop. 1990: 594,875; 12% age 65+; 42% White; 14% Black; 5% Asian; 14% Other; 41% Hispanic origin. Voting age pop.: 453,979; 12% Black; 38% Hispanic origin. Households: 45% married couple families; 21% married couple fams. w. children; 31% college educ.; median household income: $28,721; per capita income: $13,028; median gross rent: $505; median house value: $142,700.

1992 Presidential Vote

Clinton (D)	94,651	(53%)
Bush (R)	64,358	(36%)
Perot (I)	14,981	(8%)

1988 Presidential Vote

Dukakis (D)	95,237	(54%)
Bush (R)	80,681	(46%)

Rep. Robert Menendez (D)

Elected 1992; b. Jan. 1, 1954, New York, NY; home, Union City; St. Peter's Col., B.A. 1976, Rutgers Law Schl., J.D. 1979; Catholic; married (Jane Jacobsen-Menendez)

Career: Union City Board of Educ., 1974–82; Union City Mayor, 1986–92; NJ Assembly, 1987–91; NJ Senate 1991–92.

DC Office: 1730 LHOB 20515, 202-225-7919; Fax: 202-226-0792.

District Offices: 911 Bergen Ave., Jersey City 07306, 201-222-2828; and 654 Ave. C, Bayonne 07002, 201-823-2900.

Committees: *International Relations* (13th of 19 D): Western Hemisphere. *Transportation & Infrastructure* (20th of 27 D): Aviation; Water Resources and Environment.

Group Ratings

	ADA	ACLU	COPE	CFA	LCV	CON	NSI	COC	ACU	NTLC	CHC
1994	90	70	89	100	100	23	22	50	5	15	7
1993	90	—	100	90	86	32	—	18	9	—	—

National Journal Ratings

	1993 LIB — 1993 CONS		1994 LIB — 1994 CONS	
Economic	67% —	32%	67% —	29%
Social	68% —	29%	72% —	27%
Foreign	63% —	34%	72% —	25%

Key Votes of the 103d Congress

1. Clinton Deficit Plan	Y	3. Brady Handgun Purchase	Y	5. Lmt. UN Cmnd. of Forces	N
2. NAFTA	N	4. Strike Race/Death Pnlty.	N	6. Cut Missile Funds	N

Key Votes of the 104th Congress

1. Congressional Compliance	Y	6. Reform Crime Grant	N	11. Loser Pays Court Reform	N
2. Balanced Budget Amndmt.	N	7. National Security Act	N	12. Product Liability Reform	N
3. Bar Unfunded Mandates	Y	8. Moratorium on Regs.	N	13. Welfare Reform	N
4. Pass Line Item Veto	Y	9. Risk Assessment on Regs.	N	14. Term Limits Amndmt.	N
5. Relax Exclusionary Rule	N	10. Expnd. Priv. Prop. Rights	N	15. Tax Cuts	N

Election Results

1994 general	Robert Menendez (D)	67,688	(71%)	($488,448)
	Fernando A. Alonso (R)	24,071	(25%)	($6,159)
	Others	3,708	(4%)	
1994 primary	Robert Menendez (D)	unopposed		
1992 general	Robert Menendez (D)	93,670	(64%)	($645,640)
	Fred J. Theemling, Jr. (R)	44,529	(31%)	($7,499)
	Others	7,515	(5%)	

NEW MEXICO

America's oldest settlements and its newest technologies can be found, in unusual and even surrealistic form, in New Mexico. For the oldest permanently inhabited city in the United States is not Plymouth, Massachusetts, or Jamestown, Virginia, or even St. Augustine, Florida; it is probably Acoma, New Mexico. Probably, because Acoma, inhabited by the Anasazi, "an agricultural, settled and architecturally sophisticated people," said historian Roger Kennedy in *Rediscovering America*, had perhaps 1,000 years of unrecorded history before Spanish conquistadors came upon it in 1540. Some 450 years later, much of what makes New Mexico distinctive derives from the people found here by the first European explorers—something true of no other state but Hawaii. While the Pilgrims built flimsy wood houses, the Indians in New Mexico were living in extensive dwellings hundreds of years old, made with the adobe that is still the characteristic building material here.

Other state cultures are generally based on what early white settlers brought to the land; natives, except in Hawaii and Alaska, have mostly disappeared. Not in New Mexico. The English-speaking culture here is superimposed, at times rather lightly, on a society whose written history dates back to the Spanish settlement of Santa Fe in 1609, and to centuries long past when the Pueblo Indians set up stable agricultural societies on the sandy, rocky lands of northern New Mexico, using small pebbles as mulch to retain scarce moisture. Pueblo culture is still celebrated in the Indian pottery that commands premium prices in Santa Fe and in the annual Gathering of Nations pow-wow in Albuquerque which attracts 30,000 Indians. Today, a very substantial minority of New Mexicans are descendants of these Indians or the Spanish, or both. New Mexico had the highest percentage of Hispanics (38%) in the U.S. after the 1990 Census. Nearly one-third of the people in this state speak Spanish in everyday life, and only a few are recent migrants from Mexico. The Hispanic roots go very deep, as witnessed by the recent discovery of Hebrew symbols left on Christian gravestones by the *conversos*, Jews who hid their religion after it was outlawed by the Spanish in 1492; there are families here who have secretly maintained Jewish practices for centuries.

New Mexico is the northernmost salient of the great Indian-Spanish civilizations of the Cordillera, which extend along the mountain chain through Mexico and Central America to South America, as far away as Chile and Argentina. Yet New Mexico also is a civilization built on modern technology. It was to a remote mesa called Los Alamos that General Leslie Groves brought his Manhattan Project scientists during World War II to build a secret town and develop a secret weapon that would in two explosions end World War II and change the course of history. Los Alamos remains a government high-tech laboratory, and New Mexico has others as well—the White Sands Missile Range near Alamogordo, where the first atomic bomb was detonated, and the Sandia Laboratories near Albuquerque, run by Lockheed-Martin for the government, a non-nuclear high-tech weapons research facility. And if New Mexico was in on the takeoff of nuclear power, it has also come in for part of the landing. Near Carlsbad, New Mexico, is the site of the federal Waste Isolation Pilot Plant (WIPP), where the Energy Department wants to conduct a seven-year test of radioactive waste storage; the Energy Department wanted to use 1% of WIPP's capacity, while some of the state's congressional delegation held out for .5% and ultimately prevailed in 1992 legislation.

These two kinds of New Mexicos, very old and very young, intermingle with others of intermediate age in different proportions in this land of majestically vast vistas. The Hispanic-Indian culture predominates north and west of Albuquerque, with picturesque old towns and some still-functioning pueblos. "Little Texas," in the south and east, has small cities, plenty of oil wells, vast cattle ranches and desolate military bases and resembles, economically and

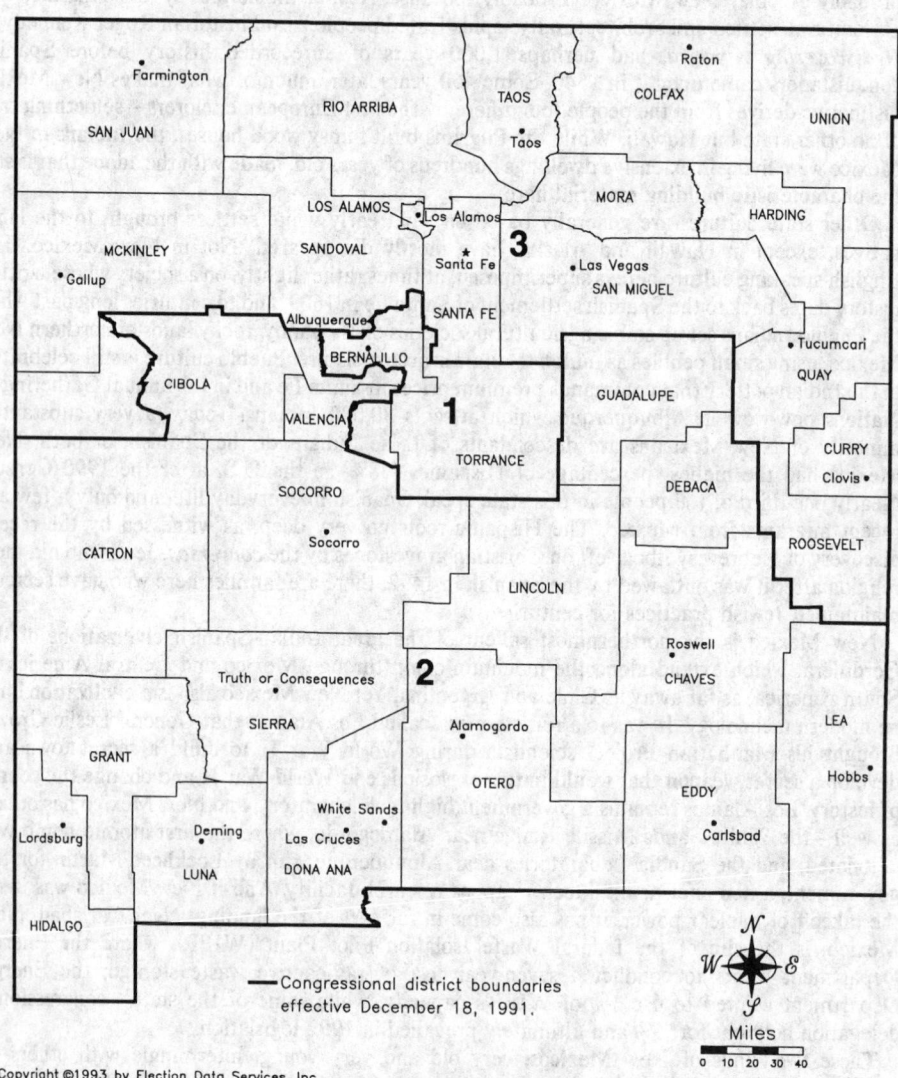

Congressional district boundaries
effective December 18, 1991.

Miles
0 10 20 30 40

Copyright ©1993 by Election Data Services, Inc.

culturally, the adjacent west Texas High Plains. Here, as everywhere in New Mexico, government is a prime employer (accounting for 27% of jobs, one of the highest figures in the country) and often the moving force in the local economy. In the middle is Albuquerque which, with the arrival of airconditioning, grew from a small desert town of 35,000 in 1940 into a Sun Belt metropolis of 600,000 today. Albuquerque has a large Hispanic minority, as do many fast-growing U.S. cities. Its economy is based heavily on high tech, especially nuclear power; but it has relatively low income and education levels—the downscale Sun Belt. Each of these three areas has about one-third of the state's population, and their impressionistic boundaries are followed pretty closely by the boundaries of New Mexico's three congressional districts.

For many years, New Mexico politics was a somnolent business. Local bosses—first Republican, later Democratic—controlled the large Hispanic vote. Elections in many counties featured irregularities that would have made a Chicago ward committeeman blush. New Mexico also had for years another feature of boss-controlled politics, the balanced ticket: one Spanish and one Anglo senator, with the offices of governor and lieutenant governor split as well. But for all its distinctiveness, in national politics New Mexico was a bellwether, voting for every winning presidential candidate from 1912, when it became a state, until 1976, when it backed Gerald Ford. In 1988 it voted 52%–47% for George Bush, close to the national average; in 1992, 46% for Bill Clinton, 37% for Bush and 16% for Ross Perot, 3% more for Clinton and less for Perot than the nation. Democrats usually have a solid base in the Hispanic areas, but there is little harsh ethnic polarization. New Mexico's relatively downscale newcomers—low-skill laborers and retirees who can afford a trailer but not a Scottsdale condominium—are culturally conservative, and if anything lean a bit Republican. Of all the border states, New Mexico has the least immigration from Mexico and Latin America; most Hispanic growth is from high birth and low death rates. But the Cordillera civilization not so far away is never entirely out of the minds of New Mexicans.

New Mexico never had much of an environmental movement nor a sagebrush rebellion—until the mid-1990s. New Mexico now has a Green Party, based in Santa Fe, which ran former Lieutenant Governor Roberto Mondragon for governor in 1994; he got 10% of the vote and may have cost incumbent Democrat Bruce King the election. And New Mexico also has its landowners rebellion. Catron County, west of the Rio Grande, passed ordinances making it illegal for the U.S. Forest Service to regulate grazing, and federal employees have been threatened by local ranchers.

Governor. The governor of New Mexico is a political newcomer, Gary Johnson, elected in 1994 over a grizzled veteran of state politics, Bruce King. King is a rancher from Santa Fe County, bilingual, with a cowboy walk and a proclivity towards malapropisms; he was first elected governor in 1970, elected again in 1978, elected a third time in 1990. He ran again in 1994, the first time governors were allowed a second consecutive term here. But despite the state's economic growth and his increased education spending, he was pressed in the Democratic primary and won with only 39% over his own lieutenant governor Casey Luna with 36% and former Clinton Administration Interior Department official Jim Baca with 25%. Meanwhile, Johnson was winning the Republican primary with 34% to 33% for Dick Cheney (no, not the former Defense Secretary), 19% for John Dendahl and 13% for long ago (1966–70) Governor David Cargo.

Johnson's great strength was in Albuquerque, where he moved when he was in junior high. In 1974, at 21, while still a student at the University of New Mexico, he started a construction business, and built a door-to-door solicitation business into Big J Enterprises, one of the largest construction companies in the state, with 600 employees. He served on civic boards, sponsored children's athletic events and was himself a competitor: he won the 1993 Bump, Bike and Bolt competition in Taos and completed a Triathlon in Hawaii in October 1993. He ran on vague slogans—"people before politics," "citizen service" and promised to hold the line on government growth, to give teachers more power to set priorities and to roll back a six cent gas tax increase. Johnson was widely criticized in April 1995 for meeting with representatives of a New Mexico militia just nine days after the Oklahoma City bombing, characterizing them as "responsible, reasonable, lawful," and saying, "they're here to help in time of emergency.

Senators. Pete Domenici is in his third decade in the Senate and is chairman of the Senate Budget Committee in a second decade. Certainly he is the giant political figure in New Mexico. Domenici grew up in an Italian-American family in Albuquerque, practiced law, was elected to the city commission in 1966; he ran for governor in 1970, and lost to Bruce King, his only loss. In 1972, when a Senate seat opened up in a Republican year, he ran and won, beating a Democrat named Jack Daniels. In his last two Senate races, Domenici set New Mexico records, winning 72% of the vote in 1984 and 73% in 1990.

Domenici's great work in the Senate is on the budget. He chaired the Budget Committee from 1981 to 1987, was ranking Republican on it from 1987 to 1995, now is chairman again: no other Republican need apply. In 1990 he turned down the ranking minority position on Energy and Natural Resources, an important committee for New Mexico, in order to keep Budget. At least until 1995, Domenici has found more frustration than satisfaction in his work. He is genuinely appalled at the federal budget deficits of the 1980s and 1990s, and ready to recommend the bitterest of medicine—entitlement cuts, tax increases—to reduce them; but for years he found others unwilling to follow his lead. In 1981, he supported the Reagan budget and tax cuts, but was dismayed by the resulting deficits and in 1982 backed Bob Dole's TEFRA tax increase. In May 1985, Dole and Domenici got Republican senators to pass a freeze on Social Security cost of living adjustments, wheeling in a post-surgery Pete Wilson to establish a tie vote, broken by then-Vice President Bush; but a few months later Senate Republicans were left politically exposed when President Reagan dropped the COLA freeze in a compromise with House Speaker Tip O'Neill. Then Domenici backed the Gramm-Rudman Act, whose mechanisms, along with Reagan Budget Director Jim Miller's fixation on holding down spending, did in fact cut the deficit by about half, at least in the short term. Always wary of tax cuts and often welcoming tax increases, Domenici advised President Bush to drop the capital gains tax cut and supported the 1990 budget summit agreement, which contained many of his long sought goals.

Domenici opposed the Clinton budget and tax package in 1993, and called Clinton defense decreases overlarge. But he supported the administration budget in 1994. He hailed the drop in the deficit, but pointed out that most of it was due to sales of savings and loan assets and unanticipated drops in medical costs. His own alternative, proposed with Sam Nunn in a Center for Strategic and International Studies report, was for a 10-year plan to balance the budget, with $476 billion in tax increases and $1.4 trillion in spending cuts, plus a consumption-based tax to replace the income tax. In mid-1994 he presented his own healthcare reform, but by August he introduced the Rowland-Bilirakis alternative and worked to defeat the Clinton plan.

After Republicans won majorities in 1994, he was leery of the House's tax cuts and wary of House plans to change budget scoring. But he was ready and willing to propose deep cuts in spending increases and hurried to rebuild the firewalls between defense and domestic spending. He favored a line-item veto that would allow a simple majority of one house to override the president, but was overridden by most Republicans who favored the House-passed two-thirds override. The conservative tide has moved Domenici some distance, but he and Finance Chairman Bob Packwood have been restraining forces on Newt Gingrich's House Republicans. The test of wills between Domenici and House Budget Chairman John Kasich will be one of the keys to which way Republicans head in the 104th Congress.

Domenici has brought his intensity to other issues. He fears "the social fabric has broken down" and called on Hollywood and business to take responsibility for the morality of their products; his bill for character education grants became law in October 1994. He tends to New Mexico affairs: he threatened a filibuster against a proposed 85% increase in grazing fees in October 1993; he passed a technology transfer act, to allow the national laboratories to share their knowledge; he helped found the Joint Economic Development Initiative for New Mexico. As the new chairman of the Energy and Water Development subcommittee of Appropriations, he is well-positioned to protect local interests. In 1993, with outgoing Democrat David Boren, he sponsored the Joint

Committee on the Organization of Congress, but the panel gained no traction in the notoriously reform-averse Senate and Domenici was left to propose a package of 32 reforms in January 1995. He co-sponsored the bill to discourage "strike suits" against corporations in 1995. Domenici comes up for reelection in 1996, and it would be astonishing if he did not win by a large margin.

New Mexico's junior senator, Jeff Bingaman, is a Democrat with good political lineage: his father was a professor at Western New Mexico University in Silver City, and his uncle was campaign manager for longtime Senator Clinton Anderson. A year out of law school, Bingaman was counsel to the state constitutional convention; a few years later, he went into law practice in Santa Fe with former Governor Jack Campbell. Bingaman's wife, Anne, started a highly successful law practice of her own that helped finance his first campaigns; she is now U.S. assistant attorney general for antitrust. In a small state, bright young people are not nearly as numerous as they are in New York or Washington or Los Angeles, and Jeff Bingaman rose fast. He ran for attorney general in 1978 and won; in 1982, he ran against Senator Harrison Schmitt, the former astronaut, also from Silver City, and won with 54%, partly because it was a recession year, but also because of Schmitt's misleading and negative ads.

Bingaman became a member of the Armed Services Committee and a protege of former Chairman Sam Nunn, who created a subcommittee tailored to his interests, now called Acquisition and Technology. This gave Bingaman lots of say over New Mexico's Los Alamos and Sandia labs but that influence has become more problematic with the Republican majority; he also has worked on superconductivity research and chartering the Technology Reinvestment Program and the Sematech consortium. He sponsored a $1.6 billion defense conversion package which passed in 1992 and $100 million in seed money for regional partnerships of small technology firms. He wants to make government research more accessible to the private sector and wants to expedite the process for government labs to enter into partnerships with private companies to develop new technologies. He worked on a procurement reform which passed the Senate in 1994. He works to promote computers and interactive television in schools and supported the Goals 2000 national standards in education.

Bingaman also serves on the Energy Committee, where he has worked to protect the archaeological sites of the Mimbres Indians and the Jemez Mountains. He joined other western senators in opposing higher federal grazing fees but pledged to work with Interior Secretary Bruce Babbitt on revising the 1872 Mining Act. On the Labor Committee in 1994, he produced a compromise to reduce healthcare benefit packages automatically if costs go up; the larger bill went nowhere, however, and he lost his committee seat in 1995. He also worked on the 1994 crime bill.

Bingaman was targeted by Republicans as one of the most vulnerable Democrats in 1994 and Colin McMillan—rancher and oilman, former Assistant Defense Secretary, sponsor of the "Big Mac" 1981 tax cut in the legislature—ran an aggressive campaign. McMillan spent over $1 million of his own money and charged that Bingaman had supported the Clinton budget and tax package and had voted three times for grazing fee increases. Bingaman ads boasted of his work on defense conversion, national education standards and education technology. The race tightened up in October, and Bingaman won 54%–46%, a decisive margin but a notable drop from 1988. He carried Albuquerque with wide margins among Hispanics and Indians, but lost Little Texas. Bingaman made his first headlines in 1995 when he was one of six Democrats who switched from yes a year earlier to no on the balanced budget amendment, and it lost by one vote.

Presidential politics. New Mexico, the most Democratic of the Rocky Mountain states and seriously contested in 1988, went for Bill Clinton in 1992. Its bellwether status—it has voted for the winner in every presidential election since statehood in 1912, except for 1976—seems more accidental than anything else; it's hard to think of a state more atypical of the nation.

Congressional districting. The boundaries of New Mexico's three congressional districts were slightly redesigned for 1992, with the apparent aim of making the Republican-held 1st and 2d both marginally more Democratic.

The People: Est. Pop. 1994: 1,654,000; Pop. 1990: 1,515,069, up 9.1% 1990–1994. 0.6% of U.S. total, 36th largest; 27% rural. Median age: 31.3 years. 10.8% 65 years and over. 75.6% White, 38.2% Hispanic origin, 8.9% American Indian, 2.0% Black, 12.6% Other. Households: 56.0% married couple families; 29% married couple fams. w. children; 46% college educ.; median household income: $24,087; per capita income: $11,246; 67.4% owner occupied housing; median house value: $70,100; median monthly rent: $312. 6.8% Unemployment. 1994 Voting age pop.:1,167,000. 1994 Turnout: 453,645; 39% of VAP. Registered voters (1994): 724,858; 415,324 D (57%), 247,214 R (34%), 62,320 unaffiliated and minor parties (9%).

Political Lineup: Governor, Gary E. Johnson (R); Lt. Gov., Walter Bradley (R); Secy. of State, Stephanie Gonzales (D); Atty. Gen., Thomas Udall (D); Treasurer, Michael A. Montoya (D); Auditor, Robert E. Vigil (D). State Senate, 42 (27 D and 15 R); State House of Representatives, 70 (46 D and 24 R). Senators, Pete V. Domenici (R) and Jeff Bingaman (D). Representatives, 3 (2 R and 1 D).

1992 Presidential Vote

Clinton (D)	261,617	(46%)
Bush (R)	212,824	(37%)
Perot (I)	91,895	(16%)

1988 Presidential Vote

Bush (R)	270,341	(52%)
Dukakis (D)	244,497	(47%)

1992 Democratic Presidential Primary

Clinton	95,933	(53%)
Brown	30,705	(17%)
Tsongas	11,315	(6%)
Other	8,221	(5%)
Uncommitted	35,269	(19%)

1992 Republican Presidential Primary

Bush	55,522	(64%)
Buchanan	7,871	(9%)
Uncommitted	23,574	(27%)

GOVERNOR

Gov. Gary E. Johnson (R)

Elected 1994, term expires Jan. 1999; b. Jan. 1, 1953, Minot, ND; home, Santa Fe; U. of NM, B.A. 1975; Lutheran; married (Dee).

Career: Pres. & CEO, Big J Enterprises, Inc., 1976–present.

Office: State Capitol, #417, Santa Fe 87503, 505-827-3000; Fax: 505-827-3026.

Election Results

1994 gen.	Gary E. Johnson (R)	232,945	(50%)
	Bruce King (D)	186,686	(40%)
	Roberto Mondragon (Green)	47,990	(10%)
1994 prim.	Gary E. Johnson (R)	32,091	(34%)
	Dick Cheney (R)	30,811	(33%)
	John Dendahl (R)	18,007	(19%)
	David F. Cargo (R)	12,105	(13%)
1990 gen.	Bruce King (D)	224,564	(55%)
	Frank M. Bond (R)	185,692	(45%)

SENATORS

Sen. Pete V. Domenici (R)

Elected 1972, seat up 1996; b. May 7, 1932, Albuquerque; home, Albuquerque; U. of NM, B.S. 1954, Denver U., LL.B. 1958; Catholic; married (Nancy).

Career: Practicing atty., 1958–72; Albuquerque City Comm., 1966–70, Mayor Ex-Officio, 1967–70.

DC Office: 328 HSOB 20510, 202-224-6621.

State Offices: 625 Silver SW, #120, Albuquerque 87102, 505-766-3481; New Postal Bldg., 120 S. Federal Pl., Santa Fe 87501, 505-988-6511; Sun Belt Plz., 1065 S. Main St., Bldg. #D-13, Las Cruces 88005, 505-526-5475; and Fed. Bldg. #140, Roswell 88201, 505-623-6170.

Committees: *Appropriations* (5th of 15 R): Commerce, Justice, State and Judiciary; Defense; Energy and Water Development (Chmn.); Interior; Transportation. *Budget* (Chmn. of 12 R). *Energy & Natural Resources* (3rd of 10 R): Energy Research and Development (Chmn.); Forests and Public Land Management; Oversight and Investigations. *Indian Affairs* (4th of 9 R).

Group Ratings

	ADA	ACLU	COPE	CFA	LCV	CON	NSI	COC	ACU	NTLC	CHC
1994	25	32	13	25	15	59	90	77	84	80	79
1993	20	—	9	30	6	57	—	100	80	—	—

National Journal Ratings

	1993 LIB — 1993 CONS	1994 LIB — 1994 CONS
Economic	30% — 67%	29% — 68%
Social	16% — 81%	25% — 74%
Foreign	29% — 70%	33% — 66%

Key Votes of the 103d Congress

1. Clinton Deficit Plan	N	3. Brady Handgun Purchase N	5. Lmt. UN Cmnd. of Forces Y
2. NAFTA	Y	4. Strike Race/Death Pnlty. Y	6. Cut Missile Funds N

Key Votes of the 104th Congress

1. Congressional Compliance Y	3. Balanced Budget Amndt. Y	5. Product Liability Reform Y
2. Bar Unfunded Mandates Y	4. Pass Line Item Veto Y	6. FY96 Budget Y

Election Results

1990 general	Pete V. Domenici (R)	296,712	(73%)	($2,250,086)
	Tom R. Benavides (D)	110,033	(27%)	($38,510)
1990 primary	Pete V. Domenici (R)	unopposed		
1984 general	Pete V. Domenici (R)	361,371	(72%)	($2,658,008)
	Judith A. Pratt (D)	141,253	(28%)	($301,661)

Sen. Jeff Bingaman (D)

Elected 1982, seat up 2000; b. Oct. 3, 1943, El Paso, TX; home, Santa Fe; Harvard, B.A. 1965, Stanford, LL.B. 1968; United Methodist; married (Anne).

Career: Army Reserves, 1968–74; NM Asst. Atty. Gen., 1969; Practicing atty., 1970–78; NM Atty. Gen., 1979–82.

DC Office: 703 HSOB 20510, 202-224-5521; Fax: 202-224-2852; e-mail: senator_bingaman@bingaman.senate.gov.

State Offices: 119 E. Marcy St., #101, Santa Fe 87501, 505-988-6647; 625 Wilver Ave., SW, #130, Albuquerque 87102, 505-766-3636; 505 S. Main St., Las Cruces 88001, 505-523-6561; and 114 E. 4th St., #103, Roswell 88201, 505-622-7113.

Committees: *Armed Services* (5th of 10 D): Acquisition and Technology (RMM); Readiness; Strategic Forces. *Energy & Natural Resources* (5th of 8 D): Energy Production and Regulation (RMM); Forests and Public Land Management. *Joint Economic Committee* (7th of 10 Sen.)

Group Ratings

	ADA	ACLU	COPE	CFA	LCV	CON	NSI	COC	ACU	NTLC	CHC
1994	60	63	75	67	69	44	60	35	16	24	21
1993	70	—	73	90	56	37	—	36	20	—	—

National Journal Ratings

	1993 LIB — 1993 CONS	1994 LIB — 1994 CONS
Economic	68% — 30%	61% — 35%
Social	52% — 46%	53% — 40%
Foreign	53% — 39%	51% — 46%

Key Votes of the 103d Congress

1. Clinton Deficit Plan	Y	3. Brady Handgun Purchase	Y	5. Lmt. UN Cmnd. of Forces	N
2. NAFTA	Y	4. Strike Race/Death Pnlty.	Y	6. Cut Missile Funds	N

Key Votes of the 104th Congress

1. Congressional Compliance	Y	3. Balanced Budget Amndt.	N	5. Product Liability Reform	N
2. Bar Unfunded Mandates	Y	4. Pass Line Item Veto	N	6. FY96 Budget	N

Election Results

1994 general	Jeff Bingaman (D).................	249,989	(54%)	($3,652,899)
	Colin R. McMillan (R)...............	213,025	(46%)	($1,537,563)
1994 primary	Jeff Bingaman (D).................	unopposed		
1988 general	Jeff Bingaman (D).................	321,983	(63%)	($2,808,659)
	Bill Valentine (R)	186,579	(37%)	($659,624)

FIRST DISTRICT

The future and the past of New Mexico come together in its single metropolis, Albuquerque. Its Spanish and Indian past is memorialized in its name (for a 17th Century Spanish grandee) and age (founded in 1706) and its quaint Old Town; its high-tech future is symbolized by Sandia Laboratories and Kirtland Air Force Base, the government installations that are the city's biggest employers. When rocket scientist Robert Goddard moved here in 1930 and nuclear scientist J. Robert Oppenheimer reconnoitered the site in 1940, Albuquerque was still a town of

35,000 sitting at the junction of the Rio Grande and the old U.S. 66 that paralleled the Santa Fe Railroad—"a dirty red sod-hut tortilla desert highway city," Tom Wolfe wrote. Since then, Albuquerque has grown more than any place in New Mexico and, with a metro population of 600,000, has as many people as all New Mexico did when the scientists first arrived. Albuquerque's prosperous neighborhoods have climbed the gently rising heights to the east; poorer residents have spread north and south along the Rio Grande. To the northwest is the new town of Rio Rancho, with Intel, Olympus, U.S. Cotton and Pepsico installations. Albuquerque is counted as part of the Sun Belt, but its climate is closer to that of the High Plains of west Texas: hot in the summer, sometimes very cold in the winter, with high winds most of the time. Nor is its economy like that of other Sun Belt cities. It has lower income levels; its recent growth has lagged behind Phoenix, Dallas, even El Paso. Albuquerque has some white-collar job growth and diversification and has become something of a tourist center (it is home of the International Balloon Fiesta), but it still depends primarily on government, which fortunately has come through, as with the 1990 designation of Kirtland Air Base as site of one of four "superlabs."

The 1st Congressional District of New Mexico is, for all practical purposes, the city of Albuquerque and its suburbs; it also includes largely empty Torrance County and communities north and south along the Rio Grande. Albuquerque is one Sun Belt city which is not solidly Republican, and in 1992 it went by a decisive margin for Bill Clinton after voting Republican for president in the 1980s—not far off the national average. The 1st District in 1990 was 38% Hispanic, with both descendants of longtime New Mexicans and recent immigrants.

The congressman from the 1st District is Steven Schiff, a Republican first elected in 1988. Schiff grew up in Chicago and came to Albuquerque to attend law school. He is an unusual New Mexico figure. He is Jewish in a state made up mostly of Anglo Protestants and Hispanic Catholics; he is aggressive and a stickler for doing things by the book in a state often tolerant of lax practices. He served in the New Mexico Air National Guard, and is now a colonel in the Air Force Reserves. After law school, he became a prosecutor and, after a few years of private practice, in 1980 was elected district attorney of Albuquerque's Bernalillo County, where he was proud of the death penalty convictions he obtained.

Schiff is the sort of man who goes where his sense of right and wrong take him, regardless of politics, as shown by his opposition to key parts of the Contract With America. He is pro-choice on abortion but believes the Freedom of Choice Act goes too far. He opposed a bill allowing military personnel to sue military physicians for malpractice, because they may already qualify for disability. He opposed a bill to criminalize animal rights terrorism. He voted against the flag amendment because of its technical language. He wrote an amendment barring criminals from evading obligations to repay their victims by filing for bankruptcy, and an amendment allowing 16- and 17-year-olds accused of violent federal crimes to be tried as adults. In 1995 he sponsored the Sexual Crimes Against Children Prevention Act, which increased sentences for child pornography and prostitution; it passed 417–0. In 1993, he was put on the Ethics Committee, which became a hot seat after Democrats filed complaints against Speaker Gingrich. He also sits on the Science and Judiciary Committees. He worked to create the Petroglyph National Monument on the west side of Albuquerque and to buy land for the Tres Pistolas animal preserve.

Schiff's toughest race was his first, when he beat two big names in 1988. In the primary, he edged Edward Lujan, the brother of his predecessor in the House and later Interior Secretary Manuel Lujan, by 41%–37%; in the general, he beat Tom Udall, son of former Interior Secretary Stewart Udall and nephew of former House Interior Committee Chairman Morris Udall, and now New Mexico Attorney General, by 51%–47%. He has won easily since; his 1994 opponent said, "I'm a long enough shot that instead of conducting a campaign I can go on a lecture tour."

The People: Pop. 1990: 505,329; 8% rural; 10% age 65+; 56% White; 3% Black; 3% Amer. Indian; 1% Asian; 15% Other; 38% Hispanic origin. Voting age pop.: 371,549; 2% Black; 34% Hispanic origin. Households: 53% married couple families; 26% married couple fams. w. children; 54% college educ.; median household income: $27,074; per capita income: $13,373; median gross rent: $400; median house value: $83,800.

1992 Presidential Vote

Clinton (D) 95,754 (45%)
Bush (R) 81,038 (38%)
Perot (I). 33,034 (16%)

1988 Presidential Vote

Bush (R) 97,414 (54%)
Dukakis (D). 82,867 (46%)

Rep. Steven H. Schiff (R)

Elected 1988; b. Mar. 18, 1947, Chicago, IL; home, Albuquerque; U. of IL, B.A. 1968, U. of NM, J.D. 1972; Jewish; married (Marcia).

Career: Air Natl. Guard, 1969–91; Air Force Reserves, 1991–present; Asst. Dist. Atty., Bernalillo Cnty., 1972–77; Practicing atty., 1977–79; Asst. City Atty. and Cnsl., Albuquerque Police Dept., 1979–81; Dist. Atty., Bernalillo Cnty., 1981–89.

DC Office: 2404 RHOB 202-225-6316; Fax: 202-225-4975.

District Offices: 625 Silver Ave. SW, #140, Albuquerque 87102, 505-766-2538.

Committees: *Government Reform & Oversight* (6th of 27 R): Human Resources and Intergovernmental Affairs; National Security, Intl. Affairs and Criminal Justice. *Judiciary* (8th of 20 R): Crime. *Science* (8th of 27 R): Basic Research (Chmn.); Energy and Environment. *Standards of Official Conduct* (5th of 5 R).

Group Ratings

	ADA	ACLU	COPE	CFA	LCV	CON	NSI	COC	ACU	NTLC	CHC
1994	15	27	44	20	12	67	100	83	80	93	64
1993	5	—	8	20	31	59	—	91	88	—	—

National Journal Ratings

	1993 LIB — 1993 CONS	1994 LIB — 1994 CONS
Economic	30% — 68%	0% — 80%
Social	34% — 65%	35% — 65%
Foreign	17% — 76%	30% — 67%

Key Votes of the 103d Congress

1. Clinton Deficit Plan	N	3. Brady Handgun Purchase	N	5. Lmt. UN Cmnd. of Forces	Y
2. NAFTA	Y	4. Strike Race/Death Pnlty.	Y	6. Cut Missile Funds	N

Key Votes of the 104th Congress

1. Congressional Compliance	Y	6. Reform Crime Grant	Y	11. Loser Pays Court Reform	Y
2. Balanced Budget Amndmt.	Y	7. National Security Act	Y	12. Product Liability Reform	Y
3. Bar Unfunded Mandates	Y	8. Moratorium on Regs.	Y	13. Welfare Reform	Y
4. Pass Line Item Veto	Y	9. Risk Assessment on Regs.	Y	14. Term Limits Amndmt.	Y
5. Relax Exclusionary Rule	Y	10. Expnd. Priv. Prop. Rights	N	15. Tax Cuts	N

Election Results

1994 general	Steven H. Schiff (R)	119,996	(74%)	($458,653)
	Peter Zollinger (D)	42,316	(26%)	($5,944)
1994 primary	Steven H. Schiff (R) .... unopposed			
1992 general	Steven H. Schiff (R)	128,426	(63%)	($589,743)
	Robert J. Aragon (D)	76,600	(38%)	($81,541)

SECOND DISTRICT

The plains of southern and eastern New Mexico are about as disparate a landscape as can be imagined: miles of sagebrush-strewn acreage, and then, suddenly, 9,000-foot mountain peaks rising in the distance. The eastern part of this region, Little Texas, is an extension of the Texas civilization that filled up empty counties when irrigation was developed. Oil has long been the economic mainstay here; cattle ranching is common; cotton is grown on irrigated land. The little cities are full of people with Texas twangs, not the lilt of northern New Mexico. West from Clovis and Portales, Lovington and Hobbs, the towns become fewer and farming mostly disappears. The scrub land shades into desert, and people in the area are crammed into small cities, protected from an environment that is burning hot in the summer and sometimes deathly cold in winter.

The 2d Congressional District of New Mexico includes the entire southern half of the state—most of Little Texas, plus the desert on either side of the Rio Grande and the mining territory in the mountains just north of the Mexican border and just short of the Arizona line. The largest city here is Las Cruces, home of New Mexico State University and only 45 miles north of the million-plus metropolis of El Paso, Texas, and Chihuahua, Mexico. These places today vote the opposite of their partisan tradition: Little Texas, settled by yellow dog Democrats from the Lone Star state, is now solidly Republican; Las Cruces, long leaning Republican, has become Democratic. In most recent elections, the 2d District has gone Republican. But redistricting subtracted Republican and added Democratic counties. In 1992 Bill Clinton narrowly carried the 2d; in 1994 it went for Republican Senate candidate Colin McMillan.

The congressman from the 2d District is Republican Joe Skeen. Skeen has been a sheep rancher for more than 40 years; he was elected to the New Mexico Senate in 1960 and ran two narrowly losing races for governor in 1974 and 1978. He was elected to the House in 1980, the hard way, as a write-in, with 61,000 votes, when Democratic incumbent Harold "Mud" Runnels died and the Democrats put Governor Bruce King's nephew on the ballot. Skeen got 38% of the vote to 34% for King and 28% for Runnels's widow, also a write-in; in 1986, Skeen beat Runnels's son Mike 63%–37%.

When Skeen became Minority Leader of the state Senate 30 years ago, there were only three other Republicans there. Now, for the first time in his career, he is in the majority. He is something of an old-fashioned conservative, generally voting against domestic spending, but working to benefit his district. He has staunchly opposed efforts to increase grazing fees for livestock producers, battling then-Congressman Mike Synar in 1992 and the Clinton Administration in 1993 and 1994, successfully. He worked to bring the WIPP nuclear waste disposal site to a salt cavern near Carlsbad and the F-117A Stealth fighter plane from Tonopah, Nevada, to Holloman Air Force Base near Alamogoro. He worked to revise the formula for federal payments in lieu of taxes to local governments. Skeen is now chairman of the Appropriations Subcommittee on Agriculture—one of the members of the "College of Cardinals" and a position held for more than three decades by Jamie Whitten, until Democrats replaced him in 1993—and he has shown Appropriations solidarity: in 1993 he was one of a very few Republicans to vote against the Penny-Kasich budget cuts. His work in 1995 will be watched closely by the farm community and could have a big political impact on Republicans representing rural districts across the nation.

Skeen has generally won reelection easily. In 1992 he won by just 56%–44%, but in 1994 he won 63%–32%, with 5% for a Green Party candidate.

The People: Pop. 1990: 504,767; 33% rural; 12% age 65+; 52% White; 2% Black; 4% Amer. Indian; 1% Asian; 9% Other; 42% Hispanic origin. Voting age pop.: 350,322; 2% Black; 37% Hispanic origin. Households: 61% married couple families; 31% married couple fams. w. children; 40% college educ.; median household income: $21,456; per capita income: $9,672; median gross rent: $325; median house value: $52,200.

1992 Presidential Vote

Clinton (D) 70,630 (41%)
Bush (R) 68,754 (40%)
Perot (I).................... 31,780 (18%)

1988 Presidential Vote

Bush (R) 94,585 (57%)
Dukakis (D)................. 72,760 (43%)

Rep. Joe Skeen (R)

Elected 1980; b. June 30, 1927, Roswell; home, Picacho; TX A&M U., B.S. 1950; Catholic; married (Mary).

Career: Navy, 1945–46 (WWII), Air Force Reserves, 1949–52; Engineer, Zuni and Ramah Navajo Indian Reservations, 1950–51; Sheep rancher, 1951–present; NM Senate, 1960–70, Minority Ldr., 1965–70.

DC Office: 2367 RHOB 20515, 202-225-2365; Fax: 202-225-9599.

District Offices: 1065 S. Main St., #A, Las Cruces 88005, 505-527-1771; and 257 Fed. Bldg., Roswell 88201, 505-622-0055.

Committees: *Appropriations* (9th of 32 R): Agriculture, Rural Development, FDA, and Related Agencies (Chmn.); Interior; National Security.

Group Ratings

	ADA	ACLU	COPE	CFA	LCV	CON	NSI	COC	ACU	NTLC	CHC
1994	0	24	11	20	0	43	90	75	95	75	86
1993	5	—	17	30	17	39	—	91	87	—	—

National Journal Ratings

	1993 LIB — 1993 CONS		1994 LIB — 1994 CONS	
Economic	20%	80%	34%	64%
Social	23%	77%	20%	77%
Foreign	9%	85%	33%	67%

Key Votes of the 103d Congress

1. Clinton Deficit Plan	N	3. Brady Handgun Purchase	N	5. Lmt. UN Cmnd. of Forces	Y
2. NAFTA	Y	4. Strike Race/Death Pnlty.	Y	6. Cut Missile Funds	N

Key Votes of the 104th Congress

1. Congressional Compliance	Y	6. Reform Crime Grant	Y	11. Loser Pays Court Reform	Y
2. Balanced Budget Amndmt.	Y	7. National Security Act	Y	12. Product Liability Reform	Y
3. Bar Unfunded Mandates	Y	8. Moratorium on Regs.	Y	13. Welfare Reform	Y
4. Pass Line Item Veto	Y	9. Risk Assessment on Regs.	Y	14. Term Limits Amndmt.	N
5. Relax Exclusionary Rule	Y	10. Expnd. Priv. Prop. Rights	Y	15. Tax Cuts	Y

Election Results

1994 general	Joe Skeen (R)	89,966	(63%)	($384,687)
	Benjamin Anthony Chavez (D)	45,316	(32%)	($221,676)
	Rex R. Johnson (Green)	6,898	(5%)	
1994 primary	Joe Skeen (R)	unopposed		
1992 general	Joe Skeen (R)	94,838	(56%)	($493,406)
	Dan Sosa, Jr. (D)	73,157	(44%)	($40,973)

THIRD DISTRICT

"The dancing ground of the sun" the Pueblo Indians called the land of northern New Mexico, where the long, empty vistas stretch for miles, detailed in pinpoint clarity in the cold light and clear air. For 100 years, artists have been coming here, attracted by the scenery and by a unique civilization that is part Indian, part Spanish, only a little Mexican (for northern New Mexico was Mexican only briefly, from 1821–46), part Anglo-American. The Spanish language, Indian pottery and dances, the adobe pueblos give the impression that life has gone on for centuries on this rocky desert soil in much the same way. Actually, the civilization hasn't been so stable. The pueblos were built in sudden spurts; the Spanish conquistadors and priests brought the Catholic religion, the baroque accents of the adobe buildings and the Spanish language in a rush; successive waves of American settlement have changed New Mexico in different ways. The Indian crafts which are thriving today nearly died out in the 1880s, and the Palace of the Governors, built in 1610, had its Victorian balustrade torn off in 1913 to restore its original appearance; the unchanged look is carefully maintained. Yet up the back roads in Rio Arriba or Taos Counties, one can find a religion that mixes Catholicism with adaptations of Indian festivals, buildings not that much different from the old pueblos, and a standard of living reminiscent of the Indian past—quite a contrast to Santa Fe, with its thousands of affluent, bohemian migrants, its 300 restaurants and the second-largest art market in the country.

The politics of northern New Mexico is a unique blend. For years, debate was conducted and votes bartered in Spanish, not by separatists, but by Republican and Democratic politicos, often cynically, sometimes corruptly; loyalties ran to families and communities more than to principles or parties. In the back country, you can still find more than just vestiges of the old communities and the old politics—though no one is going to let you in on them, even if you speak good Spanish—while in Santa Fe and Los Alamos, or in the new subdivisions along the Rio Grande north of Albuquerque, voters put a premium on environmentalism.

The 3d Congressional District of New Mexico contains most of the state's historic Spanish-speaking and Indian parts. Its largest and most dominant city is Santa Fe, but the district runs from the High Plains along the Texas border, past the haunting Sangre de Cristo Mountains, through the vast ridges and isolated buttes in the center (on one of which the government built Los Alamos in World War II to create the atomic bomb), to the windy and dusty desert-like plains, dotted occasionally by mountains, with Indian reservations in the west. The population is 34% Hispanic origin and 20% Indian (with at least 6% overlap between the categories). Politically, it is heavily Democratic, with 1980s newcomers to Santa Fe and Taos moving it farther in that direction.

The congressman from the 3d District is Bill Richardson, a hyperactive politician and a national policymaker of note on issues both domestic and foreign. Richardson is a unique politician—an Hispanic with an Anglo name, a relative newcomer to New Mexico where families go back 300 years, a seemingly cynical politician who has taken solid stands on issues and stuck with them in good times and bad. Richardson was born in California and raised by his Mexican mother in Mexico City; he has always been bilingual. He moved to New Mexico in 1978 after holding staff jobs on Capitol Hill, worked as executive director of the state Democratic Party for a month and started running against Republican Congressman Manuel Lujan in a district that then included Albuquerque and most of northern New Mexico, raising $200,000 and winning 49% in Republican 1980. New Mexico gained a seat in 1982 and Lujan was quite happy to give up the Hispanic counties to the new 3d; Richardson beat former Lieutenant Governor Roberto Mondragon 36%–31% in the primary and clobbered a Republican with 64% to become, in just four years, New Mexico's only Democrat in the House. Richardson has worked his district hard and has been reelected without difficulty.

In the House, Richardson is a chief deputy Democratic whip who has taken his own initiatives on important issues. The most important was probably NAFTA, of which he was an ardent booster. In 1992, he was working with the Bush Administration with an eye toward getting approval. In early 1993, when Bill Clinton was underplaying and Dick Gephardt was undermining NAFTA, Richardson was lobbying hard for it, trying to line up votes and to mollify those with doubts in this country and to gain concessions from groups in Mexico. Richardson saw the upside potential of a Mexico more closely aligned with the United States economically and otherwise and the downside potential of a Mexico spurned and rejected. On that issue Richardson stood against organized labor, and on others his voting record is by no means stereotypically liberal. One of his great causes in the 103d Congress was freeing manufacturers of dietary supplements from being required to get Food and Drug Administration approval of their claims. He opposed cable TV reregulation in 1992 and has backed product liability laws, although he said that the Republicans went too far with their 1995 proposal. He has relinquished his seat on the Commerce Committee, where he promoted reformulated gasoline, wrote amendments on accidental release of air toxins and established an environmental entity to study pollution on the U.S.-Mexican border. He has supported some immigration reform bills, but opposed employer sanctions.

As part of the Democratic leadership, Richardson worked loyally and hard for the 1993 budget and tax package and for the 1994 crime bill—both measures that got pretty badly mauled before being passed by one vote and after major concessions respectively. He was chairman of the Native Americans Subcommittee of Resources, and worked for Indian self-governance and reform of the Bureau of Indian Affairs, which *U.S. News & World Report* has called "the worst government agency." In 1995 he moved to ranking position on the Resources Subcommittee on National Parks, Forests and Lands. Naturally he has worked on New Mexico projects. Back in 1992, he got a compromise on the Waste Isolation Pilot Project, which he has long opposed and Joe Skeen had long favored; it was opened under tougher standards and with less waste than planned.

Richardson came close to being named Bill Clinton's Secretary of the Interior, and was ultimately passed over for Bruce Babbitt. Interestingly, much of his work in 1994 was on foreign affairs. In February 1994, he traveled to Myanmar (formerly Burma) and met with imprisoned dissident Aung Sna Suu Kyi, the afternoon after meeting with a head of the military junta—an important statement of American support for human rights. In July 1994 he traveled to Haiti and met with General Raoul Cedras, and in a five-hour conversation tried to get him to cede power to President Jean Baptiste Aristide, while urging Aristide to abjure violence; if Richardson's advice had been heeded, there might have been no need to send U.S. troops. In December 1994 he was travelling in North Korea when two U.S. helicopter pilots were gunned down for allegedly trespassing into North Korean airspace. He negotiated for the release of the surviving pilot but ended up returning with remains of the one airman who died. The other pilot was soon released. Richardson would be an attractive Senate candidate but he probably will have to wait for a retirement. He also could be a candidate to move up the House Democratic leadership ladder, especially if there is support for a shake-up.

The People: Pop. 1990: 504,973; 40% rural; 10% age 65+; 44% White; 1% Black; 20% Amer. Indian; 1% Asian; 13% Other; 34% Hispanic origin. Voting age pop.: 346,759; 1% Black; 33% Hispanic origin. Households: 58% married couple families; 31% married couple fams. w. children; 45% college educ.; median household income: $23,610; per capita income: $10,689; median gross rent: $372; median house value: $68,400.

1992 Presidential Vote

Clinton (D)	95,233	(51%)
Bush (R)	63,032	(34%)
Perot (I)	27,081	(15%)

1988 Presidential Vote

Dukakis (D)	88,870	(53%)
Bush (R)	78,342	(47%)

Rep. Bill Richardson (D)

Elected 1982; b. Nov. 15, 1947, Pasadena, CA; home, Santa Fe; Tufts U., B.A. 1970, Fletcher Schl. of Law and Diplomacy, M.A. 1971; Catholic; married (Barbara).

Career: Congressional rel., U.S. Dept. of State, 1973–75; Staff, Senate Foreign Relations Subcmte., 1975–78; Exec. Dir., NM Dem. Party, 1978; Pres., Richardson Trade Group, 1978–82.

DC Office: 2209 RHOB 20515, 202-225-6190.

District Office: 1494 S. St. Francis Dr., Santa Fe 87505, 505-988-7230; Gallup City Hall, 2d & Aztec, Gallup 87301, 505-722-6522; San Miguel Cnty. Crthse., P.O. Box 1805, Las Vegas 87701, 505-425-7270; and P.O. Box 1108, Clovis 88102, 505-769-3380.

Committees: *Chief Deputy Minority Whip. Resources* (7th of 20 D): Energy and Mineral Resources; National Parks, Forests and Lands (RMM); Water and Power Resources. *Intelligence (Permanent Select)* (2nd of 7 D): Human Intelligence, Analysis, and Counterintelligence.

Group Ratings

	ADA	ACLU	COPE	CFA	LCV	CON	NSI	COC	ACU	NTLC	CHC
1994	55	71	78	50	100	23	56	55	26	25	7
1993	75	—	92	90	93	4	—	27	17	—	—

National Journal Ratings

	1993 LIB — 1993 CONS		1994 LIB — 1994 CONS	
Economic	75%	— 25%	71%	— 29%
Social	63%	— 36%	58%	— 41%
Foreign	51%	— 42%	57%	— 37%

Key Votes of the 103d Congress

1. Clinton Deficit Plan	Y	3. Brady Handgun Purchase	N	5. Lmt. UN Cmnd. of Forces	N
2. NAFTA	Y	4. Strike Race/Death Pnlty.	N	6. Cut Missile Funds	N

Key Votes of the 104th Congress

1. Congressional Compliance	Y	6. Reform Crime Grant	N	11. Loser Pays Court Reform	N
2. Balanced Budget Amndmt.	Y	7. National Security Act	N	12. Product Liability Reform	N
3. Bar Unfunded Mandates	Y	8. Moratorium on Regs.	N	13. Welfare Reform	N
4. Pass Line Item Veto	Y	9. Risk Assessment on Regs.	N	14. Term Limits Amndmt.	N
5. Relax Exclusionary Rule	N	10. Expnd. Priv. Prop. Rights	N	15. Tax Cuts	N

Election Results

1994 general	Bill Richardson (D)	99,900	(64%)	($579,737)
	F. Gregg Bemis Jr. (R)	53,515	(34%)	($110,575)
	Others	3,697	(2%)	
1994 primary	Bill Richardson (D)	unopposed		
1992 general	Bill Richardson (D)	122,850	(67%)	($600,683)
	F. Gregg Bemis (R)	54,569	(30%)	($48,064)
	Other	4,798	(3%)	

NEW YORK

New York is a place of miracles and disasters. The state still has America's largest city, its financial capital, its center of arts and letters and entertainment, the number one immigrant destination for more than 100 years. But none of this was inevitable. These things happened because New Yorkers—and not least those people from elsewhere who opted to become New Yorkers—chose to make them happen, worked to make sure they would happen. Yet if there is nothing inevitable about New York City, there is a certain enduring character to the place which in its earliest incarnation was the 17th Century Dutch colony of Nieuw Amsterdam. Simon Schama's *The Embarrassment of Riches* paints a picture of the old world Amsterdam: the richest city in the world; full of people who work hard all day and stay up late partying, smoke too much tobacco and drink too much coffee and gin, but are dazzlingly smart and shrewd; people who know their way around every corner of the globe and can make fine aesthetic discriminations, but are attached to their uncomfortable, crowded, bad-smelling city; merchants and manipulators with no aristocratic pedigree, welcoming any religious or ethnic group who can achieve and accumulate and show good taste, cherishing education and culture but indifferent to credentials. This could be a portrait of the New York of today, of Tom Wolfe and Tina Brown, or the New York of Alexander Hamilton and Aaron Burr, or the New York of Edith Wharton and Theodore Dreiser, or the New York of Harold Ross' *New Yorker* magazine Algonquin Round Table and Henry Luce's early *Time*. Probably fewer than 2% of today's New Yorkers are descended from the Dutch of Nieuw Amsterdam, but the character of the place endures in daily life and in the workings of its great institutions, and helps explain its miraculous and entirely uninevitable growth. Combine Amsterdam and America: Dutch character with British-born political freedoms and American military invulnerability—something the Dutch have never enjoyed except perhaps in the last few years—and you have the opportunity to build a city-state that can lead the world.

But New York was not always the nation's leader. In 1776, New York was the seventh most populous colony. Only in the 19th Century did the descendants of Dutch patroons, Huguenot refugees, British West Indies traders and Yankee farmers become the nation's most successful merchants and capitalists, forging the first routes to the great American interior through the valleys of the Hudson and the Mohawk, over the Finger Lakes and the Great Lakes, and building grand brownstone mansions on broad midtown Manhattan avenues. That early diversity provides one clue to New York's success: if New York has been cynical, ready to cooperate with Loyalists and Revolutionaries, depending on who was ahead, it has also been tolerant, ready to accept anyone smart or rich enough to be counted a success. It has been propelled upward at each stage—forging ahead of London as a financial and manufacturing center by the First World War, and staying ahead of surging Chicago—by incorporating every wave of immigrants and consistently rewarding intelligence and hard work, unconcerned about preserving hierarchies.

New York's success has been a product not only of market economics, but of government—and politics. The Iroquois, the most deeply-rooted and militarily strong Native Americans, kept in place for 100 years by an alliance with British troops, were driven out of New York by the Revolution. The Erie Canal, which connected western New York state with the Hudson River, was the project of Governor DeWitt Clinton's state government. The railroads were subsidized by land grants and favorable laws. And New York led the nation in political innovation: Martin Van Buren's Albany Regency was the first state political machine, an ally of New York City's Tammany Hall, and Van Buren himself invented the Democratic Party, the national convention and the inaugural parade. His adversaries, Thurlow Weed and William Seward, formed the

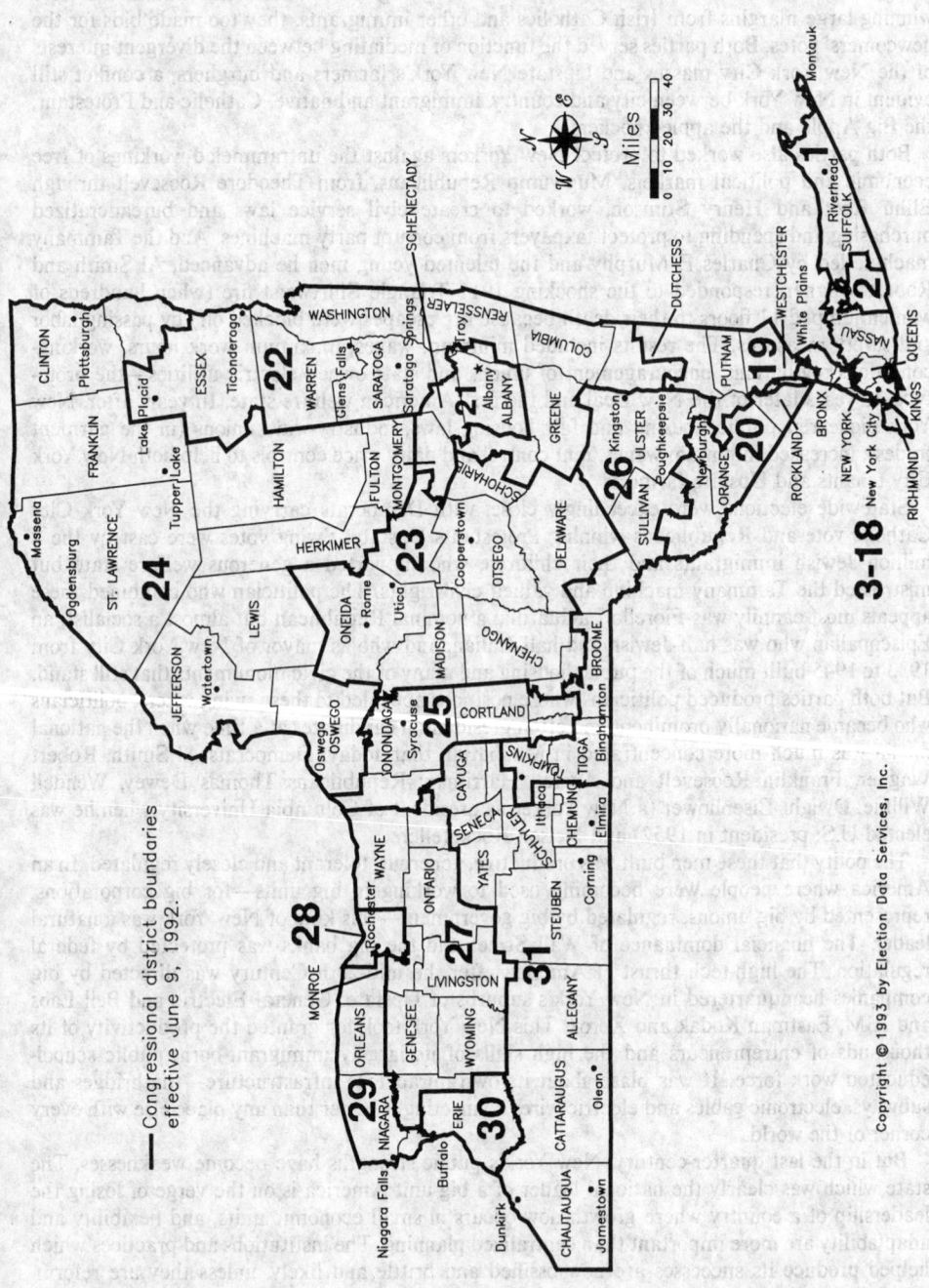

— Congressional district boundaries
effective June 9, 1992.

Whig Party and ultimately became Republicans; noting that Van Buren's Democrats were winning large margins from Irish Catholics and other immigrants, they too made bids for the newcomers' votes. Both parties served the function of mediating between the divergent interests of the New York City masses and Upstate New York's farmers and burghers, a conflict still evident in New York between city and country, immigrant and native, Catholic and Protestant, the Big Apple and the apple-knockers.

Both parties also worked to protect New Yorkers against the untrammeled workings of free economic and political markets. Mugwump Republicans, from Theodore Roosevelt through Elihu Root and Henry Stimson, worked to create civil service laws and bureaucratized purchasing and spending to protect taxpayers from corrupt party machines. And the Tammany machine led by Charles F. Murphy and the talented young men he advanced, Al Smith and Robert Wagner, responded to the shocking 1911 Triangle Shirtwaist fire (when hundreds of women jumped 11 floors to their death because fire escapes were blocked off) by passing labor and safety measures. The results included minimum wages, maximum work hours, working-conditions regulations, encouragement of unions and state-owned electric utilities—the proto-type 20 years later of the New Deal and the first American welfare state. In years after, New York pioneered public housing and fair housing laws, industry-wide unions (in the garment trades), increased minimum wages, rent control and dairy price controls to help both New York City tenants and Upstate farmers.

Statewide elections were exceedingly close, with Democrats carrying the New York City Catholic vote and Republicans winning Protestants Upstate. Swing votes were cast by the 2 million Jewish immigrants and their children, who supported a generous welfare state but mistrusted the Tammany machine and valued civil rights. The politician who combined these appeals most cannily was Fiorello LaGuardia: a nominal Republican but almost a socialist, an Episcopalian who was half-Jewish and half-Italian, and who as mayor of New York City from 1933 to 1945 built much of the public housing and many of the civic monuments that still stand. But both parties produced politicians whose positions appealed to these swing voters, politicians who became nationally prominent and often presidential candidates at a time when the national media was much more concentrated in Manhattan than today: Democrats Al Smith, Robert Wagner, Franklin Roosevelt and Averell Harriman; Republicans Thomas Dewey, Wendell Willkie, Dwight Eisenhower (a New Yorker as president of Columbia University when he was elected U.S. president in 1952) and Nelson Rockefeller.

The polity that these men built was productive, generous, tolerant and closely regulated. In an America where people were becoming used to working in big units—for big corporations, represented by big unions, regulated by big government—this kind of New York was a natural leader. The financial dominance of Wall Street and the big banks was protected by federal regulation. The high-tech thrust of America after the mid-20th Century was directed by big companies headquartered in New York's suburbs or Upstate: General Electric and Bell Labs and IBM, Eastman Kodak and Xerox. This New York took for granted the productivity of its thousands of entrepreneurs and the high skills of its largely immigrant-born, public school-educated work force. It was blase about its own miraculous infrastructure—the bridges and subways, electronic cables and electric wires connecting it better than any place else with every corner of the world.

But in the last quarter-century, New York's public strengths have become weaknesses. The state which was clearly the national leader of a big-unit America is on the verge of losing the leadership of a country where growth now occurs in small economic units, and flexibility and adaptability are more important than centralized planning. The institutions and practices which helped produce its successes are now ossified and brittle and likely, unless they are reform-minded, to induce decline. Welfare state benefits have become too expensive, measures meant to protect against corruption stifle innovation, and both have failed to achieve their objectives—ghettos throb with the pains of disorganization, and payoffs and rackets are part of the everyday cost of doing business in New York as in no other place in the country. The noble aim of creating a public sector which would guarantee cheap rents, topnotch public schools and colleges, and public hospitals, instead guarantees that none of these will be available: rent control keeps housing scarce, school bureaucracies stifle good teaching, public hospitals ration care down to nothing. The attempt to create a fail-safe government has produced a government that is sure to fail. The government that intended to aid growth now seems to be cutting it off—not completely, but enough to explain why New York state, which grew 32% in population from 1940 to 1965, grew only 1% from 1965 to 1990, while California was growing 60%.

People and businesses started voting with their feet, especially during the terms of Mayor John Lindsay, a liberal Republican hailed when he was elected in 1965 by the powerful New York-based liberal media of the day as the next John Kennedy, though about all he shared with Kennedy was good looks. Lindsay denounced Democrats for being too cozy with municipal unions, but gave up more to them than any mayor before or since. He institutionalized the practice of borrowing against next year's revenues to pay this year's bills, bringing city government to the brink of bankruptcy two years after he left office. He skillfully convinced New York's blacks that he cared about them, while allowing the institutions that had taught previous generations' immigrants to embrace middle-class values, to scorn those values. "The confluence of radical spite, absurd legal extrapolations and liberal disdain for white ethnics that led to forced busing, the bloating of welfare rolls and the mau-mauing of white teachers broke the spine of New York's civic culture," writes liberal Jim Sleeper in *The Closest of Strangers*. Antagonized middle-class New Yorkers fled not just to the suburbs, but by the hundreds of thousands to (then) low-tax New Jersey, Connecticut and Florida. In the 1970s, the population of New York, city and state, dropped by one million—an unprecedented hemorrhage of talent and productivity, a flight of the middle class away from a polity that seemed to be dying.

Retrenchment followed the mid-1970s bankruptcy crisis. Private financiers and the state government took control of city government, cut spending and negotiated cutbacks in jobs and salaries with public employees' unions. Citizens endured the loss of services and deterioration of streets, bridges and subways. With the financial boom of 1981–87, New York once again brimmed with confidence, and the buzzing of economic growth and cultural innovation could again be heard over the never-ending blare of car horns. Manhattan boomed as an office center and remained the center of America's financial, clothing, entertainment, media and publishing industries. Its population was rising and it was attracting immigrants once again. The outer boroughs attracted migrants from Latin America, the eastern Mediterranean, Asia, even Russia, injecting youth and vitality into what had been aging, listless communities.

Yet all was not well. New York's old welfare state measures left clever members of the middle class in comfortable niches, on public payrolls protected from accountability, in rent-controlled apartments paying a fraction of market rent. These same measures left newcomers and the lower classes out in the cold (literally, in the case of the homeless, because of rent control's incentives for tearing down buildings). Two brilliant Democratic executives led New York during those years—Edward Koch, mayor from 1977 to 1989, and Mario Cuomo, governor from 1982 to 1994—making genuine contributions but also covering over some of the rot. Koch rationalized and disciplined city government in many ways; Cuomo appointed some fine administrators and cut some taxes. But Koch succumbed to higher spending as revenues rolled in during the mid-1980s, and Cuomo allied himself with the public employee unions, many of which have been the most effective enemies of reform. New York's legislature—"the worst governmental institution in the western world," writes former city official William Stern—is unusually tightly controlled by the two chambers' leaders, with the Assembly dominated by New York City Democrats and the state Senate by suburban Republicans engaged in classic political logrolling, lavishing taxpayers' dollars on each other's pet projects, with no incentives to hold spending down or deliver services. Independent agencies set up to evade public scrutiny borrow huge sums and lavish them on politically connected contractors, with the taxpayers eventually paying the bill. Government and the public sector continued to grow robustly in the Cuomo years, even when the private economy did not. New York ranked 47th of the 50 states in job growth in those 12 years, as Cooper Union professor Fred Siegel points out, and its recovery from the recession of 1990–91 was so sluggish as to be invisible.

Now New York has two Republican executives, both elected on similar, government-cutting platforms, though they are not political allies and for a time were the bitterest of political enemies: Mayor Rudolph Giuliani, who in 1993 defeated David Dinkins, New York City's first black mayor and its most principled defender of big government for many years, and Governor George Pataki, who in 1994 defeated Mario Cuomo, with the conspicuous aid of Senator Alfonse D'Amato and despite the vociferous opposition of most of the state's mainstream media and articulate opinion leaders. Their victories cannot be explained as anything other than a deep revulsion against New York's big government and high taxes. In 1989, Dinkins was elected by narrow margins—51%–42% over Koch in the primary, 50%–48% over Giuliani in the general— by New Yorkers who were tired of racial tension and eager for interracial harmony. But Dinkins' hesitation before denouncing a black boycott of a Korean-owned Brooklyn grocery store and his visit to comfort relatives after a suspected drug dealer was shot by a policeman kept tensions high and convinced many he had a double standard. Giuliani insisted that government needed to be cut sharply, services privatized and crime harshly combated, and won 51%–48%.

Pataki ran on a similar platform in 1994, for lower taxes, for capital punishment. Cuomo, despite his personal magnetism, trailed for months in the polls. Then in October Giuliani endorsed Cuomo, patronage-rich Nassau County Republicans ostentatiously snubbed Pataki and the media, led by *The New York Times*, cheered for "our governor." Cuomo surged in the polls but never topped the 50% mark, and media cheers counted for less than policy fundamentals in the end. Pataki won 49%–45%, losing badly in New York City (28%–70%), but carrying the suburbs 54%–43% and annihilating Cuomo 59%–32% Upstate. The Giuliani endorsement hurt there: the suspicion was widespread that the payoff would be higher taxes Upstate for more aid to the city. Interestingly, this result was not so different from New York's last high-turnout gubernatorial election, in 1982, when Cuomo beat supply-sider Lewis Lehrman 51%–47%— only this time Cuomo's margin was bigger in the city and the Republicans' very much bigger Upstate. Republican Dennis Vacco was elected attorney general over Democrat Karen Burstein by 49%–47%; Republicans won 47% of the votes for U.S. House as compared to Democrats' 48%; and Senator Daniel Patrick Moynihan's winning margin was reduced to 55%–42%, though he ran 15% ahead of Cuomo Upstate.

Giuliani's victory can be summed up as a near-unanimous decision by outer-borough white ethnics, Asians and Hispanics that the huge city government hailed by *New York Times* writers as "the New York tradition" was destroying jobs and neighborhoods. Pataki's victory can be summed up as a near-unanimous decision by Upstaters and farther-out suburbanites that the huge state and city governments were destroying jobs and communities. The New York version of the welfare state, for all the attractiveness of its champions, was repudiated. And in truth there does seem to be a battle between New York's bubbling economic vitality and the ponderous load put on it by big government. The city's population rose 3.5% in the 1980s, the first significant rise in a decade since the 1940s, as immigrants streamed in, reviving sagging neighborhoods in the outer boroughs and creating new businesses. Some 28% of New York City residents are foreign born. The Caribbean blacks of Brooklyn, the Hispanics of Jackson Heights, Corona and Queens, the Koreans of Flushing, the Greeks of Astoria are living the American dream. Even that sore spot, the South Bronx, is filling in, thanks to some innovative Koch housing programs. But there are still horrifying problem neighborhoods—much of Harlem and Brownsville in Brooklyn—rent control continues to destroy housing, and high taxes continue to destroy jobs. The financial business no longer provides acceleration to the New York economy, as it did before 1987, and big corporations have abandoned Manhattan by the hundreds. According to Fred Siegel, 45% of jobs in the Bronx and 33% in Brooklyn are in the public sector, broadly defined: the public sector is crowding out the private. New York still has far more vitality than central cities like Detroit or Newark, but it is in danger of squelching what has for two centuries been its great strengt—its creative and surging private economy.

Not all of New York state is New York City, by any means. But the city's strengths and its problems flow beyond its limits. New York suburbs are still outvoted by the city because so much suburban overflow is in New Jersey or Connecticut. The suburbs have by national standards very large and well-paid local governments, with high property taxes and a hunger for state school aid that in the Cuomo years kept the suburban-dominated Republican state Senate a faithful ally in maintaining New York's big government apparatus. Beyond the New York City orbit is Upstate, with 47% of the state's voters, historically Protestant and Republican, now heavily Catholic and increasingly Republican. Upstate no longer has central transportation arteries as in the days of the New York Central's water level route, and so is off the beaten path; its population has not risen much since the 1950s. The largest city, Buffalo, is one of those Great Lakes factory cities where old steel mills have closed and is now growing as a low-wage back-office adjunct to Toronto. Upstate's biggest employer, IBM, lost money in the 1980s and layed off thousands, while healthier big Upstate companies—General Electric, Kodak, Xerox—have not been hiring in large numbers. Upstate has great assets: a fine physical environment—green hills, majestic mountains, glistening lakes, a plentiful water supply—and winters are no colder than those in booming Minnesota or New Hampshire. It has a highly-skilled labor force and high-tech experience. The North American Free Trade Agreement put Upstate on the doorstep of the most prosperous part of Canada: the Golden Horseshoe of Ontario from Niagara Falls to Toronto is just across the river from Buffalo's Niagara Frontier, and Interstate 87 runs straight from Albany to Montreal. This was one of America's first frontiers, with fine colleges and cultural institutions going back to the early 1800s wave of Yankee settlements. It set the dominant cultural tone of the Yankee America that won the Civil War, settled the West and stretched the United States all the way to the Pacific Ocean. But now Upstate is struggling to adapt to a new economy and to reduce New York's strangling high taxes.

For years New York has been counted as a Democratic state, indeed the stronghold of the national Democratic Party. Compared to Texas or Ohio, perhaps even to California, it still is. Yet the Republican surge evident in the 1994 election results had underpinnings that go back some time, and if New York still gives the nation the Democratic Party's wisest philosopher, Senator Daniel Patrick Moynihan, and several conspicuously useful members of the House, the maestro of its politics in 1994 and 1995 has been a Republican, Senator Alfonse D'Amato, a man recently threatened with political extinction (it was almost universally assumed he would lose for reelection in 1992 and in fact he won by only 49%–48%).

In retrospect, New York's election of nothing but Democratic governors for two decades reflected the strength of the party's candidates more than its message: Cuomo won narrowly in 1982 and in 1986 won with 53% against split opposition. And if it has been the most Democratic of the 10 biggest states since Massachusetts fell off that list (actually, Pennsylvania was 0.2% more for Walter Mondale than was New York), its 50% for Bill Clinton in 1992 was only slightly ahead of Cuomo's losing 46%, and the 1994 Upstate results suggest that Clinton will have a hard time duplicating his 40% there in 1996. D'Amato seems to have taken shrewd advantage of opportunities that in hindsight are now perceptible. He could see that Cuomo, who did not oppose him vigorously in 1992, was weak and could be beaten, that his opposition to capital punishment and deep tax cuts were fatal weaknesses. He accurately perceived that Pataki, then little known, would be smart and cool enough not to wither under Cuomo's and the media's attacks. He was proved right in estimating that Pataki could appeal directly to the voters over the hostility of Giuliani and the avidity of his former Nassau County allies. In early 1995, D'Amato lined up Pataki and all of New York's Republican Congressmen, as well as every Republican in the state Senate, in endorsing Bob Dole for president. As one shrewd New York politico put it, "The lesson of 1994 is never get in the way between Al D'Amato and what he wants."

Governor. George Pataki began 1994 as a state senator hardly recognized outside his Hudson Valley district, even in the Capitol complex in Albany. He began 1995 as the governor of New York. He grew up in Peekskill, a small industrial city on the Hudson in northern Westchester

County, at the cusp of metropolitan New York City and Upstate New York. His father was the son of Hungarian immigrants, his mother is of Italian and Irish ancestry; his parents had a farm in Peekskill and built it into a business. Pataki went to Yale and Columbia Law School, practiced law with a big Wall Street firm, then moved to a Westchester firm in 1974. In 1982 he was elected mayor of Peekskill, where he converted tax-exempt property to taxpaying housing, held taxes down, opened an industrial plant and approved 1,000 new housing units. In 1984 he ran against an incumbent Democratic assemblyman and won. In 1992, after eight years as a member of a powerless minority, he challenged an incumbent Republican state senator, and beat her by 558 votes. In the state Senate he chafed at the leadership of Nassau County's Ralph Marino, voted against the budget—a major rebellion in Albany—and was supported by a conservative group called Change/NY (which had tried to defeat Marino in 1992).

In 1993, the almost unknown Pataki began running for governor, taking on one of America's best-known politicians, Mario Cuomo. After his narrow 1982 victory, Cuomo became known nationally for his 1984 keynote speech to the Democratic convention and for a speech at Notre Dame defending his pro-choice position on abortion, despite his personal opposition to it. With deep roots in the outer borough of Queens, he defended liberal positions with an eloquence and force that few Manhattan politicians could summon. He cut New York's top tax rates but also created other taxes and increased spending robustly; he claimed credit for a workfare program but tended to support the public employee unions. Twice Cuomo was the subject of presidential speculation. In 1988, when the nomination ultimately went to an Eastern ethnic governor, he confounded reporters by saying he wouldn't run and then not running. In late 1991, he seemed poised to run, as he aimed sharp barbs at Bill Clinton. But he said he would not run if he could not get a budget agreement from Marino. When that didn't happen, he left a plane idling in the Albany airport ready to take him to New Hampshire and bowed out. At the New York convention he delivered a handsome nominating speech for Clinton and stayed close to him up through 1994, though in 1993 he said he didn't want to be considered for a Supreme Court nomination. Cuomo portrayed himself as the champion of *The New York Idea*, the title of a book he published in 1994. But by early 1994, despite all his strengths, Cuomo was in trouble, vulnerable because he opposed capital punishment and had not cut taxes as much as voters wanted.

Pataki provided a clear contrast on both issues, and he also showed political skill. He got the support of Senator Alfonse D'Amato, inheriting his backers as well as his enemies. He easily won the May 1994 convention and prevented a primary challenge and a Conservative Party candidacy from 1990 Conservative nominee Herb London, who was nominated instead for comptroller. He chose as his running mate Elizabeth McCaughey, a constitutional scholar whose devastating critique of the Clinton healthcare plan helped do it in. In the general election, Cuomo attacked Pataki for having raised taxes in Peekskill and Democrats charged that he was a puppet of D'Amato. But Pataki led in polls until Rudolph Giuliani in late October endorsed Cuomo and bitterly criticized Pataki. Cuomo went into the lead in polls but never reached 50%. He gained votes in New York City and in Nassau County, with its revenue-hungry Republican machine. Thomas Golisano, a Rochester businessman, was spending millions as an independent, advised by pro-Perot pollster Gordon Black; Perot endorsed him and polls showed him with 8%. But Golisano's share of the vote fell to 4%, and Cuomo got 45%, about where he was running in polls. Pataki won 49% of the vote, losing New York City 70%–28% but carrying the suburbs 54%–43% and Upstate (where Giuliani's endorsement hurt Cuomo) 59%–32%.

As governor, Pataki has shown determination and even ruthlessness in seeking his goals. After the election, he declined to take a congratulatory phone call from Giuliani for three weeks and engineered a coup ousting Marino as Senate Leader that was executed (like an insurance fire in a failing store) while he was on vacation in Florida; Marino resigned from the legislature in February 1995. In office, Pataki called for a cut in the state income tax and an actual reduction in state spending, including a cut in AFDC payments and Medicaid. But Pataki faces fierce budget battles with the Democratic controlled Assembly, led by Sheldon Silver who represents the Lower East Side, and even among some members of the Republican held state Senate who would opt to spend more. After Silver dragged out the death penalty debate, Pataki finally signed it into law in March 1995 and transferred to Oklahoma an inmate scheduled to be executed there—two steps that Cuomo had stubbornly resisted. He faced down Republican Governor Christine Todd Whitman of New Jersey and appointed as head of the two-state Port Authority George Marlin, the Conservative nominee for mayor of New York City in 1993. Pataki joined all of New York's Republican congressional delegation and most other leading Republicans, with the pointed exception of Giuliani, in supporting Bob Dole for president, a move obviously orchestrated by D'Amato. But it is wrong to say that Pataki is D'Amato's puppet. Pataki has shown competence, aggressiveness and nerve aplenty on his own and bids fair to become, if not a national leader, then at least a politician with a profound influence on government in New York—the redefiner of "the New York Idea."

Senators. Daniel Patrick Moynihan, the nation's best thinker among politicians since Lincoln and its best politician among thinkers since Jefferson, remains even in the minority at the summit of a long career in public life. He is New York's senior senator, the ranking Democrat on the Finance Committee, crucially positioned in a still closely balanced Senate to advance his own ideas and retard others. And for all his academic credentials, Moynihan has a range of experience in American government as broad as any member of Congress. He worked for Governor Averell Harriman in the 1950s, served as assistant secretary of labor in the Kennedy and Johnson Administrations, was chief domestic adviser to President Nixon and was ambassador to the United Nations under President Ford—the only person in American history, he likes to note, who has served in the cabinet or subcabinet of four successive presidents. As Finance chairman, he helped shepherd the 1993 budget and tax package to passage by one vote. And he advised Bill and Hillary Rodham Clinton early and often to give priority to welfare reform over healthcare reform. Had his advice been taken, it might have changed the course of their administration and the fortunes of the Democratic Party.

Moynihan is known rightly for his ability to spot emerging issues long before anyone else, qualities that were apparent at least as early as 1965, when he wrote "The Negro Family: The Case for National Action." The long expanse of his career has underlined the consistency of his ideas and interests and the persistence with which he has kept at his causes. Every summer Moynihan spends several weeks in an old one-room schoolhouse in Pindars Corners, deep in the hills of Upstate New York, writing in distinctive prose another book on any of a dozen subjects. Then he returns to Washington, to converse with colleagues in the peculiar languid atmosphere of the Senate floor and then rise in anger to challenge a bad idea. This is the kind of philosopher-politician who the Founding Fathers hoped would people the Senate—although they would have been surprised to see one spring, as Moynihan did, from the Manhattan slum of Hell's Kitchen.

Moynihan's preoccupations are many and enduring. Three decades ago, he bemoaned the dilapidated state of Pennsylvania Avenue. A redevelopment corporation was set up, and now it is a splendid boulevard, with buildings restored and new, in one of which he keeps an apartment. He is also the father of the graceful new Thurgood Marshall Federal Judiciary Center, next door to Union Station, and has set his eye on the Capitol employees' parking lots, with a view to putting gardens or parks there. For New York he worked to rebuild the Brooklyn courthouse (he can recite the history of all of New York's courthouses) and to get funding to make the Manhattan Post Office into a new Penn Station. From 1973 to 1975, he was ambassador to India and he is an expert on things Indian. Tying these subjects together is his wife Elizabeth Moynihan's scholarly work on the gardens of the great Moguls. She has also managed his campaigns in New York.

In the early 1960s, before Ralph Nader, Moynihan was arguing that traffic deaths could be reduced by redesigning car interiors. Later he became almost the nation's transportation czar. As chairman of the Water Resources, Transportation and Infrastructure Subcommittee, he produced "Ice Tea," insider language for the Intermodal Surface Transportation Efficiency Act of 1991 (ISTEA), which provided vast new sums for transportation and gave states the choice of whether to use money for highways or mass transit. It made funding formulas more favorable to New York—a pet Moynihan cause on which he publishes yearly data to show how New York is shortchanged—and got New York reimbursed for building its Thruway and funded magnetic levitation trains, also a favorite cause.

In 1993 Moynihan became the first New Yorker to chair the Senate Finance Committee in 155 years. He also became a kind of senior tutor to Bill and Hillary Rodham Clinton, often counseling them privately and sometimes rebuking them publicly, treating them like bright but sometimes wayward students. The two major Clinton initiatives, the 1993 budget and tax package and the 1994 healthcare reform, had to go through Finance, and Moynihan played a pivotal role on each. Initially the Clinton White House was contemptuous. One staffer said to *Time* in early 1993, "He's not one of us. He can't control Finance like Bentsen did. He's cantankerous, but we'll roll right over him if we have to." But Moynihan got the budget and tax package through the Senate and in August when the White House needed one last vote it was Elizabeth Moynihan who persuaded Bob Kerrey (whose presidential candidacy Moynihan supported in 1992) to cast the critical vote. Moynihan had other accomplishments. Largely because of his efforts, the nanny tax was reformed and the Social Security Administration was made an independent agency.

Health care went differently. In January 1993 Moynihan criticized HHS Secretary Donna Shalala sharply for not mentioning welfare reform in her opening statement to the committee, and for months he pressed the Clintons to emphasize welfare reform, but to no great avail. In January 1994, when the Clintons produced a vast healthcare bill, Moynihan called their puny efforts on welfare "boob bait for bubbas." On *Meet the Press* he insisted, "We don't have a healthcare crisis in this country. We do have a welfare crisis." He called the original Clinton financing mechanism "a fantasy," and he threatened to hold health care hostage to a welfare bill. He got Shalala to admit that the "few" who would pay more under the Clinton plan were actually 40% of insured families. Nonetheless Moynihan stood ready to cobble a compromise with Bob Dole, who seemed at the beginning of 1994 to be interested. But the Clintons, backed by Majority Leader George Mitchell and Finance member Jay Rockefeller, said it wasn't time to compromise yet. Finance did produce a bill, and Mitchell got ready to introduce his own version on the floor. But in August 1994, House Democrats lost a crucial procedural vote on the crime bill and had to delay action on health care, and the Mitchell effort ran out of steam.

Moynihan's great cause on health care was preserving teaching hospitals, and not just because New York has several of them. For him it was "a sin against the Holy Ghost" to threaten the existence of these institutions. One of his great causes on the Finance Committee was preserving the deductibility of gifts of appreciated property to nonprofit entities such as universities and museums. This was Moynihan using the tax code to become a Maecenas, channeling more money to America's Tocquevillian cultural institutions than the National Endowments for the Humanities and Arts will ever give.

Surprisingly for one whose critique of society can be so radical, in the sense of going to the root of things, Moynihan's approach to some issues can be cautious and, in the literal sense of aversion to change, conservative. In 1981, he was the first Democrat to jump to defend Social Security from any Reagan Administration attack; he got the Senate to vote 96–0 against any cut in benefits. In 1991, he got both Democrats and Republicans in a tizzy with his "Moyniplan" to cut the Social Security payroll tax 1%. His concern was that we finance current deficit spending out of the surpluses of Social Security taxes over benefits. In 1993, he put a quick stop to talk about delaying Social Security cost-of-living adjustments, calling it a "death wish" for Democrats. In the 1986 tax reform debate, his great cause was preserving the deductibility of state taxes, worth more in high-tax New York than any other state. But Moynihan seems pessimistic about the prospects for government. He sees it as afflicted by "Baumol's disease"— the condition noted by economist William Baumol of inevitably increasing costs of personal services—because "activities with cost disease tend to migrate to the public sector." As a result, Moynihan says, it seems that welfare states are always broke, running perpetual huge deficits as the United States has since the Reagan tax cuts in 1981 were unaccompanied by promised spending cuts. Hence his anger that the Social Security surplus is being ransacked, that healthcare research and training are threatened, that childrens' well-being is threatened by welfare reform.

Welfare reform is the idea he has been most closely associated with since 1965, when he wrote "The Negro Family." For that he was harshly criticized for years for "blaming the victim;" in fact, he was blaming fatherlessness. Since then, family breakdown among blacks has reached harrowing proportions, and family breakdown overall is now about as common as it was among blacks in 1965. His response was the Welfare Reform Act of 1988, which recognized the responsibilities of fathers to provide for their children and encouraged workfare experiments. It was opposed, incidentally, by the Children's Defense Fund, whose board members included Hillary Rodham Clinton and Donna Shalala. But enforcement of child support and work incentives produced disappointing results. In 1992, the Clinton campaign promised to "end welfare as we know it." In 1993, Moynihan pressed for an administration bill, in vain. In early 1995 Moynihan criticized the House Republicans' Contract With America welfare bill, which removed the entitlement to AFDC and left the states to write the changes.

Moynihan has also been a force in foreign policy. In 1975 and 1976, he was ambassador to the United Nations, where he denounced the Soviet Union and some Third World nations, opposing their resolution declaring Zionism as racism. Moynihan was criticized harshly by liberals for not being more conciliatory toward Communists and their allies. He argued that he was only taking international law seriously. Once considered a foreign policy hawk, in the late 1970s he became convinced that the Soviet Union was not a strong enemy and would come apart through ethnic conflict. Moynihan believes ethnic allegiances and rivalries are more important in politics than economic differences: that is the theme of his and Nathan Glazer's *Beyond the Melting Pot*, a description of New York's ethnic groups that was published in 1963 and still rings true today, and it is the theme of his 1993 book *Pandemonium*, which describes how ethnic conflicts produce war and genocide. In the 1980s, Moynihan continued to denounce the Soviet Union though not always in agreement with the Reagan Administration. Though he is generally classed now with foreign policy doves, there is a great difference between them: most doves believed that the Soviet Union was dangerous but not evil, while Moynihan believed that the Soviet Union was evil but, because it was economically weak, not dangerous. Today, Moynihan believes the United States should have a far smaller military and should basically abolish the CIA. He opposed the North American Free Trade Agreement because of his feeling that Mexico remains a "Leninist" society, but he was very much for the new General Agreement on Tariffs and Trade and was one of the few members of Congress to support the Mexico bailout in early 1995.

Electoral politics has proved surprisingly congenial to Moynihan. After beating Bella Abzug in the 1976 primary, he won a party-line victory against incumbent James Buckley in a year when Republicans were hurt by President Ford's opposition to federal loan guarantees for New York City. For 1982, Moynihan's opposition to Reagan programs prevented the emergence of opposition from the left, and he eliminated the main Republican candidate, Bruce Caputo, when it became known that Caputo had falsified his military record. Moynihan won 65%–34% in 1982 and 67%–31% in 1988, both records for New York. He is a partisan Democrat with an affection for old-time party bosses but also has many ties with reformers. In 1994 he insisted that the 1994 Democratic state convention not give perennial candidate Al Sharpton the 25% of its votes needed to put him on the primary ballot; it did not. His general election opponent was Bernadette Castro, heiress of the Castro convertible sofabed fortune. She was little known, but the election's last week surge toward Republicans almost made her a contender. Moynihan's share of the vote was sharply down from 1988. He carried New York City 73%–25%, but won in the suburbs by only 49%–48% and split the Upstate vote evenly, for a 55%–42% victory. Now Moynihan is in the minority again, with less institutional power but just as much moral stature. He is now ranking Democrat on Finance, with good relations with chairman Bob Packwood. He replaced Max Baucus as ranking member on the Trade Subcommittee, while Baucus replaced him on the Transportation subcommittee from which he wrote ISTEA.

Alfonse D'Amato, New York's junior senator, in October 1992 seemed to be a political goner. In November 1994, he was the most powerful politician in one of the nation's larger states, ready to play a lead role on national issues. And not a quiet one: he is loud, persistent, he pinches cheeks and puts his arms around shoulders and stands just a little too close when he speaks, he uses lushly vulgar expressions and is utterly shameless in his bids for popularity. His style owes something to his origins in the Long Island suburb of Island Park, where he was part of the Nassau County Republican machine from the 1960s. He was supervisor of the Town of Hempstead, which has some 700,000 people, from 1971 to 1977, and vice chairman of the Nassau County Board of Supervisors from 1977 to 1980. These are big-spending governments and no place for the naive. In 1980, he had the insight that he could win the Republican primary against Senator Jacob Javits, who was, as D'Amato's ads bluntly pointed out, 76, ailing and liberal, and that he could beat a liberal Democrat in a year when voters were turning against liberals. That is what happened: D'Amato first beat Javits 56%–44% and then beat Elizabeth Holtzman, former New York City comptroller, 45%–44%.

D'Amato quickly set out to establish a reputation as "Senator Pothole," with manically aggressive constituency service and shameless devotion to causes dear to New York constituencies—mass transit, AIDS funding, Israel, the death penalty for drug dealers, and Wall Street brokerage firms in their fights against the big banks. Yet he gets along well enough with Pat Moynihan, and their interests overlap more than one might think: Moynihan really does care about getting New York reimbursed for the Thruway and D'Amato really does care about human rights in Lithuania. Indeed, D'Amato was prescient in condemning Saddam Hussein, and his stands, sometimes with cameras rolling, for human rights in the former Soviet Union have been vindicated by history. But staying in favor by doing favors has downside risks. D'Amato is widely suspected of violating ethical standards—suspicions that have more basis in his personal style and background than in any proven facts. If he was a product of the redolent Nassau County machine, that was during the reign of party chairman Joseph Margiotta; he has had a more distant relationship with current party chairman Joseph Mondello. D'Amato was rebuked by the Senate Ethics Committee for allowing his brother Armand to use his office while representing a defense contractor, and his brother was convicted of mail fraud. But a rebuke is the mildest sanction, and his brother's conviction was overturned by a federal appeals court in a blistering opinion which said the prosecution was unjust.

D'Amato was easily reelected in 1986 over Mark Green, now New York City advocate (the post used to be council chairman). His tough race came in 1992, in a Democratic state in a Democratic year, against a strong field of Democrats. But D'Amato got some luck and made some luck. Geraldine Ferraro, who before her 1984 vice presidential nomination had been thinking about a race against D'Amato in 1986, ran in 1992 on a moderate platform (against single-payer health insurance, for the death penalty) and appealed to Manhattan feminists and outer borough Italian-Americans. Ferraro ran into trouble in the primary, though. Elizabeth Holtzman, then New York city comptroller, attacked her for not throwing out a pornography distributor tenant from a building she and her husband owned in 1985, as they had promised, and a Holtzman ad showed a *Village Voice* headline, "What You Don't Know About Ferraro And The Mob." Ferraro attacked this as "ethnic slurs" and Mario Cuomo said he was "disappointed," but Ferraro was clearly hurt. But the beneficiary was not Holtzman but Attorney General Robert Abrams. He won the September primary by some 11,000 votes, winning 37%, to 36% for Ferraro; Holtzman had 12% and the ever-telegenic black protester Al Sharpton 14%.

D'Amato immediately pounced on Abrams for making anti-Italian slurs and wrote a verse: "Lizzie Holtzman took an ax/She gave Geraldine 40 whacks/When Bobby Abrams saw what she done/He took the ax and gave her 41." Ferraro, clearly bitter, refused to concede the race for two weeks, awaiting absentee votes. D'Amato, vastly better financed, attacked Abrams as "hopelessly liberal," and touted his constituency service with ads saying, "Gettin' it done.

Makin' waves. Takin' 'em on." To pound home the point, he staged a 14-hour filibuster in mid-October to save 875 jobs at a Smith-Corona factory in the Upstate town of Cortland. Mid-October is also when Abrams made the mistake that cost him the election: after being heckled by D'Amato supporters in Binghamton, Abrams called D'Amato a "fascist." D'Amato demanded an apology; Abrams said his remark was "unfortunate" but for several days refused to apologize for calling D'Amato one of the few bad things he clearly is not. D'Amato took this, with some basis, as an anti-Italian slur and ran an ad attacking Abrams, showing Mussolini. Cuomo, whom D'Amato had never striven to beat, evidently took umbrage, saying "Bobby's race is all negative." D'Amato called Abrams "Mudslide Bob" and a "sleazebag," citing a commission that criticized him for taking money from developers whom he regulated. When it was revealed that Abrams was late in paying taxes on a $400,000 country home, D'Amato said, "He wants to raise other people's taxes . . . Let him pay his own." Meanwhile, he highlighted issues—defense cuts, health insurance—where he was closer to Bill Clinton's positions than Abrams was. From all this D'Amato squeaked out a 49%–48% victory. Exit polls showed D'Amato with high percentages among Italian descent voters (66%, 25% ahead of George Bush: the fascist slur hurt), Irish descent (63%) and white Protestants (62%); Abrams did well with blacks (84%) and those with no religious affiliation (74%), but not as well with Jews (59%).

Having survived 1992, D'Amato thrived in 1993 and 1994. His voting record on non-economic issues grew more conservative; he pressed for death penalties in the crime bill for major drug dealers. As ranking minority member of the Banking Committee, he pressed the case against Deputy Treasury Secretary Roger Altman for giving the White House a "heads up" on Whitewater; Altman resigned. His questions at the summer 1994 Whitewater hearings were sharp and penetrating. At home, his relations with Cuomo soured, and he contemplated running for governor; instead, in early 1994 he backed George Pataki, then a little-known state senator. Pataki was nominated at the state convention, led in the polls for months, then fell when Cuomo was endorsed by Rudolph Giuliani—a fierce enemy of D'Amato, at least since D'Amato supported Ron Lauder's primary race against him in 1989. But Pataki stayed cool and won, and promptly hired many D'Amato staffers. It would be wrong to see him as D'Amato's puppet, but it would be wrong to say that D'Amato has no influence in Albany either.

In Washington D'Amato became even more active on all fronts. Majority Leader Bob Dole appointed him head of the National Republican Senatorial Committee, in which capacity he criticized his predecessor, Phil Gramm, who was running for president against Dole. As chairman of the Banking Committee, he first threatened immediate Whitewater hearings, then said he would hold off in deference to independent counsel Kenneth Starr; Democrats feared he would swoop down when it would hurt the most. He introduced a bill to let banks merge with securities firms, insurance companies and commercial businesses, with firewalls to cabin off insured deposits and requirements to report on derivative trades. He not only endorsed Bob Dole, but engineered a joint Dole endorsement by Pataki and all 14 New York Republicans in Congress—but, pointedly, not Giuliani. He has also won regular attention in the tabloids—first, for his press-conference announcement that he intended to marry celebrity gossip columnist Claudia Cohen and then, not so positively, for his offensive ethnic parody on the Don Imus radio program of Judge Lance Ito. After pressure from Norm Mineta and others, D'Amato issued a reticent apology on the Senate floor. D'Amato also has his more appealing causes: a trade embargo on Iran, $15 million to fight Soviet organized crime, a law to help breast cancer detection, and demands for a monthly accounting of (and a demagogic denunciation of) the Mexican bailout: a lot more than just potholes.

Presidential politics. For more than 100 years, New York was a pivotal state in presidential politics: it was the nation's largest state and closely divided first between Whigs and Jacksonians, then Democrats and Republicans. But now California, with 54 electoral votes, is much larger than New York, with 33. California's moods are also much more changeable, thus attracting candidates' attention, while New York typically is the most Democratic large state. Back in the 1960s New York's Democratic margins came from middle-income Jews and

Catholics in the outer boroughs of New York City. Today they come primarily from blacks and Puerto Ricans in the outer boroughs and liberal whites in Manhattan. Manhattan liberals tend to be young singles, affluent childless couples, feminists, gays and lesbians, the often underpaid highly-educated people who flock to this center of arts and letters—the nation's prime leftish voting bloc. Bill Clinton's 69%–24% margin over George Bush in New York City gave him an insurmountable lead; by much smaller margins, he carried the suburbs (44%–40%) and Upstate (40%–37%). His 50% total was not impressive, but Bush's 34% total was, in a negative sense— almost as low a percentage as Barry Goldwater got in 1964, at the high water mark of faith and smug confidence in the New York welfare state.

New York has had bossed politics for years, and it never had a presidential primary until 1968. Turnout is low—for Democrats 1.0 million in 1980 and 1992, 1.3 million in 1984 and 1.5 million 1988—and convoluted petition requirements make it hard for some candidates to qualify. Pat Buchanan wasn't on the ballot here, and Alfonse D'Amato and George Pataki may well hope that no one but Bob Dole gets on the Republican ballot in 1996. Such primaries as do occur have an ethnic cast. Jewish voters, turning out heavily, set the tone of Democratic primaries from 1976 to 1984. Black voters, turning out heavily partly out of enthusiasm for Jesse Jackson but also because of anger at Mayor Edward Koch, set the tone in 1988. In 1992, the local press hyped the New York primary as a make-or-break test of Clinton, when in fact he had clinched the nomination in Illinois and Michigan three weeks before. Paul Tsongas had withdrawn, Jerry Brown was not going to win, Mario Cuomo was not running. Clinton played along with the charade, appearing on *Imus in the Morning* and parrying questions from Gabe Pressman, and sighed when it was over as if it were a great ordeal: he won with 41% to 26% for Brown and 29% for the withdrawn Tsongas.

New York's minor parties no longer much matter, except occasionally the Conservatives. The Liberal Party and its predecessor, the American Labor Party, were founded to give Jewish garment workers a line on which to vote for Franklin Roosevelt and against local Tammany Hall candidates; it garnered 1.8% of the gubernatorial vote in 1994. The Conservative Party was founded to withhold votes from liberal Republicans like Nelson Rockefeller and John Lindsay and encourage the Republican Party to nominate more conservative candidates; now it almost always does, though withdrawal of the Conservative line locally can hurt.

Congressional districting. When John Kennedy was elected president in 1960, New York elected 43 Congressmen and California 30. When Bill Clinton was elected in 1992, New York elected 31 and California 52. This is what happens when one state grows rapidly and another grows not at all. Redistricting is carnage time: New York lost five districts in the 1980 Census and another three in 1990. In 1992, New York was the last state to redistrict, in June. The plan has many districts with convoluted lines, all drawn for good political reasons.

The People: Est. Pop. 1994: 18,169,000; Pop. 1990: 17,990,455, up 1.0% 1990–1994. 7.0% of U.S. total, 3d largest; 16% rural. Median age: 33.9 years. 13.1% 65 years and over. 74.4% White, 15.9% Black, 12.3% Hispanic origin, 3.9% Asian, 5.5% Other. Households: 49.9% married couple families; 23% married couple fams. w. children; 45% college educ.; median household income: $32,965; per capita income: $16,501; 52.2% owner occupied housing; median house value: $131,600; median monthly rent: $428. 8.5% Unemployment. 1994 Voting age pop.: 13,646,000. 1994 Turnout: 5,062,404; 37% of VAP. Registered voters (1994): 8,818,691; 4,140,794 D (47%); 2,708,791 R (31%); 1,969,106 unaffiliated and minor parties (22%).

Political Lineup: Governor, George E. Pataki (R); Lt. Gov., Elizabeth McCaughey (R); Secy. of State, Alexander Treadwell (R); Atty. Gen., Dennis C. Vacco (R); Comptroller, H. Carl McCall (D). State Senate, 61 (36 R and 25 D); State Assembly, 150 (94 D and 56 R). Senators, Daniel Patrick Moynihan (D) and Alfonse M. D'Amato (R). Representatives, 31 (14 R and 17 D).

1992 Presidential Vote

Clinton (D) 3,444,450 (50%)
Bush (R) 2,346,649 (34%)
Perot (I)................. 1,090,721 (16%)

1992 Democratic Presidential Primary

Clinton.................. 412,349 (41%)
Tsongas 288,330 (29%)
Brown 264,278 (26%)
Other.................... 42,769 (4%)

1988 Presidential Vote

Dukakis (D).............. 3,347,882 (51%)
Bush (R) 3,081,871 (48%)

GOVERNOR

Gov. George E. Pataki (R)

Elected 1994, term expires Jan. 1999; b. June 24, 1945, Peekskill; home, Garrison; Yale U., B.A. 1967, Columbia U. Law Schl., J.D. 1970; Roman Catholic; married (Libby).

Career: Practicing atty., 1970–89; Peekskill Mayor, 1982–84; NY Assembly, 1985–92; NY Senate, 1993–95.

Office: Executive Chamber, State Capitol, Albany 12224, 518-474-8418; Fax: 518-473-7669.

Election Results

1994 gen.	George E. Pataki (R)	2,538,702	(49%)
	Mario M. Cuomo (D-L)	2,364,904	(45%)
	B. Thomas Golisano (INF).....	217,490	(4%)
	Others......................	82,666	(2%)
1994 prim.	George E. Pataki (R)	273,620	(76%)
	Richard M. Rosebaum (R)	88,302	(24%)
1990 gen.	Mario M. Cuomo (D-L)	2,157,087	(53%)
	Pierre A. Rinfret (R)	865,948	(21%)
	Herbert I. London (C)	827,614	(20%)
	Others......................	206,247	(5%)

SENATORS

Sen. Daniel Patrick Moynihan (D)

Elected 1976, seat up 2000; b. Mar. 16, 1927, Tulsa, OK; home, Pindars Corners; City Col. of NY, 1943, Tufts U., B.A. 1948, M.A. 1949, Ph.D. 1961; Catholic; married (Elizabeth).

Career: Navy, 1944–47; Aide, NY Gov. Averell Harriman, 1955–58; U.S. Asst. Secy. of Labor, 1963–65; Dir., Joint Ctr. for Urban Studies, MIT and Harvard, 1966–69; Asst. to Pres. Nixon, Urban Affairs, 1969–71; Prof., Harvard, 1971–73; U.S. Ambassador to India, 1973–75; Ambassador to the U.N., 1975–76.

DC Office: 464 RSOB 20510, 202-224-4451.

State Offices: 405 Lexington Ave., #4101, New York 10174, 212-661-5150; Guaranty Bldg., 28 Church St., Buffalo 14202, 716-846-4097; and 214 Main St., Oneonta 13820, 607-433-2310.

Committees: *Environment & Public Works* (2nd of 7 D): Superfund, Waste Control and Risk Assessment; Transportation and Infrastructure. *Finance* (RMM of 9 D): International Trade (RMM); Social Security and Family Policy; Taxation and IRS Oversight. *Rules & Administration* (5th of 7 D). *Joint Committee on Taxation* (4th of 5 Sen.)

Group Ratings

	ADA	ACLU	COPE	CFA	LCV	CON	NSI	COC	ACU	NTLC	CHC
1994	100	74	88	83	92	16	0	28	0	12	0
1993	90	—	91	80	75	37	—	27	4	—	—

National Journal Ratings

	1993 LIB — 1993 CONS		1994 LIB — 1994 CONS	
Economic	83%	— 0%	84%	— 0%
Social	82%	— 15%	85%	— 7%
Foreign	71%	— 24%	78%	— 15%

Key Votes of the 103d Congress

1. Clinton Deficit Plan	Y	3. Brady Handgun Purchase	Y	5. Lmt. UN Cmnd. of Forces	N
2. NAFTA	N	4. Strike Race/Death Pnlty.	N	6. Cut Missile Funds	Y

Key Votes of the 104th Congress

1. Congressional Compliance	Y	3. Balanced Budget Amndt.	N	5. Product Liability Reform	N
2. Bar Unfunded Mandates	Y	4. Pass Line Item Veto	N	6. FY96 Budget	N

Election Results

1994 general	Daniel Patrick Moynihan (D-L)	2,646,541	(55%)	($6,705,482)
	Bernadette Castro (R-C)	1,988,308	(42%)	($1,581,901)
	Others	155,487	(3%)	
1994 primary	Daniel Patrick Moynihan (D)	526,766	(75%)	
	Al Sharpton (D)	178,231	(25%)	
1988 general	Daniel Patrick Moynihan (D-L)	4,048,649	(67%)	($4,809,810)
	Robert R. McMillan (R-C)	1,875,784	(31%)	($528,989)

Sen. Alfonse M. D'Amato (R)

Elected 1980, seat up 1998; b. Aug. 1, 1937, Brooklyn; home, Island Park; Syracuse U., B.S. 1959, J.D. 1961; Catholic; divorced.

Career: Practicing atty., 1962–65; Nassau Cnty. Public Admin., 1965–68; Hempstead Town Receiver of Taxes, 1969; Hempstead Supervisor, 1971–77; Vice Chmn., Nassau Cnty. Bd. of Supervisors, 1977–80.

DC Office: 520 HSOB 20510, 202-224-6542; Fax: 202-224-5871.

State Offices: 420 Fed. Bldg., Albany 12207, 518-472-4343; Fed. Bldg., 111 W. Huron, #620, Buffalo 14202, 716-846-4111; 7 Penn Plz., 7th Ave., #600, New York 10001, 212-947-7390; 1259 Fed. Bldg., 100 S. Clinton St., Syracuse 13260, 315-423-5471; and 100 State St., 304 Fed. Bldg., Rochester 14614, 716-263-5866.

Committees: *National Republican Senatorial Committee Chairman. Banking, Housing & Urban Affairs* (Chmn. of 9 R). *Finance* (9th of 11 R): International Trade; Long-Term Growth, Debt and Deficit Reduction; Taxation and IRS Oversight.

Group Ratings

	ADA	ACLU	COPE	CFA	LCV	CON	NSI	COC	ACU	NTLC	CHC
1994	20	32	38	42	0	65	90	65	92	92	71
1993	35	—	50	30	19	86	—	91	80	—	—

National Journal Ratings

	1993 LIB — 1993 CONS		1994 LIB — 1994 CONS	
Economic	38% —	61%	39% —	60%
Social	31% —	68%	19% —	80%
Foreign	0% —	92%	6% —	86%

Key Votes of the 103d Congress

1. Clinton Deficit Plan	N	3. Brady Handgun Purchase N	5. Lmt. UN Cmnd. of Forces Y
2. NAFTA	N	4. Strike Race/Death Pnlty. Y	6. Cut Missile Funds N

Key Votes of the 104th Congress

1. Congressional Compliance Y	3. Balanced Budget Amndt. Y	5. Product Liability Reform N
2. Bar Unfunded Mandates Y	4. Pass Line Item Veto Y	6. FY96 Budget Y

Election Results

1992 general	Alfonse M. D'Amato (R-C-RTL) 3,166,994	(49%)	($11,550,958)
	Robert Abrams (D-L) 3,086,200	(48%)	($6,408,981)
	Others 205,632	(3%)	
1992 primary	Alfonse M. D'Amato (R) . . . . unopposed		
1986 general	Alfonse M. D'Amato (R-C-RTL) 2,378,197	(57%)	($12,914,822)
	Mark Green (D) 1,723,216	(41%)	($1,635,676)

FIRST DISTRICT

Long Island—the Island to most New Yorkers—is America's largest, most populous and in some ways most troubled island: 103 miles long, 12 to 20 miles wide, with sandspit beaches fronting the Atlantic Ocean and gentle hills and cliffs above Long Island Sound. Nearly seven million people live here, more than in all but nine states, 4.3 million in the New York City boroughs of Brooklyn and Queens and 2.6 million in the suburban counties of Nassau and Suffolk. Brooklyn, at the western end of the island, is urban and thickly settled, while the Hamptons at the east end are carefully manicured countryside, preserved by a stylish New York elite. The Hamptons and the old whaling village of Sag Harbor, originally settled by New Englanders, were left behind in the rush of westward migration; today they appear more comfortable than grand, a shingled and windmilled portion of middle America kept more pristine than workaday middle America ever was.

But demographically, the Hamptons are only a small (though growing) part of Long Island. More important are the (no longer growing) suburbs created in the rush eastward after World War II. Developers looked for cheaper land for aircraft factories and shopping centers, subdivisions and office parks, and found them first in Nassau County just east of Queens and then in Suffolk County even farther east. Suffolk attracted young families, of Irish and Italian descent more often than Jewish or black, looking for more ground and trees and less crime and tension than in their City neighborhoods. Politically, Suffolk County is one of the most conservative parts of New York. It has also become turbulent political territory, as life in Long Island has turned sour in the last decade. Defense plants shut down and jobs evaporated as the defense buildup and then the Cold War ended. Lilco, the local utility, had cost overruns on its nuclear plant in Shoreham, and then went into bankruptcy after Governor Mario Cuomo shut the plant down, giving Long Island the nation's highest electric rates.

The 1st Congressional District covers eastern Suffolk County, running east from Smithtown on the North Shore and Patchogue on the South Shore. It includes the Hamptons but, more important politically, the Brookhaven National Laboratory and the defense plants in the center of the Island. Politically, this is a Republican area willing in times of discontent to vote for Democrats with some special claim on support.

The congressman from the 1st District is Michael Forbes, a natural politician who upset a Democratic incumbent in 1994. Forbes has roots in the East End, and a certain theatricality. One grandfather founded *The News Review* in Riverhead, other grandparents were a vaudeville song and dance team. He was voted the "most spirited" member of his class at West Hampton Beach High School. Though he grew up in a Democratic household, he got the political bug early, as a Republican. In 1971, at 19, he started working in the Suffolk County legislature; he worked for Speaker Perry Duryea of Montauk in the mid-1970s, then for Florida Congressman (now Senator) Connie Mack, Upstate conservative Democrat Sam Stratton, Senator Alfonse D'Amato and for the 1988 and 1992 Bush campaigns. He was a Small Business Administration regional director in the Bush Administration, then a New York area staffer for the U.S. Chamber of Commerce.

Despite all these political credentials, Forbes was not a favorite when he started running in the 1st District in 1994. He had competition in the primary, and Democratic incumbent George Hochbrueckner had strong claims. Hochbrueckner was a Grumman engineer elected to the Assembly in 1974 and to the House in 1986 because of his opposition to the Shoreham plant. He got a seat on the National Security Committee, where he worked to save jobs at Grumman and other Long Island contractors; on the side, he promoted composting. In three races for reelection he won with 51%, 57% and 52%. Hochbrueckner had a huge financial advantage in 1994, outspending Forbes $698,000 to $238,000, and he argued as before that voters needed him to protect defense jobs. But in late September, Grumman announced another 3,500 layoffs, and voters turned to other issues. Forbes called for a 10% across-the-board cut in the federal government and campaigned against unfunded mandates. He said he wanted to connect the East End by wire with with business opportunities in New York City and beyond, and to give tax incentives for small business and jobs. He campaigned on a solidly conservative line. "We don't have actual poverty. We have behavioral poverty. Very few people out there go to bed hungry."

Forbes won 53%–47%, as national issues overcame local. "I know my way around. I can hit the ground running," he claimed, and his 10-year acquaintance with Newt Gingrich proved that by helping him win a seat on the Appropriations Committee—an unusual feat for a freshman. Forbes proved his party loyalty early when he refused to support the plan to build a new Penn Station in Manhattan's old Post Office; this is a pet project of Senator Daniel Patrick Moynihan, supported by practically the entire New York delegation. Forbes has great energy and is one of those freshmen whose family remains in the district and who spends as little time in Washington as possible. He seems to have a strong potential for reelection.

The People: Pop. 1990: 580,076; 8% rural; 12% age 65+; 89% White; 4% Black; 2% Asian; 1% Other; 4% Hispanic origin. Voting age pop.: 433,094; 4% Black; 4% Hispanic origin. Households: 67% married couple families; 33% married couple fams. w. children; 49% college educ.; median household income: $45,464; per capita income: $17,614; median gross rent: $782; median house value: $158,400.

1992 Presidential Vote			1988 Presidential Vote		
Bush (R)	101,160	(40%)	Bush (R)	134,518	(61%)
Clinton (D)	96,890	(38%)	Dukakis (D)	87,389	(39%)
Perot (I)	54,128	(21%)			

Rep. Michael P. Forbes (R)

Elected 1994; b. July 16, 1952, Riverhead; home, Quogue; S.U.N.Y. Albany, B.A. 1983; Roman Catholic; married (Barbara).

Career: Staff asst., U.S. Sen. Alfonse D'Amato, 1980–83; Staff asst., U.S. Rep. Sam Stratton, 1983–84; Admin. Asst., U.S. Rep. Connie Mack, 1984–87; Owner, Forbes & Co. PR firm, 1987–89; Regional Admin., Small Business Admin., 1989–93; Regional Dir., U.S. Chamber of Commerce, 1993–94.

DC Office: 502 CHOB 20515, 202-225-3826; Fax: 202-225-3143; e-mail: mpforbes@hr.house.gov.

District Office: 1500 William Floyd Pkwy., #303, Shirley 11967, 516-345-9000.

Committees: *Appropriations* (29th of 32 R): Commerce, Justice, State, and Judiciary; Foreign Operations, Export Financing, and Related Programs; Treasury, Postal Service, and General Government.

Group Ratings and 103rd Congress Votes: Newly Elected

Key Votes of the 104th Congress

1. Congressional Compliance Y	6. Reform Crime Grant Y	11. Loser Pays Court Reform Y
2. Balanced Budget Amndmt. Y	7. National Security Act Y	12. Product Liability Reform Y
3. Bar Unfunded Mandates Y	8. Moratorium on Regs. Y	13. Welfare Reform Y
4. Pass Line Item Veto Y	9. Risk Assessment on Regs. Y	14. Term Limits Amndmt. Y
5. Relax Exclusionary Rule Y	10. Expnd. Priv. Prop. Rights Y	15. Tax Cuts Y

Election Results

1994 general	Michael P. Forbes (R-C-RTL)	90,491	(53%)	($265,930)
	George J. Hochbrueckner (D-LIF)	80,146	(47%)	($719,102)
	Others	1,603	(1%)	
1994 primary	Michael P. Forbes (R)	7,562	(55%)	
	John Scott Prudenti (R)	4,564	(33%)	
	Michael Strong (R)	1,533	(11%)	
1992 general	George Hockbrueckner (D-LIF)	117,940	(52%)	($606,190)
	Edward P. Romaine (R-C-RTL)	110,043	(48%)	($226,283)

SECOND DISTRICT

Following World War II, hundreds of thousands of New York City residents—people who had trouble imagining they would live anywhere but the close-packed city streets—moved to what had been the potato fields of central Long Island. The highways that Robert Moses built to connect Jones Beach with the city masses were the routes of that migration—and often the daily commuter paths back into New York—as young veterans and their families found they could afford to leave the row-house neighborhoods where they had grown up for the single-family houses of Levittown and other Long Island subdivisions. The first wave of postwar migration moved into Nassau County, and it was largely a cross-section of all but the poorest New Yorkers: about half Catholic, with the other half split almost evenly between Jews and Protestants. As Long Island developed its own employment base, another wave moved farther east into Suffolk County. This group was more Catholic and less Jewish than the first, and more blue-collar. It was ancestrally Democratic, but firmly traditional and culturally conservative.

The 2d Congressional District includes most of western Suffolk County. The bulk of the district's population is concentrated in the South Shore townships of Babylon and Islip, each of which contains numerous communities separated only by name. There are some spacious houses with views of Great South Bay, and, across the bay—but still within the district—lie the beaches of Fire Island, where many of the homes are weekend retreats owned by affluent New York City residents. But, for the most part, the 2d is the lower-income part of Long Island, beyond the more fashionable and expensive commuter suburbs to the west and well south of the picturesque North Shore. This area filled up with people in the 1950s and 1960s but has grown little in the past quarter century. However, with some of the lowest-priced housing on the Island, it continues to attract young families. Almost 10 percent of the 2d is Hispanic, the largest percentage of any of the Long Island districts.

The congressman from the 2d District is Rick Lazio, a Republican first elected in 1992 when he upset Democratic incumbent Tom Downey—a kind of preview of what soon would take place nationally. Downey was first elected in 1974, at 25, served on Ways and Means and worked the district hard: the kind of natural politician who helped Democrats maintain majorities for 20 years. But Lazio also had political skills and local roots. He grew up on the South Shore. After Vassar and law school in Washington, he was a prosecutor and, after 1989, a legislator in Suffolk County; he has been in the public sector since age 25. In a campaign in 1992 that echoed Downey's in 1974, Lazio attacked the incumbent Congressman as part of the Washington culture out of touch with Long Island, for junketing and for his 151 overdrafts on the House bank. Downey spent $1.4 million to Lazio's $276,000, but Lazio won 53%–47%.

This was a presage of 1994 Republican victories, but Lazio is not necessarily a Contract With America Republican. He did call for congressional reform and promised to serve no more than six consecutive terms. But he styles himself part of the party's "centrist wing" and is an active member of the Tuesday Group of moderate Republicans. Lazio was named to the Budget Committee as a freshman after campaigning for a capital gains cut, and his economic views are fairly conservative. On cultural issues he is less conservative, and he voted for family and medical leave, the Brady bill, the assault weapons ban and the striker replacement bill (he was one of just 17 Republicans on this) in the 103d Congress.

Lazio has a seat on the Banking Committee, and the large turnover in the House in the 1990s plus his early start yielded a happy dividend for him in early 1995. In only his second term he became chairman of the important Housing and Community Opportunity Subcommittee, where he is well-positioned to help reshape major parts of domestic policy. In contrast to many Republican newcomers, he brings a savvy knowledge of local government and the political arts to that task. He also became part of the party leadership: he was named a deputy whip after the Republicans gained control of the House. Like several other Republicans elected in 1992 in previously Democratic districts, he did very well in the 1994 election, winning 68%–28%. He now seems safely ensconced in the 2d District for the remaining four terms he has declared he will seek. Look for him to emerge with the kind of influence that Downey once showed.

The People: Pop. 1990: 580,303; 10% age 65+; 79% White; 10% Black; 2% Asian; 3% Other; 9% Hispanic origin. Voting age pop.: 437,905; 9% Black; 9% Hispanic origin. Households: 68% married couple families; 33% married couple fams. w. children; 45% college educ.; median household income: $50,076; per capita income: $17,515; median gross rent: $817; median house value: $158,600.

1992 Presidential Vote		
Bush (R)	92,762	(40%)
Clinton (D)	91,430	(40%)
Perot (I)	44,603	(19%)

1988 Presidential Vote		
Bush (R)	128,359	(61%)
Dukakis (D)	82,713	(39%)

Rep. Rick A. Lazio (R)

Elected 1992; b. Mar. 13, 1958, West Islip; home, Brightwaters; Vassar Col., B.A. 1980, American U., J.D. 1983; Catholic; married (Patricia Moriarty).

Career: Asst. Dist. Atty., Suffolk Cnty., 1983–88; Suffolk Cnty. legislator, 1989–92; Practicing atty., 1989–92.

DC Office: 314 CHOB 20515, 202-225-3335; Fax: 202-225-4669; e-mail: lazio@hr.house.gov.

District Offices: 126 W. Main St., Babylon 11702, 516-893-9010.

Committees: *Banking & Financial Services* (7th of 27 R): Capital Markets, Securities and Government Sponsored Enterprises; Housing and Community Opportunity (Chmn.). *Budget* (11th of 24 R).

Group Ratings

	ADA	ACLU	COPE	CFA	LCV	CON	NSI	COC	ACU	NTLC	CHC
1994	20	35	33	40	39	49	90	100	57	71	64
1993	40	—	58	70	64	29	—	73	71	—	—

National Journal Ratings

	1993 LIB — 1993 CONS		1994 LIB — 1994 CONS	
Economic	35%	— 63%	37%	— 61%
Social	43%	— 56%	42%	— 57%
Foreign	37%	— 60%	25%	— 71%

Key Votes of the 103d Congress

1. Clinton Deficit Plan	N	3. Brady Handgun Purchase	Y	5. Lmt. UN Cmnd. of Forces Y
2. NAFTA	Y	4. Strike Race/Death Pnlty.	Y	6. Cut Missile Funds	N

Key Votes of the 104th Congress

1. Congressional Compliance	Y	6. Reform Crime Grant	Y	11. Loser Pays Court Reform	N
2. Balanced Budget Amndmt.	Y	7. National Security Act	Y	12. Product Liability Reform	Y
3. Bar Unfunded Mandates	Y	8. Moratorium on Regs.	Y	13. Welfare Reform	Y
4. Pass Line Item Veto	Y	9. Risk Assessment on Regs.	Y	14. Term Limits Amndmt.	Y
5. Relax Exclusionary Rule	Y	10. Expnd. Priv. Prop. Rights	N	15. Tax Cuts	Y

Election Results

1994 general	Rick A. Lazio (R-C)	100,107	(68%)	($484,133)
	James L. Manfre (D-LIF)	41,102	(28%)	($87,156)
	Others	5,567	(4%)	
1994 primary	Rick A. Lazio (R)	unopposed		
1992 general	Rick A. Lazio (R-C)	109,386	(53%)	($276,191)
	Thomas J. Downey (D-L)	96,328	(47%)	($1,446,911)

THIRD DISTRICT

It was a pivotal moment in American suburban history: in September 1947, families moved into 300 tiny 750-square-foot houses, built in record time by mass production. They sold for $6,990, with no down payment for veterans. This was Levittown, and by the time the last new house was sold for $9,500 in November 1951, the name had become a synonym for rapid suburban development. Developer William Levitt recognized that many young veterans and their families were eager to move out of crowded New York City neighborhoods, so he bought a Nassau County potato field, planted trees, designed floor plans to allow easy additions and built a community of 65,000 people. The postwar surge and then the trend toward empty nesters can be seen in Nassau County population figures: 450,000 in 1940, 1.3 million in 1960, 1.4 million in 1970, then back to around 1.3 million by 1990 as youngsters moved out.

Nassau County also is home to what may be the nation's premier county Republican machine. It was the creation of Nassau Republican chairman J. Russell Sprague before the post-war population boom. Sprague managed to carry the county for Alf Landon in 1936 and that same year, persuaded the voters to adopt a county executive form of government in which control of political patronage would center in one man, responsible to the county Republican chairman.

The 3d Congressional District includes nearly half of Nassau County, made up of two distinct areas. Most people here live in towns strung out on either side of Sunrise Highway or just off the Southern or Northern State Parkways from Levittown and Hicksville, east to the county line. About one-fifth of the district's population lives in its northern geographic half, in the less densely populated old estate areas around Oyster Bay, Old Westbury and Manhasset. The 3d also includes Bethpage, home to the old Grumman aircraft company, once a big employer here and now part of Northrop Grumman. Not many of greater New York's wealthiest live in the 3d, but the overall level of affluence is high, and the district has the third highest median income of any in the nation, just behind the New Jersey 11th and Maryland 8th. The 3d, which contains the Island Park home of New York Senator Alfonse D'Amato, tends to be pretty solidly Republican, although Democrats have been competitive here, most recently in 1992.

The congressman from the 3d is Peter King, a Republican elected by a narrow margin that year who has made a distinctive record in the House. King is a product of the Nassau County Republican machine. He started working as a lawyer and staffer in county government in 1972, at 28; in 1981 he became Nassau County comptroller. When 22-year incumbent Republican Norman Lent announced his retirement in June 1992, King ran, emphasizing his record of holding down spending and of spotting the county government's fiscal crisis in 1991. He won the Republican primary 2–1. In the general he faced Democrat Steve Orlins, who grew up in Nassau County and made his career far afield, starting a law firm in Beijing in 1979 and his own Asian trading company; he sold it to Lehman Brothers, moved back to Long Island, and in 1992 spent over $700,000 of his own money on this race. King campaigned as a political insider and fiscal conservative, Orlins as a reformer and supporter of abortion rights. King won, but by only 50%–47%.

King's voting record has been conventionally conservative, but he is best known on Capitol Hill for his involvement in a series of controversial causes and initiatives. His initial election to Congress was greeted with trepidation in Great Britain: during his years in Nassau County government, he was widely viewed as a one of the U.S.'s strongest supporters of the Irish Republican Army. Within days of his election, he flew to Belfast to meet with leaders of Sinn Fein, the IRA's political arm. His longtime support of Gerry Adams, Sinn Fein's leader, bore fruit in 1994 and 1995 as Britain and the U.S. dropped travel and fundraising restrictions on Adams and his party. King looked on approvingly on St. Patrick's Day 1995 as President Clinton greeted Adams in the White House. As a member of the Banking Committee, King has gone after HUD's practice of contracting with firms associated with the Nation of Islam to provide security at housing projects. He also is pushing legislation to make English the country's official language. And, in a spat that garnered national publicity in mid-1994, King's tough questioning of Maggie Williams, First Lady Hillary Rodham Clinton's chief of staff, during Whitewater hearings got him into a confrontation with another outspoken member, Democrat Maxine Waters of California—who at one point told King to "shut up."

In 1994, King was opposed by another rich lawyer, Norma Grill, advocate of a state law barring discrimination in private clubs. But she spent less of her own money than Orlins ($225,000) and it was a more Republican year. King won 59%–40% and has reason to believe that such a showing is the norm in this district.

The People: Pop. 1990: 580,468; 13% age 65+; 91% White; 2% Black; 3% Asian; 1% Other; 4% Hispanic origin. Voting age pop.: 455,852; 2% Black; 4% Hispanic origin. Households: 70% married couple families; 30% married couple fams. w. children; 55% college educ.; median household income: $56,060; per capita income: $23,702; median gross rent: $811; median house value: $204,900.

1992 Presidential Vote			1988 Presidential Vote		
Clinton (D)	126,112	(44%)	Bush (R)	164,426	(60%)
Bush (R)	121,176	(42%)	Dukakis (D)	111,286	(40%)
Perot (I)	40,450	(14%)			

Rep. Peter T. King (R)

Elected 1992; b. Apr. 5, 1944, Manhattan; home, Seaford; St. Francis Col., B.A. 1965, U. of Notre Dame, J.D. 1968; Catholic; married (Rosemary).

Career: Army Natl. Guard, 1968–73; Practicing atty., 1968–72, 1978–81; Dep. Atty., Nassau Cnty., 1972–74; Exec. Asst., Nassau Cnty. Exec., 1974–76, Gen. Cnsl., 1977; Hempstead Town Cncl., 1977–81; Nassau Cnty. Comptroller, 1981–92.

DC Office: 224 CHOB 20515, 202-225-7896; Fax: 202-226-2279.

District Office: 1003 Park Blvd., Massapequa Park 11762, 516-541-4225.

Committees: *Banking & Financial Services* (10th of 27 R): Financial Institutions and Consumer Credit; General Oversight and Investigations. *International Relations* (16th of 23 R): International Operations and Human Rights; Western Hemisphere.

Group Ratings

	ADA	ACLU	COPE	CFA	LCV	CON	NSI	COC	ACU	NTLC	CHC
1994	5	13	22	30	11	72	100	83	81	86	93
1993	15	—	42	40	43	29	—	82	92	—	—

National Journal Ratings

	1993 LIB — 1993 CONS		1994 LIB — 1994 CONS	
Economic	34% —	65%	0% —	80%
Social	19% —	77%	27% —	72%
Foreign	9% —	85%	25% —	71%

Key Votes of the 103d Congress

1. Clinton Deficit Plan	N	3. Brady Handgun Purchase	N	5. Lmt. UN Cmnd. of Forces	Y
2. NAFTA	Y	4. Strike Race/Death Pnlty.	Y	6. Cut Missile Funds	N

Key Votes of the 104th Congress

1. Congressional Compliance	Y	6. Reform Crime Grant	Y	11. Loser Pays Court Reform	N
2. Balanced Budget Amndmt.	Y	7. National Security Act	Y	12. Product Liability Reform	N
3. Bar Unfunded Mandates	Y	8. Moratorium on Regs.	Y	13. Welfare Reform	Y
4. Pass Line Item Veto	Y	9. Risk Assessment on Regs.	Y	14. Term Limits Amndmt.	N
5. Relax Exclusionary Rule	Y	10. Expnd. Priv. Prop. Rights	Y	15. Tax Cuts	Y

Election Results

1994 general	Peter T. King (R-C) 115,236	(59%)	($516,548)
	Norma Grill (D) 77,774	(40%)	($415,561)
	Others 1,522	(1%)	
1994 primary	Peter T. King (R) 10,391	(73%)	
	Robert Previdi (R) 3,896	(27%)	
1992 general	Peter T. King (R-C) 124,727	(50%)	($263,345)
	Steve A. Orlins (D)................... 116,915	(46%)	($1,127,239)
	Others 9,980	(4%)	

FOURTH DISTRICT

Garden City is one of America's first suburbs, created more than a century ago by New York retailer A.T. Stewart at a time when reformers wanted to maintain the commercial vitality and social interaction of the city, but in a setting that preserved the healthful openness of the countryside. Garden City's wide avenues and single-family homes, connected to New York City by the Long Island Railroad, were intended to be middle-income territory, but its amenities have made it one of the highest-income parts of Long Island. In the century after its founding, the rest of Nassau County has changed from almost entirely rural to suburban. The big rush came after World War II, as one town ran into another, freeways replaced strip highways, and shopping centers sprang up at intersections. Today, many of the middle- and upper-income residents of the 4th Congressional District still depend on the Long Island Railroad (the "LIRR") to get them to jobs in New York City. But once-removed Garden City now sits amid Nassau County's civic institutions just south of the county seat of Mineola and the site of Roosevelt Field, where Charles Lindbergh took off for Paris. Almost 60 years later, Roosevelt Field is a large suburban shopping center, with the Nassau Coliseum—home to hockey's New York Islanders—nearby.

The 4th District includes Garden City and the civic center of Nassau County. It includes half of Levittown and the neat and conservative suburbs along the Queens line from New Hyde Park to Valley Stream; it takes in the "Five Towns"—Lawrence, Inwood, Cedarhurst, Hewlett and Woodmere—near Kennedy Airport's flight paths. While most of the 4th is traditionally Republican, it voted for Bill Clinton in 1992, and its demographics have made it an appealing target for Democratic strategists. The 4th is almost one-quarter black and Hispanic, and the Five Towns area, predominantly Jewish, is heavily Democratic. On the other hand, residents of Irish and Italian ancestry make up well over 40 percent of the district, and heavily Irish and Italian communities, like Elmont and East Meadow, vote mostly Republican.

The congressman from the 4th is Daniel Frisa, who has the distinction of being the only member elected in 1994 who ousted a Republican incumbent; he is a Republican himself, and did the ousting in the primary. The victim was David Levy, who had won the seat just two years before. Behind the contest is a story of rivalry and feuding within the once-monolithic Nassau County Republican organization. Frisa and Levy both are Baby Boomers who grew up in the machine. Frisa became a Republican committeeman at 18 and starting in 1984 served eight years in the state Assembly, where he sat next to Governor-to-be George Pataki; Levy was a Hempstead town councilman who held a variety of patronage jobs during the decade prior to his election to Congress. In 1992, when Republican Raymond McGrath decided to retire, leaving his Ways and Means seat to become chief lobbyist for the beer industry, Frisa claimed to have been promised the backing of the organization, but county party chairman Joseph Mondello endorsed Levy, suggesting that Frisa was a tool of the previous party chairman, Joseph Margiotta. Levy won the primary by only 53%–41%, and then had a close race against Democrat Philip Schiliro, a Long Island native and top aide to California Congressman Henry Waxman. Levy was outspent and won by just 50%–46%.

Levy served quietly on Capitol Hill, but there was political turmoil back in Nassau County.

Frisa, who gave up his Assembly seat to run for Congress, bolted the party and supported the Democratic candidate for Nassau County executive in 1993. He went into the direct mail business and decided to challenge Levy in the September 1994 primary. Using direct mail and foot soldiers from his old Assembly district in the East Meadow area, but eschewing media attention, he flew under the radar screen of the Republican machine. Initial results showed him defeating Levy by 276 votes in a low turnout; the margin dropped to 54 after a recount. Charging irregularities, Levy sued in state court to hold another election, but lost. He remained on the general election ballot as the candidate of the state's Conservative Party but did not actively campaign, though he won 9% of the vote. The Democrats gave their initial candidate a judicial nomination (a classic boss's maneuver in New York) and put in a call to Schiliro, who—given the fund-raising prowess of his boss, Henry Waxman—was in a position and willing to mount a well-funded campaign in a hurry. Schiliro was nominated and outspent Frisa by better than $200,000. But Frisa, having attacked Levy in the primary for inaction on congressional reform, continued to play the outsider in the general election, and hit Schiliro for having spent a decade in Washington and away from Nassau County. The party machine only tepidly supported Frisa, but he won comfortably, 50%–37%.

In Washington, Frisa—who campaigned on the Contract With America's term limits and a capital gains tax cut—showed his insider skills by gaining a seat on the powerful Commerce Committee. Ironically, this is the panel on which Waxman was an influential subcommittee chairman for 16 years. Frisa serves on the subcommittee regulating securities and communications, perhaps the best assignment in Congress for raising campaign money. It is possible that Mondello and company may oppose Frisa again in 1996, or that he may have serious Democratic opposition. But, in his sometimes invisible manner, he has shown great aggressiveness and appears to be in a strong position to repel challenges.

The People: Pop. 1990: 580,492; 15% age 65+; 74% White; 16% Black; 3% Asian; 2% Other; 7% Hispanic origin. Voting age pop.: 451,532; 15% Black; 7% Hispanic origin. Households: 65% married couple families; 28% married couple fams. w. children; 50% college educ.; median household income: $50,887; per capita income: $20,349; median gross rent: $705; median house value: $197,000.

1992 Presidential Vote		
Clinton (D)	119,947	(47%)
Bush (R)	106,016	(41%)
Perot (I)	30,476	(12%)

1988 Presidential Vote		
Bush (R)	144,338	(57%)
Dukakis (D)	106,968	(43%)

Rep. Dan Frisa (R)

Elected 1994; b. Apr. 27, 1955, Westburg; home, Westbury; St. John's U., B.S. 1977; Roman Catholic; married (Jane).

Career: Salesman, Johnson & Johnson Co., 1977–78; Retail Exec., Fortunoff, 1979–84; NY Assembly, 1985–92; Direct mail consultant, 1984–94.

DC Office: 1529 LHOB 20515, 202-225-5516; Fax: 202-225-3187.

District Office: 250 Old Country Rd., #506, Mineola 11501, 516-739-1800.

Committees: *Commerce* (23rd of 26 R): Commerce, Trade and Hazardous Materials; Oversight and Investigations; Telecommunications and Finance.

Group Ratings and 103rd Congress Votes: Newly Elected

Key Votes of the 104th Congress

1. Congressional Compliance Y	6. Reform Crime Grant Y	11. Loser Pays Court Reform Y
2. Balanced Budget Amndmt. Y	7. National Security Act Y	12. Product Liability Reform Y
3. Bar Unfunded Mandates Y	8. Moratorium on Regs. Y	13. Welfare Reform Y
4. Pass Line Item Veto Y	9. Risk Assessment on Regs. Y	14. Term Limits Amndmt. Y
5. Relax Exclusionary Rule Y	10. Expnd. Priv. Prop. Rights Y	15. Tax Cuts Y

Election Results

1994 general	Dan Frisa (R)	87,815	(50%)	($231,931)
	Philip M. Schilro (D)	65,286	(37%)	($447,955)
	David A. Levy (C)	15,173	(9%)	($216,992)
	Others	6,689	(4%)	
1994 primary	Dan Frisa (R)	12,487	(50%)	
	David A. Levy (R)	12,433	(50%)	
1992 general	David A. Levy (R-C)	110,710	(50%)	($209,225)
	Philip Schiliro (D-L)	100,386	(46%)	($502,513)
	Vincent Garbitelli (RTL)	9,548	(4%)	

FIFTH DISTRICT

The North Shore of Long Island is "Gatsby country," where peninsulas jutting out into the Sound are covered with vast green lawns leading to the mansions of America's great capitalists. Nineteenth century millionaires commuted by steam yacht from Manhattan to their estates in what now is Queens or Nassau County. In the early 20th Century the richest people in business and entertainment spent their leisure time here, playing croquet while their servants unloaded bootleggers' boats at their private docks during Prohibition. Inland, behind the expansive lawns, Long Island was still farm country, with little villages clustered at railroad stations, occasional colonial era houses, and acres of billboard-strewn wasteland on the highways to New York City. But The City grew out. Affluent neighborhoods developed in Douglaston and Bayside on the water, just beyond the middle-class Flushing area of Queens inland. The Great Neck peninsula became a very affluent, mostly Jewish suburb. Farther out, on Sands Point and Oyster Bay, old estates alternated with more modest homes, originally built for servants, and newer subdivision mansions. Further east, in Suffolk County, affluent subdivisions grew up on hilly land above the bays and points.

The 5th Congressional District ties together a disparate collection of New York City neighborhoods and suburbs on or within a few miles of the North Shore. At several points the district is connected across open water, and anyone wishing to traverse its boundaries from one end of it to the other better be a good swimmer. About one-third of its votes are cast in Suffolk County, where the political leanings are conservative on cultural and economic issues. In the middle, with about one-quarter of the votes, are the North Shore communities of Nassau: the Jewish areas Democratic and liberal, the WASPy areas Republican but culturally liberal also. Half the district's population and about 40% of its voters are in the borough of Queens. Here along the Sound are the affluent double-house Bayside neighborhood, and higher-income Douglaston and Little Neck, next to the Nassau border—all Republican territory. A few blocks inland is Flushing, an old Dutch settlement from the 17th Century, with the Queens numbered-street grid superimposed on old Dutch trails. Its newer apartment buildings, mostly Jewish since the 1950s, by the 1980s were becoming heavily Asian, especially Chinese and Korean, their future politics unclear. The 5th also goes south almost to the Long Island Expressway, to pleasant homeowner neighborhoods like Fresh Meadows and Oakland Gardens. But even here, far from Manhattan and in relatively affluent areas, there are plenty of high-rises.

The Congressman from the 5th District is Democrat Gary Ackerman, a good-humored survivor of a couple of serious contested races in the 1990s. Ackerman grew up in Flushing, taught junior high school, ran an advertising agency, started the *Queens Tribune* in 1970 and sold it to publisher Jerry Finkelstein in 1978. That same year he was elected to the New York Senate, where Democrats seem permanently in the minority. In a March 1983 special election, he won his seat in the House, from a district centered in the heavily Jewish apartment complexes in central Queens. Ackerman is a colorful character, who always wears a white carnation and lives on a boat in Washington. His great cause in Congress has been the rescue of Ethiopian Jews and relieving government-caused famines in Ethiopia and Sudan. He has voted faithfully for the interests of public employees, of whom there are many in Queens. Acerbic but humorous, he is a pungent speaker: his comment on the Gulf war resolution (on which he voted yes) was "Slam, bam, thanks Saddam. You should have took the letter. Now take the loss, reverse the course, 'cause it ain't going to get no better." On the roll call for Speaker in January 1995, when he was second in alphabetical order, after Neil Abercrombie of Hawaii voted for Dick Gephardt, Ackerman said, "Move to close the roll!"

The 1992 election was Ackerman's great challenge. He had represented only 9% of the people in the new 5th District, and it was the only district in which three incumbent House members could run. But one, Robert Mrazek from Suffolk County, was running for the Senate, and then dropped out when it was revealed he had 920 overdrafts on the House bank. Another, James Scheuer, the Flying Dutchman of New York politics—who for all but two years from 1964 represented districts including parts of the Bronx, Brooklyn, Queens and Nassau, though his original residence was in Manhattan—had 133 overdrafts and decided to retire at 72. Ackerman had 111 overdrafts but had not been on the list of worst abusers which had been leaked in March 1992. He was the Ethics Committee member widely assumed to have leaked that list, and resigned from the committee in July 1992 before an investigation could be launched. In the primary, Ackerman was opposed by Rita Morris, a retired librarian from Nassau County (and mother of Democratic campaign consultant Hank Morris). She was furious that there were not more women in Congress when Anita Hill's charges against Clarence Thomas surfaced and decided to spend her life savings of $500,000 on the race. Just before the primary, *Newsday* reported that Ackerman had negotiated a $45,000 yearly consulting contract for his wife with the *Queens Tribune*'s Finkelstein, which Morris said was an attempt to evade outside income restrictions. Ackerman, in turn, charged that Morris's son had turned her into a "mud wrestler." Ackerman won by 60%–40%. The Republican candidate was Allan Binder, a 31-year-old county legislator from Suffolk County who had worked for Texas Congressman Tom DeLay; he called Ackerman a "typical tax and spend" liberal and called for tax cuts. Binder won in Suffolk 58%–38%, but Ackerman won Nassau 59%–40% and Queens 61%–38%, for an overall 52%–45% victory.

Ackerman became chairman of the Asian and Pacific Affairs Subcommittee (he told *CongressDaily*, "I love Asian food. That's probably the overriding reason for becoming chairman. Lots of good restaurants"). In October 1993, he met with Kim Il Sung in North Korea; he also worked on Africa and local issues. In 1994, conservative Grant Lally beat Binder in the Republican primary and waged a vigorous campaign. But Ackerman, better known in new territory, was one of the few Democrats to improve his showing in 1994: he lost Suffolk 57%–40%, but carried Nassau 62%–37% and Queens 63%–36%, for a 55%–43% victory. Without the demands of his chairmanship, he will have more time to solidify his still-shaky new district.

The People: Pop. 1990: 581,073; 1% rural; 15% age 65+; 79% White; 3% Black; 11% Asian; 2% Other; 7% Hispanic origin. Voting age pop.: 462,648; 3% Black; 7% Hispanic origin. Households: 63% married couple families; 27% married couple fams. w. children; 58% college educ.; median household income: $50,103; per capita income: $24,296; median gross rent: $660; median house value: $255,000.

1992 Presidential Vote			1988 Presidential Vote		
Clinton (D)	131,042	(52%)	Bush (R)	123,097	(51%)
Bush (R)	88,505	(35%)	Dukakis (D)	119,339	(49%)
Perot (I)	30,459	(12%)			

Rep. Gary L. Ackerman (D)

Elected Mar., 1983; b. Nov. 19, 1942, Brooklyn; home, Queens; Queens Col., B.A. 1965; Jewish; married (Rita).

Career: Jr. high schl. teacher, 1966–70; Editor and publisher, *Queens Tribune*, 1970–78; Pres, advertising agcy., 1972–78; NY Senate, 1979–83.

DC Office: 2243 RHOB 202-225-2601; Fax: 202-225-1589.

District Offices: 218–14 Northern Blvd., Bayside 11361, 718-423-2154; and 229 Main St., Huntington 11743, 516-423-2154.

Committees: *Banking & Financial Services* (21st of 22 D): Capital Markets, Securities and Government Sponsored Enterprises. *International Relations* (6th of 19 D): Africa (RMM); Asia and the Pacific.

Group Ratings

	ADA	ACLU	COPE	CFA	LCV	CON	NSI	COC	ACU	NTLC	CHC
1994	90	71	71	90	69	18	30	50	0	12	7
1993	80	—	100	100	85	25	—	20	13	—	—

National Journal Ratings

	1993 LIB	—	1993 CONS	1994 LIB	—	1994 CONS
Economic	78%	—	12%	73%	—	17%
Social	73%	—	27%	74%	—	26%
Foreign	66%	—	34%	85%	—	0%

Key Votes of the 103d Congress

1. Clinton Deficit Plan	Y	3. Brady Handgun Purchase	Y	5. Lmt. UN Cmnd. of Forces	N
2. NAFTA	N	4. Strike Race/Death Pnlty.	N	6. Cut Missile Funds	N

Key Votes of the 104th Congress

1. Congressional Compliance	Y	6. Reform Crime Grant	N	11. Loser Pays Court Reform	N
2. Balanced Budget Amndmt.	N	7. National Security Act	N	12. Product Liability Reform	N
3. Bar Unfunded Mandates	Y	8. Moratorium on Regs.	N	13. Welfare Reform	N
4. Pass Line Item Veto	N	9. Risk Assessment on Regs.	N	14. Term Limits Amndmt.	N
5. Relax Exclusionary Rule	N	10. Expnd. Priv. Prop. Rights	N	15. Tax Cuts	N

Election Results

1994 general	Gary L. Ackerman (D-L)	93,896	(55%)	($1,376,467)
	Grant M. Lally (R-C)	73,884	(43%)	($442,726)
	Others	2,862	(2%)	
1994 primary	Gary L. Ackerman (D)	unopposed		
1992 general	Gary L. Ackerman (D-L)	110,476	(52%)	($917,483)
	Allan E. Binder (R-C)	94,907	(45%)	($123,206)
	Other	5,448	(3%)	

SIXTH DISTRICT

New York City's largest middle-class black neighborhoods are not in Harlem or Brooklyn, but in the southeast corner of Queens. Here, in the "architectural monotony of block upon block of boxlike frame and brick houses," as one critic described them, built mostly from the 1920s to the 1950s, are the neighborhoods of Springfield, Laurelton, St. Albans and Rosedale, near Kennedy Airport and the tidal marsh of Jamaica Bay, just west of the Nassau County line. There was a small black community in South Jamaica half a century ago, and since then black families who have accumulated savings have bought houses and raised their families in neighborhoods on the streets fanning east from Jamaica. They fought to maintain the relatively spacious streets, relishing unrefracted light in their windows, enjoying safe schools and parks and good neighborhood stores: people who have, in Bill Clinton's felicitous phrase, "worked hard and played by the rules."

Neighborhoods like these form most of the 6th Congressional District, a district of uncharacteristic (for New York) geographic compactness. It includes almost all of southern Queens, roughly south of the Interborough and Grand Central Parkways, including half of the Rockaway Peninsula across Jamaica Bay. The heavily black neighborhoods in the southeast, plus white ethnic Richmond Hill and Ozone Park, are in the district. In 1990, 56% of the people here were black, 16% Hispanic, 6% Asian and 23% non-Hispanic white. While there are pockets of poverty, the district is mostly middle-class country: the median income was $36,200, far ahead of the $23,000 to $26,000 of New York's other black-majority districts—indeed ahead of the $30,300 of Queens's white-majority 7th District.

The congressman from the 6th is Floyd Flake, a black leader who gained prominence by a different route than The City's other black Congressmen (though similar to the path taken by its first, Adam Clayton Powell). Flake, one of 13 children whose father was a janitor, went to college and then divinity school. In 1976, at 31, he became a minister at Allen A.M.E. Church in Queens. In 10 years, he built it up from 1,400 to 6,000 members and from 3 to 743 employees, built a $12 million housing project for the elderly and a private school for 480 students, and handled a budget with annual revenues over $17 million. While many public institutions did not serve middle-class blacks well, Flake created a private institution that did. In 1986, he ran in a special primary against the Queens Democratic organization choice, Alton Waldon, after Congressman Joseph Addabbo died. While he won by 167 votes at the polls, he lost the special primary by 276 votes because his name had been kept off the absentee ballots by one of New York's endless election law technicalities. Flake understandably felt cheated and, with the support of many local blacks and the endorsement of Mayor Edward Koch, he then beat Waldon in the September 1986 primary for the next full term and was elected without difficulty in this overwhelmingly Democratic district.

Flake has had a turbulent time in the 1990s but has remained politically strong. He was the subject of a federal prosecution on charges—based on complaints by a disgruntled former church employee—that he embezzled funds from a church-sponsored housing project and from the church itself. In the middle of the April 1991 trial, prosecutors dropped the case after the judge suggested that the evidence against Flake was shaky. In 1992, he was the object of a challenge by the Queens Democratic organization, which endorsed Simeon Golar, an unsuccessful House candidate in 1982 and 1984 in Queens and in 1990 in the Bronx. Golar said Flake was arrogant and was using his church as a political machine that "evokes scary reminders of Jonestown." But Flake won the primary 77%–23%. He had no serious opposition in 1994.

In the 103d Congress, Flake chaired a Banking subcommittee and sponsored the Bank Enterprise Act of 1994, to provide incentives for banks to invest in "underserved" areas. He has also worked on the Community Reinvestment Act, which has similar aims, on minority set-aside contracts and on encouraging U.S. investment in emerging economies around the world. But that type of legislation, like his chairmanship, has become a distant memory under the new regime—leaving Flake to hope for a Democratic revival or to carve out a new role for himself.

The People: Pop. 1990: 581,812; 11% age 65+; 23% White; 56% Black; 1% Amer. Indian; 6% Asian; 7% Other; 16% Hispanic origin. Voting age pop.: 433,982; 54% Black; 15% Hispanic origin. Households: 52% married couple families; 25% married couple fams. w. children; 38% college educ.; median household income: $36,223; per capita income: $13,150; median gross rent: $565; median house value: $157,900.

1992 Presidential Vote

Clinton (D)	115,526	(75%)
Bush (R)	28,033	(18%)
Perot (I)	9,380	(6%)

1988 Presidential Vote

Dukakis (D)	105,816	(73%)
Bush (R)	39,511	(27%)

Rep. Floyd H. Flake (D)

Elected 1986; b. Jan. 30, 1945, Los Angeles, CA; home, Rosedale; Wilberforce U., B.A., 1967, Payne Theological Seminary, M.A. 1970, Northeastern U., 1974–76; United Theological Sem., Ph.D., 1994; African Methodist Episcopal; married (Elaine).

Career: Social worker, Head Start, 1968–69; Mktg. analyst, Xerox Corp., 1969–70; Assoc. Dean of Students, Lincoln U. 1970–73; Boston U., Dean of Students and Chaplain, Dir., MLK Afro-American Ctr., 1973–76; Pastor, Allen A.M.E. Church, 1976–present; Founder and Chmn., Allen Christian Schl., 1982–present, Allen Home Care Agcy., 1983–present.

DC Office: 1035 LHOB 202-225-3461; Fax: 202-226-4169.

District Offices: 196-06 Linden Blvd., St. Albans 11412, 718-849-5600; and 20-80 Seagirt Blvd., Far Rockaway 11691, 718-327-9791.

Committees: *Banking & Financial Services* (8th of 22 D): Capital Markets, Securities and Government Sponsored Enterprises; Domestic and International Monetary Policy (RMM). *Small Business* (5th of 19 D): Procurement, Exports and Business Opportunities.

Group Ratings

	ADA	ACLU	COPE	CFA	LCV	CON	NSI	COC	ACU	NTLC	CHC
1994	95	86	78	90	75	19	10	45	0	8	7
1993	90	—	92	90	79	16	—	22	5	—	—

National Journal Ratings

	1993 LIB — 1993 CONS		1994 LIB — 1994 CONS	
Economic	75% —	22%	83% —	0%
Social	73% —	27%	90% —	6%
Foreign	79% —	16%	85% —	0%

Key Votes of the 103d Congress

1. Clinton Deficit Plan	Y	3. Brady Handgun Purchase	Y	5. Lmt. UN Cmnd. of Forces	N
2. NAFTA	Y	4. Strike Race/Death Pnlty.	N	6. Cut Missile Funds	Y

Key Votes of the 104th Congress

1. Congressional Compliance	Y	6. Reform Crime Grant	N	11. Loser Pays Court Reform	*
2. Balanced Budget Amndmt.	N	7. National Security Act	N	12. Product Liability Reform	N
3. Bar Unfunded Mandates	Y	8. Moratorium on Regs.	N	13. Welfare Reform	N
4. Pass Line Item Veto	N	9. Risk Assessment on Regs.	N	14. Term Limits Amndmt.	N
5. Relax Exclusionary Rule	N	10. Expnd. Priv. Prop. Rights	N	15. Tax Cuts	N

Election Results

1994 general	Floyd H. Flake (D)	68,596	(80%)	($227,256)
	Denny D. Bhagwandin (R-C)	16,675	(20%)	
1994 primary	Floyd H. Flake (D)	unopposed		
1992 general	Floyd H. Flake (D)	96,972	(81%)	($281,172)
	Denny D. Bhagwandin (R-C)	22,687	(19%)	($45,015)

SEVENTH DISTRICT

Home of Shea Stadium and Forest Hills Stadium, site of the 1939 and 1964 World's Fairs, home base of noted political figures Mario Cuomo and Geraldine Ferraro, Queens doesn't get much attention or respect, even though this 2 million-person borough on its own would be the nation's fourth-largest city. But Queens does not have well-known history. It started as nondescript farmland in the 17th Century, with villages growing into urban nodes that grew quickly as the subways reached the borough. And Queens has no obvious center, unlike downtown Brooklyn or the Grand Concourse in the Bronx. Even Queens Boulevard is just another arterial street, starting in the industrial mishmash around the Queensborough Bridge (usually referred to by its Manhattan name, 59th Street) and ending near the unimpressive brick Borough Hall, sited by the Grand Central Parkway overpass, across from the Pastrami King and Crossroads Drugs.

Queens has grown around dozens of small hubs, not from a central point outward or directly from Manhattan. More than any other area of New York City, this is a borough of neighborhoods. Some are of genuine distinction, like the old Tudor-mansioned Forest Hills. Others, like Irish Sunnyside and College Point, still show their immigrant origins. Astoria, on the tip of Queens near the Triborough Bridge, is Greek-American and effervescently prosperous. Today, Jackson Heights and Corona are filled with new immigrants from Colombia and the Dominican Republic. Before World War II, Queens was filled with of one- and two-family frame house neighborhoods that were Yankee, German or Irish. The residents considered Manhattan as The City (a locution still used in many Queens neighborhoods), and they voted defiantly Republican. As the subway lines were built out farther after World War II, Queens became a borough of high-rise apartments, like giant Lefrak City near the intersection of Queens Boulevard and the Long Island Expressway. With good public schools, low rents and easy access to Manhattan, Queens was an airier place to live and raise a family than Manhattan, and central Queens became heavily settled and heavily Jewish.

The 7th Congressional District, loosely connected by narrow corridors, is a collection of Queens neighborhoods plus, over the Bronx-Whitestone Bridge, a salient of land running far into the Bronx. To describe the boundaries here would take the rest of this book. The major neighborhoods are Long Island City, just across from Manhattan, its single Citicorp tower a stark contrast with warehouses and housing projects, peopled by many ethnic groups; Sunnyside, Maspeth and Middle Village, working class neighborhoods off the Long Island Expressway; the (as of 1990) non-Hispanic parts of Corona, Elmhurst and Jackson Heights, three-story apartment neighborhoods; the expanse of Flushing Meadow, site of the still-remembered Trylon and Perisphere rising over the 1939 World's Fair; and Whitestone and College Point, working class villages on Long Island Sound. It also includes the Italian East Bronx neighborhoods, the giant Parkchester apartment complex and the area around Yeshiva University: mostly white ethnics between the Hispanic South Bronx and black Williamsbridge. About one-fifth Hispanic and one-tenth black, the 7th is fairly solidly white working class and is fairly solidly Democratic.

The congressman here is Thomas Manton, the son of Irish immigrants. He is a former police officer and IBM salesman who worked his way up to Queens Democratic chairman—a position that he continues to hold, in the long but dying tradition of urban politicians—and to Congress. He was first elected to the City Council in 1969, when he represented a conservative district opposed to liberal Republican Mayor John Lindsay. He first ran for Congress in 1972, unsuccessfully challenging conservative Democratic Congressman James Delaney in the primary. When Delaney retired in 1978, Manton ran and lost to Geraldine Ferraro. Ferraro had planned to represent Queens until she ran against Senator Alfonse D'Amato in 1986, but those plans were upset when she became the 1984 Democratic nominee for vice president and then when her husband had legal problems in 1985. She ran for the Senate in 1992 but narrowly lost the primary. Manton was well prepared to move up when Ferraro moved out. He ran in the 1984 primary and won with 30% of the vote; three other candidates got 27%, 22% and 21%. In the general he beat Conservative Party stalwart (and now state Senator) Serphin Maltese 53%–47%.

Manton showed his skill as an insider early by winning a seat on Dingell's Commerce Committee, a position that gives him less influence now that his party is in the minority. But his legislative initiatives often are geared toward solving local problems: an amendment to the hazardous waste law designed to stop the Long Island Railroad's plans to build a Long Island City waste transfer site, prohibition of sewage sludge composting plants in New York City, Clean Air Act amendments to help New York businesses. He opposed cable reregulation as a member of the Telecommunications Subcommittee; Time Warner is a big employer here. As a former cop, he worked to guarantee that disability payments to law enforcement personnel injured in the line of duty were on par with those killed on duty. During the 103d Congress, Manton pushed an amendment to competitiveness legislation to restrict foreign-owned companies' access to U.S. research and development grants. Manton wanted to pressure foreign companies to adopt U.S. standards on issues like intellectual property and national treatment. But the Clinton Administration and business groups feared retaliation; between the two arguments, the bill died. In the 104th Congress, Manton sponsored an amendment to kill the "English rule" loser-pays plank from the Contract With America; that failed as well. Manton also serves as co-chairman of the Congressional Ad-Hoc Committee on Irish Affairs.

Usually reelected easily, in 1992 Manton got a scare from Senator Bob Dole's aide Dennis Shea, who returned to the district, attacked Manton's 17 overdrafts on the House bank totaling $22,000 and hit him for his liberalism. Manton won 59%–41% in Queens but only 52%–48% in the Bronx, for a total 57%–43% win. In 1994, he received only token opposition from a Conservative Party candidate.

The People: Pop. 1990: 580,116; 17% age 65+; 58% White; 10% Black; 12% Asian; 8% Other; 21% Hispanic origin. Voting age pop.: 473,059; 9% Black; 19% Hispanic origin. Households: 46% married couple families; 19% married couple fams. w. children; 36% college educ.; median household income: $30,324; per capita income: $14,905; median gross rent: $520; median house value: $205,900.

1992 Presidential Vote			1988 Presidential Vote		
Clinton (D)	91,319	(56%)	Dukakis (D)	87,565	(54%)
Bush (R)	57,343	(35%)	Bush (R)	75,069	(46%)
Perot (I)	14,979	(9%)			

Rep. Thomas J. Manton (D)

Elected 1984; b. Nov. 3, 1932, New York City; home, Sunnyside; St. John's U., B.B.A. 1958, LL.B. 1962; Catholic; married (Diane).

Career: Marine Corps, 1951–53; NYC Police Officer, 1955–60; IBM salesman, 1960–64; Practicing atty., 1964–84; NYC Cncl., 1969–84.

DC Office: 2235 RHOB 20515, 202-225-3965; Fax: 202-225-1909; e-mail: tmanton@hr.house.gov

District Offices: 46–12 Queens Blvd., Sunnyside 11104, 718-706-1400; and 2114 Williamsbridge Rd., Bronx 10461, 718-931-1400.

Committees: *Commerce* (9th of 21 D): Commerce, Trade and Hazardous Materials; Energy and Power; Telecommunications and Finance.

Group Ratings

	ADA	ACLU	COPE	CFA	LCV	CON	NSI	COC	ACU	NTLC	CHC
1994	70	43	75	70	72	8	44	45	15	12	28
1993	70	—	100	90	79	11	—	9	17	—	—

National Journal Ratings

	1993 LIB — 1993 CONS	1994 LIB — 1994 CONS
Economic	75% — 22%	73% — 27%
Social	47% — 52%	61% — 38%
Foreign	51% — 42%	68% — 29%

Key Votes of the 103d Congress

1. Clinton Deficit Plan	Y	3. Brady Handgun Purchase Y	5. Lmt. UN Cmnd. of Forces N
2. NAFTA	N	4. Strike Race/Death Pnlty. N	6. Cut Missile Funds N

Key Votes of the 104th Congress

1. Congressional Compliance Y	6. Reform Crime Grant N	11. Loser Pays Court Reform N
2. Balanced Budget Amndmt. N	7. National Security Act N	12. Product Liability Reform N
3. Bar Unfunded Mandates Y	8. Moratorium on Regs. N	13. Welfare Reform N
4. Pass Line Item Veto Y	9. Risk Assessment on Regs. N	14. Term Limits Amndmt. N
5. Relax Exclusionary Rule Y	10. Expnd. Priv. Prop. Rights N	15. Tax Cuts Y

Election Results

1994 general	Thomas J. Manton (D)	58,935	(87%)	($360,940)
	Robert E. Hurley (C)	8,698	(13%)	
1994 primary	Thomas J. Manton (D)	unopposed		
1992 general	Thomas J. Manton (D)	72,280	(57%)	($1,013,635)
	Dennis C. Shea (R-C)	54,639	(43%)	($182,737)

EIGHTH DISTRICT

For the last 200 years, New York has been a heavily Jewish city. New York's Dutch founders came from the European country most tolerant of Jews, and so Jews settled in Nieuw Amsterdam as they had in old. German Jews came in large numbers in the 19th Century, some insisting they were more German than they were Jewish; some founded great merchant banking dynasties. Around 1890, Ashkenazi Jews from Eastern Europe started coming from what were then the Romanov and Hapsburg Empires—now Poland, Lithuania, Belarus, Ukraine, Hungary and Romania. Then, after being persecuted in the years after World War I, as many as 400,000 Jews came past the Statue of Liberty to Ellis Island every year in the early 1920s, until a 1924 law virtually shut down immigration. Had a malapportioned, rural-dominated, nativist Congress not done that, perhaps 2 million of the 6 million who perished in the Holocaust would instead have become Americans.

Ashkenazi Jews initially lived on the Lower East Side but moved out the subways to Brooklyn and the Bronx almost as soon as they were built. Their children moved up faster and farther than any new group in memorable history, rising despite prejudice to the top of almost every profession that would let them in. They invented vast new businesses from the rag trade to show biz: second-caste people from third-rate countries almost immediately becoming elite in the world's foremost country. Their descendants live all over the country, but New York remains America's most heavily Jewish city and has the largest Jewish population of any city in the world.

While there are no reliable figures, as the Census does not record religion, the 8th Congressional District of New York may be the most heavily Jewish district in the nation. About three-fifths of its population is in Manhattan, two-fifths in Brooklyn. Bizarre boundaries isolate blacks and Hispanics in nearby majority-minority districts. As it was drawn, it included the homes of then-Congressmen Ted Weiss on the Upper West Side of Manhattan and Stephen Solarz in Brighton Beach, Brooklyn. The Upper West Side from 59th Street north to Morningside Heights and Columbia University is one of the heavy voting areas here: the venerable apartments along Central Park West and West End Avenue and Riverside Drive, and the brownstones on the cross streets which house some of America's most idealistic and dedicated liberal-to-radical voters. These professional people include the wealthy, as well as the struggling who enjoy the grittiness of the Upper West Side, the almost European atmosphere of boulevarded upper Broadway and the fierce struggle that is daily life in New York. People on the West Side took up the reform issue in the 1950s and eventually eviscerated the old Tammany Hall Democratic machine. In the 1960s, the same people took up the cause of peace, attempting to end U.S. involvement in Vietnam. The cause had changed to feminism by the late 1980s, when they attempted the ending of gender-incorrect speech and the preservation of abortion rights. Greenwich Village, America's original Bohemia in the 1910s, is another big voting area. It is now a neighborhood of expensive apartments and houses interlaced with much cheaper dwellings, and New York's most conspicuously gay center; politically the Village has long had a taste for what it regards as radical. Then there are new Village-type residential areas to the south: SoHo, where old factory buildings have been refurbished as lofts; TriBeCa, where commercial space now houses artists; Battery Park City, the attractive modern apartments built on a landfill west of the now-crumbled West Side Highway.

The district includes two Brooklyn neighborhoods: Brighton Beach and Coney Island, long gone to seed but spruced up by the Russian Jewish immigrants who flocked here in the 1980s; and Borough Park, with many militantly pro-Israel Orthodox Jews. While they are connected to the heavily Jewish Manhattan neighborhoods by a narrow land bridge running along the Brooklyn waterfront and the massive Bush Terminal buildings, these areas are politically very different. The Russians favor free enterprise and are anti-socialist. Borough Park is extremely hostile to racial preferences and favors tough police treatment of crime. People here are willing to vote Republican and look askance at liberal Democrats.

The congressman from the 8th District is Jerrold Nadler, a West Side liberal Democrat. He grew up in New York and was a veteran of the late 1960s antiwar movement; he was a junior at Columbia during the 1968 campus riots. He worked as a legislative staffer before being elected to the Assembly himself in 1976: politics has been his life. In the Assembly he was known as an expert on mass transit and advocate of rail freight into New York City. He voted there against the big tax cut of 1987. His election in 1992 was something of a surprise. Stephen Solarz, with his Brooklyn Jewish base, had been expected to run here after redistricting, but his strong positions for the Gulf war and U.S. engagement in Asia probably would have hurt him in Manhattan. He decided to run in the majority-Hispanic 12th District instead, where he narrowly lost, and failed in efforts to win a job in the Clinton Administration. Ted Weiss, with his big Upper West Side base and his leftish voting record, was expected to win the seat, but he died the day before the September 1992 primary (which he won anyway).

That meant that the new congressman would be chosen by a convention of almost 1,000 county Democratic committee members. The Democrats were faced with six candidates: Nadler, Weiss's widow Sonya Weiss, Assemblyman Richard Gottfried (elected in 1970 at 23), state Senator Franz Leichter, Councilwoman Ronnie Eldridge and former Congresswoman (1970–76) Bella Abzug. The convention was as tumultuous as can be imagined. Abzug withdrew in favor of Eldridge, the wife of columnist Jimmy Breslin; neither Gottfried nor Leichter, who had expressed doubt about whether he had the energy for the job, had many votes. The key vote was procedural, for a system of weighted voting under which Nadler won 62% of the votes and Eldridge 21%; opponents decried this system (after they lost), perhaps with some reason. Nadler became the Democratic nominee and the general election was automatic. For the last two months of Weiss's term, Nadler also represented his old Manhattan-Bronx 17th District.

Nadler entered the House with a two-month seniority advantage over other freshmen and immediately called for a comprehensive transportation bill, though Congress had just passed that in the form of Senator Pat Moynihan's ISTEA in 1991. His voting record is among the House's most liberal, as one would expect; the newspaper *Roll Call* rated him in 1994 as Congress's second most liberal member. Not surprisingly he calls for large defense cuts and gay and lesbian rights. In the 1994 Democratic primary, he was opposed by City Councilman Thomas Duane, who is openly gay and announced in 1991 that he was HIV positive. Nadler won that contest 62%–29%, and then won the general election easily. But in a Republican House he is unlikely to be influential. In early 1995 he called on Republicans to include in their tax cut bill a provision to cut taxes for people living in high cost-of-living areas like New York City. It is hard to imagine something that the Republican majority would be less likely to adopt. He did demonstrate some effectiveness in his own party, however, when he pushed to passage the so-called "Nadler rule" which restricted ranking members on full committees from taking any ranking subcommittee posts on their panels as well. Nadler took the loudly protesting John Dingell head on over this, and won.

The People: Pop. 1990: 581,453; 15% age 65+; 74% White; 8% Black; 6% Asian; 5% Other; 12% Hispanic origin. Voting age pop.: 486,890; 8% Black; 11% Hispanic origin. Households: 32% married couple families; 13% married couple fams. w. children; 59% college educ.; median household income: $32,784; per capita income: $26,168; median gross rent: $544; median house value: $223,100.

1992 Presidential Vote

Clinton (D)	168,838	(77%)
Bush (R)	37,558	(17%)
Perot (I)	12,197	(6%)

1988 Presidential Vote

Dukakis (D)	147,922	(73%)
Bush (R)	55,239	(27%)

Rep. Jerrold Nadler (D)

Elected 1992; b. June 13, 1947, Brooklyn; home, New York City; Columbia U., B.A. 1970, Fordham U., J.D. 1978; Jewish; married (Joyce Miller).

Career: Legis. Asst., NY Assembly, 1972, Law Clerk, 1976; NY Assembly, 1977–92.

DC Office: 109 CHOB 20515, 202-225-5635; Fax: 202-225-6923.

District Offices: 1841 Broadway, #800, New York 10023, 212-489-3530; and 2875 W. 8th St., Brooklyn 11224, 718-373-3198.

Committees: *Judiciary* (9th of 15 D): Commercial and Administrative Law; Courts and Intellectual Property. *Transportation & Infrastructure* (18th of 27 D): Aviation; Railroads.

Group Ratings

	ADA	ACLU	COPE	CFA	LCV	CON	NSI	COC	ACU	NTLC	CHC
1994	100	90	100	100	100	9	0	17	5	11	0
1993	95	—	100	90	100	30	—	9	8	—	—

National Journal Ratings

	1993 LIB — 1993 CONS		1994 LIB — 1994 CONS	
Economic	88%	— 0%	83%	— 0%
Social	87%	— 0%	86%	— 14%
Foreign	93%	— 0%	83%	— 15%

Key Votes of the 103d Congress

1. Clinton Deficit Plan	Y	3. Brady Handgun Purchase	Y	5. Lmt. UN Cmnd. of Forces	N
2. NAFTA	N	4. Strike Race/Death Pnlty.	N	6. Cut Missile Funds	Y

Key Votes of the 104th Congress

1. Congressional Compliance	Y	6. Reform Crime Grant	N	11. Loser Pays Court Reform	N
2. Balanced Budget Amndmt.	N	7. National Security Act	N	12. Product Liability Reform	N
3. Bar Unfunded Mandates	N	8. Moratorium on Regs.	N	13. Welfare Reform	N
4. Pass Line Item Veto	N	9. Risk Assessment on Regs.	N	14. Term Limits Amndmt.	N
5. Relax Exclusionary Rule	N	10. Expnd. Priv. Prop. Rights	N	15. Tax Cuts	N

Election Results

1994 general	Jerrold Nadler (D-L)	109,946	(82%)	($791,767)
	David L. Askren (R)	21,132	(16%)	($16,172)
	Others	3,008	(2%)	
1994 primary	Jerrold Nadler (D)	33,658	(62%)	
	Thomas K. Duane (D)	15,820	(29%)	
	Deborah A. Green (D)	4,803	(9%)	
1992 general	Jerrold Nadler (D-L)	138,296	(81%)	($45,505)
	David L. Askren (R)	25,548	(15%)	($2,150)
	Others	6,404	(4%)	

NINTH DISTRICT

Brooklyn. The single word used to arouse laughter in a comedian's monologue, applause when someone said they were from there. It evoked an accent that twisted the English language almost to non-recognition, a raucous and brusque confrontational style, a sense of humor with an edge, the chip-on-the-shoulder assertiveness of those sure they will always be in second place. Brooklyn would never be more important than Manhattan; the Dodgers would always lose the series to the Yankees or the playoffs to the Giants, and when they finally did win, in 1955, they moved to Los Angeles two years later. Brooklyn, as its Dutch name testifies, was a separate community from the 17th Century on, one of the largest cities in the country in the 19th Century, with its own celebrities (Henry Ward Beecher, Walt Whitman, John Roebling). By 1898, when the five boroughs were welded into Greater New York, one million people lived in Brooklyn, but the Brooklyn of the comedians really came into being as the subways were built in the early 20th Century. Suddenly workers in all the little Manhattan factories no longer had to live in Lower East Side tenements. They moved out the subway lines, into neighborhoods of three- to five-story apartments and four-family houses. Brooklyn grew from 1.1 million in 1900 to 1.6 million in 1910 to 2.0 million in 1920 and 2.6 million in 1930. The old Brooklynites were mostly Protestant—Dutch, Yankee, German—plus some Catholic Irish. The new Brooklynites were heavily Italian and Jewish, the people who peopled sports and entertainment for a long generation, making their home town and its impenetrable accent nationally famous. In 1940, as the nation was about to go to war, Brooklyn had 2.7 million people: one in every 49 Americans lived in this one borough.

Today, 2.3 million people, one in every 108 Americans, live in Brooklyn, and it is no longer a staple of national comedy. Some of its old neighborhoods—Jewish Brownsville, Italian East New York—have been ravaged by crime and stand empty and toothless. But there is great vitality in much of Brooklyn, among upwardly mobile Hispanic immigrants and a hard-working black middle class, and in neighborhoods of the grandchildren of the earlier Jews and Italians. The farther reaches of Ocean Parkway and the expanse of Flatlands and Canarsie, the quiet corners of Sheepshead Bay and Gerritsen are such places. Here young Orthodox Jews raise families within walking distance of school, and neighbors patrol the streets at night to keep down the crime which has wrecked neighborhoods just a few miles away.

The 9th Congressional District includes many such neighborhoods in Brooklyn and in the borough of Queens as well. Its geography is grotesque, its demography more comprehensible. This is where descendants of the 1890–1924 migrants live. In Brooklyn it extends from Prospect Park south along Ocean Parkway to Coney Island and Sheepshead Bay: still one of the most Jewish areas in the United States. It extends east over Flatlands and much of Canarsie and then across Jamaica Bay south to the Rockaway Peninsula and north to a collection of Queens neighborhoods: Howard Beach, next to Kennedy Airport; the old German neighborhoods of Glendale and Ridgewood, still orderly and spotlessly clean; Italian Woodhaven and Tudor-trimmed Forest Hills; much of the heavily Jewish high-rise area along Queens Boulevard. The political balance here is Democratic but not overwhelmingly so. Jewish portions of the 9th are heavily Democratic, the other ethnic areas are often Republican.

The congressman from the 9th District is Charles Schumer, one of the most creative and active—if not hyperactive—members of the House. He has made important contributions to public policy without a traditional House power base, through energy, imagination, good humor and, not least, a certain amount of *chutzpah*: the old Brooklynite, derumpled a bit at Harvard. Schumer seems well aware that there is a country west of the Brooklyn Bridge. His outlook is optimistic but tempered by the memories of one just barely old enough to recall the Dodgers leaving town, and he has the brains and creativity that have enabled so many Brooklyn-born people to institute change.

The year he graduated from Harvard Law, 1974, Schumer was elected to the New York

Assembly, at 23; in 1980, just before he turned 30, he was elected to the House. Immediately he raised a campaign treasury of over $1 million, lest he and Brooklyn neighbor Stephen Solarz be redistricted together in 1982; they weren't, and Schumer went on to concentrate on legislation. From the unlikely venue of the Banking Committee, a panel that most talented members lobby to get off of, Schumer spotted the perverse incentives set up by the combination of deposit insurance and letting S&Ls make risky investments. He fought Banking chairman Fernand St. Germain, calling early on for higher capital requirements, and helped shape the 1989 S&L bailout bill. He has also worked on housing programs, building on the success of the Nehemiah projects in Brooklyn. But he did even more work as a junior member of Judiciary and, eventually, chairman of its Crime and Criminal Justice Subcommittee. He ranged far afield, coming up with a key compromise regarding farm laborers in the immigration reform law of 1986, and another in 1990 on employment-sponsored immigration. With free marketeer (now Majority Leader) Dick Armey, he launched an unsuccessful 1990 effort to prohibit subsidy payments to farmers with adjusted gross incomes over $100,000. He worked hard to increase funding for tuberculosis control and amended the energy bill to phase out exports of highly enriched nuclear fuel. He wrote an auto theft law to reduce the market for resale of stolen parts. Other causes include the Violence Against Women Act and a federal law against impeding access to abortion clinics.

Schumer has managed several crime bills. Unlike many Democrats, he favors the death penalty; he also strongly backs gun control. He steered to passage the Brady bill, with its waiting period for handgun purchases, over strong opposition from the National Rifle Association. He supported the inclusion of the assault weapons ban in the 1994 crime bill, and also the provisions for crime prevention, from drug counseling to midnight basketball. But Schumer was caught short in August 1994 when on the crime bill rule vote, 59 Democrats voted no, many because of the gun control provisions, and all but 11 Republicans voted no as well. Many supporters of the bill were outraged by the heavyhanded tactics and pork-barrel projects of then-Judiciary chairman Jack Brooks. Schumer, who saw Brooks's conference report only when Republicans did, insisted that his bill was good legislation. But it was caught up in the much greater partisan struggle that resulted in the Republican takeover in November 1994. Before then, the bill was revised and passed, with the gun control measures.

The Republican Congress creates a new problem for Schumer: how can this talented compromiser and maker of unlikely alliances get things done in a House where most issues divide members on partisan lines and there is little frank communication across the center aisle? Initially, his response was to work to protect New York against what he considered harmful Contract With America provisions and Republican budget proposals. He also has said that he would fight efforts to repeal gun control laws he has helped pass. But in April 1995, Schumer urged postponement of any gun vote in light of the Oklahoma City bombing.

Looking ahead to redistricting in 1992, he accumulated a $2.1 million campaign treasury. But Stephen Solarz ran in a Hispanic-majority district and Schumer, despite the Republican-leaning neighborhoods in Queens, has no problems in the 9th District, winning handily in 1994. But he has his eyes on statewide office. Had Mario Cuomo retired in 1994, Schumer would probably have run for governor. He is a likely candidate, and one who must be taken seriously, against Governor George Pataki in 1998. That helps to explain why he has begun to spend time in Buffalo as well as in Brooklyn.

The People: Pop. 1990: 579,876; 20% age 65+; 82% White; 3% Black; 6% Asian; 3% Other; 8% Hispanic origin. Voting age pop.: 469,387; 3% Black; 7% Hispanic origin. Households: 52% married couple families; 21% married couple fams. w. children; 44% college educ.; median household income: $34,758; per capita income: $17,918; median gross rent: $534; median house value: $208,300.

1992 Presidential Vote

Clinton (D) 121,361 (59%)
Bush (R) 67,034 (32%)
Perot (I) 17,606 (9%)

1988 Presidential Vote

Dukakis (D) 105,372 (52%)
Bush (R) 95,705 (48%)

Rep. Charles E. Schumer (D)

Elected 1980; b. Nov. 23, 1950, Brooklyn; home, Brooklyn; Harvard, B.A. 1971, J.D. 1974; Jewish; married (Iris).

Career: NY Assembly, 1974–80.

DC Office: 2211 RHOB 20515, 202-225-6616; Fax: 202-225-4183.

District Offices: 1628 Kings Hwy., Brooklyn 11229, 718-627-9700.

Committees: *Banking & Financial Services* (4th of 22 D): Capital Markets, Securities and Government Sponsored Enterprises; Financial Institutions and Consumer Credit. *Judiciary* (4th of 15 D): Crime (RMM); Immigration and Claims.

Group Ratings

	ADA	ACLU	COPE	CFA	LCV	CON	NSI	COC	ACU	NTLC	CHC
1994	90	83	75	100	100	42	20	58	5	26	7
1993	95	—	100	100	92	39	—	9	9	—	—

National Journal Ratings

	1993 LIB — 1993 CONS		1994 LIB — 1994 CONS	
Economic	78%	— 12%	63%	— 36%
Social	80%	— 13%	77%	— 21%
Foreign	70%	— 30%	80%	— 17%

Key Votes of the 103d Congress

1. Clinton Deficit Plan	Y	3. Brady Handgun Purchase	Y	5. Lmt. UN Cmnd. of Forces	N
2. NAFTA	N	4. Strike Race/Death Pnlty.	N	6. Cut Missile Funds	N

Key Votes of the 104th Congress

1. Congressional Compliance	Y	6. Reform Crime Grant	N	11. Loser Pays Court Reform	N
2. Balanced Budget Amndmt.	N	7. National Security Act	*	12. Product Liability Reform	N
3. Bar Unfunded Mandates	Y	8. Moratorium on Regs.	N	13. Welfare Reform	N
4. Pass Line Item Veto	Y	9. Risk Assessment on Regs.	N	14. Term Limits Amndmt.	N
5. Relax Exclusionary Rule	N	10. Expnd. Priv. Prop. Rights	N	15. Tax Cuts	N

Election Results

1994 general	Charles E. Schumer (D-L)	95,139	(73%)	($157,108)
	James P. McCall (R-C)	35,880	(27%)	($13,831)
1994 primary	Charles E. Schumer (D)	unopposed		
1992 general	Charles E. Schumer (D-L)	116,545	(89%)	($387,059)
	Alice G. Gaffrey (C)	14,985	(11%)	

TENTH DISTRICT

Bedford, a century ago one of Brooklyn's fashionable neighborhoods, has given its name to half of what is Brooklyn's best known black neighborhood. It is not the most downtrodden. If Bedford's and Stuyvesant's brownstones looked bedraggled even before modern urban decay, they also remain solid and, on many streets, well-tended. The black community settled here well before World War II, but they were then one of the smaller of dozens of Brooklyn ethnic enclaves. It grew in the years after World War II as crime and crowding moved people out of Harlem and busloads of blacks came north from the Carolinas in the 1950s and early 1960s. Sluggish job growth has meant less migration, but Brooklyn's black community, with some of New York's highest birth rates, has grown rapidly and far beyond the original bounds of Bedford-Stuyvesant.

The 10th Congressional District of New York is centered on Bedford-Stuyvesant and is entirely contained within Brooklyn; there, regularity ends. It is shaped something like a set of barbells, with one end including gentrified Brooklyn Heights and downtown Brooklyn, plus part of the mixed Fort Greene and Williamsburg neighborhoods. To the east it extends to Jamaica Bay, including much of East New York and Canarsie and Brownsville. The landscape varies widely, from utterly bombed-out blocks to secure and hardy blocks of rowhouses or high-rise rent-supplemented apartments. The district in 1990 was 61% black and 19% Hispanic, with some blocks of Italians and Hasidic Jews. Politically, it is overwhelmingly Democratic.

The congressman from the 10th is Ed Towns, a black Democrat from East New York who is as experienced in government as in politics. Towns has been a teacher, social worker and hospital administrator, and he is active in the civic affairs of this racially changing community. He served as Brooklyn's deputy borough president for six years and became widely popular. He was elected to the House in 1982. Towns's two best known legislative initiatives are the Student Athlete Right-to-Know Act, which requires colleges to report the graduation rates of student athletes, and strengthening the National Health Service Corps and the Minority Health Initiative, especially for Native Americans (not too many of them in Brooklyn!). In 1990 he got a seat on the Commerce Committee, where he has quickly moved up in seniority. In 1993 he became chairman of a Government Reform and Oversight subcommittee with a long history of superintending the Food and Drug Administration and pressing for more-stringent regulation. In the 103d Congress, Towns sought to ban waste exports and to save poison prevention centers. He also chaired hearings on Agriculture Department food inspection services and FDA rulings on medical devices. Despite his very liberal voting record, he does not support every liberal cause. A native of North Carolina, he was part of an alliance of inner-city and tobacco-state members that has defended the tobacco industry against efforts led by Henry Waxman on the Commerce Committee to impose additional controls on cigarettes. With the Republican takeover of the House, the tobacco industry no longer has to worry about such legislation; unfortunately for Towns, he is unlikely for some time to be in a position to exert much influence.

Towns had a vigorous primary challenge in 1992, after he had 408 overdrafts on the House bank, from Councilwoman Susan Alter; but he won 63%–28%. His son Darryl Towns is a member of the New York Assembly. He had no primary challenge in 1994, and whomped his Republican opponent with 89% in the general.

The People: Pop. 1990: 581,311; 10% age 65+; 21% White; 61% Black; 2% Asian; 10% Other; 19% Hispanic origin. Voting age pop.: 416,561; 60% Black; 18% Hispanic origin. Households: 34% married couple families; 16% married couple fams. w. children; 35% college educ.; median household income: $23,164; per capita income: $11,479; median gross rent: $441; median house value: $165,200.

1992 Presidential Vote			1988 Presidential Vote		
Clinton (D)	125,300	(83%)	Dukakis (D)	113,210	(82%)
Bush (R)	19,200	(13%)	Bush (R)	24,620	(18%)
Perot (I)	5,720	(4%)			

Rep. Edolphus Towns (D)

Elected 1982; b. July 21, 1934, Chadbourn, NC; home, Brooklyn; NC A&T U., B.S. 1956, Adelphi U., M.S.W. 1973; Presbyterian; married (Gwendolyn).

Career: Army, 1956–58; Prof., Medgar Evers Col.; NY public schl. teacher; Dep. hospital admin., 1965–71; Brooklyn Dep. Borough Pres., 1976–82.

DC Office: 2232 RHOB 20515, 202-225-5936; Fax: 202-225-1018.

District Offices: 545 Broadway, #200, Brooklyn 11206, 718-387-8696.

Committees: *Government Reform & Oversight* (6th of 22 D): Human Resources and Intergovernmental Affairs (RMM). *Commerce* (10th of 21 D): Health and Environment; Telecommunications and Finance.

Group Ratings

	ADA	ACLU	COPE	CFA	LCV	CON	NSI	COC	ACU	NTLC	CHC
1994	85	91	100	80	88	8	0	25	0	9	0
1993	95	—	100	90	91	39	—	10	5	—	—

National Journal Ratings

	1993 LIB — 1993 CONS		1994 LIB — 1994 CONS	
Economic	88%	— 0%	83%	— 0%
Social	87%	— 0%	94%	— 0%
Foreign	84%	— 13%	85%	— 0%

Key Votes of the 103d Congress

1. Clinton Deficit Plan	Y	3. Brady Handgun Purchase	Y	5. Lmt. UN Cmnd. of Forces	N
2. NAFTA	N	4. Strike Race/Death Pnlty.	N	6. Cut Missile Funds	Y

Key Votes of the 104th Congress

1. Congressional Compliance	Y	6. Reform Crime Grant	N	11. Loser Pays Court Reform	N
2. Balanced Budget Amndmt.	N	7. National Security Act	N	12. Product Liability Reform	*
3. Bar Unfunded Mandates	N	8. Moratorium on Regs.	N	13. Welfare Reform	N
4. Pass Line Item Veto	N	9. Risk Assessment on Regs.	Y	14. Term Limits Amndmt.	N
5. Relax Exclusionary Rule	N	10. Expnd. Priv. Prop. Rights	N	15. Tax Cuts	N

Election Results

1994 general	Edolphus Towns (D-L)	77,026	(89%)	($453,427)
	Amelia Smith Parker (R)	7,995	(9%)	($7,059)
	Others	1,489	(2%)	
1994 primary	Edolphus Towns (D)	unopposed		
1992 general	Edolphus Towns (D-L)	97,509	(96%)	($699,589)
	Owen Augustin (C)	4,315	(4%)	

ELEVENTH DISTRICT

When Jackie Robinson suited up for the Brooklyn Dodgers in 1947, becoming the first black major league baseball player, the borough didn't have many blacks. Manhattan's Harlem was the center of black life and entertainment in New York, though Brooklyn's Bedford-Stuyvesant had a scattering of blacks in cheap apartments. Then a subway line, built to replace the El, connected Bed-Stuy with Harlem, and inspired Duke Ellington's "Take the A Train."

Since then, Harlem has lost population and dozens of blocks have been emptied out, their brownstone townhouses vacant or vanished. But Brooklyn's black neighborhoods have grown and to a certain degree have prospered. Many of New York's black families came from the south, but large numbers, particularly in Flatbush, the area south of the Hasidic Jewish outposts in Crown Heights, come from what New Yorkers call "the Islands"—Haiti, the Dominican Republic, Jamaica, Barbados, Guyana, Trinidad and Tobago. Speaking deeply accented English, French, Spanish or various forms of creole, they bring spiced bread, peanut punch, Matouk's Special Hot Calypso Sauce, reggae and calypso music. These Caribbean immigrants tend to stay in families more often than low-income American-born blacks; they work hard and are commercially and civically inclined. Coming from places where life and property are not always respected by governments, they are working, like so many other immigrants to America, to build new communities.

The 11th Congressional District, in central Brooklyn, extends from downtown Brooklyn and Prospect Park across Crown Heights—the scene of violent clashes between blacks and Hasidic Jews—and covers most of Flatbush, East Flatbush and Brownsville. This area had the largest concentration of Jews in America from the 1920s to the 1960s. But today, the 11th is 74% black, the highest percentage of any congressional district in the nation, with probably as many blacks with roots in the Islands as in the American South. Like depopulated Brownsville, some neighborhoods here are in dreadful shape, while others, like much of Flatbush, seem to have considerable strength.

The congressman from the 11th, Major Owens, started out as a librarian but has had a long career in New York politics and government. He is part of the district's southern-based tradition, growing up and attending school in the region before heading north for various public-sector and civil-rights jobs. He worked in the Brownsville Community Council and with CORE, and served in Mayor John Lindsay's Administration from 1968 to 1973 as commissioner of the city's Community Development Agency. Critic Charles Morris called Owens "the most capable and canny" of New York's anti-poverty program directors. It was a high-pressure job, with few guidelines to draw on, and Owens may have been relieved when he was elected to serve in the antique chamber of the New York Senate in 1974. When Congresswoman Shirley Chisholm, an immigrant from Barbados and presidential candidate in 1972, announced her retirement in 1982, Owens entered the primary to succeed her and beat Chisholm's choice. Traditionally, Owens has had only nominal opposition, and 1994 was no exception.

Owens has one of the most liberal voting records in the House. During the 103d Congress, he chaired the Economic and Educational Opportunities Subcommittee on Select Education and Civil Rights. He worked on the Americans With Disabilities Act and, fittingly for a librarian, the Literacy Corps and library funding in the child care bill. He shepherded legislation to reauthorize the Education Department's Office of Educational Research and Improvement, attempting to restructure the office to conduct research that responded to the needs of parents and teachers. He also pushed legislation that increased federal child abuse and domestic violence programs. During the 104th Congress, now that he has little influence on his revamped committees, he has emerged as an outspoken critic on the House floor of Republican attempts to dismantle many of the programs he supports. And he criticized the Clinton Administration for their early spending initiatives on infrastructure rather than programs like Head Start. Owens chaired the Black Caucus' Haiti task force, and was arrested with five other Members in 1994 at the White House protesting Clinton's repatriation of Haitian refugees.

The People: Pop. 1990: 582,332; 9% age 65+; 16% White; 74% Black; 3% Asian; 4% Other; 11% Hispanic origin. Voting age pop.: 416,159; 72% Black; 11% Hispanic origin. Households: 36% married couple families; 20% married couple fams. w. children; 40% college educ.; median household income: $26,148; per capita income: $11,706; median gross rent: $482; median house value: $181,100.

1992 Presidential Vote

Clinton (D) 104,584 (86%)
Bush (R) 11,686 (10%)
Perot (I).................... 3,907   (3%)

1988 Presidential Vote

Dukakis (D)................. 88,925 (83%)
Bush (R) 18,265 (17%)

Rep. Major R. Owens (D)

Elected 1982; b. June 28, 1936, Memphis, TN; home, Brooklyn; Morehouse Col., B.A. 1956, Atlanta U., M.L.S. 1957; Baptist; married (Maria).

Career: Brooklyn Public Library, 1958–65, Community Coord., 1964–65; V.P., Metro. Cncl. of Housing, 1964; Chmn., Brooklyn Congress on Racial Equality; Exec. Dir., Brownsville Community Cncl., 1966–68; NYC Community Devel. Commissioner, 1968–73, Dep. Admin., 1972–74; Dir., Community Media Library Program, Columbia U., 1973–74; NY Senate, 1974–82.

DC Office: 2305 RHOB 20515, 202-225-6231; Fax: 202-226-0112.

District Offices: 289 Utica Ave., Brooklyn 11213, 718-773-3100; and 1310 Cortelyon Rd., Brooklyn 11226, 718-940-3213.

Committees: *Economic & Educational Opportunities* (6th of 19 D): Employer-Employee Relations; Workforce Protections (RMM). *Government Reform & Oversight* (5th of 22 D): Government Management, Information and Technology; Postal Service.

Group Ratings

	ADA	ACLU	COPE	CFA	LCV	CON	NSI	COC	ACU	NTLC	CHC
1994	90	90	100	90	80	11	0	18	0	4	0
1993	95	—	100	90	79	19	—	0	0	—	—

National Journal Ratings

	1993 LIB — 1993 CONS	1994 LIB — 1994 CONS
Economic	88% — 0%	83% — 0%
Social	87% — 0%	94% — 0%
Foreign	93% — 0%	85% — 0%

Key Votes of the 103d Congress

1. Clinton Deficit Plan	Y	3. Brady Handgun Purchase Y	5. Lmt. UN Cmnd. of Forces N
2. NAFTA	N	4. Strike Race/Death Pnlty. N	6. Cut Missile Funds Y

Key Votes of the 104th Congress

1. Congressional Compliance Y
2. Balanced Budget Amndmt. N
3. Bar Unfunded Mandates N
4. Pass Line Item Veto N
5. Relax Exclusionary Rule N
6. Reform Crime Grant N
7. National Security Act N
8. Moratorium on Regs. N
9. Risk Assessment on Regs. N
10. Expnd. Priv. Prop. Rights N
11. Loser Pays Court Reform N
12. Product Liability Reform N
13. Welfare Reform N
14. Term Limits Amndmt. N
15. Tax Cuts N

Election Results

1994 general	Major R. Owens (D-L)	61,945	(89%)	($295,986)
	Gary S. Popkin (R).................	6,605	(9%)	
	Others	1,150	(2%)	
1994 primary	Major R. Owens (D)...............	unopposed		
1992 general	Major R. Owens (D-L)	80,028	(94%)	($177,235)
	Michael Gaffney (C)................	4,287	(5%)	
	Other.............................	1,179	(1%)	

TWELFTH DISTRICT

Amid a vast wave of migration that seemed destined to make Puerto Ricans the majority in New York, Leonard Bernstein in 1957 wrote his musical, *West Side Story*, with Romeo as an Italian-American and Juliet as a Manhattan Puerto Rican. While the flow of Puerto Ricans balanced out by the early 1960s, ever since the 1965 immigration act, New York has had a vast influx of Hispanics from places not under U.S. control. They include Dominicans, most of whom are black; and Colombians, largely of Indian ancestry, Panamanians, who like Puerto Ricans are products of a polyglot society; and those from other parts of Latin America.

The 12th Congressional District of New York, designed to join these diverse people together, is a serpentine-shaped entity in which, by Census definition, 57% of the residents are Hispanic. Stitched together, often by the thinnest of threads, are the heavily Puerto Rican Sunset Park neighborhood in Brooklyn and on the other side of the borough, Bushwick, once German, now with mixed Latins and a political machine run by Assemblyman Vito Lopez. The Dominican neighborhood of East Elmhurst and Corona, Queens are in the 12th, as are the Colombian blocks a few miles west in Jackson Heights, plus some black neighborhoods in East New York. It also includes the Puerto Rican parts of Williamsburg in Brooklyn and, across the bridges in Manhattan, Puerto Rican blocks in the Lower East Side. The district is connected by cemeteries or parks in at least three places.

The congresswoman from the 12th is Nydia Velazquez, elected when this district was created for the 1992 elections. Velazquez was born in Puerto Rico, taught at the University of Puerto Rico in the 1970s and at Hunter College in the 1980s, worked for Congressman Ed Towns in 1983 and served on the New York City Council in 1984. Then she worked for Puerto Rico's government offices in New York. When the 12th was created, she was one of three major candidates who ran; the others were the liberal Elisabeth Colon and incumbent Congressman Stephen Solarz. By most measures Solarz was one of the leading members of Congress: chairman of the Asia Subcommittee of International Relations, with a deep and nuanced knowledge of foreign policy, and the chief Democratic advocate of the Gulf war resolution. But Solarz also had 743 overdrafts on the House bank and, when Assembly Speaker Mel Miller was removed from office in December 1991 following his own legal problems, Solarz lost the ally who would have created a favorable district for him. He had to choose between a race in the mostly-Manhattan 8th against the leftish Ted Weiss and a multicandidate contest in the 12th; ironically, Weiss died the day before the September primary. Solarz had $2 million to spend (money he had husbanded against the possibility of running against Charles Schumer), but Velazquez got the endorsements of Mayor David Dinkins and Jesse Jackson, and beat Solarz 34%–28%, with 26% for Colon.

After the primary, confidential hospital records were leaked to a New York tabloid showing that in September 1991 Velazquez had attempted suicide, was hospitalized and later underwent counseling. Evidently, that was of little concern to voters: she won in November with 77%. In her first term, Velazquez used her seat on the Banking Committee to push legislation to require credit bureaus to let people talk with live operators and to provide consumers with a free copy of their credit report after information is corrected. She wanted insurance companies to disclose their investments so that consumers could decide whether they were putting money in their neighborhoods. She has compiled one of the most liberal voting records in the House. For 1994, Republicans did not even field a candidate here, and Velazquez trounced her Conservative Party candidate with 92%.

The People: Pop. 1990: 577,757; 8% age 65+; 14% White; 14% Black; 20% Asian; 32% Other; 57% Hispanic origin. Voting age pop.: 416,223; 13% Black; 54% Hispanic origin. Households: 42% married couple families; 23% married couple fams. w. children; 25% college educ.; median household income: $20,444; per capita income: $8,534; median gross rent: $454; median house value: $175,100.

1992 Presidential Vote

Clinton (D)	67,274	(68%)
Bush (R)	25,664	(26%)
Perot (I)	5,133	(5%)

1988 Presidential Vote

Dukakis (D)	66,079	(71%)
Bush (R)	27,587	(29%)

Rep. Nydia M. Velazquez (D)

Elected 1992; b. Mar. 28, 1953, Yabucoa, PR; home, Brooklyn; U. of PR, B.A. 1974, N.Y.U., M.A. 1976; Catholic; divorced.

Career: Instructor, U. of PR, 1976–81; Adjunct prof., Hunter Col., 1981–83; Special Asst., U.S. Rep. Edolphus Towns, 1983; NYC Cncl., 1984; Migration Dir., PR Dept. of Labor and Human Resources, 1986–89; Secy., Dept. of PR Community Affairs in the U.S., 1989–92.

DC Office: 132 CHOB 20515, 202-225-2361; Fax: 202-226-0327.

District Offices: 815 Broadway, Brooklyn 11206, 718-599-3658.

Committees: *Banking & Financial Services* (16th of 22 D): General Oversight and Investigations; Housing and Community Opportunity. *Small Business* (9th of 19 D): Regulation and Paperwork (RMM).

Group Ratings

	ADA	ACLU	COPE	CFA	LCV	CON	NSI	COC	ACU	NTLC	CHC
1994	100	87	100	100	88	13	0	17	0	0	0
1993	95	—	100	100	93	32	—	0	0	—	—

National Journal Ratings

	1993 LIB — 1993 CONS		1994 LIB — 1994 CONS	
Economic	88% —	0%	83% —	0%
Social	87% —	0%	94% —	0%
Foreign	79% —	16%	85% —	0%

Key Votes of the 103d Congress

1. Clinton Deficit Plan	Y	3. Brady Handgun Purchase	Y	5. Lmt. UN Cmnd. of Forces	N
2. NAFTA	N	4. Strike Race/Death Pnlty.	N	6. Cut Missile Funds	Y

Key Votes of the 104th Congress

1. Congressional Compliance	Y	6. Reform Crime Grant	N	11. Loser Pays Court Reform	N
2. Balanced Budget Amndmt.	N	7. National Security Act	N	12. Product Liability Reform	N
3. Bar Unfunded Mandates	N	8. Moratorium on Regs.	N	13. Welfare Reform	N
4. Pass Line Item Veto	N	9. Risk Assessment on Regs.	N	14. Term Limits Amndmt.	N
5. Relax Exclusionary Rule	N	10. Expnd. Priv. Prop. Rights	N	15. Tax Cuts	N

Election Results

1994 general	Nydia M. Velazquez (D-L)	39,929	(92%)	($11,360)
	Genevieve R. Brennan (C)	2,747	(6%)	
	Others	589	(1%)	
1994 primary	Nydia M. Velazquez (D)	13,208	(82%)	
	Pedro L. Velazquez (D)	2,949	(18%)	
1992 general	Nydia Velazquez (D)	55,926	(77%)	($461,749)
	Angel Diaz (R-C-RTL)	14,976	(20%)	($5,390)
	Others	2,165	(3%)	

THIRTEENTH DISTRICT

Staten Island is one corner of America that has pondered secession—not from the United States, but from New York City. Geographically, Staten Island has always been closer to New Jersey than New York, though it became part of New York City in 1898. For two-thirds of a century it was connected to the rest of The City only by ferry (5-cent toll for many years) or through Bayonne, New Jersey, until the 5-mile-long Verrazano Narrows Bridge was finished in 1965. It is far less densely populated than the rest of New York. With about as much acreage as Brooklyn has for 2.3 million people, Staten Island has 379,000—and that's after recent robust population growth. Some of Staten Island is almost rural, though not bucolic. It has the highest point on the eastern seaboard, Todt Hill, and the vast Fresh Kills dump. Culturally, Staten Islanders are deeply conservative—more so than in most of New York's suburbs—quite a contrast from Manhattan at the other end of the ferry. New York City income taxes, the highest in the nation, pay for many programs opposed by most Staten Islanders; in November 1993, Staten Islanders voted for secession, but the legislature did not act. One who must surely oppose it is New York Mayor Rudolph Giuliani, who carried Staten Island heavily over David Dinkins and would have lost without it.

The 13th Congressional District of New York is made up of Staten Island plus a couple of adjacent neighborhoods over the Verrazano Narrows Bridge in Brooklyn. The largest of these is Bay Ridge, heavily Catholic and Italian, mostly middle-class, with thick New York accents and resentment of high New York taxes and welfare payments: large single-family houses and small apartment buildings by the looming towers of the Bridge. The 13th also includes most of heavily Italian Bensonhurst, where in 1989 the murder of a black youth transfixed the city and altered its politics. This district may have more Italian-Americans and may also be home to more police officers than any other district in America.

The 13th is represented by Susan Molinari, the youngest member of Congress when she was chosen in a March 1990 special election, and now one of the Republican leaders of the House. Molinari has a political pedigree: her grandfather S. Robert Molinari was an Assemblyman from Staten Island in the 1940s, and her father Guy Molinari represented the district from 1980 until he was elected Staten Island Borough president in November 1989. Susan Molinari's first jobs out of school were at the Republican Governors Association and Republican National Committee. In 1985 she was elected to the New York City Council, where she quickly became the Minority Leader (because she was the only Republican). In March 1990 she won her father's House seat by defeating a vocal but ineffectual Democrat, Robert Gigante, by 59%–35%.

Molinari quickly became one of the most distinctive members of the House, combining her father's concentration on local issues with loyalty to the party leadership and a zest and quickspeakingness typical of New York City. Almost immediately, she bucked senior National Security members and senior New York liberals and got the House to vote 230–188 to designate Staten Island as a Navy homeport. She got on well with then-Minority Whip Newt Gingrich, even as she vocally opposed restrictions on abortion and voted for the Americans with Disabilities Act. She sponsored a sexual assault prevention law and promoted crime victim rights. She chaired a party task force on Bosnia and called for U.S. leadership to solve the crisis without sending American ground troops. She fought the high ($6) tolls on the Verrazano Narrows Bridge. She spoke on solid waste legislation "as a representative of the world's largest landfill" and, when the homeport was finally closed despite her efforts, worked to find new uses for the property. She supported the assault weapons ban and opposed the Hyde amendment to stop funding abortions. She played a key role in forging a compromise on the 1994 crime bill, voting against the rule, then working with Gingrich and Mike Castle of Delaware to extract concessions from Democrats.

Young, energetic, with postmodern style and perfect political pitch, Molinari in 1994 and 1995 became one of the most visible voices for her party. In New York, she has appeared on

Channel 2 in "Chuck and Sue" debates with Brooklyn Democrat Charles Schumer; she stands on a box so they'll be the same height for camera angles. Locally and nationally, she was a prominent spokesman for the Contract With America. And she made news in July 1994 when, on neutral turf in Bucks County, Pennsylvania, she married Congressman Bill Paxon from Upstate New York, who is more conservative politically and the chairman of the National Republican Congressional Committee; they made dozens of appearances for party candidates across the country. "I think we have a lot less problems in our balancing act than you might expect," she said of her marriage. "We understand each other and the time pressures of our schedules and our different commitments, so juggling for us is easier." Some pro-choice Democrats complained that Molinari campaigned for anti-abortion candidates, but her priority was clearly the party, and that paid off in December 1994 when, despite her views on cultural issues, she was elected Republican Conference vice chair over Cliff Stearns of Florida by 124–100. She also has shown her interest in moving up the political ladder when she encouraged talk that she might run for governor in 1994. The election of a Republican President could open an opportunity for further advancement.

In 1992, Democrat Sal Albanese ran a serious campaign and carried the Brooklyn part of the district, but Molinari won 56%–38%. Then he brought a mischievous lawsuit charging he had a constitutional right to equal campaign funds which was dismissed in April 1995. In 1994 Molinari won easily, 71%–25%.

The People: Pop. 1990: 579,521; 14% age 65+; 82% White; 6% Black; 6% Asian; 2% Other; 7% Hispanic origin. Voting age pop.: 449,131; 5% Black; 6% Hispanic origin. Households: 57% married couple families; 26% married couple fams. w. children; 40% college educ.; median household income: $38,437; per capita income: $17,143; median gross rent: $553; median house value: $188,800.

1992 Presidential Vote			1988 Presidential Vote		
Bush (R)	100,761	(48%)	Bush (R)	113,701	(60%)
Clinton (D)	82,796	(39%)	Dukakis (D)	74,642	(40%)
Perot (I)	26,317	(12%)			

Rep. Susan Molinari (R)

Elected Mar. 1990; b. Mar. 27, 1958, Staten Island; home, Staten Island; S.U.N.Y., B.A. 1980, M.A. 1981; Catholic; married (U.S. Rep. Bill Paxon).

Career: Finance asst., Natl. Repub. Govs. Assn. 1981–82; Ethnic Liaison, RNC, 1983–84; NYC Cncl., 1985–90.

DC Office: 2435 RHOB 20515, 202-225-3371; Fax: 202-226-1272.

District Offices: 14 New Dorp Ln., Staten Island 10306, 718-987-8400; and 9818 4th Ave., Brooklyn 11209, 718-630-5277.

Committees: *Republican Conference Vice Chairman. Budget* (16th of 24 R). *Transportation & Infrastructure* (10th of 33 R): Coast Guard and Maritime Transportation; Railroads (Chmn.).

Group Ratings

	ADA	ACLU	COPE	CFA	LCV	CON	NSI	COC	ACU	NTLC	CHC
1994	20	43	44	30	17	56	90	92	71	85	64
1993	25	—	42	20	64	69	—	100	71	—	—

National Journal Ratings

	1993 LIB — 1993 CONS		1994 LIB — 1994 CONS	
Economic	35% —	65%	30% —	67%
Social	44% —	55%	38% —	61%
Foreign	17% —	76%	14% —	80%

Key Votes of the 103d Congress

1. Clinton Deficit Plan	N	3. Brady Handgun Purchase	Y	5. Lmt. UN Cmnd. of Forces	Y
2. NAFTA	Y	4. Strike Race/Death Pnlty.	Y	6. Cut Missile Funds	N

Key Votes of the 104th Congress

1. Congressional Compliance	Y	6. Reform Crime Grant	Y	11. Loser Pays Court Reform	Y
2. Balanced Budget Amndmt.	Y	7. National Security Act	Y	12. Product Liability Reform	Y
3. Bar Unfunded Mandates	Y	8. Moratorium on Regs.	Y	13. Welfare Reform	Y
4. Pass Line Item Veto	Y	9. Risk Assessment on Regs.	Y	14. Term Limits Amndmt.	N
5. Relax Exclusionary Rule	Y	10. Expnd. Priv. Prop. Rights	Y	15. Tax Cuts	Y

Election Results

1994 general	Susan Molinari (R-C)	96,491	(71%)	($481,588)
	Tyrone G. Butler (D-L)	32,060	(24%)	($21,618)
	Others	6,532	(5%)	
1994 primary	Susan Molinari (R)	unopposed		
1992 general	Susan Molinari (R-C)	107,903	(56%)	($507,962)
	Sal F. Albanese (D-L)	73,520	(38%)	($247,739)
	Kathleen M. Murphy (RTL)	10,825	(6%)	($24,514)

FOURTEENTH DISTRICT

Hardly any remnant can be found of early 19th Century New York, the city that diarists Philip Hone and George Templeton Strong said was continually being torn down and rebuilt, its earlier structures expendable after a generation or so on the high-priced real estate of this small, compact island. Yet the mayor of this quintessentially 20th Century city lives and works in two buildings of 19th Century scale: City Hall, built in 1803–11, where his ground floor office, dwarfed by the Municipal and Woolworth Buildings, overlooks City Hall Park; and Gracie Mansion, built in 1799, which looks across East End Avenue to high-rise apartments.

The 14th Congressional District, running irregularly from 14th Street north to 96th street, covers most of the East Side of Manhattan. The district also includes small salients on the Lower East Side and Upper West Side of Manhattan, although it gave up most of its black and Hispanic residents, especially on the lower East Side; 5% of its votes are cast in the Brooklyn neighborhood of Greenpoint—Hispanic and industrial and polyglot—and 7% in the Queens neighborhood of Astoria—Greek and boisterous and prosperous. The 14th is the direct descendant of the famous Silk Stocking District, originally created in 1918, then consisting of the few blocks east of Fifth Avenue along Central Park. In the years since, rich and articulate Manhattan, with its securities, publishing, advertising, entertainment, broadcasting and communications industries, has spread from this narrow enclave and taken over the greater part of the island. Meanwhile, the political leanings of this larger upper class—defined partly by income, but also by tastes in the arts, fashion, letters, all the things in which New York remains clearly the nation's capital—have changed, from elite Republican to cultural liberal.

Historically, the Silk Stocking tradition was Republican, and more tolerant than the rest of New York City and the rest of the nation—the politics of Theodore Roosevelt and the old *New York Herald-Tribune* and Henry Luce's *Time* magazine. While it did not trust union leaders and Democratic Party politicians, it accepted much of the New Deal. The district believed that the nation should be led by the well-educated Protestant gentlemen one saw strolling down

Madison Avenue to their clubs, who continued to hold high government posts, though not the presidency, since the era of Franklin D. Roosevelt. But the district changed during the tenure of John Lindsay, who first served as a congressman from 1958 to 1965 and then as mayor from 1965 to 1973. Lindsay changed from being a liberal Republican to a radical Democrat. While mayor, he ran up the huge debts that led the city to the brink of bankruptcy in 1975, while neighborhoods deteriorated so much that the city lost 1 million people during the 1970s. He was succeeded as congressman and ultimately as mayor by Edward Koch, whose political travels were the reverse of Lindsay's. Koch started as a liberal and became more conservative and in the process lost the support of Manhattan by backing capital punishment, opposing racial quotas and questioning poverty programs. But he left the city in far better shape, economically and fiscally and governmentally.

The Silk Stocking district proves that economics is not necessarily the basis of American politics. Its residents have the highest average household income in America, $74,780, but they also are solidly Democratic: 69% for Bill Clinton and 23% for George Bush in 1992. While the district is affluent, it also is full of gays, singles and others who consider anything past the canyons of Manhattan's east-west grid streets and the Hudson hostile country. In 1992, voters in this district elected a liberal Democrat who voted, albeit reluctantly, for the Clinton budget and tax package—which raised taxes by more dollars here than in any other district in the country—and then reelected her in 1994.

The congresswoman is Carolyn Maloney. Born and educated in the South, she visited New York in 1970 at the age of 22, loved it and "just stayed." She worked on welfare education programs during the 1970s, and from 1977 to 1982 she was a legislative staffer in Albany. She was elected to the City Council in 1982; one observer of her term there described her as "a little spacey" until she found a cause, but then she became "a pit bull." The 1991 state redistricting created a district that was even more Democratic than its predecessor and forced the veteran incumbent, Republican Bill Green, to sell himself to Democratic voters who knew little about him. Among those Maloney defeated in the primary was Abe Hirschfeld, who made a complete fool of himself in early 1993 when he briefly owned but did not run the New York Post. Though her net worth is well into seven figures, her campaign had little money and she talked of running against millionaires. (Green was also independently wealthy.) She campaigned personally with brio, sampling baklava in Astoria and accusing Green in Greenpoint, where residents were opposed to a new trash incinerator, of being part owner of a company that owns an incinerator.

Most observers assumed she would lose to Green, probably the most liberal Republican in the House, a thoughtful legislator first elected in 1978 and reelected with 61% in 1988 and 1990. But he had two problems in 1992. One was the enthusiasm of a Democratic Party dominated by the feminist left for woman candidates. The other was redistricting: voters in Astoria and Greenpoint did not know him and he was exactly the opposite of the kind of Republican people in those two areas like (conservative on culture, perhaps liberal on economics). Green won the Manhattan part of the district, but only by 50%–44%, below his previous showings; Maloney carried Greenpoint 60%–34% and Astoria 64%–35%, for a 50%–48% upset victory.

Maloney brought a certain naivete to Washington, telling people she had no second choice to a seat on Appropriations and, when she didn't get it, ending up on Banking and Government Operations. She called for larger cuts in defense than almost any member and supported the balanced budget amendment. She alienated some western lawmakers in her first term, when she brought in singer Carole King to stump for her legislation to protect and restrict development in the Northern Rockies; one critic wrote a bill designating Manhattan as a wilderness area. She also was not immune from criticism back home. The New York Times mentioned her reputation in the capital as a "lightweight." But Maloney was active as a freshman on congressional and campaign finance reform, serving as a co-chair of freshman task forces on reform issues. She also pushed to eliminate wasteful spending, taking a leading role in trying to slash spending for the controversial Civilian Marksmanship Program. Her vote for the Clinton budget and tax package was clearly risky, but the President remains far more popular in New York City than in almost any other part of the country.

Maloney had serious opposition in 1994 from Manhattan Councilman Charles Millard; the two candidates together spent almost $2 million. Millard received almost $1 million in contributions, making him the sixth most successful challenger in raising money. Millard said he opposed the North American Free Trade Agreement and the Clinton budget, whose tax increases he said hit the district hard. He described himself as a fiscal conservative but agreed with Maloney on cultural issues like abortion and gun control. Maloney blasted Millard for refusing to say he would not vote for Newt Gingrich as House Speaker. Millard had the Liberal as well as the Republican line—the same combination that worked for Mayor Rudolph Giuliani in 1993. But as pollster Fred Steeper pointed out, the 1994 movement toward Republicans was not uniform. Strong liberal districts became even more liberal, and the Silk Stocking District was foremost among these. It voted 78% for Mario Cuomo, even as he was losing statewide by 49%–45%. Millard came nowhere close to bucking that tide, as Maloney won 64%–35%, a result that reportedly stunned both candidates. The Silk Stocking District has clearly declared its identity, and it is hard to see how Maloney could lose this seat.

The People: Pop. 1990: 578,639; 16% age 65+; 80% White; 5% Black; 6% Asian; 4% Other; 11% Hispanic origin. Voting age pop.: 514,290; 4% Black; 10% Hispanic origin. Households: 30% married couple families; 10% married couple fams. w. children; 69% college educ.; median household income: $42,184; per capita income: $41,151; median gross rent: $678; median house value: $242,500.

1992 Presidential Vote			1988 Presidential Vote		
Clinton (D)	160,596	(69%)	Dukakis (D)	144,657	(65%)
Bush (R)	53,830	(23%)	Bush (R)	76,527	(35%)
Perot (I)	16,467	(7%)			

Rep. Carolyn B. Maloney (D)

Elected 1992; b. Feb. 19, 1948, Greensboro, NC; home, Manhattan; Greensboro Col, A.B. 1968; Presbyterian; married (Clifton).

Career: NYC Bd. of Educ., 1970–77; Legis. aide, NY Assembly, NY Senate, 1977–82; NYC Cncl., 1982–92.

DC Office: 1504 LHOB 20515, 202-225-7944; Fax: 202-225-4709.

District Offices: 110 E. 59th St., 2d Fl., New York 10022, 212-832-6531; 28–11 Astoria Blvd., Long Island City 11102, 718-932-1804; and 619 Lorimer St., Brooklyn 11211, 718-349-1260.

Committees: *Banking & Financial Services* (12th of 22 D): Domestic and International Monetary Policy; Financial Institutions and Consumer Credit. *Government Reform & Oversight* (13th of 22 D): Government Management, Information and Technology (RMM).

Group Ratings

	ADA	ACLU	COPE	CFA	LCV	CON	NSI	COC	ACU	NTLC	CHC
1994	100	87	78	90	100	37	20	58	0	21	7
1993	95	—	100	100	93	52	—	27	4	—	—

National Journal Ratings

	1993 LIB	—	1993 CONS		1994 LIB	—	1994 CONS
Economic	61%	—	37%		59%	—	37%
Social	73%	—	23%		82%	—	15%
Foreign	74%	—	22%		72%	—	25%

Key Votes of the 103d Congress

1. Clinton Deficit Plan	Y	3. Brady Handgun Purchase	Y	5. Lmt. UN Cmnd. of Forces	N
2. NAFTA	N	4. Strike Race/Death Pnlty.	N	6. Cut Missile Funds	Y

Key Votes of the 104th Congress

1. Congressional Compliance	Y	6. Reform Crime Grant	N	11. Loser Pays Court Reform	N
2. Balanced Budget Amndmt.	N	7. National Security Act	N	12. Product Liability Reform	N
3. Bar Unfunded Mandates	N	8. Moratorium on Regs.	N	13. Welfare Reform	N
4. Pass Line Item Veto	N	9. Risk Assessment on Regs.	N	14. Term Limits Amndmt.	N
5. Relax Exclusionary Rule	N	10. Expnd. Priv. Prop. Rights	N	15. Tax Cuts	N

Election Results

1994 general	Carolyn B. Maloney (D-IDN)............	98,479	(64%)	($1,032,181)
	Charles Millard (R-L).................	54,277	(35%)	($988,112)
1994 primary	Carolyn B. Maloney (D)................	29,944	(79%)	
	Rob Rosenthal (D)	8,145	(21%)	
1992 general	Carolyn B. Maloney (D-L)	101,652	(50%)	($277,223)
	Bill Green (R-IDN)	97,215	(48%)	($1,141,470)
	Other................................	2,970	(2%)	

FIFTEENTH DISTRICT

Harlem, for many years America's most famous black ghetto, has fallen on grim times. Actually, Harlem as the central focus of black America was only a moment in history, and Harlem itself has not always been black. Its five-story tenements were built almost 100 years ago for working-class whites, and central Harlem became all black only around 1920—the beginning of the decade when black entertainers and night clubs on 125th Street became world-famous. This Harlem was a wondrous place, as the *WPA Guide* described 50 years ago: "To whites seeking amusement, it is an exuberant, original and unconventional entertainment center; to Negro college graduates, it is an opportunity to practice a profession among their own people; to those aspiring to racial leadership, it is a domain where they may advocate their theories unmolested; to the mass of Negro people, it is the spiritual capital of Black America." It was around this time, in 1944, that Harlem first got its own congressional district and a congressman, Adam Clayton Powell Jr., who won national fame for his Powell Amendments banning racial discrimination in government programs.

Today, Harlem's brownstones are often abandoned and empty, if they haven't been pulled down; family structure has deteriorated so much that the father-and-mother household is a rarity; drugs and crime and AIDS infection and infant mortality are at horrifying levels. Its population is down more than 200,000 since the 1940s. The boom in jobs and economic growth in the rest of Manhattan has not touched Harlem. Its high school graduates may get into City College because of its open admissions policy, but sadly, they seldom have the basic skills needed for white-collar work. There is some vitality now on 125th Street, with its state office building and Empowerment Zone designation, and perhaps some hope. But this is a community deeply wounded.

The 15th Congressional District includes all of Harlem, indeed almost all of northern Manhattan, from approximately East 96th Street and West 91st Street on up. That means the district takes in some of the white liberal Upper West Side and the precincts around Columbia University. It includes the once Irish and now Dominican Inwood neighborhood at the north tip of Manhattan; Washington Heights, with many Dominicans and Haitians; East Harlem, Italian in the days of Fiorello LaGuardia, now Puerto Rican and Latino. Overall the district is 47% black and 45% Hispanic—figures testifying to black flight from Harlem and the continuing rush of Western Hemisphere immigrants to fill it in.

The congressman from the 15th is Charles Rangel, first elected in 1970 when he narrowly beat the legendary but fading Adam Clayton Powell Jr.. Rangel is the senior member of the New York delegation and second ranking Democrat on Ways and Means. He served in the Army in Korea, then went to college and law school, got some government legal jobs and was elected to the Assembly in 1966; in 1970 he challenged Powell and won. Like most Harlem politicians, he has long argued that government aid and racial preferences are needed to solve Harlem's problems, and indeed has so insisted with great vehemence in the 104th Congress. Yet much in his own career suggests otherwise. Rangel's main emphasis for at least ten years has been denunciation of the drug trade. From 1983 until it was abolished in 1993 with the other House select committees, Rangel chaired the Select Committee on Narcotics Abuse and Control, and seldom missed a chance to relate other problems to drugs; after all, he has seen how they can destroy a community. Rangel wants money spent on rehabilitation programs as much as interdiction and police work, and he was a scathing critic of Republican administrations' anti-drug efforts. But he also worked with the Bush Justice Department to create the Weed and Seed program, combining intensive law enforcement with social services. And he takes sharp issue with those who call for legalization of marijuana or provision of free needles to curtail AIDS or even giving heroin to terminal cancer patients.

Rangel does skillful work on other issues. He worked, with considerable success, to protect state and local tax deductibility in the 1986 tax reform and is a prime defender of Section 936, the tax exemption that has created many jobs in Puerto Rico. He is an author of the Federal Empowerment Zone demonstration, the Low Income Housing tax credit (which he says financed 90% of affordable housing from 1984–94) and the Targeted Jobs tax credit. He supported sending troops to Haiti.

For years Rangel had no serious competition at home and was in the majority in Washington. Not so in the mid-1990s. In 1994, he was opposed in the primary by Councilman Adam Clayton Powell IV, son of the man he beat 24 years earlier. Powell had a desultory record in the Council, and grew up in Puerto Rico hardly knowing his father. But Rangel felt threatened enough to spend $1.4 million in the campaign, the 17th highest among House candidates. He won 58%–33%, a margin which may or may not deter serious challengers in the future. He returned to a House dominated by Republicans and a Ways and Means Committee that voted 26–10 to repeal a tax break for broadcast properties sold to minority owners; the repeal measure was prompted by a Viacom Inc. deal that would have cost the government $4 billion in lost revenues. Rangel's response was to lash out, in the same tones that he had used against Mayor Edward Koch and in support of Jesse Jackson in New York. "Mr. Chairman, in America we cannot afford to be colorblind," he wrote in a letter to Ways and Means chairman Bill Archer. "Just like under Hitler, people say they don't mean to blame any particular individuals and groups, but in the U.S. those groups always turn out to be minorities and immigrants." This of course was inaccurate—Hitler did single out Jews and other groups for persecution—but it also coarsened political discourse, as Archer noted. "Invoking the name of Adolf Hitler injects an utterly invalid and totally uncalled for extremism into a legitimate congressional debate." Rangel may continue to encounter problems in defining a role for himself in the much-changed House, but his influential committee assignment and his proven skills should give him opportunities.

The People: Pop. 1990: 580,354; 12% age 65+; 14% White; 47% Black; 1% Amer. Indian; 2% Asian; 22% Other; 45% Hispanic origin. Voting age pop.: 437,373; 47% Black; 42% Hispanic origin. Households: 26% married couple families; 12% married couple fams. w. children; 35% college educ.; median household income: $19,238; per capita income: $10,367; median gross rent: $402; median house value: $162,600.

1992 Presidential Vote

Clinton (D)	123,846	(85%)
Bush (R)	15,505	(11%)
Perot (I)	4,700	(3%)

1988 Presidential Vote

Dukakis (D)	122,071	(87%)
Bush (R)	18,860	(13%)

Rep. Charles B. Rangel (D)

Elected 1970; b. June 11, 1930, New York City; home, New York City; N.Y.U., B.S. 1957, St. John's U., LL.B. 1960; Catholic; married (Alma).

Career: Army, 1948–52 (Korea); Asst. U.S. Atty., S. Dist. of NY, 1961; Legal Cnsl., NYC Housing and Redevel. Bd., Neighborhood Conservation Bureau, 1963–68; Gen. Cnsl., Natl. Advisory Comm. on Selective Svc., 1966; NY Assembly, 1966–70.

DC Office: 2354 RHOB 20515, 202-225-4365; Fax: 202-225-0816.

District Offices: 163 W. 125th St., New York 10027, 212-663-3900; 601 W. 181st St., New York 10033, 212-927-5333; and 2110 1st Ave., New York 10029, 212-348-9830.

Committees: *Ways & Means* (2nd of 15 D): Human Resources; Trade (RMM). *Joint Committee on Taxation* (5th of 5 Reps.).

Group Ratings

	ADA	ACLU	COPE	CFA	LCV	CON	NSI	COC	ACU	NTLC	CHC
1994	95	91	100	90	71	7	0	18	5	7	0
1993	95	—	100	100	85	32	—	0	0	—	—

National Journal Ratings

	1993 LIB — 1993 CONS	1994 LIB — 1994 CONS
Economic	88% — 0%	83% — 0%
Social	87% — 0%	79% — 20%
Foreign	84% — 13%	85% — 0%

Key Votes of the 103d Congress

1. Clinton Deficit Plan	Y	3. Brady Handgun Purchase	Y	5. Lmt. UN Cmnd. of Forces	N
2. NAFTA	N	4. Strike Race/Death Pnlty.	N	6. Cut Missile Funds	*

Key Votes of the 104th Congress

1. Congressional Compliance	Y	6. Reform Crime Grant	N	11. Loser Pays Court Reform	*
2. Balanced Budget Amndmt.	N	7. National Security Act	N	12. Product Liability Reform	*
3. Bar Unfunded Mandates	N	8. Moratorium on Regs.	N	13. Welfare Reform	N
4. Pass Line Item Veto	N	9. Risk Assessment on Regs.	N	14. Term Limits Amndmt.	N
5. Relax Exclusionary Rule	N	10. Expnd. Priv. Prop. Rights	*	15. Tax Cuts	N

Election Results

1994 general	Charles B. Rangel (D-L)	77,830	(97%)	($1,437,297)
	Others	2,812	(3%)	
1994 primary	Charles B. Rangel (D)	28,379	(61%)	
	Adam Clayton Powell IV (D)	15,500	(33%)	
	Albert Davis (D)	2,655	(6%)	
1992 general	Charles B. Rangel (D-L)	105,011	(95%)	($669,095)
	Jose A. Suero (C-INF)	4,345	(4%)	
	Other	1,337	(1%)	

SIXTEENTH DISTRICT

It may not quite be "the beautiful Bronx," as borough historian Lloyd Utlan calls it, but the Bronx seems to be coming back. The beautiful days were in the 1930s and 1940s, when Presidents Roosevelt and Truman rode down 138th Street, when Babe Ruth and Lou Gehrig and Joe DiMaggio hit home runs in Yankee Stadium, when Art Deco apartment buildings went up along the Grand Concourse, when shoppers thronged Tremont Avenue stores and New Yorkers from all over flocked to the Bronx Zoo. This Bronx was built in a trice, starting in 1906 when the first subway came in, bringing the children of immigrants from dimly lit Lower East Side tenements to comparatively spacious quarters. The Bronx's population grew from 200,000 in 1900 to 430,000 in 1910, 732,000 in 1920, and 1.3 million in 1930—more than the 1.2 million of 1990.

The Bronx fell rapidly in the dozen years after John Lindsay was elected mayor in 1965. One reason was rent control, insisted on by tenants, which guarantees that owners of low-rent property won't maintain it: the result is empty vandalized shells and venues for drug deals. Another was the drop in low-income, low-skill jobs in Manhattan and the Bronx, abetted by high union and minimum wages, restrictive work rules and the tolls exacted by organized crime. A third reason was the disintegration of family structure: stable, law-abiding males became scarce in these parts. But most important was crime. With no community institutions and little parental supervision, poor teenagers here committed an alarming number of crimes, with seeming impunity. Arson became increasingly common, perpetrated by kids for kicks or on behalf of landlords who wanted to get insurance money for rent controlled buildings. A vicious cycle was created: crime drove away jobs, which drove away fathers, which produced more crime. A section of the South Bronx with 476,000 people in 1960 and 460,000 in 1970 dropped to 233,000 in 1980, a stunning change. As people left, presidents and presidential candidates came in— Jimmy Carter in 1977, Ronald Reagan in 1980—promising help.

Now the South Bronx seems to have turned around. It is still one of the lowest income parts of America, and it still is high crime; but it is beginning to be possible for low-income families here to work their way up. Government has helped, particularly the city government under Mayor Edward Koch, which provided more-intensive police patrols and housing subsidies. Rent control was phased out, criminals held in prison longer, pocket parks were built and graffiti painted over. But citizens here did much of the work, forming community groups called Banana Kelly or Mid-Bronx Desperadoes (now MBD Housing) to build single-family pastel bungalows and small-scale apartment projects for the elderly, single-parent families and former homeless. Local institutions, notably Bronx-Lebanon Hospital, remained in operation, employing area residents and becoming a strong force for neighborhood stability; warehousing and truck terminals opened up as the streets became safer. Population rose in the South Bronx in the 1980s more than almost anywhere else in New York City. There are now $150,000 ranch houses on Charlotte Street, where Jimmy Carter spoke in 1977.

The 16th Congressional District includes most of the Bronx south of the Bronx Zoo. It includes the Art Deco apartments of the Grand Concourse and the narrow commercial strips of Westchester Avenue, Boston Road and the Hub. It includes the industrial flatlands of Bruckner Boulevard and Hunts Point and the hard-rock ridges through which the original subways bore. This is still a low-income district, with 42% of residents below the poverty line—the most in the country—and the lowest median family income, the second lowest per capita income and the third lowest median household income of any congressional district. The people here are 59% Hispanic—though not all of them are Puerto Rican, the district has New York City's largest Puerto Rican community—and 43% black (the categories aren't mutually exclusive). Politically, this is quite possibly the most heavily Democratic district in the country.

The congressman from the 16th is Jose Serrano, chosen in a March 1990 special election. A native of Mayaguez, Puerto Rico, who grew up in the Millbrook project in the South Bronx,

Serrano has moved up while other Bronx politicians have fallen by the wayside due to corruption. He was elected to the New York Assembly in 1974 and chaired its Education Committee beginning in 1983; in 1985, he ran for Bronx borough president, bucking the Bronx Democratic organization, and nearly won. His disparaging remarks about corruption in the Bronx were remembered in 1987 when the man who beat him had to be replaced after a criminal conviction in the Wedtech scandal. Then, Congressman Robert Garcia, long the co-sponsor of Jack Kemp's enterprise zones, was convicted for accepting money from the defense contractor Wedtech and resigned in January 1990 (the conviction was later reversed but far too late to help him politically). Serrano was the obvious choice for the Democratic nomination and won the seat easily.

Serrano has one of the most liberal voting records in the House and moved up rapidly when Democrats were in control. In the 103d Congress he got a seat on Appropriations and chaired the Hispanic Caucus. When the caucuses were defunded in 1995, Serrano said Republicans were trying to "silence" voices of opposition to their agenda. He sponsored amendments on bilingual education, victim counseling and conflict resolution in schools, pediatric AIDS and the School-to-Work Act. In 1995 he became a vice chairman of the Democratic Steering Committee. But the shrinkage of Democratic seats on Appropriations made Serrano the most senior of seven Democrats forced to relinquish their Appropriations seats. He got a slot on Judiciary but, presumably, he will demand the next available seat on Appropriations.

The People: Pop. 1990: 581,053; 7% age 65+; 4% White; 43% Black; 1% Amer. Indian; 2% Asian; 35% Other; 59% Hispanic origin. Voting age pop.: 385,226; 43% Black; 57% Hispanic origin. Households: 28% married couple families; 15% married couple fams. w. children; 22% college educ.; median household income: $15,060; per capita income: $7,102; median gross rent: $398; median house value: $148,000.

1992 Presidential Vote

Clinton (D)	101,195	(81%)
Bush (R)	19,029	(15%)
Perot (I)	4,123	(3%)

1988 Presidential Vote

Dukakis (D)	98,339	(85%)
Bush (R)	17,534	(15%)

Rep. Jose E. Serrano (D)

Elected Mar. 1990; b. Oct. 24, 1943, Mayaguez, PR; home, Bronx; Lehman Col.; Catholic; married (Mary).

Career: Army Medical Corps, 1964–66; Banker 1961–69; Dist. 7 Schl. Bd., 1969–74; NY Assembly, 1974–90.

DC Office: 2342 RHOB 20515, 202-225-4361; Fax: 202-225-6001.

District Offices: 890 Grand Concourse, Bronx 10451, 718-538-5400.

Committees: *Judiciary* (13th of 15 D): Constitution.

Group Ratings

	ADA	ACLU	COPE	CFA	LCV	CON	NSI	COC	ACU	NTLC	CHC
1994	95	86	78	90	89	13	0	42	0	7	7
1993	100	—	100	100	77	32	—	0	4	—	—

National Journal Ratings

	1993 LIB — 1993 CONS		1994 LIB — 1994 CONS	
Economic	88% —	0%	83% —	0%
Social	80% —	13%	87% —	13%
Foreign	93% —	0%	85% —	0%

Key Votes of the 103d Congress

1. Clinton Deficit Plan	Y	3. Brady Handgun Purchase	Y	5. Lmt. UN Cmnd. of Forces	N
2. NAFTA	N	4. Strike Race/Death Pnlty.	N	6. Cut Missile Funds	Y

Key Votes of the 104th Congress

1. Congressional Compliance	Y	6. Reform Crime Grant	N	11. Loser Pays Court Reform	N
2. Balanced Budget Amndmt.	N	7. National Security Act	N	12. Product Liability Reform	N
3. Bar Unfunded Mandates	N	8. Moratorium on Regs.	N	13. Welfare Reform	N
4. Pass Line Item Veto	N	9. Risk Assessment on Regs.	N	14. Term Limits Amndmt.	N
5. Relax Exclusionary Rule	N	10. Expnd. Priv. Prop. Rights	N	15. Tax Cuts	N

Election Results

1994 general	Jose E. Serrano (D-L)................	58,572	(96%)	($125,441)
	Others.............................	2,257	(4%)	
1994 primary	Jose E. Serrano (D)................	unopposed		
1992 general	Jose E. Serrano (D-L)................	85,222	(91%)	($96,339)
	Michael Walters (R-C)................	7,975	(9%)	

SEVENTEENTH DISTRICT

The Bronx, a product almost entirely of the first half of the 20th Century, was originally a collection of middle-class neighborhoods clustered around subway stops, a borough where children of immigrants left gloomy Manhattan for the sunlight of wide Bronx avenues and the vistas of a city where the street grid bent to adapt to nature's ridges and hills. Different ethnic groups were clustered here and there: Irish in Kingsbridge, in the valley between Riverdale and the Grand Concourse; Italians in Bedford Park, north of Fordham University and Bronx Park; well-to-do WASPs and Jews in Riverdale, on the palisades above the Hudson River; Jews with less education and advantages originally in the Art Deco apartments on the Grand Concourse, then in a rush to Co-op City, the giant union-built apartment complex, with 35 35-story buildings, built in 1965 on marshland between the Hutchinson River Parkway and I-95.

The 17th Congressional District includes much of these Bronx neighborhoods plus several in the Westchester County suburbs just to the north. Co-op City is one anchor, and perhaps the largest political bloc in the district. Just to the west is the heavily black, middle-income neighborhood of Williamsbridge. The 17th's portions of Yonkers, Mount Vernon and New Rochelle in Westchester are carefully drawn to include most blacks there. The district also dips south along the Harlem River to take in some housing projects in the South Bronx. The 17th is, in Voting Rights Act argot, a minority-influence district, 40% black and 25% Hispanic.

Eliot Engel, the congressman from the 17th District, is a son of the Bronx and a resident of Co-op City, a teacher and guidance counselor who got elected to the New York Assembly in 1976, at 29. He was elected to the House in 1988 to replace Democrat Mario Biaggi, once the most decorated member of the New York Police Department, after he was convicted in two tawdry bribery cases. (Engel replaced a convicted incumbent in the Assembly, too; like Jose Serrano of the next-door 16th, he has risen politically when others fell.) Engel filed to run against Biaggi in June, giving up his Assembly seat; he won 48%, while Biaggi and Vincent Marchiselli each got 26%. In November, Biaggi was on the ballot again, this time as the Republican nominee, and Engel beat him 56%–27%. Biaggi ran again in the 1992 Democratic primary; Engel beat him yet again, 74%–26%.

Engel has one of the most liberal voting records in the House. On the Economic and Educational Opportunities Committee he backs the public sector programs that are part of the fabric of New York life—public housing, education spending, mental health services. On the International Relations Committee he has supported policies popular among ethnic groups in the district—recognizing Jerusalem as the capital of Israel (he is the prime sponsor of this resolution), opposing British policy in Northern Ireland, watching Africa policy, and co-chairing the Albanian Issues Caucus. He can be aggressive: he supported the Gulf war resolution and wants a tough war on drugs. But his basic tendencies are liberal: he sponsored the Democrats' amendment to the Contract With America to allow U.S. troops to serve under United Nations commanders.

In 1994 Engel had serious primary opposition from salsa singer Willie Colon. Colon portrayed himself as a son of the streets (Engel grew up in a public housing project) and was supported by Rev. Al Sharpton and Assemblyman Larry Seabrook. Engel won 61%–39%, but that is not a reassuring margin for a primary and suggests he may have a serious challenge again.

The People: Pop. 1990: 578,424; 14% age 65+; 29% White; 42% Black; 4% Asian; 14% Other; 28% Hispanic origin. Voting age pop.: 437,836; 40% Black; 25% Hispanic origin. Households: 38% married couple families; 18% married couple fams. w. children; 38% college educ.; median household income: $27,227; per capita income: $13,155; median gross rent: $483; median house value: $174,200.

1992 Presidential Vote			1988 Presidential Vote		
Clinton (D)	119,964	(75%)	Dukakis (D)	117,153	(73%)
Bush (R)	30,215	(19%)	Bush (R)	42,546	(27%)
Perot (I)	7,961	(5%)			

Rep. Eliot L. Engel (D)

Elected 1988; b. Feb. 18, 1947, Bronx; home, Bronx; Hunter-Lehman Col., B.A. 1969; City U. of NY, Lehman Col., M.A. 1973; NY Law Schl., J.D. 1987; Jewish, married (Patricia).

Career: Teacher, guidance counselor, NYC public schl., 1969–77; NY Assembly, 1977–88.

DC Office: 1433 LHOB 20515, 202-225-2464; Fax: 202-225-5513; e-mail: engeline@hr.house.gov.

District Offices: 3655 Johnson Ave., Bronx 10463, 718-796-9700.

Committees: *Economic & Educational Opportunities* (13th of 19 D): Early Childhood, Youth and Families; Workforce Protections. *International Relations* (8th of 19 D): Africa; International Economic Policy and Trade.

Group Ratings

	ADA	ACLU	COPE	CFA	LCV	CON	NSI	COC	ACU	NTLC	CHC
1994	100	87	100	100	100	13	10	18	0	7	0
1993	90	—	100	80	82	11	—	0	5	—	—

National Journal Ratings

	1993 LIB — 1993 CONS		1994 LIB — 1994 CONS	
Economic	88%	0%	83%	0%
Social	87%	0%	82%	15%
Foreign	93%	0%	85%	0%

Key Votes of the 103d Congress

1. Clinton Deficit Plan	Y	3. Brady Handgun Purchase	Y	5. Lmt. UN Cmnd. of Forces	N
2. NAFTA	N	4. Strike Race/Death Pnlty.	N	6. Cut Missile Funds	Y

Key Votes of the 104th Congress

1. Congressional Compliance	Y	6. Reform Crime Grant	N	11. Loser Pays Court Reform	N
2. Balanced Budget Amndmt.	N	7. National Security Act	N	12. Product Liability Reform	N
3. Bar Unfunded Mandates	N	8. Moratorium on Regs.	N	13. Welfare Reform	N
4. Pass Line Item Veto	N	9. Risk Assessment on Regs.	N	14. Term Limits Amndmt.	N
5. Relax Exclusionary Rule	N	10. Expnd. Priv. Prop. Rights	N	15. Tax Cuts	N

Election Results

1994 general	Eliot L. Engel (D-L)	73,321	(78%)	($464,001)
	Edward T. Marshall (R)	16,896	(18%)	($211,374)
	Others	4,262	(5%)	
1994 primary	Eliot L. Engel (D)	23,719	(62%)	
	Willie Colon (D)	14,256	(38%)	
1992 general	Eliot L. Engel (D-L)	98,068	(80%)	($469,220)
	Martin Richman (R)	16,511	(14%)	
	Others	7,802	(6%)	

EIGHTEENTH DISTRICT

The great granite ridges that form the spine of Manhattan and the Bronx move north into the thin peninsula of land between Long Island Sound and the Hudson River that is lower Westchester County. Blessed with some of America's loveliest scenery, easily accessible to Manhattan by train since the mid-19th Century, this became some of the country's first suburban terrain, with grand estates built by great millionaires, like Jay Gould's Gothic revival Lyndhurst or John D. Rockefeller's spectacular Kykuit, and with villages for retainers clustered around the railroad stations.

Today Westchester still looks suburban, perhaps more than ever before, now that it has a nice patina of age. It has little commuter railroad stations across from faux Tudor drugstores, soda fountains and cobblestone post offices; it also has shopping malls and galleries and corporate headquarters. The county does have its share of homeless and racial ghettos, its seedy neighborhoods if not slums. Intensive development has not proceeded too far north of White Plains, for just to the north Westchester is crossed by the first of several mountain ridges—the closest the Appalachians come to the ocean. Historically Republican, Westchester is now intensely marginal political territory. More than Nassau or Suffolk County or northern New Jersey, it has attracted liberal-minded professionals, often Jews, who have made very high-income places like Scarsdale Democratic strongholds. In addition, blue-collar voters and blacks in places like Mount Vernon make this a mixed constituency. Westchester votes a lot like the comfortable central city neighborhoods it physically resembles—Cambridge's Brattle Street, Washington's Cleveland Park, Philadelphia's Chestnut Hill.

The 18th Congressional District contains the heart of suburban Westchester County but actually has less than half the county's population; it also includes a little territory in the Bronx and widely scattered areas in Queens. Politics, as one might expect, is at work here; this is a district designed for Congresswoman Nita Lowey, a Democrat first elected in 1988 and a favorite of Governor Mario Cuomo. The 18th includes most of southern Westchester, but not the black neighborhoods of Yonkers, Mount Vernon and New Rochelle, which are in the minority-influence 17th District. It includes the rich, Catholic and conservative suburbs of Pelham, Eastchester and Bronxville, and the more Jewish and liberal Scarsdale, plus some of the Long Island Sound towns. The 18th also contains the southern half of White Plains, the county seat-corporate headquarters-shopping mall center. From there the 18th goes on its odyssey, picking up a few thousand people in Bronx communities facing the Sound and the urban resort of City Island. Then it crosses the Throgs Neck Bridge and is connected by a block-wide land-bridge through Flushing to two distinct areas of Queens. One is Lefrak City and other high-rise apartments in Rego Park, along Queens Boulevard where the first condominium conversion in New York took place in 1966; this area is heavily Jewish and very Democratic. The other is the heavily Italian neighborhoods around St. John's University, including the longtime home of its most famous alumnus, Mario Cuomo, in the pleasant winding streets of Hollis Wood, a more politically mixed area.

Nita Lowey was born in the Bronx, raised her family in Queens, and now lives in upper-crust Harrison in Westchester. She went to work for Cuomo in 1975, after he was appointed secretary of state by Governor Hugh Carey; she was an assistant secretary of state when she decided to run for Congress in 1988. In the primary, she faced Hamilton Fish III, son and grandson of Republican Hudson River Congressmen, and as a former publisher of The Nation considerably more leftish than Lowey; she won 44%–36%. Her opponent in the general was Joseph DioGuardi, a two-term incumbent who trumpeted his experience as a CPA but was dogged by charges of illicit contributions; she won 50%–47%. Each spent spent over $1 million, with Lowey spending $657,000 in personal funds. (In 1994, Fish and DioGuardi ran and lost in the 19th District, just to the north, where Fish's father was retiring after 26 years.)

In the House Lowey has made a mostly liberal record. On the Appropriations Committee she boosted biomedical and breast cancer research, worker retraining and aid to Israel. She chairs the bipartisan Congressional Women's Caucus and in 1994 organized 72 members, mostly Democrats, who pledged not to vote for a healthcare plan that did not cover abortions. In 1995 she called a press conference to bolster the endangered nomination of Henry Foster as surgeon general. She has often been a Clinton Administration loyalist when it is tough, voting for the 1993 budget and tax package in this high-income district, splitting with most New York Democrats and organized labor to support the North American Free Trade Agreement.

The 18th District voted the same as the country in the 1988 presidential election; since then it has moved left. But it is divided enough that Lowey has received serious opposition. In 1992, DioGuardi came back and ran; she carried Westchester 53%–47% and won 71% in Queens for a 56%–44% win overall. In 1994 she faced attorney Andy Hartzell, who put $247,000 of his own money into the campaign. But Lowey is a prodigious fundraiser: she has never spent less than $911,000, and in 1994 she raised over $1 million, the fourth highest in the House, and spent $1.3 million. She is proof that the Democratic feminist left can be as politically effective as the Republican religious right.

The People: Pop. 1990: 581,021; 17% age 65+; 74% White; 7% Black; 8% Asian; 3% Other; 10% Hispanic origin. Voting age pop.: 469,196; 7% Black; 10% Hispanic origin. Households: 56% married couple families; 23% married couple fams. w. children; 54% college educ.; median household income: $43,754; per capita income: $24,392; median gross rent: $594; median house value: $286,000.

1992 Presidential Vote			1988 Presidential Vote		
Clinton (D)	117,572	(50%)	Bush (R)	123,526	(53%)
Bush (R)	94,652	(40%)	Dukakis (D)	107,548	(47%)
Perot (I)	21,986	(9%)			

Rep. Nita M. Lowey (D)

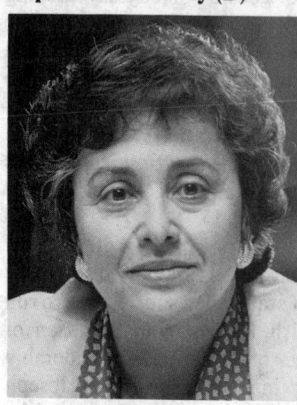

Elected 1988; b. July 5, 1937, New York City; home, Harrison; Mt. Holyoke Col., B.A. 1959; Jewish, married (Stephen).

Career: Asst. for Econ. Devel. and Neighborhood Preservation, NY Secy. of St., and Dep. Dir., Division of Econ. Opportunity, 1975–85; NY Asst. Secy. of St., 1985–87.

DC Office: 2421 RHOB 20515, 202-225-6506; Fax: 202-225-0546.

District Offices: 222 Mamaroneck Ave., White Plains 10605, 914-428-1707; and 97–45 Queens Blvd., #505, Rego Park 11374, 718-897-3602.

Committees: *Appropriations* (23rd of 24 D): Agriculture, Rural Development, FDA, and Related Agencies; Labor, Health and Human Services, and Education.

Group Ratings

	ADA	ACLU	COPE	CFA	LCV	CON	NSI	COC	ACU	NTLC	CHC
1994	85	87	89	100	94	9	30	42	10	11	7
1993	90	—	92	90	86	30	—	18	4	—	—

National Journal Ratings

	1993 LIB — 1993 CONS		1994 LIB — 1994 CONS	
Economic	68%	— 26%	73%	— 17%
Social	80%	— 13%	82%	— 15%
Foreign	84%	— 13%	72%	— 25%

Key Votes of the 103d Congress

1. Clinton Deficit Plan	Y	3. Brady Handgun Purchase	Y	5. Lmt. UN Cmnd. of Forces	N
2. NAFTA	Y	4. Strike Race/Death Pnlty.	N	6. Cut Missile Funds	Y

Key Votes of the 104th Congress

1. Congressional Compliance	Y	6. Reform Crime Grant	N	11. Loser Pays Court Reform	N
2. Balanced Budget Amndmt.	N	7. National Security Act	N	12. Product Liability Reform	N
3. Bar Unfunded Mandates	Y	8. Moratorium on Regs.	N	13. Welfare Reform	N
4. Pass Line Item Veto	N	9. Risk Assessment on Regs.	N	14. Term Limits Amndmt.	N
5. Relax Exclusionary Rule	N	10. Expnd. Priv. Prop. Rights	N	15. Tax Cuts	N

Election Results

1994 general	Nita M. Lowey (D)	91,663	(57%)	($1,343,347)
	Andrew C. Hartzell Jr. (R-C)	65,517	(41%)	($427,491)
	Others	2,873	(2%)	
1994 primary	Nita M. Lowey (D)	unopposed		
1992 general	Nita M. Lowey (D)	115,841	(56%)	($1,277,433)
	Joseph J. DioGuardi (R-C-RTL)	92,687	(44%)	($583,905)

NINETEENTH DISTRICT

The great interior of America can be said to begin where the Hudson River squeezes through the chain of Appalachian ridges at the Hudson Highlands. This chokepoint was the barrier to British military power during the Revolutionary War, when American forces built a chain across the river to keep the British from sailing north. It was over control of this part of the Hudson that Benedict Arnold betrayed his country, and it was here that the new nation built its Military

Academy high on the cliffs at West Point. The Hudson was the impetus for the builders of the Erie Canal and the water-level New York Central Railroad, the great projects that made New York City the port of the American interior, as well as the builders of the Croton Aqueduct not far away, which provided the water without which New York could not grow—and also provided a way for the first cockroaches to reach the city.

The lower Hudson was Dutch country, with Washington Irving country in Tarrytown and ancient estates like now restored Philipsburg Manor. In the late 19th Century, the ridges east of the Lower Hudson were first the site of great estates of New York's very rich and then became high-income suburbs: colonial-style Bedford, woodsy Chappaqua, John Cheever's Ossining. And in the mid-20th Century, these hills became home to some of America's leading corporations. *Reader's Digest* had built its colonial-style campus north of Pleasantville as early as the 1930s; General Foods moved to the north side of White Plains in the 1950s; soon after, not far from the Cross-Westchester Expressway, IBM and Pepsico and Texaco built headquarters.

The 19th Congressional District of New York covers much of the lower Hudson. It reaches south to take in part of White Plains and the corporate territory nearby, and includes northern Westchester County—now, for all its rural look, with almost as many people as the population-losing suburbs nearer New York City. The 19th runs north across towns filling up with middle-income public and corporate employees seeking reasonably priced housing in safe areas, up to the old city of Poughkeepsie on the Hudson and the valleys of Millbrook and Amenia and the Innisfree gardens. It crosses the Hudson where the rebels' chain did, by West Point and the Storm King Highway, and runs inland in Orange County. IBM, with its headquarters in Armonk, a research center in Yorktown Heights, and major operations in Wappingers Falls, has been a major area employer, and its growth and policy of lifetime employment have contributed greatly to local prosperity; now, with IBM's huge losses and layoffs, times have been tougher. Politically, sentiments here run counter to what might be expected. The older communities, with their well-educated and liberally inclined residents, have been historically Republican but are more inclined now to the Democrats. The newer communities, with upwardly striving people often disgusted by the crime and cultural disorder of New York City, may be filled with ancestral Democrats but are trending Republican.

The congresswoman from this district is Sue Kelly, a Republican elected in 1994 after the retirement of Hamilton Fish, a moderate Republican Congressman for 26 years, son of another Congressman Hamilton Fish and descendant of Ulysses S. Grant's Secretary of State Hamilton Fish. Kelly is not a Hudson Valley aristocrat but the daughter of a Lima, Ohio, doctor. She met her husband while she was a botany researcher at Harvard; they raised their family in Katonah, where she volunteered in many organizations, worked as a patient advocate, rape crisis counselor and educator, and sang in a church choir. She had a business renovating buildings and owned and ran a florist shop. She also had political experience as campaign manager for Assemblyman Jon Fossel in the 1970s. When Fish announced his retirement for health reasons in March 1994, Kelly decided to use the $150,000 she had saved to buy a new business to help finance a campaign for Congress instead.

It was a crowded field, in which Kelly emerged as the only candidate who was both for lower taxes and "huge" budget cuts and pro-choice on abortion. Her chief opponent in the primary was Joseph DioGuardi, elected in 1984 and 1986 in the Westchester district to the south and defeated there by Nita Lowey in 1988 and 1992; he said Kelly wasn't a real Republican, but he had to dodge charges of district-shopping. Kelly won with 23% to DioGuardi's 20%, and state Representative Glenn Warren and marketing executive Paul Bucha were a close third and fourth with 19% and 18%, respectively. On the Democratic side, two men who lost to Lowey in the 1988 primary sparred: corrugated box company founder Dennis Mehiel spent liberally of his own money, buying a New York TV ad charging his opponent, as publisher of *The Nation*, with responsibility for anti-Israel articles. But the opponent was Hamilton Fish, Jr., son of the incumbent congressman, known as III until the death of his grandfather, Franklin Roosevelt's least favorite congressman, in January 1991 at age 102. Fish won the primary with 49%, to 29%

for Mehiel and 22% for attorney Neil McCarthy.

Kelly and Fish presented a fine contrast in the general election. Kelly, campaigning in her "Kellyvan," stressed her involvement in business and community life and insisted that "government should be both smaller and smarter." Fish talked of his work on Human Rights Watch and his support of healthcare reform and opposition to capital punishment. "I saw my life in the public sector," he said. "I'm ambitious about making a contribution." DioGuardi continued running as the nominee of the Conservative and Right-to-Life parties and lobbed bitter criticisms at Kelly.

This was expected to be a close race; it turned out to be a blowout for Kelly. She led more narrowly in Westchester than to the north, but won overall 52%–37%, with 10% for DioGuardi. It helped perhaps that this district includes Peekskill and Garrison, the home bases of Governor George Pataki. Kelly was the only pro-choice Republican woman in the freshman class and became the only florist in Congress. Despite some demurs, she was a strong and consistent supporter of the Contract With America—one of only six New Yorkers with a perfect record in the first 100 days. She also defended the Republican welfare-reform plan against attacks that it was unfair to women.

The People: Pop. 1990: 580,386; 30% rural; 11% age 65+; 86% White; 7% Black; 2% Asian; 1% Other; 5% Hispanic origin. Voting age pop.: 444,175; 7% Black; 5% Hispanic origin. Households: 64% married couple families; 31% married couple fams. w. children; 57% college educ.; median household income: $50,239; per capita income: $22,458; median gross rent: $653; median house value: $198,300.

1992 Presidential Vote			1988 Presidential Vote		
Bush (R)	109,965	(42%)	Bush (R)	142,996	(60%)
Clinton (D)	104,949	(40%)	Dukakis (D)	94,387	(40%)
Perot (I)	45,088	(17%)			

Rep. Sue W. Kelly (R)

Elected 1994; b. Sept. 26, 1936, Lima, OH; home, Katonah; Denison U., B.A. 1958, Sarah Lawrence Col., M.A. 1985; Presbyterian; married (Edward).

Career: Owner/Mgr., Kelly & Assoc. bldg. rehab., 1960–present; Researcher, Harvard, 1958–60; Owner/Mgr., Kelly Florist, 1980–83; Prof., Sarah Lawrence Col., 1988–91.

DC Office: 1037 LHOB 20515, 202-225-5441; Fax: 202-225-3289.

District Offices: 21 Old Main St., #205, Fishkill 12524, 914-897-5200.

Committees: *Banking & Financial Services* (27th of 27 R): Capital Markets, Securities and Government Sponsored Enterprises; Domestic and International Monetary Policy. *Small Business* (11th of 22 R): Government Programs; Regulation and Paperwork. *Transportation & Infrastructure* (31st of 33 R): Aviation; Railroads.

Group Ratings and 103rd Congress Votes: Newly Elected

Key Votes of the 104th Congress

1. Congressional Compliance Y	6. Reform Crime Grant Y	11. Loser Pays Court Reform Y
2. Balanced Budget Amndmt. Y	7. National Security Act Y	12. Product Liability Reform Y
3. Bar Unfunded Mandates Y	8. Moratorium on Regs. Y	13. Welfare Reform Y
4. Pass Line Item Veto Y	9. Risk Assessment on Regs. Y	14. Term Limits Amndmt. Y
5. Relax Exclusionary Rule Y	10. Expnd. Priv. Prop. Rights Y	15. Tax Cuts Y

Election Results

1994 general	Sue W. Kelly (R)	100,173	(52%)	($570,821)
	Hamilton Fish, Jr. (D)	70,696	(37%)	($566,601)
	Joseph J. DioGuardi (C-RTL)	19,761	(10%)	($278,490)
	Others	1,679	(1%)	
1994 primary	Sue W. Kelly (R)	5,842	(23%)	
	Joseph J. DioGuardi (R)	5,067	(20%)	
	Glenn E. Warren (R)	4,964	(19%)	
	Paul W. Bucha (R)	4,598	(18%)	
	Guy Parisi (R)	3,845	(15%)	
	John F. Flanagan Jr. (R)	1,364	(5%)	
	Others	267	(1%)	
1992 general	Hamilton Fish, Jr. (R-C)	139,610	(60%)	($617,832)
	Neil McCarthy (D)	92,854	(40%)	($132,279)

TWENTIETH DISTRICT

From Sunnyside, the whimsical house that Washington Irving built in Tarrytown near the country he immortalized as Sleepy Hollow, you can see across the waters of the Tappan Zee, the widest point of the Hudson, and get a sense of how the land looked when first settled by Dutchmen. All around is Irving country—the old towns of Tarrytown, Irvington, Dobbs Ferry and Hastings-on-Hudson, now comfortably affluent suburbs. On the other side of the Tappan Zee is Rockland County, a stretch of suburbs between the Hudson and the Ramapos, the first Appalachian chain west of New York. First settled by Dutchmen, Rockland then was studded by little towns that grew up as if 1,000 miles from Gotham, but have thrived on the actual proximity: the town of Nyack here was the home of the actress Helen Hayes, and James A. Farley, Franklin Roosevelt's chief political major domo and Democratic National chairman, was from Stony Point just below the Hudson Highlands.

The 20th Congressional District of New York spans the Tappan Zee, connecting most of the Irving suburbs with Rockland County and stepping over the Ramapos 120 miles inland to the border of Pennsylvania. Past the Ramapos is most of Orange County, New York's second fastest-growing county in the 1980s, where old villages between mountains and farms on the nation's biggest deposit of muck soil outside the Everglades have been flanked with new modest-income subdivisions. Farther out, past the Shawangunk Mountains, is Sullivan County and the Catskills Borscht Belt district, a Jewish resort area with huge kosher hotels since the late 19th Century. Politically, this area has been trending Republican, as old Upstate-minded residents are joined by newcomers fleeing the city.

The 20th's congressman, Republican Benjamin Gilman, is now chairman of the International Affairs Committee. He grew up in Middletown; he traveled with his father to Nazi Germany in 1933, at 10, and remembers Hitler's storm troopers. After service in World War II, he became a lawyer, working for the state and bringing habeas corpus cases for mental hospital patients. In 1966 he was elected to the Assembly, and in 1972 to the House; that makes him the eighth ranking Republican in seniority today. Gilman is moderate on economics and cultural issues, rather more conservative on foreign policy; he is pleasant and ordinarily arouses little animosity. In the 1970s he worked, often with East German lawyer Wolfgang Vogel, to arrange spy swaps. He visited editor Jacobo Timmerman in jail in Argentina and helped secure his release; he championed the human rights of Pentecostals, Ukrainians, Poles and Jews in the Soviet empire. For a dozen years he was ranking Republican on the Select Committee on Narcotics, until junior Republicans in 1993 launched a drive to eliminate four select committees. He has long been a supporter of Israel, and he strongly backed the Gulf war resolution.

Gilman became ranking Republican on the committee in 1993, a position of potential influence since he could help bestow or withhold the "bipartisan" label on administration foreign policy. Despite his pleasant demeanor, he often withheld. He faulted Bill Clinton for not expanding NATO fast enough, for favoring Russia over the other former Soviet republics, and for not following through on threats to lift the Bosnian arms embargo and take action against the Bosnian Serbs. He opposed changing the mission of U.S. troops in Somalia, and he blocked the merger of the State Department counterterrorism office just after the World Trade Center bombing. He wanted to delay full recognition of Vietnam pending a full accounting of American POWs. As he summed it up after the November 1994 election, "Instead of a strong, steady signal on foreign policy coming from Washington, regrettably the world has heard a series of wavering notes sounded by an uncertain trumpet, leaving our allies concerned and our adversaries confused." And, he said, "We intend to make certain that the Congress will be fully and openly consulted about future involvements of any U.S. military intervention overseas."

A few Republicans urged Newt Gingrich to pass over Gilman for the chairmanship, but the New Yorker had strong support from conservatives like Robert Dornan. With no credible alternative available, there was never any chance that he would not get it. It became then his task to get the Contract With America foreign policy planks through committee—a process so contentious that he brought a baseball bat to the third day of markup. Gilman altered the Contract provisions a bit and then defended them stoutly on the floor. Indeed, despite his moderate reputation he voted for most of the Contract, switching to support the balanced budget amendment, dissenting on term limits. But he took care to caution freshman conservatives—and Senate foreign-policy barons Jesse Helms and Mitch McConnell—that foreign aid serves good American purposes and to warn that "one-half of the Congress has less than four years of institutional memory and little experience in foreign affairs."

After more than 20 years Gilman continues to work his district hard, often spending Saturdays riding around in his mobile home-office. In March 1995 he marched next to Sinn Fein leader Gerry Adams in the St. Patrick's Day parade in Pearl River, the third largest St. Pat's parade in the world. He won the district fairly easily in 1972 against ultraliberal John Dow and has had only one difficult reelection race, after redistricting in 1982, when he faced Republican-turned-Democrat Peter Peyser; Gilman won 53%–42%. In 1994 he won 67%–29%.

The People: Pop. 1990: 580,025; 23% rural; 11% age 65+; 83% White; 8% Black; 3% Asian; 2% Other; 6% Hispanic origin. Voting age pop.: 428,788; 8% Black; 6% Hispanic origin. Households: 65% married couple families; 32% married couple fams. w. children; 54% college educ.; median household income: $47,107; per capita income: $19,680; median gross rent: $659; median house value: $193,500.

1992 Presidential Vote

Clinton (D)	116,694	(45%)
Bush (R)	107,107	(41%)
Perot (I)	37,014	(14%)

1988 Presidential Vote

Bush (R)	135,464	(58%)
Dukakis (D)	99,201	(42%)

Rep. Benjamin A. Gilman (R)

Elected 1972; b. Dec. 6, 1922, Poughkeepsie; home, Middletown; U. of PA, B.S. 1946, NY Law Schl., LL.B. 1950; Jewish; separated.

Career: Army Air Corps, 1942–45 (WWII); NY Asst. Atty. Gen., 1953–55; Practicing atty., 1955–72; Atty., NY Temporary Comm. on the Courts; NY Assembly, 1967–72.

DC Office: 2449 RHOB 20515, 202-225-3776; Fax: 202-225-2541.

District Offices: 407 E. Main St., P.O. Box 358, Middletown 10940, 914-343-6666; 377 Rte. 59, Monsey 10952, 914-357-9000; and 32 Main St., Hastings-on-Hudson 10706, 914-478-5550.

Committees: *Government Reform & Oversight* (2nd of 27 R): Civil Service; Postal Service. *International Relations* (Chmn. of 23 R): International Operations and Human Rights.

Group Ratings

	ADA	ACLU	COPE	CFA	LCV	CON	NSI	COC	ACU	NTLC	CHC
1994	35	61	89	70	78	33	80	67	52	64	21
1993	55	—	83	80	71	52	—	45	46	—	—

National Journal Ratings

	1993 LIB	—	1993 CONS	1994 LIB	—	1994 CONS
Economic	44%	—	55%	54%	—	45%
Social	58%	—	41%	47%	—	52%
Foreign	17%	—	76%	34%	—	63%

Key Votes of the 103d Congress

1. Clinton Deficit Plan	N	3. Brady Handgun Purchase Y	5. Lmt. UN Cmnd. of Forces Y
2. NAFTA	N	4. Strike Race/Death Pnlty. Y	6. Cut Missile Funds N

Key Votes of the 104th Congress

1. Congressional Compliance Y	6. Reform Crime Grant Y	11. Loser Pays Court Reform Y
2. Balanced Budget Amndmt. Y	7. National Security Act Y	12. Product Liability Reform Y
3. Bar Unfunded Mandates Y	8. Moratorium on Regs. Y	13. Welfare Reform Y
4. Pass Line Item Veto Y	9. Risk Assessment on Regs. Y	14. Term Limits Amndmt. N
5. Relax Exclusionary Rule Y	10. Expnd. Priv. Prop. Rights Y	15. Tax Cuts Y

Election Results

1994 general	Benjamin A. Gilman (R)	120,334	(67%)	($547,731)
	Gregory B. Julian (D)	52,345	(29%)	($35,766)
	Others	5,612	(3%)	
1994 primary	Benjamin A. Gilman (R)	unopposed		
1992 general	Benjamin A. Gilman (R)	150,301	(66%)	($576,538)
	Jonathan L. Levine (D)	66,826	(29%)	($27,833)
	Robert F. Garrison (RTL)	10,204	(5%)	

TWENTY-FIRST DISTRICT

Albany, as readers of its novelist laureate William Kennedy know, is within living memory an antique city. Its solid rowhouses show its 19th-Century prosperity; its once teeming lumberyards and railroad car shops, old restaurants and hotels have the patina of age and the accumulated grime of decades of coal smoke burned during six-month-long winters. Its history is traceable to 1624, when the Dutch built Fort Orange on the banks of the Hudson so seagoing ships could dock at the edge of the great gloomy forests near the confluence of the Hudson and the Mohawk—the natural crossroads of Upstate New York even before the building of the Erie Canal and the New York Central Railroad. This was one of America's early industrial centers. Troy, a few miles upriver, was a steel town rivaling Pittsburgh in the 1840s, and later the leading producer of detachable collars; Cohoes, at the junction of the Hudson and the Mohawk, became a leading textile producer; Schenectady, a few miles up the Mohawk, was the site of Charles Steinmetz's fabled General Electric laboratories and has been a big GE town ever since. Albany was one of America's biggest lumber towns as well as the state capital.

Albany continues to have one of the nation's most famed Democratic political machines, dating back to 1921, when Daniel O'Connell and his brothers and local aristocrat Edwin Corning took control of City Hall. They never really relinquished it: Daniel O'Connell died in 1977 at age 91, still boss after 56 years, and his early partner's son, Erastus Corning II, was mayor from 1942 until his death in 1983. The machine was sustained by legions of city and county employees, by a certain creativity when it came to counting votes and by the raffish atmosphere that was found in the speakeasies of so many cities during Prohibition and lingered in Albany for decades after. Curiously, the machine made possible the transformation of antique Albany into the shiny new metropolis it is today. Mayor Corning provided financing for Nelson Rockefeller's monumental South Mall, expressways were built, the old Union Station was spruced up, and yuppies began buying and renovating old townhouses. These days, the Albany machine is battered in some elections and can't always control the suburbs as it once could Albany, but it clings to power in the H. H. Richardson City Hall facing the gaudy State House.

The 21st Congressional District includes all of Albany and Schenectady Counties, plus Troy on the Hudson's east bank, and the depressed factory town of Amsterdam on the Mohawk. More than half its votes are cast in Albany County, and it is a solidly Democratic district. It has also been a Democratic machine district, as was shown in 1988, the last time the seat changed hands. Four days after the July filing deadline and on the last day for withdrawal, 30-year incumbent Democrat Samuel Stratton announced he was retiring for health reasons, giving the Democratic machine a chance to name a replacement. It promptly picked Assemblyman Michael McNulty, whose roots in Albany politics go back to his grandfather, who served as Albany County sheriff, as did his father, who was also mayor. Michael McNulty was first elected to office in 1969, at 22, and served 13 years as town supervisor and mayor in the industrial suburb of Green Island; he was elected to the Assembly in 1982. Being in Congress is a fulfillment of his family's and his own ambition. McNulty won the 1988 general election by 62%–38% against a venture capital specialist who attacked him for avoiding the issues and for having been chosen by party bosses rather than primary voters. He has not been seriously challenged since.

McNulty is hard-working, serious, abstemious, pleasant and a conscientious campaigner. For a New York Democrat, his voting record is quite conservative on foreign and cultural issues; he is one New York Democrat endorsed by the Conservative, not the Liberal, Party. He is pro-life on abortion and for the amendment allowing penalties for desecration of the flag. He had qualms about the Clinton Administration's health care and welfare plans. Still, given the strong performance of Democratic presidential candidates in his district, it was a bit surprising that he was the northern Democrat with the highest support for the Contract with America—voting for everything except welfare reform and the tax cut. He collected signatures on a petition to Speaker Thomas Foley to make the House schedule more family-friendly; Newt Gingrich promised to do so, but didn't deliver during the first 100 days of the 104th Congress. The Democrats' loss of control hurt McNulty. He can no longer preside in the speaker's chair, where he performed ably—and where he announced the on-the-floor engagement of New York Republicans Bill Paxon and Susan Molinari. And, more importantly, he lost the seat he won in 1993 on Ways and Means.

The People: Pop. 1990: 580,320; 15% rural; 15% age 65+; 90% White; 6% Black; 2% Asian; 1% Other; 2% Hispanic origin. Voting age pop.: 451,451; 5% Black; 2% Hispanic origin. Households: 50% married couple families; 22% married couple fams. w. children; 48% college educ.; median household income: $31,489; per capita income: $15,304; median gross rent: $453; median house value: $98,800.

1992 Presidential Vote			1988 Presidential Vote		
Clinton (D)	140,251	(48%)	Dukakis (D)	154,308	(56%)
Bush (R)	99,094	(34%)	Bush (R)	121,617	(44%)
Perot (I)	51,086	(17%)			

Rep. Michael R. McNulty (D)

Elected 1988; b. Sept. 16, 1947, Troy; home, Green Island; Holy Cross Col., B.A. 1969; Catholic; married (Nancy Ann).

Career: Green Island Supervisor, 1969–77; Green Island Mayor, 1977–83; NY Assembly, 1983–88.

DC Office: 2442 RHOB 20515, 202-225-5076; Fax: 202-225-5077.

District Offices: U.S. Post Office, Jay St., Schenectady 12305, 518-374-4547; O'Brien Fed. Bldg., #827; Albany 12207, 518-465-0700; 9 Market St., Amsterdam 12010, 518-843-3400; and 33 2d St., Troy 12180, 518-271-0822.

Committees: *International Relations* (18th of 19 D): International Economic Policy and Trade.

Group Ratings

	ADA	ACLU	COPE	CFA	LCV	CON	NSI	COC	ACU	NTLC	CHC
1994	55	30	63	60	71	29	40	60	42	11	64
1993	60	—	100	90	79	29	—	18	21	—	—

National Journal Ratings

	1993 LIB — 1993 CONS		1994 LIB — 1994 CONS	
Economic	78% —	12%	67% —	29%
Social	44% —	55%	52% —	48%
Foreign	40% —	60%	43% —	56%

Key Votes of the 103d Congress

1. Clinton Deficit Plan	Y	3. Brady Handgun Purchase	Y	5. Lmt. UN Cmnd. of Forces	Y
2. NAFTA	N	4. Strike Race/Death Pnlty.	*	6. Cut Missile Funds	N

Key Votes of the 104th Congress

1. Congressional Compliance	Y	6. Reform Crime Grant	Y	11. Loser Pays Court Reform	Y
2. Balanced Budget Amndmt.	Y	7. National Security Act	Y	12. Product Liability Reform	Y
3. Bar Unfunded Mandates	Y	8. Moratorium on Regs.	Y	13. Welfare Reform	N
4. Pass Line Item Veto	Y	9. Risk Assessment on Regs.	Y	14. Term Limits Amndmt.	Y
5. Relax Exclusionary Rule	Y	10. Expnd. Priv. Prop. Rights	Y	15. Tax Cuts	N

Election Results

1994 general	Michael R. McNulty (D-C)	147,804	(67%)	($217,642)
	Joseph A. Gomez (R)	68,745	(31%)	($25,773)
	Others	4,125	(2%)	
1994 primary	Michael R. McNulty (D)	unopposed		
1992 general	Michael R. McNulty (D-C)	166,371	(63%)	($252,821)
	Nancy Norman (R-L)	91,184	(34%)	
	Other	7,723	(3%)	

TWENTY-SECOND DISTRICT

The Hudson River, an arm of the ocean and an avenue of commerce in colonial days, an inspiration to artists, is still one of America's great sights, though it is no longer central, as it was until not so long ago, in the nation's consciousness and politics. The classic mansions overlooking the River, like Clermont, whose builder Robert Livingston financed Robert Fulton's first steamboat, and Montgomery Place, built by Janet Livingston Montgomery, the widow of the general who captured Quebec in 1775, are reminders of the cool serenity of the 18th Century mind and the daring nature of its spirit. Robert Livingston administered the first oath of office to George Washington in 1789 and helped negotiate the Louisiana Purchase in 1803. It was on a visit to his lands in the 1790s that James Madison and Aaron Burr welded the Virginia-New York alliance that set the course of American political history. The Hudson was also a center of America in the romantic era: from Frederick Church's Moorish mansion, Olana, you can see the still unspoiled river landscape that inspired his art and that of others of the Hudson River school of painters. The Hudson gave birth also to our passionate party politics: nearby is Kinderhook, home of Martin Van Buren, the innkeeper's son who in alliance with Andrew Jackson invented the torchlight parade, the national party convention and, some argue, the Democratic Party itself. Later in the 19th Century, the Hudson was lined with the palaces of the nation's first great millionaires and the comfortable country houses of New York's gentry. In one of the latter, Springwood in Hyde Park, Franklin Roosevelt was born and lived; this politician, who expanded government at home and was the victorious commander-in-chief of American military forces throughout the world, was most comfortable looking out over his sloping lawn down to the river that he remembered iceboating on in the winters of the 1880s.

The 22d Congressional District of New York includes much of the Hudson Valley, the grand river south of Albany and the smaller river, freshly fed by the Adirondacks, to the north; for 1992 it extends even further north to include most of Essex County and Lake Placid. Much of the district, just outside the old manufacturing city of Troy and the still grandly 19th Century racing center Saratoga Springs, is essentially suburban Albany, and has been heavily Republican since the late 19th Century (Roosevelt never carried his home territory except when he ran for state Senate in 1910).

The congressman from the 22d, Gerald Solomon, is a strong partisan Republican, an insurance businessman in Glens Falls who was elected township supervisor in 1966, New York Assemblyman in 1972 and Congressman in 1978. Now he is chairman of the House Rules Committee. Solomon is an aggressive conservative, but not a free-market purist: in the 103d Congress he submitted a budget plan calling for higher taxes on incomes over $200,000, and he staunchly opposed the North American Free Trade Agreement and favored an end to China's most-favored-nation status. Tapped by Minority Leader Robert Michel as ranking Republican on the Rules Committee from 1991–94, he denounced the Democrats' plan to give floor votes to five representatives of territories and the District of Columbia; Democrats partially retreated, and it was summarily repealed in 1995 when Republicans took control. He denounced as utterly insufficient Democrats' versions of the line-item veto and internal House reform; his line-item veto was rejected 218–205 in July 1994, but he saw Republican versions of both passed in early

1995. In March 1994 Solomon came forward with a draconian plan to balance the budget within five years; it got only 73 votes.

Solomon, who left college and then enlisted in the Marine Corps when the Korean war began, fought to maintain the Selective Service System and sponsored several laws aimed at young people who flout their obligations. His Marine bearing survives in several efforts: the Solomon Amendment in the early 1980s cut off college aid for young men who had not registered for the draft; a 1990 amendment cut off highway funding for states that don't suspend drug offenders' driver's licenses; a 1994 amendment prohibited federal grants to colleges that bar military recruiters. He is also chief sponsor of the amendment to allow penalties for those who burn the flag. Solomon can also be generous to those who do right. As ranking Republican on Veterans' Affairs he helped pass the 1984 G.I. Bill of Rights, which creatively increased veterans' benefits and helped attract quality recruits to the volunteer military that performed so well in the Gulf.

As ranking Republican on Rules, Solomon was a major spokesman for his party on almost all issues. When Bob Michel announced his retirement in October 1993, Solomon stepped forward in the same room and announced he was running for Republican leader. But he dropped his bid 10 days later, conceding that Newt Gingrich already had pledges from most Republican members. That led to speculation that Solomon would be passed over for Rules chairman, but he was not; Gingrich seems to prize his aggressiveness and to bear him no ill will. Ever the loyal Marine, Solomon sponsored the Republicans' reorganization of committees, and he made some of the procedural changes in House debate he had sought in vain before. One was to replace "king of the hill" (in which the final majority vote on several alternatives prevails) with "queen of the hill" (in which the alternative with the most votes prevails). But as Democrats started offering dozens of amendments, Solomon resorted to the closed rules he had so often denounced: a necessity in a large body when the minority operates without self-restraint. He was criticized by black members for hanging a portrait of former Rules Chairman Howard Smith, a Virginia segregationist and a Democrat (he later had it removed). He would have done better to hang Clarence Brown of Ohio, ranking Republican in Smith's day, and a supporter of civil rights.

Solomon is reelected every two years by wide margins.

The People: Pop. 1990: 580,522; 67% rural; 13% age 65+; 96% White; 2% Black; 1% Asian; 2% Hispanic origin. Voting age pop.: 434,410; 2% Black; 2% Hispanic origin. Households: 62% married couple families; 30% married couple fams. w. children; 46% college educ.; median household income: $33,306; per capita income: $14,646; median gross rent: $465; median house value: $99,600.

1992 Presidential Vote		
Bush (R)	116,283	(41%)
Clinton (D)	99,984	(36%)
Perot (I)	62,533	(22%)

1988 Presidential Vote		
Bush (R)	146,610	(60%)
Dukakis (D)	98,001	(40%)

Rep. Gerald B. H. Solomon (R)

Elected 1978; b. Aug. 14, 1930, Okeechobee, FL; home, Queensbury; Siena Col., 1948–49, St. Lawrence U., 1953–54; Presbyterian; married (Freda).

Career: Marine Corps, 1951–52; Founding partner, Assoc. of Glens Falls Insurance co., 1964–78; Queensbury Town Supervisor, 1966–77; NY Assembly, 1972–78.

DC Office: 2206 RHOB 20515, 202-225-5614; Fax: 202-225-6234.

District Offices: Gaslight Sq., Saratoga Springs 12866, 518-587-9800; 337 Fairview Ave., Hudson 12534, 518-828-0181; and 21 Bay St., Glens Falls 12801, 518-792-3031.

Committees: *Rules* (Chmn. of 9 R); Legislative and Budget Process; Rules of the House.

Group Ratings

	ADA	ACLU	COPE	CFA	LCV	CON	NSI	COC	ACU	NTLC	CHC
1994	0	13	38	20	7	86	100	67	95	93	100
1993	15	—	40	20	29	89	—	80	96	—	—

National Journal Ratings

	1993 LIB — 1993 CONS		1994 LIB — 1994 CONS	
Economic	29%	— 71%	0%	— 80%
Social	11%	— 82%	0%	— 89%
Foreign	0%	— 91%	0%	— 88%

Key Votes of the 103d Congress

1. Clinton Deficit Plan	N	3. Brady Handgun Purchase N	5. Lmt. UN Cmnd. of Forces Y
2. NAFTA	N	4. Strike Race/Death Pnlty. Y	6. Cut Missile Funds N

Key Votes of the 104th Congress

1. Congressional Compliance Y	6. Reform Crime Grant Y	11. Loser Pays Court Reform Y
2. Balanced Budget Amndmt. Y	7. National Security Act Y	12. Product Liability Reform Y
3. Bar Unfunded Mandates Y	8. Moratorium on Regs. Y	13. Welfare Reform Y
4. Pass Line Item Veto Y	9. Risk Assessment on Regs. Y	14. Term Limits Amndmt. Y
5. Relax Exclusionary Rule Y	10. Expnd. Priv. Prop. Rights Y	15. Tax Cuts Y

Election Results

1994 general	Gerald B. H. Solomon (R-C-RTL)	157,717	(73%)	($444,067)
	L. Robert Lawrence Jr. (D)	57,064	(27%)	($17,363)
1994 primary	Gerald B. H. Solomon (R)	unopposed		
1992 general	Gerald B. H. Solomon (R-C-RTL)	164,436	(65%)	($286,286)
	David Roberts (D)	86,896	(35%)	($32,189)

TWENTY-THIRD DISTRICT

One of the first American frontiers was the Mohawk River Valley of Upstate New York, and it remained static for 150 years. From the establishment of Fort Orange in 1624 in what now is Albany until the Revolutionary War, white settlers did not dare move west along the Mohawk. The British used their Iroquois allies as a buffer against the French and in return kept New England Yankees from moving westward. Only after the French were driven from the colonies in

1759 did the pressures for westward settlement prevail; the British tried to keep their word to the Indians, but once the Revolutionary War started, the Iroquois dominion ended.

This is the background of *Drums Along the Mohawk* and of James Fenimore Cooper's Leatherstocking Tales. But there is little in these rolling hills today to evoke the bloody violence whose conclusion made possible the digging of the Erie Canal and the building of the New York Central Railroad. As migration slowed and trade increased, the Mohawk Valley became one of the nation's early industrial centers. The little Oneida County hamlets of Utica and Rome, where the canal builders had to dig through the route's highest ground, became sizable factory towns. Even the utopian Oneida Community, believers in plural marriage and communal ownership, kept open a stainless steel factory. First settled by New England Yankees, these towns attracted a new wave of immigration from the Atlantic coast in the early 20th Century. Today they are the most heavily Italian and Polish-American communities between Albany and Buffalo; politically, they are marginally Republican, nearly voting for Bill Clinton in 1992.

The 23d Congressional District, in the Mohawk Valley, is centered on Utica and Rome in Oneida County and includes a row of more sparsely settled counties to the south. Here the hilly land has an early 19th Century cast, in places like Cooperstown, certainly one of the loveliest and best-preserved small towns in America, and Pindars Corners, the crossroads where Senator Daniel Patrick Moynihan has a farm and a 19th Century schoolhouse to which he repairs periodically. The 23d District is ancestrally Republican; Madison County here was one of the hotbeds of abolitionism in the 1850s. But it is also an area that feels bypassed by more recent economic growth and in need of government assistance and sustenance.

The congressman from the 23d is Sherwood Boehlert, a Republican with deep roots in Oneida County and a distinctively moderate record in Washington. Boehlert worked for his two predecessors in Congress, then was elected Oneida County executive in 1978 and won the House seat in 1982. He has worked in government as much as politics, and does not share the free market economists' disdain for its works. His moderate views left him voting with his party 72% of the time in the 103d Congress, the third lowest rating of any Republican (behind Ben Gilman with 64% and Connie Morella with 63%). His votes against four pieces of the Contract With America—opposing chiefly the regulatory-reform agenda—were the second highest for House Republicans, behind only Connie Morella of Maryland. Some of Boehlert's votes have a local angle: he supports dairy subsidies (the 23d is part of New York City's milkshed), he favors baseball's antitrust exemption (Cooperstown is where baseball was supposedly invented in 1839 and Boehlert is part owner of a minor league team); he sponsored Pledge of Allegiance Day (the Pledge was written by Francis Bellamy in Rome in 1892). While he sometimes decried Republicans' confrontational tactics, Boehlert gave crucial support to Newt Gingrich in his race for Minority Whip in March 1989, when he won by two votes. Despite his subsequent votes, he signed the Contract With America, and in October 1994 he said, "There's a feeling that's prevalent among Republicans that our finest hour is upon us . . . that the next Congress is going to be different."

Boehlert's greatest success in Congress was in leading the fight against the superconducting supercollider, a giant atom smasher that was to be built in Texas. During the Bush years he attacked it as "siphoning money from the bulk of American science"; in the Clinton years, it was "simply not affordable science," and in October 1993 the House voted 280–150 to kill it. Boehlert was less successful in working to reauthorize the Clean Water Act and reform the Superfund program. He tends to be in the minority of his party in resisting measures to limit regulation of wetlands; his May 1995 amendment to broaden the definition of wetlands garnered support of only 34 Republicans. Boehlert is not always predictable. He was one of three Republicans to vote for the Clinton economic stimulus package in March 1993; he was one of the last undecideds on the North American Free Trade Agreement, ultimately voting yes; he voted for the Brady bill, not a plus locally; and he has questioned on budgetary grounds the Commerce Department's advanced technology program, which he originally backed. Despite his efforts, Griffiss Air Force Base, with 5,000 local jobs, wound up on the base closing list.

Boehlert has been reelected easily by very large margins.

The People: Pop. 1990: 580,259; 55% rural; 15% age 65+; 95% White; 3% Black; 1% Asian; 1% Other; 1% Hispanic origin. Voting age pop.: 435,794; 3% Black; 1% Hispanic origin. Households: 58% married couple families; 27% married couple fams. w. children; 40% college educ.; median household income: $26,155; per capita income: $11,792; median gross rent: $366; median house value: $67,800.

1992 Presidential Vote			1988 Presidential Vote		
Bush (R)	99,495	(40%)	Bush (R)	128,287	(55%)
Clinton (D)	92,554	(37%)	Dukakis (D)	103,327	(45%)
Perot (I)	55,887	(22%)			

Rep. Sherwood Boehlert (R)

Elected 1982; b. Sept. 28, 1936, Utica; home, New Hartford; Utica Col., B.A. 1961; Catholic; married (Marianne).

Career: Army, 1956–58; P.R. Mgr., Wyandotte Chemicals Corp., 1961–64; A.A., U.S. Rep. Alexander Pirnie, 1964–72; A.A., U.S. Rep. Donald Mitchell, 1973–79; Oneida Cnty. Exec., 1978–82.

DC Office: 2246 RHOB 202-225-3665; Fax: 202-225-1891; e-mail: boehlert@hr.house.gov.

District Offices: 10 Broad St., #200, Utica 13501, 315-793-8146; 41 S. Main St., Oneonta 13820, 607-432-5524; and 42 S. Broad St., Norwich 13815 607-336-7160.

Committees: *Science* (3rd of 27 R): Basic Research. *Transportation & Infrastructure* (5th of 33 R): Railroads; Water Resources and Environment (Chmn.).

Group Ratings

	ADA	ACLU	COPE	CFA	LCV	CON	NSI	COC	ACU	NTLC	CHC
1994	50	65	67	60	88	48	70	75	38	50	21
1993	60	—	83	80	85	16	—	55	38	—	—

National Journal Ratings

	1993 LIB — 1993 CONS			1994 LIB — 1994 CONS		
Economic	47%	—	53%	42%	—	57%
Social	63%	—	36%	53%	—	46%
Foreign	35%	—	63%	40%	—	59%

Key Votes of the 103d Congress

1. Clinton Deficit Plan	N	3. Brady Handgun Purchase	Y	5. Lmt. UN Cmnd. of Forces	Y
2. NAFTA	Y	4. Strike Race/Death Pnlty.	N	6. Cut Missile Funds	N

Key Votes of the 104th Congress

1. Congressional Compliance	Y	6. Reform Crime Grant	Y	11. Loser Pays Court Reform	Y
2. Balanced Budget Amndmt.	Y	7. National Security Act	Y	12. Product Liability Reform	Y
3. Bar Unfunded Mandates	Y	8. Moratorium on Regs.	N	13. Welfare Reform	Y
4. Pass Line Item Veto	Y	9. Risk Assessment on Regs.	N	14. Term Limits Amndmt.	N
5. Relax Exclusionary Rule	Y	10. Expnd. Priv. Prop. Rights	N	15. Tax Cuts	Y

Election Results

1994 general	Sherwood Boehlert (R)	124,486	(71%)	($336,183)
	Charles W. Skeele Jr. (D)	40,786	(23%)	($12,774)
	Donald J. Thomas (RTL)	11,216	(6%)	
1994 primary	Sherwood Boehlert (R)	unopposed		
1992 general	Sherwood Boehlert (R)	139,774	(64%)	($372,109)
	Paula DiPerna (D)	61,835	(28%)	($63,220)
	Randall A. Terry (RTL)	8,688	(4%)	
	Geoffrey Grace (C)	8,011	(4%)	
	Other	1,354	(1%)	

TWENTY-FOURTH DISTRICT

The North Country of Upstate New York, some early 19th Century visionaries thought, was the land of the future. Financier Gouverneur Morris, French slave trader James Leray, and Dutch silver speculator David Parish bought up thousands of acres between the Adirondacks and the St. Lawrence River and tried to unload them on farmers unaware of the shortness of the growing season and the unnavigability of the river. They left behind grand mansions, but their hopes for huge profits were frustrated when the Erie Canal turned the stream of settlement westward, and Canadians built their new capital far north of the river and away from the Americans. But northern New York was not without its business successes: It was in Watertown in 1878 that 26-year-old Frank Woolworth put a sign over a table of odds and ends that read "Any Article 5 Cents," starting America's first retail chain and inventing the concept of discount stores.

More recently, the North Country has looked to government for help. The St. Lawrence Seaway proved too small for most ocean-going freighters and remains frozen three months of the year; the locks are slow and icebreakers would wreck the shoreline. The state government has built prisons in Ogdensburg and Cape Vincent, and private developers have built big malls in Watertown and Massena (attracting Canadians, as even New York has lower taxes than Ontario). The state maintains Indian reservations, with gambling operations. But the biggest initiative has been the enlargement of Fort Drum, near Watertown, where despite the Army's preference for warm weather training sites, a 10,000-person light infantry division was stationed in 1985. The 24th Congressional District, covering most of the North Country, from Plattsburgh on Lake Champlain along the St. Lawrence Seaway and over the Adirondacks Forest Preserve to Watertown and Oswego on Lake Ontario, is geographically one of the largest districts in the East.

The congressman from the 24th is John McHugh, a Republican who was chosen almost without incident in 1992. McHugh has long been in government: he worked for the Watertown city manager in 1971, at 23; for eight years he was a staffer for state Senator Douglas Barclay; in 1984 he was elected to succeed Barclay in Albany. McHugh specialized in dairy issues (New York has long price-fixed dairy products to help farmers) and military bases—both part of the North Country's economic lifeblood. When incumbent David Martin announced his retirement in June 1992, just when the district lines were drawn, McHugh ran, with plenty of financing plus Martin's endorsement. He won the Republican primary with 70%, then won the general 61%–24%. In 1994, he won 79%–21%.

McHugh appears much like his two low-key Republican predecessors: Martin, who held the seat for 12 years, and Robert McEwen, who held it for 16. Like them he combines a conservative voting record with a concern about the economic needs of the district, not surprising given his district's dependence on federal largess. McHugh's legislative focus has been heavily tilted to the needs of the district. In 1993 he got a seat on National Security and hired none other than Martin to monitor the Defense Base Closure and Realignment Commission. In that year's base closure round, McHugh found himself pitted in a fierce lobbying battle against his colleague to the south, Republican Sherwood Boehlert. Griffiss Air Force Base, a major employer in Boehlert's district, and Plattsburgh Air Force Base, in McHugh's, were competing for a similar mission. In the end, the commission voted to close both bases.

The Republican victory brought McHugh the chairmanship of the Government Reform and Oversight Subcommittee with jurisdiction over the Postal Service, a somewhat dubious honor since it gives him responsibility for one of Congress' perennial headaches. He was also elected Republican whip for the New York delegation; another mixed blessing perhaps, as New York Republicans are among the least conservative in the House.

The People: Pop. 1990: 580,376; 65% rural; 12% age 65+; 95% White; 3% Black; 1% Amer. Indian; 1% Asian; 1% Other; 2% Hispanic origin. Voting age pop.: 426,600; 3% Black; 2% Hispanic origin. Households: 60% married couple families; 31% married couple fams. w. children; 36% college educ.; median household income: $25,687; per capita income: $11,060; median gross rent: $368; median house value: $56,700.

1992 Presidential Vote			1988 Presidential Vote		
Bush (R)	86,311	(38%)	Bush (R)	114,754	(56%)
Clinton (D)	85,078	(37%)	Dukakis (D)	89,384	(44%)
Perot (I)	54,537	(24%)			

Rep. John M. McHugh (R)

Elected 1992; b. Sept. 29, 1948, Watertown; home, Pierrepont Manor; Syracuse U., B.A. 1970, S.U.N.Y., M.P.A. 1977; Catholic; married (Katharine).

Career: Confidential Asst., Watertown City Mgr., 1971–76; Research and Liaison Chief, NY Sen. Douglas Barclay, 1976–84; NY Senate, 1984–92.

DC Office: 416 CHOB 20515, 202-225-4611; Fax: 202-226-0621.

District Offices: 404 Key Bank Bldg., 200 Washington St., Watertown 13601, 315-782-3150.

Committees: *Government Reform & Oversight* (9th of 27 R): District of Columbia; National Economic Growth, Natural Resources and Regulatory Affairs; Postal Service (Chmn.). *National Security* (15th of 30 R): Military Installations and Facilities; Military Research and Development.

Group Ratings

	ADA	ACLU	COPE	CFA	LCV	CON	NSI	COC	ACU	NTLC	CHC
1994	10	30	33	20	17	67	100	92	90	89	93
1993	20	—	58	20	29	91	—	73	83	—	—

National Journal Ratings

	1993 LIB — 1993 CONS		1994 LIB — 1994 CONS	
Economic	35% —	63%	0% —	80%
Social	27% —	72%	16% —	81%
Foreign	0% —	91%	0% —	88%

Key Votes of the 103d Congress

1. Clinton Deficit Plan	N	3. Brady Handgun Purchase	N	5. Lmt. UN Cmnd. of Forces	Y
2. NAFTA	N	4. Strike Race/Death Pnlty.	Y	6. Cut Missile Funds	N

Key Votes of the 104th Congress

1. Congressional Compliance Y	6. Reform Crime Grant Y	11. Loser Pays Court Reform Y
2. Balanced Budget Amndmt. Y	7. National Security Act *	12. Product Liability Reform Y
3. Bar Unfunded Mandates Y	8. Moratorium on Regs. Y	13. Welfare Reform Y
4. Pass Line Item Veto Y	9. Risk Assessment on Regs. Y	14. Term Limits Amndmt. N
5. Relax Exclusionary Rule Y	10. Expnd. Priv. Prop. Rights Y	15. Tax Cuts Y

Election Results

1994 general	John M. McHugh (R-C)	124,645	(79%)	($53,187)
	Danny M. Francis (D)	34,032	(21%)	
1994 primary	John M. McHugh (R)	unopposed		
1992 general	John M. McHugh (R-VRP)	122,257	(61%)	($170,749)
	Margaret M. Ravenscroft (D)	47,675	(24%)	
	Morrison J. Hosley, Jr. (C-RTL)	26,763	(13%)	($149,493)
	Other	4,374	(2%)	

TWENTY-FIFTH DISTRICT

Syracuse is a middle American city in the middle of Upstate New York, halfway between Albany and Buffalo on the Erie Canal and the old New York Central Railroad, for years the nation's major east-west transportation routes. Built on a swamp that was a salt spring, Syracuse is the home of many inventions: the dental chair, Stickley mission furniture, the drive-in bank teller, the foot measuring devices used in shoe stores. It was one of the first big manufacturers of typewriters and is the site of the New York State Fair. Its agricultural hinterland is rich with specialty crops like wine grapes, and its industrial jobs are mostly high-skill. Syracuse has spread out slowly across the countryside, but there is redevelopment of the Erie Canal waterfront where the city got its start.

The 25th Congressional District includes all of Syracuse and Onondaga County. It goes west to include part of Auburn, the home town of Governor, Senator and Secretary of State William Seward, and south to Cortland County and almost to Binghamton. Seward was the first great Republican politician of Upstate New York, and historically Syracuse is heavily Republican, partly out of antipathy to New York City. But it is also one of the most heavily Catholic cities in the United States and very ethnic, and it has elected Democratic mayors and gave a plurality to Bill Clinton in 1992.

The Congressman from the 25th District is James Walsh, son of a Syracuse mayor and former congressman. He came to the House as almost a professional civic activist: he was a Peace Corps volunteer, a social worker, then worked for New York Telephone and NYNEX, which detailed him to a local university. He was elected five times to the Syracuse Common Council, then ran for Congress in 1988 when a Republican incumbent nearly beaten two years earlier decided to retire. In the general, Walsh beat Democrat Rosemary Pooler by a solid 57%–42%. Like other Republicans from economically sluggish Upstate areas, he is open to government intervention in the economy; he voted for the Clinton stimulus package in March 1993, for the Americans with Disabilities Act and to maintain many current food programs. But he also supports the balanced budget amendment and the line-item veto.

Walsh's most prominent position now is as chairman of the District of Columbia Appropriations Subcommittee, a position which makes him virtually the surrogate mayor of the Nation's Capitol. In the 103d Congress, he lost many votes on his efforts to deny the District government funds. In the 104th, he is one of the key players who forced a financial control board on the District, working in cooperation with Northern Virginia Republican Tom Davis and D.C.'s Eleanor Holmes Norton. Walsh expressed dismay at ex-Mayor Marion Barry's September 1994 primary victory in his return to City Hall ("any progress we might have made with the District in recent years is now gone," he said) and noted that in the past the District failed to send Congress required quarterly financial reports, borrowed $250 million from Wall Street banks and spent it without implementing $140 million in promised cuts. Citing his own experience as council president in Syracuse, he argues that the District government is too large and should concentrate on its core businesses, like garbage collection and policing, and get out of others like corrections, health and post-secondary education. "The middle class is leaving the District in droves and the only response has been to raise taxes," he has said.

In this basically Republican district, Walsh beat music teacher Rhea Jezer with 56% and 58% in 1992 and 1994.

The People: Pop. 1990: 580,233; 26% rural; 13% age 65+; 90% White; 7% Black; 1% Amer. Indian; 1% Asian; 1% Hispanic origin. Voting age pop.: 435,738; 5% Black; 1% Hispanic origin. Households: 54% married couple families; 25% married couple fams. w. children; 48% college educ.; median household income: $31,080; per capita income: $14,148; median gross rent: $433; median house value: $77,600.

1992 Presidential Vote			1988 Presidential Vote		
Clinton (D)	108,335	(41%)	Bush (R)	128,873	(53%)
Bush (R)	95,476	(36%)	Dukakis (D)	113,625	(47%)
Perot (I)	58,232	(22%)			

Rep. James T. Walsh (R)

Elected 1988; b. June 19, 1947, Syracuse; home, Syracuse; St. Bonaventure U., B.A. 1970; Catholic; married (Diane).

Career: Peace Corps, 1970–72; Social worker, Onondaga Cnty. Dept. of Social Svcs., 1972–74; Marketing exec., NYNEX, 1974–88; Syracuse Common Cncl., 1978–88, Pres. 1986–88.

DC Office: 1330 LHOB 20515, 202-225-3701; Fax: 202-225-4042.

District Offices: P.O. Box 7306, Syracuse 13261, 315-423-5657; and 1 Lincoln St., Auburn 13021, 315-255-0649.

Committees: *Appropriations* (17th of 32 R): Agriculture, Rural Development, FDA, and Related Agencies; District of Columbia (Chmn.); VA, HUD, and Independent Agencies.

Group Ratings

	ADA	ACLU	COPE	CFA	LCV	CON	NSI	COC	ACU	NTLC	CHC
1994	20	22	44	20	47	38	90	91	67	69	93
1993	35	—	67	50	36	74	—	64	67	—	—

National Journal Ratings

	1993 LIB — 1993 CONS			1994 LIB — 1994 CONS		
Economic	39%	—	61%	41%	—	59%
Social	29%	—	69%	35%	—	64%
Foreign	24%	—	72%	38%	—	61%

Key Votes of the 103d Congress

1. Clinton Deficit Plan	N	3. Brady Handgun Purchase	Y	5. Lmt. UN Cmnd. of Forces	Y
2. NAFTA	N	4. Strike Race/Death Pnlty.	N	6. Cut Missile Funds	N

Key Votes of the 104th Congress

1. Congressional Compliance Y	6. Reform Crime Grant Y	11. Loser Pays Court Reform Y
2. Balanced Budget Amndmt. Y	7. National Security Act Y	12. Product Liability Reform Y
3. Bar Unfunded Mandates Y	8. Moratorium on Regs. Y	13. Welfare Reform Y
4. Pass Line Item Veto Y	9. Risk Assessment on Regs. Y	14. Term Limits Amndmt. Y
5. Relax Exclusionary Rule Y	10. Expnd. Priv. Prop. Rights Y	15. Tax Cuts Y

Election Results

1994 general	James T. Walsh (R-C).................	113,949	(58%)	($415,314)
	Rhea Jezer (D-CCP)..................	83,853	(42%)	($205,818)
1994 primary	James T. Walsh (R)................	unopposed		
1992 general	James T. Walsh (R-C)...............	135,076	(56%)	($294,850)
	Rhea Jezer (D-CSP).................	107,310	(44%)	($96,083)

TWENTY-SIXTH DISTRICT

New York's Southern Tier is territory not often explored by today's Americans. In colonial days, the Catskills looming over the Hudson were a great barrier, a mysterious zone in which phantom Dutchmen played nine pins and Indians lurked in the days of James Fenimore Cooper. The area then became part of a great pathway west, along the Erie Lackawanna and Delaware & Hudson Railroad lines, with engines steaming over giant viaducts and along narrow river valleys through these hills and mountains. But today, this quarter of Upstate New York has little passenger rail service and is bypassed by major air travel networks. Its interstates are lightly traveled, particularly as the once-famous kosher resorts in the "Borscht Belt" of the Catskills have lost their popularity in the past quarter century.

The sprawling 26th Congressional District includes much of the Southern Tier. The district stretches from the city of Beacon on the east side of the Hudson—where commuters board the train daily for jobs in New York City—west and north across the still-mysterious Catskills, past Bethel, site of the misnamed 1969 Woodstock music festival, to the industrial city of Binghamton in Broome County on the upper Susquehanna River, and finally to the university town of Ithaca, with Cornell University looming high above Cayuga Lake's waters. Along the west bank of the Hudson in Ulster County lies Kingston, settled by Dutchmen more than 300 years ago. This was Rip van Winkle country, and in the 19th Century was the political base of Governor and Vice President George Clinton. There are two population centers, widely separated: Binghamton-Ithaca in the west has about half the district's votes, and the Hudson Valley has about one-third. Politically, the heritage is Republican, but the Ithaca area, like so many university communities, is heavily Democratic, and Binghamton trends that way as well.

The congressman from the 26th is Maurice Hinchey, a leftish Democrat who has beaten Republican Bob Moppert in two close races. Both candidates came from humble backgrounds; both enlisted in the Navy in the 1950s, right after high school. But then their paths diverged, Moppert to small businesses and civic involvement, Hinchey to graduate school (while he supported himself as a Thruway toll collector) and politics. Hinchey was elected Assemblyman from Ulster County in 1974, a great Democratic year, and held on for nine terms; he was proud of more than 600 bills passed—on, among other things, acid rain, toxic waste, illegal dumping (and organized crime's influence on it), groundwater and wetlands protection. When he ran for Congress in 1992, Hinchey called for national health insurance, a repeal of Reagan-Bush tax cuts for the rich and corporations, and "reindustrializating America." He put forth a 29-page "demilitarization" plan that would eliminate 2.6 million military and defense jobs and create 3.4 million civilian jobs. By contrast, Moppert, a Binghamton moving company owner elected as a Broome County legislator in 1986, called for less government spending and bureaucracy. In a contest that was not only partisan but geographic, Hinchey beat Moppert 50%–47%. Hinchey carried Ulster and Moppert carried the Binghamton area; Ithaca and Tompkins County decided it, going for Hinchey by 30 points.

In the House, Hinchey joined the Progressive Caucus and compiled one of the most liberal voting records. Assigned to the Resources and Banking Committees, he supported environmental measures and took potshots at the Federal Reserve. One issue that caused Hinchey both political and personal discomfort was gun control. He backed the Brady Bill on handguns. But, facing a tough reelection campaign in a heavily non-metropolitan district, he agonized over the assault weapons ban, deciding at the last minute to vote against it, despite a call from Bill Clinton. Then, just weeks after his 1994 re-election victory, Hinchey was boarding a plane at Washington's National Airport when his carry-on bag was found to contain a loaded handgun. Hinchey has a license to carry a gun in New York. He says he was the subject of death threats while conducting probes of organized crime in the 1980s. He told a local court he had forgotten the gun was in his luggage; he pleaded no contest and was given a suspended sentence.

The 1994 campaign virtually began on election night 1992. Moppert spent much of 1993 attacking Hinchey, trying to tie him to Clinton while embracing the House Republicans' Contract with America, particularly a cut in the capital gains tax and a $500-per-child tax credit for families. If Moppert, like many Republicans in 1994, sought to nationalize the election, Hinchey, like many Democrats, sought to localize it. He ran ads alleging conflicts-of-interest on Moppert's behalf while the latter was in the Broome County Legislature, and pointed to tax increases during Moppert's tenure there. Hinchey also boasted of his efforts at local economic development, such as his role in the successful transfer of a former Air Force facility in Broome County to private industry. The result was one of the nation's closest races, even closer than two years earlier. Hinchey finally won 49%–48%, with the outcome uncertain until almost two weeks after the election. Ironically, the geographic breakdown was a reverse of 1992. Hinchey lost Ulster County and carried only the counties containing Ithaca and Binghamton. He spent almost $740,000, twice what he spent in 1992; Moppert spent just under $280,000.

Hinchey was among three dozen liberals aggressively challenging the new Republican majority in early 1995. But that majority means that he is unlikely to have anything like his 1994 financial advantage when he runs in 1996. Although Moppert has ruled out a third race, Republicans have made Hinchey there number one New York congressional target in 1996.

The People: Pop. 1990: 580,540; 43% rural; 13% age 65+; 88% White; 6% Black; 2% Asian; 1% Other; 4% Hispanic origin. Voting age pop.: 446,955; 5% Black; 4% Hispanic origin. Households: 54% married couple families; 25% married couple fams. w. children; 47% college educ.; median household income: $30,335; per capita income: $13,786; median gross rent: $449; median house value: $94,400.

1992 Presidential Vote

Clinton (D)	116,450	(44%)
Bush (R)	91,462	(35%)
Perot (I)	53,675	(20%)

1988 Presidential Vote

Bush (R)	125,479	(52%)
Dukakis (D)	114,749	(48%)

Rep. Maurice D. Hinchey (D)

Elected 1992; b. Oct. 27, 1938, New York City; home, Saugerties; S.U.N.Y. New Paltz, B.S. 1968, M.A. 1969; Catholic; married (Ilene).

Career: Navy, 1956–59; Cement plant worker, 1959–1964; NY St. Thruway toll collector, 1959–68; Analyst, NY St. Dept of Educ., 1971–74; NY Assembly, 1974–92.

DC Office: 1524 LHOB 20515, 202-225-6335; Fax: 202-226-0774.

District Offices: 291 Wall St., Kingston 12401, 914-331-4466; 100A Fed. Bldg., Binghamton 13901, 607-773-2768; and 114 Prospect St., Ithaca 14850, 607-273-1388.

Committees: *Banking & Financial Services* (20th of 22 D): Capital Markets, Securities and Government Sponsored Enterprises. *Resources* (18th of 20 D): National Parks, Forests and Lands; Water and Power Resources.

Group Ratings

	ADA	ACLU	COPE	CFA	LCV	CON	NSI	COC	ACU	NTLC	CHC
1994	95	87	100	90	100	21	0	33	5	11	7
1993	95	—	100	100	100	30	—	18	4	—	—

National Journal Ratings

	1993 LIB — 1993 CONS		1994 LIB — 1994 CONS	
Economic	68%	— 26%	83%	— 0%
Social	80%	— 13%	82%	— 15%
Foreign	87%	— 7%	85%	— 0%

Key Votes of the 103d Congress

1. Clinton Deficit Plan	Y	3. Brady Handgun Purchase	Y	5. Lmt. UN Cmnd. of Forces	N
2. NAFTA	N	4. Strike Race/Death Pnlty.	N	6. Cut Missile Funds	Y

Key Votes of the 104th Congress

1. Congressional Compliance	Y	6. Reform Crime Grant	N	11. Loser Pays Court Reform	N
2. Balanced Budget Amndmt.	N	7. National Security Act	N	12. Product Liability Reform	N
3. Bar Unfunded Mandates	N	8. Moratorium on Regs.	N	13. Welfare Reform	N
4. Pass Line Item Veto	N	9. Risk Assessment on Regs.	N	14. Term Limits Amndmt.	N
5. Relax Exclusionary Rule	N	10. Expnd. Priv. Prop. Rights	N	15. Tax Cuts	N

Election Results

1994 general	Maurice D. Hinchey (D-L)	95,492	(49%)	($738,098)
	Bob Moppert (R-C)	94,244	(48%)	($278,962)
	Others	4,772	(2%)	
1994 primary	Maurice D. Hinchey (D)	unopposed		
1992 general	Maurice D. Hinchey (D-L)	119,557	(50%)	($368,777)
	Bob Moppert (R-C)	110,738	(47%)	($203,274)
	Other	6,821	(3%)	

TWENTY-SEVENTH DISTRICT

Across the Finger Lakes of New York, the long, thin, deep-blue lakes in glacier-carved folds between rolling hillsides thick with grapevines, ran one of the first paths of westward migration. Cut off from white settlement by the British and the Iroquois, Upstate New York opened up after the Revolution, and streams of New England Yankees moved west. They followed the Mohawk River and the Erie Canal, dug by hand labor and finished in 1825, connecting the Hudson River and Lake Erie, the East Coast and the vast interior of America. The Finger Lakes region became one of the fastest-growing and most dynamic parts of America. Town squares here today have monuments to the enthusiasms of the 1830s and 1840s, when these new communities were full of young families on the rise, and religious revivals were so fervent that the area was known as the Burnt-Over district. Here in the village of Palmyra, near the Erie Canal, Joseph Smith had his vision of the angel Moroni and saw the golden tablets that led him to found the Mormon Church. Preachers fanned enthusiasm for abolition of slavery, greater here than anywhere else in the country. This was the birthplace of the women's movement: in Seneca Falls in 1848, Elizabeth Cady Stanton and Lucretia Mott produced a Declaration of Sentiments that started the women's suffrage movement. Upstate was also the birthplace of the temperance movement, another women's cause in those days.

The 27th Congressional District of New York covers much of this territory, now economically less dynamic and politically calmer than in its heyday. After the 1992 redistricting, the 27th starts at Aurelius, one of the many Upstate towns with classical names, and includes Seneca Falls and Palmyra, then passes south of Rochester and through Batavia and Attica to the Buffalo suburb of Amherst. Most of this is part of America's Republican heartland, though the Buffalo area, with its historic heavy industry base, has leaned Democratic.

The congressman from the 27th is Bill Paxon, a Republican who is one of his party's best natural politicians. Paxon's roots are in Buffalo's Erie County, where his father was a family court judge. Paxon volunteered in 1970, at 15, in the first congressional campaign of Jack Kemp, then famous as a quarterback for the Buffalo Bills and not yet known as an advocate of sweeping tax cuts. In 1974, he saw his father and the Assembly candidate he was working for defeated in a Democratic landslide. But in 1977, the same year he graduated from Canisius College (almost a prerequisite for a Buffalo political career), Paxon was elected to the Erie County legislature at 23, the youngest member ever, and in 1982 he was elected to the New York Assembly. In 1988, when Kemp ran for president and left his House seat open, Paxon won the Republican nomination without opposition and then spent $688,000 and won the general election with 53%.

In the few years since, Paxon has moved from being an imperiled local politician to a triumphant national leader, from facing seeming political extinction in the redistricting process to chairing the House Republicans' campaign committee as they gained 52 seats and won control of the chamber for the first time in 40 years. In the process, Paxon has played only a limited role on legislation. He fought against the gas tax increase in the 1991 energy bill and tried to stop imports of solid waste from Canada by resisting bans of waste exports across state lines. He started off with a seat on Banking and in 1993 moved to the plummier Commerce Committee. Redistricting menaced him in his second term, since his district spread across several Upstate counties and could easily have been cut in slices. But in 1991 he contributed to Republican state senators who with their majority would have a say in redistricting, and he was reported to have promised $10,000 a year for state Senate Republicans as long as he held his seat. It was money well-spent: Paxon's district gained territory from 30-year veteran Republican Frank Horton, who decided in June 1992 to retire. That meant easy renomination for Paxon and a solid 63% victory in a district more Republican than before.

At that point Paxon turned his love of campaigning and fundraising to the national scale. By lobbying hard, campaigning and raising money for fellow members, he undercut others interested in chairing the National Republican Congressional Committee and won it unanimously. He inherited the chairmanship of a committee that was $4.5 million in debt, bloated with staff and devoid of credibility after predicting several Republican gains that never occurred. He installed young vice-chairmen, fired scores of staffers, reexamined consulting contracts, worked to recruit candidates—and camouflaged the fact that the committee had much less money to contribute than in the past. He worked closely with Newt Gingrich and Dick Armey in formulating the terms and the strategy for the Contract With America and getting near-unanimous support for it from Republican candidates. Also, in August 1993, he proposed on the floor of the House to his fellow New York Republican, Susan Molinari; they were married in July 1994. Young, energetic, enthusiastic, the couple went around the country recruiting candidates and campaigning for them, belying the image of Republicans as grim old fogies.

On election night 1994, Paxon savored victory and looked forward to more gains in the future. He predicts that Republicans will gain 20-to-30 more House seats in 1996. "Now that there's a level playing field, we'll keep winning. Democrats will be retiring, because they're afraid of losing. We'll win a vast majority of those seats. Then we'll defeat the Democrats from the marginal districts," he said. He has pledged to serve only two terms as campaign chairman, but already he has contributed importantly to revolutionary change in the House.

For all their national acclaim and bright futures as party leaders, Paxon and Molinari go back to their districts, at opposite ends of New York state, every weekend, and hold town meetings. Both did well in 1994: Paxon won 75%–25%, Molinari 71%–25%.

The People: Pop. 1990: 580,317; 55% rural; 13% age 65+; 92% White; 2% Black; 1% Asian; 1% Hispanic origin. Voting age pop.: 433,859; 2% Black; 1% Hispanic origin. Households: 63% married couple families; 30% married couple fams. w. children; 48% college educ.; median household income: $34,573; per capita income: $14,934; median gross rent: $434; median house value: $81,100.

1992 Presidential Vote			1988 Presidential Vote		
Bush (R)	115,432	(42%)	Bush (R)	142,464	(59%)
Clinton (D)	90,194	(33%)	Dukakis (D)	100,338	(41%)
Perot (I)	67,721	(25%)			

Rep. Bill Paxon (R)

Elected 1988; b. Apr. 29, 1954, Buffalo; home, Amherst; Canisius Col., B.A. 1977; Catholic; married (U.S. Rep. Susan Molinari).

Career: Erie Cnty. Legislature, 1978–82; NY Assembly, 1982–88.

DC Office: 2436 RHOB 20515, 202-225-5265; Fax: 202-225-5910; e-mail: bpaxon@hr.house.gov.

District Offices: 5500 Main St., Williamsville, 14221, 716-634-2324; and 10 E. Main St., Victor 14564, 716-742-1600, 800-453-8330.

Committees: *National Republican Congressional Committee Chairman. Commerce* (11th of 26 R): Telecommunications and Finance.

Group Ratings

	ADA	ACLU	COPE	CFA	LCV	CON	NSI	COC	ACU	NTLC	CHC
1994	0	13	0	10	17	90	100	92	100	96	100
1993	5	—	0	10	29	82	—	100	100	—	—

National Journal Ratings

	1993 LIB	—	1993 CONS	1994 LIB	—	1994 CONS
Economic	14%	—	80%	0%	—	80%
Social	0%	—	89%	0%	—	89%
Foreign	9%	—	85%	0%	—	88%

Key Votes of the 103d Congress

1. Clinton Deficit Plan	N	3. Brady Handgun Purchase N	5. Lmt. UN Cmnd. of Forces Y
2. NAFTA	Y	4. Strike Race/Death Pnlty. Y	6. Cut Missile Funds N

Key Votes of the 104th Congress

1. Congressional Compliance Y	6. Reform Crime Grant Y	11. Loser Pays Court Reform Y
2. Balanced Budget Amndmt. Y	7. National Security Act Y	12. Product Liability Reform Y
3. Bar Unfunded Mandates Y	8. Moratorium on Regs. Y	13. Welfare Reform Y
4. Pass Line Item Veto Y	9. Risk Assessment on Regs. Y	14. Term Limits Amndmt. Y
5. Relax Exclusionary Rule Y	10. Expnd. Priv. Prop. Rights Y	15. Tax Cuts Y

Election Results

1994 general	Bill Paxon (R-C-RTL)...............	152,610	(75%)	($642,531)
	William A. Long Jr. (D)...............	52,160	(25%)	($62,746)
1994 primary	Bill Paxon (R)....................	unopposed		
1992 general	Bill Paxon (R-C-RTL)...............	156,596	(63%)	($1,017,327)
	W. Douglas Call (D)..................	89,906	(37%)	($71,370)

TWENTY-EIGHTH DISTRICT

Rochester, with a metro area just over one million, is one of the major cities of Upstate New York, strung out along the man-made artery that made the region's fortune: the Erie Canal. Located where the canal crosses the Genesee River, Rochester became a major industrial city, the "Flour City" in the 1830s, as it milled the wheat produced by western New York farmers, and then a high-tech city, when a bank clerk named George Eastman began making photographic dry plates and marketed the first still camera and film for Thomas Edison's motion picture camera in 1888 and 1889. Later, Bausch & Lomb developed its lens business here. Rochester, the home of Susan B. Anthony and Frederick Douglass, has lived on high-tech versions of the eye. Its great industries—Bausch & Lomb, Eastman Kodak, and Xerox, which started here as Haloid—have thrived on technical innovation, precision workmanship, high reliability and customer service, giving Rochester an affluent and well-educated population that maintains fine civic institutions and traditions. This was the city that in 1918 invented the Community Chest and still has the nation's highest United Way contributions; it is also the home of Wegman's, quite possibly the nation's best supermarket chain.

The 28th Congressional District includes Rochester and most of its Monroe County suburbs—a compact district in a state whose redistricting produced a dozen grotesqueries. For the first time in 50 years, the heart of Monroe County isn't separated into two districts. Traditionally Republican, the Rochester area was opened to Democrats in the 1970s and 1980s. It was also the base in 1994 of the independent gubernatorial candidacy of local businessman B. Thomas Golisano, who spent millions in the hope of being a New York state Ross Perot: he won 20% of the vote in Monroe County but only 4% statewide.

The congresswoman from the 28th District is Louise Slaughter, who is both a strong partisan Democrat and an assiduous worker for Rochester area interests. With an accent and occasional fieriness that are evidence of her roots in the Kentucky mountains ("I would wrestle alligators for a cause"), Slaughter has become a seasoned political professional. She worked as a local staffer for Mario Cuomo when he was lieutenant governor in the 1970s and won a seat on the

Monroe County Legislature; she was elected to the New York Assembly in 1982 and 1984. In 1986, she beat a one-term conservative Republican congressman 51%–49%, by charging that he did nothing to free Lebanon hostage Terry Anderson, a reporter and native of Rochester. She has held the seat by tending carefully to local problems, by winning the support of area businessmen and the local newspaper—ironically, the flagship of Gannett, a chain founded by a diehard Upstate Republican—and by energizing core constituencies of the Democratic Party.

Slaughter has been a member of the Rules Committee, a proponent of her party's House reforms (and a disparager of the Republicans'), an insider who used her skills behind the scenes when Democrats held the majority. The changes in committee ratios following the Republican takeover deprived her of the influential Rules Committee seat but she retained a seat on the Budget Committee. She has used these ties to get funding for the Rochester International airport and the harbor, for the Center for Integrated Manufacturing Studies and for a high-tech business incubator. In 1993 she sponsored a permanent extension of industrial development bonds that she says have helped Rochester, and in 1994 she got Rochester's pioneering managed care health plans exempted from the Clinton healthcare reform proposal. Slaughter also has tended to her party's core constituencies. The North American Free Trade Agreement might have helped Rochester exports, but she pleased organized labor by voting against it. She strongly backs feminist causes: in 1991 she was one of the seven women House members who marched on the Senate to protest its treatment of Anita Hill, in 1994 she sponsored the law to ban blockades of abortion clinics and in 1995 she spoke out loudly for Surgeon General Henry Foster. She is also co-chair of the Congressional Arts Caucus.

Slaughter has had spirited competition in the 1990s but has won convincingly. In 1992, although her district became about 6% more Democratic from redistricting, her percentage fell from 59% to 55%. Her 1994 opponent, Monroe County legislator Renee Forgensi Davison, promised to "stand up to Bill Clinton," but her campaign fizzled and Slaughter won 57%–40%, one of the few Democrats to improve her standing that year. But Democratic losses, especially in the South, were probably the reason she lost her December 1994 race for vice chairman of the Democratic Caucus to Barbara Kennelly by a 93–90 margin.

Slaughter continued to fight Republicans fiercely in the 104th Congress, initially in mostly losing causes. But she also adapted her tactics: rather than relying on her leadership ties to get favors, she went to Republicans to make her case. Sometimes it worked. She got John Porter of Illinois to block rescission of the education program for homeless children that she wrote, and she got Republicans to exempt a database on "sexual predators"'from their unfunded mandates bill. But out in the open, she was less successful: her amendment to the line-item veto bill that would have allowed the president to rescind targeted tax benefits lost on party lines, 231–196.

The People: Pop. 1990: 580,347; 4% rural; 13% age 65+; 80% White; 14% Black; 2% Asian; 2% Other; 4% Hispanic origin. Voting age pop.: 439,077; 12% Black; 3% Hispanic origin. Households: 50% married couple families; 23% married couple fams. w. children; 53% college educ.; median household income: $33,899; per capita income: $16,205; median gross rent: $477; median house value: $90,000.

1992 Presidential Vote

Clinton (D)	119,055	(44%)
Bush (R)	103,544	(38%)
Perot (I)	48,467	(18%)

1988 Presidential Vote

Dukakis (D)	128,982	(52%)
Bush (R)	121,214	(48%)

Rep. Louise M. Slaughter (D)

Elected 1986; b. Aug. 14, 1929, Harlan Cnty., KY; home, Fairport; U. of KY, B.S. 1951, M.S. 1953; Episcopalian; married (Robert).

Career: Monroe Cnty. Legislature, 1976–79; Regional Coord., Lt. Gov. Mario Cuomo, 1976–79; NY Assembly, 1982–86.

DC Office: 2347 RHOB 20515, 202-225-3615; Fax: 202-225-7822.

District Offices: 3120 Fed. Bldg., 100 State St., Rochester 14614, 716-232-4850.

Committees: *Budget* (3rd of 18 D). *Government Reform & Oversight* (8th of 22 D): National Economic Growth, Natural Resources and Regulatory Affairs; National Security, International Affairs and Criminal Justice.

Group Ratings

	ADA	ACLU	COPE	CFA	LCV	CON	NSI	COC	ACU	NTLC	CHC
1994	95	83	75	90	94	23	10	50	0	14	7
1993	100	—	100	80	86	32	—	27	4	—	—

National Journal Ratings

	1993 LIB — 1993 CONS		1994 LIB — 1994 CONS	
Economic	75%	22%	73%	17%
Social	80%	13%	90%	6%
Foreign	66%	31%	85%	0%

Key Votes of the 103d Congress

1. Clinton Deficit Plan	Y	3. Brady Handgun Purchase Y	5. Lmt. UN Cmnd. of Forces N
2. NAFTA	N	4. Strike Race/Death Pnlty. N	6. Cut Missile Funds Y

Key Votes of the 104th Congress

1. Congressional Compliance Y	6. Reform Crime Grant N	11. Loser Pays Court Reform N
2. Balanced Budget Amndmt. N	7. National Security Act N	12. Product Liability Reform Y
3. Bar Unfunded Mandates N	8. Moratorium on Regs. N	13. Welfare Reform N
4. Pass Line Item Veto N	9. Risk Assessment on Regs. N	14. Term Limits Amndmt. N
5. Relax Exclusionary Rule N	10. Expnd. Priv. Prop. Rights N	15. Tax Cuts N

Election Results

1994 general	Louise M. Slaughter (D)	110,987	(57%)	($790,778)
	Renee Forgensi Davison (R-C)	78,516	(40%)	($165,922)
	Others	6,464	(3%)	
1994 primary	Louise M. Slaughter (D)	unopposed		
1992 general	Louise M. Slaughter (D)	140,908	(55%)	($526,345)
	William P. Polito (R-C)	112,273	(44%)	($245,526)
	Other	1,897	(1%)	

TWENTY-NINTH DISTRICT

The Niagara Frontier is the romantic name for the Buffalo metropolitan area and the northwest corner of Upstate New York facing Lake Ontario. This really was the frontier once, between the United States and British-held Upper Canada, when American troops crossed the raging Niagara River in the War of 1812 to fight the Battle of Lundys Lane. Not many years later, Niagara Falls became a prime vacation spot, a must-see sight for European tourists and American honeymooners. By the mid-20th Century, Niagara Falls vacations had become routine, and few tourists took notice of the huge water intakes farther up the river, the hydroelectric power lines strung out on giant pylons fanning out in every direction, providing cheap public power for the chemical and steel factories that made the Niagara Frontier one of the heavy industry capitals of America. Nor did they notice the school and the 200 frame houses which had been built on a toxic waste dump near Love Canal, land sold by Hooker Chemical to the city of Niagara Falls with a warning that no one should live there—and where children were born with horrifying birth defects and some died.

The 29th Congressional District of New York includes the heart of the Niagara Frontier: the Falls; the Buffalo suburbs of Tonawanda and Kenmore; and the northwest one-third of Buffalo itself, with the city's downtown and its fine but financially beleaguered cultural institutions. The 29th also runs east to include towns and farm country along the southern shore of Lake Ontario to the Rochester suburb of Gates. Like most of Upstate New York, this was once Republican territory; as heavy industries declined, it trended Democratic. Its most famous Congressman was William Miller, the Republican National Committee chairman in 1961–64 and Barry Goldwater's 1964 vice presidential nominee. But it hasn't elected a Republican since 1974.

The congressman from the 29th is John LaFalce, a son of Buffalo who attended Canisius College and was elected to the New York Senate in 1970, at 31, and to the Assembly in 1972. Temperamentally an activist, he was chairman of the Small Business Committee from 1987 until the Republican takeover in 1995. LaFalce used his seats there and on Banking to push for government to spur development of industrial areas. In 1983 and 1984, he used his Banking subcommittee chairmanship to champion industrial policy—a hot subject of discussion among Democrats for a time that was shot down by the skepticism of Republicans and some Democrats as well. Later in the 1980s LaFalce took up the banner of promoting competitiveness. He strongly backed the U.S.-Canada Free Trade Agreement, which enabled the Niagara Frontier, with its low land costs and rents, to partake of the prosperity of Ontario's Toronto-based Golden Horseshoe, but he voted against the North American Free Trade Agreement. He superintended the various Small Business Administration loan programs which, of course, represent only a minuscule percentage of total lending to small business, and he has called for a government-sponsored enterprise, to be named Velda Sue, to provide a secondary market for SBA loans. LaFalce's small business interests have led him to draw up his own family and medical leave, disabilities and civil rights bills, and he was a leader in the fight to repeal the Section 89 employee-benefits tax provisions that small business owners detested.

In 1994, LaFalce was weighing whether to give up the Small Business chair for the chairmanship of the Financial Institutions Subcommittee. The decision was mooted by the 1994 election results. He remains ranking member of Small Business, where he had often worked on a bipartisan basis with the new chairman, Jan Meyers of Kansas. He is the second ranking Democrat on Banking, but no crony of former chairman Henry Gonzalez of Texas.

LaFalce has been closely pressed in the past three elections. In 1990 he was held to 55% of the vote, though the Republican candidate had only 31% and a Conservative candidate had 14%. In 1992 and 1994 he faced William Miller, Jr., son of the former Congressman. Both times LaFalce carried Erie County 60%–36%; in 1992 he narrowly won and in 1994 even more narrowly lost the rest of the district, for wins of 55%–42% and 55%–43%. This volatile district could be seriously contested again in 1996.

The People: Pop. 1990: 579,831; 23% rural; 15% age 65+; 91% White; 4% Black; 1% Amer. Indian; 1% Asian; 1% Other; 3% Hispanic origin. Voting age pop.: 441,240; 4% Black; 2% Hispanic origin. Households: 54% married couple families; 24% married couple fams. w. children; 43% college educ.; median household income: $28,951; per capita income: $13,350; median gross rent: $383; median house value: $71,200.

1992 Presidential Vote

Clinton (D)	103,528	(40%)
Bush (R)	86,730	(33%)
Perot (I)	70,231	(27%)

1988 Presidential Vote

Dukakis (D)	123,639	(51%)
Bush (R)	117,293	(49%)

Rep. John J. LaFalce (D)

Elected 1974; b. Oct. 6, 1939, Buffalo; home, Tonawanda; Canisius Col., B.S. 1961, Villanova U., J.D. 1964; Catholic; married (Patricia).

Career: Army, 1965–67; Law Clerk, U.S. Navy Gen. Cnsl., 1963; Lecturer, George Washington U., 1965–66; Practicing atty., 1967–74; NY Senate, 1971–72; NY Assembly, 1973–74.

DC Office: 2310 RHOB 20515, 202-225-3231; Fax: 202-225-8693.

District Offices: Fed. Bldg., 111 W. Huron St., Buffalo 14202, 716-846-4056; Main P.O. Bldg., 615 Main St., Niagara Falls 14302, 716-284-9976; and 409 S. Union St., Spencerport 14559, 716-352-4777.

Committees: *Banking & Financial Services* (2nd of 22 D): Capital Markets, Securities and Government Sponsored Enterprises; Financial Institutions and Consumer Credit. *Small Business* (RMM of 19 D).

Group Ratings

	ADA	ACLU	COPE	CFA	LCV	CON	NSI	COC	ACU	NTLC	CHC
1994	80	30	78	80	83	41	40	58	15	15	57
1993	75	—	100	100	85	30	—	9	17	—	—

National Journal Ratings

	1993 LIB — 1993 CONS			1994 LIB — 1994 CONS	
Economic	78%	—	12%	71%	— 28%
Social	42%	—	58%	64%	— 35%
Foreign	79%	—	16%	83%	— 15%

Key Votes of the 103d Congress

1. Clinton Deficit Plan	Y	3. Brady Handgun Purchase	Y	5. Lmt. UN Cmnd. of Forces	N
2. NAFTA	N	4. Strike Race/Death Pnlty.	N	6. Cut Missile Funds	Y

Key Votes of the 104th Congress

1. Congressional Compliance	Y	6. Reform Crime Grant	N	11. Loser Pays Court Reform	N
2. Balanced Budget Amndmt.	N	7. National Security Act	N	12. Product Liability Reform	N
3. Bar Unfunded Mandates	N	8. Moratorium on Regs.	N	13. Welfare Reform	N
4. Pass Line Item Veto	N	9. Risk Assessment on Regs.	N	14. Term Limits Amndmt.	N
5. Relax Exclusionary Rule	N	10. Expnd. Priv. Prop. Rights	N	15. Tax Cuts	N

Election Results

1994 general	John J. LaFalce (D-L)	103,053	(55%)	($825,314)
	William E. Miller Jr. (R-C)	80,355	(43%)	($219,273)
	Others	3,296	(2%)	
1994 primary	John J. LaFalce (D)	16,393	(81%)	
	John A. Basar Jr. (D)	3,882	(19%)	
1992 general	John J. LaFalce (D-L)	128,230	(55%)	($467,841)
	William E. Miller, Jr. (R-C)	98,031	(42%)	($83,110)
	Others	9,197	(4%)	

THIRTIETH DISTRICT

Buffalo has hopes of being one of America's success stories of the 1990s. The city has had its successes before. The butt of many jokes about the snow that piles up at the eastern end of Lake Erie and that supposedly keeps it immobilized half the year, Buffalo also should be credited with building a heavy industrial base in the late 19th and early 20th Centuries, as America's number one grain milling center and a major steel producer. Today, the Lackawanna mills are cold, and grain milling waned when the St. Lawrence Seaway opened in the 1950s. Buffalo is eclipsed economically by the bigger Great Lakes industrial cities of Cleveland, Detroit and Chicago, and its architecturally bold 1920s City Hall and downtown skyscrapers are far overshadowed by the high-rise horizon of Toronto, not many miles away. And though it is still one of the nation's 50 largest municipalities, Buffalo's population plummeted by almost 30% during the 1970s and another 9% in the 1980s.

But Buffalo has considerable assets which went unnoticed until the late 1980s. It has a high-skill labor force that works for reasonably low wages; it has cheap real estate; it has spruced up and gentrified its rather handsome waterfront on what is now a fairly clean Lake Erie. The key to Buffalo's recent resurgence can be summed up in one word: Canada. Canada is right across the Peace Bridge, and Buffalo is the major metropolitan area on the doorstep of the richest part of the nation whose free trade agreement with the United States was signed in late 1988. Toronto's wages, real estate prices and (with a quasi-socialist provincial government in Ontario) taxes are much higher than Buffalo's; its labor market is much tighter and its unions more militant. Canadian investment has flowed into Buffalo as the city has made the transition from an industrial to an increasingly services-oriented economy.

The 30th Congressional District of New York consists of the eastern and southern two-thirds of Buffalo, plus most of the Erie County suburbs east and south of the city, from working-class Cheektowaga and the steel-mill town of Lackawanna to higher-income Hamburg on Lake Erie. This is a solidly Democratic district, by any measure the most Democratic in Upstate New York, although some of the suburbs are Republican. But as Buffalo has fitfully revived in the late 1980s and early 1990s, it has been politically volatile, lashing out against some usual favorites. Ross Perot got a high 28% here in 1992, his best showing in a central city anywhere, and in 1994 Mario Cuomo, who had always run well in Buffalo, lost Erie County to George Pataki.

The congressman from the 30th District is another product of a political upset: Jack Quinn, a Republican and a former teacher and coach who had been the Town of Hamburg supervisor (a full-time job) since 1983. Seeing his chance when 18-year Democratic incumbent Henry Nowak retired in 1992, Quinn created his own Change Congress Party, so his name would appear under this as well as the Republican label. In anti-incumbent 1992, he ran on an 11-point program of congressional reform, including term limits and a reduction in House staff. This was a vivid contrast with his Democratic opponent, Erie County Executive Dennis Gorski, an organization man who returned from service in Vietnam to be elected to the county legislature and the New York Assembly before becoming county executive in 1987. In a stunning upset, Quinn beat Gorski by 52%–46%; in effect, Quinn got the Perot vote while Gorski ran only barely ahead of

Clinton's 45% plurality.

Quinn's fans and foes alike have compared him to another Republican who had strong appeal to working class Democrats: Ronald Reagan. The handsome Quinn is known for an affable personality that has made him extremely well-liked on Capitol Hill as well as in Buffalo. And if critics suggest that, like Reagan, Quinn's grasp of the details of governing occasionally show some gaps, his first term demonstrated that he is highly skilled in the art of political survival. Tagged almost immediately by House Democratic strategists as their number one target for a while in 1994, Quinn went to work to reach out to some key constituencies in his Democratic district. Despite the positive impact on Buffalo of the free trade agreement with Canada, Quinn in November 1993 split from most House Republicans and voted against the North American Free Trade Agreement. This, plus the fact that he was one of the few Republicans to support the 1993 striker replacement bill, won him the endorsement of the local AFL-CIO.

Then, in August 1994, as most House Republicans were voting to kill the Clinton crime bill, Quinn proposed changes that helped attract support for the measure—meeting with Clinton once and talking with him twice on the phone. The White House wooing of Quinn enraged many prominent Buffalo Democrats, but they had greater problems: several strong contenders declined to run, and the local Democratic endorsement went to City Councilman David Franczyk, who had to face two other aspirants in the primary; he emerged with just 50%. In the general election, Quinn rolled over Franczyk 67%–33%. The Democrats are certain to keep this seat high in their sights. But Quinn's showing indicates that, like another long-time Hamburg resident—former Congressman Jack Kemp—he is well-positioned to enjoy a prolonged stay in nominally hostile territory.

The People: Pop. 1990: 580,818; 13% rural; 15% age 65+; 81% White; 17% Black; 1% Amer. Indian; 1% Asian; 1% Other; 1% Hispanic origin. Voting age pop.: 441,257; 15% Black; 1% Hispanic origin. Households: 51% married couple families; 22% married couple fams. w. children; 39% college educ.; median household income: $26,263; per capita income: $12,176; median gross rent: $374; median house value: $68,000.

1992 Presidential Vote			1988 Presidential Vote		
Clinton (D)	119,115	(45%)	Dukakis (D)	149,485	(60%)
Perot (I)	73,333	(28%)	Bush (R)	100,470	(40%)
Bush (R)	68,174	(26%)			

Rep. Jack Quinn (R)

Elected 1992; b. Apr. 13, 1951, Buffalo; home, Hamburg; Siena Col., B.A. 1969, S.U.N.Y., M.A. 1973; Catholic; married (Mary Beth).

Career: Teacher and coach, Orchard Park Central Schl., 1973–83; Hamburg Town Supervisor, 1984–92.

DC Office: 331 CHOB 20515, 202-225-3306; Fax: 202-226-0347.

District Offices: 403 Main St., #240, Buffalo 14203, 716-845-5257.

Committees: *Transportation & Infrastructure* (21st of 33 R): Railroads; Surface Transportation; Water Resources and Environment. *Veterans' Affairs* (8th of 18 R): Hospitals and Health Care. *Joint Economic Committee* (3rd of 10 Reps.).

Group Ratings

	ADA	ACLU	COPE	CFA	LCV	CON	NSI	COC	ACU	NTLC	CHC
1994	30	17	56	30	12	73	100	91	76	85	93
1993	30	—	67	40	29	74	—	64	83	—	—

National Journal Ratings

	1993 LIB — 1993 CONS		1994 LIB — 1994 CONS	
Economic	40% —	58%	30% —	67%
Social	25% —	73%	38% —	61%
Foreign	17% —	76%	34% —	63%

Key Votes of the 103d Congress

1. Clinton Deficit Plan	N	3. Brady Handgun Purchase	Y	5. Lmt. UN Cmnd. of Forces	Y
2. NAFTA	N	4. Strike Race/Death Pnlty.	N	6. Cut Missile Funds	N

Key Votes of the 104th Congress

1. Congressional Compliance	Y	6. Reform Crime Grant	N	11. Loser Pays Court Reform	Y
2. Balanced Budget Amndmt.	Y	7. National Security Act	Y	12. Product Liability Reform	Y
3. Bar Unfunded Mandates	Y	8. Moratorium on Regs.	Y	13. Welfare Reform	Y
4. Pass Line Item Veto	Y	9. Risk Assessment on Regs.	Y	14. Term Limits Amndmt.	Y
5. Relax Exclusionary Rule	Y	10. Expnd. Priv. Prop. Rights	N	15. Tax Cuts	Y

Election Results

1994 general	Jack Quinn (R-C)	124,738	(67%)	($488,083)
	David A. Franczyk (D-L)	61,392	(33%)	($193,717)
1994 primary	Jack Quinn (R)	unopposed		
1992 general	Jack Quinn (R-CCP)	125,734	(52%)	($199,257)
	Dennis T. Gorski (D-C)	111,445	(46%)	($459,349)
	Other	6,025	(3%)	

THIRTY-FIRST DISTRICT

The Southern Tier of New York is one of the nation's forgotten stretches of territory, yet it has an interesting and distinctive history. Elmira was once the home of Mark Twain and, though far from the Mississippi, was where he wrote *Huckleberry Finn*. On Lake Chautauqua, not far from Lake Erie, a training camp for Methodist Sunday school teachers was founded in 1874, where in summers, on wide green lawns and on porches and in gazebos decorated with Victorian gingerbread, some 25,000 people heard educational talks and inspirational lectures from the likes of William Jennings Bryan. Corning is the headquarters of Corning Glass Works, one of America's long-successful and also artistically distinguished manufacturing companies. In between are two small Indian reservations, miles and miles of dairy farms, and much of New York's wine country. Sheltered by hills, the lands at the edge of Upstate's deep lakes are the nation's largest grape-growing area outside California, and the leader in Concord grapes, with headquarters of prime New York State wineries and Welch's grape juice.

The Southern Tier's western half forms the 31st Congressional District. Politically, this has been Republican country since the party's founding. The towns and countryside are no longer homogeneously Protestant, but they remain solidly Republican in most elections, though occasionally willing to consider a Democrat. In fact, the area was represented by Democrat Stan Lundine, onetime mayor of Jamestown, from 1976 until he was tapped to become Mario Cuomo's lieutenant governor 10 years later.

The 31st District's congressman carries his familiar name with considerable grace: He is Amory Houghton, scion of the very rich family that owns the Corning Glass Works. He was a top executive at Corning for 25 years and had considered retiring to be a missionary in Africa, but instead ran for Congress. The Houghtons are not just rich folks in a small town, they are charter members of the American establishment: Houghton's father was an ambassador to France; his grandfather, a Congressman in the 1920s, built one of the biggest mansions on Washington's Embassy Row; his family endowed the rare books library at Harvard; and this latest Houghton sat on boards of companies like IBM, Citicorp and Procter and Gamble. Cheerful, articulate, used to being in comfortable command, Amo Houghton ran a chipper and well-financed campaign in 1986; he chatted with voters, competed with a serious Democratic opponent and won 60% of the vote. Houghton is not just a leader. He joined the Marine Corps in 1945, at 18, and in his campaigns did "work days" as a disc jockey at an Elmira radio station, as a cook at the Texas Hots restaurant in Wellsville, and as a man-on-the-street reporter for the *Olean Times-Herald*. He has been reelected by wide margins.

Houghton is the only former CEO of a *Fortune* 500 company in Congress, and he brings that perspective to government—he finds it wasteful and foolish, but he also wants to preserve some programs with little public support. He dislikes adversariness (most CEOs hear little but praise) but also is ready to listen to complaints (the up-to-date CEO had better know if the organization is not working). If he was not a typical freshman Congressman, he may be more what the Founding Fathers had in mind than the politically adept youngsters who win in so many districts. His roots go way back: his namesake founded Corning Glass Works in 1851. By *Roll Call*'s estimate, he is the richest member of Congress, with $400 million; but that includes the wealth of many members of a rather large family. Anyway, he is the only member of Congress who pays for his foreign travel out of personal funds. He seems to have the cheerful unassuming nature of one to whom much is given, who has been living up to his responsibilities and has mostly enjoyed himself in the process.

Houghton's CEO attitude stands in contrast to most other Republicans on many issues. He is a staunch advocate of the National Endowment of the Arts and of public television; with Jerry Nadler of Manhattan, he organized America For the NEA. He produced a bill settling a local Seneca Indian dispute; he supported the assault weapons ban, though he is a member of the National Rifle Association; he backed the plant closing law and spoke out for the beleaguered catastrophic healthcare program. He balks at declaring he will oppose new taxes and was prominent in early 1995 in demanding (unsuccessfully) that his party leaders reduce to $95,000 the ceiling for families who could take advantage of the $500 per child tax credit in the Contract With America. "When you look at the numbers, it will be a humongous problem to try to balance the budget and cut taxes. It will be difficult enough to balance the budget." His CEO experience also was in evidence during the crime bill fight in August 1994—the issue that broke the back of the Democratic majority—when he asked, "Why not try something different, the almost-unheard-of approach of working together? Who knows? It might just work." Yet his economic experience also led him to propose letting firms with 50 employees self-insure—a rent in the fabric of the Clinton healthcare plan—and to bitterly oppose New York state's community rating plan. With his seat on the Ways and Means Committee, he is a force for bipartisanship and consensus, seeking to season the inexperience of the many junior Republicans on the committee. On balance, like most corporate CEOs, he has supported Newt Gingrich's Contract With America policies, despite economic qualms and a distaste at the Gingrichites' views on cultural issues.

The People: Pop. 1990: 580,400; 60% rural; 15% age 65+; 95% White; 2% Black; 1% Amer. Indian; 1% Asian; 1% Other; 1% Hispanic origin. Voting age pop.: 428,466; 2% Black; 1% Hispanic origin. Households: 58% married couple families; 27% married couple fams. w. children; 39% college educ.; median household income: $25,124; per capita income: $11,382; median gross rent: $341; median house value: $48,300.

1992 Presidential Vote

Bush (R)	97,447	(40%)
Clinton (D)	82,671	(34%)
Perot (I)	62,325	(25%)

1988 Presidential Vote

Bush (R)	132,922	(59%)
Dukakis (D)	91,462	(41%)

Rep. Amo Houghton (R)

Elected 1986; b. Aug. 7, 1926, Corning; home, Corning; Harvard, B.A. 1950, M.B.A. 1952; Episcopalian; married (Priscilla).

Career: Marine Corps, 1945–46 (WWII); Corning Glass Works, 1951–86, Chmn. and CEO, 1964–86.

DC Office: 1110 LHOB 20515, 202-225-3161; Fax: 202-225-5574.

District Offices: 700 W. Gate Plz., W. State St., Olean 14760, 716-372-2127; 32 Denison Pkwy. W., Corning 14830, 607-937-3333; and Fed. Bldg., #122, Prendergast & 3d Sts., Jamestown 14701, 716-484-0252.

Committees: *International Relations* (23rd of 23 R); Africa. *Ways & Means* (7th of 21 R): Health; Trade.

Group Ratings

	ADA	ACLU	COPE	CFA	LCV	CON	NSI	COC	ACU	NTLC	CHC
1994	20	45	11	30	13	56	100	100	68	85	57
1993	20	—	33	20	21	65	—	100	79	—	—

National Journal Ratings

	1993 LIB	—	1993 CONS		1994 LIB	—	1994 CONS
Economic	14%	—	80%		30%	—	67%
Social	48%	—	51%		52%	—	48%
Foreign	31%	—	67%		34%	—	63%

Key Votes of the 103d Congress

1. Clinton Deficit Plan	N	3. Brady Handgun Purchase	N	5. Lmt. UN Cmnd. of Forces	Y
2. NAFTA	Y	4. Strike Race/Death Pnlty.	*	6. Cut Missile Funds	N

Key Votes of the 104th Congress

1. Congressional Compliance	Y	6. Reform Crime Grant	Y	11. Loser Pays Court Reform	Y
2. Balanced Budget Amndmt.	Y	7. National Security Act	Y	12. Product Liability Reform	Y
3. Bar Unfunded Mandates	Y	8. Moratorium on Regs.	Y	13. Welfare Reform	Y
4. Pass Line Item Veto	Y	9. Risk Assessment on Regs.	Y	14. Term Limits Amndmt.	Y
5. Relax Exclusionary Rule	Y	10. Expnd. Priv. Prop. Rights	Y	15. Tax Cuts	N

Election Results

1994 general	Amo Houghton (R-C)	121,178	(85%)	($356,525)
	Gretchen S. McManus (RTL)	21,747	(15%)	
1994 primary	Amo Houghton (R)	unopposed		
1992 general	Amo Houghton (R-C)	150,696	(71%)	($444,296)
	Joseph P. Leahey (D)	52,010	(24%)	($5,850)
	Gretchen S. McManus (RTL)	10,848	(5%)	

NORTH CAROLINA

North Carolina, one of the 13 original states, for many years a quiet if arguably progressive backwater, now has claims to be on the nation's leading edge, a state whose growing economy, booming demography and vibrant culture are in many ways typical of the way the nation is going—or would like to go. This was mostly unanticipated. Few people 20 years ago picked North Carolina as a state that would chart a path to the future. It had no great central city, no Atlanta primed to become another Chicago or Los Angeles, but rather a series of small metropolitan areas spaced out over thickly-settled countryside. It did not have what seemed to be cutting-edge industries: the biggest employer was textiles, typically an underdeveloped nation's first industry, and the other two were stolid furniture and soon-to-be-disfavored tobacco. It seemed to be off the nation's main lines of commerce; a south Atlantic state, too steamy to be businesslike in the summer and too cold to be a resort in the winter. It did not seem socially advanced, with a population made up almost entirely of native-born Anglo-Saxons and blacks and with an attachment to traditional and sometimes fundamentalist religion.

Yet North Carolina has emerged as one of America's leading growth states. Its population grew 13% in the 1980s, making it the tenth largest state, and has continued to grow robustly in the 1990s. It boasts one of the nation's lowest unemployment rates. That happened even though the number of textile and tobacco jobs has declined. North Carolina's economy has diversified, with huge job growth around the two metro areas whose airports became major airline hubs in the 1980s, Charlotte and Raleigh-Durham. North Carolina firms have become national leaders: headquartered in Charlotte are NationsBank, formerly NCNB, the nation's fourth largest bank, and Nucor, the nation's leading minimill steelmaker; in the midst of Raleigh-Durham is Research Triangle Park. Professional and high-tech job sectors have been growing rapidly. While Carolina politicians were seeking protection for textiles, this more advanced economy was coming into being so quietly and quickly that one of its biggest problems was a labor shortage: not enough people were migrating to the state.

But not everything is changed. There is still a low-wage economy here, with old factories and almost no unions and little regulation. This dark side of North Carolina was revealed when the chicken plant in Hamlet caught fire in 1991 due to lax safety standards and 25 workers died. North Carolina still has high infant mortality and one of the nation's largest percentage of trailers as housing units. But plenty of green space and reminders of rural roots, from barbecue stands to country Baptist churches, remain in North Carolina's "countrified cities": Tarheels can live surrounded by forests or farms and yet be within an hour's drive of huge shopping centers and thousands of workplaces.

Change has not been directed from any single establishment; the forces that have produced it are decentralized—and sometimes hostile. North Carolina does have a small and articulate elite, which looks for guidance to the University of North Carolina at Chapel Hill and the resolutely progressive editors of the state's newspapers, most prominently the *Raleigh News & Observer* and the *Charlotte Observer*. Quite different attitudes are nurtured by tradition-minded churches in a state where churchgoing is deeply ingrained, endorsed for years through Sunday blue laws and strengthened periodically by religious revivals. North Carolina's Billy Graham remains a strong voice for revealed religion, appearing in Bill Clinton's inauguration as he had in Dwight Eisenhower's 40 years before. In the economically backward state North Carolina was when infant mortality was common and indoor plumbing was not, religion was a fountain of hope and a source of discipline; and it is still for a great many, in this now bustling air-conditioned, cable-wired commonwealth.

North Carolina has grown with the aid of both its progressive and tradition-minded citizens,

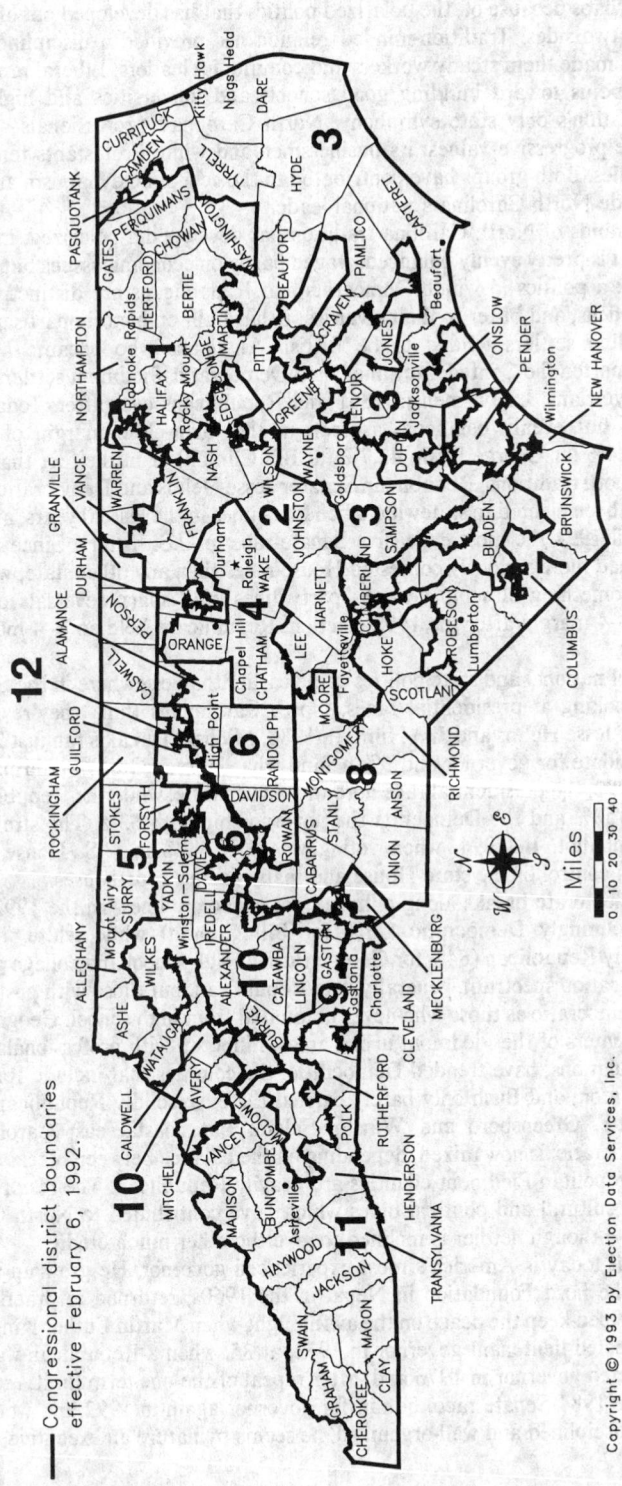

Congressional district boundaries
effective February 6, 1992.

Copyright © 1993 by Election Data Services, Inc.

and in spite of, or perhaps because of, the polarized politics that has developed out of a series of battles between the two sides. Tradition-minded religion has provided a discipline for many churchgoers that has made them steady workers and community leaders. Liberal progressivism has provided an impetus toward building good schools and universities and highways and amenities like the nation's only state symphony. North Carolina's professionals—white and black—tend to share progressive values; its businessmen and white Protestants tend to share tradition-minded values. Both groups have contributed to the economic dynamism and cultural energy that have made North Carolina a national leader.

From these two strands of North Carolina tradition has developed a polarized, increasingly party-line politics that is pretty evenly balanced, waged partly on economic issues but even more on cultural attitudes; a politics in which Democrats and Republicans are distinctive, seldom overlapping in their ideas, and bitter in their rivalries. It has built on historic partisan patterns: coastal North Carolina settlers tended to be British Anglicans who became Methodists, slaveholders who supported the Confederacy and voted Democratic; Piedmont settlers tended to be Scots-Irish Presbyterians, Union men in 1861 and Republicans ever after. Today the two sides are differently but evenly balanced, as seen in the razor-close margin of the 1992 presidential race (43.4% for George Bush, 42.7% for Bill Clinton) or in the fact that the most effective paladins of both traditions, Republican Senator Jesse Helms and Democratic Governor Jim Hunt, have each been elected to statewide office four times in the last 20 years, and in 1984 waged what was until 1994 the most expensive Senate race in U.S. history. Since the 1970s, North Carolina has had more seriously contested House races than any other state, with results tending to heel to something close to straight party lines, and sharp reversals of fortune: Democrats held an 8–4 margin after the 1992 election; Republicans held an 8–4 margin after 1994.

This convergence of national and state politics came earlier than elsewhere in the South. It is almost as if, when looking at presidential races, North Carolinians think they're looking at another race between Jesse Helms and Jim Hunt. In 1988, Michael Dukakis ran just 2% behind the Democratic candidate for governor and 5% behind what Harvey Gantt would poll against Helms in 1990. By 1992, the presidential race here was a virtual tie, while the Republicans won the Senate seat with 50% and the Democrats the governorship with 53%. The straight party voting goes far downballot. In 1994, when voting was 57%–43% in U.S. House elections, Republicans also won control of the state House and many county courthouses.

North Carolina's electorate breaks along cultural, not economic lines. In the 1992 exit poll blacks were overwhelmingly Democratic (91% for Bill Clinton) while white, born-again Christians were heavily Republican (64% for George Bush). High school and college graduates, the middle of the education spectrum, generally vote Republican, but those with post-graduate degrees are just as Democratic as those who never graduated from high school. Geographically, this means that the centers of the Piedmont urban areas, filling up with professionals and with significant black populations, have trended Democratic: the counties that include Raleigh and Durham went for Clinton, and Bush only barely carried the once solidly Republican counties that include Charlotte, Greensboro and Winston-Salem. But coastal east Carolina, once overwhelmingly Democratic, is now mixed, depending on the balance between blacks and white born-agains; non-metropolitan Piedmont counties are heavily Republican. The result is a close balance between two cultural and political blocs which have contributed to North Carolina's unanticipated growth—though neither is inclined to give the other much credit.

Governor. Jim Hunt today is America's most experienced governor. He grew up in Wilson County, worked for the Ford Foundation in Nepal in the 1960s, returned to practice law in Wilson County and helped keep the peace on the awful night when Martin Luther King, Jr., was murdered. He was elected lieutenant governor in 1972, at 35, when a Republican was elected governor. He was elected governor in 1976 and, after repeal of the one-term limit, reelected in 1980. After losing the 1984 Senate race, he ran for governor again in 1992 and won handily. Forceful, articulate, disciplined and well-organized, he seems by nature an executive; he might not have found the Senate congenial. He became governor here two years before Bill Clinton did in Arkansas, and had successes much sooner than Clinton, with education reform that included student and teacher competency tests as well as higher teacher pay, part of an effort to attract high-tech jobs to Research Triangle Park and elsewhere, and stern backing of capital punishment. In 1984, he was replaced by Republican Jim Martin, who reduced business taxes, recruited out-of-state companies, started a highway improvement program and followed through on Hunt's education program with his "career ladder" $397 million merit pay program.

In 1992, Hunt had to beat two older rivals. He whipped Attorney General Lacy Thornburg in the primary, winning 65%–27%. In the general, Hunt faced Lieutenant Governor Jim Gardner, a colorful character who was elected to Congress in 1966 at age 33, and who ran for governor in 1968 and 1972, losing the latter runoff by 1,782 votes in a year the Republican ticket swept the top offices. Gardner founded the Hardees hamburger chain and made a fortune, then lost it, then started several more companies, some of which went bankrupt (one bumper sticker read, "Honk if Jim Gardner owes you money"). Gardner opposed Martin's tax increase proposals and attacked Hunt as soft on crime; Hunt called for school-based apprenticeship programs and more spending on day care and education reform, and said he would apply ideas from David Osborne's *Reinventing Government*.

Hunt won by a 53%–43% margin. In office, he pushed through tougher crime sentences, started a volunteer drive for after-school activities for at-risk children and initiated "Smart Start" to provide day care and health care to 10,000 children in 33 counties. For 1995, he announced a $483 million tax relief package and a zero tolerance policy on violence in schools, and said he expected the Republican legislature to cooperate. If Hunt had been elected to the Senate in 1984, he might have been the southern moderate elected president in 1992. But he seems unrueful, and as governor, with a high approval rating, sets a course for activist government informed by strong moral values in a state that often sets an example for America. He seems sure to run for reelection in 1996; possible Republican candidates include Charlotte Mayor Richard Vinroot, Congressman Charles Taylor, and Raleigh Mayor Tom Fetzer.

Senators. No American politician is more controversial, beloved in some quarters and hated in others, than Jesse Helms, now completing his fourth term in the Senate and chairman of the Senate Foreign Relations Committee. Helms grew up the son of the police chief of Monroe, North Carolina, 15 miles from the birthplace of Andrew Jackson—a breeding ground, it seems, for true-believing, contentious leaders. With Jacksonian tenacity he has stuck to his early convictions—respect for elders and law and order, traditional religious faith and moral principles, patriotism, the order imposed by racial segregation—with the exception of the last, and his abandonment of it has often seemed grudging and halfhearted. In a time of relativism and ambiguity, Jesse Helms has stood out for the clarity of his views and his steadfast insistence on articulating them. Helms has always been an advocate, not a principal; a talker rather than a doer. He has never held or sought executive office: before he ran for the Senate in 1972, he was a television commentator who served on the Raleigh city council in the 1950s. When Senate Republicans had a majority in the 1980s, he had little success managing legislation; nor is he expected to in the 1990s. Helms's percentages in his four races have been in a narrow range— 54%, 55%, 52%, 53%—and he makes no attempt to mollify voters who disagree with him.

Helms believes in free market economics, but has never much emphasized economic issues. He supports tobacco benefits on the Agriculture Committee, and textile import limits, but not with great verve. He was bailed out of difficulties managing farm bills in the 1980s by Bob Dole. What energizes Helms are foreign and cultural issues—foreign wars and culture wars. Usually Helms sounds the notes of a Jeremiah who knows doom is around the corner but hopes to delay it a minute longer. "What is really at stake," he said in debating arts funding in 1990, "is whether or not America will allow the cultural high ground in this nation to sink slowly into an abyss of slime to placate people who clearly seek or are willing to destroy the Judaic-Christian foundations of this republic." For years, Helms has insisted on roll call votes on issues like abortion and the fetal tissue research ban, school busing, Japanese American redress, AIDS funding and, perhaps with greatest visibility, on the National Endowment of the Arts. His causes are by no means all loony—why should the government finance art that is offensive to most of the American public?—but he manages often to offend colleagues who want to mask unpopular positions or smooth over conflicts between different groups of supporters.

Even when in the minority, Helms used his seat on Foreign Relations to conduct something like his own foreign policy. In the Reagan and Bush years he and aides James P. Lucier, Christopher Manion and Deborah DeMoss developed their own sources and attempted to manipulate State Department appointments to help the contras in Nicaragua and rightists in El Salvador. Helms's great cause in the 1970s was to defeat the Panama Canal treaties—a cause which helped defeat a dozen liberal senators and kept alive Ronald Reagan's candidacy when it threatened to die in the North Carolina primary in 1976. Helms has proven a better prophet than many of his critics, decrying the Ceausescu dictatorship in Romania when most mainstreamers wanted to overlook it; arguing against low-interest loans to the foundering Soviet republics and arming the Iraqis; opposing the Sandinistas in Nicaragua long before free elections belied congressional Democrats' assurance that they were the people's choice; backing freedom in Eastern Europe and the Baltic States when others said it was an impossible dream.

But this Jeremiah has had to deal with the challenge of success. Helms became ranking minority member of Foreign Relations in 1987. He had pledged in the 1984 campaign not to take the chairmanship, and to remain chairman of Agriculture. But when Republicans lost their majority he considered himself no longer bound by that promise, and got fellow Republicans to follow seniority and place him ahead of former committee Chairman Richard Lugar. In 1992 Helms fired his top staffers and, dogged by illness, seemed to be taking a more passive role. But the 1994 election restored him to chairman of Foreign Relations, and liberals shuddered. They made much of his caustic post-election comments on Bill Clinton—that the president was not respected by many in the military and, "jokingly," Helms insisted, that when visiting North Carolina, "Mr. Clinton had better watch out if he comes down here. He better have a bodyguard." The suggestion was that Helms posed some grave danger to the republic. But his off-the-cuff comments are less daffy than many by his predecessor as chairman, Claiborne Pell, during whose term the republic survived, and Helms is far less capable of rallying a Senate majority on foreign issues than is Bob Dole or Richard Lugar or Mitch McConnell. Not likely to write a foreign aid reauthorization, Helms is likely to pursue particular causes. Like Dole, he favors lifting the arms embargo on Bosnia; he opposed the U.S. military intervention in Haiti and criticized President Aristide as a thug; he opposes the use of U.S. troops as peacekeeping forces in the Golan Heights; he may be leery of the U.S. agreement with North Korea; he looks askance at the operations of the United Nations. He responded to Secretary of State Warren Christopher's courtly courtesy with courtly courtesy of his own. But after promising a thorough review of State Department operations and of foreign aid, he made moves to overhaul both. To the administration's dismay, Helms even suggested that he would take a proposed streamlining advocated by Christopher but rejected by the White House. He promised not to obstruct most nominations, but even before the election stopped Robert Pastor from becoming Ambassador to Panama, and forced Clinton to withdraw his nomination of Robert Hormel, who is openly gay, as Ambassador to Fiji, which in fact has strict laws against homosexuality.

Helms's political obituary has been written many times, but the copy has always had to be reset. He turns 75 in 1996, he remains under attack by the state's newspapers as few politicians anywhere have been, he has let his ties with his old Congressional Club organization wither and he has many dedicated opponents. But then he was behind in polls during most of the 1990 contest, and came back to win. It was an extraordinary election for many reasons, only one of which was that his opponent, Harvey Gantt, is black. This was probably the most watched Senate race in the country, a contest between an obdurate opponent of the Martin Luther King holiday and a black liberal who refused to trim on issues, proclaiming his support of more federal spending in TV spots and in personal appearances on the steps of each of North Carolina's 100 county courthouses. Gantt's personal story was inspiring: he was educated in segregated schools and was admitted to Clemson University by court order; he made a successful living as an architect; he was twice elected mayor of Charlotte; far from harboring resentments or seeking reparations, he seemed exuberant and optimistic. Rather than suggest whites were prejudiced, he sought their votes, and won a runoff primary against a white moderate 57%–43%. In the general, he did a superb job of framing the issues, dismissing Helms's preoccupation with the NEA and abortion as unimportant.

But Helms, armed with money raised by a nationwide direct mail campaign, seized the initiative in mid-October with three ads. One attacked racial quotas by showing white hands crumpling a rejection slip while the announcer said the man had lost his job to a minority though he was better qualified, and then accused Gantt of supporting quotas. A radio spot attacked Gantt for "secret" campaigning because he ran ads on black radio stations (a similar charge could be made against Helms and most other candidates in this segmented society). The third attacked Gantt for using "his office and minority status" to make a $450,000 profit on a $679 investment in a TV station license which was then sold to a white corporation—a charge Democrats and journalists cried was racist but which was in fact true: Gantt had not resisted the temptation to take financial advantage of a law providing for racial preference for blacks. Gantt fell in the polls, and there was reason all along to think some of the Helms vote was hidden, concealed by conservative voters who would not speak openly to pollsters of the hated liberal media. Gantt carried young voters and Helms the elderly, the opposite of partisan patterns elsewhere in the nation. Gantt won solidly in Charlotte but ran behind in much of east Carolina. Overall, the result was almost the same as in the Helms-Hunt contest: Helms won with 53%. Gantt long ago announced he was running again in 1996. Charles Sanders, chairman of the pharmaceutical firm Glaxo, announced formally in March 1995—and resigned his chair at Glavo to focus on the campaign. Two other blacks have expressed interest, former Chapel Hill Mayor Howard Lee and former House Speaker Dan Blue. And former Congressman David Price might run.

North Carolina's junior senator is Lauch Faircloth, a longtime Democrat who in 1992 ran as a Republican and an ally of Jesse Helms. (His first name is short for McLauchlin and pronounced *lock*.) Faircloth is a farmer and textile mill owner who served on the Highway Commission under Governors Terry Sanford and Dan Moore and was Jim Hunt's Commerce Commissioner for seven years. In 1984, he ran third in the Democratic gubernatorial primary; there was talk he'd wanted the 1986 Senate nomination and was angry it went to Sanford, then President of Duke University. Sanford won that seat narrowly, but his outspoken opposition to the Gulf war and his reluctance to condemn the Keating Five were clear liabilities. Faircloth switched parties in February 1991 and with the support of Helms allies ran against former Charlotte Mayor Sue Myrick for the Republican nomination. Myrick attacked Faircloth for his millionaire status and as a two-timer who backed both Helms and Hunt in 1984, but Faircloth won the primary by a 48%–30% margin (40% is enough to win without a runoff here), carrying even Charlotte. In the general Faircloth was a stealth candidate, making few appearances but running lots of ads, accusing Sanford of voting like Ted Kennedy, for supporting welfare over workfare and funding for a Boston harbor tunnel. In early October, Sanford, 75, had heart surgery. This raised the age issue against the incumbent, and in the end Faircloth, no youngster himself, won 50%–46%.

In the Senate Faircloth has proved his party switch wasn't insincere and has one of the most conservative voting records. He has been a thorn in the side of the Clinton Administration, although not always successfully: he fell short when he opposed the Justice Department nomination of Duke law professor Walter Dellinger and the Commerce Department nomination of Ron Brown crony Lauri Fitz-Pegado, whose husband had been involved in business dealings with Brown. Faircloth also tried unsuccessfully to block the nomination of Arkansan Ricki Tigert-Helfer to head the FDIC. He demanded that the Commodity Futures Trading Commission deliver records of Hillary Rodham Clinton's cattle-futures investments. And he sharply criticized independent counsel Robert Fiske for his leniency on the Whitewater affair, and in turn was criticized for impropriety after he and Helms had lunch with Judge David Sentelle, a

North Carolinian who headed the panel selecting independent counsels, although no rule was violated. Pugnacious, alert for Democratic scandals, hostile to the press, Faircloth gives signs that he is interested not simply in one term but in winning a second in 1998 at age 70.

Presidential politics. North Carolina was as competitive as any state in the country in the 1992 general election: polls showed the race close all fall and Ross Perot was a less serious factor than almost anywhere else in the country. George Bush ended up winning by the narrowest of edges, a result similar to the 1992 and 1990 Senate races and not so different from the governor and House races. North Carolina's straight-ticket politics shows great durability.

North Carolina, which switched its primary to Super Tuesday in 1988, switched it back to May in 1992—the 1996 primary here is set for May 7. Bill Clinton and George Bush, two southerners who had already clinched their parties' nominations, won overwhelmingly. Clinton's victory recalled Albert Gore's win here in 1988; Bush's recalled his narrow win over Bob Dole. North Carolina has been really crucial only once: in 1976, when after five straight losses, Ronald Reagan started denouncing the Panama Canal Treaty and won his first victory over Gerald Ford. That kept Reagan's candidacy alive not just for 1976 but for 1980. What would history have done without North Carolina?

Congressional districting. North Carolina's robust growth in the 1980s gave it a 12th congressional district in the 1990 Census, its first new seat in 60 years. It had one of the most turbulent districting processes in the nation, thanks to application of the Voting Rights Act, whose 1982 amendments were interpreted by the Justice Department as requiring the creation of not one but two black-majority districts in a state that had none before. In December 1991, a Democratic plan was struck down which would have created only one new black-majority 1st District; Republicans chortled, but Democratic legislators drew a plan with a second black district consisting of a thin line of territory, in some places no wider than I-85, linking black precincts from Durham west to Charlotte; the plan also appeared to strengthen several Democratic incumbents. Though it violated the age-old principle of contiguity, the Justice Department in 1992 ruled the plan was acceptable. But in June 1993 the Supreme Court in *Shaw v. Reno* ordered it reexamined. On remand the federal court in August 1994 upheld the plan, which Democrats defended as politically rather than racially driven. Its fate will likely be decided anew by the Supreme Court in 1995. If the legislature has to draw new lines, they will likely be much more favorable to Republicans, who control the state House. On the other hand, the Republicans' four-seat gain in 1994 showed that the old lines did not work out as Democrats had intended. North Carolina's House and Senate passed a bill in March 1995 making it the 50th state to adopt the veto for its governor, giving that power to Democrat Jim Hunt. But the constitutional amendment, which will be on the 1996 ballot, probably would not be in place soon enough to respond to a Supreme Court call for a new map.

The People: Est. Pop. 1994: 7,070,000; Pop. 1990: 6,628,637, up 6.6% 1990–1994. 2.7% of U.S. total, 10th largest; 50% rural. Median age: 33.1 years. 12.1% 65 years and over. 75.6% White, 22.0% Black, 1.2% American Indian, 1.2% Hispanic origin. Households: 56.6% married couple families; 26% married couple fams. w. children; 41% college educ.; median household income: $26,647; per capita income: $12,885; 68.0% owner occupied housing; median house value: $65,800; median monthly rent: $284. 5.9% Unemployment. 1994 Voting age pop.: 5,364,000. 1994 Turnout: 1,482,658; 28% of VAP. Registered voters (1994): 3,635,875; 2,129,159 D (59%), 1,191,878 R (33%), 314,838 unaffiliated and minor parties (9%).

Political Lineup: Governor, James B. Hunt, Jr. (D); Lt. Gov., Dennis A. Wicker (D); Secy. of State, Rufus L. Edmisten (D); Atty. Gen., Michael F. Easley (D); Treasurer, Harlan E. Boyles (D); Auditor, Ralph Campbell (D). State Senate, 50 (26 D, 23 R and 1 vacant); State House of Representatives, 120 (68 R and 52 D). Senators, Jesse A. Helms (R) and Lauch Faircloth (R). Representatives, 12 (8 R and 4 D).

1992 Presidential Vote

Bush (R) 1,134,661 (43%)
Clinton (D) 1,114,042 (43%)
Perot (I). 357,864 (14%)

1992 Democratic Presidential Primary

Clinton. 443,498 (64%)
Brown 71,984 (10%)
Tsongas 57,589 (8%)
No Preference 106,697 (15%)

1988 Presidential Vote

Bush (R) 1,237,258 (58%)
Dukakis (D). 890,167 (42%)

1992 Republican Presidential Primary

Bush 200,387 (71%)
Buchanan. 55,420 (20%)
No Preference 27,764 (10%)

GOVERNOR

Gov. James B. Hunt, Jr. (D)

Elected 1992, term expires Jan. 1997; b. May 16, 1937, Greensboro; home, Rock Ridge; NC St., B.S. 1959, M.S. 1962, U. of NC at Chapel Hill, J.D. 1964; Presbyterian; married (Carolyn).

Career: Cattle rancher; Ford Foundation Econ. Advisor to Nepal, 1964–66; Practicing atty., 1966–92; NC Lt. Gov., 1972–76; NC Gov., 1976–84.

Office: State Capitol, Raleigh 27603, 919-733-4240; Fax: 919-733-5166.

Election Results

1992 gen.	James B. Hunt, Jr. (D)	1,368,246	(53%)
	Jim Gardner (R).	1,121,955	(43%)
	Scott McLaughlin (Lib).	104,983	(4%)
1992 prim.	James B. Hunt, Jr. (D)	459,300	(65%)
	Lacy H. Thornburg (D)	188,806	(27%)
	Marcus W. Williams (D)	25,660	(4%)
	Others.	27,840	(4%)
1988 gen.	James G. Martin (R)	1,222,338	(56%)
	Robert G. Jordan III (D).	957,687	(44%)

SENATORS

Sen. Jesse A. Helms (R)

Elected 1972, seat up 1996; b. Oct. 18, 1921, Monroe; home, Raleigh; Wingate Col., Wake Forest U.; Baptist; married (Dorothy).

Career: Navy, 1942–45; City Editor, *Raleigh Times*; A.A., U.S. Sens. Willis Smith, 1951–53 and Alton Lennon, 1953; Exec. Dir., NC Bankers Assn., 1953–60; Raleigh City Cncl., 1957–61; Exec. V.P., WRAL-TV and Tobacco Radio Network, 1960–72.

DC Office: 403 DSOB 20510, 202-224-6342; Fax: 202-224-7588.

State Offices: P.O. Box 2888, Raleigh 27602, 919-856-4630; and P.O. Box 2944, Hickory 28601, 704-322-5170.

Committees: *Agriculture, Nutrition & Forestry* (3rd of 10 R): Forestry, Conservation and Rural Revitalization; Marketing, Inspection and Product Promotion (Chmn.); Production and Price Competitiveness. *Foreign Relations* (Chmn. of 10 R): International Operations; Western Hemisphere and Peace Corps Affairs. *Rules & Administration* (3rd of 9 R).

Group Ratings

	ADA	ACLU	COPE	CFA	LCV	CON	NSI	COC	ACU	NTLC	CHC
1994	0	16	14	8	0	63	100	89	100	96	100
1993	10	—	18	0	6	68	—	80	100	—	—

National Journal Ratings

	1993 LIB — 1993 CONS		1994 LIB — 1994 CONS	
Economic	0% —	87%	0% —	88%
Social	0% —	92%	0% —	85%
Foreign	0% —	92%	0% —	94%

Key Votes of the 103d Congress

1. Clinton Deficit Plan	N	3. Brady Handgun Purchase N	5. Lmt. UN Cmnd. of Forces Y
2. NAFTA	N	4. Strike Race/Death Pnlty. Y	6. Cut Missile Funds N

Key Votes of the 104th Congress

1. Congressional Compliance Y	3. Balanced Budget Amndt. Y	5. Product Liability Reform Y
2. Bar Unfunded Mandates Y	4. Pass Line Item Veto Y	6. FY96 Budget Y

Election Results

1990 general	Jesse A. Helms (R).................	1,088,331	(53%)	($17,761,579)
	Harvey B. Gantt (D).................	981,573	(47%)	($7,811,520)
1990 primary	Jesse A. Helms (R)...................	157,345	(84%)	
	L. C. Nixon (R)	15,355	(8%)	
	George Wimbish (R).................	13,895	(8%)	
1984 general	Jesse A. Helms (R).................	1,156,768	(52%)	($16,917,559)
	James B. Hunt, Jr. (D)	1,070,488	(48%)	($9,461,924)

Sen. Lauch Faircloth (R)

Elected 1992, seat up 1998; b. Jan. 14, 1928, Concord; home, Clinton; Presbyterian; divorced.

Career: Army, 1954–55; Farmer, businessman; Owner, Faircloth Farms, Coharie Mills, Coharie Farms; NC Highway Commissioner, 1961–64, Chmn., 1967–73; NC Secy. of Commerce, 1977–83.

DC Office: 317 HSOB 20515, 202-224-3154; Fax: 202-224-7406.

State Offices: Fed. Bldg., #120, 310 New Bern Ave., Raleigh 27601, 919-856-4791; Fed. Bldg., #219, 401 W. Trade St., Charlotte 28202, 704-375-1993; Fed. Bldg., #251, 151 Patton Ave., Asheville 28801, 704-244-3099; and Fed. Bldg., #422, 251 Main St., Winston-Salem 27101, 919-631-5313.

Committees: *Banking, Housing & Urban Affairs* (6th of 9 R): HUD Oversight and Structure (Chmn.); International Finance; Securities. *Environment & Public Works* (4th of 9 R): Clean Air, Wetlands, Private Property and Nuclear Safety (Chmn.); Drinking Water, Fisheries and Wildlife; Transportation and Infrastructure.

Group Ratings

	ADA	ACLU	COPE	CFA	LCV	CON	NSI	COC	ACU	NTLC	CHC
1994	5	16	0	17	0	92	100	79	100	92	100
1993	15	—	9	0	13	89	—	67	100	—	—

National Journal Ratings

	1993 LIB — 1993 CONS		1994 LIB — 1994 CONS
Economic	20% — 78%		0% — 88%
Social	0% — 92%		0% — 85%
Foreign	8% — 86%		0% — 94%

Key Votes of the 103d Congress

1. Clinton Deficit Plan	N	3. Brady Handgun Purchase	N	5. Lmt. UN Cmnd. of Forces	Y
2. NAFTA	N	4. Strike Race/Death Pnlty.	Y	6. Cut Missile Funds	N

Key Votes of the 104th Congress

1. Congressional Compliance	Y	3. Balanced Budget Amndt.	Y	5. Product Liability Reform	Y
2. Bar Unfunded Mandates	Y	4. Pass Line Item Veto	Y	6. FY96 Budget	Y

Election Results

1992 general	Lauch Faircloth (R)	1,297,892	(50%)	($2,952,102)
	Terry Sanford (D)	1,194,015	(46%)	($2,486,380)
	Others	85,984	(3%)	
1992 primary	Lauch Faircloth (R)	129,159	(48%)	
	Sue Myrick (R)	81,801	(30%)	
	Eugene (Gene) Johnston (R)	46,112	(17%)	
	Larry E. Harrington (R)	13,496	(5%)	
1986 general	Terry Sanford (D)	823,662	(52%)	($4,168,509)
	James T. Broyhill (R)	767,668	(48%)	($5,188,244)

FIRST DISTRICT

Eastern North Carolina in colonial days was a smaller version of the Chesapeake Bay colonies of Virginia and Maryland—a fertile land intersected by dozens of rivers and inlets, with tobacco plantations and farms with docks on the water accessible to the ocean and so to London. North Carolina was settled later than the Chesapeake colonies, and was poorer, with smaller landholdings. But vestiges of its 18th Century past can still be seen in New Bern with its Tryon Palace, the governor's house when this was the capital, and the tiny well-preserved town of Edenton on Albemarle Sound. Today, east Carolina is still tobacco country, indeed the major tobacco-producing land in the United States. It is also a place inhabited almost entirely by the descendants of the original white settlers and black slaves of 200 years ago. They live in small towns and cities and in some of the most thickly-settled rural land in the United States. For tobacco is a labor-intensive crop which can produce yields of $4,000 an acre. A family can make a living off 40 acres of tobacco land; with a tobacco allotment, part of a government program dating back 60 years, many here do. But fewer than in the past. No-smoking laws and anti-smoking campaigns have cut cigarette sales, and many old east Carolina tobacco fields are planted with cucumbers, sweet potatoes and blueberries.

The 1st Congressional District of North Carolina winds through tobacco country, with tortuous boundaries totalling 2,039 miles, taking in parts of 28 counties, although only nine in their entirety. This was one of two black-majority districts created for 1992 and under attack in court since; most areas of concentrated black population in east Carolina are in this seat. Some are urban—black ghettos of Fayetteville, Rocky Mount, New Bern—but more are rural, and there are plenty of black tobacco farmers here. The largest city here is Greenville, home of East Carolina University, but the surrounding county has only 11% of the district's population. This is ancestral Democratic country and, though many whites have become Jesse Helms Republicans, the new 1st District is solidly Democratic.

The Congresswoman from the 1st District is Eva Clayton, a Democrat with a long record in public life. In the mid-1970s, she was director of the Soul City Foundation, civil rights leader Floyd McKissick's attempt to form a black "new town." That foundered, but Clayton backed Jim Hunt in 1976 and became an assistant secretary for community development in his first term as governor. She was elected to the Warren County Board of Commissioners and chaired it from 1982 to 1991. She then started her own consulting firm and in 1992 ran for the 1st District seat when the boundaries were drawn. The incumbent, 78-year-old Walter Jones, Chairman of the Merchant Marine and Fisheries Committee since 1980 and Chairman of the Peanuts and Tobacco Subcommittee before that, had decided to retire; he died in September. His son, state legislator Walter Jones, Jr., ran and won 38% in the first Democratic primary—just 2% away from the 40% which under North Carolina law would have given him the nomination—ahead of Clayton, who had 31%. In the runoff in this 57% black district, Clayton won 55%–45%, and she won in November with 67%. Thus she became the first black member of Congress from North Carolina since George White served in the late 1890s, and the first woman from North Carolina to serve a full term.

Clayton is part of the black middle class who have worked their way up in government or worked closely with it. In the campaign, she backed more public investment and job training and lower defense spending to cut the deficit; in office she earned one of the most liberal voting records, according to *National Journal*, in the House."I would hasten to say I'm not for cutting for cutting's sake," she said in 1993. Freshman Democrats elected her to chair their class. She was proud of working for WIC and food stamp extension, for crop disaster assistance, for the Section 515 affordable housing program. She was alert to district interests, voting for a new nuclear carrier (many constituents work in the Newport News, Virginia shipyard). To urban Black Caucus members seeking her support for bills, she responds, "Does it include rural areas?" Her reelection in 1994 was assured, though against the same opponent her percentage fell to 61%; she lost Greenville in the center of the district but carried both north and south ends.

The People: Pop. 1990: 553,426; 58% rural; 14% age 65+; 41% White; 57% Black; 1% Amer. Indian; 1% Hispanic origin. Voting age pop.: 399,949; 53% Black; 1% Hispanic origin. Households: 48% married couple families; 21% married couple fams. w. children; 28% college educ.; median household income: $18,226; per capita income: $8,918; median gross rent: $290; median house value: $45,600.

1992 Presidential Vote

Clinton (D)	109,657	(61%)
Bush (R)	53,019	(29%)
Perot (I)	18,266	(10%)

1988 Presidential Vote

Dukakis (D)	96,501	(61%)
Bush (R)	62,023	(39%)

Rep. Eva M. Clayton (D)

Elected 1992; b. Sept. 16, 1934, Savannah, GA; home, Littleton; Johnson C. Smith U., B.S. 1955, NC Central U., M.S. 1962, U. of NC Law Schl., 1967–69; Presbyterian; married (Theaoseus).

Career: Exec. Dir., Soul City Foundation, 1974–76; NC Asst. Secy., Community Development, 1977–81; Pres., & Owner, Technical Resources Intl. Inc., 1981–92; Warren Cnty. Commissioner, 1982–90, Chmn., 1982–90.

DC Office: 222 CHOB 20515, 202-225-3101; Fax: 202-225-3354.

District Offices: 400 W. 5th St., Greenville 27834, 800-274-8672; and P.O. Box 676, Warrenton 27589, 919-257-4800.

Committees: *Agriculture* (10th of 22 D): Resource Conservation, Research and Forestry; Risk Management and Specialty Crops. *Small Business* (7th of 19 D): Procurement, Exports and Business Opportunities (RMM).

Group Ratings

	ADA	ACLU	COPE	CFA	LCV	CON	NSI	COC	ACU	NTLC	CHC
1994	100	83	89	100	88	26	0	42	0	0	0
1993	100	—	100	100	93	32	—	9	0	—	—

National Journal Ratings

	1993 LIB — 1993 CONS		1994 LIB — 1994 CONS	
Economic	88%	0%	83%	0%
Social	87%	0%	90%	6%
Foreign	87%	7%	83%	15%

Key Votes of the 103d Congress

1. Clinton Deficit Plan	Y	3. Brady Handgun Purchase	Y	5. Lmt. UN Cmnd. of Forces	N
2. NAFTA	N	4. Strike Race/Death Pnlty.	N	6. Cut Missile Funds	Y

Key Votes of the 104th Congress

1. Congressional Compliance	Y	6. Reform Crime Grant	N	11. Loser Pays Court Reform	N
2. Balanced Budget Amndmt.	N	7. National Security Act	N	12. Product Liability Reform	N
3. Bar Unfunded Mandates	N	8. Moratorium on Regs.	N	13. Welfare Reform	N
4. Pass Line Item Veto	N	9. Risk Assessment on Regs.	N	14. Term Limits Amndmt.	N
5. Relax Exclusionary Rule	N	10. Expnd. Priv. Prop. Rights	N	15. Tax Cuts	N

Election Results

1994 general	Eva M. Clayton (D)	66,827	(61%)	($417,700)
	Ted Tyler (R)	42,602	(39%)	($16,572)
1994 primary	Eva M. Clayton (D)	unopposed		
1992 general	Eva M. Clayton (D)	116,078	(67%)	($551,028)
	Ted Tyler (R)	54,457	(31%)	($6,131)
	Other	2,727	(2%)	

SECOND DISTRICT

The coastal plain of North Carolina was long bypassed by history. It was settled after Virginia and South Carolina, and only filled in with English settlers as Scots-Irish families were streaming down the valley of Virginia to the western Piedmont. This has always been tobacco country, with life organized around a crop high-yield enough that a 40-acre plot of land can support a family (if it has a tobacco allotment). Tobacco was an important colonial crop, even more so after James B. Duke, a farmer from Durham County, created Bull Durham tobacco and Lucky Strike cigarettes. Cigarette factories grew up in Durham and eventually, from Duke's fortune, so did the gothic buildings of Duke University. But otherwise this was a backward area. Its small farms and little cities were homes mainly to tenant farmers and mill hands, people raising families in thin-walled frame houses often with no electricity or running water.

Today, life is much better in the coastal plain. Not just because incomes are up, but because this is now one of America's fastest-growing metropolitan areas; Raleigh-Durham, with a dynamic economy, provides many counties around it with jobs. Most farmers here now own the land they farm and textile workers are better paid. And the four-lane roads and interstates enable people to live where they have family roots and church affiliations, moral principles are valued and where traditional religion remains strong, and still partake of one of the nation's boom economies. Yet there remains a cultural divide. The Research Triangle area anchored by Durham, Raleigh and Chapel Hill has more Ph.D.s than any other area in the nation, and has been moving left politically despite rising incomes. The once rural counties, whose people are prosperous beyond their dreams but not highly educated, are moving to the right.

North Carolina's 2d Congressional District, as it was drastically redrawn for the 1992 election, consists of about three-quarters of a circle of rural counties, centered around Raleigh, in the state's coastal plain. It includes about half of Durham, but none of Raleigh; also Rocky Mount, Wilson, Sanford and Roanoke Rapids. Its oddly shaped boundaries are designed in part to maximize the black population in the 1st District just to the east. As a result, the 2d District has a far lower black percentage than it did in the 1980s (22% versus 40%), and is much less Democratic. While the Research Triangle counties have long voted solidly against Jesse Helms, these outer counties give him 60% of their votes.

The congressman from the 2d, elected in 1994, is David Funderburk, a Republican and a protege of Helms, a history professor by trade and former Ambassador to Romania. Funderburk grew up in small town North Carolina, studied eastern Europe at Wake Forest, learned Romanian and spent two years there studying. With Helms's help, he became Ambassador to Bucharest from 1981 to 1985. Funderburk hated the tyranny of the Ceausescu regime and fought Lawrence Eagleburger and other State Department officials who favored Ceausescu because of his anti-Soviet gestures; Funderburk's book *Pinstripes and Reds* describes this fight. Back in North Carolina, he ran in 1986 against appointed Senator James Broyhill and, despite the backing of the Jesse Helms network, lost the bitter primary 67%–30%.

In July 1993 Funderburk announced he was running against 2d District Congressman Tim Valentine, a moderate who often voted with the Clinton Administration and who won 54%–44% in 1992. His message then was an early statement of what would become the 1994 themes. "America's government has become too big and impersonal, taxing too much and spending too much and regulating people's lives too much. We have to put a stop to it. Someone has to say, 'This is crazy'." In November 1993 Valentine announced he was retiring. Funderburk won the four-candidate Republican primary with 54% of the vote. Many more voters—a vestige of history—voted in the bitter Democratic primary, which was won 47%–35% by state Representative Richard Moore. Moore is the kind of Democratic candidate who has captured southern districts for 20 years: young, handsome and charming, politically well-connected (his grandfather, Franklin Hancock Jr., was a congressman in the 1930s) and talented. He campaigned as a moderate with the support of Valentine and popular Governor Jim Hunt. Funderburk, not as smooth, hammered on issues: attacking "Moore-Clinton," linking Moore with then-Surgeon General Joycelyn Elders and anti-tobacco Health Subcommittee Chairman Henry Waxman. He attacked Moore for absenteeism and was endorsed by Moore's primary opponent, state Representative Bobby Ray Hall.

Funderburk won by a solid 56%–44% margin, carrying nearly 60% in Johnston and Harnett Counties south of Raleigh and losing only the heavily black counties around Moore's home. Two weeks later Funderburk made a triumphal trip to Romania, meeting President Ion Iliescu and worshipping at a Baptist church in Bucharest. In the House, he is a solid conservative vote. And his two chief committee assignments reflect his professional interests. But, given the shifting tides in North Carolina, he cannot take this seat for granted.

The People: Pop. 1990: 552,529; 58% rural; 13% age 65+; 77% White; 22% Black; 1% Amer. Indian; 1% Asian; 1% Hispanic origin. Voting age pop.: 420,023; 20% Black; 1% Hispanic origin. Households: 58% married couple families; 26% married couple fams. w. children; 41% college educ.; median household income: $27,271; per capita income: $13,172; median gross rent: $376; median house value: $67,000.

1992 Presidential Vote

Bush (R)	99,256	(45%)
Clinton (D)	88,141	(40%)
Perot (I)	30,669	(14%)

1988 Presidential Vote

Bush (R)	106,485	(61%)
Dukakis (D)	67,661	(39%)

Rep. David Funderburk (R)

Elected 1994; b. Apr. 28, 1944, Langley Field, VA; home, Buies Creek; Wake Forest U., B.A. 1966, M.A. 1967, U. of SC, Ph.D. 1974; Baptist; married (Betty).

Career: Assoc. Prof., Hardin-Simmons U., 1972–1978; Prof., Campbell U., 1978–81, 1985–86; U.S. Ambassador to Romania, 1981–85; Lecturer/Author, 1986–94.

DC Office: 427 CHOB 20515, 202-224-4531; Fax: 202-225-3191.

DC Office: 1207 W. Cumberland St., Dunn 28334, 910-891-1114.

Committees: *Economic & Educational Opportunities* (21st of 24 R): Postsecondary Education, Training and Life-Long Learning; Workforce Protections. *International Relations* (19th of 23 R): Africa; International Operations and Human Rights. *Small Business* (21st of 22 R): Government Programs; Procurement, Exports and Business Opportunities.

Group Ratings and 103rd Congress Votes: Newly Elected

Key Votes of the 104th Congress

1. Congressional Compliance Y	6. Reform Crime Grant Y	11. Loser Pays Court Reform Y
2. Balanced Budget Amndmt. Y	7. National Security Act Y	12. Product Liability Reform Y
3. Bar Unfunded Mandates Y	8. Moratorium on Regs. Y	13. Welfare Reform Y
4. Pass Line Item Veto Y	9. Risk Assessment on Regs. Y	14. Term Limits Amndmt. Y
5. Relax Exclusionary Rule Y	10. Expnd. Priv. Prop. Rights Y	15. Tax Cuts Y

Election Results

1994 general	David Funderburk (R)	79,207	(56%)	($725,357)
	Richard Moore (D).....................	62,122	(44%)	($918,909)
1994 primary	David Funderburk (R)	7,521	(54%)	
	Hal Sharpe (R)........................	2,453	(18%)	
	Larry Ellis Norman (R)	2,102	(15%)	
	Ted Stone (R)	1,779	(13%)	
1992 general	Tim Valentine (D).....................	113,693	(54%)	($457,958)
	Don Davis (R)........................	93,893	(44%)	($180,484)
	Other...............................	3,983	(2%)	

THIRD DISTRICT

Nearly 500 years ago, Giovanni de Verrazano sailed past the Gulf Stream and landed on a sandspit island he thought was the outer edge of China. He was wrong. It was the Outer Banks of North Carolina. These are probably America's most unstable barrier islands, constantly changing shape and cut by new inlets as they are battered by the ocean currents and storm winds. They were settled early by Europeans: Sir Walter Raleigh's Roanoke colony was founded here in 1587 then vanished shortly thereafter; Edward Teach—Blackbeard—and other pirates lurked in Pamlico and Albemarle Sounds behind the islets. History is still much with the Outer Banks: an antique form of English is spoken on Ocracoke Island, reachable only by ferry; the 208-foot lighthouse on Cape Hatteras looks out on some of the most treacherous currents in the Atlantic which have claimed a hundred ships; the sands along Kitty Hawk, with their constant winds, are where the Wright Brothers made mankind's first heavier-than-air flight in 1903.

Today, the Outer Banks have become vacation and retirement country, with affluent beachfront communities around Kitty Hawk, Nags Head and Duck and, much farther south, around Beaufort (*BOWfort*, not *BEWfort* as in South Carolina) and Morehead City. Inland, amid swamps, are some of America's biggest military bases, the Marine Corps's Camp Lejeune, the Army's Fort Bragg and Seymour Johnson Air Force Base. The flat lands of east Carolina have long been tobacco- and peanut-raising country; in recent years they have also taken to raising hogs, and Sampson County became America's number one hog county. And hogs are of course the basis of North Carolina's famous barbecue—now an export item, from an operation called Carolina Oink Express.

The 3d Congressional District of North Carolina covers the Outer Banks and much of the coastal plain. This is one of the state's irregularly shaped districts, with boundaries designed to put heavily black areas in the 1st District and leave mostly white territory in the 3d. This means that Fort Bragg and Camp Lejeune are outside the 3d, and the Seymour Johnson base is inside. It means the 3d shares the towns of Greenville, Elizabeth City, Kinston and New Bern with the 1st. It also means the 3d is not really contiguous: Wayne and Sampson Counties are connected to the rest only by a line. This made for a more Republican district than the old 3d, and a Republican gain in 1994, in a contest between two candidates of impressive local strength.

The winner was Walter Jones, Jr., who like many of his constituents is a former Democrat—a Jessecrat, as followers of Jesse Helms like to say. Jones's father was Democratic congressman from the 1st District, which included most of northeast North Carolina, from 1966 until his death in September 1992, and chairman of the Merchant Marine and Fisheries Committee for a dozen years. The younger Jones was elected in 1982 to the state legislature, where he voted to oust the Democratic speaker and often broke with Democratic leaders. In 1992, he ran as a Democrat in the new black-majority 1st District after his father retired, winning 38% in the first primary, just 2% shy of the 40% needed to avoid a runoff in North Carolina, then losing the runoff to Eva Clayton 55%–45%. In April 1993, Jones switched to the Republican Party, and in May 1994, he announced he was running for Congress in the 3d District: "My old party has changed and so has the world. Sadly, in my opinion, both are not for the best in far too many circumstances."

This pitted Jones against four-term Congressman Martin Lancaster, a Democrat who served on the senior Jones's committee and also on National Security. Lancaster grew up on a tobacco farm, was an ally of Governor Jim Hunt in the legislature and worked hard on local projects. Both men are earnest, attuned to local values, hard-working, politically knowledgeable. In 1992, issues and incumbency worked for Lancaster; though half the district was new to him, he won 54%–43%. In 1994, issues worked the other way. Lancaster voted for the Clinton budget and tax package. He argued plaintively, but with no effect on the Clintons, against only using a cigarette tax to finance the healthcare plan; he opposed the assault weapon ban but then turned around and supported the 1994 crime bill. Lancaster ran an ad showing a former top aide to Jones's father endorsing him and another saying he took on his own party and president. But Jones hit home with an ad showing Lancaster jogging with Bill Clinton ("How'd Martin Lancaster get so out of touch? Well, look who he's running around with in Washington") and a headline reading "Lancaster: Hillary, Bill Win Him Over." In a district where Jesse Helms won 59% of the vote, Jones won 53%–47%. He ran especially strong in Greenville and Kinston and carried the areas around Camp Lejeune and Morehead City. In Washington, he was rewarded with a seat on the National Security Committee, where he can look after local bases and military personnel, and he strongly supported the Contract With America. His seat on the Resources Committee, which now has jurisdiction over his father's Merchant Marine and Fisheries issues, should help him tend to the needs of Outer Banks constituents.

The People: Pop. 1990: 551,918; 62% rural; 12% age 65+; 76% White; 22% Black; 1% Amer. Indian; 1% Asian; 1% Other; 1% Hispanic origin. Voting age pop.: 412,775; 20% Black; 1% Hispanic origin. Households: 61% married couple families; 28% married couple fams. w. children; 40% college educ.; median household income: $24,553; per capita income: $11,567; median gross rent: $359; median house value: $62,600.

1992 Presidential Vote

Bush (R) 89,877 (47%)
Clinton (D) 74,702 (39%)
Perot (I)................... 28,195 (15%)

1988 Presidential Vote

Bush (R) 98,397 (61%)
Dukakis (D)................. 62,412 (39%)

Rep. Walter B. Jones, Jr. (R)

Elected 1994; b. Feb. 10, 1943, Farmville; home, Farmville; NC St. U., 1962–65, Atlantic Christian College, B.A. 1967; Catholic; married (Joe Anne).

Career: Mgr., Walter B. Jones Office Supply Co., 1967–73; Salesman, Dunn Assoc., 1973–82; NC House of Reps., 1982–92; Pres., Benefit Reserves Inc., 1989–94; Pres., Judson Co., 1990–94.

DC Office: 214 CHOB 20515, 202-225-3415; Fax: 202-225-3286.

District Offices: 102-C Eastbrook Dr., Greenville 27858, 919-931-1003.

Committees: *National Security* (27th of 30 R): Military Installations and Facilities; Military Research and Development. *Resources* (20th of 25 R): Fisheries, Wildlife and Oceans; Native American and Insular Affairs. *Small Business* (14th of 22 R): Regulation and Paperwork; Tax and Finance.

Group Ratings and 103rd Congress Votes: Newly Elected

Key Votes of the 104th Congress

1. Congressional Compliance Y	6. Reform Crime Grant Y	11. Loser Pays Court Reform Y
2. Balanced Budget Amndmt. Y	7. National Security Act Y	12. Product Liability Reform Y
3. Bar Unfunded Mandates Y	8. Moratorium on Regs. Y	13. Welfare Reform Y
4. Pass Line Item Veto Y	9. Risk Assessment on Regs. Y	14. Term Limits Amndmt. Y
5. Relax Exclusionary Rule Y	10. Expnd. Priv. Prop. Rights Y	15. Tax Cuts Y

Election Results

1994 general	Walter B. Jones Jr. (R) 72,464	(53%)	($477,463)
	H. Martin Lancaster (D) 65,013	(47%)	($941,901)
1994 primary	Walter B. Jones Jr. (R) .... unopposed		
1992 general	H. Martin Lancaster (D) 101,739	(54%)	($548,584)
	Tommy Pollard (R).................... 80,759	(43%)	($236,233)
	Other................................ 4,552	(2%)	

FOURTH DISTRICT

Back in the 1950s, few people would have predicted that the countryside around Raleigh and Durham, North Carolina, would be one of America's high-tech boom areas. But Governor Luther Hodges did, when he started Research Triangle Park as an R&D industrial park between the musty state capital of Raleigh, the Lucky Strike-manufacturing city of Durham and the tiny university town of Chapel Hill. With the drawing power of three universities (North Carolina State in Raleigh, Duke in Durham and the University of North Carolina in Chapel Hill), Research Triangle Park slowly began attracting big research outfits like Burroughs-Wellcome, Glaxo, IBM, Northern Telecom and the Environmental Protection Agency; today it has more than 34,000 people working for more than 65 major companies, stimulating hundreds of small startups and service businesses. Raleigh-Durham airport, which had four gates in the early 1970s, became a major national hub. Its metro area grew by more than 30% in the 1980s, the fastest metropolitan growth north and east of Atlanta, and for years has had one of the lowest unemployment rates in the nation.

The 4th Congressional District of North Carolina includes most of this area—it has grown too big for one district—though not the park itself. It includes Raleigh and all but one Wake County precinct and most of Chapel Hill and surrounding Orange County. Durham County is outside the district, but the 4th includes still largely rural Chatham County to the west. Politics here revolves around cultural issues; economic issues play little role in this booming environment where both tradition-minded and liberal-minded cultural views are vividly articulated by Jesse Helms and by university liberals and progressives like Jim Hunt. The two Democratic bases here are blacks and whites with post-graduate degrees. The big Republican base is whites with traditional religious beliefs. For much of the last decade, the balance has gone the Democrats' way. Jesse Helms, a winner statewide, repelled young and highly educated voters and the 4th District gave large margins to Jim Hunt and Harvey Gantt. In 1992, Bill Clinton beat George Bush here 47%–39%, possibly his best showing in any majority white southern metro area. But in the mid-1990s the pendulum has swung the other way. Helms became less visible and Bill Clinton more so, and young family voters evidently became dismayed with what they regarded as the excesses of liberalism. Tom Fetzer, a longtime Helms supporter, was elected mayor of Raleigh in 1993 campaigning on an anti-crime platform and even winning some black votes. And in November there was a major upset in the race for the House.

The winner was Fred Heineman, a Republican with roots in New York City. He was a New York cop, with a master's degree from John Jay College of Law, who was hired as Raleigh's police chief in the late 1970s and retired in February 1994 after 15 years. He immediately ran for Congress and in a light-turnout Republican primary beat a local investment banker 51%–49%. Heineman was nevertheless very much the underdog against incumbent Congressman David Price. Price is an interesting blend of political scientist and practical politician, and a lay Baptist preacher as well. As state Democratic chairman and an ally of Governor Jim Hunt, Price helped develop North Carolina's robust straight-ticket two-party politics, holding Democrats together in support of progressive policies and winning more victories than he lost over the years. He made a rather liberal record on issues and generally supported the Democratic leadership. He served on Appropriations, and got money for local projects. A professor of political science at Duke, he has written thoughtfully on his service in Congress. As a political scientist and as party chairman, he believed in party responsibility, and that was evidently his downfall in 1994. He carried Orange County 2–1 and led in Chatham as well. But in Wake County, which casts 83% of the district's votes, he lost 55%–45%, for a 1,215–vote loss overall. This was one of the big election-night surprises of 1994, a 20% drop for Price from 1992.

Heineman, like so many Republican freshmen, does not seek a lifetime career as so many young Democrats have. He entered the House at the age of 65, as the capstone of a long public career, and seems content to vote his conservative principles for a term or two and take the risk of defeat, as Price did, or just retire. With its strong Democratic base and many Democratic activists, the 4th is likely to produce a strong opponent for him in 1996, and Price may very well run again; indeed, he first won the seat in 1986 against a Republican elected in the Reagan landslide year of 1984. Heineman has a seat on the Judiciary Committee, and with his long career in law enforcement (he is the only first-term sheriff in the 104th Congress, his office likes to point out) he may be active in debate on crime legislation.

The People: Pop. 1990: 552,441; 31% rural; 8% age 65+; 77% White; 20% Black; 2% Asian; 1% Hispanic origin. Voting age pop.: 429,326; 19% Black; 1% Hispanic origin. Households: 54% married couple families; 26% married couple fams. w. children; 62% college educ.; median household income: $34,569; per capita income: $16,708; median gross rent: $477; median house value: $95,500.

1992 Presidential Vote		
Clinton (D)	126,577	(47%)
Bush (R)	105,612	(39%)
Perot (I)	38,878	(14%)

1988 Presidential Vote		
Bush (R)	102,372	(53%)
Dukakis (D)	90,808	(47%)

Rep. Fred Heineman (R)

Elected 1994; b. Dec. 28, 1929, New York, NY; home, Raleigh; St. Francis Col., B.B.A. 1970; John Jay Col., M.A. 1975; Lutheran; married (Linda).

Career: Marine Corps., 1951–54; NYC Police Dept., 1955–79; Raleigh Police Chief 1979–94.

DC Office: 1440 LHOB 20515, 202-225-1784; Fax: 202-225-3269.

District Offices: 16 E. Rowan St., Raleigh 27609, 919-856-4611.

Committees: *Banking & Financial Services* (23rd of 27 R): General Oversight and Investigations; Housing and Community Opportunity. *Judiciary* (16th of 20 R): Crime; Immigration and Claims.

Group Ratings and 103rd Congress Votes: Newly Elected

Key Votes of the 104th Congress

1. Congressional Compliance Y	6. Reform Crime Grant Y	11. Loser Pays Court Reform Y
2. Balanced Budget Amndmt. Y	7. National Security Act Y	12. Product Liability Reform Y
3. Bar Unfunded Mandates Y	8. Moratorium on Regs. Y	13. Welfare Reform Y
4. Pass Line Item Veto Y	9. Risk Assessment on Regs. Y	14. Term Limits Amndmt. Y
5. Relax Exclusionary Rule Y	10. Expnd. Priv. Prop. Rights Y	15. Tax Cuts Y

Election Results

1994 general	Fred Heineman (R)...................	77,773	(50%)	($264,869)
	David E. Price (D)....................	76,558	(50%)	($675,680)
1994 primary	Fred Heineman (R).....................	6,807	(51%)	
	Rob Romaine (R)......................	6,564	(49%)	
1992 general	David E. Price (D)	171,299	(65%)	($444,259)
	Lavinia (Vicky) Goudie (R)	89,345	(34%)	($12,270)
	Other................................	4,416	(2%)	

FIFTH DISTRICT

From the coastal plain of North Carolina, the terrain rises slowly through modest hills cut by rivers in the Piedmont, until finally the first mountain ridges appear, their mysterious blue haze filling the crevasse valleys or clinging to the steep hillsides. The Piedmont, in between the plain and the mountains, was first settled by independent-minded Scots-Irish farmers and by followers of British and German sects like the Moravians. This was hardscrabble farm country at the time of the Civil War, with few slaves. By the late 19th Century, it was becoming industrialized, with textile mills alongside streams, furniture factories not far from hardwood forests and the R. J. Reynolds cigarette factories in Winston-Salem (the only city to be honored by the name of two cigarette brands). This Piedmont economy was hailed as the basis of a progressive New South, although textile mills paid low wages and tobacco employed few workers. In fact, only in the last two decades has the North Carolina economy taken off and grown substantially more affluent. Today this area has the country's most advanced tire recycling plant in Winston-Salem, a custom furniture making operation in Kernersville, the Hanes family's Moravian cookie business in Clemmons.

All these are within or just outside the new boundaries of the 5th Congressional District of North Carolina, which sweeps along the northern edge of the state from the coastal plain to the main Appalachian chain, stopping along the way to include a little more than half of the Winston-Salem area. However, that metro area casts only 30% of the district's votes; the rest are sprinkled across the countryside and in small industrial cities like Reidsville, Eden and Mt. Airy (the setting for the Andy Griffith Show's fictional town of Mayberry). With jagged lines drawn to maximize its Democratic vote, except for black precincts assigned to the black-majority 12th District, the 5th also takes in some mountain country around Boone and Morganton.

An earlier 5th District was represented for 42 years by Robert "Muley" Doughton, a stubborn man who chaired the Ways and Means Committee for 18 years during much of the New Deal and refused to set foot on the Senate side of the Capitol. More recently, the 5th was represented for 20 years by Stephen Neal, a grandnephew of R. J. Reynolds and a high-ranking Democrat on the Banking Committee, first elected in 1974 and reelected, usually by narrow margins in this Republican-leaning district, until he retired in 1994. Now the congressman is Richard Burr, onetime Wake Forest football player who ran against Neal in 1992 and lost 53%–46%, and came back to run again in 1994. Burr's good showing in 1992 came even though he was outspent 3–1. He was unopposed in the Republican primary. The Democratic nominee, winning a six-candidate primary with 43%, was state Senator Sandy Sands, a rural trial lawyer whose district took in about half of the 5th. Sands talked of "frustration with Washington taking action without concern for the impact on local government" and attacked Burr for using Jerry Falwell's Liberty University studios to produce his ads for the 1992 campaign. Sands gained national publicity when he called on North Carolina to tax citrus crops in retaliation for Florida's cigarette tax. Burr headed North Carolina Taxpayers United and supported the Contract With America, and promised to make defense of tobacco his number one issue. He worked hard to tie Sands to the Clinton Administration.

In November, Burr's national issues prevailed over Sands's local connections. Burr won a solid 57%, carrying all but two counties and carrying the Winston-Salem area by nearly 2–1. He was assigned to his first choice committee, Commerce, where he is well-placed to work for the interests of tobacco even though the change in party control means that the major congressional threats to the industry have been muffled.

The People: Pop. 1990: 552,337; 60% rural; 14% age 65+; 84% White; 15% Black; 1% Hispanic origin. Voting age pop.: 428,296; 14% Black; 1% Hispanic origin. Households: 58% married couple families; 25% married couple fams. w. children; 36% college educ.; median household income: $25,543; per capita income: $12,716; median gross rent: $348; median house value: $59,000.

1992 Presidential Vote

Bush (R)	99,408	(43%)
Clinton (D)	98,056	(43%)
Perot (I)	30,631	(13%)

1988 Presidential Vote

Bush (R)	112,259	(58%)
Dukakis (D)	82,564	(42%)

Rep. Richard M. Burr (R)

Elected 1994; b. Nov. 30, 1955, Charlottesville, VA; home, Winston-Salem; Wake Forest U., B.A. 1978; Presbyterian; married (Brooke).

Career: Natl. Sales Mgr., Carswell Distributing, 1978–95.

DC Office: 1431 LHOB 20515, 202-225-2071; Fax: 202-225-2995.

District Offices: 2000 W. 1st St., #508, Winston-Salem 27104, 910-631-5125.

Committees: *Commerce* (19th of 26 R): Energy and Power; Health and Environment; Oversight and Investigations.

Group Ratings and 103rd Congress Votes: Newly Elected

Key Votes of the 104th Congress

1. Congressional Compliance	Y	6. Reform Crime Grant	Y	11. Loser Pays Court Reform	Y
2. Balanced Budget Amndmt.	Y	7. National Security Act	Y	12. Product Liability Reform	Y
3. Bar Unfunded Mandates	Y	8. Moratorium on Regs.	Y	13. Welfare Reform	Y
4. Pass Line Item Veto	Y	9. Risk Assessment on Regs.	Y	14. Term Limits Amndmt.	Y
5. Relax Exclusionary Rule	Y	10. Expnd. Priv. Prop. Rights	Y	15. Tax Cuts	Y

Election Results

1994 general	Richard M. Burr (R)	84,741	(57%)	($741,986)
	A. P. (Sandy) Sands (D)	63,194	(43%)	($759,742)
1994 primary	Richard M. Burr (R)	unopposed		
1992 general	Stephen L. Neal (D).................	117,835	(53%)	($517,594)
	Richard M. Burr (R)	102,086	(46%)	($188,130)
	Others	3,762	(2%)	

SIXTH DISTRICT

For more than half a century furniture store managers and owners from all over the country twice a year have converged on the huge Furniture Mart in High Point, the center of the U.S. furniture business, for the giant trade show put on by manufacturers. High Point sits amidst rolling farmland originally settled by Quakers, the site of the Battle of Guilford Courthouse in the Revolutionary War, then slaveholding country in the years before the Civil War. The furniture business grew here early in the 20th Century because of the proximity of hardwoods in the mountains not far west and the abundance of low-wage labor in the flatlands not far east. Soon it was said of High Point that there were so many factories, "only a wise man knows his own factory whistle." Today, employment in furniture continues to grow, unlike employment in North Carolina's other basic industries of textiles and tobacco, and wages have risen. Race relations are now outwardly pleasant in the city where in 1960 black students at North Carolina A&T started the first lunch counter sit-in at a local Greensboro five-and-dime.

The 6th Congressional District of North Carolina in its 1990s bounds is a relatively regularly shaped seat—except that the threadlike 12th District slices it in half in order to pick up black-majority precincts from Durham to Charlotte. The 6th includes most of Guilford County with High Point and Greensboro, furniture-manufacturing Davidson County to the west, textile-producing Alamance County to the east and Quaker-settled Randolph County to the south. This area has enjoyed solid economic growth, but many here still feel dependent on textiles which, as the classic cheap-labor industry, are always vulnerable to competition from abroad.

The congressman from the 6th District is Howard Coble, a lawyer and Coast Guard veteran who served seven years in the legislature and four as commissioner of the state department of revenue. He is a friendly and affable man who asks visitors if they mind if he smokes. Coble was first elected to the House in 1984, the third time the 6th District had ousted an incumbent in three contests, and he was reelected in 1986 by just 79 votes; but his own popularity plus the 1991 redistricting have made it a safe seat for him. He is solidly conservative, with interesting twists. He is tightfisted, calling for limits on Secret Service protection for former presidents and for reforming congressional pensions; he says he won't take his. He is proud he didn't have a single overdraft on the House bank; "I'll wear a suit two years too long. I'll drive a car 10 years too long. I'm also very fastidious when it comes to maintaining my check balance." Like many of his constituents, he is leery of free trade. He opposed fast-track for NAFTA, but finally voted for it in 1993 (without visiting the White House or selling his vote, he said); but he opposed GATT. He also opposes expansion of the Federal Prison Industries program, which has federal prisoners producing 20% of federal government furniture. He opposes a tobacco tax, naturally, and called for the resignation of Joycelyn Elders because she had taken stands "outside the mainstream of American thought."

Coble was reelected without opposition in 1994; he is for term limits, but reluctantly. He lost his seat on Merchant Marine when the committee was abolished, but got a place on Transportation and Infrastructure. He was named chairman of the Coast Guard subcommittee, which will allow him to address issues where he has personal expertise but won't provide much opportunity to tend to the local concerns of this inland district.

The People: Pop. 1990: 552,663; 53% rural; 12% age 65+; 91% White; 7% Black; 1% Asian; 1% Hispanic origin. Voting age pop.: 427,871; 7% Black; 1% Hispanic origin. Households: 62% married couple families; 27% married couple fams. w. children; 42% college educ.; median household income: $30,628; per capita income: $14,942; median gross rent: $403; median house value: $72,900.

1992 Presidential Vote			1988 Presidential Vote		
Bush (R)	119,874	(51%)	Bush (R)	133,247	(70%)
Clinton (D)	75,651	(32%)	Dukakis (D)	56,511	(30%)
Perot (I)	38,180	(16%)			

Rep. Howard Coble (R)

Elected 1984; b. Mar. 18, 1931, Greensboro; home, Greensboro; Appalachian St. U., 1949–50; Guilford Col., A.B. 1958, U. of NC, J.D. 1962; Presbyterian; single.

Career: Coast Guard, 1952–56, 1977–78, Coast Guard Reserves, 1960–82; NC House of Reps., 1969, 1978–84; Asst. U.S. Atty., NC Middle Dist., 1969–73; Commissioner, NC Dept. of Revenue, 1973–77; Practicing atty., 1979–83.

DC Office: 403 CHOB 20515, 202-225-3065; Fax: 202-225-8611.

District Offices: 324 W. Market St., Greensboro 27401, 919-333-5005; P.O. Box 1813, 1404 Piedmont Dr., Lexington 27293, 704-246-8230; P.O. Box 814, 124 W. Elm St., Graham 27253, 919-228-0159; 241 Sunset Ave., #101, Asheboro 27203, 919-626-3060; and 1912 Eastchester Dr., High Point 27265, 919-886-5106.

Committees: *Judiciary* (6th of 20 R): Courts and Intellectual Property; Crime. *Transportation & Infrastructure* (8th of 33 R): Aviation; Coast Guard and Maritime Transportation (Chmn.).

Group Ratings

	ADA	ACLU	COPE	CFA	LCV	CON	NSI	COC	ACU	NTLC	CHC
1994	5	17	22	0	17	88	60	83	95	96	100
1993	5	—	0	0	29	98	—	91	96	—	—

National Journal Ratings

	1993 LIB — 1993 CONS	1994 LIB — 1994 CONS
Economic	0% — 88%	0% — 80%
Social	0% — 89%	0% — 89%
Foreign	33% — 65%	12% — 87%

Key Votes of the 103d Congress

1. Clinton Deficit Plan	N	3. Brady Handgun Purchase N	5. Lmt. UN Cmnd. of Forces Y
2. NAFTA	Y	4. Strike Race/Death Pnlty. Y	6. Cut Missile Funds Y

Key Votes of the 104th Congress

1. Congressional Compliance Y	6. Reform Crime Grant Y	11. Loser Pays Court Reform Y
2. Balanced Budget Amndmt. Y	7. National Security Act Y	12. Product Liability Reform N
3. Bar Unfunded Mandates Y	8. Moratorium on Regs. Y	13. Welfare Reform Y
4. Pass Line Item Veto Y	9. Risk Assessment on Regs. Y	14. Term Limits Amndmt. Y
5. Relax Exclusionary Rule Y	10. Expnd. Priv. Prop. Rights Y	15. Tax Cuts Y

Election Results

1994 general	Howard Coble (R)	unopposed		($350,981)
1994 primary	Howard Coble (R)	unopposed		
1992 general	Howard Coble (R)	162,822	(71%)	($435,093)
	Robin Hood (D)	67,200	(29%)	($27,822)

SEVENTH DISTRICT

Southernmost North Carolina, where the state boundary dips down along the Atlantic coast, is tobacco country, economically dependent on this crop for more than 200 years. Tobacco can be cultivated profitably in only a few places in the world; it is labor intensive, requiring close tending and serial picking (one leaf on a stalk matures before the one above it); and it is valuable enough that North Carolina farmers today, if they have one of the tobacco allotments handed out in the 1930s or have bought the rights to one, can make a living off 40 acres. Tobacco produces more voters per federally assisted acre than any other crop. This tobacco country, it should be added, is racially diverse, the home of many blacks as well as the Lumbee Indians, whose origins have been lost in antiquity, but who were treated by state segregation laws—and still are treated by continuing custom—as a race distinct from whites and blacks; each race makes up about one-third of the population of Robeson County around Lumberton.

Southernmost North Carolina is also military country. The port city of Wilmington is home of the World War II battleship U.S.S. *North Carolina*, which runs a 70-minute show on its history every night during the summer. Eastward, in swampland, is Camp Lejeune, home base of one-fifth of the Marine Corps. Inland, near Fayetteville, is the huge complex of Fort Bragg and Pope Air Force Base, whence 39,000 troops left for the Persian Gulf in 1990. As the site of one of the biggest bases in the country, Fayetteville has developed the strip highway to an art form, with strip joints, fast food galore and the world's first Putt-Putt golf course.

North Carolina's 7th Congressional District covers much of this territory, from Camp Lejeune to Wilmington to Fayetteville; many black areas are cordoned off in the black-majority 1st District, but the 7th still includes some 100,000 blacks and almost all of Robeson County's Lumbees. This is an ancestrally Democratic area, and its boundaries were carefully sculpted to protect Democratic Congressman Charlie Rose, whose seat the Republicans had hoped to obliterate. Rose was hurt by the removal of many blacks, but redistricters avoided expanding the 7th to Republican coastal areas by including the big military bases, which swell its population but don't contain many voters.

Charlie Rose is a politically adept veteran who became a prosecutor in 1967, at 28, ran for the House in 1970 and nearly beat the incumbent in the primary, then ran again two years later and held the seat easily for 20 years. From the beginning he aimed at being a power in the House. From his seat on the House Administration Committee, he directed the design of the House's computer systems, telephone system upgrades and the House television system installation. (He is an avid video-taker and electronic gadget lover himself.) After the Democratic Caucus in December 1990 voted out House Administration Chairman Frank Annunzio by 127–125, Rose ran and won the chair 158–64 over the more senior Joseph Gaydos. There Rose passed the motor-voter bill, supported the opening of Kennedy assassination documents and urged reform of the Capitol Police. He replaced the contractor at the House restaurants, to whom members owed $250,000, and superintended the investigation of the House Post Office on charges of embezzlement and drug dealing among its employees and mysterious massive stamp sales to certain members. He worked for campaign finance reform. Rose became a vitriolic critic of both Speaker Thomas Foley and his wife and unpaid assistant Heather Foley, sending out rumors that Foley would be appointed Ambassador to Britain. And Rose made it clear he was running for speaker himself, a precarious mission when the incumbent remains healthy and in office. But Rose was also having other problems. He gave control of one House restaurant to an old friend from Fayetteville; workers eventually went out on strike over benefits coverage. He refused to give the new House administrator functions that the House had voted him. He tried to avoid the imposition of mandated staff cuts for House members' offices.

This came on top of Rose's long work on the Agriculture Committee, where he rose to chair the Tobacco and Peanuts Subcommittee by 1990, and helped preserve the tobacco allotment system by convincing the Democratic leadership that changes in tobacco supports could defeat every member of the cohesive and leadership-supporting North Carolina Democratic delegation. He also investigated the alleged misuse of agricultural loans by Saddam Hussein's regime to pay for arms. And he promises to continue working for Tibetan independence (he has known the Dalai Lama for years). Locally, he has vowed to work to get federal recognition of the Lumbees.

1994 turned out to be an *annus horribilis* for Rose. He has had ethics problems for some time. In 1986 he was accused of diverting $64,000 of campaign funds for personal use over seven years; the House Ethics Committee in March 1988 said he violated the law, rebuked him, but recommended no discipline because of mitigating circumstances. In May 1989, the Justice Department filed a civil suit charging him with failing to report over $138,000 in personal loans from his campaign on disclosure forms; in April 1992 a federal judge upheld $30,000 in fines and rejected the claim by Rose and Speaker Foley that Congress was immune; Rose settled the suit in October 1994 for $12,500. But by then he was in terrible trouble at home. Rose was one of the top Clinton supporters in the House, even though of course he opposed solely taxing cigarettes to finance the healthcare package, and like other southern Democrats wanted a tax on alcohol as well. Robert Anderson, a retired Air Force lieutenant colonel, ran against him in 1990 and lost 66%–34%. But Rose's margin in the new district was reduced to 57%–41% in 1992. And in 1994 Rose's vote fell disastrously. Anderson ran 60% or better around Camp Lejeune and Wilmington and carried the Fayetteville area as well. Rose won 52%–48% only because of a 69%–31% margin in Robeson County, and Anderson filed suit to challenge the results there; House Republicans were only too glad to launch their own investigation of the outcome.

Rose nonetheless carried on his futile battle against the Democratic leadership. With Foley defeated, he ran for Minority Leader against Dick Gephardt and claimed he had 110 votes. Gephardt won 150–58, then denied Rose the ranking Democratic slot on the House Oversight Committee (a stripped-down version of Rose's old House Administration Committee) and replaced him with leadership loyalist Vic Fazio. Stripped of his power internally, in electoral trouble at home, with little or no leverage left on Agriculture because he was no longer in the majority and with only four Democrats left in the North Carolina delegation whose redistricting map he had helped to draw, Rose seems to be a man whose career is on the brink. Will his political skills enable him to rebound?

The People: Pop. 1990: 552,037; 41% rural; 9% age 65+; 70% White; 19% Black; 7% Amer. Indian; 1% Asian; 1% Other; 3% Hispanic origin. Voting age pop.: 414,739; 17% Black; 3% Hispanic origin. Households: 61% married couple families; 31% married couple fams. w. children; 43% college educ.; median household income: $24,708; per capita income: $11,663; median gross rent: $391; median house value: $63,600.

1992 Presidential Vote		1988 Presidential Vote	
Clinton (D)	71,334 (43%)	Bush (R)	74,456 (56%)
Bush (R)	70,159 (43%)	Dukakis (D)	57,660 (44%)
Perot (I)	22,194 (14%)		

Rep. Charlie Rose (D)

Elected 1972; b. Aug. 10, 1939, Fayetteville; home, Fayetteville; Davidson Col., A.B. 1961, U. of NC, LL.B. 1964; Presbyterian; married (Stacye Hefner).

Career: Practicing atty., 1964–72; Chief 12th Dist. Court Prosecutor, 1967–70.

DC Office: 242 CHOB 20515, 202-225-2731; Fax: 202-225-0345; e-mail: crose@hr.house.gov.

District Offices: 208 P.O. Bldg., Wilmington 28401, 919-343-4959; and 218 Fed. Bldg., Fayetteville 28301, 919-323-0260.

Committees: *Agriculture* (3rd of 22 D): General Farm Commodities; Risk Management and Specialty Crops (RMM).

Group Ratings

	ADA	ACLU	COPE	CFA	LCV	CON	NSI	COC	ACU	NTLC	CHC
1994	75	59	100	90	65	26	56	50	14	14	21
1993	70	—	92	90	69	1	—	40	8	—	—

National Journal Ratings

	1993 LIB — 1993 CONS		1994 LIB — 1994 CONS	
Economic	68%	— 26%	73%	— 17%
Social	68%	— 32%	62%	— 37%
Foreign	63%	— 37%	67%	— 33%

Key Votes of the 103d Congress

1. Clinton Deficit Plan	Y	3. Brady Handgun Purchase	Y	5. Lmt. UN Cmnd. of Forces	N
2. NAFTA	Y	4. Strike Race/Death Pnlty.	N	6. Cut Missile Funds	N

Key Votes of the 104th Congress

1. Congressional Compliance	Y	6. Reform Crime Grant	N	11. Loser Pays Court Reform	N
2. Balanced Budget Amndmt.	Y	7. National Security Act	N	12. Product Liability Reform	N
3. Bar Unfunded Mandates	Y	8. Moratorium on Regs.	Y	13. Welfare Reform	Y
4. Pass Line Item Veto	Y	9. Risk Assessment on Regs.	Y	14. Term Limits Amndmt.	Y
5. Relax Exclusionary Rule	N	10. Expnd. Priv. Prop. Rights	Y	15. Tax Cuts	Y

Election Results

1994 general	Charlie Rose (D)...................	62,670	(52%)	($823,282)
	Robert C. Anderson (R)...............	58,849	(48%)	($91,027)
1994 primary	Charlie Rose (D).................	unopposed		
1992 general	Charlie Rose (D)...................	92,414	(57%)	($254,579)
	Robert C. Anderson (R)...............	66,536	(41%)	($17,374)
	Other...............................	4,151	(3%)	

EIGHTH DISTRICT

From Atlanta to Durham in the Carolina Piedmont, along Interstate 85, is the thickest concentration of America's textile industry—the mills are so thick you can almost see the lint. Within North Carolina, I-85 passes through the nation's leading textile-producing area, past Salisbury, Concord and Kannapolis—named for its founding company, Cannon Mills. East Carolina was settled by Englishmen from the coast. This Piedmont land was settled primarily by Scots and diverse groups like Quakers and Moravian sects, coming down the Blue Ridge from Pennsylvania through Virginia. These migratory patterns were reflected in Civil War divisions and continue in current voting habits. The coastal counties all the way up through the Sand Hills were Confederate and are now Democratic. The textile mill towns along I-85 were anti-secession and are now Republican.

The 8th Congressional District of North Carolina, as redistricted, combines the area around Kannapolis with Sand Hill counties extending east almost to Fayetteville. Nearly two-thirds of the people are in the textile areas, including some urban overflow from Charlotte. Except on the very west, the 8th is not bordered by one of North Carolina's two black-majority districts, and Democratic legislators were careful to maximize the number of blacks here. The intended beneficiary, Bill Hefner, is an adept Democratic politico who has operated shrewdly in the Democratic Caucus in Washington since 1974, and also kept happy the folks back home.

When Hefner first ran in the Watergate year of 1974, voters here were hungry for reform but not liberalism. Hefner, who once sang in a gospel group called Harvesters Quartet and owned a radio station in Kannapolis, promised to "help restore Christian morality in the federal government" and to protect "human-oriented programs." In the House, Hefner continued to press for school prayer and for what he considered human-oriented programs. With other North Carolina Democrats, he stuck with the House Democratic leadership on the Reagan budget and tax votes in 1981 and on other tough partisan issues. In return, North Carolina got leadership support on textiles and tobacco. Hefner also got a seat on Appropriations, which he unabashedly used to help the district. In 1982, after only eight years in the House, he became chairman of the Appropriations Military Construction Subcommittee and claims credit for funneling an average of $152 million a year into North Carolina between 1987 and 1995. Hefner is proud of his work for the Carolinas Medical Center, Fort Bragg, the Uwharrie National Forest and four different airport projects. Hefner has been less successful in his own leadership aspirations: in 1986 he ran a distant third for whip. But he has continued to support the Democratic leadership, while calling vaguely for "meaningful" welfare reform and "a moderate, bipartisan approach" to healthcare reform.

Hefner has always had serious opposition. With the large Republican vote in the textile counties, he has topped 60% of the vote only once, in 1976, and came close to losing in 1984 and 1988. In 1994, he was opposed by Sherrill Morgan, a Stanly County Honda dealer, who said, "Morality has decayed and we are quickly becoming a country far unlike that envisaged by our founding fathers." But Morgan's charges that Hefner's Uwharrie Forest and Stanly County Airport projects were meant to enhance the value of his own land fell flat, as local mayors of both parties and editorialists endorsed the hard-working Hefner.

Hefner won narrowly, 52%–48%. He lost the textile counties 53%–47% and carried the Sand

Hills by 61%–39%, though he did carry Morgan's home county of Stanly. He is no longer subcommittee chairman and cannot as plausibly claim to bring home the bacon, though Republicans are likely not to cut military construction as fiercely as most domestic programs. Whether Hefner will relish another tough contest in 1996, when he turns 66, is unclear.

The People: Pop. 1990: 552,039; 55% rural; 12% age 65+; 72% White; 23% Black; 3% Amer. Indian; 1% Asian; 1% Other; 1% Hispanic origin. Voting age pop.: 403,584; 21% Black; 1% Hispanic origin. Households: 61% married couple families; 29% married couple fams. w. children; 34% college educ.; median household income: $26,180; per capita income: $11,462; median gross rent: $359; median house value: $56,700.

1992 Presidential Vote			1988 Presidential Vote		
Bush (R)	86,493	(44%)	Bush (R)	93,130	(58%)
Clinton (D)	81,736	(42%)	Dukakis (D)	66,494	(42%)
Perot (I)	27,296	(14%)			

Rep. W. G. (Bill) Hefner (D)

Elected 1974; b. Apr. 11, 1930, Elora, TN; home, Concord; Baptist; married (Nancy).

Career: Entertainer, radio business, 1954–74.

DC Office: 2470 RHOB 20515, 202-225-3715; Fax: 202-225-4036.

District Offices: P.O. Box 385, 101 Union St. S., Concord 28025, 704-786-1612; P.O. Box 4220, 507 W. Innes St., #225, Salisbury 28144, 704-636-0635; and P.O. Box 1503, 230 E. Franklin St., Rockingham 28379, 910-997-2070.

Committees: *Appropriations* (11th of 24 D): Military Construction (RMM); National Security.

Group Ratings

	ADA	ACLU	COPE	CFA	LCV	CON	NSI	COC	ACU	NTLC	CHC
1994	65	52	89	60	67	27	60	45	19	19	43
1993	65	—	92	90	79	19	—	27	13	—	—

National Journal Ratings

	1993 LIB — 1993 CONS		1994 LIB — 1994 CONS	
Economic	66% —	33%	67% —	29%
Social	59% —	40%	59% —	41%
Foreign	51% —	42%	64% —	33%

Key Votes of the 103d Congress

1. Clinton Deficit Plan	Y	3. Brady Handgun Purchase	Y	5. Lmt. UN Cmnd. of Forces	N
2. NAFTA	Y	4. Strike Race/Death Pnlty.	N	6. Cut Missile Funds	N

Key Votes of the 104th Congress

1. Congressional Compliance	Y	6. Reform Crime Grant	N	11. Loser Pays Court Reform	N
2. Balanced Budget Amndmt.	Y	7. National Security Act	N	12. Product Liability Reform	Y
3. Bar Unfunded Mandates	Y	8. Moratorium on Regs.	Y	13. Welfare Reform	N
4. Pass Line Item Veto	N	9. Risk Assessment on Regs.	Y	14. Term Limits Amndmt.	N
5. Relax Exclusionary Rule	N	10. Expnd. Priv. Prop. Rights	Y	15. Tax Cuts	N

Election Results

1994 general	W. G. (Bill) Hefner (D)	62,845	(52%)	($669,622)
	Sherrill Morgan (R)	57,140	(48%)	($320,520)
1994 primary	W. G. (Bill) Hefner (D)	39,828	(65%)	
	Don Dawkins (D)	21,275	(35%)	
1992 general	W. G. (Bill) Hefner (D)	113,162	(58%)	($594,617)
	Coy C. Privette (R)	71,842	(37%)	($108,332)
	J. Wendell Drye (L)	10,447	(5%)	

NINTH DISTRICT

"An agreeable village but in a damn rebellious country," recorded General Cornwallis when, before the unpleasantness at Yorktown, he visited Charlotte, North Carolina. "A veritable nest of hornets." This town, settled by Scots-Irish who came down the Blue Ridge from Pennsylvania, is now the biggest metro area between Washington and Atlanta, with 1.2 million people. It has grown as a banking and distribution center for much of the Piedmont South, as the center of the nation's biggest textile manufacturing region and as an airline hub for USAir. It has become home to the NBA Hornets and NFL Panthers. The 60-story tower of NationsBank, the nation's fourth largest bank, sits next to a $50 million performing arts center. "Charlotte is always on the verge ... ," writes *The Washington Post*'s Henry Allen—the verge of not looking over its shoulder at Atlanta any more. The rebelliousness Cornwallis noted can still be seen in this home of one of the nation's biggest stock car race tracks. But Charlotte has also built a boosterish pride in its capacity for accommodation. It is proud that it responded amicably to a busing order approved in a landmark Supreme Court case in 1971; that it uncovered the shenanigans of its nearby South Carolina neighbors Jim and Tammy Fae Bakker; that it elected Harvey Gantt, who is black, mayor several times and then replaced him with Sue Myrick, a Republican woman whose grievance wasn't race but traffic.

The 9th Congressional District of North Carolina includes most of Charlotte and Mecklen-burg Counties—black precincts are in the black-majority 12th District—and extends west to include most of Gaston and Cleveland Counties, with their many textile mills. If the 9th included whole counties, it would be politically marginal and in fact, with different boundaries, came close to electing a Democrat in 1984 and 1986. But with few blacks, the 9th is heavily Republican.

The congresswoman from the 9th District is former Charlotte Mayor Sue Myrick, a Republican elected in 1994 after an up-and-down political career. The seat came open in late 1993 when incumbent Alex McMillan, whom Republicans had passed over for the ranking position on the Budget Committee in favor of John Kasich, announced his retirement. A serious deficit-fighter who backed the Brady bill and legal abortion, McMillan attacked Congress's "apparent inability or unwillingness to focus on the substance of tough issues" and his own party's "anti-everything" attitude. Myrick, the owner of an advertising agency and an Amway distributorship, ran for the Charlotte Council in 1981 and lost. She ran again and won in 1983, ran for mayor and lost in 1985, then beat Harvey Gantt in 1987. Despite nasty personal charges, she was reelected in 1989. Myrick ran for the Senate in 1992, but was beaten by Lauch Faircloth in the primary 48%–30%, losing Charlotte in the process. In the 1994 primary she faced House Minority Leader David Balmer, a 31-year-old ambitious politician. Both ran tough crime ads, and just a few weeks before the election Myrick led only 30%–26%. But before the runoff, scheduled for three weeks later, it was revealed that Balmer had embellished his resume, which said he graduated in the top 20% of his law school class and had played varsity soccer—neither is true. Not stopping there, Balmer blamed a non-existent campaign aide for the fabrications. Myrick won 68%–32%. In the general, she easily beat Democratic businessman Rory Blake, who lost 2–1 to McMillan in 1992.

"We understand what the American people want," said Myrick after easily winning the general. "And we definitely have a mandate to deliver it." Myrick, who proudly recalled that she had no increases in property taxes as mayor, enthusiastically backed the Contract With America. Republican freshmen appointed her Freshman Class Liaison to the Leadership; Newt Gingrich named her to the 104th Congress Transition Team; and she got a seat on the Budget Committee. With her political background, she quickly became a visible and enthusiastic member of the Republican freshman class.

The People: Pop. 1990: 552,490; 24% rural; 10% age 65+; 88% White; 9% Black; 1% Asian; 1% Hispanic origin. Voting age pop.: 421,244; 8% Black; 1% Hispanic origin. Households: 60% married couple families; 28% married couple fams. w. children; 55% college educ.; median household income: $35,346; per capita income: $17,234; median gross rent: $472; median house value: $83,200.

1992 Presidential Vote

Bush (R) 130,798 (52%)
Clinton (D) 81,731 (33%)
Perot (I). 36,454 (15%)

1988 Presidential Vote

Bush (R) 134,304 (69%)
Dukakis (D). 59,191 (31%)

Rep. Sue Myrick (R)

Elected 1994; b. Aug. 1, 1941, Tiffin, OH; home, Charlotte; Heidelberg Col.; Methodist; married (Ed).

Career: Charlotte City Cncl., 1983–85; Pres. & CEO, Myrick Advertising, 1985–94; Charlotte Mayor, 1987–91; Pres. & CEO, Myrick Enterprises, 1992–94.

DC Office: 509 CHOB 20515, 202-225-1976; Fax: 202-225-3389.

District Offices: 1901 Roxborough Rd., Charlotte 28211, 704-362-1060; and 224 S. New Hope Rd., Gastonia 28054, 704-861-1976.

Committees: *Budget* (20th of 24 R). *Science* (27th of 27 R): Basic Research; Technology. *Small Business* (20th of 22 R): Government Programs.

Group Ratings and 103rd Congress Votes: Newly Elected

Key Votes of the 104th Congress

1. Congressional Compliance Y
2. Balanced Budget Amndmt. Y
3. Bar Unfunded Mandates Y
4. Pass Line Item Veto Y
5. Relax Exclusionary Rule Y
6. Reform Crime Grant Y
7. National Security Act Y
8. Moratorium on Regs. Y
9. Risk Assessment on Regs. Y
10. Expnd. Priv. Prop. Rights Y
11. Loser Pays Court Reform Y
12. Product Liability Reform Y
13. Welfare Reform Y
14. Term Limits Amndmt. Y
15. Tax Cuts Y

Election Results

1994 general	Sue Myrick (R)............................	82,374	(65%)	($663,405)
	Rory Blake (D)............................	44,379	(35%)	($85,458)
1994 runoff	Sue Myrick (R)............................	17,713	(68%)	
	David Balmer (R)..........................	8,278	(32%)	
1994 primary	Sue Myrick (R)............................	12,173	(34%)	
	David Balmer (R)..........................	9,894	(28%)	
	Neil Williams (R).........................	6,613	(19%)	
	Don Reid (R)	6,094	(17%)	
	Others	539	(2%)	
1992 general	Alex McMillan (R).........................	153,650	(67%)	($236,315)
	Rory Blake (D)............................	74,583	(33%)	($30,914)

TENTH DISTRICT

Wreathed in the haze that gave them the name "Smoky," the heavily wooded mountains of North Carolina seem placid and ancient. Geologically, they are some of the oldest ranges in the world; economically, they are churning with activity. The North Carolina counties where the hills of the Appalachians rise from the Piedmont are not just countryside. Nestled in their valleys is perhaps the largest concentration of furniture factories in the world, where skilled craftsmen create from the hardwoods of Carolina forests both high quality and mass market furniture. Other industries are here as well—textiles, though not as much as in the I-85 corridor in the Piedmont, and chickens in the Holly Farms complex (acquired by Tyson) in Wilkes County.

The 10th Congressional District of North Carolina covers much of this hill and mountain country, roughly between I-85 and the Blue Ridge Parkway. Very roughly, in fact, for the Democratic legislators drew the lines carefully to connect various cities' black communities in the next-door 12th District and to maximize the vote for Democrats in the 5th District to the north and the 11th District to the west. As a result, the 10th wiggles around Democratic strongholds such as the late Senator Sam Ervin's hometown of Morganton and the college town of Boone, and instead includes heavily Republican areas deep in the hills. The result is a district that is by most measures the most Republican in North Carolina, although the Republicans here tend not to be Jesse Helms fans, but rough-hewn hill Republicans, unsympathetic to government regulators, from factory inspectors to revenuers on the lookout for illegal stills.

The congressman from this district is Cass Ballenger, a Republican who started his own business in 1957 making plastic wrappings for J.C. Penney underwear. Ballenger served on the Catawba County Board of Commissioners for eight years and in the state legislature for 12. He ran for Congress in 1986 after James Broyhill, scion of a furniture family and congressman for 24 years, was appointed to the Senate. In the House primary, Ballenger promised to be a "Broyhill Republican" and beat an opponent backed by Helms's Congressional Club. He has won general elections without difficulty.

Ballenger combines a solidly conservative voting record with a sense of civic responsibility. He and his wife have organized humanitarian trips to Central and South America, delivering donated medical supplies and other necessities. He worked hard against the Clinton healthcare plan and when he asked whether companies with 5,000 workers could arrange their own healthcare plans, heard Hillary Rodham Clinton respond, "That's a good question. We will get you an answer specifically." He has fought the Democrats on family leave and the ban on striker replacement, and amended an OSHA law by exempting employers when violations are caused by employees breaking company work rules. On the old Education and Labor Committee, he was part of a outvoted minority. On the renamed Economic and Educational Opportunities Committee, he should be on the winning side most of the time and his Workforce Protections

Subcommittee chairmanship should make him an ally of business as Congress seeks to shift the balance away from the no-longer-so-powerful labor unions.

The People: Pop. 1990: 552,303; 71% rural; 12% age 65+; 93% White; 5% Black; 1% Hispanic origin. Voting age pop.: 421,043; 5% Black; 1% Hispanic origin. Households: 65% married couple families; 29% married couple fams. w. children; 35% college educ.; median household income: $28,511; per capita income: $13,434; median gross rent: $352; median house value: $63,700.

1992 Presidential Vote			1988 Presidential Vote		
Bush (R)	127,910	(53%)	Bush (R)	142,283	(70%)
Clinton (D)	76,262	(32%)	Dukakis (D)	61,070	(30%)
Perot (I)	35,572	(15%)			

Rep. Cass Ballenger (R)

Elected 1986; b. Dec. 6, 1926, Hickory; home, Hickory; U. of NC, Amherst Col., B.A. 1948; Episcopalian; married (Donna).

Career: Naval Air Corps, 1944–45; Businessman; Pres., Hickory Paper Box Co., 1948–70; Founder & Pres., Plastic Packaging Inc., 1957–present; Catawba Cnty. Bd. of Commissioners, 1966–74, Chmn. 1970–74; NC House of Reps., 1974–76; NC Senate, 1976–86.

DC Office: 2238 RHOB 20515, 202-225-2576; Fax: 202-225-0316.

District Offices: P.O. Box 1830, Hickory 28603, 704-327-6100; and P.O. Box 1881, Clemmons 27012, 919-766-9455.

Committees: *Economic & Educational Opportunities* (6th of 24 R): Oversight and Investigations; Workforce Protections (Chmn.). *International Relations* (12th of 23 R): International Economic Policy and Trade; Western Hemisphere.

Group Ratings

	ADA	ACLU	COPE	CFA	LCV	CON	NSI	COC	ACU	NTLC	CHC
1994	5	13	0	10	6	86	100	92	90	93	100
1993	11	—	0	0	21	82	—	100	87	—	—

National Journal Ratings

	1993 LIB — 1993 CONS		1994 LIB — 1994 CONS	
Economic	0% —	88%	0% —	80%
Social	11% —	82%	16% —	81%
Foreign	33% —	65%	14% —	80%

Key Votes of the 103d Congress

1. Clinton Deficit Plan	N	3. Brady Handgun Purchase	N	5. Lmt. UN Cmnd. of Forces	Y
2. NAFTA	Y	4. Strike Race/Death Pnlty.	Y	6. Cut Missile Funds	N

Key Votes of the 104th Congress

1. Congressional Compliance	Y	6. Reform Crime Grant	Y	11. Loser Pays Court Reform	Y
2. Balanced Budget Amndmt.	Y	7. National Security Act	Y	12. Product Liability Reform	Y
3. Bar Unfunded Mandates	Y	8. Moratorium on Regs.	Y	13. Welfare Reform	Y
4. Pass Line Item Veto	Y	9. Risk Assessment on Regs.	Y	14. Term Limits Amndmt.	Y
5. Relax Exclusionary Rule	Y	10. Expnd. Priv. Prop. Rights	Y	15. Tax Cuts	Y

Election Results

1994 general	Cass Ballenger (R)	107,829	(72%)	($221,536)
	Robert Wayne Avery (D)	42,939	(28%)	
1994 primary	Cass Ballenger (R)	unopposed		
1992 general	Cass Ballenger (R)	149,033	(63%)	($278,963)
	Ben Neill (D)	79,206	(34%)	($23,101)
	Other	6,888	(3%)	

ELEVENTH DISTRICT

Western North Carolina, the protrusion of the Tarheel state deep into the fastness of the eastern United States' highest and oldest mountains, is a land of long and ornery traditions. First settled by whites not long after the Revolutionary War, it still has tiny Indian communities and hollows where people are descended from the first white settlers. Its biggest city, Asheville, is memorialized in Thomas Wolfe's novels and was a retreat for lung patients in the early 20th Century. It was also the home of the brilliant eccentric George Vanderbilt, who built the chateau-like Biltmore mansion and its vast forests, on which he pioneered scientific forestry. Over a ridge is the Smoky Mountains National Park, the nation's most heavily visited, 20 degrees cooler in the summer than the lowland towns an hour or so away. The climate and the forested, green, fog-wisped mountains have attracted millions of tourists and thousands of retirees to this area.

The orneriness of the mountain country has come out in its politics. This part of the state was reluctant to secede in the Civil War. There were few slaves and many small farmers loyal to the Union, and those who took up the Confederate cause did so out of loyalty to Governor Zebulon Vance, an Asheville native and reluctant secessionist himself. Ancestral party loyalties remain strong; local notables, like the Ponder family of Madison County, hold power for years; the retirees in the mountains south of Asheville haven't tipped things much. This western end of the state, with erose boundaries drawn by legislators for 1992, makes up the 11th Congressional District of North Carolina. For years it was one of the most closely contested in the nation, throwing out incumbents in five of six elections between 1980 and 1990.

The current congressman is Charles Taylor, a Republican tree farmer and one of the biggest private landholders in the area, who served in the legislature from 1966 to 1974 and ran for Congress in 1988. He narrowly lost then, and in 1990 won when the incumbent voted for the bipartisan budget-summit agreement. Taylor worked to delay draw-downs of area lakes each year by the TVA until August 1, and later October 1, to keep waters high for tourist season. He worked to get the Asheville veterans' hospital refurbished and obtained funding for the I-26 highway. Taylor was also one of the members of 1991's Gang of Seven, the Republican freshmen who pushed for full disclosure of overdrafts on the House bank and other congressional reforms. He got a seat on Appropriations in 1993. The House the next year passed his property-rights protection amendment to the National Biological Survey and an amendment to stop EEOC guidelines that he believed would promote religious harassment in workplaces (such as discrimination against workers who wear religious paraphernalia on the job).

The 11th was expected to have close races in the 1990s, but Taylor won by solid margins in 1992 and 1994. Under the current lines, Taylor would have lost the district by 931 votes in 1990, but in 1992—after redistricting—Taylor outspent his opponent 3–1 and won 55%–45%, the best margin here since 1974. In 1994, Maggie Lauterer, a television reporter who often sang "Amazing Grace" at rallies, seemed strong and was actively promoted by national Democrats. But Taylor linked her to the Clinton crime bill and he won 60%–40%, carrying every county.

The People: Pop. 1990: 552,497; 69% rural; 18% age 65+; 90% White; 7% Black; 1% Amer. Indian; 1% Hispanic origin. Voting age pop.: 430,423; 6% Black; 1% Hispanic origin. Households: 60% married couple families; 24% married couple fams. w. children; 38% college educ.; median household income: $23,564; per capita income: $11,923; median gross rent: $333; median house value: $59,500.

1992 Presidential Vote

Clinton (D) 105,006 (43%)
Bush (R) 103,849 (43%)
Perot (I). 34,643 (14%)

1988 Presidential Vote

Bush (R) 119,845 (58%)
Dukakis (D). 87,880 (42%)

Rep. Charles H. Taylor (R)

Elected 1990; b. Jan. 23, 1941, Brevard; home, Brevard; Wake Forest U., B.A. 1963, J.D. 1966; Baptist; married (Elizabeth).

Career: Tree farmer; NC House of Reps., 1966–72, Minority Ldr., 1968–72; NC Senate, 1972–74, Minority Ldr., 1972–74.

DC Office: 231 CHOB 20515, 202-225-6401; Fax: 202-225-0519; e-mail: chtaylor@hr.house.gov.

District Offices: 22 S. Pack Sq., #330, Asheville 28801, 704-251-1988; Cherokee Cnty. Cthse., 201 Peachtree St., Murphy 28906, 704-837-3249; and 200 S. Lafayette St., Shelby 28150, 704-484-6971.

Committees: *Appropriations* (18th of 32 R): Commerce, Justice, State, and Judiciary; Interior; Legislative.

Group Ratings

	ADA	ACLU	COPE	CFA	LCV	CON	NSI	COC	ACU	NTLC	CHC
1994	5	14	33	10	0	64	100	75	100	89	100
1993	5	—	8	0	7	63	—	82	100	—	—

National Journal Ratings

	1993 LIB — 1993 CONS	1994 LIB — 1994 CONS
Economic	12% — 87%	0% — 80%
Social	0% — 89%	0% — 89%
Foreign	24% — 72%	0% — 88%

Key Votes of the 103d Congress

1. Clinton Deficit Plan	N	3. Brady Handgun Purchase	N	5. Lmt. UN Cmnd. of Forces Y
2. NAFTA	N	4. Strike Race/Death Pnlty.	Y	6. Cut Missile Funds	Y

1. Clinton Deficit Plan   N   3. Brady Handgun Purchase N   5. Lmt. UN Cmnd. of Forces Y
2. NAFTA   N   4. Strike Race/Death Pnlty. Y   6. Cut Missile Funds   Y

Key Votes of the 104th Congress

1. Congressional Compliance Y   6. Reform Crime Grant   Y   11. Loser Pays Court Reform Y
2. Balanced Budget Amndmt. Y   7. National Security Act   Y   12. Product Liability Reform Y
3. Bar Unfunded Mandates Y   8. Moratorium on Regs.   Y   13. Welfare Reform   Y
4. Pass Line Item Veto Y   9. Risk Assessment on Regs. Y 14. Term Limits Amndmt.   Y
5. Relax Exclusionary Rule N   10. Expnd. Priv. Prop. Rights Y 15. Tax Cuts   Y

Election Results

1994 general	Charles H. Taylor (R)...............	115,826	(60%)	($999,467)
	Maggie Palmer Lauterer (D)	76,862	(40%)	($607,128)
1994 primary	Charles H. Taylor (R)...............	unopposed		
1992 general	Charles H. Taylor (R)...............	130,158	(55%)	($1,212,765)
	John S. Stevens (D)	108,003	(45%)	($431,722)

TWELFTH DISTRICT

"This is perhaps the Negros' temporary farewell to Congress," said George White, a Tarboro, North Carolina lawyer and Republican, in his last days in the House of Representatives in 1901. Segregation was being imposed by law, and blacks informally but effectively were being stricken from the voting rolls in the rural South. But White was confident that "Phoenix-like he will rise up some day and come again." It was 28 years until another black was elected to Congress and 70 years until another black won in the South. In North Carolina, although blacks have been politically influential since the Voting Rights Act of 1965, George White's prediction did not come true until 1992, when two blacks were elected. One, Eva Clayton, was from the mostly rural and small town 1st District—the kind of country where most blacks lived in George White's day. The other, Melvin Watt, represents the new 12th District, whose notorious boundaries connect several of North Carolina's urban centers, like those where most American blacks live today.

The 12th District is the most egregious example in the nation of the interpretation, urged by blacks and Republicans, that the 1982 revisions of the Voting Rights Act require the maximization of black percentages in congressional districts. It is called the I-85 district, because it consists of a series of urban black areas, many of them poor, mostly connected by a line sometimes no wider than I-85, splitting adjacent districts in two. "I love the district because I can drive down I-85 with both car doors open and hit every person in the district," said candidate Mickey Michaux. "In one county, northbound drivers on I-85 would be in the 12th District, but southbound drivers would be in another," harrumphed *The Wall Street Journal.* "The next county over, the district would 'change lanes,' and southbound drivers would be in the 12th District." There is an argument for connecting voters with some sense of affinity and common interest. But there is also an argument that such districts amount to a form of apartheid, and their shape eerily resembles those of some of South Africa's homelands.

The contest for the new seat turned out to be the kind of friends-and-neighbors Democratic primary common in the old segregated South. Michaux, a former state legislator who won 46% in the runoff in the old 2d District in 1982, got 76% in Durham County, which cast 28% of Democratic primary votes. But he won no more than 22% elsewhere, for 29% district-wide. Larry Little, based in Winston-Salem, won 66% there but no more than 20% elsewhere, for 15%. The winner was Melvin Watt of Charlotte. He won 86% of the vote in Mecklenburg County, where 27% of the votes were cast, plus 59% in Greensboro-High Point, which had no strong favorite son, and carried most of the small counties. Overall, he won 47%, well over the 40% which in North Carolina gives victory without a runoff. He won the general election easily, and on election night said, "I'm proud to be a part of George Henry White's prophecy. But I am saddened that it took 92 years. And I'm disappointed, because I know that thousands and thousands of people, but for the color of their skin, would have been just as qualified to fill this office."

Watt had served only two years in the state Senate, but was rich in experience. He grew up in a place called Dixie outside Charlotte, now overgrown with woods, in a tin-roofed house with no electricity or running water. His dream was to attend the University of North Carolina, and he was one of the first black students there; he went on to Yale Law School and then a civil rights law practice in Charlotte. He managed Harvey Gantt's campaigns for city council and mayor in the 1980s and for U.S. Senate in 1990. In the latter race, against Jesse Helms, he and Gantt pursued their strategy with a steely consistency and good humor under fierce pressure.

Watt's tenure is threatened by a lawsuit brought against the district lines. In June 1993 the Supreme Court condemned lines drawn for racial reasons, and sent the North Carolina map back to a three-judge panel. In August 1994, it split 2–1 and upheld the lines. That case was appealed, and the Supreme Court may rule again in 1995. Watt seemed outraged by the case and regarded the lines as the only way blacks can have a chance to be elected: "You go down into North Carolina and you take a poll and 30% to 35% of the population will tell you under no circumstances, regardless of how qualified, would I vote for a black candidate. So there is a need for something that will equalize the playing field." The poll data may be right, but most candidates face a large bloc of determined opponents. Gantt's success, in which Watt had a major part, in winning 47% in 1990, with many white votes, suggests a black could win statewide in North Carolina. And Watt himself took care to appeal to white voters and in fact won 70% of the vote in the general election in a district where only 53% of adults are black.

If the lines have to be redrawn, Watt will be in a difficult position, for it will be hard to design a district in the Charlotte area willing to support a candidate with his stands on issues. In his first term he had one of the most liberal voting records in Congress, voting proudly for the Clinton budget and tax package, against the crime bill because of its death penalty provisions, against NAFTA, and against the limited line-item veto. He is scrupulous in following his convictions and taking stands unpopular even in the current 12th, opposing a bill to increase penalties for hate crimes, and opposing gun bans in urban housing projects. He sponsored an amendment to delete the death penalty for drug kingpins when they are not directly responsible for a murder. He refused to join other North Carolinians in fighting the tobacco tax in the Clinton healthcare plan and supports a Canadian-style single payer system. He takes some more popular stands as well, for repeal of baseball's antitrust exemption and an amendment to allow Goals 2000 education grants to go to private parental information centers, in coordination with federal health, nutrition and crime programs. But he would have to depend on his hard constituency work and his admirable personal qualities to win in a district with a significantly lower national Democratic percentage than the current 12th. Meanwhile, he has emerged as one of the House's most articulate and forceful liberals and critics of Republican policies—black or white.

The People: Pop. 1990: 551,957; 14% rural; 12% age 65+; 41% White; 57% Black; 1% Asian; 1% Hispanic origin. Voting age pop.: 410,871; 53% Black; 1% Hispanic origin. Households: 43% married couple families; 19% married couple fams. w. children; 37% college educ.; median household income: $23,068; per capita income: $10,878; median gross rent: $381; median house value: $57,800.

1992 Presidential Vote

Clinton (D)	125,189	(66%)
Bush (R)	48,406	(25%)
Perot (I)	16,886	(9%)

1988 Presidential Vote

Bush (R)	58,457	(37%)
Dukakis (D)	101,415	(63%)

Rep. Melvin L. Watt (D)

Elected 1992; b. Aug. 26, 1945, Mecklenburg; home, Charlotte; U. of NC, Chapel Hill, B.S. 1967, Yale, J.D. 1970; Presbyterian; married (Eulada).

Career: NC Senate, 1985–86; Campaign Mgr., Harvey Gantt for Senate, 1990; Practicing atty., 1971-92; Co-developer, co-owner, East Town Manor nursing home, 1989-present.

DC Office: 1230 LHOB 20515, 202-225-1510; Fax: 202-225-1512; e-mail: melmail@hr.house.gov.

District Offices: 214 N. Church St., #130, Charlotte 28202, 704-344-9950; 315 E. Chapel Hill, #202, Durham 27702, 919-688-3004; 301 S. Greene St., #210, Greensboro 27401, 919-375-9402.

Committees: *Banking & Financial Services* (19th of 22 D): Domestic and International Monetary Policy; Financial Institutions and Consumer Credit. *Judiciary* (11th of 15 D): Constitution; Crime.

Group Ratings

	ADA	ACLU	COPE	CFA	LCV	CON	NSI	COC	ACU	NTLC	CHC
1994	100	91	100	100	100	31	0	17	10	7	0
1993	100	—	100	100	93	32	—	9	0	—	—

National Journal Ratings

	1993 LIB — 1993 CONS		1994 LIB — 1994 CONS	
Economic	88%	— 0%	83%	— 0%
Social	87%	— 0%	80%	— 19%
Foreign	87%	— 7%	85%	— 0%

Key Votes of the 103d Congress

1. Clinton Deficit Plan	Y	3. Brady Handgun Purchase	Y	5. Lmt. UN Cmnd. of Forces	N
2. NAFTA	N	4. Strike Race/Death Pnlty.	N	6. Cut Missile Funds	Y

Key Votes of the 104th Congress

1. Congressional Compliance	Y	6. Reform Crime Grant	N	11. Loser Pays Court Reform	N
2. Balanced Budget Amndmt.	N	7. National Security Act	N	12. Product Liability Reform	N
3. Bar Unfunded Mandates	N	8. Moratorium on Regs.	N	13. Welfare Reform	N
4. Pass Line Item Veto	N	9. Risk Assessment on Regs.	N	14. Term Limits Amndmt.	N
5. Relax Exclusionary Rule	N	10. Expnd. Priv. Prop. Rights	N	15. Tax Cuts	N

Election Results

1994 general	Melvin L. Watt (D).....................	57,655	(66%)	($253,715)
	Joseph A. (Joe) Martino (R).............	29,933	(34%)	($14,700)
1994 primary	Melvin L. Watt (D).................	unopposed		
1992 general	Melvin L. Watt (D)..................	127,262	(70%)	($480,713)
	Barbara Gore Washington (R)	49,402	(27%)	($22,761)
	Other...............................	4,160	(2%)	

NORTH DAKOTA

More than a century after statehood, North Dakota is still probably closer to its roots than any other state. There are North Dakotans alive today who knew the men and women that settled this land and saw the state enter the Union in 1889. As children, they walked in the ruts left by the early settlers' wagon trains; they saw the Indians, recently defeated, herded onto reservations; they saw still shining new the rails that brought the world's commerce to these desolate prairies. This was the frontier to which Teddy Roosevelt came in 1884, determined to shoot one of the fast-disappearing buffalo, a place where settlers were only then breaking the sod and plowing under the natural prairies that some environmentalists, much to North Dakotans' disgust, want to restore. In those days, the land was rich with promise. Once the soil was broken, this was some of the best wheat land in the world, empty by then of Indians and buffalo, connected to markets by rail, ready to become a cog in the industrial world being created by entrepreneurs and to raise its living standards to unparalleled heights.

And so, in a sudden rush of settlement during the 20 years before World War I, North Dakota filled up to pretty much its present population. There were 632,000 people here in 1920 and in counts since, the number has fluctuated between 617,000 and 680,000; in 1990 it was 639,000 (cumulatively, the state with the lowest growth rate since 1950). Wheat is not the only crop here; as the plains become more arid to the west, ranching and livestock grazing—along with strip mining and oil production—are important, and hardy root crops like potatoes and sugar beets grow as well. But wheat is still number one. Typically the state produces about one-tenth of the U.S. crop, and a fair percentage of the world's; its durum wheat is the main ingredient of American pasta. At the same time, wondrous increases in productivity have meant that it takes far fewer farmers to produce far more crops, and so over the years North Dakotans have moved off farms and into towns or, more often, to other states altogether. Its four biggest counties, containing Fargo, Grand Forks, Bismarck and Minot, grew from 134,000 in 1930 to 291,000 in 1990, while the state's other 48 counties dropped from 546,000 to 347,000. Yet more than one in five North Dakotans still live on farms and ranches, and many living in town own land or depend on farming for their livelihood: farming is more important here than in any other state.

This dependence on agriculture has naturally had political ramifications, for farmers are not always happy with their place in the industrial or post industrial economy. For one thing, farm economies depend not on wages but on profits: the North Dakota economy is heavily leveraged. And while farmers have no compunction about making gains from upswings in the market, they want to be protected against the downswings—especially since the physical environment is as demanding as it is on the northern Great Plains. The boosterish optimism of the first settlers was soon followed by cries reverberating with varying intensity for government protection against market forces. Since commodity prices tend to fall during periods of economic growth, there has been a countercyclical element in North Dakota politics, a tendency to vote against the national trends, and a radical strain going back to the 1910s and still lively in recent years. That radical strain also owes much to the immigrant origins of so many of North Dakota's early settlers: Norwegians in the eastern part of the state, Canadians along the northern border, Volga Germans in the west, colonies of Poles and Czechs and Icelanders, and native Germans throughout the state. (Volga Germans are descendants of early 19th Century German migrants to Russia who kept their German language and character.) These immigrant traditions also explain the orderliness of North Dakota's small cities and the communitarian tradition of cooperative action that is very much a part of the state's heritage.

Another product of the radical tradition, chronicled colorfully and with admirable frankness in the North Dakota Heritage Museum in Bismarck, was the Non-Partisan League (NPL)

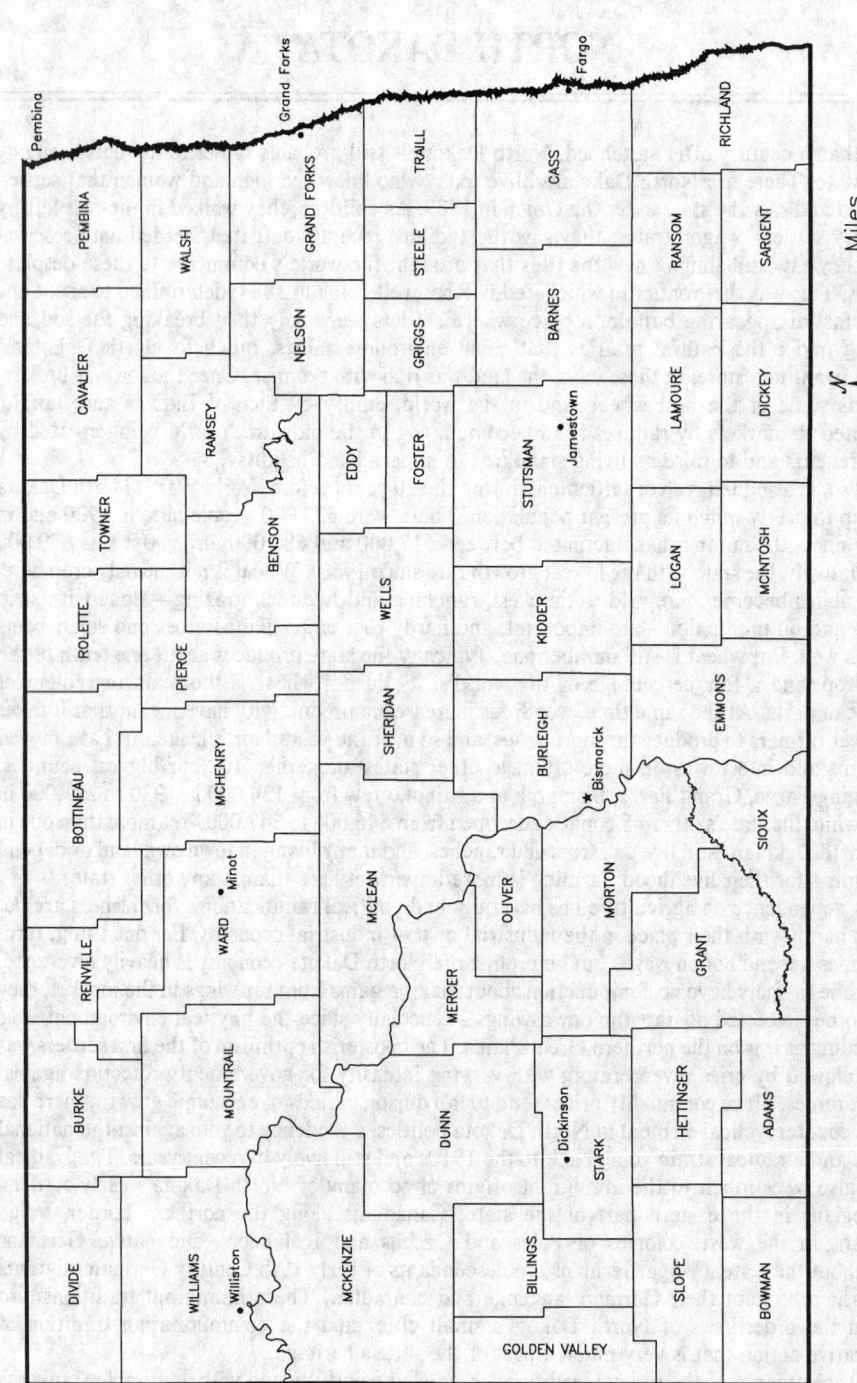

U.S. Representative elected at large.

Miles

Copyright © 1993 by Election Data Services, Inc.

formed in 1915. Its constituency was lonely marginal farmers, cut off in many cases from the wider American culture by language barriers and seemingly at the mercy of the grain millers in Minneapolis, the railroads of St. Paul, the banks of New York and the commodity traders of Chicago. The NPL's program was socialistic—government ownership of railroads and grain elevators—and, like most North Dakota ethnics, it opposed going to war with Germany. The NPL often determined the outcome of the usually decisive Republican primary and sometimes swung its support to the otherwise heavily outnumbered Democrats, instituting reforms and creating a state-owned bank. One NPL favorite was "Wild Bill" Langer, governor intermittently in the 1930s, elected to the Senate in 1940 but allowed to take his seat only after a lengthy investigation of campaign irregularities. By 1960, the NPL had more or less merged into the Democratic Party, a merger symbolized by the election of the late Democratic Senator Quentin Burdick, whose father, Usher Burdick, served 20 years in the House as an NPL-endorsed Republican. "Young Burdick," as he was long known, continued NPL tradition, supporting wheat subsidies and pork barrel projects and avoiding controversial cultural issues until his death in 1992. North Dakota's leading Democrats of recent decades, Senators Kent Conrad and Byron Dorgan, have championed a politics clearly of NPL lineage: for government farm programs, wary if not hostile to American military involvement abroad, and cheerfully championing the little guy from North Dakota against out-of-state corporations.

But a radical strain is not the only political product of North Dakota's heritage. The orderliness and closeness of life in small communities nurtures a conservative strain. This is a place where everyone knows everyone else, where divorce is as uncommon as anywhere in the United States and the two-parent family is still very much the norm, and where abortions are available in only one clinic in the whole state. There is no voter registration because poll watchers would obviously spot anyone not eligible. North Dakota is proud that its students achieve some of the nation's highest math scores, even though its teacher pay is 49th in the country—parents and neighbors make sure students work hard and teachers are able to keep track of students from kindergarten to high school—and that it has among the lowest rates of student loan defaults and strikes. Politics is personal, too, in a state where every politician is personally known to voters. North Dakota is one of only three states with an all-Democratic congressional delegation (West Virginia and Hawaii are the others), but that is as much due to the personal appeal of Senators Kent Conrad and Byron Dorgan and Congressman Earl Pomeroy as it is to their political stands, since this was one of Bill Clinton's weakest states.

There are signs now that the state's radical tradition and the Democrats' personal appeal are being overshadowed by a Republican trend. If the typical elderly North Dakotan is a hard-working retired farmer, with fond memories of NPL agitation and a belief in government programs, the typical young North Dakotan is a family person with a college education (49% of the state's households are college graduates) more trusting of markets and the private sector. They may have noticed that nearby South Dakota has attracted white-collar jobs with low tax rates and that North Dakota, with its higher taxes and pro-government traditions, is the one Great Plains state that has lost population in the 1990s as well as the 1980s. Exit polls showed older North Dakotans heavily for the Democrats in the two Senate and one House race in 1992, and young North Dakotans Republican enough to provide the nucleus for margins for George Bush and Republican Governor Ed Schafer. There was no exit poll here in 1994, but Republicans now hold most statewide offices and have big margins in both houses of the legislature. Of course many North Dakotans move away, and there may be a metaphor in the fact that the most powerful North Dakota native in the 103d Congress was House Budget Committee Chairman Martin Sabo, liberal Democrat from Minneapolis, while the most powerful North Dakota native in the 104th is House Majority Leader Dick Armey, conservative Republican from the booming Dallas-Fort Worth Metroplex. It's too soon to say that North Dakota has moved away from its radical political roots, but a conservative strain in its heritage is asserting itself as well.

Governor. North Dakota's skyscraper Capitol, towering over neatly-kept Bismarck and the rolling plains beyond, housed Republican governors for only four years from 1960 to 1992. But now it has a Republican governor, Ed Schafer, and Republican majorities among statewide officials and in the legislature—the best Republican showing since the Non-Partisan League allied with the Democrats. Schafer bears a famous name in North Dakota: his father founded the Gold Seal company, makers of Gold Seal glass wax, Snowy Bleach and Mr. Bubble; Schafer worked for the firm, in New Jersey and North Dakota, and more recently headed both a classic car dealership, Dakota Classics, and an aquaculture fish farm, Fish 'N Dakota. He ran for Congress in 1990 and won 35% against Byron Dorgan; he was not the favorite in 1992 when popular Governor George Sinner retired and Democrats had a primary fight between Attorney General Nick Spaeth and state Senate leader Bill Heigaard. Heigaard, pro-choice, won the party convention; Spaeth, antiabortion and for state investment in economic development, won the June primary 65%–35%. Economic development was a major issue. Spaeth favored the state government's "Growing North Dakota" plan, which he accused Schafer of taking advantage of its loans and tax breaks for his own business. Schafer favored more local and private sector involvement. Schafer won by a solid 58%–41%, carrying all the major towns and all but seven counties, winning over 60% with voters under 60, while Spaeth got 55% from those 60 and over.

After two years in office, Schafer pursued policies of lowering taxes and "rightsizing" government. He claimed credit for the 15,000 new jobs created in North Dakota and for the fact that Census estimates showed it gained population for the first year in more than a decade. Republicans gained smartly in 1994 state elections, winning control of the state Senate. Schafer has been popular, but the critical verdict will come when Schafer runs for reelection in 1996, and his approval rating in March 1995 was 59%—down from 68% in the fall of 1994.

Senators. North Dakota has two Democratic senators, one of whom—now the senior—once worked for the other in Bismarck, then succeeded him in elective office. It's a bit complicated: Byron Dorgan holds the seat Kent Conrad initially won, because Conrad decided to honor a campaign pledge not to run again in 1992 if the budget deficit was not cut by 80%. But Conrad then was persuaded to run for the other seat when Senator Quentin Burdick died in September 1992. Dorgan and Conrad have much in common. Both were elected state tax commissioner, and both used the office to seek greater revenues from out-of-state corporations. Both are direct heirs of the state's radical economic tradition, its faith that North Dakotans need government protection from the vagaries of farm prices and that government regulations and subsidies can help ordinary people. They also played crucial roles in the Senate's March 1995 one-vote defeat of the balanced budget amendment, with Dorgan abandoning his support of a year earlier and Conrad engaging in futile last-minute negotiations to try to prevent use of Social Security trust-fund surpluses to mask the federal deficit. And there is more: Lucy Calautti, Conrad's wife, is Dorgan's chief of staff and the chief political strategist to both Senators.

Conrad grew up in North Dakota; tragically, his parents were killed in an auto accident when he was five. He went away to school, then returned in 1974 to work for Dorgan. When Dorgan ran for Congress in 1980, he ran for tax commissioner and won; when Dorgan declined the opportunity, in 1986 he ran against Senator Mark Andrews, and won 50%–49%. Since then he has won two Senate elections, in difficult circumstances. One of Conrad's assets is earnestness, and in 1986 he promised not to run again unless "the federal deficit, the trade deficit and real interest rates will be brought under control." The latter two arguably were, and he could argue that he had worked to cut the former: he favored crackdowns on tax cheats, higher taxes on the top income brackets and across-the-board freezes in some discretionary spending; he pushed spending cut amendments on the Budget Committee and called for repealing income tax indexing. He had taken many stands popular in North Dakota and arguably inconsistent with his tight-spending advocacy: he was one of the few Democrats to support most favored nation status for China, a major buyer of North Dakota wheat; he backed coal and alternative fuels research, to help North Dakota's lignite deposits. On the Agriculture Committee, he backed far more expensive farm bills than most other senators have been willing to support. Early 1992 polls showed him with 60% when paired against Republicans. But in April 1992, after ruminating on the issue and after his wife had been mugged and dragged down the street near their Capitol Hill home, Conrad rose and shocked the Senate by saying that he was not running because he had not kept his pledge.

In September, Burdick died. Under state law, the special election could not be held in November but had to be held before January, so Conrad had to run for this seat while still serving the last month of his first term in the other. But he overcame this awkwardness by arguing that circumstances had changed, and that was evidently enough for a man many voters had seen personally in his more than 1,000 town meetings. He was nominated unanimously at a Democratic convention. Republican opponent Jack Dalrymple, chairman of the Dakota Growers Pasta cooperative, called for a vastly expensive new ($5 per bushel) wheat program, which even Conrad called unrealistic. Conrad was attacked strongly by Darold Larsen, an independent antiabortion candidate, but had far more money and won by a 63%–34% margin. So for a few hours in December 1992, Conrad technically held both Senate seats. He was sworn in December 14 to fill the remainder of Burdick's term; then a few hours later Dorgan was sworn in to fill the remainder of Conrad's seat, giving Dorgan a jumpstart in seniority on his fellow freshman Senators.

In his truncated second term, Conrad got a seat on the Finance Committee, where he might have been a pivotal vote on health care. But he did not embrace the Clinton healthcare plan, and also opposed the administration by voting against NAFTA. His voting record had a distinctly moderate tinge on most issues. The seat came up again in 1994, and his Republican opponent was Dr. Ben Clayburgh, 70-year-old former head of the state medical association. When Clayburgh accused him of voting most of the time with Bill Clinton, Conrad ran an ad asserting that he had voted with Senate Republican Leader Bob Dole more than 50% of the time; Dole responded with an endorsement of Clayburgh. Conrad ran far ahead in most polls, but in the Republican tide wasn't able to match his poll percentages at the voting booth, as he won 58%–42%. Back in the Senate, he is now in the minority, trading the chairmanship of the credit subcommittee for the ranking minority position on the marketing subcommittee as the 1995 farm bill approaches.

Byron Dorgan, who first held statewide office in 1969 and was long rated the most popular politician in the state, was finally elected to the Senate in 1992. Dorgan's career was built on his inspiration to use the tax commissioner post to bring highly publicized actions to get out-of-state corporations to pay more North Dakota taxes: this struck a chord in a state always hostile to big out-of-state money. To this work Dorgan brought the zest and cornball good humor that New Deal enthusiasts liked to summon up when liberals thought they represented the ordinary, inarticulate little guy, in contrast to the conservatives seen as old stuffed shirts. But despite his popularity, he was reluctant to take on the giants. He was elected to Congress in 1980 when incumbent Mark Andrews ran for the Senate. After extensive thought, he declined to challenge Andrews in 1986 or Quentin Burdick in 1988. Only with Conrad's surprise decision not to run for reelection in 1992 did he finally run for the Senate. In Congress Dorgan has continued to attack out-of-state economic powers. On the House Ways and Means Committee, he called for more tax audits, opposed intangibles write-offs for corporate takeovers; in the Senate, he opposed NAFTA and fast-track for trade agreements, and took aim at the independence of the Federal Reserve. He worked with Conrad to get limits on Canadian wheat exports to the United States and for rural enterprise zones. He sponsored gun-free schools and victim's rights bills.

Dorgan has been running statewide in North Dakota for a quarter-century, and his vote percentages have been going a bit down—though they remain at an impressive level. In 1988 he won 71% against Steve Sydness for the House seat; in 1990, he won 65%, his lowest ever, against now-Governor Ed Schafer. In 1992, he faced Sydness again, for the Senate, with the handicap of 98 overdrafts on the House bank. Both were for most favored nation status for China, both were wary of free trade and both wanted relaxation of the wetlands law which has classified hundreds of seasonal puddles in North Dakota as protected wetlands. With the most editorial endorsements (here, as elsewhere in America, editorials are no longer written by crusty old conservatives but by baby boom liberals), Dorgan won by a solid but not overwhelming 59%–39%—similar to Conrad's margin in 1994. He was a leading supporter of his long-time friend South Dakotan Tom Daschle for Democratic leader and was named Assistant Democratic Floor Leader. In that new role, he became an increasingly active party spokesman and Republican critic.

Representative-At-Large. North Dakota's congressional delegation has a complex history: in 1974, when Byron Dorgan challenged Congressman Mark Andrews and Kent Conrad managed his campaign, Earl Pomeroy was Dorgan's driver. In 1980, when Dorgan and Conrad won statewide elections, Pomeroy at 28 won a seat in the legislature; in 1984 and 1988 he was elected insurance commissioner. In 1992, he was planning to retire from politics and serve in the Peace Corps in Russia; then Dorgan ran for Conrad's seat in the Senate and Pomeroy ran for Dorgan's seat in the House. Articulate, cheerful, sincere and undevious, a critic of insurance companies yet unabrasive, he was the obvious choice for the House seat and was nominated unanimously by the Democratic convention. He won the general 57%–39%, almost a carbon copy of Dorgan's margin in the Senate race.

In the 103rd Congress, Pomeroy was one of two freshman Democrats on the House Budget Committee. He voted for the Clinton budget and tax plan but supported the Penny-Kasich spending cuts in 1993; he opposed the Clinton healthcare plan. He backed many reforms other freshman Democrats shied away from. With Conrad and Dorgan, he helped get limits on Canadian wheat imports. He also serves on the Agriculture Committee, where he obviously looks out for North Dakota interests; he also wants to save North Dakota's two Air Force bases; Grand Forks is on the 1995 closure list, but Minot seems to have missed the ax for now. In 1994 he had tough opposition from state legislator and businessman Gary Porter, who used his own money to match the incumbent's spending; the Republican took moderate positions but attacked Pomeroy for supporting the 1994 crime bill with its gun control provisions. Pomeroy won 52%–45%, down from 1992; he carried the four most-populated counties by only 50%–48%, winning almost all his margin in the older rural areas. That such an attractive incumbent was pressed was a measure of the Democrats' trouble in 1994. It also may explain his notable support for the Contract With America. With a moderate voting record on most issues and a proven commitment to reform, Pomeroy said he expected to work well with Republicans in the 104th House. On the Agriculture Committee, scheduled to report a 1995 farm bill, he said he was closer to Republican Chairman Pat Roberts of Kansas than to many suburban Democrats. Pomeroy is capable of being an able and useful legislator if his party label doesn't pull him down.

Presidential politics. West Virginia and Hawaii, the two other states with all-Democratic congressional delegations, lean heavily Democratic in presidential politics; North Dakota does not. Its prairie populism has seldom carried over into an enthusiasm for Democratic presidential candidates, and certainly not in 1992. Ross Perot got 23% here, running perceptibly stronger in some media markets (Bismarck, Minot) than others (Fargo, Grand Forks), suggesting a selective market-by-market time buy.

With tiny delegations, an out-of-the-way location and frigid weather in the early primary season, North Dakota does not loom large in choosing presidential nominees. In 1992 about 5,000 North Dakotans voted in Democratic Party caucuses and gave Bill Clinton, supported by then-Governor George Sinner, a solid margin. The Republicans had a primary June 9, which George Bush handily won.

The People: Est. Pop. 1994: 638,800; Pop. 1990: 638,800, down 0.1% 1990–1994. 0.2% of U.S. total, 47th largest; 47% rural. Median age: 32.4 years. 14.3% 65 years and over. 94.6% White, 4.1% American Indian. Households: 59.1% married couple families; 30% married couple fams. w. children; 49% college educ.; median household income: $23,213; per capita income: $11,051; 65.6% owner occupied housing; median house value: $50,800; median monthly rent: $266. 4.9% Unemployment. 1994 Voting age pop.: 467,000. 1994 Turnout: 233,737; 50% of VAP. No state voter registration.

Political Lineup: Governor, Edward T. Schafer (R); Lt. Gov., Rosemarie Myrdal (R); Secy. of State, Al Jaeger (R); Atty. Gen., Heidi Heitkamp (D); Treasurer, Kathi Gilmore (D); Auditor, Robert W. Peterson (R). State Senate, 49 (29 R and 20 D); State House of Representatives, 98 (75 R and 23 D). Senators, Kent Conrad (D) and Byron L. Dorgan (D). Representative, 1 D at large.

1992 Presidential Vote

Bush (R)	136,244	(44%)
Clinton (D)	99,168	(32%)
Perot (I)	71,084	(23%)

1992 Republican Presidential Primary

Bush	39,863	(83%)
Paulsen	4,093	(9%)
Perot (write-in)	3,852	(8%)

1988 Presidential Vote

Bush (R)	166,559	(56%)
Dukakis (D)	127,739	(43%)

GOVERNOR
Gov. Edward T. Schafer (R)

Elected 1992, term expires Dec. 1996; b. August 8, 1946, Bismarck; home, Bismarck; U. of ND, B.A. 1969, U. of Denver, M.B.A. 1970; Episcopalian; married (Nancy).

Career: Gold Seal Co., 1971–86, Pres., 1978–86; Founder & Secy-Treasurer, American Eagle beverage distributorship, 1976–present; Pres. & owner, Dakota Classics auto dealership, and TRIESCO Properties real estate, 1986–present; Pres. & owner, Fish 'N Dakota aquaculture, 1990–94.

Office: State Capitol, 600 E. Boulevard, Bismarck 58505, 701-224-2200; Fax: 701-328-2205.

Election Results

1992 gen.	Edward T. Schafer (R)	176,398	(58%)
	Nicholas Spaeth (D)	123,845	(41%)
1992 prim.	Edward T. Schafer (R)	unopposed	
1988 gen.	George A. Sinner (D)	179,094	(60%)
	Leon Mallberg (R)	119,986	(40%)

SENATORS
Sen. Kent Conrad (D)

Elected 1986, seat up 2000; b. Mar. 12, 1948, Bismarck; home, Bismarck; Stanford U., B.A. 1971; George Washington U., M.B.A. 1975; Unitarian; married (Lucy Calautti).

Career: Asst., ND Tax Commissioner, 1974–80; Dir., Mgmt. Planning and Personnel, ND Tax Dept., 1980; ND Tax Commissioner, 1981–86.

DC Office: 724 HSOB 20510, 202-224-2043; Fax: 202-224-7776.

State Offices: Fed. Bldg., #228, 3d & Rosser Ave., Bismarck 58501, 701-258-4648; 657 2d Ave. N., Fargo 58102, 701-232-8030; 100 1st St. SW, #105, Minot 58701, 701-852-0703; and Fed. Bldg., 102 N. 4th St., #104, Grand Forks 58201, 701-775-9601.

Committees: *Agriculture, Nutrition & Forestry* (5th of 8 D): Forestry, Conservation and Rural Revitalization; Marketing, Inspection and Product Promotion (RMM). *Budget* (6th of 10 D). *Finance* (7th of 9 D): International Trade; Medicare, Long-Term Care and Health Insurance; Taxation and IRS Oversight. *Indian Affairs* (2nd of 8 D).

Group Ratings

	ADA	ACLU	COPE	CFA	LCV	CON	NSI	COC	ACU	NTLC	CHC
1994	85	42	75	67	62	37	30	31	12	12	21
1993	80	—	82	60	44	68	—	9	24	—	—

National Journal Ratings

	1993 LIB — 1993 CONS		1994 LIB — 1994 CONS	
Economic	59%	— 34%	55%	— 40%
Social	49%	— 50%	53%	— 40%
Foreign	78%	— 13%	58%	— 40%

Key Votes of the 103d Congress

1. Clinton Deficit Plan	Y	3. Brady Handgun Purchase	Y	5. Lmt. UN Cmnd. of Forces	N
2. NAFTA	N	4. Strike Race/Death Pnlty.	Y	6. Cut Missile Funds	Y

Key Votes of the 104th Congress

1. Congressional Compliance	Y	3. Balanced Budget Amndt.	N	5. Product Liability Reform	Y
2. Bar Unfunded Mandates	Y	4. Pass Line Item Veto	N	6. FY96 Budget	N

Election Results

1994 general	Kent Conrad (D)	137,157	(58%)	($1,927,866)
	Dr. Ben Clayburgh (R)	99,390	(42%)	($941,192)
1994 primary	Kent Conrad (D)	unopposed		
1992 special	Kent Conrad (D)	103,246	(63%)	($2,479,021)
	Jack Dalrymple (R)	55,194	(34%)	($282,104)
	Other	4,871	(3%)	

Sen. Byron L. Dorgan (D)

Elected 1992, seat up 1998; b. May 14, 1942, Dickinson; home, Bismarck; U. of ND, B.S. 1965, U. of Denver, M.B.A. 1966; Lutheran; married (Kimberly).

Career: Martin-Marietta Exec. Develop. Prog., 1966–68; ND Dep. Tax Commissioner, 1968–69, Tax Commissioner, 1969–80; U.S. House of Reps., 1980–92.

DC Office: 713 HSOB 20510, 202-224-2551; Fax: 202-224-1193.

State Offices: 312 Fed. Bldg., 3rd & Rosser Ave., Bismarck 58502, 701-250-4618; 112 Robert St., Fargo 58107, 701-239-5389.

Committees: *Commerce, Science & Transportation* (9th of 9 D): Aviation; Science, Technology & Space; Surface Transportation & Merchant Marine. *Energy and Natural Resources* (9th of 9 D): Forests & Public Land Management. *Ethics* (3rd of 3 D). *Governmental Affairs* (7th of 7 D): Investigations; Post Office & Civil Service. *Indian Affairs* (7th of 8 D). *Veterans' Affairs* (5th of 5 D).

Group Ratings

	ADA	ACLU	COPE	CFA	LCV	CON	NSI	COC	ACU	NTLC	CHC
1994	85	44	75	58	69	47	20	30	8	12	31
1993	65	—	78	60	56	77	—	10	23	—	—

National Journal Ratings

	1993 LIB — 1993 CONS		1994 LIB — 1994 CONS	
Economic	59% —	34%	61% —	35%
Social	51% —	48%	63% —	35%
Foreign	78% —	13%	66% —	29%

Key Votes of the 103d Congress

1. Clinton Deficit Plan	Y	3. Brady Handgun Purchase	*	5. Lmt. UN Cmnd. of Forces	N
2. NAFTA	*	4. Strike Race/Death Pnlty.	Y	6. Cut Missile Funds	Y

Key Votes of the 104th Congress

1. Congressional Compliance	Y	3. Balanced Budget Amndt.	N	5. Product Liability Reform	Y
2. Bar Unfunded Mandates	Y	4. Pass Line Item Veto	Y	6. FY96 Budget	N

Election Results

1992 general	Byron L. Dorgan (D)	179,347	(59%)	($1,124,512)
	Steve Sydness (R)	118,162	(39%)	($498,107)
	Other	6,448	(2%)	
1992 primary	Byron L. Dorgan (D)	unopposed		
1986 general	Kent Conrad (D)	143,932	(50%)	($908,374)
	Mark Andrews (R)	141,797	(49%)	($2,270,557)

REPRESENTATIVE

Rep. Earl Pomeroy (D)

Elected 1992; b. Sept. 2, 1952, Valley City; home, Valley City; U. of ND, B.A. 1974, J.D., 1979; Presbyterian; married (Laurie Kirby).

Career: Practicing atty., 1979–84; ND House of Reps., 1980–84; ND Insurance Commissioner, 1984–92; VP, Natl. Assn. of Insurance Commissioners, 1989, Pres., 1990.

DC Office: 1533 LHOB 20515, 202-225-2611; Fax: 202-226-0893; e-mail: epomeroy@hr.house.gov.

District Offices: Fed. Bldg., 657 2nd Ave., #266, Fargo 58102, 701-235-9760; Fed. Bldg., 220 East Rosser Ave., #376, Bismarck 58501, 701-224-0355.

Committees: *Agriculture* (13th of 22 D): General Farm Commodities; Resource Conservation, Research and Forestry. *Budget* (11th of 18 D).

Group Ratings

	ADA	ACLU	COPE	CFA	LCV	CON	NSI	COC	ACU	NTLC	CHC
1994	65	52	38	80	50	28	50	75	14	22	36
1993	65	—	92	70	55	65	—	20	21	—	—

National Journal Ratings

	1993 LIB — 1993 CONS		1994 LIB — 1994 CONS	
Economic	64% —	34%	54% —	45%
Social	55% —	45%	61% —	38%
Foreign	70% —	26%	51% —	47%

Key Votes of the 103d Congress

1. Clinton Deficit Plan	Y	3. Brady Handgun Purchase	N	5. Lmt. UN Cmnd. of Forces	N
2. NAFTA	N	4. Strike Race/Death Pnlty.	N	6. Cut Missile Funds	Y

Key Votes of the 104th Congress

1. Congressional Compliance	Y	6. Reform Crime Grant	N	11. Loser Pays Court Reform	N
2. Balanced Budget Amndmt.	N	7. National Security Act	N	12. Product Liability Reform	N
3. Bar Unfunded Mandates	Y	8. Moratorium on Regs.	Y	13. Welfare Reform	N
4. Pass Line Item Veto	Y	9. Risk Assessment on Regs.	Y	14. Term Limits Amndmt.	*
5. Relax Exclusionary Rule	Y	10. Expnd. Priv. Prop. Rights	Y	15. Tax Cuts	N

Election Results

1994 general	Earl Pomeroy (D)	123,134	(52%)	($813,900)
	Gary Porter (R)	105,988	(45%)	($818,392)
	Others	6,267	(3%)	
1994 primary	Earl Pomeroy (D)	unopposed		
1992 general	Earl Pomeroy (D)	169,273	(57%)	($430,228)
	John T. Korsmo (R)	117,442	(39%)	($150,639)
	Others	11,183	(4%)	

OHIO

Ohio was the first entirely American state, and one which ever since has seemed an epitome of American normalcy. Unlike the original 13 states, which started as British colonies, or the next three, Vermont, Kentucky and Tennessee, which were spun off from New York, Virginia and North Carolina, Ohio was created anew, the first state formed from the Northwest Territory established by Congress in 1787. The Northwest Ordinance established 6 by 6 mile square townships, which imposed geometric order on diverse American landscapes west to the Pacific; it set aside one square mile per township for public schools and the landscape was soon peppered with schoolhouses and small colleges, the foundation stones of a literate republic. The Ordinance prohibited slavery, opening the way for free labor to clear fields, raise crops, build mills and factories, and in less than half a century make this wilderness one of the most productive parts of western civilization. Ohio, in the years after the Civil War, became one of the great industrial states, the longtime headquarters of John D. Rockefeller's Standard Oil, the site of major steel mills along the narrow and languidly flowing Cuyahoga and Mahoning Rivers, and home of the biggest soap companies, machine tool makers, tire manufacturers and producers of safety glass. Settled by Virginians in the southwest around Cincinnati, by New Englanders in the northeast in the Western Reserve around Cleveland, Ohio has always been regionally split between cultures: between the southern-accented counties south of the National Road and U.S. 40 and the northern-accented cities and towns to the north; between Butternut and Copperhead territory that didn't want to fight the Civil War and Yankee territory that fiercely prosecuted the War and Reconstruction afterwards.

All this left Ohio politically a closely divided state—and a nationally pivotal one. Just a century ago it was Ohio that produced the candidate and campaign manager—Governor and former Ways and Means Chairman William McKinley and iron and coal industrialist Marc Hanna—who won the Presidency in 1896 and inaugurated a 34-year period of Republican national majorities. McKinley's Republicans were for high tariffs and hard money, had a friendly regard for workers and even some unions, but no patience with large union combinations and nascent socialism—a nationalist Americanism coupled with a wariness about making major commitments abroad. Republicans were the majority in this increasingly industrial Ohio, losing rural Butternut counties but carrying the big industrial cities of the north.

Then came the Depression of the 1930s, and Ohio became the scene of something like class warfare, with sitdown strikes and victories for the CIO industrial unions in autos, steel and tires. CIO cities—Cleveland, Akron, Youngstown, Toledo—moved sharply toward the Democrats, while places with few CIO members—Cincinnati, Columbus, the dozens of small factory towns dotting the flat limestone plains of northern Ohio—stayed Republican. The political fighting was fierce and the stakes seemed big. CIO leaders hoped to organize the entire work force and build a Scandinavian-style welfare state; Republican leaders like Ohio Senator Robert Taft feared union control of business would imperil freedoms and throttle the economy. In the 1930s and 1940s, the unions made great gains. But Taft held them off, reducing union power with the Taft-Hartley Act of 1947, his own reelection to the Senate in 1950, and—his eventual rival—Dwight Eisenhower's presidential election in 1952.

Now, in the 1990s, Ohio seems to have turned sharply toward the Republicans again, perhaps only temporarily, but with results more reminiscent of the McKinley era than of the half-century after the New Deal and the rise of the CIO unions. If this trend is sustained, it spells further trouble for Democrats not only in Ohio, but nationally, for in income levels, urban-rural balance, and ethnic mix, as well as presidential percentages, this is a state near the national average. The 1994 headline event was the reelection of Republican Governor George Voinovich by a 72%–25% margin—by far the biggest margin since 1826, when neither Republican nor Democratic parties existed. And Republicans in 1994 won up and down the line: Mike DeWine was elected senator over Democrat Joel Hyatt 53%–39%, in a race that initially seemed even, and in a state that had not elected a Republican senator since 1970. Republicans won every one of the statewide offices, dominated by Democrats since 1970; they won large margins in both houses of the legislature, replacing the nation's longest-serving state House Speaker, Vern Riffe, with Jo Ann Davidson; they gained four seats in the U.S. House—an increase for a state that was topped only by Washington. The new lieutenant governor, Nancy Putnam Hollister, a woman with an old Yankee pedigree, ran with the Serbo-Croatian Voinovich, who had served 10 years as mayor of Cleveland. Republicans also elected a woman Attorney General (Betty Montgomery), a black Treasurer (Kenneth Blackwell), and Ohio's first Hispanic legislator (John Garcia of Toledo).

Most significantly, Republicans won in north-and-east Ohio, the traditionally Democratic area along Lake Erie and reaching south to the coal-mining counties across the Ohio River from West Virginia. This was the heartland of the CIO unions, the United Steelworkers in Youngstown and Cleveland, United Rubber Workers in Akron, United Mine Workers in the coal country, United Auto Workers in Toledo and Lordstown. It was heavily ethnic, with hundreds of thousands of Poles, Hungarians, Slovaks, Serbs, and Croatians streaming in throughout the early 20th Century. North-and-east Ohio was heavily Democratic from the New Deal on. And when its auto, steel, rubber and glass factories lost hundreds of thousands of jobs in the five years after the oil shock of 1979, it was one of the most Democratic parts of the country. As a separate state, it would have come as close to voting against Ronald Reagan in 1980 and 1984 as Massachusetts or New York. It voted solidly for Michael Dukakis in 1988 (54%–46%) and Bill Clinton in 1992 (47%–31%). But as the shock of the early 1980s wore off, and it became clear that CIO industries' high-wage, low-skill jobs were gone for good, attitudes began changing. Voters gave up on trying to recreate the old factory economy and began building a new, more supple and adaptable manufacturing economy, with smaller factories, less rigid management and fewer union members, fewer low-skill jobs with high wages and more medium-skill, high-flexibility jobs with chances for advancement. And, as the country's two coasts fell into recession, north-and-east Ohio began to grow again. Cleveland's new downtown is gleaming, Akron is proud of the polymer technologies which have replaced tire manufacturing, the Cuyahoga River is clean and the valleys carved by rivers in the limestone are a source of pride.

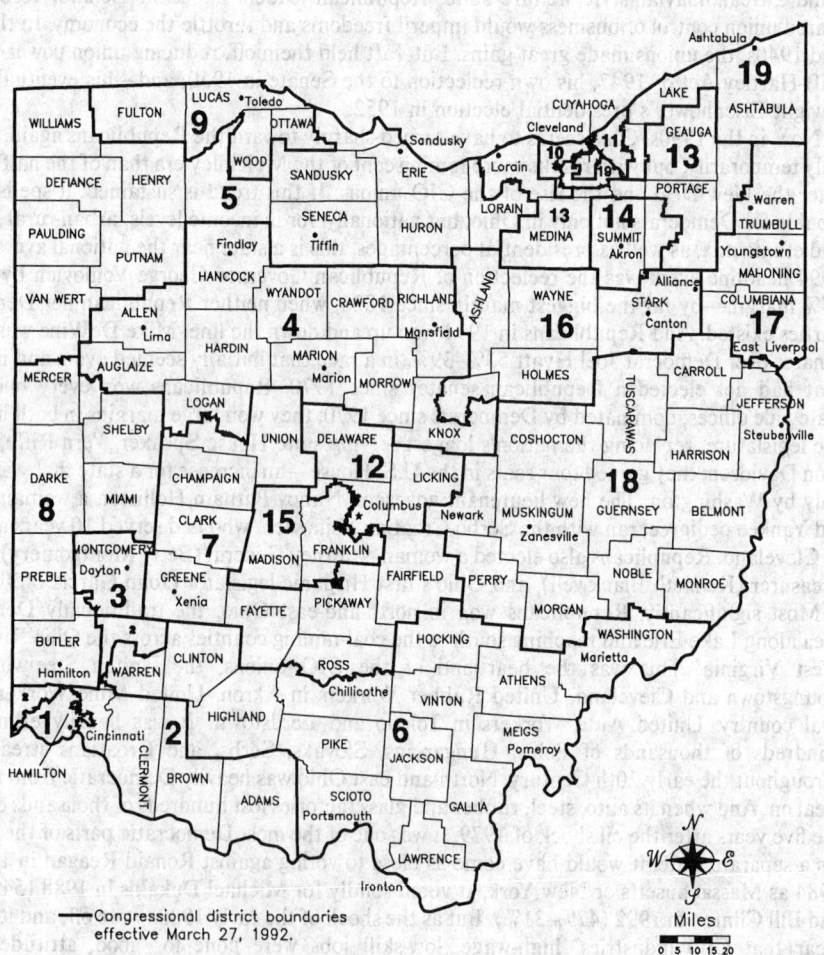

—Congressional district boundaries
effective March 27, 1992.

Miles
0 5 10 15 20

George Voinovich, long familiar to the Cleveland TV market, lost north-and-east Ohio 64%–36% in the 1988 Senate race, but two years later running for governor he carried it 55%–45%. In 1994, against a little-known opponent, he won 69%–29%, the kind of Republican margin not seen in this area of Ohio since the 1920s. Even more startlingly, Republican Mike DeWine carried the area over Democrat Joel Hyatt 47%–45% in the 1994 Senate race. Hyatt's percentage was slightly below the Democratic presidential percentages of 1992, 1984, and 1980—suggesting that Democrats have lost the natural majority they had here from the 1930s to the 1980s. The politics of union-management struggle, class warfare and economic redistribution seems dead in one of its American heartlands. Another politics is growing in its place, hostile to federal taxes and central direction but hospitable to activist local government and market economic growth.

The rest of Ohio has long been a Republican area, a stronghold for Robert Taft and for James Rhodes, governor for 16 of the 20 years between 1962 and 1982, who favored low taxes in order to attract jobs. In the 1980s, this larger part of Ohio's cultural conservatism and patriotic nationalism, plus faith in a growing economy, made it heavily Republican, 67%–32% for Ronald Reagan in 1984 and 63%–36% for George Bush (whose grandfather owned a steel factory in Columbus) in 1988. In 1992, support for Bush fell off disastrously, and he carried it by only 44%–35%, with 20% for Perot. But in 1994 Voinovich and DeWine carried it overwhelmingly.

For Voinovich, the Republicans' 1994 sweep in Ohio may signal only his momentary popularity: no well-known Democrat wanted to run against him, leaving the nomination to an obscure state senator, Robert L. Burch Jr., backed by the state AFL-CIO. But the Democrats' inability to field winning candidates up and down the ticket—in contrast to the 1970s and 1980s, when their politically sharp candidates won most statewide and legislative races—suggests demoralization. Looking ahead, there is only one major Ohio Democrat left in office, Senator John Glenn, who turns 77 in 1998, when his seat comes up—the same age at which Senator Howard Metzenbaum chose to retire in 1994. It is hard to see, absent a conspicuous Republican failure, where a Democrat can get the institutional resources or the ideas needed for a serious statewide race. Voinovich may not be an inspiring figure with a captivating vision of the future, but there was no such political figure either in the age of McKinley. The Ohioans who captured Americans' imaginations and helped shape our national image were mechanical tinkerers and can-do manufacturers, adaptive businessmen and hard-working employees, struggling to work hard, raise families and serve communities that felt little class conflict or economic envy. They were inventors like Thomas Edison and Wilbur and Orville Wright, and the men who invented the cash register and auto safety glass and the automatic starter. That is what Ohio seems to be again today and, if it continues to match the national political profile, what the nation may be heading for.

Governor. George Voinovich is an unassuming man who shines his own shoes and brownbags lunch, a Republican who has over and again won the votes of Democrats, a career politician who cast himself successfully as a reformer while mayor of Cleveland and an adversary of the insiders in Columbus, a pleasant man capable of aggressive politicking on occasion. Mayor of Cleveland for 10 years and governor for four, he seems to enjoy public policymaking, and has had great success balancing competing values. He slowed state budget growth from 8% annually to 6%, but backed one tax increase in 1992. He put a six month limit on General Assistance, but didn't zero it out, as did Michigan's John Engler. Voinovich boasts that his JOBS program has enrolled more welfare recipients than any other state's, and that he cut welfare rolls. He cut higher education spending but raised it for Head Start and primary and secondary schools, and brags of higher test scores; his current focus is an Equity Fund, to equalize resources for school districts. He sponsored a managed healthcare plan, OhioCare, for Medicaid and the uninsured, and continued Democratic Governor Richard Celeste's program for state investment in businesses. He is opposed to abortion but recognizes *Roe v. Wade* as the law and says, "Let's deal in the real world." He is a strong advocate of allowing state governments more leeway, and his own record is evidence that states can cut costs and improve services better on their own than under federal dictation.

Voinovich has had setbacks. He lost a Senate race in 1988 (the apparently obligatory statewide loss required for success in Ohio). And in 1979, when he was first running for mayor of Cleveland, his young daughter was killed in an auto accident. But in 1994, he raised $7 million and, when it became clear he had only nuisance opposition, gave $2.7 million to other Republicans, to help produce their statewide sweep. He was able to boast not only of innovative programs, but of 150,000 new private sector jobs: "The Rust is off the Belt," he likes to say. He carried virtually every demographic group, running weaker among those with no high school diplomas and those with graduate degrees: the recipients and providers of government services. Voinovich does not seem to have presidential ambitions, but has been mentioned as a vice presidential nominee. His government activism and demeanor might attract moderates, but his tax increases have led *The Wall Street Journal* to call him the "nation's premier Republican tax raiser." His popularity would help in Ohio though, whose 21 electoral votes both parties must target to win.

In Ohio, where term limits taking effect in 2000 have already squelched career politicians' ambitions, Voinovich will likely continue to dominate the public scene. The frontrunner for the Republican gubernatorial nomination for 1998 is Secretary of State Robert A. Taft II, son and grandson of senators of that name, who bowed out of the 1990 primary for Voinovich. Democrats have no clear favorite. Former Governor Richard Celeste might run, though his work as the Democratic National Committee's healthcare plan coordinator was not successful. Attorney General Lee Fisher, a winner in 1990, lost in 1994; former Attorney General William Brown, who lost the 1982 primary to Celeste, and Congressman Sherrod Brown, who lost the secretary of State job to Taft in 1990 but survived the 1994 Republican sweep in the House, might run; both have a last name that was magic in statewide races from the 1950s to the 1980s.

Senators. Ohio is represented by two senators of two parties of two generations, who both lost their first Senate races and have run against each other: veteran Democrat John Glenn and freshman Republican Michael DeWine. Both come from small towns and retain an aw-shucks tone, but have long since learned to navigate the shoals of bigtime politics.

John Glenn is now the grand old man of Ohio politics. Many voters have no living memory of the event that thrust him into national fame, when he became the first American astronaut to orbit the earth in a space capsule in February 1962; many are not even familiar with the movie *The Right Stuff*, whose release in October 1983 was expected to boost Glenn's presidential candidacy in 1984. His 22-year career in the Marine Corps, which included heroic service in World War II and Korea, is about to be equalled in length by his career in the Senate. Glenn came to politics as the authentic embodiment of the small town virtues of family, God-fearing religion, duty, patriotism and hard work typical of his home town of New Concord, Ohio; he also brought the aggressiveness that made him a brilliant fighter pilot, earned him fame as an astronaut, and then propelled him into running for the Senate in 1964. He left that race after injuring himself in a household accident; in 1970, he ran again and lost in the primary to Howard Metzenbaum, the beginning of a long rivalry that ultimately became a friendship; in 1974, he beat Metzenbaum in the primary and then easily won the general. In those days, Glenn was a moderate Democrat, with issue positions and a personal demeanor at odds with the liberal activists of the time—which helps account for the coolness of the response to his presidential candidacy in 1984. Glenn's difficulty that year was not just ideological. He did not shine in debates, and his decision to stay in the race one more week to compete in southern primaries helped pile up a campaign debt of some $3 million, the bulk of which he has never been able to pay off—and which became a liability in his 1992 election.

In the 1980s, Glenn became less of an above-the-fray hero and more of a partisan politician, in Washington and with Ohio voters. He was solidly pro-choice on abortion and dovish on the Gulf war resolution. As chairman of the Governmental Affairs Committee from 1986–94, he questioned Vice President Dan Quayle's Competitiveness Council and then sponsored legislation to support Vice President Al Gore's "reinventing government." He sponsored Cabinet rank for the Environmental Protection Agency which failed in the House and Hatch Act repeal which Clinton signed into law. He also successfully sponsored a government paperwork reduction act and a streamlined purchasing law. After failing to gain passage when Democrats were in control of an unfunded mandates ban and congressional compliance with workplace laws, he rankled some of his party seniors by joining the new Republican majority as a vocal advocate of those measures in early 1995. Glenn investigations of IRS employees snooping and of government releases of radiation into the air seem to have prompted action. He argues that his sponsorship of Inspectors General and Chief Financial Officers for government agencies has saved billions. He has worked to clean up the government's nuclear materials plants, notably the Fernald plant just outside Cincinnati.

Less visible, but arguably more important, has been Glenn's detailed work for two decades on nuclear proliferation. He has kept careful watch of, and has tried to reduce or eliminate, U.S. exports of nuclear technology and materials to Pakistan, Iraq and other countries. It is uphill work, for the violators are ingenious and foreign policy makers always have arguments why specific cases should be exempted from the anti-proliferation rules. How much difference Glenn has made is unclear, but the significance of the cause and the fact that it has no natural institutional backer has made his work on it important.

Unfortunately for Glenn, his antiproliferation work produced many fewer headlines than the Keating Five scandal, in which he played a part. For years Glenn had known Charles Keating, once a prominent Cincinnatian and later a flamboyant savings and loan owner, and was one of five senators present at the extraordinary meeting with federal regulators in the spring of 1987. After regulators told Glenn they were referring the case against Keating to the Justice Department for criminal investigation, Glenn turned down a Keating aide's offer to raise any further money for his PAC; but he did set up a January 1988 meeting between Keating and House Speaker Jim Wright, after which Glenn said he had no further contact with Keating. Many thought the Senate Ethics Committee should have dismissed Glenn's case and Senator John McCain's altogether; but committee Democrats, apparently to keep McCain, the lone Republican in the case, refused to do so. They ultimately recommended the same lack of punishment for Glenn and McCain as for the more culpable Dennis DeConcini and Donald Riegle, although specifying that Glenn was guilty only of poor judgment.

In 1992 Glenn faced his strongest general election contest from Michael DeWine, who raised the Keating Five issue and, given the obscurity of some of Glenn's legislative work, asked "What on earth has John Glenn done?" Until September, DeWine held Glenn under 50% in polls, but DeWine's 31 overdrafts on the House bank, the time he fell asleep during the Iran-contra hearings, and his anti-abortion stand were recollected by the Glenn campaign, and Glenn won 51%–42%. For the first time, he needed his margin (58%–35%) in north-and-east Ohio, because he lost the rest of the state, which he once carried 65%–32%, by 47%–45%. There are any number of statewide officials and House members—current and past—who may run for this seat in 1998.

It has long been a rule in Ohio politics that, before you can win an election for senator or governor, you must run once and lose: it applies to George Voinovich and every other governor or senator but one elected in the last 40 years. The latest example is Michael DeWine, defeated for the Senate in 1992, elected in 1994. DeWine is short, gap-toothed, bespectacled, and youthful looking; he is also nearing 50, the father of eight, and the holder of public office for nearly 20 years. DeWine grew up in Yellow Springs, Ohio, the home of liberal Antioch College, where his family owned a successful seed business; after school, he and his wife moved to nearby Cedarville, in a part of the state with rolling hills, winding creeks and covered bridges, where he now hosts an annual ice cream social. There he was elected Greene County Prosecutor at 29, where he resisted plea bargaining, and in order to nail a drug dealer once put up the collateral to get $50,000 cash to stage a buy. At 33 he was elected to the Ohio Senate; two years later, he won a six-candidate Republican primary with 69% of the vote and was elected to a U.S. House seat. He worked for tougher drunk driving penalties, mandatory sentencing, and aid to child crime victims, with more success in Republican Columbus than on Democratic Capitol Hill. Elected lieutenant governor in 1990, he sought better and more responsive teenage offender facilities and an Ohio DNA analysis lab.

DeWine's loss to Glenn didn't stop him from running again in 1994, but this time there was serious competition in both the primary and general. The contest was to succeed Howard Metzenbaum, the hard-fighting liberal Democrat whose political career goes back half a century and who for 30 years either won the seat himself or managed the campaign of the man who did. Metzenbaum was the toughest opponent of Clarence Thomas, and the lead sponsor of gun control and plant closing notification laws; Metzenbaum's last cause was to try to relieve any impediments against cross-racial adoptions. Having beaten George Voinovich in 1988, he hoped to be succeeded by his son-in-law, Joel Hyatt, founder of the storefront Hyatt Legal Services chain. But in the May primary, Hyatt defeated Cuyahoga County Commissioner Mary Boyle by only a 47%–43% margin, while DeWine by a 53%–32%–10% margin dispatched Dr. Bernadine Healy, former director of the National Institutes of Health, and state Senator Gene Watts.

From then on, DeWine had solid leads in most polls. He spent much time in the Cleveland area, cutting into the Democrats' base; in a year of anti-politician rhetoric, he cited his experience and said, mimicking a Hyatt Legal Services TV ad, with Hyatt "all you have is his 'word on it.' " Liabilities—rather than assets—included Hyatt's relationships to Metzenbaum (the Senator's job approval in the exit poll was 40% positive and 51% negative) and to the Clintons, whom he knew at Yale Law School and whose healthcare principles he supported. Also, two incidents from his past hurt Hyatt with core Democratic constituencies. A Hyatt Legal Services office in Philadelphia in 1987 fired a lawyer with AIDS, in one of the cases that inspired the movie *Philadelphia*, which premiered the spring of the primary. And while a student at Dartmouth, Hyatt had opposed admitting women to the college. DeWine's anti-crime planks, his backing of term limits and the line-item veto helped him; his support of NAFTA did not hurt (the exit poll showed voters thought it was good for Ohio by a 26%–23% margin). Nor did former Operation Rescue leader Joseph Slovenec, who ran as an Independent, siphoning off many Republican votes; Sovenec's highest percentages were in counties across from West Virginia, where he took Democratic votes. The 23% of voters in union households split evenly, while the 29% who were gun owners voted 58%–31% for the almost always plaid-shirt-clad DeWine. DeWine won statewide 53%–39%, by 47%–45% in north-and-east Ohio and 58%–35% in the rest of the state. In the Senate he is likely to remain solidly, but not stridently conservative, with a particular interest in crime and justice issues.

Presidential politics. With 21 electoral votes and a tradition of close partisan competition, Ohio is a crucial state in presidential politics. It matched the national average in 1984 and 1988 and was the closest (40%–38% Clinton, with 21% for Perot) of the six non-southern megastates in 1992, when it received the most fall visits from the Clintons and Gores (45) and the Bushes and Quayles (28). No Republican has ever been elected president without carrying Ohio; no Democrat, in the electoral vote arithmetic of the 1990s, could hope to win without it. Richard Nixon advised Reagan and Bush managers Ed Rollins and Lee Atwater to put extra money and special ads into Ohio, to make it a roadblock for Walter Mondale and Michael Dukakis. In 1992, that strategy was reversed, since the West Coast was lost to Bush and the South in jeopardy; then James Carville made Ohio a roadblock. Now, if 1994 trends continue, with the South solidly Republican and California up for grabs, Republicans may try to make Ohio their roadblock again in 1996. Many of the state's Republican leadership, including Governor Voinovich have already endorsed Bob Dole.

Ohio's primary for 1996 has been switched from May to the same Tuesday in mid-March when Illinois and Michigan vote, thus setting up a sort of regional Great Lakes primary. Just weeks after Iowa and New Hampshire and seven days after southern Super Tuesday, these contests could clinch the Republican nomination for someone—and determine the fate of any Democrat who might challenge President Clinton.

Congressional districting. Ohio lost two districts in the 1990 Census; this state that elected 24 congressmen in 1970 elected 19 in 1992. The contorted district lines, with at least three grotesque barbell-shaped districts, are the product of a late bipartisan compromise in 1992. But already six contests have been won by the party that redistricters thought would lose: so much for the plans of mice and men. More partisan instability is likely. Term limits, unless the U.S. Supreme Court overturns them, take effect for House members in 2000; reshuffling will begin before that. And, with odd timing, former Congressman Clarence Miller and the state Libertarian party filed suit in November 1994 against the current lines; if they win, they will have to be redrawn for 1996.

The People: Est. Pop. 1994: 11,102,000; Pop. 1990: 10,847,115, up 2.4% 1990–1994. 4.3% of U.S. total, 7th largest; 26% rural. Median age: 33.3 years. 13.0% 65 years and over. 87.8% White, 10.6% Black, 1.3% Hispanic origin. Households: 56.1% married couple families; 27% married couple fams. w. children; 39% college educ.; median household income: $28,706; per capita income: $13,461; 67.5% owner occupied housing; median house value: $63,500; median monthly rent: $296. 7.2% Unemployment. 1994 Voting age pop.: 8,313,000. 1994 Turnout: 3,417,249; 41% of VAP. Registered voters (1994): 6,211,161; no party registration.

Political Lineup: Governor, George V. Voinovich (R); Lt. Gov., Nancy Putnam Hollister (R); Secy. of State, Robert Taft (R); Atty. Gen., Betty D. Montgomery (R); Treasurer, J. Kenneth Blackwell (R); Auditor, Jim Petro (R). State Senate, 33 (20 R and 13 D); State House of Representatives, 99 (56 R and 43 D). Senators, John H. Glenn, Jr. (D) and Mike DeWine (R). Representatives, 19 (13 R and 6 D).

1992 Presidential Vote

Clinton (D)	1,984,942	(40%)
Bush (R)	1,894,310	(38%)
Perot (I)	1,036,426	(21%)

1992 Democratic Presidential Primary

Clinton	638,347	(61%)
Brown	197,449	(19%)
Tsongas	110,773	(11%)
Other	95,765	(9%)

1988 Presidential Vote

Bush (R)	2,416,549	(55%)
Dukakis (D)	1,939,629	(44%)

1992 Republican Presidential Primary

Bush	716,766	(83%)
Buchanan	143,687	(17%)

GOVERNOR

Gov. George V. Voinovich (R)

Elected 1990, term expires Jan. 1999; b. July 15, 1936, Cleveland; home, Columbus; Ohio U., B.A. 1958, Ohio State U., J.D. 1961; Catholic; married (Janet).

Career: OH Asst. Atty. Gen., 1963–64; OH House of Reps., 1967–71; Cuyahoga Cnty. Auditor, 1971–76; Cuyahoga Cnty. Commissioner, 1977–78; OH Lt. Gov., 1979; Cleveland Mayor, 1979–89.

Office: Office of the Governor, 77 S. High St., 30th Fl., Columbus 43266, 614-466-3555; Fax: 614-644-0951.

Election Results

1994 gen.	George V. Voinovich (R)	2,401,572	(72%)
	Robert L. Burch, Jr. (D)	835,849	(25%)
	Others	108,817	(3%)
1994 prim.	George V. Voinovich (R)	unopposed	
1990 gen.	George V. Voinovich (R)	1,938,103	(56%)
	Anthony J. Celebrezze, Jr. (D)	1,539,416	(44%)

SENATORS

Sen. John H. Glenn Jr. (D)

Elected 1974, seat up 1998; b. July 18, 1921, Cambridge; home, Columbus; Muskingum Col., B.S. 1943; Presbyterian; married (Annie).

Career: Marine Corps, 1943–65 (WWII & Korea); NASA astronaut, 1959–65, first American to orbit the Earth, 1962; V.P., Royal Crown Cola Co., 1966–68, Pres., Royal Crown Intl., 1967–69.

DC Office: 503 HSOB 20510, 202-224-3353; Fax: 202-224-7983.

State Offices: 200 N. High St., #600, Columbus 43215, 614-469-6697; 1240 E. 9th St., #2957, Cleveland 44199, 216-522-7095; 550 Main St., #10407, Cincinnati 45202, 513-684-3265; and 234 N. Summit St., #726, Toledo 43604, 419-259-7592.

Committees: *Armed Services* (6th of 10 D): Airland Forces; Readiness (RMM); Strategic Forces. *Governmental Affairs* (RMM of 7 D): Investigations. *Intelligence (Select)* (2nd of 8 D). *Aging (Special)* (2nd of 9 D).

Group Ratings

	ADA	ACLU	COPE	CFA	LCV	CON	NSI	COC	ACU	NTLC	CHC
1994	80	72	75	67	77	6	70	33	4	16	7
1993	85	—	73	90	63	32	—	27	13	—	—

National Journal Ratings

	1993 LIB — 1993 CONS		1994 LIB — 1994 CONS	
Economic	71%	17%	68%	29%
Social	92%	0%	85%	7%
Foreign	44%	52%	58%	40%

Key Votes of the 103d Congress

1. Clinton Deficit Plan	Y	3. Brady Handgun Purchase	Y	5. Lmt. UN Cmnd. of Forces	N
2. NAFTA	N	4. Strike Race/Death Pnlty.	N	6. Cut Missile Funds	N

Key Votes of the 104th Congress

1. Congressional Compliance	Y	3. Balanced Budget Amndt.	N	5. Product Liability Reform	Y
2. Bar Unfunded Mandates	Y	4. Pass Line Item Veto	N	6. FY96 Budget	N

Election Results

1992 general	John H. Glenn, Jr. (D)	2,444,419	(51%)	($4,974,109)
	Mike DeWine (R)	2,028,300	(42%)	($3,053,156)
	Martha Kathryn Grevatt (I)	321,670	(7%)	
1992 primary	John H. Glenn, Jr. (D)	unopposed		
1986 general	John H. Glenn, Jr. (D)	1,949,208	(62%)	($1,319,026)
	Thomas N. Kindness (R)	1,171,893	(38%)	($657,908)

Sen. Mike DeWine (R)

Elected 1994, seat up 2000; b. Jan. 5. 1947, Springfield; home, Cedarville; Miami U. of OH, B.S. 1969, OH Northern U., J.D. 1972; Roman Catholic; married (Frances).

Career: Practicing atty; Greene Cnty. Asst. Prosecuting atty., 1973–75, Prosecuting atty., 1977–81; OH Senate, 1981–82; U.S. House of Reps., 1982–90; OH Lt. Gov., 1990–94.

DC Office: 140 RSOB 20510, 202-224-2315; Fax: 202-224-6519.

State Offices: 200 N. High St., #405, Columbus 43215, 614-469-6774; 550 Main St., #10411, Cincinnati 45202, 513-684-3894; 234 N. Summit St., #716, Toledo 43604, 419-259-7535; 1240 E. 9th St., #2915, Cleveland 44199, 216-522-7272; and 200 Putnam St., #522, Marietta 45750, 614-373-2120.

Committees: *Intelligence (Select)* (4th of 9 R). *Judiciary* (9th of 10 R): Administrative Oversight and the Courts; Constitution, Federalism and Property Rights. *Labor & Human Resources* (6th of 9 R): Children and Families; Disability Policy; Education, Arts and Humanities.

Group Ratings and 103rd Congress Votes: Newly Elected

Key Votes of the 104th Congress

1. Congressional Compliance Y	3. Balanced Budget Amndt. Y	5. Product Liability Reform Y
2. Bar Unfunded Mandates Y	4. Pass Line Item Veto Y	6. FY96 Budget Y

Election Results

1994 general	Mike DeWine (R)	1,836,556	(53%)	($6,084,663)
	Joel Hyatt (D)	1,348,213	(39%)	($4,921,223)
	Joseph J. Slovenec (I)	252,031	(7%)	($192,867)
1994 primary	Mike DeWine (R)	422,366	(52%)	
	Bernadine Healy (R)	263,559	(32%)	
	Eugene J. Watts (R)	83,103	(10%)	
	George H. Rhodes (R)	42,633	(5%)	
1988 general	Howard M. Metzenbaum (D).	2,480,038	(57%)	($8,547,545)
	George V. Voinovich (R).	1,872,716	(43%)	($8,233,859)

FIRST DISTRICT

Cincinnati, Ohio's first major metropolis, looks down on the curves of the Ohio River from seven hills. This was the Queen City of the West in the 19th Century, the nation's fourth largest city at the outbreak of the Civil War, a heavily German beehive of riverboats and sausage factories, known as Porkopolis (it celebrated its bicentennial in 1988 with a sculpture topped by four flying pigs). Cincinnati has long given off an air of the recent past; Mark Twain said he'd like to be there for the apocalypse because everything in Cincinnati is 20 years behind. Today the city seems to be stepping, stylishly and gracefully, into the mid-1970s. Growing slowly over many decades, Cincinnati has long-settled good looks and an urbanity somehow consistent with its natural terrain: the bottomlands along the river, the hills and rolling terrain above. In the middle of Cincinnati is Mill Creek, lined with factories; on the hills to the west are the modest streetcar suburbs of the last century and the early years of this one. On Mount Adams and toward the northeast are set a string of affluent neighborhoods, with stately mansions like the William Howard Taft house, and the comfortable Tudors and colonials of the 20th Century bourgeoisie—Reform Jewish as well as WASP and German.

Cincinnati was the site of great innovations: the first iron suspension bridge, in 1867, connected Cincinnati to northern Kentucky and was designed by John Roebling who later built the Brooklyn Bridge; the first baseball team, the Red Stockings, in 1869; the country's leading Reform Jewish seminary, Hebrew Union College, in 1875. And if over the past century Cincinnati has not had the growth spurts of cities like Cleveland or Houston, neither has it had their sharp contractions. It has spawned not flashy but solid industries, like the Procter & Gamble soap business, now headquartered in a striking two-towered office complex at the edge of downtown, and it has America's biggest concentration of machine tool makers. Its Cincinnati Reds have been one of America's most exciting teams in recent decades, though hurt by the gambling of star Pete Rose and the racist rants of owner Marge Schott. Downtown Cincinnati's spruced-up Fountain Square shows off the well-maintained skyscrapers of the past, its first class restaurants still attract a dressy clientele. Old ethnic neighborhoods, crowded with brick row houses on steep hills, keep their thick local accents and special local foods, from German sauerbrauten to Cincinnati chili (try it "four way," served with spaghetti, onions and grated cheese).

The 1st Congressional District of Ohio includes almost all of Cincinnati, except for its affluent eastern edge, plus the middle-class suburbs that cling to the woody hills north and west, all the way to North Bend, the home of President William Henry Harrison, and the Indiana border. Ancestrally Republican, when it was a German anti-slavery island in a southern-stock pro-Confederate sea, this territory is now competitive between the parties, as Cincinnati's affluent population heads east and northeast. City elections here have long been competitive between the old line Republicans and a combination of Democrats and Charterites (the latter started by Charles Taft, liberal brother of Senator Robert Taft, Sr.) and council members become celebrities in the entire media market. One or both Cincinnati area congressional districts have been seriously contested in almost every election since 1964, and for 44 years were represented by nothing but former Cincinnati council members with the understandable exception of Robert Taft, Jr. (One former council member and mayor, Jerry Springer, has even become a national talk show host.)

That record was broken, after a series of close and heated contests, in 1994, with the victory of Republican Steve Chabot, a member of the Hamilton County Commission who was unopposed in the primary. This was significant perhaps as a symbol of suburbanization, and as a victory for a conservative Republican. But it was also an example of how a moderate Democrat was squeezed out by competition from both left and right. Incumbent David Mann had served on the City Council since 1974, and had twice been mayor. When incumbent Charles Luken retired suddenly after the June 1992 primary ("basically, I just feel I belong at home," he explained), Mann entered the special primary and won by 416 votes, 33%–32%, over black state Senator William Bowen. In the general, Mann beat Republican Steve Grote, who ran as an Independent because he failed to get enough signatures to get on the GOP ballot, 51%–43%. In the House, Mann quickly compiled the least liberal voting record of any Ohio Democrat on economic issues: he opposed the 1993 stimulus package and Clinton budget and tax plan; he voted against extension of unemployment benefits; he said he was against the Clinton healthcare plan. And, the last straw to the unions, he voted for NAFTA. He argued that NAFTA would be good for Cincinnati's strong export economy, but AFL-CIO officials accused him of betrayal, and Bowen, saying "It's despicable what he has done," ran against him again. Bowen had support from black, gay and union activists; Mann spent $200,000 on TV ads and brought in Vice President Gore, while insisting "I'm independent on behalf of my constituents and do not take instructions from anybody." It was enough only for a 49%–48%, 667-vote Mann victory.

In the fall, Mann's financial advantage was not enough. Chabot called for reforming welfare by letting states make more decisions; he backed the balanced budget amendment and strongly opposed abortion. He attacked Mann's support of Clinton; Mann, after a September poll showed Chabot ahead, attacked his support of the Contract With America. Mann, who served in the Navy before the Vietnam war, pointed out that Chabot was never in uniform; Chabot responded, "I didn't dodge the draft like the President did." Chabot won comfortably, 56%–44%. Although he found it tough in the early going to establish a niche that would allow him to stand out in the state's burgeoning Republican delegation, he seems likely to be a solid conservative vote in Speaker Newt Gingrich's Republican House and to have a good chance for reelection, given the Democrats' local splits and absent a sharp change in national opinion. He was particularly vocal on the welfare reform provisions of the Contract, pushing for states to have direct administration over school lunch programs. "My view is while we need nutritious lunches in our schools, we need a whole lot less baloney in Washington," he said.

The People: Pop. 1990: 571,052; 1% rural; 13% age 65+; 68% White; 30% Black; 1% Asian; 1% Hispanic origin. Voting age pop.: 420,762; 27% Black; 1% Hispanic origin. Households: 44% married couple families; 20% married couple fams. w. children; 43% college educ.; median household income: $25,405; per capita income: $12,616; median gross rent: $336; median house value: $64,300.

1992 Presidential Vote			1988 Presidential Vote		
Clinton (D)	104,494	(43%)	Bush (R)	126,174	(55%)
Bush (R)	104,339	(43%)	Dukakis (D)	101,336	(45%)
Perot (I)	34,531	(14%)			

Rep. Steve Chabot (R)

Elected 1994; b. Jan. 22, 1953, Cincinnati; home, Cincinnati; Col. of William & Mary, B.A. 1975, N. KY U. Chase Col. of Law, J.D. 1978; Catholic; married (Donna).

Career: Elem. Schl. Teacher, 1975–76; Practicing atty., 1978–94; Cincinnati City Cncl., 1985–90; Hamilton Cnty. Comm., 1990–94.

DC Office: 1641 LHOB 20515, 202-225-2216; Fax: 202-225-3012.

District Offices: 105 W. 4th St., #1115, Cincinnati 45202, 513-684-2723.

Committees: *International Relations* (20th of 23 R): Africa; International Economic Policy and Trade. *Judiciary* (18th of 20 R): Commercial and Administrative Law; Crime. *Small Business* (19th of 22 R): Procurement, Exports and Business Opportunities.

Group Ratings and 103d Congress Votes: Newly Elected

Key Votes of the 104th Congress

1. Congressional Compliance	Y	6. Reform Crime Grant	Y	11. Loser Pays Court Reform	Y
2. Balanced Budget Amndmt.	Y	7. National Security Act	Y	12. Product Liability Reform	Y
3. Bar Unfunded Mandates	Y	8. Moratorium on Regs.	Y	13. Welfare Reform	Y
4. Pass Line Item Veto	Y	9. Risk Assessment on Regs.	Y	14. Term Limits Amndmt.	Y
5. Relax Exclusionary Rule	Y	10. Expnd. Priv. Prop. Rights	Y	15. Tax Cuts	Y

Election Results

1994 general	Steve Chabot (R)	92,997	(56%)	($542,829)
	David Mann (D)	72,822	(44%)	($1,001,393)
1994 primary	Steve Chabot (R)	unopposed		
1992 general	David Mann (D)	120,190	(51%)	($278,294)
	Stephen Grote (I)	101,498	(43%)	($83,038)
	Jim Berns (I)	12,734	(5%)	($1,817)

SECOND DISTRICT

The most Republican major metro area in the nation, by some measures at least, is Cincinnati. Back in the 1850s, when Harriet Beecher Stowe wrote *Uncle Tom's Cabin* here, Cincinnati was an island of German, pro-Union, Republican sentiment in a southern, Democratic, pro-slavery sea. Later Cincinnati attracted fewer southern and eastern European immigrants than Great Lakes industrial cities like Cleveland, Detroit and Chicago; its ethnic character (like its physical appearance) and its political preference have remained pretty well fixed. Even many of the Appalachians here are Republicans, from Civil War Republican counties in the hills. Democratic constituencies here never got very large: economically, it was never a strong CIO town; culturally, it is home to a strong anti-pornography movement that, among other things, canceled a Robert Mapplethorpe exhibit here. Cincinnati's Republican record remains intact in the 1990s: it was the only million-plus metro area which George Bush carried with more than 50% in 1992; in 1994 it voted 77%–20% for Republican Governor George Voinovich.

For 140 years after 1852, Cincinnati and surrounding Hamilton County were divided by a north-south line into two congressional districts. After the 1990 Census, redistricters created one mostly urban district which leaned a bit to the Democrats and a mostly suburban district that spread out into the countryside and was heavily Republican. This 2d Congressional District of Ohio includes the affluent eastern suburbs around elite Indian Hill and newer Montgomery, plus a few affluent precincts of Cincinnati itself; it includes recent growth areas like northeastern Hamilton County and Anderson Township south of the Little Miami River, plus the far west part of the county, all heavily Republican; it heads east along the Ohio River to include Clermont County, a fast-growth area for 20 years, plus two rural counties and an oddly-shaped sliver of Warren County between Cincinnati and Dayton.

The 2d has been the most Republican district in Ohio in the last two presidential elections. For nearly 20 years it was represented by Bill Gradison, first elected in 1974, who, after losing the race for a party leadership post, resigned in January 1993 to become head of the Health Insurance Association of America, which produced the "Harry and Louise" ads that so successfully raised questions about the Clinton healthcare plan. Rob Portman, the Republican elected in March 1993 to replace Gradison, entered the House with the lowest seniority of any member of the minority and in less than two years is positioned to emerge as one of the bright operators of the majority.

Portman entered the 1993 primary with advantages and disadvantages. He had campaigned for Gradison before he was 21 and went to work for Patton, Boggs & Blow, an influential Washington lobbying law firm, right after law school. He practiced law in Cincinnati for two years and then went to work in the Bush White House. Portman got Gradison's endorsement and had impressive financial backing from the Cincinnati establishment, starting with mega-financier Carl Lindner. But Portman also could have been attacked in his initial bid as a Washington insider, which could easily have been fatal had the year been 1994. But neither of his two opponents was perfectly positioned to make that charge. Bob McEwen had spent 12 years representing the next-door 6th District, which he lost to a Democrat in 1992 after he was reported to have 166 overdrafts on the House bank; he had represented some of Clermont County before, though, and emphasized his proven conservative record. And Jay Buchert, though he had made his career in business and campaigned as "not a politician," was politically savvy enough to have ended up as president of the Washington-based National Association of Home Builders. Buchert ran a vitriolically negative campaign against both Portman and McEwen. Portman spent gobs of money and, with solid support in Cincinnati, won 36% of the vote; McEwen, carrying counties he had once represented, had 30%; Buchert had 25%. Portman then beat the Democratic nominee with 70% and won in November 1994 with 77%. The only limit to his tenure in the 2d District is the Ohio term limits law which, if constitutional, will bar him from being listed on the ballot in 2000.

Like many Republicans, Portman was campaigning on Contract With America planks before the Contract was written and signed. In line with anti-Washington sentiment, he kept his casework operations back home, and not in a downtown Cincinnati office, but in offices in Kenwood and Batavia. He sponsored in 1993 and 1994 amendments to cut unfunded federal mandates and voted against appropriations bills that didn't reduce spending in actual dollars. With his new seat on the Ways and Means Committee, he is well-positoned to gain the influence on tax and social-policy issues that Gradison had once wielded on that panel. He interpreted the 1994 vote as a mandate for "a more accountable Congress and a leaner, more responsive federal government." He backs the balanced budget amendment, the line-item veto, and a "spending reduction commission," which if enacted would tend to ratchet federal spending downward rather than, as current procedures tend to do, upward. The interesting question now is whether Portman and his Republican majority colleagues can make these changes effective, or at least make a record on them on which voters can render a verdict in 1996.

The People: Pop. 1990: 570,779; 29% rural; 11% age 65+; 96% White; 2% Black; 1% Asian. Voting age pop.: 417,438; 2% Black. Households: 63% married couple families; 31% married couple fams. w. children; 46% college educ.; median household income: $34,688; per capita income: $16,813; median gross rent: $409; median house value: $79,000.

1992 Presidential Vote			1988 Presidential Vote		
Bush (R)	143,964	(52%)	Bush (R)	167,011	(71%)
Clinton (D)	78,117	(28%)	Dukakis (D)	69,311	(29%)
Perot (I)	51,356	(19%)			

Rep. Rob Portman (R)

Elected May, 1993; b. Dec. 19, 1955, Cincinatti; home, Cincinatti; Dartmouth Col., B.A. 1979, U. of MI, J.D. 1984; Methodist; married (Jane).

Career: Practicing atty., 1984–88; Assoc. Cnsl., White House, 1989; Dep. Asst. and White House Legis. Affairs Dir., 1990–91; Alternate U.S. Rep. to UN Human Rights Comm., 1992.

DC Office: 238 CHOB 20515, 202-225-3164; Fax: 202-225-1992; e-mail: portmail@hr.house.gov.

District Offices: 8010 Fed. Bldg., 550 Main St., Cincinatti 45202, 513-684-2456.

Committees: *Ways & Means* (18th of 21 R): Oversight; Social Security.

Group Ratings

	ADA	ACLU	COPE	CFA	LCV	CON	NSI	COC	ACU	NTLC	CHC
1994	10	14	0	20	18	96	90	100	86	83	100
1993	6	—	0	14	23	*	—	89	94	—	—

National Journal Ratings

	1993 LIB —	1993 CONS	1994 LIB —	1994 CONS
Economic	0% —	88%	0% —	80%
Social	0% —	89%	20% —	77%
Foreign	17% —	76%	14% —	80%

Key Votes of the 103d Congress

1. Clinton Deficit Plan	N	3. Brady Handgun Purchase	N	5. Lmt. UN Cmnd. of Forces	Y
2. NAFTA	Y	4. Strike Race/Death Pnlty.	Y	6. Cut Missile Funds	N

Key Votes of the 104th Congress

1. Congressional Compliance	Y	6. Reform Crime Grant	N	11. Loser Pays Court Reform	Y
2. Balanced Budget Amndmt.	Y	7. National Security Act	Y	12. Product Liability Reform	Y
3. Bar Unfunded Mandates	Y	8. Moratorium on Regs.	Y	13. Welfare Reform	Y
4. Pass Line Item Veto	Y	9. Risk Assessment on Regs.	Y	14. Term Limits Amndmt.	Y
5. Relax Exclusionary Rule	Y	10. Expnd. Priv. Prop. Rights	Y	15. Tax Cuts	Y

Election Results

1994 general	Rob Portman (R)	150,128	(77%)	($250,860)
	Les Mann (D)	43,730	(23%)	($2,503)
1994 primary	Rob Portman (R)	unopposed		
1993 spec. gen.	Rob Portman (R)	53,020	(70%)	($807,571)
	Lee Hornberger (D)	22,652	(30%)	($36,043)
1993 spec.prim.	Rob Portman (R)	17,432	(36%)	
	Bob McEwen (R)	14,495	(30%)	
	Jay Buchert (R)	12,441	(25%)	
	Robert Dorsey (R)	2,939	(6%)	
	Others	1,714	(4%)	
1992 general	Willis D. (Bill) Gradison (R)	177,720	(70%)	($96,108)
	Thomas R. Chandler (D)	75,924	(30%)	($105)

THIRD DISTRICT

The ingenuity and inventiveness of America a century ago is nowhere on better display than in Dayton, Ohio. Here, just south of the old National Road that spans the Midwest, was the home of James Ritty, who in 1879 invented the cash register—that indispensable instrument of mass retail trade—and of John Henry Patterson, who bought it from Ritty for $6,500 in 1884 and established the National Cash Register company (NCR). It was home for a while of a former Patterson subordinate Tom Watson, Sr., who feuded with him and went off and founded IBM. It was in Dayton in the 1890s that Wilbur and Orville Wright, tinkering in their bicycle shop and observing the horseless carriages driven through Dayton's streets, experimented with kites and gliders and constructed the first wind tunnel in the world and the first heavier-than-air flying machine which they took to ever-windy Kitty Hawk, North Carolina, to fly in 1903. A few years later, Dayton's Charles Kettering would invent the automatic starter for cars—another example of how Dayton could not only invent but also market. In recent years Dayton's technologies have not had complete success in commerce. NCR has been buffeted by the volatility of the office and personal computer markets. The Big Three auto firms and their suppliers have gone through a decade of downsizing their work forces, adapting technologies and work patterns to supply products on a "just in time" basis. The Dayton area has Wright-Patterson Air Force Base—one of the largest and most complex Air Force bases in the world, with 23,000 workers on 8,000 acres—but defense also has been in decline. Dayton's spirit of tinkering and innovation, of practical organization and mechanical dreaming, has not entirely vanished, but it's not clear if it can produce enough new industry growth to balance job losses in the old.

Dayton has been known as a bellwether since Richard Scammon and Ben Wattenberg's *The Real Majority* of 1970. From 1982 to 1990, Dayton's Montgomery County has tracked the nation fairly well, voting Republican for president and Democratic for Congress. It gave a narrow margin to Bill Clinton in 1992 and big margins to Republicans at the top and bottom of the ticket in 1994. The 3d Congressional District of Ohio includes Dayton and all but a small corner of Montgomery County. Its congressman, Tony Hall, is a Democrat who has managed to buck national trends: he was first elected to Congress in 1978, when Republicans gained 15 seats, and was reelected in 1994, when they were carrying the 3d for other offices and gaining 53 seats nationally. Hall comes from a political background—his father was once mayor of Dayton—and he was first elected to the Ohio legislature in 1968. But he is not always a conventional politician. His views owe much, as do those of many elected officials of his generation, to his service in the Peace Corps, in his case by-no-means-primitive, but also rather cynical, Thailand in 1966 and 1967, when the Vietnam war was raging not far away. Hall became a born-again Christian in the early 1980s and opposes abortion. But his number one cause has been to alleviate world hunger. When Mickey Leland died in a plane crash in Ethiopia, Hall succeeded him as chairman of the Select Committee on Hunger, and decried the civil wars and infrastructural deficiencies that obstructed food delivery in so much of Africa (although he glosses over how African socialism has reduced food supplies). Early on he was working to send food and medical help to Somalia and Haiti, and in February 1992 called for UN intervention in Somalia. In Dayton and Washington, he launched programs to use leftover hotel and restaurant food to feed the poor. In April 1993, after the House voted not to reauthorize his, or other, select committees, Hall embarked on a fast which lasted 22 days, which resulted in Agriculture Secretary Mike Espy agreeing to hold a "National Summit on Hunger." In March 1994 he went on a three-day fast—he calls his fasts "spiritual"—and later in the year toured refugee camps in Africa to push for more hunger funding. In early 1995, however, his anti-hunger crusade suffered another blow when the Gingrich-led Republican House voted to eliminate all of the so-called legislative service organizations, including the Caucus—with its office and staff—that Hall had created two years earlier.

After years of easy reelection, Hall has had more serious opposition in the 1990s. In 1992, NCR attorney and Gulf war veteran Pete Davis attacked him harshly; Hall won 60%–40%. In 1994, prominent physician David Westbrock argued that government was interfering too much with people's lives; Hall won 59%–41%. Third District voters evidently are willing to cut this unusual politician some slack, but given local Republican successes it is possible he will have serious competition in 1996.

The People: Pop. 1990: 570,913; 5% rural; 13% age 65+; 80% White; 18% Black; 1% Asian; 1% Hispanic origin. Voting age pop.: 428,764; 16% Black; 1% Hispanic origin. Households: 53% married couple families; 23% married couple fams. w. children; 47% college educ.; median household income: $30,083; per capita income: $14,500; median gross rent: $403; median house value: $64,200.

1992 Presidential Vote

Clinton (D)	107,659	(41%)
Bush (R)	104,215	(40%)
Perot (I)	47,465	(18%)

1988 Presidential Vote

Bush (R)	131,119	(58%)
Dukakis (D)	95,502	(42%)

Rep. Tony P. Hall (D)

Elected 1978; b. Jan. 16, 1942, Dayton; home, Dayton; Denison U., A.B. 1964; Presbyterian; married (Janet).

Career: Peace Corps, Thailand, 1966–67; Real estate broker, 1968–78; OH House of Reps., 1968–72; OH Senate, 1972–78.

DC Office: 1432 LHOB 20515, 202-225-6465; Fax: 202-225-9272.

District Offices: 501 Fed. Bldg., 200 W. 2d St., Dayton 45402, 513-225-2843.

Committees: *Rules* (4th of 4 D): Rules of the House.

Group Ratings

	ADA	ACLU	COPE	CFA	LCV	CON	NSI	COC	ACU	NTLC	CHC
1994	85	24	78	80	76	7	50	33	19	15	57
1993	70	—	100	89	54	27	—	11	19	—	—

National Journal Ratings

	1993 LIB — 1993 CONS		1994 LIB — 1994 CONS	
Economic	63% —	36%	73% —	17%
Social	39% —	60%	61% —	38%
Foreign	79% —	16%	80% —	17%

Key Votes of the 103d Congress

1. Clinton Deficit Plan	Y	3. Brady Handgun Purchase	Y	5. Lmt. UN Cmnd. of Forces	N
2. NAFTA	N	4. Strike Race/Death Pnlty.	N	6. Cut Missile Funds	Y

Key Votes of the 104th Congress

1. Congressional Compliance	Y	6. Reform Crime Grant	N	11. Loser Pays Court Reform	N
2. Balanced Budget Amndmt.	N	7. National Security Act	N	12. Product Liability Reform	Y
3. Bar Unfunded Mandates	Y	8. Moratorium on Regs.	N	13. Welfare Reform	N
4. Pass Line Item Veto	N	9. Risk Assessment on Regs.	N	14. Term Limits Amndmt.	N
5. Relax Exclusionary Rule	N	10. Expnd. Priv. Prop. Rights	Y	15. Tax Cuts	N

Election Results

1994 general	Tony P. Hall (D)	105,342	(59%)	($292,838)
	David A. Westbrock (R)	72,314	(41%)	($218,384)
1994 primary	Tony P. Hall (D)	unopposed		
1992 general	Tony P. Hall (D)	146,072	(60%)	($596,272)
	Pete Davis (R).	98,733	(40%)	($174,058)

FOURTH DISTRICT

To the motorist driving through, central Ohio looks mostly like farmland; yet most people here make their living off factories in small towns and on rural highways. These places seem far from anywhere important, yet are on one of the great east-west routes—the old rail lines and newer highways—that cross the country. They seem old-fashioned and rooted in an older technological time, yet here, in Wapakoneta, a typically Ohioan-Indian name, is the home town of Neil

Armstrong, first man on the moon. Not far away, in Lima, Abrams M-1 tanks continue to roll off the assembly line—one instance of continuing defense production after the Cold War. Politically, this crossroads on the flat limestone plains of northern Ohio is one of the Republican heartlands of the United States. On the B&O tracks from Dayton to Toledo that intersect the east-west rail lines used by Richard Nixon in 1968, Ronald Reagan in 1984 and George Bush in 1992 to make whistle-stop campaign tours, one can summon up memories of past campaign styles and loyalties.

Much of central Ohio makes up the 4th Congressional District, oddly regular in shape for an Ohio district. It includes Wapakoneta; Lima, which got its name when it was pulled from a hat, and famous when John Dillinger's gang murdered the sheriff in 1933; Bucyrus, which gave its name to a company producing giant earth-moving equipment; Marion, where young Socialist-to-be Norman Thomas delivered newspapers edited by President-to-be Warren Harding; and Mansfield, home of John Sherman, one of Ohio's great 19th Century Republican statesmen, and his brother General William Tecumseh Sherman, who marched through Georgia for the Union and refused to be considered for president. This has been a Republican stronghold since the Civil War, industrial since the late 19th Century, quietly prosperous over most of the years since World War II, though shaken by the collapse of the auto-steel-coal industries after the oil shock of 1979. Through all this, it has remained mostly Republican, giving George Bush a solid margin and Bill Clinton less than one-third of its votes in 1992.

Michael Oxley, first elected in a 1981 special election by the surprisingly narrow margin of 378 votes, is now the holder of a safe seat and Ohio's second-most senior Republican in the House. He brought to the office a small city background, a stint as an FBI agent, work for previous local Republican congressmen and a reputation as a moderate—he was for George Bush over Ronald Reagan in 1980. In the House, Oxley transcended all these labels and became, even before Republicans won control of the House, one of the most important members of the Commerce Committee. There he has been a strong opponent of regulation and supporter of markets, and an ingenious one as well. Oxley was a major player on the 1990 Clean Air Act, working with Ohioans of both parties to protect that state's high-sulfur power plants and big factories from being saddled with high costs. He successfully pushed his "auction" proposal, a market approach to pollution reduction, which, by allowing firms to sell polluting rights, lets supple and adaptive firms rather than rule-bound federal bureaucrats figure out how to best deal with pollution. On the Telecommunications Subcommittee, over opposition from Democrats, he also required that new frequencies of the radio spectrum be allocated not by lottery but by auction; as a result, the 1992 reconciliation bill put 200 megahertz of the spectrum up for auction for personal communications systems, wireless telephones, pagers and air-to-ground phones. When complete, these are or will be the largest auctions in history, with $1.7 billion raised by late 1994 and much more to come. On a bipartisan basis he co-sponsored the bill passed by the House in 1994 allowing the regional Bell companies (RBOCs) into video programming. Now, as a leading member of the Commerce Committee's majority, he is in an even stronger position to press Ohio's traditional pro-business mindset on these and other issues. Oxley chairs the subcommittee with jurisdiction over the Superfund and the Resource Conservation and Recovery Act (RCRA), regulating interstate transport of solid waste. He is likely to push for more free trade, fewer protections for unions and greater decision-making by state governments.

Oxley was one of three Ohio Republicans reelected without opposition in 1994.

The People: Pop. 1990: 570,917; 46% rural; 13% age 65+; 94% White; 5% Black; 1% Hispanic origin. Voting age pop.: 417,175; 4% Black; 1% Hispanic origin. Households: 63% married couple families; 30% married couple fams. w. children; 31% college educ.; median household income: $27,312; per capita income: $12,009; median gross rent: $337; median house value: $50,300.

1992 Presidential Vote

Bush (R) 118,142 (46%)
Clinton (D) 77,975 (30%)
Perot (I). 58,900 (23%)

1988 Presidential Vote

Bush (R) 150,999 (66%)
Dukakis (D). 76,200 (34%)

Rep. Michael G. Oxley (R)

Elected June 1981; b. Feb. 11, 1944, Findlay; home, Findlay; Miami U. of OH, B.A. 1966, OH St. U., J.D. 1969; Lutheran; married (Patricia).

Career: FBI Spec. Agent, 1969–72; OH House of Reps., 1972–81; Practicing atty., 1972–1981.

DC Office: 2233 RHOB 20515, 202-225-2676; Fax: 202-226-1160.

District Offices: 3121 W. Elm Plz., Lima 45805, 419-999-6455; 24 W. 3d St., #314, Mansfield 44902, 419-522-5757; and 100 E. Main Cross St., Findlay 45840, 419-423-3210.

Committees: *Commerce* (4th of 26 R): Commerce, Trade and Hazardous Materials (Chmn.); Telecommunications and Finance.

Group Ratings

	ADA	ACLU	COPE	CFA	LCV	CON	NSI	COC	ACU	NTLC	CHC
1994	0	13	0	30	13	72	100	92	95	89	100
1993	5	—	9	20	21	63	—	100	88	—	—

National Journal Ratings

	1993 LIB — 1993 CONS		1994 LIB — 1994 CONS	
Economic	0%	— 88%	26%	— 70%
Social	25%	— 73%	19%	— 80%
Foreign	28%	— 70%	25%	— 71%

Key Votes of the 103d Congress

1. Clinton Deficit Plan	N	3. Brady Handgun Purchase Y	5. Lmt. UN Cmnd. of Forces Y
2. NAFTA	Y	4. Strike Race/Death Pnlty. Y	6. Cut Missile Funds N

Key Votes of the 104th Congress

1. Congressional Compliance Y	6. Reform Crime Grant Y	11. Loser Pays Court Reform Y
2. Balanced Budget Amndmt. Y	7. National Security Act Y	12. Product Liability Reform Y
3. Bar Unfunded Mandates Y	8. Moratorium on Regs. Y	13. Welfare Reform Y
4. Pass Line Item Veto Y	9. Risk Assessment on Regs. Y	14. Term Limits Amndmt. N
5. Relax Exclusionary Rule Y	10. Expnd. Priv. Prop. Rights Y	15. Tax Cuts Y

Election Results

1994 general	Michael G. Oxley (R)	.... unopposed		($279,829)
1994 primary	Michael G. Oxley (R)	 46,958	(74%)	
	James R. Stahl (R)	 16,769	(26%)	
1992 general	Michael G. Oxley (R).	 147,346	(61%)	($648,337)
	Raymond Ball (D).	 92,608	(39%)	($68,324)

FIFTH DISTRICT

Northwestern Ohio, undergirded by limestone, as flat and fertile as any part of the country, sits astride the land routes from the parts of the country which were economically the most productive in the years they were settled. Here were the "Firelands," reserved for Connecticut Yankees whose farms were burned in the Revolution, and the neat and substantial small towns built by German Protestants in the mid-19th Century. Northwest Ohio is the beginning of the great corn and hog belt that stretches through Indiana and Illinois into Iowa, and was long one of the heartlands of the Republican Party. Fremont, settled by abstemious Yankees, was the home of President Rutherford B. Hayes, whose wife Lucy served only lemonade in the White House; nearby Sandusky, settled by Germans who built big wineries and breweries, now has its own Merry-Go-Round Museum. Not far away is Milan, birthplace of the great inventor and capitalist Thomas Edison.

This is prime industrial country: its limestone, rail connections and location near the Great Lakes have spurred the growth of a factory economy which in dollar terms is far more important than agriculture. Since the first settlement, northwest Ohio hasn't had spectacular population growth, but it grew steadily for many decades, surging ahead in the 1950s and 1960s as its small factories supplied the big auto plants in Detroit and Ohio cities. Growth lagged noticeably in the early 1980s as the collapse of the auto industry cast a pall over the whole area. But northwest Ohio has quietly come back and showed itself capable of competing with bigger cities and lower-wage regions and countries.

Ohio's 5th Congressional District sweeps across northwest Ohio, from Grafton, just beyond the westward expansion of metropolitan Cleveland, across the limestone plains through Sandusky, its harbor on Lake Erie, home of the giant Cedar Point amusement park. It continues through Milan and Fremont, past part of the university town of Bowling Green and the Toledo suburb of Perrysburg, to the western Ohio towns of Defiance and Napoleon (wonderful names!). It avoids Toledo and its suburbs directly east and west. Historically, this was a solidly Republican district from the Civil War through the New Deal and up through the 1970s. In the early 1980s, it was competitive; now it is pretty solidly Republican again.

The current congressman from the 5th is Paul Gillmor, a 22-year veteran of the Ohio legislature when he was first elected in 1988, a professional though not especially provocative politician. Gillmor had been long eying the seat, but had to win it over the wishes of his predecessor, Delbert Latta, who wanted to pass it along to his son. Gillmor passed a state law blocking Latta from resigning to have his son designated the party nominee; then Gillmor beat the junior Latta in the 1988 primary by exactly 27 votes out of 63,000 cast. Now Gillmor may be creating a family dynasty of his own. In 1992 his wife Karen was elected to the state Senate from the 26th District, which overlaps the 5th Congressional in Sandusky and Seneca Counties; all the more strikingly, she had a baby (Paul Michael, known as Little P.M.) just before the primary, and went on to win the general with 61%. Paul Gillmor had an easier year: he did not give birth, he did not have an opponent in the general election, and he had no overdrafts at the House bank. In 1994 he easily beat a 26-year-old student; his wife's seat doesn't come up till 1996.

In his first years in the House, Gillmor focused on internal reform issues, working to freeze committee funding, and on local issues, repealing the Coast Guard recreational boating user fees. Drawing on his experience in state government, he was one of the lead House Republicans in the fight against unfunded federal mandates, which was one of the first items to move through the new Republican-controlled House. On the Commerce Committee, he backed limits on out-of-state solid waste and greater competition for cable TV and telephone companies. Gillmor's most original idea is to repeal the 12th Amendment which provides that the House, with each state casting just one vote, choose the president if there is no electoral college majority; instead, there would be a runoff. It's a cumbersome solution, but the 12th Amendment could produce an absurd result in today's republic and a majority-forcing mechanism like Gillmor's might well make sense.

The People: Pop. 1990: 570,946; 54% rural; 13% age 65+; 94% White; 2% Black; 1% Other; 3% Hispanic origin. Voting age pop.: 410,950; 2% Black; 2% Hispanic origin. Households: 65% married couple families; 32% married couple fams. w. children; 32% college educ.; median household income: $30,117; per capita income: $12,755; median gross rent: $351; median house value: $57,800.

1992 Presidential Vote

Bush (R)	108,421	(41%)
Clinton (D)	88,773	(34%)
Perot (I)	66,051	(25%)

1988 Presidential Vote

Bush (R)	143,846	(62%)
Dukakis (D)	87,268	(38%)

Rep. Paul E. Gillmor (R)

Elected 1988; b. Feb. 1, 1939, Tiffin; home, Old Fort; Ohio Wesleyan U., B.A. 1961, U. of MI, J.D. 1964; Methodist; married (Karen).

Career: Air Force, 1965–66; OH Senate, 1966–88.

DC Office: 1203 LHOB 20515, 202-225-6405; Fax: 202-225-1985.

District Offices: 120 Jefferson St., Port Clinton 43452, 800-541-6446; and 148 E. South Boundary St., Perrysburg 43551, 419-872-2500.

Committees: *Commerce* (12th of 26 R): Commerce, Trade and Hazardous Materials; Telecommunications and Finance.

Group Ratings

	ADA	ACLU	COPE	CFA	LCV	CON	NSI	COC	ACU	NTLC	CHC
1994	15	23	33	20	33	63	100	100	86	74	79
1993	15	—	30	30	50	52	—	100	82	—	—

National Journal Ratings

	1993 LIB —	1993 CONS	1994 LIB —	1994 CONS
Economic	32% —	68%	30% —	67%
Social	29% —	71%	29% —	71%
Foreign	24% —	72%	14% —	80%

Key Votes of the 103d Congress

1. Clinton Deficit Plan	N	3. Brady Handgun Purchase	N	5. Lmt. UN Cmnd. of Forces	Y
2. NAFTA	Y	4. Strike Race/Death Pnlty.	Y	6. Cut Missile Funds	N

Key Votes of the 104th Congress

1. Congressional Compliance	Y	6. Reform Crime Grant	Y	11. Loser Pays Court Reform	Y
2. Balanced Budget Amndmt.	Y	7. National Security Act	Y	12. Product Liability Reform	Y
3. Bar Unfunded Mandates	Y	8. Moratorium on Regs.	Y	13. Welfare Reform	Y
4. Pass Line Item Veto	Y	9. Risk Assessment on Regs.	Y	14. Term Limits Amndmt.	Y
5. Relax Exclusionary Rule	Y	10. Expnd. Priv. Prop. Rights	Y	15. Tax Cuts	Y

Election Results

1994 general	Paul E. Gillmor (R) 135,879	(73%)	($210,789)
	Jarrod Tudor (D) 49,335	(27%)	
1994 primary	Paul E. Gillmor (R) .... unopposed		
1992 general	Paul E. Gillmor (R) .... unopposed		($254,988)

SIXTH DISTRICT

The first settlers of Ohio came from the south, where the Ohio River and its tributaries were pathways through the woods. Yankee settlers came down the Ohio from Pittsburgh and founded Marietta in 1788 as Ohio's first town. About the same time, George Washington procured for his Revolutionary War veterans bounty lands in the Virginia Military District of Ohio between the Scioto and Miami Rivers, centered on Chillicothe. In Marietta the Yankees built New England style churches; in Chillicothe the young Virginian Thomas Worthington who became governor of Ohio built his home, Adena, designed by architect Benjamin Latrobe. Virginians soon outnumbered New Englanders, and their traces remain on the landscape, which is laid out in irregular-shaped parcels as in Virginia, not the Northwest Ordinance's checkerboard grid imposed on most of the Midwest. There have been lasting political effects too. These rolling lands south of U.S. 40 have never attracted much industry; most people here speak with an accent that sounds southern to northwest Ohioans; they retain, with conservative cultural attitudes, a Democratic heritage that manifests itself on occasion. It was one sign of the shrewdness of Bill Clinton's 1992 campaign that the Clinton-Gore bus trip out of the New York convention went through just this part of Ohio, and that Clinton ultimately carried the state in part by running just about even here.

The 6th Congressional District of Ohio covers most of southern Ohio, from Marietta down the Ohio River to the gritty industrial towns of Ironton and Portsmouth; it runs across the hilly landscape to include part of Chillicothe and all of Piketon, and west over to the Warren County suburbs of Dayton and Cincinnati. It has no large central cities and almost entirely avoids metropolitan areas. Politically, this has been not just a battlefield but a killing ground: in the two elections in which the 6th District existed in its present form, three incumbent congressmen have been defeated. The first two were Republicans who were thrown together in 1992 by redistricting. One was Clarence Miller, an old-fashioned conservative Republican first elected in 1966 who proposed usually futile percentage cuts on the Appropriations Committee; the other was Bob McEwen, elected at 30 in the Reagan year of 1980. In 1992, McEwen hoped that Miller would step aside, but Miller was offended by McEwen's brashness and the revelation that he had 166 overdrafts on the House bank. In a close and bitter primary McEwen won by 286 votes out of 66,000 cast. Then, not too surprisingly, McEwen was beaten in the general election, by Democrat Ted Strickland, candidate for Congress three times before and winner of 46% against McEwen in 1990. This time Strickland won 51%–49%.

That result was reversed in 1994, when Republican Frank Cremeans beat Strickland by the same margin. The two provide an interesting contrast of their two parties' propensities toward therapy and discipline. Strickland, son of a steelworker and eighth of nine children, is a Methodist minister, was director of a children's home, and then a prison psychologist (at Lucasville, site of an April 1993 riot) and psychology professor at Shawnee State College. He and his wife have both made their way up as counseling professionals. In 1992, Strickland campaigned for more highways and school spending, and for countering alcohol and drug abuse, school dropouts and teen pregnancy. "Building communities where children are nurtured and educated and protected and cared for," he said. In the House Strickland voted for the Clinton budget and tax package, but against the 1994 crime bill because of its gun control provisions and against NAFTA. He refused to spend all his franking allowance and turned down federal health insurance, but lobbied for road projects and "good pork."

Frank Cremeans came from a poor family in rural Cheshire, worked as a teacher, principal and school superintendent—but is not a fuzzy-headed academic. "Education is a way to work," he says. "If you don't have saleable skills, you can't get a job." He started a concrete, crane, and rigging business and made millions: "I work six days a week. My message is, hey, you can do it with your own hands. Don't look for handouts." The 1994 election, he said, was a "referendum on President Clinton and his administration," also known as "Bill and Ted's not-so-excellent adventure." He attacked Strickland's budget and tax votes, and said Strickland supported health benefits for illegal aliens, and called him a champion of homosexuals. With help from a TV spot with sausage magnate Bob Evans, he beat state Senator Cooper Snyder 50%–39% in the primary. In the general, Cremeans spent over $600,000 of his own money, enough to counterbalance Strickland's more than $250,000 in PAC contributions. Democrats hoped that Cremeans's provocative remarks and support of the Contract With America would hurt him. But he carried his home area around Gallipolis narrowly and Warren County by a wide margin, enough for a win. Cremeans seems likely to be a loyal member of Newt Gingrich's Republican Conference, and his electoral fate, like Strickland's, should depend heavily on trends in national opinion.

The People: Pop. 1990: 570,804; 60% rural; 13% age 65+; 97% White; 2% Black. Voting age pop.: 420,945; 2% Black. Households: 61% married couple families; 29% married couple fams. w. children; 30% college educ.; median household income: $21,761; per capita income: $10,349; median gross rent: $315; median house value: $46,200.

1992 Presidential Vote

Bush (R)	102,481	(40%)
Clinton (D)	99,761	(39%)
Perot (I)	50,532	(20%)

1988 Presidential Vote

Bush (R)	128,989	(59%)
Dukakis (D)	90,322	(41%)

Rep. Frank A. Cremeans (R)

Elected 1994; b. April 5, 1943, Cheshire; home, Gallipolis; U. of Rio Grande, B.A. 1966, OH U., M.A. 1969; Methodist; married (Carol).

Career: High Schl. Teacher, 1967–71; Schl. Superintendent, 1971–75, Founder & Mgr., Cremeans Concrete Co., 1971–present.

DC Office: 1107 LHOB 20515, 202-225-5705; Fax: 202-225-3054.

District Offices: 200 Putnam St., #524, Marietta 45750, 614-373-2120; 301 N. High St., Hillsboro 45133, 513-393-8688; and 308 Bank One Plz., Portsmouth 45662, 614-353-4006.

Committees: *Banking & Financial Services* (21st of 27 R): Capital Markets, Securities and Government Sponsored Enterprises; Housing and Community Opportunity. *Resources* (14th of 25 R): Energy and Mineral Resources; Water and Power Resources.

Group Ratings and 103d Congress Votes: Newly Elected

Key Votes of the 104th Congress

1. Congressional Compliance	Y	6. Reform Crime Grant	Y	11. Loser Pays Court Reform	Y
2. Balanced Budget Amndmt.	Y	7. National Security Act	Y	12. Product Liability Reform	Y
3. Bar Unfunded Mandates	Y	8. Moratorium on Regs.	Y	13. Welfare Reform	Y
4. Pass Line Item Veto	Y	9. Risk Assessment on Regs.	Y	14. Term Limits Amndmt.	Y
5. Relax Exclusionary Rule	Y	10. Expnd. Priv. Prop. Rights	Y	15. Tax Cuts	Y

Election Results

1994 general	Frank A. Cremeans (R)	91,263	(51%)	($862,015)
	Ted Strickland (D)	87,861	(49%)	($533,425)
1994 primary	Frank A. Cremeans (R)	26,365	(50%)	
	Cooper Snyder (R)	20,318	(39%)	
	Bob Kelley (R)	3,055	(6%)	
	James E. Weisman (R)	2,492	(5%)	
1992 general	Ted Strickland (D)	122,720	(51%)	($237,082)
	Bob McEwen (R)	119,252	(49%)	($716,672)

SEVENTH DISTRICT

The hills and plains of central Ohio are dotted with towns and small cities that have been manufacturing centers almost since they were settled in the early 19th Century, when the dominant technologies were the waterwheel and the open forge. In the decades since, they have been replaced by one after another new technology, and the local manufacturing economy, sometimes with uncomfortable fits and starts, has adjusted and advanced. There were painful job losses here in the early 1980s, but there has been small business growth in the years since. As old factories are shut down, new ones open that are more productive; the result is higher incomes and, though not often remembered, far less of the backbreaking hard work and drudgery that were the lot of almost everyone in supposedly better times.

The 7th Congressional District of Ohio is made up of a capital G-shaped slice of the central part of the state. Its largest city is Springfield, where International Harvester was the biggest employer for years; in the 1980s the firm went bankrupt, downsized drastically, and is now named Navistar. To the south are the eastern suburbs of Dayton around Wright-Patterson Air Force Base, whose name recalls the Dayton-based fathers of the airplane and the cash register. In the northern end of the 7th District are Bellefontaine, site of the first concrete street in America, and, a few miles away, Marysville, the site of Honda's first U.S. plant, where all Honda Accords sold here and abroad are assembled by American workers.

The 7th District has always been Republican territory. It backed the policies of Ohio Republicans President William McKinley—tariff protection, railroad regulation, antitrust suits against monopolies, discouragement of labor unions—and Governor James Rhodes—low taxes, encouragement of new businesses and jobs. It is culturally conservative and economically mostly satisfied with free markets. Solidly Republican in 1994, it was one of the few Ohio districts to give a good margin to George Bush in 1992.

The 7th District's current congressman is David Hobson, a Republican from Springfield first elected in 1990 after eight years in the state Senate. Hobson has been in real estate and until 1993 owned two Japanese steakhouses. He is conservative but not a partisan firebrand. In the House his first bill was the National Child Abuser Registration Act, which established a registered network of convicted child abusers. From his days in Columbus he has been interested in healthcare issues, and introduced his own plans to implement uniform standards for healthcare data networks and to encourage states to use Medicaid funds to enroll individuals in private healthcare plans. He was lobbied by none less than Hillary Rodham Clinton on health care, but opposed the Clinton plan because he said it would require a large federal bureaucracy. He worked with Dayton Democrat Tony Hall to secure a federal waiver for the Dayton Area Health Plan and to establish Dayton's National Aviation Historic Park.

Hobson has a front-line position in the Republican effort to control federal spending and reduce the deficit. He ranks second on the Budget Committee, chaired now by his Ohio neighbor John Kasich, and supported Kasich's budget alternative to the Clinton packages. He also serves on Appropriations. His two predecessors in the district ran for statewide office: Clarence Brown lost the governor's race in 1982, but Mike DeWine was elected Lieutenant Governor in 1990 and U.S. Senator in 1994. Hobson, however, seems to have no such ambitions. He has been reelected easily in the 7th District, in 1994 with no opposition.

The People: Pop. 1990: 570,939; 43% rural; 12% age 65+; 93% White; 5% Black; 1% Asian; 1% Hispanic origin. Voting age pop.: 421,434; 5% Black; 1% Hispanic origin. Households: 64% married couple families; 30% married couple fams. w. children; 37% college educ.; median household income: $30,364; per capita income: $12,919; median gross rent: $376; median house value: $62,400.

1992 Presidential Vote			1988 Presidential Vote		
Bush (R)	112,701	(45%)	Bush (R)	141,450	(66%)
Clinton (D)	84,098	(33%)	Dukakis (D)	73,604	(34%)
Perot (I)	54,307	(22%)			

Rep. David L. Hobson (R)

Elected 1990; b. Oct. 17, 1936, Cincinnati; home, Springfield; OH Wesleyan U., B.A. 1958, OH St. Col. of Law, J.D. 1963; Methodist; married (Carolyn).

Career: OH Natl. Guard, 1958–63; Real estate agent, 1969–present; Restaurant owner, 1977–93; OH Senate, 1982–90, Majority Whip, 1986–88, Pres. Pro Tem, 1988–90.

DC Office: 1514 LHOB 20515, 202-225-4324; Fax: 202-225-1984.

District Offices: 220 P.O. Bldg., 150 N. Limestone St., Springfield 45501, 513-325-0474; and 212 S. Broad St., Lancaster 43130, 614-654-5149.

Committees: *Appropriations* (19th of 32 R): National Security; VA, HUD, and Independent Agencies. *Budget* (2nd of 24 R). *Standards of Official Conduct* (4th of 5 R).

Group Ratings

	ADA	ACLU	COPE	CFA	LCV	CON	NSI	COC	ACU	NTLC	CHC
1994	20	22	22	20	28	74	100	83	67	79	71
1993	15	—	17	30	36	74	—	91	79	—	—

National Journal Ratings

	1993 LIB — 1993 CONS			1994 LIB — 1994 CONS		
Economic	14%	—	80%	26%	—	70%
Social	34%	—	66%	41%	—	58%
Foreign	33%	—	65%	25%	—	71%

Key Votes of the 103d Congress

1. Clinton Deficit Plan	N	3. Brady Handgun Purchase	N	5. Lmt. UN Cmnd. of Forces	Y
2. NAFTA	Y	4. Strike Race/Death Pnlty.	Y	6. Cut Missile Funds	Y

Key Votes of the 104th Congress

1. Congressional Compliance	Y	6. Reform Crime Grant	Y	11. Loser Pays Court Reform	Y
2. Balanced Budget Amndmt.	Y	7. National Security Act	Y	12. Product Liability Reform	Y
3. Bar Unfunded Mandates	Y	8. Moratorium on Regs.	Y	13. Welfare Reform	Y
4. Pass Line Item Veto	Y	9. Risk Assessment on Regs.	Y	14. Term Limits Amndmt.	Y
5. Relax Exclusionary Rule	Y	10. Expnd. Priv. Prop. Rights	Y	15. Tax Cuts	Y

Election Results

1994 general	David L. Hobson (R) .... unopposed		($191,660)
1994 primary	David L. Hobson (R) .... unopposed		
1992 general	David L. Hobson (R) 164,195	(71%)	($298,896)
	Clifford S. Heskett (D)................ 66,237	(29%)	

EIGHTH DISTRICT

The far west end of Ohio, where U.S. 40, the old National Road, heads straight as an arrow in its last miles across Ohio to Indiana, and the rail lines criss-cross the land from Cincinnati to Dayton, has since the early 20th Century been some of the nation's prime industrial country. Here the Great and Little Miami Rivers drain south into the Ohio; here U.S. 40 jogs southward twice to go over the Miami and Stillwater River dams, built after the great flood of 1913 that killed 361 people in Dayton and caused $1 billion in damage. Between Dayton and Cincinnati grew up large factory towns like Middletown and Hamilton, as well as smaller ones. In recent years, these towns have adapted more quickly than the huge factory cities of the Great Lakes region to the changing industrial markets of the late 20th Century, and comfortable suburban tracts have grown up in what were once open fields.

The 8th Congressional District of Ohio covers much of this territory, including most of four counties north of Dayton and U.S. 40, Preble County west of Dayton, and Butler County between Dayton and Cincinnati. About half its people live in Butler, around Hamilton and Middletown, which has become part of what is essentially a single metropolitan strip from northern Kentucky to U.S. 40 north of Dayton. Politically, this is solidly Republican territory, with its representative selected in the Republican primary.

The current congressman, John Boehner (pronounced *bayner*), has become in a very short time one of his party's leaders and a driving force in the House—a considerable feat for a man who as recently as 1990 was a packaging company president and three-term Ohio minority party legislator. But Boehner showed his aggressiveness by beating not one but two of his predecessors—incumbent Buz Lukens, who inexplicably ran after being convicted of having sex with a 16-year-old girl whose mother accused him of offering her a government job to keep her silent, and Thomas Kindness, who gave up the seat to run against Senator John Glenn in 1986 and then, as Boehner put it, deserted the district to become a Washington lobbyist. Boehner beat Kindness 49%–32%, with 17% for Lukens. In the House, Boehner quickly became part of the Gang of Seven, young freshman Republicans who joined together to insist that House leaders reveal the names of all the 355 members who had overdrafts at the House bank, and then went on to assail Democratic leaders and Republican go-alongers on the pay raise, the House Post Office scandal and what they called the speaker's "slush fund." They also argued that members of Congress should be subject to regulatory laws they impose on other citizens; in 1992 Boehner invited OSHA inspectors to his office, where they found what would have been 15 violations if Congress were covered by OSHA. That same month Boehner took the lead in adopting the 27th Amendment to the Constitution, proposed by James Madison with the original Bill of Rights in 1789, to prohibit Congress from varying its pay during its current term. Six states ratified it between 1789 and 1791, Ohio did so in 1873, and from 1978 to 1992, 32 more states followed suit. Boehner argued that these 39 states were the three-quarters required for ratification; Archivist of the United States certified the amendment as ratified and Congress voted nearly unanimously to accept it.

The Gang of Seven struck a chord around the nation. All but Boehner had serious challenges in the 1992 general election; six out of the seven won, Boehner with 74%; and the seventh, Frank Riggs of California, came back to win in 1994. In the 103d Congress Boehner was one of Whip Newt Gingrich's top lieutenants, working to raise money for Republican House candidates, lobbying the U.S. Chamber of Commerce to oppose the Clinton healthcare plan, offering unsuccessful amendments on health care, cutting funds for preschool transition programs, a Native Hawaiian education program and for the House itself. He led Gingrich's campaign for the GOP leader's post—which ultimately propelled Gingrich to Speaker— when Robert Michel announced his retirement, a fight quickly won when the only opponent left the field. During the 1994 campaign, he was a major player in drafting and advocating the 10-piece Contract With America, which played a vital role in allowing Republicans to promise change. For the 104th Congress, Boehner ran for chairman of the Republican Conference and—with Gingrich's backing— beat California's Duncan Hunter 122–102; he set out aggressively to use that post to sell the partisan message and accomplishments of the new majority. Boehner is poised to be one of the guiding spirits in the House, not so much because he holds a committee or leadership post, but because of his aggressiveness and willingness to take the initiative. He has been mentioned as a possible candidate for John Glenn's Senate seat in 1998, but is more likely to remain in the House and move up in the Republican leadership.

The People: Pop. 1990: 570,837; 38% rural; 12% age 65+; 96% White; 3% Black; 1% Asian. Voting age pop.: 415,686; 3% Black. Households: 65% married couple families; 32% married couple fams. w. children; 36% college educ.; median household income: $31,171; per capita income: $13,355; median gross rent: $389; median house value: $65,900.

1992 Presidential Vote			1988 Presidential Vote		
Bush (R)	121,174	(47%)	Bush (R)	151,025	(69%)
Clinton (D)	75,375	(29%)	Dukakis (D)	67,060	(31%)
Perot (I)	60,172	(23%)			

Rep. John A. Boehner (R)

Elected 1990; b. Nov. 17, 1949, Cincinnati; home, West Chester; Xavier U., B.S. 1977; Catholic; married (Debbie).

Career: Navy, 1969; Pres., Nucite Sales, Inc., 1976–90; Union Township Bd. of Trustees, 1981–85, Pres., 1984; OH House of Reps., 1984–90.

DC Office: 1011 LHOB 20515, 202-225-6205; Fax: 202-225-0704.

District Offices: 5617 Liberty-Fairfield Rd., Hamilton 45011, 513-894-6003; and 12 S. Plum St., Troy 45373, 513-339-1524.

Committees: *Republican Conference Chairman. Agriculture* (7th of 27 R): General Farm Commodities; Livestock, Dairy and Poultry. *House Oversight* (4th of 7 R).

Group Ratings

	ADA	ACLU	COPE	CFA	LCV	CON	NSI	COC	ACU	NTLC	CHC
1994	5	13	0	20	6	87	100	83	100	93	100
1993	0	—	0	0	7	74	—	91	100	—	—

National Journal Ratings

	1993 LIB — 1993 CONS		1994 LIB — 1994 CONS	
Economic	0% —	88%	0% —	80%
Social	0% —	89%	0% —	89%
Foreign	17% —	76%	14% —	80%

Key Votes of the 103d Congress

1. Clinton Deficit Plan	N	3. Brady Handgun Purchase	N	5. Lmt. UN Cmnd. of Forces	Y
2. NAFTA	Y	4. Strike Race/Death Pnlty.	Y	6. Cut Missile Funds	N

Key Votes of the 104th Congress

1. Congressional Compliance	Y	6. Reform Crime Grant	Y	11. Loser Pays Court Reform	Y
2. Balanced Budget Amndmt.	Y	7. National Security Act	Y	12. Product Liability Reform	Y
3. Bar Unfunded Mandates	Y	8. Moratorium on Regs.	Y	13. Welfare Reform	Y
4. Pass Line Item Veto	Y	9. Risk Assessment on Regs.	Y	14. Term Limits Amndmt.	Y
5. Relax Exclusionary Rule	Y	10. Expnd. Priv. Prop. Rights	Y	15. Tax Cuts	Y

Election Results

1994 general	John A. Boehner (R) .... unopposed			($713,223)
1994 primary	John A. Boehner (R) .... unopposed			
1992 general	John A. Boehner (R).................	176,362	(74%)	($530,835)
	Fred Sennet (D)	62,033	(26%)	($6,730)

NINTH DISTRICT

Toledo, Ohio, was one of America's boom towns 70 years ago. The 1920s here was "a decade of fabulous figures," Harlan Hatcher wrote: the Willys-Overland plant employed 25,000 workers and turned out an auto every 30 seconds; the city built $20 million coal and iron ore docks; the Libbey-Owens-Ford merger made Toledo, with good local supplies of natural gas and sand, the nation's biggest glass manufacturer; the city built a new museum and transcontinental airport. Toledo had long been well-situated, where the Maumee River empties into Lake Erie, where two dozen rail lines connected it with the East Coast and Chicago and the coal fields of Kentucky and West Virginia. It was well-positioned to be one of the centers of the brash rising auto industry, a national leader when it first produced the Jeep in the 1940s. But by the late 1970s and early 1980s, auto company management had allowed the unions to bid wages and benefits too high while watching quality decline, to the point that consumers would not buy enough American-made cars for the industry to survive without vast subsidy or major shrinkage. Subsidy, beyond the temporary Chrysler loan and a few small trade barriers, was not forthcoming, and so Toledo and other auto-dependent cities went through tough times: contrast the confident, growing city of the 1920s with the Toledo that sadly saw the tasteful Portside Festival Marketplace close in 1990. Yet Toledo has also had its successes: its factories now produce the Jeep Cherokee, one of America's hottest vehicles.

Ohio's 9th Congressional District is centered on Toledo; as the city's population has stagnated, it has spread east to the flatlands of Ottawa County, south to Bowling Green State University, and west to rural Fulton County. Toledo has been heavily Democratic since CIO unions organized the plants in the late 1930s; the collapse of the auto industry so unnerved the district that in 1980 it voted for Ronald Reagan and elected a Republican congressman. But in 1982, it became solidly Democratic again, electing Marcy Kaptur, who has held the seat ever since.

Kaptur is one of the most fervent and principled members of the Democratic Caucus. Almost her entire career has been in the public sector: she spent eight years as an urban planner in Toledo, then got a job in the Carter White House; she was shrewd enough to return to Toledo in 1982 when no one else wanted to run for the House seat. She has seen Toledo's economy nosedive, and feels intensely the pain of ordinary people who played by the rules but ended up losing because of the operation of larger economic forces. Her great cause is trade. She has long been convinced that Toledo and places like it have lost jobs and industry because of unfair trade practices by the Japanese and low-wage competition in countries like Mexico. If "capitalism laughs at boundaries," as the historian Fernand Braudel wrote, Kaptur, with her faith in the public sector, has worked hard to make those boundaries stronger, and not something to be snickered at. She has pressured the Japanese to buy more American auto parts, but is leery of Japanese investment in the United States. She has worked for laws to prohibit top government officials from representing foreign interests for a period after they leave government, and would like to ban them permanently from representing a foreign government or political party. She co-chaired the Competitiveness Caucus and the Congressional Auto Parts Caucus. They, like all other caucuses, no longer receive funding.

Kaptur was probably Congress's most vocal and dedicated opponent of the North American Free Trade Agreement. She visited the Mexican border in spring 1993, and returned home with soil and water samples to demonstrate the pollution there. She argued that 100,000 jobs had been transferred from Ohio to Mexico, and cited the 1993 shutdown of a Toledo auto parts plant followed by transfer of some of its jobs to Matamoros, Mexico. She criticized President Clinton for doing nothing for sagging U.S. industries and for not listening to her and other Democrats opposing NAFTA. She brought to this issue a level of commitment that was genuinely moving, one that clearly arose from a desire to restore what she considers as a vibrant economy that could provide a reliable basis for ordinary people to live decent lives. In 1994 she also opposed GATT, though not with quite the same fervor, perhaps because the outcome in the House was never much in question. In early 1995, she revived her old passion by arguing forcefully against Clinton's proposal to bail out the Mexican peso with $40 billion of U.S. loan guarantees; the President was forced to abandon the legislation and proceed with an administrative rescue. At the risk of intra-party warfare, surely she will continue to resist what she considers harmful free trade, even as the Toledo area works to deal with it.

Kaptur has a seat on the Appropriations Committee, and before the 1994 election could reasonably look forward to a subcommittee chairmanship; now the best she can hope for soon is the ranking minority position. She will surely keep working on local projects, like restoring Toledo's Farmers' Market and the Central Union Terminal, though in the minority it may be tougher. She took a lead initiative on building a World War II Memorial in Washington and minting 50th anniversary coins to pay for it.

Kaptur's hard work and evident sincerity have been rewarded by overwhelming margins at the polls. She gave serious thought to running for the Senate, but in January 1994 decided that it would take too much money to run against Joel Hyatt and Mary Boyle in the primary, and then go into the general.

The People: Pop. 1990: 570,911; 14% rural; 13% age 65+; 83% White; 12% Black; 1% Asian; 2% Other; 3% Hispanic origin. Voting age pop.: 421,038; 11% Black; 2% Hispanic origin. Households: 53% married couple families; 25% married couple fams. w. children; 42% college educ.; median household income: $28,856; per capita income: $13,477; median gross rent: $392; median house value: $58,000.

1992 Presidential Vote			1988 Presidential Vote		
Clinton (D)	118,713	(47%)	Dukakis (D)	117,368	(52%)
Bush (R)	81,784	(32%)	Bush (R)	107,658	(48%)
Perot (I)	50,151	(20%)			

Rep. Marcy Kaptur (D)

Elected 1982; b. June 17, 1946, Toledo; home, Toledo; U. of WI, B.A. 1968, U. of MI, M.A. 1974, M.I.T., 1981–82; Catholic; single.

Career: Urban planner, Toledo, Lucas Cnty. Planning Comm., 1969–75; Urban planning consultant, 1975–77; White House Asst. Dir. for Urban Affairs, 1977–80; Dep. Secy., Natl. Consumer Coop. Bank, 1980–81; Author.

DC Office: 2104 RHOB 20515, 202-225-4146; Fax: 202-225-7711.

District Offices: Fed. Bldg., 234 Summit St., #719, Toledo 43604, 419-259-7500.

Committees: *Appropriations* (17th of 24 D): Agriculture, Rural Development, FDA, and Related Agencies; District of Columbia; VA, HUD, and Independent Agencies.

Group Ratings

	ADA	ACLU	COPE	CFA	LCV	CON	NSI	COC	ACU	NTLC	CHC
1994	60	39	100	80	69	28	60	40	20	32	50
1993	70	—	92	80	57	65	—	18	26	—	—

National Journal Ratings

	1993 LIB — 1993 CONS		1994 LIB — 1994 CONS	
Economic	57% —	42%	71% —	28%
Social	60% —	38%	58% —	42%
Foreign	50% —	50%	64% —	33%

Key Votes of the 103d Congress

1. Clinton Deficit Plan	Y	3. Brady Handgun Purchase	Y	5. Lmt. UN Cmnd. of Forces	Y
2. NAFTA	N	4. Strike Race/Death Pnlty.	N	6. Cut Missile Funds	N

Key Votes of the 104th Congress

1. Congressional Compliance	Y	6. Reform Crime Grant	N	11. Loser Pays Court Reform	N
2. Balanced Budget Amndmt.	Y	7. National Security Act	N	12. Product Liability Reform	Y
3. Bar Unfunded Mandates	Y	8. Moratorium on Regs.	Y	13. Welfare Reform	N
4. Pass Line Item Veto	N	9. Risk Assessment on Regs.	N	14. Term Limits Amndmt.	N
5. Relax Exclusionary Rule	N	10. Expnd. Priv. Prop. Rights	N	15. Tax Cuts	N

Election Results

1994 general	Marcy Kaptur (D)	118,120	(75%)	($309,247)
	R. Randy Whitman (R)	38,665	(25%)	($9,500)
1994 primary	Marcy Kaptur (D)	unopposed		
1992 general	Marcy Kaptur (D)	178,879	(74%)	($335,095)
	Kenny Brown (R)	53,011	(22%)	($43,930)
	Ed Howard (I)	11,162	(5%)	

TENTH DISTRICT

Cleveland, one of America's great cities at the beginning of the 20th Century, is on its way back as the century ends. It grew early in this century as a center of heavy industry: this was the original home base of John D. Rockefeller's Standard Oil; the city's twisting and deep Cuyahoga River was the site of several of the nation's largest steel mills; great industrial fortunes here built civic institutions like the museums in Wade Park, Case Western University and the Cleveland

Symphony, and financed the campaigns of northeast Ohio Republican Presidents James Garfield and William McKinley. On the old Public Square, designed like a New England town green by the Yankees who settled this Western Reserve (the northeast corner of Ohio) in the early 19th Century, the two eccentric Van Sweringen brothers, trolley magnates of the early 20th, built the Terminal Tower, the highest skyscraper in interior America for many years. This yeasty, ethnic city, with more than 40 nationalities—Czechs, Hungarians, Poles, Italians, Germans: the Hapsburg Empire and more—and with many distinct ethnic neighborhoods, produced a robust two-party politics. Then, in the 1930s, after the New Deal and when CIO unions organized the steel factories and auto assembly plants, Cleveland became solidly Democratic, though with some affluent Republican suburbs.

But Cleveland never led the nation as it hoped: the nation's fourth largest city in 1910, it was overtaken in size first by Detroit, then by Los Angeles, eventually by the likes of Houston and Dallas; today, it's the center of the nation's 14th largest metropolitan area. The central city declined from 914,000 in 1950 to 503,000 in 1992, as the children who grew up in those tightly-packed neighborhoods made more money and moved to the suburbs. Movement was especially great in wards east of the Cuyahoga River, which were almost entirely ethnic in 1950 and almost entirely black by 1970. The 1970s were a bad decade for Cleveland, which became an object of ridicule by national sophisticates. Its heavy industries were fast declining, Lake Erie and the Cuyahoga River were badly polluted (the river caught fire in June 1969). City politics became racially polarized with the election of black Mayor Carl Stokes in 1967 and 1969, and was dominated in the late 1970s by Mayor Dennis Kucinich, a demagogue who bankrupted the city treasury. But the city government was rescued by George Voinovich, elected mayor in 1979 and governor in 1990. And the current mayor, Michael White, who is black, broke down racial polarization and first won municipal office in 1979 by carrying white wards west of the Cuyahoga while losing the black wards east of the river to black machine politician George Forbes. Downtown Cleveland revived, with a new headquarters for British Petroleum (here because it bought Standard Oil of Ohio), the fourth-largest performing arts center in the nation at Playhouse Square, a new baseball stadium, a new basketball arena and the Rock and Roll Hall of Fame. Restaurants and pleasure boat docks line the river now. Cleveland continues to be headquarters of several of the nation's largest law firms, and some of its businesses, like iron-ore giant Cleveland-Cliffs, have sharply revived; the city's number one employer is now health services, and the Cleveland Clinic handles 700,000 outpatients a year.

The 10th Congressional District of Ohio includes most of the west side of Cleveland and the western suburbs in Cuyahoga County. Excluded is one salient of mostly black Cleveland precincts attached to the 11th District across the Cuyahoga; also several western suburbs—Brook Park, Middleburg Heights—are in the convoluted suburban 19th District. Suburbs in the 11th include Lakewood, well-established by the 1920s and still comfortable middle-class territory, and Rocky River and Bay Village, growing more affluent as one moves westward along the lake. Inland is Parma, a creation of the 1950s, when second- and third-generation ethnics moved out to subdivision houses set amid what was once calculated to be America's densest concentration of bowling alleys. The political tradition here is almost entirely Democratic, but George Voinovich, popular from his decade as mayor, carried the area in 1990 and 1994.

The congressman from the 10th District is an unlikely one: Martin Hoke, Republican, cellular telephone entrepreneur, an accomplished pianist, the descendant both of colonial era German ministers and of a Romanian immigrant who opened a west side restaurant. He went through a period as a flower child, then he started a law practice in his basement; he started a business providing auto repair service for travelers flying out of Cleveland-Hopkins airport and then started Red Carpet Cellular in 1985. Hoke's political career began in 1992 and has benefited from the pecadilloes of his Democratic opponents. The first was Mary Rose Oakar, first elected to the House in 1976, an ethnic Democrat who made mammography a Medicare benefit. Back in 1987 Oakar was criticized for keeping a former aide and housemate on salary for two years after the woman moved to New York and for giving another woman staffer a $10,000 raise one month after she and Oakar bought a house together. Then in 1991 it was revealed that she had 213 overdrafts on the House bank and in 1992 the Cleveland *Plain Dealer* aired allegations, later disproved, that she put "ghost employees" on the House Post Office payroll; "damnable lies," she said, and sued. Oakar survived the June primary against County Commissioner Tim Hagan, who may be one of the last true-believing white liberal Democrats in the country, by a 39%–30% margin, while Hoke won a five candidate primary 33%–28% over the mayor of Rocky River. Hoke called Oakar "the most persuasive argument for term limits" and handed out matchbooks with aspirins attached saying, "Congress giving you a headache? Take two of these and vote for Martin R. Hoke." He tromped her in an appearance on *This Week with David Brinkley* and won 57%–43%.

Controversy abounded also in the 1994 race. While six candidates were lining up in the Democratic primary, Hoke made a *faux pas* while being miked for a post-State of the Union interview on Cleveland TV. A woman producer asked 14th District Democratic freshman Eric Fingerhut to unbutton his jacket, and he said, "You can ask me to do anything you want." Hoke added, "She has-ah beeg breasts." This went out on live mike, and grave denunciations were made by Democratic politicians and disapproving journalists. Cuyahoga County Treasurer Frank Gaul, who won the Democratic primary over Brook Park Mayor Tom Coyne and Cleveland Council member Helen Knipe Smith by a 35%–27%–23% margin, seemed to be the only one not making this comment an issue. The 68-year-old Gaul was running about even with Hoke in polls when in early October Gaul announced he was putting his campaign "on hold" because of charges aired in the *Plain Dealer* that the Cuyahoga County $1.8 billion Secured Assets Fund Earnings (SAFE) investment pool had been mismanaged. Ten days later Gaul returned to the race, denouncing Hoke's vote against the crime bill and support of the Contract With America; Hoke charged Gaul's mismanagement would cost taxpayers $100 million. Hoke won 52%–39%.

In the House Hoke has favored term limits, eliminating congressional pensions, reducing franked mailings, cutting staff and banning PAC contributions. He worked to cut government backed research-and-development for private joint ventures and his voting record has made few concessions to the Democratic heritage of the 10th District. With Republicans in the majority, he will have a chance to prevail on some previously futile issues; Although he failed in his effort to win a seat on a prime committee, he has become an increasingly public advocate of the new House majority, promoting every Contract item at great length on the House floor.

The People: Pop. 1990: 570,530; 15% age 65+; 92% White; 2% Black; 1% Asian; 2% Other; 4% Hispanic origin. Voting age pop.: 435,093; 2% Black; 3% Hispanic origin. Households: 52% married couple families; 23% married couple fams. w. children; 43% college educ.; median household income: $30,323; per capita income: $14,813; median gross rent: $388; median house value: $72,600.

1992 Presidential Vote

Clinton (D) 107,465 (41%)
Bush (R) 92,846 (36%)
Perot (I) 58,092 (22%)

1988 Presidential Vote

Bush (R) 131,372 (52%)
Dukakis (D) 119,818 (48%)

Rep. Martin R. Hoke (R)

Elected 1992; b. May 18, 1952, Lakewood; home, Cleveland; Amherst Col., B.A. 1973, Case Western Reserve U., J.D. 1980; Presbyterian; divorced.

Career: Founder & Pres., Red Carpet Car Care, 1980–present, Red Carpet Cellular, 1985–present; Practicing atty., 1982–92.

DC Office: 212 CHOB 20515, 202-225-5871; Fax: 202-226-0994; e-mail: hokemail@hr.house.gov.

District Offices: 21270 Lorraine Rd., Fairview Park 44126, 216-356-2010.

Committees: *Budget* (15th of 24 R). *Judiciary* (14th of 20 R): Constitution; Courts and Intellectual Property.

Group Ratings

	ADA	ACLU	COPE	CFA	LCV	CON	NSI	COC	ACU	NTLC	CHC
1994	15	29	13	20	11	96	80	91	80	81	64
1993	15	—	25	20	25	88	—	91	83	—	—

National Journal Ratings

	1993 LIB — 1993 CONS	1994 LIB — 1994 CONS
Economic	25% — 72%	0% — 80%
Social	31% — 68%	34% — 66%
Foreign	17% — 83%	14% — 80%

Key Votes of the 103d Congress

1. Clinton Deficit Plan	N	3. Brady Handgun Purchase N	5. Lmt. UN Cmnd. of Forces Y
2. NAFTA	N	4. Strike Race/Death Pnlty. Y	6. Cut Missile Funds N

Key Votes of the 104th Congress

1. Congressional Compliance Y	6. Reform Crime Grant Y	11. Loser Pays Court Reform Y
2. Balanced Budget Amndmt. Y	7. National Security Act Y	12. Product Liability Reform Y
3. Bar Unfunded Mandates Y	8. Moratorium on Regs. Y	13. Welfare Reform Y
4. Pass Line Item Veto Y	9. Risk Assessment on Regs.Y	14. Term Limits Amndmt. Y
5. Relax Exclusionary Rule Y	10. Expnd. Priv. Prop. Rights Y	15. Tax Cuts Y

Election Results

1994 general	Martin R. Hoke (R)	95,226	(52%)	($675,825)
	Francis E. Gaul (D)	70,918	(39%)	($494,467)
	Joseph J. Jacobs (I)	17,495	(10%)	
1994 primary	Martin R. Hoke (R)	unopposed		
1992 general	Martin R. Hoke (R)	136,433	(57%)	($682,166)
	Mary Rose Oakar (D)	103,788	(43%)	($1,292,286)

ELEVENTH DISTRICT

Like most great American cities, Cleveland has grown in great bursts of migration, when capitalists' investments suddenly were paying off beyond their wildest dreams and low-wage workers were attracted from ready corners of the country and the world. Cleveland's greatest surge of growth started in the 1890s and lasted through the 1920s, as tens of thousands of immigrants from central and southern Europe arrived here, looking for jobs in steel and auto and other factories. Bohemians came to the tight-packed neighborhoods along Broadway, Hungarians a bit to the northeast, Jews north of University Circle along East 105th Street, Italians to Little Italy along Mayfield Road.

As the nation's heavy industries geared up for World War II and enjoyed years of unexpected prosperous growth afterward, a second surge of immigrants came, this time blacks from the American South. From Cleveland's old black ghetto, south of Carnegie Avenue downtown to East 105th, the rapidly increasing number of blacks covered most of the east side by the middle 1960s, with only a few Bohemian and Italian enclaves left east of the Cuyahoga and west of the city limits. Migration stopped around 1965, but blacks have continued to move out beyond the city limits to the east side suburbs, including modest East Cleveland and Warrensville Heights and upper-income Shaker Heights, laid out in 1905 on broad boulevards by streetcar magnates, the Van Sweringen brothers. These surges of migration led to political changes. A string of ethnic mayors—Frank Lausche, Anthony Celebrezze, Ralph Locher—was followed by the election in 1967 and 1969 of Carl Stokes, the nation's first big city black mayor, and Cleveland had racially polarized city politics for much of the 1970s. Ironically, Cleveland has never had a black majority and elected its second black mayor, Michael White, in 1989, because white voters preferred his accommodating politics to the more polarizing ways of longtime City Council Chairman George Forbes.

The 11th Congressional District of Ohio includes most of the east side of Cleveland, plus the suburbs just to the east, which together have about as many people as the city now. Some of these—East Cleveland, Warrensville Heights—are mostly black; some, notably Shaker Heights, have stable black percentages in carefully maintained neighborhoods. Others are the natural destination of blacks seeking low-crime neighborhoods and middle-class schools not often found on the city side of Cleveland's impressive set of museums and medical centers. This is a heavily Democratic district, with a solid black majority, and it has been represented since 1968 by Louis Stokes, Carl Stokes's brother. The Stokeses come from a humble background. "I want you to study and get an education," their mother said. "Get something in your head so you will never have to work with your hands the way I have." Louis Stokes served in the segregated Army in World War II, got a law degree when practically no law firm would hire blacks, and challenged the Ohio congressional district lines when it was considered unthinkable that a black could be elected to Congress.

Stokes is now one of the senior members of the House—and for the first time in the minority. It is a new role—perhaps his fourth and least comfortable—for a man who started off as part of a small, rebellious Black Caucus, who then was given a series of tough assignments by the leadership, and who more recently has been an Appropriations subcommittee chairman. His first tough assignment was to replace Henry Gonzalez as chairman of the Select Committee on Presidential Assassinations in 1977, on which he supervised responsible hearings and produced a report that disputed the Warren Commission findings and concluded that President Kennedy "was probably assassinated as a result of a conspiracy." Following the chagrin caused by the film *J.F.K.*, Stokes returned to the subject in 1992, setting up a special commission to look into the matter, and despite Justice Department objections was able to secure release of most of the still secret files on the assassination. In 1980, Stokes became chairman of the House Ethics Committee, where he handled the Abscam scandal, the abuse of congressional pages and the charges made against Geraldine Ferraro when she was nominated for vice president in 1984. In 1987 and 1988, he chaired the House Intelligence Committee and was a member of the special committee investigating the Iran-contra scandal. In 1991, as all but one other member rotated off, Stokes was called again to head up Ethics—just in time for the House Bank and Post Office scandals. Not unsinged himself, Stokes recused himself from investigating the bank and admitted he had overdrawn his account "on occasion"; it turned out he had 551 overdrafts.

In 1993, after 24 years in the House, Stokes became chairman of the VA-HUD-Independent Agencies Appropriations Subcommittee; now he is ranking minority member. This covers an odd hybrid of agencies, which tend to get played off against one another: Stokes tends to favor housing over space, but in 1993 backed the space station in a crucial vote at the urging of the Clinton Administration. Stokes has shepherded minority set-aside programs, like his minority scholarship program for the CIA and NSA. He tried to keep earmarked projects off his bills, and succeeded in 1993, only to be flooded with requests in 1994; his bill ended up with, among others, $10 million worth of projects for the Cleveland area. He tried unsuccessfully to abolish Selective Service. As ranking minority member, Stokes of course will have less influence, even as court decisions and political trends emperil his minority set-asides, just as the congressional districting law he challenged was a quarter-century ago. It would be ironic if his most memorable achievement as chairman was the rescue of the space station.

Stokes is regularly reelected without difficulty.

The People: Pop. 1990: 571,295; 15% age 65+; 39% White; 59% Black; 1% Asian; 1% Other; 1% Hispanic origin. Voting age pop.: 424,100; 55% Black; 1% Hispanic origin. Households: 38% married couple families; 16% married couple fams. w. children; 41% college educ.; median household income: $22,459; per capita income: $12,629; median gross rent: $376; median house value: $58,100.

1992 Presidential Vote			1988 Presidential Vote		
Clinton (D)	169,870	(73%)	Dukakis (D)	176,683	(78%)
Bush (R)	37,886	(16%)	Bush (R)	48,767	(22%)
Perot (I)	23,428	(10%)			

Rep. Louis Stokes (D)

Elected 1968; b. Feb. 23, 1925, Cleveland; home, Shaker Heights; Western Reserve U., 1946–48, Cleveland Marshall Law Schl., J.D. 1953; A. M. E. Zion; married (Jeanette).

Career: Army, 1943–46 (WWII); Practicing atty., 1954–68.

DC Office: 2365 RHOB 20515, 202-225-7032; Fax: 202-225-1339.

District Offices: 3645 Warrensville Ctr. Rd., #204, Shaker Heights 44122, 216-522-4900.

Committees: *Appropriations* (3rd of 24 D): Labor, Health and Human Services, and Education; VA, HUD, and Independent Agencies (RMM).

Group Ratings

	ADA	ACLU	COPE	CFA	LCV	CON	NSI	COC	ACU	NTLC	CHC
1994	100	90	100	90	81	11	11	18	10	19	0
1993	90	—	100	100	71	10	—	0	4	—	—

National Journal Ratings

	1993 LIB — 1993 CONS			1994 LIB — 1994 CONS	
Economic	88%	—	0%	83%	—	0%
Social	87%	—	0%	80%	—	19%
Foreign	87%	—	7%	85%	—	0%

Key Votes of the 103d Congress

1. Clinton Deficit Plan	Y	3. Brady Handgun Purchase	Y	5. Lmt. UN Cmnd. of Forces	N
2. NAFTA	N	4. Strike Race/Death Pnlty.	N	6. Cut Missile Funds	Y

Key Votes of the 104th Congress

1. Congressional Compliance Y	6. Reform Crime Grant N	11. Loser Pays Court Reform N
2. Balanced Budget Amndmt. N	7. National Security Act *	12. Product Liability Reform N
3. Bar Unfunded Mandates N	8. Moratorium on Regs. N	13. Welfare Reform N
4. Pass Line Item Veto N	9. Risk Assessment on Regs. N	14. Term Limits Amndmt. N
5. Relax Exclusionary Rule N	10. Expnd. Priv. Prop. Rights N	15. Tax Cuts N

Election Results

1994 general	Louis Stokes (D)	114,220	(77%)	($382,332)
	James J. Sykora (R)	33,705	(23%)	
1994 primary	Louis Stokes (D)	58,709	(80%)	
	Sheldon R. Goldstine (D)	14,767	(20%)	
1992 general	Louis Stokes (D)	154,718	(69%)	($449,248)
	Beryl E. Rothschild (R)	43,866	(20%)	($79,232)
	Ed Gudenas (I)	19,773	(9%)	($15,102)
	Others	5,267	(2%)	

TWELFTH DISTRICT

Columbus is on the verge of joining the big leagues. With its city limits stretching out toward farmland at each point of the compass, Columbus is geographically the largest city in Ohio; its metropolitan area, though far less popoulated than Cleveland and a bit smaller than Cincinnati, is growing more rapidly and has some time since passed the magic million mark. Columbus has the advantages of being a state capital, the home of Ohio State University, and a major white-collar employment town: it is the home base of The Limited's Leslie Wexner and Wendy's Dave Thomas, of Nationwide Insurance and multistate giant Banc One. This does not make Columbus quite recession-proof (Banc One had to cut payrolls in 1994, but actually increased jobs here), but it has attracted the kind of upscale, enterprising people who have produced most of America's growth in recent years. Columbus likes to brag of its airfreight operations at Port Columbus, the airport, among the best in the country, and about the $43 million Wexner Center for the Visual Arts, a post-post-modern structure by architect Peter Eisenman that has evoked vast controversy.

Columbus politically has always been a Republican city, with an even more Republican hinterland. It had few of the Eastern European immigrants and CIO unions that made Cleveland so Democratic; for most of the last 30 years, its mayor has been a Republican with support from a machine redolent of the era of William McKinley (whose statue sits in front of the flat-domed Capitol). Recently, local Republicans have had spirited competition from Democrats in the city, but the suburbs are heavily Republican and the countryside even more so. The Columbus area dominates two of Ohio's congressional districts: the 12th extends east to the small industrial town of Newark and north to bucolic Delaware County, and includes black areas and the affluent east side of the city around Bexley; the 15th includes most of the territory within the city limits and extends south and west to include Madison County.

The 12th District elects one of the most important members of the Republican 104th Congress, John Kasich, chairman of the House Budget Committee. Boyish-looking but hard-working, aggressive but ingratiating, with a command of fact and argument that can only come from perseverence together with a competitive drive colleagues see on the basketball court, Kasich puts a cheerful yet earnest face on Republican policies and priorities. Kasich has been in politics just about all his adult life. He is the son of a mail carrier who grew up in working class McKees Rocks, Pennsylvania, of Hungarian, Czech and Croatian descent; after graduating from Ohio State he worked for a state legislator. In 1978, at 26, Kasich ran a strenuous door-to-door campaign and beat a Democratic state senator. In 1982, he ran for the House and, with the help of a favorable districting plan, beat a Democrat who had upset an incumbent in 1980. In the House he made his first commotion on National Security, where he was the leading Republican opponent of the B-2 bomber and succeeded in drastically reducing its production to 20 new planes from the requested 132 in 1989. He also stopped a $110 million expansion of the Pentagon building just after the end of the Cold War. He was one of the tigers who pushed through the military base closing bill (chief sponsor Dick Armey of Texas wasn't on the committee).

Kasich was appointed to the Budget Committee in 1989 and by late 1992 successfully bucked seniority—and then-Minority Leader Bob Michel—to become ranking Republican. In 1993, he led the Republicans' charge to "cut spending first," which helped defeat the Clinton stimulus package. And more importantly, he prepared a Republican budget alternative with no tax increases or Social Security cuts, but means-testing of Medicare and serious cuts in discretionary spending. It didn't succeed—some Republicans didn't back it—but it showed that greater cuts than Clinton proposed were possible. That October, Kasich, with Minnesota Democrat Tim Penny, presented a list of $90 billion in spending cuts over five years, in contrast to Clinton's $11 billion package; this proposal, known as Penny-Kasich I, lost by only 219–213, as the Democratic leadership pulled all the stops out. In March 1994, Kasich's alternative budget was rejected 243–165; in April, Penny-Kasich II lost 216–202. But Kasich had a few modest wins, cutting off dollars to the World Bank 216–210 and zeroing out during House debate the Interstate Commerce Commission's $43 million appropriation 243–194 ("a dinosaur that just absolutely refuses to die").

The margins in these votes showed the strength of Kasich's ideas in even a Democratic House, and that even a 20-seat Republican gain in 1994 would have shifted the balance in 1995. Now that the House is Republican, he has an excellent chance of getting his budget resolutions through and of reshaping the nation's fiscal policy. He is willing to talk to anyone (he invited Hillary Rodham Clinton over for dinner in 1993 and chatted up Ross Perot) and he sometimes miffs conservatives (many were angry when he voted for the final 1994 crime bill); but his philosophic thrust is clear. "The enemy of the American people is the status quo. It takes us on the road to bankruptcy," he says, and he is ready to attack "programs so bloated and waterlogged that they don't work." He sees the balanced budget amendment as "the catalyst for truly reforming the operation of the federal government," and is prepared to publically discuss hard choices. He seems to realize that, at 43, he is positioned to make a major difference in the place of government in American life. As one of the few members of Newt Gingrich's inner circle, he also has shown a brash willingness to challenge the top Republicans and to make sure that the new Speaker, as well as other senior Republicans, do not back away from the politically painful medicine of deficit reduction. *National Journal* calls Kasich "one of the most innovative and daring budget-meisters in Congress."

Kasich seems widely popular at home, and has carried the solidly Republican 12th District by sound margins. He has been mentioned as a candidate for John Glenn's Senate seat, which comes up in 1998.

The People: Pop. 1990: 571,341; 15% rural; 9% age 65+; 74% White; 23% Black; 1% Asian; 1% Hispanic origin. Voting age pop.: 416,926; 21% Black; 1% Hispanic origin. Households: 52% married couple families; 26% married couple fams. w. children; 49% college educ.; median household income: $30,859; per capita income: $14,723; median gross rent: $417; median house value: $74,700.

1992 Presidential Vote		
Bush (R)	108,359	(41%)
Clinton (D)	105,852	(40%)
Perot (I)	47,080	(18%)

1988 Presidential Vote		
Bush (R)	129,438	(59%)
Dukakis (D)	90,077	(41%)

Rep. John R. Kasich (R)

Elected 1982; b. May 13, 1952, McKees Rocks, PA; home, Westerville; OH St. U., B.A. 1974; Christian; divorced.

Career: A.A., OH Sen. Donald Lukens, 1975–77; OH Senate, 1978–82.

DC Office: 1131 LHOB 20515, 202-225-5355; Fax: 202-225-7695.

District Offices: 200 N. High St., #500, Columbus 43215, 614-469-7318.

Committees: *Budget* (Chmn. of 24 R). *National Security* (4th of 30 R): Military Readiness; Military Research and Development.

Group Ratings

	ADA	ACLU	COPE	CFA	LCV	CON	NSI	COC	ACU	NTLC	CHC
1994	10	9	11	30	6	90	100	92	76	89	100
1993	0	—	8	0	21	82	—	100	92	—	—

National Journal Ratings

	1993 LIB — 1993 CONS	1994 LIB — 1994 CONS
Economic	14% — 80%	21% — 76%
Social	19% — 77%	31% — 68%
Foreign	17% — 76%	14% — 80%

Key Votes of the 103d Congress

1. Clinton Deficit Plan	N	3. Brady Handgun Purchase N	5. Lmt. UN Cmnd. of Forces Y
2. NAFTA	Y	4. Strike Race/Death Pnlty. Y	6. Cut Missile Funds N

Key Votes of the 104th Congress

1. Congressional Compliance Y	6. Reform Crime Grant Y	11. Loser Pays Court Reform Y
2. Balanced Budget Amndmt. Y	7. National Security Act Y	12. Product Liability Reform Y
3. Bar Unfunded Mandates Y	8. Moratorium on Regs. Y	13. Welfare Reform Y
4. Pass Line Item Veto Y	9. Risk Assessment on Regs. Y	14. Term Limits Amndmt. Y
5. Relax Exclusionary Rule Y	10. Expnd. Priv. Prop. Rights Y	15. Tax Cuts Y

Election Results

1994 general	John R. Kasich (R)	114,608	(67%)	($560,117)
	Cynthia L. Ruccia (D)	57,294	(33%)	($258,299)
1994 primary	John R. Kasich (R)	40,288	(92%)	
	Ramona Whisler (R)	3,401	(8%)	
1992 general	John R. Kasich (R)...................	170,297	(71%)	($242,096)
	Bob Fitrakis (D)	68,761	(29%)	($44,659)

THIRTEENTH DISTRICT

On the southern shore of Lake Erie in northern Ohio the imprint of the westward track of New England Yankee migration is still apparent today. The Yankees, cooped up in New England for 200 years, shot across the country through Upstate New York, west across Ohio and Michigan to Chicago, and then to Kansas and southern California in just two or three generations, providing inspiration, manpower and technical might for the Union victory in the Civil War, and leaving their impress along the way. One place they stopped was the Western Reserve, the northeast corner of Ohio along Lake Erie, created for the excess population of Connecticut, whose towns, colleges and cultural institutions were mostly established by Yankees. A prime example of Western Reserve Yankee-ism is Oberlin College, founded in 1832 as the first co-educational college in the world, though no women dared apply until 1837; it accepted black students a few years later, and the town of Oberlin became a center of the Underground Railroad. Or consider Hiram, home of another college and of James Garfield, who once represented the area in Congress when it was the most Republican part of Ohio, and who was the only president elected directly from the House, in 1880.

Politically, the lands of the Yankee diaspora, with their reformist ideas and dislike of slavery and the South, were naturally Republican territory. But the great masses of immigrants lured to Cleveland and the smaller industrial cities built by Yankee capital provided a base for labor unions and Progressive politics. After the New Deal and the bloody CIO organizing drives of the late 1930s, the Western Reserve had something like class-warfare politics for 30 years, with the Democrats usually winning. Northern Ohio, like New England, moved away from the Republicans and toward the Democrats. Now the Western Reserve may be moving toward a post-industrial economy as are Connecticut and Massachusetts. Factory employment has been falling, but total jobs are rising again; small, adaptive business units with highly skilled workers are the growth sectors. That leaves the Western Reserve, like New England, leaning Democratic—but not reliably so. Bill Clinton carried it solidly in 1992; but so did George Voinovich in 1990, and even more so in 1994, when it also favored Republican Mike DeWine over Democrat Joel Hyatt for senator.

The 13th Congressional District of Ohio is grotesquely shaped—something like a barbell—with two large segments of Western Reserve lands connected by a sort of land bridge between Cleveland and Akron. The western end includes the factory towns of Lorain and Elyria, where, in the Cleveland *Plain Dealer*'s words, "portable roadside toilets are painted to resemble the Japanese flag and auto workers curse at passing Toyotas," plus Oberlin and Medina County, once rural and now filling up with outmigrants from Cleveland along I-71. The eastern, less heavily populated area includes all of Geauga County, high-income hilly townships with many reminders of New England origins, and rural parts of Trumbull and Portage Counties. This end of the district tends to vote Republican, while on the west end Lorain County is Democratic and Medina County Republican. This was an ungainly product of redistricting, represented until they retired in 1992 by two Democrats, Don Pease of Oberlin and Dennis Eckart of suburban Cleveland.

The congressman now is Sherrod Brown, one of the Democratic Party's remaining successful career politicians, who ran and won a seat in the state House the year he graduated from Yale, in 1974, and has never stopped running since. In 1982 he was elected secretary of state (while his brother, Charlie Brown, was elected attorney general of West Virginia) and worked hard to increase voter registration and turnout. He lost that office to Robert Taft in 1990, and Republican redistricters took care to keep Brown's home town of Mansfield outside the 13th. But in 1992 Brown moved into a rented lake cottage in Medina County and in the primary beat by 45%–22% a former aide to Cleveland Congresswoman Mary Rose Oakar. In the general Brown faced Republican Margaret Mueller, a millionaire social worker from Geauga County, who had run three times against Eckart. Brown showed great flair in the general election campaign, taking a 200-mile bicycle tour around the district; with solid labor support, he campaigned loud and hard against the North American Free Trade Agreement and championed universal health care. Mueller defended NAFTA, attacked Brown's record as secretary of state, and pointed out that his ex-wife had accused him of abuse in her divorce papers. Brown won 53%–35%, winning 61% in Lorain County.

In the House Brown showed his usual political adeptness, winning a seat on the now-renamed Commerce Committee. He supported the Clinton economic plan and early on said that both healthcare and welfare reform was needed. "We have talked too much to step back." But he concentrated even more on trade and was one of the most voluble liberal-labor members from the Great Lakes area attacking NAFTA and GATT. He backed a single-payer healthcare plan like the one in Canada, across Lake Erie, but he was careful never to sign onto the Clinton plan. By fall 1994, Brown was relying on pork barrel projects for local popularity: "I've delivered for the voters . . . I didn't promise that I'd change the healthcare system." Brown was facing a serious challenge from Republican Gregory White, Lorain County Prosecutor since 1980, who differed with him on the Clinton budget and tax plan, NAFTA and GATT and the crime bill. As a Vietnam war hero, White criticized Brown for attending Yale and studying in Russia.

Brown won 49%–46%, with majorities in Lorain County and much of the east end of the district. This was one of several examples of a liberal-labor Democrat who survived because of business and labor PAC money: by mid-October White outraised Brown in individual contributions, $400,000 to $269,000, but Brown had $571,000 in PAC contributions while White had $48,000. Whether Brown can enjoy such an advantage in Speaker Newt Gingrich's House is unclear: Democrats are finding it harder to raise money now that they are in the minority. But as the survivor of a tsunami, and a man who has shown no interest in a nonpolitical career, he is surely hoping to win again in 1996 and then go statewide, for governor or possibly John Glenn's Senate seat, in 1998.

The People: Pop. 1990: 570,838; 36% rural; 11% age 65+; 92% White; 4% Black; 1% Other; 3% Hispanic origin. Voting age pop.: 412,451; 4% Black; 2% Hispanic origin. Households: 66% married couple families; 32% married couple fams. w. children; 41% college educ.; median household income: $34,725; per capita income: $14,307; median gross rent: $403; median house value: $76,700.

1992 Presidential Vote

Clinton (D)	101,854	(38%)
Bush (R)	96,037	(35%)
Perot (I)	72,038	(27%)

1988 Presidential Vote

Bush (R)	122,863	(54%)
Dukakis (D)	106,085	(46%)

Rep. Sherrod Brown (D)

Elected 1992; b. Nov. 9, 1952, Mansfield; home, Lorain; Yale U., B.A. 1974, OH St. U., M.A. 1979, M.A. 1981; Lutheran; divorced.

Career: OH House of Reps. 1974–82; Prof., Ohio State U. Mansfield, 1979–81; OH Secy. of State 1982–90.

DC Office: 1019 LHOB 20515, 202-225-3401; Fax: 202-225-2266.

District Offices: 5201 Abbe Rd., Elyria 44035, 216-934-5100.

Committees: *Commerce* (13th of 21 D): Commerce, Trade and Hazardous Materials; Health and Environment. *International Relations* (14th of 19 D): Asia and the Pacific.

Group Ratings

	ADA	ACLU	COPE	CFA	LCV	CON	NSI	COC	ACU	NTLC	CHC
1994	75	74	78	70	83	55	10	67	14	19	21
1993	95	—	100	100	86	32	—	18	9	—	—

National Journal Ratings

	1993 LIB	—	1993 CONS		1994 LIB	—	1994 CONS
Economic	75%	—	22%		50%	—	46%
Social	68%	—	29%		70%	—	28%
Foreign	74%	—	22%		75%	—	23%

Key Votes of the 103d Congress

1. Clinton Deficit Plan	Y	3. Brady Handgun Purchase Y	5. Lmt. UN Cmnd. of Forces N
2. NAFTA	N	4. Strike Race/Death Pnlty. N	6. Cut Missile Funds Y

Key Votes of the 104th Congress

1. Congressional Compliance Y	6. Reform Crime Grant N	11. Loser Pays Court Reform N
2. Balanced Budget Amndmt. Y	7. National Security Act N	12. Product Liability Reform N
3. Bar Unfunded Mandates N	8. Moratorium on Regs. N	13. Welfare Reform N
4. Pass Line Item Veto Y	9. Risk Assessment on Regs. N	14. Term Limits Amndmt. Y
5. Relax Exclusionary Rule N	10. Expnd. Priv. Prop. Rights Y	15. Tax Cuts N

Election Results

1994 general	Sherrod Brown (D)	93,147	(49%)	($974,225)
	Gregory A. White (R)	86,422	(46%)	($570,331)
	Howard Mason (I)	7,777	(4%)	($11,593)
	Others	2,430	(1%)	
1994 primary	Sherrod Brown (D)	unopposed		
1992 general	Sherrod Brown (D)	134,486	(53%)	($486,354)
	Margaret R. Mueller (R)	88,889	(35%)	($864,338)
	Mark Miller (I)	20,320	(8%)	
	Others	8,563	(3%)	

FOURTEENTH DISTRICT

Akron is the center of what at least some Ohioans today call the Polymer Valley, and what formerly was known as Rubber Town. (Akron itself comes from the Greek word for high, the same root as Acropolis, because the city sits on a ridge between the Great Lakes and Mississippi watersheds.) Twenty years ago, Akron was as synonymous with tires as Detroit was with cars: Firestone, Goodyear, General Tire, and B. F. Goodrich all had their headquarters and big tire factories here; the United Rubber Workers had been the big union since the 1930s. But after the oil shocks of the 1970s, Akron's antiquated auto tire plants were closed, and the last truck and airplane tire plants closed in 1984 and 1985; several big firms were sold to out-of-town companies, though Goodyear remains as a leading employer. Akron began specializing in polymers, plastics and other hydrocarbons that can be formed or shaped like rubber into useful industrial products. The first polymer, polyvinyl chloride (PVC), was invented in 1926 when B. F. Goodrich chemist Waldo Semon, looking to make synthetic rubber, found a mysterious goo in the bottom of his test tube; the company did not bother to patent it until 1933, but now PVC is everywhere, in pipes and siding and shoes and toys and car tops and stadium covers. Polymers were a natural extension of the rubber companies' business, and now the Akron area and the Cuyahoga Valley north to Cleveland are called Polymer Valley. Ohio ships more plastic resins than any other state but Texas and employs more people in the field than any other state but California.

This change in the local economy has had political effects. Akron's population is largely descended from migrants from Eastern Europe and, especially, West Virginia, who thronged here in the 1910s and 1920s to snap up jobs in the tire factories for 10 or 12 hours a day at the price of smelling burning rubber for 24. In the 1930s, these people joined the new United Rubber Workers and started voting Democratic, opposing the Republican candidates fielded by longtime Akron resident and also National Republican Chairman Ray Bliss in the 1950s and 1960s. But as the smell of rubber vanished from Akron's air, the language of class conflict had mostly passed from its politics. Now Akron has more flexible businesses and a more upscale work force, and it no longer produces the heavy Democratic margins it did in the 1970s and much of the 1980s.

Ohio's 14th Congressional District has long been made up of Akron and surrounding Summit County, with some variation in district boundaries; currently it also includes the area around Kent (and Kent State University, site of the May 1970 shooting of four students by National Guard troops) just to the east. The current congressman, Tom Sawyer, has spent most of his adult life in public office: he was elected to the state House in 1976, became mayor of Akron in 1984, and was elected in the 14th District when the incumbent retired in 1986. In that election and in 1994, he faced tough competition from Summit County Prosecutor Lynn Slaby.

Sawyer has been a party loyalist—he ranked second only to Speaker Tom Foley in party loyalty in 1993 and 1994 roll call votes—but he has shown some original interests and cast some votes out of line with other northern Ohio Democrats. Among his original issues is the Census. He inherited the chair of the Census Subcommittee in 1989, and charged that the 1990 Census undercount was even larger than in 1980. His solution: an adjustment, which theoretically would be closer to accurate but which, because politicians could select between several defensible methods, would tilt toward the majority party—perhaps less attractive to him now than it was before November 1994. Sawyer encouraged court review of the Bush Administration's decision not to adjust the count—which if successful would channel more money to states with many immigrants like California and New York, rather than to Ohio. Sawyer also worked on the Economic and Educational Opportunities Committee to adjust formulas for federal aid—work that may be irrelevant if Republicans have the nerve to block-grant the program, in which case, a state's special needs would become less relevant than its population. He promoted the National Literacy Act of 1991 to increase adult literacy, and the Eisenhower bill for technical assistance to schools that revise their science and math programs.

Sawyer attracted the most interest, in the Akron area and beyond, in 1993 when he agonized over the North American Free Trade Agreement and, in between conferring with local labor leaders and taking phone calls from Ohio's George Stephanopoulos of the White House staff, decided to vote for it. "I don't foresee a large-scale movement of capital to Mexico," he said, noting that Akron had already made the transition from tires to polymers. Labor leaders threatened retribution and some supported plumber Kenneth Mack in the primary; but Sawyer won 69%–31%. Slaby, like most Ohio Republicans, also favored NAFTA, and, despite this, a local pipe fitters' union endorsed him. President Clinton paid a five-hour campaign visit to Akron in late October and either helped or did not decisively hurt Sawyer: he won 52%–48%, with most of his numerical margin coming from Kent and Portage County rather than Akron and Summit.

Sawyer cannot hope to be as active a legislator in the 104th Congress as the 103d, and his opinions on the Census will carry far less weight, if any. He has beaten a strong opponent twice, in difficult circumstances; but given the changing economy of the Akron area, he cannot be considered entirely safe. Nor does he seem likely to be a strong contender for statewide office, given his NAFTA stand and the continuing large role labor unions play in Ohio Democratic statewide politics. And the Ohio term limits law, if upheld, will limit his tenure in the 14th District to two more terms. So it is not clear just where this talented and articulate politician's career is headed.

The People: Pop. 1990: 570,987; 8% rural; 13% age 65+; 87% White; 11% Black; 1% Asian; 1% Hispanic origin. Voting age pop.: 433,109; 10% Black; 1% Hispanic origin. Households: 55% married couple families; 24% married couple fams. w. children; 44% college educ.; median household income: $28,184; per capita income: $13,931; median gross rent: $394; median house value: $59,800.

1992 Presidential Vote

Clinton (D)	118,715	(45%)
Bush (R)	81,232	(31%)
Perot (I)	60,000	(23%)

1988 Presidential Vote

Dukakis (D)	122,836	(53%)
Bush (R)	108,364	(47%)

Rep. Tom Sawyer (D)

Elected 1986; b. Aug. 15, 1945, Akron; home, Akron; U. of Akron, B.A. 1968, M.A. 1970; Presbyterian; married (Joyce).

Career: OH House of Reps., 1976–82; Akron Mayor, 1984–86.

DC Office: 1414 LHOB 20515, 202-225-5231; Fax: 202-225-5278.

District Offices: 411 Wolf Ledges Pkwy., #105, Akron 44311, 216-375-5710; and 250 Chestnut St., #14, Ravenna 44266, 216-296-9810.

Committees: *Economic & Educational Opportunities* (7th of 19 D): Employer-Employee Relations; Oversight and Investigations (RMM). *Standards of Official Conduct* (5th of 5 D).

Group Ratings

	ADA	ACLU	COPE	CFA	LCV	CON	NSI	COC	ACU	NTLC	CHC
1994	90	77	78	90	78	29	30	50	5	18	7
1993	85	—	92	100	71	16	—	30	9	—	—

National Journal Ratings

	1993 LIB — 1993 CONS		1994 LIB — 1994 CONS	
Economic	68% —	26%	73% —	17%
Social	80% —	13%	86% —	13%
Foreign	70% —	26%	75% —	23%

Key Votes of the 103d Congress

1. Clinton Deficit Plan	Y	3. Brady Handgun Purchase	Y	5. Lmt. UN Cmnd. of Forces	N
2. NAFTA	Y	4. Strike Race/Death Pnlty.	N	6. Cut Missile Funds	Y

Key Votes of the 104th Congress

1. Congressional Compliance	Y	6. Reform Crime Grant	N	11. Loser Pays Court Reform	N
2. Balanced Budget Amndmt.	N	7. National Security Act	N	12. Product Liability Reform	N
3. Bar Unfunded Mandates	Y	8. Moratorium on Regs.	N	13. Welfare Reform	N
4. Pass Line Item Veto	N	9. Risk Assessment on Regs.	N	14. Term Limits Amndmt.	N
5. Relax Exclusionary Rule	N	10. Expnd. Priv. Prop. Rights	N	15. Tax Cuts	N

Election Results

1994 general	Tom Sawyer (D)	96,274	(52%)	($595,448)
	Lynn Slaby (R)	89,106	(48%)	($256,758)
1994 primary	Tom Sawyer (D)	46,800	(69%)	
	Kenneth A. Mack (D)	20,594	(31%)	
1992 general	Tom Sawyer (D)	165,335	(68%)	($209,155)
	Robert Morgan	78,659	(32%)	

FIFTEENTH DISTRICT

Columbus, smack in the center of the state, was founded in 1812 to be Ohio's capital. It became a regional mid-sized city as well by the early 20th Century and in the last couple of decades has become the center of a major metropolitan area, the headquarters of major research centers like the Batelle Memorial Institute and of Ohio State University, of financial powers like Nationwide Insurance and Banc One, of retailers like The Limited and fast food chains like Wendy's. Its flat-domed Capitol at Broad and High, with the statue of William McKinley out front, is surrounded by high-rises, public and private, while the city grows out in all directions into the countryside.

Ohio's 15th Congressional District is made up of most of Columbus, all but the east side, plus southern and western Franklin County and rural Madison County directly to the west. The 15th includes most of Columbus's black population, some white working-class areas on the south side of the city and in nearby Grove City, and the Ohio State University campus area. Politically, these Democratic areas are more than balanced by the heavily Republican suburb of Upper Arlington, across the Olentangy River from Ohio State, and by Republican subdivisions sprouting up in rural land between the old villages.

The 15th District is represented in the House by Deborah Pryce, a Republican whose curriculum vitae as a relatively non-partisan local judge, by being atypical, is typical of the 1990s House and whose electoral performance reflects in exaggerated form the national partisan trends of the decade. The seat came open in 1992, when Chalmers Wylie, World War II hero, congressman for 26 years and ranking minority member on the Banking Committee for 10, decided to retire. Pryce, a former prosecutor and for eight years an elected judge, won the Republican nomination but had serious competition on two sides—from Democrat Richard Cordray, who had just the sort of political adeptness that had won so many Republican-leaning seats for Democrats over the past two decades, and from pro-life independent Linda Reidelbach, who was angry when Pryce announced after the primary she would support a Freedom of Choice Act which would restrict states' power to limit abortions. Pryce talked much about congressional reform—term limits, rotating chairmanships, line-item veto—and called for limiting spending increases to 3%. She won with 44% of the vote to Cordray's 38% and Reidelbach's 18%.

Immediately after the election, Pryce attended the Omaha meeting of Republican freshmen and was elected interim-president of the freshman Republican class. She was one of many freshmen of both parties to vote in October 1993 against the Superconducting Supercollider, thus killing this high-tech project. "It's a fiscal reform issue. It's what the freshman class stands for," she said. With freshmen of both parties, she backed a $103 billion budget cutting package in November 1993. She opposed the Clinton healthcare plan and new taxes: "I don't feel we can ask the American people for another red cent before we lower spending."

That same spirit was reflected in the 1994 Democratic primary, where the party-endorsed candidate was beaten by librarian Bill Buckel, who had a 20-year plan to increase taxes to eliminate the federal debt. Pryce, after her three-way victory in Democratic 1992, won easily in Republican 1994, with 71% of the vote. As an active ally of Newt Gingrich during the 1994 campaign, when she helped to prepare the Contract With America, she seems likely to be an active and visible member of the majority. The new speaker awarded her with a seat on the front-line Rules Committee for the 104th Congress.

The People: Pop. 1990: 570,740; 10% rural; 10% age 65+; 92% White; 5% Black; 2% Asian; 1% Hispanic origin. Voting age pop.: 442,506; 5% Black; 1% Hispanic origin. Households: 52% married couple families; 24% married couple fams. w. children; 51% college educ.; median household income: $31,020; per capita income: $15,076; median gross rent: $438; median house value: $73,000.

1072   OHIO

1992 Presidential Vote

Bush (R) 119,588 (45%)
Clinton (D) 94,232 (35%)
Perot (I) 52,316 (20%)

1988 Presidential Vote

Bush (R) 147,250 (66%)
Dukakis (D) 77,393 (34%)

Rep. Deborah Pryce (R)

Elected 1992; b. July 29, 1951, Warren; home, Columbus; Ohio State U., B.A. 1973, Capital U. Law Schl., J.D. 1976; Presbyterian; married (Randy Walker).

Career: Admin. Law Judge, OH Dept. of Insurance, 1976; Sr. Asst. Columbus City Prosecutor, 1978; Franklin Cnty. Munic. Court Judge, 1985–1992; Practicing atty., 1992.

DC Office: 221 CHOB 20515, 202-225-2015; Fax: 202-226-0986.

District Offices: 200 N. High St., #400, Columbus, OH 43215, 614-469-5614.

Committees: *Rules* (6th of 9 R): Legislative and Budget Process.

Group Ratings

	ADA	ACLU	COPE	CFA	LCV	CON	NSI	COC	ACU	NTLC	CHC
1994	15	22	78	30	12	94	100	100	67	85	79
1993	10	—	8	20	29	74	—	82	88	—	—

National Journal Ratings

	1993 LIB — 1993 CONS	1994 LIB — 1994 CONS
Economic	0% — 88%	0% — 80%
Social	35% — 64%	36% — 62%
Foreign	24% — 72%	21% — 78%

Key Votes of the 103d Congress

1. Clinton Deficit Plan	N	3. Brady Handgun Purchase N
2. NAFTA	Y	4. Strike Race/Death Pntly. Y

5. Lmt. UN Cmnd. of Forces Y
6. Cut Missile Funds   N

Key Votes of the 104th Congress

1. Congressional Compliance Y
2. Balanced Budget Amndmt. Y
3. Bar Unfunded Mandates   Y
4. Pass Line Item Veto   Y
5. Relax Exclusionary Rule Y

6. Reform Crime Grant   Y
7. National Security Act   Y
8. Moratorium on Regs.   Y
9. Risk Assessment on Regs. Y
10. Expnd. Priv. Prop. Rights Y

11. Loser Pays Court Reform Y
12. Product Liability Reform Y
13. Welfare Reform   Y
14. Term Limits Amndmt.   Y
15. Tax Cuts   Y

Election Results

1994 general	Deborah Pryce (R)	112,912	(71%)	($443,007)
	Bill Buckel (D)	46,480	(29%)	
1994 primary	Deborah Pryce (R)	unopposed		
1992 general	Deborah Pryce (R)	110,390	(44%)	($556,741)
	Richard Cordray (D)	94,907	(38%)	($312,366)
	Linda Reidelbach (I)	44,906	(18%)	($41,841)

SIXTEENTH DISTRICT

Just a century ago Canton, Ohio, was at the center of American politics. Canton was already an industrial city then, though not with the huge steel factories being built in Youngstown or Cleveland; its high-skill workers were fashioning new kinds of plows and reapers and making watches and, beginning in 1899, roller bearings. Canton did not attract masses of immigrants; its factories did not run on harsh stopwatch discipline; there was none of the class-warfare politics here that would be seen later in other northern Ohio industrial cities. Instead, Canton was united a century ago in admiring its first citizen, William McKinley, who rose to the rank of major at 22 in the Civil War, was elected congressman and governor, and sponsored high tariffs as chairman of the House Ways and Means Committee. As Republican candidate for president in 1896, McKinley conducted his campaign from his front porch in Canton, meeting with delegations brought in by train from all over the country, totalling more than 500,000 people during the fall. This spectacle, with its display of technological virtuosity and personal modesty, sounds an appealing and reverberating note in American politics, as does the McKinley platform—the "full dinner pail," the gold standard, the enforcement of law and order in labor relations—which was long seen as antiquated but which still provides useful instruction.

The 16th Congressional District of Ohio includes Canton and surrounding Stark County, plus three-and-a-half counties to the west: Wayne, site of the College of Wooster, Holmes, with its Amish communities, and Ashland and part of Knox, both new territory in 1992. This has remained mostly Republican country since McKinley's time; even when Stark County has gone Democratic, as in 1992, the others have usually kept the 16th's territory in the Republican column. The congressman from the 16th is Ralph Regula, first elected in 1972 and one of the senior Republicans in the House. A leading member of the Appropriations Committee, he has worked closely there with Democrats to craft legislation. As ranking Republican on the Interior Subcommittee, he had much to say about environmental issues. He is dubious about Clean Air provisions that stop road-building in Ohio and bans on offshore drilling. On western lands issues, he wants to reform the Mining Act which allows miners to "patent" federal lands for the low fees set in 1872 and he is a longtime advocate of higher grazing fees; these stands infuriate western Republicans seething over the Clinton Administration's "war on the West," though Regula has never gone as far as some Democrats. After the 1994 election, some conservatives wanted to keep Regula out of the subcommittee chairmanship, but Newt Gingrich saw that he got the job; he was, however, passed over for full committee chairman for the more junior Bob Livingston. Because his subcommittee's jurisdiction extends not only to environmental programs but also to agencies such as the National Endowment for the Arts and the Humanities, Regula will be on the front line of many high-profile spending battles.

Regula, a graduate of the William McKinley School of Law, does not stint Canton area issues. He has long been promoting an Ohio & Erie Canal Heritage Area and worked successfully to put pro-steel provisions into the 1994 GATT treaty to restrict the dumping of imports from other nations. He wants federal aid for cleaner coal technology and development of "brownfields" in central cities. He wrote a 1992 law to provide technical assistance to small firms for teaching employees basic skills. Regula's moderate record has not produced serious primary opposition, and he wins general elections by wide margins.

The People: Pop. 1990: 570,705; 37% rural; 14% age 65+; 94% White; 5% Black; 1% Hispanic origin. Voting age pop.: 419,413; 4% Black; 1% Hispanic origin. Households: 62% married couple families; 29% married couple fams. w. children; 33% college educ.; median household income: $27,524; per capita income: $12,413; median gross rent: $353; median house value: $58,000.

1992 Presidential Vote			1988 Presidential Vote		
Bush (R)	98,824	(39%)	Bush (R)	131,961	(58%)
Clinton (D)	95,157	(37%)	Dukakis (D)	94,491	(42%)
Perot (I)	60,639	(24%)			

Rep. Ralph S. Regula (R)

Elected 1972; b. Dec. 3, 1924, Beach City; home, Navarre; Mt. Union Col., B.A. 1948, William McKinley Schl. of Law, LL.B. 1952; Episcopalian; married (Mary).

Career: Navy, 1944–46 (WWII); Teacher and schl. principal, 1948–52; Practicing atty., 1952–73; OH Bd. of Educ., 1960–64; OH House of Reps., 1964–66; OH Senate, 1966–72.

DC Office: 2309 RHOB 20515, 202-225-3876; Fax: 202-225-3059.

District Offices: 4150 Belden Village St., NW, Canton 44718, 216-489-4414.

Committees: *Appropriations* (5th of 32 R): Commerce, Justice, State, and Judiciary; Interior (Chmn.); Transportation.

Group Ratings

	ADA	ACLU	COPE	CFA	LCV	CON	NSI	COC	ACU	NTLC	CHC
1994	15	35	11	20	33	61	100	92	86	79	86
1993	30	—	50	40	36	59	—	73	71	—	—

National Journal Ratings

	1993 LIB — 1993 CONS	1994 LIB — 1994 CONS
Economic	38% — 61%	34% — 64%
Social	29% — 69%	20% — 77%
Foreign	24% — 72%	23% — 76%

Key Votes of the 103d Congress

1. Clinton Deficit Plan	N	3. Brady Handgun Purchase Y	5. Lmt. UN Cmnd. of Forces Y
2. NAFTA	N	4. Strike Race/Death Pnlty. Y	6. Cut Missile Funds N

Key Votes of the 104th Congress

1. Congressional Compliance Y	6. Reform Crime Grant Y	11. Loser Pays Court Reform Y
2. Balanced Budget Amndmt. Y	7. National Security Act Y	12. Product Liability Reform Y
3. Bar Unfunded Mandates Y	8. Moratorium on Regs. Y	13. Welfare Reform Y
4. Pass Line Item Veto Y	9. Risk Assessment on Regs. Y	14. Term Limits Amndmt. Y
5. Relax Exclusionary Rule Y	10. Expnd. Priv. Prop. Rights Y	15. Tax Cuts Y

Election Results

1994 general	Ralph S. Regula (R)	137,322	(75%)	($120,279)
	J. Michael Finn (D)	45,781	(25%)	
1994 primary	Ralph S. Regula (R)	49,942	(86%)	
	Vince Yambrovich (R)	7,939	(14%)	
1992 general	Ralph S. Regula (R)	158,489	(64%)	($209,305)
	Warner Mendenhall (D)	90,224	(36%)	($105,293)

SEVENTEENTH DISTRICT

The Mahoning River on a relief map is just a trickle of water in the lowlands of eastern Ohio. But on an economic map it is, or was, one of the major waterways of the United States. For the Mahoning was one of America's prime steel valleys. The first coal mine here opened in 1826, canals followed, and in 1892 the first steel mill was built in Youngstown. "Soon," writes historian Harlan Hatcher, "the banks of the river were lined with Bessemer converters, open-hearth furnaces, strip and rolling mills, pipe plants, and manufacturers of steel accessories and products." For nearly a century, the Mahoning Valley, centered on Youngstown, between the Lake Erie docks that unload iron ore from Great Lakes freighters and the coalfields of western Pennsylvania and West Virginia, was one of the steel capitals of the United States. Now, in the late 20th Century, the steel mills stand empty and smokeless and silent—except those that have been dynamited and torn down. Big steel management allowed foreign producers to gain a technological edge back in the 1950s and 1960s; worldwide overcapacity in steel grew as almost every developing country decided it needed its own steel mills, while cooperation between the United Steelworkers and management after the 119-day strike in 1959 boosted wages and fringe benefits to price domestic steel out of the market. Import restrictions kept the furnaces hot for a while, but the oil shock of 1979 produced sharply higher energy prices and a collapse in U.S. autos and steel. Every plant in Youngstown and the Mahoning Valley closed and in the early 1980s metro Youngstown—Mahoning and Trumbull Counties—had one of the nation's highest unemployment rates.

Steel has since revived, but elsewhere: in decentralized minimills or in huge new rolling plants in northern Indiana. The biggest business headquartered in Youngstown is not steel, but the shopping center empire of Edward DeBartolo. The high-wage standard of living of the 1970s has vanished; young people looking for opportunities routinely leave; population has declined. Politically, the Mahoning Valley writhed in anger. Republican in the 1920s, solidly Democratic for years after the United Steelworkers organized the plants following sometimes bloody skirmishes in the late 1930s, the area wobbled toward Republicans in the Carter 1970s, then was one of the most Democratic parts of the country in the Reagan 1980s and the Clinton 1990s.

The 17th Congressional District of Ohio includes all of the Mahoning Valley, running south from Youngstown to the Ohio River across from West Virginia and north past Warren halfway to Lake Erie. The congressman from the 17th is a man who speaks in the authentic demotic accents of the Mahoning Valley. James Traficant is loud and angry and earthy—and, in his own way, creative and consistent and compassionate. He was first elected in 1984, with 56% of the vote in a seven-candidate Democratic primary and 53%–46% over a Republican incumbent, amid controversy that went back to his campaign for Mahoning County sheriff in 1980. Traficant admitted taking large bribes from mobsters to overlook gambling, loan-sharking, drug trafficking and prostitution in Mahoning County and argued, when presented with tapes of some of these transactions, that this was part of his own sting operation. The charges did not come out during the 1980 sheriff's campaign, which Traficant won; when he was tried on criminal charges in 1983 he acted as his own lawyer and persuaded the jury to find him not guilty.

Traficant is known to C-SPAN viewers for his loud speeches—tirades, some say—against foreign aid, free trade and the oppression visited on citizens by the Internal Revenue Service. In one vivid exchange in 1994, he said the CIA should use its $300 million National Reconnaissance Office as "a prison and start by locking up these lying, thieving, stealing CIA nincompoops." Like the Republicans here in the 1920s, Traficant is protectionist and isolationist, vitriolically opposed to aid to Israel and the Gulf war, as outspoken a critic as any in the Congress of the NAFTA and GATT treaties. He constantly sponsors "Made in America" amendments; seeks to ban smoking in federal buildings (he used to chair the public buildings and grounds subcommittee); he pressured the Ways and Means Committee into considering his taxpayers' rights amendments by standing on the floor for 10 hours and raising points of order against every section of the Treasury bill. He has his own creative legislation—a flat tax bill coupled with a consumption tax, an 800 number for information on American-made products, a bill to create 435 college scholarships, one in each congressional district, to be repaid by four years of federal government service. Loud and abrasive on the floor, he is one of the kindest and most thoughtful members to House employees and pages.

Traficant survived redistricting nicely in 1992. His district could have been carved up, but evidently no one wanted to take him on. His popularity was such that in 1988, when he ran in the Ohio presidential primary, he won 18% of the vote in the 17th District, running just behind Jesse Jackson.

The People: Pop. 1990: 570,963; 26% rural; 16% age 65+; 88% White; 10% Black; 1% Other; 1% Hispanic origin. Voting age pop.: 427,856; 8% Black; 1% Hispanic origin. Households: 58% married couple families; 25% married couple fams. w. children; 33% college educ.; median household income: $25,220; per capita income: $11,938; median gross rent: $337; median house value: $48,400.

1992 Presidential Vote			1988 Presidential Vote		
Clinton (D)	131,983	(50%)	Dukakis (D)	148,987	(60%)
Bush (R)	67,858	(26%)	Bush (R)	98,250	(40%)
Perot (I)	64,339	(24%)			

Rep. James A. Traficant, Jr. (D)

Elected 1984; b. May 8, 1941, Youngstown; home, Poland; U. of Pittsburgh, B.S. 1963; Youngstown St. U., M.S. 1973, M.S. 1976; Catholic; married (Patricia).

Career: Dir., Mahoning Cnty. Drug Program, 1971–81; Mahoning Cnty. Sheriff, 1980–84.

DC Office: 2446 RHOB 20515, 202-225-5261; Fax: 202-225-3719.

District Offices: 125 Market St., Youngstown 44503, 216-743-1914; 5555 Youngstown-Warren Rd., #503, Niles 44406, 216-652-5649; and 109 W. 3d St., E. Liverpool 43920, 216-385-5921.

Committees: *Transportation & Infrastructure* (7th of 27 D): Coast Guard and Maritime Transportation (RMM); Public Buildings and Economic Development. *Science* (3rd of 23 D): Space and Aeronautics.

Group Ratings

	ADA	ACLU	COPE	CFA	LCV	CON	NSI	COC	ACU	NTLC	CHC
1994	65	61	11	100	44	5	40	42	33	22	50
1993	75	—	92	80	64	0	—	45	21	—	—

National Journal Ratings

	1993 LIB — 1993 CONS			1994 LIB — 1994 CONS		
Economic	52%	—	48%	64%	—	35%
Social	50%	—	49%	48%	—	50%
Foreign	44%	—	55%	42%	—	57%

Key Votes of the 103d Congress

1. Clinton Deficit Plan	N	3. Brady Handgun Purchase	Y	5. Lmt. UN Cmnd. of Forces	Y
2. NAFTA	N	4. Strike Race/Death Pnlty.	N	6. Cut Missile Funds	N

Key Votes of the 104th Congress

1. Congressional Compliance	Y	6. Reform Crime Grant	Y	11. Loser Pays Court Reform	N
2. Balanced Budget Amndmt.	N	7. National Security Act	Y	12. Product Liability Reform	Y
3. Bar Unfunded Mandates	Y	8. Moratorium on Regs.	Y	13. Welfare Reform	Y
4. Pass Line Item Veto	N	9. Risk Assessment on Regs.	Y	14. Term Limits Amndmt.	Y
5. Relax Exclusionary Rule	Y	10. Expnd. Priv. Prop. Rights	Y	15. Tax Cuts	Y

Election Results

1994 general	James A. Traficant, Jr. (D)	149,004	(77%)	($145,793)
	Mike G. Meister (R)	43,490	(23%)	($8,522)
1994 primary	James A. Traficant, Jr. (D)	unopposed		
1992 general	James A. Traficant, Jr. (D)	216,503	(84%)	($98,740)
	Salvatore Pansino (R)	40,743	(16%)	($3,488)

EIGHTEENTH DISTRICT

The hills of east central Ohio have been industrial country for 200 years, from their earliest settlement in the 1790s. The local clay was used to make pottery, the coal that lies near the surface was dug up, a green vitriol works was built, and a nail factory went into operation, all before 1814. For more than 100 years, this area has been part of the great coal and steel belt that centers on Pittsburgh and Cleveland and stretches from the coal mines of West Virginia to Lake Erie, the destination of Great Lakes freighters filled with iron ore from Minnesota's Mesabi Range. This area is filled with small cities, each with its little steel mill or factory, most of them old towns whose storefronts and wooden, working-class houses bear the unmistakable imprint of the early 20th Century. For a time the pay was good, but after the oil shock of 1979, the coal and steel economy went into collapse; the impact here was cushioned by continuing demand for coal from electric utilities, but that threatens to be reduced by the 1990 Clean Air Act. Wage levels have sagged and the hopes many had of getting ahead have been disappointed.

The 18th Congressional District of Ohio covers much of this land along the Ohio River, just west of West Virginia, and spreads west over hilly farmland pockmarked by strip mines, from Steubenville on the Ohio, which used to have the nation's worst air quality, to New Rumley, the birthplace of General Custer, and Zanesville, the birthplace of writer Zane Grey and architect Cass Gilbert and home of a famous Y-shaped bridge, and Newark—almost all the way across the old National Road and U.S. 40 to Columbus. As one goes west, the territory is less industrial, but overall the 18th is, sociologically and politically, a kind of ethnic working-class neighborhood. For 40 years after the New Deal and World War II, it leaned Democratic; in 1994, mostly by narrow margins, it went Republican.

The beneficiary of this trend is the 18th District's new congressman, Republican Bob Ney. He grew up in Belleaire, just across the Ohio from Wheeling, West Virginia, worked as a teacher and safety director for the city of Belleaire, was elected to the state House in 1980, at 26, in quite an upset, beating Wayne Hays, the longtime (1948–76) congressman from the 18th and power in the House who lost his seat due to scandal in 1976 and then won a state House seat in 1978. Ney lost that seat in this Democratic area in Democratic 1982, but in 1984 was elected to the state Senate. There, he backed a bill encouraging electric power plants to install scrubbers so they could use high-sulfur Ohio coal and sponsored a bill to help people get or keep health insurance. When Douglas Applegate, the practical-minded Democrat who had replaced Hays, announced his retirement, Ney ran for Congress giving up his chair of the Finance Committee at home. The Democrats had a serious primary, in which state Representative Greg DiDonato beat Applegate aide James Hart 49%–36%; 1994 was not a good year to have Capitol Hill connections. DiDonato criticized Ney for accepting honoraria from lobbyists; Ney criticized DiDonato for sharing an apartment with a cable TV lobbyist. Most unions backed DiDonato, except for teachers' unions who backed ex-teacher Ney.

Ney's home base of Belmont County turned out to be the key; only 35% for Republican Senate candidate Mike DeWine, it voted 67% for Ney, enough to clinch a 54%–46% victory. Although he comported himself initially as a team player, this is one Republican freshman with a strong incentive to support old-style government programs and to work for pork barrel projects. That will be no small challenge under the new regime.

1078   OHIO

The People: Pop. 1990: 570,784; 60% rural; 15% age 65+; 97% White; 2% Black. Voting age pop.: 421,278; 2% Black. Households: 61% married couple families; 28% married couple fams. w. children; 25% college educ.; median household income: $22,808; per capita income: $10,531; median gross rent: $298; median house value: $44,000.

1992 Presidential Vote

Clinton (D)	110,491	(43%)
Bush (R)	87,512	(34%)
Perot (I)	58,605	(23%)

1988 Presidential Vote

Bush (R)	120,109	(52%)
Dukakis (D)	110,141	(48%)

Rep. Bob Ney (R)

Elected 1994; b. July 5, 1954, Wheeling, WV; home, St. Clairsville; OH St. U., B.S. 1976; Catholic; married (Candy).

Career: Teacher, Iran, 1978; Bellaire Safety Dir.; OH House of Reps., 1980–84; OH Senate, 1984–94.

DC Office: 1605 LHOB 20515, 202-225-6265; Fax: 202-225-3394.

District Offices: 3201 Belmont St., #604, Bellaire 43906, 614-676-1960; 152 2nd St., NE, New Philadelphia 44663, 216-364-6380; 500 Market St., #610, Steubenville 43952, 614-283-1915; and 225 Underwood St., #4000, Zanesville 43701, 614-452-8598.

Committees: *Banking & Financial Services* (17th of 27 R): Domestic and International Monetary Policy; Financial Institutions and Consumer Credit; Housing and Community Opportunity. *House Oversight* (7th of 7 R). *Veterans' Affairs* (11th of 18 R): Compensation, Pension, Insurance and Memorial Affairs; Hospitals and Health Care.

Group Ratings and 103rd Congress Votes: Newly Elected

Key Votes of the 104th Congress

1. Congressional Compliance Y	6. Reform Crime Grant Y	11. Loser Pays Court Reform Y
2. Balanced Budget Amndmt. Y	7. National Security Act Y	12. Product Liability Reform Y
3. Bar Unfunded Mandates Y	8. Moratorium on Regs. Y	13. Welfare Reform Y
4. Pass Line Item Veto Y	9. Risk Assessment on Regs. Y	14. Term Limits Amndmt. Y
5. Relax Exclusionary Rule Y	10. Expnd. Priv. Prop. Rights Y	15. Tax Cuts Y

Election Results

1994 general	Bob Ney (R)	103,115	(54%)	($600,426)
	Greg A. DiDonato (D)	87,926	(46%)	($434,905)
1994 primary	Bob Ney (R)	26,850	(69%)	
	Michael J. Craig (R)	4,627	(12%)	
	John Holland Jones (R)	2,284	(6%)	
	Van Slack (R)	1,872	(5%)	
	Charles L. Graber (R)	1,571	(4%)	
	Others	1,501	(4%)	
1992 general	Douglas Applegate (D)	166,189	(68%)	($102,335)
	Bill Ress (R)	77,229	(32%)	($26,810)

NINETEENTH DISTRICT

The Western Reserve—the northeast corner of Ohio that belonged to Connecticut until 1800—still bears a distinctive New England Yankee imprint. This land was on the direct westward trail of Yankee settlement in the years before the Civil War; here, amid the low hills which produced the steel streams of the Cuyahoga and the Mahoning, they established New England-style townships, churches and schools. This area produced some of the strongest opposition to slavery and support of the Union armies and the Republican Party in the nation. Its thrifty, hard-working, well-educated citizens built communities with fine schools and, with their accumulated savings, invested in what became some of the nation's leading industries. That brought great masses of immigrants to Cleveland and the other cities of northeast Ohio, which remained solidly Republican until the Great Depression and the bloody CIO organizing drives of the late 1930s; then, for 30 years, the Western Reserve was Democratic during Ohio's class-warfare politics. In the early 1980s, when the auto and steel industries lost thousands of jobs, northeast Ohio went heavily Democratic; in the early 1990s, as the economy has diversified and recovered, it has moved toward the Republicans.

The 19th Congressional District of Ohio takes in an irregularly-shaped hunk—a very irregularly-shaped hunk—of northeast Ohio and the old Western Reserve. It includes all of Lake County, with mixed middling-to-affluent suburbs and industrial Ashtabula County in the northeast corner of the state. It also includes a motley collection of the Cuyahoga County suburbs of Cleveland. East of Cleveland are affluent Italian, Jewish and WASP suburbs, Beachwood, Pepper Pike and Chagrin Falls. Directly south of Cleveland are more working-class suburbs on either side of the Cuyahoga River gorge and west to Brook Park around the convention center and airport.

The 19th has existed in this form for only two elections, and each time it has seen serious contests between talented young politicians of both parties. In 1992, two Democratic incumbents who had represented much of the district decided to retire, Dennis Eckart, who at 42 had served 12 years, and Ed Feighan, who at 45 had served 10. They were succeeded by another Democratic prodigy, Eric Fingerhut, a 33-year-old state senator who had chaired Common Cause Ohio, headed a job training program, managed Michael White's successful (and biracially supported) campaign for mayor of Cleveland in 1989 and won a seat in the Ohio Senate in 1990. There he helped oust the oldtime Democratic leader, wrote a recycling bill, created an Ohio Energy Strategy Task Force and advanced a gun safety bill. Fingerhut won the primary against four serious opponents with 24% of the vote and then beat Lake County Commissioner Robert Gardner in the general 53%–47%.

Fingerhut sounded reform themes in the campaign and when elected he became one of two chairmen of the freshman class task force on reform. But the results were underwhelming. Speaker Tom Foley convened meetings of freshmen weeks after the election and persuaded them not to work for wholesale changes. Fingerhut was persuaded also to vote for the Clinton budget and tax plan and got sidetracked on his fight for a tough ban on lobbyists gifts to members and staff. He came out with a stringent welfare bill that didn't go anywhere. And he was embarrassed when, after he had long denounced franked mail, he decided to send out his own in the election year. "The level of misunderstanding of what we did and didn't do is astounding. The positive aspects got overwhelmed by the painful parts," Fingerhut said. *The News Herald* of Lake County was more caustic: "Fingerhut . . . talks a great game about being in favor of change and heading in new directions, but his votes reveal the fundamental hypocrisy of his words."

Steve LaTourette, Lake County Prosecutor, won the 3-candidate Republican primary with 54%. He attacked Fingerhut in the general for supporting the Clinton budget, for being soft on crime, and hypocritically using the frank. Fingerhut attacked LaTourette for opposing gun control and said, "Washington will never change me." But evidently some voters thought it already had. LaTourette won 48%–43%, even though he did not raise nearly as much PAC money as Fingerhut, and carried Lake County 58%–33%. Although he initially had a low profile in the rambunctious House Republican freshman class, his background in public office and his committee assignments will give LaTourette an opportunity to show that he can make a difference on the nitty-gritty of legislative work. In March 1995, while promoting the tort reform item of the Contract, LaTourette solicited the help of humorist Dave Barry in a speech to the House floor. "As a lawyer, I am the last person to suggest that everybody in my profession is a money-grubbing, scum-sucking toad . . . The vast majority of lawyers are responsible professionals, as well as, in many ways, human beings." LaTourette also will focus on winning a solid reelection in 1996, in hopes of putting a lock on this swing district.

The People: Pop. 1990: 570,834; 12% rural; 15% age 65+; 96% White; 2% Black; 1% Asian; 1% Hispanic origin. Voting age pop.: 436,395; 2% Black; 1% Hispanic origin. Households: 62% married couple families; 26% married couple fams. w. children; 43% college educ.; median household income: $34,385; per capita income: $16,609; median gross rent: $464; median house value: $77,200.

1992 Presidential Vote

Clinton (D)	114,358	(40%)
Bush (R)	106,947	(37%)
Perot (I)	66,424	(23%)

1988 Presidential Vote

Bush (R)	129,904	(53%)
Dukakis (D)	115,147	(47%)

Rep. Steven C. LaTourette (R)

Elected 1994; b. July 22, 1954, Cleveland; home, Madison Village; U. of MI, B.A. 1976, Cleveland St. U., J.D. 1979; Methodist; married (Susan).

Career: Lake Cnty. Asst. Public Defender, 1980–83; Practicing atty., 1983–88; Lake Cnty. Prosecuting atty., 1988–94.

DC Office: 1508 LHOB 20515, 202-225-5731; Fax: 202-225-3307.

District Offices: 1 Victoria Pl., #320, Painesville 44077, 216-352-3939.

Committees: *Government Reform & Oversight* (25th of 27 R): District of Columbia. *Transportation & Infrastructure* (28th of 33 R): Public Buildings and Economic Development; Surface Transportation; Water Resources and Environment.

Group Ratings and 103rd Congress Votes: Newly Elected

Key Votes of the 104th Congress

1. Congressional Compliance Y	6. Reform Crime Grant Y	11. Loser Pays Court Reform N
2. Balanced Budget Amndmt. Y	7. National Security Act Y	12. Product Liability Reform Y
3. Bar Unfunded Mandates Y	8. Moratorium on Regs. Y	13. Welfare Reform Y
4. Pass Line Item Veto Y	9. Risk Assessment on Regs. Y	14. Term Limits Amndmt. Y
5. Relax Exclusionary Rule Y	10. Expnd. Priv. Prop. Rights Y	15. Tax Cuts Y

Election Results

1994 general	Steven C. LaTourette (R)	99,997	(48%)	($712,925)
	Eric D. Fingerhut (D)	89,701	(43%)	($981,882)
	Ronald E. Young (I)	11,364	(6%)	($42,785)
	Others	5,180	(3%)	
1994 primary	Steven C. LaTourette (R)	23,581	(54%)	
	Tucker Markston (R)	15,985	(37%)	
	Randall Paul Lundi (R)	4,187	(10%)	
1992 general	Eric D. Fingerhut (D)	138,465	(53%)	($611,478)
	Robert A. Gardner (R)	124,606	(47%)	($450,117)

OKLAHOMA

"In the middle of nowhere": that is how Oklahoma was described in the moments after the terrible bomb blast in Oklahoma City in April 1995. How strange it was, the thought went, that this terrible thing happened out here where nothing ever seems to happen. But Oklahoma is not in the middle of nowhere, but in the middle of America, and the idea that nothing ever seems to happen there is both wrong—for Oklahoma has had exhilarating highs and sickening lows several times in its history—and misleading: the very creation of an orderly yet energetic society in which ordinary people can do great things is an achievement often taken for granted in this country, yet yearned for throughout the course of human history.

Oklahoma's success has come from a most improbable history. It was settled in a rush, first by the Five Civilized Tribes driven west by Andrew Jackson's troops over the Cherokees' Trail of Tears in the 1830s. Then came white settlers one morning in April 1889, when, in the great land rush memorialized in an Edna Ferber novel, the Rodgers and Hammerstein musical and half a dozen Hollywood movies, thousands of would-be homesteaders drove their wagons across the territorial line at the sound of a gunshot, the most adventurous or unscrupulous of them literally jumping the gun—the Sooners. The heritage of these rushes remains. Oklahoma celebrated the Year of the Indian in 1992, honoring the state's 67 tribes and spotlighting their council houses, historic sites and festivals. Oklahoma has the largest Indian population of any state, 253,000 in the 1990 Census, though there is just one reservation (however, the status of may other tribal entities is often disputed). But there has been much intermarriage over the years, and many Oklahomans proudly claim some Indian blood; assimilation into everyday life plus commemoration of historic traditions and efforts to keep the Cherokee, Choctaw, Chickasaw and Seminole languages from dying out seem to have provided a better life for Native Americans here than approaches elsewhere.

Statehood came to Oklahoma late, in 1907, at which point it filled up with farmers, rising from 1.5 million people in 1907 to 2.4 million in 1930. Then, a decade of bust. Oklahoma literally went up in smoke, or rather dust, as soil loosened by erosion was whipped into giant swirling clouds: the Dust Bowl. "On a single day, I heard, 50 million tons of soil were blown away," John Gunther reported later. "People sat in Oklahoma City, with the sky invisible for three days in a row, holding dust masks over their faces and wet towels to protect their mouths at night, while the farms blew by." Okies headed in droves west out U.S. 66 to the green land of California and Oklahoma's population sank to 2.3 million in 1940 and 2.2 million in 1950, not to reach its 1930 level again until 1970.

Then another boom—this time from oil. As the oil shocks of 1973 and 1979 sent oil prices up, Oklahoma's population rose from 2.5 million in 1970 to 3 million in 1980 and 3.3 million in 1983.

Then, with the collapse of oil prices and of Oklahoma's farm economy as well, bust again. A giddy rise was followed by a giddier fall: the rig count fell from 882 in January 1982 to 232 in February 1983, 128 in 1986 and 93 in 1989. Just as the dust cloud symbolized Oklahoma's 1930s bust, so the auction of oil drilling equipment was a symbol of the 1980s calamity. The 1990 Census reported just 3.1 million Oklahomans. The nation's lowest unemployment state in the early 1980s recession, Oklahoma suffered during the late 1980s boom, but it was hurting less than most states by the early 1990s recession and unemployment actually declined in 1992. It was performing well in other ways, with rising test scores in its tradition-minded schools.

But in the meantime, Oklahoma has gone through extraordinary political turbulence. Its partisan patterns had seemed well-set: most of its early settlers were southerners, and historically it was Democratic. Little Dixie in the south was always strong for the Democrats, the wheat counties of the northwest leaned Republican; metro Tulsa and Oklahoma City have been trending Republican since the 1950s. The post-oil boom years saw an oscillation of parties, with stubborn budgetary crises and scandals; Oklahoma voters were among the first in the nation to impose term limits on state legislators in 1990.

Then, after two years of Bill Clinton, Oklahoma shifted very sharply to the Republicans. The House delegation, which consisted of four Democrats and two Republicans in January 1994, was five Republicans and one conservative Democrat by January 1995. Republicans held both Senate seats and the governorship as well. And this was not just a loss of seats but of talent. David Boren, frustrated when his campaign finance reform was beaten by Republicans and his moderate policies were rejected by Democrats, resigned from the Senate to become President of the University of Oklahoma. Mike Synar and Dave McCurdy, classmates at OU in the class of 1972, congressmen since 1978 and 1980 and national leaders on important issues, were both beaten—Synar in the Democratic runoff, McCurdy in the general election for Senate. Any party can recover from one bad year, but from losses like these the Oklahoma Democratic Party may need years to recover.

Governor. The governor of Oklahoma, suddenly a nationally visible official after the bombing of April 1995, is Frank Keating, a Republican elected in 1994 after a career in public office, elective and appointive. Keating grew up in Tulsa, graduated from Georgetown University—where he overlapped with Bill Clinton—and Oklahoma Law, then worked two years as an FBI agent. In 1972, he was elected to the Oklahoma House, in 1974 to the Oklahoma Senate, where he became minority leader. In 1981, he became U.S. attorney in Tulsa, in 1986, assistant Treasury secretary, in 1988, associate attorney general—all posts overseeing law enforcement agencies. After that, he went on to be Jack Kemp's general counsel at HUD. After Senate Democrats refused to act on President Bush's nomination of him for a federal judgeship, Keating returned to Oklahoma in 1993 and ran for governor, clearly the party leaders' choice; he was peppered in the primary by state Senator Jerry Pierce's charges that he had been out of town too long, but won 57%–29%.

The Democrats were in more disarray. Incumbent Governor David Walters, after a fairly successful first two years of gaining support for an education reform package, was beset by tragedy and scandal. His 19-year-old son committed suicide after being arrested on drug paraphernalia charges, and Walters himself was charged with violating campaign finance laws in his unsuccessful 1986 and narrowly successful 1990 campaigns. Walters was indicted in 1993 for conspiracy and perjury. He pleaded guilty in October 1993 to accepting $18,500 from a 1990 contributor, well over the $5,000 limit; in return, the judge dismissed the other counts, fined Walters $1,000 and gave him a one-year deferred sentence. This light punishment left Walters in political limbo; eventually he confirmed the obvious and said he wasn't running. That left Lieutenant Governor Jack Mildren as the leading Democrat. But he failed to get an absolute majority in the primary, leading state Senator Bernice Shedrick 49%–37%, and was forced into a September runoff, which he won with 59%. Mildren had an additional problem, the independent candidacy of Wes Watkins, former Democratic congressman from Little Dixie, who lost the 1990 runoff to Walters by only 51%–49%. Mildren led right after the primary, and Watkins and

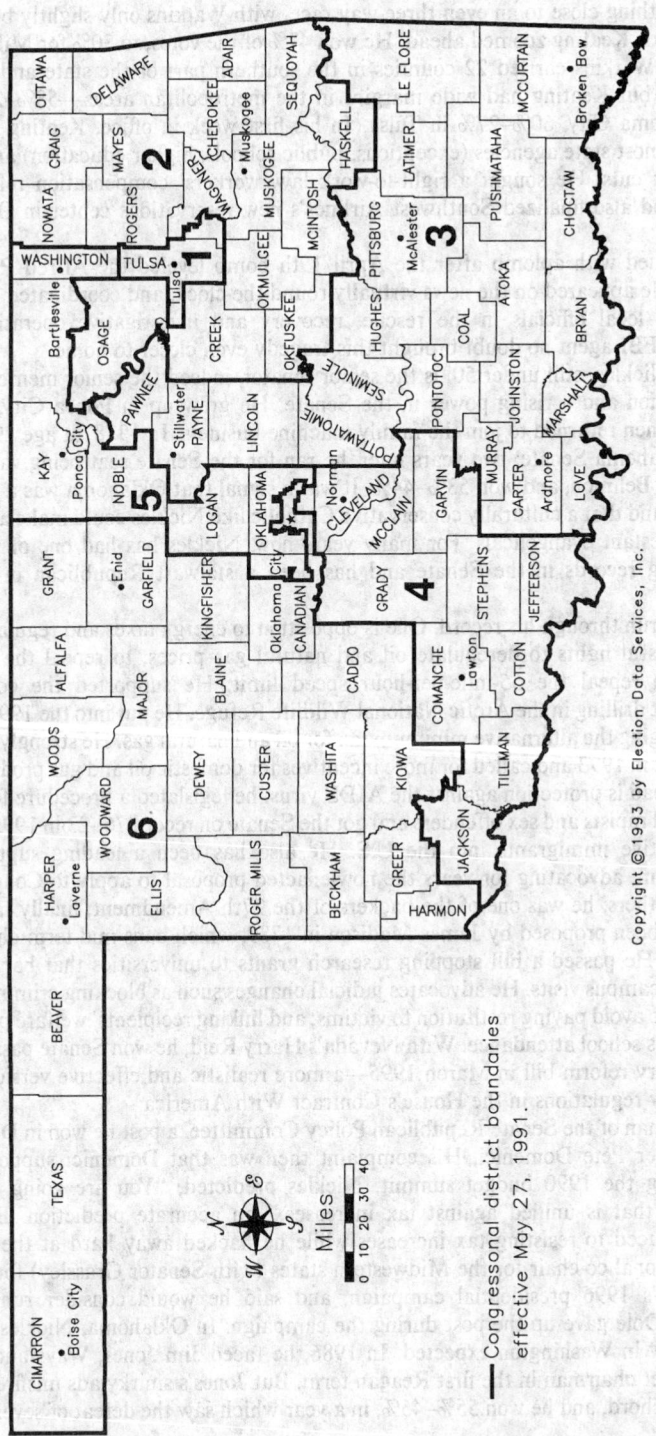

Congressional district boundaries
effective May 27, 1991.

Mildren both lambasted Keating's proposal to cut business and other taxes. But by October, the polls showed something close to an even three-way race, with Watkins only slightly behind.

In the final weeks, Keating zoomed ahead. He won 47% of the votes, to 30% for Mildren and 23% for Watkins; Watkins carried 22 counties in the southern part of the state and Mildren carried 12 others, but Keating had wide margins in the metropolitan areas—58%–27% over Mildren in Oklahoma City, 60%–27% in Tulsa. In his first week in office, Keating proposed spending cuts for most state agencies (exceptions: public schools, higher education) and nearly $65 million in tax cuts. He sought a right-to-work law, workers' compensation reform and welfare reform, and also finalized Southwest Airlines's new reservations center in Oklahoma City.

Keating performed with aplomb after the April 19th bomb leveled the Alfred P. Murrah federal building. He appeared on the news virtually round-the-clock, and coordinated efforts of federal, state and local officials in the rescue, recovery and investigative operations. His background as an FBI agent no doubt brought this tragedy even closer to home.

Senators. Don Nickles, still under 50, is the senior senator, indeed the senior member of the Oklahoma delegation and a rising power in the Senate. He grew up in Ponca City, went to Oklahoma State, then returned to join the family machine business. In 1978, at age 29, he was elected to the Oklahoma Senate; two years later, he ran for the Senate seat being vacated by Republican Henry Bellmon, and won 53%–44%. It was a signal that Oklahoma was a basically Republican state, and that a culturally conservative Catholic like Nickles could make a political alliance with Protestant evangelicals. For many years now, Nickles has had one of the most conservative voting records in the Senate and has been a stalwart Republican in partisan controversy.

Several threads run through his record. One is opposition to energy taxes and regulations; he backed the successful fights to deregulate oil and natural gas prices, to repeal the windfall profits tax and to repeal the 55-mile-per-hour speed limit. He supported the continuing campaign to permit drilling in the Arctic National Wildlife Refuge. He put into the 1992 energy bill measures changing the alternative minimum tax for oil and natural gas. He strongly opposed the Clinton Btu tax in 1993 and called for more incentives for domestic oil and gas production in 1995. Another thread is protection against the AIDS virus: he legislated a procedure for AIDS testing of convicted rapists and sex offenders and got the Senate on record 76–23 in 1993 against allowing HIV-positive immigrants into the U.S. He also has been a leading supporter of congressional reform, advocating for years the now-enacted proposal to apply to Congress the laws it applies to others; he was one of the backers of the 27th Amendment, finally ratified in 1992 after having been proposed by James Madison in 1789, which bans mid-term changes in congressional pay. He passed a bill stopping research grants to universities that bar military recruiters from on-campus visits. He advocates judicial changes such as blocking criminals from using bankruptcy to avoid paying restitution to victims, and linking recipients' welfare payments with their children's school attendance. With Nevada's Harry Reid, he won Senate passage of a bipartisan regulatory reform bill in March 1995—a more realistic and effective version of the moratorium on new regulations in the House's Contract With America.

Nickles is chairman of the Senate Republican Policy Committee, a post he won in December 1990 by 23–20 over Pete Domenici. His complaint then was that Domenici supported tax increases, including the 1990 budget summit. Nickles predicted, "You are going to see a Republican Party that is unified against tax increases," an accurate prediction. By 1995, Domenici was reduced to resisting tax increases while he hacked away hard at the budget. Nickles also is regional co-chair for the Midwestern states (with Senator Grassley) for Kansas Senator Bob Dole's 1996 presidential campaign, and said he would consider running for majority leader if Dole gave up the post during the campaign. In Oklahoma, Nickles has run stronger than many in Washington expected. In 1986, he faced Jim Jones, Ways and Means member and Budget chairman in the first Reagan term. But Jones's smirky ads misfired, while Nickles's struck a chord, and he won 55%–45%, in a year which saw the defeat of several other southern Republicans first elected in 1980; incidentally Nickles supported Jones's nomination to be ambassador to Mexico in 1993. In 1992, Nickles's Democratic opponent was Steve Lewis, who had worked his way up from poverty to become speaker of the state House, and had run unsuccessfully for governor in 1990. Nickles attacked Lewis as a Ted Kennedy clone who would raise taxes, and won 59%–38%, the best showing for a Republican Senator in Oklahoma since 1924.

Oklahoma's junior Senator is James Inhofe, a Republican from Tulsa, often beset and sometimes defeated in a 30-year political career, but triumphantly elected in 1994 to fill the vacancy created by the resignation of David Boren to become president of the University of Oklahoma. Boren's loss was a grave one for Democrats: his conservatism and performance as governor in the 1970s made him overwhelmingly popular in Oklahoma (in 1990 he carried 2,352 of 2,354 precincts), and his work for campaign finance reform and moderate stands on taxes and health care would, if followed by other Democrats, have helped the party's fortunes more than following Bill Clinton's programs did. Inhofe grew up in Tulsa, worked in real estate and insurance, has for years regularly flown planes and is Congress's only certified commercial pilot. He was elected to the Oklahoma House as long ago as 1966, at age 31, and to the Oklahoma Senate in 1970; he ran for governor in 1974 and lost to David Boren, 64%–36%. In 1976, Inhofe ran for the U.S. House against Jim Jones and lost; from 1978 to 1984 Inhofe was mayor of Tulsa. He won the heavily Republican 1st District House seat in 1986, but held it with uninspiring margins. He was hurt by negative publicity about a family business lawsuit (he eventually was awarded $3.6 million), charges of campaign finance irregularities, an order to pay the FDIC $588,000 on promissory notes to an insurance company and for lying about when he received his college degree; the liberal-leaning *Tulsa World* made sure to pepper him with criticism. In Washington, Inhofe seemed to be somewhere on the right margin of the House. He was active on aviation issues, pushing for bills to preserve American Airlines's Tulsa-based SABRE reservations system, to have the National Transportation Safety Board rather than the Federal Aviation Administration judge civil cases brought by the FAA, to establish visual flight rule routes in crowded airspace.

Then in 1993, Inhofe found a cause that captured the nation's attention: the arcane discharge petition. For years House rules kept secret the names of signers of petitions to discharge bills stuck in committees; members could lie and claim they had worked to bring legislation to the floor when they hadn't. Inhofe found a way to attack this rule institutionalizing hypocrisy: he proposed to change House rules and make public the names of members who had signed each petition, making it easy for others to put the spotlight on those who said they had or would sign but hadn't. With vocal support from Rush Limbaugh, Ross Perot and the *Wall Street Journal* editorial page, Inhofe's strategy worked. In September 1993, the Democratic leaders caved in and with the spotlight on, the Inhofe resolution making public discharge petitions passed.

When Boren announced his retirement, Inhofe jumped into the race and easily won the Republican nomination. He faced the toughest possible Democrat, Dave McCurdy, congressman since 1980, from southwest Oklahoma, chairman of the moderate Democratic Leadership Council, expert on military and intelligence affairs, critic of the House Democratic leadership (Speaker Thomas Foley maneuvered to remove him as Intelligence chairman in 1993). An extrapolation from their past electoral showings would put Inhofe far behind: he had won by small margins in a heavily Republican district, while McCurdy had won by large margins by a district that gave Bill Clinton only one-third of its votes in 1992.

But in Oklahoma in 1994 the Clinton burden was too heavy for even McCurdy to carry. He ran on welfare reform and support for defense spending; Inhofe attacked McCurdy for voting with Clinton 90% of the time—including the Clinton budget and tax package with its original energy tax and the 1994 crime bill with its assault weapon ban. McCurdy argued that as a Democrat he could be more effective on national issues and on saving Oklahoma's Tinker Air Force Base; but he was reminded that he had campaigned for Clinton in his darkest days in New Hampshire in early 1992 and in 36 states thereafter. McCurdy could argue, and often did to reporters, that Clinton had betrayed the cause of the DLC—which he had chaired a few years before McCurdy. Inhofe ads humorously but effectively showed McCurdy as Pinocchio, with his nose growing, reflecting his shifts on some issues. McCurdy did not satisfactorily explain his stand on allowing gays in the military; an ad on the crime bill showed thuggish convicts ballet dancing in pink tutus, an apparent reference to crime legislation masquerading as social policy. "Dave McClinton," as Republicans called him, was beaten, one Democrat said, by "God, guns and gays." Inhofe won by a solid 55%–40%, carrying the Tulsa area by a higher percentage that ever before (60%–37%) and Oklahoma City by even more (61%–35%); he also bested McCurdy in the rest of Oklahoma (52%–42%), carrying even McCurdy's old congressional district.

In the Senate, Inhofe was chairman of the 11 freshman Republicans, all but Olympia Snowe solid conservatives. He backs tax incentives to domestic oil and gas production and regulatory reform. He was elected to fill just the last two years of Boren's term, and must run for a full term in 1996. But given the 1994 result, the main question is whether he will have a serious Democratic opponent. Oklahoma Democrats have mentioned George Nigh, president of the University of Central Oklahoma, as a candidate to possibly challenge Inhofe. In 1982, Nigh was the first Oklahoma governor to be elected to a second term, carrying every county; his instant credibility would certainly be a benefit.

Presidential politics. Oklahoma is usually the most Republican of southern states; in 1992, it voted for 43%–34% for George Bush over Bill Clinton, with 23% for Ross Perot. There are no large blocs of voters here who back national Democrats and almost everyone finds national Republicans acceptable. Oklahoma is thus not on anyone's list of target states in October, nor is it the subject of much attention as one of the southern Super Tuesday primaries. In 1988 and 1992, it voted predictably for southerners, George Bush in the Republican primaries, Al Gore (a distant relation of onetime Oklahoma Senator Thomas Gore, grandfather of writer Gore Vidal) and Bill Clinton on the Democratic side.

Congressional districting. For the 1990s, Oklahoma narrowly missed losing a seat. Democrats drew up an "incumbent protection plan," which was supposed to strengthen the four Democratic congressmen by concentrating Republican votes in the other two districts. But that failed abysmally. By November 1994, three of the four Democrats were gone, and Democrats' chances of regaining two of those three seats seem negligible. With only one Democrat in the delegation, Oklahoma is a metaphor of that party's southern problems.

The People: Est. Pop. 1994: 3,258,000; Pop. 1990: 3,145,585, up 3.6% 1990–1994. 1.2% of U.S. total, 28th largest; 32% rural. Median age: 33.2 years. 13.5% 65 years and over. 82.1% White, 8.0% American Indian, 7.4% Black, 2.7% Hispanic origin, 1.1% Asian, 1.3% Other. Households: 57.7% married couple families; 28% married couple fams. w. children; 44% college educ.; median household income: $23,577; per capita income: $11,893; 68.1% owner occupied housing; median house value: $48,100; median monthly rent: $259. 5.7% Unemployment. 1994 Voting age pop.: 2,394,000. 1994 Turnout: 995,012; 42% of VAP. Registered voters (1994): 2,302,279; 1,452,949 D (63%), 775,754 R (34%), 73,576 unaffiliated and minor parties (3%).

Political Lineup: Governor, Frank Keating (R); Lt. Gov., Mary Fallin (R); Secy. of State, John Kennedy (D); Atty. Gen., Drew Edmondson (D); Treasurer, Robert Butkin (R); Auditor, Clifton Scott (D). State Senate, 48 (35 D and 13 R); State House of Representatives, 101 (64 D and 37 R). Senators, Don Nickles (R) and James M. Inhofe (R). Representatives, 6 (5 R and 1 D).

1992 Presidential Vote

Bush (R)	592,929	(43%)
Clinton (D)	473,066	(34%)
Perot (I)	319,878	(23%)

1992 Democratic Presidential Primary

Clinton	293,266	(70%)
Brown	69,624	(17%)
Woods	16,828	(4%)
Other	36,411	(9%)

1988 Presidential Vote

Bush (R)	678,367	(58%)
Dukakis (D)	483,423	(41%)

1992 Republican Presidential Primary

Bush	151,612	(70%)
Buchanan	57,933	(27%)
Other	8,176	(4%)

GOVERNOR
Gov. Frank Keating (R)

Elected 1994, term expires Jan. 1999; b. Feb. 10, 1944, St. Louis, MO; home, Oklahoma City; Georgetown U., B.A. 1966, U. of OK, J.D. 1969; Roman Catholic; married (Catherine).

Career: FBI Agent, 1969–71; Asst. Dist. Atty. Tulsa Cnty., 1971–72; OK House of Reps., 1972–74; OK Senate, 1974–81; US Atty., N. OK Dist., 1981–84; U.S. Asst. Secy. of Treasury., 1986–88; U.S. Assoc. Atty. Gen., 1988–89; Gen. Cnsl. & Acting Dpty. Secy. of HUD, 1989–93; Practicing Atty., 1993–95;

Office: 212 State Capitol Bldg., Oklahoma City 73105, 405-521-2342; Fax: 405-521-3353.

Election Results

1994 gen.	Frank Keating (R)	466,740	(47%)
	Jack Mildren (D)	294,936	(30%)
	Wes Watkins (I)	233,336	(23%)
1994 prim.	Frank Keating (R)	117,265	(57%)
	Jerry Pierce (R)	60,280	(29%)
	Virginia Hale (R)	15,229	(7%)
	Others	13,173	(6%)
1990 gen.	David Walters (D)	523,196	(57%)
	Bill Price (R)	297,584	(33%)
	Thomas Ledgerwood (I)	90,534	(10%)

SENATORS
Sen. Don Nickles (R)

Elected 1980, seat up 1998; b. Dec. 6, 1948, Ponca City; home, Ponca City; OK St. U., B.A. 1971; Catholic; married (Linda).

Career: OK Natl. Guard, 1970–76; Vice Pres. and Gen. Mgr., Nickles Machine Co., 1976–80; OK Senate, 1979–80.

DC Office: 133 HSOB 20510, 202-224-5754; Fax: 202-224-6008.

State Offices: 1820 Liberty Tower, 100 N. Broadway, Oklahoma City 73102, 405-231-4941; 3310 Mid-Continent Tower, 401 S. Boston, Tulsa 74103, 918-581-7651; 1916 Lake Rd., Ponca City 74601, 405-767-1270; and American Natl. Bank Bldg., 601 D Ave., #206, Lawton 73501, 405-357-9878.

Committees: *Republican Policy Committee Chairman. Budget* (3rd of 12 R). *Energy & Natural Resources* (4th of 10 R): Energy Production and Regulation (Chmn.); Parks, Historic Preservation and Recreation. *Finance* (11th of 11 R): Medicaid and Health Care for Low-Income Families; Social Security and Family Policy; Taxation and IRS Oversight. *Indian Affairs* (6th of 9 R). *Rules & Administration* (9th of 9 R).

Group Ratings

	ADA	ACLU	COPE	CFA	LCV	CON	NSI	COC	ACU	NTLC	CHC
1994	5	16	0	25	8	65	100	88	100	96	100
1993	5	—	0	0	13	89	—	91	96	—	—

National Journal Ratings

	1993 LIB — 1993 CONS		1994 LIB — 1994 CONS	
Economic	0% —	87%	12% —	82%
Social	0% —	92%	15% —	84%
Foreign	8% —	86%	6% —	86%

Key Votes of the 103d Congress

1. Clinton Deficit Plan	N	3. Brady Handgun Purchase	N	5. Lmt. UN Cmnd. of Forces	Y
2. NAFTA	Y	4. Strike Race/Death Pnlty.	Y	6. Cut Missile Funds	N

Key Votes of the 104th Congress

1. Congressional Compliance	Y	3. Balanced Budget Amndt.	Y	5. Product Liability Reform	Y
2. Bar Unfunded Mandates	Y	4. Pass Line Item Veto	Y	6. FY96 Budget	Y

Election Results

1992 general	Don Nickles (R)	757,876	(59%)	($3,492,603)
	Steve Lewis (D)	494,350	(38%)	($1,455,848)
	Others	42,197	(3%)	
1992 primary	Don Nickles (R)	unopposed		
1986 general	Don Nickles (R)	493,436	(55%)	($3,252,965)
	James R. Jones (D)	400,230	(45%)	($2,564,982)

Sen. James M. Inhofe (R)

Elected 1994, seat up 1996; b. Nov. 17, 1934, Des Moines, IA; home, Tulsa; U. of Tulsa, B.A. 1973; Presbyterian; married (Kay).

Career: Army, 1955–56; Businessman, land developer, 1962–86; OK House of Reps., 1966–69; OK Senate, 1969–77, Repub. Ldr., 1975–77; Tulsa Mayor, 1978–84; U.S. House of Reps., 1987–94.

DC Office: 453 RSOB 20510, 202-224-4721; Fax: 202-228-0380.

State Offices: 1924 S. Utica St., #530, Tulsa 74104, 918-748-5111; and 204 N. Robinson, #2701, Oklahoma City 73102, 405-231-4381.

Committees: *Armed Services* (10th of 11 R): Acquisition and Technology; Airland Forces; Readiness. *Environment & Public Works* (6th of 9 R): Clean Air, Wetlands, Private Property and Nuclear Safety; Superfund, Waste Control and Risk Assessment. *Intelligence (Select)* (6th of 9 R).

Group Ratings (as Member of U.S. House of Representatives)

	ADA	ACLU	COPE	CFA	LCV	CON	NSI	COC	ACU	NTLC	CHC
1994	0	18	0	10	7	82	100	83	100	100	100
1993	10	—	8	0	14	82	—	91	100	—	—

National Journal Ratings (as Member of U.S. House of Representatives)

	1993 LIB — 1993 CONS			1994 LIB — 1994 CONS		
Economic	13%	—	86%	0%	—	80%
Social	0%	—	89%	11%	—	85%
Foreign	0%	—	91%	0%	—	88%

Key Votes of the 103rd Congress (as Member of U.S. House of Representatives)

1. Clinton Deficit Plan	N	3. Brady Handgun Purchase	N	5. Lmt. UN Cmnd. of Forces	Y
2. NAFTA	N	4. Strike Race/Death Pnlty.	Y	6. Cut Missile Funds	N

Key Votes of the 104th Congress

1. Congressional Compliance	Y	3. Balanced Budget Amndt.	Y	5. Product Liabiliy Reform	Y
2. Bar Unfunded Mandates	Y	4. Pass Line Item Veto	Y	6. FY96 Budget	Y

Election Results

1994 general	James H. Inhofe (R)	542,390	(55%)	($1,920,227)
	Dave McCurdy (D)	392,488	(40%)	($1,872,160)
	Danny Corn (I)	47,552	(5%)	
1994 primary	James M. Inhofe (R)	159,001	(78%)	
	Tony Caldwell (R)	45,359	(22%)	
1990 general	David Lyle Boren (D)	735,684	(83%)	($1,591,093)
	Stephen Jones (R)	148,814	(17%)	($140,912)

FIRST DISTRICT

Tulsa was one of America's oil boom towns in the early 20th Century, settled not just by people from the immediate hinterland but by Midwesterners and New Englanders of Yankee stock. In the 1920s, as its skyscrapers rose in downtown on heights above the Arkansas River, it was a raw town, but intent on culture. It was optimistic and ready to seek economic change, yet culturally and politically conservative—with a Yankee elite and an Indian heritage recalled today in the Gilcrease Museum, left by one-eighth Creek Indian oil millionaire Thomas Gilcrease, and an ethnic variety suggested by the Gershon & Rebecca Fenster Museum of Jewish Art. In the decades since, Tulsa has boomed and occasionally busted; it has remained cosmopolitan and conservative; it is one of America's leading petroleum centers, and also is the headquarters of Oral Roberts and his university and 60-story City of Faith hospital.

The 1st Congressional District of Oklahoma includes all of Tulsa County plus a bit of Wagoner County to the southeast: essentially metropolitan Tulsa. The political tradition here is heavily Republican, even more so than in Oklahoma City, and accentuated in recent decades by national Democrats' cultural liberalism and penchant for petroleum taxes. Despite the collapse of oil prices in the 1980s, Tulsa is still full of a contagious enthusiasm for new business enterprises and innovations. Ordinary people here do not resent and attack the oil companies or the new rich; they identify with them. They see not class conflict, but a coincidence of economic interests. They see government as interfering with efforts to produce desired goods and services and are ready to pay for them—although Tulsans are pleased that the federal government built the McClellan-Kerr Waterway that has made the Catoosa suburb a seaport.

The congressman from the 1st District is Steve Largent, a Republican freshman elected in 1994, one of two famed football players to win an Oklahoma House seat. Largent is a native of Tulsa, who played football for the University of Tulsa in the mid-1970s; he went on to be a record-setting wide receiver with the Seattle Seahawks, retiring after 14 years in 1989, at age 34. Largent is an active Christian conservative, and when incumbent Congressman Jim Inhofe decided to run for David Boren's Senate seat, Largent ran for Congress. He won the Republican nomination with an impressive 51% in the six-candidate primary. His Democratic opponent, oil man Stuart Price, was Bill Clinton's state finance chairman in 1992. Price spent almost as much as Largent, and insisted that "all politics are local. If we take care of our district, the nation and world will take care of itself." Tulsa wasn't buying: Largent won 63%–37%.

January 1995 was a big month for Largent: he was sworn in as a member of Congress and inducted into the National Football Hall of Fame. At the latter, he said: "I thank my Lord and Savior, Jesus Christ. Football is what he gave me the physical gifts to do for a time. But my faith really defines who I am, as a husband, a father and a man." The son of divorced parents, he wants to strengthen the family and enforce child support. He quickly introduced a bill to encourage domestic oil and gas production. He supports a flat tax, a radical overhaul and eventual end of Social Security. "People my age and younger have to say we're willing to continue paying into Social Security, with the understanding that we're never going to get a benefit from it—not one penny. That's my generation's sacrifice." As a Budget Committee Republican, he got a quick immersion into legislative politics and became an active proponent of John Kasich's leadership. He seems likely to be easily reelected.

The People: Pop. 1990: 524,135; 6% rural; 11% age 65+; 82% White; 10% Black; 5% Amer. Indian; 1% Asian; 1% Other; 2% Hispanic origin. Voting age pop.: 386,430; 8% Black; 2% Hispanic origin. Households: 55% married couple families; 26% married couple fams. w. children; 54% college educ.; median household income: $27,472; per capita income: $14,695; median gross rent: $366; median house value: $60,700.

1992 Presidential Vote

Bush (R)	122,137	(49%)
Clinton (D)	73,509	(30%)
Perot (I)	52,077	(21%)

1988 Presidential Vote

Bush (R)	131,350	(65%)
Dukakis (D)	71,086	(35%)

Rep. Steve Largent (R)

Elected 1994; b. Sept. 28, 1954, Tulsa; home, Tulsa; Tulsa U., B.S. 1976; Protestant; married (Terry).

Career: Pro football player, Seattle Seahawks, 1976–89; Owner, adv. & mktg. co., 1989–present;

DC Office: 410 CHOB 20515, 202-225-2211; Fax: 202-225-9817.

District Offices: 2424 E. 21st St., #510, Tulsa 74114, 918-749-0014.

Committees: *Budget* (19th of 24 R). *Science* (23rd of 27 R): Energy and Environment; Space and Aeronautics.

Group Ratings and 103rd Congress Votes: Newly Elected

Key Votes of the 104th Congress

1. Congressional Compliance	Y	6. Reform Crime Grant	Y	11. Loser Pays Court Reform	Y
2. Balanced Budget Amndmt.	Y	7. National Security Act	Y	12. Product Liability Reform	Y
3. Bar Unfunded Mandates	Y	8. Moratorium on Regs.	Y	13. Welfare Reform	Y
4. Pass Line Item Veto	Y	9. Risk Assessment on Regs.	Y	14. Term Limits Amndmt.	Y
5. Relax Exclusionary Rule	Y	10. Expnd. Priv. Prop. Rights	Y	15. Tax Cuts	Y

Election Results

1994 general	Steve Largent (R)	107,085	(63%)	($610,211)
	Stuart Price (D)	63,753	(37%)	($546,570)
1994 primary	Steve Largent (R)	25,760	(51%)	
	Rob Johnson (R)	8,561	(17%)	
	Paula Unruh (R)	7,084	(14%)	
	Joan King Hastings (R)	3,988	(8%)	
	Dick Crawford (R)	3,310	(7%)	
	Others	1,682	(3%)	
1992 general	James M. Inhofe (R)	119,211	(53%)	($418,928)
	John Selph (D)	106,619	(47%)	($328,960)

SECOND DISTRICT

The land that is now northeast Oklahoma was less than a century ago the Indian Territory, the place where in the 1830s, the Five Civilized Tribes were driven from Georgia and Alabama over the Trail of Tears. More than one in six people here report their race as American Indian, and many more claim some Indian blood. The Indian percentage is highest in the hilly counties just west of the Ozarks of Arkansas, where county names—Cherokee, Delaware, Sequoyah—recall the Civilized Tribes. Much national attention is focused on the problems of Indians in states where there are large reservations. But no one seems to be asking if the experience of the Indians in Oklahoma—where they are now relatively prosperous and living comfortably as part of a larger community—has any useful lessons for Native Americans elsewhere. The northeast is the one non-metropolitan part of Oklahoma that has been growing rapidly since 1980, from overspill from Tulsa, but even more from retirees and young families moving onto land around the area's large man-made lakes and into peaceful hills where crime and the cost of living are low.

The 2d Congressional District of Oklahoma is made up of the northeast corner of the state, minus Tulsa County. Its geographic enter is Muskogee, subject of Merle Haggard's song, "Okie from Muskogee." It includes Will Rogers's home town of Claremore in Rogers County. It reaches far northeast where the TV signal is from Joplin, Missouri, not Oklahoma; it reaches west of Tulsa to include Osage County, still an Indian reservation and site of a revived tallgrass prairie where buffalo again roam. Most of this area is ancestrally Democratic, especially the Little Dixie counties south of Muskogee; but it is also conservative on cultural, foreign and most economic issues.

The congressman from the 2d District is Tom Coburn, a Republican elected in 1994 to replace Mike Synar, the liberal Democrat who represented the 2d for 16 years despite serious primary challenges, until he finally was upset in the 1994 Democratic primary runoff. Synar had a liberal voting record, pushed hard for gun control and higher grazing fees on federal lands, for public financing of campaigns and bans on tobacco advertising, against the flag-burning amendment and the Gulf War resolution. He was a college classmate of former Congressman Dave McCurdy. Synar won the 2d District seat in 1978, a year after graduating from law school, and had many close calls, winning narrowly in 1992 after spending $1.2 million. His ardent support of Bill Clinton and his healthcare plan in 1994 were too much. In the primary, Synar was held under 50%, leading 47%–26% over Virgil Cooper, a previously unknown 71-year-old retired principal, who spent little money, calling himself a "Will Rogers Democrat" and stating, "I'm running against Mike Synar." But unlike in 1992, Synar's heavy spending failed to improve his standing in the runoff: Cooper won 51%–49%. Coburn, expecting Synar to take the primary, ran TV ads showing Bill Clinton's face morphing into Synar's.

Synar in any case would surely have lost to Tom Coburn, the Republican who beat Synar's 1992 opponent 64%–31% in the Republican primary. Coburn grew up in Muskogee and after college worked in his father's optical business; its lens manufacturing operation grew to 35% of the U.S. market and in 1978 was sold to Revlon. Coburn, then age 30, went to medical school, then practiced medicine in Muskogee, delivering some 3,000 babies (he still delivers babies when in the district) and embarking on medical missionary trips to Haiti and Iraq. He is a deacon in the Southern Baptist Church, anti-abortion and a strong conservative on most issues. In 1994, he decided to take on Synar and was a bit surprised when Synar lost the nomination; Cooper was more conservative and thus less objectionable. Coburn vastly outspent the Democrat, but Cooper's folksy humor and Little Dixie's Democratic heritage held the Republican's margin to 52%–48%. Coburn ran strong in the northeast part of the district, where Synar had been very weak, and won counties in the south and northwest. His local popularity enabled him to carry Muskogee County with 58%, the key to his win.

Coburn was one of the few Republican candidates not to sign the Contract With America in September 1994. But he supported most Contract provisions with enthusiasm. And he won a seat on the Commerce Committee, a prime slot for a lawmaker with a medical background. He was an early signer of Iowa freshman Republican Greg Ganske's letter urging Republican leaders to reduce the $200,000-income cap on child care credits to $95,000, but then he changed his mind, took his name off and urged others to do so. He was opposed to Dr. Henry Foster's nomination as surgeon general, although he says an anti-abortion stance should not be a litmus test for the job. Of the three Oklahoma Republicans first elected to the House in 1994, the Democratic base in Coburn's district probably means that he will have the toughest fight for reelection.

The People: Pop. 1990: 524,389; 63% rural; 15% age 65+; 77% White; 5% Black; 17% Amer. Indian; 1% Hispanic origin. Voting age pop.: 381,772; 5% Black; 1% Hispanic origin. Households: 63% married couple families; 29% married couple fams. w. children; 35% college educ.; median household income: $20,633; per capita income: $9,914; median gross rent: $289; median house value: $40,800.

1992 Presidential Vote			1988 Presidential Vote		
Clinton (D)	96,486	(42%)	Dukakis (D)	98,940	(51%)
Bush (R)	81,432	(36%)	Bush (R)	95,865	(49%)
Perot (I)	49,124	(22%)			

Rep. Tom Coburn (R)

Elected 1994; b. Mar. 14, 1948, Casper, WY; home, Muskogee; OK State U., B.S. 1970; OK U., M.D. 1983; Southern Baptist; married (Carolyn).

Career: Mgr., Coburn Optical Industies, 1970–1978; Practicing physician, 1983–present.

DC Office: 511 CHOB 20515, 202-225-2701; Fax: 202-225-3038.

District Offices: 215 State St., #815, Muskogee 74401, 918-687-2533.

Committees: *Commerce* (26th of 26 R): Energy and Power; Health and Environment; Telecommunications and Finance.

Group Ratings and 103rd Congress Votes: Newly Elected

Key Votes of the 104th Congress

1. Congressional Compliance Y	6. Reform Crime Grant Y	11. Loser Pays Court Reform Y
2. Balanced Budget Amndmt. Y	7. National Security Act Y	12. Product Liability Reform Y
3. Bar Unfunded Mandates Y	8. Moratorium on Regs. Y	13. Welfare Reform Y
4. Pass Line Item Veto Y	9. Risk Assessment on Regs. Y	14. Term Limits Amndmt. Y
5. Relax Exclusionary Rule Y	10. Expnd. Priv. Prop. Rights Y	15. Tax Cuts Y

Election Results

1994 general	Tom Coburn (R)	82,479	(52%)	($604,924)
	Virgil R. Cooper (D)	75,943	(48%)	($75,202)
1994 primary	Tom Coburn (R)	14,847	(64%)	
	Jerry Hill (R)	7,181	(31%)	
	T.J. Tipton (R)	1,345	(6%)	
1992 general	Mike Synar (D)	118,542	(56%)	($1,190,197)
	Jerry Hill (R)	87,657	(41%)	($30,312)
	Other	7,314	(3%)	

THIRD DISTRICT

West of Arkansas and just north of Texas, Little Dixie is the most recognizably southern part of Oklahoma. It was settled between 1889 and 1907 by white southerners, most of them poor; some county names (Leflore, Pontotoc) were taken directly from Mississippi. It remains mostly rural today but no longer poor. A private economy that has produced jobs is one reason; another is government, which built interstate highways and turnpikes connecting many people to jobs in more vibrant metropolitan areas. Dam-made lakes have spurred the creation of resort and retirement communities. But traditional cultural attitudes are still strong here: people listen to religious radio and read the Bible twice as frequently as the average American, they serve more often in the military, they stay married and raise large families more than most.

The 3d Congressional District of Oklahoma includes most of the Little Dixie counties, and juts up into the center of the state into the old university town of Stillwater, which is Republican territory, to include enough people to meet the population standard. It has long been solidly Democratic, voting for Bill Clinton in 1992, though it responded to Clinton by going Republican in the 1994 Senate race. The 3d has never had a Republican congressman; from 1947 to 1976 it was represented by Carl Albert, speaker of the House his last six years and majority leader during the Kennedy-Johnson years.

The current congressman, Bill Brewster, is a conservative Democrat who grew up in Little Dixie, became a registered pharmacist and cattle rancher, and was elected to the Oklahoma House in 1982. In 1990, when incumbent Wes Watkins ran for governor and lost, Brewster ran for the House and in the primary won 51%–41% over Lieutenant Governor Robert Kerr III, grandson of Senator Robert Kerr (1949–63) who was legendary for his political clout and boldness in using his position to enrich himself and his Kerr-McGee company. Now, he is an endangered species, the only congressional Democrat from Oklahoma.

In the House, Brewster compiled a fairly conservative voting record. Brewster got a seat on the Ways and Means Committee in 1993 and became a vital vote on some issues, who was willing to do business with Dan Rostenkowski. He voted against the Clinton economic stimulus package and fought against the Btu tax. He co-founded an Oil and Gas Caucus. He invented the Deficit Reduction Lock Box, a proposal to insure that spending cuts go to reduce the deficit rather than to pay for new programs or tax cuts. A pharmacist, Brewster got Ways and Means to include Medicare prescription drug coverage in its version of health care, but he was against the larger bill. Brewster was reelected easily in 1994, but the next year lost his Ways and Means seat due to the drop in Democratic numbers, and was bounced to Transportation and Infrastructure.

He was one of the founders of The Coalition, a group of 23 conservative Democrats (down to 22 after Nathan Deal of Georgia switched parties) intent on achieving bipartisanship in the House. One of the leading Democratic supporters of the Contract With America, he favored the balanced budget amendment, risk-assessment and cost-benefit analysis for federal regulations and he vowed to repeal the assault weapons ban; but he stuck with his party on its centrist welfare reform alternative. Although Brewster is safe in his district, he bears watching on Capitol Hill as a sign of the inclinations among conservative Democrats.

The People: Pop. 1990: 524,287; 56% rural; 16% age 65+; 83% White; 4% Black; 11% Amer. Indian; 1% Asian; 1% Other; 1% Hispanic origin. Voting age pop.: 388,151; 4% Black; 1% Hispanic origin. Households: 60% married couple families; 27% married couple fams. w. children; 35% college educ.; median household income: $18,394; per capita income: $9,635; median gross rent: $294; median house value: $35,800.

1992 Presidential Vote			**1988 Presidential Vote**		
Clinton (D)	94,753	(41%)	Bush (R)	98,425	(50%)
Bush (R)	77,040	(34%)	Dukakis (D).	97,357	(50%)
Perot (I).	55,973	(24%)			

Rep. Bill Brewster (D)

Elected 1990; b. Nov. 8, 1941, Ardmore; home, Marietta; Southwestern OK St. U., B.S. 1964; Baptist; married (Mary Sue).

Career: Army Reserves, 1968–71; Co-owner, Brewster Angus Farms, 1968–present; Pharmacist, Owner, Colleyville Drug Inc., 1964–77; OK House of Reps., 1982–90.

DC Office: 1727 LHOB 20515, 202-225-4565; Fax: 202-225-9029.

District Offices: 201 Post Office Bldg., Ada 74820, 405-436-1980; 118 Fed. Bldg., McAlester 74501, 918-423-5951; 123 W. 7th Ave., #206, Stillwater 74074, 405-743-1400; and 101 W. Main St., Ardmore 73401, 405-266-6300.

Committees: *Transportation & Infrastructure* (27th of 27 D): Coast Guard and Maritime Transportation; Surface Transportation.

Group Ratings

	ADA	ACLU	COPE	CFA	LCV	CON	NSI	COC	ACU	NTLC	CHC
1994	30	36	33	50	39	32	70	80	60	48	57
1993	25	—	50	50	64	19	—	64	63	—	—

National Journal Ratings

	1993 LIB — 1993 CONS			1994 LIB — 1994 CONS	
Economic	43%	—	56%	55% — 44%	
Social	46%	—	53%	33% — 66%	
Foreign	47%	—	50%	44% — 56%	

Key Votes of the 103d Congress

1. Clinton Deficit Plan	N	3. Brady Handgun Purchase	N	5. Lmt. UN Cmnd. of Forces	N
2. NAFTA	Y	4. Strike Race/Death Pnlty.	Y	6. Cut Missile Funds	N

Key Votes of the 104th Congress

1. Congressional Compliance Y	6. Reform Crime Grant Y	11. Loser Pays Court Reform Y
2. Balanced Budget Amndmt. Y	7. National Security Act N	12. Product Liability Reform Y
3. Bar Unfunded Mandates Y	8. Moratorium on Regs. Y	13. Welfare Reform N
4. Pass Line Item Veto N	9. Risk Assessment on Regs. Y	14. Term Limits Amndmt. Y
5. Relax Exclusionary Rule Y	10. Expnd. Priv. Prop. Rights Y	15. Tax Cuts Y

Election Results

1994 general	Bill Brewster (D)	115,731	(74%)	($833,456)
	Darrel DeWayne Tallant (R)	41,147	(26%)	
1994 primary	Bill Brewster (D)	78,997	(71%)	
	Mike Newport (D)	32,777	(29%)	
1992 general	Bill Brewster (D)	155,934	(75%)	($386,144)
	Robert W. Stokes (R)	51,725	(25%)	($6,338)

FOURTH DISTRICT

The very lightly treed hills west of Oklahoma City and north of the Red River filled up rapidly with farmers in the early years of this century, filtering north from Texas, past the well-watered green lands of the east toward the bare brown pasturelands of the southwest. These were young people with large families, and in the years since, this land has emptied out, as children have grown up and moved elsewhere and fewer hands are needed for farming. People in southwest Oklahoma instead have accumulated around major government institutions: the state capital of Oklahoma City; Norman, home of the University of Oklahoma; Lawton, to the southwest, home of the Army's Fort Sill.

These are major landmarks for the 4th Congressional District of Oklahoma, which begins a few miles from the oil-derrick-surrounded state Capitol in Oklahoma City, smack dab in the middle of the state, and proceeds south and west to cover half of Oklahoma's Red River Valley. Demographically, this seat is becoming more suburban, but the cultural tone remains rural. That is true even in the actual suburbs, stretching out over the midwestern mile grid roads, where in new subdivisions dust still gets tracked indoors, and people still prefer chicken-fried steak to stir-fried chicken (though they eat both). Politically, this country is ancestrally Democratic, but Norman, Lawton and the Oklahoma City fringe now tend to vote Republican, and George Bush even carried this district in 1992.

The congressman from the 4th District is J. C. Watts, a Republican, former college and professional football player, conservative Christian and African-American. He won the seat in 1994 when 14-year incumbent Dave McCurdy, one of the Democrats' most competent and politically skillful moderates, ran for the Senate and lost. Watts grew up in Eufaula, Oklahoma (named after the largest town in the Alabama county where George Wallace grew up), son of a Baptist minister who was also a policeman and traded cattle. J. C. Watts was a quarterback at the University of Oklahoma and led the team to Big Eight championships and Orange Bowl wins in 1979–80. From 1981–86, he played in the Canadian Football League. In Oklahoma, Watts owned real estate and petroleum marketing companies. He became a Republican in 1989 and in 1990, he ran for state corporation commissioner and won, serving as chairman from 1992–94.

In 1994, Watts decided to run for McCurdy's seat, and had plenty of competition. He led in the Republican primary, 49%–35% over state Representative Ed Apple, but was forced into a runoff in which he was accused of business improprieties. He barely won—by just 757 votes. In both these contests, Watts's strongest support was from around Norman. The Democratic nomination was won by David Perryman, a Chickasha lawyer who stressed his lack of experience in public office. In late October, Perryman ran an ad opening with a picture of Watts in high school with an Afro haircut, followed by Perryman as a Future Farmer of America holding a pig:

an ad that some in the national press suggested was racist. Watts won by a comfortable 52%–43%; though he lost most of the rural counties, he won 60% in Norman's Cleveland County and 58% in Oklahoma City.

The fact that Watts is one of two black Republicans in the House inevitably attracts attention. Newt Gingrich asked him to give the response to President Clinton's Saturday radio address five days after the election, and it became news that Watts declined to join the Congressional Black Caucus ("I didn't come to Congress to be a black leader or a white leader, but a leader"). Watts's views seem firmly anchored in his religious faith. "I will submit to you if we advocate family, church, morality and responsibility as much as we do more government, we'd have a much sounder and safer society." He doesn't discount racism: "We can't stick our heads in the sand and say racism doesn't exist. I felt it four months ago in our campaign." But he believes that current welfare and quota programs haven't worked. "Look at the statistics. They haven't worked. Who did affirmative action help? It didn't help the people in public housing, the poor people; it helped the upper-income minorities." He warned Republican leaders to use caution on the issue of affirmative action: "I don't think the 30-second sound bite is the arena to talk about affirmative action." He adds, "I came here with no grand plans of being reelected," and hopes to move toward a balanced budget amendment and some kind of welfare reform. Back home, Watts will have to fight for Tinker Air Force Base, the district's largest employer, which was listed for further review in the May 1995 base closure commission report. In April 1995, he became one of 12 national co-chairs for Senator Bob Dole's presidential campaign.

The People: Pop. 1990: 524,407; 26% rural; 11% age 65+; 83% White; 7% Black; 5% Amer. Indian; 2% Asian; 2% Other; 4% Hispanic origin. Voting age pop.: 382,399; 6% Black; 3% Hispanic origin. Households: 62% married couple families; 31% married couple fams. w. children; 47% college educ.; median household income: $25,391; per capita income: $11,554; median gross rent: $364; median house value: $50,800.

1992 Presidential Vote			1988 Presidential Vote		
Bush (R)	90,975	(42%)	Bush (R)	99,336	(59%)
Clinton (D)	72,551	(33%)	Dukakis (D)	70,080	(41%)
Perot (I)	53,894	(25%)			

Rep. J. C. Watts, Jr. (R)

Elected 1994; b. Nov. 18, 1956, Eufala; home, Norman; U. of KS, B.S. 1981; Baptist; married (Frankie).

Career: Pro football player, Canadian League, 1981–86; Businessman, 1986–94; OK Corp. Comm., 1990–94, Chmn., 1992–94.

DC Office: 1713 LHOB 20515, 202-225-6165; Fax: 202-225-3512.

District Offices: 2420 Springer Dr., #120, Norman 73069, 405-329-6500; and 601 S.W. D Ave., #205, Lawton 73501, 405-357-2131.

Committees: *National Security* (21st of 30 R): Military Personnel; Military Procurement. *Banking & Financial Services* (26th of 27 R): Capital Markets, Securities and Government Sponsored Enterprises; Domestic and International Monetary Policy.

Group Ratings and 103rd Congress Votes: Newly Elected

Key Votes of the 104th Congress

1. Congressional Compliance *	6. Reform Crime Grant Y	11. Loser Pays Court Reform Y
2. Balanced Budget Amndmt. Y	7. National Security Act Y	12. Product Liability Reform Y
3. Bar Unfunded Mandates Y	8. Moratorium on Regs. Y	13. Welfare Reform Y
4. Pass Line Item Veto *	9. Risk Assessment on Regs. Y	14. Term Limits Amndmt. Y
5. Relax Exclusionary Rule N	10. Expnd. Priv. Prop. Rights Y	15. Tax Cuts Y

Election Results

1994 general	J.C. Watts, Jr. (R)	80,251	(52%)	($568,942)
	David Perryman (D)	67,237	(43%)	($222,946)
	Bill Tiffee (I)	7,913	(5%)	
1994 runoff	J.C. Watts, Jr. (R)	11,258	(52%)	
	Ed Apple (R)	10,501	(48%)	
1994 primary	J.C. Watts, Jr. (R)	12,489	(49%)	
	Ed Apple (R)	8,881	(35%)	
	Howard Bell (R)	2,292	(9%)	
	Mike Warkentin (R)	1,502	(6%)	
	Others	457	(2%)	
1992 general	Dave McCurdy (D)	140,841	(71%)	($584,409)
	Howard Bell (R)	58,235	(29%)	

FIFTH DISTRICT

Oklahoma City, suddenly the center of the nation's attention in April 1995 when a bomb explosion destroyed the Alfred P. Murrah federal building killing 168 and injuring more than 500 people, has for a century been the center of Oklahoma. It was sited near the geographic center of the state and was intended to be the capital; the Capitol building, surrounded by oil rigs which were pumping crude until 1989, was opened in 1917 without a dome because money ran out, and only in recent years, a local group called the Capitol Domers started a campaign to raise $14 million to finish the dome. But the initiative seems to have faltered. Oklahoma City, like many state capitals, was not the spontaneous creation of commerce but the deliberate creation of government, built on land that is browner and more eroded by creeks than the greener, rolling Oklahoma farther east. It nonetheless has a strong oil- and gas-based economy, and has grown far out into the countryside, followed, like so many southwestern cities, by expanding city limits so that it extends into five counties and four congressional districts and covers 624 square miles.

The 5th Congressional District of Oklahoma includes most of Oklahoma City, but it is a carefully chosen part: the most Democratic sections of the city, including its black areas, are chopped off and included in other districts. This is a solidly Republican area as a result. The 5th proceeds north through wheat country, to the onetime state capital of Guthrie and the market town of Ponca City, areas as Republican as any similar place in nearby Kansas. Connected by a strip of mostly uninhabited Osage County is Bartlesville, headquarters of Phillips Petroleum, solidly conservative in the Oil Patch manner. The 5th is by far Oklahoma's most Republican district: a constituency created by Democratic legislatures to corral solidly Republican precincts and give Democrats a chance to win the five other districts, as they have at one time or another over the past decade.

The congressman from the 5th District is Ernest Istook, first elected in 1992, in his views and attitudes a forerunner of the Republican freshmen of 1994. Amazingly, in two years, he became the most senior of the state's five House Republicans. Istook is the grandson of Hungarian immigrants; while attending law school in the mid 1970s, he was a political reporter on Oklahoma City radio. He attracted attention as Governor David Boren's head of the alcohol control board, where he refused to stop an investigation of liquor distributors and the state Senate denied him confirmation to complete his term in that post. He practiced law and was elected to the Oklahoma House in 1986. In the 1992 primary, he started off the most obscure of the three candidates. One was Bill Price, the party's 1990 nominee for governor; the other was Mickey Edwards, incumbent congressman for 16 years, articulate conservative and member of the Republican leadership, who had 386 overdrafts on the House bank. Price attacked Edwards; Istook attacked pork barrel spending. In the August primary, Price won 37% of the vote, Istook 32% and Edwards only 26%. In the September runoff, Istook won 56%–44%, probably picking up many Edwards supporters irritated by Price's intense criticism of the incumbent. The general election he won by only 53%–47% over oil and gas lawyer Laurie Williams, who attacked Istook for his anti-abortion stance.

In the House, Istook got Edwards's old seat on the Appropriations Committee and compiled a mostly conservative voting record. He made his presence known quickly: He pushed for a House post office investigation, voted against a bill with money for Oklahoma City's threatened-with-closure Tinker Air Force Base and pressed for information on the cost of Hillary Rodham Clinton's healthcare task force. He introduced a compromise on school prayer, stating that prayer can't be prohibited or required and that the state can't compose the words of any school prayer. He dogged Treasury Secretary Robert Rubin in early 1995 for information on his role in supporting the Mexico peso bailout. In March 1995, Istook was the center of an intra-party fracas over abortion, when 30 pro-choice Republicans successfully prevailed on Speaker Gingrich to prevent Istook from offering an amendment in the 1995 rescissions bill to allow states to refuse to use federal funds to pay for abortion in cases of rape and incest. Said Istook, "Life is about a lot more than just financial issues." Speaker Gingrich promised Istook a vote on the issue after the first 100 Days. Istook won easy reelection in 1994 and can certainly count on winning in the future.

The People: Pop. 1990: 523,729; 13% rural; 13% age 65+; 85% White; 6% Black; 5% Amer. Indian; 2% Asian; 2% Other; 3% Hispanic origin. Voting age pop.: 387,789; 5% Black; 2% Hispanic origin. Households: 57% married couple families; 26% married couple fams. w. children; 56% college educ.; median household income: $28,348; per capita income: $15,024; median gross rent: $370; median house value: $58,200.

1992 Presidential Vote

Bush (R)	129,379	(51%)
Clinton (D)	62,251	(25%)
Perot (I)	59,542	(24%)

1988 Presidential Vote

Bush (R)	134,015	(65%)
Dukakis (D)	70,918	(35%)

Rep. Ernest J. Istook, Jr. (R)

Elected 1992; b. Feb. 11, 1950, Ft. Worth, TX; home, Oklahoma City; Baylor U., B.A. 1971, Oklahoma City U. Law Schl., J.D. 1976; Mormon; married (Judy).

Career: Political reporter, Oklahoma City KOMA-radio, 1972–73, WKY-radio, 1973–76; Dir., OK Alcohol Beverage Control Bd., 1977; Practicing atty., 1977–92; OK House of Reps., 1986–92.

DC Office: 119 CHOB 20515, 202-225-2132; Fax: 202-226-1463; e-mail: istook@hr.house.gov.

District Offices: 5400 N. Grand Blvd., #505, Oklahoma City 73112, 405-942-3636; First Court Pl., #205, Bartlesville 74003, 918-336-5546; and 5th and Grand Sts., Ponca City 74601, 405-762-6778.

Committees: *Appropriations* (20th of 32 R): Labor, Health and Human Services, and Education; Military Construction; Treasury, Postal Service, and General Government.

Group Ratings

	ADA	ACLU	COPE	CFA	LCV	CON	NSI	COC	ACU	NTLC	CHC
1994	5	23	11	10	13	94	70	83	95	100	93
1993	10	—	0	0	29	97	—	100	100	—	—

National Journal Ratings

	1993 LIB — 1993 CONS		1994 LIB — 1994 CONS	
Economic	0% —	88%	21% —	76%
Social	0% —	89%	16% —	81%
Foreign	28% —	70%	21% —	78%

Key Votes of the 103d Congress

1. Clinton Deficit Plan	N	3. Brady Handgun Purchase	N	5. Lmt. UN Cmnd. of Forces	Y
2. NAFTA	Y	4. Strike Race/Death Pnlty.	Y	6. Cut Missile Funds	N

Key Votes of the 104th Congress

1. Congressional Compliance	Y	6. Reform Crime Grant	Y	11. Loser Pays Court Reform	Y
2. Balanced Budget Amndmt.	Y	7. National Security Act	Y	12. Product Liability Reform	N
3. Bar Unfunded Mandates	Y	8. Moratorium on Regs.	Y	13. Welfare Reform	Y
4. Pass Line Item Veto	Y	9. Risk Assessment on Regs.	Y	14. Term Limits Amndmt.	Y
5. Relax Exclusionary Rule	Y	10. Expnd. Priv. Prop. Rights	Y	15. Tax Cuts	Y

Election Results

1994 general	Ernest J. Istook, Jr. (R)	136,877	(78%)	($274,179)
	Tom Keith (I)	38,270	(22%)	($9,666)
1994 primary	Ernest J. Istook, Jr. (R)	unopposed		
1992 general	Ernest J. Istook, Jr. (R)	123,237	(53%)	($364,915)
	Laurie Williams (D)	107,579	(47%)	($336,418)

SIXTH DISTRICT

First settled less than a century ago, western Oklahoma is a fertile land forever at the mercy of the elements. The western plains are scorching hot under the summer sun and snow-blown in winter; this is one of the windiest parts of America. The rural counties here have far fewer people than before the dust bowl of the 1930s, and the once booming oil and natural gas exploration here in the Anadarko Basin and other fields has in recent years done little for the region.

The 6th Congressional District of Oklahoma is made up of the western plains of Oklahoma, plus blue-collar and black neighborhoods in Oklahoma City. This land was settled by farmers moving south from Kansas, starting when the gun went off the morning of the great land rush in 1889. A few of its counties in the south have always been heavily Democratic; most of the rest are heavily Republican, and always have been. These divisions are as permanent as if Oklahoma had been split down the middle during the Civil War, except that of course there were no whites in the state at the time. The bigger fact here is depopulation: counties wholly within the 6th Congressional District had 423,000 people in 1930 and 282,000 in 1990. Nearly 40% percent of the district's votes in 1994 were cast in metropolitan Oklahoma City.

The congressman from the 6th District is Frank Lucas, a Republican chosen in the May 1994 special election to replace 19-year incumbent Glenn English, a conservative Democrat who resigned to become head of the National Rural Electric Cooperative Association—in effect, to lobby the subcommittee he had served on and chaired for years. English's retirement was one— Senator David Boren's was the other—of two conservative Democrats' resignations in 1994 opening up the path for conservative Republicans. Lucas's roots are in western Oklahoma; he owns a farm and cattle ranch in Roger Mills County and was elected to the Oklahoma House in 1988. The Republican primary was a battle between Brooks Douglass and Lucas. As a teenager,

Douglass had witnessed the murder of his family and was left for dead. He campaigned from an Oklahoma City base with a western accent. Douglass spent more money and led the first primary 36%–34%. But Lucas ridiculed "some Johnny-come-lately dressed up like a drugstore cowboy" and carried all the rural areas to win the runoff 56%–44%. The Democratic nomination went to Dan Webber, a 27-year-old press secretary to outgoing Senator David Boren. But in the weeks before the May special, Lucas ran an ad showing the Capitol ("this is where Dan Webber has worked his entire adult life") and Oklahoma farmland ("this is where Frank Lucas has worked his entire adult life"). Lucas benefited from ads by the Oklahoma Taxpayers Union and Christian Coalition voting guides, and won 54%–46%.

In his first year in the House, Lucas returned home every weekend but one—when he had to stay to vote on the 1994 crime bill. He got a seat on the Agriculture Committee, an obvious place to help Oklahoma wheat farmers on the 1995 farm bill. He asked Attorney General Janet Reno not to withdraw a federal grant for 15 officers at three public housing projects in his district. His family got an SBA loan in the 1970s and he said, "I'm not ready to abolish the SBA." Lucas was elected to a full term in November 1994 with an impressive 70% of the vote—a 38% Republican rise in just two years. As a lawmaker whose special-election victory was a harbinger of the dramatic election results six months later, he was an enthusiastic supporter of the Contract With America and appears likely to make this a safe seat.

The People: Pop. 1990: 524,638; 30% rural; 15% age 65+; 77% White; 13% Black; 5% Amer. Indian; 1% Asian; 2% Other; 4% Hispanic origin. Voting age pop.: 382,199; 12% Black; 3% Hispanic origin. Households: 57% married couple families; 26% married couple fams. w. children; 38% college educ.; median household income: $21,797; per capita income: $10,540; median gross rent: $323; median house value: $39,500.

1992 Presidential Vote			1988 Presidential Vote		
Bush (R)	91,966	(43%)	Bush (R)	119,376	(61%)
Clinton (D)	73,516	(34%)	Dukakis (D)	75,042	(39%)
Perot (I)	49,268	(23%)			

Rep. Frank D. Lucas (R)

Elected May 1994; b. Jan. 6, 1960, Cheyenne; home, Cheyenne; OK St. U., B.S. 1982; Baptist; married (Lynda).

Career: Farmer & rancher; OK House of Reps., 1989–1994.

DC Office: 107 CHOB 20515, 202-225-5565; Fax: 202-225-8698.

District Offices: 215 Dean A. McGee, #109, Oklahoma City 73102, 405-231-5511; P.O. Box 3612, Enid 73701, 405-237-9224; and 1007 Main St., Woodward 73802, 405-256-5752.

Committees: *Agriculture* (15th of 27 R): General Farm Commodities; Livestock, Dairy and Poultry; Resource Conservation, Research and Forestry. *Banking & Financial Services* (12th of 27 R): Domestic and International Monetary Policy; Financial Institutions and Consumer Credit.

Group Ratings and 103rd Congress Votes: Served Only Partial Term

Key Votes of the 104th Congress

1. Congressional Compliance	Y	6. Reform Crime Grant	Y	11. Loser Pays Court Reform	Y
2. Balanced Budget Amndmt.	Y	7. National Security Act	Y	12. Product Liability Reform	Y
3. Bar Unfunded Mandates	Y	8. Moratorium on Regs.	Y	13. Welfare Reform	Y
4. Pass Line Item Veto	Y	9. Risk Assessment on Regs.	Y	14. Term Limits Amndmt.	Y
5. Relax Exclusionary Rule	Y	10. Expnd. Priv. Prop. Rights	Y	15. Tax Cuts	Y

Election Results

1994 general	Frank D. Lucas (R)	106,961	(70%)	($146,806)
	Jeffrey S. Tollett (D)	45,399	(30%)	($22,760)
1994 primary	Frank D. Lucas (R)	unopposed		
1994 spec. gen.	Frank D. Lucas (R)	71,354	(54%)	($547,350)
	Dan Webber Jr. (D)	60,411	(46%)	($491,966)
1994 spec. runoff	Frank D. Lucas (R)	11,364	(56%)	
	Brooks Douglass (R)	8,856	(44%)	
1994 spec. prim.	Brooks Douglass (R)	5,510	(36%)	
	Frank D. Lucas (R)	5,281	(34%)	
	Thom Holmes (R)	2,549	(17%)	
	Tim Pope (R)	1,570	(10%)	
	Others	531	(3%)	
1992 general	Glenn English (D)	134,734	(68%)	($553,316)
	Bob Anthony (R)	64,068	(32%)	($375,794)

OREGON

Oregon is New England on the Pacific Rim, a quintessentially American state far removed from where most Americans live, an experimental commonwealth and laboratory of reform, home of angry spotted owl-hating loggers and crusaders against homosexuality and of more bike trails than any other state and the Oregon Peace Institute, the home base of the nine volunteer firefighters from Prineville who died fighting a Colorado forest fire and of Tonya Harding and her thuggish entourage. Oregon is an affluent high-tech civilization where one can still see much the same land and water—and rain—that Lewis and Clark saw in 1805 when they came down the Columbia River gorge, past what is now Portland, to the Pacific Coast port of Astoria. This Oregon was settled by Americans when John Jacob Astor set up his fur trading post at Astoria in 1811 and when New England Yankees rode the Oregon Trail and down the Columbia to the well-watered Willamette Valley. In this remote land, nearly 2,000 miles from the Mississippi River frontier and 700 miles from the small settlements of California, the orderly, productive society of Oregon was established. It grew steadily over the years, with a few booms—when timber, always its first industry, surged in 1900–10, during the war and after in the 1940s, and in the 1970s when homebuilding boomed and Oregon's natural environment began to be widely appreciated. Too widely for some, like Governor Tom McCall (1966–74), who used to urge people to visit Oregon, "but for heaven's sake don't come to live here."

But of course many have, and Oregon has developed its own special style—look at postmodern downtown Portland—and politics. Founded by New England churchmen, Oregon today is America's most unchurched state, with the lowest rate of church membership, with large numbers of believers in astrology, New Age lore and the like. To the innovations of this cultural left the public voices of Oregon's big institutions, like those of New England, have been friendly. Oregon a generation ago produced one of the first bottle-deposit laws, decriminalized marijuana, legalized most abortions before *Roe v. Wade* and backed limits on development and use of property. More recently, it has produced an Oregon Health Plan which rations medical care, denying specified low-priority treatments to Medicaid recipients, and adopted a measure legalizing physician-assisted suicide. State government voted to limit development and use of property; a gun control law passed which banned semiautomatic weapons; and weekly betting on professional sports games was legalized.

But against this confident liberalism, based in Portland, some of its suburbs and the university towns of Eugene and Corvallis, there has come a furious counterattack, from the open range and desert of Oregon east of the Cascades and from towns beneath the tree-clad mountains near the coast. One spark came in June 1990, when the Fish and Wildlife Service declared the spotted owl an endangered species; court rulings followed that banned further logging in much of the federally owned tracts of old growth forests. Loggers were furious that the owls were protected while efforts to prohibit exports of unmilled logs have failed; and in April 1993, Bill Clinton convened a "timber summit" in Portland. But forest products employment fell by 15,000. The good news was that the local economy was strong enough to generate 20,000 new high-tech jobs and 100,000 jobs overall. Another spark of conservative opposition was the Oregon Citizens' Alliance (OCA), which sponsored referenda to turn back liberal laws, mostly without success. Oregonians in 1990 voted 68% against an abortion ban and 52% against requiring parental consent for abortions for minors. In 1992 Oregonians voted 56% against a measure to declare homosexuality "abnormal, wrong, unnatural and perverse" and "to be discouraged and avoided"; in 1994, they voted 52% against a repeal of laws which gay groups called gay rights and OCA called special rights. And in 1994, Oregon adopted, by a 51%–49% margin, a measure to allow physician-assisted suicide. Voting on all these measures followed similar patterns, with Portland and the university towns taking liberal positions and counties east of the Cascades and outside the metro reach voting against. In daily life, each region goes its own way. Portland is as proud of its Metropolitan Greenspaces and light rail lines as it is of its Rose Festival, and its mayor, former Speaker Vera Katz, is an energetic and politically shrewd liberal. But as of May 1994, 24 other cities and counties have passed measures prohibiting "special rights" for homosexuals. The cultural gap between liberal and conservative Oregon seems to be growing wider, and in its three seriously contested U.S. House races this year the candidates were almost stereotypes: liberal female Democrats versus conservative male Republicans.

The narrow but steady majorities for liberal stands on referenda are matched by Oregon's choices in state politics. Presidentially, it voted 51%–47% for Michael Dukakis and 43%–33% for Bill Clinton (Ross Perot got 24%, his largest percentage in a state this big). For governor it has elected three Portland-backed liberal Democrats in a row. Former Portland Mayor Neil Goldschmidt won in 1986, 52%–48%; Secretary of State and former legislator Barbara Roberts won in 1990, 46%–40%, as an OCA-backed third candidate won 13% of the vote; John Kitzhaber, physician and sponsor of the Oregon Health Plan, won in 1994, 51%–42%, as American and Libertarian candidates won 5% and 2%. Oregon has stayed Republican in Senate races, but only because two embattled veterans with significant personal strengths overcame great difficulties to win their fifth terms, Mark Hatfield in 1990 and Bob Packwood in 1992. But the tenuousness of the Democrats' statewide majorities is suggested by the fact that Republicans now have majorities in both houses of the legislature, and control the Senate for the first time in 40 years.

Pervading all of Oregon is a sense that this splendid place is very far from almost all of the rest of the United States. Oregon is very conscious that it is on the Pacific Rim; most Japanese cars sold in the United States are unloaded in Portland, and this is one state which usually backs free trade. You can fly nonstop from Portland to Tokyo, but not to Washington, D.C. Which is why many Oregon congressmen have found it hard to get reelected: it is just too hard to get home every weekend. Oregon, together with Washington and California, seems to backlash against incumbent presidents who seem out of touch with the Pacific Rim: Jimmy Carter won only 36% of the West Coast vote in 1980 and George Bush won a devastatingly low 33% in 1992. In 1994 Republicans came rebounding back in California and Washington, but not so much in Oregon; it seems that the battle lines here are hardened, as the culture wars go on.

Governor. Oregon's Governor John Kitzhaber is a physician who spent 16 years in the state legislature. After medical school at the University of Oregon, he practiced emergency medicine in Roseburg from 1974–88. In 1978, he was elected to the state House, in 1980, to the state Senate; he was Senate president from 1985–93. By far, his greatest achievement was the Oregon

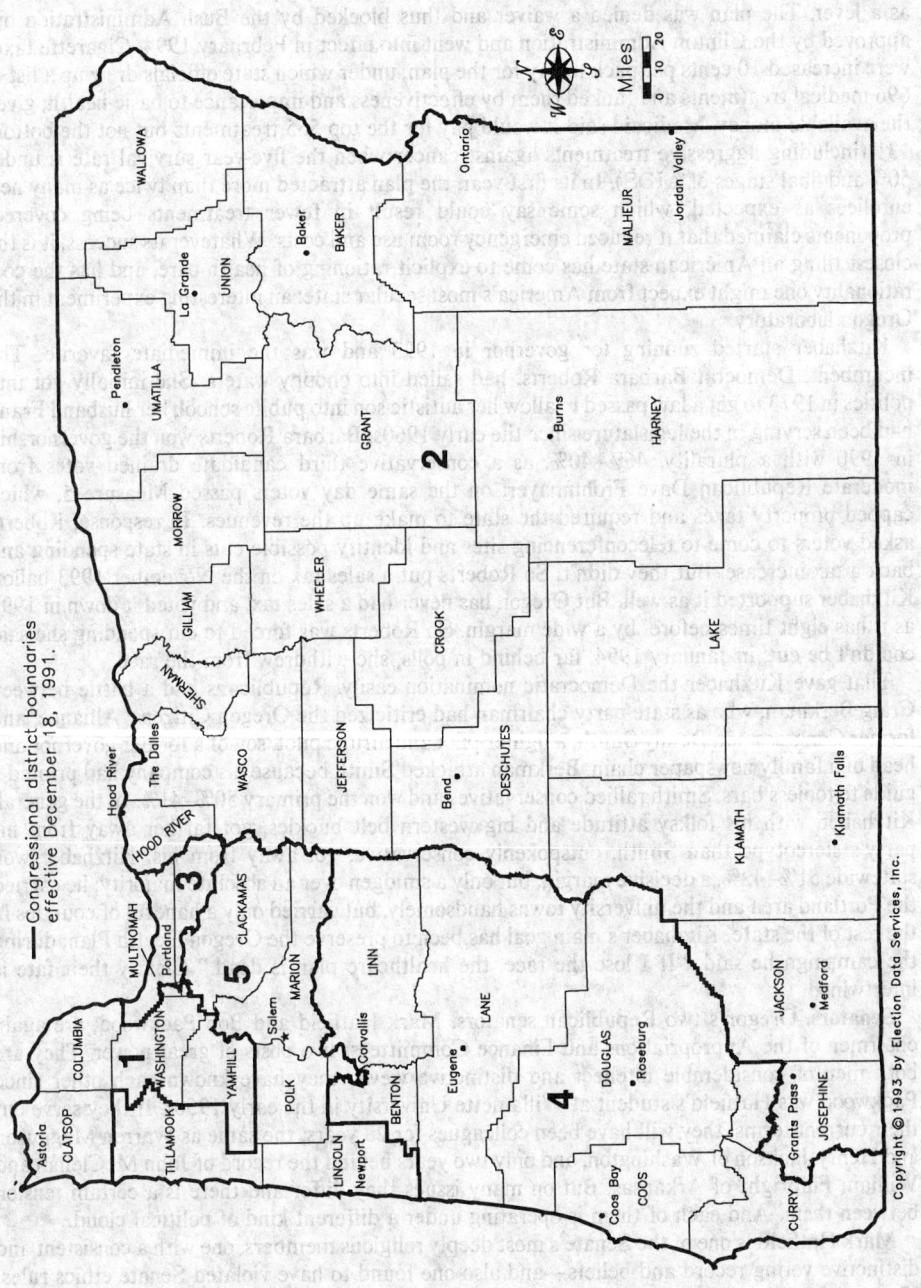

Congressional district boundaries
effective December 18, 1991.

Miles
0 10 20

Copyright © 1993 by Election Data Services, Inc.

Health Plan (the other physician-governor, Howard Dean of Vermont, is a healthcare reformer too). Its strategy is to ration treatments in order to cover more people, using the Medicaid system as a lever. The plan was denied a waiver and thus blocked by the Bush Administration but approved by the Clinton Administration and went into effect in February 1994. Cigarette taxes were increased 10 cents per pack to pay for the plan, under which state officials drew up a list of 696 medical treatments and ranked them by effectiveness and importance to basic health; given the available money, Medicaid said it would pay for the top 565 treatments but not the bottom 131 (including aggressive treatments against cancer when the five-year survival rate is under 50% and final stages of AIDS). In its first year, the plan attracted more than twice as many new enrollees as expected, which some say could result in fewer treatments being covered; proponents claimed that it reduced emergency room use and costs. Whatever its success, it is the closest thing an American state has come to explicit rationing of health care, and has the cool rationality one might expect from America's most secular state: an interesting experiment in the Oregon laboratory.

Kitzhaber started running for governor in 1993 and was the immediate favorite. The incumbent, Democrat Barbara Roberts, had sailed into choppy waters. She initially got into politics in 1973 to get a law passed to allow her autistic son into public school; her husband Frank had been serving in the legislature since the early 1960s. Barbara Roberts won the governorship in 1990 with a plurality, 46%–40%, as a conservative third candidate drained votes from moderate Republican Dave Frohnmayer; on the same day voters passed Measure 5, which capped property taxes and required the state to make up the revenues. In response, Roberts asked voters to come to teleconferencing sites and identify possible cuts in state spending and back a tax increase. But they didn't. So Roberts put a sales tax on the November 1993 ballot; Kitzhaber supported it as well. But Oregon has never had a sales tax, and voted it down in 1993 as it has eight times before, by a wide margin. So Roberts was forced to cut spending she said couldn't be cut; in January 1994, far behind in polls, she withdrew from the race.

That gave Kitzhaber the Democratic nomination easily. Republicans had a battle between Craig Berkman, who as state party chairman had criticized the Oregon Citizens' Alliance, and former Congressman Denny Smith, a fighter pilot and airline pilot, son of a former governor and head of a family newspaper chain. Berkman attacked Smith because his company had printed a guide to topless bars; Smith rallied conservatives and won the primary 50%–41%. In the general, Kitzhaber, with his folksy attitude and big western belt buckles, got farther away from his party's stereotype than Smith, outspokenly conservative, got away from his. Kitzhaber won statewide 51%–42%, a decisive margin, but only a smidgen over an absolute majority; he carried the Portland area and the university towns handsomely, but carried only a handful of counties in the rest of the state. Kitzhaber's main goal has been to preserve the Oregon Health Plan; during the campaign he said, "If I lose the race, the healthcare plan is dead." Clearly their fate is intertwined.

Senators. Oregon's two Republican senators, Mark Hatfield and Bob Packwood, are again chairmen of the Appropriations and Finance Committees, two posts of great power. They are both men of considerable intellect and distinctive views; they have known each other since Packwood was Hatfield's student at Willamette University in the early 1950s. If they serve out their current terms, they will have been colleagues for 28 years, the same as Warren Magnuson and Henry Jackson of Washington, and only two years behind the record of John McClellan and William Fulbright of Arkansas. But on many issues they differ and there is a certain tension between them. And each of them is operating under a different kind of political cloud.

Mark Hatfield is one of the Senate's most deeply religious members, one with a consistent and distinctive voting record and beliefs—and also one found to have violated Senate ethics rules. He taught political science at Willamette University and was elected Oregon's secretary of state in 1956, at age 34; in 1958, he was elected governor and served for eight years; in 1966, he was elected to the Senate and has been there ever since. As a young serviceman, he was one of the first Americans to see Hiroshima after it was bombed, and for years has been the most dovish senator. He was the co-sponsor of the McGovern-Hatfield amendment to end the Vietnam War in the early 1970s; he was an enthusiastic backer of the nuclear freeze in the 1980s; he has never voted for a defense authorization bill, though while Appropriations chairman, he witnessed unhappily the huge defense buildup of the 1980s. He voted against the Gulf war resolution (one of two Republican senators to do so) and against the alternative measure of economic sanctions. In 1992, he had the satisfaction of seeing the Senate finally adopt a moratorium on nuclear testing for one year, something he had long sought. After the 1994 election, as Republicans were poised to return to power, he said he was "proudly guilty" of backing defense spending cuts and called for knocking down the budget firewalls between defense and domestic spending. He is dovish as well on other foreign issues, and skeptical about, if not hostile to, Israel. He opposes the death penalty, even against terrorists, and calls for life imprisonment instead.

Hatfield is a man of Appropriations, which helps to explain why he was the one Senate Republican to oppose the balanced budget amendment in March 1995. He wants to maintain the prerogatives of his committee, not box it in. He has used its powers to legislate. For example he has pushed to allow more roads and logging in federal forests in past years and to fund Oregon projects—Portland's popular light rail—for a downtown Portland courthouse, for "urban-grants" for Portland State University, for Columbia River salmon, for Oregon Indian tribes. At a time when other Republicans want to privatize the facility, he has a plan to refinance the Bonneville Power Administration, in which electric customers would pay the federal government $100 million in return for guarantees that the costs of repaying the federal investment in Columbia River hydroelectricity wouldn't change. Hatfield has been known to roll his eyes at mention of the Contract With America. Yet he has his own set of proposals allowing more flexibility and initiative in state governments—a bill with Bob Graham of Florida to allow states to fashion their own healthcare plans and proposals, drawing on Oregon experience, that he calls Local Flex, which would grant states greater flexibility in administering funds.

For all his idealism, Hatfield knows how to operate politically, and has gotten into some ethics trouble. He was embarrassed in 1984 when it was revealed his wife, a realtor, had received $55,000 as a fee from a real estate developer whose plan for a $15 billion trans-Africa oil pipeline Hatfield was promoting. But he avoided reprimand and won reelection that year. In 1990, he was opposed by eastern Oregon businessman Harry Lonsdale, who touted his lack of experience in an anti-incumbent year and said that "24 years in Washington has changed Mark Hatfield." Lonsdale promised to ban log exports, attacked Hatfield for opposing abortion and backing a gay discrimination ban, called him a "timber beast" for his pro-lumber stance in the owl dispute. When a late September poll showed Hatfield leading by only 49%–43%, he suddenly returned from Washington and hit Lonsdale as an environmental zealot, and said his company dumped waste water with toxic chemicals. The final issue revolved around cult leader Bhagwan Shree Rajneesh, whose takeover of an eastern Oregon town led to a federal prosecution of his commune. Hatfield ran an ad quoting a letter Lonsdale wrote in 1984, after charges that Rajneesh followers poisoned a U.S. attorney, to Attorney General Dave Frohnmayer: "I conclude that Rajneeshpuram just may be the happiest town in America. They must be doing something right!" Hatfield won 54%–46%, carrying most parts of the state and cutting into the cultural liberal vote in the Portland area.

Hatfield was fortunate that it was not until spring 1991 that the FBI and Senate began investigating his failure to list on disclosure statements the gifts of $9,000 in artwork and $5,000 in air travel he received from the University of South Carolina president, who resigned his post because of criticism over spending university funds on lavish travel expenses. It was also revealed that Hatfield secured appropriations for the school (which had granted a full scholarship to his son) as well as for the Oregon Health Sciences University (whose president personally admitted Hatfield's daughter to medical school). In August 1992, the Senate Ethics Committee formally rebuked Hatfield for accepting and failing to report nearly $43,000 in gifts from 1983 to 1988. The committee found no link between the gifts and Hatfield's role in legislation, but Hatfield admitted, "my mistakes were many and my omissions serious." At the time, it was considered likely he would retire in 1996, when he turns 74. But after Republicans won their majority and he regained the chairmanship he held from 1981–87, he announced he might very well run again.

But his iconoclastic standing among Republicans took an odd twist when Hatfield held fast and voted against the balanced budget amendment in March 1995. Connie Mack of Florida and Rick Santorum of Pennsylvania demanded that the Republican Conference consider stripping Hatfield of his chairmanship; no vote was held, and Hatfield was unflinching: "I've been out of step most of my political life. What else is new?" Hatfield was hailed as a hero and a man of conscience by both Washington insiders and independent Oregonians. But new-breed Senate Republicans communicated the idea that chairmen may be held accountable for their votes, as they have been in the House. In any case, Hatfield will be accountable to voters, if he runs, and might well have opposition in Oregon's increasingly conservative Republican primary as well as from a strong Democrat in the general election. That could leave Democrats in a quandary on whether to run a strong candidate, such as Congressman Ron Wyden, with the prospect that a contest against Hatfield would be far more difficult than one against a conservative insurgent. Hatfield promised a decision by summer 1995 on whether he will seek a sixth term.

Bob Packwood, has had a career of many ups and downs. He is chairman of the Senate Finance Committee, as he was in 1985 and 1986, when he fashioned the great tax reform bill. He also stands accused before the Senate of sexual harassment on charges he denied right up to election day 1992, when he won his fifth term, but which were spelled out by *The Washington Post* within days after the election. In May 1995, the Senate Ethics Committee detailed the lurid charges in a way that suggested that Packwood faced an uphill road to escape unscathed.

Packwood grew up in Portland, the son of a longtime lobbyist of the Oregon legislature; he practiced law for a few years, then was elected to the Oregon House in 1962, at age 30. Six years later, he took on four-term Senator Wayne Morse, a maverick in both parties who supported public hydroelectric power and opposed the Vietnam war; Packwood won a 50.2%–49.8% upset. Environmental issues were just starting to be important in Oregon, and Packwood established himself as the Senate's champion of zero population growth. In the late 1970s, he was among the Senate's chief opponents of abortion bans; in 1980, most of his campaign money came from pro-abortion rights contributors. In the 1980s, he led fights to fund Title X family planning programs and to write *Roe v. Wade* into federal law; he was the first Senate Republican to oppose the nomination of Robert Bork and only one of two Senate Republicans to oppose Clarence Thomas.

On foreign policy, Packwood has long been a staunch supporter of Israel and opponent of Arab arms sales, and quietly supported the Gulf war resolution. Despite his long record of environmentalism, he came down pretty harshly against the spotted owl. On economics, he tends to oppose regulations, favors free trade and wants to lower taxes, and played a key role on one of the key laws of the 1980s, the 1986 tax reform. As chairman of the Finance Committee, he started off with a bill that catered to Oregon interests. But he was in trouble at home, opposed in the May 20 primary by a young conservative, and he was ridiculed as "Senator Hackwood." In late April, he and an aide started pencilling figures and came up with a bill that stripped away most tax preferences and lowered the top rate all the way to 27%—an approach that, with changes in details and some "Perils of Pauline" maneuvering, carried the Finance Committee, the Senate and the conference committee to become law. In the meantime, Packwood won renomination by the none too huge margin of 58%–42%.

In his fourth term, in the minority, he fought against tax increases and for a capital gains cut, backed free trade (but got concessions to protect Oregon plywood), opposed reregulation of cable TV and continued to back women's causes. He worked to ban driftnet fishing and to abolish the import tariff on minivans. His reelection victory in 1992 was an artful exercise in skillful—and cynical—politics. He managed to persuade the conservative Oregon Citizens' Alliance not to support a primary opponent or an independent candidate, even while marshaling feminist support and contributions for the general election. He muted—but did not retract—his pro-choice stands and avoided any stand on anti-gay rights Measure 9 until after he had no opposition from the right. He watched in the primary while 1990 Democratic nominee Harry Lonsdale attacked Congressman Les AuCoin as a Washington insider with 83 overdrafts on the House bank, then ran an anti-AuCoin ad himself before the primary. AuCoin won by only 330 votes out of 362,000 cast, 42.2%–42.1%. With $8 million raised mainly from his Finance Committee perch and from womens groups and Israel supporters, Packwood hit AuCoin for protecting "bugs and birds," for opposing NAFTA, and for not saying how he would raise taxes to pay for his national healthcare plan. After 24 years, Packwood pinned the burdens of incumbency on his opponent.

On October 29, Packwood coolly denied six women's charges of sexual harassment to *The Washington Post* and asked for time to review records and gather information about the charges; on October 31, the *Post* told Packwood it wouldn't run a story before election day. Packwood won 52%–47%, losing metro Portland 54%–46% but carrying the rest of the state 56%–44%. Three weeks later, the *Post* story ran, with the suggestion that it was odd that a supporter of women's issues and causes should be a sexual harasser. Packwood no longer denied the charges, asked for an Ethics Committee investigation and sought alcohol counseling. The Portland *Oregonian*, which had endorsed Packwood for reelection, called for his resignation; oddly, it turned out that he had kissed an *Oregonian* reporter after drinking wine in his office but that never came up in the story the *Post* published. Over the following months more women, ultimately 48, came forward with charges, and an excruciating investigation followed. Then Packwood slipped by referring to 8,200 pages of diaries that he had compiled; the committee demanded them; Packwood refused; the full Senate voted 94–6 that they must be turned over. The case went to court, but Packwood lost and dropped his appeal in March 1994.

In fall 1993, Packwood considered resigning from the Senate; when Ethics Committee staffers leaked that, he decided to stay. For a time, things appeared to turn up for him. He seemed to have weathered charges that he had used undue influence to try to get a job for his former wife. By spring 1994, he could make appearances in Oregon without jeering crowds. His fellow Republicans resisted moves to oust him. When Republicans won a Senate majority in November, Packwood was suddenly Finance Committee chairman again. He took up with some relish the challenge presented by House Republicans' Contract With America, saying that a balanced budget amendment would force vast cuts in expected spending increases and that he supported sending welfare to the states as a block grant. He seemed dubious about immediate tax cuts, but supported free trade measures like NAFTA and GATT; on the Commerce Committee he fought hard for a less regulatory telecommunications bill.

In May 1995, the ethics case once again came to the fore—and with a vengeance. The Ethics Committee released a report graphically detailing the charges against him by several women. And it is possible, though with Republican control it seems unlikely, that Packwood could leave office. On the charges regarding his efforts to get lobbyists to give a job to his ex-wife, the Justice Department continued to investigate. But the charge that could prove to be the most dangerous is that Packwood altered his diaries before handing them over to the Ethics Committee, an action that could qualify as an obstruction of justice. In the event of his resignation (or expulsion), an Oregon law passed by referendum in 1986 requires an election and bars the governor from appointing a successor; if scheduled more than 80 days in advance of an election, party primaries are held, otherwise candidates are nominated by party caucus. Whatever happens—including the possibility of public hearings or a backroom deal to settle the charges— the situation seemed like a mess for Majority Leader Bob Dole, who needed a steady hand at the pivotal Finance Committee. It is widely assumed Packwood will not run for reelection in 1998, but he has said he will not decide until 1997.

Presidential politics. Oregon shows its New England ancestry in presidential politics. It was traditionally Republican enough to have voted for Thomas Dewey over Harry Truman in 1948, and postmodernly liberal enough to have voted for Michael Dukakis over George Bush in 1988. Now it seems well on the left of the national political spectrum, though its recently galvanized conservative bloc keeps liberals from ever winning large majorities. It is a must state for Bill

Clinton and the Democrats in 1996.

The halcyon days of Oregon's late May presidential primary are long gone. Oregon ended Harold Stassen's serious presidential career in 1948, when he lost 52%–48% to Dewey; it gave Robert Kennedy his only defeat in 1968. Oregon in those days was part of a West Coast campaign swing, just before the California primary; at a time when campaigners were not yet used to flying all over the country they, like National Football League teams in the 1950s, scheduled West Coast contests together to minimize travel time. Now nominations are sewed up by the time Oregon votes.

Interestingly, Crook County, a sparsely populated lumbering area east of the Cascades, had been up through November 1992 the nation's bellwether county. The only county to vote through all its legal existence only for winning presidential candidates, it voted for George Bush on November 3. Another victim of the spotted owl? Anyway, there won't be any national political reporters poking around Prineville in 1996.

Congressional districting. Oregon's divided legislature sought a bipartisan approach to redistricting, but a smoothing out of the lines necessarily had a partisan effect, reducing the Democratic percentage in the 1st District—which may have helped persuade Congressman Les AuCoin to run against Bob Packwood. Congressional politics here has a certain volatility, because distance and the lack of nonstop flights make it hard for even the most conscientious congressman to get back to the district very often. In contrast to its two Senators, the Oregon House delegation averaged less than six years of seniority as the 104th Congress convened.

The People: Est. Pop. 1994: 3,086,000; Pop. 1990: 2,842,321, up 8.6% 1990–1994. 1.2% of U.S. total, 29th largest; 30% rural. Median age: 34.5 years. 13.8% 65 years and over. 92.8% White, 4.0% Hispanic origin, 2.4% Asian, 1.6% Black, 1.4% American Indian, 1.8% Other. Households (1980): 55.6% married couple families; 25% married couple fams. w. children; 53% college educ.; median household income: $27,250; per capita income: $13,418; 63.1% owner occupied housing; median house value: $67,100; median monthly rent: $344. 7.5% Unemployment. 1994 Voting age pop.: 2,311,000; 1994 Turnout: 995,012; 41% of VAP. Registered voters (1994): 1,832,774; 786,990 D (43%); 665,956 R (36%); 379,828 unaffiliated and minor parties (21%).

Political Lineup: Governor, John A. Kitzhaber (D); Secy. of State, Phil Keisling (D); Atty. Gen., Ted Kulongoski (D); Treasurer, Jim Hill (D). State Senate, 30 (19 R and 11 D); State House of Representatives, 60 (34 R and 26 D). Senators, Mark O. Hatfield (R) and Bob Packwood (R). Representatives, 5 (2 R and 3 D).

1992 Presidential Vote

Clinton (D)	621,314	(43%)
Bush (R)	475,757	(33%)
Perot (I)	354,091	(24%)

1992 Democratic Presidential Primary

Clinton	159,802	(45%)
Brown	110,494	(31%)
Tsongas	37,139	(10%)
Other	13,357	(4%)
Miscellaneous	33,540	(9%)

1988 Presidential Vote

Dukakis (D)	616,206	(51%)
Bush (R)	560,126	(47%)

1992 Republican Presidential Primary

Bush	203,957	(67%)
Buchanan	57,730	(19%)
Miscellaneous	35,805	(12%)

GOVERNOR

Gov. John A. Kitzhaber (D)

Elected 1994, term expires Jan. 1999; b. Mar. 5, 1947, Colfax, WA; home, Eugene; Dartmouth Col., B.S. 1969; U. of OR Med. Schl., M.D. 1973; no religious affiliation; married (Sharon).

Career: Practicing physician, 1974–88; Health & environment consultant, 1988–93; OR House of Reps., 1978–80; OR Senate, 1980–94, Senate Pres. 1985–93.

Office: State Capitol, #254, Salem 97310, 503-378-3111; Fax: 503-378-6075.

Election Results

1994 gen.	John A. Kitzhaber (D)	622,083	(51%)
	Denny Smith (R)	517,874	(42%)
	Ed Hickman (American)	58,449	(5%)
	Others	22,604	(2%)
1994 prim.	John A. Kitzhaber (D)	250,514	(88%)
	Paul Damian Wells (D)	30,052	(11%)
	Others	2,570	(1%)
1990 gen.	Barbara Roberts (D)	508,749	(46%)
	Dave Frohnmayer (R)	444,646	(40%)
	Al Mobley (I)	144,062	(13%)
	Other	14,583	(1%)

SENATORS

Sen. Mark O. Hatfield (R)

Elected 1966, seat up 1996; b. July 12, 1922, Dallas; home, Portland; Willamette U., B.A. 1943, Stanford, M.A. 1948; Baptist; married (Antoinette).

Career: Navy, 1943–46 (WWII); Prof., Willamette U., 1949–57; OR House of Reps., 1951–55; OR Senate, 1955–57; OR Secy. of State, 1956–58; OR Gov., 1958–66.

DC Office: 711 HSOB 20510, 202-224-3753; Fax: 202-224-0276.

State Offices: 727 Center St., NE, #305, Salem 97301; and One World Trade Ctr., 121 SW Salmon St., #1420, Portland 97204.

Committees: *Appropriations* (Chmn. of 15 R): Transportation (Chmn.). *Energy & Natural Resources* (2nd of 10 R): Energy Production and Regulation; Forests and Public Land Management. *Rules & Administration* (2nd of 9 R).

Group Ratings

	ADA	ACLU	COPE	CFA	LCV	CON	NSI	COC	ACU	NTLC	CHC
1994	80	63	63	75	46	41	20	56	29	60	50
1993	65	—	45	60	25	32	—	91	44	—	—

National Journal Ratings

	1993 LIB — 1993 CONS		1994 LIB — 1994 CONS	
Economic	40% —	58%	49% —	50%
Social	66% —	33%	46% —	53%
Foreign	70% —	29%	87% —	6%

Key Votes of the 103d Congress

1. Clinton Deficit Plan	N	3. Brady Handgun Purchase	Y	5. Lmt. UN Cmnd. of Forces	Y
2. NAFTA	Y	4. Strike Race/Death Pnlty.	N	6. Cut Missile Funds	Y

Key Votes of the 104th Congress

1. Congressional Compliance	Y	3. Balanced Budget Amndt.	N	5. Product Liability Reform	Y
2. Bar Unfunded Mandates	Y	4. Pass Line Item Veto	N	6. FY96 Budget	Y

Election Results

1990 general	Mark O. Hatfield (R)	590,095	(54%)	($2,714,661)
	Harry Lonsdale (D)	507,743	(46%)	($1,479,099)
1990 primary	Mark O. Hatfield (R)	220,449	(78%)	
	Randy Prince (R)	59,970	(21%)	
1984 general	Mark O. Hatfield (R)	808,152	(67%)	($671,167)
	Margie Hendriksen (D).	406,122	(33%)	($257,512)

Sen. Bob Packwood (R)

Elected 1968, seat up 1998; b. Sept 11, 1932, Portland; home, Portland; Willamette U., B.A. 1954, NY U., LL.B. 1957; Unitarian; divorced.

Career: Law Clerk, OR Supreme Court, 1957–58; Practicing atty., 1958–68; OR House of Reps., 1963–69.

DC Office: 259 RSOB 20510, 202-224-5244; Fax: 202-228-3576; e-mail: senator_packwood@packwood.senate.gov.

State Offices: 101 SW Main St., #240, Portland 97204-3210, 503-294-3370.

Committees: *Commerce, Science & Transportation* (2nd of 10 R): Communications (Chmn.); Oceans and Fisheries; Surface Transportation and Merchant Marine. *Finance* (Chmn. of 11 R): International Trade; Medicare, Long-Term Care and Health Insurance; Taxation and IRS Oversight. *Joint Committee on Taxation* (Vice Chmn. of 5 Sens.).

Group Ratings

	ADA	ACLU	COPE	CFA	LCV	CON	NSI	COC	ACU	NTLC	CHC
1994	50	74	38	50	38	84	90	57	67	79	50
1993	35	—	36	10	6	80	—	100	60	—	—

National Journal Ratings

	1993 LIB — 1993 CONS		1994 LIB — 1994 CONS	
Economic	33% —	65%	37% —	61%
Social	55% —	42%	60% —	38%
Foreign	32% —	60%	34% —	62%

Key Votes of the 103d Congress

1. Clinton Deficit Plan	N	3. Brady Handgun Purchase	Y	5. Lmt. UN Cmnd. of Forces	N
2. NAFTA	Y	4. Strike Race/Death Pnlty.	N	6. Cut Missile Funds	N

Key Votes of the 104th Congress

1. Congressional Compliance	Y	3. Balanced Budget Amndt.	Y	5. Product Liability Reform	N
2. Bar Unfunded Mandates	Y	4. Pass Line Item Veto	Y	6. FY96 Budget	Y

Election Results

1992 general	Bob Packwood (R)	717,455	(52%)	($8,034,249)
	Les AuCoin (D)	639,851	(47%)	($2,629,397)
	Others	18,727	(1%)	
1992 primary	Bob Packwood (R)	176,939	(59%)	
	John De Zell (R).....................	61,128	(20%)	
	Stephanie Jones Salvey (R)	27,088	(9%)	
	Randy Prince (R)	20,358	(7%)	
	Valentine Christian (R)................	10,501	(4%)	
	Others	3,397	(1%)	
1986 general	Bob Packwood (R)	656,317	(63%)	($6,523,492)
	Rick Bauman (D)	375,735	(36%)	($64,139)

FIRST DISTRICT

Postmodern skyscrapers rising above the riverfront and below a range of hills: this is downtown Portland. The city—which would have been named Boston if a coin toss had gone the other way—started here, along the Willamette River just before it flows into the Columbia, and downtown was built on the narrow margin of land west of the river and below the hills, not on the flat expanse that stretches east to the snow-capped peak of Mount Hood. Downtown Portland was once a dowdy place, proper in a New Englandish way, with a few formal buildings above the warehouses and factories. But in the last decade there has been an explosion of creativity here, symbolized by handsome postmodern high-rises—the pyramid-crested brick KOIN Tower, the wedge-shaped Justice Center—and restored Victorian storefronts and a downtown transit trolley, the new light rail line know as MAX (Metropolitan Area Express), and just across the river the new Oregon Museum of Science and Industry.

Similarly, the affluent neighborhoods in the hills overlooking downtown are full of old lumber barons' mansions with splendid views, as well as postmodern houses with hot tubs. Just over the hills are the valleys and interstices between green mountains of suburban Washington County. Not so long ago, this was a farm county, with 39,000 people in 1940; now it has 311,000 and is an integral part of metro Portland. This is an affluent area with a high-tech, healthy-lifestyle aura; the biggest employers here are Tektronix, Intel, Nike and Sequent Computer Systems. Like Silicon Valley, the Silicon Forest has an environment—at the foot of mountains, woodsy and even rustic but outfitted with all the comforts and services of modern civilization—that appeals to a high-skill work force.

Downtown Portland and its western hills, plus a bit of the residential areas east of the Willamette, and Washington County make up the bulk of Oregon's 1st Congressional District. The 1st also proceeds northwest along the Columbia to Astoria and the Pacific Coast, and southwest to Yamhill County, where metro growth is spreading. Like Oregon, the 1st District is historically New England Republican, electing only Republican congressmen from 1892 to 1972; like New England, it then trended sharply left on cultural issues, even as its high-tech economy brought new affluence, and since 1974 it has elected leftish Democrats. But the political balance is close here: there are Republican blocs, to some extent in high-income Lake Oswego and west Portland, even more so in middle-income Beaverton and Hillsboro, and the appeal of Portland-style liberalism thins as one heads down the Columbia to the sea.

The Congresswoman from the 1st District is Elizabeth Furse, the Kenya-born founder of the Oregon Peace Institute, who has won two close elections in a district that for 18 years elected by wider margins Les AuCoin, a quintessential Watergate-era Democrat, who lost narrowly to Senator Bob Packwood in 1992. Furse was born a colonist, the daughter of British parents in Kenya; she grew up in South Africa, and at 15 marched as a member of Black Sash, an anti-apartheid group founded by her mother. She became a U.S. citizen in 1972 and taught self-sufficiency to women in Watts, California and volunteered for the United Farm Workers. She moved to Oregon in 1978, where she and her husband own a vineyard in Washington County. For six years, she lobbied Congress to restore legal status to three Oregon Indian tribes. In 1985, she co-founded the Peace Institute and in 1988, lead a 300-person "Citizens' Train" to lobby Congress for a more liberal budget. These are not perhaps conventional credentials but they were assets in 1992. In the primary, Furse faced former AuCoin staffer and lobbyist Gary Conkling, but was able to raise more money and appeal to the enthusiasm of the so-called "year of the woman," and won 60%–40%. She also outraised her Republican opponent, state Treasurer Tony Meeker, sponsor of Oregon's successful bottle bill, and made her support of legal abortion her key issue. As Bill Clinton was carrying the district, Furse won 52%–48%.

Furse is far to the left in the House on foreign and cultural issues, rather more moderate on economics, although she voted for the Clinton budget and tax package and backed single payer health insurance. She was proud of getting funding for the Westside Light Rail Project and authorization for a Hillsboro extension, for putting community teams to deal with domestic violence in the 1994 crime bill, for sponsoring national "Year of the Girl Child," and for being the first congressional office with full computer access for constituents. She co-authored an unsuccessful amendment to force allies to pay 75% of non-salary costs of U.S. troops in Europe.

Given the close result in 1992, it was no surprise there was a spirited race here in 1994. Republicans had a hot three-candidate primary; the winner, with a solid 51% was Bill Witt. Witt owns a graphic equipment marketing company and helped establish the Oregon Christian Coalition in 1992; he was endorsed by the Oregon Citizens' Alliance, which also endorsed Republican primary winners in the 2d and 5th Districts and the governor's race. Furse painted Witt's views in sinister tones—"Oregon has become a real test case for the religious right. If they can do it here, they can do it anywhere"—but in fact he is probably no farther to the right than she is to the left of the American political spectrum. And Witt is likely to run again. He has threatened to challenge Mark Hatfield in the primary, or he may run against Furse again in 1996.

This was one of a couple dozen districts Democratic incumbents retained more through force of money than through strength of argument. Furse spent $1.1 million, raising an impressive $688,000 from individuals plus $431,000 from PACs. Witt, with a primary as well as general to contest, spent $541,000, with an impressive $304,000 from individual contributions and $128,000 from himself, but only a piddling $84,000 from PACs. With all that advantage, Furse won by only 319 votes on the initial count, and 301 on recount; she carried the Portland portion of the district 67%–30%, but lost every other county. Furse has limited herself to four terms, but she will probably have serious competition to win a third in 1996; even with her new seat on the Commerce Committee, it's not likely she'll be able to raise so much PAC money this time.

The People: Pop. 1990: 568,501; 18% rural; 12% age 65+; 91% White; 1% Black; 1% American Indian; 3% Asian; 2% Other; 4% Hispanic origin. Voting age pop.: 425,759; 1% Black; 3% Hispanic origin. Households: 56% married couple families; 26% married couple fams. w. children; 64% college educ.; median household income: $33,227; per capita income: $17,120; median gross rent: $453; median house value: $84,500.

1992 Presidential Vote

Clinton (D) 136,630 (44%)
Bush (R) 99,304 (32%)
Perot (I) 73,134 (24%)

1988 Presidential Vote

Dukakis (D) 119,198 (50%)
Bush (R) 116,864 (50%)

Rep. Elizabeth Furse (D)

Elected 1992; b. Oct. 13, 1936, Nairobi, Kenya; home, Hillsboro; Evergreen St. Col., B.A. 1974; Protestant; married (John Platt).

Career: Owner, Helvetia Vineyards, 1983-present; Founder & Dir., Oregon Peace Instit., 1985–1991; Oregon Legal Services, 1980–86.

DC Office: 316 CHOB 20515, 202-225-0855; Fax: 202-225-9497; e-mail: furseor1@hr.house.gov.

District Offices: 2701 NW Vaughn, #860, Portland 97210, 503-326-2901.

Committees: *Commerce* (16th of 21 D): Commerce, Trade and Hazardous Materials; Oversight and Investigations.

Group Ratings

	ADA	ACLU	COPE	CFA	LCV	CON	NSI	COC	ACU	NTLC	CHC
1994	95	86	78	100	94	44	0	67	5	21	0
1993	95	—	100	100	100	32	—	10	4	—	—

National Journal Ratings

	1993 LIB — 1993 CONS		1994 LIB — 1994 CONS	
Economic	88%	0%	59%	37%
Social	87%	0%	89%	10%
Foreign	74%	22%	85%	0%

Key Votes of the 103d Congress

1. Clinton Deficit Plan	Y	3. Brady Handgun Purchase	Y	5. Lmt. UN Cmnd. of Forces	N
2. NAFTA	N	4. Strike Race/Death Pnlty.	N	6. Cut Missile Funds	Y

Key Votes of the 104th Congress

1. Congressional Compliance	Y	6. Reform Crime Grant	N	11. Loser Pays Court Reform	N
2. Balanced Budget Amndmt.	N	7. National Security Act	N	12. Product Liability Reform	N
3. Bar Unfunded Mandates	Y	8. Moratorium on Regs.	N	13. Welfare Reform	N
4. Pass Line Item Veto	Y	9. Risk Assessment on Regs.	N	14. Term Limits Amndmt.	Y
5. Relax Exclusionary Rule	N	10. Expnd. Priv. Prop. Rights	N	15. Tax Cuts	N

Election Results

1994 general	Elizabeth Furse (D)	121,147	(48%)	($1,132,394)
	Bill Witt (R)	120,846	(48%)	($541,456)
	Others	11,996	(5%)	
1994 primary	Elizabeth Furse (D)	unopposed		
1992 general	Elizabeth Furse (D)	152,917	(52%)	($778,290)
	Tony Meeker (R)	140,986	(48%)	($719,611)

SECOND DISTRICT

The Cascade Mountains that wall eastern Oregon off from the rest of the state are a magnificent chain of once (and quite possibly still) active volcanic mountains that drain almost every drop of moisture out of the air coming in from the Pacific and so separate green, wet western Oregon from the brown, parched east. Eastern Oregon has 70% of the state's land, but only 365,000 of its 2.8 million people, most of whom still make their living off the land: beef and dairy cattle, timber and lumber, fish from the Columbia River and wheat from the irrigated plains. The effect of the Cascades can be felt in the one place they are breached—by the Columbia River Gorge. Here, surrounded by brown hills on both sides, funneled winds pound in steadily from the west, making the Columbia the best windsurfing site in the United States.

The 2d Congressional District of Oregon covers all of the state east of the Cascades and the southernmost valley between the Cascades and the Coast Range. Population concentrations here are far apart: Pendleton in the northeastern wheat fields; La Grande in the rich Grande Ronde Valley; The Dalles where the Columbia River Gorge begins; Bend in the center of the state, near Crook County, which until it voted for George Bush in 1992 was the only county in the country to have voted for the winning presidential candidate in every election. In the southwestern corner, separated from other areas by the Cascades and the once huge volcano whose blown-off cone is now 2,000-foot deep Crater Lake, is the lumber and pear orchard country around Medford, Ashland, Klamath Falls and Grants Pass.

Politically, the 2d District has grown increasingly Republican. Most people here are furious with federal government intrusions—the federal government owns three quarters of the 2d District's land—particularly with the designation of the spotted owl as an endangered species, which shut much of Oregon's timber industry out of federal lands, forcing the businesses to resort to heavily logging state and private lands. They are unhappy as well with the cultural liberalism of Portland and the East Coast, as measured in their votes for initiatives to deny what advocates say is special treatment for homosexuals.

The congressman from the 2d District is Wes Cooley, a Republican chosen in 1994 to replace 12-year incumbent (and 22-year legislator before that) Bob Smith, a strong conservative with impressive legislative skills. Cooley was born in California, served in the Special Forces in Korea, then after college worked for Viratek as director of drug regulatory affairs. Then he and his wife started Rose Laboratories, a firm selling nutritional supplements and moved to Crook County, Oregon. In 1992, at 60, he ran for state Senator and won; when Smith announced his retirement in November 1993, Cooley ran as "the most conservative state senator." He had some competition for that distinction in the Republican primary, from one current and another former state Senator, the sheriff in Jackson County (Medford) and a former Christian Coalition board member. The key was probably Cooley's endorsement by the Oregon Citizens' Alliance: two Medford area candidates split the vote west of the Cascades and another candidate carried Bend; but Cooley won all but one other county, and took the seven-candidate contest with 23%. Who knows what would have happened if Oregon had a runoff?

"If you like Bob Smith, you'll like Wes Cooley," Cooley said in the primary. "When will our laws protect our people?" he asked. He decried "the enormous human suffering federal policies have enacted on the people of eastern, central and southern Oregon. The Democratic nominee was Jackson County Commissioner Sue Kupillas, a former teacher and bookkeeper, who sought "workable solutions for complex problems." "I think we're smart enough to manage for wood products as well as manage for a good environment." Kupillas actually spent more money and attacked Cooley for falsely claiming to have been in Phi Beta Kappa. But Cooley proved he was in sync with the district and won convincingly, 57%–39%, carrying even Jackson County.

In the House, Cooley became an enthusiastic backer of the Contract With America. He got seats on the Agriculture and Resources Committees and on Newt Gingrich's task forces to eliminate the Department of Commerce and to rewrite the Endangered Species Act that had environmentalists up in arms—all key spots for a conservative member from this conservative district.

The People: Pop. 1990: 568,437; 50% rural; 16% age 65+; 91% White; 2% American Indian; 1% Asian; 3% Other; 5% Hispanic origin. Voting age pop.: 417,866; 4% Hispanic origin. Households: 61% married couple families; 26% married couple fams. w. children; 44% college educ.; median household income: $23,949; per capita income: $11,704; median gross rent: $363; median house value: $62,400.

1992 Presidential Vote		
Bush (R)	106,696	(38%)
Clinton (D)	97,458	(35%)
Perot (I)	74,346	(27%)

1988 Presidential Vote		
Bush (R)	126,631	(56%)
Dukakis (D)	100,624	(44%)

Rep. Wes Cooley (R)

Elected 1994; b. Mar. 28, 1932, Los Angeles, CA; home, Power Butte; U. of S. CA, B.S. 1958; Christian; married (Rosemary).

Career: U.S. Army, 1952–54 (Korea); Businessman, Rancher; OR Senate 1992–94.

DC Office: 1609 LHOB 20515, 202-225-6730; Fax: 202-225-3046.

District Offices: 259 Barnett Rd., #E, Medford 97501, 503-776-4646.

Committees: *Agriculture* (24th of 27 R): General Farm Commodities; Livestock, Dairy and Poultry. *Resources* (16th of 25 R): National Parks, Forests and Lands; Water and Power Resources. *Veterans' Affairs* (17th of 18 R): Education, Training, Employment and Housing.

Group Ratings and 103rd Congress Votes: Newly Elected

Key Votes of the 104th Congress

1. Congressional Compliance	Y	6. Reform Crime Grant	Y	11. Loser Pays Court Reform	Y
2. Balanced Budget Amndmt.	Y	7. National Security Act	Y	12. Product Liability Reform	Y
3. Bar Unfunded Mandates	Y	8. Moratorium on Regs.	Y	13. Welfare Reform	Y
4. Pass Line Item Veto	Y	9. Risk Assessment on Regs.	Y	14. Term Limits Amndmt.	Y
5. Relax Exclusionary Rule	Y	10. Expnd. Priv. Prop. Rights	Y	15. Tax Cuts	Y

Election Results

1994 general	Wes Cooley (R)	134,255	(57%)	($298,053)
	Sue C. Kupillas (D)	90,822	(39%)	($369,790)
	Others	9,304	(4%)	
1994 primary	Wes Cooley (R)	14,246	(23%)	
	Perry A. Atkinson (R)	13,306	(21%)	
	C.W. Smith (R)	12,149	(19%)	
	Dan Skotte (R)	11,361	(18%)	
	Peter A. Brockman (R)	6,520	(10%)	
	Jim Bradley (R)	2,870	(5%)	
	Others	2,295	(4%)	
1992 general	Robert F. (Bob) Smith (R)	184,163	(67%)	($401,670)
	Denzel Ferguson (D)	90,036	(33%)	($87,361)

THIRD DISTRICT

Postmodern Portland, the Rose City set between Mount Hood on the east and the Tualatin Mountains on the west, spanning the Willamette River with its airport and industrial back to the Columbia, is still one of America's least known major cities. It has its own urban style and lifestyle, a light rail system that runs down the middle of the Banfield Freeway and postmodern buildings set amid classic masonry piles in the downtown west of the Willamette. It has a Metropolitan Greenspaces program, which is expanding its inventory of natural areas. Portland is proud of its New England beginnings (it almost was called Boston) and its traditional Rose Festival. It also boasts of its local microbreweries (the most in the country, it is said) and its bicycle paths. Much of the central city of Portland has a middle-class, white-bread look; but it has attracted the hip and the culturally liberal, young people who dislike suburbs and want an urban atmosphere.

Portland's economy, to be sure, is more basic than boutique: it is in many ways a muscular, blue-collar town where Oregon unloaded autos from Japan on the dock or supplies from the east in rail yards, and where it shipped out Oregon's products, mainly lumber and fruit. Portland has been particularly conscious for the last two decades that it is on the Pacific Rim, living more and more on foreign trade, seeing East Asians as customers rather than competitors, a role that was placed at risk by President Clinton's May 1995 decision to impose huge tariffs on high-end Japanese cars. This is the one major U.S. metro area from which you cannot fly nonstop to Washington, D.C., but you can to Tokyo.

The 3d Congressional District of Oregon takes in most of Portland and Multnomah County east of the Willamette River, extending over suburban plains and hills to the splendid scenery of the Bonneville Dam in the Columbia River Gorge and Mount Hood high in the Cascades. It is middle-income, largely white, not a glaringly ethnic place, but also one which reflects a cultural liberalism which sets Portland apart even from its suburbs and the rest of Oregon. In 1994, for example, when the rest of Oregon voted 48%–46% for Democratic Governor John Kitzhaber, Portland's Multnomah County went 65%–28% for him.

The congressman from the 3d District is Ron Wyden, a Democrat first elected in 1980, one of his party's most creative legislators and one who may even manage to be influential in a Republican House. Wyden got his start in public life when he graduated from law school in 1974 and formed the Gray Panthers, an advocacy group for the elderly; his first foray into electoral politics was sponsoring a successful referendum to reduce the price of dentures. In 1980, he beat an incumbent congressman in the Democratic primary 60%–40%, and has since won reelection by impressive margins, most recently 73%–19% in the Republican 1994. In his first term in the House he got a seat on Commerce Committee and became an ally of both Chairman John Dingell and Henry Waxman, chairman of its Health and the Environment Subcommittee. Working closely under Dingell's direction on Investigations, Wyden sponsored health measures that were not Waxman's prime concern and used his Small Business subcommittee chair to spotlight others. He has a genius for coming up with sensible-sounding ideas no one else has thought of and a knack for making the counter-intuitive political alliances which are so helpful in passing unfamiliar measures through the House.

His achievements include a law, co-sponsored with Connecticut Republican Nancy Johnson, that reduced federally-funded community health clinics' malpractice insurance premiums by requiring the Justice Department to defend them in malpractice cases. He also passed a law to conserve the Pacific yew, a rare tree needed to produce a cancer-fighting drug, and a WIC Infant Formula Act to prohibit manufacturers from engaging in anti-competitive bidding practices. He produced a law, with Senator Tom Daschle, to regulate Medigap policies. He got a Fertility Clinic Success Rate and Certification Act through the House in 1992. In the 103d Congress he worked with Majority Leader Richard Gephardt to construct the Democratic healthcare plan, without success; his own approach was to set up a managed competition system with overall caps on spending if costs get too high. He was more successful on other causes. He backed NAFTA and its environmental side agreements. He passed a law to allow some unemployed workers to use part of their checks to start small businesses. He worked hard to get the Clinton Administration to issue a waiver the Bush Administration denied for John Kitzhaber's Oregon Health Plan. He also worked hard to bring the abortifacient drug RU-486 to the United States, and teamed up with Waxman to orchestrate the 1994 hearings at which top executives of tobacco companies were excoriated. The tobacco inquiry, which abruptly shut down after the 1994 election, got Wyden into a nasty lawsuit with tobacco companies over the alleged theft of industry documents by a disgruntled employee, who turned them over to the Democrats.

Wyden responded to the Democratic defeat in November 1994 by calling on President Clinton to cooperate with Republicans on welfare, crime and international trade and to develop a new and thoughtful agenda on health care and campaign reform. He fought the Republican effort to change the Consumer Price Index (which would cut Social Security COLAs). But, like the two other Oregon Democrats, he voted for both unfunded mandates and the line-item veto in the Contract With America. He has a proposal for a targeted capital gains tax cut, allowing investors in small enterprises tax-deferred rollovers of profits, and an "Employee Partnership Reward Act," rewarding workers with partially tax-free cash benefits based on achieving specific company targets. He wants to require accountants to disclose financial fraud they discover; he wants to allow state fees to recover the costs of storing out-of-state solid waste; he wants to let states use adult prison money on tougher juvenile justice; he wants to allow people who just want basic telephone service to opt out of the information superhighway. With his record of cooperating with Republicans on specific projects, he has a better chance of achieving these goals in a Republican House than many more partisan Democrats.

Wyden was mentioned, not implausibly, as a candidate for the Senate in 1986, 1990 and 1992 but he backed away each time. After the 1994 election he ranked 18th among House members in campaign cash-on-hand, and could conceivably be a candidate for Mark Hatfield's Senate seat in 1996, especially if the incumbent retires.

The People: Pop. 1990: 568,276; 6% rural; 13% age 65+; 86% White; 6% Black; 1% Amer. Indian; 4% Asian; 1% Other; 3% Hispanic origin. Voting age pop.: 427,976; 5% Black; 3% Hispanic origin. Households: 49% married couple families; 22% married couple fams. w. children; 53% college educ.; median household income: $27,150; per capita income: $13,167; median gross rent: $414; median house value: $59,300.

1992 Presidential Vote			1988 Presidential Vote		
Clinton (D)	146,835	(53%)	Dukakis (D)	151,683	(62%)
Bush (R)	72,338	(26%)	Bush (R)	93,690	(38%)
Perot (I)	58,900	(21%)			

Rep. Ron Wyden (D)

Elected 1980; b. May 3, 1949, Wichita, KS; home, Portland; Stanford U., B.A. 1971, U. of OR, J.D. 1974; Jewish; married (Laurie).

Career: Co-Dir. & Co-Founder, OR Gray Panthers, 1974–80; Dir., OR Legal Svcs. for the Elderly, 1977–79; Prof. of Gerontology, U. of OR, 1976, Portland St. U., 1979, U. of Portland, 1980.

DC Office: 1111 LHOB 20515, 202-225-4811; Fax: 202-225-8941.

District Offices: 500 NE Multnomah, #205, Portland 97232, 503-231-2300.

Committees: *Commerce* (5th of 21 D): Health and Environment; Oversight and Investigations (RMM). *Small Business* (2nd of 19 D): Government Programs.

Group Ratings

	ADA	ACLU	COPE	CFA	LCV	CON	NSI	COC	ACU	NTLC	CHC
1994	80	83	78	90	94	33	0	58	0	21	7
1993	95	—	92	100	93	39	—	18	4	—	—

National Journal Ratings

	1993 LIB	—	1993 CONS		1994 LIB	—	1994 CONS
Economic	78%	—	12%		73%	—	17%
Social	80%	—	13%		66%	—	34%
Foreign	70%	—	26%		85%	—	0%

Key Votes of the 103d Congress

1. Clinton Deficit Plan	Y	3. Brady Handgun Purchase	Y	5. Lmt. UN Cmnd. of Forces	N
2. NAFTA	Y	4. Strike Race/Death Pnlty.	N	6. Cut Missile Funds	Y

Key Votes of the 104th Congress

1. Congressional Compliance	Y	6. Reform Crime Grant	N	11. Loser Pays Court Reform	N
2. Balanced Budget Amndmt.	N	7. National Security Act	N	12. Product Liability Reform	N
3. Bar Unfunded Mandates	Y	8. Moratorium on Regs.	N	13. Welfare Reform	N
4. Pass Line Item Veto	Y	9. Risk Assessment on Regs.	N	14. Term Limits Amndmt.	N
5. Relax Exclusionary Rule	Y	10. Expnd. Priv. Prop. Rights	N	15. Tax Cuts	N

Election Results

1994 general	Ron Wyden (D).........................	161,624	(73%)	($437,586)
	Everett Hall (R)	43,211	(19%)	
	Mark Brunelle (I)	13,550	(6%)	($29,516)
	Others................................	4,437	(2%)	
1994 primary	Ron Wyden (D)....................	unopposed		
1992 general	Ron Wyden (D).........................	208,028	(77%)	($357,402)
	Al Ritter (R)..........................	50,235	(19%)	($3,036)
	Blair Bobier (LIB).....................	11,413	(4%)	

FOURTH DISTRICT

In the last bit of lowland at the south end of Oregon's Willamette Valley sits Eugene, surrounded by mountains on three sides—farming center, lumber metropolis and, most notably, university town. Settlers first arrived here in 1846, farming in the valley and cutting timber in the hills. In 1876, the University of Oregon was established, a symbol of Oregon's strong Yankee cultural ethic and sparse settlement: its first graduating class had just five students. Thousands of miles from most Americans, Eugene and next-door Springfield have grown steadily into the comfortable middle-sized towns in which many Americans would like to live. The university gives this part of Oregon a special bean-sprout tone. Eugene has bicycle paths along the river banks and on main streets and likes to bill itself as the Running Capital of the Universe.

Beyond the Eugene city limits is a different atmosphere. This is timber country: surrounded by green-clad mountains, southwestern Oregon around Eugene and the southwest coast cuts more timber than any other place in the country. But demand for wood is volatile, dependent on the vagaries of interest rates; and the demand from East Asia is increasingly for unprocessed logs rather than milled lumber, which means fewer jobs for Oregon. The early 1980s, when recession reduced the demand for housing, were tough on southern Oregon; the late 1980s, when cutting of old-growth forests was banned to protect the endangered spotted owl, was even worse. In between, many big lumber companies switched their major operations to the pinelands of the Southeastern U.S., while sawmills ran short of work because of log exports to the Far East. In the early 1990s, it seemed that federal restrictions of logging to save the spotted owl would destroy the area's economy. But an otherwise robust local economy and active job retraining has resulted in local job gains and far less unemployment than almost everyone forecast.

The 4th Congressional District of Oregon includes Eugene and Springfield and surrounding Lane County; it goes south to include Roseburg Douglas County, once perhaps the premier logging county in the United States; it extends north to Albany and part of Corvallis, home of Oregon State University; and includes two counties on the southwest coast. Eugene is now heavily Democratic, and so is Corvallis. Roseburg and Albany tend to be Republican, but the overall balance here is toward the cultural left.

The congressman from the 4th District is Peter DeFazio, a Democrat first elected in 1986, but who was working as long ago as 1977 for 4th District Democratic Congressman Jim Weaver. He was raised in Massachusetts, but went to graduate school in Oregon, and in 1977 went to work for 4th District Congressman Jim Weaver; in 1982, he moved to Springfield and won a seat on the county commission, and then his House seat in a 1986 three-way race. In Congress, DeFazio has compiled a record that seems to satisfy both Eugene and the rest of the district—liberal on some issues, moderate or even conservative on others. On foreign policy he vociferously opposed the Gulf war and has called for an end to draft registration and a strengthening of the War Powers Act. On the spotted owl issue, he produced a middle position which would reduce the no-logging buffer zone in return for what he calls "a much more sensitive form of management." He was one of three Northwest members who opposed NAFTA, and in fact has proposed legislation to repeal NAFTA, charging that the recent proposed U.S. loan to Mexico constitutes a "massive taxpayer funded bailout." He also opposed GATT. He is for log export restrictions, against factory trawler ships, for oversight of water pollution by federal facilities like the Hanford Works: local issues. He has co-sponsored Senator Mark Hatfield's bill to allow states to experiment in healthcare reform. Also with Hatfield, he has a plan to refinance the Bonneville Power Administration, in which electric customers would pay the federal government $100 million in return for guarantees that the costs of repaying the federal investment in Columbia River hydroelectricity wouldn't change.

DeFazio has been spectacularly successful in winning reelection in a district that has often been highly marginal—maybe partly because it takes long to fly to Washington, D.C., from here than from any other district in the lower 48 states. He considered running against Senator Bob

Packwood in 1992, but deferred to colleague Les AuCoin; he makes no secret of his contempt for Packwood. But he has worked closely with Hatfield, and has said he will not run against him in 1996, though he may run for the seat if Hatfield retires.

The People: Pop. 1990: 568,395; 39% rural; 15% age 65+; 95% White; 1% American Indian; 1% Asian; 1% Other; 2% Hispanic origin. Voting age pop.: 425,193; 2% Hispanic origin. Households: 58% married couple families; 25% married couple fams. w. children; 49% college educ.; median household income: $24,593; per capita income: $11,919; median gross rent: $390; median house value: $60,400.

1992 Presidential Vote			1988 Presidential Vote		
Clinton (D)	123,593	(42%)	Dukakis (D)	126,545	(55%)
Bush (R)	94,032	(32%)	Bush (R)	105,487	(45%)
Perot (I)	74,640	(25%)			

Rep. Peter A. DeFazio (D)

Elected 1986; b. May 27, 1947, Needham, MA; home, Springfield; Tufts U., B.A. 1969, U. of OR, M.S. 1977; Catholic; married (Myrnie).

Career: Air Force, 1967–71; Dist. Office Dir., U.S. Rep. James Weaver, 1977–82; Lane Cnty. Bd. of Commissioners, 1982–86.

DC Office: 2134 RHOB 20515, 202-225-6416; Fax: 202-225-0373; e-mail: pdefazio@hr.house.gov.

District Offices: P.O. Box 1557, Coos Bay 97420, 503-269-2609; 151 W. 7th Ave., Eugene 97401, 503-465-6732; and P.O. Box 2460, Roseburg 97470, 503-440-3523.

Committees: *Resources* (8th of 20 D): Water and Power Resources (RMM). *Transportation & Infrastructure* (8th of 27 D): Aviation; Surface Transportation.

Group Ratings

	ADA	ACLU	COPE	CFA	LCV	CON	NSI	COC	ACU	NTLC	CHC
1994	70	87	75	70	93	48	0	75	29	32	7
1993	100	—	100	90	93	47	—	9	13	—	—

National Journal Ratings

	1993 LIB — 1993 CONS			1994 LIB — 1994 CONS		
Economic	68%	—	26%	50%	—	46%
Social	68%	—	29%	68%	—	31%
Foreign	59%	—	38%	68%	—	29%

Key Votes of the 103d Congress

1. Clinton Deficit Plan	Y	3. Brady Handgun Purchase	Y	5. Lmt. UN Cmnd. of Forces	N
2. NAFTA	N	4. Strike Race/Death Pnlty.	N	6. Cut Missile Funds	Y

Key Votes of the 104th Congress

1. Congressional Compliance	Y	6. Reform Crime Grant	N	11. Loser Pays Court Reform	N
2. Balanced Budget Amndmt.	Y	7. National Security Act	N	12. Product Liability Reform	N
3. Bar Unfunded Mandates	Y	8. Moratorium on Regs.	N	13. Welfare Reform	N
4. Pass Line Item Veto	Y	9. Risk Assessment on Regs.	N	14. Term Limits Amndmt.	N
5. Relax Exclusionary Rule	N	10. Expnd. Priv. Prop. Rights	N	15. Tax Cuts	N

Election Results

1994 general	Peter A. DeFazio (D)	158,981	(67%)	($221,178)
	John D. Newkirk (R)	78,947	(33%)	(10,767)
1994 primary	Peter A. DeFazio (D)	unopposed		
1992 general	Peter A. DeFazio (D)	199,372	(71%)	($301,116)
	Richard L. Schulz (R)	79,733	(29%)	($6,348)

FIFTH DISTRICT

The Willamette Valley was the great promised land at the end of the Oregon Trail, one of America's most fertile valleys, shielded by the Coast Range from the cold storms of the Pacific but squeezing most of the moisture out of the clouds in the form of rain, fog and persistent mist. Here, New England Yankees planted small towns they called Salem and Albany and Oregon City, founded schools and colleges, built high-spired churches and eventually Salem's cylindri-cal-domed Art Deco state Capitol. This was one of the few valleys in the West which settlers found readily suitable for agriculture. California's great valleys depend on irrigation as does the cultivation of wheat in eastern Washington. But in the Willamette Valley the soil is fertile, the plain created by the waters of the Willamette sweeping down from the mountains is broad, and the rains everyone hears about in Oregon are dependable. But this is not only farming country now: metro Portland is spreading south and young people seeking a pleasant environment are moving into the neat little cities and towns between the two mountain ranges.

The 5th Congressional District of Oregon includes much of the northern Willamette Valley. Near Portland it has the old pioneer town of Oregon City, and spreads south to the state capital of Salem (rather conservative) and Corvallis (home of Oregon State University and quite liberal). Then the district hops over the Coast Range to take in Lincoln and Tillamook Counties, fishing and logging and cheesemaking communities (strongly Democratic) and now also includes all of Polk County. Historically, the Willamette Valley was Republican, like the New England whence most of its settlers came, but, also like New England, it has been trending Democratic, and now is prime marginal territory.

The congressman from the 5th District is Jim Bunn, a Republican who won the seat narrowly in 1994 after incumbent Democrat Mike Kopetski retired after two terms, even though he had just gotten a seat on Ways and Means. Bunn was raised on a Willamette Valley farm, one of 13 children; he has his own family farm now. In 1986 he was elected to the state Senate (one of his brothers serves there too). He is a strong conservative—for the 1990 property tax limit, for the 1992 and 1994 anti-gay rights initiatives. He was one of two state senators to run for the 5th District seat when Kopetski retired: Bunn won his primary 42%–26%, one of several notable conservative wins in 1994 Republican primaries, while state Senator Catherine Webber beat Kopetski's choice Ed Lindquist in the Democratic primary 39%–31%. Webber was well-financed—she spent $668,000, almost twice as much as Bunn—and said she wanted to be on the Clinton team. She decried "violence in the streets, schools that are ill equipped to produce graduates ready for the 21st Century workplace, and the lack of jobs that pay wages that can support a family," and said voters were "appalled" at Bunn's stand on gay rights. Bunn campaigned as a conservative who, however, declined to sign the Contract With America, because he feared its welfare bill cutting off aid to unwed mothers under 18 would encourage abortions. Bunn's politics may have seemed exotic to Webber, but it proved acceptable to most voters. Webber carried Corvallis and the coastal counties, but Bunn won both Salem and the Portland suburbs—enough, when the absentee ballots came in, for a 50%–47% victory.

In the House Bunn continued aggressively to press his case against the Contract's welfare provision and presented an 18-year-old mother from Clackamas County as his witness. He also pressed successfully to keep funds for meals for seniors from being put into block grants, and led a successful effort to save the Yaquina Head Ecological Interpretive Center in Newport. He got a committee to approve a "salvage" plan, attacked by environmentalists, to let timber companies harvest dead or decaying trees from the federal forests for two years. With a seat on the Appropriations Committee, he will be challenged to accommodate both local needs and his budget-cutting philosophy. Given this closely-balanced district, he will need to keep closely in touch back home.

The People: Pop. 1990: 568,712; 35% rural; 13% age 65+; 91% White; 1% Black; 1% American Indian; 2% Asian; 2% Other; 5% Hispanic origin. Voting age pop.: 421,120; 1% Black; 4% Hispanic origin. Households: 60% married couple families; 27% married couple fams. w. children; 53% college educ.; median household income: $28,608; per capita income: $13,180; median gross rent: $403; median house value: $69,100.

1992 Presidential Vote		
Clinton (D)	116,798	(40%)
Bush (R)	103,387	(35%)
Perot (I)	73,071	(25%)

1988 Presidential Vote		
Dukakis (D)	118,156	(50%)
Bush (R)	117,454	(50%)

Rep. Jim Bunn (R)

Elected 1994; b. Dec. 12, 1956, McMinnville; home, Gleneden; Chemeketa Comm. Col., A.A. 1977, NW Nazarene Col., B.A. 1979; Nazarene; married (Cindy).

Career: OR Natl. Guard Reserve, 1987–93; Farmer; OR Senate, 1987–94.

DC Office: 1517 LHOB 20515, 202-225-5711; Fax: 202-225-2994.

District Office: 738 Hawthorne Ave. NE, Salem 97301, 503-588-9100.

Committees: *Appropriations* (31st of 32 R): Energy and Water Development; Foreign Operations, Export Financing, and Related Programs; Interior.

Group Ratings and 103rd Congress Votes: Newly Elected

Key Votes of the 104th Congress

1. Congressional Compliance Y	6. Reform Crime Grant Y	11. Loser Pays Court Reform Y
2. Balanced Budget Amndmt. Y	7. National Security Act Y	12. Product Liability Reform Y
3. Bar Unfunded Mandates Y	8. Moratorium on Regs. Y	13. Welfare Reform N
4. Pass Line Item Veto Y	9. Risk Assessment on Regs. Y	14. Term Limits Amndmt. Y
5. Relax Exclusionary Rule Y	10. Expnd. Priv. Prop. Rights Y	15. Tax Cuts Y

Election Results

1994 general	Jim Bunn (R)	121,369	(50%)	($362,620)
	Catherine Webber (D)	114,015	(47%)	($668,534)
	Others	8,232	(3%)	
1994 primary	Jim Bunn (R)	24,695	(42%)	
	Fred Girod (R)	15,073	(26%)	
	Stan Ash (R)	11,648	(20%)	
	David H. Miller (R)	6,719	(12%)	
1992 general	Mike Kopetski (D)	174,443	(64%)	($325,620)
	Jim Seagraves (R)	97,984	(36%)	($39,612)

PENNSYLVANIA

Pennsylvania, long a backwater in American politics, the megastate least transformed economically and culturally over the last half-century, in the 1990s has been a political leader and a political laughingstock. It was a leader in 1991, when a special Senate election produced a surprise victory for Democrat Harris Wofford, who campaigned heavily for national healthcare reform: this race put that issue on the national agenda for three years. Pennsylvania is a national leader as well in restricting abortion rights; its anti-abortion laws, shepherded to passage by then-Governor Bob Casey, were upheld by the Supreme Court in June 1992. At the same time, Republican Senator Arlen Specter's reelection race was becoming something of a referendum on the charges Anita Hill made against Clarence Thomas the year before. Lynn Yeakel's surprise victory in the April Democratic primary was the leadoff in what reporters labelled "the year of the woman," and Specter was attacked for having questioned Hill and supported Thomas in the Judiciary Committee hearings. The politically nimble Specter won another term, though. These characters continued to play a national role. Wofford was defeated in 1994, after national healthcare reform failed in Congress; Specter announced in March 1995 that he was running for president, targeting the religious right; and Casey, the survivor of a heart and liver transplant in June 1993 (whose party refused to let him even speak at the 1992 Democratic National Convention), made moves to challenge President Bill Clinton.

Pennsylvania has had its moments of political farce as well. A Democratic state senator who gave his party a one-vote edge was ousted in early 1994 for blatant vote fraud; a Democratic state representative, switched parties and gave Republicans a 102–101 edge in the House. Republicans seem to be in political control, with the legislature, the governorship and two U.S. Senate seats. But their control is scarcely secure: Governor Tom Ridge was elected with 45% in a race in which an anti-abortion candidate got 13%, and Republican Senators Specter and Rick Santorum were both elected with 49% pluralities. If Pennsylvania is a bellwether, it does not ring very clearly.

Pennsylvania started off as the center of America: Philadelphia was the 13 colonies' largest city when it hosted the Continental Congress in 1776 and the Constitutional Convention in 1787. This was one of the newer colonies, founded 50 years after Massachusetts and 70 years after Virginia. Under the benevolent rule of the Penns and with its Quaker traditions, Pennsylvania soon became the major settlement in the Middle Colonies: its tolerance attracted Englishmen of all religious sects as well as Germans. The rich green farmlands west to the first Appalachian chain filled rapidly. Bordermen from Scotland, Yorkshire and Northern Ireland crossed the corduroy-like ridges and settled the mountainous interior where General Braddock had been beaten by the French and Indians not long before, and where a decade later George Washington would again lead troops when the Whiskey Rebellion flared up. On the banks of a wide estuary, with its thriving commerce and rich hinterland, Philadelphia seemed destined to be the London of America, the metropolis of government and commerce and culture. But Philadelphia, and Pennsylvania, failed to hold the central position the Founders had expected. The nation's capital was put on the Potomac rather than the Delaware as part of a political deal, and the Erie Canal and the water-level railroad from the Hudson to Lake Erie channeled trade away from Philadelphia to New York. Philadelphia's Quaker tradition, tolerant of diversity and indifferent to others' behavior, was overshadowed in intellectual life by New England's Puritan tradition, angrily intolerant and ready to use the state to impose cultural values from abolitionism to prohibition and women's rights. In antebellum America, Philadelphia was eclipsed by Washington in government, New York in commerce and Boston in education and literature.

Instead, Pennsylvania became America's energy and heavy industry capital. The key was

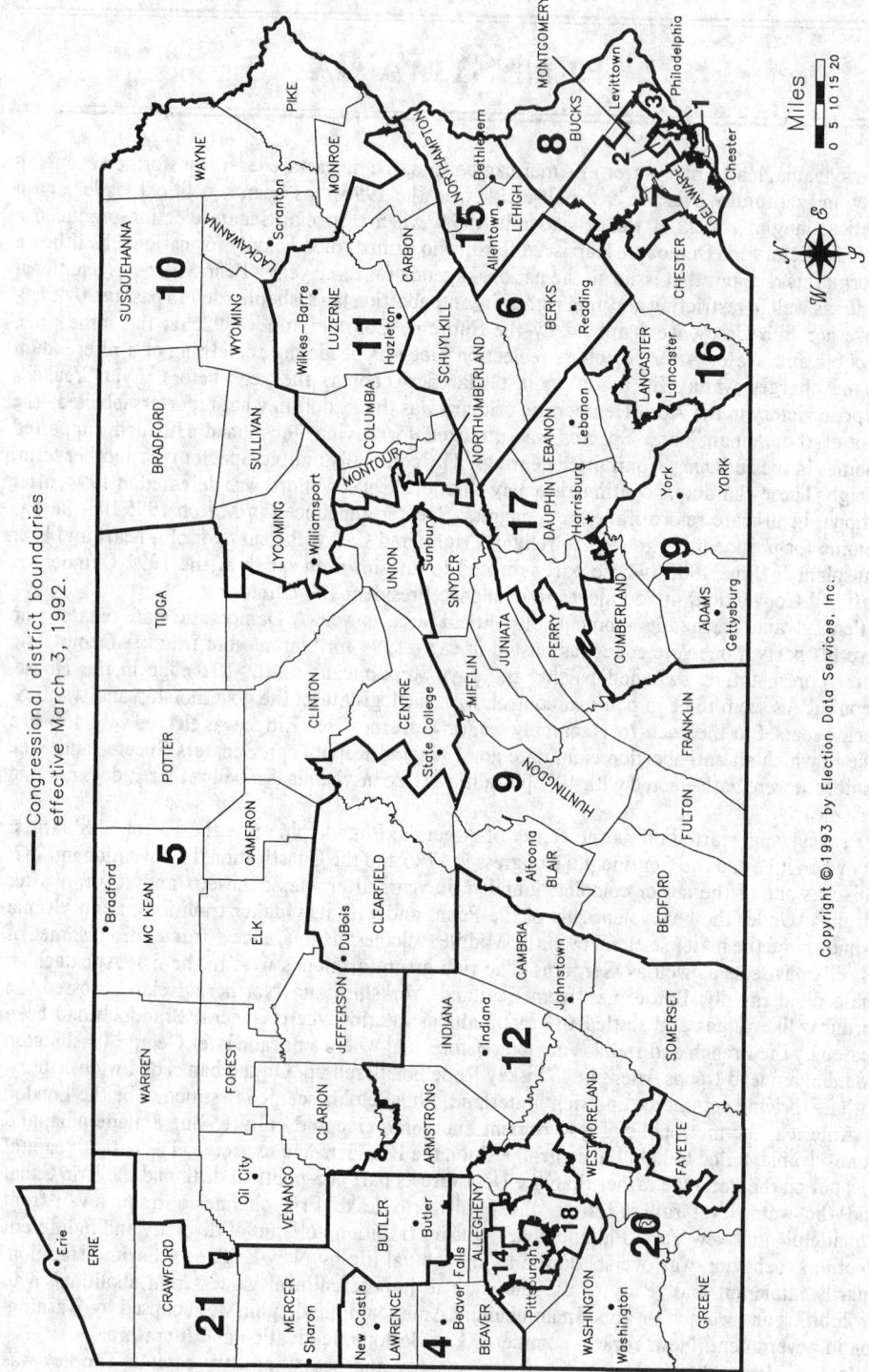

— Congressional district boundaries
effective March 3, 1992.

Copyright © 1993 by Election Data Services, Inc.

coal. Northeast Pennsylvania was the nation's primary source of anthracite, the hard coal used for home heating, and western Pennsylvania became a major source of bituminous coal, the soft coal used in steel production. Connected with Philadelphia by the Pennsylvania Railroad, the area around Pittsburgh, where the Allegheny and Monongahela rivers join to become the Ohio, was the center of the nation's steel industry by 1890. Immigrants poured in from Europe and from the surrounding hills to work in the mines and factories. Pittsburgh became synonymous with industrial prosperity, the inspiration behind the civic pride that celebrated chuffing smokestacks. In 1900, Pennsylvania was the nation's second largest state and growing rapidly. The boom ended conclusively with the Depression of the 1930s, though, and in parts of Pennsylvania it has never returned. After World War II, both home heating and industry switched away from coal. John L. Lewis's United Mine Workers traded higher pay and benefits for payroll cuts. Even when coal prices boomed in the 1970s, strip mining created relatively few new jobs. Similarly, Pennsylvania steel ceased to be a growth industry three decades ago, when big company managers made some bad technological decisions and agreed to big wage and benefit increases in the mistaken confidence that they could always pass the costs along. Big steel got import quotas in 1969—Pennsylvania has been the nation's most protectionist state since the first Bessemer converter furnaces were lit—but they didn't create jobs. By the time quotas lapsed in the 1990s, the industry had modernized, but mostly in huge new Indiana mills and small mini-mills scattered far from the cold or bulldozed factories that had lined the Monongahela.

The result has been the slowest population growth in the nation: there were 9.5 million Pennsylvanians in 1930, 11.9 million in 1990. Pennsylvania cast 36 electoral votes for Franklin Roosevelt in 1940 and 23 for Bill Clinton in 1992; it had as many congressmen (30) as California in 1960, but now has 21 while California has 52. People growing up here are as likely to leave the state as stay, and few out-of-staters move in. Pennsylvania looks and sounds today more like it did in the 1940s than any other major state. The 1980s boom did produce some new Pennsylvania growth. Southeast of the first Appalachian ridge, metro Philadelphia partook of the upscale boom that was more spectacular up and down the East Coast. Center City Philadelphia sprouted new office towers, the edge city around King of Prussia blossomed, and pharmaceutical and biotech jobs replaced those of the Fairless steel plant. Outlet stores proliferated around Reading and new jobs sprung up in the Dutch country. West of the first mountain ridge, growth was slower and spottier, radiating outward from Pittsburgh, where a high-tech, research-oriented economy was growing. But in mill towns tucked in river valleys between mountains farther from the Golden Triangle, there was little growth, and overall population loss continued. Then the white-collar recession of 1990–91 attacked real estate values and suburbanites' jobs, sharply changing the economic picture in eastern Pennsylvania. The change was less sharp in western Pennsylvania, but optimism was about as scarce.

Traditionally, Pennsylvania was the most Republican of the mega-states—for Lincoln and the Union, for the steel industry and the high tariff. Its malodorous Republican machines built parties which were not representative of one ethnic segment but organizations with places for just about everyone: in Philadelphia's huge City Hall, a knockoff of Paris's Hotel de Ville; in Pittsburgh's massive, Roman-columned City-County Building; in Harrisburg's grandiose Capitol with its rotunda modeled on St. Peter's in Rome and staircase modeled on the Paris Opera. In 1932, Pennsylvania was the only big state that stuck with Herbert Hoover and voted against Franklin Roosevelt. But the New Deal, John L. Lewis's United Mine Workers and CIO industrial union movement, and a series of bloody strikes made industrial Pennsylvania almost as Democratic in the 1930s and 1940s as it had been Republican from the 1860s to the 1920s. Even then, parts of Pennsylvania not heavy with big steel factories and coal mines—the northern tier of counties along the New York border, the central part of the state around the Welsh railroad town of Altoona, and the Pennsylvania Dutch country around Lancaster—remained the strongest Republican voting bloc in the East. Philadelphia became a mostly Democratic city, but in the suburban counties the antique Republican machines, anchored in old courthouse and railroad station towns, stayed in control. The result was a key marginal state in presidential elections from the 1950s to the 1980s.

Diverse economic trends divided Pennsylvania politically in the 1980s, when prosperous eastern Pennsylvania gave decisive margins to Ronald Reagan and George Bush while greater Pittsburgh produced some of the nation's highest percentages for Walter Mondale and Michael Dukakis. The fall in suburban real estate prices was followed by Wofford's victory in 1991, when he ran even in the usually Republican Philadelphia suburbs. More recently, western Pennsylvania has responded favorably to anti-government populism: it cast 20% of its votes for Ross Perot, and it delivered most of the victory margins for westerners Tom Ridge and Rick Santorum in 1994. But these are tentative verdicts. Pennsylvania has no major statewide contests scheduled in 1996, but it will be a key battleground in the presidential race.

Governor. Tom Ridge was scarcely known statewide when he started his 1994 campaign for governor. He is from Erie, off in the far northwestern corner of the state, where he grew up in a Catholic, Slovak-Irish, working-class family and once lived in a housing project. He went to Harvard and—an unusual combination—served as a sergeant in Vietnam. He returned to Erie, practiced law for 10 years and was elected to the House in 1982, at 37. There he made a mixed voting record by the lights of almost every rating group—not always market-oriented on economics, sometimes dovish on defense and foreign policy, liberal on some cultural issues and tradition-minded on others. He worked on banking and home finance legislation; he sponsored a bill to pay for mail service for Desert Storm personnel out of the congressional franking funds; he favored more spending for homeless veterans and treatment of Post Traumatic Stress Disorder. In February 1993, long before anyone dreamed there would be a Republican House, he announced for governor. Outside his district he was hardly known, though the addition of a new county in his 1992 district race gave him an excuse to run ads on Pittsburgh TV.

This turned out to be a crowded race. Ridge's best known opponent in the Republican primary was Attorney General Ernie Preate, a statewide winner in 1990 who was hurt when, a month before the primary, the Crime Commission said he had taken money from illegal video poker operators. Ridge, with backing from party leaders, won the May primary with 35% to 29% for Preate, 16% for Philadelphia businessman Sam Katz, campaigning as tough on crime and for school vouchers, and 14% for Pittsburgh legislator Mike Fisher, an opponent of abortion and gun control. The Democrats had an even more crowded primary. The leader was Lieutenant Governor Mark Singel, acting governor for six months during Casey's illness; he had switched stands on abortion in 1992 and lost the Senate primary 45%–32% to Lynn Yeakel. In 1994, Yeakel campaigned unimpressively and received only 14% to Singel's 31%. In between were black state Representative Dwight Evans with 21% and state Treasurer Catherine Baker Knoll with 20%.

In the general, Ridge campaigned for tough crime measures, citizens rights' to statewide initiatives and referenda, less-strict environmental regulation and a lower corporate tax. "I have not been part of the Harrisburg problem," he said. Both Ridge and Singel were pro-choice on abortion, which probably hurt both of them: Singel, because Casey was lukewarm to him; Ridge, because of the independent candidacy of antiabortion Peg Luksik, who won 13% of the vote, and over 20% in heavily Republican Lancaster and in Republican counties in western Pennsylvania. But the defining issue was probably crime. Singel hit Ridge for voting against the 1994 crime bill. Ridge attacked Singel for his votes as chairman of the Pardons Board to recommend for release 55 prisoners serving life sentences. Only eight releases were approved by Casey, but one of them kidnapped, raped and robbed a woman in New York, and Ridge made that a major issue. Singel apologized: "one of the worst decisions of my career—no, I mean the worst decision of my career," he said, as Ridge overtook him in the polls. The result was a 45%–40% Ridge victory, and a continuation of Pennsylvania's 40-year practice of alternating the two parties in the governorship every eight years. Ridge seems likely to be a more conservative governor than his voting record in the House suggests. He pushed for cutting the corporate tax and holding spending increases to 2.3%, school choice through grants to lower-income families and charter public schools.

A few words should be said about Bob Casey, who retired from the governorship in 1994 and formed a presidential exploratory committee in March 1995. With his deep Catholic beliefs, his roots in the coal town of Scranton and his confidence that government can make the lives of ordinary people better, Casey is the lineal descendant of those practical New Dealers who believed in a government compassionate to the helpless and supportive of traditional values. He backed an activist government: an aggressive recycling program and tough landfill regulations; measures helping children, from health care to enforcing child support decrees; an Industrial Resource Center using public seed money to spur private investments of $140 million in small manufacturers; the Ben Franklin Partnership, which has provided over $100 million funding for high-tech R&D. He is best known for his fervent opposition to abortion, which produced Pennsylvania's abortion restrictions and got him barred from speaking at the 1992 Democratic National Convention. In April 1995, Casey decided not to make a bid for the presidency, but his actions clearly reinforced Clinton's political image as beleaguered.

Senators. Arlen Specter, Pennsylvania's senior senator, is one of the nation's most durable "career politicians"—a characterization he accepted and survived even in anti-incumbent 1992. Specter has held public office and has been an important national figure off and on for three decades, from his service as a top staffer to the Warren Commission in 1964, when he helped develop the single-assassin theory, up through 1991, when he was attacked by Oliver Stone for that theory in Stone's fantasy movie *J.F.K.* and by feminists for his questioning of Anita Hill in the Clarence Thomas hearings. In March 1995 he announced he was running for president. Specter grew up in Russell, Kansas—astonishingly, also the home town of Bob Dole—and came to Philadelphia at 17 to attend the University of Pennsylvania. After the Warren Commission, he returned to his law practice, switched to the Republican party, and was elected district attorney in Democratic Philadelphia in 1965 and 1969. He lost for D.A. in 1973, for the Senate in 1976, and for governor in 1978, before narrowly edging a former state Republican chairman in the 1980 primary and beating a low-spending Democrat 50%–48% in the general for his Senate seat. In 1986, he won reelection by a 56%–43% margin against a low-profile House Democrat.

Specter's assets have always been brains and hard work. He is respected by colleagues and constituents, though not always well-liked. He sides with conservatives on some divisive issues, with liberals on others, building up no permanent credit with either. He is aggressive and prosecutorial, well-prepared and persuasive once he takes a stand. These traits are both his strength and weakness: they explain why he was vulnerable in 1992, and why he won; they suggest why his presidential candidacy initially seemed implausible, and why his prospects should not be dismissed. His voting record is at the midpoint of the Senate, and he has played key roles on a variety of issues. He is solidly pro-choice on abortion—an issue he is featuring in his presidential campaign, in defiance of the views of most Republican activists and primary voters. He pushes tough penalties for crime and supports capital punishment. He argued vigorously and persuasively for the Gulf War resolution. On a closely divided and rancorous Judiciary Committee, he has played a key role on several Supreme Court nominations. More than anyone else, he defeated Robert Bork in 1987 and, more than anyone but John Danforth, he confirmed Clarence Thomas in 1991. In the latter case he caught the nation's attention. When Anita Hill came before the committee with charges against Thomas that were both serious and unsubstantiated, he questioned her with the rigor that Senators skeptical or disbelieving of the truth of testimony are ordinarily entitled to use. Politically, this evoked a firestorm from people enraged that Hill's testimony had not been received earlier and was not being accepted without demur—responses that were emotionally understandable but blithely ignorant of the lessons taught by the history of Joe McCarthy and Titus Oates. Specter's most aggressive moment in the hearings came when he accused Hill of contradicting herself and committing perjury; examination of the record shows there was a basis for his charge.

Under attack from two sides, Specter did not retreat in 1992. He weathered a vitriolic primary assault from antiabortion legislator Stephen Freind, and won 65%–35%. He watched Lynn Yeakel, daughter of a former Virginia congressman and head of a charity called Women's Way, upset Lieutenant Governor Mark Singel in the Democratic primary after she aired a videoclip of Specter questioning Hill which asked, "Did this make you as mad as it made me?" But in the general Specter exploited Yeakel's weaknesses—she had forked over $17,000 in back income taxes to Philadelphia just before she filed to run, and she performed poorly in debate—and used his hard work and brains to deny her the AFL-CIO endorsement. In the Citizens Jury process, in which randomly selected citizens hear both candidates' positions in detail, Specter outpaced Yeakel in eastern and western Pennsylvania on almost all issues. His years of constituency service and visits to all 67 counties paid off with a 49%–46% margin; he ran about even in metro Philadelphia and Pittsburgh, far ahead of usual Republican showings, and carried most smaller areas.

For a time, Specter seemed eclipsed in Bill Clinton's Washington, and in June 1993 he had surgery for a non-malignant brain tumor. But he made news with a chart showing devastatingly the complexity of the Clinton healthcare plan; he also worked to fund health research and the Human Genome Project. He sponsored many provisions of the 1994 crime bill and supported it when Bob Dole tried to kill it, passed an amendment allowing private firms to run public schools, and fought cuts in the low-income heating assistance program. With the Republican victory in 1994, he became more prominent. He became chairman of the Appropriations Labor Subcommittee funding many large domestic spending programs. And, after rotating off the Intelligence Committee in 1991, he rejoined it as its chairman, quickly voicing tough criticism of Clinton Administration policies. He called for war crimes trials on Serbian atrocities. He also argued before the Supreme Court against the base-closing law that is responsible for closing the Philadelphia Navy Yard (he lost 9–0).

Specter has evidently been thinking of running for president for some time before officially declaring his candidacy in April 1995. In June 1994, he attended an Iowa straw poll and, while fellow moderate Thomas Kean of New Jersey was trying to get to know conservative Christian delegates, Specter confrontationally attacked the religious right. A week after the Republican victory in November 1994, Specter again attacked the religious right and announced he was considering running for president. He was obviously hoping for feminist support: he took to calling the Thomas hearings "a learning experience for me" and supported Dr. Henry Foster for Surgeon General against his critics. His call for a "politics of inclusion" was curious, given that he was the one attacking his fellow Republicans. Specter called himself a fiscal conservative and cultural moderate—not quite accurately, since he has been economically more liberal than almost all other Republicans. In March 1995 he called for a flat tax with a 20% rate and limited mortgage interest and charitable deductions. Specter's obvious strategy is to try to win Iowa or New Hampshire with pluralities in a multi-candidate field, then target Florida and the big northern states that vote immediately afterward. It is unclear, however, whether the Republican Party will nominate a candidate who has made such a point of how he differs from most Republicans on important issues.

Rick Santorum is the youngest Senator, elected from one of the oldest states, a hard-sell conservative elected in a state that still has many New Deal voters. Santorum is the son of an Italian immigrant who was a clinical psychologist for the Veterans Administration. He had just finished college when Ronald Reagan was elected in 1980; he spent half the decade as a staffer for state Senate Republicans in Harrisburg; he worked for a blue chip law firm in Pittsburgh for four years. In 1990 he challenged seven-term incumbent Doug Walgren, who outspent him $717,000 to $251,000. But Santorum knocked on 25,000 doors, amassed an army of volunteers including many right-to-lifers, attacked Walgren for voting "for a pay raise seven times" and for living in the Washington suburbs. Santorum opposed the congressional pay raise, backed the line-item veto and came out for limits on PAC contributions. He won 51%–49%. In the House he had a solid conservative voting record and was one of the "Gang of Seven" freshman Republicans who helped expose the House bank scandal. Redistricting gave him a seat shorn of many Republican suburbs and centered on the industrial Monongahela Valley, historically very Democratic. George Bush got only 30% in this new district, but Santorum beat a state Senator 61%–38%—an astonishing victory. Brash and confident, Santorum immediately contemplated running for the Senate, and in May 1994 easily won the Republican nomination against an African-American minister from Philadelphia.

The incumbent was Harris Wofford, a Democrat with a long public career and a short but significant electoral one. Wofford was active in the civil rights movement in the 1950s, worked as a staffer for John Kennedy and persuaded him to phone Coretta Scott King when her husband was jailed in Georgia during the 1960 campaign, and helped set up the Peace Corps. He came to Pennsylvania as president of Bryn Mawr College, then became a department head for Governor Bob Casey. After Senator John Heinz was killed in a plane crash in April 1991, Casey appointed Wofford to the Senate. He was widely expected to lose the November 1991 special election to former Governor and U.S. Attorney General Dick Thornburgh, who led 65%–21% in an early poll. But Thornburgh was a reluctant candidate, and Wofford came up with an issue that cut to the quick in a year when recession was eroding the value of voters' homes: health care. "If criminals have the right to a lawyer," he said, in a line suggested by a local doctor, "I think working Americans should have the right to a doctor." That may have conflated two kinds of rights, but it helped Wofford win a 55%–45% victory, and to establish healthcare reform as a major issue for Democrats. Bill Clinton in 1992 put Wofford on his list of vice presidential possibilities and in 1993 decided that health care would be his administration's major initiative in its first two years. Wofford had some successes—he sponsored the national service bill in 1993—but the crash-and-burn of the Clinton healthcare plan left him politically imperiled in 1994.

This was a race of sharp contrasts in issues and style: Santorum, brashly eager to chop government, backing medical savings accounts, opposing gun control; Wofford, earnestly working for government healthcare financing, backing the 1994 crime bill and gun control, supporting Clinton. Wofford appealed to a long liberal tradition; Santorum scoffed at him for championing 1960s ideas in the 1990s. Wofford was endorsed in the last week by Teresa Heinz, widow of John Heinz. But with home town appeal, Santorum ran behind only 50%–47% in metro Pittsburgh, where Wofford had won 61% in 1991. Santorum did not go over so well in metro Philadelphia, which Wofford carried 54%–42%. But in the the rest of the state—where half the votes are cast and where gun control hurt Wofford—Santorum won 55%–41%, for a statewide victory of 49%–47%.

In the Senate he will not be an entirely orthodox conservative: he opposed the North American Free Trade Agreement in 1993 and hesitated to oppose striker replacement, in deference to union strength in the Mon Valley. But he remains a rebel: on the balanced budget amendment he was unafraid to debate for hours with Robert Byrd and willing to threaten Mark Hatfield's Appropriations chairmanship over Hatfield's support of the proposal. As part of the crew that shook up the House, this brash and savvy youngster who has come a long way since 1990 now promises to change the tradition-laden Senate.

Presidential politics. In 1992, Pennsylvania voted Democratic for president as it did in 1948, 1960, 1968 and 1976, and came close to doing in 1984 and 1988: it now seems one of the more Democratic states but not necessarily willing to give up its swing-state status. With its older, deeply-rooted population, it tends to be culturally conservative; with its long-dying blue-collar communities, it tends to be economically more liberal—though both tendencies are being muted with time. Pennsylvania's late April presidential primary has not been crucial since the 1976 Democratic race, when Jimmy Carter clinched the Democratic nomination by beating Henry Jackson and Morris Udall here. In early 1995, both parties favored moving it to March 19, when Illinois, Michigan and Ohio also vote and when home-state favorite Specter may be looking for a boost.

Congressional districting. Pennsylvania lost three congressional districts in the 1950 Census and two in each of the following four decades, reducing its delegation to 21. Control of redistricting was split between the parties, but the plan seemed to eliminate two Republican seats. In fact, anticipations here, as in many other states, were confounded as both parties in 1992 and 1994 lost seats they were expected to win and won some they seemed sure to lose. But enough veteran Republicans have survived in safe seats so that the state has four committee chairmen and would have a fifth had not one incumbent been removed from his post because of a criminal indictment.

The People: Est. Pop. 1994: 12,052,000; Pop. 1990: 11,881,643, up 1.4% 1990–1994. 4.6% of U.S. total, 5th largest; 31% rural. Median age: 35.0 years. 15.4% 65 years and over. 88.5% White, 9.2% Black, 2.0% Hispanic origin, 1.2% Asian, 1.0% Other. Households: 55.7% married couple families; 25% married couple fams. w. children; 36% college educ.; median household income: $29,069; per capita income: $14,068; 70.6% owner occupied housing; median house value: $69,700; median monthly rent: $322. 7.5% Unemployment. 1994 Voting age pop.: 9,212,000. 1994 Turnout: 3,571,402; 39% of VAP. Registered voters (1994): 5,879,093; 2,955,594 D (50%), 2,534,087 R (43%), 389,412 unaffiliated and minor parties (7%).

Political Lineup: Governor, Tom Ridge (R); Lt. Gov., Mark Schwieker (R); Secy. of Commonwealth, Robert Grant (D); Atty. Gen., Ernie Preate (R); Treasurer, Catherine Baker Knoll (D); Auditor General, Barbara Hafer (R). State Senate, 50 (29 R and 21 D); State House of Representatives, 203 (102 R and 101 D). Senators, Arlen Specter (R) and Rick Santorum (R). Representatives, 21 (10 R and 11 D).

1992 Presidential Vote		
Clinton (D)	2,239,164	(45%)
Bush (R)	1,791,841	(36%)
Perot (I)	902,667	(18%)

1988 Presidential Vote		
Bush (R)	2,300,087	(51%)
Dukakis (D)	2,194,944	(48%)

1992 Democratic Presidential Primary		
Clinton	715,031	(57%)
Brown	325,543	(26%)
Tsongas	161,572	(13%)
Other	63,349	(5%)

1992 Republican Presidential Primary		
Bush	774,865	(77%)
Buchanan	233,912	(23%)

GOVERNOR

Gov. Tom Ridge (R)

Elected 1994, term expires Jan. 1999; b. Aug. 26, 1945, Munhall; home, Erie; Harvard, B.A. 1967, Dickinson Law Sch., J.D. 1972; Catholic; married (Michele).

Career: Army, 1968–70 (Vietnam); Practicing atty., 1972–82; Erie Cnty. Asst. Dist. Atty., 1979–81; U.S. House of Reps., 1983–94.

Office: 225 Capitol Bldg., Harrisburg 17120, 717-787-2500; Fax: 717-783-1396.

Election Results

1994 gen.	Tom Ridge (R)	1,627,976	(45%)
	Mark S. Singel (D)	1,430,099	(40%)
	Peg Luksik (Constitutional)	460,269	(13%)
	Others	67,182	(2%)
1994 prim.	Tom Ridge (R)	344,708	(35%)
	Ernie Preate (R)	287,400	(29%)
	Sam Katz (R)	156,895	(16%)
	Mike Fisher (R)	139,712	(14%)
	John F. Perry (R)	68,069	(7%)
1990 gen.	Robert P. Casey (D)	2,065,244	(68%)
	Barbara Hafer (R)	987,516	(32%)

SENATORS

Sen. Arlen Specter (R)

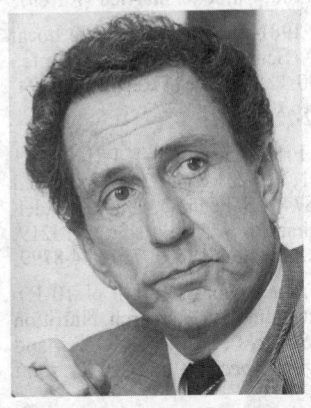

Elected 1980, seat up 1998; b. Feb. 12, 1930, Wichita, KS; home, Philadelphia; U. of PA, B.A. 1951, Yale, LL.B. 1956; Jewish; married (Joan).

Career: Air Force, 1951–53; Practicing atty., 1955–56, 1974–80; Asst. Cnsl., Warren Comm., 1964; PA Asst. Atty. Gen., 1964–65; Philadelphia Dist. Atty., 1966–74.

DC Office: 530 HSOB 20510, 202-224-4254; Fax: 202-224-1893.

State Offices: 600 Arch Street, #9400, Philadelphia 19106, 215-597-7200; Fed. Bldg., #2031, Liberty Ave. & Grant St., Pittsburgh 15222, 412-644-3400; 1159 Fed. Bldg., #18, 6th & State Sts., Erie 16501, 814-453-3010; 1159 Fed. Bldg, Harrisburg 17101, 717-782-3951; Park Plaza, #503, Scranton 18503, 717-346-2006; and P.O. Bldg., #102, 5th & Hamilton Sts., Allentown 18101, 610-434-1444.

Committees: *Appropriations* (4th of 15 R): Agriculture, Rural Development and Related Agencies; Defense; Foreign Operations; Labor, Health and Human Services, Education (Chmn.); Transportation. *Intelligence (Select)* (Chmn. of 9 R). *Judiciary* (5th of 10 R): Antitrust, Business Rights and Competition; Immigration; Terrorism, Technology and Government Information (Chmn). *Veterans' Affairs* (4th of 7 R).

Group Ratings

	ADA	ACLU	COPE	CFA	LCV	CON	NSI	COC	ACU	NTLC	CHC
1994	55	56	38	58	54	88	100	55	46	63	50
1993	85	—	45	33	38	53	—	100	57	—	—

National Journal Ratings

	1993 LIB — 1993 CONS	1994 LIB — 1994 CONS
Economic	39% — 60%	41% — 58%
Social	59% — 40%	49% — 50%
Foreign	48% — 51%	38% — 61%

Key Votes of the 103d Congress

1. Clinton Deficit Plan	N	3. Brady Handgun Purchase	N	5. Lmt. UN Cmnd. of Forces	*
2. NAFTA	Y	4. Strike Race/Death Pnlty.	Y	6. Cut Missile Funds	N

Key Votes of the 104th Congress

1. Congressional Compliance	Y	3. Balanced Budget Amndt.	Y	5. Product Liablity Reform	N
2. Bar Unfunded Mandates	Y	4. Pass Line Item Veto	Y	6. FY96 Budget	Y

Election Results

1992 general	Arlen Specter (R)	2,358,125	(49%)	($10,454,793)
	Lynn Yeakel (D)	2,224,966	(46%)	($5,028,669)
	John F. Perry (Lib)	219,319	(5%)	($53,690)
1992 primary	Arlen Specter (R)	683,118	(65%)	
	Stephen F. Freind (R)	366,608	(35%)	
1986 general	Arlen Specter (R)	1,906,537	(56%)	($5,993,230)
	Robert W. Edgar (D)	1,448,219	(43%)	($3,968,994)

Sen. Rick Santorum (R)

Elected, 1994, seat up 2000; b. May 10, 1958, Winchester, VA; home, Pittsburgh; PA St. U., B.A. 1980, U. of Pittsburgh, M.B.A. 1981, Dickinson Law Sch., J.D. 1986; Catholic; married (Karen).

Career: A.A., PA Sen. J. Doyle 1981–86; Dir., PA Senate Local Govt. Cmte., 1981–84; Dir., PA Senate Transportation Cmte., 1984–86; Practicing atty., 1986–90; U.S. House of Reps., 1990–94.

DC Office: 120 RSOB 20510, 202-224-6324.

State Offices: 130 Fed. Bldg., Erie 16501, 814-454-7114; 221 Strawberry Sq., Harrisburg 17101, 717-231-7540; 2019 Industrial Dr., Bethlehem 18017, 610-865-1874; 1 S. Penn Sq., #960, Philadelphia 19107, 215-597-9914; 1 Station Sq., #250, Pittsburgh 15219, 412-562-0533, and 527 Linden St., Scranton 18503, 717-344-8799.

Committees: *Agriculture, Nutrition & Forestry* (8th of 10 R): Marketing, Inspection and Product Promotion; Research, Nutrition and General Legislation. *Armed Services* (11th of 11 R): Airland Forces; Personnel; Readiness. *Rules & Administration* (8th of 9 R). *Aging (Special)* (9th of 10 R). *Joint Economic Committee* (5th of 10 Sen.)

Group Ratings (as Member of U.S. House of Representatives)

	ADA	ACLU	COPE	CFA	LCV	CON	NSI	COC	ACU	NTLC	CHC
1994	15	23	22	10	7	71	100	100	81	85	79
1993	20	—	50	20	21	82	—	73	70	—	—

National Journal Ratings (as Member of U.S. House of Representatives)

	1993 LIB — 1993 CONS		1994 LIB — 1994 CONS	
Economic	34%	— 65%	0%	— 80%
Social	27%	— 72%	29%	— 71%
Foreign	37%	— 60%	33%	— 66%

Key Votes of the 103d Congress (as Member of U.S. House of Representatives)

1. Clinton Deficit Plan	N	3. Brady Handgun Purchase N	5. Lmt. UN Cmnd. of Forces Y
2. NAFTA	N	4. Strike Race/Death Pnlty. Y	6. Cut Missile Funds Y

Key Votes of the 104th Congress

1. Congressional Compliance Y		3. Balanced Budget Amndt. Y	5. Product Liability Reform Y
2. Bar Unfunded Mandates Y		4. Pass Line Item Veto Y	6. FY96 Budget Y

Election Results

1994 general	Rick Santorum (R)	1,735,691	(49%)	($6,732,849)
	Harris Wofford (D)	1,648,481	(47%)	($6,300,560)
	Others	129,189	(4%)	
1994 primary	Rick Santorum (R)	667,115	(82%)	
	Joe Watkins (R)	150,969	(18%)	
1991 special	Harris Wofford (D)	1,860,760	(55%)	($3,241,556)
	Dick Thornburgh (R)	1,521,986	(45%)	($3,993,070)

FIRST DISTRICT

In Center City Philadelphia, the 1680s look out on the 1780s, 1880s and 1980s. The statute of William Penn, who founded the city in 1682, stands 37 feet high atop the 548-foot tower of the 1880s Second Empire-style City Hall at Market and Broad; east is Independence Hall, where Americans in the 1780s drew up the nation's Constitution; west is the tower of One Liberty Place, with its "romantic modernist" spire, the 1980s building that broke tradition to rise above City Hall. Philadelphia is built on a certain order. Earlier American colonies were settled by practical men, out to make money or replicate a farm settlement back home. But Penn was a Quaker, a member of one of those rationalizing sects of the 17th century, who intended to impose order on his new environment, and did. Hence Philadelphia was designed not with the cowpath street patterns of Boston or Charleston, but with a grid of numbered and named streets, with occasional open squares, replicated in dozens of American cities.

Penn's city of brotherly love has turned out to be a commercial and industrial metropolis that has grown steadily over the years, spreading out over the countryside and now the nation's fifth largest urban area. Yet there are still places in which you can see the distant past: in the restored townhouses of Society Hill and the tree-shaded public buildings around Independence Hall, and, on the way to the ornate City Hall, the Federal and Greek Revival buildings, little temples of commerce, built when Philadelphia was the nation's largest city. Interspersed are I.M. Pei's modernist Society Hill Towers (though the rich in Philadelphia, unlike New York or Chicago, don't much like apartments) and the 1920s masonry-faced skyscrapers and 1970s glass-and-steel towers built around City Hall and in Center City farther west.

For all the grandness of City Hall, Philadelphia has seldom had a city government to be proud of. Corruption has reigned here off and on for more than a century, and so has incompetence. While the city's private economy grew robustly in the 1980s, the city government, swollen with overpaid employees, committed to a costly, union-run health plan and mismanaged with ferocious ineptitude, lurched unknowingly toward bankruptcy under Mayor Wilson Goode. Then in 1991 Democrat Ed Rendell was elected Mayor. Ebullient and energetic, he immediately set to work, literally scrubbing City Hall's grimy steps. He cut spending sharply, privatized government functions and faced down unions in a strike threat. At the same time, he improved performance and sponsored innovative new programs, took over the closed-down Philadelphia Navy Yard and found new employers to save at least half of the jobs there. Rendell, who in early 1995 seemed headed for easy reelection, showed national Democrats the viable future for their politics: not increasing spending and defending public employees against constituents, but cutting spending and producing more and better services for less money.

City Hall lies at the geographic center of the 1st Congressional District. The 1st runs north on both sides of the Broad Street corridor to include much of black North Philadelphia and south through most of heavily Italian South Philadelphia, where Italian families, groceries and restaurants have been pressed tightly into narrow English and Indian-named streets under a tangle of overhead wires; this is the neighborhood where the various *Rockys* were filmed and the original Philadelphia cheesesteaks are sold. The district also includes the oil tank farms where the Schuylkill River flows into the Delaware, the Navy Yard, Philadelphia airport, and a swath of industrial suburbs along the river to the black-majority city of Chester. This was created as a black-majority district, in the argot of the Voting Rights Act, but also includes many Hispanics, and is overwhelmingly Democratic.

The 1st is represented by Thomas Foglietta, whose long career embodies Philadelphia's traditions of family politics and party switching. Foglietta, whose father was a Republican politician, was once a Republican himself during the 20 years he served as councilman from South Philadelphia. He first won his House seat in 1980 as an independent, beating convicted Abscam defendant Ozzie Myers 38%–34%. He held the seat as a Democrat in the 1982 primary against another incumbent, Joseph Smith, 52%–48%, and in 1984 and 1986 weathered serious primary challenges from South Philadelphia politico James Tayoun, 52%–45% and 62%–38%. The 1st got a black majority in 1992, but Foglietta was unopposed in the primary that year and in the 1994 primary beat former TV reporter Harvey Clark 69%–31% after winning endorsements from many black ministers and the black-owned *Philadelphia Tribune*. Foglietta is now the nation's only white representative of a black majority district.

Foglietta has one of the most liberal voting records in Congress. He is head of the Congressional Urban Caucus and works closely with Black Caucus members. He attacked the Penny-Kasich budget cuts fiercely in 1993 and 1994. In 1995 he harshly attacked the Contract With America, claiming that Philadelphia would lose $15 billion if it were passed and that it would stop the transformation of the Navy Yard. Foglietta has worked hard on that project, transferring the base to the city and attracting new tenants. He has also been very close to President Aristide of Haiti. He was one of the first to urge the Clinton Administration to use force to restore Aristide to power and accompanied him on his return to Haiti.

Foglietta could conceivably be vulnerable to a black challenger in a primary, but his roots in South Philadelphia and his liberal record make him formidable.

The People: Pop. 1990: 566,133; 13% age 65+; 36% White; 52% Black; 2% Asian; 7% Other; 9% Hispanic origin. Voting age pop.: 413,321; 50% Black; 7% Hispanic origin. Households: 35% married couple families; 15% married couple fams. w. children; 25% college educ.; median household income: $20,372; per capita income: $9,703; median gross rent: $404; median house value: $36,700.

1992 Presidential Vote			1988 Presidential Vote		
Clinton (D)	150,091	(72%)	Dukakis (D)	158,262	(73%)
Bush (R)	39,086	(19%)	Bush (R)	59,095	(27%)
Perot (I)	17,052	(8%)			

Rep. Thomas M. Foglietta (D)

Elected 1980; b. Dec. 3, 1928, Philadelphia; home, Philadelphia; St. Joseph's Col., B.A. 1949, Temple U., J.D. 1952; Catholic; single.

Career: Practicing atty., 1952–80; Philadelphia City Cncl., 1955–75; Reg. Dir., U.S. Dept. of Labor, 1976.

DC Office: 341 CHOB 20515, 202-225-4731; Fax: 202-225-0088.

District Offices: Green Fed. Bldg., 600 Arch St., #10402, Philadelphia 19106, 215-925-6840; 1806 S. Broad St., Philadelphia 19125, 215-463-8702; and 2630 Memphis St., Philadelphia 19125, 215-426-4616.

Committees: *Appropriations* (21st of 24 D): Military Construction; Transportation.

Group Ratings

	ADA	ACLU	COPE	CFA	LCV	CON	NSI	COC	ACU	NTLC	CHC
1994	95	82	89	100	88	21	0	25	0	4	7
1993	95	—	92	100	64	39	—	0	0	—	—

National Journal Ratings

	1993 LIB — 1993 CONS			1994 LIB — 1994 CONS		
Economic	68%	—	26%	83%	—	0%
Social	68%	—	29%	79%	—	21%
Foreign	84%	—	13%	85%	—	0%

Key Votes of the 103d Congress

1. Clinton Deficit Plan	Y	3. Brady Handgun Purchase Y	5. Lmt. UN Cmnd. of Forces N
2. NAFTA	N	4. Strike Race/Death Pnlty. N	6. Cut Missile Funds Y

Key Votes of the 104th Congress

1. Congressional Compliance Y	6. Reform Crime Grant N	11. Loser Pays Court Reform N
2. Balanced Budget Amndmt. N	7. National Security Act N	12. Product Liability Reform N
3. Bar Unfunded Mandates N	8. Moratorium on Regs. N	13. Welfare Reform N
4. Pass Line Item Veto N	9. Risk Assessment on Regs. N	14. Term Limits Amndmt. N
5. Relax Exclusionary Rule N	10. Expnd. Priv. Prop. Rights N	15. Tax Cuts N

Election Results

1994 general	Thomas M. Foglietta (D)	99,669	(82%)	($486,812)
	Roger F. Gordon (R)	22,595	(18%)	
1994 primary	Thomas M. Foglietta (D)	40,830	(69%)	
	Harvey Clark (D)	18,364	(31%)	
1992 general	Thomas M. Foglietta (D)	150,172	(81%)	($366,203)
	Craig Snyder (R)	35,419	(19%)	($41,210)

SECOND DISTRICT

The story of politics in Pennsylvania's 2d Congressional District is the story of black Philadelphia politics, with all its historic nuances and overtones. The black percentage of the district was reduced in redistricting in 1992, from 80% to a little over 60%. But the landscape of the 2d District still resembles the Philadelphia that 19th century painter Thomas Eakins memorialized, with tightly-packed but formidable rowhouses, the old fieldstone houses of Germantown, the Schuylkill River quietly flowing past boat houses below the small Greek temples of the Water Works and the larger temple of the Museum of Art and the skyscraper towers looming behind. Concentrated in neighborhoods that radiate outward from Center City, Philadelphia's black communities lie in West Philadelphia, across the Schuylkill on either side of Market Street; in North Philadelphia, on either side of Broad Street; and to the northwest, off the narrow diagonal of Germantown Avenue that ran through open fields in Benjamin Franklin's time. The 2d also includes many Center City skyscrapers, affluent Chestnut Hill and upper-class Rittenhouse Square, where the district's white voters tend to congregate. Pennsylvania never had slavery—thanks to William Penn's Quaker legacy—and Philadelphia had a large black community before the Civil War. While succeeding generations of the city's black politicians have included persons of both greater and lesser talent, the political atmosphere in the district has always been energized and intense.

That atmosphere has historically been almost wholly Democratic. The 2d will dole out some votes to Republicans: Senator Arlen Specter, who has a long record of support for civil rights, won enough black votes to make the difference in his reelection campaign in 1992, which he won by a 49%–47% statewide margin. But the Democratic primary is where House careers are made or lost in the 2d District, and Congressman Chaka Fattah, who won the primary (and the general election) in 1994, knows that fact very well.

A Philadelphia native, Fattah became the youngest person ever elected to the state House of Representatives when he won a seat there in 1982 at age 25. Six years later he was elected to the state Senate, where in 1990 he led a group of business owners in a campaign to raise $34 million to fend off Philadelphia's impending bankruptcy. Shortly after that, William Gray, a Democrat who had represented the 2d District since 1978, made the surprise decision to retire from Congress to become president of the United Negro College Fund. Gray had been a shining light in the Philadelphia political firmament: he had served as House Budget Committee chairman from 1984 to 1988 and was elected Majority Whip in 1989. When local ward leaders decided to nominate Lucien E. Blackwell, a longtime city councilman and labor union stalwart, as the Democratic candidate in the special House election to fill Gray's seat, Fattah temporarily quit the party to run against Blackwell. He lost the special, winning 28% to Blackwell's 39%; state welfare secretary John White, running as an independent, pulled in 28% of the vote.

Fattah passed up the 1992 election—which Blackwell won by a narrow margin—and then challenged Blackwell again in 1994. The primary campaign began on a combative note, when Fattah questioned the authenticity of a page in Blackwell's nominating petition. "The page is striking for its neatness and the similarity of the script in which all 50 names, addresses, occupations and dates are written. The addresses are listed in sequential order and are located in Tasker Homes, a battered housing development" in South Philadelphia, the *Philadelphia Inquirer* reported in March of that year. Fattah filed suit challenging the petition in a Pennsylvania court, but dropped the challenge a few days later rather than reveal the name of a confidential informant who had alerted him to the alleged forgeries. As the May 10 primary drew near, Blackwell and Fattah battled for endorsements from established local politicians and prominent citizens. Blackwell won the nod from Philadelphia Mayor Ed Rendell and City Council President John Street, while Fattah lined up ward- and precinct-level supporters and distinguished community leaders such as the United Black Clergy of Philadelphia. State Senator Hardy Williams, whose district abutted Fattah's state Senate district, also endorsed the upstart challenger over the seasoned politico who delighted in being dubbed "Lucien the Solution" for his skill in delivering favors and protecting local interests.

The contest came down to a choice between generational styles. Blackwell kept to the campaign tactics that had made him a fixture of Philadelphia politics for two decades, emphasizing door-to-door contact with voters and tending to the needs of party loyalists. Fattah, on the other hand, ran a high-brow campaign buttressed by policy papers on education, crime, housing and the plight of the inner city. He beat Blackwell handily in the primary 58%–42% and went on to capture 86% of the general election vote.

Fattah's momentum continued upon his arrival on Capitol Hill, where he was appointed to the House Democratic Policy Committee and the Democratic Congressional Campaign Committee and was elected whip of the Black Caucus—the only freshman to serve in the caucus's leadership ranks. Observers say House Democrats are counting on Fattah, who was a Democrat in a state legislature dominated by Republicans, to provide badly-needed insight. Shortly after Fattah's election, *Time* magazine named him one of America's most promising leaders under the age of 40. That honor could prove prophetic.

The People: Pop. 1990: 565,242; 15% age 65+; 34% White; 62% Black; 2% Asian; 1% Other; 1% Hispanic origin. Voting age pop.: 438,250; 58% Black; 1% Hispanic origin. Households: 32% married couple families; 12% married couple fams. w. children; 40% college educ.; median household income: $24,880; per capita income: $13,121; median gross rent: $479; median house value: $42,300.

1992 Presidential Vote			1988 Presidential Vote		
Clinton (D)	183,758	(79%)	Dukakis (D)	192,671	(79%)
Bush (R)	31,878	(14%)	Bush (R)	51,458	(21%)
Perot (I)	14,514	(6%)			

Rep. Chaka Fattah (D)

Elected 1994; b. Nov. 21, 1956, Philadelphia; home, Philadelphia; U. of PA, M.A. 1986; Baptist; married (Patricia).

Career: PA House of Reps., 1982–1988; PA Senate, 1988–1994.

DC Office: 1205 LHOB 20515, 202-225-4001; Fax: 202-225-3127.

District Offices: 4104 Walnut St., Philadelphia 19104, 215-387-6404.

Committees: *Government Reform & Oversight* (22nd of 22 D): District of Columbia; Human Resources and Intergovernmental Affairs. *Small Business* (15th of 19 D): Procurement, Exports and Business Opportunities; Regulation and Paperwork.

Group Ratings and 103rd Congress Votes: Newly Elected

Key Votes of the 104th Congress

1. Congressional Compliance Y	6. Reform Crime Grant N	11. Loser Pays Court Reform N
2. Balanced Budget Amndmt. N	7. National Security Act N	12. Product Liability Reform N
3. Bar Unfunded Mandates N	8. Moratorium on Regs. N	13. Welfare Reform N
4. Pass Line Item Veto N	9. Risk Assessment on Regs. N	14. Term Limits Amndmt. N
5. Relax Exclusionary Rule N	10. Expnd. Priv. Prop. Rights N	15. Tax Cuts N

Election Results

1994 general	Chaka Fattah (D)	120,553	(86%)	($492,348)
	Lawrence R. Watson II (R)	19,824	(14%)	($2,828)
1994 primary	Chaka Fattah (D)	55,103	(58%)	
	Lucien E. Blackwell (D)	39,836	(42%)	
1992 general	Lucien E. Blackwell (D)	164,355	(77%)	($228,229)
	Larry Hollin (R)	47,906	(22%)	($170,007)
	Other	1,666	(1%)	

THIRD DISTRICT

Known as the Great Northeast, the 3d District—lying to the north and east of Center City Philadelphia—is the only district lying entirely within the city limits and is far more racially homogeneous than the rest of Philadelphia. The 3d stretches more than a dozen miles along the Delaware River and back along the parklands by Frankford, Tacony and Pennypack Creeks. It includes most of the white residential neighborhoods of Philadelphia, starting with the 19th century homes of Kensington, where descendants of Irish and Italian immigrants live in inelegant frame houses and often earn less than those in many African-American neighborhoods. Farther out is northeast Philadelphia, a more suburban area the size of a major city itself. Here, when the alley-wide streets of North and South Philadelphia and the river wards were already teeming with houses and people and the Main Line suburbs were already well-settled, the workers of Philadelphia's docks and factories and Center City offices were just starting to move out and fill up vacant land. They settled in neighborhoods like the one near Pennypack Park, where the man who has become a symbol of Philadelphia, Sylvester Stallone, grew up. Unlike much of Philadelphia, with its high crime rate and struggling city government, northeast Philadelphia is still new urban territory, with more than half of its dwellings built after 1950. The area, which contains about one-third of the city's population, is still growing.

Politically the district appears to be a throwback to an earlier era, when you would expect to see ward heelers walking through the neighborhoods of Kensington and Frankford, distributing coal for the winter. Most people here are Catholic, but there are many Jews, living in neighborhoods like neither Brooklyn nor Scarsdale. The houses are pleasant, but modest. Many residents are part of the hard-pressed lower middle-class and are Democrats, but they also are conservative on many cultural issues. Northeast Philadelphia recoiled from the national Democrats in the 1970s. While many in the area are union members, with traditional ties to the Democratic Party, they abandoned the national party when they began to equate it with providing preferential treatment for minorities. The district voted for Ronald Reagan and George Bush in the 1980s, and then returned to give Bill Clinton an absolute majority in 1992.

Like many politicians, the congressman from the 3d, Robert Borski, first gained fame as an athlete: he was captain of the Frankford High basketball and baseball teams in 1966 and became a coach after graduating from college with an athletic scholarship. Contacts made as an athlete certainly helped him get a job as a floor manager at the Philadelphia Stock Exchange, and in 1976 he was elected to the state House of Representatives, where he served until his election to Congress in 1982. Borski was the political beneficiary of a chain of events: the indictment of northeast Philadelphia Democratic Congressman Joshua Eilberg in 1978 and the election of Republican Charles Dougherty in 1980. When other politicians showed little interest in a race against Dougherty in 1982, Borksi took on the incumbent, won and has been easily reelected since. Redistricting added Kensington to the district and a bit of gentrified Society Hill and Center City, which didn't hurt Borski. Borski also wasn't hurt by having 33 bad checks at the House bank and had no trouble being reelected in 1992. In 1994, he was opposed by Republican James Hasher, owner of a realty group, director of the Philadelphia Board of Realtors and a local committeeman for 10 years. Borksi won handily with 63% of the vote.

Borski has a low profile and a labor-liberal voting record in the House. With retirements, he had been in line to chair the Transportation and Infrastructure Committee's Water Resources Subcommittee, which authorizes projects across the country. When the Republicans took the House, Borski became the panel's ranking member—and with Republicans slashing spending, it remains to see how influential he can be in that position. Borski also is swimming against the tide in his push for the federal government to spend lots more on highways and mass transit, especially greater Philadelphia's financially-troubled SEPTA. In 1992, he introduced the Infrastructure Reinvestment and Economic Revitalization Act, which calls for bonds to finance a one-time nationwide investment in infrastructure construction. He has sponsored bills to ban backhauling of garbage in food trucks and specifying Coast Guard responsibilities in oil spills. He also has pushed the federal government to reevaluate how it manages the upper Mississippi River and its flood plain, in light of the 1993 flood. Borski gained some attention in 1993 when he and then-House Speaker Thomas Foley demonstrated their martial arts talents by breaking boards with their bare hands in an exhibition. In 1995, Borksi was reappointed to the politically sensitive House Ethics Committee.

The People: Pop. 1990: 565,884; 18% age 65+; 87% White; 5% Black; 3% Asian; 3% Other; 4% Hispanic origin. Voting age pop.: 437,308; 4% Black; 4% Hispanic origin. Households: 51% married couple families; 22% married couple fams. w. children; 29% college educ.; median household income: $29,157; per capita income: $13,429; median gross rent: $472; median house value: $64,900.

1992 Presidential Vote

Clinton (D)	125,078	(52%)
Bush (R)	75,388	(31%)
Perot (I)	39,582	(16%)

1988 Presidential Vote

Bush (R)	127,736	(52%)
Dukakis (D)	119,379	(48%)

Rep. Robert A. Borski (D)

Elected 1982; b. Oct. 20, 1948, Philadelphia; home, Philadelphia; U. of Baltimore, B.A. 1972; Catholic; married (Karen).

Career: Stockbroker, 1972–76; PA House of Reps., 1976–82.

DC Office: 2182 RHOB 20515, 202-225-8251; Fax: 202-225-4628.

District Offices: 7141 Frankford Ave., Philadelphia 19135, 215-335-3355; and 2630 Memphis St., Philadelphia 19125, 215-426-4616.

Committees: *Transportation & Infrastructure* (4th of 27 D): Railroads; Water Resources and Environment (RMM). *Standards of Official Conduct* (4th of 5 D).

Group Ratings

	ADA	ACLU	COPE	CFA	LCV	CON	NSI	COC	ACU	NTLC	CHC
1994	65	41	89	80	81	1	50	33	29	14	36
1993	70	—	100	90	77	30	—	20	13	—	—

National Journal Ratings

	1993 LIB — 1993 CONS		1994 LIB — 1994 CONS	
Economic	64%	— 34%	73%	— 17%
Social	51%	— 48%	60%	— 39%
Foreign	59%	— 38%	64%	— 33%

Key Votes of the 103d Congress

1. Clinton Deficit Plan	Y	3. Brady Handgun Purchase Y	5. Lmt. UN Cmnd. of Forces N
2. NAFTA	N	4. Strike Race/Death Pnlty. Y	6. Cut Missile Funds N

Key Votes of the 104th Congress

1. Congressional Compliance Y	6. Reform Crime Grant N	11. Loser Pays Court Reform N
2. Balanced Budget Amndmt. N	7. National Security Act N	12. Product Liability Reform N
3. Bar Unfunded Mandates Y	8. Moratorium on Regs. N	13. Welfare Reform N
4. Pass Line Item Veto N	9. Risk Assessment on Regs. N	14. Term Limits Amndmt. N
5. Relax Exclusionary Rule Y	10. Expnd. Priv. Prop. Rights N	15. Tax Cuts N

Election Results

1994 general	Robert A. Borski (D)	92,702	(63%)	($323,957)
	James C. Hasher (R)	55,209	(37%)	($120,616)
1994 primary	Robert A. Borski (D)	44,231	(86%)	
	John R. Kates (D)	4,236	(8%)	
	Dennis Jerome Gesker (D)	2,676	(5%)	
1992 general	Robert A. Borski (D)	130,828	(59%)	($664,231)
	Charles F. Dougherty (R)	86,787	(39%)	($215,321)
	Other	4,356	(2%)	

FOURTH DISTRICT

For 100 years, the area along the banks of the Beaver and Ohio Rivers, near where they join in westernmost Pennsylvania, was one of America's great heavy industrial zones. It was steel country, with mills rising black and brooding from the bottomlands and filling the narrow river valleys with smoke. The sinewy sons of immigrant families worked hard in the hot mills. Looking down on riverscapes lined with piles of iron ore, limestone and coal and littered with cranes, stocks and furnaces, the families lived in small frame houses on the hillsides. Although not an environmentalist's idea of perfection, this was a land of opportunity for thousands whose lives were far worse before moving to steel country. For a few heady years, the high union wages and early retirement plans seemed to make working in the mills the way to affluence. But the industry crashed after the oil shock of 1979, when whole mills were closed and thousands of jobs vanished. Today, thousands of workers who long ago exhausted their unemployment benefits have given up and left the Beaver and Ohio valleys. Forty years ago, the western Pennsylvania steel country had 11 House Members; it now has six.

The 4th Congressional District, as redrawn after the 1990 Census, contains much of the classic steel country: Beaver and Lawrence Counties; the northern tier of townships in Pittsburgh's Allegheny County, suburban territory with a rough, rural air to it; and western Westmoreland County, with affluent suburbs on the hills between more steel towns. Although its 1980 predecessor had more than half of the same territory and was intended to tilt Republican, this is now a heavily Democratic seat. What the district has tilted to, at least up to 1992, is electing a string of incompetent congressmen. For 20 years, the area had been represented by Democrat Frank Clark, who bucked the tide and lost in the Watergate landslide of 1974. His conqueror was Gary Myers, a Republican who after four years in Congress decided to go back to being a foreman in a steel mill. Democrat Eugene Atkinson, who had lost to Myers in 1976, won unimpressively in 1978, then switched to the Republican Party just as the steel industry headed for its worst tailspin and the steel country was about to be the one part of the country trending Democratic: bad political moves every one. The craziest district lines in the world couldn't save a politician like this, and didn't. In 1982, Atkinson lost 60%–39% to Joe Kolter, a 13-year veteran of the legislature. He was a solid labor-liberal given to malapropisms ("some of the people taking over defunct S&Ls are people who have defuncted themselves") and worse. He drew three serious primary opponents in 1992 and in March lost the AFL-CIO endorsement after he missed a key vote on unemployment benefits. The big surprise of the primary was not that Kolter lost— he got only 20%, a devastating result for an incumbent—but that the two other state representatives, one of whom had labor's endorsement, lost as well.

The easy winner, with 45%, was Ron Klink, a reporter and anchor for KDKA-TV, who issued a 39-page "Ron Klink Plan for Jobs." His non-political background and his promise to create industrial jobs in this area where their lack is so painfully obvious gave him 79% of the vote in the general election. In 1994, Klink was opposed by small business owner and engineer Edward Peglow, a political newcomer. Peglow espoused the traditional Republican planks of less government, tax cuts, support for the death penalty and welfare reform. Klink won handily, 64%–36%.

In his first term, Klink demonstrated some independence from the Democratic leadership and the White House. He vigorously opposed the North American Free Trade Agreement and as a member of the freshman fiscal caucus, he supported the Penny-Kasich spending cut plan. He also broke with most Democrats on the Economic and Educational Opportunities Committee on abortion. During the panel's markup of healthcare reform legislation, he unsuccessfully pushed an amendment that would have prohibited the federal government from requiring health insurers to include abortion coverage as part of a basic benefits package in the Clinton health plan. Klink also proposed an amendment that would have subjected Congress to occupational and safety laws. While the Committee adopted his proposal, the legislation eventually stalled in the Senate; it was not until 1995 that Congress adopted a similar proposal. Klink also proposed the novel idea of having Congress hire its own pollster to provide members with better information on which to base decisions. As a new Democrat on the Commerce Committee, his conservative social views could give him an opportunity to have an impact on health-care issues.

The People: Pop. 1990: 565,809; 33% rural; 16% age 65+; 96% White; 3% Black. Voting age pop.: 431,775; 3% Black. Households: 63% married couple families; 27% married couple fams. w. children; 36% college educ.; median household income: $26,792; per capita income: $12,684; median gross rent: $332; median house value: $55,400.

1992 Presidential Vote			1988 Presidential Vote		
Clinton (D)	118,701	(48%)	Dukakis (D)	128,445	(59%)
Bush (R)	76,291	(31%)	Bush (R)	90,923	(41%)
Perot (I)	50,654	(21%)			

Rep. Ron Klink (D)

Elected 1992; b. Sept. 23, 1951, Canton, OH; home, Jeannette; Protestant; married (Linda).

Career: Businessman; Restaurant Owner; Reporter and Anchor, KDKA-TV, Pittsburgh, 1978–92.

DC Office: 125 CHOB 20515, 202-225-2565; Fax: 202-226-2274.

District Offices: 11279 Center Hwy., N. Huntingdon 15642, 412-864-8681; Beaver Trust Bldg., #305, 250 Insurance St., Beaver 15009, 412-728-3005; Cranberry Municipal Bldg., 2525 Rochester Rd., #207, Cranberry Township 16066, 412-772-6080; 2692 Leechburg Rd., Lower Burrell 15068, 412-335-4518; and 134 N. Mercer St., New Castle 16101, 412-654-9036.

Committees: *Commerce* (20th of 21 D): Oversight and Investigations; Telecommunications and Finance.

Group Ratings

	ADA	ACLU	COPE	CFA	LCV	CON	NSI	COC	ACU	NTLC	CHC
1994	50	26	100	80	67	28	50	33	43	21	57
1993	65	—	92	70	50	65	—	30	25	—	—

National Journal Ratings

	1993 LIB — 1993 CONS			1994 LIB — 1994 CONS		
Economic	64%	—	34%	73%	—	17%
Social	42%	—	58%	42%	—	57%
Foreign	70%	—	26%	64%	—	33%

Key Votes of the 103d Congress

1. Clinton Deficit Plan	Y	3. Brady Handgun Purchase	N	5. Lmt. UN Cmnd. of Forces	N
2. NAFTA	N	4. Strike Race/Death Pnlty.	Y	6. Cut Missile Funds	Y

Key Votes of the 104th Congress

1. Congressional Compliance	Y	6. Reform Crime Grant	N	11. Loser Pays Court Reform	N
2. Balanced Budget Amndmt.	N	7. National Security Act	N	12. Product Liability Reform	N
3. Bar Unfunded Mandates	Y	8. Moratorium on Regs.	N	13. Welfare Reform	N
4. Pass Line Item Veto	N	9. Risk Assessment on Regs.	N	14. Term Limits Amndmt.	N
5. Relax Exclusionary Rule	Y	10. Expnd. Priv. Prop. Rights	N	15. Tax Cuts	N

Election Results

1994 general	Ron Klink (D)	119,115	(64%)	($467,285)
	Ed Peglow (R)	66,509	(36%)	($88,576)
1994 primary	Ron Klink (D)	unopposed		
1992 general	Ron Klink (D)	186,684	(79%)	($240,419)
	Gordon R. Johnston (R)	48,484	(20%)	($13,993)
	Other	2,754	(1%)	

FIFTH DISTRICT

North central Pennsylvania—isolated from the rest of the country by chains of mountains, off the main east-west rail and highway lines until the 1970s—is one of those empty spaces that make even the northeastern states seem lightly populated to someone used to the densely packed terrain of Western Europe or East Asia. In narrow valleys, pressed tightly by mountains and fast-flowing rivers, connected by roads that switch back and wind precariously over mountains, there are few population concentrations. The largest is in the Nittany Valley, the home of Pennsylvania State University, long known for its powerful football teams coached by Joe Paterno. This is one major node of the 5th Congressional District, which includes the geographically largest swath of this empty quarter. Another is to the west, around Oil City, where Colonel Edwin Drake sunk the first successful oil well in 1859, and where Pennsylvania crude is still an economic asset; and Lewisburg, home of Bucknell University and one of the more famous federal prisons, Allenwood. The solidly built courthouses and banks in the center of each county seat testify to the long history of prosperity in this part of the country. Yet today, even with the main east-west truck line, Interstate 80, it is a low-wage area. The 5th remains a rural and small-town district, populated mainly by descendants of the English stock farmers who moved here in the early 19th century. It is one part of America that no later wave of immigration has reached.

Pennsylvania's Republican tradition goes back to the Civil War and remains strong here. State College has sometimes trended Democratic (despite Paterno's Republicanism), and Bill Clinton did not run far behind George Bush here in 1992.

The congressman from the 5th District is Bill Clinger, a Republican first elected in 1978, the same year as Newt Gingrich. He is now chairman of the far-flung Government Reform and Oversight Committee, which in 1995 absorbed the defunct District of Columbia and Post Office and Civil Service Committees. Clinger is from the town of Warren. He served in the Navy during the Korean war, practiced law and worked in the Economic Development Administration in the 1970s. Returning home, he ran for Congress in 1978 and beat a Democratic incumbent. Despite his moderate demeanor, his voting record has been rather conservative. He also is the third-ranking member of the Transportation and Infrastructure Committee and has spent much time on local issues and projects. He got the upper Allegheny designated a Wild and Scenic River. He stopped a Clinton Administration move to cut in half the timber harvest in the Allegheny National Forest. He sought to require "rural community impact statements" for proposed hazardous waste landfills and incinerators, to keep East Coast waste out of central Pennsylvania, and he passed an anti-backhauling bill, barring trucks from using the same containers to carry garbage in one direction and food in the other.

On Government Reform and Oversight and its predecessor, Clinger labored in vain for years on issues little noticed. Suddenly, with Republicans in control, his causes became central and successful. They included prohibition of unfunded mandates, the line-item veto, paperwork reduction, regulatory moratorium and reform—all passed by the House in the first 100 days of the 104th Congress, with Clinger taking a lead role in each case. To further his goals, and with the encouragement of Speaker Gingrich, he took the unusual step of naming freshmen to head two subcommittees—David McIntosh, formerly a top aide to Dan Quayle's Competitiveness

Council, to head the regulatory reform panel, and Tom Davis of northern Virginia to handle the District of Columbia. Clinger has also taken a strong role in investigating alleged Clinton Administration scandals, including Commerce Secretary Ron Brown's finances and the White House travel office firings. He attacked Hillary Rodham Clinton's healthcare task force for meeting behind closed doors and otherwise violating open meeting laws. He criticized the Clinton drug policies because of recent rises in youth drug use. Clinger does not always take a radical tone. "We can't just abolish Cabinet-level departments without pretty careful considerations," he said. But his legislative production in just his first few months as chairman was as impressive as that of many members over a whole career.

The People: Pop. 1990: 565,736; 66% rural; 14% age 65+; 97% White; 1% Black; 1% Asian; 1% Hispanic origin. Voting age pop.: 431,401; 1% Black; 1% Hispanic origin. Households: 60% married couple families; 27% married couple fams. w. children; 31% college educ.; median household income: $23,934; per capita income: $10,946; median gross rent: $334; median house value: $47,800.

1992 Presidential Vote			1988 Presidential Vote		
Bush (R)	89,385	(41%)	Bush (R)	113,978	(60%)
Clinton (D)	78,057	(36%)	Dukakis (D)	76,882	(40%)
Perot (I)	48,100	(22%)			

Rep. William F. (Bill) Clinger, Jr. (R)

Elected 1978; b. Apr. 4, 1929, Warren; home, Warren; Johns Hopkins U., B.A. 1951, U. of VA, LL.B. 1965; Presbyterian; married (Julia).

Career: Navy, 1951–55; Marketing, Blair Co., 1955–62; Practicing atty., 1965–75, 1977–78; Chief Cnsl., Econ. Devel. Admin., U.S. Dept. of Commerce, 1975–77.

DC Office: 2160 RHOB 20515, 202-225-5121; Fax: 202-225-4681.

District Offices: 315 S. Allen St., #116, State College 16801, 814-238-1776; and 605 Integra Bank Bldg., Warren 16365, 814-726-3910.

Committees: *Government Reform & Oversight* (Chmn. of 27 R). *Transportation and Infrastructure* (3rd of 33 R): Aviation; Surface Transportation.

Group Ratings

	ADA	ACLU	COPE	CFA	LCV	CON	NSI	COC	ACU	NTLC	CHC
1994	15	16	33	40	6	53	100	100	95	88	79
1993	5	—	18	14	45	65	—	100	80	—	—

National Journal Ratings

	1993 LIB — 1993 CONS			1994 LIB — 1994 CONS		
Economic	23%	—	77%	26%	—	70%
Social	32%	—	67%	27%	—	73%
Foreign	17%	—	76%	33%	—	66%

Key Votes of the 103d Congress

1. Clinton Deficit Plan	N	3. Brady Handgun Purchase	N	5. Lmt. UN Cmnd. of Forces	Y
2. NAFTA	Y	4. Strike Race/Death Pnlty.	Y	6. Cut Missile Funds	N

Key Votes of the 104th Congress

1. Congressional Compliance Y	6. Reform Crime Grant Y	11. Loser Pays Court Reform Y
2. Balanced Budget Amndmt. Y	7. National Security Act Y	12. Product Liability Reform Y
3. Bar Unfunded Mandates Y	8. Moratorium on Regs. Y	13. Welfare Reform Y
4. Pass Line Item Veto Y	9. Risk Assessment on Regs. Y	14. Term Limits Amndmt. Y
5. Relax Exclusionary Rule Y	10. Expnd. Priv. Prop. Rights Y	15. Tax Cuts Y

Election Results

1994 general	William F. (Bill) Clinger, Jr. (R)...... unopposed		($340,709)
1994 primary	William F. (Bill) Clinger, Jr. (R)......... 45,621	(80%)	
	Larry P. Gourley (R).................. 11,755	(20%)	
1992 general	William F. (Bill) Clinger, Jr. (R)...... unopposed		($266,090)

SIXTH DISTRICT

Largely settled in the 18th century by Quaker townsmen, Welsh farmers, German peasants and members of pietistic sects who became known as the Pennsylvania Dutch, the gentle hills of southeastern Pennsylvania were America's first polyglot interior. A diverse lot looking for tolerance in the area above Philadelphia and the Delaware River and below the first chains of the Appalachians, they found a land that yielded up riches, first in crops, then in ironworking and other industry. In time this civilization poured over the mountain chains, where the farmers were rough-hewn and more violence-prone, and where the towns existed solely to mine rich veins of anthracite and bituminous coal, the primary energy source of late 19th and early 20th century America. These mountain towns were less orderly, filled with tough-talking miners and factory workers who stayed menacingly in the background unless a character stumbled into the wrong roadhouse at night or the wrong diner at dawn: this was the Pennsylvania John O'Hara grew up in and described in his 1930s and 1940s novels and stories.

The area was linked together by the Reading Railroad in 1842 and became one of America's prime industrial sites for a century after. But the anthracite country around Pottsville and the hat and textile mills of Reading were left behind by the economic growth of the late 20th century. The anthracite country, nestled amid mountains, has never rebounded from the switch from coal to oil for home heating: Schuylkill County around Pottsville had 228,000 people in 1940 and 153,000 in 1990. But Reading has come back, starting in 1970, when a company called Vanity Fair began selling seconds and overruns of stockings and lingerie at wholesale prices in what had been the Berkshire Knitting Mills; this was the first of the factory outlets. Reading was home to some 300 outlets by 1992, selling deep-discounted goods on the polished wood floors of converted brick mills, bringing in more than half a billion dollars a year, generating 5,000 jobs and 2,000 motel rooms.

The 6th Congressional District includes Berks and Schuylkill Counties centered on Reading and Pottsville, plus an almost unconnected sliver of Northumberland County, an industrial area between mountains and the upper Susquehanna River. It is politically divided between the rough mining tradition of the anthracite country and the quietism of the Pennsylvania Dutch. For three decades, this has been a potentially marginal district, but it was represented for 24 years by Democrat Gus Yatron, who chose to retire in 1992. The obvious successor was state Senator Michael O'Pake, who kept Berks and Schuylkill together during redistricting; but he decided not to run either.

The congressman now is Tim Holden, a Democrat who won close contests in 1992 and was reelected in Republican 1994. Holden comes from a political family from the coal mining hamlet of St. Clair; his great-grandfather was a coal miner who founded the forerunner to the United Mine Workkers, and his father served four terms as Schuylkill County commissioner. Holden gained fame as a football player; he says he has been around athletics all his life and has always gone to church and fire company block parties. In 1985, at age 28, he became the first Democrat to be elected Schuylkill County sheriff in 75 years; he was reelected with 75%. Holden and his 1992 opponent, Republican John Jones III, could have been two characters from O'Hara. Jones is from one of those families who seem to have been running things since O'Hara's times, keeping the mines open and unstruck and keeping the county Republican in most elections. He went to boarding school, became a lawyer and runs a family business operating public golf courses. Jones called Holden "idealess, clueless" and called for term limits and congressional salary cuts; Holden said he represented "the hardworking men and women" of the district and endorsed magnetic levitation trains. In culturally conservative but economically polarized Schuylkill County, this appeal sold, and, despite winning Republican margins for other offices, Holden won 52%–48%.

Holden got a seat on the Agriculture Committee, though this area has few subsidized crops. He compiled a record fairly liberal on economics and moderate on cultural and foreign policy; he opposed the North American Free Trade Agreement and the Clinton healthcare plan. In the 1994 election, he got lucky and benefited from disarray in the Republican Party. The party-endorsed candidate, Carl Cronrath, dropped out of the primary due to illness, but his name remained on the ballot, and he won. Republican party officials then gave the nomination to real estate broker Frederick Levering, who had served as a member of the Wyomissing Borough Council for one year. Levering pointed to his business background and his membership in two conservation groups as evidence of his well-balanced background. But Holden won 68% in Schuylkill County, plus narrow margins elsewhere, for a 57%–43% victory.

The People: Pop. 1990: 565,923; 44% rural; 17% age 65+; 92% White; 2% Black; 1% Asian; 2% Other; 3% Hispanic origin. Voting age pop.: 435,058; 2% Black; 2% Hispanic origin. Households: 59% married couple families; 25% married couple fams. w. children; 28% college educ.; median household income: $28,766; per capita income: $13,349; median gross rent: $367; median house value: $65,900.

1992 Presidential Vote

Bush (R)	90,140	(41%)
Clinton (D)	78,776	(36%)
Perot (I)	50,333	(23%)

1988 Presidential Vote

Bush (R)	117,434	(62%)
Dukakis (D)	73,464	(38%)

Rep. Tim Holden (D)

Elected 1992; b. Mar. 5, 1957, Pottsville; home, St. Clair; U. of Richmond, 1976–78, Bloomsburg St. U., B.A. 1980; Catholic; married (Gwen).

Career: Insurance broker/real estate agent, Holden Insurance Agency, 1980–85; Schuylkill Cnty. Sheriff, 1985–92.

DC Office: 1421 LHOB 20515, 202-225-5546; Fax: 202-226-0996.

District Offices: Berks Cnty. Ctr., 633 Court St., Reading 19801, 610-371-9931; Meridian Bank Bldg., #303, 101 N. Centre St., Pottsville 17901, 717-662-4212; and Northumberland Cnty. Cthse., Market Sq., Sunbury 17801, 717-988-1902.

Committees: *Agriculture* (14th of 22 D): Livestock, Dairy and Poultry; Resource Conservation, Research and Forestry.

Group Ratings

	ADA	ACLU	COPE	CFA	LCV	CON	NSI	COC	ACU	NTLC	CHC
1994	45	22	100	60	67	36	60	58	43	39	64
1993	60	—	92	70	77	74	—	27	38	—	—

National Journal Ratings

	1993 LIB	—	1993 CONS		1994 LIB	—	1994 CONS
Economic	57%	—	42%		73%	—	17%
Social	31%	—	68%		41%	—	58%
Foreign	87%	—	7%		51%	—	47%

Key Votes of the 103d Congress

1. Clinton Deficit Plan	Y	3. Brady Handgun Purchase	N	5. Lmt. UN Cmnd. of Forces	N
2. NAFTA	N	4. Strike Race/Death Pnlty.	Y	6. Cut Missile Funds	Y

Key Votes of the 104th Congress

1. Congressional Compliance	Y	6. Reform Crime Grant	N	11. Loser Pays Court Reform	N
2. Balanced Budget Amndmt.	N	7. National Security Act	Y	12. Product Liability Reform	Y
3. Bar Unfunded Mandates	Y	8. Moratorium on Regs.	N	13. Welfare Reform	N
4. Pass Line Item Veto	Y	9. Risk Assessment on Regs.	Y	14. Term Limits Amndmt.	Y
5. Relax Exclusionary Rule	Y	10. Expnd. Priv. Prop. Rights	Y	15. Tax Cuts	Y

Election Results

1994 general	Tim Holden (D)	90,023	(57%)	($675,274)
	Fred Levering (R).....................	68,610	(43%)	($132,889)
1994 primary	Tim Holden (D)	unopposed		
1992 general	Tim Holden (D)	108,312	(52%)	($284,349)
	John E. Jones III (R)	99,694	(48%)	($442,058)

SEVENTH DISTRICT

The close-in suburbs of the great eastern cities are homes to some of the most curious and most long-lasting political machines in America. They are Republican; they conduct business in the accents of ordinary people, ethnic as well as WASP; they have a tolerance for patronage, and for what city reform liberals would call corruption, that is sharply at odds with their embodiment of middle-class morality; they are old, going back to the days when political machines were as much part of the urban landscape as trolley lines or overhead electrical wires; and, unlike most big-city Democratic machines, they are still in business. One such machine is the War Board of Pennsylvania's Delaware County. This is a diverse area, mostly but not entirely white, predominantly Catholic where it was predominantly Protestant two generations ago. Its housing stock is aging but still well-maintained; its population is above average in income but differs from the affluent Main Line commuter towns. People here treasure traditional cultural values but also feel pinched by family obligations and worry about retirement; they have deep roots in greater Philadelphia, but also deep fears about crime in nearby city neighborhoods.

The 7th Congressional District includes almost all of Delaware County, except for a few towns appended to Philadelphia districts, and extends north to include Main Line suburbs and King of Prussia, the edge city where the Schuylkill Expressway intersects the Pennsylvania Turnpike. This remains a solidly Republican district, enough so to have stuck with George Bush in 1992.

The congressman from the 7th is Curt Weldon, a Republican backed by the War Board and with anything but an aristocratic pedigree. A teacher and personnel trainer, he first came to public attention as mayor of Marcus Hook, Pennsylvania's southernmost town on the Delaware River, the home of oil tank farms and a rusty-looking steel mill. Weldon was elected to the county council, ran in 1984 against liberal Democrat Bob Edgar (who got to Congress when the War Board split 10 years before), lost by 412 votes, and ran again (with no primary opposition) in 1986, this time successfully, when Edgar ran unsuccessfully for the Senate.

Weldon prides himself on attending every Eagle Scout induction in the district and just about every conceivable other event; as one newspaper wrote, Weldon seems to be "everywhere." He fought the closing of the Philadelphia Navy Yard and sought new work for it, including dismantling Russian ships. He has been a big cheerleader for the V-22 Osprey tilt-rotor aircraft—one of whose major contractors, Boeing Vertol, is in the district—and kept it funded for five years. He favors closure and relocation of an Army reserve facility in Marcus Hook and is working to attract business to the site. Weldon takes on national issues as well. As an active member of the National Security Committee, he strongly supports missile defense and opposes Clinton-style technology reinvestment—positions that have taken on new importance now that he chairs the Military Research and Development Subcommittee. With other Republicans, he started a Hollow Forces Update Committee to monitor military readiness. He is concerned about ocean dumping, especially dumping of nuclear waste by nations of the former Soviet Union; he claims that there is 700,000 times more radiation in Murmansk harbor in waste containment than was emitted in the Three Mile Island accident.

Weldon is also interested in disaster management. He has pushed, on a bipartisan basis, for reform of the oft-troubled Federal Emergency Management Agency. And he is the founder of the Congressional Fire Services Caucus, which most members laughed at at first but then joined; it sponsored measures calling for new alarm systems in congressional offices and a new fire training center in Illinois. Weldon personally helped to put out a fire in former Speaker Jim Wright's office, and he had the satisfaction of seeing George Bush come to Delaware County in October 1992 to sign Weldon's fire service bill into law.

Weldon is a partisan Republican but not always a free-market enthusiast; like Pennsylvanian Republicans of yore, he tends to support trade restrictions. Politically, the one threat to his tenure came when redistricting put him in with another suburban Republican, Richard Schulze, in 1992. But after 18 years in office Schulze decided to retire. Weldon seems a good fit for the 7th, and in the 1990s has been reelected with 65% to 70% of the vote. He has a promising future as a power-broker in the Republican-controlled House.

The People: Pop. 1990: 565,815; 5% rural; 15% age 65+; 93% White; 4% Black; 2% Asian; 1% Hispanic origin. Voting age pop.: 440,656; 4% Black; 1% Hispanic origin. Households: 60% married couple families; 26% married couple fams. w. children; 53% college educ.; median household income: $41,710; per capita income: $20,175; median gross rent: $568; median house value: $133,000.

1992 Presidential Vote			1988 Presidential Vote		
Bush (R)	124,751	(43%)	Bush (R)	167,029	(64%)
Clinton (D)	111,511	(39%)	Dukakis (D)	94,532	(36%)
Perot (I)	49,798	(17%)			

Rep. Curt Weldon (R)

Elected 1986; b. July 22, 1947, Marcus Hook; home, Aston; West Chester St. Col., B.A. 1969; Protestant; married (Mary).

Career: Elem. schl. teacher, Vice principal, 1969–76; Dir., Training and Manpower Devel., CIGNA Corp., 1976–81; Marcus Hook Mayor, 1977–82; Delaware Cnty. Cncl., 1981–86, Chmn. 1985–86.

DC Office: 2452 RHOB 20515, 202-225-2011; Fax: 202-225-8137.

District Offices: 1554 Garrett Rd., Upper Darby 19082, 610-259-0700.

Committees: *National Security* (7th of 30 R): Military Readiness; Military Research and Development (Chmn.). *Science* (6th of 27 R): Basic Research; Energy and Environment.

Group Ratings

	ADA	ACLU	COPE	CFA	LCV	CON	NSI	COC	ACU	NTLC	CHC
1994	10	13	33	20	63	70	100	92	74	81	79
1993	25	—	55	40	57	91	—	55	73	—	—

National Journal Ratings

	1993 LIB — 1993 CONS		1994 LIB — 1994 CONS	
Economic	32%	66%	24%	75%
Social	24%	76%	32%	67%
Foreign	9%	85%	30%	67%

Key Votes of the 103d Congress

1. Clinton Deficit Plan	N	3. Brady Handgun Purchase	Y	5. Lmt. UN Cmnd. of Forces	Y
2. NAFTA	N	4. Strike Race/Death Pnlty.	Y	6. Cut Missile Funds	N

Key Votes of the 104th Congress

1. Congressional Compliance	Y	6. Reform Crime Grant	Y	11. Loser Pays Court Reform	Y
2. Balanced Budget Amndmt.	Y	7. National Security Act	Y	12. Product Liability Reform	Y
3. Bar Unfunded Mandates	Y	8. Moratorium on Regs.	Y	13. Welfare Reform	Y
4. Pass Line Item Veto	Y	9. Risk Assessment on Regs.	Y	14. Term Limits Amndmt.	Y
5. Relax Exclusionary Rule	Y	10. Expnd. Priv. Prop. Rights	Y	15. Tax Cuts	Y

Election Results

1994 general	Curt Weldon (R)	137,480	(70%)	($349,639)
	Sara Nichols (D)	59,845	(30%)	($149,028)
1994 primary	Curt Weldon (R)	59,109	(80%)	
	Deborah LaFountain (R)	14,497	(20%)	
1992 general	Curt Weldon (R)	180,648	(66%)	($565,974)
	Frank Daly (D)	91,623	(34%)	($173,865)
	Other	1,627	(1%)	

EIGHTH DISTRICT

One of William Penn's three original settlements, Bucks County had a split personality from the beginning: it was a paradise of bucolic hills and creeks running into the Delaware, and then in 1727 James Logan, Penn's secretary, established the Durham Furnace iron works there. In the 1920s, the county's well-settled farmland, old fieldstone houses and covered bridges in its northern parts captured the imagination of writers and artists, attracting a theatrical crowd—Oscar Hammerstein, Moss Hart, Dorothy Parker, S. J. Perelman—who gave it a certain celebrity status. After World War II, its location between Philadelphia and industrial Trenton, New Jersey, brought industrial Bucks to the forefront. The ocean-navigable Delaware River and several rail lines resulted in huge new developments: U.S. Steel's Fairless Works, one of the few big postwar steel plants, down by the river, and the Levitt organization's second Levittown, in what had been farmland and swamp between U.S. 13 and U.S. 1. In recent years, parts of the district have experienced industrial and economic problems, as demonstrated by massive layoffs at the USX Fairless Works.

Politically, Bucks County, like all of Pennsylvania, was once solidly Republican: it was the home of Senator Joseph Grundy, longtime head of the Pennsylvania Manufacturers Association, who opposed the 1930 Smoot-Hawley tariff on the grounds that it was not protectionist enough. Development in Bucks came after the New Deal, unlike other suburban Philadelphia counties where most blue-collar immigration occurred years ago, when county political organizations were ready to enroll new residents in their party. So Lower Bucks, around the Fairless Works and Levittown, with its tightly-packed homes filled with ethnic Democrats, is fairly solidly

Democratic. And Upper Bucks, fast-growing in the 1980s and once again attracting trendy New Yorkers such as Calvin Klein and Billy Joel, is Republican but environment-conscious. Perkasie, for example, encourages recycling by requiring residents to pay $1.50 for every 40 pounds of trash picked up from their homes.

The 8th Congressional District includes all of Bucks County plus Horsham Township in Montgomery County. With its boundaries changing only slightly during much of the past two decades, the district for a dozen years was one of the country's prime marginal districts and still is closely contested in statewide contests. But it seems to have returned to its Republican roots in House races.

The congressman here is Republican James Greenwood, an area native who worked for a state legislator and was a social worker in the 1970s, supervising emotionally troubled youths at a school in Langhorne. As a county caseworker, he helped decide when to place abused children with foster families. He was elected to the state House in 1980 and the state Senate in 1986. In 1992 he ran against Peter Kostmayer, an environment-minded, defense-cutting liberal, who first won the seat in 1976 at age 30, lost it in 1980 but won it back two years later, and held it with varying margins through 1990. Kostmayer concentrated on local environmental issues and was able to raise money nationally with his liberal environmental and foreign policy positions. While he ran an amazingly good constituency service operation, by 1992 he was plainly in trouble. He had at least 50 overdrafts on the House bank and there were charges of more, including a $23,000 check to his father. Greenwood won with 52%, after spending much of the fall reminding voters of Kostameyer's bounced checks and charging that the incumbent was out of touch with his district.

Greenwood came to Washington a fervent tax-cutter and budget-shrinker, but also as an experienced legislator, with a deliberate approach to the job: "You do it by paying attention to detail. You do it by amendments in committee . . . And you do it by offering good ideas that are hard to resist." As a House moderate, he supported the 1994 crime bill, as well as the Penny-Kasich spending cuts. In February 1995, he joined 24 House Republicans breaking party ranks to oppose making a priority of a national missile defense system. Elected on a 10-point health reform plan of his own, Greenwood won a seat on the Commerce Committee, which had a piece of health reform jurisdiction. He refused to endorse either his own party's leadership health plan or the Clinton Administration plan and joined efforts to seek a bipartisan alternative, but the panel eventually deadlocked and was unable to produce a comprehensive proposal. Greenwood also pushed a plan to allow major waste-recipient states, including Pennsylvania, to reduce the amount of waste they accept, as well as a proposal urging the Centers for Disease Control and Prevention and other agencies to study the incidence of traumatic brain injuries.

Local Democrats hoped that Kostmayer would run again in 1994. But he did not, and they could not come up with a candidate of his skills or money-raising ability. Greenwood won 66%–27%, an impressive win in a district held by Democrats for 14 of the past 20 years.

The People: Pop. 1990: 565,820; 18% rural; 11% age 65+; 94% White; 3% Black; 2% Asian; 1% Other; 2% Hispanic origin. Voting age pop.: 421,289; 3% Black; 1% Hispanic origin. Households: 66% married couple families; 32% married couple fams. w. children; 49% college educ.; median household income: $43,483; per capita income: $18,374; median gross rent: $608; median house value: $139,700.

1992 Presidential Vote			1988 Presidential Vote		
Clinton (D)	101,630	(39%)	Bush (R)	133,893	(61%)
Bush (R)	99,269	(38%)	Dukakis (D)	85,452	(39%)
Perot (I)	56,261	(22%)			

Rep. Jim Greenwood (R)

Elected 1992; b. May 4, 1951, Philadelphia; home, Erwinna; Dickinson Col., B.A. 1973; Protestant; married (Christina).

Career: Legis. Asst., PA Rep. John Renninger, 1972–76; Caseworker, Bucks Cnty. Child & Youth Social Svcs., 1977–80; PA House of Reps., 1980–86; PA Senate, 1986–93.

DC Office: 430 CHOB 20515, 202-225-4276; Fax: 202-225-9511.

District Offices: 69 E. Oxford Ave., Doylestown 18901, 215-348-7511; and One Oxford Valley, #800, Langhorne 19047, 215-752-7711.

Committees: *Economic & Educational Opportunities* (15th of 24 R): Early Childhood, Youth and Families; Workforce Protections. *Commerce* (15th of 26 R): Commerce, Trade and Hazardous Materials; Health and Environment; Oversight and Investigations.

Group Ratings

	ADA	ACLU	COPE	CFA	LCV	CON	NSI	COC	ACU	NTLC	CHC
1994	20	27	11	30	44	62	100	100	70	93	57
1993	20	—	8	30	71	85	—	82	83	—	—

National Journal Ratings

	1993 LIB — 1993 CONS		1994 LIB — 1994 CONS	
Economic	14%	— 80%	21%	— 76%
Social	41%	— 58%	39%	— 60%
Foreign	31%	— 67%	38%	— 62%

Key Votes of the 103d Congress

1. Clinton Deficit Plan	N	3. Brady Handgun Purchase Y	5. Lmt. UN Cmnd. of Forces Y
2. NAFTA	Y	4. Strike Race/Death Pnlty. Y	6. Cut Missile Funds N

Key Votes of the 104th Congress

1. Congressional Compliance Y	6. Reform Crime Grant Y	11. Loser Pays Court Reform Y
2. Balanced Budget Amndmt. Y	7. National Security Act Y	12. Product Liability Reform Y
3. Bar Unfunded Mandates Y	8. Moratorium on Regs. Y	13. Welfare Reform Y
4. Pass Line Item Veto Y	9. Risk Assessment on Regs. Y	14. Term Limits Amndmt. Y
5. Relax Exclusionary Rule Y	10. Expnd. Priv. Prop. Rights N	15. Tax Cuts Y

Election Results

1994 general	Jim Greenwood (R).................	110,499	(66%)	($360,600)
	John P. Murray (D)....................	44,559	(27%)	($29,945)
	Jay Russell (Lib)......................	7,925	(5%)	
	Others..............................	4,191	(3%)	
1994 primary	Jim Greenwood (R).................	unopposed		
1992 general	Jim Greenwood (R).................	129,593	(52%)	($717,249)
	Peter H. Kostmayer (D)..............	114,095	(46%)	($1,242,355)
	Other..............................	5,850	(2%)	

NINTH DISTRICT

Like a series of vertebrae through central Pennsylvania, the Appalachian mountain chain has been a formidable barrier throughout most of the state's history. Up close the mountains look tantalizingly low: you imagine that you could hike over them in an hour or so. But they are much more daunting than they seem. The colonials and British regulars led by General Braddock to defeat near Pittsburgh in 1754 found it hard going, despite guidance from George Washington; 19th century pioneers in Conestoga wagons found it not much easier, for there are few gaps in the ridges and unless you build a tunnel you have to climb over the top.

During the 18th Century, the mountains provided Quaker Pennsylvania with a rampart against Indian attacks and allowed the commonwealth to become the richest and most populous of the colonies. But in the 19th Century, when people wanted to open up and trade with the vast interior, the mountains proved to be a barrier, so they went over New York's Erie Canal and New York Central Railroad instead. It took the aggressive capitalists who built the Pennsylvania Railroad to get trains over these ridges and a nation facing war in 1940 to build the first highway, the Pennsylvania Turnpike, that could dependably get trucks over them. Today, the old towns look much as they did 60 years ago; the farmhouses and red barns still sit on rolling hills in the shadow of the ridges, isolated and out of touch with the pulsing rhythms of the America of the 1990s.

Pennsylvania's 9th Congressional District lies wholly within these mountains. This part of the Alleghenies (the term is often used interchangeably with Appalachians in Pennsylvania), was settled by poor Scottish and Ulster Irish farmers just after the Revolutionary War. They were fiercely independent and proud, as the Whiskey Rebellion demonstrated—corn was not an article of commerce out here unless distilled into easily portable, if not very potable, alcohol. The settlers worked their hardscrabble farms and built little towns. The 9th is mostly not coal country and was thus spared the boom-bust cycles of northeastern Pennsylvania and West Virginia. This was an important area for the Pennsylvania Railroad, however. Near Altoona was the railroad's famous Horseshoe Curve, and in Altoona the nation's largest car yards were built. As rail transportation became less important and the prosperous Pennsylvania Railroad became the bankrupt Penn Central, Altoona's population fell from 82,000 in 1930 to 52,000 in 1990; it is 99% white, the highest percentage of any metro area.

This part of Pennsylvania has been solidly Republican since the election of 1860 and has not come close to electing a Democrat to Congress for years. Today its congressman is Bud Shuster, chairman of the House Transportation and Infrastructure Committee, formerly Public Works and Transportation. Shuster made his fortune building a computer business, then settled in the southern Pennsylvania mountains. He became interested in local affairs, ran for Congress and beat the favorite, a local state senator, in the 1972 Republican primary. In the 1970s, Shuster was a hard-driving partisan and conservative firebrand, the House's most vociferous opponent of the automobile air bag, and chairman of the Republican Policy Committee until 1980. Then he ran for minority whip against Trent Lott and lost. He abruptly shifted course and spent most of his time on Public Works, working with Democrats to craft bipartisan highway and water projects bills with national scope—and with plenty of pork for the 9th District. Shuster has obviously taken a long journey from doctrinaire conservatism, although his work is arguably in line with the 19th century Republican tradition of subsidizing canals and railroads and the World War II subsidies for the Pennsylvania Turnpike—transportation arteries that made most commerce possible in these mountains. There are plenty of local monuments to him in central Pennsylvania, which budget-conscious Republicans might find objectionable in the future— U.S. 220 between Altoona and the Turnpike, christened the Bud Shuster Highway by Democratic Governor Bob Casey; the $934 million in new projects Pennsylvania got from the 1991 Intermodal Surface Transportation Act (ISTEA), including $287 million for 13 projects in the 9th District; and the nation's first federally funded bus testing center, in Blair County.

But Shuster is also a serious national policy maker. ISTEA was landmark legislation, setting policy on many transportation issues. Shuster, working with then-chairman Norman Mineta of California, helped deregulate interstate trucking, phase out the Interstate Commerce Commission and pass the National Highway System through the House. He also helped delay reauthorization of the Clean Water Act and the Superfund program while Democrats were in control—all actions consistent with conservative principles. As chairman, Shuster set out an ambitious program with a tightly organized schedule designed to produce bills ready fo floor action from every subcommittee by the 101st day of the Congress, right after the Contract With America. One goal is designation of the National Highway System, with an October 1995 deadline. Otherwise, $6.5 billion stops flowing to the states. Another is a new Clean Water Act, with a less-stringent definition of wetlands, which is designed to appeal to the growing number of property-rights advocates. Others are Superfund reform, Coast Guard reauthorization and final abolition of the ICC. Shuster says he has an open mind on privatization of air traffic control. His most ambitious goal is to take off-budget the four transportation trust funds (highway, aviation, inland waterways, harbor maintenance) now totalling $33 billion. Shuster argues that these accounts funded by user-fees should be applied to dedicated purposes, not used to balance the budget, and he points out that most Republicans in the past have voted to take them off-budget. It is "a hypocrisy test" for them, he says, citing 1987 arguments from Newt Gingrich. Opponents argue that this would lead to funding of unworthy projects and larger deficits.

Since 1988, Schuster has been reelected without opposition in the primary or general elections.

The People: Pop. 1990: 565,858; 70% rural; 15% age 65+; 98% White; 1% Black. Voting age pop.: 425,141; 1% Black. Households: 63% married couple families; 28% married couple fams. w. children; 23% college educ.; median household income: $24,309; per capita income: $11,229; median gross rent: $305; median house value: $49,200.

1992 Presidential Vote			1988 Presidential Vote		
Bush (R)	97,764	(48%)	Bush (R)	117,717	(64%)
Clinton (D)	66,923	(33%)	Dukakis (D)	65,663	(36%)
Perot (I)	40,200	(20%)			

Rep. E. G. (Bud) Shuster (R)

Elected 1972; b. Jan. 23, 1932, Glassport; home, Everett; U. of Pittsburgh, B.S. 1954, Duquesne U., M.B.A. 1960, American U., Ph.D. 1967; United Church of Christ; married (Patricia).

Career: Army, 1954–56; Vice Pres., Electronic Computer Div., RCA, 1965–8; Founder and Chmn., computer software co., 1968–72.

DC Office: 2188 RHOB 20515, 202-225-2431.

District Offices: RD 2, Box 711, Altoona 16601, 814-946-1653; and 179 E. Queen St., Chambersburg 17201, 717-264-8308; 1214 Oldtown Rd., #4, Clearfield 16830, 814-765-9106.

Committees: *Transportation & Infrastructure* (Chmn. of 33 R): *Intelligence (Permanent Select)* (7th of 9 R): Human Intelligence, Analysis, and Counterintelligence; Technical and Tactical Intelligence.

Group Ratings

	ADA	ACLU	COPE	CFA	LCV	CON	NSI	COC	ACU	NTLC	CHC
1994	0	13	0	20	0	58	100	92	100	96	100
1993	10	—	8	10	29	69	—	70	96	—	—

National Journal Ratings

	1993 LIB — 1993 CONS			1994 LIB — 1994 CONS		
Economic	20%	—	77%	26%	—	70%
Social	18%	—	82%	0%	—	89%
Foreign	0%	—	91%	0%	—	88%

Key Votes of the 103d Congress

1. Clinton Deficit Plan	N	3. Brady Handgun Purchase	*	5. Lmt. UN Cmnd. of Forces	Y
2. NAFTA	N	4. Strike Race/Death Pnlty.	Y	6. Cut Missile Funds	N

Key Votes of the 104th Congress

1. Congressional Compliance	Y	6. Reform Crime Grant	Y	11. Loser Pays Court Reform	Y
2. Balanced Budget Amndmt.	Y	7. National Security Act	Y	12. Product Liability Reform	Y
3. Bar Unfunded Mandates	Y	8. Moratorium on Regs.	Y	13. Welfare Reform	Y
4. Pass Line Item Veto	N	9. Risk Assessment on Regs.	Y	14. Term Limits Amndmt.	Y
5. Relax Exclusionary Rule	Y	10. Expnd. Priv. Prop. Rights	Y	15. Tax Cuts	Y

Election Results

1994 general	E. G. (Bud) Shuster (R)	unopposed	($776,175)
1994 primary	E. G. (Bud) Shuster (R)	unopposed	
1992 general	E. G. (Bud) Shuster (R)	unopposed	($556,385)

TENTH DISTRICT

"Coal is the theme song of this city in the hills," the *WPA Guide* said of Scranton 50 years ago. But as those words were written, the anthracite kingdom was dying, or dead. Demand for hard coal as a home heating fuel started to decline in the 1920s and plummeted in the 1940s; the three major anthracite counties fell in population from 991,000 in 1930 to 699,000 in 1990, and Scranton's Lackawanna County fell from 310,000 to 219,000. In the process, the coal dust and air pollution vanished, the ethnic groups—Irish and Poles, Ukrainians and Welsh—became less distinctive, and what had been communities of young families became communities of old people. In the 1960s and 1970s, there was an influx of textile and apparel mills, bringing low-wage, non-union jobs to what had once been a high-wage, unionized area. But the anthracite kingdom, created by unbridled free enterprise, had continued to look to government for sustenance.

That is the basis of the politics of the 10th Congressional District, which is centered on Scranton and includes most of the northeast corner of Pennsylvania—green hills with little towns in crevassed river valleys, criss-crossed by giant viaducts built for the railroads linking coal and iron mines with great cities' factories, the outer-borough New Yorkers' resorts of the Poconos and new condominiums and vacation homes springing up on inexpensive real estate. Historically, this is very Republican territory; the anthracite mines brought some Democrats, but their numbers have declined. The 10th went narrowly for George Bush in 1992. But congressional politics here depends less on party than on pork. For years the benefactor of the anthracite kingdom was Daniel Flood of neighboring Wilkes-Barre and the 11th District, an Appropriations subcommittee chairman. When scandal forced him to resign in 1980, the new benefactor was Joseph McDade, the Appropriations Committee Republican with the most seniority, who was himself indicted in May 1992 but has remained an active House member.

McDade is short, chunky, white-haired, good-humored. He comes from a Scranton Irish family and was city solicitor when he was first elected to the House in 1962. Those were the days when Republicans could hold such seats only by propitiating organized labor with liberal votes. McDade's predecessor, William Scranton, had done so and was elected governor in 1962. On Appropriations, McDade naturally worked with members of both parties to bring home the bacon. He and fellow Pennsylvanian John Murtha, with the top seats on Defense Appropriations, continued Flood's law requiring the military to buy tons of unneeded and expensive Pennsylvania coal. He extended the Wilkes-Barre airport runway, got a grant to make the old Scranton train station into a luxury hotel, funded the McDade Center for Technology at the University of Scranton and got $10 million for a Military Family Institute at Marywood College. He claims credit for funding the Tobyhanna Army Depot, now the district's biggest employer. His biggest and most controversial monument is Steamtown, where the locomotive collection of a Vermont millionaire is housed in a restored railyard. McDade snuck funds into a 1986 omnibus appropriations bill and has nursed it along ever since, commanding the Park Service to spend money on a project that specialists think has no historic merit or relevance to Scranton.

McDade's 1992 indictment came after a long investigation, beginning in December 1988 when *The Wall Street Journal* detailed how he had received $45,000 in campaign contributions and speaking fees from officials involved in United Chem-Con, a company with a plant in Lancaster for which he arranged a Defense Department minority set-aside contract. It was charged that some of the employees were illegally reimbursed by the company for their campaign contributions to McDade. In May 1992, McDade was indicted on these charges and for allegedly accepting $100,000 in bribes and illegal gratuities—Lear jet trips to Florida, expense-paid vacations at posh resorts, sham "scholarships" for his son—from six defense contractors and lobbyists in the 1980s. McDade accused the prosecutor, a protegé of Senator Arlen Specter, of being politically biased; he attacked the RICO law under which he was indicted, said he was unaware of illegal contributions, and reimbursed donors for any questionable expenditures. McDade also argued that the indictment violated his constitutional immunity from prosecution for words and acts on the House floor, but a federal appeals court ruled against him in June 1994, and the Supreme Court turned down his argument in March 1995. House Republicans (unlike the Democrats) had no rule forcing McDade to step down from his ranking position on Appropriations or its Defense Subcommittee after his indictment. The Republican Conference passed such a rule in August 1993 but exempted McDade. After the Republican victory in 1994, however, the pressure from junior Republicans led Newt Gingrich to change the party's rules so that McDade could not become Appropriations chairman; Bob Livingston of Louisiana got the job instead.

McDade's legal problems have not perceptibly hurt him in the 10th District. In 1992, he not only was renominated but won the Democratic primary as a write-in; in 1994, he beat a Democrat 66%–31%. But his career is still in jeopardy from the indictment, and his popularity could suffer if Republicans' fiscal stringency prevents him from channeling money to northeast Pennsylvania as he did in the Democratic House for 32 years.

The People: Pop. 1990: 565,777; 54% rural; 17% age 65+; 98% White; 1% Black; 1% Hispanic origin. Voting age pop.: 428,610; 1% Black; 1% Hispanic origin. Households: 60% married couple families; 26% married couple fams. w. children; 33% college educ.; median household income: $25,648; per capita income: $12,005; median gross rent: $339; median house value: $70,100.

1992 Presidential Vote			**1988 Presidential Vote**		
Bush (R)	95,803	(41%)	Bush (R)	118,139	(59%)
Clinton (D)	88,193	(38%)	Dukakis (D)	83,728	(41%)
Perot (I)	46,881	(20%)			

Rep. Joseph M. McDade (R)

Elected 1962; b. Sept. 29, 1931, Scranton; home, Clarks Summit; U. of Notre Dame, B.A. 1953, U. of PA, LL.B. 1956; Catholic; married (Sarah).

Career: Clerk, Chief Fed. Judge John W. Murphy, 1956–57; Practicing atty., 1957–62; Scranton City Solicitor, 1962.

DC Office: 2107 RHOB 20515, 202-225-3731; Fax: 202-225-9594.

District Offices: 514 Scranton Life Bldg., Scranton 18503, 717-346-3834; and 240 W. Third St., #230, Williamsport 17701, 717-327-8161.

Committees: *Appropriations* (2nd of 32 R): Interior; Military Construction; National Security.

Group Ratings

	ADA	ACLU	COPE	CFA	LCV	CON	NSI	COC	ACU	NTLC	CHC
1994	20	25	38	30	14	47	90	89	83	71	64
1993	20	—	56	60	46	47	—	82	74	—	—

National Journal Ratings

	1993 LIB — 1993 CONS		1994 LIB — 1994 CONS	
Economic	40% —	60%	26% —	74%
Social	28% —	72%	32% —	68%
Foreign	17% —	83%	29% —	70%

Key Votes of the 103d Congress

1. Clinton Deficit Plan	N	3. Brady Handgun Purchase Y	5. Lmt. UN Cmnd. of Forces *
2. NAFTA	Y	4. Strike Race/Death Pnlty. *	6. Cut Missile Funds *

Key Votes of the 104th Congress

1. Congressional Compliance Y	6. Reform Crime Grant Y	11. Loser Pays Court Reform *
2. Balanced Budget Amndmt. Y	7. National Security Act Y	12. Product Liability Reform Y
3. Bar Unfunded Mandates Y	8. Moratorium on Regs. Y	13. Welfare Reform Y
4. Pass Line Item Veto *	9. Risk Assessment on Regs. Y	14. Term Limits Amndmt. N
5. Relax Exclusionary Rule Y	10. Expnd. Priv. Prop. Rights Y	15. Tax Cuts Y

Election Results

1994 general	Joseph M. McDade (R)	106,992	(66%)	($263,752)
	Daniel J. Schreffler (D).	50,635	(31%)	($12,395)
	Others	5,196	(3%)	
1994 primary	Joseph M. McDade (R)	unopposed		
1992 general	Joseph M. McDade (R)	189,414	(90%)	($343,892)
	Albert A. Smith (Lib).	20,134	(10%)	

ELEVENTH DISTRICT

One of the major industrial centers of America grew up in the 19th Century, nestled in the valley of the East Branch of the Susquehanna River, surrounded by mountain ridges. The mountains were laced with anthracite coal, the main home-heating fuel of the time. Thousands of immigrants, attracted by the high wages paid to scrape out the coal, flocked to this valley, in the chain of little cities north and south of Wilkes-Barre, named for two financial backers of the

American revolution. While the supply was endless—the area produced 40% of the world's hard coal—the demand was not. The peak year of anthracite production was 1917, and long strikes in 1922 and 1925 quickened the conversion to oil and gas. By the 1930s, the valley around Wilkes-Barre was in decline; surrounding Luzerne County's population, 445,000 in 1930, was 328,000 in 1990.

This is Pennsylvania's 11th Congressional District, including all of Luzerne County and similar land east to the town of Jim Thorpe and the Poconos and west almost to the Susquehanna. A large Democratic voting bloc—consisting of miners—has been here since the 1930s, but there also were a lot of white-collar Republicans, as well as ancestral Republicans in a myriad of occupations. While party registration gives Democrats a definite advantage, the district voted for Ronald Reagan in 1980 and 1984 and for George Bush in 1988. In 1992, Bill Clinton carried two counties but lost the rest of the district. For more than three decades, the district was represented by Daniel Flood, a mustachioed and theatrical Democrat who, from his perch on the Appropriations Committee, brought millions of federal dollars to the anthracite country. But in 1980, he resigned amid scandal, and over the next six years the 11th District had a series of bizarre elections and no less than four different congressmen of both parties, who served in their order of finish in the 1980 special election.

Now, a Democratic with deep roots in the Wilkes-Barre area, Paul Kanjorski, appears safely entrenched in the seat. He served nine years as a workmen's compensation administrative law judge and 12 years as Nanticoke city solicitor. He effectively won the seat in the 1984 primary, by pointing out that the then-incumbent congressman was traveling in Central America while flood-soaked Wilkes-Barre area residents had to boil their tap water because it was contaminated. Kanjorski held the seat in 1986 against a 25-year-old former Reagan White House aide who raised $1.3 million from Reagan connections but won only 29% of the vote. In 1994, he won easily with 67% of the vote against Jurij Podolak, a consultant for small businesses and defense contractors.

With his economically liberal and culturally moderate record and his skepticism about foreign commitments and Washington lobbyists, Kanjorski is one of those congressmen who are always looking to benefit local areas and who seem suspicious of the outside. While chairing Human Resources Subcommittee of the now-defunct Post Office and Civil Service Committee, he sharply attacked White House perquisites and expenses and called for full public disclosure of all taxpayer-financed White House spending. President Bush once apologized at a breakfast meeting for the skimpy meal and blamed Kanjorski's investigations. More recently, Kanjorski has led efforts to shut down the National Endowment for Democracy, which he said was making its own foreign policy. However, his parsimony does not apply to his own district. *The New York Times* has cited Kanjorski as a master of earmarking for capturing millions of dollars for the Earth Conservancy Applied Research Center, a public-private project for developing new technologies to reclaim the mine-ravaged northeastern area of Pennsylvania. When the Defense Department attempted to fund a technology project elsewhere, Kanjorski, in what he told the newspaper was a "straight earmark," made sure funds went to his project. *The Times* pointed out that the funding allowed a nonprofit company run by Kanjorski's brother, friends and allies to buy thousands of acres of land in the district for far less than their appraised value. During the 103rd Congress, Kanjorski used his chairmanship of the Banking Committee's Economic Growth and Credit Formation Subcommittee to push legislation reauthorizing the Economic Development Administration and streamlining the method by which government-developed technologies become available to the public. He also spearheaded efforts to create a secondary market to make loans available to small businesses, led a floor fight to bar former Iraqi soldiers from settling in the United States and established the Reinventing Government Caucus to assist the Clinton Administration in its executive branch reorganization efforts. In 1995, shorn of the majority but feisty as ever, Kanjorski entered the fray over Speaker Newt Gingrich's book deal by introducing legislation that would bar members from receiving book royalties. He also tried unsuccessfully to attach a sunset provision to the line-item veto bill.

The People: Pop. 1990: 565,802; 40% rural; 19% age 65+; 98% White; 1% Black; 1% Hispanic origin. Voting age pop.: 441,019; 1% Black; 1% Hispanic origin. Households: 57% married couple families; 24% married couple fams. w. children; 29% college educ.; median household income: $24,310; per capita income: $11,937; median gross rent: $327; median house value: $57,600.

1992 Presidential Vote			1988 Presidential Vote		
Clinton (D)	91,616	(42%)	Bush (R)	104,667	(53%)
Bush (R)	84,199	(38%)	Dukakis (D)	92,717	(47%)
Perot (I)	42,950	(20%)			

Rep. Paul E. Kanjorski (D)

Elected 1984; b. Apr. 2, 1937, Nanticoke; home, Nanticoke; Temple U., 1957–61, Dickinson U., 1962–65; Catholic; married (Nancy).

Career: Army Reserves, 1960–61; Practicing atty., 1966–85; Nanticoke City Solicitor, 1969–81; Admin. Law Judge, 1971–80.

DC Office: 2429 RHOB 20515, 202-225-6511.

District Offices: 10 E. South St., Wilkes-Barre 18701, 717-825-2200.

Committees: *Banking & Financial Services* (6th of 22 D): Capital Markets, Securities and Government Sponsored Enterprises (RMM); Financial Institutions and Consumer Credit. *Government Reform & Oversight* (9th of 22 D): Government Management, Information and Technology; National Economic Growth, Natural Resources and Regulatory Affairs.

Group Ratings

	ADA	ACLU	COPE	CFA	LCV	CON	NSI	COC	ACU	NTLC	CHC
1994	55	39	89	70	78	23	30	42	29	14	50
1993	70	—	100	90	64	39	—	18	21	—	—

National Journal Ratings

	1993 LIB — 1993 CONS			1994 LIB — 1994 CONS		
Economic	78%	—	12%	67%	—	29%
Social	41%	—	58%	55%	—	44%
Foreign	51%	—	42%	72%	—	25%

Key Votes of the 103d Congress

1. Clinton Deficit Plan	Y	3. Brady Handgun Purchase	N	5. Lmt. UN Cmnd. of Forces	N
2. NAFTA	N	4. Strike Race/Death Pnlty.	Y	6. Cut Missile Funds	N

Key Votes of the 104th Congress

1. Congressional Compliance	Y	6. Reform Crime Grant	N	11. Loser Pays Court Reform	N
2. Balanced Budget Amndmt.	N	7. National Security Act	N	12. Product Liability Reform	N
3. Bar Unfunded Mandates	Y	8. Moratorium on Regs.	N	13. Welfare Reform	N
4. Pass Line Item Veto	N	9. Risk Assessment on Regs.	N	14. Term Limits Amndmt.	N
5. Relax Exclusionary Rule	Y	10. Expnd. Priv. Prop. Rights	N	15. Tax Cuts	N

Election Results

1994 general	Paul E. Kanjorski (D)................	101,966	(67%)	($304,520)
	J. Andrew Podolak (R)................	51,295	(33%)	($57,006)
1994 primary	Paul E. Kanjorski (D)..............	unopposed		
1992 general	Paul E. Kanjorski (D)...............	138,875	(67%)	($342,314)
	Michael A. Fescina (R)	68,112	(33%)	($54,724)

TWELFTH DISTRICT

The area within a 100-mile radius of Pittsburgh, including the steel and coal country of southwestern Pennsylvania, northern West Virginia and eastern Ohio, is one of America's most troubled industrial regions. Even as central Pittsburgh upgrades its economy, the small factory and mining towns know that steel and coal are no longer job-growth industries. This area was first settled by Scots-Irish farmers in the 1790s. In the 19th century bituminous coal was discovered here, and immigrants from other parts of Europe were attracted to work the mines and the blast furnaces. The region was long a land of economic class conflict, but through the 1920s it was one of the most Republican parts of America. Republican policies, including high tariffs and discouragement of labor unions, were thought to have contributed greatly to steel's growth. That has changed and people in these parts now see the Democrats, with their support for unions, trade restrictions and perhaps for industrial policies, as their tribunes: the steel and coal country is one part of America where Republican policies grew steadily more unpopular during the 1980s and where deeply embedded cultural conservatism did not produce many votes for Republicans in the 1990s. This is pretty solid Democratic territory now.

The 12th Congressional District of Pennsylvania includes much of this coal and steel country. Its best known community is Johnstown, the steel town that was ravaged by the disastrous flood of May 31, 1889, when a dam broke and a 75-foot wall of water half a mile wide swept through the town killing more than 2,200 people. Johnstown had 67,000 people in 1920, 28,000 in 1990. From Johnstown, the redistricted 12th reaches south to the West Virginia border and west to take in Armstrong and Indiana Counties northeast of Pittsburgh. It also includes the hills around Ligonier, green with prosperity, where Mellons and others of Pittsburgh's elite have vast estates. For all its distinctiveness, the 12th proved in 1990 to be a distant early warning—the canary in the coal mine, to use a local image—of the discontent with incumbents in Congress expressed so sharply in 1992.

The local congressman, John Murtha, seemed well in line with district opinion, and he undeniably occupies a position where he can help an economically ailing district. First elected in one of those 1974 special elections that helped topple Richard Nixon, Murtha was a Marine who had reenlisted to fight in Vietnam. He is a member of the Appropriations Committee and was the chairman of the Defense Subcommittee until the Republicans captured the House. His voting record—hawkish and patriotic on foreign policy, interventionist on economics and usually tradition-minded on cultural issues—seemed perfectly suited to the steel and coal country. Murtha is also one of those old-time politicians who operate best in secret, standing at the back of the House chamber and trading gossip and votes, avoiding national and local reporters and appearing on television only when he is presiding over the chamber. He has depended on fellow members, not the press, to transmit his messages. His audience was the House Democratic Caucus, nothing wider, though he would work with White House lobbyists from time to time.

For many years, Murtha was reelected without trouble. Then, suddenly, he found himself pressed in the April 1990 primary by Westmoreland County lawyer Kenneth Burkley, who held Murtha to only 51% of the vote. After that close call, Murtha started visiting the district more, spending whole days in single communities, stressing local issues like his bill to exempt the Rolling Rock brewery in Latrobe from having to label its recyclable bottles with alcohol health warnings. He hired a press secretary, and if he still remains secluded from national reporters he is now courting the local press. He did not quit using his skills as an insider: the 1992 redistricting removed most of Westmoreland County, which Burkley had carried, from the district and added Armstrong and Indiana, which have much in common with the Johnstown area. In 1992, he had no opposition; in 1994 he won 69%–31%.

On foreign issues, Murtha voted for the Gulf war resolution and opposed intervention in Bosnia and deployment in Somalia, arguing that U.N. officials lacked the know-how to command U.S. troops. He also pushed a proposal that would have barred funds for U.N. peacekeeping missions unless the president gave Congress 15 days advance-notice of deployment; that was added as non-binding language to a defense appropriations bill. In 1994, Murtha forged an unlikely alliance with members of the Congressional Black Caucus to push a resolution requiring the Clinton Administration to report on the progress of its mission in Haiti. He is proud of having reduced foreign military aid by $1 billion and the Bush defense budget request by $7 billion. He led a move to slash 10,000 Navy jobs as punishment for the Tailhook scandal and spoke out against a Navy plan to build a $250 million office building in northern Virginia. However, he also has argued that large new cuts in the defense budget would result in the kind of "hollow force" that developed after the Vietnam War.

When Appropriations Chairman William Natcher was dying in February 1994, some thought Murtha might have designs on the chairmanship. Instead, Murtha threw his support behind Neal Smith of Iowa, who was in line for the position under a strict seniority system but was being challenged by David Obey of Wisconsin, a blunt-talking liberal; Obey easily won the post in the Democratic Caucus election. Murtha also found himself in a tussle in 1994 with Science Committee Chairman George Brown of California. Brown sought Defense Department documents on earmarking of funds to academic institutions and charged that Murtha's district was receiving more than its share of such funds, buried in the defense appropriations bill. Then-House Speaker Thomas Foley had to step in and referee the battle.

In 1995, Minority Leader Richard Gephardt named Murtha to a newly formed leadership advisory team that will help formulate and publicize Democratic positions. In the 104th Congress, Murtha finds himself caught between his inclination to work for a strong defense and the Democratic Party's objections to Republicans' cutting domestic programs to help pay for increased defense.

The People: Pop. 1990: 565,760; 70% rural; 17% age 65+; 98% White; 1% Black. Voting age pop.: 431,625; 1% Black. Households: 61% married couple families; 27% married couple fams. w. children; 25% college educ.; median household income: $22,024; per capita income: $10,586; median gross rent: $293; median house value: $44,300.

1992 Presidential Vote			1988 Presidential Vote		
Clinton (D)	102,768	(47%)	Dukakis (D)	112,739	(55%)
Bush (R)	72,664	(33%)	Bush (R)	92,372	(45%)
Perot (I)	44,846	(20%)			

Rep. John P. Murtha (D)

Elected Feb., 1974; b. June 17, 1932, New Martinsville, WV; home, Johnstown; U. of Pittsburgh, B.A. 1962, Indiana U. of PA, 1963–64; Catholic; married (Joyce).

Career: Marine Corps, 1952–55, 1966–67 (Vietnam), Marine Corps Reserves, 1955–65, 1968–90; Owner, Johnstown Minute Car Wash; PA House of Reps., 1969–74.

DC Office: 2423 RHOB 20515, 202-225-2065; Fax: 202-225-5709.

District Offices: Vine and Walnut Sts., Centre Town Mall, Johnstown 15907, 814-535-2642.

Committees: *Appropriations* (5th of 24 D): National Security (RMM).

Group Ratings

	ADA	ACLU	COPE	CFA	LCV	CON	NSI	COC	ACU	NTLC	CHC
1994	50	38	78	60	47	0	90	55	38	15	36
1993	50	—	100	90	57	1	—	27	22	—	—

National Journal Ratings

	1993 LIB — 1993 CONS		1994 LIB — 1994 CONS	
Economic	78%	— 12%	73%	— 17%
Social	47%	— 52%	52%	— 47%
Foreign	51%	— 42%	54%	— 45%

Key Votes of the 103d Congress

1. Clinton Deficit Plan	Y	3. Brady Handgun Purchase	N	5. Lmt. UN Cmnd. of Forces	N
2. NAFTA	N	4. Strike Race/Death Pnlty.	N	6. Cut Missile Funds	N

Key Votes of the 104th Congress

1. Congressional Compliance	Y	6. Reform Crime Grant	N	11. Loser Pays Court Reform	N
2. Balanced Budget Amndmt.	N	7. National Security Act	N	12. Product Liability Reform	N
3. Bar Unfunded Mandates	Y	8. Moratorium on Regs.	N	13. Welfare Reform	N
4. Pass Line Item Veto	N	9. Risk Assessment on Regs.	N	14. Term Limits Amndmt.	N
5. Relax Exclusionary Rule	Y	10. Expnd. Priv. Prop. Rights	N	15. Tax Cuts	N

Election Results

1994 general	John P. Murtha (D)..................	117,825	(69%)	($913,004)
	Bill Choby (R)	53,147	(31%)	($35,782)
1994 primary	John P. Murtha (D)................	unopposed		
1992 general	John P. Murtha (D)................	unopposed		($794,097)

THIRTEENTH DISTRICT

Montgomery County, Pennsylvania, is the hinterland of Philadelphia: rolling hills cut on one side by the Schuylkill River and at intervals by the Pennsylvania and Reading Railroad lines radiating outward from Center City. Older suburbs, the rich Main Line towns and more modest places like Glenside and Ambler, grew up around rail stations, with comfortable houses within walking distance for commuters. Here and there are the old Schuylkill River factory towns, Conshohocken and Norristown and towns established 200 years ago by German sects. Farther out are 18th and

19th century villages, once surrounded by farm fields, now encroached on by subdivisions where people depend on cars, not rail lines, to get to work, and office complexes in places like Blue Bell, the headquarters of Unisys. Statistically, Montgomery County is the most affluent part of metro Philadelphia, but as in most suburban counties there is much variety here—economically, with high income enclaves like Gladwyne, and ethnically, with Jewish suburbs out York Road.

Most of Montgomery County makes up the 13th Congressional District; parts of the county are nibbled off by the 6th, 7th, 8th and 15th Districts. It is one of those quintessentially Republican seats, where the style of politics was set for years by Ivy-educated Republican men, and where Republicans with more modest and sometimes ethnic backgrounds manned the local precincts and staffed local offices. But now the suburbs are as multiethnic as the central city, if not more so, and with varied cultural attitudes. They were a land of discontent in the recession of the early 1990s, which hit harder at residential real estate and other forms of wealth than at incomes, and which saw more permanent layoffs of white-collar and professional workers than temporary layoffs of blue-collar and factory workers. They remained a land of discontent in the mid-1990s economic recovery as well, as taxes seemed to increase and government provided services poorly and in ways that seemed to undercut hard work and traditional values. George Bush, who in 1988 carried the 13th District 60%–40%, lost to Bill Clinton in 1992 by 44%–39%.

This turmoil has had political effects. When Republican Lawrence Coughlin retired in 1992 after representing the district for 24 years, he was replaced by Democrat Marjorie Margolies-Mezvinsky, a longtime television news reporter and mother of 11, who was inspired to run by the Clarence Thomas hearings and was elected 50%–49% over Republican Jon Fox, a longtime local officeholder. But in a 1994 rematch with Fox, MMM (as she is called) lost 49%–45%. Her personal story was attractive: she grew up in Philadelphia and went into television news; covering a story on Korean adoptions in Philadelphia, she decided at 28 to adopt a Korean 6-year-old; four years later, she adopted a Vietnamese child. In 1975, on assignment in Washington, she met and married Iowa Congressman Edward Mezvinsky. When he was defeated in 1976, they moved with their large family to Montgomery County.

In the House, MMM proved herself not at all a political outsider—she got a seat on Commerce—but a person who makes sudden decisions on impulse and then follows through with great effort. Such was the case on the Clinton budget and tax package in 1993. She initially announced her opposition and taped a television interview explaining why she would vote against it. Then, as Democrats were just short of their majority, she voted yes, casting the decisive 218th vote as Republicans chanted, "Goodbye, Marjorie." MMM realized that her vote could well be "political suicide"—there are more high-income taxpayers here than in all but a dozen or so other districts in the country—but defended it doggedly.

Fox made a nice contrast with MMM because he had voted to cut county taxes by 3%. Fox is in many ways a typical suburban politician. He was class president at Penn State, worked in Washington while attending law school, became a Montgomery County assistant DA in 1976, at 29. He was elected Abington Township commissioner in 1980, state representative in 1984, member of the Montgomery County Board of Commissioners in 1990. Fox is Jewish and won in constituencies with many Jewish Democratic voters; the *Philadelphia Inquirer* called him a "zen master of constituency service." After he won the 1992 Republican primary, MMM attacked him as "a political animal who runs and runs and runs from political feeding to political feeding" and for waffling ("pro-choice, that's me; multiple choice, that's Jon Fox"). He had aggressive primary opposition from legislator Ellen Harley, who had contemplated running for Senate; the party favorite, state Senator Stewart Greenleaf, decided not to run. Fox won the primary with 37%, to 25% for Harley and 18% for self-financing businessman Jack Murray. MMM raised vast sums from feminists around the country and spent $1.6 million in all. But Fox had his own volunteers and local backing. In the House, he seemed to fit in comfortably with the Republican majority, frequently taking to the House floor to talk up the Contract With America. It will be interesting to see whether Democrats can muster a serious challenge to him in 1996 on this historically Republican turf.

1162   PENNSYLVANIA

The People: Pop. 1990: 565,663; 8% rural; 15% age 65+; 90% White; 6% Black; 2% Asian; 1% Hispanic origin. Voting age pop.: 439,398; 6% Black; 1% Hispanic origin. Households: 61% married couple families; 27% married couple fams. w. children; 55% college educ.; median household income: $44,764; per capita income: $22,786; median gross rent: $600; median house value: $146,600.

1992 Presidential Vote			1988 Presidential Vote		
Clinton (D)	118,579	(44%)	Bush (R)	145,609	(60%)
Bush (R)	107,439	(39%)	Dukakis (D)	95,710	(40%)
Perot (I)	44,148	(16%)			

Rep. Jon D. Fox (R)

Elected 1994; b. Apr. 22, 1947, Abington; home, Abington; PA St. U., B.A. 1969, DE Law Schl., J.D. 1975; Jewish; married (Judithanne).

Career: Air Force Reserves, 1969–75; Montgomery Cnty. Asst. Dist. Atty., 1976–80; Abington Township Bd. of Commissioners, 1980–84; PA House of Reps., 1984–91; Montgomery Cnty. Bd. of Commissioners, 1991–94.

DC Office: 510 CHOB 20515, 202-225-6111; Fax: 202-225-3155.

District Offices: 1768 Markley St., Norristown 19401, 610-272-8400; and Easton & Edge Hill Rds., Abington 19001, 215-885-3500.

Committees: *Banking & Financial Services* (22nd of 27 R): Capital Markets, Securities and Government Sponsored Enterprises; Domestic and International Monetary Policy; Housing and Community Opportunity. *Government Reform & Oversight* (15th of 27 R): Government Management, Information and Technology; National Economic Growth, Natural Resources and Regulatory Affairs. *Veterans' Affairs* (12th of 18 R): Hospitals and Health Care.

Group Ratings and 103rd Congress Votes: Newly Elected

Key Votes of the 104th Congress

1. Congressional Compliance Y	6. Reform Crime Grant	Y	11. Loser Pays Court Reform Y
2. Balanced Budget Amndmt. Y	7. National Security Act	Y	12. Product Liability Reform Y
3. Bar Unfunded Mandates Y	8. Moratorium on Regs.	Y	13. Welfare Reform Y
4. Pass Line Item Veto Y	9. Risk Assessment on Regs. Y		14. Term Limits Amndmt. Y
5. Relax Exclusionary Rule Y	10. Expnd. Priv. Prop. Rights Y		15. Tax Cuts Y

Election Results

1994 general	Jon D. Fox (R)	96,254	(49%)	($1,015,330)
	Marjorie Margolies-Mezvinsky (D)	88,073	(45%)	($1,620,110)
	Others	10,461	(5%)	
1994 primary	Jon D. Fox (R)	24,929	(37%)	
	Ellen Harley (R)	16,868	(25%)	
	John J. Murray (R)	12,529	(18%)	
	Michael J. Becker (R)	10,576	(15%)	
	Gayle Michael (R)	3,388	(5%)	
1992 general	Marjorie Margolies-Mezvinsky (D)	127,685	(50%)	($559,060)
	Jon D. Fox (R)	126,312	(49%)	($719,618)
	Other	3,513	(1%)	

FOURTEENTH DISTRICT

The Golden Triangle that is the inevitable center of Pittsburgh, the tip of land where the Allegheny and Monongahela Rivers come together to form the Ohio, has been a strategic site for more than 200 years. It was there, to Fort Duquesne, that Braddock's army was headed (with George Washington helping lead the way) when it was ambushed and defeated in 1754. A few years later, trees were felled, and a city was carved out of the wilderness here and named after the English statesman William Pitt—the first urban center in the American interior. Pittsburgh grew rapidly in those days when most of the nation's commerce moved over water. When traffic switched to railroads, Pittsburgh still did nicely, since rail lines had to run at riverside rather than scale the mountains. Then came Andrew Carnegie—and steel. A Scottish immigrant working as a telegrapher for the Pennsylvania Railroad, he saw that steel would replace iron for railroad bridges and built a steel factory in Pittsburgh—then a rail junction with large deposits of coal nearby and ready access to iron ore from the Great Lakes. With associates like Henry Clay Frick and Henry Phipps, Carnegie built his capacity to the point that when he sold out in 1901, the resulting U.S. Steel Corporation had a near-monopoly of the business.

The Pittsburgh that Carnegie and his steel men built is one of giant mills in the bottomlands along the rivers and massive buildings downtown like the classic City-County Building next to the Richardsonian jail. There were 12 cable cars going up the Duquesne Incline and other routes, connecting mills with the neighborhoods above, and the ever-present grime of coal smoke in the air. The Pittsburgh smog—a word used here before it was in Los Angeles—was so bad that street lights stayed on all day downtown, and photographs circa 1947 show a midnight-like darkness at nine in the morning. In the years after World War II, Pittsburgh's business leaders and Mayor David Lawrence were determined to clean up the smog and did so: Pittsburgh is one of our cleaner-aired cities today. They also cleaned up the riverfront and created a grand park at the junction of the three rivers. Pittsburgh ranks high, though not as high as it used to, as a headquarters of major corporations (USX, Westinghouse, Heinz, Alcoa, Koppers, PPG) and has fine cultural institutions, from Carnegie-Mellon University and the University of Pittsburgh with its "cathedral of learning" to its public television station (home of *Mr. Rogers' Neighborhood*) and the recently opened Andy Warhol museum. In the early 1980s, Pittsburgh formed a high-tech council to encourage start-up businesses. By the early 1990s, it had a robust high-tech, white-collar sector, replacing the manufacturing jobs which had declined in the metropolitan area from 265,000 in the mid-1970s to 112,000 by 1995. The old millworker towns in the outer metro ring continued to lose population and jobs, but much of the central city is vital, with yuppie-like growth in Mount Washington and Manchester and fine homes still maintained in Shadyside and Squirrel Hill.

The 14th Congressional District includes all of the city of Pittsburgh plus suburban territory to the west and north. It takes in the city's black neighborhoods and Shadyside and its depopulated white working class areas. To the west it goes out along a new expressway up to the airport, which is USAir's major hub (Bill Clinton's opposition to the USAir-British Airways merger cost him some votes here in 1992), to the north through middle-income townships and northeast along the Ohio River to some of the hilly high-income precincts of Sewickley. The 14th has its Republican neighborhoods and a Republican heritage, but that has not been very lively since the New Deal, and this is a solidly Democratic district today. Though unhappy with the Democrats' cultural liberalism in the 1970s, it became more Democratic in the years of the steel industry's collapse in the 1980s.

Democrat William Coyne has been the 14th's congressman since 1980. With a characteristic Irish-American knack for politics, this onetime accountant has moved up. He was elected to the legislature at age 34 in 1970, to the city council in 1973, to the chairmanship of the Democratic Party in Pittsburgh in 1978, and then to Congress in 1980 when he beat the son of his predecessor in the Democratic primary by a 65%–35% margin. After the 1984 election, he won a seat on the Ways and Means Committee. Philosophically, Coyne wants the government to spend more on transportation, education and energy conservation, which he sees as producing economic growth. Legislatively, he produced funds for home dialysis treatments and more medicare reimbursement. In the 103d Congress he made permanent the tax-exempt Industrial Development Bond program, which he says has created or preserved 26,000 Pennsylvania jobs in five years; his measure deemed that money from tax-exempt municipal bonds could be used for high-speed rail or magnetic levitation systems. He opposed the proposed $1 increase in the federal fuel tax for inland waterways and supported paying the earned income tax credit on a monthly basis. He has secured funding for many local projects—the Software Engineering Institute, Children's Hospital, restructuring the former Hays Ammunition Plant.

Coyne is, in short, a locally oriented congressman who seldom, if ever, attracts national attention, the eighth ranking Democrat on Ways and Means who could escape notice at a Washington cocktail party. He has been reelected easily every two years.

The People: Pop. 1990: 565,838; 17% age 65+; 80% White; 18% Black; 1% Asian; 1% Hispanic origin. Voting age pop.: 449,679; 16% Black; 1% Hispanic origin. Households: 44% married couple families; 17% married couple fams. w. children; 42% college educ.; median household income: $24,751; per capita income: $14,255; median gross rent: $379; median house value: $50,900.

1992 Presidential Vote			1988 Presidential Vote		
Clinton (D)	145,419	(58%)	Dukakis (D)	160,379	(66%)
Bush (R)	66,016	(26%)	Bush (R)	84,066	(34%)
Perot (I)	38,460	(15%)			

Rep. William J. Coyne (D)

Elected 1980; b. Aug. 24, 1936, Pittsburgh; home, Pittsburgh; Robert Morris Col., B.S. 1965; Catholic; single.

Career: Army, 1955–57; Accountant, 1957–70; PA House of Reps., 1971–72; Pittsburgh City Cncl., 1974–80.

DC Office: 2455 RHOB 20515, 202-225-2301; Fax: 202-225-1844.

District Offices: 2009 Fed. Bldg., 1000 Liberty Ave., Pittsburgh 15222, 412-644-2870.

Committees: *Budget* (5th of 18 D). *Ways & Means* (8th of 15 D): Trade.

Group Ratings

	ADA	ACLU	COPE	CFA	LCV	CON	NSI	COC	ACU	NTLC	CHC
1994	100	87	89	100	89	31	0	25	0	7	0
1993	95	—	100	100	79	32	—	0	4	—	—

National Journal Ratings

	1993 LIB — 1993 CONS			1994 LIB — 1994 CONS		
Economic	88%	—	0%	83%	—	0%
Social	87%	—	0%	94%	—	0%
Foreign	87%	—	7%	85%	—	0%

Key Votes of the 103d Congress

1. Clinton Deficit Plan	Y	3. Brady Handgun Purchase	Y	5. Lmt. UN Cmnd. of Forces	N
2. NAFTA	N	4. Strike Race/Death Pnlty.	N	6. Cut Missile Funds	Y

Key Votes of the 104th Congress

1. Congressional Compliance	Y	6. Reform Crime Grant	N	11. Loser Pays Court Reform	N
2. Balanced Budget Amndmt.	N	7. National Security Act	N	12. Product Liability Reform	N
3. Bar Unfunded Mandates	N	8. Moratorium on Regs.	N	13. Welfare Reform	N
4. Pass Line Item Veto	N	9. Risk Assessment on Regs.	N	14. Term Limits Amndmt.	N
5. Relax Exclusionary Rule	N	10. Expnd. Priv. Prop. Rights	N	15. Tax Cuts	N

Election Results

1994 general	William J. Coyne (D)	105,310	(64%)	($185,539)
	John Robert Clark (R)	53,221	(32%)	($9,747)
	Others	5,645	(3%)	
1994 primary	William J. Coyne (D)	unopposed		
1992 general	William J. Coyne (D)	165,633	(72%)	($323,937)
	Byron W. King (R)	61,311	(27%)	($73,936)
	Others	2,094	(1%)	

FIFTEENTH DISTRICT

For much of the 1980s the economy in the Lehigh Valley, tucked among the rolling hills of eastern Pennsylvania, grew vigorously despite the odds against it. In 1982 singer Billy Joel painted a grim picture of the unemployment rampant in Allentown, the Valley's largest city, in a popular song of the same name. When Mack Trucks, Allentown's major employer, moved one of its main assembly plants to South Carolina five years later in search of nonunion wages, the Valley's future looked dicey. But AT&T was building a major facility in Allentown and smaller companies in the city were thriving, so the region absorbed the shock and moved on. Nestle Foods has since located in the Valley, and the makers of Crayola crayons and Dixie cups, two of America's best-known products, are still going strong. Even the Mack Truck plant has been turned into a busy warehouse. In 1994 Allentown's unemployment rate stood at the national average, and jobs were more plentiful in the Lehigh Valley than in central and western Pennsylvania. Another hardship may be on the horizon for the Valley, however. Bethlehem Steel has announced that it will shut down its last operating blast furnace in Bethlehem, the Valley's second-largest city, in 1995. The closing of the Bethlehem plant (the company will retain its 21-story headquarters building in the city) has historical as well as economic impact: the company has been making steel there since its founding, as Saucona Iron, in 1857.

The 15th Congressional District consists of the Lehigh Valley plus a small adjacent portion of Montgomery County. For generations, Democratic politics held sway in this heavy-industrial region, where the steel smokestacks rose up on the horizon like iron pikes. In 1978, however, the district elected a Republican Congressman, Don Ritter, an opponent of tax increases and a strong backer of local historic renovation projects, and then re-elected him six more times. The tide turned back to the Democrats in 1992, though, when the district went for Bill Clinton 41%–37%, and Democrat Paul McHale toppled Ritter 52%–47%. McHale, a Lehigh Valley native, had joined the Marine Corps after college and then practiced law before being elected to the state House in 1982. After the invasion of Kuwait in 1990, he volunteered for active duty in the Gulf War; he resigned from the legislature, and his wife won his seat. Campaigning for Congress in 1992, he attacked Ritter for accepting honoraria and free trips; he also supported a line-item veto and a phased-in balanced budget amendment. Promising to find a solution to the healthcare issue was McHale's ace in the hole. "There will be no excuse for inaction," he declared during the campaign. But in the House, McHale found himself increasingly drawn into the vortex of conflicting reform proposals. He backed President Clinton's goal of universal coverage, but when the White House produced its much-vaunted healthcare plan he announced at a meeting with district hospital officials that he would oppose it because it would give rise to a new government bureaucracy and thus damage the economy. That announcement didn't sit well with some of McHale's powerful constituents, including Bethlehem Steel, which backed comprehensive reform as a way of realigning medical costs, and the unions, who contributed nearly half of the $222,000 McHale spent on his 1992 campaign. McHale insisted, however, that by refusing to back either the Administration's plan or the plan substituted for it by the House Democratic leadership, he was simply conforming to the wishes of voters in his district, many of whom had come to fear big government more than higher insurance premiums. "The center of gravity has shifted," he told *The Wall Street Journal* in August 1994.

McHale also made a name for himself in his first term as an outspoken critic of Pentagon plans that he believed would cut combat readiness in some sectors of the military. He expressed outrage at reports that about 500 former Iraqi soldiers had been admitted to the United States as refugees following the Gulf war. He opposed plans by the Joint Chiefs of Staff to create "pre-positioning" ships loaded with tanks and supplies for quick-response Army divisions on the grounds that the Marine Corps was already equipped to carry out that function. And while he rejected Republican claims that Clinton's fiscal 1994 budget—which McHale voted for—made keeping a fighting edge impossible, he warned that increased demands on overworked military personnel hurt troop morale and could pose a risk to combat readiness.

McHale's struggle to prove himself a "new Democrat" and walk a moderate-to-conservative line in Congress paid off meagerly in the 1994 election. He drew not only a strong Republican challenger, Jim Yeager, a fuel oil dealer who raised $330,000 to McHale's $285,000, but also a third-party candidate, Victor Mazziotti, the general manager of a computer software company, who ran on the ballot of the Patriot Party, an outgrowth of Ross Perot's 1992 presidential campaign. The vote was so close that Yeager paid for a recount; the final tally showed McHale winning by 471 votes. Given the 15th District's recent predilection for electing Republicans, McHale could find himself with a tough campaign on his hands in 1996.

The People: Pop. 1990: 565,818; 26% rural; 15% age 65+; 92% White; 2% Black; 1% Asian; 3% Other; 5% Hispanic origin. Voting age pop.: 434,459; 2% Black; 4% Hispanic origin. Households: 61% married couple families; 26% married couple fams. w. children; 37% college educ.; median household income: $33,049; per capita income: $15,073; median gross rent: $458; median house value: $101,400.

1992 Presidential Vote

Clinton (D)	92,363	(41%)
Bush (R)	81,349	(37%)
Perot (I)	47,740	(21%)

1988 Presidential Vote

Bush (R)	104,773	(55%)
Dukakis (D)	84,834	(45%)

Rep. Paul McHale (D)

Elected 1992; b. July 26, 1950, Bethlehem; home, Bethlehem; Lehigh U., B.A. 1972, Georgetown U. Law Sch., J.D. 1977; Catholic; married (Katherine).

Career: Marine Corps, 1972–74, 1990–91 (Persian Gulf); Marine Reserves, 1974–80, 1984–present; Practicing atty., 1977–92; PA House of Reps., 1982–91.

DC Office: 217 CHOB 20515, 202-225-6411; Fax: 202-225-5320.

District Offices: 26 E. 3d St., Bethlehem 18015, 215-866-0916; Hamilton Financial Ctr., One Center Sq., #203, Allentown 18101, 215-439-8861; and 168 Main St., Pennsburg 18073, 215-541-0614.

Committees: *National Security* (19th of 25 D): Military Readiness; Military Research and Development. *Science* (10th of 23 D): Energy and Environment; Technology.

Group Ratings

	ADA	ACLU	COPE	CFA	LCV	CON	NSI	COC	ACU	NTLC	CHC
1994	45	48	67	80	78	47	70	83	24	36	43
1993	65	—	92	90	86	59	—	36	25	—	—

National Journal Ratings

	1993 LIB — 1993 CONS	1994 LIB — 1994 CONS
Economic	54% — 45%	50% — 46%
Social	58% — 41%	48% — 50%
Foreign	63% — 34%	57% — 37%

Key Votes of the 103d Congress

1. Clinton Deficit Plan	Y	3. Brady Handgun Purchase Y	5. Lmt. UN Cmnd. of Forces N
2. NAFTA	N	4. Strike Race/Death Pnlty. Y	6. Cut Missile Funds Y

Key Votes of the 104th Congress

1. Congressional Compliance Y	6. Reform Crime Grant N	11. Loser Pays Court Reform N
2. Balanced Budget Amndmt. Y	7. National Security Act N	12. Product Liability Reform N
3. Bar Unfunded Mandates Y	8. Moratorium on Regs. N	13. Welfare Reform N
4. Pass Line Item Veto Y	9. Risk Assessment on Regs. N	14. Term Limits Amndmt. N
5. Relax Exclusionary Rule Y	10. Expnd. Priv. Prop. Rights Y	15. Tax Cuts N

Election Results

1994 general	Paul McHale (D)	72,073	(48%)	($284,930)
	Jim Yeager (R)	71,602	(47%)	($325,713)
	Victor Mazziotti (Patriot)	7,227	(5%)	
1994 primary	Paul McHale (D)	unopposed		
1992 general	Paul McHale (D)	111,419	(52%)	($221,935)
	Don Ritter (R)	99,520	(47%)	($865,974)
	Other	2,385	(1%)	

SIXTEENTH DISTRICT

The Pennsylvania Dutch country, settled by Germans in the 18th Century when it was Pennsylvania's frontier, remains a distinctive part of America. These Germans were Amish, Mennonites, members of pietistic sects seeking religious liberty and determined to farm their rich lands in the same intensive way they had in Germany. Today, many of their descendants—the Eisenhower family is the most famous example—have blended into mainstream America, but in the Dutch area around Lancaster, many "Plain People" still live. Tourists can still see Amish families clad in black, clattering over the back roads in horse-drawn carriages, with scrupulously tended farms set amid rolling hills, the barns decorated with hex signs. Farmers here continue to produce some of the highest per-acre yields on earth, with simple equipment and limited use of chemical fertilizers. But efficient farming is not all that is happening here economically. Lancaster is the headquarters of Armstrong, and nearby Hershey is where Milton Hershey built his chocolate firm back in 1903—the main street is Chocolate Avenue and the lampposts are topped with ceramic Hershey Kisses. The Dutch area also has many small firms; new startups prosper, profiting from the skills and work habits of the labor force. Lancaster County grew robustly in the 1980s, and so did western Chester County, technically part of metro Philadelphia, but with its own Pennsylvania Dutch communities.

The 16th Congressional District includes most of Lancaster County and part of Chester County, ranging east from the Dutch country through the small towns and spreading suburbs of greater Philadelphia, including America's leading mushroom-growing center around Kennett Square (fragrant with the compost needed for the crop) and on to the Wyeth country around Chadds Ford. The latter area is a new addition to the district, resulting from the collapse of three Republican districts into two; but the new 16th, like the old, is by most measures the most Republican district in Pennsylvania and the whole Northeast. It has favored the party of Lincoln since it abandoned the party of Pennsylvania's only President, Lancaster resident James Buchanan, in the years just before the Civil War.

The 16th District's congressman, Robert Walker, is chairman of the Science Committee and, though he does not hold a major party leadership position, one of the true Republican leaders in the House. Indeed, as much as anyone, he is the father of the revolution that led to the Republican victory of 1994. He grew up near Lancaster, taught high school and worked 10 years for Congressman Edwin Eshleman; when he retired in 1976, Walker ran for the seat and at 33 won, with 16% of the vote in an 11-candidate primary. This was two years before Newt Gingrich came to the House, when Democrats had the presidency and a 2–1 majority: no Republican revolution was in sight. But Walker—scrappy, good-humored, ready to push his principles forward even at the cost of being mocked—set out to make one. He was the first to see the potential of using the House's "special orders" procedure, which allows speechmaking after the legislative business of the day, to reach a wide public on C-SPAN. He was also the one caught at the podium, gesturing and asking rhetorical questions, when Speaker Tip O'Neill ordered the C-SPAN cameras to show that the Republicans were speaking to an empty House. And during debate he stayed on the floor, good-humored but vigilant, ready to pounce on Democrats' mistakes or spotlight what he regarded as injustices. He became the Republicans' leading expert on House rules, willing to use irritating tactics, objecting to unanimous consent requests for one-minute speeches, demanding roll calls and even teller votes on routine matters. He was Gingrich's first recruit for his Conservative Opportunity Society of young conservative rebels; he played a major role in Gingrich's March 1989 campaign for majority whip, which prevailed by the history-making margin of 87–85.

Walker also spent some time on substantive legislation, usually with a political angle. His debt buydown proposal was backed by George Bush at the 1992 Houston convention, to no effect; his drug-free workplace law got into the 1990 crime bill. On the Science Committee, he worked to create the National Space Council, giving Vice Presidents Dan Quayle and Al Gore superintendency over the space program. He objected to some science spending as pork barrel, but he wanted to spend more on hydrogen energy, rural growth research, earthquake R&D and research about possible global weather changes. He successfully sponsored risk-assessment amendments in 1994. As Science Committee chairman, he wants to emphasize basic research and scale back applied research, which he feels should be market-driven and handled by the private sector—an immediate target was the Commerce Department's Advanced Technology Program. He also opposes academic earmarking. He sees space as a new economic frontier to be developed and would allow space commercialization.

Walker's effort to win the number-three leadership post, majority whip, failed in December 1994. He refused to set up a leadership PAC to contribute to other Republicans and spent much time on the House floor, while his rival Tom DeLay of Texas contributed generously and campaigned indefatigably for others, especially freshmen. Gingrich stated his support for Walker but did not twist arms for him. DeLay won 119 votes to 80 for Walker and 28 for Bill McCollum of Florida. But Walker remained probably the Republican most knowledgeable about House rules and procedure, and he stays on easy terms with Gingrich and part of his inner circle, helping to enforce discipline and maintain order on the House floor. It was Walker's recounting of the words of a Lancaster party committeeman—"Tell our new Speaker we all worked for this victory and he should not take advantage of our efforts"—that persuaded Gingrich to turn down his $4.5 million book advance. Gingrich made him vice chairman of the Budget Committee.

Walker has been reelected without difficulty in the 16th District.

The People: Pop. 1990: 565,908; 44% rural; 12% age 65+; 90% White; 5% Black; 1% Asian; 4% Hispanic origin. Voting age pop.: 417,051; 5% Black; 3% Hispanic origin. Households: 64% married couple families; 31% married couple fams. w. children; 42% college educ.; median household income: $37,553; per capita income: $16,321; median gross rent: $500; median house value: $115,300.

1992 Presidential Vote

Bush (R)	109,019	(48%)
Clinton (D)	72,724	(32%)
Perot (I)	43,271	(19%)

1988 Presidential Vote

Bush (R)	128,968	(69%)
Dukakis (D)	58,526	(31%)

Rep. Robert S. Walker (R)

Elected 1976; b. Dec. 23, 1942, Bradford; home, East Petersburg; Millersville U., B.S. 1964, U. of DE, M.A. 1968; Presbyterian; married (Sue).

Career: PA Natl. Guard, 1967–73; High schl. teacher, 1964–67; A.A., U.S. Rep. Edwin D. Eshleman, 1967–77.

DC Office: 2369 RHOB 20515, 202-225-2411; Fax: 202-225-1116; e-mail: pa16@hr.house.gov.

District Offices: Lancaster Cnty. Crthse., 50 N. Duke St., Lancaster 17603, 717-393-0666; Exton Commons, #595, Exton 19341, 215-363-8409.

Committees: *Budget* (3rd of 24 R). *Science* (Chmn. of 27 R).

Group Ratings

	ADA	ACLU	COPE	CFA	LCV	CON	NSI	COC	ACU	NTLC	CHC
1994	0	13	0	0	6	76	100	92	100	96	100
1993	5	—	0	0	21	82	—	100	100	—	—

National Journal Ratings

	1993 LIB	—	1993 CONS	1994 LIB	—	1994 CONS
Economic	0%	—	88%	0%	—	80%
Social	0%	—	89%	0%	—	89%
Foreign	9%	—	85%	0%	—	88%

Key Votes of the 103d Congress

1. Clinton Deficit Plan	N	3. Brady Handgun Purchase	N	5. Lmt. UN Cmnd. of Forces	Y
2. NAFTA	Y	4. Strike Race/Death Pnlty.	Y	6. Cut Missile Funds	N

Key Votes of the 104th Congress

1. Congressional Compliance	Y	6. Reform Crime Grant	Y	11. Loser Pays Court Reform	Y
2. Balanced Budget Amndmt.	Y	7. National Security Act	Y	12. Product Liability Reform	Y
3. Bar Unfunded Mandates	Y	8. Moratorium on Regs.	Y	13. Welfare Reform	Y
4. Pass Line Item Veto	Y	9. Risk Assessment on Regs.	Y	14. Term Limits Amndmt.	Y
5. Relax Exclusionary Rule	Y	10. Expnd. Priv. Prop. Rights	Y	15. Tax Cuts	Y

Election Results

1994 general	Robert S. Walker (R)	109,759	(70%)	($242,192)
	Bill Chertok (D)	47,680	(30%)	($71,547)
1994 primary	Robert S. Walker (R)	unopposed		
1992 general	Robert S. Walker (R)	137,823	(65%)	($158,564)
	Robert Peters (D)	74,741	(35%)	($10,507)

SEVENTEENTH DISTRICT

Through the center of Pennsylvania flows the Susquehanna, the longest river in the East if you include the Chesapeake Bay, which is actually the flooded lower Susquehanna Valley. Starting in the mountain fastness of central Pennsylvania, emptying into the Chesapeake next to the antique town of Havre de Grace, Maryland, the Susquehanna is the one river strong enough to break through the Appalachian chains of central Pennsylvania. But few songs are written to celebrate the Susquehanna; it occupies nothing like the place of the Hudson or even the Schuylkill in art; it has not given a name to a fever (Potomac), a school of painting (Hudson) or economics (Charles), or to a state (Delaware, Connecticut, Ohio, Mississippi, Alabama, Illinois, Missouri, Colorado).

The 17th Congressional District of Pennsylvania covers much of the lower Susquehanna Valley, where the river breaks through the mountains and drains the fertile plains of the Pennsylvania Dutch Country, one of colonial America's great frontiers. Its big population center is Harrisburg, the central city huddled around the marvelous Capitol building, the metro area spreading over various valleys, not far upstream from the Three Mile Island nuclear power plant. From there the district spreads east to the Pennsylvania Dutch country, including Lebanon County and part of Lancaster County. Here the black buggies of the "Plain People" click-clack over the roads of some of the most fertile farmland in the world.

This is a solidly Republican area. Harrisburg has been a Republican town from the days when the party seemed to conquer all in Pennsylvania; Republicans held the governorship for all but eight years from 1860 to 1934 and filled the ornate halls of the Capitol—its dome is modeled after St. Peter's in Rome, its stairway on the Paris Opera—with Republican patronage hacks. The Pennsylvania Dutch country is even more Republican. Although the 17th District had elected a Democratic congressman as recently as 1980, when it stretched north from Harrisburg along the Susquehanna; it is now a safe Republican seat.

The current congressman is George Gekas who, as state senator from Harrisburg, helped draw the district boundaries and won the seat easily in 1982. Conservative in fiscal impulse and on crime issues, Gekas has been an active legislator, leading the Republican ranks on some issues, starting his own crusades on others. In the legislature, Gekas sponsored the state's mandatory sentencing and child abuse laws, and in the House Judiciary Committee he has backed tough anti-crime laws. He sponsored the death penalty for drug dealers convicted of murder and has led the fight for most death penalty provisions in federal crime bills. He sponsored a law preventing international kidnapping of children and another preventing evictions of the elderly after being prompted by constituents' experiences. For years, he unsuccessfully tried to prohibit legal services lawyers from taking any abortion cases and to bar Congressmen elected before 1980 from converting leftover campaign funds to personal use. He is a supporter of biomedical research and has sought to protect labs from "animal rights terrorists" (not as much an overstatement as it sounds) and secured passage of a Farm Animal and Research Facilities Protection Act. He was the lead Republican seeking to apply the procedures of the Independent Counsel law to Members of Congress.

Gekas is now chairman of the Judiciary Subcommittee on Commercial and Administrative Law and shepherded to passage Contract With America provisions on regulatory reform. He aims to put a moratorium on the EPA's centralized auto inspection program and to discourage litigation that is keeping raw materials out of the biomedical device industry. He has been reelected routinely.

The People: Pop. 1990: 565,702; 39% rural; 13% age 65+; 90% White; 7% Black; 1% Asian; 1% Other; 2% Hispanic origin. Voting age pop.: 427,392; 6% Black; 1% Hispanic origin. Households: 59% married couple families; 27% married couple fams. w. children; 33% college educ.; median household income: $31,841; per capita income: $14,434; median gross rent: $415; median house value: $76,500.

1992 Presidential Vote			1988 Presidential Vote		
Bush (R)	114,245	(50%)	Bush (R)	122,558	(64%)
Clinton (D)	72,594	(32%)	Dukakis (D)	67,751	(36%)
Perot (I)	40,495	(18%)			

Rep. George W. Gekas (R)

Elected 1982; b. Apr. 14, 1930, Harrisburg; home, Harrisburg; Dickinson Col., B.A. 1952, Dickinson Law Sch., J.D. 1958; Greek Orthodox; married (Evangeline).

Career: Army, 1953–55; Asst. Dist. Atty., Dauphin Cnty., 1960–66; PA House of Reps., 1967–75; PA Senate, 1977–83.

DC Office: 2410 RHOB 20515, 202-225-4315; Fax: 202-225-8440.

District Offices: 3605 Vartan Way, Harrisburg 17110, 717-541-5507; 222 S. Market St., #102-A, Elizabethtown 17022, 717-367-6731; and 108-B Municipal Bldg., 400 S. 8th St., Lebanon 17042, 717-273-1451.

Committees: *Judiciary* (5th of 20 R): Commercial and Administrative Law (Chmn.); Courts and Intellectual Property.

Group Ratings

	ADA	ACLU	COPE	CFA	LCV	CON	NSI	COC	ACU	NTLC	CHC
1994	10	23	11	20	6	72	90	92	95	93	86
1993	5	—	0	0	21	91	—	91	92	—	—

National Journal Ratings

	1993 LIB — 1993 CONS			1994 LIB — 1994 CONS		
Economic	29%	—	71%	20%	—	79%
Social	25%	—	73%	20%	—	77%
Foreign	0%	—	91%	14%	—	80%

Key Votes of the 103d Congress

1. Clinton Deficit Plan	N	3. Brady Handgun Purchase	N	5. Lmt. UN Cmnd. of Forces	Y
2. NAFTA	Y	4. Strike Race/Death Pnlty.	Y	6. Cut Missile Funds	N

Key Votes of the 104th Congress

1. Congressional Compliance	Y	6. Reform Crime Grant	Y	11. Loser Pays Court Reform	Y
2. Balanced Budget Amndmt.	Y	7. National Security Act	Y	12. Product Liability Reform	Y
3. Bar Unfunded Mandates	Y	8. Moratorium on Regs.	Y	13. Welfare Reform	Y
4. Pass Line Item Veto	Y	9. Risk Assessment on Regs.	Y	14. Term Limits Amndmt.	Y
5. Relax Exclusionary Rule	*	10. Expnd. Priv. Prop. Rights	Y	15. Tax Cuts	Y

Election Results

1994 general	George W. Gekas (R)	unopposed		($86,839)
1994 primary	George W. Gekas (R)	unopposed		
1992 general	George W. Gekas (R)	150,158	(70%)	($190,885)
	Bill Sturges (D).......................	65,881	(30%)	($47,217)

EIGHTEENTH DISTRICT

Pittsburgh is surely the hilliest of the large metropolitan areas of the United States; it is indicative of the nerve of its founders that they were willing to build on such steep terrain. In its years of great growth, from the mid-1800s to the early 1900s, with the steel mills lining the riverbanks, Pittsburgh and its suburbs spread up and down hills, through the interstices of river valleys and over gaps to the next nearly level spot. Then, as growth resumed in mid-20th Century, the spreading-out process continued. One result is that there are no clusters of rich and poor suburbs, no one middle-class zone: they are spread out around the irregular terrain. The richest Pittsburghers, for example, live in Fox Chapel and Sewickley to the northeast and northwest; there are upper-middle-income suburbs like Mount Lebanon south of the Golden Triangle, but also some north of the Allegheny; working class enclaves, now greatly depopulated, are strung along the Monongahela River, near the mostly cold steel mills, but are found in other pockets as well. Pittsburgh does not yet have an edge city, though there are new housing and a few office developments to the north and to the west around the airport, now a major hub for USAir.

When John Kennedy was elected president, there were four congressional districts in Pittsburgh's Allegheny County, numbered 27th through 30th; now all of Pennsylvania has only 21 districts, and there are only two fully in Allegheny County. One, the 14th, is made up primarily of the city of Pittsburgh; the other, the 18th, includes suburbs to the north, south and east, plus most of the industrial Mon Valley to the southeast. This is a new creation of redistricting, containing much of the old Republican-leaning suburban 18th and some of the heavily Democratic Mon Valley 20th. It was expected to be a Democratic district, but in fact has been seriously contested.

The congressman now is Mike Doyle, a Democrat who won in 1994 while the 18th District's Republican incumbent, 36-year-old brash conservative Rick Santorum, was being elected to the U.S. Senate. Santorum's defeat of an incumbent Democrat in 1990 was one of the big upsets of that year; his reelection in the more-Democratic 18th over Republican-turned-Democrat state Senator Frank Pecora was one of the important Republican victories of 1992. To all this Doyle was an interested bystander. Of Irish and Italian descent, he grew up in the Mon Valley town of Swissvale, returned there after Penn State, worked as an insurance agent and for a nonprofit agency and was elected to the Swissvale Borough Council in 1977, at 24.

In 1979 he became chief of staff to Pecora. When Santorum ran for the Senate, Doyle was one of seven Democrats and four Republicans to run for the seat. The Democrats were close to evenly matched: all won between 10% and 20% of the vote. Doyle, who had switched parties only recently, was helped by endorsements from unions and community leaders he had worked with over the years; he, like Santorum in his first campaign, knocked on 40,000 doors. He boasted that he is not a lawyer: "Sending another lawyer to Washington is like trying to put out a fire with gasoline." In the general, he faced John McCarty, a former aide to the late Senator John Heinz; McCarty was endorsed heartily by Teresa Heinz, who attacked Santorum and endorsed Democratic Senator Harris Wofford. An interesting twist in their campaign was that McCarty is pro-choice and Doyle anti-abortion. Doyle campaigned for sweeping healthcare reform, against the new General Agreement on Tariffs and Trade, and for rebuilding the Mon Valley's industrial base. McCarty made it a close race, but Doyle still won 55%–45%.

The People: Pop. 1990: 565,771; 2% rural; 19% age 65+; 91% White; 8% Black; 1% Asian. Voting age pop.: 447,649; 7% Black. Households: 55% married couple families; 21% married couple fams. w. children; 43% college educ.; median household income: $29,003; per capita income: $15,251; median gross rent: $394; median house value: $55,000.

1992 Presidential Vote		1988 Presidential Vote	
Clinton (D)	137,507 (52%)	Dukakis (D)	147,588 (58%)
Bush (R)	80,795 (30%)	Bush (R)	104,800 (42%)
Perot (I)	46,754 (18%)		

Rep. Mike Doyle (D)

Elected 1994; b. Aug. 5, 1953, Pittsburgh; home, Swissvale; Penn St. U., B.S. 1975; Catholic; married (Susan).

Career: Insurance agent, 1975–77; Exec. Dir., Turtle Creek Valley Citizens Union, 1977–79; Swissvale Borough Cncl., 1977; Chief of Staff, PA St. Sen. Frank Pecora, 1978–94; Co-Founder, Eastgate Insurance Agency, 1983–present.

DC Office: 1218 LHOB 20515, 202-225-2135; Fax: 202-225-3084.

District Offices: 11 Duff Rd., Pittsburgh 15235, 412-241-6055; 541 5th Ave., McKeesport 15132, 412-664-4049.

Committees: *Science* (21st of 23 D): Basic Research; Energy and Environment. *Veterans' Affairs* (14th of 15 D): Hospitals and Health Care.

Group Ratings and 103rd Congress Votes: Newly Elected

Key Votes of the 104th Congress

1. Congressional Compliance	Y	6. Reform Crime Grant	N	11. Loser Pays Court Reform	N
2. Balanced Budget Amndmt.	Y	7. National Security Act	N	12. Product Liability Reform	N
3. Bar Unfunded Mandates	Y	8. Moratorium on Regs.	N	13. Welfare Reform	N
4. Pass Line Item Veto	Y	9. Risk Assessment on Regs.	Y	14. Term Limits Amndmt.	Y
5. Relax Exclusionary Rule	Y	10. Expnd. Priv. Prop. Rights	Y	15. Tax Cuts	N

Election Results

1994 general	Mike Doyle (D)	101,784	(55%)	($381,733)
	John McCarty (R)	83,881	(45%)	($362,091)
1994 primary	Mike Doyle (D)	16,571	(20%)	
	Mike Adams (D)	15,055	(18%)	
	Richard Edward Caligiuri (D)	12,077	(14%)	
	Jon Delano (D)	10,930	(13%)	
	Chris McNally (D)	10,720	(13%)	
	Arthur J. Murphy Jr. (D)	10,202	(12%)	
	Joseph Rudolph (D)	7,947	(10%)	
1992 general	Rick Santorum (R)	154,024	(61%)	($626,793)
	Frank A. Pecora (D)	96,655	(38%)	($284,757)
	Other	3,650	(1%)	

NINETEENTH DISTRICT

The Mason-Dixon Line, the historic boundary between Maryland and Pennsylvania, runs through some of the country's most pleasant rolling farmlands, west of the Susquehanna River up through the first of the Appalachian chains. It was over this invisible line that Robert E. Lee's Confederate troops crossed and were then repulsed in the Confederacy's northernmost advance in the Battle of Gettysburg in July 1863. Nearby was the westernmost capital of the United States during the Revolutionary War, the small city of York, capital from September 1777 to June 1778. This is where the Continental Congress passed the Articles of Confederation, received word from Benjamin Franklin in Paris that the French would help the colonies with money and ships and issued the first proclamation calling for a national day of thanksgiving. Little today reminds you that it was once the frontier and later fiercely fought over: the rolling green farmland looks peaceful, prosperous and mostly undisturbed by the commercial trappings and stylistic excesses of the late 20th Century.

Some 50 miles of the Mason-Dixon Line is the southern boundary of the 19th Congressional District of Pennsylvania, which is centered on York, including the suburbs of Harrisburg across the Susquehanna, the old town of Carlisle with Dickinson College and Carlisle Barracks and President Eisenhower's retirement home near Gettysburg. Eisenhower was of Pennsylvania Dutch stock himself; his father migrated in the late 19th century, with a group of Mennonite brethren, to Kansas and Texas. The district has the look of deeply contented land and has been, with just occasional exceptions, heavily Republican.

The congressman from the 19th District is Bill Goodling, chairman of the Economic and Educational Opportunities Committee, formerly Education and Labor. Goodling was a public school teacher, coach and principal in a small town in York County for 22 years; his father was 19th District Congressman for 12 years, elected every two years from 1960 to 1972 except in 1964. When George Goodling retired in 1974, Bill Goodling ran and won both the primary and general by rather narrow margins. He has had only one tough election year since, in 1992, after it was revealed that he had 430 overdrafts on the House bank totalling $188,000. Democrat Paul Kilker, owner of a local graphics company, ran an aggressive campaign, and so did Tom Humbert, whose family started the Snyder's of Hanover pretzel company and who worked as an aide to Housing and Urban Development Secretary Jack Kemp; Humbert missed the filing deadline for the primary and ran in November as an independent. Attacked from the moderate left and reformist right, Goodling was happy to have campaign appearances from Newt Gingrich and Dan Quayle and won with 45% to 34% for Kilker and 20% for Humbert—almost the same percentages as in the presidential race here.

In the Democratic 103d Congress, as ranking Republican on Economic and Educational Opportunities, Goodling made contributions to the reauthorization of the Elementary and Secondary Act, the Goals 2000 program, national service and direct college loans. But he also attacked unfunded mandates and intrusive government policies. "We need programs that are less restrictive and more supportive of the genius of our local school programs," he said. He even questioned the oft-praised Head Start program: The problem, he told *National Journal* in 1994, is "They keep pumping in more money, more money, more money, and everybody says [Head Start] is wonderful, and yet it's not cutting the mustard."

Now, as chairman, Goodling is in a position to make great changes, and he took early steps to deliver. Organized labor had controlled the committee since the 1950s and made efforts to put pro-union Republicans on it as well as keep anti-union Democrats off. But today there are few pro-union Republicans left, and not many who sympathize with teachers' unions. Goodling is something of a moderate here: he says he wants to shrink, not eliminate, the Department of Education; he wants to make a systematic review of education programs, not just zero many out. In helping to write the welfare-reform bill in the Contract With America, he has started to deliver on his goal of giving states flexibility through block grants, starting with food programs, perhaps going to special education and vocational education.

Goodling has spent less time on labor issues and takes a tougher conservative line on them. He has opposed family and medical leave and minimum wage increases. And he tends to favor the pro-management agenda of the Labor Policy Association. He wants to encourage worker-management teams, currently not allowed except through unions; he contrasts the cooperative teams at Harley-Davidson with the strike at Caterpillar in plants in the 19th District. He may also try to ease labor laws to encourage flexible time and compensatory time rather than overtime premium pay, and seek alternative dispute resolution and repeal of the Davis-Bacon Act. Opponents charge this would allow management to oppress workers; proponents say it would allow management and workers to be more creative and productive. President Clinton would likely veto such measures, but that would create issues for 1996 and make the formerly obscure Goodling into a national policy maker.

The People: Pop. 1990: 565,789; 50% rural; 13% age 65+; 95% White; 3% Black; 1% Asian; 1% Other; 1% Hispanic origin. Voting age pop.: 431,983; 2% Black; 1% Hispanic origin. Households: 63% married couple families; 28% married couple fams. w. children; 33% college educ.; median household income: $32,424; per capita income: $14,539; median gross rent: $416; median house value: $80,200.

1992 Presidential Vote

Bush (R) 105,647 (47%)
Clinton (D) 75,515 (33%)
Perot (I).................. 44,373 (20%)

1988 Presidential Vote

Bush (R) 123,621 (66%)
Dukakis (D)............... 64,277 (34%)

Rep. Bill Goodling (R)

Elected 1974; b. Dec. 5, 1927, Loganville; home, Jacobus; U. of MD, B.S. 1953, Western MD Col., M.A. 1957; Methodist; married (Hilda).

Career: Army, 1946–48; Public schl. teacher, admin., 1952–74; Pres., Dallastown School Bd., 1966–67.

DC Office: 2263 RHOB 20515, 202-225-5836; Fax: 202-226-1000.

District Offices: Fed. Bldg., 200 S. George St., York 17405, 717-843-8887; 212 N. Hanover St., Carlisle 17013, 717-243-5432; 140 Baltimore St., Gettysburg 17325, 717-334-3430; 2020 Yale Ave., Camp Hill 17011, 717-763-1988; and 44 Frederick St., Hanover 17331, 717-632-7855, 800-631-1811.

Committees: *Economic & Educational Opportunities* (Chmn. of 24 R): Early Childhood, Youth and Families; Oversight and Investigations; Postsecondary Education, Training and Life-Long Learning. *International Relations* (2nd of 23 R): International Operations and Human Rights.

Group Ratings

	ADA	ACLU	COPE	CFA	LCV	CON	NSI	COC	ACU	NTLC	CHC
1994	10	22	33	20	12	85	90	92	90	96	86
1993	10	—	17	20	36	88	—	82	87	—	—

National Journal Ratings

	1993 LIB — 1993 CONS		1994 LIB — 1994 CONS	
Economic	32%	— 66%	30%	— 67%
Social	29%	— 69%	35%	— 65%
Foreign	30%	— 69%	14%	— 80%

Key Votes of the 103d Congress

1. Clinton Deficit Plan	N	3. Brady Handgun Purchase Y	5. Lmt. UN Cmnd. of Forces Y
2. NAFTA	Y	4. Strike Race/Death Pnlty. Y	6. Cut Missile Funds *

Key Votes of the 104th Congress

1. Congressional Compliance Y	6. Reform Crime Grant Y	11. Loser Pays Court Reform Y
2. Balanced Budget Amndmt. Y	7. National Security Act Y	12. Product Liability Reform Y
3. Bar Unfunded Mandates Y	8. Moratorium on Regs. Y	13. Welfare Reform Y
4. Pass Line Item Veto Y	9. Risk Assessment on Regs. Y	14. Term Limits Amndmt. Y
5. Relax Exclusionary Rule Y	10. Expnd. Priv. Prop. Rights Y	15. Tax Cuts Y

Election Results

1994 general	Bill Goodling (R) .... unopposed			($50,718)
1994 primary	Bill Goodling (R) .... unopposed			
1992 general	Bill Goodling (R)	98,599	(45%)	($201,951)
	Paul V. Kilker (D)...................	74,798	(34%)	($238,346)
	Thomas M. Humbert (I)...............	44,190	(20%)	($122,486)

TWENTIETH DISTRICT

The area south of Pittsburgh and next to the deceptively straight-edged West Virginia state line is one of the industrial backlands of America. The Scots and Irish bordermen who came here 200 years ago were wild settlers who were never tamed by townsmen in their native countries or here; this was the land of the Whiskey Rebellion of 1794. In the 19th Century, more or less never-ending seams of bituminous coal were discovered under these never-ending ridges. The offspring of the original settlers were joined by immigrants from Italy, Poland and Czechoslovakia, living in little frame houses packed into the towns on interstices between hills and rivers, within walking distance of steel factories, foundries and coal mine shafts. While life was never easy here, it seems to have gotten harder in the last two decades. The recession that followed the 1979 oil price increase hit the area hard and coal has never recovered from the battering it took after oil prices fell in 1982–83. While young people had been leaving the area for years, people in their prime family years are now fleeing, often leaving only the elderly who can find no market for their houses. Living standards and working conditions are much better than a generation ago, but there is less work and less of the hope for the advancement that makes the burdens of everyday living more bearable.

The 20th Congressional District of Pennsylvania consists of most of this southwest corner of the state, southwest of Pittsburgh, with erose boundary lines after the 1992 redistricting. Population here fell 7% in the 1980s, but the district's political leanings have remained strongly Democratic, as they have been since the United Mine Workers backed the New Deal and established the United Steelworkers as the bargaining agent in the steel mills. Recent decades made the 20th even more Democratic, more than almost any other non-central city district.

The congressman from the 20th District is Frank Mascara, a Democrat who came close to ousting incumbent Austin Murphy in 1992 and was elected after the incumbent retired in 1994. Murphy's problem was scandal: in 1987 he was reprimanded for letting someone else cast his vote, in 1990 he was charged with keeping a second family in the Washington area, in 1992 he had records subpoenaed because of extensive purchases of stamps from the House Post Office; he beat Mascara in the primary by only 36%–34% and beat an underfunded Republican in the general by only 51%–49%. Mascara grew up in this rough industrial country and knows its risks personally: his father died in a steel mill accident and his grandfather was killed in a mining accident. He served in the Army and was an accountant and small businessman before being elected Washington County controller in 1973; he was elected chairman of the county board of commissioners in 1980 and held that post through 1994. Mascara ran for the House on a labor-liberal platform, stressing the links among job creation, job training, education, health reform and crime prevention; he opposed the NAFTA and the new General Agreement on Tariffs and Trade. The Republican candidate, political newcomer Michael McCormick, owner of an investment and financial services business, called for a one-third reduction in federal jobs through a five-year hiring freeze, eliminating the Environmental Protection Agency and other agencies and privatizing of some government services. Astonishingly, he won 47% of the vote in this historically heavily Democratic district; Mascara won with just 53%.

In the House, Mascara sought a seat on the Economic and Educational Opportunities Committee, which handles job safety issues, or on Transportation and Infrastructure. But because of the shift in party control, there were no open slots on either committee for Democratic freshmen, and Mascara received a seat on the less active Government Reform and Veterans' Affairs panels, where he says he will concentrate on ensuring that budget cuts do not cause "undue" harm to veterans' benefits.

The People: Pop. 1990: 565,789; 40% rural; 17% age 65+; 96% White; 3% Black. Voting age pop.: 436,821; 3% Black. Households: 61% married couple families; 26% married couple fams. w. children; 36% college educ.; median household income: $26,294; per capita income: $13,349; median gross rent: $332; median house value: $56,600.

1992 Presidential Vote

Clinton (D) 121,823 (51%)
Bush (R) 69,811 (29%)
Perot (I) 48,251 (20%)

1988 Presidential Vote

Dukakis (D). 127,283 (59%)
Bush (R) 89,992 (41%)

Rep. Frank R. Mascara (D)

Elected 1994; b. Jan. 19, 1930, Belle Vernon; home, Charleroi; CA U. of PA., B.S. 1972; Roman Catholic; married (Delores).

Career: Army, 1946–47; Businessman, 1956-74; Washington Cnty. Controller, 1974–80; Chmn., Bd. of Cnty. Commissioners, 1980–94.

DC Office: 1531 LHOB 20515, 202-225-4665; Fax: 202-225-3377.

District Offices: 96 N. Main St., Washington 15301, 412-228-4326; 47 E. Penn St., Uniontown 15401, 412-437-5078; and 93 E. High St., Waynesburg 15370, 412-852-2182.

Committees: *Government Reform & Oversight* (21st of 22 D): Civil Service; Government Management, Information and Technology. *Veterans' Affairs* (15th of 15 D): Education, Training, Employment and Housing.

Group Ratings and 103rd Congress Votes: Newly Elected

Key Votes of the 104th Congress

1. Congressional Compliance Y	6. Reform Crime Grant	N	11. Loser Pays Court Reform N
2. Balanced Budget Amndmt. N	7. National Security Act	N	12. Product Liability Reform N
3. Bar Unfunded Mandates Y	8. Moratorium on Regs.	N	13. Welfare Reform N
4. Pass Line Item Veto Y	9. Risk Assessment on Regs. N		14. Term Limits Amndmt. Y
5. Relax Exclusionary Rule Y	10. Expnd. Priv. Prop. Rights Y		15. Tax Cuts N

Election Results

1994 general	Frank R. Mascara (D)	95,251	(53%)	($489,508)
	Mike McCormick (R)...................	84,156	(47%)	($363,080)
1994 primary	Frank R. Mascara (D)	41,252	(54%)	
	Charlie Kelly (D)	23,451	(31%)	
	Alan Benyak (D).......................	11,791	(15%)	
1992 general	Austin J. Murphy (D).................	114,898	(51%)	($309,425)
	Bill Townsend (R)...................	111,591	(49%)	($51,775)

TWENTY-FIRST DISTRICT

The best natural harbor on Lake Erie is in a state that few think of as a Great Lakes state. It is the harbor of Erie, Pennsylvania, protected by the Presque Isle peninsula, up in the remotest corner of Pennsylvania, 428 miles from Center City Philadelphia. This is heavy industry country: there is farmland here, and even some woods, but this land between the Great Lakes and the basin of the Ohio River has been prime heavy industry territory for more than 100 years.

The 21st Congressional District occupies this corner of Pennsylvania. About half its people are in Erie County. To the south are the farming areas of Crawford County, the steel-producing town of Sharon in Mercer County—on the Ohio border and part of the Youngstown-Warren area—and Butler County, a suburban and country area directly north of Pittsburgh. Politically this is closely balanced territory: Erie and Mercer Counties usually vote Democratic, and Butler and Crawford Counties usually vote Republican. The result was one of the classic marginal seats in the nation from 1964 to 1982 and again in 1994. The exception came during the tenure of

Tom Ridge, a Republican from a Catholic working class family in Erie, a Harvard graduate and Vietnam veteran, who was first elected here in 1982 and then won easily until he was elected governor in 1994.

The new congressman from the 21st is Phil English, who calls himself a Ridge Republican. English grew up in Erie and has worked at little else but politics and government. At 20, he was an alternate to the 1976 Republican National Convention, and he worked during the early 1980s as a Republican staffer in Harrisburg. In 1985 he became Erie controller; in 1988, he was the Republican nominee for state treasurer, losing to Democrat Catherine Baker Knoll. In 1990 he helped produce Rick Santorum's upset win in the Pittsburgh-area 18th District, the first step on Santorum's path to the Senate, and went on to other Republican staff jobs. In 1994, when Ridge ran for governor, English ran for the House and won 66% of the votes in the Republican primary—which attracted almost as many voters (61,000) as the Democratic (62,000). Nonetheless, the attention was on the Democratic primary, in which five candidates competed, four of them from Erie, two of them the men beaten by Ridge in 1982 and 1984. The race was close, with totals ranging from 16% to 23%, but the winner was the one candidate from outside Erie, Bill Leavens, who won 70% in Mercer, 40% in Butler and 6% in Erie. He had worked six years for the General Accounting Office and then four years for the Shenango Valley Chamber of Commerce. He campaigned as a moderate Democrat, against abortion; one of his primary opponents, Buzz Andrezeski, threatened to run as a write-in, then pulled back, saying, "Half a Democrat is better than no Democrat at all." In the general, three of the four counties voted on party lines. But Erie, English's home—and probably more important, Tom Ridge's—voted for the Republican, giving English a 49%–47% victory.

In the House English has been a spirited voice for the Contract With America. One of three freshman Republicans to gain a seat on the Ways and Means Committee, which he gained with help from Santorum and Bob Walker, he showed early that he will be a Gingrich loyalist. The committee assignment also leaves him well-positioned to focus on his personal agenda. He listed his priorities as reforming welfare, cutting wasteful spending and creating jobs for northwestern Pennsylvania, with an 18-point plan for revitalizing small business and manufacturing. Democrats obviously see English as highly vulnerable in 1996: In April 1995, he was one of two Republicans (along with Jay Dickey of Arkansas) targeted by the Democratic Congressional Campaign Committee in local ads that sought to link his votes with Gingrich's views.

The People: Pop. 1990: 565,806; 44% rural; 15% age 65+; 95% White; 4% Black; 1% Hispanic origin. Voting age pop.: 424,816; 3% Black; 1% Hispanic origin. Households: 58% married couple families; 26% married couple fams. w. children; 33% college educ.; median household income: $25,845; per capita income: $11,884; median gross rent: $326; median house value: $50,200.

1992 Presidential Vote

Clinton (D)	105,538	(45%)
Bush (R)	80,902	(34%)
Perot (I)	48,004	(20%)

1988 Presidential Vote

Dukakis (D)	104,662	(51%)
Bush (R)	101,259	(49%)

Rep. Philip S. English (R)

Elected 1994; b. June 20, 1956, Erie; home, Erie; U. of PA., B.A. 1978; Roman Catholic; married (Christiane).

Career: Staff Mbr., PA Senate; 1980–84; Erie City Controller, 1986–90; Chief of Staff, PA Sen. Melissa Hart 1990–92; Exec. Dir., PA Senate Finance Cmte., 1990–94.

DC Office: 1721 LHOB 20515, 202-225-5406; Fax: 202-225-3103.

District Offices: 310 French St., #107, Erie 16507, 814-456-2038; 306 Chestnut St., Meadville 16335, 814-724-8414; City Annex Bldg., Hermitage 16148, 412-342-6132; 327 N. Main St., Butler 16001, 412-285-5616.

Committees: *Ways & Means* (19th of 21 R): Human Resources; Social Security.

Group Ratings and 103rd Congress Votes: Newly Elected

Key Votes of the 104th Congress

1. Congressional Compliance Y	6. Reform Crime Grant Y	11. Loser Pays Court Reform Y
2. Balanced Budget Amndmt. Y	7. National Security Act Y	12. Product Liability Reform Y
3. Bar Unfunded Mandates Y	8. Moratorium on Regs. Y	13. Welfare Reform Y
4. Pass Line Item Veto Y	9. Risk Assessment on Regs. Y	14. Term Limits Amndmt. Y
5. Relax Exclusionary Rule Y	10. Expnd. Priv. Prop. Rights Y	15. Tax Cuts Y

Election Results

1994 general	Philip S. English (R)	89,439	(49%)	($450,795)
	Bill Leavens (D)	84,796	(47%)	($465,191)
	Others	6,588	(4%)	
1994 primary	Philip S. English (R)	40,770	(66%)	
	Mary Ann McConnell (R)	20,769	(34%)	
1992 general	Tom Ridge (R)	150,729	(68%)	($705,861)
	John C. Harkins (D)	70,802	(32%)	($15,800)

RHODE ISLAND

The tiny little city-state with a mouthful of an official name, Rhode Island and Providence Plantations, has as turbulent a political history as any state in the Union. A successful trading community since the 1600s, a leader in manufacturing since Samuel Slater replicated from memory an English water-powered cotton textile mill in Pawtucket in 1791, Rhode Island also had its beginning as an upstart community, a refuge for religious dissenters, "the sewer of New England," as the orthodox Cotton Mather put it. Rhode Island profited from slavery (two-thirds of America's slaves arrived on ships owned by Rhode Islanders) and war (the state boomed during the Civil War), and carried its tradition of tolerating just about anything into politics. Rhode Island refused to pay its share for the Revolutionary War, declined to send delegates to the 1787 Constitutional Convention, and delayed joining the Union until the other 12 states had, prompting George Washington to say, "Rhode Island still perseveres in that impolitic, unjust— and one might add without much impropriety—scandalous conduct, which seems to have marked all her public counsels of late." Later the new nation's first bank failure occurred here in 1809, when a bank capitalized at $45 issued $800,000 in bank notes. In the 1840s, conflict between hard money merchants and soft money farmers resulted in two state governments and a conflict known as Dorr's War, with the outcome determined when merchant Dorr's two ancient cannons failed to fire.

Then, in the 1930s, Rhode Island had something resembling a political revolution. Thousands of immigrants from French Canada, Ireland and Italy had come to Rhode Island to work in the textile mills; by the early 1900s, this colony of dissident Protestants had become the most heavily Catholic state in the nation. Yankee Republicans were able to appeal to Catholics by running French Canadians for high office for example. But national events—Al Smith's candidacy in 1928, when he carried Rhode Island, and Franklin Roosevelt's New Deal—moved the Catholics toward the Democrats. Then came the revolution: in 1935, the Democrats under Governor Theodore Green, although they had won only 20 of the 42 state Senate seats, refused to seat two Republicans. With the lieutenant governor's tie-breaker, they voted Democrats into the seats, and proceeded in 14 minutes to declare the state Supreme Court seats vacant, abolish state boards that controlled Democratic cities, strengthen the power of the governor and reorganize state government to purge Republicans. This ended the direct political control of Rhode Island's "Five Families"—the Browns, Metcalfs, Goddards, Lippitts and Chafees—who owned or ran many of the textile mills, the Rhode Island Hospital Trust (long the largest bank), the *Providence Journal*, Brown University, the Rhode Island School of Design and the state Republican Party; they ultimately lost the leadership of Rhode Island politics to the heirs of the 1935 Green revolution. The Democrats have won most elections with the lion's share of votes from Rhode Island's 64% Catholic majority, starting with Green's election in 1936 at age 69 to the first of his four terms as U.S. senator. From 1940–80, Democrats won every election for the U.S. House seat; its Democratic percentages in presidential elections from 1968–92 were rivalled only by Massachusetts. Republicans have won when they've been able to capitalize on scandal or Democratic disarray, as Governor Lincoln Almond was able to do in 1994. But the only really durable Republican politician has been John Chafee, elected governor in 1962, 1964 and 1966, senator in 1976, 1982 and 1988; and even he has lost twice statewide, in 1968 and 1972.

But Rhode Island political patterns were destabilized by economic transformation in the 1970s and 1980s. Manufacturing was reduced from almost half of Rhode Island jobs to one-quarter, with twice as many jobs in services, trade and finance. For years, the unions remained politically powerful, though they represented fewer and fewer workers. The state economy was

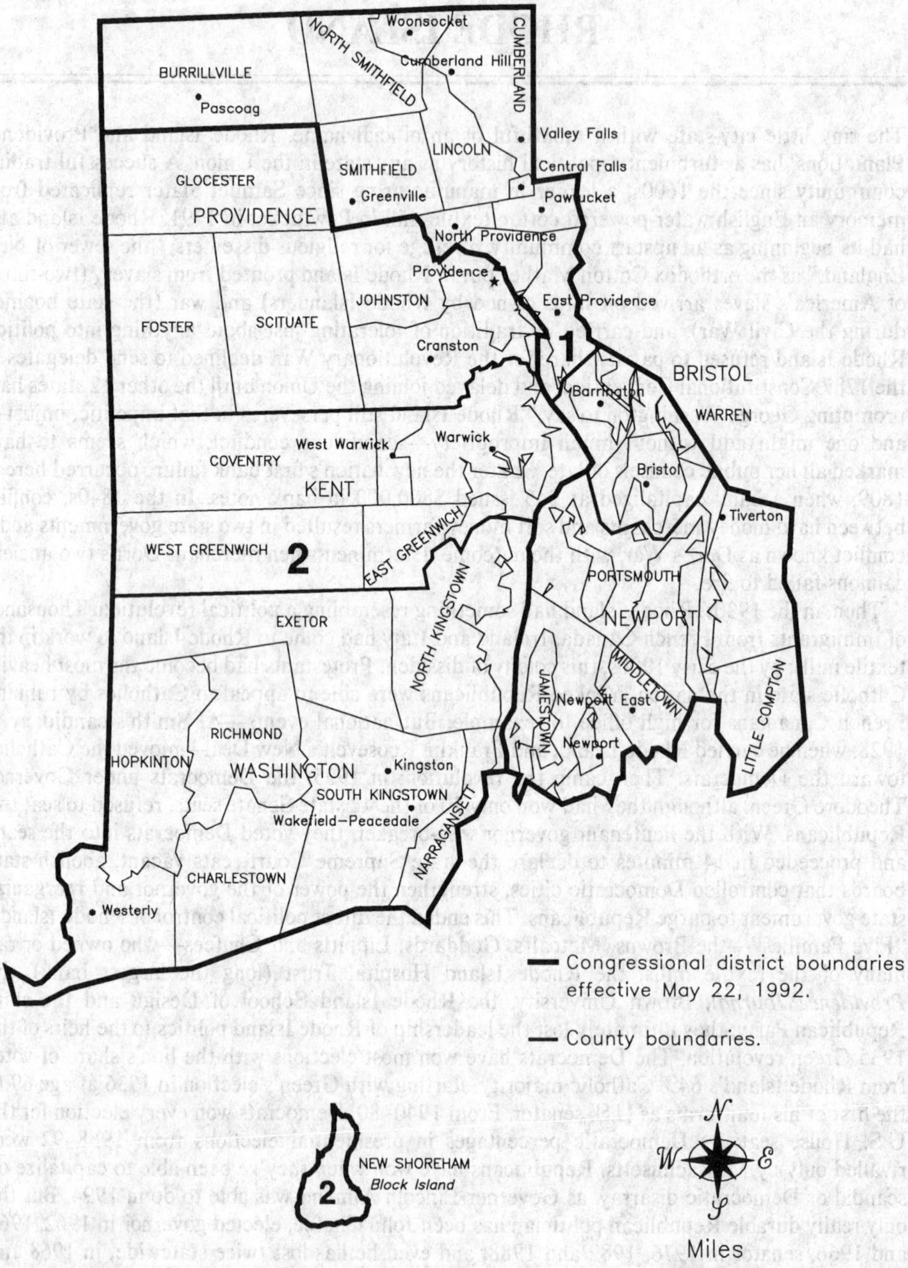

BURRILLVILLE

Pascoag

NORTH SMITHFIELD

Woonsocket

Cumberland Hill

CUMBERLAND

Valley Falls

LINCOLN

Central Falls

SMITHFIELD

GLOCESTER

Greenville

Pawtucket

PROVIDENCE

North Providence

Providence ★

FOSTER

SCITUATE

JOHNSTON

East Providence

Cranston

BRISTOL

Barrington

WARREN

West Warwick

Warwick

COVENTRY

Bristol

KENT

Tiverton

WEST GREENWICH

2

EAST GREENWICH

PORTSMOUTH

NEWPORT

EXETER

NORTH KINGSTOWN

MIDDLETOWN

JAMESTOWN

Newport East

LITTLE COMPTON

RICHMOND

HOPKINTON

WASHINGTON

Kingston

Newport

SOUTH KINGSTOWN

Wakefield–Peacedale

NARRAGANSETT

CHARLESTOWN

Westerly

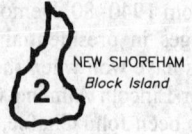
—— Congressional district boundaries
      effective May 22, 1992.

—— County boundaries.

NEW SHOREHAM
Block Island

N
W   E
S

Miles
0 1 2 3 4

quietly upgraded from blue-collar to white-collar, from textiles to high tech. The electorate, instead of being a mass of Catholic factory workers pressed into neighborhoods of three-story three-family houses, became comfortably affluent and suburban. Old political ties frayed, tolerance of scandal and sleaze diminished, and in the 1980s there were wild oscillations around the political spectrum. In 1984, after eight years of apparent satisfaction with Democratic Governor Joseph Garrahy, voters rejected his Greenhouse Compact 80%–20%, a policy conceived by Bill Clinton health plan deviser Ira Magaziner that would use government to encourage and incubate industry. The new governor, Republican businessman Edward DiPrete, promised to encourage private sector growth, but personal scandal and fallout from the late 1980s New England recession turned voters against him. Democrat Bruce Sundlun, running against him in successive years, won 32% in 1986, 49% in 1988, 74% in 1990. When he took office in January 1991 he immediately closed 45 state-backed credit unions and banks because of the collapse of the Rhode Island Share and Deposit Indemnity Corporation triggered by the disappearance of one mob-connected bank executive with $13 million. Scandal struck elsewhere as well: Chief Justice Thomas Fay was forced off the bench in 1993 and pled guilty to crimes in 1994; former Rhode Island House Speaker Matthew Smith was indicted in the same case; former Governor DiPrete was fined $30,000 for steering state contracts to friends and then indicted in 1994 on 23 counts of soliciting and accepting bribes for state contracts. Yet scandal can descend into farce. Providence Mayor Buddy Cianci was convicted in 1984 of a felony after he assaulted and burned a man he accused of having an affair with his wife; his political career ended, but he has since become a popular talk show host. And Governor Sundlun got bad publicity in 1993 when he illegally shot three racoons who, he said, were attacking a vixen fox and her cubs on his Newport property.

Governor. Governor Lincoln Almond grew up in the mill town of Central Falls, not the usual venue for a Republican, and got involved in local government in Lincoln in 1963, at 26. He ran for Congress in 1968 and lost, then served as U.S. Attorney from 1969 to 1977, ran for governor in 1978 and lost, and was U.S. Attorney again from 1981 to 1993. He ran for governor again in 1994, and this time won. It was an upset not only in the general but in the primary. For 1st District Congressman Ron Machtley, a career military veteran who in 1988 beat Banking Chairman Fernand St Germain, the man whose lax savings and loan laws led to the collapse of the industry and hundreds of billions in losses to taxpayers, was the favorite, leading incumbent Democrat Bruce Sundlun 61%–20% in one poll and Almond 63%–28% in another. But Almond rallied more party support and won the primary 58%–42%. Meanwhile, Sundlun, who had been unpopular since his first-term tax increases and had only won his 1992 primary by 52%–48% over Warwick Mayor Frank Flaherty, fell before liberal state Senator Myrth York by a humiliating 57%–27% margin. In the general election, the two disagreed on casino gambling; Almond was totally opposed, York said it was up to the people; curiously, the Mashantucket Pequot's Foxwoods casino in Connecticut has become a major employer of Rhode Islanders. Ultimately, Almond won by the narrow margin of 47%–44%. This was the first time Rhode Island has elected a governor to a four-year term, with a two-term limit. Almond attracted national attention in May 1995 when he signed into law a comprehensive gay rights bill banning discrimination towards homosexuals in housing, employment, credit and public accommodation.

Senators. Ethnic, Catholic Rhode Island has two blue-blooded WASPs as U.S. senators, both enduring political figures of great popularity. Claiborne Pell, first elected to the Senate in 1960, is now not only Rhode Island's senior politician, but one of the nation's: in the Senate, only Strom Thurmond and Robert Byrd have served longer. Pell's father was a one-term congressman from New York, a friend of Franklin Roosevelt and minister to Portugal and Hungary. Pell himself served in the Coast Guard and as a foreign service officer for several years, then settled on Bellevue Avenue in Newport, where you find the Vanderbilt and Auchincloss "cottages." (Rhode Island's Five Families tend to live on Providence's College Hill, with comfy summer places on Rhode Island Sound; the oceanfront palaces of Newport were built mostly by New Yorkers.) In 1987 Pell became what he long wanted to be, chairman of the Senate Foreign

Relations Committee, until Republicans regained control in 1995. But Pell tended to be an inactive, passive chairman—diffident, polite, but often tongue-tied—of a committee that wields much less influence than it once did. Ranking Republican, now-Chairman Jesse Helms spent much of his time monitoring Bush and Clinton Administration appointments, keeping track of policy in peripheral areas in which he is interested. Pell gave Democratic subcommittee chairmen larger budgets and more leeway. Most committee Democrats were longtime doves, reflexively opposed to the exertion of American military power almost anywhere, up through and including the Gulf war, whose outcome they spectacularly failed to foresee. In fall 1990, Pell called for the War Powers Act to be invoked during the Persian Gulf crisis, but did not pursue the point; almost entirely ignored, this statutory legacy of the Vietnam era has become effectively a dead letter. In June 1992, Pell called for consideration of military action to enforce UN sanctions in Bosnia; in early 1993, he was almost entirely silent on the issue. He and Helms did have one achievement, a 1992 bill penalizing countries trading in chemical weapons. Pell has other interests: banning nuclear weapons on the ocean floor, banning environmental alteration as a weapon of war, repealing Cold War laws. But as ranking minority member he seems unlikely to be a major force.

Over the years, Pell has accomplished more on education. He has one of the most liberal voting records in the Senate, and has been active on the Labor Committee and its Education subcommittee. His Pell grants for needy college and university students have become a household word over a generation; they have never been fully funded, and Pell has backed off from attempts to make them an entitlement not subject to annual appropriations. Pell was for many years the congressional father of the National Endowments for the Arts and the Humanities, but has played little role in controversies over their funding in the 1990s. He has also been one of the main promoters of ocean research (Rhode Island's license plates call it the "Ocean State"). He has made the Foreign Service a career service and sponsored early laws against drunk driving.

For all of Pell's singularities, he has been a formidable figure in Rhode Island, an iron fist in a velvet glove. He has received everything he wanted in politics, and by whipping the toughest competition this little state could offer. In the 1960 Democratic primary, he beat former Governor Dennis Roberts and former Governor, Senator and U.S. Attorney General J. Howard McGrath; this was the first time since Theodore Green's governorship that a candidate won who was not endorsed by the Democratic organization. In 1972, while Rhode Island was going Republican for president, Pell faced John Chafee, then a popular former governor and secretary of the navy, and beat him decisively. In 1990 he faced another tough challenge from Congresswoman Claudine Schneider, who had a strong environmental record and a great deal of energy. Her popularity ratings were as high as Pell's, and she shared most of his issue positions and a bit of his oddity. At a Pell-Schneider forum televised in August, Pell was asked to identify a piece of legislation he'd sponsored recently to help people in Rhode Island; he replied, "I couldn't give you a specific answer. My memory's not as good as it should be." The next day, however, Iraq invaded Kuwait, and Pell was soon getting coverage, on Rhode Island TV if not so much nationally, opining on the crisis and visiting the Persian Gulf. It was an exquisitely polite race, with Pell praising Schneider ("You've done a fine job . . . in the Congress, and I would congratulate you") and Schneider ads conceding Pell's strong points ("We all love Claiborne Pell," she said). "Quiet accomplishments that make a world of difference," Pell's ads proclaimed, and Rhode Islanders gave him a 62%–38% victory in what he indicated at the time would be his final campaign. There is widespread speculation Pell will retire in 1996, when he turns 78; he announced in April 1995 that he has Parkinson's disease. If he does not run, Democratic Congressman Jack Reed is interested and would be the favorite for the seat (Patrick Kennedy would not meet the constitutional requirement of age 30 to seek the seat in 1996); former Providence Mayor Joseph Paolino and Republican Attorney General Jeffrey Pine might also run. But it should be noted that Pell succeeded Theodore Green, another former Foreign Relations Committee chairman, who was first elected in 1936 at 69 and retired in 1960 at 93; if

Pell waits until that age, he will serve until 2012.

Senator John Chafee, a scion of one of Rhode Island's Five Families and a Marine veteran of World War II and Korea, has been a statewide elected official for most of the last three decades. He was elected to the legislature as a young lawyer, in 1956; ran for governor in 1962, and beat a Democratic incumbent by 398 votes; was reelected by wide margins in 1964 and 1966. For all his popularity, this Republican has had electoral setbacks in this Democratic state: he was defeated for a fourth term as governor in 1968 and, after several years as Richard Nixon's Secretary of the Navy, he lost the 1972 Senate race to Pell. But he won an open Senate seat in 1976, was reelected with just 51% in the recession year of 1982, then won with 55% in 1988 over Lieutenant Governor Richard Licht, whose uncle had defeated him 20 years before. Chafee turned out not to have strong opposition in 1994. He was opposed by a Pat Buchanan backer in the primary and won 69%–31% and, against Democratic legislator Linda Kushner, won in November 65%–35%, carrying every city and town. In his last three races he has received substantial backing, in endorsements and money, from environmental groups, who regard him as their most loyal Republican ally in Congress.

Chafee's voting record makes him a liberal Republican, by many measures the most liberal in the Senate, because of the cumulation of individual stands on various issues. But he can also be a stubborn and angry Republican partisan. From a state where labor unions were politically dominant when he started off in politics, he could not have hoped to rise without some sympathy for union positions. He has a mixed record on economics: he was a strong supporter of family and medical leave and opposed President Bush's school choice plan. But he bucked unions and many Democrats by backing NAFTA, the investment tax credit and reducing regulation to make more credit available from banks. He sided with the Clinton Administration on three of eight early budget votes, but he joined with relish the Republican filibuster against the Clinton stimulus package. On foreign policy he is moderate to liberal: he shares some of the caution about American military intervention of post-Vietnam doves and was cautious in 1992 and early 1993 about going into Bosnia. He also came out for repealing the ban on gays in the military. From a part of the country where Catholics have large families and Protestants preach birth control, he is pro-choice and was a vehement opponent of the "gag rule." Not leaving Rhode Island issues unaddressed, he worked to save the Seawolf submarine, produced just over the line in Connecticut, and to repeal the luxury tax which has destroyed Rhode Island's boat-building industry (boatbuilders are not themselves rich: see John Casey's Rhode Island novel *Spartina*). He inserted into the 1991 banking bill a provision helping Rhode Island finance the RISDIC payouts.

In recent years Chafee has concentrated on two areas—the environment and health care. Chafee is a Republican in the conservationist tradition that goes back to Theodore Roosevelt. He now chairs the Environment and Public Works Committee after 8 years as ranking Republican. He strongly supported the 1987 water projects bill passed over President Reagan's veto, the 1988 ocean dumping law, the 1989 oil spill law and, especially, the 1990 Clean Air Act, of which he was often the effective manager in the Senate. He has been a major force for protection of wetlands and barrier islands. He wants to toughen the Clean Water Act. He has also backed billboard control, commercial fishing safety, state partnerships for wildlife preservation and the Rio treaties on global climate change and biodiversity. On gun control, he favors a ban on the manufacture, sale and possession of handguns. Most or all of these stands are anathema to conservative Republicans, especially from western states, and just after Republicans regained control in November 1994 there was talk of challenging Chafee for the chairmanship. No challenge materialized, partly because the next Republican in line, John Warner, would not be much more reliable to westerners, and the next, Bob Smith, does not have great clout. The Senate's near-reverence for seniority also protected him.

Chafee's other great specialty is health care. In 1990 Bob Dole made him head of a Republican task force on the issue, well before it was raised to national attention by Harris Wofford's victory in Pennsylvania in November 1991. He has been a backer of managed competition, naturally refining his proposals as the facts on the ground and the terms of debate change; as he put it in a letter to Bill Clinton in early 1993, "Refining this theory so that it will work in practice will take much thought and creativity." In November 1991, Chafee came up with a Republican healthcare package, with tax incentives for workers and employers, beefed-up preventive care, and overhaul of medical malpractice. In September 1992, he prepared a compromise with then-Senate Finance Chairman Lloyd Bentsen, with group purchasing cooperatives, small group insurance reform, a cost containment commission, more portability of insurance, managed care and 100% tax deductibility for the self-employed: not all that much different from the Rowland-Bilirakis bill which could have passed Congress in 1994 if the Clintons had given the go-ahead. In 1993 and 1994 it was widely expected in Washington that Chafee's proposals would be at the center of a bipartisan compromise embraced by everyone from Hillary Rodham Clinton to Bob Dole. But Clinton declined any effort at compromise until the summer of 1994, while Dole became convinced during early 1994 not to seek compromise but to try to defeat the Clinton bill instead. That left little room for Chafee, who nonetheless convened bipartisan meetings and worked seriously on alternative legislation. As the last moment for legislating glimmered, in August 1994, Chafee infuriated Dole by supporting the Clinton crime bill, which Newt Gingrich had bottled up in the House but Dole could not bottle up in the Senate. By November 1994 the fulcrum point on health care had shifted far to the right of John Chafee.

So, long ago, had the fulcrum point of opinion in the Republican Conference. The hearty liberal Chafee was elected Republican Conference chairman over conservative Jake Garn in 1984 by 28–25. But Chafee, who describes himself as proud of being a "coalition builder, striving to end gridlock and move the legislative process forward," was far to the left of most Republicans, and he lost the post to the personable, conservative Thad Cochran in 1990, 22–21.

Presidential politics. Rhode Island is always among the most Democratic states in presidential elections—over the last generation, the most Democratic on average. The ancestral Democratic preference of the nearly two-thirds of Rhode Islanders who are Catholic has played a role. It should be added that abortion is not a big issue here, and Rhode Island overall is pro-choice: in states where Catholics are beleaguered minorities they may stand together and strongly oppose abortion; in Rhode Island, where they're the strong majority and where the mostly Mediterranean Catholics have never paid much attention to the mostly Irish priests anyway, they come out on this issue like Americans generally.

Rhode Island holds a presidential primary the same day as Massachusetts and has the lowest turnout in the nation, a vestige of the days when Democratic Party bosses had sway. Massachusetts neighbor Paul Tsongas and Maine neighbor George Bush won their primaries in 1992, but Bill Clinton carried the state in November.

Congressional Districting. The boundaries of Rhode Island's two congressional districts were altered only slightly for 1992. Providence is split and both districts are overwhelmingly Democratic.

The People: Est. Pop. 1994: 997,000; Pop. 1990: 1,003,464, down 0.7% 1990–1994. 0.4% of U.S. total, 43d largest; 14% rural. Median age: 34.0 years. 15.0% 65 years and over. 91.4% White, 4.6% Hispanic origin, 3.9% Black, 1.8% Asian, 2.5% Other. Households: 53.5% married couple families; 24% married couple fams. w. children; 43% college educ.; median household income: $32,181; per capita income: $14,981; 59.5% owner occupied housing; median house value: $133,500; median monthly rent: $416. 8.9% Unemployment. 1994 Voting age pop.: 764,000. 1994 Turnout: 348,099; 46% of VAP. Registered voters (1994): 552,638; no party registration.

Political Lineup: Governor, Lincoln Almond (R); Lt. Gov., Robert A. Weygand (D); Secy. of State, James Langevin (D) Atty. Gen., Jeffrey B. Pine (R); General Treasurer, Nancy J. Mayer (R). State Senate, 50 (40 D and 10 R); State House of Representatives, 100 (83 D and 17 R). Senators, Claiborne Pell (D) and John H. Chafee (R). Representatives, 2 (2 D).

1992 Presidential Vote

Clinton (D)	213,299	(47%)
Bush (R)	131,601	(29%)
Perot (I)	105,045	(23%)

1992 Democratic Presidential Primary

Tsongas	26,825	(53%)
Clinton	10,762	(21%)
Brown	9,541	(19%)
Other	2,878	(6%)
Uncommitted	703	(1%)

1988 Presidential Vote

Dukakis (D)	225,123	(56%)
Bush (R)	177,761	(44%)

1992 Republican Presidential Primary

Bush	9,853	(63%)
Buchanan	4,967	(32%)

GOVERNOR

Gov. Lincoln Almond (R)

Elected 1994, term expires Jan. 1999; June 16, 1936, Pawtucket; home, Lincoln; U. of RI, B.S. 1958, Boston U., J.D. 1961; Episcopalian; married (Marilyn).

Career: Naval Reserves, 1953–61; Practicing atty., 1962–94; Lincoln Town Admin., 1963–68; U.S. Atty. for RI, 1969–78, 1981–93; Pres., Blackstone Valley Land Develop. Foundation, 1982–94.

Office: The State House, #222, Providence 02903, 401-277-2080; Fax: 401-272-0860.

Election Results

1994 gen.	Lincoln Almond (R)	171,194	(47%)
	Myrth York (D)	157,361	(44%)
	Robert J. Healey, Jr. (I)	32,822	(9%)
1994 prim.	Lincoln Almond (R)	24,873	(58%)
	Ronald K. Machtley (R)	18,150	(42%)
1992 gen.	Bruce Sundlun (D)	261,484	(62%)
	Betty Leonard (R)	145,590	(34%)
	Others	17,744	(4%)

SENATORS

Sen. Claiborne Pell (D)

Elected 1960, seat up 1996; b. Nov. 22, 1918, New York, NY; home, Newport; Princeton, A.B. 1940, Columbia U., A.M. 1946; Episcopalian; married (Nuala).

Career: Coast Guard, 1941–45 (WWII), Coast Guard Reserves, 1945–78; Foreign Svc., U.S. Dept. of State, Czechoslovakia and Italy, 1945–52; Exec. Asst., RI Dem. St. Chmn., 1952, 1954; Consultant, DNC, 1953–60.

DC Office: 335 RSOB 20510, 202-224-4642; Fax: 202-224-4680.

State Offices: 418 Fed. Bldg., Providence 02903, 401-528-5456.

Committees: *Foreign Relations* (RMM of 8 D): European Affairs; International Economic Policy, Export and Trade Promotion; International Operations; Western Hemisphere and Peace Corps Affairs. *Labor & Human Resources* (2nd of 7 D): Children and Families; Education, Arts and Humanities (RMM). *Rules & Administration* (2nd of 7 D).

Group Ratings

	ADA	ACLU	COPE	CFA	LCV	CON	NSI	COC	ACU	NTLC	CHC
1994	95	74	75	75	92	24	0	23	0	12	7
1993	85	—	82	90	88	22	—	30	0	—	—

National Journal Ratings

	1993 LIB — 1993 CONS		1994 LIB — 1994 CONS	
Economic	83%	0%	72%	18%
Social	87%	8%	93%	0%
Foreign	92%	0%	87%	6%

Key Votes of the 103d Congress

1. Clinton Deficit Plan	Y	3. Brady Handgun Purchase	Y	5. Lmt. UN Cmnd. of Forces	N
2. NAFTA	Y	4. Strike Race/Death Pnlty.	N	6. Cut Missile Funds	Y

Key Votes of the 104th Congress

1. Congressional Compliance	Y	3. Balanced Budget Amndt.	N	5. Product Liability Reform	Y
2. Bar Unfunded Mandates	Y	4. Pass Line Item Veto	N	6. FY96 Budget	N

Election Results

1990 general	Claiborne Pell (D)	225,105	(62%)	($2,363,904)
	Claudine Schneider (R)	138,947	(38%)	($2,056,923)
1990 primary	Claiborne Pell (D)	unopposed		
1984 general	Claiborne Pell (D)	286,780	(73%)	($430,739)
	Barbara M. Leonard (R)	108,492	(27%)	($143,842)

Sen. John H. Chafee (R)

Elected 1976, seat up 2000; b. Oct. 22, 1922, Providence; home, Warwick; Yale, B.A. 1947, Harvard, LL.B. 1950; Episcopalian; married (Virginia).

Career: Marine Corps, 1942–45 (WWII), 1951–53 (Korea); Practicing atty., 1952–63, 1973–75; RI House of Reps., 1957–63, Minority Ldr., 1959–63; RI Gov., 1963–69; Secy. of the Navy, 1969–72.

DC Office: 505 DSOB 20510, 202-224-2921.

State Offices: 10 Dorrance St., Providence 02903, 401-528-5294.

Committees: *Environment & Public Works* (Chmn. of 9 R). *Finance* (4th of 11 R): Medicaid and Health Care for Low-Income Families (Chmn.); Medicare, Long-Term Care and Health Insurance; Social Security and Family Policy.

Group Ratings

	ADA	ACLU	COPE	CFA	LCV	CON	NSI	COC	ACU	NTLC	CHC
1994	65	65	25	42	85	65	70	57	30	64	28
1993	55	—	27	60	69	68	—	82	52	—	—

National Journal Ratings

	1993 LIB — 1993 CONS			1994 LIB — 1994 CONS	
Economic	42%	—	57%	35%	—	64%
Social	75%	—	24%	74%	—	25%
Foreign	51%	—	47%	45%	—	54%

Key Votes of the 103d Congress

1. Clinton Deficit Plan	N	3. Brady Handgun Purchase	Y	5. Lmt. UN Cmnd. of Forces	N
2. NAFTA	Y	4. Strike Race/Death Pnlty.	N	6. Cut Missile Funds	N

Key Votes of the 104th Congress

1. Congressional Compliance	Y	3. Balanced Budget Amndt.	Y	5. Product Liability Reform	Y
2. Bar Unfunded Mandates	Y	4. Pass Line Item Veto	Y	6. FY96 Budget	Y

Election Results

1994 general	John H. Chafee (R)	222,856	(65%)	($2,086,236)
	Linda J. Kushner (D)	122,532	(35%)	($805,867)
1994 primary	John H. Chafee (R)	27,906	(69%)	
	Thomas Post (R).....................	12,517	(31%)	
1988 general	John H. Chafee (R)	217,273	(55%)	($2,841,985)
	Richard A. Licht (D)	180,717	(45%)	($2,735,917)

FIRST DISTRICT

The 1st Congressional District is the eastern half of Rhode Island, east of Narragansett Bay, a line that cuts through Providence and then proceeds west and north to the Massachusetts-Connecticut-Rhode Island border. It includes much of Providence (elite College Hill around Brown University) and all of next-door Pawtucket; the onetime textile mill towns of the Blackstone Valley, Woonsocket and Central Falls; high income Barrington and Bristol and, south on the ocean, the old city of Newport, with its restored 18th Century houses and the "cottages" that are really palaces. Ethnically, this is the more French Canadian and less Italian of the two Rhode Island districts; politically, it is strongly Democratic in most elections.

The congressman from the 1st District is Patrick Kennedy, the youngest member of the 104th Congress, one of the growing number of grandchildren of Joseph P. Kennedy who are seeking political constituencies in corners of New England. Patrick Kennedy was born in 1967, his father's fifth year in the Senate; a week after his second birthday came the terrible accident at Chappaquiddick. He had a somewhat troubled youth, spending time in a drug rehabilitation clinic in 1986 before enrolling at Providence College, at 20, in 1987. Almost immediately, in 1988, he ran for a seat in the legislature and, in one of Rhode Island's tiny districts beat the longtime incumbent with the help of his name. He became chairman of the Rules Committee in 1992, a year after spending the now-infamous Easter weekend in Palm Beach with his father and cousin William Kennedy Smith. In 1994, when the 1st District's Congressman Ron Machtley ran for governor, Kennedy decided to run for Congress. He had to brush aside Scott Wolf, the Democrat who might have beaten Fernand St Germain in the 1988 primary had not the Republican Justice Department held back evidence of his wrongdoing and who then ran a strong race against Machtley in 1990.

Kennedy's Republican opponent was Kevin Vigilante, a physician who grew up on Long Island, worked in emergency rooms, with handicapped orphans in Romania and with female prison inmates infected with HIV. Vigilante was a moderate on issues, and raised enough to spend $803,000. But of course Kennedy, blessed with contacts on both coasts, could raise far more, and spent $1,070,000. And his margins in Providence, Pawtucket and the suburbs turned out to be enough for a 54%–46% victory.

Rather awkwardly Kennedy took his place in the Republican 104th Congress. His father, regarded as a lightweight when first elected Senator at 30, was able to demonstrate in a Democratic Senate that he was capable of managing serious legislation and making serious arguments. In a Republican House Patrick Kennedy may have a harder time demonstrating that he is something more than one of the minor players in a family dedicated politically to redistributing others' income. One must assume he is interested in becoming senator from Rhode Island. In 1996 he will only be 29, not old enough to take his place in the Senate if he were to be elected to Claiborne Pell's seat; but he must be assumed to be a candidate for the Senate seat now held by John Chafee, who turns 78 when it comes up in 2000.

The People: Pop. 1990: 501,696; 9% rural; 16% age 65+; 91% White; 3% Black; 1% Asian; 2% Other; 4% Hispanic origin. Voting age pop.: 393,122; 3% Black; 3% Hispanic origin. Households: 55% married couple families; 24% married couple fams. w. children; 42% college educ.; median household income: $31,675; per capita income: $15,224; median gross rent: $482; median house value: $136,400.

1992 Presidential Vote			1988 Presidential Vote		
Clinton (D)	107,141	(48%)	Dukakis (D)	115,562	(57%)
Bush (R)	62,758	(28%)	Bush (R)	85,619	(43%)
Perot (I)	50,842	(23%)			

Rep. Patrick J. Kennedy (D)

Elected 1994; b. July 14, 1967, Brighton, MA; home, Providence; Providence Col., B.A. 1991; Catholic; single.

Career: RI House of Reps., 1988–94.

DC Office: 1505 LHOB 20515, 202-225-4911; Fax: 202-225-3290.

District Offices: 286 Main St., Pawtucket 02860, 401-729-5600; 320 Thames St., Newport 02840, 401-841-0440; also, 127 Social St., Woonsocket 02895, 401-762-2288.

Committees: *National Security* (25th of 25 D): Military Research and Development. *Small Business* (19th of 19 D): Tax and Finance.

Group Ratings and 103rd Congress Votes: Newly Elected

Key Votes of the 104th Congress

1. Congressional Compliance	Y	6. Reform Crime Grant	N	11. Loser Pays Court Reform	N
2. Balanced Budget Amndmt.	N	7. National Security Act	N	12. Product Liability Reform	N
3. Bar Unfunded Mandates	N	8. Moratorium on Regs.	N	13. Welfare Reform	N
4. Pass Line Item Veto	Y	9. Risk Assessment on Regs.	N	14. Term Limits Amndmt.	N
5. Relax Exclusionary Rule	N	10. Expnd. Priv. Prop. Rights	N	15. Tax Cuts	N

Election Results

1994 general	Patrick J. Kennedy (D)	89,832	(54%)	($1,065,597)
	Kevin Vigilante (R)	76,069	(46%)	($803,371)
1994 primary	Patrick J. Kennedy (D)	33,215	(78%)	
	Norman J. Jacques (D)	9,390	(22%)	
1992 general	Ronald K. Machtley (R)	135,982	(70%)	($564,588)
	David R. Carlin, Jr. (D)	48,092	(25%)	($90,459)
	Others	9,801	(5%)	

SECOND DISTRICT

The 2d Congressional District is the western half of Rhode Island. While the 1st includes many mill towns, the 2d has most of its population in working and middle-class towns like Cranston and Warwick which, despite their Anglo-Saxon names, are inhabited mostly by people with Irish, Italian, French and Portuguese surnames. The 2d also has the affluent suburbs to the south along Narragansett Bay and the area around Westerly, where many residents work at the Electric Boat shipyards in Groton, Connecticut.

The congressman from the 2d is Jack Reed, a Democrat who won the seat in 1990 when its Republican incumbent Claudine Schneider ran against Senator Claiborne Pell and lost. Reed is from working-class Cranston, the son of a school custodian, a graduate of West Point who served in the 82d Airborne and taught at West Point; in 1979 he retired from the Army and went to Harvard Law School. In 1984, at 35, he was elected to the state Senate, where he served for six years, was close to the party leadership and built a good reputation. In the 1990 primary, he beat several better known Democrats, with the help of the state party endorsement and $350,000, much of which he held back for a TV barrage in the last three weeks; he won 49%–27% over Edward Beard, the incumbent Schneider beat in 1980. In the general, he faced Republican Trudy Coxe, executive director of Save the Bay. Reed talked in idealistic terms of the laws he pushed to help children, and of the volunteer work he did for the homeless, and he played up his military background, though he called for substantial defense cuts. Reed won with 59%.

Reed has compiled a substantially, though not quite totally, liberal record in the House. In 1991 he worked successfully for a $180 million loan guarantee package for Rhode Island in its banking crisis. He welcomed the Clinton Administration: "I sense with Clinton a reality and a pragmatism to deal with the problems. I would hate to see a return to the unrealities of the '80s," he said in 1993. On the Goals 2000 bill he insisted on a requirement that states show gradual progress in meeting educational standards; he also insisted on the "opportunity to learn" standards backed by teachers' unions. In on-the-scene reports, he criticized UN efforts in the Balkans as trying to be "all things to all people" and, before American Rangers were killed, said the Somalia mission was hampered by "poor intelligence" and "an awkward command structure." In summer 1994, after a trip to Haiti, he called for tougher economic sanctions and no military involvement; in March 1995 he said he was "pleasantly surprised" about Aristide's "apparent commitment to democratic reform."

Reed was reelected by a large margin in Republican 1994, and he is considered a very strong candidate for the Senate if Claiborne Pell retires in 1996.

The People: Pop. 1990: 501,768; 19% rural; 14% age 65+; 88% White; 4% Black; 1% Amer. Indian; 2% Asian; 3% Other; 5% Hispanic origin. Voting age pop.: 384,337; 4% Black; 4% Hispanic origin. Households: 55% married couple families; 25% married couple fams. w. children; 43% college educ.; median household income: $32,729; per capita income: $14,739; median gross rent: $498; median house value: $129,500.

1992 Presidential Vote

Clinton (D)	106,158	(46%)
Bush (R)	68,843	(30%)
Perot (I)	54,203	(23%)

1988 Presidential Vote

Dukakis (D)	109,561	(54%)
Bush (R)	92,142	(46%)

Rep. Jack Reed (D)

Elected 1990; b. Nov. 12, 1949, Cranston; home, Cranston; U.S. Military Acad., West Point, B.S. 1971, Harvard, M.P.P. 1973, J.D. 1982; Catholic; single.

Career: Army, 1967–79; Assoc. Prof., U.S. Military Acad. Dept. of Soc. Sciences, 1978–79; Practicing atty., 1982–90; RI Senate, 1984–90.

DC Office: 1510 LHOB 20515, 202-225-2735; Fax: 202-225-9580.

District Offices: Garden City Ctr., 100 Midway Place, #5, Cranston 02920, 401-943-3100.

Committees: *Economic & Educational Opportunities* (11th of 19 D): Oversight and Investigations; Postsecondary Education, Training and Life-Long Learning. *Judiciary* (8th of 15 D): Commercial and Administrative Law (RMM).

Group Ratings

	ADA	ACLU	COPE	CFA	LCV	CON	NSI	COC	ACU	NTLC	CHC
1994	85	78	78	80	89	16	30	50	5	15	7
1993	90	—	100	100	100	39	—	18	9	—	—

National Journal Ratings

	1993 LIB — 1993 CONS		1994 LIB — 1994 CONS	
Economic	78%	— 12%	73%	— 17%
Social	80%	— 13%	82%	— 15%
Foreign	78%	— 21%	75%	— 23%

Key Votes of the 103d Congress

1. Clinton Deficit Plan	Y	3. Brady Handgun Purchase Y	5. Lmt. UN Cmnd. of Forces N
2. NAFTA	N	4. Strike Race/Death Pnlty. N	6. Cut Missile Funds Y

Key Votes of the 104th Congress

1. Congressional Compliance Y	6. Reform Crime Grant N	11. Loser Pays Court Reform N
2. Balanced Budget Amndmt. N	7. National Security Act N	12. Product Liability Reform N
3. Bar Unfunded Mandates Y	8. Moratorium on Regs. N	13. Welfare Reform N
4. Pass Line Item Veto N	9. Risk Assessment on Regs. N	14. Term Limits Amndmt. N
5. Relax Exclusionary Rule N	10. Expnd. Priv. Prop. Rights N	15. Tax Cuts N

Election Results

1994 general	Jack Reed (D)	119,659	(68%)	($604,267)
	A. John Elliot (R)	56,348	(32%)	($224,743)
1994 primary	Jack Reed (D)	unopposed		
1992 general	Jack Reed (D)	144,450	(71%)	($815,622)
	James W. Bell (R)	49,998	(24%)	($39,260)
	Others	9,965	(5%)	

SOUTH CAROLINA

South Carolina stands as one of America's great success stories. Not so long ago this state looked like an underdeveloped country: beneath a thin veneer of rich people, this was among the poorest of states in the union, with income levels less than half the national average and with high levels of illiteracy and disease. South Carolina was founded by planters from Barbados and even today there are reminders of the West Indies—the semitropical climate, the lush foliage and trademark palmettos, and the $4 billion of destruction wreaked by Hurricane Hugo's 135 mile-per-hour winds in September 1989 all are reminiscent of the Caribbean. But economically and culturally, South Carolina is now securely part of the booming South Atlantic region from Maryland south into Florida, filling up with new retirement condominiums, factories and office buildings, giant shopping centers, and leading the nation's economic growth in the 1990s.

In South Carolina, this growth occurs atop the plantation economy built on the swampy Low Country below the Fall Line, where the great 18th and 19th Century planters built rice paddies and cultivated exotic crops like indigo in the days before cotton was king. The great wealth of these Low Country planters was destroyed by the Civil War which they, more than any other southerners, provoked. But their pride and way of life continued as did that of former slaves. As late as 1940, 43% of South Carolinians were black, most living in conditions incomprehensible today. South Carolina's economic growth had started only in the 1920s, with that lowest-wage of industries, textiles. Mills were built in the Up Country above Columbia, hiring poor whites (never blacks) from the hardscrabble farms in the area. Politics remained a rough business, with harsh appeals to racial fear and economic envy, and with limited participation: in 1940, just 99,000 South Carolinians voted for president, 96% of them Democratic—the highest Democratic percentage in the nation. In the Democratic primary the year Strom Thurmond ran for governor, 1946, only 271,000 people voted in this state of more than two million.

Now this once underdeveloped country has joined the First World. Personal incomes are near national levels; health standards are like those in the rest of the nation; education levels have been rising toward the national average. South Carolina was helped for some years by the military bases clustered around Charleston, by the big textile mills around Greenville and Spartanburg, and by the outmigration of Low Country blacks to big cities of the northeast. Then, starting in the 1970s, South Carolina became the most aggressive state in the South in attracting new industry. It enticed French and German firms to set up major operations in the Piedmont and the Low Country. It advertised its business climate (one of the lowest rates of unionization), its taxes (low), and its willingness to meet local employers' needs (very high).

But it also used some of its new affluence to upgrade the quality of its local work force through public expenditures on schools as well as highways, teachers as well as police. Capping its success symbolically was German car manufacturer BMW's decision in 1992 to build its first U.S. assembly plant off I-85 in Spartanburg County, a decision prompted in part by $130 million in incentives from Governor Carroll Campbell. But even more typical are the decisions of hundreds of small employers to open plants, rent offices and create jobs in what has become one of America's more vibrant economic environments.

Much of this was possible because South Carolina was relieved, quite against the will of its white majority, of the burdens and stigma of racial segregation. Beginning in the 1950s, fewer people were kept from voting by the poll tax, and turnout surged as South Carolina became competitive in the presidential elections of 1952, 1956 and 1960. Then the Civil Rights Act of 1964 and the Voting Rights Act of 1965 ended legal segregation of public accommodations and workplaces and brought blacks suddenly into the electorate.

Politically, this new South Carolina has been moving, more than any other state in the South,

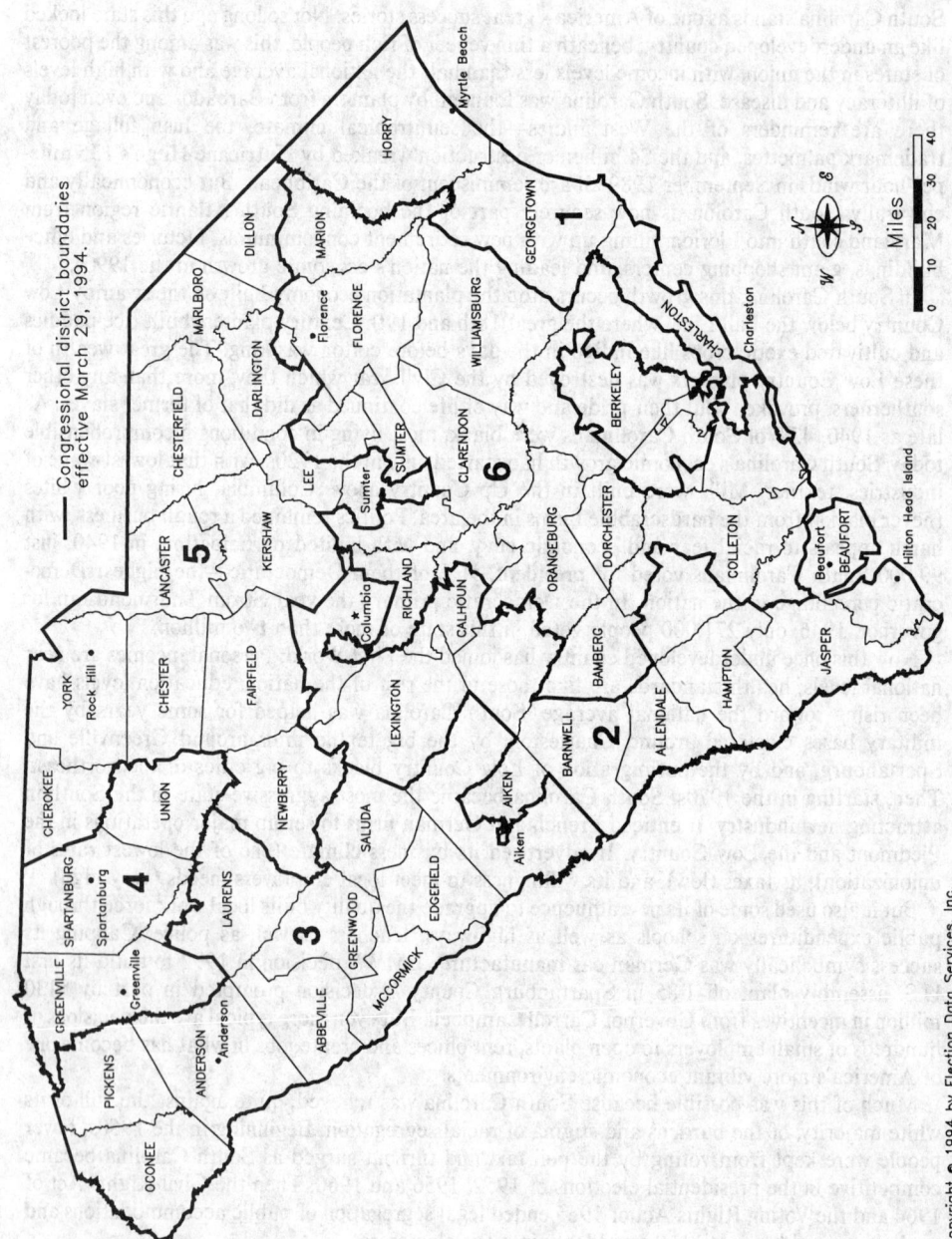

Congressional district boundaries
effective March 29, 1994.

toward the Republicanism exemplified by its native son, the late Lee Atwater, former Republican National Committee chairman and 1988 Bush campaign manager. Republicans hold the governorship and one Senate seat and came close to winning the other in 1992; they hold four of the state's six House seats, and came close to a fifth in 1994, when they led Democrats in votes for the House 64%–36%; they won six of eight downballot state offices in 1994 and elected a Republican Speaker of the House in 1995. South Carolina cast the second highest percentage for George Bush in 1992 (after Mississippi) and the third highest in 1988 (after Utah and New Hampshire). This Republican trend continues even though the 30% of South Carolinians who are black remain heavily Democratic.

Republican gains were limited in the 1960s and 1970s by opposition to busing; most white southerners didn't want to rally to a past they were proud to have overcome. One who understood this instinctively was Senator Strom Thurmond, the once fierce segregationist who left the Democratic Party in 1964 to become a Republican and then, in the early 1970s, became the first southern senator to hire black staffers and make black patronage appointments. Another is Carroll Campbell, an Atwater ally elected congressman in 1978 and governor in 1986, a policy activist who rather than play the race card stressed race-free issues. He sought black votes while gaining near-unanimous white support by emphasizing economic growth and education reform, against a background of a relaxed acceptance of patriotism and traditional values in a world that, even in South Carolina, has been moving away from old traditions. Democrats had once hoped to unite blacks plus enough whites to make a bare majority, but Republicans have come closer to doing it the other way around, uniting almost all whites with enough blacks to make a huge majority. The results can be seen in the numbers: Republicans Campbell and Thurmond were reelected in 1990 with 69% and 64% of the vote, while the state's leading Democrat, Senator Ernest Hollings, won by a bare 50%–47% margin in 1992. The current Republican Governor, David Beasley, was elected by only a 50%–48% margin. But his Democratic opponent, Lieutenant Governor Nick Theodore, started the race much better known, and Republicans ran well ahead of Beasley in other contests. Bill Clinton has spent the first days of recent years in South Carolina, at the New Year's Renaissance Weekend at Hilton Head, sponsored by onetime Democratic gubernatorial candidate Phil Lader—and now head of the Small Business Administration—with former Governor and now Education Secretary Richard Riley; but these Democrats, despite their activist policies and personal strengths, now seem in the minority here.

Not everything has gone well for South Carolina. Despite Thurmond's influence, the Navy has pretty much pulled out of the Charleston area; the Savannah River nuclear plant, with the only tritium plant in the country, was shut down in 1993; Hurricane Hugo inflicted much damage here in 1989; the nationally publicized murders in Union by Susan Smith of her two young sons showed the underside of American life. South Carolina may present more starkly than most states the contrast between belief in traditional religion and morals and a daily life in which these seem to be honored less and less. But it is also a state proud of its Confederate heritage and its civil rights progress—it flies the Confederate flag over the Capitol but also seeks to honor civil rights pioneers—proud of Charleston's Spoleto Festival music and arts celebration as it is of Darlington's annual Southern 500 Stock Car Race, proud that it is a national leader after so many years of lagging behind.

Governor. In 1994, South Carolina had to choose a new governor with Carroll Campbell having completed his term. Campbell had produced lower taxes; he built on the education reforms of his predecessor Democrat Richard Riley and chaired the National Governors' Association Task Force on Education from 1989–90 that set national goals for achievement; he boasted of programs to reduce infant mortality and of reforming Medicaid with managed care; he did much to attract the BMW plant to Spartanburg. Campbell also took a role in national politics. He and Atwater were the architects of moving the 1988 South Carolina presidential primary to the Saturday before Super Tuesday, in order to give George Bush a jump-start in the South; he got one, beating Bob Dole 49%–21%. Highly popular at home, Campbell contemplated running for president, but in 1994 announced that he would not. He remains a possible vice presidential nominee (and he has all but announced his endorsement for Dole) in 1996 or a Cabinet appointee in 1997. He may have some interest in running for Ernest Hollings's Senate seat in 1998 or for Strom Thurmond's if and when it becomes open.

South Carolina's new governor is David Beasley, like Thurmond a Democrat-turned-Republican. Beasley was elected to the state House in 1978 at age 20 and served 14 years, rising to majority leader and becoming chairman of the Education and Public Works Committee. In 1992, he resigned and ran for governor, with covert support (dictated by party decorum) from Campbell and open support from the Christian right. In the Republican primary, Beasley faced flamboyant Charleston Congressman Arthur Ravenel and former Congressman Tommy Hartnett, who had won 47% against Senator Ernest Hollings in 1992. Beasley made no secret that he had a born-again religious experience in 1984, and got attention when a Democrat joked that he had two skills needed by a Republican, how to handle snakes and speak in tongues. But this was an asset in a state where 55% of Beasley's voters identified themselves as supporting his religious views. In a Republican primary that attracted 253,000 voters, almost as many as the Democrats' 261,000, Beasley won 47% to 32% for Ravenel and 21% for Hartnett; among Democrats, Theodore had 49.6% to 38% for Charleston Mayor Joe Riley, Jr. Ravenel called the runoff a battle "for the soul" of the Republican Party; Beasley said this was "Christian-bashing," and won the runoff 58%–42%, while Theodore finished only microscopically ahead of Riley in the Democratic primary. The general election was a battle between the affable, mature Theodore and the fervent, young Beasley. The Democrat carried Charleston County and Columbia—cities where Republicans usually run strong—but Beasley made inroads in rural areas and carried the Greenville-Spartanburg I-85 corridor solidly. This was a battle along cultural lines: Theodore carried 92% of blacks, Beasley 80% of the white religious right; Beasley carried young voters, while Theodore won those with graduate school degrees. Beasley's margin may have been only 50%–48%, but the Republican tide extended to most statewide offices and resulted in the election of Republican House Speaker David Wilkins.

In office, Beasley called for state term limits and unfunded mandate laws, property tax cuts, efforts to encourage small business job creation and encouragement of exports, a work requirement and two-year limit for welfare and tougher prison sentences.

Senators. The most enduring figure in American politics today is Strom Thurmond. The man who became chairman of the Senate Armed Services Committee in 1995 was elected to the legislature as a Democrat in 1932, was elected governor in 1946, ran for president in 1948 as a "States' Rights Democrat" and won 39 electoral votes. He was elected senator as a write-in in 1954, resigned and ran for the seat again in 1956; he has served as both a Democrat and a Republican, and was elected in 1990 to a seventh term which, if he serves it out, will make him the oldest person ever to serve in Congress. He switched to the Republican Party to support Barry Goldwater in 1964, a move that seemed unwise at the time but proved sentient about the direction of opinion; in 1968, Thurmond provided key backing to hold the South for Richard Nixon at the Republican National Convention. Thurmond has combined a reputation for steadfastness with a flexibility and adroitness that have enabled this onetime symbol of racial segregation to prosper politically in an era of integration. In 1957, he set a record, filibustering for over 24 hours against a fair housing bill. But when South Carolina blacks started voting in large numbers after the Voting Rights Act of 1965, Thurmond shifted gears and became the first Southern senator to hire black staffers and appoint blacks to high positions (including a federal judgeship). He voted for renewal of the 1982 Voting Rights Act and the Martin Luther King Holiday. He probably gets few black votes, but those who are adamantly against him don't form a strong enough political base for a possible opponent.

Thurmond's party switch was an example of his mind at work; there are no baroque embellishments to his thoughts and he is not interested in nuance or qualification. His intellect is simple but strong: he decides where he wants to go, figures out how to get there, and then does it. His health seems good. He has been a proud teetotaler and physical fitness buff all his life, and always an appreciator of beautiful women. His first wife was 23 years his junior; after she died, he married a South Carolina beauty queen 44 years younger; the first of his four children was born when he was 69. In hearings and on the Senate floor, Thurmond usually seems heavily scripted and has slowed some physically, but he responds aptly to arguments and interjections and is always polite and courtly.

As the senior member of the Senate, Thurmond is president pro tempore, a position that puts him theoretically fourth in line for the presidency. He chaired the Judiciary Committee from 1981–87, and was at the center of the fights over Supreme Court nominees Robert Bork and Clarence Thomas. He has sponsored many bills to extend the death penalty and reduce federal courts' jurisdiction over collateral attacks on state criminal convictions. He has supported some gun control measures endorsed by police, such as bans on cop-killer bullets and plastic guns. He is a stickler for ethics, supporting outside income limits for senators, bans on lobbying for federal projects on a contingent fee basis and lobbying for foreign countries by former federal officials. He backs the use of fetal tissue in research; one of his daughters has diabetes, research on which requires such material.

In 1993, Thurmond exercised his option to switch to the ranking position on Armed Services, replacing John Warner there; this meant that when Republicans won control in 1995, Thurmond became chairman of Armed Services—leading to some private grumbling and preliminary maneuvering by Republicans who felt that he was not up to the job but no change in the seniority-reverential Senate—and Orrin Hatch assumed the Judiciary chairmanship. Thurmond's identification with things military is strong. He landed in Normandy on D-Day and by 1995 had served on Armed Services for 36 years. He clearly wants to reverse the slide in the Pentagon budget and increase defense spending, and wants the Pentagon to spend less on non-military matters. He is worried about the readiness of U.S. troops and supports a missile defense system. Interestingly, the budget realities and the base closing bill written by Dick Armey limit severely what Thurmond and House Chairman Floyd Spence can do to protect South Carolina's military bases, many of which are already closing. Thurmond appears to lack the votes to turn the trends around but he may be able to help his state's facilities at the margin.

Thurmond's almost non-stop politicking in South Carolina has helped keep his popularity exceedingly high. His last tough challenge was from businessman Charles Ravenel in 1978, when he got 56%; he won with 67% and 64% in 1984 and 1990. Despite doubts about whether he will follow through, he said that he plans to run for reelection in 1996, for a term that would take him to 2002, when he turns 100. Oddly, Democrats might have a better (though not great) chance running against Thurmond on the basis of his age than against a would-be successor, such as Campbell; an early 1995 poll showed that 66 per cent of voters think that he should retire in 1996. He stands to become the oldest member of Congress ever in February 1996. He continues to raise campaign money, although he has also donated $733,000 to scholarships and endowed university chairs in South Carolina.

Approaching 30 years in the Senate, and into his 70s, Ernest (Fritz) Hollings is still the junior senator from South Carolina. But Hollings has always done things at unusual ages. He was first elected to the legislature in 1948, at 26, was a member of the leadership two years later, was elected governor in 1958 at 36, serving as South Carolina first faced school desegregation, and then spent four years out of office until he beat another former governor in the 1966 Senate race. Hollings may look like an aristocrat, but he is from a middle-class family, got his education at The Citadel in Charleston and made his living as a trial lawyer, a profession he continues to avidly support; he has one of the quickest and sharpest tongues in the Senate. He is "the Senate bully," wrote his former colleague the late John Tower, and Hollings' instinct for zeroing in on others' weaknesses can be directed at the strong as well as the weak. Hollings has had his disappointments. His campaign for president fell flat in 1984, and after he was the only South Carolinian to vote against the Gulf war, he suddenly found himself supported by far less than half his state's voters after enjoying years of top-level, positive visibility.

For much of the 1980s and 1990s, he has concentrated on budget issues. In the early 1980s he favored a budget freeze; in 1985, he co-sponsored the Gramm-Rudman-Hollings deficit-cutting bill, which in fact did lead to the lowest deficits in the post-1980 era. He strongly backs the line-item veto and was one of 19 Senate Democrats to vote for it in 1995. When Democrats were in the majority, his votes typically have left him in the Senate's ideological middle, according to *National Journal* vote ratings. But, along with other Senate Democrats, he stood aside taking potshots when the new Republican majority launched the largest deficit-reduction package ever. In 1993, he advocated replacing the proposed energy tax and the tax increase on social security benefits favored by the Clinton Administration with a value-added tax; the VAT revenue would go to reduce the deficit. This is typical Hollings: he believes in an activist federal government, but one subject to strict discipline. His frustration is that the dominant political forces for a dozen years believed in neither.

As chairman of the Commerce, Science and Transportation Committee from 1987–1994, Hollings was an activist and a regulator, the major opponent of deregulating broadcasting and a major proponent of the 1992 cable reregulation act, the one law on which Congress overrode President Bush's veto. In 1994, after the House near-unanimously passed a telecommunications bill, Hollings opposed it, insisting that the regional Bell companies get actual competition in local service before they were permitted to enter the long distance or cable markets. The result was that no bill passed. Now, as ranking minority member, Hollings has less power, but still sought to work with new chairman Larry Pressler to exercise considerable leverage on what he terms his effort to protect consumers on an issue on which most senators feel more comfortable with a bipartisan approach. He has worked on various ocean issues on the committee, including the 1988 ocean dumping law, and has championed a National Global Climate Change Research Act. On trade issues, he proudly proclaims himself a "hawk," shepherding the textile trade bill to passage in 1990, but President Bush's veto was sustained. In early 1991, he led opposition to fast-tracking NAFTA and in 1993 opposed NAFTA itself based on what he saw as Mexico's questionable political system. In 1994, his objections required the bill to be referred to his committee and the vote on GATT to be postponed until after the election over George Mitchell's opposition, depriving President Clinton and Democrats of a needed legislative victory; then he opposed it, although it eventually passed with little difficulty.

Hollings's vote against the Gulf war resolution was a break from his usual hawkish record on foreign and military issues, though he did lead opposition to the MX missile in the early 1980s; he seemed guided by his disgust with the rulers of Kuwait. Fully 70% of voters disagreed with Hollings, and he seemed hard-pressed in the 1992 race by former Republican Congressman Tommy Hartnett. But Hartnett proved a weak campaigner and let Hollings argue he was the true "outsider" and ran an ad showing himself being praised at a White House ceremony by President Reagan. Hartnett called for term limits and the line-item veto, charged Hollings with supporting hiring quotas for gays, and hit Hollings for inspecting his own beachfront property while on a helicopter surveying wreckage from Hurricane Hugo. Hollings won by the unimpressive margin of 50%–47%, but he at least survived while the Democrats from the two adjoining states who also voted against the Gulf war resolution, Terry Sanford and Wyche Fowler, were defeated. This was Hollings's closest margin by far since 1966 and suggests that he may not run for reelection in 1998, when he turns 76.

Presidential politics. South Carolina is one of the top three Republican states, with Utah and Idaho, to judge from the 1992 and 1988 presidential vote—a tribute to the late Lee Atwater. This is also evidence of the expanding South Carolina private sector economy, the strength of its traditional cultural values and the fact that so much of its growth has been in Hilton Head-style condominium communities on the coast and suburban areas well away from the cities.

Also, South Carolina's Republican primary has become more important than its Democratic contest. Atwater purposefully scheduled the Republican primary here for the Saturday before Super Tuesday, and in 1988, George Bush won a smashing victory over Bob Dole and Pat Robertson, forecasting the southern sweep that clinched his nomination. In 1992, Bush won with two-thirds of the vote, squashing Pat Buchanan's claims to represent the South and reducing

David Duke to the single-digit crank candidate he had been before winning a Louisiana legislative seat by a few dozen votes in 1989. The Democrats, in contrast, scheduled their 1988 caucus after Super Tuesday, to deflect attention; it was won by Jesse Jackson, who was born in South Carolina, and was briefly registered to vote there after his 1984 campaign. In 1992, the Democratic primary was moved to the same day as the Republicans, giving a huge victory to Bill Clinton over the several Yankees in the race.

Congressional districting. The Voting Rights Act amendments of 1982 were interpreted to require creation of a black-majority district in South Carolina, and the plan adopted in May 1992 stitches together black majority areas in the Low Country (but not the condominium-glutted coast) and in Columbia and Charleston to create the 6th District. The plan made the 1st, 2d, 3d and 5th Districts more Republican. After the Supreme Court's *Shaw v. Reno* case, that plan was overturned by a federal court in July 1993; the legislature passed a plan the following March with only minor changes for 1994.

The People: Est. Pop. 1994: 3,664,000; Pop. 1990: 3,486,703, up 5.1% 1990–1994. 1.4% of U.S. total, 25th largest; 45% rural. Median age: 32.0 years. 11.4% 65 years and over. 69.0% White, 29.8% Black. Households: 56.4% married couple families; 27% married couple fams. w. children; 39% college educ.; median household income: $26,256; per capita income: $11,897; 69.8% owner occupied housing; median house value: $61,100; median monthly rent: $276. 6.2% Unemployment. 1994 Voting age pop.: 2,740,000. 1994 Turnout: 930,279; 34% of VAP. Registered voters (1994): 1,499,589; no party registration.

Political Lineup: Governor, David M. Beasley (R); Lt. Gov., Bob Peeler (R); Secy. of State, Jim Miles (R); Atty. Gen., Charles M. Condon (R); Treasurer, Richard Eckstrom (R); Comptroller General, Earle E. Morris, Jr. (D). State Senate, 46 (27 D and 18 R); State House of Representatives, 124 (63 R, 58 D, and 3 I). Senators, Strom Thurmond (R) and Ernest F. (Fritz) Hollings (D). Representatives, 6 (4 R and 2 D).

1992 Presidential Vote

Bush (R)	577,508	(48%)
Clinton (D)	479,514	(40%)
Perot (I)	138,782	(12%)

1992 Democratic Presidential Primary

Clinton	73,221	(63%)
Tsongas	21,338	(18%)
Harkin	7,657	(7%)
Brown	6,961	(6%)
Other	7,237	(6%)

1988 Presidential Vote

Bush (R)	606,443	(62%)
Dukakis (D)	370,554	(38%)

1992 Republican Presidential Primary

Bush	99,558	(67%)
Buchanan	38,247	(26%)
Duke	10,553	(7%)

GOVERNOR

Gov. David M. Beasley (R)

Elected 1994, term expires Jan. 1999. b. Feb. 26, 1957, Lamar; home, Society Hill; Clemson U., 1975–78; U. of SC, B.A. 1979, J.D. 1983; Baptist; married (Mary).

Career: Practicing atty., 1983–94; SC House of Reps., 1979–92

Office: P.O. Box 11369, The State House, Columbia 29211, 803-734-9818; Fax: 803-734-1598.

Election Results

1994 gen.	David M. Beasley (R)	470,756	(50%)
	Nick A. Theodore (D)	447,002	(48%)
	Others	17,128	(2%)
1994 runoff	David M. Beasley (R)	134,297	(58%)
	Arthur Ravenel, Jr. (R)	98,915	(42%)
1994 prim.	David M. Beasley (R)	119,724	(47%)
	Arthur Ravenel, Jr. (R)	81,129	(32%)
	Tommy Hartnett (R)	52,866	(21%)
1990 gen.	Carroll A. Campbell, Jr. (R) . . .	528,831	(69%)
	Theo Mitchell (D)	212,034	(27%)
	Others	20,100	(3%)

SENATORS

Sen. Strom Thurmond (R)

Elected 1956, seat up 1996; b. Dec. 5, 1902, Edgefield; home, Aiken; Clemson U., B.S. 1923; Baptist; separated.

Career: Army, 1942–46 (WWII), Army Reserves, 1923–59; Teacher and coach, 1923–29; Edgefield Cnty. Supervisor of Educ., 1929–33; Practicing atty., 1930–38, 1951–55; SC Senate, 1933–38; Circuit Judge, 1938–42; SC Gov., 1947–51; States' Rights candidate for U.S. Pres., 1948; U.S. Senate, 1954–56; Pres. Pro Tem, U.S. Senate, 1981–87.

DC Office: 217 RSOB 20510, 202-224-5972; Fax: 202-224-1300.

State Offices: 1835 Assembly St., #1558, Columbia 29201, 803-765-5494; 334 Meeting St., #600, Charleston 29493, 803-724-4282; 211 York St. NE, #29, Aiken 29801, 803-649-2591; and 401 W. Evans St., Florence 29501, 803-662-8873.

Committees: *President Pro-Tempore. Armed Services* (Chmn. of 11 R) *Judiciary* (2nd of 10 R): Administrative Oversight and the Courts; Antitrust, Business Rights and Competition (Chmn.); Terrorism, Technology and Government Information. *Veterans' Affairs* (2nd of 7 R).

Group Ratings

	ADA	ACLU	COPE	CFA	LCV	CON	NSI	COC	ACU	NTLC	CHC
1994	5	17	13	25	0	65	100	88	•96	83	93
1993	10	—	10	10	6	57	—	82	83	—	—

National Journal Ratings

	1993 LIB	—	1993 CONS	1994 LIB	—	1994 CONS
Economic	19%	—	80%	29%	—	68%
Social	25%	—	74%	0%	—	85%
Foreign	16%	—	77%	0%	—	94%

Key Votes of the 103d Congress

1. Clinton Deficit Plan	N	3. Brady Handgun Purchase	Y	5. Lmt. UN Cmnd. of Forces	Y
2. NAFTA	N	4. Strike Race/Death Pnlty.	Y	6. Cut Missile Funds	N

Key Votes of the 104th Congress

1. Congressional Compliance	Y	3. Balanced Budget Amndt.	Y	5. Product Liability Reform	Y
2. Bar Unfunded Mandates	Y	4. Pass Line Item Veto	Y	6. FY96 Budget	Y

Election Results

1990 general	Strom Thurmond (R)	482,032	(64%)	($2,333,689)
	Robert H. Cunningham (D)	244,112	(33%)	($6,232)
	Others	24,122	(3%)	
1990 primary	Strom Thurmond (R)	unopposed		
1984 general	Strom Thurmond (R)	644,815	(67%)	($1,682,962)
	Melvin Purvis (D)..................	306,982	(32%)	($9,023)

Sen. Ernest F. (Fritz) Hollings (D)

Elected 1966, seat up 1998; b. Jan. 1, 1922, Charleston; home, Charleston; The Citadel, B.A. 1942, U. of SC, LL.B. 1947; Lutheran; married (Peatsy).

Career: Army, 1942–45 (WWII); Practicing atty., 1947–55, 1963–66; SC House of Reps., 1948–54, Speaker Pro Tem, 1951–54; SC Lt. Gov., 1954–58; SC Gov., 1958–62.

DC Office: 125 RSOB 20510, 202-224-6121; Fax: 202-224-4293.

State Offices: 1835 Assembly St., Columbia 29201, 803-765-5731; 112 Custom House, 200 E. Bay St., Charleston 29401, 803-727-4525; and 126 Fed. Bldg., Greenville 29304, 803-233-5366; 103 Fed. Bldg., Spartanburg 29301, 803-585-3702.

Committees: *Appropriations* (3rd of 13 D): Commerce, Justice, State and Judiciary (RMM); Defense; Energy and Water Development; Interior; Labor, Health and Human Services, Education. *Budget* (2nd of 10 D). *Commerce, Science & Transportation* (RMM of 9 D): Communications (RMM).

Group Ratings

	ADA	ACLU	COPE	CFA	LCV	CON	NSI	COC	ACU	NTLC	CHC
1994	50	53	71	58	77	35	40	46	22	21	43
1993	55	—	91	50	56	37	—	27	42	—	—

National Journal Ratings

	1993 LIB	—	1993 CONS	1994 LIB	—	1994 CONS
Economic	66%	—	33%	52%	—	47%
Social	48%	—	51%	48%	—	51%
Foreign	44%	—	52%	50%	—	49%

Key Votes of the 103d Congress

1. Clinton Deficit Plan	Y	3. Brady Handgun Purchase	N	5. Lmt. UN Cmnd. of Forces	Y
2. NAFTA	N	4. Strike Race/Death Pnlty.	Y	6. Cut Missile Funds	N

Key Votes of the 104th Congress

1. Congressional Compliance	Y	3. Balanced Budget Amndt.	N	5. Product Liability Reform	N
2. Bar Unfunded Mandates	N	4. Pass Line Item Veto	Y	6. FY96 Budget	N

Election Results

1992 general	Ernest F. (Fritz) Hollings (D)	591,030	(50%)	($4,188,829)
	Tommy Hartnett (R)	554,175	(47%)	($886,816)
	Other	35,233	(3%)	
1992 primary	Ernest F. (Fritz) Hollings (D)	unopposed		
1986 general	Ernest F. (Fritz) Hollings (D)	456,500	(63%)	($2,233,843)
	Henry D. McMaster (R)	262,886	(36%)	($584,288)

FIRST DISTRICT

Looking out across the harbor to Fort Sumter are the glorious mansions of the Battery, gazing on the same view that the hot-blooded young swells of Charleston saw in 1861 when they fired the shots that began the Civil War. Today there are few more beautiful urban scenes in America than the pastel "single houses" of Charleston, built flush with the sidewalk, turning their shoulders to the streets, with open piazzas inside their gateways facing south to catch the breeze, lovingly restored and maintained. Charleston, founded in 1670, was blessed with one of the finest harbors on the Atlantic, at the point where, Charlestonians say, the Ashley and Cooper Rivers meet to form the Atlantic Ocean. It was one of the South's two leading cities through the Civil War. Across its docks went cargoes of rice, indigo and cotton—all cultivated by black slaves, enriching the white planters and merchants who dominated the state's economic and political life. In the years following the Civil War, Charleston became an economic backwater, enabling the old buildings to survive; now the prosperity of recent years—metropolitan Charleston grew 18% in the 1980s—has financed their restoration.

This old society, descended from Barbados planters and French Huguenots, Sephardic Jews and English gentry second sons, was once a leading force in American political life. The hotheads in the gallery disrupted the 1860 Democratic National Convention here so boisterously that it was adjourned and reconvened in Baltimore, while southern Democrats split off and nominated their own candidate, enabling Abraham Lincoln to win with 38% of the popular vote. South Carolina's blacks also have a lively history. There were free blacks here before the Civil War (some even owned slaves themselves), and Charleston's historic black culture was memorialized in George Gershwin's *Porgy and Bess*. The local accent, which seems to outsiders to have a touch of New Jersey and which can be incomprehensible when rapidly spoken, is best appreciated in the speech of Charlestonian Senator Ernest Hollings.

Some 25 years ago, the Charleston area depended heavily on its big Navy and Air Force bases, which accounted for 20% of regional payrolls. But in the years since, it has built a vibrant private economy with lots of small companies, and jobs rose significantly over the 1980s. The tourist attractions of Charleston and beach communities have helped. Overall, the South Carolina beach from the high rises of the Grand Strand around Myrtle Beach through the eponymous hammocks of Pawleys Island south to Hilton Head with its tasteful condos, has become one of the South's favorite vacation and second home areas. With all this growth, the Charleston area handily survived the 1993 round of military base closings, but there are more to come in 1995.

The 1st Congressional District of South Carolina, as designed in 1992, is the Charleston and

Low Country district, drawn to maximize the black population of the next-door 6th; but, given the plantation heritage here, it is still 20% black. It includes the old houses of the Battery of Charleston and the beachfront and affluent suburbs strung out on high ground in all directions. It proceeds north past Pawleys Island to the Grand Strand; it runs south to Kiawah Island, but stops short of Hilton Head. About two-thirds of the voters are in metropolitan Charleston, which has produced notable leaders like Mayor Joe Riley, Jr., who made a run at the 1994 Democratic gubernatorial nomination but won 38% to Theodore's 50%, and Police Chief Reuben Greenberg, who is both black and Jewish and who is known to be very shrewd about preventing crime. Represented into the 1970s by House Armed Services Chairman Mendel Rivers, this is now a solidly Republican district, and when incumbent Arthur Ravenel—a colorful figure who said drug agents should shoot down drug-carrying planes and machine-gun the survivors—ran for governor in 1994, it was clear the next congressman would be chosen in the Republican primary.

It also seemed fairly clear at the outset who that person would be—Van Hipp, Republican state chairman in 1987, at 26; a Pentagon official who joined his Reserve unit in Desert Storm, a candidate with top level support from the start (from the wife of former Governor James Edwards and the father of then-Governor Carroll Campbell). "Running for Congress is something I dreamed of and planned for since I was 15," Hipp said. He took solid conservative stands on issues and had serious backing from Christian right groups. Hipp had some well-known opponents, but this was 1994, and the ultimate winner came from the political outside. Hipp led the primary with 31% of the vote; Mendel Rivers, Jr., son of the former congressman, who said he didn't run until now because of "confusion about what kind of person I was," got only 12%; former state Highway Commissioner Bob Harrell and state Senator Mike Rose ran just five votes apart, with 17% each.

A little more than 1,000 votes ahead, with 19% of the vote, was the previously unknown Mark Sanford. At 34, Sanford was two years older than Hipp, but had never run for office or worked in politics. He was a successful real estate developer, who gave his own campaign $100,000 and ran against Congress. He called for term limits and cutting the deficit; he said citizen-legislators needed to replace career politicians; he pledged to serve only three terms, to take no PAC money, to vote for no tax increases and to refuse any salary increase until the budget was balanced. There was an obvious contrast with Hipp, who had held only political jobs and who had only recently moved to the district. It was close, but with 55% in Charleston County, Sanford won the runoff 52%–48%.

Sanford's campaign theme and some of his spots copied those of Bob Inglis, the upset winner in the 4th District in 1992. Even before the election, Inglis and 3d District Republican nominee Lindsey Graham started holding conference calls with Sanford each week. It was a good formula: Sanford won 66% of the vote, Graham 61% and Inglis 74% in 1994. After the election, like each South Carolina Republican, he was an unqualified supporter of the Contract with America. He took on Henry Hyde in advocating that Republicans set a limit of three-terms for House service. Arguing that Congressional experience is overrated, Sanford said, "It's not like we're dealing with brain surgery." In Washington, Sanford has followed Inglis's practice (sternly denounced by Congresswoman Patricia Schroeder of Colorado but defended by Speaker Newt Gingrich) of sleeping in his office rather than finding other local accommodations. "From a practical standpoint, you save a lot of time," Sanford explains. "I do not have a commute. From a philosophical standpoint, it's less comfortable. The whole idea of getting up in the morning and walking three flights of stairs with your shampoo is not exactly the greatest, and I think the discomfort level is important, because it makes you all that much more anxious to head home." Which, evidently, he will do, having voted for the Contract With America, every weekend until 2000.

The People: Pop. 1990: 581,445; 25% rural; 9% age 65+; 77% White; 20% Black; 1% Asian; 1% Hispanic origin. Voting age pop.: 427,621; 18% Black; 1% Hispanic origin. Households: 60% married couple families; 30% married couple fams. w. children; 48% college educ.; median household income: $28,705; per capita income: $13,112; median gross rent: $441; median house value: $75,400.

1992 Presidential Vote

Bush (R) 101,830 (53%)
Clinton (D) 63,318 (33%)
Perot (I).................. 26,620 (14%)

1988 Presidential Vote

Bush (R) 102,935 (69%)
Dukakis (D)............... 46,787 (31%)

Rep. Marshall (Mark) Sanford, Jr. (R)

Elected 1994; b. May 28, 1960, Ft. Lauderdale, FL; home, Charleston; Furman U. B.A. 1983; U. of VA, M.B.A. 1988; Episcopalian; married (Jenny).

Career: Owner, Norton & Sanford real estate investment firm, 1992–present.

DC Office: 1223 LHOB 20515, 202-225-3176.

District Offices: 640 Federal Bldg., Charleston 29043, 803-727-4175; 206 Laurel St., Conway 29526, 803-248-2660; 829-E Frost St., Georgetown 29440, 803-527-6868.

Committees: *Government Reform & Oversight* (26th of 27 R): Human Resources and Intergovernmental Affairs; Postal Service. *International Relations* (21st of 23 R): Africa; Asia and the Pacific. *Joint Economic Committee* (5th of 10 Reps.).

Group Ratings and 103rd Congress Votes: Newly Elected

Key Votes of the 104th Congress

1. Congressional Compliance Y	6. Reform Crime Grant Y	11. Loser Pays Court Reform Y
2. Balanced Budget Amndmt. Y	7. National Security Act Y	12. Product Liability Reform Y
3. Bar Unfunded Mandates Y	8. Moratorium on Regs. Y	13. Welfare Reform Y
4. Pass Line Item Veto Y	9. Risk Assessment on Regs. Y	14. Term Limits Amndmt. Y
5. Relax Exclusionary Rule Y	10. Expnd. Priv. Prop. Rights Y	15. Tax Cuts Y

Election Results

1994 general	Marshall (Mark) Sanford, Jr. (R).........	97,803	(66%)	($544,574)
	Robert Barber (D)	47,769	(32%)	($437,530)
	Others.................................	1,899	(1%)	
1994 runoff	Marshall (Mark) Sanford, Jr. (R).........	30,304	(52%)	
	Van Hipp (R)	27,921	(48%)	
1994 primary	Van Hipp (R)	17,066	(31%)	
	Marshall (Mark) Sanford, Jr. (R).........	10,568	(19%)	
	Mike Rose (R)	9,424	(17%)	
	Bob Harrell (R).......................	9,419	(17%)	
	L. Mendel Rivers Jr. (R)	6,604	(12%)	
	Others.................................	2,392	(4%)	
1992 general	Arthur Ravenel, Jr. (R).................	121,938	(66%)	($561,793)
	Bill Oberst, Jr. (D)	59,908	(33%)	($56,902)
	Other.................................	2,703	(1%)	

SECOND DISTRICT

In 1786, just after the Revolutionary War, the South Carolina legislature decided to move the state's capital away from the Charleston aristocracy and into the Up Country interior, away from a city named after a king to a new city named after a discoverer of America: so began Columbia. The State House was built on high ground above the Congaree River in a town of one-and-a-half story houses with first floor porticoes, dormers and raised brick basements—

"Columbia cottages." In 1865, General William Tecumseh Sherman's army burned everything here but the State House. In the post-Sherman years, Columbia grew slowly, with state government and the university, the Army's Fort Jackson and local insurance companies proving steady employers. In the 1970s and 1980s, it started to boom, attracting plants such as Michelin, Allied Chemical, United Technologies, FN of Belgium, DuPont and Square D. Approaching half a million in metro area population in the 1990s, Columbia is becoming a true city, and not just a village-capital.

The Columbia to which Jimmy Byrnes, after years in top posts in Democratic Washington, returned as governor to lament the *Brown v. Board of Education* decision in 1954, has trended Republican in the years since. Upwardly mobile South Carolinians, transplanted from underdeveloped rural areas to comfortable subdivisions with two-car garages, preferred Republicans first in national and then in state and local elections. Columbia voted for Eisenhower in the 1950s; in the late 1960s and 1970s, blacks were usually outnumbered by increasingly Republican whites in Columbia's Richland County and fast-growing Lexington County across the river.

South Carolina's 2d Congressional District includes most of metropolitan Columbia, except for black neighborhoods lopped off in 1992 to create a black-majority 6th District. It contains the city's affluent white neighborhoods and the spread-out towns of Richland and Lexington Counties, with their shopping centers and many churches and the Army's huge training center, Fort Jackson. The district extends south through the horse-farm area around Aiken and several lightly populated black-majority rural counties, and then includes Beaufort and Hilton Head on the coast—the former is an old town, with wonderful mansions and a history intertwined with slave plantations and the Marine Corps's Parris Island training base; the latter, made famous by Pat Conroy's novel, *The Prince of Tides*, has been developed with much meticulous attention to its natural environment, a model now for Atlantic coast condominium and vacation communities. This is a heavily Republican district: few whites vote Democratic, and since this new 2d is only 25% black, Republicans carry it almost every time.

The congressman from the 2d District is Floyd Spence, a Republican first elected in 1970 who is now chairman of the National Security Committee. Spence was a star football player and student body president at the University of South Carolina; he served as an officer in the Navy and Naval Reserve until 1985. When he graduated from law school in 1956, he started running for office, became a Republican in 1962, two years before Strom Thurmond, narrowly lost a House race that year to a Democrat who later switched parties and, when the man ran for governor in 1970, Spence ran again for the House seat and won. Spence has been easily reelected ever since, by safe pluralities; in 1994 he was unopposed.

Spence was the first House member to sponsor the balanced budget constitutional amendment, in 1971; he was the first House member to survive a double-lung transplant, in 1988. He served for many years on the House Ethics Committee. But his greatest energy has been devoted to military issues. He favored the defense buildup of the 1980s and called for "responsible downsizing of defense expenditures rather than drastic cuts" in the 1990s. He probes in great detail into readiness and charged in late 1994 that one-quarter of units had readiness problems. He welcomed Bill Clinton's December 1994 call for a $25 billion defense spending increase over six years, and called for more. Spence became ranking Republican on National Security in 1993, and thus chairman in 1995—a stunning change from Democratic chairman Ron Dellums. Spence of course uses his committee slots to service local bases and installations, but—as Strom Thurmond has also learned—the base closing law limits his ability to keep bases open; he may have an easier time helping the local veterans' hospital and historically black colleges and the Congaree Swamp National Monument. As shown by the early 1995 defeat, albeit symbolic, for the Republicans' long-prized space-based missile defense system, Spence will have a hard time attempting to restore the glories of the Reagan era's lavish defense build-up. He also was unhappy about Speaker Gingrich's one-third downsizing of the committee's staff and the end of the panel's traditional staff bipartisanship. Like other old-guard Republicans, however, he was in no position to challenge Gingrich and he was grateful finally to become Mr. Chairman.

The People: Pop. 1990: 580,624; 40% rural; 10% age 65+; 72% White; 25% Black; 1% Asian; 1% Other; 1% Hispanic origin. Voting age pop.: 430,168; 23% Black; 1% Hispanic origin. Households: 59% married couple families; 28% married couple fams. w. children; 50% college educ.; median household income: $30,500; per capita income: $13,807; median gross rent: $435; median house value: $73,400.

1992 Presidential Vote		
Bush (R)	119,658	(52%)
Clinton (D)	82,652	(36%)
Perot (I)	25,853	(11%)

1988 Presidential Vote		
Bush (R)	122,981	(69%)
Dukakis (D)	56,205	(31%)

Rep. Floyd D. Spence (R)

Elected 1970; b. Apr. 9, 1928, Columbia; home, Lexington; U. of SC, A.B. 1952, LL.B. 1956; Lutheran; married (Deborah).

Career: Navy, 1952–54, Naval Reserves, 1947–52, 1954–85; SC House of Reps., 1956–62; Practicing atty., 1956–70; SC Senate, 1966–70, Minority Ldr., 1966–70.

DC Office: 2405 RHOB 20515, 202-225-2452; Fax: 202-225-2455.

District Offices: 220 Stoneridge Dr., #202, Columbia 29210, 803-254-5120; 1681 Chestnut St., P.O. Box 1609, NE Orangeburg 29115, 803-536-4641; 66 E. Railroad Ave., P.O. Box 550, Estill 29918, 803-625-3177; 807 Port Republic St., #2, P.O. Box 1538, Beaufort 29901, 803-521-2530; 1 Town Center Ct., Hilton Head Island 29928, 803-842-7212.

Committees: *National Security* (Chmn. of 30 R): Military Procurement. *Veterans' Affairs* (4th of 18 R): Hospitals and Health Care.

Group Ratings

	ADA	ACLU	COPE	CFA	LCV	CON	NSI	COC	ACU	NTLC	CHC
1994	5	13	33	20	6	49	100	82	95	89	100
1993	5	—	17	20	23	39	—	82	96	—	—

National Journal Ratings

	1993 LIB — 1993 CONS		1994 LIB — 1994 CONS	
Economic	25% —	72%	24% —	75%
Social	11% —	82%	16% —	81%
Foreign	0% —	91%	0% —	88%

Key Votes of the 103d Congress

1. Clinton Deficit Plan	N	3. Brady Handgun Purchase	N	5. Lmt. UN Cmnd. of Forces	Y
2. NAFTA	N	4. Strike Race/Death Pnlty.	Y	6. Cut Missile Funds	N

Key Votes of the 104th Congress

1. Congressional Compliance	Y	6. Reform Crime Grant	Y	11. Loser Pays Court Reform	Y
2. Balanced Budget Amndmt.	Y	7. National Security Act	Y	12. Product Liability Reform	Y
3. Bar Unfunded Mandates	Y	8. Moratorium on Regs.	Y	13. Welfare Reform	Y
4. Pass Line Item Veto	Y	9. Risk Assessment on Regs.	Y	14. Term Limits Amndmt.	Y
5. Relax Exclusionary Rule	Y	10. Expnd. Priv. Prop. Rights	Y	15. Tax Cuts	Y

Election Results

1994 general	Floyd D. Spence (R)............... unopposed		($149,321)
1994 primary	Floyd D. Spence (R)............... unopposed		
1992 general	Floyd D. Spence (R).................. 148,667	(88%)	($179,539)
	Gebhard Sommer (Lib) 20,816	(12%)	

THIRD DISTRICT

The South Carolina Up Country, many days' travel by wagon from the Low Country plantations, was first settled by Scots-Irish farmers, like the family of John C. Calhoun in the years around the Revolutionary War. The pioneers wanted to make big plantations of these forests, but the land did not always cooperate: it was often too hilly for the labor-intensive rice crop grown in the Low Country and sometimes too cold for cotton. So relatively few slaves were brought here, and the land was mostly small farms owned by whites. Today, the racial and cultural tone of Up Country South Carolina shows traces of these roots. This is a mostly white part of the South, with a hell-of-a-fella tone to daily life, an economically growing and culturally tradition-minded slice of Middle America.

The 3d Congressional District of South Carolina covers much of this territory, following the Georgia border from the government's troubled Savannah River Plant all the way north to mountains on the North Carolina border. In the southern part of the 3d are a few heavily black communities, like Edgefield, where Strom Thurmond grew up and first won public office in the 1930s. But the major population center here is the increasingly affluent suburban strip linking Aiken and Augusta, Georgia. In the northern part of this district, Calhoun had his mansion and his son-in-law created Clemson University nearby. Here today, the Savannah River intersects Interstate 85, the main street of America's textile belt, one of the nation's prime economic growth areas. The politics of this area, ancestrally Democratic, has been trending Republican for years. Yankified Aiken started voting Republican for Dwight Eisenhower in the 1950s, well before Thurmond switched parties in 1964; Anderson skittered around, supporting Jimmy Carter for a while but then veering Republican again; Pickens and Oconee Counties around Clemson and the mountains are heavily Republican. A Jimmy Carter district in 1976 and 1980 became a George Bush district in 1988 and 1992. This may have prompted the retirement in 1994 of 20-year Congressman Butler Derrick. He was part of the Democratic leadership as number-two Democrat on the Rules Committee and one of four chief deputy whips. And although he won by large margins, he relied on vastly outspending opponents and, with the Clinton Administration locally very unpopular, he could see stronger opposition coming and the time to begin a new career—as a Washington lawyer.

Both parties here had contested primaries, but the Republican contest attracted more voters—41,000 versus 35,000—and produced a clear winner, state Representative Lindsey Graham, who won 52% of the vote. Graham had served in the legislature for only two years. After law school he served in the Air Force from 1982–1988, then returned home to Oconee County and became an assistant county attorney; he continued in the Air Force National Guard and was called to service in Desert Storm. Graham called for term limits and was for more defense spending and against gays in the military. His attitude toward the Clinton Administration and the House Democratic leadership was unequivocal: "I'm one less vote for an agenda that makes you want to throw up." Meanwhile, state Senator Jim Bryan won the Democratic runoff against Deborah Dorn Pracht, daughter of longtime Congressman William Jennings Bryan Dorn. In the general, Bryan, with a strong Laurens County base, campaigned as a conservative—pro-life, anti-gays in the military, against employer mandates in health care, against defense cuts. He had more money and boasted more experience in the legislature. But those may have been liabilities in 1994. Graham modeled his campaign after Bob Inglis's successful 1992 race in the 4th District.

Graham won a very impressive 61% in a district Democratic since Reconstruction; Bryan carried Laurens County handsomely, but Graham won over 70% in Oconee and Pickens Counties and 67% in Aiken. With his strong support of the Contract With America, he became an ally of the House Republican leadership.

The People: Pop. 1990: 580,873; 58% rural; 13% age 65+; 78% White; 21% Black. Voting age pop.: 434,796; 19% Black. Households: 60% married couple families; 27% married couple fams. w. children; 34% college educ.; median household income: $25,897; per capita income: $11,813; median gross rent: $326; median house value: $54,100.

1992 Presidential Vote

Bush (R)	101,962	(51%)
Clinton (D)	69,161	(35%)
Perot (I)	26,424	(13%)

1988 Presidential Vote

Bush (R)	107,999	(67%)
Dukakis (D)	54,344	(33%)

Rep. Lindsey Graham (R)

Elected 1994; b. July 9, 1955, Seneca; home, Seneca; U. of SC, B.A. 1977, J.D. 1981; Baptist; single.

Career: Air Force, 1982–88; Air Force Reserves, 1988–present (Persian Gulf), Air Natl. Guard, 1989–present; Air Force Chief Prosecutor, 1984–88; Asst. Oconee Cnty. Atty., 1988–92; Practicing atty., 1988–94; Central SC City Atty., 1990–94; SC House of Reps., 1992–94.

DC Office: 1429 LHOB 20515, 202-225-5301; Fax: 202-225-3216.

District Offices: P.O. Box 4126, Anderson 29622, 803-224-7401; 5 Fed. Bldg., 211 York St., NE, Aiken 29801, 803-649-5571; and 129 Fed. Bldg., 120 Main St., Greenwood 29646, 803-223-8251.

Committees: *Economic & Educational Opportunities* (19th of 24 R): Employer-Employee Relations; Workforce Protections. *Science* (16th of 27 R): Basic Research; Energy and Environment.

Group Ratings and 103rd Congress Votes: Newly Elected

Key Votes of the 104th Congress

1. Congressional Compliance	Y	6. Reform Crime Grant	Y	11. Loser Pays Court Reform	Y
2. Balanced Budget Amndmt.	Y	7. National Security Act	Y	12. Product Liability Reform	Y
3. Bar Unfunded Mandates	Y	8. Moratorium on Regs.	Y	13. Welfare Reform	Y
4. Pass Line Item Veto	Y	9. Risk Assessment on Regs.	Y	14. Term Limits Amndmt.	Y
5. Relax Exclusionary Rule	Y	10. Expnd. Priv. Prop. Rights	Y	15. Tax Cuts	Y

Election Results

1994 general	Lindsey Graham (R)	90,123	(60%)	($551,212)
	James E. Bryan Jr. (D)	59,932	(40%)	($443,965)
1994 primary	Lindsey Graham (R)	21,562	(52%)	
	Bob Cantrell (R)	13,609	(33%)	
	Ed Allgood (R)	6,235	(15%)	
1992 general	Butler C. Derrick (D)	119,119	(61%)	($673,677)
	Jim Bland (R)	75,660	(39%)	($17,339)

FOURTH DISTRICT

A century ago, northern investors looking for sites for textile mills, looked at the Up Country of South Carolina and "were attracted by the mild climate, abundant water power, proximity to the cotton fields and plenty of native [white] labor already accustomed to a low standard of living." As mills fled New England, the textile industry became concentrated along the Southern Railway and Seaboard Coast Line tracks between Charlotte and Atlanta, especially in the Piedmont of South Carolina. The textile country could look bucolic, but Greenville, Spartanburg and the dozens of mill towns thick in the surrounding countryside were as industrial as Lancashire or the Ruhr, with mills rising up on what were once twisting woodland paths.

Today, this same stretch of land along South Carolina's Interstate 85, which parallels the Southern Railway, remains the number one textile-producing area in the United States. But it is much more than that. The number of textile and apparel jobs declined from 57,000 in the early 1970s to 42,000 in the late 1980s, from 27% of all jobs to 14%, but new businesses include domestic companies like Digital Computer, Procter & Gamble, where the world's supply of Pepto-Bismol is made, and Wal-Mart, which has its largest distribution center here. Foreign companies include Adidas, Hitachi and, part of the largest concentration of German investment in the United States, Hoechst. Michelin's North American headquarters is near Greenville and BMW built and is operating its North American plant next to the airport just off I-85, on a site assembled by Governor Carroll Campbell with a $130 million package of tax incentives and airport expansion to accommodate 747s loaded with auto parts.

What attracts all these businesses? Sometimes big tax concessions, as with BMW. More important, overall tax levels are low, with good state-built infrastructure—the airport, the Interstate highways, the port of Charleston, now one of the busiest on the East Coast. Unions are almost nonexistent. The work ethic here is strong; as public schools elsewhere in America seem to concentrate on inculcating multiculturalism and self-esteem, South Carolina public schools strive to teach reading, mathematics and good work habits. Culturally this area ranges from conservative to very conservative, with a strong influence by Greenville's Bob Jones University and many evangelical and fundamentalist churches. But the culture of mainstream churches and civic boosters has a certain bedrock conservatism to it as well.

South Carolina's 4th Congressional District, only slightly revised by the 1990s redistricting, fits almost perfectly around the Greenville-Spartanburg area. Republican in national elections, it elected Republican Carroll Campbell from 1978–84, then voted from 1986–92 for Democrat Liz Patterson, former state senator and daughter of Governor and Senator Olin Johnston. The congressman now is Bob Inglis, who typifies many of the new Republican members nationally and especially in South Carolina. Inglis grew up in the Low Country, then excelled at Duke and the University of Virginia law school, and moved to Greenville to practice commercial law; he started a family and became involved in civic and church affairs. In 1992, he challenged Patterson, who had a moderate voting record but often supported the Democratic leadership. Inglis campaigned hard for term limits and against PAC contributions; he pledged to serve only three terms and to never take PAC money. He inspired a huge door-to-door effort, targeting key precincts with many volunteers; volunteers hung tens of thousands of doorknobs fliers attacking the House bank and post office scandals. He benefited as well from a 200,000-person mailing of comparative issue stands by the Christian Coalition. Inglis won 57% in Greenville County and 43% in Spartanburg County, for a 50%–48% district-wide victory.

In the House, Inglis kept his promises. He refused PAC money and pushed for internal House reform and he worked unsuccessfully to have Republican leaders embrace six-year term limits. He kept his family in South Carolina and slept (and still does) in his office on an air mattress. He has had almost a totally conservative voting record and became close to the not-yet-as-famous Newt Gingrich, Dick Armey and John Kasich. He voted against funding for the Southern Connector between I-85 and I-385 because it was part of what he considered a pork-laden bill.

He voted against the Supercollider and space station, despite pleas from local suppliers. He voted against NAFTA and GATT, though he supported free trade generally. He scorned seeking pork barrel projects for his district, explaining, "It reflects a change in South Carolina's situation. There was a day when we were the nation's redheaded step-child and we had to depend on seniority to bring us goodies. Now the situation has changed, dramatically. What we need is a sound economy and the key to that is right-sizing the federal government."

In 1994, Inglis was successful not only in his district but beyond. He spent only modestly and won reelection with a stunning 74% of the vote. And his 1992 race inspired many of the campaign tactics and promises of 1st and 3d District Republican nominees Mark Sanford and Lindsey Graham, with whom he held regular teleconferences and both of whom won handsomely. In the 104th Congress Inglis, told reporters he was less interested in a plum committee or subcommittee chairmanship than in advancing the Contract With America, much of which his 1992 campaign anticipated; he played an active role in achieving this goal as a member of Kasich's Budget Committee. He seems a clear favorite for a third term in 1996.

The People: Pop. 1990: 581,385; 36% rural; 12% age 65+; 79% White; 20% Black; 1% Asian; 1% Hispanic origin. Voting age pop.: 437,750; 18% Black; 1% Hispanic origin. Households: 58% married couple families; 26% married couple fams. w. children; 39% college educ.; median household income: $27,703; per capita income: $13,011; median gross rent: $367; median house value: $58,900.

1992 Presidential Vote			1988 Presidential Vote		
Bush (R)	107,970	(54%)	Bush (R)	114,778	(68%)
Clinton (D)	65,106	(33%)	Dukakis (D)	54,814	(32%)
Perot (I)	24,131	(12%)			

Rep. Bob Inglis (R)

Elected 1992; b. Oct. 11, 1959, Savannah, GA; home, Greenville; Duke U., B.A. 1981, U. of VA Law Schl., J.D. 1984; Presbyterian; married (Mary Anne).

Career: Practicing atty., 1984–92.

DC Office: 1237 LHOB 20515, 202-225-6030; Fax: 202-226-1177.

District Offices: 201 Magnolia St., #108, Spartanburg 29301, 803-582-6422; 300 E. Washington St., #101, Greenville 29601, 803-232-1141; and 405 W. Main St., Union 29379, 803-427-2205.

Committees: *Budget* (14th of 24 R). *Judiciary* (11th of 20 R): Commercial and Administrative Law; Constitution.

Group Ratings

	ADA	ACLU	COPE	CFA	LCV	CON	NSI	COC	ACU	NTLC	CHC
1994	5	17	22	10	17	88	100	67	100	100	100
1993	10	—	8	0	36	82	—	82	100	—	—

National Journal Ratings

	1993 LIB	—	1993 CONS	1994 LIB	—	1994 CONS
Economic	12%	—	87%	0%	—	80%
Social	0%	—	89%	24%	—	73%
Foreign	0%	—	91%	0%	—	88%

Key Votes of the 103d Congress

1. Clinton Deficit Plan	N	3. Brady Handgun Purchase	N	5. Lmt. UN Cmnd. of Forces	Y
2. NAFTA	N	4. Strike Race/Death Pnlty.	Y	6. Cut Missile Funds	N

Key Votes of the 104th Congress

1. Congressional Compliance	Y	6. Reform Crime Grant	Y	11. Loser Pays Court Reform	Y
2. Balanced Budget Amndt.	Y	7. National Security Act	Y	12. Product Liability Reform	Y
3. Bar Unfunded Mandates	Y	8. Moratorium on Regs.	Y	13. Welfare Reform	Y
4. Pass Line Item Veto	Y	9. Risk Assessment on Regs.	Y	14. Term Limits Amndt.	Y
5. Relax Exclusionary Rule	Y	10. Expnd. Priv. Prop. Rights	Y	15. Tax Cuts	Y

Election Results

1994 general	Bob Inglis (R)	109,626	(73%)	($184,079)
	Jerry L. Fowler (D)	39,396	(26%)	($6,311)
1994 primary	Bob Inglis (R)	unopposed		
1992 general	Bob Inglis (R)	99,879	(50%)	($215,364)
	Liz Patterson (D)	94,182	(48%)	($348,528)
	Others	4,349	(2%)	

FIFTH DISTRICT

Some of the fiercest battles of the Revolutionary War were fought in South Carolina's Up Country, on hilly lands just being settled by Scots-Irish farmers moving up from the Low Country or down the Virginia Piedmont valley. This was a country of violent passions and unclear lines; Carolinians have long argued over which side of the North and South Carolina boundary Andrew Jackson was born in 1767. Ever since, the fighting spirit and Calvinist faith of Up Country Carolinians have never wavered. This "Olde English District" remains intensely religious and pro-military. But it is no longer impoverished. For many years, the dominant industry here was textiles, traditionally the first factory enterprise of industrializing countries, with low pay and poor working conditions. But in the 1980s the number of textile jobs declined, and small-business prosperity more recently has been barreling out the interstates from Greenville-Spartanburg and Columbia and Charlotte, to transform counties once dependent on tobacco fields and textile mills.

The 5th Congressional District of South Carolina consists of all or part of 13 counties, mostly in the Up Country. It includes none of the three area metropolitan centers, but much of their growing fringe. In the east, the 5th includes Darlington, site of the Southern 500 stock car race every Labor Day, and verges on lowland tobacco country, including Marlboro and Chesterfield Counties, although heavily black areas here have been lopped off and placed in the new black-majority 6th District. In the west, they include Fort Mill and Rock Hill in York County, just south of Charlotte, ready for fast development now that a land settlement with the Catawba Indians has been reached. Politically, this homeland of Andrew Jackson is ancestrally Democratic. But in recent years, first the more affluent towns and now increasingly the countryside have been trending Republican.

The congressman from the 5th District is John Spratt, a Democrat who is well-respected in the House as well as back home. He comes from a prominent York County family and has degrees from Davidson, Yale Law and Oxford; he first got involved in politics in Charles Ravenel's unsuccessful 1974 campaign for governor. Spratt was elected to the House in 1982, when the incumbent retired a week before the filing deadline; Spratt put a campaign together fast and won 38% in the primary, 55% in the runoff against a candidate who spent $929,000, and 68% in the general. For 10 years he was reelected easily; then in 1994 he had a tough race, and won by just 52%–48%, carrying the rural counties and running even in York County. It is a measure of the strength of the Republican tide that a Democrat with so many political assets could be so hard pressed.

Spratt started off specializing in military issues and in the 1990s has also worked on budget reforms. He served in the Pentagon during the Vietnam war and has a senior seat on the National Security Committee. In the 1980s, he worked with then-Chairman Les Aspin and, in his thick Carolina accent and with impressive knowledge of details, stitched together compromises on the MX missile, binary nerve gas weapons, the Strategic Defense Initiative, and the Savannah River and other nuclear plants—keeping military projects flowing through the House, many of whose members were temperamentally inclined to zero out military spending. Even after Democrats lost control, Spratt won an important symbolic victory in 1995, when the House voted to limit further production of the space-launched missile defense system.

Frustrated by "our feckless inability to do something about the deficit," Spratt passed through the House in 1990 a bill that would require the administration and both Houses of Congress to submit balanced budgets. In 1991, he got on the Budget Committee; after the 1992 election, he ran for chairman as a more conservative alternative to Minnesotan Martin Sabo and, in a campaign that stayed on the issues and avoided rancor, lost by 149–112. Spratt left Budget, but introduced his version of a line-item veto in 1993. In 1994, he presented a bill to require budgeters to use two baselines, the current one which grants each department inflation increases or more and one that simply shows the amount of dollars spent, and another bill to require that emergency appropriations be limited to emergencies. If the Democratic leadership had advanced and supported such measures, it might have undercut the demands for reform that resulted in the Contract With America in 1994 and the Republican House in 1995.

Indeed, such stands did not prevent Spratt from getting strong opposition for the first time in a decade in 1994. Larry Bigham, graduate of The Citadel, owner of Thursday's Too restaurant in Rock Hill, school board member for 10 years, was angry at government mandates. He called the Family and Medical Leave Act an example of "expensive mandates for small business" imposed by the government. "I will work to get government out of our lives, out of our schools, out of our homes, out of our businesses." he said, calling Spratt a "tax and spend" Democrat and arguing that "a vote for John Spratt is a vote for Bill Clinton." He made some clumsy errors, attacking Spratt on provisions of the Clinton healthcare plan which Spratt did not support and attacking Spratt for negotiating a settlement with the Catawba Indians, which he said would bring gambling. This was a 15-year controversy which Spratt succeeded in settling just before a 1992 deadline would have triggered an Indian lawsuit against 62,000 landowners. Spratt was hailed by Republican Governor Carroll Campbell as well as Democrats, and Bigham had to back off his criticism; the only gambling it allowed was the bingo and video poker already legal in South Carolina. There were some clear issue differences. Spratt voted for the Clinton budget and tax package and for the 1994 crime bill, which Bigham said was "stuffed with pork." Bigham promised to serve only four terms and backed term limits; Spratt said, "The longer you serve here, if you enjoy the work and are effective at it, then you can accomplish more." Spratt argued that there was no way states could compensate for Bigham's Medicare and Medicaid cuts, and contrasted Bigham's support from free-marketeer Dick Armey with his own support of farm programs. Spratt voted for NAFTA, which was supported by Springs Industries and most other local textile firms.

Spratt's work on local issues—he is head of the Congressional Textile Caucus and works to protect Shaw Air Force Base in Sumter—helped, and so did money; he outraised Bigham among PACs and spent $180,000 of his own money. But the closeness of the result suggests this seat may be seriously contested again. Spratt responded with support for much of the Contract With America. But by early 1995, Republicans already were targeting him for defeat, with Bigham and state senator Wes Hayes expressing interest in the nomination.

The People: Pop. 1990: 581,174; 63% rural; 12% age 65+; 68% White; 31% Black. Voting age pop.: 422,161; 28% Black. Households: 59% married couple families; 28% married couple fams. w. children; 32% college educ.; median household income: $25,215; per capita income: $11,009; median gross rent: $327; median house value: $52,800.

1992 Presidential Vote

Bush (R) 86,118 (45%)
Clinton (D) 81,192 (42%)
Perot (I). 23,462 (12%)

1988 Presidential Vote

Bush (R) 92,919 (61%)
Dukakis (D). 60,559 (39%)

Rep. John M. Spratt, Jr. (D)

Elected 1982; b. Nov. 1, 1942, Charlotte, NC; home, York; Davidson Col., A.B. 1964, Oxford U., M.A. 1966, Yale U., LL.B. 1969; Presbyterian; married (Jane).

Career: Army Operations, U.S. Dept. of Defense, 1969–71; Practicing atty., 1971–82; Pres., Bank of Ft. Mill, 1973–82; Pres., Spratt Insurance Agcy., 1973–82.

DC Office: 1536 LHOB 20515, 202-225-5501; Fax: 202-225-0464.

District Offices: 305 Fed. Bldg., Rock Hill 29731, 803-327-1114; 39 E. Calhoun St., Sumter 29150, 803-773-3362; and 88 Public Sq., Darlington 29532, 803-393-3998.

Committees: *Government Reform & Oversight* (7th of 22 D): Government Management, Information and Technology; National Economic Growth, Natural Resources and Regulatory Affairs. *National Security* (6th of 25 D): Military Readiness; Military Research and Development (RMM).

Group Ratings

	ADA	ACLU	COPE	CFA	LCV	CON	NSI	COC	ACU	NTLC	CHC
1994	65	52	88	70	65	31	70	50	24	25	28
1993	55	—	83	100	85	7	—	45	25	—	—

National Journal Ratings

	1993 LIB — 1993 CONS		1994 LIB — 1994 CONS	
Economic	54%	— 45%	67%	— 29%
Social	58%	— 42%	58%	— 42%
Foreign	59%	— 38%	57%	— 37%

Key Votes of the 103d Congress

1. Clinton Deficit Plan	Y	3. Brady Handgun Purchase	Y	5. Lmt. UN Cmnd. of Forces	N
2. NAFTA	Y	4. Strike Race/Death Pnlty.	N	6. Cut Missile Funds	N

Key Votes of the 104th Congress

1. Congressional Compliance	Y	6. Reform Crime Grant	N	11. Loser Pays Court Reform	N
2. Balanced Budget Amndmt.	Y	7. National Security Act	N	12. Product Liability Reform	Y
3. Bar Unfunded Mandates	Y	8. Moratorium on Regs.	N	13. Welfare Reform	N
4. Pass Line Item Veto	Y	9. Risk Assessment on Regs.	N	14. Term Limits Amndmt.	N
5. Relax Exclusionary Rule	Y	10. Expnd. Priv. Prop. Rights	Y	15. Tax Cuts	N

Election Results

1994 general	John M. Spratt, Jr. (D).................	77,311	(52%)	($643,947)
	Larry Bigham (R).....................	70,967	(48%)	($213,775)
1994 primary	John M. Spratt, Jr. (D).............	unopposed		
1992 general	John M. Spratt, Jr. (D)................	112,031	(61%)	($381,942)
	Bill Horne (R).......................	70,866	(39%)	($102,728)

SIXTH DISTRICT

South Carolina was first settled by planters from Barbados, bringing with them a tropical plantation economy, which they transferred to the not quite tropical climate of the Carolina coastal lowlands. Here the flat Low Country and many islands are laced with sluggish-flowing rivers and swamps, and here the planters brought thousands of slaves directly from Africa. Colonial South Carolina was one of the richest parts of North America, with dazzling Georgian architecture in Charleston and classic plantation gardens; the planters built great irrigation systems and grew rice and cotton and the dye-plant indigo, all heavily in demand in Britain and elsewhere. And of course all this wealth was built on the slave labor of thousands of African-Americans, many of them still speaking their ancestral languages, or a patois mixing them with English. A majority of colonial South Carolinians were black slaves; so were most residents of the lowlands when the Civil War started with the bombardment of Fort Sumter in Charleston Harbor, although by that time there were also many free blacks in Charleston, some of whom owned slaves themselves.

South Carolina's black heritage has left an imprint on American culture, still apparent in the lowlands today. The special accents and dialects of lowland blacks were long retained: traces of Gullah and others still can be found on lowland islands and the Charleston accent, which to outsiders seems often incomprehensible (should C-SPAN run subtitles when Senator Hollings speaks?). The poverty that was the almost universal lot of lowland blacks after the Civil War has only in the last generation been alleviated, as development comes to the coast and the long cultural isolation of people here is dissipated. But many blacks who grew up here have long since left, leaving after high school graduation on the bus for New York, nicknamed "the chicken-bone special" because of the fried chicken their families packed for the journey.

The 6th Congressional District of South Carolina, created for 1992 to have a black majority, and modified slightly for 1994, includes very little of the coast, now mostly lined with affluent condominium communities; but it does include most of the geographic expanse of Low Country South Carolina. Its erose and irregular boundaries are designed to include the black central city neighborhoods of Charleston and Columbia but leave in the adjacent 1st and 2d Districts their affluent white city and suburban areas. The 6th district includes much of Orangeburg, home of the historically black South Carolina State University, and Florence, at the center of the Pee Dee tobacco-growing country in eastern South Carolina. This last area was the center of the old, 39% black 6th District, represented for 10 years by Democrat Robin Tallon, a genial clothing store owner who won mostly black votes in the general and courted tobacco farmers on the Agriculture Committee. Tallon filed to run for reelection in 1992, and might have won a multi-candidate primary; but on the last possible day he withdrew, saying that he wanted to avoid what might be a racially divisive contest in this new black majority district.

The current congressman from the 6th is James Clyburn, former state human affairs commissioner, who effectively won the seat in the 1992 Democratic primary, with 56% of the vote against four black opponents, all with serious claims for the nomination. Each of the others had regional strengths. But Clyburn, well known from nearly two decades as human rights commissioner and two nearly-successful statewide races for secretary of state, ran first or second in each major center and piled up huge margins in others (88% in his home county of Sumter).

In November, Clyburn won 65% of the vote and became the first black to represent South Carolina in Congress since 1897. He has been active in the civil rights movement since his youth and also has good working relationships with leading businessmen and Republicans. He has a knack for accommodating people of different backgrounds—note his support for the balanced-budget and term-limits amendments—and at the same time a successful record of lobbying the legislature for civil rights laws. He had a solidly liberal record on economic and cultural though not on foreign issues in the 103d Congress. He was reelected easily in 1994, and the main threat to his tenure is the possibility that lawsuits will give the 6th District more regular boundaries and a white majority. House Democrats praise him as potentially a future party leader.

The People: Pop. 1990: 581,202; 51% rural; 12% age 65+; 37% White; 62% Black; 1% Hispanic origin. Voting age pop.: 412,159; 58% Black. Households: 49% married couple families; 24% married couple fams. w. children; 30% college educ.; median household income: $19,254; per capita income: $8,628; median gross rent: $314; median house value: $47,900.

1992 Presidential Vote

Clinton (D)	118,085	(62%)
Bush (R)	59,970	(31%)
Perot (I)	12,292	(6%)

1988 Presidential Vote

Dukakis (D)	97,845	(60%)
Bush (R)	64,831	(40%)

Rep. James E. Clyburn (D)

Elected 1992; b. July 21, 1940, Sumter; home, Columbia; SC St. U., B.A. 1962; African Methodist Episcopal; married (Emily).

Career: Teacher, 1962–66; Dir., Charleston Neighborhood Youth Corps, 1966–68; Exec. Dir., SC Commission for Farm Workers, 1968–71; Asst., SC Gov. West, 1971–74; SC Human Affairs Commissioner, 1974–92.

DC Office: 319 CHOB 20515, 202-225-3315; Fax: 202-225-2313.

District Offices: 1703 Gervais St., Columbia 29201, 803-799-1100; 181 E. Evans St., Florence 29502, 803-622-1212; and 4900 LaCrosse Rd., N. Charleston 29418, 803-747-9660.

Committees: *Transportation & Infrastructure* (21st of 28 D): Aviation; Surface Transportation. *Veterans' Affairs* (12th of 15 D): Education, Training, Employment and Housing.

Group Ratings

	ADA	ACLU	COPE	CFA	LCV	CON	NSI	COC	ACU	NTLC	CHC
1994	75	82	88	90	82	1	20	45	15	14	0
1993	90	—	100	100	71	30	—	27	13	—	—

National Journal Ratings

	1993 LIB	—	1993 CONS	1994 LIB	—	1994 CONS
Economic	88%	—	0%	83%	—	0%
Social	77%	—	22%	90%	—	6%
Foreign	63%	—	34%	57%	—	37%

Key Votes of the 103d Congress

1. Clinton Deficit Plan	Y	3. Brady Handgun Purchase	Y	5. Lmt. UN Cmnd. of Forces	N
2. NAFTA	N	4. Strike Race/Death Pnlty.	N	6. Cut Missile Funds	Y

Key Votes of the 104th Congress

1. Congressional Compliance	Y	6. Reform Crime Grant	N	11. Loser Pays Court Reform	N
2. Balanced Budget Amndmt.	Y	7. National Security Act	N	12. Product Liability Reform	N
3. Bar Unfunded Mandates	Y	8. Moratorium on Regs.	N	13. Welfare Reform	N
4. Pass Line Item Veto	N	9. Risk Assessment on Regs.	N	14. Term Limits Amndmt.	Y
5. Relax Exclusionary Rule	N	10. Expnd. Priv. Prop. Rights	N	15. Tax Cuts	N

Election Results

1994 general	James E. Clyburn (D)................. 88,635	(64%)	($445,461)
	Gary McLeod (R).................... 50,259	(36%)	($13,047)
1994 primary	James E. Clyburn (D)................. 50,476	(86%)	
	Ben Frasier (D)....................... 8,419	(14%)	
1992 general	James E. Clyburn (D)................ 120,647	(65%)	($324,379)
	John Chase (R)..................... 64,149	(35%)	($114,289)

SOUTH DAKOTA

In 1890, the Census Bureau proclaimed the closing of the American frontier. One of the last places it closed was the southern part of the Dakota Territory, admitted to the Union in 1889 as the state of South Dakota. For years this land had been the home of the Oglala Sioux, one of the largest Native American tribes, who had built a buffalo hunting civilization by becoming masters of the horses the Spaniards had imported to North America 350 years earlier. It was the Sioux warrior chief Sitting Bull, now buried on a bluff above the Missouri River, who destroyed Custer at Little Big Horn in 1876; it was Oglala Sioux who were the victims at the massacre of Wounded Knee in 1890. After half a century of horrifying disease and a decade of defeat, the Sioux were a traumatized people, and still are today, living on reservations with proud traditions but also terrible poverty. Isolated in reservations, Indians are far from mainstream economic participation. Alcoholism and suicide, in some way the after-effects of wounds suffered 100 years ago, remain persistent problems. There have been clashes between the civilizations in recent memory—the killings of government agents by Indian rebels at Wounded Knee in 1975—but also moves toward reconciliation. In 1989 the legislature renamed Pioneer Day (which had been Columbus Day) as Native American Day, and Governor George Mickelson declared 1990 a Year of Reconciliation, with a peace pipe ceremony at the Capitol involving leaders of nine Sioux nations. And in 1994 the Sioux took heart from the birth of a white buffalo in a preserve in Wisconsin, the first white buffalo known of since 1959, a sign of great hope in the Sioux religion.

The settlement of South Dakota a century ago was a rapid and sometimes violent process. The first gold strikes in the Black Hills came in 1876, and soon the mountains swarmed with settlers; Deadwood became a city of 20,000 where Calamity Jane ruled the saloons and Wild Bill Hickock was shot in the back while holding two pair—aces and eights. Ranchers, knowing that the buffalo could not be contained by barbed wire fences, massacred them so thoroughly that when Teddy Roosevelt got to the Dakota Territory in 1884, he had a hard time finding one to shoot. It was not long before the railroad came through, and before enough settlers, many of them German and Scandinavian immigrants recruited by the railroads, had built sodhouses, broken the land and set down enough roots to justify making two Dakota states.

But South Dakota never entirely filled up. In the 25 years between statehood and World War I, the eastern third of the state, sectioned off Midwestern style into 640 acre square miles, was settled by farmers. But moving westward, before a traveler reaches the Missouri River in the middle of the state, green turns to brown, cultivation grows sparse and then stops; the plains are open grazing land, scarcely touched by the white men who were so eager to establish dominion over them a century ago. The land is punctuated, not by roads meeting every mile at precise angles, but by buttes, gullies and grasslands sweeping to the horizon with no sign of human habitation except the occasional missile silos which once were pointed at the Soviet Union and which by 1994 were all empty.

South Dakota's political patterns were fairly well set by the early 1900s. Its early settlers were mostly Midwesterners who brought their Republicanism with them. Voters here never had much use for the Non-Partisan League, which caught on in the more Scandinavian soil of North Dakota, and there was never anything here comparable to the Farmer-Labor Party of Minnesota. But the nature of the farm economy—its dependence on the great railroads and milling companies, and on the vagaries of international markets—meant that South Dakota was subject to periodic farm revolts. It voted for Populists and William Jennings Bryan in the 1890s; it supported the early New Deal; it revolted against the Eisenhower Administration in the 1950s by electing a young congressman named George McGovern. South Dakota also shared the isolationist impulse of much of the Great Plains, and McGovern's opposition to the Vietnam war in the late 1960s was not a liability here. In the early 1970s, Democrats seemed on the verge of becoming the majority party.

But reaction to the Wounded Knee uprising moved South Dakotans sharply to the Republicans in the late 1970s. And the policies of Governor William Janklow, first elected in 1978, moved them further in that direction. It was Janklow who sparked repeal of the state usury law, after which Citicorp moved its credit card operations to Sioux Falls. The Citibank operation here grew from 50 employees to 2,700 in 1981 to 3000 today; other banks followed; shopping centers burgeoned as Sioux Falls grew and shoppers started driving more than 200 miles for the selection a big mall could provide; medical centers grew, as South Dakotans sought the better care large hospitals could provide. Metro Sioux Falls grew 13% in the 1980s—amazing growth in a state which often lost population between censuses—and in the 1990s had the nation's lowest unemployment rate; Rapid City, with a similar economic boost plus tourism, grew 16%; Watertown and Brookings, mid-sized freeway towns, grew as well, while almost every other county in the state lost population. There are still some 35,000 farms in South Dakota, but population patterns here on the Plains now look more like those in the Rockies, with most people concentrated in a few areas, while vast acreage remains vacant, punctuated with infrequent ranches and resort areas—a landscape that would not have been totally alien to Sitting Bull.

South Dakota keeps its sales tax low and has no state property or income tax. Wages are low too—teacher's salaries are the lowest in the country; but defenders point out that living costs are also low, and low-wage jobs are better than none. South Dakota also works hard to court tourists. The lure of natural attractions in the Black Hills and the huge and varyingly unfinished sculptures of Mount Rushmore and the Crazy Horse Memorial are augmented by such commercial enterprises as gold-panning creeks and gambling casinos in Deadwood and on Indian reservations. And Wall Drug, the 46,000-square foot emporium between the Badlands and Rapid City snares three-quarters of the freeway traffic. Janklow's reelection in 1994, after eight years out of office, signifies a continued approval of this regimen, and Republicans also won control of the state Senate. Yet South Dakota is happy to send Democrats to Washington to vote for more spending even as it keeps Republicans in Pierre to hold down taxes.

Governor. Probably no governor in South Dakota's history has had as great an impact as Bill Janklow; yet he remains as controversial in victory as in defeat. Janklow started off as a lawyer on a Sioux Indian reservation. Then, elected attorney general in 1974, he reacted sharply to the militants' uprisings of 1975, insisting that the law be enforced. Elected governor in 1978, he got Citibank into the state—the first of many credit card operations—and set the state on a low-tax course. Reelected in 1982, he ran for the Senate in 1986, and lost the primary 55%–45% to the inarticulate but personally popular incumbent Senator Jim Abdnor. The new governor, Republican George Mickelson, was proud of his revolving economic development fund, financed by a temporary one-cent sales tax increase, to attract jobs and industry. He died in a plane crash in April 1993, and was succeeded by 67-year-old Walter Dale Miller, a rancher from near Rapid City who served 20 years in the legislature and six as lieutenant governor. Janklow challenged him in the 1994 Republican primary and won by a 54%–46% margin, carrying most of eastern South Dakota and losing much of the west. In the general election he won easily, 55%–41%, over

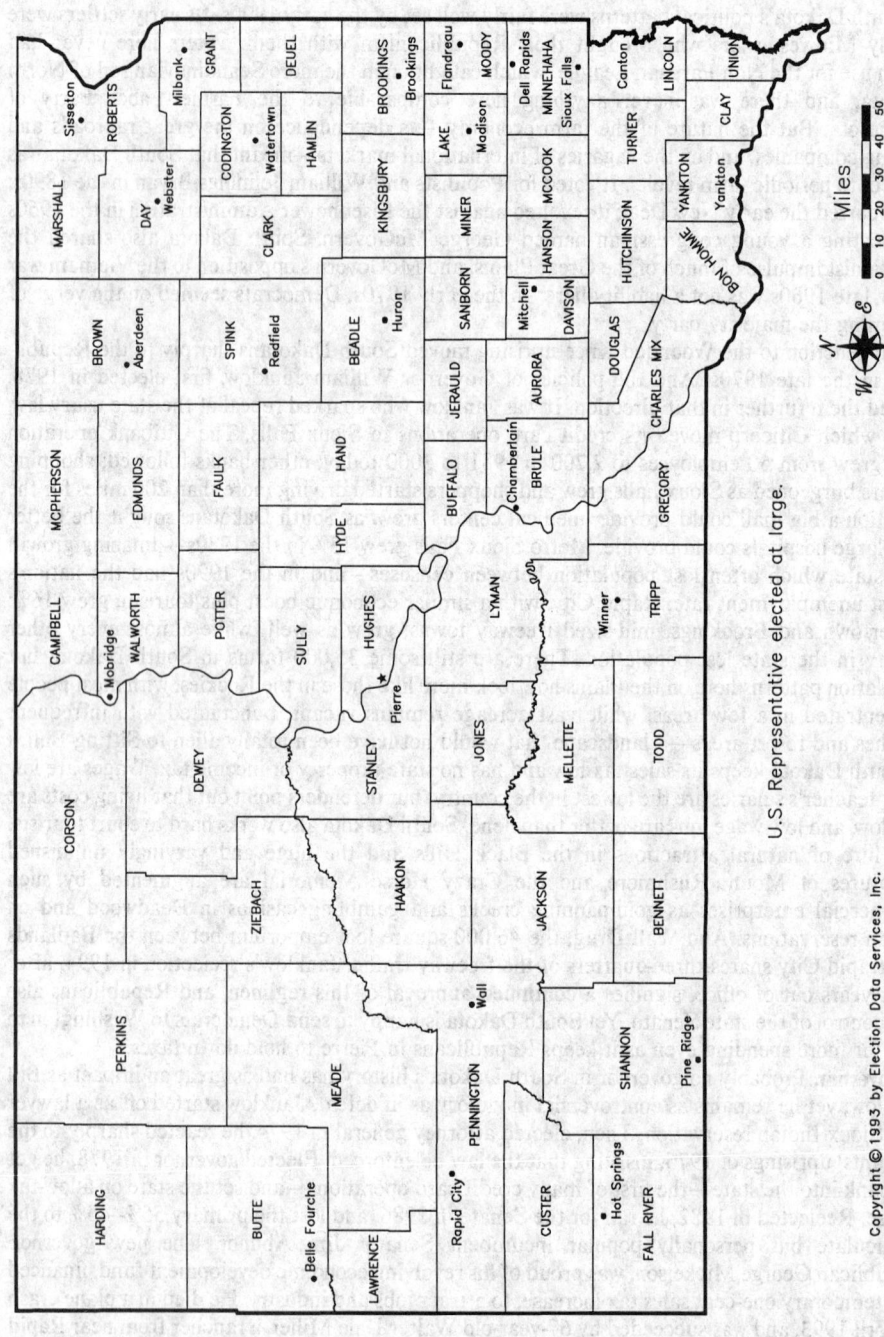

U.S. Representative elected at large.

Jim Beddow, the former president of McGovern's alma mater, Dakota Wesleyan University. Feisty and sometimes abrasive, Janklow's critics say he runs state government like a dictator. But Janklow pledges to keep South Dakota's economy strong and to be tough on crime and drug abuse. He would like to see "two strikes and you're out."

Senators. South Dakota's two senators, both former representatives, were on election day 1994 largely unknown nationwide. But they emerged, thanks to the defeat of many Democrats, as prominent national figures by January 1995. Republican Larry Pressler is chairman of the Commerce Committee, where he superintends consideration of some of the most heavily lobbied issues in Washington. Democrat Tom Daschle is Senate minority leader. Adding to the spice is the fact that, as much as any two Senators from the same state, they don't get along and each makes clear his minimal regard for the other.

Larry Pressler is now 13th in seniority among Republican senators and has impressive credentials: Vietnam veteran (the first elected to the Senate), Rhodes scholar, Harvard lawyer. He was first elected to the House by beating an incumbent Democrat in the Democratic year of 1974, easily elected to the Senate in 1978, and reelected by the widest margin in South Dakota history in 1984. But for years he was not taken seriously by colleagues; he seemed a classic example of the 1970s congressman who hustled to please the folks back home, opposing every congressional pay raise and voting for farm price supports and export subsidies galore. For a time in the 1980s he seemed to wobble from conservative to liberal—more in response to opposition back home than to any clear philosophic bent. But in the 1990s he has become a staunch ally of Bob Dole, hewing pretty straight to a conservative voting record. He has made some important if controversial legislative achievements, and has worked hard to master some of the most heavily-lobbied and bafflingly difficult issues before Congress. And all this while facing sharp attacks from his home town newspaper, the *Sioux Falls Argus-Leader*, whose coverage of Pressler is almost as partisan and hostile as Ted Kennedy's from the *Boston Herald* or Jesse Helms's from the *Raleigh News & Observer*.

Pressler has been successful legislatively when he seizes on an issue others have ignored, sometimes because it's in his committees' jurisdiction, sometimes because of a South Dakota angle, sometimes apparently just because something catches his eye. Take the 1985 Pressler amendment requiring a cutoff of aid to Pakistan if it develops nuclear weapons. This was passed although the Reagan Administration was depending on Pakistan to funnel aid to Afghan rebels; Pressler, from his seat on Foreign Relations, has pressured successive administrations to enforce it. In 1992 he conditioned aid to Russia on its withdrawal from the Baltics, pressure which worked. He has also attacked China for its military buildup and violations of human rights in Tibet, and has pressed for reform of internal United Nations operations and appointment of a UN inspector general. Foreign policymakers must regard him as an interloper, yet he does push for core American values which have little political constituency.

For years on the Commerce Committee he worked on peripheral issues: an outage prevention agency for telecommunications networks, an AM stereo standard, a law to let citizens stop telephone solicitations, a Landsat law. He was not the major Republican player on telecommunications reform in 1994—Bob Packwood was—but the bill died in September 1994 and, despite the many formidable policy and interest-group obstacles, Pressler moved quickly to take over the issue in the 104th Congress. He initially opposed the restrictions that then-Chairman Ernest Hollings had insisted on and said, "Our goal here is complete free enterprise, complete competition." But his efforts to cut a deal with Hollings in early 1995 led to complaints from the free-marketers. He also said he would "revisit" the 1992 cable reregulation law, which he voted for, and he launched a high-profile bid to reduce government funding of the Corporation for Public Broadcasting, despite the popularity of its services in rural areas. (A bumper sticker in the state read: "Let's keep PBS and Privatize Pressler.") He admitted a tactical error after sending a questionnaire to NPR employees, which asked them detailed personal and political questions. Pressler has been a free trader, voting for NAFTA and GATT, but backed actions against Canada for allegedly unfair agricultural subsidies. On the Aviation Subcommittee, he attacked the FAA for slipshod safety regulation after Governor George Mickelson was killed in a small plane crash and he followed up by encouraging an investigation into Senate colleague Tom Daschle's efforts to intervene with federal regulators on behalf of a South Dakota commuter aircraft firm whose plane crashed in a snow storm. He questions whether bilingual education keeps kids from learning English and opposed employer mandates in healthcare reform. He also weighs in on South Dakota issues: he is concerned about Indian tribal jurisdiction, wants state control of food stamps, favors lots of federal Impact Aid, favors ethanol development, wants wetlands reform, and works for the Mni Wiconi Rural Water System. Pressler is still far from being regarded as one of the large figures, the "whales," in the Senate. But his committee positions and his willingness to use the Senate's obstructionist rules to advance causes he believes in make him a figure to be reckoned with.

Pressler had his toughest Senate race in 1990, when Democrat Ted Muenster, cheered on by the *Sioux Falls Argus-Leader* and by Daschle ("a Senate seat is a terrible thing to waste,") raised money in Washington and nationally for cheap South Dakota TV time and held Pressler to a 52%–45% victory. Pressler was weak in fast-growing Sioux Falls and Watertown but was helped by Muenster's poor showing among Indians. In 1996, he faces another serious challenge, likely from Congressman-at-Large Tim Johnson, though Pressler's committee chairmanship and the recent Republican trend in South Dakota both work in his favor.

In 1995, Tom Daschle was elected Senate Democratic Leader at 48 by a 24–23 margin (over Connecticut's Chris Dodd), after spending almost all his adult life in politics—and after winning each important position he has held by narrow margins. Daschle returned from service in the Air Force in 1972 at the high point of South Dakota Democratic fortune and became a Washington staffer to Senator James Abourezk; in 1978, as Abourezk was about to retire, Daschle returned to South Dakota, ran for the eastern House district that Larry Pressler was vacating, and won by exactly 139 votes over the former P.O.W. who had come close to beating George McGovern in 1974. In 1982, when South Dakota returned to a single at-large district, Daschle beat fellow incumbent Clint Roberts by 52%–48%. In 1986, he was elected to the Senate by 52%–48% over incumbent James Abdnor, who was hurt by primary competition from then Governor Bill Janklow. Two years later, in January 1989, new Senate Majority Leader George Mitchell named Daschle co-chairman of the Senate Democratic Policy Committee—in effect, though not in title, the number two man in the Senate leadership. Mitchell announced his retirement in March 1994, and Daschle immediately started running for the spot—too quickly, as far as some Senate traditionalists were concerned. He had varied opposition: Pat Leahy, Wendell Ford and Harry Reid declined to run; Jim Sasser, who was an early favorite, ran hard but lost his own reelection race in Tennessee. After Sasser's defeat, Christopher Dodd was encouraged to run by many more-senior Democrats, and he nearly won. The result left Daschle in an awkward position in which he had to prove himself to most of the senior Democrats who had voted against him. Not only did he have to contend with Republican Leader Bob Dole, but Daschle also faced an early testing period with Robert Byrd, the former old-style Democratic leader and acknowledged master of Senate procedure. His narrow victory also led to an unusual decision by Daschle to relinquish his Finance Committee seat to Carol Moseley-Braun of Illinois, a late supporter who eagerly wanted a seat on the committee.

Daschle's strengths are a liberal voting record on farm and economic issues that resonate in South Dakota, a wariness of foreign involvements and moderate stands on some cultural issues, plus hard work and team playing. Until 1994, he was always part of a legislative majority, voting with the Democratic leadership in the House for eight years, then working with the other Democrats whose election in 1986 returned their party to control of the Senate; they were the nucleus of his support for minority leader. On some farm issues, he has not always succeeded. As a "prairie populist," he has resisted cuts in farm subsidies; but they were reduced in the farm bills of 1985 and 1990, and are likely to be slashed again in 1995. He had more success in cutting legislative deals to get breaks for reformulated gas and ethanol—both use South Dakota grain. Despite a Centers for Disease Control study showing no connection between exposure and cancer, Daschle was the leader in getting the Senate to agree to compensate Vietnam veterans exposed to Agent Orange. He was one of the Democrats' leaders in 1994 for healthcare reform; he worked closely with Mitchell to craft a version of the Clinton plan that could pass the Senate, and at least publicly was optimistic that they could get most senators to swallow an employer mandate and comprehensive federal control of health care decisions. A strong and unyielding partisan like Mitchell, he surely did not anticipate, and was dismayed by, the legislative fiasco on health care and the Republican election victories of 1994.

As minority leader, Daschle cannot hope to pass much legislation immediately, but, with the Senate's obstruction-loving rules, he can be instrumental in stopping some. His primary goal is "to ensure economic security," an indication that he has not abandoned the traditional Democratic willingness to use government to help people, but adds that he also wants to "repair the social fabric" and "redesign government." That internal tension was evident in his handling of the balanced-budget constitutional amendment, which he had earlier supported but turned against in early 1995 because of his fear of how Republicans would apportion their spending cuts. Burned on his efforts at healthcare before, Daschle made it clear he planned to keep some distance from the Clinton Administration. He has called for small changes in Senate rules, noting how desultory the Senate looks on C-SPAN during endless quorum calls. But, with Byrd's prodding, he stands ready to use the filibuster, the chief weapon of a 46-member minority, as George Mitchell did on capital gains in 1989. In March 1995, he played a key role in handing a stinging defeat to the Republican bid to pass the balanced budget amendment, when they refused his demands to specify how they would balance the budget over seven years. He obviously hopes to become majority leader before too long, but the early outlook for 1996 makes that seem improbable.

After close initial victories in House and Senate races, Daschle was reelected comfortably in 1992, testimony to his hard work and detailed attention to South Dakota issues from farm programs to fetal alcohol syndrome. In 1992, Republicans tried to get Bill Janklow to run against him. When Janklow declined, Republican nominee Charlene Haar was depicted locally as a second choice and ignored or scorned by feminists and reporters busy celebrating "the year of the woman" elsewhere. With a huge financial edge, Daschle won 65%–33%. He is not up for reelection until 1998, and at this point must be regarded as a favorite. But he ran into trouble with national press coverage, including negative pieces in *The New York Times* and on CBS-News's *60 Minutes* as the result of an early 1994 plane crash by B&L Aviation, a commuter aircraft operated by a friend on whose behalf Daschle had earlier intervened with federal safety regulators. Although even his critics acknowledged that it was difficult to prove a connection to the B&L crash, which killed three local doctors plus the pilot, the paper trail of Daschle's pleas on behalf of his friend made the Senator a target of the grieving widows and opened a window on the often unsavory ways in which business is transacted in Washington. In addition to his letters on behalf of B&L, Daschle also sought unsuccessfully in 1994 to move the Forest Service's jurisdiction over aircraft inspection to the Federal Aviation Administration, where (by seeming coincidence) Daschle's wife Linda has been the deputy administrator.

Representative-at-Large. The House member representing the nation's second most populous district is South Dakota's Representative-at-Large Tim Johnson. Johnson is a Democrat with a similarly youthful demeanor but a more moderate voting record than Daschle. His early political career was spent in South Dakota: he was elected to the legislature in 1978, at 31, and ran for the House in 1986 when Daschle ran for the Senate. He beat fellow state Senator Jim Burg in the Democratic primary, 48%–45%, with big margins in his southeastern home area and in Sioux Falls and Rapid City, and won the general 59%–41%, a better mark than Daschle made against the same candidate two years before.

Johnson has done much of his work on the Agriculture Committee, chairing two subcommittees before the Republicans took over. He worked on crop subsidies and crop insurance reform, and he claims credit for crop relief after the disastrous 1993 floods, price supports for sunflowers and other oilseeds, and a fund to encourage use of vegetable oils. He also pushed for action against Canadian and European Community agricultural subsidies. He voted against the 1990 farm bill and as sixth ranking Democrat on Agriculture is likely to push hard against a Republican 1995 farm bill. On the Resources Committee he has worked successfully for South Dakota water projects, the most recent of which is the Mni Wiconi Rural Water System. He seeks establishment of the Chief Big Foot National Memorial Park at the Wounded Knee massacre site and a Northern Great Plains Rural Development Commission. On some issues he splits from other Democrats, notably abortion, on which he backed the Hyde amendment, and the line-item veto and voted for the balanced budget amendment.

Against lightly funded Republicans, Johnson has won reelection by impressive margins, better than 2–1 in 1990 and 1992, 60%–37% in Republican-leaning 1994. He made no move to run against Senator Larry Pressler in 1990 but, after Daschle, Johnson is by far the best known Democrat in the state. He made moves in early 1995 to prepare for what would be an expensive, bitter and probably close challenge to Pressler in 1996. If Johnson makes the move, expect a wide-open contest in both parties for his House seat.

Presidential politics. With only three electoral votes, South Dakota is not a glittering prize in presidential contests. Nevertheless, it has been close in four of the last six elections. With typical Farm Belt contrariness, it has tilted against the party in power, giving good, though losing, votes to Democrats in 1972, 1976, 1988 and 1992 and going heavily Republican in 1980. George Bush narrowly won here twice, 53%–47% in 1988 and 41%–37% in 1992: Democrats have a chance here in any close race.

South Dakota's presidential primary for years was held on the same day as California's, and eclipsed by it. Since 1988 it has been held in February, just one week after New Hampshire. So far it has been not a trendsetter, but a booster of Great Plains candidates who do not fare well elsewhere: Bob Dole and Dick Gephardt in 1988, Bob Kerrey and Tom Harkin in 1992. When Pat Buchanan missed the filing deadline in 1992, George Bush beat an uncommitted slate. In 1996, the Republican favorite here is obviously Dole.

The People: Est. Pop. 1994: 721,000; Pop. 1990: 696,004, up 3.6% 1990–1994. 0.3% of U.S. total, 45th largest; 50% rural. Median age: 32.5 years. 14.7% 65 years and over. 91.6% White, 7.3% American Indian. Households (1980): 58.9% married couple families; 29% married couple fams. w. children; 43% college educ.; median household income: $22,503; per capita income: $10,661; 66.1% owner occupied housing; median house value: $45,200; median monthly rent: $242. 3.1% Unemployment. 1994 Voting age pop.: 522,000. 1994 Turnout: 311,577; 60% of VAP. Registered voters (1994): 431,873; 176,881 D (41%); 212,544 R (49%); 42,448 unaffiliated and minor parties (10%).

Political Lineup: Governor, William J. Janklow (R); Lt. Gov., Carole Hillard (R) Secy. of State, Joyce Hazeltine (R); Atty. Gen., Mark Barnett (R); Treasurer, Richard Butler (D); Auditor, Vernon L. Larson (R). State Senate, 35 (19 R and 16 D); State House of Representatives, 70 (46 R and 24 D). Senators, Larry Pressler (R) and Thomas A. Daschle (D). Representative, 1 D at large.

1992 Presidential Vote

Bush (R)	136,718	(41%)
Clinton (D)	124,888	(37%)
Perot (I)	73,295	(22%)

1988 Presidential Vote

Bush (R)	165,415	(53%)
Dukakis (D)	145,560	(47%)

1992 Democratic Presidential Primary

Kerrey	23,892	(40%)
Harkin	15,023	(25%)
Clinton	11,375	(19%)
Tsongas	5,729	(10%)
Brown	2,300	(4%)

1992 Republican Presidential Primary

Bush	30,964	(69%)
Uncommitted	13,707	(31%)

GOVERNOR

Gov. William J. Janklow (R)

Elected 1994, term expires Jan. 1999; b. Sept. 13, 1939, Chicago, IL; home, Brandon; U. of SD, B.S. 1964, LL.B 1966; Lutheran; married (Mary).

Career: Marine Corps, 1956–59; Legal Aid, Rosebud Indian Reservation, 1966–73; Practicing atty., 1973; SD Special Prosecutor, 1973–75; SD Atty. Gen., 1975–78; SD Gov., 1979–86.

Office: Executive Office, State Capitol, Pierre 57501, 605-773-3212; Fax: 605-773-5844.

Election Results

1994 gen.	William J. Janklow (R)	172,515	(55%)
	Jim Beddow (D)	126,273	(41%)
	Nathan A. Barton (Lib)	12,825	(4%)
1994 prim.	William J. Janklow (R)	57,221	(54%)
	Walter D. Miller (R)	48,754	(46%)
1990 gen.	George S. Mickelson (R)	151,198	(59%)
	Bob L. Samuelson (D)	105,525	(41%)

SENATORS

Sen. Larry Pressler (R)

Elected 1978, seat up 1996; b. Mar. 29, 1942, Humboldt; home, Humboldt; U. of SD, B.A. 1964, Rhodes Scholar, Oxford U., 1966, Harvard, M.A., J.D. 1971; Catholic; married (Harriet).

Career: Army, 1966–68 (Vietnam); U.S. House of Reps., 1974–78.

DC Office: 243 RSOB 20510, 202-224-5842; e-mail: larry_pressler@pressler.senate.gov.

State Offices: 1923 6th Ave., #105-A, Aberdeen 57402, 605-226-7471; 112 Rushmore Mall, Rapid City 57701, 605-341-1185; and 309 Minnesota Ave., Sioux Falls 57102, 605-335-1990.

Committees: *Commerce, Science & Transportation* (Chmn. of 10 R): Aviation; Communications; Consumer Affairs, Foreign Commerce and Tourism; Science, Technology and Space. *Finance* (8th of 11 R): International Trade; Long-Term Growth, Debt and Defict Reduction (Chmn.); Taxation and IRS Oversight. *Small Business* (2nd of 10 R). *Aging (Special)* (2nd of 10 R).

Group Ratings

	ADA	ACLU	COPE	CFA	LCV	CON	NSI	COC	ACU	NTLC	CHC
1994	0	16	13	33	8	78	90	71	96	88	100
1993	10	—	0	20	0	57	—	91	96	—	—

National Journal Ratings

	1993 LIB — 1993 CONS		1994 LIB — 1994 CONS	
Economic	0% —	87%	12% —	82%
Social	0% —	92%	21% —	75%
Foreign	8% —	86%	18% —	80%

Key Votes of the 103d Congress

1. Clinton Deficit Plan	N	3. Brady Handgun Purchase	N	5. Lmt. UN Cmnd. of Forces	Y
2. NAFTA	Y	4. Strike Race/Death Pnlty.	Y	6. Cut Missile Funds	N

Key Votes of the 104th Congress

1. Congressional Compliance	Y	3. Balanced Budget Amndt.	Y	5. Product Liability Reform	Y
2. Bar Unfunded Mandates	Y	4. Pass Line Item Veto	Y	6. FY96 Budget	Y

Election Results

1990 general	Larry Pressler (R)	135,682	(52%)	($2,124,359)
	Ted Muenster (D)	116,727	(45%)	($1,323,770)
	Other	6,567	(3%)	
1990 primary	Larry Pressler (R)	unopposed		
1984 general	Larry Pressler (R)	235,176	(74%)	($1,155,683)
	George V. Cunningham (D)	80,537	(26%)	($166,426)

Sen. Thomas A. Daschle (D)

Elected 1986, seat up 1998; b. Dec. 9, 1947, Aberdeen; home, Aberdeen; SD St. U., B.A. 1969; Catholic; married (Linda).

Career: Air Force, 1969–72, Air Force Reserves, 1975–78; Legis. Asst., U.S. Sen. James Abourezk, 1972–77; U.S. House of Reps., 1978–86.

DC Office: 509 HSOB 20510, 202-224-2321; Fax: 202-224-2047; e-mail: tom_daschle@daschle.senate.gov.

State Offices: P.O. Box 1274, Sioux Falls 57101, 605-334-9596; P.O. Box 1536, Aberdeen 57401, 605-225-8823; and P.O. Box 8168, Rapid City 57709, 605-348-3551.

Committees: *Minority Leader. Democratic Conference Chairman. Democratic Policy Committee Chairman. Agriculture, Nutrition & Forestry* (6th of 8 D): Production and Price Competitiveness; Research, Nutrition and General Legislation.

Group Ratings

	ADA	ACLU	COPE	CFA	LCV	CON	NSI	COC	ACU	NTLC	CHC
1994	80	53	63	75	77	17	20	37	4	0	28
1993	75	—	91	90	56	8	—	20	12	—	—

National Journal Ratings

	1993 LIB — 1993 CONS			1994 LIB — 1994 CONS		
Economic	71%	—	17%	72%	—	18%
Social	63%	—	35%	81%	—	16%
Foreign	92%	—	0%	66%	—	29%

Key Votes of the 103d Congress

1. Clinton Deficit Plan	Y	3. Brady Handgun Purchase	Y	5. Lmt. UN Cmnd. of Forces	N
2. NAFTA	Y	4. Strike Race/Death Pnlty.	N	6. Cut Missile Funds	N

Key Votes of the 104th Congress

1. Congressional Compliance	Y	3. Balanced Budget Amndt.	N	5. Product Liability Reform	N
2. Bar Unfunded Mandates	Y	4. Pass Line Item Veto	Y	6. FY96 Budget	N

Election Results

1992 general	Thomas A. Daschle (D)	217,095	(65%)	($3,981,548)
	Charlene Haar (R)	108,733	(33%)	($478,421)
	Others	8,667	(3%)	
1992 primary	Thomas A. Daschle (D)	unopposed		
1986 general	Thomas A. Daschle (D)	152,657	(52%)	($3,485,870)
	James Abnor (R)...................	143,173	(48%)	($3,410,387)

REPRESENTATIVE

Rep. Tim Johnson (D)

Elected 1986; b. Dec. 28, 1946, Canton; home, Vermillion; U. of SD, B.A. 1969, M.A. 1970, J.D. 1975; Lutheran; married (Barbara).

Career: Practicing atty., 1975–85; Clay Cnty. Dep. State Atty., 1985; SD House of Reps., 1978–82; SD Senate, 1982–86.

DC Office: 2438 RHOB 20515, 202-225-2801; Fax: 202-225-2427.

District Offices: 515 S. Dakota Ave., Sioux Falls 57102, 605-332-8896; 809 South St., #104, Rapid City 57701, 605-341-3990; and 20 6th Ave., SW, #C, Aberdeen 57401, 605-226-3440.

Committees: *Agriculture* (6th of 22 D): Resource Conservation, Research and Forestry (RMM). *Resources* (10th of 20 D): Native American and Insular Affairs.

Group Ratings

	ADA	ACLU	COPE	CFA	LCV	CON	NSI	COC	ACU	NTLC	CHC
1994	55	48	67	60	67	44	30	75	24	21	28
1993	65	—	92	100	86	55	—	36	21	—	—

National Journal Ratings

	1993 LIB — 1993 CONS			1994 LIB — 1994 CONS		
Economic	55%	—	45%	59%	—	37%
Social	60%	—	38%	55%	—	44%
Foreign	43%	—	57%	64%	—	33%

Key Votes of the 103d Congress

1. Clinton Deficit Plan	Y	3. Brady Handgun Purchase	Y	5. Lmt. UN Cmnd. of Forces	N
2. NAFTA	N	4. Strike Race/Death Pnlty.	Y	6. Cut Missile Funds	N

Key Votes of the 104th Congress

1. Congressional Compliance	Y	6. Reform Crime Grant	N	11. Loser Pays Court Reform	N
2. Balanced Budget Amndmt.	Y	7. National Security Act	N	12. Product Liability Reform	N
3. Bar Unfunded Mandates	Y	8. Moratorium on Regs.	Y	13. Welfare Reform	N
4. Pass Line Item Veto	Y	9. Risk Assessment on Regs.	Y	14. Term Limits Amndmt.	Y
5. Relax Exclusionary Rule	Y	10. Expnd. Priv. Prop. Rights	Y	15. Tax Cuts	N

Election Results

1994 general	Tim Johnson (D).....................	183,036	(60%)	($480,230)
	Jan Berkhout (R)	112,054	(37%)	($144,356)
	Others...........................	10,832	(4%)	
1994 primary	Tim Johnson (D)...................	unopposed		
1992 general	Tim Johnson (D)...................	230,070	(69%)	($376,741)
	John Timmer (R)	89,375	(27%)	($170,143)
	Others...........................	13,457	(4%)	

TENNESSEE

Tennessee was the scene in 1994 of the most thoroughgoing political revolution in a politically revolutionary year: revolution, that is, in the 18th Century sense as a turning over, not a 20th Century destructive spasm. Surely it was a revolution in office: Tennessee entered 1994 with a Democratic governor, two Democratic senators, a House delegation 6–3 Democratic; by early 1995 it had a Republican governor, two Republican senators, a House delegation 5–4 Republican. All this occurred, moreover, in a state without great economic grievance— Tennessee has the fastest-growing economy of any state in the Mississippi Valley South—and not because of dissatisfaction with any visible Tennessee executive—Governor Ned McWherter left office after two terms admired and liked, and Vice President Al Gore maintains high ratings in the polls. The Republican tide here has to be taken as a stinging rebuke to the Clinton Administration and its policies, from a state that had voted for Bill Clinton in 1992 and has been part of every enduring Democratic majority in American history.

The Republican revolution in Tennessee was all the more striking because political loyalties run deep in this state, imprinted in the soil over many years of sometimes bloody history. Many Tennesseans today live in the same counties where their ancestors settled in the years from 1796, when Tennessee was admitted to the Union, to 1829, when its first president, Andrew Jackson, rode off from the Hermitage on his way to the White House. The state was as feisty and quick to take umbrage as Old Hickory; it peopled the armies of our early wars so eagerly it became known as the Volunteer State. And it took sides so strongly in the Civil War that most of its counties today still vote their 1860s loyalties: the Union counties, mainly in the east but with a scattering to the west, vote solidly Republican, while the Confederate counties in middle and west Tennessee are heavily Democratic.

Within the limits of these enduring party loyalties, political entrepreneurs have set the tone for the state. From the 1920s to 1948, Edward Crump, longtime mayor of Memphis, used his total control of Democratic primary votes there to elect governors and senators. The Tennessee Valley Authority and the cheap electric power it generated provided an institutional base for reform liberal Democrats Estes Kefauver and Albert Gore, Sr., elected to the Senate in 1948 and 1952. They were soon national figures, with reliable enough backing from Tennessee's yellow-dog Democratic majority to vote for civil rights bills and to refuse to sign the segregationist Southern Manifesto, and still thrive electorally. Tennessee has never had a large black population—about 16% in the 1990s, half of whom live in and around Memphis—and the state was not riven by the racial animosity that seared so much of the South in the 1950s and 1960s, thanks in large part to the actions of its leading politicians, but also to the continuing hold of ancestral partisan preferences.

Eventually, the Democrats' cultural liberalism on issues other than race moved west

Tennessee voters away from their ancestral party, and moderate east Tennessee Republicans Howard Baker and Bill Brock, elected to the Senate in 1966 and 1970, set the state's tone; Baker protege Lamar Alexander, elected governor in 1978, instituted education reforms and attracted Japanese investment that have changed and strengthened the state over the last dozen or so years. But starting with the Jimmy Carter sweep in 1976, Tennessee reverted to its old basic divisions, and Democrats were mostly on top again—until the Clinton Administration laid bare national policies which most Tennesseans were unwilling to endorse, even with Al Gore's support.

Tennessee's regional personalities remain distinct: the east is feisty and Republican, middle Tennessee has been devoutly Democratic since the days of Nashville's Andrew Jackson, the west is the one part that has long been racially polarized. The persistence of these differences is matched by the musical traditions which have made Tennessee, for many Americans, the music capital of the nation. Tennessee is associated with country music, but there are several strains to it. East Tennessee country music has been influenced by bluegrass and the mountain fiddling tradition, with string bands and vocal harmony. The country music first developed in Nashville 50 years ago, featuring solo singers in bands, seems rooted in the gospel music also centered in that city—which, as it happens, is also the nation's leading center of religious publishing. (Nashville's Grand Ole Opry, broadcast since 1925, and Knoxville's Tennessee Barn Dance, broadcast since 1942, have names suggesting the difference.) West Tennessee, the Mississippi lowlands around Memphis, is a northern extension of the Mississippi Delta, the part of America that gave birth to the blues in the 1890–1920 period. Memphis produced many musicians who drew on the blues tradition, from the jazz musicians of Beale Street in the 1920s, to Elvis Presley of Graceland mansion in the 1950s and 1960s. The primacy of music in Tennessee is witnessed by the fact that its 1996 presidential candidate, Lamar Alexander, uses music as a trademark, remembering soft gospel songs, playing "Rocky Top" the electric keyboard at his announcement, trying to learn to play still more instruments as he goes around the campaign trail.

Those traditions have remained as Tennessee has grown and prospered. While other states in the Mississippi Valley barely grew or even lost population, Tennessee gained 8% in the 1980s, and its boom town, metro Nashville, gained 16%, the biggest major metro growth between Atlanta and Dallas-Fort Worth. Tennessee has attracted more Japanese investment than any other state but California—starting in 1977 with a Nissan forklift distribution center, including the big Nissan pickup plant in Smyrna, amounting by 1990 to 56 factories and 34 distribution centers throughout Tennessee. The Japanese were attracted to Tennessee not just by financial concessions, but by its respect for tradition and hard work, its lack of strong unions and state corporate income taxes and (though they won't say so) its few minorities. They like the fact that Tennesseans do business with less lawyering and more ceremony than Americans in bigger states, and they were impressed when Lamar Alexander showed them satellite photos of the United States taken at night, indicating how many Americans live within a day's drive of Tennessee. It was Tennessee's lack of change—its absence of the institutions that sprang from the labor strife of the 1930s and the civil rights strife of the 1960s—that attracted the Japanese, and they in turn helped to attract General Motors' Saturn project to Spring Hill near Nashville.

The election of Vice President Albert Gore, Jr., elevated to national prominence the success of scions of famous families in Tennessee politics. They include Gore, Congressmen Jimmy Duncan and Bob Clement, former Congressman Jim Cooper and former Senator Howard Baker, among others. But Tennessee has also generated ideas. Lamar Alexander enacted education reforms here, primarily merit pay for teachers and teacher competency tests, and amplified these into a broader agenda as chairman of the National Governors' Association in 1986 and as George Bush's hard-charging secretary of education in 1991. Governor Ned McWherter's proposed TennCare health plan, putting Medicaid recipients and the uninsured into managed care, has made Tennessee an interesting laboratory of reform on that issue. Tennessee is also the headquarters of Columbia/HCA, the nation's biggest private hospital company, whose leading stockholder is the family of Senator Bill Frist, himself a heart

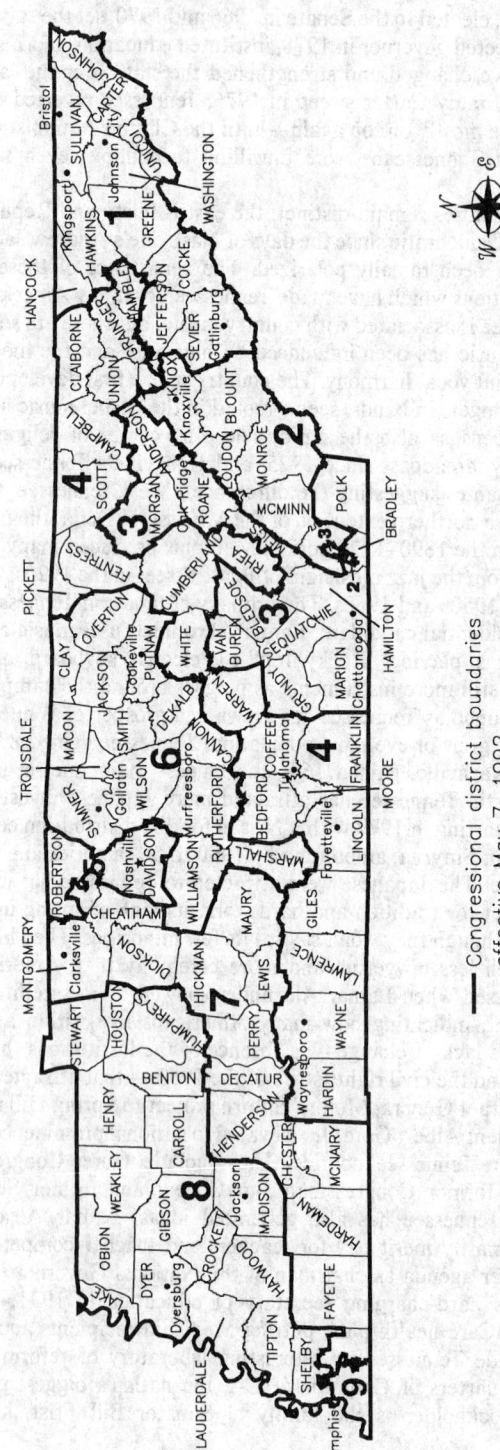

— Congressional district boundaries
effective May 7, 1992.

Copyright © 1993 by Election Data Services, Inc.

transplant surgeon. From a state where the American past is vividly present may come harbingers of the American future.

Governor. Tennessee's governor is Don Sundquist, a Republican elected in 1994, who quite unusually for this state is not from Tennessee at all. He was born in Illinois, the son of a welder, was the first in his family to go to college and served in the Navy. He worked for Jostens, a college and high school ring maker, in Shelbyville, Tennessee, for 10 years; in 1972, he started his own graphics and printing firm in Memphis. He volunteered for Howard Baker as early as 1964, when Baker lost a Senate race, and became active in the national Young Republicans organization. In 1982, Sundquist ran for Congress from the 7th District, which stretched from Memphis all the way to Nashville; he won 51%–49% over current 5th District Congressman Bob Clement, carrying the white Memphis suburbs but losing the rural counties. Sundquist served on the Ways and Means Committee and opposed tax increases; he worked his rural counties with 100 "community days" a year. He was reelected easily.

Sundquist had no trouble winning the Republican nomination for governor in 1994. The Democrats, not atypically, had a riproaring primary, won by Nashville Mayor Phil Bredesen with 53%; he was helped when criminal charges were filed (though they were soon dropped) against Shelby County (Memphis) Mayor Bill Morris. Bredesen was a formidable candidate, popular in Nashville—and in the state's largest media market—rich enough to self-finance his campaign generously. Moreover, the record of Democratic incumbent Ned McWherter was impressive: the passage of TennCare; 21st Century Schools, with teacher salary raises and more leeway for superintendents and principals in choosing teachers; no income tax (Tennessee is one of seven states without one). Sundquist was boosted by Alexander, Baker and east Tennessee Congressman Jimmy Quillen. Bredesen attacked Sundquist for indulging in the perquisites of Congress and for serving on the board of a retirement community that hired a felon to run it. But Sundquist swept in by a solid 54%–45% margin, losing Nashville but carrying the other big metro areas handily. He began office by seeking to close a budget cap caused by TennCare, while insisting on no tax increase.

Senators. Tennessee elected two new Republican senators in 1994, rejecting the chairman of the Senate Budget Committee and the formulator of the Democratic Leadership Council's healthcare reform in favor of a heart transplant surgeon who had not voted most of his adult life, and a former Watergate investigator who has acted in more than a dozen movies and drove around the state in a red pickup truck.

The senior senator now is Fred Thompson, advocate of and advertisement for the idea of the citizen-politician. He grew up in Lawrenceburg, Tennessee, son of a used car dealer, worked his way through school rearing a young family. After Vanderbilt Law, he became an assistant U.S. attorney in Nashville, handling moonshine and stolen car cases. In 1973, Howard Baker made Thompson chief Republican counsel to the Senate Watergate Committee, where he helped uncover the scandal that drove a Republican president from office. Back in Tennessee, incoming Governor Lamar Alexander appointed Thompson special counsel to investigate clemency-selling by outgoing Governor Ray Blanton, who went to jail. In the process, Thompson defended parole board chairman Marie Ragghianti, whose plight was the subject of the movie *Marie*, Thompson's first movie role. He took a couple of more special counsel assignments in Washington and acted in 16 more movies, including box office hits like *The Hunt for Red October*, playing a CIA chief, FBI director and White House chief of staff, as well as some villains. Well connected politically, but without ever having run for office, he decided to run in 1994 for the Senate seat Al Gore had vacated to become vice president and which was held for two years by Harlan Mathews, longtime top aide to outgoing Governor Ned McWherter.

The initial favorite for the seat, and with some good reason, was Congressman Jim Cooper. His father Prentice Cooper was governor of Tennessee from 1939–45; Jim Cooper was a Rhodes Scholar who after Harvard Law School practiced law in Shelbyville briefly and then was elected to the House in 1982 from the elongated 4th District, beating Howard Baker's daughter and becoming the youngest member of Congress. Youthful-looking and serious, he worked on difficult issues in the Commerce Committee, forging compromise positions on complex issues from the Clean Air Act to cable TV reregulation to telecommunications. Cooper's biggest issue was health care: he became a proponent of managed competition early in the debate, and produced a healthcare reform bill in 1993 which was endorsed by the Democratic Leadership Council but opposed with some frenzy by the Clinton White House. In retrospect, it might have passed had the Clinton Administration embraced it. Cooper went into the Senate race well funded, ultimately with $4 million, though he accepted no PAC money; Thompson eventually spent $3.8 million. In most other years in recent times, Cooper would have been the clear favorite for the seat.

But Thompson stressed some issues which caught voters' attention and found a device to symbolize his message. One of his issues has long been advocated by Howard Baker and was featured by Lamar Alexander: limiting congressional sessions to half the year and allowing lawmakers to make their livings in their home communities. To this he coupled strong advocacy of term limits. The symbol—gimmick, Democrats said—for this was the red pickup truck which Thompson leased and drove all around Tennessee, speaking to small groups over coffee or fried chicken. Ads also captured a personal contrast between the candidates: the six foot five Thompson appeared in workshirts, speaking confidently to the camera while walking up porch stairs (not so easy to do: his acting experience helped); the much shorter and youthful-looking Cooper appeared before a church in starched white shirt and tie. In early October, Thompson zoomed to a lead. Cooper responded by citing his opposition to the Clinton healthcare plan. But Cooper got squeezed out of the middle ground he had long worked to occupy. Tennesseans decided to vote against the Clinton Administration and career politicians, and Thompson won 60%–39%.

No sooner had Thompson taken office than Republican leaders appointed him to respond to President Clinton's December 1994 speech urging a tax cut. Thompson's strong words and delivery made him seem the more presidential: "We welcome the President to help us lead America in a new direction, but if he will not, we will welcome the President to follow—because we are moving ahead." Thompson continued to strongly support term limits, despite many senators' doubts, while he dissented from some of the legal reform planks of the Contract With America. He will surely seek a full term in 1996, and Democrats will be hard put to come up with a challenger stronger than the one he defeated by such a wide margin. But Thompson insists he does not intend to make the Senate a lifetime career.

Tennessee's junior senator is Bill Frist, a heart and lung transplant surgeon elected in 1994, when he defeated Senate Budget Committee Chairman Jim Sasser. Frist is from a medical family famous in Tennessee: his father practiced medicine for 50 years, was internist and cardiologist to seven successive governors; his brother, Tom Frist, Jr., and his father started HCA and is now vice-chairman of Columbia/HCA, the nation's leading owner of hospitals, with stock worth an estimated $800 million; his brother Bob is a cardiac surgeon in Nashville. Bill Frist graduated from Harvard Medical School, studied at Mass General, in England and at Stanford, and in 1986 started the heart and lung transplant program at Vanderbilt. He wrote a book, *Transplant*, on the social and ethical issues of these surgeries; he has performed 250 transplants. He was not, however, politically active: he did not vote until he returned to Nashville at age 34, and never voted in a Republican primary until 1994; the Frists were not known as Republicans, and Democratic Governor Ned McWherter appointed Bill Frist in 1992 to chair a task force on Medicaid.

In 1994, Frist decided to challenge Jim Sasser, who was seeking his fourth term. Sasser was first elected in 1976, beating Senator Bill Brock, as Jimmy Carter swept the South; he grew up the son of a Department of Agriculture official, practiced law, and became Tennessee Democratic chairman in 1972. He compiled a liberal voting record with some significant exceptions. As Budget Committee chairman from 1989, he worked closely with Majority Leader George Mitchell, helping engineer the budget summit tax increases in 1990 and pass the Clinton budget and tax package in 1993. Sasser kept in touch with local issues and was reelected by wide margins in 1982 and 1988. In 1994, he spent much time running for Senate majority leader, seeking commitments from colleagues; he also raised and spent $5 million, with $1.8 million from PACs. He watched the Republicans have a fractious primary, with east Tennessee businessman Bob Corker attacking Frist for not voting for years and for obtaining cats from animal shelters for experiments as a medical student. But Frist, spending liberally, carried the Nashville and Memphis media markets and beat Corker 44%–32% (Tennessee is the one former Confederate state without a runoff primary).

In the fall campaign, Sasser emphasized the conservative parts of his record: school prayer, the balanced budget amendment, cracking down on illegal immigrants. His campaign ridiculed Frist as a bored, rich surgeon, showing pictures of his Nashville and Nantucket mansions; Sasser said Frist probably had never heard of the minimum wage. Frist said he wanted to "give communities and individuals the freedom to solve problems and return to our basic conservative values," and backed term limits, welfare reform, federal spending cuts and school prayer. "Term limits for career politicians and the death penalty for career criminals," one ad said. Frist charged that Sasser "never met a tax he didn't like" and as majority leader would be "the official water boy to Bill Clinton." Frist's campaign was managed by Tom Perdue, the same man who helped Georgia's Paul Coverdell unseat Wyche Fowler, another liberal-leaning senator who talked southern at election time; it helped that Frist could outspend Sasser, with $7 million total, $3.7 million of it his own money to $5 million for Sasser. Sasser led in polls up through October, but in November Frist won 56%–42%, carrying all the large metro areas and losing only scattered traditionally Democratic rural counties.

In the Senate, Frist is likely to back most of the conservative program, and can be expected, as the chamber's only physician, to take a hand in healthcare issues. Indeed, on one he played a key role, the nomination of Nashville physician Henry Foster to be surgeon general. Many Republicans initially opposed him because he performed abortions and responded inaccurately to several questions. But Frist led him carefully through his testimony before the Labor Committee in May 1995, eliciting information about standard medical practice; although Foster faced additional obstacles, his fellow Nashville physician had given him a big boost.

Presidential politics. The existence of two strong partisan traditions with the Democrats' base somewhat larger over the years has made for unusual stability in Tennessee presidential politics. While other southern states went Republican, Tennessee stayed about evenly divided—in the Eisenhower 1950s and the Carter-Reagan race of 1980—with similar percentages in almost every county. When southern Democrats have run strong races, they have carried Tennessee handily, as in 1964, 1976 and 1992. And when Republicans are strong, they have won similarly: Ronald Reagan and George Bush both won 58% here in 1984 and 1988, and the Republican percentage in the three major statewide races in 1994 ranged between 54% and 60%. Does this mean Tennessee is out of reach for Bill Clinton and Al Gore in 1996? Yes, say professionals of both parties, barring some major shift in opinion.

Tennessee's presidential primary is held on Super Tuesday; the easy winners in 1992 were those two southern moderates, Bill Clinton and George Bush. The Democratic legislature in early 1995 was threatening not to fund the primary, because Sundquist had left it out of the state budget, but Republicans, eager to help Lamar Alexander, will surely find a way to do so.

Congressional districting. Tennessee needed only minor changes to get its districts back to equal population after the 1990 Census. Democrats controlled the process, and tried to help their prospects marginally, but the 1994 Republican revolution swept any advantage away.

The People: Est. Pop. 1994: 5,175,000; Pop. 1990: 4,877,185, up 6.1% 1990–1994. 2.0% of U.S. total, 17th largest; 39% rural. Median age: 33.6 years. 12.7% 65 years and over. 83.0% White, 16.0% Black. Households: 57.2% married couple families; 26% married couple fams. w. children; 37% college educ.; median household income: $24,807; per capita income: $12,255; 68.0% owner occupied housing; median house value: $58,400; median monthly rent: $273. 6.4% Unemployment. 1994 Voting age pop.: 3,913,000. 1994 Turnout: 1,476,747; 38% of VAP. Registered voters (1994): 2,683,422; no party registration.

Political Lineup: Governor, Don Sundquist (R); Secy. of State, Riley C. Darnell (D); Atty. Gen., Charles W. Burson (D); Treasurer, Steve Adams (D); Comptroller, William Snodgrass (D). State Senate, 33 (18 D and 15 R); State House of Representatives, 99 (59 D and 40 R). Senators, Fred Thompson (D) and William H. Frist (R). Representatives, 9 (5 R and 4 D).

1992 Presidential Vote

Clinton (D)	933,521	(47%)
Bush (R)	841,300	(42%)
Perot (I)	199,968	(10%)

1992 Democratic Presidential Primary

Clinton	214,485	(67%)
Tsongas	61,717	(19%)
Brown	25,560	(8%)
Uncommitted	12,551	(4%)

1988 Presidential Vote

Bush (R)	947,233	(58%)
Dukakis (D)	679,794	(42%)

1992 Republican Presidential Primary

Bush	178,219	(73%)
Buchanan	54,585	(22%)
Other, Uncommitted	12,849	(5%)

GOVERNOR

Gov. Don Sundquist (R)

Elected 1994, term expires Jan. 1999; b. Mar. 15, 1936, Moline, IL; home, Memphis; Augustana Col., B.A. 1957; Lutheran; married (Martha).

Career: Navy, 1957–59; Jostens, Inc., 1961–72; Pres. & Partner, Graphic Sales of Amer., 1972–82; Co-founder, Red, Hot & Blue Restaurant, 1989; U.S. House of Reps., 1982–94.

Office: State Capitol, 7th Ave. & Charlotte, Nashville 37243, 615-741-2001; Fax: 615-741-1416.

Election Results

1994 gen.	Don Sundquist (R)	807,104	(54%)
	Phil Bredesen (D)	664,252	(45%)
	Others	15,774	(1%)
1994 prim.	Don Sundquist (R)	386,696	(83%)
	David Y. Copeland (R)	69,773	(15%)
	Others	7,978	(2%)
1990 gen.	Ned McWherter (D)	480,885	(61%)
	Dwight Henry (R)	289,348	(37%)
	Other	20,148	(3%)

SENATORS

Sen. Fred Thompson (R)

Elected 1994; seat up 1996; b. Aug. 19, 1942, Sheffield, AL; home, Nashville; Memphis St. U., B.S. 1964; Vanderbilt U. Schl. of Law, J.D. 1967; Church of Christ; divorced.

Career: Practicing Atty,. 1967–94; Asst. US Atty., Middle TN Dist., 1969–72; Minority Cnsl., U.S. Sen. Watergate Cmte., 1973–74; Special Cnsl., TN Gov. Lamar Alexander, 1980; Special Cnsl., U.S. Sen. Foreign Relations Cmte., 1980–81; Special Cnsl., U.S. Sen. Intelligence Cmte., 1982; TN Appellate Court Nom. Comm., 1985–87; Author; Actor.

DC Office: 523 DSOB 20515, 202-224-4944; Fax: 202-228-3679.

State Office: 3322 West End Ave., #120, Nashville 37230, 615-736-5129; 403 Fed. Bldg., 167 N. Main St., Memphis 38103, 901-544-4224; 315 Post Office Bldg., 501 Main St., Knoxville 37902, 615-545-4253; B-9 Fed. Bldg., 109 S. Highland St., Jackson 38301, 901-423-9344.

Committees: *Foreign Relations* (7th of 10 R): European Affairs; International Economic Policy, Export and Trade Promotion (Chmn.); Near Eastern and South Asian Affairs; Western Hemisphere and Peace Corps Affairs. *Governmental Affairs* (4th of 8 R): Oversight of Government Management and the District of Columbia; Investigations. *Judiciary* (7th of 10 R): Terrorism, Technology and Government Information; Youth Violence (Chmn). *Aging (Special)* (10th of 10 R).

Group Ratings and 103rd Congress Votes: Newly Elected

Key Votes of the 104th Congress

1. Congressional Compliance Y	3. Balanced Budget Amndt. Y	5. Product Liability Reform Y
2. Bar Unfunded Mandates Y	4. Pass Line Item Veto Y	6. FY96 Budget Y

Election Results

1994 general	Fred Thompson (R)	885,998	(60%)	($3,793,813)
	Jim Cooper (D)	565,930	(39%)	($3,979,425)
	Others	13,934	(1%)	
1994 primary	Fred Thompson (R)	235,386	(64%)	
	John Baker (R)	131,431	(36%)	
1990 general	Albert Gore, Jr. (D)	530,898	(68%)	($1,905,865)
	William R. Hawkins (R)	233,703	(30%)	($6,510)
	Other	19,321	(2%)	

Sen. William H. Frist (R)

Elected 1994, seat up 2000; b. Feb. 22, 1952, Nashville; home, Nashville; Princeton U., A.B. 1974; Harvard Medical Schl., M.D. 1978; Presbyterian; married (Karyn).

Career: Practicing Surgeon, 1978–94; Dir., Vanderbilt Medical Ctr. Heart-Lung Transplant Program, 1986–93.

DC Office: 565 DSOB 20510, 202-224-3344; Fax: 202-228-1264.

State Offices: U.S. Cthse., 801 Broadway, #569, Nashville 37203, 615-736-7353.

Committees: *Banking, Housing & Urban Affairs* (9th of 9 R): Financial Institutions and Regulatory Relief; Housing Opportunity and Community Development; International Finance. *Budget* (12th of 12 R). *Labor & Human Resources* (5th of 9 R): Disability Policy (Chmn.); Education, Arts and Humanities. *Small Business* (9th of 10 R).

Group Ratings and 103rd Congress Votes: Newly Elected

Key Votes of the 104th Congress

1. Congressional Compliance Y	3. Balanced Budget Amndt. Y	5. Product Liability Reform Y
2. Bar Unfunded Mandates Y	4. Pass Line Item Veto Y	6. FY96 Budget Y

Election Results

1994 general	William H. Frist (R)	834,226	(56%)	($7,017,424)
	James R. (Jim) Sasser (D)	623,164	(42%)	($5,020,515)
	Others	23,001	(2%)	
1994 primary	William H. Frist (R)	197,734	(44%)	
	Bob Corker (R)	143,808	(32%)	
	Steve Wilson (R)	50,274	(11%)	
	Harold Sterling (R)	28,425	(6%)	
	Others	25,410	(6%)	
1988 general	James R. (Jim) Sasser (D)	1,020,061	(65%)	($3,069,615)
	Bill Andersen (R)	541,033	(35%)	($612,421)

FIRST DISTRICT

Between the corduroy-like ridges of the Appalachian chains, as they bend west and then south, the valley of Virginia extends far into northeastern Tennessee. The communities of this region—a hilly patchwork of industrial centers, small farms and federal land—were largely shaped by the building of railroads in the 1850s. The land rush immediately after the Revolutionary War populated the area; here in tiny Jonesborough the early settlers established the free state of Franklin in 1784, and many pioneer cabins, federal mansions and Greek Revival churches are lovingly preserved. It was the railroads, however, that determined the winners and losers. Other Appalachian areas were cut off from the rest of America, with tracks running only to the coal mines, but the small industrial cities that had grown up here—Johnson City, Kingsport, Bristol—were on the main lines of national commerce even before the Civil War. The War had a different political effect here than in most of the South: northeast Tennessee, the home of wartime Governor and then Vice President Andrew Johnson, had few slaves and with its connection to northern industry was Union territory. It remains heavily Republican to this day.

The political continuity is all the more surprising because this area has had continuous economic growth and has developed the sort of industrial economy which produced unions and Democrats in the North. Its growth has been helped by modest wage levels, a skilled and hard-working labor force, low electric power rates because of the TVA and good transportation routes (rail lines and now Interstate 81). Its small cities boast major paper and printing plants, and have the look of comfortable, clean, 1920s factory towns. Growth has been rapid only in Sevier County, where Gatlinburg and Pigeon Forge are the main tourist centers—5,000 motel rooms and numerous attractions—for travelers to the Great Smoky Mountains National Park. And even there, the small-town flavor lingers: Pigeon Forge's big scandal of 1994 was the mysterious killing of some 80 rabbits at Bunnyland Mini Golf.

The far northeastern end of the state forms the 1st Congressional District of Tennessee, a district so heavily Republican that it has not elected a Democrat to the House for more than 100 years. Nonetheless, it has had turbulent politics on occasion. For almost 40 years (1921–61, with one two-year hiatus), the seat was held by B. Carroll Reece, a fierce mountain politician who was once Republican National Committee chairman. After Reece died in 1961, and his widow was elected to fill out his term, there was a hotly contested primary here, the winner of which, Jimmy Quillen, has held the seat ever since. Quillen is a bread-and-butter politician, a former owner of the *Johnson City Times* who is focused on the needs of his district. He takes great pride in the establishment of what now is the James H. Quillen College of Medicine at East Tennessee State University and in the James H. and Cecile C. Quillen Center for Rehabilitative Medicine, both in Johnson City. The medical school seems to be his pride and joy: Quillen remembered that the 1986 Republican gubernatorial nominee, Winfield Dunn, had vetoed the College of Medicine when he was governor in the early 1970s, and his conspicuous coolness toward Dunn helped Democrat Ned McWherter carry the 1st District, a key to his 54% statewide victory. Quillen also maintained a good relationship with ousted Democratic Senator Jim Sasser; he had supported Sasser outright in 1988 and appeared with Sasser days before the 1994 election at a local renovation project.

Quillen is now tied with northeast Pennsylvania's Joseph McDade as the most senior Republican in the House, but he is not a committee chairman. He ceded the ranking minority position on the Rules Committee to Gerald Solomon back in 1990, and in early 1995, at 78, did not seem as active as in the past. Republicans did name him chairman emeritus of Rules—the first in House history. He remains capable of maintaining his "open door" policy of taking his entire district staff to each county in the district during offyears and of continuing to boost district projects. Most of his contemporaries have left the House now, and he definitely is not a Gingrich-style revolutionary. In 1994 he seemed about to retire, donating some $800,000 of campaign money to charity. But he changed his mind and was reelected, as usual, by a huge margin.

The People: Pop. 1990: 541,978; 53% rural; 14% age 65+; 97% White; 2% Black. Voting age pop.: 419,046; 2% Black. Households: 63% married couple families; 27% married couple fams. w. children; 31% college educ.; median household income: $21,952; per capita income: $11,024; median gross rent: $295; median house value: $51,200.

1992 Presidential Vote

Bush (R)	107,515	(51%)
Clinton (D)	76,113	(36%)
Perot (I)	24,358	(12%)

1988 Presidential Vote

Bush (R)	120,132	(68%)
Dukakis (D)	55,907	(32%)

Rep. James H. (Jimmy) Quillen (R)

Elected 1962; b. Jan. 11, 1916, Wayland, VA; home, Kingsport; United Methodist; married (Cecile).

Career: Navy, 1942–46 (WWII); *Kingsport Press*, 1934–35; *Kingsport Times*, 1935–36; Founder, publ., *Johnson City Times*, 1939–44; TN House of Reps., 1955–62, Minority Ldr., 1959–60.

DC Office: 102 CHOB 20515, 202-225-6356; Fax: 202-225-7812.

District Offices: Fed. P.O. Bldg., #157, Kingsport 37662, 615-247-8161.

Committees: *Rules* (2nd of 9 R): Legislative and Budget Process.

Group Ratings

	ADA	ACLU	COPE	CFA	LCV	CON	NSI	COC	ACU	NTLC	CHC
1994	5	14	43	20	6	49	80	100	95	77	92
1993	5	—	30	10	29	19	—	89	95	—	—

National Journal Ratings

	1993 LIB — 1993 CONS	1994 LIB — 1994 CONS
Economic	37% — 62%	30% — 70%
Social	23% — 76%	19% — 81%
Foreign	0% — 91%	0% — 88%

Key Votes of the 103d Congress

1. Clinton Deficit Plan	N	3. Brady Handgun Purchase N	5. Lmt. UN Cmnd. of Forces Y
2. NAFTA	Y	4. Strike Race/Death Pnlty. Y	6. Cut Missile Funds N

Key Votes of the 104th Congress

1. Congressional Compliance Y	6. Reform Crime Grant Y	11. Loser Pays Court Reform Y
2. Balanced Budget Amndmt. Y	7. National Security Act Y	12. Product Liability Reform Y
3. Bar Unfunded Mandates Y	8. Moratorium on Regs. Y	13. Welfare Reform Y
4. Pass Line Item Veto Y	9. Risk Assessment on Regs. Y	14. Term Limits Amndmt. N
5. Relax Exclusionary Rule Y	10. Expnd. Priv. Prop. Rights Y	15. Tax Cuts Y

Election Results

1994 general	James H. (Jimmy) Quillen (R)	102,947	(73%)	($1,117,126)
	J. Carr (Jack) Cristian (D)	34,691	(25%)	
	Others	3,589	(3%)	
1994 primary	James H. (Jimmy) Quillen (R)	52,088	(79%)	
	Dan H. Perry (R)	7,977	(12%)	
	Larry Gaudet (R)	6,172	(9%)	
1992 general	James H. (Jimmy) Quillen (R)	114,797	(68%)	($325,383)
	J. Carr (Jack) Christian (D)	47,809	(28%)	
	Others	7,552	(4%)	

SECOND DISTRICT

Knoxville, the largest city in east Tennessee, is nestled between mountain ridges where the Holston and French Broad Rivers join to form the Tennessee. It was established not long after the first wave of pioneers came through the gaps and down between the mountains of the Appalachian chain. During the Civil War it was Union territory, and has remained Republican in allegiance ever since: the ancestral tug of Tennessee politics. But its Republican heritage is tempered by another tradition, that of the Tennessee Valley Authority. A venturesome program when created in the 1930s, it is now part of the fabric of life in east Tennessee, sometimes criticized as its cheap hydroelectric power capacity was filled and more of its production came from expensive and sometimes poorly functioning nuclear plants. TVA cut its payroll from 35,000 to 21,000 from 1988 to 1992 and hasn't raised rates since 1987: but it still may be threatened by Republican budget cuts in the 104th Congress.

The 2d Congressional District of Tennessee, which includes Knoxville and several mountainous counties to the south, is one of the most reliably Republican districts in the nation—but also one of the more practical-minded. The congressman, Jimmy Duncan, is similarly inclined; his father represented the district from 1964 until his death in 1988. John Duncan, Jr.—his formal name—was educated in Knoxville and Washington, practiced law and was a trial judge in the 1980s. When his father died, he won the seat despite a spirited challenge from Democrat Dudley Taylor, also from a family long prominent in east Tennessee politics, who attacked Duncan for signing up with the National Guard in 1970 and for his ties to convicted banker Jake Butcher. Duncan won anyway with 57% in the special and 56% in November. He has been reelected easily in the 1990s.

Duncan is now chairman of the Aviation Subcommittee of Transportation and Infrastructure. He has maintained one of the most fiscally conservative voting records in recent years, questioning such projects as NASA's $12 million to search for extraterrestrial intelligence, and the Army Corps of Engineers proposal to restore Florida's Kissimmee River to its original shape after spending millions to straighten it out. In 1994, Duncan criticized what he called lavish expenditures for federal courthouses, notably the Boston Fan Pier courthouse planned by Stephen Breyer, whose Supreme Court nomination was then pending. In 1995, Duncan questioned how a company once headed by Transportation Secretary Federico Pena got a contract to manage $5 million in Los Angeles transit pension funds shortly after Pena's swearing-in as secretary. Pena has since been cleared of wrondoing following a Justice Department review. But Duncan has sought funding for local projects—resurfacing the Foothills Parkway in the Great Smoky Park, a $40 million federal judicial center in Knoxville, a $1.25 million grant to help Kimberly-Clark expand its operation in Loudon County, a $1 million grant to help put local public TV Channel 15 on the air. Duncan is also cautious about making commitments abroad, and was one of several members who introduced a resolution that questioned the Mexico economic bailout in February 1995.

The People: Pop. 1990: 541,780; 36% rural; 13% age 65+; 92% White; 6% Black; 1% Asian; 1% Hispanic origin. Voting age pop.: 416,979; 6% Black. Households: 59% married couple families; 26% married couple fams. w. children; 41% college educ.; median household income: $25,267; per capita income: $13,118; median gross rent: $337; median house value: $59,400.

1992 Presidential Vote		
Bush (R)	107,920	(48%)
Clinton (D)	92,752	(41%)
Perot (I)	25,157	(11%)

1988 Presidential Vote		
Bush (R)	118,578	(65%)
Dukakis (D)	64,249	(35%)

Rep. John J. Duncan, Jr. (R)

Elected 1988; b. July 21, 1947, Lebanon; home, Knoxville; U. of TN, B.S. 1969, George Washington U., J.D. 1973; Presbyterian; married (Lynn).

Career: Army Natl. Guard & Army Reserves, 1970–87; Practicing atty., 1973–81; St. Trial Judge, 1981–88.

DC Office: 2400 RHOB 20515, 202-225-5435; Fax: 202-225-6440.

District Offices: 501 W. Main St., #318, Knoxville 37902, 615-523-3772; 200 E. Broadway, #419, Maryville 37801, 615-984-5464; and Crthse., Athens 37303, 615-745-4671.

Committees: *Resources* (5th of 25 R): Energy and Mineral Resources; National Parks, Forests and Lands. *Transportation & Infrastructure* (9th of 33 R): Aviation (Chmn.); Public Buildings and Economic Development.

Group Ratings

	ADA	ACLU	COPE	CFA	LCV	CON	NSI	COC	ACU	NTLC	CHC
1994	20	17	22	10	17	99	50	75	76	89	100
1993	20	—	17	10	36	95	—	73	92	—	—

National Journal Ratings

	1993 LIB — 1993 CONS		1994 LIB — 1994 CONS	
Economic	14% —	80%	0% —	80%
Social	11% —	82%	0% —	89%
Foreign	40% —	57%	34% —	63%

Key Votes of the 103d Congress

1. Clinton Deficit Plan	N	3. Brady Handgun Purchase	N	5. Lmt. UN Cmnd. of Forces	Y
2. NAFTA	Y	4. Strike Race/Death Pnlty.	Y	6. Cut Missile Funds	Y

Key Votes of the 104th Congress

1. Congressional Compliance	Y	6. Reform Crime Grant	Y	11. Loser Pays Court Reform	Y
2. Balanced Budget Amndmt.	Y	7. National Security Act	Y	12. Product Liability Reform	Y
3. Bar Unfunded Mandates	Y	8. Moratorium on Regs.	Y	13. Welfare Reform	Y
4. Pass Line Item Veto	Y	9. Risk Assessment on Regs.	Y	14. Term Limits Amndmt.	Y
5. Relax Exclusionary Rule	Y	10. Expnd. Priv. Prop. Rights	Y	15. Tax Cuts	Y

Election Results

1994 general	John J. Duncan Jr. (R)	128,937	(90%)	($200,332)
	Randon J. Krieg (I)	6,854	(5%)	
	Greg Samples (I)	6,682	(5%)	
1994 primary	John J. Duncan Jr. (R)	unopposed		
1992 general	John J. Duncan, Jr. (R)	148,377	(72%)	($170,836)
	Troy Goodale (D)	52,887	(26%)	($6,471)
	Other	4,137	(2%)	

THIRD DISTRICT

Through some of the most vivid scenery of the Appalachian chain, etching its way through the serrated ridges of east Tennessee, is the river that gave Tennessee its name. From Knoxville, the river cuts through a ridge and then plunges down a long valley to the city of Chattanooga at the Georgia line. There it switches course again, winding around the table-top Lookout Mountain and then moving into northern Alabama. This is the land of the 3d Congressional District of Tennessee. Chattanooga, its largest city, was just a village when it was a Civil War battlefield; it grew into an industrial city after the War. A quarter-century ago it was labeled America's most polluted city. But it has cleaned up its air with the use of smokestack scrubbers and battery-power buses, and it has spruced up its river banks. It is now the proud home of the 12-story-high Tennessee Aquarium, the world's largest fresh water aquarium, with an exhibit in which you can follow the course of a drop of rain from the headwaters of the Tennessee until it flows out the Mississippi River into the ocean.

The 3d Congressional District of Tennessee is centered on Chattanooga, with an irregular shape that has a political provenance. It reaches far north to take in the Democratic area around Oak Ridge, site of the nuclear laboratory, but avoids heavily Republican counties on either side of this salient; it reaches east to the North Carolina line and west to the Cumberland Plateau to take in more Democratic areas. All this is necessary because Chattanooga has been trending Republican in recent years, evidently pinning its hopes for growth more on the private sector, which developed the Aquarium among other attractions, and less on public sector institutions like the Tennessee Valley Authority, which has laid off more than a third of its work force. That was enough to make this part of the Republican tsunami of 1994.

The congressman from the 3d District now is Zach Wamp, a Republican elected after two turbulent campaigns to replace retiring 20-year moderate Democrat Marilyn Lloyd, a strong backer of the failed Clinch River breeder reactor. Wamp left college before graduating to become a real estate developer back in Chattanooga, selling $22 million in real estate in five years. In 1987, at 30, he was county Republican chairman. In 1992 he ran for Congress as a conservative against Lloyd in a high-voltage race. At the start, Wamp revealed he had used cocaine and had treatment for it 10 years before. Lloyd referred to Wamp's "criminal" past (two bad checks for $20 written while he was in college) and litigation against his real estate firm; Wamp called these "vicious, personal attacks." Wamp carried Chattanooga and Hamilton County 51%–44%; overall Lloyd won by just 49%–47%, the closest margin of her career, and she decided to retire in 1994.

In 1994, Wamp ran again as a strong conservative; one proposal was to pay members of Congress the same as a lieutenant colonel and billet them in officer housing. The seven-candidate Democratic primary was won by Randy Button, a land appraiser from Oak Ridge and the Roane County assessor; he led three other opponents 25%–23%–22%–20%. Button attacked Wamp's character, bringing up his past cocaine use and accusing him of lying when he said he had a "Q" security clearance at the Oak Ridge Reservation and only had a "Secret" clearance instead. Wamp accused Button of flip-flopping on issues and attacked him for taking PAC money. Like many Republicans, Wamp ran an ad showing his opponent's face morphing into Bill Clinton's. Button complained, saying his six-year-old daughter was upset: "She said it turned her father into a monster." Wamp ran behind the statewide Republican ticket, but still won, carrying Hamilton County 54%–43% and losing the Oak Ridge area only narrowly, for an overall win of 52%–46%.

In the House, Wamp was elected the freshman representative on the Republican Steering Committee and was made the number two Republican on the subcommittee overseeing the Tennessee Valley Authority.

The People: Pop. 1990: 542,065; 35% rural; 14% age 65+; 87% White; 12% Black; 1% Asian; 1% Hispanic origin. Voting age pop.: 410,463; 11% Black; 1% Hispanic origin. Households: 59% married couple families; 26% married couple fams. w. children; 38% college educ.; median household income: $24,687; per capita income: $12,338; median gross rent: $348; median house value: $55,000.

1992 Presidential Vote			1988 Presidential Vote		
Clinton (D)	97,112	(44%)	Bush (R)	119,222	(61%)
Bush (R)	97,073	(44%)	Dukakis (D)	75,533	(39%)
Perot (I)	25,719	(12%)			

Rep. Zach Wamp (R)

Elected 1994; b. Oct. 28, 1957, Fort Benning, GA; home, Chattanooga; U. of NC, 1976–77, 1979–80; U. of TN, 1978–79; Baptist; married (Kim).

Career: Regional Sales Super., 1981–82; Partner, Wamp Alliance Architectural Development Co., 1983–89; Real estate broker, 1989–94.

DC Office: 423 CHOB 20515, 202-225-3271; Fax: 202-225-3494.

District Offices: 6100 Eastgate Ctr., #400, Chattanooga 37411, 615-894-7400; and 55 Jefferson Cir., #231-D, Oak Ridge 37830, 615-483-3366.

Committees: *Science* (14th of 27 R): Basic Research; Energy and Environment. *Small Business* (10th of 22 R): Regulation and Paperwork. *Transportation & Infrastructure* (26th of 33 R): Water Resources and Environment.

Group Ratings and 103rd Congress Votes: Newly Elected

Key Votes of the 104th Congress

1. Congressional Compliance	Y	6. Reform Crime Grant	Y	11. Loser Pays Court Reform	Y
2. Balanced Budget Amndmt.	Y	7. National Security Act	Y	12. Product Liability Reform	Y
3. Bar Unfunded Mandates	Y	8. Moratorium on Regs.	Y	13. Welfare Reform	Y
4. Pass Line Item Veto	Y	9. Risk Assessment on Regs.	Y	14. Term Limits Amndmt.	Y
5. Relax Exclusionary Rule	Y	10. Expnd. Priv. Prop. Rights	Y	15. Tax Cuts	Y

Election Results

1994 general	Zach Wamp (R)	84,583	(52%)	($704,220)
	Randy Button (D)	73,839	(46%)	($502,668)
	Others	3,431	(2%)	
1994 primary	Zach Wamp (R)	39,123	(67%)	
	Kenneth J. (Ken) Meyer (R)	14,561	(25%)	
	Kenneth W. Gross (R)	3,213	(6%)	
	Others	1,284	(2%)	
1992 general	Marilyn Lloyd (D)	105,693	(49%)	($637,790)
	Zach Wamp (R)	102,763	(47%)	($267,844)
	Other	8,077	(4%)	

FOURTH DISTRICT

The invisible line between Civil War Republican and Civil War Democratic territory runs along the Cumberland Plateau, the westernmost upswelling of the Appalachians, west of the valley where the Tennessee River runs south from Knoxville to Chattanooga. It separates the Tennessee valley, which had few slaves and whose economic ties were with the North, from the rolling farmlands of middle Tennessee, first settled by Andrew Jackson in the 1790s and resolutely Democratic from the time he became the first president to call himself a Democrat in the 1830s. And not only is this line invisible, it is also irregular: some counties in west Tennessee, where the Tennessee River runs north from Alabama to Kentucky, are Union Republican.

The 4th Congressional District of Tennessee runs across this line and crosses the state northeast to southwest, from Lee County, Virginia, all the way to Tishomingo County, Mississippi. It is some 300 miles long, yet seldom more than one county wide, and contains such spots as Lynchburg, home of the Jack Daniels distillery since 1860, and Dayton, where in 1925 John Scopes was prosecuted by William Jennings Bryan and defended by Clarence Darrow for teaching Darwin's theory of evolution.

The congressman from the 4th District is Van Hilleary, a Republican elected in 1994 after the Democratic incumbent for all 12 years of the district's existence, Jim Cooper, ran for the Senate and lost. Cooper combined local roots (his father Prentice Cooper was once governor) with policy brains and political smarts, but he was crushed in 1994 between Bill Clinton's opposition to his moderate healthcare plan and Tennesseans' angry rejection of Clinton. In that unsettled context, five Democrats and three Republicans ran for the seat. Hilleary is from Dayton, where he helped start the family textile company; after college he served in the Air Force, went to law school and volunteered for duty in the Persian Gulf, where he flew 24 missions on a C-130. In 1992, at 33, he ran for the state Senate against 18-year incumbent Anna Belle Clement O'Brien, sister of former Governor Frank Clement, and lost by only 52%–48% despite her much greater fame and financing. In 1994, he ran for the House, supporting term limits, welfare reform with a two-year limit, tougher crime sentences and limiting PACs to the same amount as individual contributions and 10% of a candidate's total campaign funds. Hilleary won the Republican primary easily, with 58%.

The Democratic nominee was Jeff Whorley. At 34, he had long political experience: he worked for Bob Clement's gubernatorial campaign in 1978, for Jim Cooper for Congress in 1982, for Bart Gordon in the 6th District in 1984; Whorley was Gordon's chief of staff before he returned to Bedford County to teach creative writing. From the middle of the district, Whorley won the primary with 31% to 27% for Lincoln Davis, who is from east Tennessee, and 24% and 15% for two candidates from the west. Whorley was for the death penalty, school vouchers, school prayer, gun control: mostly a conservative platform. His political connections were obviously helpful in fund raising. He spent $842,000 in all, with $196,000 from PACs and $312,000 from his own funds; Hilleary spent $614,000, with nothing from PACs and $126,000 from his own funds. But in this Republican year that was enough. Hilleary carried the eastern Republican counties by wide margins; he carried the far western counties, where Davis was still smarting at Whorley's attacks; and he lost the middle Tennessee counties rather narrowly, for a 57%–42% victory.

In the House, Hilleary achieved his greatest notice as the deviser of an alternative term limits proposal. Republicans were buffeted between Bill McCollum's 12-year limit and U.S. Term Limits's insistence on a six-year limit. Hilleary proposed a 12-year limit nationally on both House and Senate service, but a shorter limit if states so decide, as many already have. His amendment garnered only 164 votes to 265 against, a much poorer showing than McCollum's 227–204, though that too was far short of the two-thirds requirement. But Hilleary was the first freshman to have a constitutional amendment reach the floor since 1897, although his formula, now that the Supreme Court has declared state term limits unconstitutional, is moot. But he has pledged to continue the fight on what is no doubt a winning political issue for him. Meanwhile, he is taking advantage of his Air Force experience in his work on the National Security Committee.

The People: Pop. 1990: 541,650; 74% rural; 14% age 65+; 96% White; 4% Black. Voting age pop.: 405,647; 3% Black. Households: 65% married couple families; 29% married couple fams. w. children; 24% college educ.; median household income: $20,685; per capita income: $9,886; median gross rent: $277; median house value: $44,400.

1992 Presidential Vote

Clinton (D)	100,292	(48%)
Bush (R)	83,923	(40%)
Perot (I)	23,838	(11%)

1988 Presidential Vote

Bush (R)	94,190	(58%)
Dukakis (D)	66,940	(42%)

Rep. Van Hilleary (R)

Elected 1994; b. June 20, 1959, Dayton; home, Grandview; U. of TN, B.S. 1981; Samford U. Cumberland Schl. of Law, J.D. 1990; Presbyterian; single.

Career: Air Force, 1982–84; Air Force Reserves, 1984–present (Persian Gulf); Dir., Planning & Business Devel., SSM Industries, Inc, 1984–86, 1992–94.

DC Office: 114 CHOB 20515, 202-225-6831; Fax: 202-225-3272.

District Offices: 1502 N. Main St., Crossville 38555, 615-484-1114; 400 W. Main St., #304, Morristown 37814, 615-587-0396; and 300 S. Jackson St., Tullahoma 37388, 615-393-4764.

Committees: *National Security* (25th of 30 R): Military Installations and Facilities; Military Research and Development. *Science* (24th of 27 R): Basic Research; Space and Aeronautics. *Small Business* (16th of 22 R): Regulation and Paperwork.

Group Ratings and 103rd Congress Votes: Newly Elected

Key Votes of the 104th Congress

1. Congressional Compliance Y	6. Reform Crime Grant Y	11. Loser Pays Court Reform Y
2. Balanced Budget Amndmt. Y	7. National Security Act Y	12. Product Liability Reform Y
3. Bar Unfunded Mandates Y	8. Moratorium on Regs. Y	13. Welfare Reform Y
4. Pass Line Item Veto Y	9. Risk Assessment on Regs. Y	14. Term Limits Amndmt. Y
5. Relax Exclusionary Rule Y	10. Expnd. Priv. Prop. Rights Y	15. Tax Cuts Y

Election Results

1994 general	Van Hilleary (R)	81,539	(57%)	($613,648)
	Jeff Whorley (D)	60,489	(42%)	($842,445)
	Others	1,948	(1%)	
1994 primary	Van Hilleary (R)	20,798	(58%)	
	Keith Hayworth (R)	9,913	(28%)	
	Clairborne Sanders (R)	5,112	(14%)	
1992 general	Jim Cooper (D)	98,984	(64%)	($195,279)
	Dale Johnson (R)	50,340	(33%)	
	Other	5,187	(3%)	

FIFTH DISTRICT

Nashville is the home of country music, the buckle of the Bible Belt, and in almost every way the heart of Tennessee. This was one of the first American cities established west of the Appalachians; Andrew Jackson built his Hermitage nearby above the banks of the Cumberland River, and his political home base has remained Democratic ever since. It was the capital of Tennessee early on, just as it was—and still is—the center of the state's political life and discourse: the *Tennessean* and the *Nashville Banner* still present more or less Democratic and Republican views of Tennessee politics, and Nashville is the biggest television market in the state. Nashville is proud of its universities and of its columned Capitol and its Parthenon; this is perhaps the greatest center of Greek Revival architecture in America. Nashville is also firmly established as the religious publishing center of the country, producing more Bibles probably than any city in the world. And of course, Nashville is home to a $6 billion entertainment industry centered on the Country Music Hall of Fame and the Grand Ole Opry, now broadcast from the giant theme park on the banks of the Cumberland in Opryland U.S.A.

Nashville was also the boom city of Tennessee in the 1980s, with metropolitan growth of 16%, the highest of any major metro area between Atlanta and Dallas-Fort Worth. Country music and Bible publishing flourished, Ingram grew as the nation's largest book wholesaler and the Goo-Goo Cluster candy factory churned out its product, Nissan built a big plant in nearby Smyrna and General Motors set its Saturn plant in nearby Spring Hill, and many smaller businesses started up. There were commercial and apartment real estate booms as well, though followed as booms usually are by some busts. But the overall picture is of growth and, for those who can remember back more than a generation, a lifestyle of comfort mostly undreamed of—air conditioning everywhere, shopping malls and supermarkets overflowing with affordable goods. An agreeable quality of life, plenty of medium-wage, high-skill labor, a central location, and absence of urban strife and militant unions have all helped Nashville grow.

The 5th Congressional District of Tennessee includes all but one precinct of Nashville and Davidson County plus the bulk of increasingly suburban Robertson County to the north—but this is not all of metropolitan Nashville now that development has spread into once rural areas. The 5th is usually reliably Democratic in statewide elections, and to Congress it has long elected rather liberal Democrats: this is, after all, the home of the first Democratic president. It was also for several years the home of Al Gore, when he was a divinity student at Vanderbilt and reporter for the *Tennessean*, and as much his home base as is his ancestral home near Carthage in Smith County.

The congressman from the 5th District is Bob Clement, a Democrat whose father was a three-term governor of Tennessee and memorably keynoted the 1956 Democratic National Convention. The younger Clement won the seat after the incumbent, Bill Boner, resigned in October 1987 just ahead of an ethics investigation, to begin a tumultuous term as mayor of Nashville. Clement took the Democratic primary with 40% (Tennessee has no runoff), and easily won the January 1988 special election.

In the House, Clement has compiled a moderate voting record. He has worked on airport noise abatement and on obtaining improvements for Nashville's airport; he pushed to replace the Bordeaux railroad bridge over the Cumberland River and to finish the Natchez Trace Parkway into Nashville; he has worked hard on nuclear plant design standards and increasing penalties for drug sales at truck stops. Off the House floor, Clement has served as an occasional sounding board for President Clinton, particularly on the damage control surrounding Dr. Henry Foster's nomination as surgeon general. Clement, who has a mixed record on abortion rights, introduced Foster, who is from the 5th District at his Senate hearing.

Clement has been reelected fairly easily in the 5th. He considered running for governor in 1994 but wisely, in light of the Republican sweep here, decided to run for reelection instead, and ran far enough ahead of the statewide ticket to win 60%–39%. Like the two other remaining white Democrats from Tennessee, he had a conspicuous record of support for the Contract With America.

The People: Pop. 1990: 541,878; 5% rural; 12% age 65+; 75% White; 23% Black; 1% Asian; 1% Hispanic origin. Voting age pop.: 416,608; 21% Black; 1% Hispanic origin. Households: 48% married couple families; 21% married couple fams. w. children; 47% college educ.; median household income: $28,208; per capita income: $14,874; median gross rent: $430; median house value: $74,200.

1992 Presidential Vote

Clinton (D)	112,795	(53%)
Bush (R)	79,398	(37%)
Perot (I)	21,531	(10%)

1988 Presidential Vote

Bush (R)	100,268	(52%)
Dukakis (D)	93,139	(48%)

Rep. Bob Clement (D)

Elected Jan. 1988; b. Sept. 23, 1943, Nashville; home, Nashville; U. of TN, B.S. 1967, Memphis St. U., M.B.A. 1968; United Methodist; married (Mary).

Career: Army, 1969–71, Army Natl. Guard, 1971–present; TN Public Svc. Comm., 1973–79; Bd. of Dir., TN Valley Authority, 1979–81; Founder and owner, Bob Clement & Assoc., 1981–83; Owner and partner, Charter Equities real estate, 1981–83; Pres., Cumberland U., 1983–87.

DC Office: 2229 RHOB 20515, 202-225-4311; Fax: 202-226-1035.

District Offices: 552 U.S. Crthse., Nashville 37203, 615-736-5295; 2701 Jefferson St., N. Nashville 37208, 615-320-1363; and 101 5th Ave. W., Springfield 37172, 615-384-6600.

Committees: *Transportation & Infrastructure* (10th of 27 D): Aviation; Railroads. *Veterans' Affairs* (6th of 15 D): Hospitals and Health Care.

Group Ratings

	ADA	ACLU	COPE	CFA	LCV	CON	NSI	COC	ACU	NTLC	CHC
1994	35	36	56	50	56	46	60	92	35	36	57
1993	55	—	75	80	71	8	—	50	29	—	—

National Journal Ratings

	1993 LIB — 1993 CONS		1994 LIB — 1994 CONS	
Economic	49%	50%	47%	51%
Social	56%	44%	39%	61%
Foreign	47%	50%	68%	29%

Key Votes of the 103d Congress

1. Clinton Deficit Plan	N	3. Brady Handgun Purchase Y	5. Lmt. UN Cmnd. of Forces N
2. NAFTA	Y	4. Strike Race/Death Pnlty. Y	6. Cut Missile Funds N

1. Clinton Deficit Plan   N   3. Brady Handgun Purchase Y   5. Lmt. UN Cmnd. of Forces N
2. NAFTA   Y   4. Strike Race/Death Pnlty. Y   6. Cut Missile Funds   N

Key Votes of the 104th Congress

1. Congressional Compliance Y   6. Reform Crime Grant   N   11. Loser Pays Court Reform N
2. Balanced Budget Amndmt. Y   7. National Security Act   N   12. Product Liability Reform Y
3. Bar Unfunded Mandates   Y   8. Moratorium on Regs.   Y   13. Welfare Reform   N
4. Pass Line Item Veto   Y   9. Risk Assessment on Regs. Y   14. Term Limits Amndmt.   Y
5. Relax Exclusionary Rule   Y   10. Expnd. Priv. Prop. Rights N   15. Tax Cuts   Y

Election Results

1994 general	Bob Clement (D).....................	95,953	(60%)	($486,214)
	John Osborne (R)	61,692	(39%)	($102,251)
	Others................................	1,659	(1%)	
1994 primary	Bob Clement (D)..................	unopposed		
1992 general	Bob Clement (D)....................	125,233	(67%)	($600,244)
	Tom Stone (R)	49,417	(26%)	($10,590)
	Steven L. Edmondson (I)	6,724	(4%)	($122)
	Other................................	6,216	(3%)	

SIXTH DISTRICT

The rolling countryside of middle Tennessee, west of the Cumberland Plateau and the last chain of Appalachians, has been called "the dimple of the universe." This is hilly and fertile land, cut by deep rivers ambling along in S-curves. The terrain here was never much suited for plantation crops; this has long been a land of small farmers and small county seat towns, nestled amid what people here regard as some of the loveliest scenery on earth. Middle Tennessee has also been one of the heartlands of the Democratic Party. It was the political home base of Andrew Jackson and supported him nearly unanimously; during the Civil War, though it had very few slaves, it resisted the invading Union armies. For 140 years after Jackson, it voted solidly Democratic and elected as its congressmen some of the luminaries of the national Democratic Party: James K. Polk (1825–39), speaker of the House and later president; Cordell Hull (1907–21, 1923–31), later senator and secretary of State; Albert Gore Sr., (1939–53), later senator; and Albert Gore Jr., (1977–85), later senator and now vice president.

The 6th Congressional District of Tennessee includes 14 middle Tennessee counties east and south of Nashville, plus a bit of Nashville itself. The heritage here is old and rural, but economic growth has fanned out into the farmland from Nashville—symbolized most vividly by the huge Nissan plant in Smyrna and General Motors's Saturn plant in Spring Hill (actually a mile outside the district), but also evident in thousands of jobs created by Japanese companies and American startups, firms fleeing the North and entrepreneurs fleeing Texas. Many new voters here are Republican, not only in the affluent suburbs of Williamson County just south of Nashville, but in the more modest suburbs spreading to the east. The 6th is now competitive in national elections, and Republicans have won seats in the legislature from Williamson, Sumner and Rutherford Counties in the ring around Nashville.

The congressman from the 6th District is Bart Gordon, a Democrat first elected in 1984 when Al Gore left the House seat to run for the Senate. Gordon grew up in Murfreesboro in Rutherford County and went to college there. He practiced law and became Tennessee Democratic chairman in 1981: politics is most of his life. In 1984, he ran a computerized fundraising operation and voter contact system—then a novelty in this district where a personal handshake from a candidate was the norm. He won a multicandidate primary with 28% of the vote—there is no runoff in Tennessee—and won the general election 63%–37%.

In the House, Gordon used his insider skills to build a close relationship with Speaker Jim Wright and Majority Whip Tony Coelho, and got a seat on the Rules Committee in 1987. Gordon went after trade schools with high student loan default rates, even posing in 1991 as a student (though he was 42 at the time) with an NBC investigative unit. He passed new accountability provisions for the federal financial aid system in 1992, which are intended to eliminate almost $1 billion in losses. He sponsored family and medical leave and opposed construction of a temporary nuclear waste dump in middle Tennessee. In the 103d Congress he served on the Budget Committee, where he supported the Clinton budget and tax package though urging more spending cuts.

In 1992, Gordon won by 57%–41%, despite outspending his opponent $988,000 to $181,000: a danger sign. In 1994, he had even more opposition. His top aide Jeff Whorley left to run in the 4th District, where he lost to Republican Van Hilleary. And Gordon had a serious opponent in Steve Gill, a lawyer from Williamson County but better known as a member of a championship basketball team at the University of Tennessee. Gill dressed in his trademark maroon shirt, and spread his anti-Clinton message—balanced budget amendment, tougher sentences, term limits—around the district. Gordon had the accumulated goodwill from years of reaching out to constituents and, probably more important, had accumulated money. Gordon spent $1,386,000, some $608,000 of it raised from PACs; Gill spent $533,000, with just 11% from PACs. Gill ran ahead in the ring of counties around Nashville, where most of the votes are cast, 52%–48%. But Gordon carried the smaller rural counties 58%–42%, for a slim overall victory margin of 51%–

49%.

In the 104th Congress, Gordon was forced to give up his seat on the Rules panel but ended up with a decent substitute: the Commerce Committee. His first priority is legislation to ban 900-number "teleporn lines." He will presumably spend even more time with constituents to attempt to reestablish his firm control of the seat. But with Republicans in control and with PACs and lobbyists watched carefully, it is hardly likely that Gordon will be able to spend $1 million again; and it is not clear that he knows how to beat a serious opponent without a huge financial advantage

The People: Pop. 1990: 542,002; 54% rural; 11% age 65+; 93% White; 6% Black; 1% Asian; 1% Hispanic origin. Voting age pop.: 399,552; 5% Black; 1% Hispanic origin. Households: 66% married couple families; 33% married couple fams. w. children; 38% college educ.; median household income: $29,234; per capita income: $13,286; median gross rent: $378; median house value: $71,300.

1992 Presidential Vote		
Clinton (D)	109,895	(47%)
Bush (R)	93,036	(40%)
Perot (I)	28,151	(12%)

1988 Presidential Vote		
Bush (R)	103,630	(61%)
Dukakis (D)	65,686	(39%)

Rep. Bart Gordon (D)

Elected 1984; b. Jan. 24, 1949, Murfreesboro; home, Murfreesboro; Middle TN St. U., B.S. 1971, U. of TN, J.D. 1973; United Methodist; single.

Career: Practicing atty., 1974–84; Chmn., TN Dem. Party, 1981–83.

DC Office: 2201 RHOB 20515, 202-225-4231; Fax: 202-225-6887.

District Offices: P.O. Box 1986, 106 S. Maple St., Murfreesboro 37133, 615-896-1986; and 17 S. Jefferson, Cookeville 38501, 615-528-5907.

Committees: *Commerce* (15th of 21 D): Energy and Power; Telecommunications and Finance.

Group Ratings

	ADA	ACLU	COPE	CFA	LCV	CON	NSI	COC	ACU	NTLC	CHC
1994	55	39	25	50	72	52	70	83	24	39	57
1993	60	—	83	80	71	59	—	27	21	—	—

National Journal Ratings

	1993 LIB — 1993 CONS		1994 LIB — 1994 CONS	
Economic	61% —	37%	44% —	54%
Social	56% —	42%	48% —	50%
Foreign	63% —	34%	83% —	15%

Key Votes of the 103d Congress

1. Clinton Deficit Plan	Y	3. Brady Handgun Purchase	Y	5. Lmt. UN Cmnd. of Forces	N
2. NAFTA	Y	4. Strike Race/Death Pnlty.	N	6. Cut Missile Funds	Y

Key Votes of the 104th Congress

1. Congressional Compliance Y	6. Reform Crime Grant N	11. Loser Pays Court Reform N
2. Balanced Budget Amndmt. Y	7. National Security Act N	12. Product Liability Reform Y
3. Bar Unfunded Mandates Y	8. Moratorium on Regs. Y	13. Welfare Reform N
4. Pass Line Item Veto Y	9. Risk Assessment on Regs. Y	14. Term Limits Amndmt. Y
5. Relax Exclusionary Rule Y	10. Expnd. Priv. Prop. Rights Y	15. Tax Cuts Y

Election Results

1994 general	Bart Gordon (D)	90,933	(51%)	($1,385,995)
	Steve Gill (R)	88,759	(49%)	($533,704)
1994 primary	Bart Gordon (D)	50,751	(68%)	
	Dan Rudd (D)	23,446	(32%)	
1992 general	Bart Gordon (D)	120,777	(57%)	($988,920)
	Marsha Blackburn (R)	86,289	(41%)	($181,515)
	Other	5,962	(3%)	

SEVENTH DISTRICT

Rural Tennessee north of Mississippi is one of the most sparsely settled areas in the state. Along each side of the Tennessee River, as it flows north and widens out into Kentucky Lake amid heavy forests, are small rural communities that go back to pre-Civil War days and have not grown much since. Farther west the land is flatter and more open, a northward extension economically and demographically of the northern Mississippi farmlands, with cotton fields and a large black rural population. This mostly empty land is bounded on two sides by large metropolitan areas, Nashville to the east and Memphis to the west.

The 7th Congressional District of Tennessee spans this territory, from the Cheatham County suburban fringe of Nashville, west across the Tennessee River and south to the Mississippi border and finally to the white neighborhoods on the east side of Memphis and Shelby County. It is a mixed district politically. Most of the rural counties are traditionally Democratic, with a few Republican exceptions, while the fringe of Nashville is mixed and the 7th District's portion of Memphis is, like all white parts of Memphis, heavily Republican. The balance has usually tipped toward Republicans, though the lines in Memphis and Shelby County were altered by 1990s redistricting to help the Democrats.

The congressman from the 7th District is Ed Bryant, a Republican elected in 1994 to replace Republican Don Sundquist, who was elected governor. Bryant is from Jackson in west Tennessee, went to school at Ole Miss, served six years in the Army and practiced law in Tennessee since 1978. In 1991, President Bush, on the recommendation of Don Sundquist, made him U.S. attorney in West Tennessee; he left that post in a dispute over jury selection in the bank fraud trial of Memphis Democratic Congressman Harold Ford. This was a hugely visible and controversial case, with many irregularities, which ultimately reflected credit on no one involved but the judge and the jury in the second trial. Bryant was frustrated when a Memphis jury split along racial lines 8–4 for acquittal of Ford, who is black. Jurors for a second trial were picked from mostly white Jackson by a black judge; when Bush holdover acting Attorney General Stuart Gerson, after a meeting with then-White House liaison Webster Hubbell and members of the Congressional Black Caucus, backed Ford's request for a Memphis jury, Bryant resigned. That gave him celebrity all over the area. In the 1994 Republican primary, he lost Shelby County to Germantown Mayor Charles Salvaggio. But he won in all but one of the rural counties by enough votes to win overall 35%–33%. The Democratic nomination went to Harold Byrd, former state legislator and former aide to Senator Jim Sasser, owner of a family farm, travel agency, bank and mortgage company. His four opponents ran well only in their geographic bases, which sometimes overlapped; Byrd carried Shelby County handily and half the rural counties for a 36% win.

One omen for the general election is that more votes were cast in the Republican primary (62,000) than in the Democratic (57,000), not the usual pattern in Tennessee. Bryant called for *habeas corpus* reform, converting closed military bases into prisons, term limits and cuts in congressional staff; he proposed that half of all congressional campaign contributions must be from in-state—which helps Tennessee Republicans, who have developed marvelous in-state fund-raising networks. Byrd called for market-oriented healthcare reform, the balanced budget amendment and line item veto: a pretty conservative platform. This was a close race, 51%–48% for Bryant outside Shelby County; the western counties near Jackson went for Bryant, while counties along the Tennessee River and near Nashville were marginally for Byrd. But Bryant carried Shelby County with 72%, for an overall solid 60%–39% win—despite national Demo-crats' initial strong hopes for a win. In the House, he serves on the Agriculture Committee as well as on the Judiciary Committee, where he has seats, which should play to his background, on its Immigration and Crime Subcommittees. Early in the 104th Congress, he sponsored a bill increasing penalties for escaping from prison. An articulate speaker, he became an early freshman presence on the House floor.

The People: Pop. 1990: 542,270; 43% rural; 10% age 65+; 86% White; 12% Black; 1% Asian; 1% Hispanic origin. Voting age pop.: 397,089; 12% Black; 1% Hispanic origin. Households: 65% married couple families; 32% married couple fams. w. children; 42% college educ.; median household income: $29,242; per capita income: $13,758; median gross rent: $412; median house value: $69,500.

1992 Presidential Vote

Bush (R)	114,544	(50%)
Clinton (D)	91,644	(40%)
Perot (I)	22,486	(10%)

1988 Presidential Vote

Bush (R)	109,719	(65%)
Dukakis (D)	57,919	(35%)

Rep. Ed Bryant (R)

Elected 1994; b. Sept. 7, 1948, Jackson; home, Henderson; U. of MS, B.A. 1970, J.D. 1972; Protestant; married (Cyndi).

Career: Army, 1973–78; Practicing atty., 1978–90; US Atty. for West TN, 1991–92.

DC Office: 1516 LHOB 20515, 202-225-2811; Fax: 202-225-2989.

District Offices: 5909 Shelby Oaks Dr., Memphis 38134, 901-382-5811; 330 N. 2nd St., #111, Clarksville 37040, 615-503-0391; and 810 1/2 S. Garden St., Columbia 38401, 615-381-8100.

Committees: *Agriculture* (22nd of 27 R): Department Opera-tions, Nutrition and Foreign Agriculture; Risk Management and Specialty Crops. *Judiciary* (17th of 20 R): Crime; Immigration and Claims.

Group Ratings and 103rd Congress Votes: Newly Elected

Key Votes of the 104th Congress

1. Congressional Compliance Y	6. Reform Crime Grant Y	11. Loser Pays Court Reform Y
2. Balanced Budget Amndmt. Y	7. National Security Act Y	12. Product Liability Reform Y
3. Bar Unfunded Mandates Y	8. Moratorium on Regs. Y	13. Welfare Reform Y
4. Pass Line Item Veto *	9. Risk Assessment on Regs. Y	14. Term Limits Amndmt. Y
5. Relax Exclusionary Rule Y	10. Expnd. Priv. Prop. Rights Y	15. Tax Cuts Y

Election Results

1994 general	Ed Bryant (R)	102,587	(60%)	($493,712)
	Harold Byrd (D)	65,851	(39%)	($608,768)
	Others	1,945	(1%)	
1994 primary	Ed Bryant (R)	21,776	(35%)	
	Charles Salvaggio (R)	20,269	(33%)	
	Maida Pearson (R)	10,157	(16%)	
	Aaron F. Tatum (R)	3,410	(5%)	
	Scott Kelly (R)	3,370	(5%)	
	Others	3,365	(5%)	
1992 general	Don Sundquist (R)	125,101	(62%)	($1,001,217)
	David R. Davis (D)	72,062	(36%)	($106,774)
	Others	5,685	(3%)	

EIGHTH DISTRICT

West of Nashville and the TVA lakes along the Tennessee River and north of Memphis, the rivers roll lazily through flat or gently rolling land that almost could be the northern end of Mississippi. Cotton and soybeans are the main crops; more blacks remain in rural areas here than in any other part of Tennessee, a reminder of its old plantation economy. The towns here are small, edged in by farm fields; the river bottoms, often flooded, are heavily forested. Here is Henning, the home town of Alex Haley, where he used to sit on his porch and listen to his aunts tell him stories about slave ships and the Civil War that in time became *Roots*.

The 8th Congressional District of Tennessee includes much of this west Tennessee farmland, from the TVA lakes west to the Mississippi; its largest city is Jackson, but it includes the northern suburban fringe of Memphis. Historically, this is Democratic country; Republicans haven't represented most of the counties that make up the 8th since the end of Reconstruction. The region trended Republican in national races in the 1960s and 1970s, then turned back toward the Democrats with the help of some smart local politicians. One of them is Ned McWherter, first elected to the legislature from Weakley County in 1968, Speaker from 1973 to 1986, then governor until 1994. Another is Congressman John Tanner who, when 19-year incumbent Ed Jones retired in 1988, won the seat with a whopping 66% in a four-candidate primary and 62% in the general.

Tanner is a businessman and lawyer from Obion County, exactly the sort of local notable who traditionally runs things in southern politics; after law school and service in the Judge Advocate Corps, he came back to west Tennessee, was elected to the legislature in 1976 and became chairman of the Commerce Committee. He combines political shrewdness with a country demeanor; when his Republican opponent said Tanner would be a liberal national Democrat, his reply was: "Bull. Ed Jones has been his own man and John Tanner will be his own man." Tanner's voting record was right at the midpoint of the Democratic House. He sits on the National Security Committee and is generally pro-defense—Memphis Naval Air Station is the district's largest employer—but questioned the C-17 transport; he also came up with a "Medi-Guard" program to have National Guard personnel provide medical services in underserved urban and rural areas, and supports using the military to counter drug trafficking. On the Science Committee, he probed the Justice Department handling of an investigation of alleged environmental mismanagement at the Rocky Flats nuclear weapons factory near Denver. He also directed attention to the New Madrid Fault, which produced three great earthquakes from 1811–12, and got $2 million for a silt retention basin in Reelfoot Lake, created by the New Madrid quake.

In 1992, Tanner could have been a senator for the asking. Governor McWherter was ready to appoint him to succeed Al Gore, but Tanner refused the post and chose instead to stick with the

8th District, where he had held 650 public meetings in his first three terms. Against Republican opponent Neal Morris in 1994, Tanner won 64%–36%.

In the 104th Congress, Tanner was one of the conservative Democrats who formed The Coalition and became its vice chairman for eastern states. And while Nathan Deal, who later switched parties, was the name sponsor of The Coalition's welfare reform proposal, Tanner was a primary author. He has long backed a balanced budget amendment and the line-item veto, but voted against the version that passed the House in 1995. On such issues, Tanner says, "the biggest difference" caused by the 1994 elections "is that we are winning these votes instead of losing them." But his position is also frustrating: his own well-meant reforms, like the Deal welfare proposal, are accepted only grudgingly by many Democrats and are rejected en bloc by Republicans.

The People: Pop. 1990: 541,852; 52% rural; 14% age 65+; 79% White; 20% Black; 1% Hispanic origin. Voting age pop.: 402,271; 17% Black; 1% Hispanic origin. Households: 60% married couple families; 27% married couple fams. w. children; 30% college educ.; median household income: $22,622; per capita income: $10,712; median gross rent: $311; median house value: $47,200.

1992 Presidential Vote			1988 Presidential Vote		
Clinton (D)	101,328	(48%)	Bush (R)	101,448	(58%)
Bush (R)	89,533	(42%)	Dukakis (D)	74,249	(42%)
Perot (I)	19,328	(9%)			

Rep. John Tanner (D)

Elected 1988; b. Sept. 22, 1944, Halls; home, Union City; U. of TN, B.S. 1966, J.D. 1968; Disciples of Christ; married (Betty Ann).

Career: Navy, 1968–72; TN Natl. Guard, 1974–present; Practicing atty., 1973–88; TN House of Reps., 1976–88.

DC Office: 1127 LHOB 20515, 202-225-4714; Fax: 202-225-1765.

District Offices: 203 W. Church St., Union City 38261, 901-885-7070; Fed. Bldg., #B-7, Jackson 38301, 901-423-4848; and 2836 Coleman Rd., Memphis 38128, 901-382-3220.

Committees: *National Security* (10th of 25 D): Military Procurement; Military Research and Development. *Science* (5th of 23 D): Technology (RMM).

Group Ratings

	ADA	ACLU	COPE	CFA	LCV	CON	NSI	COC	ACU	NTLC	CHC
1994	30	43	44	20	29	53	90	83	67	68	57
1993	50	—	75	60	57	88	—	36	50	—	—

National Journal Ratings

	1993 LIB — 1993 CONS		1994 LIB — 1994 CONS	
Economic	50% —	49%	44% —	54%
Social	45% —	54%	40% —	59%
Foreign	43% —	57%	49% —	49%

Key Votes of the 103d Congress

1. Clinton Deficit Plan	Y	3. Brady Handgun Purchase	N	5. Lmt. UN Cmnd. of Forces	Y
2. NAFTA	Y	4. Strike Race/Death Pnlty.	Y	6. Cut Missile Funds	N

Key Votes of the 104th Congress

1. Congressional Compliance Y	6. Reform Crime Grant Y	11. Loser Pays Court Reform N
2. Balanced Budget Amndmt. Y	7. National Security Act Y	12. Product Liability Reform Y
3. Bar Unfunded Mandates Y	8. Moratorium on Regs. Y	13. Welfare Reform N
4. Pass Line Item Veto N	9. Risk Assessment on Regs. Y	14. Term Limits Amndmt. N
5. Relax Exclusionary Rule Y	10. Expnd. Priv. Prop. Rights Y	15. Tax Cuts Y

Election Results

1994 general	John Tanner (D)	97,951	(64%)	($251,431)
	Neal R. Morris (R)	55,573	(36%)	($14,906)
1994 primary	John Tanner (D)	unopposed		
1992 general	John Tanner (D)	136,852	(84%)	($167,669)
	Lawrence J. Barnes (I)	9,605	(6%)	
	David L. Ward (I)	6,930	(4%)	
	Other	10,045	(6%)	

NINTH DISTRICT

Memphis, the largest city in Tennessee, is in the far southwestern corner of the state, 500 miles from Tennessee's Appalachian border with Virginia and only 20 miles from a Mississippi cotton field. Memphis is symbolized by its musical tradition, entirely separate from Nashville's country music: Beale Street, near downtown Memphis, gave birth to jazz in the 1920s, rooted in the blues music of the lower Mississippi Valley, particularly the Delta; Elvis Presley, Mississippi-born but a Memphis resident most of his adult life, drew on the blues and black music generally to produce the rock-and-roll which made him a star in his lifetime and a strong presence years after his death. Some 40% of metro Memphis's residents are black, more than any other major American city—evidence of the city's economic heritage as a capital of the Cotton Kingdom; today it still has the world's largest spot cotton market. For some years Memphis tried to live this heritage down, redeveloping Beale Street; now it recognizes its history as an asset, and is proud of its old fountains and the courtyard of the Peabody Hotel, where you can get a sense of the days when big Mississippi planters came north to sell their crop and make financial arrangements for the next growing season. Memphis's heritage also includes the Lorraine Motel, where Martin Luther King was assassinated in 1968, now site of a civil rights museum; Graceland, the grandiosely decorated mansion where Elvis Presley lived and, contrary to sightings, died August 16, 1977, is now one of the nation's biggest tourist attractions.

Memphis has become more than a cotton center and it has more than just history. Geographically central in the U.S., it is the home of the first supermarket (Piggly Wiggly) and the first Holiday Inn. It calls itself "America's distribution center": by far its biggest employer is Federal Express, which ships all of its domestic packages in and out of Memphis Airport every night. Just north of Mud Island in the Mississippi, near the old downtown, is the 32-story Great American Pyramid sports and events arena.

Like Mississippi, Memphis has not had an entirely happy political life. The hard edge of racial animosity may have now worn off, but racial polarization, to most people's discomfort, remains. Blacks still vote almost unanimously Democratic; whites vote by percentages almost as high for Republicans in seriously contested races. The 9th Congressional District of Tennessee consists of most of the city of Memphis and a bit of its suburban fringe; in 1992, 54% of its residents were black.

The congressman from the 9th District, Harold Ford, has been in office for two decades and has had a career full of ups and downs. The ups included his election to the House in 1974, at 29, after four years in the state legislature; he is part of a politically prominent Memphis family, well-established as morticians, and came of age just as black majority districts were first being created. Ford moved up quickly in the House, winning a seat on the Ways and Means Committee and in 1981 becoming chairman of the subcommittee handling welfare programs. But he did relatively little with this assignment until early 1987, when it marked up a welfare reform bill. Then—here was one of his downs—Ford was indicted in April 1987 and automatically lost his chairmanship, pending the trial outcome.

Ford's indictment was on federal charges of bank and tax fraud stemming from money he had received from C.H. Butcher, Jr., an east Tennessee banker and brother and partner of Jake Butcher, the 1982 Democratic candidate for governor. But the Butcher banking empire collapsed in 1983. In 1985, C.H. Butcher was sentenced to 20 years in jail for defrauding depositors of $20 million. The indictment said that more than $1 million in sham loans were made by a C.H. Butcher firm to a corporation controlled by Ford, who then used the money for personal purposes. Ford said he expected to repay the loans when he sold his interest in the family funeral home to Butcher. Ford charged that the assistant U.S. attorney bringing the case was politically motivated, and the case was ordered transferred to Memphis. Trial there resulted in a hung jury in April 1990, with the jury split along racial lines 8–4 for acquittal. Charges of alleged jury misconduct prompted black Judge Odell Horton to pick jurors for the second trial from mostly white Jackson; Ford appealed that to the Supreme Court and lost in October 1992. A second judge, Jerome Turner, then presided over a jury selection that resulted in 11 whites and one black; then in February 1993, Bush holdover acting Attorney General Stuart Gerson backed Ford's request for a Memphis jury, at which point the U.S. attorney in Memphis—now 7th District Congressman Ed Bryant—resigned; Turner angrily denied the request for a new jury, and Ford left the court complaining of chest pains.

It turned out that Gerson and White House liaison Webster Hubbell, had met with 26 members of the Congressional Black Caucus delegation the day before Gerson's decision. Republican leaders called for an investigation of this obvious political pressure. Then, to the surprise of many in Washington, Ford was acquitted in April 1993. Overall, this six-year episode reflects discredit on just about everyone; only the judges and the members of the second jury seem to have acted responsibly.

In 1993, Ford returned to his Human Resources Subcommittee chair after a six-year hiatus. He had remained active on some issues in the meantime, working for special accounting rules for cotton warehouse owners and for allowing public housing residents to qualify for jobs programs currently limited to welfare recipients; he got funding for a Job Corps center in Memphis, for Central Station renovation, for a local HUD grant. The bipartisan 1988 welfare reform contained few of Ford's initiatives, and he has opposed both the kind of workfare suggested by Bill Clinton during the 1992 campaign and—even more strongly the welfare bill of House Republicans in 1995. Without much enthusiasm, he did hold hearings on the 1994 Clinton welfare reform proposal; he was a co-sponsor but said he couldn't vote for it without a provision for more public jobs.

Ford has won reelection largely on racial lines, with a consistent 58% of the vote in 1990, 1992 and 1994. His 388 overdrafts on the House bank evidently made no difference to anyone. Interestingly, in 1994 he did not back his brother, state Senator John Ford, for Shelby County Mayor, but instead put his support behind Independent Jack Sammons whom he felt had a better chance at beating a Republican.

The People: Pop. 1990: 541,710; 12% age 65+; 39% White; 59% Black; 1% Asian; 1% Hispanic origin. Voting age pop.: 393,874; 54% Black; 1% Hispanic origin. Households: 40% married couple families; 18% married couple fams. w. children; 42% college educ.; median household income: $22,117; per capita income: $11,296; median gross rent: $362; median house value: $54,900.

1992 Presidential Vote

Clinton (D)	151,590	(66%)
Bush (R)	68,358	(30%)
Perot (I)	9,400	(4%)

1988 Presidential Vote

Dukakis (D)	126,171	(61%)
Bush (R)	80,047	(39%)

Rep. Harold E. Ford (D)

Elected 1974; b. May 20, 1945, Memphis; home, Memphis; TN St. U., B.S. 1967, John Gupten Col., A.A. 1969; Howard U., M.P.A. 1982; Baptist; married (Dorothy).

Career: Mortician, 1969–75; TN House of Reps., 1971–75.

DC Office: 2111 RHOB 20515, 202-225-3265; Fax: 202-225-9215.

District Offices: 369 Fed. Bldg., 167 N. Main St., Memphis 38103, 901-544-4131.

Committees: *Ways & Means* (5th of 15 D): Human Resources (RMM).

Group Ratings

	ADA	ACLU	COPE	CFA	LCV	CON	NSI	COC	ACU	NTLC	CHC
1994	75	83	88	90	77	30	0	45	0	15	0
1993	80	—	86	70	91	*	—	20	5	—	—

National Journal Ratings

	1993 LIB — 1993 CONS		1994 LIB — 1994 CONS	
Economic	*	*	83%	0%
Social	87%	0%	81%	19%
Foreign	87%	13%	83%	17%

Key Votes of the 103d Congress

1. Clinton Deficit Plan	Y	3. Brady Handgun Purchase	Y	5. Lmt. UN Cmnd. of Forces	N
2. NAFTA	Y	4. Strike Race/Death Pnlty.	N	6. Cut Missile Funds	Y

Key Votes of the 104th Congress

1. Congressional Compliance	Y	6. Reform Crime Grant	N	11. Loser Pays Court Reform	N
2. Balanced Budget Amndmt.	Y	7. National Security Act	N	12. Product Liability Reform	N
3. Bar Unfunded Mandates	Y	8. Moratorium on Regs.	N	13. Welfare Reform	N
4. Pass Line Item Veto	Y	9. Risk Assessment on Regs.	N	14. Term Limits Amndmt.	N
5. Relax Exclusionary Rule	N	10. Expnd. Priv. Prop. Rights	N	15. Tax Cuts	N

Election Results

1994 general	Harold E. Ford (D)	94,805	(58%)	($366,683)
	Rod DeBerry (R)	69,226	(42%)	($181,980)
1994 primary	Harold E. Ford (D)	49,959	(79%)	
	Mark Flanagan (D)	13,655	(21%)	
1992 general	Harold E. Ford (D)	123,276	(58%)	($194,631)
	Charles L. Black (R)	60,606	(29%)	
	Richard Lipstock (I)	14,075	(7%)	
	James Vandergriff (I)	12,265	(6%)	
	Other	2,533	(1%)	

TEXAS

Texas, the second largest state in acreage and, since it passed New York in 1994, second in population, is one of two states that was once an independent republic and, like the other, California, continues to be a sort of empire in its own right. Texas, like most of America, has no aristocratic past. This was a place settled by dirt farmers, without lineage or much in the way of manners. It provided only a chance to scratch a hard living out of soil and then, with the discovery of oil, the chance, and the risks, of sudden riches. Now it has become one of the most productive and creative commonwealths in the world. But its success is not just economic. There are large elements of heroism—some mythical, some genuine—in the Texas history that every high school student here learns. "What Texans dream, Texans can do," as its new Governor, George W. Bush, often says.

Texas has also had great and sometimes heroic political strength. Forty years ago, the two houses of Congress were led by two Texas Democrats who had risen from modest roots, House Speaker Sam Rayburn and Senate Majority Leader Lyndon Johnson. Today, Texas has a presidential candidate for 1996, Senator Phil Gramm, and in 1992 two of the three leading candidates were Texans, President George Bush and billionaire Ross Perot. And though they both lost, together they won 56% of the votes to Arkansan Bill Clinton's 43%. In the years since the era of Johnson and Rayburn, Texas has moved from ancestral Democratic to conservative Republican. As recently as 1992 many of its major political figures were Democrats, but now almost all are Republicans. Senator Kay Bailey Hutchison's smashing 67%–33% victory in the June 1993 special election signalled the unpopularity of Clinton Administration policies here and foreshadowed the Republican sweep of 1994. Those elections also changed the lineups of Texas's national leaders. Only a few years before, Texas boasted Jim Wright as Speaker of the House and Lloyd Bentsen as Senate Finance Chairman and 1988 vice presidential nominee; up until 1994 it had three Democratic House committee chairmen, and Governor Ann Richards was a politician of national stature. Now Texas boasts the number two and three House Republicans, Majority Leader Dick Armey and Whip Tom DeLay, and Ways and Means Chairman Bill Archer; it has two Republican senators, Phil Gramm, who is running for president in 1996, and Kay Bailey Hutchison; it has a Republican governor, George W. Bush, referred to everywhere as George W. to distinguish him from his father. It should be added that leading Texans made all the difference on one national issue of especial importance to Texas: the North American Free Trade Agreement would not have happened without them. President George Bush proposed NAFTA and supervised the negotiations, with support from his Secretary of State James Baker; Treasury Secretary Lloyd Bentsen played a key role in getting Bill Clinton to support it; Governor Ann Richards provided important vocal support here and cultivated friendly relations with Mexico. With luck, history may well record that NAFTA prevented the emergence of a revolutionary, hostile Mexico, the greatest threat to the quality of life in the United States in the 21st Century.

With a significant boost from NAFTA, Texas's economy today is booming, and it has less of the tension over immigration, legal and illegal, found in California or Florida. This is all the more impressive because over the last decade Texas has encountered great setbacks. Oil prices plummeted in 1985, the savings and loan scandal had its epicenter and more than half its losses here in the late 1980s, the defense spending cuts of the early 1990s hit hard here, and in 1993 the $8 billion Superconducting Supercollider, set by George Bush to be located in Waxahachie, was zeroed out by Congress. But Texas rebounds. Texans remember the Alamo, the nine years of the independent Texas Republic, the Confederate veterans who returned from the war to scratch a living out of the hard soil or headed west to become cowboys. They may notice that the Alamo

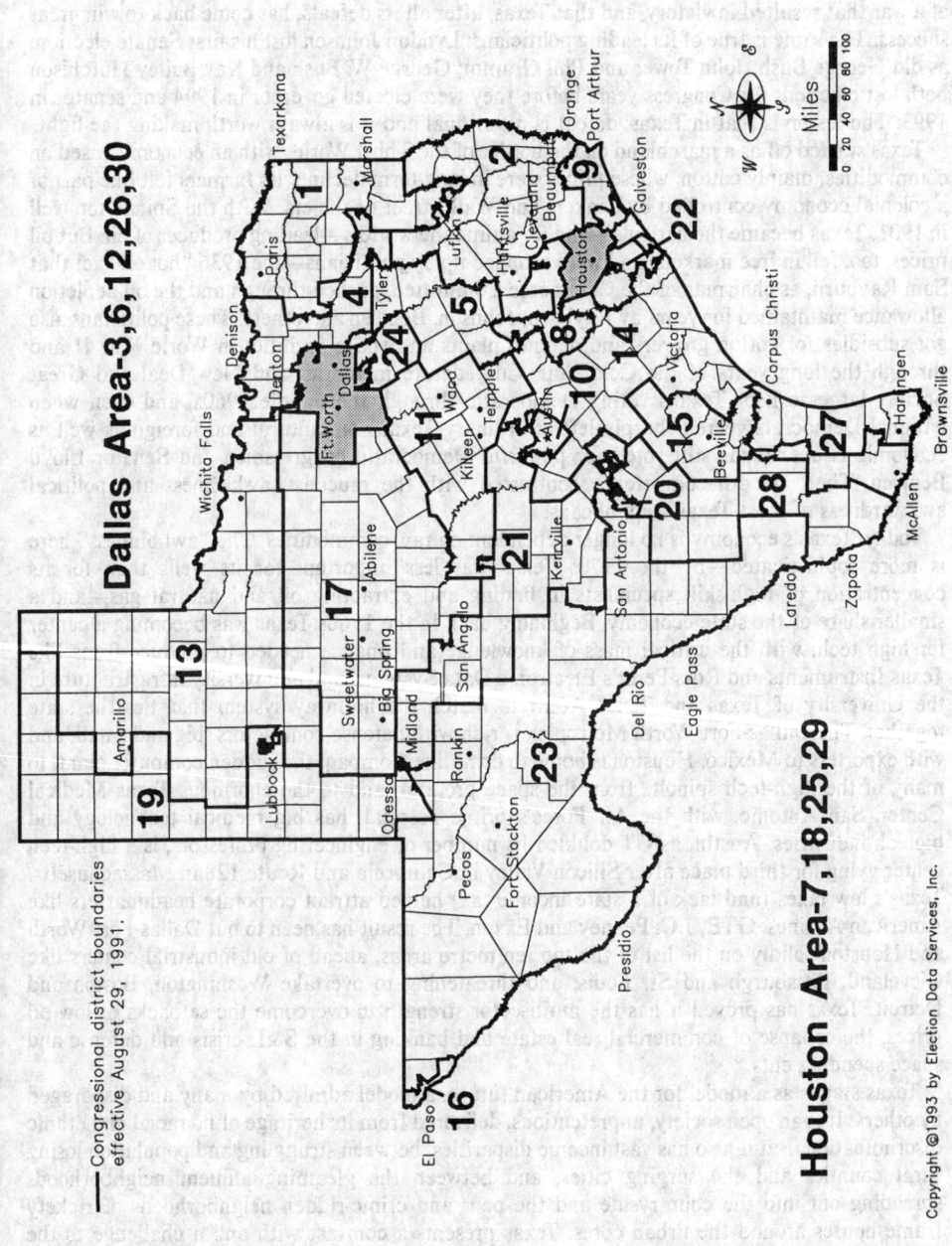

Dallas Area-3,6,12,26,30

Houston Area-7,18,25,29

— Congressional district boundaries
  effective August 29, 1991.

Copyright ©1993 by Election Data Services, Inc.

was not a victory, the Republic did not last, the Confederacy was a lost cause, and the *Lonesome Dove* cattle drives lasted only a few years. But they also learn that the Alamo was the beginning of a war that resulted in victory, and that Texas, after all its defeats, has come back to win great success. The same is true of its leading politicians: Lyndon Johnson lost his first Senate election, as did George Bush, John Tower and Phil Gramm; George W. Bush and Kay Bailey Hutchison both lost elections for Congress years before they were elected governor in 1994 and senator in 1993. The lesson is that in Texas, defeat is never final and it is always worth making the fight.

Texas started off as a marchland on the border of the Third World, with an economy based on commodities, mainly cotton, whose prices were in long-term decline. Its farmers felt like part of a colonial economy controlled by bankers and Wall Street financiers. With the Spindletop well in 1901, Texas became the nation's—and for a time the world's—leading producer of oil. But oil prices, too, fell in free markets, and were propped up by politicians—the 1936 "hot oil" act that Sam Rayburn, as chairman of the Commerce Committee, pushed through and the oil depletion allowance maintained for years by Rayburn, Johnson, Bentsen and others. These politicians also got subsidies for cotton growers and defense plants and space facilities in World War II and through the long years of the Cold War. Confederate memories and New Deal and Great Society largesse kept Texans voting Democratic through the middle 1960s, and even when national Democrats veered sharply left of ordinary Texans on cultural and foreign as well as economic issues, Texas still voted for powerful Democratic congressmen and Senator Lloyd Bentsen. Their smooth competence contrasted with the raucous hawkishness and political awkwardness of most Texas Republicans.

Today, Texas's economy is no longer dependent on raw commodities. The "awl bidness" here is more sophisticated—by the 1970s Texas was less important for its wells than for its concentration of high-skill specialists in finding and extracting oil and natural gas—and a smaller share of the state economy. Beginning back in the 1960s Texas was becoming a center for high tech, with the critical mass of knowledge and finance needed to produce firms like Texas Instruments and Ross Perot's Electronic Data Systems, and a university infrastructure in the University of Texas and Texas A&M to match the highway system that ties the state together. The Dallas-Fort Worth Metroplex is rich with defense contractors, big and small, and with exporters to Mexico. Houston is home to firms like Compaq, the sudden computer giant, to many of the high-tech spinoffs from the space program and to the enormous Texas Medical Center. San Antonio, with the Air Force's prime hospital, has big medical technology and biotech industries. Austin, as UT doubled its number of engineering professors, is a high-tech center vying for third place after Silicon Valley in California and Route 128 in Massachusetts. Texas's low taxes (and lack of a state income tax) helped attract corporate headquarters like American Airlines, GTE, J.C. Penney and Exxon. The result has been to put Dallas-Fort Worth and Houston solidly on the list of the top ten metro areas, ahead of old industrial centers like Cleveland, Pittsburgh and St. Louis, and threatening to overtake Washington, Boston and Detroit. Texas has proved it has the multisector strength to overcome the setbacks of low oil prices, the collapse of commercial real estate and banking in the S&L crisis and defense and space spending cuts.

Texas stands as a model for the American future, a model admired by many and disparaged by others. It is an open society, unpretentious, delivered from its heritage of no racial and ethnic discrimination. But it also has vast income disparities, between struggling and population-losing rural counties and the surging cities, and between the gleaming affluent neighborhoods spreading out into the countryside and the poor and crime-ridden neighborhoods of rickety frame houses around the urban cores. Texas presents a contrast with and a challenge to the traditions of other megastates—New York which pioneered the American welfare state, California which used high taxes to build highways and schools, the Great Lakes industrial states with their big labor unions. For Texas has some of the lowest taxes in the country and some of the lowest welfare levels; it has few union members and a relatively small public sector; it has resisted court-ordered moves to equalize spending among school districts; it continues to be a violent state, with a high crime rate and the nation's most executions. For years, out-of-state elites and liberals in Texas have called on the state to become more like New York or California or Michigan. But Texas's Republican victories—and none more than George W. Bush's 53%–46% win over the personally popular Ann Richards—indicate that most Texans prefer their own model. Indeed, in important respects New York and California and Michigan are choosing to become more like Texas; so is Mexico. Low taxes and high tech, few barriers to opportunity but only a weak safety net, moving away from reliance on agriculture and oil, bypassing the era of big factories and big unions of the Great Lakes and eschewing the liberal cultural values of the two coasts: this is Texas's way, and increasingly North America's.

Politically, Texas is now an indisputably Republican state. One-party Democratic dominance ended in the 1960s, and for two decades Democratic victories since then have been largely the product of Lloyd Bentsen, when he was on the ballot in 1976, 1982 and 1988 and when he exerted his influence for Ann Richards for governor in 1990. The old Democratic strength in the Texas countryside is gone—in 1994 George W. Bush carried 189 counties to Richards's 65—and the Republican hold on the big cities is solid—Bush carried 55% in the Dallas-Fort Worth Metroplex and in greater Houston, which together cast 45% of the state's votes. Republicans won the vote for U.S. House 56%–42% in 1994. That gave them only 11 of 30 seats, thanks to brilliant Democratic redistricting, but a federal court ruled that some of the boundaries designed to ensure minority districts were constitutionally unacceptable and it required that plan to be changed for 1996. Republicans won three of seven downballot offices and all the contested statewide judgeships in 1994; they are moving close to majorities in the state Senate and House. The Democratic primary electorate has shrunk, from 1.8 million in 1978 to just over 1.0 million in 1994, to a more liberal, minority-dominated constituency. The Republican primary electorate has grown, from 158,000 in 1978 to 855,000 for their last real contest in 1990. George Bush carried Texas even in 1992, and the 1994 VNS exit poll showed Bill Clinton's approval rating at 36% and disapproval at 59%, one of his lowest marks in the country.

Pockets of Democratic strength in Texas are increasingly isolated. Their best vote is in the Border counties, which cast 7% of the state's votes; they voted 60%–39% for Richards in 1994, 53%–33% for Clinton in 1992. Exit polls showed Hispanics voted 71% for Richards, a tribute to the close attention she paid them and her strong support of NAFTA—a mark hard for other Democrats to match. Another Democratic area, but not as strong as liberals have hoped, is the urban strip from San Antonio to Austin. In 1990 Richards, who served as a Travis County commissioner in Austin before she was state treasurer, carried it 57%–40%; but in 1994, by just 51%–48%. Austin's cultural liberals are not as dominant as they once were. This is now a high-tech town, with lots of free market enthusiasts in new subdivisions running north of the pink marble Capitol and the UT campus. And in San Antonio, where Anglos are heavily Republican, Republicans are also competing for Hispanic votes. Rural Texas, historically Democratic, now seems solidly Republican. George Bush carried it 42%–35% in 1992, with Ross Perot getting 22%; George W. Bush in 1994 carried it 57%–43%, a similar margin to his father's over Michael Dukakis in 1988. Cultural attitudes are conservative here, and there is little of the economic populism of Sam Rayburn's day. In East Texas, once the home of yellow dog Democrats, most counties voted for Bush over Richards. In West Texas, Richards carried only sparsely populated ranch territory. In the vast triangle from Waco (Richards's home town) to Midland (Bush's) and Victoria near the Gulf of Mexico, Bush carried practically every county.

Nearly half of Texas's votes are cast in the two big metro areas. The Dallas-Fort Worth Metroplex is more volatile. Here, Richards led oilman Clayton Williams in 1990, winning the votes, especially, from working women which were critical to her election; here, local boy Ross Perot won 28% in 1992. But in 1994, Bush beat Richards here 55%–45%. There is a large black vote and central Dallas has a liberal professional enclave. But the new subdivisions around the Metroplex's edge cities are overwhelming Republican. Metro Houston also gave Richards a narrow margin in 1990. But Perot got only 20% there, and George W. Bush in his parents' home town won 55%–44%.

It is risky to predict future elections, but the future political course of Texas seems plain. The retirement of Lloyd Bentsen and the defeat of Ann Richards removes from the scene two giant Democratic figures, capable of winning the loyalty of the party's liberal core while appealing to rural and metropolitan conservatives; no replacements are apparent. Nor are the Democrats likely to profit in an economic downturn. Indeed in recent years, they have run best when times were good, as in 1982, while voters returned to free market Republicans when the economy sagged, as in 1986. But Democrats lost in the good times of 1994, which Ann Richards in Austin and Bill Clinton in Washington could arguably claim credit for. Generational change also works for the Republicans. George W. Bush lost voters over 60; but not by a large margin and, unlike in Florida, where his brother Jeb Bush lost the elderly but won all age groups under 45, over 60s here are only 20% of the electorate. George W. Bush won voters under 30 by 59%–41%, an impressive margin indeed. On the major issues, and on the overriding question of whether to continue Texas's traditions of cultural conservatism and minimalist government, Bush and the Republicans seem very much on the majority side. The future in Texas appears to be theirs and, if this state is as attractive a model as it thinks, perhaps in the nation as well.

Governor. In January 1994, George W. Bush was known as the former president's son, a spottily successful businessman and onetime unsuccessful candidate for Congress, and managing director of the Texas Rangers baseball team, helpful in commissioning its charmingly old-fashioned The Ballpark in Arlington; in January 1995, he was inaugurated as governor of the nation's second largest state. Bush was raised in a modest ranch house in Midland, when it was a rough and tumble Permian Basin oil boom town. Soon after his parents moved to Houston in 1960, he went east to school, where he was uncomfortable with the radicalism of late 1960s and early 1970s Yale (undergraduate) and Harvard (business school). He returned to Texas, became a fighter pilot in the National Guard, got into the oil business in Midland and ran for Congress in 1978. He lost that race 53%–47% to Kent Hance, then a Democrat from Lubbock: rural West Texas wasn't yet ready for a Midland Republican. Bush's business career wasn't especially successful. He did better as a political adviser to his father in 1988 and after, and as the 2% owner and managing director of the Rangers. After his father's defeat in 1992, George W. decided to run for governor. He brought his nervous intensity to the race and a determination to discuss specifics of state issues in a way that illustrated sensitivity to the texture of everyday life—just the opposite of his father's perceived disinterest in domestic issues and distance from ordinary life. In heavy personal campaigning he consistently called for tougher sentences for criminals, including adult prison incarceration for violent offenders beginning at age 14. He favored letting school districts opt out of control by the Texas Education Agency, limiting AFDC benefits to two years and requiring job training for welfare beneficiaries. He also was for limiting punitive damages to $200,000 or three times the actual economic damage incurred, whichever is greater, and barring frivolous lawsuits.

Bush took on a tough opponent in Ann Richards. She first came on the national scene in 1988, when as Democratic National Convention keynoter she attacked George Bush with perfect timing and a thick Waco accent: "Poor George. He just can't help it. He was born with a silver foot in his mouth." She was already a veteran of Austin politics, elected County Commissioner in 1976 and state Treasurer in 1982; it was well known she was a recovering alcoholic. In 1990, she persevered through one of the most grueling gubernatorial races ever, skewering former Governor Mark White in the spring primary, attacked by former Attorney General Jim Mattox as a drug user in the runoff, which she won 57%–43%. For months she ran behind oil man Clayton Williams, whose ads had him promising boot camps to teach teenage violators "the joys of busting rocks." But Williams made several impolitic remarks and, when attacked on his business ethics, refused to shake Richards's hand. Richards won 49%–47%. In office, Richards pushed through a state lottery and a corporate income tax, but stoutly opposed any income tax; she got increased minimum sentences for murder and a new school finance formula to respond to court orders. She hosted Mexico's then-President Salinas and campaigned for NAFTA. She did make a few missteps. Her appointee to chair the Railroad Commission, Lena Guerrero, turned out to have falsified her credentials. Her appointee to fill Lloyd Bentsen's Senate seat, Bob Krueger, lost the June 1993 special election to Kay Bailey Hutchison by a 67%–33% margin. Later in the year, Richards seemed smug when Democratic District Attorney Ronnie Earle prosecuted Hutchison for using office perquisites for political purposes. Then it was revealed during the trial that Richards's office phones had been used for such purposes. Soon after, the case against Hutchison was dismissed.

Still, Richards was personally liked and her record was popular. This was, as early polls showed, a race, unusual for 1994, in which both candidates had strong positive ratings. Yet Richards unaccountably failed to sound the positive, triumphalist note she might have. In public she called George W. Bush "shrub" and referred to him as "some jerk who's running for public office," apparently resentful of being challenged by someone with less experience than she so painfully had gained. He was careful always to speak of her respectfully as Governor Richards. In June, speaking to Texas Girls State camp, she said, "You cannot count on Prince Charming to make you feel better about yourself and take care of you . . . Prince Charming may be driving a Honda and telling you that you have no equal, but that won't do you much good when you've got kids and a mortgage—and he has a beer gut and a wandering eye." Some in the media reprinted this as feminist wisdom, but Bush denounced it as an unduly negative view of marriage.

In many ways, this race was an example of 1994 politics as an argument between therapy and discipline, symbolized by the way the two candidates quit alcohol, Richards through the 12-step AA group therapy process, Bush by stopping drinking after waking up with a hangover on the morning after his 40th birthday. In Texas, discipline proved more popular. Late in the campaign, Richards ads attacked Bush's business record, as they had Clayton Williams's in 1990 (Bush was heartily endorsed by Williams); she poked fun when Bush went out to shoot doves but instead shot an endangered killdeer; she worked to relieve flood victims in east Texas; she was endorsed by Ross Perot. But Bush continued to stay with his message, "take a stand for Texas values." The polls, consistently within margin of error from April, suggested Bush was edging ahead, and he won by a greater than expected 53%–46%.

In office Bush has the advantage of having popular positions on issues and a legislature where Republicans have greater strength than ever. Bob Bullock, the durable Democrat who as Lieutenant Governor in effect runs the state Senate, started off pledging cooperation and helped Bush put Republicans in control of the confirmation panel, in effect vetoing some late Richards appointments. But now that he is governor, Bush must deliver. He seems to have no ambitions to run for national office, but his performance in office in this nation-sized state will have national significance.

Senators. Texas now has two Republican senators, neither of them from the mold of the talented, powerful men who were elected from rural backgrounds and with business backing—the John Connallys, Lyndon Johnsons and Lloyd Bentsens of the past. Phil Gramm grew up in Columbus, Georgia, and became an economics professor at Texas A&M. Kay Bailey Hutchison grew up near Houston and, unable to get into a law firm after law school, became a reporter for a Houston television station.

Phil Gramm is Texas's senior senator and a politician of presidential stature in his own eyes—and those of many others. The son of an Army sergeant, he flunked third, seventh and ninth grades, and went on to earn his Ph.D. from the University of Georgia. His field was economics, the one discipline that has moved to the right since the mid-1960s, due to the growing belief in the efficacy of free markets; and Gramm certainly is a believer in free markets. He moved to Texas in 1967 to teach economics at Texas A&M. There he met and married his second wife, Wendy Lee, granddaughter of Korean immigrants and also an economics Ph.D. In the Texas of Lyndon Johnson's time, where Democrats held almost all offices and while preaching conservatism concentrated on funneling federal money into what was then considered an underdeveloped economy, Gramm conceived political ambitions, though he had no local connections, no personal money and little to none of the good ol' boy charm which was long an ingredient of political success in the state. Seething with energy and conviction, he started giving speeches around the state, boosting free market economics and decrying the grasping hand of government. One of his first fans was Dicky Flatt, a print shop owner in Mexia who became a staple in Gramm speeches, the hard-working American whose money the government is taking away to spend on someone else. In 1976, at 34, Gramm ran as a Democrat in the primary against Senator Lloyd Bentsen and lost 64%–28%. Undaunted, Gramm ran for an open House seat in 1978, making the runoff by 115 votes over current Congressman Chet Edwards, and then winning the primary runoff 53%–47% and easily beating the Republican in the general. One sign of future races: he spent the very considerable sum of $480,000. Within three years, Gramm was a major national figure. He got a seat on the Budget Committee, promising Majority Leader Jim Wright to be a team player. But, while he kept attending Democratic strategy meetings, he became co-sponsor of the Gramm-Latta budget resolution, the 1981 Reagan budget cuts, which passed the House over the opposition of the Democratic leadership.

For that apostasy and because Democrats decided that they could not trust him with confidential information, Speaker Tip O'Neill kicked Gramm off the Budget Committee in 1983. But Gramm turned that to his advantage by switching parties, resigning and triumphantly running in a special election campaign that gave him exposure in both the Houston and Dallas-Fort Worth media markets. "I had to choose between Tip O'Neill and y'all," he said, showing his capacity for attractively framing issues, "and I decided to stand with y'all." He won with 55% and in 1984 easily won the Republican Senate nomination when John Tower announced his retirement from Congress. The Democratic winner in an epic three-way primary was Lloyd Doggett, then a liberal state senator from Austin and now congressman from the 10th District, whom Gramm attacked for holding a fundraiser at a gay male strip joint in San Antonio. Gramm won 59%–41%.

In his first year in the Senate Gramm had two major initiatives. First, he engineered a vacancy in the east Texas 1st District seat by securing a federal judgeship for the incumbent Democrat and, with the aid of a young operative named Lee Atwater, came close to having his Republican candidate win in that yellow dog Democratic territory. His idea was to encourage Republicans to run in rural southern districts. If he had succeeded, they might have captured the House in 1988 or 1990, rather than 1994. Gramm's second initiative, advanced immediately after his first, was the Gramm-Rudman deficit reduction law requiring automatic budget cuts if the deficit was not reduced to specific levels. Politically, Gramm-Rudman swept all before it and passed both houses. Fiscally, under the lead of OMB Director James Miller (who earned his economics Ph.D. from the University of Georgia at the same time as Phil Gramm and who has run for the Senate), it did in fact result in lowering the deficit. Gramm was one of the Republican negotiators at the 1990 budget summit, but did not resist a tax increase, as some conservatives had hoped. After George Bush caved in on the issue, Gramm ended up negotiating the final package of budget cuts, spending caps and tax increases. In 1991, he opposed New York Senator Daniel Patrick Moynihan's plan to cut Social Security taxes; here too Gramm supported the Bush Administration rather than follow free market principles. Texas loyalty, perhaps: Gramm gave the nominating speech for Bush in New Orleans in 1988 and the keynote speech in Houston in 1992. Texas loyalty works other ways too: critics on both sides of the aisle also noted that he has worked hard to keep money for big government projects flowing into Texas—Houston's space program, Waxahachie's now-canceled Supercollider, Austin's Sematech research center, Ingleside's Navy base. But Gramm's government-cutting initiatives kept coming. He has long opposed "baseline" and "current services" budgeting that gives government automatic spending increases; these fell victim to the 1994 Contract With America. In 1991, he joined with Newt Gingrich to propose a series of tax cuts; in 1992 he argued for a 5% defense spending cut, with proceeds to increase the dependent exemption on the federal income tax; that same year, he held up Senate business to press for the balanced budget amendment; in 1995, he demanded that the Senate vote on the large House-passed tax cut.

Gramm was also all business at politics. In 1991, he was elected chairman of the National Republican Senatorial Committee by 26–17; he hoped initially to gain seats, but watched in

1992 as the press ballyhooed "the year of the woman" (there were no such articles when most of the women candidates were Republicans in 1990), then ended up seeing Republicans gain just one seat on election day and then another weeks later in the Georgia runoff. Gramm then sought, despite the usual practice, to win a second term at the NRSC, and was opposed by Mitch McConnell of Kentucky. Gramm won by 20–19, with key support from megastate incumbents who narrowly won their races and four grateful freshmen. "I did not come to Washington to be loved, and I have not been disappointed," Gramm says. Although fund raising was initially disappointing, Gramm ended up having a splendid record: Republicans gained seven seats on November 8, 1994, and an eighth a day later when Richard Shelby of Alabama switched parties. In his four years as chairman, Gramm travelled thousands of miles, worked with all the party's leading consultants, met and solicited its leading fundraisers ("I love raising money. I believe in what I am doing and don't mind asking for help")—all with the transparent intention of strengthening his run for the presidency in 1996.

But his intent also was strengthened by his deployment of ideas. "I have always felt on budget issues the party that defines the parameters of the debate almost always wins the debate," Gramm once said, and he is as good as anyone in American politics at tightly defining issues to steer the public his way. When other Republicans, including perhaps Bob Dole, were mulling compromise with the Clinton healthcare plan, Gramm was preaching root and branch opposition, threatening to filibuster the plan if it came to the floor. In 1994, he also vociferously opposed the Clinton crime bill: he is for much tougher penalties and adds, "If social spending stopped crime, this would be the safest nation on earth." He has proposed doubling the dependent tax exemption from $2,500 to $5,000. A convinced free trader, he was a strong supporter of the North American Free Trade Agreement, widely popular in Texas; he was a quieter and later supporter of the General Agreement on Tariffs and Trade, suspect in some Republican quarters. In the 1994 campaign, Gramm as Senate campaign chairman was making many of the same arguments and stressing the same issues as the House Republicans' Contract With America.

Gramm has never tried to hide his national ambitions. "I think anybody who's ever been a city councilman, much less a United States Senator, is interested in being President of the United States," he said in 1992. His 1992 convention keynote for a moment seemed to mention Dicky Flatt more than George Bush. Gramm's ambitions naturally arouse his colleagues' jealousy, and it does not help that he is less than cooperative in trading political favors. After the 1994 election his putative presidential rival Bob Dole was clearly looking askance at Gramm (and making sure that a Dole ally, New York Senator Alfonse D'Amato, took over the campaign committee), and allies also made sure Gramm did not get his publicly expressed desire for a spot on the Finance Committee. (In the Senate, Gramm ended up with a nice consolation prize: the chairmanship of the Appropriations Subcommittee which writes the budget for the Commerce, Justice and State Departments, among others. He quickly called for a doubling of the Border Patrol's budget in order to combat illegal immigration.) But in February 1995, he announced his candidacy and set about methodically collecting his $25 million campaign treasury. He brings to the race a bullish aggressiveness, a strong and well-disciplined mind, a gift for pungent phrase, the ability to frame issues favorably for his cause. Gramm sees himself as a man with a mission to change the role of government in American life and as the logical successor to fellow party-switcher Ronald Reagan. But he does not have Reagan's geniality. There is a note of anger to him—a hard edge of hostility toward those whose view of America differs from his. He is, some think, a walking gender gap, attractive to the angry white males who voted Republican in 1994, off-putting to women who have wavered between the parties in the 1990s. Wendy Lee Gramm could be an asset here: she served as chairwoman of the Commodities Futures Trading Commission in the Reagan and Bush years, demonstrating in a politically accountable office the competence and independence of judgment many now attribute to Hillary Rodham Clinton. It is also not clear whether Gramm can engage the core constituency of today's Republican Party, the religious right, which finds his views acceptable, but can't help noticing that most issues that engage this economist are economic.

Gramm's voting record is almost impeccably conservative, but his energies seem most engaged on economics and crime and welfare. Other than to state his antiabortion views with a caveat that the nation does not agree, he has relatively little to say about abortion and explicitly religious issues and, though well-informed, he is not tremendously interested in foreign policy. But he begins the campaign prodigiously well-organized and well-financed, prepared for the 44-day contest between New Hampshire and California that will decide the nomination. He obviously hopes for a victory in low-tax New Hampshire and in the Arizona primary that his supporters Senator John McCain and Governor Fife Symington engineered. Colorado, Maryland and his native Georgia vote on March 5. Can he beat Bill Clinton, or whoever else is in the race? Not on charm, as he readily admits, but quite possibly on issues, certainly if voters are in the same frame of mind as in November 1994.

Gramm's Senate seat comes up in 1996, but under a law written by Democrats first for Lyndon Johnson and used by Lloyd Bentsen, he can run for both offices. His 1990 numbers suggest he is in good shape: he won 60% of the vote then, carrying rural Texas and the two big metro areas with more than 60%, and he ran ahead even in the Border counties; only inner city districts and Austin rejected him. Historic precedent also works in his favor: both Johnson and Bentsen were reelected when they were running for vice president in 1960 and 1988. If he is elected president, his successor in the Senate will be picked by George W. Bush and would face the voters in a spring 1997 special election—the same scenario that led the Johnson and Bentsen seats to switch to the Republicans.

Texas's junior senator is Kay Bailey Hutchison, a Republican who won a stunning June 1993 victory over the man Governor Ann Richards appointed to fill Lloyd Bentsen's seat. And then, after undergoing what appeared to be a political prosecution, Hutchison was reelected triumphantly in November 1994 to serve a full term. Kay Bailey grew up in LaMarque, near the refinery town of Texas City, a prom queen who went to college and then law school at the University of Texas and then, unable to get a law job, in 1967 worked for a Houston TV station as a reporter. In 1972, she won a seat in the legislature, its first Republican woman. In 1976 she went to Washington to fill the number two position at the National Transportation Safety Board. She married, moved to Dallas and went into banking and became a small business owner in 1978. In 1982, she lost a House race to Steve Bartlett, later mayor of Dallas, but in 1990 she was elected state Treasurer, a breakthrough race for state Republicans. Hutchison has been mocked by liberals for her tight-lipped good manners, but she remembers when being a woman was much more of a career handicap than today's younger generation has ever encountered, and she has passed through political ordeals as searing as those endured by her predecessor as Treasurer—and political non-friend—former Governor Ann Richards.

Hutchison quickly became one of four major candidates for the Senate seat vacated by Treasury Secretary Lloyd Bentsen and to which Richards appointed former Congressman Bob Krueger. Krueger is a Shakespeare-quoting former professor and congressman who worked to deregulate energy prices in the 1970s, nearly beat Senator John Tower in 1978, then ran third in a three-way Senate primary in 1984 and was elected Railroad Commissioner (actually, oil regulator) in 1990. A market conservative, he opposed the Clinton budget and tax plan. Even so, the Democratic label was so deadly that he took only 29% of the vote in the May 1993 open general, and finished second to Hutchison, who also had 29%. Krueger's cause was obviously doomed, and his campaign flailed around, running absurd ads in which Krueger, dressed in an Arnold Schwarzenegger Terminator outfit, claimed to be a lousy politician. Meanwhile, Hutchison weathered charges she had hit a Treasury employee (the daughter of former Governor John Connally), and kept the focus on Bill Clinton, whose Texas job rating was 73% negative. Hutchison won the runoff by an astonishing 67%–33%, ahead of any Senate candidate here since the 1950s, when Republicans did not put up serious candidates. She won the Dallas-Fort Worth Metroplex 71%–29% and greater Houston 70%–30%, carried the usually Democratic San Antonio-Austin corridor and the Border counties; rural Texas, once heavily Democratic, went for Hutchison 68%–32%. Yellow dog Democratic counties went Republican in droves: Krueger carried 15 counties, Hutchison 239. Her victory echoed with greater resonance the defeat of the last Texas senator appointed by a Democratic governor to replace a Texan taking a high position in Washington: the 1961 loss of conservative Democrat "Dollar Bill" Blakeley to Republican John Tower, replacing then-Vice President Lyndon Johnson. Tower's victory was a sign that Republicans could be competitive in Texas; Hutchison's victory was a sign that Republican policies were ascendant nationally.

Hutchison started her Senate career articulate and pleasant but willing to be partisan, pro-choice on abortion but opposing taxpayer funding and a Freedom of Choice Act that would wipe out state parental consent laws, opposing the Clinton tax increase but supporting NAFTA and voting with two other women senators to deny Admiral Frank Kelso, of Tailhook notoriety, retirement with his four-star rank. But immediately after her win in 1993, Austin District Attorney Ronnie Earle, a liberal Democrat, worked to indict Hutchison for using office employees for political purposes and for destroying some records. It was a rotten prosecution from the beginning: the law imposes limits on state elected officials, which at times seem absurd, and Hutchison had purged mailing lists from her Texas computer on the advice of the Democratic attorney general. Then, in February 1994, Earle dropped the charges when the trial judge refused to rule on the admissibility of evidence seized in a June 1993 raid on Hutchison's office, in effect admitting he had no case.

Hutchison's job rating had declined, but not disastrously, and Phil Gramm helped her avoid any serious Republican primary opposition. Three serious Democrats were running for her seat. The potentially strongest candidate, moderate Houston Congressman Mike Andrews, was eliminated in the March primary with 16%. In the April runoff, former Attorney General and bitter Richards enemy Jim Mattox lost 54%–46% to Richard Fisher, a free-spending moderate who campaigned extensively in the Border counties in Spanish. In the general, Fisher's credentials seemed a bit fishy—he claimed to have been an adviser to former British Prime Minister Margaret Thatcher, though Thatcher said their acquaintance was minor—and Hutchison cruised to a solid 61%–38% victory. This time she lost the Border, but won the San Antonio-Austin corridor and took over 60% in the big metro areas and the rural counties.

Hutchison now has a solid Senate seat and good committee assignments on the majority side, a clean reputation and the ability, as one of three Republican women senators, to command national attention.

Presidential politics. Texas is now a major player in presidential politics, a source of candidates, a fount of campaign funds and a dynamo in the electoral college with 32 electoral votes, more than any state except California or New York, with more national candidates than both put together. George Bush, Ross Perot, Lloyd Bentsen, Phil Gramm—all have run in the last dozen years or may well in 1996, or both. The most stereotypically Texan of them is the billionaire Perot, though the stereotype is not precise. Perot is indeed a billionaire, with a deep east Texas accent and a Texas gift for the memorable sound bite ("I'm not gonna sound bite this"). But he is also a rebel against some things Texan, a school reformer who helped impose a no-pass-no-play rule regarding school athletics. A seeming traditionalist (he used to insist that his male employees cut their hair and marry their girlfriends), he sent signals that he was the most secular of the fall 1992 candidates. Perot's penchant for conspiracy was especially obvious in his persuading the FBI in Dallas in 1992 to approach Bush state chairman Jim Oberwetter and offer to sell him wiretaps of Perot. Oberwetter of course would have no part of it, though no one asked why the FBI initiated a sting that involved it in a political campaign and was based on a charge relayed by Perot that originated with an obvious crank. Perot did run a strong 28% in the Dallas-Fort Worth Metroplex, his home since leaving the Navy. But in Bowie County, which includes his home town of Texarkana, perhaps the single jurisdiction in which all three candidates were best known—it is Perot's boyhood home, right next door to Clinton's Arkansas and has voted yes or no on Bush in six elections—Perot got just 22% of the vote, to 39% each for Bush and Clinton.

For all the ruckus and commotion, Texas remained a Republican state presidentially, as it did in 1988 when Lloyd Bentsen's presence on the Democratic ticket got its percentage up to only 43%. In 1992, Bill Clinton stumped Texas in his bus and on LBJ's birthday, and George Bush had to campaign in his home state and had trouble raising money there. But Clinton's cultural liberalism and Bush's opposition to trial lawyers (an issue familiar because it dominates state Supreme Court races, which trial lawyer candidates mostly lose) helped Bush carry his home state 41%–37%. No Democratic candidate has carried the Dallas-Fort Worth Metroplex or greater Houston since LBJ, and no Democratic candidate has carried rural and small town Texas since Jimmy Carter in 1976. The good news for the Democrats in 1992 was that they no longer needed Texas to win. For nearly 150 years, since Texas was admitted to the Union in 1845, Democrats never won the presidency without carrying Texas; in 1992, they did. The bad news for Democrats is that for the foreseeable future, they no longer have a chance to win Texas.

Texas's March 1992 Super Tuesday primary produced big victories for Bill Clinton and George Bush. For 1996, Phil Gramm is obviously counting on a big win here, and it's not clear that any rival will want to spend the time and money to seriously challenge him. On the Democratic side, Bill Clinton's strength among black and Latino voters will help him against a challenge from the right or even the left, since they make up a large share of the Democratic primary electorate.

Congressional districting. Texas's 1991 redistricting plan, the product of Bob Mansker, aide to Democratic Congressman Martin Frost, wins the Phil Burton Award for the decade for its creatively drawn lines in unlikely places; for the convoluted boundaries of its districts which, snakelike, seem to be threatening to swallow each other; for the ingenuity with which white urban Democrats, long dependent on black votes, were given districts where Democratic rural counties were substituted for urban black neighborhoods. This was a Democratic gerrymander, and its partisan effect was clear in the two elections when it was in effect. In 1992, Democrats carried the popular vote for House by only 50%–48%, but they won 21 of 30 districts. In 1994, Democrats lost the popular vote for House resoundingly, with only 42% of the votes to the Republicans' 56%. But they won 19 of 30 seats anyway.

This may not happen again. In August 1994, a federal court ruled that three urban minority districts were racially gerrymandered and therefore unconstitutional; 1991 boundaries were left in place for 1994. In December 1994, Justice Antonin Scalia said the legislature did not have to redraw district lines until the Supreme Court decides to hear the state's appeal. Theoretically, new lines could actually help Democrats, by giving white urban incumbents like Frost more black and Hispanic constituents. But the lines are so intricate that any tinkering is likely to change every district. Plus, Governor George W. Bush is not likely to sign any plan as favorable to the Democrats as Mansker's. That would leave it to the court to draw the lines, which would surely help Republicans. Or—in the unlikely event of a deadlock—it might invoke the historic remedy of requiring all members to run at-large through the whole state, which could mean a 19-seat Republican gain. In any case, there is a good likelihood of Republican gains through redistricting for 1996. There seems no likely impact on Texas's now powerful Republican Congressmen—Majority Leader Dick Armey, Majority Whip Tom DeLay, Ways and Means Chairman Bill Archer—who represent some of the most heavily Republican districts in the country, for almost all the area adjacent to their districts is heavily Republican as well.

The People: Est. Pop. 1994: 18,378,000; Pop. 1990: 16,986,510, up 8.2% 1990–1994. 7.1% of U.S. total, 2d largest; 20% rural. Median age: 30.8 years. 10.1% 65 years and over. 75.2% White, 25.5% Hispanic origin, 11.9% Black, 1.9% Asian, 10.6% Other. Households: 56.6% married couple families; 30% married couple fams. w. children; 47% college educ.; median household income: $27,016; per capita income: $12,904; 60.9% owner occupied housing; median house value: $59,600; median monthly rent: $328. 7.5% Unemployment. 1994 Voting age pop.: 13,166,000. 1994 Turnout: 4,393,418; 33% of VAP. Registered voters (1994): 8,929,397; no party registration.

Political Lineup: Governor, George W. Bush (R); Lt. Gov., Bob Bullock (D); Secy. of State, John Hannah, Jr. (D); Atty. Gen., Dan Morales (D); Treasurer, Martha Whitehead (D); Comptroller of Public Accounts, John Sharp (D); Auditor, Lawrence Alwin (D). State Senate, 31 (17 D and 14 R); State House of Representatives, 150 (89 D and 61 R). Senators, Phil Gramm (R) and Kay Bailey Hutchison (R). Representatives, 30 (11 R and 19 D).

1992 Presidential Vote

Bush (R)	2,496,071	(41%)
Clinton (D)	2,281,815	(37%)
Perot (I)	1,354,781	(22%)

1992 Democratic Presidential Primary

Clinton	972,151	(66%)
Tsongas	285,191	(19%)
Brown	118,923	(8%)
Other	106,710	(7%)

1988 Presidential Vote

Bush (R)	3,036,829	(56%)
Dukakis (D)	2,352,748	(43%)

1992 Republican Presidential Primary

Bush	556,280	(70%)
Buchanan	190,572	(24%)
Uncommitted	27,936	(4%)

GOVERNOR

Gov. George W. Bush (R)

Elected 1994, term expires Jan. 1999; b. July 6, 1946, New Haven, CT; home, Austin; Yale U., B.A. 1968; Harvard U., M.B.A. 1975; Methodist; married (Laura).

Career: TX Air Natl. Guard, 1968–73; Founder & CEO, Bush Exploration oil & gas co., 1975–87; Sr. Advisor, Bush presidential camp., 1988; Managing General Partner, Texas Rangers baseball org., 1989–94.

Office: State Capitol, P.O. Box 12428, Austin 78711, 512-463-2000; Fax: 512-463-1847.

Election Results

1994 gen.	George W. Bush (R)	2,350,994	(53%)
	Ann W. Richards (D)	2,016,928	(46%)
	Others	28,320	(1%)
1994 prim.	Geroge W. Bush (R)	520,130	(93%)
	Ray Hollis (R)	37,210	(7%)
1990 gen.	Ann W. Richards (D)	1,925,670	(49%)
	Clayton Williams (R)	1,826,431	(47%)
	Twenty Others	140,645	(4%)

SENATORS

Sen. Phil Gramm (R)

Elected 1984, seat up 1996; b. July 8, 1942, Ft. Benning, GA; home, College Station; U. of GA, B.A. 1964, Ph.D. 1967; Episcopalian; married (Wendy).

Career: Prof., TX A&M U., 1967–78; U.S. House of Reps., 1978–84.

DC Office: 370 RSOB 20510, 202-224-2934; Fax: 202-228-2856.

State Offices: 2323 Bryan, Dallas 75201, 214-767-3000; 222 E. Van Buren., #404, Harlingen 78550, 512-423-6118; 712 Main, Houston 77002, 713-229-2766; 113 Fed. Bldg., 1205 Texas Ave., Lubbock 79401, 806-743-7533; 123 Pioneer Plz., #665, El Paso 79901, 915-534-6896; 9311 San Pedro, #565, San Antonio 78216, and InterFirst Plz., 102 N. College St., #201, Tyler 75702, 903-593-0902.

Committees: *Appropriations* (6th of 15 R): Commerce, Justice, State and Judiciary (Chmn.); Defense; Foreign Operations; Transportation; VA, HUD and Independent Agencies. *Banking, Housing & Urban Affairs* (2nd of 9 R): Financial Institutions and Regulatory Relief; HUD Oversight and Structure; Securities (Chmn). *Budget* (4th of 12 R).

Group Ratings

	ADA	ACLU	COPE	CFA	LCV	CON	NSI	COC	ACU	NTLC	CHC
1994	5	18	0	17	0	93	100	87	100	87	86
1993	5	—	0	10	6	50	—	100	92	—	—

National Journal Ratings

	1993 LIB — 1993 CONS		1994 LIB — 1994 CONS	
Economic	0%	— 87%	24%	— 75%
Social	0%	— 92%	20%	— 79%
Foreign	30%	— 69%	6%	— 86%

Key Votes of the 103d Congress

1. Clinton Deficit Plan	N	3. Brady Handgun Purchase	N	5. Lmt. UN Cmnd. of Forces	N
2. NAFTA	Y	4. Strike Race/Death Pnlty.	Y	6. Cut Missile Funds	N

Key Votes of the 104th Congress

1. Congressional Compliance	Y	3. Balanced Budget Amndt.	Y	5. Product Liability Reform	Y
2. Bar Unfunded Mandates	*	4. Pass Line Item Veto	*	6. FY96 Budget	Y

Election Results

1990 general	Phil Gramm (R)	2,302,357	(60%)	($12,349,397)
	Hugh Parmer (D)	1,429,986	(37%)	($1,677,087)
	Other.............................	89,814	(2%)	
1990 primary	Phil Gramm (R)	unopposed		
1984 general	Phil Gramm (R)	3,111,348	(59%)	($9,452,360)
	Lloyd Doggett (D)	2,202,557	(41%)	($5,887,858)

Sen. Kay Bailey Hutchison (R)

Elected June 1993, seat up 2000; b. July 22, 1943, Galveston; home, Dallas; U of TX, B.A. 1992, J.D. 1967; Episcopalian; married (Ray).

Career: Political & legal corresp., KPRC-TV, 1967–70; TX House of Reps., 1972–76; Vice Chmn., Natl. Transp. Safety Bd., 1976–78; V.P. & Gen. Cnsl., RepublicBank Corp., 1978–82; Owner, McCraw Candies, 1984–88; TX Treasurer, 1990–93.

DC Office: 283 RSOB 20510, 202-224-5922; Fax: 202-224-0776; e-mail: senator@hutchison.senate.gov.

State Offices: 10440 N. Central Expressway, #1160, Dallas 75231, 214-361-3500; 8023 Vantage Dr., #460, San Antonio 78230, 210-340-2885; and 500 Chestnut St., #1570, Abilene 79602, 915-676-2839.

Committees: *Armed Services* (9th of 11 R): Acquisition and Technology; Airland Forces; Strategic Forces. *Commerce, Science & Transportation* (8th of 10 R): Aviation; Science, Technology and Space; Surface Transportation and Merchant Marine. *Intelligence (Select)* (7th of 9 R). *Small Business* (7th of 10 R).

Group Ratings

	ADA	ACLU	COPE	CFA	LCV	CON	NSI	COC	ACU	NTLC	CHC
1994	10	33	0	17	0	95	100	100	96	82	78
1993	13	—	0	20	0	48	—	100	94	—	—

National Journal Ratings

	1993 LIB —	1993 CONS	1994 LIB —	1994 CONS
Economic	*	*	25% —	74%
Social	33% —	66%	0% —	85%
Foreign	8% —	86%	6% —	86%

Key Votes of the 103d Congress

1. Clinton Deficit Plan	N	3. Brady Handgun Purchase	Y	5. Lmt. UN Cmnd. of Forces	Y
2. NAFTA	Y	4. Strike Race/Death Pnlty.	Y	6. Cut Missile Funds	N

Key Votes of the 104th Congress

1. Congressional Compliance	Y	3. Balanced Budget Amndt.	Y	5. Product Liability Reform	Y
2. Bar Unfunded Mandates	Y	4. Pass Line Item Veto	Y	6. FY96 Budget	Y

Election Results

1994 general	Kay Bailey Hutchison (R)	2,604,218	(61%)	($6,114,755)
	Richard Fisher (D)	1,639,615	(38%)	($3,360,850)
	Others	36,107	(1%)	
1994 primary	Kay Bailey Hutchison (R)	467,975	(84%)	
	Stephen Hopkins (R)	34,703	(6%)	
	Others	52,660	(9%)	
1993 runoff	Kay Bailey Hutchison (R)	1,188,716	(67%)	($6,255,765)
	Bob Krueger (D)	576,538	(33%)	($4,582,323)
1993 special	Kay Bailey Hutchison (R)	593,338	(29%)	
	Bob Krueger (D)	593,239	(29%)	
	Joe L. Barton (R)	284,135	(14%)	
	Jack M. Fields, Jr. (R)	277,560	(14%)	
	Richard Fisher (D)	165,564	(8%)	
	Nineteen Others	131,923	(6%)	

FIRST DISTRICT

Texarkana, with a population of 50,000 and a rural and small town hinterland somewhat larger, for years was noteworthy mainly because its neat grid streets cross the Texas-Arkansas state line. The downtown post office straddles the boundary, with the west wing serving Texarkana, Texas, 75501 and the east wing Texarkana, Arkansas, 75502. Yet this small city and its hinterland produced not one but two presidential candidates in 1992: Ross Perot grew up in Texarkana, while Bill Clinton's boyhood home of Hope, Arkansas, is only 30 miles east on Interstate 30. Both grew up in comfortable but not lavish circumstances: Perot's father was a cotton broker, Clinton's stepfather a Buick dealer. Both lived in town, where the houses were shaded from the pounding summer sun by trees and most people had electricity and indoor plumbing—a vivid contrast with the countryside when Perot was growing up in the 1930s and even when Clinton was young in the late 1940s.

Did the particular atmosphere of the Texarkana area have an effect on these men's politics? One can guess that it did. Both were taught that they had obligations to those less fortunate, even while they were obliged themselves to work hard to get ahead. Texarkana was populist country then, a place where farmers producing cotton and crops felt themselves at the mercy of Dallas cotton brokers, Wall Street financiers and railroad magnates who were grabbing all the gains of their hard work. Outside Texarkana, in landscape littered with small houses amid lazily winding rivers, there was little protection from the sun and wind, and precious little ornament. The politics here was always Democratic: Clinton, who remembers his grandfather as a FDR fan, has never been anything else, while Perot seems more at ease with moderate Democrats Lloyd Bentsen and Ann Richards than with Republicans. And in Texarkana this politics was surely affected by Wright Patman, congressman from the 1st District of Texas from 1928 until his death in 1976, a populist who began his career in the House by moving to impeach Treasury Secretary Andrew Mellon, punctuated it by calling constantly for low interest rates and ended it after years as Banking Committee chairman. But culture here was always traditional: this is an area of heavy churchgoing and proud patriotism. Traces of that can be seen in Perot's military bearing and Clinton's religious cadences.

The 1st Congressional District of Texas includes most of the northeastern corner of the state—east Texas from Texarkana west to within two counties of Dallas and south almost to Lufkin. In 1985, the 1st was the scene of one of the pivotal political battles of the decade. To shake the Democrats' hold on rural southern districts, Republican Senator Phil Gramm contrived a special election in the Texas 1st by appointing the Democratic congressman, Sam Hall, to a federal judgeship and recruiting former Texas A&M and pro quarterback Edd Hargett to run as a Republican. Both national and Texas Democrats responded by pouring in money—some raised by House Speaker Jim Wright from unscrupulous S&L operators. It was a battle of giants, with Gramm and Lee Atwater on one side, Wright, Senator Lloyd Bentsen and Democratic Congressman Tony Coelho on the other. In the first contest, Hargett just missed the 50% needed to avoid a runoff. Then his miscues on trade and Social Security gave Democrat Jim Chapman a 51%–49% win. Gramm's gambit lost, but the Democrats paid a price. After S&L operators made their crucial contributions here, Jim Wright began intervening with federal regulatory agencies and bottling up S&L bills on their behalf, at an ultimate cost to government above $100 billion and an incalculable toll of public cynicism.

Jim Chapman is an able politician and a natural insider. A loyal follower of Wright, he got a seat on Appropriations in 1989. There he has been the chief Texas proponent of two very big Texas projects, the Supercollider and the Space Station Freedom. He worked hard for both, helping to save the space station in 1993 and 1994. But the scientifically more significant Supercollider was killed in late 1993. He also works on smaller local projects. With a voting record at the ideological center of the 103d Congress, he never took a solid stand on the Clinton healthcare plan and, although he sponsored a provision for more prison construction and voted for the final 1994 Crime Bill, cast four procedural votes prior to the final vote against the bill because of its ban on assault weapons.

Chapman's statewide ambitions have so far been frustrated. He hoped for Ann Richards's appointment to Lloyd Bentsen's Senate seat in 1993, but was passed over, perhaps because of his amendment to allow restaurants to transfer workers with AIDS from food-handling jobs. There is no proof the disease is spread this way and gay rights leaders opposed Chapman. He publicly mulled challenging Attorney General Dan Morales for reelection in the 1994 primary, but didn't. He was mentioned as a Senate candidate for 1994 and has been for 1996. But in 1994, Chapman got caught up in the "Movinggate" scandal, in which he admitted not paying, until 1994, Sherwood moving company for his 1986 move to Washington. Chapman was granted partial immunity by prosecutors looking into whether two other Texas congressional colleagues, Bill Sarpalius and Greg Laughlin, received favors from the company.

That did not prevent Chapman from winning in 1994, over Dr. Mike Blankenship, a kidney specialist, whom one newspaper called "memorable, in the same sense one awakens in a flash from a bad dream." Two policemen charged Blankenship with misconduct during a messy divorce. And Blakenship proudly announced, "I am probably the only candidate who owns an AK-47." Chapman won 55%–41%, a lower margin than in his last two contested races, as George W. Bush was carrying the 1st District over Ann Richards. That's not a victory that suggests Chapman has special electoral strength, and it will be harder for him to raise money now that he is in the minority. So his Senate candidacy must be regarded as iffy and it is possible he will have more serious competition in the 1st—and that Phil Gramm someday may get his way with this district.

The People: Pop. 1990: 565,594; 56% rural; 16% age 65+; 78% White; 18% Black; 1% Amer. Indian; 2% Other; 3% Hispanic origin. Voting age pop.: 415,855; 16% Black; 3% Hispanic origin. Households: 60% married couple families; 27% married couple fams. w. children; 37% college educ.; median household income: $21,697; per capita income: $10,785; median gross rent: $334; median house value: $43,600.

1992 Presidential Vote

Clinton (D) 85,771 (39%)
Bush (R) 84,545 (38%)
Perot (I) 50,567 (23%)

1988 Presidential Vote

Bush (R) 110,323 (55%)
Dukakis (D). 92,008 (45%)

Rep. Jim Chapman, Jr. (D)

Elected Aug. 1985; b. Mar. 8, 1945, Washington, D.C.; home, Sulphur Springs; U. of TX, B.A. 1968, Southern Methodist U., J.D. 1970; United Methodist; married (Betty).

Career: Practicing atty., 1970–76, 1984–85; Dist. Atty., 8th TX Judicial Dist., 1976–84.

DC Office: 2417 RHOB 202-225-3035; Fax: 202-225-7265.

District Offices: P.O. Box 538, Sulphur Springs 75482, 903-885-8682; Fed. Bldg., #G-15, 100 E. Houston St., Marshall 75670, 903-938-8386; and P.O. Box 248, New Boston 75510, 903-628-5594.

Committees: *Appropriations* (16th of 24 D): Energy and Water Development; VA, HUD, and Independent Agencies.

Group Ratings

	ADA	ACLU	COPE	CFA	LCV	CON	NSI	COC	ACU	NTLC	CHC
1994	45	45	75	20	24	35	80	67	45	29	50
1993	45	—	83	70	67	0	—	50	25	—	—

National Journal Ratings

	1993 LIB	—	1993 CONS		1994 LIB	—	1994 CONS
Economic	53%	—	46%		57%	—	43%
Social	54%	—	45%		50%	—	50%
Foreign	44%	—	55%		40%	—	59%

Key Votes of the 103d Congress

1. Clinton Deficit Plan	N	3. Brady Handgun Purchase	Y	5. Lmt. UN Cmnd. of Forces	N
2. NAFTA	Y	4. Strike Race/Death Pnlty.	N	6. Cut Missile Funds	N

Key Votes of the 104th Congress

1. Congressional Compliance	Y	6. Reform Crime Grant	N	11. Loser Pays Court Reform	N
2. Balanced Budget Amndmt.	Y	7. National Security Act	Y	12. Product Liability Reform	N
3. Bar Unfunded Mandates	Y	8. Moratorium on Regs.	Y	13. Welfare Reform	N
4. Pass Line Item Veto	Y	9. Risk Assessment on Regs.	Y	14. Term Limits Amndmt.	N
5. Relax Exclusionary Rule	Y	10. Expnd. Priv. Prop. Rights	Y	15. Tax Cuts	N

Election Results

1994 general	Jim Chapman, Jr. (D)	86,480	(55%)	($752,189)
	Mike Blankenship (R)	63,911	(41%)	($519,586)
	Others	6,001	(4%)	
1994 primary	Jim Chapman, Jr. (D)	unopposed		
1992 general	Jim Chapman, Jr. (D)	unopposed		($208,815)

SECOND DISTRICT

East Texas is thick with landmarks of Lone Star history. There's still an Indian reservation in Polk County and the Big Thicket National Preserve to remind you of what this land once looked like. Over near Beaumont is the site of Spindletop, where the world's first gusher spewed out in 1901 and started the Texas oil boom. Not far away is the huge oil field that wildcatter H. L. Hunt found in 1931, the foundation of a billion dollar fortune. Much of east Texas looks little different from the wildcat days of 50 years ago: the town squares with courthouses and churches; the stands of cheap, quick-growing pine; the rough farmland. Yet much has changed. Real incomes have tripled over 50 years, endemic diseases have been wiped out and racial segregation has been abolished, despite vestiges found in tiny Vidor. Small-town isolation has been ended by television, the interstate highway and the regional shopping mall, and metropolitan growth, sprinting outward from Houston's loop freeways, is spreading in between the pine forests and reservoirs.

The 2d Congressional District of Texas includes all or part of 19 east Texas counties, most of them still seemingly rural; it runs from the oil port of Orange past Lufkin and Nacogodoches to Jacksonville. The political tradition here is Democratic and populist, devoted to traditional values but with a taste for military posture and a certain Texas rowdiness. This is the kind of district Democrats must carry to win Texas: Ann Richards won it in 1990 and Bill Clinton in 1992 but in 1994 it voted for George W. Bush.

The 2d District's congressman is Charlie Wilson—his campaign signs just say "Charlie," with a Texas lone star dotting the 'i'—one of the genuine characters in the House. He is tall, with an aggressive military bearing, flamboyant and pleasure-loving, always ready with a wisecrack or quip, yet also serious-minded when he wants to be and even idealistic. He graduated from the Naval Academy, served four years in the Navy, then returned to east Texas and got elected to the legislature. His record in the Texas Senate got him labeled a liberal—a high-risk label then as now—but he won the House seat of a scandal-plagued conservative in the 1972 Democratic primary; a term later, he shoved aside a fellow Texan for a seat on Appropriations. Somewhat liberal on economics, he is a hawk on matters military. On Appropriations he is on the National Security Subcommittee, now under the Republicans one of the few panels charged with increasing rather than reducing spending. As the new senior Democrat on the Foreign Operations, he also will have more opportunities to influence events in trouble spots overseas. Already, he has made his mark in American, perhaps in world, history as a champion of the Afghan rebels, the man who probably more than any other member of Congress is responsible for U.S. aid to the *mujaheddin*, which helped them to force the Soviets out of their country. Wilson traveled 14 times to Afghanistan, Pakistan and South Asia in the 1980s, at least once accompanied by a former Miss USA. He started sponsoring secret appropriations for the Afghans in 1982 and kept close relations with Pakistan's leaders. More recently he has traveled in Kuwait and Somalia, dispensing advice and aid.

Wilson has had more than usual opposition in the 2d District in the 1990s, all from Donna Peterson, a West Point graduate returned to help run a family business in east Texas. Peterson has attacked Wilson for his high living, which he cheerfully admits, and his liberal votes on some issues. In 1990, capitalizing on local opposition to Wilson's backing for expansion of the Big Thicket National Preserve, she held Wilson to 56% of the vote. In 1992, she had more money and Wilson had the problem of 81 overdrafts on the House bank. "If my constituents didn't forgive sloppiness and a certain amount of eccentricity, I wouldn't be here in the first place," Wilson said, and again won with 56%. In 1994 Wilson was again dogged by charges of overusing military helicopters and womanizing. He replied, "As long as I represent them well, they don't care so much if I am a single man and have dinner with a pretty lady every now and then, although as you get to be 61, that becomes less of a concern." Republicans put little money into the race and in a dreadful Democratic year Wilson won with 57%. Having voted for the constitutional amendment to impose limits, he said that he wants to serve at least three more terms, which would take him to 2000. Since he keeps winning in adverse circumstances—and since his recent votes for the Republican Contract have shown that he has kept his bases covered—he may well do so.

The People: Pop. 1990: 565,906; 61% rural; 14% age 65+; 77% White; 17% Black; 3% Other; 5% Hispanic origin. Voting age pop.: 413,391; 15% Black; 5% Hispanic origin. Households: 61% married couple families; 28% married couple fams. w. children; 32% college educ.; median household income: $21,216; per capita income: $10,113; median gross rent: $333; median house value: $41,800.

1992 Presidential Vote			1988 Presidential Vote		
Clinton (D)	91,731	(43%)	Dukakis (D)	101,986	(52%)
Bush (R)	76,365	(35%)	Bush (R)	95,806	(48%)
Perot (I)	47,157	(22%)			

Rep. Charles Wilson (D)

Elected 1972; b. June 1, 1933, Trinity; home, Lufkin; Sam Houston St. U., 1950–51, U. of TX, 1951–52, U.S. Naval Acad., Annapolis, B.S. 1956; United Methodist; divorced.

Career: Navy, 1956–60; Mgr., lumber store & building co., 1961–72; TX House of Reps., 1960–66; TX Senate, 1966–72.

DC Office: 2256 RHOB 20515, 202-225-2401; Fax: 202-225-1764; e-mail: cwilson@hr.house.gov.

District Offices: 701 N. 1st St., #201, Lufkin 75901, 409-637-1770.

Committees: *Appropriations* (6th of 24 D): Foreign Operations, Export Financing, and Related Programs (RMM); National Security.

Group Ratings

	ADA	ACLU	COPE	CFA	LCV	CON	NSI	COC	ACU	NTLC	CHC
1994	55	55	67	38	38	36	90	67	53	36	50
1993	60	—	100	80	67	11	—	40	29	—	—

National Journal Ratings

	1993 LIB — 1993 CONS		1994 LIB — 1994 CONS	
Economic	61%	— 39%	59%	— 37%
Social	54%	— 45%	51%	— 49%
Foreign	43%	— 56%	53%	— 47%

Key Votes of the 103d Congress

1. Clinton Deficit Plan	Y	3. Brady Handgun Purchase	N	5. Lmt. UN Cmnd. of Forces	N
2. NAFTA	N	4. Strike Race/Death Pnlty.	N	6. Cut Missile Funds	N

Key Votes of the 104th Congress

1. Congressional Compliance	Y	6. Reform Crime Grant	N	11. Loser Pays Court Reform	N
2. Balanced Budget Amndmt.	Y	7. National Security Act	*	12. Product Liability Reform	N
3. Bar Unfunded Mandates	Y	8. Moratorium on Regs.	Y	13. Welfare Reform	N
4. Pass Line Item Veto	Y	9. Risk Assessment on Regs.	Y	14. Term Limits Amndmt.	Y
5. Relax Exclusionary Rule	Y	10. Expnd. Priv. Prop. Rights	Y	15. Tax Cuts	Y

Election Results

1994 general	Charles Wilson (D)	87,709	(57%)	($848,019)
	Donna Peterson (R)	66,071	(43%)	($136,188)
1994 primary	Charles Wilson (D)	55,676	(68%)	
	Edgar J. (Bubba) Groce (D)	26,635	(32%)	
1992 general	Charles Wilson (D)	118,625	(56%)	($1,193,599)
	Donna Peterson (R)	92,176	(44%)	($344,065)

THIRD DISTRICT

North Dallas's history is full of irony. This is one of America's most famous affluent, educated and Republican areas, famed as the locus of the most successful television program of the 1980s and the eponymous football novel of the 1970s, but it grew up in one of the poorest, least educated and most Democratic parts in the nation. Dallas, named for the Philadelphia lawyer who was James K. Polk's vice president, got its commercial start as the place where the first railroad in Texas stopped at the three forks of the Trinity River, surrounded by dirt-poor farm country. "Its wealth originally came from cotton," John Gunther wrote in 1946, "but primarily it is a banking and jobbing and distributing center, the headquarters of railroads and utilities." Then Dallas became one of the nation's leading high-tech cities, the home of Texas Instruments and Ross Perot's EDS, and one of the nation's major defense centers. As Dallas's private sector has demanded and rewarded expertise, it has attracted high-skill people from all over the world, and they tend to move to the north side.

On the rolling, scrub-covered hills north of downtown Dallas, this growth has built a vast affluent metropolis, extending now 30 miles out into the countryside, from the mansion-lined streets of Highland Park and Southern Methodist University's larger-than-life copy of Thomas Jefferson's University of Virginia. One of the nation's first upscale shopping centers was built here, around the Neiman Marcus store in North Park, as was the nation's first cluster of singles apartments (The Village) along Greenville Avenue. Alongside the Central Expressway, now so choked it may be double-decked, is the office tower where Ross Perot's operations are headquartered. North Dallas has long since spread east to White Rock Lake (where Stanley Marcus of Neiman Marcus lived for years) and north far past the LBJ Freeway. It has moved north beyond fast-growing Plano in Collin County. With its giant modernist office towers looming over freeways, north Dallas has become the business center of the Dallas-Fort Worth Metroplex, and indeed of a much larger territory. This is the big city nearest to the population center of the North American free trade area. With its huge airport, and its well-developed business services, north Dallas is poised to be the center of a continent.

Politically, north Dallas has moved about as far from the area's traditional populist Democrats as it could. In 1944, it backed the Texas Regular campaign against Franklin Roosevelt; in 1954 Dallas County elected Republican Bruce Alger to Congress; in 1960 its bitter, angry conservatism became notorious when Alger and others manhandled Lyndon and Lady Bird Johnson in the lobby of the Adolphus Hotel. Unanchored to traditional politics, angry that their money was being taken away by political fixers in Washington, north Dallas millionaires financed odd ducks and fanatics and made laughingstocks of themselves. But the raucousness of Dallas politics changed to remorse after President Kennedy was shot there in 1963. Today, north Dallas is no longer so alienated. Its continued economic optimism, its belief in old-fashioned hard work and new-fangled technological competence, and its entrepreneurialism have spread outward toward large parts of the rest of the nation.

The 3d Congressional District of Texas is the north Dallas district, though its boundaries are so convoluted as to defy easy description. It includes the Park Cities of Highland Park and University Park, the homes of much of the Dallas elite, and the affluent neighborhoods fanning out from the Dallas North Tollway, where Ross Perot now lives. Across town it includes the

1274   TEXAS

affluent area around White Rock Lake to the east. A narrow corridor connects most of the upscale suburbs of Garland and Richardson. From there, one salient heads south and takes in the eastern Dallas County suburbs of Mesquite and Sunnyvale, while another heads north to add Plano and other fast-growing, affluent communities that make up about half the population of Collin County. Politically, these areas are all among the most heavily Republican territory in the country, and this is one of the most Republican districts in the nation.

The congressman from the 3d District is Sam Johnson, former Air Force fighter pilot and prisoner of war in Vietnam for seven years. He won the seat in a May 1991 special election when incumbent Steve Bartlett, frustrated with being in the minority, became mayor of Dallas. Johnson had served in the Texas state house since 1984, and he ran second in the primary, with 20%, to 28% for two-time 5th District House candidate and former Peace Corps head Tom Pauken. In the runoff Johnson emphasized his war record, tended to stay above the fray and, although he showed limited knowledge of issues in debate, won by a 53%–47% margin over Pauken, who is now Texas Republican Chairman.

In the House, Johnson has had an unblemished conservative record, opposing pork barrel projects of all kinds, voting for more IRAs and against extending unemployment benefits. In October 1993, after a U.S. airman was dragged through the streets of Mogadishu, Johnson, who had visited Somalia, called for the resignation of Defense Secretary Les Aspin for his mismanagement of U.S. involvement there. Johnson sponsored a successful amendment to require school districts to permit voluntary prayer. In 1995, with his new seat on Ways and Means, he showed early support for chairman Bill Archer, his fellow Texan. Serving on the powerful committee gives Johnson many more opportunities to redirect federal policy. But—as with many other Republicans new to the majority—Johnson must show that he can take on the tough issues.

In 1994 Johnson tried to help Republicans in neighboring districts, but he could not give his most valuable commodity—his huge margin of votes—and the Democrats survived.

The People: Pop. 1990: 565,581; 2% rural; 8% age 65+; 86% White; 4% Black; 3% Asian; 2% Other; 6% Hispanic origin. Voting age pop.: 420,115; 4% Black; 5% Hispanic origin. Households: 61% married couple families; 31% married couple fams. w. children; 72% college educ.; median household income: $45,232; per capita income: $22,946; median gross rent: $534; median house value: $100,100.

1992 Presidential Vote			1988 Presidential Vote		
Bush (R)	133,834	(48%)	Bush (R)	169,019	(74%)
Perot (I)	84,097	(30%)	Dukakis (D)	58,077	(26%)
Clinton (D)	58,398	(21%)			

Rep. Sam Johnson (R)

Elected May 1991; b. Oct. 11, 1930, San Antonio; home, Dallas; Southern Methodist U., B.A. 1951, George Washington U., M.S. 1974; Methodist; married (Shirley).

Career: Air Force, 1951–79 (Korea & Vietnam); Builder; TX House of Reps., 1984–91.

DC Office: 1030 LHOB 20515, 202-225-4201; Fax: 202-225-1485; e-mail: samtx03@hr.house.gov.

District Offices: 9400 N. Central Expressway, #610, Dallas 75231, 214-767-4848.

Committees: *Economic & Educational Opportunities* (14th of 24 R): Early Childhood, Youth and Families. *Ways & Means* (15th of 21 R): Health; Oversight; Social Security.

Group Ratings

	ADA	ACLU	COPE	CFA	LCV	CON	NSI	COC	ACU	NTLC	CHC
1994	0	13	11	0	6	78	100	83	100	100	100
1993	0	—	0	10	21	74	—	100	96	—	—

National Journal Ratings

	1993 LIB — 1993 CONS		1994 LIB — 1994 CONS	
Economic	0% —	88%	0% —	80%
Social	0% —	89%	0% —	89%
Foreign	0% —	91%	0% —	88%

Key Votes of the 103d Congress

1. Clinton Deficit Plan	N	3. Brady Handgun Purchase	N	5. Lmt. UN Cmnd. of Forces	Y
2. NAFTA	Y	4. Strike Race/Death Pnlty.	Y	6. Cut Missile Funds	N

Key Votes of the 104th Congress

1. Congressional Compliance	Y	6. Reform Crime Grant	Y	11. Loser Pays Court Reform	Y
2. Balanced Budget Amndmt.	Y	7. National Security Act	Y	12. Product Liability Reform	Y
3. Bar Unfunded Mandates	Y	8. Moratorium on Regs.	Y	13. Welfare Reform	Y
4. Pass Line Item Veto	Y	9. Risk Assessment on Regs.	Y	14. Term Limits Amndmt.	Y
5. Relax Exclusionary Rule	Y	10. Expnd. Priv. Prop. Rights	Y	15. Tax Cuts	Y

Election Results

1994 general	Sam Johnson (R).....................	157,011	(91%)	($417,039)
	Tom Donahue (Lib)	15,611	(9%)	
1994 primary	Sam Johnson (R).....................	29,546	(89%)	
	David Corley (R)	2,063	(6%)	
	Dave Schum (R)......................	1,680	(5%)	
1992 general	Sam Johnson (R).....................	201,569	(86%)	($481,802)
	Noel Kopala (Lib).....................	32,570	(14%)	

FOURTH DISTRICT

The Red River Valley is one of the hearts of Texas. It is hardscrabble farm country along an unnavigable river. First settled in the 1830s, in the days of the Texas Republic, many counties here reached their population peak around 1900, when every 160 acres was worked by a large farm family with skads of children and aunts and grandparents. This was the part of Texas that first sent Speaker Sam Rayburn to Congress in 1912. The Red River then was one of the strongest Democratic parts of the country, with a sentimental regard for Confederate veterans and a seething hatred of Wall Street bankers. Today, that economic populism is muted, but traditional religious values remain strong, even as people head for work on the interstate, listen to country music on their Walkmans and shop at Wal-Marts.

The 4th Congressional District of Texas is the lineal descendant of the seat represented by Sam Rayburn for 49 years, and still includes his home town of Bonham in Fannin County. But about one-quarter of the district's people now live in the Dallas-Fort Worth Metroplex, with one-third in the small oil cities of Tyler and Longview. These are the homes of upwardly mobile families, still conservative in their cultural values, far more trusting of free markets than of government regulation. Politics here has changed as well. In 1940, when Rayburn first became speaker, his 4th Congressional District voted 90% for Franklin Roosevelt. In 1992, only 28% voted for Bill Clinton, who finished behind both Bush and Perot.

The Congressman from the 4th is Ralph Hall, a conservative Democrat of the old Tory mold, one of the few left in the House. He was first elected in 1980 after a 30-year career in local politics and business. He has one of the most conservative voting records of any House

1276　　TEXAS

Democrat, and usually does not back the leadership except on purely party matters—as shown by his unqualified voting support for the Contract With America. He once declined to vote for Tip O'Neill for speaker. He was one of two Democrats voting to expel Barney Frank on ethics charges in 1990 and he opposed the Clinton budget and tax package in 1993. But he is not a free market ideologue: he opposed NAFTA too.

Hall has been mentioned often as a possible party-switcher, but hasn't made the jump—perhaps because he had invested too much in his party label. Before 1994, that would have meant giving up majority status on the Commerce Committee, where he worked especially on telecommunications issues (he is skeptical of expansion of the baby Bells and favored cable reregulation), and the chairmanship of a space subcommittee, important for Texas. He sees no limit to the possibilities of space: "I fully and firmly believe that we're going to find some cures for the dreaded diseases, cancer and diabetes, there, because we can't find them on Earth." Hall seems to share his older constituents' mistrust of free markets as well as his younger constituents' anger at government.

Remaining a Democrat is not without risk back home. Hall has won the last two elections over the same Republican 58%–38% and 59%–40%—comfortable but not unanimous. He saw 1994 as a "wakeup call from the country to the members of Congress to get off people's back and straighten up its act." Now that he is in the minority, with less clout on committees and fewer possibilities to be the deciding vote, he is less pivotal than he used to be. Given the changing political dynamics, the *Dallas Morning News* said this should be his last term; in addition, redistricting could change the boundaries. It is possible he will retire in 1996 at 73. If he does, Democrats will be hard-pressed to keep his seat.

The People:　Pop. 1990: 567,231; 49% rural; 14% age 65+; 86% White; 8% Black; 1% Amer. Indian; 2% Other; 4% Hispanic origin. Voting age pop.: 414,229; 8% Black; 3% Hispanic origin. Households: 63% married couple families; 30% married couple fams. w. children; 45% college educ.; median household income: $26,974; per capita income: $12,724; median gross rent: $385; median house value: $57,100.

1992 Presidential Vote			1988 Presidential Vote		
Bush (R)	95,182	(41%)	Bush (R)	122,019	(63%)
Perot (I)	69,648	(30%)	Dukakis (D)	71,887	(37%)
Clinton (D)	65,522	(28%)			

Rep. Ralph M. Hall (D)

Elected 1980; b. May 3, 1923, Fate; home, Rockwall; U. of TX, TX Christian U., Southern Methodist U., LL.B. 1951; United Methodist; married (Mary Ellen).

Career:　Navy, 1942–45 (WWII); Rockwall Cnty. Judge, 1950–62; TX Senate, 1962–72; Practicing atty.; Pres. and CEO, TX Aluminum Corp.; Spec. Cnsl., Howmet Corp.

DC Office: 2236 RHOB 20515, 202-225-6673; Fax: 202-225-3332.

District Offices:　104 N. San Jacinto St., Rockwall 75087, 214-771-9118; 119 N. Fed. Bldg., Sherman 75090, 214-892-1112; 211 Fed. Bldg., Tyler 75702, 214-597-3729; and Cooke Cnty. Cthse., Gainesville 76240, 819-668-6370.

Committees:　*Commerce* (6th of 21 D): Energy and Power; Health and Environment; Telecommunications and Finance. *Science* (2nd of 23 D): Space and Aeronautics (RMM).

Group Ratings

	ADA	ACLU	COPE	CFA	LCV	CON	NSI	COC	ACU	NTLC	CHC
1994	10	22	44	30	22	65	90	92	95	79	86
1993	20	—	33	50	31	55	—	73	79	—	—

National Journal Ratings

	1993 LIB	—	1993 CONS	1994 LIB	—	1994 CONS
Economic	32%	—	66%	26%	—	70%
Social	24%	—	75%	24%	—	73%
Foreign	37%	—	60%	24%	—	75%

Key Votes of the 103d Congress

1. Clinton Deficit Plan	N	3. Brady Handgun Purchase	N	5. Lmt. UN Cmnd. of Forces	Y
2. NAFTA	N	4. Strike Race/Death Pnlty.	Y	6. Cut Missile Funds	N

Key Votes of the 104th Congress

1. Congressional Compliance	Y	6. Reform Crime Grant	Y	11. Loser Pays Court Reform	Y
2. Balanced Budget Amndmt.	Y	7. National Security Act	Y	12. Product Liability Reform	Y
3. Bar Unfunded Mandates	Y	8. Moratorium on Regs.	Y	13. Welfare Reform	Y
4. Pass Line Item Veto	Y	9. Risk Assessment on Regs.	Y	14. Term Limits Amndmt.	Y
5. Relax Exclusionary Rule	Y	10. Expnd. Priv. Prop. Rights	Y	15. Tax Cuts	Y

Election Results

1994 general	Ralph M. Hall (D)	99,303	(59%)	($559,157)
	David L. Bridges (R)	67,267	(40%)	($46,375)
	Others	2,377	(1%)	
1994 primary	Ralph M. Hall (D)	27,081	(79%)	
	Doug Dudley (D)	7,250	(21%)	
1992 general	Ralph M. Hall (D)	128,008	(58%)	($739,979)
	David L. Bridges (R)	83,875	(38%)	($34,412)
	Steven Rothacker (Lib)	8,450	(4%)	($6,283)

FIFTH DISTRICT

Not all of Dallas is glitz and postmodern marble. From each side of downtown, on one of the three street grids that run skew to each other, is an older Dallas, with neighborhoods of high-ceilinged old mansions, modest bungalows and shotgun houses running out toward the old airport at Love Field or the State Fair Grounds and the Cotton Bowl in east Dallas, or south to the desolate treeless parks along the cement-lined Trinity River. Some of this older Dallas is being renovated and rebuilt, with chic cafes and trendy stores serving those who make their livings catering to the rich farther north. Other once middle-class neighborhoods are filling up with immigrants from Mexico and other parts of Latin America, once again noisy with children as they were in the 1950s when their parents were migrants not from Mexico or Central America but from the almost all-Anglo counties of north and central Texas.

Texas's 5th Congressional District under the creative 1991 redistricting combines east Dallas, except for its black and Latino precincts, with rural central Texas into a constituency designed to reelect a Democratic congressman. In Dallas the 5th includes part of the singles neighborhood of Oak Lawn, much of the eastern edge of the city and parts of the suburbs of Garland, Mesquite and Seagoville; 56% of the district's population is in Dallas County. Then, through a narrow corridor which avoids many new subdivisions, the district goes southeast to include seven rural and small town counties about halfway between Dallas and Houston. It also reaches out to bring in black neighborhoods in Tyler and Bryan. The Dallas County precincts were chosen because they are reliably, though not overwhelmingly, Democratic; the central Texas counties have a

Democratic tradition and voted for Ann Richards in 1990.

The congressman from the 5th is John Bryant, an old-fashioned Democrat from Dallas who was born in small town Texas. He is a career politician, elected to the Texas House in 1974 two years after finishing law school. He was elected to the U.S. House in 1982 with 65% against a well-known opponent in the Democratic primary. In his first term, Bryant won a seat on the most coveted legislative committee, Commerce. In his work can be discerned a reasonably coherent set of values. He sees government as a protector of children and young people: he pushed for the Children's Television Act which limits the amount of advertising time on children's programming and passed a Children of Substance Abusers Act. He believes in greater federal regulation: of stock trading, of baby Bell long distance market access, of violent television programming, though—this is Texas—he is opposed to regulation of oil and natural gas prices. He also shares the desire rural Texans felt for years to insulate themselves against the outside world. He is hostile to immigration, doubtful that the country can produce enough jobs for its citizens if more immigrants are allowed in. As the new ranking Democrat on the Immigration Subcommittee, he is in a good position to influence an issue that historically has ignored partisan lines and that has become a hot legislative topic. He was chief sponsor of a bill to require foreign owners of U.S. companies to disclose assets, a less onerous version of which passed. On both immigration and foreign investment, Bryant seems a tribune of a native-born working class that sees demographic and economic change as a threat and that wants to maintain its current place rather than take chances on economic growth. But, like most other Texans, he backed NAFTA and GATT.

Bryant has backed Democratic versions of reform. He was one of the leading Democrats pushing the independent counsel bill, which ended up hurting the Clinton Administration. He sponsored the lobby registration bill which passed the Democratic-controlled House, which he accused then-Minority Whip Newt Gingrich of killing in 1994. In April 1992, Bryant harshly attacked Speaker Tom Foley for not being more partisanly aggressive: "Political leadership is not a responsibility he relishes." But if he is an aggressive partisan in Washington, Bryant got aggressive opposition back home in 1994 from Pete Sessions, son of former FBI Director William Sessions. Pete Sessions made a two-day, 12-city tour of the rural portions of the district with a livestock trailer full of horse manure with a sign saying, "the Clinton healthcare plan stinks worse than this trailer." ("A vulgar thing," Bryant sniffed.) He supported Dick Armey's 17% flat tax. Bryant said Sessions was too close to Newt Gingrich; Sessions said Bryant was too close to Bill Clinton.

In a district that voted for Bill Clinton in 1992, Bryant won just 50% of the vote to Sessions's 47%. Bryant had a 51%–46% lead in Dallas County and ran only 735 votes ahead in the rest of the district. In the 104th Congress, Bryant has argued that the Republicans' refusal to embrace his lobby reform bill vitiated their claims that the Contract With America constituted genuine reform of Washington. He also joined the band of Democrats harshly criticizing the ethics of Speaker Gingrich. But Bryant remains very much on the defensive. The Texas redistricting case pending in federal court in 1995 could mean everything to him. If the lines are redrawn to give him more black and Latino voters—something he says he doesn't want—so that minorities will have more minority representatives, he would be strengthened. But if the lines are redrawn to give him a geographically regular part of Dallas County and the Metroplex, this politically competent and strongly partisan Democrat could easily lose to Sessions or another Republican.

The People: Pop. 1990: 565,916; 25% rural; 12% age 65+; 64% White; 16% Black; 1% Asian; 10% Other; 17% Hispanic origin. Voting age pop.: 414,120; 15% Black; 15% Hispanic origin. Households: 53% married couple families; 26% married couple fams. w. children; 38% college educ.; median household income: $24,045; per capita income: $11,219; median gross rent: $401; median house value: $52,900.

1992 Presidential Vote

Clinton (D) 70,298 (40%)
Bush (R) 59,588 (34%)
Perot (I)................... 45,131 (26%)

1988 Presidential Vote

Bush (R) 89,284 (53%)
Dukakis (D)................ 80,495 (47%)

Rep. John Bryant (D)

Elected 1982; b. Feb. 22, 1947, Lake Jackson; home, Dallas; Southern Methodist U., B.A. 1969, J.D. 1972; United Methodist; married (Janet).

Career: Practicing atty., 1972–82; Chief Cnsl., TX Senate Consumer Affairs Subcmte., 1973; TX House of Reps., 1974–82.

DC Office: 2330 RHOB 20515, 202-225-2231; Fax: 202-225-0327.

District Offices: 8035 E. R.L.Thornton Freeway, #518, Dallas 75228, 214-767-6554.

Committees: *Commerce* (7th of 21 D): Health and Environment; Telecommunications and Finance. *Judiciary* (7th of 15 D): Commercial and Administrative Law; Immigration and Claims (RMM).

Group Ratings

	ADA	ACLU	COPE	CFA	LCV	CON	NSI	COC	ACU	NTLC	CHC
1994	80	73	67	70	78	51	11	67	5	14	14
1993	90	—	91	100	93	32	—	27	4	—	—

National Journal Ratings

	1993 LIB — 1993 CONS		1994 LIB — 1994 CONS	
Economic	68%	— 26%	67%	— 29%
Social	79%	— 20%	68%	— 31%
Foreign	93%	— 0%	85%	— 0%

Key Votes of the 103d Congress

1. Clinton Deficit Plan	Y	3. Brady Handgun Purchase	Y	5. Lmt. UN Cmnd. of Forces	N
2. NAFTA	Y	4. Strike Race/Death Pnlty.	N	6. Cut Missile Funds	Y

Key Votes of the 104th Congress

1. Congressional Compliance	Y	6. Reform Crime Grant	N	11. Loser Pays Court Reform	N
2. Balanced Budget Amndmt.	Y	7. National Security Act	N	12. Product Liability Reform	N
3. Bar Unfunded Mandates	Y	8. Moratorium on Regs.	N	13. Welfare Reform	N
4. Pass Line Item Veto	N	9. Risk Assessment on Regs.	N	14. Term Limits Amndmt.	N
5. Relax Exclusionary Rule	N	10. Expnd. Priv. Prop. Rights	*	15. Tax Cuts	N

Election Results

1994 general	John Bryant (D)	61,877	(50%)	($799,511)
	Pete Sessions (R)	58,521	(47%)	($394,401)
	Others	3,218	(3%)	
1994 primary	John Bryant (D) .... unopposed			
1992 general	John Bryant (D)	98,567	(59%)	($795,462)
	Richard Stokley (R)	62,419	(37%)	($44,542)
	William H. Walker (Lib)	6,344	(4%)	

SIXTH DISTRICT

The Dallas-Fort Worth Metroplex—yes, the name is part of everyday speech there—has spread outward from its two, different-sized historic nodes in downtown Dallas and Fort Worth and although the larger population center is in the east, in Dallas, much of the development has moved west, across the dusty plains where one crosses the barely perceptible Balcones Escarpment, the geologist's boundary between green and grassy east Texas and the brown and barren West. This was empty territory a few decades ago; now it is filling in, though with subdivisions and shopping centers that leave some feeling of the shape of this land under the enormous Texas sky.

The 6th Congressional District takes in much of this territory. It is the descendant of a district that stretched across rural territory from Dallas-Fort Worth to Houston and was represented from 1978–84 by Phil Gramm, who shifted from Boll Weevil Democrat to Reagan Republican even as the population balance shifted from rural to urban. Now the district, under the complex lines drawn in 1991, is entirely within the Metroplex. Its political center may well be Waxahachie, chosen just after Texas's George Bush was elected president to be the site of the Superconducting Supercollider, which was killed the year Bush left the White House. Waxahachie was the home base of 6th District Republican Congressman Joe Barton, who promised to stay with the giant science project, despite the outcome of redistricting. That made it unattractive to Martin Frost, the Democratic congressman whose aide drew the Texas district lines, so he gave Barton a new 6th District with convoluted lines which starts with parts of Waxahachie, then goes north through a narrow corridor to include the bulk of Arlington, its largest community and one with many defense engineers. The 1990s district includes an affluent area on the east side of Fort Worth and the Bible Belt suburbs north of Fort Worth and west of DFW Airport—Bedford, Euless, Grapevine, Colleyville. The 6th then crosses a couple of reservoirs to bypass Fort Worth on the west, except for its most affluent neighborhood around Texas Christian University, to include the rural country around Joshua. This is a collection of heavily Republican territory, and one of the two dozen most Republican districts in the nation.

Joe Barton is a feisty, aggressive, true-believing conservative who had to fight hard for this seat. In 1984, he won the Republican runoff by only 10 votes, got 57% in the general election, then won with 56% in 1986 against the well-financed Democrat Pete Geren, who since 1989 has represented the Fort Worth-based 12th District. Barton has had two great causes. One was the Supercollider, of which he was the House's most enthusiastic advocate. But despite all his efforts the House voted 282–143 to zero it out in October 1993. He has since spent much time trying to get more funding for the Supercollider closing—a big project by itself. The other cause is the constitutional balanced budget amendment. He has been the chief House sponsor of the version requiring a three-fifths vote to raise taxes. When the House took up the issue in early 1995, the issue threatened to cause a schism among House Republicans as many of the freshmen complained that party leaders were not doing enough to support that version, even though it was apparent that the three-fifths measure could not gain the needed 290 votes. Barton played a vital role in assuring that all but two Republicans voted for the final version, without tax limitation, and in gaining a promise from Speaker Gingrich to schedule the three-fifths measure for another vote in April 1996, as a possible prelude to a national campaign debate on tax limitation. He has other causes. He has pushed hard to allow sales of the F-16 fighter plane (made in Fort Worth) to Taiwan. He opposed cable regulation on the Commerce Committee. With the notable exception of his opposition to term limits, he has an almost perfectly conservative voting record.

Barton has not had success in getting other jobs. He ran for the Senate in 1993 after Lloyd Bentsen resigned to be Treasury Secretary. Despite the support of former Governor Bill Clements and strong opposition to the then-hot issue of gays in the military, he finished third with just 14% of the vote in the May all-party primary and was eliminated. In June 1994 he was outgoing Republican state Chairman Fred Meyer's choice to succeed him. But Clements opposed his candidacy, saying that Barton lacked the time and experience to do both jobs, and Barton lost at the convention to Tom Pauken. The November 1994 elections put Barton in the majority for the first time and put the spotlight both on his version of the balanced budget amendment and his efforts, as an active Commerce Committee member, to cut back federal regulation. So despite his disappointments he has become an important legislator. Also an unbeatable one: he was reelected with 76% of the vote.

The People: Pop. 1990: 566,256; 9% rural; 6% age 65+; 88% White; 5% Black; 2% Asian; 2% Other; 5% Hispanic origin. Voting age pop.: 412,594; 4% Black; 5% Hispanic origin. Households: 64% married couple families; 34% married couple fams. w. children; 67% college educ.; median household income: $41,697; per capita income: $18,824; median gross rent: $470; median house value: $92,300.

1992 Presidential Vote		
Bush (R)	127,158	(46%)
Perot (I)	83,633	(30%)
Clinton (D)	65,846	(24%)

1988 Presidential Vote		
Bush (R)	150,576	(72%)
Dukakis (D)	58,345	(28%)

Rep. Joe L. Barton (R)

Elected 1984; b. Sept. 15, 1949, Waco; home, Ennis; Texas A&M U., B.S. 1972, Purdue U., M.S. 1973; United Methodist; married (Janet).

Career: Asst. to V.P., Ennis Business Forms, 1973–81; White House Fellow, U.S. Dept. of Energy, 1981–82; Consultant, Atlantic Richfield Co., 1982–84.

DC Office: 2264 RHOB 20515, 202-225-2002; Fax: 202-225-3052; e-mail: barton06@hr.house.gov.

District Offices: 2019 E. Lamar Blvd., Arlington 76006, 817-543-1000.

Committees: *Commerce* (7th of 26 R): Health and Environment; Oversight and Investigations (Chmn.); Telecommunications and Finance. *Science* (9th of 27 R): Basic Research.

Group Ratings

	ADA	ACLU	COPE	CFA	LCV	CON	NSI	COC	ACU	NTLC	CHC
1994	0	17	13	10	13	95	100	90	100	96	93
1993	0	—	0	0	29	59	—	100	100	—	—

National Journal Ratings

	1993 LIB — 1993 CONS	1994 LIB — 1994 CONS
Economic	0% — 88%	0% — 80%
Social	18% — 81%	15% — 84%
Foreign	28% — 70%	0% — 88%

Key Votes of the 103d Congress

1. Clinton Deficit Plan	N	3. Brady Handgun Purchase N	5. Lmt. UN Cmnd. of Forces Y
2. NAFTA	Y	4. Strike Race/Death Pnlty. Y	6. Cut Missile Funds N

Key Votes of the 104th Congress

1. Congressional Compliance Y	6. Reform Crime Grant Y	11. Loser Pays Court Reform Y
2. Balanced Budget Amndmt. Y	7. National Security Act Y	12. Product Liability Reform Y
3. Bar Unfunded Mandates Y	8. Moratorium on Regs. *	13. Welfare Reform Y
4. Pass Line Item Veto Y	9. Risk Assessment on Regs. Y	14. Term Limits Amndmt. N
5. Relax Exclusionary Rule Y	10. Expnd. Priv. Prop. Rights Y	15. Tax Cuts Y

Election Results

1994 general	Joe L. Barton (R)	152,038	(76%)	($574,897)
	Terry Jesmore (D)	44,286	(22%)	($33,383)
	Others	4,688	(2%)	
1994 primary	Joe L. Barton (R)	23,063	(90%)	
	Jerry Goode (R)	2,707	(11%)	
1992 general	Joe L. Barton (R)	189,140	(72%)	($1,423,644)
	John Dietrich (D)	73,933	(28%)	($13,751)

SEVENTH DISTRICT

When George Bush moved from Midland in West Texas to Houston in 1960, he bought a house in Briarwood, in what was then near the western edge of the fast-growing city, beyond Memorial Park and Loop 610, long before the Galleria and high-rises went up around the intersection of Post Oak and Westheimer. Bush returned to Houston in 1993 and built a new house a mile from his old one. The territory is familiar: Memorial Park, the largest in Houston, is just to the east. Bush's favorite shopping mall is nearby on Sage and San Felipe and his favorite barbecue joint a mile east on Memorial; his new office is atop the Park Laureate building at 10000 Memorial. But now all these landmarks are not at the edge of the vastly bigger Houston metropolitan area, but near its epicenter, certainly its retail center and not far from its commercial center, though the industrial center of gravity remains far to the east, near the Ship Channel.

The 7th Congressional District of Texas is the lineal descendant of the district that elected George Bush its first member of the House in 1966 and 1968. It occupied far more territory then, and its boundaries have been pared back as the population of the west side of Houston has skyrocketed. There are more than 1.5 million people today in the area that had 350,000 when Bush was first elected. Indeed, in 1990 the then-7th District had 784,000 people, the second most in Texas. The district was pared back for 1992, so that it now starts just outside Memorial Park and extends west on Westheimer and the Katy Freeway and occupies part of Harris County west of Hillcroft and Bingle. It remains hyper-Republican, quite possibly the most Republican district in the nation.

The congressman from the 7th District is Bill Archer, chairman of the House Ways and Means Committee, who was elected to the House in 1970 when Bush ran for the Senate. Archer is a native Houstonian, who after service in the Air Force ran a feed business and participated in civic affairs. He was elected to the state House in 1966 as a Democrat, a very conservative one; in 1968 he switched parties and in 1970 was easily elected to the House as a Republican. His devotion to free market economics, cultural conservatism and an assertive foreign policy give him one of the most conservative voting records in the House. He joined Ways and Means in 1973, when Chairman Wilbur Mills let Republicans participate as much as Democrats. From 1975–94, when Al Ullman and Dan Rostenkowski were chairmen, Archer was given little say on most issues. Sometimes he was even a minority within his party. He opposed the 1983 Social Security bailout and was one of the Republicans who nearly scuttled the 1986 tax reform in December 1985. He opposed the budget summit agreement of 1990. In some ways his own platform is more conservative than the Contract With America. When a reporter, mistaking affability for moderation, suggested that Speaker-designate Newt Gingrich might pass over Archer for chairman because he wasn't conservative enough, Archer replied, "Surely you jest."

As chairman, Archer quickly blended his congenial style with a no-nonsense approach to meet the House's demanding schedule. "He has the ability to control with a smile on his face," Jennifer Dunn of Washington, a new committee member, told *National Journal*. "He doesn't overpower people the way that Rostenkowski might have." Under Republican control, committee meetings and legislative drafting became much more open than they had been under the Democratic majority. Archer conceded that some issues were handled at "a higher pay grade," namely by Speaker Gingrich and Majority Leader Dick Armey—a concession that it is hard to imagine from the lips of Dan Rostenkowski. For example, Gingrich worked with Governors Engler, Weld and others to craft the outlines of the welfare bill shifting most decision-making to the state, leaving Archer and his committee to write the details. Still, Archer was hardly without influence. After Gingrich briefly suggested that Republicans might rethink their opposition to welfare benefits for legal aliens, Archer later complimented the Speaker for being "willing to admit he has made a mistake." Many Democrats complained that the fix was in and that they had little opportunity to shape outcomes. Their frustration was exhibited by displays on the House floor such as Sam Gibbons, the committee's senior Democrat, yelling that Republicans should "Shut up," and normally mild-mannered John Lewis of Georgia using the word "Nazi" in reference to legislation drafted by Ways and Means Republicans.

Archer's unmistakable imprint can be seen in the Contract. Among the features of the tax cuts that the House easily passed in April was his longtime call to eliminate the alternate minimum tax, a change that would substantially benefit oil and gas producers in the Houston area plus other heavy industries. He is an ardent backer of capital gains tax cuts, higher estate and gift tax credits and expanded IRAs—all of which were part of the Contract. Other Archer goals were saved for subsequent legislation. They include higher deductions for home offices and a measure to allow homeowners who sell their homes at a loss to deduct that against a future gain from a home sale. He was less enthusiastic about the $500 per child tax credit, which Speaker Gingrich made the centerpiece of the tax bill, partly in response to pressure from the conservative pro-family coalition. As chairman, he reduced Ways and Means's membership and its budget and staff (though not as much as he had hoped) and he promised to treat Democrats respectfully—a return, he said, to Mills's day. (Not only Wilbur, but also Roger Q. Mills, the last Texas Ways and Means chairman, back in 1889.) But Archer has an even more ambitious long-term agenda. As the first Ways and Means chairman in years who fills out his own tax forms, he dislikes the complexity of the income tax, and has said, "I strongly embrace the idea of replacing it with a broad-based consumption tax." He does not seek that immediately and Congress clearly is not prepared to pass such a bill before the 1996 election. But he planned hearings on alternatives to the progressive income-tax system, in hopes of sparking discussion that could lead to a consumption tax by the end of the century.

In the meantime Archer weighs in on other issues. He strongly opposed the Clinton healthcare plan and was a major advocate of medical savings accounts. He strongly supported NAFTA, but in early 1995 seemed wary of a broad-based fast track bill authorizing trade negotiations with all of Latin America. He has proposed lowering the legal immigration level from 675,000 to 320,000. Back home, Archer has always won easily, often unopposed. He accepts no contributions from PACs or from outside Texas, and he is proud that the 7th District is one of the lowest recipients of federal funds—and intends to keep it that way. Although he voted against the term limits proposal in the Contract, he announced at that time that he would serve a maximum of three more terms. But that would give him plenty of time to make radical changes in tax and social policy before he caps a late-blooming 30-year House career.

The People: Pop. 1990: 566,440; 4% rural; 6% age 65+; 77% White; 6% Black; 6% Asian; 5% Other; 12% Hispanic origin. Voting age pop.: 413,369; 5% Black; 11% Hispanic origin. Households: 57% married couple families; 31% married couple fams. w. children; 71% college educ.; median household income: $42,157; per capita income: $23,171; median gross rent: $475; median house value: $88,000.

1992 Presidential Vote			1988 Presidential Vote		
Bush (R)	137,541	(57%)	Bush (R)	150,889	(78%)
Clinton (D)	52,501	(22%)	Dukakis (D)	41,363	(22%)
Perot (I)	49,201	(21%)			

Rep. Bill Archer (R)

Elected 1970; b. Mar. 22, 1928, Houston; home, Houston; Rice U., 1945–46, U. of TX, B.B.A. 1949, LL.B. 1951; Catholic; married (Sharon).

Career: Air Force, 1951–53; Pres., Uncle Johnny Mills Inc., 1953–61; Hunters Creek Village Cncl., Mayor Pro Tem, 1955–62; TX House of Reps., 1966–70; Dir., Heights State Bank, Houston, 1967–70; Practicing atty., 1968–71.

DC Office: 1236 LHOB 20515, 202-225-2571; Fax: 202-225-4381.

District Offices: 1003 Wirt Rd., #311, Houston 77055, 713-467-7493.

Committees: *Ways & Means* (Chmn. of 21 R). *Joint Committee on Taxation* (Chmn. of 5 Reps.).

Group Ratings

	ADA	ACLU	COPE	CFA	LCV	CON	NSI	COC	ACU	NTLC	CHC
1994	0	13	0	0	6	79	100	92	100	100	100
1993	5	—	0	0	21	69	—	91	100	—	—

National Journal Ratings

	1993 LIB — 1993 CONS		1994 LIB — 1994 CONS	
Economic	0%	— 88%	0%	— 80%
Social	0%	— 89%	0%	— 89%
Foreign	0%	— 91%	0%	— 88%

Key Votes of the 103d Congress

1. Clinton Deficit Plan	N	3. Brady Handgun Purchase	N	5. Lmt. UN Cmnd. of Forces	Y
2. NAFTA	Y	4. Strike Race/Death Pnlty.	Y	6. Cut Missile Funds	N

Key Votes of the 104th Congress

1. Congressional Compliance	Y	6. Reform Crime Grant	Y	11. Loser Pays Court Reform	Y
2. Balanced Budget Amndmt.	Y	7. National Security Act	Y	12. Product Liability Reform	Y
3. Bar Unfunded Mandates	Y	8. Moratorium on Regs.	Y	13. Welfare Reform	Y
4. Pass Line Item Veto	Y	9. Risk Assessment on Regs.	Y	14. Term Limits Amndmt.	N
5. Relax Exclusionary Rule	Y	10. Expnd. Priv. Prop. Rights	Y	15. Tax Cuts	Y

Election Results

1994 general	Bill Archer (R)	unopposed	($215,637)
1994 primary	Bill Archer (R)	unopposed	
1992 general	Bill Archer (R)	unopposed	($121,751)

EIGHTH DISTRICT

When Houston Intercontinental Airport opened in 1969, it was located far north of the city, in vacant ground near the small town of Humble (named for the oil company that was the predecessor of Exxon)—much too far, said many, from downtown Houston or from just about any other concentration of population. Today, Intercontinental is still a long way from downtown Houston—traffic jams on the way to the airport are still common—but Intercontinental is no longer in the middle of nowhere. It's in the middle of a zone of rapid metropolitan expansion and growth, of commercial office space and upscale residential subdivisions rising on land that once held roadside stands and barbecues and unpainted farmhouses with water pooling on low swampy fields. Greater Houston has spread far out into the countryside, past Loop 610 in the inner city, past the Sam Houston Tollway, past the now mislabeled Farm-Market 1960, out past Conroe and Woodbranch Village in once rural Montgomery County.

The 8th Congressional District occupies most of this territory. A district that once covered the docks along the Houston Ship Channel has moved out with the people, so that its southern boundary runs roughly along the Sam Houston Tollway. It includes almost all of Montgomery County and two still mostly rural counties to the west and takes in College Station, home of Texas A&M University. This institution deserves more notice than it usually gets: it is one of Texas's two major state universities, with quite a different atmosphere from the University of Texas at Austin. A&M, which stands for Agriculture and Mining, specializes in technical subjects, though it has other topnotch departments. It has a military lineage, though students are no longer required to serve in the cadet corps. It attracts a strongly credentialed student body that is much more conservative culturally and politically than UT's. Senator Phil Gramm used to teach economics at A&M and it is the site of the George Bush Presidential Library. College Station, and almost all the rest of the 8th District, is staunchly Republican: defiantly free market on economics, respectful of tradition on cultural issues, firmly hawkish on military policy.

The congressman from the 8th District is Jack Fields, who first won the seat when he upset a liberal Democratic incumbent in 1980. Now he is chairman of the Telecommunications and Finance Subcommittee of the Commerce Committee—arguably the most important subcommittee in Congress, charged with shaping new policies that will affect vast flows of investment and the progress of technology far into the 21st Century. Fields has kept his roots in this area even as it has changed. He lives on land his family has owned since the 1860s; he returned to Humble after being student body president at Baylor; he comes home every weekend where his family still has its business, the Rosewood Cemetery and Funeral Home, in Humble.

Even before the Republican takeover of the House in 1994, Fields was an active legislator. Telecommunications issues were often bipartisan, and he worked to forge alliances with conservative committee Democrats even when John Dingell was Commerce Committee chairman. Working with then-chairman of the subcommittee Edward Markey, Fields got the House in 1994 to pass 423–4 a telecommunications bill allowing the regional Bells and cable TV companies into the long distance market and encouraging competition in local phone service. He promised to pass a similar telecommunications bill in 1995, and called on the different interests to negotiate an agreement. He criticized Vice President Al Gore for saying that Regional Bells and cable shouldn't be allowed in long distance until their local monopolies have actually ended. Here as elsewhere Fields is a free marketeer, but not quite a perfect one. With Markey and Commerce Chairman Thomas Bliley, he supports some provisions to guard against the possibility of monopolies in an unregulated market. He launched an effort to modify the 1992 cable reregulation bill, the one law passed over President Bush's veto.

Fields has other legislative achievements and projects. Before he joined the Telecommunications and Finance Subcommittee, he worked on Clean Air legislation, and helped to pass an amendment requiring the use of reformulated gasoline in 1995 in the nine smoggiest cities. He was ranking Republican on the old Merchant Marine and Fisheries Committee, abolished for 1995, and there looked after the interests of the huge port of Houston, opposing new insurance requirements on oil tankers, for example. More important, he sponsored a private property rights bill with Louisiana Democrat Billy Tauzin, to ease intrusive regulations under the Endangered Species and Wetlands Protection Acts. He strongly supported oil drilling in the Arctic National Wildlife Refuge but in 1994 passed a law for rhino and tiger conservation and has urged sanctions against Taiwan for importing rhino horns. He has an eye for popular proposals: making prisoners ineligible for certain education grants, granting tax credits for child safety seats in cars, and laws for child boat safety. He backed the Mickey Leland satellite education program in Africa but opposed Al Gore's GLOBE program to pay schoolchildren to monitor air quality.

When Fields was first elected, the 8th District was centered on Houston's port, and leaned

Democratic. Now it has moved outward, and it is heavily Republican, in part to allow creation of heavily black and Hispanic districts in the city. Fields has shown he can raise very large sums, and has won reelection without difficulty. However, when he ran for the Senate to fill Lloyd Bentsen's seat in 1993, he finished fourth with 14% in the May all-party primary, just behind 6th District Congressman Joe Barton. But that may be the only blemish in a still-young career that may before long land him in the powerful position of Commerce Committee chairman.

The People: Pop. 1990: 566,572; 35% rural; 7% age 65+; 85% White; 5% Black; 2% Asian; 3% Other; 7% Hispanic origin. Voting age pop.: 408,402; 5% Black; 6% Hispanic origin. Households: 64% married couple families; 35% married couple fams. w. children; 58% college educ.; median household income: $35,454; per capita income: $15,998; median gross rent: $439; median house value: $78,200.

1992 Presidential Vote			1988 Presidential Vote		
Bush (R)	134,184	(55%)	Bush (R)	134,412	(73%)
Clinton (D)	55,917	(23%)	Dukakis (D)	49,815	(27%)
Perot (I)	55,199	(23%)			

Rep. Jack M. Fields, Jr. (R)

Elected 1980; b. Feb. 3, 1952, Humble; home, Humble; Baylor U., B.A. 1974, J.D. 1977; Baptist; married (Lynn).

Career: Practicing atty., 1977–80; Vice Pres., Rosewood Memorial Funeral Home, 1977–80.

DC Office: 2228 RHOB 20515, 202-225-4901; Fax: 202-225-2772.

District Offices: 111 E. University Dr., #216, College Station 77840, 409-846-6068; 300 W. Davis, #507, Conroe 77301, 409-756-8044; and 9810 FM1960 Bypass W., #165, Deerbrook Plz., Humble 77338, 409-540-8000.

Committees: *Commerce* (3rd of 26 R): Commerce, Trade and Hazardous Materials (Vice Chmn.); Telecommunications and Finance (Chmn.).

Group Ratings

	ADA	ACLU	COPE	CFA	LCV	CON	NSI	COC	ACU	NTLC	CHC
1994	0	13	11	20	0	62	100	91	100	100	100
1993	0	—	0	0	21	74	—	90	100	—	—

National Journal Ratings

	1993 LIB — 1993 CONS		1994 LIB — 1994 CONS	
Economic	0% —	88%	30% —	70%
Social	0% —	89%	0% —	89%
Foreign	0% —	91%	0% —	88%

Key Votes of the 103d Congress

1. Clinton Deficit Plan	N	3. Brady Handgun Purchase	N	5. Lmt. UN Cmnd. of Forces	Y
2. NAFTA	Y	4. Strike Race/Death Pnlty.	Y	6. Cut Missile Funds	N

Key Votes of the 104th Congress

1. Congressional Compliance	Y	6. Reform Crime Grant	Y	11. Loser Pays Court Reform	Y
2. Balanced Budget Amndmt.	Y	7. National Security Act	Y	12. Product Liability Reform	Y
3. Bar Unfunded Mandates	Y	8. Moratorium on Regs.	Y	13. Welfare Reform	Y
4. Pass Line Item Veto	Y	9. Risk Assessment on Regs.	Y	14. Term Limits Amndmt.	Y
5. Relax Exclusionary Rule	Y	10. Expnd. Priv. Prop. Rights	Y	15. Tax Cuts	Y

Election Results

1994 general	Jack M. Fields, Jr. (R)	148,473	(92%)	($709,896)
	Russ Klecka (I)	12,831	(8%)	
1994 primary	Jack M. Fields, Jr. (R)	unopposed		
1992 general	Jack M. Fields, Jr. (R)	179,349	(77%)	($746,361)
	Charles Robinson (D)	53,473	(23%)	

NINTH DISTRICT

The spongy land of the Texas Gulf Coast, where the French explorer LaSalle and the Spanish colonizer Galvez dreamed of thriving settlements, remained mostly unsettled until well into the 20th Century. The elements here are not gentle, as Galveston learned when a hurricane in 1900 destroyed this city on a sandspit; the summer heat is ferocious and the rains torrential; few crops grow well here. But this is a land of oil. Ever since the Spindletop strike in Beaumont in 1901, southeast Texas has grown. First oil exploration, then petroleum refining, then petrochemicals: the straight-edged metal of oil rigs and the intricate curving metalwork of refineries shine through the swampy landscape of southeast Texas. And the rig workers and mechanical engineers they brought here have given a kind of permanent roughneck air to the region.

The 9th Congressional District of Texas occupies much of this territory. About half its people live in and around Beaumont and Port Arthur, still very much oil country, and one of the few places in Texas where labor unions have ever had much strength. The other half live south of Houston—in Galveston, now restoring its grand historic buildings (and the unlikely site of a Dickensian Christmas celebration every year), and the refinery town of Texas City, where more than 500 died in a huge liquefied natural gas tanker explosion in 1947, and the Lyndon B. Johnson Space Center, where America's probes into space are planned, brought here originally by then-Vice President Lyndon Johnson and longtime Houston Congressman Albert Thomas.

The congressman from the 9th District is Steve Stockman, a Republican and the slayer of one of the most fearsome congressional dragons, the man who would have been dean of the House had he been reelected, Jack Brooks. With his thick accent, unlit cigar, the chair of the Judiciary Committee and the confidence of a man who went one-on-one with Lyndon Johnson, Brooks had the strengths and weaknesses of the old congressional order. He butted heads with John Dingell over telecommunications and looked after the interests of trial lawyers. His last major bill, the crime bill, proved to be his undoing. He supported and helped to draft the Democrats' version, though he had long opposed gun control, so that he could add pork barrel measures. The announcement of a $10 million grant to his alma mater, Lamar University in Beaumont, before Republicans or even Democrats had a chance to see the bill he reported out of conference committee, fueled Republicans' rage and enabled Newt Gingrich to get enough pro-gun control moderates to vote against the rule on the crime bill in August 1994—the pebble that sent the Democrats' House fortress tumbling down. Brooks tumbled too. Although he had voted against the assault weapons ban in separate legislation, his support for a bill including gun control was used heavily against him.

Stockman is an unlikely Texas politician, an accountant who grew up in Michigan. He was one of the many "black tag" (from their license plates) unemployed men from Michigan who came to Texas in 1980 seeking a job; for a time he was unemployed and homeless. Only at age 34 did he get his bachelor's degree, and by then, a convinced conservative, he was running for Congress. Jack Brooks was not an easy target. In 1990, he spent $885,000 and beat Stockman 58%–42%. In 1992, though redistricting strengthened Brooks slightly and Bill Clinton was carrying the district, Stockman narrowed the margin to 54%–44%. In 1994, Brooks, strongly supported by trial lawyers, spent $1.1 million. But the man George Will called "the number one stumbling block for term limits and the number one argument for them" was defeated 52%–46%. Brooks carried Beaumont and Jefferson County, but only barely, 52%–46%, and lost usually Democratic Galveston County and was whipped 2–1 in the Harris County area around the Space Center.

Stockman quickly gained attention in the House, not all of it favorable: he told *Roll Call*, the Capitol Hill newspaper, that he and his staff prayed together each morning before their regular meeting. Although the move surely played well back home, he antagonized Speaker Gingrich by opposing the U.S. bailout of the Mexican peso, which had been delicately crafted in a high-level bipartisan deal. Stockman was thrust onto the national stage in the days following the bombing of an Oklahoma City federal building when it was revealed that his office received a fax regarding the bombing on the day of the tragedy from a woman affiliated with militia organizations. Stockman criticized media reports implying that he contacted the NRA about the fax before sending it to the FBI. It was later confirmed that he sent the fax to the FBI within hours of receiving it, but he was hurt by acknowledging that he wrote Attorney General Janet Reno a letter expressing concern about planned raids in Texas on militia organizations. In this Democratic-leaning district, he is likely to have a serious challenge in 1996, but unlike Brooks he is not looking to serve 42 years.

The People: Pop. 1990: 566,154; 13% rural; 11% age 65+; 67% White; 22% Black; 2% Asian; 3% Other; 9% Hispanic origin. Voting age pop.: 410,542; 20% Black; 8% Hispanic origin. Households: 56% married couple families; 27% married couple fams. w. children; 47% college educ.; median household income: $29,420; per capita income: $13,745; median gross rent: $398; median house value: $52,700.

1992 Presidential Vote			1988 Presidential Vote		
Clinton (D)	98,959	(44%)	Dukakis (D)	104,860	(54%)
Bush (R)	80,813	(36%)	Bush (R)	90,445	(46%)
Perot (I)	47,418	(21%)			

Rep. Steve Stockman (R)

Elected 1994; b. Nov. 14, 1956, Bloomfield Hills, MI; home, Friendswood; U. of Houston, B.S. 1990; Baptist; married (Patti).

Career: Accountant, 1990–94.

DC Office: 417 CHOB 20515, 202-225-6565; Fax: 202-225-1584.

District Offices: 2490 McFadin, Beaumont 77702, 409-838-0061; and 2102 Mechanic, #107, Galveston 77550, 409-766-3608.

Committees: *Banking & Financial Services* (24th of 27 R): Capital Markets, Securities and Government Sponsored Enterprises; General Oversight and Investigations. *Science* (19th of 27 R): Energy and Environment; Space and Aeronautics.

Group Ratings and 103rd Congress Votes: Newly Elected

Key Votes of the 104th Congress

1. Congressional Compliance	Y	6. Reform Crime Grant	Y	11. Loser Pays Court Reform	Y
2. Balanced Budget Amndmt.	Y	7. National Security Act	Y	12. Product Liability Reform	Y
3. Bar Unfunded Mandates	Y	8. Moratorium on Regs.	Y	13. Welfare Reform	Y
4. Pass Line Item Veto	Y	9. Risk Assessment on Regs.	Y	14. Term Limits Amndmt.	*
5. Relax Exclusionary Rule	N	10. Expnd. Priv. Prop. Rights	Y	15. Tax Cuts	Y

Election Results

1994 general	Steve Stockman (R)	81,353	(52%)	($245,547)
	Jack Brooks (D)	71,643	(46%)	($1,202,868)
	Others	3,801	(2%)	
1994 primary	Steve Stockman (R)	8,644	(73%)	
	John LeCour (R)	2,468	(21%)	
	James C. Milburn (R)	802	(7%)	
1992 general	Jack Brooks (D)	118,690	(54%)	($471,285)
	Steve Stockman (R)	92,270	(44%)	($98,622)
	Other	6,401	(3%)	

TENTH DISTRICT

Austin, the capital of the second largest state in the United States and site of its largest Capitol building, is also the southernmost capital in the continental 48 states. It is one of many capitals with a first-rate university, the University of Texas, but one of the few (Nashville is the obvious other) with its own musical tradition, symbolized by Willie Nelson. Not so long ago Austin seemed as laid-back and countrified as Nelson himself. There has never been much commerce here, and for much of the year the Capitol basked in a sun that seemed to ban gainful employment. Its skies were untainted with the smoke of industry, its ground unpocked with pumping oil rigs, its main street lined not with business offices but with buildings holding a few lobbyists and the antique Driskill Hotel.

Today Austin is quite different: if not bustling, it is busy; if it is still laid-back, it is everywhere air-conditioned; if the Driskill still stands, glass high-rises have popped up all over downtown, to the south and far to the north in what was once lonely hill country. Sparking the change is the University of Texas. Endowed with thousands of west Texas acres that turned out to sit on top of oil, the nation's largest single university campus is here in Austin. With some 50,000 students, it has a tower at its symbolic center that looms high over the campus, and houses the exemplary LBJ Presidential Library with its 35 million documents. The University has spawned a community of liberal intellectuals since the 1950s and a high-tech industry that started booming in the 1980s, symbolized when Austin was selected in 1983 as the site of the Microelectronics and Computer Technology Corporation research consortium. Austin is now one of America's four or five leading high-tech centers. The Austin metropolitan area grew 46% in the 1980s—the fastest pace of growth of any similar-sized or larger metro area outside of Florida and Las Vegas—and has continued to grow in the 1990s. The Austin city limits have expanded, and vast new tracts of houses have been built north of the old town, far beyond the Capitol and the University, and south of the Colorado River. Soon-to-be-closed Bergstrom Air Force Base has been suggested as the site for a larger, much needed new airport.

Historically Democratic, Austin moved toward the Republicans in the 1980s, but not all the way. The new subdivisions in the north vote Republican, though less than similar places in Houston or Dallas. The University area is still heavily Democratic. In 1992, Austin's Travis County voted for Bill Clinton over George Bush by a 47%–32% margin; in 1994, it voted 59%–41% for former Travis County Commissioner Ann Richards over George W. Bush. The new affluent techie residents have built a bigger Republican base than in the old Austin. But as in other high-tech areas, Research Triangle and Silicon Valley, the cultural politics of the 1990s has driven voters back to the Democrats.

The 10th District of Texas, which once spread over the Hill Country to the west and south, now is entirely within Travis County: essentially Austin and its suburban fringe. It is the descendant of the 10th District which in April 1937 elected a gangly-looking 29-year-old New Dealer named Lyndon Johnson. Johnson gave up the seat to make his second, and successful, run for the Senate in 1948. His friend Homer Thornberry won the seat and held it until he became a federal judge in December 1963. Another LBJ backer, Jake Pickle, was elected that month and served until he retired in 1994—57 years of representation from three political allies, all born between 1908 and 1913. Pickle, kindly and conscientious, but tough when pressed, played a key role in the 1983 Social Security bailout and was consistently reelected without trouble.

The current congressman is Lloyd Doggett, a liberal Democrat with a dream resume and an up-and-down political career. Doggett grew up in Austin, finished first in his class and was president of the student body at UT in 1967. In 1972, he was elected to the state Senate at 26: he is the same age as Bill Clinton, who spent that fall in Austin as the Texas McGovern coordinator. Doggett was part of the surprisingly large bloc of liberals in the Texas Senate and pushed laws against job discrimination and copkiller bullets and for generic drugs. He had a certain flair. He was one of the "killer bees" who hid out to prevent a quorum on changing the rules in the Democratic primary and filibustered—wearing sneakers—against what he called an anti-consumer bill.

Doggett, vastly popular in Austin, is somewhat less so in the rest of the state. In 1984 he ran for the U.S. Senate, narrowly edging out future Senator Bob Krueger in the primary and conservative Congressman Kent Hance in the runoff. Then, despite the campaign help of James Carville, Doggett lost the general by a resounding 59%–41% to party-switching Congressman Phil Gramm, who attacked him sharply for holding a fund raiser at a San Antonio gay strip bar. Doggett came back and, with strong support from trial lawyers, was elected to the Texas Supreme Court in 1988. When Pickle retired, Doggett left that position and ran for Congress. He won the Democratic primary with only token opposition and in the general outpolled black Republican Jo Baylor. Campaigning strongly on the 1994 crime bill, endorsing its death penalties and assault weapons ban, Doggett won by the solid, but not quite overwhelming, margin of 56%–40%. This seems likely to be a safe seat for him, and he has the seniority edge that goes to members who first win in years that are bad for their party. With his significant experience, he emerged quickly as a party spokesman and Gingrich-basher. But he must enter the House with some disappointment that the causes which he has championed so ably and so long are so much on the defensive, and that his vision of the future appeals to so few in the rest of Texas, and by no means to everyone in Austin.

The People: Pop. 1990: 566,357; 8% rural; 7% age 65+; 65% White; 11% Black; 3% Asian; 13% Other; 21% Hispanic origin. Voting age pop.: 430,048; 10% Black; 18% Hispanic origin. Households: 45% married couple families; 23% married couple fams. w. children; 64% college educ.; median household income: $27,280; per capita income: $14,978; median gross rent: $415; median house value: $76,700.

1992 Presidential Vote		
Clinton (D)	128,813	(48%)
Bush (R)	84,560	(32%)
Perot (I)	54,304	(20%)

1988 Presidential Vote		
Dukakis (D)	126,311	(55%)
Bush (R)	102,287	(45%)

Rep. Lloyd Doggett (D)

Elected 1994; b. Oct. 6, 1946, Austin; home, Austin; U. of TX, B.B.A. 1967, J.D. 1970; Methodist; married (Libby).

Career: Practicing atty., 1970–89; TX Senate, 1973–85; Adjunct Prof., U. of TX Law Schl., 1989–94; TX Supreme Ct. Justice, 1989–94.

DC Office: 126 CHOB 20515, 202-225-4865; Fax: 202-225-3073; e-mail: doggett@hr.house.gov.

District Offices: 763 Fed. Bldg., 300 E. 8th St., Austin 78701, 512-482-5921.

Committees: *Budget* (18th of 18 D). *Science* (20th of 23 D): Basic Research.

Group Ratings and 103rd Congress Votes: Newly Elected

Key Votes of the 104th Congress

1. Congressional Compliance Y	6. Reform Crime Grant N	11. Loser Pays Court Reform N
2. Balanced Budget Amndmt. N	7. National Security Act N	12. Product Liability Reform N
3. Bar Unfunded Mandates Y	8. Moratorium on Regs. N	13. Welfare Reform N
4. Pass Line Item Veto Y	9. Risk Assessment on Regs. N	14. Term Limits Amndmt. N
5. Relax Exclusionary Rule N	10. Expnd. Priv. Prop. Rights N	15. Tax Cuts N

Election Results

1994 general	Lloyd Doggett (D)	113,738	(56%)	($567,552)
	A. Jo Baylor (R)	80,382	(40%)	($374,706)
	Others	7,866	(4%)	
1994 primary	Lloyd Doggett (D)	33,682	(83%)	
	John Longsworth (D)	7,130	(17%)	
1992 general	J.J. (Jake) Pickle (D)	177,233	(68%)	($363,561)
	Herbert Spiro (R)	68,646	(26%)	($117,934)
	Others	16,013	(6%)	

ELEVENTH DISTRICT

Waco, Texas, at the intersection of lines from Dallas to Austin and Houston to Amarillo, is arguably the geographic and cultural heart of Texas. The accent here may be the purest Texas accent around: listen to former Governor Ann Richards, a Waco native. Waco is now a city of over 100,000, but the farm fields and small towns all around recall the state as it was years ago, before the growth of the oil industry transformed Texas from a rural backwater into one of the centers of western capitalism, while the latest extravagances of affluent metropolitan Texas can be sampled at gallerias of the Dallas-Fort Worth Metroplex, a little more than an hour away on I-35. Some of Texas's characteristic institutions cluster around Waco: Baylor University, the oldest college in Texas and the largest Baptist university in the world, and Fort Hood, the Army's second largest installation, which occupies much of next-door Bell and Coryell Counties and employs just under 50,000 military personnel and civilians. The odd-duck violence which is also part of Texas's history flared here in February 1993 when agents of the Bureau of Alcohol, Tobacco and Firearms moved in on David Koresh's Branch Davidian compound, Ranch Apocalypse, near Waco, until agents stormed the compound and Koresh and his followers immolated themselves.

The 11th Congressional District of Texas is centered on Waco and the Fort Hood area. It includes all or most of 12 counties, most of them still rural, which are ancestrally Democratic. But that loyalty has slowly waned. Ann Richards carried the 11th with 51% in 1990, but lost it to George W. Bush 52%–47% in 1994. In congressional politics the 11th has remained Democratic thanks to strong candidates—Marvin Leath, who won the seat after 42-year incumbent Bob Poage retired in 1978, and Chet Edwards, who was elected to succeed Leath in 1990.

Edwards is one of those highly skilled and motivated Democrats who has made politics his life—and who made the House ever Democratic until 1994. In 1978, after three years as a staffer to Congressman Olin Teague, Edwards ran at age 27 for the 6th District House seat Teague was vacating. In the first Democratic primary, Edwards wound up in third place, just 115 votes behind his former Texas A&M economics professor Phil Gramm, who went on to win the seat; if Edwards had won just 116 more votes, a lot of Texas and national political history would be different. Edwards went off to Harvard to get an M.B.A., returned and moved to Duncanville in southwest Dallas County, and at age 31 ran for the state Senate in 1982 and won. There he made a moderate-to-liberal record, helping to incorporate Texas into the Super Tuesday primary and working to attract the Supercollider, bucking the unions and trial lawyers on workmen's compensation reform.

In 1990, when Leath retired, Edwards dropped his race for lieutenant governor, moved his residence to Waco (the Senate district overlapped), and ran for the 11th District seat unopposed in the Democratic primary. In the Republican primary, Bell County legislator Hugh Shine beat two former mayors of Waco despite being a party-switcher who was a Mondale delegate in San Francisco in 1984. In the general, Shine emphasized his military experience and attacked Edwards for attending a gay and lesbian fund raiser. Edwards got a promise of an National Security Committee slot from Speaker Foley and strong support from Leath. Shine carried Bell County, but Edwards got 56% in Waco's McLennan County and carried all the rural counties.

In the House, with the promised seat on National Security and one on Veterans' Affairs, Edwards immediately bucked the Democratic leadership and voted for the Gulf war resolution. He was also one of the Democratic "Gang of Six" who launched an effort for the balanced budget amendment and tried to get 1992 freshmen Democrats to initiate reform. They dropped the ball; he hasn't. He turned back over $200,000 in office funds, regularly voted for the balanced budget amendment—including 1995—and opposed the Clinton budget and tax package. He worked on National Security for Fort Hood and the Veterans' Committee helped with the large number of veterans here. He joined others in killing a proposal to designate parts of 33 Texas counties as a critical habitat for the endangered golden-cheeked warbler and supports the Private Property Owners Bill of Rights. He voted against the Brady bill but for the assault weapons ban and the 1994 crime bill. In 1992, he managed the campaign of Sonny Montgomery to retain the Veterans chair over the younger Lane Evans.

His efforts to blend party loyalty with the votes of a southern conservative left Edwards as part of a diminishing breed but also made him a logical candidate for one of the Democrats' four chief deputy whip posts, a symbol of his rising influence but a challenging task given the Democratic Caucus's steady move leftward. When Minority Leader Dick Gephardt in December 1994 appointed Edwards to the job, he characteristically replied, "I did not ask for this job and I will not change my political independence to keep it." In another era, when Texas was less Republican, he would have been an obvious candidate for statewide office. Edwards works the district hard, and his voting record and personality clearly have struck a chord. He won in 1992 with 67% of the vote and in 1994 with 59%, running 12% ahead of Richards in her home area.

The People: Pop. 1990: 566,280; 29% rural; 13% age 65+; 70% White; 16% Black; 2% Asian; 6% Other; 12% Hispanic origin. Voting age pop.: 413,467; 15% Black; 10% Hispanic origin. Households: 60% married couple families; 30% married couple fams. w. children; 43% college educ.; median household income: $22,283; per capita income: $10,630; median gross rent: $362; median house value: $49,700.

1992 Presidential Vote

Bush (R) 75,545 (41%)
Clinton (D) 66,440 (36%)
Perot (I). 42,305 (23%)

1988 Presidential Vote

Bush (R) 97,765 (58%)
Dukakis (D). 70,916 (42%)

Rep. Chet Edwards (D)

Elected 1990; b. Nov. 24, 1951, Corpus Christi; home, Waco; TX A&M U., B.A. 1974, Harvard, M.B.A. 1981; Methodist; married (Lea Ann).

Career: Legis. and Dist. Dir., U.S. Rep. Olin Teague, 1975–77; Marketing rep., Trammell Crow Co., 1981–85; TX Senate, 1982–90; Pres., Edwards Communications, 1985–90.

DC Office: 328 CHOB 20515, 202-225-6105; Fax: 202-225-0350.

District Offices: 710 University Tower, 700 S. University Parks Dr., Waco 76706, 817-752-9600.

Committees: *Chief Deputy Minority Whip. National Security* (14th of 25 D): Military Procurement; Military Readiness. *Veterans' Affairs* (4th of 15 D): Hospitals and Health Care (RMM).

Group Ratings

	ADA	ACLU	COPE	CFA	LCV	CON	NSI	COC	ACU	NTLC	CHC
1994	45	30	44	60	33	41	90	75	38	46	64
1993	35	—	67	70	64	4	—	55	33	—	—

National Journal Ratings

	1993 LIB — 1993 CONS		1994 LIB — 1994 CONS	
Economic	42%	— 57%	50%	— 46%
Social	55%	— 45%	47%	— 52%
Foreign	51%	— 42%	57%	— 37%

Key Votes of the 103d Congress

1. Clinton Deficit Plan	N	3. Brady Handgun Purchase	N	5. Lmt. UN Cmnd. of Forces	N
2. NAFTA	Y	4. Strike Race/Death Pnlty.	Y	6. Cut Missile Funds	N

Key Votes of the 104th Congress

1. Congressional Compliance	Y	6. Reform Crime Grant	N	11. Loser Pays Court Reform	N
2. Balanced Budget Amndmt.	Y	7. National Security Act	N	12. Product Liability Reform	Y
3. Bar Unfunded Mandates	Y	8. Moratorium on Regs.	Y	13. Welfare Reform	N
4. Pass Line Item Veto	Y	9. Risk Assessment on Regs.	Y	14. Term Limits Amndmt.	N
5. Relax Exclusionary Rule	Y	10. Expnd. Priv. Prop. Rights	Y	15. Tax Cuts	N

Election Results

1994 general	Chet Edwards (D).	76,667	(59%)	($420,832)
	Jim Broyles (R).	52,876	(41%)	($52,992)
1994 primary	Chet Edwards (D).	unopposed		
1992 general	Chet Edwards (D).	119,999	(67%)	($420,880)
	Jim Broyles (R).	58,033	(33%)	($17,150)

TWELFTH DISTRICT

Fort Worth, Texas, has a fair claim to being the quintessential mid-American city: halfway across the continent, midway between the oceans, just west of the Balcones Escarpment that divides the dry treeless grazing lands of west Texas from the humid green croplands of the east. It is southern in heritage and northern in its advanced post-industrial economy. It has the nation's biggest row of Western wear shops and one of the nation's richest families, the Basses, whose steel-sheen skyscrapers, outlined at night by lights, dominate the skyline. This is where the West begins, Fort Worth boosters say, adding, as Will Rogers said, that Dallas is "where the East peters out." This is not a primitive West. Fort Worth has a high-tech economy, though one hard hit by defense cuts. The big General Dynamics plant that produced so many U.S. bombers has been sold to Lockheed; next-door Carswell Air Force Base, the home of B-52s for years, was slated for closure in 1993 but was turned into a Joint Reserve Base in late 1994. The assembly lines at Bell Helicopter's nearby plant were kept going only when the Texas delegation and others overruled the cancellation of the V-22 Osprey. Fort Worth also has some of the nation's premier small museums, the Amon Carter Museum of Western Art, Louis Kahn's gem The Kimbell Museum and the Will Rogers Coliseum with exhibits of Texas history. Other cities have their claims, but the visitor from abroad who wants to see what is quintessentially American would be well advised to head to Fort Worth.

The 12th District of Texas is still centered on Fort Worth. Its highly convoluted boundaries for 1992 and 1994 include much of the city, though not its poorest black or richest white areas, which are in the 24th and 6th Districts. It also extends south and west in a whorl around Fort Worth, taking in much of rural Johnson and Parker Counties, including Weatherford, where Speaker Jim Wright got his start in politics. Fort Worth's political heritage is Democratic, but lately it has been trending Republican. For 34 years the 12th District was represented by Wright, speaker of the House from 1987 until he was forced to resign in June 1989. Wright was first elected to Congress in 1954 after a primary victory over an anti-labor Democrat in this still dusty blue-collar town, in contrast to white-collar Dallas, which was electing its first Republican congressman the same year. Now Fort Worth is more diverse, with extensive rich as well as poor neighborhoods, and Tarrant County, with a population boom in Arlington between Fort Worth and Dallas, has become as Republican as Dallas County if not more so.

The congressman from the 12th now is Pete Geren, one of the more conservative Democrats in the House. Geren is from a prominent Fort Worth family. In the mid-1980s he served on Senator Lloyd Bentsen's staff, then returned to Fort Worth, invested in a restaurant and ran against 6th District Congressman Joe Barton in 1986, and held Barton to a 56%–44% win. After Wright's resignation, Geren ran again, and was opposed on all sides. Democrat Jim Lane was supported by labor and attacked Geren's support of a capital gains tax cut; Republican Bob Lanier, a pediatric allergist known as "Dr. Bob" for his Dallas-Forth Worth Metroplex TV appearance on *60 Second Housecall*, was running as a Republican with Senator Phil Gramm's support. Lanier led the first primary, 39%–32%. But Geren capitalized on Lanier's mistakes—he hadn't voted in 1988 and couldn't identify the Second Amendment as granting the right to bear arms while backing some limits on gun ownership—and won the runoff by just 51%–49%.

Geren is fiscally cautious, pro-defense, opposed to "blindly issuing rules and regulations without regard to their costs" and was the unofficial leader of the "Gang of Six" Democrats backing the balanced budget constitutional amendment. His strong support for the Contract With America didn't win many plaudits in the Democratic Caucus but it likely will help to keep him in office. With the help of a National Security Committee seat, he has worked to promote the Fort Worth-built F-16 and to get the Pentagon to designate it as the primary suppression of enemy air defenses (SEAD) platform. On foreign affairs, he has traveled to northwest India and in August 1993, introduced a resolution in the House supporting the Sikhs and calling for a United Nations plebiscite for Punjab independence.

Geren won reelection with an impressive 69% in 1994 and does not seem likely to be targeted by Republicans in 1996. But redistricting could change the boundaries of the 12th to his disadvantage.

The People: Pop. 1990: 565,988; 13% rural; 12% age 65+; 74% White; 8% Black; 1% Amer. Indian; 2% Asian; 9% Other; 16% Hispanic origin. Voting age pop.: 412,521; 7% Black; 14% Hispanic origin. Households: 57% married couple families; 28% married couple fams. w. children; 43% college educ.; median household income: $27,366; per capita income: $12,641; median gross rent: $402; median house value: $57,200.

1992 Presidential Vote

Clinton (D)	76,637	(38%)
Bush (R)	70,522	(35%)
Perot (I)	55,951	(28%)

1988 Presidential Vote

Bush (R)	102,339	(56%)
Dukakis (D)	80,239	(44%)

Rep. Pete Geren (D)

Elected Sept. 1989; b. Jan. 29, 1952, Ft. Worth; home, Ft. Worth; U. of TX, B.A. 1974, J.D. 1978; Baptist; married (Beckie).

Career: Practicing atty., 1979–84, 1985–89; Exec. asst., U.S. Sen. Lloyd Bentsen, 1984–85; Restaurant owner, 1986–91.

DC Office: 2448 RHOB 20515, 202-225-5071; Fax: 202-225-2786.

District Offices: 1600 W. 7th St., #740, Ft. Worth 76102, 817-338-0909.

Committees: *National Security* (20th of 25 D): Military Procurement; Military Research and Development. *Science* (6th of 23 D): Basic Research (RMM).

Group Ratings

	ADA	ACLU	COPE	CFA	LCV	CON	NSI	COC	ACU	NTLC	CHC
1994	15	35	33	40	17	63	100	92	67	68	93
1993	20	—	33	50	43	57	—	91	75	—	—

National Journal Ratings

	1993 LIB — 1993 CONS		1994 LIB — 1994 CONS	
Economic	34%	— 65%	41%	— 58%
Social	38%	— 61%	20%	— 77%
Foreign	47%	— 50%	45%	— 54%

Key Votes of the 103d Congress

1. Clinton Deficit Plan	N	3. Brady Handgun Purchase	N	5. Lmt. UN Cmnd. of Forces	N
2. NAFTA	Y	4. Strike Race/Death Pnlty.	Y	6. Cut Missile Funds	N

Key Votes of the 104th Congress

1. Congressional Compliance	Y	6. Reform Crime Grant	Y	11. Loser Pays Court Reform	Y
2. Balanced Budget Amndmt.	Y	7. National Security Act	Y	12. Product Liability Reform	Y
3. Bar Unfunded Mandates	Y	8. Moratorium on Regs.	Y	13. Welfare Reform	N
4. Pass Line Item Veto	Y	9. Risk Assessment on Regs.	Y	14. Term Limits Amndmt.	N
5. Relax Exclusionary Rule	Y	10. Expnd. Priv. Prop. Rights	Y	15. Tax Cuts	Y

Election Results

1994 general	Pete Geren (D)	96,372	(69%)	($345,739)
	Ernest J. Anderson Jr. (R)	43,959	(31%)	($20,471)
1994 primary	Pete Geren (D)	unopposed		
1992 general	Pete Geren (D)	125,492	(63%)	($812,234)
	David Hobbs (R)	74,432	(37%)	($384,635)

THIRTEENTH DISTRICT

Heading west in Texas, the population thins out, the land becomes browner, until you can travel through a whole county with only a few hundred people—plus quite a few more head of cattle. And then the land rises nearly 1,000 feet in elevation, up steep gullies that surround the rivers which for most of the year are just tiny trickles, to the tilted tableland that is the High Plains of west Texas. The winds here sweep down from the Rockies, the land is barren except where irrigated, often with the now dangerously depleted waters of the Ogallala Aquifer. But here and there in this demanding environment—sticky-hot in the summer, swept by north winds from Canada in winter, always threatened here in "Tornado Alley"—comfortable cities have been built to house the people and businesses that bring forth oil, natural gas, helium and other elements from the earth.

The 13th Congressional District of Texas spans much of this territory. Population declined here in the 1980s, in some rural counties by as much as 30%, with only small gains in and around two of the three biggest cities, Wichita Falls and Amarillo. Around Wichita Falls, in the eastern part of the district, is the agricultural land of the Red River Valley—dusty land with empty skylines, like Archer City, the boyhood home of novelist Larry McMurtry, chronicled in *The Last Picture Show* and *Texasville* and where he lives now in the biggest mansion in town. This is white Anglo Texas: few blacks got this far west and few Mexican-Americans go this far north. Up on the High Plains, the economy is different: it is based on minerals. The largest city here is Amarillo, the helium capital of North America and, pace Chicago, the windiest city in the United States. Just outside town is the Pantex factory that made thousands of nuclear warheads—the epicenter of American defense in the Cold War, and its 16,000 acres are now scheduled (pending lawsuits) to be used to store the disarmed weapons. The political traditions here differ. The Red River Valley, settled by Confederate veterans, was until very recently Democratic. The High Plains, settled overland from Kansas wheatlands, is more Republican. The lines were changed for the 1990s: not all of Amarillo is in the 13th any more, and black portions of Lubbock have been added. The purpose was to subtract Republicans and help Democratic Congressman Bill Sarpalius.

But it was not enough: Sarpalius was defeated in 1994 by Republican Mac Thornberry. The newcomer is a farmer and rancher who claims roots in both ends of the district. He also is a veteran of Capitol Hill, working from 1983–88 for Texas Republican Congressmen Tom Loeffler and Larry Combest. In 1988, Thornberry became the State Department's congressional lobbyist, and in he 1989 returned to West Texas. Well-connected, Thornberry easily won the Republican primary in 1994, with 75% of the vote, and campaigned hard on Contract With America issues. And, he was helped by the problems of Bill Sarpalius.

Sarpalius was the upwardly mobile product of a broken home. He was elected to the House in 1988 and, with a conservative voting record, increased his percentage to 57% and 60% in 1990 and 1992. But in 1993 he voted for the Clinton budget and tax package—according to Bob Woodward's *The Agenda*—after being urged by Treasury Secretary Lloyd Bentsen to do so. Sarpalius also was hurt by "Movinggate." When he was first elected, he hired Sherwood Van Lines to move his family to Washington. Sherwood, a firm that did most of its business moving the military, billed Sarpalius, but did not receive payment until 1994, Sarpalius said, because of damage to his goods. In 1989, the head of Sherwood paid Sarpalius an honorarium for speaking at a Las Vegas convention, which Sarpalius did not report until four years later—after Sherwood's president became the target of an FBI investigation. "Movinggate" first made news in December 1993. In October 1994, the story flared on the eve of the election as the FBI investigated Sarpalius and Texas colleagues Greg Laughlin and Jim Chapman. This was, if not fatal, certainly not helpful.

Thornberry won a solid 55%–45% victory, carrying the northern panhandle by wide margins and carrying Wichita Falls as well, trailing only in sparsely populated ranching counties. He supported all the provisions of the Contract With America, which in this Republican district should be a political plus.

The People: Pop. 1990: 566,682; 27% rural; 14% age 65+; 71% White; 8% Black; 1% Amer. Indian; 1% Asian; 11% Other; 19% Hispanic origin. Voting age pop.: 409,705; 7% Black; 15% Hispanic origin. Households: 58% married couple families; 28% married couple fams. w. children; 37% college educ.; median household income: $20,907; per capita income: $10,344; median gross rent: $334; median house value: $38,100.

1992 Presidential Vote

Bush (R)	87,492	(43%)
Clinton (D)	73,454	(36%)
Perot (I)	41,187	(20%)

1988 Presidential Vote

Bush (R)	106,620	(57%)
Dukakis (D)	81,789	(43%)

Rep. Mac Thornberry (R)

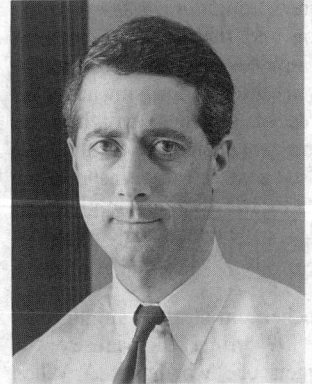

Elected 1994; b. July 15, 1958, Clarendon; home, Clarendon; TX Tech. U., B.A. 1980, U. of TX Schl. of Law, J.D. 1983; Presbyterian; married (Sally).

Career: Legis. Cnsl., U.S. Rep. Tom Loeffler, 1983–85; Chief of Staff, Rep. Larry Combest, 1985–88; Dep. Asst. Secy. of State for Legis. Affairs, 1988–89; Practicing atty., 1989–94.

DC Office: 1535 LHOB 20515, 202-225-3706; Fax: 202-225-3846.

District Offices: 724 S. Polk St., #400, Amarillo 79101, 806-371-8844; and 811 6th St., #130, Wichita Falls 76301, 817-767-0541.

Committees: *National Security* (22nd of 30 R): Military Personnel; Military Procurement. *Resources* (21st of 25 R): Energy and Mineral Resources; Water and Power Resources. *Joint Economic Committee* (4th of 10 Reps.).

Group Ratings and 103rd Congress Votes: Newly Elected

Key Votes of the 104th Congress

1. Congressional Compliance Y	6. Reform Crime Grant Y	11. Loser Pays Court Reform Y
2. Balanced Budget Amndmt. Y	7. National Security Act Y	12. Product Liability Reform Y
3. Bar Unfunded Mandates Y	8. Moratorium on Regs. Y	13. Welfare Reform Y
4. Pass Line Item Veto Y	9. Risk Assessment on Regs. Y	14. Term Limits Amndmt. Y
5. Relax Exclusionary Rule Y	10. Expnd. Priv. Prop. Rights Y	15. Tax Cuts Y

Election Results

1994 general	Mac Thornberry (R)	79,466	(55%)	($442,237)
	Bill Sarpalius (D)	63,923	(45%)	($540,096)
1994 primary	Mac Thornberry (R)	11,568	(75%)	
	Wayne Collins (R)	2,147	(14%)	
	Flavious Smith (R)	1,714	(11%)	
1992 general	Bill Sarpalius (D)	117,892	(60%)	($521,328)
	Beau Boulter (R)	77,514	(40%)	($370,582)

FOURTEENTH DISTRICT

Retreating east from the Alamo, the ragtag army led by Sam Houston passed over what would become, after their bloody and conclusive victory at San Jacinto, some of the prime cropland in the new Republic and later the state of Texas. The hilly and river-crossed land between Houston and Austin, both named after Texas's first leaders, was settled early. The flat coastal plains, steamy and humid so much of the year, were settled later when the railroads came in. The Gulf of Mexico coastline, though it has plenty of inlets, never had any important ports in the stretch between Houston and Corpus Christi until the discovery of oil here made it worthwhile to build channels to ship the oil out.

This is the land of the 14th Congressional District of Texas. Made up of rural countrysides, small towns and a couple of small cities, it runs along the Gulf coast and inland toward the old Texas German country. Its eastern and northern edges bring it within metropolitan range of Houston, Austin and San Antonio; more than one-third of its people live in these areas. Redistricting in 1991 changed its shape somewhat, adding Blanco County in the Hill Country west of Austin, the birthplace and first political base of Lyndon B. Johnson. This country is ancestrally Democratic except for a couple of counties settled by Texas Germans, who were pro-Union in the Civil War and have remained Republican ever since. But it voted Republican in the 1980s and favored George Bush over Bill Clinton.

The congressman from the 14th District is Greg Laughlin, a Democrat who won the seat in unusual circumstances and has held it through some difficult times. Laughlin is a lawyer from Brazoria County, a former intelligence officer in the Pentagon and the National Security Agency, and a former prosecutor in Houston. He ran in the 14th in 1986 and lost narrowly; two years later, in a rematch, he won by beating an incumbent who was criticized for lying about his resume, his opponents and his mostly nonexistent legislative record. In office, Laughlin has compiled a moderate record—in the midpoint of the 103d Congress on economic, cultural and foreign issues, according to *National Journal* ratings—and used his seat on the Transportation and Infrastructure Committee to support road and beach projects for the district. Laughlin has served in the Army since he graduated from Texas A&M, and as a lieutenant colonel in the Army Reserve volunteered for two weeks of duty in the Persian Gulf in 1991. The next year he won 68%–27%.

Laughlin had spirited opposition in 1994 from Republican rancher Jim Deats. Laughlin had voted against the Clinton budget and tax package and against the 1994 crime bill because of the assault weapon ban. But in October he was one of three targets of "Movinggate." When Laughlin was first elected, at the advice of a Jim Wright aide, he hired Sherwood Van Lines to move his family to Washington. But Sherwood, a firm that did most of its business moving the military, never billed him. In 1990 Laughlin signed a letter supporting a bidding system for military moves that favored Sherwood. Subsequently, the head of Sherwood was indicted for funneling illegal contributions into Laughlin's and others campaigns and for paying them higher-than-legal honorarium at a Las Vegas convention. "Movinggate" first made news in December 1993; in January 1994 Laughlin paid the bill to then bankrupt Sherwood.

Late in the campaign, the story flared as the FBI investigated Laughlin and Texas colleagues Bill Sarpalius and Jim Chapman in October 1994. Deats printed literature saying: "Jim Deats. Because the only place Greg Laughlin shouldn't be serving time is Congress." Laughlin's campaign manager said the timing indicated it was just "a political ploy." In fact Laughlin was not formally charged with wrongdoing, though he certainly was guilty, at least, of sloppiness. Evidently his accumulated goodwill in the district worked for him: he ran well ahead of Governor Ann Richards and won 56%–44%, with Deats carrying his home area around Blanco County in the western corner of the district. But this does not absolutely guarantee him an easy race in 1996 and Laughlin's votes for most of the Contract suggested that he was looking over his shoulder to deter potential opponents.

The People: Pop. 1990: 566,008; 51% rural; 13% age 65+; 65% White; 11% Black; 1% Asian; 11% Other; 23% Hispanic origin. Voting age pop.: 407,091; 10% Black; 20% Hispanic origin. Households: 61% married couple families; 30% married couple fams. w. children; 37% college educ.; median household income: $23,812; per capita income: $11,127; median gross rent: $344; median house value: $52,300.

1992 Presidential Vote		1988 Presidential Vote	
Bush (R)	86,225 (41%)	Bush (R)	103,065 (53%)
Clinton (D)	78,706 (37%)	Dukakis (D).	92,141 (47%)
Perot (I).	47,119 (22%)		

Rep. Greg Laughlin (D)

Elected 1988; b. Jan. 21, 1942, Bay City; home, West Columbia; TX A&M U., B.A. 1964, U. of TX, LL.B. 1967; Methodist; married (Ginger).

Career: Army, 1964–69, 1991 (Persian Gulf), Army Reserves, 1969–present; Asst. Dist. Atty., Harris Cnty., 1970–74; Practicing atty., 1974–88.

DC Office: 236 CHOB 20515, 202-225-2831; Fax: 202-225-1108.

District Offices: 312 S. Main St., Victoria 77901, 512-576-1231; and 221 E. Main St., #203, Round Rock 78664, 512-244-3765.

Committees: *Intelligence (Permanent Select)* (7th of 7 D): Human Intelligence, Analysis, and Counterintelligence; Technical and Tactical Intelligence. *Transportation & Infrastructure* (13th of 27 D): Surface Transportation; Water Resources and Environment.

Group Ratings

	ADA	ACLU	COPE	CFA	LCV	CON	NSI	COC	ACU	NTLC	CHC
1994	50	42	63	30	27	41	90	83	60	50	43
1993	20	—	45	50	43	8	—	55	52	—	—

National Journal Ratings

	1993 LIB — 1993 CONS			1994 LIB — 1994 CONS	
Economic	42%	—	57%	58%	— 41%
Social	48%	—	52%	51%	— 49%
Foreign	51%	—	42%	48%	— 51%

Key Votes of the 103d Congress

1. Clinton Deficit Plan	N	3. Brady Handgun Purchase	N	5. Lmt. UN Cmnd. of Forces	N
2. NAFTA	Y	4. Strike Race/Death Pnlty.	Y	6. Cut Missile Funds	N

Key Votes of the 104th Congress

1. Congressional Compliance	Y	6. Reform Crime Grant	Y	11. Loser Pays Court Reform	N
2. Balanced Budget Amndmt.	Y	7. National Security Act	Y	12. Product Liability Reform	Y
3. Bar Unfunded Mandates	Y	8. Moratorium on Regs.	Y	13. Welfare Reform	N
4. Pass Line Item Veto	Y	9. Risk Assessment on Regs.	Y	14. Term Limits Amndmt.	N
5. Relax Exclusionary Rule	Y	10. Expnd. Priv. Prop. Rights	Y	15. Tax Cuts	Y

Election Results

1994 general	Greg Laughlin (D)	86,175	(56%)	($789,201)
	Jim Deats (R)	68,793	(44%)	($271,551)
1994 primary	Greg Laughlin (D)	unopposed		
1992 general	Greg Laughlin (D)	135,930	(68%)	($540,139)
	Huberto J. (Bert) Garza (R)............	54,412	(27%)	($13,550)
	Vic Vreeland (I)	9,329	(5%)	

FIFTEENTH DISTRICT

The Lower Rio Grande Valley of south Texas is one of America's 20th Century frontiers. A century ago, there was little here but desert wilderness. Only a handful of people lived anywhere near the shallow, sluggish Rio Grande; there was no Border patrol, because in this desert land no one bothered to cross it. Then in the early days of this century came pioneers like Lloyd Bentsen, Sr., father of the former Senator and Treasury secretary, who arrived after World War I with five dollars in his pocket and became one of the biggest Valley landowners, remaining active in his business until he died in an auto accident in 1989 at age 95. Bentsen and others cleared the land and dug canals, hired Mexican and Mexican-American workers, planted citrus groves and cornfields and palm windbreaks, ran cattle and drilled for oil and gas. Along U.S. 83 north of the Rio Grande these pioneers built a string of towns with Anglo names and storefronts. But most of the people here were Latino in culture and language. Wage levels higher than in Mexico (though low by U.S. standards) brought more Mexicans over the border. But if wages are low, so is the cost of living—which makes this a haven for low-income "winter Texan" retirees, coming down from the North in their RVs. The days are past when ranchers and oil men wielded absolute political power here. There is instead a robust, mostly Hispanic politics, often with big Democratic majorities but with genuine two-party competition on occasion.

The 15th Congressional District of Texas is one of three districts dividing up the Lower Rio Grande Valley. Some two-thirds of its residents and 56% of its voters live in Hidalgo County, in or near the string of towns from Mercedes through McAllen to Los Ebanos, just north of the river. The 15th then moves north through a narrow corridor of land between Corpus Christi and San Antonio to meet the population requirement, including Goliad, where 352 captured Texans were massacred by Santa Ana's troops in 1836, and Beeville, the big town nearby where George Bush, as President, would go for barbecue after shooting quail at each year's end. The 15th's population is 74% Hispanic and mostly Democratic. This is the descendant of a district that in 1948, 1950 and 1952 elected Lloyd Bentsen, Jr., to the House, before he went to Houston to make his fortune and then on to national office.

The congressman from the 15th District is Eligio (Kika) de la Garza, for 14 years chairman of the House Agriculture Committee. Though de la Garza's family was given part of the 18th Century Santa Gertrudis de la Garza Spanish land grant, he grew up poor, working as a shoeshine boy on the streets of McAllen, then went to law school at St. Mary's in San Antonio (which has educated many outstanding Texas Hispanics). He served 12 years in the legislature, where he was a favorite of big landowners and was sometimes attacked by Austin-based liberals. His voting record for years was rather conservative; he is somewhat liberal on economic issues and has always supported civil rights, but is more moderate on foreign policy and cultural matters. But this meshes well with the pro-military and culturally traditional views of Mexican-American voters. De la Garza is an earnest, pleasant man, who takes the trouble to learn new languages so that he can surprise foreign visitors by speaking to them in their native tongue. But he is capable of a little more guile than is first apparent.

De la Garza served as Agriculture chairman for a longer uninterrupted period than anyone else in history and superintended three major farm bills, in 1981, 1985 and 1990. The 1981 farm bill boosted program costs enormously by setting target prices above world levels and stimulating vast overproduction while discouraging exports and letting farm land prices decline. In response, the 1985 bill cut subsidies sharply. In 1990, he worked to protect farm programs from further cuts, opposing a modest proposal to cut two cents out of the sugar subsidy and beating the Armey-Schumer proposal to ban subsidies for farmers with incomes over $100,000. De la Garza shrewdly marshalled environmentalists, unions (who were against cargo preference) and the textile industry (which wanted support for textile import quotas), and prevailed. He also worked on drought relief and pesticide bills and to make sure NAFTA included 15-year phaseouts of tariffs on fruits and vegetables. In his last month as chairman, and on the day before former committee member Mike Espy announced his resignation as Agriculture Secretary, de la Garza led the full House in passing by voice vote a measure with two important reforms: it reorganized the USDA in line with Vice President Al Gore's "reinventing government" recommendations, the first department to be so realigned, and it overhauled the federal crop insurance program, to be paid for from the mandatory accounts for three years after enactment.

De la Garza has not gone totally unchallenged at the polls. In 1992, he had 284 overdrafts on the House bank, and won 60%–40%. In 1994 he was challenged in the primary by his godson, Eli Ochoa, and won 60%–26%; in the general he won 59%–39%. All solid margins, but not unanimous. With Espy resigning and Republicans controlling the House, de la Garza saw two committee members ascend in farm policy: Democrat Dan Glickman as Agriculture Secretary and Republican Pat Roberts as Agriculture Committee chairman. Both are from Kansas, with its own agricultural interests; both are practical men, knowledgeable about farm programs, aware that they are under attack and probably must be cut. Assuming the committee continues its bipartisan tradition, de la Garza is likely to play an important, though diminished, role in shaping the 1995 farm bill.

The People: Pop. 1990: 566,805; 29% rural; 11% age 65+; 24% White; 1% Black; 23% Other; 74% Hispanic origin. Voting age pop.: 369,686; 1% Black; 69% Hispanic origin. Households: 66% married couple families; 38% married couple fams. w. children; 29% college educ.; median household income: $17,866; per capita income: $7,407; median gross rent: $290; median house value: $36,900.

1992 Presidential Vote

Clinton (D)	80,135	(53%)
Bush (R)	52,102	(34%)
Perot (I)	19,995	(13%)

1988 Presidential Vote

Dukakis (D)	87,323	(59%)
Bush (R)	59,541	(41%)

Rep. E (Kika) de la Garza (D)

Elected 1964; b. Sep. 22, 1927, Mercedes; home, Mission; Edinburg Jr. Col., St. Mary's U., LL.B. 1952; Catholic; married (Lucille).

Career: Navy, 1945–46; Army, 1951–52 (Korea); Practicing atty., 1952–64; TX House of Reps., 1952–64.

DC Office: 1401 LHOB 20515, 202-225-2531; Fax: 202-225-2534.

District Offices: 1418 Beech St., McAllen 78501, 210-682-5545; and Alice Fed. Bldg., #210, 401 E. 2d St., Alice 78332, 512-664-2215.

Committees: *Agriculture* (RMM of 22 D).

Group Ratings

	ADA	ACLU	COPE	CFA	LCV	CON	NSI	COC	ACU	NTLC	CHC
1994	50	23	56	70	53	33	90	67	45	25	57
1993	35	—	83	90	64	4	—	40	39	—	—

National Journal Ratings

	1993 LIB — 1993 CONS		1994 LIB — 1994 CONS	
Economic	55%	— 45%	56%	— 44%
Social	36%	— 64%	53%	— 47%
Foreign	45%	— 54%	57%	— 37%

Key Votes of the 103d Congress

1. Clinton Deficit Plan	Y	3. Brady Handgun Purchase	N	5. Lmt. UN Cmnd. of Forces	N
2. NAFTA	Y	4. Strike Race/Death Pnlty.	N	6. Cut Missile Funds	N

Key Votes of the 104th Congress

1. Congressional Compliance	Y	6. Reform Crime Grant	N	11. Loser Pays Court Reform	Y
2. Balanced Budget Amndmt.	Y	7. National Security Act	N	12. Product Liability Reform	N
3. Bar Unfunded Mandates	Y	8. Moratorium on Regs.	Y	13. Welfare Reform	N
4. Pass Line Item Veto	N	9. Risk Assessment on Regs.	Y	14. Term Limits Amndmt.	*
5. Relax Exclusionary Rule	Y	10. Expnd. Priv. Prop. Rights	Y	15. Tax Cuts	N

Election Results

1994 general	E (Kika) De La Garza (D)	61,527	(59%)	($701,528)
	Tom Haughey (R)	41,119	(39%)	($30,193)
	Others	1,720	(2%)	
1994 primary	E (Kika) De La Garza (D)	40,513	(60%)	
	Eli Ochoa (D)	17,481	(26%)	
	Rigo Martinez (D)	8,998	(13%)	
1992 general	E (Kika) de la Garza (D)	86,351	(60%)	($267,600)
	Tom Haughey (R)	56,549	(40%)	($13,452)

SIXTEENTH DISTRICT

El Paso, Texas, and Juarez, Mexico, sit across from each other on the narrow Rio Grande, their tree-shaded streets spread out below the rough brown face of Comanche Peak, two border cities surrounded by hundreds of miles of some of the most desolate landscape in the country, 400 miles from Phoenix and 600 from Dallas-Fort Worth. There is much history here: Texas claims the first Thanksgiving took place in San Elizario near El Paso in 1598. Fifty years ago, there were still only 140,000 people in both cities; now there are over two million, 600,000 in El Paso, 1.5 million in Juarez. This is a bilingual, bicultural pair of cities, where most people have a Mexican heritage; the thrust of growth is from Spanish-speaking people and an English-speaking economy. El Paso is one of the lowest wage cities in the U.S., Juarez one of the highest wage in Mexico; *maquiladora* plants pioneered a cross-border economy and the North American Free Trade Agreement seems sure to strengthen it. But free trade doesn't necessarily mean porous borders. In September 1993, El Paso Immigration and Naturalization Service leader Silvestre Reyes started Operation Hold the Line, wangling $300,000 extra and positioning 400 officers on the border instead of trying to intercept illegal crossers after they have gotten inside El Paso. Before that, 8,000 illegals had crossed the border each day; that was drastically reduced to near zero. Mexico complained about threats to its sovereignty, merchants worried about loss of sales, homeowners fretted about finding domestic help. But the law was finally being enforced, by an agency which had long said it was impossible; Californians began asking why the INS couldn't hold the line there.

The 16th Congressional District of Texas is made up of most of the city of El Paso and communities up and down the Rio Grande, and giant Fort Bliss to the north. Well over 60% of the people here are Latino, and for many years politics divided people on ethnic lines, with most Anglos Republican and Latinos Democratic. But today it seems voters respond across ethnic lines. Operation Hold the Line was almost universally popular in El Paso, for example.

The congressman from the 16th District, Ron Coleman, is a Texas political type: the tough-guy liberal, practical and aggressive, profane and unprincipled if you believe *Hill Rat* (a book by a former staffer who was attacked by his colleagues as scurrilous), a guy who has made a good but always risky political career by backing labor unions and trial lawyers and getting support from them in return. Coleman was the lawyer for strikers in the major walkout against the Farah slacks company in the 1970s; he ran for the open 16th in 1982, and won a tough primary against a Mexican-American and a tough general against a Republican. In the 1980s House, things went swimmingly for him. From the National Security Committee and then the Appropriations Military Construction Subcommittee, he has funneled money to Fort Bliss. He commended President Carlos Salinas's Mexico for its market-oriented economic reforms and strongly backed NAFTA, even as he kept an eye on local air quality and urged tougher Mexican environmental rules and enforcement and called for $1 billion for new border infrastructure.

Then in early 1992 it was revealed that an El Paso area businessman assumed $65,000 in debts for Coleman and, weeks later, that he had 673 overdrafts on the House bank, totalling $275,000, making him one of the worst abusers of the House bank. The Republican nominee, newscaster Chip Taberski, ran an ad on the check-bouncing showing a jail door swinging shut. Coleman responded with characteristic feistiness. He ran a TV spot apologizing and then another, with an out of focus shot of Taberski, accusing him of being ignorant of Hispanic concerns and hitting him for supporting the English-language-only movement. Coleman vastly outspent Taberski, and wound up winning 52%–48%.

Coleman remained busy in the House as Democrats there imploded in 1994. He chaired the Intelligence subcommittee on legislation. He switched from his opposition to gun control measures to support the assault weapons ban. He passed Border Health Commission legislation and obtained $175 million for water and sewer projects on the border. Texas Republican incumbent congressmen, hoping to attract Latino votes to oppose Coleman, endorsed Bobby Ortiz in the Republican primary; he won 65% of only 5,248 votes. Ortiz immigrated from Mexico at 10, served in the Air Force, became an executive at Farah, where he negotiated a wage freeze contract. From there, he went on to manage apparel factories in Central America. Ortiz was highly touted by the national party, and was a presenter on the Capitol steps in September 1994 of the Contract With America. But Coleman, although he lost NRA support in 1994, raised more money and his relative liberalism evidently appealed to more voters. Ortiz's campaign was not well-run, and Coleman won with 57%—about the same as Governor Ann Richards. After the election, he remained consistent, with the least support for the Contract of any Anglo Democrat from Texas. It seems risky to say that Coleman has a firm hold on the seat, but he has shown the ability to survive tough opposition and difficult circumstances.

The People: Pop. 1990: 566,238; 2% rural; 8% age 65+; 25% White; 4% Black; 1% Asian; 18% Other; 70% Hispanic origin. Voting age pop.: 383,578; 4% Black; 66% Hispanic origin. Households: 61% married couple families; 36% married couple fams. w. children; 41% college educ.; median household income: $22,632; per capita income: $9,195; median gross rent: $345; median house value: $57,000.

1992 Presidential Vote

Clinton (D) 65,614 (51%)
Bush (R) 45,367 (35%)
Perot (I) 18,779 (14%)

1988 Presidential Vote

Dukakis (D) 61,247 (53%)
Bush (R) 53,619 (47%)

1304 TEXAS

Rep. Ronald D. Coleman (D)

Elected 1982; b. Nov. 19, 1941, El Paso; home, El Paso; U. of TX, B.A. 1963, J.D. 1967; Presbyterian; married (Amy).

Career: Army, 1967–69; Teacher, El Paso public schls., TX School for Deaf; Legis. Asst., TX House and Senate, 1965–67; Asst. El Paso Cnty. Atty., 1969; Practicing atty., 1969–82; 1st Asst. El Paso Cnty. Atty., 1971; TX House of Reps., 1973–82.

DC Office: 2312 RHOB 20515, 202-225-4831; Fax: 202-225-4825.

District Offices: Fed. Bldg., 700 E. San Antonio St., #723, El Paso 79901, 915-534-6200; and P.O. Bldg., #304, Pecos 79772, 915-445-6218.

Committees: *Appropriations* (14th of 24 D): Transportation (RMM); Treasury, Postal Service, and General Government. *Intelligence (Permanent Select)* (5th of 7 D): Human Intelligence, Analysis, and Counterintelligence (RMM).

Group Ratings

	ADA	ACLU	COPE	CFA	LCV	CON	NSI	COC	ACU	NTLC	CHC
1994	80	57	78	80	75	11	70	58	19	19	14
1993	65	—	92	90	69	11	—	27	21	—	—

National Journal Ratings

	1993 LIB — 1993 CONS		1994 LIB — 1994 CONS	
Economic	66%	— 33%	73%	— 17%
Social	64%	— 34%	69%	— 30%
Foreign	51%	— 42%	64%	— 33%

Key Votes of the 103d Congress

1. Clinton Deficit Plan	Y	3. Brady Handgun Purchase N	5. Lmt. UN Cmnd. of Forces N
2. NAFTA	Y	4. Strike Race/Death Pnlty. N	6. Cut Missile Funds N

Key Votes of the 104th Congress

1. Congressional Compliance	Y	6. Reform Crime Grant N	11. Loser Pays Court Reform N
2. Balanced Budget Amndmt.	N	7. National Security Act N	12. Product Liability Reform N
3. Bar Unfunded Mandates	Y	8. Moratorium on Regs. N	13. Welfare Reform N
4. Pass Line Item Veto	N	9. Risk Assessment on Regs. N	14. Term Limits Amndmt. N
5. Relax Exclusionary Rule	N	10. Expnd. Priv. Prop. Rights N	15. Tax Cuts N

Election Results

1994 general	Ronald D. Coleman (D)	49,815	(57%)	($704,186)
	Bobby Ortiz (R)	37,409	(43%)	($324,335)
1994 primary	Ronald D. Coleman (D)	20,990	(62%)	
	Mike Crowley (D)	12,871	(38%)	
1992 general	Ronald D. Coleman (D)	66,731	(52%)	($780,038)
	Chip Taberski (R)	61,870	(48%)	($209,271)

SEVENTEENTH DISTRICT

West from Fort Worth, the West Texas plains stretch miles beyond the horizon, thousands and thousands of acres of rolling grazing land punctuated occasionally by oases of irrigated farmland (often in circles that show the reach of the sprinklers). This is primarily cattle country, although there is some oil here, and cotton and grain. On the interstate straight west of Fort Worth, settlements start thinning out quickly. Before long, you are on open plains, with enormous skies and no people to be seen. Then in the distance is a good-sized town, an oasis of busyness. The largest town here is Abilene, with a high concentration of bankers, lawyers and professionals. Settled by Confederate veterans suspicious of eastern bankers and Yankee businessmen, this was one of the Democratic heartlands of America up through the 1970s; now it is voting Republican in major statewide races. In the sparsely populated counties that seem utterly left behind, the few hundred voters may tilt crazily left and resoundingly right.

The 17th Congressional District of Texas takes up much of this "God's country," starting a few miles from Fort Worth and including most of three tiers of counties westward almost to New Mexico. This is ancestral Democratic country, but it preferred George Bush to Bill Clinton in 1992 and George W. Bush to Ann Richards in 1994.

The congressman from the 17th District is Charles Stenholm, one of several conservative Texas Democrats elected in 1978, and the only one still a Democratic member of the House. Stenholm is a farmer from a small town settled by Swedes near Abilene, a natural politician who went to Congress after running the Rolling Plains Cotton Growers Association and the Stamford Electric Co-op (Stamford is the home town also of Democratic super-lobbyist Robert Strauss). He became a Democrat because in the 1970 Senate race Lloyd Bentsen was interested in his issues and George Bush wasn't. In 1978, when 32-year incumbent Omar Burleson retired, Stenholm ran for the seat and won, easily beating a Republican. In the House, he and Phil Gramm were leaders of the "Boll Weevils" backing the 1981 Reagan budget and tax cuts. He threatened momentarily to run against Speaker Tip O'Neill in 1985, but desisted when conservatives were promised more attention. His voting record is conservative, especially on cultural issues, but not always market-oriented. On the Agriculture Committee, he has worked on farm credit, disaster relief, animal product safety and pesticide bills; he is for relaxing environmental restrictions and against caps on subsidies. He has pressed for boosts to rural health care, and put together a healthcare bill with more rural health care plus insurance reform and Medicaid reform.

Stenholm has been head of the Conservative Democratic Forum, which boasted 54 members in the 103d Congress but quite a bit fewer after the Democratic losses in 1994. In 1994, he helped to organize FROG (Fair Rules and Openness Group), which pressed the Democratic leadership for less closed rules and more votes on proposed amendments. But he was also a chief deputy whip and, in the opinion of then-Minority Whip Newt Gingrich, a conservative talker who always ended up cooperating with the Democratic leaders. But he did oppose the Clinton budget and tax package in 1993 and was a leading sponsor of the balanced budget amendment. He presented a Common Cents Budget Reform proposal in 1994, attacking inflated baseline spending and current services budget-measuring tools, which the Republicans gutted in 1995. He backed, after some concessions were made to him, the A-to-Z spending cut mechanism (which would have forced the full House to consider virtually any spending cut proposal a member wanted to offer) in June 1994. He tried to attack entitlements, including cuts in Social Security, but lost this battle in July 1994 by 392–37. He supported the Republican welfare reform in March 1994 but then opposed it a year later after the Republicans took control and moved their proposal to the right.

In the Democratic House, Stenholm was often a crucial vote and, because he talked a lot with like-minded colleagues, one who could round up others. With the Republican victory in 1994, he suddenly became less pivotal on most issues. His immediate reaction to November 1994 was:

1306   TEXAS

"We have to make some changes in the Democratic Party. We have lost touch with Middle America. Our base is eroding, and we're losing the young vote." But he added that he wasn't quitting the Democratic Party and was worried about the 1995 farm bill. Stenholm ran for Minority Whip against David Bonior and, predictably, lost 145–60.

Why does Stenholm seem unlikely to leave the Democratic Party? One reason is that he does not entirely believe in free market economics; he is concerned about likely cutbacks in the new farm bill. Another is that as a Republican he might get lost in the herd, while among Democrats he is distinctive, and his vote is sought—if less often now, at least still when Republicans need two-thirds of the vote on key issues. Thus Stenholm was co-sponsor of the balanced budget amendment which passed 300–132 in January 1995, an effort that won him bipartisan plaudits. A third reason may just be stubbornness: he started off this way, he keeps trying to move the party his way, and danged if he's going to give up on it. And in the past, staying a Democrat seemed good electoral politics: few Republicans rose up to run against him, while there always seemed to be plenty of local Democrats who might challenge a Republican. Now that balance may be shifting. Unopposed in general elections from 1980 to 1990, the winner in 1992 with 66%, Stenholm was much more closely challenged in 1994. Republican Phil Boone was outspent and outendorsed, but he carried Abilene and seven other counties and held Stenholm to a 54%–46% win. That suggests that remaining a Democrat is no longer a no-risk strategy at home, and that the 17th District may be seriously contested again in the 1990s.

The People: Pop. 1990: 566,255; 38% rural; 16% age 65+; 79% White; 4% Black; 1% Asian; 10% Other; 17% Hispanic origin. Voting age pop.: 412,115; 3% Black; 14% Hispanic origin. Households: 62% married couple families; 29% married couple fams. w. children; 36% college educ.; median household income: $21,532; per capita income: $10,642; median gross rent: $329; median house value: $38,400.

1992 Presidential Vote			1988 Presidential Vote		
Bush (R)	86,490	(40%)	Bush (R)	116,567	(58%)
Clinton (D)	73,388	(34%)	Dukakis (D)	84,865	(42%)
Perot (I)	55,834	(26%)			

Rep. Charles W. Stenholm (D)

Elected 1978; b. Oct. 26, 1938, Stamford; home, Avoca; TX Tech. U., B.S. 1961; M.S. 1962; Lutheran; married (Cynthia).

Career: Farmer; Vocational educ. teacher, 1962–65; Exec. V.P., Rolling Plains Cotton Growers, 1965–68; Mgr., Stamford Electric Coop., 1968–76.

DC Office: 1211 LHOB 20515, 202-225-6605; Fax: 202-225-2234.

District Offices: 903 E. Hamilton St., Stamford 79553, 915-773-3623; 341 Pine St., Abilene 79604, 915-673-7221; and 33 E. Twohig Ave., #318, San Angelo 76903, 915-655-7994.

Committees: *Agriculture* (4th of 22 D): General Farm Commodities (RMM); Resource Conservation, Research and Forestry. *Budget* (2nd of 18 D).

Group Ratings

	ADA	ACLU	COPE	CFA	LCV	CON	NSI	COC	ACU	NTLC	CHC
1994	5	17	0	20	17	99	90	100	90	79	100
1993	10	—	17	20	36	96	—	73	78	—	—

National Journal Ratings

	1993 LIB — 1993 CONS		1994 LIB — 1994 CONS	
Economic	35% —	63%	36% —	63%
Social	24% —	76%	11% —	85%
Foreign	59% —	38%	40% —	59%

Key Votes of the 103d Congress

1. Clinton Deficit Plan	N	3. Brady Handgun Purchase	N	5. Lmt. UN Cmnd. of Forces	N
2. NAFTA	Y	4. Strike Race/Death Pnlty.	Y	6. Cut Missile Funds	N

Key Votes of the 104th Congress

1. Congressional Compliance	Y	6. Reform Crime Grant	Y	11. Loser Pays Court Reform	Y
2. Balanced Budget Amndmt.	Y	7. National Security Act	N	12. Product Liability Reform	Y
3. Bar Unfunded Mandates	Y	8. Moratorium on Regs.	Y	13. Welfare Reform	N
4. Pass Line Item Veto	N	9. Risk Assessment on Regs.	Y	14. Term Limits Amndmt.	N
5. Relax Exclusionary Rule	Y	10. Expnd. Priv. Prop. Rights	Y	15. Tax Cuts	N

Election Results

1994 general	Charles W. Stenholm (D)	83,497	(54%)	($712,156)
	Phil Boone (R)	72,108	(46%)	($192,079)
1994 primary	Charles W. Stenholm (D)	unopposed		
1992 general	Charles W. Stenholm (D)	136,213	(66%)	($377,949)
	Jeannie Sadowski (R)	69,958	(34%)	($17,791)

EIGHTEENTH DISTRICT

Houston contains, within its vast bounds, disparities of income and wealth as striking as any city in the United States. This is not accidental: Houston has had exceedingly rapid economic growth for several decades now, plus huge flows of immigration, lack of centralized planning and the cultural diversity of a large Third World city. Such rapid growth does not pull everybody up at the same rate. The contrast is glaringly apparent at the edge of Houston's gleaming downtown with its keynote Pennzoil, Heritage Plaza and NationsBank buildings and the few blocks of Freedman's Village. Yet a few streets away are the slums where blacks and Mexican-Americans live in unpainted frame houses full of cracks wide enough to let in Houston's humid, smoggy air. When the great builders of Houston like Jesse Jones, millionaire cotton broker, newspaper publisher, and distributor of government capital as Franklin Roosevelt's head of the Reconstruction Finance Corporation, started erecting downtown skyscrapers, they were operating in a town with a Third World economy, a low-skill producer of basic commodities. Today, Houston is much more than that, a high-tech mecca as well as the petroleum-servicing center of the world. And much of that growth is now filtering down: many of Houston's blacks and Hispanics are moving up economically and moving out geographically, fleeing the horrifyingly high crime rates and disorganization in what were once stable if poor inner city neighborhoods. But the disparities still glare.

The 18th Congressional District of Texas has some of the most irregular boundaries of any congressional district in the country. It was drawn as Houston's black majority district, the descendant of the district first created for Barbara Jordan in 1972. But blacks have scattered outward in Houston, and Mexican-Americans and other Latinos have moved into neighborhoods in north central and southeast Houston in great numbers. Accordingly, the 18th District, even with boundaries that squiggle north toward Intercontinental Airport and northwest out radial highways, then spur south on one side toward the port and on the other toward the Astrodome, still enclose an area that in 1990 was only 49% black and 14% Hispanic. It is quite a contrast, however, with the 29th District, with which it interlocks like a jigsaw puzzle (indeed, one in which it might be impossible to get the pieces apart); the 29th is 10% black and 55% Hispanic. These numbers, and the boundaries, will probably change for 1996. A federal court ruled in 1994 that the 18th and 29th are racially discriminatory, and the result for 1996 may be two districts with similar percentages of blacks and Hispanics.

The congresswoman from the 18th District is Sheila Jackson Lee, a Houston City Council member who won the seat in 1994. Jackson Lee was educated at Yale and Virginia Law School, worked on Capitol Hill and practiced law in Houston, served as a local judge and on the Houston Council. After a term limits law took effect, in January 1994, she ran for Congress in the March Democratic primary. The incumbent was Craig Washington, a talented but storm-tossed legislator, elected to the legislature in 1972 and to Congress in 1989 to replace Mickey Leland, who was killed in a plane crash in Ethiopia. Washington had the worst attendance record in Congress (absent on 24% of roll calls in 1993), was sentenced at one point to 30 days in jail for leaving two legal clients "in the lurch," and filed for personal bankruptcy, claiming to owe $205,000 in federal taxes. He often was an iconoclast: He voted against thanking U.S. military personnel for serving in Operation Desert Storm, and against the Space Station and NAFTA, both of which are big pluses for the Houston area economy. Jackson Lee supported NAFTA and raised lots of money from business interests who favored it. Washington went to the unusual length of asking Republican as well as Democratic House colleagues to support him in the primary. Jackson Lee won by the astonishing margin of 63%–37%.

Like many new legislators of both parties, Jackson Lee is not moving her family to Washington. Her husband is a vice president at the University of Houston and her children remain in local schools. She did not get her first choice of a seat on the Commerce Committee—always a popular slot for a Texan, no matter their party or ideology. But, elected in a bad year for her party, she may have an edge in seniority later.

The People: Pop. 1990: 564,708; 1% rural; 9% age 65+; 31% White; 51% Black; 3% Asian; 8% Other; 15% Hispanic origin. Voting age pop.: 413,519; 49% Black; 13% Hispanic origin. Households: 40% married couple families; 19% married couple fams. w. children; 40% college educ.; median household income: $22,531; per capita income: $11,091; median gross rent: $375; median house value: $46,400.

1992 Presidential Vote			1988 Presidential Vote		
Clinton (D)	118,493	(66%)	Dukakis (D)	115,057	(70%)
Bush (R)	40,208	(22%)	Bush (R)	50,107	(30%)
Perot (I)	20,416	(11%)			

Rep. Sheila Jackson Lee (D)

Elected 1994; b. Jan. 12, 1950, Queens, NY; home, Houston; Yale U., B.A. 1972, U. of VA Law Schl., J.D. 1975; Seventh Day Adventist; married (Elwyn).

Career: Practicing atty., 1975–77, 1978–87; Staff Cnsl., U.S. House Select Assassinations Cmte., 1977–78; Houston Assoc. Municipal Judge, 1987–90; Houston City Cncl., 1990–94.

DC Office: 1520 LHOB 20515, 202-225-3816; Fax: 202-225-3317.

District Offices: 1919 Smith St., #1180, Mickey Leland Bldg., Houston 77002, 713-655-0050.

Committees: *Judiciary* (15th of 15 D): Crime. *Science* (22nd of 23 D): Basic Research; Space and Aeronautics.

Group Ratings and 103rd Congress Votes: Newly Elected

Key Votes of the 104th Congress

1. Congressional Compliance Y	6. Reform Crime Grant N	11. Loser Pays Court Reform N
2. Balanced Budget Amndmt. N	7. National Security Act N	12. Product Liability Reform N
3. Bar Unfunded Mandates Y	8. Moratorium on Regs. N	13. Welfare Reform N
4. Pass Line Item Veto N	9. Risk Assessment on Regs. N	14. Term Limits Amndmt. N
5. Relax Exclusionary Rule N	10. Expnd. Priv. Prop. Rights N	15. Tax Cuts N

Election Results

1994 general	Sheila Jackson Lee (D).................	84,790	(73%)	($593,740)
	Jerry Burley (R)	28,153	(24%)	($113,182)
	Others...............................	2,447	(2%)	
1994 primary	Sheila Jackson Lee (D).................	26,672	(63%)	
	Craig Washington (D).................	15,381	(37%)	
1992 general	Craig Washington (D)................	111,422	(65%)	($184,742)
	Edward Blum (R)	56,080	(33%)	($209,453)
	Other................................	4,706	(3%)	

NINETEENTH DISTRICT

Up on the High Plains of Texas, separated from the dusty cattlelands further east by rising gullies astride wide river courses, is some of the most productive cotton and wheat land in the United States, centered around the city of Lubbock. This fertility is a triumphant work of man. For this is irrigated land, which gets its water from the giant Ogallala Aquifer that undergirds so much of the western Great Plains, making this part of Texas a sort of green island in a vast brown sea of arid grazing land. The area was settled relatively late, with most growth after World War II. Lubbock grew from 31,000 in 1940 to 128,000 in 1960 and 191,020 in 1994. But the 1980s were tough on the High Plains. The aquifer seemed to be going dry, populations declined in almost every rural county, hospitals were closed in small towns. Lubbock, with an economy that includes Texas Tech University as well as agribusiness, has continued to grow. Politically this was once Democratic territory, and Lubbock elected George Mahon, chairman of the House Appropriations Committee from 1964 to 1979. Now Lubbock has indeed become heavily Republican, so much so that George Bush always liked to refer to it as a bellwether of public opinion. Lubbock County preferred President Bush over Bill Clinton 60%–23% and voted for George W. Bush over Ann Richards 63%–37% in 1994—even though, as a Republican candidate for Congress, the younger Bush lost Lubbock to then-Democrat Kent Hance in 1978.

The 19th Congressional District of Texas covers the western edge of the High Plains of Texas, from the northern edge of the Panhandle south to the Permian Basin. Tantalizingly, it includes only part of each of its four widely separated major cities. In 1992, the Democratic legislature took the black area of Lubbock and the lower income areas of Amarillo and put them in the 13th District to help Democrat Bill Sarpalius; the Permian Basin oil towns of Midland and Odessa, where George and Barbara Bush moved in the pre-air conditioning days of 1948, were split to help 23d District Democrat Albert Bustamante (they didn't—Bustamante lost in 1992 and Sarpalius in 1994). This makes the 19th District overwhelmingly Republican, possibly one of the dozen most Republican districts in the country.

The congressman here is Larry Combest, originally an electronics distributor in Lubbock, now chairman of the House Intelligence Committee. Combest served on Senator John Tower's staff, specializing in farm issues. He moved back to Lubbock in 1978, then ran for Congress when Hance ran for the Senate in 1984. Combest had a tough primary, runoff and general election then, and has since won easily. Now holding a senior seat on Agriculture, he has specialized in farm issues; with an impeccably conservative voting record, he nevertheless opposed cutting target prices and ending subsidies in the 1990 farm bill, and looks forward to working on the

1995 farm bill as well. He supports the Conservation Reserve Program to retain topsoil in areas exposed to wind erosion and research funding for the Plant Stress and Water Conservation Laboratory at Texas Tech. But he insists that the prime farm issue is protecting property rights against government intervention to enforce environmental laws.

Combest's most important assignment is as chairman of the Intelligence Committee. He joined the committee in 1989, became ranking Republican in 1993 and, with Speaker Newt Gingrich waiving the usual six-year term limit for service on the committee, became chairman in 1995. Combest has always supported high defense spending, and believes there are many threats lurking: "Just as many varied intelligence assets (electronic, signal and human) are still needed in a world where the Soviet bear is gone, many poisonous snakes remain." In 1993 and 1994, unlike their Senate counterparts, Combest and Chairman Dan Glickman were relatively supportive of CIA Director James Woolsey. Combest does confess dismay at the Aldrich Ames spying case, and argues that agency personnel never accurately answered his questions on counter-espionage. The Ames case left Combest concerned about "the compartmented culture of the intelligence community." At the same time, he believes that cuts hidden from the public can be harmful, and intelligence successes hidden from the public are too readily discounted. He says that budget cuts forced the withdrawal of American intelligence from Somalia six months before Marines hit the beach; after the World Trade Center bombing in New York, he credited the intelligence agencies for foiling a plan to set off five simultaneous bombs elsewhere. Combest's immediate objectives for the committee are oversight in the wake of the Ames case and "our own 'bottom-up' review of the economic application of intelligence assets and objectives." He began his chairmanship by requesting that Congress block resurrection of the "Blackbird" strategic reconnaissance aircraft in the 1995 budget in an effort to save $100 million.

The People: Pop. 1990: 565,925; 18% rural; 10% age 65+; 77% White; 2% Black; 1% Amer. Indian; 1% Asian; 10% Other; 19% Hispanic origin. Voting age pop.: 402,873; 2% Black; 16% Hispanic origin. Households: 62% married couple families; 32% married couple fams. w. children; 50% college educ.; median household income: $27,267; per capita income: $13,184; median gross rent: $366; median house value: $55,000.

1992 Presidential Vote			1988 Presidential Vote		
Bush (R)	130,639	(60%)	Bush (R)	147,596	(74%)
Clinton (D)	50,815	(23%)	Dukakis (D)	51,195	(26%)
Perot (I)	36,068	(17%)			

Rep. Larry Combest (R)

Elected 1984; b. Mar. 20, 1945, Memphis; home, Lubbock; W. TX St. U., B.B.A. 1969; United Methodist; married (Sharon).

Career: Farmer; Teacher, 1970–71; Dir., U.S. Agric. Stabilization and Conservation Svc., Graham TX, 1971; Aide, U.S. Sen. John Tower, 1971–78; Founder & Pres., Combest Distrib. Co., 1978–1985.

DC Office: 1511 LHOB 20515, 202-225-4005; Fax: 202-225-9615.

District Offices: 1205 Texas Ave., #611, Lubbock 79401, 806-763-1611; 5809 S. Western, #205, Amarillo 79110, 806-353-3945; and 3800 E. 42d St., #205, Odessa 79762, 915-362-2631.

Committees: *Agriculture* (4th of 27 R): General Farm Commodities; Risk Management and Specialty Crops. *Intelligence (Permanent Select)* (Chmn. of 9 R).

Group Ratings

	ADA	ACLU	COPE	CFA	LCV	CON	NSI	COC	ACU	NTLC	CHC
1994	0	13	11	10	0	67	90	83	100	89	93
1993	5	—	8	20	29	10	—	91	96	—	—

National Journal Ratings

	1993 LIB — 1993 CONS		1994 LIB — 1994 CONS	
Economic	23% —	75%	0% —	80%
Social	0% —	89%	0% —	89%
Foreign	0% —	91%	0% —	88%

Key Votes of the 103d Congress

1. Clinton Deficit Plan	N	3. Brady Handgun Purchase	N	5. Lmt. UN Cmnd. of Forces	Y
2. NAFTA	Y	4. Strike Race/Death Pnlty.	Y	6. Cut Missile Funds	N

Key Votes of the 104th Congress

1. Congressional Compliance	Y	6. Reform Crime Grant	Y	11. Loser Pays Court Reform	Y
2. Balanced Budget Amndmt.	Y	7. National Security Act	Y	12. Product Liability Reform	Y
3. Bar Unfunded Mandates	Y	8. Moratorium on Regs.	Y	13. Welfare Reform	Y
4. Pass Line Item Veto	Y	9. Risk Assessment on Regs.	Y	14. Term Limits Amndmt.	Y
5. Relax Exclusionary Rule	Y	10. Expnd. Priv. Prop. Rights	Y	15. Tax Cuts	Y

Election Results

1994 general	Larry Combest (R).................	unopposed		($148,894)
1994 primary	Larry Combest (R).................	unopposed		
1992 general	Larry Combest (R)..................	162,057	(77%)	($197,657)
	Terry Lee Moser (D).................	47,325	(23%)	($5,198)

TWENTIETH DISTRICT

San Antonio, with its antique past and theme park future, its Hispanic heritage, its military superstructure and its high-tech hopes, is unlike any other city in the United states. Here on a plaza is the Alamo, preserved by the Daughters of the Republic of Texas, where Davy Crockett, Jim Bowie and 184 others were wiped out in 1836 (Crockett was a Tennessee congressman for three terms; if he had not lost his bid for reelection in 1835, he never would have left Tennessee for Texas). The Spanish architecture, recalling San Antonio's days as the most important town in Texas when the state was part of Mexico, contrasts with the 31-story Tower Life Building, which contrasts with the armadillo-like Alamodome; the stark terrain contrasts with the lushness of the Paseo, the 1970s-redeveloped Riverwalk along the tiny San Antonio River. The city also includes old neighborhoods redolent of the Texas Germans who were its chief Anglo citizens for many years. For most of this century, San Antonio's economy has been built on the military: this is the home of four Air Force bases and the Brooks Army Medical Center at Fort Sam Houston, contributing some $3 billion to the local economy; San Antonio also has 30,000 military retirees, second highest in the country. Behind them as a local employer is the medical complex centered on the Health Science Center. And San Antonio is also becoming a tourist center: for generations Texas schoolchildren have made pilgrimages to the Alamo, and in recent decades, they stop at the nearby HemisFair, preserved from the 1968 World's Fair, and the Riverwalk.

San Antonio had an estimated 940,000 people in 1995 and is the third largest city in Texas, though its metro area is barely more than one third the size of metro Houston or the Dallas-Fort Worth Metroplex. San Antonio is also notable as the only Hispanic-majority major city in the country, and it has the low education and income levels one might expect from a city whose economy is affected by the proximity of the Mexican border. Yet it has avoided the polarized politics and ethnic anger that was manifested in the urban black-white tensions of the 1960s and has made notable progress as a kind of low-wage, high-tech center, making some linkage with nearby Austin. Much of the credit is due Henry Cisneros, mayor from 1981–89, educated at Texas A&M and Harvard, who sparked high-tech and tourism growth but dropped out of Texas politics in 1989 over bad publicity from an extramarital affair, and in 1993 became Bill Clinton's secretary of Housing and Urban Development.

It was quite a different San Antonio that first elected Henry B. Gonzalez to the House in 1961. Then Texas's 20th District included all of Bexar County and it seemed unthinkable to Anglos in comfortable north side neighborhoods that a Mexican-American could represent them. Today, the 20th District includes just central San Antonio, roughly the part of the city within the I-410 loop, which has a large Hispanic majority and is solidly Democratic. It is hard now to imagine the prejudice against Mexican-Americans that existed in Texas decades ago, or how it affected Gonzalez, who learned to speak English by reading Carlyle and Stevenson. Gonzalez began serving on the San Antonio Council in 1953 and was elected to the Texas Senate in 1956—and had the nerve to run for governor in 1958 and for the Senate in the 1961 special election (against John Tower and Jim Wright, among others). Gonzalez ran poorly in those races, but later in 1961, when Congressman Paul Kilday, part of a long-successful San Antonio machine, was appointed to a federal judgeship, he got into the race for Congress—and won. In his early days in Congress, Gonzalez was the patron saint of Texas liberalism, as he compiled a record of support for the administration and civil rights. Always, Gonzalez has brought a determination to do right and an indifference to what others may think. He is not afraid to show his temper: in 1963, he took a swing at Texas Republican Congressman Ed Foreman who accused him of being a Communist; in 1986, he punched a 40-year-old man in a San Antonio restaurant for the same offense—one which must particularly rankle a man who has served his country loyally for many years.

From 1989 to 1994, Gonzalez was chairman of the Banking Committee, the lone-wolf head of a fractious, divisive pack. His first major task was the savings and loan bailout bill, made necessary by the failures of his predecessor Fernand St Germain. Gonzalez hammered out a version that may have cracked down too hard on some S&L investments but which enabled regulators to wind up most of their work by 1993. Gonzalez also held hearings on the Charles Keating scandal. Gonzalez's first love has been housing programs, and after some tussles with HUD Secretary Jack Kemp he passed a housing bill that included his National Housing Trust proposal. Gonzalez's go-it-alone style can prompt opposition. Bruce Vento of Minnesota challenged him for chairman in December 1990; Gonzalez won 163–89, but most Democratic chairmen were never challenged at all. And in 1991 a jurisdictional squabble with Commerce Chairman John Dingell ended up in a major banking bill going down 324–89.

Perhaps in response to legislative disappointments, Gonzalez started investing more energy in partisan responses to alleged scandal. In 1991 he started probing "Iraqgate," citing evidence that the Bush Administration knew or should have known that federal farm product guarantees were being used by Iraq and the Atlanta branch of Banca Nazionale del Lavoro to generate cash to pay for weapons before the Gulf war. Gonzalez went so far out on a limb as to call for Bush's impeachment on the issue. The administration cut him off from documents and Republicans sought an Ethics Committee investigation of leaking by Gonzalez; in time the issue died. In late 1993 he angrily blocked any investigation of the Whitewater scandals and accused ranking Republican Jim Leach, who like Gonzalez had proved his nonpartisan bona fides on S&Ls, of acting as a shill for the Republican Caucus. Gonzalez canceled a March 1994 hearing at which Leach would have raised Whitewater and refused to endorse Leach's efforts to get government documents, accusing Republicans of a "witch hunt." In June 1994 he agreed to hearings, but under absurd conditions. Most issues were declared out of bounds, questioning was limited and Democrats used wisecracks and ridicule to discredit the entire hearing—and may have contributed to the discrediting of their party's stewardship of the House, which produced the results of November. In the meantime, the committee's big legislative issue—consolidating bank regulators—went nowhere.

In 1994 Gonzalez was, as always, easily reelected in the overwhelmingly Democratic 20th. But the Republican takeover removed Gonzalez from the chair and gave Leach control of the Whitewater investigation. Unlike his Senate Banking Committee counterpart Al D'Amato, Leach was content to wait for independent counsel Kenneth Starr to complete much of his work. Gonzalez may still play some role on banking legislation on which bipartisan agreement is needed, and he will certainly protest what he considers partisan unfairness by Republicans. But, as he approaches 80, he is unlikely to have great influence again, unless he holds on until Democrats regain control of the House.

The People: Pop. 1990: 564,865; 3% rural; 10% age 65+; 32% White; 6% Black; 1% Asian; 21% Other; 60% Hispanic origin. Voting age pop.: 398,058; 6% Black; 56% Hispanic origin. Households: 51% married couple families; 28% married couple fams. w. children; 44% college educ.; median household income: $22,372; per capita income: $9,672; median gross rent: $362; median house value: $48,500.

1992 Presidential Vote

Clinton (D)	81,381	(48%)
Bush (R)	57,977	(34%)
Perot (I)	28,968	(17%)

1988 Presidential Vote

Dukakis (D)	80,307	(57%)
Bush (R)	61,599	(43%)

Rep. Henry B. Gonzalez (D)

Elected Nov. 1961; b. May 3, 1916, San Antonio; home, San Antonio; San Antonio Jr. Col., A.A. 1937, U. of TX, St. Mary's U., LL.B., J.D. 1943; Catholic; married (Bertha).

Career: Military Intelligence, 1941–44; Bexar Cnty. Chief Probation Officer, 1946; Dpty. Dir., San Antonio Housing Authority, 1950–51; San Antonio City Cncl., 1953–56, San Antonio Mayor Pro Tem, 1955–56; TX Senate, 1956–61.

DC Office: 2413 RHOB 20515, 202-225-3236; Fax: 202-225-1915.

District Offices: #B-124 Fed. Bldg., 727 E. Durango St., San Antonio 78206, 512-229-6195.

Committees: *Banking & Financial Services* (RMM of 22 D): Housing and Community Opportunity.

Group Ratings

	ADA	ACLU	COPE	CFA	LCV	CON	NSI	COC	ACU	NTLC	CHC
1994	75	87	100	100	83	0	50	25	15	7	7
1993	80	—	100	100	71	7	—	9	8	—	—

National Journal Ratings

	1993 LIB — 1993 CONS			1994 LIB — 1994 CONS		
Economic	78%	—	12%	72%	—	27%
Social	78%	—	21%	94%	—	0%
Foreign	51%	—	42%	57%	—	37%

Key Votes of the 103d Congress

1. Clinton Deficit Plan	Y	3. Brady Handgun Purchase	Y	5. Lmt. UN Cmnd. of Forces	N
2. NAFTA	N	4. Strike Race/Death Pnlty.	N	6. Cut Missile Funds	N

Key Votes of the 104th Congress

1. Congressional Compliance Y	6. Reform Crime Grant N	11. Loser Pays Court Reform N
2. Balanced Budget Amndmt. N	7. National Security Act N	12. Product Liability Reform N
3. Bar Unfunded Mandates Y	8. Moratorium on Regs. *	13. Welfare Reform N
4. Pass Line Item Veto N	9. Risk Assessment on Regs. *	14. Term Limits Amndmt. N
5. Relax Exclusionary Rule N	10. Expnd. Priv. Prop. Rights *	15. Tax Cuts N

Election Results

1994 general	Henry B. Gonzalez (D)	60,114	(63%)	($55,382)
	Carl Bill Colyer (R)	36,035	(37%)	
1994 primary	Henry B. Gonzalez (D)	unopposed		
1992 general	Henry B. Gonzalez (D)	unopposed		($43,147)

TWENTY-FIRST DISTRICT

The Texas German country, on the gently rolling plains between San Antonio and Austin and west into the Hill Country, is one of this nation's lesser known ethnic enclaves. First settled by refugees from the failed democratic revolutions of 1848, the German country has always been a set of orderly communities in riproaring Texas, economically prosperous in a state that considered itself poor until it struck oil. It has been antislavery and politically Republican in a state whose enthusiasm for the Democratic party had roots in Confederate loyalties and populist rebellions. The Texas Germans in political history are entwined with the career of Lyndon Johnson: the death of Republican Congressman Harry Wurzbach of Guadalupe County enabled the Democrats to elect John Nance Garner of Uvalde speaker in 1931, while Wurzbach's replacement in the House, Democrat Richard Kleberg (of the King ranch family) hired the then 23-year-old Johnson to his first Washington job. And, though Johnson never emphasized this, his LBJ Ranch was not in Blanco County or near poor Johnson City, where he grew up, but west in Gillespie County near the prosperous town of Fredericksburg, historically Texas German and heavily Republican.

The 21st Congressional District has its demographic center in the old Texas German country. But, as with so many Texas districts under the 1991 redistricting, its boundaries are quite complex. And this is now a metropolitan district, with most of its population technically in the San Antonio or Austin metropolitan areas. About 40% is on the north side of San Antonio and Bexar County (pronounced like a drawn-out *bear*), mostly Anglo neighborhoods around Alamo Heights and out Interstate 35, and in Guadalupe and Comal Counties just beyond—Texas German country now classified as part of metro San Antonio; all this is heavily Republican. Another 20% is in Williamson County, just north of Austin—suburban overspill subdivisions full of high-tech and white-collar workers who are much more Republican than the liberals who live in older neighborhoods near downtown Austin and UT. These two areas are connected by sparsely populated Hill Country and Texas German counties, including Fredericksburg and the LBJ Ranch, the almost mountainous country around Kerrville, sheep and goat ranching country reaching west to San Angelo, the mohair capital of America, all the way to Midland, headquarters of the high-income, oil-rich Permian Basin, where George Bush lived from 1949 to 1960.

The congressman from the 21st District is Lamar Smith, a Republican first elected in 1986, now suddenly powerful as chairman of the Judiciary Committee's Immigration Subcommittee and member of the Budget Committee. Smith is from an old San Antonio and south Texas ranching family and served both in the legislature and on the Bexar County Commission. When he first ran, the 21st ranged far wider and had more acreage than Ohio; he won by beating two other San Antonio-based candidates in the primary 31%–25%–20% and then winning the runoff, with help from Senator Phil Gramm, against a religious conservative. He has been reelected easily since.

In his first three terms, Smith earned a conservative record and pursued some original initiatives. One Smith bill added 100,000 acres to Big Bend National Park along the Rio Grande; another sponsored the Bush Administration's government-wide ethics act. By 1991, Smith was proposing cuts in every appropriation bill, with special emphasis on cutting government overhead costs, especially travel; often Democrats prevented them from coming to a vote. Appointed to Budget in 1993, he worked on now-Chairman John Kasich's alternative budget and has pointed out that the budget could be balanced with a one-year spending freeze and inflation rate increases only thereafter. Standing out from the crowd among the influential Texas Republicans has not been easy. In April 1993 he was appointed head of the Republicans' "theme team," organizing more than 800 one-minute speeches by Republican members. He also was active in drafting parts of the Contract With America dealing with legal and regulatory issues. Meanwhile, he pursued other interests: stopping designation of part of Texas as "critical habitat" for the golden-cheeked warbler, funding programs to promote teen abstinence, stopping HIV-positive aliens from attending the Gay Games.

In 1995, Smith became chairman of the Judiciary Committee's Immigration Subcommittee, on which he had been ranking Republican since 1991. On the 1990 immigration bill he worked hard and with little success to hold down legal quotas and grants of refugee status against an Irish-Hispanic-Asian alliance at a time of little public concern. He did win a provision preventing illegal aliens from using Legal Service Corporation lawyers except in employment, housing or transportation cases. Now anti-immigration feeling is much greater and Smith is well positioned to advance his views. He seems likely to support lower quotas for legal immigrants, perhaps with more emphasis on skills and less on family unification. He is also likely to support stricter border enforcement, perhaps of the kind pioneered in El Paso in 1993. Immigration is a difficult issue, and even determined chairmen have often found it impossible to pass any bill at all. But it is possible that Smith will play a major role in reducing legal immigration to the U.S. for the first time since the 1920s.

The People: Pop. 1990: 566,105; 29% rural; 13% age 65+; 82% White; 3% Black; 1% Asian; 5% Other; 14% Hispanic origin. Voting age pop.: 420,543; 2% Black; 12% Hispanic origin. Households: 63% married couple families; 29% married couple fams. w. children; 59% college educ.; median household income: $32,103; per capita income: $16,086; median gross rent: $434; median house value: $79,400.

1992 Presidential Vote

Bush (R)	144,073	(52%)
Clinton (D)	70,677	(25%)
Perot (I)	63,454	(23%)

1988 Presidential Vote

Bush (R)	169,319	(70%)
Dukakis (D)	71,647	(30%)

Rep. Lamar S. Smith (R)

Elected 1986; b. Nov. 19, 1947, San Antonio; home, San Antonio; Yale, B.A. 1969, Southern Methodist U., J.D. 1975; Christian Scientist; married (Beth).

Career: U.S. Small Business Admin., 1969–70; Business writer, *Christian Science Monitor*, 1970–72; Practicing atty., 1975–76; TX House of Reps., 1981–82; Bexar Cnty. Commissioner, 1982–85.

DC Office: 2443 RHOB 20515, 202-225-4236; Fax: 202-225-8628.

District Offices: 1st Federal Bldg., 1100 NE Loop 410, #640, San Antonio 78209, 210-821-5024; 201 W. Wall St., #104, Midland 79701, 915-687-5232; 1006 Junction Hwy., Kerrville 78028, 512-895-1414; 221 E. Main, #318, Round Rock 78664, 512-218-4221; and 33 E. Twohig, #302, San Angelo 76903, 915-653-3971.

Committees: *Budget* (8th of 24 R). *Judiciary* (7th of 20 R): Constitution; Immigration and Claims (Chmn.).

Group Ratings

	ADA	ACLU	COPE	CFA	LCV	CON	NSI	COC	ACU	NTLC	CHC
1994	5	18	11	20	0	84	100	92	95	92	93
1993	5	—	8	20	21	69	—	100	96	—	—

National Journal Ratings

	1993 LIB — 1993 CONS		1994 LIB — 1994 CONS	
Economic	14%	— 80%	0%	— 80%
Social	0%	— 89%	0%	— 89%
Foreign	0%	— 91%	0%	— 88%

Key Votes of the 103d Congress

1. Clinton Deficit Plan	N	3. Brady Handgun Purchase N	5. Lmt. UN Cmnd. of Forces Y
2. NAFTA	Y	4. Strike Race/Death Pnlty. Y	6. Cut Missile Funds N

Key Votes of the 104th Congress

1. Congressional Compliance Y	6. Reform Crime Grant Y	11. Loser Pays Court Reform Y
2. Balanced Budget Amndmt. Y	7. National Security Act Y	12. Product Liability Reform Y
3. Bar Unfunded Mandates Y	8. Moratorium on Regs. Y	13. Welfare Reform Y
4. Pass Line Item Veto Y	9. Risk Assessment on Regs. Y	14. Term Limits Amndmt. Y
5. Relax Exclusionary Rule Y	10. Expnd. Priv. Prop. Rights Y	15. Tax Cuts Y

Election Results

1994 general	Lamar S. Smith (R)	165,595	(90%)	($538,347)
	Kerry L. Lowry (I)	18,480	(10%)	
1994 primary	Lamar S. Smith (R)	44,600	(82%)	
	Scott Campbell (R)	10,050	(18%)	
1992 general	Lamar S. Smith (R)	190,979	(72%)	($476,501)
	James M. Gaddy (D)	62,827	(24%)	($5,694)
	William E. Grisham (Lib)	10,847	(4%)	

TWENTY-SECOND DISTRICT

Spreading out in all directions from its historic center at Allen's Landing on Buffalo Bayou, Houston has become one of the great metropolises of North America. A half-century ago, the steaming flatlands south of Houston running down to the Gulf of Mexico did not seem a likely site of one of the world's most advanced civilizations. But they are today. On Clear Lake, not far from the sluggish and oily shores of Galveston Bay, is the Johnson Space Center, where NASA's top engineers plan space flights. Farther south, where the narrow Brazos River enters the Gulf of Mexico, is the Brazosport complex of towns, with some of the biggest oil refinery and petrochemical operations anywhere—an example of the petroleum engineering expertise that makes greater Houston an oil capital even though less and less oil is actually drilled in these parts. Back up Route 288 are the outlying parts of central Houston—the Texas Medical Center and Rice University, the art museum complex and the 30- and 60-story high-rises that tower over the Southwest Freeway, where all manner of business genius is being employed. The success and sophistication is testimony to human—and Texan—creativity, and to the triumph of air conditioning. For who supposed that all these people would move here if they had to sweat through Houston's steamy five-month summer?

Put all these areas together, roughly, and you have the 22d Congressional District of Texas. First established in the 1950s, when it included all the south side of Houston, it has moved farther out each decade. In the 1991 redistricting, only 45% of its people were in Houston's Harris County—most in a jagged corridor running along the Southwest Freeway, where many of Houston's business and creative leaders live, and in a separate corridor around the Space Center and Galveston Bay. The 22d also includes most of Fort Bend County just southwest of Houston—starting with Sugar Land, a series of suburbs growing in what was once farming country. The 22d finally moves directly south to include most of Brazoria County, including land along 288 not yet filled in with suburbs, and most of the Brazosport area. The 22d is a heavily Republican district. You will be hard pressed to find many national Democrats among the people who have come from other parts of Texas and the nation to live in these new, mostly affluent subdivisions. Even in local elections the historic Democratic leanings of the rural areas are usually overwhelmed by the strong Republican allegiance of the newcomers. Its boundaries may be much altered by redistricting, depending on the courts and perhaps the legislature. But there are enough Republican voters in this southwest quadrant of metropolitan Houston to guarantee there will be a Republican 22d.

The congressman from the 22d District is Tom DeLay, the House Majority Whip, number three member of the House Republican leadership—an aggressive political operator, strong ideological conservative and key member of the new leadership team. DeLay was born in the border town of Laredo and spent much of his childhood in Venezuela, where his father drilled oil wells. Settling in Sugar Land, DeLay built a pest control business and was elected to the state legislature in 1978, the first Republican legislator from Fort Bend County this century. DeLay easily won the 1984 Republican primary and the general election for this seat. His voting record is almost purely conservative, but he sought posts that usually appeal to more practical pols. In his first term, he was the freshman representative on the Republican Committee on Committees. In his second term he got a seat on the Appropriations Committee, where he has been known to seek money for his district, including grants for a bus system to ease traffic on the choked Southwest Freeway. But he opposed former Mayor Kathy Whitmire's $1.2 billion monorail (which surely would never pay its way in this automobile culture) and took on Senators Lloyd Bentsen and Phil Gramm in 1991 when they sought $30 million for it, and was successful in getting a provision postponing spending until there was a "consensus" on the type of transit system to build.

DeLay is an ardent booster of the space program and has worked mightily to save the Space Station from demise. Partly through his efforts this scientifically unadventurous venture survived in 1994, winning 278–155 in the House, while the scientifically much more interesting Supercollider was killed in October 1993. Another issue DeLay heavily weighs in on is regulation—or overregulation, as he would put it. He was an ardent backer of Vice President Dan Quayle's Competitiveness Council and drafted the regulatory section of the Contract With America. In early 1995, working with committee leaders on Capitol Hill and with lobbyists from downtown, he was taking a lead role on regulatory relief designed to halt and reverse the steady growth and power of the federal bureaucracy, especially as it affects corporate decisions in the free market. Through increased use of risk assessment and cost-benefit analyses and a moratorium on new regulations, DeLay's goal has been to change Washington's regulatory culture, particularly as it affects pest controllers and other small businesses around the nation. In doing that, he also has sought to make the downtown lobbyists more sympathetic to what he considers their natural allies among Republicans and to end their alliance of convenience with Democrats. He is a solid supporter of NAFTA and market-based healthcare reform.

DeLay may talk issues, but leadership positions—in which politicking usually overshadows issue talk—seem to suit him best. Not all his moves are deft. In March 1989, when Minority Whip Dick Cheney became Defense Secretary, DeLay actively supported Robert Michel's Illinois colleague Edward Madigan over Newt Gingrich, indeed managed his campaign: DeLay's attempt to get on the inside. But Gingrich won 87–85, and DeLay adapted. In December 1992, he ran against Ohio's Bill Gradison for the post of Republican Conference Secretary and won 95–71. At the start of the 103d Congress, DeLay, who had earlier tried to overturn funding of the District of Columbia's domestic partnership law, zeroed in on the gays in the military issue. And at the end of the session, he organized the effort to defeat the Democrats' lobby reform bill. In between and afterward he was running very hard for the number three leadership position. If Republicans had remained in the minority, as almost everyone in Washington expected, DeLay would have run for Whip, leapfrogging Dick Armey, who had described him as his best friend. When Republicans won the majority, Armey became the natural candidate for majority leader and DeLay for whip. He had strong opposition: Bob Walker, Newt Gingrich's best friend in the House and probably the Republicans' best expert on House rules, was running; so was Bill McCollum of Florida, one of the Republicans' most active legislators, especially on crime issues.

But DeLay was the best organized. He campaigned in 25 states in 1994, and contributed to large numbers of Republican candidates, responsible for the dispersal of $2 million in campaign funds by his own count. He schmoozed his colleagues even when it hurt ("It's like walking on eggs for a year. Any time anybody argues with you about an issue, they always bring it up," he said.) DeLay showed his vote-counting acumen by proclaiming that he was not interested in the second-ballot votes he would need if no one had a majority: "We are locked into winning this outright." He won with 119 votes to 80 for Walker and 28 for McCollum. And he quickly assembled a whip organization, mostly from supporters led by Dennis Hastert of Illinois, but including some leadership race opponents as well. There was surely some tension here with Gingrich, who remembers the 1989 whip race. While Gingrich raised his and Dick Armey's budgets for the 104th from those of their predecessors, Thomas Foley and Dick Gephardt, DeLay's budget was cut. DeLay acquiesced gracefully, and persevered in his legislative work to overturn two generations of presumptions in favor of federal regulations. And there also is tension with Republican Conference Chairman John Boehner, as the two disagreed over which of them should control outside-group coalitions. Whether he will ascend higher into the leadership is unclear; but he already is having great impact.

The People: Pop. 1990: 567,852; 14% rural; 6% age 65+; 69% White; 8% Black; 7% Asian; 8% Other; 16% Hispanic origin. Voting age pop.: 407,903; 7% Black; 14% Hispanic origin. Households: 63% married couple families; 35% married couple fams. w. children; 63% college educ.; median household income: $40,654; per capita income: $17,608; median gross rent: $453; median house value: $75,100.

1992 Presidential Vote

Bush (R)	116,557	(51%)
Clinton (D)	63,092	(27%)
Perot (I)	50,705	(22%)

1988 Presidential Vote

Bush (R)	123,211	(69%)
Dukakis (D)	54,775	(31%)

Rep. Tom DeLay (R)

Elected 1984; b. Apr. 8, 1947, Laredo; home, Sugar Land; U. of Houston, B.S. 1970; Baptist; married (Christine).

Career: Owner, Albo Pest Control, 1973–84; TX House of Reps., 1978–84.

DC Office: 203 CHOB 20515, 202-225-5951; Fax: 202-225-5241.

District Offices: 12603 Southwest Frwy., #285, Stafford 77477, 713-240-3700.

Committees: *Majority Whip. Appropriations* (11th of 32 R): Transportation; VA, HUD, and Independent Agencies.

Group Ratings

	ADA	ACLU	COPE	CFA	LCV	CON	NSI	COC	ACU	NTLC	CHC
1994	0	17	0	0	0	76	100	92	100	96	100
1993	0	—	0	0	14	64	—	100	100	—	—

National Journal Ratings

	1993 LIB — 1993 CONS	1994 LIB — 1994 CONS
Economic	0% — 88%	0% — 80%
Social	0% — 89%	0% — 89%
Foreign	0% — 91%	0% — 88%

Key Votes of the 103d Congress

1. Clinton Deficit Plan	N	3. Brady Handgun Purchase N	5. Lmt. UN Cmnd. of Forces Y
2. NAFTA	Y	4. Strike Race/Death Pnlty. Y	6. Cut Missile Funds N

Key Votes of the 104th Congress

1. Congressional Compliance Y	6. Reform Crime Grant Y	11. Loser Pays Court Reform Y
2. Balanced Budget Amndmt. Y	7. National Security Act Y	12. Product Liability Reform Y
3. Bar Unfunded Mandates Y	8. Moratorium on Regs. Y	13. Welfare Reform Y
4. Pass Line Item Veto Y	9. Risk Assessment on Regs. Y	14. Term Limits Amndmt. N
5. Relax Exclusionary Rule Y	10. Expnd. Priv. Prop. Rights Y	15. Tax Cuts Y

Election Results

1994 general	Tom DeLay (R)	120,302	(74%)	($701,245)
	Scott Douglas Cunningham (D)	38,826	(24%)	($149,385)
	Others	4,016	(2%)	
1994 primary	Tom DeLay (R)	unopposed		
1992 general	Tom DeLay (R)	150,221	(69%)	($371,362)
	Richard Konrad (D)	67,812	(31%)	($39,836)

TWENTY-THIRD DISTRICT

The border country of Texas is a zone all its own. It is part of the United States but its culture and economy are not entirely Yanqui or Latino, a local economy that fluctuates depending on, among other things, the strength of the peso and the aggressiveness of INS patrols. Years ago, movements like La Raza Unida—which got its beginnings here in 1969 when Hispanic youngsters wanted to elect high school cheerleaders in Crystal City—wanted the border country to become more like Mexico, with its union and party apparatchiks. More recently, with former President Salinas's economic reforms and NAFTA, it seems that Mexico has sought to become more like the United States, and particularly like Texas, with open markets and privatized companies, fewer local political or labor bosses, even while so-called Mexican food has become a staple all over the United States. Border towns like Laredo have seen great growth, as Mexico opens up, and then bust, when Mexico devalues the peso, as in 1982 and again in 1994, which raised anxieties on both sides of the border. In the early 1990s Laredo was the second fastest-growing U.S. metro area, with one of the largest Wal-Marts and the busiest railroad crossing on the border. The bustle does not go very far from the Rio Grande. This is quiet ranching and oil country and places like Loving County, the smallest U.S. county with 141 people in 1990, are not changing much from one decade to another.

The 23d Congressional District of Texas includes the longest portion of the 2,500-mile U.S.-Mexico border, following the Rio Grande almost from El Paso south past Laredo. The 23d begins in the Anglo neighborhoods on the north side of San Antonio and goes all the way to the Big Bend territory, where 7,000-foot peaks tower over stony desert. It covers miles of arid hills and rugged desert, of cattle grazing, sheep ranching and oil well country. Yet most of its people live in a few widely scattered metropolitan areas, about one-third in or near San Antonio, with others in Laredo, Midland and Odessa, and the fringes of El Paso. Politically, the border counties around Laredo and Eagle Pass are heavily Democratic, while many of the grazing counties inland are Republican. Some 63% of the residents here in 1990 were Hispanic, as were something approaching 50% of its voters.

The congressman from the 23d is Henry Bonilla, a Republican who beat an incumbent in 1992 and held on to the seat impressively in 1994. He was brought up in a Latino neighborhood in San Antonio; his grandmother worked as a maid and his father worked two jobs. Bonilla went to the University of Texas and then worked as a TV reporter, news producer and executive at local stations in San Antonio, New York, Philadelphia and in 1986 San Antonio again, where he appeared on TV as did his wife, news anchor Deborah Knapp Bonilla. In 1991, Bexar County Republican leaders recruited Bonilla to run for Congress against incumbent Democrat Albert Bustamante, who was an attractive target. In 1990 the *San Antonio Light* reported that the FBI was investigating Bustamante and a local bingo operator for racketeering. Then Bustamante was revealed to have 30 overdrafts on the House bank, was attacked for junkets to Europe and Asia and was accused of connections with a law firm which received delinquent tax collection contracts and had at one time employed Bustamante's wife. Bustamente was eventually convicted of 2 counts of misuse of office for racketeering and bribery.

Bonilla, who has said that "Newt inspired me to run for office," backed standard conservative planks—term limits, the line-item veto and a congressional ethics committee made up of private citizens. But he made his own issues as well. He opposed two new hazardous waste dumps near Del Rio and hit Bustamante for preventing a visiting Mexican legislator from attending an event at which Bonilla was scheduled to sign a U.S.-Mexico anti-toxic waste pledge. Bonilla backed tax and environmental policies more favorable to the oil industry and sided with water users over the allegedly endangered fountain darter fish in a dispute over Comal Springs. Bustamante called Bonilla "a eunuch for the plantation owners" for opposing a minimum wage bill, but Bonilla won by a whopping 59%–38%, with most of his margin in San Antonio's Bexar County, which he won 81%–16%. Three months later Bustamante was indicted on bribery and racketeering charges and in 1994 went to prison.

Republicans, ecstatic at electing their first Mexican-American representative in Texas, gave Bonilla a seat on the Appropriations Committee and he has grown close to Gingrich. He had a conservative voting record, with some exceptions. He pushed for money for Hispanic schools and a Laredo bridge and was successful in delaying tighter rules on trade schools. He voted enthusiastically for NAFTA and against gun control.

Democrats dearly wanted the seat back and the 1994 Democratic nominee, Rolando Rios, a voting rights attorney, hit Bonilla hard for opposing the Clinton budget, the earned income tax credit and gun control. Bonilla attacked Rios as "one of those pseudo-intellectuals who think that all Mexican-American voters want to hear about is food stamps and welfare ... They're insulted ... They want to be free to run their lives the way they want." Bonilla won by a striking 63%–37%, winning 76% in Bexar County but, more important for the longer run, carrying most of the border counties and losing Laredo by only 59%–41%. Bonilla ran well ahead of his ticket, but even George W. Bush ran about even here, suggesting that the area that La Raza Unida thought would be the launching ground for a revolution is instead a breeding ground for Newt Gingrich Republicans. For it was Bonilla who nominated Gingrich for speaker at the House Republican Conference and who can give personal testimony to its philosophy: "You can have anything you ask for, if you are willing to step forward and work."

The People: Pop. 1990: 566,736; 25% rural; 9% age 65+; 34% White; 3% Black; 1% Asian; 22% Other; 62% Hispanic origin. Voting age pop.: 375,375; 3% Black; 58% Hispanic origin. Households: 66% married couple families; 38% married couple fams. w. children; 39% college educ.; median household income: $21,555; per capita income: $9,764; median gross rent: $322; median house value: $47,900.

1992 Presidential Vote

Clinton (D)	72,452	(42%)
Bush (R)	70,576	(41%)
Perot (I)	28,846	(17%)

1988 Presidential Vote

Dukakis (D)	78,900	(51%)
Bush (R)	76,884	(49%)

Rep. Henry Bonilla (R)

Elected 1992; b. Jan. 2, 1954, San Antonio; home, San Antonio; U. of TX, B.A. 1976; Baptist; married (Deborah).

Career: TV reporter, 1976–80; Asst. Press Secy., PA Gov. Thornburgh, 1981; Writer/producer, WABC, New York, 1982–85; Asst. News Dir., WATF-TV, Philadelphia, 1985–86; KENS-TV, San Antonio, Exec. News Producer, 1986–89, Public Affairs, 1989–92.

DC Office: 1427 LHOB 20515, 202-225-4511; Fax: 202-225-2237.

District Offices: 11120 Wurzbach, #300, San Antonio 78230, 210-697-9055; 1300 Matamoros St., #113B, Laredo 78040, 210-726-4682; 100 E. Broadway, #101, Del Rio 78840, 210-774-6547; 4400 N. Big Spring, #211, Midland 79705, 915-686-8833.

Committees: *Appropriations* (21st of 32 R): District of Columbia; Labor, Health and Human Services, and Education; National Security.

Group Ratings

	ADA	ACLU	COPE	CFA	LCV	CON	NSI	COC	ACU	NTLC	CHC
1994	0	13	0	20	6	76	90	100	95	96	93
1993	5	—	0	10	21	88	—	100	96	—	—

National Journal Ratings

	1993 LIB	—	1993 CONS	1994 LIB	—	1994 CONS
Economic	28%	—	72%	26%	—	70%
Social	27%	—	72%	20%	—	77%
Foreign	0%	—	91%	0%	—	88%

Key Votes of the 103d Congress

1. Clinton Deficit Plan	N	3. Brady Handgun Purchase	N	5. Lmt. UN Cmnd. of Forces Y
2. NAFTA	Y	4. Strike Race/Death Pnlty.	Y	6. Cut Missile Funds N

Key Votes of the 104th Congress

1. Congressional Compliance Y	6. Reform Crime Grant Y	11. Loser Pays Court Reform Y
2. Balanced Budget Amndmt. Y	7. National Security Act Y	12. Product Liability Reform Y
3. Bar Unfunded Mandates Y	8. Moratorium on Regs. Y	13. Welfare Reform Y
4. Pass Line Item Veto Y	9. Risk Assessment on Regs. Y	14. Term Limits Amndmt. Y
5. Relax Exclusionary Rule Y	10. Expnd. Priv. Prop. Rights Y	15. Tax Cuts Y

Election Results

1994 general	Henry Bonilla (R)	73,815	(63%)	($758,591)
	Rolando L. Rios (D)	44,101	(37%)	($426,042)
1994 primary	Henry Bonilla (R)	unopposed		
1992 general	Henry Bonilla (R)	98,259	(59%)	($594,032)
	Albert G. Bustamante (D)	63,797	(38%)	($758,453)
	Other	4,291	(3%)	

TWENTY-FOURTH DISTRICT

The geographical heart of the Dallas-Fort Worth Metroplex was open country as late as the 1950s, when the Dallas-Fort Worth Turnpike was built to link the two downtowns. Then, over the next three decades, the bottomlands of the West Fork of the Trinity River and the barren hills overlooking them filled up. Whole new Dallases and Fort Worths, with as many people as the central cities had in the 1940s—Grand Prairie and Arlington and Irvington—grew up in these once impoverished lands and became central to one of America's richest and most productive metropolitan areas. Major landmarks have arisen here as well, from Six Flags Over Texas to The Ballpark in Arlington, the new old-style major league baseball stadium that replaced the old modern Turnpike Stadium. New subdivisions are going up here, but one can still see barren hills above the Metroplex. These new towns are taking on a graceful aging air, as trees grow and houses are renovated and added onto and commercial buildings are adapted to new and unexpected uses. Not that the oldest areas are all left behind: there are slums in the Metroplex, but also neighborhoods like Oak Cliff, across the Trinity River south of Dallas, large parts of which are being redeveloped by Texans appreciating their prairie architectural heritage.

When the Mid-Cities area, as it is sometime known, started filling up in the 1950s, Dallas was Republican and Fort Worth Democratic; in the years since, the white Anglo majority in the Metroplex has tilted heavily Republican, and most Democratic votes have come from blacks and Hispanics. But there were and still are pockets of blue-collar whites who give Democrats at least sizeable minorities—in the lower income areas of Grand Prairie or around the GM assembly plant in Arlington.

The 24th Congressional District of Texas, in the boundaries used for 1992 and 1994, collects as many such areas as possible, plus a black neighborhood in southeast Fort Worth. The first 24th District was established in 1972; as the population between Dallas and Fort Worth grew, the 26th was added in 1982; now the 6th includes much of this area. The boundaries of all of these are as convoluted as any in America, thanks to the 24th's congressman since 1978,

Democrat Martin Frost. Frost's tenure was threatened more than anyone else's by the interpretation of the 1982 amendments to the Voting Rights Act requiring a maximum number of black-majority districts. He had been getting most—perhaps all—of his comfortable majorities in black precincts, but most of those would be taken to create a new black-majority district anchored in Dallas, to comply with the law and because the Texas Senate redistricting committee was headed by Eddie Bernice Johnson, a black woman from Dallas who is now the congresswoman from the 30th District.

Frost and his staffer Bob Mansker responded with a plan of breathtaking creativity, not just for the Metroplex but for the whole state, creating a new seat for Johnson and winnable districts for Frost and John Bryant, a white Democrat from the east side of Dallas, whose 24th and 5th Districts were attached by the thinnest of tentacles to rural areas far beyond the Metroplex. This all succeeded, but only barely. Frost's old district was 29% black and 21% Hispanic; the new district, which included large parts of Fort Worth, Oak Cliff, Grand Prairie and Arlington, is 19% black and 21% Hispanic. In 1994, Frost was reelected 53%–47%; Bryant by 50%–47%. But neither is home free. A federal court has ruled that the Frost-Mansker plan must be changed, and once Johnson's 30th District is altered, the 24th and 5th must change as well, and probably the whole state. Frost could conceivably be helped by getting more black precincts; indeed, he was saved in 1994 by black precincts in Fort Worth which were too far away from Johnson's grasp. But geographically regular boundaries could easily bring into the 24th enough overwhelmingly Republican precincts to change the result.

It is not surprising that Frost fought hard and creatively for his seat. Politics has been practically his whole professional life. He first ran for Congress in 1974 at 32 and, except for a few years in school and a stint as a public broadcasting commentator and a lawyer, has spent all his adult life in Congress. He first won the seat in 1978 by reversing the 1974 result and beating conservative Democratic incumbent Dale Milford. As a freshman he got a seat on the Rules Committee, thanks to then-Majority Leader Jim Wright of Fort Worth. Frost was a stalwart supporter of Wright to the end and has been a Democratic leadership man ever since. He worked in tandem with Wright to kill measures that would have tightened lending and investment requirements for S&Ls and would have increased capital requirements. He lost two leadership bids in the 1980s, backing off a bid to chair the Budget Committee in 1984 and losing the race for Caucus Vice Chairman to Vic Fazio in 1989 by 147–74. But he came back to chair the IMPAC 2000 redistricting panel from 1991–94 and, as a loyal backer of Minority Leader Dick Gephardt, he was appointed chairman of the Democratic Congressional Campaign Committee after the debacle of 1994. His goal of regaining the Democrats' control of the House in 1996 surely will be a demanding challenge, with Frost working to keep down the number of retirees from his side, finding quality challengers for the large corps of Republican freshmen and ensuring that the House Democrats' financial base remains in place despite their minority status. He also works hard on local issues: keeping the V-22 Osprey and the C-17 transport, securing some $720 million in cash, land and equipment to close down the Supercollider site after the project was defeated (despite his strong advocacy) in October 1993, expanding the DFW Airport runways, getting funds for the Dallas Area Rapid Transit system.

Despite all his strengths, Frost has had tough competition in the 1990s. In the new 24th he designed, he spent $1.5 million, most of it raised from business PACs, in 1992 and won with 60%—only 53% in Dallas County but 68% in Fort Worth, Arlington and Tarrant County. In 1994, he was opposed by Ed Harrison, a homebuilder who had supported himself from age 16, who gave $85,000 of his own money to his campaign and attacked Frost for voting with President Clinton 91% of the time. Frost raised well over $1 million again, scampered on the crime issue (switching to oppose the assault weapon ban, then voting for the crime bill rule) and had the chutzpah, after his years of leadership loyalty, to accuse Harrison of kowtowing to Newt Gingrich. This time Frost lost Dallas County 54%–46% but carried Tarrant 62%–38%, for a 53%–47% victory—his lowest general election percentage ever.

Frost continues to persevere. At home, redistricting could hurt (or help, by restoring some of his minority voters) him and, as part of the minority, he will surely have a harder time raising the business PAC money that has been his financial mainstay. But he also has taken on the campaign committee chairmanship. Chipperly, he notes that Democrats need only 15 seats to regain control. Optimistically, he minimizes losses of business PAC money while promising to raise more through direct mail. Always the team player, he continues to favor the Voting Rights Act interpretation requiring more minority districts, which has jeopardized his career. Always the dedicated partisan, he seems willing to risk going down with his ship, but looks forward to serving as first or second mate when it returns to port in the lead.

The People: Pop. 1990: 565,779; 9% rural; 9% age 65+; 57% White; 19% Black; 1% Amer. Indian; 2% Asian; 14% Other; 21% Hispanic origin. Voting age pop.: 395,763; 18% Black; 18% Hispanic origin. Households: 57% married couple families; 31% married couple fams. w. children; 41% college educ.; median household income: $27,535; per capita income: $11,534; median gross rent: $417; median house value: $58,800.

1992 Presidential Vote			1988 Presidential Vote		
Clinton (D)	73,635	(41%)	Bush (R)	82,082	(52%)
Bush (R)	59,372	(33%)	Dukakis (D)	77,167	(48%)
Perot (I)	46,571	(26%)			

Rep. Martin Frost (D)

Elected 1978; b. Jan. 1, 1942, Glendale, CA; home, Dallas; U. of MO, B.A., 1964, Georgetown U., J.D. 1970; Jewish; married (Valerie).

Career: Army Reserves, 1966–72; Legal commentator, KERA-TV, Dallas, 1971–72; Practicing atty., 1972–78.

DC Office: 2459 RHOB 20515, 202-225-3605; Fax: 202-225-4951.

District Offices: 3020 S.E. Loop 820, Ft. Worth 76140, 817-293-9231; 400 S. Zang Blvd., #506, Dallas 75208, 214-948-3401; and 100 N. Main St., #534, Corsicana 75110, 903-874-0760.

Committees: *Democratic Congressional Campaign Committee Chairman. Rules* (3rd of 4 D): Legislative and Budget Process (RMM).

Group Ratings

	ADA	ACLU	COPE	CFA	LCV	CON	NSI	COC	ACU	NTLC	CHC
1994	55	55	67	70	54	46	70	75	25	23	21
1993	65	—	91	90	69	19	—	36	21	—	—

National Journal Ratings

	1993 LIB — 1993 CONS			1994 LIB — 1994 CONS		
Economic	68%	—	26%	59%	—	37%
Social	64%	—	34%	61%	—	38%
Foreign	58%	—	41%	63%	—	37%

Key Votes of the 103d Congress

1. Clinton Deficit Plan	Y	3. Brady Handgun Purchase	Y	5. Lmt. UN Cmnd. of Forces	N
2. NAFTA	Y	4. Strike Race/Death Pnlty.	N	6. Cut Missile Funds	N

Key Votes of the 104th Congress

1. Congressional Compliance Y	6. Reform Crime Grant N	11. Loser Pays Court Reform N
2. Balanced Budget Amndmt. Y	7. National Security Act N	12. Product Liability Reform N
3. Bar Unfunded Mandates Y	8. Moratorium on Regs. N	13. Welfare Reform N
4. Pass Line Item Veto *	9. Risk Assessment on Regs. Y	14. Term Limits Amndmt. *
5. Relax Exclusionary Rule N	10. Expnd. Priv. Prop. Rights Y	15. Tax Cuts N

Election Results

1994 general	Martin Frost (D)......................	65,019	(53%)	($1,589,612)
	Ed Harrison (R)	58,062	(47%)	($562,260)
1994 primary	Martin Frost (D)...................	unopposed		
1992 general	Martin Frost (D)....................	104,174	(60%)	($1,549,556)
	Steve Masterson (R)..................	70,042	(40%)	($109,306)

TWENTY-FIFTH DISTRICT

Houston is, among other things, a blue-collar city: the Ship Channel which made it a great port is lined with petrochemical plants and refineries and surrounded by port facilities, factories, truck terminals and railroad offloading platforms. And many of the neighborhoods that have sprouted up in and around Houston's wide city limits in the last three decades, with their plain, contemporary houses and commercial strip highways, could be called working class. Some of these neighborhoods have been close-knit places for decades, but others have sprouted up recently, moved into by whites as Mexican-Americans fill their former streets. After all, physical mobility is easy in spread-out Houston and many people keep in touch through churches though they are miles apart.

The 25th District of Texas includes many such neighborhoods on the east and south sides of Houston. The boundaries as established in 1991 are complex beyond description: on the map the 25th forms a curlicue around central Houston. It includes blue-collar neighborhoods on both sides of the Houston Ship Channel, Highlands and Channelview on the north, Deer Park and Pasadena on the south. It includes a strip of southern Houston from Hobby Airport west toward the Astrodome and beyond, with a salient reaching north to the more affluent, in some cases Jewish, neighborhoods near Rice University and the giant Texas Medical Center. The 25th also proceeds south into Missouri City and Fort Bend County, to make up for heavily black and Hispanic precincts lost to the 18th and 29th Districts in redistricting. These seemingly erose boundaries were carefully crafted to produce a district 27% black and 16% Hispanic and, more to the point, pretty solidly Democratic.

The 25th was intended for Mike Andrews, Democratic moderate and politically skillful Ways and Means Committee member, who was first elected in 1982. Its current representative is Ken Bentsen, nephew of the former Senator and Treasury Secretary, who won the seat after Andrews ran for the Senate (and finished third in the all-party primary, with 14%) in 1994. Ken Bentsen's grandfather, Lloyd Bentsen Sr., was a pioneer landowner in the Lower Rio Grande Valley, amassing fortunes in cotton, cattle, citrus and oil. His father is a Houston architect and Ken Bentsen grew up and went to college in Houston. He spent four years as a staffer on Capitol Hill for Ron Coleman, spending much of his time at the Appropriations Committee; then, he joined an investment banking firm in Houston and was elected Harris County Democratic Chairman in 1990 and 1992. But for all that, he was not the outstanding candidate when Andrews retired. The best known was probably Dolly Madison McKenna, a pro-choice Republican who held Andrews to a 56%–41% win in 1992, or perhaps Dr. Eugene Fontenot, a conservative Republican who spent $853,000 of his own money in the primary. Also spending more than Bentsen was Democrat Carrin Patman, daughter and granddaughter of congressmen, who spent nearly as much was former Democratic legislator Paul Colbert. Fontenot won the Republican primary 56%–44%. The leader in the Democratic primary was low-spending Beverley Clark, a black former Houston Council member, elected in 1989 and defeated in 1991, anti-abortion and supported by the Christian right. In a light-turnout (25,945) Democratic primary, Clark won 37%, Bentsen 26%, Colbert 23% and Patman 13%. Bentsen, pro-choice on abortion, concentrated on crime issues, supporting boot camps and more death penalties, and won the runoff 64%–36%. In the general election Fontenot spent more than any other candidate in the nation in 1994—$4.7 million overall. Bentsen spent a comparatively modest $973,000, attacking Fontenot as "radical right," and offering his own stand that combined a budget freeze with a pledge of universal healthcare coverage.

Bentsen won 52%–45%, getting only 50% in Harris County but adding nearly 6,000 votes to his margin from the heavily black portion of Fort Bend County. Having won as a nonincumbent, Bentsen is probably well positioned for 1996. But redistricting looms. If the boundaries of the next-door 18th and 29th Districts are changed, that could help Bentsen. But any additions from the next-door 7th or 22d Districts, or any regularly shaped lines, could hurt him severely.

The People: Pop. 1990: 565,202; 1% rural; 7% age 65+; 53% White; 27% Black; 4% Asian; 8% Other; 16% Hispanic origin. Voting age pop.: 404,772; 25% Black; 15% Hispanic origin. Households: 52% married couple families; 28% married couple fams. w. children; 52% college educ.; median household income: $30,614; per capita income: $14,269; median gross rent: $403; median house value: $57,000.

1992 Presidential Vote			1988 Presidential Vote		
Clinton (D)	85,412	(47%)	Bush (R)	78,504	(51%)
Bush (R)	64,962	(36%)	Dukakis (D)	76,478	(49%)
Perot (I)	32,515	(18%)			

Rep. Ken Bentsen (D)

Elected 1994; b. June 3., 1959, Houston; home, Houston; U. of St. Thomas., B.A. 1982, American U., M.P.A., 1985; Presbyterian; married (Tamra).

Career: Legis. Asst., U.S. Rep. Ronald Coleman, 1983–87; Staff Assoc., U.S. House Approprations Cmte., 1985–87; Investment Banker, 1987–94.

DC Office: 128 CHOB 20515, 202-225-7508; Fax: 202-225-2947.

District Offices: 515 Rusk St., #12102 Fed. Bldg., Houston 77002, 713-229-2244; and 100 E. Southmore St., #810, Pasadena 77502, 713-473-4334.

Committees: *Banking & Financial Services* (22nd of 22 D): Capital Markets, Securities and Government Sponsored Enterprises. *Small Business* (16th of 19 D): Regulation and Paperwork; Tax and Finance.

Group Ratings and 103rd Congress Votes: Newly Elected

Key Votes of the 104th Congress

1. Congressional Compliance	Y	6. Reform Crime Grant	N	11. Loser Pays Court Reform	N
2. Balanced Budget Amndmt.	N	7. National Security Act	N	12. Product Liability Reform	N
3. Bar Unfunded Mandates	Y	8. Moratorium on Regs.	N	13. Welfare Reform	N
4. Pass Line Item Veto	N	9. Risk Assessment on Regs.	N	14. Term Limits Amndmt.	N
5. Relax Exclusionary Rule	Y	10. Expnd. Priv. Prop. Rights	Y	15. Tax Cuts	N

Election Results

1994 general	Ken Bentsen (D)	61,959	(52%)	($972,688)
	Gene Fontenot (R)	53,321	(45%)	($4,658,585)
	Others	3,249	(3%)	
1994 runoff	Ken Bentsen (D)	11,812	(64%)	
	Beverley Clark (D)	6,684	(36%)	
1994 primary	Beverley Clark (D)	9,614	(37%)	
	Ken Bentsen (D)	6,778	(26%)	
	Paul Colbert (D)	5,914	(23%)	
	Carrin Patman (D)	3,373	(13%)	
	Others	266	(1%)	
1992 general	Michael A. Andrews (D)	98,975	(56%)	($1,397,469)
	Dolly Madison McKenna (R)	73,192	(41%)	($585,616)
	Other	4,710	(3%)	

TWENTY-SIXTH DISTRICT

On the northern edge of the Dallas-Fort Worth Metroplex, one of America's most affluent and fastest-growing metropolitan areas heads out into hardscrabble countryside. Here is a clash of cultures, and not least politically. North of the line of advancing subdivisions is the old Red River Valley of Sam Rayburn, where farmers for 125 years eked out meager livings. Far west of the great centers of capital and trade, more than a day's journey for many years even from Dallas and Fort Worth, they felt beset by some of the continent's harshest weather and at the mercy of market forces they had no chance of controlling. This was one of the centers of populism in the United States, and one of the hotbeds of the Democratic Party. Counties in or near the Red River Valley gave the country three Democratic speakers of the House: Sam Rayburn of Bonham, Texas, Jim Wright originally from Weatherford, Texas, and Carl Albert from McAlester, Oklahoma.

An entirely different spirit is apparent now in the advancing Metroplex. Here is optimism and promise of advance as symbolized by the huge Dallas-Fort Worth Regional Airport, opened in 1972 with hopes of knitting the Dallas-Fort Worth area together and stimulating growth, and by the office buildings, shopping centers, subdivisions and condominiums of the new communities to the north; the lavish Las Colinas development, the almost wholly new city of Plano, and the golden triangle between I-35E and I-35W stretching toward Denton. These are full of people whose talents and skills have made the Dallas-Fort Worth Metroplex a ranking high-tech and defense industry center. They seem safe and secure against the urban ills that afflict many neighborhoods. Politically, these areas are overwhelmingly Republican, receptive to the message of free enterprise and respectful of traditional moral values.

The 26th Congressional District of Texas occupies much of the northern marchland of the Metroplex. About half its people are in Dallas County, on the far north side of Dallas, or in Irving, which includes Las Colinas and Texas Stadium where the Dallas Cowboys play, and the large suburbs of Carrollton, Farmers Branch, Richardson, and Coppell. The 26th also includes much of Plano in Collin County and most of Denton County to the west—Lewisville, Flower Mound and the county seat of Denton. The district lines were much adjusted for the 1990s. Thanks to explosive growth, the old 26th had 895,000 people, the second most populous district in the country and far above the requisite 566,000. This is a very Republican district, but people do not necessarily feel moored to the party. It cast the second highest percentage for Ross Perot (32%) of any district in 1992. (The first was far away in nothern Maine.)

The congressman from the 26th is Dick Armey, the House Majority Leader, a free market economist who a decade ago was a political nonentity who did not even attend the 1984 Republican National Convention in nearby Dallas where Ronald Reagan was renominated. His political career could never have happened before the 1980s. He grew up on a farm in Cando, North Dakota—pronounced affirmatively as *can do*. At 18, working atop an electric pole at night, he decided to become the first in his family to go to college. By 1984, Armey was an economics professor at North Texas State University in Denton, a northern-accented academic in the Red River Valley of Texas: not a likely candidate for anything. But as he was watching the House sessions on C-SPAN, it occurred to him that he could do as well as or better than the people he was watching on the screen. And he has proceeded to do just that. He got the Republican nomination in the 26th in 1984 unopposed, because no one thought incumbent Tom Vandergriff, the longtime mayor of Arlington, then the largest city in the 26th, could be unseated. But Armey won 51%–49%. He arrived in Washington in such modest circumstances that he saved money by sleeping first in the House gym and, when forced to stop, on his office couch—a practice that had been abandoned by Armey but was okayed for others by Speaker Gingrich in 1995.

Armey brought to the House a sometimes impolitic bluntness but also fine political instincts and an appreciation of how to sell his principles to his colleagues. His first major achievement was the military base closing bill. In 1987, Armey proposed a base closing commission operating outside of politics, but neither Congress nor then-Defense Secretary Caspar Weinberger were ready to delegate such power. After a long debate, Armey worked with the Pentagon, the Joint Chiefs of Staff and then-Armed Services Chairman Les Aspin to create an independent commission that would draw up a list of base closings which Congress would have to approve or reject in its entirety. The result: in 1988 Congress approved the first base closings in 12 years. The 1990 round of closings was rejected, but in 1993 the second round of base closings was approved. In 1995, a more modest third round was proposed by the Clinton Administration. Armey's bill had changed political incentives so that they ratcheted government spending down, not up. Rather than compete for House committee positions which would allow them to save uneconomic bases, members are forced to maneuver to make bases economically defensible. Armey has had less success with his next target, farm subsidies. He argued persuasively that subsidies are no more needed to maintain supplies of the six large subsidized crops than they are for the hundreds of crops which manage to be produced without subsidies and that farmers no more deserve subsidies than any other small businessmen. He forged an alliance on the issue with Brooklyn Democrat Charles Schumer, but was never able to prevail on the floor. With Republicans now in control, he may do better, and as 1995 began Farm Belt congressmen were trying to pare down subsidies to protect against an Armey assault.

Armey had little success for his first decade as a minority back-bencher on the Economic & Educational Opportunities or Budget Committees, where he was outvoted by committed partisans of expanded domestic programs, which he attacked. But he found more sympathizers in the Republican Conference. He strongly opposed President Bush's budget summit tax increase and determined he wanted "a seat at the table." So after the 1992 election, Armey ran for Republican Conference chairman against incumbent Jerry Lewis, who had supported the budget summit. Armey won the number-three leadership position 88–84, winning the lion's share of the 47 freshman Republicans and gaining crucial support from Lewis's California delegation as well. This put Armey into leadership meetings at the White House, at one of the first of which he told President Clinton that passage of his budget and tax plan would make him a "one-term president"—not the first or last Armey breach of Washington's collegial etiquette, and not the first or last prediction he has made that has proved more insightful than almost anyone in conventional Washington believed. Later in 1993 he called the Clinton health plan "a Kevorkian prescription for the jobs of American men and women." Then at a committee hearing, Hillary Rodham Clinton compared Armey to Dr. Kevorkian, to which he replied, "I have been told about your charm and wit, and let me say, the reports on your charm are overstated and the reports on your wit are understated." He was capable of even more bitter riposte: during the 1994 crime bill debate, when Democrats talked of the need to support President Clinton, Armey said, "Your president is just not that important for us"—for which he soon apologized, after then Minority Leader Bob Michel took him to task.

But when Newt Gingrich came up with the idea of having all Republican incumbents and candidates sign a pledge on the steps of the Capitol in September 1994, Armey spearheaded the effort to draw up and then sell—including to some doubters within his own party, let alone other parts of Washington's political class—many of the specifics of the Contract With America. Along with Gingrich, he then travelled virtually non-stop across the nation in the month before the election to raise money and enthusiasm for Republican candidates. After they won control in November, Armey gained his just reward of being elected Majority Leader without opposition. And he then surprised many with his legislative skill in commanding the 100-day schedule that delivered on the Republicans' campaign promise to debate each item of the Contract, with the House passing everything except for term limits. Gingrich and others credited Armey as instrumental with the impressive legislative performance.

There is some tension between Armey's personal stands and his leadership responsibilities. He seems to have deferred his crusade against farm subsidies. And he has not pressed for early consideration of the flat-tax proposal he advanced in June 1994, and thought too ambitious to include in the Contract With America. His idea, which has run up against the call by Ways and Means Committee chairman Bill Archer and other senior Republicans to replace the income tax altogether with a consumption-based tax, is to tax at a flat rate—20%, then 17% after two years—all personal and corporate income, with no deductions but generous personal allowances ($13,100 for individuals, $26,200 for married couples, $5,300 deduction per child). There would be no taxes on capital gains, dividends, interest or inheritances. Opponents immediately claimed it would cut revenues hugely, but Armey convincingly refuted their doomsday estimates. Armey says a flat tax would have major effects: stopping distortion of economic decisions, eliminating the need for tax accountants and avoidance. Interestingly, Minority Leader Dick Gephardt advanced with only sketchy details his own flat tax idea in January 1995. The flat tax, which seemed wildly visionary when proposed in 1994, could end up a reality. To try to resolve party differences and to move the debate, Speaker Gingrich and Senate Majority Leader Bob Dole named Jack Kemp, the original Republican tax reformer, to develop a consensus position by the fall of 1995.

Armey still has a rough and ready style. He drives a red pickup truck, wears cowboy boots with House patches stitched into the leather, and loves to go fishing, often with Justice Clarence Thomas (whose wife Virginia is an Armey staffer). He said that he has never tried to bring home pork, and in fact his base-closing law closed Carswell Air Force Base in Fort Worth. Representing a district with one of the highest percentages of women working outside the home, he called family leave "yuppie welfare." But he has turned out to be suited to his district. His ebullience matches its mood and his faith in market economics reflects its settled convictions, and he has been reelected overwhelmingly, in 1994 with 76% of the vote.

The People: Pop. 1990: 566,722; 5% rural; 5% age 65+; 82% White; 4% Black; 1% Amer. Indian; 4% Asian; 4% Other; 9% Hispanic origin. Voting age pop.: 422,805; 4% Black; 8% Hispanic origin. Households: 57% married couple families; 30% married couple fams. w. children; 68% college educ.; median household income: $40,533; per capita income: $20,675; median gross rent: $509; median house value: $99,000.

1992 Presidential Vote		
Bush (R)	118,519	(47%)
Perot (I)	81,424	(32%)
Clinton (D)	52,727	(21%)

1988 Presidential Vote		
Bush (R)	138,883	(73%)
Dukakis (D)	50,703	(27%)

Rep. Richard K. (Dick) Armey (R)

Elected 1984; b. July 7, 1940, Cando, ND; home, Cooper Canyon; Jamestown Col., B.A. 1963, U. of ND, M.A. 1964, U. of OK, Ph.D. 1969; Presbyterian; married (Susan).

Career: Prof., West TX St. U., 1967–68, Austin Col., 1968–72, North TX St. U., 1972–77, Chmn., Dept. of Economics, 1977–83.

DC Office: 301 CHOB 20515, 202-225-7772; Fax: 202-225-7614.

District Offices: 9901 Valley Ranch Pkwy. E., #3050, Irving 75063, 214-556-2500.

Committees: *Majority Leader.*

Group Ratings

	ADA	ACLU	COPE	CFA	LCV	CON	NSI	COC	ACU	NTLC	CHC
1994	0	13	0	0	6	87	100	83	100	96	100
1993	0	—	0	0	23	74	—	100	100	—	—

National Journal Ratings

	1993 LIB — 1993 CONS		1994 LIB — 1994 CONS	
Economic	0%	— 88%	0%	— 80%
Social	0%	— 89%	0%	— 89%
Foreign	17%	— 76%	0%	— 88%

Key Votes of the 103d Congress

1. Clinton Deficit Plan	N	3. Brady Handgun Purchase	N	5. Lmt. UN Cmnd. of Forces	Y
2. NAFTA	Y	4. Strike Race/Death Pnlty.	Y	6. Cut Missile Funds	N

Key Votes of the 104th Congress

1. Congressional Compliance	Y	6. Reform Crime Grant	Y	11. Loser Pays Court Reform	Y
2. Balanced Budget Amndmt.	Y	7. National Security Act	Y	12. Product Liability Reform	Y
3. Bar Unfunded Mandates	Y	8. Moratorium on Regs.	Y	13. Welfare Reform	Y
4. Pass Line Item Veto	Y	9. Risk Assessment on Regs.	Y	14. Term Limits Amndmt.	Y
5. Relax Exclusionary Rule	Y	10. Expnd. Priv. Prop. Rights	Y	15. Tax Cuts	Y

Election Results

1994 general	Richard K. (Dick) Armey (R)	135,398	(76%)	($900,871)
	LeEarl Ann Bryant (D)................	39,763	(22%)	($13,131)
	Others	2,030	(1%)	
1994 primary	Richard K. (Dick) Armey (R)	unopposed		
1992 general	Richard K. (Dick) Armey (R)	150,209	(73%)	($475,756)
	John Wayne Caton (D)................	55,237	(27%)	($9,589)

TWENTY-SEVENTH DISTRICT

South from Corpus Christi, the southernmost natural port on Texas's Gulf Coast, with its big petrochemical plants, to the Rio Grande and the Mexican border, are two Texan versions of dreamland. One, fronting the Gulf of Mexico, is the sandspit of Padre Island, for most of its length a national seashore, at the southern tip of which is a high-rise resort to which college students throng for Spring break. Remains of a 1554 Spanish shipwreck have been found here, and it is here that Portuguese settlers began cattle ranching. The other, inland from the Laguna Madre, are the vast grazing and oil lands of the 825,000-acre (that's 1,289 square miles, partner) King Ranch. This still seemingly vacant land between the Nueces and the Rio Grande was the territory in contention in the Mexican-American War. The United States won that war and established its sovereignty, but today most of the people here are of Mexican ancestry, and if their culture and economy are, ultimately, thoroughly Norteamericano, they also are pronouncedly Mexican.

The 27th Congressional District of Texas includes this land from Corpus Christi south to the Rio Grande. The population is not spread out evenly here. Over half the 27th's voters live in and around Corpus (as it is called locally). Most of the other half live some 150 miles south in the Lower Rio Grande Valley around Brownsville and Harlingen. With a 66% Hispanic majority, the 27th is a Democratic district, though not quite so Democratic as some may suspect, since many Hispanics here are not citizens and those who are by no means vote solidly Democratic.

The congressman from the 27th, since its creation following the 1982 redistricting, has been Solomon Ortiz. He grew up in the Canta Ranas (singing frogs) neighborhood of Robstown, inland from Corpus. His father died when he was 14, leaving him the eldest of four children who scratched out a living as migrant farm workers, sometimes as far away as Colorado and Michigan. "I know what it is being poor, going home and nothing to eat," he says. As a boy he shined policemen's shoes, and wanted to be a policeman himself. When his father died, his employer at the local newspaper raised his wage, and then urged him to join the Army. Ortiz worked as an Army investigator and translator, using his Spanish to learn French, then took a correspondence course in police work and returned home to run for constable. "If it wasn't for the military, I wouldn't be here today," he has said. In 1976 he was elected Nueces County Sheriff. In 1982, when the new 27th lines were drawn, he ran for Congress; after receiving 26% in the initial primary, he made a propitious alliance with party leaders in the Brownsville area and won the runoff.

Ortiz's voting record was middle of the road in the Democratic House. He served on the now-defunct Merchant Marine Committee, where he was subcommittee chairman. He is on the National Security Committee and worked to save the Ingleside Navy home port in Corpus Christi. His successful legislation includes funding for the Palo Alto Battlefield, the Lower Rio Grande wildlife range and the Brownsville wetlands bill. He supported NAFTA, wants more border patrol officers to stop illegal immigration and heads the Coastal Bend Area Joint Military Task Force to keep four local bases open. Ortiz had a closer than usual call in 1992, when redistricting took away some heavily Democratic precincts in the Lower Rio Grande Valley, and he won with 56% of the vote; in 1994 he won 59%–41%.

The People: Pop. 1990: 565,992; 14% rural; 10% age 65+; 31% White; 2% Black; 1% Asian; 18% Other; 66% Hispanic origin. Voting age pop.: 380,498; 2% Black; 61% Hispanic origin. Households: 61% married couple families; 34% married couple fams. w. children; 38% college educ.; median household income: $21,552; per capita income: $9,366; median gross rent: $343; median house value: $47,000.

1992 Presidential Vote			1988 Presidential Vote		
Clinton (D)	78,441	(48%)	Dukakis (D)	83,007	(53%)
Bush (R)	58,780	(36%)	Bush (R)	72,507	(47%)
Perot (I)	27,468	(17%)			

Rep. Solomon P. Ortiz (D)

Elected 1982; b. June 3, 1937, Robstown; home, Corpus Christi; Del Mar Col., Natl. Sheriffs Training Inst., 1977; Methodist; divorced.

Career: Army, 1960–62; Nueces Cnty. Constable, 1965–68, Commissioner, 1969–76, Sheriff, 1977–82.

DC Office: 2136 RHOB 20515, 202-225-7742; Fax: 202-225-1134.

District Offices: 3649 Leopard St., #510, Corpus Christi 78408, 512-883-5868; and 3505 Boca Chica Blvd., Brownsville 78521, 512-541-1242.

Committees: *National Security* (7th of 25 D): Military Installations and Facilities (RMM); Military Research and Development. *Resources* (14th of 20 D): Energy and Mineral Resources; Fisheries, Wildlife and Oceans.

Group Ratings

	ADA	ACLU	COPE	CFA	LCV	CON	NSI	COC	ACU	NTLC	CHC
1994	45	26	56	60	33	8	80	55	48	23	64
1993	40	—	83	90	57	1	—	50	39	—	—

National Journal Ratings

	1993 LIB — 1993 CONS		1994 LIB — 1994 CONS	
Economic	55%	— 43%	59%	— 37%
Social	39%	— 60%	48%	— 52%
Foreign	51%	— 42%	46%	— 53%

Key Votes of the 103d Congress

1. Clinton Deficit Plan	Y	3. Brady Handgun Purchase	N	5. Lmt. UN Cmnd. of Forces	N
2. NAFTA	Y	4. Strike Race/Death Pnlty.	N	6. Cut Missile Funds	N

Key Votes of the 104th Congress

1. Congressional Compliance	Y	6. Reform Crime Grant	N	11. Loser Pays Court Reform	Y
2. Balanced Budget Amndmt.	Y	7. National Security Act	N	12. Product Liability Reform	N
3. Bar Unfunded Mandates	Y	8. Moratorium on Regs.	*	13. Welfare Reform	N
4. Pass Line Item Veto	N	9. Risk Assessment on Regs.	Y	14. Term Limits Amndmt.	N
5. Relax Exclusionary Rule	Y	10. Expnd. Priv. Prop. Rights	Y	15. Tax Cuts	N

Election Results

1994 general	Solomon P. Ortiz (D)	65,325	(59%)	($469,694)
	Erol A. Stone (R)	44,693	(41%)	($42,282)
1994 primary	Solomon P. Ortiz (D)	unopposed		
1992 general	Solomon P. Ortiz (D)	87,022	(56%)	($343,904)
	Jay Kimbrough (R)	66,853	(43%)	($57,832)
	Other	2,969	(2%)	

TWENTY-EIGHTH DISTRICT

The Mexican-American tradition in the part of south Texas radiating from San Antonio is anchored in two culturally conservative but adaptive institutions, the Roman Catholic Church and the United States military. They are a major presence in San Antonio, which for many years had the largest Mexican-American population of any American city, a place just 150 miles north of the border where Spanish was widely spoken and political refugees from Mexico's revolution could be sure of freedom. The church in San Antonio was led for years by liberal bishops who also ran St. Mary's University, which educated many Hispanic politicians and leaders, including two longtime chairmen of U.S. House committees, Henry B. Gonzalez and Kika de la Garza. Just as visible a presence in San Antonio are the Army and Air Force, with huge Fort Sam Houston, Lackland Air Force Base, Kelly Air Force Base, Randolph Air Force Base, and the Brooks Air Medical Center, all in or near the city limits. Mexican-Americans have long volunteered for military service in numbers far higher than most ethnic groups, and for many years Mexican-Americans in San Antonio (among them, the father of HUD Secretary and former Mayor Henry Cisneros) worked in civilian jobs for the military service—Uncle Sam was long an equal opportunity employer. San Antonio's Mexican-American community has produced many politicians who are liberal on economic issues and on civil rights and civil liberties. But it has not produced many who are hostile to the military or to traditional religious and cultural values.

The 28th Congressional District of Texas stretches from the southern half of San Antonio to the Mexican border. Some 63% of its people are in San Antonio and Bexar County, on the south and east sides of the city. It has a salient north to Hispanic precincts in Guadalupe County and also heads south, through thinly settled ranch and oil well country, to the Lower Rio Grande. There it includes Starr County, home of many blatant and wealthy drug smugglers, and, not far north, Duval County, often the most Democratic county in the United States, whose then-boss George Parr provided the key votes Lyndon Johnson needed for his disputed 87-vote victory in the 1948 Democratic Senate runoff. This was a new district for 1992, 60% Hispanic and solidly Democratic.

Frank Tejeda, congressman from the 28th, is a good example of San Antonio's military and Catholic traditions. He left school at 17, volunteered for the Marine Corps and was sent to Vietnam. "I was a grunt, and proud of it. I wouldn't have it any other way," he told *Roll Call*. Two weeks before his tour was up, in 1966, he was hit with shrapnel and was later awarded a Bronze Star. He got the highest grades ever in Marine Officers Candidate School. Tejeda went back to San Antonio and graduated from St. Mary's, and then embarked on graduate law study at Berkeley and Yale and graduate school at Harvard even while building a political base in San Antonio. He was elected to the state House in 1976 and to the state Senate in 1986. As a Democrat he was part of the majority, but not a reliable liberal. He is against abortion. And in the legislature he opposed legalized parimutuel betting in the early 1980s and later opposed a state lottery. He voted against trial lawyers and with business on workers' compensation. He attracted much attention investigating a state House committee chairman and two state Supreme Court justices who were later disciplined. By 1991, Tejeda's clout was such that he was able to draw the boundaries of the 28th District to his liking. His popularity was great enough that he had no opposition in the Democratic primary. He also won some political chits, after Bill Clinton was attacked for evading the draft, by forming a Veterans for Clinton movement.

In the House, Tejeda has seats on National Security and Veterans' Affairs—naturals for San Antonio. His voting record in the 103d Congress was at about midpoint of the House, but was among the top four in voting for spending according to a study by the National Taxpayers Union Foundation. He favors greater veterans' educational benefits and has worked on local projects like the Mission San Jose Visitors Center, a public health clinic in Duval County and an aircraft contract in San Antonio.

The People: Pop. 1990: 566,447; 21% rural; 11% age 65+; 30% White; 9% Black; 1% Asian; 22% Other; 60% Hispanic origin. Voting age pop.: 382,367; 9% Black; 56% Hispanic origin. Households: 61% married couple families; 34% married couple fams. w. children; 30% college educ.; median household income: $20,276; per capita income: $8,050; median gross rent: $328; median house value: $39,900.

1334 TEXAS

Rep. Frank M. Tejeda (D)

Elected 1992; b. Oct. 2, 1945, San Antonio; home, San Antonio; St. Mary's U., B.A. 1970, U. of CA at Berkeley, J.D. 1974, Harvard, M.P.A. 1980, Yale, LL.M., 1989; Catholic; divorced.

Career: Marines Corps, 1963–67 (Vietnam), Marine Reserves, 1967-present; Practicing atty., 1974–1992; TX House of Reps., 1976–86; TX Senate, 1986–92.

DC Office: 323 CHOB 20515, 202-225-1640; Fax: 202-225-1641.

District Offices: 1313 SE Military Dr., #115, San Antonio 78214, 210-924-7383; and 202 E. St. Joseph St., #5, San Diego 78384, 512-279-3907.

Committees: *National Security* (15th of 25 D): Military Installations and Facilities; Military Readiness. *Veterans' Affairs* (8th of 15 D): Hospitals and Health Care.

Group Ratings

	ADA	ACLU	COPE	CFA	LCV	CON	NSI	COC	ACU	NTLC	CHC
1994	50	30	67	50	33	1	80	50	43	22	64
1993	45	—	83	90	64	1	—	45	33	—	—

National Journal Ratings

	1993 LIB — 1993 CONS		1994 LIB — 1994 CONS	
Economic	59%	— 40%	57%	— 42%
Social	39%	— 60%	45%	— 54%
Foreign	51%	— 42%	49%	— 49%

Key Votes of the 103d Congress

1. Clinton Deficit Plan	Y	3. Brady Handgun Purchase	N	5. Lmt. UN Cmnd. of Forces	N
2. NAFTA	Y	4. Strike Race/Death Pnlty.	N	6. Cut Missile Funds	N

Key Votes of the 104th Congress

1. Congressional Compliance	Y	6. Reform Crime Grant	N	11. Loser Pays Court Reform	N
2. Balanced Budget Amndt.	N	7. National Security Act	N	12. Product Liability Reform	N
3. Bar Unfunded Mandates	Y	8. Moratorium on Regs.	Y	13. Welfare Reform	N
4. Pass Line Item Veto	N	9. Risk Assessment on Regs.	Y	14. Term Limits Amndt.	N
5. Relax Exclusionary Rule	Y	10. Expnd. Priv. Prop. Rights	Y	15. Tax Cuts	N

Election Results

1994 general	Frank M. Tejeda (D) 73,986	(71%)	($224,124)
	David C. Slatter (R) 28,777	(28%)	
	Others 1,612	(2%)	
1994 primary	Frank M. Tejeda (D) .... unopposed		
1992 general	Frank M. Tejeda (D) 122,457	(87%)	($304,286)
	David C. Slatter (Lib) 18,128	(13%)	($1,401)

TWENTY-NINTH DISTRICT

"What built Houston," wrote John Gunther in *Inside U.S.A.*, "was a combination of cotton, oil, and the ship canal." The cotton and oil were gifts of nature, though they require much human effort and ingenuity to produce in commercial quantities; the Houston Ship Channel was almost totally man's creation. After the sand-spit port of Galveston was destroyed by a hurricane and tidal wave in 1900, Houston's town fathers decided to dredge out Buffalo Bayou and make their inland city a seaport, and they succeeded. And so a sluggish creek became a harbor and this small city built on a swamp became a major port by the 1940s and a world-class metropolis of 3.7 million people by 1990. On the west side of town, Houston seems entirely a white-collar, office-bound city. But on the east and north, around the turning basin in the port and through the maze of refinery towers and tubing, Houston is plainly blue collar, with blacks, Mexican-Americans and large numbers of whites from the rural South and even Michigan and California, who came here to move up in the world.

The 29th Congressional District of Texas might be called the Houston Ship Channel District. It was created in 1991 as Houston's Hispanic district, but has not elected a Hispanic representative. Its eastern half pretty much parallels the canal, including working class neighborhoods on both sides, and its western extremities, with their extremely intricate boundaries, follow radial highways north and northwest from the industrial area. Paul Burka's description in the *Texas Monthly* cannot be improved on: "The 29th District looks like a sacred Mayan bird, with its body running eastward along the Ship Channel from downtown Houston until the tail terminates in Baytown. Spindly legs reach south to Hobby Airport, while the plumed head rises northward almost to Intercontinental. In the western extremity of the district, an open beak appears to be searching for worms in Spring Branch. Here and there, ruffled feathers jut out at odd angles." The population here is 55% Hispanic and 10% black—almost precisely the opposite of the 14% Hispanic and 49% black of the 18th, with which the 29th interlocks like an exceedingly complex jigsaw piece. But most Latinos in the Houston area do not live here—they have dispersed too widely. And most voters here are not Latinos—many residents are not citizens and others, hard-working but not particularly civic-minded, do not bother to vote. All this may well change by 1996. In 1994 a federal court ruled that the 29th and 18th Districts' boundaries are unconstitutional, and their boundaries—and probably the boundaries of surrounding districts—will have to be smoothed out. So it's possible that a new 29th will elect a black or a white, but almost certainly not a Republican.

Whatever happens, the current 29th has had two lively Democratic primaries, between two now longtime political enemies, Gene Green and Ben Reyes. Green, the winner both times, is an Anglo Houstonian who worked as a printer's apprentice and was admitted to the bar at age 30; he was elected to the state House in 1972, at 25, and to the state Senate in 1984. He has been a faithful union and trial-lawyer man in Austin and Washington, and also an opponent of gun control—a politician whose natural base is Texas's small union, blue-collar class. He is a compulsive campaigner who goes door to door, with lawn signs and a hammer in his trunk. Ben Reyes is more tempestuous: a former union organizer and an eight-term Houston Councilman who once pleaded no contest to a misdemeanor theft charge. To protest official inaction, he and friends demolished a crack house, after which they carted off a magnolia tree from its front yard and planted it on Reyes's property. He filed for bankruptcy in 1990 and pleaded no contest to campaign law violations, but he had a strong base in the Denver Harbor area around the Shipping Channel.

These two squared off in 1992. In the crucial Democratic primary in this district of 566,000 people, only 30,989 voters showed up; Reyes led with 34% to 28% for Green. In the April runoff, Green ran ads showing Reyes's face with "GUILTY" pasted over it; Reyes appealed to the district's Hispanic base and attacked Green for switching from anti-abortion to pro-choice just before filing. Green came out ahead by 180 votes out of 31,508 cast. Then Reyes went to court and charged that Republican voters had illegally crossed over and voted in the runoff. That got him a July re-runoff, but to no avail. This time Green won with 52%, by 1,132 votes out of 36,722 cast. In the general election, Clark Kent Ervin, a black Rhodes Scholar who worked on George Bush's 1,000 Points of Light, got Reyes's angry endorsement. But Green won with 65%.

In the House, Green cast two controversial votes: against NAFTA and against the Brady bill. That got him strong support from unions and the National Rifle Association, and he campaigned at *panchagas*, political gatherings that include as part of the festivities tamales, guacamole and mariachi bands. In the 1994 campaign, Reyes, pro-NAFTA and gun control, got downtown business money and had the backing of most Latino politicians. Only 30,726 voted in the Democratic primary. Green won 55%–45%, winning 80% of Anglos and 30% of Latinos. In the fall, he was helped by announcements of local grants to Houston; he won with 73%. Green is not well positioned to exert influence in the 104th Congress; he will have to hustle and hope to survive redistricting. But politics is his life, and he has shown he knows how to win unlikely victories.

The People: Pop. 1990: 566,937; 7% age 65+; 28% White; 10% Black; 2% Asian; 34% Other; 60% Hispanic origin. Voting age pop.: 377,824; 10% Black; 54% Hispanic origin. Households: 54% married couple families; 33% married couple fams. w. children; 22% college educ.; median household income: $20,612; per capita income: $7,898; median gross rent: $339; median house value: $38,000.

1992 Presidential Vote

Clinton (D)	54,344	(52%)
Bush (R)	31,839	(30%)
Perot (I)	18,427	(18%)

1988 Presidential Vote

Dukakis (D)	67,793	(58%)
Bush (R)	48,971	(42%)

Rep. Gene Green (D)

Elected 1992; b. Oct. 17, 1947, Houston; home, Houston; U. of Houston, B.A., 1971, Bates College of Law at U. of Houston, 1973–77; Methodist; married (Helen).

Career: TX House of Reps., 1972–84; Practicing atty., 1977–92; TX Senate, 1984–92.

DC Office: 1024 LHOB 20515, 202-225-1688; Fax: 202-225-9903; e-mail: ggreen@hr.house.gov.

District Offices: 5502 Lawndale, Houston 77023, 713-923-9961; and 420 N. 19th St., Houston 77008, 713-880-4364.

Committees: *Economic & Educational Opportunities* (16th of 19 D): Oversight and Investigations; Postsecondary Education, Training and Life-Long Learning. *Government Reform & Oversight* (19th of 22 D): Human Resources and Intergovernmental Affairs; Postal Service.

Group Ratings

	ADA	ACLU	COPE	CFA	LCV	CON	NSI	COC	ACU	NTLC	CHC
1994	80	62	88	80	65	35	30	55	16	19	14
1993	85	—	100	90	86	11	—	18	13	—	—

National Journal Ratings

	1993 LIB — 1993 CONS			1994 LIB — 1994 CONS		
Economic	88%	—	0%	83%	—	0%
Social	56%	—	42%	69%	—	31%
Foreign	69%	—	30%	46%	—	53%

Key Votes of the 103d Congress

1. Clinton Deficit Plan	Y	3. Brady Handgun Purchase	N	5. Lmt. UN Cmnd. of Forces	N
2. NAFTA	N	4. Strike Race/Death Pnlty.	N	6. Cut Missile Funds	Y

Key Votes of the 104th Congress

1. Congressional Compliance	Y	6. Reform Crime Grant	N	11. Loser Pays Court Reform	N
2. Balanced Budget Amndmt.	N	7. National Security Act	*	12. Product Liability Reform	N
3. Bar Unfunded Mandates	Y	8. Moratorium on Regs.	N	13. Welfare Reform	N
4. Pass Line Item Veto	Y	9. Risk Assessment on Regs.	Y	14. Term Limits Amndmt.	N
5. Relax Exclusionary Rule	Y	10. Expnd. Priv. Prop. Rights	Y	15. Tax Cuts	N

Election Results

1994 general	Gene Green (D)	44,102	(73%)	($594,375)
	Harold (Oilman) Eide (R)	15,952	(27%)	($10,065)
1994 primary	Gene Green (D)	16,934	(55%)	
	Ben T. Reyes (D)...................	13,795	(45%)	
1992 general	Gene Green (D)	64,064	(65%)	($691,275)
	Clark Kent Ervin (R).................	34,609	(35%)	($509,818)

THIRTIETH DISTRICT

Dallas is, among other things, the westernmost city of the Deep South. Cotton was the major crop originally in this part of Texas, and many of Dallas's first enterprising businessmen, when the railroad reached the Trinity River here in the 1870s, were cotton brokers. Geographically, Dallas is directly west of the Black Belt of Alabama and the Mississippi Delta, both heavy cotton-producing areas in the days before the boll weevil. Many blacks and whites came west on U.S. 80—and now Interstate 20—to this metropolis, which is now larger than any such area in the Deep South, including Atlanta. Dallas has never had nearly as big a Mexican-American population as Houston, much less San Antonio. But it has always had a larger percentage of blacks than both those cities. Indeed, south Dallas, south and west of the Trinity River, is predominately black, and black neighborhoods are scattered through other parts of the city and suburbs as well.

To see where, just look at a map of the 30th Congressional District of Texas as designed in 1991: attached to the central body in south and east Dallas are tentacles that appear as complex and attenuated as a series of DNA molecules. The 30th is one of those majority-black districts whose creation was inspired by the 1982 amendments to the Voting Rights Act. But its creation also was insisted upon by Eddie Bernice Johnson, in 1991 chairwoman of the state Senate committee on redistricting, now congresswoman from the 30th District. For 10 years, Dallas's blacks were split between two Democratic congressman, Martin Frost and John Bryant. In 1992, it was understood that a majority-black district would be created, and Frost and an aide came up with an ingenious plan that stretched the 5th and 24th outward from urban bases safely past Republican suburbia into rural Democratic territory to concede Johnson a district. Geographically, it covers most of south Dallas, takes in vacant land alongside various freeways, curves around Irving and takes in neighborhoods behind the Dallas-Fort Worth Regional Airport, and then curves around north Dallas out to black neighborhoods in Plano. In 1992, it was 50% black and 17% Hispanic, one of two majority-black seats in Texas.

The 30th's odd shape and obvious racial motivation sparked a Republican lawsuit, and in August 1994 a federal court ruled the district an unconstitutional gerrymander. The lines stayed in place for the 1994 election. An appeal was pending in early 1995 in the Supreme Court. Johnson is not likely to be imperiled. She pointed out that a much more regularly-shaped black-dominated district could have been created, but that the convoluted lines were drawn to accommodate Frost and Bryant. If the legislature redraws the lines, it must now please

Republican Governor George W. Bush, who will probably not object to a regularly-shaped heavily black district but will certainly veto lines designed to protect the white Democrats.

Eddie Bernice Johnson was the first black woman elected to anything in Dallas when she won a seat in the state House in 1972. She became a regional HEW director in the Carter Administration and then was elected to the state Senate in 1986. Johnson is a registered nurse and is said to be the first RN elected to Congress. She effectively won the seat in the 1992 primary with 92%. In her first term, she had a liberal voting record. She was attacked by union leaders for reneging on a pledge to vote against NAFTA. She denied the pledge, but did vote for the agreement. Dallas probably exports more to Mexico than does any other American city, and many jobs depend on exports to Mexico. She has had no difficulty winning here, and is not likely to unless redistricting takes an unexpected turn.

The People: Pop. 1990: 566,977; 8% age 65+; 31% White; 50% Black; 2% Asian; 10% Other; 17% Hispanic origin. Voting age pop.: 408,030; 47% Black; 15% Hispanic origin. Households: 39% married couple families; 20% married couple fams. w. children; 42% college educ.; median household income: $23,144; per capita income: $11,416; median gross rent: $402; median house value: $59,300.

1992 Presidential Vote			1988 Presidential Vote		
Clinton (D)	98,103	(62%)	Dukakis (D)	105,903	(63%)
Bush (R)	33,764	(21%)	Bush (R)	61,007	(37%)
Perot (I)	25,192	(16%)			

Rep. Eddie Bernice Johnson (D)

Elected 1992; b. Dec. 3, 1935, Waco; home, Dallas; St. Mary's at Notre Dame, B.A. 1955, Texas Christian U., B.S. 1967, Southern Methodist U., M.B.A. 1976; Baptist; divorced.

Career: TX House of Reps., 1972–1977; Regional Dir., U.S. Dept. of HEW, 1977–81; Mgmt. consultant, Sammons Corp., 1979–1981; Owner, Eddie Bernice Johnson & Assoc., 1981–present; TX Senate, 1986–92.

DC Office: 1123 LHOB 20515, 202-225-8885; Fax: 202-226-1477.

District Offices: 2525 McKinney Ave., #1565, Dallas 75201, 214-922-8885.

Committees: *Science* (12th of 23 D): Energy and Environment; Technology *Transportation & Infrastructure* (26th of 27 D): Surface Transportation.

Group Ratings

	ADA	ACLU	COPE	CFA	LCV	CON	NSI	COC	ACU	NTLC	CHC
1994	85	77	78	100	78	78	40	33	19	0	0
1993	90	—	92	100	79	10	—	27	0	—	—

National Journal Ratings

	1993 LIB — 1993 CONS		1994 LIB — 1994 CONS	
Economic	78% —	12%	83% —	0%
Social	87% —	0%	87% —	11%
Foreign	79% —	16%	64% —	33%

Key Votes of the 103d Congress

1. Clinton Deficit Plan	Y	3. Brady Handgun Purchase	Y	5. Lmt. UN Cmnd. of Forces N
2. NAFTA	Y	4. Strike Race/Death Pnlty.	N	6. Cut Missile Funds	N

Key Votes of the 104th Congress

1. Congressional Compliance Y	6. Reform Crime Grant N	11. Loser Pays Court Reform N
2. Balanced Budget Amndmt. N	7. National Security Act N	12. Product Liability Reform N
3. Bar Unfunded Mandates Y	8. Moratorium on Regs. N	13. Welfare Reform N
4. Pass Line Item Veto N	9. Risk Assessment on Regs. N	14. Term Limits Amndmt. N
5. Relax Exclusionary Rule N	10. Expnd. Priv. Prop. Rights N	15. Tax Cuts N

Election Results

1994 general	Eddie Bernice Johnson (D)	73,166	(73%)	($240,577)
	Lucy Cain (R)	25,848	(26%)	($1,060)
	Others	1,728	(2%)	
1994 primary	Eddie Bernice Johnson (D)	unopposed		
1992 general	Eddie Bernice Johnson (D)	107,831	(72%)	($282,734)
	Lucy Cain (R)	37,853	(25%)	($1,754)
	Other	5,063	(3%)	

UTAH

Utah is a triumph of man over nature, the creation of a productive and orderly civilization in a remote expanse of desert and mountain, arrayed around a desolate salt sea. Today's Utah and Mormonism have their roots in a very different landscape of more than 150 years ago, when a wave of religious enthusiasm, prophecy and utopianism swept across the "burnt-over district" of Upstate New York in the 1820s and 1830s. There Joseph Smith, a young farmer, experienced a vision in which the angel Moroni appeared and told him where to unearth several golden tablets inscribed with hieroglyphic writings. With the aid of special spectacles, Smith translated the tablets and published them as the Book of Mormon in 1831. He later declared himself a prophet and founded the Church of Jesus Christ of Latter-day Saints. The Mormons, as they were called, attracted thousands of converts and created their own communities; persecuted for their beliefs, they moved west to Ohio, Missouri and then Illinois. In 1844, the Mormon colony at Nauvoo, Illinois, had some 15,000 members living under the strict theocratic rule of Joseph Smith. It was here that Smith received a revelation sanctioning the practice of polygamy, which led to his death at the hands of a mob in 1844. After the murder, the new church president Brigham Young, decided to move the faithful, "the saints," farther west into territory that was still part of Mexico and far beyond white settlement. Young led a well-organized march across the Great Plains and into the Rocky Mountains. In 1847, they stopped on the western slope of the Wasatch Range and, as Brigham Young gazed over the valley of the Great Salt Lake spread out below, he uttered the now famous words, "This is the place."

The place was Utah. Young was governor of the territory for many years, and it is the only state that largely continues to live by the teachings of a church. The early pioneers laid out towns foursquare to the points of the compass, with huge city blocks, built sturdy houses and planted dozens of trees. Brigham Young's home still stands a block away from Temple Square, where the Temple, closed to non-Mormons, stands in gleaming marble, topped by the golden angel Moroni, across from the oval Mormon Tabernacle where its great choir sings. For more than 100 years this "Zion" has attracted thousands of converts from the Midwest, the north of England and Scandinavia. The object of religious fear and prejudice, Utah was not granted statehood until 1896, after the church renounced polygamy. Utah has grown steadily since then, and remains heavily Mormon, its basic character is stamped on the desert, mountain-shadowed, often surrealistic landscape which would have been, without the Mormons, mostly unpopulated.

The Church remains distinctive in many ways. It cares deeply about its past: in caves in the mountains of Utah, the Church preserves America's most complete genealogical records. It tries to spread the faith: young Mormons spend missionary years abroad, and their experiences in turn give Utah the biggest inventory of people with knowledge of obscure foreign languages of any state in the union, a nice commercial advantage. It prohibits the consumption of tobacco, alcohol and caffeine; it encourages hard work and large families, and Utah has by far the nation's highest birth rates; its members are healthier than the average American, better educated, they work longer hours and earn more money. In an individualist country, it fosters communitarian attitudes: the LDS Church has no clergy, but members serve in positions for which they are chosen, conducting religious services but also keeping in touch with members and counseling them when they need help. And the Church also maintains its own social service organizations. It evidently works. While American mainline denominations are losing members, the Mormon Church is growing, with more members than either the Presbyterian or Episcopalian churches. There were 2.9 million Mormon in 1970 and 7.7 million in 1990: 4.3 million in the United States and 3.4 million abroad.

The Church's influence in Utah is great—it owns one of the two leading Salt Lake City newspapers and a TV station, it has holdings in an insurance company, several banks, real estate and owns ZCMI, the largest department store in Salt Lake City—and it is sometimes resented. The conservative hold that the Church has over the state can appear in political issues. In 1991 Utah passed the strictest abortion law of any state, banning abortion except in cases of rape and incest, or if the mother's life is endangered. Also in 1990, it became the first state to ban the sale of vending machine cigarettes, although earlier in the year it became the last state to abolish the provision which stated that hard liquor could not be served in public. And the Church itself, financed by the tradition of tithing, runs its own high-quality welfare programs: this is a society that favors market economics and free enterprise, but also has a lively tradition of communal effort and responsibility. Utah's state workfare program, started in 1983, requires one adult in a welfare family to spend 32 hours a week in community service or training, plus job search, and benefits are paid only after performance; social workers here seem to strengthen middle-class values rather than lead rebellions against them.

But if the moral underpinnings of life in Utah have not changed in 50 years, Utah's view of its place in the nation has. Before World War II, Utah saw itself as a colonial victim of East Coast bankers and financiers and Mormons saw themselves as suffering religious discrimination and bigotry—all with some cause. Its income levels were well below the national average, its cost of living higher, the prices paid for the things it produced seemed to be controlled elsewhere. Politically, this perspective translated into a Democratic allegiance: in 1940, Utah was represented by staunch New Dealers in Congress and cast 62% of its votes for Franklin Roosevelt. Today, Utah is more likely to see itself as a busy generator of wealth, with a raft of successful businesses and a knack for high-tech innovation. It has the youngest and highest-productivity work force of any in the nation, leading the nation in job creation in 1992 with 3.2% growth. Workers here work an average of 48 hours a week, more than Japan, far more than the 39 elsewhere in America. And Utah has the second largest concentration of information technology firms, after California. WordPerfect, long the favorite word processing software, was invented in Orem; Novell is headquartered in Provo; the University of Utah in Salt Lake City and Brigham Young University in Provo are producing hundreds of computer engineers. Utah has over 60,000 jobs in information technology; the state government has a Centers of Excellence program to fund small high-tech startups. Utah believes in the coexistence of high-tech and traditional values.

Politically, this perspective translates into a strong Republican preference; Utah was pretty solidly Republican by the middle 1960s. In the last 20 years, as traditional values thriving in Utah have come under attack elsewhere, it has become arguably the most Republican of states—standing out in national statistics politically just as it does demographically. In 1960,

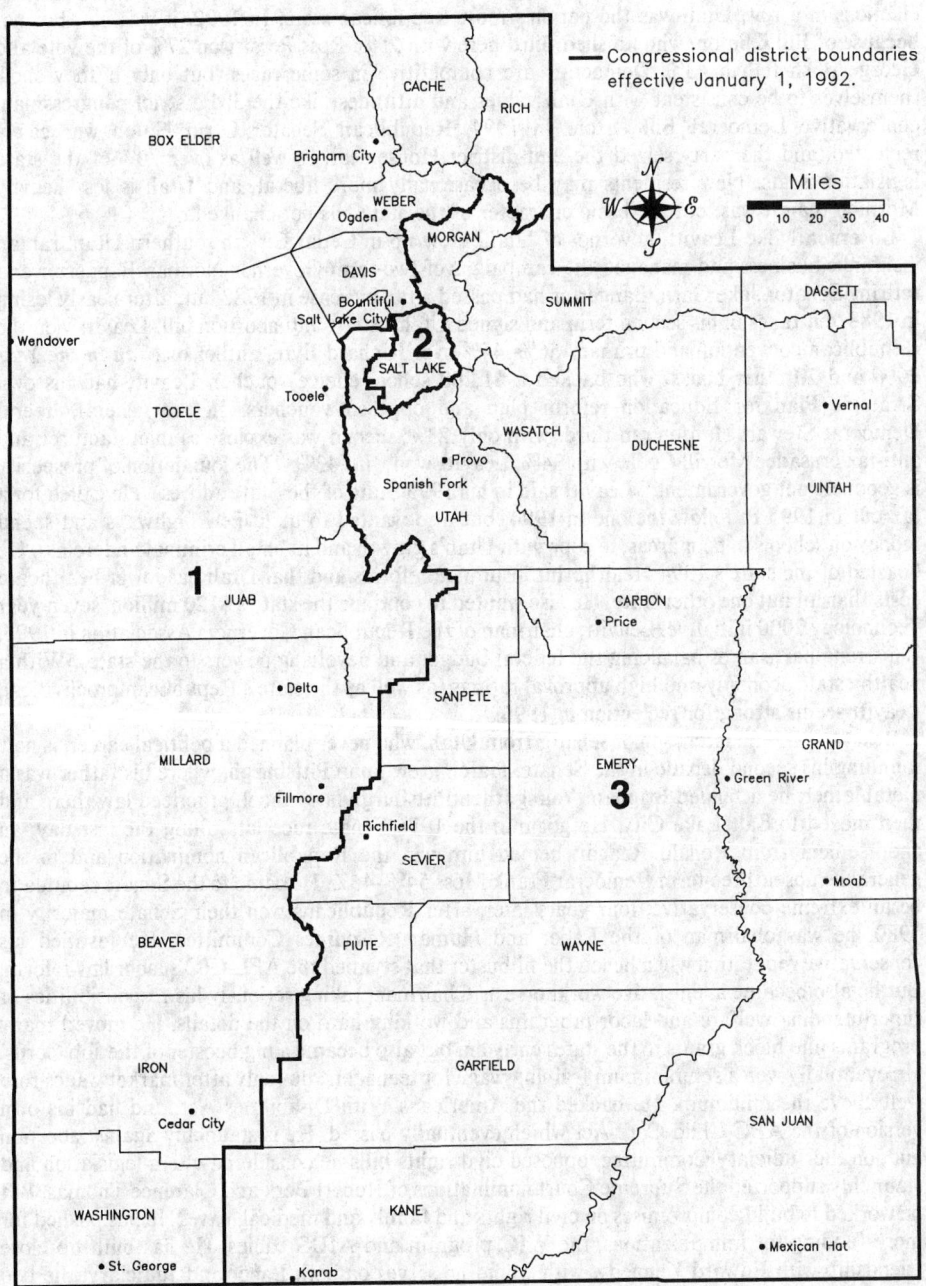

Congressional district boundaries
effective January 1, 1992.

Miles
0 10 20 30 40

CACHE
RICH
BOX ELDER
Brigham City
WEBER
Ogden
MORGAN
DAVIS
Bountiful
Salt Lake City
SUMMIT
DAGGETT
Wendover
SALT LAKE
2
Tooele
TOOELE
Vernal
WASATCH
DUCHESNE
Provo
Spanish Fork
UTAH
UINTAH
1
JUAB
CARBON
Price
Delta
SANPETE
GRAND
MILLARD
EMERY
Green River
Fillmore
3
Richfield
SEVIER
Moab
BEAVER
PIUTE
WAYNE
IRON
GARFIELD
Cedar City
SAN JUAN
WASHINGTON
KANE
St. George
Kanab
Mexican Hat

Richard Nixon carried Utah with 55% of the vote; by 1972, he won with 72%. Ronald Reagan won 73% and 75% of Utah's votes; George Bush won 66% here in 1988: for four presidential elections in a row, Utah was the nation's most Republican state. In 1992, it was not, but not because of Bill Clinton, who finished third here with 25%: Ross Perot won 27% of the vote and George Bush fell to 43%. Democrats are competitive in some races, but only if they show themselves to be consistent with Utah values and attitudes, like the 3rd district congressman, conservative Democrat Bill Orton. In 1994, Republican Senator Orrin Hatch was easily reelected, and the party seized the 2nd district House seat, as well as over 70% of the state legislature seats. New residents may be occasionally more liberal, and Utah is less heavily Mormon than it was, but the basic character of the state has not changed.

Governor. Mike Leavitt, governor of Utah, grew up in Cedar City in southern Utah, ran an insurance business and managed the campaigns of two-term Governor Norman Bangerter and retiring Senator Jake Garn. Bangerter had passed a tax increase in 1987 but, after nearly losing in 1988, cut taxes in his second term and signed Utah's strict anti-abortion bill. Leavitt won the Republican convention and primary 56%–44% over Richard Eyre, author of *Utah in the Year 2000* and 20 other books, who backed a $1,200 school choice voucher. Leavitt had his own Strategic Plan for Education reform plan and opposed vouchers. In the general, liberal Democrat Stewart Hanson ran third, with only 23%; second was explosives manufacturer and anti-tax crusader Merrill Cook, with 34%; Leavitt won with 42%. "The foundation of prosperity is goodness not government," Leavitt said in his 1995 State of the State address. He called for a tax cut in 1995 to follow the one in 1994, but also wanted to build new highways and spend money on schools in poor areas, to cope with Utah's growth and its small criminal underclass. He boasted of the state's 1994 Healthprint insurance reforms and that Utah has lower healthcare costs than all but one other state. He also wanted to continue the state's $120 million, seven-year Technology 2000 initiative. Leavitt, chairman of the Republican Governors Association in 1995, is a strong partisan of balancing the federal budget and devolving powers to the states. With a healthy state economy and high approval ratings (as well as the state's Republican proclivities), Leavitt seems strong for reelection in 1996.

Senators. Orrin Hatch, senior senator from Utah, who never planned a political career, is now rounding his second decade in the Senate. Hatch grew up in Pittsburgh, where his father was a metal lather; he attended Brigham Young, then Pittsburgh law school, practiced law there and then moved to Salt Lake City. He got into the 1976 Senate race late, filing the last day; an endorsement from Ronald Reagan helped him win the Republican nomination and in the general he upset three-term Democrat Frank Moss 54%–45%. He came to the Senate reputed to be an extreme conservative; four years later, after Republicans won their Senate majority in 1980, he was chairman of the Labor and Human Resources Committee. He justified his conservative reputation when he led the filibuster that stymied the AFL-CIO's labor law reform. But he also became a legislative workhorse as Chairman, taking seriously his responsibilities of superintending welfare and labor programs and working hard on the details. He moved many programs into block grants to the states early on, but also became a big booster of the Job Corps. He eventually won a subminimum training wage for teenagers, but only after market wages rose well above the minimum. He backed the Americans With Disabilities Act, and had his own version of the ABC Child Care Act which eventually passed. He is staunchly against abortion and, on the Judiciary Committee, opposed civil rights bills he considered quota legislation and staunchly supported the Supreme Court nominations of Robert Bork and Clarence Thomas. But he worked to build compromises on civil rights and family and medical leave. He has pushed for more funding for immunizations, the WIC program and AIDS babies. He has built up close friendship with Edward Kennedy, with whom he serves on both Labor and Judiciary; the two have worked together on issues from AIDS legislation to immigration reform. But Hatch remains a vigorous opponent of striker replacement and laws to strengthen labor unions.

Hatch has spent much time on technical rather than headline issues: railway labor disputes, bankruptcy reform, sovereign immunity of states for patents and trademarks, and compensation for exposure to radiation during nuclear tests (which affects southern Utah). He worked on home health care, food safety, family leave, organ transplants, orphan drugs and smoking bans. He has worked hard to get a user fee for drug companies seeking quick FDA approval of new drugs; FDA Commissioner David Kessler, appointed by George Bush and held over by Bill Clinton, is a former Hatch staffer. He wants to allow exports of FDA-regulated products regardless of their FDA status. In 1993, Hatch switched from ranking Republican on Labor to the same post on Judiciary, when it was vacated by Strom Thurmond; he got a seat on Finance in 1991 which he kept rather than take Garn's Appropriations spot in 1993.

But first came the 1994 election. Hatch had been reelected fairly easily every six years; even in 1982, when he was opposed by popular Salt Lake City Mayor Ted Wilson, he won 58%–41%. But in 1993 he was dogged by stories that he had tried to help a business associate get a loan from the scandal-plagued BCCI and that he defended the bank on the Senate floor following its guilty plea on charges of laundering drug money, and for a time he was only running even in polls against 3d District Congressman Bill Orton. But in November 1993 Hatch was cleared by the Senate Ethics Committee on all the BCCI charges, and in the months that followed strong Democrats—Orton, Attorney General Jan Graham, activist Grethe Peterson—decided not to make the race. At the last minute, former Democratic state chairman Pat Shea stepped in and ran and recalled how Hatch had beaten a three-term incumbent after filing on the last day 18 years before. But in Utah having Ronald Reagan's endorsement in 1976 and being a member of Bill Clinton's party in 1994 were two very different things. Shea ran a respectable but underfinanced campaign, and Hatch won 69%–28%.

Once again in the majority, Hatch, as chairman of Judiciary, has a full plate. He pledged to give Clinton judicial appointees a fair hearing. He was heavily involved in tort reform and regulatory reform and was the floor manager of the by-one-vote unsuccessful drive to pass the balanced budget amendment, spending hours on the floor trying to formulate compromises. He worked hard to move Contract legislation through his committee and the Senate by trying to offer proposals that a more moderate Senate could stomach.

Utah's junior senator is Bob Bennett, first elected in 1992 but no stranger to the Senate. He grew up in Salt Lake City, and was 17 when his father Wallace Bennett was first elected to the Senate in 1950; he served four terms and retired in 1974. Bob Bennett was a congressional staffer and the Transportation Department's chief lobbyist during the Nixon Administration. He also headed the public relations firm (and CIA front) that employed Watergate burglar Howard Hunt, but was involved in no wrongdoing himself; author Bob Woodward has denied that Bennett was his "Deep Throat" source. Back in Utah, he headed Microsonics Corporation, which makes audio disks for talking toys, for three years and then became head of Franklin Quest, which produces the Franklin day planners and organizers; he increased it from four to 700 employees and sales of $80 million; he sold his interest in 1991 for a reported $25 million. He headed a commission that produced Utah's Strategic Plan for Education and wrote *Gaining Control*, a book on the forces that control daily life.

In 1992, when Jake Garn retired from the Senate, Bennett decided to run for the seat his father held for four terms. He was not the only millionaire in the race. The initial favorite was Republican Joseph Cannon, who had taken over the old Geneva Steel plant and made it profitable; he is a great-grandson of Utah's first territorial delegate, George Q. Cannon, who "had five wives and a lot of progeny." Cannon spent $5 million of his own money on an expensive media campaign, but Bennett spent $1.4 million of his own money and effectively attacked Geneva's environmental record. Bennett won 51%–49%. The Democratic primary was won 61%–39% by Congressman Wayne Owens, a familiar figure since winning an upset House victory in 1972 and a candidate for this seat in 1974, over businessman Doug Anderson who spent $1 million of his own money.

The general election provided a clear contrast. Owens, a staffer for Edward Kennedy in the 1960s, is an environmentalist, and liberal on many issues; on the House Judiciary Committee, he voted to impeach Richard Nixon. He lost a race for governor in 1984 but was returned to the

House in 1986. Bennett campaigned as an outsider, despite his Washington experience; it helped that Owens had 87 overdrafts on the House bank. He won on election day 55%–40%, with exit polls showing Owens carrying only the elderly—not a good omen for Utah Democrats.

In the Senate Bennett compiled a pretty solidly conservative record. With healthcare reform seemingly dying, He introduced the Rowland-Bilirakis health insurance reform in the Senate in 1994 along with Senators Nunn, Boren and Domenici. Dole appointed him chairman of the Republican Healthcare Task Force for the 104th Congress. Bennett will be in the thick of Glass-Steagal reform and the budget battle from his seats on both the Banking and Appropriations Committees. He is also considered a possible supporter of a consumption or flat tax.

Presidential politics. Utah is one of the most Republican states in the country—the most Republican from 1976 to 1988—and so sees little presidential campaigning. For the national conventions, its relatively few delegates are chosen in caucuses. The Democratic caucus in March preferred Paul Tsongas and Jerry Brown to Bill Clinton.

Congressional districting. The Republican legislature drew new lines for Utah's three congressional districts for 1992. Salt Lake County, the most Democratic part of the state now, had to be split between districts, and the legislature gave some of the less Republican portions to the 1st and 3d Districts.

The People: Est. Pop. 1994: 1,908,000; Pop. 1990: 1,722,850, up 10.7% 1990–1994. 0.7% of U.S. total, 34th largest; 13% rural. Median age: 26.2 years. 8.7% 65 years and over. 93.8% White, 4.9% Hispanic Origin, 1.9% Asian, 1.4% American Indian, 2.1% Other. Households: 64.8% married couple families; 38% married couple fams. w. children; 58% college educ.; median household income: $29,470; per capita income: $11,029; 68.1% owner occupied housing; median house value: $68,900 median monthly rent: $300. 4.9% Unemployment. 1994 Voting age pop.: 1,246,000. 1994 Turnout: 520,136; 42% of VAP. Registered voters (1994): 921,981; no party registration.

Political Lineup: Governor, Michael O. Leavitt (R); Lt. Gov., Olene S. Walker (R); Atty. Gen., Jan Graham (D); Treasurer, Edward T. Alter (R); Auditor, Tom L. Allen (R). State Senate, 29 (19 R and 10 D); State House of Representatives, 75 (55 R and 20 D). Senators, Orrin G. Hatch (R) and Robert F. Bennett (R). Representatives, 3 (2 R and 1 D).

1992 Presidential Vote		
Bush (R)	322,632	(43%)
Perot (I)	203,400	(27%)
Clinton (D)	183,429	(25%)
Other	34,607	(5%)

1992 Democratic Presidential Primary		
Tsongas	10,582	(33%)
Brown	8,971	(28%)
Clinton	5,780	(18%)
Kerrey	3,447	(11%)
Harkin	1,274	(4%)
Other, Uncommitted	1,584	(5%)

1988 Presidential Vote		
Bush (R)	428,442	(66%)
Dukakis (D)	207,343	(32%)

GOVERNOR

Gov. Michael O. Leavitt (R)

Elected 1992, term expires Jan. 1996; b. Feb. 11, 1951, Cedar City; home, Salt Lake City; S. UT U., B.A. 1976; Mormon; married (Jacalyn).

Career: Army Natl. Guard, 1969–78; Pres. & CEO, Leavitt Group Insurance Co., 1984–92; Chmn., S. UT U. Bd. of Trustees, 1985–89; UT Board of Regents, 1989–92.

Office: 210 State Capitol, Salt Lake City 84114, 801-538-1000. Fax: 801-538-1528.

Election Results

1992 gen.	Michael O. Leavitt (R)	321,713	(42%)
	Merrill Cook (I)	255,733	(34%)
	Stewart Hanson(D).	177,181	(23%)
1992 prim.	Michael O. Leavitt (R)	143,647	(56%)
	Richard Eyre (R)............	112,881	(44%)
1988 gen.	Norman H. Bangerter (R)	260,462	(40%)
	Ted Wilson (D)..............	249,321	(38%)
	Merrill Cook (I)	136,651	(21%)

SENATORS

Sen. Orrin G. Hatch (R)

Elected 1976, seat up 2000; b. Mar. 22, 1934, Pittsburgh, PA; home, Salt Lake City; Brigham Young U., B.S. 1959, U. of Pittsburgh, J.D. 1962; Mormon; married (Elaine).

Career: Practicing atty., 1962–76.

DC Office: 135 RSOB 20510, 202-224-5251; Fax: 202-224-6331.

State Offices: 8402 Fed. Bldg., Salt Lake City 84138, 801-524-4380; 109 Fed. Bldg., 51 S. University Ave., #320, Provo 84601, 801-375-7881; 1410 Fed. Bldg., 325 25th St., Ogden 84401, 801-625-5672; and 10 N. Main, P.O. Box 99, Cedar City 84720, 801-586-8435.

Committees: *Finance* (6th of 11 R): International Trade; Medicare, Long-Term Care and Health Insurance; Taxation and IRS Oversight (Chmn). *Judiciary* (Chmn. of 10 R): Antitrust, Business Rights and Competition; Constitution, Federalism and Property Rights; Youth Violence. *Indian Affairs* (9th of 9 R). *Joint Committee on Taxation* (3rd of 5 Sen.)

Group Ratings

	ADA	ACLU	COPE	CFA	LCV	CON	NSI	COC	ACU	NTLC	CHC
1994	5	21	0	17	0	72	100	91	100	92	100
1993	5	—	0	0	13	48	—	100	88	—	—

1346   UTAH

National Journal Ratings

	1993 LIB — 1993 CONS			1994 LIB — 1994 CONS		
Economic	13%	—	81%	18%	—	77%
Social	16%	—	81%	0%	—	85%
Foreign	24%	—	71%	26%	—	71%

Key Votes of the 103d Congress

1. Clinton Deficit Plan	N	3. Brady Handgun Purchase	N	5. Lmt. UN Cmnd. of Forces	N
2. NAFTA	Y	4. Strike Race/Death Pnlty.	Y	6. Cut Missile Funds	N

Key Votes of the 104th Congress

1. Congressional Compliance	Y	3. Balanced Budget Amndt.	Y	5. Product Liability Reform	Y
2. Bar Unfunded Mandates	Y	4. Pass Line Item Veto	Y	6. FY96 Budget	Y

Election Results

1994 general	Orrin G. Hatch (R)...............	357,297	(69%)	($4,209,993)
	Pat Shea (D).....................	146,938	(28%)	($311,491)
	Others	15,088	(3%)	
1994 primary	Orrin G. Hatch (R)...............	unopposed		
1988 general	Orrin G. Hatch (R)...............	430,089	(67%)	($3,706,381)
	Brian H. Moss (D)	203,364	(32%)	($153,475)

Sen. Robert F. Bennett (R)

Elected 1992, seat up 1998; b. Sept. 18, 1933, Salt Lake City; home, Salt Lake City; U. of UT, B.S. 1957; Mormon; married (Joyce).

Career: Chaplain, Army Natl. Guard, 1957–60; Cong. Liaison, U.S. Dept. of Transportation, 1969–70; Pres., Robert Mullen P.R., 1970–74; P.R. Dir., Summa Corp., 1974–78; Pres., Osmond Communications, 1978–79; Chmn., American Computers Corp., 1979–81; Pres., Microsonics Corp., 1981–84; Chmn., UT Educ. Strategic Plng. Comm., 1988; C.E.O., Franklin Quest Co., 1984–91.

DC Office: 431 DSOB 20510, 202-224-5444; Fax: 202-224-6717.

State Offices: 4225 Wallace F. Bennett Fed. Bldg., Salt Lake City 84138, 801-524-5933; 51 S. University Ave., #310, Provo 84601, 801-379-2525; 324 24th St., #1410, Ogden 84401, 801-625-5676; and Fed. Bldg., 196-E Tabernacle St., #22, St. George 84770, 801-628-5514.

Committees: *Appropriations* (15th of 15 R): District of Columbia; Energy and Water Development; Interior; Legislative Branch; VA, HUD and Independent Agencies. *Banking, Housing & Urban Affairs* (7th of 9 R): Financial Institutions and Regulatory Relief; International Finance; Securities. *Small Business* (6th of 10 R). *Joint Economic Committee* (4th of 10 Sen.)

Group Ratings

	ADA	ACLU	COPE	CFA	LCV	CON	NSI	COC	ACU	NTLC	CHC
1994	5	21	0	17	0	72	100	95	100	92	92
1993	5	—	0	30	13	79	—	100	88	—	—

National Journal Ratings

	1993 LIB — 1993 CONS			1994 LIB — 1994 CONS	
Economic	13%	—	81%	18%	—	77%
Social	19%	—	78%	0%	—	85%
Foreign	16%	—	77%	29%	—	70%

Key Votes of the 103d Congress

1. Clinton Deficit Plan	N	3. Brady Handgun Purchase	N	5. Lmt. UN Cmnd. of Forces	Y
2. NAFTA	Y	4. Strike Race/Death Pnlty.	Y	6. Cut Missile Funds	N

Key Votes of the 104th Congress

1. Congressional Compliance	Y	3. Balanced Budget Amndt.	Y	5. Product Liability Reform	Y
2. Bar Unfunded Mandates	Y	4. Pass Line Item Veto	Y	6. FY96 Budget	Y

Election Results

1992 general	Robert F. Bennett (R)	420,069	(55%)	($3,339,325)
	Wayne Owens (D)	301,228	(40%)	($1,904,750)
	Others	37,182	(5%)	
1992 primary	Robert F. Bennett (R)	135,514	(51%)	
	Joe Cannon (R)	128,125	(49%)	
1986 general	Edwin Jacob (Jake) Garn (R)	314,608	(72%)	($752,944)
	Craig S. Oliver (D)	115,523	(27%)	($24,508)

FIRST DISTRICT

In May 1869, a motley crowd of Irish and Chinese laborers, teamsters, engineers, train crews, officials and guests from California and Salt Lake City gathered in Promontory Point, Utah, to watch the opening of the transcontinental railroad. The Union Pacific train was late and Leland Stanford raised his hammer and totally missed the golden spike, but an alert telegrapher mimicked the sound over the wire and a photographer recorded the scene for posterity: united at last were the civilized East and the mostly untamed West. Here, beyond sight of the snow-capped mountains crossed by the Mormon pioneers, the salt flats still stretch out endlessly; the rail lines now pass north of here, and Promontory Point lies on uninhabited flat land beside the rising Great Salt Lake. The lake kept rising into the middle 1980s, despite state legislation forbidding it from going above a certain level. The local county commissioners called for a day of prayer for drought in May 1986, the lake finally obeyed the law, and the state didn't have to pump water through canals which would have formed a vast new lake in the salt flats to the west.

The 1st Congressional District of Utah includes the western half of the state, from Promontory Point down to the Arizona and Nevada borders near Las Vegas, where the Colorado River flows south through Glen Canyon into Arizona; Zion National Park is in the south, there is mining country in the center and the desert lies west of the lake. But 75% of the people in this district live along the Wasatch Front, a thin strip of land on the east side of the Lake between the salt flats and the Wasatch Mountains. It takes in Brigham City and Logan near the Idaho border, goes south through Ogden, an old working-class town on the Union Pacific line and the nearest station stop to Promontory Point, and then proceeds through a strip of suburbs to the salt flats northwest of downtown Salt Lake City near the airport. The rest of the 1st's voters live in small communities, many entirely Mormon, in central and southern Utah.

The congressman from this district is James Hansen, a Republican with as solidly conserva-tive a record as anyone in the House. He grew up in Farmington, Utah, served in the Navy, was elected to the Council in Farmington and then to the Utah House in 1972, at 40; he was Speaker in 1979 and 1980, when he ran for Congress. He is on the National Security Committee and chairs the National Parks, Forests and Lands Subcommittee of Resources. This makes him one of the Republicans' leaders in attacking what many westerners consider the Clinton Administration's "war on the West." In the past, he worked to complete the Central Utah Project to bring Colorado River water to the Wasatch Front in 1992, helped crack down on cheap water rates in the Central Valley of California and backed the 65 mile per hour speed limit. On National Security, he has tried to save Hill Air Force Base, though it seemed doomed for closure, and in 1993 stoutly defended the Tooele Army Depot, with its stockpiles of nerve gas, against threatened closure. He wants to amend education funding formulas that hurt Utah, which has many schoolchildren. Much of Hansen's time in the 103d Congress was spent at his post as ranking Republican on the Ethics Committee; he is a stickler for ethics and worked to disclose overdrafts on the House bank and malfeasance at the House post office. But he has rotated off the committee.

Hansen initially won this district in 1980 by beating an incumbent Democrat, Gunn McKay. He had relatively close races in 1986 and 1990, but in 1994 against an active Democrat, Bobbie Coray, who raised almost as much money as he did, he won with 65%.

The People: Pop. 1990: 574,205; 16% rural; 9% age 65+; 92% White; 1% Black; 1% Amer. Indian; 2% Asian; 2% Other; 5% Hispanic origin. Voting age pop.: 360,724; 1% Black; 4% Hispanic origin. Households: 69% married couple families; 40% married couple fams. w. children; 57% college educ.; median household income: $30,563; per capita income: $10,856; median gross rent: $364; median house value: $68,800.

1992 Presidential Vote		
Bush (R)	115,627	(47%)
Perot (I)	68,884	(28%)
Clinton (D)	50,622	(20%)
Other	12,989	(5%)

1988 Presidential Vote		
Bush (R)	156,533	(73%)
Dukakis (D)	59,228	(27%)

Rep. James V. Hansen (R)

Elected 1980; b. Aug. 14, 1932, Salt Lake City; home, Farmington; U. of UT, B.A. 1960; Mormon; married (Ann).

Career: Navy, 1951–55; Farmington City Cncl., 1962–72; UT House of Reps., 1972–80, Speaker, 1978–80.

DC Office: 2466 RHOB 20515, 202-225-0453; Fax: 202-225-5857.

District Offices: 1017 Fed. Bldg., 324 25th St., Ogden 84401, 801-625-5677; and 435 E. Tabernacle, #301, St. George 84770, 801-628-1071.

Committees: *National Security* (6th of 30 R): Military Installations and Facilities; Military Research and Development. *Resources* (2nd of 25 R): National Parks, Forests and Lands (Chmn.); Water and Power Resources. *Intelligence (Permanent Select)* (4th of 9 R): Technical and Tactical Intelligence.

Group Ratings

	ADA	ACLU	COPE	CFA	LCV	CON	NSI	COC	ACU	NTLC	CHC
1994	0	17	0	20	0	96	100	92	95	89	100
1993	0	—	8	0	8	57	—	100	96	—	—

National Journal Ratings

	1993 LIB — 1993 CONS			1994 LIB — 1994 CONS		
Economic	14%	—	80%	0%	—	80%
Social	11%	—	82%	23%	—	76%
Foreign	0%	—	91%	0%	—	88%

Key Votes of the 103d Congress

1. Clinton Deficit Plan	N	3. Brady Handgun Purchase	N	5. Lmt. UN Cmnd. of Forces	Y
2. NAFTA	Y	4. Strike Race/Death Pnlty.	Y	6. Cut Missile Funds	N

Key Votes of the 104th Congress

1. Congressional Compliance	Y	6. Reform Crime Grant	Y	11. Loser Pays Court Reform	Y
2. Balanced Budget Amndmt.	Y	7. National Security Act	Y	12. Product Liability Reform	Y
3. Bar Unfunded Mandates	Y	8. Moratorium on Regs.	Y	13. Welfare Reform	Y
4. Pass Line Item Veto	Y	9. Risk Assessment on Regs.	Y	14. Term Limits Amndmt.	Y
5. Relax Exclusionary Rule	Y	10. Expnd. Priv. Prop. Rights	Y	15. Tax Cuts	Y

Election Results

1994 general	James V. Hansen (R)	104,954	(65%)	($348,036)
	Bobbie Coray (D)	57,664	(35%)	($276,892)
1994 primary	James V. Hansen (R)	unopposed		
1992 general	James V. Hansen (R)	160,037	(65%)	($240,969)
	Ron Holt (D)	68,712	(28%)	($64,451)
	William J. Lawrence (I)	16,505	(7%)	

SECOND DISTRICT

The center of Utah and of the Mormon Church is Temple Square, illuminated by 300,000 lights during Christmas week, and nestled beneath the towering, snow-capped mountains that flank Salt Lake City. Here you can find the Mormon Tabernacle, home of the famous choir, and the Temple itself, crowned with the golden angel Moroni. Two long blocks north is the state Capitol, four blocks south is City Hall and all around are Salt Lake City's impressive skyscrapers. Ironically, Salt Lake City is the least Mormon and most cosmopolitan part of Utah, with the state university and businesses bringing in outsiders. Some think it now has a non-Mormon majority, but most likely it doesn't; it grew nearly 18% in the 1980s, and the metro area has 1.1 million people now, but that growth is in large part internally generated by Utah's large Mormon families.

Utah's 2d Congressional District, which includes most of Salt Lake County, has somewhat fewer families and children than the other two Utah districts. Its boundaries exclude the western suburbs on the flats out toward the Great Salt Lake, which lean toward the Democrats—an attempt by the Republican legislature to help Republican chances. The 2d has most of Utah's affluent people, living in Salt Lake City and suburbs like East Millcreek, Holladay and Cottonwood, right next to the Wasatch Mountains which rise at that point to 9,000 feet. It's just a 20-minute drive—well, 30—from offices to ski slopes, as Utah boosters like to tell prospective new residents. The district also includes a string of suburbs south of Salt Lake City—West Jordan, South Jordan, Murray, Sandy, Draper, Riverton, Bluffdale. By national standards, this is a Republican district, but it is the most Democratic of Utah's three House seats, and in fact has been seriously contested in 11 of the last 13 elections.

The congresswoman from the 2d District is Enid Greene Waldholtz, a Republican elected in 1994 when she beat the Democrat who beat her in 1992. Waldholtz typifies Utah in many ways: she is Mormon and conservative, a successful professional with wide experience. She grew up in Utah, attended the University of Utah and Brigham Young Law School, from 1983 to 1990 was a litigator with a Salt Lake law firm. In 1990 she became deputy chief of staff to Governor Norman Bangerter, in 1992 she lost the House race to Democrat Karen Shepherd, and in 1993 she became corporate counsel to Novell, the computer giant, in Provo. She ran as Enid Greene in 1992 and was married in August 1993. Initial prospects for her 1994 race were not propitious. Shepherd had outspent her in 1992 and won 51%–47%, helped by what appeared to be Greene's negative campaigning; Shepherd had campaigned as a congressional reformer and was one of the leaders of the freshman Democrat reformers. But she made three terrible mistakes. After promising not to vote for a tax increase, she voted for the Clinton budget and tax package in August 1993; the reaction in Utah was so negative she was accompanied by police to town meetings in the district. She and her reformers allowed Speaker Tom Foley and the Democratic leadership to talk them out of most of their reforms. And she voted for the Brady bill, the assault weapons ban and the 1994 crime bill. Suddenly the contrast between cultural attitudes, between therapy and discipline—the non-Mormon Shepherd was a teacher and public relations person, the Mormon Waldholtz was a litigator and a business executive—worked very much the Republicans' way, as therapy came to be associated with the sloppiness and mendacity of Bill Clinton and discipline with the hard work and tough love that have made Utah prosperous and happy.

The 1994 race was not without its complications. Merrill Cook, owner of an explosives company and a losing independent candidate five times, most recently for governor in 1992, ran again. He backed a term limits proposition which he put on the ballot, but which also provided for runoffs, in which he as a minority candidate obviously had an interest; it lost, making Utah only the second state so far (Washington in 1990) to reject term limits. Democrats hoped that Cook would siphon votes from Republicans, although Waldholtz maintained Cook would hurt Shepherd with voters in low-income west side neighborhoods. Shepherd, with money from feminists and PACs, started off outspending Waldholtz again, and highlighted her support of term limits and a gift ban on lobbyists as well as an early call for a Whitewater independent counsel: "Utah's independent voice in Congress." But in September Waldholtz launched a massive campaign, using mostly her own money, with ads featuring "ENID," showing her tough on crime, cautious on healthcare reform, against abortion, strong for the balance budget amendment and against Bill Clinton. This was a big-spending campaign, with the three candidates spending $3.9 million in all. Shepherd spent $1 million; Cook $879,000, almost all of it his own money; Waldholtz spent $1,976,000, some $1,644,000 of it her own. Waldholtz won 46% of the vote, 1% less than 1992, but Shepherd won only 36%, down 15% from two years before—a very big drop for a competent incumbent. Cook, who said he would not run for office again if he lost, won 18%.

Waldholtz made her mark early in the 104th Congress. In January 1995 she became a member of the Rules Committee, the first Republican freshman to do so in 80 years. And in March 1995 she announced she was pregnant, only the second member of Congress in history to give birth while in office; the other, Yvonne Brathwaite Burke, gave birth in November 1973, and sent her best wishes from her current office as a Los Angeles County Supervisor.

The People: Pop. 1990: 574,412; 9% age 65+; 92% White; 1% Black; 1% Amer. Indian; 2% Asian; 2% Other; 5% Hispanic origin. Voting age pop.: 378,723; 1% Black; 4% Hispanic origin. Households: 60% married couple families; 34% married couple fams. w. children; 62% college educ.; median household income: $30,960; per capita income: $12,971; median gross rent: $379; median house value: $76,700.

1992 Presidential Vote			**1988 Presidential Vote**		
Bush (R)	101,169	(38%)	Bush (R)	138,467	(62%)
Clinton (D)	81,233	(31%)	Dukakis (D)	85,967	(38%)
Perot (I)	75,921	(29%)			

Rep. Enid G. Waldholtz (R)

Elected 1994; b. Oct. 5, 1958, Salt Lake City; home, Salt Lake City; U. of UT, B.S. 1980; Brigham Young U., J.D. 1983; Mormon; married (Joseph).

Career: Practicing atty., 1983–90; Deputy Chief of Staff, UT Gov. Norm Bangerter, 1990–92; Corp. Cnsl., Novell Inc., 1993–94.

DC Office: 515 CHOB 20515, 202-225-3011; Fax: 202-225-3491; e-mail: enidutah@hr.house.gov.

District Offices: 125 S. State St., #2311, Salt Lake City 84138, 801-524-4394.

Committees: *Rules* (9th of 9 R): Rules of the House.

Group Ratings and 103rd Congress Votes: Newly Elected

Key Votes of the 104th Congress

1. Congressional Compliance Y	6. Reform Crime Grant Y	11. Loser Pays Court Reform Y
2. Balanced Budget Amndmt. Y	7. National Security Act Y	12. Product Liability Reform Y
3. Bar Unfunded Mandates Y	8. Moratorium on Regs. Y	13. Welfare Reform Y
4. Pass Line Item Veto Y	9. Risk Assessment on Regs. Y	14. Term Limits Amndmt. Y
5. Relax Exclusionary Rule Y	10. Expnd. Priv. Prop. Rights Y	15. Tax Cuts Y

Election Results

1994 general	Enid G. Waldholtz (R)	85,507	(46%)	($1,976,289)
	Karen Sheperd (D)	66,911	(36%)	($1,009,176)
	Merrill Cook (I)	34,167	(18%)	($878,528)
1994 primary	Enid G. Waldholtz (R)	unopposed		
1992 general	Karen F. Shepherd (D)	127,738	(51%)	($617,594)
	Enid Greene (R)	118,307	(47%)	($446,334)
	Others	6,924	(3%)	

THIRD DISTRICT

The heartland of the Mormon Church in America is in a geographically isolated valley between 11,000-foot peaks of the Wasatch Range and the shores of Utah Lake. Here is Provo, the home of Brigham Young University, an institution long known for the rigorously conservative views of its faculty, the old-fashioned moral standards it encourages and its welcoming of technological innovation. The Mormon commonwealth, after all, started off with a terrific shortage of both labor and water and was eager to use technology to make up for this and prosper in this fearsome terrain. Today this is one of America's high-tech centers, the home of WordPerfect and Novell and hundreds of other firms, some fleeing California's high taxes and cultural liberalism.

The 3d Congressional District of Utah includes Provo and Utah County and most of the west side of Salt Lake City and its suburb of West Valley, connected by a strip of desert along the Great Salt Lake. These two urban areas cast more than two-thirds of the district's votes; the rest are cast in towns scattered amid huge mountains, florid rock formations and deep canyons from Wyoming down to the Arizona border. Its northernmost point is in the Wasatch Range, and it includes the depressed uranium country in eastern Utah around Moab and the surreal rock formations of Canyonlands and Capitol Reef National Parks. Utah County is one of the most heavily Republican areas in the United States, and the 3d District was the number one

Republican district in the 1980 presidential election. Republican redistricters for 1992, however, added the Democratic west side of Salt Lake County to make the 2d District more Republican, which strengthened Democrats marginally in the 3d.

That makes a difference, since against considerable odds the 3d District has a Democratic Congressman, Bill Orton, a tax lawyer and former Internal Revenue Service agent, who won the seat in 1990 when the incumbent retired. Orton was helped by a fractious Republican primary, by Republican nominee Karl Snow's business ties to a convicted stock manipulator, and by a Snow newspaper ad that juxtaposed a picture of Snow and his family with a picture of Orton, who was then single, labeled "Bill Orton and his family." Even in the Mormon heartland of large families, this was thought to be dirty pool. Orton won a stunning 58%–36% victory, carrying every county but one tiny rural enclave.

In the House Orton has had a voting record about as conservative as any Democrat. He started off voting for the Gulf war resolution, he opposed the Brady bill and he did not support the Clinton budget and tax package in 1993. On local matters he worked for the Central Utah Project, defended ranchers' grazing rights federal lands and supported mandatory alcohol label warnings. He passed a "Veteran Teacher Corps" bill to provide teaching opportunities for retiring military personnel; and this horse owner and resident of Provo drew up his own Utah wilderness bill. In 1994 he negotiated with the Democratic leadership on budget and fiscal issues, agreeing to keep several Democrats' signatures off the discharge petition for the A-to-Z spending votes reform in return for House votes on budgetary process. But he was not entirely vindicated by the result, and frustrated when the House overwhelmingly rejected his motion, 339–83, to consider means-testing entitlements.

Orton was easily reelected in 1992, when Republicans kept entering and leaving the race in a farcical manner. In Utah County, which cast almost half the votes, Orton won by only 50%–46%. But he carried the Salt Lake County portion added by the Republican legislature 70%–24% and the smaller counties 64%–31% for a 59%–37% victory. With a high job rating, he considered running against Senator Orrin Hatch in early 1994. Grethe Peterson would not leave the race and, perhaps not relishing a primary, Orton decided not to run. Instead he won reelection to the House by 59%–40%, once again only narrowly carrying Utah County (52%–47%), but running far better in Salt Lake County (69%–29%) and the rest of the district (61%–37%). In the 104th Congress he was part of The Coalition, the group of independent-minded conservative Democrats who presented their own budget proposal. Orton, once called "single and socialist," also evoked bipartisan applause when he asked permission to announce how he would have voted on roll calls he missed because his wife was giving birth to their first child.

The People: Pop. 1990: 574,233; 23% rural; 8% age 65+; 90% White; 3% Amer. Indian; 2% Asian; 2% Other; 5% Hispanic origin. Voting age pop.: 355,475; 5% Hispanic origin. Households: 68% married couple families; 41% married couple fams. w. children; 54% college educ.; median household income: $26,570; per capita income: $9,259; median gross rent: $358; median house value: $59,800.

1992 Presidential Vote			1988 Presidential Vote		
Bush (R)	105,836	(46%)	Bush (R)	133,442	(68%)
Perot (I)	58,595	(25%)	Dukakis (D)	62,148	(32%)
Clinton (D)	51,574	(22%)			
Other	14,245	(6%)			

Rep. William H. Orton (D)

Elected 1990; b. Sept. 22, 1948, North Ogden; home, Provo; Brigham Young U., B.S. 1973, J.D. 1979; Mormon; married (Jacquelyn).

Career: Tax auditor, Internal Revenue Svc., 1976–77; Adjunct prof., Portland St. U., Portland Commun. Col., 1974–76, Brigham Young U., 1984–85; Practicing atty., 1980–90.

DC Office: 440 CHOB 20515, 202-225-7751; Fax: 202-226-7683.

District Offices: 51 S. University Ave., #317, Provo 84601, 801-379-2500; and 3540 S. 40th St., #410, West Valley City 84119, 801-964-5828.

Committees: *Banking & Financial Services* (11th of 22 D): Capital Markets, Securities and Government Sponsored Enterprises; Financial Institutions and Consumer Credit. *Budget* (10th of 18 D).

Group Ratings

	ADA	ACLU	COPE	CFA	LCV	CON	NSI	COC	ACU	NTLC	CHC
1994	25	30	33	30	18	97	60	92	79	69	57
1993	25	—	67	40	36	91	—	55	54	—	—

National Journal Ratings

	1993 LIB — 1993 CONS		1994 LIB — 1994 CONS	
Economic	44% —	56%	44% —	54%
Social	29% —	69%	35% —	64%
Foreign	46% —	53%	49% —	49%

Key Votes of the 103d Congress

1. Clinton Deficit Plan	N	3. Brady Handgun Purchase	N	5. Lmt. UN Cmnd. of Forces	N
2. NAFTA	N	4. Strike Race/Death Pnlty.	Y	6. Cut Missile Funds	N

Key Votes of the 104th Congress

1. Congressional Compliance	Y	6. Reform Crime Grant	N	11. Loser Pays Court Reform	N
2. Balanced Budget Amndmt.	Y	7. National Security Act	N	12. Product Liability Reform	N
3. Bar Unfunded Mandates	Y	8. Moratorium on Regs.	Y	13. Welfare Reform	N
4. Pass Line Item Veto	Y	9. Risk Assessment on Regs.	Y	14. Term Limits Amndmt.	Y
5. Relax Exclusionary Rule	Y	10. Expnd. Priv. Prop. Rights	Y	15. Tax Cuts	N

Election Results

1994 general	Bill Orton (D)	91,505	(59%)	($278,477)
	Dixie Thompson (R)	61,839	(40%)	($114,884)
	Others	1,802	(1%)	
1994 primary	Bill Orton (D)	unopposed		
1992 general	William H. Orton (D)	135,029	(59%)	($241,403)
	Richard R. Harrington (R)	84,019	(37%)	($71,074)
	Others	10,013	(4%)	

VERMONT

Vermont is an antique state, carefully preserved. Consider the Shelburne Museum, with its barn and jail, railroad station and blacksmith shop and covered bridge, 37 buildings of folk art, established by New Yorkish Havemeyers and Vanderbilts to preserve the past in better-than-ever condition. Vermont, wrote Vermonter Dorothy Canfield Fisher half a century ago, "represents the past, is a piece of the past in the midst of the present and future." Today, reverence for that past has made Vermont, for many Americans approaching the 21st Century, a guide to a congenial future. Vermont's closeness to nature, the intimacy of its small communities, its lack of unattractive accoutrements of early 20th Century industrialism have all made it a kind of promised land for urban expatriates: the state that missed out on U.S. Steel now produces Ben & Jerry's Ice Cream. By the 1980s, for the first time in nearly 200 years, Vermont became a growth area: in an era when Americans are increasingly ill-served by the rigidities of big organizations and repelled by big-city congestion, small businesses and computers enable more and more Americans to make their livings where they want, which often means Vermont.

Vermont began as an agricultural state, a target of America's northward and eastward migration (as important, for a while, as westward movement), a place where starting in the 1790s, second sons and daughters from small New England farms went to scratch out livings from the rocky soil. Agriculture has remained important, especially dairy farming, but Vermont has commerce as well. With its legendary thriftiness, it has accumulated capital that, invested wisely, was used to build the solid stone office buildings and courthouses, the thick-timbered houses and gold-topped state Capitol that have remained long after ramshackle wooden buildings of the 1880s have crumbled into dust. But Vermont never developed labor-intensive industry, and so over the years it exported people, and aged. Today, millions of Americans have Vermont blood—far more than the half million who live here now, many of whom have no Vermont roots at all. Two presidents were born here, but both made their careers elsewhere—Chester Arthur in New York, Calvin Coolidge in Massachusetts—while Vermont made no visible impression on two great writers who lived here for years—Rudyard Kipling and Aleksander Solzhenitsyn. As a result of continuous outmigration, Vermont's population hovered between 300,000 and 400,000 from 1850 to 1960.

Since then—perhaps the key date was 1963, when people started outnumbering cows—Vermont has changed rapidly. Its economy has boomed, led by leisure-time industries—ski resorts, summer homes—and IBM, with several big high-tech facilities around the Burlington area on the mostly undeveloped shores of glorious Lake Champlain. Vermont's tradition of cottage industries continues, with knitters seeking to overturn union-inspired federal bans on home production. Home-grown firms started by erstwhile Baby Boom rebels—Ben & Jerry's Ice Cream is the archetype—have flourished. Ben & Jerry's continues to move ahead: in order to reenergize the company, Ben and Jerry chose a new CEO after a celebrated and unusual search by essay contest in 1994. The population rose from 390,000 in 1960 to 444,000 in 1970, 511,000 in 1980 and 580,000 in 1994, and it hasn't been random settlement. While next-door New Hampshire, trumpeting its low taxes and aversion to government, has attracted right-leaning migrants from Massachusetts happy to live in spanking-new developments and ravenous for low taxes, Vermont, proclaiming its desire to preserve the environment and the past, has attracted left-leaning migrants from New York and elsewhere, willing to pay higher taxes and higher prices for the privilege of living in a seemingly pristine setting and in 1995, the only state without a Wal-Mart (Vermonters continue to fight efforts by Wal-Mart to change this).

Another key point may have been in 1970, when Republican Governor Deane Davis, facing a primary challenge, pushed through a sweeping land use law (Act 250) that helped give Vermont

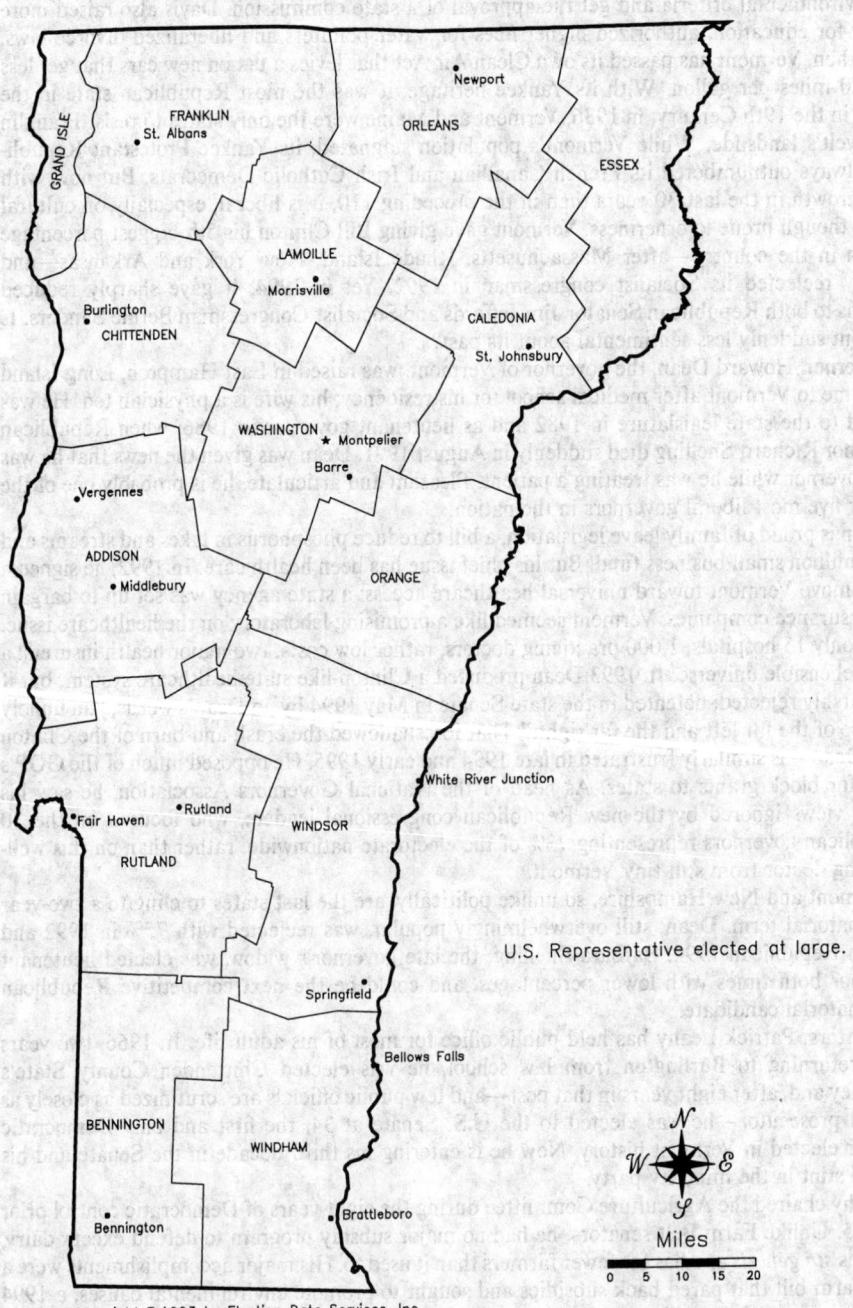

GRAND ISLE

FRANKLIN
St. Albans

ORLEANS

Newport

ESSEX

LAMOILLE

Morrisville

CALEDONIA

Burlington

CHITTENDEN

St. Johnsbury

WASHINGTON ★ Montpelier

Barre

Vergennes

ADDISON

Middlebury

ORANGE

White River Junction

Rutland

Fair Haven

WINDSOR

RUTLAND

U.S. Representative elected at large.

Springfield

Bellows Falls

BENNINGTON

WINDHAM

Brattleboro

Bennington

W E

Miles

0 5 10 15 20

its environmental reputation. Housing developments and new ski resorts were required to meet ten environmental criteria and get the approval of a state commission. Davis also raised more money for education, authorized higher fines for water polluters and liberalized divorce laws. Since then, Vermont has passed its own Clean Air Act that levies a tax on new cars that get less than 20 miles per gallon. With its Yankee heritage, it was the most Republican state in the nation in the 19th Century; in 1936, Vermont and Maine were the only states to resist Franklin Roosevelt's landslide. While Vermont's population stagnated, its Yankee Protestant Republicans always outnumbered its French Canadian and Irish Catholic Democrats. But now, with more growth in the last 30 years than in the preceding 110, it is liberal, especially on cultural issues, though prone to orneriness. Vermont gave giving Bill Clinton his 5th biggest percentage margin in the country—after Massachusetts, Rhode Island, New York and Arkansas—and handily reelected its Socialist congressman in 1992. Yet in 1994, it gave sharply reduced margins to both Republican Senator Jim Jeffords and Socialist Congressman Bernie Sanders. Is Vermont suddenly less sentimental about its past?

Governor. Howard Dean, the governor of Vermont, was raised in East Hampton, Long Island and came to Vermont after medical school for his residency; his wife is a physician too. He was elected to the state legislature in 1982 and as lieutenant governor in 1986; when Republican Governor Richard Snelling died suddenly in August 1991, Dean was given the news that he was now governor while he was treating a patient. Pleasant and articulate, he is probably one of the four or five most liberal governors in the nation.

Dean is proud of family leave legislation, a bill to reduce phosphorus in lakes and streams and a $14 million small business fund. But his chief issue has been health care. In 1992, he signed a bill to move Vermont toward universal healthcare access; a state agency was set up to bargain with insurance companies. Vermont seemed like a promising laboratory on the healthcare issue. It has only 15 hospitals, 1,000 practicing doctors, rather low costs, two major health insurers: a comprehensible universe. In 1993 Dean produced a Clinton-like state healthcare system, but it was harshly rejected, defeated in the state Senate in May 1994 by, in Dean's words, "an unholy alliance of the far left and the far right." That foreshadowed the crash-and-burn of the Clinton plan. Dean was similarly frustrated in late 1994 and early 1995. He opposed much of the GOP's plans for block grants to states. As head of the National Governors Association, he saw his liberal views ignored by the new Republican congressional leaders, who focused on the 30 Republican governors representing 73% of the electorate nationwide, rather than on this well-meaning doctor from still tiny Vermont.

Vermont and New Hampshire, so unlike politically, are the last states to cling to a two-year gubernatorial term. Dean, still overwhelmingly popular, was reelected with 75% in 1992 and 69% in Republican 1994. Barbara Snelling, the late governor's widow, was elected lieutenant governor both times with lower percentages, and could be the next competitive Republican gubernatorial candidate.

Senators. Patrick Leahy has held public office for most of his adult life. In 1966, two years after returning to Burlington from law school, he was elected Chittenden County State's Attorney and, after eight years in that post—and few public officials are scrutinized as closely as a local prosecutor—he was elected to the U.S. Senate at 34, the first and only Democratic senator elected in Vermont history. Now he is entering his third decade in the Senate and his second stint in the minority party.

Leahy chaired the Agriculture Committee during the eight years of Democratic control prior to 1995. Unlike Farm Belt senators, he had no major subsidy program to defend except dairy, which is *sui generis* and has far fewer farmers than it used to. His major accomplishments were a 1990 farm bill that pared back subsidies and sought to promote environmental causes, a 1994 crop insurance reform and the 1994 Leahy-Lugar Act that closed down 1100 USDA offices and promises to save $3.5 billion over the next several years—the first of Vice President Al Gore's Reinventing Government initiatives to be passed. Leahy said that he will cooperate with new Chairman Richard Lugar's plans to cut farm spending further, but he will surely fight

Republican attempts to block-grant or cut food stamps and other nutrition programs. As ranking Democrat on the Foreign Operations Appropriations Subcommittee, he is involved in many foreign policy issues, indicating occasional skepticism about the motives behind Israeli settlements, the staying power of Russian leaders and the wisdom of providing agricultural export credits to Saddam Hussein's Iraq. He has led a movement to outlaw landmines and remove the 100 million that are emplaced around the world; in 1992 he got a moratorium on U.S. exports of landmines and in 1994 he got the United Nations to approve unanimously their eventual elimination. On Judiciary, Leahy is part of the liberal bloc, the earliest opponent of Justice Clarence Thomas; he worked to get the U.S. to join the Bern Convention on international copyright laws, favored the Digital Telephony Act and weighed in against the Clinton Administration's Clipper Chip Encryption, a program he thought might violate property rights. After George Mitchell announced his retirement, he thought about running for majority leader, but opted out of the race and supported Tom Daschle in April 1994—the most senior Democrat to back him. He has the youth and political staying power to remain a Senate power for years to come—perhaps, Appropriations Committee chairman sometime in the next decade.

To his record, among the most liberal in the Senate in some years, Leahy brings the parsimony consonant with Vermont tradition, and a quiet, thoughtful temperament. But he also has a zest for life and a puckish sense of humor, part of the Yankee heritage of Vermont, though his Irish and Italian ethnic origin is certainly not standard Yankee. His standing in Vermont has been strong over the years: he survived the Republican sweep in 1980 and beat popular Governor Richard Snelling 63%–35% in 1986. In 1992, Republican Jim Douglas, secretary of state from 1980 and in 1994 elected treasurer, campaigned against special interest money and accused Leahy of not doing enough for dairy farmers or getting enough federal money for Vermont. In response, Leahy put his PAC money into escrow and championed Governor Howard Dean's healthcare plan. In late October 1992, a Republican flier hit Leahy for voting for the congressional pay raise and for the loss of dairy jobs; Leahy attacked this as "sleazeball negative campaigning," and Douglas, who was heavily outspent, disavowed the flier. Leahy won with 54%–43%—a decisive margin, but no landslide.

Vermont's junior senator is Jim Jeffords, known since he was first elected to the House in 1974 for having one of the most liberal records of all Republicans. Jeffords, son of a Vermont chief justice, returned home from law school to Shrewsbury, was elected state Senator at 32 in 1966 and then state attorney general in 1968 and 1970. In 1974, he was elected to the House; in 1988, when Robert Stafford retired, to the Senate. There he has had a moderate record on economic issues and a decidedly liberal one on cultural and foreign issues. Before 1992 he voted against the Reagan budget and tax cuts, against Clarence Thomas, against the B-2 and SDI. He opposed the Clinton budget and tax package in 1993, but voted for family and medical leave, motor voter, national service, the Brady bill and the 1994 crime package, despite anti-gun control feeling in Vermont. In July 1993 he announced he was supporting the not-yet-written Clinton healthcare plan—the only Republican who ever did—and he voted for Edward Kennedy's plan in the Labor Committee and supported George Mitchell's version on the Senate floor. In 1995, he bucked his party by supporting Henry Foster for Surgeon General and opposing tax cuts until the budget was balanced. A Civil War buff interested in a Vermont regiment's critical role in the Shenandoah Valley Battle of Cedar Creek, and inspired by murals in the Vermont Capitol, he has a bill to catalogue and study unprotected Civil War sites to avoid repeating the imbroglio over Virginia's Manassas battlefield, in which Congress paid millions to save part of the battle site from becoming a shopping center.

Jeffords's toughest hurdle in originally winning the seat in 1988 was the Republican primary, in which conservative Mike Griffes attacked him on gun control, abortion, and church and family issues, as well as for accepting $5,000 from the Teamsters' PAC after asking the Justice Department not to take over the union. Jeffords won 61%–39%. In contrast, in 1994 his serious competition was in the general. State Senator Jan Backus upset the favored Douglas Costle, Carter Administration EPA Director, in the Democratic primary, and then proceeded to attack

Jeffords from both left and right. Much of the energy in the Democratic Party here, even more than nationally, comes from the women's groups and though Backus was not endorsed by NOW she clearly benefited from her symbolism as a woman and a political outsider running against the political establishment. Ultimately, after an unexpected scare, Jeffords won 50%–41%—a decent margin, but not showing the kind of invincibility liberal Republicans used to have in the Northeast. He remains one of the Senate Republicans most likely to dissent from his party, as when he supported the Democrats on campaign finance reform in 1994, which was rumored to cause Texan Phil Gramm, then chairman of the National Republican Senatorial Committee, to rip Jeffords' portrait off the committee's lobby wall.

Representative-At-Large. The 1990s will go down as the decade in which socialism was rejected all over the world—except in Vermont. At least in House elections: for Vermont has three times now elected Bernie Sanders, self-proclaimed Socialist, to Congress. Sanders is not just a Socialist, but also very much a modern Vermonter: the son of a Flatbush paint salesman, he came here as part of the hippie invasion of 1968. His rumpled, tieless, sincere persona helped him win election as mayor of Burlington in 1981 by 10 votes, after losing four statewide races. There he governed ably for eight years, using the city's prosperity to start a municipal day care center, expand low- and moderate-income housing, put a pollution control facility on Lake Champlain and switch the tax base from property to hotel and restaurant fees and a utility tax on companies using certain public facilities. In 1990, he ran for Congress and reversed his defeat by Republican Peter Smith two years before, by capitalizing on Smith's support of the 1990 budget summit agreement and his vote for the ban on semiautomatic weapons. The National Rifle Association came out against Smith, with bumper stickers reading, "Smith & Wesson, Yes. Peter Smith, No." Gun control probably made the most difference as the urban-based Socialist carried 227 of Vermont's 251 cities and towns, and three gores and one grant. Sanders became only the third Socialist elected to the House, after Victor Berger of Milwaukee (1911–13, 1923–29) and Meyer London of Manhattan's Lower East Side (1915–23).

In the House Sanders has actually functioned as a liberal Democrat, with committee slots and seniority, plus plenteous contributions, up through 1994, from PACs. He voted against the Gulf war resolution and the Brady bill, and generally had one of the most liberal voting records in the House—including active opposition to the Contract With America. He moved without success to require on-budget, cash payoff of S&L and possible bank bailouts, to be funded by progressive taxes: Vermont thrift and Fabian socialism, all in one breath. He favors higher dairy prices and a ban on bovine growth hormone.

Sanders won reelection in 1992 over the Republican by the impressive margin of 58%–31% and in late 1993, trailing by only 47%–41% in one poll, considered taking on Republican Senator Jim Jeffords. Instead he ran for reelection, and had a tougher race than before. One reason was better opposition: John Carroll, in six years in the state Senate, had become Appropriations Chairman and Majority Leader, and criticized Sanders's opposition to NAFTA and support of a Canadian-style single-payer healthcare plan, while Carroll refused to sign the Contract With America. "People sent Bernie Sanders to make a point; send John Carroll to make a difference," ran his slogan and he attacked Sanders's "gloomy, angry vision of the class struggle." The other reason was gun control. Sanders voted for the assault weapons ban and the 1994 crime bill after having voted against the Brady Bill a second time in 1993; the NRA-supported Vermont Sportsmen's Coalitions put out "Bye, Bye, Bernie" bumper stickers and ran radio ads against him. Sanders outspent Carroll $599,000 to $381,000, but he outpolled him by only 50%–47%. Much rural support had vanished—and Sanders carried only 136 cities and towns. Sanders remains an energetic, active fighter for his principles, and vows to be part of a group of about 30 members—the Progressive Caucus—to "provide intelligent alternatives" to the Republicans and "fight an almost guerrilla war." But Carroll has indicated he plans to run again, and Sanders may have to fight another tough political battle in Vermont.

Presidential politics. James A. Farley had a good laugh on Vermont in 1936 when he updated an adage to say "As goes Maine, so goes Vermont." But today's Vermont, liberal on cultural and foreign issues, not tremendously conservative on economics, has little use for conservative Republicans. Back in 1980, Ronald Reagan got his seventh lowest percentage here and John Anderson his best, 15%; in 1984 and 1988 Vermont was more Democratic than the nation, and in 1992 it gave Bill Clinton one of his largest margins. It is one state he can carry in 1996, though gun control won't help.

In May 1991, Vermont axed its presidential primary to save money; coming after New Hampshire, it never got much attention anyway. The state's caucuses went 80% for George Bush among Republicans and 46% for Jerry Brown among Democrats.

The People: Est. Pop. 1994: 580,000; Pop. 1990: 562,758, up 3.1% 1990–1994. 0.2% of U.S. total, 49th largest; 68% rural. Median age: 33.0 years. 11.8% 65 years and older. 98.6% White. Households: 56.4% married couple families; 28% married couple fams. w. children; 46% college educ.; median household income: $29,792; per capita income: $13,527; 69.0% owner occupied housing; median house value: $95,500; median monthly rent: $378. 6.6% Unemployment. 1994 Voting age pop.: 429,000. 1994 Turnout: 206,050; 48% of VAP. Registered voters (1994): 373,442; no party registration.

Political Lineup: Governor, Howard Dean (D); Lt. Gov., Barbara W. Snelling (R); Secy. of State, Jim Milne (R); Atty. Gen., Jeffrey L. Amestoy (R); Treasurer, James H. Douglas (R); Auditor, Edward S. Flanagan (D). State Senate, 30 (18 R and 12 D); State House of Representatives, 150 (86 D, 61 R, 2 I, and 1 Progressive Coalition). Senators, Patrick J. Leahy (D) and James M. Jeffords (R). Representative, 1 I at large.

1992 Presidential Vote		
Clinton (D)	133,592	(46%)
Bush (R)	88,122	(30%)
Perot (I)	65,991	(23%)

1988 Presidential Vote		
Bush (R)	124,331	(51%)
Dukakis (D)	115,775	(48%)

GOVERNOR

Gov. Howard Dean (D)

Assumed office, Aug. 1991, term expires Jan. 1997; b. Nov. 17, 1948, New York, NY; home, Burlington; Yale., B.A. 1977, Albert Einstein Col. of Medicine, M.D. 1978; Congregationalist; married (Judith).

Career: Practicing physician, 1981–91; VT House of Reps, 1983–86; VT Lt. Gov., 1987–91.

Office: Pavilion State Office Bldg., 109 State St., Montpelier 05609, 802-828-3333. Fax: 802-828-3339.

Election Results

1994 gen.	Howard Dean (D)	145,661	(69%)
	David F. Kelley (R)	40,292	(19%)
	Thomas J. Morse (I)	15,000	(7%)
	Others	11,093	(5%)
1994 prim.	Howard Dean (D)	unopposed	
1992 gen.	Howard Dean (D)	213,523	(75%)
	Richard McClaughry (R)	105,191	(23%)

SENATORS

Sen. Patrick J. Leahy (D)

Elected 1974, seat up 1998; b. Mar. 31, 1940, Montpelier; home, Burlington; St. Michael's Col., B.A. 1961, Georgetown U., J.D. 1964; Catholic; married (Marcelle).

Career: Practicing atty., 1964–74; VT St. Atty., Chittenden Cnty., 1966–74.

DC Office: 433 RSOB 20510, 202-224-4242; Fax: 202-224-3595; e-mail: senator_leahy@leahy.senate.gov.

State Offices: 199 Main St., Burlington 05401, 802-863-2525; and Fed. Bldg., Box 933, Montpelier 05602, 802-229-0569.

Committees: *Agriculture, Nutrition & Forestry* (RMM of 8 D): *Appropriations* (5th of 13 D): Defense; Foreign Operations (RMM); Interior; VA, HUD and Independent Agencies. *Judiciary* (3rd of 8 D): Antitrust, Business Rights and Competition (RMM); Terrorism, Technology and Government Information.

Group Ratings

	ADA	ACLU	COPE	CFA	LCV	CON	NSI	COC	ACU	NTLC	CHC
1994	95	79	100	92	92	21	10	27	0	12	0
1993	95	—	82	90	100	22	—	27	8	—	—

National Journal Ratings

	1993 LIB — 1993 CONS		1994 LIB — 1994 CONS	
Economic	83%	— 0%	84%	— 0%
Social	73%	— 25%	93%	— 0%
Foreign	78%	— 13%	94%	— 0%

Key Votes of the 103d Congress

1. Clinton Deficit Plan	Y	3. Brady Handgun Purchase	N	5. Lmt. UN Cmnd. of Forces	N
2. NAFTA	Y	4. Strike Race/Death Pnlty.	N	6. Cut Missile Funds	Y

Key Votes of the 104th Congress

1. Congressional Compliance	Y	3. Balanced Budget Amndt.	N	5. Product Liability Reform	N
2. Bar Unfunded Mandates	N	4. Pass Line Item Veto	N	6. FY96 Budget	N

Election Results

1992 general	Patrick J. Leahy (D)	154,762	(54%)	($1,202,445)
	James H. Douglas (R)	123,854	(43%)	($195,737)
	Other	7,123	(2%)	
1992 primary	Patrick J. Leahy (D)	unopposed		
1986 general	Patrick J. Leahy (D)	124,123	(63%)	($1,705,099)
	Richard Snelling (R)	67,798	(35%)	($1,502,304)

Sen. James M. Jeffords (R)

Elected 1988, seat up 2000; b. May 11, 1934, Rutland; home, Shrewsbury; Yale U., B.S. 1956, Harvard, LL.B. 1962; Congregationalist; married (Elizabeth Daley).

Career: Navy, 1956–59, Naval Reserves, 1959–90; Law clerk, 1962–63; Practicing atty., 1963–69, 1973–75; Shrewsbury Repub. Chmn., 1963–74, Town Agent, Grand Juror, 1964; VT Senate, 1966–68; VT Atty. Gen., 1968–72; U.S. House of Reps. 1974–1988.

DC Office: 513 HSOB 20515, 202-224-5141; e-mail: vermont@jeffords.senate.gov.

State Offices: P.O. Box 676, 138 Main St., Montpelier 05601, 802-223-5273; 95 St. Paul St., #100, Burlington 05401, 802-658-6001; and P.O. Box 397, 2 S. Main St., Rutland 05702, 802-773-3875.

Committees: *Appropriations* (13th of 15 R): District of Columbia (Chmn.); Foreign Operations; Labor, Health and Human Services, Education; Legislative Branch; Treasury, Postal Service and General Government. *Energy & Natural Resources* (9th of 10 R): Energy Production and Regulation (Vice Chmn.); Parks, Historic Preservation and Recreation. *Labor & Human Resources* (2nd of 9 R): Children and Families; Disability Policy; Education, Arts and Humanities (Chmn). *Veterans' Affairs* (5th of 7 R). *Aging (Special)* (5th of 10 R).

Group Ratings

	ADA	ACLU	COPE	CFA	LCV	CON	NSI	COC	ACU	NTLC	CHC
1994	85	63	50	67	100	56	50	54	12	40	28
1993	60	—	40	80	69	7	—	64	38	—	—

National Journal Ratings

	1993 LIB — 1993 CONS		1994 LIB — 1994 CONS	
Economic	43%	— 56%	43%	— 55%
Social	81%	— 18%	85%	— 7%
Foreign	78%	— 13%	72%	— 22%

Key Votes of the 103d Congress

1. Clinton Deficit Plan	N	3. Brady Handgun Purchase Y	5. Lmt. UN Cmnd. of Forces N
2. NAFTA	Y	4. Strike Race/Death Pnlty. N	6. Cut Missile Funds	Y

Key Votes of the 104th Congress

1. Congressional Compliance Y		3. Balanced Budget Amndt. Y	5. Product Liability Reform Y
2. Bar Unfunded Mandates Y		4. Pass Line Item Veto N	6. FY96 Budget	Y

Election Results

1994 general	James M. Jeffords (R)	106,505	(50%)	($1,174,973)
	Jan Backus (D)	85,868	(41%)	($308,069)
	Gavin T. Mills (I)	12,465	(6%)	
	Others	6,834	(3%)	
1994 primary	James M. Jeffords (R)	unopposed		
1988 general	James M. Jeffords (R)	163,183	(70%)	($876,877)
	Bill Gray (D)	71,460	(30%)	($549,908)

REPRESENTATIVE

Rep. Bernard Sanders (I)

Elected 1990; b. Sept. 8, 1941, New York, NY; home, Burlington; U. of Chicago, B.A. 1964; Jewish; married (Jane).

Career: Writer; Dir., Amer. People's History Soc.; Burlington Mayor, 1981–89; Lecturer, Harvard, 1989; Prof., Hamilton Col., 1989–90.

DC Office: 213 CHOB 20515, 202-225-4115; Fax: 202-225-6790; e-mail: bsanders@igc.apc.org.

District Offices: 1 Church St., Burlington 05401, 802-862-0697.

Committees: *Banking & Financial Services* (1st of 1 I): Domestic and International Monetary Policy; Housing and Community Opportunity. *Government Reform & Oversight* (1st of 1 I): Civil Service; Human Resources and Intergovernmental Affairs.

Group Ratings

	ADA	ACLU	COPE	CFA	LCV	CON	NSI	COC	ACU	NTLC	CHC
1994	100	87	100	100	93	26	0	33	0	11	0
1993	95	—	100	80	93	39	—	0	13	—	—

National Journal Ratings

	1993 LIB — 1993 CONS	1994 LIB — 1994 CONS
Economic	88% — 0%	83% — 0%
Social	71% — 28%	90% — 6%
Foreign	70% — 26%	72% — 25%

Key Votes of the 103d Congress

1. Clinton Deficit Plan	Y	3. Brady Handgun Purchase	N	5. Lmt. UN Cmnd. of Forces	N
2. NAFTA	N	4. Strike Race/Death Pnlty.	N	6. Cut Missile Funds	Y

Key Votes of the 104th Congress

1. Congressional Compliance	Y	6. Reform Crime Grant	N	11. Loser Pays Court Reform	N
2. Balanced Budget Amndmt.	N	7. National Security Act	N	12. Product Liability Reform	N
3. Bar Unfunded Mandates	N	8. Moratorium on Regs.	N	13. Welfare Reform	N
4. Pass Line Item Veto	N	9. Risk Assessment on Regs.	N	14. Term Limits Amndmt.	N
5. Relax Exclusionary Rule	N	10. Expnd. Priv. Prop. Rights	N	15. Tax Cuts	N

Election Results

1994 general	Bernard Sanders (I)	105,502	(50%)	($622,351)
	John Carroll (R)	98,523	(47%)	($387,767)
	Others	7,424	(4%)	
1994 primary	Bernard Sanders (I)	unopposed		
1992 general	Bernard Sanders (I)	162,724	(58%)	($575,791)
	Tim Philbin (R)	86,901	(31%)	($72,958)
	Lewis Young (D)	22,729	(8%)	
	Other	9,799	(3%)	

VIRGINIA

In Virginia traditions endure. Through nearly 400 years of history, Virginians have honored, and sometimes been fixated by, traditions going back to the Revolution and before. Virginia has been growing lustily. But the first state in the nation to elect a black governor still hews to a course close to its roots. For Virginia's recent growth, unlike that in the years after World War II, came less from an expanding government than from a vibrant private sector. The first Virginia was a commonwealth ruled by a landed gentry which was, in the words of historian David Hackett Fischer, "elitist and libertarian." From the tobacco-growing counties emerged in the 1770s a group of leaders—George Washington, Patrick Henry, Thomas Jefferson, Richard Henry Lee, James Madison, James Monroe—who in learning, wisdom and strength of character, equal any such group from any similarly-sized polity since Periclean Athens: slaveholders who insisted on liberty, armed men living on the marches of civilization who insisted on the rule of law, racists who propounded principles of equality to form the basis of a nonracist society. The Virginia they led into the American Revolution was not only the most populous and richest of the 13 colonies, it also was the indispensable creator of the Republic and the Constitution that has held together the world's greatest nation.

After the Revolutionary War, gentry control continued even as Virginia was eclipsed in population and wealth by Pennsylvania and New York and, its tobacco fields all but exhausted, became a breeding ground for slaves. But Virginia had two more great heroes, Robert E. Lee and Stonewall Jackson, both of whom reluctantly and brilliantly fought for their state rather than their country. The state's leadership class was impoverished and embittered by the Civil War, so much of which was fought on Virginia soil. Industrialization was haphazard: railroads were constructed to ship cotton up from the South and coal east to the seaports; textile mills were built in Southside towns and tobacco factories in Richmond; the giant Newport News Shipbuilding & Drydock Company was built by railroad magnate Collis Huntington.

But most of Virginia remained agricultural, sunk in a low-wage economy and ruled by a local gentry who had become a small class of landowners, bankers and lawyers worshipping their Revolutionary past and their Lost Cause. They were pessimists, looking not for economic growth but for stability, bent on maintaining Virginia's segregation and content with its second-class economy, determined that the poor masses not use government to pillage the rich as Yankee troops once had done. County courthouse organizations became the political machine of Harry Byrd, who ran Virginia politics from 1925, when he was elected governor, until 1965, when he retired from the Senate.

In national politics, this machine lost battles more often than Lee lost on the field, and less gallantly. But the machine succeeded in keeping most vestiges of the welfare state and racial equality out of Virginia, to the point of closing public schools in the 1950s rather than obey federal court integration orders. This "massive resistance," however, generally collapsed in the late 1950s, and Governor Mills Godwin, though a Byrd loyalist, accepted integration and reformed state government in the late 1960s.

Meanwhile, demographics changed the Old Dominion. As the 20th Century progressed, the peripheral parts of the state grew: the coal-mining counties of the southwest, the Tidewater area around the Navy bases in Norfolk and the shipbuilding yards in Newport News, and the government employee-filled suburbs across the Potomac from Washington, D.C. Courthouse politicians no longer carried the vote for the Byrd machine by the middle 1960s: Harry Byrd Jr., appointed to his father's Senate seat, was nearly beaten in the 1966 Senate primary, and 20-year Senate veteran A. Willis Robertson—father of 1988 presidential candidate Pat Robertson—was beaten in his primary. In 1969, Linwood Holton, a believer in integration, was elected the first

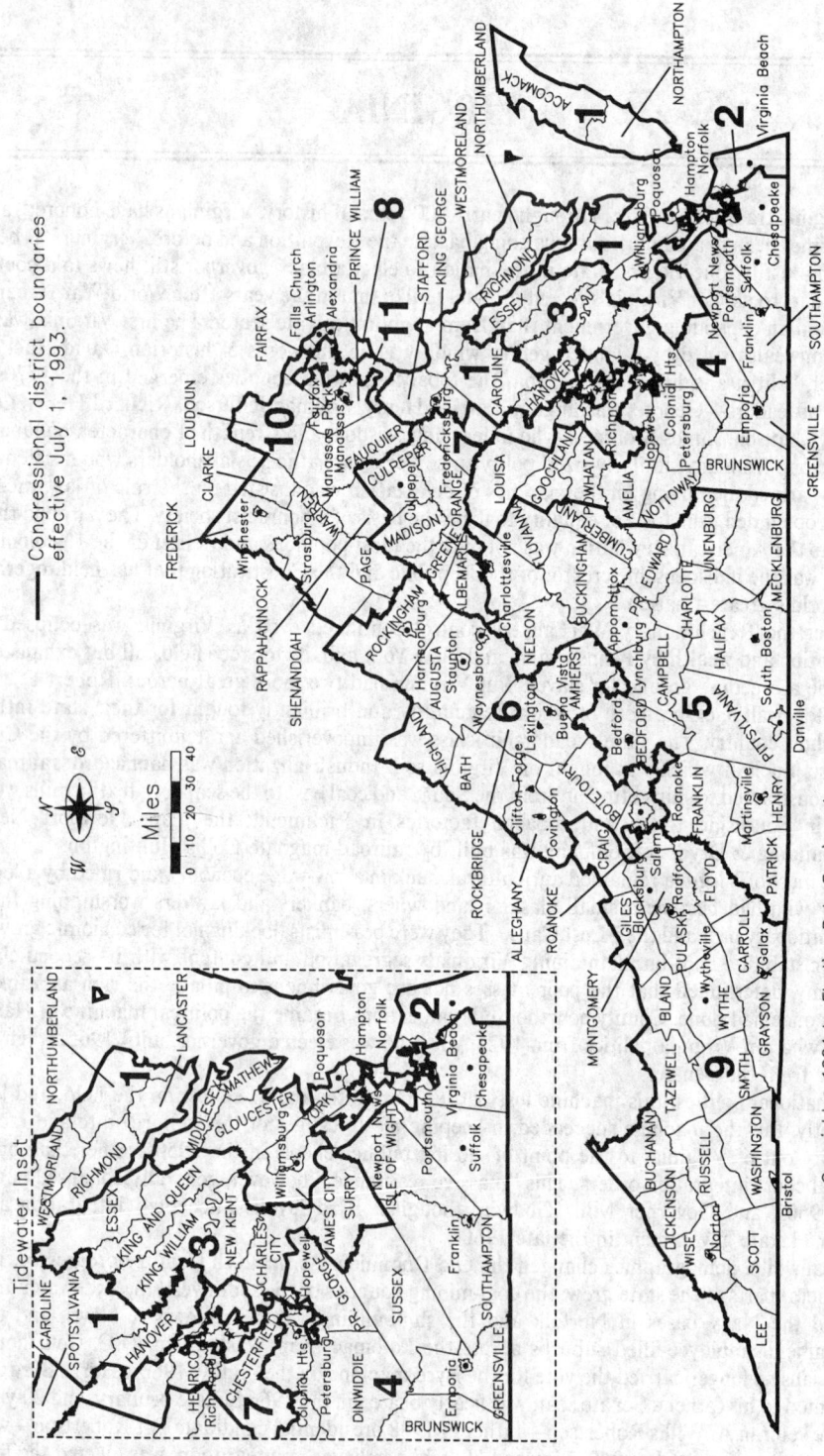

Congressional district boundaries
effective July 1, 1993.

Copyright © 1994 by Election Data Services, Inc.

Republican governor of Virginia. But over the next decade, most victories were won by conservatives, some of them Byrd stalwarts turned Republican (like Mills Godwin, who returned to the governorship in 1973), some the sons of former insurgent Republicans (like John Dalton, elected governor in 1977) or Republicans with no deep local roots (like John Warner, elected Senator in 1978).

In the 1980s, things began going the other way. The Democrats won the governorship in 1981 after a 16-year political drought and proceeded not only to hold on to it in 1985, but to elect a black lieutenant governor and a woman attorney general. These Democrats had strong black support, and carried the Washington suburbs, the Tidewater and the far western mountains; more importantly, they carried or ran even in the Richmond area and the rural counties that geographically and historically are the heart of the state. Democrats Charles Robb, Gerald Baliles and Douglas Wilder won the statehouse in 1981, 1985 and 1989 because they no longer represented an attempt to impose a labor-liberal agenda on an unwilling Virginia, and because they argued they could use government effectively to improve education and build Virginia's economy. Wilder's election was in some sense a national breakthrough, an attempt by a black politician to campaign and govern on equal terms; he won largely because of his margins in the Tidewater and Northern Virginia, where his pro-choice stand on abortion clearly helped, but he also ran solidly across the state. His fiscal conservatism, which resulted in sharp spending cuts in the early 1990s, like his elegant manners and thick Richmond accent, echoed Virginia's elitist and libertarian tradition.

Now Virginia may be heading in other directions. In 1993, it elected by a wide margin Republican George Allen as governor, a believer in fundamentals of lower taxes, longer prison sentences and no parole. Discord between Wilder and Senator Charles Robb and Robb's personal scandal left his Senate seat open to Republican capture; but Republican activists nominated a candidate incapable of winning a majority, Iran contra ringleader Oliver North. Senator John Warner refused to endorse North and frequent Republican candidate Marshall Coleman ran as an Independent: a politically crippled Robb won a second term. Yet underneath this turbulence was something fairly close to a consensus on public policy. Virginia has more faith in growth through market economics than the Byrd machine did, and more commitment to racial equality than the Founders imagined possible. But amid its growth, most of its voters are seeking affirmation of traditional cultural values and a stable and orderly framework within which to live their lives.

Governor. George Allen came into Virginia politics with a congenial manner and hard-line conservative proposals. He grew up in California, son of the football coach fondly remembered in Virginia for his winning seasons with the Washington Redskins. During those years, the younger George Allen was at college and law school at the University of Virginia. He moved to a home in the country near Charlottesville and practiced law—wearing boots and chewing tobacco. In 1982, he was elected to the Virginia Assembly, where he was a conservative backbencher; in a 1991 special election, he won a seat in the U.S. House, which was promptly redistricted out from under him. So he started running for governor. The initial favorite was Attorney General Mary Sue Terry, a moderate from Southside Virginia, who backed some forms of gun control (like Governor Douglas Wilder's one-handgun-a-month purchase limit) and was pro-choice on abortion. Allen opposed gun control and called for abolishing parole; he is anti-abortion, though thinks states should decide the issue, and for cutting taxes and government spending. Allen maneuvered smartly to get the support of religious conservatives at the 13,000-delegate June 1993 state convention, perhaps the largest deliberative body in the history of democracy, whose real enthusiasm was reserved for its lieutenant governor nominee, home schooling advocate Michael Farris. Democrats thought gun control and association with the religious right would hurt Republicans. But Allen won by a whopping 58%–41% margin, Republican James Gilmore was elected attorney general and Farris lost to Democratic Lieutenant Governor Don Beyer, who outspent him 10–1, by only 54%–45%.

Allen also proved more successful in office with his agenda than many had expected. His achievements included a more permissive concealed weapons law, abolition of parole, parental notification for abortions, a $163 million incentive package for Disney's northern Virginia theme park (plans which Disney later cancelled) and welfare reform that requires recipients to work after 90 days and cuts off benefits after two years. But in 1995, the legislature rejected Allen's proposed tax cuts, his education initiatives and most of his prison construction program. Allen evidently believes he will have the last laugh, however, since Republicans need to win only three seats in each chamber in the November 1995 elections to take control for the first time this century.

Senators. Virginia is represented in the Senate by two residents of the greater Washington area, neither with deep Virginia roots, both of whom first came to public notice because of the women they married. Both have since shown more talent and accomplished more than most observers expected, but each has had some recent setbacks.

John Warner, one of the luckiest men in politics, has made his mark with a pleasant personality and hard work; if he is not the Senate's strongest intellect, and is sometimes prone to cliche, he does have a stubbornness and strength of character. He grew up in Washington, D.C., and volunteered for the Navy in 1944, at age 17. He volunteered again after college and law school for service in the Marine Corps in Korea. He practiced law in Washington and had a house in the horse country in Middleburg, Virginia; in the Nixon-Ford years, he was secretary of the Navy. He ran for the Senate in 1978 with few political assets other than his then-wife, Elizabeth Taylor. Finishing second at the huge Republican state convention, he graciously supported winner Richard Obenshain; then, when Obenshain died in a plane crash, Republican leaders reluctantly named Warner to fill his place. Warner won the general over Democrat Andrew Miller by a 4,721-vote margin. He made few enemies, and was easily reelected over a liberal Democrat in 1984 and had no serious opposition in 1990.

Warner has had a conservative-to-moderate voting record, generally sticking within Republican ranks, but occasionally diverging. He is pro-choice on abortion, but favors parental consent laws. Representing a state which still has a large number of public employees (though the proportion is dropping), Warner favors higher federal pay and supported repeal of the Hatch Act. He has sponsored a new National Highway System. He also wants to build an extension of the National Air and Space Museum at Dulles Airport in northern Virginia.

Warner has specialized in military issues, occupying the ranking Republican position on the Armed Services Committee from 1987 until 1993, when he was bumped from it by the more senior Strom Thurmond. Accordingly, Thurmond and not Warner now chairs Armed Services. In the late 1980s and early 1990s Warner worked closely with then-Chairman Sam Nunn, even when Nunn set out to defeat the nomination of former Senator John Tower as secretary of Defense or in 1991 when Nunn opposed the Gulf war resolution. On other defense issues, Warner is, as Virginia senators usually are, a booster of Newport News Shipbuilding & Drydock as the nation's chief submarine builder. He warned against U.S. military involvement in Bosnia. For credibility in defending Virginia bases, he made a point of opposing NASA's space station, even as NASA employed hundreds of Northern Virginians at the time. In early 1995, he and John McCain of Arizona proposed a Republican blueprint for defense spending, cutting funds for the B-2 bomber, National Guard expansion and some construction in order to fully fund readiness.

Warner has also taken a hand in Intelligence. In 1993, he was about to lose his ranking position on Intelligence when Arlen Specter invoked a 1990 promise that he could return to the committee and have the post, but Warner protested and prevailed with Republican Leader Bob Dole; two years later, however, the eight-year limitation on committee service forced Warner off the committee, denying him the chairmanship. In May 1994, Warner urged President Clinton to set up a presidential commission on the CIA to rethink the role of the CIA in the post-Cold War era; that passed, and Dole named him to the commission.

Warner has become controversial politically because of his active opposition to some in his own party. In 1993, he refused to endorse lieutenant governor candidate Michael Farris. In

1994, Warner aroused more hackles when he announced that he would not support Oliver North. What stuck in Warner's craw, apparently, were North's frequent contradictions—some said lies—and the conviction on Iran-contra charges which was overturned on the grounds of inadmissibility of some critical evidence. Warner went on to actively oppose North and to back Marshall Coleman, losing Republican gubernatorial nominee in 1981 and 1989, who was running as an Independent. "My conscience is clear, and I'm just not going to change. I'm going to fight for what I think is correct. And I'm not spending one second a day thinking about '96," Warner said. Many active Republicans were furious at Warner, including former OMB Director James Miller, who lost to North narrowly at the convention and then supported him, and if the Republican nomination were to be determined by convention in 1996, Warner would surely not get it. But according to Virginia law, because Warner filed primary papers in 1990, the Republicans can hold a nominating convention only with his approval, and Warner would surely choose a primary instead. Warner was confident he would get on the ballot: "I will find a way of getting my name in front of the voters of Virginia. I hope to do it through the party structure. But a small, tiny group is not going to stop me." Even in a primary he would not be an overwhelming favorite. Soon after the 1994 election, both North and Farris announced they would not run for senator in 1996. But Miller clearly was running, and cannot be dismissed as a tool of the religious right or any small group; he is an economics Ph.D. and as budget director, cut the deficit in half in the late Reagan years. Possible Democratic candidates include Congressman Owen Pickett and former state Chairman Mark Warner, and no one can ever be sure what former Governor Douglas Wilder will do (he ran for president in 1991 and for senator in 1994 and withdrew both times). It is possible there will be a three-way race, and Warner could conceivably win as an Independent, as Harry Byrd, Jr., did in 1970 and 1976.

Senator Charles Robb has had a roller coaster of a career and won his second term against great odds and despite serious misdeeds. Robb first came to national attention in 1967, when he married Lynda Bird Johnson in the White House, where he had been one of the Marine guards; he then served a year of combat duty in Vietnam. He began his political career in 1977 when, working in Washington and living across the river in McLean, he ran for lieutenant governor and won, while Republicans were carrying other offices. In 1981, he ran for governor and beat Marshall Coleman 54%–46%. As governor, he was widely popular and was given credit for much of Virginia's dynamic growth; he added $1 billion to the education budget, worked to boost Virginia's coal export industry and appointed blacks and women to top posts in large numbers. Out of office, he was the second chairman of the Democratic Leadership Council, after Dick Gephardt. He was easily elected to the Senate in 1988: incumbent Paul Trible decided to retire at age 42, and Robb's only opponent was a hapless Republican black minister.

Robb's troubles first surfaced in August 1988, when newspaper stories reported that, while governor, he was present at parties in Virginia Beach where cocaine was used. Charges of a sexual encounter with a former Miss Virginia were aired by NBC in April 1991. That same month, Robb aides played for reporters a tape of Governor Douglas Wilder in a car phone conversation gloating over Robb's problems; in July 1991, three Robb aides resigned by "mutual consent," and later pleaded guilty to charges of conspiracy. In May 1992, Robb was notified he was the object of a grand jury investigation of the incident, but despite wide speculation, the grand jury voted in January 1993 not to indict him. He immediately announced that he would run for reelection in 1994, but Wilder continued to attack him and this episode placed Robb in anything but an appealing light.

The 1993 session saw a liberal shift in Robb's voting record, though he remained middle-of-the-road on defense and foreign issues. He had managed to remain something of a partisan Democrat while voting conservatively, for the Gulf war resolution and Clarence Thomas while chairing the Democratic Senatorial Campaign Committee in 1991 and 1992. Budget Committee Chairman Jim Sasser reduced the size of the committee in 1991 to keep Robb out, since he supported the Nunn-Domenici deficit reduction proposal. But in 1993 and 1994, Robb was a pretty faithful supporter of the Clinton Administration, even on gays in the military, the 1993 budget and tax package and the 1994 crime bill. All of which made him vulnerable to almost any Republican opponent except his eventual challenger: Oliver North.

North was a candidate who stirred more emotions, pro and con, than any other in the 1994 cycle, a retired lieutenant colonel with a sincere manner who lied to even his own associates in government as well as to Congress. North's believers saw him almost as a man who would save western civilization, and the scorn of inside-the-Beltway experts annealed his support in the far-beyond-the-Beltway hinterlands where he was strongest. These included not just the rural Virginia counties that produced the delegates that nominated him at the Republican state convention, but direct mail recipients in remote zip codes all over the country, who made North's campaign the second best financed in the country. North was nominated by just 55%–45% at the June convention, with many religious right delegates supporting Miller.

Robb also had primary opponents but, fortunately for him, the sharp-tongued Wilder had decided not to make the race, and Robb bested Delegate Virgil Goode by the unspectacular margin of 58%–34%. Support for Marshall Coleman's candidacy fizzled down toward 10%. Even former President Reagan weighed in, with a letter saying he was "getting pretty steamed" about North's misstatements; North then changed his story and said Reagan did not know all about Iran-contra. North raised and spent over $20 million; but much of this went to generating more direct mail campaigns; Robb spent $5.9 million, enough for a formidable campaign in Virginia.

Most voters said no to both candidates. Robb won with 46% to North's 43%; Coleman had 11%. Northern Virginia's Washington suburbs—Fairfax, Arlington and Alexandria—voted overwhelmingly for Robb (55%–33%) and so did the black-majority 3d Congressional District (72%–22%); the rest of the state went for North (48%–40%). Nonetheless, North did not delude himself, and soon after said he would not run for the Senate in 1996 and got a talk radio program instead. And Robb, after two years of moving to the left, moved perversely back to the right again—the only Democratic Senator to vote for all six of the early Republican major initiatives.

Presidential politics. Virginia remains one of the most Republican states in presidential races, and it picks its delegates by conventions. Accordingly, Virginia, so near the White House and the Capitol, sees relatively little presidential politicking.

Congressional districting. For all its genteel traditions, Virginia has one of the most partisan—in this case, Democratic—redistricting plans of the 1990s, a rival of Texas and North Carolina in this regard. But as often happens, partisan plans go awry. The new 11th District in northern Virginia, designed for a Democrat, went Republican in 1994; the 7th District which threw two Republicans in together put one of them, George Allen, into the governor's race, where he thrashed the Democrats; except for the black-majority 3d and maybe the inside-the-Beltway 8th, none is out of reach of the Republicans.

The People: Est. Pop. 1994: 6,552,000; Pop. 1990: 6,187,358, up 5.9% 1990–1994. 2.5% of U.S. total, 12th largest; 31% rural. Median age: 32.6 years. 10.7% 65 years and over. 77.4% White, 18.8% Black, 2.6% Hispanic origin, 2.6% Asian. Households: 56.8% married couple families; 27% married couple fams. w. children; 49% college educ.; median household income: $33,328; per capita income: $15,713; 66.3% owner occupied housing; median house value: $91,000; median monthly rent: $411. 6.4% Unemployment. 1994 Voting age pop.: 4,967,000. 1994 Turnout: 2,031,732; 41% of VAP. Registered voters (1994): 3,000,560; no party registration.

Political Lineup: Governor, George F. Allen (R); Lt. Gov., Donald S. Beyer, Jr. (D); Secy. of Commonwealth, Betsy Beamer (R), Atty. Gen., James S. Gilmore, III (R); Treasurer, Ronald Tillett (R); Comptroller, William E. Landsidle [no party]. State Senate, 40 (22 D and 18 R); State House of Delegates, 100 (52 D, 47 R, and 1 I). Senators, John W. Warner (R) and Charles S. Robb (D). Representatives, 11 (5 R and 6 D).

1992 Presidential Vote

Bush (R) 1,150,517 (45%)
Clinton (D) 1,038,650 (41%)
Perot (I). 348,639 (14%)

1988 Presidential Vote

Bush (R) 1,309,162 (60%)
Dukakis (D). 859,799 (39%)

GOVERNOR

Gov. George F. Allen (R)

Elected 1993, term expires Jan. 1998; b. Mar. 8, 1952, Whittier, CA; home, Earlysville; U. of VA, B.A. 1974, J.D. 1977; Presbyterian; married (Susan).

Career: Practicing atty., 1977–91; VA House of Delegates, 1982–91; U.S. House of Reps., 1990–92.

Office: State Capitol, Richmond 23219, 804-786-2211; Fax: 804-371-6351.

Election Results

1993 gen.	George F. Allen (R)	1,045,319	(58%)
	Mary Sue Terry (D)	733,527	(41%)
	Others	15,070	(1%)
1993 prim.	George F. Allen (R)	nom. by convention	
1989 gen.	L. Douglas Wilder (D)	896,936	(50%)
	J. Marshall Coleman (R)	890,195	(50%)

SENATORS

Sen. John W. Warner (R)

Elected 1978, seat up 1996; b. Feb. 18, 1927, Washington, D.C.; home, Middleburg; Washington and Lee U., B.S., 1949, U. of VA, LL.B. 1953; Episcopalian; divorced.

Career: Navy, 1944–46 (WWII), Marine Corps, 1950–52 (Korea); Law Clerk, U.S. Court of Appeals Chief Judge Barrett Prettyman, 1953–54; Practicing atty., 1954–56, 1960–69; Asst. U.S. Atty., 1956–60; Undersecy. of the U.S. Navy, 1969–72, Secy., 1972–74; Dir., Amer. Rev. Bicentennial Comm., 1974–76.

DC Office: 225 RSOB 20510, 202-224-2023; Fax: 202-224-6295; e-mail: senator@warner.senate.gov.

State Offices: 600 E. Main St., Richmond 23219, 804-771-2579; 4900 World Trade Ctr., Norfolk 23510, 804-441-3079; 235 Fed. Bldg., 180 W. Main St., Abingdon 24210, 703-628-8158; and 1003 First Union Bank Bldg., 213 S. Jefferson St., Roanoke 24011, 703-857-2676.

Committees: *Agriculture, Nutrition & Forestry* (9th of 10 R): Forestry, Conservation and Rural Revitalization; Production and Price Competitiveness. *Armed Services* (2nd of 11 R): Airland Forces (Chmn.); Seapower; Strategic Forces. *Environment & Public Works* (2nd of 9 R): Drinking Water, Fisheries and Wildlife; Superfund, Waste Control and Risk Assessment; Transportation and Infrastructure (Chmn). *Rules & Administration* (4th of 9 R). *Small Business* (8th of 10 R).

Group Ratings

	ADA	ACLU	COPE	CFA	LCV	CON	NSI	COC	ACU	NTLC	CHC
1994	20	26	25	33	23	65	100	84	80	87	71
1993	10	—	9	30	25	96	—	91.	84	—	—

National Journal Ratings

	1993 LIB — 1993 CONS	1994 LIB — 1994 CONS
Economic	22% — 75%	18% — 77%
Social	22% — 77%	34% — 65%
Foreign	32% — 60%	34% — 62%

Key Votes of the 103d Congress

1. Clinton Deficit Plan	N	3. Brady Handgun Purchase	Y	5. Lmt. UN Cmnd. of Forces	N
2. NAFTA	Y	4. Strike Race/Death Pnlty.	Y	6. Cut Missile Funds	N

Key Votes of the 104th Congress

1. Congressional Compliance	Y	3. Balanced Budget Amndt.	Y	5. Product Liability Reform	*
2. Bar Unfunded Mandates	Y	4. Pass Line Item Veto	Y	6. FY96 Budget	Y

Election Results

1990 general	John W. Warner (R)	876,782	(81%)	($1,219,726)
	Nancy B. Spannaus (I)	196,755	(18%)	
	Other	10,153	(1%)	
1990 primary	John W. Warner (R) ..... nominated by convention			
1984 general	John W. Warner (R)	1,406,194	(70%)	($2,974,498)
	Edythe C. Harrison (D)	601,142	(30%)	($492,201)

Sen. Charles S. Robb (D)

Elected 1988, seat up 2000; b. June 26, 1939, Phoenix, AZ; home, McLean; U. of WI, B.B.A. 1961, U. of VA, J.D. 1973; Episcopalian; married (Lynda).

Career: Marine Corps, 1961–1970 (Vietnam), Marine Corps Reserves, 1970–91; Law Clerk, Judge John Butzner, U.S. Court of Appeals, 1973–74; Practicing atty., 1974–77, 1986–88; VA Lt. Gov., 1978–82; VA Gov., 1982–86.

DC Office: 154 RSOB 20515, 202-224-4024; Fax: 202-224-8689; e-mail: senator_robb@robb.senator.gov.

State Offices: 1001 E. Broad St., Richmond 23219, 804-771-2221; 310 1st St., SW, #102, Roanoke 24011, 703-985-0103; Signet Bank Bldg., 530 Main St., Danville 24541, 804-791-0330; Dominion Towers, 999 Waterside Dr., Norfolk 23510, 804-441-3124; 8229 Boone Blvd., #888, Vienna 22182, 703-356-2006; and First Union Bank Bldg., Main St., Clintwood 24288, 703-926-4104.

Committees: *Armed Services* (8th of 10 D): Personnel; Readiness; Seapower. *Foreign Relations* (6th of 8 D): East Asian and Pacific Affairs (RMM); Near Eastern and South Asian Affairs; Western Hemisphere and Peace Corps Affairs. *Intelligence (Select)* (8th of 8 D). *Joint Economic Committee* (10th of 10 Sen.)

Group Ratings

	ADA	ACLU	COPE	CFA	LCV	CON	NSI	COC	ACU	NTLC	CHC
1994	60	74	63	67	69	62	90	34	12	28	7
1993	75	—	82	80	75	83	—	36	12	—	—

National Journal Ratings

	1993 LIB — 1993 CONS	1994 LIB — 1994 CONS
Economic	49% — 47%	72% — 18%
Social	77% — 21%	76% — 19%
Foreign	49% — 49%	46% — 51%

Key Votes of the 103d Congress

1. Clinton Deficit Plan	Y	3. Brady Handgun Purchase Y	5. Lmt. UN Cmnd. of Forces N
2. NAFTA	Y	4. Strike Race/Death Pnlty. N	6. Cut Missile Funds N

Key Votes of the 104th Congress

1. Congressional Compliance Y	3. Balanced Budget Amndt. Y	5. Product Liability Reform Y
2. Bar Unfunded Mandates Y	4. Pass Line Item Veto Y	6. FY96 Budget Y

Election Results

1994 general	Charles S. Robb (D)	938,376	(46%)	($5,501,697)
	Oliver L. (Ollie) North (R)	882,213	(43%)	($20,607,367)
	J. Marshall Coleman (I)	235,324	(11%)	($813,409)
1994 primary	Charles S. Robb (D)	154,561	(58%)	
	Virgil H. Goode Jr. (D)	90,547	(34%)	
	Sylvia L. Clute (D)	17,329	(6%)	
	Others	4,507	(2%)	
1988 general	Charles S. Robb (D)	1,474,086	(71%)	($2,881,666)
	Maurice A. Dawkins (R)	593,652	(29%)	($282,229)

FIRST DISTRICT

When the first British settlers sailed up the estuaries that flow into the Chesapeake Bay, they were searching for gold, hoping to sail back soon with fortunes. But they couldn't help noticing that the spot where the James River feeds into the Bay, now Hampton Roads, was a fine natural harbor, with calm, deep water and good anchorages. There they established a civilization whose elegance is recalled in the craftsmanship of restored Williamsburg and whose coarseness and brutality is brought to life by the story of Jamestown and the other beleaguered settlements. Tidewater Virginia brought slavery to America and tobacco to the world, and slave-raised tobacco was the center of its economy in the colonial era and in the years afterward, when its most talented sons left its depleted soil for better opportunities elsewhere.

Now the economy and tone of life in Tidewater Virginia are set by the American military. Fifty years ago, as America was on the brink of world war, the Navy base at Norfolk and the Newport News Shipbuilding and Drydock Company across Hampton Roads became the center of American naval might in the Atlantic. Just before World War II, there were some 369,000 people living on both sides of Hampton Roads. Today there are 1.4 million—a population collected not just from the local rural hinterland but from all over the country, making this a metropolitan area that is not so much southern in atmosphere as it is, in the manner of military bases abroad, national. But you can still see this area's origins in the Shipbuilding and Drydock Company that lies over the flat neighborhoods lining the baysides, with its ships looming larger than life, their turrets and superstructures bristling with armored might. This is, among other things, the biggest private employer in Virginia. At the height of 1980s naval expansion, 30,000 people worked here, and the Defense Department spent $1.2 billion a year in this area.

Virginia's 1st Congressional District—America's First District, Congressman Herb Bateman calls it—contains much of this territory. Its boundaries are convoluted in order to accommodate the black-majority 3d District. About 45% of the district's residents live on the Peninsula, in and around Newport News, Williamsburg and other Hampton Roads area towns. It also includes the southern tip of the Delmarva Peninsula—Virginia's Eastern Shore, site of the annual roundup of wild Chincoteague ponies, and much of the Northern Neck between the Rappahannock and Potomac Rivers, where Robert "King" Carter, one of the great landowners of colonial Virginia, reigned, and where George Washington and Robert E. Lee were born; the Northern Neck is now growing again for the first time in two centuries. The 1st also dips south to the Hanover County suburbs outside of Richmond. Ancestrally, most of this area is Democratic, but with black precincts shorn away, the 1st now is reliably Republican, voting 49%–34% for George Bush over Bill Clinton in 1992.

The congressman from the 1st District is Herb Bateman, who has deep roots in the area—deeper indeed than many Hampton Roads area locals, who were brought here by the military. He grew up in Newport News, went to William and Mary, enlisted in the Air Force in the Korean war, practiced law and was elected to the Virginia Senate in 1967. He switched parties in 1976, and was outmaneuvered for the congressional nomination that year. But when the district became open again in 1982, he easily won the nomination and then won the seat over a substitute after the first Democratic opponent withdrew. Bateman has a moderate-conservative record on economics and cultural issues (he opposed term limits and supports gun control, for example) and is more conservative on foreign policy and defense. He has served on the National Security Committee since 1985, backing higher defense spending in the middle 1980s and warning after the end of the Cold War that America must "maintain a flexible military capability that can quickly respond to a crisis anywhere in the world." In 1989, he led the successful effort to build two new Nimitz-class aircraft carriers at Newport News for $6.3 billion and the September 1994 approval of the $4.5 billion CVN-76 carrier. He has also sought subsidies to support U.S. flagship lines and federal loan guarantees for foreign customers of the shipbuilders. He supports more pay for military personnel and pushes for NASA research at the Langley space center in Hampton. He has sought money for dredging in Hampton and cleanup of the Chesapeake Bay. He has also worked to set aside funds for the nation's only Continuing Electron Beam Accelerator Facility, which is being built in Newport News.

Bateman has had some serious electoral challenges in the past. Bobby Scott, now congressman from the 3d District, held him to 56% in 1986 and former TV anchorman Andy Fox held him to 51% in 1990. But Bateman beat Fox soundly in the new district lines in 1992 and won easily in 1994, for what he had said would be his last term. But on election night he said, "It has been my desire, my preference, that it be my last term. But if the Republicans become a majority, I won't walk away from making a meaningful and specific contribution." He is now the fifth ranking Republican on the National Security Committee and chairman of the Military Readiness Subcommittee.

The People: Pop. 1990: 563,126; 44% rural; 11% age 65+; 79% White; 18% Black; 1% Asian; 2% Hispanic origin. Voting age pop.: 419,128; 17% Black; 1% Hispanic origin. Households: 63% married couple families; 30% married couple fams. w. children; 47% college educ.; median household income: $33,285; per capita income: $14,675; median gross rent: $491; median house value: $92,700.

1992 Presidential Vote		
Bush (R)	120,131	(49%)
Clinton (D)	81,826	(34%)
Perot (I)	39,307	(16%)

1988 Presidential Vote		
Bush (R)	133,877	(68%)
Dukakis (D)	63,738	(32%)

Rep. Herbert H. Bateman (R)

Elected 1982; b. Aug. 7, 1928, Elizabeth City, NC; home, Newport News; William and Mary, B.A. 1949, Georgetown U., LL.B. 1956; Protestant; married (Laura).

Career: Air Force, 1951–53; Teacher, Hampton Schl., 1949–51; Law Clerk, Judge Bastian, 1956–57; Practicing atty., 1957–82; VA Senate, 1968–82.

DC Office: 2350 RHOB 20515, 202-225-4261; Fax: 202-225-4382.

District Offices: 739 Thimble Shoals Blvd., Newport News 23606, 804-873-1132; 4712 Southpoint Pkwy., Fredericksburg 22407, 703-898-2975; and P.O. Box 447, Accomac 23301, 804-787-7836.

Committees: *National Security* (5th of 30 R): Military Readiness (Chmn.); Military Research and Development. *Transportation & Infrastructure* (6th of 33 R): Surface Transportation; Water Resources and Environment.

Group Ratings

	ADA	ACLU	COPE	CFA	LCV	CON	NSI	COC	ACU	NTLC	CHC
1994	10	14	22	20	6	81	100	92	90	86	86
1993	5	—	8	20	21	29	—	100	92	—	—

National Journal Ratings

	1993 LIB — 1993 CONS		1994 LIB — 1994 CONS	
Economic	30%	— 68%	34%	— 64%
Social	19%	— 77%	30%	— 69%
Foreign	24%	— 76%	14%	— 80%

Key Votes of the 103d Congress

1. Clinton Deficit Plan	N	3. Brady Handgun Purchase Y	5. Lmt. UN Cmnd. of Forces *
2. NAFTA	Y	4. Strike Race/Death Pnlty. Y	6. Cut Missile Funds N

Key Votes of the 104th Congress

1. Congressional Compliance Y	6. Reform Crime Grant Y	11. Loser Pays Court Reform N
2. Balanced Budget Amndmt. Y	7. National Security Act Y	12. Product Liability Reform N
3. Bar Unfunded Mandates Y	8. Moratorium on Regs. Y	13. Welfare Reform Y
4. Pass Line Item Veto Y	9. Risk Assessment on Regs. Y	14. Term Limits Amndmt. N
5. Relax Exclusionary Rule Y	10. Expnd. Priv. Prop. Rights Y	15. Tax Cuts Y

Election Results

1994 general	Herbert H. Bateman (R)	142,930	(74%)	($423,501)
	Mary F. Sinclair (D)	45,173	(23%)	($80,435)
	Others	4,393	(2%)	
1994 primary	Herbert H. Bateman (R) . nominated by convention			
1992 general	Herbert H. Bateman (R)	133,537	(58%)	($764,820)
	Andrew H. (Andy) Fox (D)	89,814	(39%)	($419,878)
	Donald J. MacLeay, Jr. (I)	8,677	(4%)	($7,755)

SECOND DISTRICT

The United States Navy Atlantic fleet berthed in its home port of Norfolk is one of the great awe-inspiring sights in America, or anywhere. The aggregation of destructive power in the line of towering gray ships is probably greater than in any other single port in history—over 100 ships are based here, with some 100,000 sailors and Marines, some $2 billion in annual spending. Norfolk has been a Navy port since 1801, and has long been recognized as one of the best natural harbors on the East Coast, one that never freezes, has a channel 50 feet deep and is within 750 miles of three-quarters of U.S. manufacturing activity.

Norfolk, once a small city, is now the center of a metropolitan area on both sides of Hampton Roads with over 1.4 million people—fourfold growth since Pearl Harbor, double the national growth rate in the 1980s. One-fourth of the jobs here are with the military, but with its skilled labor force and lack of unions the Hampton Roads area has also attracted a lot of private employment; the port has taken a great deal of business away from the labor-torn piers of Baltimore. To the Hampton Roads area, this growth over the last 45 years has brought a wider cross-section of people than is usually found in the South. There is no heavy accent here: the brothy Tidewater accent is heard more often farther up the rivers toward Richmond. And Norfolk preserves its antique past more carefully now, developing cultural institutions and commercial amenities appropriate to a major metro area. Older parts of Norfolk have the look and feel of a working-class town, with shipyard workers and many blacks (35% of the total), but most of it is white middle-class suburbia, except perhaps for Virginia Beach's string of oceanfront motels.

The 2d Congressional District of Virginia is made up of most of Norfolk and most of Virginia Beach, with boundaries carefully drawn to put heavily black neighborhoods in the black-majority 3d District. The politics here has changed as the area has become more heavily suburban, and the Democrats more associated with defense policy critics. In 1968, the 2d District voted for Hubert Humphrey, as Norfolk cast 65,000 votes and Virginia Beach 37,000. In 1992, the 2d District voted 48%–35% for George Bush, as its portion of Norfolk cast 45,000 votes and Virginia Beach 134,000.

The congressman from the 2d District is Owen Pickett, a conservative Democrat first elected in 1986. An accountant and lawyer with little personal magnetism, a legislator since 1972, he was known as a fiscal conservative and for his hard work restructuring the state retirement system. He was Democratic state chairman in 1981, when Charles Robb won the governorship, beginning a string of Democratic victories. In 1982, he was Robb's choice for the Senate but withdrew after Governor Douglas Wilder, then state senator, threatened to run as an independent against him. But by the time he ran for Congress in 1986, the quiet and methodical Pickett had Wilder's support and that of Jesse Jackson's Norfolk coordinator. Pickett carried Norfolk heavily, and won 49%–42%.

In the House, Pickett showed his political acumen by getting a new seat created for him on the National Security Committee and getting a seat on the old Merchant Marine as well—two crucial committees for any Norfolk congressman. His voting record stood at the midpoint of the Democratic House, but conservative on defense. He voted for the Gulf war resolution and against family and medical leave; he opposed the Clinton budget and tax package in 1993.

In 1992 and 1994, Pickett was challenged by aggressive conservative Jim Chapman, who tried to nationalize the race. He was not entirely successful: Pickett won with 56% the first time and 59% the second. But the trajectory of Pickett's career may now be different. The new House Republican majority, and its abolition of the Merchant Marine Committee, made it harder for Pickett to argue that he could bring benefits to the district. But he is ranking minority member of the Military Personnel Subcommittee—very important to this district. In March 1995, he was one of the 23 conservative Democrats to form The Coalition, to signal their dissent from their party. Pickett has been mentioned as a candidate for John Warner's Senate seat in 1996, and positioning himself as a clear conservative would probably be helpful for that race. But Pickett has announced he has no plans to run for that seat. And certainly, he remains well-poised for the next race in the 2d District.

The People: Pop. 1990: 562,789; 1% rural; 7% age 65+; 77% White; 17% Black; 4% Asian; 1% Other; 3% Hispanic origin. Voting age pop.: 420,036; 15% Black; 3% Hispanic origin. Households: 60% married couple families; 31% married couple fams. w. children; 55% college educ.; median household income: $32,576; per capita income: $14,492; median gross rent: $528; median house value: $92,500.

1992 Presidential Vote			1988 Presidential Vote		
Bush (R)	85,773	(48%)	Bush (R)	99,266	(66%)
Clinton (D)	62,946	(35%)	Dukakis (D)	51,918	(34%)
Perot (I)	30,587	(17%)			

Rep. Owen Pickett (D)

Elected 1986; b. Aug. 31, 1930, Richmond; home, Virginia Beach; VA Polytechnic Inst., B.S. 1952, U. of Richmond, LL.B. 1955; Baptist; married (Sybil).

Career: Accountant; Practicing atty., 1955–86; VA House of Delegates, 1972–86; Chmn., VA Dem. Party, 1980–82.

DC Office: 2430 RHOB 20515, 202-225-4215; Fax: 202-225-4218; e-mail: opickett@hr.house.gov.

District Offices: 112 E. Little Creek Rd., Norfolk 23505, 804-583-5892; and 2710 VA Beach Blvd., Virginia Beach 23452, 804-486-3710.

Committees: *National Security* (8th of 25 D): Military Personnel (RMM); Military Readiness.

Group Ratings

	ADA	ACLU	COPE	CFA	LCV	CON	NSI	COC	ACU	NTLC	CHC
1994	35	35	56	30	12	19	80	92	48	50	50
1993	20	—	42	50	57	0	—	73	50	—	—

National Journal Ratings

	1993 LIB — 1993 CONS		1994 LIB — 1994 CONS	
Economic	40%	— 58%	46%	— 53%
Social	58%	— 41%	41%	— 58%
Foreign	51%	— 42%	43%	— 57%

Key Votes of the 103d Congress

1. Clinton Deficit Plan	N	3. Brady Handgun Purchase	N	5. Lmt. UN Cmnd. of Forces	N
2. NAFTA	Y	4. Strike Race/Death Pnlty.	Y	6. Cut Missile Funds	N

Key Votes of the 104th Congress

1. Congressional Compliance	Y	6. Reform Crime Grant	N	11. Loser Pays Court Reform	N
2. Balanced Budget Amndmt.	N	7. National Security Act	N	12. Product Liability Reform	N
3. Bar Unfunded Mandates	Y	8. Moratorium on Regs.	Y	13. Welfare Reform	N
4. Pass Line Item Veto	N	9. Risk Assessment on Regs.	Y	14. Term Limits Amndmt.	N
5. Relax Exclusionary Rule	N	10. Expnd. Priv. Prop. Rights	Y	15. Tax Cuts	N

Election Results

1994 general	Owen B. Pickett (D)	81,372	(59%)	($386,469)
	J.L. (Jim) Chapman (R)	56,375	(41%)	($433,587)
1994 primary	Owen B. Pickett (D) . . . . . nominated by convention			
1992 general	Owen Pickett (D)	99,253	(56%)	($373,047)
	J.L. (Jim) Chapman (R)	77,797	(44%)	($190,447)

THIRD DISTRICT

The history of African-American slavery literally began along the tidal expanse of the James River. In 1607, the first English colonists chose one of the marshiest, least healthy spots along the broad river as the site of their settlement at Jamestown. Only a dozen years later, the first slave ship sailed up the James and offloaded its human cargo, giving birth to the biracial society of the American South. In the 20th Century, the great plantation houses of the Tidewater, entire communities once adorned by the most impressive architecture and learning of the day and attended by hundreds of slaves, still dot the banks of the James. Charles City County, the site of William Byrd II's Westover, Benjamin Harrison III's Berkeley, and John Carter's Shirley, also was the birthplace of two successive presidents, William Henry Harrison and John Tyler. The county's population continues to be heavily black—the demography of the plantation remains.

The 3d Congressional District of Virginia is the black-majority district formed in 1991. It strings together black precincts and communities along the James River from Norfolk and Newport News upriver on the Peninsula past Jamestown and Charles City County, with spindly extensions into black neighborhoods of Richmond and Petersburg and their suburban fringes. It also includes several rural counties to the north with high black percentages. Overall, the district's population is 64% black. Politically, the 3d is by far the most Democratic in Virginia—65% for Bill Clinton in 1992. But it also is sensitive to the needs of the businesses that supply its economic base—notably Newport News Shipbuilding and Drydock Co., the state's largest private employer with 19,500 workers—and to the ravages of crime on its urban core. In 1994, voters in Richmond, which comprises one quarter of the district, replaced most of the City Council because of its failure to control the city's spiraling homicide rate, hold on to disappearing jobs and revitalize the deteriorating downtown area. Blacks still hold six seats on the council, but most are from a generation with little connection to the black leaders of the civil rights era who once ran Richmond.

Bobby Scott, a native of Newport News and a former state senator, is the congressman from the 3d District. The son of a doctor, Scott went to Harvard, where he was a classmate of Al Gore, and then to Boston College Law School. He served in the National Guard and Army Reserves and returned home to practice law in 1973. In 1977, he was elected to the House of Delegates and in 1983 to the state Senate, representing a multiracial district in a community where, because of the military tradition of integration, biracial politics comes more naturally than in other places. In 1992, Scott ran for the newly created 3d District, and with his base in the Peninsula, and against two Richmond-based candidates, won the crucial Democratic primary with 67% of the vote. The general election made him the first black Member of Congress to be elected from Virginia since Reconstruction. Cautious on economic and foreign policy issues during his first year in Congress, Scott became more liberal on economics as his term progressed. On the Economic and Educational Opportunities Committee, he jumped into the healthcare debate: remembering how his father had been denied staff privileges in a Newport News hospital, he vowed that any healthcare bill would prohibit racial discrimination against patients and healthcare providers. Scott was one of 10 members of the Congressional Black Caucus who refused to support the Democrats' 1994 crime bill; they insisted that its death penalty provisions be balanced by requirements that death sentences not be disproportionately applied by race. "I'd like to see a crime bill passed," he said. "I'm just not going to accept 60 new death penalties and no provisions they be applied fairly." But his provision obviously lacked majority support, and Scott voted no.

Scott won reelection easily in 1994, but still wound up with $125,000 in campaign debts. In the debate over crime and welfare provisions of the Contract With America, Scott spoke frequently and his passions showed no sign of cooling. When the House Judiciary Committee wrangled over efforts to expand the rights of police to gather evidence, Republican Sonny Bono of California accused Democrats of ignorance of "what's out on the street." Scott shot back that black motorists in many places are being routinely stopped for drug searches simply because of their race, and said, "Some people are getting tired of police misconduct." Expect to hear more from this savvy Democrat.

The People: Pop. 1990: 560,640; 11% rural; 12% age 65+; 33% White; 64% Black; 1% Asian; 1% Other; 1% Hispanic origin. Voting age pop.: 413,025; 61% Black; 1% Hispanic origin. Households: 42% married couple families; 19% married couple fams. w. children; 36% college educ.; median household income: $22,556; per capita income: $10,558; median gross rent: $398; median house value: $61,700.

1992 Presidential Vote			1988 Presidential Vote		
Clinton (D)	124,857	(65%)	Dukakis (D)	114,002	(65%)
Bush (R)	48,843	(25%)	Bush (R)	62,435	(35%)
Perot (I)	16,779	(9%)			

Rep. Robert C. (Bobby) Scott (D)

Elected 1992; b. Apr. 30, 1947, Washington, D.C.; home, Newport News; Harvard, B.A. 1969, Boston Col. Law Schl., J.D. 1973; Episcopalian; divorced.

Career: Army Natl. Guard, 1970–73; Army Reserves, 1973–76; Practicing atty., 1973–91; VA House of Delegates, 1977–82; VA Senate, 1983–92.

DC Office: 501 CHOB 20515, 202-225-8351; Fax: 202-225-8354.

District Offices: 2700 Washington Ave., Newport News 23607, 804-380-1000.

Committees: *Economic & Educational Opportunities* (15th of 19 D): Early Childhood, Youth and Families; Oversight and Investigations. *Judiciary* (10th of 15 D): Commercial and Administrative Law; Crime.

Group Ratings

	ADA	ACLU	COPE	CFA	LCV	CON	NSI	COC	ACU	NTLC	CHC
1994	80	91	89	80	82	1	40	42	24	18	7
1993	90	—	100	100	79	11	—	18	8	—	—

National Journal Ratings

	1993 LIB — 1993 CONS		1994 LIB — 1994 CONS	
Economic	68% —	26%	83% —	0%
Social	80% —	13%	77% —	23%
Foreign	66% —	31%	54% —	45%

Key Votes of the 103d Congress

1. Clinton Deficit Plan	Y	3. Brady Handgun Purchase	Y	5. Lmt. UN Cmnd. of Forces	N
2. NAFTA	N	4. Strike Race/Death Pnlty.	N	6. Cut Missile Funds	N

Key Votes of the 104th Congress

1. Congressional Compliance Y	6. Reform Crime Grant N	11. Loser Pays Court Reform N
2. Balanced Budget Amndmt. N	7. National Security Act N	12. Product Liability Reform N
3. Bar Unfunded Mandates N	8. Moratorium on Regs. N	13. Welfare Reform N
4. Pass Line Item Veto N	9. Risk Assessment on Regs. N	14. Term Limits Amndmt. N
5. Relax Exclusionary Rule N	10. Expnd. Priv. Prop. Rights Y	15. Tax Cuts N

Election Results

1994 general	Robert C. (Bobby) Scott (D)	108,532	(79%)	($252,350)
	Thomas E. (Tom) Ward (R)	28,080	(21%)	($77,642)
1994 primary	Robert C. (Bobby) Scott (D) .. nom. by convention			
1992 general	Robert C. (Bobby) Scott (D)	132,432	(79%)	($500,359)
	Daniel (Dan) Jenkins (R)	35,780	(21%)	($16,318)

FOURTH DISTRICT

The clash of arms resounds through much of the history of Tidewater Virginia. This was the scene of the first permanent English settlement in North America, at Jamestown, and of its first revolution, Bacon's Rebellion, in 1676. In 1781, George Washington's tattered and exhausted army finally pushed General Cornwallis to the sea, where the French Navy waited at Yorktown: the final victory of the Revolutionary War. The Tidewater also was the scene of bitter fighting more than 80 years later in the Civil War, as Union troops invested the battlements of the small industrial city of Petersburg, 25 miles south of Richmond. Today, the Tidewater region boasts one of the densest concentrations of military power in the world: the Hampton Roads area has the United States' largest accumulation of Navy bases, while Fort Lee, the big Army base near Petersburg, south of Richmond, provides an estimated 17,000 jobs for the local economy.

The 4th Congressional District of Virginia includes much of the Tidewater. Nearly half its people are in the Hampton Roads area, in Portsmouth—a Navy port and industrial town with a charming old town section—and in the suburban expanse of Chesapeake and Suffolk Counties. The district also takes in the flat lands of Southside Virginia fanning south from the James River. These were tobacco lands when the English first settled them in the 17th Century; today they also produce Virginia's peanut crop and its Smithfield hams. The district then loops around most of Petersburg and Hopewell, with its Allied Chemical plant facing 18th Century plantations, and juts to the growing suburbs north and west of Richmond. Historically, this was a solidly Democratic area, and the 4th's Democratic percentages are buoyed up by the 32% of its residents who are black. But in national and increasingly in state elections this area is trending Republican: it voted 61% for George Bush in 1992 and 60% for George Allen in 1993.

The congressman from the 4th District, however, is a Democrat, Norman Sisisky, a Richmond native who transformed a small Pepsi bottling company in Petersburg into one of the largest soft drink bottling operations in the South. In 1973, when he had owned his firm 24 years, Sisisky was first elected to the House of Delegates. He ran for Congress in 1982, financing a solid campaign with his own money. Once in the House, he immediately got a seat on the National Security Committee, where he built a reputation over the years as a conservative who could be counted on to support increased defense spending. In 1993 he joined six other House Democrats calling themselves "Democrats for a Strong Defense" who mobilized against further defense cuts. He played a major role in an all-hands-on-deck lobbying effort by the Tidewater's congressional delegation and in 1994 won approval of the $4.5 billion Nimitz-class aircraft carrier, CVN-76, in Hampton Roads. So popular have Sisisky's efforts been in his district that in 1994, while other Democrats were in trouble, he won reelection with 62% of the vote over the minister of a 4,000-member Baptist church. But Sisisky had to spend $290,000 of his own money, considerably more than he has in other recent contests (in 1992 he spent none of his own money).

Sisisky chaired the Military Oversight Subcommittee in the 103d Congress; in the 104th, he is ranking minority member of Military Readiness. He also sponsored a paperwork reduction act, signed into law, that cuts the number of government forms small businesses are required to file. Sisisky has been mentioned as a possible party-switcher, but he has a middle of the road voting record and has seemed inclined to stay where he is. Were he not running, a Republican would have a good chance of capturing this district.

The People: Pop. 1990: 563,206; 37% rural; 12% age 65+; 66% White; 32% Black; 1% Asian; 1% Hispanic origin. Voting age pop.: 415,363; 31% Black; 1% Hispanic origin. Households: 61% married couple families; 29% married couple fams. w. children; 38% college educ.; median household income: $30,425; per capita income: $12,887; median gross rent: $424; median house value: $72,900.

1992 Presidential Vote			1988 Presidential Vote		
Bush (R)	106,392	(46%)	Bush (R)	118,408	(60%)
Clinton (D)	90,641	(39%)	Dukakis (D)	77,544	(40%)
Perot (I)	31,467	(14%)			

Rep. Norman Sisisky (D)

Elected 1982; b. June 9, 1927, Baltimore, MD; home, Petersburg; VA Commonwealth U., B.A. 1949; Jewish; married (Rhoda).

Career: Navy, 1945–46; Pres., Pepsi-Cola Bottling Co. of Petersburg, 1949–82; VA House of Delegates, 1973–82.

DC Office: 2371 RHOB 20515, 202-225-6365; Fax: 202-226-1170.

District Offices: Emporia Exec. Ctr., 425-H S. Main St., Emporia 23847, 804-634-5575; 43 Rives Rd., Petersburg 23805, 804-732-2544; and 309 County St., #204, Portsmouth 23704, 804-393-2068.

Committees: *National Security* (5th of 25 D): Military Procurement; Military Readiness (RMM). *Small Business* (3rd of 19 D): Procurement, Exports and Business Opportunities.

Group Ratings

	ADA	ACLU	COPE	CFA	LCV	CON	NSI	COC	ACU	NTLC	CHC
1994	35	50	67	20	18	36	90	75	48	54	36
1993	45	—	75	70	69	19	—	45	42	—	—

National Journal Ratings

	1993 LIB — 1993 CONS		1994 LIB — 1994 CONS	
Economic	46% —	54%	50% —	46%
Social	55% —	45%	36% —	62%
Foreign	51% —	42%	49% —	49%

Key Votes of the 103d Congress

1. Clinton Deficit Plan	Y	3. Brady Handgun Purchase	N	5. Lmt. UN Cmnd. of Forces	N
2. NAFTA	N	4. Strike Race/Death Pnlty.	Y	6. Cut Missile Funds	N

Key Votes of the 104th Congress

1. Congressional Compliance Y	6. Reform Crime Grant N	11. Loser Pays Court Reform N
2. Balanced Budget Amndmt. Y	7. National Security Act N	12. Product Liability Reform Y
3. Bar Unfunded Mandates Y	8. Moratorium on Regs. Y	13. Welfare Reform N
4. Pass Line Item Veto N	9. Risk Assessment on Regs. Y	14. Term Limits Amndmt. N
5. Relax Exclusionary Rule Y	10. Expnd. Priv. Prop. Rights Y	15. Tax Cuts N

Election Results

1994 general	Norman Sisisky (D)	115,055	(62%)	($741,224)
	A. George Sweet III (R)...............	71,678	(38%)	($329,607)
1994 primary	Norman Sisisky (D) ..... nominated by convention			
1992 general	Norman Sisisky (D)	147,649	(68%)	($466,010)
	A. J. (Tony) Zevgolis (R)	68,286	(32%)	($82,068)

FIFTH DISTRICT

Southside Virginia is a geographic name which for years was shorthand for a state of mind. Here is Appomattox Court House, in the serene little hamlet where Robert E. Lee surrendered to his onetime subordinate Ulysses S. Grant; here is Danville, where the tobacco auction originated in 1858; here also is Prince Edward County, where Harry Byrd's massive resistance shut down public schools in 1957 rather than obey a federal court desegregation order. This land north of the dividing line Colonel William Byrd surveyed in 1728 has some variety. Its eastern counties are flat and humid—frontier in the late colonial period, plantation country by 1800, now peanut fields and pine forests. To the west, into the Piedmont, the land gradually gets hillier. Here are textile mill towns and furniture manufacturing centers—Danville, Martinsville and a dozen smaller towns. Westward, nearer to the mountains, is more livestock and less tobacco, and the thick syrupy tones of the Southside Virginia accent turn to mountain twangs.

The 5th Congressional District consists of much of Southside Virginia, west of metropolitan Richmond and at some points up to the Blue Ridge. It includes Charlottesville and much of surrounding Albemarle County, but skirts around Lynchburg. Historically, politics here was Democratic, segregationist and conservative, run by chain-smoking local bankers and court-house lawyers, personified by the late House of Delegates Speaker A. L. Philpott. But those Democrats are a rare breed these days, and younger and sleeker politicians are now competing for office in Southside; conservative Republicans Oliver North and Michael Farris carried the district in their losing bids for Senate and lieutenant governor, respectively.

The congressman from the 5th District is L. F. Payne, a Democrat with a middle-of-the-road record in the Democratic Congress, developer of the Wintergreen ski resort, which accounts for about half of the jobs in rural Nelson County. Payne, the son of a school teacher and a highway patrolman, grew up in Amherst County, went to Virginia Military Institute and served in the Army, started with Wintergreen in 1973, at age 28. He won the seat in a June 1988 special election over a Reagan appointee, Linda Arey; he self-financed much of his campaign and won with 59%. Payne started off on the Transportation and Infrastructure Committee and switched to the Ways and Means Committee in 1993. He says he wants to "increase the economic pie not redistribute it," and supports the balanced budget amendment. Payne was a supporter of Tennessean Jim Cooper's managed competition healthcare plan and voted for the Clinton budget and tax package. On Ways and Means, he fought to hold the healthcare plan's tobacco tax down to 45 cents from $1.25 a pack—he represents some 5,000 tobacco growers in his district. He was the only Virginia Democrat to support the Hyde amendment on abortion in the 103d Congress, and also opposed the crime bill and striker replacement. He did support NAFTA.

Payne had a closer race than expected in 1994. He outspent Republican George Landrith,

$915,000 to Landrith's $356,000, with the help of $601,000 in PAC contributions. But he won by only 53%–47%. He is one of the 23 members of The Coalition, a conservative Democrats' group, and was one of the Democrats' top supporters of the Contract With America. Payne has been mentioned as a candidate for John Warner's Senate seat in 1996, and the race may look especially tempting if Republicans seek to dry up his PAC money, now that they hold the majority; otherwise his alternatives would be to spend his own money again and take a serious risk of defeat. If Payne does not run here, the 5th becomes a prime target for Republicans, who undoubtedly will make this seat a priority either way.

The People: Pop. 1990: 562,273; 67% rural; 14% age 65+; 74% White; 25% Black; 1% Asian; 1% Hispanic origin. Voting age pop.: 432,813; 23% Black. Households: 58% married couple families; 24% married couple fams. w. children; 32% college educ.; median household income: $24,807; per capita income: $11,675; median gross rent: $325; median house value: $55,400.

1992 Presidential Vote			1988 Presidential Vote		
Bush (R)	104,236	(46%)	Bush (R)	118,464	(61%)
Clinton (D)	90,769	(40%)	Dukakis (D)	77,130	(39%)
Perot (I)	26,978	(12%)			

Rep. L. F. Payne (D)

Elected June 1988; b. July 9, 1945, Amherst; home, Nellysford; VA Military Inst., B.S. 1967, U. of VA, M.B.A. 1973; Presbyterian; married (Susan).

Career: Army Corps of Engineers, 1967–69; Engineering Assoc., C&P Telephone, 1970–71; Mgr., Wintergreen Development Inc., 1973–75, Pres., 1976–85, Chmn. 1985–88.

DC Office: 2412 LHOB 20515, 202-225-4711; Fax: 202-226-1147.

District Offices: 301 P.O. Bldg., 700 Main St., Danville 24541, 804-792-1280; Abbitt Fed. Bldg., 103 S. Main St., Farmville 23901, 804-392-8331; and 103 E. Water St., #302, Charlottesville 22902, 804-295-6372.

Committees: *Ways & Means* (14th of 15 D): Social Security; Trade.

Group Ratings

	ADA	ACLU	COPE	CFA	LCV	CON	NSI	COC	ACU	NTLC	CHC
1994	25	35	33	40	61	59	90	83	57	50	64
1993	30	—	50	70	79	64	—	45	42	—	—

National Journal Ratings

	1993 LIB — 1993 CONS		1994 LIB — 1994 CONS	
Economic	47% —	53%	44% —	54%
Social	52% —	47%	33% —	66%
Foreign	51% —	42%	57% —	37%

Key Votes of the 103d Congress

1. Clinton Deficit Plan	Y	3. Brady Handgun Purchase	N	5. Lmt. UN Cmnd. of Forces	N
2. NAFTA	Y	4. Strike Race/Death Pnlty.	Y	6. Cut Missile Funds	N

Key Votes of the 104th Congress

1. Congressional Compliance	Y	6. Reform Crime Grant	N	11. Loser Pays Court Reform	Y
2. Balanced Budget Amndmt.	Y	7. National Security Act	Y	12. Product Liability Reform	Y
3. Bar Unfunded Mandates	Y	8. Moratorium on Regs.	Y	13. Welfare Reform	N
4. Pass Line Item Veto	Y	9. Risk Assessment on Regs.	Y	14. Term Limits Amndmt.	N
5. Relax Exclusionary Rule	Y	10. Expnd. Priv. Prop. Rights	Y	15. Tax Cuts	N

Election Results

1994 general	L. F. Payne (D)	95,308	(53%)	($915,224)
	George C. Landrith III (R)	83,555	(47%)	($356,574)
1994 primary	L. F. Payne (D)	nominated by convention		
1992 general	L. F. Payne (D)	133,031	(69%)	($414,696)
	W. A. (Bill) Hurlburt (R)	60,030	(31%)	($54,705)

SIXTH DISTRICT

The sturdy men and women who settled the Valley of Virginia west of the Blue Ridge could hardly have differed more from the "second sons" of the European aristocracy who cleared the marshy forests of the Tidewater and built grand plantations there. Even before the Revolutionary War, Englishmen and Scots, German Protestants and Mennonites and Moravians—members of religious communities and fiercely independent farmers—poured down the great Wagon Road from Pennsylvania to the Valley. They were looking not for the flat, mahoganybrown land that eastern tobacco growers sought, but for fields which could support wheat, corn and hay, crops which could be rotated and which an individual farmer and his family could handle. That same independent spirit nurtured the growth of higher education here. In Lexington alone are Washington and Lee University, which Robert E. Lee headed, and the Virginia Military Institute, where Stonewall Jackson taught philosophy and artillery tactics. A quartet of the South's most distinguished women's private colleges are only a short drive away: Mary Baldwin College at Staunton, Randolph-Macon Woman's College at Lynchburg, Sweet Briar College at Sweet Briar, and Hollins College at Roanoke, farther south in the Valley. Meanwhile, industry flourished here more than in most of Virginia east of the Blue Ridge. In the 19th Century the Norfolk and Southern Railroad established its chief junction at Roanoke; as the years passed the city became the railroad's headquarters, and many major companies have plants here.

The 6th Congressional District of Virginia covers the heart of the Valley of Virginia, from Harrisonburg south to Roanoke, and crosses over the Blue Ridge to take in Lynchburg. Politically, this area has a Republican tradition almost as venerable as the Wagon Road, a tradition which is hospitable to economic assistance for the little guy, and fiercely opposed to Byrd Democrats. But in more recent years, the ancestral conservatism of Byrd Democrats and the feisty politics of the mountain rebels have melded into a single conservative Republicanism, more populist than elite in tone, as concerned with moral values as economic freedom, prickly about interference from Washington or even Richmond.

The congressman from the 6th District is Bob Goodlatte, a Republican first elected in 1992. Goodlatte grew up in Maine, attended college there and then law school at W&L, then went to work in Congressman Caldwell Butler's office in Roanoke. Goodlatte then practiced law and stayed active in politics; in 1992, when Democratic Congressman Jim Olin retired, Goodlatte was nominated by convention and won the general 60%–40%.

In his first term, Goodlatte got seats on the Judiciary and Agriculture committees and developed a reputation of being, along with Thomas Bliley, one of Virginia's two most conservative members. But the assertive Goodlatte was no meek follower of the party line: early in his first term, he was one of the Republican freshmen who pushed successfully for committee term limits on ranking minority members—which now applies to committee chairmen. His performance was so well received, that in 1994, he was re-elected without opposition.

Goodlatte gained widespread attention in the opening days of the 104th Congress by tangling with White House budget director Alice Rivlin at a hearing on the balanced budget amendment. Rivlin said the amendment would force spending cuts that would "boggle the imagination." Goodlatte retorted, "The administration is not only not willing to specify *how* you would balance the budget, you're not even willing to specify that you *would* balance the budget"—a reasonably prescient prediction. Goodlatte showed a bit of mountain Republican orneriness by opposing a measure to streamline the deportation of criminal aliens after they served their sentences. He served as floor leader for the House debate on his compromise version of the "loser pays" requirement in the Contract With America legal reform legislation. "A star is born," gushed Judiciary Chairman Henry Hyde, long one of the Republicans' few stars himself, after watching Goodlatte perform on the floor.

The People: Pop. 1990: 562,426; 34% rural; 15% age 65+; 87% White; 11% Black; 1% Asian; 1% Hispanic origin. Voting age pop.: 437,645; 11% Black; 1% Hispanic origin. Households: 57% married couple families; 24% married couple fams. w. children; 39% college educ.; median household income: $27,155; per capita income: $13,017; median gross rent: $358; median house value: $64,600.

1992 Presidential Vote				1988 Presidential Vote			
Bush (R)		111,405	(49%)	Bush (R)		122,874	(62%)
Clinton (D)		84,037	(37%)	Dukakis (D)		74,994	(38%)
Perot (I)		29,207	(13%)				

Rep. Bob Goodlatte (R)

Elected 1992; b. Sept. 22, 1952, Holyoke, MA; home, Roanoke; Bates Col., B.A. 1974, Washington and Lee Law Schl., J.D. 1977; Christian Scientist; married (Maryellen).

Career: Dist. Dir., U.S. Rep. Caldwell Butler, 1977–79; Practicing atty., 1979–92.

DC Office: 123 CHOB 20515, 202-225-5431; Fax: 202-225-9681; e-mail: talk2bob@hr.house.gov.

District Offices: 540 Crestar Plz., 10 Franklin Rd., SE, Roanoke 24011, 703-857-2672; 114 N. Central Ave., Staunton 24401, 703-885-3861; 2 S. Main St., #A, Harrisonburg 22801, 703-432-2391; and 916 Main St., #300 Lynchburg 24504, 804-845-8306.

Committees: *Agriculture* (10th of 27 R): Department Operations, Nutrition and Foreign Agriculture; Livestock, Dairy and Poultry. *Judiciary* (12th of 20 R): Constitution; Courts and Intellectual Property.

Group Ratings

	ADA	ACLU	COPE	CFA	LCV	CON	NSI	COC	ACU	NTLC	CHC
1994	10	9	0	20	11	88	90	92	90	93	100
1993	5	—	8	20	29	74	—	91	96	—	—

National Journal Ratings

	1993 LIB — 1993 CONS		1994 LIB — 1994 CONS	
Economic	14% —	80%	0% —	80%
Social	11% —	82%	0% —	89%
Foreign	31% —	67%	21% —	78%

Key Votes of the 103d Congress

1. Clinton Deficit Plan	N	3. Brady Handgun Purchase	N	5. Lmt. UN Cmnd. of Forces	Y
2. NAFTA	Y	4. Strike Race/Death Pnlty.	Y	6. Cut Missile Funds	Y

Key Votes of the 104th Congress

1. Congressional Compliance Y	6. Reform Crime Grant	Y	11. Loser Pays Court Reform	Y
2. Balanced Budget Amndmt. Y	7. National Security Act	Y	12. Product Liability Reform	Y
3. Bar Unfunded Mandates Y	8. Moratorium on Regs.	Y	13. Welfare Reform	Y
4. Pass Line Item Veto Y	9. Risk Assessment on Regs.	Y	14. Term Limits Amndmt.	Y
5. Relax Exclusionary Rule Y	10. Expnd. Priv. Prop. Rights	Y	15. Tax Cuts	Y

Election Results

1994 general	Bob Goodlatte (R) .... unopposed			($211,653)
1994 primary	Bob Goodlatte (R) ...... nominated by convention			
1992 general	Bob Goodlatte (R)	127,309	(60%)	($452,048)
	Stephen Alan Musselwhite (D)...........	84,618	(40%)	($597,020)

SEVENTH DISTRICT

In the center of Virginia, on a hill in downtown Richmond above the James River, is Thomas Jefferson's Capitol, one of the first classical-style buildings in North America, chaste and simple in the Jefferson style. Monument Avenue, Richmond's grand 140-foot wide boulevard, is punctuated by circles, each with a statue of a Confederate hero—Robert E. Lee (62 feet tall, dedicated Memorial Day 1890), Jeb Stuart, Jefferson Davis, Stonewall Jackson, Matthew Fountain Maury, "the Pathfinder of the Sea." On the grid streets of Church Hill, on the other side of the Capitol, Douglas Wilder grew up in a segregated neighborhood, working as a waiter in a hotel he could not check into, looking up the downtown streets at office buildings he could only dream of working in, staring at the Capitol where it was assumed he could never hold office. It is not surprising that there eventually was a clash between the whites who occupied the leading places in Richmond's great institutions—the Virginia Electric and Power Company, the big Main Street banks and the big law firms, the Philip Morris tobacco company and the Richmond newspapers—and the blacks who have become a majority within the Richmond city limits. When blacks first won a majority on the Richmond council in the 1970s, the outgoing administration feared the newcomers would tear down the statue of Lee, and so deeded it to the state. Now, the state has had a black governor, and the Martin Luther King holiday law pays homage to Confederate heroes as well as to the civil rights leader. But there remains a gulf between these two separate cultures, connected but still not unified.

That gulf now is reflected in the Richmond metropolitan area congressional districts. Most black precincts, including downtown Richmond and the Capitol, are collected in the black-majority 3d District, which extends downriver along the James to Newport News and Norfolk. The mostly white precincts on the west side of Richmond, most of suburban Henrico, Chesterfield and Hanover Counties are in the 7th District, which extends north past James Madison's home at Montpelier to Culpeper County and the Blue Ridge Mountains. But some 80% of the 7th's population is in metro Richmond. Demographically, the 7th District is only 10% black; politically, it is overwhelmingly Republican, 69% for Governor George Allen in 1993.

The congressman from the 7th District is Thomas Bliley, one of the House's new powers as chairman of the Commerce Committee. Bliley grew up in Richmond, where his family owned a funeral home; he started off in politics as a conservative Democrat and was mayor of Richmond from 1970–77. In 1980, he was elected to this seat as a Republican by a 53%–33% margin, and has been reelected easily every two years; he was redistricted in with George Allen in 1992, but Bliley had represented 80% of the constituency and Allen decided to run for governor—and both won. Bliley got a seat on the Commerce Committee, and became ranking Republican on John Dingell's Oversight Committee; in 1993, he switched to ranking Republican on Henry Waxman's Health and Environment Subcommittee. Even before Bliley gained seniority, he worked skillfully on a wide variety of issues, from the electric utility grid and Medicaid formulas to home medical services and drug discounts for veterans. He favors free broadcasting time for political candidates. He was co-chairman of the Adoption Caucus. He passed an amendment to bar immigrants with the HIV virus from entering the country. As ranking member of the District of Columbia Committee in 1991, he cooperated with D.C. Delegate Eleanor Holmes Norton in providing aid to Mayor Sharon Pratt Kelly; unfortunately, she did not keep her commitments to Congress.

Bliley's rise to chair the Commerce Committee was predicted almost nowhere; few expected Republicans to win a majority ("it was like we caught lightning in a bottle," Bliley said), and fewer still expected Speaker-designate Newt Gingrich to sweep aside more senior Republican Carlos Moorhead of California to make way for Bliley. But Bliley's skills obviously impressed Gingrich. The press focused initially on tobacco issues: there would be no more inquisitions of tobacco company presidents, for Bliley opposes federal restrictions on tobacco and cigarettes. This is hardly surprising, since Richmond has been a tobacco center for 250 years and the Philip Morris plant on the south side of the James River is one of the largest in the world. But Bliley has many other interests. He had sharply questioned the Clinton healthcare plan in 1993 and said he was looking only for modest reform in 1995. Bliley's priorities, after the Contract With America, were Clean Water legislation (in the past he has sought fewer unfunded mandates on localities), food safety laws and regulation of "orphan drugs" developed to treat rare diseases (Bliley wants longer patent protection than does Henry Waxman). He questions EPA's centralizing auto emissions inspections. He wants to limit liability on Superfund sites. He wants to speed up approval of drugs by the FDA. He has strong views, but is willing to talk and perhaps compromise: "You can stand like the oak or you can bend like the pine. If you choose to stand like the oak, you'll probably fall like the oak. If you stand like the pine and bend a little bit, you'll usually come out of the storm in pretty good shape."

Within the Commerce Committee, Bliley created something of a revolution by moving power away from the subcommittees, where Henry Waxman and Ed Markey had once called the shots, and centralized power and staff in the full committee. Though that ruffled some feathers, especially early in the session, Bliley demonstrated that he had the full loyalty of his troops by winning overwhelming passage, 38–5, of a sweeping telecommunications bill in May. It would deregulate most cable television rates and establish rules designed to lead to competition in the local telephone industry and set a framework for freeing the baby Bells to get into long distance.

The People: Pop. 1990: 562,729; 26% rural; 11% age 65+; 87% White; 10% Black; 2% Asian; 1% Hispanic origin. Voting age pop.: 424,682; 9% Black; 1% Hispanic origin. Households: 59% married couple families; 29% married couple fams. w. children; 56% college educ.; median household income: $38,865; per capita income: $18,360; median gross rent: $520; median house value: $91,300.

1992 Presidential Vote

Bush (R)	154,575	(54%)
Clinton (D)	85,357	(30%)
Perot (I)	42,724	(15%)

1988 Presidential Vote

Bush (R)	164,525	(73%)
Dukakis (D)	61,268	(27%)

Rep. Thomas J. Bliley, Jr. (R)

Elected 1980; b. Jan. 28, 1932, Chesterfield Cnty.; home, Richmond; Georgetown U., B.A. 1952; Catholic; married (Mary Virginia).

Career: Navy, 1952–55; Funeral home Dir., 1955–80; Richmond City Cncl. 1968–77, Vice Mayor 1968–70, Mayor, 1970–77.

DC Office: 2241 RHOB 20515, 202-225-2815; Fax: 202-225-0011.

District Offices: 4914 Fitzhugh Ave., #101, Richmond 23230, 804-771-2809.

Committees: *Commerce* (Chmn. of 26 R).

Group Ratings

	ADA	ACLU	COPE	CFA	LCV	CON	NSI	COC	ACU	NTLC	CHC
1994	0	18	11	20	0	74	100	100	100	96	100
1993	5	—	17	10	21	74	—	100	100	—	—

National Journal Ratings

	1993 LIB — 1993 CONS		1994 LIB — 1994 CONS	
Economic	0%	— 88%	26%	— 70%
Social	11%	— 82%	0%	— 89%
Foreign	17%	— 76%	25%	— 71%

Key Votes of the 103d Congress

1. Clinton Deficit Plan	N	3. Brady Handgun Purchase N	5. Lmt. UN Cmnd. of Forces Y
2. NAFTA	Y	4. Strike Race/Death Pnlty. Y	6. Cut Missile Funds N

Key Votes of the 104th Congress

1. Congressional Compliance Y	6. Reform Crime Grant Y	11. Loser Pays Court Reform Y
2. Balanced Budget Amndmt. Y	7. National Security Act Y	12. Product Liability Reform Y
3. Bar Unfunded Mandates Y	8. Moratorium on Regs. Y	13. Welfare Reform Y
4. Pass Line Item Veto Y	9. Risk Assessment on Regs. Y	14. Term Limits Amndmt. N
5. Relax Exclusionary Rule Y	10. Expnd. Priv. Prop. Rights Y	15. Tax Cuts Y

Election Results

1994 general	Thomas J. Bliley, Jr. (R)	176,941	(84%)	($572,427)
	Gerald E. (Jerry) Berg (I)	33,220	(16%)	
1994 primary	Thomas J. Bliley, Jr. (R) . . nominated by convention			
1992 general	Thomas J. Bliley, Jr. (R)	211,618	(83%)	($698,964)
	Gerald E. (Jerry) Berg (I)	43,267	(17%)	

EIGHTH DISTRICT

Two hundred years ago, when George Washington trod the brick sidewalks of Alexandria, Virginia, on his way to market or court or church, this was the largest city in northern Virginia, and dwarfed Georgetown, Maryland, just up the Potomac River; what is now Capitol Hill and downtown Washington were just hills above the river's mud flats. As Washington grew, Northern Virginia seemed left behind. The District of Columbia retroceded its land south of the

Potomac—now Alexandria and Arlington—to Virginia in 1846 because it seemed obvious that the federal government would never need it, and it was 97 years before the first federal building was built on the Virginia side—the Pentagon; Franklin Roosevelt wondered out loud what they would do with all that space after the war. When the Pentagon was built, Alexandria and the rural countryside of Northern Virginia were represented in Congress by Judge Howard W. Smith, a Byrd Democrat, who saw as his mission the maintenance of the standards of George Washington, Thomas Jefferson and Robert E. Lee. Yet by the 1960s, even as Judge Smith kept his law offices in Old Town, Alexandria, the area was changing around him. New subdivision dwellers with white-collar jobs and lots of children wanted schools with good academic programs—not the segregated schoolhouses Judge Smith's friends were willing to finance. They wanted freeways and traffic lights, planning instituted to regulate development, parks and recreation facilities. Smith's district was moved farther out into the countryside, two-party politics came to the suburbs, and local governments got to work. The congressional seat here, though often bitterly contested, was held from 1952–74 by Republican Joel Broyhill, a real estate developer who ran a fine constituency service operation in a district more than one-third of whose residents were federal employees. But Democrats won many legislative and local offices .

Now the onetime suburbs of Arlington and Alexandria have become central cities of a sort—edge cities, in Joel Garreau's term—themselves. Giant office developments sprang up from rail yards in Crystal City and from used car lots in Rosslyn. Vietnamese and other Asian-Americans have moved into these neighborhoods, and one of America's biggest Vietnamese commercial districts is in Clarendon, about a mile from Arlington National Cemetery and Fort Myer. Politically, this once hotly-contested territory is now solidly Democratic; Arlington and Alexandria voted for Chuck Robb over Oliver North 67%–24% in 1994.

The 8th Congressional District of Virginia consists of Arlington County and the cities of Alexandria and Falls Church. It also takes in two separate parts of Fairfax County—the portion of high-income McLean inside the Capital Beltway and several areas south of Alexandria's Old Town: the gentle landscapes of Mount Vernon, lower-income Groveton along the old U.S. 1, suburban Springfield and the more rural areas around Lorton prison and Fort Belvoir. This district was designed for the 1990s by a Democratic legislature and governor to be solidly Democratic. Where formerly, there had been two marginal Northern Virginia districts, now there is the safely Democratic 8th, the safely Republican 10th and the toss-up (Democratic in 1992, Republican in 1994) 11th.

The congressman from the 8th District is Jim Moran, an oft-embattled Alexandria politician with traces in his accent of his Massachusetts roots. He was elected to the Alexandria Council in 1979 and vice mayor in 1982; in 1984 he pleaded no contest to a conflict of interest charge and resigned from the Council. The charges were eventually dropped (the law he supposedly violated was even changed), and in 1985 Moran was elected mayor. In 1990, he ran for Congress in what had become one of the most populous districts in the country, stretching from Alexandria south almost to Fredericksburg; the incumbent was Stanford Parris, an old battler himself, elected congressman in 1972 and then again throughout the 1980s, candidate for governor of Virginia in 1989, and the Republican nominee in 1995 for a Northern Virginia Senate seat. It was one of the nastiest-tempered races of 1990: Parris said Moran was a supporter of Saddam Hussein; Moran said he wanted to "break [Parris's] nose," and called him "a deceitful, fatuous jerk." The major substantive issue was abortion, on which Moran ran a pro-choice ad portraying Lady Liberty behind bars. With a big margin in Alexandria, Moran won 52%–45%.

In the House, Moran was freshman class whip, but flip-flopped on his first big vote, the Gulf war resolution, which he ultimately voted against. He has engaged in a long and mostly unsuccessful fight to stop 11,000 Navy employees from being relocated out of Crystal City but he successfully fought Redskins owner Jack Kent Cooke's plan to build a football stadium at Potomac Yards in Alexandria. In 1992 he was greatly strengthened by redistricting but nevertheless had vigorous and acrimonious opposition from conservative Republican Kyle McSlarrow, in which both were prompted to confess youthful drug use; Moran won 56%–42%, a margin similar to the 14% by which Bill Clinton carried the district.

In the Clinton years Moran has sometimes been on the spot. In 1993 he voted for the Clinton budget and tax package, despite its one-year pay freeze on federal employees—a tough vote in a district where 21% of workers are federal employees, the second highest in the country (although it was much higher in this area, over 30%, 20 years ago). He switched his vote at the last minute in June 1994 to save NASA's space station. But he balked at the Clinton healthcare reform because it threatened federal employees' plan and blasted as "politically expedient" and based on "sound bites" the reinventing government plan as threatening the most talented federal employees. His proudest achievement in the 103d Congress was a law prohibiting state motor vehicle departments from disclosing information to people without legitimate business interests.

In 1994, Moran again was opposed by McSlarrow. But the tone was much less nasty. In August, Moran's three-year-old daughter was diagnosed with a malignant brain tumor. Campaigning became relatively low key for a while, and both candidates agreed on maintaining the existing federal healthcare plan; but McSlarrow and Moran both used negative ads in the closing days of the campaign. Moran won 59%–39%, with a vote paralleling Charles Robb's 60%–29% margin over Oliver North in the district. After the election, McSlarrow went to work as counsel for Senator Bob Dole. Moran went on to fight on 8th District issues, hoping to defend federal COLAs from budget cuts and restore military COLAs to civilian levels and working with area Republicans Frank Wolf and Tom Davis to close the District of Columbia's Lorton prison in Fairfax County. Moran was acting chairman of the moderate Mainstream Forum, but he also took occasional shots at the Contract With America. In January 1995, he got an amendment passed by voice vote barring suits that alleged unfunded mandates were halting the implementation of federal regulations; in March 1995, with Davis and Maryland Republican Connie Morella, he defeated a Republican effort to cut $12 billion in costs for the federal pension system that they said would amount to a tax hike for the average federal employee of $750 a year. The Republican takeover of the House was especially unpleasant for Moran, forcing him to give up his seat on the Appropriations Committee and redirecting his attention to the mundane but locally vital interests of the civil service.

The People: Pop. 1990: 562,808; 9% age 65+; 71% White; 13% Black; 7% Asian; 4% Other; 9% Hispanic origin. Voting age pop.: 454,220; 13% Black; 8% Hispanic origin. Households: 48% married couple families; 21% married couple fams. w. children; 71% college educ.; median household income: $48,839; per capita income: $24,799; median gross rent: $729; median house value: $210,200.

1992 Presidential Vote

Clinton (D)	133,183	(51%)
Bush (R)	96,799	(37%)
Perot (I)	28,967	(11%)

1988 Presidential Vote

Bush (R)	120,173	(53%)
Dukakis (D)	108,658	(47%)

Rep. James P. Moran, Jr. (D)

Elected 1990; b. May 16, 1945, Buffalo, NY; home, Alexandria; Col. of Holy Cross, B.A. 1967, City U. of NY, 1968, U. of Pittsburgh, M.P.A. 1970; Catholic; married (Mary).

Career: Budget analyst, auditor, U.S. Dept. of H.E.W., 1968–74; Fiscal policy spec., Library of Congress, 1974–76; Staff, U.S. Senate Approp. Cmte., 1976–80; Alexandria City Cncl., 1979–82; Alexandria Vice Mayor, 1982–84, Alexandria Mayor, 1984–90; Investment broker, 1980–88.

DC Office: 405 CHOB 20515, 202-225-4376; Fax: 202-225-0017.

District Offices: 5115 Franconia Rd., #B, Alexandria 22310, 703-971-4700.

Committees: *Government Reform & Oversight* (18th of 22 D): Civil Service (RMM). *International Relations* (19th of 19 D): International Operations and Human Rights.

Group Ratings

	ADA	ACLU	COPE	CFA	LCV	CON	NSI	COC	ACU	NTLC	CHC
1994	55	78	67	70	78	26	40	55	29	12	7
1993	80	—	92	100	86	27	—	27	8	—	—

National Journal Ratings

	1993 LIB — 1993 CONS		1994 LIB — 1994 CONS	
Economic	61%	— 37%	66%	— 33%
Social	80%	— 13%	63%	— 36%
Foreign	63%	— 34%	56%	— 44%

Key Votes of the 103d Congress

1. Clinton Deficit Plan	Y	3. Brady Handgun Purchase	Y	5. Lmt. UN Cmnd. of Forces	N
2. NAFTA	Y	4. Strike Race/Death Pnlty.	Y	6. Cut Missile Funds	N

Key Votes of the 104th Congress

1. Congressional Compliance	Y	6. Reform Crime Grant	N	11. Loser Pays Court Reform	N
2. Balanced Budget Amndmt.	Y	7. National Security Act	N	12. Product Liability Reform	Y
3. Bar Unfunded Mandates	Y	8. Moratorium on Regs.	N	13. Welfare Reform	N
4. Pass Line Item Veto	N	9. Risk Assessment on Regs.	Y	14. Term Limits Amndmt.	N
5. Relax Exclusionary Rule	Y	10. Expnd. Priv. Prop. Rights	N	15. Tax Cuts	N

Election Results

1994 general	James P. Moran Jr. (D)	120,281	(59%)	($910,239)
	Kyle E. McSlarrow (R)	79,568	(39%)	($643,979)
	Others	2,824	(1%)	
1994 primary	James P. Moran Jr. (D) . . . nominated by convention			
1992 general	James P. Moran Jr. (D)	138,542	(56%)	($923,999)
	Kyle E. McSlarrow (R)	102,717	(42%)	($424,895)
	Other	5,867	(2%)	

NINTH DISTRICT

One of the first areas to be settled from the seacoast to the great American interior was in what is now southwest Virginia. As early as 1765, settlements were carved out in the great Valley of Virginia, which bends westward and south toward Tennessee and the Cumberland Gap. Most settlers were of Scots-Irish lineage, and the mountainous area where they moved developed almost apart from the rest of Virginia. The fiercely independent settlers were first farmers, later often coal miners, as in West Virginia, which wasn't a separate state until 1863. Politically, this virtually all-white area opposed slavery and was skeptical if not hostile to the Confederacy. Out of the crucible of struggle between secessionists and unionists, southwest Virginia developed a robust two-party politics after the Civil War, with both parties resembling their national counterparts more closely than the rest of Virginia.

The 9th Congressional District of Virginia covers all of southwest Virginia west of Roanoke. Over the years, the district became known as the "Fighting Ninth," because of its taste for raucous politics, culturally conservative and economically populist. It is becoming somewhat more like the rest of Virginia, as development has moved down Interstate 81 to, and even past, Blacksburg, home of Virginia Tech. But mountain counties farther west have lost population and otherwise not changed much, and a bitter coal strike in 1990 showed that the old economic order and antagonisms had not entirely vanished.

The congressman from the 9th is Rick Boucher, a Democrat first elected in 1982 over a Republican incumbent. Boucher grew up in the antique town of Abingdon, went to the University of Virginia and practiced law, was elected to the Virginia Senate in 1975, at 29. In 1982 he ran against veteran incumbent William Wampler and won with big margins in the coal counties on the Kentucky border. Boucher, like other Fighting Ninth Democrats, tends to vote along national party lines, fairly liberal on economics and cultural issues, more conservative on foreign and defense policy. He has also taken a hand on major policy issues in the Commerce Committee. On telecommunications he has supported the baby Bells in their drive to erase the restrictions that keep them out of long distance, cable television and manufacturing, and he has worked to give investor-owned utilities the right to compete on a level field with cable companies and others offering an array of voice, video and data services over cooper or fiber-optic wires. He supported fellow Virginian and Commerce Chairman Tom Bliley's telco bill in committee in May 1995.

Given the robust partisan divisions in the Fighting Ninth, Boucher has been reelected pretty easily, partly because of the PAC fundraising prowess he has enjoyed as a Commerce Committee member. In 1994 he outspent his opponent $779,000 to $209,000, primarily because he raised $466,000 from PACs to the Republican's $7,000—and Boucher had $324,000 cash left over afterwards. With that advantage, Boucher won 59%–41%, impressive in a district where Oliver North led Charles Robb. But that advantage may not be as great in the future, and in the 104th Congress, Boucher parted company with Democrats on two major issues, product liability and crime—the only Democrat on the Judiciary Committee to do so. On product liability, he voted for national standards to limit litigation and for a cap on damages. On crime, while national Democrats were attacking Republicans for scaling back the 1994 bill, Boucher backed Republican proposals for block grants for police, backed, he said, by departments in his district, which got only four new police officers out of the 1994 bill. Whether those votes will keep Republicans away from his door remains to be seen.

The People: Pop. 1990: 562,508; 71% rural; 13% age 65+; 96% White; 2% Black; 1% Asian. Voting age pop.: 434,028; 2% Black. Households: 62% married couple families; 28% married couple fams. w. children; 30% college educ.; median household income: $20,857; per capita income: $10,097; median gross rent: $315; median house value: $49,100.

1992 Presidential Vote

Clinton (D) 99,099 (45%)
Bush (R) 93,673 (42%)
Perot (I)................... 26,676 (12%)

1988 Presidential Vote

Bush (R) 108,448 (55%)
Dukakis (D)................. 88,263 (45%)

Rep. Rick Boucher (D)

Elected 1982; b. Aug. 1, 1946, Abingdon; home, Abingdon; Roanoke Col., B.A. 1968, U. of VA, J.D. 1971; United Methodist; single.

Career: Practicing atty., 1971–83; VA Senate, 1975–1983.

DC Office: 2245 RHOB 20515, 202-225-3861; Fax: 202-225-0442; e-mail: ninthnet@hr.house.gov.

District Offices: 188 E. Main St., Abingdon 24210, 703-628-1145; 311 Shawnee Ave., Big Stone Gap 24219, 703-523-5450; and 112 N. Washington Ave., Pulaski 24301, 703-980-4310.

Committees: *Commerce* (8th of 21 D): Commerce, Trade and Hazardous Materials; Telecommunications and Finance. *Judiciary* (6th of 15 D): Courts and Intellectual Property.

Group Ratings

	ADA	ACLU	COPE	CFA	LCV	CON	NSI	COC	ACU	NTLC	CHC
1994	65	55	67	70	67	1	50	42	30	15	21
1993	60	—	100	90	69	4	—	30	13	—	—

National Journal Ratings

	1993 LIB — 1993 CONS	1994 LIB — 1994 CONS
Economic	75% — 22%	73% — 17%
Social	62% — 38%	57% — 43%
Foreign	66% — 31%	48% — 51%

Key Votes of the 103d Congress

1. Clinton Deficit Plan	Y	3. Brady Handgun Purchase	N	5. Lmt. UN Cmnd. of Forces	N
2. NAFTA	N	4. Strike Race/Death Pnlty.	N	6. Cut Missile Funds	N

Key Votes of the 104th Congress

1. Congressional Compliance	Y	6. Reform Crime Grant	N	11. Loser Pays Court Reform	N
2. Balanced Budget Amndmt.	N	7. National Security Act	N	12. Product Liability Reform	Y
3. Bar Unfunded Mandates	Y	8. Moratorium on Regs.	N	13. Welfare Reform	N
4. Pass Line Item Veto	N	9. Risk Assessment on Regs.	N	14. Term Limits Amndmt.	N
5. Relax Exclusionary Rule	N	10. Expnd. Priv. Prop. Rights	N	15. Tax Cuts	N

Election Results

1994 general	Rick Boucher (D) 102,876	(59%)	($779,616)
	S. H. (Steve) Fast (R)................. 72,133	(41%)	($209,235)
1994 primary	Rick Boucher (D) .... nominated by convention		
1992 general	Rick Boucher (D) 133,284	(63%)	($660,452)
	L. Garrett (Gary) Weddle (R) 77,985	(37%)	($100,089)

TENTH DISTRICT

Even as the Constitution was being hammered out in Philadelphia, the rolling green Piedmont of northern Virginia and the fertile mountain-bound lands of the Shenandoah Valley were buzzing with new settlers. They came up the rivers that flow into the Chesapeake, into the Valley from the great Wagon Road south from Pennsylvania, moving onto lands speculated on by George Washington and his peers. During the Civil War, this was some of the most heavily contested land on the continent; afterwards, the surge of movement having propelled new settlers much farther west, this part of Virginia was well-settled and became prime fox hunting country. Subdivisions are sprouting up on fields, and the horse farms of the Piedmont, long first or second homes of some of the richest people in America, are attracting a growing population of Washington, D.C. commuters and weekend residents. What looked like marginal farmlands to the settlers of the early 19th Century now looks like heaven for city-dwellers: bucolic green hills with views of the Blue Ridge and other mountains, antique houses and tiny crossroads communities. There is still an old-fashioned air in the narrow streets of the old county seat towns, but a McDonald's culture has developed on the bypass roads on their outskirts.

The 10th Congressional District of Virginia covers much of this territory. This district has expanded as people have moved outward; today it is entirely, in the familiar phrase, outside the Beltway. About one-third of its people live in suburban Fairfax County, by many measures the most affluent county in the United States: 61% of its households had incomes over $50,000 in 1989, number one in the country, though it was only number seven in percentage of over $100,000 households. Also, 49% of its adults over 25 were college graduates, more than double the national figure. Fairfax, and especially the 10th's portion of it—affluent and woodsy Great Falls and parts of McLean, the new subdivisions around the old crossroads of Centreville and the upscale Fair Oaks shopping mall area—is full of high-salaried, two-earner families, young and well-educated, employed more often by the private sector than by government, frazzled by commuting on clogged roads. Beyond Fairfax, another one-third of 10th District residents live in Loudoun and parts of Prince William County, once rural—the Manassas battlefield is here—but now heavily settled, not as high-income or well-educated as Fairfax nor as culturally liberal. The last third of the 10th's residents are in smaller, still rural-appearing Fauquier and Rappahannock Counties and west of the Blue Ridge in the Shenandoah Valley. Politically, this is a very Republican district. The Shenandoah tradition of Harry Byrd Democrats switched seamlessly to Republicanism, as indeed many local politicians switched parties themselves; the new suburbanites are if anything more determinedly Republican.

The congressman from the 10th District is Frank Wolf, now chairman of the Transportation Appropriations Subcommittee. Wolf is a native of Philadelphia who went to school at Georgetown University, was an appointee in the Nixon and Ford Administrations, then ran for Congress in 1980, when most of the 10th District was inside the Beltway. He beat a Democratic incumbent and as the 10th has moved outward, and as he has worked hard on federal employee, transportation and other issues, he has become unbeatable. His overall voting record is mostly conservative. He has long maintained a crackerjack constituency service operation and has been key in promoting federal employee causes. He has promoted on-site child care centers at federal workplaces and pushed federal telecommuting (the first center was in Winchester). He opposed the Clinton budget and tax package because of general tax issues and limits on federal pay increases. But he stood up against Hatch Act repeal, saying it would politicize the federal work force. He opposed the Clinton healthcare reform in 1994 because it would have gutted the federal employees healthcare plan, and he opposed the Contract With America tax cut in 1995 because it would have required higher pension payments by federal employees; he and Tom Davis and Maryland's Connie Morella were three of only 11 Republicans who voted against the tax cut.

Wolf has long labored hard to improve transportation in traffic-choked northern Virginia. He used his Transportation Appropriations seat to get funding for the 103-mile Metro subway system, for I-66 from the Beltway to Gainesville, for the Route 234 interchange in Manassas, for express buses in the Dulles Airport corridor. He led the move to put National and Dulles Airports under a regional authority and pushed to get the National Air and Space Museum annex located at Dulles. He worked to get the National Science Foundation relocated to a high-rise in Arlington and, with Davis and Democrat Jim Moran, is working to phase out the District of Columbia's Lorton Prison in Fairfax County. Wolf protests that he is not a believer in pork barrel projects. He forced Senator Robert Byrd, from next-door West Virginia, to scale way back the highway demonstration projects earmarked for West Virginia in 1994—Wolf called it "highway robbery"—and in 1995 he announced that as subcommittee chairman he would recommend funding no demonstration projects—putting him on a crash course with Byrd and House Transportation and Infrastructure Committee Chairman Bud Shuster.

Wolf has gone afield, to China and Serbia, to back human rights, and has sought to increase penalties on businesses who knowingly import prison-made goods from such countries and successfully worked to withdraw most favored nation status from Serbia in 1992. He worked doggedly to find out how many non-employees had White House passes and to get campaign consultants with passes to make financial disclosures. He was prime sponsor of the move to increase the personal tax exemption for children under 18 from $2,050 to $3,500, with a goal of $6,000 by 2000. This would move the deduction back toward the value it had in real dollars following World War II, when it was the functional equivalent of a children's allowance and helped stimulate the postwar baby boom, with the family stability and economic growth many Americans would like to see again.

The People: Pop. 1990: 562,257; 44% rural; 7% age 65+; 89% White; 6% Black; 3% Asian; 1% Other; 2% Hispanic origin. Voting age pop.: 411,700; 6% Black; 2% Hispanic origin. Households: 67% married couple families; 35% married couple fams. w. children; 55% college educ.; median household income: $46,205; per capita income: $20,065; median gross rent: $657; median house value: $155,000.

1992 Presidential Vote			1988 Presidential Vote		
Bush (R)	124,783	(50%)	Bush (R)	132,359	(69%)
Clinton (D)	83,214	(33%)	Dukakis (D)	59,465	(31%)
Perot (I)	41,228	(16%)			

Rep. Frank R. Wolf (R)

Elected 1980; b. Jan. 30, 1939, Philadelphia, PA; home, Vienna; PA St. U., B.A. 1961; Georgetown, LL.B. 1965; Presbyterian; married (Carolyn).

Career: Army, 1962–63, Army Reserves 1963–67; Legis. Asst., U.S. Rep. Edward Biester, 1968–71; Asst., U.S. Interior Secy. Rogers Morton, 1971–74; Dep. Asst. Secy., U.S. Dept. of Interior, 1974–75; Practicing atty., 1975–80.

DC Office: 241 CHOB 20515, 202-225-5136; Fax: 202-225-0437.

District Offices: 13873 Park Center Rd., Herndon 22075, 703-709-5800; and 110 N. Cameron St., Winchester 22601, 703-667-0990.

Committees: *Appropriations* (10th of 32 R): Foreign Operations, Export Financing, and Related Programs; Transportation (Chmn.); Treasury, Postal Service, and General Government.

Group Ratings

	ADA	ACLU	COPE	CFA	LCV	CON	NSI	COC	ACU	NTLC	CHC
1994	0	13	33	20	22	63	100	83	86	89	100
1993	10	—	0	30	14	57	—	91	92	—	—

National Journal Ratings

	1993 LIB	—	1993 CONS		1994 LIB	—	1994 CONS
Economic	23%	—	75%		34%	—	64%
Social	27%	—	72%		20%	—	77%
Foreign	9%	—	85%		30%	—	70%

Key Votes of the 103d Congress

1. Clinton Deficit Plan	N	3. Brady Handgun Purchase	Y	5. Lmt. UN Cmnd. of Forces	Y
2. NAFTA	Y	4. Strike Race/Death Pnlty.	Y	6. Cut Missile Funds	N

Key Votes of the 104th Congress

1. Congressional Compliance	Y	6. Reform Crime Grant	Y	11. Loser Pays Court Reform	Y
2. Balanced Budget Amndmt.	Y	7. National Security Act	N	12. Product Liability Reform	Y
3. Bar Unfunded Mandates	Y	8. Moratorium on Regs.	Y	13. Welfare Reform	Y
4. Pass Line Item Veto	Y	9. Risk Assessment on Regs.	Y	14. Term Limits Amndmt.	Y
5. Relax Exclusionary Rule	Y	10. Expnd. Priv. Prop. Rights	Y	15. Tax Cuts	N

Election Results

1994 general	Frank R. Wolf (R)	153,311	(87%)	($222,532)
	Alan R. Ogden (I)	13,687	(8%)	
	Robert L. (Bob) Rilee (I)	8,267	(5%)	
1994 primary	Frank R. Wolf (R)	nominated by convention		
1992 general	Frank R. Wolf (R)	144,471	(64%)	($431,829)
	Raymond E. (Ray) Vickery, Jr. (D)	75,775	(33%)	($191,260)
	Other	6,945	(3%)	

ELEVENTH DISTRICT

When author and *Washington Post* reporter Joel Garreau coined the term "edge city" some years ago to describe the autonomous urban centers developing on the rims of some of the nation's oldest municipalities, his prime example was Tysons Corner, Virginia. Rising on a hill west of Washington, Tysons Corner was a back-country intersection 50 years ago and a junction of several suburban roads 25 years ago; today it is home to the largest concentration of office space to be found anywhere between Washington and Atlanta, with a modern skyline and busy multi-lane avenues that serve as arteries to the nearby Capital Beltway. Fairfax County, which includes all of Tysons Corner, has changed just as dramatically since the end of World War II. At first only a few District of Columbia residents seeking breathing room in the suburbs trickled into Northern Virginia; initially they went to Arlington and Alexandria. But that trickle became a rush as young marrieds with large families and whites avoiding the increasingly high-crime District pushed farther out into Fairfax. Now Fairfax County is no longer Washington's country cousin. It has the nation's highest median household income—$59,284 in 1990, almost half its residents have a bachelor's degree or more, and nearly 70% of its households have two or more vehicles. Gradually but inexorably, Fairfax has been transformed from a suburban county where people commute to Washington to government jobs, to a 21st Century urban county where people work somewhere around the Beltway and mostly for private sector employers.

The 11th Congressional District of Virginia, the new seat gained in the 1990 Census, went to fast-growing Fairfax County and its neighbor just to the south, Prince William County. The 11th straddles the Beltway; its inner portion includes older but still affluent areas like Annandale, which has an increasing Asian-American population, while the outer portion spans Tysons Corner and the office corridor out the Dulles Access Road, to Dulles Airport. The 11th also runs south through new subdivision areas like Burke and covers the somewhat lower-income Woodbridge and Dale City areas of Prince William. This is a cosmopolitan district: 8% black, 7% Hispanic, 8% Asian; 19% of residents speak a language other than English at home. The district is also made up largely of two-income families, with at least one spouse employed in one of the many divisions of high-tech companies like Computer Sciences, AT&T or Honeywell, that dot Fairfax County. The federal government is also a presence here, sometimes a spooky one: in 1994 the Senate Intelligence Committee revealed that a $310 million, 3,500-employee four-building complex near Dulles Airport was being built not for Rockwell International but for the National Reconnaissance Office, our spy satellite agency. Politically, the 11th's educated, mobile electorate produces a robust two-party politics. In the 1980s, it voted Republican for president, with both Democratic and Republican state legislators; in the 1990s it voted by the narrowest of margins for George Bush, but again for legislators of both parties.

The congressman from the 11th District is Thomas Davis III, formerly chairman of the Fairfax County Board of Supervisors, a Republican who won the seat in 1994 from Virginia's first woman representative, Democrat Leslie Byrne, who was elected in 1992. Davis grew up in northern Virginia, was a friend of David Eisenhower at Amherst College, served on active duty in the Army before earning a law degree, and was first elected to the Board of Supervisors, a high visibility position here, in 1979. Over the years, he gained a reputation for financial savvy in municipal matters and for seeking compromise over confrontation. Nonetheless, he was willing to challenge the aggressive Byrne, who won the seat by treating Republican Henry Butler with contempt and labelling him an "extremist," and then voted solidly for Clinton Administration positions and called for discipline against members of the Democratic Caucus who did not. Byrne had solid support from labor and feminist groups, and spent $1.1 million, $455,000 of it raised from PACs. But Davis, with his connections, was able to raise and spend even more, $1.4 million. Byrne blasted Davis for not forcefully condemning efforts by conservative Christian activists to restrict youngsters' library access to books on homosexuality and the occult and stop the distribution of a homosexual newspaper in Fairfax County libraries. Davis, in turn, accused Byrne of overstating her support from the business community and of falsely claiming to be a fiscal conservative in a desperate attempt not to fall behind in fund raising. Davis won 53%–45%, a considerable achievement in these straight-ticket times, since Republican Oliver North trailed Democrat Charles Robb in the 11th by 51%–36%. It may also be a harbinger of what will happen when Republican challengers no longer have to battle against the huge PAC money advantage most Democratic incumbents enjoyed in 1994 but will surely not in 1996.

As soon as he arrived on Capitol Hill, Davis was handed by Speaker Newt Gingrich one of the hottest potatoes to fall into the hands of the new Congress: staunching the District of Columbia's ever-deepening river of red ink. As chairman of the House Government Reform and Oversight Committee's District of Columbia subcommittee, Davis first rejected D.C. Mayor Marion Barry's request for massive federal aid, insisting instead on a specific plan to cut District spending and payrolls. In this he worked closely with Gingrich and District Delegate Eleanor Holmes Norton; together they backed in March 1995 a law creating a five-member financial control board to oversee District of Columbia finances. Davis made his mark in other ways as well. He opposed the Contract With America tax cut in 1995 because it would have required higher pension payments by federal employees; he and suburban Washington's Frank Wolf and Connie Morella were three of only 11 Republicans who voted against the tax cut. Also, with Wolf and Democrat Jim Moran, he backed a bill to close the District of Columbia's Lorton Prison in Fairfax County.

Byrne is reportedly considering a rematch in 1996, although she might challenge John Warner for the Senate instead. The 11th may be seriously contested again, but if 1994 is any indication, Davis should have great strength going into the race.

The People: Pop. 1990: 562,596; 2% rural; 6% age 65+; 76% White; 8% Black; 8% Asian; 3% Other; 7% Hispanic origin. Voting age pop.: 420,391; 7% Black; 7% Hispanic origin. Households: 62% married couple families; 33% married couple fams. w. children; 71% college educ.; median household income: $54,369; per capita income: $22,202; median gross rent: $797; median house value: $190,400.

1992 Presidential Vote			1988 Presidential Vote		
Bush (R)	103,907	(43%)	Bush (R)	128,333	(61%)
Clinton (D)	102,721	(42%)	Dukakis (D)	82,819	(39%)
Perot (I)	34,719	(14%)			

Rep. Tom Davis (R)

Elected 1994; b. Jan. 5, 1949, Minot, ND; home, Falls Church; Amherst Col. B.A. 1971; U. of VA, J.D. 1975; Christian Scientist; married (Peggy).

Career: Army, 1971–72; Army Reserves, 1972–79; Vice Pres. & Gen. Cnsl., PRC Inc., 1977–94; Fairfax Cnty. Bd. of Supervisors, 1979–94, Chmn., 1991–94.

DC Office: 415 CHOB 20515, 202-225-1492; Fax: 202-225-3071.

District Offices: 7018 Evergreen Ct., Annandale 22003, 703-916-9610.

Committees: *Government Reform & Oversight* (13th of 27 R): District of Columbia (Chmn.); Government Management, Information and Technology; Human Resources and Intergovernmental Affairs. *Science* (18th of 27 R): Energy and Environment; Space and Aeronautics.

Group Ratings and 103rd Congress Votes: Newly Elected

Key Votes of the 104th Congress

1. Congressional Compliance	Y	6. Reform Crime Grant	Y	11. Loser Pays Court Reform	Y
2. Balanced Budget Amndmt.	Y	7. National Security Act	Y	12. Product Liability Reform	Y
3. Bar Unfunded Mandates	Y	8. Moratorium on Regs.	Y	13. Welfare Reform	Y
4. Pass Line Item Veto	Y	9. Risk Assessment on Regs.	Y	14. Term Limits Amndmt.	Y
5. Relax Exclusionary Rule	Y	10. Expnd. Priv. Prop. Rights	Y	15. Tax Cuts	N

Election Results

1994 general	Tom Davis (R)	98,216	(53%)	($1,430,272)
	Leslie L. Byrne (D)	84,104	(45%)	($1,136,669)
	Others	3,360	(2%)	
1994 primary	Tom Davis (R)	nominated by convention		
1992 general	Leslie L. Byrne (D)	114,172	(50%)	($773,128)
	Henry N. Butler (R)	103,119	(45%)	($844,695)
	Others	10,981	(5%)	

WASHINGTON

From Starbuck's coffee to grunge music, from America's leading exporter Boeing to America's leading software maker Microsoft, Washington—the state at the far northwest corner of the continental United States, not Washington, D.C.—has become a national trend-setter. An unusual environment and human creativity have combined to produce these achievements: Seattle's cold misty air stimulates the appetite for strong aromatic coffee and the shapeless blue jeans and sweatshirts that are worn year-round in this moist climate created a trend made famous by Nirvana and Soundgarden and other grunge groups. Boeing's airframe business took off in World War II because of the Pacific Northwest's cheap hydroelectric power and cheap aluminum, and through booms and busts Boeing has just kept growing. Microsoft, founded by the usually tieless and tousle-haired Bill Gates and based in Redmond, Washington, became one of America's great success stories as its software business boomed, while the hardware business soured and IBM, with its white shirts and plain ties, laid off thousands. With its flannel shirts and umbrellas, its blue-collar types working off a hangover as if in a Raymond Carver story and its professionals relaxing on woodsy acreage, Washington has set a tone for the 1990s, a style plainly Middle American but with attitude, an ordinariness that is so apt it is no longer ordinary.

All this comes to a state barely a century old, which in the two decades after statehood in 1889 built a new civilization, as transcontinental railroads reached the great ports of Puget Sound, the wheat-processing city of Spokane inland, orchard towns and fishing ports and lumber settlements. Shielded from the heavy rains and storms of the Pacific by the Olympic Mountains and the Sound, Seattle quickly became a serious American city, a lusty town full of lumbermen and railroad workers. When gold was struck in the Klondike and Alaska, it became a metropolis of miners, prospectors and get-rich-quick operators, the site of the original "Skid Road" (skid row is a corruption propagated by a 1937 magazine article), where logs were rolled downhill to the port; today it's the center of the restored Pioneer Square area. This booming, young Seattle had a turbulent class-warfare politics in the years before World War I, pitting the Industrial Workers of the World (the IWW, or Wobblies) against city business and civic leaders; the businessmen, brutally, prevailed. Adding to the area's distinctiveness was its large numbers of Scandinavian immigrants, more favorable to cooperative enterprises and government ownership than other Americans.

Over time, Washington was transformed by a series of national decisions which set the course of its development for decades. One was government development of hydroelectric power. The Columbia River and its tributary, the Snake, falling thousands of feet in a relatively short distance, had far greater hydroelectric potential than any other American river system, and Franklin Roosevelt was always interested in these river valley projects. In 1937, Bonneville Dam was completed on the lower Columbia; in 1940, Grand Coulee Dam, the largest man-made structure in the world at the time, was opened where the Columbia cuts through the arid, surrealistically contoured plains of eastern Washington. Washington proved hospitable to the industrial union movement of the 1930s and became one of the nation's most heavily unionized states. When war came, Washington's hydroelectric power—the cheapest electricity in the country—made it the natural site for huge aluminum production plants, which require vast amounts of electricity, and the Seattle area became the home not only of shipbuilders, but of the biggest aircraft manufacturer in the country, Boeing. After the war, the Hanford plant on the Columbia was one of the government's main nuclear weapons manufacturing sites. Cheap power, aluminum, aircraft, nuclear weapons and high unionized wages: these became Washington's economic foundations in the post-World War II years.

Today, Washington is a commonwealth of more than five million, economically booming,

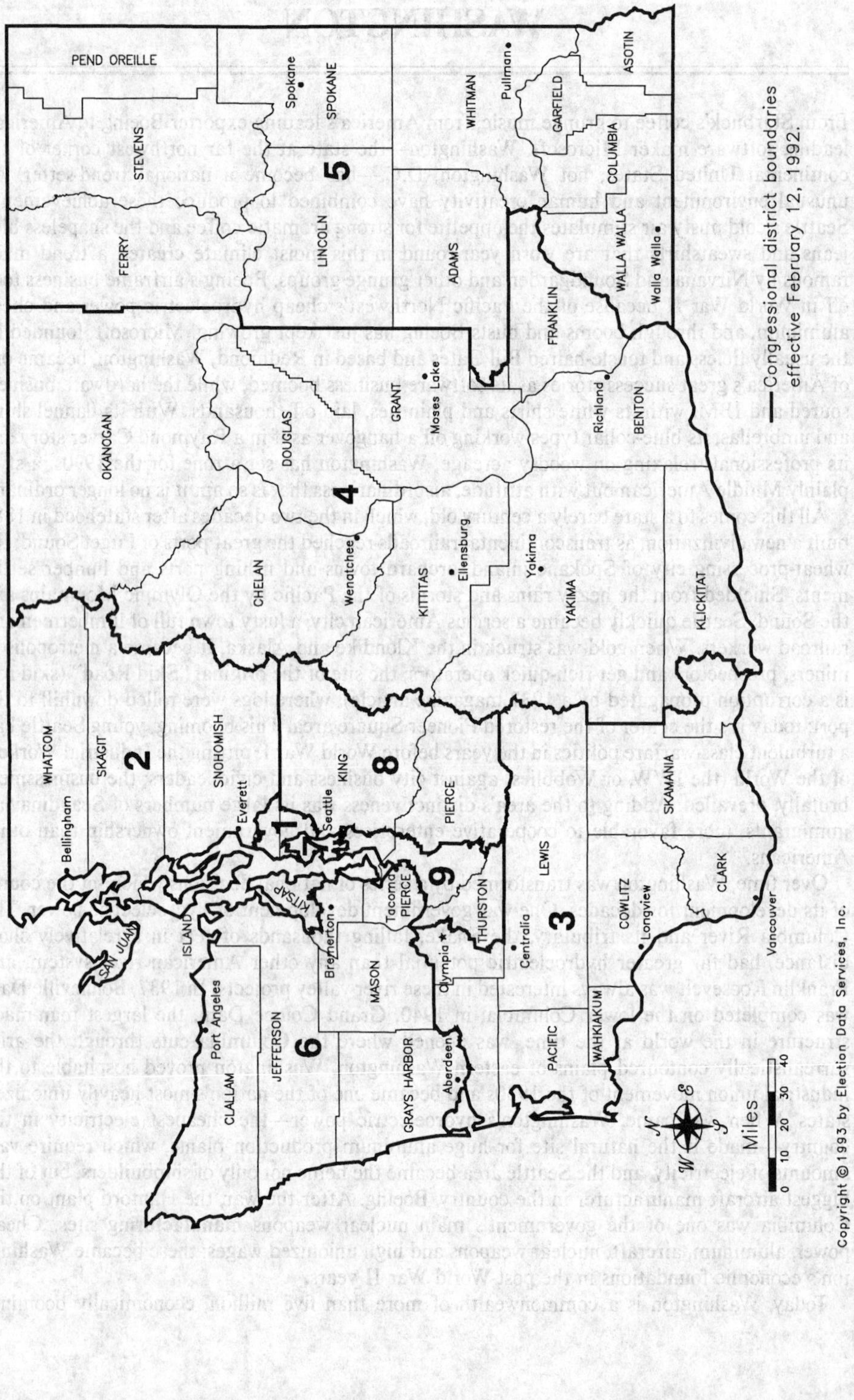

Congressional district boundaries
effective February 12, 1992.

PEND OREILLE

STEVENS

FERRY

OKANOGAN

WHATCOM

SKAGIT

Bellingham

SNOHOMISH

Everett

KING

Seattle

ISLAND

SAN JUAN

CLALLAM

Port Angeles

JEFFERSON

MASON

Bremerton

KITSAP

Tacoma

PIERCE

Olympia

THURSTON

GRAYS HARBOR

Aberdeen

MASON

PACIFIC

WAHKIAKUM

Longview

COWLITZ

LEWIS

Centralia

CLARK

Vancouver

SKAMANIA

KLICKITAT

YAKIMA

Yakima

KITTITAS

Ellensburg

CHELAN

Wenatchee

DOUGLAS

GRANT

Moses Lake

LINCOLN

Spokane

SPOKANE

ADAMS

FRANKLIN

BENTON

Richland

WALLA WALLA

Walla Walla

COLUMBIA

GARFIELD

ASOTIN

WHITMAN

Pullman

Miles

0   10   20   30   40

N
W   E
S

pleased to the point of smugness with its physical environment. But it has potential problems: it remains uncomfortably dependent on Boeing and the inherently unstable airframe business; payrolls can go up and down and many people here still remember how Boeing pared its payroll from 100,000 to 38,000 between 1967 and 1971. There were 12,000 layoffs projected for 1995. The Columbia basin's hydroelectric capacity has been used up, and electricity rates are now above national levels. The Hanford Works for years leaked radioactive waste, which must now be cleaned up at the cost of billions, while new underground storage procedures have been criticized as unsafe. Washington's apples, half the nation's production, are barred from obvious markets like Japan and China. Then there is the spotted owl. After a federal judge in Seattle ruled that old growth forests must be left uncut to preserve the apparently endangered spotted owl, thousands of logging jobs have been lost and whole communities left idle; President Clinton's April 1993 timber summit in Portland produced a compromise which kept production low.

Yet these are footnotes to what is mainly the story of success. Look at a map that shows elevation of mountains and density of population. On both sides of the Pacific, vast numbers of people are squeezed into small margins of level land between steeply rising volcanic mountains and the sea, or tucked into valleys. These islands of settlement are surrounded by vast wildernesses—desert and mountains, open sea and Arctic lands. Yet the inhabitants of these pockets of the Pacific Rim have, over the past two or three decades, produced more economic growth than anywhere else in the world. This has happened despite the widely diverse, sometimes hostile, ethnic groups: the Japanese and Koreans, the Chinese of Taiwan, Hong Kong and Singapore, the Malays and Filipinos; and Washington's ethnic mix of Scandinavians, Yankees and new migrants.

Politically, Washington, with its Scandinavian and labor union heritage, was once one of the most Democratic states: Roosevelt campaign manager James Farley used to refer to "the 47 states and the Soviet of Washington." Its mainstream Democrats, notably Warren Magnuson and Henry Jackson who represented the state in Congress for a total of 87 years, believed in an active and compassionate federal government that built dams, aluminum plants and the Hanford Works at home, and pursued an internationalist, anti-Communist foreign policy abroad. Their political strength was built on a blue-collar base, augmented by the respect the leaders of the state's big businesses had for their clout in the capital. In today's Washington, the fulcrum of the electorate has moved from blue-collar to white-collar, from economic class warfare to cultural wars between liberals and conservatives. Washington moved toward the Democrats in the 1980s, and Michael Dukakis's 50%–48% victory here foreshadowed Bill Clinton's 43%–32% win in 1992, with a big 24% for Ross Perot. The Democratic trend swept down the ballot: Seattle liberal Patty Murray was elected senator and Mike Lowry governor, and Democrats won eight out of nine House seats, winning the House vote 56%–41%. Then in 1994 the pendulum went the other way. Republican Senator Slade Gorton was reelected 56%–44% and Republicans won seven of the nine House seats, carrying the House vote 51%–49%—a 10% gain. Most startling was the defeat after 30 years of House Speaker Thomas Foley.

Yet it should be added that in this cultural war Washington remains closely divided. The central city of Seattle is increasingly the liberal bastion, as old blue-collar strongholds have soured on the Democrats; Republicans run best, but not way ahead, in the arid country east of the Cascades. Referenda show how closely Washington can be divided. In 1991 it rejected a "death with dignity" measure heavily opposed by Catholic and traditionalist Protestant churches, 54%–46%; in 1992 it narrowly approved a measure codifying *Roe v. Wade*. In 1991 it rejected a term limits initiative which would have applied limits immediately to incumbents; but in 1992 it adopted 52%–48% the prospective term limits which Foley challenged in court—a case that became a major issue in his defeat. Republicans now seem in the ascendancy, but only by narrow margins; results in 1996 may depend on which side has the enthusiasm and elan that Democrats had in 1992 and Republicans in 1994.

Governor. Washington is one of the few states with an avowedly liberal Democratic governor,

Mike Lowry, elected in 1992. He is a political veteran, a state legislative staffer in 1969, at 30, then a King County councilman, elected to Congress from the liberal Seattle district for a decade starting in 1978, a loser in Senate races to Daniel Evans in 1983 and Slade Gorton in 1988, then a 52% winner in the Democratic *annus mirabilis* of 1992. In his first two years in office, he enacted a liberal platform, with a tax increase, a Youth Agenda that tried to get at the roots of youth violence and a healthcare reform aimed at covering the uninsured, especially children. But his job rating languished in the 30s and in 1994 Republicans captured the state House.

The new Republican legislature rolled back Lowry's tax increases and healthcare program, which was similar to the Clinton plan. The legislature repealed key provisions (employer mandates and insurance premium caps) but kept provisions for the portability of coverage and increased services to the poor. Passed with a veto proof majority and faced with a new political reality, Lowry signed the bill. The legislature also passed its own welfare reform, with a two-year limit on benefits and denial of aid to teenage welfare mothers. But the biggest headlines came in February 1995 when Lowry was accused by a former staffer of sexual harassment. He denied the charges and asked for an independent investigation; in the days that followed two other aides, both women, also resigned, one of whom had represented the accuser of former Senator Brock Adams, who after sexual harassment charges declined to run for reelection in 1992. The 51-page report concluded that Lowry was not guilty of sexual harassment, though he had "touched her in ways she found offensive." The staffer, expecting to be vindicated by the report, attempted suicide by taking prescription drugs. Her lawyer said that if Lowry's actions (repeated touching of her leg, neck and midriff) does not constitute sexual harassment, what does? In May 1995, Lowry was severely criticized by womens' groups who either did not believe the report or thought him "too cocky in his insistence that the report cleared him."

A raft of Republicans lined up to oppose Lowry in 1996, and there was talk that he might have a primary opponent as well. Possible candidates include Nona Brazier, a black businesswoman who sees "the liberal establishment as the cause, not the cure for the inner cities"; former state Senator Ellen Craswell, a former anti-tax crusader and now religious-inspired conservative; former Attorney General Ken Eikenberry, who lost to Lowry in 1992 and became state party chairman; House Majority Leader Dale Foreman, with a base in agricultural eastern Washington; Senate Republican Leader Dan McDonald; and King County Prosecutor Norman Maleng.

Senators. Slade Gorton, a Republican first elected in 1980, defeated in 1986, then elected again in 1988 and 1994, is Washington's senior senator. He moved to the state in the 1950s, was elected to the legislature in 1958, at 30, was elected attorney general for 12 years starting in 1968, and in 1980 challenged and beat 75-year-old Senator Warren Magnuson. During all of that time Gorton had a reputation as a liberal Republican, with a political base in Seattle. But starting in 1988, when his opponent was Mike Lowry, now governor, he appealed more to rural and working class areas, stressing his sympathy for loggers whose jobs were endangered by environmental rules and calling for conversion of the Hanford nuclear power plant to an environmental clean-up facility.

Gorton thus favors major revision of the Endangered Species Act, but he takes positions backed by environmentalists—stronger laws against driftnet fishing, federal funding of recreational trails. He supports some increased regulation—CAFE standards for higher gas mileage for autos, requiring airbags in all cars, banning trucks from carrying toxic materials on one trip and foodstuffs the next. But he is also the leading Republican sponsor of the product liability bill, setting uniform standards for the states, which after being blocked in 1994 passed the Senate in May 1995. He tends to Washington state issues: he is against an airline fuel tax increase and Airbus unfair trade practices (these are Boeing gripes), he is for tug escorts for oil tankers in Puget Sound, he found a new buyer to keep the Mariners baseball team in Seattle, and he worked to open an Olympic Peninsula summer camp closed by "an overzealous, uncaring federal bureaucracy." He favored banning the federal standards in history because they were "ideology masquerading as history." In May 1995, he urged colleagues to participate in a meaningful debate on the budget and called the House proposal for cutting raxes, "a dead horse."

Gorton's overall voting record is about two-thirds conservative, enough to leave him at risk in liberal western Washington, but not enough to be trusted by conservative Republican senators: he lost a race for Republican whip to incumbent Alan Simpson in December 1992 by 25–14, and in early 1993 he looked to be in trouble for reelection at home. But Democrats' best-known candidates—former Governor Booth Gardner, Seattle Mayor Norm Rice—declined to run. He ran as "an independent voice," an implicit concession that his views were by no means universally popular. Washington's open primary, which allows voters to switch between parties, often gives a good forecast of the election: Gorton, with only nuisance Republican opposition, won 53% of total vote, while the Democratic nomination went to King County Councilman Ron Sims over talk show host Mike James by 17%–14%. Sims is black, a New Democrat, a fiscal conservative who kept a total of adds and would not close the county budget until it was matched by deletes; he claimed hands-on experience with social problems from street kids to day care. But he was no match for the articulate Gorton in debate and the incumbent outspent him by $4.8 million to $1.2 million. Gorton won 56%–44%, losing King County but carrying working class enclaves in most of the rest of the state and running very strong in the east.

Washington's junior senator is Patty Murray, one of those 1992 winners who would have seemed an unlikely victor in any previous year, but was an unstoppable force in what many called "the year of the woman." A dozen years earlier, when she was in Olympia trying to save a parent education class she was teaching at Shoreline Community College from being cut from the budget, a state legislator told her gruffly, "You're just a mom in tennis shoes; you can't make a difference." But, like many committed public employees, she won her fight; then she ran for the school board, lost, was appointed and then elected, and served as president. In 1988, she challenged a Republican state senator, knocked on 17,000 doors, and won the seat. Her first great cause there was extending a family leave bill to include leave for a parent whose child is sick or dying; she threatened to put the issue on the ballot, and won the issue; she worked on school bus safety, "negative option" mail orders, accidental pesticide exposure—the warp and woof of everyday life. Then in late 1991, she decided to run against U.S. Senator Brock Adams, who was under a cloud from charges of sexual harassment and molestation; but he decided not to run.

Suddenly Murray was, if not a favorite, in a position of visibility in what was starting to look like a Democratic year. She was joined in the primary by former Congressman Don Bonker, who had run and narrowly lost a Senate nomination in 1988; he brought a record on trade and a home base in the logging country in western Washington. Republican Congressman Rod Chandler, a booming voiced former TV reporter and 10-year congressman, had a moderate image and backing in Washington, D.C. Onetime Vietnam POW Leo Thorsness, who nearly beat Senator George McGovern in 1974 when he lived in South Dakota, was also in the Washington Senate, where he turned back his pay raise. King County Executive Tim Hill, a Seattle moderate, brought a record on local issues and defiance of anti-abortion delegates at the state party convention. But it was Murray, with her flat accent and her "mom in tennis shoes" line who attracted voters' attention, even while she captured union endorsements. In the September primary, she had 28% of the vote to 19% for Bonker; on the Republican side, Chandler's 20% edged Thorsness's 16% and Hill's 11%. Murray sprinted to a big lead in polls, and in November won 54%–46%, carrying 60% in King County and winning Puget Sound and the west. Her margins over Chandler were similar to Bill Clinton's over George Bush, except in eastern Washington, which Clinton nearly carried but where Murray ran 10% behind.

Murray has compiled an almost solid liberal voting record. She has called, as have other senators, for a more "family-friendly" legislative schedule and for action against sexual harassment in Congress; she has strongly denounced Bob Packwood for the sexual harassment charges against him. With other Democratic women senators, she pushed successfully to allow abortion coverage in federal workers' health plans. Bucking tradition, pro-choice Murray (along with Tennessee Congressmen Bob Clement and Harold Ford) introduced Surgeon General nominee Henry Foster to the Senate Labor and Human Resources Committee, when Tennessee Senators Bill Frist and Fred Thompson declined to introduce him. Murray acted as Foster's sponsor throughout the nomination process.

Presidential politics. Bill Clinton and the Democrats must hope that their victory in Washington in 1992 does not turn out to be part of its historical pattern. For this is one of the most contrarian of states in presidential elections. It voted for Richard Nixon in 1960, Hubert Humphrey in 1968, Gerald Ford in 1976 and Michael Dukakis in 1988. It was also a better than average Perot state in 1992, especially in the outer edges of metro Seattle, where young voters with few roots in local institutions responded to his appeal.

Washington switched from a caucus system to primaries after 1988, when Pat Robertson won among Republicans and Jesse Jackson finished a solid second among Democrats. Counting the results from the 1992 primary as they would be in Washington's all-party primary for state office, Bush had 43% of the votes to Clinton's 31% and Perot's 27%; this was not a good forecast of Clinton's eventual 43%–32% victory, but may have reflected opinion accurately at that time, when Clinton was running third in national polls.

Congressional districting. Washington gained a seat in each of the last two censuses, and both new districts went to fast-growing suburban areas east and south of Seattle. A nonpartisan commission drew the district lines for the 1990s and most of the districts are evenly balanced—so much so that Democrats won eight of nine districts in 1992 and Republicans seven of nine in 1994.

The People: Est. Pop. 1994: 5,343,000; Pop. 1990: 4,866,692, up 9.8% 1990–1994. 2.1% of U.S. total, 15th largest; 24% rural. Median age: 33.1 years. 11.8% 65 years and over. 88.5% White, 4.4% Hispanic origin, 4.3% Asian, 3.1% Black, 1.7% American Indian, 2.4% Other. Households: 55.0% married couple families; 26% married couple fams. w. children; 56% college educ.; median household income: $31,183; per capita income: $14,923; 62.6% owner occupied housing; median house value: $93,400; median monthly rent: $383. 7.5% Unemployment. 1994 Voting age pop.: 4,000,000. 1994 Turnout: 1,467,231; 37% of VAP. Registered voters (1994): 2,896,519; no party registration.

Political Lineup: Governor, Michael Lowry (D); Lt. Gov., Joel Pritchard (R); Secy. of State, Ralph Munro (R); Atty. Gen., Christine Gregoire (D); Treasurer, Dan Grimm (D); Auditor, Brian Sonntag (D). State Senate, 49 (25 D and 24 R); State House of Representatives, 98 (61 R and 37 D). Senators, Slade Gorton (R) and Patty Murray (D). Representatives, 9 (7 R and 2 D).

1992 Presidential Vote

Clinton (D)	993,037	(43%)
Bush (R)	731,234	(32%)
Perot (I)	541,780	(24%)

1992 Democratic Presidential Primary

Clinton	62,171	(42%)
Brown	34,111	(23%)
Write-In (Perot)	28,311	(19%)
Tsongas	18,981	(13%)

1988 Presidential Vote

Dukakis (D)	933,516	(50%)
Bush (R)	903,835	(48%)

1992 Republican Presidential Primary

Bush	86,839	(67%)
Write-In (Perot)	25,423	(20%)
Buchanan	13,273	(10%)

GOVERNOR

Gov. Michael Lowry (D)

Elected 1992, term expires Jan. 1997; b. Mar. 8, 1939, St. John; home, Olympia; WA St. U., B.A. 1961; Baptist; married (Mary).

Career: Staff Dir., WA Senate Ways & Means Cmte., 1969–74; PR Dir., Group Health Coop. of Puget Sound, 1974–75; King Cnty. Cncl., 1975–78, Chmn., 1977–78; U.S. House of Reps., 1978–88; Prof., Seattle U. Inst. for Public Svc., 1989–92.

Office: Office of the Governor, P.O. Box 40002, Olympia 98504, 360-753-6780; Fax: 360-753-4110.

Election Results

1992 gen.	Michael Lowry (D)	1,184,315	(52%)
	Ken Eikenberry (R)	1,086,216	(48%)
1992 prim.	Michael Lowry (D)	337,783	(29%)
	Ken Eikenberry (R)	258,553	(22%)
	Sid Morrison (R)	250,418	(22%)
	Dan McDonald (R)	144,050	(12%)
	Joe King (D)	96,480	(8%)
	Six Others	68,321	(8%)
1988 gen.	William Booth Gardner (D)	1,166,448	(62%)
	Bob Williams (R)	708,481	(38%)

SENATORS

Sen. Slade Gorton (R)

Elected 1988, seat up 2000; b. Jan. 8, 1928, Chicago, IL; home, Seattle; Dartmouth, A.B. 1950, Columbia U., LL.B. 1953; Episcopalian; married (Sally).

Career: Army, 1946–47, Air Force Reserves, 1953–56; WA House of Reps., 1959–69, Majority Ldr., 1967–69; WA Atty. Gen., 1969–80; Pres., Natl. Assn. of Attys. Gen., 1976–78; U.S. Senator, 1980–86.

DC Office: 730 HSOB 20510, 202-224-3441; Fax: 202-224-9393.

State Offices: 1350 Grandridge Blvd., #212, Kennewick 99336, 509-783-0640; 15600 Redmond Wy., #300, Redmond 98052, 206-883-6072; and 402 E. Yakima Ave., Box 4083, Yakima 98901, 509-248-8084.

Committees: *Appropriations* (8th of 15 R): Agriculture, Rural Development and Related Agencies; Energy and Water Development; Interior (Chmn.); Labor, Health and Human Services, Education; Transportation. *Budget* (8th of 12 R). *Commerce, Science & Transportation* (6th of 10 R): Aviation; Communications; Consumer Affairs, Foreign Commerce and Tourism (Chmn.); Oceans and Fisheries. *Labor & Human Resources* (9th of 9 R): Disability Policy; Education, Arts and Humanities. *Indian Affairs* (3rd of 9 R).

Group Ratings

	ADA	ACLU	COPE	CFA	LCV	CON	NSI	COC	ACU	NTLC	CHC
1994	30	32	13	25	31	64	100	75	80	88	64
1993	20	—	27	20	13	80	—	100	84	—	—

National Journal Ratings

	1993 LIB — 1993 CONS			1994 LIB — 1994 CONS		
Economic	35%	—	64%	26%	—	72%
Social	32%	—	67%	27%	—	71%
Foreign	14%	—	85%	26%	—	71%

Key Votes of the 103d Congress

1. Clinton Deficit Plan	N	3. Brady Handgun Purchase	Y	5. Lmt. UN Cmnd. of Forces	Y
2. NAFTA	Y	4. Strike Race/Death Pnlty.	Y	6. Cut Missile Funds	N

Key Votes of the 104th Congress

1. Congressional Compliance	Y	3. Balanced Budget Amndt.	Y	5. Product Liability Reform	Y
2. Bar Unfunded Mandates	Y	4. Pass Line Item Veto	Y	6. FY96 Budget	Y

Election Results

1994 general	Slade Gorton (R)	947,821	(56%)	($4,792,764)
	Ron Sims (D)	752,352	(44%)	($1,228,098)
1994 primary	Slade Gorton (R)	492,251	(53%)	
	Ron Sims (D)	162,382	(17%)	
	Mike James (D)	138,005	(15%)	
	Others	136,965	(15%)	
1988 general	Slade Gorton (R)	944,359	(51%)	($2,851,591)
	Michael Lowry (D)	904,183	(49%)	($2,191,187)

Sen. Patty Murray (D)

Elected 1992, seat up 1998; b. Oct. 11, 1950, Seattle; home, Seattle; WA St. U., B.A. 1972; no religious affiliation; married (Rob).

Career: Shoreline Schl. Bd., 1985–89, Pres., 1985–86; WA Senate, 1988–92.

DC Office: 111 RSOB 20510, 202-224-2621; Fax: 202-224-0238.

District Offices: 2988 Jackson Fed. Bldg., 915 2nd Ave., Seattle 98174, 206-553-5545; 601 1st Ave., Spokane 99201, 509-624-9515; and 140 Fed. Bldg., 500 W. 12th St., Vancouver 98660, 206-696-7797.

Committees: *Appropriations* (13th of 13 D): Energy and Water Development; Foreign Operations; Interior; Legislative Branch (RMM). *Banking, Housing & Urban Affairs* (7th of 7 D): HUD Oversight and Structure; International Finance; Securities. *Budget* (10th of 10 D).

Group Ratings

	ADA	ACLU	COPE	CFA	LCV	CON	NSI	COC	ACU	NTLC	CHC
1994	90	79	88	83	92	8	0	18	0	5	0
1993	90	—	91	89	81	12	—	14	0	—	—

National Journal Ratings

	1993 LIB — 1993 CONS			1994 LIB — 1994 CONS		
Economic	68%	—	30%	84%	—	0%
Social	92%	—	0%	85%	—	7%
Foreign	71%	—	24%	86%	—	13%

Key Votes of the 103d Congress

1. Clinton Deficit Plan	Y	3. Brady Handgun Purchase	Y	5. Lmt. UN Cmnd. of Forces	N
2. NAFTA	Y	4. Strike Race/Death Pnlty.	N	6. Cut Missile Funds	Y

Key Votes of the 104th Congress

1. Congressional Compliance	Y	3. Balanced Budget Amndt.	N	5. Product Liability Reform	N
2. Bar Unfunded Mandates	Y	4. Pass Line Item Veto	N	6. FY96 Budget	N

Election Results

1992 general	Patty Murray (D)	1,197,973	(54%)	($1,342,038)
	Rod Chandler (R)	1,020,829	(46%)	($2,504,777)
1992 primary	Patty Murray (D)	318,455	(28%)	
	Rod Chandler (R)	228,083	(20%)	
	Don Bonker (D)	208,321	(19%)	
	Leo K. Thorsness (R)	185,498	(16%)	
	Tim Hill (R)	128,232	(11%)	
	Six Others	56,042	(5%)	
1986 general	Brock Adams (D)	677,471	(51%)	($1,912,307)
	Slade Gorton (R)	650,937	(49%)	($3,290,072)

FIRST DISTRICT

In the last 20 years metropolitan Seattle has spread out to the north and the east, as an influx of newcomers—it became a tidal wave in the late 1980s—have arrived seeking this area's distinctive blend of natural environmental beauty, free-wheeling culture and briskly expanding economy. But with growth, Seattle has lost some of its distinctiveness: the fishy odor of its docks does not permeate the new subdivisions built on what were once vegetable fields or vineyards; the Scandinavian heritage of old neighborhoods like Ballard has been mixed into a Pacific Northwest blend; the hoboes who used to hang around Yesler Way, the original "Skid Road," with its cast iron buildings and its street clocks, aren't allowed in the shopping malls off I-5 or I-405. The excesses spawned by the city's unrelenting high-tech boom of the last decade are also beginning to show. Bill Gates, the 39-year-old chairman of the Redmond-based computer software behemoth Microsoft and the richest man in America, is building a 37,000-square-foot home in the "Gold Coast" suburb of Medina, just across Lake Washington from Seattle. The massive house, which will include a trampoline room with vaulted ceilings, video walls that can be electronically programmed with art from the world's great museums, and a garage large enough to hold 20 cars, was originally in 1991 expected to cost $15 million; by early 1995 the estimates were up to $30 million and the completion date pushed back to 1996.

The 1st Congressional District of Washington includes Medina and a small part of Seattle, then stretches north to take in much of the northern and eastern suburbs of Seattle in Snohomish and King counties. It also runs west across Puget Sound, to Kitsap County, and gathers in Bainbridge Island, where you can commute by ferry to downtown Seattle each day and then return home to what looks like the perfect American small town in the evening. The eastern part of the district includes part of Bellevue, a onetime Seattle suburb that is now a thriving edge city, and Redmond, the American headquarters of the computer game dynamo Nintendo as well as Microsoft. Politically, this is an area torn by forces of roughly equal strength between the two parties. Most Seattle-area residents appreciate, and want to preserve, the region's unique natural aura: the evergreen smell of a well-watered land; the subtle cultural patterns that are plainly American yet geographically distant from most of the nation. But it is impossible not to recognize the spectacular success of market economics in the 1st District—and to predict which way the district will lean if that success goes sour, as recent events indicate it could. Microsoft still hums along busily in its campus of offices in pine-shaded, low-rise, turquoise buildings, despite attacks by competitors and antitrust threats by the government and the courts.

The congressman from the 1st District is Rick White, one of six freshman Republicans from Washington and perhaps the biggest surprise winner. He grew up in Indiana, went to college and law school in the east, then joined Seattle's largest law firm in 1983—a typical 1980s migrant to the area. Not quite so typically, he soon became active in local Republican politics. In 1990 White helped found the "Farm Team" to recruit young professionals to the party, and served on the finance committee for state Senator Dan McDonald's 1992 campaign for governor.

In 1994, when White decided to run for Congress, few local experts thought he had a chance. The incumbent, Maria Cantwell, when elected in 1992 was the first Democrat to win in the 1st District for 40 years, but with a moderate record she seemed well suited to the district and she was treated well in the House—appointed to the Democrats' Steering and Policy Committee, rare for a freshman. She had even been encouraged to challenge Republican Senator Slade Gorton in 1994. In the all-party open primary, White worked for the backing of party leaders, and with 28% ran well ahead of King County prosecutor Anthony Lowe, a former Gorton aide, and minister Bill Tinsley; more significantly, Cantwell won only 44% of the total vote. In the general election White emphasized his extensive involvement in church and community activities, and contrasted his own attractive family—he and his wife have four children and a home on Bainbridge Island—against the fact that Cantwell was single and had no family in the district. At the end, the race grew acrimonious. White released a poll in early October showing him tied with Cantwell 40%–40%—"intentionally peddling phony numbers," sniffed Cantwell aides. Cantwell ran a widely-criticized ad insinuating that because White took money from oil interests and his father is an oil executive, voters could expect to see drilling platforms in Puget Sound. This was an expensive race: Cantwell spent $876,000 to White's $878,000, with Cantwell raising $472,000 from PACs and with White spending $26,000 of his own money. But White had the most votes, winning 52%–48%.

White strongly supports term limits and pledged to serve no more than five terms. He seems to be one of the rising stars in Republican ranks: he received a plum appointment to the Commerce Committee with seats on the Commerce, Trade and Hazardous Materials and Telecommunications and Finance Subcommittees, panels with wide-ranging jurisdiction over complex issues. He enthusiastically backed the Contract With America, from the balanced budget amendment (including the version requiring a three-fifths vote to raise taxes) to the moratorium on new federal regulations. White will work hard to retain this seat, but there is a large Democratic base here, and he will likely receive a serious challenge in 1996.

The People: Pop. 1990: 540,315; 10% rural; 9% age 65+; 90% White; 1% Black; 1% Amer. Indian; 5% Asian; 1% Other; 2% Hispanic origin. Voting age pop.: 400,376; 1% Black; 2% Hispanic origin. Households: 60% married couple families; 29% married couple fams. w. children; 67% college educ.; median household income: $40,390; per capita income: $18,687; median gross rent: $587; median house value: $147,900.

1992 Presidential Vote			1988 Presidential Vote		
Clinton (D)	118,386	(42%)	Bush (R)	124,695	(52%)
Bush (R)	90,537	(32%)	Dukakis (D)	113,237	(48%)
Perot (I)	70,340	(25%)			

Rep. Rick White (R)

Elected 1994; b. Nov. 6, 1953, Bloomington, IN; home, Bainbridge Island; Dartmouth Col., B.A. 1975, Georgetown U., J.D. 1980; Presbyterian; married (Vikki).

Career: Practicing atty., 1980–94.

DC Office: 116 CHOB 20515, 202-225-6311; Fax: 202-225-3524.

District Offices: 21905 64th Ave., Mountlake Terrace 98043, 206-640-0233.

Committees: *Commerce* (25th of 26 R): Commerce, Trade and Hazardous Materials; Telecommunications and Finance.

Group Ratings and 103rd Congress Votes: Newly Elected

Key Votes of the 104th Congress

1. Congressional Compliance Y	6. Reform Crime Grant Y	11. Loser Pays Court Reform Y
2. Balanced Budget Amndmt. Y	7. National Security Act Y	12. Product Liability Reform Y
3. Bar Unfunded Mandates Y	8. Moratorium on Regs. Y	13. Welfare Reform Y
4. Pass Line Item Veto Y	9. Risk Assessment on Regs. Y	14. Term Limits Amndmt. Y
5. Relax Exclusionary Rule Y	10. Expnd. Priv. Prop. Rights Y	15. Tax Cuts Y

Election Results

1994 general	Rick White (R)	100,554	(52%)	($877,570)
	Maria Cantwell (D)	94,110	(48%)	($875,756)
1994 primary	Maria Cantwell (D)	45,308	(44%)	
	Rick White (R)	28,425	(28%)	
	Anthony Lowe (R)	13,855	(14%)	
	Bill Tinsley (R)	10,239	(10%)	
	Others	4,821	(5%)	
1992 general	Maria Cantwell (D)	148,844	(55%)	($621,961)
	Gary Nelson (R)	113,897	(42%)	($114,546)
	Others	8,533	(3%)	

SECOND DISTRICT

The 172 San Juan Islands, in the waters of Puget Sound at the far northwest corner of Washington, were the last part of the continental United States to be turned over to this country; this was once a whaling area, and not until 1860 did the British relinquish the islands. Today, ferry boats ply the waters of the Sound, connecting the islands to mainland Washington, and to British Columbia directly to the west. This is some of the most beautiful land and water of North America, the steely blue Sound with green forested hills rising behind; it is wet country, shielded from the full force of Pacific rains by the Olympic Mountains but still seldom dry. The little towns have the look of pristine New England villages or Midwestern historic towns, but are better preserved than the original; the stores are full of fresh produce and local seafood. Here the Seattle metropolitan area has marched north along the shore of Puget Sound, to the old port and railroad terminus of Everett, with its huge Boeing 747 plant, and beyond.

The 2d Congressional District of Washington includes the San Juan Islands, Whidbey Island and most of Puget Sound from Everett north, plus the margin of mainland along the Sound and the huge mountains, topped by snow-capped Mount Baker, behind. The political tradition in most of the lumbering and fishing areas here is Democratic, while the agricultural areas are more Republican; overall, this is a pretty evenly balanced district which tends to vote as the state does.

The congressman from the 2d District is Jack Metcalf, oldest member of the freshman Republican class, successful at last in his efforts to become a member of Congress that stretch back 26 years. Metcalf grew up in Washington, was a teacher, and was first elected to the legislature in 1960, at 33. He lost his seat in the anti-Goldwater landslide of 1964, was elected to a four-year term to the Washington Senate in 1966, then was the Republican candidate against Senator Warren Magnuson in 1968 and 1974. Metcalf was elected to the state Senate again in 1980, and he and his wife ran the Log Castle Bed and Breakfast on Whidbey Island. His opportunity in 1994 came on the long-announced retirement of Al Swift, the latest in a line of Democrats who represented the district for 52 of 54 years stretching back to the election of 28-year-old Henry Jackson in 1940. Swift was a member of the Commerce Committee who worked hard on public power, recycling and campaign finance issues; Metcalf ran against him in 1992 and lost 52%–42%.

Metcalf began 1994 with what seemed to be disadvantages. He once described himself as "a guy willing to take some kamikaze runs," and some of his stands seemed eccentric: he is for the gold standard and believes the Federal Reserve is illegal because Congress can't delegate its power to coin money. But in 1994 some of his other longtime stands suddenly seemed apropos: that Congress is corrupt, the federal government out of control, the budget deficit will result in economic collapse. If running at 67 was a handicap, he promised to serve no more than three terms. His stands against gun control and court decisions giving Indians half the harvestable salmon catch were probably an asset. It may also have helped that his chief Republican opponent, Tim Erwin, was named by Seattle newspapers as the state's worst legislator, made extravagant charges and claimed endorsements he didn't have. In the all-party primary Metcalf beat Erwin 26%–12% to capture the Republican nomination.

The Democratic nomination went by a narrow 23%–18% margin to state Senator Harriet Spanel, who was endorsed by the Washington State Labor Council and by environmentalist and feminist groups. A legislator since 1986 with a liberal record, her approach was reminiscent of Bill Clinton's in 1992. "I'm a person who is not going to go to Congress with my own agenda. I define Jack as someone who is going to march off in his direction. I'm known for listening and working with people." She called for affordable health care, though not necessarily the Clinton plan, and supported the Brady bill, and said, "Congress must be focused on the needs of families and communities, not only on issues outside our borders. We need to adopt a more holistic approach to these needs, recognizing that our country's problems cannot be overcome by repairing just one link in a chain." That may have been too liberal or perhaps just too touchy-feely a tone for the 2d District in 1994. Metcalf won 55%–45%, running despite his outspoken conservatism close to Senator Slade Gorton's run in the district.

Metcalf has seats on the Resources and Banking Committees and is surely one of the most committed conservatives on the Republican side, as well as the oldest. Given the Democratic pedigree of the district, he can probably expect serious competition in 1996.

The People: Pop. 1990: 540,861; 42% rural; 12% age 65+; 92% White; 1% Black; 2% Amer. Indian; 2% Asian; 1% Other; 3% Hispanic origin. Voting age pop.: 396,615; 1% Black; 2% Hispanic origin. Households: 60% married couple families; 28% married couple fams. w. children; 52% college educ.; median household income: $31,305; per capita income: $14,419; median gross rent: $468; median house value: $100,100.

1992 Presidential Vote

Clinton (D)	103,405	(39%)
Bush (R)	85,876	(33%)
Perot (I)	71,794	(27%)

1988 Presidential Vote

Bush (R)	93,159	(51%)
Dukakis (D)	88,525	(49%)

Rep. Jack Metcalf (R)

Elected 1994; b. Nov. 30, 1927, Marysville; home, Marysville; Pacific Lutheran U., B.A. 1951, U. of WA, M.A. 1966; Protestant; married (Norma).

Career: Army 1946–47; U.S. Marshal Patrol Boat Skipper, 1947–48; High Schl. Teacher, 1951–81; WA House of Reps., 1960–64; WA Senate, 1966–74, 1980–92; Owner, Log Castle Bed & Breakfast, 1978–present.

DC Office: 507 CHOB 20515, 202-225-2605; Fax: 202-225-4420.

District Offices: 2930 Wetmore Ave., #901, Everett 98201, 206-252-3188; and 322 N. Commercial St., #203, Bellingham 98225, 206-733-4500.

Committees: *Banking & Financial Services* (15th of 27 R): Domestic and International Monetary Policy; Financial Institutions and Consumer Credit. *Resources* (23rd of 25 R): Fisheries, Wildlife and Oceans; Native American and Insular Affairs. *Small Business* (22nd of 22 R): Tax and Finance.

Group Ratings and 103rd Congress Votes: Newly Elected

Key Votes of the 104th Congress

1. Congressional Compliance Y	6. Reform Crime Grant Y	11. Loser Pays Court Reform Y
2. Balanced Budget Amndmt. Y	7. National Security Act Y	12. Product Liability Reform Y
3. Bar Unfunded Mandates Y	8. Moratorium on Regs. Y	13. Welfare Reform Y
4. Pass Line Item Veto Y	9. Risk Assessment on Regs. Y	14. Term Limits Amndmt. Y
5. Relax Exclusionary Rule N	10. Expnd. Priv. Prop. Rights Y	15. Tax Cuts Y

Election Results

1994 general	Jack Metcalf (R)	107,430	(55%)	($407,902)
	Harriet A. Spanel (D)	89,096	(45%)	($613,063)
1994 primary	Jack Metcalf (R)	29,984	(26%)	
	Harriet A. Spanel (D)	26,124	(23%)	
	Paull Shin (D)	20,030	(18%)	
	Tim Erwin (R)	14,036	(12%)	
	John Sandifer (D)	10,337	(9%)	
	Jim Andrews (R)	6,502	(6%)	
	Others	7,080	(6%)	
1992 general	Al Swift (D)	133,207	(52%)	($1,060,650)
	Jack Metcalf (R)	107,365	(42%)	($201,029)
	Others	15,348	(6%)	

THIRD DISTRICT

From the Pacific Ocean to the majestic row of active and inactive volcanoes from Mount Rainier to Mount St. Helens to Oregon's Mount Hood, southwest Washington is one of America's most productive lumber areas. The moist air and almost constant rains blown in from the Pacific keep the trees on the coast growing rapidly; in the valleys just past the Coast Range, there is still plenty of precipitation and fast-growing forest. Then come the high mountains: the Cascades are a genuine divide, wrenching almost all the precipitation out of the air, so that the climate eastward for a thousand miles is arid. Americans were reminded of the force of the volcanoes when Mount St. Helens, dormant for 123 years, erupted in 1980, killing 65 people, pouring lava and mud down the rivers, damming lakes and flooding 160,000 acres, ruining the land in its path. The land and mountain reconfigured, nature has repaired itself, as it must have done dozens of times before.

The 3d Congressional District of Washington covers the land between the Ocean and the Cascades, from the state capital of Olympia on an inlet of Puget Sound, south to Vancouver, site of the Hudson Bay company headquarters in the 19th Century and now an industrial suburb across the Columbia River from Portland, Oregon. Despite its lumberjack, flannel shirt look, this is one of America's great international trading districts, with big exports of fish and, in the port of Portland, offloading of imported cars. But lumber has always been the biggest industry here, and one that has constantly roiled its politics. In the 1970s and 1980s, there were ferocious demands to stop the export of unprocessed timber to East Asia; local sawmills wanted the work. In the early 1990s, the raging issue was the spotted owl, or rather the court decision closing off old-forest logging to save the seldom seen bird's habitat. The owls' habitat covers a vast territory, and the court's interpretation of the Endangered Species Act not only endangered but destroyed thousands of logging jobs in this area; the political outcry was loud enough to draw President Clinton to hold a timber summit in Portland in April 1993. But the outcry died down less because of politicians' acts than because the surging Pacific Northwest economy generated more new jobs than the court decision could kill.

The 3d District in 1994 was the scene of a lively, even rollicking, House race, in which Republican Linda Smith, a favorite of the religious right, soundly beat three-term incumbent Jolene Unsoeld, a favorite of the environmentalist and feminist left. Both were improbable politicians. Unsoeld is a mountaineer whose daughter and husband died in climbing accidents. Smith grew up poor in Colorado, never went to college, married young, raised a family and started a tax preparation business in Vancouver. In 1983, at 32, she was elected to the Washington House, beating an appointed incumbent in a special election; she went on to the Washington Senate in 1987, giving Republicans control of the chamber. There she became known for her strong opposition to gay rights and gay adoption laws. Frustrated in efforts to promote campaign ethics and tax reforms, she sponsored ballot measures: Initiative 134 on campaign ethics passed in 1992, Initiative 601 on requiring voter approval for tax increases passed in 1993, after Governor Mike Lowry's tax increase.

But as late as August 1994 Smith was not a candidate for Congress at all. Challenging Unsoeld strong was businessman Timothy Moyer, who spent $1.5 million of his own money—not so far out of line with the $1.3 million Unsoeld spent in the heatedly contest 1990 race. Then a newspaper story accused Moyer of dodging taxes on his luxury automobiles, and on August 31 he dropped out of the race. Republican activists did not want the nomination to go to the other active Republican candidate, chiropractor Paul Phillips, so they drafted Smith. In less than three weeks her write-in campaign called 50,000 voters and sent out 145,000 mailers. In the September 20 all-party primary, Unsoeld won the Democratic nomination with 40% of the total vote—not impressive, since incumbents' totals are often good forecasts of their general election percentages. Smith won 34,038 write-in votes (did it help that her name is easy to spell?), 29% of the total, well ahead of Phillips's 15%.

Smith had the enthusiastic supported of Christian right activists and opponents of the Endangered Species Act, and she brought a strength of convictions and steadiness under attack that was impressive. A Smith ad showed her walking through a crowd and said, "We're the people of Washington, taking back our government." Unsoeld, who had almost twice as large a campaign budget, tried to get voters to fear Smith. An Unsoeld ad quoted her as saying, "You can definitely force your narrow views on people," and charged that Smith would means-test Social Security. Unsoeld also stressed her opposition to two Clinton causes—gun control, which she has steadily opposed, and NAFTA. But her charges of extremism didn't work. Unsoeld carried the heavily Democratic counties on and near the Pacific coast and, though only narrowly, the state capital of Olympia. But Smith carried the ordinarily Democratic Vancouver area and the inland lumbering area around Centralia, for a 52%–45% victory overall.

In the House, Smith has been one of the most strong-minded supporters of the Contract With

America and a vibrant opponent of Democrats. But she has not neglected traditional district interests. Her early bills included the National Family Enterprise Preservation Act and the Grays Harbor Navigation Project, and when Wisconsin's Scott Klug suggested privatizing the Bonneville Power Administration, which is required to sell hydroelectric power for cost in the Pacific Northwest, Smith strongly opposed it. "I've always supported privatization, but not if it is going to destroy the economy of our region." She serves on the Resources Committee and on Newt Gingrich's Endangered Species Task Force and chairs the Small Business Subcommittee on Tax and Finance. In April 1995, after the Oklahoma City bombing, Smith was identified as one of three members of Congress with close ties to militia organizations, but clashed with Washington state militia members who chastised her for voting for a Republican-backed bill easing restrictions on federal prosecutors' use of evidence found in searches. Given her strong views and the strong opposition she evokes from many Democrats, she may very well have strong opposition in 1996.

The People: Pop. 1990: 540,658; 38% rural; 13% age 65+; 93% White; 1% Black; 1% Amer. Indian; 2% Asian; 1% Other; 2% Hispanic origin. Voting age pop.: 392,660; 1% Black; 2% Hispanic origin. Households: 59% married couple families; 28% married couple fams. w. children; 50% college educ.; median household income: $29,154; per capita income: $13,328; median gross rent: $414; median house value: $70,300.

1992 Presidential Vote			1988 Presidential Vote		
Clinton (D)	104,682	(42%)	Dukakis (D)	101,683	(52%)
Bush (R)	82,648	(33%)	Bush (R)	93,833	(48%)
Perot (I)	61,609	(25%)			

Rep. Linda Smith (R)

Elected 1994; b. July 16, 1950, LaJunta, CO; home, Vancouver; Assembly of God; married (Vern).

Career: Mgr., Tax Consulting firm, 1968–82; WA House of Reps., 1983–87; WA Senate, 1987–94.

DC Office: 1217 LHOB 20515, 202-225-3536; Fax: 202-225-3478.

District Office: 1220 Main St., #310, Vancouver 98660, 360-695-6292; and 719 Sleater-Kinney Rd., Lacey 98503, 360-923-9393.

Committees: *Resources* (18th of 25 R): Fisheries, Wildlife and Oceans; National Parks, Forests and Lands. *Small Business* (8th of 22 R): Procurement, Exports and Business Opportunities; Tax and Finance (Chmn.).

Group Ratings and 103rd Congress Votes: Newly Elected

Key Votes of the 104th Congress

1. Congressional Compliance Y	6. Reform Crime Grant Y	11. Loser Pays Court Reform Y
2. Balanced Budget Amndmt. Y	7. National Security Act Y	12. Product Liability Reform Y
3. Bar Unfunded Mandates Y	8. Moratorium on Regs. Y	13. Welfare Reform Y
4. Pass Line Item Veto Y	9. Risk Assessment on Regs. Y	14. Term Limits Amndmt. Y
5. Relax Exclusionary Rule Y	10. Expnd. Priv. Prop. Rights Y	15. Tax Cuts Y

Election Results

1994 general	Linda Smith (R)	100,188	(52%)	($515,316)
	Jolene Unsoeld (D)	85,826	(45%)	($987,242)
	Others	6,620	(3%)	
1994 primary	Jolene Unsoeld (D)	47,346	(40%)	
	Linda Smith (R)	34,038	(29%)	
	Paul J. Phillips (R)	18,350	(15%)	
	Tim Moyer (R)	14,782	(12%)	
	Others	4,665	(4%)	
1992 general	Jolene Unsoeld (D)	138,043	(56%)	($619,947)
	Pat Fiske (R)	108,583	(44%)	($212,192)

FOURTH DISTRICT

The rugged peaks of the Cascade Mountains divide Washington state into two starkly different climates zones and two different political cultures. West of the Cascades, Washington is moist, green, full of watery inlets; to the east, it is barren and brown, except where irrigation ditches feed the waters of the Columbia River into thirsty valleys, or where mountaintop waters fall east, as they do to water the apple orchards in the Yakima Valley. The federal government has been a presence in the East-of-the-Cascades since the 1930s, when it began to build dams that provided cheap power and boosted economic development in this forbidding, often surreal, landscape: a giant bust of Franklin Roosevelt gazes from a bluff on the Columbia out over 550-foot-high Grand Coulee Dam, which Roosevelt initiated and which was one of his favorite projects. Other dams are strung along downriver, like beads on the necklace of the Columbia, all the way to Bonneville Dam near Portland, where the river breaks through the Cascades.

The 560-square mile Hanford Nuclear Reservation lies between these dams, near the Tri-Cities of Richland, Kennewick and Pasco. Established by the Army Corps of Engineers in 1943 to provide plutonium for the Manhattan Project, it was the site of the construction of the Nagasaki bomb. The Hanford Works eventually became the primary producer of materials for America's nuclear weapons and is still the area's largest private employer. In 1988, however, the federal government shut down Hanford's plutonium plant because of hazardous leaks and contaminated waste, causing a loss of 1,000 jobs. And despite an estimated $50 billion Department of Energy project begun a year later to clean up the toxic wastes that have seeped out of the Hanford Works over the past half century, people are unhappy with proposals to shut more of the Hanford operation.

The 4th Congressional District covers the western half of this portion of central Washington, running from the Canadian border past Grand Coulee and through the Hanford Works down to The Dalles Dam. Sentiment toward the federal government has soured in other parts of the district almost as much as it has around the Tri-Cities. The Yakima Valley, which produces more than half of the nation's apples, is angry that the apparently groundless Alar scare in 1989 hurt sales. Lumber towns in the Cascades are furious that those who want to preserve the spotted owl from extinction may shut down their logging businesses. And district residents are proud of their economic heritage, even if it no longer fits the political correctness of the 1990s: when they settled on Richland as the site of the 1994 state Democratic convention, party leaders were dismayed to discover that the high school where delegates would meet has athletic teams named the Bombers in honor of the Hanford Works, and the school's auditorium is decorated with a large mosaic of a mushroom cloud.

The congressman from the 4th District is Republican Richard "Doc" Hastings, a Republican who lost here in 1992 to Democrat Jay Inslee and then beat him in 1994. Hastings is a paper company executive from the Tri-Cities who was elected to the state House back in 1979 and quickly rose to become assistant majority leader. Inslee's 1992 51%–49% victory was something of a surprise, for this is by most measures Washington's most Republican district; he compiled a moderate voting record but, working with Speaker Thomas Foley of the next-door 5th District, cast key votes for the Clinton budget and tax package in 1993 and the crime bill in 1994. Hastings began running by fall 1993, attacking Inslee's pro-Clinton votes. In the September 1994 all-party primary, Hastings won 50% of the vote and Inslee only 41%, with a nuclear engineer who belonged to the John Birch Society winning 9%. Since an incumbent's showings in this primary are usually a good forecast for November, Inslee was obviously in trouble, and October polls showed the race about even. Despite the remoteness of the district, Hastings got visits from big Republican names like Bob Dole and Newt Gingrich; Inslee had to make do with Special Trade Representative Mickey Kantor. Outraged at Inslee's backing of the assault weapons ban, the National Rifle Association put Hastings's picture on the cover of the 4th District edition of its monthly magazine, and organized a "Meet and Greet, Shoot Skeet" for him. Inslee fought back by attacking Hastings' antiabortion position and his backing from conservative religious groups. Hastings campaigned heavily in Chelan, Douglas and Okanogan counties in the north of the district, where Inslee had eked out his victory margin in 1992. This time Hastings carried all three, swept the Tri-Cities and despite losing Yakima won overall 53%–47%.

In the House Hastings got a seat on the Resources Committee, where he will have the opportunity to amend the Endangered Species Act, one of his top legislative priorities. He is also on National Security. After a Senate committee study concluded in March 1995 that the federal government has gotten "far too little in return" for the $7.5 billion spent so far to clean up Hanford, Hastings and Senator Slade Gorton introduced bills to privatize clean-up operations at the site.

The People: Pop. 1990: 540,701; 39% rural; 12% age 65+; 79% White; 1% Black; 3% Amer. Indian; 1% Asian; 12% Other; 16% Hispanic origin. Voting age pop.: 380,860; 1% Black; 12% Hispanic origin. Households: 59% married couple families; 29% married couple fams. w. children; 44% college educ.; median household income: $25,055; per capita income: $11,578; median gross rent: $333; median house value: $60,100.

1992 Presidential Vote			1988 Presidential Vote		
Bush (R)	87,995	(42%)	Bush (R)	105,894	(59%)
Clinton (D)	71,914	(35%)	Dukakis (D)	74,951	(41%)
Perot (I)	45,256	(22%)			

Rep. Doc Hastings (R)

Elected 1994; b. Feb. 7, 1941, Spokane; home, Pasco; Columbia Basin Col., Central Washington U.; Catholic; married (Claire).

Career: Army Reserves, 1964–69; Pres., Columbia Basin Paper & Supply, 1967–present; WA House of Reps., 1979–87.

DC Office: 1229 LHOB 20515, 202-225-5816; Fax: 202-226-1137.

District Offices: 320 N. Johnson, #500, Kennewick 99336, 509-783-0310; 302 E. Chestnut, Yakima 98901, 509-452-3243; and 25 N. Wenatchee Ave., #202, Wenatchee 98801, 509-662-4294.

Committees: *National Security* (30th of 30 R): Military Personnel; Military Research and Development. *Resources* (22nd of 25 R): Native American and Insular Affairs; Water and Power Resources.

Group Ratings and 103rd Congress Votes: Newly Elected

Key Votes of the 104th Congress

1. Congressional Compliance Y	6. Reform Crime Grant Y	11. Loser Pays Court Reform Y
2. Balanced Budget Amndmt. Y	7. National Security Act Y	12. Product Liability Reform Y
3. Bar Unfunded Mandates Y	8. Moratorium on Regs. Y	13. Welfare Reform Y
4. Pass Line Item Veto Y	9. Risk Assessment on Regs. Y	14. Term Limits Amndmt. Y
5. Relax Exclusionary Rule Y	10. Expnd. Priv. Prop. Rights Y	15. Tax Cuts Y

Election Results

1994 general	Doc Hastings (R)	92,828	(53%)	($619,963)
	Jay Inslee (D)	81,198	(47%)	($496,638)
1994 primary	Doc Hastings (R)	50,343	(50%)	
	Jay Inslee (D)	41,917	(41%)	
	Craig L. Williams (D)	9,431	(9%)	
1992 general	Jay Inslee (D)	106,556	(51%)	($255,159)
	Doc Hastings (R)	103,028	(49%)	($355,859)

FIFTH DISTRICT

Eastern Washington is a land of great rivers and bare parched land, where the Columbia, Spokane and Snake Rivers wind among vast plateaus, bringing water from the Rockies to the desert. Spokane grew up at the falls of the Spokane River when the railroads first came through, and became a major wheat, mining, electrical and railroad center early in this century, the center of the so-called "Inland Empire"; it celebrated with the 1974 World's Exposition on the downtown riverfront. Nearby are some of the most fascinating landscapes in the United States: surreally undulating yellow wheatfields, the ridges of the Palouse where the topsoil is 200 feet deep, the bare-rock coulees rising above dammed-up lakes and barren desert. It is remote, a spot of Middle America set off by itself. This is not hospitable land: the summers are blazing hot and winters bitter cold; the rivers run wildly. But it has been tamed by man, and the water from the Grand Coulee and other dams irrigates some of the richest farmland in the country.

The 5th Congressional District of Washington covers the easternmost segment of the state. Some two-thirds of the people here live in greater Spokane, a city whose voting habits are a fairly good proxy of the nation's. Its heritage leans toward the Republicans, but it is not nearly as Republican as most of the nearby Rocky Mountain states, though it veers toward them angrily at times; it is open also to Democrats, and Spokane County gave Bill Clinton a smart margin in 1992. It helped that Clinton made a well-received campaign appearance in not very centrally located Spokane, but with good reason: Spokane and the 5th District were the home of Speaker of the House Thomas Foley, and Clinton, campaigning as an outsider and after keeping congressional leaders out of the spotlight at his convention, wanted to woo the man who would have much to do with his success or failure on Capitol Hill.

Today the congressman from the 5th District is George Nethercutt, the Republican who beat Foley in 1994—the first time a speaker of the House has been defeated in his home district since Galusha Grow lost in Pennsylvania in 1862. Ironically, Foley had won the seat himself, in 1964, as a lawyer and former congressional staffer who took on a 22-year Republican incumbent and beat him. In the following years Foley looked after district interests—wheat growers appreciated his work as chairman of the Agriculture Committee and he looked after Spokane's Fairchild Air Force Base and the quasi-government agencies that provided the cheapest electricity in America. But he also became a legislator national in scope: as chairman of the Democratic Study Group in 1972, when it was preparing for liberal dominance of the Democratic Caucus and the House; as Democratic whip, appointed in 1981; as Majority Leader, elected unanimously in 1986; and as Speaker, taking over in June 1989 when Jim Wright resigned under a cloud of scandal. As speaker, Foley retained his reputation for scrupulous personal fairness and intellectual elegance; but he also was a tough, disciplined partisan, willing to use and reshape the rules in order to prevent a Democratic loss. He was willing also to defy popular opinion on some issues he deemed important—on the flag-burning amendment and the Gulf war resolution, both of which he spoke eloquently against. But he was hurt by House scandals—the bank and post office—not of his making, and he was hurt by the unpopularity of the Clinton budget and tax package in 1993 and the healthcare plan of 1994. Then, when Washington voters passed term limits on congressmen in 1992, he was hurt when he filed a lawsuit to overturn their decision. In the 5th District Foley for many years ran ahead of his party, but in 1992 he ran closer to Clinton—part of a national trend toward straight-ticket voting—winning just 53% of the vote in the all-party primary and 55% in the general election; he carried Spokane solidly but lost four rural counties in November.

In April 1994 Nethercutt announced his candidacy. His moderate image, deep family roots in Spokane and his civic work—representing clients in adoptions, heading the local Diabetes Foundation (his daughter was diagnosed with the disease), starting a crisis nursery for abused children—made him more attractive than the hard-edged ideological candidates who had run against Foley before. But two of them entered the race in May, Duane Alton, owner of a chain of tire stores who ran in 1976 and 1978, and John Sonneland, a physician who ran in 1980, 1982 and 1992, and the last time spent $400,000 of his own money and won 45% of the vote. For a time the contest among Republicans seemed more intense than the race against Foley; Nethercutt won with 29%, to 20% for Alton and 15% for Sonneland. But the big news was that in the all-party primary, which often forecasts the incumbent's November percentage, Foley took only 35% of the votes. Immediately Foley began spending heavily, emphasizing the work he had done for the district and what he could do in the future. But he had to buck not only Nethercutt's ads but campaigns by the National Rifle Association (furious that Foley, a longtime gun control opponent, backed the 1994 crime bill) and the National Taxpayers Union. Nethercutt in an ad promised never to sue the people of Washington—a swipe at Foley's lawsuit against the term limits initiative. When attacked for his conservatism and support for the Kasich budget cuts, Nethercutt responded with sensitive ads showing him walking out of a crisis nursery holding a baby and one with his family walking in a park; he was helped also by a November 4th campaign appearance by Ross Perot. This was one of the most expensive House races in the nation: Foley spent $2.1 million, Nethercutt $1.1 million. Foley did carry Spokane County, but not by much, and lost all but one of the smaller counties; that gave Nethercutt a 51%–49% win.

Nethercutt brought to the House experience in the 1970s as a staffer to Alaska Senator Ted Stevens. He got a seat on the Appropriations Committee, unusual for a freshman; he was one of the framers of Tennessee Representative Van Hilleary's version of the term limits amendment. His prospects for reelection in this basically Republican district seem good.

The People: Pop. 1990: 540,865; 29% rural; 13% age 65+; 92% White; 1% Black; 2% Amer. Indian; 2% Asian; 2% Other; 3% Hispanic origin. Voting age pop.: 398,951; 1% Black; 3% Hispanic origin. Households: 55% married couple families; 26% married couple fams. w. children; 54% college educ.; median household income: $25,107; per capita income: $12,177; median gross rent: $345; median house value: $57,400.

1992 Presidential Vote			1988 Presidential Vote		
Clinton (D)	99,676	(40%)	Bush (R)	105,489	(51%)
Bush (R)	90,294	(36%)	Dukakis (D)	99,555	(49%)
Perot (I)	56,472	(23%)			

Rep. George R. Nethercutt, Jr. (R)

Elected 1994; b. Oct. 7, 1944, Spokane; home, Spokane; WA St. U., B.A. 1967; Gonzaga U. Schl. of Law, J.D. 1971; Presbyterian; married (Mary Beth).

Career: Law Clerk, Fed. Judge Ralph Plumer, 1971–72; Chief of Staff & Cnsl., U.S. Sen. Ted Stevens, 1972–76; Practicing atty., 1976–94.

DC Office: 1527 LHOB 20515, 202-225-2006; Fax: 202-225-3392.

District Offices: W. 920 Riverside, #594, Spokane 99201, 509-353-2374.

Committees: *Appropriations* (30th of 32 R): Agriculture, Rural Development, FDA, and Related Agencies; Interior; National Security.

Group Ratings and 103rd Congress Votes: Newly Elected

Key Votes of the 104th Congress

1. Congressional Compliance Y	6. Reform Crime Grant	Y	11. Loser Pays Court Reform N
2. Balanced Budget Amndmt. Y	7. National Security Act	Y	12. Product Liability Reform Y
3. Bar Unfunded Mandates Y	8. Moratorium on Regs.	Y	13. Welfare Reform Y
4. Pass Line Item Veto Y	9. Risk Assessment on Regs. Y		14. Term Limits Amndmt. Y
5. Relax Exclusionary Rule Y	10. Expnd. Priv. Prop. Rights Y		15. Tax Cuts Y

Election Results

1994 general	George R. Nethercutt, Jr. (R)	110,057	(51%)	($1,067,185)
	Thomas S. Foley (D)	106,074	(49%)	($2,144,579)
1994 primary	Thomas S. Foley (D)	44,829	(35%)	
	George R. Nethercutt, Jr. (R)	37,844	(29%)	
	Duane Alton (R)	25,177	(20%)	
	John Sonneland (R)	19,415	(15%)	
	Others	1,085	(1%)	
1992 general	Thomas S. Foley (D)	135,965	(55%)	($913,647)
	John Sonneland (R)	110,443	(45%)	($477,806)

SIXTH DISTRICT

The rainiest part of the continental United States is at its far northwest corner, where the Olympic Mountains of Washington thrust into the Pacific Ocean. The cold waters of the Pacific evaporate, condense and then mist or rain down on the hills and mountains that jut up from the ocean and Puget Sound. The mountains here are always green, the trees that line the inlets towering, and during heavy rainfalls the rivers can rise six feet a day. This has long been lumbering and fishing country, where men go out to work at 6 a.m. in air cold enough to see your breath year round, and where dependence on the vagaries of nature and the unpredictable requirements of environmentalists—like the ban on old-growth logging to protect the habitat of the spotted owl—have strengthened a traditional surly independence and suspicion of authority.

The inlets of Puget Sound, winding sinuously through the mountains, are among America's most picturesque waterways and strategically quite important. Here during World War II, shipyards built and sheltered much of the U.S. Navy's Pacific fleet, and here during the Cold War much of the nuclear submarine fleet anchored at the Bremerton Navy base, which today is home to great relics of those conflicts, the *U.S.S. Missouri* where the Japanese surrendered to General MacArthur in September 1945, and the *Turner Joy* which was the alleged object of attack in the Gulf of Tonkin incident in July 1965.

The 6th Congressional District of Washington contains the Olympic Peninsula, Bremerton and most of surrounding Kitsap County amid various inlets of Puget Sound and about half the city of Tacoma just to the east, over the bridge that replaced the Tacoma Straits suspension bridge that, in a scene preserved on newsreel (and still viewed by civil engineering students), started vibrating on the wrong harmonic in high winds and collapsed in 1940. Politically, the Olympic Peninsula and Bremerton are working-class Democratic; Tacoma, a port and paper mill town, is traditionally Democratic, though the 6th's portion of it is the more white-collar side of town. On balance the 6th is, after the central Seattle 7th, Washington's most Democratic district.

The congressman from the 6th District is Norman Dicks, a onetime University of Washington football player who was on Senator Warren Magnuson's staff when it was one of the best staffs ever seen on Capitol Hill. Dicks returned home to Kitsap County to run for Congress in 1976, when the 6th District incumbent finally got the judgeship he had been hankering after for 12 years. Dicks was elected easily that year, and in every year since except 1980, when Magnuson lost. In anti-incumbent 1992, Dicks won 58% in the all-party primary and 64% in the general; in anti-Democratic 1994, he won 59% in the primary and 58% in the general. Dicks passed up possible chances to run for the Senate in 1983, 1986 and 1988, and seems firmly committed to the House.

In the House, Dicks has shown an aggressiveness and political shrewdness that were hallmarks of the Magnuson staff in its golden days, plus an interest in defense and intelligence reminiscent of Magnuson's congressional colleague for 40 years, Henry Jackson. Dicks has a seat on the Appropriations Committee and is on both the National Security Subcommittee—a vital post for Kitsap County, where most workers depend on Pentagon payrolls, and for Washington generally, because of Boeing. He is now also ranking Democrat on the Select Committee on Intelligence. In these posts Dicks even in the minority can, as he has for years, exerted pivotal influence on important policies, usually operating quietly and behind the scenes. For example, in the early 1980s, Dicks took the lead on restoring Export-Import Bank loan authority—Boeing is America's biggest exporter and user of the loans—when the Reagan Administration wanted to cut it, and led a campaign that switched 80 House votes overnight. In the middle 1980s, working with Les Aspin, he helped keep the MX missile alive in return for arms control commitments from the Reagan Administration. During the post-Cold War downsizing of the Pentagon, he has looked out for the F-117 Stealth aircraft and the B-2 Stealth bomber, arguing in 1994 that the B-2 has an increased "potential for providing critical conventional capability as the United States makes reductions in its defense budget." He used his Appropriations seat when Democrats held control to channel federal money to localities hurt by the ban on logging in old-growth forests and he used Appropriations again when Republicans held control to authorize a vastly increased harvest of timber on federal lands, arguing it was needed to salvage timber from rotting. Naturally he looks after the interests of the Bremerton waterfront and has pushed for funding of a Tacoma waterfront development from which visitors can gaze upon Mount Rainier.

Dicks owes his seat on Intelligence to former Speaker Thomas Foley, who was obviously grooming him for chairman when he gave him a seat there in 1991. Now he is the ranking minority member, but this body often runs on a bipartisan manner, and in addition to his post there he was named to the 17-member Commission on the Roles and Capability of Intelligence. He is always ready to use political circumstance for political advantage, and is keenly aware that Republicans may be more willing to fund intelligence efforts and defense projects than many Democrats.

The People: Pop. 1990: 540,836; 26% rural; 14% age 65+; 86% White; 5% Black; 2% Amer. Indian; 4% Asian; 1% Other; 3% Hispanic origin. Voting age pop.: 403,683; 5% Black; 2% Hispanic origin. Households: 55% married couple families; 24% married couple fams. w. children; 51% college educ.; median household income: $27,882; per capita income: $13,403; median gross rent: $415; median house value: $74,400.

1418   WASHINGTON

Rep. Norm Dicks (D)

Elected 1976; b. Dec. 16, 1940, Bremerton; home, Bremerton; U. of WA, B.A. 1963, J.D. 1968; Lutheran; married (Suzanne).

Career: Legis. Asst., U.S. Sen. Warren Magnuson, 1968–73, A.A., 1973–76.

DC Office: 2467 RHOB 20515, 202-225-5916; Fax: 202-226-1176.

District Offices: 1717 Pacific Ave., #2244, Tacoma 98402, 206-593-6536; and 500 Pacific Ave., #301, Bremerton 98310, 206-479-4011.

Committees: *Appropriations* (7th of 24 D): Interior; National Security. *Intelligence (Permanent Select)* (RMM of 7 D): Technical and Tactical Intelligence.

Group Ratings

	ADA	ACLU	COPE	CFA	LCV	CON	NSI	COC	ACU	NTLC	CHC
1994	65	76	78	90	61	5	60	58	14	21	0
1993	83	—	92	90	85	1	—	30	13	—	—

National Journal Ratings

	1993 LIB	—	1993 CONS		1994 LIB	—	1994 CONS
Economic	68%	—	26%		72%	—	27%
Social	87%	—	0%		67%	—	33%
Foreign	51%	—	42%		57%	—	37%

Key Votes of the 103d Congress

1. Clinton Deficit Plan	Y	3. Brady Handgun Purchase	Y	5. Lmt. UN Cmnd. of Forces	N
2. NAFTA	Y	4. Strike Race/Death Pnlty.	N	6. Cut Missile Funds	N

Key Votes of the 104th Congress

1. Congressional Compliance	Y	6. Reform Crime Grant	N	11. Loser Pays Court Reform	N
2. Balanced Budget Amndmt.	N	7. National Security Act	N	12. Product Liability Reform	N
3. Bar Unfunded Mandates	Y	8. Moratorium on Regs.	N	13. Welfare Reform	N
4. Pass Line Item Veto	N	9. Risk Assessment on Regs.	N	14. Term Limits Amndmt.	N
5. Relax Exclusionary Rule	Y	10. Expnd. Priv. Prop. Rights	N	15. Tax Cuts	N

Election Results

1994 general	Norm Dicks (D)	105,480	(58%)	($629,161)
	Benjamin Gregg (R)	75,322	(42%)	($60,721)
1994 primary	Norm Dicks (D)	67,750	(59%)	
	Benjamin Gregg (R)	46,803	(41%)	
1992 general	Norm Dicks (D)	152,933	(64%)	($617,460)
	Lauri J. Phillips (R)	66,664	(28%)	($6,438)
	Tom Donnelly (I)	14,490	(6%)	($15,810)
	Other	4,075	(2%)	

SEVENTH DISTRICT

Seattle is no longer a secret. It zoomed into the national consciousness with the 1897 Klondike gold strike, has been a major American city since around 1910, had its own World's Fair in 1962, yet not until the late 1980s did it begin to make an impression as one of America's most booming cities, while remaining one of the most beautiful. Seattle rises from the Puget Sound harbor of Elliott Bay on steep hills, once covered with 300-foot-high Douglas firs; behind the hills and buildings you can see on a clear day, from almost anywhere, the nimbus of Mount Rainier. On the waterfront, below gleaming high-rises, is the Pike Place market, where you can get fresh salmon and Dungenesse crab; nearby is Pioneer Square, where stores and warehouses from the turn of the century have been restored and renovated; and Yesler Way, America's original "Skid Road," now has upscale shops but still some homeless too. Seattle's upper class, like San Francisco's, continues to be anchored downtown, which has a certain formality; but there is a high-tech Technology Corridor east of Lake Washington, and many comfortable old working-class neighborhoods of frame houses on steep hillsides. The old ethnic groups are not very distinctive to the untrained eye, because so many people are of Scandinavian ancestry; but Seattle is now getting an influx of Asians and Hispanics. Generally, blue-collar workers live on the south side of the city and in valleys, or midway between Puget Sound and Lake Washington; the factories, warehouses and railroad yards are concentrated in a flat plain near Puget Sound and south of downtown. The big Boeing factories are located farther south, and younger blue-collar workers have followed them into the suburban areas directly south of the city: Burien, Tukwila, Kent and Renton, which lie at the southern end of Lake Washington.

More affluent, white-collar workers and better-educated people tend to live on the hills and near the water, and are more likely to be found on the north side; here is Capitol Hill, though Seattle is not the state capital, and Queen Anne, with late Victorian and early prairie houses arrayed on grid streets with marvelous overlooks of the harbor, downtown and, on clear days, the Mountain. All this is knit together by infrastructure that was high-tech for its time: the pontoon bridge across Lake Washington, the Lake Washington Ship Canal, connecting the Sound and the Lake, whose Chittenden Locks are the second-largest locks in this hemisphere, behind Panama's. Seattle has been booming, and exporting its own institutions—Boeing airplanes have been the world's best sellers for many years; Nordstrom's department stores with their famously polite service, even in the New York area; Seattle espresso bars—especially Starbuck's, named after the coffee-crazed first mate in Herman Melville's *Moby Dick*, have been bringing caffe latte across America.

The 7th Congressional District of Washington includes almost all the city of Seattle, a little industrial suburban fringe to the south, plus rural-looking Vashon Island in Puget Sound. This is the Seattle area's minority district, 10% black and 12% Asian. The 7th has the highest education levels of any Washington district (37% of adults are college grads), but not at all the highest household income; it has the oldest housing and by far the highest percentage of householders living alone (39%) and the fewest households with families (49%). Central Seattle, in other words, shares more with central San Francisco than hills and scenery: it is heavily populated by singles and gays, young professionals and elderly pensioners. A generation ago, the city of Seattle was roughly split between the parties; today, it is heavily Democratic and liberal, proud of its black mayor, Norman Rice, its vote rejecting an antibusing referendum, its vote in favor of a 70-mile light rail system which was nixed by the suburbs.

The congressman from the 7th District is Jim McDermott, one of the most liberal members of the House and its only (credentialed) psychiatrist. McDermott was the first in his family to attend college, and went to conservative religious Wheaton College; after service in the Navy and stints in New York and Illinois hospitals, he came to the University of Washington Hospital in Seattle. Almost immediately, he was elected to the state House in 1970 and state Senate in 1974, where he worked on issues from clean water to comparable worth to health care. He retired from the legislature in 1987 and went to Zaire as a medical officer in the Foreign Service. But when Congressman Mike Lowry ran for the Senate in 1988 (he lost, but in 1992 was elected governor), McDermott returned home and ran for the 7th District seat and easily won, beating Norm Rice 38%–29% in the primary and winning 76% in the general. He has been reelected without difficulty.

McDermott is one of the most thoughtful liberals in the House, idealistic and realistic all at the same time. He was the House's chief proponent of a single-payer, Canadian-type national health insurance program in the 103d Congress, financed by a $2 cigarette tax and 50 cent handgun and ammunition excise. He got some 90 co-sponsors, and could have got more had the Clinton Administration not discouraged it; he maintained a benign attitude toward the changing Clinton plan, even while making the point that his was simpler to administer and more comprehensible to voters. But by early August 1994 he was disgusted enough with the Gephardt and Mitchell plans to urge Congress to abandon all healthcare bills that year.

McDermott has worked on other matters as well. He had the thankless task of chairing the House Ethics Committee in 1993 and 1994; he led an effort to restore most favored nation status to China—an important market for Washington products. Selflessly, he gave the state's Democrats $118,000 of his campaign money in 1994; he expected Democratic losses, but not as great as occurred. His explanation: "Since the end of the Cold War, this country has not figured out where it's going and what its role is going to be. We've fallen into fighting among ourselves. It has made people angry." He recognized that his healthcare plan has no chance in this environment, but insisted, "We'll be back."

The People: Pop. 1990: 541,202; 2% rural; 15% age 65+; 74% White; 10% Black; 1% Amer. Indian; 12% Asian; 1% Other; 3% Hispanic origin. Voting age pop.: 448,939; 8% Black; 3% Hispanic origin. Households: 38% married couple families; 14% married couple fams. w. children; 66% college educ.; median household income: $29,707; per capita income: $18,021; median gross rent: $462; median house value: $132,100.

1992 Presidential Vote

Clinton (D)	191,781	(65%)
Bush (R)	54,478	(18%)
Perot (I)	45,167	(15%)

1988 Presidential Vote

Dukakis (D)	170,301	(70%)
Bush (R)	72,349	(30%)

Rep. Jim McDermott (D)

Elected 1988; b. Dec. 28, 1936, Chicago, IL; home, Seattle; Wheaton Col., B.S. 1958; U. of IL, M.D. 1963; Episcopalian; divorced.

Career: U.S. Navy Medical Corps., 1968–70; Asst. Prof., U. of WA, Practicing psychiatrist, 1970–83; WA House of Reps., 1970–72; WA Senate, 1974–87; Medical Officer, U.S. Foreign Svc., Zaire, 1987–88.

DC Office: 2349 RHOB 20515, 202-225-3106; Fax: 202-225-6197.

District Offices: 1212 Tower Bldg., 1809 7th Ave., Seattle 98101, 206-553-7170.

Committees: *Standards of Official Conduct* (RMM of 5 D). *Ways & Means* (11th of 15 D): Health; Oversight.

Group Ratings

	ADA	ACLU	COPE	CFA	LCV	CON	NSI	COC	ACU	NTLC	CHC
1994	95	87	78	100	89	20	0	33	5	15	0
1993	85	—	92	100	93	27	—	27	4	—	—

National Journal Ratings

	1993 LIB — 1993 CONS			1994 LIB — 1994 CONS		
Economic	78%	—	12%	83%	—	0%
Social	87%	—	0%	94%	—	0%
Foreign	93%	—	0%	80%	—	17%

Key Votes of the 103d Congress

1. Clinton Deficit Plan	Y	3. Brady Handgun Purchase	Y	5. Lmt. UN Cmnd. of Forces	N
2. NAFTA	Y	4. Strike Race/Death Pnlty.	N	6. Cut Missile Funds	Y

Key Votes of the 104th Congress

1. Congressional Compliance	Y	6. Reform Crime Grant	N	11. Loser Pays Court Reform	N
2. Balanced Budget Amndmt.	N	7. National Security Act	N	12. Product Liability Reform	N
3. Bar Unfunded Mandates	N	8. Moratorium on Regs.	N	13. Welfare Reform	N
4. Pass Line Item Veto	N	9. Risk Assessment on Regs.	N	14. Term Limits Amndmt.	N
5. Relax Exclusionary Rule	N	10. Expnd. Priv. Prop. Rights	N	15. Tax Cuts	N

Election Results

1994 general	Jim McDermott (D)	148,353	(75%)	($275,259)
	Keith Harris (R)	49,091	(25%)	
1994 primary	Jim McDermott (D)	67,639	(71%)	
	Keith Harris (R)	22,836	(24%)	
	Paul Glumaz (D)	4,436	(5%)	
1992 general	Jim McDermott (D)	222,604	(78%)	($191,472)
	Glenn C. Hampson (R)	54,149	(19%)	($30,317)
	Other	7,197	(2%)	

EIGHTH DISTRICT

Half a century ago the land east of Seattle's Lake Washington was bucolic and tranquil. Orchards and vineyards flourished in the rich, moist soil that predominates west of the Cascades Mountains, while farms and broad pasturelands spread toward 14,410-foot Mount Rainier like a living green quilt. But a business boom in the Seattle area in the 1980s, and the population growth that accompanied it, transformed that peaceful scene. Today this area, known locally as Overlake, has become thoroughly suburban, with all the aspects of urbanness but with high crime and unpleasant poverty. Subdivisions have spread almost to the base of the Cascades, wiping out most of the rural expanses that earlier drew many people weary of the closed-in feeling they got living nearer to Seattle. Bellevue, once merely a Seattle suburb, now has a population of more than 100,000, with enough office space to make it an edge city. While downtown Seattle specialized in banks and law firms and trading companies, Bellevue and other communities in Overlake specialized in high-tech startups. Microsoft, the software giant, and the American headquarters of Nintendo, the computer game maker, are located close by in what was once the farm town of Redmond; but they are only two computer-related businesses in an area that boasts of dozens.

The 8th Congressional District of Washington includes most of the eastern edge of metro Seattle, as well as the scarcely inhabited territory of the Cascades. It includes almost three-quarters of Bellevue, as well as the exclusive community of Mercer Island, located in the middle of Lake Washington, and part of Pierce County, which stretches south to the suburban fringe east of Tacoma. Mount Rainier, 60 miles southeast of Seattle, is also part of the district—a fact that could spell trouble for the 8th: a 1994 National Academy of Sciences study warned that Mount Rainier is an active volcano and could erupt in the foreseeable future. This is the most affluent district in Washington, rivaled only by the 1st, market-oriented on economics, more liberal on the environment, tolerant on cultural issues; in partisan terms, it is also one of the two most Republican districts in the state.

Indeed after the 1992 election the 8th was the only Washington district represented by a Republican. Jennifer Dunn, a former IBM systems engineer, a lobbyist on property tax issues for the King County Assessor's office, and chairman of the Washington state Republican Party for 12 years, won the seat in 1992 in a walkaway. In her first term, Dunn was a vocal deficit hawk, backing the Penny-Kasich budget cut package and the "A to Z" appropriation-cutting procedure. She was also tough on crime: the House passed the aptly-named "Dunn-Deal" proposal she submitted with Nathan Deal of Georgia, then a Democrat, to allow local communities to track "sexual predators" who pose a danger to children. Dunn was also the only freshman picked by then-Minority Leader Robert Michel to serve on the Joint Committee on the Organization of Congress.

Dunn easily won reelection in this Republican district against a Democratic backer of Lyndon LaRouche. After the election she was invited to join the "working group" of advisers to House Speaker Newt Gingrich of Georgia; Gingrich later appointed her to his 10-member transition team. She also worked hard to win a seat on the powerful Ways and Means Committee, where her priorities will be international trade—greater Seattle is arguably the United States's number one export metro area—and lowering the capital gains tax rate. Dunn was also considered partisanly reliable enough to be named to the three-member task force investigating the 21-vote victory of Connecticut Democrat Sam Gejdenson (the challenge to him was dropped). She has also introduced legislation to privatize government printing and lay off employees of the Governemnt Printing Office. The buzz in state political circles is that Dunn might challenge Democratic Senator Patty Murray in 1998. But Dunn has dismissed such speculation—perhaps because she hopes to leave the door open to a possible Administration job if a Republican wins the presidency in 1996.

The People: Pop. 1990: 540,735; 21% rural; 8% age 65+; 91% White; 2% Black; 1% Amer. Indian; 5% Asian; 1% Other; 2% Hispanic origin. Voting age pop.: 389,198; 1% Black; 2% Hispanic origin. Households: 65% married couple families; 33% married couple fams. w. children; 63% college educ.; median household income: $42,379; per capita income: $18,432; median gross rent: $550; median house value: $142,100.

1992 Presidential Vote		1988 Presidential Vote	
Clinton (D)	102,859 (38%)	Bush (R)	122,431 (56%)
Bush (R)	92,274 (34%)	Dukakis (D)	97,524 (44%)
Perot (I)	72,523 (27%)		

Rep. Jennifer B. Dunn (R)

Elected 1992; b. July 29, 1941, Seattle; home, Bellevue; U. of WA, 1960–62, Stanford, B.A. 1963; Episcopalian; divorced.

Career: Systems Engineer, IBM, 1964–69; P.R., King Cnty. Assessors Office, 1978–80; Delegate, U.N. Comm. on Status of Women, 1984, 1990; Chmn., WA St. Repub. Party, 1981–92.

DC Office: 432 CHOB 20515, 202-225-7761; Fax: 202-225-8673; e-mail: dunn@hr.house.gov.

District Offices: 50-116th Ave., SE, Bellevue 98004, 206-460-0161.

Committees: *House Oversight* (5th of 7 R). *Ways & Means* (16th of 21 R): Human Resources; Trade.

Group Ratings

	ADA	ACLU	COPE	CFA	LCV	CON	NSI	COC	ACU	NTLC	CHC
1994	5	30	11	20	0	64	100	92	86	93	86
1993	5	—	0	10	21	69	—	100	91	—	—

National Journal Ratings

	1993 LIB — 1993 CONS		1994 LIB — 1994 CONS	
Economic	25% —	72%	0% —	80%
Social	23% —	77%	29% —	70%
Foreign	24% —	72%	34% —	63%

Key Votes of the 103d Congress

1. Clinton Deficit Plan	N	3. Brady Handgun Purchase	N	5. Lmt. UN Cmnd. of Forces	Y
2. NAFTA	Y	4. Strike Race/Death Pnlty.	Y	6. Cut Missile Funds	N

Key Votes of the 104th Congress

1. Congressional Compliance	Y	6. Reform Crime Grant	Y	11. Loser Pays Court Reform	Y
2. Balanced Budget Amndmt.	Y	7. National Security Act	Y	12. Product Liability Reform	Y
3. Bar Unfunded Mandates	Y	8. Moratorium on Regs.	Y	13. Welfare Reform	Y
4. Pass Line Item Veto	Y	9. Risk Assessment on Regs.	Y	14. Term Limits Amndmt.	Y
5. Relax Exclusionary Rule	Y	10. Expnd. Priv. Prop. Rights	Y	15. Tax Cuts	Y

Election Results

1994 general	Jennifer B. Dunn (R)	140,409	(76%)	($685,083)
	Jim Wyrick (D)......................	44,165	(24%)	
1994 primary	Jennifer B. Dunn (R)	57,410	(71%)	
	Jim Wyrick (D)......................	23,300	(29%)	
1992 general	Jennifer B. Dunn (R)	155,874	(60%)	($704,674)
	George O. Tamblyn (D)	87,611	(34%)	($410,465)
	Bob Adams (I)	14,686	(6%)	($14,104)

NINTH DISTRICT

The misty shores of Puget Sound have seen some of America's most vibrant economic growth over the last decade. It has spread south from Seattle, over the mixed suburban territory, south and west to the once industrial city of Tacoma. The subdivisions along the Sound, which have some of the loveliest views in America, tend to be high-income. But much of greater Seattle's prime industrial territory lies between the ridges that run north and south inland. Weyerhaeuser, the world's largest private owner of softwood timber, has its headquarters here in Federal Way, a suburb of Tacoma that recently incorporated in an attempt to manage its growth. Boeing is also a major presence in Renton, a suburb southeast of Seattle; its aircraft and electronic components plants and its business services division, employing more than 14,000 people, have helped make the company America's number one exporter. A host of smaller factories cluster near the rail lines that run from Minneapolis-St. Paul across the Great Plains to Puget Sound. The military has influenced this area too. Fort Lewis is just west of Tacoma and active-duty and retired military personnel and their families make up perhaps one-fifth of the population in this area.

The 9th Congressional District of Washington covers much of this area. It is a new seat created after the 1990 Census and confirmed by a June 1992 Supreme Court decision that upheld the counting of servicemen abroad in their state of residence (otherwise, this seat would have gone to Massachusetts). The 9th District's northern end wraps around Sea-Tac International Airport and Renton, which lies on the southern shore of Lake Washington. Then the district winds south past Kent, Auburn and Federal Way and reaches the shipyards and docks of Tacoma. It covers half of Tacoma, including McChord Air Force Base, and then proceeds west, taking in the Army's vast Fort Lewis in Pierce County and stopping just shy of the boundaries of the state capital of Olympia. Politically, this is a district balanced almost at equipoise: in its two elections it went Democratic in 1992 and Republican in 1994.

The congressman from the 9th now is Randy Tate, elected at 29, the youngest of the 73 Republican freshmen in the House. But Tate is no newcomer to politics. In 1988, at 22, while he was completing a degree in economics and political science at Western Washington University, he was elected to the state House, where he worked his way up to Republican caucus chairman. Tate is strongly motivated by his religious faith, and he supported the presidential candidacy of Pat Robertson in 1988; that year he also distributed a brochure which many Democrats thought insinuated his opponent was a child molester. All this made Tate a *bete noire* for Washington Democrats. In 1994 he decided to challenge Congressman Mike Kreidler, who was elected in a 52%–43% upset in 1992. Immediately the Democratic state chairman called Tate "the poster boy of the radical right." Despite the bombardment of local Democrats and a visit from First Lady Hillary Rodham Clinton at an August $1,000-per-person reception for Kreidler, Tate won 52% of the vote in Washington's all-party open primary to Kreidler's 48%. These results are often a good forecast of the November results, and Kreidler responded shrilly: "In Randy Tate's world, women will have no reproductive choices, worse healthcare security, ... less help when they are pregnant and less help with raising their children," one of his October TV ads proclaimed. Kreidler spent $880,000 to Tate's $617,000, and outraised him among PACs by $536,000 to $140,000. But even so, in November Tate again won 52%–48%.

Tate got off to a high-profile start in the House. He was one of eight freshmen-elect invited to advise House Speaker Newt Gingrich of Georgia on the formation of a transition team, and soon after he was appointed one of three freshman deputy whips. A balanced budget activist, Tate worked hard to a pass proposal dear to the hearts of many of his freshman colleagues: a requirement in the balanced budget constitutional amendment that any tax increase must have the approval of three-fifths of the House and Senate. That effort failed, but the Republican first-termers gained in the end, Tate said. "We have learned to stick to our beliefs, even when there is pressure," he noted. "We are the conscience of the Republican Conference, hot off the campaign trail." Tate is clearly part of the cutting edge of American politics. But in this closely divided district, he may very well be challenged for that position in 1996.

The People: Pop. 1990: 540,519; 9% rural; 9% age 65+; 84% White; 5% Black; 2% Amer. Indian; 6% Asian; 1% Other; 4% Hispanic origin. Voting age pop.: 396,950; 5% Black; 3% Hispanic origin. Households: 57% married couple families; 27% married couple fams. w. children; 52% college educ.; median household income: $32,194; per capita income: $14,264; median gross rent: $478; median house value: $93,300.

1992 Presidential Vote		
Clinton (D)	93,964	(42%)
Bush (R)	69,593	(31%)
Perot (I)	58,037	(26%)

1988 Presidential Vote		
Bush (R)	93,554	(52%)
Dukakis (D)	86,839	(48%)

Rep. Randy Tate (R)

Elected 1994; b. Nov. 23, 1965, Puyallup; home, Puyallup; Tacoma Commun. Col., A.A. 1986, Western WA U., B.A. 1988; Baptist; married (Julie).

Career: WA House of Reps., 1988–94.

DC Office: 1118 LHOB 20515, 202-225-8901; Fax: 202-225-3484.

District Offices: 33305 1st Way, S., #B-210, Federal Way 98003, 206-661-1459; and 10925 Canyon Rd., #C-1, Puyallup 98373, 206-539-1322.

Committees: *Government Reform & Oversight* (16th of 27 R): Government Management, Information and Technology; National Economic Growth, Natural Resources and Regulatory Affairs. *Transportation & Infrastructure* (30th of 33 R): Aviation; Surface Transportation.

Group Ratings and 103rd Congress Votes: Newly Elected

Key Votes of the 104th Congress

1. Congressional Compliance Y	6. Reform Crime Grant Y	11. Loser Pays Court Reform Y
2. Balanced Budget Amndmt. Y	7. National Security Act Y	12. Product Liability Reform Y
3. Bar Unfunded Mandates Y	8. Moratorium on Regs. Y	13. Welfare Reform Y
4. Pass Line Item Veto Y	9. Risk Assessment on Regs. Y	14. Term Limits Amndmt. Y
5. Relax Exclusionary Rule Y	10. Expnd. Priv. Prop. Rights Y	15. Tax Cuts Y

Election Results

1994 general	Randy Tate (R)	77,833	(52%)	($617,127)
	Mike Kreidler (D)	72,451	(48%)	($880,262)
1994 primary	Randy Tate (R)	42,590	(52%)	
	Mike Kreidler (D)	38,832	(48%)	
1992 general	Mike Kreidler (D)	110,902	(52%)	($430,476)
	Pete von Reichbauer (R)	91,910	(43%)	($414,594)
	Others	10,107	(5%)	

WEST VIRGINIA

Things are finally looking up for West Virginia. It's about time: this is a state that has had more than its share of tragedy and heartbreak, but whose people have never lost their sense of hope or their affection for the hills and mountains that make this the most unhorizontal state in the nation. West Virginia was born out of the tragedy of the Civil War, when 55 mountain counties with few slaves seceded from Virginia, and has made its living since mostly on that cruelest of commodities, coal. Coal kept the sons of large mountaineer families here for much of the 20th Century, men who would otherwise have left for big cities; coal brought immigrants in, a few from odd corners of Europe, but more from adjacent areas of the South where the local farming economies were stagnant when West Virginia's coal economy was booming. Coal and local rock salt and brines brought the large concentration of chemical plants 50 years ago to the Kanawha Valley around Charleston; it built the steel mills in the panhandle and the Monongahela River valley, not far south of Pittsburgh.

But coal did not build a self-sustaining economy. When America was beleaguered abroad, demand for coal increased and energy prices rose, and West Virginia boomed, during World War II (the state reached its all-time population peak of 2 million in 1950) and the oil shocks of the 1970s. Coal changed West Virginia's politics too. West Virginia's heritage from the Civil War days was Republican, though some counties tilted toward the Confederacy and the Democrats. But after John L. Lewis's United Mine Workers organized most of the West Virginia mines in the 1930s, with the help of Franklin Roosevelt's Democrats, the coal country shifted toward the Democrats, and West Virginia for half a century has been one of the most Democratic states, deserting the ticket only in Republican landslide years (1956, 1972, 1984).

But neither Democratic administrations nor the pensions and medical benefits the UMW negotiated for retired miners have been able to provide the economic growth to keep thousands of West Virginians from leaving their mountains to find work elsewhere—now more often south on I-77 to the booming Carolinas than north to the Great Lakes' industrial cities. As underground miners were replaced by strip-mining machines, coal tonnage went way up but coal mine employment dropped from 22% of the state's work force in 1950 to 10% in 1980 and 5% in 1990. The state's population, 1.95 million in 1980, fell to 1.8 million in 1990—the largest decrease, absolutely and in percentage terms, of any state. But West Virginians have a strong attachment to their unique state, where the accent sounds southern and the early 20th Century factories and houses look northern, where the landscape is rural and the economy industrial.

Now in the 1990s there are finally signs of a rebound, and not because of upward spikes of energy prices. Population is up in the 1990s, most notably in the eastern panhandle counties now part of the Washington, D.C., metropolitan area, but elsewhere as well. Government has played a role. Senator Robert Byrd achieved his career goal of the chairmanship of the Appropriations Committee in 1989, and before his six year tenure was up, delivered on his promise to channel $1 billion of federal projects into West Virginia, and more: over $1.5 billion. As ranking minority member, his efforts continue: new highways, grants to college, offices for the FBI and the Fish and Wildlife Service, the list goes on and on. West Virginia has also attracted private sector investment from Georgia Pacific, Swearingen Aircraft, Weyerhaueser, NGK Sparkplugs and Shinsei Harness, and it hopes to persuade others to move backoffice operations to low-wage, good-work-habits, electronically-accessible West Virginia. By early 1995 unemployment was down to 7.1%, the lowest rate in 15 years. West Virginia's efforts to market itself as a tourist center have not reached goals, but historic Harper's Ferry and the outlet malls around Martinsburg have attracted visitors, and when Disney gave up on its theme park plans in Virginia, West Virginia invited it in, and in early 1995 the legislature considered, but did not pass, riverboat gambling. The state has moved from 49th to 31st in teacher's salaries, and is adding computers to every classroom from kindergarten to high school; it hopes these measures will enable West Virginia students to compete in a worldwide high-tech economy. West Virginia's problems are by no means solved. There will always be a need for better roads in a place where people are scattered over constant hills and hollows. In the southern coal counties, wages are low, infant mortality is high and many jobs are controlled by some of America's most corrupt local politicians. But West Virginia seems to have turned around.

Governor. Taking some of the credit for West Virginia's turnaround is Governor Gaston Caperton. He grew up in Charleston, in a prominent family; after college he went into the family insurance business and over 25 years transformed it into a firm of national scale. He ran for governor in 1988 and spent $2 million on a media campaign and won 38% in a seven-candidate primary; in the general, he faced Arch Moore, elected in 1968, 1972 and 1984, but under a cloud on corruption charges for which in 1990 he was sentenced to five years in jail; Caperton won 59%–41%. Also, the state treasurer lost $279 million in state funds through bad investments, and two former state Senate presidents were convicted of political corruption. Once in office, Caperton's job rating plunged when he broke his no-new-taxes pledge and steered to passage a $392 million tax increase, restoring the food sales tax former Governor (now Senator) Jay Rockefeller had repealed. Then came a soap opera episode, as his wife divorced him and ran for

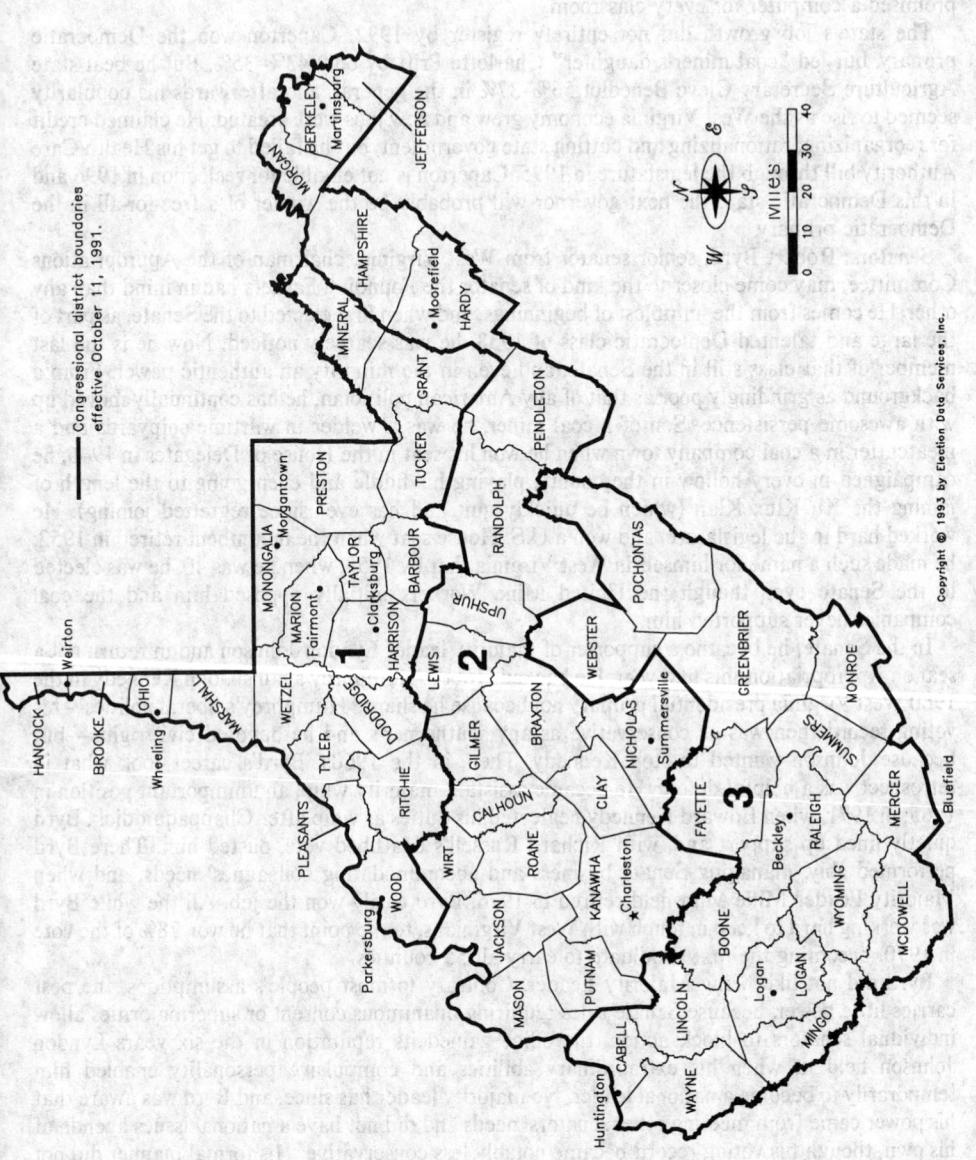

state Treasurer; Caperton's second wife, Racheal Worby, is the conductor of the Wheeling Symphony. But he had positive achievements, including an ethics bill, a road building package and, most important, an education bill that raised teacher pay, set performance standards and promised a computer for every classroom.

The state's job growth did not entirely register by 1992. Caperton won the Democratic primary, but led "coal miner's daughter" Charlotte Pritt by only 43%–35%. But he beat state Agriculture Secretary Cleve Benedict 56%–37% in the general, and afterwards his popularity seemed to rise as the West Virginia economy grew and new jobs were created. He claimed credit for reorganizing, rationalizing and cutting state government; but he failed to get his Health Care Authority bill through the legislature in 1995. Caperton is not eligible for reelection in 1996 and in this Democratic state the next governor will probably be the winner of a free-for-all in the Democratic primary.

Senators. Robert Byrd, senior senator from West Virginia, chairman of the Appropriations Committee, may come closer to the kind of senator the Founding Fathers had in mind than any other. He comes from the humblest of beginnings, and when first elected to the Senate, as part of the large and talented Democratic class of 1958, he was scarcely noticed. Now he is the last member of that class still in the Senate, and even in the minority an authentic power. From a background as grindingly poor as that of any American politician, he has continually moved up with awesome persistence. Son of a coal miner, he was a welder in wartime shipyards and a meatcutter in a coal company town when he won his seat in the House of Delegates in 1946; he campaigned in every hollow in the county, playing his fiddle and even going to the length of joining the Ku Klux Klan (which he quickly quit and has ever since regretted joining). He worked hard in the legislature, and won a U.S. House seat when the incumbent retired in 1952; he made such a name for himself in West Virginia that by 1958, when he was 40, he was elected to the Senate even though the United Mine Workers initially opposed him and the coal companies never supported him.

In the Senate, he became a supporter of majority leader Lyndon Johnson and in return got a seat on Appropriations his first year. He backed Hubert Humphrey against John Kennedy in the 1960 West Virginia presidential primary not because he shared Humphrey's liberal politics—his voting record then was as conservative as any southerner's and he opposed civil rights—but because Johnson wanted to stop Kennedy. Then, in the 1960s, Byrd's career took what in retrospect was a helpful detour. He became assistant majority whip, an unimportant position in 1965; in 1971, when Edward Kennedy neglected his duties as whip after Chappaquiddick, Byrd quietly lined up support and, with Richard Russell's deathbed vote, ousted him. There Byrd performed ably, managing Senate business and accommodating colleagues' needs, and when Majority Leader Mike Mansfield retired in 1976, Byrd easily won the job. All the while Byrd was working hard to keep in touch with West Virginians, to the point that he won 78% of the vote in 1970, becoming the first candidate to carry all 55 counties.

Byrd did not like being Majority Leader. Contrary to most people's assumptions, the post carries little power, because Senate rules requiring unanimous consent or supermajorities allow individual senators to block action; the office gained its reputation in the six years Lyndon Johnson held it, when his extraordinary abilities and compulsive personality enabled him temporarily to become a national leader. No majority leader has since, and Byrd was aware that his power came from meeting other senators' needs and did not have a national issues agenda of his own, though his voting record became notably less conservative. His formal manner did not project well on television, and Byrd was challenged in 1984 by then-Florida Senator (now Governor) Lawton Chiles. In 1987, with Democrats back in the majority after six years out of power, Byrd established some legislative priorities and then announced he would leave the post after the 1988 election.

So in 1989 Byrd got the position he had been aiming for all along, chairman of the Appropriations Committee. "I want to be West Virginia's billion dollar industry," he announced in 1990, and in six years as chairman succeeded handsomely. An FBI office went to Clarksburg,

Treasury and IRS offices To Parkersburg, the Fish and Wildlife Training Center in Harper's Ferry, a Bureau of Alcohol, Tobacco and Firearms in Martinsburg, a NASA Research center in Wheeling. "All roads, they say, lead to Rome," he said in 1994 in Logan, West Virginia. "They haven't seen anything yet. All roads lead to Logan." Byrd does not always deliver: a GAO report helped defeat his attempt to build a $1.2 billion CIA facility in Jefferson County; and he lost by one vote, despite personally lobbying every senator, his amendment to compensate coal miners who lose their jobs because of the Clean Air Act. But Byrd usually wins. And, while he insists that he does not retaliate against those who oppose his projects, no one doubts he remembers how every senator voted. "You might as well slap my wife as take the highway money from West Virginia."

It should be added that Byrd's positions are not just parochial but are the product of serious study of the Constitution and of history. With the assistance of Senate historian Richard Baker, he wrote *The Senate 1789-1989*, which he delivered as a series of speeches; based on impressive research, gracefully written, full of arresting anecdotes and sound insights, it surpasses any previous work on the subject. Byrd, who earned his law degree while in the Senate and had his diploma presented to him by President Kennedy at the 1963 American University commencement where Kennedy delivered his most important foreign policy speech, has read the classics as well, and takes to quoting Shakespeare, Thucydides or Cato the Younger in debates on the balanced budget amendment and the line-item veto. These two measures he opposed obdurately, as destructive of the constitutional prerogatives of the Senate, and his objections in early 1995 forced the Senate to devise an ungainly version of the line-item veto and stalled consideration of the balanced budget amendment long enough that Democratic leaders could get enough of their followers to welsh on their commitments to defeat it by one vote.

Byrd's insistence on Senate prerogatives have not always worked well. His refusal to allow Republican amendments led to a successful filibuster of the Clinton stimulus package in March 1993, he blocked putting the healthcare package in the 1993 budget reconciliation and his sustained opposition to unfunded mandates failed. But Byrd's prominence also showed that in important ways he, and not Majority Leader George Mitchell or Minority Leader Tom Daschle, led Democrats in the Senate. He raised his voice in stentorian tones to denounce misdeeds, calling on Bob Packwood to resign from the Senate, calling for withdrawal of U.S. forces from Somalia.

In 1994 Byrd became the third senator to be elected to seven six-year terms (the others were Carl Hayden of Arizona and Strom Thurmond of South Carolina). Republican Stan Klos said Byrd was changing the state motto from "Mountaineers are Always Free" to "Mountaineers are Always Dependent" but contributed $50 for his statue to be unveiled in the state Capitol in 1996, his 50th anniversary of holding public office; Don Marsh, retired editor of the *Charleston Gazette*, called him "our greatest economic asset," and *The Daily Athenaeum*, wrote "Senator Byrd deserves to win his Senate race unanimously." Almost: he won with 69%, again carrying all 55 counties, the only man in West Virginia history to do so.

West Virginia's junior senator is Jay Rockefeller. His full name, John D. Rockefeller, IV, has a familiar ring to most older voters, who remember his great-grandfather as the oil billionaire who was once America's richest man, and his grandfather as the heir who had more than enough money to build Rockefeller Center, restore Colonial Williamsburg and found the Museum of Modern Art in the Depression years. Jay Rockefeller's father and uncles were men of impressive achievement, each in a different field, and in two cases in politics. His uncle Winthrop Rockefeller moved to an impoverished state in the southern hills—in his case Arkansas—ran for governor and lost, ran again and won two terms and ran an honest and reforming administration: the same could be said of Jay Rockefeller's career in West Virginia. There are interesting comparisons between the careers of Jay Rockefeller and his other governor-uncle: Nelson Rockefeller in his 30s became head of Franklin Roosevelt's Latin American policy program; Jay Rockefeller in his 20s studied for three years in Japan. Nelson Rockefeller became governor of the nation's then-biggest state and spent money expansively on generous welfare and gigantic monuments; Jay Rockefeller became governor of what turned out to be America's number one population-losing state of the 1980s, leaving behind a network of roads and highways and a progressive tax structure that removed the sales tax on food (since restored). Nelson Rockefeller was a Republican at a time when the party's Ivy League establishment believed it could soon resume its status as the majority party. Jay Rockefeller broke family tradition and became a Democrat at a time when the party's Ivy League ideologues believed it would always retain what seemed then its natural status as the majority party. Both Rockefellers were mentioned early on as presidential candidates: Nelson, never very shy about running, finally did so in 1964 at 56, and again in 1968; Jay for years avoided projecting his name forward, then almost decided to run in the summer of 1991 at 54, but now as an ally of Bill Clinton and Al Gore seems unlikely to run until 2000.

The parallels stop here, for Jay Rockefeller lacks the aloof, imperial bearing of his uncle Nelson; he is affable, full of self-deprecating humor, tall enough so that he stoops to get through doorways and uses hearing aids because of noise damage from frequent helicopters travel. He was careful to work his way up the political ladder. Originally coming to West Virginia as a VISTA volunteer, he was elected to the house of delegates in Kanawha County in 1966 and as secretary of state in 1968, and then had the chastening experience of losing to Governor Arch Moore in 1972. He served four years as president of West Virginia Wesleyan College in Buckhannon, and his politics became more practical: he dropped his opposition to strip mining, for example. He was not shy about spending his own millions and was elected governor in 1976 and, against Moore, in 1980, after which the state was plunged into deep recession. In 1984, he ran for the U.S. Senate and beat Republican businessman John Raese by just 52%–48% after spending $12 million. Every penny helped, especially the huge sums needed to air ads on Washington and Pittsburgh TV: in most counties in the state, Rockefeller ran between 1% and 7% ahead of Walter Mondale's 45% showing; in all but one of the dozen or so panhandle counties in these hugely expensive media markets, he ran 12% to 18% ahead of Mondale.

Initially in the Senate Rockefeller deferred to Robert Byrd, compiled a conventional liberal voting record, somewhat more inclined to free trade because of his experience in East Asia. Then he began his concentration on health care. With a seat on the Finance Committee, he got a place on the Pepper Commission on long-term health care; when George Mitchell became majority leader, he gave his seat to Rockefeller, who became chairman when Pepper died in June 1989. He got an 11–4 vote for long-term care for all Americans regardless of age and an 8–7 margin for universal medical insurance coverage, with a "pay or play" plan, of which Rockefeller soon became the Senate's most conspicuous proponent. During his own out-loud thinking about running for president in spring and summer 1991, he talked mostly about health care. His biggest legislative achievement in 1992 was inserting into the energy bill, over furious opposition from western coal states, a tax on non-union coal operators to bail out the United Mine Workers' healthcare trust funds.

Rockefeller endorsed Clinton with an enthusiasm that seemed undimmed by regret that he had not run himself; he was fueled in part by an angry disdain for George Bush who had not, in his view, lived up to the patrician's obligation to be generous to those less fortunate (with taxpayers' money, critics might add). In 1993, he strongly supported the Clintons' healthcare reform efforts, assembling bipartisan groups of senators, speaking out publicly of the benefits, recommending privately that Democrats avoid compromise and push for a maximalist bill. He was motivated in part by anger at his mother's treatment during a long terminal illness—an experience that would be much worse for people of ordinary incomes, he thought—and he worked to increase the number of general practitioners, especially in states like West Virginia and Arkansas, at the risk of harming the major teaching hospitals. That earned him strong opposition from Finance Chairman Daniel Patrick Moynihan, but Rockefeller, like some young White House aides, evidently thought they could roll over him. "We're going to push through healthcare reform regardless of the views of the American people," he said at one point. That turned out to be poor political judgment. Efforts at compromise came far too late, after voters had turned against a government takeover of health care, and the healthcare bill crashed and burned in September 1994.

Rockefeller has other causes. He has been the Senate's leading promoter of uniform federal product liability laws, to reduce the burden of lawsuits on manufacturers; foiled in the Democratic Congress, he led passage of a bill in the Republican Senate in May 1995. As ranking minority member on the Veterans' Committee, he wants to reform the VA hospital system to provide medical care for everyone who has served in the military. He backed compensation for veterans suffering from the vaguely-defined Gulf war syndrome, and in October 1994 Congress passed legislation that will enable Gulf War veterans to receive compensation for illnesses that doctors have been unable to diagnose. He has worked with House Minority Leader Richard Gephardt on the framework bill for Japan-U.S. trade relations. He wants to prevent higher telecommunications costs for rural areas on the information superhighway.

Rockefeller is in strong shape politically. He won reelection easily in 1990 with a (for him) bargain basement campaign costing $2.7 million; he prides himself now on raising money from others rather than spending his own, but of course he could spend millions if he felt the need to.

Presidential politics. "We do kind of feel like an island of Democrats in a sea of Republicans," said Democratic state chairman George Carenbauer after the November 1994 election. West Virginia is one of the most Democratic states in national elections, solidly Democratic in the close elections of 1948, 1960, 1968, 1976 and 1988: a safe Democratic state for any Democrat who has a chance to win. West Virginia's presidential primary was important here only once, in 1960, when John Kennedy seized it as an opportunity to prove he could beat Hubert Humphrey in a virtually all-Protestant state, spending money freely and in ways that would not be legal today.

Congressional districting. West Virginia lost one of its four House seats for 1992, and so one of its four Democratic congressmen had to go. This game of musical chairs was played out lustily in the legislature, and the loser turned out to be Harley Staggers, whose 2d District was divided up among the other three, in any of which he would have been at a severe disadvantage; he ran against Alan Mollohan in the 1st District primary and lost. In Republican 1994 the Democratic congressmen were reelected easily; in all three races, the incumbent Democrats lost a total of two counties.

The People: Est. Pop. 1994: 1,822,000; Pop. 1990: 1,793,477, up 1.6% 1990–1994. 0.7% of U.S. total, 35th largest; 64% rural. Median age: 35.4 years. 15.0% 65 years and over. 96.2% White, 3.1% Black. Households: 59.0% married couple families; 28% married couple fams. w. children; 29% college educ.; median household income: $20,795; per capita income: $10,520; 74.1% owner occupied housing; median house value: $47,900; median monthly rent: $221. 11.3% Unemployment. 1994 Voting age pop.: 1,389,000. 1994 Turnout: 417,811; 30% of VAP. Registered voters (1994): 884,315; 576,448 D (65%); 269,217 R (30%); 38,650 unaffiliated and minor parties (4%).

Political Lineup: Governor, Gaston Caperton (D); Senate Pres., Earl Ray Tomblin (D); Secy. of State, Ken Hechler (D); Atty. Gen., Darrell V. McGraw, Jr. (D); Treasurer, Larrie Bailey (D); Auditor, Glen Gaynor (D). State Senate, 34 (26 D and 8 R); State House of Delegates, 100 (71 D and 29 R). Senators, Robert C. Byrd (D) and John D. (Jay) Rockefeller IV (D). Representatives, 3 D.

1992 Presidential Vote		
Clinton (D)	331,001	(48%)
Bush (R)	241,974	(35%)
Perot (I)	108,829	(16%)

1988 Presidential Vote		
Dukakis (D)	341,016	(52%)
Bush (R)	310,065	(48%)

1992 Democratic Presidential Primary		
Clinton	227,815	(74%)
Brown	36,505	(12%)
Tsongas	21,271	(7%)
Other	21,275	(7%)

1992 Republican Presidential Primary		
Bush	99,994	(81%)
Buchanan	18,067	(15%)
Fellure	6,096	(5%)

GOVERNOR

Gov. Gaston Caperton (D)

Elected 1988, term expires Jan. 1997; b. Feb. 21, 1940, Charleston; home, Charleston; U. of NC, B.A. 1963; Protestant; married (Rachael Worby).

Career: Pres., McDonough Caperton Ins. Group, 1963–88.

Office: State Capitol, Charleston 25305, 304-558-2000; Fax: 304-342-7025.

Election Results:

1992 gen.	Gaston Caperton (D)	368,302	(56%)
	Cleve Benedict (R)	240,390	(37%)
	Charlotte Jean Pritt (I)	48,501	(7%)
1992 prim.	Gaston Caperton (D)	142,261	(43%)
	Charlotte Jean Pritt (D)	115,498	(35%)
	Mario J. Palumbo (D)	66,984	(20%)
	Others	8,534	(3%)
1988 gen.	Gaston Caperton (D)	382,421	(59%)
	Arch A. Moore, Jr. (R)	267,172	(41%)

SENATORS

Sen. Robert C. Byrd (D)

Elected 1958, seat up 2000; b. Nov. 20, 1917, North Wilkesboro, NC; home, Sophia; American U., J.D. 1963; Baptist; married (Erma).

Career: WV House of Delegates, 1946–50; WV Senate, 1950–52; U.S. House of Reps., 1953–58; U.S. Senate Majority Whip, 1971–76, Majority Ldr., 1977–80, Minority Ldr., 1981–86, Pres. Pro-tem, 1989–94; Book Author.

DC Office: 311 HSOB 20510, 202-224-3954; Fax: 202-228-0002.

State Offices: Fed. Bldg., 500 Quarrier St., #1019, Charleston 25301, 304-342-5855.

Committees: *Appropriations* (RMM of 13 D): Defense; Energy and Water Development; Interior (RMM); Labor, Health and Human Services, Education; Transportation. *Armed Services* (7th of 10 D): Airland Forces; Personnel (RMM). *Rules & Administration* (3rd of 7 D).

Group Ratings

	ADA	ACLU	COPE	CFA	LCV	CON	NSI	COC	ACU	NTLC	CHC
1994	75	32	75	50	54	5	50	30	40	8	57
1993	55	—	100	70	69	8	—	18	24	—	—

National Journal Ratings

	1993 LIB — 1993 CONS			1994 LIB — 1994 CONS		
Economic	71%	—	17%	55%	—	40%
Social	45%	—	52%	35%	—	63%
Foreign	67%	—	30%	54%	—	43%

Key Votes of the 103d Congress

1. Clinton Deficit Plan	Y	3. Brady Handgun Purchase	Y	5. Lmt. UN Cmnd. of Forces	N
2. NAFTA	N	4. Strike Race/Death Pnlty.	Y	6. Cut Missile Funds	Y

Key Votes of the 104th Congress

1. Congressional Compliance	N	3. Balanced Budget Amndt.	N	5. Product Liability Reform	N
2. Bar Unfunded Mandates	N	4. Pass Line Item Veto	N	6. FY96 Budget	N

Election Results

1994 general	Robert C. Byrd (D).................	290,495	(69%)	($1,550,354)
	Stan Klos (R)......................	130,441	(31%)	($267,165)
1994 primary	Robert C. Byrd (D).................	190,061	(85%)	
	John M. Fuller (D).................	20,057	(9%)	
	Paul Nuchims (D)...................	12,381	(6%)	
1988 general	Robert C. Byrd (D).................	410,983	(65%)	($1,282,746)
	M. Jay Wolfe (R)..................	223,564	(35%)	($115,284)

Sen. John D. (Jay) Rockefeller IV (D)

Elected 1984, seat up 1996; b. June 18, 1937, New York, NY; home, Charleston; Harvard, B.A. 1961, Intl. Christian U., Tokyo, Japan, 1957–60; Presbyterian; married (Sharon).

Career: Natl. Advisory Cncl., Peace Corps, 1961; Asst., Peace Corps Dir. Sargent Shriver, 1962–63; VISTA worker, 1964–66; WV House of Delegates, 1966–68; WV Secy. of State, 1968–72; Pres., WV Wesleyan Col., 1973–75; WV Gov., 1976–84.

DC Office: 109 HSOB 20510, 202-224-6472; Fax: 202-224-7665.

State Offices: 405 Capitol St., #608, Charleston 25301, 304-347-5372; 115 S. Kanawha St., #1, Beckley 25801, 304-253-9704; and 200 Adams St., #A, Fairmont 26554, 304-367-0122.

Committees: *Commerce, Science & Transportation* (5th of 9 D): Aviation; Communications; Consumer Affairs, Foreign Commerce and Tourism; Science, Technology and Space (RMM). *Finance* (5th of 9 D): International Trade; Medicaid and Health Care for Low-Income Families; Medicare, Long-Term Care and Health Insurance (RMM). *Veterans' Affairs* (RMM of 5 D)

Group Ratings

	ADA	ACLU	COPE	CFA	LCV	CON	NSI	COC	ACU	NTLC	CHC
1994	95	56	75	67	92	13	20	28	0	4	21
1993	70	—	91	70	75	22	—	18	12	—	—

National Journal Ratings

	1993 LIB — 1993 CONS		1994 LIB — 1994 CONS	
Economic	83% —	0%	84% —	0%
Social	71% —	28%	69% —	30%
Foreign	65% —	33%	85% —	14%

Key Votes of the 103d Congress

1. Clinton Deficit Plan	Y	3. Brady Handgun Purchase	Y	5. Lmt. UN Cmnd. of Forces	N
2. NAFTA	N	4. Strike Race/Death Pnlty.	N	6. Cut Missile Funds	Y

Key Votes of the 104th Congress

1. Congressional Compliance	*	3. Balanced Budget Amndt.	N	5. Product Liability Reform	Y
2. Bar Unfunded Mandates	Y	4. Pass Line Item Veto	N	6. FY96 Budget	N

Election Results

1990 general	John D. (Jay) Rockefeller IV (D)........	276,234	(68%)	($2,709,665)
	John Yoder (R)......................	128,071	(32%)	($22,904)
1990 primary	John D. (Jay) Rockefeller IV (D)........	200,161	(85%)	
	Ken Buchanon Thompson (D)	21,669	(9%)	
	Paul Nuchims (D).....................	14,467	(5%)	
1984 general	John D. (Jay) Rockefeller IV (D)........	374,233	(52%)	($12,055,043)
	John R. Raese (R)....................	344,680	(48%)	($1,147,123)

FIRST DISTRICT

The northern part of West Virginia is in many ways an extension of the Pittsburgh metropolitan area. People here are Steelers and Pirates fans, they drink Iron City and Rolling Rock beer, they watch Pittsburgh TV, they live in the crevasses between hills cut by the Monongahela and Ohio Rivers, on terrain that seems forbidding to industrial and urban development. Yet this has been one of America's prime industrial areas; northern West Virginia is part of the same coal-and-steel economy that made Pittsburgh one of the nation's largest cities and filled the narrow bottomlands along the rivers with steel and glass factories, foundries and coal yards. In the 1980s and 1990s these have been declining industries, or rather industries becoming far less labor-intensive, shedding many jobs, leaving the fabric of everyday life badly frayed in these parts.

The 1st Congressional District of West Virginia includes the northern third of the state. On the panhandle along the Ohio River are the old steel towns of Wheeling, once one of the richest cities in the country with its steel company investors and executives, and Weirton, a steel company town and site of one of the most visible experiments with employee ownership, where steelworkers decided to cut their own pay in order to produce profits. South of Pittsburgh on the Monongahela are Morgantown, site of West Virginia University, and Clarksburg and Fairmont. Far to the west, the district includes Parkersburg and the surrounding hills on the Ohio River. To the east, it extends to the upper Potomac River opposite Cumberland, Maryland. Politically, most of this territory is solidly Democratic, except for some mountain countries never heavily industrialized which have remained Republican since the Civil War.

The congressman from the 1st District is Alan Mollohan, a Democrat whose father Robert Mollohan was elected congressman in 1952 and 1954, ran for governor and lost in 1956, and then won the seat again when Arch Moore was elected governor in 1968 and kept it until he retired in 1982. Alan Mollohan, a Washington lawyer for Consolidation Coal among other clients, returned home in 1982 and won the seat. His one major challenge came in the 1992 primary, after he was redistricted in with another congressman who was the son of a congressman, Harley Staggers, Jr. The younger Staggers made his name as chief sponsor of the National Rifle Association-supported substitute for the Brady bill seven-day handgun purchase waiting period, to establish a computerized list of felons which gun sellers could check before sales. The younger Mollohan made his name as a member of the Appropriations Committee who hustled to bring jobs to northern West Virginia. But the key was that only 20% of the Democratic primary vote here was cast in Staggers's old district. He carried that part with 73%, but Mollohan won 70% in his old district and won overall, 62%–38%.

Mollohan has compiled a moderately liberal voting record and concentrated on bringing projects to the district. He claims credit for a West Virginia High-Technology Consortium and a First District Federal Procurement Team; he has worked to fund waterways, education projects, a flight simulator for Fairmont State College and a defense procurement center in Parkersburg, historic sites, the Morgantown federal prison, the Orbital Science Corporation's satellite tracking station. In April 1994 Mollohan moved up to the "college of cardinals" when he became chairman of the Commerce, Justice, State, and Judiciary Appropriations Subcommittee. But power can be fleeting, and with Republican control of Congress Mollohan is now ranking minority member.

The People: Pop. 1990: 598,056; 55% rural; 16% age 65+; 97% White; 2% Black; 1% Asian; 1% Hispanic origin. Voting age pop.: 456,485; 1% Black; 1% Hispanic origin. Households: 59% married couple families; 27% married couple fams. w. children; 32% college educ.; median household income: $21,903; per capita income: $10,920; median gross rent: $307; median house value: $46,400.

1992 Presidential Vote			1988 Presidential Vote		
Clinton (D)	113,756	(46%)	Dukakis (D)	117,705	(50%)
Bush (R)	86,131	(35%)	Bush (R)	115,989	(49%)
Perot (I)	45,856	(19%)			

Rep. Alan B. Mollohan (D)

Elected 1982; b. May 14, 1943, Fairmont; home, Fairmont; Col. of William & Mary, A.B. 1966, WV U., J.D. 1970; Baptist; married (Barbara).

Career: Army, 1970, Army Reserves, 1970–83; Practicing atty., 1970–82.

DC Office: 2427 RHOB 20515, 202-225-4172; Fax: 202-225-7564.

District Offices: 213 Fed. Bldg., Morgantown 26505, 304-292-3019; 1117 Fed. Bldg., Parkersburg 26101, 304-428-0493; 316 Fed. Bldg., Wheeling 26003, 304-232-5390; and 209 P.O. Bldg., Clarksburg 26301, 304-623-4422.

Committees: *Appropriations* (15th of 24 D): Commerce, Justice, State, and Judiciary (RMM); VA, HUD, and Independent Agencies. *Budget* (6th of 18 D).

Group Ratings

	ADA	ACLU	COPE	CFA	LCV	CON	NSI	COC	ACU	NTLC	CHC
1994	60	30	89	70	59	0	80	33	38	14	50
1993	45	—	100	80	50	1	—	20	29	—	—

National Journal Ratings

	1993 LIB — 1993 CONS		1994 LIB — 1994 CONS	
Economic	78% —	12%	73% —	17%
Social	36% —	62%	55% —	45%
Foreign	51% —	42%	57% —	37%

Key Votes of the 103d Congress

1. Clinton Deficit Plan	Y	3. Brady Handgun Purchase	N	5. Lmt. UN Cmnd. of Forces	N
2. NAFTA	N	4. Strike Race/Death Pnlty.	N	6. Cut Missile Funds	N

Key Votes of the 104th Congress

1. Congressional Compliance	Y	6. Reform Crime Grant	N	11. Loser Pays Court Reform	N
2. Balanced Budget Amndmt.	N	7. National Security Act	N	12. Product Liability Reform	N
3. Bar Unfunded Mandates	N	8. Moratorium on Regs.	N	13. Welfare Reform	N
4. Pass Line Item Veto	N	9. Risk Assessment on Regs.	Y	14. Term Limits Amndmt.	N
5. Relax Exclusionary Rule	N	10. Expnd. Priv. Prop. Rights	Y	15. Tax Cuts	N

Election Results

1994 general	Alan B. Mollohan (D)...................	103,177	(70%)	($315,389)
	Sally Rossy Riley (R)...................	43,590	(30%)	($7,245)
1994 primary	Alan B. Mollohan (D).............. unopposed			
1992 general	Alan B. Mollohan (D).............. unopposed			($629,436)

SECOND DISTRICT

Not all of West Virginia is coal country, not all of its valleys are industrial hollows choked with workingmen's homes and small factories, not all of its hills are scarred with strip mining wounds or piled with tailings. For miles you can see gentle hills and rugged mountains, stands of green trees and vistas stretching to far horizons. Yet over another hill you may find, amid scenery primeval and rural, sudden evidence of industrialization: a pulp mill or charcoal factory in a clearing scraped out of the forest; a small factory town, built close to a river in a cleft bordered with hills, its houses built in the same 1910s style as in the factory towns of Pittsburgh; the entrance to an underground coal mine or the exposed brown earth of a strip mine scar. Large parts of this naturally beautiful state look as verdant and unchanged as they must have when George Washington was speculating in land here or taking the waters in Berkeley Spring or when John Brown launched his assault at the federal arsenal at Harper's Ferry or when the Civil War pitted brother against brother.

The 2d Congressional District of West Virginia is the central part of the state, a belt of land from Berkeley Springs and Harper's Ferry all the way west to the Ohio River town of Point Pleasant where the Kanawha River (pronounced *kaNAW*) flows into the Ohio. It could easily take a full day to drive through this district which, if ironed out, would probably spread across the country. The one major urban center here is Charleston, where on the banks of the Kanawha rises West Virginia's Capitol, built in 1932 and designed by Cass Gilbert with a dome higher than the U.S. Capitol and a chandelier with 10,000 pieces of cut glass. Charleston is the state capital, and, with its two partisan newspapers, the Democratic *Gazette* and the Republican *Daily Mail*, the center of the state's political culture. Charleston is also a major industrial center, with coal in the hills all around and, downriver from the Capitol, huge petrochemical plants that convert coal tar and other feedstocks into everyday products. This was a center of American high tech in the 1940s, when it produced all the nation's lucite, polyethylenes and nylon as well as much of its artificial rubber and antifreeze. More recently, these factories are seen as heavy polluters in a valley that has well above average rates of cancer. Yet Charleston is also West Virginia's white-collar and professional center, with a few downtown skyscrapers and some pleasant affluent residential districts. Politically, the 2d has some mountain Republican counties, and Charleston's Kanawha County sometimes goes Republican too; but in national terms this is a solidly Democratic seat.

The congressman from the 2d District is Bob Wise, a Democrat from an affluent Charleston family, who returned home after law school to start a law practice geared to low- and middle-income clients and led a movement to force coal companies to pay higher taxes. A strong advocate of West Virginia culture he urges West Virginia students to make their careers, as he did, in their home state. But he is not a total traditionalist. In a state where past politicians got ahead by relying on ancestral loyalties and smoothing relations with big economic institutions, he has made his way by emphasizing issues on which he opposes the big interests. Wise, elected to the state Senate in 1980, was shrewd and popular enough to beat the state House majority leader and a former Kanawha County sheriff in the 1982 primary and then to beat a Republican incumbent soundly in November. He has been reelected easily ever since.

In the House Wise is an enthusiastic and articulate partisan Democrat. Early in his career he bucked local power, taking to the floor in 1983 to oppose a dam favored by the rest of the West Virginia delegation; he is one of the House's biggest boosters of alternative fuels and has championed compressed natural gas as an auto fuel; he has had two CNG-powered cars (though one broke down on I-64 with transmission problems). He became the first West Virginian on the Budget Committee in 1989, and became a supporter of the balanced budget amendment; but in 1994 he made his support contingent on putting Social Security off budget, and in 1995 he opposed the Republican version strenuously. His biggest legislative success was his 1990 amendment, adopted 274–146, to provide benefits for workers displaced by compliance with the Clean Air Act; this was similar to Senator Robert Byrd's amendment, which lost in the Senate by one vote, but Wise's amendment had a five-year spending cap of $250 million and was passed partly to forestall Byrd's.

At the beginning of the 104th Congress, the Democratic leadership asked Wise and Massachusetts's Barney Frank to lead opposition to Republican proposals on the floor. Witty, cheerful, energetic, Wise responded with gusto. "If you liked Reagan's supply side economics, you will love this riverboat gamble," he said of the Republicans' tax cuts. And so this sometime critic of Democratic policies has become, now that they are so fundamentally threatened, one of their most vigorous and articulate defenders.

The People: Pop. 1990: 597,921; 62% rural; 14% age 65+; 96% White; 3% Black. Voting age pop.: 448,503; 3% Black. Households: 61% married couple families; 28% married couple fams. w. children; 30% college educ.; median household income: $22,253; per capita income: $11,083; median gross rent: $321; median house value: $55,200.

1992 Presidential Vote

Clinton (D)	104,257	(45%)
Bush (R)	90,375	(39%)
Perot (I)	36,813	(16%)

1988 Presidential Vote

Bush (R)	111,398	(51%)
Dukakis (D)	104,450	(48%)

Rep. Robert E. (Bob) Wise, Jr. (D)

Elected 1982; b. Jan. 6, 1948, Washington, D.C.; home, Clendenin; Duke U., B.A. 1970, Tulane U., J.D. 1975; Episcopalian; married (Sandy).

Career: Practicing atty., 1975–80; Dir., WV for Fair and Equitable Assessment of Taxes, 1977–80; WV Senate, 1980–82.

DC Office: 2434 RHOB 20515, 202-225-2711; Fax: 202-225-7856.

District Offices: Elk Office Ctr., 4710 Chimney Dr., Charleston 25302, 304-342-7170; and 222 W. John St., Martinsburg 25401, 304-264-8810.

Committees: *Government Reform & Oversight* (4th of 22 D): Government Management, Information and Technology; National Security, International Affairs and Criminal Justice. *Transportation & Infrastructure* (6th of 27 D): Aviation; Public Buildings and Economic Development (RMM).

Group Ratings

	ADA	ACLU	COPE	CFA	LCV	CON	NSI	COC	ACU	NTLC	CHC
1994	75	55	89	70	59	5	56	42	30	25	28
1993	70	—	100	90	86	11	—	20	21	—	—

National Journal Ratings

	1993 LIB	—	1993 CONS	1994 LIB	—	1994 CONS
Economic	78%	—	12%	73%	—	17%
Social	59%	—	40%	63%	—	37%
Foreign	51%	—	42%	57%	—	37%

Key Votes of the 103d Congress

1. Clinton Deficit Plan	Y	3. Brady Handgun Purchase	N	5. Lmt. UN Cmnd. of Forces	N
2. NAFTA	N	4. Strike Race/Death Pnlty.	N	6. Cut Missile Funds	N

Key Votes of the 104th Congress

1. Congressional Compliance	Y	6. Reform Crime Grant	N	11. Loser Pays Court Reform	N
2. Balanced Budget Amndmt.	N	7. National Security Act	N	12. Product Liability Reform	N
3. Bar Unfunded Mandates	Y	8. Moratorium on Regs.	N	13. Welfare Reform	N
4. Pass Line Item Veto	N	9. Risk Assessment on Regs.	N	14. Term Limits Amndmt.	N
5. Relax Exclusionary Rule	Y	10. Expnd. Priv. Prop. Rights	N	15. Tax Cuts	N

Election Results

1994 general	Robert E. (Bob) Wise, Jr. (D)	90,757	(64%)	($271,315)
	Sam Cravotta (R)	51,691	(36%)	($43,897)
1994 primary	Robert E. (Bob) Wise, Jr. (D)	unopposed		
1992 general	Robert E. (Bob) Wise, Jr. (D)	143,988	(71%)	($330,052)
	Samuel A. Cravotta (R)	59,102	(29%)	($36,405)

THIRD DISTRICT

Early in this century, the coalfields of southern West Virginia were one of America's boom areas. Into rural farmland and hollows, inhabited by the same families since they first arrived at these mountains 100 years before, came coal company lawyers with mineral rights' leases to sign, coal company engineers to design and sink the mineshafts, and men from other mountain counties, as well as Europe, to work the mines. Company houses were built, company stores stocked with goods as the company dictated and company paymasters kept close tabs on the finances of every employee. These conditions bred dull discontent, ignited into the fire of industrial unionism by the tongue of John L. Lewis, president of the United Mine Workers, who organized most of the mines in the 1930s. Lewis was not only a militant unionist, but an isolationist, and during and after World War II he called out his coal miners on strikes, to the fury of Franklin Roosevelt and Harry Truman. The entire national war effort and postwar economic recovery seemed gravely threatened by these labor stoppages involving perhaps 300,000 workers, centered in back corners of the country like southern West Virginia.

All that is history now. Coal is no longer central to our economy and there are only a few thousand coal miners left in southern West Virginia—and many are not UMW members anymore. In 1950, when coal area population peaked, there were 579,000 people in the eight counties that made up the heart of southern West Virginia's coal country. Their population fell to 437,000 in 1970, then spurted up after energy prices were raised by the two oil shocks of the 1970s to 487,000 in 1980, but went down by 1990 to only 421,000. Most of the old underground mines have been abandoned, leaving behind mineshafts and piles of tailings—and lives that were snuffed out by cave-ins or simple carelessness in America's deadliest industry.

The 3d Congressional District of West Virginia includes most of the coal country in the southern part of the state, the mountainous counties directly south of Charleston that are among America's most heavily Democratic—and in some cases most politically corrupt—jurisdictions: Mingo County, where in the 1980s a sheriff bought his job for $100,000 and other politicos bought votes for $2 or a half-pint of bourbon. But the coal mining counties are no longer populous enough for a full congressional district and now make up about half the 3d District. About one-quarter is in and around the industrial city of Huntington on the Ohio River, and another quarter is to the east, in the farming uplands around the resort of White Sulphur Springs, where President John Tyler honeymooned in 1844, and the interstate junction at Beckley, which has become a popular whitewater rafting area. These two areas as a whole are much less Democratic than the coal counties.

The congressman here is Nick Joe Rahall, a Democrat first elected in 1976. He comes from the thin economic upper crust of the coal country; his family owns radio and TV stations in Beckley and in St. Petersburg, Florida. Rahall has concentrated on bringing public works projects and jobs to his district. He got a seats on Transportation and Infrastructure and Resources early on, and is now high-ranking on both. After negative publicity for gambling debts and a drunk driving arrest, he had close calls in 1990: his predecessor, then 75-year-old Secretary of State (and onetime Adlai Stevenson speechwriter) Ken Hechler, won 43% of the vote in the primary; an underfinanced Republican in the general won 48%. Rahall evidently took heed from this narrow escape. He used his senior position on Transportation and Infrastructure to help West Virginia get $1.3 billion in highway projects in the 1991 transportation bill (Senator Robert Byrd helped, of course). He used his chairmanship of the Mining Subcommittee of Resources to push for reform of the 1872 mining bill that allowed companies to cheaply purchase rights to mine federal land. With Senators Rockefeller and Byrd, he pushed for a tax on non-union coal operators to bail out the United Mine Workers healthcare funds. He worked on water and sewer projects, a trout hatchery in McDowell County and protection against development of the New River. He introduced new black lung legislation, pressed for tamper-proof coal mine dust sampling devices, tried to create disincentives for U.S. companies to import coal from abroad.

All this paid off when Rahall emerged from redistricting without any serious opposition in 1992. As chairman of the Transportation and Infrastructure Subcommittee on Surface Transportation, he sponsored a National Highway System bill which passed the House, but was never reconciled with a Senate version. He was similarly frustrated on reforming the Mining Act of 1872 ("the Jurassic Park of all federal laws"). He was more successful in establishing a Coal Heritage Area, but this required no significant federal funding.

Rahall was easily reelected in 1994 and seems to have tightened his hold on this seat. But with Republican control, he lost his chairmanships, and Republican budgets threaten his ability to channel money to the coal country. He is under no illusions: he argued against the balanced budget amendment on the grounds it could cost West Virginians $1 billion.

The People: Pop. 1990: 597,500; 74% rural; 15% age 65+; 95% White; 4% Black. Voting age pop.: 444,283; 4% Black. Households: 60% married couple families; 29% married couple fams. w. children; 26% college educ.; median household income: $18,166; per capita income: $9,557; median gross rent: $284; median house value: $41,700.

1992 Presidential Vote		
Clinton (D)	112,988	(55%)
Bush (R)	65,468	(32%)
Perot (I)	26,160	(13%)

1988 Presidential Vote		
Dukakis (D)	118,861	(59%)
Bush (R)	82,678	(41%)

Rep. Nick J. Rahall (D)

Elected 1976; b. May 20, 1949, Beckley; home, Beckley; Duke U., A.B. 1971; Presbyterian; divorced.

Career: Civil Air Patrol, 1977–88; Staff Asst., U.S. Sen. Robert Byrd, 1971–74; Bd. of Dir., Rahall Communications Corp. 1974–76; Pres., Mountaineer Tour & Travel Agency, 1974–76; Pres., WV Broadcasting Corp. 1980–present.

DC Office: 2269 RHOB 20515, 202-225-3452; Fax: 202-225-9061.

District Offices: 110½ Main St., Beckley 25801, 304-252-5000; 815 5th Ave., Huntington 25701, 304-522-6425; 1005 Fed. Bldg., Bluefield 24701, 304-325-6222; R.K. Bldg., 45 Washington Ave., Logan 25601, 304-752-4934; and P.O. Box 5, 101 N. Court St., Lewisburg 24901, 304-647-3228.

Committees: *Resources* (2nd of 20 D): Energy & Mineral Resources; Natl. Parks, Forests & Lands. *Transportation & Infrastructure* (3rd of 27 D): Railroads; Surface Transportation (RMM).

Group Ratings

	ADA	ACLU	COPE	CFA	LCV	CON	NSI	COC	ACU	NTLC	CHC
1994	75	39	100	60	61	15	30	25	24	15	57
1993	70	—	100	80	77	11	—	18	30	—	—

National Journal Ratings

	1993 LIB — 1993 CONS	1994 LIB — 1994 CONS
Economic	88% — 0%	73% — 17%
Social	36% — 62%	55% — 45%
Foreign	70% — 26%	68% — 29%

Key Votes of the 103d Congress

1. Clinton Deficit Plan	Y	3. Brady Handgun Purchase	N	5. Lmt. UN Cmnd. of Forces	N
2. NAFTA	N	4. Strike Race/Death Pnlty.	N	6. Cut Missile Funds	Y

Key Votes of the 104th Congress

1. Congressional Compliance	Y	6. Reform Crime Grant	N	11. Loser Pays Court Reform	N
2. Balanced Budget Amndmt.	N	7. National Security Act	N	12. Product Liability Reform	N
3. Bar Unfunded Mandates	Y	8. Moratorium on Regs.	N	13. Welfare Reform	N
4. Pass Line Item Veto	N	9. Risk Assessment on Regs.	N	14. Term Limits Amndmt.	N
5. Relax Exclusionary Rule	Y	10. Expnd. Priv. Prop. Rights	N	15. Tax Cuts	N

Election Results

1994 general	Nick J. Rahall (D)	74,967	(64%)	($389,323)
	Ben Waldman (R)	42,382	(36%)	($41,838)
1994 primary	Nick J. Rahall (D)	unopposed		
1992 general	Nick J. Rahall (D)	122,279	(66%)	($309,313)
	Ben Waldman (R)	64,012	(34%)	($150,822)

WISCONSIN

Wisconsin, tucked off north of the main east-west routes across the country and squeezed between Lake Michigan and the Mississippi River, almost a century ago was one of America's premier "laboratories of reform," in Justice Louis Brandeis's phrase—and, some argue, is again today: a state originating new public policies, seeing how they work, serving as an example for others. Wisconsin's first fame as a laboratory came during the Progressive era that began around 1900, and its primacy was due to an extraordinary Governor, Robert LaFollette, Sr., and to the state's unique history and German heritage. For Wisconsin is the first state of the Old Northwest, that vast stretch of the United States reaching all the way to the Pacific, settled first by New England Yankees but even more by immigrants from Germany and Scandinavia. The German language is seldom heard now, the once plainly German beer brands now seem quintessentially American and few ties remained with the old country after two world wars. But in the late 19th and early 20th Centuries, Germans were among America's most numerous immigrants and until the 1890s probably the most distinctive. They established, on the rolling dairyland of Wisconsin and the orderly streets of Milwaukee, their separate religions, often keeping their language and maintaining old customs, from country weddings to drinking beer— a source of friction in temperance-minded America—to eating bratwurst.

Politically, the Germans were not monolithic. Their origins were diverse and they were spread too widely across the nation. But where they were concentrated, there was a distinctive politics, basically American, but with echoes of progressive ideas current in German-speaking countries in Europe. Nowhere was the politics of German-Americans more apparent than in Wisconsin. This is one of the two states that gave birth to the Republican Party in 1854 (the other is Michigan), and Germans, then arriving in America in vast numbers, heavily favored it. They abhorred slavery and welcomed the free lands Republicans advocated in the Homestead Act, the free education promised by setting up land grant colleges and the transportation routes constructed by subsidizing railroad builders. Then came the Progressive movement of Robert LaFollette, elected governor of Wisconsin in 1900. Up to that time a conventional Republican politician, LaFollette completely revamped the state government before going to the Senate in 1906. At a time when Germany was Europe's leader in graduate education and the application of science to government, LaFollette had professors from the University of Wisconsin, just across town in Madison, help develop the state workmen's compensation system and income tax. The Progressive movement favored rational use of government to improve the lot of the ordinary citizen—an idea borrowed partly from German liberals and adopted by the New Dealers a generation later. All these programs were an attempt to bring bureaucratic rationality— Germanic systematization—to the seemingly disordered America of free markets and multiple cultures, gigantic fortunes and vast open spaces.

LaFollette became a national figure. He tried to run for president in 1912 as a Progressive, but was shoved aside by Theodore Roosevelt. He did run in 1924 on his Progressive ticket and won 18% of the votes, the best third-candidate showing between 1912 and 1992. He was strongest in the northern tier of states from Wisconsin west and along the West Coast—the same area of strength of later liberals George McGovern, Walter Mondale and Michael Dukakis. After LaFollette died in 1925, his sons carried on his tradition, progressive at home and isolationist abroad: Robert LaFollette, Jr., for 22 years in the Senate; Philip, elected governor in 1930, 1934 and 1936. Philip created his own Progressive Party in 1934, with ominous overtones: with a Cross in Circle symbol his critics called a circumcised swastika, huge rally-like parades reminiscent of some in Europe at the time and a call for the governor to propose all legislation. But Philip lost in 1938 and did not run again, and Robert, Jr. decided to run for reelection in

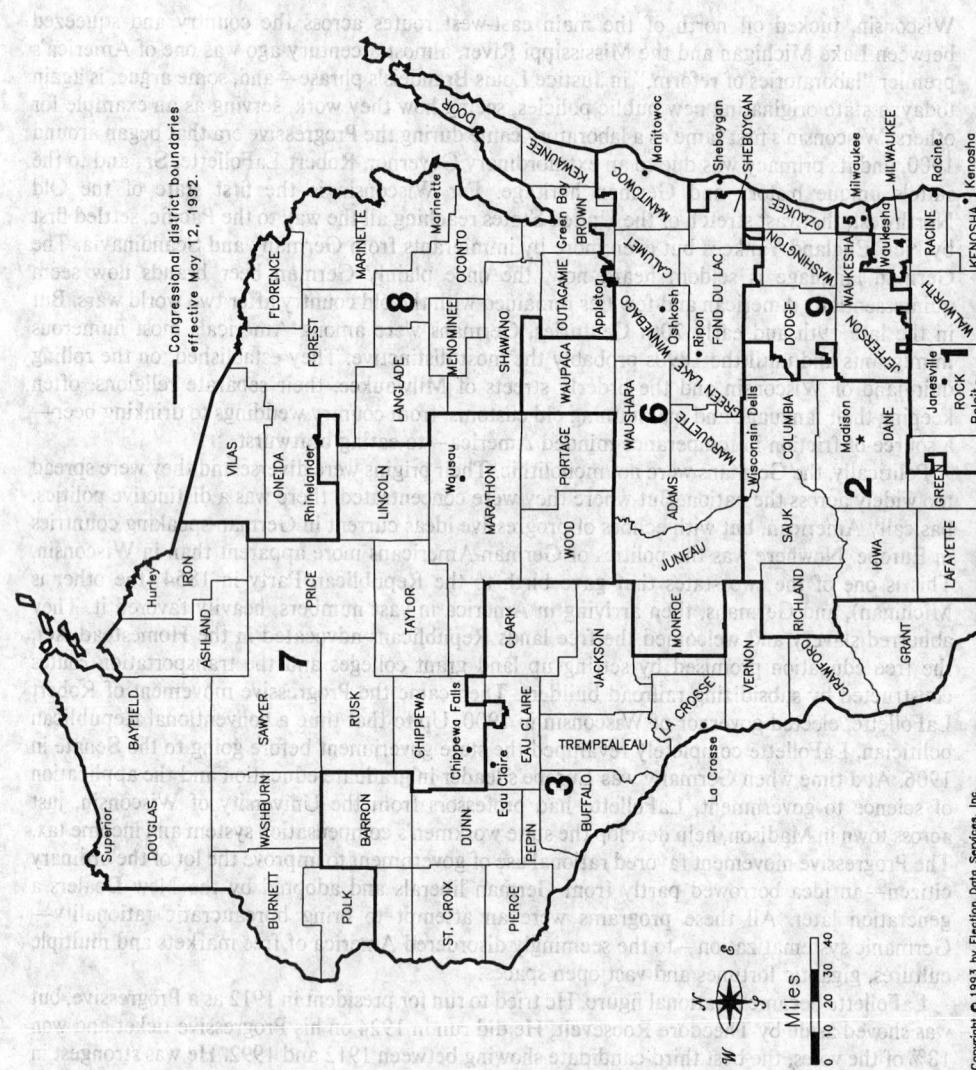

Congressional district boundaries
effective May 12, 1992.

1946 as a Republican but lost the primary to Joseph McCarthy. McCarthy's charges that Communists were influencing American foreign policy fed on the inarticulate convictions of many in Wisconsin and elsewhere that the U.S. should have been fighting Russia as well as Germany in World War II.

McCarthy's national prominence made Wisconsin seem like a Republican state. But he won by narrow margins and the LaFollette progressive tradition was taken up by liberal Democrats like Senators William Proxmire and Gaylord Nelson and Governor Patrick Lucey. Like most liberals of their era, these progressives saw Washington rather than Madison as the main site of their laboratory of reform. Wisconsin, a mostly Republican state in the mostly Democratic years from 1944–64, became a mostly Democratic state in the mostly Republican years from 1968–88. It was one of the most dovish states, as if many Wisconsin voters were hit by the same impulse that led so many West German voters in the early 1980s to fear the presence of nuclear weapons and to favor disarmament.

Now Wisconsin seems to have turned in another direction, and is a laboratory for different kinds of reforms. The motivating force comes, as it did in the early 1900s, from the Governor, in this case Republican Tommy Thompson, who beat a liberal Democrat in 1986 and has become one of the nation's most popular governors. He has cut taxes, sponsored a school choice program championed by Milwaukee black activist Polly Williams, implemented a "learnfare" program which ties a parent's welfare grants to children's school attendance, passed a "bridefare" law paying welfare recipients more if they get married and less if they have more children and signed a law making a parent or guardian, rather than the state, responsible for supporting children of unmarried teenagers. He also signed what has been called the nation's most comprehensive recycling law. Wisconsin's high-skill, precision manufacturing economy—its biggest companies include Johnson Controls, Harnischfeger, Briggs & Stratton, Harley-Davidson—jumped into gear in the late 1980s, as its factories helped lead the nation's export boom. Wisconsin gained more jobs than other midwestern states and was hurt relatively little by the early 1990s recession.

Thompson has not carried all before him. Wisconsin has two Democratic U.S. Senators and it voted for Bill Clinton in 1992. But Thompson has been reelected handsomely, with 58% against Speaker Tom Loftus in 1990 and with 67% against state Senator Chuck Chvala in 1994. In this as in other races, the Milwaukee area is no Democratic stronghold; Thompson's percentage there was actually higher than in the rest of the state in 1994. Wisconsin has one of the nation's most highly partisan legislatures, and Thompson's Republicans won control of the state Senate in 1993 and the state House in 1994. Milwaukee Mayor John Norquist, a New Democrat, echoes some though not all of Thompson's themes. He prides himself on lowering taxes while providing better services, and argues that central cities should see themselves not as hovels full of victims but as shining examples of excellence. And Thompson's laboratory of reform, like LaFollette's, has attracted attention across the country. State officials and members of Congress strive to match his welfare reforms and even President Clinton seems to cite Thompson with favor. Most of all, however, Thompson has worked closely with Speaker Newt Gingrich, who often cites Wisconsin as a laboratory for the nation and whose House-passed bill responded to the Governor's call to turn federal welfare assistance into a block grant program that gives broad flexibility to the states. Thompson and Wisconsin seem to have decided that the bureaucratic, supposedly rational state which the LaFollettes championed is now dysfunctional, and that individuals making their own choices, in the framework of a fair and orderly society, can achieve more than planners can ever conceive. It helps perhaps now as it did then that Wisconsin with its Yankee and German traditions tends to be more fair and orderly than many other states. But once again it seems experiments in this laboratory matter.

Governor. From the small town of Elroy, 85 miles south to Madison, Wisconsin's Governor Tommy Thompson has been commuting most of his life, first as a student at the University of Wisconsin, where he was a Goldwater Republican on a campus full of liberal Democrats, then to the legislature when he was elected in 1966 just after finishing law school, and now as governor.

For years he was part of a minority in Madison; "Dr. No," his liberal critics called him. Now he is the dominant political figure in the state. He has used Wisconsin's extraordinary "partial veto" more than 1,200 times. He can strike not only lines from the budget, but words and numbers, enabling him to cut a program by 90% by dropping one zero, or to restore his "bridefare" experiment by writing it back in. He cut income and capital gains taxes and repealed the inheritance tax; he funded a property tax cut with spending cuts; he improved the business climate. Those reforms helped Wisconsin gain 450,000 jobs and reach full employment since Thompson took office. He instituted and spotlighted school choice and sponsored the nation's first "work not welfare" experiment. Wisconsin welfare rolls dropped by 25% from 1987–95; a Thompson law ends the current welfare system by 1999 and he has promised a new system by 1997. He pushed for tough crime bills and an Information Technology Fund which will make government services more efficient and cost effective through expanded technology. In early 1995 he pledged "a new government for a new century"—the LaFollette example is very much on his mind.

The secrets of Thompson's success have been hard work, good political instincts and a common touch. He refers constantly to his home town of Elroy, and refers to the rest of the state as "greater metropolitan Elroy." "Let's face it," he likes to say, "It's hard to be humble when you're from Wisconsin." He has had some disappointments: he lost the primary for a vacant congressional seat to Tom Petri in 1979, and he was not taken as seriously as a force at the 1992 Republican National Convention as he had hoped to spotlight his achievements in Wisconsin. But in early 1995 he seemed interested in running for president. He does not have many national political or fundraising contacts, though he has raised large sums in Wisconsin. He will have neither the time nor the money to win a nomination the way Jimmy Carter did in 1976. He must depend on the fame of his experiments in the laboratory of reform that is Wisconsin, and it is not negligible.

Senators. Wisconsin has had two Democratic senators since 1992, as it did from 1962–80, and there is a certain symmetry between then and now, with Herb Kohl resembling William Proxmire and Russ Feingold closer to Gaylord Nelson.

Herb Kohl is one of the richest members of Congress, and one of the least flamboyant, a mild-mannered but stubborn and politically successful politician. His parents immigrated to Milwaukee from Russia and Poland in the 1920s and opened a food store. Kohl's ultimately became a Wisconsin supermarket chain and was sold in 1979, for great profit; Kohl's fortune has been estimated at $250 million. In 1985 he became a local celebrity in a city smarting from sports franchises that too often were often losers, both financially and competitively, when he bought the Milwaukee Bucks basketball team to keep it from moving out of the city. When William Proxmire—famous for his pinchpenny ways opposing federal spending and spending nothing on his own campaigns—announced he was retiring in 1988, Kohl decided to run. He spent his own money liberally, running an extensive ad campaign with the theme, "Nobody's senator but yours." He won 47% in the primary to 38% for former Governor Tony Earl. In the general, against moderate Republican Susan Engeleiter, Kohl stressed his support of defense cuts—popular in dovish Wisconsin—and for requiring businesses to provide medical insurance; Engeleiter stressed her environmental stands, her legislative experience and her status as a wife and mother—in contrast to Kohl, a bachelor. This turned out to be one of the closest Senate races in the country, with Kohl winning 52%–48%, after spending $7 million of his own money.

Kohl is a pleasant, shy, almost painfully earnest man, of transparent good will and seemingly little guile. He dislikes the crunch of partisan politics, which he encountered in the Judiciary Committee fight over the nomination of Justice Clarence Thomas, and in 1992 decried "gridlock, polarized politics, and legislative inaction accompanied by frenzied finger pointing and blame placing." Kohl's chief focus seems to be on holding down federal spending. His record on economic issues is quite conservative for a Democrat, like Proxmire's; he is rather more liberal on cultural and foreign issues. He is unfazed in challenging colleagues and co-partisans, as he did in early 1993 when he pushed an ultimately successful amendment requiring the

Clinton stimulus package to be paid for by spending cuts. Later in 1993 he insisted that he would support a gas tax increase of no greater than 4.3 cents in the Clinton budget and tax package; Clinton, needing his vote, agreed on 4.3 cents, which meant that his package increased taxes on ordinary people but didn't raise much money in doing so. Kohl voted against the Supercolider, the space station, and Trident II missiles. He supports the balanced budget amendment, most recently during the unsuccessful March 1995 vote. In 1994, with Charles Grassley of Iowa, Kohl sponsored a welfare-to-work bill.

Kohl's other major accomplishments are on crime and gun issues. Acting from the unusual perspective of a non-lawyer on the Judiciary Committee, he was a chief sponsor of the Brady bill requiring a waiting period to buy handguns; he saw it killed under George Bush but later signed into law by Bill Clinton. Kohl also drafted a law banning possessing of handguns by people under 18, and loudly decried violence on television and in video games. As ranking minority member on the Terrorism Subcommittee, Kohl labeled the Oklahoma City bombing "a grim wake-up call," and with Senators Arlen Specter and Joe Biden, introduced the Administration's anti-terrorism legislation designed to improve the federal government's ability to deal swiftly with terrorists. He succeeded in getting a measure allowing phone customers to block caller ID. After the Tiananmen Square massacre, he sponsored the measure to allow Chinese students to remain in the United States, on which a Bush veto was upheld by appeals to Republican partisanship. He also supports Wisconsin causes. As a subcommittee chairman, he stood stoutly against adjustment of the 1990 Census figures—a worthy stand against a measure that, as it happens, would have cost Wisconsin a congressional seat. He has worked on Great Lakes issues, from requiring that farm commodities be shipped from Great Lakes ports to preventing oil spills and controlling the harmful and predatory zebra mussel. Additionally, he has worked for higher dairy prices, funds for Milwaukee harbor and Lake Superior and for research into cryptosporidium in municipal water systems. He backs spending $8 million to restore Frank Lloyd Wright's famous house, Taliesin, in Spring Green, Wisconsin. And he personally funds the Herb Kohl Educational Foundation which has given $1.5 million in scholarships and grants to students, teachers and schools, and in April 1995, gave $25 million to his alma mater, the University of Wisconsin.

In his 1994 reelection campaign, Kohl stressed his work against spending and crime and also his own sincere, unprepossessing demeanor. He was able to get his message across: with far less press criticism than in 1988, he spent $6.5 million of his own money on the campaign (far more per voter, incidentally, than Michael Huffington was spending in California). His Republican opponent, Robert Welch, a land surveyor and a young conservative firebrand in the state legislature, raised many of the issues Republicans were winning on elsewhere, but did not have the funds to get much of a hearing. Meanwhile, Kohl joked with voters by asking them to contribute to meet basketball player Glenn Robinson's demands for the Bucks to give him a $100 million contract. Kohl won 58%–41%.

Wisconsin's junior senator, Russ Feingold, first elected in 1992 at age 39 after a riproaring and sometimes amusing campaign, is what might be called a postmodern liberal. Feingold wanted to be a senator when he was growing up in Janesville. He nurtured his ambition at the University of Wisconsin, as a Rhodes Scholar, and at Harvard Law School; he moved to Middleton, a not-so-academic suburb of Madison, and beat an incumbent state senator in 1982, at 29. Feingold has a flair for publicity, and for making novel arguments for liberal stands. His great goal in the legislature was to ban bovine growth hormone, a luddite measure aimed at keeping in business Wisconsin's numerous and overly subsidized dairy farmers (their problem is that Americans drink less milk today than in the 1950s. Feingold also opposed Thompson's welfare reforms and tax cuts and opposed capital punishment. Feingold's goal for 1992 was the Senate seat held by Bob Kasten, a free-market conservative who pushed tort reform and capital gains tax cuts, and who narrowly beat Senator Gaylord Nelson in 1980 and was reelected 51%–47% in 1986.

In the 1992 Democratic senatorial primary, Feingold faced Milwaukee businessman Joseph Checota, who had more money, and Milwaukee Congressman Jim Moody, who had better name recognition. But while his opponents battered each other with negative ads, Feingold ran clever, humorous spots: one showing Elvis, alive and endorsing Feingold; another showing Feingold at home, opening up a closet and saying, "No skeletons"; another showing his three key pledges written out on his garage door. He also had detailed position papers, including an 82-point plan for reducing the deficit. Near primary day, Checota apologized for his ads and asked voters to vote for Feingold if they didn't vote for him. Feingold, already ahead in polls, zoomed to an astonishing 70% win in this three-way primary. Feingold also bounced way ahead of Kasten, who ran his own Elvis ads attacking Feingold on issues; Feingold attacked Kasten's negativity and avoided engaging on specifics. For all his issue papers, this was a campaign not of issues but of attitude. The race narrowed, but Feingold won 53%–46%.

In the Senate, Feingold made a very liberal record on cultural and foreign issues while acting more moderate on economics. He pushed through a moratorium and study on bovine growth hormone, worked with others to dispatch the mohair subsidy and forced a consolidation of government overseas broadcasting by attacking Radio Free Europe/Radio Liberty as obsolete, despite the remaining strife, repression and uncertainty in former Communist areas. He attacked spending virtually wherever he could find it: the Pentagon's medical school, helium subsidies and the Supercollider. He was one of the crusaders against lobbyists' gifts to lawmakers. He attacked the national milk-marketing system as anti-Midwest and moved to eliminate the Extremely Low Frequency radio system—"a cold war relic" in his words—embedded in northern Wisconsin. But for all his anti-spending measures, he is scarcely anti-government. He backed a single-payer healthcare system. He sponsored bills to prohibit insurance company redlining and to prevent employees from agreeing to arbitrate discrimination cases. On the Foreign Relations Committee, he moved to condition aid to Indonesia on human rights in East Timor and favored lifting the Bosnian arms embargo. He has shown an unpredictable streak, such as his early opposition to Tom Daschle in the 1994 race for Democratic Leader, despite his closer generational and geographic ties to Daschle than to Jim Sasser and then Chris Dodd.

Feingold is one of many young members who has not moved his family to Washington and who spends most of his time in his state. He kept his promise to hold public listening meetings in all 72 Wisconsin counties each year. With his political skills, he seems likely to be a strong candidate for reelection in 1998.

Presidential politics. Wisconsin formerly had one of the nation's most influential presidential primaries. It knocked Wendell Willkie out of the race in 1944, helped John Kennedy establish his lead over Hubert Humphrey in 1960, and prompted Lyndon Johnson to withdraw as Eugene McCarthy was about to beat him here in 1968. But now there are many early primaries and Wisconsin's, in April, tends to get lost. In 1992, Wisconsin's primary was held the same day as New York's, but by then Clinton had already clinched the nomination and beat Jerry Brown in Wisconsin 38%–35%. The national Democrats, incidentally, have allowed Wisconsin to continue its open primary, one of Bob LaFollette's reforms.

Wisconsin has been competitive in the past two presidential elections, and arguably in four of the last five. Wisconsin becomes one of the most liberal Democratic states when Democrats nominate a liberal from the northern tier. When they nominate a southerner, it votes much like the nation: Wisconsin was Michael Dukakis's 7th best state in 1988, Bill Clinton's 27th best in 1992. The low Clinton percentage and the relatively small drop in George Bush's percentage (10% versus 16% nationally) may reflect the absence here of two phenomena which worked for Clinton and against Bush on the East and West Coasts: falling real estate prices and a large singles population. Wisconsin housing prices have held steady or risen, and the divorce rate here is one of the lowest in the country.

Congressional districting. Wisconsin did not lose a congressional district in the 1990 Census, and its population grew evenly enough that no major changes were needed in the current district lines to meet the equal-population standard. The Democratic legislature's plan, signed by Thompson, shifted a few dozen townships between districts.

The People: Est. Pop. 1994: 5,082,000; Pop. 1990: 4,891,769, up 3.9% 1990–1994. 2.0% of U.S. total, 18th largest; 34% rural. Median age: 32.9 years. 13.3% 65 years and over. 92.2% White, 5.0% Black, 1.9% Hispanic origin, 1.1% Asian. Households: 57.5% married couple families; 28% married couple fams. w. children; 42% college educ.; median household income: $29,442; per capita income: $13,276; 66.7% owner occupied housing; median house value: $62,500; median monthly rent: $331. 5.1% Unemployment. 1994 Voting age pop.: 3,777,000. 1994 Turnout: 1,565,339; 41% of VAP. No state voter registration.

Political Lineup: Governor, Tommy G. Thompson (R); Lt. Gov., Scott McCallum (R); Secy. of State, Douglas LaFollette (D); Atty. Gen., James Doyle (D); Treasurer, Jack Voight (R). State Senate, 30 (17 R, 15 D, and 1 vacant). State Assembly, 99 (51 R and 48 D). Senators, Herb Kohl (D) and Russell D. Feingold (D). Representatives, 9 (6 R and 3 D).

1992 Presidential Vote

Clinton (D)	1,041,066	(41%)
Bush (R)	930,855	(37%)
Perot (I)	544,479	(22%)

1992 Democratic Presidential Primary

Clinton	287,356	(38%)
Brown	266,207	(35%)
Tsongas	168,619	(22%)
Other	36,764	(5%)

1988 Presidential Vote

Dukakis (D)	1,126,794	(51%)
Bush (R)	1,047,499	(47%)

1992 Republican Presidential Primary

Bush	364,507	(78%)
Buchanan	78,516	(17%)
Other	17,699	(4%)

GOVERNOR

Gov. Tommy G. Thompson (R)

Elected 1986, term expires Jan. 1999; b. Nov. 19, 1941, Elroy; home, Elroy; U. of WI, B.A. 1963, J.D. 1966; Catholic; married (Sue Ann).

Career: Practicing atty; WI Assembly, 1966–86, Asst. Minority Ldr., 1973–81, Floor Ldr., 1981–86; Chmn., Repub. Govs. Assn., 1991–92; Chmn., Natl. Govs. Assn., 1995–present.

Office: State Capitol, 115 E. State Capitol, Madison 53702, 608-266-1212. Fax: 608-267-8983.

Election Results

1994 gen.	Tommy G. Thompson (R)	1,051,326	(67%)
	Chuck Chvala (D)	482,850	(31%)
	Others	29,659	(2%)
1994 prim.	Tommy G. Thompson (R)	unopposed	
1990 gen.	Tommy G. Thompson (R)	802,321	(58%)
	Thomas Loftus (D)	546,280	(42%)

SENATORS

Sen. Herb Kohl (D)

Elected 1988, seat up 2000; b. Feb. 7, 1935, Milwaukee; home, Milwaukee; U. of WI, B.A. 1956, Harvard, M.B.A. 1958; Jewish; single.

Career: Army Reserves, 1958–64; Businessman; Pres., Kohl Corp., 1970–79; Chmn., WI St. Dem. Party, 1975–77; Pres., Herbert Kohl Investments 1979–88; Owner, Milwaukee Bucks basketball team.

DC Office: 330 HSOB 20510, 202-224-5653; Fax: 202-224-9787.

State Offices: 310 W. Wisconsin Ave., Milwaukee 53202, 414-297-4451; 14 W. Mifflin St., #312, Madison 53703, 608-264-5338; 402 Graham Ave., #206, Eau Claire 54701, 715-832-8424; and 4321 W. College Ave., #235, Appleton 54914, 414-738-1640.

Committees: *Appropriations* (12th of 13 D): Agriculture, Rural Development and Related Agencies; District of Columbia (RMM); Labor, Health and Human Services, Education; Military Construction. *Judiciary* (6th of 8 D): Administrative Oversight and the Courts; Terrorism, Technology and Government Information (RMM); Youth Violence. *Aging (Special)* (7th of 9 D).

Group Ratings

	ADA	ACLU	COPE	CFA	LCV	CON	NSI	COC	ACU	NTLC	CHC
1994	90	63	63	67	85	98	20	30	12	36	21
1993	95	—	73	70	75	63	—	45	24	—	—

National Journal Ratings

	1993 LIB	—	1993 CONS	1994 LIB	—	1994 CONS
Economic	46%	—	51%	48%	—	51%
Social	77%	—	21%	63%	—	35%
Foreign	78%	—	13%	78%	—	15%

Key Votes of the 103d Congress

1. Clinton Deficit Plan	Y	3. Brady Handgun Purchase	Y	5. Lmt. UN Cmnd. of Forces	N
2. NAFTA	N	4. Strike Race/Death Pnlty.	N	6. Cut Missile Funds	Y

Key Votes of the 104th Congress

1. Congressional Compliance	Y	3. Balanced Budget Amndt.	Y	5. Product Liability Reform	Y
2. Bar Unfunded Mandates	Y	4. Pass Line Item Veto	Y	6. FY96 Budget	N

Election Results

1994 general	Herb Kohl (D)	912,662	(58%)	($8,249,531)
	Robert T. Welch (R)	636,989	(41%)	($1,180,382)
	Others	15,977	(1%)	
1994 primary	Herb Kohl (D)	135,982	(90%)	
	Edmond Galileo Hou-Seye (D)	15,579	(10%)	
1988 general	Herb Kohl (D)	1,128,625	(52%)	($7,491,600)
	Susan Engeleiter (R)	1,030,440	(48%)	($2,853,842)

Sen. Russell D. Feingold (D)

Elected 1992, seat up 1998; b. Mar. 2, 1953, Janesville; home, Middleton; U. of WI, B.A. 1975, Rhodes Scholar, Oxford U., 1977, Harvard Law Schl., J.D. 1979; Jewish; married (Mary).

Career: Practicing atty., 1979–83; WI Senate, 1983–92;

DC Office: 502 HSOB 20510, 202-224-5323; Fax: 202-224-2725.

State Offices: 517 E. Wisconsin Ave., Milwaukee 53202, 414-276-7282; 8383 Greenway Blvd., Middleton 53562, 608-828-1200; 317 1st St., #107, Wausau 54403, 715-848-5660; and 425 State St., #232, LaCrosse 54603, 608-782-5585.

Committees: *Foreign Relations* (7th of 8 D): African Affairs (RMM); European Affairs; International Operations. *Judiciary* (8th of 8 D): Administrative Oversight and the Courts; Antitrust, Business Rights and Competition; Constitution, Federalism and Property Rights. *Aging (Special)* (8th of 9 D).

Group Ratings

	ADA	ACLU	COPE	CFA	LCV	CON	NSI	COC	ACU	NTLC	CHC
1994	100	89	100	83	100	56	0	5	4	16	0
1993	100	—	91	80	94	68	—	0	12	—	—

National Journal Ratings

	1993 LIB — 1993 CONS		1994 LIB — 1994 CONS	
Economic	59%	— 34%	61%	— 35%
Social	92%	— 0%	71%	— 26%
Foreign	87%	— 8%	78%	— 15%

Key Votes of the 103d Congress

1. Clinton Deficit Plan	Y	3. Brady Handgun Purchase Y	5. Lmt. UN Cmnd. of Forces N
2. NAFTA	N	4. Strike Race/Death Pnlty. N	6. Cut Missile Funds Y

Key Votes of the 104th Congress

1. Congressional Compliance Y		3. Balanced Budget Amndt. N	5. Product Liability Reform N
2. Bar Unfunded Mandates Y		4. Pass Line Item Veto Y	6. FY96 Budget N

Election Results

1992 general	Russell D. Feingold (D)	1,290,662	(53%)	($2,056,079)
	Robert W. Kasten, Jr. (R).............	1,129,599	(46%)	($5,427,163)
	Other..................................	34,863	(1%)	
1992 primary	Russell D. Feingold (D)	367,746	(70%)	
	Jim Moody (D)	74,472	(14%)	
	Joseph Checota (D)...................	71,570	(13%)	
	Other..................................	14,056	(3%)	
1986 general	Robert W. Kasten, Jr. (R).............	1,754,537	(51%)	($3,433,870)
	Edward Garvey (D)	1,702,963	(47%)	($1,702,963)

FIRST DISTRICT

Rolling dairy country, blanketed by snow during most of the winter, gloriously green under sunny blue skies in summer, the southern tier of Wisconsin from Lake Michigan inland to the Rock River valley is some of America's prime industrial country. Settled by Yankee and German farmers 150 years ago, it was once primarily dairyland. By the early 20th Century, the steady habits and high skills of the local dairy farmers provided a good labor pool for factories. Today, there are still major plants here: the operations center for Johnson Wax (and its Frank Lloyd Wright-designed tower and Wingspread Center) in Racine; the old Nash plant, later run by American Motors and Chrysler but finally shut down, in Kenosha; and the Parker Pen operation in Janesville. In between on lakes are resorts, most notably Lake Geneva, a favorite of rich Chicagoans. To the untrained eye, this part of southern Wisconsin looks much the same as nearby northern Illinois; but politically there is a vast difference. The dotted line on the map is the boundary between the corruption-prone machine politics of Illinois and squeaky-clean progressive politics of Wisconsin.

This is the land of the 1st District of Wisconsin, from Lake Michigan west to the Rock River and beyond, a politically marginal area in Wisconsin politics and a marginal district in congressional politics from 1958–68. Then, from 1970–93, it was the home base of the late Les Aspin, chairman of the House Armed Services Committee from 1985–93 and Secretary of Defense from 1993–94. Now once again, this is prime marginal territory politically, with two different results in two different races between the same two candidates in less than two years.

The congressman from the 1st now is Republican Mark Neumann, who lost to Aspin in November 1992 and to Democrat Peter Barca in the May 1993 special to succeed Aspin, then came back to beat Barca in November 1994. Neumann was a math teacher who decided to become a homebuilder on the side in 1980. In 1986 he started his own homebuilding business and made a fortune by using computers to make quick and accurate estimates on custom-built houses. He sold the business in 1992 and, deciding that he must do something about the national debt and high taxes, he ran for Congress. He had support from the Christian right, spent more than $700,000 of his own money, and held Aspin to a 58%–41% win. Neumann ran again in the special, but spent less of his own money and minimized his connection with the religious right and sharply attacked the Clinton budget and tax package. One Democrat, former state party chairman Jeff Neubauer, came forward and defended it, but he lost the primary 49%–34% to Peter Barca, a state legislator with a solid base in Kenosha and strong labor union support. Barca said he would not vote for many of the new taxes proposed by Clinton, but backed healthcare and welfare reform, while labor unions conducted a heavy "negative persuasion" phone bank campaign against Neumann, especially against his proposal to invest some Social Security trust funds. Barca won 50%–49%; Neumann demanded a recount, which delayed Barca's swearing in until June, allowing him to skirt the first tough vote on Clinton's tax-increase proposal.

Neumann was reluctant to run again in 1994, but was pressed by national Republican leaders. Again he argued that taxes and regulations were strangling small companies like his; he attacked Barca for voting for the Clinton budget and tax package after having pledged to vote against the gas tax it contained. Barca soon moved to cut spending, supporting the Penny-Kasich spending cuts, and sponsored amendments that cut spending on consulates, new courthouses, and elevator operators in the House's Longworth Building. "When his vote doesn't count, he votes conservative," Neumann said, and attacked him for getting most of his campaign money from PACs. Neumann ran ads featuring Governor Tommy Thompson and supported the Contract With America. Barca carried Kenosha County and led in Rock County, Neumann's home area. But Neumann carried Racine and the area around Lake Geneva, for a 49.4%–48.8% victory. He became a strong supporter of House Speaker Newt Gingrich but with a seat on Appropriations—generally considered a good assignment for a freshman—he will find himself having to cast some tough votes to cut federal programs. How he will fare in 1996 is uncertain, but in this close bellwether district both parties seem to be moving to the right. And Barca is one of several former House members said to be mulling a comeback bid.

The People: Pop. 1990: 543,380; 29% rural; 12% age 65+; 90% White; 5% Black; 1% Asian; 2% Other; 3% Hispanic origin. Voting age pop.: 396,994; 4% Black; 2% Hispanic origin. Households: 60% married couple families; 28% married couple fams. w. children; 39% college educ.; median household income: $31,431; per capita income: $13,567; median gross rent: $401; median house value: $61,200.

1992 Presidential Vote			1988 Presidential Vote		
Clinton (D)	109,790	(41%)	Dukakis (D)	115,873	(51%)
Bush (R)	94,712	(35%)	Bush (R)	109,474	(49%)
Perot (I)	62,465	(23%)			

Rep. Mark W. Neumann (R)

Elected 1994; b. Feb. 27, 1954, Mukwonago; home, Janesville; U. of WI, B.S. 1975, M.S., 1977; Lutheran; married (Sue).

Career: High Schl. teacher, 1977–80; Realtor, 1980–86; Homebuilder, 1986–92; Owner, Neumann Corp. Real Estate & Devel., 1992–93.

DC Office: 1725 LHOB 20515, 202-225-3031; Fax: 202-225-3393.

District Offices: 1 Parker Pl., #720, Janesville 53525, 608-752-4050.

Committees: *Appropriations* (32nd of 32 R): District of Columbia; National Security; VA, HUD, and Independent Agencies.

Group Ratings and 103rd Congress Votes: Newly Elected

Key Votes of the 104th Congress

1. Congressional Compliance	Y	6. Reform Crime Grant	Y	11. Loser Pays Court Reform	Y
2. Balanced Budget Amndmt.	Y	7. National Security Act	Y	12. Product Liability Reform	Y
3. Bar Unfunded Mandates	Y	8. Moratorium on Regs.	Y	13. Welfare Reform	Y
4. Pass Line Item Veto	Y	9. Risk Assessment on Regs.	Y	14. Term Limits Amndmt.	Y
5. Relax Exclusionary Rule	Y	10. Expnd. Priv. Prop. Rights	Y	15. Tax Cuts	Y

Election Results

1994 general	Mark W. Neumann (R)	83,937	(49%)	($512,091)
	Peter W. Barca (D)	82,817	(49%)	($671,438)
	Others	3,101	(2%)	
1994 primary	Mark W. Neumann (R)	unopposed		
1993 spec. gen.	Peter W. Barca (D)	55,605	(50%)	($742,069)
	Mark W. Neumann (R)	54,930	(49%)	($910,278)
	Other	941	(1%)	
1993 spec. prim.	Peter W. Barca (D)	31,073	(49%)	
	Jeffrey Neubauer (D)	21,610	(34%)	
	Wayne W. Wood (D)	8,254	(13%)	
	Others	2,927	(5%)	
1992 general	Les Aspin (D)	147,495	(58%)	($1,355,737)
	Mark W. Neumann (R)	104,352	(41%)	($941,674)
	Other	4,433	(2%)	

SECOND DISTRICT

On a narrow isthmus between Lakes Mendota and Monona is the center of Madison and, in many ways, the center of Wisconsin. Here the state Capitol rises at the one end of State Street; at the other end of several commercial blocks is the main campus of the University of Wisconsin, on a beautiful, parklike, sometimes windswept setting above Lake Mendota. For most of this century, Wisconsin politics was dominated by the Madison-based LaFollettes and their liberal Democratic successors. And the traffic on State Street was two-way, with university faculty devoted to Bob LaFollette's "Wisconsin idea" of an enlightened, apolitical bureaucracy, his Wisconsin Tax Commission and workmen's compensation law—both firsts in the nation. The *Progressive* magazine is still published here, and the *Madison Capital-Times* continues to be one of the nation's most explicitly liberal newspapers, though its Republican rival, the *Wisconsin State Journal*, has a much larger circulation; the two newspapers practice the kind of partisan journalism still seen in only a few major cities and state capitals (Nashville, Sacramento, Boston, Detroit).

Madison is the center of Wisconsin's 2d Congressional District, and with surrounding Dane County casts about 70% of the district's votes. The rest are in several rural dairy counties which are more Republican and conservative; they include such picturesque Wisconsin scenes as Frank Lloyd Wright's home, Taliesin, the Swiss-settled town of New Glarus, and the headquarters of Lands' End in Dodgeville. Madison was LaFollette country for the first half of the century, and very liberal and Democratic for most of the second, enough so that despite the Republican leanings of the rural counties, the 2d District voted for George McGovern in 1972 and Walter Mondale in 1984. It also spawned an activist and sometimes violent student movement (during the Vietnam War, a graduate student was killed in a laboratory by a bomb set off by a protester) and a permanent postgraduate proletariat. But the tone of life seems to be mellowing lately. Even as the Madison campus produces more Peace Corps volunteers than any other in the country, it also produced a student government victory for a party organized by Republicans and celebrated the Wisconsin Badgers victory over UCLA in the 1994 Rose Bowl. And in the 1990s Madison and the 2d District have been voting Republican. The locals embraced Governor Tommy Thompson and his innovative conservatism, voting for his reelection in 1994, even though Thompson had been in the minority in Madison ever since he was a Goldwater Republican as a University student in the early 1960s. And they voted even earlier for Congressman Scott Klug, a more moderate and conciliatory Republican, who captured the district from 32-year liberal incumbent Robert Kastenmeier in 1990 and, despite Democrats' efforts, has held it by wide margins ever since.

Klug is a Wisconsin native who after college worked as an investigative TV reporter in Washington; in 1988 he returned to Madison to work as an anchor at Channel 27. His 1990 campaign was deft. He treated Kastenmeier respectfully but said his ideas were "stuck in the '60s" and he ran as his campaign logo the number 32 in a circle with a line drawn through it. He showed candor in calling for means-testing Social Security and moderation in calling for early intervention programs for at-risk children. Klug lost Madison's Dane County by only 52%–48% and won 63% in the smaller counties, for a 53%–47% victory, slightly ahead of Republican Governor Tommy Thompson's strong showing there.

Klug is one of those young congressmen who has kept his family home in the district, and he spends more days in Wisconsin than in Washington. In his first term in the House, he compiled a moderate voting record on issues but made waves as one of the freshman Republican "Gang of Seven" who insisted on full disclosure of House bank overdrafts. He joined the Porkbusters' Coalition identifying $1 billion in recommended cuts. But he also worked on preserving details of federal dairy programs, tried to restrict cheese imports, boosted ethanol fuels and supported University of Wisconsin Chancellor Donna Shalala as Bill Clinton's secretary of Health and Human Services. He got a law changed so that U.S. soldiers killed by friendly fire can receive the Purple Heart. In 1992 Klug faced—now Interior Assistant Secretary for Indian Affairs—Ada Deer, an American Indian (that term is her preference) who in the 1970s helped to reestablish the tribal status of her fellow Menominees, and who beat a veteran state Senator in the primary. Deer said she would have voted against the Gulf war resolution and was not sure if she would have voted for declaring war against Germany and Japan in 1941. She held a fundraiser at a clinic that performs abortions, with a basket full of condoms next to her basket of bumper stickers. Bill Clinton carried the 2d district by a big margin, but Klug did even better, carrying Dane County with 60% of the vote and winning 69% in the smaller counties, for a striking 63%–37% victory.

Klug continued to have a moderate voting record in his second term. He sponsored successful amendments to kill the Advanced Solid Rocket Motor (passed 379–43) and against experiments that he referred to as "pigs in space" (333–98). He worked to curtail the Trident II, to cut Radio Free Europe/Radio Liberty, and to zero out the International Fund for Ireland. He opposed the Haiti invasion and called for lifting the Bosnian arms embargo. He opposed the Clinton vaccine program and supported the healthcare plan sponsored by Tennessee Representative Jim Cooper, working with a bipartisan group of House members on the issue. With Ron Wyden, he proposed a national data bank on medical malpractice. He also bucked most of his party, by supporting the assault weapons ban and the 1994 crime bill. He voted for NAFTA and against the striker replacement ban. He got new regulations to protect against the ticket fraud that many Wisconsin fans complained about at the Rose Bowl.

Klug approached the 1994 election with great strength. His Democratic opposition was so unimpressive the *Cap Times* endorsed Klug, while he ran soft-focus ads showing his family with his dog, Watson. Klug won an amazing 66% in Dane County and 78% in the smaller counties, for a 69%–29% victory. With that performance in the formerly Democratic bastion, Klug is increasingly mentioned as a candidate for governor or senator. Meanwhile, new House assignments have piled up. In the 104th Congress he has been one of Speaker Newt Gingrich's main liaisons with Republican moderates, and as a member of the Commerce Committee and its Health and Telecommunications Subcommittees, he prepared for an active role on major economic legislation, co-sponsoring Chairman Tom Bliley's and subcommittee Chairman Jack Fields' Telco bill. He also took an assignment from Gingrich to head the House Republicans' effort to identify federal programs that are ripe for privatization—from the Government Printing Office to public-power agencies.

The People: Pop. 1990: 543,625; 36% rural; 11% age 65+; 95% White; 2% Black; 2% Asian; 1% Hispanic origin. Voting age pop.: 412,215; 2% Black; 1% Hispanic origin. Households: 55% married couple families; 26% married couple fams. w. children; 53% college educ.; median household income: $30,625; per capita income: $14,319; median gross rent: $441; median house value: $69,800.

1992 Presidential Vote		
Clinton (D)	149,340	(50%)
Bush (R)	94,368	(32%)
Perot (I)	52,552	(18%)

1988 Presidential Vote		
Dukakis (D)	139,552	(56%)
Bush (R)	108,929	(44%)

Rep. Scott Klug (R)

Elected 1990; b. Jan. 16, 1953, Milwaukee; home, Madison; Lawrence U., B.A. 1975, Northwestern U., M.S.J. 1976, U. of WI, M.B.A. 1990; Catholic; married (Theresa).

Career: Investigative reporter, WJLA-TV Washington, D.C., 1976–88; News anchor, WKOW-TV Madison, 1988–90.

DC Office 1113 LHOB 20515, 202-225-2906; Fax: 202-225-6942.

District Offices: 16 N. Carroll St., #600, Madison 53703, 608-257-9200.

Committees: *Commerce* (13th of 26 R): Health and Environment; Telecommunications and Finance.

Group Ratings

	ADA	ACLU	COPE	CFA	LCV	CON	NSI	COC	ACU	NTLC	CHC
1994	45	48	44	30	67	97	60	75	43	82	64
1993	40	—	33	70	71	94	—	73	58	—	—

National Journal Ratings

	1993 LIB — 1993 CONS		1994 LIB — 1994 CONS	
Economic	30% —	68%	30% —	67%
Social	50% —	49%	47% —	52%
Foreign	40% —	57%	40% —	59%

Key Votes of the 103d Congress

1. Clinton Deficit Plan	N	3. Brady Handgun Purchase	Y	5. Lmt. UN Cmnd. of Forces	Y
2. NAFTA	Y	4. Strike Race/Death Pnlty.	Y	6. Cut Missile Funds	Y

Key Votes of the 104th Congress

1. Congressional Compliance	Y	6. Reform Crime Grant	Y	11. Loser Pays Court Reform	Y
2. Balanced Budget Amndmt.	Y	7. National Security Act	Y	12. Product Liability Reform	Y
3. Bar Unfunded Mandates	Y	8. Moratorium on Regs.	Y	13. Welfare Reform	Y
4. Pass Line Item Veto	Y	9. Risk Assessment on Regs.	Y	14. Term Limits Amndmt.	Y
5. Relax Exclusionary Rule	Y	10. Expnd. Priv. Prop. Rights	N	15. Tax Cuts	N

Election Results

1994 general	Scott Klug (R)	133,734	(69%)	($689,215)
	Thomas C. Hecht (D).................	55,406	(29%)	($281,783)
	Others	4,109	(2%)	
1994 primary	Scott Klug (R)	unopposed		
1992 general	Scott Klug (R)	183,366	(63%)	($829,378)
	Ada E. Deer (D)	108,291	(37%)	($522,956)

THIRD DISTRICT

On the rolling land of western Wisconsin, in the knobby hills just east of the Mississippi River, on some of the most beautiful river landscape in the country, is where Laura Ingalls Wilder's family built the "little house in the big woods" in the 1870s, before the first railroad came steaming up the narrow floodplain alongside the Mississippi River. Today, it is hard to imagine the big woods: the trees have long since been cut and the hillsides are covered with grass grazed by placid dairy cattle. Where pioneers tried to scratch out diversified crops, farmers soon made America's premier dairying region, producing milk, butter and especially cheese. Today the dairy industry is in trouble. Cows are more productive, while demand for milk has decreased because there are fewer children in America today than in the 1950s, and fewer Americans are descended exclusively from the northern European stock that carries the genes for the enzymes adults need to digest milk. And Wisconsin has trouble competing against the European Common Market's hugely subsidized cheese and butter. Many communities here are losing population, as has the factory town of LaCrosse, where the locally owned Trane Company and Heileman Brewing have been bought by outsiders. But there is also growth in these beautiful hills, evidence of mobility and prosperity despite problems in the dairy industry.

The 3d Congressional District of Wisconsin follows the Mississippi and St. Croix River counties from the southern border of the state almost to Lake Superior, and here and there reaches east a county or two. This is probably the nation's number one dairy district—it has more cows than people. It was settled largely by German and Scandinavian immigrants (Laura's Yankee family moved away as Swedes were moving into the area), and it once voted for LaFollette progressives. More recently, it has been sharply contested partisan territory, Democratic in the Watergate years, Republican around 1980, Democratic again in the late 1980s, and trending Republican more cautiously than most of Wisconsin in the 1990s.

The congressman from the 3d District is Steve Gunderson, a Republican who first won the seat in 1980 at 29 and has said he will not run for reelection in 1996. Gunderson is a natural political operator who served in the state legislature, worked on Governor Lee Dreyfus's campaign in 1978, and then ran on his own. In Congress he immediately interested himself in dairy issues. He is now chairman of Agriculture's Livestock, Dairy and Poultry Subcommittee, where he was ranking Republican from 1989–95. In the 1990 farm bill, he got a provision imposing assessments on dairy farmers who overproduce milkfat, an attempt at supply control. He also won elimination of a higher support price for California, and wants to eliminate a formula that prices all milk as if it is shipped from Eau Claire, in the 3d District, a policy that works against Midwest dairy farmers. For the 1995 farm bill, he said there will be no "sacred cows." He is in a strong position to oppose current programs, such as those he believes would require higher assessments from farmers. He wants a level playing field domestically, which would mean getting rid of Eau Claire prices, and he wants U.S. dairy producers to become competitive in world markets, which would mean changing European Community rules. One choice, he says, is to deregulate the U.S. dairy industry.

Gunderson has had other causes in Congress. He sponsored a bill to equip House offices with telecommunications for the deaf, introducing it with sign language, which he has learned through a deaf cousin; he has served on the board of Gallaudet University, a renowned school for the deaf, which is on Capitol Hill. He is proud of the Environmental Management System he is sponsoring for the upper Mississippi River. He wants federal job training loans to be backed up by the government's Sallie Mae. He sponsored a national school-to-work act modeled on Wisconsin's and embraced by the Clinton Administration. In 1995, as a senior member of the committee with jurisdiction over the agencies, he took the lead in proposing to fold the Education and Labor Departments together with the EEOC.

Not all of Gunderson's career has gone smoothly. In March 1989, after Gunderson provided key help in the successful campaign for Minority Whip, Newt Gingrich named him one of two chief deputy Republican whips, despite (or perhaps because of) his moderate stands on many cultural and foreign issues. But he was uncomfortable with what he called the Republican Party's "growing image of intolerance" at the Republican National Convention in Houston, and in January 1993, after Jerry Lewis lost his leadership post to Dick Armey, Gunderson resigned his leadership post, which was then abolished. "I do not believe our present leadership represents mainstream Republicans in this country or even in the Congress," he said. At the same time, his own percentages were declining, from well over 60% to 56%–42% in 1992. In February 1994 he announced he would seek one more term and then retire from Congress. The Democrats had a four-way primary, and Gunderson—after comfortably surviving a scare in the Republican primary—had vigorous opposition from state legislator Harvey Stower, a United Methodist minister. In October 1994 the *New York Times Magazine* published an article entitled "Congressman (R), Wisconsin. Fiscal Conservative. Social Moderate. Gay," with pictures of Gunderson and his companion of 11 years. He said the account was essentially accurate, his campaign manager said it was "pretty much old news," and Stower said he wouldn't discuss personal issues. Gunderson won 56%–41%, an indication either that his sexual preference made no difference or that voters had taken it into account some time ago. It has caused some friction with some members of the Republican Conference, but Gunderson seems determined, and is well positioned, to make his last term a legislatively busy one. Nevertheless, he has usually kept on good terms with Gingrich, who has gone out of his way to stand by Gunderson, and he has kept up the pressure to ensure that conservative Republicans don't move the Speaker too far to the right. Despite reservations, Gunderson said, he supported the Contract with America so that he could save his battles for the tougher issues that lay ahead. "Newt is a visionary," he told *National Journal* in early 1995. "But he is caught up with a power base that is conservative populist." Assuming Gunderson keeps his retirement pledge, look for a wide-open contest to succeed him. His brother Matt Gunderson, who ran in the 1994 Republican Senate primary, could be in the field; and Republican former state Senator Jim Harsdorf and state Representative Rob Kreibich are also exploring the race.

The People: Pop. 1990: 543,447; 56% rural; 14% age 65+; 98% White; 1% Asian. Voting age pop.: 398,244. Households: 60% married couple families; 30% married couple fams. w. children; 39% college educ.; median household income: $25,758; per capita income: $11,505; median gross rent: $336; median house value: $52,400.

1992 Presidential Vote			1988 Presidential Vote		
Clinton (D)	119,721	(43%)	Dukakis (D)	125,756	(53%)
Bush (R)	90,813	(33%)	Bush (R)	111,583	(47%)
Perot (I)	67,134	(24%)			

Rep. Steve Gunderson (R)

Elected 1980; b. May 10, 1951, Eau Claire; home, Osseo; U. of WI, B.A. 1973, Brown Schl. of Broadcasting, 1974; Lutheran; single.

Career: WI Assembly, 1974–79.

DC Office: 2185 RHOB 20515, 202-225-5506; Fax: 202-225-6195.

District Offices: P.O. Box 247, 622 E. State Hwy. 54, Black River Falls 54615, 715-284-7431.

Committees: *Agriculture* (3rd of 27 R): Livestock, Dairy and Poultry (Chmn.); Resource Conservation, Research and Forestry. *Economic & Educational Opportunities* (4th of 24 R): Early Childhood, Youth and Families; Postsecondary Education, Training and Life-Long Learning.

Group Ratings

	ADA	ACLU	COPE	CFA	LCV	CON	NSI	COC	ACU	NTLC	CHC
1994	10	48	33	20	24	60	70	83	81	86	57
1993	30	—	42	40	36	69	—	91	83	—	—

National Journal Ratings

	1993 LIB — 1993 CONS			1994 LIB — 1994 CONS	
Economic	25%	—	72%	30%	—	67%
Social	49%	—	51%	40%	—	59%
Foreign	33%	—	65%	37%	—	63%

Key Votes of the 103d Congress

1. Clinton Deficit Plan	N	3. Brady Handgun Purchase	N	5. Lmt. UN Cmnd. of Forces	Y
2. NAFTA	Y	4. Strike Race/Death Pnlty.	Y	6. Cut Missile Funds	Y

Key Votes of the 104th Congress

1. Congressional Compliance	Y	6. Reform Crime Grant	Y	11. Loser Pays Court Reform	Y
2. Balanced Budget Amndmt.	Y	7. National Security Act	Y	12. Product Liability Reform	Y
3. Bar Unfunded Mandates	Y	8. Moratorium on Regs.	Y	13. Welfare Reform	Y
4. Pass Line Item Veto	Y	9. Risk Assessment on Regs.	Y	14. Term Limits Amndmt.	Y
5. Relax Exclusionary Rule	Y	10. Expnd. Priv. Prop. Rights	Y	15. Tax Cuts	Y

Election Results

1994 general	Steve Gunderson (R)	89,338	(56%)	($658,181)
	Harvey Stower (D)	65,758	(41%)	($217,460)
	Others	5,217	(3%)	
1994 primary	Steve Gunderson (R)	21,307	(63%)	
	Donald M. Brill (R)	12,320	(37%)	
1992 general	Steve Gunderson (R)	146,903	(56%)	($458,846)
	Paul Sacia (D)	108,664	(42%)	($33,109)
	Other	4,768	(2%)	

FOURTH DISTRICT

The world's largest clock faces outward from all sides of the tower on the Allen-Bradley factory, looking out over the manufacturing city of Milwaukee. It is an apt symbol, a piece of precision engineering, in this high-skill manufacturing town, with its skyline of smokestacks and church steeples, the closest thing in America to the factory cities of the Germany whence so many Milwaukeeans' ancestors came. Chicago, just 90 miles away, provides much of the banking, advertising, insurance, accounting and legal services Milwaukee businesses need, and the retail and entertainment base as well, and Madison has the big research university. But Milwaukee leads the nation in industrial control equipment, mining gear, cranes and independent foundries. The work force, with German, Polish, Mitteleuropean work habits, is highly skilled and hard-working. German-Americans made Milwaukee the nation's major beer brewer for years, though brewing employs fewer than 4,000 here today. Milwaukee lost 60,000 manufacturing jobs in the 1979–82 recession years, but it stuck to its high-skill manufacturing strength and eventually prospered. Since that recession, Allen-Bradley has spent millions on improvements and new facilities, Rockwell International doubled sales to $1.5 billion, and Harnischfeger spent $39 million on machine tools for its mining shovels and papermaking machinery after nearly going bankrupt in 1983. Milwaukee was responsible for much of the nation's late 1980s export boom and, with help from Wisconsin's tax cuts, weathered the early 1990s recession better than many American cities.

Prospering quietly from this growth, for this is still a union, high-wage town, are the residents of Milwaukee's traditionally blue-collar south side. Here, in neighborhoods with sturdy houses that withstand northern winters and streets lined with bars emblazoned with beer signs, are Milwaukee's prototypical Polish neighborhoods and its even larger number of German-Americans. The 4th Congressional District of Wisconsin, which has been the south-side district since 1892, has spread out with the population into the suburbs. Now, over 100 years later, only one-third of its voters are in Milwaukee, another 40% in the Milwaukee County suburbs and one-quarter farther west in suburban Waukesha County. Historically this was the only securely Democratic part of Wisconsin, and still is, though the Waukesha portion is Republican.

Gerald Kleczka, congressman from the 4th District, is one of the state's three highly skilled Democratic congressmen who have spent almost all their adult lives as legislators in Madison and Washington. Kleczka is a product of the south side, the sort of man who has remodeled his house from top to bottom and maintains the best lawn in the neighborhood. But he is also, says the *Milwaukee Sentinel*, "the sort of guy you wouldn't want on the other side in a tavern brawl," with a temper known to flare up even in the halls of Congress. He was elected to the Wisconsin assembly in 1968 at 24, to the state Senate in 1974 where he chaired several committees, and to the U.S. House in April 1984, after the death of Clement Zablocki, who had represented the district for 35 years and chaired the Foreign Affairs Committee.

In the House Kleczka has worked hard to repair flaws in the welfare state he generally supports. In the new Republican-controlled Ways and Means Committee, he is often the only Democrat to whom the majority party looks for support. On the Banking Committee he worked for higher capital requirements for S&Ls and for protecting elderly tenants of public housing. On Ways and Means he supported California Representative Pete Stark's 1994 healthcare bill after including a provision for people without children to pay lower premiums. Kleczka has looked hard at the Supplemental Security Income program, charging that SSI for children is "failing" because of loose definitions of disabilities. With Senator William Cohen of Maine, he got passed a law to cut off benefits from those with alcohol and drug disabilities after 36 months. Treatment theorists moaned, but Kleczka, quoting from a letter from an approving constituent, made the common-sense point: "I don't think addicts should be on the government dole. It only encourages them to continue." Ironically, Kleczka entered an alcohol-abuse treatment center after being arrested for drunken driving in May 1995.

Kleczka first won the seat in the April 1984 Democratic primary, beating the Milwaukee County district attorney, a former Zablocki aide and a well-known state senator. Kleczka won reelection easily until the 1994 Republican tsunami held him to 54% (58% in Milwaukee County and 42% in Waukesha County), while Governor Thompson was carrying the district overwhelmingly. But it would be astonishing if he were to lose.

The People: Pop. 1990: 543,482; 2% rural; 13% age 65+; 91% White; 1% Black; 1% Amer. Indian; 1% Asian; 3% Other; 6% Hispanic origin. Voting age pop.: 410,091; 1% Black; 5% Hispanic origin. Households: 56% married couple families; 25% married couple fams. w. children; 43% college educ.; median household income: $32,260; per capita income: $14,177; median gross rent: $448; median house value: $71,400.

1992 Presidential Vote

Clinton (D)	116,048	(41%)
Bush (R)	108,761	(38%)
Perot (I)	59,263	(21%)

1988 Presidential Vote

Dukakis (D)	140,615	(56%)
Bush (R)	111,335	(44%)

Rep. Gerald D. Kleczka (D)

Elected Apr. 1984; b. Nov. 26, 1943, Milwaukee; home, Milwaukee; U. of WI; Catholic; married (Bonnie).

Career: Air Natl. Guard, 1963–69; Accountant; Milwaukee Cnty. Cncl., 1965–68; WI Assembly, 1968–74; WI Senate, 1974–84, Asst. Majority Ldr., 1977–82.

DC Office: 2301 RHOB 20515, 202-225-4572; Fax: 202-225-8135.

District Offices: 5032 W. Forest Home Ave., Milwaukee 53219, 414-297-1140; and 414 W. Moreland Blvd., #105, Waukesha 53188, 414-549-6360.

Committees: *Ways & Means* (12th of 15 D): Health.

Group Ratings

	ADA	ACLU	COPE	CFA	LCV	CON	NSI	COC	ACU	NTLC	CHC
1994	85	65	78	100	88	47	20	67	5	32	21
1993	80	—	100	100	79	27	—	18	13	—	—

National Journal Ratings

	1993 LIB — 1993 CONS		1994 LIB — 1994 CONS	
Economic	78%	— 12%	64%	— 35%
Social	63%	— 36%	73%	— 26%
Foreign	59%	— 38%	80%	— 17%

Key Votes of the 103d Congress

1. Clinton Deficit Plan	Y	3. Brady Handgun Purchase	Y	5. Lmt. UN Cmnd. of Forces	N
2. NAFTA	N	4. Strike Race/Death Pnlty.	N	6. Cut Missile Funds	N

Key Votes of the 104th Congress

1. Congressional Compliance	Y	6. Reform Crime Grant	N	11. Loser Pays Court Reform	N
2. Balanced Budget Amndmt.	Y	7. National Security Act	N	12. Product Liability Reform	Y
3. Bar Unfunded Mandates	Y	8. Moratorium on Regs.	N	13. Welfare Reform	N
4. Pass Line Item Veto	Y	9. Risk Assessment on Regs.	N	14. Term Limits Amndmt.	N
5. Relax Exclusionary Rule	N	10. Expnd. Priv. Prop. Rights	N	15. Tax Cuts	N

Election Results

1994 general	Gerald D. Kleczka (D)	93,789	(54%)	($495,371)
	Tom Reynolds (R)	78,225	(45%)	($111,356)
	Others	2,675	(2%)	
1994 primary	Gerald D. Kleczka (D)	unopposed		
1992 general	Gerald D. Kleczka (D)	173,482	(66%)	($309,036)
	Joseph L. Cook (R)	84,872	(32%)	($67,267)
	Other	5,449	(2%)	

FIFTH DISTRICT

Milwaukee is America's most German city, with an ethnic heritage noticeable not just in the names of its beers and its old German restaurants but in the solidness of its houses and the orderliness of its streets. Until the World Wars made this German character seem un-American, German was spoken on the streets and read in newspapers, German beer was brewed in dozens of breweries and German cultural traditions breathed in churches, union halls and parlors. There was a German-type politics, with a Socialist mayor and an efficient, honest city government. Wisconsin's 5th Congressional District, which since 1892 has included the north side of Milwaukee, elected Socialist Victor Berger to Congress in 1910 and again from 1918 through 1926, even though he was denied his House seat after the 1918 and 1920 elections because of his opposition to World War I; in 1919, he was sentenced to 20 years in prison for writing antiwar articles. Though some ghetto neighborhoods here are beset by crime and drug use, most of Milwaukee is solid and upstanding, and some of it—Brewers Hill near the old Schlitz brewery—is gentrifying. There is an Oktoberfest (as well as an Irish Fest, summerfest, etc.), and there are large and efficiently run factories that pay high wages to highly-skilled and well-disciplined workers. This is also the place where state legislator Polly Williams, a Jesse Jackson backer in 1988, joined forces with Republican Governor Tommy Thompson to oppose the Democratic education bureaucracy and institute an educational choice system, to give young blacks access to better schools.

The 5th Congressional District of Wisconsin includes the northern half of Milwaukee and Milwaukee County, including its black neighborhoods and the high-income suburbs on Lake Michigan. Overall, its tone is sturdily blue and white collar. Once Socialist and LaFollette Progressive, the 5th is now the most heavily Democratic district in Wisconsin.

The congressman from the 5th District is Tom Barrett, who has spent most of his adult life in politics. He was elected to the state House in 1984, at 30; in 1988 he was overwhelmingly elected to the state Senate in a district that conveniently was one of only two entirely within the 5th District. His legislation in Madison included bringing 911 emergency call service to Milwaukee and passing a state version of the Brady bill. Running for the House in 1992 when the 5th District's Jim Moody ran for the Senate, Barrett presented detailed position papers on the economy and healthcare reform. He also called for large defense cutbacks, a national police corps and federal encouragement of direct investment in "microenterprises" in depressed city neighborhoods. He won the primary with 41%, to 23% for County Supervisor Terrance Pitts, who was based in the north side black wards, 19% for former Circuit Judge Fred Kessler, who spent $200,000 of his own money, and 16% for former Marquette basketball star Marc Marotta. The general election was easy; Barrett won with 69%.

Barrett has been rather moderate on economics, more liberal on cultural and foreign issues. In contrast to his 1992 concern with broad national issues, Barrett has worked since then on targeted problems. He wants a healthcare deduction for the self-employed, and a bill to prevent federal block grants from being used to move jobs away, as Briggs & Stratton did in Milwaukee. He wants to prevent insurance redlining and provide full disclosure on rent-to-own contracts. He also wants to prevent members of Congress from using frequent flyer miles for family trips. But that idea was nixed by Speaker Newt Gingrich. Barrett sought unsuccessfully to extend the Republicans' line-item veto to targeted tax breaks. He backed the Brady bill and introduced a ban on Black Talon bullets. With the diminished supply of talented liberal Democrats, Barrett has an opportunity to make his mark, though he won't win many battles for a while. In Republican 1994 he was reelected 62%–36%.

The People: Pop. 1990: 543,607; 13% age 65+; 60% White; 35% Black; 1% Amer. Indian; 2% Asian; 1% Other; 2% Hispanic origin. Voting age pop.: 395,627; 29% Black; 2% Hispanic origin. Households: 41% married couple families; 18% married couple fams. w. children; 49% college educ.; median household income: $26,267; per capita income: $13,277; median gross rent: $435; median house value: $62,400.

1992 Presidential Vote

Clinton (D)	142,047 (56%)
Bush (R)	76,935 (30%)
Perot (I)	32,138 (13%)

1988 Presidential Vote

Dukakis (D)	152,975 (63%)
Bush (R)	89,509 (37%)

Rep. Thomas M. Barrett (D)

Elected 1992; b. Dec. 8, 1953, Milwaukee; home, Milwaukee; U. of WI, B.A. 1976, J.D., 1980; Catholic; married (Kristine).

Career: FDIC bank examiner, 1977; Law Clerk, Fed. Dist. Judge Robert Warren 1980–82; Practicing atty., 1982–84; WI Assembly, 1984–88; WI Senate, 1988–92.

DC Office: 1224 LHOB 20515, 202-225-3571; Fax: 202-225-2185.

District Offices: 135 W. Wells St., #618, Milwaukee 53203, 414-297-1331.

Committees: *Banking & Financial Services* (15th of 22 D): Domestic and International Monetary Policy; Financial Institutions and Consumer Credit. *Government Reform & Oversight* (14th of 22 D): Human Resources and Intergovernmental Affairs.

Group Ratings

	ADA	ACLU	COPE	CFA	LCV	CON	NSI	COC	ACU	NTLC	CHC
1994	95	78	89	90	100	44	20	58	0	29	21
1993	90	—	92	90	93	74	—	27	13	—	—

National Journal Ratings

	1993 LIB — 1993 CONS		1994 LIB — 1994 CONS	
Economic	64% —	34%	59% —	37%
Social	68% —	29%	76% —	23%
Foreign	79% —	16%	85% —	0%

Key Votes of the 103d Congress

1. Clinton Deficit Plan	Y	3. Brady Handgun Purchase Y	5. Lmt. UN Cmnd. of Forces N
2. NAFTA	N	4. Strike Race/Death Pnlty. N	6. Cut Missile Funds Y

Key Votes of the 104th Congress

1. Congressional Compliance Y	6. Reform Crime Grant N	11. Loser Pays Court Reform N
2. Balanced Budget Amndmt. N	7. National Security Act N	12. Product Liability Reform N
3. Bar Unfunded Mandates Y	8. Moratorium on Regs. N	13. Welfare Reform N
4. Pass Line Item Veto Y	9. Risk Assessment on Regs. N	14. Term Limits Amndmt. N
5. Relax Exclusionary Rule N	10. Expnd. Priv. Prop. Rights N	15. Tax Cuts N

Election Results

1994 general	Thomas M. Barrett (D)	87,806	(62%)	($239,418)
	Stephen B. Hollingshead (R)	51,145	(36%)	($115,791)
	Others	1,689	(1%)	
1994 primary	Thomas M. Barrett (D)	unopposed		
1992 general	Thomas M. Barrett (D)	162,344	(69%)	($387,469)
	Donalda A. Hammersmith (R)	71,085	(30%)	($98,338)

SIXTH DISTRICT

Central Wisconsin is solid country, a producer of basic commodities—milk, butter and cheese, paper and paper products, Oshkosh overalls and Mirro-Foley pots and pans, Mercury outboard motors and Kleenex. Settled first by Yankee Protestants, it was one of the birthplaces of the Republican Party in February 1854, when a group of Whigs, Free Soilers and Democrats met in a small white schoolhouse in Ripon, Wisconsin, and proclaimed themselves Republicans; Jackson, Michigan, also claims to be the birthplace of the party. Whichever, the party grew rapidly, winning a near-majority in the House in the 1854 elections. But Republican roots here are not just Yankee. The 1850s brought the first surge of German migration into the United States, and central Wisconsin was a favorite destination. Here they built the dairy farms and factory towns that seemed steadfastly prosperous 50 years ago, and still seem solid and successful today.

The 6th Congressional District of Wisconsin, which cuts a swath across the state from Manitowoc on Lake Michigan through Oshkosh and Ripon west almost to the Mississippi River, includes country which has voted Republican almost without interruption since that first meeting in Ripon. It has also elected Republican congressmen who have come up with thoughtful and original solutions to problems. One was William Steiger, first elected in 1966, whose chief monuments are the all-volunteer military and the 1978 Steiger amendment cutting capital gains tax rates—considerable accomplishments for a member of the minority party, and for one who died at age 40 in 1978. Another is Thomas Petri, who won the 1979 special election to succeed Steiger by a narrow margin and has also specialized in proposals that cut across ideological and party lines.

Petri grew up in Fond du Lac. He was a Peace Corps volunteer in Somalia and was elected to the state Senate in 1972, at 32. In April 1979, after Steiger died, Petri ran for the House, beating Tommy Thompson (now governor) in the primary 35%–19% and then winning the special with 50.4%. Some of Petri's ideas have been adopted. He long boosted the Earned Income Tax Credit, which results in payments to low-income people who work, arguably targeting aid to families much better than the minimum wage. Eventually he picked up support from the Democratic Leadership Council and the Clinton Administration, and the EITC was expanded in 1993. Now he wants to expand it to middle income families and those with more children. One of the strongest congressional opponents of spending bills, Petri has succeeded in blocking the Auburn Dam in California and the $250 million Washington, D.C., International Cultural and Trade Center. Other Petri plans remain unadopted. One he calls IDEA (Income-Dependent Education Assistance), to guarantee student loans to be repaid at rates based on incomes after school. Another is federal deposit insurance reform, to privatize deposit insurance with risk-related rates. Another is encouraging multi-employer health insurance pools.

Petri is now chairman of the Surface Transportation Subcommittee, which handles highway legislation—a different type of leader for this traditionally pork-laden position. He finds himself torn between cost-cutting pressures and the public-works lobby, including some of his committee colleagues, who want to keep the gravy train rolling. He has changed the highway spending formula to deliver more money to Wisconsin and got more funding for recreational trails out of gas taxes (Wisconsin has extensive snowmobile trails). Nationally he helped to privatize Conrail.

Petri, usually reelected easily, had a tough race in 1992, primarily because of his 77 overdrafts on the House bank—seemingly out of character for a congressman who has given all his honoraria and pay increases to charity. His opponent, Peg Lautenschlager, had been District Attorney in Winnebago County and an assembly member from Fond du Lac County. Juggling family and legislative duties with supermom zest, she campaigned as an "ordinary citizen," although she tended to back state employees and bureaucracies against Governor Tommy Thompson's reforms. Lautenschlager carried Manitowoc, and Petri had big margins in the western counties and carried Fond du Lac and Winnebago narrowly, for a 53%–47% victory. In

1994 he was unopposed. If House Republicans keep their majority a few more years, this unassuming lawmaker has a good chance to become a committee chairman.

The People: Pop. 1990: 543,531; 47% rural; 15% age 65+; 98% White; 1% Asian; 1% Hispanic origin. Voting age pop.: 399,900; 1% Hispanic origin. Households: 63% married couple families; 29% married couple fams. w. children; 34% college educ.; median household income: $28,038; per capita income: $12,400; median gross rent: $349; median house value: $54,800.

1992 Presidential Vote

Bush (R)	114,517	(41%)
Clinton (D)	97,121	(34%)
Perot (I)	69,339	(25%)

1988 Presidential Vote

Bush (R)	127,016	(54%)
Dukakis (D)	106,937	(46%)

Rep. Tom Petri (R)

Elected Apr. 1979; b. May 28, 1940, Marinette; home, Fond du Lac; Harvard, B.A. 1962, J.D. 1965; Lutheran; married (Anne).

Career: Peace Corps, Somalia, 1966–67; Law Clerk, Fed. Judge James Doyle, 1965–66; White House aide, 1969; Practicing atty., 1970–79; WI Senate, 1972–79.

DC Office: 2262 RHOB 20515, 202-225-2476; Fax: 202-225-2356.

District Offices: 845 S. Main St., #160, Fond du Lac 54935, 414-922-1180; and 115 Washington Ave., Oshkosh 54901, 414-231-6333.

Committees: *Economic & Educational Opportunities* (2nd of 24 R): Employer-Employee Relations; Postsecondary Education, Training and Life-Long Learning. *Transportation & Infrastructure* (4th of 33 R): Surface Transportation (Chmn.); Water Resources and Environment.

Group Ratings

	ADA	ACLU	COPE	CFA	LCV	CON	NSI	COC	ACU	NTLC	CHC
1994	25	13	11	20	28	98	60	100	76	82	93
1993	20	—	36	50	36	85	—	73	83	—	—

National Journal Ratings

	1993 LIB — 1993 CONS		1994 LIB — 1994 CONS	
Economic	23%	— 75%	21%	— 76%
Social	24%	— 76%	0%	— 89%
Foreign	40%	— 60%	41%	— 58%

Key Votes of the 103d Congress

1. Clinton Deficit Plan	N	3. Brady Handgun Purchase N	5. Lmt. UN Cmnd. of Forces Y
2. NAFTA	Y	4. Strike Race/Death Pnlty. Y	6. Cut Missile Funds Y

Key Votes of the 104th Congress

1. Congressional Compliance Y	6. Reform Crime Grant Y	11. Loser Pays Court Reform Y
2. Balanced Budget Amndmt. Y	7. National Security Act *	12. Product Liability Reform Y
3. Bar Unfunded Mandates Y	8. Moratorium on Regs. Y	13. Welfare Reform Y
4. Pass Line Item Veto Y	9. Risk Assessment on Regs. Y	14. Term Limits Amndmt. N
5. Relax Exclusionary Rule Y	10. Expnd. Priv. Prop. Rights Y	15. Tax Cuts Y

Election Results

1994 general	Tom Petri (R) .... unopposed		($326,635)
1994 primary	Tom Petri (R) .... unopposed		
1992 general	Tom Petri (R) 143,875	(53%)	($775,594)
	Peggy A. Lautenschlager (D) 128,232	(47%)	($319,363)

SEVENTH DISTRICT

In the late 19th Century, on the rail lines radiating northwest from Chicago and Milwaukee, came thousands of migrants whose descendants have made the northern reaches of Wisconsin the most thickly settled land this far north in the United States and east of the Mississippi. What brought people up so far was not cropland—there are no industrial-sized wheat farms as in the Red River Valley of North Dakota—but trees and iron and cows. This was one of America's largest virgin timberlands, and the river towns are still dotted with paper mills. Farther north, iron brought Finns and Italians to the port of Superior, Wisconsin, right next to Duluth, Minnesota, and to smaller towns on the chilly lake. Then, on the cleared forestlands, came dairy farms: dairy cattle, properly cared for, thrive in these northern uplands, and the sons of Wisconsin dairymen, many of them immigrants from Germany and Norway, moved their dairy herds even farther north. On this base, small cities grew, some with big enterprises. Wausau has paper mills and Wausau Insurance, Wisconsin Rapids has Nekoosa Papers and Stevens Point has Sentry Insurance.

All these places are in Wisconsin's 7th Congressional District, which stretches from a point not far from Green Bay and Madison in the south up to Lake Superior in the north. The politics of northern Wisconsin and the 7th District has a rough-hewn quality, a certain lumberjack populist flavor. Ancestrally Republican, this area favored the progressivism of the LaFollettes. Today Superior and Stevens Point are heavily Democratic, while much of the country in between leans Republican.

The congressman from the 7th District is David Obey, chairman of the Appropriations Committee from March 1994 to January 1995, one of the ablest and mostly strongly motivated legislators now on the minority side of the aisle. He grew up in Wausau, where his father worked in a roofing factory. Obey is a natural politician, who in 1962, the year he got his master's degree, was elected to the Wisconsin Assembly, at 24. When Melvin Laird resigned his House seat to become Richard Nixon's Defense Secretary, Obey won in an upset in the April 1969 special election. In the state legislature he was inspired by older New Deal Democrats who fought hard for the little guy. In the House Obey entered, the driving energy came from liberal Democrats opposed to the Vietnam war. Obey preserves something of the force of each. He is not a sentimental liberal: he has a prickly personality and a vigorous temper and does not suffer gladly those he considers fools or knaves. Even as he has moved to the top of the seniority ladder, he has retained his sense of outrage and his eagerness to fight for what he believes in—a quality that even some Democrats complain has been too intense. But he continues to display abundant energy and leadership on a host of fronts. In the mid-1970s he chaired a special committee on ethics, pushing through a code requiring detailed disclosure of personal finances and limiting outside income: this was not forgiven by some of the oldtimers. From 1979 well into the 1980s he was the chief sponsor of campaign finance bills to limit PAC contributions, reduce individual donations and provide public financing. He had his disappointments. He lost the Budget Committee chairmanship to Jim Jones in 1980 by 121–116. In 1984 he wanted to become Caucus Chairman, but demurred when it became clear that Dick Gephardt had the votes. Even so, informally Obey became a key leader of liberal Democrats, in 1989 pushing Gephardt for majority leader when Jim Wright and Tony Coelho were resigning, in 1990 pushing a rules change requiring Ways and Means subcommittee chairmen to be elected by the whole caucus.

Obey remains a true believer in traditional liberalism, in Keynesian economics and economic redistribution. He thinks that government should provide economic security, create jobs and build infrastructure through public investment, that it should control healthcare costs and guarantee coverage with choice of physician for everyone. In 1994 he wanted to give the president power to lower taxes to counterbalance Federal Reserve interest rate increases and stood ready to back middle class tax cuts even as the economy by some measures was growing smartly. In two stints as chairman of the Joint Economic Committee, he prepared studies arguing that Reagan-Bush policies enriched the rich and hurt the middle class. He has bucked the Democratic leadership on behalf of principle, leading the opposition to the 1990 budget summit package. He also has bucked the Clinton Administration, vocally opposing NAFTA and, when Clinton seemed to be backing away from universal healthcare coverage in July 1994, said "then I will walk away from the Clinton healthcare plan" and support his real preference, a single-payer system. In recent years Obey has had the most liberal voting record in the Wisconsin delegation, although he voted for the Hyde Amendment on abortion and opposed entry of immigrants who are HIV-positive.

When Obey first joined Appropriations, he did not hesitate to insult members of its "college of cardinals," the subcommittee chairmen; he became one himself after 16 years, in 1985, chairing the Foreign Operations Subcommittee. This was a frustrating post for him, for several reasons. One is that he has little sympathy for the structure of foreign aid produced by the Camp David agreement, with huge percentages of aid going to Israel and Egypt. He would like to see more money for humanitarian assistance, such as the Peace Corps, UNICEF and the vitamin A deficiency program. He has often taken on the Israel lobby, insisting evenhandedly on conditioning more aid to Israel on recognition of a Palestinian homeland, and more aid to Arab countries on recognition of Israel. Usually he has opposed U.S. military involvement abroad; he was against aid to the government in El Salvador and the contras in Nicaragua in the 1980s and voted against the Gulf war resolution in 1991. But he supported the dispatch of U.S. troops to Somalia in 1992, declaring potential need for "UN trusteeships in several areas of the world, including Somalia," and he supported U.S. intervention in Haiti in March 1994, saying "I believe Haiti is a special circumstance."

In January 1993, as he looked forward to a new Democratic administration (Bill Clinton's victory made him "feel like a 1,000-pound weight has been lifted from my shoulders"), he still ranked only fifth among Appropriations Democrats, after 24 years. But Jamie Whitten, his health impaired, was voted out of the chairmanship, and his successor William Natcher, after performing ably for a year, was visibly failing in January 1994, and had to be wheeled in to make his last vote in February. By that time both the next senior Democrat, Neal Smith of Iowa, and Obey were campaigning for the job, which fell vacant when Natcher died. Smith, 74, had the support of other cardinals such as Sidney Yates and John Murtha, but Obey had the backing of Democrats who wanted a more activist, partisan leader, and the support of most of the freshmen. Well organized, he won 152–106. That made Obey, at 55, the youngest Appropriations chairman since James Good of Iowa in 1919. Obey immediately replaced the longtime chief staffer with his own able aide, Scott Lilly. But Obey was not as partisan as some may have hoped. "Our mission has been fairly well defined by circumstances," he said. "We've been trying to dig out of the Reagan era deficits and manage the downsizing of programs while freeing up a tiny bit for the president's programs, and I want to do that in the most collegial and bipartisan way." With leeway for argument limited by spending caps and political factors, Appropriations bills were reported and passed in an orderly manner.

Yet even as Obey ascended the heights in Washington, he was facing more trouble than usual at home. Over the years he tended to local matters, working to improve the highway spending formula for Wisconsin, trying to settle the sticky issue of Chippewa Indian fishing rights. For years he had been reelected by wide margins, and his 1994 opponent, Scott West, a 32-year-old admissions counselor at UW-Stevens Point, did not seem a serious threat. Obey, fortified by $312,000 of the PAC contributions he had long worked to limit, spent $589,000 on his 1994 campaign, next to the Republican's $98,000. Yet such was the strength of the Republican tsunami that Obey won by only 54%–46%. He carried the northern part of the district by very solid margins. But he lost his home county around Wausau and lost the southern half of the district 52%–48%.

This no more than anything else seems to daunt Obey. With experience in the minority party from his days in Madison, he switched to take the ranking position on the Labor-HHS-Education Subcommittee, where he can try to spend more on education, health research, worker training and occupational safety and health. His fighting spirits seemed aroused. When Republicans were busy passing the line-item veto—a body blow against the institutional interests of Appropriations Committee heads—Obey said he had a hit list for President Clinton to zero out, including Alaska Natives culture studies and 96th Street upgrading in Indianapolis—projects with strong Republican constituencies. "I know where the bones are buried," Obey said, and this still active warrior, though he seems as much on the defensive today against the new congressional forces as his adversaries were against his allies in the first years after he was elected, seems still eager to fight. Despite his partisan tendencies, his strong institutional loyalty could lead him to provide occasional key support for the Republican leaders of Appropriations.

The People: Pop. 1990: 543,569; 59% rural; 15% age 65+; 97% White; 2% Amer. Indian; 1% Asian. Voting age pop.: 395,664. Households: 62% married couple families; 29% married couple fams. w. children; 34% college educ.; median household income: $25,277; per capita income: $11,427; median gross rent: $327; median house value: $48,400.

1992 Presidential Vote

Clinton (D) 117,203 (42%)
Bush (R) 93,156 (33%)
Perot (I) 67,558 (24%)

1988 Presidential Vote

Dukakis (D) 132,110 (54%)
Bush (R) 111,206 (46%)

Rep. David R. Obey (D)

Elected Apr. 1969; b. Oct. 3, 1938, Okmulgee, OK; home, Wausau; U. of WI, B.S. 1960, M.A., 1962; Catholic; married (Joan).

Career: Real estate broker; Owner, family supper club and motel; WI Assembly, 1962–69.

DC Office: 2462 RHOB 20515, 202-225-3365.

District Offices: Fed. Bldg., 317 First St., Wausau 54401, 715-842-5606.

Committees: *Appropriations* (RMM of 24 D): Labor, Health and Human Services, and Education (RMM); *Joint Economic Committee* (8th of 10 Reps.).

Group Ratings

	ADA	ACLU	COPE	CFA	LCV	CON	NSI	COC	ACU	NTLC	CHC
1994	80	73	89	70	85	11	20	18	10	8	14
1993	90	—	100	90	79	32	—	27	13	—	—

National Journal Ratings

	1993 LIB — 1993 CONS		1994 LIB — 1994 CONS	
Economic	78%	— 12%	73%	— 17%
Social	64%	— 34%	77%	— 23%
Foreign	87%	— 7%	80%	— 17%

Key Votes of the 103d Congress

1. Clinton Deficit Plan	Y	3. Brady Handgun Purchase	N	5. Lmt. UN Cmnd. of Forces	N
2. NAFTA	N	4. Strike Race/Death Pnlty.	N	6. Cut Missile Funds	Y

Key Votes of the 104th Congress

1. Congressional Compliance	Y	6. Reform Crime Grant	N	11. Loser Pays Court Reform	N
2. Balanced Budget Amndt.	N	7. National Security Act	N	12. Product Liability Reform	N
3. Bar Unfunded Mandates	Y	8. Moratorium on Regs.	N	13. Welfare Reform	N
4. Pass Line Item Veto	N	9. Risk Assessment on Regs.	N	14. Term Limits Amndt.	N
5. Relax Exclusionary Rule	N	10. Expnd. Priv. Prop. Rights	Y	15. Tax Cuts	N

Election Results

1994 general	David R. Obey (D)	97,184	(54%)	($607,058)
	Scott West (R)	81,706	(46%)	($98,781)
1994 primary	David R. Obey (D)	unopposed		
1992 general	David R. Obey (D)	166,200	(64%)	($524,574)
	Dale R. Vannes (R)	91,772	(36%)	($20,327)

EIGHTH DISTRICT

In 1673, the French explorer and priest Father Marquette (a statue of whom resides in the U.S. Capitol) sailed from the open waters of Lake Michigan into what is now Green Bay. He had hoped to find the Northwest Passage to the Pacific. He actually found the Fox River, which leads to Lake Winnebago and, after a not-too-difficult portage, the Wisconsin River that flows into the Mississippi. Green Bay and the Fox River Valley remained mostly wilderness and Indian country for more than 150 years. But once settled by Europeans, they became, as Father Marquette would have liked, one of the most heavily Catholic parts of the United States (he might be surprised, however, to see that disputes over Chippewa Indians spearfishing rights were a media circus for 17 years). Economically, Green Bay and the towns clustered around Appleton at the head of Lake Winnebago live off paper mills and high-skill manufacturing. Psychically, they live for the triumphs of the Green Bay Packers, America's only municipally-owned National Football League franchise.

Green Bay and the Fox River Valley make up most of the 8th Congressional District of Wisconsin. It also includes several north woods and dairy counties inland, plus the Door County peninsula that juts out into Lake Michigan, a favorite summer vacation spot for Chicago and Milwaukee families. Politically, this has often been malleable country. Democrats, especially Catholics, can win here: John Kennedy carried the Fox River Valley in the primary and general election in 1960, and the most recent Democratic congressman was Robert Cornell, a priest elected in 1974 and 1976. But the 8th District can turn almost ferociously Republican: Appleton was the home of Senator Joseph McCarthy, who did much to tar the good names of politics, Congress, conservatism and the Republican Party in the early 1950s.

The congressman from the 8th District today is Toby Roth, a Republican whose first victory in 1978 was a little noticed precursor of the conservative tide that swept the country in 1980. Roth built a real estate business in Appleton in the 1960s and was elected to the Wisconsin Assembly in 1972; after three terms he ran for Congress. His record has been solidly conservative, except perhaps on foreign issues where he sometimes opposes U.S. involvement abroad: a hint of old-fashioned Midwestern isolationism. He insisted on tough export controls during the Cold War and still questions some military sales to countries like Saudi Arabia. In 1995 he became chairman of the International Relations Subcommittee on International Economic Policy and Trade. Roth is an advocate of "fair trade" and believes the U.S. will have to battle aggressively for markets with the Pacific Rim and the European Economic Community. He opposed U.S. military intervention in Somalia in 1992 and Bosnia in 1993; he wants to bring home troops from Europe and station them to patrol the U.S.-Mexico border. He strongly backs declaring English as the official language and wants to eliminate bilingual education programs. When a Wisconsin sailor was drowned during a naval training exercise, he sparked an investigation of Navy training procedures. Solidly conservative on economics, he hailed the repeal of the luxury boat tax. He is also proud of bringing a veterans' clinic to Grand Chute.

Roth has had a couple of serious challenges, and was held to 54% as recently as 1990. In 1994 he had spirited opposition from state Assemblyman Stan Gruszynski, who made blistering attacks on Governor Tommy Thompson and moved from Stevens Point to make the race. But in this Republican year, Roth won 64%–36%.

The People: Pop. 1990: 543,526; 44% rural; 14% age 65+; 96% White; 3% Amer. Indian; 1% Asian; 1% Hispanic origin. Voting age pop.: 396,416. Households: 62% married couple families; 30% married couple fams. w. children; 37% college educ.; median household income: $28,169; per capita income: $12,628; median gross rent: $357; median house value: $57,800.

1992 Presidential Vote			**1988 Presidential Vote**		
Bush (R)	115,128	(40%)	Bush (R)	129,440	(53%)
Clinton (D)	101,493	(35%)	Dukakis (D)	113,361	(47%)
Perot (I)	69,373	(24%)			

Rep. Toby Roth (R)

Elected 1978; b. Oct. 10, 1938, Strasburg, ND; home, Appleton; Marquette U., B.A. 1961; Catholic; married (Barbara).

Career: Army Reserves, 1962–69; Realtor; WI Assembly, 1972–78.

DC Office: 2234 RHOB 20515, 202-225-5665; Fax: 202-225-0087.

District Offices: 2301 S. Oneida St., Green Bay 54304, 414-494-2800; and 126 N. Oneida St., Appleton 54911, 414-739-4167.

Committees: *Banking & Financial Services* (5th of 27 R): Financial Institutions and Consumer Credit. *International Relations* (4th of 23 R): Africa; International Economic Policy and Trade (Chmn.).

Group Ratings

	ADA	ACLU	COPE	CFA	LCV	CON	NSI	COC	ACU	NTLC	CHC
1994	15	14	11	20	29	94	40	92	81	81	86
1993	25	—	17	30	29	50	—	73	83	—	—

National Journal Ratings

	1993 LIB — 1993 CONS			1994 LIB — 1994 CONS		
Economic	23%	—	75%	0%	—	80%
Social	11%	—	82%	0%	—	89%
Foreign	40%	—	57%	37%	—	62%

Key Votes of the 103d Congress

1. Clinton Deficit Plan	N	3. Brady Handgun Purchase	N	5. Lmt. UN Cmnd. of Forces	Y
2. NAFTA	Y	4. Strike Race/Death Pnlty.	Y	6. Cut Missile Funds	Y

Key Votes of the 104th Congress

1. Congressional Compliance Y	6. Reform Crime Grant Y	11. Loser Pays Court Reform *
2. Balanced Budget Amndmt. Y	7. National Security Act Y	12. Product Liability Reform Y
3. Bar Unfunded Mandates Y	8. Moratorium on Regs. Y	13. Welfare Reform Y
4. Pass Line Item Veto Y	9. Risk Assessment on Regs. Y	14. Term Limits Amndmt. Y
5. Relax Exclusionary Rule Y	10. Expnd. Priv. Prop. Rights Y	15. Tax Cuts Y

Election Results

1994 general	Toby Roth (R).....................	114,319	(64%)	($683,149)
	Stan Gruszynski (D)..................	65,065	(36%)	($215,831)
1994 primary	Toby Roth (R)........................	49,544	(68%)	
	Nancy J. Nusbaum (R)	23,274	(32%)	
1992 general	Toby Roth (R).....................	191,704	(70%)	($444,548)
	Catherine L. Helms (D)	81,792	(30%)	($42,827)

NINTH DISTRICT

For decades, the orderly, heavily German-American factory city of Milwaukee has been spreading slowly, mostly west and north, into Wisconsin dairy country. There are high-income enclaves here, like close-in Elm Grove and Oconomowoc spread out around its lakes. There is office development in Brookfield; subdivisions spread out in Mequon and Menomonee Falls and farther, to reach small towns with roots deep in the 19th Century. This is comfortable but not fancy territory, and the economy here is still based heavily on skilled manufacturing. Not far from Milwaukee are Sheboygan, home of Kohler plumbing fixtures; Port Washington, with Allen-Edmonds shoes; West Bend, with West Bend kitchen appliances; Pewaukee, with QuadriGraphics printing.

The 9th Congressional District of Wisconsin includes most of the western, northwestern and northern suburbs of Milwaukee and spreads out into rich dairy farm country and to these factory towns. Almost every precinct here votes Republican, and this is usually the most Republican district in the state.

The congressman from the 9th District, James Sensenbrenner, first elected in 1978, is one of the most senior Republicans in the House. His Wisconsin roots are strong—his great-grandfather was a top executive at Kimberly-Clark—and Sensenbrenner is one of the richest members of Congress and the most scrupulous (he discloses a complete list of his investments). He has spent most of his adult life in politics, briefly as a U.S. House staffer, and then serving 10 years in the Wisconsin legislature from 1968–78. For almost all that time, Sensenbrenner has been in the minority, gamely undertaking the Sisyphean task of moving amendments certain to lose. But he has persevered out of a dogged sense of principle. Though he backed the Brady bill, he was the House's leading opponent of the assault weapon ban, for example, losing 216–214 after President Clinton infuriated him by publicizing a Wisconsin policeman killed with such a weapon; Sensenbrenner argued they accounted for very few murders and were mostly used lawfully. But the ban is what caused the setback for the crime bill in August 1994, at which point Democrats lost working control of the House. Sensenbrenner also opposed the crime bill and wrote a block grant proposal, rebating to states 2% of their personal income tax revenues. Sensenbrenner now chairs the Space and Aeronautics Subcommittee, on which he has been a strong backer of the space station, which survived by a one-vote margin in 1993 and by 278–155 in 1994. He seriously questioned the joint U.S.-Russia space agreement and got assurances from the White House that NASA was prepared to complete the space station within budget regardless of what Russia did.

Sensenbrenner is a stickler for rules and ethics, one of the first to urge that Congress apply to itself the laws it imposes on the rest of the country. He has insisted on impeachment action against federal judges convicted of crimes. He prepared motions to censure or expel Dan Rostenkowski if he had pleaded guilty to any crimes—one reason, perhaps, why he did not. Sensenbrenner upholds the principle of colorblindness, opposing race-based standards in crime bills and arguing strongly against racial quotas until George Bush negotiated the issue away in 1991. He was rated the nation's top spending-cutter by the National Taxpayers Union Foundation in 1994.

Sensenbrenner's only tough race was the 1978 primary. He is routinely reelected by overwhelming margins, and was unopposed in 1994.

The People: Pop. 1990: 543,602; 36% rural; 12% age 65+; 96% White; 1% Asian; 1% Hispanic origin. Voting age pop.: 395,884; 1% Hispanic origin. Households: 69% married couple families; 33% married couple fams. w. children; 46% college educ.; median household income: $37,579; per capita income: $16,187; median gross rent: $430; median house value: $82,500.

1992 Presidential Vote

Bush (R) 142,465 (48%)
Clinton (D) 88,303 (30%)
Perot (I). 64,657 (22%)

1988 Presidential Vote

Bush (R) 149,007 (60%)
Dukakis (D). 99,615 (40%)

Rep. F. James Sensenbrenner, Jr. (R)

Elected 1978; b. June 14, 1943, Chicago, IL; home, Menomonee Falls; Stanford U., A.B. 1965, U. of WI, J.D. 1968; Episcopalian; married (Cheryl).

Career: Practicing atty., 1968–69; Staff asst., U.S. Rep. Arthur Younger, 1965; WI Assembly, 1968–74; WI Senate, 1974–78.

DC Office: 2332 RHOB 20515, 202-225-5101; Fax: 202-225-3190.

District Offices: 120 Bishops Way, #154, Brookfield 53005, 414-784-1111.

Committees: *Judiciary* (3rd of 20 R): Constitution; Courts and Intellectual Property. *Science* (2nd of 27 R): Space and Aeronautics (Chmn.).

Group Ratings

	ADA	ACLU	COPE	CFA	LCV	CON	NSI	COC	ACU	NTLC	CHC
1994	20	13	22	0	22	99	50	67	76	96	100
1993	20	—	0	30	43	98	—	82	92	—	—

National Journal Ratings

	1993 LIB — 1993 CONS		1994 LIB — 1994 CONS	
Economic	0% —	88%	0% —	80%
Social	19% —	77%	0% —	89%
Foreign	37% —	60%	34% —	63%

Key Votes of the 103d Congress

1. Clinton Deficit Plan	N	3. Brady Handgun Purchase	Y	5. Lmt. UN Cmnd. of Forces	Y
2. NAFTA	Y	4. Strike Race/Death Pnlty.	Y	6. Cut Missile Funds	Y

Key Votes of the 104th Congress

1. Congressional Compliance Y	6. Reform Crime Grant Y	11. Loser Pays Court Reform Y
2. Balanced Budget Amndmt. Y	7. National Security Act Y	12. Product Liability Reform Y
3. Bar Unfunded Mandates Y	8. Moratorium on Regs. Y	13. Welfare Reform Y
4. Pass Line Item Veto Y	9. Risk Assessment on Regs. Y	14. Term Limits Amndmt. N
5. Relax Exclusionary Rule Y	10. Expnd. Priv. Prop. Rights Y	15. Tax Cuts Y

Election Results

1994 general	F. James Sensenbrenner, Jr (R) .... unopposed			($161,986)
1994 primary	F. James Sensenbrenner, Jr (R) .... unopposed			
1992 general	F. James Sensenbrenner, Jr. (R)	192,898	(70%)	($457,292)
	Ingrid K. Buxton (D)	77,362	(28%)	($27,125)
	Other...............................	6,527	(2%)	

WYOMING

Wyoming is "the land of the cowboy" the *WPA Guide* proclaimed 50 years ago. "Its mountains, plains, and valleys are essentially livestock country. A cowboy astride a bucking bronco greets the visitor from enameled license plates, from newspapers, magazines and painted signs." The cowboy is still on the license plates, and Wyoming remains the most western of states in spirit—largely unsettled, the least populous state, a thin veneer of civilization stretched over a forbidding and beautiful land. "Wyoming seems to be the doing of a mad architect," writes Gretel Ehrlich, "tumbled and twisted, ribboned with faded, deathbed colors, thrust up and pulled down as if the place had been startled out of a deep sleep and thrown into a pure light." Wyoming "has a 'lean-to' look," says Ehrlich. "Instead of big, roomy barns and Victorian houses, there are dugouts, low sheds, log cabins, sheep camps and fence lines that look like driftwood blown haphazardly into place. People here still feel pride because they live in such a harsh place, part of the glamorous cowboy past."

But the economic life of Wyoming now depends less on cowboys and more on mining and minerals. The mining bust and population losses of the 1980s have been succeeded by new mining and job growth in the 1990s; new processing plants have come on line, and there are new demands for Wyoming's low-sulfur coal. The big strip mines around Gillette now make Wyoming the nation's leading coal-producing state; its oil industry, centered in Casper, pumps along; there are large natural gas deposits in the southwest, around Evanston, and soda ash around Green River. Wyoming has also had glamour growth, notably around Jackson Hole, which made headlines during the Bush Administration as the vacation home of Secretary of State James Baker and Secretary of Defense and former Wyoming Congressman Dick Cheney. And there has been growth in the scenic and pastoral country on the eastern slope of the Big Horn mountains around Buffalo and Sheridan. Meanwhile, tourists still flock to Yellowstone and Teton national parks: tourist dollars are crucial to the local economy.

Wyoming, for all its Old West atmosphere, has depended on new technology working on age-old nature. Cattle ranches after the open-range era were made possible only by the barbed wire that could fence in roaming herds, and the steam locomotives that could carry cattle to market back east. This 19th Century high tech was brought to Wyoming by large capitalist operators, some of them onetime Texas cowhands or second sons of English landed gentry, who started the first big operations and consolidated their power in the Johnson County land war of 1890. More recently, Wyoming has boomed and busted as geologists and engineers have discovered and developed minerals in demand on world markets. The 1970s spikes in energy prices brought in big operators who found oil and natural gas in the Overthrust belt near Evanston. Huge deposits of coal in the north became economically feasible to mine when transportation improved and clean air laws were changed to remove the advantage for high-sulfur West Virginia coal. The result was not always a pretty picture. Workers who flocked here lived in grimy trailers, linked only precariously to civilization's utilities and unprotected against the winds and snows that come out of the enormous sky; these communities had an atmosphere redolent of 19th Century mining camps like Virginia City, Nevada, or Deadwood, South Dakota. In the 1990s, wolves were returned, despite local ranchers' objections, to the Yellowstone area and were seen elsewhere—nature edging man back just a little bit. Wyoming still is a kind of frontier: it was until recently one of the few states with more men than women—the reason it was the first part of the United States, when it was a territory in 1869, to give women the vote.

There is a settled part of Wyoming as well, in the medium-sized towns that are the state's largest cities, and among sheep and cattle ranches, sugar beet farmers and denizens of tiny settlements. This is a small state, a single community really, where people remember who played what position, when and how well, for what high-school football team; where because all locals know who your father's cousins married, you mostly live on the straight and narrow. Yet there is a sharp economic and regional split traditionally reflected in partisan politics. The big economic interests—cattle ranchers, organized in the Wyoming Stock Growers' Association, and the Union Pacific Railroad management always favored the Republicans, as do the wildcatters, independent producers and oil company geologists. The main Democratic constituency has been the Union Pacific Railroad workers who built the first transcontinental line across southern Wyoming in the 1860s and have maintained it ever since; the southern tier of counties, from Cheyenne through Laramie to Evanston, often votes Democratic. The balance of population has long favored the Republicans, and in the 1970s and 1980s this was one of the most Republican states. In 1992, Wyoming was full of discontent and flirted with Ross Perot, giving him 26% of its votes. That held down George Bush's vote to 40%, not so far ahead of Bill Clinton's 34%.

But the Clinton Administration produced a sharp Republican reaction. Interior Secretary Bruce Babbitt's proposed grazing fees were received here as an assault not only on people's livings but on their lifestyle; the federal government's reintroduction of grey wolves into Yellowstone National Park didn't help. Other federal restrictions were seen more than ever as alien Eastern intrusions, a "war on the West." By November 1994, Wyoming voters felt Clinton environmental policies hurt rather than helped the state by a 60%–12% margin. Personal campaigning has always remained important here: there aren't many people—not even half a million, less than the size of an average congressional district, in 1990—and Wyoming voters expect to talk person-to-person with their governors, senators and congressmen every few years. But in 1994, even strong Democratic candidates were unable to prevent a Republican sweep. Governor Mike Sullivan, with a very high job rating after two terms, nonetheless lost the Senate race 59%–39% to Congressman-at-Large Craig Thomas; people didn't mind having a Democratic governor, but couldn't bear giving Clinton's Democrats one more vote in the Senate. Barbara Cubin won the House seat 53%–41% despite the big spending of Democrat Bob Schuster. And Republican Jim Geringer, winner of a multicandidate primary, beat the initially better-known Secretary of State Kathy Karpan for governor 59%–40%.

Governor. Mike Sullivan, with his trademark Stetson with a hole in it and his fiscal austerity which earned him a top rating from the libertarian Cato Institute, could probably have won a third term in 1994; but he ran for the Senate instead. Secretary of State Kathy Karpan was the obvious Democratic nominee, and in another year might well have won.

Instead, the key contest was the Republican primary, won by Jim Geringer. He grew up in Wheatland, where his father, a Volga German, had emigrated early in the century. That was his Old West background; his high-tech came from service in the Air Force, where he worked on Air Force and NASA space boosters for 10 years. In 1977, Geringer returned to Wyoming, starting from scratch and buying his own farm. He was elected to the state legislature in 1982. In the

U.S. Representative elected at large.

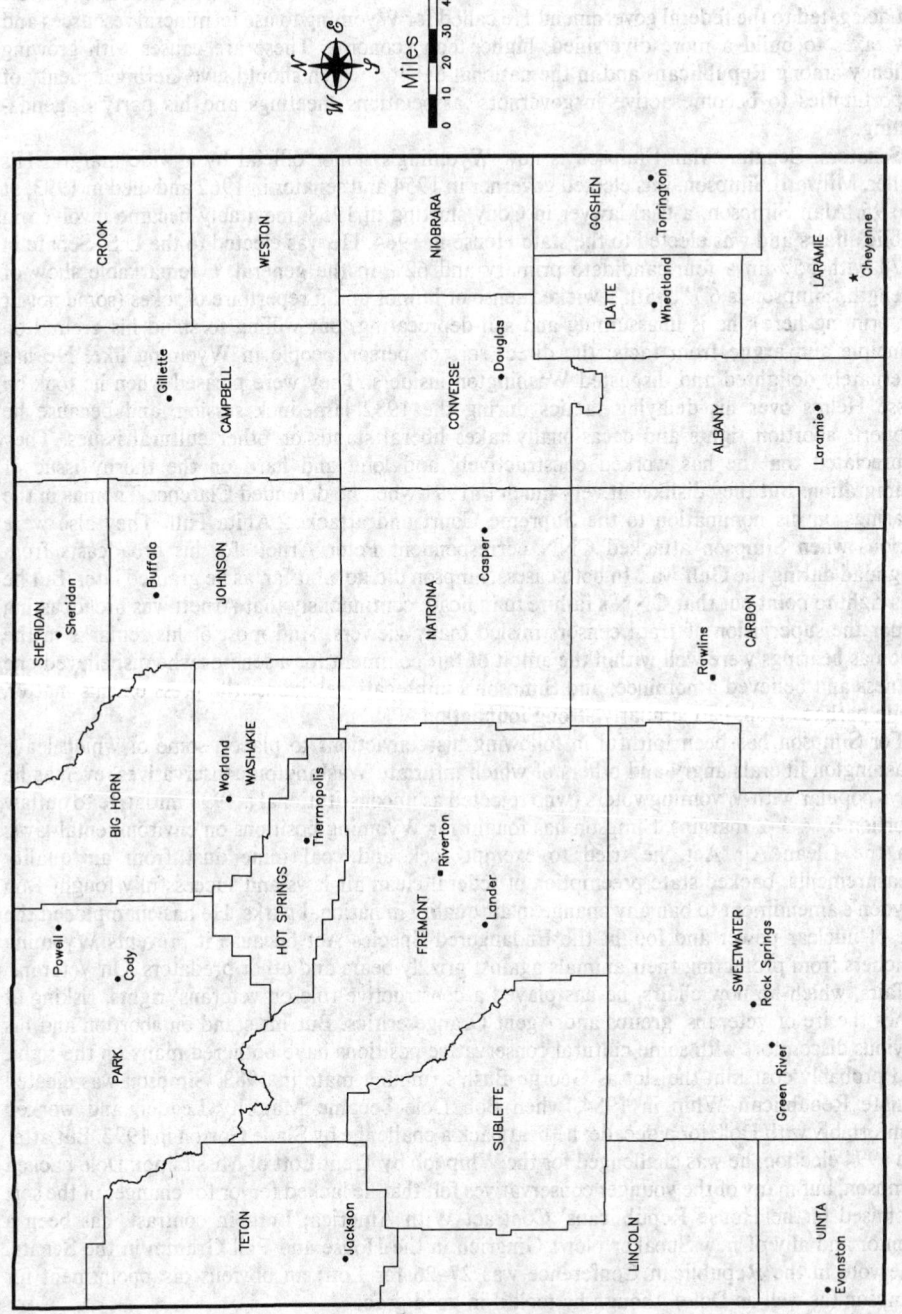

anti-Clinton atmosphere of November 1994, he easily prevailed over Karpan, carrying all but one county. Geringer complains of "the increasing imbalance of power between federal and state governments" and wants to give life to the 10th Amendment which reserves to the states powers not delegated to the federal government. He called for Wyoming to use its mineral resources and low taxes to build a more diversified, higher-tech economy. These are causes with growing saliency among Republicans and in the national debate, which should give Geringer plenty of opportunities to become active in governors' associations meetings and his party's agenda-setting.

Senators. Senator Alan Simpson is now Wyoming's senior official by a wide margin. His father, Milward Simpson, was elected governor in 1954 and senator in 1962 and died in 1993, at age 95. Alan Simpson, a trial lawyer in Cody starting in 1958, inevitably became involved in public affairs and was elected to the state House in 1964. He was elected to the U.S. Senate in 1978 with 55% in a four-candidate primary and 62% in the general, a remarkable show of strength. Simpson is 6'7", with a wicked sense of humor and a repertoire of jokes (some not fit for printing here); he is unassuming and self-deprecating, but willing to stand his ground on principle and argue from facts: the direct sort of person people in Wyoming like. He has alternately delighted and disgusted Washington insiders. They were pleased when he took on Jesse Helms over his delaying tactics during the 1982 lameduck session, and because he supports abortion rights and occasionally takes liberal stands on other cultural issues. They appreciated that he has worked constructively and long and hard on the thorny issue of immigration. But they disliked it very much in 1991 when he defended Clarence Thomas in the hearings on his nomination to the Supreme Court and attacked Anita Hill. They also were furious when Simpson attacked CNN correspondent Peter Arnett for his broadcasts from Baghdad during the Gulf war. In both cases, Simpson did go a bit far, as he granted later. But he was right to point out that CNN's failure to indicate continuously that Arnett was broadcasting under the supervision of Iraqi censors misled many viewers. And most of his remarks in the Thomas hearings were well within the ambit of fair comment for a senator who disbelieved one witness and believed a nominee; and Simpson's imprecations against the press on this matter, while perhaps rash, had similarly strong foundation.

For Simpson has been faithful in following his convictions to places, some of which leave Washington liberals angry and others of which infuriate Washington conservatives, even as he stays popular with Wyoming voters (who rejected as unconstitutional a 1994 initiative to outlaw abortion by a 3–2 margin). Simpson has fought for Wyoming positions on environmental laws. On the Clean Air Act, he tried to exempt rock and coal mine dust from air quality measurements, backed state preemption of federal clean air laws and successfully fought Ron Wyden's amendment to ban any change in air quality in national parks. He has championed the use of nuclear power and fought the Endangered Species Act because it prevents Wyoming ranchers from protecting their animals against grizzly bears and other predators. On Veterans' Affairs, which he now chairs, he has played a constructive role on veterans' rights, risking at times the ire of veterans' groups and Agent Orange critics. But his stand on abortion and his obvious discomfort with some cultural conservative positions have bothered many on the right, and probably cost him the slot as George Bush's running mate in 1988. Simpson was elected Senate Republican Whip in 1984, when Bob Dole became Majority Leader, and worked comfortably with Dole for a decade; he beat back a challenge by Slade Gorton in 1992. But after the 1994 election, he was challenged for the Whip job by Trent Lott of Mississippi. Dole backed Simpson, but many of the younger conservatives felt that he lacked fervor for changes of the sort promised in the House Republicans' Contract With America; Lott, in contrast, has been a mentor and ally of new Speaker Newt Gingrich in the House and Phil Gramm in the Senate. The vote in the Republican Conference was 27–26 for Lott: an obvious disappointment for Simpson (as well as Dole), though he took it in good grace.

Simpson reclaimed the Veterans' Affairs chairmanship. And he moved to devote most of his attention to the issue on which he made his first major legislative achievement, immigration.

Simpson had inherited the Judiciary Immigration Subcommittee chair back in 1981 and with his then-counterpart in the House, Romano Mazzoli, fashioned bills to discourage illegal immigration by imposing sanctions on employers who hire illegal immigrants and to legitimize migrants already here for some years; he pushed this through the Senate three times and finally got agreement with the House at the end of the 1986 session. He lost leverage on the issue when Democrats regained control of the Senate, and subcommittee chairman Edward Kennedy, largely at the behest of Irish groups, helped shape the immigration law of 1990 which increases legal immigration quotas. Simpson now thinks that a mistake, and in early 1995 advanced his own measure, lowering total legal immigration from 675,000 to 500,000, and setting up an electronic verification system for legal immigrants to establish their eligibility for employment and government benefits, a form of the identity card recommended by Barbara Jordan's commission in September 1994. This time the House is much more restrictive than Simpson, with immigration skeptic Lamar Smith of Texas chairing the immigration subcommittee and the Contract With America calling for a cutoff of government aid to legal immigrants. It will be interesting to see whether the government can regain control of its borders, and whether lower legal immigration limits can prevail against the economic incentives of work, if not welfare, that bring immigrants here. In addition, Simpson has turned his attention to reducing the rate of growth in entitlement spending. With his new seat on the Finance Committee, he held hearings to take on the American Association of Retired Persons, one of Washington's most powerful interest groups. And he joined Bob Kerrey in filing a bipartisan proposal to make long-term cuts in Social Security spending, including an eventual increase in the retirement age to 70.

Simpson has remained highly popular in Wyoming and was reelected with 78% in 1984 and 64% in 1990 against a 32-year-old anti-abortion Democrat and political unknown. He had been the subject of speculation that he would retire at the end of his current term. But, with the Republicans' recapture of the majority, he seems rejuvenated and is an overwhelming favorite to win a fourth term in 1996.

Wyoming's junior senator is Craig Thomas, elected in 1994 to fill the seat vacated after three terms by Malcolm Wallop, a descendant of one of Wyoming's 19th Century British aristocrats. Wallop had championed a hard line on foreign policy and defense and opposed tax increases like the 1990 budget summit agreement, and he had worked on some environmental issues. Thomas grew up in Cody with Al Simpson; he worked for the Farm Bureau and the Wyoming Rural Electric Association, organizations with conservative political leanings that kept him in touch with hundreds of people active in their communities. He served five years in the state legislature. In March 1989, Congressman-at-Large Dick Cheney was appointed Secretary of Defense; and the contest to succeed him proved close, even in this Republican state, as is often the case with special elections early in a president's term in districts long held by his party. Democrat John Vinich just a few months before had nearly beaten Malcolm Wallop. When Republican campaign committee honchos said they couldn't afford to lose Wyoming after dropping seats in Indiana and Alabama, Vinich sounded a powerful Wyoming theme—don't let outsiders make decisions for Wyoming. But Thomas rallied and won with 53% of the vote. His campaign attacked Vinich's heavy labor funding, unpopular in this right-to-work state, and a TV ad suggesting that Thomas had voted against an anti-crime measure which was denounced by the *Casper Star-Tribune*.

In the House, Thomas had a solidly conservative voting record. He concentrated on Wyoming issues: working for Wyoming nuclear radiation victims' compensation, cleaning up uranium tailings, opposing reintroducing wolves in Yellowstone Park, backing reclamation programs, and limiting federal land acquisition. He won reelection with 55% in 1990 and 58% in 1992. When Wallop stepped down in 1994, he was the obvious Republican candidate and had no primary opposition. In the general, he faced Governor Mike Sullivan, personally popular and with a conservative record, but handicapped by his association with Bill Clinton. Sullivan was a FOB from their governors' conference days together and campaigned for Clinton when he was in trouble in the 1992 New Hampshire primary; Clinton personally asked him to run for the

Senate. Thomas relentlessly attacked Sullivan as a FOB and ally of Interior Secretary Bruce Babbitt; he hammered Sullivan for being willing to bargain with Babbitt. "I'm not willing to bargain with Bruce Babbitt," Thomas said. "I'm not afraid to stand up and say no." Thomas won 59%–39%, losing only one southern tier county, and that by only six votes.

Thomas serves on the Energy Committee, where he can work against Babbitt's policies, and also on Environment, Indian Affairs and Foreign Relations—heavy assignments for a freshman, even one who takes a serious approach to many issues.

Representative-At-Large. Wyoming's roughest and readiest contest in 1994 was the race for representative-at-large: five Republicans and two Democrats filed, all but one serious candidates. The ultimate winner, state Senator Barbara Cubin, is the great-great-granddaughter of one of Wyoming's original homesteaders. She grew up in Casper, where she worked as a teacher, social worker, chemist and realtor; for 19 years she managed her husband's medical practice. She was divorced after an early first marriage, worked as a single mother, was subjected to sexual harassment, but insists: "I am not a feminist. I am not gender sensitive." She worked in Casper charities and was elected to the legislature in 1986, where she was prime sponsor of a 1994 ballot measure authorizing life without parole sentences. In the legislature Cubin's specialty was energy law, and in the campaign for Congress, she sharply attacked "the Clinton-Babbitt war on the West," though she said she would accept an increase in some grazing fees and slightly higher mining royalties. In the Republican primary, she won 39% to 25% for House staffer Rob Wallace, 18% for sheep farmer Jim Magagna and 17% for state House Speaker Doug Chamberlain.

The Democratic nominee was Bob Schuster, a law partner of high-profile trial lawyer Gerry Spence, and a Democratic National committeeman. Schuster beat 1992 candidate Jon Herschler in the 1994 primary by charging that Herschler would abolish VA hospitals and favored higher taxes for health care, charges which Herschler angrily denied. But Schuster spent over $500,000 on saturation advertising and altogether spent $2.4 million, most of it his own money, on what was the third-highest spending campaign in the country. Schuster's big issue in the general was abortion; he was pro-choice, Cubin anti-abortion, and he hammered her even as the anti-abortion initiative was going down to defeat. He had been a Clinton delegate in 1992 in New York, and she called him a "a slick trial-lawyer Clinton Democrat." He countered by praising the "Wyoming approach" of a panel appointed by Democratic Governor Mike Sullivan to streamline government. But in anti-Clinton Wyoming that was not enough. Schuster carried only four counties, three in the southern tier and the other in Jackson Hole, and Cubin won 53%–41%. She serves on the Resources and Science committees. Along with several other recently elected women from the West, she has brought a fresh voice to the House and Republican politics.

Presidential politics. Wyoming is one of the least likely states in the nation to be seriously contested in presidential general elections: it is too Republican, too remote and has only three electoral votes. The high Perot vote here and disenchantment with Bush made Wyoming competitive in some 1992 polls, and Clinton actually made a stop here on October 24—the first time Wyoming has seen a presidential nominee in the stretch in a long time. That's not likely to happen again: Clinton had just a 30% job approval rating here in November 1994, and will do well to equal the 34% he won in 1992.

In 1992 Wyoming's Democrats held a caucus March 7, just before Super Tuesday; Clinton emerged the marginal winner over Jerry Brown and Paul Tsongas; its winner four years before was Albert Gore. The Republicans met later and routinely backed George Bush.

The People: Est. Pop. 1994: 475,000; Pop. 1990: 453,588, up 4.9% 1990–1994. 0.2% of U.S. total, 51st largest; 35% rural. Median age: 32.0 years. 10.4% 65 years and over. 94.2% White, 5.7% Hispanic origin, 2.1% American Indian, 2.3% Other. Households: 59.7% married couple families; 31% married couple fams. w. children; 50% college educ.; median household income: $27,096; per capita income: $12,311; 67.8% owner occupied housing; median house value: $61,600; median monthly rent: $270. 5.6% Unemployment. 1994 Voting age pop.: 343,000. 1994 Turnout: 201,228; 59% of VAP. Registered voters (1994): 237,836; 79,326 D (33%), 135,245 R (57%), 23,212 unaffiliated and minor parties (10%).

Political Lineup: Governor, Jim Geringer (R); Secy. of State, Diana Ohman (R); Atty. Gen., Joseph B. Meyer (R); Treasurer, Stanford Smith (R); Auditor, David Ferrari (R). State Senate, 30 (20 R and 10 D), State House of Representatives, 60 (47 R and 13 D). Senators, Alan K. Simpson (R) and Craig Thomas (R). Representative, 1 R at large.

1992 Presidential Vote			**1988 Presidential Vote**		
Bush (R)	79,347	(40%)	Bush (R)	106,867	(61%)
Clinton (D)	68,160	(34%)	Dukakis (D)	67,113	(38%)
Perot (I)	51,263	(26%)			

GOVERNOR

Gov. Jim Geringer (R)

Elected 1994, term expires Jan. 1999; b. Apr. 24, 1944, Wheatland; home, Wheatland; KS St. U., B.S. 1967; Lutheran; married (Sherri).

Career: Air Force, 1967–77, Air Force Reserves, 1977–91; Contract Admin., Missouri Basin Power Project, 1977–79; Farmer, Rancher; WY House of Reps., 1982–88; WY Senate, 1988–94.

Office: State Capitol Bldg., #124, Cheyenne 82002, 307-777-7434; Fax: 307-632-3909.

Election Results

1994 gen.	Jim Geringer (R)	118,016	(59%)
	Kathy Karpan (D)	80,747	(40%)
	Others	2,227	(1%)
1994 prim.	Jim Geringer (R)	37,847	(43%)
	John Perry (R)	28,019	(32%)
	Charles K. Scott (R)	19,305	(22%)
	Others	3,442	(4%)
1990 gen.	Michael J. (Mike) Sullivan (D)	104,638	(65%)
	Mary Mead (R)	55,471	(35%)

SENATORS

Sen. Alan K. Simpson (R)

Elected 1978, seat up 1996; b. Sept. 2, 1931, Denver, CO; home, Cody; U. of WY, B.S. 1954, J.D. 1958; Episcopalian; married (Ann).

Career: Army, 1954–56; Practicing atty., 1959–78; WY Asst. Atty. Gen., 1959; Cody City Atty., 1959–69; WY House of Reps., 1964–77, Majority Floor Ldr., 1975–76, Speaker Pro-Tem, 1977.

DC Office: 105 DSOB 20510, 202-224-3424; Fax: 202-224-1315.

State Offices: P.O. Box 430, Cody 82414, 307-527-7121; Fed. Ctr., #3201, Casper 82601, 307-261-5172; Fed. Ctr., #2007, Cheyenne 82001, 307-772-2477; 2201 S. Douglas Hwy., P.O. Box 3155, Gillette 82716, 307-682-7091; 2020 Grand Ave., #411, Laramie 82070, 307-745-5303; 2515 Foothills Blvd., #220, Rock Springs 82901, 307-382-5097; and 1731 Sheridan Ave., Cody 82414, 307-527-7121.

Committees: *Finance* (7th of 11 R): Long-Term Growth, Debt and Defict Reduction; Medicare, Long-Term Care and Health Insurance; Social Security and Family Policy (Chmn). *Judiciary* (3rd of 10 R): Antitrust, Business Rights and Competition; Immigration (Chmn.); Youth Violence. *Veterans' Affairs* (Chmn. of 7 R) *Aging (Special)* (4th of 10 R).

Group Ratings

	ADA	ACLU	COPE	CFA	LCV	CON	NSI	COC	ACU	NTLC	CHC
1994	15	33	14	42	8	91	100	85	88	87	71
1993	20	—	0	30	13	83	—	100	86	—	—

National Journal Ratings

	1993 LIB — 1993 CONS		1994 LIB — 1994 CONS	
Economic	20% —	78%	12% —	82%
Social	27% —	71%	35% —	63%
Foreign	23% —	76%	20% —	78%

Key Votes of the 103d Congress

1. Clinton Deficit Plan	N	3. Brady Handgun Purchase N	5. Lmt. UN Cmnd. of Forces Y
2. NAFTA	Y	4. Strike Race/Death Pnlty. Y	6. Cut Missile Funds N

Key Votes of the 104th Congress

1. Congressional Compliance Y	3. Balanced Budget Amndt. Y	5. Product Liability Reform N
2. Bar Unfunded Mandates Y	4. Pass Line Item Veto Y	6. FY96 Budget Y

Election Results

1990 general	Alan K. Simpson (R)	100,784	(64%)	($1,435,814)
	Kathy Helling (D)	56,848	(36%)	($6,243)
1990 primary	Alan K. Simpson (R)	69,142	(84%)	
	Douglas W. Crook (R)	6,201	(8%)	
	Nora Marie Lewis	6,577	(8%)	
1984 general	Alan K. Simpson (R)	146,373	(78%)	($862,039)
	Victor A. Ryan (D)	40,525	(22%)	

Sen. Craig Thomas (R)

Elected 1994, seat up 2000; b. Feb. 17, 1933, Cody; home, Casper; U. of WY, B.S. 1954, LaSalle U., LL.B. 1968; Methodist; married (Susan).

Career: Marine Corps, 1955–59; V.P., WY Farm Bureau, 1960–66; Legis. staff, Amer. Farm Bureau, 1966–75; Gen. Mgr., WY Rural Electric Assn., 1975–89; WY House of Reps., 1984–89; U.S. House of Reps., 1989–94.

DC Office: 302 HSOB 20515, 202-224-6441; Fax: 202-224-1724.

State Offices: 2201 Fed. Bldg., Casper 82601, 307-261-5413; 2120 Capitol Ave., #2009, Cheyenne 82009, 307-772-2451; 2632 Foothills Blvd., #101, Rock Springs 82901, 307-362-5012; and 325 W. Main St., #F, Riverton 82501, 307-856-6642.

Committees: *Energy & Natural Resources* (6th of 10 R): Forests and Public Land Management; Parks, Historic Preservation and Recreation; Oversight and Investigations (Chmn.). *Environment & Public Works* (7th of 9 R): Clean Air, Wetlands, Private Property and Nuclear Safety; Drinking Water, Fisheries and Wildlife. *Foreign Relations* (8th of 10 R): East Asian and Pacific Affairs (Chmn.); International Economic Policy, Export and Trade Promotion; Near Eastern and South Asian Affairs. *Indian Affairs* (8th of 9 R).

Group Ratings (as Member of U.S. House of Representatives)

	ADA	ACLU	COPE	CFA	LCV	CON	NSI	COC	ACU	NTLC	CHC
1994	5	23	0	20	0	81	100	100	89	88	86
1993	10	—	17	20	7	89	—	91	87	—	—

National Journal Ratings (as Member of U.S. House of Representatives)

	1993 LIB — 1993 CONS		1994 LIB — 1994 CONS	
Economic	14%	80%	0%	80%
Social	19%	77%	28%	71%
Foreign	30%	69%	0%	88%

Key Votes of the 103d Congress (as Member of U.S. House of Representatives)

1. Clinton Deficit Plan	N	3. Brady Handgun Purchase N	5. Lmt. UN Cmnd. of Forces Y
2. NAFTA	Y	4. Strike Race/Death Pnlty. Y	6. Cut Missile Funds	Y

Key Votes of the 104th Congress

1. Congressional Compliance Y	3. Balanced Budget Amndt. Y	5. Product Liability Reform Y
2. Bar Unfunded Mandates Y	4. Pass Line Item Veto Y	6. FY96 Budget Y

Election Results

1994 general	Craig Thomas (R)...................... 118,754	(59%)	($1,068,335)
	Mike Sullivan (D)..................... 79,287	(39%)	($712,991)
	Others.............................. 3,669	(2%)	
1994 primary	Craig Thomas (R).................. unopposed		
1988 general	Malcolm Wallop (R)................... 91,143	(50%)	($1,344,185)
	John P. Vinich (D)..................... 89,821	(50%)	($490,230)

REPRESENTATIVE

Rep. Barbara Cubin (R)

Elected 1994; b. Nov. 30, 1946, Salinas, CA; home, Casper; Creighton U., B.S. 1969; Episcopalian; married (Frederick).

Career: Office Mgr., Dr. Frederick Cubin, 1975–94.

DC Office: 1114 LHOB 20515, 202-225-2311; Fax: 202-225-3057.

District Offices: 4003 Fed. Bldg., 100 E. B St., Casper 82601, 307-261-5595; 2015 Fed. Bldg., 2120 Capitol Ave., Cheyenne 82001, 307-772-2595; and 2515 Foothills Blvd., #202, Rock Springs 82901, 307-362-4095.

Committees: *Resources* (15th of 25 R): Energy and Mineral Resources; National Parks, Forests and Lands. *Science* (25th of 27 R): Energy and Environment; Technology.

Group Ratings and 103rd Congress Votes: Newly Elected

Key Votes of the 104th Congress

1. Congressional Compliance Y	6. Reform Crime Grant Y	11. Loser Pays Court Reform Y
2. Balanced Budget Amndmt. Y	7. National Security Act Y	12. Product Liability Reform *
3. Bar Unfunded Mandates Y	8. Moratorium on Regs. Y	13. Welfare Reform Y
4. Pass Line Item Veto Y	9. Risk Assessment on Regs. Y	14. Term Limits Amndmt. Y
5. Relax Exclusionary Rule Y	10. Expnd. Priv. Prop. Rights Y	15. Tax Cuts Y

Election Results

1994 general	Barbara Cubin (R)	104,426	(53%)	($511,119)
	Bob Schuster (D)	81,022	(41%)	($2,429,346)
	Dave Dawson (Lib)	10,749	(5%)	
1994 primary	Barbara Cubin (R)	33,752	(39%)	
	Rob Wallace (R)	21,582	(25%)	
	Jim Magagna (R)	15,746	(18%)	
	Doug Chamberlain (R)	15,038	(17%)	
	Others	986	(1%)	
1992 general	Craig Thomas (R)	113,882	(58%)	($459,523)
	Jon Herschler (D)	77,418	(39%)	($348,361)
	Other	5,677	(3%)	

PUERTO RICO, VIRGIN ISLANDS, GUAM, AMERICAN SAMOA

Four American insular territories—Puerto Rico, Virgin Islands, Guam, American Samoa—are represented in Congress by elected delegates who, like the District of Columbia's delegate, have floor privileges, votes on committees but not votes on the floor (though House Democrats let them vote in committee of the whole proceedings in the 103d Congress). Each territory's status, its relationship to the United States is different, governed by a separate law, and status is often the pivot around which territorial politics turn.

PUERTO RICO

Puerto Rico has a unique history. For four centuries, from Columbus's landing here in 1493 until the Spanish-American War of 1898, Puerto Rico was a Spanish colony and the port of San Juan the gathering place for its annual convoy of gold and silver from the Americas to Spain. Today, with 3.6 million people, it is the largest American territory—about the same population as South Carolina or Arizona (with perhaps an additional two million Puerto Ricans on the mainland). Fifty years ago, it was "the poorhouse of the Caribbean," heavily populated, devoted almost entirely to sugar cultivation. Then in the 1940s, 1950s and early 1960s, Puerto Rico was transformed by Governor Luis Munoz Marin and his Popular Democratic Party. Munoz initiated "Operation Bootstrap" to lure businesses to Puerto Rico with promises of low-wage labor and government assistance. Munoz also developed Puerto Rico's commonwealth form of government—better understood in Spanish, Estado Libre Asociado (ELA): Free Associated State—which came into effect in 1952. Under commonwealth, Puerto Rico is part of the United States for purposes of international trade, foreign policy and war, but has its own separate laws, taxes and representative government, and is not subject to federal income taxes. Puerto Rico has also developed its own political parties: Munoz's Popular Democrats, the New Progressives who favor statehood, and two Independence parties.

But Munoz's solution, by its own terms, was open to amendment; and ever since his voluntary retirement in 1964, the central issue in Puerto Rico's politics has been status: should this island continue or modify ELA, should it seek statehood, should it seek independence? Both parties when in power have tried to move opinion in their direction. But over time there clearly has been slow movement toward statehood. In the July 1967 referendum, Puerto Ricans voted for ELA over statehood by 60%–39%; in the November 1993 referendum, the vote was 49% for ELA, 46% for statehood. In other words, neither side has a majority: there is nothing like consensus. Independence has negligible support—4% in 1993—primarily from university students; nor are there many pro-independence abstentions, for voter turnout in the enthusiastic politics of Puerto Rico is the highest under the American flag, higher than in even the most affluent, long-settled suburbs of the mainland. Support for ELA has always been strongest among peasants in rural Puerto Rico, who are declining in numbers; the San Juan metro area, expanding over verdant hills from the old city and the harbor, is heavily pro-statehood. ELA supporters are proud of Puerto Rico's Spanish culture, its own Olympic team, and seek to replace the Commonwealth statute with a treaty, which could only be changed by mutual consent of Congress and Puerto Rico—a step toward independence. Statehood supporters are proud of Puerto Rico's economic progress and of Puerto Ricans' frequent and heroic service in the American military, and feel sure it could advance even more rapidly as an integral part of the United States.

Statehood's failure to win a plurality probably averted a crisis in Puerto Rico-mainland relations. Successive presidents have promised to support statehood. Historically, the PNP has been associated with mainland Republicans, and in 1989 George Bush called for statehood, fulfilling a promise he made to win Puerto Rico's delegates to the national convention in 1988. But Rafael Hernandez Colon, the PPD governor elected in 1972, 1984 and 1990, would not call a referendum, and Congress could not agree on defining the choices for Puerto Rico voters. Then in 1992 Hernandez Colon retired, and the PNP's Pedro Rosello was elected governor and his party won two-thirds majorities in the House and Senate. This allowed the PNP to frame the choices in the July 1993 referendum. The party's two major leaders, though feuding on many issues, agreed in affiliating with the national Democratic party: Resident Commissioner (i.e., delegate to Congress) Carlos Romero-Barcelo, elected governor in 1976 and 1980, had been a Jimmy Carter supporter at Democratic conventions; Rosello supported Hillary Rodham Clinton's health care proposal even before he reaffiliated as a Democrat in March 1994. President Clinton announced he would support whatever status Puerto Ricans voted for. Had statehood won, Congress would have been presented with a difficult choice: for most Puerto Ricans expect they would be welcomed into statehood if they sought it, and would get a phase-out over time of their tax exemptions and federal aid, and could continue to use Spanish as well as English as an official language. But it is doubtful that a Congress of either party would vote for such a statehood bill. The problem has been avoided for now. But if Rosello is reelected in 1996, he may well have another referendum and, if opinion keeps moving glacially toward statehood, this time it may win.

Governor Pedro Rosello is the son of a psychiatrist, educated at Notre Dame and Yale Medical School, trained at Harvard and Boston teaching hospitals; he returned to Puerto Rico in 1976, specialized in surgery and wrote scholarly articles, played championship tennis. In 1988 he ran for delegate and lost 49%–47%; in 1992 he ran for governor against Senator Victoria "Melo" Munoz, the daughter of Luis Munoz Marin, and won 50%–46%. Puerto Rico's straight ticket voting swept his party to large majorities in both the Senate (20–8) and House (36–16). Rosello quickly reversed one Hernandez Colon law and restored English as one of Puerto Rico's official languages. In spring 1993 he lobbied Congress to save Section 936, the provision that shelters earnings of some Puerto Rico manufacturing from federal taxes and allows their products into the U.S. duty-free: this is one of the cornerstones of ELA and remains responsible, boosters say, for some 300,000 Puerto Rican jobs, a great many in the pharmaceutical industry. With help from Senate Finance Chairman Daniel Patrick Moynihan, Rosello scaled down the proposed change. But he has said that he expected 936 will be gone in 10 years—one reason he is for statehood. Possibly sooner: in spring 1995, 936 was being identified as an instance of "corporate welfare" which Republicans were being challenged to eliminate; and the revenue gain could prove tempting.

In Puerto Rico Rosello has been a policy innovator. He sent the National Guard in with local police on raids systematically targeting public housing projects where drug dealing was common; afterwards the projects were cordoned off and only residents allowed in. Civil libertarians protested, but project residents overwhelmingly approved. Rosello also advanced a school choice law, but it was blocked by the courts. He has also promised to free Puerto Rico from its Latin American-style centralized bureaucratic regulations, which though often unenforced nonetheless choke off small business growth. For Puerto Rico, despite all its advances, still has a high unemployment rate and remains dependent on welfare programs such as food stamps, for which most Puerto Ricans are eligible. Much of Latin America is now deregulating, privatizing and growing rapidly; Puerto Rico will have to move in that direction if it is to continue to have the highest living standards south of the 48 continental states.

Carlos Romero-Barcelo, two-term governor, was elected resident commissioner in 1992, in a party-line vote; he is the only member of Congress with a four-year term. He was educated at Exeter and Yale and earned a law degree in Puerto Rico; he was elected mayor of San Juan in 1968 and 1972 and Governor in 1976 and 1980; he lost to his longtime rival Rafael Hernandez Colon in 1984. He has worked to get federal funding for Puerto Rico projects: nutritional programs, Medicaid, Tren Urbano, drug-fighting projects, El Portal de El Yunque tropical research center at the Caribbean National Forest. He backs a plan under which Puerto Ricans would pay federal taxes in return for federal funds; Governor Rosello opposes it. But Romero-Barcelo and Rosello, though both Progresistas and both mainland Democrats, are not at all allies; if Romero stayed close to the Carter Administration, Rosello has stayed close to the Clintons.

Puerto Rico does not vote for president in November, but it does choose delegates to the parties' national conventions. It elects only a few Republicans, but its Democratic delegation is larger than that of 25 states and, since it is invariably made up of backers of a single leader, it casts a bigger margin for its candidate than all but a few large states. The Democratic delegation naturally belonged to Rafael Hernandez Colon in 1988 and 1992; in 1996 it will probably belong to Pedro Rosello, unless he is challenged by Carlos Romero-Barcelo.

Del. Carlos A. Romero-Barcelo (D)

Elected 1992; b. Sept. 4, 1932, San Juan; home, San Juan; Yale, B.A. 1951, U. of PR Law Schl., LL.B. 1956; Catholic; married (Kathleen).

Career: Practicing atty., 1956–68, 1985–92; San Juan Mayor, 1968–76; PR Gov., 1976–84; Pres., New Progressive Party, 1989–91.

DC Office: 428 CHOB 20515, 202-225-2615; Fax: 202-225-2154.

District Offices: P.O. Box 4751, San Juan 00902, 809-723-6333; and P.O. Box 946, Ponce 00733, 809-841-3300

Committees: *Economic & Educational Opportunities* (18th of 19 D): Early Childhood, Youth and Families; Workforce Protections. *Resources* (16th of 20 D): National Parks, Forests and Lands; Native American and Insular Affairs.

VIRGIN ISLANDS

The United States' other insular area in the Caribbean is the Virgin Islands, a very different sort of place than Puerto Rico. It is much smaller, with a resident population of only 101,000, mainly on the three islands of St. Thomas, St. John and St. Croix. Puerto Rico is multiracial and not self-conscious about it; most Virgin Islanders are black, with a clear divide between the races much resented by the blacks. While Puerto Rico has attracted all kinds of light industry, the Virgin Islands live off tourism and refineries, industries that have produced higher income levels for its few citizens but have not provided the basis for a mature economy. St. Croix, in particular, with less tourism and more residents, has a faltering economy; it voted for casino gambling in 1995. And crime has been high everywhere.

The Virgin Islands was the scene in 1994 of a minor political revolution, the replacement by Independents of two longtime Democratic officeholders—Governor Alexander Farrelly, first elected in 1986, and Congressional Delegate Ron de Lugo, first elected in 1968 and in office since except for one two-year interval. The new Governor is Roy Schneider, an oncologist, a Virgin Island native who worked at Howard Medical School and Sloan-Kettering Institute, then came back to be Governor Cyril King's health director in 1977. In 1994 Farrelly stepped down, and Schneider ran against his protege Lieutenant Governor Derek Hodge. He called for smaller government and getting tough on drugs; he was accused of accepting money to testify that smoking does not cause cancer, but was elected anyhow. In office Schneider said the deficit was far worse than he thought, and called for spending cuts, a war against drugs and an enterprise zone in St. Croix. He called for reducing the Virgin Islands' dependence on ad hoc appropriations from Congress, given its desire for spending cuts, and to rely instead on local revenues.

The Delegate from the Virgin Islands is Victor Frazer, elected as an Independent in 1994. He is a Virgin Islands native, educated at Fisk and Howard Law, a banker in New York and congressional staffer in Washington where he helped set up a Caribbean Action Lobby. In the four-way 1994 race he ran just behind Democrat Eileen Petersen, a former judge, on November 8; two weeks later he won the runoff 55%–45%, though he spent far less. In the House he decided after some weeks to caucus with the Democrats.

Del. Victor O. Frazer (I)

Elected 1994; b. May 24, 1943, St. Thomas; home, St. Thomas; Fisk U., B.S. 1964, Howard U., J.D. 1971; Christian; single.

Career: Practicing atty., 1971–74, 1983–87, 1992–94; Admin. Asst., U.S. Rep. Mervyn Dymally, 1981–83, 1989–92; Spec. Asst., U.S. Rep. John Conyers, 1983; Gen. Cnsl., VI Water & Power Co., 1987–89.

DC Office: 1711 LHOB 20515, 202-225-1790; Fax: 202-225-3171.

District Offices: 2 Vitraco Mall, #3, St. Thomas 02802, 809-774-4408

Committees: *International Relations* (1st of 1 I). Africa; Western Hemisphere.

GUAM

Some 3,700 miles west of Hawaii, 19 hours of flying time to Washington, D.C., is Guam, the place where, as viewers of political conventions over the years were informed, America's day begins. Guam lies just west of the International Date Line, and it is indeed the early hours of Tuesday there when the rest of us are just trying to get through Monday afternoon. Geographically in the center of the Mariana Islands, Guam is legally separate: the Marianas were administered by the U.S. as a trust territory until they became a commonwealth in 1978. Guam was ruled by a Navy captain from 1898 to 1950, except for years of Japanese occupation during World War II; in 1950 the Organic Act made Guamanians U.S. citizens and allowed them to elect a local government, but Congress still retained final power over the territory. Guam is 30 miles long by five miles wide, with 150,000 people; in 1990, 47% were Chamorro, descendants of the original islanders, 25% Filipino, 18% other Asian and 10% Caucasian; almost everyone is Catholic. In 1990 Guam passed a law banning almost all abortions, which was overturned by a federal court in April 1992, as clearly contrary to *Roe v. Wade*; in November 1992 the Supreme Court declined to review the case, thus dodging a direct challenge to that landmark decision. Economically, Guam depended for years on American military bases; now its economy is diversifying, with tourism from Japan, and Guamanians welcomed a Base Closing Commission decision to phase out Agana Naval Air Station.

The major issue in Guam's politics is status. In a 1982 plebiscite, Guamanians voted for commonwealth status and Governor Joseph Ada, a Republican elected in 1986, appointed a Commission on Self-Determination which drafted a status bill. The two major provisions of its commonwealth status were immigration control—Chamorros want to block others from coming in and making them a minority—and "mutual consent," which would bar Congress from changing laws and treaties that affect Guam without Guam's consent. Guamanians remembered that its just-created watch and garment industries were destroyed by congressional action in the 1970s and 1980s. The bill was endorsed by Governor Ada and introduced in Congress by Guam's Delegate Robert Underwood, a Democrat first elected in 1992. The Bush Administration had rejected this as inconsistent with the Constitutional provision giving Congress full powers over territories. The Clinton Interior Department, perhaps sympathetic to native claims and perhaps alert to implied threats to U.S. military bases in Guam which have become our major forward staging point in the western Pacific with the shutdown of Clark Air Force Base and the Subic Bay Navy base in the Philippines, appointed former University of California Chancellor Michael Heyman as its negotiator. In October 1994 Heyman and Ada agreed on "mutual consent," and prepared a bill that, as Underwood pointed out, would establish a relation similar to that of New Zealand and the Cook Islands. But the election of the Republican Congress abruptly changed its prospects. The new House Territories Subcommittee chairman, Elton Gallegly of California, announced in January 1995 that he would block any mutual consent bill that seeks to bind future Congresses; in February 1995, Heyman, newly appointed head of the Smithsonian Institution, resigned his negotiating post. It did not soothe feelings when in November 1994 Clinton top advisers Anthony Lake and Robert Rubin laughed out loud (they later apologized) when they heard a suggestion that Guam take part in the APEC summit.

All that has left Guam's top officials seeking common understandings with congressional Republicans that will get them some distance toward their goals. Ada retired in 1994, and the new governor is a Democrat, Carl Gutierrez. He went to high school in California, served in the Air Force, then set up the first data processing center in Guam and started a construction business; he was elected to the Guam Senate for all but four years starting in 1972. He campaigned for commonwealth status, for exemption from the requirement that goods from the U.S. be shipped in U.S.-registered ships and for return of federal lands for Guam. But after the election he attacked Republican-style the high-handedness of federal bureaucrats: "Guam has to survive with minor federal luminaries who operate with no apparent adult supervision," he said, and complained that the Fish and Wildlife Service seized 20% of Guam's land for a wildlife refuge.

Delegate Robert Underwood was also educated in California. He started teaching at the University of Guam in 1976 and was known for his efforts promoting and preserving Chamorro culture. By 1990 he had become the university's academic vice president, and he ran against

Republican Delegate Ben Blaz, a former Marine general. Personal connections are often more important than party in Guam, and Underwood explained his victory thus: "I have a lot of relatives. His grandfather and my great-grandfather are first cousins. So I cut into his action when I ran—more of the relatives are closer to me." In January 1994 he pushed through the House a bill transferring 3,200 acres from federal to GovGuam control; he called for a land summit, not the Interior Department, to parcel out the territory. He also made progress in getting reparations for Guamanians harmed by Japanese during their occupation in World War II. In 1995 he bucked efforts to lower his seniority on the National Security and Resources Committees, and questioned whether Republicans who wanted to devolve power to the states wanted to devolve it to territories as well. He called for Endangered Species Act reform to allow local people to handle predators: Guam has few native species, and has been ravaged by the imported tree snake. He stressed that Resources Committee Chairman Don Young grew up in what once was a territory, Alaska, and he welcomed Gallegly's omnibus territories legislation which addresses crimes by the Japanese against the Chamorros and acknowledges Guam's claim for a role in APEC. He cheered with Republicans when the head of Interior's OTIA, unpopular in Guam, announced her agency would be terminated by September 1995. Guam's Democrats, perhaps reflecting that even now large base-closings could unemploy 10% or more of the island's work force, seem to be gaining a sympathetic hearing from House Republicans for at least some of their proposals.

Del. Robert A. Underwood (D)

Elected 1992; b. July 13, 1948, Tamuning; home, Baza Gardens; CA St. U., B.A. 1969, M.A. 1971, U. of S. CA, Ed.D. 1987; Catholic; married (Lorraine Aguilar).

Career: Teacher, Admin., Guam Public Schls., 1972–76; Prof., U. of Guam, 1976–88, Dean, 1988–90, Academic V.P., 1990–92.

DC Office: 424 CHOB 20515, 202-225-1188; Fax: 202-226-0341.

District Offices: 120 Father Duenas Ave., #107, Agana 96910, 671-477-4272.

Committees: *National Security* (17th of 25 D): Military Installations and Facilities; Military Research and Development. *Resources* (19th of 20 D): National Parks, Forests and Lands; Native American and Insular Affairs.

AMERICAN SAMOA

American Samoa obtained representation in Congress for the first time in 1980. That has not been an entirely happy experience for this Southern Pacific island which, unlike Guam, has been little influenced by western settlers and remains almost as Polynesian as it was when the United States took possession in 1900: its first delegate went to jail for payroll fraud. American Samoa has 53,000 people, 89% of them Polynesian, mostly Christian (50% Congregationalist, 20% Catholic); it is an unincorporated territory administered by the Interior Department. The Governor is A. P. Lutali, who spent many years as a teacher, legislator and judge in American Samoa. He was elected in 1984 and defeated in 1986, then elected again in 1992 for a four-year term at the end of which he will be 77.

The delegate from American Samoa is Eni F. H. Faleomavaega, a Democrat first elected in 1988; he won reelection in 1994 with 63% of the vote. He went to high school in Hawaii, to Brigham Young University, then to law school in Houston and Berkeley; he served in Vietnam in the Army. In 1981 he became deputy attorney general in American Samoa, in 1985 lieutenant governor. He serves on the Resources Committee where in 1995 he became ranking Democrat on the Native Americans and Insular Affairs Subcommittee—Indians and Islands, insiders call it—obviously the most important possible assignment for his constituents. There he supported, with Chairman Elton Gallegly, a bill penalizing American Samoa if it flunks federal audits.

American Samoa stages a Democratic presidential primary, but in 1988 only 36 people actually voted. Not surprisingly, none of the candidates campaigned in person here.

Del. Eni F. H. Faleomavaega (D)

Elected 1988; b. Aug. 15, 1943, Vailoatai; home, Pago Pago; Brigham Young U., B.A. 1972, U. of CA, LL.M. 1973; Mormon; married (Hinanui).

Career: Army, 1966–69; A.A., U.S. Del. from AS, 1973–75; Cnsl., U.S. House Interior Cmte., 1975–81; AS Dep. Atty. Gen., 1981–84; AS Lt. Gov., 1984–89.

DC Office: 2422 RHOB 20515, 202-225-8577; Fax: 202-225-8757.

District Offices: P.O. Drawer X, Pago Pago, AS 96799, 684-633-1372.

Committees: *International Relations* (9th of 19 D): Asia and the Pacific; International Operations and Human Rights. *Resources* (9th of 20 D): National Parks, Forests and Lands; Native American and Insular Affairs (RMM).

SENATE COMMITTEES

This committee section includes all Standing, Special and Select committees of the U.S. Senate in alphabetical order.

AGING (Special)   G-31 Dirksen, 202-224-1467

Majority (10 R): Cohen (ME), Chmn.; Pressler (SD), Grassley (IA), Simpson (WY), Jeffords (VT), Craig (ID), Burns (MT), Shelby (AL), Santorum (PA), Thompson (TN).
Minority (9 D): Pryor (AR), RMM; Glenn (OH), Bradley (NJ), Johnston (LA), Breaux (LA), Reid (NV), Kohl (WI), Feingold (WI), Moseley-Braun (IL).

NO SUBCOMMITTEES

AGRICULTURE, NUTRITION & FORESTRY   328-A Russell, 202-224-2035

Majority (10 R): Lugar (IN), Chmn.; Dole (KS), Helms (NC), Cochran (MS), McConnell (KY), Craig (ID), Coverdell (GA), Santorum (PA), Warner (VA), Campbell (CO).
Minority (8 D): Leahy (VT), RMM; Pryor (AR), Heflin (AL), Harkin (IA), Conrad (ND), Daschle (SD), Baucus (MT), Kerrey (NE).

SUBCOMMITTEES

FORESTRY, CONSERVATION & RURAL REVITALIZATION

Majority (4 R): Craig, Chmn.; Coverdell, Warner, Helms, Campbell.
Minority (3 D): Heflin, RMM; Harkin, Conrad, Kerrey.

MARKETING, INSPECTION & PRODUCT PROMOTION.

Majority (5 R): Helms, Chmn.; Dole, Cochran, McConnell, Santorum.
Minority (4 D): Conrad, RMM; Pryor, Baucus, Heflin.

PRODUCTION & PRICE COMPETITIVENESS

Majority (5 R): Cochran, Chmn.; Warner, Helms, Coverdell, Dole.
Minority (4 D): Pryor, RMM; Daschle, Baucus, Kerrey.

RESEARCH, NUTRITION & GENERAL LEGISLATION

Majority (4 R): McConnell, Chmn.; Dole, Santorum, Craig, Campbell.
Minority (3 D): Harkin, RMM; Heflin, Daschle, Pryor.

APPROPRIATIONS   S-128 The Capitol, 202-224-4594

Majority (15 R): Hatfield (OR), Chmn.; Stevens (AK), Cochran (MS), Specter (PA), Domenici (NM), Gramm (TX), Bond (MO), Gorton (WA), McConnell (KY), Mack (FL), Burns (MT), Shelby (AL), Jeffords (VT), Gregg (NH), Bennett (UT).
Minority (13 D): Byrd (WV) RMM; Inouye (HI), Hollings (SC), Johnston (LA), Leahy (VT), Bumpers (AR), Lautenberg (NJ), Harkin (IA), Mikulski (MD), Reid (NV), Kerrey (NE), Kohl (WI), Murray (WA).

SUBCOMMITTEES

AGRICULTURE, RURAL DEVELOPMENT & RELATED AGENCIES
Majority (6 R): Cochran, Chmn.; Specter, Bond, Gorton, McConnell, Burns.
Minority (5 D): Bumpers, RMM; Harkin, Kerrey, Johnston, Kohl.

COMMERCE, JUSTICE, STATE & JUDICIARY
Majority (6 R): Gramm, Chmn.; Stevens, Hatfield, Domenici, McConnell, Gregg.
Minority (5 D): Hollings, RMM; Inouye, Bumpers, Lautenberg, Kerrey.

DEFENSE
Majority (9 R): Stevens, Chmn.; Cochran, Specter, Domenici, Gramm, Bond, McConnell, Mack, Shelby.
Minority (8 D): Inouye, RMM; Hollings, Johnston, Byrd, Leahy, Bumpers, Lautenberg, Harkin.

DISTRICT OF COLUMBIA
Majority (2 R): Jeffords, Chmn.; Bennett.
Minority (1 D): Kohl, RMM

ENERGY & WATER DEVELOPMENT
Majority (7 R): Domenici, Chmn.; Hatfield, Cochran, Gorton, McConnell, Bennett, Burns.
Minority (6 D): Johnston, RMM; Byrd, Hollings, Reid, Kerrey, Murray.

FOREIGN OPERATIONS
Majority (7 R): McConnell, Chmn.; Specter, Mack, Gramm, Jeffords, Gregg, Shelby.
Minority (6 D): Leahy, RMM; Inouye, Lautenberg, Harkin, Mikulski, Murray.

INTERIOR & RELATED AGENCIES
Majority (8 R): Gorton, Chmn.; Stevens, Cochran, Domenici, Hatfield, Burns, Bennett, Mack.
Minority (7 D): Byrd, RMM; Johnston, Leahy, Bumpers, Hollings, Reid, Murray.

LABOR, HEALTH & HUMAN SERVICES, & EDUCATION
Majority (8 R): Specter, Chmn.; Hatfield, Cochran, Gorton, Mack, Bond, Jeffords, Gregg.
Minority (7 D): Harkin, RMM; Byrd, Hollings, Inouye, Bumpers, Reid, Kohl.

LEGISLATIVE BRANCH
Majority (3 R): Mack, Chmn.; Bennett, Jeffords.
Minority (2 D): Murray, RMM; Mikulski.

MILITARY CONSTRUCTION
Majority (4 R): Burns, Chmn.; Stevens, Shelby, Gregg.
Minority (3 D): Reid, RMM; Inouye, Kohl.

TRANSPORTATION
Majority (6 R): Hatfield, Chmn.; Domenici, Specter, Gramm, Bond, Gorton.
Minority (5 D): Lautenberg, RMM; Byrd, Harkin, Mikulski, Reid.

TREASURY, POSTAL SERVICE & GENERAL GOVERNMENT
Majority (3 R): Shelby, Chmn.; Jeffords, Gregg.
Minority (2 D): Kerrey, RMM; Mikulski.

VA, HUD & INDEPENDENT AGENCIES
Majority (6 R): Bond, Chmn.; Gramm, Burns, Stevens, Shelby, Bennett.
Minority (5 D): Mikulski, RMM; Leahy, Johnston, Lautenberg, Kerrey.

ARMED SERVICES

228 Russell, 202-224-3871

Majority (11 R): Thurmond (SC), Chmn.; Warner (VA), Cohen (ME), McCain (AZ), Lott (MS) Coats (IN), Smith (NH), Kempthorne (ID), Hutchison (TX), Inhofe (OK), Santorum (PA).

Minority (10 D): Nunn (GA), RMM; Exon (NE), Levin (MI), Kennedy (MA), Bingaman (NM), Glenn (OH), Byrd (WV), Robb (VA), Lieberman (CT), Bryan (NV).

SUBCOMMITTEES

ACQUISITION & TECHNOLOGY

Majority (4 R): Smith, Chmn.; Kempthorne, Hutchison, Inhofe.
Minority (3 D): Bingaman, RMM; Levin, Kennedy.

AIRLAND FORCES

Majority (7 R): Warner, Chmn.; Cohen, Coats, Kempthorne, Hutchison, Inhofe, Santorum.
Minority (6 D): Levin, RMM; Exon, Glenn, Byrd, Lieberman, Bryan.

PERSONNEL

Majority (4 R): Coats, Chmn.; McCain, Lott, Santorum.
Minority (3 D): Byrd, RMM; Kennedy, Robb.

READINESS

Majority (5 R): McCain, Chmn.; Cohen, Coats, Inhofe, Santorum.
Minority (4 D): Glenn, RMM; Bingaman, Robb, Bryan.

SEA POWER

Majority (5 R): Cohen, Chmn.; Warner, McCain, Lott, Smith.
Minority (4 D): Kennedy, RMM; Exon, Robb, Lieberman.

STRATEGIC FORCES

Majority (6 R): Lott, Chmn.; Warner, Cohen, Smith, Kempthorne, Hutchison.
Minority (5 D): Exon, RMM; Levin, Bingaman, Glenn, Bryan.

BANKING, HOUSING & URBAN AFFAIRS

534 Dirksen, 202-224-7391

Majority (9 R): D'Amato (NY), Chmn.; Gramm (TX), Shelby (AL), Bond (MO), Mack (FL), Faircloth (NC), Bennett (UT), Grams (MN), Frist (TN).

Minority (7 D): Sarbanes (MD), RMM; Dodd (CT), Kerry (MA), Bryan (NV), Boxer (CA), Moseley-Braun (IL), Murray (WA).

SUBCOMMITTEES

FINANCIAL INSTITUTIONS & REGULATORY RELIEF

Majority (7 R): Shelby, Chmn.; Grams, Frist, Gramm, Bennett, Bond, Mack.
Minority (5 D): Bryan, RMM; Moseley-Braun, Dodd, Kerry, Boxer.

HUD OVERSIGHT & STRUCTURE

Majority (3 R): Faircloth, Chmn.; Gramm, Grams.
Minority (2 D): Moseley-Braun, RMM; Murray.

HOUSING OPPORTUNITY & COMMUNITY DEVELOPMENT

Majority (4 R): Mack, Chmn.; Bond, Frist, Shelby.
Minority (3 D): Kerry, RMM; Dodd, Bryan.

INTERNATIONAL FINANCE
Majority (5 R): Bond, Chmn.; Mack, Faircloth, Bennett, Frist.
Minority (4 D): Boxer, RMM; Moseley-Braun, Kerry, Murray.

SECURITIES
Majority (5 R): Gramm, Chmn.; Bennett, Shelby, Faircloth, Grams.
Minority (4 D): Dodd, RMM; Murray, Boxer, Bryan.

BUDGET   621 Dirksen, 202-224-0642

Majority (12 R): Domenici (NM), Chmn.; Grassley (IA), Nickles (OK), Gramm (TX), Bond (MO), Lott (MS), Brown (CO), Gorton (WA), Gregg (NH), Snowe (ME), Abraham (MI), Frist (TN).
Minority (10 D): Exon (NE), RMM; Hollings (SC), Johnston (LA), Lautenberg (NJ), Simon (IL), Conrad (ND), Dodd (CT), Sarbanes (MD), Boxer (CA), Murray (WA).

NO SUBCOMMITTEES

COMMERCE, SCIENCE & TRANSPORTATION   508 Dirksen
202-224-5115

Majority (10 R): Pressler (SD) Chmn.; Packwood (OR), Stevens (AK), McCain (AZ), Burns (MT), Gorton (WA), Lott (MS), Hutchison (TX), Snowe (ME), Ashcroft (MO).
Minority (9 D): Hollings (SC), RMM; Inouye (HI), Ford (KY), Exon (NE), Rockefeller (WV), Kerry (MA), Breaux (LA), Bryan (NV), Dorgan (ND).

SUBCOMMITTEES

AVIATION
Majority (8 R): McCain, Chmn.; Pressler, Stevens, Gorton, Burns, Lott, Hutchison, Ashcroft.
Minority (7 D): Ford, RMM; Exon, Inouye, Bryan, Rockfeller, Breaux, Dorgan.

COMMUNICATIONS
Majority (8 R): Packwood, Chmn.; Pressler, Stevens, McCain, Burns, Gorton, Lott, Ashcroft.
Minority (7 D): Hollings, RMM; Inouye, Ford, Exon, Kerry, Breaux, Rockefeller.

CONSUMER AFFAIRS, FOREIGN COMMERCE & TOURISM
Majority (5 R): Gorton, Chmn.; Pressler, McCain, Snowe, Ashcroft.
Minority (4 D): Exon, RMM; Ford, Bryan, Rockefeller.

OCEANS & FISHERIES
Majority (4 R): Stevens, Chmn.; Packwood, Gorton, Snowe.
Minority (3 D): Kerry, RMM; Inouye, Breaux.

SCIENCE, TECHNOLOGY & SPACE
Majority (5 R): Burns, Chmn.; Pressler, Hutchison, Stevens, Lott.
Minority (4 D): Rockefeller, RMM; Kerry, Bryan, Dorgan.

SURFACE TRANSPORTATION & MERCHANT MARINE
Majority (6 R): Lott, Chmn.; Hutchison, Packwood, Stevens, Burns, Snowe.
Minority (5 D): Inouye, RMM; Exon, Breaux, Dorgan, Bryan.

ENERGY & NATURAL RESOURCES

304 Dirksen, 202-224-4971

Majority (11 R): Murkowski (AK), Chmn.; Hatfield (OR), Domenici (NM), Nickles (OK), Craig (ID), Campbell (CO), Thomas (WY), Kyl (AZ), Grams (MN), Jeffords (VT), Burns (MT).
Minority (9 D): Johnston (LA), RMM; Bumpers (AR), Ford (KY), Bradley (NJ), Bingaman (NM), Akaka (HI), Wellstone (MN), Heflin (AL), Dorgan (ND).

SUBCOMMITTEES

ENERGY PRODUCTION & REGULATION

Majority (4 R): Nickles, Chmn.; Jeffords, Hatfield, Burns.
Minority (3 D): Bingaman, RMM; Ford, Akaka.

ENERGY RESEARCH & DEVELOPMENT

Majority (4 R): Domenici, Chmn.; Craig, Kyl, Grams.
Minority (3 D): Ford, RMM; Wellstone, Heflin.

FORESTS & PUBLIC LAND MANAGEMENT

Majority (6 R): Craig, Chmn.; Kyl, Hatfield, Domenici, Campbell, Thomas.
Minority (4 D): Bradley, RMM; Bumpers, Bingaman, Dorgan.

PARKS, HISTORIC PRESERVATION, & RECREATION

Majority (5 R): Campbell, Chmn.; Grams, Nickles, Thomas, Jeffords.
Minority (4 D): Bumpers, RMM; Bradley, Wellstone, Heflin.

OVERSIGHT & INVESTIGATIONS

Majority (5 R): Thomas, Chmn.; Burns, Domenici, Craig, Campbell.
Minority (1 D): Akaka, RMM.

ENVIRONMENT & PUBLIC WORKS

410 Dirksen, 202-224-8832

Majority (9 R): Chafee (RI), Chmn.; Warner (VA), Smith (NH), Faircloth (NC), Kempthorne (ID), Inhofe (OK), Thomas (WY), McConnell (KY), Bond (MO).
Minority (7 D): Baucus (MT), RMM; Moynihan (NY), Lautenberg (NJ), Reid (NV), Graham (FL), Lieberman (CT), Boxer (CA).

SUBCOMMITTEES

CLEAN AIR, WETLANDS, PRIVATE PROPERTY & NUCLEAR SAFETY

Majority (4 R): Faircloth, Chmn.; Inhofe, Thomas, McConnell.
Minority (3 D): Graham, RMM; Lieberman, Boxer.

DRINKING WATER, FISHERIES & WILDLIFE

Majority (5 R): Kempthorne, Chmn.; Faircloth, Thomas, Bond, Warner.
Minority (4 D): Reid, RMM; Lautenberg, Lieberman, Boxer.

SUPERFUND, WASTE CONTROL, & RISK ASSESSMENT

Majority (4 R): Smith, Chmn.; Warner, Inhofe, McConnell.
Minority (3 D): Lautenberg, RMM; Moynihan, Boxer.

TRANSPORTATION & INFRASTRUCTURE

Majority (5 R): Warner, Chmn.; Smith, Kempthorne, Bond, Faircloth.
Minority (4 D): Baucus, RMM; Moynihan, Reid, Graham.

ETHICS (Select)   220 Hart, 202-224-2981

Majority (3 R): McConnell (KY), Chmn.; Smith (NH), Craig (ID).
Minority (3 D): Bryan (NV), Vice Chmn.; Mikulski (MD), Dorgan (ND).

NO SUBCOMMITTEES

FINANCE   205 Dirksen, 202-224-4515

Majority (11 R): Packwood (OR), Chmn.; Dole (KS), Roth (DE), Chafee (RI), Grassley (IA),
  Hatch (UT), Simpson (WY), Pressler (SD), D'Amato (NY), Murkowski (AK), Nickles (OK).
Minority (9 D): Moynihan (NY), RMM; Baucus (MT), Bradley (NJ), Pryor (AR), Rockefeller
  (WV), Breaux (LA), Conrad (ND), Graham (FL), Moseley-Braun (IL).

SUBCOMMITTEES

INTERNATIONAL TRADE

Majority (7 R): Grassley, Chmn.; Packwood, Roth, Hatch, Pressler, D'Amato, Murkowski.
Minority (7 D): Moynihan, RMM; Baucus, Bradley, Rockefeller, Breaux, Conrad, Graham.

LONG-TERM GROWTH, DEBT & DEFICIT REDUCTION

Majority (4 R): Pressler, Chmn.; Simpson, D'Amato, Murkowski.
Minority (2 D): Pryor, RMM; Bradley.

MEDICAID & HEALTH CARE FOR LOW-INCOME FAMILIES

Majority (3 R): Chafee, Chmn.; Roth, Nickles.
Minority (3 D): Graham, RMM; Rockefeller, Moseley-Braun.

MEDICARE, LONG-TERM CARE & HEALTH INSURANCE

Majority (6 R): Dole, Chmn.; Packwood, Chafee, Grassley, Hatch, Simpson.
Minority (6 D): Rockefeller, RMM; Baucus, Pryor, Conrad, Graham, Moseley-Braun.

SOCIAL SECURITY & FAMILY POLICY

Majority (4 R): Simpson, Chmn.; Dole, Chafee, Nickles.
Minority (4 D): Breaux, RMM; Moynihan, Baucus, Moseley-Braun.

TAXATION & IRS OVERSIGHT

Majority (9 R): Hatch, Chmn.; Packwood, Roth, Dole, Grassley, Pressler, D'Amato,
  Murkowski, Nickles.
Minority (5 D): Bradley, RMM; Moynihan, Pryor, Breaux, Conrad.

FOREIGN RELATIONS   450 Dirksen, 202-224-4651

Majority (10 R): Helms (NC), Chmn.; Lugar (IN), Kassebaum (KS), Brown (CO), Coverdell
  (GA), Snowe (ME), Thompson (TN), Thomas (WY), Grams (MN), Ashcroft (MO).
Minority (8 D): Pell (RI), RMM; Biden (DE), Sarbanes (MD), Dodd (CT), Kerry (MA), Robb
  (VA), Feingold (WI), Feinstein (CA).

SUBCOMMITTEES

AFRICAN AFFAIRS
Majority (3 R): Kassebaum, Chmn.; Snowe, Ashcroft.
Minority (2 D): Feingold, RMM; Feinstein.

EAST ASIAN & PACIFIC AFFAIRS
Majority (5 R): Thomas, Chmn.; Lugar, Kassebaum, Coverdell, Grams.
Minority (4 D): Robb, RMM; Biden, Kerry, Feinstein.

EUROPEAN AFFAIRS
Majority (5 R): Lugar, Chmn.; Kassebaum, Brown, Snowe, Thompson.
Minority (4 D): Biden, RMM; Pell, Sarbanes, Feingold.

INTERNATIONAL ECONOMIC POLICY, EXPORT & TRADE PROMOTION
Majority (4 R): Thompson, Chmn.; Thomas, Grams, Ashcroft.
Minority (3 D): Sarbanes, RMM; Pell, Biden.

INTERNATIONAL OPERATIONS
Majority (5 R): Snowe, Chmn.; Helms, Brown, Coverdell, Ashcroft.
Minority (4 D): Kerry, RMM; Pell, Biden, Feingold.

NEAR EASTERN & SOUTH ASIAN AFFAIRS
Majority (5 R): Brown, Chmn.; Snowe, Thompson, Thomas, Grams.
Minority (4 D): Feinstein, RMM; Sarbanes, Kerry, Robb.

WESTERN HEMISPHERE & PEACE CORPS AFFAIRS
Majority (4 R): Coverdell, Chmn.; Helms, Lugar, Thompson.
Minority (3 D): Dodd, RMM; Pell, Robb.

GOVERNMENTAL AFFAIRS   340 Dirksen, 202-224-4751

Majority (8 R): Roth (DE), Chmn.; Stevens (AK), Cohen (ME), Thompson (TN), Cochran (MS), Grassley (IA), McCain (AZ), Smith (NH).
Minority (7 D): Glenn (OH), RMM; Nunn (GA), Levin (MI), Pryor (AK), Lieberman (CT), Akaka (HI), Dorgan (ND).

SUBCOMMITTEES

OVERSIGHT OF GOVERNMENT MANAGEMENT & THE DISTRICT OF COLUMBIA
Majority (5 R): Cohen, Chmn.; Thompson, Cochran, Grassley, McCain.
Minority (4 D): Levin, RMM; Pryor, Lieberman, Akaka.

PERMANENT SUBCOMMITTEE ON INVESTIGATIONS
Majority (8 R): Roth, Chmn.; Stevens, Cohen, Thompson, Cochran, Grassley, McCain, Smith.
Minority (7 D): Nunn, RMM; Glenn, Levin, Pryor, Lieberman, Akaka, Dorgan.

POST OFFICE & CIVIL SERVICE
Majority (4 R): Stevens, Chmn.; Cochran, McCain, Smith.
Minority (3 D): Pryor, RMM; Akaka, Dorgan.

INDIAN AFFAIRS
838 Hart, 202-224-2251

Majority (9 R): McCain (AZ), Chmn.; Murkowski (AK), Gorton (WA), Domenici (NM), Kassebaum (KS), Nickles (OK), Campbell (CO), Thomas (WY), Hatch (UT).
Minority (7 D): Inouye (HI), Vice Chmn.; Conrad (ND), Reid (NV), Simon (IL), Akaka (HI), Wellstone (MN), Dorgan (ND).

NO SUBCOMMITTEES

INTELLIGENCE (Select)
211 Hart, 202-224-1700

Majority (9 R): Specter (PA), Chmn.; Lugar (IN), Shelby (AL), DeWine (OH), Kyl (AZ), Inhofe (OK), Hutchison (TX), Mack (FL), Cohen (ME).
Minority (8 D): Kerrey (NE), Vice Chmn.; Glenn (OH), Bryan (NV), Graham (FL), Kerry (MA), Baucus (MT), Johnston (LA), Robb (VA).

NO SUBCOMMITTEES

JUDICIARY
224 Dirksen, 202-224-5225

Majority (10 R): Hatch (UT), Chmn.; Thurmond (SC), Simpson (WY), Grassley (IA), Specter (PA), Brown (CO), Thompson (TN), Kyl (AZ), DeWine (OH), Abraham (MI).
Minority (8 D): Biden (DE), RMM; Kennedy (MA), Leahy (VT), Heflin (AL), Simon (IL), Kohl (WI), Feinstein (CA), Feingold (WI).

SUBCOMMITTEES

ADMINISTRATIVE OVERSIGHT & THE COURTS

Majority (4 R): Grassley, Chmn.; Thurmond, Brown, DeWine.
Minority (3 D): Heflin, RMM; Kohl, Feingold.

ANTITRUST, BUSINESS RIGHTS & COMPETITION

Majority (4 R): Thurmond, Chmn.; Hatch, Specter, Simpson.
Minority (3 D): Leahy, RMM; Heflin, Feingold.

CONSTITUTION, FEDERALISM & PROPERTY RIGHTS

Majority (5 R): Brown, Chmn.; Hatch, Kyl, DeWine, Abraham.
Minority (4 D): Simon, RMM; Kennedy, Feingold.

IMMIGRATION

Majority (4 R): Simpson, Chmn.; Grassley, Kyl, Specter.
Minority (3D): Kennedy, RMM; Simon, Feinstein.

TERRORISM, TECHNOLOGY & GOVERNMENT INFORMATION

Majority (4 R): Specter, Chmn.; Thompson, Abraham, Thurmond.
Minority (3 D): Kohl, RMM; Leahy, Feinstein.

YOUTH VIOLENCE

Majority (3 R): Thompson, Chmn.; Hatch, Simpson.
Minority (2 D): Biden, RMM; Kohl.

LABOR & HUMAN RESOURCES 835 Hart, 202-224-6770

Majority (9 R): Kassebaum (KS), Chmn.; Jeffords (VT), Coats (IN), Gregg (NH), Frist (TN), DeWine (OH), Ashcroft (MO), Abraham (MI), Gorton (WA).
Minority (7 D): Kennedy (MA), RMM; Pell (RI), Dodd (CT), Simon (IL), Harkin (IA), Mikulski (MD), Wellstone (MN).

SUBCOMMITTEES

AGING
Majority (4 R): Gregg, Chmn.; Kassebaum, Coats, Ashcroft.
Minority (3 D): Mikulski, RMM; Simon, Wellstone.

CHILDREN & FAMILY
Majority (5 R): Coats, Chmn.; Jeffords, DeWine, Ashcroft, Abraham.
Minority (4 D): Dodd, RMM; Pell, Harkin, Wellstone.

DISABILITY POLICY
Majority (4 R): Frist, Chmn.; Jeffords, DeWine, Gorton.
Minority (3 D): Harkin, RMM; Kennedy, Simon.

EDUCATION, ARTS & HUMANITIES
Majority (9 R): Jeffords, Chmn.; Kassebaum, Coats, Gregg, Frist, DeWine, Ashcroft, Abraham, Gorton.
Minority (7 D): Pell, RMM; Kennedy, Dodd, Simon, Harkin, Mikulski, Wellstone.

RULES & ADMINISTRATION 305 Russell, 202-224-6352

Majority (9 R): Stevens (AK), Chmn.; Hatfield (OR), Helms (NC), Warner (VA), Dole (KS), McConnell (KY), Cochran (MS), Santorum (PA), Nickles (OK).
Minority (7 D): Ford (KY), RMM; Pell (RI), Byrd (WV), Inouye (HI), Moynihan (NY), Dodd (CT), Feinstein (CA).

NO SUBCOMMITTEES

SMALL BUSINESS 428-A Russell, 202-224-5175

Majority (10 R): Bond (MO), Chmn.; Pressler (SD), Burns (MT), Coverdell (GA), Kempthorne (ID), Bennett (UT), Hutchison (TX), Warner (VA), Frist (TN), Snowe (ME).
Minority (9 D): Bumpers (AR), RMM; Nunn (GA), Levin (MI), Harkin (IA), Kerry (MA), Lieberman (CT), Wellstone (MN), Heflin (AL), Lautenberg (NJ).

NO SUBCOMMITTEES

VETERANS' AFFAIRS
414 Russell, 202-224-9126

Majority (7 R): Simpson (WY), Chmn.; Thurmond (SC), Murkowski (AK), Specter (PA), Jeffords (VT), Campbell (CO), Craig (ID).
Minority (5 D): Rockefeller (WV), RMM; Graham (FL), Akaka (HI), Dorgan (ND), Wellstone (MN).

NO SUBCOMMITTEES

HOUSE COMMITTEES

This committee section includes all Standing, Special and Select committees of the U.S. House in alphabetical order.

AGRICULTURE
1301 LONGWORTH 202-225-2171

Majority (27 R): Roberts (KS) Chmn.; Emerson (MO), Gunderson (WI), Combest (TX), Allard (CO), Barrett (NE), Boehner (OH), Ewing (IL), Doolittle (CA), Goodlatte (VA), Pombo (CA), Canady (FL), Smith (MI), Everett (AL), Lucas (OK), Lewis (KY), Baker (LA), Crapo (ID), Calvert (CA), Chenoweth (ID), Hostettler (IN), Bryant (TN), Latham (IA), Cooley (OR), Foley (FL), Chambliss (GA), LaHood (IL).
Minority (22 D): de la Garza (TX), RMM; Brown (CA), Rose (NC), Stenholm (TX), Volkmer (MO), Johnson (SD), Condit (CA), Peterson (MN), Dooley (CA), Clayton (NC), Minge (MN), Hilliard (AL), Pomeroy (ND), Holden (PA), McKinney (GA), Baesler (KY), Thurman (FL), Bishop (GA), Thompson (MS), Farr (CA), Pastor (AZ), Baldacci (ME).

SUBCOMMITTEES

DEPARTMENT OPERATIONS, NUTRITION & FOREIGN AGRICULTURE

Majority (12 R): Emerson, Chmn.; Allard, Ewing, Goodlatte, Canady, Calvert, Hostettler, Bryant, Latham, Foley, LaHood, Crapo.
Minority (10 D): Condit RMM; Brown, McKinney, Hilliard, Baesler, Thurman, Bishop, Thompson, Farr, Baldacci.

GENERAL FARM COMMODITIES

Majority (10 R): Barrett, Chmn.; Emerson, Combest, Boehner, Smith, Baker, Latham, Cooley, Chambliss, Lucas.
Minority (8 D): Stenholm, RMM; Minge, Pomeroy, Thompson, Rose, Volkmer, Dooley, Pastor.

LIVESTOCK, DAIRY & POULTRY

Majority (7 R): Gunderson, Chmn.; Boehner, Goodlatte, Pombo, Smith, Lucas, Cooley.
Minority (5 D): Volkmer, RMM; Peterson, Dooley, Hilliard, Holden.

RESOURCE CONSERVATION, RESEARCH & FORESTRY

Majority (12 R): Allard, Chmn.; Gunderson, Barrett, Doolittle, Pombo, Smith, Lucas, Lewis, Crapo, Chenoweth, Hostettler, LaHood.
Minority (10 D): Johnson, RMM; Baldacci, Brown, Stenholm, Condit, Peterson, Clayton, Minge, Pomeroy, Holden.

RISK MANAGEMENT & SPECIALTY CROPS

Majority (9 R): Ewing, Chmn.; Combest, Doolittle, Pombo, Everett, Lewis, Bryant, Foley, Chambliss.
Minority (7 D): Rose, RMM; Clayton, Baesler, Thurman, Bishop, Farr, Pastor.

APPROPRIATIONS   SH-218 The Capitol, 202-225-2771

Majority (32 R): Livingston (LA), Chmn.; McDade (PA), Myers (IN), Young (FL), Regula (OH), Lewis (CA), Porter (IL), Rogers (KY), Skeen (NM), Wolf (VA), DeLay (TX), Kolbe (AZ), Vucanovich (NV), Lightfoot (IA), Packard (CA), Callahan (AL), Walsh (NY), Taylor (NC), Hobson (OH), Istook (OK), Bonilla (TX), Knollenberg (MI), Miller (FL), Dickey (AR), Kingston (GA), Riggs (CA), Frelinghuysen (NJ), Wicker (MS), Forbes (NY), Nethercutt (WA), Bunn (OR), Neumann (WI).
Minority (24 D): Obey (WI), RMM; Yates (IL), Stokes (OH), Bevill (AL), Murtha (PA), Wilson (TX), Dicks (WA), Sabo (MN), Dixon (CA), Fazio (CA), Hefner (NC), Hoyer (MD), Durbin (IL), Coleman (TX), Mollohan (WV), Chapman (TX), Kaptur (OH), Skaggs (CO), Pelosi (CA), Visclosky (IN), Foglietta (PA), Torres (CA), Lowey (NY), Thornton (AR).

SUBCOMMITTEES

AGRICULTURE, RURAL DEVELOPMENT, FDA & RELATED AGENCIES

Majority (7 R): Skeen, Chmn.; Myers, Walsh, Dickey, Kingston, Riggs, Nethercutt.
Minority (4 D): Durbin, RMM; Kaptur, Thornton, Lowey.

COMMERCE, JUSTICE, STATE & JUDICIARY

Majority (5 R): Rogers, Chmn.; Kolbe, Taylor, Regula, Forbes.
Minority (3 D): Mollohan, RMM; Skaggs, Dixon.

DISTRICT OF COLUMBIA

Majority (5 R): Walsh, Chmn.; Bonilla, Kingston, Frelinghuysen, Neumann.
Minority (3 D): Dixon, RMM; Durbin, Kaptur.

ENERGY & WATER DEVELOPMENT

Majority (6 R): Myers, Chmn.; Rogers, Knollenberg, Riggs, Frelinghuysen, Bunn.
Minority (3 D): Bevill, RMM; Fazio, Chapman.

FOREIGN OPERATIONS, EXPORT FINANCING & RELATED PROGRAMS

Majority (9 R): Callahan, Chmn.; Porter, Livingston, Lightfoot, Wolf, Packard, Knollenberg, Forbes, Bunn.
Minority (4 D): Wilson RMM; Yates, Pelosi, Torres.

INTERIOR

Majority (8 R): Regula, Chmn.; McDade, Kolbe, Skeen, Vucanvoich, Taylor, Nethercutt, Bunn.
Minority (4 D): Yates, RMM; Dicks, Bevill, Skaggs.

LABOR, HEALTH & HUMAN SERVICES, & EDUCATION

Majority (8 R): Porter, Chmn.; Young, Bonilla, Istook, Miller, Dickey, Riggs, Wicker.
Minority (5 D): Obey, RMM; Stokes, Hoyer, Pelosi, Lowey.

LEGISLATIVE

Majority (5 R): Packard, Chmn.; Young, Taylor, Miller, Wicker.
Minority (3 D): Fazio, RMM; Thornton, Dixon.

MILITARY CONSTRUCTION

Majority (7 R): Vucanovich, Chmn.; Callahan, McDade, Meyers, Porter, Istook, Wicker.
Minority (4 D): Hefner, RMM; Foglietta, Visclosky, Torres.

NATIONAL SECURITY

Majority (9 R): Young, Chmn.; McDade, Livingston, Lewis, Skeen, Hobson, Bonilla, Nethercutt, Neumann.
Minority (5 D): Murtha, RMM; Dicks, Wilson, Hefner, Sabo.

TRANSPORTATION

Majority (8 R): Wolf, Chmn.; DeLay, Regula, Rogers, Lightfoot, Packard, Callahan, Dickey.
Minority (3 D): Coleman, RMM; Durbin, Foglietta.

TREASURY, POSTAL SERVICE, & GENERAL GOVERNMENT

Majority (5 R): Lightfoot, Chmn.; Wolf, Istook, Kingston, Forbes.
Minority (3 D): Hoyer, RMM; Visclosky, Coleman.

VA, HUD, & INDEPENDENT AGENCIES

Majority (8 R): Lewis, Chmn.; DeLay, Vucanovich, Walsh, Hobson, Knollenberg, Frelinghuysen, Neumann.
Minority (4 D): Stokes, RMM; Mollohan, Chapman, Kaptur.

BANKING & FINANCIAL SERVICES　　2129 Rayburn, 202-225-7502

Majority (27 R): Leach (IA), Chmn.; McCollum (FL), Roukema (NJ), Bereuter (NE), Roth (WI), Baker (LA), Lazio (NY), Bachus (AL), Castle, (DE), King, (NY), Royce (CA), Lucas (OK), Weller (IL), Hayworth (AZ), Metcalf (WA), Bono (CA), Ney (OH), Ehrlich (MD), Barr (GA), Chrysler (MI), Cremeans (OH), Fox (PA), Heineman (NC), Stockman (TX), LoBiondo (NJ), Watts (OK), Kelly (NY).
Minority (22 D): Gonzalez (TX), RMM; LaFalce (NY), Vento (MN), Schumer (NY), Frank (MA), Kanjorski (PA), Kennedy (MA), Flake (NY), Mfume (MD), Waters (CA), Orton (UT), Maloney (NY), Gutierrez (IL), Roybal-Allard (CA), Barrett (WI), Velazquez (NY), Wynn (MD), Fields (LA), Watt (NC), Hinchey (NY), Ackerman (NY), Bensten (TX).
Independent (1): Sanders (VT).

SUBCOMMITTEES

CAPITAL MARKETS, SECURITES & GOVERNMENT SPONSORED ENTERPRISES

Majority (11 R): Baker, Chmn.; Hayworth, Cremeans, Fox, Stockman, LoBiondo, Watts, Kelly, Roukema, Lazio, Bachus.
Minority (9 D): Kanjorski, RMM; Hinchey, Ackerman, Bensten, LaFalce, Schumer, Flake, Waters, Orton.

DOMESTIC & INTERNATIONAL MONETARY POLICY

Majority (11 R): Castle, Chmn.; Royce, Lucas, Metcalf, Barr, Chrysler, LoBiondo, Watts, Kelly, Ney, Fox.
Minority (8 D): Flake, RMM; Frank, Kennedy, Maloney, Roybal-Allard, Barrett, Fields, Watt.
Independent (1): Sanders.

FINANCIAL INSTITUTIONS & CONSUMER CREDIT

Majority (12 R): Roukema, Chmn.; McCollum, Bereuter, Roth, King, Royce, Lucas, Weller, Metcalf, Bono, Ney, Ehrlich.
Minority (10 D): Vento, RMM; LaFalce, Schumer, Kanjorski, Mfume, Maloney, Barrett, Orton, Wynn, Watt.

GENERAL OVERSIGHT & INVESTIGATIONS

Majority (6 R): Bachus, Chmn.; Barr, Chrysler, Heineman, King, Stockman.
Minority (4 D): Mfume, RMM; Velazquez, Gutierrez, Wynn.

HOUSING & COMMUNITY OPPORTUNITY

Majority (12 R): Lazio, Chmn.; Bereuter, Baker, Castle, Weller, Hayworth, Bono, Ney, Ehrlich, Cremeans, Fox, Heineman.
Minority (9 D): Kennedy, RMM; Gonzalez, Waters, Gutierrez, Roybal-Allard, Velazquez, Fields, Vento, Frank.
Independent (1): Sanders.

BUDGET   309 Cannon, 202-226-7270

Majority (24 R): Kasich (OH), Chmn.; Hobson (OH), Walker (AZ), Kolbe (AZ), Shays (CT), Herger (CA), Bunning (KY), Smith (TX), Allard (CO), Miller (FL), Lazio (NY), Franks (NJ), Smith (MI), Inglis (SC), Hoke (OH), Molinari (NY), Nussle (IA), Hoekstra (MI), Largent (OK), Myrick (NC), Brownback (KS), Shadegg (AZ), Radanovich (CA), Bass (NH).
Minority (18 D): Sabo (MN), RMM; Stenholm (TX), Slaughter (NY), Parker (MS), Coyne (PA), Mollohan (WV), Costello (IL), Johnston (FL), Mink (HI), Orton (UT), Pomeroy (ND), Browder (AL), Woolsey (CA), Olver (MA), Roybal-Allard (CA), Meek (FL), Rivers (MI), Doggett (TX).

NO SUBCOMMITTEES

COMMERCE   2125 Rayburn, 202-225-2927

Majority (26 R): Bliley (VA), Chmn.; Moorhead (CA), Fields (TX), Oxley (OH), Bilirakis (FL), Schaefer (CO), Barton (TX), Hastert (IL), Upton (MI), Stearns (FL), Paxon (NY), Gillmor (OH), Klug (WI), Franks (CT), Greenwood (PA), Crapo (ID), Cox (CA), Deal (GA), Burr (NC), Bilbray (CA), Whitfield (KY), Ganske (IA), Frisa (NY), Norwood (GA), White (WA), Coburn (OK).
Minority (21 D): Dingell (MI), RMM; Waxman (CA), Markey (MA), Tauzin (LA), Wyden (OR), Hall (TX), Bryant (TX), Boucher (VA), Manton (NY), Towns (NY), Studds (MA), Pallone (NJ), Brown (OH), Lincoln (AR), Gordon (TN), Furse (OR), Deutsch (FL), Rush (IL), Eshoo (CA), Klink (PA), Stupak (MI).

SUBCOMMITTEES

COMMERCE, TRADE & HAZARDOUS MATERIALS

Majority (12 R): Oxley, Chmn.; Fields; Upton, Gillmor, Greenwood, Crapo, Bilbray, Whitfield, Ganske, Frisa, White.
Minority (10 D): Tauzin, RMM; Furse, Markey, Boucher, Manton, Brown, Lincoln, Deutsch, Stupak.

ENERGY & POWER

Majority (11 R): Schaefer, Chmn.; Franks, Moorhead, Bilirakis, Hastert, Upton, Stearns, Crapo, Deal, Burr, Norwood, Coburn.
Minority (9 D): Pallone, RMM; Tauzin, Gordon, Rush, Markey, Hall, Manton, Lincoln, Deutsch.

HEALTH & ENVIRONMENT

Majority (14 R): Bilirakis, Chmn.; Hastert, Barton, Upton, Stearns, Klug, Franks, Greenwood, Burr, Bilbray, Whitfield, Ganske, Norwood, Coburn.
Minority (11 D): Waxman, RMM; Brown, Lincoln, Deutsch, Stupak, Wyden, Hall, Bryant, Towns, Studds, Pallone.

OVERSIGHT & INVESTIGATIONS

Majority (7 R): Barton, Chmn.; Cox, Franks, Greenwood, Crapo, Burr, Frisa.
Minority (5 D): Wyden, RMM; Waxman, Furse, Eshoo, Klink.

TELECOMMUNICATIONS & FINANCE

Majority (14 R): Fields, Chmn.; Oxley, Moorhead, Schaefer, Barton, Hastert, Stearns, Paxon, Gillmor, Klug, Cox, Deal, Frisa, White, Coburn.
Minority (11 D): Markey, RMM; Hall, Bryant, Boucher, Manton, Towns, Studds, Gordon, Rush, Eshoo, Klink.

ECONOMIC & EDUCATIONAL OPPORTUNITIES   2181 Rayburn
202-225-4527

Majority (24 R): Goodling (PA), Chmn.; Petri (WI), Roukema (NJ), Gunderson (WI), Fawell (IL), Ballenger (NC), Barrett (NE), Cunningham (CA), Hoekstra (MI), McKeon (CA), Castle (DE), Meyers (KS), Johnson (TX), Talent (MO), Greenwood (PA), Hutchinson (AR), Knollenberg (MI), Riggs (CA), Graham (SC), Weldon (FL), Funderburk (NC), Souder (IN), McIntosh (IN), Norwood (GA).
Minority (19 D): Clay (MO), RMM; Miller (CA), Kildee (MI), Williams (MT), Martinez (CA), Owens (NY), Sawyer (OH), Payne (NJ), Mink (HI), Andrews (NJ), Reed (RI), Roemer (IN), Engel (NY), Becerra (CA), Scott (VA), Green (TX), Woolsey (CA), Romero-Barcelo (PR), Reynolds (IL).

SUBCOMMITTEES

EARLY CHILDHOOD, YOUTH & FAMILIES

Majority (10 R): Cunningham, Chmn.; Goodling, Gunderson, Castle, Johnson, Greenwood, Riggs, Weldon, Souder, McIntosh.
Minority (8 D): Kildee, RMM; Miller, Williams, Payne, Mink, Engel, Scott, Romero-Barcello.

EMPLOYER-EMPLOYEE RELATIONS

Majority (8 R): Fawell, Chmn.; Petri, Roukema, Talent, Meyers, Knollenberg, Weldon, Graham.
Minority (6 D): Martinez, RMM; Kildee, Owens, Sawyer, Payne, Reynolds.

OVERSIGHT & INVESTIGATIONS

Majority (9 R): Hoekstra, Chmn.; Barrett, Ballenger, Cunningham, McKeon, Castle, Weldon, Goodling, Fawell.
Minority (7 D): Sawyer, RMM; Martinez, Reed, Roemer, Scott, Green, Reynolds.

POSTSECONDARY EDUCATION, TRAINING & LIFE-LONG LEARNING

Majority (9 R): McKeon, Chmn.; Gunderson, McIntosh, Goodling, Petri, Roukema, Riggs, Funderburk, Souder.
Minority (7 D): Williams, RMM; Andrews, Reed, Roemer, Becerra, Green, Woolsey.

WORKFORCE PROTECTIONS

Majority (9 R): Ballenger, Chmn.; Hutchinson, Graham, Funderburk, Norwood, Fawell, Barrett, Hoekstra, Greenwood.
Minority (7 D): Owens, RMM; Miller, Mink, Andrews, Engel, Woolsey, Romero-Barcelo.

GOVERNMENT REFORM & OVERSIGHT   2157 Rayburn, 202-225-5074

Majority (27 R): Clinger (PA), Chmn.; Gilman (NY), Burton (IN), Morella (MD), Shays (CT), Schiff (NM), Ros-Lehtinen (FL), Zeliff (NH), McHugh (NY), Horn (CA), Mica (FL), Blute (MA), Davis (VA), McIntosh (IN), Fox (PA), Tate (WA), Chrysler (MI), Gutknecht (MN), Souder (IN), Martini (NJ), Scarborough (FL), Shadegg (AZ), Flanagan (IL), Bass (NH), LaTourette (OH), Sanford (SC), Ehrlich (MD).
Minority (22 D): Collins (IL), RMM; Waxman (CA), Lantos (CA), Wise (WV) Owens (NY), Towns (NY), Spratt (SC), Slaughter (NY), Kanjorski (PA), Condit (CA), Peterson (MN), Thurman (FL), Maloney (NY), Barrett (WI), Taylor (MS), Collins (MI), Norton (DC), Moran (VA), Green (TX), Meek (FL), Mascara (PA), Fattah (PA).
Independent (1): Sanders (VT).

SUBCOMMITTEES

CIVIL SERVICE

Majority (5 R): Mica, Chmn.; Bass, Gilman, Burton, Morella.
Minority (2 D): Moran, RMM; Mascara.
Independent (1): Sanders.

DISTRICT OF COLUMBIA

Majority (5 R): Davis, Chmn.; Gutknecht, McHugh, LaTourette, Flanagan.
Minority (3 D): Norton, RMM; Fattah, Collins (MI).

GOVERNMENT MANAGEMENT, INFORMATION & TECHNOLOGY

Majority (8 R): Horn, Chmn.; Flanagan, Blute, Davis, Fox, Tate, Scarborough, Bass.
Minority (6 D): Maloney, RMM; Owens, Mascara, Wise, Spratt, Kanjorski.

HUMAN RESOURCES & INTERGOVERNMENTAL AFFAIRS

Majority (9 R): Shays, Chmn.; Souder, Schiff, Morella, Davis, Chrysler, Martini, Scarborough, Sanford.
Minority (6 D): Towns, RMM; Lantos, Barrett, Green, Fattah, Waxman.
Independent (1): Sanders.

NATIONAL ECONOMIC GROWTH, NATURAL RESOURCES & REGULATORY AFFAIRS

Majority (8 R): McIntosh, Chmn.; Fox, McHugh, Tate, Gutknecht, Scarborough, Shadegg, Ehrlich.
Minority (6 D): Peterson, RMM; Waxman, Spratt, Slaughter, Kanjorski, Condit.

NATIONAL SECURITY, INTERNATIONAL AFFAIRS & CRIMINAL JUSTICE

Majority (8 R): Zeliff, Chmn.; Ehrlich, Shiff, Ros-Lehtinen, Mica, Blute, Souder, Shadegg.
Minority (7 D): Thurman, RMM; Wise, Taylor, Meek, Lantos, Slaughter, Condit.

POSTAL SERVICE

Majority (6 R): McHugh, Chmn.; Sanford, Gilman, Shays, McIntosh, Ehrlich.
Minority (4 D): Collins (MI), RMM; Owens, Green, Meek.

HOUSE OVERSIGHT   1309 Longworth, 202-225-8281

Majority (7 R): Thomas (CA), Chmn.; Ehlers (MI), Roberts (KS), Boehner (OH), Dunn (WA), Diaz-Balart (FL), Ney (OH).
Minority (5 D): Fazio (CA), RMM; Gejdenson (CT), Hoyer (MD), Jefferson (LA), Pastor (AZ).

NO SUBCOMMITTEES

INTELLIGENCE (Permanent Select)   H-405 The Capitol, 202-225-4121

Majority (9 R): Combest (TX), Chmn.; Dornan (CA), Young (FL), Hansen (UT), Lewis (CA), Goss (FL), Shuster (PA), McCollum (FL), Castle (DE).
Minority (7 D): Dicks (WA), RMM; Richardson (NM), Dixon (CA), Torricelli (NJ), Coleman (TX), Pelosi (CA), Laughlin (TX).

SUBCOMMITTEES

HUMAN INTELLIGENCE, ANALYSIS, & COUNTERINTELLIGENCE

Majority (6 R): Lewis, Chmn.; Young, Goss, Shuster, McCollum, Castle.
Minority (4 D): Coleman, RMM; Richardson, Dixon, Laughlin.

TECHNICAL & TACTICAL INTELLIGENCE

Majority (6 R): Dornan, Chmn.; Hansen, Lewis, Shuster, McCollum, Castle.
Minority (4 D): Pelosi, RMM; Dicks, Torricelli, Laughlin.

INTERNATIONAL RELATIONS
2170 Rayburn, 202-225-5021

Majority (23 R): Gilman (NY), Chmn.; Goodling (PA), Leach (IA), Roth (WI), Hyde (IL), Bereuter (NE), Smith (NJ), Burton (IN), Meyers (KS), Gallegly (CA), Ros-Lehtinen (FL), Ballenger (NC), Rohrabacher (CA), Manzullo (IL), Royce (CA), King (NY), Kim (CA), Brownback (KS), Funderburk (NC), Chabot (OH), Sanford (SC), Salmon (AZ), Houghton (NY).

Minority (19 D): Hamilton (IN), RMM; Gejdenson (CT), Lantos (CA), Torricelli (NJ), Berman (CA), Ackerman (NY), Johnston (FL), Engel (NY), Faleomavaega (AS), Martinez (CA), Payne, (NJ), Andrews (NJ), Menendez (NJ), Brown (OH) McKinney (GA), Hastings, (FL), Wynn (MD), McNulty (NY), Moran (VA).

Independents (1): Frazer (VI).

SUBCOMMITTEES

AFRICA

Majority (7 R): Ros-Lehtinen, Chmn.; Roth, Brownback, Funderburk, Chabot, Sanford, Salmon.
Minority (5 D): Ackerman, RMM; Johnston, Engel, Payne, Hastings.
Independent (1): Frazer.

ASIA & THE PACIFIC

Majority (8 R): Bereuter, Chmn.; Royce, Rohrabacher, Leach, Kim, Sanford, Burton, Manzullo.
Minority (6 D): Berman RMM; Faleomavaega, Brown, Andrews, Gejdenson, Ackerman.

INTERNATIONAL ECONOMIC POLICY & TRADE

Majority (8 R): Roth, Chmn.; Meyers, Manzullo, Brownback, Chabot, Rohrabacher, Bereuter, Ballenger.
Minority (6 D): Gejdenson, RMM; Martinez, McNulty, Torricelli, Johnston, Engel.

INTERNATIONAL OPERATIONS & HUMAN RIGHTS

Majority (8 R): Smith, Chmn.; Gilman, Goodling, Hyde, King, Funderburk, Salmon, Royce.
Minority (6 D): Lantos, RMM; McKinney, Moran, Berman, Faleomavaega, Payne.

WESTERN HEMISPHERE

Majority (6 R): Burton, Chmn.; Ros-Lehtinen, Ballenger, Smith, Gallegly, King.
Minority (5 D): Torricelli, RMM; Menendez, Wynn, Lantos, Martinez.
Independent (1): Frazer.

JUDICIARY
2138 Rayburn, 202-225-3951

Majority (20 R): Hyde (IL), Chmn.; Moorhead (CA), Sensenbrenner (WI), McCollum (FL), Gekas (PA), Coble (NC), Smith (TX), Schiff (NM), Gallegly (CA), Canady (FL), Inglis (SC), Goodlatte (VA), Buyer (IN), Hoke (OH), Bono (CA), Heineman (NC), Bryant (TN), Chabot (OH), Flanagan (IL), Barr (GA).

Minority (15 D): Conyers (MI), RMM; Schroeder (CO), Frank (MA), Schumer (NY), Berman (CA), Boucher (VA), Bryant (TX), Reed (RI), Nadler (NY), Scott (VA), Watt (NC), Becerra (CA), Serrano (NY), Lofgren (CA), Jackson Lee (TX).

SUBCOMMITTEES

COMMERCIAL & ADMINISTRATIVE LAW

Majority (6 R): Gekas, Chmn.; Hyde, Inglis, Chabot, Flanagan, Barr.
Minority (4 D): Reed, RMM; Bryant, Nadler, Scott.

CONSTITUTION

Majority (8 R): Canady, Chmn.; Hyde, Inglis, Flanagan, Sensenbrenner, Hoke, Smith, Goodlatte.
Minority (5 D): Frank, RMM; Watt, Serrano, Conyers, Schroeder.

COURTS & INTELLECTUAL PROPERTY

Majority (9 R): Moorhead, Chmn.; Sensenbrenner, Coble, Goodlatte, Bono, Gekas, Gallegly, Canady, Hoke.
Minority (6 D): Schroeder, RMM; Conyers, Berman, Becerra, Boucher, Nadler.

CRIME

Majority (8 R): McCollum, Chmn.; Schiff, Buyer, Coble, Heineman,, Bryant, Chabot, Barr.
Minority (5 D): Schumer, RMM; Scott, Lofgren, Jackson Lee, Watt.

IMMIGRATION & CLAIMS

Majority (7 R): Smith, Chmn.; Gallegly, Moorhead, McCollum, Bono, Heineman, Bryant.
Minority (5 D): Bryant, RMM; Frank, Schumer, Berman, Becerra.

NATIONAL SECURITY   2120 Rayburn, 202-225-4151

Majority (30 R): Spence (SC), Chmn.; Stump (AZ), Hunter (CA), Kasich (OH), Bateman (VA), Hansen (UT), Weldon (PA), Dornan (CA), Hefley (CO), Saxton (NJ), Cunningham (CA), Buyer (IN), Torkildsen (MA), Fowler (FL), McHugh (NY), Talent (MO), Everett (AL), Bartlett (MD), McKeon (CA), Lewis (KY), Watts (OK), Thornberry (TX), Hostettler (IN), Chambliss (GA), Hilleary (TN), Scarborough (FL), Jones (NC), Longley (ME), Tiahrt (KS), Hastings (WA).
Minority (25 D): Dellums (CA), RMM; Montgomery (MS), Schroeder (CO), Skelton (MO), Sisisky (VA), Spratt (SC), Ortiz (TX), Pickett (VA), Evans (IL), Tanner (TN), Browder (AL), Taylor (MS), Abercrombie (HI), Edwards (TX), Tejeda (TX), Meehan (MA), Underwood (GU), Harman (CA), McHale (PA), Geren (TX), Peterson (FL), Jefferson (LA), DeLauro (CT), Ward (KY), Kennedy (RI).

SUBCOMMITTEES

MILITARY INSTALLATIONS & FACILITIES

Majority (10 R): Hefley, Chmn.; McHugh, Hostettler, Hilleary, Jones, Stump, Hunter, Hansen, Saxton, Fowler.
Minority (8 D): Ortiz, RMM; Montgomery, Browder, Abercrombie, Tejeda, Underwood, Peterson, Ward.

MILITARY PERSONNEL

Majority (9 R): Dornan, Chmn.; Buyer, Lewis, Watts, Thornberry, Chambliss, Tiahrt, Hastings, Hunter.
Minority (7 D): Pickett, RMM; Montogmery, Skelton, Harman, Jefferson, DeLauro, Ward.

The Almanac of American Politics 1996

order form

Yes, send me *The Almanac of American Politics 1996* — the most comprehensive, insightful political reference available.

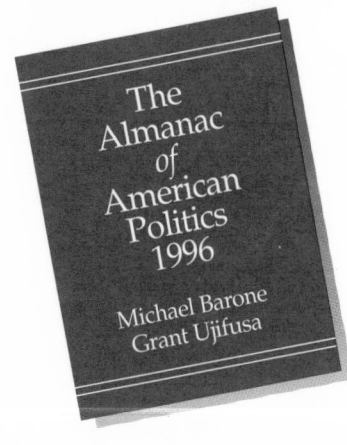

Quantity

_____	Hardcover copies @ $64.95 each ISBN: 0-89234-057-6	$ _____
_____	Softcover copies @ $49.95 each ISBN: 0-89234-058-4	$ _____
_____	Shipping & Handling @ 10% **FREE** for credit card & check orders!	$ _____
	Sales Tax (6% DC, MO add appropriate)	$ _____
	TOTAL ORDER	$ _____

For orders of 10 or more: call 800-356-4838
for additional special discounts.

CHECK ONE:

Check enclosed, payable to National Journal.
Free Shipping & Handling

Charge my:
VISA   MasterCard   American Express
Free Shipping & Handling

Acct# _____   Exp. Date _____

Signature _____

Bill me. P.O.# _____

Please make this a standing order. I will receive a 5%
discount on future editions.

Name

Title

Organization

Address

City   State   Zip

Phone   Fax

Signature

3 easy ways to order

1. Mail this completed order form.

or

2. Fax this order form to (202) 739-8540

or

3. Call toll-free 800-356-4838.

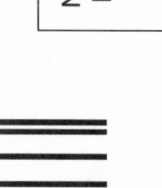

BUSINESS REPLY MAIL

POSTAGE WILL BE PAID BY ADDRESSEE

National Journal

1501 M ST NW
WASHINGTON DC 20005

MILITARY PROCUREMENT

Majority (15 R): Hunter, Chmn.; Spence, Stump, Saxton, Buyer, Torkildsen, Talent, Everett, Bartlett, McKeon, Lewis, Watts, Thornberry, Chambliss, Longley.
Minority (12 D): Skelton, RMM; Dellums, Sisisky, Evans, Tanner, Taylor, Abercrombie, Edwards, Geren, Peterson, Jefferson, DeLauro.

MILITARY READINESS

Majority (11 R): Bateman, Chmn.; Kasich, Cunningham, Fowler, Scarborough, Weldon, Torkildsen, Talent, Everett, Bartlett, McKeon.
Minority (9 D): Sisisky, RMM; Spratt, Pickett, Evans, Browder, Edwards, Tejeda, Meehan, McHale.

MILITARY RESEARCH & DEVELOPMENT

Majority (14 R): Weldon, Chmn.; Hansen, Tiahrt, Hastings, Kasich, Bateman, Dornan, Hefley, Cunningham, McHugh, Hostettler, Hilleary, Scarborough, Jones.
Minority (11 D): Spratt, RMM; Schroeder, Ortiz, Tanner, Taylor, Meehan, Underwood, Harman, McHale, Geren, Kennedy.

RESOURCES   1324 Longworth, 202-225-2761

Majority (25 R): Young (AK), Chmn.; Hansen (UT), Saxton (NJ), Gallegly (CA), Duncan (TN), Hefley (CO), Doolittle (CA), Allard (CO), Gilchrest (MD), Calvert (CA), Pombo (CA), Torkildsen (AZ), Hayworth (AZ), Cremeans (OH), Cubin (WY), Cooley (OR), Chenoweth (ID), Smith (WA), Radanvoich (CA), Jones (NC), Thornberry (TX), Hastings (WA), Metcalf (WA), Longley (ME), Shadegg (AZ).
Minority (20 D): Miller (CA), RMM; Rahall (WV) Vento (MN), Kildee (MI), Williams (MT), Gejdenson (CT), Richardson (NM), DeFazio (OR), Faleomavaega (AS), Johnson (SD), Abercrombie (HI), Studds (MA), Tauzin (LA), Ortiz (TX), Dooley (CA), Romero-Barcelo (PR), Hinchey (NY), Underwood (GU), Farr (CA), one vacancy.

SUBCOMMITTEES

ENERGY & MINERAL RESOURCES

Majority (8 R): Calvert, Chmn.; Duncan, Hefley, Hayworth, Cremeans, Cubin, Chenoweth, Thornberry.
Minority (6 D): Abercrombie, RMM, Rahall, Richardson, Tauzin, Ortiz, Dooley.

FISHERIES, WILDLIFE & OCEANS

Majority (8 R): Saxton, Chmn.; Young, Gilchrest, Torkildsen, Smith, Jones, Metcalf, Longley.
Minority (6 D): Studds, RMM; Miller, Gejdenson, Tauzin, Ortiz, Farr.

NATIONAL PARKS, FORESTS & LANDS

Majority (14 R): Hansen, Chmn.; Duncan, Hefley, Doolittle, Allard, Pombo, Torkildsen, Hayworth, Cubin, Cooley, Chenoweth, Smith, Radanovich, Shadegg.
Minority (11 D): Richardson, RMM; Rahall, Vento, Kildee, Williams, Faleomavaega, Studds, Romero-Barcelo, Hinchey, Underwood, one vacancy.

NATIVE AMERICAN & INSULAR AFFAIRS

Majority (7 R): Gallegly, Chmn.; Young, Gilchrest, Jones, Hastings, Metcalf, Longley.
Minority (5 D): Faleomavaega, RMM, Williams, Johnson, Romero-Barcelo, Underwood.

WATER & POWER RESOURCES

Majority (11 R): Doolittle, Chmn.; Hansen, Allard, Pombo, Cremeans, Cooley, Chenoweth, Radanovich, Thornberry, Hastings, Shadegg.
Minority (9 D): DeFazio, RMM; Miller, Vento, Gejdenson, Richardson, Dooley, Hinchey, Farr, one vacancy.

RULES   H-312 The Capitol, 202-225-9191

Majority (9 R): Solomon (NY), Chmn.; Quillen (TN), Dreier (CA), Goss (FL), Linder (GA), Pryce (OH), Diaz-Balart (FL), McInnis (CO), Waldholtz (UT).
Minority (4 D): Moakley (MA), RMM; Beilenson (CA), Frost (TX), Hall (OH).

SUBCOMMITTEES

LEGISLATIVE & BUDGET PROCESS

Majority (5 R): Goss, Chmn.; Quillen, Linder, Pryce, Solomon.
Minority (2 D): Frost, RMM; Moakley.

RULES & ORGANIZATION OF THE HOUSE

Majority (5 R): Dreier, Chmn.; Diaz-Balart, McInnis, Waldholtz, Solomon.
Minority (2 D): Beilenson, RMM; Hall.

SCIENCE   2320 Rayburn, 202-225-6371

Majority (27 R): Walker (PA), Chmn.; Sensenbrenner (WI), Boehlert (NY), Fawell (IL), Morella (MD), Weldon (PA), Rohrabacher (CA), Schiff (NM), Barton (TX), Calvert (CA), Baker (CA), Bartlett (MD), Ehlers (MI), Wamp (TN), Weldon (FL), Graham (SC), Salmon (AZ), Davis (VA), Stockman (TX), Gutknecht (MN), Seastrand (CA), Tiahrt (KS), Largent (OK), Hilleary (TN), Cubin (WY), Foley (FL), Myrick (NC).
Minority (23 D): Brown (CA), RMM; Hall (TX), Traficant (OH), Hayes (LA), Tanner (TN), Geren (TX), Roemer (IN), Cramer (AL), Barcia (MI), McHale (PA), Harman (CA), Johnson (TX), Minge (MN), Olver (MA), Hastings (FL), Rivers (MI), McCarthy (MO), Ward (KY), Lofgren (CA), Doggett (TX), Doyle (PA), Jackson Lee (TX), Luther (MN).

SUBCOMMITTEES

BASIC RESEARCH

Majority (14 R): Schiff, Chmn.; Boehlert, Barton, Baker, Ehlers, Gutknecht, Morella, Weldon (PA), Bartlett, Wamp, Weldon (FL), Graham, Hilleary, Myrick.
Minority (11 D): Geren, RMM; Hastings, Rivers, Doggett, Luther, Olver, Lofgren, Doyle, Jackson Lee, two vacancies.

ENERGY & ENVIRONMENT

Majority (15 R): Rohrabacher, Chmn.; Fawell, Weldon (PA), Bartlett, Wamp, Graham, Salmon, Davis, Largent, Cubin, Foley, Schiff, Baker, Ehlers, Stockman.
Minority (12 D): Hayes, RMM; Minge, Olver, Ward, Doyle, Roemer, Cramer, Barcia, McHale, Johnson, Rivers, McCarthy.

SPACE & AERONAUTICS

Majority (13 R): Sensenbrenner, Chmn.; Calvert, Weldon (FL), Stockman, Seastrand, Tiahrt, Hilleary, Rohrabacher, Salmon, Davis, Largent, Foley, one vacancy.
Minority (10 D): Hall, RMM; Traficant, Roemer, Cramer, Barcia, Harman, Jackson Lee, Hastings, Ward, Luther.

TECHNOLOGY

Majority (7 R): Morella, Chmn.; Myrick, Calvert, Gutknecht, Seastrand, Tiahrt, Cubin.
Minority (5 D): Tanner, RMM; McHale, Johnson, McCarthy, Lofgren.

SMALL BUSINESS   2361 Rayburn, 202-225-5821

Majority (22 R): Meyers (KS), Chmn.; Hefley (CO), Zeliff (NH), Talent (MO), Manzullo (IL), Torkildsen (MA), Bartlett (MD), Smith (WA), LoBiondo (NJ), Wamp (TN), Kelly (NY), Chrysler (MI), Longley (ME), Jones (NC), Salmon (AZ), Hilleary (TN), Souder (IN), Brownback (KS), Chabot (OH), Myrick (NC), Funderburk (NC), Metcalf (WA).
Minority (19 D): LaFalce (NY), RMM; Wyden (OR), Sisisky (VA), Mfume (MD), Flake (NY), Poshard (IL), Clayton (NC), Meehan (MA), Velazquez (NY), Fields (LA), Tucker (CA), Hilliard (AL), Peterson (FL), Thompson (MS), Fattah (PA), Bensten (TX), McCarthy (MO), Luther (MN), Kennedy (RI).

SUBCOMMITTEES

GOVERNMENT PROGRAMS

Majority (7 R): Torkildsen, Chmn.; Hefley, Myrick, Kelly, Chrysler, Funderburk, one vacancy.
Minority (5 D): Poshard, RMM; Wyden, Mfume, Fields, Thompson.

PROCUREMENT, EXPORTS & BUSINESS OPPORTUNITIES

Majority (8 R): Manzullo, Chmn.; Chrysler, Salmon, Brownback, Chabot, Funderburk, Bartlett, Smith.
Minority (6 D): Clayton, RMM; Sisisky, Flake, Hilliard, Fattah, Luther.

REGULATION & PAPERWORK

Majority (8 R): Talent, Chmn.; LoBiondo, Wamp, Kelly, Longley, Jones, Hilleary, Souder.
Minority (6 D): Velazquez, RMM; Peterson, Fattah, Bensten, McCarthy, Luther.

TAX & FINANCE

Majority (8 R): Smith, Chmn.; Metcalf, LoBiondo, Jones, Souder, Brownback, Bartlett, one vacancy.
Minority (6 D): Meehan, RMM; Tucker, Bensten, McCarthy, Kennedy, one vacancy.

STANDARDS OF OFFICIAL CONDUCT   HT-2 The Capitol, 202-225-7103

Majority (5 R): Johnson (CT), Chmn.; Bunning (KY), Goss (FL), Hobson (OH), Schiff (NM).
Minority (5 D): McDermott (WA), RMM; Cardin (MD), Pelosi (CA), Borski (PA), Sawyer (OH).

NO SUBCOMMITTEES

TRANSPORTATION & INFRASTRUCTURE 2165 Rayburn, 202-225-9446

Majority (33 R): Shuster (PA), Chmn.; Young (AK), Clinger (PA), Petri (WI), Boehlert (NY), Bateman (VA), Emerson (MO), Coble (NC), Duncan, Jr. (TN), Molinari (NY), Zeliff (NH), Ewing (IL), Gilchrest (MD), Hutchinson (AR), Baker (CA), Kim (CA), Horn (CA), Franks (NJ), Blute (MA), Mica (FL), Quinn (NY), Fowler (FL), Ehlers (MI), Bachus (AL), Weller (IL), Wamp (TN), Latham (IA), LaTourette (OH), Seastrand (CA), Tate (WA), Kelly (NY), LaHood (IL), Martini (NJ).

Minority (27 D): Mineta (CA), RMM; Oberstar (MN), Rahall (WV), Borski (PA), Lipinski (IL), Wise (WV), Traficant (OH), DeFazio (OR), Hayes (LA), Clement (TN), Costello (IL), Parker (MS), Laughlin (TX), Poshard (IL), Cramer (AL), Collins (MI), Norton (DC), Nadler (NY), Danner (MO), Menendez (NJ), Clyburn (SC), Brown (FL), Barcia (MI), Filner (CA), Tucker (CA), Johnson (TX), Brewster (OK).

SUBCOMMITTEES

AVIATION

Majority (15 R): Duncan, Chmn.; Weller, Clinger, Coble, Zeliff, Ewing, Hutchinson, Kim, Ehlers, Bachus, Seastrand, Tate, Kelly, LaHood, Martini.
Minority (12 D): Oberstar, RMM; Costello, Lipinski, Wise, DeFazio, Hayes, Clement, Collins, Nadler, Danner, Menendez, Clyburn.

COAST GUARD & MARITIME TRANSPORTATION

Majority (6 R): Coble, Chmn.; Fowler, Young, Molinari, Baker, Ehlers.
Minority (5 D): Traficant, RMM; Tucker, Brewster, Oberstar.

PUBLIC BUILDINGS & ECONOMIC DEVELOPMENT

Majority (5 R): Gilchrest, Chmn.; Seastrand, Duncan, Blute, LaTourette.
Minority (4 D): Wise, RMM; Norton, Traficant, Brown.

RAILROADS

Majority (8 R): Molinari, Chmn.; Kelly, Boehlert, Kim, Franks, Mica, Quinn, Bachus.
Minority (6 D): Lipinski, RMM; Clement, Nadler, Rahall, Borski, Cramer.

SURFACE TRANSPORTATION

Majority (20 R): Petri, Chmn.; LaHood, Clinger, Bateman, Emerson, Zeliff, Hutchinson, Baker, Kim, Horn, Franks, Blute, Mica, Quinn, Fowler, Weller, Latham, LaTourette, Tate, Martini.
Minority (16 D): Rahall, RMM; DeFazio, Laughlin, Poshard, Cramer, Danner, Clyburn, Tucker, Johnson, Parker, Collins, Brown, Barcia, Filner, Brewster.

WATER RESOURCES & ENVIRONMENT

Majority (15 R): Boehlert, Chmn.; Wamp, Young, Petri, Bateman, Emerson, Zeliff, Ewing, Gilchrest, Horn, Franks, Quinn, Latham, LaTourette, Martini.
Minority (12 D): Borski, RMM; Hayes, Menendez, Oberstar, Costello, Parker, Laughlin, Poshard, Norton, Barcia, Filner.

VETERANS' AFFAIRS
335 Cannon, 202-225-3527

Majority (18 R): Stump (AR), Chmn.; Smith (NJ), Bilirakis (FL), Spence (SC), Hutchinson (AR), Everett (AL), Buyer (IN), Quinn (NY), Bachus (AL), Stearns (FL), Ney (OH), Fox (PA), Flanagan (IL), Barr (GA), Weller (IL), Hayworth (AZ), Cooley (OR), Schaefer (CO).
Minority (15 D): Montgomery (MS), RMM; Evans (IL), Kennedy (MA), Edwards (TX), Waters (CA), Clement (TN), Filner (CA), Tejeda (TX), Gutierrez (IL), Baesler (KY), Bishop (CA), Clyburn (SC), Brown (FL), Doyle (PA), Mascara (PA).

SUBCOMMITTEES

COMPENSATION, PENSION INSURANCE & MEMORIAL AFFAIRS

Majority (6 R): Everett, Chmn.; Weller, Hayworth, Barr, Ney, one vacancy.
Minority (4 D): Evans, RMM; Montgomery, Filner, Kennedy.

EDUCATION, TRAINING, EMPLOYMENT & HOUSING

Majority (6 R): Buyer, Chmn.; Barr, Cooley, Hutchinson, Schaefer, one vacancy.
Minority (4 D): Waters, RMM; Clyburn, Mascara, Evans.

HOSPITALS & HEALTH CARE

Majority (11 R): Hutchinson, Chmn.; Stump, Smith, Bilirakis, Spence, Quinn, Bachus, Stearns, Ney, Fox, Flanagan.
Minority (9 D): Edwards, RMM; Kennedy, Clement, Tejeda, Gutierrez, Baesler, Bishop, Brown, Doyle.

WAYS & MEANS
1102 Longworth, 202-225-3625

Majority (21 R): Archer (TX), Chmn.; Crane (IL), Thomas (CA), Shaw (FL), Johnson (CT), Bunning (KY), Houghton (NY), Herger (CA), McCrery (LA), Hancock (MO), Camp (MI), Ramstad (MN), Zimmer (NJ), Nussle (IA), Johnson (TX), Dunn (WA), Collins (GA), Portman (OH), English (PA), Ensign (NV), Christensen (NE).
Minority (15 D): Gibbons (FL), RMM; Rangel (NY), Stark (CA), Jacobs (IN), Ford (TN), Matsui (CA), Kennelly (CT), Coyne (PA), Levin (MI), Cardin (MD), McDermott (WA), Kleczka (WI), Lewis (GA), Payne (VA), Neal (MA),

SUBCOMMITTEES

HEALTH

Majority (8 R): Thomas, Chmn.; Johnson (CT), McCrery, Ensign, Christensen, Crane, Houghton, Johnson (TX).
Minority (5 D): Stark, RMM; Cardin, McDermott, Kleczka, Lewis.

HUMAN RESOURCES

Majority (8 R): Shaw, Chmn.; Camp, McCrery, Collins, English, Nussle, Dunn, Ensign.
Minority (5 D): Ford, RMM; Kennelly, Levin, Rangel, Stark.

OVERSIGHT

Majority (7 R): Johnson (CT), Chmn.; Herger, Hancock, Johnson (TX), Portman, Ramstad, Zimmer.
Minority (4 D): Matsui, RMM; Levin, Cardin, McDermott.

SOCIAL SECURITY

Majority (7 R): Bunning, Chmn.; Johnson (TX), Collins, Portman, English, Christensen, Hancock.

Minority (4 D): Jacobs, RMM; Kennelly, Payne, Neal.

TRADE

Majority (9 R): Crane, Chmn.; Thomas, Shaw, Houghton, Hancock, Camp, Ramstad, Zimmer, Dunn.

Minority (6 D): Rangel, RMM; Gibbons, Matsui, Coyne, Payne, Neal.

JOINT COMMITTEES

JOINT ECONOMIC COMMITTEE   G-01 Dirksen, 202-224-5171

Senate (10): Mack (FL), Chmn.; Roth (DE), Craig (ID), Bennett (UT), Santorum (PA), Grams (MN), Bingaman (NM), Sarbanes (MD), Kennedy, (MA), Robb (VA).

House (10): Saxton (NJ), Vice Chmn.; Ewing (IL), Quinn (NY), Manzullo (IL), Sanford (SC), Thornberry (TX), Stark (CA), Obey (WI), Hamilton (IN), Mfume (MD).

JOINT COMMITTEE ON TAXATION   1015 Longworth, 202-225-3621

Senate (5): Packwood (OR), Vice Chmn.; Roth (DE), Hatch (UT), Moynihan (NY), Baucus (MT).

House (5): Archer (TX), Chmn.; Crane (IL), Thomas (CA), Gibbons (FL), Rangel (NY).

CAMPAIGN FINANCE CHARTS

All data are derived from candidate and party reports as well as other official studies available from the Federal Election Commission (FEC) located at 999 E Street, N.W., Washington, DC 20463. Telephone 202-219-4140 (or toll-free 800-424-9530).

U.S. SENATE

The following charts show the top 15 1994 Senate candidates in terms of the highest total net receipts, net expenditures, political action committee (PAC) contributions, individual contributions, cash on hand and candidate contributions during the 1988–94 election cycle.

1994 Senate: Top Raisers

1.	*Michael Huffington (R-CA)*	$29,992,884
2.	*Oliver L. (Ollie) North (R-VA)*	20,770,879
3.	Dianne Feinstein (D-CA)	14,597,791
4.	Edward M. Kennedy (D-MA)	9,816,808
5.	Bill Frist (R-TN)	9,679,522
6.	*W. Mitt Romney (R-MA)*	7,628,061
7.	Herb Kohl (D-WI)	7,388,348
8.	Rick Santorum (R-PA)	6,850,767
9.	Kay Bailey Hutchison (R-TX)	6,790,930
10.	Frank R. Lautenberg (D-NJ)	6,443,199
11.	Mike DeWine (R-OH)	6,344,528
12.	*Harris Wofford (D-PA)*	5,918,433
13.	Charles S. Robb (D-VA)	5,502,523
14.	Daniel Patrick Moynihan (D-NY)	5,245,823
15.	*Chuck Haytaian (R-NJ)*	5,110,518

1994 Senate: Top Spenders

1.	*Michael Huffington (R-CA)*	$29,969,695
2.	*Oliver L. (Ollie) North (R-VA)*	20,607,367
3.	Dianne Feinstein (D-CA)	14,407,179
4.	Edward M. Kennedy (D-MA)	10,540,244
5.	Bill Frist (R-TN)	9,517,424
6.	*W. Mitt Romney (R-MA)*	7,624,491
7.	Herb Kohl (D-WI)	7,374,312
8.	Frank R. Lautenberg (D-NJ)	7,278,332
9.	Rick Santorum (R-PA)	6,732,849
10.	*Harris Wofford (D-PA)*	6,300,560
11.	Mike DeWine (R-OH)	6,274,663
12.	Kay Bailey Hutchison* (R-TX)	6,114,755
13.	Daniel Patrick Moynihan (D-NY)	5,784,736
14.	Charles S. Robb (D-VA)	5,501,697
15.	*Chuck Haytaian (R-NJ)*	5,110,378

1994 Senate: Top PAC Recipients

1.	*Jim Sasser (D-TN)*	$1,723,494
2.	Dianne Feinstein (D-CA)	1,570,773
3.	Kent Conrad (D-ND)	1,429,114
4.	Kay Bailey Hutchison (R-TX)	1,424,109
5.	Mike DeWine (R-OH)	1,423,379
6.	Conrad Burns (R-MT)	1,316,194
7.	Orrin G. Hatch (R-UT)	1,293,621
8.	Robert J. Kerrey (D-NE)	1,275,087
9.	Charles S. Robb (D-VA)	1,272,597
10.	Daniel Patrick Moynihan (D-NY)	1,260,776
11.	Richard H. Bryan (D-NV)	1,250,009
12.	Frank R. Lautenberg (D-NJ)	1,248,189
13.	Rick Santorum (R-PA)	1,237,564
14.	Slade Gorton (R-WA)	1,172,322
15.	Joseph I. Lieberman (D-CT)	1,122,269

1994 Senate: Top Individual Contributions

1.	*Oliver L. (Ollie) North (R-VA)*	$20,555,200
2.	Dianne Feinstein (D-CA)	9,271,008
3.	Edward M. Kennedy (D-MA)	8,201,215
4.	Rick Santorum (R-PA)	5,291,676
5.	Kay Bailey Hutchison (R-TX)	5,166,298
6.	*Chuck Haytaian (R-NJ)*	4,542,417
7.	Mike DeWine (R-OH)	4,504,962
8.	*W. Mitt Romney (R-MA)*	4,482,702
9.	*Harris Wofford (D-PA)*	4,450,489
10.	Charles S. Robb (D-VA)	4,005,353
11.	Frank R. Lautenberg (D-NJ)	3,833,549
12.	Spencer Abraham (R-MI)	3,588,646
13.	*Jim Copper (R-TN)*	3,545,077
14.	*Robert Krueger* (D-TX)*	3,328,082
15.	Slade Gorton (R-WA)	3,325,996

1994 Senate: Top Cash-on-Hand

1. Kay Bailey Hutchison (R-TX) — $1,568,900
2. Joseph I. Lieberman (D-CT) — 1,335,036
3. Connie Mack (R-FL) — 1,042,915
4. Trent C. Lott (R-MS) — 735,472
5. John H. Chafee (R-RI) — 438,257
6. Robert C. Byrd (D-WV) — 427,362
7. Richard G. Lugar (R-IN) — 405,212
8. Orrin G. Hatch (R-UT) — 402,359
9. Craig Thomas (R-WY) — 326,804
10. Daniel Patrick Moynihan (D-NY) — 315,411
11. James M. Jeffords (D-VT) — 310,336
12. Olympia J. Snowe (R-ME) — 268,077
13. Daniel K. Akaka (D-HI) — 254,488
14. Dianne Feinstein (D-CA) — 239,515
15. Richard H. Bryan (D-NV) — 209,688

1994 Senate: Top Candidate Contributions

1. *Michael Huffington (R-CA)* — $28,382,489
2. Herb Kohl (D-WI) — 6,935,000
3. *W. Mitt Romney (R-MA)* — 3,082,406
4. *John R. Lakian (R-MA)* — 2,804,528
5. Dianne Feinstein (D-CA) — 2,530,053
6. *Richard Fisher* (D-TX)* — 2,010,490
7. *William Brock (R-MD)* — 1,581,739
8. Edward M. Kennedy (D-MA) — 1,350,000
9. Bill Frist (R-TN) — 1,265,000
10. *Charles Woods (R-NV)* — 1,182,761
11. *Bernadette Castro (R-NY)* — 1,099,056
12. *Bob Corker (R-TN)* — 1,090,020
13. *Joel Ferguson (D-MI)* — 1,030,278
14. Frank R. Lautenberg (D-NJ) — 750,000
15. *Jack M. Fields, Jr. (R-TX)* — 670,000

U.S. HOUSE OF REPRESENTATIVES

The following charts show the top 25 1994 House candidates in terms of the highest total net receipts, net expenditures, political action committee (PAC) contributions, individual contributions, cash on hand and candidate contributions during the 1992–94 election cycle.

1994 House: Top Raisers

1. *Gene Fontenot (R-TX)* — $4,659,466
2. Richard A. Gephardt (D-MO) — 2,509,186
3. *Bob Schuster (D-WY)* — 2,420,786
4. Robert K. (Bob) Dornan (R-CA) — 2,327,930
5. Enid Waldholtz (R-UT) — 2,175,815
6. *Thomas S. Foley (D-WA)* — 2,104,164
7. *Timothy P. Moyer (R-WA)* — 2,032,723
8. Newt Gingrich (R-GA) — 2,012,572
9. *John Sonneland (R-WA)* — 1,783,062
10. Vic Fazio (D-CA) — 1,757,508
11. *Richard Sybert (R-CA)* — 1,697,243
12. *Peter G. Fitzgerald (R-IL)* — 1,653,627
13. *M. Margolies-Mezvinsky (D-PA)* — 1,609,938
14. Martin Frost (D-TX) — 1,608,720
15. Sander M. Levin (D-MI) — 1,458,644
16. *Dan Rostenkowski (D-IL)* — 1,449,757
17. Tom Davis (R-VA) — 1,435,382
18. Steny H. Hoyer (D-MD) — 1,427,122
19. Sam Gejdenson (D-CT) — 1,415,185
20. Joseph P. Kennedy II (D-MA) — 1,396,555
21. *Lynn Schenk (D-CA)* — 1,388,353
22. Gary L. Ackerman (D-NY) — 1,358,352
23. Charles B. Rangel (D-NY) — 1,350,357
24. Nita M. Lowey (D-NY) — 1,314,605
25. *Frederick C. Overby (D-GA)* — 1,294,536

1994 House: Top Spenders

1. *Gene Fontenot (R-TX)* — $4,658,585
2. Richard A. Gephardt (D-MO) — 2,621,479
3. *Dan Rostenkowski (D-IL)* — 2,495,222
4. *Bob Schuster (D-WY)* — 2,429,346
5. Robert K. (Bob) Dornan (R-CA) — 2,261,696
6. *Thomas S. Foley (D-WA)* — 2,144,579
7. *Timothy P. Moyer (R-WA)* — 2,032,722
8. Enid Waldholtz (R-UT) — 1,976,289
9. Vic Fazio (D-CA) — 1,972,033
10. Newt Gingrich (R-GA) — 1,817,792
11. *John Sonneland (R-WA)* — 1,773,472
12. *Richard Sybert (R-CA)* — 1,687,166
13. *Peter G. Fitzgerald (R-IL)* — 1,653,431
14. *M. Margolies-Mezvinsky (D-PA)* — 1,620,110
15. Martin Frost (D-TX) — 1,589,612
16. Sander M. Levin (D-MI) — 1,536,445
17. Charles B. Rangel (D-NY) — 1,437,297
18. Tom Davis (R-VA) — 1,430,272
19. Sam Gejdenson (D-CT) — 1,422,126
20. *Lynn Schenk (D-CA)* — 1,392,948
21. Bart Gordon (D-TN) — 1,385,995
22. Gary L. Ackerman (D-NY) — 1,376,467
23. Nita M. Lowey (D-NY) — 1,343,347
24. Jane Harman (D-CA) — 1,300,855
25. Steny H. Hoyer (D-MD) — 1,295,542

1994 House: Top PAC Recipients

1.	*Thomas S. Foley (D-WA)*	$1,158,072
2.	Vic Fazio (D-CA)	1,069,170
3.	Richard A. Gephardt (D-MO)	1,010,316
4.	Steny H. Hoyer (D-MD)	860,152
5.	Sam M. Gibbons (D-FL)	829,967
6.	*Dan Rostenkowski (D-IL)*	799,119
7.	*Peter Hoagland (D-NE)*	778,250
8.	David E. Bonior (D-MI)	768,648
9.	Newt Gingrich (R-GA)	768,480
10.	Martin Frost (D-TX)	767,215
11.	Charles B. Rangel (D-NY)	763,025
12.	John D. Dingell (D-MI)	752,610
13.	Jack M. Fields Jr. (R-TX)	683,399
14.	Sander M. Levin (D-MI)	658,315
15.	*M. Margolies-Mevinsky (D-PA)*	656,716
16.	*Lynn Schenk (D-CA)*	655,566
17.	Bill Brewster (D-OK)	652,002
18.	*Richard H. Lehman (D-CA)*	627,959
19.	Sherrod Brown (D-OH)	619,932
20.	L. F. Payne (D-VA)	615,192
21.	Bart Gordon (D-TN)	608,490
22.	Dale E. Kildee (D-MI)	605,558
23.	Robert T. Matsui (D-CA)	582,794
24.	Charles Wilson (D-TX)	581,100
25.	Norman Y. Mineta (D-CA)	571,112

1994 House: Top Individual Contributions

1.	Robert K. (Bob) Dornan (R-CA)	$2,262,125
2.	Newt Gingrich (R-GA)	1,182,887
3.	Joseph P. Kennedy II (D-MA)	1,158,211
4.	Nita M. Lowey (D-NY)	1,029,817
5.	Lloyd Doggett (D-TX)	979,403
6.	Richard A. Gephardt (D-MO)	972,722
7.	Tom Davis (R-VA)	969,008
8.	Edward J. Markey (D-MA)	957,935
9.	*Charles Millard (R-NY)*	955,312
10.	*M. Margolies-Mevinsky (D-PA)*	884,282
11.	Richard K. (Dick) Armey (R-TX)	883,494
12.	Richard A. Zimmer (R-NJ)	868,449
13.	George R. Nethercutt Jr. (R-WA)	867,736
14.	*Thomas S. Foley (D-WA)*	848,800
15.	Martin T. Meehan (D-MA)	842,868
16.	*Michael L. (Mike) Synar (D-OK)*	814,734
17.	Jon D. Fox (R-PA)	808,868
18.	Peter I. Blute (R-MA)	797,278
19.	Martin Frost (D-TX)	795,676
20.	Gary L. Ackerman (D-NY)	789,734
21.	Jay Dickey (R-AR)	776,086
22.	Jon Christensen (R-NE)	744,995
23.	Jane Harman (D-CA)	744,356
24.	Peter G. Torkildsen (R-MA)	734,901
25.	Frank A. LoBiondo (R-NJ)	733,074

1994 House: Top Cash-on-Hand

1.	David Dreier (R-CA)	$2,306,513
2.	Charles E. Schumer (D-NY)	2,221,979
3.	Robert G. Torricelli (D-NJ)	1,291,421
4.	Joseph P. Kennedy II (D-MA)	785,807
5.	Bill Archer (R-TX)	739,772
6.	Dan Burton (R-IN)	728,606
7.	Fortney (Pete) Stark (D-CA)	719,618
8.	Lloyd Doggett (D-TX)	684,119
9.	Nick J. Rahall II (R-IN)	668,033
10.	Richard K. (Dick) Armey (R-TX)	627,869
11.	Jim Ramstad (R-MN)	577,577
12.	John Lewis (D-GA)	569,881
13.	James H. Saxton (R-NJ)	535,075
14.	Jack M. Fields Jr.(R-TX)	531,990
15.	Thomas P. Lantos (D-CA)	503,228
16.	James H. (Jimmy) Quillen (R-TN)	490,192
17.	Richard A. Zimmer (R-NJ)	488,554
18.	Jerry Lewis (D-CA)	478,451
19.	Ron Wyden (D-OR)	475,769
20.	W.J. (Billy) Tauzin, Jr. (D-LA)	457,578
21.	Lamar S. Smith (R-TX)	428,554
22.	Henry A. Waxman (D-CA)	420,929
23.	Pete Geren (D-TX)	417,734
24.	Patricia Schroeder (D-CO)	416,453
25.	Tom Bevill (D-AL)	415,460

1994 House: Top Candidate Contributions

1.	*Gene Fontenot (R-TX)*	$2,413,651
2.	Enid Waldholtz (R-UT)	1,644,089
3.	*Timothy P. Moyer (R-WA)*	1,461,984
4.	*Bob Schuster (D-WY)*	1,452,232
5.	*Peter G. Fitzgerald (R-IL)*	1,437,395
6.	*John Sonneland (R-WA)*	1,044,982
7.	*Merrill A. Cook (I-UT)*	854,815
8.	*Charles L. Owen (D-KY)*	797,196
9.	Greg Ganske (R-IA)	618,427
10.	*Peter James Tsakanikas (R-FL)*	582,123
11.	*Richard Sybert (R-CA)*	506,685
12.	*Frederick C. Overby (D-GA)*	504,005
13.	*Dennis M. Blankenship (R-TX)*	499,153
14.	*Gilbert L. Ziegler (R-MI)*	476,000
15.	*Dennis Mehiel (D-NY)*	469,180
16.	*Michael G. Maxfield (R-MI)*	458,970
17.	*John J. Murray* (R-PA)*	380,055
18.	Frank A. Cremeans (R-OH)	364,677
19.	*Paul W. Bucha (R-NY)*	354,804
20.	*Gary Dale Porter (R-ND)*	347,999
21.	*Grant M. Lally (R-NY)*	329,991
22.	*Stuart Price (D-OK)*	328,316
23.	Mark W. Neumann* (R-WI)	324,195
24.	*John Whorley (D-TN)*	312,123
25.	*Ronald M. Florance (R-CA)*	295,054

DEMOGRAPHICS CHARTS

Population. All population figures are from the Bureau of the Census, U.S. Department of Commerce, Washington, D.C. 20233, 301-763-4040. Figures for 1970, 1980 and 1990 are final Census Bureau population counts as of April 1 of those years. Figures for 1994 are estimates as of July 1. (The District of Columbia is included as a state in all the following charts.)

Voting Age Population. This figure indicates all persons at least 18 years of age who are eligible to vote, including the Armed Forces, aliens and institutional members.

Chart I shows the total U.S. population and total U.S. voting age population for 1994, 1990, 1980 and 1970.

Chart I

Total U.S. Population		Total U.S. Voting Age Population	
July 1, 1994 (est.)	280,341,000	July 1, 1994(est.)	192,322,000
April 1, 1990	248,709,873	April 1, 1990	185,105,441
April 1, 1980	226,545,805	April 1, 1980	163,997,000
April 1, 1970	203,302,031	April 1, 1970	135,290,000

Chart II indicates the range of highest and lowest state population changes in percentage growth and absolute change for 1980–90.

Chart II

1980–90 Population Change
(National Avg.: up 9.8%)

State	Highest		State	Lowest	
Nevada	50.1%	401,340	West Virginia	−8.0%	−156,167
Alaska	36.9	148,192	District of Columbia	−4.9	−31,433
Arizona	34.8	947,013	Iowa	−4.7	−137,053
Florida	32.7	3,191,602	Wyoming	−3.4	−15,969
California	25.7	6,092,119	North Dakota	−2.1	−13,917

Chart III shows the ten highest and the ten lowest state populations.

Chart III

1994 (Est.) U.S. Population: Ten Highest and Lowest States

State	Highest	State	Lowest
California	31,431,000	Wyoming	476,000
Texas	18,378,000	District of Columbia	570,000
New York	18,169,000	Vermont	580,000
Florida	13,953,000	Alaska	606,000
Pennsylvania	12,052,000	North Dakota	638,000
Illinois	11,752,000	Delaware	706,000
Ohio	11,102,000	South Dakota	721,000
Michigan	9,496,000	Montana	856,000
New Jersey	7,904,000	Rhode Island	997,000
North Carolina	7,070,000	Idaho	1,133,000

Chart IV lists the states with the highest and lowest median age.

Chart IV

Median Age
(National Avg.: 32.8 years)

State	Highest	State	Lowest
Florida	36.4 years	Utah	26.2 years
West Virginia	35.4	Alaska	29.4
Pennsylvania	35.0	Texas	30.8
New Jersey, Oregon	34.5	Louisiana	31.0
Connecticut	34.4	Mississippi	31.2

Chart V illustrates the states with the highest and lowest average percentages of married-couple family households.

Chart V

Married-Couple Family Households
(National Avg.: 55.9%)

State	Highest	State	Lowest
Utah	64.8%	District of Columbia	25.3%
Idaho	62.2	New York	49.9
Wyoming, New Hampshire	59.7	Nevada	51.4
Arkansas, Iowa, Kentucky	59.2	Massachusetts	52.1
North Dakota	59.1	California	52.7

Chart VI illustrates the states with the highest and lowest average percentages of population over 65 years of age.

Chart VI

Population Over 65 Years of Age
(National Avg.: 12.5%)

State	Highest	State	Lowest
Florida	18.3%	Alaska	4.1%
Pennsylvania	15.4	Utah	8.7
Iowa	15.3	Colorado	10.0
W. Virginia, Iowa	15.0	Texas, Georgia	10.1
Arkansas	14.9	Wyoming	10.4

Chart VII illustrates the states with the highest and lowest average percentages of Owner Occupied Housing.

Chart VII

Owner Occupied Housing
(National Avg.: 65.4%)

State	Highest	State	Lowest
West Virginia	74.1%	District of Columbia	38.9%
Minnesota	71.8	New York	52.2
Mississippi	71.5	Hawaii	53.9
Michigan	71.0	Nevada	54.8
Pennsylvania	70.6	California	55.6

Chart VIII illustrates the states with the highest and lowest median house value.

Chart VIII

Median House Value
(National Avg.: $84,209)

State	Highest	State	Lowest
Hawaii	$245,300	South Dakota	$45,200
California	195,500	Mississippi	45,600
Connecticut	177,800	Iowa	45,900
Massachusetts	162,800	Arkansas	46,300
New Jersey	162,300	West Virginia	47,900

Chart IX illustrates the states with the highest and lowest median monthly rent.

Chart IX

Median Monthly Rent
(National Avg.: $350)

State	Highest	State	Lowest
Hawaii	$599	Mississippi	$215
California	561	West Virginia	221
New Jersey	521	Alabama	229
Connecticut	510	Arkansas	230
Massachusetts	506	South Dakota	242

Chart X shows the states with the highest and lowest per capita income.

Chart X

1990 Per Capita Income
(National Avg.: $18,685)

State	Highest	State	Lowest
Connecticut	$25,358	Mississippi	$12,735
New Jersey	24,968	West Virginia	13,747
District of Columbia	23,491	Utah	14,083
Massachusetts	22,642	Arkansas	14,218
New York	21,975	New Mexico	14,228
Maryland	21,864	Louisiana	14,391
Alaska	21,761	Alabama	14,826
California	20,795	Kentucky	14,929
New Hampshire	20,789	S. Carolina	15,099
Illinois	20,303	Montana	15,110

Chart XI shows the states with the highest and lowest average unemployment rates for 1990. These figures are from the U.S. Department of Labor, Bureau of Labor Statistics, and were compiled independently of the Census Bureau figures.

Chart XI

1990 Average Unemployment Rate

(National Avg: 5.4%)

Highest		Lowest	
West Virginia	8.3%	Nebraska	2.2%
Mississippi	7.5	Hawaii	2.8
Michigan	7.5	South Dakota	3.7
Arkansas	6.9	North Dakota	3.9
Alaska	6.9	North Carolina	4.1
Alabama	6.8	Iowa	4.2
Rhode Island	6.7	Virginia	4.3
District of Columbia	6.6	Utah	4.3
New Mexico	6.3	Kansas	4.4
Texas	6.2	Wisconsin	4.4

Ethnic Breakdown. The racial and ethnic breakdowns illustrate the potential ethnic vote as opposed to the overall population. The concepts of race and ethnicity as defined by the Census Bureau reflect self-identification and not clear-cut biological definitions.

Chart XII lists voting age and total state population figures for the fourteen states with black populations well above the national average of 12.1% in 1990. Black ethnic classification refers to those persons who indicated their race as Black on the Census questionnaire.

Chart XII

1990 Black Population: Total State Population

State	% of voting age pop.	% of total state pop.	State	% of voting age pop.	% of total state pop.
District of Columbia	62.4%	65.8%	North Carolina	20.1%	22.0%
Mississippi	31.6	35.6	Virginia	17.6	18.8
Louisiana	27.9	30.8	Delaware	15.3	16.9
South Carolina	26.9	29.8	Tennessee	14.4	16.0
Georgia	24.6	27.0	New York	14.7	15.9
Alabama	22.7	25.3	Arkansas	13.7	15.9
Maryland	23.5	24.9	Illinois	13.4	14.8

Chart XIII illustrates the voting age and total population figures for the fourteen states with American Indian concentrations well above the national average of 0.8% in 1990. The American Indian classification includes persons who classified themselves as American Indian, Eskimo, or Aleut.

Chart XIII

1990 American Indian: Total State and Voting Age Population

State	% of voting age pop.	% of total state pop.	State	% of voting age pop.	% of total state pop.
Alaska	13.5%	15.6%	Wyoming	1.8%	2.1%
New Mexico	7.5	8.9	Washington	1.4	1.7
Oklahoma	6.9	8.0	Nevada	1.5	1.6
South Dakota	5.4	7.3	Utah	1.2	1.4
Montana	4.8	6.0	Oregon	1.2	1.4
Arizona	4.4	5.6	Idaho	1.2	1.4
North Dakota	3.1	4.1	North Carolina	1.1	1.2

Chart XIV illustrates the voting age and total state population figures for the eight states with Asian concentrations at or above the national average of 2.9% in 1990. The Asian classification includes persons who classified themselves as Asian or Pacific Islander.

Chart XIV

1990 Asian Origin: Total State and Voting Age Population

State	% of voting age pop.	% of total state pop.	State	% of voting age pop.	% of total state pop.
Hawaii	61.3%	61.8%	Alaska	3.6%	3.6%
California	9.2	9.6	New Jersey	3.2	3.5
Washington	4.1	4.3	Nevada	3.1	3.2
New York	3.8	3.9	Maryland	2.8	2.9

Chart XV illustrates voting age and total state population figures for the eight states with Hispanic origin concentrations well above the national average of 9.0% in 1990. The Hispanic origin classification includes three specific categories—Mexican, Puerto Rican and Cuban—as well as those who indicated that they were of other Spanish or Hispanic origin (origin can be viewed as ancestry, nationality group, lineage or country of birth of the person or the person's parents or ancestors prior to their arrival in the United States). Persons of Hispanic origin may be of any race.

Chart XV

1990 Hispanic Origin: Total State and Voting Age Population

State	% of voting age pop.	% of total state pop.	State	% of voting age pop.	% of total state pop.
New Mexico	33.0%	38.2%	Colorado	11.2%	12.9%
California	22.5	25.8	New York	11.2	12.3
Texas	22.4	25.5	Florida	11.7	12.2
Arizona	15.8	18.8	Nevada	9.1	10.4

INDEX

The names of Governors, Senators and Representatives appear in boldface type. The number of the page that includes their corresponding biographical, voting and campaign finance information also appears in bold.

THE AUTHORS

MICHAEL BARONE, senior editor for *U.S. News and World Report*, is a graduate of Harvard College and Yale Law School. He has been affiliated with the polling group of Peter D. Hart Research Associates, Inc. and was an editorial writer and columnist for *The Washington Post*. Barone is also author of *Our Country: The Shaping of America from Roosevelt to Reagan*. He has appeared as an analyst and commentator on numerous television and radio news shows. He lives with his daughter Sarah in Washington, DC.

GRANT UJIFUSA is a senior editor at *Reader's Digest* magazine in Pleasantville, New York. Ujifusa, a native of Worland, Wyoming and a graduate of Harvard College, lives with his wife Amy and sons Steven and Andrew in Chappaqua, New York. He is also the Strategy Chair for a group associated with the Japanese American Citizens League.

THE PUBLISHER

"The nation's most respected nonpartisan source of information about how Washington policymaking machinery really works."

That's how *Newsweek* described *National Journal*. For more than 25 years, *National Journal* has reached subscribers with an award-winning weekly magazine noted for its dedication to "facts only" reporting. *National Journal* speaks to people who make it their business to know what's going on in the world's largest business—the United States Government.

Only *National Journal* is exclusively devoted to the coverage and analysis of what the government is doing today, what it's going to do tomorrow, and how its actions affect every facet of our lives.

This 1996 edition of *The Almanac of American Politics* marks the seventh volume to be published by National Journal Inc. In addition to the *Almanac* and *National Journal*, National Journal Inc. publishes the monthly *Government Executive* magazine; *CongressDaily*, a daily fax newsletter covering Congress; the semi-annual directory, *The Capital Source*; and the *National Journal Convention Daily*, in conjunction with the Democratic and Republican Conventions.

National Journal Inc. is a wholly-owned subsidiary of the Los Angeles-based Times Mirror Company.

1501 M Street, NW, Washington, DC 20005 Telephone (202) 739-8400